Indonesia

Peter Turner
Marie Cambon Paul Greenway
Brendan Delahunty Emma Miller

LONELY PLANET PUBLICATIONS
Melbourne • Oakland • London • Paris

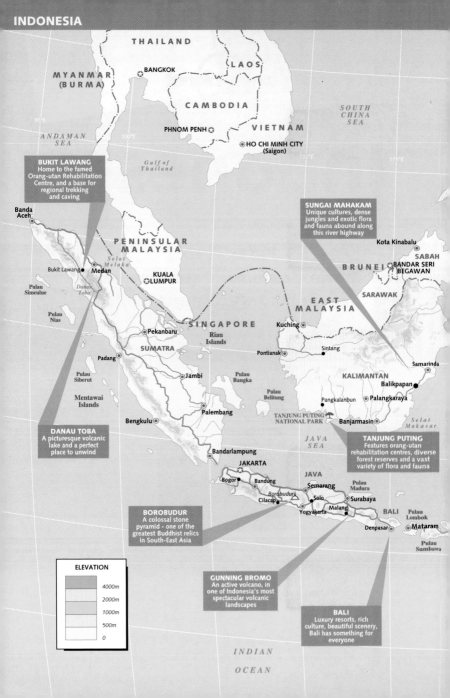

INDONESIA

THAILAND

LAOS

MYANMAR
(BURMA)

BANGKOK

CAMBODIA

SOUTH
CHINA
SEA

PHNOM PENH

VIETNAM

ANDAMAN
SEA

HO CHI MINH CITY
(Saigon)

Gulf of
Thailand

BUKIT LAWANG
Home to the famed
Orang-utan Rehabilitation
Centre, and a base for
regional trekking
and caving

SUNGAI MAHAKAM
Unique cultures, dense
jungles and exotic flora
and fauna abound along
this river highway

Banda
Aceh

PENINSULAR
MALAYSIA

Kota Kinabalu

SABAH

Selat
Melaka

BANDAR SERI
BEGAWAN

BRUNEI

Bukit Lawang   Medan

KUALA
LUMPUR

SARAWAK

EAST
MALAYSIA

Pulau
Simeulue

Danau
Toba

Pulau
Nias

SINGAPORE

Kuching

Pekanbaru

Riau
Islands

Sintang

Samarinda

Padang

SUMATRA

Jambi

Pontianak

Pulau
Bangka

KALIMANTAN

Balikpapan

Pulau
Siberut

Mentawai
Islands

Palembang

Pulau
Belitung

Pangkalanbun

Palangkaraya

Bengkulu

DANAU TOBA
A picturesque volcanic
lake and a perfect
place to unwind

TANJUNG PUTING
NATIONAL PARK

Banjarmasin

Selat
Makasar

TANJUNG PUTING
Features orang-utan
rehabilitation centres, diverse
forest reserves and a vast
variety of flora and fauna

Bandarlampung

JAVA
SEA

JAKARTA

JAVA

Pulau
Madura

Bogor

Bandung

Semarang

Borobudur

Solo

Surabaya

Cilacap

Malang

BALI

Pulau
Lombok

BOROBUDUR
A colossal stone
pyramid - one of the
greatest Buddhist relics
in South-East Asia

Yogyakarta

Denpasar

Mataram

Pulau
Sumbawa

ELEVATION

4000m

2000m

1000m

500m

0

GUNNING BROMO
An active volcano, in
one of Indonesia's most
spectacular volcanic
landscapes

BALI
Luxury resorts, rich
culture, beautiful scenery,
Bali has something for
everyone

INDIAN

OCEAN

Contents – Text

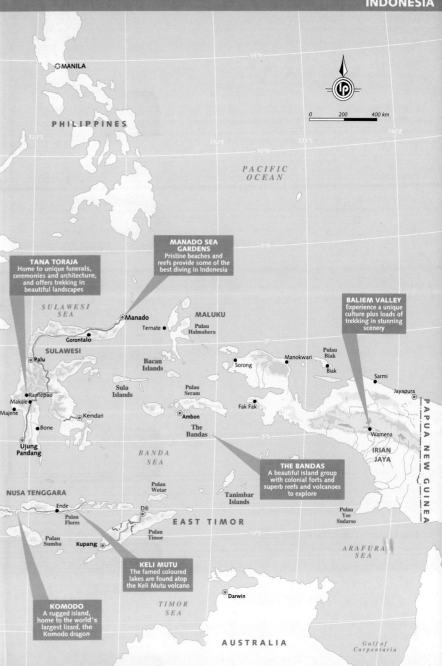

Indonesia
6th edition – January 2000
First published – September 1986

Published by
Lonely Planet Publications Pty Ltd A.C.N. 005 607 983
192 Burwood Rd, Hawthorn, Victoria 3122, Australia

Lonely Planet Offices
Australia PO Box 617, Hawthorn, Victoria 3122
USA 150 Linden St, Oakland, CA 94607
UK 10a Spring Place, London NW5 3BH
France 1 rue du Dahomey, 75011 Paris

Photographs
Many of the images in this guide are available for licensing from
Lonely Planet Images.
email: lpi@lonelyplanet.com.au

Front cover photograph
Nocturnal activities in the bat cave – Padangbai, Bali (Greg Elms)

ISBN 0 86442 690 9

text & maps © Lonely Planet 2000
photos © photographers as indicated 2000

Printed by The Bookmaker Pty Ltd
Printed in China

Contents – Text

THE AUTHORS

THIS BOOK

FOREWORD

INTRODUCTION

FACTS ABOUT INDONESIA

INDONESIAN CRAFTS

FACTS FOR THE VISITOR

GETTING THERE & AWAY

GETTING AROUND

JAVA

SUMATRA

NUSA TENGGARA

EAST TIMOR   771

KALIMANTAN   784

SULAWESI   857

MALUKU 957

IRIAN JAYA 1007

LANGUAGE 1061

GLOSSARY 1068

ACKNOWLEDGMENTS 1075

INDEX 1086

MAP LEGEND back page

METRIC CONVERSION inside back cover

Contents – Maps

EAST TIMOR

KALIMANTAN

SULAWESI

MALUKU

IRIAN JAYA

MAP INDEX

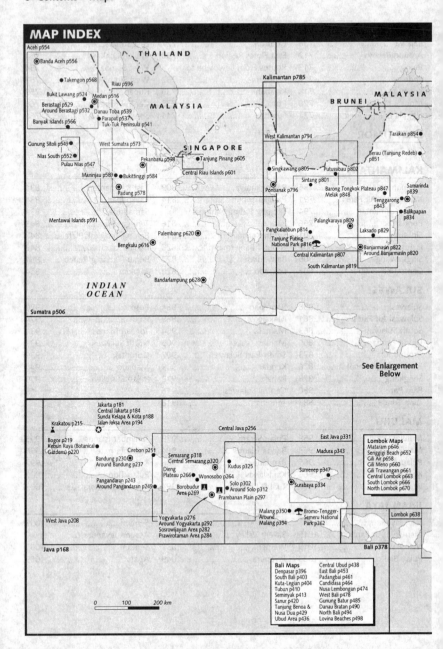

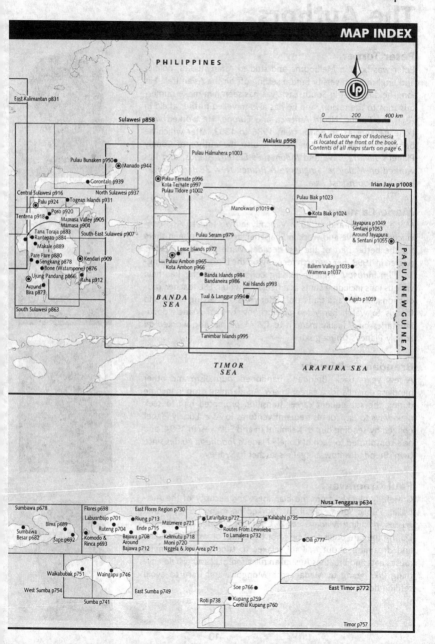

MAP INDEX

PHILIPPINES

A full colour map of Indonesia is located at the front of the book. Contents of all maps starts on page 6.

0   200   400 km

The Authors

Peter Turner

Peter was born in Melbourne and studied Asian studies, politics and English at university before setting off on the Asian trail. His long-held interest in South-East Asia has seen him make numerous trips to the region, and he has also travelled further afield in Asia, the Pacific, North America and Europe. He worked with Lonely Planet as an editor from 1986 to 1993, after which he became a full-time writer. Peter is also the author of Lonely Planet's *Jakarta*, *Java* and *Indonesia's Eastern Islands*, and has worked on *Malaysia, Singapore & Brunei*, *New Zealand*, *Singapore* and *South-East Asia*.

Marie Cambon

Marie was born and raised in Vancouver. Two trips to Asia convinced her to live and work in Shanghai, and she has been there for the better part of the last decade. Marie gained a Masters degree in 1993, her research focusing on the history of the Shanghai film industry. Prior to joining Lonely Planet, she has held various jobs including stints as a freelance writer, ESL teacher, production assistant and translator. After years of coercing family and friends to watch her video productions, two of Marie's documentaries have finally made it to TV. Marie has also worked on Lonely Planet's *China* guide.

Brendan Delahunty

A few years back, Brendan abandoned journalism and other mindless pursuits for a career in law. An alarming drop in income during the subsequent career transition prompted him to seek new ways to pay for his frequent ventures to Asia. Lonely Planet obliged by sending him to Kalimantan and Sulawesi in 1994, and he's contributed to each of Lonely Planet's *Indonesia* guides since then. Brendan is now a legal researcher in Sydney.

Paul Greenway

Gratefully plucked from the blandness and security of the Australian Public Service, Paul has worked on many Lonely Planet guides including *Madagascar & Comoros*, *Mongolia* and *Iran*. During the rare times that he's not travelling, or writing, reading and dreaming about it, Paul relaxes to tuneless heavy metal music, eats and breathes Australian rules football, and will do anything (like going to Madagascar, Mongolia and Iran) to avoid settling down.

Emma Miller
Born and bred in the 'burbs of Melbourne, Emma was infected with the common Australian travel bug at an early age, when she fled Indonesian classes to Java and Bali. Several trips to Asia and Europe followed, interrupted by a BA in Journalism and life as a reporter on a metro daily tabloid. When she tired of fires, car crashes, exorcist trials, police shootings, inquests and state politics, Emma switched to Lonely Planet, where she now works as the condensed guides editor. On this her fourth trip to Indonesia, Emma battled landslides, pickpockets, a couple of riots and a nasty case of dengue fever in Sumatra.

FROM THE AUTHORS
Peter Turner Of the many people who helped with the preparation of this book, in Jakarta, special thanks to Agus, Ibu Tuti from the Jakarta Tourist Office and Jeffery Pradjanata. Thanks also to the staff of the West Java Deparpostal, particularly the ever helpful Pak Amir. In Pangandaran, thanks to Kristina and Jajang Nurjaman, and in Mojokerto, cheers to Owen and the Westinghouse gang. In East Java, thanks to the very knowledgable Martin Tyson for help with Baluran and other parks, and to Mark Grantham for all the help in Alas Purwo National Park.

Marie Cambon In West Kalimantan, thanks to David Djunaidi, Daniel Madu, Femke Kroes and Chris for all their info and advice. In Central Kalimantan, many thanks to the Baso family, Yusuf Kawaru, Sri Utami, Mr Tono and Muskin Hussein. Also, many thanks to Heather Hope and Jo for details on their trek from Central Kalimantan to East Kalimantan. In South Kalimantan, *terima kasih* to Johan Yasin, and Ryan for his wheels and invaluable assistance. In East Kalimantan, thanks to Mokhta, Rusli, Lucas Zwaal, Ir Senoadji S, Erwin Tjioz and the ghost of Joseph Conrad in Berau. Many thanks to Steve Stuart for his companionship at Tanjung Puting and ongoing supply of information, and Michell Huillier for information on Tanjung Puting and the Mahakam. Thanks also to Peter Turner for editorial advice and patience, and my mother for keeping her eye out for Kalimantan news and orang-utan facts.

Brendan Delahunty Wild applause for 'Adventure Boy' Jeff, whose patient interest in my misadventures on the road makes travelling a lot more fun. Three cheers for Karina, Babe Chris, and Peter and Tracey Duncan, whose enthusiasm for life in Indonesia is delightfully infectious. And a huge terima kasih to Frans Mola, Pak Darmawan, Eben Unu and others along the way who steered me in the right direction, especially the many ordinary people whose amazing hospitality belies the extraordinary hardships currently affecting everyday life in Indonesia and Timor.

Paul Greenway Thanks to the following people. In Indonesia: Sari Surjadi, and the gang from Conservation International; the guys from the NGOs at Ampana and Bomba working in the Togean Islands – keep up the excellent work; the immigration office in Palu for (eventually) granting me a visa extension; Redzky Mahakena at the tourist office in Ambon; Graeme Fay at the Australian Consulate, Denpasar; and Martin Davies, Kim Ohashi, Anne Price-Beglin and Neil Beglin, who were stranded with me in the heavenly Bandas.

Elsewhere: Lindsay Warren and Paula McDonell from Operation Wallacea; my 'Dutch connection', Anne-Marie van Dam; Irena and George Palenicek from the Czech Republic – good luck with the new book; the unknown people at Bali Online; and, finally, all the readers who send letters and emails.

Back home in Adelaide, thanks to my family and friends for worrying about me. At Lonely Planet, thanks to Sue Galley and Kristin Odijk for sending me to Bali; the previous author, James Lyon, for creating the opportunity for me to go there; Peter Turner, for the information about Gunung Rinjani; and the unsung cartographers, editors and designers who have to deal with my work.

Emma Miller Heartfelt thanks to: Adi, Zulkarnain and Henri at the Medan Tourist Office; all the guys at Merpati in Medan; Fraser Cargill, Australia's Consul-General in Medan, for trashy literature and timely assistance; Idam Darma Waty Halawa for introducing me to the top dogs in Gunung Sitoli; Rohasi Naibaho for companionship on the bumpy road to Danau Toba; Belinda Syme on Nias for the fish, the megaliths and the repellent; Firdaus and friends in Bengkulu; Gie and Nele at Danau Maninjau for the spaghetti, tips and pics; Khadijah in Bukit Lawang for rambutans and religion; Niar in Banda Aceh; Novita and Devi in Palembang; Dr Ong for tales of black urine; and my folks, my sister, the wonder twins, Miss Behaviour, Nadine, KristinO and Chris for your emails, calls and support.

This Book

The monumental task of compiling this 1st edition was the collective work of Alan Samalgaski, who roamed the far reaches of the archipelago, Ginny Bruce, who covered Java, and Mary Covernton, who wrote Sumatra and Bali. For the 2nd edition, Alan went to Sumatra and Sulawesi, Tony Wheeler explored Bali, Lombok and Sumatra, John Noble and Susan Forsyth island-hopped through Nusa Tenggara and Maluku, and Joe Cummings went to Java and Kalimantan. For the 3rd edition, Robert Storey oversaw the project and researched Nusa Tenggara, Maluku and Sulawesi. Dan Spitzer updated Java and Kalimantan, Richard Nebesky went to Sumatra and Bali was covered by Tony Wheeler and James Lyon, who also explored Lombok. For the 4th edition, Peter Turner was the coordinating author and researched Java. James Lyon covered Bali and Lombok, Brendan Delahunty explored Kalimantan and Sulawesi, Paul Greenway went to Maluku and Irian Jaya, Chris MacAsey updated Nusa Tenggara and David Willett updated Sumatra. For the 5th edition, Peter Turner was again the coordinating author and updated the introductory chapters and Java and Nusa Tenggara. James Lyon updated Bali and the Lombok section of Nusa Tenggara, Brendan Delahunty researched the Sulawesi chapter, Paul Greenway worked on the Maluku and Irian Jaya chapters, Chris Taylor covered Kalimantan and David Willett updated Sumatra.

For this edition, Peter Turner was once again the coordinating author, updating the introductory chapters and Java. Paul Greenway updated Bali and the Lombok section of Nusa Tenggara as well as Sulawesi, Maluku and Irian Jaya. Marie Cambon updated Kalimantan and Brendan Delahunty updated Nusa Tenggara. Emma Miller updated Sumatra.

From the Publisher

This 6th edition of *Indonesia* was produced in Lonely Planet's Melbourne office. Leanne Peake coordinated the mapping and was responsible for the design and layout. Kusnander, Adrian Persoglia, Glenn Beanland, Maree Styles and Jack Gavran assisted with the mapping. Kate Daly was the coordinating editor, with assistance from Lara Morcombe, Martin Heng, Russ Kerr, Lyn McGaurr, Joanne Newell, Kristin Odjik, Cherry Prior, Jane Thompson and Lucy Williams. The cover was designed by Guillaume Roux. Quentin Frayne compiled the Language chapter, and Kusnandar was a great help throughout production with Bahasa Indonesia queries. Many thanks also to contributors Chris Eisinger, Audra Kunciunas, Stefan Merker, Tim Rock and Andrew Tudor. Thanks also to Paul King and Peter Neely for assistance with the 'Surfari Indonesia' section.

THANKS
Many thanks to the travellers who used the last edition and wrote to us with helpful hints, advice and interesting anecdotes. Your names appear in the back of this book.

Foreword

ABOUT LONELY PLANET GUIDEBOOKS

The story begins with a classic travel adventure: Tony and Maureen Wheeler's 1972 journey across Europe and Asia to Australia. Useful information about the overland trail did not exist at that time, so Tony and Maureen published the first Lonely Planet guidebook to meet a growing need.

From a kitchen table, then from a tiny office in Melbourne (Australia), Lonely Planet has become the largest independent travel publisher in the world, an international company with offices in Melbourne, Oakland (USA), London (UK) and Paris (France).

Today Lonely Planet guidebooks cover the globe. There is an ever-growing list of books and there's information in a variety of forms and media. Some things haven't changed. The main aim is still to help make it possible for adventurous travellers to get out there – to explore and better understand the world.

At Lonely Planet we believe travellers can make a positive contribution to the countries they visit – if they respect their host communities and spend their money wisely. Since 1986 a percentage of the income from each book has been donated to aid projects and human rights campaigns.

Updates Lonely Planet thoroughly updates each guidebook as often as possible. This usually means there are around two years between editions, although for more unusual or more stable destinations the gap can be longer. Check the imprint page (following the colour map at the beginning of the book) for publication dates.

Between editions up-to-date information is available in two free newsletters – the paper *Planet Talk* and email *Comet* (to subscribe, contact any Lonely Planet office) – and on our Web site at www.lonelyplanet.com. The *Upgrades* section of the Web site covers a number of important and volatile destinations and is regularly updated by Lonely Planet authors. *Scoop* covers news and current affairs relevant to travellers. And, lastly, the *Thorn Tree* bulletin board and *Postcards* section of the site carry unverified, but fascinating, reports from travellers.

Correspondence The process of creating new editions begins with the letters, postcards and emails received from travellers. This correspondence often includes suggestions, criticisms and comments about the current editions. Interesting excerpts are immediately passed on via newsletters and the Web site, and everything goes to our authors to be verified when they're researching on the road. We're keen to get more feedback from organisations or individuals who represent communities visited by travellers.

Lonely Planet gathers information for everyone who's curious about the planet – and especially for those who explore it first-hand. Through guidebooks, phrasebooks, activity guides, maps, literature, newsletters, image library, TV series and Web site we act as an information exchange for a worldwide community of travellers.

Research Authors aim to gather sufficient practical information to enable travellers to make informed choices and to make the mechanics of a journey run smoothly. They also research historical and cultural background to help enrich the travel experience and allow travellers to understand and respond appropriately to cultural and environmental issues.

Authors don't stay in every hotel because that would mean spending a couple of months in each medium-sized city and, no, they don't eat at every restaurant because that would mean stretching belts beyond capacity. They do visit hotels and restaurants to check standards and prices, but feedback based on readers' direct experiences can be very helpful.

Many of our authors work undercover, others aren't so secretive. None of them accept freebies in exchange for positive write-ups. And none of our guidebooks contain any advertising.

Production Authors submit their raw manuscripts and maps to offices in Australia, USA, UK or France. Editors and cartographers – all experienced travellers themselves – then begin the process of assembling the pieces. When the book finally hits the shops, some things are already out of date, we start getting feedback from readers and the process begins again ...

WARNING & REQUEST

Things change – prices go up, schedules change, good places go bad and bad places go bankrupt – nothing stays the same. So, if you find things better or worse, recently opened or long since closed, please tell us and help make the next edition even more accurate and useful. We genuinely value all the feedback we receive. Julie Young coordinates a well travelled team that reads and acknowledges every letter, postcard and email and ensures that every morsel of information finds its way to the appropriate authors, editors and cartographers for verification.

Everyone who writes to us will find their name in the next edition of the appropriate guidebook. They will also receive the latest issue of *Planet Talk*, our quarterly printed newsletter, or *Comet*, our monthly email newsletter. Subscriptions to both newsletters are free. The very best contributions will be rewarded with a free guidebook.

Excerpts from your correspondence may appear in new editions of Lonely Planet guidebooks, the Lonely Planet Web site, *Planet Talk* or *Comet*, so please let us know if you *don't* want your letter published or your name acknowledged.

Send all correspondence to the Lonely Planet office closest to you:

Australia: PO Box 617, Hawthorn, Victoria 3122
USA: 150 Linden St, Oakland, CA 94607
UK: 10A Spring Place, London NW5 3BH
France: 1 rue du Dahomey, 75011 Paris

Or email us at: talk2us@lonelyplanet.com.au

For news, views and updates see our Web site: www.lonelyplanet.com

HOW TO USE A LONELY PLANET GUIDEBOOK

The best way to use a Lonely Planet guidebook is any way you choose. At Lonely Planet we believe the most memorable travel experiences are often those that are unexpected, and the finest discoveries are those you make yourself. Guidebooks are not intended to be used as if they provide a detailed set of infallible instructions!

Contents All Lonely Planet guidebooks follow roughly the same format. The Facts about the Destination chapters or sections give background information ranging from history to weather. Facts for the Visitor gives practical information on issues like visas and health. Getting There & Away gives a brief starting point for researching travel to and from the destination. Getting Around gives an overview of the transport options when you arrive.

The peculiar demands of each destination determine how subsequent chapters are broken up, but some things remain constant. We always start with background, then proceed to sights, places to stay, places to eat, entertainment, getting there and away, and getting around information – in that order.

Heading Hierarchy Lonely Planet headings are used in a strict hierarchical structure that can be visualised as a set of Russian dolls. Each heading (and its following text) is encompassed by any preceding heading that is higher on the hierarchical ladder.

Entry Points We do not assume guidebooks will be read from beginning to end, but that people will dip into them. The traditional entry points are the list of contents and the index. In addition, however, some books have a complete list of maps and an index map illustrating map coverage.

There may also be a colour map that shows highlights. These highlights are dealt with in greater detail in the Facts for the Visitor chapter, along with planning questions and suggested itineraries. Each chapter covering a geographical region usually begins with a locator map and another list of highlights. Once you find something of interest in a list of highlights, turn to the index.

Maps Maps play a crucial role in Lonely Planet guidebooks and include a huge amount of information. A legend is printed on the back page. We seek to have complete consistency between maps and text, and to have every important place in the text captured on a map. Map key numbers usually start in the top left corner.

Although inclusion in a guidebook usually implies a recommendation we cannot list every good place. Exclusion does not necessarily imply criticism. In fact there are a number of reasons why we might exclude a place – sometimes it is simply inappropriate to encourage an influx of travellers.

Introduction

Like a string of jewels in a coral sea, the 13,000-plus islands of the Indonesian archipelago stretch almost 5000km from the Asian mainland into the Pacific Ocean. And like jewels, the islands have long represented wealth. A thousand years ago, the Chinese sailed as far as Timor to load up cargoes of sandalwood and beeswax; by the 16th century the spice islands of the Moluccas (Maluku) were luring European navigators in search of cloves, nutmeg and mace, once so rare and expensive that bloody wars were fought for the control of production and trade. The Dutch ruled for almost 350 years, drawing their fortunes from the islands where rich volcanic soil can produce two crops of rice a year, as well as support commercially valuable crops like coffee, sugar, tobacco and teak.

Endowed with a phenomenal array of natural resources and unique cultures, Indonesia became a magnet for every shade of entrepreneur from the west – a stamping ground for proselytising missionaries, unscrupulous traders, wayward adventurers and inspired artists. The country has been overrun by Dutch and Japanese armies; surveyed, drilled, dug up and shipped off by foreign mining companies; littered with the 'transmigrants' of Java and Bali; and poked and prodded by ethnologists, linguists and anthropologists turning fading cultures into PhD theses.

More recently Indonesia has attracted a new breed of visitor – the modern-day tourist. Places like Bali, Lombok, Tana Toraja in Sulawesi, and the Hindu-Buddhist monuments of Borobudur and Prambanan in Central Java have attracted huge numbers of visitors. On the other hand, much of the country remains barely touched by mass tourism, despite great improvements in communications and transport connections. Indonesia's thousands of islands and myriad

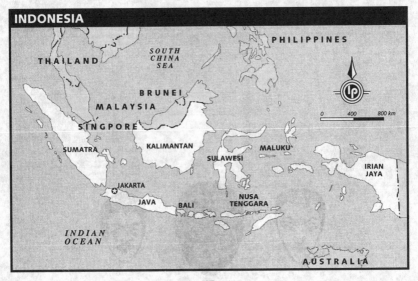

cultures offer adventure that is hard to find in the modern world.

In the wake of the economic and political turmoil following the downfall of Soeharto, tourism plummeted everywhere except Bali. Despite TV images of the Jakarta riots that rocked the world, most of Indonesia goes on as normal. All the attractions are still there but the currency devaluation means that they can be experienced for a fraction of the price.

Indonesia possesses some of the most remarkable sights in South-East Asia and there are things about this country you will never forget: the flaming red and orange sunsets over the mouth of the Sungai Kapuas (Kapuas River) in Kalimantan; standing on the summit of Kelimutu in Flores and gazing at the coloured lakes filling its volcanic craters; the lumbering leather-skinned dragons of Komodo; the funeral ceremonies of the Toraja in the highlands of Central Sulawesi; the Dani tribesmen of Irian Jaya wearing little more than feathers and penis gourds; the wooden *wayang golek* puppets manipulated into life by the puppet-masters of Yogyakarta; and the brilliant coral reefs off Manado on the north coast of Sulawesi.

You can relax on Kuta Beach in Bali, paddle a canoe down the rivers of Kalimantan, surf at Nias off the coast of Sumatra, trek in the high country of Irian Jaya, eat your way through a kaleidoscope of fruit from one end of the archipelago to the other, stare down the craters of live volcanoes, learn the art of batik in Yogyakarta, or kite-making from any Indonesian kid – almost anything you want, Indonesia has it.

Facts about Indonesia

HISTORY
Prehistory

The Indonesian archipelago was first inhabited by *Pithecanthropus erectus*, or Java Man, one of the earliest human ancestors that migrated via land bridges to Java at least one million years ago. Java Man became extinct or mingled with later migrations, as the people of Indonesia today are of Malay origin – closely related to the peoples of Malaysia and the Philippines – and are descendants of much later migrations from South-East Asia that began around 4000 BC.

The Dongson culture, which originated in Vietnam and southern China about 3000 years ago, spread to Indonesia, bringing with it techniques of irrigated rice growing, ritual buffalo sacrifice, bronze casting, the custom of erecting large monumental stones and some of the peculiar *ikat* weaving methods found in pockets of Indonesia today. Some of these practices have survived only in isolated areas which were little touched by later arrivals and cultural currents – such as the Batak areas of Sumatra, Tana Toraja in Sulawesi, parts of Kalimantan and several islands of Nusa Tenggara.

From the 7th century BC there were well developed and organised societies in the Indonesian archipelago. The inhabitants knew how to irrigate rice fields, domesticate animals, use copper and bronze, and were noted seafarers. There were villages – often permanent ones – where life was linked to the production of rice, the staple crop.

Early Indonesians were animists, believing that all animate and inanimate objects have their own particular *semangat* (life force or soul). The spirits of the dead had to be honoured because their semangat could still help the living; there was a belief in the afterlife, and weapons and utensils would be left in tombs for use in the next world. Supernatural forces were held responsible for natural events, and evil spirits had to be placated by offerings, rites and ceremonies.

Villages, at least in Java, developed into embryonic towns and, by the 1st century AD, small kingdoms (little more than collections of villages subservient to petty chieftains) evolved with their own ethnic and tribal religions. The climate of Java, with its hot, even temperature, plentiful rainfall and volcanic soil, was ideal for the wet-field method of rice cultivation known as *sawah* cultivation. The well organised society it required may explain why the people of Java developed a seemingly more sophisticated civilisation than those of the other islands. The dry-field, or *ladang*, method of rice cultivation is a much simpler form of agriculture and requires no elaborate social structure.

Coming of Hinduism & Buddhism

The oldest works of Hindu art in Indonesia, statues from the 3rd century AD, come from Sulawesi and Sumatra. The earliest Hindu inscriptions, in Sanskrit, have been found in West Java and eastern Kalimantan, and date from the early 5th century AD.

How Hinduism and Buddhism came to Indonesia remains a topic of speculation. One likely theory holds that the developing courts invited Brahman priests from India to advise on spirituality and ritual, thereby providing occult powers and a mythological sanction for the new Indonesian rulers. In the Hindu period the kings were seen as incarnations of Vishnu.

Another factor was undoubtedly trade. Traders from South India, the conduit for Hinduism, established early contact and provided Indonesia's main link with the outside world. Indonesia's strategic position on the sea lanes between India and China meant that trade between the two main Asian civilisations was firmly established in Indonesia by the 1st century AD. Though Indonesia had its own products to trade, such as spices, gold and benzoin (an aromatic gum particularly valued by the

Chinese), it owed its growing importance to its position at the crossroads of trade.

Early Kingdoms

The Sumatran Hindu-Buddhist kingdom of Sriwijaya rose in the 7th century AD and maintained a substantial international trade – run by Tamils and Chinese. It was the first major Indonesian commercial sea power, able to control much of the trade in South-East Asia by virtue of its strategic position on the Straits of Melaka between Sumatra and the Malay peninsula.

Merchants from Arabia, Persia and India brought goods to the coastal cities in exchange for goods from China and for local products, such as spices from the spice islands of Maluku (the Moluccas) in the eastern archipelago.

Meanwhile, the Buddhist Sailendra and the Hindu Mataram dynasties flourished on the plains of Central Java between the 8th and 10th centuries. While Sriwijaya's trade brought it wealth, these land-based states had far more human labour at their disposal and left magnificent remains, particularly the vast Buddhist monument at Borobudur and the huge Hindu temple complex at Prambanan.

Thus two types of states evolved in Indonesia. The first, typified by Sriwijaya, were the mainly Sumatran coastal states – commercially oriented, their wealth derived from international trade and their cities highly cosmopolitan. In contrast, the inland kingdoms of Java, separated from the sea by volcanoes (like the kingdom of Mataram in the Sungai Solo (Solo River) region), were agrarian cultures – bureaucratic and conservative, with a marked capacity to absorb and transform the Indian influences.

By the end of the 10th century the monuments at Borobudur and Prambanan were abandoned and Mataram mysteriously declined. The centre of power shifted from Central to East Java, where a series of kingdoms held sway until the rise of the Majapahit kingdom. This is the period when Hinduism and Buddhism were syncretised, and when Javanese culture began to come

into its own, finally spreading its influence to Bali. By the 12th century Sriwijaya's power had declined, and the empire broke up into smaller kingdoms.

Hindu Majapahit Kingdom

One of the greatest Indonesian states and the last great Hindu kingdom was the Majapahit. Founded in East Java in 1294, Majapahit grew to prominence during the reign of Hayam Wuruk, though its territorial expansion can be credited to its brilliant military commander, Gajah Mada. Gajah Mada put down an anti-royalist revolt in the 1320s, and then brought parts of Java and other areas under control. Majapahit went on to claim control over much of the archipelago, extracting trading rights and suzerainty from smaller kingdoms.

Hayam Wuruk's reign is usually referred to as an Indonesian golden age, comparable with the Tang dynasty of China. One account, by the court poet Prapanca, credits the Majapahits with control over much of the coastal regions of Sumatra, Borneo, Sulawesi, Maluku, Sumbawa and Lombok, and also states that the island of Timor sent tribute. Such claims are greatly exaggerated, but the kingdom is said to have maintained regular relations with China, Vietnam, Cambodia, Annam and Siam. However, after Hayam

Gajah Mada assumed virtual leadership of the Mahajapit kingdom from 1336.

Wuruk's death in 1389, the kingdom rapidly declined and the coastal dependencies in northern Java were in revolt.

Spread of Islam

Islam first took hold in north Sumatra, where traders from Gujarat (a state in western India) stopped en route to Maluku and China. Settlements of Arab traders were established in the latter part of the 7th century, and in 1292 Marco Polo noted that the inhabitants of the town of Perlak (present-day Aceh) in Sumatra's northern tip had been converted to Islam.

The first Muslim inscriptions found in Java date to the 11th century, and there may even have been Muslims in the Majapahit court at the zenith of its power in the mid-14th century. But it was not until the 15th and 16th centuries that Indonesian rulers turned to Islam, making it a state religion. It was then superimposed on the mixture of Hinduism and indigenous animist beliefs to produce the peculiar hybrid religion that predominates in much of Indonesia, especially Java, today.

By the time of Majapahit's final collapse at the beginning of the 16th century, many of its old satellite kingdoms had declared themselves independent Muslim states. Much of their wealth was based on their position as transhipment points for the growing spice trade with India and China. Islam spread across the archipelago from west to east, following the trade routes. It was, at least initially, a peaceful transformation, but once established it was carried further by the sword.

Rise of Melaka & Makassar

By the 15th century the centre of power in the archipelago had moved to the Malay peninsula, where the trading kingdom of Melaka (also spelt Malacca) was reaching the height of its power and had embraced Islam. The rise of Melaka, and of trading cities along the north coast of Java, coincided with the spread of Islam through the archipelago. The Melaka kingdom controlled the trading lanes of the Melaka Straits, and gathered the ports of northern Java within its commercial orbit. By the 16th century it was the principal port of the region.

By the end of the 16th century, a sea power had risen in the Indonesian archipelago – the twin principalities of Makassar and Gowa in south-western Sulawesi. These regions had been settled by Malay traders who also sailed to Maluku and beyond. In 1607 when Torres sailed through the strait which now bears his name, he met Makassar Muslims in western New Guinea. Other Makassar fleets visited the northern Australian coast over several hundred years, introducing the Aborigines to metal tools, pottery and tobacco.

Arrival of the Portuguese

When the first Europeans arrived in the Indonesian archipelago they found a varying collection of principalities and kingdoms. These kingdoms were occasionally at war with each other, but were also linked by the substantial inter-island and international trade, over which successive powerful kingdoms – Sriwijaya, Majapahit and Melaka – had been able to exert control by virtue of their position or sea power.

Marco Polo and a few early missionary travellers aside, the first Europeans to visit Indonesia were the Portuguese. Vasco de Gama had led the first European ships around the Cape of Good Hope to Asia in 1498; by 1510 the Portuguese had captured Goa on the west coast of India and then pushed on to South-East Asia. They came seeking to dominate the valuable spice trade in Maluku. Under Alfonso d'Albuquerque they captured Melaka in 1511, and the following year arrived in Maluku.

Portuguese control of trade in Indonesia was based on their fortified bases, such as Melaka, and on their superior firepower at sea. This allowed them to exercise a precarious control over the strategic trading ports that stretched from Maluku to Melaka, Macau, Goa, Mozambique and Angola.

Soon other European nations sent ships to the region in search of wealth – notably the Spanish, then the Dutch and English. By the time these new forces appeared on the horizon, the Portuguese had suffered a military defeat at Ternate and, though they had taken Melaka, they could not control trade in the region. Islamic Banten became the main port in the region, attracting Muslim merchants such as Arabs, Persians and Gujaratis away from Melaka. Of the newcomers, it was the Dutch who would eventually lay the foundations of the Indonesian state we know today.

Coming of the Dutch

A disastrous expedition of four Dutch ships, led by Cornelius de Houtman in 1596 lost half its crew, killed a Javanese prince and lost a ship in the process. Nevertheless, it returned to The Dutch Republic (Holland) with boat loads of spices that made a profit for the expedition's backers, and soon others followed.

Recognising the potential of the East Indies trade, the Dutch government amalgamated the competing merchant companies into the United East India Company or Vereenigde Oost-Indische Compagnie (VOC). This government monopoly soon became the main competitor in the bid to secure the spice trade.

The intention was to create a force to bring military pressure to bear on the Portuguese and the Spanish. Dutch trading ships were replaced by heavily armed fleets with instructions to attack Portuguese bases. By 1605 the Dutch had defeated the Portuguese at Tidore and Ambon, and occupied the territory themselves.

The Dutch then looked for a base closer to the important shipping lanes of the Melaka and Sunda straits. The ruler of Jayakarta (present-day Jakarta) in West Java granted permission for the Dutch to build a warehouse in 1610, but he also granted the English trading rights. The Dutch warehouse became a fort, and as relations between the Dutch and the English came to the boil, skirmishes resulted in a siege of the fort by the English and the Jayakartans. The Dutch retaliated, razing

THE MALAY ARCHIPELAGO, ALFRED WALLACE

An early 19th century sketch of Dobo in the Aru Islands, Maluku, then under Dutch control.

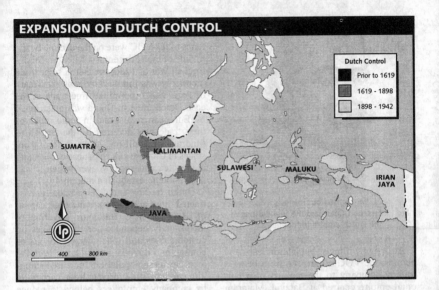

EXPANSION OF DUTCH CONTROL

Dutch Control
- Prior to 1619
- 1619 - 1898
- 1898 - 1942

SUMATRA

KALIMANTAN

SULAWESI

MALUKU

IRIAN JAYA

JAVA

0   400   800 km

the town in 1619. They renamed their new headquarters Batavia.

Foundation of a Dutch Empire

The founder of the Dutch Empire in the Dutch East Indies was Jan Pieterszoon Coen, an imaginative but ruthless man. Among his 'achievements' was the near-total extermination of the indigenous population of the Banda Islands in Maluku. Coen developed a grandiose plan to make Batavia, his capital in Java, the centre of intra-Asian trade from Japan to Persia, and to develop the spice plantations using Burmese, Madagascan and Chinese labourers.

While the more grandiose plans were rejected, he was instrumental in realising Dutch plans to monopolise the spice trade. An alliance with the sultan of Ternate in Maluku in 1607 gave the Dutch control over the production of cloves, and their occupation of the Bandas from 1609-21 gave them control of the nutmeg trade.

The capture of Melaka from the Portuguese in 1641 completed the Dutch mastery of the seas in the region. The spice trade monopoly was supplemented by important trade from China. South-East Asia had become the great trading bazaar of the east, the crossroads for trade between India and China.

Batavia lived in constant fear of attack in its early years, but by the mid-16th century it was an important centre of trade after successfully repelling attacks from the Mataram empire of Central Java. The Dutch defeated Makassar in 1667 and secured a monopoly over its trade, and eventually brought the Sumatran ports under their sway. The last of the Portuguese were expelled in 1660. At Banten in 1680, the Dutch helped the ruler's ambitious son to overthrow his father in return for a monopoly over the pepper trade and expulsion of the British.

The VOC's policy at this stage was to keep to its trading posts and to avoid expensive territorial conquests. An accord with the *susuhunan* (king) of Mataram, the dominant kingdom in Java, was established. It permitted only Dutch ships, or those with permission from the VOC, to trade with the spice islands and the regions beyond.

Far-sighted but ruthless,
Jan Pieterszoon Coen laid the foundations of
the Dutch empire in Indonesia.

At first unwillingly, but later in leaps and bounds, the VOC progressed from being a trading company to the masters of a colonial empire centred at Batavia. Mataram declined after the death of its greatest leader, Sultan Agung (1613-46); while warring principalities and court intrigues allowed the Dutch to persue a successful 'divide and rule' strategy.

Java was beset by wars from the end of the 17th century as Mataram fragmented. The VOC were only too willing to lend military support to contenders to the throne, in return for compensation and land concessions. The death knell for Mataram followed the Third Javanese War of Succession (1746-57), when Prince Mangkubumi and Mas Said contested the throne of the susuhunan, Pakubuwono II, largely because of his concessions and capitulation to Dutch demands.

In 1755 the Dutch split the Mataram kingdom into two – Yogyakarta and Surakarta (Solo). These new states and the other smaller states in Java were only nominally sovereign; in reality they were dominated by the VOC. Fighting among the princes was halted, and peace was brought to East Java by the forced cessation of invasions and raids from Bali.

Thus Java was finally united under a foreign trading company with an army comprising only 1000 Europeans and 2000 Asians.

Decline of the VOC

Despite some dramatic successes, the fortunes of the VOC were on the decline by the middle of the 18th century. After the Dutch-English War of 1780, the Dutch spice trade monopoly was finally broken by the Treaty of Paris which permitted free trade in the east. Dutch trade in China was outstripped by European rivals, and in India much of their trade was diverted by the British to Madras. In addition, trade shifted from spices to Chinese silk, Japanese copper, and coffee, tea and sugar – over which it was impossible to establish a monopoly.

Dutch trading interests gradually contracted more and more around their capital of Batavia. The Batavian government increasingly depended for its finances on customs dues and tolls charged for goods coming into Batavia, and on taxes from the local Javanese population. Increased smuggling and the illicit private trade carried on by company employees helped to reduce profits. The mounting expense of wars within Java and of administering the additional territory acquired after each new treaty also played a part in the decline.

The VOC turned to the Dutch government at home for support, and the subsequent investigation of VOC affairs revealed corruption, mismanagement and bankruptcy. In 1799 the VOC was formally wound up, its territorial possessions became the property of the Dutch government and the trading empire became a colonial empire.

British Occupation & the Java War

In 1811, during the Napoleonic Wars when France occupied Holland, the British occupied several Dutch East Indies posts, including Java. Control was restored to the Dutch in 1816, and a treaty was signed in 1824 under which the British exchanged their Indonesian settlements (such as Bengkulu in Sumatra) for Dutch holdings in India and the Malay peninsula. While the two European powers may have settled their differences to their own satisfaction, the Indonesians were of another mind. There were a number of wars and disturbances in various parts of the archipelago during the early 19th century, but the most prolonged struggles were the Paderi War in Sumatra (1821-38) and the famous Java War (1825-30) led by Prince Diponegoro. In one sense the Java War was yet another war of succession, but both wars are notable because Islam became the symbol of opposition to the Dutch.

In 1814 Diponegoro, the eldest son of the Sultan of Yogya, had been passed over for succession to the throne in favour of a younger claimant who had the support of the British. Having bided his time, Diponegoro eventually vanished from court and in 1825 launched a guerrilla war against the Dutch. The courts of Yogya and Solo largely remained loyal to the Dutch but many of the Javanese aristocracy supported the rebellion. Diponegoro had received mystical signs that convinced him that he was the divinely appointed future king of Java. News spread among the people that he was the long-prophesied Ratu Adil, the prince who would free them from colonial oppression.

The rebellion finally ended in 1830 when the Dutch tricked Diponegoro into peace negotiations, arrested him and exiled him to Sulawesi. The five year war had cost the lives of 8000 European and 7000 Indonesian soldiers of the Dutch army. At least 200,000 Javanese died, most from famine and disease, and the population of Yogyakarta was halved.

Dutch Exploitation of Indonesia

For 350 years, from the time the first Dutch ships arrived in 1596 to the declaration of independence in 1945, Dutch rule was always tenuous. Throughout the 17th century the VOC, with its superior arms and Buginese and Ambonese mercenaries, fought everywhere in the islands. Despite Dutch domination of Java, many areas of the archipelago – including Aceh, Bali, Lombok and Borneo – remained independent throughout this time.

Fighting continued to flare up in Sumatra and Java, and between 1846 and 1849 expeditions were sent to Bali in the first attempts to subjugate the island. In southeastern Borneo, the violent Banjarmasin War saw the Dutch defeat the reigning sultan. The longest and most devastating war was in Aceh, which lasted 35 years from the Dutch invasion in 1873 until the Aceh guerrilla leaders eventually surrendered in 1908.

Even into the 20th century, Dutch control outside Java was still incomplete. Large-scale Indonesian piracy continued right up until the middle of the 19th century, and the Dutch fought a war in Sulawesi against the Buginese. Dutch troops occupied southwestern Sulawesi between 1900 and 1910, and Bali in 1906. The Bird's Head Peninsula of West Irian did not come under Dutch administration until 1919-20.

The concerted exploitation of Indonesian resources by the Dutch really only began in 1830. The cost of the Java and Paderi wars meant that despite increased returns from the Dutch system of land tax, Dutch finances were severely strained. When the Dutch lost Belgium in 1830, the home country itself faced bankruptcy and any government investment in the East Indies *had* to make quick returns. From here on Dutch economic policy in Indonesia falls into three overlapping periods: the period of the so-called 'Culture System'; the Liberal Period; and the Ethical Period.

JENNY BOWMAN

Prince Diponegoro, the leader of a bloody guerilla war against the Dutch from 1825-30.

Throughout all three periods, the exploitation of Indonesia's wealth contributed to the industrialisation of the Netherlands. Large areas of Java became plantations whose products, cultivated by Javanese peasants and collected by Chinese intermediaries, were sold on the overseas markets by European merchants. Before WWII, Indonesia supplied most of the world's quinine and pepper, over a third of its rubber, a quarter of its coconut products, and almost a fifth of its tea, sugar, coffee and oil. Indonesia made the Netherlands one of the major colonial powers.

Culture System A new governor-general, Johannes Van den Bosch, fresh from experiences of the slave labour of the West Indies, was appointed in 1830 to make the East Indies pay their way. He succeeded by introducing a new agricultural policy called the Cultuurstelsel, or Culture System. It was a system of government-controlled agriculture or, as Indonesian historians refer to it, Tanam Paksa (Compulsory Planting).

Instead of land taxes, peasants had to either cultivate government-owned crops on 20% of their land or work in the government plantations for nearly 60 days of the year. Much of Java became a Dutch plantation, generating great wealth in the Netherlands.

For the Javanese peasantry, this forced-labour system brought hardship and resentment. Forced to grow crops such as indigo and sugar instead of rice, famine and epidemics swept Java in the 1840s, first at Cirebon in 1843 and then Central Java. In strong contrast, the Culture System was a boon to the Dutch and the Javanese aristocracy. The profits made Java a self-sufficient colony and saved the Netherlands from bankruptcy.

Liberal Period Public opinion in the Netherlands began to decry the treatment and suffering of Indonesians under the colonial government. The so-called Liberal Policy was introduced by liberals in the Dutch parliament in an attempt to reform and eliminate the excesses of the Culture System.

Agrarian reform in 1870 freed producers from the compulsion to provide export crops but opened the Indies to private enterprise, which developed large plantations. As the population increased dramatically, especially in Java, less land was available for rice production, bringing further hardship. Dutch profits grew dramatically in the latter part of the 19th century.

Sugar production doubled between 1870 and 1885, new crops like tea and cinchona (a medicinal bark which yields quinine) flourished, and rubber was introduced. At the same time, oil produced in south Sumatra and Kalimantan became a valuable export – a response to the new industrial demands of the European market.

The exploitation of Indonesian resources was no longer limited to Java but had filtered through to the other islands. As Dutch commercial interests expanded, so did the need to protect them. More and more territory was taken under direct control of the Dutch government, and most of the outer islands came under firm Dutch sovereignty.

Ethical Period The 20th century heralded a new approach to colonial government as the Ethical Policy was introduced in 1901. Under this policy it became the Dutch government's duty to further the welfare of the Indonesian people in health, education and other social programs. Direct government control was exerted on the outer islands, most of which appeared as Dutch territory on the map; in fact these regions had been left to go about their business, free of colonial control. Minor rebellions broke out everywhere from Sumatra to Timor, but were easily crushed as the Dutch assumed control from traditional leaders, establishing a true Indies empire for the first time.

New policies were to be implemented, foremost among them irrigation, transmigration (transmigrasi) from heavily populated Java to lightly populated islands, and education. There were also plans for improved communications, agriculture, flood control, drainage, health programs, industrialisation and the protection of native industry. Other policies aimed for the decentralisation of authority with greater autonomy for the Indonesian government, as well as greater power to local government units within the archipelago.

The humanitarian policies were laudable but ultimately inadequate. Increases in public health expenditure were simply not enough. While education possibilities for Indonesians increased, the vast majority of Indonesians were illiterate. Though primary schools were established and education was open to all, by 1930 only 8% of school age children received an education. Industrialisation was never seriously implemented, and Indonesia remained an agricultural colony.

Indonesian Nationalism

Though the Ethical Period failed to deliver widespread educational opportunities, it did provide a Dutch education for the children of the Indonesian elite, largely to supply clerical labour for the growing bureaucracy. Western education brought with it western political ideas of freedom and democracy, but the first seeds of Indonesian nationalism were sown by the Islamic movements.

Sarekat Islam was an early, pre-modern nationalist movement, inspired more by Islamic and Javanese mysticism than by notions of independent self-rule. It rallied Indonesians under the traditional banner of Islam, in opposition to Dutch influence, but had no national agenda and was often more anti-Chinese than anti-colonial.

The Indonesian Communist Party (PKI) on the other hand was a fully fledged, pro-independence party inspired by European politics. It was formed in 1920 and found support among workers in the industrial cities. The PKI presumptuously decided to start the revolution in Indonesia in 1926 with isolated insurrections across Java. The panicked and outraged Dutch government arrested and exiled thousands of Communists, effectively putting them out of action for the rest of the Dutch occupation.

Despite Dutch repression of nationalist organisations and the arrest of their leaders, the nationalist movement was finding a unified voice. In an historic announcement, the All Indonesia Youth Congress proclaimed its Youth Pledge in 1928, adopting the notions of the one fatherland (Indonesia), one united country and one language (Bahasa Indonesia). In Bandung in 1929, Achmed Soekarno founded the Partai Nasional Indonesia (PNI), the most significant nationalist organisation. It was the first all-Indonesia secular party devoted primarily to independence and not ideology.

Soekarno was educated in East Java and went on to receive a European education before studying at the Bandung Institute of Technology, where he was active in the Bandung Study Club. Bandung was a hotbed of political intellectualism, where the PKI and radical Muslim thought flowered. Soekarno was widely influenced by Javanese, western, Muslim and socialist ideals, and blended these various influences towards a national ideology.

Soekarno was soon arrested and a virtual ban placed on the PNI. Nationalist sentiment remained high in the 1930s, but with many nationalist leaders in jail or exiled, independence seemed a long way off. Even when Germany invaded the Netherlands in May 1940, the colonial government in exile was determined to continue its rule in the East Indies.

All was to change when the Japanese attacked Pearl Harbour and then stormed down through South-East Asia. After the fall of Singapore, many Europeans fled to Australia, and the colonial government abandoned Batavia, surrendering to the Japanese on 8 March 1942.

Japanese Occupation

The Japanese imperial army marched into Batavia on 5 March 1942, carrying the red-and-white Indonesian flag alongside that of the Japanese rising sun. The city's name was changed to Jakarta, Europeans were arrested and all signs of the former Dutch masters eliminated.

Though greeted initially as liberators, public opinion turned against the Japanese as the war wore on and Indonesians were expected to endure more hardship for the war effort. The Japanese were keen to impress their superiority on the Indonesian population and soon developed a reputation as cruel masters.

Undoubtedly though, the Japanese gave Indonesians more responsibility and participation in government. The very top administrative positions were held by Japanese, but Indonesians from the top down ruled themselves for the first time. The Japanese also gave prominence to nationalist leaders, such as Soekarno and Mohammed Hatta, and trained youth militias to defend the country. Apart from giving Indonesia a military

psyche that has endured in Indonesian politics, these militias gave rise to the *pemuda* (youth) of the independence movement who would later form the independence army.

Independence Struggle

As the war ended, the nationalist leadership of Soekarno and Hatta was in effect kidnapped and pressured by radical youth groups to immediately declare Indonesia's independence before the Dutch could return. On 17 August 1945, with tacit Japanese backing, Soekarno proclaimed the independence of the Republic of Indonesia from his Jakarta home.

Street Names & Indonesian Heroes

In every city, town and *kampung* (village) in Indonesia, streets (as well as airports, parks and so on) are named after Indonesian heroes who, invariably, helped fight the Dutch during the colonial period or after independence was declared by Indonesia in 1945. Some of the more well known are:

Cokroaminoto, HOS (1883-1934) was from East Java and helped establish the Islamic Federation, also known as the PSII.

Diponegoro, Pangeran (1785-1855) was a prince from Yogyakarta. He was a leader in the Java War of 1825-30 against the Dutch, during which he was captured, and later exiled to Ujung Pandang where he died.

Gajah Mada was prime minister and a brilliant military commander in the Javanese Majapahit kingdom in the 14th century. He helped defeat rebels who fought King Jayanegara (but Gajah Mada later arranged the king's murder because he took Gajah Mada's wife!).

Hasanuddin, Sultan (1631-70) was born in South Sulawesi and helped with the resistance against the Vereenigde Oost-Indische Compagnie (VOC).

Hatta, Mohammed (1902-80) was a Sumatran who was arrested in 1927 for promoting resistance against the Dutch. He was sent to the notorious prison, Boven Digul, and then to Banda, but was later released by the Japanese. On 17 August 1945, he declared Indonesian independence with Soekarno, and served as vice-president and/or prime minister from 1945 to 1956.

Imam Bonjol (1772-1864) was an important Islamic leader, as well as a leader of the resistance against the Dutch in the Paderi War of 1821-38. He was captured by the Dutch, sent to Ambon and then Manado.

Kartini, Raden Ajeng (1879-1905) was a Javanese writer and activist who became famous for her promotion of education and women's rights, especially through her letters, which were discovered after her death (see the boxed text 'Kartini' in the Java chapter).

Monginsidi, Wolter (1925-49) was captured and shot at only 24 years of age by the Dutch during the period of resistance.

Indonesians throughout the archipelago rejoiced, but the Netherlands refused to accept the proclamation and still claimed sovereignty over Indonesia. British troops entered Java in October 1945 to accept the surrender of the Japanese. Under British auspices, Dutch troops gradually returned to Indonesia and it became obvious that independence would have to be fought for.

Clashes broke out with the new Republican army, and came to a head in the bloody Battle for Surabaya. As Europeans and Dutch internees returned to the city, skirmishes developed with armed youth militia. The situation deteriorated when British Indian troops landed in the city. When General Mallaby, leader of the British forces, was killed by a bomb, the British launched a bloody retribution. On 10 November (now celebrated as 'Heroes Day') the British began to take the city under cover of air attacks. Thousands of Indonesians died as the population fled to the countryside, but though poorly armed, the numerous Republican forces fought a pitched battle for three weeks. The brutal retaliation of the British and the spirited defence of Surabaya by the Republicans galvanised Indonesian support and helped turn world opinion.

Street Names & Indonesian Heroes

Sisingamangaraja (1849-1907) was the last of a long line of Batak kings, who had ruled since the 16th century. His ancestors were spiritual leaders, but he became a leader of the resistance against the Dutch, which cost him his life.

Subroto, Gatot (1907-62) fought for Indonesian independence in the 1940s, and helped quell Communist rebels in 1948. He became Military Governor of Surakarta, then a general and later a member of Soeharto's early cabinet.

Sudarso, Yos (1925-62) was a senior naval officer who died when his ship, the *Macan Tutul*, was sunk by the Dutch during the liberation of Irian Jaya.

Sudirman (1916-50) was a leader of the resistance against the Dutch between 1945 and 1950. After independence, he was appointed General and Commander-in-Chief of the Indonesian Republic.

Supratman, WR (1903-38) composed the Indonesian national anthem, *Indonesia Raya*, which was first performed by Supratman at the 2nd Indonesian Youth Congress in 1928.

Syahrir, Sutan (1909-66), also referred to as Sjahrir, was a leading nationalist leader in Java in the 1930s, but was opposed to Soekarno. Syahrir was arrested by the Dutch, exiled to the prison Boven Digul, and later denounced the Japanese Occupation. He served as prime minister from 1945 to 1947, and was instrumental in obtaining former Dutch territories for the new Indonesia.

Thamrin, Mohammed (1894-1941) was a nationalist leader and politician in the 1920s and 1930s. He was arrested by the Dutch in 1941, after cooperating with the Japanese, and died soon after.

Yamin, Mohammed (1903-62) was a Sumatran writer, poet, lawyer and politician; he helped to form the Youth Pledge in 1928. He was arrested in 1946 by the Dutch, then became a cabinet minister and later the instigator of 'Guided Democracy'.

Yani, Ahmad (1922-65) was responsible for suppressing Sumatran rebels in 1958. He was commander of the 'liberation' of Irian Jaya three years later, and became Army Chief of Staff in 1962. He was among the six high-ranking generals killed in the ill-fated coup of September 1965, which was backed by elements of the armed forces.

The Dutch dream of easy reoccupation was shattered, while the British were keen to extricate themselves from military action and broker a peace agreement. The last British troops left at the end of November 1946, by which time 55,000 Dutch troops had landed in Java. In Bogor in Java and Balikpapan in Kalimantan, Indonesian republican officials were imprisoned. Bombing raids on Palembang and Medan in Sumatra prepared the way for the Dutch occupation of these cities. In southern Sulawesi, a Captain Westerling was accused of pacifying the region – by murdering 40,000 Indonesians in a few weeks. Elsewhere, the Dutch were attempting to form puppet states among the more amenable ethnic groups.

In Jakarta the republican government, with Soekarno as president and Hatta as vice-president, tried to maintain calm. On the other hand, youth groups advocating armed struggle saw the old leadership as prevaricating and betraying the revolution.

Outbreaks occurred across the country, and Soekarno and Hatta were outmanoeuvred in the Republican government. Sultan Syahrir became prime minister, and as the Dutch assumed control in Jakarta, the Republicans moved their capital to Yogyakarta. Sultan Hamengkubuwono IX, who was to become Yogyakarta's most revered and able sultan, played a leading role in the revolution. In Surakarta, on the other hand, Pakubuwono XII was ineffectual, to the detriment of Surakarta come independence.

The battle for independence wavered between warfare and diplomacy. Under the Linggarjati Agreement of November 1946, the Dutch recognised the Republican government and both sides agreed to work towards an Indonesian federation under a Dutch commonwealth. The agreement was soon swept aside as the war escalated. The Dutch mounted a large offensive in July 1947, causing the United Nations to step in.

During these uncertain times, the main forces in Indonesian politics regrouped. The PKI and Soekarno's old party, the PNI, reformed, while the main Islamic parties remained Masyumi and Nahdatul Ulama.

The army also emerged as a force, though it was split by many factions. The Republicans were far from united, and in Java, civil war threatened to erupt when the PKI staged a rebellion in Surakarta and then in Madiun. In a tense threat to the revolution, Soekarno galvanised opposition to the Communists, who were massacred by army forces.

In February 1948, the Dutch launched another full scale attack on the Republicans, breaking the UN agreement and turning world opinion. Under pressure from the USA, which threatened to withdraw its postwar aid to the Netherlands, and a growing realisation at home that this was an unwinnable war, the Dutch negotiated for independence. On 27 December 1949, the Indonesian flag, the *sang merah putih* (the Red and the White) was raised at Jakarta's Istana Merdeka (Freedom Palace) as power was officially handed over.

Economic Depression & Disunity

The threat of external attacks from the Dutch helped keep the nationalists united in the first years after the proclamation of independence. However, with the Dutch gone, the divisions in Indonesian society began to appear. Soekarno had tried to hammer out the principles of Indonesian unity in his Pancasila speech of 1945 (see the boxed text 'Pancasila – The Five Principles' in this chapter) and while these, as he said, may have been 'the highest common factor and the lowest common multiple of Indonesian thought', the divisive elements in Indonesian society could not be swept away by a single speech. Regional differences in *adat* (customs), morals, tradition, religion, the impact of Christianity and Marxism, and fears of political domination by the Javanese all contributed to disunity.

Separatist movements battled the new republic. They included the militant Darul Islam (Islamic Domain), which proclaimed an Islamic State of Indonesia and waged guerrilla warfare in West Java against the new Indonesian republic from 1949 to 1962. In Maluku, the Ambonese members of the former Royal Dutch Indies Army tried to establish an independent republic, and there were revolts in Minahasa (the northern limb of Sulawesi) and in Sumatra.

Against this background lay the sorry state of the new republic's economy, and divisions in the leadership elite. When the Republic of Indonesia came into being, the economy was in tatters after almost 10 years of Japanese occupation and war with the Dutch. The population was increasing and the new government was unable to boost production of food and other necessities to keep pace. Most of the population was illiterate, and there was a dearth of skilled workers and management. Inflation was chronic, smuggling cost the central government badly needed foreign currency, and many of the plantations had been destroyed during the war.

Political parties proliferated and deals between parties for a share of cabinet seats resulted in a rapid turnover of coalition governments. There were 17 cabinets for the period 1945 to 1958. The frequently postponed elections were finally held in 1955 and the PNI – regarded as Soekarno's party – topped the poll. There was also a dramatic increase in support for the PKI but no party managed more than a quarter of the votes and short-lived coalitions continued.

Soekarno Takes Over – Guided Democracy

By 1956, President Soekarno was openly criticising parliamentary democracy, stating that it was 'based upon inherent conflict' which ran counter to the Indonesian concept of harmony as the natural state of human relationships.

Soekarno sought a system based on the traditional village system of discussion and consensus, which occurred under the guidance of the village elders. He proposed a threefold division – nationalism *(nasionalisme)*, religion *(agaman)* and Communism *(komunisme)* – to be blended into a cooperative *'Nas-A-Kom'* government, thereby appeasing the three main factions of Indonesian political life – the army, Islamic groups and the Communists.

Soekarno, founder of the Indonesian Nationalist Party (PNI), first president of the Republic and father of 'guided democracy'.

In February 1957, with support from the military, Soekarno then proclaimed 'guided democracy' and proposed a cabinet representing all the political parties of importance (including the PKI). Western-style democracy was finished in Indonesia, though the parties were not abolished.

Sumatra & Sulawesi Rebellions

Clashes broke out in Sumatra and Sulawesi in 1958 as a reaction against Soekarno's usurpation of power, the growing influence of the PKI, and the corruption, inefficiency and mismanagement of the central government. There were also rebellions against Java, whose leaders and interests dominated Indonesia, despite the fact that the other islands provided most of the country's export income.

The rebellions were effectively smashed by mid-1958, though guerrilla activity continued for three years. Rebel leaders were granted amnesty, but their political parties were banned and some of the early nationalist leaders were discredited. Syahrir and others were arrested in 1962.

Soekarno was now able to exercise enormous personal influence and set about re-organising the political system in order to give himself *real* power. In 1960 the elected parliament was dissolved, and replaced by a parliament appointed by, and subject to, the will of the president. The Supreme Advisory Council, another non-elected body, became the chief policy-making body and the National Front was set up in September 1960 to 'mobilise the revolutionary forces of the people'. The Front was presided over by the president and became a useful adjunct to the government in organising 'demonstrations', such as sacking embassies during the period of 'Confrontation' with Malaysia.

Soekarno – Revolution & Nationalism

With his assumption of power, Soekarno set Indonesia on a course of stormy nationalism. His speeches were those of a romantic revolutionary. They held his people spellbound, uniting them against a common external threat. *Konfrontasi* became the buzz word as Indonesia confronted Malaysia (and their imperialist backers, the UK), the USA and indeed the whole western world.

Soekarno was popularly referred to as *bung* (older brother), a man of the people who carried the dreams and aspirations of his nation and dared to take on the west.

Soekarno is best remembered for his flamboyance and his contradictions. Abstinence, monogamy and temperance were conspicuously undervalued by Soekarno. He was a noted womaniser, claimed to be a pious Muslim and also a Marxist, yet he was also very much a mystic in the Javanese tradition. His contradictions were those of his nation, which he somehow held together through the force of his oratory and personality.

Economic Deterioration

What Soekarno could not do was create a viable economic system that would lift Indonesia out of its poverty. Soekarno's corrosive vanity burnt money on a spate of status symbols meant to symbolise the new Indonesian identity. They included the Merdeka (Freedom) Monument, Jakarta's Istiqlal mosque (reputedly the biggest in South-East Asia), and a vast sports stadium, Senayan, built with Russian money. Unable to advance beyond revolution to the next stage of rebuilding, Soekarno's monuments became substitutes for real development.

Richard Nixon, who became the US president in 1968, visited Indonesia in 1953 and presented this image of Indonesia under Soekarno:

> In no other country we visited was the conspicuous luxury of the ruler in such striking contrast to the poverty and misery of his people. Jakarta was a collection of sweltering huts and hovels. An open sewer ran through the heart of the city, but Soekarno's palace was painted a spotless white and set in the middle of hundreds of acres of exotic gardens. One night we ate off gold plate to the light of a thousand torches while musicians played on the shore of a lake covered with white lotus blossoms and candles floating on small rafts.

Soekarno's increased authority also resulted in a more aggressive stance on foreign affairs. Soekarno believed that Asia had been humiliated by the west and he sought recognition for a 'nation of coolies and a coolie amongst nations'. From Soekarno's view, Indonesia was surrounded and threatened by the remnants of western imperialism: the British and their new client state of Malaysia; the hated Dutch who continued to occupy West Irian (now Irian Jaya); and the Americans and their military bases in the Philippines.

First on the agenda was West Irian, which Indonesia had claimed in August 1945. An arms agreement with the Soviet Union in 1960 enabled the Indonesians to begin a diplomatic and military confrontation with the Dutch over West Irian, though US pressure on the Dutch finally led to the Indonesian takeover in 1963.

In the same year, Indonesia embarked on Confrontation with the new nation of Malaysia. The northern states in Borneo, which bordered on Indonesian Kalimantan, wavered in their desire to join Malaysia. Indonesia saw itself as the rightful leader of the Malay peoples and supported an attempted revolution in Brunei. Soekarno railed against British imperialism and revived the glories of Indonesia's revolution. The army increased its budget and mounted offensives along the Kalimantan-Malaysia border, and the PKI demonstrated in the streets in Jakarta. The west became increasingly alarmed at Indonesian foreign policy.

Confrontation took the spotlight, but Indonesia's main concerns were economic. Foreign aid dried up after the USA withdrew its aid because of Confrontation. The cash-strapped government abolished subsidies in several areas of the public sector, leading to massive increases in public transport, electricity, water and postal charges. Economic plans had failed miserably and inflation was running at 500%.

Soekarno, the Army & the Communists

Though Soekarno often talked as if he held absolute power, his position depended on maintaining a balance between the different political powers in Indonesia, primarily the army and the PKI. Soekarno is often described as the great *dalang*, or puppet master, who balanced the forces of the left and right just as competing forces are balanced in the Javanese shadow puppet shows.

Confrontation alienated western nations, and Indonesia came to depend more on support from the Soviet Union, then increasingly from Communist China. Meanwhile, tensions grew between the Indonesian Army and its mortal enemy, the PKI.

By 1965, the three million-strong PKI was the largest Communist Party in the world, other than those in the Soviet Union and China. Affiliate organisations of the PKI claimed membership of 20 million. Except for the inner cabinet, it penetrated the government apparatus extensively.

After the success of the PKI in the 1955 election, Soekarno realised that he had to give it prominence in his guided democracy government. Increasingly the PKI gained influence ahead of the army, which had been the main power base of Indonesian politics since independence.

Guided democracy under Soekarno was marked by an attempt to give the peasants better social conditions, but attempts to give tenant farmers a fairer share of their rice crops and to redistribute land led to more confusion. The PKI pushed for reforms and encouraged peasants to seize land without waiting for decisions from land-reform committees. In 1964 these tactics led to violent clashes in Central and East Java, and Bali.

The pressure increased in 1965 with growing tension between the PKI and the army. In a visit to Jakarta in April 1965, Zhou Enlai (the then Premier of China) proposed a 'fifth force' – an armed people's militia independent of the four branches of the armed forces (the army, navy, air force and police). Soekarno supported this proposal to arm the Communists, the army opposed it, and rumours of an army takeover became rife in Jakarta.

Slaughter of the Communists

On the night of 30 September 1965, six of Indonesia's top generals were taken from their Jakarta homes and executed in an attempted coup. Led by Colonel Untung of the palace guard and backed by elements of the armed forces, they took up positions around the presidential palace and later seized the national radio station. The coup group claimed they had acted against a plot organised by the generals to overthrow the president.

This bumbling exercise appears to have had little or no coordination with revolt in the rest of Java, let alone the rest of the archipelago. Within a few hours of the coup, General Soeharto, head of the army's Strategic Reserve, was able to mobilise army forces to take counteraction. By the evening of 1 October, the coup had clearly failed.

Exactly who had organised the coup and what it had set out to achieve remains shrouded in mystery. The Indonesian army asserted that the PKI plotted the coup and used discontented army officers to carry it out. Other theories are that it was primarily an internal army affair, led by younger officers against the older leadership. And then there are those who believe that Soekarno himself was behind the coup – and yet another story that Soeharto was in the confidence of the conspirators.

Certainly, civilians from the PKI's People's Youth organisation accompanied the army battalions that seized the generals, but whatever the PKI's real role in the coup, the effect on its fortunes was devastating.

Soeharto orchestrated a counter coup, and an anti-Communism purge swept Indonesia. Hundreds of thousands of Communists and their sympathisers were slaughtered or imprisoned, primarily in Java and Bali. The party and its affiliates were banned and its leaders were killed, imprisoned or went into hiding. Estimates of the death toll vary widely. Adam Malik, who was to become Foreign Minister under Soeharto, said that a 'fair figure' was 160,000. Independent commentators estimate the figure to be closer to 500,000.

Following the army's lead, anti-Communist civilians went on the rampage. In Java, where long-simmering tensions between pro-Muslim and pro-Communist factions erupted in the villages, both sides believed that their opponents had drawn up death lists to be carried out when they achieved power. The anti-Communists, with encouragement from the government, carried out their list of executions. On top of this uncontrolled slaughter, perhaps 250,000 people were arrested and sent to prison camps for alleged involvement with the coup.

Soekarno's Fall & Soeharto's Rise

Soeharto took over leadership of the armed forces and set about manoeuvring Soekarno from power. Soekarno continued as president, maintaining that he was still in charge. Meanwhile the army-orchestrated campaign of killings in the countryside was accompanied by violent demonstrations in Jakarta between Soekarnoists and anti-Soekarnoists.

Despite the chaos, Soekarno still had supporters in all the armed forces and it seemed unlikely that he would topple. Then on 11 March 1966, after troops loyal to Soeharto surrounded the Presidential Palace, Soekarno signed the 11 March Order giving Soeharto the power to restore order. While always deferring to the name of Soekarno, Soeharto rapidly consolidated his power. The PKI was officially banned. Pro-Soekarno soldiers and officers and a number of cabinet ministers

The head of 'Soeharto Family Inc' – after more than 30 years in power, Soeharto was forced to resign as president in 1998.

were arrested. A new six-man inner cabinet, including Soeharto and two of his nominees, Adam Malik and Sultan Hamengkubuwono of Yogyakarta, was formed.

Soeharto then launched a campaign of intimidation to blunt any grassroots opposition to his power. Thousands of public servants were dismissed as PKI sympathisers, putting thousands more in fear of losing their jobs.

By 1967 Soeharto was firmly enough entrenched to finally cut Soekarno adrift. The People's Consultative Congress, after the arrest of many of its members and the infusion of Soeharto appointees, relieved Soekarno of all power and elected Soeharto acting president. On 27 March 1968 it 'elected' Soeharto as president.

The New Order

Under Soeharto's 'New Order' government, Indonesia looked to the west in foreign policy, and western-educated economists set about balancing budgets, controlling inflation and attracting foreign investment.

In 1971 general elections were held to give a veneer of democracy to the new regime. Soeharto used the almost defunct Golkar Party as the spearhead of the army's election campaign. Soeharto having appointed his election squad, the old parties were then crippled by being banned, by the

army killings in Aceh and the abduction and murder of opposition activists.

As the government stalled on announcing an election date, it became obvious that it was also stalling on full political reform, preferring to keep democracy within the framework of the old system. The students returned to the streets, demanding elections and Habibie's resignation.

As IMF money flowed into Indonesia, the currency strengthened, but widespread poverty resulted in continuing food riots. People sold their meagre possessions to buy food, while others simply took it, and in uncertain times, old grudges resurfaced. The Chinese continued to be the main scapegoats, while in East Java, bizarre serial killings of black magicians and Muslim clerics claimed the lives of over 200 people. See the boxed text 'Ninja Killers' in the Java chapter.

Student protests came to a head again in November 1998, when thousands rallied as the Indonesian parliament met to discuss terms for the new election. Student demands for immediate elections and the abolition of military appointees to parliament were ignored.

Tension on the streets of Jakarta was fuelled by thousands of pro-government youth militia employed by the authorities. The military, with presidential orders to crack down on dissent, did just that. Three days of skirmishes peaked on 13 November when a student march on parliament was met by military force and gunfire. Clashes left 12 dead and hundreds injured. Jakarta again was in flames, as shopping centres and Chinese businesses were looted and burnt by Jakarta *preman* (thugs) and other opportunists.

Before the smoke had settled, new disturbances in Jakarta took on an even more worrying trend. A local dispute involving Christians from Maluku resulted in Muslims rampaging through the Ketapang district of Jakarta burning churches. Christians throughout Indonesia were outraged, and in eastern Indonesia, Christians attacked mosques and the minority Muslim community. Riots in Kupang, West Timor, were followed by prolonged Muslim/Christian violence in Maluku province and then in Kalimantan in early 1999.

Java, which had seen the majority of violence at the onset of the economic crisis, returned to relative order while the outlying areas of Indonesia erupted. The real possibility of independence from a weakened Jakarta, also saw renewed trouble in the separatist-minded regions of Aceh, Irian Jaya and East Timor.

Moves to reach a resolution for East Timor came in early 1999, when after a continual refusal to grant autonomy, let alone independence, President Habibie did an about turn. Indonesia prepared a ballot, overseen by UN observers, with the choice of autonomy or independence. Despite these laudable moves by Jakarta, pro-integration militia launched a bloody campaign of intimidation, with the tacit backing of the army. Even with the militia ruling the streets, the 78.5% majority vote in favour of independence on August 30 proved that their was little popular support for their case. East Timorese celebrations soon turned to despair as independence through the ballot box failed to secure peace. See the East Timor chapter for more information.

Violence is historically the handmaiden of political change in Indonesia, and democracy will be a rocky road. The problem, as always, will be how to reconcile the disparate groups in Indonesian society. In such a diverse country, with separate Christian and Hindu regions that have always been resentful of Javanese dominance, Balkanisation is possible.

Despite widespread predictions of violence in the lead up to the June 1999 national elections, few problems were experienced. In the first free election in over 40 years, thousands took to the streets in support of the new political parties in what was largely a joyous celebration of democracy. The elections, however, are only the first step to real democratic change.

Megawati Soekarnoputri emerged as the most popular choice for president, but her PDI-P (Indonesian Democractic Party for Struggle) could muster only a third of the vote. The government Golkar party, without the benefit of a rigged electoral system, had its vote slashed from over 70% to just over 20%, but with strong support from outside Java and Bali, Golkar remains a political force with a number of seats in the DPR lower house.

In August 1999 lobbying and political deals were still being made. The real struggle is the formation of a coalition that will satisfy Indonesian electors. Despite muttering's from Megawati's erstwhile opposition partners that she may not have what it takes to be president, if the opposition parties do not form a united coalition, Golkar may be back in government. Without a majority government, Indonesia's political scene may remain unstable, but there is a resurgent optimism in Indonesia after the cataclysmic events of 1998-99.

The presidential contest is due to be decided in early November 1999 by the People's Consultative Assembly, a 700-member body which includes the 500 members of the newly elected parliament. Democracy promises hope for a better future and, while the economy is still a long way from recovery, hyper-inflation has been eliminated and negative growth has been arrested.

GEOGRAPHY

The Republic of Indonesia is the world's most expansive archipelago, stretching almost 5000km from Sabang off the northern tip of Sumatra, to a little beyond Merauke in south-eastern Irian Jaya. It stretches north and south of the equator for a total of 1770km, from the border with Sabah to the small island of Roti off the southern tip of Timor.

Officially, the archipelago contains 13,677 islands – from specks of rock to huge islands like Sumatra and Borneo – 6000 of which are inhabited. The five main islands are Sumatra (473,606 sq km), Java (132,107 sq km), Kalimantan (Indonesian Borneo, 539,460 sq km), Sulawesi (189,216 sq km) and Irian Jaya (the western part of New Guinea, 421,981 sq km). Most of the country is water; the Indonesians refer to their homeland as Tanah Air Kita (literally, Our Earth and Water). While the total land and sea area of Indonesia is about 2½ times greater than the land area of Australia, Indonesia's total land area is only 1,900,000 sq km, a little larger than Queensland, or about three times the size of Texas.

Most of the country's islands are mountainous; in Irian Jaya there are peaks so high they're snowcapped year-round. North-central Kalimantan and much of central Sulawesi are also mountainous, but in most other parts of Indonesia volcanoes dominate the skyline. Running like a backbone down the western coast of Sumatra is a line of extinct and active volcanoes, which continues through Java, Bali and Nusa Tenggara, and then loops around through the Banda Islands of Maluku to north-eastern Sulawesi. Some of these have erupted, with devastating effects – the 1963 eruption of Gunung Agung (Mt Agung) devastated large areas of Bali.

To many Balinese the eruption of this sacred mountain was a sign of the wrath of the gods; in East Java the Tenggerese people still offer a propitiatory sacrifice to the smoking Bromo crater which dominates the local landscape. However, it is the ash from these volcanoes that has provided Indonesia with some of the most fertile stretches of land on the planet.

Indonesia is a country of plentiful rainfall, particularly in west Sumatra, northwest Kalimantan, West Java and Irian Jaya. A few areas of Sulawesi and some of the islands closer to Australia – notably Sumba and Timor – are considerably drier, but they're exceptions. The high rainfall and the tropical heat make for a very humid climate – but also for a very even one. The highlands of Java and Irian Jaya can get very cold indeed, but on the whole most of Indonesia is warm and humid year-round.

High rainfall and year-round humidity mean that nearly two-thirds of Indonesia is covered in tropical rainforest – most of it in Sumatra, Kalimantan, Sulawesi and Irian Jaya. Most of the forests of Java disappeared centuries ago as land was cleared for agriculture. Today the rest of Indonesia's rainforest, which is second only to Brazil's in area, is disappearing at an alarming rate as local and foreign timber companies plunder the forests. Other contributing factors are the clearing of forest for agriculture, transmigration and mining.

Along the east coast of Sumatra, the south coast of Kalimantan, Irian Jaya and much of the northern coast of Java, there is swampy, low-lying land often covered in mangroves. In many areas the over-clearing of natural growth has led to continual erosion as topsoil is washed down the rivers by heavy rains, simultaneously wreaking havoc on the Indonesian roads.

The tropical vegetation, the mountainous terrain and the natural division of the country into numerous islands have always made communication difficult between islands and between different parts of each island. But it is these factors that have had a marked effect on Indonesia's history and culture, and also explain some of the peculiarities of the country and its people.

First, Indonesia straddles the equator between the Indian Ocean to the west and lies between the Pacific Ocean to the east. To the north are China and Japan, to the northwest India and beyond that the Middle East. Because of this central position, the Indonesian islands – particularly Sumatra and Java – and the Malay peninsula have long formed a stopover and staging post on the sea routes between India and China, a convenient midway point where merchants met and exchanged goods.

Second, the regular and even climate (there are some exceptions – in some of the islands east of Java and Bali the seasonal differences are pronounced, and even within Java some districts have a sufficiently marked dry season to suffer drought at times) means that the rhythm of life for many Indonesian farmers is based less on the annual fluctuations of the seasons than on the growth patterns of their crops. In areas with heavy rainfall and terraced rice-field cultivation, there is no set planting season or harvest season but a continuous flow of activity, where at any one time one hillside may demonstrate the whole cycle of rice cultivation, from ploughing to harvesting.

CLIMATE

Straddling the equator, Indonesia tends to have a fairly even climate year-round. Rather than four seasons, Indonesia has two – wet and dry – and there are no extremes of winter and summer as in some parts of Asia, such as China and northern India.

In most parts of Indonesia the wet season falls between October and April, and the dry season between May and September. Rain tends to come in sudden tropical downpours, and it is often dry for the rest of the day, but it can also rain non-stop for days. In some parts, like Kalimantan and Sumatra, the difference between the seasons is slight – the dry season just seems to be slightly hotter and not quite as wet as the wet season. In the other areas, such as Nusa Tenggara, the differences are very pronounced – droughts in the dry season and floods in the wet.

Indonesians may tell you it gets cold in their country – you'll often see them running around in long-sleeved shirts and even winter coats in the stifling heat! In fact, it's invariably hot and generally humid during the day and warm during the night. Once you get up into the hills and mountains the temperature drops dramatically – camp out at night atop Gunung Rinjani on Lombok without a sleeping bag, and you'll be as stiff as those wood carvings they sell in Bali. Sleeping out at night on the deck of a small boat or ship can also be bitterly cold, no matter how oppressive the heat may be during the day. There is a 'cold season' if you want to call it that, namely July and August, but you're only likely to notice it in the 'deep south' (about 10° south of the equator) and, again, mostly in the highlands.

At the other end of the thermometer, an hour's walk along Kuta Beach in Bali in the middle of the day will roast you a nice bright red.

See the climate charts of Ambon, Denpasar, Balikpapan, Dili, Jakarta and Danau Toba (Lake Toba) in this section.

Java

Across the island the temperature throughout the year averages 22°C to 29°C (72°F to

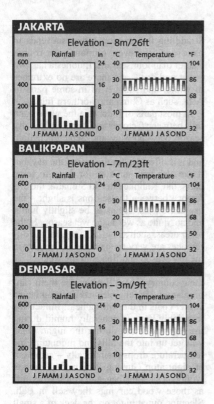

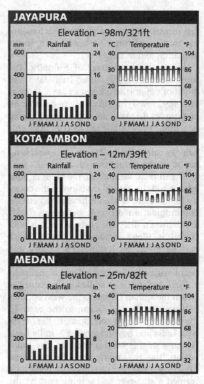

84°F) and humidity averages a high 75%, but the north coastal plains are usually hotter, up to 34°C (94°F) during the day in the dry season, and more oppressively humid than anywhere else. Generally the south coast is a bit cooler than the north, and the mountainous regions inland are very much cooler.

The wet season is from October to the end of April, so the best time to visit the island is May to September. The rain comes as a tropical downpour, falling most afternoons during the wet season and intermittently at other times of the year. The heaviest rains are usually around January and February. Regional variations occur – West Java is wetter than East Java, and the mountain regions receive a lot more rainfall. The highlands of West Java average

over 4000mm (156 inches) of rain a year, while the north-east coastal tip of East Java has a rainfall of only 900mm (35 inches).

Bali

The climate here is much like Java: the dry season is between April and September. The coolest months of the year are generally May, June and July, with the average temperature around 28°C (82°F). The rainy season is between October and March but the tropical showers alternate with clear skies and sunshine. The hottest months of the year are generally February and March, with the average temperature around 30°C (86°F).

Overall, the best time to visit the island is in the dry and cooler months between May and August, which are characterised by cool evenings and fresh breezes coming off the ocean.

Sumatra

The climate here resembles that of Java and is hot and extremely humid. The equator cuts this island into two roughly equal halves, and since the winds of northern Sumatra differ from those of the rest of the archipelago, so does the timing of the seasons – though temperatures remain pretty constant year-round. North of the equator the heaviest rainfall is between October and April, and the dry season is from May to September. South of the equator, the heaviest rainfall is from December to February, though it will have started raining in September. Heavy rains can make already bad roads impassable.

Nusa Tenggara

In the islands east of Bali the seasonal differences are more pronounced. The driest months are August and September, and the wettest months are from November to February. However, the duration of the seasons varies from island to island. The seasons on Lombok are more like those in Bali, with a dry season from April to September and a wet season from October to March. Much the same applies to Sumbawa and Flores. The duration of the dry season increases the closer you get to Australia – the rusty landscapes of Sumba and Timor are a sharp contrast to well vegetated Flores. At almost 10°S, Timor is also the only island in Indonesia far enough from the equator to experience typhoons (cyclones), but these are rare. Nearby northern Australia is not so lucky.

Kalimantan

Indonesian Borneo is permanently hot and damp; the wettest period is from October to March and the driest period is from July to September. Although the sun predominates between April and September, be prepared for heavy tropical downpours.

Sulawesi

The wettest months here tend to be from around November and December to March and April, but in central and northern Sulawesi the rainfall is slightly more evenly spread throughout the year. The mountains of central Sulawesi and the northern peninsula are wetter, and can receive rain in the dry season, while the south-eastern peninsula is the driest part of the island.

Temperatures drop quite considerably going from the lowlands to the mountains. Average temperatures along the coast range from around 26°C to 30°C (79°F to 86°F), but in the mountains the average temperature drops by 5°C.

Maluku

Maluku is the main exception to the climate rule in Indonesia. While the wet season everywhere else is from October to April, in central Maluku the wet season is from April through to July and may even carry on to the end of August. Travelling in Maluku during the wet season is more difficult; the sea is rougher, inter-island connections are fewer and heavy rainfall can interrupt travel plans. The best time to visit is from September to March.

Maluku does have regional variations. Northern and central Maluku do not have an exclusive dry season and rainfall occurs throughout the year, and it is much drier in the south. Aru in far south-eastern Maluku has its wet season from September to April.

Irian Jaya

Irian Jaya is hot and humid in the northern coastal regions. In the highlands it's warm by day but can get very cold by night – and the higher you go the colder it gets! August and September in the highlands will be gloomy and misty. In the northern part of Irian Jaya, May to October is the drier season and May is the hottest month. Southern Irian Jaya has a much more well defined dry season than the northern part of the island, and Merauke has a more distinct dry season from April to October.

ECOLOGY & ENVIRONMENT

Indonesia's economy is becoming progressively industrialised, while its large and generally poor population continues to grow. These factors point to ecological degradation in a country that does not have the resources to give environmental issues high priority. Nevertheless, there are environmental protection programs in place in Indonesia, but typically they are poorly funded and enforcement is difficult or ignored.

Despite widespread logging, and development encroaching on the jungle Indonesia still has large forest reserves representing 10% of the world's remaining tropical rainforest. The government policy of selective logging and reafforestation is all but ignored, and the forests are disappearing at up to one million hectares per year. The government has plans to control log exports to keep logging at a sustainable level, but the monetary crisis will undoubtedly put pressure on those levels.

In 1997, after prolonged dry spells, massive forest fires broke out in Kalimantan, blanketing the region in choking smoke. The fires burned for months, and were made worse by accompanying fires in Sumatra, prompting rebukes from Singapore and Malaysia, whose cities were also affected by the haze. Reported as the greatest forest fires ever recorded and the greatest ecological disaster the world has seen, the truth is they have become a regular occurrence. Huge forest fires burnt out of control in both Sumatra and Kalimantan in 1994 and 1991, and the 'Great Fire of Kalimantan' in 1983 destroyed 35,000 sq km of rainforest and was as big, if not bigger, than the 1997 fires. The government, as always, blames shifting 'slash-and-burn' cultivators, but outside experts say the fires are triggered by the waste wood and debris left by loggers, setting off peat and coal fires beneath the ground which burn for months.

In the cities, industrial pollution is increasing, mostly in Java. The increasing wealth of the middle classes has seen the number of new motor vehicles increase dramatically, and along with it vehicle emissions.

As Indonesia becomes more urbanised – over 30% of Indonesians now live in cities compared to 15% in 1970 – more strains are put on the urban environment. Waste removal services have difficulty coping with household and industrial garbage, but the worst threat to living standards is the lack of decent sewerage systems. Very few cities have a sewerage system and so rely on septic tanks or disposal of effluent through the canals and river systems. This in turn is a major source of pollution of water resources. Most Indonesians are simply not supplied with safe drinking water and must boil it before use.

FLORA & FAUNA

Indonesia has one of the world's richest natural environments, harbouring an incredible diversity of plant and animal species. Covering such a large area, Indonesia includes regions of disparate natural history and unique ecosystems.

The British naturalist Alfred Wallace, in his classic study *The Malay Archipelago*, first classified the Indonesian islands as two zones – a western, Asian ecological zone and an eastern, Australian zone. The 'Wallace Line' dividing these two zones runs along the edge of the Sunda shelf between Kalimantan and Sulawesi, and south through the straits between Bali and Lombok. West of this line, Indonesian flora and fauna show great similarities to those of the rest of Asia, while to the east the islands gradually become drier and the flora and fauna more like Australia's. Scientists have since further expanded on this classification to show distinct breaks between the ecologies of Sulawesi and Maluku, and Maluku and Irian Jaya.

Greater Sunda Islands (Sumatra, Java, Kalimantan & Bali)

The western part of the country, comprising Sumatra, Java, Kalimantan and Bali, lying on the Sunda shelf and known as the Greater Sunda Islands, was once linked to the Asian mainland. As a result some large Asian land animals still survive there, including elephants, tigers, rhinoceros and leopards, and the dense rainforests and abundant flora of Asia are in evidence.

Perhaps the most famous animal is the orang-utan (man of the forest), the long-haired red apes found only in Sumatra and Kalimantan. The Orang-utan Rehabilitation Centre in North Sumatra provides easy access to see orang-utans in their natural setting, as does the centre at the Tanjung Puting National Park (Taman Nasional Tanjung Puting) in Kalimantan. Kalimantan is also home to the proboscis monkey, identified by its pendulous, almost comical nose. Various species of the graceful gibbon also exist throughout the Greater Sundas, as do other common varieties of primate.

Elephants are not numerous, but they still exist in the wild in Sumatra and can be seen at the Way Kambas Reserve in Sumatra's Lampung province. Kalimantan also has a few wild elephants in the north-east, but they are very rare and the species is probably introduced.

The magnificent tiger once roamed freely throughout Asia, and existed in large numbers in Sumatra, Java and Bali. A few places in Java claim to be the last refuge of the tiger, but tigers in Indonesia are now known only to exist in Sumatra. Leopards (the black leopard or panther is more common in South-East Asia) are also rare but still live in Sumatra and in Java's Ujung Kulon National Park. This park is also home to the rare, almost extinct, one-horned Javan rhinoceros. Rhinos have not fared well in Indonesia and the two-horned variety, found in Sumatra, is also on the endangered species list.

Of all Indonesia's flora, the most spectacular is the rafflesia, the world's largest flower, growing up to one metre in diameter. This parasitic plant is found primarily in Sumatra, but smaller versions are found in Kalimantan and Java.

The rainforests are disappearing at an alarming rate. The mighty dipterocarp forests of Kalimantan are being logged ferociously, prized as they are for their durable tropical hardwoods, such as ironwood. Sumatran forests are also being logged and cleared as the jungle is pushed back for new settlements; however, both Sumatra and Kalimantan present some of the best opportunities in Indonesia to explore rainforest environments. The landscapes of heavily populated Java and Bali are dominated by wet-field rice cultivation, but natural forest remains in national parks and in some remote mountain regions.

Irian Jaya & Aru Islands

Irian Jaya and the Aru Islands were once part of the Australian land mass and lie on the Sahul shelf. The collision between the Australian and Pacific tectonic plates resulted in a massive mountain range running along the middle of Irian Jaya, isolating a number of unique environments, but the fauna throughout is closely related to Australia's. Irian Jaya is the only part of Indonesia to have kangaroos, marsupial mice, bandicoots and ring-tailed possums, all marsupials found in Australia. Aussie reptiles include crocodiles and frilled lizards. While the south is much drier, the mountain regions and the north are covered with dense rainforest and the flora includes Asiatic and endemic species. Irian Jaya has over 600 species of birds, the most well known being the cassowary and bird of paradise species.

The isolated Aru Islands, though administratively part of Maluku, share a common evolution with, and are more closely related to, Irian Jaya.

Sulawesi, Nusa Tenggara & Maluku

Lying between the two shelves, the islands of Sulawesi, Nusa Tenggara (also known as the Lesser Sunda Islands) and Maluku have long been isolated from the continental land masses, and have developed unique flora and fauna.

Endemic to Sulawesi is the anoa, or dwarf buffalo, a wallowing animal which looks like a cross between a deer and a cow, standing only about 80cm high. The *babi rusa* (deer pig) has great curving tusks that come out the side of the mouth and through the top of the snout. The bulbous beaked hornbills are some of Indonesia's most spectacular birds and are often considered sacred. They are found throughout most of the Greater Sundas as well as Sulawesi, but the *enggang Sulawesi*

(Buton hornbill) with its brightly coloured beak and neck, is one of the most spectacular of the species. In terms of resources, Sulawesi is noted for its ebony and teak.

Maluku shows similarities with Sulawesi, but with fewer species of flora and fauna. The babi rusa and smaller mammals are found, as are some primates, but it seems most of the migratory waves bypassed Maluku. However, it is noted for its butterflies – Pulau Seram (Seram Island) has reported some enormous species – and bird life, particularly the *nuri raja*, or Amboina king parrot, a large, magnificently coloured bird.

The Wallace Line separates Lombok, the westernmost island of Nusa Tenggara, from Bali. From East Lombok eastwards, the flora and fauna of Nusa Tenggara reflect the more arid conditions of these islands. Large Asian mammals are nonexistent and mammal species in general are smaller and less diverse. Asian bird species diminish further east and Australian birds are found on the eastern islands. Nusa Tenggara has one astonishing and famous animal, the Komodo dragon, the world's largest lizard, found only on the island of Komodo and a few neighbouring islands.

National Parks

Although environmentalists have blasted Indonesia's government for its logging and transmigration development schemes, it's only fair to mention that the past decade has seen a rapid increase in the number of national parks, nature reserves and historical sites. While it's true that loggers, farmers and hunters violate national park boundaries, there has been a sincere effort to enforce the rules – no easy task in a country with so much sparsely inhabited jungle.

Indonesian national parks *(taman nasional)* are managed by the Directorate General of Forest Protection and Nature Conservation (Perlindungan Hutan dan Pelestarian Alam), more commonly known as the PHPA. The PHPA offices that manage the parks are usually located in the towns, and go under the title of Konservasi dan Sumber Daya Alam (KSDA). Many new national parks have been proclaimed in recent years, mostly because national parks receive greater international recognition and funding than nature, wildlife and marine reserves, of which there are also many in Indonesia.

Most of Indonesia's national parks are very isolated and have minimal facilities. To explore Indonesia's magnificent wilderness areas requires time, endurance and usually a guide. Some parks have huts where visitors can stay, but most have no visitor facilities and accommodation is in the nearest town. If the wilderness is your main reason to visit Indonesia, bring a good tent, sleeping bag and kerosene stove. As a general rule, park staff spend little time in the parks and more time in the office, which will be located in the nearest town or city. Call into these offices before heading to the park to check the latest conditions.

Java The pick of Java's national parks is Ujung Kulon, on the south-west tip of the island. Though not easy to reach, it has superb coastal scenery, lush forest and coral reefs, and is home to the almost extinct Javan rhinoceros, and leopards.

In complete contrast, Baluran National Park, on the dry north-eastern tip of Java, is easily visited and has sparse, arid forest typical of Africa or Australia. This drive-through park is noted for its *banteng* (wild ox), deer, native dogs and bird life.

Bromo-Tengger-Semeru National Park is justly famous for its spectacular volcanic craters and Gunung Bromo is one of Java's main attractions. For mountain climbers, the park also contains Java's highest peak, Gunung Semeru.

The small Pangandaran National Park is right on the doorstep of a popular beach resort but the trails have been closed for conservation reasons. In the mountains south of Jakarta, Gunung Gede-Pangrango National Park offers volcano climbing through submontane forest. Gunung Halimun National Park is nearby but is undeveloped and access is difficult.

One of Java's most spectacular walks is to the active crater lake of Kawah Ijen in the plateau reserve near Banyuwangi in East Java. East Java also has some fine coastal national parks, Alas Purwo and spectacular Meru Betiri, but access is difficult. Pulau Seribu, consisting mostly of resorts, fishing villages and private islands, has rather strangely been made a marine national park.

Bali West Bali National Park (Taman Nasional Bali Barat) takes up a significant chunk of the western part of the island. Most of the park is savanna, with coastal mangroves and more tropical vegetation in the southern highlands. Over 200 species of plants inhabit the various environments, and animals include monkeys, deer, squirrels, wild pigs, buffaloes, iguanas, pythons and green snakes. The bird life is prolific, with many of Bali's 300 species represented, the most famous of which is the rare Bali starling.

Sumatra This province has some excellent national parks, Gunung Leuser being the most accessible and rewarding. Covering almost 10,000 sq km, this park contains the Orang-utan Rehabilitation Centre at Bukit Lawang on its eastern flank; from there and Berastagi it's easy to arrange treks into the park.

The Bukit Barisan Selatan National Park, in southern Sumatra is difficult to reach, but contains varied flora from coastal to rainforest and large mammal species, including tigers, elephants and tapirs. Way Kambas National Park in Lampung Province is noted for its elephants, which are protected in the park but also exploited in an elephant training show. The island of Pulau Weh in Aceh is a marine national park noted for its coral. Lembah Anai Nature Reserve between Bukittinggi and Padang is known for its rafflesia.

Other national parks are isolated and rarely visited. Siberut National Park on the island of Siberut covers 1900 sq km and is noted for its unique fauna and the Mentawai people.

Bukit Tigapuluh (Thirty Hills) National Park, straddling Riau and Jambi provinces, has significant areas of lowland forest and the area is inhabited by tribal peoples, notably the Kubu.

Kerinci Seblat National Park, covering 15,000 sq km, is one of Indonesia's largest parks and one of the last homes of the Sumatran rhinoceros. Gunung Kerinci (3805m) is the highest mountain in this diverse park.

Berbak National Park in Jambi province is noted for tiger and tapir, but is inaccessible most of the year because of flooding.

Nusa Tenggara Gunung Rinjani, at 3726m, is one of the highest mountains in Indonesia outside Irian Jaya, and dominates the island of Lombok. It's a very popular three to five day trek to the top, and the huge crater contains a large, green, crescent-shaped lake, Segara Anak (Child of the Sea), 6km across at its widest point. Some 40,000 hectares of Rinjani's slopes form a protected national park. See the special colour section 'Climbing Rinjani'.

The mostly dry savanna of Komodo National Park encompasses much of Komodo and the Rinca Islands, and is home to Indonesia's most famous beastie, the Komodo dragon. The islands also have coral reefs.

In Flores, the three coloured lakes of Keli Mutu, one of Indonesia's most impressive sights, fall inside a national park.

Many remote nature and wildlife reserves have been declared, especially on Timor and Sumba. Two-thirds of Pulau Moyo, off the north coast of Sumbawa, is a nature reserve with savanna, some forest and coral reefs.

Kalimantan Tanjung Puting is Kalimantan's most renowned national park, famous for its Camp Leakey orang-utan rehabilitation centre, and encompasses 355 sq km of tropical rainforest, mangrove forest and wetlands.

Kutai National Park in East Kalimantan is a mix of national park and logging zone; it is difficult to reach and facilities are minimal. Tangkiling National Park is another nature reserve, 35km north of Palangkaraya.

The Gunung Palung National Park in West Kalimantan has everything from beaches to mountain forest, but is one of

Kalimantan's most remote parks. Bukit Baka-Bukit Raya park straddles the border of East and Central Kalimantan and contains Bukit Raya (2278m), with tropical and montane forest.

Bentuang Karimun National Park borders Sarawak and is a catchment area for the Rejang, Lupar and Kapuas rivers. One of Kalimantan's most important parks with rich biodiversity, access is very difficult.

Kayan Mentarang National Park in the interior of East Kalimantan covers an area of 16,000 sq km and includes one of the largest tracts of rainforest in Borneo. Home to nomadic and semi-nomadic Dayak tribes, access is only by chartered flight.

The new Sebuku Sembakung National Park borders the Kayan Mentarang National Park and has lowland and mangrove forest, and Kalimantan's only elephants. It is accessed from Nunukan.

Sulawesi Lore Lindu in Central Sulawesi is a remote and untouched national park, rich in exotic plants and animal life. It is also home to several indigenous tribes, has ancient megalithic relics and great trekking, as well as a couple of mountains for peak bagging. Sulawesi's other major park is Bogani Nani Wartabone in North Sulawesi, a watershed area with intact forest.

Sulawesi has some good reserves. Tangkoko-Batuangas Dua Saudara Reserve, 30km from Bitung, is home to black apes, anoa, babi rusa and maleo birds (the maleo looks like a huge hen and lays eggs five times the size of a hen's). The reserve also includes the coastline and coral gardens offshore. The Morowali Reserve in Central Sulawesi is good for treks that can be organised out of Kolondale. Wildlife includes maleo birds.

Rawa Aopa Watumohai National Park in South-East Sulawesi is a coastal park with tracts of savanna and mangrove, and swampy lakes noted for waterbirds. Access is from Kendari and the main entrance is at Lanowulu.

Sulawesi's most famous natural attractions are its coral reefs. The easily accessible, fabulous reefs of Pulau Bunaken are famous and are part of the Bunaken Manado Tua Marine National Park, and the Togian Islands also have some fine reefs for snorkelling and diving.

Wakatobi Marine National Park, also known as Tukangbesi, is a string of islands off the far south-east coast with accommodation on Pulau Hoga, reached with some difficulty from Bau Bau. Taka Bone Rate Marine National Park is the largest atoll in Indonesia, noted for the variety of its coral and marine species. Access is from Selayar.

Maluku Manusela National Park, forming a large chunk of Pulau Seram's centre, comprises remote mountain regions, and sandy beaches and coral off the north coast. Access is not easy and facilities are limited, but it is possible to organise treks within the park.

Irian Jaya With some effort you can visit two national reserves on Pulau Biak, Wasur National Park near Merauke, the Wondiwoi Mountains Reserve and the Cenderawasih Bay Marine Park, which covers most of the island of Pulau Yos Sudarso off the coast of Merauke. The Baliem Valley is the main area for trekking in Irian Jaya.

GOVERNMENT & POLITICS

Reformasi (reform) is the new buzz word in Indonesia. After the repression of the Soeharto years, people now openly talk about what they want – and what they don't want. Demonstrations are a constant in political life, the press enjoys an unprecedented freedom and though the road to democracy is a tumultuous one, it would be very difficult to turn back. Reform still has a long way to go, and the process will be an ongoing one as the new forces in Indonesian politics set about deciding Indonesia's future.

Reform resulted in a slight rejigging of the two houses of parliament, but the new system still allows for the appointment of non-elected appointees, including 38 seats set aside for the military in the 500 seat lower house (DPR). The DPR promises to be a real forum for debate, whereas under Soeharto it had little say and power presided firmly with the autocratic president and his inner cabinet.

Political Parties

Over 100 new political parties formed with the promise of the first open elections in more than 40 years. Mindful of regional divisions, the government attempted to restrict parties to those that could claim national representation in at least 14 of the 27 provinces.

Under the old system, the government only allowed three parties: the ruling Golkar party, which had all the power and controlled the elections, and an emasculated opposition, consisting of the Partai Persatuan Pembangunan (PPP), representing Islamic groups, and Partai Demokrasi Indonesia (PDI), Soekarno's old party which became an amalgam of nationalists, Christians and 'the rest'.

Golkar, the artificial, all-encompassing government party of the Soeharto era used to be the only party of power and influence. Civil servants automatically became members of Golkar and everyone from village heads to army generals wore the yellow shirts of the party. Now Golkar is desperately trying to throw off its tarnished image as Soeharto's party of corruption and repression.

The PPP now has to compete with other Muslim parties, and if anything it has become more Islamic.

The PDI has split into two parties. After a government-backed leadership challenge removed popular opposition leader Megawati Soekarnoputri in 1996, Megawati has gone on to form her own splinter party of the PDI. Of all the opposition leaders, she has probably the widest popular support. Certainly her enthusiastic supporters, often sporting red bandannas and waving red flags, are the most noticeable. Appealing to Muslims and non-Muslims alike, Megawati's party is overtly secular. Her lack of support among the army and the old elite is both a pro and a con.

The other main forces are the Muslim-orientated parties. Amien Rais, who was the most prominent and effective opposition leader in the months leading up to Soeharto's

JENNY BOWMAN

Megawati Soekarnoputri, leader of the PDI-P, and presidential frontrunner with 33.8% of the June 1999 election vote.

demise, is a Muslim intellectual whose moderate, modernist line has wide appeal. Nahdatul Ulama, the country's largest Muslim organisation, is once again a political force appealing mostly to older, syncretic Muslims. Its ageing and ailing leader, Abdurrahman Wahid, more fondly known as Gus Dur, is more conservative but commands widespread support.

Amien Rais and Gus Dur are both moderates and very keen to keep a lid on communal divisions in multireligious, multiethnic Indonesia. The emergence of fundamentalist Islamic groups would pose the greatest threat to national unity. Though everything is now up for review and there has been talk of scrapping the national ideology of Pancasila (see the boxed text in this section), the principles for secular government remain strong.

As well as the three main opposition figures, a fourth must be added, Sri Sultan Hamengkubuwono X. Like his father, who was prominent in the independence movement, the present sultan of Yogyakarta came out strongly behind the students and the reform movement in the lead-up to Soeharto's demise. Though without a real power base, the respect he commands as both a traditional and modern leader makes him a very influential figure.

Armed Forces

'What are you going to do with your life?', an Indonesian father asks his son.

'I'm not sure', replied the boy. 'I'd like to go into government and maybe become governor or even president, but I'd also like to go into business and become rich. Or perhaps I could go into law and become a judge.'

'In that case', said the father, 'Join the army and you can do it all.'

The Indonesian military (ABRI), of which the army is the dominant wing, plays a prominent role in Indonesian politics and society. Indonesia's military psyche developed during WWII when the Japanese organised village militias to defend Indonesia in the event of reoccupation. When the Dutch returned, independence was gained only after a bloody war waged by village armies united under the banner of the new republic.

The Indonesian independence revolution was led by the *pemuda* (youth) and Indonesian freedom fighters became heroes. Their leaders' names adorn Indonesian streets (see the boxed text 'Street Names & Indonesian Heroes' in this chapter), their exploits are endlessly retold in schools and their homes have become museums. Indonesia's history has become a military one, and even the most obscure leaders of ancient, easily crushed peasant rebellions have become national heroes. The military has been a part of the political process since independence, and it hardly regards itself as having usurped power that somehow 'rightfully' belongs to civilians.

Under Soekarno's guided democracy the military's powers and aspirations intensified. In 1958 General Nasution, chief of staff of the army, expounded the doctrine of *dwifungsi* (dual function) to justify the army's expanded role in Soekarno's government after the establishment of martial law. This stated that the army not only played a security role and was responsible to the government, but it also had an independent social and political role to play as 'one of the many forces in society'.

After the 1965 coup the army became not just one of many, but a dominant force in society. The military dwifungsi role strengthened, and military support was necessary for power. As well as automatic military representation in parliament, it was involved in local government right down to the village level. In later years, Soeharto increasingly preferred a civilian image, and his cabinet contained few members of the military, but military personnel, both former and present, are still widely represented in government and in business.

The military remains a major behind-the-scenes player, and in the turmoil leading up to Soeharto's resignation, all eyes were on ABRI. The top brass came out firmly behind Soeharto, while it was rumoured the younger level of officers below were pro-reform. A coup looked possible but did not eventuate and in the aftermath, Prabowo Subianto, commander of Indonesia's special forces and son-in-law of Soeharto, was held accountable for the Jakarta riots.

Probowo was sacked, and his main rival, General Wiranto, chief of the armed forces, became top dog. Wiranto assumed a prominent role as a leader of strength and calm throughout the turmoil but, while he remains a leader to defer to, the military's influence is in decline. The newly free press soon reported atrocities committed by the army over many years.

Political leaders continue to show deference to the armed forces, but more radical reform groups are demanding that the military get out of politics. The students, Indonesia's new revolutionary pemuda, are particularly vocal, having borne the brunt of the military's law and order campaigns that have seen students killed by soldiers.

The military, historically the liberators of Indonesia and the keepers of peace, no longer command widespread public support. At best they are tolerated as a necessary evil, the only force that can keep Indonesia together in the face of disintegration, but their dwifungsi role is under review and the police have already been separated from ABRI.

A coup is never totally out of the question, especially if a new government tried to forcibly remove ABRI from politics, but without popular support ABRI could only hold power through brutal repression. ABRI has spent decades promoting its role and propagandising itself as the supporter and protector of the people. To undo that may well see splits in the ranks and the emergence of a new leadership.

Regional Government

Politically, Indonesia is divided into 27 provinces, including the three special territories of Aceh, Jakarta and Yogyakarta. Java has five provinces: Jakarta, West Java, Central Java, Yogyakarta and East Java. Sumatra has eight: Aceh, North Sumatra, West Sumatra, Riau, Jambi, Bengkulu, South Sumatra and Lampung. Kalimantan has West, Central, South and East provinces.

Pancasila – The Five Principles

Since it was first expounded by Indonesian leader Soekarno in 1945, the Pancasila (Five Principles) have remained the philosophical backbone of the Indonesian state. Soekarno's intention was to provide a broad philosophical base on which a united Indonesian state could be formed. All over Indonesia you'll see the Indonesian coat of arms with its symbolic incorporation of the Pancasila, hung on the walls of government offices and the homes of village heads, on the covers of student textbooks and immortalised on great stone tablets.

In the post-Soeharto era everything is up for re-evaluation and some have suggested that Pancasila be scrapped. Pancasila, however, is likely to continue albeit with a new interpretation, for the principles are sufficiently vague to support both democracy and autocracy. The main message of Pancasila is that religious and ethnic divisions must always take second place to the interests of the state. The principles of Pancasila are:

Faith in God – symbolised by the star. This is perhaps the most important and contentious principle. As interpreted by Soekarno and the Javanese syncretists who have ruled Indonesia since independence, this can mean any god – Allah, Vishnu, Buddha, Christ etc. For many Muslims, it means belief in the only true God, Allah, but the government goes to great lengths to suppress both Islamic extremism and calls for an Islamic state. Since independence the government's faith has been in a multiethnic and multireligious Indonesia.

Humanity – symbolised by the chain. This represents the unbroken unity of humankind, and Indonesia taking its place among this family of nations.

Nationalism – symbolised by the banyan tree. All ethnic groups in Indonesia must unite.

Representative government – symbolised by the head of the buffalo. As distinct from the western brand of parliamentary democracy, Soekarno envisaged a form of Indonesian democracy based on the village system of deliberation (*permusyawaratan*) among representatives to achieve consensus (*mufakat*). The western system of 'majority rules' is considered a means by which 51% oppress the other 49%.

Social justice – symbolised by sprays of rice and cotton. A just and prosperous society gives adequate supplies of food and clothing for all – these are the basic requirements of social justice.

Sulawesi has North, Central, South and South-Eastern provinces. Other provinces are: Bali, West Nusa Tenggara (Lombok and Sumbawa), East Nusa Tenggara (Sumba, West Timor, Flores and the Solor and Alor archipelagos), East Timor, Maluku and Irian Jaya.

Each province has its own political legislature, headed by a governor, with extensive powers to administer the province. The 27 provinces are further broken down into 241 *kabupaten* (districts) headed by a *bupati* (district head) and 56 *kotamadya* (municipalities) headed by a *walikota* (mayor). The districts are further broken down into 3625 *kecamatan* (subdistricts), each headed by a *camat* (subdistrict head). Kecamatan are further broken down into *kelurahan*, or village groupings.

Each level of government has its own bureaucracy, often with overlapping functions. Government is Indonesia's major employer, and it's a major frustration if you have to deal with it.

But despite this extended hierarchy of government, often the most relevant level of government is village level. In the *desa* or *kampung*, the day-to-day running of the village, neighbourhood disputes and local affairs are handled by an elected *lurah* or *kepala desa* (village chief), though often the position of kepala desa is virtually hereditary. The kepala desa is the government representative at the most basic level, and the person to see if you wander into a village and need to spend the night or resolve a problem. Even at this basic political level, reform has struck, with corrupt and/or pro-Soeharto village chiefs being deposed, or even chased out of the village.

The village is the main social unit, providing welfare, support and guidance. If a fire destroys a house, or a village needs a new well, then everyone pitches in. This grassroots system of mutual help and discussion is usually presided over by a traditional council of elders, but village organisations or government representatives also carry out government policies and campaigns on economic development, population control,

health etc. One of the main community organisations is the *rukun tetangga*, which organises neighbourhood security – many villages have a security post *(pos kamling)* – and the registration of families and new arrivals.

ECONOMY

Up until 1997, all was rosy as the Indonesian economy bounded along like most of Asia with an average annual growth rate of more than 6% for 20 years. Only weeks before the monetary crisis swept through Asia, the World Bank declared that Indonesian was performing well and could look forward to more years of high growth. A few months later, Indonesia was bankrupt.

Asia as a whole suffered but Indonesia, because of the accompanying political strife, was hit the hardest. When the run started on the rupiah in July 1997, the rate was 2500Rp to US$1. The Indonesian central bank was unable to defend the currency from overseas selling and the rupiah plummeted. Many large corporations had taken out US dollar loans and suddenly, with the fall in the rupiah, these loans trebled, then quadrupled and kept going. Companies went bankrupt overnight and laid off their workers. At the same time prices skyrocketed, mostly for imported items but also for essentials such as rice.

The IMF stepped in and promised a US$40 billion bail-out package of grants and soft loans to help Indonesia service its foreign debt and keep the economy afloat. In return it demanded changes in basic economic fundamentals. Those changes included the lifting of subsidies on fuel and rice, which was destined to hit the poor hardest. When the price of kerosene rose, sporadic rioting broke out in towns across Indonesia, with shops owned by Chinese-Indonesians often being the prime target.

The rupiah plummeted to almost 17,000Rp to US$1 in January 1998, recovered substantially after Soeharto's re-election, then plunged again after the Jakarta riots in May 1998. With the disbursement of IMF funds, some stability has returned to the currency, but it cannot be guaranteed.

The swiftness and scope of the human tragedy is difficult to comprehend. Millions lost their jobs overnight, the economy stalled with negative growth of 20%, and inflation hit 80%. Many were close to starvation.

Substantial progress in eliminating poverty, for so long the pride and excuse of authoritarian government, was rapidly reversed. Under the development programs of Soeharto, poverty steadily dropped until, before the crisis, it was estimated that 20 million Indonesians lived below the poverty line, down to 11% of the population from 40% in 1976. In just one year, the figure jumped to 100 million, nearly 50% of the populace, wiping out the gains of a generation. Poverty, unlike in western countries, is defined as not earning enough money to buy enough food to avoid starvation.

All is not lost, however. The country has advanced enormously in the last 30 years and has a vastly improved infrastructure of roads, energy and telecommunications. From an economy dependent on oil and gas for export income, the mid-80s saw Indonesia start to develop a substantial light industrial base. Helped by huge foreign investment in the 90s, Indonesia is now a major producer of textiles and clothing, and is an exporter of footwear, chemicals, fertilisers, cement and glassware.

The manufacturing base remains largely intact, as do oil reserves, the old mainstay of Indonesia's exports. Indonesia also exports timber and wood products, tin, coal, copper and bauxite, and substantial cash crops like rubber, coffee, copra and fish. Tourism is also a major industry, but continuing strife has seen a big downturn in visitor arrivals.

Indonesia's main stumbling block is foreign debt. Companies that borrowed overseas but receive much of their income in rupiah are in a hopeless situation. It is also estimated that US$100 billion left the country after the economic crises began. This is not just Indonesian-Chinese leaving and taking their money with them, as some Indonesian politicians portray it, but almost anyone with money in Indonesia sold their rupiah in the grab for hard currency.

Hopefully, the only way is up for Indonesia's economy. By mid-1999, hyperinflation was under control and growth had steadied, along with the exchange rate. While Indonesia is still in an economic hole, improvement is evident and the indicators should keep moving up – if lasting political stability returns.

Corruption

One of the other buzz acronyms of the new Indonesia is KKN, standing for Corruption, Collusion and Nepotism. Much talk has been made about stamping it out, but it remains to be seen how effective that will be.

The focus of KKN has been former president Soeharto and his family. For decades it was impossible to do big business in Indonesia without deferring to Soeharto Family Inc, which has interests right across the archipelago. The trip into Jakarta from the airport is a famous journey through recent economic history – down the Soeharto-owned toll road in a Soeharto-owned taxi past Soeharto-owned skyscrapers. Most of the enterprises are owned by Soeharto's children rather than Soeharto himself but they grew rich through blatant favouritism in the appointment of government contracts and monopolies.

No-one knows how much the Soeharto enterprises are worth – US$40 billion is widely quoted, but the family's wealth has been slashed by the economic crisis, and various government contracts have been cancelled or are under review.

Soeharto is under investigation only because of continued public pressure, and the investigation is less than thorough, especially as it may spread to other former and current ministers. At the same time there is little evidence to suggest that Soeharto plundered the state coffers, or at least it is difficult to prove. The main issue is cronyism, and though the Soeharto family is the biggest indigenous force in the economy, for them to collapse or have their assets seized would be an even bigger blow to the economy.

The emphasis on Soeharto has also tended to divert attention from the need for a broader examination of corruption. Corruption has been entrenched in Indonesia since Dutch times and is often accepted with resignation. It has exploded in the last decade mostly because of the huge inflow of foreign investment which, given the huge profits to be made, also grew accustomed to the system. 'Commissions' of 10% or more were regularly given to receive contracts or set up business, not all of them to the Soeharto family.

Even mid-ranking bureaucrats receive a salary of only about 400,000Rp (US$50) a month. Teachers and many other government employees receive less. Many civil servants have extra jobs or investments related to their official duties, and it is seen as acceptable. More obvious bribery takes many forms – police regularly extract traffic 'fines' on the spot, a telephone will be connected quicker with 'extra payment', students can receive extra marks with an 'appeal' to the principal.

Government contracts are the greatest source of extra revenue. Contracts are often granted according to the size of the kickbacks, and inefficient or unnecessary projects get approval simply because more can be creamed off the top.

The Indonesian bureaucracy (KORPRI) is undergoing reform. A few purges and some laudable restructuring have occurred, but a lot of the changes are in letterheads and titles.

Indonesia's problems are not unique but it will take a lot of work to reverse Indonesia's reputation as one of the world's most corrupt countries.

Poverty & Prospects for the Future

The tragedy following the economic collapse is difficult to comprehend. Millions are unemployed, the price of staple goods have skyrocketed and the hopes of a turnaround still seem a long way off. Impromptu markets have sprung up in the cities of Java, where the poor sell their clothes, work tools, cooking utensils – anything to get money to buy food.

Even when the economy recovers, many long-term effects will be also felt. School enrolments have dropped sharply because parents can't afford to send their children to school, and a significant percentage of the new generation will now struggle to be educated.

The New Order government made significant strides in improving health, education and employment opportunities. Its politics of development were based on the notion that political freedom should be suppressed to promote stability and develop the economy, and it did work for 30 years. Under a series of five-year plans known as Repelita, social services expanded and roads and communications improved throughout the country. With the economy being directed by Western-educated economists balancing budgets and reducing government restrictions, and with the return of stability after the Soekarno years, foreign investment started to flow, first in a trickle then in a flood.

The economy boomed, especially from the mid-80s on, as foreign investment spawned new industries, mostly in Java. Disparity of wealth grew, as did grumblings about cronyism and the new super-rich, but poverty was steadily reduced under Soeharto, who proudly accepted the tag of the 'father of development'. When the economy collapsed, so did tolerance of autocracy and corruption.

The influx of IMF funds has helped to shore up the rupiah and the collapsed banking system, a necessary first step and good news for Indonesian investors, but it will do little to alleviate the plight of the poor in the immediate future. The reduction of subsidies for staples has also hit hard, but at the same time rising prices increased farmers' incomes and promoted food production, which was on the decline.

The main problem will be to reverse negative growth. Indonesia needs a resumption of foreign investment, but investors are now very wary. The economy is inextricably tied to politics and everyone is waiting to see what happens. Business did well under autocracy and repression – it not only delivered stability but the lack of protective legislation and free unions was a boon for profits. The old elite keeps stressing the need for stability and talks about stifling

Rice Production

Although Indonesia produces a range of agricultural products, including some introduced from Latin America, such as corn (thanks to the early Spanish and Portuguese settlers), its staple crop remains rice.

With the exception of Bali, most of Java, and a few small patches across the archipelago, the soil is just as poor in Indonesia as it is elsewhere in the tropics. In sparsely populated areas of Sumatra, Kalimantan, Sulawesi and West Java, where the peasants moved from one place to another, a form of shifting cultivation (*ladang*) developed.

In ladang cultivation, the jungle is burned off to speed up the normal process of decomposition and to enrich the soil in preparation for planting, but the soil quickly loses its fertility. When the top cover of forest is removed, the intense heat and heavy rain soon leach the soil of its nutrients. As a result, settled agriculture is impossible without the continuous addition of fertilising agents.

On the other hand, the rich volcanic soils of most of Java, Bali and western Lombok have allowed *sawah* (wet rice) cultivation in flooded rice fields. Rice cultivation in terraced sawah fields has been practised for over 2000 years. The system has been continually refined and developed, and is widely seen as a contributing factor to the development of the prolific civilisations in Java and later in Bali. The development of the fields, particularly in the highland areas where extensive terracing took place, required great organisation, either at a co-operative village level or through the suppression of a peasant work force.

The wonder of this method of agriculture is that sawah fields can keep producing two or even three crops a year, year after year, with little or no drop in soil fertility. This is due, however, not solely to the fertility of the soil; this astonishing ecosystem depends on water to provide nutrients and on the bacteria produced in water, which also aid in the extraction of nitrogen. Other nutrients are provided by the remains of previous crops, the addition of extra organic material and the aeration of the soil through water movement in the field.

After each rice harvest, the stubble from the crop is ploughed back into the field, traditionally using bullocks. Small carpets of the best rice seed are planted and, when ready, seedlings are prized apart and laboriously transplanted in even rows in a field flooded to a depth of a few centimetres. The level of the water is crucial in the life cycle of the rice plant – the water is increased in depth as the plant grows and then drained in increments until the field is dry at harvest time. The field may also be drained during the growing period in order to weed the field or aerate the soil.

Since 1968 the government has introduced schemes, such as the introduction of high-yield varieties of rice, to improve productivity. However, the basic method of sawah farming has remained unchanged for generations.

As development has claimed farming land, the production of rice in Indonesia has fallen and the country has had to import rice. This has caused an added burden in the economic crisis. However, the main reason for the fall in production is that government subsidies had kept the price artificially low. The lifting of these subsidies saw rice double in price – a burden for the poor, but a boon for farmers as Indonesia seeks to increase its rice production.

dissent for the sake of the economy. But the politics of developmentalism have failed. The election of Megawati Soekarnoputri will not please investors, but it may well be the only way to appease public dissent and stabilise Indonesia.

POPULATION & PEOPLE

Indonesia, with 202 million people, is the world's fourth most populous nation after China, India and the USA. Java alone has a population of 128 million people.

Indonesia's population is growing at a rate of about 1.5% per year, a rate that is expected to drop to around 1.25% in the first five years of the 21st century. At those rates, Indonesia will have over 225 million people by 2005, and 327 million by 2035. Overpopulation, however, is largely a Javanese and, to some extent, a Balinese problem. Java's population was estimated as six million in 1825, 9.5 million in 1850, 18 million in 1875, 28 million in 1900, 36 million in 1925, 63 million in 1961 and 108 million in 1990.

The total area of Java and the island of Madura off Java's north coast is 132,000 sq km, or just over half the area of the UK, and Java's population density of nearly 1000 people per sq km is four times that of the UK, and double that of the Netherlands (Europe's most densely populated country). Yet population in Indonesia is very unevenly distributed, and the national population density figure is 110 people per sq km. The following table reflects the percentages of total area and population.

island(s)	area (%)	pop (%)
Java	6.89	59.99
Bali & Nusa Tenggara	4.61	5.67
Sumatra	24.67	20.33
Sulawesi	9.85	6.98
Kalimantan	28.11	5.08
Maluku	3.88	1.03
Irian Jaya	21.99	0.92

Population Control

Each year three million people are added to the Indonesian population, most of them in Java. However, Indonesia's birth control program is making inroads into population growth.

After taking power, Soeharto reversed Soekarno's policies of continued population expansion to provide a workforce to develop the outer islands. He set up a National Family Planning Co-ordinating Board which greatly expanded the network of private clinics providing free contraceptive services. Efforts were concentrated in Bali and Java at first, with noticeable drops in the birth rate. It was also reported that over 80% of the women who took part in the scheme were from the poorer end of the scale – those who normally have the most children. However, birth-control campaigns have been heeded more by better educated, urban families, and have been less successful in highly traditional and strongly Muslim areas. In poorer, isolated rural areas, large families are still common.

The campaign has been most successful in Java, where many families are now firm believers in the slogan *'dua anak cukup'* (two children is enough). As well as public awareness campaigns, coordinators are appointed at village level to advise on contraception, monitor birth rates and counsel, if not admonish, families that exceed two children.

Transmigration

The other arm of population control is *transmigrasi*, which attempts to take the pressure off heavily populated areas, particularly Java and Bali, by moving people out to less populated islands like Sumatra, Kalimantan, Irian Jaya and Maluku.

These programs started in 1905 with the Dutch, who moved some 650,000 people, mostly from Java to Sumatra as plantation labourers. In the first 18 years of independence (1950-68) only about 450,000 people were moved. However, the Soeharto government placed much more emphasis on transmigration, and from 1968 to 1994, 6.4 million people were resettled.

Since the peak five-year plan in 1984-89, when 3.2 million were resettled, transmigration has slowed. Birth control programs proved to be much more effective at reducing population growth and transmigration causes other problems.

Most government-sponsored transmigrants are not experienced farmers; two-thirds of transmigrants are landless peasants, the poorest of the countryside, and another

10% are homeless city dwellers. Up until 1973 the urban poor of Jakarta were often virtually press-ganged into moving out of Java – they turned out to be the least successful transmigrants, often returning to the towns they came from. Inexperienced farmers tended to attempt wet-rice cultivation in unsuitable areas and ended up as subsistence farmers no better off than they were back in Java, if not because of poor soil and water then because of inadequate support services and isolation from markets.

Transmigration also takes its toll on the natural environment through destruction of forest, loss of topsoil and degradation of water supplies. Tension, even conflict, with the indigenous people in some settled areas is not uncommon.

The emphasis now is on 'spontaneous' transmigrants who emigrate on their own initiative and choose their own location. Transmigration is a voluntary program, and more support is now given, such as advice on suitable crops to grow. Some transmigrants are settled on plantations, where they receive a house and land, but their land is part of a plantation and they work on the estate for wages.

People

The rugged, mountainous terrain and the fact that the country is made up of many islands has separated groups of people from each other, resulting in an extraordinary differentiation of language and culture across the archipelago. Indonesians are divided – according to one classification – into approximately 300 ethnic groups which speak some 365 languages and dialects.

Indonesia's national motto is 'Bhinneka Tunggal Ika', an old Javanese phrase meaning 'They are many; they are one', which usually gets translated as 'Unity in Diversity'. The peoples of the archipelago were not 'Indonesian' until 1949, when a line was drawn on the map enclosing a group of islands which housed a remarkably varied collection of people.

Most Indonesians are of Malay stock, descended from peoples who originated in China and Indochina, and spread into Indonesia over several thousand years. The other major grouping is the darker skinned, fuzzy-haired Melanesians who inhabit much of easternmost Indonesia.

Despite the Malay predominance, the culture and customs of the various islands are often quite different. There are different languages and dialects, different religions and differences in adat (the unwritten village law which regulates the behaviour of everyone in every village in Indonesia). The Indonesian terrain is partly responsible for the incredible diversity; mountains and jungles cut off tribes and groups on certain islands from the outside world – like the Kubu tribe of south Sumatra, thought to be descendants of the original settlers from Sri Lanka. They were barely known to outsiders until guerrillas fighting against the Dutch came into contact with them. Other isolated groups have included the Papuan Dani people of the Baliem Valley in Irian Jaya, and the Dayaks – the collective name given to the people who inhabit the interior of Borneo. There are also the Badui of West Java, who withdrew to the highlands as the Islamic religion spread through the island, and have had little contact with outsiders. Other distinctive groups, like the Balinese and Javanese, have had considerable contact with the outside world but nevertheless have managed to maintain their traditional cultures intact.

Despite the diversity of peoples, cultures, languages and religions, and the inevitable conflicts that arise because of this diversity, Indonesia is surprisingly unified. When the republic was proclaimed, Indonesia was a group of hundreds of different societies, united through their subjection to Dutch colonialism, a tenuous reason upon which to build a nation. But Indonesia has done just that, through mass culture and prolonged campaigns, all conveyed through the national language, Bahasa Indonesia. Regional conflicts and loyalties remain, but the overwhelming majority of Indonesians now identify themselves proudly with their nation, flag and language.

Chinese Of all the ethnic minorities in Indonesia, few have had a larger impact on the country than the Chinese, or 'overseas Chinese' as they are commonly known. Although comprising less than 3% of the population, the Chinese are the major force in the economy, operating everything from small shops, hotels and restaurants to major banks and industries. The Chinese are by far the wealthiest ethnic group in the country, leading to much anti-Chinese resentment in Indonesia.

The Chinese in Indonesia have long suffered repression and even slaughter. The Dutch used the Chinese as an entrepreneurial middle class, but colonial authorities restricted Chinese settlement and ownership of land. As far back as 1740, anti-Chinese feeling erupted in the massacre of Batavia, in which colonial citizens participated.

When mass Indonesian organisations emerged in the early 20th century, such as the Muslim organisation Sarekat Islam, frustration with colonialism often resulted in attacks not on the Dutch, but on the Chinese.

In post-independence Indonesia the Chinese are seen as an overly privileged group, and their culture has been discriminated against by law. Chinese characters were banned, Chinese schooling was forbidden to Indonesian citizens; thus those Chinese who had chosen citizenship were forced to drop their language. The issue of citizenship is still a contentious one, with the ever-changing government policies making it hard for Chinese to gain Indonesian citizenship.

Many Chinese took the government's integration line and have adopted Indonesian language and names and blended more readily into Indonesian society. They have their own traditions and have developed their own patois, a mixture of Indonesian and Chinese dialects such as Hokkien, but most simply speak Bahasa Indonesia.

Discrimination against the Chinese is again at high levels in the wake of Indonesia's economic crisis. The Jakarta riots of May 1998 targeted Chinese businesses, though most rioters were simply looters with little political motivation. But whenever there is unrest in Indonesia, for whatever reason, the Chinese are singled out. In 1965 they were killed for being communists, now they are killed for being capitalists.

Certainly the Chinese are an entrenched and privileged business class but the eagerness of even educated Indonesians to blame their woes on the Chinese shows deep-rooted ignorance and resentment. Unless the government can promote ethnic harmony or increase economic opportunities for ethnic Indonesians to diffuse resentment, Chinese emigration will increase and with it will go much-needed business expertise and capital.

Though many Chinese fled Indonesia, the majority stayed and many have returned. Indonesia is home to them, as it has been for many generations, and even if they wanted to leave, many Indonesian-Chinese cannot afford to and have nowhere else to go.

EDUCATION

In Indonesia, education begins with six years of primary school (Sekolah Dasar or SD), then three years of junior high school (Sekolah Menengah Pertama or SMP) and three years of senior high school (Sekolah Menengah Atas or SMA), leading on to university. Before the monetary crisis, school enrolments rose to 90% for the seven- to 12-year-old age group, but then fell dramatically. Fewer than half will make it to secondary school and fewer than half again will graduate. Schooling is not free in Indonesia, not even at the primary level. Fees are low, but when combined with uniforms and books, are a burden on the very poor. Unfortunately, many families cannot afford schooling for their children and send them out to work instead, a problem that has increased with the economic crisis. The literacy rate is around 77%.

There are plenty of private schools, many operated by mosques and churches. Private schools generally have higher standards (and higher fees), and this is where the moneyed classes educate their children.

Going to university is expensive and few can afford it. Higher education is concentrated in Java. The foremost and largest university in Indonesia is Universitas Indonesia

(UI) in Jakarta, a government-run university. Yogya is an important educational centre, famous for its Universitas Gajah Mada. Bandung has the major high-tech school, Institut Teknologi Bandung (ITB). Lesser universities are located in the other provinces, such as Sulawesi's Universitas Hasanuddin (UNHAS) in Ujung Pandang.

ARTS

Indonesia has an astonishing array of cultures and all express themselves in different ways. The most readily identifiable arts are from Java and Bali. No travel documentary on Indonesia is complete without scenes of a *wayang kulit* (shadow puppet) performance or a Balinese dance, all performed to the haunting gongs and drums of the gamelan orchestra. Yet Java and Bali are only a small part of a vast archipelago, and Indonesia has an astonishing diversity of dance, music and especially crafts (see the special colour section 'Indonesian Crafts' in this chapter).

Theatre

Javanese *wayang* (puppet) plays have their origins in the Hindu epics, the *Ramayana* and the *Mahabharata*. There are different forms of wayang: wayang kulit are the leather shadow puppets, *wayang golek* are the wooden puppets. A detailed discussion about wayang theatre can be found in the Arts section of the Java chapter.

Dance

If you spend much time in Jakarta or on Bali's Kuta Beach, you could be forgiven if you thought that disco was Indonesia's traditional folk dance. But if you get past the skyscrapers and tourist traps, you'll soon find that Indonesia has a rich heritage of traditional dance styles.

There are wayang dance dramas in Java. Yogyakarta has dance academies as well as its *Ramayana* ballet, Java's most spectacular dance drama. Solo competes with Yogyakarta with its many academies of dance. Wonosobo (Central Java) has its Lengger dance, in which men dress as women. Jaipongan is a modern dance found in West Java, with some erotic elements reminiscent of Brazil's lambada.

Central Kalimantan has the Manasai, a friendly dance in which tourists are welcome to participate. Kalimantan also has the Mandau dance, performed with knives and shields.

Some of the most colourful performances of all, including the Barong, Kecak, Topeng, Legong and Baris dances, are found in Bali. For more information on these and other dances, see Dance under Arts in the Bali chapter.

Music

Indonesia produces a lot of indigenous pop music, most of which does not suit western tastes. One thing you can be certain of is that Indonesians like their music *loud*.

Traditional gamelan orchestras are found primarily in Java and Bali. The orchestras are composed mainly of percussion instruments, including drums, gongs and shake-drums *(angklung)*, along with flutes and xylophones. See the Arts section in the Java chapter for more details.

Dangdut music is a very popular Indonesian modern music, characterised by wailing vocals and a strong beat. Though often attributed to Islamic Arabic influences, its roots lie in Indian pop music popularised by Hindi films. This is the music of Jakarta's kampungs, and is sometimes strongly Islamic in content. Seen as somewhat low class, it was popularised by performers such as Rhoma Irama in the early 1980s; its popularity continues to grow and has spread across the nation.

Western rock music – both modern and vintage stuff from the 1960s – is also popular. Michael Jackson and the Rolling Stones have given concerts to packed audiences at the Senayan football stadium in south Jakarta.

One of Indonesia's established rock idols is Iwan Fals whose anti-establishment and anti-government bent got him arrested several times; but he always seemed to get released fairly quickly, probably because his father is a general in the Indonesian army.

Literature

Pramoedya Ananta Toer, a Javanese author, is Indonesia's most well-known novelist. Toer spent over 14 years in jail under the New Order government because of his political affiliations and criticism of the government. His most famous quartet of historical realist novels set in the colonial era includes *This Earth of Mankind*, *Child of All Nations*, *Footsteps* and *House of Glass*. The quartet charts the life of Minke, a Javanese intellectual who must reconcile his Javanese beliefs with the colonial world around him.

Mochtar Lubis is another well-known Indonesian writer. His most famous novel, *Twilight in Djakarta*, is a scathing attack on corruption and the plight of the poor in Jakarta in the 1950s. The book was banned and Lubis was subsequently jailed. Much has changed, but the problems still remain.

Cinema

While television production is booming, the movie industry is ailing. Indonesia has produced hundreds of movies since independence but the chances of getting to see them, even in Indonesia, are limited. Hollywood and Hong Kong blockbusters dominate Indonesian cinemas, and contemporary Indonesian film makers who explore unacceptable themes, such as poverty, have had trouble gaining distribution for their films.

Many Indonesian films tend to be low budget tragic romances, with a bit of titillation thrown in, or glorifications of Indonesia's revolutionary spirit. In the latter category is the recent *Fatahillah*, a US$1.24 million blockbuster (that's a big budget in Indonesia) which tells the story of the national hero who defeats Portuguese incursions of present-day Jakarta.

Some good movies exploring contemporary Indonesian society have been produced in recent years. They include *Langitku Rumahku* (My Sky, My Home) a touching 1990 film directed by Slamet Rahardjo about two boys, one rich and one from the slums of Jakarta, who form a bond and set off on a journey to Yogyakarta. *Istana Kecantikan* (The Beauty Parlour, 1989) by

Wahyu Sihombing is about a gay man forced into marriage because of societal pressure.

Indonesia's best known contemporary director is Garin Nugroho, whose hard-hitting documentaries and feature films have garnered critical acclaim and international awards. His *Bulan Tertusuk Ilalang* (And the Moon Dances, 1995) was voted the best South-East Asian film and grabbed awards at Berlin, Nantes and Japanese film festivals. It is the story of a master of traditional arts and his relationship with two students, who seek to come to grips with Javanese traditions in a modern world. Other feature films by Garin Nugroho are *Cinta Dalam Sepotong Roti* (Love on a Slice of Bread, 1991) and the acclaimed *Surat Untuk Bidadari* (A Letter to an Angel, 1994). *Dongeng Kancil Tentang Kemerdekaan* (Kancil's Tale of Freedom, 1995) is a documentary following the lives of four boys who scratch a living on the streets of Yogyakarta. It drew criticism from within Indonesia for presenting the darker side of Indonesian life to the world.

SOCIETY & CONDUCT

Indonesia is comprised of a huge spectrum of societies and cultures. However, mass education, mass media and a policy of government-orchestrated nationalism have created a definite Indonesian national culture, using Bahasa Indonesia as its medium.

Though Indonesia is predominantly Islamic, in many places Islam is infused with traditional customs and Hindu-Buddhism, making it barely recognisable from the more orthodox Middle Eastern variety. In terms of area rather than population, most of Indonesia is in fact Christian or animist. Just to leaven the mix, Bali has its own unique brand of Hinduism.

The relatively small but dominant island of Java is increasingly modern, but even here thousand-year-old traditions remain alive, as they do in the rest of the archipelago. While Java is the most developed, and Bali is one of the richest provinces due to tourism receipts, parts of the outer islands have barely emerged from the Neolithic Age. This rift is a great source of resentment,

Dari Mana?

Dari mana? Where do you come from? You will be asked this question frequently, in Bahasa Indonesia or English, along with many other things like *Sudah kawin?* (Are you married?) and *Mau kemana?* (Where are you going?). Visitors can find these questions intrusive, irritating and even infuriating, but Indonesians regard them as polite conversation.

An Indonesian approaching a friend might ask, in their local language, 'What are you doing?', even if it's perfectly obvious. Similarly, someone obviously going to the market might be asked 'Where are you going?', simply as a form of greeting. Indonesians are a curious and very friendly people, and seemingly inane questions are used as small talk and to express positive feelings for others. Indonesians will ask foreign visitors such questions in English (it may be their only English!), and you should not get annoyed – a smile and a 'hello', or a greeting in Indonesian is generally a polite and adequate response. If the questions continue, which is likely, you will need to take a different approach, as one new arrival in Indonesia found out ...

The newcomer was introduced to a young man, who immediately began asking her all manner of personal questions – Where did she come from?, Was she married?, Where was she staying?, Did she like Indonesia? Anxious to be friendly and polite, she tried to answer every question, while becoming increasingly dubious about his motives. But he never seemed to be satisfied with her responses, because as soon as she answered one question, he would ask her another, but he seemed to become more morose with each exchange. Finally, and with a note of utter despondency in his voice, the young man announced, 'I have five children'.

The message is that you don't really have to answer every question, but you should ask some questions yourself to show a polite interest in the other person. If the questioning becomes too nosy, try responding with an equally nosy question and you might be surprised at the warmth of the response. When you've had enough chatter, you can answer the question 'Where are you going?', even if it wasn't asked.

particularly in the eastern islands, where development is slow and Java's neglect, except as a distant ruler, is most noticed.

Indonesia is rent by opposing forces – orthodox Muslim versus syncretist Muslim, Muslim versus Christian versus Hindu, country versus city, modern versus traditional, rich versus poor, 'inner' (ie Java) versus 'outer'. In the current political uncertainty, these age-old opposing forces are threatening to erupt again, but somehow the country still manages to hang together. With notable exceptions like Irian Jaya, East Timor and Aceh, the bonds have grown stronger and an Indonesian as opposed to regional identity has emerged.

Despite the changes and modernisation, Indonesia remains one of the most traditional countries in South-East Asia. Traditional values of the family and religion are maintained. The head of the family is accorded great respect, and children acquiesce to their parents and elders. Beyond the extended family, the main social unit is the village. The concerns of the individual are of less importance than they are in western society, and western notions of individualism are seen as odd or selfish.

'Keeping face' is important to Indonesians and they are generally extremely courteous – criticisms are not spoken directly and they will often agree with what you say rather than offend. They will also prefer to say something rather than appear as if they don't know the answer. They mean well but when you ask how to get somewhere, you may often find yourself being sent off in the wrong direction!

Dos and Don'ts

Indonesians make allowances for western ways, especially in the main tourist areas, but there are a few things to bear in mind when dealing with people.

Never hand over or receive things with the left hand. It will cause offence – the left hand is used to wash after going to the toilet and is considered unclean. To show great respect to a high-ranking or elderly person, hand something to them using both hands.

Talking to someone with your hands on your hips is impolite and is considered a sign of contempt, anger or aggression.

Many Asians resent being touched on the head – the head is regarded as the seat of the soul and is therefore sacred. In Javanese culture, traditionally a lesser person should not have their head above that of a senior person, so you may sometimes see Javanese duck their heads when greeting someone, or walk past with dropped shoulders as a mark of respect.

The correct way to beckon to someone is with the hand extended and a downward waving motion of all the fingers (except the thumb). It looks almost like waving goodbye. The western method of beckoning with the index finger crooked upward won't be understood and is considered rude. It is fine to point at something or to indicate direction, but rude to point at someone – gesture with the whole hand.

Handshaking is customary for both men and women on introduction and greeting. It is customary to shake hands with everyone in the room when arriving or leaving.

Hospitality is highly regarded, and when food or drink is placed in front of you, wait until asked to begin by your host, who will usually say *silahkan* (please). It is impolite to refuse a drink.

While places of worship are open to all, permission should be requested to enter, particularly when ceremonies or prayer are in progress, and you should ensure that you're decently dressed. Always remove footwear before entering a mosque. When entering someone's house, it is polite to remove your shoes.

Indonesians will accept any lack of clothing on the part of poor people who cannot afford them; but for westerners, thongs, bathing costumes, shorts or strapless tops are considered impolite, except perhaps around places like Kuta. Elsewhere you should look respectable.

RELIGION

The early Indonesians were animists, and practised ancestor and spirit worship. The social and religious duties of the early agricultural communities that developed in the archipelago were gradually refined to form a code of behaviour which became the basis of adat, or customary law. When Hindu-Buddhism spread into the archipelago it was overlaid on this spiritual culture. There are still a few areas where the practice of animism survives virtually intact, such as in West Sumba and some parts of Irian Jaya.

Although Islam eventually became the predominant religion of the archipelago, it was really only a nominal victory. What we see in ostensibly Islamic Indonesia today is often Islam rooted in Hindu-Buddhism, adat and animism. Old beliefs persist and in Java, for example, there are literally hundreds of holy places where spiritual energy is said to be concentrated. Meditators and pilgrims flock to these areas and to the graves of saints, despite the proscription against saint worship by Islam.

As for Christianity, despite the lengthy colonial era, missionaries have only converted pockets of the Indonesian population. The Christian beliefs that have been absorbed are also usually fused with indigenous religious beliefs and customs.

Since independence, religious tolerance has been vigorously promoted in Indonesia. However, the rise of militant Islamic groups, such as Darul Islam in the 1950s, threaten Indonesian's 'Unity in Diversity' and are summarily crushed.

Hinduism

Outside India, Hindus predominate only in Nepal and Bali. However, the Hinduism of Bali is far removed from that of India.

Hinduism came to Bali from Java, which Islam overran in the 17th century. (A few isolated pockets of Hinduism remain, notably the Tengger people around Gunung Bromo.)

Hinduism is a complex religion, but at its core is the mystical principle that the physical world is an illusion *(maya)* and until this is realised through enlightenment *(moksha)*, the individual is condemned to a cycle of rebirths and reincarnations. Brahma is the ultimate god and universal spirit, but Hinduism has a vast pantheon of gods who are worshipped on a daily basis.

The two main gods are Shiva, the destroyer, and Vishnu, the preserver. Shivaism represents a more esoteric and ascetic path, and with Shiva's *shakti* or female energy (represented by his wives Kali and Parvati), destruction and fertility are intertwined. Shivaism generally found greater acceptance in Indonesia, perhaps because it was closer to existing fertility worship and the appeasement of malevolent spirits. Vishnuism places greater emphasis on devotion and duty, and

LPP
The Hindu god, Ganesh, Shiva's elephant-headed son.

Vishnu's incarnations, Krishna and Rama, feature heavily in Indonesian art and culture through the stories of the *Ramayana*.

Hinduism and Buddhism were often intertwined in Indonesia and many empires accepted the principles and iconography of both religions. Hinduism's rigid caste system had much less relevance, but the notions of the god-king and the elitist nature of Hindu society were readily accepted by Indonesian rulers.

Buddhism

Buddhism was founded by Siddhartha Gautama, an Indian prince, in the 6th century BC. His message is that the cause of life's suffering is the illusory nature of desire, and that by overcoming desire we can free ourselves from suffering. Desire can be conquered by following the Eightfold Path, consisting of right understanding, thought, speech, conduct, livelihood, effort, attentiveness and concentration. The ultimate goal is nirvana, the escape from the endless round of births and rebirths, and their lives of suffering.

Buddhism is essentially a Hindu reform movement, and its philosophy owes much to the Hindu notions of maya and moksha. The big difference is that Buddhism shunned the Hindu pantheon of gods and the caste system. It was initially not so much a religion but a practical, moral philosophy free from the priestly Brahman hierarchy.

Buddhism gained wide adherence in India with its adoption by Emperor Ashoka in the 3rd century BC, but later split into two sects: Mahayana (greater path) and Hinayana (lesser path), also known as Theravada (teaching of the elders). Mahayana Buddhism incorporates greater mysticism and the *bodhisattva* (saint who attained nirvana) reintroduced the idea of divinity to Buddhism.

Most Buddhists in Indonesia are Chinese. Though Chinese religion typically blends Buddhism with Taoism, Confucianism and ancestor worship, most Chinese profess to be Buddhist, to satisfy the Pancasila's tenet of 'belief in one god'.

Hinduism & Buddhism in Indonesia

Sanskrit inscriptions date back to the 5th century AD, and many ancient Hindu and Buddhist shrines and statues have been found in the archipelago. The two religions were often intertwined and fused with older religious beliefs.

Indian religion and culture has had more influence in royal courts and government, and one prevalent theory is that the emerging kingdoms of Indonesia invited Brahman priests from India to confer mythological sanction to the new rulers. The Indian concept of the god-king, the use of Sanskrit as the language of religion and courtly literature, and the introduction of Indian mythology were all concentrated in the courts, while ordinary people followed traditional religions.

Indonesia adapted Indian religion to its needs. Even the events and people recorded in epics like the *Ramayana* and *Mahabharata* have been shifted out of India to Java. Various Hindu and Buddhist monuments were built in Java. The Sumatran-based Sriwijaya kingdom, which arose in the 7th century, was the centre of Buddhism in Indonesia.

Bali's establishment as a Hindu enclave dates from the time when the Javanese Hindu kingdom of Majapahit, in the face of Islam, evacuated Java to the neighbouring island. The Balinese probably already had strong religious beliefs and an active cultural life, and the new influences were simply overlaid on the existing practices – hence the peculiar Balinese variant of Hinduism.

Islam

In the early 7th century in Mecca, Mohammed received the word of Allah (God) and called on the people to submit to the one true God. His teachings appealed to the poorer levels of society and angered the wealthy merchant class. In 622 Mohammed and his followers were forced to flee Medina, and this migration – the *hijrah* – marks the beginning of the Islamic calendar, year 1 AH or 622 AD. In 630 Mohammed returned to take Mecca.

Islam is the Arabic word for submission, and the duty of every Muslim is to submit themselves to Allah. This profession of faith (the *Shahada*) is the first of the Five Pillars of Islam, the five tenets in the Koran which guide Muslims in their daily life. The other four are to pray five times a day, give alms to the poor, fast during the month of Ramadan, and make the pilgrimage to Mecca at least once in a lifetime.

In its early days Islam suffered a major schism into two branches – the Sunnis (or Sunnites) and the Shi'ites – after a struggle to overtake the Caliphate. The Sunnis comprise the majority of Muslims today, including most Muslims in Indonesia.

Islam in Indonesia

The first contact with Islam came through Muslim traders, primarily from India, who introduced a less orthodox form of Islam than that of Arabia. The state of Perlak in Aceh adopted Islam near the end of the 13th century, then the ruler of Melaka accepted the faith in the early part of the 15th century. Melaka, on the Malay peninsula, became the centre of South-East Asian trade, and a centre of Islamic study, and trading ships carried the new religion to Java, from where it spread to the spice islands of eastern Indonesia via Makassar (now Ujung Pandang) in Sulawesi. Islam caught hold in Java in the 16th and 17th centuries. At about the same time, Aceh developed as a major Islamic power and the religion took root in west and south Sumatra, and in Kalimantan and Sulawesi.

By the 15th and 16th centuries, centres for the teaching of Islam along the northern coast of Java played an important role in disseminating the new religion, and established centres of Hinduism also adopted elements of Islam. Javanese tradition holds that the first propagators of Islam in Java were nine holy men, the *wali songo*, who possessed a deep knowledge of Islamic teaching as well as exceptional supernatural powers. Another theory holds that Islam was adopted by the rulers of the coastal trading ports, who broke with the dominant Hindu kingdoms of the interior that claimed suzerainty over the north. The common people followed suit in much the same way as Europeans adopted the religions

Indonesian Mosques

A mosque is an enclosure for prayer. The word *mesjid* means 'to prostrate oneself in prayer'. Mosques can be differentiated according to function: the *jami mesjid* is used for the Friday prayer meetings; the *musalla* is one that is used for prayer meetings but not for those on Friday; the 'memorial mosque' is for the commemoration of victorious events in Islamic history; and the *mashad* is found in a tomb compound. There are also prayer houses that are used by only one person at a time, not for collective worship – you'll often find that larger hotels and airport terminals in Indonesia have a room set aside for this purpose.

The oldest mosques in Indonesia – in Cirebon and Demak in Java, and Palembang in Sumatra, for example – have rooms with two, three or five storeys. It is thought that these multistorey rooms were based on Hindu meru (shrines) that you see on Bali. Today's mosques are often built with a high dome over an enclosed prayer hall. Inside these are five main features. The *mihrab* is a niche in a wall marking the direction to Mecca. The *mimbar* is a raised pulpit, often canopied, with a staircase. There is also a stand to hold the Koran, a screen to provide privacy for important worshippers, and a fountain, pool or water jug for ablutions. Outside the building there is often a menara – a minaret, or tower, from which the muezzin summons the community to prayer. Apart from these few items the interior of the mosque is empty. There are no seats and no decorations – if there is any ornamentation at all it will be quotations of verses from the Koran. The congregation sits on the floor.

Friday afternoons are officially set aside for believers to worship, and all government offices and many businesses are closed as a result. All over Indonesia you'll hear the call to prayer from the mosques, but the muezzin of Indonesia are now a dying breed – the wailing is now usually recorded on a cassette tape.

Because of the preponderance of Muslims in Indonesia, especially in Java, very large mosque complexes, such as the Istiqlal Mosque in Jakarta, have been built. These complexes have the space to accommodate tens of thousands of worshippers, and depart from typical Javanese mosque-building traditions in response to global influences and technological advances.

of their kings, and these Islamic kingdoms went on to overrun and sack the Hindu courts.

Whatever the reasons for the spread of Islam, today it is the professed religion of 90% of Indonesians, and its traditions and rituals affect all aspects of their daily life. Like Hinduism and Buddhism before it, Islam also had to come to terms with older existing traditions and customs.

Customs in Indonesia often differ from those of other Muslim countries. Respect for the dead throughout most of Indonesia is not expressed by wearing veils but by donning traditional dress. Muslim women in Indonesia are allowed more freedom than their counterparts in other Muslim countries. They do not have to wear *jilbab* (head covering), nor are they segregated. Muslim men in Indonesia are allowed to marry only two women and even then must have the consent of their first wife – Muslims in other parts of the world can have as many as four wives. Throughout Indonesia it is the women who initiate divorce proceedings. The Minangkabau society of Sumatra, for example, is a strongly Muslim group but their adat allows matriarchal rule, which conflicts strongly with the assumption of male supremacy inherent in Islam.

Like other Muslims, Indonesian Muslims practise circumcision. The laws of Islam require that all boys be circumcised, and in Indonesia this is usually done somewhere between the ages of six and 11.

One of the most important Islamic festivals is Ramadan, a month of fasting prescribed by Islamic law.

Islam not only influences routine daily living but also Indonesian politics. It was with the Diponegoro revolt in the 19th century that Islam first became a rallying point in Indonesia. In the early part of the 20th century Sarekat Islam became the first mass political party. Its philosophy was derived from Islam and its support was derived from the Muslim population. In post-independence Indonesia it was an Islamic organisation, Darul Islam, which launched a separatist movement in West Java.

Islam has always followed a tolerant path in Indonesia, and a majority have never been too concerned about following Islam to the letter. That said, millions of Indonesians have made the pilgrimage to Mecca. Islam in Indonesia is becoming more orthodox, as can be seen by the growing number of women who wear the jilbab. Militant Muslim groups exist, but most Indonesians are very suspicious of them, and any attempts to incite religious division are quickly crushed by the government.

Christianity in Indonesia

The Portuguese introduced christianity in the 16th century. Though they dabbled in religious conversion in Maluku and sent Dominican friars on religious/colonising expeditions to Timor and Flores, their influence was never strong and they were soon supplanted by the Dutch.

For the Dutch, trade was paramount and interference in religion was strictly avoided in Java and other Muslim areas. Missionary efforts only came when the Dutch set about establishing direct colonial rule in the rest of Indonesia at the end of the 19th century. Animist areas were up for grabs in Indonesia, and missionaries set about their work with zeal in East Nusa Tenggara, Maluku,

Kalimantan, Irian Jaya and parts of Sumatra (notably among the Batak) and Sulawesi (among the Minahasans).

Thus Christianity is a relatively new religion in Indonesia, and it often exists over a base of animist beliefs. Protestants form a slight majority because of the work of Dutch Calvinist and Lutheran missions, but Catholics are also numerous. East Timor is almost 100% Catholic because of Portuguese colonisation, and Flores is predominantly Catholic because of the work of priests from the Dutch SVD mission.

Muslims and Christians generally coexist in harmony, but religious conflict has spiralled in recent times. Church authorities estimate that over 600 churches were attacked in Indonesia in 1997-98, mostly in Java. Though the Muslim *ulama* (religious leaders) and church authorities persistently stress tolerance, rumours point to small numbers of clandestine Muslim militants whipping up trouble. At the same time, in majority Christian areas, any rumours about an affront to Christianity can result in mobs attacking mosques.

The conflict is often not strictly one of religion. In Java, the attacks often go hand in hand with the senseless violence against the Chinese, because many Chinese, in the face of discrimination against their traditions, have converted to Christianity. In majority Christian areas, there may be resentment against Javanese settlers, who dominate the marketplaces.

Christians are very aware of their minority status. There is often resentment of the central government and many Christians feel excluded from mainstream power. Attacks on churches have engendered retaliation, such as the anti-Muslim riots in Kupang in 1998 following attacks on churches in Jakarta. Though few in number, Indonesia's Christian communities are spread over a large part of the country.

INDONESIAN
CRAFTS

Indonesia's crafts reflect the regional histories, religions and influences of the archipelago's mind-boggling array of ethnic groups. Its crafts can be classified into three major groupings, which loosely parallel the three cultural streams within Indonesia.

The first is that of 'outer' Indonesia, the islands of Sumatra, Kalimantan, Sulawesi, Nusa Tenggara, Maluku and Irian Jaya, which have strong animist traditions. Crafts such as carving, weaving and pottery have developed from tribal religious art.

The second stream is that of 'inner' Indonesia – the islands of Java and Bali – which have come under the greatest influence from Hindu-Buddhist tradition. The techniques and styles that built Borobudur temple and the Indian epics such as the *Mahabharata*, which form the basis for *wayang* theatre, are still a major influence on arts and crafts.

The third influence is that of Islam, which not so much introduced its own artistic tradition, but modified existing traditions. Its more rigid style and its ban on human and animal representation restricted art, yet because of it, existing artistic traditions became more stylised.

These days the religious influence or magic associated with many traditional objects is disappearing. For example, *sahan*, the Batak medicine holder made from a buffalo horn, line Danau Toba (Lake Toba) craft shops. These copies have no significance to the maker apart from the sale value.

While one can lament at the passing of traditional meaning and methods, it would be wrong to assume that the tourist trade is destroying traditional crafts. The sophistication and innovation of the craft 'industry' is growing. For example, Batak carvers now produce sahan that are bigger and more intricately carved than the original. While they lack spiritual meaning, they are fine pieces of craftwork. The designs have changed to suit the market – small, simple sahan just don't sell, and anyway, the spiritual meaning of an original sahan has no relevance for most buyers.

Of course, many of the trinkets turned out for the tourist trade are of poor quality and there is an increasing cross-fertilisation of craft styles. The 'primitif' Asmat or Kalimantan statues, so in vogue in Balinese art shops, may well have been carved just up the road in Peliatan. On the other hand, Javanese woodcarvers are turning out magnificent traditional panels and innovative furniture commissioned by large hotels, and Balinese jewellers influenced by western designs are producing new work of stunning quality.

RICHARD I'ANSON

Title Page: Hand-crafted Javanese *wayang golek* puppets feature beaten metal adornments (photograph by Gregory Adams).

Left: Carved mask.

WOODCARVING

Woodcarving is the most enduring and widespread medium for artistic expression in Indonesia. Each culture has its own style, and the diversity and sophistication of Indonesia's woodcarvers is remarkable.

In Indonesia, a house not only protects its inhabitants from the elements, but repels unwanted spirits. Examples include the horned *singa* (lion) heads that protect Batak houses, the water buffalo representations on Toraja houses signifying prosperity, and the serpent and magical dog carvings on Dayak houses in Kalimantan.

Woodcarvings and statues are an important expression of the spirits in the outer islands. Statues of the ancestors are an integral part of

BERNARD NAPTHINE

SIMON BRACKEN

JULIET COOMBE

EMMA MILLER

ADAM McCROW

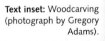
Text inset: Woodcarving (photograph by Gregory Adams).

Right: Woodcarving adorns religious objects, such as temple guardians, and furniture, such as a Javanese *jodang* (solid rectangular box with higher ends).

spiritual life on Nias and Sumba islands. The Toraja's famed funerals are important events for the artist also; a realistic statue is carved of the dead and the coffin is adorned with animal heads. In Ngaju and Dusun villages in Kali-

ERIC L WHEATER

mantan, giant carved ancestor totems *(temadu)* depict the dead.

Perhaps the most famous and mythologised of Indonesia's woodcarvers are the Asmat of south-west Irian Jaya. Shields, canoes, spears, drums and everyday objects are carved, but the most distinctive and easily recognisable Asmat woodcarvings are the ancestor poles *(mbis)*. These poles show the dead one above the other, and the open carved 'wing' at the top of the pole is a phallic symbol expressing fertility and power. The poles are also an expression of revenge and were traditionally carved to accompany a feast following a head-hunting raid.

Woodcarving also has a decorative as well as spiritual function, and everyday objects from the outer islands are often intricately carved. Some of the most common objects are the baby carriers and ironwood stools from Kalimantan, lacquered bowls from South Sumatra, carved bamboo containers from Sulawesi, and even doors from Timor and horse effigies from Sumba.

Bali and Java also have strong woodcarving traditions, with Balinese woodcarving the most ornamental and intricate in Indonesia. Carved statues, temple doors and relief panels are decorated with the gods and demons of Balinese cosmology. While religion still plays an important part in traditional Balinese woodcarving, nowhere in Indonesia has western art

BERNARD NAPTHINE

and souvenir demand made so much impact. Western influence saw a revolution in woodcarving akin to that in Balinese painting (see the special colour section 'Balinese Painting' in the Bali chapter). Many years ago Balinese woodcarvers began producing simpler, elongated statues of purely ornamental design with a natural finish. Nowadays Bali also produces its own interpretations of Asmat totems or Kalimantan fertility statues, as well as unique modern statues.

The centre for woodcarving in Java is Jepara on the north coast of

Top: Dayak Spirit House, Kalimantan.

Bottom: Carved wooden door panel, Agung Rai Museum of Art (ARMA), Ubud.

Central Java. The intricate style is obviously of the same tradition as the Balinese, but Islamic and other influences have seen human representation replaced by heavily carved and stylised motifs. Heavily carved furniture is the main business in Jepara. Other centres in Java are Kudus, which mostly produces intricate panels seen in traditional houses, and Madura.

The most favoured and durable wood in Indonesia is teak *(jati)*, though this is an increasingly expensive commodity. Sandalwood, which is grown in East Timor, is also occasionally seen in Balinese carvings. Mahogany is also used, though not common, while ebony imported from Sulawesi and Kalimantan is used in Bali. This very heavy wood is also very expensive. Jackfruit is a common, cheap wood, though it tends to warp and split. Above all, local carvers use woods at hand so, for example, heavy ironwood and meranti are used in Kalimantan woodcarving, and *belalu*, a quick growing light wood, is used in Bali.

Carved Masks

Masks are also a specialised form of woodcarving. Though they exist throughout the archipelago and may be used in funerary rites and the like, the most readily identifiable form of mask is the topeng used in the wayang *topeng* dances of Java and Bali. Dancers perform tales from Indian epics such as the *Mahabharata*, or from distinctly local tales, and the masks are used to represent the characters. Masks vary from the stylised but plain masks of Central and West Java to the heavily carved masks of East Java. Balinese topeng masks are less stylised and more naturalistic – the Balinese save their love of colour and detail for the masks of the Barong dance, which is more strongly pre-Hindu in influence.

RICHARD I'ANSON

RICHARD I'ANSON

Right: Carved masks, Lombok.

TEXTILES

Indonesian textiles come in a dazzling variety of fabrics, materials, techniques, colours and motifs. Basically there are three major textile groupings.

The first is *ikat*, a form of tie-dyeing patterns onto threads before weaving them together; this technique is associated with the proto-Malay people of the archipelago such as the ethnic groups of Nusa Tenggara (see the Nusa Tenggara chapter for more information on ikat). The second is *songket*, where gold or silver threads are woven into silk cloth. This is strongest where Islam has made the most impact, such as Aceh on Sumatra and among the Malays of coastal Kalimantan. The third group is *batik*, the alternate waxing and dyeing technique most clearly associated with those parts of central Java where the great Javanese kingdoms were established. It was also taken up in Bali, Madura and in Jambi on Sumatra, all of which have been subject to considerable Javanese influence.

Ikat

The Indonesian word ikat, which means to tie or bind, is the name for the intricately patterned cloth of threads which are tie-dyed in a very painstaking and skilful process *before* they are woven together.

Ikat cloth is made in many scattered regions of the archipelago, from Sumatra to Maluku, but it's in Nusa Tenggara that this ancient art form thrives. Ikat garments are still in daily use in many areas, and there's an incredible diversity of colours and patterns. The spectacular ikat of Sumba and the intricate patterned work of Flores are the best known, but Timor and Lombok and small islands like Roti, Sawu, Ndao and Lembata all have their own varied and high-quality traditions, as do Sulawesi, Kalimantan and Sumatra. In Bali the rare double-ikat method, in which both warp and weft threads are pre-dyed, is used in the weavings of Gringseng.

PETER TURNER

Text inset: Cottons used in *batik*, Lombok (photograph by Juliet Coombe)

Left: Young girl, Umabara, Sumba.

Making Ikat

Ikat cloth is nearly always made of cotton, still often hand spun, though factory-made threads have come into use. Dyes are traditionally handmade from local plants and minerals, and these give ikat its characteristically earthy tones, as well as the blue of indigo.

Ikat comes in a variety of shapes and sizes, including *selendang* (shawls); sarongs; 2m-long tubes which can be used as a cloak or rolled down to the waist to resemble a sarong; *selimut* (blankets); and 4m-long pieces (known as *kapita* in Flores) used as winding cloths for burial of the dead.

Some aspects of ikat production are changing with the use of manufactured dyes and thread. A description of the traditional method follows.

Ikat production is performed by women – they produce the dyes and plant, harvest, spin, dye and weave the cotton. Spinning is generally done with a spindle. The thread is strengthened by immersion in stiffening baths of grated cassava, finely stamped rice or a meal made of roasted maize, and then is threaded onto a winder. The product is usually thicker and rougher than machine-spun cotton.

Traditional dyes are made from natural sources. The most complex processes are those involved with the production of the bright rust colour, known on Sumba as *kombu*, which is produced from the bark and roots of the kombu tree. Blue dyes come from the indigo plant, and purple or brown can be produced by dyeing the cloth deep blue and then overdyeing it with kombu.

Each time the threads are dipped in dye, the sections that are not due to receive colour are bound together ('ikatted') beforehand with dye-resistant fibre. A separate tying-and-dyeing process is carried out for each colour that will appear in the finished cloth – and the sequence

RICHARD I'ANSON

Right: Ikat weaving.

of dyeing has to consider the effect of over-dyeing. This stage requires great skill, as the dyer has to work out – *before* the threads are woven into cloth – exactly which parts of the thread are to receive each colour in order to create the complicated pattern of the final cloth. After dyeing, the cloth is woven on a simple hand loom.

There is a defined time for the traditional production of ikat. On Sumba the thread is spun between July and October, and the patterns bound between September and December. After the rain ends in April, the blue and kombu dyeing is carried out. In August the weaving starts – more than a year after work on the thread began.

Origins & Meaning of Ikat

The ikat technique probably came to Indonesia over 2000 years ago with migrants bringing the Dongson culture from southern China and Vietnam. It has survived in more isolated areas that were bypassed by later cultural influences.

Ikat styles vary according to the village and gender of the wearer, and some types of cloth are reserved for special purposes. In parts of Nusa Tenggara, high quality ikat is part of a bride's dowry. On Sumba, less than 90 years ago, only members of the highest clans could make and wear ikat textiles. Certain motifs were traditionally reserved for noble families (as on Sumba and Roti) or members of a particular tribe or clan (Sawu or among the Atoni of Timor).

Motifs & Patterns

In the 20th century traditional motifs have blended with some of European origin, and ikat's function in indicating its wearer's role or rank has declined.

Top: Elements of the ikat production process including dyed cotton drying and pots of dyes.

Some experts believe that motifs found on Sumba, such as front-views of people, animals and birds stem from an artistic tradition even older than Dongson. The main Dongson influence was in geometric motifs like diamond and key shapes (which often go together), meanders and spirals.

A particularly strong influence was cloth known as *patola* from Gujurat in India. In the 16th and 17th centuries these became highly prized in Indonesia and one characteristic motif was copied by local ikat weavers. It's still a favourite today – a hexagon framing a four pronged star. On the best patola and geometric ikat, repeated small patterns combine to form larger patterns and the longer you look at it the more patterns you see – rather like a mandala.

Judging Ikat

Not so easy! Books on the subject aren't much use when you're confronted with a market trader telling you that yes, this cloth is definitely hand-spun and yes, of course the dyes are natural. Taking a look at the process is informative: you can see women weaving in many places, and at the right time of year you may see dye-making, thread-spinning or tie-dyeing. Cloths made in villages will nearly always be hand spun and hand woven. Here are some tips on recognising the traditional product:

Thread Hand-spun cotton has a less perfect 'twist' to it than factory cloth.

Weave Hand-woven cloth, whether made from hand-spun or factory thread, feels rougher and, when new, stiffer than machine-woven cloth. It will probably have imperfections (perhaps minor) in the weave.

Top: Ikat examples from Nusa Tenggara.

INDONESIAN CRAFTS

Dyes Until you've seen enough ikat to get a feel for whether colours are natural or chemical, you often have to rely on your instincts as to whether they are 'earthy' enough. Some cloths contain both natural and artificial dyes.

Dyeing Method The patterns on cloths which have been individually tie-dyed by the authentic method will rarely be perfectly defined, but they're unlikely to have the detached specks of colour that often appear on mass-dyed cloth.

Age No matter what anybody tells you, there are very few antique cloths around. Most of what you'll be offered for sale will be new or newly second-hand. There are several processes to make cloth look old.

Songket

Songket is silk cloth with gold or silver threads woven into it, although these days imitation silver or gold is often used. Songket is most commonly found in West Sumatra, but can be seen in parts of Kalimantan and Bali. Gold thread is also used in embroidery in the more Islamic areas of Indonesia.

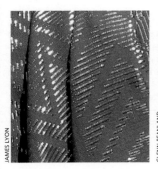
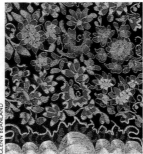

JAMES LYON

GLENN BEANLAND

Batik

The technique of applying wax or some other type of dye-resistant substance (like rice paste) to cloth to produce a design is found in many parts of the world. The Javanese were making batik cloth as early as the 12th century, but its origins are hard to trace. Some think the skills were brought to Java from India, others that the Javanese developed the technique themselves. The word 'batik' is an old Javanese word meaning 'to dot'.

The development of batik in Indonesia is usually associated with the flowering of the creative arts around the royal courts – it's likely that the use of certain motifs was the preserve of the aristocracy. The rise of Islam in Java probably contributed to the stylisation of batik patterns and to the absence of representations of living things. More

Left to right: Silver threaded *songket*; Minankabau wedding scarf, Bukittinggi, Sumatra.

recently batik has grown from an art mainly associated with the royal courts into an important industry.

In the older method of making batik is known as *batik tulis* or 'written batik'. The wax is applied hot to the smooth cloth with a *canting*, a pen-like instrument with a small reservoir of liquid wax. The design is first traced out onto the prepared white cloth (or onto a cloth previously dyed to the lightest colour required in the finished product) and the patterns are then drawn in wax. The wax-covered areas resist colour change when immersed in a dye bath. The waxing and dyeing are continued with increasingly dark shades until the final colours are achieved. Wax is added to protect previously dyed areas or scraped off to expose new areas to the dye. Finally, all the wax is scraped off and the cloth boiled to remove all traces of the wax.

From the mid-19th century, production was speeded up by applying the wax with a metal stamp called a *cap*. The cap technique can usually be identified by the repetition of identical patterns, whereas in batik tulis, even repeated geometric motifs vary slightly. Some batik combines the cap technique with canting work for fine detail. It's worth noting that batik cap is true batik; don't confuse it with screen-printed cloth which completely bypasses the waxing process and is often passed off as batik.

Java is the home of Indonesian batik and each district produces its own style. The court cities of Yogyakarta and Solo in Central Java are major batik centres. Traditional court designs are dominated by brown, yellow and indigo blue. These days both cities produce a wide range of modern as well as traditional batiks. Solo is also a major textile centre.

Batik from the north coast of Java has always been more colourful and innovative in design – as the trading region of Java, the north coast came in contact with many influences. Pekalongan is the other major batik centre on the north coast, and traditional floral designs are brightly coloured and show a Chinese influence. Many modern designs and bird motifs are now employed and some of Indonesia's most interesting batik comes from Pekalongan. Cirebon also produces very colourful and fine traditional batik tulis.

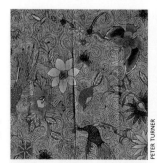

Left to right: *Batik* sarong, Cirebon, West Java; Modern mass-produced *batik* sarongs.

PETER TURNER

RICHARD I'ANSON

CERAMICS

Indonesia's position on the trade routes saw the import of large amounts of ceramics from China, making it a fertile hunting ground for antique Chinese ceramics dating back to the Han dynasty. The best examples of truly indigenous ceramics are the terracottas from the Majapahit empire of East Java.

Indonesian pottery is usually unglazed and hand-worked, although the wheel is also used. It may be painted, but is often left natural. Potters around Mojokerto, close to the original Majapahit capital, still produce terracottas, but the best known pottery centre in Java is just outside Yogyakarta at Kasongan, where intricate, large figurines and pots are produced.

In the Singkiwang area of West Kalimantan, the descendants of Chinese potters produce a unique style of utilitarian pottery.

Lombok pottery has an earthy 'primitive' look with subtle colourings. Balinese ceramics show a stronger western influence and are more inclined to be glazed.

Text inset: Utilitarian Lombok ceramics (photograph by Richard I'Anson).

Left: The distinctive ceramics of Lombok – Penujak, 6km south of Praya, Banyumulok and Masbagik are all centres for the production of traditional pottery.

BASKETWORK & BEADWORK

Some of the finest basketwork in Indonesia comes from Lombok. The spiral woven rattan work is very fine and large baskets are woven using this method, while smaller receptacles topped with wooden carvings are also popular.

In Java, Tasikmalaya is a major cane-weaving centre, often adapting baskets and vessels to modern uses with the introduction of zips and plastic lining. The Minangkabau people, centred around Bukittinggi, also produce interesting palm leaf bags and purses, while the lontar palm is used extensively in weaving on Timor, Roti and other outer eastern islands. The Dayak of Kalimantan produce some superb woven baskets and string bags, and they also produce some fine beadwork which can be seen on their baby carriers.

Some of the most colourful and attractive beadwork is produced by the Toraja of Sulawesi, and beadwork can be found throughout Nusa Tenggara from Lombok to Timor. Small, highly prized cowrie shells are used like beads and are found on Dayak and Lombok artefacts, though the best application of these shells is in the Sumbanese tapestries intricately beaded with shells.

RICHARD I'ANSON

RICHARD I'ANSON

GLENN BEANLAND

RICHARD I'ANSON

Text inset: Rattan bundles, Kalimantan (photograph by Marie Cambon).

Right: Lombok is noted for its fine spiral-woven basketware.

PUPPETS

The most famous puppets of Indonesia are the carved leather *wayang kulit* puppets. The intricate lace figures are cut from buffalo hide with a sharp, chisel-like stylus and then painted. They are produced in Bali and Java, particularly Central Java. The leaf-shaped *kayon* representing the 'tree' or 'mountain of life' is used to end scenes in the wayang and is also made of leather.

Wayang golek are the three dimensional wooden puppets found in Central Java, but are most popular among the Sundanese of West Java. The *wayang klitik* puppets are a rarer flat wooden puppet of East Java.

GREGORY ADAMS

GREGORY ADAMS

Text inset: *Wayang kuli* shadow puppet, Yogya-karta (photograph by Sara-Jane Cleland).

Top: In the shadow puppet theatre of Java, stories are usually based on the Hindu epics, the *Ramayana* and the *Mahabarata*.

Bottom: Javanese *wayang golek* puppets.

METALWORK

The Bronze age in Indonesia began with the metalworking introduced from Dongson culture (present-day Vietnam). Bronze work peaked with the Hindu-Buddhist empires of Java. Brassware was mostly of Indian and Islamic influence. Today, some of the best workmanship is that of the Minangkabau in Sumatra, but brassware is also produced in Java, South Kalimantan and Sulawesi.

The most important ironwork objects are knives and swords. As well as kris, Kalimantan *parang* are sacred weapons used in everything from jungle clearance to head-hunting. Scabbards for ceremonial parang are intricately decorated with beads, shells and feathers.

Kris

Some think the Javanese kris (*iris* – to cut) is derived from the bronze daggers produced by the Dongson around the 1st century AD. Bas-reliefs of a kris appear in the 14th century Panataran temple-complex in East Java, and the carrying of the kris as a custom in Java was noted in 15th century Chinese records. Even today, the kris is still an integral part of men's formal dress on ceremonial and festive occasions.

The kris is no ordinary knife. It is said to be endowed with supernatural powers; *adat* (traditional law) requires that every father furnish his son with a kris upon his reaching manhood, preferably an heirloom kris enabling his son to draw on the powers of his ancestors which are stored in the sacred weapon.

Distinctive features, the number of curves in the blade and the damascene-design on the blade are read to indicate good or bad

Text inset: Kris for sale (photograph by Sara-Jane Cleland).

Left to right: Kris worn to a funeral ceremony, West Sumba; kris, Lombok.

SARA-JANE CLELAND

JULIET COOMBE

fortune for its owner. The number of curves in the blade also has symbolic meaning: five curves symbolise the five Pandava brothers of the *Mahabharata* epic; three represents fire, ardour or passion. Although the blade is the most important part of the kris, the hilt and scabbard are also beautifully decorated.

Before the arrival of Islam, Hindu-inspired images were often used to decorate the wooden hilts – the mythological Garuda was a popular figure. After the spread of Islam such motifs were discouraged, but were often preserved in stylised forms – the origins and symbolism of the kris lay too deep in Javanese mysticism to be eradicated by the laws of Islam.

Although the kris is mostly associated with Java and Bali, it is also found in Sumatra, Kalimantan and Sulawesi. Kris from the outer islands are larger and less ornate than those in Java and Bali.

Jewellery

Gold and silver work has long been practised in Indonesia. Some of the best gold jewellery comes from Aceh in the very north of Sumatra where fine filigree work is produced, and chunky bracelets and earrings are produced in the Batak lands. Gold jewellery can be found all over Indonesia and, while some interesting traditional work can be found throughout the islands, the ubiquitous *toko mas* (gold shop) found in every Indonesian city is mostly an investment house selling gold jewellery by weight, while design and workmanship take a back seat.

The best known jewellery is the silver jewellery of both Bali and the ancient city of Kota Gede within the city boundaries of Yogyakarta. Balinese work is nearly always hand-worked and rarely involves casting techniques. Balinese jewellery is innovative, employing traditional designs but, more often than not, adapting designs or copying from other jewellery presented by western buyers. The traditional centre for Balinese jewellery is Cleek.

Kota Gede in Yogyakarta is another major silver centre, famous for its fine filigree work. Silverware tends to be more traditional, but is also starting to branch out and adapt new designs. As well as jewellery, Kota Gede produces a wide range of silver tableware.

Left to right: A bride adorned in traditional Balinese handbeaten gold jewellery; Girl at Usaba Sambah Festival, Tenganan, Bali.

GREGORY ADAMS

RICHARD I'ANSON

Facts for the Visitor

SUGGESTED ITINERARIES

It is impossible to see all of Indonesia in the 60 days allowed by a tourist pass, if not in a lifetime. If you are prepared to fly extensively you can easily visit a funeral in Tana Toraja, lie on the beach on Bali, hear a *gamelan* orchestra at the sultan's palace in Yogyakarta, see Danau Toba (Lake Toba) and the Komodo dragons – all in one month. This requires stamina and a great deal of luck, especially for travel to remote regions where transport is limited, subject to cancellation and bookings often go astray.

Most visitors to Indonesia have only a few weeks to explore the vast archipelago, and it pays to choose only one, two or a maximum of three regions to explore.

The most visited islands are Bali, Java and Sumatra, and it is possible to see the main highlights of these three islands in one hectic month. The other regions are less inaccessible these days, though travel costs are higher because air travel is essential unless you have large amounts of time.

Always allow extra time. Travel can sometimes be hard, flight schedules are less reliable due to the *krisis moneter* (monetary crisis) and you may need extra time to rest. You may also find yourself sidetracked to some wonderful place that you never knew existed. Schedules in Indonesia are flexible, and you may be forced to bend your own.

Bali

Compact Bali, with good infrastructure and travel services, is the easiest island to explore. Based at the beach resorts of southern Bali, you can see most of the island on day trips. Ubud is a good base for Central Bali, with Gunung Kawi (Mt Kawi), Goa Gaja (Gaja Cave) and many nearby craft villages. Gunung Batur is a popular attraction in the central mountains, while Lovina is a popular budget beach in the north. Bali has plenty of attractions to keep you busy for a few days or to a month or more.

Highlights

Indonesia has fine beaches, volcanoes, ancient cultures, magnificent wilderness, vibrant cities, archaeological wonders – too many highlights to visit in a limited time. Perhaps Indonesia's greatest attraction is its people, in a country of many varied cultures, each presents a unique face.

- Bali's beaches, including Kuta/Legian, Sanur, Nusa Dua, Lovina and Candidasa, have excellent tourist facilities.

- In the central mountains of Bali, Ubud is a centre for traditional art and culture. Tourism now competes with art, but it makes a good base for exploring the 'real Bali'.

- The Buddhist temple of Borobudur in Java is one of the world's wonders.

- Java's main tourist destination, Yogyakarta, is a centre for Javanese culture with good facilities and many nearby attractions.

- The huge crater lake of Danau Toba, with Pulau Samosir rising from the middle, is the most spectacular of Sumatra's natural wonders.

- Bali's less-touristed neighbour, Lombok, has fine beaches, good facilities and the towering volcano of Gunung Rinjani to climb.

- Komodo in Nusa Tenggara is home to the famous Komodo dragons, Indonesia's beasts from the dinosaur age.

- Tana Toraja's communal funerals reveal a unique culture in Sulawesi.

- The remote Banda Islands in Maluku receive only a trickle of visitors, but have a lot to offer – colonial forts, a volcano, and snorkelling and diving.

- The Baliem Valley in Irian Jaya offers unique culture and trekking among stunning scenery.

Java

Starting from Bali, the typical route is to head to Surabaya via the impressive volcanic landscapes of Gunung Bromo. Then it's on to Yogyakarta, the cultural heartland of Java and main base to visit the temples at Borobudur and Prambanan. From Yogya to Jakarta is usually done via the beach resort of Pangandaran and then Bandung. Count on two to three weeks, and if time is very limited, head straight to Yogya. Solo, Dieng Plateau and Bogor are other popular detours on this route.

Sumatra

Sumatra's big attractions are in the north from Padang to Medan, so many visitors skip southern Sumatra through a long bus trip or quicker ship or flight from Jakarta to Padang. First stop on this route is the mountain town of Bukittinggi, a cultural centre for the Minangkabau people. From there, it's a long bus journey to the other main travellers centre at Danau Toba. From Toba to Medan, popular stops are the mountain town of Berastagi and the famous orangutan centre at Bukit Lawang.

This route can be done in two weeks, but three weeks is less gruelling. Of the many side trips, Aceh in the far north is increasingly popular. Pulau We (We Island) is the main area of interest.

Nusa Tenggara

Lombok is a very popular, easily reached side trip from Bali and is worth at least a week's visit. Senggigi is a less frenetic, Bali-style beach resort, and the coral atolls of the Gili Islands have great beaches and budget accommodation. The climb to the top of Gunung Rinjani is one of Indonesia's best hikes.

Further east, Sumbawa has fine surf beaches but is usually just a transit island on the way to see the dragons of Komodo. Flores is home to the famous coloured lakes of Kelimutu, but it also has beaches and traditional villages between Labuanbajo and Maumere to break up the tiring bus journeys. From Maumere, you can fly to Bali or head to Kupang (and Australia). Sumba's fascinating traditional culture makes an interesting detour. You'll need a month to explore Nusa Tenggara in some depth.

Kalimantan

This vast island has relatively few roads, and unless you fly, boat travel is time consuming. Banjarmasin and its river life is one of the main attractions, and is a good starting point. From Banjarmasin you can head to Tanjung Puting National Park, famous for its orang-utan centres. A road runs from Banjarmasin to Balikpapan, the main air hub on the west coast, and further north is Samarinda, where boats go up Sungai Mahakam (Mahakam River) into the interior.

Balikpapan and Tanjung Puting can be visited in a rushed week, but a month is needed to see more of Kalimantan.

Sulawesi

From the main city of Ujung Pandang, most travellers head straight to Rantepao in Tana Toraja. Some don't travel beyond it, but you can head up through Central Sulawesi via Danau Poso to Lore Lindu National Park (Taman Nasional Lore Lindu) or detour to the beautiful Togean Islands. Sulawesi has other good wildlife reserves but is more famous for its beaches and coral, such as at Pulau Bunaken near Manado in the north-east.

You can fly or sail to Ujung Pandang and visit Tana Toraja in less than a week, though at least three weeks is needed to explore more of Sulawesi.

Maluku

The main travel hub, Pulau Ambon, has some good beaches and reefs, and is easy to reach by air from Bali, Sulawesi or Irian Jaya. The main attraction is the Banda Islands, but flights from Ambon are not always reliable, so allow at least a week and consider the Pelni boats. Northern Maluku boasts the interesting islands of Ternate and Tidore (the original 'spice islands'), and Maluku has many other difficult to reach islands perfect for adventurers. Allow at least a month to see more of Maluku.

Irian Jaya

Jayapura is easily reached by plane from the rest of Indonesia. Nearby Danau Sentani is worth exploring but the Baliem Valley, reached only by air from Jayapura, is the major tourist attraction. Cancellations and overbooking can occur, so allow another week or more. Biak, with regular air and boat connections, is popular for diving, beaches and WWII relics. Other areas of interest also require air or boat travel – allow at least a month.

PLANNING
When to Go

Though travel in the wet season is not usually a major problem in most parts of Indonesia, mud-clogged back roads can be a deterrent. The best time to visit Indonesia is in the dry season between May and October (see Climate in the Facts about Indonesia chapter).

Bali is Australia's favourite Asian getaway. The Christmas holiday period until the end of January brings a wave of migratory Australians, as do the school breaks during the year. An even bigger tourist wave during the northern summer brings crowds of Europeans in July and August to Bali, Java, Sumatra and Sulawesi.

The main Indonesian holiday periods are the end of Ramadan (see Public Holidays & Special Events later in this chapter), when some resorts are packed to overflowing and prices skyrocket; Christmas and the end of the school year from mid-June to mid-July when graduating high school students take off by the bus-load to tourist attractions, mainly in Java and Bali.

So that leaves May-June and September-October as the pick of the months to visit Indonesia – although in peak tourist months you can always find a place away from the crowds.

Maps

Locally produced maps are often inaccurate. Periplus produces excellent maps of most of the archipelago and includes maps of the major cities. The Nelles Verlag map series covers Indonesia in a number of separate sheets, and they're usually very reliable. Both series are available in Indonesia and overseas.

The Directorate General of Tourism publishes a free, useful information booklet, the *Indonesia Tourist Map*, which includes maps of Java, Bali, Sumatra and Sulawesi, and a good overall map of Indonesia. Maps of major Javanese, Sumatran and Balinese cities are easy enough to come by – ask at a tourist office or try bookshops, airports and major hotels. Elsewhere in Indonesia, maps can be hard to find.

What to Bring

Before deciding what to pack, first decide what you're going to carry it in. For budget travellers, the backpack is still the best item of luggage; however, make sure that it can be locked. A small day pack is also handy. If you're not taking a backpack, you'll still be using public transport – remember that space is very limited and that it's best to be able to keep a watchful eye on your luggage, so small is good. See Theft under Dangers & Annoyances later in this chapter.

Temperatures are uniformly tropical year-round in Indonesia, so light and loose, wash-and-wear natural fibre clothes are the order of the day, as are a sturdy pair of walking sandles. If you intend to travel by motorcycle at some stage, you'll need some heavier clothing, such as a pair of jeans.

Bring at least one long-sleeved top or shirt for the cool evenings. Mountain areas are cold – jeans, closed walking shoes and a jacket are definitely worth taking; a sleeping bag is really only necessary if you intend to do a lot of high altitude trekking (see Hiking & Trekking under Activities later in this chapter). Probably one of the most important items, and one that most people forget, is a hat – the Indonesian sun is relentless. Sunglasses are also essential, and don't forget sunscreen lotion.

Clothing is very cheap in Indonesia, so you can always buy extra items, but larger sizes for both men and women can sometimes be hard to find.

Be aware of local customs and standards of dressing when deciding what to pack. Beach attire is only tolerated in heavily touristed areas such as Kuta in Bali (see Dos & Don'ts under Society & Conduct in the Facts about Indonesia chapter).

Higher dress-standards apply particularly when visiting a government office – have a smart but casual outfit ready for this and other more formal occasions.

You'll doubtless purchase a sarong while you're in Indonesia – it's an all-purpose fashion marvel. Not only can you wear it, but it can serve as a blanket, beach mat, top sheet, mattress cover and even a towel, or as head protection against the pounding sun.

Toiletries such as soap, shampoo, conditioner, toothpaste and toilet paper are all readily available in Indonesia. Dental floss, tampons and shaving cream are hard to find – bring your own.

The following is a checklist of things you might consider packing:

- namecards
- Swiss army knife, flashlight with batteries, compass, padlock
- camera and accessories
- sunglasses, sunhat, sunscreen
- alarm clock
- leakproof water bottle, cup, spoon
- thongs
- rain jacket or poncho, raincover for backpack
- sewing kit
- toilet paper, tampons, nail clippers, tweezers, mosquito repellent and any special medications you use, plus a copy of the prescription.

RESPONSIBLE TOURISM

Tourism provides much-needed foreign income and on the whole it is encouraged and accepted; however, it can have a negative impact that you can help lessen.

Tourism in developing countries attracts much patronising writing, but the key word is respect. If you respect culture, its customs and environment and, most importantly, respect and show an interest in the people that you meet, not only will your own travels will be more rewarding, so will the experience of your hosts.

Customs & Culture

Indonesia is a relatively conservative country where religious, family and social values are still highly respected. Learn something of the customs and culture, and avoid behaviour that contradicts those values. Brief beach attire, public displays of affection and aggressive behaviour are poor form in Indonesia. They may be tolerated in tourist resorts such as Kuta in Bali, but that doesn't mean they are acceptable.

Take your cues from Indonesians. Be aware of religious customs and always ask permission before entering a mosque, temple, church or sacred site.

Tourist Economy

Staying in family-owned budget hotels, eating at *warungs* (food stalls) and travelling on local transport means your dollars will flow more directly into the local economy. It should also mean that you will meet more Indonesians and gain a wider knowledge of Indonesian society, but how you travel is up to you. Staying in better hotels, travelling 1st class or taking tours contributes just as much, if not more, to the economy, which is the main benefit tourism offers. How you interact is more important than how much money you spend.

Bargaining is an essential social skill for Indonesians, and you will gain more respect if you're aware of local prices and can bargain for goods. At the same time, while overcharging becomes annoying after a while, tourism is a luxury item that attracts a premium – for rich Indonesians as well as foreign tourists. It may be the case that increased wealth from tourism and paying a little over the odds can 'distort' local economies (though this complaint is open to the charge of assuming that poverty is a natural state).

Visiting Villages

Some villages receive bus-loads of visitors and are almost tourist theme parks, but in general wandering into a village is like wandering into someone's home, and a few rules of etiquette apply. It is polite to first introduce yourself to the *kepala desa* (village head) or another senior person.

Those that are used to visitors will often have a visitors' book, where you sign in and make a donation – a few thousand rupiah is usually sufficient. In more remote villages, bring a guide, especially if a language difficulty is likely. A guide can make the introductions, teach you protocol and greatly enhance your visit by explaining points of interest.

It is possible to stay with the kepala desa in most villages (see Staying in Villages under Accommodation later in this chapter).

Environmental Concerns

Environmental issues often seem to be alien in Indonesia, and Indonesians are wont to say to Europeans: 'We are a poor country that needs to exploit our natural resources, and how can you tell us not to cut down our forests when you have already cut down all your own?'. That said, Indonesia has a growing environmental awareness and environmental laws, even if they are poorly enforced.

You can lecture all you like and even report violations to the local authorities, but the best you can hope for is not to add to environmental degradation. Tourist areas are most sensitive to environmental criticism because they may lose their livelihood.

Snorkellers and divers should never stand on corals and should avoid touching or otherwise disturbing living marine organisms (see the boxed text 'Considerations for Responsible Diving' under Activities). Hikers should follow the maxim posted in every Indonesian national park: 'take nothing but photos, leave nothing but footprints'. Minimise disposable waste and take it with you, even though the trails may already be littered. See Hiking & Trekking under Activities for more information.

Laws are in place to protect endangered species, but you can still see such creatures for sale in local bird markets. Many souvenirs are made from threatened species. Turtle shell products, sea shells, snake skin, stuffed birds, framed butterflies etc are all-too-readily available in Indonesia. Not only

does buying them encourage ecological damage, their import into most countries is banned and they will be confiscated by customs. See the CITES (Convention on International Trade in Endangered Species) Web site (www.wcmc.org.uk:80/CITES) for more information.

TOURIST OFFICES
Local Tourist Offices

The Indonesian national tourist organisation, the Directorate General of Tourism, maintains offices in each province. These produce some literature but are generally not the place to get specific queries answered. The head office of the Directorate General of Tourism (☎ 021-383 8412) is at Jl (Jalan) Merdeka Barat 16-19, Jakarta.

Each provincial government has a tourist office called Departemen Pariwisata Daerah (DIPARDA or DIPARTA), usually in the capital cities. In addition, many *kabupaten* (districts) have their own tourist departments, and city governments may have their own tourist offices. The sign on the building is usually written only in Indonesian – look for *dinas pariwisata* (tourist office).

The usefulness of tourist offices varies greatly from place to place. Tourist offices in places that attract lots of tourists, like Bali or Yogya, provide good maps and information, while offices in the less-visited areas may have nothing to offer at all. They'll always try to help, but many offices are a long way out of town and staffed by career bureaucrats with little interest or idea of tourism, and unfortunately many don't speak English.

Tourist Offices Abroad

Indonesian Tourist Promotion Offices (ITPO) abroad can supply brochures and information. Useful publications are the *Travel Planner*, *Tourist Map of Indonesia* and the *Calendar of Events*. ITPO offices are listed below. Garuda Indonesia offices overseas can also be worth contacting for information.

Germany
    (☎ 069-233677) Wiessenhuttenstrasse 17
    D6000, Frankfurt am Main 1

Japan
  (☎ 03-3585 3588) 2nd floor, Sankaido bldg,
  1-9-13 Akasaka, Minato-ku, Tokyo 107
Singapore
  (☎ 534 2837) 10 Collyer Quay, Ocean bldg,
  Singapore 0104
Taiwan
  (☎ 02-537 7620) 5th floor, 66 Sung Chiang
  Rd, Taipei
UK
  (☎ 020-7493 0030) 3-4 Hanover St, London
  W1R 9HH
USA
  (☎ 213-387 2078) 3457 Wilshire Blvd, Los
  Angeles, CA 90010

VISAS & DOCUMENTS
Passport
Check your passport expiry date. Indonesia
requires that your passport is valid for six
months following your date of arrival.

Visas
Tourist Pass For many nationalities, a visa
is not necessary for entry and a stay of up to
60 days. These are: Argentina, Australia,
Austria, Belgium, Brazil, Brunei Darussalam, Canada, Chile, Denmark, Egypt, Finland, France, Germany, Greece, Hungary,
Iceland, Ireland, Italy, Japan, Kuwait, Liecht-
enstein, Luxembourg, Malaysia, Maldives,
Malta, Mexico, Monaco, Morocco, Netherlands, New Zealand, Norway, Philippines,
Saudi Arabia, Singapore, South Korea,
Spain, Sweden, Switzerland, Taiwan, Thailand, Turkey, United Arab Emirates, UK,
USA and Venezuela.

For nationals of these countries a 60 day
tourist pass is issued on arrival, as long as
you enter and exit through recognised entry
ports. Officially (but not always in practice), you must have a ticket out of the
country when you arrive and you may be
asked to show sufficient funds for your stay.
Officially (and almost certainly), you cannot extend your visa beyond 60 days.

The best answer to the ticket-out requirement is to buy a return ticket to Indonesia or
to include Indonesia as a leg on a through
ticket. Medan-Penang and Singapore-Jakarta
tickets are cheap, popular options for satis-

> ### Short-Hop Option
>
> If your tourist pass is running out and
> you'd like to return to Indonesia, Darwin is
> not your only Australian short-hop des-
> tination option. Christmas Island is only
> 360km away from Jakarta with direct
> flights on Thursday, Friday and Sunday
> (A$450 return).
>
> Contact PT Wabaru (☎ 021-392 6966,
> fax 392 6965, email xch@cbn.net.id) in
> Jakarta for flight bookings. Contact the
> Christmas Island Visitor Information Centre
> for info and reservations (☎ 61-8-9164
> 8382, email cita@christmas.net.au) or check
> its Web site: www.christmas.net.au.

fying the requirement. Though immigration
officials often won't even ask to see an onward ticket, if you don't have one, you may
be forced to buy one on the spot. Jakarta has
the worst reputation in this regard, whereas
the busy tourist ports of Bali and Batam
(Sumatra) cater to short-stay package trips,
so you're unlikely to be troubled.

In addition to (sometimes in lieu of) an
onward ticket, you may be asked to show
evidence of sufficient funds. US$1000 is
the magic number. Travellers cheques are
best to flash at immigration officials; credit
cards sometimes work but are not guaranteed. Imigrasi in Kupang like to see cash,
and have been known to try to extract some
of it.

Recognised Entry/Exit Points The Indonesian government produces an official
list of recognised entry/exit ports where
tourist passes are issued, but it is rarely updated and your carrier will often be better
informed than an Indonesian embassy. In
general, entry by air on a regular flight or
scheduled international ferry does not require a visa. This 'no visa' list includes all
the main airports and regular entry points,
including ferries to/from Sumatra: Penang-
Medan, Penang-Belawan, Melaka-Dumai
and Singapore-Batam/Bintan. The only

recognised no-visa land crossing is at Entikong in West Kalimantan, between Pontianak and Kuching.

The main crossings that require a visa are between Jayapura (Irian Jaya) and Vanimo (Papua New Guinea), and between Tarakan (Kalimantan) and Tawau (Sabah, Malaysia). Even if you only want to exit through these points, officially you must enter the country on a visitor visa. See the Irian Jaya and Kalimantan chapters for more details.

Visitor Visa For citizens of countries not on the visa-free list, a visitor visa must be obtained from any Indonesian embassy or consulate before entering the county. Visitor visas are only valid for one month, not 60 days as for visa-free entry, and are usually only extendable for two weeks.

A visitor visa is also required for entry *or exit* via an obscure port that is not a recognised entry/exit point.

Study & Work Visas Visas for overseas students, short-term research, visiting family and similar purposes can be arranged if you have a sponsor, such as an educational institution. These social/cultural *(sosial/ budaya)* visas, must be applied for at an Indonesian embassy or consulate overseas. Normally valid for three months on arrival, they can be extended every month after that for up to six months without leaving the country.

Limited stay visas (Kartu Izin Tinggal Terbatas, KITAS), valid for one-year periods are also issued, usually for those given permission to work. Work permits must first be obtained from the Ministry of Manpower and should be arranged by your employer. Those granted limited stay are issued a KITAS card, often referred to as the KIMS card.

The 60 day tourist pass supposedly also covers business travel where the holder is not employed in Indonesia. Visits for conventions or exhibitions are not a problem, but you may be asked a lot of questions if you put 'business' as a reason for travel on your embarkation card. Inquire at an Indonesian embassy before departure.

Visa Extensions Tourist passes are not extendable beyond 60 days. You may get a few extra days in special circumstances, like missed flight connections or illness on presentation of written evidence, but whatever you do, do not simply show up at the airport with an expired visa or tourist pass and expect to be able to board your flight. You may be sent back to the local immigration office to clear up the matter.

Extensions for visitor, social and work visas have to applied for at immigration offices in Indonesia.

Travel Permits

For political and bureaucratic reasons, foreigners must obtain a travel permit known as a *surat jalan* before they can visit many places in Irian Jaya, including the Baliem Valley (see Surat Jalan under Visas & Documents in the Irian Jaya chapter).

Travel Insurance

A travel insurance policy to cover theft, loss and medical problems is a wise idea. There is a wide variety of policies, and your travel agent will have recommendations. Some policies offer lower and higher medical expenses options – a mid-range one is usually recommended for South-East Asia where medical costs are not so high. Check the small print to see if it excludes 'dangerous activities' that you may be contemplating, such as scuba diving, motorcycling or even trekking. Check that the policy covers ambulances or an emergency flight home, which may be useful.

Theft is a potential problem in Indonesia, so make sure that your policy covers expensive items adequately. Many policies have restrictions on laptop computers and expensive camera gear, or refunds are often for depreciated value, not replacement value.

Driving Licence

To drive in Indonesia, officially you need an International Driving Permit from your local automobile association. In fact this is often not required but police may ask to see it. Take your home-country driving licence, which may be useful as identification even if you won't be driving.

Hostel Cards

A Hostelling International (HI) card will give you a tiny discount at the few hostels in Indonesia, but it is of very limited use given the abundance of good, cheap alternatives.

Student & Youth Cards

The International Student Identity Card (ISIC) is useful for discounts on domestic flights, though maximum age limits (usually 26) often apply; some attractions offer student discounts.

Photocopies

All important documents (passport data page and visa page, credit cards, travel insurance policy, airline tickets, driving licence etc) should be photocopied before you leave home. Leave one copy with someone at home and keep another with you, separate from the originals, with a stash of cash (US$100 or more) for emergency use.

EMBASSIES & CONSULATES
Indonesian Embassies & Consulates

Indonesia embassies and consulates abroad include:

Australia
   Embassy:
   (☎ 02-6250 8600) 8 Darwin Ave, Yarralumla, ACT 2600
   Consulates:
   Adelaide, Darwin, Melbourne, Perth and Sydney
Canada
   Embassy:
   (☎ 613-231 0186) 55 Parkdale Ave, Ottawa, Ontario K1Y 1E5
   Consulates:
   Vancouver and Toronto
France
   Embassy:
   (☎ 01-45 03 07 60) 47-49 Rue Cortambert 75116, Paris
   Consulate:
   Marseilles
Germany
   (☎ 0228-382990) 2 Bernakasteler Strasse, 53175 Bonn

   Consular offices:
   Berlin, Bremen, Dusseldorf, Hamburg, Hannover, Kiel, Munich and Stuttgart
Japan
   (☎ 03-3441 4201) 5-9-2 Higashi Gotanda, Shinagawa-ku, Tokyo
Malaysia
   Embassy:
   (☎ 03-984 2011) 233 Jalan Tun Razak, Kuala Lumpur
   Consulates:
   Penang, Kuching, Kota Kinabalu and Tawau
Netherlands
   (☎ 070-310 8100) 8 Tobias Asserlaan, 2517 KC Den Haag
New Zealand
   (☎ 04-475 8697) 70 Glen Rd, Kelburn, Wellington
Papua New Guinea
   (☎ 675-325 3116) 1+2/410, Kiroki St, Sir John Guise Drive, Waigani, Port Moresby
Philippines
   Embassy:
   (☎ 02-892 5061) 185 Salcedo St, Legaspi Village, Makati, Manila
   Consular office in Davao
Singapore
   (☎ 737 7422) 7 Chatsworth Rd, Singapore
Thailand
   (☎ 02-252 3135) 600-602 Petchburi Rd, Bangkok
UK
   (☎ 020-71 499 7661) 38 Grosvenor Square, London W1X 9AD
USA
   Embassy:
   (☎ 202-775 5200) 2020 Massachussetts Ave NW, Washington DC 20036
   Consulates:
   Chicago, Honolulu, Houston, Los Angeles, New York and San Francisco

Embassies in Indonesia

Foreign embassies are located in the capital, Jakarta. Australia, France, Germany, the Netherlands and the USA also have consular representatives in Bali (see Embassies & Consulates in the Bali chapter). A number of countries also have consulates in Medan in Sumatra (see Foreign Consulates in the Sumatra chapter) and Surabaya in Java. Embassies in Jakarta include:

Australia
   (☎ 5227111) Jl Rasuna Said, Kav 15-16

Brunei
  (☎ 5712180) 8th floor, Wisma BCA, Jl
  Jenderal Sudirman Kav 22-23
Canada
  (☎ 5250709) 5th floor, Wisma Metropolitan
  I, Jl Jenderal Sudirman, Kav 29
France
  (☎ 3142807) Jl Husni Thamrin 20
Germany
  (☎ 3901750) Jl Husni Thamrin 1
Japan
  (☎ 324308) Jl Husni Thamrin 24
Malaysia
  (☎ 5224947) Jl Rasuna Said Kav X/6 No 1
Myanmar
  (☎ 3140440) Jl H Augus Salim 109
Netherlands
  (☎ 5251515) Jl Rasuna Said, Kav S-3,
  Kuningan
New Zealand
  (☎ 5709460) Jl Diponegoro 41
Papua New Guinea
  (☎ 7251218) 6th floor, Panin Bank Centre, Jl
  Jenderal Sudirman No 1
Philippines
  (☎ 3100334) Jl Imam Bonjol 6-8
Singapore
  (☎ 5201489) Jl Rasuna Said, Block X,
  Kav 2 No 4
Thailand
  (☎ 3904055) Jl Imam Bonjol 74
UK
  (☎ 3907484) Jl Husni Thamrin 75

USA
  (☎ 3442211) Jl Merdeka Selatan 5
Vietnam
  (☎ 3100357) Jl Teuku Umar 25

CUSTOMS

Customs allows you to bring in a maximum of 1L of alcohol, 200 cigarettes or 50 cigars or 100g of tobacco.

Prohibited items include narcotics, arms and ammunition, explosives, laser guns, transceivers, cordless telephones, pornography, printed matter in Chinese characters and Chinese medicines. Film, pre-recorded video tape, video laser disc or records must be declared and censored.

Duty is payable on goods obtained overseas and should be declared if the goods exceed US$250, or US$1000 per family. Personal effects are not a problem. Customs officials rarely worry about how much gear tourists bring into the country – if you have a western face.

No restrictions apply on the import/export of foreign currency, but the import/export of rupiah is limited to 5,000,000Rp. Amounts between 5,000,000Rp and 10,000,000Rp must be declared. Import/export above that amount requires prior written permission from the Bank of Indonesia.

Your Own Embassy

It's important to realise what your own embassy – the embassy of the country of which you are a citizen – can and can't do to help you if you get into trouble.

Generally speaking, it won't be much help in emergencies if whatever trouble you're in is remotely your own fault. Remember that you are bound by the laws of the country you are in. Your embassy will not be sympathetic if you end up in jail after committing a crime locally, even if such actions are legal in your own country.

In genuine emergencies you might get some assistance, but only if other channels have been exhausted. For example, if you need to get home urgently, a free ticket home is exceedingly unlikely – the embassy would expect you to have insurance. If you have all your money and documents stolen, it might assist with getting a new passport, but a loan for onward travel is out of the question.

Some embassies used to keep letters for travellers or have a small reading room with home newspapers, but these days the mail holding service has usually been stopped and even newspapers tend to be out of date.

MONEY

Currency

The unit of currency in Indonesia is the rupiah (Rp). Coins of 25, 50, 100 and 500 rupiah are in circulation in both the old silver-coloured coins and the newer bronze-coloured coins. A 1000Rp coin is also minted but rarely seen, and the 25Rp coin has almost vanished. Notes come in 500, 1000, 5000, 10,000, 20,000 and 50,000 rupiah denominations.

Exchange Rates

For many years the Indonesian rupiah was a relatively stable currency based primarily on the US dollar and traded at around 2000Rp to 2400Rp to the dollar. Since the 1997 Asian monetary crises and the turmoil in Indonesia, the currency has been on a roller coaster ride, trading as low as 17,000Rp to US$1, though it appears to be settling in at around 7500Rp to 8000Rp.

country	unit		rupiah
Australia	A$1	=	5263Rp
euro	€1	=	6873Rp
France	1FF	=	1305Rp
Germany	DM1	=	4378Rp
Japan	¥100	=	6650Rp
Malaysia	RM1	=	2134Rp
Netherlands	G1	=	3886Rp
Singapore	S$1	=	4691Rp
Switzerland	SFr1	=	5371Rp
UK	UK£1	=	12,991Rp
USA	US$1	=	8110Rp

Exchanging Money

Cash & Travellers Cheques US dollars are the most widely accepted foreign currency in Indonesia, but you can change all major currencies in the main cities and tourist areas. Currencies other than US dollars usually bring reasonable rates in Jakarta and Bali; however, US dollars are always more reliable – either in cash or preferably travellers cheques from a major US company such as American Express (the most widely accepted), Citicorp or Bank of America – especially if you intend to travel farther afield in Indonesia. If you bring currencies other than US dollars, be prepared to put in more legwork – first to find a bank that will accept them and secondly to find one that gives a good rate.

Rates vary, so it pays to shop around. The best rates of exchange are found in Jakarta and Bali. Touristy places have lots of moneychangers as well as banks, but banks usually have better exchange rates, though moneychangers may offer the best rates for cash. When changing cash, bigger notes are better – a US$100 note will attract a better exchange rate than a US$20 note.

Moneychangers in Bali offer some of the best rates in Indonesia *if* you don't get short-changed or charged commission. Signboard rates are often a fabrication, and after signing your travellers cheque you may find that a 10% (or higher) commission applies. Double check the conversion rate and beware that these thieves even rig their calculators.

Always count your rupiah before you hand over your travellers cheques or foreign currency. Several readers letters have warned of being short-changed through sleight of hand:

There are heaps of moneychangers in Kuta and elsewhere that offer really good rates but will rip you off ... Count the rupiah in front of them. DON'T GIVE THE MONEY BACK TO THEM TO COUNT – they will recount and some will (likely) disappear. Once you have double checked that you have received the correct amount, hand over the US$ or whatever. If they start messing you about and not giving you the right amount the first time, leave with your cash. There will be another moneychanger next door.

Beren Patterson

While the chances of getting short-changed at a bank are perhaps 50 to 1, at a Kuta moneychanger the odds are more like 50-50. Moneychangers elsewhere are much less problematic but offer lower rates.

It pays to change enough money to tide you over until you reach another major centre. Away from the big cities, rates can be very poor. For really remote places, carry stacks of rupiah because foreign exchange may be impossible. Have a mix of notes – breaking even a 10,000Rp note in a warung can be a major hassle out in the villages.

ATMs Many Indonesian banks have ATMs linked to international banking networks, such as Cirrus and Plus, allowing withdrawals from overseas savings accounts. Cash advances on Visa and MasterCard can also be made through many ATMs which display the relevant symbols (and sometimes those that don't show the symbols). Cards and networks accepted by ATMs among Indonesia's main banks include:

Bank Bali
    MasterCard, Cirrus, Alto
Bank Central Asia (BCA)
    Visa, Plus
Bank Duta
    MasterCard, Visa
Bank Internasional Indonesia (BII)
    MasterCard, Visa, Cirrus, Plus, Alto
Bank Negara Indonesia (BNI)
    MasterCard, Cirrus
Lippobank
    MasterCard, Cirrus, Alto

Check with your bank at home to see if you can use ATM facilities in Indonesia, and also check to see what charges apply.

ATMs in Indonesia have a maximum withdrawal limit, sometimes 600,000Rp or 1,000,000Rp, sometimes as low as 400,000 Rp, which is not much in foreign currency terms. Problems can occur if your bank has a minimum withdrawal limit that may well be higher than the ATM's maximum. In this case your transaction will be refused.

Indonesian ATMs also experience a lot of downtime. Except in major cities with many ATMs, don't rely on them. These days, most large towns have banks with ATMs, but they can be hard to find and do not always accept foreign cards.

Credit Cards If you have a credit card, don't leave home without it. If you are travelling on a low budget, credit cards are of limited use for day-to-day travel expenses, as only expensive hotels, restaurants and shops accept them; but they are very useful for major purchases like airline tickets (though smaller offices in the back blocks may not accept them).

MasterCard and Visa are the most widely accepted credit cards. American Express is a distant third. Cash can be obtained at Amex agents, usually PT Pacto, in major cities only.

Credit cards can be a convenient way to carry money, especially if your account is always in the black. Cash advances on Visa and MasterCard can be obtained over the counter at many banks (as well as from ATMs), though some charge transaction fees of around 5000Rp – always ask first.

Cash advances are readily obtainable in the main cities, and many regional towns have banks that accept credit cards, but as a general rule, credit cards may be a good way to carry some of your cash, but don't rely on them solely. You could get away with it in Java and Bali, but even there cash and travellers cheques are more convenient and reliable. In more remote areas, you're asking for trouble if all you have is a credit card.

Banks are also charging increasing transaction fees for the use of credit cards overseas, often much higher than the 1% commission charged on travellers cheques; check this with your bank. However, credit-card cash advances are the way to go when there are sudden fluctuations in the rupiah. When this happens, Indonesian banks offer conservative rates for cash or travellers cheques and the interbank exchange rates are often better.

Other Methods Dutch travellers with a Dutch post office account can conveniently obtain cash from Indonesian post offices. These *girobetaalkaarten* are useful in the many Indonesian towns where there is no bank.

Costs

Indonesian costs vary depending on where you go, but the devaluation in the rupiah makes Indonesia one of the cheapest travel destinations in Asia. Hotels, food and transport are all very cheap in US dollar terms.

With rampant inflation occurring during the economic crisis, expect costs quoted in this book to rise, but within a week or two of arrival you should get an idea of price rises and be able to estimate current prices. Goods and services with a high import quota, such as air travel, are likely to rise the most, but transport prices have already risen rapidly and these are expected to moderate.

Travellers centres with lots of competition like Danau Toba and Yogyakarta are superb value for accommodation and food. Bargains can still be found in Bali, but many places try to charge inflated US dollar rates.

Elsewhere, transport costs rise, budget accommodation can be limited and prices are higher because competition is less fierce. Sulawesi and Nusa Tenggara are cheap enough, but accommodation in Maluku and Irian Jaya can be twice as high, and transport costs on Kalimantan are high.

Transport expenses also increase once you get into the outer provinces. In Bali, Java, Sumatra and Nusa Tenggara there's very little need to take to the air, while in the interior of Irian Jaya you have no choice but to fly. Flying is much more expensive than other forms of transport, though still relatively cheap in dollar terms.

If you confine yourself to Sumatra, Java, Bali and Nusa Tenggara, a shoestring traveller can get around for as little as US$10 per day. A mid-range budget starts at around US$30, which will get you an air-conditioned hotel room, occasional tours and car hire. However, mid-range accommodation is much more expensive in Balinese resorts. Unless you insist on top-end hotels and the finest restaurants, you can travel in real comfort for US$50 a day.

Tipping & Bargaining

Tipping is not normal practice in Indonesia, but is often expected for special service. Someone who carries your bag or guides you around a tourist attraction will naturally expect a tip. Jakarta taxi drivers expect a tip

– the fare is usually rounded up to the next 1000Rp. Hotel porters expect a few 100Rp per bag.

Many everyday purchases in Indonesia require bargaining. This applies particularly to handicrafts, artwork and any tourist items, but can also apply to almost anything you buy. Restaurant meals, transport and, sometimes, accommodation are generally fixed price. However, when supply exceeds demand, hotels may be willing to bend their prices, and you can be overcharged on transport. As a general rule, if prices are displayed, prices are fixed; otherwise, bargaining may be possible. The exception is tourist shops, especially those selling artwork, where price tags are often absurdly inflated for the unwary – hard bargaining is required.

When bargaining, it's usually best to ask the seller their price rather than make an initial offer, unless you know very clearly what you're willing to pay. As a rule of thumb, your starting price could be anything from a third to two-thirds of the asking price – assuming that the asking price is not completely crazy, which it can be in tourist areas. Then with offer and counteroffer you move closer to an acceptable price. Don't show too much interest when bargaining and if you can't get an acceptable price, walk away. You will often be called back and offered a lower price.

A few rules apply to good bargaining. First of all, it's not a question of life or death, where every rupiah you chisel away makes a difference. Don't pass up something you really want that's expensive or unobtainable at home because the seller won't come down a few hundred rupiah – it is nothing compared with the hundreds of dollars you spent on the air fare. Secondly, when your offer is accepted you have to buy it – don't then decide you don't want it after all. Thirdly, while bargaining may seem to have a competitive element in it, it's a mean victory knocking a poor *becak* driver down from 1000Rp to 800Rp for a ride.

Bargaining is sometimes fun – and often not. Equanimity is the name of the game. If the seller likes you, you might get a better price, if you are too aggressive or offensive, forget about it.

For everyday items, ask Indonesian friends or hotel staff for information about correct prices. If you don't know the right price for transport, you might try asking another passenger the regular price *(harga biasa)*. There's not much point doing this when you're buying something in a shop or at a market – onlookers naturally side with their own people.

Don't get hassled by bargaining and don't go around feeling that you're being ripped off all the time – too many people do. There is a nauseating category of westerner on the Asian trail who will launch into lengthy bitch sessions about being overcharged five cents for a mango. It is very easy to become obsessed with getting the 'local' price. Even locals don't always get the local price – Indonesian visitors to Bali will be overcharged on the *bemos* just like westerners. In Indonesia, if you are rich it is expected that you pay more, and *all* westerners are rich when compared to the grinding poverty of most Indonesians. Above all, keep things in perspective. The 500Rp you may overpay for a becak ride wouldn't buy a newspaper at home, but it's a meal for a becak driver.

POST & COMMUNICATIONS
Postal Rates
Examples of international airmail *(pos udara)* rates are:

	Australia	Europe	USA
Postcards	3400Rp	6400Rp	8000Rp
Aerograms	3200Rp	8500Rp	10,600Rp
Letters (up to 20g)	6800Rp	12,800Rp	15,900Rp
Parcels (500g to 1kg)	162,500Rp	295,000Rp	348,000Rp

Sending Mail
Post offices *(kantor pos)* are usually open Monday to Friday from 8 am to 3 pm, and Saturday until around 1 pm. In the larger cities, main post offices are often open extended hours – until 8 pm or later including Sunday – for basic postal services. Go during normal hours for poste restante. *Warpostels* and *warparpostels* are private post and telephone agencies that are open extended hours and provide an efficient postal service for slightly higher rates.

Though the postal service has improved enormously, international mail is still quite slow. Mail to Australia or the USA takes anywhere from one to two weeks, usually around 10 days. Mail to Europe is a little faster.

Parcels up to a maximum weight of 7kg can be sent by air mail, or up to 10kg by cheaper sea mail.

Letters and small packets bound for overseas or domestic delivery may be registered *(terdaftar)* for an extra fee.

Mail within Indonesia can take forever and it is better to pay an extra 600Rp for the *kilat* domestic express service. *Kilat khusus* provides overnight domestic delivery (a maximum of two days to even the most remote destination) for 1000Rp to 2000Rp. Kilat khusus envelopes, plus aerograms, can be bought at all post offices.

Post offices also offer Express Mail Service to 46 countries, with a maximum of three days delivery time. Tariffs are reasonable compared to courier services. Mail is registered and traceable.

Receiving Mail
Poste restante at post offices is reasonably efficient. Expected mail always seems to arrive – eventually. Have your letters addressed to you with your surname in capitals and underlined. 'Lost' letters may have been misfiled under your first name, so always check under both your names.

Telephone
Telkom, the government-run telecommunications company, has offices *(kantor Telkom)* in many cities and towns. They are usually open 24 hours, and often offer fax service as well as telephone. These are the cheapest places to make international and long-distance *(inter-lokal)* phone calls, and they often have Home Country Direct phones or allow collect calls.

Telecommunications agencies, either Telkom or privately run, are called *wartel*, warpostal or warparpostel and offer the same services. They may be marginally more expensive but are often more convenient. They are usually open from around 7 am until midnight, but sometimes 24 hours. As a rule, wartels don't offer a collect-call service – in the rare cases that they do, an initial first minute charge may apply.

Domestic calls are charged according to a system of zones – the cost jumps dramatically if ringing to other provinces.

Public Phones Public phones are either coin phones, card phones (the most common), chip-card phones (not numerous but multiplying rapidly) and credit card phones (still rare). Coin and card phones do not support International Direct Dialling, except for a few (very rare) card phones at big hotels and outside Telkom offices. The new chip-card phones do allow international calls.

Most public coin phones are blue, and take 50Rp and 100Rp. You can make a local call with a 100Rp coin, but you will have to keep feeding coins in or risk being cut off. Newer coin phones are grey, and accept 50Rp, 100Rp and 500Rp coins.

For the grey card phones *(telepon kartu)*, you can buy Telkom telephone cards *(kartu telepon)* in a variety of unit denominations – 100, 125, 250 up to 640 units. They currently cost 170Rp per unit, plus 10%, so a 100 unit card is 18,700Rp. They are sold at Telkom offices, wartels, supermarkets and other retail outlets that display the *Sedia kartu telepon* sign. Some retailers put a bigger commission on the cards.

The grey chip-card *(kartu chip)* phones use a hard plastic card embedded with an electronic chip, unlike the normal card phones that take a flexible card with a magnetic strip. The chip cards can also be bought from wartels and retail outlets for the same price. Chip-card phones are found in the big cities but are not yet common in the countryside.

There are also light-green coloured phones that take both the normal and chip cards.

Home Country Direct phones can also be found at some Telkom offices, airports and luxury hotels. Just press the button for your country (Australia, USA etc) and an operator from that country will come on the line for a reverse-charge or international telephone card call.

International Calls For International Direct Dialling (IDD) – dial ☎ 001 or ☎ 008, then the country code, area code (minus the initial zero if it has one) and then the number you want to reach. Two companies provide international connections: ☎ 001 is for Indosat and ☎ 008 is for Satelindo. All top-end and many mid-range hotels offer IDD dialling on room phones, but their surcharges can be hefty. Calls from a wartel are cheaper.

International calls operate on a zoning system. Zone 1 covers Malaysia and Singapore (3250Rp per minute), Zone II covers most of the rest of South-East Asia (4875Rp), Zone III covers Thailand, Australia and the US (8750Rp), Zone IV includes Canada and the UK (6875Rp) and Zone V covers most of Europe (7725Rp). Rates are what you'll pay at a Telkom office, and an extra 10% tax is charged. They are subject to change and are variable, depending on currency fluctuations. Wartel rates are similar but it pays to check – some charge a big premium.

It's cheaper to ring on weekends and public holidays, when a 25% discount applies, or on weekdays from 9 pm to 6 am for Asia and Oceania, or midnight to 7 am for North America, Europe and Africa.

Collect Calls Making reverse-charge calls isn't easy. Wartels usually don't allow collect calls because they don't make money on them, or in the rare cases that they do, 5000Rp or so is charged. Many hotels are similarly unhelpful.

The main answer is to use public phones. You can make a collect call via the Indonesian operator (☎ 101), but make sure it is collect rather than the more expensive person-to-person service. Alternatively, the Home Country Direct service allows you to

Telephone Codes

Ambon	0911	Kudus	0291	Prapat	0625
Ampenan	0370	Kupang	0380	Probolinggo	0335
		Kuta (Bali)	0361		
Bajawa	0384	Kuta (Lombok)	0370	Rantepao	0423
Balikpapan	0542	Kutacane	0629	Ruteng	0385
Banda Aceh	0651				
Bandaneira	0910	Labuanbajo	0385	Sabang	0652
Bandar Lampung	0721	Labuha	0927	Samarinda	0541
Bandung	022	Lagundri	0630	Samosir	0625
Banjarmasin	0511	Lahat	0731	Sanur	0361
Batam	0778	Lovina Beach	0362	Sapura	0911
Bengkulu	0736			Semarang	024
Berastagi	0628	Malang	0341	Senggigi	0370
Biak	0961	Manado	0431	Sentani	0967
Bima	0374	Maninjau	0752	Sibolga	0631
Bitung	0438	Manokwari	0962	Singaraja	0362
Bogor	0251	Masohi	0914	Singkawang	0562
Bukittinggi	0752	Mataram	0370	Soe	0388
		Maumere	0382	Solo	0271
Cilacap	0282	Medan	061	Sorong	0951
Cirebon	0231	Merauke	0971	Sulu Islands	0929
Curup	0732	Meulaboh	0655	Sumbawa Besar	0371
		Minahasa	0436	Sungaipenuh	0748
Denpasar	0361			Surabaya	031
Dili	0391	Nabire	0964		
Dumai	0765	Nusa Dua	0361	Tanimbar Islands	0918
				Tanjung Karang	0271
Ende	0381	Padang	0751	Tanjung Pinang	0771
		Padangbai	0363	Tarakan	0551
Fak Fak	0956	Padangpanjang	0758	Ternate	0921
		Palangkaraya	0514	Tidore	0920
Garut	0262	Palembang	0711	Timika	0979
Gorontalo	0435	Palu	0451	Tobelo	0924
Gunung Sitoli	0639	Pangandaran	0265		
		Pangkalanbun	0532	Ubud	0361
Jakarta	021	Pangkalpinang	0717	Ujung Pandang	0411
Jambi	0741	Parapat	0625		
Jayapura	0967	Pare-Pare	0421	Wahai	0914
Jember	0311	Pekalongan	0285	Waikabubak	0387
		Pekanbaru	0761	Wamena	0969
Kai Islands	0916	Pelabuhan Ratu	0266	Wiangapu	0386
Kaimana	0957	Pontianak	0561	Wonosobo	0286
Kalianda	0727	Poso	0452	Yapen	0963
Kendari	0401			Yogyakarta	0274
Kerinci	0748				

dial directly to an operator from that country for a reverse-charge or international telephone card call. This service may be convenient but it is rarely cheaper than phoning from a wartel.

Apart from special Home Country Direct phones, the service can also be used from any phone with IDD capability (such as a chip-card public phone). Dial ☎ 001 801 and then the country code. Codes for countries with multiple phone companies are listed in Indonesian phone books.

Cellular Phones Indonesia has three GSM networks – Telkomsel, Satelindo, and Excelcomindo – with wide coverage in Java and Bali and in the main regional centres elsewhere. Telkomsel has the most extensive network.

If your phone company offers international roaming for Indonesia, you can use your 'handphone' (as it's called in Indonesia) and home SIM card in Indonesia. Mobile calls are cheap in Indonesia, but check the roaming rates charged by your company. Some, such as Telstra in Australia, charge many times higher than Indonesian companies.

Indonesian telephone companies sell SIM cards that you can plug into your phone. This is usually cheaper, especially if you will be making a lot of local calls, and it will give you a local number. Telkomsel's simPATI cards are readily available in the big cities (many Fuji photo shops stock them).

Useful Numbers

Police	☎ 110
Fire Brigade	☎ 113
Ambulance	☎ 118
Indonesia country code	☎ 62
Directory assistance, local	☎ 108
Directory assistance, long-distance	☎ 106
Directory assistance, international	☎ 102
Operator assisted domestic calls	☎ 100
Operator assisted international calls	☎ 101
International Direct Dial	☎ 001 or ☎ 008

Fax

Government-run telecommunications offices in most cities and many mid-sized towns offer a fax service, as do wartels. Many hotels also offer a fax service.

Email & Internet Access

Indonesia has the lowest per capita rate of Internet penetration in Asia at just 1%; nonetheless, you'll find plenty of opportunity to check and send email or surf the World Wide Web (WWW). Post offices in main cities throughout the country have a Warposnet, which is a privately contracted Internet service, usually open until 8 pm. Its rates are the cheapest at around 10,000Rp per hour. Even some surprisingly small towns have a Warposnet, but they may be open office hours only.

Internet cafes are also popular in the main cities and tourist areas. Rates are higher and cafe service is usually limited to drinks, if anything, but the atmosphere is less business-like than the Warposnet. Almost all luxury hotel business centres offer Internet connection at high rates.

As a rule, Indonesian servers are very slow. It can take forever to log onto popular Web sites and email services such as Hotmail.

INTERNET RESOURCES

The WWW is a rich resource for travellers. You can research your trip, hunt down bargain air fares, book hotels, check on weather conditions or chat with locals and other travellers about the best places to visit (or avoid). The Lonely Planet Web site (www.lonelyplanet.com) has succinct summaries to most places on earth, postcards from other travellers, the Thorn Tree bulletin board, travel news and updates, and links to useful travel resources.

Some of the more interesting sites include:

Academic Internet Resources on Indonesia
  www.arts.auckland.ac.nz/indo/links.html
  (useful links site from the University of
  Auckland including a link to Indonesia Daily
  News Online)
ANTARA
  www.antara.co.id/index-ENG.html
  (the official Indonesian news agency; searchable database)

Indonesia
  coombs.anu.edu.au/WWWVLPages/Indon-
  Pages/WWWVL-Indonesia.html
  (Australian National University's links site,
  the 'grand daddy' of links to everything
  Indonesian)
Indonesia Home Page
  Indonesia.elga.net.id
  (a good general introduction to Indonesia
  with a range of links)
Jakarta City Government Tourist Office
  discover-jakarta.com
  (official tourism site of Jakarta city, but not
  regularly updated)
Living in Indonesia, A Site for Expats
  www.expat.or.id
  (information, advice and links to the expatriate community)
Nature Conservation in Indonesia
  www.noord.bart.nl/~edcolijn/index.html
  (amazing site for information on nature
  conservation)
Royal Institute of Linguistics and Anthropology
  (KITLV)
  gopher://oasis.leidenuniv.nl:70/11/.kitlv/.da
  ily-report
  (news service in Indonesian and English from
  Leiden University in the Netherlands, with
  reports you won't find in the regular press;
  plenty of East Timor news)
TEMPO Interaktif
  www.tempo.co.id/
  (one of Indonesia's most respected magazines, it offers good daily news articles in
  Indonesian and English)

BOOKS

Indonesia is not a straightforward country. Its
history, economics, politics and culture – and
their bizarre interactions – are wide open to
interpretation, and different writers come up
with astoundingly different interpretations of
events. If you want to read about Java or
Bali, you'll be suffocated beneath the literature, but trying to find out anything about the
other islands is like putting together bits and
pieces of a jigsaw puzzle.

Most books are published in different editions by different publishers in different
countries. As a result, a book might be a hard-
cover rarity in one country while it's readily
available in paperback in another. Fortunately, bookshops and libraries search by title
or author, so your local bookshop or library

is best placed to advise you on the availability
of the following recommendations.

For information on dictionaries and other
Bahasa Indonesia language references, see
the Language chapter.

Lonely Planet

Lonely Planet's *Bali & Lombok*, *Indonesia's
Eastern Islands* (covering Nusa Tenggara)
and *Java* are more detailed guides for exploring those islands in depth. Lonely
Planet's *Jakarta* covers the capital with in-
sider information and detailed colour maps.
Lonely Planet also produces the *Indonesian
phrasebook*.

Guidebooks

Periplus Editions produces a number of
beautifully illustrated, detailed books about
Indonesia, including regional guides, and
more specialised guides, such as *Underwater Indonesia*, a diving guide and *Surfing
Indonesia*. See the special section 'Surfing
in Indonesia' for more specialised surfing
publications.

Travel

If you think travel through the eastern islands
of Indonesia is time-consuming now, read
Helen & Frank Schreider's *Drums of Tonkin*
(published 1965). The pair island-hopped all
the way from Java to Timor and overcame
everything from landslides to soldiers shooting at vehicles making illegal turns.

While the Schreiders took only their pet
dog with them, zoologist and TV personality
David Attenborough left the UK with practically nothing and returned from the archipelago with a menagerie. The whole saga of
the enterprise is recounted in his book *Zoo
Quest for a Dragon*, published in 1957.

The Malay Archipelago by Alfred Russel
Wallace is an 1869 classic of this famous
naturalist's wanderings throughout the
Indonesian islands.

More recent travelogues include Gavin
Young's *In Search of Conrad*, an interesting account of this British author's re-
tracing of Joseph Conrad's journeys by
boat around Sumatra, Java, Kalimantan,

Bali and Sulawesi. *Distant Islands – Travels Across Indonesia* is by Charles Corn, who island-hops his way from Jakarta across to Timor and back to Sumatra in a light but engaging narrative. *An Empire of the East* by Norman Lewis visits Indonesia's hotspots – Aceh, East Timor and Irian Jaya – in a partly successful travelogue.

History

An excellent general history is *A History of Modern Indonesia* (1981) by MC Ricklefs. It covers Indonesian history from the rise of Islam (circa 1300) to the present. It mainly covers Java, but ties in with events on other islands. For an introduction to all the major empires, movements and currents in Javanese history, this book is a must.

Of the many general histories on the country, a readable, popular history is *Indonesia – Land Under the Rainbow* (1990) by the noted Indonesian writer Mochtar Lubis. It provides an interesting view of the country through modern Indonesian eyes.

Indonesian Trade and Society by JC van Leur is a classic academic study of Indonesian social and economic history, looking at the early influences that shaped the history of the archipelago.

For the serious student of Indonesian history, *The History of Java* by Thomas Stamford Raffles (1817) is a classic work covering all aspects of Javanese history and society. It is available in two hefty and very expensive volumes with numerous illustrations.

People & Society

A compilation of some of the intriguing religious, social and mystical customs of the diverse peoples of Indonesia is Lee Khoon Choy's *Indonesia – Between Myth & Reality*. It's a journalistic travelogue, derived from the author's short spells in the country as a journalist and politician, and his position as Singapore's ambassador to Indonesia from 1970 to 1975.

Indonesia in Focus, edited by Peter Homan, *et al*, is a Dutch publication with glossy photos and well illustrated articles exploring Indonesia's rich ethnic diversity.

Various books explore regional cultures in detail. *The Religion of Java* by Clifford Geertz is not only a classic book on Javanese religion, culture and values, but revolutionised the study of social anthropology. Robin Hanbury-Tenison's *A Pattern of Peoples* was based on his trip to Indonesia in 1973, visiting minority groups like the Dani of Irian Jaya and the Toraja of Sulawesi. It comments on the effects that tourism and other developments have had on what were, until recently, isolated peoples.

For a good general introduction to Indonesian culture, customs, language and food, useful for both expats and travellers, *Culture Shock – Indonesia* by Cathie Draine & Barbara Hall is part of a well-known travel series. Another excellent general guide to living in Indonesia is *Introducing Indonesia – A Guide to Expatriate Living* by the American Women's Association of Indonesia.

General

Christopher Koch's *The Year of Living Dangerously* is an evocative reconstruction of life in Jakarta during the final chaotic months of the Soekarno period, and a sympathetic portrayal of Indonesian culture and society. The movie by Australian director Peter Weir packs a feel for the city that few other movies could ever hope to achieve.

Much of Joseph Conrad's *Victory* is set in Borneo and Surabaya. Though not particularly evocative of Indonesia, it gives a wonderful account of the sea traders of the time. Many of his other books are set in region, such as *Almayer's Folly*, set in eastern Borneo.

Max Havelaar by Multatuli (the pseudonym of Douwes Dekker) is a classic Dutch novel first published in 1860. Written by a Dutch official based in West Java, it focuses on the inhumane treatment of the Javanese under the Dutch Culture System (see History in the Facts about Indonesia chapter). The ensuing public outcry in the Netherlands helped to change government policy.

Two good illustrated books on Indonesian wildlife are *The Wildlife of Indonesia* by Kathy MacKinnon and *Wild Indonesia* by Tony & Jane Whitten. *The Birds of Java and Bali* by Derek Holmes & Stephen Nash is one of the best birding guides available. *The Birds of Sulawesi* by Derek Holmes & Karen Phillipps is also worthwhile.

Periplus produces *The Ecology of Indonesia* in eight regional volumes. These scholarly books cover everything from flora and fauna to population distribution.

Claire Holt's *Art in Indonesia – Continuities and Change* is an excellent introduction to the arts of Indonesia, focusing on traditional dance, *wayang* and literature. For an overall guide to Indonesian crafts, *Arts and Crafts of Indonesia* by Anne Richter is detailed and beautifully illustrated.

Glossy coffee table books on Indonesia abound. Of the more interesting is *Bali Style* by Barbara Walker & Rio Helmi, a lavishly photographed look at Balinese design, architecture and interior decoration. In the same series is *Java Style*.

Eat Smart in Indonesia by Joan Peterson, David Peterson & SV Medaris is a good, well illustrated introduction to Indonesian dishes and their ingredients.

For books by Indonesian authors, see Literature in the Facts About Indonesia chapter.

Bookshops

Books in English, usually only cheap novels, can be found in bookshops in the main cities, airports and in some of the large hotels, although they're generally expensive. Good bookshops are hard to find, impossibly so in the outer islands and smaller cities. Jakarta has the best bookshops in the country. Well touristed places like Ubud and Yogya have second-hand bookshops, and these are the best bet for books in other languages, such as Dutch, French and German.

FILMS

A few foreign films have been shot in Indonesia and might be available in video stores. *Jakarta* (1988), directed by Charles Kaufman, is a rousing action film starring Christopher Noth. It provides little insight into Indonesia, but was filmed in and around the capital. The best of the foreign movies is

Max Havelaar (1976), a Dutch/Indonesian co-production directed by Fons Rademakers. Based on the classic novel by Multatuli (see Books earlier), it is about a Dutch official in 19th century Java who is confronted by the injustices of colonialism. See also Cinema in the Facts About Indonesia chapter.

NEWSPAPERS & MAGAZINES

The news media now openly publishes stories that could only be hinted at during the Soeharto era. Now the media rails against Soeharto, but other figures are treated with more care, especially those in the army. The press is now remarkably free, but though the government talks about 'transparensi', it may be some time before repressive press laws are fully repealed and old habits die hard, especially the desire of government to control information.

Local

The English-language press is limited mostly to the daily *Jakarta Post*. In a country where, until very recently, self-censorship applied and stories of corruption and repression never saw the light of day, the *Jakarta Post* was surprisingly open. As well as forthright reporting, it also gives a useful rundown of events in Jakarta and further afield.

The other main English-language newspaper is the *Indonesian Observer*, but its coverage of local politics is a long way behind that of the *Jakarta Post*.

Two of the leading Indonesian-language newspapers are the Jakarta dailies *Pos Kota* and the respected *Kompas*, each with a circulation of around 3 million per day. The other main newspapers, in terms of readership, are *Jawa Pos*, *Suara Pembaruan*, *Republika*, *Pikiran Rakyat*, *Harian Terbit* and *Media Indonesia*.

Popular tabloids include *Nova*, a women's paper, and *Bola* (as in soccer ball), while post-reform political tabloids such as *Adil* and *Aksi* are also strong performers. *Femina* is a top selling women's magazine, while *Gatra* is a general news and features magazine, as is the once banned *Tempo*.

Foreign

The *International Herald-Tribune*, *Asian Wall Street Journal* and major Asian dailies are sold in Indonesia. Western magazines like *Time*, *Newsweek*, the *Economist* and the excellent Hong Kong-published *Far Eastern Economic Review* are also available in Indonesia.

For information on current events (including Indonesian politics, history and culture) take out a subscription to *Inside Indonesia*, published in Australia by IRIP (☎ 03-9419 4504, fax 9419 4774, email admin@insideindonesia.org), PO Box 1326, Collingwood Vic 3066, Australia. Excellent articles cover everything from power plays within the army to the environment, and it discusses issues not raised in the Indonesian media and rarely covered overseas.

RADIO & TV

Radio Republik Indonesia (RRI) is the national radio station and broadcasts 24 hours in Indonesian from every provincial capital. Indonesia also has plenty of privately run stations.

Thanks to satellite broadcasting, TV can be received everywhere in Indonesia. You'll see plenty of Indonesians gathered around the TV set of any hotel – they are among the world's foremost TV addicts.

Televisi Republik Indonesia (TVRI) is the government-owned Indonesian-language TV station, which is broadcast in every province. It broadcasts on two channels, but the second channel is not available in more remote areas.

Private stations are Rajawali Citra Televisi Indonesia (RCTI), Andalas Telvisi (AN-TV), Indosair, Surya Citra Televisi (SCTV) and Televisi Pendidikan Indonesia (TPI), originally an educational station but now much the same as the rest.

Most programming revolves around interminable government news broadcasts. Local news is broadcast in English at 6.30 am on TVRI, 7 am on SCTV and 7.30 am on RCTI. Foreign movies, mostly B-grade US adventure flicks, are screened most evenings with Indonesian subtitles (a good way to pick up the language) and an amazing number of advertisements to interrupt the action at the most inappropriate moments.

Satellite dishes also pick up overseas stations transmitting in the region. CNN, BBC, Television Australia, Malaysian and French television can all be received. Some large hotels also have cable television access for HBO and Discovery Channel, among others.

VIDEO SYSTEMS

VCR recorders are outdated technology in Indonesia – VCDs (video CDs) are all the rage.

Almost every shopping centre in the big cities has a shop or stalls selling cheap pirate VCDs, but the quality is often poor. Some hunting will turn up a good selection of recent-release movies, and they are not censored in a country that cuts just about anything more risque than *Bambi*.

Laser discs are also popular and they can be bought or rented in the main cities. The quality is better than VCDs.

PHOTOGRAPHY & VIDEO
Film

Film is cheap and Indonesia is an incredibly photogenic country, so you can easily whip through large quantities of film. Colour print film is preferred to anything else; slide film and B&W film are not as readily available. In Jakarta and Bali you can usually find most types of film and video tape. Fuji is by far the most widely available brand for prints and slides.

Developing and printing is cheap. Slide film can be developed in two or three days, and colour print film can be done the same day through photographic shops in major towns all across the archipelago. Try them out with one roll before you commit all your holiday snaps. The quality is variable but often good; Fuji shops are usually reliable.

In the small towns or towns, few tourists visit, many types of film aren't available at all, particularly slide film. Also, turnover of stock is slow, so it's best to check the expiry date of the film.

Camera batteries and other accessories are available from photographic shops in major cities only.

Technical Tips

Photography Shoot photos early or late, as between 10 am and 1 or 2 pm the sun is uncomfortably hot and high overhead, and you're likely to get a bluish, washed-out look to your pictures. A polarising filter helps reduce glare and darkens an otherwise washed-out sunlit sky. A lens hood will reduce your problems with reflections and direct sunlight on the lens. Beware of the sharp differences between sun and shade – if you can't get reasonably balanced overall light, you may have to opt for exposing only one area correctly; alternatively, use a fill-in flash.

Those lush, green rice fields come up best if backlit by the sun. For those sunset shots at Kuta, Kalibukbuk or Pontianak, set your exposure on the sky without the sun making an appearance – then shoot at the sun. Photography from fast-moving trains and buses doesn't work well unless you use a fast shutter speed. Dust can be a problem – hazy days will make it difficult to get sharp shots.

Video Properly used, a video camera can give a fascinating record of your holiday. As well as shooting the obvious things – sunsets, spectacular views – remember to record some of the ordinary everyday details of life in Indonesia.

Video cameras these days have amazingly sensitive microphones, and you might be surprised how much sound will be picked up. This can also be a problem if there is lots of ambient noise – filming by the side of a busy road might seem OK when you do it, but viewing it back home might simply give you a deafening cacophony of traffic noise. One good rule to follow for beginners is to try to film in long takes, and don't move the camera around too much. Otherwise, your video could well make your viewers seasick! If your camera has a stabiliser, you can use it to obtain good footage while travelling on various means of transport, even on bumpy roads.

Make sure you keep the batteries charged, and have the necessary charger, plugs and transformer suitable for Indonesia. It is possible to obtain video cartridges easily in Jakarta and Denpasar and the main tourist areas, but make sure you buy the correct format; it's usually worth buying at least a few cartridges duty free to start off your trip.

Photographing People

You get a fantastic run for your money in Indonesia – not only are there 200 million or so portraits to choose from, the variation in ethnic types is phenomenal.

Few people expect payment for their photos, the Baliem Valley on Irian Jaya being the exception. What Indonesians *will* go for is a copy of the photo – if you hang around Indonesia long enough, you'll wind up with a pocketful of bits of paper with addresses of people to send photos.

Some Indonesians will shy away from having their photo taken and duck for cover, some are shy but only too pleased to be photographed, some are proud and ham it up for the camera and others won't get out of the way of the lens when you want them too!

Whatever you do, photograph with discretion and manners. It's always polite to ask first and if the person says no, don't take the photo. A gesture, a smile and a nod are all that is usually necessary. In some places you may come up against religious barriers to taking photographs – such as trying to photograph Muslim women in the more devoutly Islamic parts of the archipelago. The taboo might also apply to the minority groups. Don't take photographs at public bathing places – intruding with your camera is no different to sneaking up to someone's bathroom window. Remember, wherever you are in Indonesia, the people are *not* exotic birds of paradise and the village priest is *not* a photographic model. And finally, don't be surprised if Indonesian people turn the tables on you – they have become fond of sneaking up on westerners and shooting a few exotic photos to show their friends!

Video users should follow the same rules regarding people's sensitivities as for a photograph – having a video camera shoved in their face is probably even more annoying and offensive for locals than a still camera. Always ask permission first.

TIME

There are three time zones in Indonesia. Sumatra, Java, and west and Central Kalimantan are on Western Indonesian Time, which is seven hours ahead of GMT/UTC (Greenwich Mean Time/Universal Time Coordinated). Bali, Nusa Tenggara, South and East Kalimantan, and Sulawesi are on Central Indonesian Time, which is eight hours ahead of GMT. Irian Jaya and Maluku are on Eastern Indonesian Time, nine hours ahead of GMT. In a country straddling the equator, there is of course no daylight-saving time.

Allowing for variations due to daylight saving, when it is noon in Jakarta it is 9 pm the previous day in San Francisco or Los Angeles, midnight in New York, 5 am in London, 1 pm in Singapore and Ujung Pandang, 2 pm in Jayapura and 3 pm in Melbourne or Sydney.

Strung out along the equator, Indonesian days and nights are approximately equal in length, and sunrises and sunsets occur very rapidly with almost no twilight. Sunrise is around 5.30 to 6 am and sunset is around 5.30 to 6 pm, varying slightly depending on distance from the equator.

ELECTRICITY

Electricity is 220V/50Hz AC. Indonesia switched over from 110V years ago, and some places may still possibly be wired for 110V.

Sockets accommodate two round prongs, the same as in most European countries. Recessed sockets are designed to take earth (ground) facilities, but most appliances and the wiring in many cheap hotels aren't earthed, so take care. Electricity is usually reliable in cities, but occasional blackouts occur. It's wise to keep a flashlight (torch) or candles handy.

Safe adaptors for foreign plugs are hard to find, so bring your own. The voltage supply is not stable in many parts of Indonesia,

and a voltage stabiliser/surge guard is recommended for computers.

WEIGHTS & MEASURES

Indonesia has fully adopted the international metric system.

LAUNDRY

Virtually every hotel – from the smallest to the largest – has a laundry service, and in most places it is very inexpensive. About the only thing you need to be concerned about is the weather – clothes are dried on the line, so a hot, sunny day is essential. Give staff your laundry in the morning – they like to wash clothes before 9 am so it all has sufficient time to dry before sunset.

MANDI & TOILETS

One thing you'll have to learn to deal with is the *mandi*. The word mandi simply means to bathe or to wash. A mandi is a large water tank with a plastic saucepan. The popularity of the mandi is mainly due to a frequent lack of running water in Indonesia – sometimes the tank is refilled by a hose attached to a hand-pump.

Climbing into the mandi is very bad form indeed – it's your water supply and it's also the supply for every other guest that comes after you, so the idea is to keep the water clean. What you're supposed to do is to scoop water out of the mandi and pour it over yourself. Most of the tourist hotels have showers, and the more expensive ones have hot water and bathtubs.

Another thing which may require adjustment are Indonesian toilets. These are basically holes in the ground with footrests on either side, over which you squat and aim. In some tourist areas, Asian toilets are fading away as more places install western-style toilets. The lack of running water makes flushing toilets a problem, so what you do is reach for that plastic saucepan again, scoop water from the mandi and flush it away.

As for toilet paper, it is seldom supplied in public places, though you can easily buy your own. Indonesians seldom use the stuff and the method is to use the left hand and copious quantities of water – again, keep that saucepan handy. Some westerners easily adapt to this method, but many do not. If you need to use toilet paper, see if there is a wastebasket next to the toilet. If there is, that's where the paper should go, not down the toilet. If you plug up the hotel's plumbing with toilet paper, the management is going to get really angry.

Kamar kecil is Bahasa Indonesia for toilet, but people usually understand 'waysay' (WC). *Wanita* means women and *pria* means men.

HEALTH

As a tropical country with a low sanitation standards, Indonesia is a fairly easy place to get ill. The climate provides a good breeding ground for malarial mosquitoes, but the biggest hazards come from contaminated food and water. Don't worry excessively about all this – with some basic precautions and adequate information, few travellers experience more than upset stomachs.

Predeparture Planning

Immunisations Plan ahead for getting your vaccinations: some of them require more than one injection, while some vaccinations should not be given together. Note that some vaccinations should not be given during pregnancy or to people with allergies – discuss with your doctor.

It is recommended you seek medical advice at least six weeks before travel. Be aware that there is often a greater risk of disease with children and during pregnancy. Also carry some proof of your vaccinations.

Discuss your requirements with your doctor, but vaccinations you should consider for this trip include the following (for more details about the diseases themselves, see the individual disease entries later in this section).

Diphtheria & Tetanus Vaccinations for these two diseases are usually combined and are recommended for everyone. After an initial course of three injections (usually given in childhood), boosters are necessary every 10 years.

Polio Everyone should keep up to date with this vaccination, which is normally given in

Medical Kit Check List

Following is a list of items you should consider including in your medical kit – consult your pharmacist for brands available in your country.

☐ **Aspirin** or **paracetamol** (acetaminophen in the USA) – for pain or fever
☐ **Antihistamine** – for allergies, eg hay fever; to ease the itch from insect bites or stings; and to prevent motion sickness
☐ **Antibiotics** – consider including these if you're travelling well off the beaten track; see your doctor, as they must be prescribed, and carry the prescription with you
☐ **Loperamide** or **diphenoxylate** –'blockers' for diarrhoea; **prochlorperazine** or **metaclopramide** for nausea and vomiting
☐ **Rehydration mixture** – to prevent dehydration, eg due to severe diarrhoea; particularly important when travelling with children
☐ **Insect repellent, sunscreen, lip balm** and **eye drops**
☐ **Calamine lotion, sting relief spray** or **aloe vera** – to ease irritation from sunburn and insect bites or stings
☐ **Antifungal cream** or **powder** – for fungal skin infections and thrush
☐ **Antiseptic** (such as povidone-iodine) – for cuts and grazes
☐ **Bandages, Band-Aids (plasters)** and other wound dressings
☐ **Water purification tablets** or **iodine**
☐ **Scissors, tweezers** and a **thermometer** (note that mercury thermometers are prohibited by airlines)
☐ **Syringes** and **needles** – in case you need injections in a country with medical hygiene problems. Ask your doctor for a note explaining why you have them.
☐ **Cold** and **flu tablets, throat lozenges** and **nasal decongestant**
☐ **Multivitamins** – consider for long trips, when dietary vitamin intake may be inadequate

childhood. A polio booster every 10 years maintains immunity.

Hepatitis A Hepatitis A vaccine (eg Avaxim, Havrix 1440 or VAQTA) provides long-term immunity (possibly more than 10 years) after an initial injection and a booster at six to 12 months.

Alternatively, an injection of gamma globulin can provide short-term protection against hepatitis A – two to six months, depending on the dose given. It is not a vaccine, but is ready-made antibody collected from blood donations. It is reasonably effective and, unlike the vaccine, it is protective immediately – but because it is a blood product, there are current concerns about its long-term safety.

Hepatitis A vaccine is also available in Twinrix, a combined form with hepatitis B vaccine. Three injections over a six month period are required, the first two providing substantial protection against hepatitis A.

Typhoid Vaccination against typhoid may be required if you are travelling for more than a couple of weeks in Indonesia. It is now available either as an injection or as capsules to be taken orally.

Cholera The current injectable vaccine against cholera is poorly protective and has many side effects, so it is not generally recommended for travellers.

Hepatitis B People who should consider vaccination against hepatitis B include any long-term travellers, as well as those visiting countries where there are high levels of hepatitis B infection, where blood transfusions may not be adequately screened or where sexual contact or needle sharing is a possibility. Vaccination involves three injections, with a booster at 12 months. More rapid courses are available if necessary.

Rabies Vaccination should be considered by those who will spend a month or longer in a country where rabies is common, especially if they are cycling, handling animals, caving or travelling to remote areas, and for children (who may not report a bite). Pretravel rabies vaccination involves having three injections over 21 to 28 days. If someone who has been vaccinated is bitten or scratched by an animal, they will require two booster injections of vaccine; those not vaccinated require more.

Japanese B Encephalitis Consider vaccination against this disease if spending a month or longer in a high risk area (parts of Asia), making repeated trips to a risk area or visiting during an epidemic. It involves three injections over 30 days.

Tuberculosis The risk of TB to travellers is usually very low, unless you will be living with or closely associated with local people in high risk areas such as Asia, Africa and some parts of the Americas and Pacific. Vaccination with the BCG vaccine (against TB) is recommended for children and young adults living in these areas for three months or more.

Malaria Medication

Antimalarial drugs do not prevent you from being infected but kill the malaria parasites during a stage in their development and significantly reduce the risk of becoming very ill or dying. Antimalarials are generally recommended for Indonesia, but expert advice on medication should be sought, as there are many factors to consider, including the area to be visited, the risk of exposure to malaria-carrying mosquitoes, the side effects of medication, your medical history and whether you are a child or an adult or pregnant. Travellers to isolated areas in Indonesia may like to carry a treatment dose of medication for use if symptoms occur.

Health Insurance Ensure you have adequate health insurance. See Travel Insurance under Visas & Documents earlier in this chapter for details.

Travel Health Guides If you are planning to be away or travelling in remote areas for a long period of time, you may like to consider taking a more detailed health guide.

CDC's Complete Guide to Healthy Travel (1997). The US Centers for Disease Control & Prevention recommendations for international travel.

Healthy Travel, Asia & India by Dr Isabelle Young, Lonely Planet, 2000. This first edition of the Healthy Travel series provides practical advice from basic first aid to alternative travel remedies.

Staying Healthy in Asia, Africa & Latin America, by Dirk Schroeder (1994). Detailed and well organised.

Travellers' Health, by Dr Richard Dawood, (1995). Comprehensive, easy to read, authoritative and highly recommended, although it's rather large to lug around.

Where There Is No Doctor, David Werner, (1994). A very detailed guide intended for someone, such as a Peace Corps worker, going to work in an underdeveloped country.

Travel with Children, by Maureen Wheeler, Lonely Planet, 1995. This book includes advice on travel health for younger children.

There are also a number of excellent travel health Web sites on the Internet. The Lonely Planet home page has links at www.lone lyplanet.com/health/health.htm to the World Health Organization (WHO) and the Centers for Disease Control & Prevention.

Other Preparations Make sure you're healthy before you start travelling. If you are going on a long trip, make sure your teeth are in reasonable condition. If you wear glasses, take a spare pair and your prescription.

If you require a particular medication, take an adequate supply, as it may not be available locally. Take part of the packaging showing the generic name rather than the brand, which will make getting replacements easier. It's a good idea to have a legible prescription or letter from your doctor to show that you legally use the medication to avoid any problems.

Basic Rules

Food There is an old saying: 'If you can cook it, boil it or peel it, you can eat it ... otherwise, forget it'. Vegetables and fruit should be washed with purified water or peeled where possible. Beware of ice cream sold in the street or anywhere it might have been melted and refrozen; if there's any doubt (eg a power cut in the last day or two), steer well clear. Shellfish such as mussels, oysters and clams should be avoided, as well as undercooked meat, particularly in the form of mince. Steaming does not make shellfish safe for eating.

If a place looks clean and well run and the vendor also looks clean and healthy, the food is probably safe. In general, places that are packed with travellers or locals will be fine. The food in busy restaurants is cooked and eaten quite quickly with little standing around and is probably not reheated.

Water The No 1 rule is *be careful of the drinking water* and especially ice. If you don't know for certain that the water is safe, assume the worst. Reputable brands of bottled water or soft drinks are generally fine. Only use water from containers with a serrated seal – not with tops or corks. Take care with fruit juice, particularly if water may have been added. Milk should be treated with suspicion, as it is often unpasteurised, though boiled milk is fine if it is stored hygienically. Tea or coffee should also be OK, since the water should have been boiled.

Water Purification The simplest way of purifying water is to boil it. Vigorous boiling should be satisfactory; however, at high altitude water boils at a lower temperature, so germs are less likely to be killed. Boil it for longer in these environments.

Consider purchasing a water filter for a long trip or if you intend to go trekking. There are two main kinds of filter. Total filters take out all parasites, bacteria and viruses and make water safe to drink. They are often expensive, but they can be more cost effective than buying bottled water. Simple filters (which can even be a nylon mesh bag) take out dirt and larger foreign bodies from the water so that chemical solutions work much more effectively; if water is dirty, chemical solutions may not work at all. It's very important when buying a filter to read the specifications, so that you know exactly what it removes from the water and what it doesn't. Simple filtering will not remove all dangerous organisms, so if you cannot boil water it should be treated chemically. Chlorine tablets (Puritabs, Steritabs or other brand names) will kill many pathogens, but not some parasites like *Giardia* and amoebic cysts. Iodine is more effective in purifying water and is available in tablet form (such as Potable Aqua). Follow the directions carefully and remember that too much iodine can be harmful.

Medical Problems & Treatment

Self-diagnosis and treatment can be risky, so you should always seek medical help. Although we do give drug dosages in this section, they are for emergency use only. Correct diagnosis is vital.

In most cases you can buy virtually any medicine across the counter in Indonesia without a prescription. If you need some special medication, take it with you. However, you shouldn't have any trouble finding common western medicines in Indonesia, at least in big cities like Jakarta and Denpasar where there are lots of well stocked pharmacies *(apotik)*. In rural areas pharmacies are scarce, but grocery shops will gladly sell you all sorts of dangerous drugs, which are often long beyond their expiry dates (check them). Many of the big tourist hotels also have pharmacies (drugstores).

In each apotik there is an English-language copy of the Indonesian Index of Medical Specialities (IIMS), a guide to pharmaceutical preparations available to doctors in Indonesia. It lists drugs by brand name, generic name, manufacturer's name and therapeutic action. Drugs may not be of the same strength as in other countries, or may have deteriorated due to age or poor storage conditions.

As for medical treatment, Catholic or missionary hospitals or clinics are often of a reasonable standard and in remote areas they may be your only hope other than prayer beads and chanting; missionary hospitals also often have English-speaking staff. Back in the developed world, you can often locate a competent doctor *(dokter)*, dentist *(dokter gigi)* and hospital *(rumah sakit)* by asking at hotels, embassies or offices of foreign companies in places where large expatriate communities work. In towns and cities there seems to be a fair supply of doctors and dentists to choose from. In remote areas such as Irian Jaya there are clinics set up by missionaries. There are also public hospitals in cities and towns.

Hospitals are open during the day, but private clinics operate mostly in the evening from 6 pm. It's first come, first served, so go early and be prepared to wait. Medical costs are generally very cheap, but drugs are expensive.

Jakarta has the best medical facilities in the country, but a lot of people still prefer to go to Singapore for serious ailments that require hospitalisation. Alternatively, Darwin is close for eastern Indonesia.

Rumah Sakit Pondok Indah
(☎ 7500157) Jl Metro Duta Kav UE. This perfectly modern hospital in South Jakarta rivals the best hospitals in the west, although it charges modern prices.
Rumah Sakit Cipto Mangunkusumo
(☎ 330808) Jl Diponegoro 71. Near Jl Jaksa, this is a government public hospital. It is reasonably priced with good emergency facilities but is often very crowded.
St Carolus Hospital
(☎ 3904441) Jl Salemba Raya 41. This is a private Catholic hospital in Central Jakarta charging mid-range prices.

Jakarta also has well equipped, modern medical clinics that provide a full range of services, including specialists, emergency and dental care. Two that are popular with expatriates are:

AEA International Clinic/SOS Medika
(☎ 7505980)
Jl Puri Sakti 10, Cipete
Medical Scheme
(☎ 5201034, 5255367)
Setiabudi bldg 2, Jl Rasuna Said, Kuningan

Environmental Hazards

Heat Exhaustion Dehydration and salt deficiency can cause heat exhaustion. Take time to acclimatise to high temperatures, drink sufficient liquids and do not do anything too physically demanding.

Salt deficiency is characterised by fatigue, lethargy, headaches, giddiness and muscle cramps; salt tablets may help, but adding extra salt to your food is better.

Anhidrotic heat exhaustion is a rare form of heat exhaustion that is caused by an inability to sweat. It tends to affect people who have been in a hot climate for some time, rather than newcomers. It can progress to heatstroke. Treatment involves removal to a cooler climate.

Heatstroke This serious, occasionally fatal, condition can occur if the body's heat-regulating mechanism breaks down and the body temperature rises to dangerous levels. Long, continuous periods of exposure to high temperatures and insufficient fluids can leave you vulnerable to heatstroke.

The symptoms are feeling unwell, not sweating very much (or at all) and a high body temperature (39°C to 41°C, or 102°F to 106°F). Where sweating has ceased, the skin becomes flushed and red. Severe, throbbing headaches and lack of coordination will also occur, and the sufferer may be confused or aggressive. Eventually the casualty will become delirious or convulse. Hospitalisation is essential, but in the interim get the casualty out of the sun, remove their clothing, cover them with a wet sheet or towel and then fan continually. Give fluids if they are conscious.

Jet Lag Jet lag is experienced when a person travels by air across more than three time zones (each time zone usually represents a one hour time difference). It occurs because many of the functions of the human body (such as temperature, pulse rate and emptying of the bladder and bowels) are regulated by internal 24-hour cycles. When we travel long distances rapidly, our bodies take time to adjust to the 'new time' of our destination, and we may experience fatigue, disorientation, insomnia, anxiety, impaired concentration and loss of appetite. These effects will usually be gone within three days of arrival, but to minimise the impact of jet lag:

- Rest for a couple of days prior to departure.
- Try to select flight schedules that minimise sleep deprivation; arriving late in the day means you can go to sleep soon after you arrive. For very long flights, try to organise a stopover.
- Avoid excessive eating (which bloats the stomach) and alcohol (which causes dehydration) during the flight. Instead, drink plenty of non-carbonated, nonalcoholic drinks such as fruit juice or water.
- Avoid smoking.

- Make yourself comfortable by wearing loose-fitting clothes and perhaps bringing an eye mask and ear plugs to help you sleep.
- Try to sleep at the appropriate time for the time zone you are travelling to.

Motion Sickness Eating lightly before and during a trip will reduce the chances of motion sickness. If you are prone to motion sickness, try to find a place that minimises movement – near the wing on aircraft, close to midship on boats, near the centre on buses. Fresh air usually helps; reading and cigarette smoke don't. Commercial motion-sickness preparations, which can cause drowsiness, have to be taken before the trip commences. Ginger (available in capsule form) and peppermint (including mint-flavoured sweets) are natural preventatives.

Prickly Heat Prickly heat is an itchy rash caused by excessive perspiration trapped under the skin. It usually strikes people who have just arrived in a hot climate. Keeping cool, bathing often, drying the skin and using a mild talcum or prickly heat powder, or resorting to air-conditioning, may help.

Sunburn In the tropics you can get sunburnt surprisingly quickly, even through cloud. Use a sunscreen, a hat, and a barrier cream for your nose and lips. Calamine lotion or Stingose are good for mild sunburn. Protect your eyes with good quality sunglasses, particularly if you will be near water or sand.

Infectious Diseases

Diarrhoea Simple things like a change of water, food or climate can all cause a mild bout of diarrhoea, but a few rushed toilet trips with no other symptoms is not indicative of a major problem.

Dehydration is the main danger with any diarrhoea, particularly in children or the elderly, as dehydration can occur quite quickly. Under all circumstances *fluid replacement* (at least equal to the volume being lost) is the most important thing to remember. Weak black tea with a little sugar, soda water, or soft drinks allowed to go flat and diluted by 50% with clean water are all good. With severe diarrhoea, a rehydrating solution is preferable to replace minerals and salts lost. Commercially available oral rehydration salts (ORS) are very useful; add them to boiled or bottled water. In an emergency you can make up a solution of six teaspoons of sugar and a half teaspoon of salt to 1L of boiled or bottled water. You need to drink at least the same volume of fluid that you are losing in bowel movements and/or vomiting. Urine is the best guide to the adequacy of replacement – if you have small amounts of concentrated urine, you need to drink more. Keep drinking small amounts often. Stick to a bland diet as you recover.

Gut-paralysing drugs such as Lomotil or Imodium can be used to bring relief from the symptoms, although they do not actually cure the problem. Only use these drugs if you do not have access to toilets (eg if you *must* travel). For children under 12 years Lomotil and Imodium are not recommended. Do not use these drugs if the person has a high fever or is severely dehydrated.

In certain situations antibiotics may be required: diarrhoea with blood or mucus (dysentery), any diarrhoea with fever, profuse watery diarrhoea, persistent diarrhoea not improving after 48 hours and severe diarrhoea. These suggest a more serious cause of diarrhoea, and gut-paralysing drugs should be avoided.

In these situations, a stool test may be necessary to diagnose what bacteria is causing your diarrhoea, so you should seek medical help urgently. Where this is not possible the recommended drugs for bacterial diarrhoea (the most likely cause of severe diarrhoea in travellers) are norfloxacin 400mg twice daily for three days or ciprofloxacin 500mg twice daily for five days. These are not recommended for children or pregnant women. The drug of choice for children would be cotrimoxazole (Bactrim, Septrin or Resprim) with dosage dependent on weight. Ampicillin or amoxycillin may be given in pregnancy, but medical care is necessary.

Two other causes of persistent diarrhoea in travellers are giardiasis and amoebic dysentery.

Giardiasis is caused by a common parasite, *Giardia lamblia*. Symptoms include stomach cramps, nausea, a bloated stomach, watery, foul-smelling diarrhoea and frequent gas. Giardiasis can appear several weeks after you have been exposed to the parasite. The symptoms may disappear for a few days and then return; this can go on for several weeks.

Amoebic dysentery, caused by the protozoan *Entamoeba histolytica*, is characterised by a gradual onset of low-grade diarrhoea, often with blood and mucus. Cramping abdominal pain and vomiting are less likely than in other types of diarrhoea, and fever may not be present. It will persist until treated, and can recur and cause other health problems.

You should seek medical advice if you think you have giardiasis or amoebic dysentery, but where this is not possible, tinidazole or metronidazole are the recommended drugs. Treatment is a 2g single dose of tinidazole or 250mg of metronidazole three times daily for five to 10 days.

Fungal Infections Fungal infections occur more commonly in hot weather and are usually found on the scalp, between the toes (athlete's foot) or fingers, in the groin and on the body (ringworm). You get ringworm (which is a fungal infection, not a worm) from infected animals or other people. Moisture encourages these infections.

To prevent fungal infections, wear loose, comfortable clothes, avoid artificial fibres, wash frequently and dry yourself carefully. If you do get an infection, wash the infected area at least daily with a disinfectant or medicated soap and water, and rinse and dry well. Apply an antifungal cream or powder like tolnaftate. Try to expose the infected area to air or sunlight as much as possible, and wash all towels and underwear in hot water, change them often and let them dry in the sun.

Hepatitis This is a general term for inflammation of the liver. It is a common disease worldwide. There are several different viruses that cause hepatitis, and they differ in the way they are transmitted. The symptoms are similar in all forms of the illness, and include fever, chills, headache, fatigue, feelings of weakness and aches and pains, followed by loss of appetite, nausea, vomiting, abdominal pain, dark urine, light-coloured faeces, jaundice (yellowed skin and yellowing of the whites of the eyes). People who have had hepatitis should avoid alcohol for some time after the illness, as the liver needs time to recover.

Hepatitis A is transmitted by contaminated food and drinking water. You should seek medical advice, but there is not much you can do apart from resting, drinking lots of fluids, eating lightly and avoiding fatty foods. **Hepatitis E** is transmitted in the same way as hepatitis A.

There are almost 300 million chronic carriers of **hepatitis B** in the world and it is estimated that over a third of the Indonesia population are carriers. It is spread through contact with infected blood, blood products or body fluids (eg through sexual contact, unsterilised needles and blood transfusions, or contact with blood via small breaks in the skin). Other risk situations include sharing shaving equipment, or tattoo or body piercing with contaminated equipment. The symptoms of hepatitis B may be more severe than type A and the disease can lead to long-term problems such as chronic liver damage, liver cancer or a long-term carrier state. **Hepatitis C** and **hepatitis D** are spread in the same way as hepatitis B and can also lead to long term-complications.

There are vaccines against hepatitis A and B, but there are currently no vaccines against the other types of hepatitis. Following the basic rules about food and water (hepatitis A and E) and avoiding risk situations (hepatitis B, C and D) are important preventative measures.

HIV & AIDS Infection with the human immunodeficiency virus (HIV) may lead to acquired immune deficiency syndrome (AIDS), which is a fatal disease. Any exposure to blood, blood products or body fluids may put the individual at risk. The disease is often transmitted through sexual contact or dirty needles – vaccinations, acupuncture, tattooing and body piercing can be potentially as dangerous as intravenous drug use. HIV/AIDS can also be spread through infected blood transfusions; some developing countries cannot afford to screen blood used for transfusions and though blood screening occurs in Indonesia, it is not reliable.

If you do need an injection, ask to see the syringe unwrapped in front of you, or take a needle and syringe pack with you. Fear of HIV infection should never preclude treatment for serious medical conditions.

Intestinal Worms These parasites are most common in rural, tropical areas. The different worms have different ways of infecting people. Some may be ingested on food such as undercooked meat (eg tapeworms) and some enter through your skin (eg hookworms). Infestations may not show up for some time, and although they are generally not serious, if left untreated some can cause severe health problems later. Consider having a stool test when you return home to check for these and determine the appropriate treatment.

Schistosomiasis Also known as bilharzia, this disease is transmitted by minute worms. They infect certain varieties of freshwater snails found in rivers, streams, lakes and particularly behind dams. The worms multiply and are eventually discharged into the water. Schistosomiasis mostly occurs in Africa but is cited as being present in central Sulawesi, but it is very rare.

Sexually Transmitted Diseases Gonorrhoea, herpes and syphilis are among these diseases; sores, blisters or rashes around the genitals and discharges or pain when urinating are common symptoms. In some STDs, such as wart virus or chlamydia, symptoms may be less marked or not observed at all, especially in women. Chlamydia infection can cause infertility in men and women before any symptoms have been noticed. Syphilis symptoms eventually disappear completely but the disease continues and can cause severe problems in later years. While abstinence from sexual contact is the only 100% effective prevention, using condoms is also effective. The treatment of gonorrhoea and syphilis is with antibiotics. The different sexually transmitted diseases each require specific antibiotics. There is no cure for herpes.

Typhoid Typhoid fever is a dangerous gut infection caused by contaminated water and food. Medical help must be sought.

In its early stages sufferers may feel they have a bad cold or flu on the way, as early symptoms are a headache, body aches and a fever which rises a little each day until it is around 40°C (104°F) or more. The victim's pulse is often slow relative to the degree of fever present – unlike a normal fever where the pulse increases. There may also be vomiting, abdominal pain, diarrhoea or constipation.

In the second week the high fever and slow pulse continue and a few pink spots may appear on the body; trembling, delirium, weakness, weight loss and dehydration may occur. Complications such as pneumonia, perforated bowel or meningitis may occur.

Insect-Borne Diseases

Filariasis and typhus are insect-borne diseases, but they do not pose a great risk to travellers. For more information on them see Less Common Diseases later in this section.

Malaria This serious and potentially fatal disease is spread by mosquito bites. Bali officially falls within the malarial zone but if you are travelling only to the main tourist resorts, the risk is very minimal. Similarly, the main cities of Java are very low risk, as is most of the rest of Java, but the risk is higher in less populated areas, especially the south coast and the national parks. Jakarta is one of the few places in Indonesia that has been classified as malaria free, but nowhere in Indonesia can it be guaranteed an outbreak

will never occur. The risk is generally higher in rural areas of Indonesia and some areas, like Irian Jaya, are definitely high-risk areas.

Symptoms range from fever, chills and sweating, headache, diarrhoea and abdominal pains to a feeling of ill health. Seek medical help immediately if malaria is suspected. Without treatment malaria can rapidly become more serious and can be fatal.

If medical care is not available, malaria tablets can be used for treatment. You need to use a malaria tablet which is different from the one you were taking when you contracted malaria. The standard treatment dose of mefloquine is two 250mg tablets and a further two six hours later. For Fansidar, it's a single dose of three tablets. If you were previously taking mefloquine and cannot obtain Fansidar, then other alternatives are Malarone (atovaquone-proguanil; four tablets once daily for three days), halofantrine (three doses of two 250mg tablets every six hours) or quinine sulphate (600mg every six hours). There is a greater risk of side effects with these dosages than in normal use if used with mefloquine, so medical advice is preferable. Be aware also that halofantrine is no longer recommended by WHO as emergency stand-by treatment, because of side effects, and should only be used if no other drugs are available.

Travellers are advised to prevent mosquito bites at all times:

- Wear light-coloured clothing.
- Wear long trousers and long-sleeved shirts.
- Use mosquito repellents containing the compound DEET on exposed areas (prolonged overuse of DEET may be harmful, especially to children, but its use is considered preferable to being bitten by disease-transmitting mosquitoes).
- Avoid perfumes or aftershave.
- Use a mosquito net impregnated with mosquito repellent (permethrin) – it may be worth taking your own.
- Impregnating clothes with permethrin effectively deters mosquitoes and other insects.

Dengue Fever This viral disease is transmitted by mosquitoes and occurs throughout

Indonesia. Generally, there is only a small risk to travellers except during epidemics, which are usually seasonal (during and just after the rainy season). Minor outbreaks occur every year in Indonesia but a major outbreak occurred in 1998 and over 500 people died of the more serious dengue haemorrhagic fever.

The *Aedes aegypti* mosquito, which transmits the dengue virus, is most active during the day, unlike the malaria mosquito, and is found mainly in urban areas, in and around human dwellings.

Signs and symptoms of dengue fever include a sudden onset of high fever, headache, joint and muscle pains (hence its old name, 'breakbone fever') and nausea and vomiting. A rash of small red spots appears three to four days after the onset of fever. Dengue is commonly mistaken for other infectious diseases, including influenza.

You should seek medical attention if you think you may be infected. Infection can be diagnosed by a blood test. There is no specific treatment for dengue. Aspirin should be avoided, as it increases the risk of haemorrhaging. Recovery may be prolonged, with tiredness lasting for several weeks. Severe complications are rare in travellers but include dengue haemorrhagic fever (DHF), which can be fatal without prompt medical treatment. DHF is thought to be a result of second infection due to a different strain (there are four major strains) and usually affects residents of the country rather than travellers.

There is no vaccine against dengue fever. The best prevention is to avoid mosquito bites at all times – see the earlier malaria entry for more details.

Japanese B Encephalitis This viral infection of the brain is transmitted by mosquitoes. Most cases occur in rural areas, as the virus exists in pigs and wading birds, but it is rare in Indonesia. Symptoms include fever, headache and alteration in consciousness. Hospitalisation is needed for correct diagnosis and treatment. There is a high mortality rate among those who have symptoms; of those who survive, many are intellectually disabled.

Cuts, Bites & Stings

See Less Common Diseases for details of rabies, which is passed through animal bites.

Bedbugs & Lice Bedbugs live in various places, but particularly in dirty mattresses and bedding, evidenced by spots of blood on bedclothes or on the wall. Bedbugs leave itchy bites in neat rows. Calamine lotion or Stingose spray may help.

All lice cause itching and discomfort. They make themselves at home in your hair (head lice), your clothing (body lice) or in your pubic hair (crabs). You catch lice through direct contact with infected people or by sharing combs, clothing and the like. Powder or shampoo treatment will kill the lice, and infected clothing should then be washed in very hot, soapy water and left in the sun to dry.

Bites & Stings Bee and wasp stings are usually painful rather than dangerous. However, in people who are allergic to them, severe breathing difficulties may occur and require urgent medical care. Calamine lotion or Stingose spray will give relief, and ice packs will reduce the pain and swelling. There are some spiders with dangerous bites but antivenenes are usually available. Scorpion stings are notoriously painful. The insects often shelter in shoes or clothing.

Cuts & Scratches Wash well and treat any cut with an antiseptic such as povidone-iodine. Where possible avoid bandages and Band-Aids, which can keep wounds wet. Coral cuts are notoriously slow to heal and if they are not adequately cleaned, small pieces of coral can become embedded in the wound.

Jellyfish Avoid contact with these sea creatures because of their stinging tentacles – seek local advice. Dousing in vinegar will de-activate any stingers which have not 'fired'. Calamine lotion, antihistamines and analgesics may reduce the reaction and relieve the pain.

Marine Life to Watch Out For

Most venomous fish, including sting rays, stonefish and scorpionfish are found in salt water. If you do come in contact with these species, it will usually be through stepping on them by accident.

Sting Rays

These creatures like to lie half-submerged in mud or sand in the shallows. You'll know if you step on one because they whip their tails up in defence. This can cause a nasty ragged wound, but they also have venomous spines which can sometimes be fatal. Shuffle along in the shallows to give sting rays plenty of warning of your approach.

Stonefish & Scorpionfish

With sharp dorsal fins through which they inject a venom, these species are the most dangerous of all venomous fish. They occur throughout Indonesia.

Stonefish are generally reef dwellers, and as their name suggests, they are masters of disguise and lie half-submerged in sand, mud or coral debris. Their stings are extremely painful and may lead to collapse and coma. There is a stonefish antivenin which should be given as soon as possible after the sting. Scorpionfish are very distinctive and much easier to avoid. The chances of being stung by one is remote. There's no antivenin available.

Sea Snakes

These beautiful creatures are found throughout coastal Indonesia. They're often inquisitive, although not aggressive. However, their venom is extremely toxic, so give them a wide berth. Symptoms of poisoning may not appear for several hours, and include anxiety and restlessness, dry throat, nausea and, eventually, paralysis.

Sea Urchins & Other Stingers

Avoid stepping on sea urchins, as their spines can break off and are very difficult to remove. Some species can cause a severe reaction that may result in paralysis and breathing difficulties. Sometimes you can get an itchy skin rash (sea urchin dermatitis) for several months after.

Treatment

Hot (nonscalding) water can help break down the toxins in fish venom and can be surprisingly effective at relieving pain from stings. The procedure is as follows:

- If any spines are poking out, try to remove them gently (be sure to protect your own hands).
- Wash any surface venom off with water.
- Bathe the wound in hot (nonscalding) water for up to 90 minutes or until the pain has gone, or apply hot packs.
- Wash the wound thoroughly once the pain is under control and apply a clean dressing.
- Rest with the limb raised.
- Seek medical help for antivenin if necessary, eg for a stonefish sting.

Leeches & Ticks Leeches may be present in damp rainforest conditions; they attach themselves to your skin to suck your blood. Trekkers often get them on their legs or in their boots. Salt or a lighted cigarette end will release them; do not pull them off, as the bite is then more likely to become infected. Clean and apply pressure if the point of attachment is bleeding. An insect repellent may keep them away.

You should always check all over your body if you have been walking through a potentially tick-infested area as ticks can cause skin infections and other more serious diseases. If a tick is found attached, press down around the tick's head with tweezers, grab the head and gently pull upwards. Avoid pulling the rear of the body as this may squeeze the tick's gut contents through the attached mouth parts into the skin, increasing the risk of infection and disease. Smearing chemicals on the tick will not release it and is not recommended.

Snakes To minimise your chances of being bitten always wear boots, socks and long trousers when walking through undergrowth where snakes may be present. Don't put your hands into holes and crevices, and be careful when collecting firewood.

Snake bites do not cause instantaneous death and antivenenes are usually available. Immediately wrap the bitten limb tightly, as you would for a sprained ankle, and then attach a splint to immobilise it. Keep the victim still and seek medical help, if possible with the dead snake for identification. Don't attempt to catch the snake if there is a possibility of being bitten again. Tourniquets and sucking out the poison are now comprehensively discredited.

Less Common Diseases

The following diseases pose a small risk to travellers, and so are only mentioned in passing. Seek medical advice if you think you may have any of these diseases.

Cholera This is the worst of the watery diarrhoeas, and medical help should be sought.

Outbreaks of cholera are generally widely reported, so you can avoid such problem areas. *Fluid replacement is the most vital treatment* – the risk of dehydration is severe, as you may lose up to 20L a day. If there is a delay in getting to hospital, begin taking tetracycline. The adult dose is 250mg four times daily. It is not recommended for children under nine years or for pregnant women. Tetracycline may help shorten the illness, but adequate fluids are required to save lives.

Filariasis This is a mosquito-transmitted parasitic infection found in parts of Indonesia. Possible symptoms include fever, pain and swelling of the lymph glands; inflammation of lymph drainage areas; swelling of a limb or the scrotum; skin rashes; and blindness. Treatment is available to eliminate the parasites from the body, but some of the damage already caused may not be reversible. Medical advice should be sought promptly if the infection is suspected.

Rabies This fatal viral infection occurs in Indonesia. Many animals can be infected (dogs are the main carriers of the disease, but cats, bats and monkeys should also be treated circumspectly), and it is their saliva which is infectious. Any bite, scratch or even lick from an animal should be cleaned immediately and thoroughly. Scrub with soap and running water, and then apply alcohol or iodine solution. Medical help should be sought promptly to receive a course of injections to prevent the onset of symptoms and death.

Tetanus This disease is caused by a germ which lives in soil and in the faeces of animals. It enters the body via breaks in the skin. The first symptom may be discomfort in swallowing, or stiffening of the jaw and neck; this is followed by painful convulsions of the jaw and whole body. The disease can be fatal. It can be prevented by vaccination.

Tuberculosis (TB) TB is a bacterial infection usually transmitted from person to person by coughing, but which may be transmitted through consumption of unpasteurised milk. Milk that has been boiled is safe to drink, and the souring of milk to make yoghurt or cheese also kills the bacilli. Travellers are usually not at great risk, as close household contact with the infected person is usually required before the disease is passed on. You may need to have a TB test before you travel, as this can help diagnose the disease later if you become ill.

Typhus This disease is spread by ticks, mites or lice. It begins with fever, chills, headache and muscle pains followed a few days later by a body rash. There is often a large painful sore at the site of the bite and nearby lymph nodes are swollen and painful. Typhus can be treated under medical supervision. Seek local advice on areas where ticks pose a danger and always check your skin carefully for ticks after walking in a danger area such as a tropical forest. An insect repellent can help, and walkers in tick-infested areas should consider having their boots and trousers impregnated with benzyl benzoate and dibutylphthalate.

Women's Health

Gynaecological Problems Antibiotic use, synthetic underwear, sweating and contraceptive pills can lead to fungal vaginal infections, especially when travelling in hot climates. Fungal infections are characterised by a rash, itch and discharge, and can be treated with a vinegar or lemon-juice douche, or with yoghurt. Nystatin, miconazole or clotrimazole pessaries or vaginal cream are the conventional methods of treatment. Maintaining good personal hygiene and wearing loose-fitting clothes and cotton underwear may help prevent these infections.

Sexually transmitted diseases are a major cause of vaginal problems. Symptoms include a smelly discharge, painful intercourse and sometimes a burning sensation when urinating. Medical attention should be sought and male sexual partners must also be treated. Remember that in addition to these diseases, HIV or hepatitis B may also be acquired during exposure. Besides abstinence, the best preventative is to practise safer sex using condoms.

Pregnancy Check with your doctor if you plan to travel to Indonesia while pregnant, as some vaccinations normally used to prevent serious diseases are not advisable during pregnancy. In addition, some diseases are much more serious for the mother (and may increase the risk of a stillborn child) in pregnancy, such as malaria.

Most miscarriages occur during the first three months of pregnancy. Miscarriage is not uncommon and can occasionally lead to severe bleeding. The last three months should also be spent within reasonable distance of good medical care. A baby born as early as 24 weeks stands a chance of survival, but only in a well equipped, modern hospital. Pregnant women should avoid all unnecessary medication, although vaccinations and malarial prophylactics should still be taken where needed. Additional care should be taken to prevent illness, and particular attention should be paid to diet and nutrition (eg alcohol and nicotine should be avoided).

WOMEN TRAVELLERS

Indonesia is a predominantly Muslim society and very much male oriented. However, women are not cloistered or required to wear purdah, although the head scarf (jilbab) and cover-all dresses have become more common in recent years.

In many ways Indonesia is a pre-feminist society. Sexual politics are rarely on the agenda and Indonesia has few women's organisations, unlike in some Asian countries. Perhaps this is because Indonesian women have not been subjected to the extremes present in other parts of Asia. For example, suttee has never had any place in Indonesian Hindu societies, but female circumcision does occur in some Muslim areas. In Java, typically it is done soon after birth and a small incision is made, the intention being to draw a few drops of blood, not the removal of the clitoris.

Attitudes Towards Women

Wives are expected to bear children and cater to their husbands but, in the cities, many women are well educated and employed; two-income families are increasingly common and often a necessity. Women are widely represented in the bureaucracy and industry, usually at the lower end, but many hold middle management positions, though executive positions are overwhelmingly held by men. In traditional rural societies, divisions of labour are very well defined and social organisation is male dominated, but women are not excluded and some societies are matriarchal, notably the Minangkabau of Sumatra.

Hassles & Precautions

Plenty of western women travel in Indonesia either solo or in pairs, and most seem to travel through the country without major problems; however, women travelling solo will receive extra attention, and some of it will be unwanted.

Western looks are considered the pinnacle of beauty and desirability in Indonesia (for men as well as women). This, combined with the notion that the west is the home of 'free sex' and the legendary exploits of the Bali beach boy gigolos, means women travelling solo will get plenty of attention from Indonesian men trying their luck.

To avoid this, some women invent a boyfriend or, even better, a husband, who they are 'meeting soon'. A wedding ring can also be a good idea, while a photo of you and 'your partner' also works well. Sunglasses and a hat are also a good way to avoid eye contact and to stop you feeling so exposed.

While Indonesian men are generally very courteous, there is a macho element that indulges in puerile behaviour – horn honking, lewd comments etc. Ignore them totally, as do Indonesian women; they are unsavoury but generally harmless. There are some things you can do to minimise being harassed – the most important is dressing appropriately. You'll see travellers in Bali that dress with complete disregard for local standards of decency. Take your cue from Indonesian women, not other travellers.

Dressing modestly won't stop the attention but it will lessen its severity. In fundamentalist regions such as Aceh in northern Sumatra, it is essential that women cover up as much as possible (including the arms, although a loose fitting T-shirt which covers the top of your arms will do). Walk around in shorts and a singlet and you'll be literally touched and grabbed by men in the street and leered at; cover up and they'll just call out as you walk past.

GAY & LESBIAN TRAVELLERS

Gay travellers in Indonesia will experience few problems. Physical contact between same-sex couples is quite acceptable, even though a boy and a girl holding hands may be seen as improper. Homosexual behaviour is not illegal, and the age of consent for sexual activity is 16 years. Immigration officials may restrict entry to people who reveal HIV positive status. Gay men in Indonesia are referred to as *homo* or *gay*; lesbians are *lesbi*.

Indonesia's transvestite/transsexual *waria* – from *wanita* (woman) and *pria* (man) – community has always had a very public profile. Also known by the less polite term *banci*, they are often extrovert performers as stage entertainers and as street-walkers. Perhaps because of the high profile of the waria, community attitudes to the wider gay community are surprisingly tolerant in a conservative society. Islamic groups proscribe homosexuality, but such views are not dominant and there is no queer-bashing or campaigns against gays. It pays to be less overt in some orthodox areas though, and the rampage against nightclubs in the Mangga Dua/Glodok area of Jakarta in 1998 is a worrying trend.

Indonesia has a number of gay and lesbian organisations. The coordinating body is GAY a Nusantara (☎ 031-5934924, fax 5939070), Jl Mulyosari Timur 46, Surabaya, which publishes a monthly magazine *GAY a Nusantara*. Good Web sites include www .gunung.com/seasiaweb, with links to other gay Web sites, and www.utopia-asia.com, which has an extensive list of gay and lesbian venues and accommodation listings throughout Indonesia and the rest of Asia.

DISABLED TRAVELLERS

Laws covering the disabled date back to 1989, but Indonesia has very little supportive legislation or special programs for disabled people, and is a difficult destination for those with limited mobility.

At Indonesian airports, arriving and departing passengers usually have to walk across the tarmac to their planes, and that includes Ngurah Rai airport in Bali. Check with the airline to see what arrangements can be made and if they can provide skychairs. Jakarta airport has direct access and lifts, but not all flights use these facilities. International airlines are usually helpful, but domestic flights are much more problematic.

Building regulations do not specify disabled access, and even international hotels, such as the Sheraton, Hyatt and Hilton rarely have facilities; however, it might be worth contacting these corporations in your home city and asking them about disabled facilities in their Indonesian hotels. Some hotels have easy street-access, by accident rather than design – if you can get a ground floor room. Only top-end and upper midrange hotels have lifts.

Pavements are a minefield of potholes, loose manholes, parked motorcycles and all sorts of street life; and are rarely level for long until the next set of steps. Even the abled walk on roads rather than negotiate the hassle of the pavement.

Public transport is also difficult but cars with a driver can be readily hired at cheap rates and are much more common than self-drive rentals. Minibuses are easily hired but none have wheelchair access. Guides are also readily found in the tourist areas and, though not usual, they could be hired as helpers if needed.

Bali, with its wide range of tourist services and facilities, is the most favourable destination.

For unsighted travellers or those with limited vision, Indonesia would definitely be a rewarding destination. Music is heard everywhere, Indonesians are always ready to chat, and the exotic smells of incense and tropical fruit linger in the air. With a sighted companion, many places should be reasonably accessible.

SENIOR TRAVELLERS

Apart from respect, senior travellers don't receive much in the way of special treatment in Indonesia, except for discounts on domestic air tickets. Garuda, Merpati Nusantara and Bouraq airlines offer discounts of 35% to passengers aged 60 and over. Your passport must be shown and a photocopy of the front page provided.

TRAVEL WITH CHILDREN

Travelling anywhere with children requires energy and organisation. Most Indonesians adore children, especially cute western kids; however, children may find the constant attention overwhelming.

Travelling in some areas of Indonesia is hardgoing, probably too hard for most people to tackle with small children in tow. Other areas such as Bali are easy. The island is well set up with resorts, high-quality restaurants, comfortable transport, a ready supply of babysitters (often advertised as 'babysisters') and plenty for kids to do. Java doesn't have Bali's mega-tourism industry, so it caters less to children, but it is well developed with a range of amenities, transport, hotel and food options. In the more remote regions, the regional cities are easy to reach by plane, but travel outside these cities requires hardiness and experience – both for parents and kids.

Health standards are low in Indonesia compared to the rest the world, but with proper precautions, children can travel safely. As with adults, contaminated food and water present the most risks, and children are more at risk from sunstroke and dehydration. Again, it depends where and how you travel. Indonesians may have to take their toddlers on gruelling eight hour journeys in stuffy, sweltering buses, but you'd be well advised to take a luxury bus or rent a car. Similarly, many adults can comfortably sample warung food, but parents with kids will want to be more careful.

Many inoculations are contra-indicated for young children, as are the effective malarial prophylactics. If you're only travelling to the main cities and tourist areas, like the resorts of southern Bali, the malaria risk is minuscule, but in known malarial areas like Irian Jaya or Pulau Nias on Sumatra, it is probably not worth the risk.

DANGERS & ANNOYANCES
Political Strife

The monetary crisis of October 1997 and the resultant political upheaval of 1998 saw disturbances across the country. Rioting erupted in towns and cities in Java, especially Jakarta, as well as Medan in Sumatra and in southern Sulawesi. Some incidents were politically inspired, others were food riots, while others were simply old grudges that came to the surface in tumultuous times.

After this initial wave subsided, violence erupted in Christian areas in early 1999. On the island of Ambon, in Maluku, a seemingly minor incident sparked weeks of clashes between Christian and Muslim communities. Scores were killed and Ambon was closed to travel. In March 1999, in West Kalimantan's Sambas Regency, violence between Christian Dayaks and Muslim migrants from the island of Madura resulted in over 150 deaths.

The areas mentioned above are now quiet, and Indonesia in general is more stable, but it pays to keep abreast of the news if travelling extensively in Indonesia. Currently of most concern for travellers are separatist guerrilla activity in the staunchly Muslim province of Aceh and continuing violence in East Timor.

Even at the height of the troubles, Bali was quiet and experienced only peaceful demonstrations.

The economic crisis means that crime is on the rise. Violent crime (eg muggings) is very rare in Indonesia, but Jakarta is a place to be wary. Follow the usual rules (eg avoid disreputable areas and don't walk the streets alone at night).

Theft

Theft can be a problem. If you are mindful of your valuables and take precautions, the chances of being ripped off are small. Most thefts are the result of carelessness or naivety. The chances of theft are highest in crowded places and when travelling on public bemos, buses and trains.

Pickpockets are common, and crowded bus and train stations are favourite haunts, as are major tourist areas. Compared to most Indonesians, tourists are rich and this attract thieves. Bali, particularly Kuta, is No 1 in the thievery stakes, closely followed by the other main tourist areas of Yogyakarta and Lombok. The thieves are very skilful and often work in gangs – if you find yourself being hassled and jostled, check your wallet, watch and bag. The Indonesian word for thief is *pencuri*. In Kuta, the gangs of small children waving necklaces for sale are notorious pickpockets.

Don't leave valuables unattended, and in crowded places hold your handbag or day pack closely. Don't carry your passport, travellers cheques or wallet in a bag that can be pickpocketed. A money belt worn under your clothes is the safest way to carry your passport, cash and travellers cheques. We get regular letters from travellers whose passport and travellers cheques have been stolen from their bags while sitting on buses. Wear a money belt and make sure you have a separate record of important items such as travellers cheques, credit cards and your passport.

Keep an eye on your luggage if it's stored on the roof of a bus; however, bag slashing or theft from bags next to you inside the bus is also a hazard. It's good insurance to have luggage that can be locked – it can be worth sewing on tabs to hiking packs to make them lockable.

Java and Sumatra are the worst places for theft on buses. Organised gangs board the buses and take the seat behind you. If you fall asleep or put your bag on the floor, they will slash it and be gone with your gear before you know it. Chances of this happening are very slight, but the gangs target tourists. Economy buses are the worst but travelling deluxe is no guarantee.

Always lock your hotel room door and windows at night and whenever you go out, even if momentarily. If you leave small things like sunglasses, sandals and books lying around outside your room, expect them to disappear. Don't leave valuables, cash or travellers cheques lying around in open view inside your room. It is very rare for hotel staff to risk losing their jobs by stealing, but there's no need to tempt them. It is wise to keep valuables hidden and locked inside your luggage; better hotels have safe storage facilities.

Report any theft to the police, but without witnesses don't expect action. Bus companies and hotels will automatically deny any responsibility. Reported theft is usually termed ·kehilangan, or 'loss' – you lost it and it is your responsibility to prove theft. Police will provide a report, which is necessary for replacement passport and travellers cheques, and for insurance claims.

Be wary and know where your valuables are at all times – at the same time remember that the overwhelming majority of Indonesians are honest and will go out of their way to look after a visitor. Out in the villages, far removed from the big cities and tourist areas, theft is a foreign concept.

Scams
As in most poor countries, plenty of people are out to relieve you of your money in one way or another. It's hard to say when an 'accepted' practice like overcharging becomes an unacceptable rip-off, but plenty of instances of practised deceit occur.

Con artists are always to be found. Usually those smooth talkers are fairly harmless guides seeking to lead you to a shop where they receive a commission. Just beware of instant friends and watch out for excessive commissions. Yogyakarta's batik salespeople fall into this category.

As the main tourist destination, Bali is the home of many scams. Is it possible for a Kuta moneychanger not to shortchange you? Then there's the friendly local who discovers a serious problem with your car or motorbike and urgently gets one of his contacts to fix it for you, for an outrageous amount of money. Even more expensive are the holiday timeshares, often sold by a westerner. Though not illegal, many who sign up while caught in the holiday euphoria of Bali regret it later.

An invite to visit a traditional Balinese village from an instant friend may end up with a hard luck story designed to extract large amounts of money. It is almost always a con. Indonesia is full of heart-wrenching stories of hardship and poverty at the moment, and Bali is better off than most provinces. Most Indonesians suffer in silence and would never ask for money; consider giving to aid programs if you want to help.

Another scam involves being invited to someone's house, then introduced to a card game where you can't lose. Of course, you do lose – big time. This gang moves around.

Reports of police imposters searching foreigners for drugs and trying to extract money have been reported in Jakarta. Robberies of foreigners at knife-point by Jakarta taxi drivers have also occurred, but these are very rare.

Drugs
In most of Indonesia, recreational plants and chemicals are utterly unheard of. Being caught with drugs will result in jail or, if you're lucky, a large bribe. Most marijuana in Indonesia is grown in the north Sumatran province of Aceh, and some of this filters down to tourist resorts such as Danau Toba.

Hotel owners are required by law to report offenders. Bali used to be the place to float sky high, and you'll still get plenty of offers, but more often than not those 'buddha sticks' are banana leaves and 'hashish' is boot polish. Possession will land you in prison.

Indonesia has become something of an Asian centre for ecstasy, which fuels the local rave scenes in Bali, Jakarta and other big cities. When it first appeared a few years ago there was some confusion as to whether it was actually illegal. Make no mistake: it is, and possession can land you in jail.

Noise

If you're deaf, there's no problem. If you're not, you might be after a few months in Indonesia. The major sources of noise are radios and TVs – Indonesians always set the volume to maximum. You can easily escape the racket at remote beaches and other rural settings by walking away, but there isn't much you can do on a bus with a reverberating stereo system. In hotels, the lobby often contains a booming TV set, but if you choose your room carefully, you might be able to avoid the full impact. If you complain about the noise, it's likely the TV or radio will be turned down but then turned back up again five minutes later.

Another major source of noise is the mosques, which start broadcasting the calls to prayer at 4 am, repeating the procedure four more times during the day. Again, choose your hotel room carefully.

'Hello Mister' Fatigue

This is the universal greeting given to foreigners regardless of whether the person being addressed is male or female. The less advanced English students know only 'Mister', which they will enthusiastically *scream* in your ear every five seconds. Most have no idea what it means, but have been told by their schoolteachers that this is the proper way to greet foreigners. It's mainly a problem in the outer islands, not in Java, Bali or the main tourist areas, where foreigners are ubiquitous and English-speaking abilities are higher.

Beggars

Beggars are a rare but growing feature of Indonesian society, mostly in Java. Many are professionals who have been begging since long before the economic crisis, but others are simply destitute. Indonesians will tell you not to encourage them, which is probably sound but hard advice. If you do give to beggars, a few coins is usual.

Personal Space

You tend to get stared at in places where few foreigners go, but overall, Indonesians stand back and look, rather than gather around you. Those who do come right up to you are usually kids. Getting stared at is nothing new; almost 500 years ago when the first Portuguese arrived in Melaka the *Malay Annals* recorded that:

> ... the people of Melaka ... came crowding to see what the Franks (Portuguese) looked like; and they were all astonished and said, 'These are white Bengalis!' Around each Frank there would be a crowd of Malays, some of them twisting his beard, some of them fingering his head, some taking off his hat, some grasping his hand.

The other habit which is altogether ordinary to Indonesians is touching. The Indonesians are an extraordinarily physical people; they'll balance themselves on your knee as they get into a bemo, reach out and touch your arm while making a point in conversation, or simply touch you every time they mean to speak to you or when they want to lead you in a new direction if they're showing you around a house or museum. All this is considered friendly – some Indonesians just have to be friendly regardless of the time or situation, even if it means waking you from your peaceful slumber!

While casual touching among members of the same sex is regarded as OK, body contact between people of different sexes is not. Walking down the street holding hands with a member of the opposite sex may have become more acceptable among university students in the big cities in Java, but public displays of affection (like kissing) may incur the wrath of moral vigilantes.

Sometimes you'll come across young guys who hang around bus terminals, outside cinemas and ferry docks with not much else to do except stir foreigners. They'll crack jokes, laugh and sometimes make obscene gestures. Don't give them their entertainment by chucking a fit – ignore their puerile antics.

On the whole you'll find the Indonesians (including the army and the police, despite the reputation they have with the locals) are *extraordinarily* hospitable and very easy to get on with.

LEGAL MATTERS

Drugs, gambling and pornography are illegal, and it is an offence to engage in paid work or stay in the country for more than 60 days on a tourist pass. Generally, you are unlikely to have any encounters with the police unless you commit a traffic infringement while driving a motorcycle or car.

In the reform era, much has been made of stamping out KKN (Collusion, Corruption and Nepotism), but corruption is still widespread throughout the bureaucracy. Police often stop motorists on minor or dubious traffic infringements in the hope of obtaining bribes. Usually there will be talk about a trip to the police station and lengthy delays, if not court appearances. Don't become impatient, aggressive or demand your rights. Sit through the lecture and don't offer a bribe – the police may let you off on a warning or they will broach the subject after the lecture. If it looks like you will have to go to the police station, play the worried tourist and ask if it is possible to pay the fine on the spot. For minor traffic infringements, 20,000Rp is usually more than enough, but Balinese police may want more.

In the case of accidents involving property, hope you have insurance and let the rental company sort it out. You may be hassled for immediate compensation, regardless of fault, but don't lose your cool and avoid being pressured into an admission or commitment.

In the case of an accident involving serious injury or death, the best advice is to drive straight to the nearest police station, unless you are in an isolated area and can offer assistance. If you hit someone in a village, an angry mob will soon gather. The police may detain you but they will sort it out and you will be safe. A court appearance and jail sentence is not likely unless your driving was extremely negligent or you admit culpability, but you will have to pay compensation to the victim or the family.

Tourists are unlikely to come across any other problems with officialdom or requests to pay bribes. It may be different for foreign residents, but a great deal of leeway is granted visitors, and Indonesians like to give a good impression of their country. Immigration officials have a bad name, but short-term visitors are rarely hassled. Avoid any requests for 'gifts' unless you have contravened regulations and there is absolutely no alternative.

BUSINESS HOURS

Government offices opening hours are variable (sometimes very variable) but are generally open Monday to Friday from 7 or 8 am to 3 or 4 pm, with a break for Friday prayers from 11.30 am to 1.30 pm, and Saturday until noon. Go in the morning if you want to get anything done.

Private business offices have staggered hours: Monday to Friday from 8 am to 4 pm or 9 am to 5 pm, with a lunch break in the middle of the day. Many offices are also open on Saturday until noon.

Banks are open Monday to Friday, usually from 8 am to 4 pm. In some places banks open on Saturday until around 11 am. Foreign exchange hours may be more limited and some banks close their forex counter at 1 pm. Moneychangers are open longer hours.

Shops open at around 9 or 10 am and smaller shops may close at 5 pm, but in the big cities, shopping complexes, supermarkets and department stores stay open until 9 pm. Sunday is a public holiday but some shops and airline offices open for at least part of the day.

PUBLIC HOLIDAYS & SPECIAL EVENTS

Indonesia has many faiths and many festivals are celebrated on different days throughout the country. As the major religion, Islam provides many of the holidays. The most important time for Muslims is Ramadan (Bulan Puasa), the traditional Muslim month of daily fasting from sunrise to sunset.

Muslim events follow the lunar calendar; thus, dates move back 10 or 11 days each year. Ramadan falls in the ninth month of the Muslim calendar. It's a good time to avoid fervent Muslim areas of Indonesia – you may get woken up in your hotel at 3 am to have a meal before the fasting period begins. Many restaurants shut down during the day, leaving you searching the back streets for a restaurant that's open. Lebaran (Idul Fitri) marks the end of Ramadan, and is a noisy two day public holiday when half the country seems to be on the move, and hotels fill up and prices skyrocket.

National Holidays

Following are the national public holidays in Indonesia.

December/January
New Year's Day
   Celebrated on 1 January.

Ramadan

One of the most important months of the Muslim calendar is the fasting month of Ramadan. As a profession of faith and spiritual discipline, Muslims abstain from food, drink, cigarettes and other worldy desires (including sex) from sunrise to sunset. Exemptions from fasting are granted, eg to pregnant women, the ill or infirm, young children and those undertaking extreme physical labour.

Ramadan is often preceded by a cleansing ceremony, Padusan, to prepare for the coming fast *(puasa)*. Traditionally, during Ramadan people get up at 3 am or 4 am to eat (this meal is called *sahur*) and then fast until sunset. Many Muslims visit family graves and royal cemeteries, recite extracts from the Koran, sprinkle the graves with holy water and flower offerings.

Special prayers are said at mosques and at home. The first day of the 10th month of the Muslim calendar is the end of Ramadan, called Idul Fitri or Lebaran. Mass prayers are held in the early morning, followed by two days of feasting. Extracts from the Koran are read and religious processions take place. During this time of mutual forgiveness, gifts are exchanged and pardon is asked for past wrongdoings. This is the big holiday of the year, a time for rejoicing, and the whole country is on the move as everyone goes home to be with their family.

During Ramadan, many restaurants and warungs are closed in Muslim regions of Indonesia. Those owned by non-Muslims will be open, but in deference to those fasting, they may have covered overhangs or will otherwise appear shut. Ask around for open restaurants. In the big cities, many businesses are open and fasting is less strictly observed. For night owls the cities come alive for the night meal.

Though not all Muslims can keep to the privations of fasting, the overwhelming majority do and you should respect their values. Do not eat, drink or smoke in public or in someone's house. If you must, excuse yourself and go outside.

Ramadan is an interesting time to travel but it can be difficult. Apart from having to hunt out restaurants and abstain from imbibing in public, the first few weeks of Ramadan are not too restrictive, but travel is a real hassle towards the end of Ramadan.

Around a week before and a week after Idul Fitri, transport is chaotic and packed to the gunwales. Don't even consider travelling during this time. You will be better off in the non-Muslim areas – eg Bali, East Nusa Tenggara, Maluku or Irian Jaya – but even these areas have significant Muslim populations and Idul Fitri is a big national holiday of two days duration for everyone. Plan well, find yourself an idyllic spot and stay put.

Ramadan and Idul Fitri move back 10 days or so every year, according to the Muslim calendar. Approximate dates for Ramadan are:

30 November 2000 to 30 December 2000
20 November 2001 to 30 December 2001
10 November 2002 to 10 December 2002.

Idul Fitri
Held on 8-9 January 2000 and 29-30 December 2001. Also known as Lebaran, this festival marks the end of Ramadan and is a noisy celebration at the end of a month of gastronomic austerity. It is a two day national public holiday.

March
Idul Adha
Held on 16 March 2000 and 5 March 2001. This Muslim festival commemorates Abraham's willingness to sacrifice his son, Isaac, and is celebrated with prayers and feasts. Animals (usually goats) are sacrificed at mosques and the meat is distributed.

April
Nyepi (Balinese New Year)
This marks the end of the Hindu *saka* (lunar) calendar. The day before Nyepi, evil spirits are chased away with gongs, drums and flaming torches, but on Nyepi itself Balinese stay at home and all Balinese businesses close down so that bad spirits will only find deserted streets and leave. The date is announced at the start of the year – although it generally falls in April, sometimes in March.

Muharram
Islamic New Year; start of the Muslim calendar.
Good Friday
Held 21 April 2000 and 13 April 2001.

May-June
Waisak Day
Held on 1 May 1999 and 18 June 2000. Marks the Buddha's birth, enlightenment and death.
Ascension of Christ
Held 1 June 2000, 24 May 2001
Maulud Nabi Muhammed
Held 15 June 2000, 4 June 2001.This is the birthday of the Prophet Muhammed, also known as Hari Natal.

August
Independence Day
(Hari Proklamasi Kemerdekaan)
On 17 August 1945, Soekarno proclaimed Indonesian independence in Jakarta. The day is now a national public holiday, and the parades and special events are at their grandest in Jakarta.

October-December
Isra Miraj Nabi Mohammed
Held on 6 November 1999, 26 October 2000. This is a celebration of the ascension of the Prophet Muhammed.

Christmas Day
Celebrated on 25 December.

Festivals & Cultural Events
With such diversity of people, there are many local holidays, festivals and cultural events (eg on Sumba, mock battles and jousting matches harking back to the era of internecine warfare are held in February and March). The Balinese have the Galungan Festival, when according to local lore, all the gods including the supreme deity, Sanghyang Widi, come down to earth. In Tana Toraja, in central Sulawesi, the end of the harvest season from July to September is the time for funeral and house-warming ceremonies. In Java, Bersih Desa takes place at the time of the rice harvest – houses and gardens are cleaned, and village roads and paths are repaired. This festival was once enacted to remove evil spirits from the village but it's now used to express gratitude to Dewi Sri, the rice goddess.

Regional *Calendar of Events* are generally available from tourist offices. They list national holidays, regional festivals, and many of the music, dance and theatre performances held throughout the year. The *Indonesia Calendar of Events* covers holidays and festivals throughout the archipelago. You may be able to pick a copy up from any overseas ITPO, or try international Garuda Airlines offices.

ACTIVITIES
Diving
With so many islands and so much coral, Indonesia presents all sorts of possibilities for diving. See the special colour section 'Diving & Snorkelling in the Gilis' in the Nusa Tenggara chapter.

For much of Indonesia, diving may not be as good during the wet season, from about October to April, as storms tend to reduce visibility. Bring your scuba certification – most of the main qualifications are recognised, including those of PADI, NAUI, BSAC, FAUI and SSI.

Bali has the best established dive operators in Indonesia, and are found in the major resorts and hotels. Baruna Marine Sports (☎ 0361-753820, fax 752779), Jl By-pass Ngurah Rai 300B, Kuta, is one of Bali's most reliable operators. Sanur also has a good selection of dive shops.

Some of Bali's best known dive sites include Nusa Dua, Sanur, Padangbai, Candidasa, Tulamben (the big attraction is the wreck of the USS *Liberty*), Amed, Lovina Beach and Pulau Menjangan (in the West Bali National Park), and perhaps Bali's best diving is on Nusa Penida.

Diving is not as well developed on Lombok, though new diving areas are being explored, such as Gili Petangan off the east coast. Most dive operators are found on Senggigi and the Gilis. Further afield in Nusa Tenggara, Waira near Maumere has dive operators, though much of the nearby reefs suffered damage in the earthquake of 1992. Labuanbajo, Komodo and Kupang also have dive operators and good diving.

Sulawesi has brilliant coral reefs around Pulau Bunaken off Manado in the north, as well as many other good dive spots, including the Togean Islands.

In Maluku, the Banda Islands are popular, and Ambon has diving sites and well established dive operators. Increasingly popular areas are Pulau Halmahera and Pulau Morotai, as well as the WWII wrecks around Biak and Teluk Cenderawasih in Irian Jaya.

Java is not a great diving destination, as the waters aren't clear and it doesn't have well developed reefs. A number of dive operators can be found in Jakarta and on the west coast around Carita. Pulau Seribu, just off the coast north of Jakarta, has diving opportunities, as do the waters of West Java, around Krakatau and Ujung Kulon National Park.

On Sumatra, the best diving opportunities are around Pulau We and Pulau Banyak.

continued on page 135

Considerations for Responsible Diving

The popularity of diving is placing immense pressure on many sites. Consider the following tips when diving and help preserve the ecology and beauty of reefs:

- Do not use anchors on the reef, and take care not to ground boats on coral.

- Avoid touching living marine organisms with your body or dragging equipment across the reef. Never stand on corals, even if they look solid and robust. If you must hold on to the reef, only touch exposed rock or dead coral.

- Be conscious of your fins. The surge from heavy fin strokes near the reef can damage delicate organisms. When treading water in shallow reef areas, take care not to kick up clouds of sand. Settling sand can easily smother delicate reef organisms.

- Practise and maintain proper buoyancy control. Major damage can be done by divers descending too fast and colliding with the reef. Make sure you are correctly weighted and that your weight belt is positioned so that you stay horizontal.

- Resist the temptation to collect corals or shells. The same goes for marine archaeological sites (mainly shipwrecks).

- Ensure that you collect all your rubbish and any litter you find as well. Plastics in particular are a serious threat to marine life. Turtles can mistake plastic for jellyfish and eat it.

- Resist the temptation to feed fish.

- Minimise your disturbance of marine animals. In particular, do not ride on the backs of turtles as this causes them great anxiety.

SURFARI INDONESIA

Dreams of an Indonesian surf adventure often include fantasies of idyllic palm-lined beaches, small bamboo bungalows and perfect barrels peeling around an untouched coral reef. Dreams of a surfing nirvana can come true but just like anywhere else, Indonesia is subject to flat spells, onshore winds and, with every new season, more surfers.

In a relatively short time, surfing in Indonesia has experienced tremendous growth, drawing surfers from all parts of the globe. Organised yacht charters and overland tours have become common, and in the mid-1990s the pro-tour set up contest sites at Grajagan (G-Land or Pantai Plengkung) in Java and on Nias in Sumatra. These contests are now held elsewhere, although once the region stabilises they will almost certainly return. They are usually held in May, June or July.

Crowding can be a problem and, with an increasing number of locals ripping on both small beach-break waves and hollow reef breaks, it can be hard to get waves, particularly in Bali. Treat locals with respect, avoid situations with a smile and you should get lots of waves.

For most surfers Bali is the focal point and the start of their 'green room' (tube wave) search. Though, from the tip of Sumatra all the way down to West Timor there is plenty of scope for hardcore surf adventurers to seek out uncrowded waves, great tubes and a board bag full of stories to take home.

Weather Conditions

The dry season between May and September is more likely to produce solid ground swell initiated in the Indian Ocean. Trade winds are from the east/south-east, which means winds will be offshore in Bali, from Kuta to Ulu Watu.

During the wet season, between October and April, trade winds will be west/north-west, and on the other side of Bali (Sanur to Nusa Dua) will be offshore.

Traditionally the months between June and August provide the most consistent and largest swells, but along with the waves come the crowds. Outside the high season, it's still possible to find good waves without the drop-ins and jostling that can take place.

MARTIN TULLEMANS

Text inset: Surfboards Bali (photograph by Richard I'Anson).

What to Bring

Surfboards On arrival at Denpasar, it pays to carry a small amount of Indonesian rupiah as officials sometimes attempt to charge a 'surfboard tax' (import duty) for bringing two or more boards into the country – try to refuse to pay.

Indonesia's waves mostly break over shallow coral reefs and therefore break more sharply. Given this you will need to have a few more inches underneath you to avoid getting pitched over the falls on the takeoff. Taking a quiver is a good idea. Seven feet to 7 feet 6 inches are the boards most commonly used, but shorter boards are handy for Bali and you'll need every inch of a board around 8 feet if you're planning on tackling the big swells.

Board bags holding up to three boards are available. Most Bali-bound airlines are used to carrying this type of board bag, but you may be charged for excess luggage at some airports.

Accessories You can buy most surf supplies, including surfboards, at any of the many surf shops in Kuta, although it's better to bring everything you'll need from home. This should include reef boots (preferably hard soled), spare leg-ropes, wax (if you use it), a rash shirt and plenty of full strength sunblock. A set of soft roof racks will make it easier to get around with lots of boards.

Some of the waves in Indonesia break on super shallow reef, so a surfing helmet and a short-arm spring suit will provide protection not only from the reef, but also from the sun. Most surf shops sell small ding repair kits, although local ding repairers are easily found in Kuta or at most of the breaks in Bali.

Organised Tours

Yacht charters and overland tours run throughout the dry season and go to all parts of Indonesia. Yacht charters allow you to surf the breaks that are not accessible by land and that offer some of the heaviest tubes in Indonesia. They also allow you to escape the overcrowded breaks of Bali.

Your best bet is to surf the Internet for surfing agencies that organise trips to Indonesia. The Indo Surf & Lingo Web site (see More Information in this section for details) has links to all major surfing tour operators.

The longest established tour company is the Australian-based Surf Travel Company (STC, ☎ 02-9527 4722, fax 9527 4522, email surf trav@ozemail.com.au), suite 2/25 Cronulla Plaza, Cronulla, New South Wales 2230. It offers overland 'surfaries' and yacht charters to Nusa Lembongan, West Java, Lombok, West Sumbawa, Sumatra and the Mentawai Islands. The seven day G-Land, Java trip stays at Bobby's Camp and costs around A$714, including transfers and three meals a day.

STC's US agent is Waterways Travel (☎ 818-376 0341) and its contact point for all surf tours in Bali is Wanasari Wisata (☎ 0361-755588),

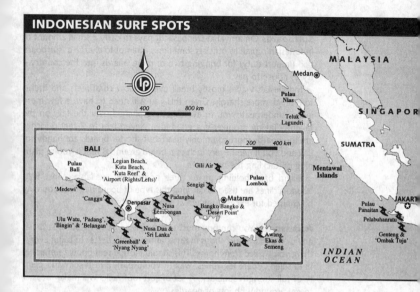

INDONESIAN SURF SPOTS

Jl Pantai 8B, Kuta. Daily services run to Nusa Lembongan, Kuta Reef, Ulu Watu, Canggu and Medewi.

Boraspati Express (☎ 061-526802, fax 567906) at Jl Dazam Raya 77 in Medan specialises in surfing tours to Pulau Nias (Nias Island).

More Information

For information on the treatment of coral cuts and rash see the Health section in the Facts for the Visitor chapter. For details and treatment relating to venomous fish, see the boxed text 'Marine Life to Watch Out For' in the Facts for the Visitor chapter.

As the popularity of surfing in Indonesia has increased, so has the demand for surfing guides. *Indo Surf & Lingo* by Peter Neely has all the information any hardcore surf explorer needs. You can find it at most surf shops in Bali, Australia and the USA. It's also available by mail order from the Indo Surf & Lingo Web site (www.indosurf .com.au) or (☎ 07-5447 2882), PO Box 950, Noosa, Queensland 4567, Australia.

The publishers of *SURFER Travel Guides*, EMAP, sells back-issues of *The Surf Report – Journal of World-wide Surfing Destinations*. It provides information on surf conditions in Indonesia, maps and the best weather conditions for surf breaks. Contact EMAP (☎ 949 496 5922), PO Box 1028, Dana Point, CA 92629, USA or email surfermag@earth link.net. See also Guidebooks under Books in the Facts for the Visitor chapter in this book.

INDONESIAN SURF SPOTS

PHILIPPINES

BRUNEI

MALAYSIA

KALIMANTAN

SULAWESI   MALUKU   Jayapura

Banjarmasin   Kota Ambon

Ujung   IRIAN JAYA
Pandang

JAVA

Surabaya   NUSA TENGGARA
          See Bali   Pulau
          Enlargement   Sumbawa
Denpasar   Bima

Grajagan   Huu   Pulau   Roti   Pulau
          Maluk   Sumba   Kupang   Timor
                    Rua &   Baing   Pulau
                    Tarimbang   Roti

Bali

Touted as a surfing Mecca, Bali has much to offer surfers. Though getting to the breaks can be an adventure in itself, the rewards at the end of the road can be well worth it. If you plan to hire a car or motorcycle, try taking a bemo the first few times you travel to the breaks, just to become familiar with the roads and wave locations. If you hire a car, don't leave anything in it.

Tubes Bar & Restaurant on Poppies Gang II is a great place for surfers to hang out. It has meals, cold beer, surfboards for sale and daily surf movies (see Entertainment under Kuta in the Bali chapter for more information).

West Coast

Ulu Watu Ulu Watu is a true surfers' paradise. *Warungs* line the cliff and look out over the break – the locals here will watch over your gear while you surf and most will let you stay the night if the surf's up.

To paddle out, you first have to negotiate the steep path and step ladder that descends down into the cave. At high tide you can paddle out from the cave, but at low tide a walk across the reef will be necessary. The current that washes down the reef can be quite strong (particularly when it's big), so start well right of the cave when you paddle in to avoid getting swept past its entrance.

The wave has three main sections and all are left-handers: The Peak, Racetracks and Outside Corner. **The Peak** is a high tide wave that handles small and big swells, and is directly in front of the cave. **Racetracks** is further down the reef. It's a hollow wave that starts to work properly on the mid-tide and gets better as it runs out. It handles up to about 6 feet and is very shallow. On a big swell and a low tide, try **Outside Corner** for a long ride on a huge face.

Padang Possibly Bali's most hollow wave, Padang is a dangerously shallow left-hander that only works when Ulu Watu is around 8 to 10 feet. Its jacking takeoff forms into a perilous tube that only experienced surfers should try to exit.

The wave is best surfed on the mid to high tide and will provide top to bottom tube action for the surfer or the spectator. Take the road from Pecatu village to Padang and Bingin.

Bingin & Impossibles Bingin is a short left-hander and its peaky takeoff provides a steep drop followed by a walling barrel section. Be careful not to ride it too far – flick off before the end section closes out on a sharp shallow reef. It will handle around 6 feet before it starts closing out. The *warungs* along the beach can provide shelter and storage for gear.

Paddle out to **Impossibles** from the south end of the warungs at Bingin. The wave looks like you can ride it forever, but it's not called Impossibles for nothing. In bigger swells at low tide you will have the best chance of making longer sections.

Belangan This left-hander is not as top to bottom as Ulu Watu or Padang and needs a high tide, but can be surfed in small or big swells.

Airport Rights & Lefts The right-hander breaks on the south side of the airport runway, while the left breaks on the north side. They are best reached by a boat ride from the beach in front of the breaks. The left is usually less crowded than Kuta Reef and a little bigger, but not as hollow.

Kuta Reef Take a boat ride from the beach in front of the break, or paddle out if you're feeling fit. The mid to high tide is best. When it gets big, the wall doubles up on the takeoff and is a fast tubing section all the way to the shoulder. On a high tide the inside reforms and is a bowling wall over a shallow reef. This place is always crowded, so you'll need patience.

Kuta & Legian Beach Breaks This is one of the few Indonesian beaches where beginners can learn how to surf, although the waves can get big and sometimes the currents are strong, so take care. Boards can be hired for about 50,000Rp a day, or less if you rent for a few days, from locals along the beach.

Kuta can provide some fast tubing waves over its sandy bottom and handles some sizeable swells. Any good peak will be crowded, but the beach is long and some less crowded peaks can be found. When Kuta

Top: Expect some damage – waves break with real force over shallow, covered coral reefs around Lakey Peak, Sumbawa; Indonesian surfers, Bali; Bingin, Bali.

Middle: All in a row, Kuta Beach, Bali.

Bottom: Padang, Bali.

MARTIN TULLEMANS

RICHARD I'ANSON

BERNARD NAPTHINE

MARTIN TULLEMANS

MARTIN TULLEMANS

Top: Bingin, Bali.

Middle: Surfboard city, Kuta Beach, Bali.

Bottom: Lakey Peak, Sumbawa.

is small, Ulu Watu will be a few feet bigger and Racetracks will be the best option on the mid to low tide.

Legian is usually 1 or 2 feet bigger than Kuta and similar peaks and tubing sections can be found on bigger swells. A long walk further north along the beach could provide some waves away from the crowds.

Canggu This is a right-hand reef break good for natural footers. The right break can be surfed from mid to high tide and holds up to about 8 feet. There is a left off the right and another left further north. Canggu will be a foot or two bigger than the Kuta beach breaks. South-east trade winds during the dry season may be side to onshore, so a dawn patrol is the best bet for glassy waves. Canggu has *warungs* and losmen-style *accommodation* close to the break.

From Canguu to Medewi, some Legian-style beach breaks and a few reef breaks are reported, but not surfed much.

Medewi This break is a long left-hander over a rock and sand bottom. Though a long ride, it's not hollow like the lefts of Ulu Watu, Padang or Bingin. Like Canggu, the trade winds are onshore, so early morning on a mid to high tide will be the best time for a surf. It's about 75km north of Kuta, so you might need to spend a couple of days while a swell is running to make the most of the break.

South Coast
Greenball & Nyang Nyang These right and left waves break over a reef and sand bottom and need small swells and north winds. During both the dry and wet seasons the wind is cross shore, so a dawn patrol is often the only solution. There can be dangerous currents facing the open ocean. The steep cliffs down to the beach also require careful negotiation, though access to Greenball is via the Bali Cliffs resort and is easier to reach.

East Coast
Nusa Dua Big, thick shifting peaks followed by fast bowl sections characterise Nusa Dua as possibly Bali's best right-hander; it's often overhead and usually picks up 1 to 2 feet more swell than elsewhere. The wave breaks over a more forgiving reef than the lefts on Bali's west coast. It can handle a swell of almost any size and provides long rides.

During the dry season the wind is onshore, so it pays to get there before sunrise. During the wet season the wind is offshore and the waves may be smaller, but good size cyclone swells can provide solid rides.

Take a boat ride to the break from the south end of the golf course as the peak is a long way out to sea.

Sri Lanka A right-hand reef break with a steep bowling takeoff that turns into a very hollow end section. Sri Lanka is more protected in the dry season, but usually smaller than Nusa Dua.

Sanur A fickle, right-hand reef break. Sanur is best on bigger swells and can be surfed on any tide, although mid to high is often better. Its end section is a super shallow almost dry reef excursion that will probably lead to injury, so avoid pulling in.

Between Nusa Dua and Sanur are the reef breaks of **Serangan, Hyatt Reef** and **Tanjung Sari**. These are a long way offshore and can be fickle as they require the right swell and wind direction.

North of Sanur Padang Galak, **Ketewel, Lebih** and **Padangbai** are right-handers and are a combination of beach break and reef waves, although Padang Galak is a sand bottom beach break. They require big swells from the right direction and even then will be smaller than Sanur, but may be a good option if you feel the need to escape the crowds.

Nusa Lembongan

East across the Badung Strait from Bali is the small island of Nusa Lembongan. The two main breaks are Shipwreck's and Lacerations. They are both right-hand reef breaks and are best surfed in the south to south-east trade winds over the dry season.

Shipwreck's is so named because of the old rusted hull that pokes out of the reef. It's known for its back door tubes and fast walling sections. You can paddle out at high tide or navigate the small sand trails through the seaweed farm out to the reef at low tide. Wear your reef boots and don't be surprised if you see the odd sea snake wriggle through the patchy seaweed.

Lacerations is also aptly named and is a super shallow tube from takeoff until you're spat into the channel. Usually smaller than Shipwreck's, it needs a bigger swell to work – when it does you should wear reef boots, some rubber and possibly a helmet. Only experienced riders should surf this break.

Lombok

 The best-known break on Lombok is Desert Point (Bangko Bangko), but waves are increasingly being surfed along the south and west coasts.

Desert Point

Although classic when it works, Desert Point is known as an inconsistent wave that needs a solid ground swell and a dry season southeasterly trade wind. The wave is a left-hander over a coral reef that can get shallow on the inside, so it's best to wear your reef boots. Starting as a smaller peak, the wave builds as it goes down the line and entices you into surprisingly makeable tube sections, but gets faster and shallower the further you go.

Desert Point is best accessed through yacht charters out of Bali or Nusa Lembongan, but it is possible to drive to the break and camp in the small primitive huts on the beach. Bring all of your own supplies.

West Coast

Like Desert Point, the waves on the west coast need a solid ground swell to work properly. **Senggigi** has a right and left reef break that works on dry season trade winds, while further north, **Gili Air** has two breaks. **Pertama** on Gili Air is a very hollow right-hander and, like most hollow Indonesian waves, breaks over shallow coral reef. The wave can be messy in strong trade winds during the wet and dry season.

South Coast

Working in a variety of changing weather conditions, it's possible to surf the south coast year-round. Some breaks work in the easterly trade winds of the dry season, others work in the westerly trade winds of the wet season, and some work on a northerly wind. Most of the waves break over coral reef, and you can choose from lefts and rights.

Kuta is on the central south coast and is a good place to begin looking for waves, with a left and a right reef break. Travelling overland by car will get you to most of the breaks, but some will require boat charters to access them or an outrigger ride out to the break.

Other places to check include **Semeng**, **Awung** and **Ekas**, all east of Kuta and accessible by car. You may need to charter a yacht and go looking for waves west of Kuta.

Sumbawa

 Most surf trips to Sumbawa's west coast (Scar Reef, Supersuck and Yo Yo's) will be organised yacht charters. To surf the south-east coast, fly or ferry to Bima and then hire a taxi or negotiate a series of buses to Huu to surf the Periscopes and Lakey Peak area.

Much of the south coast is not surfed. It's very hard to get to overland, but opportunities for hardened surf adventurers do exist.

West Coast

Scar Reef This left-hander breaks over sharp coral reef and is usually best on the high tide, but needs a solid ground swell to line up. If it's small at low tide don't despair, the wave often jacks 2 to 3 feet on the incoming tide. Beware of the unexpected and unforgiving shutdowns further down the line after the takeoff. The break holds big swells, but the dry season trade winds are mostly cross shore.

You can *camp* on the beach, but the facilities are nonexistent so you will need to bring all of your own supplies. If you are staying on the beach the paddle out is about 1km.

There are a few yacht charters doing this leg now, so don't be surprised to see another yacht anchored at the break.

Supersuck Aptly named Supersuck, this wave turns inside out and is a tube rider's dream. The steep peaky takeoff funnels into a long sucking bowl over a shallow reef. The wave can be surfed on all tides, but is super shallow at low tide. Unfortunately, Supersuck requires a big swell to turn on, but in its favour the dry season trade winds are mostly offshore.

Yo Yo's This right-hand reef break is reasonably deep compared with Supersuck, but the end section gets shallow on a mid to low tide. The wave horseshoes around the reef with some good tubes and walling sections. This bay cops any swell that's around and will be rideable even if Scar Reef is flat. It holds up to about 6 feet and is best on the high tide. The dry season trade winds are onshore, so early morning surfs are best.

The beach is accessible by land and is about a 20 minute walk off the dirt road that leads south from Maluk village. There is accommodation at Maluk.

South-East Coast

It is possible to surf here year-round as the dry season trade winds tend to cross to onshore. Surfing with fewer people in the water may mean gambling on swell size late in the wet season, but could pay off.

There are plenty of good bungalow-style *losmens* close to all the breaks.

Lakey Peak A classic A-frame peak with a left and a right. It is usually better for holding big swells and providing good hollow tube sections. Watch out for surfers trying to backdoor the peak. The wave is best surfed at low to mid tide in glassy early morning conditions.

Lakey Pipe This break is another left over a sucking rock ledge. Deep barrels can be expected.

Nungas On big swells of 8 feet plus, this place starts to get good with the sections lining up. It holds almost any size swell and provides big walls and tubing sections.

Periscopes A popular destination for natural footers looking for a right. The wave handles up to about 8 feet and can provide excellent tubes over a rock reef. Watch out for the shallow end section bowl before reaching the channel. The wave is best for surfing on the mid to high tide. It is about 2km from Lakey Peak.

Sumba & Timor

 Though these islands are being surfed more and more, take a few friends with you just in case there is no-one out. Around south-western Sumba, **Rua** is a good place to head. It is a left-hand reef break and the dry season trade winds are cross to offshore. **Tarimbang** on Sumba's central southern coast and **Baing** on the south-eastern coast also have good waves.

STC charters yachts from Kupang for surfing at **Roti** and other outer islands. This is possibly the best way to surf in Timor.

T-land is off Roti and is a big left-hander. It can be reached by travelling overland to **Nemberala**. There are several *losmens* on the beach right in front of the wave.

Java

Grajagan (G-Land)

Alas Purwo National Park on Java's south-east tip is home to what has become a world famous surfing break. G-Land is a freight train left-hander that has several takeoff sections, monster barrels and speeding walls. From the camp at Pantai Plengkung, the reef stretches east up around the headland as far as the eye can see and, when a ground swell hits and big tubing left-handers line-up all the way round, it's truly a sight to behold.

The only way to surf G-Land is with an organised tour out of Bali (see Organised Tours earlier in this section).

The break has four main sections: Kongs, Moneytrees, Launching Pads and Speedies. **Moneytrees** is probably the most consistent, but **Launching Pads** to **Speedies** starts as a wedging peak and runs into a grinding barrel over the shallow speed reef. The dry season trade winds are offshore and the wave works best when a solid ground swell of over 6 feet turns on.

A long walk further west of the camp along the beach may provide some good reef breaks if G-Land is 10 feet plus. **Twenty Twenties** is a left-hand reef break and **Tiger Tracks** is a right.

West Java

Gaining popularity among surfers, the south-west beaches of Java offer some excellent reef breaks and beachies (wave that break over a sand bank). Be wary of strong rips, sea urchins and currents, and don't surf alone.

Head for **Pelabuhanratu** where there are quite a few breaks, with **Cimaja** being the most well known. Cimaja is a right-hand reef break that holds big swells. Further south is **Genteng**, which is usually bigger than Cimaja as it is more exposed to the open ocean. **Ombak Tujuh** is a big left just north of Genteng.

Pulau Panaitan

Part of **Ujung Kulon National Park**, Pulau Panaitan is uninhabited apart from a small ranger's station and is only accessible by yacht charter.

The waves are incredibly hollow, breaking over super shallow coral reef. They often get faster and more hollow towards the end section. It's advisable to take a spring suit or even a full length wet suit. The guiding rule for all of the breaks is not to prone out and go straight in front of the white-water. The waves break so close to the reef that if you do go straight you'll be on dry coral in seconds. If the wave looks like closing down and you can't get off, tuck into the tube, it's definitely the safest place to be. *This place is for experienced surfers only.*

One Palm Point is on the south-eastern corner of the bay and is a merciless tubing left-hander that needs a bigger swell to work. It's offshore in the dry season's south-easterly trade winds. Line up with the palm for the takeoff and then flick out in front of the broken surfboard nailed to the tree further down the reef. After the flick-off spot, the wave gets faster and shallower and, though it may look makeable, there is usually no exit. The wave breaks too close to the reef to surf on a small swell, so it has to be around 6 feet before you can tackle it.

Napalm is another intense left-hander that needs a moderate swell to work and a north wind to be offshore. Best surfed in the early morning in the dry season, it also breaks close to the reef and is best at mid to high tide. The end section bowl is a makeable tube, but is really shallow.

Illusions is a right-hander over coral reef on the western side of the bay that works on a westerly wind. The spot needs a moderate swell and is often onshore in the dry season. It's a fast fun wall with tubing sections and can provide a long ride.

There are other breaks to surf, such as the beach break **Crock 'n' Rolls** and **Pee Pee's**, a left-hander on the western side of Java off Ujung Kulon National Park. Pee Pee's needs a moderate to big swell to work and is offshore in the dry season trade winds.

Sumatra

Northern Sumatra's **Pulau Nias** is the most visited surfing destination. Getting there can take a while – see the respective Getting There & Away sections in the Sumatra chapter. There are plenty of cheap *losmen* nestled among the shore at **Teluk Lagundri**, with the famous right-hander in full view.

Yacht charters booked through STC leave from Padang on the Sumatran mainland and visit the neighbouring **Talos**, **Hinakos** and **Mentawai Islands**. Fishing trawlers can also be chartered to the outer islands, but are less comfortable than an organised yacht charter.

The right-hander is a relatively short wave, but at size is a high and tight tube from takeoff to finish. The outside reef only starts to work on a solid ground swell of about 4 to 6 feet, but holds huge swells and the tubes are perfect. The water is pretty deep and the sets tend to spring up quickly, so keep your eye on **Indicators** further out.

In between the main peak and Indicators is a channel in the reef, **Keyhole**, which provides a safe paddle out to the takeoff area. West to north-westerly winds are offshore and the wave can be surfed on all tides.

On the other side of the bay is a great left-hander that is offshore in easterly winds and provides very hollow tubes. Only surfed on high tides, the famous right needs to be around 5 feet before this left starts to work.

The outer islands offer some classic tubing rights and lefts over shallow coral reef. This area has been further explored by yacht charter over recent years and new spots are being found all the time.

Andrew Tudor

continued from page 123

Snorkelling

If diving is beyond your budget, try snorkelling. Many of the dive sites can also be explored with a snorkel, and there are beautiful coral reefs on almost every coastline in Indonesia. While you can usually buy or rent the gear when you need it, packing your own snorkel, mask and fins is a good idea.

Windsurfing

Bali is the place where windsurfing is most common, followed by Lombok, although it has also caught on in Manado in North Sulawesi. Indonesians windsurf the Sungai Kapuas at Pontianak in West Kalimantan, and at Pantai Waiara (Waiara Beach), near Maumere on Flores. In Java, windsurfers can be rented at the resorts of Pulau Seribu and on the west coast around Carita.

Whitewater Rafting

The art of floating down raging rivers is not well developed in Indonesia, although a few commercial operators cater to this peculiar western custom. The Sungai Hamputung on Kalimantan offers a fairly easy float down a river with an impressive jungle canopy. The canyon of the Sungai Sa'dan in Tana Toraja, Sulawesi, is becoming popular. There are a number of other rivers in Central Sulawesi which are also attracting tour groups. Inquire with local travel agents. Bali, of course, will pump anything of tourist interest, and hotels and travel agents sell trips down the Sungai Ayung. In Java, whitewater rafting is well established on the Sungai Citarak, bordering Gunung Halimun National Park near Bogor.

Whitewater enthusiasts get quite a thrill out of being the first to raft a particular river, and in this regard Indonesia offers quite a few opportunities. There are a number of unrafted rivers in Irian Jaya, but tackling these will require expedition-style preparations – roads are nonexistent, crocodiles will probably find western food delightful and there may be unexpected surprises like waterfalls. But if you survive all this, it will certainly be the adventure of a lifetime.

Hiking & Trekking

Despite the fact that Indonesia has numerous opportunities for some superb hiking and jungle trekking, hiking is not well established. Information is lacking, and even the national parks often don't have well maintained trails. Walking in Indonesia is something that poor people have to do, not a recreational activity, though increasing numbers of university students are tackling peaks.

Good hiking can be found, and where demand exists, local guide services have sprung up. The national parks, such as Gunung Leuser on Sumatra, have good hiking possibilities. In Java, the lack of forest means that hiking is mostly limited to short climbs of volcanoes, or Ujung Kulon National Park (Java's largest wilderness area). Hiking in Bali is similarly restricted mostly to volcanoes, such as Gunung Batur. Gunung Rinjani on neighbouring Lombok is one of Indonesia's best and most popular hikes (from two to five days). See the special colour section 'Climbing Rinjani' in the Nusa Tenggara chapter. The Baliem Valley in Irian Jaya is one of Indonesia's better known walking destinations, and Tana Toraja has plenty of walking opportunities to see traditional villages.

At high altitude, like Gunung Rinjani on Lombok, you must be prepared for unstable mountain weather. Sudden rainstorms are common at high altitudes, and Indonesia is no longer tropical once you get above 3000m. The rain will not only make you wet, but freezing cold. Forget umbrellas – a good rain poncho is essential. Bring warm clothing, but dress in layers so you can peel off each item of clothing as the day warms up. Proper footwear is essential. A compass could be a real life-saver if you're caught in the fog. Don't depend on open fires for cooking – it's worth bringing a light-weight kerosene stove (other fuels are less readily available in Indonesia).

Be sure to bring sunscreen (UV) lotion – it's even more essential at high altitudes than in the lowlands. It should go without saying that you must bring sufficient food and water. Don't underestimate your need for water – figure on at least 2L per day, more in extreme heat.

If you haven't done much long-distance walking or jogging recently, work up to it gradually rather than trying to 'get in shape' all at once. Do a few practice runs at home before disappearing into the Indonesian jungles.

Guides A big decision is whether or not you need a guide. Often you do, but be prepared to haggle over the price. Guides in Indonesia sometimes ask for ridiculous amounts of money. Unless hired through a travel agency, a guide will typically cost around 15,000Rp to 20,000Rp per day. A travel agency may ask 10 times this amount. Take some time to talk to your guide to make sure he (Indonesian guides are always male) really understands the route and won't simply help you get lost.

Guides licensed by the government are commonly better than unlicensed ones. If a guide is licensed, he is almost certainly a local, not a transient just passing through looking to pick up some quick cash. If your guide claims to be licensed, you should ask to see the licence and copy down his name and number. That way, if you encounter some really big problems (eg the guide abandons you on a mountainside), you can report him. On the other hand, if your guide turns out to be exceptionally good, you can then recommend him to other travellers you meet.

COURSES

Many culture, language and cooking courses are available, particularly in the main tourist areas. In each tourist centre, look for advertisements at your hotel, and at local restaurants and bars; ask friends and hotel staff; and check out the tourist newspapers and magazines.

Bahasa Indonesia

Many students come to Indonesia to study Indonesian. The better private courses can charge US$15 or more per hour, though many offer individual tuition. Jakarta, Yogyakarta and Bali have schools geared for foreigners wishing to learn Bahasa Indonesia.

In Jakarta, reputable schools include the Indonesian Australia Language Foundation (☎ 021-5213350), Jl Rasuna Said Kav C6; and Business Communications Services (☎ 021-7941488), Jl Buncit Raya 21B, Mampang. Some embassies arrange courses, or have information on teachers and language institutes. In Yogyakarta, Realia (☎ 0274-564969), Pandega Marta V/6, Pogung Utara, is highly regarded but expensive. There are also plenty of other language schools.

In Denpasar, the Indonesia Australia Language Foundation (IALF, ☎ 0361-225243, fax 263509), Jl Kapten Agung 17, and Bali Language Training & Cultural Centre (BLTCC, ☎ 0361-239331), Jl Tukad Pakerisan, run courses. In Ubud several courses are available.

Arts & Culture

Batik courses are popular in Yogyakarta and Solo. They are generally one-day courses, but more serious study is possible. Javanese music and dance can also be studied in both these cities, but are mostly for long-term students. East Javanese dance can be studied at the Mangun Dhama Art Centre (☎ 0341-787907) at Tumpang, near Malang, along with other arts.

In Denpasar, the BLTCC and Sua Bali Culture & Information Centre (☎ 0361-98349, fax 921035), PO Box 574, run courses in dance, music and art. In and near Ubud, several places run courses in batik and music.

Meditation & Spiritual Interests

Bali's mystical ambience is an attraction for spiritually inclined foreigners. In Ubud, the Meditation Shop (☎ 0361-976206), Monkey Forest Rd, runs a number of free courses in several languages between 6 and 7 pm every evening. Meditation is also possible at Bali's only Buddhist monastery in Banjar.

In Java, Solo has several meditation centres offering courses (see Meditation under Solo in the Java chapter). Buddhist meditation courses are sometimes run at the Mendut Buddhist monastery, near Borobudur.

continued on page 141

INDONESIAN CUISINE

Food

Geographic and cultural diversity, together with a long history of visiting foreign merchants and colonists, have produced a unique cuisine. The Chinese introduced *nasi goreng* (fried rice with vegetables) and *mie* (noodles), the Indians their curries, and the Dutch have left their mark with sweets and cakes, and of course *rijsttafel* (a selection of meat, vegetable and rice dishes served in individual bowls over a hot burner). In recent times, western fast food chains together with Japanese and Thai restaurants have become a more common feature of eating out in Indonesian cities. Although some regional cuisines are becoming 'endangered species', new influences have not diminished the joy of eating in Indonesia. See the Language chapter for useful words and phrases, as well as a food and drink glossary.

Indonesians eat relatively simple but delicious meals. Eating only becomes a grand affair when communal feasts are held to celebrate family occasions, such as weddings, funerals and circumcisions, or harvest and religious feasts (such as the end of Ramadan).

Text inset: When in need of a snack, remember some handy Bahasa Indonesia – *saya mau beli satu sisir pisang*, or 'please give me a bunch of bananas' (photograph by Sara-Jane Cleland).

Top left to right: A *kaki lima* (food cart); regional food from Minado, North Sulawesi.

Bottom left to right: A market stall in Yogyakarta selling *jajanan* (snacks); a market in Flores, Nusa Tenggara.

ANDREW BROWNBILL

GREG ELMS

BERNARD NAPTHINE

SARA-JANE CLELAND

Indonesian Cuisine

RICHARD I'ANSON

GREGORY ADAMS

SARA-JANE CLELAND

LIZ THOMPSON

GLENN BEANLAND

Top left to right: Fresh produce for sale; *bakso* (meat ball soup) sold at a cremation ceremony, Bali.

Middle: Bukittinggi markets, Sumatra

Bottom left to right: Small eggplants and chillies, Wamena market, Irian Jaya; a *kaki lima* (food cart) at Blok M, Jakarta.

To discover the real delights of Indonesian food, be adventurous but be careful. Take care with uncooked vegetables and fruits, rubbery seafood, tap water and ice. The cleanliness and popularity of a restaurant provides some guide as to how clean the kitchen will be. See the Health section in the Facts for the Visitor chapter for more information.

For serious foodies, a monthly magazine, *Selera* (Taste) is available in Jakarta. Many general books on Asian food include a section on Indonesian cuisine, including *South-East Asia Food* by Rosemary Brissendon. Sri Owen's *Indonesian Regional Food & Cookery* is a straightforward cookery book, with an excellent rundown on Indonesian food, and wonderful regional recipes.

Regional Food

Many dishes served in restaurants, both within and outside Indonesia, come from Java and Sumatra. The coastal areas traditionally use a wider range of spices and flavourings. Sumatran cooking blends fresh and dry spices to produce hot and spicy dishes served with plenty of rice to ease the heat. *Rendang* (meat simmered in spices and coconut milk), is a traditional west Sumatran dish. The Javanese use a more subtle blend of fresh spices, together with chilli mellowed by the addition of sugar. The Sundanese people of West Java make a beautifully crisp, aromatic salad *(karedok)*.

The third region usually visited by tourists is Bali and Lombok, where you'll find delicious *sate* (small pieces of meat roasted on a skewer) and poultry dishes. Roasted suckling pig (*babi guling*) is a traditional Balinese dish.

There is little in the way of traditional dishes in Kalimantan, as most townspeople come from elsewhere in Indonesia, though wild boar smoked over a fire is one specialty. Sulawesi's expansive coastline has given it a resource for great fish dishes.

In Maluku, the Ambonese use sago as a staple food which is supplemented with fish, mainly tuna, and a few vegetables. In Irian Jaya, the indigenous highland people grow sweet potato *(erom)* as a staple food. Erom has significance far beyond simple sustenance – some varieties can only be eaten by a particular group, such as pregnant women or old men.

Restaurants

Indonesians eat best at home. An invitation to eat with friends you make along the way should not be missed. Outside the home, *warungs* (street stalls) and *kaki lima* (food carts) are a familiar part of Indonesian life. Warungs are simple, open-air eateries providing a small range of dishes based on rice and one meat or vegetable. Often their secret to success comes from having a reputation for cooking one dish better than anyone else. A congregation point for warungs is often the *pasar malam* (night market).

Rumah makan (eating house), refers to anything one step above a warung, although some owners prefer to use the more western-sounding

Fruit Wonders

It's almost worth making a trip to Indonesia just to sample the trop-ical fruit – apples, bananas and even papaya appear humdrum compared to the wonders of nangkas, rambutans, mangosteens and starfruit.

apel – apple. Most are imported from Australia, New Zealand and the USA, and hence are expensive. Local apples grown in moun-tain areas, such as Malang in Java, are much cheaper and fresher.

apokat – avocado. Plentiful and cheap – try an avocado and ice cream combo.

belimbing – the 'starfruit' is a cool, crispy, watery tasting fruit – if you cut a slice, you'll immediately see where the name comes from.

durian – the most infamous tropical fruit, the durian is a large green fruit with a hard, spiky exterior. Inside are pockets of creamy white fruit. Stories are often told of a horrific stench emanating from an opened durian – hotels and airlines often ban them because of their foul odour. Some don't smell so bad – unpleas-ant yes, but certainly not like holding your nose over an over-flowing sewer. The durian season is in the later part of the year.

jambu air – water apple or wax jambu. These glossy white or pink bell-shaped fruit come from a popular garden tree found throughout Indonesia. Children can often be seen selling the fruit skewered on a sliver of bamboo. The jambu air is crisp and refreshing eaten chilled, but fairly tasteless. The single seed should not be eaten.

jambu batu – guava. Also known as *jambu klutuk*, the guava comes from Central America and was brought to Asia by the Spanish. The fruit comes in many colours, shapes and sizes; the most common are light green and pear-shaped, turning yellow when fully ripe. The pinkish flesh is full of seeds. Ripe guava have a strong smell that some find overpowering. In Asia, the unripe fruit are also popular sliced and dipped in thick soy sauce with sliced chilli; mango can also be served this way.

jeruk – the all-purpose term for citrus fruit. There are several kinds available. The main ones include the huge *jeruk muntis* or *jerunga*, known in English as the pomelo. It's larger than a grape-fruit but is sweeter and has a very thick skin; it has segments that break apart very easily. Regular oranges are known as *jeruk manis* (sweet jeruk). The small tangerine-like oranges which are often quite green are *jeruk baras*. Lemons are *jeruk nipis*.

kelapa – coconut. As plentiful as you would expect! *Kelapa muda* means young coconut, and you'll often get them straight from the tree. Drink the milk and then scoop out the flesh.

Fruit Wonders

mangga – mango. The mango season is the second half of the year.

manggis – mangosteen. One of the most famous of tropical fruits, this is a small purple-brown fruit. The outer covering cracks open to reveal pure-white segments with an indescribably fine flavour. Queen Victoria once offered a reward to anyone able to transport a mangosteen back to England while still edible. Beware of stains from the fruit's casing, which can be permanent. From November to February is the mangosteen season.

nanas – pineapple

nangka – also known as jackfruit, this is an enormous yellow-green fruit that can weigh over 20kg. The flesh has individual segments of yellow fruit, each containing a roughly egg-shaped seed. The segments are held together by strong white fibres. The fruit is moist and fairly sweet, with a slightly rubbery texture. It is used mostly in cooking. The skin of a nangka is green when young, yellow when ripe. The *cempadak* is a close relative of the nangka, but smaller, sweeter and more strongly flavoured.

papaya – or paw paw, are not unusual in the west. It's actually a native of South America and was brought to the Philippines by the Spanish, and from there spread to other parts of South-East Asia.

pisang – banana. The range in Indonesia is astonishing – from midgets to specimens well over a foot long. A bunch of bananas, by the way, is *satu sisir pisang*.

rambutan – a bright red fruit covered in soft, hairy spines – the name means hairy. Break it open to reveal a delicious white fruit closely related to the lychee. Rambutan season is from November to February.

salak – found chiefly in Indonesia, the salak is immediately recognisable by its perfect, brown 'snakeskin' covering. Peel it off to reveal segments that, in texture, are similar to a cross between an apple and a walnut, but in taste are quite unique. Each segment contains a large, brown oval-shaped seed. Salaks from Bali are much nicer than any others.

sawo – brown-skinned, looks like a potato and has honey-flavoured flesh.

sirsak – the sirsak is known in the west as soursop or zurzak. Originally a native of tropical America, the Indonesian variety is one of the best. The warty green skin covers a thirst-quenching soft, white, pulpy interior with a slightly lemonish, tart taste. You can peel it off or slice it into segments. Sirsaks are ripe when the skin has begun to lose its fresh green colouring and become darker and spotty. It should then feel slightly soft.

restoran. Offerings may be as simple as a warung's, but usually include more choices of meat and vegetable dishes, and spicy accompaniments.

In most parts of Indonesia you will find a *rumah makan Padang*, named after the West Sumatran capital from which the cuisine originates. A large selection of hot and spicy dishes are placed in front of customers, who are only charged for what they eat.

Large hotels in places such as Jakarta and Bali often have extensive buffets, incorporating richly spiced and sauced dishes. This is a modern version of Dutch rijsttafel, which once fed planters and businessmen.

Main Dishes

While the arts were taken to great heights by Central Javanese courts, Indonesian food is essentially 'peasant' cuisine. Fresh, simple ingredients, combined with a subtle blend of spices, can result in a delicious, inexpensive meal.

Aromatic coriander and cumin, together with chillies, lemon grass, coconut, *kecap manis* (sweet soy sauce*)* and palm sugar are all important flavourings; sambal and *acar* (pickles) are important side dishes. Fish is a favourite with Indonesians, and seafood restaurants are often of a good standard. Indonesians traditionally eat with their fingers, hence the soft stickiness of their *nasi* (rice), the foundation of all meals. Sate, nasi goreng and *gado gado* (vegetables with spicy peanut sauce) are some of Indonesia's most famous dishes.

Markets

Indonesia markets are wonderful examples of how fresh food can feed the soul and the stomach. There is no refrigeration, so freshness is dependent on quick turnover – hopefully quicker than the flies! You'll also find a huge range of sweet and savoury snacks. In competition with local markets, supermarkets are becoming more common in major cities.

Snacks

Snacks *(jajanan)* are sold everywhere from street stalls to department stores. There are literally thousands of varieties of sweet and savoury snacks made from a range of ingredients, including peanuts, coconuts, bananas and sweet potato.

Drinks

Do your health a favour and sip on an icy fresh fruit juice *(es juice)* – they are simply delicious. Also, don't miss another pleasure, *kelapa muda*, the juice drunk straight from a young coconut, often bought at roadside stops. Many of the Dutch-built breweries still supply beer. While comparatively expensive, try one of the three popular brands of beer, Bintang, San Miguel and Anker.

Audra Kunciunas

continued from page 136

Cooking

Short courses are available in Denpasar, Ubud, Sanur and Lovina in Bali. In Java, try Yogya. In Ubud, Noni Orti restaurant on Monkey Forest Rd runs Balinese cooking courses three days a week. Casa Luna restaurant (☎/fax 96282, Jl Raya, email casaluna@ denpasar.wasnatara.net.id) also conducts classes three times a week.

WORK

A work permit is required to work in Indonesia (see Study & Work Visas under Visas & Documents earlier in this chapter). These are very difficult to procure and should be arranged by your employer.

The job market was strong before the monetary crisis and the resultant crash, especially in Jakarta. By far the best way to arrange employment is through a company outside Indonesia.

Official government policy is to hire Indonesians wherever possible. In the past, travellers have been able to pick up work as English teachers, for around 50,000Rp to 60,000Rp per hour, which used to be reasonable money but now it hardly seems worth it. Apart from expatriates employed by foreign companies, most foreigners working in Indonesia are involved in the export business.

Anyone seeking long-term paid or volunteer work may want to contact one of the following agencies:

Australian Volunteers International
(☎ 03-9279 1788, fax 9419 4280, email ozvol@ozvol.org.au)
71 Argyle St, Fitzroy 3065, Australia.
Web site: www.ozvol.org.au.
This organisation places qualified Australian residents on one to two-year contracts.

Global Volunteers
(☎ 800-487 1074, fax 651-482 0915, email@globalvolunteers.org)
375 East Little Canada Road, St Paul, MN 55117-1627 USA.
Web site: www.globalvlntrs.org
Global Volunteers coordinates teams of volunteers on short-term humanitarian and economic development projects.

United Nations Volunteers
(☎ 228-815 2000, fax 815 2001, email webmaster@unv.org)
PO Box 260 11, D-53153, Bonn Germany.
Web site: www.unv.org.
UNV places volunteers with qualifications and experience in a range of fields.

Voluntary Service Overseas, (VSO)
VSO places qualified and experienced volunteers for up to two years.
Canada:
(☎ 613-234 1364, fax 234 1444)
806-151 Slater St, Ottawa, Ontario K1P 5H3, Canada.
Web site: www.magi.com/~vsocan
The Netherlands:
(☎ 30-276 9237, fax 272 0922)
3514 AZ, Utrecht, The Netherlands.
Web site www.vso.nl
Portugal:
(☎ 1-8866139, fax 8878837)
Rua Santiago 9, 1100 Lisbon, Portugal
Web site: www.oneworld.org/vso
UK:
(☎ 20-8780 7200, fax 8780 7300, email enquiry@vso.org.uk)
317 Putney Bridge Rd, London SW15 2PN,
Web site: www.vso.org.uk

ACCOMMODATION

Camping

Camping grounds are rare, but there are opportunities for back-country camping. It is important that you camp away from civilisation, unless you want spectators all night.

You can probably do without a sleeping bag below 1000m, but at higher elevations you'll certainly need one. Rain is a possibility even in the dry season, especially as you gain altitude, so bring some sort of tent or rain-fly. You'll also want to guard against insects and other things that crawl and slither in the night, so a tent or a mosquito net would be appropriate.

Hostels

Indonesia doesn't have many hostels, mainly because there are so many inexpensive hotels. One exception is Jakarta, where there are a number of places offering dormitory accommodation. There are a handful of hostels in a few other places, such as Surabaya and Kupang, but it's entirely possible to travel through Indonesia on a tight budget without ever staying in one.

The main thing to be cautious about in hostels is security. Few places provide lockers, and it's not just the Indonesians you must worry about – foreigners have been known to subsidise their trip by helping themselves to other people's valuables. It's not a huge problem, but something to be aware of.

If you want to avoid nocturnal visits by rats, don't store food in your room, or at least have it sealed in jars or containers. Rats have a keen sense of smell, and they can and will chew through a backpack to get at food.

Bedbugs are occasionally a problem in this climate. Examine the underside of the mattress carefully before retiring for the night. If you find it crawling with bugs, ask for a different room.

See the Mandi & Toilets section earlier in this chapter for information on bathing.

Hotels

Hotels in Indonesia come in different grades of price and comfort. At the bottom end of the scale is the *penginapan* or *losmen*. *Wisma* are slightly more upmarket, but still cheap. Hotels are at the top of the scale.

The Indonesian government wants all budget-end accommodation to replace 'losmen' etc with 'hotel'. This has largely been successful, but not all hotel owners are happy about this, as the old naming system gave potential guests an idea of the price.

A hotel can be either a flower *(melati)* or *yasmin* hotel, which is relatively low standard, or a star *(bintang)* hotel, which is more luxurious. A hotel at the bottom of the barrel would be one melati *(satu melati)* whereas a five-star hotel *(bintang lima)* occupies the top end.

All hotels are required to pay a 10% tax to the government, and this may be passed on to the customer, but most cheap hotels either avoid the tax or absorb it into their room rates. Some mid-range and top-end places charge a whopping 21% tax and service charge. Why 21%? That's 10% tax, 10% service charge and a 10% tax on the service charge, which makes another 1%.

A few years ago, the government outlawed the use of foreign words in hotel names. Many hotels have changed their names, and now the thousands of 'Beach' hotels are 'Pantai' hotels – but their signs and letter heads haven't changed, and a hotel will often still be referred to by its old name. Others have simply ignored the law, and others don't have to comply because they have copyrighted trademarks.

The real budget hotels are spartan places with shared bath, costing as little as 10,000Rp per person, sometimes less. Many are good, family-run places catering primarily to travellers, while other cheap places can be real rat-holes. Mid-range hotel rooms, which can be a real bargain in the current economic climate, usually come with private bath and typically cost from 25,000Rp to 100,000Rp or more, depending on the facilities. Five-star hotels can match the best in the west, with prices breaking the US$100 level. Top-end hotels often quote prices in US dollars, and some mid-range hotels also engage in this dubious practice, though with the fall in the rupiah, US dollar prices are often meaningless and many now quote in rupiah.

The cost of accommodation varies considerably across the archipelago. If you follow the well beaten tourist track through South-East Asia, you'll find that Indonesia is one of the cheapest countries, especially with the currency devaluation. Travellers centres like Yogyakarta and Danau Toba are superb value for food and accommodation. Nusa Tenggara is marginally more expensive, but cheap by any standards. On the other hand, once you get to the outer provinces, such as Kalimantan, Maluku or Irian Jaya, where competition is less fierce, you'll pay more.

Bali has the best standards and widest range but prices in the main resorts, especially for mid- and top-end accommodation, are high. Despite the rupiah's plunge, many Balinese hotels have clung to inflated US dollar rates. Most hotels, particularly budget and some mid-range hotels, do offer discounts on the US dollar rate and then convert to rupiah at a rate much more favourable than the bank rate. Competition at the budget end means prices are still very reasonable, but the real travel bargains are outside Bali.

As a general rule, if you are quoted a price in US dollars, you are paying too much, and if the US dollar rate is then converted to rupiah at the current exchange rate, you are being ripped off. Outside of Bali, most hotels now charge rupiah rates, and you can stay at quality hotels for incredibly low prices.

Some hotels have fixed prices and display them, but prices are often flexible, especially in quiet periods. This particularly applies to mid-range and top-end hotels, where discounts of 10% to 50% are readily available. Some top-end hotels are less amenable, in which case book your room through a big city-based travel agent – they sell discounted rates.

The most polite way to get a cheaper price is to simply ask for a discount. Ask also to see the printed price list *(daftar harga)* when you front up at a hotel. For many cheap hotels, the price is often fixed to this rate, and a quick glance will allow you to see the price range available – you may have only be offered the most expensive.

On the whole, it's cheaper if two people travel together and split the cost of the room – the price for a two person room is nearly always well below the cost of two singles, if the single rate is available at all.

Staying in Villages

In many places in Indonesia you'll often be welcome to stay in the villages. If the town has no hotel, ask for the kepala desa, who is generally very hospitable and friendly, offering you not only a roof over your head but also meals. You may not get a room of your own, just a bed. In larger, more important villages, government officials visit regularly and guest rooms may be set aside.

Payment is usually expected: about the same price as a cheap losmen as a rule of thumb. The kepala desa may suggest an amount, but often it is *tersera* (up to you),

and you should always offer to pay. While the kepala desa's house may sometimes act as an unofficial hotel, you are a guest and often an honoured one. Elaborate meals may be prepared just for you. It's also a good idea to have one or two gifts to offer – cigarettes, photographs or small souvenirs from your country are popular.

In towns where no accommodation is available, you also may be able to stay with the *camat* (district head) or at the local police station. Indonesian police and military are actually quite friendly to foreigners – how they treat the locals is another matter.

Rental Accommodation

Given the wide assortment of cheap hotels, it almost doesn't pay to bother with renting a house or apartment. Trying to find a house for one or two months rental is difficult and depends on personal contacts or luck. Real estate agents are virtually nonexistent in Indonesia. Ask your Indonesian friends, staff at your hotel, restaurants etc. Negotiating a proper price may also be difficult, and it's wise to obtain the help of an Indonesian friend.

For more permanent accommodation, rents vary widely. Jakarta's rates are very high, and rent is required in advance, even for three-year leases. Prices are lower elsewhere. More than a few foreigners have taken up semi-permanent residence on Bali, either renting houses on long-term lease, or leasing the land and building their own homes with an Indonesian partner.

ENTERTAINMENT
Discos & Bars

Obviously, discos are easiest to find in large cities like Jakarta and resort areas like Kuta Beach in Bali. Some discos are independent, but many are in five-star hotels. Prices vary, but generally there's a small cover charge and expensive drinks.

Despite being a primarily Muslim country, alcohol (generally beer) is widely available, as are bars to drink it in. This applies mostly to the big cities, or resorts in Bali.

Cinemas

Indonesians are great movie fans and cinemas can be found in all the main towns. Large cities like Jakarta, Surabaya and Denpasar have cineplexes showing the latest western films, usually with English dialogue and Indonesian subtitles. They tend to be B-grade adventure flicks, but the occasional Hollywood blockbuster is shown. As you get into the backwaters, the films tend to get older and older. Besides western movies, there are plenty of violent kung fu epics from Hong Kong. Cinema admission is very cheap at 10,000Rp or less.

Traditional Performances

Traditional entertainment is easy to see in Indonesia. Wayang, gamelan, traditional theatre and dance performances are held on a regular basis and for special occasions. Tourist offices can provide information. In Bali and other touristy places like Yogya, traditional performing arts can be seen any night of the week, though they may be travesties adapted for foreign audiences.

The main cities, particularly in Java, have subsidised theatre troupes and performing arts schools where performances of the classics are regularly staged.

Traditional dance and music is alive throughout the country, and is performed at festivals and for many ceremonial occasions, everything from a harvest festival to weddings, funerals and the swearing in of a government official. Most events occur in the dry season, after the harvest, and it's simply a case of asking around. Foreigners are often welcome.

SPECTATOR SPORTS

Many of Indonesia's live spectator sports are male-oriented and associated with illegal gambling. You may get the chance to see cockfighting, especially in Bali and Kalimantan. Bull racing, horse racing, ram head-butting and other contests are staged all around the country, and are usually designed to improve the breed.

Soccer and badminton are the national sporting obsessions, and Indonesians are the world badminton champions. They fare less well in international soccer competitions, but that doesn't dampen their enthusiasm for *sepak bola*. The average Indonesian male can tell you more about Manchester United than you ever wanted to know, and regional soccer teams in the national league have their own fanatic followers. Surabaya fans are said to be the most fanatic.

Volleyball is played in villages everywhere, and you may well get an invite to join in. *Sepak takraw*, also known as *sepak raga*, is a popular, unique South-East Asian game. Played with a rattan ball, it is a cross between volleyball and soccer and, apart from serving, only the feet are used, resulting in amazing acrobatics.

Pencak silat, Indonesia's own form of martial arts, is most popular in West Java and West Sumatra. This form of fighting uses not only hands and feet, but also some weapons, including sticks and knives. Many regions, particularly those with a history of tribal warfare, also stage traditional contests to accompany weddings, harvest festivals and other ceremonial events. Mock fighting ceremonies are sometimes staged in Irian Jaya; *caci* whip fights are a specialty on Flores; men fight with sticks and shields on Lombok; but the most spectacular is the *pasola* on Sumba, where every February and March, horse riders in traditional dress hurl spears at each other.

SHOPPING

Indonesia is a great place to buy arts and crafts. The range is amazing and the prices cheap.

Souvenir vendors positively swarm around heavily touristed places. Off the beaten track, shopping is more relaxed. If you're an art collector, you'll find plenty of chances to stock up on unusual items. Wood carvings are on sale everywhere. Batik and *ikat* (a form of dyed woven cloth) attract a steady stream of foreign art enthusiasts. Good pottery is available, mostly on Lombok and in Java. See the Indonesia Crafts colour section for an overview.

If you have little or no interest in art, there are still plenty of more practical, everyday items that make good buys. You can even find jackets, ski caps and other winter clothing in Jakarta. Clothing and shoes in general are very cheap in Indonesia.

Many foreigners get addicted to Indonesian coffee, which is superb. Kapal Api is a popular brand name for packaged coffee, but the best coffee is the stone-ground stuff you buy in markets. Don't bother buying coffee beans unless you can get it ground to the fine, pulverised powder that gives Indonesian coffee its texture and flavour.

Bali is a shoppers paradise, with crafts from all over Indonesia. Jl Legian in Kuta has kilometres of shops selling crafts, antiques, clothes, shoes etc. Sanur, Ubud and other tourist centres are also worthwhile. Yogya is the best place to shop in Java, with crafts from all over Java and a smaller selection from further afield. Jakarta is expensive, although it has a wider range from all over the archipelago.

Elsewhere in Indonesia you only tend to see locally produced crafts, but of course the price for those items will be much cheaper than in the tourist shops of Bali or Jakarta.

Always bargain for handicrafts. In the more touristed areas prices can be extortionate. Even if price tags are displayed, assume you can bargain. Fixed-price art shops are very rare.

Getting There & Away

AIR

The principal gateways for entry to Indonesia are Jakarta and Bali. Jakarta is serviced by more airlines but with its huge tourist trade, Bali gets almost as much traffic. See these chapters under Getting There & Away for airline details.

There are also international flights from neighbouring countries to various cities throughout the country and a couple of possible land and sea entry routes. Singapore has some of the cheapest flights to Indonesia and is a major travel hub in the region. It may be cheaper to fly to Singapore, from where you can enter Indonesia by air or ship. The same applies to Penang in Malaysia, where you can take a short flight or ferry to Medan on Sumatra.

For bargain fares, it's usually better to go to a travel agent than to an airline, as the latter can only sell fares by the book. Budget tickets may come with lots of restrictions – check the length of ticket validity, the minimum period of stay, stopover options, cancellation fees and any amendment fees if you change your date of travel. Plenty of discount tickets are valid for six or 12 months, allowing multiple stopovers with open dates. Make sure you get details in writing of the flights you've requested (before you pay for the ticket). Round-the-World (RTW) tickets may also be worth looking into.

Fares quoted in this chapter are an approximate guide only. Fares vary depending on the season (high, shoulder or low) and special deals are often available. Fares can vary from week to week, and it pays to shop around by ringing a variety of travel agents for the best fare and ticket to suit your needs.

Airports

Indonesian airports are dull affairs. Jakarta's Soekarno-Hatta airport is spacious, modern and surprisingly efficient, but only has a few food and shopping outlets. Bali's smaller Ngurah Rai international airport is slightly more interesting. Shopping is also overpriced here but more varied. In peak tourist seasons when a few jumbos land, it is standing room only and queues are long. Standard duty-free items are on sale at both airports, but local cigarettes are much cheaper than the duty-free variety; there are no great bargains for alcohol, either.

Departure Tax

Airport tax on international flights from Jakarta and Denpasar is 50,000Rp. At other airports the charge on international flights is 25,000Rp.

For residents of Indonesia, including foreigners on KITAS (one-year temporary stay/work) visas, a *fiskal* tax of 1,000,000Rp is payable when leaving the country.

Warning

The information in this chapter is particularly vulnerable to change: prices for international travel are volatile, routes are introduced and cancelled, schedules change, special deals come and go, and rules and visa requirements are amended. Airlines and governments seem to take a perverse pleasure in making price structures and regulations as complicated as possible. You should check directly with the airline or a travel agent to make sure you understand how a fare (and ticket you may buy) works. In addition, the travel industry is highly competitive and there are many lurks and perks.

The upshot of this is that you should get opinions, quotes and advice from as many airlines and travel agents as possible before you part with your hard-earned cash. The details given in this chapter should be regarded as pointers and are not a substitute for your own careful, up-to-date research.

The USA

Some very good open tickets remain valid for six months or 12 months, but they don't lock you into any fixed dates of departure. Flights to Indonesia, either Jakarta or Denpasar, go via Taiwan, Hong Kong, Singapore, Malaysia or another Asian destination, and will include the country as a stopover (sometimes you have to stop over). Garuda used to have a Los Angeles-Honolulu-Denpasar-Jakarta flight but suspended it in the wake of the economic crisis – it may commence again.

Return fares to Jakarta or Denpasar start from around US$1000 to US$1500 return in the low season (outside summer and Christmas) from the west coast, and around US$1200 from New York. Recent discounts have seen even lower prices and some real bargains. China Airlines via Taipei is often one of the cheapest, while Singapore Airlines is one of the most direct.

If you are visiting other parts of Asia, some good deals can be organised (eg there are cheap tickets between the US west coast and Singapore with stopovers in Bangkok for very little extra money). However, be careful during the peak travel seasons (summer and Chinese New Year) because seats will be hard to come by unless reserved months in advance.

The *New York Times*, *LA Times*, *Chicago Tribune* and *San Francisco Examiner* all produce weekly travel sections in which you'll find any number of travel agents' ads. Council Travel (☎ 800-226 8624) and STA Travel (☎ 800-777-0112) have offices in major cities nationwide. Both agencies have Web sites: Council Travel is at www.ciee.org and STA Travel can be found at www.statravel.com.

Canada

Getting discount tickets in Canada is much the same as in the USA – shop around until you find a good deal. Again, you'll probably have to fly into Hong Kong or Singapore and carry on from there to Indonesia.

Travel CUTS (☎ 800-667 2887) is Canada's national student bureau and has offices in all major Canadian cities – you don't have to be a student to use its services.

Its Web site is at www.travelcuts.com. There are a number of good agents in Vancouver for cheap tickets. The *Toronto Globe & Mail* and *Vancouver Sun* advertise travel agents.

Australia

Bali is the major gateway to Australia, with almost all flights to/from Indonesia routed via Denpasar. Direct flights connect Denpasar with Sydney, Melbourne, Brisbane, Perth, Darwin, and Port Hedland. Garuda, Qantas and Ansett Australia are the main carriers and compete on most of these runs, but the Port Hedland-Denpasar flight on Friday is operated only by Merpati. From Denpasar you can connect to other Indonesian cities.

Other direct flights to Indonesia are limited. They include Darwin-Kupang, Perth-Jakarta (Qantas) and Sydney-Jakarta (Qantas). The cheapest flight is from Darwin to Kupang (in Timor) on Wednesday and Saturday. Tickets can be bought from Merpati in Darwin (☎ 08-8941 1606) or through travel agents, but there is not much discounting. If bought in Kupang, the one way fare to Darwin is around US$180. Port Hedland-Denpasar costs A$465 one way. From Kupang, regular flights go to Bali, or you can island-hop through Nusa Tenggara.

Sample fares in Australian dollars, ranging from the low season to the high season (December and January) are:

from	to	one way (A$)	return (A$)
Brisbane	Denpasar	700-900	900-1400
Darwin	Denpasar	500-600	700-850
Darwin	Kupang	244-319	396-536
Melbourne	Denpasar	700-900	900-1400
Perth	Denpasar	500-600	700-850
Sydney	Denpasar	700-900	900-1400

Flights to Jakarta normally cost around A$100 more than to Denpasar, but the drop in demand has seen big discounting.

Travel agents are the best place to shop for cheap tickets, but because Bali is such a popular destination, flight discounting is minimal and most agents prefer to sell package

Air Travel Glossary

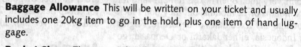

Baggage Allowance This will be written on your ticket and usually includes one 20kg item to go in the hold, plus one item of hand luggage.

Bucket Shops These are unbonded travel agencies specialising in discounted airline tickets.

Bumped Just because you have a confirmed seat doesn't mean you're going to get on the plane (see Overbooking).

Cancellation Penalties If you have to cancel or change a discounted ticket, there are often heavy penalties involved; insurance can sometimes be taken out against these penalties. Some airlines impose penalties on regular tickets as well, particularly against 'no-show' passengers.

Check-In Airlines ask you to check in a certain time ahead of the flight departure (usually one to two hours on international flights). If you fail to check in on time and the flight is overbooked, the airline can cancel your booking and give your seat to somebody else.

Confirmation Having a ticket written out with the flight and date you want doesn't mean you have a seat until the agent has checked with the airline that your status is 'OK' or confirmed. Meanwhile you could just be 'on request'.

Courier Fares Businesses often need to send urgent documents or freight securely and quickly. Courier companies hire people to accompany the package through customs and, in return, offer a discount ticket which is sometimes a phenomenal bargain. In effect, what the companies do is ship their freight as your luggage on regular commercial flights. This is a legitimate operation, but there are two shortcomings – the short turnaround time of the ticket (usually not longer than a month) and the limitation on your luggage allowance. You may have to surrender all your allowance and take only carry-on luggage.

Full Fares Airlines traditionally offer 1st class (coded F), business class (coded J) and economy class (coded Y) tickets. These days there are so many promotional and discounted fares available that few passengers pay full economy fare.

ITX An ITX, or 'independent inclusive tour excursion', is often available on tickets to popular holiday destinations. Officially it's a package deal combined with hotel accommodation, but many agents will sell you one of these for the flight only and give you phoney hotel vouchers in the unlikely event that you're challenged at the airport.

Lost Tickets If you lose your airline ticket an airline will usually treat it like a travellers cheque and, after inquiries, issue you with another one. Legally, however, an airline is entitled to treat it like cash and if you lose it then it's gone forever. Take good care of your tickets.

MCO An MCO, or 'miscellaneous charge order', is a voucher that looks like an airline ticket but carries no destination or date. It can be exchanged through any International Association of Travel Agents (IATA) airline for a ticket on a specific flight. It's a useful alternative to an onward ticket in those countries that demand one, and is more flexible than an ordinary ticket if you're unsure of your route.

No-Shows No-shows are passengers who fail to show up for their flight. Full-fare passengers who fail to turn up are sometimes entitled to travel on a later flight. The rest are penalised (see Cancellation Penalties).

Air Travel Glossary

On Request This is an unconfirmed booking for a flight.

Onward Tickets An entry requirement for many countries is that you have a ticket out of the country. If you're unsure of your next move, the easiest solution is to buy the cheapest onward ticket to a neighbouring country or a ticket from a reliable airline which can later be refunded if you do not use it.

Open Jaw Tickets These are return tickets where you fly out to one place but return from another. If available, this can save you backtracking to your arrival point.

Overbooking Airlines hate to fly empty seats and since every flight has some passengers who fail to show up, airlines often book more passengers than they have seats. Usually excess passengers make up for the no-shows, but occasionally somebody gets 'bumped' onto the next available flight. Guess who it is most likely to be? The passengers who check in late.

Point-to-Point Tickets These are discount tickets that can be bought on some routes in return for passengers waiving their rights to a stopover.

Promotional Fares These are officially discounted fares, available from travel agencies or direct from the airline.

Reconfirmation If you don't reconfirm your flight at least 72 hours prior to departure, the airline may delete your name from the passenger list. Ring to find out if your airline requires reconfirmation.

Restrictions Discounted tickets often have various restrictions on them – such as needing to be paid for in advance and incurring a penalty to be altered. Others are restrictions on the minimum and maximum period you must be away, such as a minimum of 14 days or a maximum of one year.

Round-the-World Tickets RTW tickets give you a limited period (usually a year) in which to circumnavigate the globe. You can go anywhere the carrying airlines go, as long as you don't backtrack. The number of stopovers or total number of separate flights is decided before you set off and they usually cost a bit more than a basic return flight.

Stand-by This is a discounted ticket where you only fly if there is a seat free at the last moment. Stand-by fares are usually available only on domestic routes.

Transferred Tickets Airline tickets cannot be transferred from one person to another. Travellers sometimes try to sell the return half of their ticket, but officials can ask you to prove that you are the person named on the ticket. This is less likely to happen on domestic flights, but on an international flight tickets are compared with passports.

Travel Agencies Travel agencies vary widely and you should choose one that suits your needs. Some simply handle tours, while full-service agencies handle everything from tours and tickets to car rental and hotel bookings. If all you want is a ticket at the lowest possible price, then go to an agency specialising in discounted fares.

Travel Periods Ticket prices vary with the time of year. There is a low (off-peak) season and a high (peak) season, and often a low-shoulder season and a high-shoulder season as well. Usually the fare depends on your outward flight – if you depart in the high season and return in the low season, you pay the high-season fare.

holidays. Packages including return airfare with five to 10 days accommodation can cost little more than the price of an air fare alone.

Two well known agents for cheap fares are STA Travel and Flight Centre. For STA Travel, call ☎ 131 776 Australia-wide for the location of your nearest branch or visit its Web site (www.statravel.com). Flight Centre (☎ 131 600 Australia-wide) has dozens of offices throughout Australia. Its Web address is www.flightcentre.com.

The highest demand for flights is during school holidays, especially the Christmas break – book well in advance.

New Zealand

Garuda and Ansett have direct flights between Auckland and Denpasar, with connections to Jakarta. Air New Zealand has suspended its Bali flights. The return economy air fare from Auckland to Denpasar is NZ$1245 to NZ$1499, depending on the season, or NZ$100 more to Jakarta with Garuda.

Check the latest fare developments and discounts with the airlines, or shop around for possible deals. As in Australia, STA Travel (☎ 09-309 0458) and Flight Centre are popular travel agents.

The UK

Ticket discounting is a long-established business in the UK – the various agencies advertise their fares and there's nothing under the counter about it at all. For more information, pick up a copy of the free newspapers *TNT*, *Southern Cross* or *Trailfinder*, or the weekly guide *Time Out*. Discounted tickets are available all over the UK; they're not just a London exclusive.

A couple of excellent places to look are Trailfinders and STA Travel. Trailfinders (☎ 020-7938 3939) has branches at 194 Kensington High St, London W8 and (☎ 020-7938 3366), 46 Earls Court Rd. It also has offices in Manchester (☎ 061-839 6969) and Glasgow (☎ 041-353 2224). STA Travel (☎ 020-7361 6161) is at 86 Old Brompton Rd, London SW7 3LQ.

Garuda Indonesia is one of the main discounters to Indonesia, and stops over in Bangkok or Singapore. Many of their Jakarta flights go via Denpasar. Rock-bottom fares (low season) from London to Indonesia are around £270/£395 one way/return to Bali, the same to Jakarta. The least loved airlines, such as Pakistan Airlines, usually have the cheapest fares to Jakarta. A host of other airlines fly to Indonesia, including Gulf Air to Jakarta and Lauda Air to Denpasar. These airlines regularly have cheap fares but plenty of stopovers, while Qantas, Thai Airways International (THAI) and Singapore Airlines are usually more expensive. Most tickets are valid for six months.

Continental Europe

The Netherlands, Brussels and Antwerp are good places for buying discount air tickets. In Antwerp, WATS has been recommended. In Zurich, try SOF Travel and Sindbad. In Geneva, try Stohl Travel. In the Netherlands, NBBS Reizen is a reputable agency. Many flights go to Denpasar but the cost is around the same to Jakarta. The cheapest flights often go via Bangkok or Singapore, with another stop en route.

From Amsterdam, 60-day return tickets with KLM to Jakarta cost around NL 3400 in the low season, NL 3600 in the high season (June to September). Tickets to Jakarta have been considerably cheaper recently. Garuda flies to Denpasar via Jakarta, and vice versa, for around the same price but recently has been offering substantial discounts to fill seats. Other airlines such as Royal Brunei, Kuwait Airlines, Air India and Malaysia Airlines often have cheaper fares, but go via more inconvenient routes or have more stopovers.

From Frankfurt, Garuda flies to Jakarta and Denpasar for around DM 1450. Flights with Lauda, Malaysia Airlines and Royal Brunei are often cheaper, while Lufthansa Airlines tends to be more expensive.

Garuda has flight connections between Jakarta and several other European cities, including Paris, Zurich and Rome. From Paris, Garuda flights to Denpasar are around FF5500 to FF6000, or you can fly with Cathay Pacific via Hong Kong for around the same price. Lauda is also a regular discounter on Paris-Denpasar flights.

Asia

Malaysia The most popular flight is from Penang to Medan in Sumatra with Malaysia Airlines for US$60. Malayia Airlines also flies to Kuala Lumpur for US$60. The regional Malaysian airline, Pelangi, flies Medan-Ipoh (US$60), and Padang to Kuala Lumpur and Johor Bahru. Silk Air flies from Pekanbaru in Sumatra to Melaka and Kuala Lumpur. See Getting There & Away in the Sumatra chapter.

Malaysia Airlines flies three times a week between Pontianak and Kuching in Sarawak for US$74. Bali-Air flies between Tarakan and Tawau in Sabah. Malaysia Airlines also flies between Kuala Lumpur and Ujung Pandang.

For Java, the cheapest connections are from Singapore, though Malaysia Airlines has competitively priced flights from Kuala Lumpur and Johor Bahru to Jakarta, and also flies to Surabaya.

Philippines Bouraq has a twice weekly flight from Manado on Sulawesi to Davao in the Philippines, but you need an onward or return ticket to enter the Philippines. Other airlines also fly Manila-Jakarta.

Singapore Of most interest are the numerous Singapore-Jakarta tickets which are discounted to as low as US$65.

Silk Air flies to several cities in Sumatra, such as Medan (US$93), Pekanbaru (US$100) and Padang (US$125). Silk Air also flies direct from Singapore to Sulawesi (Manado and Ujung Pandang) and to Solo in Java.

LAND

The only open land crossing is at Entikong, between Kalimantan and Sarawak (eastern Malaysia). This border post on the Pontianak-Kuching highway is now an official international entry point. Visas are not required and a 60 day tourist pass is issued on the spot. See Getting There & Away in the Kalimantan chapter.

SEA

Malaysia

Most sea connections are between Malaysia and Sumatra. The comfortable, high-speed ferries from Penang (Malaysia) to Medan (Sumatra) are one of the most popular ways to reach Indonesia. The other main ferry connection is between Dumai (Sumatra) and Melaka (Malacca). See the main Getting There & Away entry in the Sumatra chapter.

From Johor Bahru in southern Malaysia, daily ferries run to Batam and Bintan islands in Sumatra's Riau Islands, from where there are connections further afield. However, the standard way to reach these islands is from Singapore.

Papua New Guinea

With the cessation of flights in May 1998, the only way to travel between Irian Jaya and Papua New Guinea (PNG) is by boat. A regular service sails on Monday and sometimes Wednesday between Jayapura and Vanimo in PNG. Otherwise, you will have to charter a boat for the two hour journey. A visa may be obtained prior to departure for either country on this route.

Singapore

A popular way to reach Indonesia is via Sumatra's Riau Islands (see Getting There & Away in the Sumatra chapter). The main stepping stones are the islands of Batam and Bintan, both only a short high-speed ferry ride from Singapore.

Batam is the bigger travel hub, and from this island speedboats run through to Pekanbaru on the Sumatran mainland.

From Bintan, Pelni ships run to Jakarta and other destinations, and other regular ships go from Bintan to Jakarta.

Yachts

With a bit of effort it's still possible to hop on yachts around South-East Asia. Yacht owners frequently need crew members – all it usually costs is the contribution to the food kitty. As for where to look – well, anywhere that yachts pass through or in towns with western-style yacht clubs. We've had letters from people who have managed to get rides from Singapore, Penang, Phuket (Thailand) and Benoa (Bali). Other popular yachting places include the main ports in PNG and Hong Kong.

If have some sailing experience (and an Australian visa if heading to Darwin), you may be able to hitch a lift on a yacht during the annual Darwin to Ambon Yacht Race. See Yachts under Getting There & Away in the Maluku chapter.

ORGANISED TOURS

Tours tend to be oriented towards Bali. Most are accommodation and air fare only packages, and they can be good value for short stays. Choose your accommodation so that you are not too isolated and forced to rely on expensive hotel services. Other more expensive tours include sightseeing, all transfers and meals.

Tours to other parts of Indonesia range from adventure/trekking tours of Irian Jaya and Kalimantan to temple tours of Java. There are so many tours that it's impossible to list them here. The European market has the biggest selection – Dutch tour companies in particular have very competitively priced tours, ranging from big luxury groups to small, interesting off-the-beaten-track tours.

Prices vary according to the standard of accommodation. Some try so hard to maximise luxury and minimise hassles that par-

ticipants are hermetically isolated from the country. Smaller groups that provide some independence generally provide a more worthwhile experience. Some worth looking into include:

Intrepid Travel
 (☎ 03-9473 2626, fax 9419 4426, email
 info@intrepidtravel.com.au)
 11 Spring St, Fitzroy, Vic 3065
 Web site: www.intrepidtravel.com.au.
 Intrepid believes in sustainable, low impact travel. It organises a range of interesting tours covering all regions of Indonesia, including Irian Jaya.
The Imaginative Traveller
 (☎ 020-8742 8612, email info@imaginative-tra veller.com)
 1st floor, 14 Barley Mow Passage, Chiswick, London W4 4PH
 Web site: www.imaginative-traveller.com
 Acts as Intrepid Travel's UK sales agent for South-East Asia

Some of the more deluxe tours also include luxurious boat trips to neighbouring islands. The more upmarket tours may be comfortable and fun, but some of the staged ceremonies you'll be shown are basically little more than theatre. We ran into one tour group on the island of Lembata while they were attending a 'traditional ceremony' imported from Hawaii, complete with female dancers in grass skirts and flower necklaces, moving to the beat of bongo drums. Nice but not exactly authentic Indonesian culture.

Getting Around

AIR

Indonesia has a fairly extensive network of flights serviced by a variety of domestic airlines, some of which have a bizarre collection of aircraft. The main airlines are Garuda Indonesia, Merpati Nusantara Airlines, Bouraq Indonesia Airlines and Mandala Airlines, and there are several smaller ones. Ticket prices are set by the government and cost the same regardless of the airline.

Discounting is the exception rather than rule, but a few large travel agents in the main cities sell tickets at a small discount – around 5% on Garuda and Merpati tickets, and 10 to 15% on Bouraq and Mandala.

Domestic air travel in Indonesia is in a real state of flux. In the wake of the economic crisis of the late 1990s, Sempati (one of the major airlines) folded and the remainder are still in financial trouble. The main problem is that most airlines lease aircraft in US dollars but domestic flights are paid for in rupiah. Air fares have risen approximately 200% since the collapse of the rupiah in 1997, making flying many times more expensive than other forms of transport. However, for those with hard currency, air travel is still very cheap by world standards.

The main problem is that services have also been cut dramatically. Some 54 regional airports throughout Indonesia have closed due to falling passenger numbers, but many of the flights to remote airports were always unprofitable and unreliable anyway. There are still 158 regional airports that remain operational, and though the frequency of flights has also been cut, the main routes are operating. Garuda and Merpati are government-owned and have profitable international flights, and they appear to have weathered the economic storm. Another problem with Indonesian air travel is that flights that have few passengers are often cancelled.

Most airlines offer student discounts of up to 25%. You need a valid International Student Identity Card (ISIC) to take advantage of this. The age limit for claiming the student discount is usually 26.

Airlines accept credit cards, but don't expect to be able to use them in small offices in the outer islands.

Each airline publishes a nationwide timetable – definitely worth picking up if you're going to do a lot of flying, but not always easy to get. Minor changes to schedules are frequent, so always check with local airline offices to see what's available.

The number of Indonesians able to afford air travel is reasonably small so the chances of getting a seat, even on the day of departure, are good – but it pays to book as far in advance as possible during Indonesian holiday periods and the peak season around August. During these times flights may be booked on the more popular out-of-the-way routes serviced by small aircraft.

It is essential to *reconfirm*. Overbooking is another problem and if you don't reconfirm at least a few days before departure, you may well get bumped. Expect problems in the outer islands, where flights are limited, communications poor and booking procedures haphazard – you should reconfirm and reconfirm again.

Travel agents overseas can usually include discounted domestic flights with an international ticket if you enter Indonesia with Garuda. However, domestic tickets bought overseas are quoted in US dollars and cost around 50% more than if bought in Indonesia in rupiah, so it is usually just as cheap, if not cheaper, to buy them after you arrive.

Domestic Air Services

Garuda Indonesia The major national airline is Garuda, named after the mythical manbird vehicle of the Hindu god Vishnu. Garuda operates most of Indonesia's international flights and has a useful domestic network between the major cities only. Garuda operates wide-bodied jets on the domestic runs and has an efficient booking network.

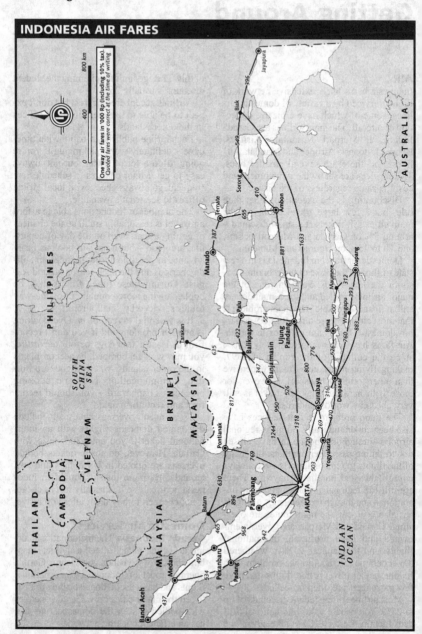

INDONESIA AIR FARES

One way air fares in '000 Rp (including 10% tax).
Quoted fares were correct at the time of writing

Merpati Nusantara Airlines Merpati runs a mind-boggling collection of aircraft – everything from modern jets to single-engine eggbeaters. It has the most extensive domestic network, and part of its charter is to cover obscure locations that would otherwise be without an air service. Merpati was a subsidiary of Garuda, then operated independently, and is now in the process of merging again to cut costs.

Merpati has a not-undeserved reputation for poor service, bungled bookings and cancelled flights. It provides a reasonable service on the main runs, but in the back blocks, flights are subject to frequent and unexplained cancellations. Hence the airline's unofficial theme song: 'It's Merpati and I'll Fly If I Want To' ...

Bouraq Airlines The network of this privately run airline is nowhere near as extensive as Merpati's or Garuda's, but it has some useful flights in Kalimantan, Maluku, Nusa Tenggara and Sulawesi, including connections between Java and Bali.

Mandala Airlines Mandala is the smallest of the all-Indonesia airlines, and apart from a few new jets, it appears to run a largely clapped-out collection of rattle traps. Its services have been cut drastically.

Other Air Services There are some intriguing possibilities for flying in Indonesia. The mission air services which operate in places such as Kalimantan, Central Sulawesi and Irian Jaya fly to some really remote parts of the interior of these islands and will take *paying* passengers if seats are available. See the respective chapters for details.

Various aircraft and helicopters are used by the foreign mining and oil companies – if you meet the right people in the right place, they like the look of your face and they're not yet sick of every self-proclaimed Marco Polo looking for a free ride, you never know where you could end up.

Other airlines include Sabang Merauke-Raya Air Charter (SMAC), Deraya and Dirgantara Air Service (DAS), which fly back routes within Sumatra and/or Kalimantan.

Air Passes
Garuda offers a 50% discount off the full fare on domestic flights – if you enter Indonesia with Garuda. There are no minimum sectors, so it works out to be a very good deal. Inquire at Garuda offices.

Domestic Departure Tax
Domestic departure tax varies from 5500Rp to 11,000Rp, depending on the airport. On top of the basic fare quoted by airlines, a 10% tax is charged as well as an insurance fee of 2500Rp. Tax and insurance is paid when you buy the ticket, but departure tax is paid at the airport. Baggage allowance is usually 20kg, or only 10kg on the smaller planes, and you may be charged for excess baggage.

BUS
Buses are the mainstay of Indonesian transport – at any time of the day, thousands of buses in all shapes and sizes are moving thousands of people throughout Indonesia.

Classes
Bus services vary throughout the archipelago but are usually dependent on the roads – eg Java has all types of buses, including luxury air-con coaches that ply the well paved highways. Luxury buses can also be found on the Trans-Sumatran Highway and on paved roads in Bali, Lombok and Sumbawa. The 'Wallace Line' for the evolution of buses lies between Sumbawa and Flores, as luxury buses don't operate on Flores and the islands further east. Only small, overcrowded rattlers ply Flores' narrow, potholed roads that would soon wreck an expensive bus. In Indonesia, the further off the beaten track you go, the more pot-holed that 'track' becomes and the less choice you have in buses.

The bottom line in buses is the ordinary, everyday *ekonomi* buses that run set routes between towns. They stop at bus terminals in every town en route, but will also stop for anyone, anywhere in the search for more paying customers – there is no such thing as 'full'. These buses are the lifeline for many communities, delivering the post and freight; passengers may include goats, pigs and chickens on the rural runs. Ekonomi buses can be hot, slow and crowded, but they are also ridiculously cheap and provide a never-ending parade of Indonesian life. They are often beat-up rattle traps with limited leg room, but if you get a seat and the road is good, they can be quite tolerable for short distances, especially on the main highways.

The next class up are the express (patas) buses. They can be much the same as the ekonomi buses, but stop only at selected bus terminals en route and don't pick up from the side of the road. Air-con patas buses are more luxurious and seating is often guaranteed. Usually there is no need to book and you can just catch one at bus terminals in the big cities.

The luxury air-con buses come in a variety of price categories, depending on whether facilities include reclining seats, toilets, TV, karaoke or snacks. These buses should be booked in advance; ticket agents often have pictures of the buses and seating plans, so check to see what you are paying for when you choose your seat. In Sumatra, Java and Bali, many of the luxury buses are night buses (bis malam), travelling the highways when the traffic is lighter.

Bring as little luggage as possible – there is rarely any room to store anything on buses. A large pack with a frame will be difficult to find space for. Many out-of-the-way places can only be reached by public bus – for real exploration it pays to leave your luggage in storage and travel with a day pack for a few days.

Reservations

Vehicles usually depart throughout the day for shorter routes over good roads; for longer routes, you'll have to get down to the bus terminal early in the morning to get a vehicle. On bad roads, there'll be fewer vehicles, so buying a ticket beforehand can be a good idea. In many towns and villages, the bus companies have a ticket/reservations office, or there are shops which act as an agent (or

own the buses). Often, hotels will act as agents or buy a ticket for you and will arrange for the bus to pick you up at the hotel – sometimes they will charge a few hundred rupiah for this service but it's easily worth it.

Costs

Ekonomi buses are ridiculously cheap, and you can travel over 100km for 3000Rp. Prices vary from region to region and with the condition of the road. The daytime buses that depart early in the morning – carrying chickens, pigs and goats – are usually the cheapest. You'll rarely have to pay more than 15,000Rp for a full day journey.

By way of comparison, the most luxurious overnight buses from Jakarta to Bali cost around 100,000Rp (including the ferry crossing). A express bus without air-con will do the same run for around half the price.

MINIBUS (BEMO)

Public minibuses are used both as local transport around cities and towns, and on short intercity runs, but their speciality is delivering people out into the hills and villages. They service the furthest reaches of the transport network.

The great minibus ancestor is the bemo, a small three-wheeled pick-up truck with a row of seats down each side, but they are more like regular minibuses these days. The word 'bemo' (a contraction of becak – three-wheeled bicycle-rickshaw and motor) is rarely used now but is still applied in Bali and is universally understood. In other regions, minibuses go by a mind-boggling array of names, such as opelet, mikrolet, angkot or angkudes. Just to make things confusing, they are called taksi in many parts of Irian Jaya, Kalimantan and East Java. Often they will be called simply by their brand name, such as Suzuki, Daihatsu or Toyota, but the most popular make by far is the Mitsubishi Colt, therefore 'Colt' is widely used.

Most minibuses operate a standard route, picking up and dropping off people and goods anywhere along the way. They can be very cramped, with even less room for luggage than buses and, if there is a choice, buses are usually more comfortable.

Within cities, there is usually a standard fare no matter how long or short the distance. On longer routes between cities you may have to bargain a bit. Minibus drivers often try to overcharge foreigners – more in some places than others. It's best to ask somebody, such as your hotel staff, about the *harga biasa* (normal price) before you get on; otherwise, see what the other passengers are paying and offer the correct fare.

Beware of getting on an empty minibus; you may end up chartering it! On the other hand, sometimes chartering a bemo is worth considering – for a few people it can work out cheaper than hiring a motorcycle by the day and much cheaper than hiring a car. Regular bemos carry around 12 people, so multiplying the usual fare by 12 should give you a rough idea of what to pay.

As with all public transport in Indonesia, the drivers wait until their vehicles are crammed to capacity before they contemplate moving, or they may go *keliling* – driving endlessly around town looking for a full complement of passengers. Often there are people, produce, chickens, baskets and even bicycles hanging out the windows and doors – at times it seems you're in danger of being crushed to death or at least asphyxiated (there's no air-con on any of these vehicles).

Door-to-Door Minibus

Express minibuses also operate between cities, mostly in Java, but tourist minibuses also run between the main tourist centres in Bali, Lombok and Sumatra. These minibuses are often luxurious seven or eight seaters with air-con and lots of leg room. Often called *travel*, they will pick you up from your hotel and drop you at your destination at the other end. Cheaper minibuses without air-con also operate, and sometimes you will have to go to a depot to catch them.

TRUCK

One of the great ironies of Indonesia is that farm animals ride in buses and people ride on the back of farm trucks! Trucks come in many different varieties. The luxurious ones operate with rows of bench seats in the tray at the back of the truck. More likely, you will have to sit on the floor or stand. It's imperative to try and get a seat in front of the rear axle; otherwise, every time the truck hits a pothole you'll find out what it's like to be a ping-pong ball. Trucks are disappearing as the roads improve, but they can still be found in places where roads are so bad that no other vehicles dare travel on them.

TRAIN

Train travel in Indonesia is restricted solely to Java and Sumatra (see Train under Getting Around in those chapters). Briefly, there is a good railway service running from one end of Java to the other – in the east it connects with the ferry to Bali, and in the west with the ferry to Sumatra. In Java, trains are one of the most comfortable and easiest ways to get around. There are a few lines tacked down in Sumatra, but most of that island is reserved for buses. There are no railways on any of the other islands.

CAR & MOTORCYCLE
Road Rules

Indonesians drive on the left of the road (sometimes the right, sometimes the pavement), as in Australia, Japan, the UK and most of South-East Asia. Indonesia has its fair share of maniacal drivers, including most bus drivers, but traffic manages to get along with relatively few accidents. The key is defensive driving. The roads are not just for cars but also pedestrians, animals, food carts etc. Opportunities for self-drive are fairly limited in Indonesia, except in Bali and Lombok – see Getting Around in the Bali chapter and Getting Around under Lombok in the Nusa Tenggara chapter. Generally when hiring a jeep or minibus, the driver is included. Punctures are usually repaired at roadside stands known as *tambal ban*.

Driving yourself is not much fun in many parts of Indonesia. It requires enormous amounts of concentration and the legal implications of accidents can be a nightmare – that is if you survive an angry mob should someone be hurt. If you do have an accident, as a foreigner it's *your* fault (see Legal Matters in the Facts for the Visitor chapter). It is more common and often cheaper to rent a car or minibus with driver.

Rental

Car Rental A car offers much the same advantages and disadvantages as a motorcycle, except for the price – hiring a car is at least five times more expensive.

The price of car hire varies according to both location and vehicle. Indonesia has regular car-rental agencies in large cities such as Jakarta, where a car without driver costs over 150,000Rp per day, or around 200,000Rp with driver. Bali is one of the cheapest places to rent a car. A Suzuki jeep costs around 60,000Rp to 75,000Rp a day, including insurance and unlimited kilometres; or a Toyota Kijang (a cross between a sedan and an off-road vehicle) costs from around 85,000Rp per day. In most cases, the price includes unlimited mileage but you supply the petrol.

The major car rental agencies, including Hertz, Avis and National, have offices in the main cities, such as Jakarta, Bandung, Yogyakarta, Medan, Surabaya and Denpasar, but they are expensive.

Car or minibus rental, including driver but excluding petrol, starts at around 90,000Rp per day. The price may include petrol if you are just sightseeing around a city. Bargaining is usually required. It is harder, but certainly possible, to find a driver for longer trips lasting a few days or even weeks. Negotiate a deal covering food and accommodation – either you provide a hotel room each night and pay a food allowance or negotiate an allowance that covers both – figure on about 25,000Rp per day. It pays to see what your driver is like on a day trip before heading off on a lengthy expedition.

Minibus Rental Renting a minibus can be a particularly good deal for a group. They are sturdy, comfortable, go-almost-anywhere vehicles, and can take up to six people plus luggage in comfort.

Travel agents in the travellers centres are good places to try for minibus rental. Go to the cheap tour operators – agents in the big hotels will charge big prices. Through the agents you have a better chance of finding a good, experienced driver that speaks some English and knows what tourists want. Failing that, ask at a tourist information centre or your hotel. There is always someone with a vehicle that is looking for work. Bali is a good place for renting on this basis. In Java, Yogyakarta is the best, and on Lombok, try around Senggigi. It is less common (and more expensive) in other parts of Indonesia, but always possible.

Motorcycle Rental Motorcycles are readily available for hire throughout Indonesia. In the tourist centres, they can be rented from around 20,000Rp per day, but in most places locals rent out their own motorcycles to earn a few extra rupiah. Rental charges vary with the type of bike and the length of hire. The longer the hire period, the lower the rate; the bigger or newer the bike, the higher the rate.

Motorcycles are almost all between 90 and 125cc, with 100cc the average size. You really don't need anything bigger – the distances are short and the roads are rarely suitable for fast speeds.

Indonesia is not the place to learn how to ride. The main highways are hectic, especially in Java and Bali. Combined with all the normal hazards of motorcycle riding are narrow roads, unexpected potholes, crazy drivers, buses and trucks that claim road ownership, children who dart onto the road, bullocks that lumber in, dogs and chickens that run around in circles, and unlit traffic at night. Take it slowly and cautiously around curves to avoid hitting oncoming traffic – this includes very large and heavy buses, buffalo, herds of stray goats and children. Keep to the back roads as much as possible, where riding can be pleasurable.

In theory you need to have a licence, especially to satisfy travel insurance in case of an accident, though you rarely need to show one. Bring your motorcycle licence if you have one. See Car & Motorcycle under Getting Around in the Bali chapter for details on obtaining a licence for Bali, Lombok and Sumbawa.

Some travel insurance policies do not cover you if you are involved in an accident while on a motorcycle. Check the small print.

Petrol The price of petrol is reasonably low in Indonesia – at the time of writing, it was 1000Rp per litre. There are petrol stations around the larger towns, but out in the villages they can be difficult to find. Small roadside shops sell small amounts of petrol – look for signs that read *press ban*, or for crates of bottles with a *bensin* sign. Some of the petrol from these stands is said to be of dubious quality, so it's probably best to refill whenever you see a petrol station *(pompa bensin)*.

BICYCLE

Bicycles can be rented in the main centres of Java, Bali and also Lombok, though they aren't used very much by Indonesians or by travellers. A few places like Solo are exceptions, with plenty of bicycles on the roads.

The main advantage of cycling is the quality of the experience. You can cover many more kilometres by bemo, bus or motorcycle but you really don't see more. Bicycles also tend to bridge the time gap between the rush of the west and the calm of rural Asia – without the noise of a motorcycle engine you can hear the wind rustling in the rice paddies or *gamelan* music as you pass a Balinese village.

The main problems with seeing Indonesia by bicycle are the traffic in Java, and the hills and enormous distances everywhere, which make it rather impractical or tough going to ride all over Indonesia. Bali is more compact, and seeing it by bicycle is reasonably popular despite the traffic on the roads. More people are giving it a try and more places are renting bikes. At all the main sights in Java there are bicycle parking areas (usually 100Rp or 200Rp), where an attendant keeps an eye on your bicycle.

For serious bicycle touring, bring your own. Good quality bicycles and components can be found in the major cities, particularly Java and Bali, but are difficult to find elsewhere.

HITCHING

Hitching is not part of the culture but if you put out your thumb, someone may give you a lift. Confusion may arise as to whether payment is required or not. On the back roads where no public transport exists, hitching may be the only alternative to walking, and passing motorists or trucks are often willing to help.

Bear in mind, however, that hitching is never entirely safe in any country in the world, and we do not recommend it. Travellers who decide to hitch should understand that they are taking a small but potentially serious risk. People who do choose to hitch will be safer if they travel in pairs and let someone know where they are planning to go.

BOAT

Regular ferries connect all the islands from Sumatra right through Java, Bali and Nusa Tenggara to Timor (see the relevant chapters for details). These ferries run either daily or several times a week, so there's no need to spend days in sleepy little port towns waiting for the elusive piece of driftwood to take you to the next island. Almost all of these ferries can transport large vehicles, and all of them will take motorcycles.

Going to and between Kalimantan, Sulawesi, Maluku and Irian Jaya, the main connections are provided by Pelni, the government-run passenger line.

Pelni Ships

Pelni is the biggest shipping line, with services almost everywhere. It has modern, all air-con passenger ships that operate set routes around the islands, either on a two weekly or monthly schedule. The ships usually stop for four hours in each port – so there's time for a quick look around.

Routes and schedules change every year, sometimes with only minor adjustments, but if new ships are added, major changes may be made. Try to find a copy of the latest

PELNI SHIPPING PORTS

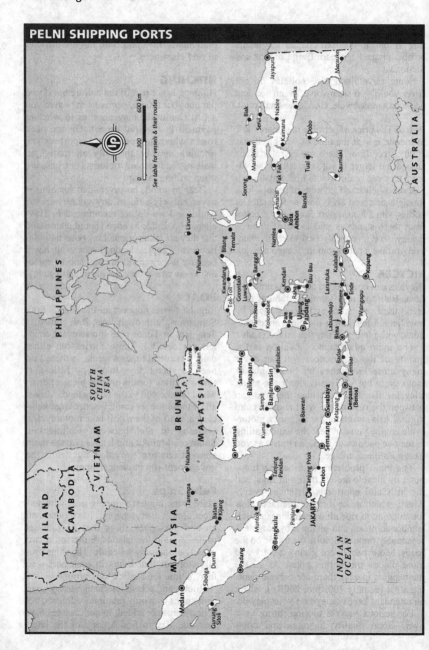

Pelni Vessels & Routes

The main Pelni ships, and the routes they ply (all fortnightly for the round trip unless otherwise indicated), are as follows:

Awu:

Benoa (B) – Lembar (NT) – Waingapu (NT) – Ende (NT) – Kupang (NT) – Kalabahi (NT) – Dili (NT) – Maumere (NT) – Ujung Pandang (Sl) – Tarakan (K) – Nunukan (K), and back via the same ports.

Bukit Siguntang:

Dumai (Sm) – Kijang (Sm) – Jakarta (J) – Surabaya (J) – Ujung Pandang (Sl) – Bau Bau (Sl) – Ambon (M) – Banda (M) – Tual (M) – Dobo (IJ) or Kaimana (IJ), and back via the same ports.

Ciremai:

Jakarta (J) – Semarang (J) – Ujung Pandang (Sl) – Bau-Bau (Sl) – Banggai (Sl) – Bitung (Sl) – Ternate (M) – Sorong (IJ) – Manokwari (IJ) – Biak (IJ) – Jayapura (IJ), and back via the same ports.

Dobonsolo:

Jakarta (J) – Surabaya (J) – Benoa (B) – Kupang (NT) – Dili (NT) – Ambon (M) – Sorong (IJ) – Manokwari (IJ) – Biak (IJ) – Jayapura (IJ), and back via the same ports.

Kambuna:

Sibolga (Sm) – Padang (Sm) – Jakarta (J) – Surabaya (J) – Ujung Pandang (Sl) – Balikpapan (K) – Pantoloan (Sl) – Toli-Toli (Sl) – Bitung (Sl), and back via the same ports.

Kelimutu:

Shuttles back and forth between Surabaya (J) and Banjarmasin (K) every two days, substituting Semarang for Surabaya twice a fortnight.

Kerinci:

Dumai (Sm) – Kijang (Sm) – Jakarta (J) – Surabaya (J) – Ujung Pandang (Sl) – Balikpapan (K) – Pantoloan (Sl) – Toli-Toli (Sl) – Tarakan (K) – Nunukan (K), and back via the same ports.

Lambelu:

Sibolga (Sm) – Padang (Sm) – Jakarta (J) – Surabaya (J) – Ujung Pandang (Sl) – Bau-Bau (Sl) – Ambon (M) – Namlea (M) – Bitung (Sl) – Ternate (M), and back via the same ports (except Bitung).

Lawit:

Kumai (K) – Semarang (J) – Pontianak (K) – Tanjung Pandan – Jakarta (J) – Tanjung Pandan – Pontianak (K) – Cirebon (J) – Pontianak (K) – Tanjung Pandan – Jakarta (J) – Tanjung Pandan – Pontianak (K) – Semarang (J) – Kumai (K).

Leuser:

Semarang (J) – Sampit (K) – Surabaya (J) – Batulicin (K) – Pare-Pare (Sl) – Samarinda (K) – Toli-Toli (Sl) – Tarakan (K) – Nunukan (K), and back via the same ports.

Pangrango:

Ketapang (J) – Semarang (J) – Sampit (K) – Bawean (off Java) – Surabaya (J) – Badas (NT) – Labuanbajo (NT) – Waingapu (NT) – Ende (NT) – Sabu (NT) – Roti (NT) – Kupang (NT), and back via the same ports.

Rinjani:

Surabaya (J) – Ujung Pandang (Sl) – Bau-Bau (Sl) – Ambon (M) – Banda (M) – Tual (M) – Fak Fak (IJ) – Sorong (IJ) – Manokwari (IJ) – Nabire (IJ) – Serui (IJ) – Jayapura (IJ), and back via the same ports.

Tatamailau:

Ketapang (J) – Bima (NT) – Labuanbajo (NT) – Larantuka (NT) – Dili (NT) – Saumlaki (M) –

Pelni Vessels & Routes

Continued from previous page

Tual (M) – Dobo (IJ) – Merauke (IJ) – Timika (IJ) – Kaimana (IJ) – Fak Fak (IJ) – Amahai (M) – Ambon (M) – Bau-Bau (Sl) – Ujung Pandang (Sl) – Badas (NT) – Benoa (B) – Ketapang (J); does the trip in the reverse order the next fortnight.

Tidar:

Surabaya (J) – Balikpapan (K) – Surabaya (J) – Pare-Pare (Sl) – Pantoloan (Sl) – Nunukan (K) – Tarakan (K) – Balikpapan (K) – Pare-Pare (Sl) – Surabaya (J) – Ujung Pandang (Sl) – Balikpapan (K) – Tarakan (K) – Pantoloan (Sl) – Ujung Pandang (Sl) – Surabaya (J).

Tilongkabila:

Benoa (B) – Surabaya (J) – Kumai (K) – Semarang (J) – Sampit (K) – Surabaya (J) – Semarang (J) – Kumai (K) – Surabaya (J) – Batulicin (K) – Surabaya (J) – Sampit (K) –

Surabaya (J) – Benoa (B) – Lembar (NT) – Bima (NT) – Labuanbajo (NT) – Ujung Pandang (Sl) – Bau-Bau (Sl) – Raha (Sl) – Kendari (Sl) – Kolonedale (Sl) – Luwuk (Sl) – Gorontalo (Sl) – Bitung (Sl) – Tahuna (Sl) – Lirung (Sl), and back to Benoa via the same ports in Sulawesi, Maluku and Nusa Tenggara; takes four weeks to complete the entire voyage.

Umsini:

Dumai (Sm) – Kijang (Sm) – Muntok (Sm) – Jakarta (J) – Surabaya (J) – Ujung Pandang (Sl) – Balikpapan (K) – Pantoloan (Sl) – Kwandang (Sl) – Bitung (Sl), and back via the same ports.

Note: The port for Jakarta is Tanjung Priok; Benoa is the port for Bali; Bitung is the port for Manado (Sulawesi). B=Bali, IJ=Irian Jaya, J=Java, K=Kalimantan, M=Maluku, NT=Nusa Tenggara, Sl=Sulawesi, Sm=Sumatra. See the Pelni Shipping Ports map for port locations.

schedule from any Pelni office, but they may only have schedules for the ships that call at their port.

Because Pelni ships operate only every two or four weeks, regular ferries are much more convenient. You can travel from Sumatra right through to Timor by land/ferry connections, but Pelni ships are often the only alternative to flying for travel to and between Kalimantan, Sulawesi, Maluku and Irian Jaya. Given the current chaos in the aviation industry, Pelni ships are often more reliable.

Pelni has four cabin classes, followed by Kelas Ekonomi, which is the modern version of deck class. It is sometimes possible to book a sleeping place in ekonomi; otherwise, you'll have to find your own empty space. Mattresses can be rented and many boats have a 'tourist deck' upstairs. Even ekonomi is air-conditioned and it can get pretty cool at night, so bring warm clothes or a sleeping bag. There are no locker

facilities, so you have to keep an eye on your gear.

Class I is luxury-plus, with only two beds per cabin. Class II is a notch down in style, with four to a cabin, but still very comfortable. Class III has six beds and Class IV has eight beds to a cabin. Class I, II, III and IV have a restaurant with good food, while in ekonomi you queue up to collect an unappetising meal on a tray and then sit down wherever you can to eat it. It pays to bring some other food with you.

Ekonomi is OK for short trips. Class IV is the best value for longer hauls, but some ships only offer Class I and II or III in addition to ekonomi. With the devaluation of the rupiah, Class I is good value for the comfort on offer. Prices quoted in this book are generally for ekonomi – as a rough approximation, Class IV is 50% more than ekonomi, Class III is 100% more, Class II is 200% more and Class I is 400% more.

It's best to book at least a few days in advance, although you can book tickets up to a week ahead. Pelni is not a tourist operation, so don't expect any special service, although there is usually somebody hidden away in the ticket offices who can help foreigners.

As well as its luxury liners, Pelni has Perinitis (Pioneer) ships that visit many of the other ports not covered by the passenger liners. The ships are often beaten-up old crates that primarily carry cargo, but they can get you to just about any of the remote islands, as well as the major ports. They offer deck class only, but you may be able to negotiate a cabin with one of the crew.

Other Ships

Sumatra, Java, Bali and Nusa Tenggara are all connected by regular ferries, and you can use them to island-hop all the way from Sumatra to Timor.

Apart from Pelni, a few regular passenger services also operate from the Sumatran mainland to Batam and Bintan islands in the Riau Islands, and between those islands and Jakarta. Kalimantan also has a few passenger services, but it is often a matter of hanging loose until something comes by. Check with shipping companies, the harbour office or travel agents.

If you're travelling deck class on these services, unroll your sleeping bag on the deck and make yourself comfortable. Travelling deck class during the wet season can prove to be extremely uncomfortable. Either get one person in your party to take a cabin or discuss renting a cabin from one of the crew (it's a popular way for the crew to make a little extra money). Bring some food of your own.

It's also possible to make some more unusual sea trips. Old Makassar schooners still sail the Indonesian waters and it's often possible to travel from Sulawesi to other islands, particularly Java and Kalimantan.

Small Boats

There's a whole range of floating tubs you can use to hop between islands, down rivers

and across lakes. Just about any sort of vessel can be rented in Indonesia. Fishing boats or other small boats can be chartered to take you to small offshore islands. Some of these boats are *not* reliable and engine trouble is an occasional problem. Check out the boat before you rent it – it would be nice if it had a two way radio and a lifeboat, but these are rare.

The *longbot* (longboat) is a long, narrow boat powered by a couple of outboard motors, with bench seats on either side of the hull for passengers to sit on. They are mainly used in Kalimantan as a standard means of transport.

Outrigger canoes powered by an outboard motor are a standard form of transport for some short inter-island hops – like the trip out from Manado in northern Sulawesi to the coral reefs surrounding nearby Pulau Bunaken (Bunaken Island). On Lombok these elegant, brilliantly painted fishing boats, which look like exotic dragonflies, are used for the short hop from Bangsal harbour to the offshore islands of Gili Air and Gili Trawangan. There are standard fares for standard routes, and you can charter these boats.

Speedboats are not all that common, although they are used on some routes on the rivers of Kalimantan or for some short inter-island hops in some parts of Indonesia. They are, of course, considerably faster than longbots or river ferries, but are considerably more expensive.

River ferries are commonly found on Kalimantan, where the rivers *are* the roads. They're large, bulky vessels that carry passengers and cargo up and down the water network.

LOCAL TRANSPORT
Bus

Large buses aren't used much as a means of city transport except in Java. There's an extensive system of buses in Jakarta and these are universally cheap, but beware of pickpockets. They usually work in gangs and can empty your pockets faster than you can say '*gado gado*'.

Minibus

Minibuses are the usual form of transport around Indonesian towns and cities – most run on standard routes with standard fares. They go under a variety of generic names – bemo, angkot – or brand names, such as Daihatsu or Colt.

Taxi

Metered taxis are readily available in major cities, especially in Java and Bali. If a taxi has a meter (argo), make sure it is used. Most drivers will use them without fuss. Jakarta has a few rogues, but taxi drivers are fairly honest. Elsewhere, meters don't exist and you will have to bargain for the fare in advance. Non-licensed taxis abound and are sometimes the only alternative; otherwise, opt for the licensed taxis.

Metered taxis charge about 1500Rp to 2000Rp for the first kilometre and around 750Rp for each additional kilometre. At airports, taxis usually operate on a coupon system, payable at the relevant booth before you board the taxi.

Becak

These are three-wheeled bicycle-rickshaws. Unlike the version found in India where the driver sits in front of you, or the Filipino version with the driver at the side, in Indonesia the driver sits at the rear, nosing your life ever forwards into the traffic.

Many drivers rent their vehicles, but those who own them add personal touches: brightly painted pictures, bells, or whirring metal discs strung across the undercarriage. In Yogyakarta one guy peddles furiously around the streets at night with a tiny flashing light-bulb on the point of his coolie hat!

While becaks are now banned from the main streets of large Javanese cities (they are banned from Jakarta altogether), in just about any town of any size in Java, as well as in some other parts of Indonesia (eg Ujung Pandang), they're the most basic form of transport – for people and anything else that has to be shifted.

Bargain your fare *before* you get in; and if there are two passengers, make sure that it covers both people – otherwise you'll be in for an argument when you get to your destination. Becak drivers are hard bargainers – they have to be to survive, but they will usually settle on a reasonable fare – around 500Rp to 1000Rp (at most) per kilometre. Fares vary from city to city and increase with more passengers, luggage, hills and night journeys. Hiring a becak for a period of time or for a round-trip often makes good sense if you're planning to cover a lot of ground in one day, particularly in large places like Yogyakarta or Solo.

Bajaj

These are noisy, smoke-belching three-wheeled vehicles with a driver at the front, a small motorcycle engine below and seats for two passengers behind. They're a common form of local transport in Jakarta, but you don't see them very often elsewhere.

Dokar

Dokars are the jingling, horse-drawn carts found throughout Indonesia. The two-wheeled carts are usually brightly coloured with decorative motifs and bells, and the small horses or ponies often have long tassels attached to their bridle. A typical dokar has bench seating on either side, which can comfortably fit three or four people. However, their owners generally pack in as many people as possible plus bags of rice and other paraphernalia. It's a picturesque way of getting around if you don't get upset by the ill-treatment of animals – although generally the ponies are well looked after. Dokars often operate on set runs and payment is per person (around 500Rp). Foreigners may have to charter – 2000Rp should get you just about anywhere around town.

In Java you also see the *andong* or *dilman*, which is a larger horse-drawn wagon designed to carry six people. In some parts of Indonesia such as Gorontalo and Manado in northern Sulawesi, you also see the *bendi*, which is basically a small dokar that carries two passengers.

Other Local Transport

There are various other ways of getting around. *Ojek* (or *ojeg*) are motorcycle riders that take pillion passengers for a bargainable price. They are found at bus terminals and markets, or just hanging around at crossroads. They will take you around town and go where no other public transport exists, or along roads that are impassable in any other vehicle. They can also be rented by the hour for sightseeing (starting at around 5000Rp).

In many of the hill resorts in Java you can hire horses. Likewise, it's often possible to hire one just about anywhere else horses are raised – this is possibly the ideal solution to getting over some of that rough terrain and actually enjoying the abominable roads!

ORGANISED TOURS

A wide range of tours can be booked from travel agents within Indonesia. Most of these take in places where tourists are numerous, such as Jakarta, Yogyakarta, Bali, Lombok and Danau Toba (Lake Toba).

You can be absolutely certain that taking a tour will work out to be more expensive than going by yourself, but some are good value: you can take a day tour to Borobudur and the Dieng Plateau from Yogyakarta, and be picked up and dropped off at your hotel for only 35,000Rp (see Organised Tours under Yogyakarta in the Java chapter). Yogya and Bali have the cheapest tours and

the best range, but cheap tours are available in all the main travellers centres.

Tours are normally less expensive if you book through a hotel rather than through a travel agent.

There are, of course, expensive all-inclusive tours available from travel agencies in Jakarta, Bali and elsewhere. Some of the Jakarta head offices of major operators are:

Natour
(☎ 021-798 2300) Jl (Jalan) Warung Buncit Raya 18
Pacto
(☎ 021-719 6550) Jl Tmn Kemang II, bldg D 2-4
Vayatour
(☎ 021-3800 202) Jl Batu Tulis 38

Other reliable companies based in Jakarta include:

Natrabu
(☎ 021-332728), Jl Agus Salim 29A
Nitour
(☎ 021-3846347), Jl Majapahit 2
Raptim Tours & Travel
(☎ 021-335585), Jl Cut Mutiah 8
Smailing Tour
(☎ 021-3864274), Jl Majapahit 28

You can find other agents in the Yellow Pages (www.yellowpages.co.id). Most travel agents have some economy tours, but they prefer to sell packages with accommodation at five star hotels that include banquet-style meals and top prices.

Java

Java is the political, geographic and economic centre of Indonesia. With an area of 132,000 sq km, Java is a little over half the size of the island of Great Britain, but its population of 120 million is almost double Britain's. With such vast human resources, Java is the powerhouse and dictator of Indonesia.

Java presents vivid contrasts of wealth and squalor, majestic open country and crowded filthy cities, quiet rural scenes and bustling modern traffic. The main cities can be overwhelming, but rural Java is still an island of astonishing beauty. A string of high volcanic mountains runs through the centre of the island, providing a smoking backdrop to the fertile green fields and terraces. The rich volcanic soils that have long been the secret to Java's abundance extend north to the flat coastal plain and the murky Java Sea, while the south coast fronts the crashing waves of the Indian Ocean.

It was in plentiful Java that the Hindu-Buddhist empires reached their zenith, producing the architectural wonders of Borobudur and Prambanan. When Islam came to Java, it absorbed rather than banished the existing influences, and Java is a blend of cultures and religion. The Indonesian images of shadow puppets, court dances and batik exist alongside the muezzin's call to the mosque.

Java is a long, narrow island, conveniently divided into three provinces: West, Central and East Java. It also includes the special territories of Jakarta, the teeming capital, and Yogyakarta (Yogya), a centre for Javanese culture and one of Indonesia's premier tourist destinations.

West Java is home to the Sundanese people and has places of interest such as Bandung in the Sundanese heartland, the court city of Cirebon, the beach at Pangandaran, famous Krakatau and the wilds of the Ujung Kulon National Park.

HIGHLIGHTS

- Yogyakarta, the cultural centre of Java, is an ideal base for trips to the awe-inspiring Buddhist pyramid of Borobudur.

- Java's cities are intense, crowded and disorienting, but to appreciate contemporary Indonesia, or its Dutch heritage, a visit is essential.

- A string of volcanoes runs through the island. Krakatau is the most famous, while Gunung Bromo is the most spectacular.

- Java's beaches don't match the superb examples elsewhere in Indonesia, but Pangandaran is deservedly Java's No 1 beach resort.

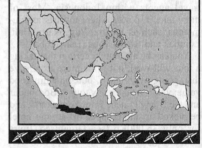

In Central Java, temples and royal cities mark the rise and fall of the Hindu, Buddhist and Muslim kingdoms, from which the present-day court cities of Yogya and Solo have evolved. Java is people and lots of them, but there are isolated places where you can find yourself out of sight and sound, such as the Dieng Plateau in the beautiful central highlands.

In East Java, spectacular Gunung Bromo (Mt Bromo) is wild and desolate, and the highlands have some of Java's best hill resorts and hiking opportunities. Off the coast, Madura retains its independent traditions.

HISTORY

The history of human habitation in Java extends back a million years to when 'Java Man' lived along the banks of Sungai Bengawan Solo (Bengawan Solo River) in Central Java. Waves of migrants followed, coming down through South-East Asia to inhabit the island. The Javanese are an Austronesian people, closely related to the people of Malaysia and the Philippines.

Early Javanese Kingdoms

The island's exceptional fertility allowed the development of an intensive *sawah* (wet-rice) agriculture, which in turn required close cooperation between villages for the maintenance of the irrigation systems. From this first need for local government small kingdoms developed, but the first major principality appears to have been that of King Sanjaya's. Around the beginning of the 8th century he founded the Mataram kingdom, which controlled much of central Java. Mataram's religion centred on the Hindu god Shiva, and the kingdom produced some of the earliest of Java's Hindu temples on the Dieng Plateau.

Sanjaya's Hindu kingdom was followed by a Buddhist interlude under the Sailendra dynasty; it was during this time that Mahayana Buddhism was established in Java and work began (probably around 780 AD) on Borobudur. Hinduism continued to exist alongside Buddhism, and the massive Hindu Prambanan complex was built and consecrated around 856 AD. Hinduism and Buddhism often fused into one religion in Java.

Mataram eventually fell, possibly as a result of conflict with the Sumatra-based Sriwijaya kingdom, which invaded Java in the 11th century. However, Sriwijaya also suffered attacks from the Chola kingdom of southern India. Javanese power revived under King Airlangga, a semi-legendary figure who brought much of Java under his control and formed the first royal link between Java and Bali. Airlangga divided his kingdom between his two sons, resulting in the formation of the Kediri and Janggala kingdoms.

Early in the 13th century, the commoner Ken Angrok usurped the throne of Singosari (a part of the Janggala kingdom), defeated Kediri and then brought the rest of Janggala under his control. His new kingdom of Singosari expanded its power during the 13th century up until its last king, Kertanegara, was murdered in a rebellion in 1292.

Majapahit Kingdom

Kertanegara's son-in-law and successor, Wijaya, established the Majapahit kingdom, the greatest kingdom of the Hindu-Javanese period. Under Hayam Wuruk, who ruled from 1350 to 1389, the Majapahit kingdom claimed sovereignty over the Indonesian archipelago, although its territorial sovereignty was probably restricted to Java, Madura and Bali. Hayam Wuruk's strongman prime minister, Gajah Mada, was responsible for many of Majapahit's territorial conquests.

While previous Javanese kingdoms based their power on the control of the rich Javanese agricultural areas, the Majapahits established the first Javanese commercial empire by taking control of Java's main ports and the shipping lanes throughout the archipelago.

The Majapahit kingdom began to decline soon after the death of Hayam Wuruk. Various principalities began breaking away from Majapahit rule and adopting Islam.

Islamic Kingdoms

Islam in Java now became a strong religious and political force opposed to Majapahit, making converts among the Majapahit elite even at the height of the kingdom's power. The 15th and 16th centuries saw the rise of new Islamic kingdoms, such as Demak, Cirebon and Banten along the north coast.

By the end of the 16th century the Muslim kingdom of Mataram had taken control of Central and eastern Java. The last remaining independent principalities, Surabaya and Cirebon, were eventually subjugated, leaving only Mataram and Banten (in West Java) to face the Dutch in the 17th century.

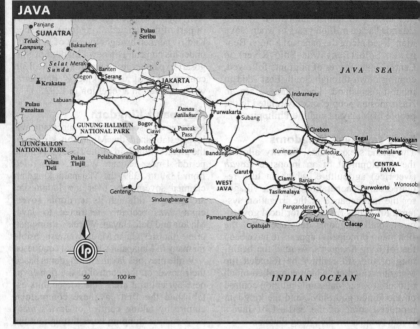

Dutch Period

The conquest of Java by the Dutch need not be recounted here, but by the end of the 18th century practically all of the island was under Dutch control. (See the History section in the Facts about Indonesia chapter for more details.)

During the Dutch period there were strong Muslim powers on Java, most notably Mataram. The Javanese were great warriors who continually opposed the Dutch, but they were never a united force because of internal conflict or battles with the Sundanese or the Madurese. The last remnants of the Mataram kingdom survived as the principalities of Surakarta (Solo) and Yogyakarta until the foundation of the Indonesian republic. Javanese kings claimed to rule with divine authority and the Dutch helped to preserve the vestiges of a traditional Javanese aristocracy by confirming them as regents, district officers or sub-district officers in the European administration.

Java Today

Java plays an extraordinary role in Indonesia today. It is more than simply the geographical centre of Indonesia. Much of Indonesian history was hacked out on Javanese soil. The major battles of the independence movement took place in Java and two of the strongest political parties in the first decade of independence – the Nationalist Party (PNI) and the Communist Party (PKI) – drew their support from the Javanese.

To a large extent the rebellions of the Sumatrans, Minahasans and Ambonese in the 1950s and 1960s were rebellions against Javanese domination. Furthermore, the Darul Islam rebellion against the new republic broke out in West Java. The abortive Communist coup of 1965 started in Jakarta,

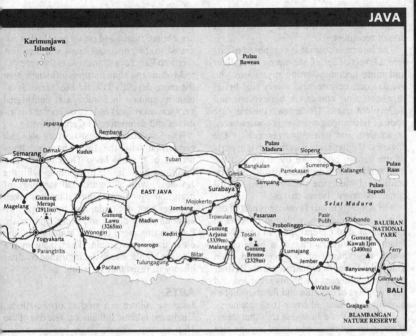

JAVA

Karimunjawa
Islands

Pulau
Bawean

Jepara

Rembang

Semarang Demak Kudus
Ambarawa   Tuban

Pulau
Madura Slopeng
Bangkalan   Sumenep Kalianget
Pamekasan
Gresik   Sampang   Pulau
Raas

EAST JAVA   Surabaya   Pulau
Sapudi

Magelang Gunung
Merapi   Mojokerto   Selat Madura
(2911m)
Solo   Gunung   Jombang
Lawu   Madiun   Trowulan   Pasaruan   Pasir
(3265m)   Putih Situbondo BALURAN
Wonogiri   Kediri   Gunung   Probolinggo   NATIONAL
Yogyakarta   Arjuna   Tosari   Gunung   PARK
(3339m)   Bondowoso Kawah Ijen
Parangtritis   Ponorogo   Malang   (2400m)   Ferry
Gunung   Lumajang
Blitar   Bromo   Banyuwangi
Tulungagung   (2329m)   Jember   Gilimanuk
Pacitan   BALI
Watu Ulo
Grajagan
BLAMBANGAN
NATURE RESERVE

and some of its most dramatic and disastrous events took place in Java. Java has provided the lead and the leadership for the republic.

Java also dominates economic life in Indonesia. Java has the bulk of Indonesia's industry and it received most of the foreign investment that poured into the country in the 1990s. The island is the most developed part of Indonesia by far, but the effects of the economic crisis have also been felt the most here. Huge numbers of urban workers lost their jobs and rising prices have hit hard right across Java, resulting in sporadic disturbances and riots across the island. With its huge population, some 60% of all Indonesia, if anything happens in Indonesia it will happen in Java first and foremost.

PEOPLE & CULTURE

Java has three main ethnic groups, each speaking their own language: the Javanese

of Central and East Java; the Sundanese of West Java; and the Madurese from Madura island off the north-east coast. The divisions are blurred – the Madurese, for example, have settled in large numbers in East Java and further afield, and Indonesians from all over the archipelago have come to seek work in the cities. Smaller pockets of pre-Islamic peoples also remain, like the Badui in the mountains of West Java and the Hindu Tenggerese centred on Gunung Bromo in East Java. Jakarta identifies its own polyglot tradition in the Betawi, the name for the original inhabitants of the city.

Today the Javanese are Muslim. Though most are *santri* (devout) Muslim, and Java is slowly becoming more orthodox, Javanese culture owes much to pre-Islamic animism and Hinduism. India has had probably the most profound and enduring influence on religion in Java, yet the Indian poet

Rabindranath Tagore, when visiting the country, said 'I see India everywhere, but I do not recognise it'.

The Javanese cosmos is composed of different levels of belief, stemming from older and more accommodating mysticism, the Hindu court culture, and a very real belief in ghosts and numerous benevolent and malevolent spirits. Underneath the unifying code of Islam, magic power is concentrated in amulets and heirlooms (especially the Javanese dagger known as the kris), in parts of the human body like the nails and the hair, and in sacred musical instruments. The traditional medicine man *(dukun)* is still consulted when illness strikes.

The *halus* (refined) Javanese is part of the Hindu court tradition, which still exists in the heartland of Central Java. In contrast to Islam, the court tradition is a hierarchical world view, based on privilege and often guided by the gods or nature spirits. Refinement and politeness are highly regarded, and loud displays of emotion and flamboyant behaviour is considered *kasar* (bad manners).

Indirectness is a Javanese trait that stems from an unwillingness to make anyone else feel uncomfortable or ashamed. It is impolite to point out mistakes, embarrassments, sensitive or negative areas, or to directly criticise authority. Even the Javanese language reinforces this deference to authority. Like Balinese, Javanese has 'high' and 'low' forms; different words are used when speaking to superiors, elders, equals or inferiors. This underlines differences in status, rank, relative age and the degree of acquaintance between the two people talking.

The Javanese of East Java speak a coarser form of Javanese but share many of the same traditions as the Central Javanese. Pockets of Hinduism still survive in East Java. The most well known group is the Tengger people of the Bromo area. The Tengger are regarded as the survivors of Majapahit, the commoners that were left behind after the Majapahit elite fled to Bali.

While the southern and central part of East Java shows a greater Hindu influence, the north coast is the stronghold of Islam

(much of the population is Madurese). From the hot dry island to the north, the Madurese are a blunt, strong and proud people that migrated to the north-east coast and then further into East Java. Surabaya is the gateway to Madura and shows strong influence from the more devoutly Islamic Madurese. Javanese as spoken in Surabaya is considered very kasar (vulgar) as it is without the intricacies and deferences of Central Java.

The Sundanese of West Java are also less concerned with the flourishes and hierarchies of Central Java. Their culture and traditions have much in common with the Javanese, with a hierarchical language of high and low forms, but Islam has taken stronger root in Sunda, and the people are earthier, more direct and more egalitarian. Even in this more Islamic atmosphere, the older traditions remain. The Badui in the western highlands are distinguished by their history of resistance to Islam.

ARTS

Javanese culture is a product of pre-Hindu, Hindu and Islamic influences. The rise of the 16th century Islamic states brought a rich new cultural heritage, but the Hindu heritage also managed to continue its influence.

Wayang

Javanese *wayang* (puppet) theatre has been a major means of preserving the Hindu-Buddhist heritage in Java. The most well known form is the *wayang kulit*, the shadow-puppet theatre using puppets made of leather (*kulit* means leather).

Wayang Kulit In the shadow-puppet theatre, perforated leather figures are manipulated behind an illuminated cotton screen. The stories are usually based on the Hindu epics, the *Ramayana* and *Mahabharata*, although other purely Javanese stories are also performed. In a traditional performance, a whole night might be devoted to just one drama *(lakon)* from a legend. A single puppeteer *(dalang)* animates the puppets, and narrates and chants through the entire night to the accompaniment of the gamelan orchestra.

Many wayang kulit figures and even whole stories have a specific mystical function; certain stories are performed for the purpose of protecting a rice crop (these incorporate the rice goddess Dewi Sri), the welfare of a village or even individuals.

Shadow-puppet theatre is not unique to Java; it can also be found in Turkey, India, China and parts of South-East Asia. Wayang kulit owes much to Indian tradition.

By the 11th century wayang performances with leather puppets flourished in Java, and by the end of the 18th century wayang kulit had developed most of the details of puppet design and performance techniques we see today. The standardisation of the puppet designs is traditionally attributed to King Raden Patah of Demak, a 16th century Islamic kingdom.

The puppets are made of leather, with water-buffalo hide from a young animal being the most favoured material. The outline of the puppet is cut using a thin knife, and the fine details are carved out using small chisels and a hammer. When the carving is finished, the movable arms are attached and the puppet is painted. Lines are drawn in and accentuated with black ink, which is also used to increase the contrast of the carved holes. The *cempurit*, the stick of horn used to hold the puppet upright, is then attached.

The leaf-shaped *kayon* represents the 'tree' or 'mountain of life', and is used to end scenes or to symbolise wind, mountains, obstacles, clouds or the sea. Made of the same flexible hide as the other puppets, the kayon might be waved softly behind the cloth screen while a puppet figure is held horizontally – a surprisingly effective way of indicating flight through the cloudy sky. Symbolic decorations on the kayon include the face in the centre of the tree, which symbolises the danger and risk that all people must confront in life.

The characters in wayang are brought to life by the dalang. To call the dalang a puppeteer belittles the extraordinary range of talents a dalang must possess. Sitting cross-legged on a mat before the white screen, the dalang might manipulate dozens of figures in the course of a performance.

The dalang recounts events spanning centuries and continents, improvising from the basic plot a complex network of court intrigues, great loves, wars, philosophy, magic, mysticism and comedy. The dalang must be a linguist, capable of speaking both the language of the audience and the ancient Kawi language spoken by the aristocratic characters of the play. The dalang must also be a mimic, capable of producing a different voice for each of the characters, and have great physical stamina to sustain a performance lasting from evening until the early hours of the morning.

The dalang must be a musician, able to direct the village's gamelan orchestra that accompanies the performance, be versed in history, and have a deep understanding of philosophy and religion. The dalang must be a poet capable of creating a warm or terrifying atmosphere, but must also be a comedian able to introduce some comic relief into the performances. Understandably, the dalang has always been regarded as a very special type of person.

The dalang directs the gamelan orchestra using a system of cues, often communicating the name of the composition to be played using riddles or puns. The player of the *kendang* (drum) liaises between the dalang and the other gamelan players by setting the proper tempo and changes of tempo for each piece, and in executing the important signals for ending pieces. The dalang may communicate with the orchestra using signals tapped out with the wooden *cempala* (mallet) held in the left hand. Or there may be other types of cues – for example, one of the clowns in the performance may announce that a singing contest is to be held, then announce the song he intends singing and the gamelan will play that song.

The mass of the audience sits in front of the screen to watch the shadow figures, but some also sit behind the screen to watch the dalang at work.

Wayang Golek These three dimensional wooden puppets have movable heads and arms, and are manipulated in the same way

Mahabharata & Ramayana

Ancient India, like ancient Greece, produced two great epics. The *Ramayana* describes the adventures of a prince who is banished from his country and wanders for many years in the wilderness. The *Mahabharata* is based on the legends of a great war. The first story is a little reminiscent of the *Odyssey*, which relates the adventures of Ulysses as he struggles to return home from Troy; the second has much in common with the *Iliad*.

When Hinduism came to Java so did the *Ramayana* and the *Mahabharata*. The Javanese shifted the locale to Java; Javanese children were given the names of the heroes and by tradition the kings of Java were descendants of the epic heroes.

The *Mahabharata* and the *Ramayana* are the basis of the most important *wayang* stories in Java and Bali. While they often come across like ripping yarns, both are essentially moral tales, which for centuries have played a large part in establishing traditional Javanese values.

They are complex tales, and the division between good and evil is never absolute. The good heroes have bad traits and vice versa. Although the forces of good usually triumph over evil, more often than not the victory is an ambivalent one; both sides suffer grievous losses and though a king may win a righteous war he may lose all his sons in the process. In the *Mahabharata*, when the great battle is over and the Pandavas are victorious, one of their enemies sneaks into the encampment and kills all the Pandava women and children.

Mahabharata

The great war portrayed in the *Mahabharata* is believed to have been fought in northern India around the 13th or 14th century BC. The war became a centre of legends, songs and poems, and at some point the vast mass of stories accumulated over the centuries was gathered together into a narrative called the 'Epic of the Bharata Nation (India)' – the *Mahabharata*. Over the following centuries more was added to it until it was seven times the size of the *Iliad* and the *Odyssey* combined!

The central theme of the *Mahabharata* is the power struggle between the Kurava brothers and their cousins the Pandava brothers. Important events along the way include: the

as shadow puppets. Although *wayang golek* is found in Central Java, it is most popular among the Sundanese of West Java. Sometimes a wayang golek puppet is used right at the end of a wayang kulit play to symbolise the transition back from the world of two dimensions.

Wayang golek uses the same stories as the wayang kulit, including the *Mahabharata* and *Ramayana*, as well as stories about the mythical Javanese king Panji and other legendary kings. It also has its own set of stories, for which there is some direct Islamic inspiration. These include the elaborate romances inspired by legends about the Prophet Muhammed's uncle, Amir Hamzah.

Wayang Klitik In East Java the wayang kulit is replaced by the *wayang klitik* or *keruchil*, which is a flat wooden puppet carved in low relief. This type of wayang is performed without a shadow screen. The wayang klitik is associated with the Damar Wulan stories that are of particular historical relevance to East Java. The stories relate the adventures of a handsome prince and his rise to become ruler of the Majapahit kingdom.

Wayang Orang Known as *wayang wong* in Javanese, the *wayang orang* is a dance drama in which real people dance the part of the wayang characters.

Mahabharata & Ramayana

appearance of Krishna, an incarnation of Lord Vishnu, who becomes the adviser of the Pandavas; the marriage of Prince Arjuna of the Pandavas to the Princess Drupadi; the Kuravas' attempt to kill the Pandavas; and the division of the kingdom into two in an attempt to end the rivalry between the cousins. Finally, after 13 years in exile and hiding, the Pandavas realise there is no alternative but war, the great war of the *Mahabharata*, which is a series of bloody clashes between the two sets of cousins.

It is at this time that the Pandava warrior Arjuna becomes despondent at the thought of fighting his own flesh and blood, so Krishna, his charioteer and adviser, explains to him the duties and obligations of the warrior in a song known as the 'Bhagavad Gita'. Krishna explains that the soul is indestructible and that whoever dies shall be reborn and so there is no cause to be sad; it is the soldier's duty to fight and he will be accused of cowardice if he runs away.

In the course of the battles many of the great heroes from both sides are slain, one by one. Many others also lose their lives, but in the end the Pandavas are victorious over the Kuravas.

Ramayana

The *Ramayana*, the story of Prince Rama, is thought to have been written after the *Mahabharata*. Long before Prince Rama was born the gods had determined that his life would be that of a hero, but as with all heroic lives it would be full of grave tests. Rama is an incarnation of the god Vishnu, and it is his destiny to kill the ogre king Rawana (also known as Dasamuka or Dasakhantha).

Due to scheming in the palace, Rama, his wife the beautiful Sita and his brother Laksamana are all exiled to the forest, where Sita is abducted by the ogre king. Rawana takes the form of a golden deer, luring Rama and Laksamana into the forest as they try to hunt the deer. Rawana then carries off Sita to his island kingdom of Lanka.

Rama begins his search for Sita and is joined by the monkey god Hanuman and the monkey king Sugriwa. Eventually a full-scale assault is launched on the evil king and Sita is rescued.

Wayang Topeng The *wayang topeng* is similar to wayang orang but uses masks. The two forms of dance drama were cultivated at varying times in the courts of Central Java. Wayang topeng is the older of the two and dates back to the Majapahit kingdom. In more recent times wayang wong was performed only as the official court dance drama, while wayang topeng was also performed outside the walls of the palace. The stylisation of human features seen in the shadow puppets is also seen in the wayang topeng masks; elongation and refinement are the key notes of the halus (noble) characters, while grotesque exaggeration denotes the kasar (vulgar) characters.

Gamelan

The musical instruments of Indonesia can be grouped into four main strata: those from pre-Hindu days; those from the Hindu period from the first centuries AD until about the 15th century; the Islamic period from about the 13th century; and from the 16th century, which is associated with Christian and European influences.

The oldest known instruments in Indonesia are the bronze 'kettle drums' belonging to the Dongson culture that developed in what is now northern Vietnam and spread into the Indonesian archipelago – they are not really drums as they have bronze rather than membrane heads. These instruments have been found in Sumatra, Java, Bali and Kalimantan and in other parts of South-East Asia; among the most curious examples are those of the island of Alor in Nusa Tenggara.

Other instruments are also thought to be very old, particularly those made of bamboo (like flutes and reed pipes). By the time of the Hindu period there was a wealth of metallic as well as wooden and bamboo instruments played in Java, and these are depicted on the stone reliefs of Borobudur and Prambanan and other shrines. On Borobudur there are reliefs of drums (waisted, hour-

Wayang Characters

The *wayang* characters are often based on figures from the *Mahabharata* and *Ramayana*. In the *Mahabharata*, the Kuravas are essentially the forces of greed, evil and destruction, while the Pandavas represent refinement, enlightenment and civilised behaviour.

At a wayang, or dance performance, if you know the plot well, it is easy to identify the characters; otherwise shape, colour, deportment and voice will help.

The noble *(halus)* characters tend to be smaller in size and more elegant in proportion; their legs are slender and close together, and their heads are tilted downwards, presenting an image of humility and self-effacement. The *kasar* (coarse, rough) characters are often enormous, muscular and hairy, with their heads upturned.

Eye shape and the colour of the figures, particularly on the faces, are of great importance. Red often indicates aggressiveness, greed, impatience, anger or simply a very forthright personality. Black and blue indicate calmness, spiritual awareness and maturity. Gold and yellow are reserved for kings and the highest nobles. White can symbolise purity or virtue, high moral purpose and the like. Hair styles, ornamentation and clothing are all important in identifying a particular character.

Pandavas

Bima Bima is the second-eldest of the Pandavas. He is big, burly, aggressive and not afraid to act on what he believes; he can be rough, even using the language of the streets to address the gods. He is able to fly and is the most powerful warrior on the battlefield, but he also has infinite kindness and a firm adherence to principle.

Arjuna Arjuna is the handsome and refined ladies' man, a representative of the noble class, whose eyes look at the ground because it's kasar to stare into people's faces. He can also be fickle and selfish, but despite his failings, he is halus – refined in manner, never speaking ill to offend others, polite and humble, patient and careful. Arjuna's charioteer is Krishna, an incarnation of the god Vishnu, a spiritual adviser, but also a cunning and ruthless politician.

Semar A purely Javanese addition to the story is Arjuna's servant, the dwarf clown Semar. An incarnation of a god, Semar is a great source of wisdom and advice to Arjuna – but his body is squat with an enormous posterior, bulging belly and he sometimes has an uncontrollable disposition for farting.

SALLY GERDAN

Semar

glass, pot and barrel-shaped), two stringed lutes, harps, flutes, mouth organs, reed pipes, a keyed metallophone *(saron)*, xylophone, cymbals and others. Some of these instruments are direct imports from India, while others resemble the instruments now used in the Javanese gamelan orchestra.

One interesting and ancient instrument is the *calung*, a Sundanese instrument that is also found in a few places in Java and southern Thailand. The basic version consists of a set of bamboo tubes, one end of each tube closed off by the natural node of the bamboo and the other end pared down for part of its

Wayang Characters

Gareng, Petruk & Bagong Semar has three sons: Gareng, with his misshapen arms, crossed eyes, limp and speech impediment; Petruk, with his hilarious long nose and enormous smiling mouth, who lacks proportion in physique and thinking; and Bagong, the youngest of the three, who speaks as though he has a mouthful of marbles. Though they are comic figures, they play the important role of interpreting the actions and speech of the heroic figures in the *wayang kulit* plays. Despite their bumbling natures and gross appearance they are the mouthpieces of truth and wisdom.

Kuravas
On the Kurava side is Duryudana, a handsome and powerful leader, but too easily influenced by the prevailing circumstances around him and thus often prey to the evil designs of his uncle and adviser, Sangkuni. Karna is the good man on the wrong side, whose loyalty is divided between the Kuravas and the Pandavas. He is actually a Pandava but was brought up a Kurava; adhering to the code of the warrior he stands by his king as a good Javanese should and, as a result, he dies at the hands of Arjuna.

Ramayana Characters
The characters of the *Ramayana* are a little more clear-cut. Like Arjuna, Rama is the epitome of the ideal man – a gentle husband, noble prince, kindly king and brave leader. His wife Sita (or sometimes Shinta) is the ideal wife who remains totally devoted to her husband. But not all characters are easily defined: Rawana's warrior brother, Kumbakarna, knows that the king is evil but is bound by the ethics of the Ksatria warrior to support his brother to the end, consequently dying a horrible death by dismemberment.

Puppets
The most famous puppets of Indonesia are the carved leather wayang kulit puppets. The intricate lace figures are cut from buffalo hide with a sharp, chisel-like stylus and then painted. They are produced on Bali and Java, particularly Central Java. The leaf-shaped *kayon* representing the 'tree' or 'mountain of life' is used to end scenes in the wayang and is also made of leather.

Wayang golek are the three-dimensional wooden puppets found in Central Java, but are most popular among the Sundanese of West Java. The *wayang klitik* puppets are a rarer, flat, wooden puppet of East Java.

Sita

length like a goose-quill pen. The instrument is played with one or two sickle-shaped wooden hammers *(panakol)* padded with cotton or rubber. The calung is still commonly found in Java.

The oldest instruments still in use include drums, gongs, and various wind and plucked string instruments. The large Javanese gamelan has sets of suspended and horizontal gongs, gong chimes, drums, flutes, bowed and plucked string instruments, metallophones and xylophones. The total complement comprises 60 to 80 instruments.

BOOKS

A classic book on Javanese religion, culture and values is *The Religion of Java* by Clifford Gertz, which is slightly dated (it was based on research done in the 1950s) but nevertheless fascinating reading.

Javanese Culture by Koentjaraningrat is one of the most comprehensive studies of Javanese society, history, culture and beliefs. This excellent reference book covers everything from Javanese toilet training to kinship lines.

Two books by Neils Mulder that explore Javanese mysticism are: *Individual & Society in Java* and *Mysticism & Everyday Life in Contemporary Java*. Though concerned primarily with the non-mainstream *kebatinan* (Javanese mysticism) mystical movements, they are useful elucidations of Javanese mysticism and world view.

Hindu Javanese: Tengger Tradition and Islam by Robert Hefner is a detailed study on the Tenggerese people of the Gunung Bromo area in East Java.

A classic book on Java's wayang traditions is *Javanese Shadow Puppets* by Ward Keeler. *Wayang Golek: The Entrancing World of Classical Javanese Puppet Theatre* by Peter Buurman is the best book on West Java's wooden puppets. It is well illustrated, covers different styles and everything from puppet making to an explanation of the different characters. *Folk Art of Java* by Joseph Fischer examines wayang puppets, masks, children's toys, ceramics and woodcarvings as they relate to village traditions.

The *Oxford in Asia* paperback series has a number of excellent books, including *Javanese Wayang Kulit – An Introduction* by Edward C van Ness & Shita Prawirohardjo, *Javanese Gamelan* by Jennifer Lindsay and *Borobudur* by Jacques Dumarcay.

GETTING THERE & AWAY
Air

Jakarta is Indonesia's busiest entrance point for overseas airlines and, though not in the same class as Singapore, it is the best place in Indonesia to shop around for cheap international air tickets. One of the most popular short-hop international connections is the Jakarta-Singapore run for around US$65. Surabaya has a few international flights, and Solo has two flights a week to Singapore.

Jakarta is also the hub of the domestic airline network. Garuda Indonesia and Merpati Nusantara are the main airlines serving the outer islands from Java, though Bouraq and Mandala also have useful services. See the Jakarta Getting There & Away section for airline office details.

Sea

Jakarta is the main hub for Pelni passenger ships that run all over Indonesia, but no international connections exist. The most direct connection from Singapore is to take a ferry from Singapore to Tanjung Pinang on Pulau Bintan (Bintan Island) in the Riau archipelago and then take a ship to Jakarta (see the Sumatra chapter for details).

Bali Ferries run round-the-clock between Banyuwangi/Ketapang harbour in Java and Gilimanuk in Bali. In Bali, buses run to Gilimanuk from where frequent ferries go to Ketapang, which has numerous buses and trains to the rest of Java. An easier alternative is take a through bus from Denpasar to any major city in Java – these buses include the ferry journey. From Denpasar you can get a bus straight to Probolinggo (7½ hours), Surabaya (nine hours), Yogyakarta (16 hours) or even Jakarta. A few buses also run between Javan cities and Lovina/Singaraja and Pandangbai in Bali.

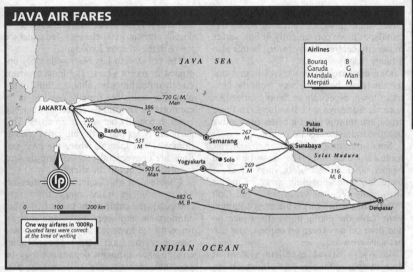

JAVA AIR FARES

Airlines

Bouraq	B
Garuda	G
Mandala	Man
Merpati	M

JAVA SEA

JAKARTA

720 G, M, Man

386 G

205 M

Bandung

500 G

531 M

Semarang

267 M

Pulau Madura

Surabaya

Selat Madura

Yogyakarta • Solo

503 G, Man

269 M

316 M, B

470 G

882 G, M, B

Denpasar

0   100   200 km

One way airfares in '000Rp
Quoted fares were correct
at the time of writing

INDIAN OCEAN

Sumatra Ferries shuttle between Merak in Java and the southern Sumatran port of Bakauheni, 24 hours a day.

Regular buses go to Merak from Jakarta's Kalideres bus terminal. In Bakauheni buses take you north to Bandarlampung's Rajabasa bus terminal, from where other buses can take you all over Sumatra. The easy option is the long-distance buses that run from Jakarta (and other cities in Java) straight through to the main Sumatran destinations. Most of these leave from Jakarta's Pulo Gadung bus terminal.

The long bus journeys in Sumatra can take their toll and as most points of interest are in North Sumatra, many travellers prefer to take a Pelni boat or to fly between Jakarta and Padang.

GETTING AROUND

Most travellers going through Java follow the well worn route from Jakarta to Bogor, Bandung, Pangandaran, Yogyakarta, Solo, Surabaya, Gunung Bromo and on to Bali, with short diversions from points along that route.

Air

There's no real need to fly around Java unless you're in a real hurry or have money to burn. Flights in and out of Yogya are the most useful but are limited. If you do take to the air you'll get some spectacular views of Java's many mountains and volcanoes – try to get a window seat!

Bus

Buses are the main form of transport in Java. As so many buses operate, you can often just front up to the bus terminal and catch one straight away, especially the big public buses that constantly shuttle between the cities and towns.

Buses are convenient, and quick and comfortable if you pay extra. Java has a huge variety of services from public, economy buses to super-luxury coaches. The economy buses can be very crowded and slow because they pick up and drop off anywhere en route, while the luxury coaches run directly between the main cities and sometimes travel at night to avoid the worst of the traffic.

Tickets for *patas* (express) and luxury buses can be bought in advance at bus terminals, or more conveniently at bus agents in the city centres. Many tourist hotels also arrange tickets.

One drawback to bus travel is that bus terminals can be a long way from the centre of town, especially in the big cities like Jakarta, Surabaya and Bandung. In these cities, the train is often a better alternative because train stations are central.

Small minibuses also cover the shorter routes and back runs. They may be called *bemos*, *opelets*, *mikrolets*, *angkots* etc – there is a mind-boggling array of names with many regional variations – but Colt (after Mitsubishi Colt) is the most common term. Like the public buses, they pick up and drop off anywhere on request, and can get very crowded.

Java also has an excellent system of door-to-door minibuses *(travel)*, which can pick you up at your hotel (though sometimes you have to go to a depot) and will drop you off wherever you want to go in the destination city. They run all over Java and are usually deluxe air-con minibuses, though some are getting old and the air-con no longer works. Air-con minibuses are almost always newer and more comfortable than those without air-con.

Be careful on the buses. Thievery has always been a problem but has increased as the economy has declined. Typically, thieves take the seat behind you, slash your bag, take your belongings and are gone before you know it. Always wear a concealed money belt for your passport, travellers cheques etc. Economy buses are certainly worse but travelling deluxe is no guarantee against theft.

Train

Java has a good rail service running from one end of the island to the other. In the east (Ketapang/Banyuwangi) it connects with the ferry to Bali and in the west (Merak) it connects with the ferry to Sumatra. The two main lines run between Jakarta and Surabaya – the longer central route goes via Yogyakarta and Solo, and the shorter northern route goes via Semarang. These main lines are serviced by dozens of trains in all classes – see under the towns in this chapter for details.

The rail system has been noticeably upgraded in recent years. The long overruns on scheduled times are almost a thing of the past. The trains are usually quicker, more comfortable and more convenient than the buses, especially between main cities. This particularly applies to the big cities such as Surabaya and Jakarta, where the train stations are conveniently central and the bus terminals are out in the sticks.

Choose your trains carefully for comfort and speed. The trains range from very cheap, squalid cattle trains to expensive but comfortable expresses. Fares and journey times for the same journey and in the same class vary from train to train. The schedules change and, although departures may be punctual, arrivals may still be late, particularly on the cheap trains.

When choosing a train, try to get one that begins in the city you are departing from. Seats are more difficult to get on a train coming through from somewhere else, and in *ekonomi* (economy) you may be a standing-room-only sardine. Try also to get a train that ends in the city of your destination. Even if you are only going part of the train's journey, the fare is almost the same for the full journey; for example, Jakarta-Yogyakarta costs the same as Jakarta-Surabaya on the *Bima*.

Classes Ekonomi trains can be no frills with bare wooden seats, hawkers, beggars and all manner of produce. They can be very crowded and slow, particularly on the back runs. Seats on these trains are hard to get and cannot be booked. However, many ekonomi runs have been upgraded – they are limited express and have padded seats that can be booked. The aisles may still fill up but, if you can get a seat, they provide an efficient service. The better trains are usually designated 'ekonomi plus'. In the larger cities, some ekonomi trains may not stop at the main station, but at another less central station.

Though ekonomi has improved, it is worth shelling out extra for the expresses that offer *bisnis* (business) and *eksekutif* (executive) carriages, which are less subject to overruns. In bisnis class you get a guaranteed, comfortable seat with plenty of room and fans (but not air-con). Eksekutif is much more luxurious and has air-con, reclining seats, video (maybe), and a snack usually included in the ticket price. Everything else you are offered – from Coke to cushions – costs extra.

Top of the range are the fast, new luxury trains that run from Jakarta, such as the *Argobromo* to Surabaya or the super luxury *Anggrek*, which has fax, telephone and other business services. Other top trains are the *Argo Gede* to Bandung, the *Argo Muria* to Semarang, and the *Argo Lawu* and the *Dwipangga* to Solo via Yogyakarta.

Tickets & Information Buying tickets is usually straightforward, but ticket windows can be crowded and trying to get information can be frustrating. Some cities, such as Yogya and Bandung, have helpful tourist information booths at the station or the *kepala stasiun* (station master) can help. Train stations display timetables on boards and you can sometimes get a printed *jadwal* (timetable) at the main stations (for that station), but all-Java timetables are impossible to get.

For basic ekonomi trains, tickets go on sale an hour before departure – just front up, buy a ticket and hope that you can get a seat. The better ekonomi services can be booked up to a week in advance for an extra 1500Rp.

Bisnis and eksekutif trains can be booked weeks in advance at the appropriate ticket window. The main stations also have a separate air-con, computerised booking office for eksekutif trains. A few travel agents and hotels can buy tickets for you, for a suitable commission, but most do not.

Though it is often possible to get a ticket in any class on the day of departure, you may have to stand in a long queue. Seats are hard to get on weekends and impossible during holiday periods. Always try to book at least a day in advance or a few days for travel on public holidays and long weekends.

Car

Self-drive cars can be hired in Jakarta, but the rates at the international companies like Avis and National are very high – typically around US$100 per day. Local companies are slightly cheaper. To hire a car you must have a valid local driving licence or an International Driving Permit. The age limit is usually 19, though it's sometimes higher.

While it is possible to drive yourself in Java, you need the patience of a saint and the concentration powers of a chess grand master. The main Jakarta-Bandung-Yogya-Solo-Surabaya route is no fun. Apart from a few toll roads and the odd quiet stretch with stunning scenery, driving along this highway is a procession of towns, villages and chaotic traffic.

The usual alternative is to rent a car or minibus with driver, which can be a lot cheaper than hiring a self-drive car. The big car-rental agencies prefer to rent cars with drivers. Much cheaper are the private operators that cost as little as 80,000Rp per day with driver. Cars can be hired through travel agents and hotels, who have regular drivers or may know of a driver looking for work. Check out the driver for experience and language ability, and get licence and identity-card details. Good places for hiring cars on this basis are the main cities and tourist destinations, such as Yogya, Jakarta, Surabaya, Bogor, Bandung, Pangandaran and Malang.

For shorter trips around town you can rent taxis or minibuses quite easily through car-rental companies, some travel agencies and the hotels in main cities. The rates vary but it's likely to be around 10,000Rp an hour for a minimum of two hours or a flat rate for a set route.

Boat

Besides ferries and boats from Java to the other islands, there is also a boat trip across the inland sea between Cilacap and Kalipucang, which is really worth doing. If you're travelling between Central Java and Pangandaran in West Java the boat is an excellent alternative to taking the bus and/or train all the way.

There are daily boat services to Pulau Seribu in the Bay of Jakarta, but trips to the small islands off the coast usually involve chartering a fishing boat – an outrigger vessel with sails or a motorised boat – which is dependent on the weather. There are regular daily ferries between Java and Madura, Bali and Sumatra.

Jakarta

☎ 021 • pop 9.3 million

Jakarta is all Indonesia rolled into one huge urban sprawl. Indonesians come from all over the archipelago to seek fame and fortune, or just to eke out a living. Bataks and Minangkabau from Sumatra, Ambonese from Maluku, Dani from Irian Jaya, Minahasans from Sulawesi, Balinese, Madurese and Timorese are all united by Bahasa Indonesia and a desire to make it in the capital. For it is in Jakarta that the latest styles and thoughts are formed, the important political decisions made. Jakarta is the main centre for the economy, the place to find work, do deals and court government officials.

In the 1990s Jakarta underwent a huge transformation as the face of the city was changed by the constant construction of more skyscrapers, flyovers, hotels and shopping centres, with development centred on the showpiece 'Golden Triangle' central business district bounded by Jalan (Jl) Thamrin/Sudirman, Jl Rasuna Said and Jl Gatot Subroto. Viewed from the Golden Triangle, Jakarta is still a boom city, but away from the centre much of the city still doesn't have sewerage or a decent water supply. Jakarta has more luxury cars than the rest of Indonesia put together, but it also has the worst slums in the country.

In 1998, in the aftermath of the economic crisis, the disparity between rich and poor erupted in Indonesia's worst violence in three decades. Areas such as Glodok provide lingering reminders of the riots but the most vivid reminders of the city's fall from grace are the abandoned cranes and building sites around the city.

JAKARTA

PLACES TO STAY
12 Kempinski Hotel Plaza
14 Hotel Mulia Senayan; CJ's Bar
15 Hilton Hotel
18 Hotel Atlet Century Park; Komodo Airways

OTHER
1 Pelni Passenger Termina
2 Pasar Pagi Mangga Dua (Market)
3 Kota Station
4 Jakarta Fair Grounds
5 Pelni Office
6 Ciputra Mall
7 Tanah Abang Station
8 Gambir Station
9 Pasar Senen Station
10 Pulo Gadung Bus Terminal
11 Jalan Jalan (Nightclub)
13 Taman Ria Senayan (Fun Park & Restaurant Complex)
16 Jamz (Nightclub)
17 Sudirman CBD; Bengkel (Nightclub)
19 Plaza Senayan
20 Planet Hollywood
21 Armed Forces Museum
22 Blok M Mall
23 Pondok Indah Mall
24 Twilite Cafe (TC)
25 Lebak Bulus Bus Terminal
26 Kampung Rambutan Bus Terminal

Jakarta is primarily a city of government and business, not a tourist destination, but the old part of the city is not to be missed. Kota is the heart of the 17th century Dutch town of Batavia, centred around the cobbled square of Taman Fatahillah. From Kota, you can wander north to the old schooner dock of Sunda Kelapa, the most impressive reminder of the age of sailing ships to be found anywhere in the world. The city also has a few interesting museums, oversized monuments, some theme parks and excellent shopping possibilities.

Jakarta is the most expensive city in Indonesia, the most polluted and the most congested, but if can you withstand it and afford to indulge in its attractions, it can also be an exciting city. For this is the 'Big Durian', the foul-smelling exotic fruit that some can't stomach but others can't resist.

JAKARTA

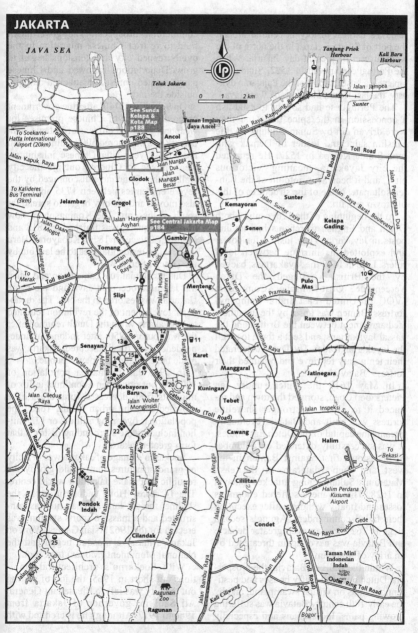

JAVA SEA

Teluk Jakarta

Tanjung Priok Harbour

Kali Baru Harbour

Jalan Jampea

Sunter

Jalan Raya Kampung Bandan

0   1   2 km

See Sunda Kelapa & Kota Map p188

Taman Impian Jaya Ancol

To Soekarno-Hatta International Airport (20km)

Toll Road

Ancol

Jalan Kapuk Raya

Toll Road

3

Jalan Mangga Dua

Jalan Mangga Besar

Gunung Sahari

Jalan Gunung Sahari

Jalan Cijah Muda

Glodok

To Kalideres Bus Terminal (3km)

Jelambar

Grogol

Jalan Hasyim Asyhari

4

Kemayoran

Jalan Sunter Jaya

Sunter

Jalan Raya Barat Boulevard

Jalan Pegangsaan Dua

Toll Road

Kelapa Gading

Jalan Perintis Kemerdekaan

Jalan Daan Mogot

6

Tomang

Jalan Tomang Raya

Banjir Canal

5

Senen

Jalan Suprapto

To Merak

Toll Road

Jalan Perjuangan

Grogol Canal

Sebrestang

See Central Jakarta Map p184

Gambir

8

Jalan Abdul Muis

Jalan Husni Thamrin

Menteng

9

Jalan Kramat Raya

Jalan Pramuka

Pulo Mas

10

Jalan Bekasi Raya

Slipi

7

Jalan Diponegoro

Jalan Matraman Raya

Rawamangun

Pesanggrahan

Jalan Perjuangan Panjang

Senayan

13

12

Toll Road

11

Jalan Rangkuti Rasuna Said

Karet

Jalan Matraman Raya

Jatinegara

Jalan Asia Afrika

14 15

18

17

16

Jalan Jenderal Sudirman

Manggarai

Jalan Ciledug Raya

19

Kebayoran Baru

20

21

Jalan Wolter Monginsidi

Gatot Subroto (Toll Road)

Kuningan

Tebet

Jalan Inspeksi Saluran

Cawang

Halim

To Bekasi

Outer Ring Toll Road

22

Jalan Panglima Polim

Kali Krukut

Cililitan

Halim Perdana Kusuma Airport

23

Pondok Indah

Jalan Metro Pondok Indah

Jalan Pangeran Antasari

24

Jalan Warung Jati Barat

Jalan Raya Pasar Minggu

Condet

Jalan Raya Pondok Gede

Jalan Ciputat Raya

Jalan Rempoa

25

Jalan Fatmawati

Cilandak

Jalan Bambu Raya

Jalan Bogor

Taman Mini Indonesia Indah

Ragunan Zoo

Ragunan

Kali Ciliwung

26

Jalan Jagorawi (Toll Road)

Outer Ring Toll Road

To Bogor

JAVA

HISTORY

Jakarta's earliest history is centred around the port of Sunda Kelapa, in the north of the Kota district of present-day Jakarta. When the Portuguese arrived in 1522, Sunda Kelapa was a bustling port of the Pajajaran dynasty, the last Hindu kingdom of West Java.

The Portuguese had sought to establish a concession in the spice trade but they were driven out by Sunan Gunungjati, the Muslim saint and leader of Demak who took Sunda Kelapa in 1527. He renamed the city Jayakarta, meaning 'victorious city', and it became a fiefdom of the Banten sultanate. None of the structures of this old town remain.

At the beginning of the 17th century both Dutch and English merchants had trading posts in Jayakarta. They jostled for power and exploited the intrigue between local rulers. Late in 1618 the Jayakartans, backed by the British, besieged the Dutch Vereenigde Oost-Indische Compagnie (VOC or United East India Company) fortress. Banten was upset by the unauthorised agreement between the British and the vassal Jayakartans, and sent a force to recall the Jayakartan leader. The Dutch celebrated their temporary reprieve and renamed their fortress 'Batavia'.

In May 1619 the Dutch, under Jan Pieterszoon Coen, stormed the town and reduced it to ashes. A stronger shoreline fortress was built and Batavia eventually became the capital of the Dutch East Indies. It was successfully defended on a number of occasions, first against Banten in the west and then Mataram in the east. Mataram's Sultan Agung attacked Batavia in 1628. The Javanese suffered enormous losses and finally withdrew after executing their failed commanders. Agung's second siege in 1629 was an even greater debacle and Batavia was never again threatened by an army of Mataram.

Within the walls of Batavia, the prosperous Dutch built tall stuffy houses and pestilential canals on virtual swampland, and by the early 18th century Batavia was suffering growing pains. Indonesians and especially Chinese flocked to the city, attracted by its commercial prospects. The government tried to restrict Chinese migration to the overburdened city and tensions began to grow. Deportations followed and Chinese gangs created unrest and attacked outposts outside the city.

On 9 October 1740, after the government ordered a search of Chinese premises for weapons, the good citizens of Batavia went berserk and massacred 5000 Chinese within the city. A year later Chinese inhabitants were moved to Glodok, outside the city walls. Other Batavians, discouraged by the severe epidemics between 1735 and 1780, also moved and the city began to spread far south of the port. The Koningsplein, now Merdeka Square, was finished in 1818 and Merdeka Palace in 1879; Kebayoran Baru was the last residential area to be laid out by the Dutch after WWII.

Dutch colonial rule came to an end when the Japanese occupied Java and the name 'Jakarta' was restored to the city. The republican government of the revolution retreated to Yogyakarta when the Dutch returned after the war, but in 1950, after Indonesian independence was finally secured, Jakarta was made the capital of the new republic.

In 1945 Jakarta had a population of 900,000, but since then a continual influx of migrants from depressed rural areas have crowded into the urban slums. Today the population is over nine million, or 17.5 million including the surrounding districts that form greater Jakarta.

Soekarno's image of Jakarta was of a city of grand structures that would glorify the republic and make Jakarta a world centre. The 14 storey Hotel Indonesia broke the skyline, the six lane Jl Thamrin was constructed and a massive sports stadium was erected for the 1962 Asian Games. Work on Jakarta's massive mosque began and the National Monument (Monas) took root.

With Soekarno's architectural ambitions cut short in 1965, the job of sorting out the city was left to Lieutenant General Ali Sadikin, governor of Jakarta from 1966 to 1977. Although he is credited with rehabilitating the roads and bridges, building several hospitals and a large number of new schools, he also began the campaign of ruthlessly cleaning up the city by clearing out slum dwellers, and banning becaks and street peddlers. He also started controlling migration to the city, to stem hopeless overcrowding and poverty.

Jakarta's astonishing growth and prosperity in the 1990s seemed destined to continue until the sudden economic collapse of 1997. With the economy in tatters, the capital became a battleground for new political aspirations. Student protests demanding Soeharto's resignation increased in intensity in the early months of 1998, but the army sent tanks on to the streets of Jakarta, determined that the riots and looting that had plagued other parts of Indonesia would not happen in Jakarta.

Then on 12 May 1998, the army cracked down on students and opened fired with live ammunition, killing four students at Trisakti University. Jakarta erupted in three days of rioting as thousands took to the streets to vent their anger or simply to loot. Over 6000 buildings were damaged or destroyed, and an estimated 1200 people died, mostly those trapped in burning shopping centres. The Chinese were hit the hardest, with shocking tales of rape and murder emerging after the riots, and businesses looted and destroyed. Jakarta's Chinatown around Glodok looked like a bomb site.

The riots lead to the overthrow of Soeharto and the promise of a more democratic Indonesia but the students returned to the streets when the government stalled on full reform. New riots erupted on 13 November 1998 when student demonstrations were met by military force and gunfire again. Clashes left 12 dead, hundreds injured and the city in flames.

ORIENTATION

Jakarta sprawls over 25km from the docks to the suburbs of south Jakarta, covering 661 sq km in all. The city centre fans out from around Merdeka Square, which contains the central landmark of Soekarno's towering gold-tipped National Monument. Merdeka Square itself is just a barren, deserted field, a product of grand urban planning gone wrong. Jakarta's main problem is that it doesn't really have a centre that can be explored on foot, but a number of centres, all separated by vast traffic jams and heat.

For most visitors, Jakarta revolves around the modern part of the city to the south of the monument. Jl Thamrin runs from the southwest corner of Merdeka Square down to the Welcome Monument roundabout and is the main thoroughfare, containing many of the big hotels and a couple of major shopping centres – the Sarinah department store and the Plaza Indonesia.

Just east of Jl Thamrin and south of the National Monument is Jl Jaksa, the main centre for cheap hotels and restaurants.

North of the National Monument, the old city of Kota is Jakarta's main tourist attraction and nearby is the schooner harbour of Sunda Kelapa. The modern harbour, Tanjung Priok, is several kilometres along the coast to the east past the Taman Impian Jaya Ancol recreation park.

The main train station, Gambir, is just to the east of the National Monument. The intercity bus terminals – Kalideres in the west, Kampung Rambutan in the south and Pulo Gadung in the east – are on the outskirts of Jakarta.

To the south, Jl Thamrin becomes Jl Jenderal Sudirman, which is home to more hotels, large banks and office blocks. Further south are the affluent suburban areas of Kebayoran Baru, Pondok Indah and Kemang, with their own centres and busy shopping districts, such as Blok M in Kebayoran Baru.

INFORMATION
Tourist Offices

The Jakarta Visitor Information Office (☎ 3142067) is opposite the Sarinah department store in the Jakarta Theatre building on Jl Thamrin. It can answer most queries and has a good giveaway map of Jakarta, and a number of excellent leaflets and publications. It is open Monday to Friday from 9 am to 5 pm and Saturday until noon. It also has a desk at the airport.

CENTRAL JAKARTA

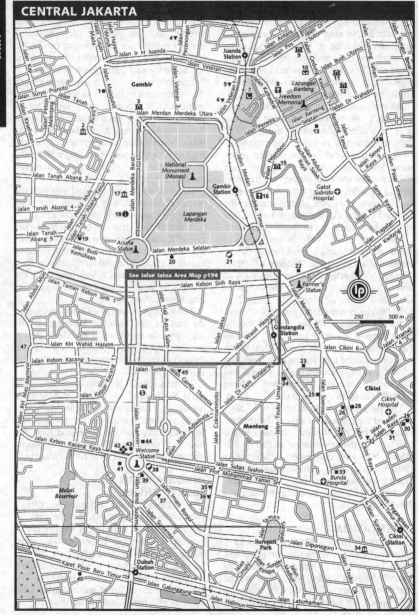

PLACES TO STAY		PLACES TO EAT		OTHER	
13	Borobudur Inter-Continental Jakarta	4	Jl Pecenongan Night Stalls	10	Main Post Office
22	Hotel Aryaduta	5	Queen's Tandoor	11	Mahkamah Agung
23	Gondia International Guesthouse	6	Sahara Restaurant	12	Ministry of Finance Building
		27	Art & Curio	14	Bharata Theatre
25	Hotel Menteng I	31	Oasis Bar & Restaurant	15	Gedung Pancasila
26	Hotel Alia Cikini	32	Raden Kuring Restaurant	16	Emanuel Church
29	Yannie International Guest House	35	Tamnak Thai	17	National Museum
		36	Gandy Steakhouse	18	Directorate-General of Tourism
30	Karya II Hotel	37	Lan Na Thai		
33	Hotel Marcopolo	45	Kafe Pisa	19	Tanamur (Disco)
39	Mandarin Oriental Jakarta; Zigolini; Harry's Bar			20	Garuda
		OTHER		21	US Embassy
40	Shangri-La Hotel; B.A.T.S	1	Smailing Tours	24	Immigration Office
		2	Taman Prasasti Museum	28	Taman Ismail Marzuki (TIM)
41	Hotel Indonesia	3	Istana Bogor	34	Adam Malik Museum
43	Grand Hyatt Jakarta	7	Istiqlal Mosque	38	British Embassy
44	President Hotel	8	Catholic Cathedral	42	Plaza Indonesia
		9	Gedung Kesenian Jakarta	46	BII Bank
				47	Pasar Tanah Abang

The headquarters of the Indonesia Tourist Promotion Organisation is the Directorate-General of Tourism (☎ 3838221) at Jl Merdeka Barat 16-19. This is not the best place to have specific travel queries answered but it has some useful publications. It is open Monday to Friday from 8 am to 4 pm (on Friday there is a prayer break from 11.30 am to 1.30 pm) and Saturday until noon.

Immigration Office

There is a central immigration office (☎ 3909744) at Jl Teuku Umar 1 in Menteng.

Money

Jakarta is crawling with banks offering the best exchange rates in Indonesia, though it pays to shop around. Most banks are open Monday to Friday from 8 am to 4 pm and Saturday until 11 am.

Handy banks to Jl Jaksa are the Lippobank and Bank Duta on Jl Kebon Sirih, both with ATMs for MasterCard withdrawals. Jl Thamrin has plenty of banks, such as the Bank Internasional Indonesia (BII), where rates are usually very good and its ATMs offer cash advances on Visa and MasterCard.

The Plaza Indonesia has a selection of banks, including the BII bank in the basement level, which has an ATM and is open Mon-

day to Friday from 10 am to 6 pm and weekends until 3 pm. The Bank Dagang Negara Indonesia (BDNI) on the 1st level is open from 10 am to 9 pm, but rates are not as good.

Moneychangers generally have much poorer rates, but one that offers good rates for cash is PT Metro Jala Masino in the car park of the Jakarta Theatre building.

Post & Communications

The main post office and efficient poste-restante service is in the octagonal building behind Jl Pos, to the north-east of the National Monument. It's a half-hour walk from the city centre or take a No 12 bus from Jl Thamrin. The poste restante at counter 53 is open daily from 8 am to 6 pm. For basic postal services, a few windows are open extended hours until 10 pm daily.

Wartels (private telephone offices) are found throughout the city and are usually open daily from around 7 am until midnight, but are sometimes open 24 hours. As a rule, wartels don't offer a collect-call service. Convenient wartels for those staying around Jl Jaksa are the Duta Perdana Raya Wartel (☎ 3143310, fax 3190460), Jl Jaksa 15a, and the Sapta Persona Wartel, Jl Kebon Sirih Dalam 41, which is near the Borneo Hostel.

Faxes can be sent from most wartels and all major hotels.

Email & Internet Access The Warung Pos Internet at the main post office has a bank of terminals that cost 2000Rp for 15 minutes or 9500Rp per hour. It is open weekdays from 8 am to 9 pm, Saturday until 7 pm and Sunday until 4 pm.

The Duta Perana Raya wartel also has a couple of terminals for 10,000Rp per hour. Click! at Jl Jaksa 29, is an Internet cafe that offers access at 8000Rp per 10 minute periods, 15,000Rp per 30 minutes and 22,000Rp per hour.

Almost all hotel business centres offer Internet connection at high rates.

Travel Agencies
The travel agencies on Jl Jaksa are convenient places to start looking for international flights; try Robertu Kencana Travel (☎ 3142926) at Jl Jaksa 20B. Plenty of other agents along Jl Jaksa also sell domestic air and bus tickets as well as tours.

Domestic air tickets usually cost the same at a travel agent as at the airline, but discounts are sometimes available. Raptim Tours & Travel (☎ 335585), Jl Cut Mutiah 8, just to the east of Jl Jaksa, is good for discount ticketing, tours and hotels. Smailing Tours (☎ 3800022), Jl Majapahit 28, is past the National Museum on the way to Kota and is one of Jakarta's biggest travel agents. It also has an office in the Skyline building (☎ 331994), Jl Thamrin 9, just next to the tourist office.

Bookshops
Times Bookshop in the Plaza Indonesia on Jl Thamrin, and another in the Pondok Indah Mall, has one of the best stocks of English-language and travel books.

Books Kinokuniya is also excellent, and is upstairs at Level 2B of the Sogo department store in the Plaza Indonesia.

Sarinah department store on Jl Thamrin has a good travel book and map section. Gramedia and Gunung Agung are the two big Indonesian chains with shops all over town.

Newspapers
The daily English-language *Jakarta Post* (1800Rp from street vendors) gives a useful rundown of what's on, temporary exhibitions and cinema programs.

Photography
Jl Agus Salim, between Jl Jaksa and Jl Thamrin, has photographic shops for film, developing and equipment, but 'tourist prices' may apply and bargaining might be necessary. Otherwise, Jakarta has plenty of places for film developing. Fuji is the most common brand of film and the Plaza Indonesia has a Fuji shop, which is good for supplies and developing.

Libraries & Useful Organisations
The various foreign cultural centres have libraries and/or regular exhibits, films and lectures:

American Cultural Centre
   (☎ 5262834) Wisma Metropolitan II, Jl Jenderal Sudirman
Australian Cultural Centre
   (☎ 5227093) Australian embassy, Jl Rasuna Said Kav C15-16
British Council
   (☎ 5206222) Widjoyo Centre, Jl Jenderal Sudirman 71
Centre Culture Français
   (☎ 3908585) Jl Salemba Raya 25
Erasmus Huis
   (☎ 5252321) Jl Rasuna Said Kav S-3; beside the Dutch embassy. It has a Dutch library and a regular program of cultural events.
Goethe Institut
   (☎ 8581139) Jl Mataram Raya 23
Indonesian/American Cultural Center (Perhimpunan Persahabatan Indonesia Amerika)
   (☎ 8583241) Jl Pramuka Kav 30. It has exhibits, films and lectures related to Indonesia, and a library.

Dangers & Annoyances
For a city with such a huge population and obvious social problems, Jakarta is surprisingly safe. That said, Jakarta is the most crime-prone city in Indonesia and violent crime, almost unheard of in the rest of the country, is reported and on the increase. Take the usual precautions – avoid disreputable

areas and don't walk the streets alone at night. Muggings by taxi drivers have been reported; those alone and drunk in the early hours of the morning seem to be most at risk. The overwhelming majority of taxis are safe, however, and you are better off taking a taxi than walking the streets alone at night.

Jakarta's buses and trains tend to be hopelessly crowded, particularly during rush hours. Pickpockets are notoriously adept and they're great bag slashers too. So take care.

KOTA

The old town of Batavia, known as Kota today, is the oldest and finest reminder of the Dutch presence in Indonesia. At one time it contained Coen's massive shoreline fortress, the Kasteel, and was surrounded by a sturdy defensive wall and a moat. In the early 19th century Governor General Daendels did a good job of demolishing much of the unhealthy city, but there is still a Dutch flavour to this old part of the town. A few of Batavia's old buildings remain in active use, although others were restored during the 1970s and have become museums.

The centre of old Batavia is the cobblestone square known as **Taman Fatahillah**. A block west of the square is the **Kali Besar**, the great canal along Sungai Ciliwung (Ciliwung River). This was once a high-class residential area and on the west bank are the last of the homes that date from the early 18th century. The **Toko Merah** (Red Shop) was formerly the home of Governor General van Imhoff and is now occupied by the Dharma Niaga company. At the north end of the Kali Besar is the last remaining Dutch drawbridge, which dates from the 17th century and is called the **Chicken Market Bridge**.

To reach Taman Fatahillah, from Jl Thamrin you can take air-con bus Nos P-01 and P-10 or normal bus No P11. Alternatively you can take a city train from Gongandia, near Jl Jaksa, to Kota train station and walk. A taxi will cost around 5000Rp from Jl Thamrin.

Jakarta History Museum

The Jakarta History Museum is housed in the old town hall of Batavia, which is on the south side of Taman Fatahillah. It's probably one of the most solid reminders of Dutch rule within Indonesia. This bell-towered hall, built in 1627 and added to between 1707 and 1710, served the administration of the city. It was also used by the city law courts and its dungeons were the main prison compound of Batavia. In 1830 the Javanese hero Prince Diponegoro was imprisoned here for a time on his way into exile in Ujung Pandang.

Today it contains lots of heavy, carved furniture and other memorabilia from the Dutch period. Among the more interesting exhibits are early pictures of Batavia and a series of gloomy portraits of all the Dutch governor generals.

In the courtyard at the back of the building is a strange memorial stone to one Pieter Erbervelt, who was put to death in 1722 for allegedly conspiring to massacre the Dutch inhabitants of Batavia.

Admission is 1000Rp. It opens daily, except Monday, from 9 am to 3 pm (Friday until 2.30 pm and Saturday until 12.30 pm).

Wayang Museum

Also on Taman Fatahillah, this museum has one of the best collections of wayang puppets in Java, and includes puppets not only from Indonesia but also China, Malaysia, India and Cambodia.

Formerly the Museum of Old Batavia, the building itself was constructed in 1912 on the site of the Dutch Church of Batavia, which was demolished by Daendels in 1808. In the downstairs courtyard there are memorials to the Dutch governor generals once buried here. These include Jan Pieterszoon Coen, founder of Batavia, who died of cholera in 1629 during the siege by Mataram, and Anthony van Diemen, the governor general after whom Abel Tasman named Van Diemen's Land (Tasmania, Australia).

Admission and opening hours are the same as the Jakarta History Museum.

Balai Seni Rupa (Fine Arts Museum)

Built between 1866 and 1870, the Palace of Justice building is now a museum. It houses

JAVA

SUNDA KELAPA & KOTA

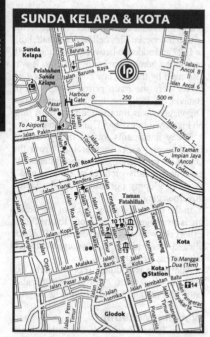

SUNDA KELAPA & KOTA

1   Phinisi Cafe
2   Luar Batang Mosque
3   Museum Bahari (Maritime Museum)
4   Watchtower
5   VOC Shipyards
6   Chicken Market Bridge
7   Omni Batavia Hotel
8   Toko Merah
9   Wayang Museum
10 Cafe Batavia
11 Cannon Si Jagur
12 Balai Seni Rupa (Fine Arts Museum)
13 Jakarta History Museum
14 Gereja Sion

contemporary paintings with works by prominent painters, including Affandi, Raden Saleh and Ida Bagus Made. Part of the building is also a ceramics museum, with Chinese ceramics and Majapahit terracottas.

Admission and opening hours are as per the Jakarta History Musuem.

Cannon Si Jagur

This huge bronze cannon on Taman Fatahillah is adorned with a Latin inscription, *'Ex me ipsa renata sum'*, which means 'Out of myself I was reborn'. The cannon tapers at one end into a large clenched fist, with the thumb protruding between the index and middle fingers. This suggestive fist is a sexual symbol in Indonesia, and childless women would offer flowers and sit astride the cannon in the hope of gaining children. Si Jagur is a Portuguese cannon brought to Batavia as a trophy of war after the fall of Melaka in 1641.

Gereja Sion

On Jl Pangeran Jayakarta, near Kota train station, this church dates from 1695 and is the oldest remaining church in Jakarta. Also known as Gereja Portugis (Portuguese Church), it was built just outside the old city walls for the so-called 'black Portuguese' – the Eurasians and natives captured from Portuguese trading ports in India and Malaya and brought to Batavia as slaves. Most of these people were Catholics, but they were given their freedom on the condition that they joined the Dutch Reformed Church. The converts became known as the Mardijkers (Liberated Ones).

The exterior of the church is very plain but inside there are copper chandeliers, the original organ and a Baroque pulpit. Although in the year 1790 alone, more than 2000 people were buried in the graveyard here, very few tombs remain. One of the most interesting is the ornate bronze tombstone of Governor General Zwaardecroon, who died in 1728 and, as was his wish, was buried among the 'ordinary' folk.

SUNDA KELAPA

Just a 10 minute walk north of Taman Fatahillah, the old port of Sunda Kelapa has many magnificent Macassar schooners *(pinisi)*. These brightly painted sailing ships are one of the finest sights in Jakarta. The ships are still an important means of transporting goods to and from the outer islands. Most of them come from Kalimantan, spending up to a week in port unloading timber, then reloading cement and other supplies for the return journey.

Entry to the dock costs 250Rp. The guides that hang around can provide some interesting insights and spin a few yarns for a bargainable price. You can also take a row boat around the schooners and across to the Pasar Ikan (Fish Market) for around 5000Rp to 6000Rp. From the Pasar Ikan you can take the footbridge to the Luar Batang mosque.

Museum Bahari (Maritime Museum)

Near the entrance to Sunda Kelapa, an old VOC warehouse built in 1645 has been turned into a maritime museum. It exhibits craft from around Indonesia and also has an interesting collection of old photographs recreating the voyage to Jakarta from Europe via Aden, Ceylon and Singapore. The building itself is worth a visit and the sentry posts outside are part of the old city wall. Admission and opening hours are the same as the Jakarta History Museum.

Just before the entrance to the museum is the old **watchtower** back near the bridge. It was built in 1839 to sight and direct traffic to the port. There are good views over the harbour, but opening hours are haphazard – ask for the caretaker if it is closed. Admission is 1000Rp.

Further along the same street from the museum is the early-morning fish market, **Pasar Ikan**. It's an intense, colourful scene of busy crowds around dawn, when the day's catch is sold. Later in the day it sells household items and a growing collection of souvenirs.

GLODOK

After the Chinese massacre of 1740, the Dutch decided there would be no repetition and prohibited all Chinese from residing within the town walls, or even from being there after sundown. In 1741 a tract of land just to the south-west of Batavia was allocated as Chinese quarters. The area became

Glodok, Jakarta's Chinatown, and the city's flourishing commercial centre.

Over two centuries later the Chinese were subjected to senseless violence again. The Jakarta riots of May and November 1998 destroyed much of the area as rioters went on the rampage, pillaging and looting shops, and then burning the buildings. It will be years before the scars are erased and the burnt buildings replaced.

Glodok is bounded to the east by Jl Gajah Mada, a busy commercial thoroughfare, but if you walk in from Jl Pancoran, old Glodok still consists of winding lanes, narrow crooked houses with balconies, slanting red-tiled roofs and tiny obscure shops. Just south of Jl Pancoran is the Chinese **Dharma Jaya Temple**, which was built in 1650.

Businesses carry on as best they can, but many have moved. Perversely, the chief reason for visiting Glodok nowadays would be to take a look at the evidence of the Jakarta riots.

NATIONAL MUSEUM

On the west side of Merdeka Square, the National Museum, built in 1862, is the best museum in Indonesia and one of the finest in South-East Asia. Its collection includes a huge ethnic map of Indonesia and an equally big relief map on which you can pick out all those volcanoes you have climbed.

The museum has an enormous collection of cultural objects of the various ethnic groups – costumes, musical instruments, model houses and so on – and numerous fine bronzes from the Hindu-Javanese period, as well as many interesting stone pieces salvaged from Central Javanese and other temples. There's also a superb display of Chinese ceramics dating back to the Han dynasty (300 BC to 220 AD), which was almost entirely amassed in Indonesia.

One of the best places to start a tour of the museum is the Treasure Room upstairs from the entrance. The gold exhibits are interesting, but if you walked to the museum the real attraction is the air-conditioning.

Just outside the museum is a bronze elephant that was presented by the King of

Thailand in 1871; thus the museum building is popularly known as the Gedung Gajah (Elephant House).

The museum is open daily, except Monday, from 8.30 am to 2.30 pm (Friday until 11 am and Saturday until 1.30 pm). Entry costs 750Rp. Conducted tours in a number of languages are organised by the Indonesian Heritage Society (☎ 360551 ext 22).

OTHER MUSEUMS

Jakarta has a number of other museums apart from the excellent National Museum and those in old Batavia. North-west of the National Museum is the **Taman Prasasti Museum** (Park of Inscription), on Jl Tanah Abang. Once the Kebon Jahe Cemetery, important figures of the colonial era are buried here, including Olivia Raffles (wife of British Governor General Sir Stamford Raffles) who died in 1814. It is open Tuesday to Thursday and Sunday from 9 am to 3 pm, Friday until 2.30 pm and Saturday until 12.30 pm.

The **Textile Museum** is in a Dutch colonial house on Jl Satsuit Tubun 4, near the Tanah Abang train station. It is open Tuesday to Thursday and Sunday from 9 am until 3 pm, Friday until 2.30 pm and Saturday until 12.30 pm. Admission is 1000Rp. The building is certainly worth a look, but the Museum Purna Bhakti Pertiwi at Taman Mini has a much better permanent exhibition of Indonesian textiles.

In the old-money suburb of Menteng, the **Adam Malik Museum**, Jl Diponegoro 29, was the home of the former vice-president and foreign minister. This Dutch villa houses his private art collection, and you can poke around the man's bedroom and even his bathroom, which remains much as he left it in 1984. This excellent museum is open daily, except Monday, from 9 am to 3 pm.

NATIONAL MONUMENT (MONAS)

This 132m high column towering over Merdeka Square is both Jakarta's principal landmark and the most famous architectural extravagance of Soekarno. Commenced in 1961, the monument was not completed until 1975, when it was officially opened by Soeharto. This phallic symbol topped by a glittering flame symbolises the nation's independence and strength (and, some would argue, Soekarno's virility). The National Monument is constructed 'entirely of Italian marbles', according to a tourist brochure and the flame is gilded with 35kg of gold leaf.

In the base of the National Monument, the **National History Museum** tells the history of Indonesia's independence struggle in 48 dramatic dioramas. The numerous uprisings against the Dutch are overstated but interesting, Soekarno is barely mentioned and the events surrounding the 1965 coup are a whitewash.

The highlight of a visit is to take the lift to the top for dramatic, though rarely clear, views of Jakarta. Avoid Sunday and holidays when the queues for the lift are long.

The National Monument is open daily from 9 am to 5 pm. Admission is 600Rp to the museum in the base, or 3100Rp including the ride to the top of the monument.

LAPANGAN BANTENG

Just east of Merdeka Square in front of the Borobudur Inter-Continental Hotel, Lapangan Banteng Square (formerly the Weltevreden) was laid out by the Dutch in the 19th century, and the area has some of Jakarta's best colonial architecture.

The **Catholic cathedral** has twin spires and was built in 1901 to replace an earlier church. Facing the cathedral is Jakarta's principal place of Muslim worship, the modernistic **Istiqlal mosque**, which was constructed under Soekarno and is reputedly the largest mosque in South-East Asia.

To the east of Lapangan Banteng is the **Mahkamah Agung** (Supreme Court), built in 1848, and next door is the **Ministry of Finance** building, formerly the Witte Huis (White House). This grand government complex was built by Daendels in 1809 as the administration centre for the Dutch government.

To the south-west, on Jl Pejambon, is the **Gedung Pancasila**, which is an imposing neoclassical building built in 1830 as the

Dutch army commander's residence. It later became the meeting hall of the Volksraad (People's Council), but is best known as the place where Soekarno made his famous Pancasila speech in 1945, laying the foundation for Indonesia's constitution. Just west along Jl Pejambon from Gedung Pancasila is the **Emanuel Church**, which is another classic building, dating from 1893.

TAMAN MINI INDONESIA INDAH

In the city's south-east, near Kampung Rambutan, Taman Mini is one of those 'whole country in one park' collections popular in Asia. The idea for the park was conceived by Madame Tien Soeharto. In 1971 the families inhabiting the land were cleared out to make way for the project (then estimated to cost the awesome total of US$26 million) and the park was opened in 1975.

This 100 hectare park has 27 full-scale traditional houses from the 27 provinces of Indonesia, with displays of regional handicrafts and clothing, and a large 'lagoon' where you can row around the islands of the archipelago or take a cable car across for a bird's eye view. There are also a host of museums, theatres, restaurants, an orchid garden and a bird park with a huge walk-in aviary. There's even a mini Borobudur. The park is quite good value and Indonesians will tell you that if you see this there's no need to go anywhere else in the country!

Other attractions include Keong Mas (Golden Snail Theatre) with its huge Imax screen. Admission is 4000Rp and screenings are every couple of hours.

You can walk or drive your own car around Taman Mini. Free shuttle buses go regularly, or take the monorail (3000Rp) or the cable car (1000Rp) that goes from one end to the other. Bicycles can be hired for 1000Rp per half-hour. Free cultural performances are staged in a selected regional house, usually around 10 am and sometimes in the afternoons. Sunday is the big day for cultural events but shows are also held during the week. Check the Taman Mini monthly program available from the Visitors Information Centre or ring ☎ 840 9237.

Taman Mini is open daily from 8 am to 5 pm, and the houses and Museum Indonesia are open from 9 am to 4 pm. Admission is 2500Rp (children 1500Rp).

Taman Mini is about 18km from the city centre; allow about 1½ hours to get there and at least three hours to look around. Take any bus to Kampung Rambutan terminal (air-con, patas bus Nos 9,10 and 11 run from Jl Thamrin) and then a T15 metro-mini to the park entrance. A taxi is much quicker and will cost around 18,000Rp from central Jakarta, plus another 4000Rp for the toll roads.

TAMAN IMPIAN JAYA ANCOL

Along the bay front between Kota and Tanjung Priok, the people's 'Dreamland' is built on land reclaimed in 1962. This huge landscaped recreation park, providing non-stop entertainment, has hotels, nightclubs, theatres and a variety of sporting facilities.

Taman Impian Jaya Ancol's prime attractions include the **Pasar Seni** (Art Market), which has sidewalk cafes, a host of craft shops, art exhibitions, and live music on Friday and Saturday nights. The **Seaworld** aquarium with its walk-through tunnel, a variety of pools and big array of sea life is worth seeing. Ancol also has the **Gelanggang Samudra**, another oceanarium with a boat ride and dolphin shows, and the impressive **Gelanggang Renang** swimming pool complex, which includes a wave pool and slide pool. **Ancol Beach** is close to the city and is not the greatest place for a swim, but you can take a boat from the marina for day trips to some of the Pulau Seribu islands.

The big drawcard at Ancol is **Dunia Fantasi** (Fantasy Land), a fun park that must have raised eyebrows at the Disney legal department. Resemblances to Disneyland start at the 'main street' entrance and the Puppet Castle is a straight 'it's a small world' replica. Dunia Fantasi is actually very well done and great for kids, with a host of fun rides. It's open Monday to Thursday from 11 am to 6 pm, Friday from 2 to 9 pm and weekends from 10 am to 9 pm. Entry costs 21,000Rp on weekdays and 25,000Rp on weekends (not including entry to Ancol).

Basic admission to Ancol is 2500Rp on weekdays and 3000Rp on weekends. The park is open 24 hours but all the attractions have their own opening hours and cost extra, except for the Pasar Seni, which is free. Student discounts are offered. For more information call ☎ 681511. The park can be very crowded on weekends, but on weekdays it's fairly quiet and a great place to escape from the hassles of the city.

Take a bus or city train to Kota train station, then bus No 64 or 65, or mikrolet No M15. A taxi will cost around 10,000Rp from Jl Thamrin.

RAGUNAN ZOO

Jakarta's Ragunan Zoo is 10km south of the city centre in the Pasar Minggu area. Apart from the usual exotica, this large zoo has a good collection of Indonesian wildlife including Komodo dragons and orang-utans. It's not San Diego or even Singapore but this is by far the best zoo in Indonesia and, though some of the enclosures are depressingly small, for the most part Ragunan is spacious. You can spend a couple of hours wandering around the extensive grounds, which have some remaining stands of bamboo and rainforest flora, and a landscaped lake. It's open daily from 7.30 am to 6 pm. Admission is 1000Rp for adults and half-price for children. From Jl Thamrin take bus No 19.

OTHER ATTRACTIONS

Indonesia's independence was proclaimed at **Gedung Perintis Kemerdekaan**, Jl Proklamasi 56, in Menteng, on the site of the former home of Soekarno. A monument to president Soekarno and vice president Hatta marks the spot.

The **Pasar Burung** on Jl Pramuka in Jatinegara is Jakarta's market for captive birds from all over Indonesia.

Taman Ria Senayan is a family recreation park with fairground rides. It's near the Olympic Stadium in Senayan, on the corner of Jl Jenderal Gatot Subroto and Jl Gerbang Pemuda. This new complex is built around an attractively landscaped laguna (lagoon) and is quite impressive, but best of all are the restaurant complexes, which have an excellent range of dining options and bars. Opening hours are Monday to Friday from 3 to 10 pm and weekends from 10 am to 10 pm. Access to the restaurants is separate and they stay open longer hours. Entry costs 4000Rp (3000Rp for children), or a 15,000Rp ticket includes entry and most of the rides.

SWIMMING

The swimming pools at Ancol are great, and some hotels let nonguests use their facilities. The Hotel Indonesia has a large pool costing 12,500Rp for nonguests (17,500Rp on weekends).

ORGANISED TOURS

Numerous travel agents offer daily tours of Jakarta, but they tend to be expensive. Bookings can be made through the tourist office and major hotels. Boca Pirento, Panorama and Buana are the main operators. All tour buses pick up from the major hotels, and tour prices and sights are very similar. A four hour morning city tour, for example, costs US$20 and includes the National Museum, National Monument, Sunda Kelapa and Kota.

There are also a variety of tours to nearby towns in West Java that basically go to Bogor, the Puncak Pass and Tangkuban Prahu volcano near Bandung. An eight hour tour to the Bogor botanical gardens and zoological museum costs US$35. A tour to the Puncak Pass costs US$40.

SPECIAL EVENTS

The Jakarta Anniversary on 22 June marks the establishment of the city by Gunungjati back in 1527, and is celebrated with fireworks and the Jakarta Fair. The latter is a fairground event held at the Jakarta Fair Grounds, north-east of the city centre in Kemayoran, from late June until mid-July.

The Jl Jaksa Street Fair features Betawi dance, theatre and music, as well as popular modern performances. Street stalls sell food and souvenirs, and art and photography exhibits are also staged. It is held for one week in August.

Indonesia's independence day is 17 August and the parades in Jakarta are the biggest in the country.

PLACES TO STAY

Jakarta is the most expensive city in Indonesia for hotels, but in US dollar terms it has to be one of the world's cheapest cities. The economic meltdown and a drop in tourism has seen big discounts available, especially at mid-range and top-end hotels.

Places to Stay – Budget

Jl Jaksa Area This strip of cheap hotels and restaurants is the main budget accommodation area. It's conveniently located near Jakarta's main drag, Jl Thamrin, and is a 10 to 15 minute walk from Gambir train station.

Wisma Delima (☎ 3923850, *Jl Jaksa 5*) was the original guesthouse and used to be hopelessly crowded and totally chaotic. Now it is quieter but still very hospitable and well run, even if a little down at heel. Dorm beds cost 9000Rp (1000Rp less for YHA/Hostelling International (HI) members) and singles/doubles with shared mandi are 15,000/ 20,000Rp. Food and cold drinks are available, and it has good travel information.

Norbek Hostel (☎ 330392, *Jl Jaksa 14*) is a dark rabbit warren with a big variety of plywood-walled rooms from 15,000Rp to 40,000Rp with attached bathroom.

Nearby is the *Jusran Hostel* (☎ 3140373, *Jl Kebon Sirih Barat VI 9*). Cramped, plywood rooms for 15,000/20,000Rp may be uninspiring but this is a cosy, friendly place.

Nick's Corner Hostel (☎ 3141988, *16 Jl Jaksa*) is a more substantial, air-con hostel, but standards have slipped. A bed costs 10,000Rp in cramped dorms, or dark and depressing rooms downstairs cost 25,000Rp to 37,000Rp. Upstairs air-con rooms with bathroom are much brighter and cost 47,000Rp and 65,000Rp, but need a good scrub.

Djody Hotel (☎ 3151404, *Jl Jaksa 35*) is another old stand-by that has lost its shine. It has a pleasant cafe, but the rooms are dreary and overpriced (even though they are more substantial than the hostel's) at 15,500/ 27,500Rp, to 55,000Rp with bathroom and

air-con. The *Djody Hostel* (*Jl Jaksa 27*) is the hotel's even drearier offshoot. The rooms are none-too-clean, it's noisy when it fills up and the showers run murky brown water. Singles/ doubles/triples with shared bathroom cost 16,000/22,400/35,000Rp.

Hotel Tator (☎ 323940, *Jl Jaksa 37*) is one of the few that lies somewhere between budget and mid-range. It has a good little cafe and other touches that set it apart but some rooms are dark and musty. The rooms have showers and toilets for 30,000/45,000Rp, or 55,000Rp with air-con and telephone, and 60,000Rp with hot water (if you're lucky).

More places can be found in the small alleys running off Jl Jaksa. Gang 1 is home to two small, quiet places: the *Kresna Homestay* (☎ 325403) at No 175; and the *Bloem Steen Homestay* (☎ 325389) next door at No 173. They're a bit cramped, but reasonable value for Jakarta. The Kresna has older rooms for 20,000/25,000Rp without/with mandi; the Bloem Steen is a touch better and has singles/doubles for 20,000/25,000Rp with shared mandi.

Just west off Jl Jaksa, *Borneo Hostel* (☎ 320095, *Jl Kebon Sirih Barat I, No 35*) is popular and friendly, with rooms from 20,000Rp up to 35,000Rp with mandi. The spartan but airy rooms in the same building as the cafe are best. The annexe next door is dank and dungeon-like with dripping plumbing and scurrying cockroaches.

Other places are dotted along this lane, such as *Bintang Kejora* (☎ 323878, *Jl Kebon Sirih Barat 52*), which has very clean rooms for 15,000/20,000Rp or 35,000Rp with mandi. *Hotel Rita*, *Pondok Wisata Kebon Sirih* and *Pondok Wisata Jaya Hostel* are all uncomfortably close to the mosque and an early morning wakeup call.

Just past Hostel Rita, turn left down the alleyway and follow the sign to *Lia's Hostel* (☎ 3162708) in the middle of the kampung at Jl Kebon Sirih Barat 8 No 47. It has a pleasant garden pavilion for sipping coffee and a hip, switched-on manager. This small hostel packs in the rooms but they're well kept and cost 20,000Rp and 25,000Rp without mandi, or 30,000Rp with mandi.

JAVA

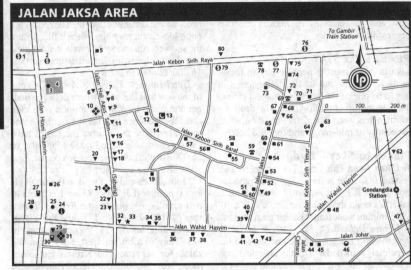

JALAN JAKSA AREA

To Gambir
Train Station

Jalan Kebon Sirih Raya

0   100   200 m

Places to Stay – Mid-Range

Jl Jaksa Area *Hotel Le Margot* (☎ 391 3830, Jl Jaksa 15) is a relatively new hotel with small but well appointed rooms for 115,500Rp (including tax and service). The service is not a strong point but it is good value.

Hotel Karya (☎ 3140484, Jl Jaksa 32-4) has been recently renovated and is the best on Jl Jaksa. The rooms are well furnished and it has a good restaurant. Posted rates of US$70 are discounted to 125,000Rp and 150,000Rp, making it a good option.

Jl Wahid Hasyim has a string of mid-range hotels. *Hotel Indra Internasional* (☎ 315 2858, Jl Jaksa 63) is the cheapest with well appointed but dark rooms for 140,000Rp to 200,000Rp.

The much more impressive *Arcadia Hotel* (☎ 2300050, Jl Jaksa 114) has modern decor and very comfortable rooms for US$90 and US$150, but even with a 50% discount it is still expensive. Its sister hotel, the *Ibis Tamarind* (☎ 3912323, Jl Wahid Hasyim 77), has a pool, fitness centre and bar. It is edging into the top end but is also overpriced at US$115 and US$160 per room, even with 50% discounts.

The *Cemara Hotel* (☎ 3149985, Jl Cemara 1) is on the corner of Jl Wahid Hasyim and is a popular hotel in this range, with good rooms and service. The rooms for 250,000Rp and 360,000Rp are competitively priced.

Next door, the *Hotel Bumi Johar* (☎ 314 5746, Jl Johar 17-19) is a small, new hotel with a Japanese restaurant. Excellent singles/doubles from 175,000/245,000Rp, even less with discount, make it one of the best buys.

The *Hotel Paragon* (☎ 3917070, Jl Wahid Hasyim 29) is a strangely designed multi-storey hotel with rooms fronting on to open corridors, but the rooms are immaculate and very good value at 165,000Rp after discount.

The *Sabang Metropolitan Hotel* (☎ 3857621, Jl Haji Agus Salim 11) is an old high-rise with a pool. Despite a recent facelift it is still dog-eared, but rooms from 140,000Rp are reasonably priced.

Cikini The Cikini area is east of Jl Thamrin and close to the TIM cultural centre, and

JAVA

JALAN JAKSA AREA

PLACES TO STAY		PLACES TO EAT		OTHER	
5	Sabang Metropolitan Hotel	6	HP Gardena	1	Bank Indonesia
12	Pondok Wisata Jaya Hostel	7	Mel's Drive-In	2	Bangkok Bank
		8	Bakwan Campur	3	Qantas Airways; Thai
14	Pondok Wisata Kebon Sirih	9	Sakura Anpan Bakery		Airways International
19	Lia's Hostel	11	Natrabu Padang Restaurant	4	BDN Building
26	Sari Pan Pacific Hotel	15	Sederhana Padang Resta-	10	Ramayana Department
34	Arcadia Hotel		raunt		Store
36	Hotel Indra Internasional	16	Sizzler	13	Mosque
37	Ibis Tamarind	17	Bakini Sabang	21	Robinson Department
41	Cipta Hotel	18	Hoka Hoka Bento		Store
44	Cemara Hotel	20	Paradiso 2001	24	Tourist Office; Jakarta
45	Hotel Bumi Johar	22	Dunkin' Donuts		Theatre;
48	Hotel Paragon	23	Lim Thiam Kie		Green Pub
50	Hotel Karya	29	McDonald's	25	Skyline Building
51	Hostel 36	32	Pho Hoa	27	Jaya Pub
52	Hotel Tator	35	Hazara	28	Jaya Building
53	Djody Hotel	38	Le Bistro	30	Hard Rock Cafe
56	Bintang Kejora	39	Mbak Merry	31	Sarinah Department Store
57	Hostel Rita	40	Romance Bar & Restaurant	33	Police Station
58	Borneo Hostel	42	Ayam Goreng Nyonya	46	Media Taxis
61	Djody Hostel		Suharti	54	Click! (Internet Cafe)
65	Nick's Corner Hostel	43	Tony Roma's	55	Mitra Marsada Utama
67	Norbek Hostel	47	Rendezvous	59	Arfina Margi Wisata
68	Hotel Le Margot;	49	Pappa Kafe		Travel
	Margot Cafe	62	Cahaya Kota	60	Roberto Kencana Travel
70	Bloem Steen Homestay	64	Pondok Ikan Gurame	63	Bimantara Building
71	Kresna Homestay	66	Warung Memori	69	RTQ Warparpostal
73	Jusran Hostel	72	Angie's Cafe	76	Bank Duta
74	Wisma Delima; BFC Cafe	75	Sate Khas Senayan	77	Lippobank
		80	Ikan Bakar Kebon Sirih	78	Telkom Wartel
			Restaurant	79	BNI Bank

has a selection of mid-range hotels and good guesthouses.

The **Gondia International Guesthouse** (☎ 3909221, Jl Gondia Kecil 22) is in a quiet side street off Jl Soeroso. Comfortable air-con rooms around a small garden area cost 140,000Rp, including breakfast. It has a pleasant, homey atmosphere.

A good value and deservedly popular guesthouse is **Yannie International Guest House** (☎ 3140012, Jl Raden Saleh Raya 35). There is no sign, just a 'Y' at the front. Very well kept rooms with air-con and hot water cost 84,000/96,000Rp for singles/doubles, including breakfast.

If the Yannie is full, the **Karya II Hotel** (☎ 3101380, Jl Raden Saleh Raya 37), next door, is cheap but drab, and has rooms from 66,000Rp to 105,000Rp.

The **Hotel Marcopolo** (☎ 2301777, Jl Teuku Cik Ditiro 19) is a quality, high-rise hotel and one of Jakarta's best options. Though old, the rooms are well maintained and it has a swimming pool, good service, and a restaurant for cheap buffet breakfasts and dinners. Well appointed rooms with fridge, TV and hot water cost from 149,000Rp, single or double.

Hotel Alia Cikini (☎ 3924444, Jl Cikini Raya 32) is opposite the TIM. Though new, it is already starting to fray, but is very good value with rooms for 115,000Rp and 127,000 Rp. The rooms have tiled rather than carpeted floors but are otherwise very well appointed. It also has a small, dirty swimming pool.

Airport The cheapest hotel near the airport is the **Hotel Bandara Jakarta** (☎ 6191964,

JAVA

Jl Jurumudi, Km 2.5, Cengkareng). There's nothing fancy about it – air-con rooms with bath start at US$35/48 for singles/doubles, and there's a 24 hour coffee shop. It usually has a representative at the airport hotel booths offering free transport and discounts as low as 89,000/99,000Rp for its rooms.

Places to Stay – Top End

The *Hotel Indonesia (☎ 2301008, fax 2301007, Jl Thamrin)* was built for the Asian Games that Jakarta hosted in 1962 and heralded a new era for hotel development in Indonesia. In 1965 it provided refuge for foreigners surrounded by the turmoil of Soekarno's 'year of living dangerously'. Increasingly shabby rooms start at US$130/140 for singles/doubles but are discounted to as little as 200,000Rp.

Also on the Welcome Statue roundabout, the opulent *Grand Hyatt Jakarta (☎ 3901234, fax 3906426)* is one of the city's best and sits above the Plaza Indonesia shopping centre. Rooms start at US$310.

Diagonally across from the Hyatt, the *Mandarin Oriental Jakarta (☎ 3141307, fax 3148680)* has rooms from US$180 to US$235. It has no grounds, but is an excellent business hotel and the well furnished rooms have good extras. The nearby *President Hotel (☎ 2301122, fax 3143631, Jl Thamrin 59)* is a smaller, fading luxury hotel with rooms from US$145/155.

The *Sari Pan Pacific Hotel (☎ 323707, fax 323650)* is conveniently located on Jl Thamrin around the corner from the Jakarta Theatre building. The rooms cost US$170/ 190 and US$200/220.

Just off Jl Jenderal Sudirman, the opulent *Shangri-La Hotel (☎ 5707440, fax 5703531, Jl Jenderal Sudirman Kav 1)* has rooms from US$245/275. Further south, the *Kempinski Hotel Plaza (☎ 2510888, fax 2511777, Jl Jenderal Sudirman Kav 10-11)* is a huge new hotel that's situated just off Jakarta's most prestigious street. Rooms cost US$190 to US$250 but discounts of 50% have been on offer.

A little further south, the *Sahid Jaya Hotel (☎ 5704444, fax 5733168, Jl Jenderal Sudirman 86)* is a rambling hotel with rooms from US$150. Further south again is *Le Meridien Jakarta (☎ 2513131, fax 5711633, Jl Jenderal Sudirman Kav 18-20)*. The rooms from US$190 have nice touches and extras.

The *Hilton Hotel (☎ 5703600, fax 5733089)* on Jl Jenderal Gatot Subroto has large grounds and a good range of facilities. The rooms cost US$180/195 to US$200/ 215. Near the Hilton, the *Hotel Atlet Century Park (☎ 5712041, fax 5712191, Jl Pintu Satu)* is a three star hotel, but it has good facilities and well appointed rooms making it a good alternative to the more expensive hotels. The rooms cost from US$95/ 105. The *Hotel Mulia Senayan (☎ 574 7777, fax 574 7888)* in the same area on Jl Asia Afrika is a new luxury hotel with low opening rates of US$99.

To the north-east of the city centre and not far from the National Monument, the *Borobudur Inter-Continental Jakarta (☎ 3805555, fax 3809595, Jl Lapangan Banteng Selatan)* is one of the older generation of luxury hotels, recently restored and with a large range of sporting facilities. Tastefully furnished rooms start at US$175 or weekend packages cost 550,000Rp per night.

Nearby, the *Hotel Aryaduta (☎ 3861234, fax 3809900, Jl Prapatan 44-8)* is another of the older breed but still a top business class hotel. The rooms start at US$180.

Other new hotels are springing up everywhere, though these tend to be less central. The *Omni Batavia Hotel (☎ 6904118, fax 6904092, Jl Kali Besar Barat 44-6)* is in the historic Kota district, which is desolate at night. The rooms cost US$120 to US$160 but expect big discounts.

Airport For transit visitors, *Quality Hotel Aspac (☎ 5590008, fax 5590018)* is right in the international terminal at the airport, upstairs in the departure area. The hotel has a small bar and restaurant, but no other facilities. The rooms for US$100 (US$50 for six hours) are good but very expensive, even with a readily offered discount.

The much more luxurious *Sheraton Bandara (☎ 5597777, fax 5597700)* is 3km east from the terminals. The rooms start at US$160 (US$125 on weekends).

PLACES TO EAT

Jakarta has the best selection of restaurants in Indonesia – everything from street fare to top international restaurants. The restaurants are expensive by Indonesian standards but the devalued rupiah means fine dining for a fraction of the price it would cost elsewhere in the world.

Jl Jaksa Area

Jl Jaksa's cafes are convivial meeting places dishing out the standard travellers' menu. They are certainly cheap and the breakfasts are very good value. Food is quasi-European or bland Indonesian.

The monetary crisis has taken its toll on the number of cafes but one survivor is *Angie's Cafe (Jl Jaksa 15)*, with a typical menu. *Mbak Merry (Jl Jaksa 40)* is a very cheap hole-in-the-wall warung with hamburgers and Indonesian dishes. *Pappa Kafe (Jl Jaksa 41)* is the pick of the restaurants, with outside tables and a varied menu that includes Indian food. *Memori* has a remarkably similar menu and screens violent American action videos in the evening. *Margot Cafe (Jl Jaksa 15C)* at the Hotel Le Margot is the main backpackers bar and also serves food. At the north end of Jl Jaksa, *Sate Khas Senayan (Jl Kebon Sirih Raya 31A)* is a newly renovated air-con restaurant with a variety of superb sate for 9000Rp to 12,000Rp, gado gado, *soto buntut* (oxtail soup) and other classic Indonesian dishes.

The next street west of Jl Jaksa, Jl H Agus Salim, but universally known by its old name of Jl Sabang, has a string of cheap to midrange restaurants. Jl Sabang is famed as the sate capital of Indonesia and dozens of sate hawkers set up on the street in the evening.

Restaurants line both sides of Jl Sabang. The most famous is *Natrabu (Jl Sabang 29A)*, Jakarta's best Padang restaurant. For standard Chinese fare, try the air-con *Lim Thiam Kie (Jl Sabang 49)*, or the *Paradiso 2001* is a small, basic Chinese vegetarian restaurant. A few modern, spotless restaurants

serve cheap noodles, such as the *Bakmi Sabang (Jl Sabang 43A)*, or the *Pho Hoa* on the Jl Wahid Hasyim corner serves Vietnamese noodles. More expensive restaurants include *Sizzler*, for chain restaurant grills, and *Mel's Drive-In*, an American diner.

At the southern end of Jl Jaksa, Jl Wahid Hasyim has a number of more expensive restaurants. *Ayam Goreng Nyonya Suharti (Jl Wahid Hasyim 51)* serves up the famous Yogyakarta-style fried chicken at very reasonable prices. *Tony Roma's (Jl Wahid Hasyim 49)* has belly-extending, melt-in-the-mouth ribs for around 50,000Rp, or there are half serves. *Hazara (Jl Wahid Hasyim 112)* is an expensive Indian restaurant, but the food is excellent and the chic decor makes this restaurant special. Although the long-running *Le Bistro (Jl Wahid Hasyim 75)* tries, it doesn't quite succeed to be French; however, the continental food is consistently good, the decor faded but pleasant and it has a piano bar.

Jl Thamrin

The *Sarinah department store* has a very good if expensive food-stall area in the basement next to the supermarket. Try the excellent *soto Betawi* (Betawi soup). Sarinah is also home to Indonesia's first *McDonald's* and the more expensive *Hard Rock Cafe* for grills. *American Chillis Bar & Grill* on the 2nd floor has Tex Mex favourites and over-indoctrinated American chain restaurant service.

The *Green Pub* is in the Jakarta Theatre, opposite the Sarinah department store, and has been pumping out Mexican food and grills for years. In the evening local bands perform in Mexican cowboy garb! *Jaya Pub* is at the back of the Jaya building, Jl Thamrin 12, and is another classic music venue that also puts on good grills and pub food.

Further down Jl Thamrin at the Welcome Statue roundabout, Plaza Indonesia is one of Jakarta's most exclusive shopping centres. The *Cira Food Court* on the 3rd floor is a Singapore-style hawker's centre with a range of good international food stalls. *Cafe Oh La La* in the basement has good pastries and cappuccinos, but *Kafe Excelso* has better espresso and light meals. Other fast-food emporia are in abundance.

Zigolini is in the Mandarin Oriental Jakarta hotel and is a superb Italian restaurant. Mains such as scaloppine or rack of lamb cost over 100,000Rp, or the big pizza oven pumps out excellent pizza and calzone for around 40,000Rp.

Other Areas

Menteng is just south of Jl Jaksa and has some good dining options. *Kafe Pisa (Jl Gereja Theresia 1)* has rustic Mediterranean decor, an outside area for al fresco dining, and decent pasta, pizza, calamari, scaloppine etc. Housed in a Dutch villa, *Lan Na Thai (Jl Kusuma Atmaja 85)* is one of Jakarta's most stylish restaurants. Rub shoulders with the Indonesian elite and expect to pay at least 100,000Rp per person. In the Menteng shopping centre, for seafood or steak try the *Gandy Steakhouse* or *Black Angus*. *Tamnak Thai* at No 78, Jl Cokroaminoto has good, moderately priced Thai cuisine and Chinese seafood.

The Pasar Baru area is near the main post office and is home to Jakarta's Indian community. Some good Indian restaurants are on Jl Veteran 1, opposite the Istiqlal mosque. *Queen's Tandoor (Jl Veteran 1 No 6)* has bare, bright decor, but the good food and reasonable prices make it very popular. *Sahara Restaurant (Jl Veteran 1 No 23)* is also good.

One of the best *warung* areas is on Jl Pecenongan, about 1km north of the National Monument. Night warungs start setting up large marquees around 5 pm, and serve excellent Chinese seafood and other dishes at cheap prices.

Right in the middle of historic Kota on Taman Fatahillah, *Cafe Batavia (Jl Pintu Besar Utara 14)* is the place to be seen. Housed in a tastefully renovated Dutch building, the restaurant is not cheap but the food is excellent.

The historic *Oasis Bar & Restaurant (Jl Raden Saleh Raya 47)* in Cikini is housed in a large, old Dutch villa and has the feel of an extravagant 1930s Hollywood film set, with prices to match. More than a dozen waitresses serve up a traditional *rijsttafel* (a selection of meat, vegetable and rice dishes), while you are serenaded by a group of Batak singers from Sumatra. Also in Cikini, *Art & Curio (Jl Cikini IV 8A)* is a delightfully old-fashioned restaurant with dark, bamboo decor and waiters in starched linen jackets. Though not exactly Dutch, it has plenty of colonial ambience, roast beef sandwiches, *bitterballen* (meat or prawn filled croquettes served with mustard), steaks and other grills, all at very reasonable prices.

Jakarta has hundreds of other fine dining establishments scattered around the Golden Triangle business district, Kebayoran Baru and especially in the wealthy, expat-favoured suburb of Menteng. Closer to the city centre, the *Taman Ria Senayan* on Jl Jenderal Gatot Subroto is not far from the Hilton Hotel and has a great selection of stylish restaurants overlooking the lagoon. Wander around to see what takes your fancy – Thai, Balinese, Italian, grills – a bit of everything.

ENTERTAINMENT

Check the entertainment pages of the *Jakarta Post* for films, concerts and special events. Films, lectures and discussions on Indonesian culture are often sponsored by foreign embassies and cultural centres.

Cultural Performances

On Jl Cikini Raya, not far from Jl Jaksa, the *Taman Ismail Marzuki (TIM, ☎ 3154087)* is Jakarta's cultural showcase. There is a performance almost every night and you might see anything from Balinese dancing to poetry readings, gamelan concerts to a New Zealand film festival. The TIM monthly program is available from the tourist office, the TIM office and major hotels. Events are also listed in the *Jakarta Post*.

The *Gedung Kesenian Jakarta (☎ 380 8283, Jl Gedung Kesenian 1)* also has a regular program (see the tourist office) of traditional dance and theatre, as well as European classical music and dance.

The *Bharata Theatre (☎ 4214937, Jl Kalilio 15)* in Pasar Senen has *ketoprak*

(Javanese folk theatre) performances from 8 pm every Monday and Thursday evening, and wayang orang on other nights.

Wayang kulit and wayang golek shows used to be a regular Sunday event at the *Jakarta History Museum* in Kota but are often cancelled because of lack of demand. The various cultural centres, particularly *Erasmus Huis*, also hold regular events.

Nightlife

Jakarta is the most sophisticated, broad-minded and corrupt city in Indonesia, and has nightlife to match. Hundreds of bars, discos, karaoke lounges and nightclubs range from sleazy to refined. Jakarta still has plenty of money and people partying to dawn in spite of, or perhaps because of, the monetary crisis. Bands start around 10 or 11 pm, and continue until 2 or 3 am, sometimes later on the weekends. During the week many places close at 1 am.

Many places don't have cover charges, though sometimes a first drink cover charge applies in the discos. A beer or a mixed drink costs from 15,000Rp, more in exclusive hotel bars.

Bars & Live Music The *Hard Rock Cafe* is on Jl Thamrin and has the usual blend of rock memorabilia, music and food. It is always lively and has decent bands or occasional top-line imports. The music starts around 11 pm, when dinner finishes, and keeps going until 2 or 3 am. The other chain cafes such as the *Fashion Cafe (Wisma 46, BMI City, Jl Jenderal Sudirman)*, near the Shangri-La Hotel, and *Planet Hollywood (Jl Jenderal Gatot Subroto 16)* also have live music and are popular on weekends.

The *Jaya Pub*, next to the car park behind the Jaya building, Jl Thamrin 12, is a Jakarta institution that has live pub music most evenings.

The historic, restored *Cafe Batavia* at Taman Fatahillah is another upmarket venue. DJs play from 10 am onwards and it is open 24 hours.

Hotel bars can be very lively, depending on the bands. Current favourites include *B.A.T.S.* in the Shangri-La Hotel, just off Jl Jenderal Sudirman; *CJ's Bar*, in the Hotel Mulia Senayan on Jl Asia Afrika; and the nearby *Komodo Airways*, Hotel Atlet Century Park, Jl Pintu Satu Senayan. On Jl Thamrin, *Harry's Bar* in the Mandarin Oriental Jakarta hotel attracts a business clientele and is one of the best bars in Jakarta for jazz, every night of the week.

The wealthy southern suburb of Kemang also has plenty of bar/restaurants with bands. For something different, *Twilite Cafe (TC, Jl Kemang Raya 24A)* is a fashionable two storey complex that houses a bar, cafe, Internet cafe, art gallery and bookshop. It is open daily from mid-morning until 11.30 pm, and Friday and Saturday until 1.30 pm.

Discos & Clubs Jakarta has some sophisticated clubs with high-tech lighting, massive sound systems and pumping dance music. The clubs open around 9 pm, but don't really get going until midnight when the bars close. On weekends they are open to 4 am or later. Cover charges are around 20,000Rp to 25,000Rp.

Jakarta's most infamous disco is the long-running *Tanamur (Jl Tanah Abang Timur 14)*. This institution is jammed nightly with gyrating revellers of every race, creed and sexual proclivity. It is unbelievably crowded after midnight on Friday and Saturday nights. Wear what you like here.

Tanamur is the benchmark of Jakarta's nightlife for most visitors, but Jakarta has other amazingly sophisticated clubs. *Bengkel* at Lot No 14 in the backblocks of the sprawling Sudirman Central Business District, off Jl Jenderal Sudirman, is a pyramidal building with a huge dance floor, big screens, dazzling light show and an eclectic mix of music. The cafe at the front has bands and a billiards area, and it's open until 6 am on weekends.

Smaller but also high-tech, *Jalan Jalan (36th floor, Menara Imperium, Jl Rasuna Said)* is another top spot for house music with the twinkling lights of Jakarta as a backdrop. It also has a sushi bar, billiard area and bands.

Jamz, at the front of Lippo Sudirman/ Lippo Suites Hotel on Jl Jenderal Sudirman, is the Hard Rock of jazz with jazz memorabilia but its music is confined to one cramped lounge, while DJs and pop bands ply the other two lounges. It is very popular and packs in a middle-class crowd every night.

SHOPPING

Shopping is one of Jakarta's biggest attractions. Clothes, shoes and many other goods are very cheap, especially those that are locally made. Brand name goods are in profusion, but are many times more expensive. Jakarta has handicrafts from almost everywhere in Indonesia. Prices are higher than the place of origin but if this is your first stop, it's a good place to get an overall view of Indonesian crafts and, if it's your last stop, it's a final chance to find something that you missed elsewhere in the country.

A good place to start is Sarinah on Jl Thamrin. The 3rd floor of this large department store is devoted to batik and handicrafts from all over the country. The handicrafts are souvenirs rather than true collectibles, but the quality is high and the prices reasonable.

In the same vein, but even bigger, is the related Pasaraya, Jl Iskandarsyah II/2, in Blok M (see later in this entry).

The Pasar Seni, at Ancol recreation park in north Jakarta, is a good place to look for regional handicrafts and to see many of them being made.

Jakarta's famous flea market is in Menteng on Jl Surabaya. It has woodcarvings, furniture, brassware, jewellery, batik, oddities like old typewriters and many (often instant) antiques. It is always fun to browse, but bargain like crazy – prices may be up to 10 times the worth of the goods.

Jl Kebon Sirih Timur, the street east of Jl Jaksa, has a number of shops that sell antiques and curios. The quality is high, but so are the prices.

Jakarta has plenty of shopping centres and markets to explore. Pasar Pagi Mangga Dua on Jl Mangga Dua is a huge wholesale market with some of the cheapest clothes, accessories and shoes, as well as a host of other goods. Across the road is the Mangga Dua Mall for computers and electronics, and the surrounding area has other shopping centres, making it South-East Asia's biggest shopping precinct.

Blok M in Kebayoran Baru is also huge and a little more upmarket. The Blok M Mall above the large bus terminal has scores of small, reasonably priced shops offering clothes, shoes, music tapes, household goods etc. More upmarket is the nearby Pasaraya department store and the multi-storey Blok M Plaza, which is just across the way. Jl Palatehan 1 is just to the north of the Blok M bus terminal, and has some interesting antique and craft shops.

Jakarta has dozens of other big, dazzling shopping centres, such as the exclusive and expensive Plaza Indonesia on Jl Thamrin. Plaza Senayan on Jl Asia Afrika is well stocked, as is the Pondok Indah Mall in the southern suburbs.

GETTING THERE & AWAY

Jakarta is the main international gateway to Indonesia; for details on arriving here from overseas see the introductory Getting There & Away section at the start of this chapter. Jakarta is also a major centre for domestic travel, with extensive bus, train, air and boat connections.

Air

International and domestic flights operate from the Soekarno-Hatta international airport. Departure tax is payable at the airport; it's 50,000Rp for international departures and 11,000Rp for domestic flights. The departure tax from Halim airport, which is little-used, costs 20,000Rp for international departures and 9000Rp for domestic flights. Flights depart from Jakarta to all the main cities across the archipelago. The main domestic airlines have offices open normal business hours, and usually Sunday morning as well. Travel agents also sell domestic tickets. Addresses for airline offices in Jakarta are as follows:

Air Canada
   (☎ 5738185) Chase Plaza, Jl Jenderal
   Sudirman Kav 21

Air France
(☎ 5202262) 9th floor, Summitmas Tower, Jl Jenderal Sudirman Kav 61-2
Air India
(☎ 3858845) Jl Abdul Muis
Air New Zealand
(☎ 5738195) Chase Plaza, Jl Jenderal Sudirman Kav 21
Bouraq
(☎ 6288815) Jl Ankasa 1-3, Kemayoran
British Airways
(☎ 5211500) 10th floor, World Trade Centre, Jl Jenderal Sudirman Kav 29
Cathay Pacific Airways
(☎ 3806664) 3rd floor, Hotel Borobudur Inter-Continental, Jl Lapangan Banteng Selatan
China Airlines
(☎ 2510788) Wisma Dharmala Sakti, Jl Jenderal Sudirman
Garuda Indonesia
(☎ 2311801) Garuda bldg, Jl Merdeka Selatan 13
Japan Airlines
(☎ 5703883) Mid Plaza, Jl Jenderal Sudirman Kav 10-11
KLM-Royal Dutch Airlines
(☎ 2526730/5) 17th floor, Summitmas Tower II, Jl Jenderal Sudirman Kav 61-2
Lufthansa Airlines
(☎ 5702005) Panin Centre bldg, Jl Jenderal Sudirman 1
Malaysia Airlines
(☎ 5229682) World Trade Centre, Jl Jenderal Sudirman Kav 29-31
Mandala
(☎ 4246100) Jl Garuda 76
Merpati Nusantara Airlines
(☎ 6544444) Jl Angkasa Blok B/15 Kav 2-3, Kemayoran;
Gambir train station
(☎ 3501433) 24 hour ticket office
Qantas Airways
(☎ 2300655) 11th floor, BDN bldg, Jl Thamrin 5
Royal Brunei Airlines
(☎ 5211842) World Trade Centre, Jl Jenderal Sudirman 29-31
Silk Air
(☎ 5208023) Chase Plaza, Jl Jenderal Sudirman Kav 21
Singapore Airlines
(☎ 5206881) Chase Plaza, Jl Jenderal Sudirman Kav 21
Thai Airways International (THAI)
(☎ 3140607) BDN bldg, Jl Thamrin 5
United Airlines
(☎ 5707520) Bank Pacific bldg, Jl Jenderal Sudirman Kav 7-8

Jakarta's Soekarno-Hatta airport is spacious, modern and surprisingly efficient, but only has a few overpriced food and shopping outlets.

Bus

Jakarta has four major bus terminals, all a long way from the city centre. In some cases it can take longer getting to the bus terminal than the bus journey itself, making the trains a better alternative for arriving at or leaving Jakarta.

Tickets can be bought from travel agents around town. The agents along Jl Jaksa not only sell tickets but can include travel to the bus terminals; although this tends to cost considerably more, it can save a lot of hassle. Advance bookings are a good idea for peak periods, but as so many buses operate to the main destinations, if you just front up at the bus terminals you won't have to wait long to find one. The main bus terminals are Kalideres, Kampung Rambutan, Pulo Gadung and Lebak Bulus.

Kalideres Buses to the west of Jakarta go from the Kalideres bus terminal, about 15km north-west of Merdeka Square. Frequent normal/air-con buses run to Merak (4000Rp, three hours), Labuan (5000Rp, 3½ hours) and Serang (3000Rp, 1½ hours). A few buses go through to Sumatra from Kalideres, but most Sumatra buses leave from Pulo Gadung bus terminal.

Kampung Rambutan The big Kampung Rambutan bus terminal handles buses to areas south and south-west of Jakarta. It was designed to carry much of Jakarta's intercity bus traffic, but it mostly handles buses to West Java, including: Bogor (2000/3000Rp normal/air-con, 40 minutes); Bandung (6500Rp to 13,000Rp, 4½ hours); Tasikmalaya (8000Rp to 15,000Rp, 7½ hours); and Banjar (6500/12,000Rp to 22,000Rp, nine hours). Buses also go to Merak, Sumatra, Cirebon, Yogya, Surabaya and other long-distance destinations, but Pulo Gadung bus terminal still has most of the long-distance services. Take the train to Bogor or Bandung.

Kampung Rambutan is about 18km to the south of the city centre and takes at least an hour by city bus.

Pulo Gadung Pulo Gadung is 12km to the east of the city centre, and has buses to Cirebon, Central and East Java, Sumatra and Bali. Many of the air-con, deluxe buses operate from here. This wild bus terminal is the busiest in Indonesia, with buses, crowds, hawkers and beggars everywhere.

The terminal is divided into two sections: one for buses to Sumatra and the other for all buses to the east.

Most buses to Sumatra leave between 10 am and 3 pm, and you can catch a bus right through to Aceh if you are crazy enough. Destinations and fares include: Palembang (45,000Rp to 80,000Rp); Bengkulu (60,000 Rp to 90,000Rp); and Padang and Bukittinggi (70,000Rp to 110,000Rp). Prices are for air-con deluxe buses with reclining seats and toilets – well worth it for those long hauls through Sumatra. For Bukittinggi, two good companies are ALS (☎ 8503446) and ANS (☎ 352411). Both charge 110,000Rp for the 30 hour plus journey.

To the east, frequent buses go to Central and East Java and on to Bali. Destinations include: Cirebon (8500Rp to 15,000Rp, four hours); Yogya (25,000Rp to 55,000Rp, 14 hours); Surabaya (30,000Rp to 68,000Rp, 18 hours); and Denpasar (60,000Rp to 100,000 Rp, 24 hours). Most buses to Yogya leave between 8 am and 6 pm. Two of the better deluxe bus companies are Raya and Muncul.

Lebak Bulus This terminal is 16km south of the city centre, and also handles long-distance deluxe buses to Yogya, Surabaya and Bali. The fares are similar to those from Pulo Gadung terminal. Most bus departures are scheduled for the late afternoon or evening.

Minibus

Door-to-door *travel* minibuses are not a good option in Jakarta because it can take hours to pick up or drop passengers in the traffic jams. Some travel agents book them, but you may have to go to a depot on the outskirts. Media Taxis (☎ 323744), Jl Johar 15, near Jl Jaksa, has minibuses to Bandung and beat-up 1970s Holdens (Australian-made cars) for 25,000Rp.

Mitra Marsada Utama (☎ 3142566), Jl Kebon Sirih Barat Dalam I No 56, near Jl Jaksa, was running a tourist bus to Pangandaran (45,000Rp) – check to see if it has started again. Jl Jaksa travel agents also offer direct minibuses to Yogya.

Train

Jakarta's four main train stations are quite central, making the trains the easiest way out of the city into Java. The most convenient and important is Gambir train station, on the eastern side of Merdeka Square, a 15 minute walk from Jl Jaksa. Gambir handles express trains to Bogor, Bandung, Yogya, Solo, Semarang and Surabaya. Some Gambir trains also stop at Kota, which is the train station in the old city area in the north. The Pasar Senen train station is to the east and mostly has *ekonomi* (economy) trains to eastern destinations. Tanah Abang train station has ekonomi trains to the west.

For long hauls, the express trains are far preferable to the ekonomi trains. Most have cheaper bisnis class in addition to air-con eksekutif class. For express trains, tickets can be bought in advance at the air-con booking offices at the northern end of Gambir train station, while the ticket windows at the southern end are for tickets bought on the day of departure. For schedules and departure times ring ☎ 8292151 or ☎ 6927843.

From Gambir train station, taxis cost a minimum of 7000Rp from the taxi booking desk. A cheaper alternative is to go out the front to the main road and hail down a bajaj, which will cost 2000Rp to 3000Rp to Jl Jaksa after bargaining.

Bogor No-frills ekonomi trains to Bogor are part of the city rail network and can be horribly crowded during rush hour (watch your gear), but at other times are quite tolerable and provide an efficient service. They can also be boarded at Gondangdia train station, only a short stroll from Jl Jaksa. They leave every 20 minutes until around 8 pm and take 1½ hours. The fare is 900Rp from Gondangdia or Gambir, 1000Rp from Kota.

The much better Pakuan Express trains (4000Rp bisnis, one hour) leave from Gambir only at 7.43, 8.23 (air-con) and 11 am, and 2.28, 2.48, 4.23 (air-con), 4.48, 6.38 (air-con) and 7.03 pm. Air-con eksekutif carriages cost 6000Rp. Seats cannot be booked and tickets go on sale one hour before departure.

Bandung The easiest way to get to Bandung is by train. The journey is very scenic as the train climbs into the hills before Bandung. It is best to book in advance, essential on weekends and public holidays unless you want to stand in a ticket queue for hours.

The efficient and comfortable *Parahyangan* service departs from Gambir train station for Bandung (20,000/32,000Rp bisnis/eksekutif, three hours) roughly every hour between 5 am and 11.30 pm. The more luxurious *Argogede* (40,000Rp eksekutif, 2½ hours) departs at 10 am and 6 pm.

Cirebon Most trains that run along the north coast or to Yogya go through Cirebon. One of the best services is the *Cirebon Express* departing from Gambir train station at 6.45 and 10.10 am, and 4.55 pm. It costs 18,000/32,000Rp in bisnis/eksekutif and takes 3½ hours.

Yogyakarta & Solo The most luxurious trains are the *Argo Lawu* (115,000Rp eksekutif; 7½ hours) departing at 9 pm, and the *Dwipangga* (160,000Rp, eight hours) departing at 8 am. These trains go to Solo and stop at Yogyakarta, 45 minutes before Solo, but cost the same to either destination.

Better value express services to Yogya are the *Fajar Utama Yogya* (36,000/76,000Rp bisnis/eksekutif; eight hours) departing from Gambir train station at 6.10 and 6.20 am, and the *Senja Utama Yogya* (36,000/72,000Rp) departing at 7.20 and 8.40 pm. Expect overruns on scheduled journey times. The *Senja Utama Solo* goes to Solo (40,000/80,000Rp, 10 hours) at 7.40 pm and also stops in Yogya.

At the other end of the comfort scale are the crowded ekonomi trains that depart from Pasar Senen station. The *Gaya Baru Malam Selatan* and *Matamaja*, or the better choice *Empujaya*, leave Pasar Senen at 9.35 pm and terminate in Yogya. The ekonomi trains cost around 14,000Rp and take 10½ hours to Yogya, but overruns are common.

Surabaya Most trains between Jakarta and Surabaya take the shorter northern route via Semarang, though a few take the longer southern route via Yogya. Express trains range from the *Jayabaya Utara* (48,000Rp bisnis, 12 hours) that departs from Kota at 3 pm to the luxurious *Argobromo* (140,000Rp eksekutif, nine hours) that departs from Gambir at 8.05 pm. The *Anggrek* train (160,000Rp, nine hours) depart from Gambir at 9.30 am and 9.30 pm, and also have a super eksekutif class (185,000Rp) with computer, telephone and fax services.

The cheapest services taking the north coast route are the ekonomi class only *Gaya Baru Malam Utara* (13,500Rp, 13 hours) from Pasar Senen to Surabaya's Pasar Turi train station at 3.40 pm and the *Parcel* at 8.35 pm.

Boat

See the Getting Around chapter for information on the Pelni shipping services that operate on a regular two week schedule to ports all over the archipelago. The Pelni ticketing office (☎ 4211921) is at Jl Angkasa 18, north-east of the city centre in Kemayoran. Tickets plus commission can also be bought through designated Pelni agents such as: Menara Buana Surya (☎ 3142464) in the Tedja Buana building, Jl Menteng Raya 29, which is about 500m east of Jl Jaksa; or Kerta Jaya (☎ 3451518), Jl Veteran I No 27, opposite the Istiqlal mosque.

Direct Pelni destinations from Jakarta include: Padang, Tanjung Pandan (Pulau Belitung), Surabaya, Semarang, Muntok (Pulau Bangka), Belawan, Kijang (Pulau Bintan) and Batam. Services on the *Lambelu* to Padang and the *Sinabong* to Batam (near Singapore) are of most interest to travellers. To

Kalimantan, the *Lawit* goes via Tanjung Pandan to Pontianak. A number of Pelni boats go to Ujung Pandang (Sulawesi) via Semarang or Surabaya but there are no direct services.

Pelni ships all arrive at and depart from Pelabuhan Satu (Dock No 1) at Tanjung Priok, 13km north-east of the city centre. Take bus No 81 from Jl Thamrin, opposite Sarinah department store, via Pasar Senen; allow at least an hour. The bus terminal is at the old Tanjung Priok train station from where it is a 600m walk to the dock or 500Rp by ojek (motorcycle or bicycle). From the Tanjung Priok terminal buses also run to Bogor. A taxi to Jl Jaksa will cost around 15,000Rp (you will have to bargain), a little less than the meter going to the harbour. The information centre (☎ 4301080 ext 2223) at the front of the Dock No 1 arrival hall is helpful.

Other passenger ships also go from Dock No 1 to Bintan and Batam islands, from where it is just a short ferry ride to Singapore. The *Samudera Jaya* is a small but reasonably comfortable air-con hydrofoil that seats up to 300 passengers. It leaves Tanjung Priok on Saturday at 1 pm and sails to Tanjung Pandan (70,000Rp, 12 hours) on Pulau Belitung, before continuing on to Tanjung Pinang (Pulau Bintan; 85,000Rp) and Batam (95,000Rp). Count on a 24 hour trip to Batam. In the reverse direction it leaves Thursday. The *Telaga Express* also leaves Jakarta every Saturday at 6 am to cover the same route.

To Kalimantan, the *Kapuas Express* departs for Pontianak every Tuesday and Thursday at 10 am, and Saturday at 4 pm.

GETTING AROUND
To/From the Airport
Jakarta's Soekarno-Hatta international airport is 35km west of the city centre. A toll road links the airport to the city and a journey between the two takes 45 minutes to an hour, longer in the rush hour.

Damri airport buses (4000Rp) depart every 30 minutes from around 3 am to 6.30 pm between the airport and Gambir train station (near Jl Jaksa) in central Jakarta. Other airport buses also go to Blok M, Kemayoran, Rawamangun and Bogor. From Gambir train station to Jl Jaksa, take a bajaj (3000Rp or less with bargaining) or taxi (7000Rp from the taxi desk), or it is just under 1km to walk.

A metered taxi from the airport to Jl Thamrin/Jl Jaksa costs about 35,000Rp and on top of the metered fare you have to pay around another 10,000Rp, which includes the airport surcharge (2300Rp, payable from but not to the airport) and 7500Rp in toll road charges. Take taxis from the booth outside the arrival area, not the private drivers that assail you, as they overcharge.

Bus
In Jakarta everything is at a distance. It's hot and humid, and hardly anybody walks – you will need to use some form of transport to get from one place to another.

Jakarta has a comprehensive city bus network. Jakarta's crowded buses have their fair share of pickpockets and bag slashers. The more expensive buses are generally safer, as well as being more comfortable.

Around town at least a dozen bus companies run a confusion of routes. Big regular city buses charge a fixed 400Rp fare. The big express 'Patas' buses charge 800Rp and the air-con Patas buses cost 2000Rp; these are usually less crowded and are the best option. These services are supplemented by orange toy-sized buses and, in a few areas, by pale blue Mikrolet buses that cost between 400Rp and 600Rp. The main terminal for mikrolet and the numerous red-and-blue Metro Mini buses is at the Pasar Senen.

The tourist office has information on buses around Jakarta. Some of the useful buses that operate along Jl Thamrin include:

P1 (air-con), **P10** (air-con) or **P11**
  Jl Thamrin to Kota
P11, **P10** or **79** (air-con)
  Kota to Kampung Rambutan via Jl Thamrin
P15
  Jl Sabang (Jl Haji Agus Salim) to Jl Ankasa
  (for Pelni, Merpati and Bouraq offices)
P14
  Tanjung Priok to Tanah Abang via Jl Kebon Sirih
78 (air-con)
  Kota to Kalideres bus terminal

Car

Jakarta has branches of major rent-a-car operators including: Avis (☎ 3142900), Jl Diponegoro 25; Bluebird (☎ 7941234), Jl Mampang Prapatan Raya 6; and National Car Rental (☎ 3143423), Kartika Plaza Hotel, Jl Thamrin 10. Alternatively, inquire at the cheaper travel agents, as a vehicle with driver may be the cheapest option.

A number of the 'transport' guys who hang out on Jl Jaksa can offer some of the best deals if you negotiate directly with them, avoiding hotel or travel agent commission. Count on around 100,000Rp to 150,000Rp for a day of driving around town.

Taxi

Taxis in Jakarta are metered and cost 2000Rp for the first kilometre and 90Rp for each subsequent 100m. Make sure the meter is used. Many taxi drivers provide a good service, but Jakarta has enough rogues to give its taxis a bad réputation. Tipping is expected, if not demanded, but not obligatory. It is customary to round the fare up to the next 1000Rp. Carry plenty of small notes – Jakarta taxi drivers rarely give change.

Bluebird cabs (☎ 7941234, 7981001) are pale blue, and have the best reputation and well maintained cars.

Typical taxi fares from Jl Thamrin are: to Kota (5000Rp); Sunda Kelapa (6000Rp); Pulo Gadung (8000Rp); and Kampung Rambutan or Taman Mini (18,000Rp). Any toll road charges are extra and paid by the passengers.

Bajaj & Other Local Transport

Bajaj (pronounced 'ba-jai') are nothing less than Indian auto-rickshaws: orange three wheelers that carry two passengers (three at a squeeze if you're all tiny) and sputter around powered by noisy two stroke engines. Short trips such as Jl Jaksa to the main post office will cost about 3000Rp. They're good value, especially during rush hours, but hard bargaining is required. Always agree on the price beforehand. Bajaj are not allowed along main streets such as Jl Thamrin, so make sure they don't simply drop you off at the border.

Jakarta has other weird and wonderful means of getting around. Bemos are the original three wheelers from the 1960s that still operate around Glodok and other parts of Jakarta. In the back streets of Kota, push-bikes with a padded 'kiddy carrier' on the back will take you for a ride! The *helicak*, cousin to the bajaj, is a green motorcycle contraption with a passenger car mounted on the front. Jakarta also has ojeks, which are motorcycles that take pillion passengers. Weaving in and out of Jakarta's traffic on the back of an ojek is decidedly risky. Becaks have been banned from the city and only a few tourist becaks remain at Ancol.

AROUND JAKARTA
Pulau Seribu

☎ 021   • pop 15,000

Scattered across the Java Sea to the north of Jakarta are the tropical islands of Pulau Seribu (Thousand Islands). Despite the name, there are actually only around 130 in number. These beautiful islands have white-sand beaches, palm trees, coral reefs and calm waters – just a short ride from Jakarta. The area is a marine national park, though 37 of the islands are permitted to be exploited for commercial purposes.

Jakarta's 'offshore' islands start only a few kilometres out in the Bay of Jakarta. The waters closest to Jakarta are murky – the islands are better the further you go from Jakarta. **Pulau Bidadari** is the closest resort island and is popular for day trips with Jakarta residents. It is one of the least interesting resorts, but you can use it to visit other islands like **Pulau Kahyangan**, **Pulau Kelor**, which has the ruins of an old Dutch fort, or **Pulau Onrust**, where the remains of an old shipyard from the 18th century can be explored.

Further north, **Pulau Ayer** is another popular day-trip destination. It has a comfortable resort with a small stretch of good beach, though the waters are still cloudy.

The entire island group has a population of around 15,000, with the district centre on **Pulau Pramuka**. Most people live on just one island, **Pulau Kelapa**, which is about 15km north of Jakarta. These poor fishing communities have yet to share in the wealth generated by the resorts. Near Pulau Kelapa, **Pulau Panjang** has the only airstrip on the islands. Around this group of islands are two more resorts on **Pulau Kotok**, which has a good reef for snorkelling and diving, and the Matahari resort on **Pulau Macan**, which is surrounded by a retaining wall.

The best resorts lie around 4km north of Pulau Kelapa, all close to each other. **Pulau Putri** is notable for its aquariums. **Pulau Sepa** is a small island surrounded by wide stretches of pristine sand. As well has having the best beach, Pulau Sepa is one of the cheapest. Nearby **Pulau Pelangi** also has some good stretches of beach, while **Pulau Bira** has a golf course and decent beaches. **Pulau Antuk Timur** and **Pulau Antuk Barat** are separated by a small channel and both house Pulau Seribu's fanciest resort.

Places to Stay All the resorts have individual bungalows with attached bathrooms and provide water sport facilities, including diving. While comfortable, none are international-standard resorts despite the high prices. Most of the resorts offer packages that include buffet-only meals and transport. Weekends are up to 50% more expensive than prices quoted here. The resorts have offices in Jakarta or at the Ancol Marina for bookings. Travel agents at the Ancol Marina also sell packages and are useful for comparing prices. Hikari Multi Sinergi (☎ 6453679) at Counter No 6 in the Marina building and Mitra Semesta Raya (☎ 6406707) at Counter No 9 book most of the resorts.

Pulau Bidadari Resort can be booked at Ancol Marina (☎ 680048), Taman Impian Jaya Ancol. It has a variety of simple cottages from 76,000Rp to 100,000Rp per person during the week, or 91,000Rp to 122,500Rp on weekends.

Coconut Island Resort (☎ 082-8134144) is on the eastern tip of Pulau Kotok and has an office in Jakarta (☎ 8295074), Jl Tebet Barat Dalam X/3, for bookings. Though very downmarket, it is reasonably priced with two-bedroom bungalows for 250,000Rp (100,000Rp more on week-

ends). Meals are extra and the boat costs 220,000Rp per person return.

Kul Kul Kotok Island Resort (☎ 082-8121862), on the western side of Kotok, can be booked through their office in Jakarta (☎ 6345507), 3rd floor, Duta Merlin shopping arcade, Jl Gajah Mada 3-5. This resort is one of the most attractive, but most bungalows are simple and have fan and cold water only. Full packages are offered at 500,000Rp per person (10% more on weekends).

Matahari Island Resort (direct ☎ 641 5332) can be booked through counter 1 and 2 (☎ 640338) at the Ancol Marina. Rooms in attractive two-storey bungalows cost from US$50/65 for singles/doubles or US$60/75 on weekends; discounted full-board packages from 390,000Rp per person are available (450,000Rp on weekends).

Pulau Putri Resort can be booked through PT Buana Bintang Samudra (☎ 8281093), Jl Sultan Agung 21. It has a swimming pool and a variety of accommodation options, old and new. Package rates that include transport and meals cost 460,000Rp per person, or 600,000Rp on weekends.

Patra Bira Cottages (☎ 5415103) on Pulau Bira Besar can be booked though PT Pulau Seribu Paradise (☎ 7975157), Gedung Multika, Mampang Prapatan Raya 71-3. Spacious, well equipped bungalows cost from 480,000Rp per person twin share full board (560,000Rp on weekends).

Pulau Pelangi Resort can also be booked through PT Pulau Seribu Paradise. Full board packages in older bungalows cost around 500,000Rp (560,000Rp on weekends), including transport.

Pulau Sepa Resort (☎ 5453375) can be booked through PT Pulau Sepa Permai (☎ 6906968), Jl Kali Besar Barat 29. Rooms have air-con and hot water but are really just a better class of losmen, while bungalows are also simple but have more character. All-inclusive room packages start at 300,000/465,000Rp for one/two nights, while bungalow packages are 343,000/523,000Rp to 468,000/773,000Rp.

Pulau Seribu Marine Resort can be booked through PT Pantara Wisata Jaya

(☎ 5723161), Jl Jenderal Sudirman Kav 3-4. It is the most upmarket resort and is popular with Japanese groups. Bungalows are very comfortable, though not really luxurious. It's the range of facilities that stand out. Full-board packages cost US$105/165/230 for singles/doubles/triples, slightly more on weekends, and the boat is an extra US$50 return.

Getting There & Away The resorts have daily speedboats from Jakarta's Ancol Marina for guests and day-trippers, usually leaving around 8 am and returning around 2 pm. Even the furthest islands take only a little over two hours to reach. Return day trip rates to the resorts with lunch include: Pulau Bidadari (40,000Rp), Pulau Ayer (80,000Rp), Pulau Kotok (250,000Rp), Pulau Putri (240,000Rp) and Pulau Sepa (200,000Rp).

West Java

The province of West Java has a population of 40 million, an area of 46,229 sq km and Bandung as its capital. It is historically known as Sunda, the home of the Sundanese people and their culture.

Away from Jakarta and the flat, hot coastline to the north, West Java is predominantly mountainous and agricultural, with lush green valleys and high volcanic peaks surrounding the capital, Bandung. West Java is also strongly Islamic, yet in the remote Kendeng mountains there is still a small isolated community known as the Badui, believed to be descendants of the ancient Sundanese who fled from Islam more than 400 years ago. The name Sunda is of Sanskrit origin and means 'pure' or 'white'.

For travellers, West Java has tended to be a place to whiz through between Jakarta and eastern destinations. However, apart from its historic and cultural centres, West Java has a good beach resort at Pangandaran and a fine backwater trip along the coastal lagoons to Central Java. Other major attractions, though remote and isolated, are the famous Krakatau and the unique Ujung Kulon National Park.

HISTORY

Early in its history, Sunda was primarily dependent on overseas trade. It was not only an important spice centre in its own right but also a transhipment point for trade with Asia. West Java was the first contact point in Indonesia for the Dutch, and earlier it was one of the first regions to come into contact with Indian traders and their culture.

Ancient stone inscriptions record an early Hindu influence during the reign of King Purnawarman of Taruma – one of his rock edicts can be seen near Bogor. In the 7th century Taruma was destroyed by the powerful Sumatran-based Buddhist kingdom of Sriwijaya. Much later, Hinduism reasserted itself alongside Buddhism when the Pajajarans ruled the region. They're chiefly remembered for constructing the first trading settlement on the site of Old Batavia and for establishing trading relations with the Portuguese.

The first half of the 16th century saw the military expansion of the Muslim state of Demak, and in 1524 Muslim power first made itself felt in West Java. In that year Demak's leader, Sunan Gunungjati, took the port of Banten and then Sunda Kelapa. Some time after 1552 he became the first of the kings of Cirebon, which today is the least visited and thus the most surprising of Java's surviving sultanates. Banten, on the other hand, was the maritime capital of the only Muslim state to remain independent of the great Javanese power, Mataram, but today is little more than a small fishing village.

After the fall of Melaka in 1511, Chinese, Arabs and Indians poured into Banten, and it became a major trading centre for Muslim merchants who made use of the Sunda Straits (Selat Sunda) to avoid the Portuguese. Gunungjati's successor, Hasanuddin, spread Banten's authority to the pepper-producing district of Lampung in south Sumatra. His son, Maulana Yusuf, finally conquered the inland Hindu kingdom of Pajajaran in 1579 and so carved out a huge slice of Sunda as Banten's own domain.

Towards the end of the century, Banten felt the first impact of a new force – the Europeans. In 1596 the Dutch made their first

WEST JAVA

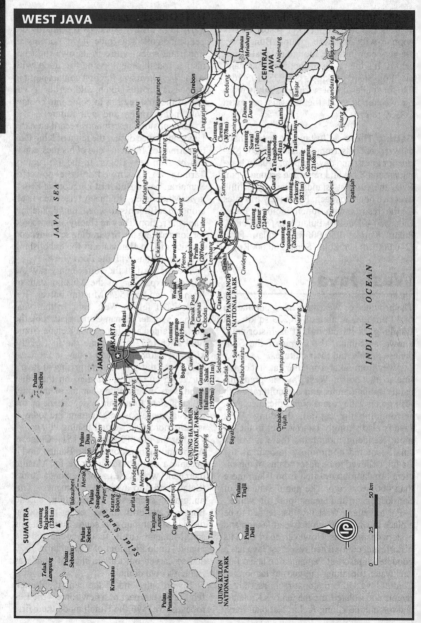

appearance at Banten, in 1600 the English established an East India Company trading post and two years later the Dutch formed a counterpart company, the VOC. Banten naturally became a centre of fierce Anglo-Dutch competition and the Dutch soon moved out and seized Jayakarta instead, henceforth to be their capital as Batavia.

The VOC's most formidable opponent was the Mataram kingdom that was extending its power over parts of West Java, but Banten, which was so close to its own headquarters, remained a troublesome rival. It not only harboured foreign competitors but a powerful ruling house. Hostilities reached their peak with the accession of Banten's greatest ruler, Sultan Agung, in 1651. With the help of European captains, Agung established an impressive trading network. He defied both Mataram and the VOC on more than one occasion before civil war within the ruling house led to Dutch intervention and his defeat and capture in 1683.

By the end of the 17th century, Dutch power had taken a great step forward in the west, and throughout the colonial era West Java remained under more direct control than the rest of the country. It was closer to Batavia but, more importantly, much of the land was ceded to the Dutch by Mataram in return for military aid, while in Central and East Java the kingdoms became Dutch protectorates.

JAKARTA TO MERAK

Most visitors just head straight through from Jakarta to Merak on their way to (or from) Sumatra, but along this route you can also branch off and head for the west coast.

The Jakarta to Merak road runs through a flat coastal area with plenty of industrial development. It's one of the busiest in Java, with a great deal of traffic of all types. Getting out of Jakarta from Kalideres can be slow but once on the toll road it is a quick journey.

Banten

Due north of Serang, on the coast, are the few fragments of the great maritime capital

of the Banten sultanate, where the Dutch and English first landed in Java to secure trade and struggle for economic supremacy.

Banten reached its peak during the reign of Sultan Agung (1651-83) but he unwisely declared war on the Dutch in Batavia in 1680. Before he could make a move, internal conflict within the royal house led to Dutch intervention on behalf of the ambitious crown prince. Agung fled Banten but finally surrendered in 1683, and his defeat marked the real beginning of Dutch territorial expansion in Java. Not only was Banten's independence at an end but the English East India Company was driven out, which effectively destroyed British interests in Java.

The Dutch maintained trading interests in Banten for a time. Banten today is just a small dusty fishing village.

The chief landmark of a prosperous era is the 16th century mosque **Mesjid Agung**, which dominates the village. This is a good example of early Islamic architecture, though its great white minaret was reputedly designed by a Chinese Muslim.

Next to the mosque is an **archaeological museum** (open daily from 9 am to 4 pm, closed Monday), which has a modest collection of clay artefacts found in the area. It also has a few of the long, iron, chained spikes for which the 'Debus players' are famous. Banten has long been a centre for practitioners of the Debus tradition, which is supposed to have come from India. These Islamic ascetics engage in masochistic activities such as plunging sharp weapons into their bodies (without drawing blood!) and are able to control the pain by the strength of their faith. It's said this was originally part of the training of the invincible special soldiers to the Banten court.

Directly across from the mosque is the large grass-covered site of Hasanuddin's fortified palace, the **Surosowan**, which was wrecked in the bloody civil war during the reign of Sultan Agung. It was rebuilt, only to be razed to the ground by the Dutch in 1832.

Other points of interest around the mosque include the massive ruins of **Fort Speelwijk** to the north-west. This fort now

Sundanese Arts

Music

The most characteristic Sundanese instrument is the *kecapi* (a type of lute that is plucked), accompanied by the *suling* (a soft-toned bamboo flute that fades in and out of the long vibrating notes of the kecapi). Another traditional instrument is the *angklung* – a device of bamboo pieces of differing lengths and diameter loosely suspended in a bamboo frame, which is shaken to produce hollow echoing sounds. In Cirebon there's a variation on Bandung-style kecapi-suling music, called *tarling* because it makes use of *guitar* and *suling*.

Another traditional Sundanese music form is *gamelan degung*. This dynamic gamelan style is played by a small ensemble similar to the Central Javanese gamelan with the addition of the *degung*, which is a set of small suspended gongs, and the suling. It is less soporific and more rhythmic than Central Javanese gamelan music, yet not as hectic as the Balinese forms.

Dance

Nowadays, West Java is famous for the more modern music and dance form called **Jaipongan**, which is found mostly in Bandung and Jakarta. Jaipongan features dynamic drumming coupled with erotic and sometimes humorous dance movements that include elements of *pencak silat* (Indonesian martial arts) and even New York-style break dancing. Jaipongan dance/music is a rather recent derivation of a more traditional Sundanese form called Ketuktilu, in which a group of professional female dancers (sometimes prostitutes) dance for male spectators. The newer form involves males and females dancing alone and together, although in lengthy performances Jaipongan songs are usually interspersed with the older Ketuktilu style.

Other dance forms include **Longser**, **Joker** and **Ogel**. Longser and Joker involve the passing of a sash between two couples. Ogel is an extremely difficult form that features very slow dance movements. Traditional Ogel is in danger of dying out, because few younger performers are patient enough to endure the many years of training required to master the subtle movements.

Wayang Golek

Although the wayang golek puppet play can be seen elsewhere on Java, it is traditionally associated with West Java and the Sundanese prefer it to the shadow play. First used in north-coast towns for Muslim propaganda, this type of puppet play was Islamic and a popular, robust parody of the stylised aristocratic wayang kulit play. In the early 19th century a Sundanese prince of Sumedang had a set of wooden puppets made to correspond exactly to the wayang kulit puppets of the Javanese courts. With these he was able to perform the Hindu epics with the traditional splendour of his rivals, but at the same time preserve his regional identity by using puppets long associated with anti-Javanese art. In West Java the stories are still usually based on the *Mahabharata* and *Ramayana* legends, and the puppets are larger and more vivid than those found in Central Java.

overlooks an expanse of sand-silt marsh, although at one time it stood on the sea's edge. The fort was built by the Dutch in 1682 and finally abandoned by Governor General Daendels at the beginning of the 19th century. Opposite the entrance to the fort is a **Chinese temple**, dating from the 18th century, which is still in use. Back along the road to Serang are the huge crumbling walls and archways of the **Kaibon** palace, and nearby is the **tomb of Maulana Yusuf**, who died in 1580.

Getting There & Away Take a bus from Jakarta's Kalideres bus station to Serang (3000Rp, 1½ hours), 10km south of Banten, from where a minibus (700Rp, half-hour) will drop you near the Mesjid Agung. Alternatively, take any bus between Jakarta and Cilegon and get off at the mosque in Kramatwatu village, from where ojek motorbike riders can take you the 5km to Banten for around 2000Rp to 3000Rp.

Pulau Dua Bird Sanctuary

Off the coast at Banten, Pulau Dua is one of Indonesia's major bird sanctuaries. The island has a large resident population – mainly herons, storks and cormorants – but peak time is between March and July when great numbers of migratory birds flock here for the breeding season.

It's a half-hour trip by chartered boat from the Karanghantu harbour in Banten but you can walk across the fishponds to the island. From Banten, take an angkot 5km east to the village of Sawahluhur. The trail to the island starts just 100m or so before the village and then it is a hot 1km walk, weaving between the fishponds – just keep heading for the trees on the horizon. There is a Perlindungan Hutan dan Pelestarian Alam (PHPA) post with a derelict hut that has bare wooden beds and not much else. If you are planning to stay bring food and water. For more information you can contact the PHPA office in Jakarta. Very expensive tours are also arranged from Carita.

MERAK
☎ 0254

Right on the north-western tip of Java, 140km from Jakarta, Merak is the terminus for ferries shuttling to and from Bakauheni on the southern end of Sumatra. Merak is just an arrival and departure point, and most people pass straight through this noisy, rapidly industrialising town. If you do have reason to stay, *Hotel Anda* (☎ 71041, Jl Raya Pulorida 5) is right opposite the ferry terminal and is a reasonable budget hotel. The *Hotel Feri Merak* (☎ 572081, Jl Raya

Pelabuhan 30) is 1.5km from the ferry terminal towards Jakarta, and is far and away the best option.

Getting There & Away

The bus terminal and train station are at the ferry dock.

Bus Frequent buses run between Merak and Jakarta (4000Rp, three hours). Most terminate at Jakarta's Kalideres bus terminal, but buses also run to/from Pulo Gadung and Kampung Rambutan. Other buses run all over Java, including Bogor (7000Rp), Bandung (10,000/15,000Rp normal/air-con, to 23,000Rp), Yogya and Solo.

Buses leave from the front of the bus terminal to Serang (1000Rp), Cilegon (700Rp), Labuan (2700Rp) and Rangkasbitung (2200 Rp). Buses to Labuan via Anyer and Carita are not frequent so you may have to take one to the Simpang Tiga turn-off on the western outskirts of Cilegon and then another bus from there.

Train An eksekutif train to Jakarta (10,000 Rp, three hours) departs at noon and stops at Kota station, otherwise a slower ekonomi train (2500Rp) goes to Tanah Abang station at 1.30 pm.

Boat Ferries to Bakauheni in Sumatra depart about every 30 minutes, 24 hours a day. Ferries cost 2900/2300Rp in ekonomi A/B class and take two hours. Motorbikes cost 5600Rp and cars 96,000Rp. Alternatively, the *Dermaga* is a fast ferry to Bagoni taking 45 minutes and costing 8000/12,000Rp. The through buses to Bandarlumpang are the easiest option.

WEST COAST BEACHES

At Cilegon, south-east of Merak, the road branches south to Anyer and runs close to the sea all the way to Labuan. The road passes Cilegon's massive steel works and chemical, cement and other industrial plants until it reaches Anyer market. From there the road runs south to Labuan along a flat, green coastal strip bordered by a rocky, reef-lined coast that is punctuated by stretches of white-sand beach.

This picturesque coast has masses of coconut palms and banana trees, and because of its easy access by toll road from Jakarta, it's a popular weekend beach strip. Though not world beaters, the beaches are good and make a fine escape from Jakarta's heat and crowds. The main place of interest is Carita, where you can arrange tours to Krakatau and Ujung Kulon National Park.

Apart from the multiplying resorts, the area is sparsely populated, perhaps simply because the land isn't suitable for intensive rice agriculture. It's also said that the survivors of the Krakatau eruption, and succeeding generations, believed it to be a place of ill omen and never returned.

Anyer
☎ 0254

Anyer is 12km south-west of Cilegon and is an upmarket beach resort that's popular with Jakarta residents. Anyer was once the biggest Dutch port in Selat Sunda before being totally destroyed by the tidal waves generated by the eruption of Krakatau. The Anyer lighthouse was built by the Dutch at the instigation of Queen Wilhelmina in 1885.

Karang Bolong
☎ 0254

There's another good beach here, 11km south of Anyer and 30km north of Labuan, where a huge stand of rock forms a natural archway from the land to the sea.

Carita
☎ 0253

Carita has a wide sandy beach that's good for swimming and wandering. It's the most popular beach for travellers because it has moderately priced accommodation and it is the best place to arrange visits to Krakatau and the Ujung Kulon National Park. That said, Carita is becoming very developed; condominiums now hog the beach and you even get hassling massage ladies, a la Bali. It's still relaxed on weekdays but this is no longer an unspoiled beach village.

About 2km from Carita across the rice paddies you can see the village of **Sindanglaut** (End of the Sea), where the giant tsunami of 1883 ended. The **Hutan Wisata Carita** is a forest reserve with walks through the hills and jungle. The **Curug Gendang** waterfall is a three hour return hike through the reserve.

Diving
The big hotels used to have dive shops but most have closed due to falling demand. Arrange equipment hire and dive trips in Jakarta. Boat hire is easily arranged all along the coast. The best diving is in Ujung Kulon National Park, and Krakatau and Pulau Sanghiang also have diving.

Organised Tours
In Carita, a number of small operators offers tours to Krakatau, Ujung Kulon and further afield. No bargains are on offer but they are cheaper than the larger travel agents in the hotels.

The Rakata Tourist Information Service (☎ 81124) at the Rakata Hostel is well run and a good place to start looking. Others offering similar services include the Black Rhino (☎ 81072) near the Sunset View Hotel and the privately run Tourist Information Service (☎ 81330), opposite the Hotel Desiana.

They all offer almost identical tours to Krakatau and Ujung Kulon (from US$175 per person for four days/three nights), as well as Badui villages (US$150), Pulau Dua (US$150) and even Jakarta (US$100). Expect a very favourable exchange rate for payment in rupiah. See under Krakatau for tours to those islands.

Places to Stay
The resorts along this stretch of coast are overpriced, but the standards are generally high. Dozens of hotels and villas (many private but some for rent) are spaced out along the 30km stretch from Anyer to Carita. Prices drop the further south you head from Anyer, and the only cheap accommodation is found in Carita.

On weekends the hotels fill up and prices are 20% to 30% more than the weekday rates quoted here, and 21% tax and service is added. During the week, discounts are often available and some bargaining may be required.

Anyer Most hotels in Anyer have swimming pools, restaurants and rooms with aircon, TV and hot-water showers. They are spaced out over a 5km stretch and start just south of the Anyer market, but the better places are past the Anyer lighthouse. The first one south of the lighthouse is *Hotel Mambruk Anyer* (☎ 601602), with a good range of facilities and excellent rooms from 315,000Rp to 730,000Rp, plus 21%, but the beach is not great.

Further south around the headland, *Ancotte* (☎ 601556) is one of the best mid-range buys and is on a fine stretch of sandy beach. Rooms cost from 150,000Rp; old but comfortable bungalows, many with kitchens, cost 275,000Rp and 325,000Rp. Rates are almost double on weekends.

Past Ancotte is the real centre of the Anyer resort strip with a number of places to stay and a good beach with almost white sand. *Patra Jasa Anyer* (☎ 602700) is at the northern end of this beach. Well appointed, older motel units start at 350,000Rp.

The biggest and best by far is the *Sol Elite Marbella* (☎ 602345) condominium/hotel. This Spanish-owned hotel has real Iberian style, swimming pools, shops, restaurants and a host of activities. The beach is good and is lined with small warungs and stalls selling cheap beachwear. The rooms start at 480,000Rp, plus 21%, and even at that price it can pack them in on weekends.

In the shadow of the Sol Elite Marbella, the small *Pondok Tubagus Resort* (☎ 601776) is one of the classiest on the coast and furnished in Asian antique style. The rooms and cottages cost 500,000Rp to 1,000,000Rp or 'tropical tents' right near the beach have open living rooms for 300,000Rp.

Karang Bolong A few hotels are clustered around the recreational park but there's not a lot of reasons to stay here. Karang Bolong has a dirty sprawling warung area around the car park where buses disgorge gawking local tourists. Six kilometres south, the friendly *Resor Prima Anyer* (☎ 650440) is away from the crowds and has good mid-range, air-con rooms facing the beach. They cost 170,000Rp to 423,000Rp but with a big discount they are reasonable value for this part of the world.

Carita Heading north from Labuan, the usual access point, Carita proper starts around the Km 8 mark. *Resor Lippo Carita/Clarion Suites Hotel* (☎ 81900) is a huge condominium/hotel complex that hogs the best stretch of beach for almost a kilometre, destroying Carita's character in the process. One/two-bedrooms suites are 150,000/225,000Rp on weekdays and 225,000/375,000Rp on weekends, plus 21%, which are good rates for the quality on offer.

Over the road is the popular *Rakata Hostel* (☎ 81171), which has a good restaurant and runs tours to Ujung Kulon and Krakatau. Bright rooms with bathroom for 40,000Rp and 70,000Rp (50,000Rp and 90,000Rp on weekends) are a reasonable deal in Carita. More expensive mid-range rooms with aircon and TV cost 100,000Rp (120,000Rp on weekends). All rates are subject to 11% tax.

At the southern end of the Resor Lippo, the small *Krakatau Surf Carita* (☎ 83849) is on the beach. It has some of the coast's best accommodation – very stylish one and two-bedroom villas cost US$150 to US$250, plus 21%, but expect big discounts (up to 50%).

Around the Km 9 mark, *Pondok Pandawa* (☎ 82193) is the only cheap place right on the beach but very basic and over-priced with rooms for 40,000Rp (more on weekends). Next along, the *Carita Baka Baka* (☎ 81126) is also on the beach and has a pleasant restaurant. Expensive rooms with shower and fan are around 60,000Rp or 90,000Rp with air-con, double that on weekends. Try bargaining.

Further north, across the road from the beach, the popular *Sunset View* (☎ 81075) is the best value on the coast for a budget room. Clean rooms with mandi cost only 25,000Rp.

Further north, *Carita Krakatau Hostel* (☎ *83027*) also caters to travellers, arranges tours and has a restaurant. The rooms are well back from the road and cost 30,000Rp or 50,000Rp with air-con.

Not far from the Km 10 mark, the *Niguadharma Hotel* (☎ *83288*) is a new mid-range hotel with a swimming pool and restaurant. It is over the road from the beach, but well appointed and very reasonably priced. Economy rooms are 25,000Rp; rooms with bathroom are 50,000Rp or 100,000Rp with air-con, including breakfast.

Places to Eat

Seafood warungs are scattered along the coast from Anyer to Karanga Bolang and provide the only cheap dining. Good hotel dining options in Anyer include the restaurant at the *Patra Jasa Anyer*, which has fabulous sea views and good Chinese, Indonesian and western food, or the restaurants at the *Sol Elite Marbella*, where you can get a good paella, among other things. Further south and just before Karang Bolong, *Marina Anyer Kafe* is part of a huge marina/real estate development. The cafe on the waterfront is a very fashionable spot for a drink or light meal and bands play on the weekend.

Carita has plenty of warungs and rumah makans. Opposite the Resor Lippo Carita, *Warung Kita* is basic but cheap, or *Rumah Makan Ibu Deni* is also cheap and does a good *ikan bakar* (grilled fish). The beachside restaurant at the *Carita Baka Baka* is very pleasant and reasonably priced, and the *Rakata Hostel* has decent food. The *Lesehan Resor Lippo* is a large Indonesian restaurant with dining on mats or at tables. It is part of the Lippoland development across the road from the condominiums among the fun rides, mini golf, trail bikes etc.

Further north on the waterfront, the Lippo Marina is home to the *Kafe Marina*, for sea breezes and seafood starting at around 20,000Rp. Around the Km 14 mark, the *Cafe de Paris* is an oddity – it has air-con and European food, and it accepts credit cards.

Getting There & Away

To get to Carita from Jakarta, take a bus to Labuan and then a Colt or angkot to Carita (1000Rp). Overcharging is common.

Most visitors to Anyer go by car from Jakarta – 2½ to three hours via the toll road and the turn-off at Cilegon. By bus from Jakarta, take a Merak bus (4000Rp) and get off at Cilegon from where infrequent buses run to Labuan via Anyer and Karang Bolong. Otherwise take more frequent minibuses from the Anyer market.

LABUAN
☎ 0252

The dreary little port of Labuan is merely a jumping-off point for Carita or the Ujung Kulon National Park. Wanawisata Alamhayati (☎ 81217) is about 1km north of town on the road to Carita and books accommodation on the islands at Ujung Kulon National Park. The Labuan PHPA office (☎ 81477) is 1km further along the same road and is more helpful for information on visiting Ujung Kulon independently.

Of the town's basic hotels, the *Citra Ayu Hotel* (☎ *81229, Jl Perintis Kemerdekaan 27*) is the best bet, but Carita is only a few kilometres up the road from Labuan and has much better accommodation.

Getting There & Away

Frequent buses depart from Kalideres bus terminal in Jakarta for Labuan (5000Rp, 3½ hours) via Serang and Pandeglang. Frequent buses also go from Labuan to Bogor (5000Rp, four hours), Rangkasbitung (2500Rp, 1½ hours) and Serang (2500Rp, 1½ hours), while buses to Merak (3000Rp, two hours), Bandung (9000Rp, seven hours) and other destinations are less frequent and usually leave in the morning only.

Angkots for Carita (1000Rp, half-hour) leave from the market, 100m from the Labuan bus terminal, as do minibuses to Sumur (4000Rp, three hours).

KRAKATAU

The legendary Krakatau lies in the Selat Sunda straits – 50km from the West Java coast and 40km from Sumatra. Today only a small part of the original volcano remains, but when Krakatau blew itself apart in 1883, in one of the world's greatest and most catastrophic eruptions, the effects were recorded far beyond Selat Sunda and it achieved instant and lasting infamy.

For centuries Krakatau had been a familiar nautical landmark for much of the world's maritime traffic that was funnelled through the narrow Selat Sunda straits. The volcano had been dormant since 1680 and was widely regarded as extinct, but from May through to early August in 1883 passing ships reported moderate activity. By 26 August Krakatau was raging and the explosions became more and more violent.

At 10 am on 27 August 1883 Krakatau erupted with the biggest bang ever recorded on earth. On the island of Rodriguez, more than 4600km to the south-west, a police chief reported hearing the booming of 'heavy guns from eastward'; in Alice Springs, Australia, 3500km to the southeast, residents also reported hearing strange explosions from the north-west.

With its cataclysmic explosions, Krakatau sent up a record column of ash 80km high and threw into the air nearly 20 cubic km of rock. Ash fell on Singapore 840km to the north and on ships as far as 6000km away; darkness covered the Selat Sunda straits from 10 am on 27 August until dawn the next day.

Far more destructive were the great ocean waves triggered by the collapse of Krakatau's cones into its empty belly. A giant tsunami more than 40m high swept over the nearby shores of Java and Sumatra, and the sea wave's passage was recorded far from Krakatau, reaching Aden (on the Arabian Peninsula) in 12 hours over a distance 'travelled by a good steamer in 12 days'. Measurable wave effects were even said to have reached the English Channel. Coastal Java and Sumatra were devastated: 165 villages were destroyed and more than 36,000 people were killed.

The following day a telegram sent to Singapore from Batavia (160km east of Krakatau) reported odd details such as 'fish dizzy and caught with glee by natives'! Three months later the dust thrown into the atmosphere caused such vivid sunsets in the USA that fire engines were being called out to quench the apparent fires, and for three years it continued to circle the earth, creating strange and spectacular sunsets.

The astonishing return of life to the devastated islands has been the subject of

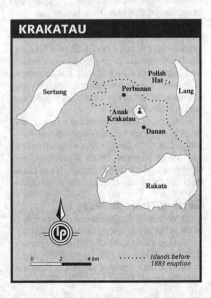

KRAKATAU

Sertung

Polish Hat

Perbunan

Lang

Anak Krakatau

Danan

Rakata

0   2   4 km

· · · · · · Islands before 1883 eruption

The Formation of Krakatau

Thousands of years ago Krakatau built up a cone-shaped mountain which eventually formed a huge caldera over 6km across and mostly beneath water level. The peaks of the rim projected as four small islands – Sertung on the north-west, Lang and the Polish Hat on the north-east, and Rakata ('Crab' in old Javanese) on the south-east. Later volcanic activity threw up two cones, Perbunan and Danan, which merged with the Rakata cone to form a single island – Krakatau – that extended almost completely across the caldera. When an eruption in 1883 ended, Lang and the Polish Hat had disappeared and only a stump of the original Krakatau, with the caldera of Rakata, remained above sea level.

scientific study ever since. Not a single plant was found on Krakatau a few months after the event; 100 years later – although the only fauna are snakes, insects, rats, bats and birds – it seems almost as though the vegetation was never disturbed.

Krakatau basically blew itself to smithereens but, roughly where the 1883 eruption began, Anak Krakatau (Child of Krakatau) has been vigorously growing ever since its first appearance in 1928. It has a restless and uncertain temperament, sending out showers of glowing rocks and belching smoke and ashes.

Krakatau is still a menacing volcano, and in its more active phases intermittent rumblings can be heard on quiet nights from the west coast beaches. Boats sometimes land on the east side, but it's not possible to climb right up the cinder cones to the caldera.

Getting There & Away

Most visitors to Krakatau come from Carita or the other beach resorts on the west coast of Java. However, Krakatau officially lies in Sumatra's Lampung Province and it is slightly shorter, and cheaper, to reach Krakatau from the small port of Kalianda, 30km north

of the ferry terminal at Bakauheni (see the Sumatra chapter for details).

Carita is the usual place to arrange a trip to Krakatau, but more than likely you will have to charter a boat. The tour operators (see under West Coast Beaches) will take down the names of interested travellers wanting to share a boat, but usually the numbers just aren't available and you will have to charter.

Prices vary depending on the quality of the boat, but the cost of chartering is now more affordable given the rupiah's devaluation. Charter the best boat you can afford. During the rainy season (November to March) there are strong currents and rough seas, but even during the dry season strong south-east winds can whip up the swells and make a crossing inadvisable. When weather conditions are fine it's a long one day trip, but having visited Krakatau we'd say it's definitely worth the effort – *if* you can hire a safe boat.

Small fishing boats may be cheap but so are the tales of travellers who spent the night, or longer, adrift in high swells. At the very least charter one of the large fishing boats that take up to 10 people for around 800,000Rp per boat. These can be organised through Carita agents or for slightly less at Carita village or Labuan.

On the other hand, speed boats from Carita Marina start at around one million rupiah. They will do the trip in just over an hour instead of three or four hours, life jackets should be provided and most have radios. The big hotels also arrange speed boats at higher rates.

UJUNG KULON NATIONAL PARK

Ujung Kulon National Park is on the remote south-western tip of Java, covering about 760 sq km of land area, including the large **Pulau Panaitan**. Because of its isolation and difficult access, Ujung Kulon has remained an outpost of primeval forest and untouched wilderness in heavily developed Java. The park was declared a World Heritage Site in 1991 and presents some fine opportunities for hiking. It also has some good beaches with intact coral reefs. Few people visit the park, but despite its remoteness, it is one of the most rewarding national parks in Java.

Ujung Kulon is best known as the last refuge in Java for the once plentiful one-horned rhinoceros, now numbering only around 60. The shy Javan rhino, however, is an extremely rare sight and you are far more likely to come across banteng (wild cattle), wild pigs, otters, squirrels, leaf monkeys and gibbons. Panthers also live in the forest and crocodiles in the river estuaries, but these are also a rare sight. Green turtles nest in some of the bays and Ujung Kulon also has a wide variety of birdlife. On Pulau Peucang, sambar deer, long-tailed macaques and big monitor lizards are common, and there is good snorkelling around coral reefs.

The main park area is on the peninsula but the park also includes the nearby island of Panaitan and the smaller offshore islands of Peucang and Handeuleum. Much of the peninsula is dense lowland rainforest and a mixture of scrub, grassy plains, swamps, pandanus palms, and long stretches of sandy beach on the west and south coasts. Walking trails follow the coast around much of the peninsula and loop round Gunung Payung on the western tip.

Information

The park office in Labuan is a useful source of information, but pay your entry fee (2500Rp) when you enter the park at the park office in Tamanjaya or on the islands. Pick up a copy of the excellent *Visitor's Guidebook to the Trails of Ujung Kulon National Park*.

Visit Ujung Kulon in the dry season (April to October) when the sea is generally calm and the reserve is not so boggy. Malaria has been reported in Ujung Kulon.

Guides must be hired for hiking in the park and cost around 15,000Rp to 20,000Rp per day. Bring lightweight food, such as packaged noodles, and drinking water if trekking. Supplies are available in Tamanjaya, but Sumur and Labuan have more choice.

Exploring the Park

The main way to reach the park, and the only cheap option, is by road to Tamanjaya, which

has accommodation and can arrange guides for the three day hike across to the west coast and on to Pulau Peucang. This is the most rewarding way to explore the park and its diversity. It can be tackled by anyone of reasonable fitness, but is not an easy walk.

Conditions on the trail are basic – there are rough shelters but some are almost derelict. If you have a tent, bring it. The trail heads to the south coast and the hut near Cibandawoh beach. The second day is a five hour walk along the beach to the hut at Sungai Cibunar – rivers have to be waded. On the third day, most hikers cross over the hills to the west coast at Cidaon, opposite Peucang. An alternative and longer trail with good coastal scenery goes from Cibunar via Sanghiang Sirah and the lighthouse at Tanjung Layar, the westernmost tip of mainland Java.

Pulau Peucang is the other main entry into the park but can only be reached by chartered boat. Good but very expensive accommodation and a restaurant are run by a private company, Wanawisata Alamhayati. Peucang also has beautiful white-sand beaches and coral reefs on the sheltered eastern coast. Hikers might be able to hitch a lift on a boat out of Peucang, but don't count on it.

Wanawisata Alamhayati also has comfortable but simple accommodation at **Pulau Handeuleum**, which is ringed by mangroves and doesn't have Peucang's attractions. Boats or canoes can be hired for the short crossing to Cigenter, on the mainland opposite Pulau Handeuleum, and other trails can be explored on this side of the park.

Large **Pulau Panaitan** is more expensive to reach, but has some fine beaches and some hiking opportunities. Panaitan is also popular with surfers – tours operate out of Bali. It is a day's walk between the PHPA posts at Legon Butun and Legon Haji, or you can walk to the top of Gunung Raksa, topped by a Hindu statue of Ganesh, from Citambuyung on the east coast.

Organised Tours

Wanawisata Alamhayati (☎ 021-641 1124) at the Ancol Marina in Jakarta has all-inclusive two day/three-night tours to Pulau Peucang from US$256 to US$323 per person, depending on accommodation, for two people.

A typical tour from Carita is four days/three nights with a transfer by car to Sumur, then a boat to Handeuleum where you camp. Then you trek to Jamang and camp overnight at the rangers' post. The next day you can explore around Tanjung Alang Alang and the nearby beaches, then return. The all-inclusive tours cost US$175 per person for a minimum of four people, but expect big discounts.

The park office at Tamanjaya can arrange boat hire for 150,000Rp return to Handeuleum, or 350,000Rp to 500,000Rp to Peucang, depending on the boat. Both islands can arrange a variety of activities, but as they are run by Wanawisata Alamhayati they are overpriced. Guides can be hired on the islands or at Tamanjaya for 15,000Rp to 20,000Rp per day.

Places to Stay

The **Wisma Cinta Alam** (Labuan ☎ 025-81477) is opposite the national park office at Tamanjaya, and has three-bedroom cottages with kitchen and sitting area for 35,000Rp per room. The village also has homestays: Pak Kumar's **Sunda Jaya** homestay has rooms for only 10,000Rp per person and meals can be arranged. Tamanjaya is a sleepy, rural village with a few shops and warungs.

The pleasant **guesthouse** at Pulau Handeuleum has doubles/triples for US$15 a double, US$25 a quad, plus 15%. It has a kitchen but bring your own food as the island has no other dining options.

Pulau Peucang has double rooms in the old **guesthouse** for US$35, which is an outrageous price for losmen standard accommodation. The much more luxurious **Flora A & B bungalows** have air-con, hot water and refrigerators for US$70 and US$90 a double. Add 15% to all rates, including food in the expensive but very good restaurant. Expect discounts for rupiah payment.

Advance bookings through Wanawisata Alamhayati (Jakarta ☎ 021-6411124, Labuan 025-81217) are recommended at both islands, particularly on weekends.

Within the park you can **camp** or stay at the primitive **huts**. Bring food for yourselves and your guide.

Getting There & Away

The cheapest way to get to the park is by bus from Labuan to Sumur (4000Rp, four hours). From Sumur to Tamanjaya it is 20km along a terrible road and only ojeks (7500Rp) tackle it. Sumur is a large fishing village and has warungs, shops and a basic losmen. The **Ciputih Beach** (☎ 021-8281093) is a midrange resort 7km from Sumur towards Tamanjaya, but it is very isolated.

The only other way to reach the park is to charter a boat. Given the long stretch of open sea, which is often subject to large swells, take a good boat. This would mean either a large fishing boat or a speed launch, which will cost around 1,000,000Rp from Labuan or Carita. Sumur is cheaper – a large fishing boat will cost around 500,000Rp return to Peucang, which can also be reached by charter boat from Tamanjaya.

BOGOR

☎ 0251   • pop 712,000

In colonial times, Bogor was the most important Dutch hill station, midway between the mountains and the hot plains of Jakarta, 60km to the north. Governor General van Imhoff built his large country estate, Buitenzorg (Without a Care), here in 1745 and it became the favoured retreat for successive governor generals. Daendels made it his semi-official residence in 1808, and during the British interregnum Sir Stamford Raffles made it his country home. Raffles judged Bogor 'a romantic little village', but Bogor has grown to become almost a Jakarta suburb.

Bogor's main attraction is its world-class botanical gardens, which is a vast expanse of luxuriant greenery in the middle of the city. The gardens can be visited as a day trip from Jakarta, or since the capital is only one hour away, Bogor can be used as a cooler and much more relaxed base from which to visit Jakarta. From Bogor you can venture to the nearby mountains that surround the city or continue on to Bandung or Pelabuhanratu.

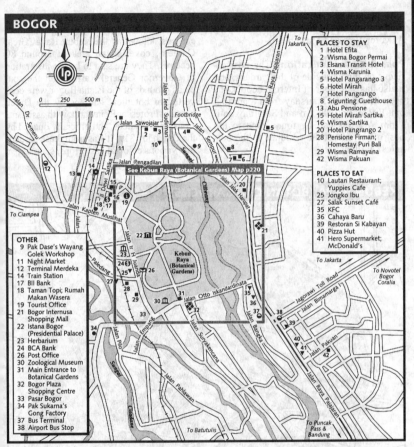

BOGOR

PLACES TO STAY
1 Hotel Efita
2 Wisma Bogor Permai
3 Elsana Transit Hotel
4 Wisma Karunia
5 Hotel Pangarango 3
6 Hotel Mirah
7 Hotel Pangrango
8 Srigunting Guesthouse
13 Abu Pensione
15 Hotel Mirah Sartika
16 Wisma Sartika
20 Hotel Pangrango 2
28 Pensione Firman;
   Homestay Puri Bali
29 Wisma Ramayana
42 Wisma Pakuan

PLACES TO EAT
10 Lautan Restaurant;
   Yuppies Cafe
25 Jongko Ibu
27 Salak Sunset Café
35 KFC
36 Cahaya Baru
39 Restoran Si Kabayan
40 Pizza Hut
41 Hero Supermarket;
   McDonald's

OTHER
9 Pak Dase's Wayang
   Golek Workshop
11 Night Market
12 Terminal Merdeka
14 Train Station
18 BII Bank
18 Taman Topi; Rumah
   Makan Wasera
19 Tourist Office
21 Bogor Internusa
   Shopping Mall
22 Istana Bogor
   (Presidential Palace)
23 Herbarium
24 BCA Bank
26 Post Office
30 Zoological Museum
31 Main Entrance to
   Botanical Gardens
32 Bogor Plaza
   Shopping Centre
33 Pasar Bogor
34 Pak Sukarna's
   Gong Factory
37 Bus Terminal
38 Airport Bus Stop

Kebun
Raya
(Botanical
Gardens)

See Kebun Raya (Botanical Gardens) Map p220

Though Bogor stands at a height of only 290m it's appreciably cooler than Jakarta, but visitors in the wet season should bear in mind the town's 'City of Rain' nickname. Bogor has probably the highest annual rainfall in Java and is credited with a record 322 thunderstorms a year.

Information

Tourist Offices The tourist office (☎ 338 052) on the west side of the gardens at Jl Ir H Juanda 10 has a rough map of the town but not much else. It is open Monday to Thursday from 7 am to 2 pm, Friday until 11 am and Saturday until noon. A branch is at the entrance to the gardens.

At Jl Ir H Juanda 15, next to the main garden gates, is the headquarters of the PHPA – the official body for administration of all of Indonesia's wildlife reserves and national parks.

Money Bogor has plenty of banks all over town. The Bank Central Asia (BCA) is at Jl

Ir H Juanda 28. The BII bank is near the train station on Jl Dewi Sartika and has an ATM for Visa and MasterCard.

Post & Communications The post office is on the west side of the gardens, and it also has a number of Internet booths. It's open Monday to Thursday from 8 am to 3 pm, Friday until 11 am and Saturday until 1 pm. Wartels can be found next to the post office and at the entrance to the botanical gardens.

Kebun Raya (Botanical Gardens)

At the heart of Bogor are the huge botanical gardens, known as the Kebun Raya (Great Garden), covering an area of around 80 hectares. They are said to be the inspiration of Governor General Raffles, but the spacious grounds of the Istana Bogor were converted to botanical gardens by the Dutch botanist Professor Reinwardt, with assistants from Kew Gardens, and officially opened by the Dutch in 1817. It was from these gardens that various colonial cash crops, such as tea,

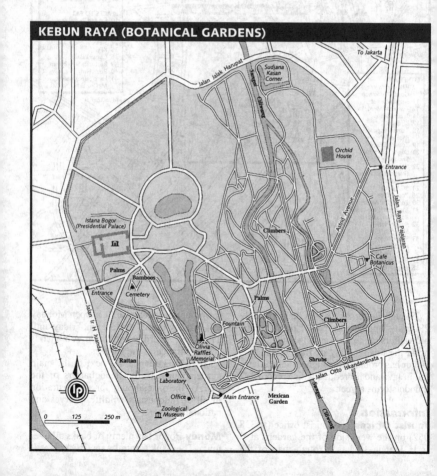

KEBUN RAYA (BOTANICAL GARDENS)

cassava, tobacco and cinchona, were developed by early Dutch researchers during the infamous Cultivation Period in the 19th century. The park is still a major centre for botanical research in Indonesia.

The gardens contain streams and lotus ponds, and more than 15,000 species of trees and plants, including 400 types of magnificent palms. The orchid houses are reputed to contain more than 3000 orchid varieties. Close to the main entrance of the gardens is a small **monument** in memory of Olivia Raffles who died in 1814 and was buried in Batavia. Further behind and near the palace is a **cemetery** with Dutch headstones. The *Cafe Botanicus* on the eastern side of the gardens has a fine view across the lawns and is a pleasant place for a snack or drink.

The gardens are open daily from 8 am to 5 pm. Entry costs 2500Rp during the week and 1500Rp on Sunday and holidays. Crowds flock on Sunday, but on other days the gardens are very peaceful and a fine place to escape from the hassles and crowds of Jakarta. The southern gate is the main entrance; other gates are only open on Sunday and holidays.

Zoological Museum

Near the botanical gardens entrance, this museum has a motley but interesting collection of zoological oddities, including the skeleton of a blue whale. If you've heard about Flores having a rat problem, one glance at the stuffed Flores version in the showcase of Indonesian rats will explain why. Admission to the museum is 500Rp, and it's open daily from 8 am to 4 pm.

Istana Bogor (Presidential Palace)

In the north-west corner of the botanical gardens, the summer palace of the president was formerly the official residence of the Dutch governor generals from 1870 to 1942. The present huge mansion is not Buitenzorg though; this was destroyed by an earthquake and a new palace was built on the site a few years later in 1856.

In colonial days, deer were raised in the parklands to provide meat for banquets, and through the gates you can still see herds of white-spotted deer roaming on the immaculate lawns. The Dutch elite would come up from the pest hole of Batavia and many huge, glamorous parties were held here. Following independence, the palace was a much favoured retreat for Soekarno, although it was ignored by Soeharto.

Today the building contains Soekarno's huge art collection, much of which lays great emphasis on the female figure, but the palace is only open to groups (minimum 10) by prior arrangement and children are not allowed inside. Contact the tourist office in advance or it may also be able to include interested individuals on a tour that is already booked.

Other Attractions

The **Batutulis** is an inscribed stone dedicated to Sri Baduga Maharaja (1482-1521), a Pajajaran king accredited with great mystical power. The stone is housed in a small shrine visited by pilgrims – remove your shoes and pay a small donation before entering. Batutulis is 2.5km south of the botanical gardens, on Jl Batutulis. It's almost opposite the former home of Soekarno, who was attracted by the stone's mystical power. His request to be buried here was ignored by Soeharto who wanted the former president's grave as far away from the capital as possible.

One of the few remaining gongsmiths in West Java is Pak Sukarna, and you can visit his **gong factory** at Jl Pancasan 17. Gongs and other gamelan instruments are smelted over a charcoal fire in the small workshop out the back. A few gongs and wayang golek puppets are on sale in the front showroom.

Pak Dase makes quality puppets at his **wayang golek workshop** in Lebak Kantin RT 02/VI, down by the river, just north of the botanical gardens. Take the footbridge to the Wisma Karunia from Jl Jen Sudirman and ask for Pak Dase in the kampung.

Places to Stay – Budget

Bogor has a good selection of family-run places. The most popular budget options are close to each other, midway between the train station and bus terminal near the botanic gardens.

Pensione Firman (☎ *323246, Jl Pale-dang 48)* is friendly, well run and cheap. A few basic rooms at the back cost from 17,000Rp and better rooms with mandi are 25,000Rp and 30,000Rp. The owner speaks excellent English, tours are offered and meals are served.

Homestay Puri Bali (☎ *317498, Jl Pale-dang 50)* is next door and is more spacious. It has large doubles with bathroom for 30,000Rp and 40,000Rp, including breakfast. It also has a Balinese-style restaurant in a pleasant garden setting.

Around the corner, across from the gardens, the *Wisma Ramayana* (☎ *320364, Jl Ir H Juanda 54)* has the most colonial charm. It has a big variety of rooms at the back, with and without bath, from 27,000Rp to 36,000Rp, or the rooms at front for 37,500Rp have the most style. A couple of huge family rooms are also available for 50,000Rp and 53,000Rp. Breakfast is included.

The other main hotel geared to the travellers' trade is *Abu Pensione* (☎ *322893)*, which is near the train station at Jl Mayor Oking 15. This clean, attractive hotel is good for information and travel services. A few basic singles cost 15,000Rp or more substantial budget doubles are 25,000Rp. Most rooms have attached bath and range from 30,000Rp up to mid-range quality rooms for 60,000Rp with air-con and hot water. Breakfast is an extra 6000Rp. It also has a good restaurant overlooking the littered river.

Other options include the *Wisma Sartika* (☎ *323747, Jl Dewi Sartika 4D)*, on the other side of the train station. This family concern is convenient, but the simple rooms for 30,000Rp, or 40,000Rp and 50,000Rp with shower, are expensive. North of the botanical gardens, *Wisma Karunia* (☎ *323411, Jl Sem-pur 33-5)* is a long way from the city centre but is a quiet and very friendly family-run place. It is reasonably priced at 15,000Rp for doubles with shared bath, and 30,000Rp to 35,000Rp for rooms with private bath.

Places to Stay – Mid-Range

Wisma Pakuan (☎ *319430, Jl Pakuan 12)* is in a large, modern family home south-east of the bus terminal. Well kept rooms with balcony cost 55,000Rp and 66,000Rp with attached bath and hot water, or bigger air-con rooms at the front are 71,500Rp. It is a good buy, breakfast is included and the family is very helpful.

One of the newest and best, halfway between a guesthouse and a hotel, is the smaller *Wisma Bogor Permai* (☎ *381633, Jl Sawojajar 38)*. Excellently appointed rooms with carpet, TV and minibar cost 100,000Rp for twin rooms or 125,000Rp for doubles. Discounts of 20% to 30% have been on offer, making it exceptional value. The rooms face a courtyard garden and there is a small coffee shop.

Nearby, the *Hotel Efita* (☎ *333400, Jl Sawojajar 5)* is bigger and not as cosy, but it is also relatively new and has very good rooms with minibar, TV etc for 86,000Rp and 110,000Rp. *Hotel Mirah Sartika* (☎ *312343, Jl Dewi Sartika 6A)* has older rooms but they are spacious and moderately priced. Rooms, all with hot water and TV, cost 55,000Rp to 75,000Rp, plus 15%.

Another good hunting ground for mid-range hotels is north-east of the botanical gardens. *Hotel Mirah* (☎ *328044, Jl Pan-grango 9A)* is a long-running hotel with a small swimming pool. The older rooms for 65,000Rp to 90,000Rp are very average but rooms in the impressive new wing for 135,000Rp are quite luxurious and are among the best in this range. Add 21% to the rates. Next door, the *Hotel Pangrango* (☎ *328670, Jl Pangrango 23)* also has a small pool and a variety of older rooms for 99,000Rp to 166,000Rp, plus 21%. It's new sister hotel, *Hotel Pangarango 3* (☎ *343433, Jl Raya Pajajaran 1)* doesn't have a pool, but the rooms are better and good value at 103,000Rp up to 133,100Rp for large suites.

Places to Stay – Top End

The best hotel in the city centre is the new *Hotel Pangrango 2* (☎ *321482, Jl Raya Pa-jajaran 32)*. This three star hotel has a pool, restaurant and good rooms for 181,500Rp and 242,000Rp.

Top of the heap is the very stylish *Novotel Bogor Coralia* (☎ 271555, *Golf Estat Bogor Raya)*, with rooms for US$110 to US$130. It's a long way from town – from the end of the Jagorawi toll road, take the side road next to the toll road for about 5km through a real estate development and then a golf course.

Places to Eat

Cheap *food stalls* appear at night along Jl Dewi Sartika and during the day you'll find plenty of food stalls and good fruit at *Pasar Bogor*, the market close to the main garden gates. In the late afternoon along Jl Raja Permas next to the train station, *street vendors* cook up delicious snacks, such as deep-fried *tahu* (tofu) and *pisang goreng* (fried banana fritters). Also near the train station, Taman Topi is a fun park with a number of good little cafes, such as the *Rumah Makan Wasera*, good for sate and *gule kambing* (goat curry).

The *Pujasera* is an air-con hawkers' centre on the top floor of the Bogor Plaza shopping centre opposite the entrance to the botanical gardens. *Es Teler KK* is one of the better stalls for inexpensive lunches and good fruit juices.

The *Salak Sunset Café (Jl Paledang 38)* is attached to the Alliance Française and is a chic, cheap little place with river views. Juices, pizzas, spaghetti and Indonesian favourites are featured.

A good restaurant for Sundanese food is the *Jongko Ibu* opposite the post office at Jl Ir H Juanda 36. The prices are moderate and you can dine buffet-style and try a number of dishes. *Restoran Si Kabayan* (☎ 311849, *Jl Bina Marga I No 2)* is one of Bogor's most pleasant Sundanese restaurants with individual bamboo huts arranged around an attractive garden. You'll need to order a number of dishes to get your fill, but this restaurant is reasonably priced.

Jl Pajajaran is near the end of the Jagorawi toll road and is a good hunting ground for restaurants. The air-con *Cahaya Baru (Jl Raya Pajajaran 7)* is Bogor's best Chinese restaurant, and it is flanked by good Padang restaurants. On the corner of Jl Otto Iskandardinata is *KFC*, or further south is a *Pizza Hut* and *McDonald's* attached to the Hero supermarket.

Getting There & Away

Bus Buses from Jakarta (2000/3000Rp for normal/air-con) depart every 15 minutes or so from the Kampung Rambutan bus terminal, and can do the trip in a little over half an hour via the Jagorawi Hwy toll road. The only problem is that it takes at least double that time to travel between Kampung Rambutan and central Jakarta.

A Damri bus goes to Jakarta's Soekarno-Hatta airport (7000Rp) hourly from 4 am to 6 pm. It leaves from Jl Bimamaga I, opposite the Restaurant Yenny, near the end of the Jagorawi toll road.

Buses depart frequently from Bogor to Bandung (4000/7000Rp, three hours). On weekends the buses are not allowed to go via the scenic Puncak Pass and therefore travel via Sukabumi (5000/8000Rp, four hours). Other bus destinations from Bogor include Pelabuhanratu (3000Rp), Rangkasbitung (3000Rp), Labuan (5000Rp) and Merak (5000Rp). To Pangandaran (15,000Rp, seven hours), the Sari Bakti Utama bus leaves at 6.30 pm.

Air-con, door-to-door minibuses go to Bandung for 20,000Rp. Dewa (☎ 653672) and Master (☎ 379184) have the best buses and you can ring for pick-up or the guesthouses can arrange them.

Angkots to villages around Bogor, including Ciampea (No 5), depart from the Terminal Merdeka near the train station.

Train The easiest way to reach central Jakarta is to take the trains, which operate every 20 minutes from around 4 am to 8 pm and take 1½ hours. They cost 900Rp to Gambir train station or 1000Rp to Kota. The ekonomi trains are reasonably efficient but best avoided during peak hours when they can be crowded with commuters. Much more comfortable *Pakuan* express trains leave Bogor at 6.22, 6.45 (air-con) and 9.36 am, and 1.12, 2.48 (air-con), 3.34, 5.24 (air-con) and 5.48 pm. Pakuan trains cost 4000Rp in bisnis and 6000Rp in air-con eksekutif.

Slow ekonomi trains between Bogor and Sukabumi depart at 7.55 am, and 1.15 and 5.40 pm, and take about two hours. There is no direct train service to Bandung.

Car Bogor is a good place to hire a car and driver. Bargaining is essential. Bogor has a number of private operators who are used to taking tourists on day trips or extended trips further afield. Many speak English, some speak Dutch. Prices start at around 100,000Rp per day for a sedan. This price includes a driver but not the petrol, and if you've booked through a hotel expect it to add on a large commission.

Getting Around
Green angkot minibuses (300Rp) shuttle around town, particularly between the bus terminal and train station. Blue angkots run to outlying districts and terminate at Terminal Merdeka. From the bus terminal, angkots leave from the street behind, Jl Bangka – angkot No 03 does an anti-clockwise loop of the botanical gardens on its way to Jl Muslihat, near the train station. To the bus terminal from the tourist office take No 06.

Becaks are banned from the main road encircling the gardens. Metered taxis are nonexistent, but you can haggle with the minivan drivers that hang out near the entrance to the botanical gardens.

AROUND BOGOR
Purnawarman Stone (Batutulis)
From the village of Ciampea, about 12km north-west of Bogor, you can take a Colt to Batutulis, where sits a large black boulder on which King Purnawarman inscribed his name and footstep around 450 AD. His inscription, in the Palawa script of South India, reads 'This is the footstep of King Purnawarman of Tarumanegara kingdom, the great conqueror of the world.'

The Ciampea boulder has been raised from its original place and embedded in the shallow water of Sungai Ciaruteun. The inscription on the stone is still remarkably clear after more than 1500 years.

Gunung Halimun National Park
This new national park is home to some primary rainforest, but the park has mixed usage and also includes plantations such as the Nirmala Tea Estate. The dominant feature of the park is the rich montane forest in the highland regions around Gunung Halimun (1929m), which is the highest peak.

Visitor facilities at the park are not developed and park administration is handled by the Gede Pangrango National Park at Cibodas. The most visited attractions of the park are the waterfalls near Cikidang and those near the Nirmala estate, but the big drawcard is **white-water rafting**. BJ's Rafting (☎ 021-9233312), Jl Duren Tiga Pav 42A, Jakarta, organises whitewater rafting on the Class III Sungai Citarak on the south-east edge of the park.

The usual access (you need your own transport) is via Cibadak on the Bogor-Pelabuhanratu road, from where you turn off to Cikadang and then on to Nirmala Tea Estate. Rainfall in the park is around 4000mm to 6000mm per year, most of which falls from October to May, when a visit is more or less out of the question.

SUKABUMI & SELABINTANA
☎ 0266
Sukabumi is a thriving commercial town of 120,000 people at the foot of Pangrango and Gede volcanoes. The main reason to visit is for bus connections to Bandung and Pelabuhanratu or to visit Selabintana, a small hill resort 7km north of town.

Selabintana is much less developed but also much less crowded than the Puncak Pass resort area to the north of Gunung Gede. It is possible to walk up the hillside to **Sawer Waterfall** and on to **Gunung Gede**, but there is no PHPA post in Selabintana. Selabintana has a golf course, swimming pools and a selection of mid-range hotels. Otherwise Selabintana is simply a quiet place to relax and soak up the mountain air.

Places to Stay
Minibuses from Sukabumi (take a No 10 from the Yogya department store) to Se-

Sunda Kelapa schooner dock, Jakarta.

Once a VOC warehouse, now Museum Bahari.

A symbol of war and fertility – Cannon Si Jagur.

Soekarno's legacy – National Monument, Jakarta.

Chinese Vihara Dharma Bhakti temple, Jakarta.

A view past Dutch-built canals to modern Jakarta.

OLIVIER CIRENDINI

Agricultural worker on the tea-carpeted slopes of Gunung Mas Tea Estate, Cisarua, West Java.

GLENN BEANLAND

Brightly coloured *perahu* (boats) in the fishing village and beach resort of Pangandaran, West Java.

labintana run straight up to the foot of Gunung Gede and terminate at the old fashioned, slightly faded *Hotel Selabintana (☎ 221501, Jl Selabintana, Km 7)*. It has a golf course, tennis and volley ball courts, two swimming pools and a bar/restaurant. The rooms cost 40,000Rp or huge bungalows with antique furniture cost 90,000Rp and 150,000Rp. Add 20% tax and service, but this hotel is still a bargain.

Although Hotel Selabintana is *the* place to stay and there is not a lot to do if you stay elsewhere, Selabintana has plenty of other hotels. Budget accommodation is available in the main village, around the Km 6 marker. Best value is the *Hotel Intan (☎ 223031)* at 27,500Rp for good rooms with carpet and attached bathroom. The upstairs rooms are lighter and have views.

PELABUHANRATU
☎ 0266

Pelabuhanratu is 90km south of Bogor and is a seaside resort that's popular with Jakarta residents. Outside this small fishing town, the large horseshoe bay has black-sand beaches and lush scenery, with rice paddies coming almost to the water's edge. Though quiet during the week, it can be crowded at weekends and holidays, and accommodation reflects Jakarta prices, ie expensive.

Swimming is possible when the sea is quiet but like most of Java's south coast, the crashing surf can be treacherous. Drownings do occur in spite of the warning signs. Legend states that Pelabuhanratu (Harbour of the Queen) actually witnessed the creation of Nyai Loro Kidul, the malevolent goddess who takes fishermen and swimmers off to her watery kingdom. Don't wear green on the beach or in the water (it's her colour), and in the Hotel Indonesia Samudra a room is set aside for meditating mystics wishing to contact the Queen of the South Seas.

Information
The tourist office (☎ 433298) is on Jl Kidang Kencana, just west of the fish market, and a wartel is next door.

BCA bank on Jl Siliwangi will change US dollars and travellers cheques, cash only for other currencies, but the rates are low. The ATM accepts Visa card.

Things to See & Do
The town of Pelabuhanratu has little interest, but the harbour is dotted with brightly painted *perahus* (outrigger boats) and the fish market is lively in the morning. The beaches to the west hold the main interest and some have good surfing. **Cimaja** is 8km west of Pelabuhanratu and has a pebble beach, and the best surf when it is working.

Pantai Karang Hawu is 13km west of Pelabuhanratu and is a towering cliff with caves, rocks and pools that were created by a large lava flow that pushed over the beach. According to legend, it was from the rocks of Karang Hawu that Nyai Loro Kidul (Queen of the South Seas) leapt into the mighty ocean to regain her lost beauty and never returned. Stairs lead up to a small *kramat* (shrine) at the top.

Further west, about 2km past Cisolok, are the **Cipanas** hot springs. Boiling water sprays into the river and you can soak downstream where the hot and cold waters mingle. It is a very scenic area and you can walk a few kilometres upstream through the lush forest to a waterfall. Cipanas has changing sheds, warungs and crowds on the weekend.

Goa Lalay is a bat cave that's about 4km south-east of Pelabuhanratu. It's of limited interest except at sunset when thousands of small bats fly out.

Places to Stay & Eat
Pelabuhanratu has plenty of mid-range accommodation and a few vaguely cheap options. The beach and the nicest accommodation starts 1km west from the town.

The cheap options in town are on Jl Siliwangi, a few hundred metres before the harbour. *Penginapan Laut Kidul (Jl Siliwangi 148)* has simple but clean rooms with bath from 22,500Rp, but there is little reason to stay in town. Pelabuhanratu has some excellent Chinese seafood restaurants, the pick of which are the *Restoran Sanggar*

Sari (Jl Siliwangi 76) and the *Queen Restaurant (Jl Kidang Kencana)*.

About 1.5km from town on a headland, *Buana Ayu (☎ 431111)* is the best value accommodation close to town. Rooms with air-con and bathroom for 75,000Rp to 85,000Rp are perched above the sea with great views. The restaurant is the sort of place you could sit all day – good seafood, great views and sea breezes.

In Citepus village, 3km from Pelabuhanratu, *Padi Padi (☎ 42124)* is the most stylish hotel on the coast with Santa Fe architecture, rustic Asian furnishings and a good restaurant. Superb rooms with private porches backing on to a fish pond maze cost US$79 to US$149, or much less at the rupiah rate.

About 5km west of town, the *Hotel Indonesia Samudra (☎ 431200)* is one of Soekarno's original luxury hotels built in the 1960s to kick start tourism in Indonesia. It has a huge pool and some wonderful 60s touches but this government-run hotel is at least a decade overdue for renovations. Down-at-heel singles/doubles cost US$70/80 but various *paket* (packages) are on offer, for as little as 150,000/250,000Rp including breakfast and dinner. Room 308 is said to be the haunt of the Queen of the South Seas.

Eight kilometres out at Cimaja, the surfing beach, there is also a range of accommodation. The *Mustika Rata (☎ 431233)* is a reasonable and cheap option with fan rooms for 20,000Rp to 90,000Rp. The *Hotel Daun Daun* in the village is another budget option with rooms from 25,000Rp, and the *Rumah Makan Mirasa* nearby is a favourite with surfers. *Pondok Kencana (☎ 431465)*, up above the main road, has a small swimming pool and the Ombak 7 pub, with surf flicks and other diversions. Villas with lounge rooms start at 120,000Rp.

A few kilometres further towards Cisolok is the *Wisma Tenang (☎ 431365)*, with so-so rooms for 40,000Rp and 60,000Rp, but it is right on the beach. On the other side of the road, the good *Pantai Mutiara (☎ 431330)* has a small swimming pool and fitness centre. The rooms cost 35,000Rp to 170,000Rp and around 30% more on weekends.

Getting There & Away

The road from Bogor cuts south over the pass between Gunung Salak and Pangrango through valleys and hillsides of rubber, coconut, cocoa and tea plantations, and terraced rice fields. By car, Pelabuhanratu can be reached in four hours from Jakarta. Local buses run throughout the day from Bogor (3000Rp, three hours) and Sukabumi (2500Rp, 2½ hours). Buses from Sukabumi continue on to Cisolok from Pelabuhanratu, and it is possible to continue right along the south coast by a variety of connections.

Getting Around

Angkots run between Pelabuhanratu and Cisolok (800Rp) and occasionally continue on to Cipanas, otherwise charter them from Cisolok to Cipanas for around 2500Rp. Ojeks at the Pelabuhanratu and Cisolok bus terminals can be hired for around 3000Rp per hour for sightseeing. Motorbikes (30,000Rp per day) can be hired at the Hotel Bayu Amrta.

BOGOR TO BANDUNG PUNCAK PASS AREA

Between Bogor and Bandung you cross over this beautiful 1500m-high pass on a narrow, winding mountain road that passes through small resort towns and tea plantations. At high altitudes it's cool and often misty but in the early mornings the views across the valleys can be superb.

Almost the whole highway is a resort strip that's crammed with hotels and villas starting about 10km out of Bogor at Ciawi and continuing up through Cibogo, Cipayung and Cisarua to the Puncak Pass and over the other side to Cipanas. The area has fine scenery, a refreshing climate and some good walks, especially from Cibodas. However, much of the main highway is an endless, tacky strip of karaoke lounges, rumah makans and overpriced mid-range hotels.

The Puncak area makes a good escape from Jakarta on a day trip or some quiet spots can be found away from the highway melee for a longer stay. Avoid the weekends when the crowds and traffic jams are horrendous.

From Jakarta's Kampung Rambutan bus terminal any Bandung bus can drop you off at any of the resort towns on the highway (but not on Sunday when they aren't allowed to use this highway). From Bogor frequent buses and Colts (which travel on Sunday) also ply the highway.

Cisarua
☎ 0251

Ten kilometres from Bogor on the slopes of the Puncak, Cisarua has budget accommodation and walks to picnic spots and waterfalls, such as **Curug Cilember**, which is about 30 minutes walk from Cisarua.

Just east of Cisarua is the turn-off to **Taman Safari Indonesia**. This drive-through game park has indigenous and African 'safari' animals, a bird park, white tiger pavilion, red pandas, children's rides and animal shows. This spacious park with its well tended animals also has a night safari (15,000Rp) on Saturday night for viewing nocturnal animals. Though best explored by car, any Bogor-Bandung bus can drop you at the turn-off, from where minibuses go to the park, 2.5km away. Entry is 12,000Rp for adults, 8000Rp for children under six; cars are 6000Rp or a minibus is 12,000Rp. A park bus does tours of the safari park for those without a car. Park facilities include a swimming pool, restaurants and accommodation.

In the foothills, 7km before the Puncak summit, you finally leave the overdevelopment behind and pass through the tea-carpeted hills of **Gunung Mas Tea Estate**. You can tour the tea factory, which is a couple of kilometres from the highway. Tourism is almost as big a business as tea these days, and the estate has excellent accommodation. Factory tours cost 1500Rp and guides expect a tip.

Almost at the top of the pass, the Rindu Alam Restaurant is a must on every tour itinerary and either has fine views of the surrounding tea estates or is surrounded by ethereal mist. Just below the restaurant is **Telaga Warna**, a small 'lake of many

colours'. The colours require sunlight, otherwise the lake is not exciting. The patch of montane forest around from the lake is an interesting example of the original flora.

Places to Stay *Kopo Hostel (☎ 254296, Jl Raya Puncak 557)* is near the *pompa bensin* (petrol station) in Cisarua. Four or six-bed dorms cost 8000Rp per person or comfortable rooms cost 22,000Rp to 49,000Rp, including breakfast. Good value walking tours, including transport, are organised to points of interest such as Gunung Gede (25,000Rp per person).

Apart from the Kopo, scores of mid-range hotels and villas are spread out along the highway from Ciawi to Cipanas. Some of the villas can be rented.

The *Gunung Mas Guesthouse (☎ 252 501)* is a truly tranquil place to stay. Well appointed rooms are 160,000Rp or huge VIP rooms with towering ceilings are 200,000Rp. A variety of bungalows sleeping four to 14 people cost 240,000Rp to 700,000Rp. Add 50,000Rp to all rates on weekends.

The top hotel in terms of facilities and elevation is the *Puncak Pass Hotel (☎ 0263-512503)*, which is right near the pass itself and has fantastic views. The rooms start at 195,000Rp and are 20% less during the week.

Getting There & Away From Bogor take a bus or Colt to Cisarua (1000Rp, 45 minutes) or a direct bus from Jakarta (1½ hours).

Cibodas
☎ 0263

At Cibodas, over the Puncak Pass, is a beautiful high-altitude extension of the Bogor botanical gardens, the **Kebun Raya Cibodas**. It's surrounded by thick tropical jungle on the slopes of the twin volcanoes of Gunung Gede and Gunung Pangrango. The 80 hectare gardens were originally planted in 1860. Entry to the gardens is 2200Rp. Beside the entrance to the gardens is the entrance to the Gede Pangrango National Park.

Cibodas has limited facilities and gets much fewer visitors, but it has fine scenery and excellent walks.

JAVA

Places to Stay & Eat In Cibodas village, 500m before the gardens, *Freddy's Homestay (☎ 515473)* is a good option. Bright clean rooms with shared mandi are 20,000Rp and 25,000Rp upstairs, including breakfast. A bed in a shared dorm room is 15,000Rp. Meals are available and good information is provided.

The *Pondok Pemuda Cibodas (☎ 512 807)* is near the PHPA office and is a HI-affiliated hostel, but it caters primarily to school groups. Groups can hire a whole dormitory block for only 80,000Rp, but otherwise a room for up to four people will cost 40,000Rp.

A truly tranquil place to lodge is right within the gardens, a 1km walk uphill from the gate. The colonial *Wisma Tamu (☎ 512 233)* costs 50,000Rp for faded but large rooms with loads of character. Meals can be ordered. Bookings are essential.

There's cheap food at the *warungs* near the gardens and in the village, 500m down the hill.

Getting There & Away The turn-off to Cibodas is on the Bogor-Bandung Hwy, a few kilometres west of Cipanas. The gardens are 5km off the main road. Angkots run from Cipanas (800Rp, 30 minutes).

Gede Pangrango National Park

The Cibodas gardens are right next to the main entrance to the Gede Pangrango National Park, the highlight of which is the climb to the 2958m peak of volcanically active Gunung Gede. From the top of Gede on a clear day you can see Jakarta, Cirebon and even Pelabuhanratu on the south coast – well, Raffles reported that he could.

Register for the climb and obtain your permit (4000Rp) from the PHPA office just outside the garden entrance. The office has an information centre and pamphlets on the park, which is noted for its alpine forest and birdlife, including the rare Javan eagle.

From Cibodas, the trail passes **Telaga Biru** (15 minutes), which is a blue/green lake. **Cibeureum Falls** (one hour away) lies just off the main trail. Most picnickers only go this far or some continue on to the **hot springs**, 2½ hours from the gate. The trail continues to climb another 1½ hours to **Kandang Badak**, where a new hut has been built on the saddle between the peaks of Gunung Gede and Gunung Pangrango (3019m). Take the trail to the right for a hard three hour climb to Pangrango. Most hikers turn left for the easier, but still steep, 1½ hour climb to Gede, which has more spectacular views. The **Gede Crater** lies below the summit, and you can continue on to the **Suryakencana Meadow**.

The 10km hike right to the top of Gunung Gede takes at least 10 hours there and back, so you should start as early as possible and take warm clothes (night temperatures can drop to 5°C), food, water and a torch (flashlight). Most hikers leave by 2 am to reach the summit in the early morning before the mists roll in. Register at the park office the day before. The main trails are easy to follow. The hike should only be undertaken in the dry season from May to October.

Cipanas

☎ 0263

Cipanas, 5km beyond the Cibodas turn-off, has hot springs noted for their curative properties. The **Istana Cipanas** is another seldom-used summer presidential palace that was favoured by Soekarno. Built in 1750, it is an elegant country house in beautiful gardens but, like the Bogor palace, it is not normally open to the public. Apart from that, Cipanas is another resort town with plenty of *hotels* and a few *restaurants*.

BANDUNG

☎ 022   • pop 2 million

Bandung is the capital of West Java and Indonesia's fourth largest city. At 750m above sea level it has a cool and comfortable climate, and it attracts people from all over Indonesia and from abroad, seeking work and higher education. The majority of the population are the Sundanese of West Java.

Bandung was originally established in the late 19th century as a Dutch garrison town of some 90,000 Sundanese, Chinese and Europeans. It rapidly acquired importance as a commercial and educational centre, renowned in particular for its Institute of Technology. Because of its agreeable climate, the Dutch had plans to make it the capital prior to WWII and many government departments set up headquarters in Bandung. Bandung's most notable entry in the history books was as host of the Asia-Africa conference in 1955, which placed Bandung in the world spotlight.

Bandung has maintained some of its European-created production centres, and its major industries include textiles, telecommunications, tea and food processing. Bandung has suffered in the monetary crisis, with the collapse of the Timor national car industry and cutbacks to the aerospace industry, but Bandung has been far removed from turmoil elsewhere in Java.

Though once described as the 'Paris of Java', due to its many fine parks and gardens, much of the city's former glamour has faded. Today it is a mish-mash of dilapidated colonial architecture and modern buildings, though the northern suburbs still have graceful residential areas. The Kebun Raja is the focus of the old colonial city and is ringed by Dutch architecture. Art Deco architecture is in abundance, one of the best examples being the Savoy Homann Hotel.

Bandung is an excellent place to visit for Sundanese culture, otherwise the main attractions lie in the beautiful countryside around the city. To the north and south there's a wild tangle of high volcanic peaks, hot springs and huge tea plantations.

Orientation

Bandung sprawls out over the northern foothills of a huge plateau surrounded by high mountain ridges. The main part of the city lies south of the train line, and is centred around Jl Asia Afrika and the *alun alun* (city square). Along Jl Asia Afrika are the tourist office, post office and most of the banks, airline offices, restaurants and top-end hotels. Jl Braga was the ritzy shopping area in Dutch times, and has a few useful shops and cafes. The budget hotel area in Bandung is on the south side of the train station.

In colonial times, the railway tracks divided the riff-raff in the south from the Dutch city in the north, and the social divide still rings true. The gracious residential areas in the north are studded with tree-lined streets and parks, and bordered on the northernmost edge by the hills of Dago.

Information

Tourist Offices The very helpful Bandung Tourist Information Centre (☎ 4206644) at the alun alun on Jl Asia Afrika is the place to go for detailed information and all the latest on cultural events in and around Bandung. It's open daily from 9 am to 5 pm.

There is a handy tourist information counter at the south side of the train station.

Money Golden Megah moneychanger has branches at Jl Oto Iskandardinata (known locally as Jl Otista) 180 and Jl Lembong 36. It usually has the best rates in town and no fees. It's open Monday to Friday from 8.30 am to 4.30 pm and Saturday until 2 pm. Banks are scattered all around town and have ATMs – try the BNI bank just west of the Kebun Raja or along Jl Merdeka, south of the Bandung Indah Plaza, for the biggest selection.

Post & Communications The main post office on the corner of Jl Banceuy and Jl Asia Afrika is open daily from 8 am to 8 pm and has an Internet service. For international telephone calls, a Telkom wartel is on the corner of Jl Tamblong and Jl Naripan, or a wartel is on Jl Asia Afrika opposite the Savoy Homann Hotel.

Medical Services For medical attention, the Adventist Hospital (☎ 234386) at Jl Cihampelas 161 is a missionary hospital with English-speaking staff.

Gedung Merdeka (Freedom Building)

If you're interested in learning more about the Asia-Africa conference of 1955, visit the Museum Konperensi (Conference Museum) in Gedung Merdeka on Jl Asia Afrika. Photographs and exhibits detail the

BANDUNG

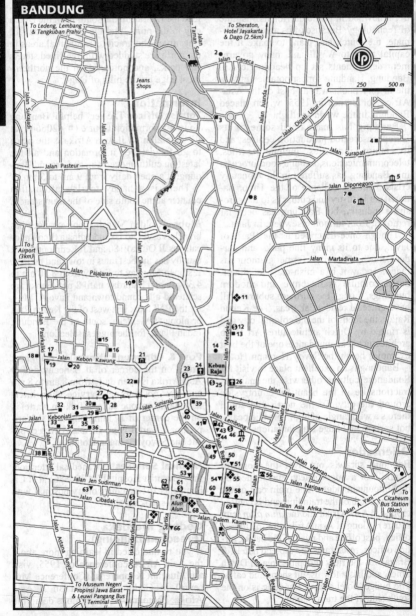

To Ledeng, Lembang
& Tangkuban Prahu

To Sheraton,
Hotel Jayakarta
& Dago (2.5km)

Jalan Taman Sari

Jalan Ganeca

Jeans
Shops

Jalan Cipaganti

Jalan Juanda

Jalan Dipati Ukur

Jalan Surapati

Jalan Pasteur

Cikapundung

Jalan Diponegoro

Jalan Martadinata

To
Airport
(3km)

Jalan Pajajaran

Jalan Cihampelas

Jalan Pasirkaliki

Jalan Kebon Kawung

Jalan Merdeka

Kebun
Raja

Jalan Jawa

Jalan Suniaraja

Jalan
Kebonjati

Jalan Garoujati

Jalan Lembong

Jalan Sumatra

Jalan Tamblong

Jalan Veteran

Jalan Braga

Jalan Jen Sudirman

Jalan Cibadak

Alun
Alun

Jalan Dewi Sartika

Jalan Dalem Kaum

Jalan Oto Iskandardinata

Jalan Naripan

Jalan Asia Afrika

Jalan A Yani

To
Cicaheum
Bus Station
(8km)

Lengkong Besar

Jalan Astana Anyar

To Museum Negeri
Propinsi Jawa Barat
& Leuwi Pangang Bus
Terminal

0   250   500 m

BANDUNG

PLACES TO STAY		
3 Hotel Sawunggaling	49 French Bakery	24 Bethel Church
4 Wisma Asri	50 Canary Bakery	25 Bank Indonesia
13 Hotel Royal Merdeka	51 Sindang Reret Restaurant	26 Catholic Church
15 Hotel Patradissa	53 Night Warungs	27 Train Station
16 Serena Hotel	54 Rumah Makan Tenda Biru	31 Bus Agents
17 Mutiara Hotel	63 Rumah Makan Sari Indah	37 Pasar Baru
18 Hotel Cemerlang	66 Warung Nasi Mang Udju	40 4848 Taxis
22 Hotel Guntur		41 Braga Disco
29 Losmen Sakardana	OTHER	42 North Sea Bar
30 Sakardana Homestay	1 Zoo	46 Golden Megah
32 Hotel Patradissa II	2 Bandung Institute of	(Moneychanger)
33 New Le Yossie	Technology (ITB)	47 Museum Mandala Wangsit
34 Hotel Surabaya	5 Museum Geologi	(Army Museum)
35 Le Yossie Homestay	(Geological Museum)	52 Ramayana Department Store;
36 By Moritz	6 Museum Prangko (Stamp	Supermarket
38 Hotel Trio	Museum)	55 Sarinah Department Store
39 Hotel Kedaton	7 Gedung Sate (Regional	56 Wartel
45 Hotel Panghegar	Government Building)	58 Merpati Office
57 Grand Hotel Preanger	8 Galael Supermarket	59 Wartel
69 Savoy Homann Hotel	9 Flower Market	60 Gedung Merdeka
70 Hotel Mawar	10 Bouraq Office	(Freedom Building)
	11 Plaza Bandung Indah	61 BRI Bank; Polo
PLACES TO EAT	Shopping Mall	62 Main Post Office
19 Rumah Makan Mandarin	12 Bank Duta	64 Golden Megah Corp
28 Warungs; Restaurants	14 Kantor Walikota	Moneychanger
43 Amsterdam Cafe	(City Hall)	65 King's Department Store
44 Braga Permai	20 4848 Taxis	67 Tourist Information Centre
48 London Bakery	21 Governor's Residence	68 Palaguna Shopping Centre
	23 BNI Bank	71 Rumentang Siang

meeting between Soekarno, Chou En-Lai, Ho Chi Minh, Nasser and other Third World leaders of the 1950s. The building itself dates from 1879 and was originally the 'Concordia Societeit', a meeting hall of Dutch associations. The museum is open Monday to Friday from 8 am to 6 pm.

Museum Geologi (Geological Museum)

North across the railway tracks at Jl Diponegoro 57, this museum is housed in the massive old headquarters of the Dutch Geological Service. It has excellent volcano exhibits and an array of fossils, including a model skull of Java Man. It's open Monday to Thursday from 9 am to 3 pm and weekends until 1 pm. From the train station you can take an angkot bound for 'Sadang Serang' and get off at the Gedung Sate, about 400m from the museum.

Other Museums

The **Museum Negeri Propinsi Jawa Barat** (West Java Provincial Museum), south-west of the city at Jl Oto Iskandardinata 638, has an interesting display of Sundanese artefacts. It is open daily, except Monday, from 8 am to 2 pm.

The **Museum Prangko** (Stamp Museum) is in the north-east corner of the Gedung Sate (Regional Government) complex on Jl Diponegoro. As well as thousands of stamps from around the world, the museum has everything from post boxes to pushcarts used since colonial times to ensure that the mail must go through. It is open Monday to Friday from 9 am to 3 pm and weekends until 1 pm, but closes for lunch and prayer breaks.

The **Museum Mandala Wangsit** (Army Museum), Jl Lembong 38, is devoted to the history and exploits of the West Java Siliwangi division (based in Bandung).

Bandung Institute of Technology (ITB)

North of town on Jl Ganeca is the Bandung Institute of Technology, built at the beginning of the century. The university has large grounds and gardens, and the main campus complex is notable for its 'Indo-European' architecture, featuring Minangkabau-style roofs atop colonial style buildings.

Opened in 1920, the ITB was the first Dutch-founded university open to Indonesians. It was here that Soekarno studied civil engineering (1920-25) and helped to found the Bandung Study Club, members of which formed a political party that grew as the Indonesian Nationalist Party (PNI), with independence as its goal. The institute's students have maintained their reputation for outspokenness and political activism, and in 1978 they published the *White Book of the 1978 Students' Struggle* against alleged corruption in high places. It was banned in Indonesia. In 1998, in the lead up to Soeharto's downfall, up to 100,000 students rallied daily, but in keeping with Bandung's laid-back reputation, the city saw no riots.

The ITB is the foremost scientific university in the country, but it also has one of the best fine arts schools, and its art gallery can be visited. Across from the main gate is a useful canteen in the *asrama mahasiswa* (student dorm complex) where many of the students congregate.

To reach the ITB, take a Lembang or Dago angkot from the train station and then walk down Jl Ganeca.

Zoo

Bandung zoo's spacious, beautifully landscaped gardens are very attractive, but the animals are few and most are housed in typically cramped conditions. The zoo is a few minutes walk from the ITB on Jl Taman Sari – the entrance is down the steps past the toy stalls opposite Jl Ganeca. It's open daily from 7 am to 5 pm, and admission costs 2000Rp.

Dago

At the end of Jl Merdeka, Jl Juanda climbs up to Dago Hill to the north, overlooking the city. The famous **Dago Thee Huis** (Dago Tea House) offers commanding vistas over the bluff and is a fine place to catch the sunset. The complex has an outdoor theatre and an indoor theatre further down the hill where cultural events are sometimes held.

On the main road, 100m past the tea house turn-off, a path leads down to the **Curug Dago** (Dago Waterfall). From here you can walk along the river to the **Taman Hutan Raya Ir H Juanda**, which is a pleasant forest park with another waterfall, 'caves' and walking paths. By road, the park entrance is 2km past the Dago bemo terminal. The **Gua Pakar** is in fact an ammunition store hacked out by the Japanese during the war. Further north is the **Gua Belanda**, which is the same deal but built by the Dutch. A tunnel leads right though the mountain to the start of the trail that leads all the way to Maribaya along Sungai Cikapundung (see under Maribaya Hot Springs in the North of Bandung section for more information).

'Jeans' Street

No discussion of Bandung's sights would be complete without mention of its famous 'jeans' street, Jl Cihampelas, in the more affluent northern side of town. Celebrating its standing as a major textile centre, shops with brightly painted humungous plaster statues of King Kong, Rambo and other legendary monsters compete with one another in kitsch. It has to be seen to be believed. The jeans are very cheap, though the quality is not fantastic. Denim jackets and T-shirts are a good buy.

Ram Fights

Noisy traditional ram-butting fights known as *adu domba* are held in Cilimus, in the northern suburbs of Bandung, and at Ciater (see Around Bandung). They are held most Sunday mornings in the dry season.

To the sound of drums, gongs and hand clapping, two rams charge at each other with a head-on clash of horns for 25 or more clashes, with a referee deciding the winner. If a ram gets dizzy they tweak his testicles and send him back into combat until he's had enough! This sport has been popular in West Java for so long that most villages have their own ram-fight societies and there are organised tournaments to encourage farmers to rear a stronger breed of ram. At village level it's just good fun; at district and provincial level there's wild betting.

To reach Cilimus, take an angkot or Lembang minibus (600Rp) to Terminal Ledeng on Jl Setiabudi, the continuation of Jl Sukajadi. Go down Jl Sersan Bajuri directly opposite the terminal, turn left at Jl Cilimus and continue to the bamboo grove.

Places to Stay – Budget
Bandung's hotels are fairly expensive but Jl Kebonjati, near the train station and the city centre, has some good travellers' guesthouses.

The *By Moritz* (☎ 4295788, fax 4207495, Kompleks Luxor Permai 35, Jl Kebonjati) is a well managed guesthouse with a good restaurant. Dorm beds cost 10,000Rp and small but spotless singles/doubles/triples with shared bathroom are 15,000/20,000/30,000Rp. Breakfast is included.

Le Yossie Homestay (☎ 4205453, Jl Kebonjati 53) tends to be overrun with local hangers-on but the rooms are light and there is a downstairs cafe. A dorm bed costs 9000Rp per person; rooms are 12,500/17,500/25,000Rp. An offshoot, the quieter *New Le Yossie* is one street south. Airy rooms around a courtyard garden are a notch above the pack and cost 15,000Rp for singles, and 20,000Rp and 25,000Rp for doubles.

Bandung's original guesthouse, *Losmen Sakardana* (☎ 4209897) is down a little alley off Jl Kebonjati beside the Hotel Melati I at No 50/7B. Singles/doubles for 12,500/15,000Rp are very basic and past their prime. *Sakardana Homestay* (☎ 4218553, Gang Babakan 55-7/B), further along the alley, is better kept but the walls are thin and the alleyway is noisy from nocturnal goings on. Rooms cost 10,000/15,000Rp.

Hotel Surabaya (☎ 436791, Jl Kebonjati 71) is a rambling old hotel with plenty of colonial ambience (check out the old photographs in the lobby). This would be

a superb hotel with renovation but is sadly neglected. Spartan rooms cost 13,000/22,500Rp without bath to 45,000Rp for better rooms with bath and a touch of style.

Places to Stay – Mid-Range
Bandung has plenty of mid-range hotels, especially north of the train station and along Jl Gardujati, but most are old and faded.

The *Hotel Patradissa* (☎ 4206680, Jl H Moch Iskat 8) is an older hotel but very well kept and friendly. Rooms with bathroom and hot water cost 25,000/30,000 for singles/doubles to 72,500Rp. Under different owners, *Hotel Patradissa II* (☎ 4202645, Jl Pasirkaliki 12) is reasonably priced but overdue for a paint job. Spotty rooms with hot water showers cost 35,000Rp.

The best deal at the moment is the new *Serena Hotel* (☎ 4207850, Jl Marjuk 6). Sparkling rooms with hot water, TV and minibar cost 88,000Rp or only 66,000Rp after discount.

Just north of the city centre near the Plaza Bandung Indah, *Hotel Royal Merdeka* (☎ 4200555, Jl Merdeka 34) is a better class of mid-range hotel with coffee shop, bar, fitness centre and well appointed rooms from 158,400Rp.

Wisma Asri (☎ 4521717, Jl Merak 5) is a more homey guesthouse/hotel out near the Gedung Sate. Comfortable rooms cost 50,000Rp to 75,000Rp, plus 20%.

Out near the ITB, *Hotel Sawunggaling* (☎ 4218254, Jl Sawunggaling 13) is an attractive hotel with colonial style. Big rooms with minibar and TV cost 110,000Rp to 155,000Rp.

Spanning the middle and top-end ranges, the *Hotel Panghegar* (☎ 432286, Jl Merdeka 2) is an older business hotel that's well positioned and has good rooms from US$100, before a massive discount. *Hotel Kedaton* (☎ 4219898, Jl Suniaraja 14) is even more central and has a pool and top facilities for the price. The rooms cost 150,000/170,000Rp.

Places to Stay – Top End
Bandung has a glut of luxury hotels, all with swimming pools. Though brochures quote

US dollars, they are meaningless, and hotels have been offering remarkable discounts to attract weekend visitors from Jakarta – 200,000Rp or less per night. Ring around for the current discount rates.

The very central *Savoy Homann Hotel* (☎ 432244, *Jl Asia Afrika 112*) is Bandung's most famous hotel, noted for its Art Deco style. Posted rates start at US$100. The hotel has a garden restaurant and superb Art Deco dining room facing the street.

Built in 1928, the *Grand Hotel Preanger* (☎ 431631, *Jl Asia Afrika 181*) competes with the Savoy Homann for colonial style. It doesn't quite match the Savoy Homann on that score but it is one of Bandung's best hotels. Most rooms are in the new tower but the best rooms are in the old wing. Discounting has seen prices drop to 245,000Rp.

Many of Bandung's new hotels are found in the north of the city. On the road to Dago, the smaller *Sheraton* (☎ 2500303, *Jl Juanda 390*) has rooms from 400,000Rp after discount, and right near the Dago Tea House, *Hotel Jayakarta* (☎ 2505888, *Jl Juanda 381*) is better value with discounted rooms from 220,000Rp.

North of the zoo on the outskirts of town, *Chedi Hotel* (☎ 230333, *Jl Ranca Bentang 56-8*) is a smaller boutique hotel with countryside views, and unique architecture and furnishings. This is one of Java's most stylish hotels and rooms start at US$150.

Places to Eat

By Moritz (*Kompleks Luxor Permai 35, Jl Kebonjati*) is the most popular travellers' bar/cafe (it's also a guesthouse). Cheap but fairly grotty *warungs* and *restaurants* can be found on the south side of the train station, or Jl Gardujati, opposite the Hotel Trio, has a good selection of *night warungs* that stay open late.

The best *night warungs* are on Jl Cikapundung Barat, across from the alun alun near the Ramayana department store. Stalls sell a bit of everything – soto, sate, gado gado, seafood – or try the *soto jeroan*, intestinal soup with various medicinal properties, mostly designed to stimulate male libido. Nearby on the ground floor in the Ramayana department store is a good, squeaky clean *food-stall area*.

Bandung also has a number of excellent Chinese restaurants. The *Rumah Makan Mandarin* on Jl Kebon Kawung is a no-frills place with excellent dishes served in steaming cast-iron pans. Seafood is a speciality and the restaurant is popular with Bandung's Chinese community.

Jl Braga is quasi-European avenue with a string of coffee shops and bakeries. The centre-piece is the *Braga Permai* (*Jl Braga 74*) sidewalk cafe, which is a more upmarket restaurant with a mixed menu, a variety of cakes and superb ice cream. On the corner of Jl Braga and Jl ABC/Naripan, *Canary Bakery* has hamburgers and western fare. The *Sumber Hidangan Bakery* and the *French Bakery* are good for a snack or light meal – croissants, Danish pastries or chicken curry puffs. Most popular is the *London Bakery*, which has an espresso machine. The *North Sea Bar* (*Jl Braga 82*) and the *Amsterdam Cafe* (*Jl Braga 74*) specialise in grills, beer and bar girls.

Further east on Jl Tamblong, *Rasa Bakery* is housed in a fine colonial building and is a pleasant spot for pastries or a light meal.

All the big hotels have restaurants. For a treat with style try the rijsttafel in the *Savoy Homann Hotel* restaurant or the revolving restaurant at the top of the *Hotel Panghegar*.

Sundanese Restaurants Bandung is a good place to try traditional Sundanese food. The *Warung Nasi Mang Udju*, on Jl Dewi Sartika just south of the alun alun, is a simple place, but the food is excellent and cheap. *Rumah Makan Tenda Biru* on Jl Braga is a no-frills, cafeteria-style place with good Sundanese food.

Rumah Makan Sari Indah (*Jl Jen Sudirman 103-7*) is much more salubrious with bamboo decor, an artificial waterfall and huts in the garden out the back for dining on mats. The food is excellent and very moderately priced.

The *Sindang Reret Restaurant* (*Jl Naripan 9*), just around the corner from Jl Braga, has Saturday night cultural performances and good, if slightly expensive, Sundanese food.

Entertainment

Cultural Performances Bandung is a good place to see Sundanese performing arts. Many performances are irregular – the visitor information office has the latest details.

Bandung's performing arts centre is the **Rumentang Siang** at Jl Baranangsiang 1. Wayang golek performances, Jaipongan (West Javanese dance), Pencak Silat (the art of self defence), *sandiwara* (traditional Javanese theatre) and ketoprak are held on Saturday nights – check with the tourist office for schedules.

You can catch a scaled-down wayang golek exhibition with a meal every Saturday night from 7 pm at the **Sindang Reret Restaurant**.

Sanggar Langen Setra (*Jl Oto Iskandardinata 541A*) is a Jaipongan dance club that features Ketuktilu and Jaipongan every evening from 8 pm to 1 am. The club is about 2km south of Jl Jen Sudirman. A cover charge applies and you pay extra to join the performers for a dance. While owing much to traditional dance, Jaipongan is a modern social dance and hostesses dance primarily to entertain male clients – something like traditional bar girls.

ASTI-Bandung is in the southern part of the city at Jl Buah Batu 212 and is a school for traditional Sundanese arts – music, dancing and pencak silat. Check with the tourist office for events or it is open to interested visitors every morning, except Sunday.

Angklung (bamboo musical instrument) with performances take place at Pak Ujo's **Saung Angklung**, Jl Padasuka 118, east of the city on the way to the Cicaheum bus terminal, where you can see the instruments being made. Performances cost 12,500Rp and are held most afternoons but they depend on tour group bookings.

Nightlife Jl Braga is a good place in the evening for less cultural pursuits. The **North Sea Bar** is at No 82 and the similar **Amsterdam Cafe** at No 74 are popular with

expats and visitors. They are crawling with bar girls but get a mixed crowd on weekends and are convivial places. Discos include the **Braga Disco**, just off Jl Braga, and **Polo**, on the 11th floor of the BRI building on Jl Asia Afrika.

North-west of the city centre at Jl Dr Junjunan 164, **Laga Pub** is a convivial place that gets some good bands and a fair smattering of expats. **S.O.B Fun Pub** (*Jl Ir H Juanda 390*) at the Sheraton has bands and gets a lively crowd on weekends.

Shopping

In the city centre, down a small alley behind Jl Pangarang 22, near the Hotel Mawar, Pak Ruhiyat at No 78/17B produces wayang golek puppets and masks, and you can see them being carved.

The Cupu Manik puppet factory is on Jl Haji Akbar, off Jl Kebon Kawung just north of the train station. Traditional Sundanese musical instruments can be bought at Pak Ujo's Saung Angklung (Bamboo Workshop; see Entertainment for details) or the Toko Musik at Gang Suniaraja 3, off Jl ABC.

Jl Cibaduyut, in south-west Bandung, is to shoes as Jl Cihampelas is to jeans, but without the gaudy statues. Dozens of shops sell shoes and bags at competitive prices.

Jl Braga used to be the exclusive shopping street of Bandung, though it is fairly quiet these days. Jakarta's Sarinah department store has a small branch here with a selection of crafts.

These days shopping centres dominate the town – Plaza Bandung Indah is the biggest and brightest mall. For everyday goods, the liveliest shopping district is on Jl Dalem Kaum and nearby streets, just west of the alun alun. Supermarkets can be found in the Ramayana department stores on Jl Cikapundung Barat and Jl Dalem Kaum, and in the Plaza Bandung Indah.

Pasar Baru is Bandung's big, somewhat grotty central market, with fruit, vegetables and all manner of goods. Bandung's title of the 'City of Flowers' comes true at the flower market on Jl Wastukencana, on the way to the zoo. Pasar Jatayu is 1km west of the train station on Jl Arjuna. It's a flea market where you may be able to find some collectibles if you sift through the junk.

Getting There & Away
Air Merpati (☎ 441226), Jl Asia Afrika 73, opposite the Savoy Homann Hotel, has direct flights to Jakarta's Halim airport (205,000Rp) and Surabaya (531,000Rp). Garuda (☎ 4209467) is in the Hotel Preanger on Jl Asia Afrika.

Bus The Leuwi Panjang bus terminal, 5km south of the city centre on Jl Soekarno Hatta, has buses west to places like Bogor (4000/7000Rp for normal/air-con, three hours), Sukabumi (3500Rp, three hours) and Jakarta's Kampung Rambutan bus terminal (6500Rp to 15,000Rp, 4½ hours). Buses to Bogor are not allowed to take the scenic Puncak Pass route on weekends. Door-to-door minibuses also go to Bogor (20,000Rp) via Puncak.

Buses to the east leave from the Cicaheum bus terminal on the eastern outskirts of the city. Normal/air-con buses include Cirebon (5000/8000Rp, 3½ hours), Garut (2000Rp, two hours), Pangandaran (10,000Rp, six hours) and Yogya (16,500/25,000Rp, 10 hours).

Sari Harum (☎ 708110) has air-con minibuses to Pangandaran (25,000Rp, five hours). The 4848 company (☎ 4208448), Jl Kebon Kawong 49, has minibuses to Pangandaran, Garut, Cirebon and other destinations, but its fleet is decrepit. Its other depot at Jl Suniaraja Timur 39 (☎ 434848) has better minibuses to Jakarta (30,000Rp air-con) or beat up taxis to Jakarta (25,000Rp).

For luxury buses to long-distance destinations, Kramatdjati (☎ 439860), Jl Kebonjati 96, and Pahala Kencana (☎ 432911), Jl Kebonjati 90, are two convenient agents in the budget accommodation area.

From the Stasiun Hall terminal outside the train station, Colts also run to Lembang and Subang (for Tangkuban Prahu and Ciater).

Train The Bandung-Jakarta *Parahyangan* (20,000/32,000Rp bisnis/eksekutif, three

hours) is the main service with departures to Jakarta's Gambir train station roughly every hour from 4 am to 10.05 pm. The *Argogede* luxury service (40,000Rp, 2½ hours) departs at 6.30 am and 2.30 pm.

Several trains operate on the Bandung-Banjar-Yogya route, most continuing on to Surabaya. Most are night expresses, such as the *Mutiara Selatan* (33,000Rp bisnis) and *Turangga* (45,000/75,000Rp).

Getting Around
To/From the Airport Bandung's Husein Sastranegara airport is 4km north-west of town; 10,000Rp by taxi.

Bus, Angkot & Taxi Bandung has a fairly good, if crowded, Damri city bus service that charges a fixed 500Rp. Bus Nos 9 and 11 run from west to east down Jl Asia-Afrika to Cicaheum bus terminal.

Angkots run set routes all over town between numerous stations. From Stasiun Hall (St Hall) on the southern side of the train station, angkots go to Dago, Ledeng and other stations. When returning, catch any angkot displaying 'St Hall'. Abdul Muis (Abd Muis), south of the alun alun on Jl Dewi Sartika, and Cicaheum are the other main angkot terminals. Angkots cost from 300Rp to 600Rp (500Rp for most destinations).

Becaks have all but disappeared from central Bandung. Taxis are numerous, both private and metered, but meters are rarely used – they want a minimum of 5000Rp for up to 5km. From the taxi booth at the train station, taxis cost 10,000Rp to any central destination, or fixed charter rates are Maribaya (35,000Rp) and Tangkuban Perahu (60,000Rp).

NORTH OF BANDUNG
Lembang
☎ 022
Lembang is on the road to Tangkuban Prahu, 16km north of Bandung. It was once a noted hill resort but is now a busy little market town and most visitors keep heading further up into the hills.

AROUND BANDUNG

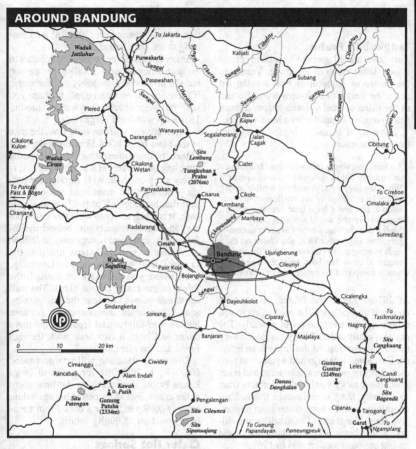

To Jakarta
Waduk Jatiluhur
Purwakarta
Sungai
Pasawahan
Kalijati
Ciacem
Subang
Plered
Sungai Cikeruh
Sungai Ciherang
Sungai Cikao
Jalan Cagak
Batu Kapur
Cibitung
Cikalong Kulon
Wanayasa
Darangdan
Segalaherang
Situ Lembang
Ciater
To Cirebon
Waduk Cirata
Cikalong Wetan
Tangkuban Prahu (2076m)
Cikole
Cimalaka
To Puncak Pass & Bogor
Panyadakan
Cisarua
Lembang
Maribaya
Sumedang
Ciranjang
Radalarang
Cikapundang
Ujungberung
Waduk Saguling
Cimahi
Bandung
Pasir Koja
Bojangloa
Cileunyi
Sindangkerta
Soreang
Dayeuhkolot
Ciparay
Cicalengka
Nagreg
To Tasikmalaya
Banjaran
Majalaya
Situ Cangkuang
Cimanggu
Ciwidey
Gunung Guntur (2249m)
Leles
Candi Cangkuang
Rancabali
Alam Endah
Kawah Putih
Danau Dangkalan
Situ Bagendit
Situ Patengan
Gunung Patuha (2334m)
Pengalengan
Situ Cileunca
Cipanas
Tarogong
Garut
To Ngamplang
Situ Sipanuajang
To Gunung Papandayan
To Pameungpeuk

0   10   20 km

Places to Stay The *Grand Hotel Lembang* (☎ 2786671, Jl Raya Lembang 272) harks back to the days when Lembang was a fashionable resort for Bandung's Dutch colonial community. It is old fashioned and comfortable, with beautiful gardens, a swimming pool and tennis courts. Rooms in the old wing, with attached sitting rooms, are neglected but have plenty of character. They cost 45,000Rp and 60,000Rp. Rooms in the new wing cost from 128,000Rp.

Maribaya Hot Springs

Maribaya, 5km east of Lembang, has a thermal spa, landscaped gardens and a thundering waterfall. It's another tourist spot, crowded on Sunday, but worth visiting. You can extend your Tangkuban Prahu trip (see the following entry) by walking from the bottom end of the gardens down through a brilliant, deep and wooded river gorge all the way to Dago. There's a good track and if you allow about two to three hours for the walk (6km) you can be at a Dago vantage point for sunset. From there it's only a short trip by Colt back into Bandung.

Tangkuban Prahu

The 'overturned perahu' volcano crater stands 30km north of Bandung. Years ago the centre of Tangkuban Prahu collapsed under the weight of built-up ash and, instead of the usual conical volcano shape, it has a flat elongated summit with a huge caldera.

There is, of course, a legend to explain this phenomenon.

An estranged young prince returned home and unwittingly fell in love with his own mother. When the queen discovered the terrible truth of her lover's identity she challenged him to build a dam and a huge boat during a single night before she would agree to marry him. Seeing that the young man was about to complete this impossible task, she called on the gods to bring the sun up early and as the cocks began to crow the boat builder turned his nearly completed boat over in a fit of anger.

At 2076m Tangkuban Prahu can be quite cool and around noon the mist starts to roll in through the trees, so try to go early. The crater is easily accessible by car, so it's very much a tourist trap. At the crater is an information centre, *warungs* and a parade of peddlers hustling postcards, souvenirs and other junk. It's a tacky jumble that detracts from the scenery, but you can escape this bedlam of activity, and the huge crater is an impressive sight. Tangkuban Prahu still emits sulphur fumes but is not particularly active and its last serious eruption was in 1969.

Kawah Ratu is the huge 'Queen Crater' at the top. Walk around the rim of the main crater for about 20 minutes for views of the secondary crater, **Kawah Upas**. The trail leads further along a ridge between the two craters and returns to the car park, but it is steep and slippery in parts – *exercise caution*. A better and less crowded walk is to **Kawah Domas**, a volcanic area of steaming and bubbling geysers that can be reached by a side trail to the top. You can also head off across country towards Ciater or Lembang. Guides can be hired for around 10,000Rp.

Getting There & Away From Bandung's minibus terminal in front of the train station, take a Subang Colt (3000Rp) via Lembang to the park entrance.

Entry is 2550Rp per person. Minibuses to the top officially cost 2500Rp per person but the drivers will probably ask for more; if there are not enough people to share you will have to charter anyway – around 15,000Rp with hard bargaining.

Alternatively, you can walk from the gate at the main road. It's 4.5km along the road or take the more interesting side trail via the bubbling hot geysers at Kawah Domas. It is a very steep one hour walk through the jungle – head up the main road and take the trail that branches off at the first small car park. It is much easier to walk this trail from the top down – it starts just behind the information centre and is very easy to follow.

Alternatively, a trail starts just past the Jayagiri fruit market, outside Lembang, from where you can walk up through the forest to the crater (about 8km). The trail starts and comes out near the bus parking area, 1.2km below the main crater. Another less easy-to-follow trail leads off the main crater to Ciater, a two hour walk through forest and tea plantations.

Drivers in Bandung will charge around 60,000Rp to 70,000Rp for a visit to Tangkuban Prahu, depending on the time spent at the crater, including petrol but excluding entry (6000Rp extra for a car). From Lembang count on 35,000Rp return.

Ciater Hot Springs

Eight kilometres north-east of Tangkuban Prahu, Ciater is a pretty little place in the middle of huge tea and clove estates. The area has good walks and a tea factory on the south side of Ciater can be visited.

At the end of the road through the village, Ciater's main attraction is the **Sari Ater Hot Spring Resort**. Although quite commercialised, the pools are probably the best of all the hot springs around Bandung. If you've been climbing around the volcano on a cool, rainy day there's no better way to get warm. There is a 2500Rp admission into the resort area and it costs extra to use the pool. Private baths cost 7500Rp. You can walk to Ciater – about 12km across country – from Tangkuban Prahu, or flag down a Colt at the entrance point.

Places to Stay The extensive *Sari Ater Hot Springs Resort* (☎ *460888*) has a variety of rustic bungalows spread out in spacious grounds. It has all the facilities of a big hotel, but the rooms are crumbling and cost 154,000Rp to 533,000Rp for family bungalows, all plus 21%.

Ciater has plenty of small *penginapans* (lodging houses) with rooms starting at around 20,000Rp – those on the main road are cheaper. *Hotel Permata Sari* (☎ *203891*) is close to the hot springs and has good views and rooms from 30,000Rp.

Waduk Jatiluhur

This artificial lake (*waduk* means dam in Indonesian) is 70km north-west of Bandung in the hills near Purwakarta, and is a popular resort for swimming, boating and waterskiing. It stretches 1200m across, is 100m high and has created a lake some 80 hectares in surface area. It's part of a hydro-electric generating system supplying Jakarta and West Java, and also providing irrigation water for a large area of the province. The original village was built by the French for their staff when they were building the dam and is now run by a government corporation as tourist accommodation. It's a very peaceful spot during the week, but you really need your own transport to get there and around. Purwakarta is the access point either from Jakarta (125km by rail or road) or from Bandung (by road).

SOUTH OF BANDUNG
☎ 022

The mountains south of Bandung also have popular weekend retreats, though the area is less developed compared with the resorts north of the city. The road south of Bandung leads to Ciwidey, which is a small town noted for its stylish Sundanese restaurants.

The road winds through the hills to the turn-off to Kawah Putih, a volcanic crater

with a beautiful turquoise lake. The turn-off is 6km before Rancabali, and then it is 8km to the small crater lake just below Gunung Patuha (2334m). Though only a small crater, Kawah Putih is exceptionally beautiful and eerily quiet when the mists roll in.

Back on the road a few kilometres further south from the turn-off to Kawah Putih are two developed hot springs at **Cimanggu**, and the newer **Walini** complex has big hot pools and a few bungalows.

Rancabali, 42km from Bandung, is a tea-estate town surrounded by the rolling green hills of the tea plantations. Just 2km south of the town is **Situ Patengan**, a pretty lake with tea rooms and boats catering to the Sunday crowds.

Also south of Bandung, **Situ Cileunca** is an artificial lake dammed for a hydro-electric scheme, outside the hill town of Pengalengan. The area's main attraction is the **Malabar Tea Estate**, where you can tour the plantations and stay at the wonderful guesthouse (see Places to Stay for details).

Places to Stay

Accommodation is limited, and empty during the week. In Ciwidey, *Penginapan Sederhana* on the main road opposite the market has dismal rooms for 11,500Rp. The *Sindang Reret Hotel* (☎ *5928205*) and *Motel Sukarasa Endah* (☎ *9958311*) are both on the highway north of town and have large Sundanese restaurants built over fish ponds. The Sindang Reret is slightly better and has comfortable rooms with hot water showers from 72,000Rp to 151,250Rp during the week, 10% more on weekends.

At Alam Endah, 5km south of Ciwidey, *Pondok Taman Unyil Lestari* (☎ *5928250*) is 1km from the main road and has simple cottages with sitting rooms for 66,000Rp, fine views, a nice garden and a good restaurant.

Pengalengan has a number of hotels, but the town is of minor interest. Stay at the Malabar Tea Estate, 5km from town. *Malabar Mess* (☎ *5979401*) is a delightful colonial guesthouse furnished with Dutch antiques. The rooms cost 75,000Rp in the outside block, but the old rooms in the main house cost 120,000Rp and 150,000Rp and are worth the extra price.

Getting There & Away

From Bandung's Leuwi Panjang terminal, frequent buses run to Ciwidey (1200Rp, 1½ hours), as do minibuses (1500Rp). From Ciwidey local angkots run to Situ Patengan (2000Rp). Kawah Putih is not serviced by regular public transport, but you'll find plenty of ojeks in Alam Endah. Buses also run directly to Pengalengan, where ojeks hang out at the bus terminal.

BANDUNG TO PANGANDARAN

Heading south-east from Bandung, the road passes through a scenic and fertile stretch of hilly countryside and volcanic peaks. This is the Bandung-Yogya road as far as Banjar; the Bandung to Yogya train line passes through Tasikmalaya and Banjar, but not Garut. The district is part of the Parahyangan highlands around Bandung.

Garut & Cipanas
☎ 0262

Sixty-three kilometres south-east of Bandung, Garut is a highland town and a centre for vegetable, orange, tea and tobacco growing. The town is ringed by impressive volcanic peaks that have provided the valley's fertility. Garut itself is just another town, but the surrounding area has a number of attractions.

On the outskirts of town, 6km north-west, are the hot springs at **Cipanas**, a small resort at the foot of **Gunung Guntur** and an ideal base to explore the area. From Cipanas, the **Curug Citiis** waterfall is a 3km walk away up the mountain and a four hour walk further on to the peak of Gunung Guntur. It is best to leave by 5 am for good views.

Ngamplang is 5km from Garut on the south-eastern outskirts, and has a nine hole golf course and resort hotel. Adu domba (ram fights) are held here on the first and third Sunday of the month.

Garut is famed for its *dodol* – a confectionery of coconut milk, palm sugar and sticky rice. At the bus terminal hawkers selling tubes of sweet dodol besiege passing buses. It's also sold at many shops around town. The 'Picnic' brand is the best quality, and it is possible to visit the Picnic factory on Jl Pasundan. Garut also has a thriving leatherwork industry, churning out amazingly cheap leather jackets from cow and softer sheep leather. Styles tend to be a bit old-fashioned but there is a big selection – check out the many shops on Jl Sukaregang in the east of town.

Places to Stay The township of Garut has plenty of hotels and guesthouses, but Cipanas is the nicest place to stay.

Cipanas has over a dozen hotels strung along Jl Raya Cipanas, the resort's single road. All have rooms with large baths with water piped in from the hot springs – pamper yourself after a hard day's trekking. Cheap hotels include the basic *Pondok Kurnia Artha* (☎ 232112), which has dark but OK rooms for 25,000Rp, perhaps less with bargaining. The *Hotel Tirta Merta* (☎ 231422) is cheerier and has doubles from 25,000Rp. Both hotels charge 10,000Rp or more on weekends. More expensive, but no better, are the *Hotel Banyu Arta* and *Penginapan Cipta Rasa*, both with rooms from 30,000Rp.

As well as hot baths, the following hotels have swimming pools heated by the springs. *Cipanas Indah* (☎ 233736) is a good mid-range hotel favoured by tour groups. Rooms start at 35,000Rp and good VIP rooms are 50,000Rp (around 10,000Rp more on weekends). The *Sumber Alam* (☎ 231027) is the most attractive hotel, with rooms built over the water from 60,000Rp to 245,000Rp (40% more on weekends). The big *Tirtagangga Hotel* (☎ 231811) is the top hotel, with rooms from 145,000Rp during the week.

Getting There & Away Buses and angkots leave from Garut's Guntur terminal, in the north of town. Garut is easily reached by bus from Bandung (2000Rp, two hours) and Tasikmalaya. For Pangandaran take another bus from Tasikmalaya. Air-con buses also go to Bogor and Jakarta.

Regular angkots run around town and to Cipanas (angkot No 4, 500Rp) and Ngamplang, and to the nearby villages.

A car or minibus with driver can be rented in Cipanas – ask around the hotels. A trip to Papandayan will cost around 40,000Rp.

Around Garut

Near Leles, about 10km north of Garut, is **Candi Cangkuang**, which is one of the few stone Hindu temples found in West Java. Dating from the 8th century, some of its stones were found to have been carved into tombstones for a nearby Islamic cemetery. The small, restored temple lies on the edge of Situ Cangkuang, a small lake. It has become something of a tourist trap, but it's a peaceful and beautiful trip. From Garut take a angkot No 10 to Leles on the highway and then another angkot or horse-drawn *delman* (two wheeled-buggy, 6000Rp to charter) for the 3km to Candi Cangkuang. Boats across the lake to the temple cost 10,000Rp.

Twenty-eight kilometres to the south-west of Garut, **Gunung Papandayan** (2662m) is one of the most active volcanoes in West Java. Papandayan has only existed since 1772, when a large piece of the mountain exploded sideways in a catastrophe that killed more than 3000 people. It last erupted in 1925. The bubbling yellow crater (Kawah Papandayan) just below the peak is an impressive sight and clearly visible from Garut valley on fine mornings. To get there, take a Cikajang minibus and get off at the turn-off on the outskirts of Cisurupan where you can catch a waiting ojek (3000Rp, 13km).

From the car park area it is an easy half-hour walk to the crater, which is riddled with bubbling mud pools, steam vents and crumbling sulphur deposits. Take care – keep well to the right when ascending through the crater or it may pay to hire a guide for closer inspection. For fine views, go very early in the morning before the clouds roll in. Gunung Papandayan's summit is a two hour walk beyond the crater, and there are fields of Javan edelweiss near the top. PHPA staff can arrange a camping permit, or there are *cottages* at the warung area for 40,000Rp.

To the east of Garut, **Gunung Telagabodas** (2201m) has a bubbling bright-green crater lake that's alive with sulphur. To get to Telagabodas, take an angkot to Wanaraja (500Rp), an ojek (2000Rp) to the parking area and then walk to the crater. Craters to the west of Garut that can be visited are **Kawah Darajat**, 26km away, and **Kawah Kamojang**, 23km away, the site of a geothermal plant that has defused the once spectacular geyser activity and replaced it with huge pipes.

Halfway between Garut and Tasikmalaya is **Kampung Naga**, which is a traditional village and museum piece of Sundanese architecture and village life. The old ways are very much preserved in Kampung Naga – the many tour groups that visit wouldn't come otherwise. Despite the fact that it can be crowded some mornings when the big bus-loads arrive, there's no denying the beauty of the place. Kampung Naga, with its thatched-roof houses, is nestled next to a river and surrounded by steep hills terraced with rice paddies – a photographer's dream. Kampung Naga is 26km from Garut. From Neglasari on the main highway, more than 300 steps lead down into the valley.

Tasikmalaya
☎ 0265

Sixty kilometres east of Garut, Tasikmalaya is the centre for the district of the same name. It is noted for rattan crafts: palm leaf and bamboo are used to make floor mats, baskets, trays, straw hats and paper umbrellas. Tasikmalaya (usually called simply Tasik) has a small batik industry and is also noted for its *bordel* lacework and *kelom geulis* (wooden sandals). For travellers, it is merely a transit town on the way to Pangandaran, but the surrounding area has a few points of interest. Tasik has plenty of hotels: *Abadi Hotel (☎ 332789, Jl Empang 58)* is a good budget option with rooms from 15,000Rp; while the *Mahkota Graha (☎ 332282, Jl Martadinata 45)* is the best in town and has rooms from 95,000Rp.

Getting There & Away From Tasikmalaya buses operate to Bandung (4000Rp, four hours), Garut (2000Rp, two hours), Pangandaran (5000Rp, three hours), Banjar, Jakarta, Cipatujah, Cirebon etc. The main bus terminal is 4km from the town centre on the eastern outskirts. Tasikmalaya is also on the main train line.

Around Tasikmalaya

For cheap rattan crafts, visit the village of **Rajapolah**, 12km north of Tasikmalaya on the road to Bandung, where many of the weavers work.

Cipanas Galunggung is 20km north-west and is a hot spring at the foot of **Gunung Galunggung**, a volcano that exploded dramatically in 1982. From the hot springs recreation park, a trail leads to a small waterfall and then on to Galunggung crater, 3km away. A steep road to the crater is an easier walk but less interesting. From Tasikmalaya's main bus terminal take an angkot to Bantar on the highway and then an ojek can take you the 14km along a rough road.

Situ Lengkong is 40km north of Tasikmalaya and 500m from the village of Panjalu. It's a serene lake that was formed when the Hindu ruler of Panjalu dammed the valley. There is a forested island in the middle and boats can be hired to take you around the island. Panjalu village has a small museum containing the heirlooms of the kings of Panjalu. Situ Lengkong can be reached by bus from Tasikmalaya or from Kawali terminal, where angkots run the 20km to Ciamis.

On the highway to Banjar and Pangandaran, 16km south-east of Ciamis, **Karang Komulyan** is the excavated site of the ancient Galuh kingdom. Local guides and tourist literature give a glorified account of the Galuh kingdom as both the first Hindu and the first Muslim kingdom in Java, but this Neolithic settlement dating from around the 5th century points to the pre-Hindu period. Only a few stone walls and foundations remain of the 'palace', store, prayer and bathing areas, but it is a beautiful walk through the jungle and bamboo groves down to the confluence of the swift Ciliwung and Citanduy rivers. A large car park and government-built cottages next to the park are attempts to make it a major tourist stop.

Banjar

Banjar, 42km east of Tasikmalaya, is the junction point where the Pangandaran road branches from the Bandung to Yogya road and rail route. It has some basic hotels if you get stuck en route to Pangandaran.

Getting There & Away The bus terminal is 4km west of town on the highway. Many buses can be caught as they come through the centre of town near the train station. From Banjar the buses go to Pangandaran (3000Rp, 1½ hours), Bandung, Purwokerto, Jakarta etc. Buses also go from the Banjarsari bus terminal, half an hour south of Banjar, to Jakarta.

Banjar is not a good place to catch trains as most are crowded through trains. To Yogya, the best options are the *Pajajaran* at 10.50 am or the slower, ekonomi *Cisadane* at 12.50 pm, but they come through from Bandung and it is hard to get a seat. Evening eksekutif trains run right through to Surabaya. Heading to Jakarta via Bandung by train, the *Galuh* originates in Banjar, so seats are easier to get. It leaves at 6.30 am and takes at least nine hours.

PANGANDARAN
☎ 0265

The fishing village of Pangandaran is Java's most popular beach resort. It lies on the narrow isthmus of a peninsula with broad sandy beaches that sweep back along the mainland. At the end of the peninsula is the Pangandaran National Park.

Pangandaran has black-sand beaches and dangerous swimming (except for the more sheltered southern end of the west beach), but despite these drawbacks it is an idyllic place to take a break from travelling; the people are exceptionally friendly, accommodation is cheap and the seafood excellent. Many other quieter beaches and attractions are nearby.

Pangandaran is popular with Bandung residents, though the monetary crisis has taken its toll and weekends are not so hectic

PANGANDARAN

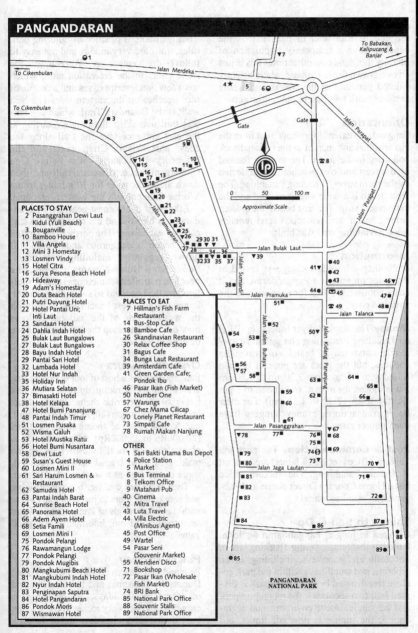

To Cikembulan

To Cikembulan

To Babakan,
Kalipucang &
Banjar

Jalan Merdeka

Gate

Gate

Jalan Parapat

Jalan Parapat

Jalan Pamugaran

Jalan Bulak Laut

Jalan Sumardi

Jalan Pramuka

Jalan Talanca

Jalan Kalen Buhaya

Jalan Kidang Pananjung

Jalan Pasanggrahan

Jalan Jaga Lautan

PANGANDARAN
NATIONAL PARK

0   50   100 m

Approximate Scale

PLACES TO STAY
2 Pasanggrahan Dewi Laut
   Kidul (Yuli Beach)
3 Bouganville
10 Bamboo House
11 Villa Angela
12 Mini 3 Homestay
13 Losmen Vindy
15 Hotel Citra
16 Surya Pesona Beach Hotel
17 Hideaway
19 Adam's Homestay
20 Duta Beach Hotel
21 Putri Duyung Hotel
22 Hotel Pantai Uni;
   Inti Laut
23 Sandaan Hotel
24 Dahlia Indah Hotel
25 Bulak Laut Bungalows
27 Bulak Laut Bungalows
28 Bayu Indah Hotel
29 Pantai Sari Hotel
32 Lambada Hotel
33 Hotel Nur Indah
35 Holiday Inn
36 Mutiara Selatan
37 Bimasakti Hotel
38 Hotel Kelapa
47 Hotel Bumi Pananjung
48 Pantai Indah Timur
51 Losmen Pusaka
52 Wisma Galuh
53 Hotel Mustika Ratu
56 Hotel Bumi Nusantara
58 Dewi Laut
59 Susan's Guest House
60 Losmen Mini II
61 Sari Harum Losmen &
   Restaurant
62 Samudra Hotel
63 Pantai Indah Barat
64 Sunrise Beach Hotel
65 Panorama Hotel
66 Adem Ayem Hotel
68 Setia Famili
69 Losmen Mini I
75 Pondok Pelangi
76 Rawamangun Lodge
77 Pondok Pelangi
79 Pondok Mugibis
80 Mangkubumi Beach Hotel
81 Mangkubumi Indah Hotel
82 Nyur Indah Hotel
83 Penginapan Saputra
84 Hotel Pangandaran
86 Pondok Moris
87 Wismawan Hotel

PLACES TO EAT
7 Hillman's Fish Farm
   Restaurant
14 Bus-Stop Cafe
18 Bamboe Cafe
26 Skandinavian Restaurant
30 Relax Coffee Shop
31 Bagus Cafe
34 Bunga Laut Restaurant
39 Amsterdam Cafe
41 Green Garden Cafe;
   Pondok Ibu
46 Pasar Ikan (Fish Market)
50 Number One
57 Warungs
67 Chez Mama Cilicap
70 Lonely Planet Restaurant
73 Simpati Cafe
78 Rumah Makan Nanjung

OTHER
1 Sari Bakti Utama Bus Depot
4 Police Station
5 Market
6 Bus Terminal
8 Telkom Office
9 Matahari Pub
40 Cinema
42 Mitra Travel
43 Luta Travel
44 Villa Electric
   (Minibus Agent)
45 Post Office
49 Wartel
54 Pasar Seni
   (Souvenir Market)
55 Meridien Disco
71 Bookshop
72 Pasar Ikan (Wholesale
   Fish Market)
74 BRI Bank
85 National Park Office
88 Souvenir Stalls
89 National Park Office

nowadays. During holidays – Christmas and the end of Ramadan in particular – the beaches have a temporary population of literally thousands. At other times this is just an overgrown fishing village, where brightly painted perahu fish the waters and whole families work together to pull in the nets.

Orientation
Pangandaran extends for about 3km from the bus terminal and market to the national park boundary in the south. The town is flanked by the west and east beaches, and dissected by the main street, Jl Kidang Pananjung. The west beach is a wide sweep of sand and the main resort strip. The east beach is a quieter, fishing beach, and not much sand remains since a retaining wall was built.

Information
A 2000Rp admission charge is levied at the gates on entering Pangandaran, and it costs another 1250Rp for each visit to the national park.

Money The Bank Rakyat Indonesia (BRI) on Jl Kidang Pananjung changes most currencies and major brands of travellers cheques, but the rates are poor. It is open Monday to Friday from 7.30 am to 4.30 pm but is closed for a 'rest' from noon to 1 pm (Friday from 12.30 to 1.30 pm). For after hours transactions, moneychangers have even poorer rates.

Post & Communications The post and Telkom offices (open 24 hours) are both on Jl Kidang Pananjung. The Telkom office has a Home Country Direct phone and Pangandaran also has wartels.

Things to See & Do
Cloaked in jungle, **Pangandaran National Park** has bantengs, *kijang* (barking deer), hornbills and monkeys, including Javan gibbons, and small bays within the park enclose tree-fringed beaches. The park is divided into two sections – the recreation park and the jungle. Due to environmental degradation, the jungle is now off limits, but

some guides still offer illegal tours. Apart from the dubious practice of ignoring park rules, trails are very muddy and not easy to follow – don't enter alone. You can walk the stone paths in the recreation park, which has a few nondescript caves and a couple of nice beaches on the eastern side. The best walk is the Boundary Trail, which is a natural trail that skirts the jungle. Starting at the east entrance take the trail along the coast past Wisma Cirengganis and the Boundary Trail starts 150m before Goa Cirengganis cave. It leads uphill and then down along the river for 30 minutes to the Wisma Cikumal and the western entrance.

Like most south coast beaches, Pangandaran has **black-sand beaches** and the surf can be treacherous. The northern end of the west beach is dangerous and people still drown regularly, including foreigners. South from Bumi Nusantara Hotel, the beach is patrolled (sometimes) and is sheltered by the headland so swimming is safer. Pangandaran's best beach, Pasir Putih, on the western side of the national park, is now off limits to stop the hordes that have destroyed the reef.

Organised Tours
Pangandaran has a host of tour operators that are constantly thinking up new tours and hyperbole to describe them. Popular tours are to Green Canyon (30,000Rp per person), and 'countryside' or 'home industry' tours (20,000Rp to 25,000Rp), which take you to plantations and local industries to see the making of tofu, *krupuk* (prawn crackers), sugar etc, as well as a wayang golek maker.

Then there are cycling, boating, walking and snorkelling tours to just about anywhere within a 50km radius of Pangandaran. Tours are usually well run, informative and good value.

Places to Stay
Pangandaran has over 100 places to stay. During the Christmas and Lebaran (the end of Ramadan) holidays, Pangandaran is crowded and prices sky rocket. It can also get busy during school holidays and in the peak

European holiday season, around August. However, for much of the year most hotels are empty and Pangandaran is quiet.

Prices are very seasonal and in busy periods may be higher than quoted here. First night prices are often higher, because of the commission system employed by becak drivers and guides. Many hotels, especially the budget places, charge a two night minimum, but like the rates this is often negotiable.

The Bulak Laut area on the west beach is the best place to stay. Though the swimming is dangerous, the beach is uncluttered and Jl Bulak Laut has good restaurants and plenty of travel services.

Places to Stay – Budget
Pangandaran Most places around Bulak Laut tend to be mid-range, but there are some budget options.

The *Holiday Inn (☎ 639285, Jl Bulak Laut 50)* is the cheapest but rough. Singles/doubles cost 7500/10,000Rp with mandi in the rundown wooden rooms or 20,000Rp in the marginally better concrete block rooms. Next door, *Mutiara Selatan (☎ 639416, Jl Bulak Laut 49)* is better. Simple rooms with a porch and attached bathroom cost 10,000/15,000Rp. The beds are lumpy, but the rooms are well kept.

Closer to the beach, *Pantai Sari Hotel (☎ 639175)* has a good restaurant and roomy doubles with fan and mandi for 25,000Rp, or brighter air-con rooms upstairs for 35,000Rp. Check a few out as the quality and price varies depending on the season and length of stay.

Further north down the alleyway next to the Bamboe Cafe, *Losmen Vindy (☎ 639 641)* is a small new place with neat bamboo rooms for 15,000Rp or 30,000Rp with mandi. Inquire at the cafe if no one is around.

On the same alley, *Mini 3 Homestay (☎ 639436)* is another good option. Slightly dark but comfortable rooms with bathroom cost 20,000/25,000Rp including breakfast or the cute bungalows in the attractive garden cost 30,000Rp. It has a pleasant dining area and good travel services.

Bamboo House (☎ 639419) is to the north and away from the beach, but this small, family-run place is well worth considering. Attractive rooms cost 15,000/20,000Rp or bungalow rooms with mandi cost 30,000Rp.

Jl Samurdi also has a few options, the pick of which is the *Hotel Kelapa (☎ 639329)*. Fairly basic but good-sized rooms with shower cost 20,000Rp. It has a wonderful, spacious garden and an attractive cafe.

Further south, cheap hotels cater mostly to the weekend crowds. The basic *Losmen Mini I* on Jl Kidang Pananjung costs 10,000/15,000Rp for rooms with mandi, or across the road the rougher but friendly *Rawamangun Lodge* has rooms for only 6000/9000Rp. Once popular with travellers, it attracts only the desperately impecunious now.

The small *Pondok Moris (☎ 639490, Gang Moris 3)* has well kept rooms with a porch facing an attractive garden for 20,000/25,000Rp. Service is very good in this friendly place – if only it wasn't so close to the mosque.

On the eastern beach, the *Panorama Hotel (☎ 639218)* has pleasant rooms with verandah from where you can watch the fishers haul in the nets. The rooms are a good deal at only 20,000Rp with attached bathroom.

Further north near the post office, the small *Pondok Ibu (☎ 639166, Jl Kidang Pananjung 116)* is attached to the tranquil Green Garden Cafe. Three simple but comfortable rooms cost 20,000/25,000Rp, including breakfast, and have their own sitting areas.

Around Pangandaran The quiet beaches outside Pangandaran are increasingly popular places to hang out and relax, especially when Pangandaran is crowded during the main holiday periods. Most of the following guesthouses are run by westerners who have settled in Pangandaran, and are on the ball with information and services.

Cikembulan is 4km along the beach road to the west and has a small enclave of guesthouses. Electricity is not yet the norm but the room lamps add to the atmosphere. *Delta Gecko (☎ 630607)* is run by the ebullient

Kristina and is a very popular travellers guesthouse with excellent information, a library and a cultural/BBQ night once a week. Individually styled bungalows with bathroom start at 10,000Rp for a bed in a share room, and from 15,000/20,000Rp up to 40,000Rp for the elevated bungalows with sea views. Full travel services and tours are offered. Its neighbour, the **Losmen Kalapa Nunggal** (☎ 630285) is another that receives rave reviews for hospitality and atmosphere. It has just four spotless rooms with bathroom for 20,000Rp and 25,000Rp, and meals are available for guests. About 500m back towards Pangandaran on the beach road, **Tono Homestay** (☎ 630371) is a friendly, small place, with rooms from 35,000Rp.

In Babakan, 4km east of Pangandaran, **Laguna Beach Bungalows** (☎ 639761) offers stylish mid-range accommodation and has a good restaurant. Delightful bungalows facing the beach cost 50,000Rp and 57,500Rp, or rooms over the fish pond are 35,000Rp and 45,000Rp. Ring for pick-up.

Places to Stay – Mid-Range & Top End

The west beach strip along Jl Pamugaran near Jl Bulak Laut is Pangandaran's Riviera, with a host of good value mid-range hotels popular with Europeans.

Bulak Laut Bungalows (☎ 639377), opposite the beach on Jl Pamugaran, is 100m north of Jl Bulak Laut and is an excellent option. Spacious rooms have TV and rock garden bathrooms (cold water) from 20,000/25,000Rp for singles/doubles, or stylish bungalows with their own sitting rooms are dotted around the lush garden at the back and cost 30,000/35,000Rp. A second **Bulak Laut Bungalows** (☎ 639171), down the street on the corner of Jl Bulak Laut, is under different management and has just four similarly styled bungalows for 35,000Rp.

Further back from the beach, the **Bimasakti Hotel** (☎ 639194, Jl Bulak Laut 12) has a restaurant, small pool and good air-con rooms with hot water and TV for 66,000Rp and 88,000Rp, and more on weekends.

The delightful **Adam's Homestay** (☎ 639164) has eclectic architecture, a book shop, cappuccino and a small pool. This excellent establishment has uniquely styled rooms from 54,000/63,000Rp up to 261,000Rp for a luxury family bungalow with its own pool. Most are in the 90,000Rp to 126,000Rp range.

Down the alley beside Adam's, the new **Villa Angela** (☎ 628641) has copied the architectural style. Though not in the same league as Adam's, this small place has attractive air-con rooms for 100,000Rp and two fan rooms downstairs for 75,000Rp, before discount.

One of Pangandaran's bigger resort hotels is the big **Surya Pesona Beach Hotel** (☎ 639428). It has a swimming pool, restaurant, and good rooms with balcony and all the trimmings for 120,000Rp – a good deal.

The **Pasanggrahan Dewi Laut Kidul** (Yuli Beach, ☎ 639375) has delightful boutique bungalows (160,000Rp) with sunken lounge areas in a lush garden with a pool. New rooms for 100,000Rp and 120,000Rp out the back also have style. All have cold water showers and fan, so expect discounts. Don't expect much in the way of service and the breakfasts are overpriced, but this is one of Pangandaran's most attractive hotels.

More mid-range hotels can be found towards the southern end of the west beach. **Susan's Guest House** (☎ 639290, Jl Kalen Buhaya 20) is a cheaper option with fan rooms for 30,000Rp or air-con rooms with hot water for 50,000Rp. A complete four-bedroom unit costs 150,000Rp. **Pondok Pelangi** (☎ 639023, Jl Pasanggrahan 7) is also good for families and has self-contained two/three-bedroom bungalows in an attractive garden for 150,000/250,000Rp. The bungalows are old but well kept and come with a fully equipped kitchen.

Hotel Bumi Nusantara (☎ 639032) faces the western beach and is a big, older hotel with a swimming pool and restaurant. Rooms range from worn bungalows for 100,000Rp to big family rooms for 300,000Rp. The best options are the stylish rooms in the new block for 175,000Rp; or 120,000Rp after discount.

Sunrise Beach Hotel (☎ *639220, Jl Kidang Pananjung 175*) on the east beach, is one of the most pleasant. It has a swimming pool, a good restaurant and attractive rooms, but tour groups stay here so rates are over the top at US$50 to US$195. Even with a discount to 260,000Rp, it is still overpriced.

Across the street from the Sunrise, the *Pantai Indah Barat* (☎ *639006*), along with its plush cousin on the east beach *Pantai Indah Timur* (☎ *630714*), offer top-of-the-range accommodation but both are usually empty. The Timur has a huge pool and tennis courts, while the Barat has a more modest pool, tennis courts and a restaurant. They also quote high rates – from 235,000Rp at the Barat and 310,000Rp at the Timur – but discounts of 40% are readily offered.

Places to Eat

Pangandaran is famous for its excellent seafood (prawns, squid and fish). For cheap Indonesian food, the town has dozens of *warungs*, especially along the southern end of the western beach. The little eateries in front of the *Pasar Seni* are very cheap and have a good selection.

The Bulak Laut area has travellers' eateries with western-style breakfasts, pancakes, and a variety of fruit juices and fruit salads. On Jl Bulak Laut, the pleasant *Pantai Sari Hotel* has a limited menu, but does a good spaghetti and is a top spot for breakfast. The popular *Holiday Inn* has a big menu and passable food at cheap prices. *Bagus Cafe* across the road is part of the Number One chain, and is a pleasant little spot for pizzas and other fare. The Swiss-run *Relax Coffee Shop* is one of Pangandaran's fanciest restaurants and, though expensive, it has superior European dishes, Indonesian selections, delicious *volkenbrot* bread and great milkshakes. For good Sundanese and Javanese food, head to the *Bunga Laut Restaurant*. The food is not blandified for western tastes and it serves good soups, chicken and tempe (fermented soybean cake) dishes.

Pangandaran's newest travellers' cafe is the *Bus-Stop Cafe* to the north on Jl Pamugaran. Run by Delta Gecko, this switched-on place overlooks the sea and has a wide range of booking services.

The main street, Jl Kidang Pananjung, also has some good restaurants. *Chez Mama Cilacap* (*Jl Kidang Pananjung 187*) is one of Pangandaran's best restaurants with an extensive menu, moderate prices, fresh fish and icy fruit juices. Further north, the ever-popular *Number One* has a varied menu and good food. The new *Green Garden Cafe* (*Jl Kidang Pananjung 116*) has a delightful garden setting and its Indonesian dishes, steak, seafood and salads are served with some style.

For seafood, the excellent *Pasar Ikan* (Fish Market) is on the east beach. Pick out what you want from the selection of fresh seafood at the front of the warungs here and pay according to weight. The market is to the north near the post office (not the wholesale fish market to the south). The main market near the bus terminal is the place to stock up on fruit and groceries.

Further south, overlooking the eastern beach, *Lonely Planet Restaurant* (no relation!) at Jl Jaga Lautan 2, comes with basic warung decor, but the seafood is excellent. Choose dishes from the menu or select fish and prawns at the front and pay by weight.

Inti Laut at the front of the Hotel Pantai Uni on Jl Pamaguran is another excellent spot for fresh seafood with a Chinese bent. Further south on the west beach, the restaurant at the *Nyur Indah Hotel* is a little expensive, but one of Pangandaran's best Chinese seafood restaurants. Nearby, the no-frills *Rumah Makan Nanjung* has sea breezes and does a mean barbecued fish.

Top of the range for seafood is *Hillman's Fish Farm Restaurant*. It's expensive and the service can be slow, but it's worth it for the serene surrounds overlooking the fish ponds (a successful seafood export business operates from here). The food is superb and this is one of the few places you can regularly get lobster.

Getting There & Away

Pangandaran lies halfway between Bandung and Yogya. Coming from Yogya by bus or rail, Banjar is the transit point. The most popular way to reach Pangandaran is via the pleasant backwater trip from Cilacap to Kalipucang. From Bandung, plenty of direct buses go to Pangandaran, or it's possible to change for connections in Tasikmalaya.

Pangandaran has a small airport at Nusawiru, 20km to the west, but no scheduled flights.

Bus Local buses run from Pangandaran's bus terminal to Tasikmalaya (5000Rp, three hours), Ciamis (4500Rp, 2½ hours), Banjar (3000Rp, 1½ hours), Kalipucang (1000Rp, 40 minutes) and Cilacap (3500Rp, 2½ hours). Buses also run along the west coast as far as Cijulang (1500Rp, 40 minutes).

The large patas (express) buses leave from the Sari Bakti Utama and Budiman bus company depots about 2km west of Pangandaran along Jl Merdeka. Frequent normal buses go to Bandung (10,000Rp, six hours) between 6 am and 9 pm, and Sari Bakti Utama also goes to Bogor (15,000Rp, nine hours) at 7.15 am and 7.30 pm. Buses to Jakarta (16,500/19,500Rp normal/aircon) terminate in Bekasi, 22km east of Jakarta, or Tangerang to the west of Jakarta.

The most comfortable way to travel to Bandung is with the Sari Harum door-to-door minibus for 25,000Rp. The Mitra (☎ 639180) door-to-door bus to Jl Jaksa in Jakarta is no longer operating but may start up again.

Agents in Pangandaran sell bus tickets for a premium, but they save a lot of hassle and usually include transport to the depots. Commission can be high – it pays to shop around.

The best way to reach Central Java is via the Kalipucang-Cilacap ferry (see the Boat entry in this section). If the boat doesn't appeal, take a bus to Cilacap from where buses go to Yogya or Wonosobo. You can take the train to Yogya from Banjar, but seats are hard to get.

Car Most travel agents rent minibuses with drivers for about 150,000Rp per day including driver and petrol. Put together your own tour and you may be able to negotiate a better rate, especially for an older vehicle. The most popular trip is a three day tour to

Yogya. The usual route is via the ferry (the driver drops you in Kalipucang then picks up in Cilacap) and on to Wonosobo for the first night. The second day goes to Dieng for the sunrise then on to Borobudur for the night. The final day is to Yogya via Prambanan.

Boat One of the highlights of a trip to Pangandaran is the interesting backwater trip between Cilacap and Kalipucang. From Pangandaran it starts with a 17km bus trip to Kalipucang (1000Rp, 40 minutes), where the ferry travels across the wide expanse of Segara Anakan and along the waterway sheltered by the island of Nusa Kambangan. It's a fascinating, peaceful trip, hopping from village to village in a rickety 25m wooden boat; a larger boat also operates if the number of passengers warrants. As well as carrying a regular contingent of tourists, it's a very popular local service.

Ferries (3200Rp, four hours) leave from Kalipucang at 8 am, noon and/or 1 pm. A car ferry also operates from the new Majinklang harbour to the south of Kalipucang but this is much less atmospheric.

From the Cilacap harbour it is about 1km to the main road (1000Rp by becak), from where bemos go to the Cilacap bus terminal (500Rp). A becak all the way to the terminal costs around 2500Rp. From Cilacap direct buses go to Yogya or Wonosobo for the Dieng Plateau. The last Yogya bus leaves at 9 pm.

Much easier are the door-to-door services between Pangandaran and Yogya. Bus-ferry-bus services (30,000Rp, 10 hours) are sold all around Pangandaran and will drop you at your hotel in Yogya. Connections to Wonosobo are also advertised, but these are on Yogya buses that will drop you in Kebumen, from where you are put on a public bus to Wonosobo.

Getting Around

Pangandaran's brightly painted becaks start at around 1000Rp and require heavy negotiation. Bicycles can be rented for as little as 5000Rp per day, or motorcycles cost around 20,000Rp per day.

AROUND PANGANDARAN

The scenic coast road west from Pangandaran to Cipatujah skirts along the surf-pounded beaches and runs through small villages and paddy fields. **Cikembulan** is 4km from Pangandaran and has accommodation (see under Pangandaran) and local industries that can be visited, including the krupuk factory and a wayang golek workshop.

Karang Tirta is a lagoon set back from the beach with *bagang* fishing platforms. It's 16km from Pangandaran and 2km from the highway. **Batu Hiu** (Shark Rock) is 23km from Pangandaran and 1km from the highway, and has a recreational park atop the cliffs with views along the coast.

Inland from Parigi, near Cigugur, **Gunung Tilu** has fine views and is included in some of the tour itineraries. The **Sungai Citumang** is reached by a rough and hard-to-find inland road from Karang Benda, and has a small dam from where you can walk upstream to a beautiful gorge – 'Green Canyon II' in Pangandaran tour parlance.

Batu Karas is 32km from Pangandaran and is a relaxed fishing village with a surf beach, one of the best on the coast, sheltered by a rocky promontory. Accommodation that's favoured by surfers can be found 1km beyond the fishing village at the headland beach. *Hotel Melati Indah* is the best value and has well kept rooms with mandi for 20,000Rp. *Alana's Bungalows* has bamboo decor, surf culture and rooms for 20,000Rp to 35,000Rp with mandi. Good rumah makans include the *Kang Avi* and *Sederhana*.

Right in the village, the new *Hotel Pondok Putri* (☎ 6650370) has a pool and very good rooms with hot water for 80,000Rp with fan or 100,000Rp and 120,000Rp with air-con. On the other side of the village to the east, the *Cijulang Permai* (☎ 0811-854359) has a pool and very good mid-range rooms for 125,000Rp before discount, but it is a long way from anywhere and the beach is ordinary. Batu Karas can be reached from Pangandaran by taking a bus to Cijulang and then an ojek for 2500Rp.

Pangandaran's No 1 tour is to **Green Canyon** (Cujang Taneuh is the real name). Many tour operators in Pangandaran run trips here for around 35,000Rp to 40,000Rp and include 'countryside' excursions on the way to make a full day tour. To get there yourself, hire a boat from the Green Canyon river harbour on the highway, 1km before the turn-off to Batu Karas. Boats cost 23,500Rp for five people and operate daily from 7.30 am to 4 pm (Friday 1.30 to 4 pm). They travel up the emerald-green river through the forest to a waterfall and a steep rock canyon, and stop for swimming. Count on around 1½ hours for this excellent trip, but it has become so popular that there can be a flotilla of boats on the river and the serenity is giving way to litter and crowds. Go as early as possible at peak times to avoid the crush.

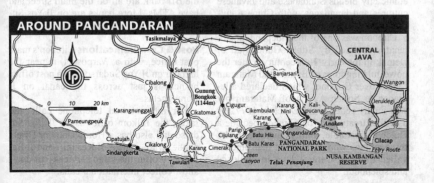

AROUND PANGANDARAN

The coast road ends at the village of **Cipatujah**, which has a wide but uninspiring beach with dangerous swimming, and a couple of cheap hotels. Five kilometres before Cipatujah is a small PHPA post that monitors the green turtles that lay their eggs at **Sindangkerta** beach. The post welcomes interested visitors.

To the east of Pangandaran, **Karang Nini** is a recreational park perched high on the cliffs. Trails lead down the cliff face to the beach and crashing surf below.

Getting There & Away

Regular buses run between Cijulang and Pangandaran (1500Rp). Buses run from Cijulang west to Cikalong (3000Rp), but buses on to Cipatujah are rare and ojeks may be the only option. Cipatujah is well serviced by buses from Tasikmalaya and some continue to Ciparanti and even Jakarta. The best way to see this stretch of coast is to hire a motorcycle in Pangandaran.

For Karang Nini, take any Kalipucang-bound bus to the Karang Nini turn-off, 9km east of Pangandaran on the highway. It is then a 3km walk to the park.

CIREBON
☎ 0231

Few people make the trip out to Cirebon, but it's an interesting seaport and the seat of an ancient Islamic kingdom with its own *kratons* (palaces). On the north coast, near the border with Central Java, this multi-ethnic city blends Sundanese and Javanese cultures and languages, with Chinese culture thrown in for good measure.

Cirebon was one of the independent sultanates founded by Sunan Gunungjati of Demak in the early 16th century. Later the powerful kingdoms of Banten and Mataram fought over Cirebon, which declared allegiance to Sultan Agung of Mataram but was finally ceded to the Dutch in 1677. By a further treaty of 1705 Cirebon became a Dutch protectorate, jointly administered by three sultans whose courts at that time rivalled those of Central Java in opulence and splendour.

Cirebon's kratons are open to visitors and, although not as large as the palaces of Yogya and Solo, are well worth visiting.

During the Dutch Culture System, forced labour produced a flourishing trade in colonial crops. Cirebon's great wealth attracted many Chinese entrepreneurs and the influence of the Chinese can still be seen in the design of Cirebon's famous batik. The countryside fared less well under the Culture System – famine and epidemics swept the region in the 1840s.

Cirebon has long been a major centre for batik, and is also famous for its *tari topeng* (a type of masked dance) and *tarling* music, blending guitar, *suling* (bamboo flute) and voice. Cirebon is also important as the major port and fishing harbour between Jakarta and Semarang, with the added bonus that it has excellent seafood.

The north coast, particularly in the dry season, can be a sweltering contrast to the cooler heights inland. Other than that, Cirebon is a well kept city that's small enough not to be overwhelming, and makes a worthwhile stopover.

Information
Tourist Offices The tourist office (☎ 208856), Jl Dharsono 5, is 5km out of town on the bypass road, near Gua Sunyaragi. It has a few brochures in Indonesian, but it's not worth the trip.

Money BCA bank, Bank Bumi Daya and the BII bank are all on the main street and have ATMs. More banks are on Jl Yos Sudarso near the main post office.

Post & Communications Cirebon's main post office, with a Warposnet, is near the harbour on Jl Yos Sudarso, and a post office branch is just across the canal on Jl Karanggetas.

For international telephone calls and faxes, the Telkom office is on Jl Yos Sudarso and also has a Home Country Direct phone. Warpostals at Jl Kartini 7 and Jl Bahagia 40 offer the same services, but don't allow collect international calls.

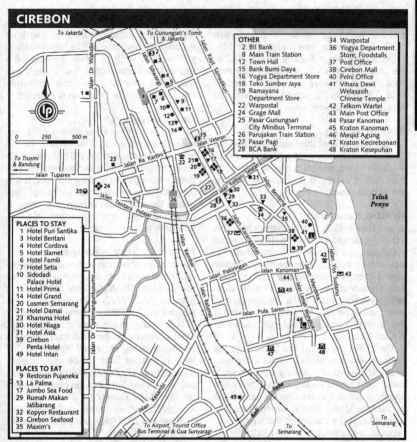

CIREBON

To Jakarta
To Gunungjati's Tomb & Jakarta

OTHER
2 BII Bank
8 Main Train Station
12 Town Hall
15 Bank Bumi Daya
16 Yogya Department Store
18 Toko Sumber Jaya
19 Ramayana Department Store
22 Warpostal
24 Grage Mall
25 Pasar Gunungsari City Minibus Terminal
26 Parujakan Train Station
27 Pasar Pagi
28 BCA Bank

34 Warpostal
36 Yogya Department Store; Foodstalls
37 Post Office
38 Cirebon Mall
40 Pelni Office
41 Vihara Dewi Welasasih Chinese Temple
42 Telkom Wartel
43 Main Post Office
44 Pasar Kanoman
45 Kraton Kanoman
46 Mesjid Agung
47 Kraton Kecirebonan
48 Kraton Kesepuhan

0   250   500 m

To Trusmi & Bandung

Teluk Penyu

To Airport, Tourist Office Bus Terminal & Gua Sunyaragi

To Semarang

PLACES TO STAY
1 Hotel Puri Santika
3 Hotel Bentani
4 Hotel Cordova
5 Hotel Slamet
6 Hotel Famili
7 Hotel Setia
10 Sidodadi Palace Hotel
11 Hotel Prima
14 Hotel Grand
20 Losmen Semarang
21 Hotel Damai
23 Kharisma Hotel
30 Hotel Niaga
31 Hotel Asia
39 Cirebon Penta Hotel
49 Hotel Intan

PLACES TO EAT
9 Restoran Pujaneka
13 La Palma
17 Jumbo Sea Food
29 Rumah Makan Jatibarang
32 Kopyor Restaurant
33 Cirebon Seafood
35 Maxim's

Kraton Kesepuhan

At the south end of Jl Lemah Wungkuk, the Kraton Kesepuhan is the oldest and best preserved of Cirebon's kratons. Built in 1527, its architectural style is a curious blend of Sundanese, Javanese, Islamic, Chinese and Dutch styles. Although this is the home of the Sultan of Kesepuhan, part of the building is open to visitors. Inside the palace is a pavilion with whitewashed walls dotted with blue-and-white Delft tiles, a marble floor and a ceiling hung with glittering French chandeliers.

The kraton museum has an interesting, if somewhat run-down, collection of wayang puppets, kris, cannons, furniture, Portuguese armour and ancient royal clothes. But the *pièce de résistance* of the collection is the Kereta Singa Barong, a 17th century gilded chariot with the trunk of an elephant (Hindu), the body and head of a dragon (Chinese-Buddhist), and wings (Islamic)! It was traditionally pulled by four white buffaloes.

Entry to the kraton is 1000Rp and includes a guided tour; camera fees are an extra

500Rp to 2000Rp. The kraton is open daily from 8 am to 4 pm, except Friday (7 to 11 am and 2 to 4 pm) and Sunday (8 am to 5 pm).

The guided tour may finish at the Museum Kereta Singa Barong, but behind in the large grounds of the palace is a new dance pavilion where practice is sometime held. There's also a pleasure palace in the same style, Gua Sunyaragi.

Mesjid Agung

On the west side of the field in front of the Kraton Kesepuhan is the Mesjid Agung. With its tiered roof, it's one of the oldest mosques in Java and is similar in style to the Mesjid Agung in Banten.

Kraton Kanoman

A short walk from Kraton Kesepuhan, this kraton was constructed in 1588. Kraton Kanoman was founded by Sultan Badaruddin, who broke away from the main sultanate after a lineage dispute with the sixth sultan's heir. Outside the kraton is a red-brick, Balinese-style compound and a massive banyan tree. Further on past the white, stone lions is the kraton, a smaller, neglected cousin of Kraton Kesepuhan.

Go to the right past the lions, sign the register and a guide will unlock the museum. It's worth it – among the museum's small holdings of mostly carved doors is a stunning sultan's chariot, in the same style as the one in the Kraton Kesepuhan. It is claimed that the chariot in the Kraton Kesepuhan is a newer copy – the rivalry for the sultanate still exists it seems. You can also visit the *pendopo* (large open-sided pavilion) and its inner altar. Antique European plates, some with Dutch Reformist scenes from the Bible, can be seen before entering.

Opening hours are haphazard and the guide's fee is by donation.

The colourful **Pasar Kanoman**, just in front of the kraton, is at its most vibrant in the morning and is worth a visit in its own right.

Kraton Kecirebonan

Although it's classed as a kraton, this is really only a house occupied by members of the current royal family, descendants of Raja Kanomin who broke away from the 10th Kesepuhan sultanate. Wander in, knock on the door and someone will be happy to show you around. Built in 1839, the house has fine colonial architecture and a small collection of swords, documents and other royal memorabilia. Donation is expected.

Gua Sunyaragi

About 4km south-west of town, a not-to-be-missed attraction is this bizarre ruined 'cave' – a grotto of rocks, red brick and plaster, honeycombed with secret chambers, tiny doors and staircases leading nowhere. It was originally a water palace for a sultan of Cirebon in the early 18th century and owes its present strange shape to the efforts of a Chinese architect who had a go at it in 1852.

Places to Stay – Budget

Inexpensive hotels can be found directly opposite the main train station, but conditions are not good. The *Hotel Setia* (☎ 207270, Jl Inspeksi PJKA 1222) is the best, but is expensive at 30,000Rp a double with mandi.

Jl Siliwangi is the main drag for hotels. On the corner near the main train station, at Jl Siliwangi 66, the *Hotel Famili* (☎ 207 935) is another basic place with singles/doubles from 17,500/22,000Rp. Other cheap but uninspiring hotels in the centre of town are the *Hotel Damai* (☎ 203045, Jl Siliwangi 130), where doubles with mandi cost 16,000Rp to 25,000Rp, and the *Losmen Semarang* (Jl Siliwangi 132) next door.

The best bet is the *Hotel Asia* (☎ 202183, Jl Kalibaru Selatan 15) alongside the tree-lined canal near the Pasar Pagi. This fine old Dutch-Indonesian inn has a terraced courtyard where you can sit and have breakfast. It's about a 15 minute walk or 2000Rp by becak from the main train station. This very well kept and friendly hotel has a variety of rooms from 17,900Rp to 37,800Rp with mandi.

Places to Stay – Mid-Range

The *Hotel Grand* (☎ 208867, Jl Siliwangi 98) is a pleasantly old-fashioned place.

Worn but large rooms with separate sitting areas have air-con, hot water and TV from 46,000Rp to 70,000Rp.

The *Hotel Cordova* (☎ 204677, Jl Siliwangi 87) is near the main train station and is one of the better buys. Good, renovated rooms with air-con and hot water cost 38,000Rp to 72,000Rp.

The *Sidodadi Palace Hotel* (☎ 202305, Jl Siliwangi 74) is a pleasant motel-style place built around a quiet courtyard. Comfortable rooms with air-con, hot water and parabola TV cost 76,000Rp to 96,000Rp. The *Hotel Slamet* (☎ 203296, Jl Siliwangi 95) is a cheaper hotel, with reasonable fan rooms with mandi from 27,000Rp, and air-con rooms with hot water from 38,500Rp.

Hotel Intan (☎ 244788, Jl Karan Anyar 36) is a new hotel with excellent rooms from only 25,000Rp, or 60,000Rp and 75,000Rp with air-con. It is one of Cirebon's best buys, but well south of the city centre.

Cirebon has a selection of more expensive mid-range hotels. Most are older hotels that have fallen from grace but offer attractive discounts. The large *Kharisma Hotel* (☎ 207668, Jl Kartini 60) is typical and has old rooms from 169,000Rp, or much better rooms in the new section from 236,000Rp.

Places to Stay – Top End
Cirebon's better hotels charge 21% tax and service, but include breakfast. Competition is stiff and large discounts (up to 50%) are readily available, making them good value.

The very central *Cirebon Penta Hotel* (☎ 203328, Jl Syarif Addurakhman 159) is small but classy with a rooftop garden and a health centre. Excellent rooms start at US$60, before big discounts. It is above the KFC.

Close to the train station, *Hotel Bentani* (☎ 203246, Jl Siliwangi 69) has a small pool and a variety of rooms from uninspiring mid-range for 190,000Rp to newer luxury for 249,000Rp.

The large *Hotel Prima* (☎ 205411, Jl Siliwangi 107) has a pool, tennis court, health centre, business centre, restaurants and bar. The rooms cost from US$50/60 and are well appointed but faded.

The *Hotel Puri Santika* (☎ 200570, Jl Dr Wahidin 32) is of a similar standard to the Prima, but newer and the best in town. Rooms start at US$85.

Places to Eat
Apart from Cirebon's fine seafood, a local speciality to try is *nasi lengko*, a delicious rice dish with bean sprouts, tahu, tempe, fried onion, cucumber and peanut sauce. The *Rumah Makan Jatibarang* on the corner of Jl Karanggetas and Jl Kalibaru Selatan has nasi lengko as well as other Indonesian dishes.

Good warungs serving seafood, *ayam goreng* (fried chicken) and sate can be found along Jl Kalibaru Selatan between the Asia and Niaga hotels. The *Moel Seafood* warung has delicious, cheap prawns in oyster sauce, and *Seafood 31* is also good. The department stores have food stall areas; the food stalls upstairs at the back of the *Ramayana department store* is the best.

Jl Bahagia has a number of seafood restaurants such as *Cirebon Seafood* (Jl Bahagia 9). One of Cirebon's best Chinese seafood restaurants is the cavernous *Maxim's* (Jl Bahagia 45). Shrimp and crab dishes are a speciality. *Jumbo Sea Food* (Jl Siliwangi 191) is next to the Yogya department store and serves great seafood grills.

Jl Siliwangi has a few good options. *Restoran Pujaneka* (Jl Siliwangi 105) is a mid-range, buffet-style eatery, with Sundanese and Cirebon specialities as well as western dishes. *La Palma* (Jl Siliwangi 86) is a very pleasant bakery in an old Dutch villa with tables where you can sit down and enjoy a snack or a drink.

Cirebon Mall and *Grage Mall* are the place for western fast food and supermarkets.

Shopping
Toko Sumber Jaya has two branches, at Jl Siliwangi 211 and 229, stocking all sorts of *oleh-oleh* (souvenirs) from Cirebon. Most oleh-oleh are of the syrup, dried prawn and krupuk variety but pottery, bamboo crafts and other interesting knick knacks are on sale. The Asia department store on Jl

Karanggetas also has a selection of woven palm and rattan goods from Tasikmalaya.

Though Cirebon is noted for its batik, the shops in town mostly sell batik from other regions. Batik Purnama, Jl Karanggetas 16, has a general selection, though the biggest concentration of batik shops is on the ground floor under the Matahari department store on Jl Pekiringan.

Getting There & Away

Road and rail routes to Cirebon from Jakarta (256km) follow the flat north coast, or from Bandung (130km) the road runs through scenic hilly country. Heading east to Pekalongan (137km) and Semarang (245km), the road runs just inland from the coast and is one of the busiest and most congested in Java.

Bus The Cirebon bus terminal is 4km southwest of the centre of town.

Normal/air-con buses run between Cirebon and Jakarta (8000/12,000Rp, five hours), Bandung (5000/8000Rp, 3½ hours), Pekalongan (4000/7000Rp, four hours) and Semarang (7500/13,000Rp, seven hours), as well as Yogya, Bogor, Solo, Merak, Surabaya and other destinations. For Pangandaran, first take a bus to Ciamis along a winding but paved, quiet and very scenic road.

For express minibuses from Cirebon, the ACC Kopyor 4848 office (☎ 204343), Jl Karanggetas 7, is next door to the Kopyor Restaurant. It has air-con minibuses to Bandung (13,500Rp, 3½ hours), Semarang (20,000Rp, six hours), Yogya (25,000Rp, eight hours) and Cilacap (12,500Rp normal, five hours). Ring to arrange pick-up from your hotel.

Train Cirebon is serviced by frequent trains on both the main northern Jakarta-Semarang-Surabaya train line and the southern Jakarta-Yogya-Surabaya line. The better services leave from Cirebon's main train station, just off Jl Siliwangi. Crowded ekonomi trains leave from the Parujakan train station further south.

To Jakarta's Gambir train station, the *Cirebon Express* (18,000/32,000Rp bisnis/eksekutif, 3½ hours) departs from Cirebon at 5.50 am, and 1 and 3.30 pm. It is much quicker and more convenient than the buses.

To Yogyakarta, the *Fajar Utama Yogya* (36,000/76,000Rp, five hours) departs at 9.20 am. To Semarang, via Tegal and Pekalongan, the *Fajar Utama Semarang* (32,000Rp bisnis, four hours) departs at 10.45 pm.

Boat The Pelni office (☎ 204300) is at the harbour past the harbour entrance. The *Lawit* stops in Cirebon when travelling to/from Pontianak in Kalimantan.

Getting Around

Cirebon's city minibus *(angkutan kota)* service operates from Pasar Gunungsari, a couple of blocks west of Jl Siliwangi and charge a fixed 400Rp fare around town – some even offer 'full music'!

Cirebon has hordes of becaks ringing through the streets. A becak from the train station to Pasar Pagi costs around 2000Rp. Taxis at the bus terminal and train station are unwilling to use their meters. From the bus terminal to the train station costs around 6000Rp.

AROUND CIREBON
Tomb of Sunan Gunungjati

In the royal cemetery, 5km north of Cirebon, is the tomb of Sunan Gunungjati, who died in 1570. The most revered of Cirebon's kings, Gunungjati was also one of the nine *wali songo* (holy men who spread Islam throughout Java) and his tomb is one of the holiest places in the country. The inner tombs are only open once a month on Kliwon Thursday of the Javanese calendar (the calendar is a combination of the normal seven day week and the five day Javanese market week), and at Idul Fitri (a public holiday marking the end of Ramadan) and Maulud Nabi Muhammed (see Public Holidays & Special Event in the Facts for the Visitor chapter for more information). Pilgrims sit in contemplation and pray outside the doors on other days. Along from Sunan Gunungjati's tomb is the tomb of his first wife, who was Chinese – this tomb attracts Chinese worshippers.

Trusmi

Some of Cirebon's finest batik is made in the village of Trusmi, 5km west of town. Take a G4 or GP angkot from Pasar Gunungsari minibus terminal to Plered, on the Bandung road. Walk past the market from the main road and down a country lane of whitewashed cottages (or take a becak). At the end of the lane, **Ibu Masina's** is the best known studio where you can see *batik tulis* (handmade batik) being made. Her air-con showroom has a wide range of colours and designs, and excellent silk batik. Also worth visiting is the workshop of **Ibu Ega Sugeng**, which is nearby at Jl Trusmi 218.

Surrounding villages, each specialising in their own crafts, include **Tegalwangi**, where rattan workshops line the Bandung road, 1km on from Plered.

Linggarjati & Sangkan Hurip

Linggarjati's place in the history books was assured when, in 1946, representatives of the Republican government and the returning Dutch occupying forces met to negotiate a British-sponsored cooperation agreement. Terms were thrashed out in a colonial hotel at the foot of Gunung Cirema (3078m), once a retreat from the heat for Cirebon's Dutch residents. Soekarno briefly attended, but the Linggarjati Agreement was soon swept aside as the war for independence escalated. The hotel is now the **Gedung Naksa**, which is a museum recreating the events.

Linggarjati is not one of Java's premier hill resorts, but it has a few mid-range hotels and makes a pleasant sojourn from the heat of the northern plains. It is possible to climb **Gunung Cirema**, which erupted dramatically last century, but a guide is necessary to negotiate the 10 hour walk through the forested slopes to the crater.

Sangkan Hurip is 3km away and is a fairly nondescript hot springs resort, with a large hot water swimming pool, hot baths and a dozen or so hotels in all price ranges.

Getting There & Away Linggarjati and Sangkan Hurip are 23km south of Cirebon, lying 2km to the west of the Kuningan road and 1km to the east respectively. From Cirebon take a Kuningan bus to Cilimus (800Rp) and then a Colt (300Rp) or andong to either resort.

Central Java

Central Java has a population of 30 million, an area of 34,503 sq km and Semarang as its capital. It's at the heart of Java and is the heart of Javanese culture. It was the centre of Java's first great Indianised civilisation and much of the island's early culture. Later, the rise of Islam created powerful sultanates centred around the kratons of Yogyakarta and Surakarta (Solo). Although the north coast was the early Muslims' first foothold in Java, further inland the new faith was gradually infused with strong Hindu-Buddhist influences and even older indigenous beliefs.

Today, the old Javanese traditions and arts, cultivated by the royal courts, are at their most vigorous here. The years of Dutch rule made little impact and even though the Indonesian revolution stripped the sultans of their political powers, the influence of kraton culture still lingers in the minds of many Javanese.

Within the province, the 'special territory' of Yogyakarta forms a triangular enclave with its base on the south coast and its apex at the volcano, Gunung Merapi (2911m). Although Semarang is the capital, the cities of Yogya and Solo are the emotional and cultural centres, having both been capitals of Javanese kingdoms and, frequently, rival cities. Most of Central Java's main attractions are within or nearby these two cities and include the magnificent Borobudur and Prambanan temples. There are also earlier temples in Central Java, particularly the ancient shrines of Dieng. The province also has some fine hill resorts, such as Kaliurang.

Despite its high population, Central Java is a relaxed, easy-going province. Yogyakarta in particular remains one of Indonesia's most important tourist destinations.

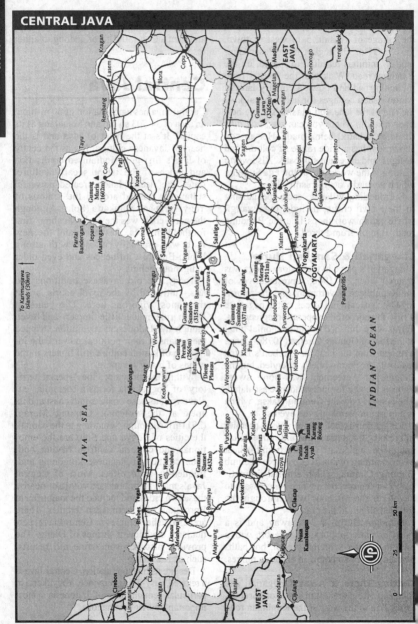

CENTRAL JAVA

FIRE MOUNTAINS

Indonesia is arguably the best place in the world for volcano enthusiasts. It has 129 active volcanoes – more than any other country – and most are easily accessible and safe for trekking (when not erupting). From the north-western tip of Sumatra to the eastern islands of Maluku, steaming *gunung api* (fire mountains) dominate the landscape. They range in elevation from well below sea level at Gunung Nieuwerkerk (-2285m), to just above 3800m at Gunung Kerinci jn Sumatra. While every volcano is shaped uniquely, most share a similar geologic past.

Indonesia lies on a significant segment of the Pacific 'Ring of Fire' where two large crustal plates, the Indian Ocean and western Pacific plates, collide with a third, the massive Eurasian plate. The denser of these plates (in this case, the Indian Ocean and western Pacific plates) are forced to descend into the earth's mantle where they begin melting at approximately 100km beneath the surface. Some of the newly melted rock (magma) then rises to the earth's surface, and erupts to form a neat line of volcanic islands from Sumatra to the Banda Sea (a distance of over 3000km). With Indonesia's volcanic activity also comes earthquakes and the occasional tsunami (large sea wave). Very few places in Indonesia are safe from the region's tectonic instability.

Of the more than 13,000 islands in Indonesia, Java has the most active volcanoes (21 have erupted since 1600), and the highest population density (more than 800 people per sq km). This makes for a particularly hazardous situation, especially when large eruptions occur.

Right: An illustration from *Zijne Gedante, Zijn Plantentooi, En Inwendige Bouw*, the journey of Dutch geologist Frans unghuhn through Java in the 19th century.

CHRIS MELLOR

PETER TURNER

Nusa Tenggara and North Sulawesi/Pulau Halmahera also have many active volcanoes (20 and 16 respectively), but these areas are more remote, and thus their eruptions generally less threatening.

Fearful Explosions

Two of the world's greatest historic eruptions occurred in Indonesia in the 19th century – one at Krakatau and the other at Tambora. Krakatau, located between Java and Sumatra, now appears very different than it did before a paroxysmal eruption in August 1883. That eruption, lasting nearly 24 hours, killed over 36,000 people, and was heard more than 4000km away. The majority of fatalities were caused

Top: Early morning mist over Gunung Bromo

Bottom: A view of the volcano, Ili Api Lembata, Nusa Tenggara

SARA-JANE CLELAND

CHRIS EISINGER

Top: Staring down into Gunung Bromo's angry crater.

Bottom: Gunung Semaru, East Java, currently one of Indonesia's most active volcanoes.

FIRE MOUNTAINS

SARA-JANE CLELAND

PETER TURNER

CHRIS EISINGER

Top: The caldera of Kelimutu in Central Flores, and its three spectacular crater lakes

Middle: Segara Ana (Child of the Sea), Gunung Rinjani – large, green crescent shaped crater lake

Bottom: Sulphur miners at Kawah Ijen, East Java

by a large tsunami, up to 40m high, which swept people, animals and even steamships several kilometres inland. Additionally, Krakatau ejected vast amounts of volcanic ash and gas high into the stratosphere, which helped to generate dramatic sunsets around the globe. In total, Krakatau's 1883 eruption displaced nearly 18 cubic kilometres of rock, and left only one-third of the original island still above sea level.

Gunung Tambora, 1600km to the east on the island of Sumbawa, makes Krakatau's eruption seem paltry. Here, in 1815, enough ash and pumice (150 to 180 cubic km) was disgorged to lower global air temperatures significantly the following year – in fact, 1816 was known in Europe and the USA as the 'year without a summer' (snow fell near London in August of that year). Tambora's death toll, while initially smaller than Krakatau, grew to more than 92,000 people as the result of famine from crop destruction on Sumbawa and Lombok.

In more recent years, Indonesia has not seen an eruption of the magnitude of Krakatau or Tambora. However, Indonesia does deal with a major volcanic event once a year, on average. Some of the more recent fatal eruptions include Galunggung (West Java) in 1982, Kolo (North Sulawesi) in 1983, Gunung Api (Maluku) in 1988, Kelut (East Java) in 1990, Lokon-Empung (North Sulawesi) in 1992, Merapi (Central Java) and Semeru (East Java) in 1994, and Karangetang (North Sulawesi) in 1997. Amazingly, death and destruction have been kept low thanks in large part to the efforts of the Indonesian government.

Keeping Close Watch:
The Volcanological Survey of Indonesia

Indonesia's Direktorat Vulkanologi (☎ 022-771402, fax 702761) at Jl Diponegoro 57, Bandung, 40122, has existed in various forms since the 1920s, after an eruption of Gunung Kelut in East Java killed more than 5000 people. Originally set up by the Dutch, and then expanded under the Indonesian government, Volcanological Survey of Indonesia (VSI) currently has more than 60 observation posts (*pos pengamatan*) strategically positioned on 60 of Indonesia's most dangerous volcanoes – over a third on the island of Java alone. These observation posts vary greatly in their size and monitoring capabilities. The observatory at Gunung Merapi, for example, boasts over 50 employees and a state-of-the-art monitoring system including real-time video. Many observation posts, however, consist of little more than a small building with two local observers, one seismograph and a transmitting radio.

There are over 170 Indonesian volcano observers whose job it is to watch the seismographs, make regular visual reports and to notify the VSI headquarters of any unusual activity. While lacking a formal volcanology education, the observers do receive extensive training and are generally very adept at noting changes at 'their' volcano. Unfortunately, in the more populated areas, even their skills may be no match for a future eruption on the scale of Krakatau or Tambora.

A Land of Fire, Destruction and Rebirth

Volcanoes are a threat to thousands of Indonesians on a daily basis. Pyroclastic flows (moving clouds of hot ash and lethal gases) have come down upon many villages with little or no warning. Known as *awan panas* in Bahasa Indonesia, these notorious hazards can travel more than 15km from a volcano at speeds approaching 250km per hour. The air temperature inside the flows can reach in excess of 500°C, and anyone caught in them is severely burned, if not killed instantly. At Gunung Merapi 60 people perished in 1994, and over 300 were injured, when several large pyroclastic flows came racing down the south-west flank of the volcano. At Gunung Karangetang in North Sulawesi, three people were killed when a much smaller pyroclastic flow caught them in a designated 'danger zone'. Because of their high speeds and low predictability pyroclastic flows are extremely dangerous.

Lahars (volcanic mudflows) are also a major hazard in Indonesia. The word 'lahar' actually comes from Bahasa Indonesia, and has been adopted by the international volcanology community. Lahars are essentially a mixture of volcanic debris and water which originate on the steep slopes of a volcano. They are gravity driven, can be either hot or cold, move very fast and usually deposit thick layers of concrete-like mud. Lahars commonly follow pre-existing river or stream channels, and can travel a great distance from a volcano (in some cases 20 to 30km). This makes them a potent hazard in highly developed areas such as Java and Bali.

In 1919 a particularly devastating eruption of Gunung Kelut, in East Java, ejected a mixture of 38 million cubic metres of water (from a crater lake) and ash over the surrounding countryside. In less than an hour, 5000 people were killed and 104 villages destroyed. In the town of Blitar, more than 10km away, lahars left mud up to 2.5m thick. After this eruption the Dutch engineered a way to drain the lake in an attempt to prevent future catastrophes at Gunung Kelut. While successful in greatly reducing the volume of water, recent eruptions have still produced fatal lahars.

Despite the destruction, Indonesian volcanoes have generally had a positive impact on the land and people. Nutrient-rich lavas and ash have enriched the soil, allowing for intense agricultural development; high volcanic peaks have helped to generate rain – an important source of water for both agriculture and human consumption; and the volcanoes support many unique ecosystems and wildlife. Also, the high volcanoes provide a refreshing escape from the tropical heat of Indonesia's lowlands.

With caution, visiting an active volcano can be the experience of a lifetime. The sulphur-rich gases combined with a barren crater and/or bubbling crater lake provide a landscape unlike any other. At the most lively volcanoes, you may witness small to large explosions of ash and volcanic ejecta, and, if lucky, observe glowing red lava. But, beware of getting too close, as Indonesian volcanoes can change their mood with little warning.

A Long Tradition

Virtually every volcano (including those recently active and those long dormant) has a story or myth about associated gods and/or supernatural beings. Offerings and rituals to pay homage to (or appease) the volcano spirits (*roh halus* or *jiwa*) are also common, especially among those living on the volcano's slopes or harvesting the near-by land. At Gunung Merapi, near Yogyakarta, many Javanese have strong beliefs that the volcano has an important connection with Sultan Hamengkubuwono X and his family. Also, there are many sacred rocks, caves and meditation places that local villagers often visit. Interestingly, the majority of people in this area are Muslim, yet still believe in the volcano's special powers. This is a common theme from one island to the next, despite the primary religion of each region.

Bali, however, uniquely integrates nature and volcano deities through the dominant Hindu faith. In fact, Gunung Agung is considered the centre of the Balinese universe, and it is an important centrepiece for many Balinese traditions, including Eka Dasa Rudra – the centennial purification festival (the most recent festival was held in 1963). Further, Gunung Agung serves as a geographic landmark for many Balinese who think spatially in terms of the mountain's location.

In Indonesia, modern and traditional volcano beliefs often intersect. In 1963, for example, Gunung Agung erupted, catastrophically killing thousands of people in Bali. To Indonesians, an important aspect of this eruption was not so much the geological cause, but rather what political event or person prompted the disaster. As it turns out, many Indonesians believe Soekarno, who was president at the time, brought on the tragedy by asking religious leaders to 'stage' an important ceremony to coincide with an international tourism conference. Even today, any large eruption prompts Indonesians to question who or what caused the event. See the boxed text 'The 1963 Eruption' in the Bali chapter for more information.

Some Practical Information

Volcanoes are certainly one of Indonesia's major attractions. They provide cool relief from the heat of the lowlands, allow you to get away from crowded cities, and give you an opportunity to see some incredible wildlife, active geology and beautiful landscapes. However, there are some important considerations to be made before planning a trek:

Check the accessibility of the volcano you plan to visit While many volcanoes in Java and Bali have roads leading to their summits, others have poorly kept trails on which you can get lost for hours. Also, transportation should be planned before starting a trek, as just getting to the trailhead can be a challenge in itself.

Find out how long it takes to ascend the volcano While some volcanoes can be visited in a few hours, others take a full day and still others require two to five days. For overnight trips, you'll probably need some camping equipment and supplies. Also, a guide and/or porter can be very helpful, if not crucial, for any extended-length trip.

Be prepared for cold temperatures and wet conditions Remember that for every 500m gained in elevation, the temperature decreases by about 3°C. By the time you're above 2000m, temperatures can easily get below 10°C at night, and above 3000m, you'll be right near freezing point. Combine the cold with lots of rain and you have a potentially dangerous situation if you're not properly prepared. In fact, several of the taller Indonesian volcanoes have claimed the lives of local climbers, not from eruptive activity but from exposure and fatigue. At the more popular volcanoes, tents, sleeping bags and warm clothing can usually be rented.

Try to plan your visit for the dry season Although most volcanoes can be climbed during the rainy season, it can be a miserably wet and cold experience.

Consider hiking with a local tour group Many of the volcanoes in Java, Bali and Sumatra can be climbed with tours that provide transportation, a guide and food all for one price. While these organised tours can be rushed and feel crowded, they can also make climbing a volcano far more convenient and enjoyable.

Check the current status of the volcano you plan to climb While most volcanoes in Indonesia are safe for trekking, there are several that have been erupting almost continuously for several years. These include Gunung Merapi, Gunung Semeru and Gunung Ruang in Java, and Gunung Karangetang in North Sulawesi. Anak Krakatau (Child of Krakatau) is, at the time of writing, very active with large explosions of ash and smoke up to several hundred metres high.

Other Indonesian volcanoes have a tendency to come alive every couple of years, so check with a reliable source before your trip. On the Internet, the Global Volcanism Program homepage (www.nmnh.si .edu/gvp/) is a good source for status reports, plus it has bulletins of past eruptive activity. Volcano World (volcano.und.nodak.edu) is an excellent source of both educational and general information about volcanoes and volcanic hazards.

In Indonesia, check with the local tourist office, other travellers or the nearest observation post for a volcano's eruption status. If it is closed, do not attempt to climb the volcano or hike into the 'danger zone'. In 1992 two German tourists were killed by volcanic bombs at Gunung Semeru, and in 1993 one tourist was killed and five others injured at Krakatau. In both cases, people were in places they should not have been. While it is an incredible experience to observe an eruption, it's an utterly terrifying experience to have to run from one. Remember to keep a safe distance and you'll be sure to enjoy Indonesia's remarkable volcanoes.

Chris Eisinger

HISTORY

Central Java has been a great religious centre for both Hindus and Buddhists. Under the Sailendra and Old Mataram kings, the Hindu-Javanese culture flourished between the 8th and 10th centuries AD, and it was during this time that Java's most magnificent religious monuments were built. The province has also been the major centre for the political intrigues and cultural activities of the Islamic states of old Java.

The renaissance of Central Java's political ascendancy began in the late 16th century with the disintegration of the Hindu Majapahit empire. Strong maritime Muslim states arose in the north, but the most powerful dynasties developed in the south. According to legend, the founder of this second Mataram empire sought the support of Nyai Loro Kidul (Queen of the South Seas), who was to become the special protector of the House of Mataram and is still very much a part of court and local traditions.

From its capital at Kota Gede, near Yogya, the Mataram empire eventually dominated Central and East Java and Madura. It reached its peak under Sultan Agung. The only permanent defeats of his career were his failure to take Dutch Batavia and the sultanate of Banten in the west. Sultan Agung's tomb at Imogiri near Yogyakarta is still revered as a holy place.

Following Agung's death in 1646, the empire rapidly began to disintegrate and ultimately fell to growing Dutch power. Amangkurat I followed Sultan Agung and devoted his reign to destroying all those he suspected of opposing him. In 1647 he moved his palace to Plered, not far from the old court. His tyrannical policies alienated his subjects and revolts soon broke out on all sides, which eventually led to the start of Dutch intervention in Javanese affairs. Rebellion broke out in 1675 and Plered fell to a predatory raid by Prince Trunojoyo of Madura, who then withdrew to Kediri, taking the Mataram treasury with him.

After Amangkurat's death in 1677 his son and successor made an alliance with the Dutch and began his reign from a new capital at Kartasura, near present-day Solo. In 1678 Dutch and Javanese troops destroyed Trunojoyo's stronghold at Kediri, and the Mataram treasury was plundered by the victors, although some of it was later restored.

In the 18th century, intrigues and animosities at the Mataram court erupted into what became known as the First and Second Javanese Wars of Succession. Later, the repercussions of the Batavian Chinese massacre in 1740 spilled into Central Java and the fighting lasted almost 17 years. The *susuhunan* (king), Pakubuwono II, unwisely joined those Chinese who escaped slaughter in their siege of Dutch headquarters along the north coast, but was forced to retreat. Madurese intervention on behalf of the Dutch added to the confusion, and in 1742 the court of Mataram was once again conquered by Madurese troops. The struggle was finally resolved by the treaty of 1743, by which Pakubuwono II was restored to his battered court but at the cost of enormous concessions to the Dutch.

Kartasura was now abandoned, and in 1745 Pakubuwono II established a new court at Surakarta, which is still occupied by his descendants. In 1746 the Third Javanese War of Succession began and continued until 1757. The Dutch, rapidly losing patience, finally adopted a policy of divide and rule – a tactic which was also adopted by the British when they took control during the five year interregnum from 1811. By 1757 the former Mataram empire had been split into three rival, self-governing principalities – the realm of Surakarta was partitioned and the Sultanate of Yogyakarta was formed in 1755 and, finally, a smaller domain called Mangkunegara was created within Surakarta (Solo).

The founder of Yogya, Hamengkubuwono I (1755-92), was the most able Mataram ruler since Sultan Agung. During his reign the sultanate was the predominant military power in Central Java. Yet, within 40 years of his death, his successor had brought about the destruction of Javanese independence and the beginning of the truly colonial period of Central Javanese history. The deterioration of

JAVA

Hamengkubuwono II's relations both with his rivals in Surakarta and the Dutch was followed by equal hostility towards the British. In 1812 European troops, supported by the sultan's ambitious brother and Mangkunegara, plundered the court of Yogya, and Hamengkubuwono was exiled to Penang. He was replaced as sultan by his son, and his brother was appointed Prince Paku Alam of a small enclave within the sultanate.

At this time Java was in a state of flux due to corruption at court, continual European interference and increased hardship among the Javanese villagers. Into this turbulent picture stepped one of the most famous figures of Indonesian history, Prince Diponegoro, to launch the Java War of 1825-30. At the end of the war the Dutch held Yogya responsible and all of its outer districts were annexed. To maintain the principle of equality, the outer districts of Surakarta were also annexed. Pakubuwono IV was so disturbed by this apparent injustice that he set out for the Indian Ocean to confer with the 'Goddess of the South Seas', but the Dutch, fearing yet more rebellion, brought him back and exiled him to Sulawesi.

The Java War was the last stand of the Javanese aristocracy. For the remainder of the colonial period the courts became ritual establishments and Dutch *residen* (head of a residency during colonial administration) exercised control. With no real room or will for political manoeuvre, the courts turned their energies to traditional court ceremonies and patronage of literature and the arts. Their cultural prestige among the masses was high and this, combined with their political impotence, possibly explains why the royal elite were not major targets for the nationalist movement which arose in the 20th century. In fact, Yogyakarta became the capital of the Republican government for a period, and the progressive sultan at that time was so popular that he later served in several government posts. The sultanate has also remained administratively autonomous from Central Java as a special territory *(daerah istimewa)* with the status of a province.

CILACAP
☎ 0282

Over the border from West Java, Cilacap is a medium-sized city in a growing industrial area, and has the only natural harbour with deep-water berthing facilities on Java's south coast. It is a pleasant town and the river is dotted with brightly painted fishing boats, but the main reason to visit is to make the backwater trip to Pangandaran.

The tourist office (☎ 34481), Jl A Yani 8, is opposite the Hotel Wijayakusuma.

Things to See
Built between 1861 and 1879, **Benteng Pendem** is an impressive Dutch fort complex at the entrance to the old harbour. With intact barracks, gun rooms and massive ramparts, it is one of the best preserved forts in Java. Bring a flashlight and wear sandals – one tunnel leads to the sea and lies in shallow water. The fort is open from 7 am to 5 pm; entry is 600Rp.

The fort overlooks a long stretch of dirty sand, **Pantai Teluk Penyu**, a popular local beach with souvenir stalls selling an array of shells and other ecologically unsound items.

Places to Stay & Eat
The friendly *Losmen Tiga (☎ 33415, Jl Mayor Sutoyo 61)* is in the centre of town and gets a steady trickle of travellers. The rooms, all with shared mandi, don't come much rougher or cheaper at 5500/7700Rp for singles/doubles; 11,000Rp for triples. The well kept *Hotel Anggrek (☎ 33835, Jl Anggrek 16)* is a better bet with decent rooms for 12,000Rp up to 40,800Rp with air-con.

Hotel Graha Indah Cilacap (☎ 33706, Jl Dr Wahidin 5) is shabby but has a pool, restaurant and disco. Rooms with air-con and hot water cost 60,000Rp to 110,000Rp. *Hotel Wijayakusuma (☎ 34871, Jl A Yani 12A)* also has a pool, restaurant and pub, and the best rooms in town for 292,000Rp and 337,000Rp (much less with a discount).

The excellent *Restaurant Perapatan/ Sien Hieng (Jl A Yani 62)*, in the very centre of town, is a Cilacap institution with a large Chinese menu.

Getting There & Away

Bus The bus terminal is 3km north of the city centre on Jl Gatot Subroto. Buses to/from Cilacap include Pangandaran (4500Rp, 2½ hours), Yogya (6000Rp, five hours, 232km), Purwokerto (2000Rp, 1½ hours) and Wonosobo (4500Rp, four hours).

For door-to-door minibuses to Yogya (15,000Rp), check Toko Djadi (☎ 33490), Jl A Yani 72, and Travel Rejeki (☎ 33371), Jl A Yani 68.

Train Cilacap's neglected but central train station (☎ 33842) is just off Jl A Yani. Only three trains operate: the *Purwojaya* to Jakarta (28,000/48,000Rp in bisnis/eksekutif) at 6 pm; the ekonomi *Capbaya* to Yogya (4500Rp) and *Seraya* to Bandung (7000Rp) both depart at 5.45 am.

Boat Boats to Kalipucang (3200Rp, four hours) leave at 8 am and noon and/or 1 pm. They depart from the jetty on the river estuary a few kilometres north-west of town. Take a bemo to the jetty turn-off (500Rp), and then a becak for the 1km or so to the jetty (1000Rp). A becak from the bus terminal all the way to jetty should cost about 2500Rp. The jetty is near the big Pertamina installations – no photography! The last ferry leaves at 1 pm, so start early if coming from Yogya or Dieng unless you want to spend the night in Cilacap. See Getting There & Away under Pangandaran earlier in this chapter for more details.

PURWOKERTO

This medium-sized city is primarily a transport hub for trains and buses; and you may find yourself here en route between Wonosobo or Cilacap, or on the way to Baturaden. Purwokerto is an unhurried, remarkably clean city with some architectural reminders of Dutch colonialism. It has plenty of hotels, but Baturaden is a better option.

The train station is close to the city centre and the bus terminal is about 2km south. Buses run to all major centres, including Cilacap, Wonosobo, Banjar and Yogya. Infrequent direct buses go to Baturaden

(1000Rp) or catch an angkot from Pasar Wage (1000Rp) in town.

BATURADEN
☎ 0281

Baturaden, 14km north of Purwokerto on the slopes of Gunung Slamet, is one of Java's most attractive mountain resorts. Savour the mountain air on quiet weekdays and go for walks through forested hills to waterfalls and hot springs. The recreation park has a swimming pool, boat rides and zoo.

Gunung Slamet (3432m), the second-highest peak in Java, is a Fujiesque volcanic cone that dominates the landscape of western Central Java. Trails lead from Baturaden to the peak, but this is a very tough route. The usual ascent is from Bambangan village to the east or Serang from the north.

Places to Stay

Wisma Kartika Asri is in a good position opposite the gates to the recreation park. Basic, clean rooms with mandi cost 20,000Rp. Nearer the bus terminal, the *Hotel Sari* is a little better, with rooms for 30,000Rp. The rock-bottom *Hotel Teluk Penyu* has rooms for 12,500Rp.

Top of the range is the big *Hotel Rosenda* (☎ 32570), with a pool and rooms from 175,000Rp (before discount). The older *Rosenda Cottages* is simpler and has rooms for 125,000Rp. The other big resort hotel is the *Queen Garden* (☎ 38388), 2km east. It also has a pool and good rooms from 190,000Rp.

GUA JATIJAJAR

This huge limestone cave, about 130km west of Yogya and 21km south-west of Gombong, is a popular local tourist attraction. From the car park, make your way past the souvenir sellers to the recreation park and up to the graffiti-spattered cave. A concrete path wends its way over natural springs and through the cave halls decorated with statues relating the story of the legendary lovers Raden Kamandaka and Dewi Ratna Ciptarasa. It's very tacky, which is unfortunate because this is an otherwise impressive natural cave.

JAVA

More difficult to explore, but larger and unspoilt, **Gua Petruk** is 7km south of Gua Jatijajar.

Several black-sand beaches lie to the south. **Pantai Indah Ayah** (aka Pantai Logending) is 5km beyond Gua Petruk. At **Pantai Karang Bolong** people make a living collecting the nests of sea swallows from the steep cliff walls.

WONOSOBO
☎ 0286 • pop 25,000
Wonosobo is the main gateway to the Dieng Plateau. At 900m above sea level in the hills of the central mountain range, Wonosobo has a comfortable climate and is a fairly typical country town with a busy market. On national holidays it comes alive as people from the surrounding villages gather for festivities held in the main square. You might see the Kuda Kepang dance from nearby Temanggung, or the local Lengger dance in which men dress as women and wear masks.

Information
The tourist office (☎ 21194), Jl Kartini 3, is open standard office hours, and has maps and brochures of Wonosobo and the Dieng Plateau. The BNI bank on Jl A Yani changes cash and travellers cheques at low rates, and has an ATM for credit card withdrawals. The Telkom office is on Jl A Yani near the alun alun (main public square) and has Home Country Direct telephones.

Places to Stay – Budget
Wisma Duta Homestay (☎ 21674, Jl Rumah Sakit 3) is the best budget option, with comfortable, bright rooms with attached mandi for 15,000Rp and 20,000Rp, 40,000Rp with shower. It provides good travel information. Another good guesthouse is the small *Citra Homestay* (☎ 21880, Jl Angkatan 45). Large rooms with shared bathroom cost 20,000Rp and it has a pleasant sitting area.

Wonosobo also has plenty of cheap, uninspiring losmen. *Hotel Petra* (☎ 27152, Jl A Yani 97) is one of the more welcoming. Singles/doubles cost 7000/20,000Rp and 11,000/25,000Rp.

If you can't be bothered heading into town, the well run *Hotel Dewi* (☎ 21813, Jl A Yani 90A) opposite the bus terminal is a good choice with economy rooms for 15,000Rp, and mid-range rooms with mandi for 30,000Rp or from 40,000Rp with hot water.

Places to Stay – Mid-Range & Top End
Hotel Nirwana (☎ 21066, Jl Resimen 18 No 34) is quiet, secure and very popular, although the staff are surly. Rooms with hot shower

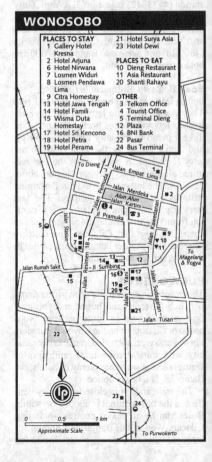

WONOSOBO

PLACES TO STAY	
1	Gallery Hotel Kresna
2	Hotel Arjuna
6	Hotel Nirwana
7	Losmen Widuri
8	Losmen Pendawa Lima
9	Citra Homestay
13	Hotel Jawa Tengah
14	Hotel Famili
15	Wisma Duta Homestay
17	Hotel Sri Kencono
18	Hotel Petra
19	Hotel Perama
21	Hotel Surya Asia
23	Hotel Dewi

PLACES TO EAT	
10	Dieng Restaurant
11	Asia Restaurant
20	Shanti Rahayu

OTHER	
3	Telkom Office
4	Tourist Office
5	Terminal Dieng
12	Plaza
16	BNI Bank
22	Pasar
24	Bus Terminal

are immaculate but overpriced at 50,000Rp, or 100,000Rp for large family rooms.

The **Hotel Sri Kencono** (☎ 21522, Jl A Yani 81) is the best of the older mid-range hotels. The tiled rooms are well kept, have hot water showers and TV for 44,000Rp.

Hotel Surya Asia (☎ 22992, Jl A Yani 137) is an excellent three star hotel with a good restaurant. Rooms cost from 136,000Rp, including tax and service and breakfast.

The only top-end hotel is the new **Gallery Hotel Kresna** (☎ 24111, Jl Pasukan Rong-golawe 30), which has a pool, restaurant and bar. This stylish hotel was built in 1921 as a retreat for Dutch planters. The original dining room remains but the rest of the hotel is new. Rooms start at US$80 (discounted to as low as 180,000Rp).

Places to Eat
The popular **Dieng Restaurant** (Jl Kawe-danan 29) has good Indonesian, Chinese and European food served buffet style. The owner is an inspirational source of information on Dieng, and his photograph albums are worth a look. This long-running institution may move closer to the new bus terminal. The **Asia**, two doors down, is one of Wonosobo's best restaurants and serves Chinese food.

Getting There & Away
Wonsobo's bus terminal in 2km south of the town centre but plans are afoot to move it 3km out of town on the Magelang road.

From Yogya take a bus to Magelang (2000Rp, one hour) and then another bus to Wonosobo (2200Rp, two hours). Rahayu Travel (☎ 21217), Jl A Yani 111, and Rama Sakti Travel (☎ 21236) have door-to-door minibuses to Yogya (8000Rp, three hours). Hotels can arrange pick-up.

Hourly buses go to Semarang (4000Rp, four hours) via Secang and Ambarawa (3000Rp).

Infrequent direct buses run to Cilacap (4500Rp, four hours). Otherwise take a bus to Purwokerto (3000Rp, three hours) and change there. Leave early in the morning to catch the ferry to Kalipucang and on to Pangandaran.

Frequent buses to Dieng (1500Rp, one hour) leave from Dieng terminal throughout the day and continue on to Batur.

Getting Around
Yellow angkots run around town and to nearby villages and cost 400Rp for most journeys. Andongs from the bus terminal to the town centre cost 500Rp per person.

DIENG PLATEAU
☎ 0286
The oldest Hindu temples in Java were discovered on this lofty plateau, 2000m above sea level. The name 'Dieng' comes from Di-Hyang (Abode of the Gods), and it is thought that this was once the site of a flourishing temple-city of priests.

Over 400 temples, mostly built between the 8th and 9th centuries, covered the highland plain, but with the mysterious depopulation of Central Java, this site, like Borobudur, was abandoned and forgotten. It was not until 1856 that the archaeologist Van Kinsbergen drained the flooded valley around the temples and catalogued the ruins. The eight remaining temples are characteristic of early Central Javanese architecture – stark, squat and box-like.

These simple temples, while of great archaeological importance, are not stunning. Rather Dieng's beautiful landscape is the main reason to make the long journey to this isolated region. Steep mountainsides terraced with vegetable plots enclose the huge volcanically active plateau, a marshy caldera of a collapsed volcano. Any number of walks to cool mineral lakes, steaming craters or other quiet, lonely places can be made around Dieng – even to the highest village in Central Java, Sembungan, if you're feeling energetic.

To really appreciate Dieng, it's best to stay in Dieng village, although Wonosobo has better facilities and can be used as a base. Yogya companies also run tours to Dieng. The temples and the main 'natural' sights can be seen in one day on foot – arrive in Dieng in the morning before the afternoon mists roll in. It is a pleasant three or four hour loop south

JAVA

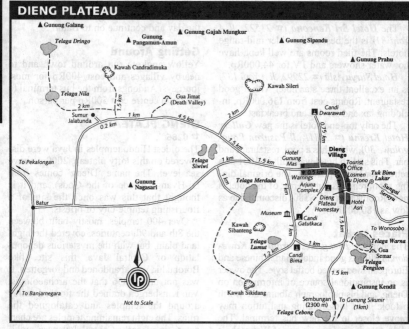

DIENG PLATEAU

▲ Gunung Galang
Telaga Dringo
Gunung Pangamun-Amun
▲ Gunung Gajah Mungkur
▲ Gunung Sipandu
▲ Gunung Prahu
Kawah Candradimuka
Kawah Sileri
Telaga Nila
Gua Jimat (Death Valley)
Candi Dwarawati
2 km
1 km
1.5 km
4.5 km
2 km
Sumur Jalatunda
0.2 km
1.5 km
0.75 km
To Pekalongan
Telaga Siwiwi
1 km
1.5 km
Hotel Gunung Mas
Dieng Village
Tourist Office
Losmen Bu Djono
Tuk Bima Lukar
Sungai Sergyu
1 km
Telaga Merdada
1 km
0.5 km
Warnngs
Arjuna Complex
Dieng Plateau Homestay
Hotel Asri
Gunung Nagasari
Batur
Museum 🏛
Candi Gatutkaca
To Wonosobo
Kawah Sibanteng
Telaga Lumut
1.2 km
Candi Bima
1 km
1.5 km
Telaga Warna
Gua
Semar
Telaga Pengilon
To Banjarnegara
Not to Scale
Kawah Sikidang
Sembungan (2300 m)
Telaga Cebong
To Gunung Sikunir (1km)
▲ Gunung Kendil

from Dieng village to Telaga Warna (Coloured Lake), Candi Bima (Bima Temple), Kawah Sikidang (Sikidang Crater), and then back to Candi Gatutkaca, the Arjuna Complex and the village. Many other lakes and craters around Dieng are scattered over a large area, but they are difficult to reach.

Information

In Dieng village, a kiosk sells tickets to Dieng for 3000Rp. BRI bank near the Hotel Gunung Mas changes US dollars cash at poor rates.

Temples

The five main temples that form the **Arjuna Complex** are clustered together on the central plain. They are Shiva temples, but like the other Dieng temples have been named after the heroes of the wayang stories of the *Mahabharata* epic – Arjuna, Puntadewa, Srikandi, Sembadra and Semar. Raised walkways link the temples (as most of this land is waterlogged), but you can see the remains of ancient underground tunnels which once drained the marshy flatlands.

Just to the south-west of the Arjuna Complex is **Candi Gatutkaca** and the small site **museum** containing statues and sculpture from the temples. The museum is open weekends – ask around for the caretaker at other times. The statuary inside reveals interesting carvings, including Shiva's carrier, Nandi the bull. With the body of a man and the head of a bull it is a unique representation in Hindu iconography found nowhere else. A gargoyle sporting an erection is distinctly animist.

Further south, **Candi Bima** is unique in Java, with its *kudu*, sculpted heads like so many spectators peering out of windows. The restored **Candi Dwarawati** is on the northern outskirts of the village. Near the entrance to Dieng at the river, **Tuk Bima Lukar** is an ancient bathing spring. It was once a holy place and is said to be a 'fountain of youth'.

Other Attractions

The road south from the Dieng Plateau Homestay passes a mushroom factory and a flower garden before the turn-off to beautiful **Telaga Warna**, which has turquoise hues from the bubbling sulphur deposits around its shores. A trail leads anticlockwise to the adjoining lake, **Telaga Pengilon**, and the holy cave of **Gua Semar**, a renowned meditational cave. Return to the main road via the indistinct trail that leads around Telaga Pengilon and up the terraced hillside before eventually returning to the road. The colours of the lakes are better viewed from up high.

A turn-off just south of here leads to a large geothermal station, which has become a major electricity supplier. Its pipes run throughout the valley.

From Telaga Warna, it is 1km along the main road to Candi Bima, and then another 1.2km to **Kawah Sikidang**, a volcanic crater with steaming vents and frantically bubbling mud ponds. Exercise extreme caution here – there are no guard rails to keep you from slipping off the sometimes muddy trails into the scalding hot waters, as one tourist discovered recently. **Kawah Sibentang** is another less spectacular crater nearby, and **Telaga Lumut** is another small lake.

South of the geothermal station, the paved road leads on to **Sembungan**, said to be the highest village in Java at 2300m. Potato farming has made this large village relatively wealthy – it sends an inordinate number of pilgrims to Mecca.

The main attraction is **Gunung Sikunir**, 1km past Sembungan, and the shallow lake of Telaga Cebong. Views from Sikunir are spectacular, stretching across Dieng and east as far as Merapi and Merbabu volcanoes on a clear day. To reach the hill for sunrise, the favoured viewing time, start at 4 am from Dieng village. It's a one hour walk to Sembungan and another 30 minutes to the top of the hill. The Dieng Plateau Homestay and Losmen Bu Djono both offer guides for 10,000Rp per person.

Other attractions to the west are more difficult to reach. **Telaga Merdada** is a large lake, with a mushroom factory alongside. **Kawah Sileri**, 2km off the main road and 6km from Dieng, is a smoking crater area with a hot lake. The cave, **Gua Jimat**, is a 1km walk through the fields from the main road.

Nine kilometres from Dieng village is the trail to **Kawah Candradimuka**, a pleasant 1.5km walk to this crater through the fields. Another trail branches off to two lakes, **Telaga Nila** and a longer two hour walk to **Telaga Dringo**. Just a few hundred metres past the turn-off to Kawah Candradimuka is **Sumur Jalatunda** (Jalatunda Well). This well is in fact a deep hole some 100m across with vertical walls plunging down to bright green waters.

Another popular spot to see the sunrise and great views of the valley is from the lookout point on the Wonosobo road, 5km towards Wonosobo. This is the 'golden sunrise' of tour parlance, while the 'silver sunrise' comes a little later to Dieng itself.

Places to Stay & Eat

Dieng has a handful of spartan hotels. The *Dieng Plateau Homestay* (☎ 92823) and the *Losmen Bu Djono* next door are perennial competitors. Both have cafes and information on Dieng. The Dieng Plateau is better maintained with singles/doubles for 10,000/15,000Rp (a couple of rooms have mandis but no water as yet). The Bu Jono is friendly, but it asks 15,000Rp for a decrepit room and it has one overpriced 'VIP' room for 50,000Rp. The *Hotel Asri* is another option with passable rooms for 20,000/25,000Rp.

Hotel Gunung Mas (☎ 92417) is the best hotel in town (only just), but the mosque is right behind it and rooms cost a ridiculous 50,000Rp and 70,000Rp.

Don't expect much in the way of culinary delights. The *Losmen Bu Jono* wins back a few points from the *Dieng Plateau Homestay* in the eats department and it has cold beer. *Warungs* opposite the Hotel Gunung Mas include a good Madurese sate stall.

Getting There & Away

Dieng is 26km from Wonosobo, which is the usual access point. Buses from Wonosobo to Dieng village take an hour and continue on to Batur. They cost 1500Rp for lowlanders, only 1200Rp for Dieng villagers and maybe 2000Rp for tourists. From Batur (750Rp by bus from Dieng), pick-ups may not be comfortable but they'll take you to Pekalongan (1500Rp, three hours, 90km). The road is steep but paved. The usual way to reach the north coast is to head down to Wonosobo and then take a bus to Semarang.

It is possible to reach Dieng from Yogya in one day, including a stop at Borobudur, provided you leave early to make all the connections. The route is Yogya-Borobudur-Magelang-Wonosobo-Dieng. Yogya travel agents have day tours that include Borobudur, but you'll spend most of your time on a bus.

YOGYAKARTA

☎ 0274   • pop 425,000

Yogyakarta is the cultural heart of Java, lying between two of Java's most potent mystical symbols – volatile Gunung Merapi in the north and the Indian Ocean, home of the Goddess of the South Seas, in the south. Yogyakarta (pronounced 'Jogjakarta'), or Yogya for short, is the most active centre for Javanese arts, and spoken Javanese is at its most halus here. It is also an intellectual centre, with many prestigious universities and academies, and Yogya's influence and importance far outweighs its size. Yogya has always strived to maintain its independence, clinging proudly to its traditions. It is still headed by its sultan whose walled palace, or kraton, remains the hub of traditional life.

The district of Yogyakarta has a population of 3.2 million and an area of 3186 sq km, while the population of the city itself is under 500,000. No longer the city of bicycles, Yogya has noisy and chaotic traffic much like any Javanese city, but just a short stroll behind the main streets to the kampungs, life is still unhurried.

The city provides easy access for an insight into Javanese culture: craft industries such as batik, silver, pottery and wayang kulit are easily visited; traditional Javanese performing arts can readily be seen; and the contemporary arts are also flourishing. Yogya is also a good base to explore nearby attractions, including Indonesia's most important archaeological sites, Borobudur and Prambanan.

Yogya is Java's premiere tourist centre and Indonesia's most popular city for visitors. It's easy to see why – apart from its many attractions, Yogya is friendly and easygoing, with an excellent range of economical hotels and restaurants.

History

Yogyakarta owes its foundation to Prince Mangkubumi who, in 1755, after a land dispute with his brother, the susuhunan of Surakarta, returned to the former seat of Mataram and built the kraton of Yogyakarta. He took the title of 'sultan' and adopted the name of Hamengkubuwono (The Universe on the Lap of the King), which all his successors have used. He created the most powerful Javanese state since the 17th century. His son was less competent, however, and during the period of British rule the Yogya kraton was sacked, Hamengkubuwono II exiled and the smaller Paku Alam principality created within the sultanate.

For the Javanese, Yogya has always been a symbol of resistance to colonial rule. The heart of Prince Diponegoro's Java War (1825-30) was in the Yogya area. More recently, Yogya was again the centre of revolutionary forces and became the capital of the Republic from 1946 until independence was achieved in 1949. As the Dutch took control of other Javanese cities, part of the kraton was turned over to the new Gajah Mada University, which opened in 1946. Thus, as one of the sultan's advisers observed, in Yogya 'the Revolution could not possibly smash the palace doors, because they were already wide open'.

continued on page 274

BOROBUDUR

From the plain of Kedu, 42km north-west of Yogya, a small hill rises up out of a pattern of palm trees and fields of rice and sugar cane. It's topped by one of the greatest Buddhist relics of South-East Asia – up there with Cambodia's Angkor Wat and Myanmar's Bagan.

Rulers of the Sailendra dynasty built the colossal pyramid of Borobudur sometime between 750-850 AD. Little else is known about Borobudur's early history, but the Sailendras must have recruited a huge workforce, as some 60,000 cubic metres of stone had to be hewn, transported and carved during its construction. The name Borobudur is possibly derived from the Sanskrit words 'Vihara Buddha Uhr', which mean 'Buddhist monastery on the hill'.

With the decline of Buddhism and the shift of power to East Java, Borobudur was abandoned soon after completion and for centuries lay forgotten, buried under layers of volcanic ash. It was only in 1815, when Sir Thomas Stamford Raffles governed Java, that the site was cleared and the sheer magnitude of the builders' imagination and technical skill was revealed. Early in the 20th century the Dutch began to tackle the restoration of Borobudur, but over the years the supporting hill had become waterlogged and the whole immense stone mass started to subside. A mammoth US$25 million restoration project was undertaken between 1973 and 1983.

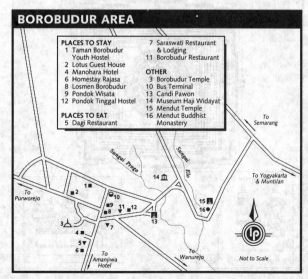

BOROBUDUR AREA

PLACES TO STAY
1 Taman Borobudur Youth Hostel
2 Lotus Guest House
4 Manohara Hotel
6 Homestay Rajasa
8 Losmen Borobudur
9 Pondok Wisata
12 Pondok Tinggal Hostel

PLACES TO EAT
5 Dagi Restaurant

7 Saraswati Restaurant & Lodging
11 Borobudur Restaurant

OTHER
3 Borobudur Temple
10 Bus Terminal
13 Candi Pawon
14 Museum Haji Widayat
15 Mendut Temple
16 Mendut Buddhist Monastery

To Semarang
Sungai Progo
Sungai Elo
To Yogyakarta & Muntilan
To Purworejo
To Amanjiwa Hotel
To Wanurejo
Not to Scale

Text inset: Borobudur Stupa (illustration by Jenny Bowman).

Although easily forgotten, standing as they do in the shadow of the great Borobudur, two smaller structures – the Mendut and Pawon temples – form a significant part of the complex.

Orientation & Information

The small village of Borobudur consists of warungs, souvenir stalls and a few hotels that face the monument. The bus terminal is less than a 10 minute walk from the monument.

The temple site is open from 6 am to 5.15 pm. Admission is 10,000Rp, which includes entrance to the archaeological museum just north of the monument. To hire one of the guides, who are usually knowledgable, costs 15,000Rp (for one to 20 people). An audiovisual show at the Manohara Hotel costs 4000Rp, and Borobudur has a few other attractions, including a children's playground and elephant rides.

Borobudur is Indonesia's single most popular tourist attraction, and it can be crowded and noisy, especially on weekends. Hawkers outside

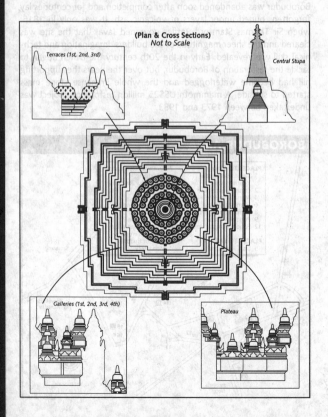

(Plan & Cross Sections)
Not to Scale

Terraces (1st, 2nd, 3rd)

Central Stupa

Galleries (1st, 2nd, 3rd, 4th)

Plateau

and inside the archaeological park are becoming increasingly aggressive. The finest time to see Borobudur and capture something of the spirit of the temple is at dawn or sunset, but you won't have it to yourself. These are also popular times for the bus-loads of tour groups.

Borobudur Temple

Borobudur is built in the form of a massive symmetrical stupa, literally wrapped around the hill. It stands solidly on its 118 x 118m base. Six square terraces are topped by three circular ones, with four stairways leading up through finely carved gateways to the top. The paintwork is long gone, but it's thought that the grey stone of Borobudur was at one time washed with a colour to catch the sun. Viewed from the air, the whole thing looks like a giant three dimensional tantric mandala. It has been suggested, in fact, that the Buddhist community that once supported Borobudur were early Vajrayana or Tantric Buddhists who used it as a walk-through mandala.

The entire monument was conceived as a Buddhist vision of the cosmos in stone, starting in the everyday world and spiralling up to nirvana – the Buddhist heaven. At the base of the monument is a series of reliefs representing a world dominated by passion and desire, where the good are rewarded by reincarnation as a higher form of life, while the evil are punished by a lowlier reincarnation. These carvings and their carnal scenes are covered by stone to hide them from view, but they are partly visible on the south side.

Starting at the main eastern gateway, go clockwise (as one should around all Buddhist monuments) around the galleries of the stupa. Although Borobudur is impressive for its sheer bulk, it is the close-up sculptural detail that is quite astounding. The pilgrim's walk is about 5km long and takes you along narrow corridors past nearly 1460 richly decorated narrative panels and 1212 decorative panels in which the sculptors have carved a virtual textbook of Buddhist doctrines as well as many aspects of Javanese life 1000 years ago – a continual procession of ships and elephants, musicians and dancing girls, warriors and kings. Some 432 serene-faced Buddha images stare out from open chambers above the galleries, while 72 more Buddha images sit only partly visible in latticed stupas on the top three terraces. Reaching in through the stupa to touch the fingers or foot of the Buddha inside is believed to bring good luck.

Candi Pawon

This tiny temple is about 1.5km east of Borobudur and is similar in design and decoration to

Right: Lion guarding the entrance to Borobudur.

JENNY BOWMAN

Mendut. It is not a stupa but resembles a Central Javanese temple, with its broad base, central body and pyramidal roof. Pot-bellied dwarfs pouring riches over the entrance to this temple suggest that it was dedicated to Kuvera, the Buddhist god of fortune.

Mendut Temple

This temple is another 2km east, back towards Muntilan. It may be small and insignificant compared with its mighty neighbour, Borobudur, but it houses the most outstanding statue of any temple in Java that can still be seen in its original setting – a magnificent 3m-high figure of Buddha, flanked by Bodhisattvas – Lokesvara on the left and Vairapana on the right. The Buddha is also notable for his posture, instead of the usual lotus position, he sits western-style with both feet on the ground.

The Mendut Temple, or the Venu Vana Mandira (Temple in the Bamboo Grove), was discovered in 1836 and attempts to restore it were made by the Dutch between 1897 and 1904. Although parts of the roof and entrance remain unfinished, it is nevertheless a fine temple and the gracefully carved relief panels on its outer walls are among the finest and largest examples of Hindu-Javanese art. Next to the temple is the new Mendut Buddhist Monastery. Meditation courses are often held here around December.

Museum Haji Widayat

Amongst the antiquities of Borobudur, halfway between the Pawon and Mendut temples on the main road, the Modern Art Museum is incongruously devoted to modern Indonesian art. This small but significant museum is open daily except Monday from 9 am to 4 pm; admission is 2000Rp.

Special Events

The Buddha's birth, his enlightenment and his reaching of nirvana are all celebrated on the full-moon day of Waisak. A great procession of saffron-robed monks travels from Mendut to Pawon then Borobudur, where candles are lit and flowers strewn about as offerings, followed by praying and chanting. This holiest of Buddhist events attracts thousands of pilgrims, and usually falls in May.

Around June, the Festival of Borobudur kicks off with a Ramayana-style dance, with a cast of over 300, but based on an episode of the Buddhist Manohara. Folk dancing competitions, handicrafts, white-water rafting and other activities add to the carnival atmosphere.

Places to Stay & Eat

The popular *Lotus Guest House* (☎ 0293-88281, Jl Medang Kamulan 2) is on the east side of the temple near the main parking area and is the place to head. Rooms with mandi cost 20,000Rp to 35,000Rp, including breakfast and free tea and coffee throughout the day. This well-run losmen has a good cafe, information on things to do in the area, bicycle rental and organises whitewater rafting trips.

In contrast to the lower galleries, the upper terraces of Borobudur, called the Arupadhatu (Sphere of Formlessness), open on to the lush Kedu plain. The Buddha images on these terraces all sit in the *mudra* position. The hands are symbolically important here and signify reasoning.

JULIET COOMBE

BERNARD NAPTHINE

BERNARD NAPTHINE

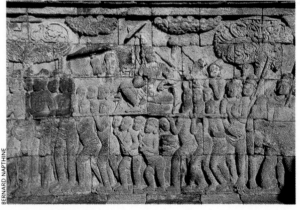

BERNARD NAPTHINE

Top and bottom: The sculptural narrative panels of Borobudur.

Middle: Sculptural reliefs of female deities.

Other cheap options on the south side directly opposite the temple are the basic **Losmen Borobudur**, with rooms for 15,000Rp to 20,000Rp, and the equally simple **Pondok Wisata** (☎ 0293-88362) with rooms from 10,000Rp to 15,000Rp.

One kilometre from Borobudur, the flash **Pondok Tinggal Hostel** (☎ 0293-88245) has bamboo-style rooms around an attractive garden. A bed in the spotless, often empty, dorms costs 7500Rp. Comfortable rooms with attached bathroom cost 33,000Rp, or larger rooms with a sitting room cost from 44,000Rp to 125,000Rp. Add 15% to all rates; it also has a good restaurant.

The **Manohara Hotel** (☎ 0293-88131) has an unbeatable position within the monument grounds. Pleasant air-con rooms, most with porches facing the monument, have private bath, hot water and TV for US$47 and US$50, but expect large discounts. Breakfast and unlimited entry to Borobudur are included. It also runs the **Taman Borobudur Youth Hostel**, primarily for groups.

A number of other hotels are scattered around the village. The most pleasant is the new **Homestay Rajasa** (☎ 0293-88276, Jl Badrawati 2), which has a small restaurant. Attractive, if slightly expensive, rooms overlook rice paddies and cost 60,000Rp/100,000Rp with fan/air-con.

Last but by no means least, the **Amanjiwa** (☎ 0293-88333) rivals Borobudur temple in architectural extravagance. Lying at the foothills of the Menoreh Hills, 3km south of Borobudur, it overlooks the monument and mimics its style with extensive use of stone. Exclusive suites, many with their own pool, cost US$665 to US$2260, making it Java's most expensive hotel.

As well as hotel restaurants, dining options include the pleasant **Borobudur Restaurant** and the more expensive **Dagi Restaurant** near the Manohara Hotel. The **Saraswati Restaurant** has good food, reasonable prices and the elderly woman who runs it is a gracious and educated host. New hotel rooms are also being built here.

Getting There & Away

From Yogya's Umbulharjo bus terminal, direct buses go to Borobudur (2000Rp, 1½ hours) via Muntilan. These buses skirt the central city but can also be caught at Jombor, about 4km north of Yogya on Jl Magelang, near the northern ring road. Bus No 5 runs from Jombor to the city centre.

From Borobudur terminal, buses also go to Muntilan (500Rp), Magelang (1000Rp) and Purworejo.

In Borobudur, the hotels are within walking distance of the bus terminal, or a becak will cost no more than 1000Rp to anywhere in the village. It's a fine walk to Mendut and Pawon, otherwise a bus or bemo is 300Rp to hop from one temple to the next; or hire a becak.

Tours of Borobudur are easily arranged in Yogyakarta at the Prawirotaman or Sosrowijayan agents for as little as 25,000Rp per person. See Organised Tours under Yogyakarta in the Java chapter.

JAVA

continued from page 268

When the Dutch occupied Yogya in 1948, the patriotic sultan locked himself in the kraton, which became the major link between the city and the guerillas who retreated to the countryside. The Dutch did not dare move against the sultan for fear of arousing the anger of millions of Javanese who looked upon him almost as a god. The sultan let rebels use the palace as their headquarters and, as a result of this support and the influence of the sultan, come independence Yogya was granted the status of a special territory. Yogya is now a self-governing district answerable directly to Jakarta and not to the governor of Central Java.

Under Soeharto's government, the immensely popular Sultan Hamengkubuwono IX was Indonesia's vice-president until he stepped down in March 1978. The sultan passed away in October 1988, and in March 1989 Prince Bangkubumi, the eldest of 16 sons, was installed as Sultan Hamengkubuwono X. The coronation involved great pomp and ceremony, and included a procession of dwarfs and albinos.

Hamengkubuwono X was an outspoken supporter of reform leading up to the overthrow of Soeharto, and when Jakarta attempted to appoint an outsider as governor in 1998, the people took to the streets demanding that the sultan become governor, forcing Jakarta to bow to popular pressure.

Orientation

It is easy to find your way around Yogya. Jl Malioboro, named after the Duke of Marlborough, is the main road and runs straight down from the train station to the kraton at the far end. The road becomes Jl A Yani further south but is generally referred to as Jalan Maliboro. The tourist office and many souvenir shops and stalls are along this street, and most of the budget places to stay are west off it, in the Jl Sosrowijayan area near the railway line.

The old, walled kraton is the centre of old Yogya, where you will also find the Taman Sari (Water Castle), Pasar Ngasem (Bird Market) and numerous batik galleries. A second mid-range hotel enclave is south of the kraton area around Jl Prawirotaman.

Information

Tourist Offices The Tourist Information Office (☎ 566000), Jl Malioboro 16, is open daily from 8 am to 8 pm except Sunday. It has useful maps of the city, produces a number of publications (including a calendar of events) and can answer most queries. Tourist office counters are also at the airport and on the eastern side of the Tugu train station, facing Jl Pasar Kembang, in the Sosrowijayan area.

Money Yogya has plenty of banks, open weekdays only, and numerous moneychangers in the tourist areas. Banks usually give better exchange rates.

BNI bank at Jl Trikora 1, opposite the main post office, and the BCA bank on Jl Mangkubumi are worth trying. Both have ATMs that accept Visa and MasterCard.

PT Baruman Abadi at the front of the Natour Garuda Hotel is one moneychanger that gives excellent rates (often better than the banks). It's open Monday to Friday from 7 am to 4 pm and Saturday until 3 pm. Rates are lower at other moneychangers, but they are open long hours. Opposite the train station, PT Haji La Tunrung, Jl Pasar Kembang 17, has so-so rates, but is open daily until 9.30 pm.

The agent for American Express is Pacto (☎ 566328) in the Natour Garuda Hotel on Jl Malioboro; it has another branch at the Radisson Hotel.

Post & Communications The main post office, on Jl Senopati near Jl A Yani, the southern continuation of Jl Malioboro, is open daily from 8 am to 10 pm. Parcel post only operates during business hours. For Internet access, the Warposnet at the post office is open Monday to Saturday from 8 am to 9 pm and Sunday from 9 am to 8 pm (1500Rp for 15 minutes).

For international calls, convenient wartels are behind the post office at Jl Trikora 2 and opposite the Tugu train station at Jl

Pasar Kembang 29. The Telkom office, 1km east of Jl Malioboro on Jl Yos Sudarso, is open 24 hours and has Home Country Direct phones. These can also be found in the lobby of the Natour Garuda Hotel on Jl Malioboro (also chip-card phones) and at the Putri Restaurant on Jl Prawirotaman.

Internet cafes are all over town. In the Sosrowijayan area, Whizz Kids and CMC on are on Gang I and Warnet is on Gang II. The going rate is around 2000Rp for 10 minutes. On Jl Prawirotaman there is Protech 8 or the slightly more expensive Metro Internet in the Metro Guest House on Jl Prawirotaman II. The Pujayo restaurant, to the north of the city, on Jl Simanjuntak, is the cheapest Internet cafe, charging 1500Rp for 15 minutes.

Dangers & Annoyances Yogya has its fair share of thieves – of the break into your room, snatch your bag, steal your bicycle and pick your pocket varieties. Be particularly wary when catching buses to Borobudur and Prambanan. Bag snatching by motorcycle riders have also been reported.

Yogya is crawling with batik salespeople, who'll strike up a conversation on Jl Malioboro or follow you around Taman Sari, pretending to be guides or simply instant friends. Inevitably you'll end up at a gallery where you'll get the hard sell and they'll rake in a big commission if you buy something. A time-honoured scam is the special batik exhibition that is being shipped to South-East Asia – this is your 'last chance' to buy, at maybe 50 times the real price. Variations on a theme are the special student or *koperasi* (co-operative) exhibitions.

Ditch anyone who steers or follows you to shops, and be wary of anyone who strikes up a conversation on the street. Becak drivers offering 'special rates' of 500Rp or 1000Rp for one hour are also trying to get you into a batik gallery.

Kraton

In the heart of the old city the huge palace of the sultans of Yogya is effectively the centre of a small walled-city within a city. Over 25,000 people live within the greater kraton compound, which contains its own market, shops, batik and silver cottage industries, schools and mosques.

The innermost group of buildings, where the current sultan still lives, were built between 1755 and 1756, although extensions were made during the long reign of Hamengkubuwono I. European-style touches to the interior were added much later in the 1920s. Structurally this is one of the finest examples of Javanese palace architecture, providing a series of luxurious halls, and spacious courtyards and pavilions. The sense of tradition holds strong in Yogya, and the palace is attended by very dignified elderly retainers who still wear traditional Javanese dress.

The centre of the kraton is the reception hall, the Bangsal Kencana (Golden Pavilion), with its intricately decorated roof and great columns of carved teak. A large part of the kraton is used as a museum and holds an extensive collection, including gifts from European monarchs, gilt copies of the sacred *pusaka* (heirlooms of the royal family) and gamelan instruments. One of the most interesting rooms contains the royal family tree, old photographs of grand mass weddings and portraits of the former sultans of Yogya.

An entire museum within the kraton is dedicated to Sultan Hamengkubuwono IX, with photographs and personal effects of the great man.

Other points of interest within the kraton include the 'male' and 'female' entrances indicated by giant-sized 'he' and 'she' dragons, although they look very similar. Outside the kraton, in the centre of the northern square, there are two sacred *waringin* (banyan trees), where, in the days of feudal Java, white-robed petitioners would patiently sit hoping to catch the eye of the king. In the *alun alun kidul* (southern square), two similar banyan trees are said to bring great fortune if you can walk between them without mishap while blindfolded.

The kraton is open from daily from 8 am to 2 pm, except Friday when it closes at 1 pm. It is closed on national holidays and for special kraton ceremonies but batik touts

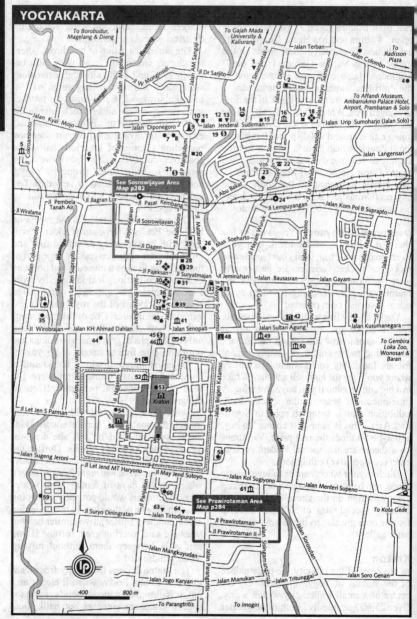

YOGYAKARTA

PLACES TO STAY		7	Merpati Office	41	Benteng Vredeburg
2	Indraloka Home Stay	8	Minibus Agents	42	Pakualaman Kraton
11	Hotel Phoenix	9	Tugu Monument	43	Batik Research Centre
12	Hotel Santika	14	Terban Colt/BusTerminal to	44	Nitour
15	Java Palace Hotel		Kaliurang & Prambanan	45	BNI Bank
17	Novotel Hotel	16	Army Museum	46	Sono-Budoyo Museum
20	New Batik Palace Hotel	18	Galeria Shopping Mall	47	Main Post Office
25	Hotel Ibis	19	Bank Exim	48	Vihara Buddha Prabha
28	Mutiara Hotel	21	BCA Bank		(Chinese Temple)
32	Melia Purosani Hotel	22	Telkom Office	49	Museum Biologi
		23	Public Swimming Pool	50	Sasmitaluka Jenderal
PLACES TO EAT		24	Lempuyangan		Sudirman
1	Pujayo; Internet Cafe		Train Station	51	Mesjid Besar
6	Pesta Perak	26	Bouraq Office	52	Museum Kareta Kraton
10	Pizza Hut	27	Matahari Department	53	Kraton Entrance
13	Rumah Makan Tio Ciu		Store	54	Pasar Ngasem
36	Cherry Cafe	29	Tourist Information Office		(Bird Market)
37	Griya Dahar Timur; Cirebon	30	Toko Ramai Department	55	Purawisata Theatre
	Restaurant		Store	56	Taman Sari (Water Castle)
63	Kedai Kebun	31	Terang Bulan Batik Shop	57	Sasono Hinggil
64	Dutch Cafe	33	Mandala Office	58	Ndalem Pujokusuman
		34	Amri Yahya's Gallery		Theatre
OTHER		35	ISI (Fine Arts Faculty)	59	Agastya Art Institute
3	ISI (Dance Faculty)	38	Mirota Batik	60	Swasthigita Wayang Kulit
4	RRI Auditorium	39	Pasar Beringharjo		Workshop
5	Museum Sasana Wiratama	40	Gedung Negara	61	Museum Perjuangan
	(Monumen Diponegoro)		(Governor's Building)	62	Umbulharjo Bus Terminal

will tell you it's closed to lure you to Taman Sari and a batik gallery.

The entrance is on the north-west side and easy to find if you are coming down Jl Malioboro but more difficult if coming on foot from the south. Admission is 3000Rp (plus a 500Rp camera free), which includes a guided tour. In the inner pavilion from 9 or 10 am to 11 am or noon, you can see performances of gamelan on Monday and Tuesday, wayang golek on Wednesday, classical dance on Thursday and Sunday, wayang kulit on Saturday and Javanese singing on Friday.

Taman Sari (Water Castle)

Just west of the kraton is the Taman Sari, or Fragrant Garden. Better known as the Water Castle, this was once a splendid pleasure park of palaces, pools and waterways for the sultan and his entourage. The architect of this elaborate retreat, built between 1758 and 1765, was a Portuguese from Batavia. The story goes that the sultan had him executed in order to keep his hidden pleasure rooms secret. They were damaged first by Diponegoro's Java War, and an earthquake in 1865 helped finish the job. Today most of the Taman Sari is in ruins among dusty alleys, small houses and batik galleries, but it's an eerie and interesting place with underground passages and a large subterranean mosque.

The bathing pools have been restored and it's possible to imagine the sultan and harem members relaxing here. From the tower overlooking the pools the sultan was able to dally with his wives and witness the goings-on below.

The entrance to the restored bathing pools are on Jl Taman and open daily from 9 am to 3 pm; entry is 1000Rp. Batik touts will try to lure you to a batik gallery or pretend to be official guides – shake them off. They can be informative guides, but even if you establish a price for a tour beforehand, they'll still take you to a batik gallery.

Gamelan Instruments

Bonang The *bonang* consists of a double row of bronze kettles (like small *kenongs*) resting on a horizontal frame. There are three kinds, although the lowest in pitch is no longer used in gamelan orchestras. The bonang is played with two long sticks bound with red cord at the striking end. Although in modern Javanese gamelan the bonang has two rows of bronze kettles, originally it had only one row, as it still has in Bali.

Celempung This is a plucked, stringed instrument, looking somewhat like a zither. It has 26 strings arranged in 13 pairs. The strings are stretched over a coffin-shaped resonator that stands on four legs; the strings are plucked with the thumbnails. The sitar is a smaller version of the *celempung*, with fewer strings and a higher pitch; the body is box-shaped and without legs.

Gambang The *gambang* is the only gamelan instrument with bars made not of bronze but of hardwood, laid over a wooden frame. It is struck with two sticks made of supple buffalo horn, each topped with a small, round, padded disc. Unlike the *gender* keys, the gambang keys do not need to be damped.

Gender This is similar to a *slentem* in structure but there are more bronze keys, and the keys and bamboo chambers are smaller. The gender is played with two disc-shaped hammers, smaller than those used for the slentem. The hand acts as a damper, so each hand must simultaneously hit a note and damp the preceding one.

Gong Ageng The *gong ageng* or *gong gede* is suspended on a wooden frame. There is at least one such gong, sometimes more, in a gamelan orchestra. The gong is made of bronze and is about 90cm in diameter. It performs the crucial task of marking the end of the largest phrase of a melody.

Kempul This is a small hanging gong and marks a smaller musical phrase than the big gong.

Kendang These drums are all double-ended and beaten by hand (with the exception of the giant drum, the *bedug*, which is beaten with a stick). The drum is an important leading instrument;

Pasar Ngasem (Bird Market)

At the edge of Taman Sari, the Pasar Ngasem is a colourful bird market crowded with hundreds of budgerigars, orioles, roosters and singing turtle-doves in ornamental cages, though pigeons are the big business here. Yogya residents are great pigeon fanciers – for training not eating. Lizards and other small animals are also on sale, as are big trays of bird feed of swarming maggots and ants. From the back of Pasar Ngasem, an alleyway leads up to the broken walls of Taman Sari for fine views across Yogya.

Pasar Beringharjo

Yogya's main market on Jl A Yani, the southern continuation of Jl Malioboro, is a lively and fascinating place. The renovated front section has a wide range of batik, mostly cheap *batik cap* (printed batik) but some good tulis (handmade batik) is available. The 2nd floor is dedicated to cheap clothes and shoes but the most interesting area is the old section behind. Crammed with warungs and stalls selling a huge variety of fruit and vegetables, this is still very much a traditional market. Check out the *rempah rempah* (spices) on the

Gamelan Instruments

it is made from the hollowed tree-trunk sections of the jackfruit (nangka) tree with cow or goat skin stretched across the two ends. There are various types of drums but the medium-sized *kendang batangan* or *kendang ciblon* is used chiefly to accompany dance and *wayang* (puppet) performances; the drum patterns indicate specific dance movements or movements of the wayang puppets.

Kenong The *kenong* is a small gong laid horizontally on crossed cord and sitting inside a wooden frame.

Ketuk The *ketuk* is a small kenong, tuned to a certain pitch, which marks subdivisions of phrases; it is played by the kenong player. The sound of the ketuk is short and dead compared with the clearer, resonant tone of the kenong.

Rebab The *rebab* is a two stringed, bowed instrument of Arabic origin. It has a wooden body covered with fine, stretched skin. The movable bridge is made of wood. The bow is made of wood and coarse horsehair which is tied loosely, unlike the bows of western instruments which are stretched tight. The rebab player sits cross-legged on the floor behind the instrument.

Saron This is the basic instrument-type of the gamelan, a xylophone with bronze bars that are struck with a wooden mallet. There are three types of *saron*: high, medium and low pitched. The high saron is called *saron panerus* or *saron peking* and is played with a mallet made of buffalo horn rather than wood.

Slentem The slentem carries the basic melody in the soft ensemble, as the saron does in the loud ensemble. It consists of thin bronze bars suspended over bamboo resonating chambers; it is struck with a padded disc on the end of a stick.

Suling The *suling*, or flute, is the only wind instrument in the gamelan orchestra, particularly Sundanese gamelan. It is made of bamboo and played vertically.

1st floor and the woven goods on the 3rd floor in the south-west corner.

The market is open from 5 am to 4 pm. And as the signs say: *awas copet* (beware pickpockets).

Other Palaces

The smaller **Pakualaman Kraton**, on Jl Sultan Agung, is also open to visitors. It has a small museum, a pendopo that can hold a full gamelan orchestra and a curious colonial house. It is open Tuesday, Thursday and Sunday from 9.30 am to 1.30 pm.

The **Ambarrukmo Palace** on Jl Solo, in the grounds of the Ambarrukmo Palace Hotel, was built in the 1890s as a country house for Hamengkubuwono VII.

Museums

On the north side of the main square in front of the kraton, the **Sono-Budoyo Museum** is the pick of Yogya's museums. Though not particularly well maintained, it has a first-rate collection of Javanese art, including wayang kulit puppets, topeng masks, kris and batik. There is also a courtyard which is packed with Hindu statuary. Artefacts from further afield are also on display, including some superb Balinese carvings. It's open Tuesday to Thursday from 8 am to 1.30 pm, Friday until 11.15 am and weekends until noon; entry is 750Rp. Wayang kulit performances are held every evening from 8 to 10 pm.

Near the kraton entrance, the **Museum Kareta Kraton** has exhibits of opulent chariots of the sultans. It's open from 9 am to 1 pm daily; entry is 500Rp.

Dating from 1765, **Benteng Vredeburg** is an old Dutch fort opposite the main post office on Jl A Yani. The restored fort is now a museum with dioramas showing the history of the independence movement in Yogya. The architecture is worth a look, but the dioramas are designed for Indonesian patriots. Opening hours are Tuesday to Thursday from 8.30 am to 1.30 pm, Friday until 11 am, weekends until noon; admission is 750Rp.

Up until his death in 1990, Affandi, Indonesia's internationally best known artist, lived and worked in an unusual tree-house studio overlooking the river, about 6km east of the town centre on Jl Solo. The **Affandi Museum** in the grounds exhibits his impressionist works, as well as paintings by his daughter Kartika and other artists. Affandi is buried in the back garden. The museum is open from 8 am to 3 pm.

The **Sasmitaluka Jenderal Sudirman** on Jl B Harun is the memorial home of General Sudirman, the commander of the revolutionary forces who died shortly after the siege of Yogya in 1948. The house is open every morning, except Monday.

The **Museum Sasana Wiratama**, also known as the Monumen Diponegoro, honours the Indonesian hero, Prince Diponegoro, leader of the bloody but futile rebellion of 1825-30 against the Dutch. A motley collection of the prince's belongings and other exhibits are kept in the small museum at his former Yogya residence; open daily from 8 am to 1 pm.

The **Museum Biologi** at Jl Sultan Agung 22 has a collection of plants and stuffed animals representative of the whole archipelago; it's open daily except Sunday. The

Museum Perjuangan, in the southern part of the city on Jl Kol Sugiyono, has a small and rather poor collection of photographs documenting the Indonesian Revolution. The large **Army Museum** (Museum Dharma Wiratama), on the corner of Jl Jenderal Sudirman and Jl Cik Ditiro, displays documents, home-made weapons, uniforms and medical equipment from the revolution years. It is open Monday to Thursday from 8 am to 1 pm and until noon on weekends.

Kota Gede

Kota Gede has been famous since the 1930s as the centre of Yogya's silver industry. However, this quiet old town, now a suburb of Yogya, was the first capital of the Mataram kingdom founded by Panembahan Senopati in 1582. Senopati is buried in the small mossy graveyard of an old mosque near the town's central market. The sacred tomb is open only on Sunday, Monday and Thursday from around 9 am to noon, and on Friday from around 1 to 3 pm. Visitors should wear conservative dress. On other days there is little to see here.

Jl Kemasan, the main street leading into town from the north, is lined with busy silver workshops. Most of the shops have similar stock, including hand-beaten bowls, boxes, fine filigree and modern jewellery (see Shopping later in this section).

Kota Gede is about 5km south-east of Jl Malioboro – take bus No 4 or 8. You can also take a becak, but andongs (about 2000Rp) are cheaper and more agreeable. Cycling is also pleasant on the back road and it is flat most of the way.

Other Attractions

In the evenings, if you are bored, you can always head along to the **Purawisata** on Jl Brigjen Katamso. This amusement park is noted more for its dance performances, but there are also rides, fun-fair games and a Pasar Seni (Art Market) with a basic collection of souvenirs.

Yogya's **Gembira Loka Zoo** has its fair share of cramped cages, but on the whole it is spacious and has some interesting exotica, such as komodo dragons. It's open daily from 8 am to 6 pm; entry is 2000Rp.

Organised Tours

Yogya is the best place in Java to arrange tours. Tour agents on Jl Prawirotaman, Jl Sosrowijayan, Jl Dagen and Jl Pasar Kembang offer a host of similar tours at competitive prices. Typical day tours and per person rates are: Borobudur (25,000Rp); Dieng (35,000Rp); Prambanan (20,000Rp); Parangtritis and Kota Gede (30,000Rp); Gunung Merapi climb from Selo (50,000Rp); and Gedung Songo and Ambarawa (50,000Rp).

Longer tours, such as to Gunung Bromo and on to Bali (100,000Rp, two days/one night) are also offered. Tours are often dependent on getting enough people to fill a minibus (usually a minimum of four), and prices vary depending on whether air-con and snacks are provided. The prices usually don't include entrance fees, and many tours also stop at batik or silver galleries to earn extra commission for tour operators.

Operators also arrange cars with driver – at some of the best rates in Java if you bargain.

Special Events

The three Garebeg festivals held each year are Java's most colourful and grand processions. Palace guards and retainers in traditional court dress and large floats of decorated mountains of rice all make their way to the mosque, west of the kraton, to the sound of prayer and gamelan music. These are ceremonies are not to be missed .

Places to Stay – Budget

Sosrowijayan Area Most of Yogya's cheap hotels are in the Sosrowijayan area, immediately south of the train line, right in the city centre near Jl Malioboro. Running between Jl Pasar Kembang and Jl Sosrowijayan, the narrow alleyways of Gang Sosrowijayan I and II are lined with cheap accommodation and popular eating places. Despite mass tourism, the gangs are quiet and still have a kampung atmosphere.

Gang Sosrowijayan I has some very basic, very cheap places but they are dingy and

cater mostly to locals. *Losmen Beta* fits into this category, but losmens don't come much cheaper at 5000/8000Rp for singles/doubles. A bit further along this gang is *Losmen Superman*, behind the restaurant of the same name. Light, clean rooms with shared mandi are 8000Rp. Darker rooms with mandi cost 10,000Rp, but have interesting rock garden bathrooms.

Just off Gang I, *Losmen Lucy* has basic rooms with mandi for 15,000Rp. The *105 Homestay* (π 582896) is more appealing and has had a makeover. Bright rooms with bathroom and pastiche tiling are better than most, and cost 15,000/20,000Rp.

On Gang Sosrowijayan II, the *Hotel Bagus* is a passable cheap place. Clean rooms with fan cost 7000/8500Rp. Further south, *Gandhi Losmen*, with its own garden, has very basic rooms but is friendly and cheap with rooms for 5000Rp per person. *Suprianto Inn*, down an alley by itself, has bright, well-kept rooms with foam mattresses for 7500/10,000Rp.

More small losmen are on Gang II and the small alleys off it. *Hotel Selekta* is popular and friendly. It's roomier and lighter than most. Rooms with mandi cost 15,000Rp, including breakfast. Nearby the *Monica Hotel* (π 580598) is a newer, more substantial hotel. Good rooms around a garden cost 25,000Rp. Of the other cheap losmen along this alley, the *Utar Pension* is more hotel-like and rooms cost 12,500Rp; or the *Lita Homestay* is a light, friendly place with rooms for 9000Rp or 12,500Rp with mandi.

Hotel Indonesia (π 587659, Jl Sosrowijayan 9) is popular and well run. It has pleasant courtyard gardens but the rooms and mattresses need an upgrade. Rooms with mandi cost 10,000Rp, 15,000Rp and 17,500Rp.

The very friendly *Hotel Karunia* (π 565057, Jl Sosrowijayan 78) straddles the budget and mid-range categories, and has a rooftop restaurant. Rooms cost 16,500/20,000Rp with fan, 22,500/25,000Rp with mandi or 40,000Rp with air-con; all plus 10% – a good deal.

JAVA

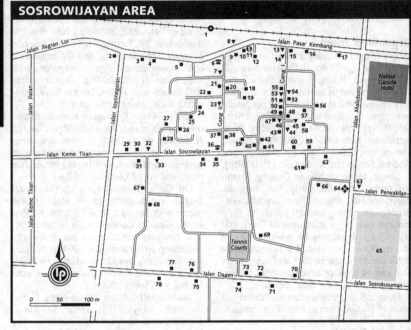

SOSROWIJAYAN AREA

Prawirotaman Area This area has some cheaper places like the very friendly *Kelana Youth Hostel (Vagabond)* (☎ 371207, Jl Prawirotaman MG III/589). Dormitory beds cost 10,000Rp and singles/doubles cost 12,500/20,000Rp with shared mandi. Student and HI card holders receive a small discount.

Jl Prawirotaman II has some cheaper options. *Post Card Guest House*, run by the bigger Metro, has rooms from 15,000/18,500Rp, or much better, quiet rooms with mandi for 22,000/27,500Rp. Some of the mid-range accommodation in Jl Prawirotaman is only marginally more expensive. *Guest House Makuta* or the *Muria Guest House* (☎ 387211) are cheaper options.

Places to Stay – Mid-Range

Sosrowijayan Area Jl Pasar Kembang, opposite the train station, has a number of mid-range hotels. *Hotel Asia-Afrika* (☎ 566219,

Jl Pasar Kembang 21) is a good place to start looking. It has a small pool, nice garden cafe and good singles/doubles with bathroom for 40,000Rp with fan, 60,000Rp with air-con, and 90,000Rp with TV and hot water.

Hotel Istana Batik (☎ 589849, Jl Pasar Kembang 29) has a nice garden, a murky pool and rooms with hot water from 78,000/94,000Rp (before discount).

At the western end of Jl Pasar Kembang, the small, renovated *Hotel Kota* (☎ 515844, Jl Jlagran Lor 1) has oodles of colonial charm. Rooms have high ceilings, original tilework, air-con and hot water. Tiny singles cost 63,000Rp or substantial rooms with all the trimmings cost 87,500/122,500Rp; at the time of writing 20% discounts were on offer.

Jl Sosrowijayan also has a number of mid-range hotels. *Bladok Restaurant & Losmen* (☎ 560452, Jl Sosrowijayan 76) is the best and has a small pool, excellent restaurant and

SOSROWIJAYAN AREA

PLACES TO STAY

2	Hotel Kota
3	Berlian Palace
4	Nusantara
5	Hotel Mendut
9	Hotel Istana Batik
10	Hotel Asia-Afrika
12	Hotel Ratna
15	Kencana Hotel
16	Trim Guest House
17	Hotel Trim
18	Suprianto Inn
19	Losmen Setia Kawan
20	Hotel Bagus
22	Losmen Setia
24	Isty Losmen
25	Utar Pension
26	Lita Homestay
27	Hotel Selekta
28	Monica Hotel
29	Yogya Inn
30	Hotel Karunia
31	Oryza Hotel
34	Wisma Gambira
35	Bakti Kasih
38	Gandhi Losmen
39	Losmen Atiep
40	Dewi Homestay
41	Losmen Rama

42	Losmen Happy Inn
43	Hotel Jogja
47	New Superman's Losmen
50	Hotel Rejeki
51	Losmen Sastrowihadi
52	Sari Homestay
55	Losmen Beta
56	105 Homestay
57	Losmen Lucy
58	Lima Losmen
59	Hotel Aziatic
60	Hotel Kartika
61	Hotel Indonesia
62	Marina Palace Hotel
66	Hotel Cahaya Kasih
67	Ella Homestay
68	Hostel Yogya Backpackers
69	Hotel Batik Yogyakarta II
70	Wisma Perdada
71	Sri Wibowo Hotel
72	Lilik Guest House
73	Blue Safir Hotel
74	Peti Mas
75	Kombokarno Hotel
76	Wisma Nendra
77	Puntodewo Guest House
78	Hotel Kristina

PLACES TO EAT

7	Cafe Sosro
8	Mama's Warung
13	Borobudur Bar & Restaurant
14	Cheap Warungs
23	Anna's Restaurant
32	Bladok Restaurant & Losmen
33	Chaterina Restaurant
37	Heru Jaya; Jaya Losmen
44	Murni Restoran
45	Bu Sis
46	New Superman's Restaurant
53	N & N
54	Superman's Restaurant & Losmen
63	Legian Restaurant

OTHER

1	Tugu Train Station
6	Wartel
11	PT Haji La Tunrung (Money-changer)
21	Warnet (Internet)
36	Warpostal
48	Whizz Kids (Internet)
49	CMC (Internet)
64	Ramayana Department Store
65	Malioboro Mall; McDonalds; Ciao

good rooms with nice touches that the others lack. Rooms cost 35,000/38,000Rp with mandi; from 52,000/55,000Rp with European bathroom to 82,000/85,000Rp for the luxurious VIP rooms with air-con, TV and minibar.

Jl Dagen, parallel to Jl Sosrowijayan, is another mid-range enclave. The stylish *Peti Mas* (☎ 561938, Jl Dagen 37) has a pool, manicured gardens and attractive restaurant. The air-con rooms around the garden for 107,500/122,500Rp and 130,000/145,000Rp are the ones to go for, while the cheaper rooms from 66,000/79,500Rp are dark and unappealing. Expect a discount.

Hotel Batik Yogyakarta II (☎ 561828) is an oasis in the quiet back alleys just north of Jl Dagen. Only a short stroll from Jl Malioboro, it has spacious grounds, a large pool and a restaurant. Plain rooms cost 104,000/124,000Rp, or attractive bunga-

lows cost 128,000/152,000Rp to 168,000/196,000Rp. The bungalows have air-con, TV, hot water and a touch of kraton style but are not luxurious so expect a discount.

Nearby, the *Hotel Cahaya Kasih* (☎ 580360, Sosromenduran GT I/280) is just 50m west of Jl Malioboro down a quiet alley. This good lower mid-range hotel has bright, tiled rooms for 44,000Rp with fan, or 52,000Rp to 69,500Rp with air-con.

Prawirotaman Area This street, a couple of kilometres south of the city centre, is a more upmarket enclave than the Sosrowijayan area but most hotels offer good value. Many are spacious converted old houses, with gardens. Swimming pools are the norm. Prices can vary markedly between hotels of the same standard. After the monetary crisis, some raised prices dramatically while others didn't. Negotiation is often possible.

The high-density *Airlangga Hotel (☎ 378 044, Jl Prawirotaman 1, 6-8)* has a restaurant and bands play on Saturday night in the bar (avoid the rooms directly above). For long the best hotel on Prawirotaman, it is now a little frayed, but good value. Comfortable singles/doubles with air-con, TV and hot water cost 50,000/60,000Rp or sunnier rooms upstairs are 60,000/70,000Rp, including breakfast.

Further down the street, the very popular *Prambanan Guest House (☎ 376167)* at No 14 has an attractive garden, good service and

rooms with nice touches. Shame about the price. It is expensive at US$11/16 to US$16/ 21 for fan rooms, and US$24/29 to US$32 for air-con rooms.

The popular *Hotel Rose (☎ 377991)* at No 28 has a larger than normal pool and a restaurant. It is good value with prices lower than the others, but so are room standards. A few rooms cost 25,000/30,000Rp with shared mandi, but most have attached mandi for 30,000/40,000Rp (5000Rp extra with hot water) to 60,000/70,000Rp for air-con and hot water.

PRAWIROTAMAN AREA

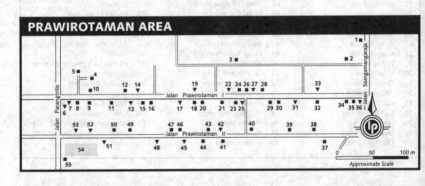

PRAWIROTAMAN AREA

PLACES TO STAY
1 Ayodya Hotel
2 Kelana Youth Hostel
3 Wisma Harto
4 Puri Pertiwi
5 Indraprastha Hotel
8 Wisma Gajah
9 Airlangga Hotel
10 Borobudur
11 Hotel Putra Jaya
12 Sriwijaya Hotel
15 Prambanan Guest House
16 Wisma Indah
18 Sumaryo
21 Hotel Duta
23 Hotel Rose
24 Mas Gun Guest House
26 Rumah Makan Asri
28 Perwita Sari Guest House
29 Wisma Parikesit
30 Prayogo Guest House

32 Galunggung Guest House
34 Hotel Kirana
35 Hotel Sartika
37 Post Card Guest House
38 Hotel Palupi
39 Wisma Kroto
40 Agung Guest House
41 Guest House Makuta
43 Metro Guest House; Metro Internet
44 Metro Guest House
46 Sumaryo
47 Muria Guest House
49 Delta Homestay
50 Mercury Guest House
55 Sunarko Guest House

PLACES TO EAT
6 Tante Lies (Warung Java Timur)
7 Laba Laba Cafe

13 Palma Restaurant
14 Hanoman's Forest Restaurant
17 La Beng Beng Restaurant
19 Griya Bujana Restaurant
22 Putri Restaurant
25 Yuri
27 French Grill Restaurant
31 Via Via
33 Dalton Family Cafe
36 Going Bananas
42 Agni Restaurant
45 Lotus Breeze
48 Restaurant Java
51 Bamboo House Restaurant
52 Lotus Garden
53 Little Amsterdam

OTHER
20 Protech 8 Internet Cafe
54 Pasar Pagi (Morning Market)

A lot of the guesthouses in the old villas are pleasant enough but the rooms can be dingy. *Sumaryo* (☎ *373507*) at No 22 is one of the better ones. It has rooms from 25,000Rp up to 60,000Rp for a big air-con room.

The next street south, Jl Prawirotaman II (sometimes called Jl Gerilya, and with an illogical numbering system), is quieter than Jl Prawirotaman I, and the hotels are not as flash. The *Metro Guest House* (☎ *372364*) at No 71 is the most popular, and has a garden area and an Internet cafe. The rooms cost 15,000/18,000Rp to 65,000/75,000Rp with air-con and hot water showers. The mid-priced rooms in the annexe across the street, where you'll find the pool, are the best value.

The inexpensive and popular *Agung Guest House* (☎ *375512*) at No 68 costs 19,000/22,500Rp to 56,000/60,000Rp with air-con (less with negotiation). The attractive *Delta Homestay* (☎ *378092*) at No 597A has simple but good rooms for 27,500/44,000Rp to 90,000/100,000Rp with air-con. (Prices are after discount.)

The *Mercury* (☎ *370846*) at No 595 has kraton-style architecture and a wonderful dining area with antique furniture and floor cushions. The rooms are simple but very well kept and cost 30,000/45,000Rp with hot water showers (before discount).

Other Areas The *Indraloka Home Stay* (☎ *564341, Jl Cik Ditiro 18*) is north of the city centre near Gajah Mada University and is popular with overseas students. Singles/doubles with air-con and hot water in this fine old colonial house are discounted as low as 50,000/60,000Rp, which is very good value. Tours are organised, and a travel agent and wartel are attached.

Places to Stay – Top End

Yogya has a glut of luxury hotels and heavy discounting has always been the norm. US$ rates are still quoted in brochures but a request for rupiah rates will readily bring big reductions. If arriving by air, the Indotel (☎ 512144) hotel booking desk at the airport usually has good deals. The following entries have swimming pools, and most include breakfast, tax and service in the price.

The *Natour Garuda Hotel* (☎ *566353*), right in the action at Jl Malioboro 60, was Yogya's premier grand hotel in Dutch times, but the rooms are now rundown. Singles/doubles cost 250,000/270,000Rp and suites start at 375,000/425,000Rp.

Right behind the Malioboro Mall, the new *Hotel Ibis* (☎ *516977, Jl Malioboro 52-58*) has small rooms with shower discounted as low as 165,000Rp plus 21%, though you might be told that these are full or only for Indonesian residents, in which case the bigger rooms with bath are 312,000Rp.

Just to the east of Jl Malioboro is the huge Spanish-owned *Melia Purosani Hotel* (☎ *589521, Jl Suryotomo 31.*) The central location and superior facilities make this one of Yogya's better hotels, but its rooms are expensive at 423,500Rp, including breakfast.

Many of Yogya's big hotels are stretched out along the road to Solo. The road changes names many times but is usually referred to simply as 'Jalan Solo'. Close to Jl Mangkubumi and the centre of town, *Hotel Phoenix* (☎ *566617, Jl Jenderal Sudirman 9-11*) is a smaller hotel with some class. Rooms cost 200,000Rp (the price is negotiable).

Nearby, *Hotel Santika* (☎ *563036*) is popular with business travellers and noted for its good service. Rooms start at US$100 but discounts may bring the price down to 300,000Rp.

Further east, the *Novotel Hotel* (☎ *580929, Jl Jenderal Sudirman 89*) is an excellent new hotel in a good position next to the Galeria shopping mall. Rooms are discounted to 240,000Rp and 301,000Rp.

Nearby, the *Radisson Plaza* (☎ *584222, Jl Gejayan*) is near the Radio Republik Indonesia (RRI) auditorium. Plush rooms start at US$110/120, discounted down to 240,000Rp.

On Jl Solo about 5km from the city centre, the *Ambarrukmo Palace Hotel* (☎ *588 488, Jl Adisucipto*) is a 1960s Soekarno-inspired construction and contains the old Ambarrukmo Palace in its grounds. At one time the most prestigious hotel in Yogya, this government-run hotel is now looking tired, but discount rates of 160,000/180,000Rp make it a good choice.

Many other big hotels are on the way to the airport, including the five star *Hotel Aquila Prambanan* and the top of the range *Sheraton*, while the new luxury *Hyatt Regency*, built in the style of Borobudur, is on Jl Palagan Pelajar on the northern outskirts of the city. All are long way from the city centre.

Places to Eat

Sosrowijayan Area This area is overrun with very cheap eating houses featuring western breakfasts and meals, as well as Indonesian dishes.

A whole host of good warungs line Jl Pasar Kembang, beside the train line, but *Mama's* is the best of them all in the evenings. On Jl Pasar Kembang at No 17, *Borobudur Bar & Restaurant* has average fare at high prices, but it has unlimited cold beer and bands after 9.30 pm.

Gang Sosrowijayan I is a favourite for cheap eats. The famous *Superman's*, one of the original purveyors of banana pancakes, has been around for decades. The owner, Pak Suparman, adapted his name, and likewise his food, to suit western sensibilities. Its offshoot, *New Superman's*, a bit further down Gang I, is more popular, and has pizzas, steak, and Indonesian and Chinese food. However, the 10% tax added to the bill gives it pretensions it doesn't deserve. The no-frills *N & N* is popular for its low prices, and the alcohol-free *Murni Restoran* serves tasty curries with flaky parathas and good ice juices.

Gang II also has a few options. *Anna's* is popular for its low prices, while the *Cafe Sosro* has the best decor and reasonable western and Indonesian food. *Heru Jaya* at the Jaya Losmen has a big menu of cheap western, Indonesian and Chinese food. The speciality 'French grills', such as steak and fries are the most expensive item on the menu at around 10,000Rp, but are good.

Jl Sosrowijayan also has some good restaurants. *Chaterina* at No 41 has a varied menu, low prices and you can dine sitting on mats at the back. One of Sosro's best is *Bladok Restaurant*, opposite at No 76, a classy little place with mainly European food.

Upstairs on the corner of Jl Malioboro and Jl Perwakilan, the classy *Legian Restaurant* has Indonesian, Chinese, French and Italian food served by Balinese waiters in a roof-garden setting. It does a great claypot *gudeg ayam* (chicken with jackfruit) and good Balinese specialities.

Nearby, Malioboro Mall is not complete without fast food and *McDonald's* takes pride of place at the front of this monument to western consumerism. The mall has some reasonable cafes inside, including *Ciao* for pizzas, pasta, cappuccino and ice cream. The top floor has a food stall area.

Jl Malioboro After 10 pm, the souvenir vendors pack up and a *lesahan* area (diners sit on straw mats) comes alive along the north end of Jl Malioboro. Food stalls serve Yogya's specialities, such as *nasi gudeg* (rice with jackfruit in coconut milk) and *ayam goreng*. Young Indonesians sit around strumming guitars and playing chess into the wee hours.

Griya Dahar Timur (Jl A Yani 57) is a cheaper place with Chinese, Indonesian and European dishes, more expensive steaks and excellent icy juices. *Cirebon Restaurant (Jl A Yani 15)*, a few doors further south, is an old fashioned Chinese restaurant with good juices and vegetarian food.

Prawirotaman Area Prawirotaman I has the bulk of restaurants. Most have virtually identical menus, from gado gado to snapper meuniere, and most are mediocre. Indonesian dishes are usually a horrible travesty but some do decent attempts at western fare.

For Indonesian food, the long-running *Tante Lies* (Aunt Lies) at the Jl Parangtritis intersection has sate, *nasi pecel* (similar to gado gado), *soto ayam* (chicken soup), and other Central and East Javanese dishes at reasonable prices.

Laba Laba Cafe (Jl Prawirotaman I, 2) has a typically mixed menu of western,

Indonesian and Chinese food and, though more expensive than most, the food is innovative. It stays open late and the bar attracts patrons until midnight.

Via Via (Jl Prawirotaman I, 24B) is a very popular Belgian-run travellers' cafe and meeting spot. As well as providing good food including Indonesian dishes, it organises a variety of activities, such as bicycle trips around Yogya, Bahasa Indonesia, batik and cooking courses.

Hanoman's Forest Restaurant has mediocre Indonesian and western cuisine, but classical Javanese dance, wayang golek or wayang kulit is performed most nights for a cover charge of 7500Rp. Jl Tirtodipuran, the continuation of Jl Prawirotaman, is home to *Dutch Cafe* at 47A, which features good steaks, a few Dutch-inspired dishes and Indonesian fare. It has a bar with good music and draught beer, and is open until 1 am. Definitely the place for homesick Hollanders, with Drum, Heineken and Dutch books on sale.

Further down the street, *Kedai Kebun* at No 3 is notable mostly for its beautiful garden setting with an art gallery at the back.

Other Areas Good eats can be found to the north of the city out towards Gajah Mada University. *Pujayo (Jl Simanjuntak 73)* is Yogya's best food stall complex. A dozen food vendors split over two floors serve an array of dishes and drinks at low prices in ultra-hygienic surrounds. It has karaoke upstairs and an Internet cafe downstairs.

The well known *Pesta Perak*, *(Jl Tentara Rakyat Mataram 8)*, about 1km north-west of Jl Malioboro, has a delightful garden ambience and occasional performances of gamelan music. Lunch and dinner buffets for 15,000Rp (plus 21%) feature a range of Javanese dishes.

The famous Yogya fried chicken leaves Colonel Sander's recipe for dead. Yogya chicken is boiled in the water of young coconuts and then deep fried – absolute heaven when done well. One of the most famous purveyors was Mbok Berek out on Jl Solo just before Prambanan, and in her wake a host of eateries have appeared nearby with similar names. *Nyonya Suharti (Jl Adisucipto 208)* just past the Ambarrukmo Palace, has restaurants all over Java and is popular with tour groups.

Some of the big hotels put on good value buffets. The *Novotel* has a Java Buffet on Sunday with a wide selection for 43,000Rp, and it also has other buffets during the week.

Entertainment

Yogya is by far the easiest place to see traditional Javanese performing arts, with performances of one sort or another held daily. Dance, wayang or gamelan are performed every morning at the kraton and provide a useful introduction to Javanese arts. Check with the tourist office for any special events.

Most famous of all performances is the spectacular *Ramayana* ballet held in the open air at Prambanan in the dry season (see Prambanan later in this chapter).

Wayang Kulit Leather puppet performances can be seen at several places around Yogya every night of the week. Most of the centres offer shortened versions for tourists but at *Sasono Hinggil*, in the alun alun selatan (south main square) of the kraton, marathon all-night performances are held every second Saturday from 9 pm to 5 am.

Abridged wayang kulit performances are held every day except Saturday at the *Agastya Art Institute*, Jl Gedong Kiwo MD III/237, where dalang are trained. The two hour show begins at 3 pm and costs 5000Rp.

The *Sono-Budoyo Museum*, near the kraton, also has popular two-hour performances nightly from 8 pm for 7500Rp. The first half-hour involves the reading of the story in Javanese so most people skip this and arrive later.

Wayang Golek Wooden puppet plays are also performed frequently. *Nitour (Jl Dahlan 71)* has tourist-oriented shows at 11 am daily, except Sunday, for 12,500Rp.

On Saturday there are wayang golek performances at the *Agastya Art Institute* from 3 to 5 pm.

Dance Most dance performances are based on the *Ramayana* or at least billed as 'Ramayana ballet' because of the famed performances at Prambanan.

The *Ramayana* story is also performed in two parts on consecutive nights at *Purawisata*, the amusement park on Jl Katamso, at the Gazebo Garden restaurant. They cost 30,000Rp, including dinner an extra 18,000Rp.

One of the finest troupes used to perform at *Ndalem Pujokusuman (Jl Katamso 45)*, but its program has been suspended. Hopefully it will start up again.

Schools You may see dance practice at the *Dance faculty of the Indonesia Institute of Arts* (ISI) on Jl Colombo in north Yogya. It's open from Monday to Saturday. *Bagong Kussudiarja*, one of Indonesia's leading dance choreographers, has a school at Padepokan, 5km south of Yogya, where he runs courses for foreign students.

Other Performances Ketoprak (folk theatre) performances are held at the *RRI auditorium* on the corner of Jl Gejayan and Jl Colombo, from 8 pm to midnight on the first Saturday of every month.

Other hotels and restaurants have gamelan or wayang performances. On Jl Prawirotaman, *Hanoman's Forest Restaurant* has different wayang performances most nights of the week (see Places to Eat – Prawirotaman Area).

Shopping

Yogya is a great place to shop for crafts and antiques, primarily from Java, but bits and pieces from all over the archipelago can be found.

Jl Malioboro is one great long colourful bazaar of souvenir shops and stalls selling cheap cotton clothes, leatherwork, batik bags, topeng masks and wayang golek puppets. Look in some of the fixed price shops on Jl Malioboro to get an idea of prices. Mirota Batik, Jl A Yani 9, is a good place to start and has a wide selection of batik and crafts at reasonable prices.

The other major area to shop is Jl Tirtodipuran, the continuation of Jl Prawirotaman. This is an interesting, more upmarket shopping stretch, with galleries and art shops and expensive batik factories. You'll find furniture, antiques and a variety of crafts and curios from Java and further afield.

For designer label clothes, Yogya is not Jakarta, but the two big malls are Malioboro Mall on Jl Malioboro and the new Galeria on Jl Solo.

Batik Batik in the markets is cheaper than in the shops, but you need to be careful about quality and should be prepared to bargain. Good fixed-price places to try include: Terang Bulan, Jl A Yani 108; Ramayana Batik, Jl Ahmad Dahlan 21; and the more expensive Batik Keris, a branch of the big Solo batik house on Jl A Yani 71. Many other reasonably priced shops are on Jl Malioboro and Jl A Yani.

Most of the batik workshops and several large showrooms are along Jl Tirtodipuran, south of the kraton. Many, such as Batik Indah (Rara Jonggrang) at No 6A and Batik Winotosastro at No 54 give free guided tours of the batik process. These places cater to tour groups so prices are very high – view the process and shop elsewhere.

Batik Painting Once an innovative and uniquely Indonesian form of art, sadly, much of the interest in batik painting has faded but the copy cat galleries and the increasingly hungry touts remain.

Given that the batik painting industry is Yogya's biggest blight, perhaps the best advice is to avoid it altogether, but batik paintings can be attractive souvenirs and small paintings (around 300mm x 300mm) can be as cheap as 20,000Rp (the asking price may be 200,000Rp). Most of the mass-production galleries are found around Taman Sari. It pays to shop around for something more unique and to always bargain hard.

A few artists who pioneered and grew famous from batik painting still produce some batik. Amri Yahya's Gallery at Jl Gampingan 67 has a few early batik works on display, though he mostly produces abstract oil paintings these days; it's open daily except Monday.

Antiques, Curios & Furniture While a few antiques can be found, they are best left to collectors who know their stuff. Yogya art shops spend an inordinate amount of time defacing wayang golek puppets and topeng masks in the name of antiquity, and many other items get similar treatment.

Jl Tirtodipuran has the best selection of artefacts from all over Java and Indonesia. Prices are generally very high here – bargain furiously, or get an idea of quality and look around for somewhere else to shop.

Furniture, mostly antique copy, can be found on Jl Tirtodipuran and in the back lanes nearby. Mirota Moesson, around the corner at Jl Parangtritis 107, has a large and interesting collection. A number of smaller shops are on Jl Sisingamangaraja at the end of Jl Prawirotaman II. The larger places can arrange shipping but prices are high.

Silver Silverwork can be found all over town, but the best area to shop is in the silver village of Kota Gede. Fine filigree work is a Yogya speciality, but many styles and designs are available. Kota Gede has some very attractive jewellery, boxes, bowls, cutlery and miniatures.

You can get a guided tour of the process, with no obligation to buy, at the large factories such as Tom's Silver, Jl Ngeski Gondo 60, HS at Jl Mandarokan I, and MD, Jl Pesegah kg 8/44, down a small alley off the street. Tom's has an extensive selection and some superb large pieces, but prices are very high. HS is marginally cheaper, as is MD, but always ask for a substantial discount off the marked prices. Kota Gede has dozens of smaller silver shops on Jl Kemesan and Jl Mondorakan, where you can get some good buys if you bargain.

Other Crafts Yogya's leatherwork can be excellent value for money and the quality is usually high, but always check the quality and stitching. Shops and street stalls on Jl Malioboro are the best places to shop for leatherwork.

Good quality wayang puppets are made at the Mulyo Suhardjo workshop at Jl Taman Sari 37 and also sold at the Sono-Budoyo Museum. Swasthigita, Ngadinegaran MJ 7/50, just north of Jl Tirtodipuran, is another wayang kulit puppet manufacturer.

Courses
Batik Plenty of places in the Sosrowijayan (such as Losmen Lucy opposite New Superman's) and Prawirotaman (ask at Via Via) areas offer short courses of one or two days' duration, and you get to make a batik T-shirt. High art they aren't but they provide a good introduction for around 25,000Rp. Tiyos (Sutiyoso Wijanarko, ☎ 0274-512812), Sosrowijayan Wetan GT1/7A, has been recommended by readers.

Hadjir Digdodarmojo (☎ 377835) has been teaching batik for years and offers three and five-day courses, but they are expensive at US$25. His studio is on the left of the main entrance to the Taman Sari at Taman Kp 3/177.

Getting There & Away
Air Garuda (☎ 565835) in the Ambarrukmo Palace Hotel has direct flights to Jakarta (503,000Rp), Denpasar (470,000Rp) and Mataram (580,000Rp), with onward domestic and international connections. Merpati (☎ 514272), Jl Dipenogoro 31, has one flight daily to Surabaya (269,000Rp). Mandala (☎ 564559), Jl Suryotomo 31, also flies to Jakarta, while Bouraq (☎ 562664), Jl Mataram 60, had cancelled all Yogya flights at the time of writing.

The big travel agents can sell domestic tickets at a small discount. Try one of the many agents in the Ambarrukmo Palace Hotel, such as Satriavi, or Pacto in the Hotel Garuda.

Bus Yogya's Umbulharjo bus terminal is 4km south-east of the city centre. From Jl Malioboro take city bus No 4. The terminal will move outside the city to the South Ring Rd but this will most likely be years away.

From Umbulharjo, buses run all over Java and to Bali. Ordinary/air-con buses include: Solo (2000/3500Rp, two hours); Magelang (2000 Rp, 1½ hours); Semarang (4000/7000 Rp, 3½ hours); Wonogiri (3000 Rp, 2½ hours); Purwokerto (6000/10,000Rp, 4½ hours); Bandung (16,500/25,000Rp, 10 hours); Jakarta (17,000/35,000 Rp, 12 hours (via Purwokerto and Bogor); Surabaya (10,000/20,000 Rp, eight hours); Probolinggo (17,000/32,000 Rp, nine hours); and Denpasar (24,000/40,000 Rp, 16 hours).

For long trips it's best to take luxury buses. It's cheaper to buy tickets at the bus terminal, but it's less hassle to simply check fares and departures with the ticket agents along Jl Mangkubumi, Jl Sosrowijayan near the Hotel Aziatic, or on Jl Prawirotaman. These agents can also arrange pick-up from your hotel. Check more than one agent – some charge excessive commission. Typical fares are: Denpasar (55,000Rp to 60,000Rp); Surabaya and Malang (30,000Rp); Bandung (35,000Rp); Bogor (40,000Rp); and Jakarta (45,000Rp to 55,000Rp).

From the main bus terminal, local buses also operate regularly to all the towns in the immediate area: Borobudur (2000Rp, 1½ hours); Parangtritis (2500Rp, one hour); and Kaliurang (1000Rp, one hour). For Prambanan (1000Rp), take the yellow Pemuda bus. For Imogiri (500Rp, 40 minutes), take a Colt or the Abadi bus No 5 to Panggang and ask the conductor to let you off at the *makam* (graves). Buses to Imogiri and Parangtritis can also be caught on Jl Sisingamangaraja at the end of Jl Prawirotaman.

Apart from the main bus terminal, Colts operate to the outlying towns from various sub-stations. The most useful is the Terban Colt terminal to the north of the city centre on Jl Simanjuntak. From here Colts go to Kaliurang (1500Rp), and Solo (3000Rp), passing the airport en route.

Buses, and Colts in particular, to the tourist attractions around Yogya are renowned for overcharging. Know the correct fare before boarding and tender the right money, but expect to pay extra if you have luggage taking up passenger space.

Minibus Door-to-door minibuses run to all major cities from Yogya. Many companies are found on Jl Diponegoro – including SAA (☎ 584976) at 9A, Rahayu (☎ 561322) at No 15 and Madya (☎ 566306) at No 27. The Sosrowijayan and Prawirotaman agents also sell tickets. Most will pick up from hotels in Yogya, but not for the short runs like Solo (they will drop off at your Solo hotel, however). They provide a good service but some of the minibuses are ageing and may not have air-con.

Minibus destinations include Solo (7000Rp air-con, two hours), Cilacap (12,500Rp, five hours), Wonosobo (8000Rp), Purwokerto (12,500Rp), Semarang (8000Rp, three hours), Kudus (9000Rp), Pekalongan (11,000Rp), Surabaya (30,000Rp), Malang (23,000Rp), Jakarta (45,000Rp, 14 hours) and Bali (60,000Rp).

Two popular tourist shuttles operate from Yogya. Direct bus-ferry-bus tickets to Pangandaran cost 30,000Rp and the less than wonderful Yogya Rental door-to-door service to Gunung Bromo costs 50,000Rp (see Gunung Bromo in the East Java section for more details).

Train Yogya's Tugu train station (☎589685) is conveniently central, and handles all bisnis and eksekutif trains. Economy trains depart from and arrive at Lempuyangan station, 1km to the east.

The *Fajar Utama Yogya* day services and *Senja Utama Yogya* night services to Jakarta (36,000/76,000Rp bisnis/eksekutif, 8½ hours) originate in Yogya, with departures at 7 and 9 am, and 6 and 8 pm. Other express services to Jakarta come via Solo or Surabaya.

For Solo, the best option is the *Prambanan Ekspres* departing at 7.25 and 10.30 am, and 1.20 and 4 pm. It costs 3000Rp in bisnis class and takes just over an hour – the quickest and most convenient way to get to Solo.

To Surabaya, the *Sancaka* (25,000/ 40,000Rp, 4½ hours) at 3.25 pm is the pick of the trains and quicker than the buses. Numerous other night trains from Jakarta, such as the *Bima* and *Mutiara Selatan*, stop in Yogya on the way to Surabaya.

Three trains operate on the Yogya-Banjar-Bandung route. Most trains come through from Surabaya. The night expresses, such as the *Mutiara Selatan* (33,000Rp bisnis) and *Turangga* (45,000/75,000Rp), provide the best services and take about 7½ hours.

From Lempuyangan train station, most ekonomi services are the through night trains between Surabaya and Jakarta (14,000Rp, 11 hours) and Bandung (9000Rp, 10 hours). The *Purbaya* provides a reasonable ekonomi service to Surabaya (6000Rp, seven hours) leaving at 10.13 am, if you can get a seat. In the other direction it goes to Cilacap. The *Sri Tanjung* at 7.30 am goes to Surabaya, Probolinggo and Banyuwangi. The *Matarmaja* to Malang (14,000Rp, seven hours) departs at 11.55 pm.

Getting Around

To/From the Airport Taxis from Yogya's Adisucipto airport, 10km to the east, cost 10,000Rp to the city centre, slightly cheaper going to the airport on the meter.

If you stroll out to the main road, only 200m from the airport, Colts run to Yogya's Terban Colt station (about 1.5km from Jl Sosrowijayan) or buses go to the Umbulharjo bus terminal for 500Rp.

Bus Yogya's city buses *(bis kota)* operate on dozens of set routes around the city for a flat 500Rp fare. They work mostly straight routes – going out and then coming back the same way – and all start and end at the Umbulharjo bus terminal.

Bus No 2 is one of the more useful services. It runs from the bus terminal and turns down Jl Sisingamangaraja, past Jl Prawirotaman, then loops around, coming back up Jl Parangtritis and on to Jl Mataram, a block from Jl Malioboro, before continuing to the university and returning.

Bus No 4 runs down from Jl Malioboro to the Umbulharjo terminal. From the terminal it goes on to Jl Ngeksigondo at Kota Gede – get off at Tom's Silver and walk 1km south to the centre of the village. Bus No 8 from the bus terminal runs through the centre of Kota Gede.

Becak & Andong Yogya is oversupplied with becaks and it is impossible to go anywhere in the main tourist areas without being greeted by choruses of 'becak'. Fares cost around 500Rp/km, but the minimum fare for tourists is usually 1000Rp and the asking rate is a lot more. The trip from Jl Prawirotaman to Jl Malioboro costs at least 2000Rp. Fares do vary – depending on the weather, whether it is uphill or downhill etc. Avoid becak drivers who offer cheap hourly rates unless you want to do the rounds of all the batik galleries that offer commission. There are also horse-drawn andongs around town, which cost about the same or cheaper than becaks.

Car & Motorcycle Travel agents on Jl Sosrowijayan and Jl Prawirotaman rent out cars with drivers for trips in and around town for 10,000Rp per hour, including petrol. They have inflated price lists for longer destinations, but you can usually get a car or small minibus with driver for 100,000Rp per day or less. Work out exactly what is included, and be prepared to bargain.

Bali Car Rental (☎ 587548) in front of the Adisucipto airport is a registered car-rental agency for self-drive hire, but rates are very high at US$26 for a Suzuki Jimney.

Motorcycles can be hired for around 15,000Rp a day. An International Driving Permit is required by law, but nobody seems to bother.

Taxi Taxis in Yogya are metered, efficient and cost 1500Rp for the first kilometre, then 750Rp for each subsequent kilometre. Waiting time is 10,000Rp per hour and some taxis have a 3000Rp minimum.

Bicycle Bicycles cost as little as 3000Rp a day from hotels; or try the shops at the southern end of Gang I in Sosrowijayan. Always lock your bike and look for bicycle *parkirs* who will look after your bike for a couple of hundred rupiah – you'll find them at the train stations, the markets and the post office.

AROUND YOGYAKARTA
Imogiri

Perched on a hilltop 20km south of Yogya, Imogiri was built by Sultan Agung in 1645 to serve as his own mausoleum. Imogiri has since been the burial ground for almost all his successors and for prominent members of the royal family, and it is still a holy place. The cemetery contains three major courtyards – in the central courtyard are the tombs of Sultan Agung and succeeding Mataram kings, to the left are the tombs of the susuhunans of Solo and to the right those of the sultans of Yogya. The tomb of Hamengkubuwono IX, the father of the present sultan, is one of the most visited graves.

Of major interest to pilgrims is the tomb of Sultan Agung. It is only open on Monday from 10 am to 1 pm, and Friday and Sunday from 1.30 to 4 pm. There is no objection to visitors joining the pilgrims at these times, although to enter the tombs you must don full Javanese court dress, which can be hired for a small fee.

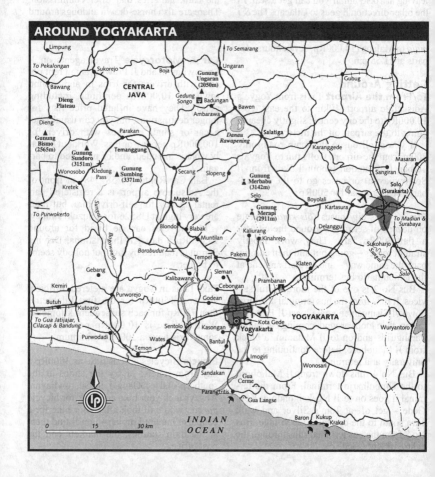

AROUND YOGYAKARTA

Limpung
To Pekalongan
Sukorejo
Boja
To Semarang
Ungaran
Gunung Ungaran (2050m)
Gubug
Bawang
CENTRAL JAVA
Dieng Plateau
Gedung Songo
Badungan
Bawen
Ambarawa
Dieng
Gunung Bismo (2565m)
Parakan
Danau Rawapening
Salatiga
Karanggede
Masaran
Gunung Sundoro (3151m)
Temanggung
Sangiran
Wonosobo
Kledung Pass
Gunung Sumbing (3371m)
Secang
Slopeng
Gunung Merbabu (3142m)
Solo (Surakarta)
Kretek
Magelang
Selo
Boyolali
Gunung Merapi (2911m)
Kartasura
To Madiun & Surabaya
To Purwokerto
Blondo
Blabak
Muntilan
Kaliurang
Kinahrejo
Delanggu
Sukoharjo
Borobudur
Tempel
Pakem
Klaten
Solo
Gebang
Sleman
Kalibawang
Cebongan
Prambanan
Kemiri
Godean
YOGYAKARTA
Butuh
Kutoarjo
Purworejo
Kota Gede
Wuryantoro
To Gua Jatijajar, Cilacap & Bandung
Sentolo
Kasongan
Yogyakarta
Purwodadi
Wates
Bantul
Temon
Imogiri
Wonosari
Sandakan
Gua Cerme
Parangtritis
Gua Langse
Baron
Kukup
Krakal
INDIAN OCEAN

0   15   30 km

It's an impressive complex, reached by an equally impressive flight of 345 steps. From the top of the stairway, a walkway circles the whole complex and leads to the actual hill summit, with a superb view over Yogya to Gunung Merapi.

Colts and buses from Yogya (500Rp) stop at the car park, from where it is about 500m to the base of the hill and the start of the steps. Like most pilgrimage sites, there will be various demands for 'donations'. The only compulsory entry charge is payable when you sign the visitors' book, inside the main compound on the hilltop.

Kasongan

This is Yogya's pottery centre. Dozens of workshops produce pots and some superb figurines, including 2m-high dragons and pony-sized horses. Kasongan pottery is sold painted or unpainted – very little glazing work is done.

Catch a Bantul-bound bus and get off on the main road at the entrance to the village, 6.5km south of Yogya. It is then about a 1km walk to the centre of the village and most of the pottery workshops.

Parangtritis
☎ 0274

Twenty-seven kilometres south of Yogya, Parangtritis has rough surf and a long sweep of shifting, black-sand dunes backed by high, jagged cliffs. Like so many places along the south coast, it's a centre for the worship of Nyai Loro Kidul. Legend has it that Senopati, the 16th century Mataram ruler, took her as his wife and thus established the strong tie between the goddess and the royal house of Mataram. Their sacred rendezvous spot is at **Parangkusumo**, 1km west down the beach, where the sultans of Yogya still send offerings every year at Labuhan, the festival, to appease this consort of kings. Just beyond Parangkusumo there are hot springs at **Parang Wedang**.

The crashing surf and undertows at Parangtritis are dangerous and a sign in Indonesian proclaims that swimming is forbidden, but those who are experienced in surf conditions may want to enter the water. Just don't wear green – the Goddess of the South Sea's favourite colour. You can swim safely in freshwater pools *(pemandian)* at the base of the hill near the village, where spring water spills out through high bamboo pipes from the hilltop.

The beach promenade of straggling warungs and souvenir stalls is nothing to rave about, but you can go for long lonely walks along the beach, or up into the sand dunes and the cliffs. This is a quiet, simple place ideal for a break from Yogya during the week when the hotels are empty. Avoid weekends and holidays when the beach is swamped by mobs from Yogya.

Trails along the hills above the sea to the east of Parangtritis lead to the meditation cave, **Gua Cerme**. A couple of kilometres from town past the Queen of the South resort is **Gua Langse**, used by mystics as a meditation cave.

Places to Stay & Eat The centre of the village is the plaza, marked by the Sudirman monument – the famous general hid out in the caves and hills here during the independence war. Leading down to the beach, the main promenade has plenty of basic cheap hotels and rumah makan. Bargaining may be required.

Hotel Widodo is a good cheap option with rooms for 15,000Rp, including breakfast and free tea and coffee. It has a good little restaurant and information on the area. Opposite, the *Agung Garden* is another hotel catering to travellers, but rooms are very basic for 15,000Rp or 40,000Rp with air-con. Next to the Widodo towards the beach, *Wisma Lukita* (no sign), has very well kept rooms with mandi for 15,000Rp.

The best hotel by far is the *Queen of the South* (Puri Ratu Kidul) *(☎ 367196)*, perched on the clifftops high above town. It has excellent views, a fine pendopo-style restaurant and a swimming pool. Comfortable bungalows cost US$82 and US$90 plus 21%, but even with a 50% discount they are very expensive.

Getting There & Away Buses from Yogya's Umbulharjo bus terminal, which can also be caught on Jl Parangtritis at the end of Jl Prawirotaman, leave throughout the day for the one hour journey. The last bus back from Parangtritis leaves at around 5.30 pm. The cost is 2500Rp, which includes the 1100Rp entry fee to Parangtritis (most tourist areas charge a small entry fee), but the price is *very* variable. You can also reach Parangtritis via Imogiri, but this is a much longer route.

Other Beaches

Yogya has several other uninspiring beaches besides Parangtritis. The only ones of minor interest are the isolated beaches to the southeast. **Baron**, 60km from Yogya, has safe swimming inside a sheltered cove. **Kukup** is a white-sand beach 1km east of Baron.

Krakal, 8km east of Baron, has a fine, usually deserted, white-sand beach, but the shallow reef rules out swimming. If you really want to be isolated, the *Krakal Beach Hotel* has a restaurant, run-down rooms for 15,000Rp and 25,000Rp, and cottages with mandi for 35,000Rp.

To reach these beaches, take a bus from Yogya to Wonosari, then an infrequent opelet to the beaches, but you will usually have to charter for around 10,000Rp.

Gunung Merapi

Gunung Merapi (Fire Mountain) is one of Java's most active and destructive volcanoes. Standing at the northern pinnacle of Yogya's borders, its towering peak, with an elevation of 2911m, can be seen from many parts of the city on a clear day. The mountain is a source of spiritual power, and every year offerings from the kraton are made to appease Merapi, in conjunction with offerings to the Queen of the South Seas at Parangtritis.

Merapi has erupted numerous times, with at least four major eruptions and dozens of minor ones this century. Some have theorised that it was a massive eruption of Merapi that caused the sudden and mysterious evacuation of Borobudur and the collapse of the old Mataram kingdom in the 11th century.

> ## WARNING
>
> ! • Check the current status of the volcano. While most volcanoes in Indonesia are safe for trekking, there are several that have been erupting almost continuously for the past several years and Gunung Merapi is one of them. *Extreme caution is advised.* Check with the local tourist office, other travellers or the nearest observation post *(pos pengamatan)* for Gunung Merapi's eruption status. If it is closed, do not attempt to climb the volcano or hike into the 'danger zone'. See the special colour section 'Fire Mountain' in this chapter for more information on climbing volcanoes.

Merapi's violent reputation was again confirmed on 22 November 1994, when it erupted killing over 60 people. Due to its proximity to heavily populated areas, the volcano is constantly monitored by the Volcanology Survey of Indonesia, with observation posts all around the volcano. In 1994 advance warnings were issued and nearby villages were evacuated, but a wedding party ignored the warning and many were killed by deadly gases escaping through fissures on the flank of the mountain. Merapi has been on the boil ever since. In June 1998 pyroclastic flows raced down its western flank damaging farm land.

The hill resort town of Kaliurang, 25km north of Yogya, is the main access point for views of Merapi and makes a wonderful break from the city. Climbing to the summit of Merapi is possible from the small village of Selo, on the other side of the mountain, but only if Merapi is quiet. Even then *extreme caution* is advised.

Merapi issues smoke and a regular stream of lava that flows away down the Sungai Boyong valley from the crater. Check the latest situation in Kaliurang, but at the time of writing, with Merapi constantly threatening more eruptions, the climb to the peak from Kaliurang is off limits. However, it is possible (and much easier) to walk part way up the mountain for unique views of Merapi's lava flows.

Yogya travel agents also sell night trips for drive-in views of the lava flows from Pos Babatan, on the western side of the mountain. You take the road to Muntilan and then it is 5km up the mountain. Unless Merapi is in full force, it is unlikely you'll see great streams of lava as shown in the tour photos.

Climbing Merapi A 1.30 am start from Selo is necessary to reach the summit for dawn (a four hour trip). After a 2km walk through the village to Pos Merapi, the abandoned volcanology post, the steady but steep climb begins. It is a tough, demanding walk but manageable by anyone with a reasonable level of fitness.

The last stages are through loose volcanic scree, but guides may stop short of the summit. Check with your guide if it is possible to go to the top before setting off. Climbs from Selo are not always well organised. Guides should advise against climbing if it looks dangerous. While they don't want to endanger lives, they may be prepared to take risks in order to be paid. Even during quieter periods, Merapi can suddenly throw out a stream of lava. There are two vents where lava can be seen, but it is not advisable to approach them.

From Kaliurang, the climb to the summit of Merapi is currently off limits because of the volcanic activity. Vogels Hostel has organised climbs for years and is an essential first reference point (See Places to Stay & Eat under Kaliurang for details). Its shorter hikes to see the lava are popular.

Kaliurang
☎ 0274
Kaliurang, 25km north of Yogya, is the nearest hill resort to the city, standing at 900m on the slopes of Gunung Merapi. Pick a clear, cloudless day during the week when it's quiet, and this is a great place to escape from the heat of the plains. There are good forest walks and superb views of the smoking, fire-spewing mountain.

Day-trippers can explore the excellent **forest park** (Hutan Wisata Kaliurang) on the slopes of the mountain. Maps at the park entrance show areas you are allowed explore. Heed them and don't venture further. In a sudden eruption lava can flow down the mountain at 300km per hour. At the time of writing you can walk 15 minutes to the Promojiwo viewpoint for great views of Merapi and on to the Tlogo Muncar waterfall, which is just a trickle in the dry season, and then back to the entrance. The park is open from 8 am to 4 pm; entry 450Rp.

Kaliurang is a delightful place to spend a day or two. Vogels Hostel arranges mountain walks to see the lava flows (see Places to Stay & Eat for details). The five hour return trek starts at 3 am to see the glowing lava at its best and costs 15,000Rp per person. Overnight camping trips, village tours and birdwatching walks can also be arranged. A minimum of four people is required for all trips.

Places to Stay & Eat Kaliurang is a down-market resort with no rated hotels, but it has over 100 places to stay. Some of the guesthouses are pleasant, older-style places.

Vogels Hostel (☎ 895208, Jl Astamulya 76) has deservedly been the travellers' favourite for years. As well as being the local tourist information office, the owner, Christian Awuy, also has a great travel library, with books on Indonesia and further afield. A dorm bed costs 5000Rp, or a variety of rooms range from doubles for 10,000Rp to good mid-range bungalows with bath for only 20,000Rp; HI card holders receive a small discount.

The nearby, modern *Christian Hostel* is a Vogel's offshoot. Spotless rooms with mandi provide excellent accommodation for 25,000Rp (22,500Rp for YHA members). The rooftop sitting area has views of Merapi and the lava flow.

Wisma Gadjah Mada (☎ 895225, Jl Wreksa 447), about 500m before the park entrance, has interesting Indo-European architecture and two-bedroom villas with hot water for 50,000Rp and 75,000Rp. On Jl

Astarengga, *Wisma Merapi Indah (☎ 895 224)* is a more basic three-bedroom colonial villa costing 30,000Rp per room (with hot water).

One kilometre south of Vogels, *Villa Taman Eden (☎ 895442)* is the most luxurious and has a swimming pool. Good rooms with TV and hot water are 75,000Rp, or a self-contained three-bedroom villa costs 300,000Rp.

The old part of *Vogels Hostel*, the former residence of a Yogya prince, has a good, inexpensive restaurant, while the *Restaurant Joyo* is a bright, clean place, with good Chinese and Indonesian food.

Getting There & Away From Yogya's Terban Colt station, a Colt to Kaliurang costs 1500Rp, or a bus from the main bus terminal costs 1000Rp. The last Colt leaves Kaliurang at 4 pm, the last bus at 6 pm. Buses and Colts pass through Pakem before Kaliurang. From Pakem buses go to Prambanan, and Tempel, where another bus goes to Borobudur.

Selo

On the northern slopes of volatile Gunung Merapi, 50km west of Solo, Selo is just a straggling village with limited amenities, but it has a few basic homestays where guides can be arranged for the Merapi climb. The views of the mountain from the village are superb.

From Selo it is a four hour trek to the volcano's summit (see Climbing Merapi under the Gungung Merapi entry earlier).

Places to Stay The hospitable Pak Darto has been guiding trips to the top for years and runs a popular homestay, known as *Pak Auto*. Accommodation is very basic but clean, and costs 9000Rp per person. Elderly Pak Darto rarely ventures far these days, but he can offer good advice and arrange other guides. Prices are very variable, depending on the guide, your fitness, how many people and the risk factor. Count on around 30,000Rp to 40,000Rp for two to three people.

The crumbling *Hotel Agung Merapi* is a slight step up in standards and has a restaurant. Rooms cost 20,000Rp or 39,000Rp with mandi. Standards are very poor for the price, so try bargaining. Alternatively, dorm beds cost 6000Rp. They ask whatever price they can get for guides and their advice is dubious.

Getting There & Away Selo is most easily reached from Solo. Take one of the Tri Karya buses from Solo to Magelang, stopping at Selo (1500Rp, two hours) on the way. The last bus leaves Solo at 5 pm. From Yogya take a Magelang bus to Blabak and then a Colt or bus to Selo. Travel agents in Solo and Yogya arrange Merapi climbing trips via Selo.

PRAMBANAN
☎ 0274

On the road to Solo, 17km north-east of Yogya, the temples at Prambanan village are the best remaining examples of Java's period of Hindu cultural development. Not only do these temples form the largest Hindu temple complex in Java, but the wealth of sculptural detail on the great Shiva Temple makes it easily the most outstanding example of Hindu art.

All the temples in the Prambanan area were built between the 8th and 10th centuries AD, when Java was ruled by the Buddhist Sailendras in the south and the Hindu Sanjayas of Old Mataram in the north. Possibly by the second half of the 9th century, these two dynasties were united by the marriage of Rakai Pikatan of Hindu Mataram and the Buddhist Sailendra princess Pramodhavardhani. This may explain why a number of temples, including those of the Prambanan temple complex and the smaller Plaosan group, reveal Shivaite and Buddhist elements in architecture and sculpture. Although, these two elements are found to some degree in India and Nepal also.

Following this creative burst over a period of two centuries, the Prambanan Plain was abandoned when the Hindu-Javanese kings moved to East Java. In the middle of the 16th century there is said to have been a great earthquake which toppled many of the temples. In the centuries that followed, their destruction was accelerated by treasure hunters

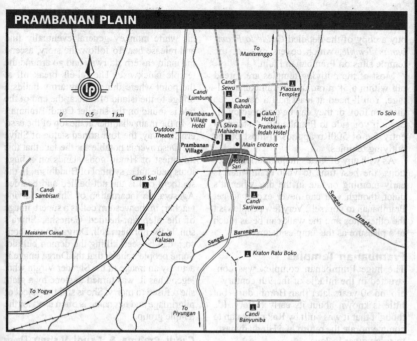

PRAMBANAN PLAIN

0   0.5   1 km

To Manisrenggo

To Solo

Candi Sewu
Candi Lumbung
Candi Bubrah
Plaosan Temples
Prambanan Village Hotel
Galuh Hotel
Shiva Mahadeva
Outdoor Theatre
Prambanan Indah Hotel
Prambanan Village
Main Entrance
Hotel Sari
Candi Sari
Candi Sambisari
Candi Sarjiwan
Mataram Canal
Candi Kalasan
Barongan
Sungai
Sungai Drankeng
Candi Banyuniba
To Yogya
To Piyungan
Kraton Ratu Boko

and local people searching for building material. Most of the restoration work of this century has gone into the preservation of the main Prambanan complex. Most temples have now been restored to some extent. People mostly only visit the temples of the main Prambanan complex, but if you have the time and energy it can be pleasant getting out into the countryside to see the other smaller temples such as Sambisari.

Orientation & Information

The Prambanan temples *(candi)* straddle the border between Yogyakarta and Central Java, and are usually visited from Yogya (17km away) but can also be visited from Solo (50km away). The main temple complex lies on the Yogya-Solo highway, opposite Prambanan village. From the main entrance on the south-eastern side, it is a short walk to Candi Shiva Mahadeva, the largest of the temples, locally called Candi Loro Jonggrang (Slender Virgin). Behind it, on the western side near the highway, is the outdoor theatre where the *Ramayana* ballet is performed on full-moon nights.

To the north of the Shiva Mahadeva, which is flanked by the smaller Brahma and Vishnu temples, is the archaeological museum and, further north, are smaller, partly renovated temples leading to Candi Sewu, 1km north. A 'mini-train' from the museum loops to Candi Sewu (1000Rp). All of these temples form the main Prambanan complex.

The temple enclosure is open daily from 6 am to 6 pm, with last admission at 5.15 pm. Entry costs 10,000Rp and, as at Borobudur, this includes camera fees and the museum. Hiring a guide can be a good investment at 15,000Rp for one to 20 people (one hour). There is also an audio-visual show every 30 minutes (2000Rp).

At the temple complex there is little in the way of free brochures or maps – you can buy a copy of the detailed *Guide to Prambanan Temple*, which covers most of the temple sites on Prambanan Plain.

Most of the outlying temples are spread out within a 5km radius of Prambanan village. You'll need at least half a day to see them on foot, or they can be explored by bicycle if you ride to Prambanan. A standard entry fee of 500Rp applies in most of the outlying temples.

As with any of Java's major tourist attractions, the best time to visit Prambanan is early morning or late in the day when it's quiet, though you can never expect to get Prambanan to yourself. Very few people visit the other sites and the walk can be as much of a pleasure as the temples themselves.

Prambanan Temples

The huge Prambanan complex was constructed in the middle of the 9th century – around 50 years later than Borobudur – but little is known about its early history. It's thought that it was built by Rakai Pikatan to commemorate the return of a Hindu dynasty to sole power in Java.

Prambanan was in ruins for years and, although efforts were made in 1885 to clear the site, it was not until 1937 that reconstruction was first attempted. Of the original group, the outer compound contains the remains of 244 temples. Eight minor and eight main temples stand in the highest central courtyard.

Candi Shiva Mahadeva The temple dedicated to Shiva is not only the largest of the temples, it is also artistically and architecturally the most perfect. The main spire soars 47m high and the temple is lavishly carved. The 'medallions' which decorate its base have a characteristic Prambanan motif – small lions in niches flanked by 'trees of heaven' *(kalpaturas)* and a menagerie of stylised half-human and half-bird heavenly beings *(kinnaras)*. The vibrant scenes carved onto the inner wall of the gallery encircling the temple are from the *Ramayana* – they tell

how Lord Rama's wife, Sita, is abducted and how Hanuman the monkey god and Sugriwa his white monkey general eventually find and release her. To follow the story, ascend the main eastern stairway and go around the temple clockwise. The reliefs break off at the point where the monkey army builds a bridge to the island of Lanka; the end of the tale is found on the smaller Candi Brahma.

In the main chamber at the top of the eastern stairway, the four armed statue of Shiva the Destroyer is notable for the fact that this mightiest of Hindu gods stands on a huge lotus pedestal, a symbol of Buddhism. In the southern cell, the pot-bellied and bearded Agastya, an incarnation of Shiva as divine teacher; in the western cell is a superb image of the elephant-headed Ganesha, Shiva's son. In the northern cell, Durga, Shiva's consort, can be seen killing the demon buffalo. Some people believe that the Durga image is actually an image of the Slender Virgin who, legend has it, was turned to stone by a giant she refused to marry. She is still the object of pilgrimage and her name is often used for the temple group.

Candi Brahma & Candi Vishnu These two smaller temples flank the large Candi Shiva Mahadeva. The Candi Brahma to the south, carved with the final scenes of the *Ramayana*, has a four headed statue of Brahma, the god of creation. Reliefs on Candi Vishnu to the north tell the story of Lord Krishna, a hero of the *Mahabharata* epic. Inside is a four armed image of Vishnu the Preserver.

Candi Nandi This small shrine, facing Candi Shiva Mahadeva, houses one of Prambanan's finest sculptures – a huge, powerful figure of the bull, Nandi, the vehicle of Shiva.

The shrines to the north and south of Nandi may once have contained Brahma's vehicle, the swan, and Vishnu's sun-bird, the Garuda.

Candi Sewu The 'Thousand Temples', dating from around 850 AD, originally consisted of a large central Buddhist temple surrounded by four rings of 240 smaller 'guard' temples. Outside the compound stood four sanctuaries

SALLY GERDAN

A sculptural relief from Candi Brahma, narrating the final scenes of the *Ramayana*.

at the points of the compass, of which the Candi Bubrah is the southern one.

The renovated main temple is interesting for the unusual finely carved niches around the inner gallery, with shapes resembling those found in the Middle East. Once these would have held bronze statues but plundering of the temple went on for many years – some of the statues were melted down and others disappeared into museums and private collections.

Candi Sewu lies about 1km north of the Shiva Mahadeva, past the small, partly renovated Candi Lumbung and Candi Bubrah.

Plaosan Temples

This north-eastern group of temples are 3km from the Prambanan complex. They can be reached on foot by taking the road north from the main gate, past the Candi Sewu at the end of the main complex, and then a right turn. Keep on this road for about 2km.

Believed to have been built at about the same time as the Prambanan temple group by Rakai Pikatan and his Buddhist queen, the Plaosan temples combine both Hindu and Buddhist religious symbols and carvings.

The temples are comprised of the main Plaosan Lor (Plaosan North) compound and the smaller Plaosan Kidul (Plaosan South), just a couple of hundred metres away.

Plaosan Lor is comprised of two restored, identical main temples, surrounded by some 126 small shrines and solid stupas, most of which are just a jumble of stone.

Two giant *dwarapalas* (temple guardian statues) stand at the front of each main temple, notable for their unusual three part design. These are two storey, three-room structures, with an imitation storey above and a tiered roof of stupas rising to a single larger one in the centre. Inside each room are impressive stone Bodhisattvas on either side of an empty lotus pedestal and intricately carved *kala* (dragon) heads above the many windows. The bronze Buddhas that once sat on the lotus pedestals have been removed.

Plaosan Kidul has more stupas and the remnants of a temple but little renovation work has been done.

Guards produce a visitors book (always a bad sign) and ask for a 2000Rp donation.

Southern Group

Sajiwan Temple Not far from the village of Sajiwan, about 1.5km south-east of Prambanan village, are the ruins of this Buddhist temple. Around the base are carvings from the *Jataka* (episodes from the Buddha's various lives).

Kraton Ratu Boko Perched on a hill overlooking Prambanan, Kraton Ratu Boko (Palace of King Boko) is believed to have been the central court of the great Mataram empire – a huge Hindu palace complex dating from the 9th century. Little remains of the original complex. Renovations, while only partially successful, have included new stonework. You can see the large gateway, walls, the platform of the main pendopo, the Candi Pembakaran (Royal Crematorium) and a series of bathing places on different levels leading down to the nearby village. The view from this site to the Prambanan Plain is magnificent, especially at sunset, and worth the walk alone.

JAVA

To get to Ratu Boko, take the road just south-west of where the river crosses, 1.5km south of Prambanan village. Near the 'Yogya 18km' signpost a steep rocky path leads up to the main site. Altogether it is about a one hour walk. The site can be reached by car or motorcycle via a much longer route that goes around the back of the mountain.

Western Group

There are three temples in this group between Yogya and Prambanan, two of them close to Kalasan village on the main Yogya road. Kalasan and Prambanan villages are 3km apart, so it is probably easiest to take a Colt or bus to cover this stretch.

Candi Kalasan Standing 50m off the main road near Kalasan village, this temple is one of the oldest Buddhist temples on the Prambanan Plain. A Sanskrit inscription of 778 AD refers to a temple dedicated to the female Bodhisattva, Tara, though the existing structure appears to have been built around the original one some years later. It has been partially restored during this century and has some fine detailed carvings on its southern side, where a huge, ornate kala head glowers over the doorway. At one time it was completely covered in coloured shining stucco, and traces of the hard, stone-like 'diamond plaster' that provided a base for paintwork can still be seen. The inner chamber of Kalasan once sheltered a huge bronze image of Buddha or Tara.

Candi Sari About 200m north of Candi Kalasan, in the middle of coconut and banana groves, the Sari Temple has the three part design of the larger Plaosan Temple but is probably slightly older. Some students believe that its 2nd floor may have served as a dormitory for the Buddhist priests who took care of Candi Kalasan. The sculptured reliefs around the exterior are similar to those of Kalasan but are in much better condition.

Candi Sambisari A country lane runs to this isolated temple, about 2.5km north of the main road. Sambisari is a Shiva temple

and possibly the latest temple at Prambanan to be erected by the Mataram empire. It was only discovered by a farmer in 1966. Excavated from under ancient layers of protective volcanic ash and dust, it lies almost 6m below the surface of the surrounding fields and is remarkable for its perfectly preserved state. The inner sanctum of the temple is dominated by a large *lingam* and *yoni* (stylised penis and vagina) typical of Shiva temples.

Places to Stay

Very few visitors stay at Prambanan given its proximity to Yogya. There are a plenty of hotels but most are very seedy. On the main highway opposite the main complex, *Hotel Sari* (☎ 496595) has basic, noisy rooms from 15,000Rp.

The quiet road on the east side of the main complex has a dozen budget hotels strung out over a kilometre or more, but they rent rooms by the hour! The big *Prambanan Indah* (☎ 497353, Jl Candi Sewu 8) at least claims to be a genuine hotel and has a few economy rooms for 20,000Rp with fan; 60,000Rp to 120,000Rp with air-con.

The sparkling new *Galuh Hotel* (☎ 496 854, Jl Manis Renggo) is one road east but over 1km from the main complex. This big hotel has good rooms from 40,000Rp to 133,100Rp, a pool and a large restaurant.

The delightful *Prambanan Village* (☎ 496435), down a quiet country lane at the north-west corner of the temple complex, has a pool, pleasant gardens and a restaurant. Attractive but overpriced bungalows next to the sawah cost 200,000/240,000Rp for singles/doubles.

Entertainment

The famous *Ramayana Ballet* held at the *outdoor theatre* is Java's most spectacular dance-drama. The story of Rama and Shinta unfolds over four successive nights, once or twice each month from May to October (the dry season), leading up to the full moon. With the magnificent flood-lit Candi Shiva Mahadeva as a backdrop, nearly 200 dancers and gamelan musicians take part in a spectacle of monkey armies, giants on stilts, clashing battles and acrobatics.

Performances last from 7.30 to 9.30 pm. Tickets are sold in Yogya through the Tourist Information Office and travel agents at the same price you'll pay at the theatre box office, but they usually offer packages that include transport direct from your hotel for 5000Rp to 10,000Rp extra. Tickets cost 10,000Rp to 35,000Rp for VIP (padded chairs up the front). There are no bad seats in the amphitheatre – all have a good view and are not too far from the stage, but the cheapest seats are stone benches side-on to the stage. Cushions can be hired for an extra 1000Rp.

Alternatively, the *Ramayana Ballet Full Story* is a good two hour performance, condensing the epic into one night, and alternates with the four-part episodic performances. It features fewer performers but is still a fine spectacle held at the same open air theatre from May to October. During the rest of the year, in the wet season, it moves indoors to Prambanan's **Trimurti covered theatre**. Performances start at 7.30 pm every Tuesday, Wednesday and Thursday throughout the year.

Getting There & Away
Bus From Yogya, take the yellow Pemuda bus (1000Rp, 30 minutes) from the main bus terminal, or from the Sosrowijayan area take a No 4 bus along Jl Mataram and get off at the Jl Cik Ditiro/Jl Terbau corner and then take a bemo to Prambanan bus station. From Solo, buses take 1½ hours and cost 1500Rp.

Bicycle By bicycle, you can visit all the temples. The most pleasant route, though a longer ride, is to take Jl Senopati out past the zoo to the eastern ring road where you turn left. Follow this right up to Jl Solo, turn right and then left at Jl Babarsari. Go past the Sahid Garden Hotel and follow the road anticlockwise around the school to the Selokan Mataram (Mataram Canal). This canal runs parallel to the Solo road, about 1.5km to the north, for around 6km to Kalasan, about 2km before Prambanan.

To view the western temples you really need to come back via the Solo road. The turn-off north to Candi Sambasari from the Solo road crosses the canal before leading another 1km to the temple. You can visit the temple, back track to the canal path and continue back to Yogya.

SOLO (SURAKARTA)
☎ 0271 • pop 517,000
Only 65km north-east of Yogya, the old royal city of Surakarta, more popularly known as Solo, competes with Yogya as a centre of Javanese culture. It has two palaces and one is even older than Yogya's, for Solo was originally the seat of the great Mataram empire before Yogyakarta separated from it.

Solo, even though it is larger than Yogya, is more traditional and unhurried. It can also rightfully claim to be more Javanese than Yogyakarta, which has a large population of non-Javanese students at its universities.

As well as its palaces, Solo attracts many students and scholars to its academies of music and dance. The city is an excellent place to see traditional performing arts. Traditional crafts are also well represented, especially batik, as Solo is a major textile centre.

Wander around the backs streets past white-washed palace walls and down alleyways through the kampungs and you will discover Solo's graciousness. It can be visited on a day trip from Yogya, but Solo is worth far more than a day, and a number of attractions lie outside the city. It has a good range of accommodation, and, though tourist services are not as developed as in Yogya, tourism is far less commercialised.

History
Surakarta's founding in 1745 has a mystical history. Following the sacking of the Mataram court at Kartasura in 1742, the susuhunan, Pakubuwono II, decided to look for a more auspicious site. According to legend, 'voices' told the king to go to the village of Solo because 'it is the place decreed by Allah and it will become a great and prosperous city'.

JAVA

SOLO (SURAKARTA)

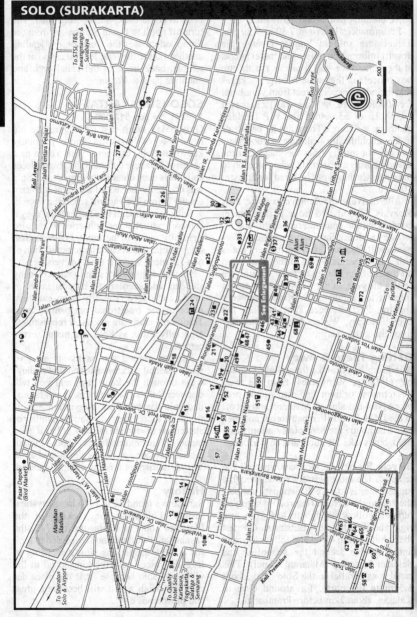

JAVA

SOLO (SURAKARTA)

PLACES TO STAY
6   Hotel Agas International
7   Hotel Bringin
8   Riyadi Palace Hotel
9   Hotel Putri Ayu
10 Ramayana Guesthouse
12 Solo Inn
16 Hotel Dana
17 Novotel Solo
18 Hotel Said Raya Solo
20 Pendhawa Homestay
23 Lucie Pension
25 Kusuma Sahid Prince Hotel
27 Hotel Asia
39 Remaja Homestay
40 Mama Homestay
41 Paradiso Guest House
42 Westerners
43 Cendana Homestay;
    Warung Biru
47 Hotel Wisata Indah
49 Hotel Cakra; Garuda
59 Hotel Kota
61 Hotel Sekar Kedaton
65 Hotel Keprabon
66 Istana Griyer
72 Hondra Guesthouse
73 Dagdan's

PLACES TO EAT
14 Adem Ayam
19 Tio Ciu 99
21 Kafe Atria; Atria Supermarket
29 Timlo Solo
44 McDonald's
46 Bu Mari
48 Cafe Wina
52 Cipta Rasa
53 Pujosari; C-21; Lezat;
    Oriental; Café Champion
54 Restoran Boga
60 Kusama Sari
62 Warung Baru
63 Cafe Gamelan
64 Monggo Pinarak; Steak
    Warung
67 Kafe Solo

OTHER
1   Tirtonadi Bus Terminal
2   Gilingan Minibus Terminal
3   Balapan Train Station
4   Radio Republik Indonesia
    (RRI)
5   Batik Semar
11 Akuarius
13 Gelael Supermarket; KFC

15 Toko Bedoyo Srimpi
22 Pasar Triwindu
24 Kraton Mangkunegara
26 SMKI School
28 Jebres Train Station
30 Nirwana
31 Pasar Gede
32 BNI Bank
33 Lojikom Internet
34 Main Post Office
35 Telkom Wartel
36 Balai Agung
37 BCA Bank; Kusuma
    Sari
38 Mesjid Agung
45 Batik Danarhadi
50 Batik Danarhadi
51 Legenda
55 Tourist Office
56 Radya Pustaka Museum
57 Sriwedari Amusement Park;
    Sriwedari Theatre
58 Wartel
68 Vihara Rahayu Chinese
    Temple
69 Pasar Klewer
70 Kraton Surakarta
71 Kraton Museum

Solo had already reached the peak of its political importance and within 10 years the realm of Mataram had crumbled, split by internal conflict into three rival courts, of which Yogya was one. From then on the ruler of Surakarta and the subsidiary prince of Mangkunegara remained loyal to the Dutch, even at the time of Diponegoro's Java War.

Pakubuwono X (1893-1938) was a mystical ruler who revived the prestige of the court. He was looked upon as the rightful king of Java and his popularity challenged Dutch authority. After WWII, the royal court fumbled opportunities to play a positive role in the revolution, and lost out badly to Yogya, which became the seat of the independence government. With the tide of democracy in the 1940s, the palaces of Solo became mere symbols of ancient Javanese feudalism and aristocracy.

Solo was a stronghold of the communists in the 60s and the atrocities following Soekarno's overthrow saw many slaughtered. Again, with the overthrow of Soeharto, Solo erupted following the Jakarta riots in May 1998. For two days rioters went on a rampage, systematically looting and burning every shopping centre and department store in Solo. The shells of burnt out buildings are dotted throughout the city and it will be years before Solo recovers.

Orientation

The oldest part of the city is centred around the Kraton Surakarta to the east. Jl Slamet Riyadi, the broad tree-lined avenue running east-west through the centre of Solo, is the main thoroughfare. Most hotels and restaurants are on or just off Jl Slamet Riyadi. Solo's Balapan train station is in the northern part of the city, about 2km from the city centre, and the main bus terminal, Tirtonadi, is over 500m north again. The Gilingan minibus terminal is near the bus terminal.

JENNY BOWMAN

Pakubuwono X (1893-1938), a ruler whose
popularity challenged Dutch authority.

Information

Tourist Offices The Solo Tourist Office
(☎ 711435), Jl Slamet Riyadi 275, has useful pamphlets, a map of Solo, and information on cultural events and places to visit.
The office is open daily from 8 am to 5 pm
except Sunday. A branch office is at the Tirtonadi bus terminal.

Post & Communications The efficient
main post office on Jl Jenderal Sudirman is
open daily from 8 am to 8 pm for most
postal services.

A Telkom wartel is on Jl Mayor Kus-
manto near the post office and has a Home
Country Direct phone. Otherwise wartels
can be found everywhere, including Hotel
Kota and Sriwedari Amusement Park.

At the time of writing, the Warposnet for
Internet access was closed, but Solo has
plenty of alternatives. Lojikom, Jl Ronggowarsito 2A, is open daily from 9 am to
9 pm. C-21, buried among the warungs at
the Pujosari warung area on Jl Slamet
Riyadi, is open from 9 am to 10 pm. Both
charge 5000Rp per hour.

For Internet cafes, Monggo Pinarak on
Jalan Dahlan (7500Rp per hour) and Kafe
Atria (11 am to 11 pm; 6000Rp per hour)
are both salubrious options.

Kraton Surakarta

In 1745 Pakubuwono II moved from Kartasura to Kraton Surakarta (also known as
Kraton Kasunanan) in a day-long procession which transplanted everything belonging to the king, including the royal banyan
trees and the sacred Nyai Setomo cannon
(the twin of Si Jagur in old Jakarta), which
now sits in the northern palace pavilion. Ornate European-style decorations were later
added by Pakubuwono X, the wealthiest of
Surakarta's rulers, from 1893 to 1939.

Entry to the kraton is through the north
entrance, fronting the alun alun. Here the
Pagelaran is the main audience hall where
the susuhunan held court in front of his
people. Crossing over the street behind the
Pagelaran is the kraton proper, though the
main gateway is not open to the public and
entry is from around the east side at the
museum/art gallery. Much of the kraton was
destroyed by fire in 1985, attributed by the
Solonese to the susuhunan's lack of observance of tradition. Many of the inner buildings, including the pendopo, were destroyed
and have been rebuilt. One that has survived is the distinctive tower known as
Panggung Songgo Buwono, built in 1782
and looking like a cross between a Dutch
clock tower and a lighthouse. Its upper
storey is a meditation sanctum where the
susuhunan is said to commune with Nyai
Loro Kidul (Goddess of the South Seas).

A heavy carved doorway leads through
from the museum across the inner courtyard
of shady trees to the pendopo, but most of the
kraton is off limits and is in fact the *dalem*
(residence) of the susuhunan. The main sight
for visitors is the Sasono Sewoko museum.
Its exhibits include fine silver and bronze
Hindu-Javanese figures, Javanese weapons,
antiques and other royal heirlooms.

Admission is 2500Rp, which includes a
guide and entry to the kraton complex and
museum. Entry is only from the north side

opposite the alun alun. The kraton is open every day from 8 am to 2 pm except Friday. Children's dance practice can be seen on Sunday from 10 am to noon, while adult practice is from 1 to 3 pm. The palace souvenir shop at the entrance sells a few craft items, crockery with the kraton emblem and even beer glasses sporting faces of the susuhunans.

Kraton Mangkunegara

In the centre of the city and dating back to 1757, this is the kraton of the second ruling house of Solo. It was founded after a bitter struggle against Pakubuwono II, launched by his nephew Raden Mas Said (an ancestor of Madam Tien Soeharto, the late wife of the former president). Though much smaller in scale and design, this kraton is better maintained and obviously wealthier than the more important Kraton Surakarta. Tours also tend to be better organised. Members of the royal family still live at the back of the palace.

The centre of the palace compound is the pendopo pavilion, bordered on its northern side by the dalem, which now forms the palace museum. The pavilion has been added to over the centuries and is one of the largest in the country. Its high rounded ceiling was painted in 1937 and is intricately decorated with a central flame surrounded by figures of the Javanese zodiac, each painted in its own mystical colour. In Javanese philosophy yellow signifies a preventative against sleepiness, blue against disease, black against hunger, green against desire, white against lust, rose against fear, red against evil and purple against wicked thoughts. The pavilion contains one of the kraton's oldest sets of gamelan known as Kyai Kanyut Mesem (Drifting in Smiles).

The museum here is a real delight and the guided tours are much less hurried and more informative than Kraton Surakarta. Most of the exhibits are from the personal collection of Mangkunegara VII. Among the items are gold-plated dresses for the royal Srimpi and Bedoyo dances, jewellery and a few oddities, including huge Buddhist rings and gold genital covers – one for a queen and a decidedly small penis cover for a king.

The kraton is open Monday to Saturday from 8.30 am to 2 pm, and Sunday until 1 pm; admission is 3500Rp. At the pavilion, you can see excellent dance practice sessions on Wednesday from 10 am until noon. The shop sells good quality wayang golek and other craft items.

Radya Pustaka Museum

This small museum, next to the tourist office on Jl Slamet Riyadi, has good displays of gamelan instruments, jewelled kris, wayang puppets from Thailand and Indonesia, a small collection of *wayang beber* (scrolls which depict wayang stories) and Raja Mala, a hairy muppet figurehead from a royal barge. Offerings must be made regularly to Raja Mala, otherwise it is said it will exude a pungent odour. Official opening hours are Tuesday, Thursday and Sunday from 8 am to 1 pm, and Friday and Saturday until 11 am, but it often closes early; entry costs 500Rp.

Markets

Pasar Klewer is the ever-crowded three storey textile market near Kraton Surakarta. This is the place to buy batik (mainly cap batik) – and it helps if you know your stuff and are prepared to bargain. It's open from 8 am to 4 pm.

Solo's flea market, **Pasar Triwindu**, is always worth a browse. It sells antiques and all sorts of bric-a-brac. Half the market is also devoted to car and motorcycle parts.

Pasar Gede is the city's largest general market selling all manner of produce, while **Pasar Depok** is Solo's bird market, at the north-west end of Jl RM Said.

Other Attractions

On the west side of the alun alun, the **Mesjid Agung** (Grand Mosque) is the largest and most sacred mosque in Solo, featuring classical Javanese architecture.

Solo's **Sriwedari** Amusement Park has fair rides, side-show stalls and other dated diversions. The main reason to come is for the nightly wayang orang performances and other regular cultural performances. Dangdut music nights on Tuesday are very popular.

Courses

Batik Mama at Mama Homestay (see Places to Stay – Budget) offers a one day introductory batik course for 20,000Rp (you supply the T-shirt); longer courses are also available. Warung Baru (Jl Ahmad Dahlan 23), never to be outdone, also offers batik courses.

Meditation Solo is a noted centre for contemporary mystical groups of different philosophies and religions, which come under the broad umbrella of Kebatinan (Mysticism). A few schools in Solo attract western followers. Some well known teachers include:

Pak Suprapto Suryodarmo (☎ 635210) at Plesungan Mojosonango follows Buddhist philosophy and practises meditation through movement, similar to Tai Chi.
Pak Suwondo, Jl Sidikoro 10A, teaches the traditional theory and practice of Javanese meditation with a Hindu perspective, and has a reputation as a patient teacher.
Ananda Suyono, Jl Ronggowarsito 60, is a Javanese 'New Age' eclectic.
Pak Hardjanto is about as Hindu and as ascetic as they come. His organisation, Pura Mandira Seta, is on the eastern side of the kraton opposite the museum.

Organised Tours

Various travel agents around town run tours, and many guesthouses, hotels and travellers' cafes can book them. Most are expensive and require a minimum of two people. They include Candi Sukuh (see the Candi Sukuh entry in the Around Solo section later) and the hill resort, Tawangmangu (50,000Rp), and trekking to the summit of Gunung Merapi (55,000Rp).

Inta Tours (☎ 56128), Jl Slamet Riyadi 96, is one conveniently located tour operator and many others are nearby. Mandira Tours & Travel (☎ 718558), Jl Gajah Mada 77, opposite the Hotel Said Raya Solo, is another well established travel agent.

Warung Baru and many of the homestays run bicycle tours of Solo and sites outside the city limits. These tours are reasonably priced and are a perennial favourite in Solo. For 20,000Rp, one full day tour takes you through beautiful countryside to see batik production, gamelan making, and tofu, arak and rice-cracker processing.

Places to Stay – Budget

Solo has an excellent selection of friendly homestays. Almost all offer good travel information, tours, bus bookings, bicycles, breakfast, and free tea and drinking water.

Westerners (☎ 633106, *Kemlayan Kidul 11*), on the first alley north of Jl Secoyudan off Jl Yos Sudarso, is spotlessly clean, well run and secure. Solo's original homestay, it is cheap and still popular, if a little cramped. Dorm beds/singles cost 6000Rp/6500Rp, and good-sized doubles with mandi are 17,500Rp.

On the same alley at No 1/3, the *Paradiso Guest House* (☎ 54111) is a classy little place with a pendopo-style sitting area. The all-white rooms are good, if expensive, at 9500Rp with shared mandi; 27,500Rp to 44,000Rp with mandi.

Off another alley to the north, the well run *Cendana Homestay* (☎ 46169, *Gang Empu Panuluh III No 4*) has well kept rooms from 9000Rp, and from 13,000/17,000Rp with bathroom for singles/doubles. The good Warung Biru restaurant is attached.

Mama Homestay (☎ 52248, *Kauman Gang III*), also off Jl Yos Sudarso, has basic rooms for 10,000/15,000Rp, or better but dark rooms with mandi for 15,000/20,000Rp including breakfast. Standards are below the others but many people enjoy the homey atmosphere. Mama gives one-day batik courses and bicycle tours are offered.

The nearby *Remaja Homestay* (☎ 47758, *Jl Cokro 1 No 1*) has extremely basic but airy rooms for 7500Rp, including breakfast. The old couple who run it don't speak much English but are natural hosts.

Istana Griyer (☎632667, *Jl A Dahlan 22*) is a friendly new homestay in a good position down a lane off Solo's main cafe strip. Rooms are spotless and hotel-like in standard and price. They cost 22,500/27,500Rp with shared mandi, or from 30,000/35,000Rp with mandi to 47,500/52,500Rp with air-con, hot water and TV.

Lucie Pension (☎ *53375, Jl Ambon 12)* is another new, switched-on homestay near Kraton Mangkunegaran. Spotless rooms have tatami-style mats and mattresses on the floor for 9000Rp to 12,000Rp.

Another option is the *Pendhawa Homestay* (☎ *52219, Jl Jawa 31A)*, but others have more appeal. Gloomy rooms cost 15,000Rp.

Solo has dozens of hotels, but they tend to be anonymous places. *Hotel Keprabon* (☎ *632811, Jl Ahmad Dahlan 8-12)* is right near Solo's travellers' cafes and is a reasonably priced option with old-style rooms from 12,500Rp. Rooms with hot water cost 25,000Rp, and air-con rooms are 30,000Rp and 40,000Rp.

Hotel Kota (☎ *632841, Jl Slamet Riyadi 125)* is very central. This double storey place built around a large open courtyard has rooms for 15,000Rp up to 45,000Rp with air-con.

Places to Stay – Mid-Range

Many of the hotels in this bracket are strung out along or just off Jl Slamet Riyadi, west of the city centre. *Hotel Putri Ayu* (☎ *711812, Jl Slamet Riyadi 331)* is a friendly place with quiet rooms around a courtyard for 34,500Rp with mandi, fan and TV, and 54,000Rp for rooms with air-con and bath.

Ramayana Guesthouse (☎ *712814, Jl Dr Wahidin 22)* is an attractive house with a garden. It has reasonable doubles with bath for 27,000Rp to 30,000Rp, or rooms with air-con and hot water for 40,000Rp to 50,000Rp; add 20% tax and service. Breakfast is included.

Hotel Sekar Kedaton (☎ *661884, Jl Ahmad Dahlan 7)* is very central but shielded from traffic noise. Spotless but simple rooms with bathroom cost 60,000Rp; with air-con 70,000Rp and 90,000Rp. Expect a big discount – 40% is about right.

Across the street from the tourist office and museum is the *Hotel Dana* (☎ *711976, Jl Slamet Riyadi 286)*. This fine colonial hotel has undergone extensive renovation, not all of it sympathetic, but it still has plenty of grace and excellent rooms, most with private sitting areas. Rooms are 102,000Rp and 150,000Rp, and suites are 150,000Rp to 270,000Rp, including breakfast. Regular discounts make it one of the best in this range.

Further west, the *Riyadi Palace Hotel* (☎ *717181, Jl Slamet Riyadi 335)* has well appointed rooms costing from 129,500Rp to 275,000Rp, but discounts to as low as 87,500Rp make it a good buy. Across the street, the new, motel-style *Hotel Bringin* (☎ *726232, Jl Slamet Riyadi 392)* has rooms a touch better than most. Air-con rooms are 75,000Rp, or fancier rooms with carpet and hot water are 95,000Rp.

Places to Stay – Top End

The following hotels all have swimming pools and restaurants. Solo has a glut of luxury hotels and relatively few visitors, so big discounts make its luxury hotels some of the cheapest in South-East Asia.

Hotel Agas International (☎ *720746, Jl Dr Muwardi 44)* is a smaller hotel with everything you need, including a heated swimming pool. Good singles/doubles cost from 245,000/277,000Rp, but the paket rates are as low as 130,000/145,000Rp.

The grand *Kusuma Sahid Prince Hotel* (☎ *46356, Jl Sugiyopranoto 20)* is designed around a former Solonese palace. Though an older hotel, most rooms are renovated, it has a large pool and more style than most. Published room rates are around US$100, but it has been discounting to as low as 175,000Rp.

Hotel Said Raya Solo (☎ *714144, Jl Gajah Mada 82)* is a big high-rise hotel with all the trimmings. Rooms cost US$110 and US$142, but expect a huge discount.

Most of the new hotels are near the airport, but the *Novotel Solo* (☎ *724555, Jl Slamet Riyadi 272)* is the most popular because of its excellent central position. Discount rates start at 240,000Rp, but because it can actually fill its rooms, discounts may be hard to get.

Solo's newest hotel is the *Quality Hotel Solo* (☎ *731312, Jl Ahmad Yani 40)*, 3km west of the city centre. This big hotel has impressive facilities, but opening rates are only 145,000Rp, which is exceptional value.

The most luxurious of all is the stylish *Sheraton Solo* (☎ *724500, Jl Adisucipto 47)*, but it is 5km from town out in the middle of nowhere on the airport road. Rooms from US$110 to US$170 are discounted to 285,000Rp.

Places to Eat

For the cheapest food listen out for the distinctive sounds that are the trademarks of the roaming street hawkers. The bread seller sings (or screeches) a high-pitched 'tee'; 'ding ding ding' is the *basko* (meat ball soup) seller; 'tic toc' is for *mie* (noodles); a wooden buffalo bell advertises sate; and a shrieking kettle-on-the-boil sound is the *kue putu* seller. These are coconut cakes, which are pushed into small bamboo tubes, cooked over a steam box and served hot, sprinkled with coconut and sugar.

Nasi gudeg (unripe jackfruit served with rice, chicken and spices) is popular, but the speciality of Solo is *nasi liwet*, rice cooked in coconut milk and served with side dishes. Another local speciality to try at night is delicious *srabi*, the small rice puddings served on a crispy pancake with banana, chocolate or jackfruit topping – best eaten piping hot.

Jl Ahmad Dahlan is the centre for budget travellers' eateries. At No 23, the most popular travellers' meeting place is the long-running *Warung Baru*. While it might not be haute cuisine, the prices are hard to beat and the menu is huge. Various travel services are also offered.

Across the street, *Monggo Pinarak* (Javanese for 'please sit down') is the most stylish of the travellers' cafes, and has a library, Internet terminals and eclectic music. The well travelled Bangladeshi owner serves excellent Indian food, western dishes and good breakfast fare. A couple of doors along, *Steak Warung* has steaks and is open late. Further down at No 28, the friendly *Cafe Gamelan* is another good travellers' cafe with a varied menu of Indonesian and western dishes, and a range of travel services.

In the main homestay area, *Warung Biru* at the Cendana Homestay has good food and vegetarian meals. The small *Cafe Wina (Jl Slamet Riyadi 183)* has a limited menu, but is a friendly meeting spot good for a drink,

and it offers a full range of travel services, including bicycle and motorbike rental.

Some of the cheapest and best food is to be found in Solo's numerous warungs dotted around the streets. The small depots on Jl Teuku Umar are good for an inexpensive taste of local specialities and most offer lesahan dining, which is very much a part of eating in Solo. On fine evenings, straw mats are laid out on the pavements all around Solo, especially on Jl Slamet Riyadi, for all sorts of goodies including sate.

Pujosari, a concentration of warungs, has a good selection. It's next to the museum and tourist office in the Sriwedari Amusement Park area. The warungs offer a wide range of Solonese and other Indonesian dishes. The biggest places are *Lezat*, a 24 hour lesahan place that does a mean *ayam kampung* (village chicken), and the more restaurant-like *Oriental* for Chinese dishes. *Cafe Champion* is another more salubrious warung serving steak and other dishes.

Cheap Chinese restaurants along Jl Slamet Riyadi include *Cipta Rasa* at 245 for cheap, filling fare, or the popular *Tio Ciu 99* is a better bet for good Chinese food.

Also on Jl Slamet Riyadi at No 342, *Adem Ayam* is split into two restaurants, one serving Chinese food and the other Javanese; gudeg is its best dish. *Timlo Solo (Jl Urip Sumohardjo 94)* is a Solo institution serving Javanese specialities, such as nasi liwet, gudeg and *nasi timlo* in its pack 'em in, move 'em out, laminex dining hall.

Kusama Sari, on the corner of Jl Slamet Riyadi and Jl Yos Sudarso, has seductive air-con, good hot platter grills and ice creams. It is also one of those rarities in Indonesia – a non-smoking restaurant. Another branch is next to the BCA bank.

In a similar vein, *Kafe Atria*, above the supermarket of the same name on the corner of Jl Ronggowosito and Jl Kartini, is a smart new restaurant serving mostly grills and some Asian dishes. It also has an Internet cafe, views over the city and live music in the evenings.

Kafe Solo (Jl Secoyudan) is Solo's most stylish restaurant, housed in a restored colonial building. The menu is vaguely Chinese and Indonesian, with a few interesting variations and a smattering of western dishes. Meals cost around 5000Rp to 22,000Rp for imported steaks.

Entertainment

Solo is an excellent place to see traditional Javanese performing arts. The *Sriwedari Theatre*, at the back of Sriwedari Amusement Park, has a long running wayang orang troupe. Though no longer a premier troupe, it only costs 1000Rp to sample this unique vaudeville style of telling the classics, complete with singing, comedy and action drama. Come and go as you please. Performances are staged nightly from 8 to 10 pm except Sunday.

Various cultural performances are held at the *RRI auditorium*, Jl Abdul Rahman Saleh 51. RRI performances are popular and often excellent. The station has all-night wayang kulit shows on the third Saturday of every month from 9 pm to around 5 am; wayang orang on the second Tuesday of the month from 8 pm to midnight; and ketoprak (folk theatre) performances on the fourth Tuesday of the month from 8 pm to midnight.

Sekolah Tinggi Seni Indonesia (STSI), the arts academy at the Kentingan campus in Jebres, in the north-east of the city, has dance practice Monday to Friday from around 7.30 am to noon. *SMKI*, the high school for the performing arts on Jl Kepatihan Wetan, also has dance practice every daily from around 9 am to noon, except Sunday.

Kraton Mangkunegara and *Kraton Surakarta* each have traditional Javanese dance practice (see individual entries earlier in this section for details).

Wayang kulit shows are performed by the famous dalang Ki Anom Suroto at Jl Gambir Anom 100, Notodiningran, in the area behind the Hotel Cakra. You can count on all-night performances there every Tuesday Kliwon, a date in the Javanese calendar occurring every five weeks. All-night wayang kulit is also held at the *Taman Budaya Surakarta* (TBS), the city's cultural centre at Jl Ir Sutami 57, to the east of the city, on Friday Kliwon of the Javanese calendar. Ki Mantep Sudarsono is one of Indonesia's most famous dalang and often performs in Solo.

Solo's title of the 'city that never sleeps' refers more to its all-night warungs than raging nightlife, but the city has a few lively nightspots. *Legenda (Jl Honggowongso 81A)* is the city's most popular pick-up spot, but it's small and incredibly dark – the strobe seems to operate on a 40W globe. Entry is 10,000Rp, as are the beers. Other nightclubs include the *Nirwana* at Jl Urip Sumoharjo, and the more modern *Freedom* on Jl Ahmad Yani, to the north-west behind the stadium at Balai Kambang. The bars at the *Novotel* and *Quality* hotels have pop cover bands and expensive beers.

Shopping

Solo is one of Indonesia's main textile centres, producing not only its own unique, traditional batik but every kind of fabric for domestic use and export.

For everyday shopping, check out the markets or the shops on Jl Secoyudan.

Solo has no big department stores – its few shopping centres were destroyed in the 1998 riots and the only modern supermarkets left are the rebuilt Gelael on Jl Slamet Riyadi and the new Atria on Jl Ronggowarsito.

Batik Pasar Klewer near Kraton Surakarta has hundreds of stalls selling fabrics (see Markets earlier in this section for more information).

The big manufacturers have showrooms with a range of sophisticated work. You can see the batik process at the Batik Keris factory in Lawiyan, west of the city; open Monday to Saturday from 8 am to 5 pm.

Another big Solonese manufacturer is Batik Danarhadi, with shops at Jl Slamet Riyadi 205 and others on Jl Gatoto Subroto and Jl Honggowongsa. It has a good range of batik fabrics and ready-made clothes. Batik Semar, Jl RM Said 148, is good for modern cotton and beautiful silk batiks.

Smaller batik industries include Batik Srimpi at Jl Dr Supomo 25 and Batik Arjuna at Jl Dr Rajiman 247.

Curios Pasar Triwindu on Jl Diponegoro is Solo's flea market. All kinds of bric-a-brac plus a few genuine antiques are sold here – fine porcelain, puppets, batik tulis pens, lamps, and furniture etc. Many of the 'antik' (antiques) are newly aged. Be prepared to bargain hard. Some of the dealers have larger collections at their homes, so it is worth asking if they have other pieces.

Toko Bedoyo Srimpi, Jl Ronggowarsito 116, is the place to buy wayang orang dancers' costumes and theatrical supplies, such as gold gilt headdresses. It also sells masks and wayang kulit puppets.

Jl Dr Rajiman (Secoyudan) is the goldsmiths' street. Buy gold in the Chinese shops and have it verified by the streetside gold testers along Jl Dr Rajiman and the side street of Jl Reksoniten. With their scale and little bottles of chemicals, gold testers can confirm the weight and purity.

Kris and other souvenirs can be purchased from street vendors at the east-side of the alun alun near Kraton Surakarta. The gem sellers have a mind-boggling array of semi-precious stones.

Vendors at Sriwedari Amusement Park also sell souvenirs. Pak Fauzan has a wide variety of kris for sale and you can see kris-making at his small home-workshop in Kampung Yosoroto Rt 09 No 21. It is in the kampung just north off Jl Slamet Riyadi, about 200m from the Riyadi Palace Hotel.

At the Balai Agung, on the north side of the alun alun in front of the Kraton Surakarta, you can see high-quality wayang kulit puppets being made. Gamelan sets are also on sale, but these are produced in the village of Bekonang, 5km east of Solo.

Getting There & Away

Air Silk Air flies to Singapore on Tuesday and Saturday for around US$160 return. At the time of writing, domestic services have been pared to the bone – Garuda (☎ 630082), in the Hotel Cakra, flies daily to Jakarta and that's it.

Bus The Tirtonadi bus terminal is 3km from the city centre. Frequent buses go to Pram-

banan (1500Rp, 1½ hours), Yogya (2000/3500Rp normal/air-con, two hours), Semarang (3000/5000Rp to 8000Rp air-con, 2½ hours) and Salatiga (1600/2800Rp, 1½ hours).

Buses to East Java include: Tawangmangu (1300Rp, one hour); Pacitan (3600Rp, four hours); Madiun (3300/6000Rp); and numerous buses go to Surabaya (six hours) and Malang. To Probolinggo (eight hours), the Mila air-con bus goes direct at 6pm. Luxury buses also do the longer runs, and agents can be found at the bus terminal and in the main tourist area around Jl Yos Sudarso/Slamet Riyadi; or the homestays and travellers' cafes also sell tickets. Luxury buses to Denpasar cost 60,000Rp, to Jakarta 45,000Rp.

Near the bus terminal, the Gilingan minibus terminal has express minibuses to nearly as many destinations as the buses. Door-to-door minibuses include: Yogya (7000Rp); Semarang (8500Rp); Blitar (21,000Rp); Surabaya or Malang (25,000); and Bandung (50,000Rp). Homestays, cafes and travel agents also sell tickets. They also sell tickets to Bromo on the Yogya Rental bus for around 40,000Rp.

Train Solo is on the main Jakarta-Yogya-Surabaya train line and most trains stop at Balapan, the main train station.

The quickest and most convenient way to get to Yogya is on the *Prambanan Ekspres* (3000Rp bisnis, one hour) departing at 6 and 9 am, noon and 2.40 pm.

For Jakarta, the express trains are far preferable to the ekonomi trains. The *Argo Lawu* (115,000Rp eksekutif, 9½ hours) is the most luxurious day train, departing at 6 am. The *Senja Utama* (40,000/80,000Rp bisnis/eksekutif, 11 hours) departs at 6 pm. The eksekutif *Bima* and bisnis class *Jayabaya* both come through Solo from Surabaya on the way to Jakarta. For Bandung, the *Senja Mataram* (30,000/52,000Rp, nine hours) departs at 8.15 pm, or the *Turangga* (45,000/75,000Rp) and the *Mutiara Selatan* (33,000Rp bisnis) are other night trains to Bandung.

Numerous trains run between Solo and Surabaya. The *Sancaka* is a good bisnis/

eksekutif train to Surabaya (25,000/ 40,000Rp, 3½ hours) at 4.30 pm. The *Sri Tanjung* (7000Rp, five hours) is a bookable ekonomi service at 8.20 am that continues on to Probolinggo and Banyuwangi (14,000Rp, 13 hours). Other ekonomi trains from Balapan run to Malang, Madiun and Kediri as well as all the big cities on the main line.

Jebres train station in the north-east of Solo has a few ekonomi services to Surabaya and others to Semarang and the north-coast – although the bus is a better option. From Purwosari train station in the west, a slow ekonomi service runs to Wonogiri, right along the main street, Jl Slamet Riyadi.

Getting Around

A taxi from Adi Sumarmo airport, 10km north-west of the city centre, costs 14,000Rp, or take a bus to Kartasura and then another to the airport. A becak from the train station or bus terminal into the city centre costs around 2000Rp, or a taxi from the taxi counter at the train station costs 7500Rp. Solo's taxis are metered, but drivers won't use them from the bus terminal or train station. The orange minibus No 06 costs 500Rp to Jl Slamet Riyadi.

The city double-decker bus runs between Kartasura in the west and Palur in the east, directly along Jl Slamet Riyadi, and costs a flat fare of 500Rp.

Many homestays and travellers' cafes can arrange bike hire for around 5000Rp or a motorbike will cost around 25,000Rp. Cars with drivers can also be arranged, but prices are higher than Yogya.

AROUND SOLO
Sangiran

Fifteen kilometres north of Solo, Sangiran is an important archaeological excavation site, where some of the best examples of fossil skulls of prehistoric 'Java Man' *(Pithecanthropus erectus)* were unearthed by a Dutch professor in 1936.

Sangiran has a small museum with a few skulls (one of *homo erectus*), various pig and hippopotamus teeth, and fossil exhibits, including huge mammoth bones and tusks.

Souvenir stalls outside sell bones, 'mammoth tusks' carved from stone and other dubious fossil junk. Guides will also offer to take you to the area where shells and other fossils have been found in the crumbling slopes of the hill.

The museum is open daily from 9 am to 4 pm except Sunday. Admission is 1000Rp. From the Solo main bus terminal, take a Purwodadi bus to Kalijambe (800Rp). Ask for Sangiran and you will be dropped at the turn-off, 15km from Solo. It is then 4km to the museum (2000Rp by ojek).

Gunung Lawu

Towering Gunung Lawu (3265m), lying on the border of Central and East Java, is one of the holiest mountains in Java. Mysterious Hindu temples dot its slopes and each year thousands of pilgrims seeking spiritual enlightenment climb its peak.

Though popular history has it that when Majapahit fell to Islam, the Hindu elite all fled east to Bali, Javanese lore relates that Brawijaya V, the last king of Majapahit, went west. Brawijaya's son, Raden Patah, was the leader of Demak and led the conquering forces of Islam against Majapahit, but rather than fight his own son, Brawijaya retreated to Gunung Lawu to seek spiritual enlightenment. There he achieved nirvana as Sunan Lawu, and today pilgrims come to seek his spiritual guidance or to achieve magic powers.

The unique temples on the mountain, the last Hindu temples built in Java before the region converted to Islam, show the influence of the later 'wayang' style of East Java, though they incorporate elements of fertility worship. Most famous is the temple of Candi Sukuh, while Candi Ceto is another large complex that still attracts Hindu worshippers. Some villages in the area have still resisted conversion to Islam.

Climbing Gunung Lawu Colts between Tawangmangu and Sarangan pass Cemoro Sewu, 5km from Sarangan on the border between East and Central Java. This small village is the starting point for the 6.7km hike to the summit. Thousands of pilgrims

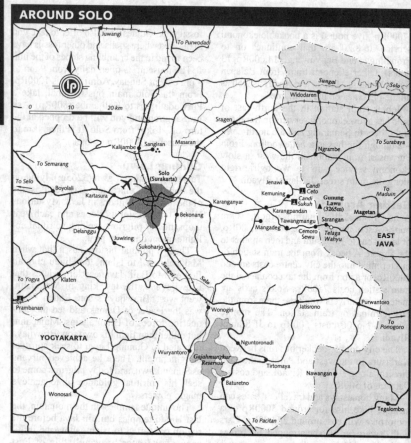

AROUND SOLO

flock to the summit on 1 Suro, the start of the Javanese new year, but pilgrims and holidaying students make the night climb throughout the year, especially on Saturday nights. Most start around 8 pm, reaching the peak at around 2 am for meditation.

To reach the top for a sunrise free of clouds, start by midnight at the latest, though superfit hikers can do the climb in as little as four hours. It is a long, steady hike, but one of the easiest mountains in Java. The stone path is easy to follow – bring a strong flash-light. Alternatively, guides can make a night climb easier and can lead you to the various pilgrimage sites along the way. Guides in Cemoro Sewu cost around 40,000Rp or try the Hotel Nusa Indah in Sarangan. Sign in at the PHPA post before starting the climb.

Candi Sukuh

One of Java's most mysterious and striking temples, Candi Sukuh stands 900m above sea level on the slopes of Gunung Lawu, 36km east of Solo. In form it is a large trun-

Java Man

Charles Darwin's *On the Origin of Species* (1859) spawned a new generation of naturalists in the 19th century, and his theories sparked acrimonious debate across the world. Ernst Haeckel's *The History of Natural Creation* (1874) expounded on Darwin's theory of evolution and surmised the evolution of primitive humans from a common ape-man ancestor, the famous 'missing link'.

One student of the new theories, Dutch physician Eugene Dubois, set sail for Sumatra in 1887, where he worked as an army doctor. In 1889 he left his position and went to Java after hearing of the uncovering of a skull at Wajak, near Tulung Agung in East Java. Dubois worked at the dig, uncovering other human fossils closely related to modern man. Later, in 1891, at Trinil in East Java's Ngawi district, Dubois unearthed an older skull and other remains that he later classified as *Pithecanthropus erectus*, a low-browed, prominent-jawed early human ancestor, dating from the Middle Pleistocene epoch. His published findings of 'Java Man' caused a storm in Europe and were among the earliest findings in support of Darwin's theories.

Since Dubois' findings, many older examples of *Homo erectus* (the name subsequently given to *Pithecanthropus erectus*) have been uncovered on Java. The most important and most numerous findings have been at Sangiran, where in the 1930s Ralph von Koenigswald found fossils dating back to around one million BC; while in 1936, at Perning near Mojokerto, the skull of a child was discovered and some, possibly sensationalist, estimates have dated it at 1.9 million years old. Most findings have been along the Sungai Bengawan Solo in Central and East Java, though Pacitan on East Java's south coast is also an important archaeological area.

Discoveries in Kenya now date the oldest hominid human ancestors, *Australopithecine*, at 4.5 million years old. Ancient man is thought to have migrated from Africa to Asia and come to Java via the land bridges that existed between the Asian mainland and the now insular Indonesian lands. It is thought that Java Man eventually became extinct, and that the present inhabitants are descendants of a much later migration.

cated pyramid of rough-hewn stone, which is curiously Inca-like and, while the sculpture is carved in the 'wayang style' found particularly in East Java, the figures are crude, squat and distorted. The temple is hardly as wildly erotic as is sometimes suggested but there are fairly explicit and humorous representations of a stone penis or two and the elements of a fertility cult are quite plain.

Built in the 15th century during the declining years of the Majapahit empire, Candi Sukuh seems to have nothing whatsoever to do with other Javanese Hindu and Buddhist temples, and the origins of its builders and strange sculptural style remain a mystery. It is the most recent Hindu-Buddhist temple in the region, yet it seems to mark a reappear-

ance of the pre-Hindu animism that existed 1500 years before. It's a quiet, isolated place with a strange, potent atmosphere.

At the gateway before the temple are a large stone lingam and yoni. Flowers are still often scattered over it and there's a story that the symbol was used mainly by villagers to determine whether a wife had been faithful or a wife-to-be was still a virgin. The woman had to wear a sarong and stride across the lingam – if the sarong tore, her infidelity was proven. Other interesting cult objects stand further in among the trees, including a tall-standing monument depicting Bima, the *Mahabharata* warrior hero, with Narada, the messenger of the gods, both in a stylised womb. This is followed by Bima

JAVA

passing through the womb at his birth. In the top courtyard three enormous flat-backed turtles stand like sacrificial altars.

From the site the views are superb, to the west and north across terrace fields and mountains. A paved trail leads downhill most of the way to Tawangmangu.

Getting There & Away From Solo, take a Tawangmangu bus to Karangpandan (1000Rp), then a Kemuning minibus to the turn-off to Candi Sukuh (750Rp). On market days (Wage and Pahing in the Javanese calendar), a 9 am bus from Karangpandan stops right beside the temple; otherwise it's a walk of a couple of kilometres uphill to the site. The trip takes about 1½ hours in total. The ubiquitous visitors' book makes an appearance.

Candi Ceto

Further up the slopes of Gunung Lawu, Candi Ceto dates from the same era as Candi Sukuh. Combining elements of Shivaism and fertility worship, it is a larger temple than Sukuh, spread over terraces leading up the misty hillside. It is a spartan complex with little carving and the closely fitted stonework, some of it new, gives the temple a medieval atmosphere. Along with Sukuh, it is reputed to be the most recent Hindu temple in Java, built when the wave of Islamic conversion was already sweeping the island.

Because of the difficulty in reaching Ceto, few visitors make it here – which is one of its attractions. Ceto is 9km by road past the Sukuh turn-off. Take a bus as far as Kemuning, then an ojek, though it is more pleasant to walk the 6km through the hills covered in tea plantations, clove trees and vegetable plots.

Tawangmangu
☎ 0271

Trekkers can make an interesting 2½ hour walk from Candi Sukuh, 6km along a paved path to Tawangmangu, a hill resort on the other side of Gunung Lawu. This path is steep in parts but also negotiable by motorbike. Or you can reach Tawanmangu by bus from Solo

via Karangpandan, which is just as fine a trip along a switchback road through magnificent tightly terraced hills. Tawangmangu is packed on Sunday – go during the week.

On the back road in Tawangmangu, about 2km from the bus terminal, **Grojogan Sewu**, a 100m-high waterfall, is a favourite playground for monkeys. This is perhaps the most famous waterfall in Java, though apart from its height, it isn't very spectacular (entry is 1500Rp). It's reached by a long flight of steps down a hillside and you can swim in the very chilly and dirty swimming pool at the bottom. From the bottom of the waterfall a walking trail leads to the path to Candi Sukuh; ojeks also hang out here on weekends.

The cave of **Gua Maria** is a 3km walk from the road. Another 2km walking trail leads up through vegetable plots from the front of the Hotel Garauda and joins the main road at the top of the village. There's a wartel about 100m uphill from the Wisma Yanti.

Places to Stay & Eat The *Pak Amat Losmen* is right by the bus terminal. Dirty rooms with disgusting mandis cost 15,000Rp (more like 10,000Rp after bargaining).

Prices and quality increase as you head up the hill, a long grunt from the bus terminal. *Pondok Garuda* (☎ 97239), about 500m uphill, is a good but expensive mid-range place. Rooms with hot water cost 35,000Rp to 125,000Rp.

Wisma Yanti (☎ 97056, Jl Raya Lawu 65) needs a thorough renovation, not to mention a good scrub, but this fine colonial villa is one of the cheapest around. Rooms at the back with mandi cost 20,000Rp and 25,000Rp. Better are the 30,000Rp rooms inside the main house, which has a wonderful sitting/dining room.

Further up the hill, the modern *Wisma Lumayan* (☎ 97481, Jl Raya Lawu 10) has good rooms with mandi for 20,000Rp and 35,000Rp. A three-bedroom villa with hot water costs 90,000Rp. Next door, the more basic *Losmen Arto Moro* has rooms for 20,000Rp.

Nearby, the friendly, good value *Pondok Indah* (☎ 97024, Jl Raya Lawu 22) has well kept rooms with sitting room, hot water and TV for 45,000Rp. Two and three-bedroom villas cost 90,000Rp to 135,000Rp.

The best in town is the *Komajaya Komaratih Hotel* (☎ 97125, *Jl Raya Lawu 150-151*) near the turn-off to the waterfall. It is favoured by tour groups, and rooms with hot water showers and TV cost 50,000Rp to 118,000Rp, plus 21%. It has a small restaurant and bar.

For good, cheap Indonesian dishes, the *Sapto Argo* is on Jl Raya Lawu opposite the Wisma Lumayan. It serves *sate kelinci* (rabbit sate), the local speciality, and also gives out rough maps of Tawangmangu. Also on Jl Raya Lawu, the tranquil *Lesahan Pondok Indah* has excellent food to enjoy while seated cross-legged on bamboo mats. At the front of the Wisma Yanti, a little no-name *warung* serves a mean *nasi goreng* and *kopi susu* (white coffee) made from *susu segar* (fresh milk).

Getting There & Away Buses go to Solo (1300Rp) and Colts to Sarangan (2500Rp). Minibuses (500Rp) loop through town from the bus terminal up the main road, across to the waterfall and back around to the bus terminal. They are frequent on Sundays but expect to wait forever on other days until they are jampacked.

Sarangan
☎ 0351

An interesting alternative to backtracking to Solo is to take a Colt to Sarangan, 18km from Tawangmangu on the mountain road to Madiun. It is just over the provincial border in East Java, though most foreign visitors come via Solo. On weekends, local crowds pack the place.

This picturesque hill town lies on the slopes of Gunung Lawu, with hotels clustered at the edge of Telaga Pasir, a **crater lake**. At 1287m the climate is refreshing and this is one of the most pleasant hill resorts in Java. It is cooler and more attractive than Tawangmangu, and the lake provides opportunities for boating, water-skiing and walks around the lake to **Tirtosari Waterfall**.

Sarangan is also a good base for tackling the ascent of Gunung Lawu.

Places to Stay Many hotels are on the main road as you enter town. A 1000Rp fee is payable at the entrance to the town.

Hotel Nusa Indah (☎ 888021, *Jl Raya Telaga 171*) is friendly, well kept and can arrange English-speaking guides (50,000Rp) to climb Gunung Lawu. Rooms with hot water cost 20,000Rp to 35,000Rp, and villas with sitting rooms are 75,000Rp to 90,000Rp.

Nearby, the *Sari Rasa Guest House* (☎ 888050) also has clean rooms from 25,000Rp, and across the road the *Hotel Asia Jaya* (☎ 888027) has rooms from 28,000Rp to 70,000Rp (before discount).

From the main street turn right at the lake and you come to the *Hotel Indah* (☎ 888 012), a more upmarket motel-style place with doubles from 59,000Rp to 89,000Rp, and family rooms from 116,000Rp; breakfast is included.

At the top of the village, with fantastic views of the lake, *Hotel Sarangan* (☎ 888022) has a colonial atmosphere and is very popular with Dutch tourists. Rooms, most sleeping four or more people, cost 95,000Rp to 145,000Rp and have their own sitting rooms with open fire places. Request a discount.

Getting There & Away Regular Colts run to Tawangmangu (2500Rp), passing Cemoro Sewu for the climb to Gunung Lawu. Buses also run to Magetan and Madiun, from where there are buses to all of Java.

Mangadeg
Near Karangpandan, a road branches south from the main Solo-Tawangmangu Hwy about 5km to Mangadeg, the burial hill of Solo's royal Mangkunegoro family. Make a small donation and visit the graves or simply take in the superb views.

A couple of kilometres away in the same sacred hills, the lavish **Astana Giribangun** is the Soeharto family burial palace where the former president's wife, Madam Tien Soeharto, is buried.

On the way to Mangadeg is **Pablengan**, the former bathing pools of the Mangkunegoro, with dilapidated, ancient bathing pavilions fed by seven types of spring water.

NORTH COAST

For many centuries Java's north coast was the centre for trade with merchants from Arabia, India and China. Through trade the north coast came in contact with different cultures and ideas, and became the birthplace of Islam in Java. During the 15th and 16th centuries Islam was adopted by the rulers of the trading principalities in opposition to the Hindu kingdoms of inland Central Java.

Islam in Indonesia has immortalised the *wali songo* (nine saints), to whom the establishment of Islam in Java is credited. With the exception of Sunan Gunungjati in Cirebon, the tombs of the saints all lie between Semarang and Surabaya, and are important pilgrimage points for devout Muslims. A number of these places lie on the road to Surabaya and can also be visited using Semarang as a base.

While the coast attracts many pilgrims, few tourists venture north. The flat, hot coastal plain bordered by low hills doesn't have fine beaches or the spectacular scenery of the central mountains. The massive monuments of ancient Java are missing, and apart from some impressive mosques, the reminders of the north coast's trading heyday are not obvious. Yet, while the north coast doesn't have any 'must see' tourist attractions and is conspicuously absent from tour group itineraries, it has an interesting mix of cultural influences, a lazy Middle Eastern atmosphere and makes an interesting diversion for the more adventurous with time to spare.

PEKALONGAN
☎ 0285   • pop 324,000

On the north coast between Semarang and Cirebon, Pekalongan is known as Kota Batik (Batik City) and its batiks are some of the most sought after in Indonesia. Positioned on the trading routes between China, India and Arabia, the city absorbed many influences and these are reflected in its style of batik. It is less formal, more colourful and innovative in design when compared to the traditional styles of Yogyakarta and Solo.

Pekalongan is a must for batik freaks, but otherwise it isn't a tourist destination. The town has a neglected, old-fashioned atmosphere and an ethnically mixed population. While the main street, Jl Gajah Mada/Hayam Wuruk, can bustle, Pekalongan is relatively quiet for its size.

Information

The tourist office (☎ 41092), Jl Jatayu 3, in the town hall (Balai Kota) will try to answer most queries.

The main post office (Kantor Pos dan Giro) is opposite the Balai Kota. For international telephone calls, the Telkom office is next door at Jl Merak 2.

Change money at Bank Expor Impor on Jl Hayam Wuruk.

Things to See

Pekalongan's small **Batik Museum**, 2km south of the train station on Jl Majapahit, exhibits examples of different batik styles, with explanations in Indonesian. It's open daily from 9 am to 1 pm except Sunday. Of more interest is the **bird market** nearby on Jl Kurinci.

The most interesting area of town is around the **Pasar Banjarsari**, a lively market and a good place for batik shopping. Nearby Jl Blimbing is the old **Chinese quarter**, and along this street is a Chinese temple and old terraced houses. To the east, Jl Patiunus and the streets leading off it, is the **Arab quarter**, and this is also a good area for batik (see Shopping in this section).

Facing the alun alun, the **Mesjid Jami Yasmaja** has impressive Arabic architecture enclosing an older Javanese-style mosque.

Places to Stay

Budget hotels are directly opposite the train station on Jl Gajah Mada. The friendly *Hotel Gajah Mada* (☎ 22185) at No 11 has doubles from 10,000/12,500Rp.

In the centre of town, a popular mid-range option is the *Hotel Hayam Wuruk* (☎ 228 23,

Jl Hayam Wuruk 152-54). It has a variety of shabby rooms with mandi from 28,500/33,000Rp to 57,000Rp for those with TV, air-con and hot water and, perhaps, hot water.

Hotel Istana (☎ 23581, Jl Gajah Mada 23), near the train station, is a better mid-range hotel with rooms from 40,000Rp with fan and 60,000Rp with air-con. It has a disco, about the only nightlife in Pekalongan.

The *Nirwana Hotel (☎ 22446, Jl Dr Wahidin 11)* is by far the best hotel in town. It has a large pool, coffee shop and restaurant. Air-con rooms cost 62,000/70,000Rp to 108,000/119,000Rp, including breakfast.

Places to Eat
On Jl Merdeka, just north of the main road near the market, *Mie Rasa* is a spotless little place with noodle dishes and icy fruit juices. At *Remaja (Jl Dr Cipto 30),* good and reasonably cheap Chinese food is available. Seafood is a served, but for the best seafood meals head 2km west of town along Jl Gaja Mada to *Bu Nani (Jl Raya Tirta).*

Purimas Bakery (Jl Hayam Wuruk) has good cakes, pastries, cold drinks and a sit-down area. A smaller branch is on Jl Gajah Mada near A Karim.

Shopping
Shop for batik, of course. Pekalongan batik is constantly evolving and new designs are more suited to western and modern Indonesian tastes. Traditional batik is still popular, however, and for formal occasions Indonesians are often required to don it.

Street peddlers casually wave batik from the doorways of hotels and restaurants – mostly cheap clothes and poor quality sarongs. Shops around town, many on Jl Hayam Wuruk, sell clothes, lengths of cloth, and sarongs in cotton and silk.

Pasar Banjarsari is a great place to browse for cheap batik, although some better pieces can be found. In the same area, Tobal, Jl Teratai 24, is a large rag trade business that produces clothes for the export market; you can view the process. Jacky, nearby at Jl Surabaya 5A, has a showroom down an alley with a large range

of clothes and lengths of good quality cloth.

Most of the traditional batik is produced in the villages around Pekalongan. In the batik village of Kedungwuni, 17km south of town, Oey Soe Tjoen's workshop is famous for its intricate batik tulis. You can see it being made every day of the week, except Friday.

Getting There & Away
Pekalongan is on the main Jakarta-Semarang-Surabaya road and rail route. There is also a road linking Pekalongan and the Dieng Plateau.

Bus Pekalongan's bus terminal is about 4km south-east of the centre of town, 500Rp by Colt or 2000Rp by becak. Buses from Cirebon can drop you off in town on their way through.

Frequent buses go to Semarang (3100/5000Rp for normal/air-con, three hours). Buses go to Cirebon (4000/7000Rp, four hours), but often you will first have to take a bus to Tegal and then another to Cirebon. The most direct route to Dieng is to take a bus to Batur and then a pick-up from there.

The agents for door-to-door minibuses are clustered together on Jl Alun Alun, just north of the square. Fares and journey times include: Jakarta (50,000Rp air-con, 10 hours); Yogyakarta (11,000Rp air-con, five hours); Semarang (13,500Rp without air-con, two hours); and Bandung (30,000Rp, eight hours). Hotels can ring for pick-up.

Train As Pekalongan is midway for most trains, it is hard to get a booking on the better express services and ekonomi trains are crowded. The *Senja Utama* and *Fajar Utama* expresses run from Semarang to Jakarta and stop in Pekalongan and Cirebon. The ekonomi *Cepat* leaves at 3.05 pm for Semarang and Solo.

Getting Around
Pekalongan has plenty of becaks, costing around 500Rp per kilometre. Orange bemos run all over town for a standard 500Rp. For Kedungwuni, take a bemo down Jl Mansyur.

SEMARANG

☎ 024   • pop 1.35 million

The north-coast port of Semarang, the provincial capital of Central Java, is a strong contrast to the royal cities of Solo and Yogyakarta. Under the Dutch it became a busy trading and administrative centre, and great numbers of Chinese traders joined the north coast Muslim entrepreneurs. Even in the depressed 1950s great wealth flowed through the city, with sugar and other agricultural produce going out, and industrial raw materials and finished goods coming in.

Today, Semarang is the main port on the central coast. Deep-water berthing facilities were built so that ocean-going vessels no longer had to anchor out in the mouth of Sungai Kali Baru. More a commercial centre than a city for tourists, Semarang's main points of interest are the old city and the Chinese Gedung Batu Temple.

The city is a good starting point for trips along the north coast or south to the central mountains and it makes a good stopover for a night or two.

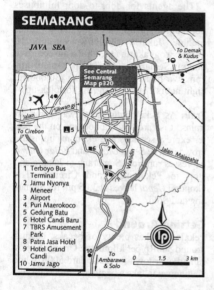

SEMARANG

JAVA SEA

To Demak & Kudus

See Central Semarang Map p320

To Cirebon

To Ambarawa & Solo

0   1.5   3 km

1 Terboyo Bus Terminal
2 Jamu Nyonya Meneer
3 Airport
4 Puri Maerokoco
5 Gedung Batu
6 Hotel Candi Baru
7 TBRS Amusement Park
8 Patra Jasa Hotel
9 Hotel Grand Candi
10 Jamu Jago

Orientation

Semarang has two parts – 'old' Semarang is on the coastal plain, sandwiched between the two Banjir canals, while the new town has spread out to the wealthy residential areas in the southern hills of Candi. An important hub in the old town is the Pasar Johar on the roundabout at the top of Jl Pemuda.

Jalan Pemuda, Semarang's premier boulevard in Dutch times, is still a major artery and shopping street, though nowadays the Simpang Lima (Five Ways) square, with its shopping malls and big hotels, is the real centre of Semarang.

Information

Tourist Offices The city tourist office (☎ 414332) has a counter tucked away on the 1st floor of the Plaza Simpang Lima in the north-east corner. It's open daily from 10 am to 2.30 pm and 3.30 to 7.30 pm, except Sunday. The head office (☎ 311220) is at Jl Siliwangi 29.

The Central Java tourist office (☎ 607 182) has maps and brochures available, including a regional *Calendar of Events*. Unfortunately, it is well out of the city in the PRPP Complex, Jl Madukoro Blok BB, near Puri Maerakaca.

Money BCA bank, Jl Pemuda 90-2, changes most currencies and its ATM accepts Visa cards. Other big banks are nearby on Jl Pemuda, including the Lippo, which has a MasterCard ATM.

Post & Communications Semarang's main post office on Jl Pemuda near the river is open from 8 am to 10 pm for basic postal services; for parcel post it is open during normal office hours. The W-Net Internet service next door is open daily from 8 am to 10 pm, and costs 2000Rp for 15 minutes. The Telkom office for international calls is at Jl Suprapto 7. It has a Home Country Direct phone. Wartels are found all over town – one is directly behind the post office.

Medical Services The best hospital and first choice of the sizeable Semarang expat community is RS Saint Elizabeth (☎ 315345) on Jl Kawi in the Candi Baru district.

Old City

Semarang's old city is fascinating to wander around. On Jl Let Jenderal Suprapto, the Dutch church, **Gereja Blenduk**, was built in 1753 and still has services. This area was the main port in Dutch times and, heading towards the river from the church, there are numerous old Dutch warehouses, many still housing shipping companies. Head south from here along the canal behind the post office for a glimpse of Amsterdam in the tropics. The imposing PT Perkebunan building in particular is a superb example of Dutch architecture.

The **market street** here is the favourite haunt of traditional masseurs and other streetside medical *ahli* (experts) who claim to fix everything from kidney disease to sexual dysfunction.

Further south you plunge into the narrow streets of Semarang's old **Chinatown**. Though Chinese characters do not grace the shops (the Chinese language is still discriminated against by law), Semarang is Indonesia's most Chinese city. Chinatown's highlight is the brightly painted **Tay Kak Sie Temple**, dating from 1772, one of the finest Chinese temples in Indonesia. The temple is on Gang Lombok, the small alley running along the river off Jl Pekojan. **Pasar Cina** (Chinese Market), also called Pasar Gang Baru, is a fascinating early morning market to wander around – it's best before 7 am. Wander along Gang Pinggir and nearby bustling streets where Chinese businesses ply their trade.

Back towards the centre of the city, **Pasar Johar** is Semarang's most intriguing market. Facing the market is Semarang's **Mesjid Besar** (Grand Mosque).

Gedung Batu (Sam Po Kong Temple)

This well known Chinese temple stands 5km south-west of the centre of the city. It was built in honour of Admiral Cheng Ho, the famous Muslim eunuch of the Ming dynasty,

who led a Chinese fleet on seven expeditions to Java and other parts of South-East and West Asia in the early 15th century. Cheng Ho has since become a saint known as Sam Po Kong and is particularly revered in Melaka, Malaysia. He first arrived in Java in 1405 and is attributed with helping to spread Islam. This temple is also revered by Muslims.

The main hall of the temple complex is built around an inner chamber in the form of a huge cave flanked by two great dragons, hence the temple's popular name, *gedung batu* (stone building). Inside the cave is an idol of Sam Po Kong.

To get to Gedung Batu, take the Damri bus No 2 from Jl Pemuda to Karang Ayu, and then a Daihatsu to the temple. It takes about half an hour from central Semarang.

Puri Maerakoco

Often referred to as 'Taman Mini Jawa Tengah', this large theme park is Semarang's version of Jakarta's Taman Mini, with traditional houses representing all of Central Java's *kabupaten* (regencies). While mostly of interest to domestic tourists, it's worth a look if you will be exploring Central Java in depth.

Puri Maerakoco is open daily from 8 am to 9 pm, and entry is 1500Rp. It is way out near the airport, and not accessible by public transport. Nearby, **Taman Rekreasi Marina**, is a large swimming pool complex, on the beach of sorts, where jet skis can be hired. It is open from 5.30 am to 8 pm; entry is 5000Rp.

Jamu (Herbal Medicines)

Semarang is known for its two large *jamu* manufacturers – **Jamu Nyonya Meneer**, Jl Raya Kaligawe, Km 4, near the bus terminal; and **Jamu Jago**, Jl Setia Budi 273, about 6km from the city on the Ambarawa road. Jamu Jago is well known for its advertisements that use a squad of dwarfs. Both have museums that are open Monday to Friday from 8 am to 3 pm. Tours of the factories are available upon request.

Other Attractions

Tugu Muda, at the southern end of Jl Pemuda, is a candle-shaped monument

CENTRAL SEMARANG

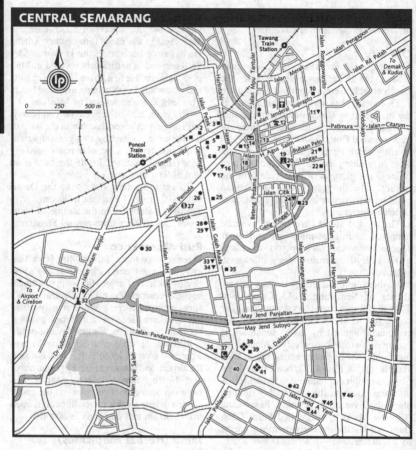

commemorating Semarang's five day battle against the Japanese military in October 1945. **Lawang Sewu** (1000 Doors) is nearby. It was formerly Dutch offices, later headquarters of the Japanese forces and is now occupied by the Indonesian army.

Simpang Lima square houses Semarang's cinema complexes and big malls. Crowds congregate in the evenings and browse aimlessly at goods they simply can't afford.

Semarang harbour is worth a look to see *pinisi* (schooners) and other traditional

ocean-going vessels that dock at Tambak Lorok wharfs.

Ronggowarsito Museum on Jl Abdul-rachman, about 2km before the airport, is a provincial museum with antiquities from all over the state. One of the most interesting exhibits is a recycled stone panel from the Mantingan mosque. One side shows Islamic motifs, while the reverse shows the original Hindu-Buddhist scene. The museuem is open daily from 8 am to 2.30 pm except Monday.

CENTRAL SEMARANG

PLACES TO STAY		PLACES TO EAT			
1	Losmen Arjuna	11	Toko Wingko Babad	14	Main Post Office; W-Net; Wartel
2	Hotel Rahayu	16	Sari Medan	18	Pasar Johar
3	Hotel Oewa Asia	17	Toko Oen	19	Tay Kak Sie Temple
4	Hotel Surya	20	Loenpia Semarang	21	Minibus Agents
5	Losmen Singapore	24	Rumah Makan Bintang Tiga	26	Merpati
6	Hotel Blambangan	29	Rumah Makan Oriental	27	BCA Bank
7	Natour Dibya Puri	33	Bintang Laut	28	Bouraq
10	Hotel Raden Patah	34	Rumah Makan Tio Cio	30	Ngesti Pandowo Theatre
15	Metro Hotel	43	Mbok Berek	31	Lawang Sewu
22	Losmen Jaya	45	Timlo Solo	32	Tugu Muda
23	Hotel Nendra Yakti	46	Istana & Matsuri Restaurants	37	Mesjid Baiturrakhman
25	Quirin Hotel			38	Ciputra Mall
35	Telomoyo	**OTHER**		40	Simpang Lima
36	Hotel Graha Santika; Garuda	8	Pelni Office	41	Plaza Simpang Lima; Tourist Office; Parkview Bar-BQ
39	Hotel Ciputra	9	Gereja Blenduk	42	RRI
44	Hotel Santika	12	Telkom Office		
		13	Pasar Cina		

Places to Stay – Budget

The friendly but noisy *Hotel Oewa Asia* (☎ 542547, Jl Kol Sugiono 12) gets a steady trickle of travellers, so you won't be a total oddity here. Large, fairly basic rooms cost 22,500Rp with fan and mandi, or darker air-con rooms cost 30,000Rp and 35,000Rp.

Hotel Raden Patah (☎ 511328, Jl Suprapto 48) is in the colonial district, near the train station. Spartan, good value rooms cost 13,500Rp, or 17,000Rp with mandi and fan.

If these two are full and you can speak some Indonesian, other options include the basic *Losmen Singapore* (☎ 543757, Jl Imam Bonjol 12) or the better *Hotel Rahayu* (☎ 542532, Jl Imam Bonjol 35).

Losmen Jaya (☎ 543604, Jl Let Jend Haryono 85-87) is a little far from the city centre but has reasonable budget rooms from 16,000Rp, or 22,500Rp with mandi.

Hotel Nendra Yakti (☎ 544202, Gang Pinggir 68) in Chinatown straddles the budget and mid-range categories. It has good service and spotless rooms with fan and mandi for 25,000Rp. Better air-con rooms with TV cost 55,000Rp or 60,000Rp with hot water.

Places to Stay – Mid-Range

In the city centre, the *Natour Dibya Puri* (☎ 547821, Jl Pemuda 11) is a hotel with loads of colonial atmosphere but it is sadly neglected. Grubby air-con doubles cost 65,000Rp to 100,000Rp, but nothing seems to work. Singles/doubles for 30,000/35,000Rp with fan, but without bathroom, have towering ceilings – savour the colonial ambience without paying for non-existent facilities.

Hotel Surya (☎ 540355, Jl Imam Bonjol 28) is a small, newly renovated hotel. It's one of the better options in central Semarang. Rooms with air-con and hot water cost 60,000Rp to 120,000Rp.

Candi Baru in the southern hills, 3km south-west of Simpang Lima, has a number of hotels. For colonial style, the *Hotel Candi Baru* (☎ 315272, Jl Rinjani 21) is a magnificent, rambling old villa with panoramic views of the city. It's shabby but good value. A few economy rooms cost 25,000Rp, or huge air-con rooms are 60,000Rp to 105,000Rp – all plus 21%.

The three star *Metro Hotel* (☎ 547371, Jl H Agus Salim 3) is right in the city centre. Once Semarang's best, it is now outclassed but its rooms from 142,800Rp are well kept and fully equipped.

Places to Stay – Top End

Most of these hotels cater to business travellers, but discounts are usually available.

The top-class *Hotel Ciputra* (☎ 449888) has an unbeatable position right on the Simpang Lima. Rooms cost from US$105 plus 21%; try a travel agent for a discount.

The nearby *Hotel Graha Santika* (☎ 318 850, Jl Pandanaran 116-120) is an older luxury hotel but well maintained with all amenities. Rooms cost 260,000Rp after discount.

The other major hotels are near each other in Candi Baru. The *Patra Jasa Hotel* (☎ 314441, Jl Sisingamangaraja) is getting a little old, but it has fine views of Semarang, good sporting facilities and discounts as low as 160,000Rp on its regular rates of 250,000/280,000Rp for singles/doubles.

The new *Hotel Grand Candi* (☎ 416222, Jl Sisingamangaraja 16) competes with the Ciputra to be Semarang's best hotel. Rates start at 500,000Rp (50% less after discount).

Places to Eat
The *Toko Oen* (Jl Pemuda 52) is a large, old-fashioned tea room where white tablecloths and basket chairs hark back to genteel colonial times. The Chinese, Indonesian and European menu includes grills and ice cream – expensive but good food.

At night dozens of kaki lima around the Simpang Lima serve a bit of everything and offer lesahan dining. Simpang Lima's malls are the place for fast food. Plaza Simpang Lima has a food court on the 4th floor, or for something more upmarket, *Parkview Bar-BQ* on the 5th floor has a bar, live music, good views and tasty grills, including Korean food.

Local specialties include *lumpia* (Chinese spring rolls), sold all around town, and *wingko babad*, delicious coconut cakes – buy them hot from the bakery, *Toko Wingko Babad* at Jl Cendrawasih 14.

Jl Gajah Mada has some excellent places for reasonably priced Chinese food, with an emphasis on seafood. *Rumah Makan Tio Cio*, opposite the Telemoyo Hotel, is an open-air restaurant, all steam and sizzling woks in the evenings. The *Bintang Laut* nearby is similar. Further north, the air-con *Rumah Makan Oriental* is more upmarket and has an ice cream parlour out the front.

Another top spot for Chinese seafood is the hole-in-the-wall *Rumah Makan Bintang Tiga (Gang Pinggir 31A)* in Chinatown. The decor is bare, but the fish is excellent.

Timlo Solo (Jl A Yani 182) has good, inexpensive Javanese food. Try the *lontong timlo* (rice steamed in banana leaf) or *nasi timlo*. A few doors away, *Mbok Berek* has Yogya-style ayam goreng.

Entertainment
The TBRS amusement park on Jl Sriwijaya, Tegalwareng has wayang orang every evening from 9 pm to midnight, and wayang kulit every Thursday Wage and ketoprak every Monday Wage of the Javanese calendar. Wayang kulit is performed at the *RRI (Jl A Yani)* on the first Saturday of the month, and in the courtyard of the *kantor bupati* (governor's office) Jl Pahlawan 10, on the 16th of the month.

Getting There & Away
Air At the time of writing, flight services have been slashed. Garuda (☎ 449331), in the Graha Santika Hotel, has direct flights to Jakarta (386,400Rp). Merpati (☎ 517 137), Jl Gajah Mada 17, has direct flights to Surabaya (267,600Rp).

Merpati has suspended its flights to Kalimantan but they may commence again. Deraya Air (☎ 604329) at the airport currently handles all flights to Kalimantan, which include: Pangkalanbun (298,600Rp); Pontianak (412,200Rp); and Ketapang (387,200Rp). It also offers charters to Karimunjawa (2,430,000Rp).

Bus Semarang's Terboyo bus terminal is 4km east of town, just off the road to Kudus. Destinations for normal/air-con buses include: Yogya (4000/7000Rp, three hours); Solo (3000/5000Rp, 2½ hours); Magelang (2500/6000Rp); Wonosobo (4000Rp, four hours); Pekalongan (3100/5000Rp, three hours); Cirebon (7500/13,000Rp, six hours); Kudus (2000/3000Rp, one hour); and Surabaya (10,000/15,000Rp, nine hours).

Agents for luxury buses and express minibuses are near the Losmen Jaya. Try the

Rahayu agent (☎ 543935), Jl Let Jend Haryono 9, and the Nusantara Indah agent (☎ 548648), Jl Let Jend Haryono 9B; or Armada Inter City (☎ 545144), around the corner at Kompleks Bubaan Baru 1-2. They each have luxury buses for all major long-haul destinations, including Jakarta or Denpasar for around 50,000Rp.

Normal/air-con minibuses go to Solo (7500/11,000Rp) and Yogya (8000/11,500Rp) every hour from 7 am to 6 pm. Other services without air-con include Kudus (11,000Rp); Wonosobo (11,000Rp); and Pekalongan (13,500Rp). Air-con buses include Surabaya (37,500Rp); Malang (35,000Rp); Bandung (35,000Rp); and Jakarta (50,000Rp).

Train Semarang is on the main Jakarta-Cirebon-Surabaya train route. Tawang is the main train station in Semarang.

Good trains between Jakarta and Semarang are the *Senja Utama* and *Fajar Utama* (36,000/72,000Rp) in bisnis/eksekutif, 7½ hours). They stop in Pekalongan and Cirebon. The luxury *Argomuria* does the run in six hours and costs 115,000Rp. The *Sembani* and a number of other trains also pass through Semarang between Surabaya and Jakarta, while the *Mahesa* goes to Bandung (40,000/70,000Rp, 12 hours).

Most of the ekonomi services depart from Poncol train station. To Jakarta, most are night trains, or the *Tawangmas* (12,000Rp, nine hours) leaves at 7 am. All ekonomi trains to Surabaya are through-night trains, such as the *Kertajaya* (14,000Rp, eight hours). A few trains go to Solo, but they take four hours – buses are much quicker.

Boat The Pelni office (☎ 555156), Jl Tantular 25, is near the Tawang train station. It's open Monday to Friday from 8 am to 4 pm, Saturday until 1 pm. Pelni's *Tilongkabila Lawit*, *Kelimutu*, *Binaiya* and *Sirimau* run between Semarang and the Kalimantan ports of Sampit (ekonomi/1st class 53,500Rp/174,000Rp), Kumai (46,000Rp to 152,000Rp), Banjarmasin (55,000Rp to 185,000Rp) and Pontianak (85,000Rp to 212,000Rp). Other Pelni boats are the *Pangrango* to Ketapang

(Banyuwangi) and the *Ciremai* to Ujung Pandang (98,500Rp to 333,500Rp). Occasional cargo boats go from Semarang to Kalimantan and take passengers – inquire in the harbour area.

Getting Around

To/From the Airport Ahmad Yani airport is 6km to the west of town. A taxi into town costs 8000Rp and less when returning to the airport using the taxi meter.

Public Transport City buses charge a fixed 300Rp fare and terminate at the Terboyo bus terminal. Bus No 1, 2 or 3 run south along Jl Pemuda to Candi Baru. Minibuses cost 500Rp and operate all around town.

Private minibuses for hire can be found at the post office and bus terminal, but bargain furiously.

A becak from Tawang train station or the bus terminal to the Oewa Asia Hotel will cost about 2000Rp, as will most rides around town. Becaks aren't allowed along Jl Pemuda.

Semarang has metered taxis, which congregate around the big hotels, the Simpang Lima and the post office.

AMBARAWA
☎ 0298

At the junction where the Bandungan road branches from the Yogya to Semarang road, this market town is the site of the **Ambarawa Train Station Museum** (Museum Kereta Api Ambarawa). Originally the Koening Willem I station, opened in 1873, the museum has exhibits of rail memorabilia and steam locomotives built between 1891 and 1928. It's open daily from 7 am to 5 pm.

Though the line has closed, groups of up to 100 passengers can charter a train for the 18km round trip from Ambarawa to Bedono at a cost of 1,300,000Rp. Book through Ambarawa train station (☎ 91035) a few days in advance. Alternatively, charter a little diesel lorry on the spot for a fun trip to Ngampin (10,000Rp return, 10km) or to Jambu (20,000Rp, 10km).

The museum is a couple of kilometres outside town, just off the road to Magelang. Ambarawa has hotels but Bandungan is a nicer place to stay.

Getting There & Away
Ambarawa can be reached by public bus from Semarang (2000Rp, one hour, 40km), and Yogya (2½ hours, 90km) via Magelang. From Solo, change buses at Salatiga.

BANDUNGAN
☎ 0298
Bandungan at 980m is a pleasant enough hill resort in which to savour the mountain air, but the main attraction is the nearby Gedung Songo temples. It's a busy little market town, noted for locally grown fruit, vegetables and cut flowers.

Places to Stay
Bandungan has dozens of losmen and more expensive hotels. The cheapest places are in town, while the better options are further out on the road to Gedung Songo.

In town, *Hotel Parahita* (☎ 711017), just down the back road to Semarang from the market, has basic rooms for 15,000Rp. *Hotel Santosa* next door is similar.

One kilometre west of town, *Hotel Rawa Pening Eltricia* (☎ 711134) is the best value. Perched on a hill with great views and a terraced garden, it has a lovely old colonial-style restaurant, a pool and tennis court. A wide variety of rooms are scattered around the grounds. It costs 45,000Rp up to 162,000Rp for a four-bedroom cottage. Further along, *Rawa Pening Pratama* (☎ 711134) has a similar aspect and facilities, but less style. Rooms start at 60,000Rp.

At the top end is the newer *Hotel Nugraha Wisata* (☎711501), with a swimming pool, restaurant and rooms for 80,000Rp to 225,000Rp (50% more on weekends).

Getting There & Away
Buses run directly from Semarang to Bandungan (2000Rp). If you are coming from the south, get off at Ambarawa and take a Colt to Bandungan (500Rp).

GEDUNG SONGO TEMPLES
These nine small Hindu temples (Gedung Songo means 'nine buildings' in Javanese) are scattered along the tops of the foothills around Gunung Ungaran. The architecture may not be overwhelming, but the setting is superb. The 1000m perch gives one of the most spectacular views in Java – south across shimmering Danau Rawa Pening to Gunung Merbabu and, behind it, smouldering Gunung Merapi; and west to Gunung Sumbing and Gunung Sundoro.

Built in the 8th and 9th century AD and devoted to Shiva and Vishnu, five of the temples are in good condition after major restoration in the 1980s; however, most of the carvings were lost. The temples were first discovered by the Dutch in 1740, and Raffles called them Gedung Pitoe (Seven Buildings) after a visit in 1804, though it wasn't until 1930 that all the ruins were catalogued.

A hill path goes past three temple groupings – the temples at the third grouping are the most impressive. Halfway up, the trail leads down to a ravine and hot sulphur springs, and then up again to the final temple and its expansive views. The 3km loop can be walked in an hour, but allow longer to savour the atmosphere. Horses can also be hired.

The site is open daily from 7 am to 5 pm. Arrive early in the morning for the best views. A couple of small hotels with rooms for 10,000Rp are just outside the gate.

Getting There & Away
The temples are about 6km from Bandungan. Take a Sumawono bus (only 100Rp) 3km to the turn-off to the temples. Buses also run from Semarang and Ambarawa (1250Rp). From the turn-off, take an ojek for the final 3km uphill to Gedung Songo (2000Rp).

DEMAK
Twenty-five kilometres east of Semarang on the road to Surabaya, Demak was once the capital of the first Javanese Islamic state and was the most important state during the early 16th century. Demak conquered the Hindu Majapahit kingdom and helped spread Islam to the interior. At that time,

Demak was a seaport but silting of the coast has now left it several kilometres inland.

One of Indonesia's most important pilgrimage sites for Muslims, **Mesjid Agung** (Grand Mosque) dominates the town. Built in 1466, it is Java's oldest mosque. Combining Javanese-Hindu and Islamic elements in its architecture, legend has it that it was constructed entirely of wood by the wali songo in a single night. Four main pillars in the central hall were originally made by four of the Muslim saints and one pillar, erected by Sunan Kalijaga, is said to be made from scraps of wood magically fused together.

The mosque was extensively restored in 1987. The history and restoration of the mosque is outlined in the small museum to the side. Some of the original woodwork, including magnificent carved doors, and the original pillars are on display; it's open from 8 am to 5 pm.

The tombs of Demak's rulers are next to the mosque, including Raden Patah, Demak's first sultan, though it is the tomb of Raden Trenggono, leader of Demak's greatest military campaigns that attracts the most pilgrims. During Grebeg Besar, when various heirlooms are ritually cleansed, thousands of pilgrims flock to Demak (the date is different each year). The mausoleum of Sunan Kalijaga is at **Kadilangu**, 2km south of Demak.

The mosque is on the main road in the centre of town. Through-buses can drop you on the doorstep. The bus fare is 750Rp to Semarang or Kudus.

KUDUS
☎ 0291

North-east of Semarang, Kudus was founded by the Muslim saint Sunan Kudus. Like Demak, it is an Islamic holy city and an important pilgrimage site. Its name comes from the Arabic *al-Quds* (holy), and it is the only place in Java that has permanently acquired an Arabic name. Although strongly Muslim, interestingly, some old Hindu customs prevail, such as the tradition that cows may not be slaughtered within the town. It is a prosperous town, noted for its woodcarving craft and its *kretek* (clove cigarette) industry.

Information
The tourist office (☎ 35958), Jl Komplek Kriday Wisata, is in a children's recreation park to the east of town. The BII bank changes cash and has an ATM (Visa and MasterCard), or try the BCA bank.

Old Town
West of the river on the road to Jepara, **Kauman**, the oldest part of town, has narrow, winding streets and a Middle Eastern atmosphere. Some of the buildings are colourful traditional houses, with ornately carved wooden fronts.

Mesjid Al-Manar (or Al-Aqsa), constructed in 1549 by Sunan Kudus, is named after the mosque in Jerusalem. Like so many of Java's early mosques, it displays elements of Islamic and Hindu-Javanese design, such as its carved split doorways. It is famous for its tall red-brick minaret

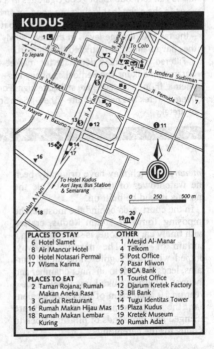

KUDUS

To Jepara / Jl Sunan Kudus / To Colo / Jl Manggar / Jl Mayor H Basuno / Jl Jenderal Sudirman / Jl Pemuda / Jalan A Yani / To Hotel Kudus Asri Jaya, Bus Station & Semarang

0   250   500 m

PLACES TO STAY	OTHER
6 Hotel Slamet	1 Mesjid Al-Manar
8 Air Mancur Hotel	4 Telkom
10 Hotel Notasari Permai	5 Post Office
17 Wisma Karima	7 Pasar Kliwon
	9 BCA Bank
PLACES TO EAT	11 Tourist Office
2 Taman Rojana; Rumah	12 Djarum Kretek Factory
Makan Aneka Rasa	13 BII Bank
3 Garuda Restaurant	14 Tugu Identitas Tower
16 Rumah Makan Hijau Mas	15 Plaza Kudus
18 Rumah Makan Lembar	19 Kretek Museum
Kuring	20 Rumah Adat

Kretek Cigarettes

One of the distinctive 'aromas' of Indonesia is the sweet, spicy smell of *kretek* (clove-flavoured cigarettes). The kretek has only been around since the early 20th century, but today the addiction is nationwide and accounts for 90% of the cigarette market, while sales of *rokok putih* (cigarettes without cloves) are languishing. So high is the consumption of cloves used in the kretek industry that Indonesia, traditionally a supplier of cloves in world markets, has become a substantial net importer from other world centres.

The invention of the kretek is attributed to a Kudus man Nitisemito, who claimed the cigarettes relieved his asthma. He mixed tobacco with crushed cloves rolled in corn leaves (*rokok klobot*) – the prototype for his Bal Tiga brand, which he began selling in 1906. Nitisemito was a tireless promoter of his product – over the radio, by air dropping advertising leaflets and by touring with a musical troupe across Java in an attempt to sell the new cigarettes.

Kudus became the centre for the kretek industry and at one stage the town had over 200 factories, though today less than 50 cottage industries and a few large factories remain. Rationalisation in the industry has seen kretek production dominated by the big producers, such as Bentoel in Malang, Gudang Garam in Kediri and Djarum in Kudus. Nitisemito became a victim of the industry he started and died bankrupt in 1953.

Although filtered kreteks are produced by modern machinery, non-filtered kreteks are still rolled by hand on simple wooden rolling machines. The manual process is protected by law; women work in pairs with one rolling the cigarettes and the other snipping ends. The best rollers can turn out about 7000 cigarettes in a day.

As to the claim that kreteks are good for smokers' cough, cloves are a natural anaesthetic and so do have a numbing effect on the throat. Any other claims to aiding health stop there – the tar and nicotine levels in the raw, slowly cured tobaccos are so high that some countries have banned or restricted their import.

Filtered kreteks now dominate the market and popular brands include Bentoel, Gudang Garam and Sukun. The Bentoel company has even produced a 'light' range of kreteks, Sampoerna, though tar levels are still quite high. For the kretek purist, the conical, crackling, non-filtered kretek has no substitute – the Dji Sam Soe ('234') brand is regarded as the Rolls Royce of kreteks.

(*menara*), which may have originally been the watchtower of the Hindu temple the mosque is said be built on.

In the courtyards behind the mosque, the imposing **Tomb of Sunan Kudus**, crafted with finely carved stone, is shrouded with a curtain of lace. The narrow doorway, draped with heavy gold-embroidered curtains, leads through to an inner chamber and the grave. During Buka Luwur, held once a year on 10 Muharram of the Islamic calendar, the curtains around the tomb are changed and thousands of pilgrims flock to Kudus for the ceremony.

Kretek Production

The main kretek companies are Djambu Bol, Nojorono, Sukun and the Chinese-owned Djarum, which started in 1952 and is now the biggest producer in Kudus. Djarum's modern factory on Jl A Yani is central, but it usually requires a week's notice to tour the factory. Sukun, outside the town, still produces *rokok klobot*, the original kretek cigarettes rolled in corn leaves. To tour one of the factories, contact the tourist office.

The **Kretek Museum** has exhibits of a number of interesting photographs and implements used in kretek production, (all explanations are in Indonesian); it's open daily from 9 am to 4 pm except Friday.

Other Attractions

Next to the Kretek Museum, **Rumah Adat** is a traditional wooden Kudus house exhibiting the fabulous carving work the town is noted for. It is said that the Kudus style originated from Ling Sing, a 15th century Chinese immigrant and Islamic teacher. Nearby Jepara has surpassed Kudas as a woodcarving centre, although a few workshops still exist.

In front of Plaza Kudus, **Tugu Identitas**, styled after the Mesjid Al-Menar minaret, can be climbed for views over Kudus.

Places to Stay

The central *Hotel Slamet (Jl Jenderal Sudirman 63)* is a colonial building with high ceilings, layers of dust and basic but cheap rooms for 11,500Rp. It's OK for a night.

The small *Wisma Karima (☎ 31712, Jl Museum Kretek Jati Kulon 3)* has very clean rooms with mandi for 24,000Rp to 29,500Rp. It would be a good option if it was closer to the town centre.

Hotel Notasari Permai (☎ 37245, Jl Kepodang 12) is a very popular, friendly midrange hotel. It has a swimming pool and restaurant. Poorly lit rooms with mandi are 25,000Rp and 30,000Rp; much better aircon rooms start at 70,000Rp.

Hotel Kudus Asri Jaya (☎ 38449, Jl Agil Kusumadya) is the best hotel but a long way from the town centre, a few hundred metres north of the bus terminal. Rooms with mandi start at 25,000Rp but most have aircon from 95,000Rp to 145,000Rp. It has a pool and a good restaurant.

Places to Eat

Local specialities to try include *soto Kudus* (chicken soup) and *jenang Kudus*, a sweet made of glutinous rice, brown sugar and coconut. The best place for cheap eats and a range of local specialties is *Taman Rojana*, a new food-stall centre with over a dozen stalls downstairs, or the breezier *Rumah Makan Aneka Rasa* upstairs.

The cheap *Rumah Makan Hijau Mas (Jl A Yani 1)*, near the Plaza Kudus shopping centre, is good for Indonesian food and super-cool fruit juices.

The *Hotel Notasari Permai* restaurant is reasonably priced, and the *Garuda (Jl Jenderal Sudirman 1)* is the town's best Chinese restaurant.

For ambience, the best restaurant is *Rumah Makan Lembar Kuring*, on Jl A Yani. Good Sundanese and Javanese dishes are served.

Getting There & Away

Kudus is on the main Semarang to Surabaya road. The bus terminal is about 4km south of town. City minibuses run from behind the bus terminal to the town centre (500Rp), or you can take an ojek or becak.

From Kudus buses go to Demak (750Rp, 30 minutes), Semarang (1500/2000Rp normal/air-con, one hour, 54km), Purwodadi (1200Rp) and Surabaya (7000/14,000Rp to 20,000Rp, 286km). Brown and yellow minibuses go to Colo for 2500Rp. For Jepara (1000Rp, 45 minutes, 35km) and Mantingan, buses leave from the Jetak sub-station, 4km west of town (500Rp by purple minibus).

AROUND KUDUS
Colo

This small hill resort lies at an altitude of 700m on the slopes of Gunung Muria, 18km north of Kudus. Colo is most famous for its **Tomb of Sunan Muria** (Raden Umar Said), a wali songo buried here in 1469. Built in the 19th century, the mosque surrounding the tomb is perched high on a ridge overlooking the plains to the south. Pilgrims regularly come to pray at the tomb and during Buka Luwur, held in Colo on 16 Muharram of the Islamic calendar, up to 10,000 pilgrims line the road to the top.

A waterfall, **Air Terjun Monthel**, is 1.5km or about a half-hour stroll from the village.

Stay at the government-run *Hotel Pesanggrahan Colo (☎ 35157)*. Rooms with mandi cost 10,000Rp to 44,000Rp.

JAVA

JEPARA
☎ 0291

Jepara, 35km north-west of Kudus, is famed as the best woodcarving centre in Java. Its booming furniture business has brought signs of wealth, such as new hotels and a supermarket. The road into Jepara ('Jeporo' in Javanese pronunciation) passes woodcarving workshops, so you should get an idea of places to visit when you arrive.

Jepara has a surprisingly colourful history. An important port in the 16th century, it had both English and Dutch factories by the early 1600s, and was involved in a violent dispute between the VOC and Sultan Agung of Mataram. After some of the Dutch reputedly compared Agung to a dog and relieved themselves on Jepara's mosque, hostilities finally erupted in 1618 when the Gujarati (from Gujarat, in west India), who governed Jepara for Agung, attacked the VOC trading post. The Dutch retaliated by burning Javanese ships and much of the town. In 1619 Jan Pieterszoon Coen paused on his way to the conquest of Batavia to burn Jepara yet again and with it the English East India Company's post. The VOC headquarters for the central north coast was then established at Jepara.

Things to See

Raden Ajeng Kartini, a 19th century writer and progressive thinker, was the daughter of the *bupati* (regent) of Jepara. She grew up in the bupati's residence, on the east side of the alun alun, and it is possible to visit Kartini's rooms – if you contact the tourist office first. It was in this residence that Kartini spent her *pingit* ('confinement' in Javanese), when girls from 12 to 16 were kept in virtual imprisonment and forbidden to venture outside the family home.

The small **Museum RA Kartini**, next to the tourist office on the north side of the alun alun, has photos and furniture from the family home. It is open daily from 7 am to 5 pm.

Heading north from the museum, cross the river and veer left up the hill to the old Dutch **Benteng VOC**. Over the last 50 years

---

Kartini – Indonesia's First Modern Feminist?

Raden Ajeng Kartini (1879-1904), a progressive thinker and reformer, is regarded as perhaps the first modern Indonesian writer. Her letters, published in 1911 in the original Dutch, are entitled *Through Darkness to Light*. The English edition is available in paperback.

Kartini was born in Mayong, 12km north-west of Kudus on the road to Jepara, the daughter of the regent of Jepara. As a child she was allowed against Indonesian custom to attend the Dutch school in Jepara along with her brothers. As a result of her education, Kartini questioned both the burden of Javanese etiquette and the practice of polygamy permitted under Islamic law. In letters to Dutch friends she criticised colonial behaviour and vocalised an 'ever growing longing for freedom and independence, a longing to stand alone'.

Kartini married the regent of Rembang, himself a supporter of progressive social policies, and together they opened a school in Rembang for the daughters of regents. In 1904 Kartini died shortly after the birth of her son.

A monument to Kartini at Mayong marks the place where her placenta was buried according to Javanese custom. The towns of Jepara and Rembang commemorate Kartini Day on 21 April.

---

the fort's stonework has been pillaged, but the site has good views across town to the Java Sea. The cemetery nearby has some Dutch graves.

Places to Stay

Budget options are rough and bargaining is required. *Menno Jaya Hotel* (☎ 91143, Jl Diponegoro 40B) used to be *the* budget place to stay but since the owner passed away his widow has had difficulty maintaining the hotel. It's friendly but sadly neglected. Rooms cost 20,000Rp.

The other budget option is *Losmen Asia* (*Jl Kartini 32*). It's passable but the asking price for basic rooms is an inflated 25,000Rp.

Mid-range choices are much better. The friendly *Ratu Shima* (☎ *91406, Jl Dr Soetomo 13-15)* is a good option. Fan rooms start at 15,000Rp, and air-con rooms are 40,000Rp to 55,000Rp. A notch up in quality is the larger *Kalingga Star* (☎ *91054, Jl Dr Soetomo 16)*. Standard rooms start at 16,500Rp, or from 37,000Rp with air-con. Both have decent restaurants.

Hotel Segoro (☎ *91982, Jl Ringin Jaya 2)* is a motel with a good restaurant. It has a range of immaculate rooms from 22,000Rp to suites for 92,000Rp. *Hotel Jepara Indah* (☎ *93548, Jl HOS Cokroaminoto 12)* is a cheaply built three star hotel, but is definitely the best and biggest in Jepara. Rooms cost US$47/55 and US$68/73, plus 21%.

Places to Eat
Pondok Makan Maribu (Jl Dr Soetomo 16-19) next to the Kalingga Star has a huge Chinese and western menu – everything from spaghetti to lamb chops. The food is excellent.

In the centre of town on Jl Diponegoro, *CFC* is a KFC clone. Just across the river from the alun alun, the *Pondok Rasa (Jl Pahlawan 2)* has a pleasant garden and good Indonesian food served lesahan style. *Rumah Makan Citra*, next to the Hotel Segoro, is Jepara's flashest restaurant and specialises in seafood.

Shopping
Intricately carved teak *(jati)* and mahogany furniture and relief panels are on display at shops and factories all around Jepara. The main furniture centre is the village of **Tahunan**, 4km south of Jepara on the road to Kudus.

Brightly coloured ikat weavings using motifs from Sumba are sold in Bali, but they are actually crafted in the village of Torso, 14km south of Jepara, 2km off the main road. Other original designs are also produced and men instead of women perform the weaving, allowing broader looms to be used. Srikandi Ratu and Lestari Indah are two workshops with fixed price showrooms.

Pecangaan, 18km south of Jepara, produces rings, bracelets and other jewellery from *monel* (stainless steel alloy).

Getting There & Away
Frequent buses run from Jepara to Kudus (1000Rp, 45 minutes) and Semarang (2500Rp, 1½ hours). A few buses also go to Surabaya, but Kudus has more connections. Night buses to Jakarta cost 25,000Rp to 35,000Rp (Bumi Nusantara buses are the best).

Becaks are cheap. From the terminal, about 1km west of the town centre, 1000Rp will get you to anywhere in town.

AROUND JEPARA
Mantingan
The mosque and tomb of Ratu Kali Nyamat, the great warrior-queen, are in Mantingan village, 4km south of Jepara. Kali Nyamat twice laid siege to Portugal's Melaka stronghold in the latter part of the 16th century. The campaigns against Melaka were unsuccessful, but posed a serious threat to the Portuguese.

The mosque, dating from 1549, was restored some years ago and the tomb lies to the side of it. The mosque is noted for its Hindu-style embellishments and medallions.

Mantingan is easily reached from Jepara. *Angkudes* (minibuses) from the bus terminal can drop you outside the mosque for 500Rp.

Beaches
Jepara has some surprisingly nice, white-sand beaches. **Pantai Bandengan** (aka Tirta Samudra), 8km north-east of town, is one of the best beaches on the north coast. The main public section can be littered and is best avoided on Sunday, but a short walk away the sand is clean, the water clear and the swimming is safe. From Jepara, take a brown and yellow bemo (500Rp) from Jl Patimura, behind the tourist office. On weekdays you will probably have to charter a whole bemo for around 5000Rp.

The only hotel, *Pondok Bougenville* (☎ *92693)*, has basic rooms with mandi (each with four beds or more), for 30,000Rp a double including breakfast; 5000Rp per extra person (not including breakfast). It has a good beachside restaurant, and an excellent stretch of sand out the front with windsurfing equipment for hire. This is a great place to relax, with views of the offshore fishing platforms (karamba).

The most popular seaside recreation park is **Pantai Kartini**, 3km west of town. It is lined with *warungs*, but doesn't have a sandy beach. However, you can rent a boat for around 30,000Rp return to **Pulau Panjang**, 1km offshore, which has excellent white-sand beaches.

KARIMUNJAWA

These 27 islands, lying around 90km northwest of Jepara, are a marine national park. Though promoted as a tropical paradise, facilities are limited, the islands are difficult to reach and few visitors make it to this forgotten part of Java.

The main island, **Pulau Karimunjawa**, has homestay accommodation but, apart from peace and quiet, the island's attractions are few. You can swim in the calm, clear waters but the island is mostly ringed by mangroves and has no decent beaches. Nearby islands do have magnificent beaches and coral reefs, but can only be reached by chartered boat.

Pulau Tengah, to the north, is a small island ringed by a reef, with beautiful sandy beaches. Its small resort has the best accommodation of all the islands. Other nearby deserted islands with good beaches are **Pulau Burung** and **Pulau Geleang** to the west.

Places to Stay & Eat

The main village of Karimunjawa has a handful of *homestays* charging around 15,000Rp, including meals. *Pak Kholik* and *Pak Abdul Mu'in* have decent accommodation, and *Pak Ipong* has rooms with mandi for 20,000Rp with meals. The government-run *Wisma Pemda* has the best accommodation. Rooms with mandi cost 20,000Rp, and food costs an extra 6000Rp per meal. For something different, *Pak Cuming* rents

a room on a fishing platform 1km offshore for 15,000Rp per night. Karimunjawa now even has a warung, *Bu Ester*, serving standard fare and beer.

Pulau Tengah has luxurious, two-bedroom *cottages*, but they are only available through expensive tours organised by Satura Tours (☎ 555555), Jl Cendrawasih A-6, Semarang.

Getting There & Away

Scheduled flights no longer operate but Deraya Air in Semarang offers charters for 2,430,000Rp to Pulau Kemujan, linked to Pulau Karimunjawa by a bridge.

Ferries to Karimunjawa (20,000Rp, five hours) leave from Pantai Kartini in Jepara (2000Rp by becak) on Wednesday and Saturday at 9 am, returning from Karimunjawa on Monday and Thursday. The *Kota Ukir* (7500Rp, seven hours) carries cargo and passengers twice a month, but it doesn't carry life jackets or rafts and the Java Sea swells can be wild.

From Pulau Karimunjawa, it costs around 70,000Rp to 100,000Rp to charter a boat for a day trip to the nearby islands.

East Java

The province of East Java, or Jawa Timur, includes the island of Madura off the northwest coast, and has a total population of 34 million and an area of 47,921 sq km. The majority of its population are Javanese, but many Madurese farmers and fishermen live in East Java. In the Bromo area there is a small population of Hindu Tenggerese.

The north-west is lowland with deltas along the Brantas and Bengawan Solo rivers – vast rice-growing plains interspersed with countless villages and towns. The rest of East Java is mountainous and contains the huge Bromo-Tengger Massif and Java's highest peak, the volcano, Gunung Semeru (3676m). This region is less populated and offers raw, natural beauty.

Major attractions include the impressive volcanic landscapes of Gunung Bromo (2392m), still one of Java's most active

EAST JAVA

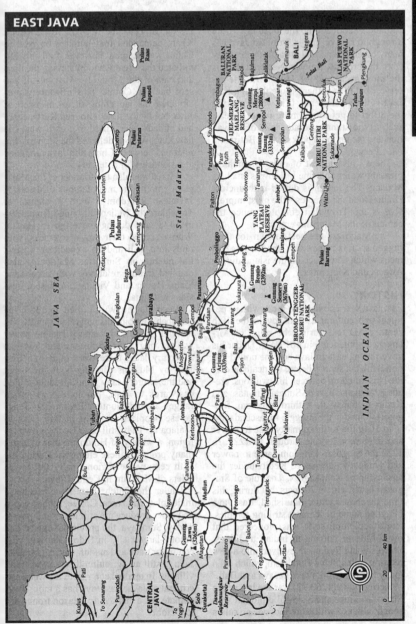

volcanoes. Most visitors only see Bromo and then scoot along the northern route through to Bali or Yogya, but East Java has many other fine natural attractions far away from the crowds. Baluran National Park is the most accessible of Java's wildlife reserves, but the southern route through East Java is the most scenic. It is worth making the effort to get to the more remote areas, such as the stunning crater lake of Kawah Ijen and the national parks, Meru Betiri and Alas Purwo.

There's also a host of other mountains, pleasant walks and fine hill towns, such as Malang. The region is dotted with ancient Hindu-Buddhist temples – the most impressive is the Trowulan complex, once the capital of the Majapahit empire.

The Madurese are best known for their rugged sport, *kerapan sapi*, the famous bull races which take place on the island during August and September.

HISTORY

East Java's past comes into focus with its political and cultural ascendancy in the 10th century AD and during the reign of Airlangga commencing in 1019 AD. Under his government, eastern Java became united and powerful, but shortly before his death he divided his kingdom between his two sons, creating Janggala, east of Sungai Brantas, and Kediri to the west. A third kingdom, Singosari, joined in the struggle for ascendancy.

In 1049 the Kediri dynasty rose to power and continued its rule through to 1222. In 1222 the Singosari kingdom came to power and gradually superseded Kediri under the leadership of Ken Angrok. The rule of Singosari lasted a mere 70 years, but during this time Javanese culture flourished. East Java inherited some of its most striking temples, and a sculptural style was pioneered that owed little or nothing to Indian traditions. Shivaism and Buddhism evolved into a new religion called Shiva-Buddhism, which even today has many followers in Java and Bali.

Kertanegara (1262-92) was the last of the Singosari kings and a skilful diplomat who sought alliance with other Indonesian rulers in the face of the threat of a Mongol invasion. In 1292 the Mongol ruler, Kublai Khan, demanded that homage be paid to China. Kertanegara, however, foolishly humiliated the Great Khan by having the nose and ears of the Mongol envoy cut off and sent back to China. This effrontery precipitated the launching of an invasion of Java, but by the time it arrived Kertanegara had already been killed in a civil war. The new king, Wijaya, defeated the Mongols but relations between China and Java remained at a standstill for a century.

Wijaya was also the founder of the Majapahit empire, the most famous of the early Javanese kingdoms. With a capital at Trowulan, the Majapahits ruled from 1294 to 1478, and during the reign of Hayam Wuruk carried their power overseas, with raids into Bali and an expedition against Palembang on Sumatra. Majapahit also claimed trading relations with Cambodia, Siam, Burma and Vietnam, and sent missions to China.

When Hayam Wuruk died in 1389, the Majapahit empire disintegrated rapidly. By the end of the 15th century Islamic power was growing on the north coast and, less than a century later, there were raids into East Java by Muslims carrying both the Koran and the sword. Many Hindu-Buddhists fled eastwards to Bali, but in the mountain ranges around Gunung Bromo the Tenggerese people trace their history back to Majapahit. They still practise their own religion, a variety of Hinduism that includes many proto-Javanese elements. During the 17th century the region finally fell to the rulers of Mataram in Central Java.

Under the Dutch, East Java became a major plantation area. Coffee, rubber, cacao and other produce are still major industries. Today, Surabaya, the provincial capital and second-largest city in Indonesia, is a vital centre for trade and manufacturing, but East Java is still an agricultural region of small villages. In marked contrast to the wet western end of Java, East Java has a monsoonal climate and a marked dry season from April to October.

SURABAYA

☎ 031 • pop 2.4 million

The provincial capital of East Java, the industrial city of Surabaya is second only to Jakarta in size and economic importance. For centuries it has been one of Java's most important trading ports. Today it is also the main base for the Indonesian navy. Surabaya is a city on the move, yet the narrow streets in the old part of the city, crowded with warehouses and jostling becaks, contrast strongly with the modern buildings and shopping centres of the showpiece central city.

For most visitors, Surabaya is merely a commercial centre or a transit point on the way to or from Bali or Sulawesi. For Indonesians, however, it has a special place as it was here that the battle for independence began. Surabaya is known as Kota Pahlawan (City of Heroes) and statues commemorating the independence are scattered all over the city.

Orientation

The centre of this sprawling city is the area around Jl Pemuda, which runs west from Gubeng train station, Plaza Surabaya and a number of big hotels and banks. Jl Pemuda runs into Jl Tunjungan/Basuki Rahmat, another main commercial street where you'll find Tunjungan Plaza.

The old city is centred around Jembatan Merah (Red Bridge) and Kota train station to the north. Further north is Tanjung Perak harbour. Surabaya's zoo is 5km south of the city centre, and the main bus terminal, Purabaya, is just outside the city limits, 10km south.

Information

Tourist Offices The Dinas Parawisata Daerah Surabaya (Surabaya Area Tourist Office, ☎ 5344710), Jl Basuki Rahmat 119, is at least central and if you wake up the staff they will try to answer your queries. It's open Monday to Saturday from 7 am to 2 pm.

For information on Madura and the greater Surabaya area, the regional tourist office (☎ 5675448), Jl Darmokali 35, is 5km south of the city, but hardly worth the effort. The East Java Regional Tourist Office

(☎ 8531822) at Jl Wisata Menanggal, further south, has a few brochures on the province.

Foreign Consulates Surabaya has a number of foreign consular representatives, such as the USA, the Netherlands and France, but in general they perform only limited functions.

Money Surabaya has more than its fair share of extravagant banking real estate. Jl Pemuda has plenty – Bank Duta and BNI bank usually have good rates and their ATMs accept credit cards. Jl Tunjungan also has a string of banks.

Post & Communications Surabaya's main post office and poste-restante service, on Jl Kebon Rojo, is 4km north of the city centre. It is open daily from 8 am to 7.30 pm. For Internet access, there's a Wasantara-net office next door. Online time costs 1500Rp for the first 15 minutes then 150Rp per minute; it's open daily from 7 am to 9 pm.

For telephone calls, a convenient wartel, open 24 hours, is in the basement level of the Tunjungan Plaza.

Useful Organisations There is a French Cultural Centre (☎ 5620079) at the French consulate, Jl Darmokali 10-12, and a Goethe Institut (☎ 5343735) at Jl Taman Ade Irma Suryani Nasution 15. The British Council (☎ 568 9958) is at Jl Cokroaminoto 12A.

Dangers & Annoyances In most large Javanese cities crossing the street is difficult, but it is almost impossible on Surabaya's big, four-lane roads, which have constant traffic and few traffic lights or pedestrian bridges. The only way to cross the street is to wait for the traffic to subside (it never stops), head out onto the road and motion with one hand for the traffic to stop. Cross yourself in prayer with the other.

Old City

This is the most interesting part of Surabaya, with fine Dutch architecture, a strong Chinese influence and an Arab quarter. If

JAVA

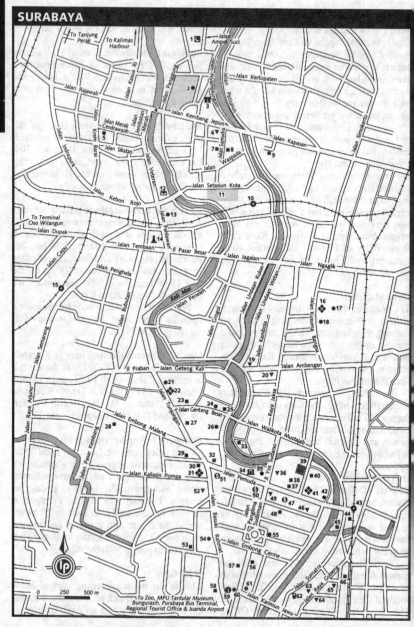

SURABAYA

To Tanjung Perak
To Kalimas Harbour

Jalan Ampel Suci
1

Jalan Kertopaten

Jalan Rajawali
Jalan Kasua Ri
Jalan Pangsud
Jalan Nyamplungan
Jalan Pattang

2

3

Jalan Kembang Jepun

Jalan Merak
Cendrawasih
Jalan Zembatan
Merah
Jalan Veteran
Jalan Samudra
Jalan Waspada
Jalan Kapasan

6

7
8
9

Krem Burai
Jalan Sikatan

5

Jalan Indrapura

Jalan Smokerto

Jalan Setasiun Kota
12
11
10

Jalan Kebon Rojo

To Terminal
Oso Wilangun
Jalan Dupak
13

Jalan Tembaan
Jalan Tembaan
14
Jl Pasar Besar

Jalan Penghela

Jalan Bubutan
Jalan Cepu
Kali Mas
Jalan Peneleh

15

Jalan Semarang

Jalan Grogol
Jalan Undaan Kulon
Jalan Undaan Wetan
Jalan Kambojo
Jalan Kusuma Bangsa

16
17
18

Jl Praban Jalan Geteng Kali
19
Jalan Ambengan
20

Jalan Raya Arjuno
Jalan Tunjungan
21
22
23
24
25
Jalan Genteng Besar
26
27
Jalan Walikota Mustajab
Raya Jaksa

Jalan Embong Malang
28
Jalan Pasar Kembang
29
32
33
Jl Yos Sudarso
34
35
39
Jalan Kaliasin Pompa
30
31
51
36
38
37
40
41
42
Jalan Pemuda
52
50
49
47
46
48
43
44
45
Panglima Sudirman
Jalan Basuki
54
55
Rahmat
Jalan Embong Cerme
53
57
56
Jalan Sumatra
Jalan Raya Gabeng
58
59
60
61
62
63
65
66
64
Jalan Karimun Jawa

To Zoo, MPU Tantular Museum,
Bungurasih, Purabaya Bus Terminal,
Regional Tourist Office & Juanda Airport

0   250   500 m

PLACES TO STAY

7	Hotel Semut
8	Hotel Irian
9	Hotel Ganefo
23	Hotel Paviljoen
25	Weta Hotel
27	Hotel Majapahit
28	Westin Hotel
29	Sheraton Hotel; Bongos
30	Hotel Tunjungan
32	Natour Simpang
33	Bamboe Denn
37	Garden Palace Hotel
38	Garden Hotel
40	Radisson Plaza Suite Hotel
44	Sahid Surabaya Hotel
45	Hotel Gubeng
48	Hotel Remaja
53	Cendana Hotel
56	Tanjung Hotel
57	Elmi Hotel
58	Hyatt Regency Surabaya; Garuda Office
66	Puri Kencana Hotel

PLACES TO EAT

6	Kiet Wan Kie
19	Soto Ambengan
20	Cafe Venezia
36	Zangrandi Ice Cream Palace
46	Turin
49	Granada Modern Bakery
52	Galael Supermarket; KFC; Swensen's
63	Boncafé
64	Ria Galeria
65	Restoran Kuningan International

OTHER

1	Mesjid Ampel
2	Pasar Pabean
3	Kong Co Kong Tik Cun Ong
4	Jembatan Merah Bridge
5	Gedung PTP XXII
10	Kota Train Station
11	Pasar Atum Market; Bandara Terminal 1
12	Main Post Office; Wasantara-Net
13	Pelni Office

14	Tugu Pahlawan
15	Pasar Turi Train Station
16	Surabaya Mall
17	Taman Hiburan Rakyat (THR)
18	Taman Remaja
21	Tunjungan Centre
22	Sarinah Department Store
24	Pasar Genteng
26	Andhika Plaza
31	Tunjungan Plaza; Wartel; Top Ten; Vagatour
34	Governor's Residence
35	Mitra Cinema
39	World Trade Centre
41	Plaza Surabaya
42	Monumen Kapal Selam
43	Gubeng Train Station; Merpati
47	BII Bank
50	BNI Bank
51	Bank Duta
54	Minibus Agents
55	Goethe Institut
59	Surabaya Area Tourist Office
60	Bouraq Office
61	Hargono Tours & Travel
62	Colors

Indonesia was a rich country, this part of the city would have been renovated years ago to become fashionable real estate. As it is, much of this culturally mixed area is sadly run-down but efforts have been made to clean it up.

It was at **Jembatan Merah** that Brigadier Mallaby, chief of the British forces, was killed in the lead up to the bloody battle of Surabaya for Indonesian independence. Run-down but worthy examples of **Dutch architecture** can be seen in the area. Jl Jembatan Merah, running south of the bus terminal along the canal, is a grungy replica of Amsterdam. The area further south around the post office and Pelni office also has some fine buildings, though the most impressive is the Indo-European-style Gedung PTP XXII government office building, just west of Jl Jembatan Merah, along Jl Cendrawasih.

To the east of Jembatan Merah is Surabaya's **Chinatown**, where hundreds of small businesses and warehouses ply their trade. Becaks and hand-pulled carts are still the best way to transport goods in the crowded, narrow streets. **Pasar Pabean** on Jl Pabean is a sprawling, darkly lit market, where you can buy everything from Madurese chickens to Chinese crockery.

Further east, on Jl Dukuh near the canal, **Kong Co Kong Tik Cun Ong** temple is primarily Buddhist but has a variety of Confucian and Taoist altars. On the full moon, wayang performances are held here.

The highlight of a visit to the old city is **Mesjid Ampel**, in the heart of the Arab quarter. From the Kong Co Kong Tik Cun Ong temple, proceed north along Jl Nyamplungan and then take the second left down Jl Sasak. A crowd of becaks marks the way to the mosque. Through the arched stone entrance is Jl Ampel Suci, a narrow, covered bazaar with perfumes, sarongs, *pecis* (hats) and other religious paraphernalia for sale. Follow the pilgrims past the beggars to the mosque. This is the most sacred mosque in Surabaya; as it was here that Sunan Ampel, one of the wali songo who brought

Islam to Java, was buried in 1481. Pilgrims chant and offer rose petal offerings at the grave behind the mosque.

From the old city you can then head north to the **Kalimas harbour**, where brightly painted pinisi schooners from Sulawesi and Kalimantan unload their wares. This is a far less touristed version of Jakarta's Sunda Kelapa.

Surabaya Zoo

On Jl Diponegoro, 4km south of Jl Pemuda, the Surabaya Zoo (Kebun Binatang) specialises in nocturnal animals, exotic birds and fish. The animals look just as bored as they do in any other zoo, but the park is quite well laid out, with large open enclosures, and a great collection of pelicans and lively otters. The dazed-looking Komodo dragons are the highlight for most visitors.

The zoo is open from 7 am to 4 pm. Entry costs 2000Rp. Sunday is crowded and entertainment is often featured in the afternoon. Any bus heading down Jl Panglima Sudirman, such as P1 (1000Rp), will take you to the zoo or take an M bemo (700Rp).

MPU Tantular Museum

Across the road from the zoo, this small historical and archaeological museum has some interesting Majapahit artefacts, and is housed in a superb example of Dutch architecture. It is open Sunday to Friday from 8 am to 2 pm, and Saturday 7 am to 1 pm.

Taman Remaja & Taman Hiburan Rakyat

This 'Youth Park' is a neglected cultural park behind the Surabaya Mall shopping centre. The Aneka Ria theatre in the park is home to a *srimulat* (East Javanese folk comedy) company, with performances held on Thursday and Saturday from 8 pm. The cost is 3000Rp for this raucous, slapstick theatre. Other dance and theatre is held at the park. On Thursday evening, transvestites perform to dangdut music.

Next door, the Taman Hiburan Rakyat (People's Amusement Park) is open from 5 to 10.30 pm; admission is 1300Rp.

Monumen Kapal Selam

On Jl Pemuda, this attempt at riverside rejuvenation revolves around the *Pasopati*, a Russian submarine commissioned into the Indonesian navy in 1962. This is yet another 'monument' glorifying the Indonesian armed forces, but the sub has some 'Boys' Own' interest. Entry is 1000Rp into the small landscaped park, which has a couple of cafes, and another 1000Rp into the sub. It's open daily from 8.30 am to 9 pm.

Places to Stay – Budget

The *Bamboe Denn* (☎ 5340333, Jl Ketabang Kali 6A), a 20 minute walk from Gubeng train station, is a Surabaya institution and has been the No 1 travellers' centre in Surabaya for over 20 years. Beds in the large dorm are 9000Rp and a few tiny, very basic singles/doubles cost 9500/17,000Rp. You may well get roped into a little English conversation with Indonesian students at the language school that operates from here.

Across the river, the *Hotel Paviljoen* (☎ 5343449, Jl Genteng Besar 94) is the next best bet. The friendly owners of this stylish old colonial building speak Dutch and English. Rooms with mandi cost 32,000Rp and 36,000Rp, or air-con rooms approaching mid-range standard cost 50,000Rp and 60,000Rp. Breakfast is included.

Most of Surabaya's other cheap accommodation is uninspiring, and some of the mid-range hotels are only slightly more expensive and much better value.

The very basic *Hotel Gubeng* (☎ 5031603, Jl Sumatra 18) is close to Gubeng train station. It has rooms with shared mandi at the back for 30,000Rp or noisy high-ceiling rooms with mandi at the front for 40,000Rp.

Plenty of cheap hotels can be found near Kota train station. It's an interesting area but it's a long way from the city centre so few travellers stay this far north. *Hotel Ganefo* (☎ 364880, Jl Kapasan 169-171) has a fantastic colonial lobby. The rooms are very simple, and cost 30,000Rp with shared mandi or big rooms with mandi are 40,000Rp. Rooms in the new section with mandi, air-con, TV and telephone are

50,000Rp. The *Hotel Irian* (☎ 20953, Jl Samudra 16) has some colonial style. Basic rooms with shared mandi around the garden cost 30,000Rp. Rooms with mandi in the old colonial building cost 40,000Rp, or 42,000Rp to 50,000Rp with air-con.

Places to Stay – Mid-Range

Surabaya has a wide selection of mid-range accommodation and competition is fierce, particularly at the top of this range. All of these hotels have rooms with air-con, hot water and TV.

Puri Kencana Hotel (☎ 5033161, Jl Kalimantan 9) is a small, well kept hotel near Gubeng train station. Standard rooms are small and some are dark, but they are a very good deal at 45,000Rp. Larger and lighter rooms are 50,000Rp and 60,000Rp.

Hotel Semut (☎ 3559850, Jl Samudra 9-15) in the old part of town dates from the Art Deco era. It has good-sized rooms facing large verandahs around a central quadrangle. Air-con rooms are good value at 50,000Rp or 65,000Rp with minibar, plus 21%.

Surabaya has some central mid-range hotels just south of Jl Pemuda. Rooms are a little dark in these older but well maintained hotels. *Hotel Remaja* (☎ 5341359, Jl Embong Kenongo 12), in a quiet street just behind Jl Pemuda, has tidy singles/doubles for 61,000/73,000Rp. Nearby, the *Tanjung Hotel* (☎ 5344032, Jl Panglima Sudirman 43-45) is a larger hotel with a variety of rooms from 81,000Rp to 127,000Rp (before discount).

Moving right up the scale, the *Hotel Tunjungan* (☎ 5466666, Jl Tunjungan 102-104) is an excellent three star hotel right next to Tunjungan Plaza. It has a pool and large rooms with all the trimmings for 150,000Rp, including buffet breakfast. Nearby, the *Cendana Hotel* (☎ 5455333, Jl Kombes Pol M Doeryat 6) is another of the newer hotels and also a good buy, though it doesn't have a pool. Well appointed rooms with minibar cost 138,000Rp after discount, including buffet breakfast.

Among the older hotels, all charging around 150,000Rp, the *Sahid Surabaya*

Hotel (☎ 5322711, Jl Sumatra 1) has no pool but good rooms and is right next to Gubeng train station. The *Elmi Hotel* (☎ 5322571, Jl Panglima Sudirman 42-44) is more expensive with rooms at 200,000Rp, but it has a fitness centre, large pool, renovated rooms and good service.

Places to Stay – Top End

Surabaya has a glut of luxury hotels and competition is cut throat.

The *Garden Palace Hotel* (☎ 5321001, Jl Yos Sudarso 11) is an older four star hotel, with rooms as low as 137,500Rp and 199,000Rp after discount.

The ritzier *Radisson Plaza Suite Hotel* (☎ 516833, Jl Pemuda 31-37) is in an excellent position. It has a variety of rooms and suites from US$180 to US$550, but discounts are as low as 300,000Rp.

The five star *Hyatt Regency Surabaya* (☎ 5311234, Jl Basuki Rahmat 124-128) has long been one of Surabaya's best hotels. Plush rooms start at US$180.

The central *Hotel Majapahit* (☎ 545 4333, Jl Tunjungan 65) is a superb colonial hotel built in 1910. Originally the Oranje Hotel, it bears a striking resemblance to Schomberg's hotel described in Joseph Conrad's *Victory*. In 1945 the returning colonial forces hoisted the Dutch flag, an incident which helped spark the independence Battle of Surabaya. Recent renovations have restored the hotel to one of Surabaya's finest. Brochure rates start at US$220 but discounts are as low as US$50.

All the big chains are represented in Surabaya – the Hilton, Shangri-La, Novotel and Westin – but the *Sheraton* (☎ 5468000, Jl Embong Malang 25) has the best position adjoining Tunjungan Plaza. Superior rooms cost from US$140/150. Weekend packages start at 350,000Rp.

Places to Eat

For cheap eats, Pasar Genteng on Jl Genteng Besar has good night warungs. Most other eateries in the city centre are mid-range shopping mall restaurants.

The ground floor of the Plaza Surabaya has the *Food Plaza*, with a range of restaurants serving Indonesian, Thai, Italian and American fast food. The best deal is the *Food Bazaar* on the 4th floor, with a large variety of moderately priced stalls.

The huge Tunjungan Plaza has a much bigger selection of restaurants and fast-food outlets starting on the lower level of Tunjungan Plaza II. The 4th and 5th floors have a number of restaurants. The 5th floor of the adjoining Tunjungan Plaza III has an excellent food court, including *Suroboyo* for East Javanese dishes and *Jimbaran* for ikan bakar.

Zangrandi Ice Cream Palace (Jl Yos Sudarso 15) is an old establishment parlour favoured by wealthy Surabayans. Relax in planters' chairs at low tables and somehow ignore the traffic noise. Another good place for ice cream and Chinese food is the *Turin* on Jl Embong Kenongo.

At *Soto Ambengan (Jl Ambengan No 3A)*, enjoy Pak Sadi's famed lemon grass and coriander Madurese chicken soup. This simple restaurant is a Surabaya institution, or if you prefer a more sanitised version an offshoot is attached to the Suroboyo restaurant on the 5th floor of Tunjungan Plaza III.

Cafe Venezia (Jl Ambengan 16) is a very classy establishment in an old villa with a delightful garden. Considering the setting, the prices are very reasonable. The menu has steaks (around 16,000Rp), Korean BBQ, Japanese dishes and ice cream.

The best area for mid-range restaurants is south of Gubeng train station along Jl Raya Gubeng. Most are housed in impressive colonial buildings, like the *Restoran Kuningan International (Jl Kalimantan 14)*, just off Jl Raya Gubeng. It has a large, mixed menu and seafood is a speciality. *Boncafé (Jl Raya Gubeng 46)* has a big menu of mostly western dishes and grills. *Ria Galeria (Jl Bangka 2)* is housed in a beautiful old villa and is a great spot for reasonably priced Indonesian food.

Entertainment
Bars at the big hotels are the happening places and often have decent bands perform-

ing. Try *Desperado's* at the Shangri-La Hotel *(Jl May Jen Sungkono 120)*, 6km south-west of the city centre, or *Bongos* in the Sheraton.

Colors (Jl Sumatra 81) is a small venue in a historic villa. It has cheaper beers than the other nightclubs and a friendly atmosphere. Bands play nightly until 2 am. Meals and snacks are served.

Surabayans are big on discos. Popular places include *Top Ten* in Tunjungan Plaza and *Bandara Terminal 1* in Pasar Atum near Kota train station.

Cinema complexes are found all around the city. *Mitra Cinema* at the back of the Balai Pemuda building on Jl Pemuda, and *Tunjungan 21* in Tunjungan Plaza show recent Hollywood releases for around 8000Rp.

Getting There & Away
Air Surabaya has a number of international connections, though services are rapidly diminishing. The most popular flights are Singapore Airlines (☎ 5319218) and Garuda flights to Singapore (US$180). Flights also go to Kuala Lumpur, Bangkok and Hong Kong.

Surabaya is an important hub for domestic flights, including Denpasar (316,000Rp); Jakarta (720,500Rp); Bandung (531,000Rp); Yogyakarta (269,000Rp); Ujung Pandang (800,500Rp); Balikpapan (749,000Rp); Banjarmasin (526,000Rp); and other connections.

Merpati (☎ 5688111), Jl Raya Darmo 111, is south of the city centre. It also has a convenient 24 hour office (☎ 5033991) at Gubeng train station. The Garuda office (☎ 5321525) is at the Hyatt Regency Surabaya, Jl Basuki Rachmat 124. Bouraq (☎ 5452918) is at Jl Panglima Sudirman 70. Mandala (☎ 5678973) is at Jl Raya Diponegoro 73.

Travel agents sell domestic tickets at a small discount and international tickets with a bigger cut. Agents include Haryono Tours & Travel (☎ 5327300), Jl Panglima Sudirman 93, opposite the Bouraq office, and Vayatour (☎ 5319235) in the Tunjungan Plaza.

Bus Most buses operate from Surabaya's main Purabaya bus terminal, 10km south of the city centre at Bungurasih. Crowded Damri buses run between the bus terminal and the city centre – the P1 service (1000Rp) from the bus terminal is best and can drop you at the Jl Tunjungan/Jl Pemuda intersection. A metered taxi costs around 12,000Rp. Buses along the north coast and to Semarang depart from the Terminal Oso Wilangun, 10km west of the city.

Normal/patas buses from Purabaya include: Pandaan (1500Rp, one hour); Malang (2500/5500Rp, two hours); Blitar (3000/4500Rp, four hours); Probolinggo (3000/6000Rp, two hours); Banyuwangi (9500/17,500Rp, six hours); Bondowoso (7500Rp, 4½ hours); Solo (9000/15,000Rp, 6½ hours); and Yogya (10,500/17,500Rp, eight hours). Buses also operate from Purabaya bus terminal to Madura and Semarang.

Luxury buses from Purabaya also do the long hauls to Solo, Yogya, Bandung, Bogor, Denpasar and further afield. Most are night buses leaving in the late afternoon/evening. Bookings can be made at Purabaya bus terminal, or travel agents in the city centre sell tickets with a mark-up. The most convenient bus agents are those on Jl Basuki Rahmat. Intercity buses are not allowed to enter the city so you will have to go to Purabaya to catch your bus.

From Oso Wilangun terminal, buses go to the north coast towns of Gresik (1000Rp), Tuban (3000Rp), Kudus (8000Rp) and Semarang (10,500/17,500Rp normal/air-con).

Minibus Door-to-door travel minibuses pick up at hotels, thus saving a long haul to the bus terminal, but they are not always quicker because it can take a long time to pick up a full load of passengers in sprawling Surabaya.

Minibuses run from Surabaya to all the major towns in East Java and to the rest of Java and Bali. Destinations and sample fares include: Malang (12,000Rp); Denpasar (50,000Rp); Solo (27,000Rp); Yogya (27,000Rp); and Semarang (37,500Rp). Hotels can make bookings and arrange pick-up or agents, such as Tirta Jaya (☎ 5468687), Jl Basuki Rahmat 64, and Tunggal (☎ 532 3069), Jl Basuki Rahmat 70, can arrange it.

Train Trains from Jakarta, taking the fast northern route via Semarang, arrive at the Pasar Turi train station. Trains taking the southern route via Yogya, and trains from Banyuwangi and Malang, arrive at Gubeng and most carry on to Kota. Gubeng train station (☎ 5340080) is much more central and sells tickets for all trains.

Most Jakarta trains leave from Pasar Turi and range from ekonomi services, such as the *Gaya Baru Malam Utara* (13,500Rp, 13 hours) to the luxury *Anggrek* (185,000Rp, nine hours) and the *Argo Bromo* (140,000Rp, nine hours). From Gubeng, night trains along the longer southern route via Yogya range from the ekonomi *Gaya Baru Malam* (13,500Rp, 16 hours) to the *Bima* (115,000Rp eksekutif, 12 hours).

The *Sancaka* is the best day train, leaving at 7.15 am to Solo (3½ hours) and Yogyakarta (4½ hours). It costs 25,000/40,000Rp in bisnis/eksekutif to either destination. The train is much faster than the buses. The 8.54 am *Purbaya* (6000Rp, seven hours) and the faster 1.14 pm *Sri Tanjung* (7000Rp, six hours) are reasonable ekonomi services to Yogya's Lempungan train station via Solo.

Apart from services to the main cities, seven trains per day go to Malang (two hours) and most continue on to Blitar. The *Mutiara* goes to Banyuwangi (18,000/28,000Rp in bisnis/eksekutif, six hours) via Probolinggo at 8.15 am and 10.15 pm, or the ekonomi *Sri Tanjung* (7000Rp, 6½ hours) departs at 2.10 pm.

Boat Surabaya is an important port and a major travel hub for ships to the other islands.

Popular Pelni connections run to Sulawesi, with several ships running direct to Ujung Pandang (67,500/228,000Rp ekonomi/1st class) and to Kalimantan: Banjarmasin (48,500Rp to 162,500Rp) and Pontianak (83,000Rp to 282,000Rp). See the Getting Around chapter for Pelni route details.

The Pelni ticket office, Jl Pahlawan 112, is open Monday to Friday from 9 am to 3 pm and on weekends until noon if there are ship departures. Boats depart from Tanjung Perak harbour – bus P1 or C will get you there.

Ferries to Kamal on Madura (550Rp, 30 minutes) leave every 40 minutes from Tanjung Perak, at the end of Jl Kalimas Baru.

Getting Around

To/From the Airport Taxis from the Juanda airport (15km) operate on a coupon system and cost 17,000Rp to the city centre. The Damri airport bus (3000Rp) runs infrequently between 8 am and 3 pm and goes to Purabaya bus terminal and then on to the city centre.

Bus Surabaya has an extensive Damri city bus network, with normal buses (300Rp flat rate) and patas buses (1000Rp per journey). They can be very crowded, especially the normal buses, and are a hassle if you have luggage.

One of the most useful services is the patas P1 bus, which runs from Purabaya bus terminal past the zoo and into the city along Jl Basuki Rahmat. It then turns down Jl Embong Malang and continues on to the Pasar Turi train station, the Pelni office and Tanjung Perak harbour. In the reverse direction, catch it on Jl Tunjungan or at the bus stop in front of the Natour Simpang hotel on Jl Pemuda. The normal C buses also cover the same route.

Surabaya also has plenty of bemos labelled A, B, C etc, and all charge 500Rp to 700Rp, depending on the length of the journey. Bemo M runs to the zoo.

Taxi Surabaya has air-con metered taxis charging 1800Rp for the first kilometre and 900Rp for subsequent kilometres. Typical fares from central Surabaya are: Pelni office (5000Rp), Tanjung Perak harbour (9000Rp), zoo (6000Rp), Bamboe Denn hotel to Gubeng train station (3500Rp), and Purabaya bus terminal (12,000Rp). Surabaya also has yellow *angguna* pick-ups that are nonmetered taxis – bargaining is required.

AROUND SURABAYA

Pandaan

Pandaan is 40km south of Surabaya on the road to Tretes. At **Candra Wilwatika** Amphitheatre (☎ 31841) modern Javanese ballet performances take place once a month from June to October, but performances have been irregular since the economic crisis. The varied program usually consists of dances based on indigenous tales and East Javanese history. To reach the amphitheatre take a bus from Surabaya, and then a Tretes-bound Colt. The theatre is 1km from Pandaan, right on the main road to Tretes.

Also on the main road to Tretes, a few kilometres from Pandaan before Pringen, **Candi Jawi** is an early 14th century Hindu temple. It is basically a Shivaite structure built to honour King Kertanegara. A Buddhist stupa was a later addition.

Tretes

☎ 0343

This hill town, standing at an 800m altitude on the slopes of Arjuna and Welirang mountains, is renowned for its cool climate and fine views. Tretes also has a reputation as a weekend red-light district. If you have to kill time in Surabaya, it can be a pleasant enough place to escape to. **Kakek Bodo** (Stupid Grandfather), **Putuh Truno** and **Alap-alap** waterfalls are nearby, and there are several interesting walks around the town, including the trek to the Lalijiwo Plateau and Gunung Arjuna.

The **PPLH Environmental Education Centre** (☎ 5614493) is near Trawas, a few kilometres north-west of Tretes. It has hiking/accommodation packages, mostly for groups, but interested volunteers are welcome to stay in the rustic bungalows and do self-guided forest walks. Take a bus to Pandaan, then a Trawas bemo (ask for PPLH) and then take an ojek.

Places to Stay & Eat Accommodation in Tretes is expensive but keep an eye out for special deals, especially at the big hotels. The best place to stay is towards the top of the hill, while hotels lower down around Prigen are cheaper. Cottages can be rented for longer stays. Unattached males looking for a room are considered an oddity, especially at the cheap hotels.

Starting near the top of the hill, the three star *Natour Bath Tretes Hotel* (☎ 81776) is an 'old money' hotel with some style and a good range of facilities. Large, slightly run-down rooms cost as little as US$20 after discount.

Opposite the Natour, the *Kalimas Hotel* (Jl Pesanggrahan 26) has small but tidy rooms with bathroom and welcome hot water for 30,000Rp and 40,000Rp.

The *Lie Mas Hotel* (☎ 82091, Jl Pesang-grahan) has fine views with rooms on different levels down the hillside. This good mid-range hotel has rooms from 80,000Rp (less during the week) with hot-water.

On the main road near the Natour Bath Tretes Hotel, *Mess Garuda* is a bottom of the barrel cheapie with rooms for 20,000Rp during the week. The *Wisma Semeru Indah* (☎ 81701, Jl Semeru 7), down from the main shopping area, has rooms from 40,000Rp.

The other luxury hotel competing with the Natour is the *Hotel Surya* (☎ 81991), a concrete-and-glass upstart with a huge heated pool, a fitness centre and tennis court. Rooms cost from US$75.

For cheap eats, *Depot Abadi* (Jl Raya 27) opposite the Mess Garuda has standard fare. A line of mid-range restaurants can be found along the road from the Natour Bath Tretes Hotel, including the *Mandarin* for Chinese food and the *Istana Ayam Goreng* for chicken.

Getting There & Away From Surabaya take a bus to Pandaan (1500Rp) and then a minibus to Tretes.

Gunung Arjuna-Lalijiwo Reserve

This reserve includes the dormant volcano Arjuna (3339m), the semi-active Gunung Welirang (3156m) and the Lalijiwo Plateau on the north slopes of Arjuna. Experienced and well equipped hikers can walk from Tretes to Selekta in two days, but you need a guide to go all the way. Alternatively, you can just climb Welirang from Tretes.

A well used hiking path, popular with students on weekends and holidays, begins in Tretes at the Kakak Bodo Recreation Reserve. Get information from the PHPA post at the entrance to the waterfall before heading off. It's a hard five hour, 17km walk to the huts, used by the Gunung Welirang sulphur collectors.

It is usual to overnight at the huts in order to reach the summit before the clouds and mist roll in around mid-morning. Bring your own camping gear, food and drinking water, and be prepared for freezing conditions. From the huts it's a 4km climb to the summit. Allow at least six hours in total for the ascent, and 4½ hours for the descent. You can also rent horses, but hard bargaining is required.

The trail passes Lalijiwo Plateau, a superb alpine meadow, from where a trail leads to Gunung Arjuna, the more demanding peak. From Arjuna a trail leads down the southern side to Junggo, near Selekta and Batu. It's a five hour descent from Arjuna this way, but a guide is essential.

Gunung Penanggungan

The remains of no less than 81 temples are scattered over the slopes of Gunung Penanggungan (1650m), a sacred Hindu mountain said to be the peak of sacred Mt Mahameru, which broke off and landed at its present site when Mt Mahameru was transported from India to Indonesia.

This was an important pilgrimage site for Hindus. Pilgrims made their way to the top of the mountain and stopped to bathe in the holy springs adorned with Hindu statuary. The two main bathing places are **Jolotundo** and **Belahan**, the best examples of remaining Hindu art. Both are difficult to reach.

TROWULAN

Trowulan was once the capital of the largest Hindu empire in Indonesian history. Founded by a Singosari prince Wijaya in 1294, it reached the height of its power under Hayam Wuruk (1350-89), who was guided by his powerful prime minister, Gajah Mada. During his time Majapahit claimed control over, or at least received tribute from, most of the regions encompassing present-day Indonesia and even parts of the Malay peninsula. The capital was a grand affair, the kraton forming a miniature city within the city, surrounded by great fortified walls and watchtowers.

Its wealth was based both on the fertile rice-growing plains of Java and on control of the spice trade. The religion was a hybrid of Hinduism, with worship of the deities Shiva, Vishnu and Brahma; however, as in earlier Javanese kingdoms, Buddhism was also prominent. It seems Muslims too were tolerated, and Koranic burial inscriptions found on the site suggest that Javanese Muslims resided within the royal court even in the 14th century when this Hindu-Buddhist state was at the height of its glory. The empire came to a sudden end in 1478 when the city fell to the north coast power of Demak and the Majapahit elite fled to Bali, thus opening up Java for conquest by the Muslims.

The remains of Majapahit are scattered over a large area around the small village of Trowulan, 12km from Mojokerto. The Majapahit temples were mainly built from red clay bricks and did not stand the test of time. Many have been rebuilt and are relatively simple compared to the glories of Central Java, such as Borobudur, but the numerous temples give a good idea of what was once a great city. It's possible to walk around the sites in one day if you start early, or you can hire a becak. Given the heat and the fact that the temples are spread over a large area, a car is ideal.

Trowulan Museum

One kilometre from the main Surabaya-Solo road, this museum houses superb examples of Majapahit sculpture and pottery from East Java. Pride of place is the splendid statue of Kediri's King Airlangga-as-Vishnu astride a huge Garuda, taken from Belahan. It should be your first port of call for an understanding of Trowulan and Majapahit history, and it includes descriptions of the other ancient ruins in East Java. The museum is open daily from 7 am to 4 pm, except Monday and public holidays.

Ruins

Some of the most interesting sites include the **Kolam Segaran** (a vast Majapahit swimming pool); the gateway of **Bajang Ratu**, with its strikingly sculptured kala heads; the **Tikus Temple** (Queen's Bath); and the **Siti Inggil Temple**, with the impressive tomb of Wijaya (people still come to meditate here and in the early evening it has a strong spiritual atmosphere). The **Pendopo Agung** is an open-air pavilion built by the Indonesian army. Two kilometres south of the pavilion, the **Troloyo cemetery** is the site of the oldest Muslim graves found in Java, the earliest dating from 1376 AD.

Places to Stay & Eat

Trowulan has a few *restaurants* on the highway but no accommodation. If you want to stay nearby, Mojokerto has plenty of cheap hotels (the *Wisma Tenera* is a good choice).

Getting There & Away

Trowulan can be visited from Surabaya, 60km to the east.

From Surabaya's Purabaya bus terminal it's a one hour trip to Trowulan. Take a Jombang bus, which can drop you at the turn-off to the museum, or a Mojokerto bus which will stop at the bus terminal on the outskirts of town, then a bemo (500Rp) to Trowulan. A becak tour of the sites will cost around 10,000Rp to 15,000Rp with bargaining.

When leaving Trowulan, flag a bus down on the road from Surabaya to Solo. Heading east to Probolinggo or south to Malang, take a bus or Colt to Gempol and continue from there by public bus, which is cheaper. For Malang, an interesting alternative is to travel by bus via Jombang and the hill town of Batu.

MADURA

● pop 3 million

Madura is a large and rugged island, about 160km long by 35km wide, separated from Surabaya on the East Java coast by a narrow channel. It is famous for its colourful bull races, kerapan sapi, but it also has several historical sites, some passable beaches and an interesting traditional culture. The sarong and *peci* are still the norm – mall fever has not found its way to Madura. Very few tourists stay beyond a day trip to the bull races.

The people of Madura have settled widely in East Java, particularly in Surabaya, on the north coast and around Banyuwangi. Up to 10 million Madurese live outside the island. Since independence, Madura has been governed as part of the province of East Java, but the island has had a long tradition of involvement with its larger neighbour, Java, and with the Dutch. The Dutch were not interested in the island itself, which was initially of little economic importance, but rather in the crucial role the Madurese played in Javanese dynastic politics.

Madurese men claim that the name Madura is derived from *madu* (honey) and *dara* (girl), and Madurese women are, so the story goes, known throughout Java for their sexual prowess. Madura is, however, a very traditional and devoutly Islamic society. The Madurese are rugged kasar (unrefined) people according to the Javanese, and are said to be adept at wielding knives when disputes arise. While the Madurese can be disconcertingly blunt at times, and in remote areas you may attract a crowd of curious onlookers, they can also be extremely hospitable.

The southern side of the island, facing Java, is shallow beach and cultivated lowland, while the northern coast alternates between rocky cliffs and great rolling sand dune beaches, the best of which is at Lombang. At the extreme east is tidal marsh and vast tracts of salt around Kalianget. The interior of this flat, arid island is riddled with limestone slopes, and is either rocky or sandy, so agriculture is limited. There are goat farms, tobacco estates, and extensive stands of coconut palms, but the main industries of this dry, sunburnt land are cattle, salt and fishing.

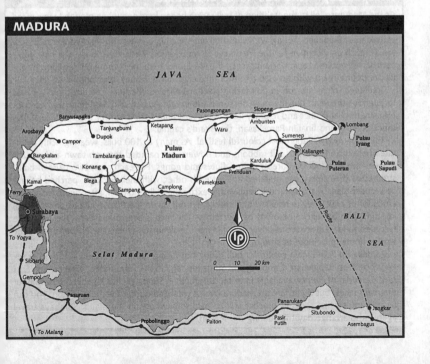

MADURA

History

In 1624 the island was conquered by Sultan Agung of Mataram and its government united under one Madurese princely line, the Cakraningrats. Until the middle of the 18th century the Cakraningrat family fiercely opposed Central Javanese rule and harassed Mataram, often conquering large parts of the kingdom. Prince Raden Trunojoyo even managed to carry off the royal treasury of Mataram in 1677, which was restored only after the Dutch intervened and stormed Trunojoyo's stronghold at Kediri.

In 1705 the Dutch secured control of the eastern half of Madura following the conflict of the First Javanese War of Succession between Amangkurat III and his uncle, Pangeran Puger. Dutch recognition of Puger was largely influenced by Cakraningrat II, the lord of West Madura. He probably supported Puger's claims simply because he hoped a new war in Central Java would give the Madurese a chance to interfere but, while Amangkurat was arrested and exiled to Ceylon, Puger took the title of Pakubuwono I and concluded a treaty with the Dutch which, along with large concessions in Java, granted them East Madura.

The Cakraningrats fared little better by agreeing to help the Dutch put down the rebellion in Central Java that broke out after the Chinese massacre in 1740. Although Cakraningrat IV attempted to contest the issue, a treaty was eventually signed in 1743 in which Pakubuwono II ceded full sovereignty of Madura to the Dutch. Cakraningrat fled to Banjarmasin and took refuge on an English ship but was robbed, betrayed by the sultan

Kerapan Sapi – the Bull Races of Madura

As the Madurese tell it, the tradition of bull racing began long ago when plough teams raced each other across the arid fields. This pastime was encouraged by Panembahan Sumolo, an early king of Sumenep. Today, with stud-bull breeding big business on Madura, *kerapan sapi* are as much an incentive for the Madurese to breed good stock. Only bulls of a high standard can be entered for important races – the Madurese keep their young bulls in superb condition, dosing them with an assortment of medicinal herbs, honey, beer and raw eggs.

Traditional races are run in bull-racing stadiums all over Madura. Practice trials are held throughout the year, but the main season starts in late August and September, when contests are held at district and regency level. The finest bulls fight it out for the big prize in October at the grand final in Pamekasan, the island's capital.

This is the biggest and most colourful festival. As many as 100 bulls, wearing richly decorated halters and yokes of gilt, ribbons and flowers, are paraded through town and around the stadium to a loud fanfare of drums, flutes and gongs. For each race, two pairs of bulls, stripped of their finery, are matched against each other, with their 'jockeys' perched behind on wooden sleds. Gamelan music is played to excite the bulls and then, after being fed a generous tot of arak, they're released and charge flat out down the track – just as often plunging right into the excited crowds of spectators! The race is over in a flash – the best time recorded so far is nine seconds over 100m. After the elimination heats the victors are proudly trotted home to be used at stud.

Pamekasan is the main centre for bull racing but racing can also be seen in the other regency centres, Bangkalan, Sampang and Sumenep, and in the surrounding villages. The *East Java Calendar of Events*, available from tourist offices in Surabaya, has a general schedule for the main races, but if you are on Madura over a weekend during the main season, you can be guaranteed that races or practice will be held somewhere on the island. Surabaya travel agents also arrange day trips during the season.

and finally captured by the Dutch and exiled to the Cape of Good Hope (South Africa).

Under the Dutch, Madura continued as four states, each with its own regent. Madura was initially important as a major source of colonial troops, but in the second half of the 19th century it acquired greater economic value as the main supplier of salt to Dutch-governed areas of the archipelago.

Getting There & Away

Ferries sail to Kamal (500Rp, 30 minutes), the port town on the western tip of Madura, roughly every half-hour around the clock from Surabaya's Tanjung Perak harbour. From the centre of town to Tanjung Perak, take the P1 express city bus (1000Rp) or a C bus. Buses go directly from Surabaya's Purabaya bus terminal via the ferry right to Sumenep (6000Rp; 10,000Rp air-con), or catch them at the harbour. Buses also run right across to Sumenep from Banyuwangi via Probolinggo, Denpasar, Malang, Semarang and Jakarta.

Another possibility, if coming from the east, is to take the passenger and car ferry from Jangkar harbour (near Asembagus) to Kalianget (6500Rp, four hours) on the eastern tip of Madura. The ferry departs from Jangkar daily at 1.30 pm. Buses run from Situbondo to Jangkar, or take a bus to Asembagus, then a becak or andong for the 4.5km trip to Jangkar. From Kalianget, the ferry departs from Kalianget at 7.30 am. To Kalianget take an 'O' Colt from Sumenep (500Rp, 11km).

Getting Around

On arrival on the ferry from Surabaya, Colts run from Kamal to Terminal Baru on the southern outskirts of Bangkalan. From here, Colts run along the main highway to Bangkalan (800Rp, 30 minutes), Pamekasan (3500Rp, 2½ hours) and Sumenep (5000Rp, four hours). If heading straight to Sumenep, try to get on a bus at Tanjung Perak in Surabaya.

From Surabaya's Purabaya bus terminal, at least a dozen buses a day go to Madura across the island to Sumenep and most continue to Kalianget. Colts are much more frequent and run all over the island but can spend a lot of time picking up passengers. Colts travel along the northern route to Arosbaya, Tanjungbumi, Pasongsongan and Ambunten.

To see something of the island, it's interesting to take a Colt from Pamekasan inland through tobacco country to Waru, and another to Pasongsongan from where you can head back to Sumenep, via Ambunten and Slopeng.

Madura's roads are almost all paved and in excellent condition with relatively little traffic. As the island is mostly flat, Madura is a good cycling destination, although it does get very hot.

Bangkalan

☎ 031

This is the next town north of Kamal along the coast, and because it is so close to Surabaya many visitors only day trip to watch the bull races. **Museum Cakraningrat** focuses on Madurese history and culture. It's open Monday to Saturday from 8 am to 2 pm.

Places to Stay & Eat The *Hotel Ningrat* (☎ 3095388, Jl Kahaji Muhammed Kholil 113) on the main road south of town is one of Madura's best hotels, though hardly luxurious. Small singles/doubles are 15,000/30,000Rp, and more comfortable rooms with mandi are 40,000Rp. More attractive air-con rooms are decorated in traditional Madurese style and cost 80,000Rp.

Closer to the centre of town, *Hotel Melati* (☎ 3096457, Jl Majen Sungkono 48) is a basic place with rooms for 15,000Rp. It is back from the street down an alleyway.

For good Chinese food, try the *Agung Restaurant (Jl Jaksa Agung Suprapto 23)*.

Sampang

Sampang, 61km from Bangkalan, is the centre of the regency of the same name and also stages bull races. It has a couple of *hotels*.

Camplong

Camplong, 9km further east, is a popular, if grungy, safe swimming beach on the south coast. The Pertamina storage tanks nearby do nothing for its visual appeal, but it is a breezy oasis from the hot interior of Madura. Impressive flotillas of perahu (twin-outrigger dugout canoes) are used for fishing along the coast and carry huge, triangular striped sails.

Places to Stay At Camplong, the *Pondok Wisata Pantai Camplong* (☎ 21569) provides some of the best accommodation on Madura. Attractive cottages on the beach cost 37,500Rp to 60,000Rp.

Pamekasan
☎ 0324

On the southern side of the island, 100km east of Kamal, the capital of Madura is a quiet and pleasant enough town, although during October each year it comes alive with the festivities of the Kerapan Sapi Grand Final. Bull races are held in and around Pamekasan every Sunday from the end of July until the big day in early October. To see tulis batik production, visit Batik Kristal, Jl Jokotole 29, across the road from the BCA bank.

About 35km east of Pamekasan before Bluto, **Karduluk** is a woodcarving centre producing mostly cupboards.

Information The BCA bank, just east of the alun alun on Jl Jokotole, changes money and allows cash advances on credit cards.

Places to Stay In the centre of town opposite the alun alun, *Hotel Garuda* (☎ 22589, *Jl Mesigit 1)* has doubles with shared mandi for 6600Rp, and big, old rooms with mandi for 11,000Rp up to 28,600Rp with air-con. It's good value but lacks atmosphere.

Nearby on the road to Bangkalan, *Hotel Trunojoyo* (☎ 22181, *Jl Trunojoyo 48)* is clean, quiet and better. Rooms cost 8000Rp up to 40,000Rp with air-con, including breakfast.

Hotel Ramayana (☎ 22406, *Jl Niaga 55)* is the best in town. A few small rooms with shared mandi cost 10,000Rp, but most are bright rooms with mandi from 20,000Rp. Air-con rooms start at 35,000Rp.

Sumenep
☎ 0328

At the eastern end of the island, Sumenep is Madura's most interesting town. It is centred around the kraton, mosque and market, and is considered to be the most refined area of Madura. This small, quiet, easy-going town makes a fine base to explore the island.

Sumenep's decaying villas with whitewashed walls, high ceilings and cool porches give the town a Mediterranean air. Sumenep is also a champion bull breeding centre, and on most Saturday mornings practice bull races can be seen at the Giling stadium.

The annual Festival of Sumenep, on 31 October, celebrates the founding of the town, with celebrations and cultural performances.

Information The post office is on the road to Kalianget, and the Telkom office is further out past the Chinese temple. The BCA bank, on Jl Trunojoyo, and the BNI bank change cash at poor rates.

Things to See The kraton and taman sari (pleasure garden) were built in 1750 by Panembahan Sumolo, son of Queen Raden Ayu Tirtonegoro and her spouse, Bendoro Saud. The architect is said to have been the grandson of one of the first Chinese to settle in Sumenep after the Chinese massacre in Batavia. The kraton is occupied by the present bupati of Sumenep, but part of the building is a small museum with an interesting collection of royal possessions, including Madurese furniture, stone sculptures and *binggels* (heavy silver anklets worn by Madurese women). Opposite the kraton, the royal carriage-house museum contains the throne of Queen Tirtonegoro and a Chinese-style bed reputedly 300 years old. Entry is 300Rp to the museum and guided tours of the kraton run from here. On the first and third Sunday of the month, traditional dance or gamelan practice is held at the kraton.

Sumenep's 18th century **Mesjid Jamik** is notable for its three tiered Meru-style roof, Chinese porcelain tiles and ceramics. Sumenep also has a **Chinese temple.**

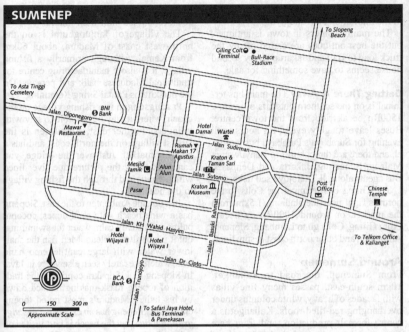

SUMENEP

To Slopeng Beach

To Asta Tinggi Cemetery

Giling Colt Terminal

Bull-Race Stadium

Jalan Diponegoro

BNI Bank

Mawar Restaurant

Hotel Damai

Wartel

Rumah Makan 17 Agustus

Jalan Sudirman

Kraton & Taman Sari

Mesjid Jamik

Alun Alun

Jalan Sutomo

Kraton Museum

Pasar

Post Office

Chinese Temple

Jalan Basuki Rahmat

Police

Jalan KH Wahid Hasyim

Hotel Wijaya II

Hotel Wijaya I

To Telkom Office & Kalianget

Jalan Dr Cipto

BCA Bank

Jalan Trunojoyo

To Safari Jaya Hotel, Bus Terminal & Pamekasan

0   150   300 m
Approximate Scale

The tombs of the royal family are at the **Asta Tinggi cemetery**, which looks out over the town from a peaceful hilltop 2km away. The main royal tombs are decorated with carved and painted panels; two depict dragons said to represent the colonial invasion of Sumenep. The biggest mausoleum is that of Panembahan Notokusomo (1762-1811), but it is the grave of Tirtonegoro that attracts pilgrims from all over Madura and Java. One of the small pavilions in the outer courtyard still bears the mark of an assassin's sword from an unsuccessful attempt to murder Bendoro Saud.

Places to Stay & Eat The best place to head for is the *Hotel Wijaya I* (☎ 62433, Jl Trunojoyo 45-47). Clean rooms cost 10,000Rp without mandi, from 17,000Rp with mandi and from 35,000Rp with air-con. The sister *Hotel Wijaya II* (☎ 62532,

Jl KH Wahid Hasyim 3) is also clean and well run. It is quieter, though many of the rooms are dark. Rooms cost 9000Rp up to 48,000Rp for air-con rooms with mandi, fridge and TV.

Safari Jaya (☎ 21989, Jl Trunojoyo 90), on the southern outskirts of town, is a big hotel with rooms from 8000Rp, and from 20,000Rp with air-con. It is also good value but dull and a long way from town.

Decent restaurants to try around town include the *Mawar Restaurant* (Jl Diponegoro 105) and *Rumah Makan 17 Agustus* (Jl Sudirman 34) serving inexpensive Chinese and Indonesian cuisine. There are good day and night *markets* in the area around the mosque. The *Hotel Wijaya I* has a good restaurant and serves ice cold beer.

Shopping Sumenep is a centre for batik on Madura, though Madurese batik isn't as fine as that in Java. Try the market or Citra Batik in the market on Jl Trunojoyo.

The main business in town is antiques, but the best antiques are carted off by the truck load to Bali and Jakarta. Every second house seems to have something for sale.

Getting There & Away The main bus terminal is on the southern outskirts of town, a 1500Rp becak ride from the town centre. Buses leave roughly every 1½ hours until evening for Surabaya's Purabaya bus terminal, and there are direct buses to Banyuwangi, Malang, Semarang, Jakarta and Denpasar. Bus agents along Jl Trunojoyo sell tickets.

The Giling bus terminal for Colts to the north is right near the stadium, 1.5km from the market, or around 1000Rp by becak. From Giling, Colts go to Lombang, Slopeng, Ambunten and other north coast destinations.

Around Sumenep

From Sumenep, the road to **Kalianget**, 10km south-east, passes many fine villas with facades of heavy, white columns under overhanging red-tiled roofs. Kalianget is a centre for salt production, and from here you can take boats to the other islands of Sumenep district. You can go **snorkelling** at Pulau Talango, just offshore. The larger islands include Sapudi, Rass and Kangean, well to the east. The ferry from Kalianget to Jangkar, on the mainland, runs every day except Wednesday and Sunday when it goes to Kangean.

North Coast

Fishing villages and their brightly painted perahus dot the north coast. The coast is lined with sandy beaches, but Madura's beaches are not brilliant.

Near Arosbaya, 27km north of Kamal, the tombs of the Cakraningrat royalty are at **Air Mata** (Tears) cemetery, superbly situated on the edge of a small ravine overlooking a river valley. The ornately carved *gunungan* (wayang mountain motif) headstone on the grave of Ratu Ibu, consort of Cakraningrat I, is the most impressive and is on the highest terrace. The turn-off to Air

Mata is shortly before Arosbaya. From the coast road it's a 4km walk inland.

The village of **Tanjungbumi** is on the north-west coast of Madura, about 60km from Kamal. Although primarily a fishing village, it is also a manufacturing centre for traditional Madurese batik and perahus. On the outskirts is **Pantai Siring Kemuning**.

Pasongsongan is a fishing village on the beach, where it may be possible to stay with villagers. Further east, **Ambunten** is the largest village on the north coast and has a bustling market. Just over the bridge, you can walk along the picturesque river lined with perahus and through the fishing village to the beach.

Just outside Ambunten to the east, **Slopeng** has a wide beach with sand dunes, coconut palms and usually calm water for swimming, but it is not always clean. Men fish the shallower water with large cantilevered hand nets, which are rarely seen elsewhere in Java. In Slopeng, Pak Supakra continues the tradition of topeng mask-making handed down by his father, Madura's most noted topeng craftsman. Slopeng has an expensive *pasanggrahan* lodge, but the beach is best visited on a day trip from Sumenep, only 20km away.

Lombang Beach, 30km north-east of Sumenep, is touted as the best beach on Madura. It has a wide stretch of sand but is nothing special.

MALANG
☎ 0341 • pop 710,000

Malang is one of Java's more attractive cities, with a hill station atmosphere. Much smaller and quieter than Surabaya, it makes a good base for exploring East Java. Situated on the banks of Sungai Brantas, Malang was established by the Dutch around the end of the 18th century when coffee was first grown as a colonial cash crop in the area. In more recent years, local farmers have grown tobacco and apples, and cigarette factories and the army have set themselves up here. It's a cool, clean place with a well planned alun alun and the central area of town is studded with parks, tree-lined streets and old Dutch architecture.

The main attractions lie outside the city, but it is also worth a day or two's visit for its own sake. Unlike many Javanese towns, which are planned on a grid pattern, this one sweeps and winds along the river bank, with surprising views and quiet backwaters to explore. The living is good and the atmosphere easy-going.

Orientation

Life in Malang revolves around the alun alun and the busy streets flowing into Jl Agus Salim and Pasar Besar near the central market. This is where you'll find the main shopping plazas, restaurants, cinemas and many of Malang's hotels. The alun alun in particular is a very popular area in the evenings, when families and students promenade and buskers perform. Banks, the Telkom office and many restaurants are north-west of the alun alun along Jl Basuki Rachmat.

Information

Tourist Offices The East Java Government tourist bureau (DIPARDA, ☎ 368473), Jl Kawi 41, has brochures on East Java.

Money Malang has plenty of banks, with ATMs and moneychangers. Compare the BNI and BCA banks on Jl Basuki Rachmat for the best rates, or try Bank Lippo opposite the alun alun.

Post & Communications The main post office is opposite the alun alun on Jl Kauman Merdeka. The Warposnet here has Internet terminals for 6000Rp per hour. It's open from 8 am to midnight. Prima Warung Internet is an Internet cafe on Jl Basuki Rachmat.

The Telkom office on Jl Basuki Rachmat is open 24 hours. It has a Home Country Direct phone, as does the Toko Oen restaurant and the Hotel Kartika Graha. A Telkom wartel is on Jl Agus Salim, near the Hotel Santosa.

Things to See & Do

The major attractions are outside town, but Malang has a few diversions to stave off boredom.

The city is noted for its **colonial architecture**. The Balai Kota (Town Hall) on Jl Tugu Circle is a sprawling Dutch administrative building, and nearby are some former old mansions, such as the Splendid Inn and the Wisma IKIP next door on Jl Majapahit. For reliving colonial dining, nothing beats the Toko Oen restaurant. Another good example of Art Deco colonial architecture is the interior of the Hotel Pelangi restaurant. Near Toko Oen, the Gereja Kathedral Kuno is the old Dutch Reform Church. Jl Besar Ijen is Malang's millionaire's row. Most of the large houses date from the colonial era, but many have been substantially renovated, losing architectural detail in the process.

On the north-west outskirts of town, **Candi Badut** is a small Shivaite temple dating from the 8th century. West of town on Jl Besar Ijen, the modern **Army Museum** is devoted to Malang's Brawijaya Division.

Malang has some good **markets**. The huge central market, the Pasar Besar, is always worth a browse. The flower market, Pasar Bunga, has a pleasant aspect down by the river, and it is the place to stroll in the morning. At the same time, take in the nearby Pasar Senggol, Malang's bird market, which also sells butterflies. Pasar Kebalen, near the Eng An Kiong Chinese temple, is the most active market in the evening, open until around 9 pm most nights.

Organised Tours

A number of operators have tours to the Singosari temples (from 50,000Rp per person, minimum two), Batu (50,000Rp) and Bromo (via Tosari for around 85,000Rp). The private Tourist Information Service (☎ 364052) at Toko Oen restaurant and the cheaper Hotel Helios are two well known operators (staff speak Dutch as well as English). They can also arrange car hire with driver from around 90,000Rp per day.

Places to Stay – Budget

The popular *Hotel Helios* (☎ 362741, Jl Pattimura 37) has doubles for 15,000Rp to 20,000Rp with shared mandi, and rooms with private bath for 27,500Rp and 37,500Rp. It's

JAVA

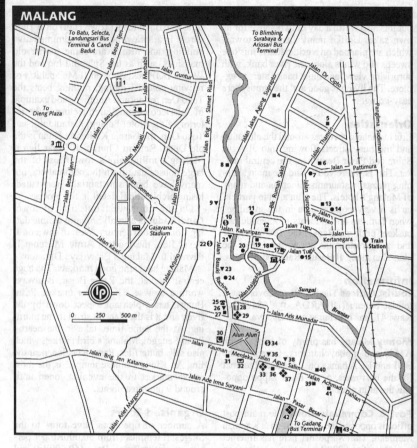

MALANG

To Batu, Selecta,
Landungsari Bus
Terminal & Candi
Badut

To Blimbing,
Surabaya &
Arjosari Bus
Terminal

To
Dieng Plaza

Jalan Besar Ijen
Jalan Merbabu
Jalan Guntur
Jalan Lawu
Jalan Besar Ijen
Jalan Merapi
Jalan Semeru
Jalan Bromo
Jalan Brig Jen Slamet Riadi
Jalan Jaksa Agung Suprapto
Jalan Dr Cipto
Panglima Sudirman
Jalan Thamrin
Jalan   Pattimura
Blk Rumah Sakit
Jalan Suropati
Jalan Pajajaran
Jalan Kahuripan
Jalan Tugu
Jalan Kertanegara
Gajayana Stadium
Jalan Kawi
Jalan Arjuno
Jalan Basuki Rachmat
Jalan Majapahit
Train Station

Sungai
Brantas

0   250   500 m

Jalan Aris Munadar

Jalan Kauman
Jalan Brig Jen Katamso
Jalan Arief Margono
Alun Alun
Jalan Merdeka
Jalan Agus Salim
Jalan Achmad Dahlan
Jalan Ade Irma Suryani
Jalan Pasar Besar

To Gadang
Bus Terminal

---

good value, clean, comfortable and all rooms have balconies overlooking the garden. Good travel information, bus bookings and tours are available.

If the Helios is full, the *Hotel Palem II* (☎ 325129, Jl Thamrin 15) is a passable hotel only a short walk away. Rooms with mandi cost 22,500Rp to 32,500Rp.

In the lively central area, the friendly *Hotel Riche* (☎ 324560, Jl Basuki Rachmat 1) is well placed near the Toko Oen restaurant. Dark rooms at the front cop the street

noise but those at the back around the courtyard are lighter, quieter and a good choice. Rooms, all with mandi, cost 25,000Rp to 40,000Rp.

Other central hotels include the *Hotel Tosari* (☎ 326945, Jl Achmad Dahlan 31), with bare but very clean rooms for 20,000Rp, or 30,000Rp to 70,000Rp with mandi.

Hotel Santosa (☎ 366889, Jl Agus Salim 24) is right in the thick of things opposite the alun alun. Clean but uninspiring budget doubles cost 22,500Rp, or 35,000Rp with

PLACES TO STAY		40	Losmen Semarang	14	Wijaya Transport
2	Hotel Graha Cakra	41	Hotel Margosuko	15	Balai Kota (Town Hall)
4	Hotel Taman Regent's			16	Wisma IKIP
5	Hotel Palem II		**PLACES TO EAT**	20	Pasar Senggol; Pasar Bunga
6	Hotel Helios	9	Rumah Makan Minang Jaya	22	BNI Bank
8	Kartika Graha	21	Jack's Cafe	24	Prima Warung Internet
12	Hotel Kartika Kusuma;	23	Minang Agung	25	Telkom Office
	Restaurant Gardena	26	Toko Oen Restaurant	28	Gereja Kathedral Kuno
13	Hotel Menara	35	Rumah Makan Agung	29	Sarinah Department Store
17	Splendid Inn	38	Gloria Restaurant	30	Mosque
18	Tugu Park Hotel; Melati			32	Main Post Office
	Pavilion Restaurant		**OTHER**	33	Mitra Department Store;
19	Montana Hotel	1	Gereja Maria Bundel Karmel		Gajah Mada Plaza
27	Hotel Riche	3	Army Museum	34	Bank Lippo
31	Hotel Pelangi	7	Wartel Suropati	37	Malang Plaza
36	Hotel Santosa	10	BCA Bank	42	Pasar Besar; Matahari
39	Hotel Tosari	11	Taman Rekreasi Senaputra		Department Store
				43	Eng An Kiong

mandi. The mid-range rooms from 45,000Rp to 80,000Rp are a much better choice.

Places to Stay – Mid-Range

Right on the alun alun, the colonial *Hotel Pelangi* (☎ 365156, *Jl Kauman Merdeka 3*) has simple 'driver's' rooms (business people and the well-to-do often have drivers, and they stay in the cheap rooms of hotels, hence the name) for 25,000Rp to 35,000Rp, or more gracious rooms with bath, hot water and TV for 75,000Rp and 80,000Rp. Modern air-con rooms cost 115,000Rp and 130,000Rp. Add 10% tax to the rates, but a discount is usually possible and a buffet breakfast in the delightful hotel restaurant is included.

Also in the city centre, the *Hotel Margosuko* (☎ 325270, *Jl Achmad Dahlan 40-42*) has a flash new lobby, a small coffee shop and good service. Older, sometimes noisy, rooms with bathroom and TV cost 40,000Rp and 50,000Rp, or the more luxurious, renovated rooms with air-con and hot water cost 65,000Rp and 85,000Rp.

The most fashionable area to stay is in the area around Jl Tugu, the old Dutch administrative district with impressive public buildings and old villas. The *Splendid Inn* (☎ 366860, *Jl Majapahit 2-4*) is a fine old Dutch villa and good value. Worn but comfortable rooms with hot water, TV and air-

con cost 60,000Rp to 70,000Rp, including breakfast. It has a small, murky swimming pool, and a good restaurant and bar.

The newer *Hotel Kartika Kusuma* (☎ 352266, *Jl Kahuripan 12*) has well kept rooms around a courtyard garden for 50,000Rp, or 65,000Rp with air-con and hot water. Some rooms are a little dark but this is an attractive smaller hotel.

For something cheaper in Tugu, try the friendly, well run *Hotel Menara* (☎ 362871, *Jl Pajajaran 5*). All rooms have hot water and TV from 33,000Rp to 67,000Rp. The tariff includes breakfast in the restaurant.

Places to Stay – Top End

Malang has a couple of faded luxury hotels and two very classy boutique hotels.

The *Hotel Taman Regent's* (☎ 363388, *Jl Jaksa Agung Suprapto 12*) has worn rooms from 175,000Rp after a 50% discount. The better maintained *Kartika Graha* (☎ 361900, *Jl Jaksa Agung Suprapto 17*) is a more modern hotel with a pool, restaurants, bar and rooms from 180,000Rp after discount.

Hotel Graha Cakra (☎ 324989, *Jl Cerme 16*) is a superbly restored Art Deco building tastefully furnished with antiques. It has a small swimming pool and restaurant. Rooms for US$60 and US$75 are a better class of mid-range room, while suites from US$95 to

US$195 are luxurious. After discount, rates still start at a hefty 355,000Rp.

The *Tugu Park Hotel* (☎ 363891, Jl Tugu 3) is one of the most delightful hotels in Java. Though neither large nor lavishly appointed, it has real style despite being a modern hotel. Rooms cost US$115, but it is worth the extra for the suites, all furnished in different Asian antique styles. They cost US$140 to US$250. It has a pool, business centre, restaurant and a tea house facing Tugu square.

Places to Eat

The *Toko Oen*, opposite the Sarinah department store, is an anachronism from colonial days, with tea tables and cane chairs. Relax, read a newspaper and be served by waiters in white sarongs and black peci. It has Chinese and western dishes, good Indonesian food and delicious home-made ice cream. It is expensive, but one of the most relaxing places for a meal and a good place for breakfast. It's open daily from 8.30 am to 9 pm.

For a drink or snack, the *Melati Restaurant* in the Hotel Pelangi is even more architecturally impressive. This cavernous colonial relic has towering pressed metal ceilings, and painted tiles around the walls feature picture postcard scenes from old Holland. While guaranteed to make any Netherlander homesick, the Indonesian and western food is only average.

The similarly named *Melati Pavilion Restaurant* in the Tugu Park Hotel serves good Indonesian, Chinese and Continental cuisine at upscale prices. Dutch dishes are featured including, of course, rijsttafel.

For cheap and varied eats, head for Jl Agus Salim. Near the alun alun, *Rumah Makan Agung* at No 2F has good Indian dishes – savoury *martabak* (pancake stuffed with meat, egg and vegetables), *biryani* (North Indian dish of basmati rice and meat, seafood or vegetables) and chicken ayam – as well as Indonesian dishes. The Chinese *Gloria Restaurant* at No 23 has a varied menu, including *pangsit mie* – a bowl of delicious noodles, meat and vegetables served with a side bowl of soup to mix it all with.

The big shopping centres have a variety of places to eat. The *food centre*, sandwiched between the Mitra department store and the Gajah Mada Plaza, has busy stalls offering a great selection of dishes, including local specialities such as *nasi rawon* (beef soup served with rice). Street vendors on Jl Agus Salim also have tasty sweets and dumplings.

Jack's Cafe (Jl Kahuripan 11A) is a hip restaurant with a varied menu, popular with students and an alternative crowd. Bands play downstairs on Thursday, Friday and Saturday.

Entertainment

Taman Rekreasi Senaputra is Malang's cultural and recreational park. Every Sunday morning at 10 am, *kuda lumping* 'horse trance' dances are held here. The dancers ride plaited cane horses until they fall into a trance, allowing them to eat glass and perform other masochistic acts without harm.

On the last Wednesday of the month, wayang kulit is performed at *Senaputra* from 10 pm. The *RRI*, Jl Candi Panggung, 5km north-west of the city, has wayang kulit from 9 pm on the first Saturday of the month.

Getting There & Away

Bus & Mikrolet Malang has three bus terminals. Arjosari, 5km north of town, is the main terminal with regular buses mostly along the northern route to destinations such as Surabaya (2500/5500Rp, two hours), Probolinggo (3000/6000Rp, 2½ hours), Jember (6000Rp, 4½ hours), Banyuwangi (9500/17,500Rp, six hours) and Denpasar (12,000/20,000Rp, 10 hours). Mikrolet run from Arjosari to nearby villages such as Singosari (800Rp) and Tumpang (1000Rp).

The Gadang bus terminal is 5km south of the city centre, and has buses along the southern routes to destinations such as Blitar (3000Rp, two hours), Kepanjan (800Rp), Lumajang (3200Rp), Dampit (1500Rp), and Trenggalek and Tulungagung.

The Landungsari bus terminal, 5km north-west of the city, has buses west to destinations such as Kediri (2500Rp) and Jombang (3000Rp). Frequent mikrolet run to Batu (700Rp, half an hour).

Numerous bus companies offer deluxe services from Arjosari for the long hauls. Buses to Bandung (around 60,000Rp), Bogor and Jakarta (43,000Rp to 70,000Rp) leave around 2 pm. Numerous buses to Solo and Yogya cost around 25,000Rp, and leave around 7 pm. Night buses also do the run to Bali for 28,000Rp to 35,000Rp, and some continue on to Padangbai and Lombok.

Buy tickets from agents on Jl Basuki Rachmat, south of the tourist office; or Wartel Suropati (☎ 353089), Jl Suropati 42, near the Hotel Helios, books a wide range of buses. The travel agent at the Toko Oen restaurant also sells tickets.

Minibus Plenty of door-to-door minibus companies operate from Malang, and hotels and travel agents can book them. Wijaya Travel (☎ 327072), Jl Pajajaran 7, next to the Hotel Menara, is a reliable agent. Destinations include: Madiun (9500Rp); Solo (25,000Rp); Yogya; Jember (12,500) via Probolinggo; Semarang (30,000Rp); and Denpasar (45,000Rp). Minibuses to Surabaya (10,000Rp to 12,000Rp) will drop off at hotels in Surabaya, thus saving the long haul from Surabaya's bus terminal.

Train Some useful services, mostly ekonomi, operate out of Malang. The bisnis/eksekutif *Jatayu* is the best train to Surabaya's Gubeng train station (6000/ 9000Rp, 1½ hours) at 3 pm. It leaves Surabaya at 7.45 am. The *Pattas* is an express ekonomi service running between Surabaya and Blitar via Malang. The ekonomi/bisnis *Matarmaja* goes west from Malang to Solo, Yogya (18,000/36,000Rp, seven hours), Cirebon and Jakarta at 4 pm. The *Regganis* goes to Banyuwangi (4500Rp ekonomi, eight hours) via Probolinggo. Most other services tend to go via Surabaya.

Getting Around

Mikrolets run all over town from the main bus terminals and to other mikrolet stations. Most run between the bus terminals through the centre of town. These are marked A-G (Arjosari to Gadung and return), A-L (Arjosari-Landungsari) or G-L

(Gadang-Landungsari). A trip anywhere around town costs 500Rp.

Becaks and metered taxis are also available around town.

AROUND MALANG
Singosari Temples

The Singosari Temples lie in a ring around Malang and are mostly funerary temples dedicated to the kings of the Singosari dynasty (1222 to 1292 AD), the precursors of the Majapahit empire.

Candi Singosari Right in Singosari village, 12km north of Malang, this temple stands 500m off the main Malang to Surabaya road. One of the last monuments erected to the Singosari dynasty, it was built in 1304 AD in honour of King Kertanegara, the fifth and last Singosari king who died in 1292 in a palace uprising. The main structure of the temple was completed but, for some reason, the sculptors never finished their task. Only the top part has any ornamentation and the kala heads have been left strangely stark, with smooth bulging cheeks and eyes. Of the statues that once inhabited the temple's chambers, only Agastya, the Shivaite teacher who walked across the water to Java, remains. Statues of Durga and Ganesha were carted off to the Netherlands, but have since been returned and are now in the Jakarta Museum.

About 200m beyond the temple there are two enormous figures of *dwarapala* (guardians against evil spirits) wearing clusters of skulls and twisted serpents. These may have been part of the original gates to the palace of the Singosari kingdom.

To reach Singosari, take a green mikrolet (800Rp) from Malang's Arjosari bus terminal and get off at the Singosari market on the highway, then walk or take a becak.

Candi Sumberawan This small, plain Buddhist stupa lies in the foothills of Gunung Arjuna, about 5km north-west of Singosari. Originating from a later period than the Singosari temples, it was built to commemorate the visit of Hayam Wuruk, the great Majapahit king, who visited the area in 1359.

JAVA

AROUND MALANG

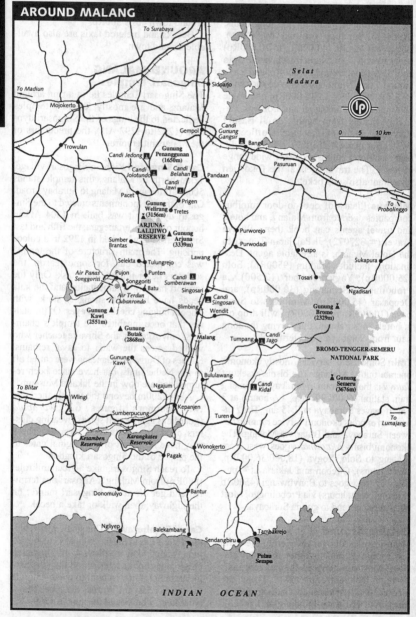

To Surabaya

To Madiun

Mojokerto

Trowulan

Selat Madura

Sidoarjo

Candi Gunung Gangsir

Gempol

Bangil

0   5   10 km

Candi Jedong

Pasuruan

Gunung Penanggunan (1650m)

Candi Jolotundo

Candi Belahan

Pandaan

Candi Jawi

Prigen

Pacet

Gunung Welirang (3156m)

Tretes

To Probolinggo

ARJUNA-LALIJIWO RESERVE

Purworejo

Gunung Arjuna (3339m)

Purwodadi

Puspo

Sumber Brantas

Lawang

Sukapura

Selekta

Tulungrejo

Tosari

Air Panas Songgoriti

Pujon

Punten

Songgoriti

Batu

Candi Sumberawan

Ngadisari

Air Terdun Cubanrondo

Singosari

Candi Singosari

Gunung Kawi (2551m)

Blimbing

Wendit

Gunung Bromo (2329m)

Gunung Butak (2868m)

Malang

Tumpang

Candi Jago

BROMO-TENGGER-SEMERU NATIONAL PARK

Gunung Kawi

Bululawang

Gunung Semeru (3676m)

To Blitar

Ngajum

Candi Kidal

Wlingi

Kepanjen

To Lumajang

Sumberpucung

Turen

Kesamben Reservoir

Karangkates Reservoir

Wonokerto

Pagak

Donomulyo

Bantur

Ngliyep

Balekambang

Sendangbiru

Tambakrejo

Pulau Sempu

INDIAN   OCEAN

Take a Colt from the Singosari market on the highway to Desa Sumberawan, and from where the Colts terminate, walk 500m down the road to the canal, turn right and follow the canal through picturesque rice paddies for 1km to the temple. This delightful walk is the highlight of the visit.

Candi Jago Along a small road near the market in Tumpang (18km from Malang), Candi Jago (or Jajaghu) was built in 1268 AD and is thought to be a memorial to the fourth Singosari king, Vishnuvardhana. The temple is in fairly poor condition but it still has some interesting decorative carving – in the two dimensional wayang kulit-style typical of East Java – from the *Jataka* and the *Mahabharata*. This primarily Buddhist temple also has Javanese-Hindu statues, including a six armed death-dealing goddess and a lingam, the symbol of Shiva's male potency.

To reach Candi Jago take a white mikrolet from Malang's Arjosari bus terminal to Tumpang (1000Rp). In Tumpang you can also visit the Mangun Dhama Art Centre (☎ 0341-787907). It is noted for its dance classes, run by an American, and it also has gamelan, wayang, batik and woodcarving courses.

If coming from Singosari, go to Blimbing where the road to Tumpang branches off the highway, and then catch a mikrolet. In Tumpang, the temple is only a short stroll from the main road.

Candi Kidal This temple, a small gem and a fine example of East Javanese art, is 7km south of Candi Jago. Built around 1260 AD as the burial shrine of King Anusapati, the second Singosari king who died in 1248 AD, it is tapering and slender, with pictures of the Garuda on three sides, bold, glowering kala heads and medallions of the *haruna* and Garuda symbols. Two *kala makara* (dragons) guard the steps – like those at the kraton steps in Yogya, one is male and the other female.

Colts run from Tumpang market to Candi Kidal but are infrequent. From Candi Kidal you can take another Colt south to Turen,

where buses go to Malang, but it is usually quicker to backtrack through Tumpang.

Batu
☎ 0341

For a day or two's outing, take a bus to Batu, one of Java's most attractive hill resorts on the slopes of Gunung Arjuna, 15km northwest of Malang. There is not a lot to do in Batu, but the mountain scenery is superb, the climate delightfully cool and a number of side trips can be made. The Kusuma Agrowisata hotel has apple orchards you can tour (6500Rp) with an attached mini-zoo.

Songgoriti, 3km west of Batu, has well known hot springs and a small ancient Hindu temple in the grounds of the Hotel Air Panas Songgoriti. Nearby, Pasar Wisata, is a tourist market selling mostly apples, bonsai plants, and stone mortar and pestles. Five kilometres south-west of Songgoriti are the falls, **Air Terjun Cubanrondo**.

Selekta is a small resort 5km further up the mountain from Batu, and 1km off the main road. Selekta's main claim to fame is the Pemandian Selekta, a large swimming pool with a superb setting in landscaped gardens.

Further up the mountain, the small mountain village of **Sumber Brantas**, high above Selekta, is at the source of Sungai Brantas. From here you can walk 2km to **Air Panas Cangar**, a hot springs high in the mountains surrounded by forest and mist.

Places to Stay Accommodation is available in Batu, Songgoriti and all along the road to Selekta at Punten and at Tulungrejo, where the road to Selekta turns off. Songgoriti is a small and quiet resort, as is Selekta higher up the mountain with better views, but Batu has better facilities and is a more convenient base.

Most hotels in Batu are scattered along Jl Panglima Sudirman, the main road to Kediri running west from the town centre. Most are mid-range hotels, but the friendly *Hotel Kawi* (☎ 591139) at No 19, 400m from the central plaza, has passable rooms for 15,000Rp, or 25,000Rp with mandi (with *cold* water). Another 500m up the hill, *Hotel*

Ragil Kuning (☎ *593051*) is a tad better and has rooms for 25,000Rp.

Hotel Perdana (☎ *591104*) at No 101 is a good mid-range choice and has a restaurant. Rooms with shower and hot water cost 30,000Rp to 50,000Rp, or large, newer rooms at the back cost 55,000Rp.

The upscale *Hotel Kartika Wijaya* (☎ *592600*) at No 127 has a delightful colonial lobby, swimming pool, fitness centre and landscaped gardens. Rooms are styled after different regions in Indonesia and start at 233,000Rp (from 275,000Rp on weekends), before a large discount. The newer *Royal Orchids Hotel* (☎ *593083*), nearby at Jl Indragiri 4, is of a similar price and standard.

Kusuma Agrowisata (☎ *593333, Jl Abdul Gani Atas*) is 3km south of the town centre. It's a sprawling place with rooms from US$56 and an 'agrotourism' apple orchard to visit.

Selekta has a couple of upper-notch hotels, such as the *Hotel Selekta* (☎ *91025*), near the swimming pool. In Tulungrejo, the *Hotel Santosa* and *Hotel New Victory* are on the main road. In Songgoriti, the *Arumdalu Hotel* (*Jl Aramdalu 2*) has been recommended by readers. It has a swimming pool, and rooms with hot water cost 24,500Rp to 70,000Rp.

Places to Eat Jl Panglima Sudirman in Batu also has plenty of restaurants. Near the Hotel Kawi, *Restoran Pelangi* (*Jl Panglima Sudirman 7*) is an attractive restaurant serving East Javanese and Chinese meals, with private dining bungalows around a garden at the back. Right next to the Hotel Kawi, *Warung Kawi* is a stylish little spot for buffet dishes and ice juices. Further west, the *Rumah Makan Cairo* has martabak and Middle-Eastern inspired fare.

Getting There & Away From Malang's Landungsari bus terminal take a Kediri bus or one of the frequent purple mikrolet to Batu (700Rp, 30 minutes). Batu's bus terminal is 2km from the centre of town – take another mikrolet (500Rp) from the bus terminal. For onward travel, buses can be caught along the main road to Pare, Kediri and Jombang. Batu Transport (☎ 592218), Jl Agus Salim 2, has door-to-door minibuses to Surabaya and Kediri.

From the bus terminal, orange mikrolet run through town to Selekta (500Rp, 30 minutes) and Sumber Brantas (1000Rp, one hour), but they often hang out endlessly for a full complement of passengers. Mikrolet turn off to Sumber Brantas at Jurangkuwali village. For Air Panas Cangar, walk 2km straight ahead.

Gunung Kawi

On Gunung Kawi (2551m), west of Malang and 18km north-west of Kepanjen, is the tomb of the Muslim sage Kanjeng Penembahan Djoego, who died in 1871. Descended from Pakubuwono I, king of the Mataram empire, the sage is better known as Mbah Jugo.

From the parking area, a long path leads up the slope past shops, souvenir stalls and beggars. Before the tombs at the top, there is a Chinese temple and the house of Mbah Jugo, which attracts non-Muslim, Chinese worshippers from as far away as Jakarta. Legend has it that the saint will answer the prayers of fortune-seeking pilgrims. Apparently he did so for one Chinese couple who went on to form one of Indonesia's biggest kretek companies.

Malam Jumat Legi in the Javanese calendar is the most propitious time, but pilgrims visit Gunung Kawi throughout the year, especially at night.

This strange cross-religious mountain resort can be experienced on a day trip, or there are plenty of basic *penginapan* (simple lodging houses) and restaurants if you want to stay the night. Gunung Kawi can be reached by taking a bus to Kepanjen, 3km east of the turn-off, and then a Colt for the final 19km.

South Coast Beaches

The coast south of Malang has some good beaches, but facilities are limited. **Sendang-gbiru** is a picturesque fishing village separated by a narrow channel from **Pulau Sempu**, a nature reserve with a lake in the centre, ringed by jungle.

A few kilometres before Sendangbiru, a rough track to the left leads 3km to **Tambakrejo**, a small fishing village with a sweeping sandy bay, which despite the surf is generally safe for swimming.

Balekambang is best known for its picturesque Hindu temple on the small island of Pulau Ismoyo, connected by a footbridge to the beach. This is Java's answer to Bali's Tanah Lot and was built by Balinese artisans in 1985 for the local Hindu communities. Balekambang is one of the most popular beaches and is crowded on weekends. Accommodation is limited to the very basic *Pesanggrahan Balekambang*.

Ngliyep further west is a popular rocky beach. It has a *pasanggrahan* offering basic accommodation.

Getting There & Away Minibuses from Malang's Gadang bus terminal go to Sendangbiru (2500Rp, two hours, 69km), past the turn-off to Tambakrejo; otherwise take a bus to Turen and then another to Sendangbiru. For Balekambang, buses run direct from Malang along the upgraded road for 2000Rp. The road to Ngliyep is also good and occasional white minibuses run direct, otherwise first take a bus to Bantur.

Lawang
☎ 0341
Lawang, 18km north of Malang on the road to Surabaya, is forgettable, but the Hotel Niagara is a notable five storey Art Nouveau mansion built in the 1900s. This once grand hotel has seen better days. Tourists aren't encouraged to poke around inside.

Of more interest, the road just south of the Hotel Niagara leads a few kilometres west to the **Kebun Wonosari** (☎ 426032) tea estate. This agro-tourism venture offers everything from tea plantation tours to tennis and a mini zoo. Best of all, accommodation is available in this peaceful setting. The old plantation guesthouses have rooms from 30,000Rp to 250,000Rp. Bicycles can be hired and the estate will provide transport to/from Lawang (15,000Rp) and Malang (30,000Rp) with advance notice.

Purwodadi
A few kilometres north of Lawang, the **Kebun Raya Purwodadi** are expansive dry-climate botanical gardens, open daily from 7 am to 4 pm. The entrance is on the main highway. If you want more information and maps of the gardens, visit the garden offices to the south of the entrance. **Air Terjun Cobanbaung** is a high waterfall next to the gardens.

BLITAR
☎ 0342   • pop 125,000
Blitar is the usual base from which to visit Panataran, and is also of interest as the site of President Soekarno's grave. It's quite a pleasant country town to stay in overnight on the southern route between Malang and Solo.

Information
Change money at the BNI bank at Jl Kenanga 9 or the BCA bank on Jl Merdeka. The post office is next to the train station and has an Internet warung (6000Rp per hour) open daily until 3 pm, expect Sunday. For international telephone calls, Telkom, at Jl A Yani 10 (the continuation of Jl Merdeka), is about 1km east of the Hotel Lestari.

Makam Bung Karno
At Sentul, about 2km north of the town centre on the road to Panataran, an elaborate monument now covers the place where former president Soekarno was buried in 1970. Soekarno is looked on by many as the 'father of his country', although he was only reinstated as a national hero in 1978 by the present regime.

Soekarno, affectionately referred to as Bung Karno, was given a state funeral but, despite family requests that he be buried at his home in Bogor, the hero of Indonesian independence was buried as far as possible from Jakarta in an unmarked grave next to his mother in Blitar. His father's grave was also moved from Jakarta to Blitar. It was only in 1978 that the lavish million-dollar monument was built over the grave and opened to visitors. Hundred of pilgrims come to all-but worship Soekarno, and the first president's recent rehabilitation means his grave is more popular than ever.

A becak from the town centre will cost about 1500Rp, or take a Panataran angkudes (yellow minibus) and ask for the *makam* (grave). Bemos turn off before the souvenir stalls from where it is a walk of a few hundred metres.

Other Attractions

The house that Soekarno lived in as a boy functions as the **Museum Soekarno**. Photos and memorabilia line the front sitting room, and you can see the great man's bedroom and check out the old Mercedes in the garage, a former state car. Still owned by relatives of Soekarno, though they now live in Jakarta, the museum is at Jl Sultan Agung 59, about 1.5km from the centre of town. The spacious new parking area is testament to Soekarno's revival in popularity.

Blitar's large **Pasar Legi**, next to the bus terminal, is also worth a look. In the northeast corner a few stalls sell kris, woodcarvings and bronze walking sticks.

Places to Stay & Eat

The most popular place to stay is *Hotel Sri Lestari (Tugu)* (☎ 802766, Jl Merdeka 173) right in the centre of town. It is undergoing renovations that will make it a fine boutique hotel but, until then, it has a few cheap rooms for 15,000Rp, or mid-range rooms from 45,000Rp to 125,000Rp. The superb, renovated rooms in the old colonial building are decked out in antique style and cost 165,000Rp.

Hotel Sri Rejeki (☎ 802770, Jl TGP 13) is a cheaper mid-range hotel with good-value rooms to suit most budgets from 9000Rp, or 30,000Rp to 60,000Rp with air-con. Further east of town, *Hotel Blitar Indah* (☎ 802779, Jl Jend Ahamad Yani 60) is similar and has rooms from 15,000Rp to 40,000Rp.

Blitar has some good restaurants on Jl Merdeka, such as the large Chinese *Ramayana (Jl Merdeka 65)*, east of the alun alun. *Rumah Makan Sarinah* has varied fare and does good *sop buntut* (oxtail soup) and ayam goreng. Further east past the Telkom office, *Depot Miranti* has breezy bamboo decor and a varied menu. *Hotel Sri Lestari* has an excellent if expensive restaurant.

Getting There & Away

Regular buses run from Blitar to Malang (3000Rp, two hours, 80km) and Surabaya (3000/4500Rp, four hours), as well as Kediri (1½ hours), Madiun (3½ hours) and Solo (six hours). The bus terminal is 4km south of town along Jl Veteran (500Rp by angkot from the central market). Angkudes run from the bus terminal and the market to Panataran for 1000Rp and stop right outside the temple. They also pass near Makam Bung Karno, but the road in front of the grave is closed and they skirt around the side streets to the east.

Rosalia Indah (☎ 802149), Jl Mayang 45, opposite the market and bemo terminal, and Restu (☎ 802583), next door at No 47, have door-to-door air-con minibuses to Solo (23,000Rp), Yogya (24,000Rp) and Semarang (30,000Rp).

The easiest way to reach Malang is by train. The express ekonomi *Pattas* departs for Malang at 11.40 am (3000Rp, 40 minutes) and Surabaya (3800Rp, 3½ hours); seats can be booked for 1500Rp. The *Dhoho* runs east to Kediri (1300Rp, 1½ hours).

PANATARAN

The Hindu temples at Panataran are the largest intact Majapahit temples, and the finest examples of East Javanese architecture and sculpture. Construction began around 1200 AD during the Singosari dynasty but the temple complex took some 250 years to complete. Most of the important surviving structures date from the great years of the Majapahit empire during the 14th century and are similar to many Balinese temples.

Around the base of the first level platform, which would once have been a meeting place, the comic-strip carvings tell the story of a test between the fat meat-eating Bubukshah and the thin vegetarian Gagang Aking.

Further on is the small Dated Temple, so called because of the date 1291 (1369 AD) carved over the entrance. On the next level are colossal serpents snaking endlessly around the Naga Temple, which once housed valuable sacred objects.

At the rear stands the Mother Temple – or at least part of it, for the top of the temple has been reconstructed alongside its three tiered base. Followed anticlockwise, panels around the base depict stories from the *Ramayana*. The more realistic people of the Krishna stories on the second tier of the base show an interesting transition from almost two dimensional representation to three dimensional figures.

Behind is a small royal mandi with a frieze of lizards, bulls and dragons around its walls.

The temple complex is open from 7 am to 5 pm, and entry is by donation. As you enter the village if you continue straight ahead past the turn-off to the temples, the **Museum Panataran** is 300m away. It contains an impressive collection of statuary taken from the complex, but the labelling is poor and the museum is only open irregular hours.

Getting There & Away Panataran is 16km from Blitar, and 3km north of the village of Nglegok. It is possible to see the Panataran temples comfortably in a day from Malang – and possibly from Surabaya also.

PACITAN
☎ 0357

On the south coast near the provincial border, the small town of Pacitan is on a horseshoe bay ringed by rocky cliffs. Pacitan's **Pantai Ria Teleng** is 4km from town and makes a good beach break from Solo. The sand is a dark yellow and the surf is rough, but it is very peaceful, and the coastline and hills surrounding Pacitan Bay are very scenic. Swimming is possible when the seas are calm – the safest area is towards the fishing boats at the south-western end of the bay, where there is also a swimming pool.

Information

The BRI bank is on Jl A Yani, the main street. Further down towards the market on the same street, the BNI bank changes cash for a number of currencies, also at poor rates.

There is a wartel next to the Hotel Remaja, or there is a Telkom office further west on Jl A Yani.

Places to Stay & Eat

The best place to stay is 4km out of town at Pantai Ria Teleng. *Happy Bay Beach Bungalows* (☎ 881474) has comfortable singles/doubles with bathroom for 25,000/30,000Rp, or private bungalows for 40,000Rp. Owned by an Australian and his Indonesian wife, Happy Bay is directly opposite the beach and has a good restaurant. It has bicycles and motorbikes for rent.

The beach is the main reason to visit, so there is not a lot of reason to stay in town. Budget hotels in Pacitan are along Jl A Yani. The *Hotel Pacitan* (☎ 881244, Jl A Yani 37) is central and has rooms with mandi from 12,500Rp to 30,000Rp. The *Srikandi* (☎ 881252, Jl A Yani 67) is the best and overlooks the rice paddies on the western edge of town. Spotless, new rooms cost 50,000Rp with TV and fan, or 70,000Rp with air-con. Attached is the town's best *restaurant*, a pleasant spot for cheap Indonesian dishes and fruit juices.

The next best dining option is *Depot Makan Bu Jabar (Jl H Samanhudi 3)*, a block behind the police station on Jl A Yani. It has excellent gado gado, nasi campur and fish, and fruit juices.

Getting There & Away

Pacitan can be approached by bus from Solo (4000Rp, four hours), or hourly buses run along the scenic road to Ponorogo (2500Rp, 2½ hours), just south of Madiun. From Ponorogo, buses run to Surabaya via Madiun, and direct buses go to Blitar (four hours) throughout the day. From Blitar to Malang take a Colt or bus.

For Yogya, head to Solo and take a bus from there.

Pacitan's bus terminal is 500m from the centre of town on the road to Solo and the beach. Buses from Solo pass the turn-off to the beach and can drop you there. Happy Bay is a 500m walk away, or a becak from the terminal costs 3000Rp.

AROUND PACITAN

At Punung village, on the Solo road 30km north-west of Pacitan, is the turn-off to the limestone caves of **Goa Putri**, 2km away, and the much more impressive **Gua Gong**, 8km from the highway. Only open to the public since 1995, Gua Gong is the largest and most spectacular in an area famed for its caves.

The more famous **Gua Tabuhan** (Musical Cave) is 4km north on the highway beyond Punung, and then another 4km to the cave. This huge limestone cavern is said to have been a refuge for the 19th century guerilla leader Prince Diponegoro. Guides will give an excellent 'orchestral' performance by striking rocks against stalactites, each in perfect pitch, and echoing pure gamelan melodies. The concert lasts about 10 minutes. You must hire a guide and lamp. This is also agate country, and hawkers sell reasonably priced polished stones and rings.

PROBOLINGGO

☎ 0355 • pop 180,000

Probolinggo, on the Surabaya-Banyuwangi coastal road, is a transit centre for people visiting Gunung Bromo. It grows the finest mangoes in Java, and its well stocked fruit stalls are a delight, but otherwise Probolinggo is forgettable.

The main post office and most of the banks, including the BCA and BNI, and government buildings are on Jl Suroyo, which leads off the main street to the train station.

Places to Stay & Eat

The *Hotel Bromo Permai* (☎ 22256, Jl Panglima Sudirman 327) is the most popular travellers hotel, and has comfortable, clean rooms from 12,500Rp; or 35,000Rp to 45,000Rp with air-con. It's on the main road close to the centre of town at the eastern end.

The very well kept *Hotel Ratna* (☎ 427886, Jl Panglima Sudirman 16) is 2km further west. It's the best hotel in town and has good economy rooms for 12,500Rp, large rooms with TV and bathroom from 30,000Rp, and air-con rooms from 55,000Rp to 70,000Rp.

The *Hotel Tampiarto Plaza* (☎21280, Jl Suroyo 16) is a fancier hotel but run-down and in need of a good scrub. It has a pool but it's open to the public and is usually full of screaming kids. Rooms start at 16,500Rp and from 32,500Rp with air-con.

Most of the hotels have restaurants and there are also some good Chinese restaurants. *Restaurant Malang (Jl Panglima Sudirman 104)* has a wide menu and the food is good. You'll find plenty of small restaurants and 'depots' at the *night market* around Pasar Gotong Royong.

Getting There & Away

Bus Probolinggo's Bayuangga bus terminal is about 5km from town on the road to Gunung Bromo. Yellow angkot run to/from the main street and the train station for 500Rp. The bus terminal is overrun with 'tourist office' bus agents offering dubious information and you'll be assailed by ticket sellers. Buses to destinations in East Java (eg Banyuwangi and Surabaya) are frequent, so avoid the agents and just pay on the bus. Advance bookings for long-distance eksekutif buses will cost a little more – shop around.

Ekonomi/air-con buses include: Surabaya (3000/6000Rp, two hours); Malang (3000/ 6000Rp, 2½ hours); Banyuwangi (6000/ 12,000Rp, five hours) via Situbondo; Bondowoso (3000/6000Rp); Yogya (13,000/ 22,000Rp, eight hours); and Denpasar (16,000/ 25,000Rp).

Thieves are very common on buses in East Java, especially out of Probolinggo.

Gunung Bromo Green Colt minibuses from Probolinggo's Bayuangga bus terminal go to Cemoro Lawang (3000Rp, two hours) via Ngadisari (2500Rp, 1½ hours) until around 5 pm, sometimes later during peak tourist periods if there is demand. The late afternoon buses charge 3500Rp to Cemoro Lawang, when fewer passengers travel beyond Ngadisari. Make sure it goes all the way to Cemoro Lawang when you board.

Train The train station is about 2km north of town and 7km from the bus terminal.

Probolinggo is on the Surabaya-Banyuwangi train line. Most services are ekonomi, or the *Mutiara Timur* costs 15,000/25,000Rp in bisnis/eksekutif to Surabaya (departing 1.40 pm) or Banyuwangi (departing 10 am). The pick of the economy services is the *Rengannis* to Banyuwangi (5500Rp) at 2.55 pm, via Jember and Kalibaru. The slow *Sri Tanjung* goes to Yogya (10,000Rp) at 10.40 am via Solo.

GUNUNG BROMO & BROMO-TENGGER-SEMERU NATIONAL PARK
☎ 0335

Gunung Bromo (2392m) is an active volcano lying at the centre of the Tengger Massif, a spectacular volcanic landscape and one of the most impressive sights in Indonesia. The Tengger crater stretches 10km across and its steep walls plunge down to a vast, flat sea of lava sand. From the crater floor emerges the smoking peak of Gunung Bromo, the spiritual centre of the highlands. This desolate landscape has a strange end-of-the-world feeling, particularly at sunrise, the favoured time to climb to the rim of Bromo's crater.

Bromo is the best known peak, and often the whole area is simply referred to as 'Mt Bromo', but it is only one of three mountains that have emerged within the caldera of the ancient Tengger volcano – Bromo is flanked by the peaks of Batok (2440m) and Kursi (2581m). Further south the whole supernatural moonscape is overseen by Gunung Semeru (3676m), the highest mountain in Java and the most active volcano in these highlands. The whole area has been incorporated as the Bromo-Tengger-Semeru National Park.

Legend has it that the great Tengger crater was dug out with just half a coconut shell by an ogre smitten with love for a princess. The ogre had to complete the task in a single night to gain the hand of the princess, but when her father, the king, saw that the ogre might succeed, he ordered his servants to pound rice. On hearing this, the cocks started to crow, thinking dawn had broken. Believing he had failed, the ogre flung away the coconut before dying of exhaustion. The coconut became Gunung Batok and the trench became the Sand Sea.

The Bromo area is also home to the Hindu Tengger people, who cultivate market vegetables on the steep mountain slopes and are found only on the high ranges of the Tengger-Semeru Massif. When the Majapahit empire collapsed and its aristocracy fled to Bali to escape the tide of Islam in Java, the Tengger highlands provided a haven for Hindus left behind. Hinduism has in fact made a resurgence in the area, evidenced by growing cultural ties with Bali and the building of a Hindu temple near the base of Gunung Bromo.

Each year, Bromo is the site for the Kasada festival, a colourful procession of Tenggerese who come to throw offerings into the crater at sunrise to pacify the god of the volcano.

Access is usually via Probolinggo, but Bromo can be approached from a number of routes. The ideal time to visit is during the dry season from April to October. At any time of year it's cold on these mountains and night temperatures can drop to around 2°C to 5°C.

Probolinggo Approach

This is the easiest and by far the most popular route. From Probolinggo, it's 28km to Sukapura, then another 14km to Ngadisari and another 3km to Cemoro Lawang. Minibuses run all the way to Cemoro Lawang from Probolinggo. Just before Cemero Lawang, you must pay the 2100Rp entrance post.

As with mountain scaling anywhere in Asia, it is all important to be at the top of Gunung Bromo for the impressive sunrise. From Cemoro Lawang, it's 3km down the crater wall and across the Sand Sea (Lautan Pasir) to Bromo, about a one hour walk. Get up at 4.30 am or earlier for an easy stroll across to Bromo. White stone markers are easy to follow in the dark, not to mention all the other climbers. Horses can also be hired for 15,000Rp. By the time you've crossed the lava plain from Cemoro Lawang and started to climb up Bromo (246 steps, one traveller reported), it should be fairly light. Bromo itself is not one of the great volcanoes

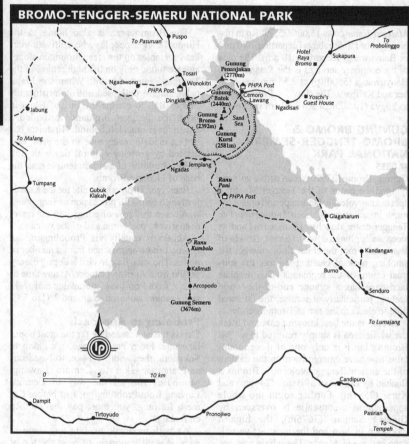

BROMO-TENGGER-SEMERU NATIONAL PARK

of Indonesia – it is the whole landscape that is breathtaking. From the top you'll get fantastic views down into the smoking crater and of the sun sailing up over the outer crater.

The colours are better at dawn but visibility is usually good throughout the day in the dry season, even though the slopes below Cemoro Lawang may be covered in mist. Later in the day you'll also avoid the dawn crowds, especially during school and other holiday periods. In the wet season the clouds and the dawn often arrive at the same time.

From Cemoro Lawang, it is also possible to visit **Gunung Penanjakan** (2770m), the highest point on the outer crater. Hired jeeps (90,000Rp to 100,000Rp) go down to the Sand Sea and up to Penanjakan for the dawn, then return via Gunung Bromo. Penanjakan is where those picture postcards shots are taken, with Bromo in the foreground and Semeru smoking in the distance. Alternatively, it is two hours on foot. Walk one hour (or charter a jeep) along the road to the 'Penanjakan II' viewpoint, itself a spectacular vantage point, but it's worth taking the walking trail behind this viewing area for another hour to reach Penanjakan proper. The trail is fairly steep but easy to follow (bring a flashlight) and comes out on the Dingklik road, 500m before the summit.

From Cemoro Lawang, trekkers can also take an interesting walk across the Sand Sea to Ngadas (8km) on the southern rim of the Tengger crater. You'd need to start early in order to get to Malang by evening.

Wonokitri Approach

Small tour groups come this way to do the trip to Gunung Penanjakan, which can be reached by sealed road, or by 4WD, which can drive all the way to the base of Bromo. Wonokitri can be approached from Pasuruan on the main northern highway, or coming from Malang you can turn off before Pasuruan at Warungdowo on the Purworejo-Pasuruan road.

From Pasuruan take a Colt to Puspo and then another to Tosari, 42km from Pasuruan. From Warungdowo take a Colt straight to Tosari (3000Rp). Tosari Colts sometimes continue on to Wonokitri, otherwise take an ojek (2000Rp, 3km). Tosari and Wonokitri have accommodation.

At Wonokitri check in at the PHPA office on the southern outskirts of town and pay your 2100Rp entry fee. In Wonokitri you can hire a jeep to Bromo for 125,000Rp return, or 150,000Rp including a side trip to Gunung Penanjakan. Cheaper ojeks can also be hired.

From Wonokitri, it's 5km along a good road to Dingklik. There are superb views from Dingklik, on the edge of the outer crater. From Dingklik the road forks – down to Bromo or 4km up along the paved road to Gunung Penanjakan for even better views. From Penanjakan a walking trail leads to Cemoro Lawang. The paved road from Dingklik, 6km down to the Sand Sea is very steep. From the bottom it is then 3km across the sand to Bromo.

Ngadas Approach

It is also possible to trek into the Tengger crater from Ngadas to the south-west of Gunung Bromo, although it is more often done in the reverse direction as a trek out from Bromo or as an approach to climbing Gunung Semeru. This is definitely a trek for those willing and able to rough it a bit, but it is very rewarding.

From Malang take a mikrolet to Tumpang, or from Surabaya take a bus to Blimbing, just north of Malang, then a mikrolet to Tumpang. From here take another mikrolet to Gubug Klakah, from where you walk 12km to Ngadas. From Ngadas it is 2km to Jemplang at the crater rim, and then three hours on foot (12km) across the floor of the Tengger crater to Gunung Bromo and on to Cemoro Lawang. From Jemplang, you can also head south for the Gunung Semeru climb.

Lumajang Approach

This route to Bromo from the south-east is rarely used because of difficult access. From Lumajang take a mikrolet to Senduro (18km), then charter an ojek to Ranu Pani (25km) via Burno, from where you can walk to Bromo (14km) or Gunung Semeru.

Climbing Gunung Semeru

Part of the huge Tengger Massif, Gunung Semeru is the highest peak in Java at 3676m. Also known as Mahameru (Great Mountain), it is looked on by Hindus as the most sacred mountain of all and the father of Gunung Agung on Bali. It's a rugged three day trek to the summit, and you must be well equipped and prepared for camping overnight. Nights on the mountain are freezing and inexperienced climbers have died of exposure. The best time to make the climb is May to October.

Hikers usually come through Tumpang in the west, from where you can charter jeeps to Ranu Pani, the start of the trek, otherwise take a Colt from Tumpang to Gubug Klakah and walk 12km to Ngadas, and then on to Jemplang. It is also possible to cross the Tengger Sand Sea from Gunung Bromo (12km) to Jemplang, 2km from Ngadas at the Tengger crater rim. From Jemplang, the road skirts around the crater rim before heading south to Ranu Pani (6km; 1½ hours on foot).

WARNING

! Check the current status of the volcano. While most volcanoes in Indonesia are safe for trekking, there are several that have been erupting almost continuously for the past several years and Gungung Semeru is one of them. Check with the local tourist office, other travellers or the nearest observation post (*pos pengamatan*) for Gunung Semeru's eruption status. If it is closed, do not attempt to climb the volcano or hike into the 'danger zone'.

Ranu Pani is a lake with a small village nearby. Pak Tasrip runs a *homestay* costing 6000Rp per person and meals are served. He can help organise a climb of Gunung Semeru, and he also rents sleeping bags, which are essential. Ranu Pani is the usual overnight rest spot, and the Ranu Pani PHPA post is towards the lake. You can also stay at the new lodge above the PHPA post. *Register with the PHPA and obtain advice on the climb*. It can also help arrange guides, which are not essential but recommended unless there are a lot of other climbers.

The main trail begins behind the PHPA post. This new trail is lined with scrubby growth, but is an easier walk than old trail which is a steeper climb. Both trails lead to Ranu Kumbolo crater lake (2400m), 13km or 3½ hours from Ranu Pani. From Ranu Kumbolo, which has a shelter, the trail climbs to Kalimati (three hours) at the foot of the mountain. From Kalimati it is a steep 1½ hour climb to Arcopodo, where there is a campsite for the second night on the mountain.

The next day from Arcopodo the real fun begins. It is a short steep climb to the start of the volcanic sands, the result of Semeru's eruption, and then a struggling three hour climb through loose scree to the peak. Semeru explodes every half-hour and sends billowing smoke upwards. These gases and belching lava make Semeru dangerous – stay well away from the vent. From the top

on a clear day, there are breathtaking views of Java's north and south coasts, as well as views of Bali. To see the sunrise it is necessary to start at 2 am for the summit. It is possible to make it back to Ranu Pani on the same day.

Places to Stay & Eat

Cemoro Lawang Right at the lip of the Tengger crater and the start of the walk to Bromo, Cemoro Lawang is the most popular place to stay. Prices for everything, including accommodation, are inflated and bargaining brings few reductions.

Cafe Lava Hostel (☎ 541020) is the most popular travellers place. Singles/doubles cost 15,000/20,000Rp, or 30,000/40,000Rp with cold water mandi. Rooms are very basic, but it's convivial and has a good restaurant.

The *Cemara Indah Hotel* (☎ 541019) is on the lip of the crater, has fantastic views and an excellent, airy restaurant. Very spartan rooms in the old block cost from 10,000/15,000Rp. Much better rooms with bathroom and hot water cost 65,000Rp, and it also has a couple of overpriced rooms with TV for 165,000Rp.

One hundred metres past the Cafe Lava Hostel, the *Hotel Bromo Permai I* (☎ 541 021) is the fanciest hotel and has a restaurant/bar but don't expect luxury rooms. Rooms with shared mandi cost from 16,000Rp and 27,000Rp, or better rooms with attached bathroom and hot water are 60,000Rp to 106,000Rp.

The popular *Lava View Lodge* (☎ 541009), the upmarket cousin of the Cafe Lava Hostel, is 500m along a side road through the parking/souvenir stall area below Hotel Bromo Permai I. It is right at the edge of the crater with great views. Rooms with cold water cost 40,000Rp, or 60,000Rp and 100,000Rp with hot water, including a substantial breakfast in the very good but expensive restaurant.

The PHPA's *Guest House Rumah Tamu* (☎ 541038), opposite the Hotel Bromo Permai I, has two comfortable cottages, each with two bedrooms, sitting room, hot water and TV for 200,000Rp.

All the hotels have restaurants. *Adas Cafe*, next to the information centre, has a limited but reasonably priced menu, while *Venus Cafe* near the bus terminal has more varied fare.

Ngadisari This village is 3km down the mountain from Cemoro Lawang, and is home to *Yoschi's Guest House* (☎ 541018). Just outside the village, it is an excellent, friendly place to stay. Singles/doubles with shared mandi cost 12,500/17,500Rp, or from 35,000/45,000Rp with shower. Comfortable family cottages with hot water are 65,000Rp to 125,000Rp. It has a great restaurant, and offers tours and transport to Bromo (4500Rp person).

A short walk away, the *Bromo Home Stay* (☎ 541022) has a restaurant and reasonable rooms with cold-water mandis for 15,000Rp, 25,000Rp and 40,000Rp. The Yogya Rental buses stop here.

Sukapura The plush *Hotel Raya Bromo* (☎ 581103) is a few kilometres up the mountain from Sukapura village and a full 9km from the crater. If you want luxury accommodation and have a car this may be your place, otherwise it's too far from the crater to be convenient. Rooms cost 242,000Rp to 726,000Rp, plus 21%, but at the time of writing it had been offering packages from 145,000Rp per room.

Tosari & Wonokitri *Bromo Cottages* (☎ Surabaya 336888) in Tosari are perched on the hillside, with fine mountain views and a restaurant. Posted room rates are an expensive US$60, plus 21%, before big discounts.

It also possible to stay with villagers in Wonokitri.

Getting There & Away
Most visitors come through Probolinggo (see Probolinggo earlier in this chapter for transport details). Hotels in Cemoro Lawang and Ngadisari can make bookings for onward bus tickets from Probolinggo for a large premium – 40,000Rp or more to Yogya or Denpasar.

Travel agents in Solo and Yogya book the Yogya Rental minibuses to Bromo for 40,000Rp to 50,000Rp. These are not luxury minibuses, and sometimes they run a bigger bus to Probolinggo and change there. Yogya Rental stops at the Bromo Homestay in Ngadisari – for Cemoro Lawang specify when you buy the ticket. It runs a similar service to/from Bali. A two day tour – Yogya/Solo to Bromo and Bali – costs around 100,000Rp from travel agents, but accommodation is at the less popular Bromo Homestay.

For Ngadas, frequent mikrolet go to Tumpang from Malang (600Rp). Jeeps can be chartered in Tumpang or Ngadas for around 150,000Rp, or Colts go as far as Gubuk Klakah.

Bromo tours are easily arranged in Malang, and you can also arrange jeep hire in hotels and travel agents there.

PASIR PUTIH
☎ 0338
On the north coast, roughly halfway between Probolinggo and Banyuwangi, Pasir Putih is East Java's most popular seaside resort and is mobbed on the weekend by sun'n'sand worshippers from Surabaya. It has picturesque perahu and safe swimming, but its name 'White Sand' is a misnomer – the sand is more grey-black than white. This reasonable beach would make a pleasant enough stopover if the accommodation was better. Pasir Putih's government-run hotels, sandwiched between the beach and the noisy main road, are dirty and overpriced.

BONDOWOSO
☎ 0332
Bondowoso, 34km south-west of Situbondo, is one of the cleanest towns in Java, in itself an attraction; otherwise it is merely a transit point for nearby attractions such as Ijen (see the following entry).

Hotel Anugerah (☎ 421870, Jl Sutoyo 12) is very friendly and can arrange transport to Ijen (150,000Rp/return). Neat and tidy rooms cost 20,000Rp and 25,000Rp with mandi; 30,000Rp with air-con. A good, cheap restaurant is attached. The nearby **Palm Hotel** (☎ *421505, Jl A Yani 32*) is the best hotel in town, with a swimming pool and good restaurant. It has a huge variety of rooms with mandi from 16,000Rp. Air-con rooms with TV and hot water start at 70,000Rp. It also arranges transport to Ijen.

On weekends in **Tapen**, 15km from Bondowoso towards Situbondo, traditional Madurese horn-locking bullfights *(aduan sapi)* are held, but at the time of writing, these were cancelled for fear of exciting the Madurese population in a region that experienced a lot of problems during the economic crisis, as well as isolated looting.

Getting There & Away

Buses from Bondowoso include: Situbondo (1500Rp, one hour); Jember (1000Rp, 45 minutes); Probolinggo (3000Rp, two hours); and Surabaya (7500/12,000Rp normal/air-con, five hours). For Tapen take any Situbondo-bound bus.

IJEN PLATEAU

The plateau, part of a reserve that stretches north-east to Baluran National Park, was at one time a huge active crater, 134 sq km in area. Today, Ijen is a quiet but active volcano, and the landscape is dominated by the volcanic cones of Ijen (2368m) and Merapi (2800m) on the north-eastern edge of the plateau, and Raung (3332m) on the south-west corner. Coffee plantations cover much of the western area of the plateau, where there are a few settlements. The plateau has a number of difficult-to-reach natural attractions, but most visitors come for the hike to spectacular Kawah Ijen. There are few people in this unspoilt area.

Kawah Ijen Hike

The magnificent turquoise sulphur lake of Kawah Ijen lies at 2148m above sea level and is surrounded by the volcano's sheer crater walls. Ijen's last major eruption was in 1936, though a minor ash eruption occurred in 1952. At the edge of the lake, smoke billows out from the volcano's vent and the lake bubbles when activity increases.

The vent is a source of sulphur and collectors work here, making the trek up to the crater and down to the lake every day. The best time to make the hike is in the dry season between April and October. Sulphur collectors hike up in the morning and return around 1 pm when the clouds roll in. Trekkers are advised to do the same, but the clouds often disappear in the late afternoon. Make it for the dawn if you can.

The starting point for the trek to the crater is the PHPA post at Pos Paltuding, which is usually reached from Bondowoso but can also be accessed from Banyuwangi. Sign in and pay your 1000Rp entry fee here. The steep well worn, 3km path up to the observation post takes about one hour. Keep an eye out for gibbons and the prolific birdlife. Just past the post the road forks – to the left is the walk to the 'safety-valve' dam, built to regulate the flow of water into Banyu Pahit (Bitter River), but the main area of interest lies along the right fork, a 30 minute walk to the top of the crater and its stunning views.

From the crater a steep, gravelly path leads down to the sulphur deposits and the steaming lake. The walk down takes about 20 minutes, double the time for the walk back up. The path is slippery in parts and the sulphur fumes towards the bottom can be overwhelming. *Take great care* – a French tourist fell and died in 1997.

Back at the lip of the crater, turn left for the climb to the highest point on the crater (2368m) and magnificent views of the lake and the surrounding mountains. Or keep walking anticlockwise around the crater for even more expansive views of the lake. On the other side of the lake opposite the vent, the trail disappears into crumbling volcanic rock and deep ravines.

Places to Stay & Eat

At Sempol, 13km before Pos Paltuding on the Bondowoso side, the Kebun Kalisat coffee plantation has a guest house, the *Arabika Homestay*, 1km from the main road. It is the best accommodation near Ijen but overpriced and run like an army camp. Rooms with attached bathrooms and hot water (if you're lucky) cost 50,000Rp to 90,000Rp, plus 10%; meals are served. Sempol village has a couple of *warungs*. You can also visit the coffee groves and see the factory of this *agro wisata* (agricultural tourism) venture.

Pos Paltuding, the PHPA post at the start of the walk, has a small shop for provisions and a cafe serving noodles and not much else. There is an open-sided shelter for campers or a bed in the cafe costs 10,000Rp per person. The new guesthouse nearby is bare but peaceful and has comfortable beds. Rooms with mandi cost 35,000Rp. Blankets are not provided, so bring a sleeping bag – it gets very cold at this altitude.

The *volcanology observation post* just below the crater allows you to throw a sleeping bag on the floor for a small donation. The staff will gladly rent you their beds if you make it worth their while. This enterprising post also sells drinks and snacks, and will cook meals.

The coffee plantation also has another guesthouse, the more luxurious *Jampit Guesthouse*, 14km south of Sempol at Jampit. The accommodation is better than the Arabika Homestay, but it is a long way from Ijen. Rooms cost 57,500Rp with outside mandi, from 86,250Rp with hot water. The guesthouses can be booked through PTP Nusantara XII in Surabaya (☎ 031-22360) and Jember (☎ 0331-86861).

Getting There & Away

It is possible to travel most of the way to Kawah Ijen by public transport but most visitors charter transport. The starting point for the hike to Kawah Ijen, Pos Paltuding, can be reached by road from Bondowoso or with more difficulty from Banyuwangi.

Bondowoso From Wonosari, 8km from Bondowoso towards Situbondo, an upgraded road runs via Sukosari and Sempol all the way to Pos Paltuding, 64km from Bondowoso. Apart from a few rough stretches, it a good paved road and takes about two hours by car. Sign in at the coffee plantation checkpoints on the way. The Hotel Palm and the Hotel Anugerah in Bondowoso arrange day tours to Ijen for around 150,000Rp per vehicle.

Two minibuses run from Bondowoso to Sempol (3000Rp, 2½ hours) at around 7.30 am and 1 pm. You should be able to find someone in Sempol who will take you the 13km to Pos Paltuding on the back of their motorbike for around 15,000Rp one way; alternatively the Arabika Homestay offers return transport, taking up to 10 people, for 75,000Rp. At the Pos Paltuding cafe there's usually a few motorbikes to take you back or on to Banyuwangi for 30,000Rp.

Banyuwangi Ijen is closer to Banyuwangi, but the road is very steep and has deteriorated badly. A 4WD is essential, although difficult to hire in Banyuwangi and outrageously expensive. Most people walk the last 8km along the road to Pos Paltuding.

From Banyuwangi's Blambangan bemo station, take a Lin 3 bemo to Sasak Perot (500Rp) on the eastern outskirts of town and then a Licin-bound Colt which can drop you off in Jambu (1000Rp) at the turn-off to Kawah Ijen, a further 17km away. Start at 5.30 am to reach the crater in time for good views. From Jambu, ojeks can take you 9km along the paved road to Sodong through the plantations for 10,000Rp maximum. Beyond Sodong it is a hair-raisingly steep ride and ojeks are not keen to do it.

Sodong is nothing more than a small parking area at the edge of the forest where the sulphur collectors bring their loads to be taken by truck to Banyuwangi. Beyond Sodong the washed out road is just a very steep, slippery, rock strewn track for about 4km, though the last 4km is paved.

The 8km walk from Sodong to Pos Paltuding is a tough three hours uphill, but is rewarded by brilliant, dense rainforest with towering ferns and palms. Halfway up, the PHPA Pos Totogan, at the edge of the reserve, is not always staffed.

Only 4WD vehicles and motorcycles can make it up, but cars and minibuses can go down from Pos Paltuding to Banyuwangi. It's a slow, bumpy ride in first gear with brakes on all the way.

JEMBER
☎ 0331

Jember is the thriving service centre for the surrounding coffee, cacao, rubber, cotton and tobacco plantations. It has all the amenities of a large city, but is relatively traffic-free and competes with Bondowoso for the tidy town award.

From Jember groups can arrange a plantation tour, though Kalibaru is the usual centre for plantation visits. PT Perkubunan Nusantara XII (☎ 86861), Jl Gajah Mada 249, is the state-owned company that controls most of the plantations. It offers day or overnight tours with accommodation on the plantations.

The *Hotel Widodo* (☎ 83650, Jl Letjen Suprapto 74), about 1km south of the town centre, is a good cheap hotel and on the ball with travel information.

Getting There & Away

The main terminal, Tawung Alun, 6km west of town, has buses to Probolinggo, Surabaya, Malang, Bondowoso, Banyuwangi and Kalibaru, but buses from Bondowoso usually terminate at the sub-terminal, 5km north of town; there are also sub-terminals to the east (for Banyuwangi) and south (for Watu Ulo). Damri city buses and yellow Lin bemos run from the terminals to the centre of town.

Jember is also on the train line for Surabaya-Banyuwangi, and the railway station is in the centre of town.

WATU ULO & PAPUMA
☎ 0331

Watu Ulo is popular on weekends, but like most of the beaches on Java's south coast, it has grey sands and crashing surf with dangerous swimming. The real surprise lies just west around the headland from Watu Ulo at Papuma – a small beach with white sand, turquoise waters and sheltered swimming. Further around from Papuma, the rugged coastline, with spectacular rocky outcrops, is again pounded by the surf, but deserted patches of white sand can be found for sunbathing. Nearby **caves** and the **Wana Wisata Londolapesan** forest area can also be explored.

At Watu Ulo, the basic *Hotel Vishnu* (☎ 81028) has rooms with mandi from 20,000Rp.

Getting There & Away

In Jember, take a city bemo (500Rp) to the Ajung sub-terminal and then a *taksi* (the confusing name for a public minibus in these parts) to Ambulu (1000Rp, 25km). From Ambulu yellow bemos go to Watu Ulo (500Rp, 12km). Papuma is then a half-hour walk along the paved road over the steep headland, though bemos can drop you at the beach.

KALIBARU
☎ 0333

The picturesque road from Jember to Banyuwangi winds around the foothills of Gunung Raung (3322m) up to the small hill town of Kalibaru. It has a refreshing climate and makes a pleasant stop on this route. The village itself is unremarkable, but Kalibaru has excellent accommodation for such a small town and makes a good base for visiting the nearby plantations around **Glenmore**, 10km east. Java's finest coffee, both *arabica* and *robusta* varieties, is produced in the Ijen Plateau area, as well as cacao, cloves and rubber. In Kalibaru town, to the north of the train station, there are smaller, easily visited plots of coffee and cloves.

Organised Tours

The area has many plantations but the main plantation of interest is Kebun Kandeng Lembu, 5km south of Glenmore. Guides can be hired (35,000Rp) for groups to see rubber tapping and processing, as well as cacao and coffee plantations, and the washing, drying and sorting processes. The Margo Utomo in Kalibaru has plantation tours for 101,000Rp for two people. It also organises transport and other fairly expensive tours to Kawah Ijen, Alas Purwo and Sukamade, as well as river rafting (100,000Rp per person) in the dry season.

The Kalibaru train station (☎ 897322) is also cashing in on the agro-tourism boom and runs a small diesel lorry that travels 35km through impressive mountain countryside,

silent gamelan orchestra – Yogyakarta.

A glimpse of one of Yogyakarta's *pasar* (markets).

A *Ramayana* dance-drama performer.

he faded glory of Taman Sari, Yogyakarta.

he waiting game – Pasar Beringharjo, Yogya.

A young agitator for change – Yogya, May 1998.

A child-wedding among the Hindu Tengger people of Gunung Bromo, West Java.

Muslim woman, Solo.

The towering Shiva temple of Prambanan.

across bridges and tunnels and past a coffee plantation (170,000Rp/eight people).

Places to Stay & Eat

Most visitors come to Kalibaru just to stay at the delightful *Margo Utomo Homestay* (☎ 897123, Jl Lapangan 10), an old Dutch inn that has maintained its colonial feel. It has newer, colonial-style cottages with private balconies built around a pretty garden for US$19/25 for singles/doubles, including breakfast. All-you-can-eat meals cost 15,000Rp for lunch or 20,000Rp for dinner.

The newer *Margo Utomo Cottages* (☎ 897420, Jl Putri Gunung 3) doesn't have the same colonial atmosphere but it is in a superb, restful setting down by a river, 3km east of town. Attractive bungalows cost US$22.50/27.50 – try to get one overlooking the river. It has a pool and a restaurant.

The *Raung View Hotel* (☎ 897214, Jl Jember 16) has a swimming pool and restaurant. Rooms with hot water for 30,000Rp are a good deal, or pleasant cottages for 47,000Rp overlook the rice paddies and are even better.

Hotel Kalibaru (☎ 897333), 4km west of town on the Jember road, is a bigger, flasher hotel and also has a pool. Rooms for 99,500Rp have pleasant, open-air bathrooms and breakfast is included.

Getting There & Away

Any bus between Jember (one hour) and Banyuwangi (two hours) can drop you near the hotels. The train station is right near the Margo Utomo Homestay and Kalibaru is on the main Banuwangi/Jember/Probolinggo/Surabaya railway line. It is a scenic run from Kalibaru to Banyuwangi (1100Rp ekonomi; 2½ hours) or the *Mutiara Timur* also runs to Banyuwangi (12,000/20,000Rp bisnis/eksekutif) and Surabaya (14,000/24,000Rp). A 6.20 am train also goes to Malang via Bangil.

MERU BETIRI NATIONAL PARK

Covering 580 sq km, the Meru Betiri National Park lies between Jember and Banyuwangi districts. With magnificent coastal rainforest, abundant wildlife and superb coastal scenery, it is one of Java's finest parks but it receives few visitors because of difficult access.

Named after Gunung Betiri (1223m) in the north of the park, the coastal mountains trap the rain and the park is very wet for much of the year. Visit in the dry season from April to October because the road into the park fords a river, which easily floods. Even in the dry season you may have to wade across the river and walk into the park.

The park's major attraction is the protected turtle beach at **Sukamade**, one of Indonesia's most important turtle spawning grounds where five species of turtle come ashore to lay their eggs. Green turtles are the most common, but the giant leatherbacks come in the wet season from December to February. The PHPA accommodation nearby, Mess Pantai, can arrange a night trip.

Wildlife, mostly in the mountain forests, include leopard, wild pigs, deer, banteng, black giant squirrels, civets and pangolin. The silvered-leaf monkey and long-tailed macaque are also common. Birdlife is prolific and hornbills, including the rhinoceros hornbill, whoosh and honk overhead. Meru Betiri is most famous as the last home of the Javan tiger, though they are now believed to be extinct.

Despite this rich biodiversity, the park is not all wilderness and two plantations lie within its boundaries: Sukamade in the eastern part of the park, and the other in the west, near

The banded linsang is a nocturnal, arboreal animal.

Bandealit. Visitors can tour the plantations, which harvest coffee, cacao, coconut and rubber.

Trails are limited in the park and a guide, arranged through the PHPA, is usually necessary. Apart from coastal walks, a trail leads about 7km north-west of the Sukamade estate to the **Sumbersari** grazing ground, part of the way through rainforest and bamboo thicket.

The area is noted for its superb coastal scenery. **Rajegwesi**, at the entrance to the park, is on a large bay with a sweeping beach and a fishing village. Past the park entrance the road climbs, giving expansive views over spectacular **Teluk Hijau** (Green Bay), with its cliffs and white-sand beach framed by deep green sea. A trail leads 1km from the road down to Teluk Hijau, or it is about a one hour walk east from Mess Pantai. From Mess Pantai other coastal walks are possible.

Places to Stay
The best place to stay when exploring the park is *Mess Pantai* in the forest back from Sukamade beach. Simple, four-bedroom cottages with shared mandi cost 20,000Rp per room. Cooking facilities are provided and the staff may be able to help but bring your own food – stock up in Sarongan, or the Sukamade estate in the plantation has a shop selling basic supplies.

About 5km north of the beach, the plantation's *Wisma Sukamade* has much more comfortable accommodation with electricity and all creature comforts. It has a variety of rooms from 60,000Rp and meals are provided. Though the accommodation is good, it not as convenient a place to stay unless you have your own transport.

Outside the park, the nearest hotels are in Jajag.

Getting There & Away
This is one of the most isolated parts of Java, and it is a long bumpy trip, even by 4WD which is how many visitors travel to the park.

From Banyuwangi first take a bus to Pesanggaran (2300Rp, 2½ hours, 87km) or from Jember take a bus to Jajag (south of the highway), then a minibus to Pesanggaran

(800Rp, 22km). From Pesanggaran take a taksi (the local name for a public minibus) to Sarongan (2000Rp, one hour; 18km). The road is paved and goes through plantations.

Sarongan is just a small town with a market and a few rumah makan. Stock up on supplies and then take an ojek (around 15,000Rp) for the 18km trip to Sukamade. After 4km you reach the Rajegwesi PHPA post at the entrance to the park. Pay your 2000Rp entry fee and also check on the condition of the river.

From Rajegwesi the very rough road runs 10km to the river crossing at Sumbosuko. This stretch climbs through brilliant dense forest before dropping down the mountain again. The views are stunning, but the road is really only for 4WD vehicles – the few cars that do tackle it wish they hadn't.

If the river is low, ojeks can take you straight on to Sukamade or Mess Pantai and 4WDs can cross. There are two river crossings – the deeper one further south and the multiple, shallower crossing further upstream. If the river is up but not flooded, you can wade across and get another ojek or walk the 4km to Mess Pantai.

ALAS PURWO NATIONAL PARK
This 43,420 hectare national park occupies the whole of the remote Blambangan Peninsula at the south-eastern tip of Java. Facilities are limited and it is not easy to reach, but Alas Purwo has fine beaches, good opportunities for wildlife spotting, and savanna, mangrove and lowland monsoon forests. Apart from day-trippers and local beach parties on weekends, the park gets few visitors.

Alas Purwo means First Forest in Javanese – according to legend this is where the earth first emerged from the ocean. It is an important Hindu spiritual centre and **Pura Giri Selokah**, a temple in the park attracts many pilgrims, especially during Pagerwesi, the Hindu new year.

More recently, the waves at Plengkung on the isolated south-eastern tip of the peninsula have reached legendary proportions among surfers. A series of huge breaks stretching almost 2km has made it world famous among surfers, who have dubbed it 'G-Land' (for Grajagan, which the area is also known as).

Surfers come by charter boat from Grajagan at the western end of the bay, but the usual park entry is by road via the village of Pasar Anyar, which has a large national park office and interpretive centre. Call in here to check on accommodation; alternatively check with the head office in Banyuwangi (☎ 424119) on Jl Agus Salim 138. The actual gateway to the park is at Rowobendo, 10km south along a bad road, where you pay your 2000Rp entry fee. From Rowobendo the road runs past the temple before hitting the beach at Trianggulasi, 2km away. Trianggulasi has hut accommodation but nothing else.

Exploring the Park
This limestone peninsula is relatively flat and the rolling hills reach a peak of only 322m. Alas Purwo has plenty of lowland, coastal forest but few trails to explore it – vast expanses of the eastern park are untrammelled, even by park staff.

Using Trianggulasi as a base, there are some interesting short walks. The white-sand beach here is beautiful, though swimming is usually dangerous.

It's common to see herds of wild banteng, kijang and peacocks in the early morning and late afternoon at the **Sadengan** grazing ground, which has a viewing tower. This beautiful meadow backed by forest is a 2km walk from Trianggulasi along a road and then a swampy trail.

Alas Purwo also has a small population of *ajag* (Asiatic wild dogs), jungle fowl, leaf monkeys, *muntjac* (barking deer), sambar deer and leopards (mostly black panthers). The park guards can arrange night leopard-spotting expeditions for around 10,000Rp and, though sightings are not guaranteed, night walks are interesting.

Guards can also arrange a motorbike trip to the turtle hatchery at **Ngagelan**, or you can walk. It's 6km from Rowobendo along a rough road, or a 7km walk along the beach at low tide from Trianggulasi.

It is also possible to walk along the beach all the way to Plengkung via **Pancur**, 3km south-east of Trianggulasi, where there is a small waterfall that flows onto the beach, another PHPA post and a camping ground.

From Pancur a trail heads 2km inland through some good forest to **Gua Istana**, a small cave, and 2km further to **Gua Padepokan**.

From Pancur it is a further 11km walk (two hours) around Grajagan Bay to the fine beach at **Plengkung**, one of Asia's premier surfing spots. Between 1995-98 the Quiksilver Pro surfing championship was held here every year around June as part of the Association of Surf Professionals World Championships. The surf camps at Plengkung are by no means five star but provide unexpected luxury in the wilderness.

Places to Stay & Eat
The PHPA's *Pesanggrahan* at Trianggulasi has elevated bungalows near the beach at 7500/12,000Rp for singles/doubles. Rooms are spartan with only a bed. Water is from a well and there is no electricity. Though primitive, this is a lovely, relaxing spot and many who come for a day or two end up staying longer.

All food and drink *must* be brought with you. Trianggulasi has no warungs and is deserted if no guests stay, but the Pesanggrahan has a kitchen with a kerosene stove and hurricane lamps. The *PHPA office* at Pasar Anyar has a shop selling basic provisions, such as Supermie packet noodles, but it is better to stock up at the two *general stores* in Dambuntung, where the bus drops you. A guard stays at Trianggulasi if there are guests and will cook for you if you share your food and, preferably, your beer (bring a few bottles with you).

There is also a *camping ground* at Pancur and a PHPA post.

The three surf camps back from the beach at Plengkung are for tours only. The biggest, *Bobby's Camp*, is run by Wanawisata Alam Hayati (☎ 0333 421485) in Banyuwangi. *Plengkung Indah* (☎ 031-53147) based in Surabaya is the other main

JAVA

operator. The elevated bungalows are comfortable and have most of the facilities a surfer could want – cold beer, surf videos, pool tables and decent restaurants. The new **Bambang Camp** is a simpler place and not yet fully established. Accommodation costs around US$30 a day at all the camps but everyone comes on a surfing package that includes all transfers, usually from Bali. Most tours are sold in Bali – try the surf shops on Jl Legian in Kuta or Tubes Bar, also in Kuta.

Getting There & Away
From Banyuwangi's southern Brawijaya bus terminal, the Putra Jaya company has buses to Kalipahit (2200Rp, 1.5 hours) via Benculuk and Tegaldelimo until 4 pm. Buses can drop you at the small village of Dambuntung, where you can stock up on food. Then take an ojek for around 10,000Rp first to the park office in Pasar Anyar, 3km from Dambuntung, to check on accommodation, and then on to the park. The 12km road from Pasar Anyar to Triangulasi is badly pot-holed but flat and negotiable by car.

From Ketapang or Bali, a number of buses take the southern highway. Any bus that goes via Jember can drop you at Rogojampi on the highway where you can pick up the bus to Kalipahit.

BANYUWANGI
☎ 0333

Although there are no particular attractions to drag you here, schedules or just the urge to be somewhere different might take you to Banyuwangi, the ferry departure point for Bali. The ferry terminus, main bus terminal and train station are all at Ketapang, 8km north of town, so most people go straight through to Gunung Bromo, Yogya or elsewhere. While Bali is teeming with tourists, Banyuwangi, just a stone's throw away, is a quiet, neglected backwater. The name Banyuwangi means 'perfumed water' from a legend that a Hindu king vanquished an evil usurper and threw him into the river, which became forever fragrant thereafter.

Information
The Banyuwangi Tourist Office, Jl Diponegoro 2, is at the cultural centre/sports field. A branch in the passenger terminal in Ketapang is open sporadically.

The post office is opposite the tourist office and has Internet terminals. It's open Monday to Saturday from 8 am to 3 pm.

Change money at the BCA bank on Jl Sudirman or the BNI bank south of the market, which has an ATM that accepts MasterCard. Another BNI branch at the Ketapang ferry terminal also has an ATM, and other banks at the ferry will change money at reasonable rates, but there are no after-hours moneychangers.

For information on Alas Purwo National Park and Kawah Ijen, the head office (☎ 424119) is at Jl A Yani 108, about 2km south of the town centre. The Baluran National Park head office (☎ 424119) is 2km further south-west at Jl Agus Salim 138.

Things to See
The main reason to stay here is to overnight on the way to Kawah Ijen or the national parks to the south. If you are desperate for something to do, the **Museum Daerah Blambangan**, opposite the alun alun on Jl Sritanjung, has a small collection of artefacts. In **Desa Temenggungan**, the kampung just behind the museum, Banyuwangi-style batik, *gajah oleng*, is produced. Ask around to see it being made. The town's market, **Pasar Banyuwangi**, with its crowded, narrow alleyways, is also worth a look.

Places to Stay
The *Hotel Baru (☎ 421369, Jl MT Haryono 82-84)* is the best of Banyuwangi's numerous cheap hotels and has a restaurant. Rooms, all with bathroom, cost 13,800Rp to 16,300Rp with fan, or 35,000Rp and 42,000Rp with air-con.

For something better, the popular *Hotel Pinang Sari (☎ 423266, Jl Basuki Rachmat 116)* is on the main road north of the Blambangan bemo station. This excellent mid-range hotel has a very attractive garden and a restaurant. Rooms with bath cost 18,900Rp

Ninja Killers

Quiet Banyuwangi hit the headlines in 1998 after mysterious serial killings claimed over 200 lives. The international press picked up on the killings and Banyuwangi made headlines around the world as the centre for the strangest story to emerge from Indonesia's turbulent economic period.

Local rumour has it that the killings began in a village south of Banyuwangi. When the identity of two *orang sakti* (black magicians) visiting the village became known, the villagers beat and tortured them before dragging them around the village until they were dead. Police found it difficult to lay charges without arresting the entire village.

Black magicians are feared throughout Indonesia. Anyone with a grudge can employ the services of a black magician who then casts a spell against the intended victim. The victim becomes sick and may die. Typically, it is said, the victim's stomach swells horrendously and the body turns black.

Soon black magicians were turning up dead throughout Banyuwangi city and the surrounding district with their throats cuts or hacked to death with knives. Then conservative Muslim clerics were targeted. Many belonged to Nahdatul Ulama, the 40 million strong Muslim organisation that belongs to the old school of syncretic Islam, with a strong slant towards mysticism. The killings had the hallmarks of an organised gang, and were dubbed the 'ninja killers' by the Indonesian media because they dressed in black and committed the killings at night.

Rumour was rife as the killings spread to Jember and continued throughout East Java. Doors were locked at night and vigilantes set up roadblocks in towns and villages, searching vehicles for suspected 'ninjas'.

In a country where the open transmission of information is a relatively new phenomenon, speculation is as much news as fact. Political leaders and newspapers, forever dreaming up conspiracy theories and blaming Indonesia's troubles on 'unknown forces', claimed it was the work of the army. In response, the army pulled the red rabbit out of the hat and claimed it was communists. Opposition leader Amien Rais even claimed Soeharto was behind the killings in an attempt to deflect anger away from himself and his cronies.

Abdurrahman Wahid, leader of Nahdatul Ulama, seemed nearer the mark when he hinted it was the work of rival Muslim groups, though many were random killings by hysterical mobs in this conservative, superstitious region. On Madura, three detectives were set upon and killed by a mob when a suspect they were chasing shouted out that the three were ninjas. In Malang, the severed head of a suspected ninja was paraded through the streets, but police had no idea of the victim's identity. In other incidents, those with mental disorders were killed.

Hundreds of suspects were arrested and a handful have been committed to trial. The violence is over but it is unlikely that the killings were the work of a single organised gang. The real truth may never be known, but the killings mirror similar incidents in this region in the 1950s and 60s. Old grudges are resurfacing in Indonesia and are a constant threat to emergent democracy.

and 22,900Rp. A variety of stylish rooms and bungalows with air-con, TV and hot water cost 44,000Rp to 145,000Rp.

Banyuwangi's top hotels are in Ketapang. The big *Manyar Hotel* (☎ 424741), 1km south of the ferry terminal on the road to Banyuwangi, is shabby but has comfortable motel units, a restaurant, disco and pool. Discounted rates cost 52,500Rp to 203,000Rp. One kilometre further south, the newer *Hotel Ketapang Indah* (☎ 422280) is marginally better and has a pool. Bungalows back from the beach cost 150,000Rp and 170,000Rp or the sea-view rooms are 300,000Rp (before a substantial discount).

Places to Eat

For snacks, Jl Pattimura has night *food stalls* where you'll find delicious *air jahe* (ginger tea), *dadak jagung* (egg and sweetcorn patties), *ketan* (sticky rice topped with coconut) and *pisang goreng* (fried banana).

Around the corner, ***Rumah Makan Surya*** *(Jl W Hasyim 94)* has moderately priced Chinese food. ***Depot Asia*** *(Jl Dr Sutomo 12)* also has good, if slightly expensive, Chinese food and boasts air-con. For the best Maduresestyle sate in town, go to Pak Amat's *warung* on Jl Basuki Rachmat in the evening.

Getting There & Away

Bus Banyuwangi has two bus terminals. The Seri Tanjung bus terminal is 3km north of the Bali ferry terminal at Ketapang, and 11km north of town. Buses from here go to northern destinations, such as Baluran (1000Rp, one hour); Probolinggo (6000/12,000Rp normal/patas, four hours) for Gunung Bromo; Surabaya (9500/17,500Rp, six hours); and Malang (9500/17,500Rp). Buses also go right through to Yogya, Jakarta and Denpasar (5000/10,000Rp to 15,000Rp, four hours including the ferry trip).

Some long-distance buses from Seri Tanjung take the southern route via Jember but Brawijaya terminal (also known as Karang Ente), 4km south of town, has most of the buses to the south, including: Kalipahit (2200Rp, 1½ hours); Pesanggaran (2300Rp, two hours); and Jember (3200/6500Rp aircon, three hours).

Train The main train station is just a few hundred metres north of the ferry terminal at Ketapang. Most trains also stop at the Argopuro and Karang Asem train stations, on the northern and eastern outskirts of Banyuwangi respectively, but it is hard to get public transport to either.

The express *Mutiara Timur* leaves at 9.30 am and 10 pm for Probolinggo (15,000/25,000Rp in bisnis/eksekutif, four hours)

and Surabaya (15,000/28,000Rp, six hours). Ekonomi trains include the *Blambangan* to Probolinggo at 1.05 pm; the *Regganis* to Malang (4500Rp, eight hours); the *Sri Tanjung* to Yogya (14,000Rp, 13 hours); and the *Pandanwangi* to Jember (1700Rp, 3½ hours) via Kalibaru (1100Rp, two hours) at 5.30 pm. All trains take the southern route via Jember and on to Probolinggo. Trains can be very crowded at peak travel times, particularly Sunday.

Boat Ferries from Ketapang depart roughly every 30 minutes around the clock for Gilimanuk on Bali. The ferry costs 1400Rp for passengers, 3600Rp for motorcycles and 18,000Rp for cars. Through buses between Bali and Java include the fare in the bus ticket and are the easiest option. Otherwise check the buses on the ferry for a spare seat.

Pelni's *Tatamailau* stops in Banyuwangi on its route to Nusa Tenggara and Irian Jaya. It docks at Ketapang, along from the Bali ferry dock.

Getting Around

Banyuwangi has a squadron of minibuses running between the bus terminals and terminating at the Blambangan minibus terminal near the centre of town. They're marked Lin 1, 2, 3 etc, and charge a fixed 500Rp fare around town, or 800Rp from the ferry terminal. Lin 6 or 12 runs from Blambangan to the ferry terminal and on to the Seri Tanjung bus terminal. Lin 2 goes from Blambangan to the Hotel Baru area. Lin 3 goes from Blambangan to Sasak Perot, where you get Colts to the Ijen Plateau. Private cars at the ferry terminal act as taxis but are expensive and not always easy to find.

KALIKLATAK

Kaliklatak, 20km north of Banyuwangi, is another agro-tourism venture, with tours available of late coffee, cocoa, rubber, coconut and clove plantations. *Wisata Irdjen Guesthouse* (☎ 424061 Kaliklatak or ☎ 424896 Banyuwangi) offers excellent accommodation but it's expensive and must be booked in advance.

BALURAN NATIONAL PARK

On the north-east corner of Java, the national park covers an area of 250 sq km. Gunung Baluran (1247m), in the park's centre, formerly overlooked extensive savanna grasslands, which led to the parks label 'Indonesia's little bit of Africa'. The park is still rich in wildlife, but the grasslands have disappeared due to encroachment by Acacia thorn scrub. The park has undertaken major programs to eliminate the species, planted as a firebreak in the late 70s.

Baluran supports internationally important populations of banteng and ajag plus sambar deer, muntjac (barking) deer, two species of monkey, wild pigs, leopards and other smaller carnivores. The birdlife is depleted, due to extensive illegal trapping for the caged-bird trade. However, green peafowl, red and green junglefowl, hornbills and bee-eaters are still easy to see.

On the hill above the guesthouses at Bekol there is a viewing tower that provides a panoramic view over a 300 hectare clearing. Banteng and sambar herds can be seen here, and wild dogs can sometimes be seen hunting sambar, usually in the early morning. There are walking trails around Bekol.

Bama, on the coast, is a 3km walk or drive from Bekol. It has accommodation and a half-decent beach where you can snorkel. The nearby coastal forest (follow the stony tracks) has numerous waterholes and is a good place to see water monitor lizards, monkeys and birds.

The main service town for Baluran is Wonorejo, on the main coast road between Surabaya and Banyuwangi, where food supplies can be bought – the PHPA office and visitor centre is on the highway. If you're not staying overnight, baggage can be left safely at the PHPA office. The park entry fee is 2000Rp.

Baluran can be visited at any time of the year, but the dry season (June to November) is usually the best time because the animals congregate near the waterholes at Bekol and Bama. Recently, park projects, particularly

one allowing villagers to harvest Acacia seeds, have disrupted wildlife. In view of this, the period between October and January (when the early rains cause new grass to grow) may be the best time to see large mammals.

Places to Stay

At Bekol, 12km into the park, *Pesanggrahan* has seven rooms and costs 6000Rp per person; there's a mandi and kitchen but you must bring your own provisions. *Wisma Tamu* next door has three very comfortable rooms with attached mandi for 10,000Rp per person; *Pondok Peneliti* costs 12,500Rp. The *canteen* at Bekol sells drinks and some provisions, but meals are cooked only for groups if advance notice is given. You might be able to arrange something with the PHPA staff, but bring your own food.

Bama Guesthouse is 3km east of Bekol on the beach and provides rooms for 6000Rp per person. It also has cooking facilities, but you must bring your own food. The newer *Rumah Panggung* is nearer the waterhole.

Bookings can be made in advance at the Baluran PHPA office in Banyuwangi or through the Baluran PHPA (☎ 0333-461650). Most visitors tend to day trip so accommodation is not usually full, but it pays to book, especially in the peak June to July holiday period when school groups visit the park.

Getting There & Away

Surabaya to Banyuwangi buses, taking the coast road via Probolinggo, can drop you right at the park entrance; and when leaving the park, buses are easily flagged down. From Banyuwangi (or Ketapang ferry, if you're coming from Bali) it's only a half-hour journey on the Wonorejo bus (1000Rp). Ask the driver to let you off at the park entrance, and ask a PHPA ranger to arrange an ojek (7500Rp) to take you the 12km to Bekol along the badly rutted road. A private car (20,000Rp) can be arranged, but the park has no vehicles of its own. Coming from the west, Baluran is 3½ hours from Probolinggo.

Bali

For many westerners, Bali doesn't extend beyond the tourist leaflet: idyllic tropical beaches, lush green forests and rice fields tripping down hillsides like giant steps. This vision of paradise has been turned into a commodity for the hundreds of thousands of tourists who flood into Bali every year. But Bali has much more than this – you can still discover the extraordinary richness of Balinese culture, which remains unique and authentic despite the tourist invasion, and it's not hard to find out-of-the-way places where tourists are a rarity.

HISTORY

It's certain that Bali has been populated since early prehistoric times, but the oldest human artefacts found in Bali are stone tools and earthenware vessels from Cekik, from about 3000 years ago. Not much is known of Bali during the period when Indian traders brought Hinduism to the Indonesian archipelago, but the earliest written records are stone inscriptions, dating from around the 9th century AD. By that time, rice was being grown with a complex irrigation system, and there were precursors of the religious and cultural tradition that can be traced to the present day.

Hindu Influence

Hindu Java began to spread its influence into Bali during the reign of King Airlangga, from 1019 to 1042. At the age of 16, when his uncle lost the throne, Airlangga fled into the forests of western Java. He gradually gained support, won back the kingdom once ruled by his uncle and went on to become one of Java's greatest kings. Airlangga's mother had moved to Bali and remarried shortly after his birth, so when he gained the throne there was an immediate link between Java and Bali. At this time, the courtly Javanese language known as Kawi came into use among the royalty of Bali, and the rock-cut memorials seen at Gunung Kawi (Mt Kawi) near Tam-

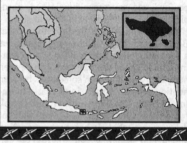

paksiring are a clear architectural link between Bali and 11th century Java.

After Airlangga's death Bali retained its semi-independent status until Kertanagara became king of the Singasari dynasty in Java two centuries later. Kertanagara conquered Bali in 1284, but his greatest power lasted only eight years until he was murdered and his kingdom collapsed. However, the great Majapahit dynasty was founded by his son. With Java in turmoil, Bali regained its autonomy and the Pejeng dynasty, centred near modern-day Ubud, rose to great power. In 1343 Gajah Mada, the legendary chief Majapahit minister, defeated the Pejeng king Dalem Bedaulu and brought Bali back under Javanese influence.

Although Gajah Mada brought much of the Indonesian archipelago under Majapahit control, this was the furthest extent of their power. In Bali the 'capital' moved to Gelgel, near modern Semarapura (once known as Klungkung), around the late 14th century and for the next two centuries this was the base for the 'king of Bali', the Dewa Agung. As Islam spread into Java the Majapahit kingdom collapsed into disputing sultanates. However, the Gelgel dynasty in Bali, under Dalem Batur Enggong, extended its power eastwards to the neighbouring island of Lombok and even crossed the strait to Java.

As the Majapahit kingdom fell apart, many of its intelligentsia moved to Bali, including the priest Nirartha, who is credited with introducing many of the complexities of Balinese religion to the island. Artists, dancers, musicians and actors also fled to Bali at this time, and the island experienced an explosion of cultural activities. The final great exodus to Bali took place in 1478.

European Contact

The first Europeans to set foot in Bali were Dutch seafarers in 1597. Setting a tradition that prevails right down to the present day, they fell in love with the island and when Cornelius Houtman, the ship's captain, prepared to set sail from Bali, some of his crew refused to leave with him. At that time, Balinese prosperity and artistic activity, at least among the royalty, were at a peak, and the king who befriended Houtman had 200 wives and a chariot pulled by two white buffaloes, not to mention a retinue of 50 dwarfs whose bodies had been bent to resemble kris handles! Although the Dutch returned to Indonesia in later years, they were interested in profit, not culture, and barely gave Bali a second glance.

Dutch Conquest

In 1710 the capital of the Gelgel kingdom was shifted to nearby Klungkung (as it was known), but local discontent was growing, lesser rulers were breaking away from Gelgel domination and the Dutch began to move in, using the old policy of divide and conquer. In 1846 the Dutch used Balinese salvage claims over shipwrecks as the pretext to land military forces in northern Bali. In 1894 the Dutch chose to support the Sasaks of Lombok in a rebellion against their Balinese rajah. After some bloody battles, the Balinese were defeated in Lombok, and with northern Bali firmly under Dutch control, southern Bali was not likely to retain its independence for long. Once again, salvaging disputes gave the Dutch the excuse they needed to move in. A Chinese ship was wrecked off Sanur in 1904 and ransacked by the Balinese. The Dutch demanded that the rajah of Badung pay 3000 silver dollars in damages – this was refused. In 1906 Dutch warships appeared at Sanur; Dutch forces landed and, despite Balinese opposition, marched the 5km to the outskirts of Denpasar.

On 20 September 1906, the Dutch mounted a naval bombardment on Denpasar and then commenced their final assault. The three princes of Badung (south Bali) realised that they were outnumbered and outgunned, and that defeat was inevitable. Surrender and exile, however, were the worst imaginable outcome, so they decided to take the honourable path of a suicidal *puputan* – a fight to the death.

The Dutch begged the Balinese to surrender rather than make their hopeless stand, but their pleas went unheard and wave after wave of the Balinese nobility marched forward to their death. In all, nearly 4000 Balinese died in the puputan. Later, the Dutch marched east towards Tabanan, taking the rajah of Tabanan prisoner, but he committed suicide rather than face the disgrace of exile.

The kingdoms of Karangasem and Gianyar had already capitulated to the Dutch and were allowed to retain some of their powers, but other kingdoms were defeated and their rulers exiled. Finally, the rajah of Klungkung followed the lead of Badung and once more the Dutch faced a puputan. With this last obstacle disposed of, all of Bali was now under Dutch control and part of the Dutch East Indies. Dutch rule over Bali was short-lived, however, as Indonesia fell to the Japanese in WWII.

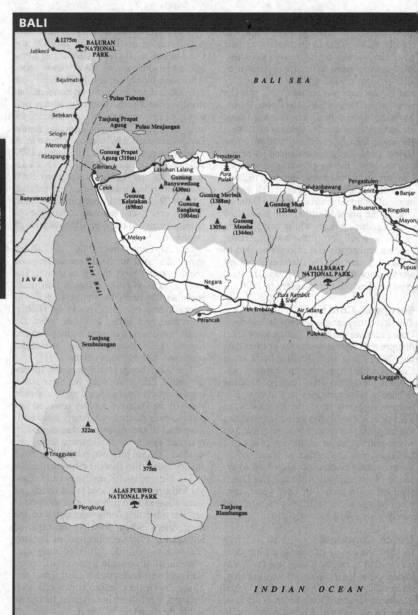

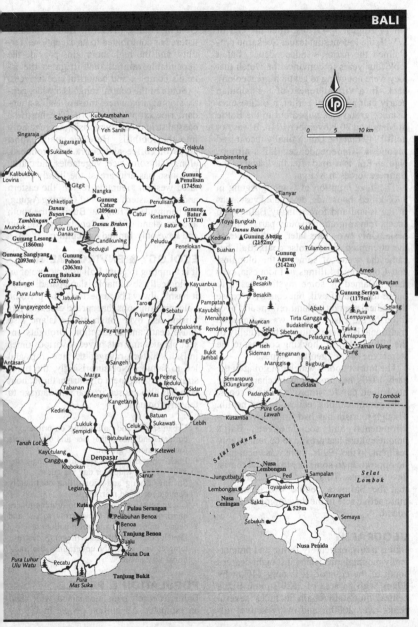

BALI

Independence
On 17 August 1945, just after the end of WWII, the Indonesian leader Soekarno proclaimed the nation's independence, but it took four years to convince the Dutch that they were not going to get their great colony back. In a virtual repeat of the puputan nearly half a century earlier, a Balinese resistance group was wiped out in the Battle of Marga on 20 November 1946. It was not until 1949 that the Dutch finally recognised Indonesia's independence. Bali's airport, Ngurah Rai, is named after the leader of the Balinese forces at Marga.

The huge eruption of Gunung Agung in 1963 killed thousands, devastated vast areas of the island and forced many Balinese to accept transmigration to other parts of Indonesia. Only two years later, in the wake of the attempted Communist coup, Bali became the scene of some of the bloodiest anti-Communist killings in Indonesia, perhaps inflamed by some mystical desire to purge the land of evil, but equally because the radical agenda of land reform and abolition of the caste system was a threat to traditional Balinese values. The brutality of the killings was in shocking contrast to the stereotype of the 'gentle' Balinese.

The tourist boom, which got going in the early 1970s, has brought many changes, and has helped pay for improvements in roads, telecommunications, education and health. Though tourism has had some adverse environmental and social effects, Bali's unique culture has proved to be remarkably resilient. In the 1990s, there was vocal public opposition to some controversial tourist developments. This may be an indication that the Balinese people will demand a more active role in the development of their island.

GEOGRAPHY
Bali is a tiny, extremely fertile and dramatically mountainous island just eight degrees south of the equator. It is only 140km by 80km, with an area of 5620 sq km. Bali's central mountain chain includes several peaks over 2000m and many active volcanoes, including the 'mother' mountain Gunung Agung (3142m). Bali's volcanic nature has contributed to its exceptional fertility, and the high mountains provide the dependable rainfall that irrigates the island's complex and beautiful rice terraces.

South of the central range is a wide, gently sloping area where most of Bali's abundant rice crops are grown. The northern coastal strip is narrower, rising more rapidly into the foothills. Here the main export crops of coffee and copra are produced, along with some rice, vegetables and cattle. Bali also has arid areas: the lightly populated western mountain region, the eastern and north-eastern slopes of Gunung Agung, the peninsula of Tanjung Bukit in the south and the island of Nusa Penida get little rain and have only limited agriculture.

ECOLOGY & ENVIRONMENT
It is tempting to paint Bali as a picture of an ecologically sustainable island paradise, but it hasn't always been perfect. The periodic volcanic eruptions that spread essential fertilising ash over much of the island also cause death and destruction. Droughts, insect plagues and rats have, at various times in Bali's history, ravaged the rice crops and led to famine. Not surprisingly, the unrestrained development of tourism throughout Bali has also caused irreparable damage to the environment:

- Urban sprawl and hotels built on prime agricultural land means that rice and other staple foods cannot be grown.
- Each top-end hotel in Bali uses a staggering 570L of fresh water per day per guest.
- Surfing, diving and snorkelling continually damage reefs and marine life.
- Cheap rental of cars and motorbikes places enormous strain on the narrow roads, and causes immense air and noise pollution.
- Development displaces villagers, destroys temples and seriously undermines the traditional way of life.

POPULATION & PEOPLE
Bali is a densely populated island, which had an estimated 2.9 million people in 1995 –

about 520 people per sq km. The population is almost all Indonesian; 95% are of Balinese Hindu religion and could be described as ethnic Balinese. Most of the other residents are from other parts of Indonesia, particularly Java, but also Sumatra and Nusa Tenggara.

The Balinese have a traditional caste system that resembles the Indian Hindu system, although there are no 'untouchables'. Nor is there an intricate division of labour based on caste, except for the Brahmana priesthood. Over 90% of the population belong to the common Sudra caste, which now includes many wealthy Balinese. The main significance of caste is in religious roles and rituals, and in the language; but its importance in other aspects of life is declining.

ARTS

The Balinese have no words for 'art' and 'artist' because traditionally, art has never been regarded as something to be treasured for its own sake. Prior to the tourist invasion, art was just something you did – you painted or carved as a part of everyday life, and what you produced went into temples or palaces or was used for festivals. Although respected, the painter or carver was not considered a member of some special elite, the artists' work was not signed and there were no galleries or craft shops.

It's a different story today, with thousands of galleries and craft shops in every possible crevice a tourist might trip into. Although much of Balinese art is churned out quickly for people who want a cheap souvenir, buried beneath the reproductions of reproductions there's still quite a lot of beautiful work to be found – if you dig deep enough.

Even the simplest activities are carried out with care, precision and artistic flair. Just glance at those little offering trays thrown down on the ground for the demons every morning – each one a throwaway work of art. Look at the temple offerings, the artistically stacked pyramids of fruit or other beautifully decorated foods. Look for the *lamaks* (long woven palm-leaf strips used as decorations), the stylised female figures known as *cili* and the intricately carved coconut-shell

wall-hangings. At funerals, you'll be amazed at the care and energy that goes into constructing huge funeral towers and exotic sarcophagi, all of which go up in flames.

Architecture

A basic element of Balinese architecture is the *bale*, a rectangular, open-sided pavilion with a steeply pitched hip roof of palm thatch. A family compound will have a number of bale for eating, sleeping and working. The focus of a community is the *bale banjar*, a large pavilion for meeting, debate, *gamelan* (Balinese orchestra) practice etc. Large, modern buildings like restaurants and the lobby areas of new hotels are often modelled on the bale – they are airy, spacious and handsomely proportioned.

Like the other arts, architecture has traditionally served the religious life of Bali. Balinese houses, although often attractive places, have never been lavished with the architectural attention that is given to temples. Even Balinese palaces are modest compared with the more important temples. Temples are designed to set rules and formulas, with sculpture serving as an adjunct, a finishing touch to these design guidelines.

Sculpture

In small or less important temples, the sculpture may be limited or even nonexistent, while in other temples – particularly some of the exuberantly detailed temples of northern Bali – the sculpture may be almost overwhelming in its detail and intricacy. A temple gateway, for example, might be carved over every square centimetre, with a diminishing series of demon faces above it as protection. Even then it's not finished without a couple of stone statues to act as guardians.

Door guardians, of legendary figures like Arjuna or other protectors, flank the steps to the gateway. Above the main entrance to a temple is the monstrous face of the guardian temple demon *kala*, sometimes a number of times – its hands reach out beside its head to catch any evil spirits that try to sneak in. The ancient swastika symbol indicates good fortune and prosperity. Carved panels on the walls may show scenes of local significance or everyday life. The front of a *pura dalem* (temple of the dead) will often feature images of the *rangda* (witch) and sculptured panels may show the horrors that await evildoers in the afterlife.

Woodcarving

Like painting, woodcarving is no longer done simply for decoration or other symbolic purposes in temples and palaces but is now created for its own sake. As with painting, influences from outside inspired new subjects and styles, and some of the same western artists provided the stimulus.

Especially around Ubud, carvers started producing highly stylised and elongated figures, leaving the wood in its natural state rather than painting it, as was the traditional practice. Others carved delightful animal figures, some totally realistic and others wonderful caricatures, while other artists carved whole tree trunks into ghostly, intertwined 'totem poles' or curiously exaggerated and distorted figures.

Dance

Music, dance and drama are all closely related in Bali. In fact, dance and drama are synonymous, though some 'dances' are more drama and less dance, and others more dance and less drama. Most dancers are not specialists, but ordinary people who dance in the evening or in their spare time. They learn the dances by long hours of practice, usually carefully following the movements of an expert.

There are rarely the soaring leaps of classical ballet or the smooth flowing movements often found in western dance. Balinese dance tends to be precise, jerky, shifting and jumpy, like the accompanying gamelan music, which has abrupt shifts of tempo and dramatic changes between silence and crashing noise. There's virtually no physical contact in Balinese dancing – each dancer moves independently, but every movement of wrist, hand and finger is important. Even facial expressions are carefully choreographed to convey the character of the dance.

The Balinese like a blend of seriousness and slapstick, and their dances show this. Basically, the dances are straightforward ripping yarns, where you cheer on the goodies and cringe when the baddies appear. Some dances have a comic element, with clowns who counterbalance the staid, noble characters. The clowns often have to convey the story to the audience, since the noble characters may use the classical Javanese Kawi language, while the clowns (usually servants of the noble characters) converse in everyday Balinese.

Dances are a regular part of almost every temple festival and Bali has no shortage of these. There are also dances virtually every night at all the tourist centres (see the boxed text 'Where are the Dances' later in this section); admission to a 1st class performance in Ubud, for example, costs 10,000Rp to 15,000Rp. Some performances are offered as entertainment at a restaurant or hotel, often with a mixture of dances – a little Topeng, a taste of Legong and some Baris to round it off. This is not a good way to see Balinese dance, so it's worth looking around for a better performance. The authenticity, quality and level of drama varies widely, but excellent dances can be seen, where the audience includes many appreciative Balinese.

Kecak Probably the best known of the many Balinese dances, the Kecak is unusual because it doesn't have a gamelan accompaniment. Instead, the background is provided by a chanting 'choir' of men who provide the 'chak-a-chak-a-chak' noise that distinguishes the dance. Originally this chanting group was known as the Kecak and was part of a Sanghyang trance dance. Then in the 1930s the modern Kecak developed in Bona, near Gianyar, where the dance is still held regularly.

The Kecak tells the tale of the *Ramayana* (see the Java chapter for a rundown of the story), the quest of Prince Rama to rescue his wife Sita after she had been kidnapped by Rawana, the King of Lanka. Rama is accompanied to Lanka by Sugriwa, the king of the monkeys, with his monkey army. Throughout the Kecak dance, the circle of men, all bare-chested and wearing checked cloth around their waists, provide a nonstop accompaniment, rising to a crescendo as they play the monkey army and fight it out with Rawana and his cronies. The chanting is accompanied by the movements of the monkey army whose members sway back and forth, raise their hands in unison, flutter their fingers and lean left and right, all with an eerily exciting coordination.

Barong & Rangda The Barong Keket is a strange creature – half shaggy dog, half lion – and is played by two men in much the same way as a circus clown-horse. Its opponent is the rangda (witch).

The barong personifies good and protects the village from the rangda, but is also a mischievous and fun-loving creature. It flounces into the temple courtyard, snaps its jaws at the gamelan, dances around and enjoys the acclaim of its supporters – a group of men with krises. Then the rangda makes her appearance, her long tongue lolling, her pendulous breasts wobbling, human entrails draped around her neck, fangs protruding from her mouth and sabre-like fingernails clawing the air.

Now the barong is no longer the clown, but the protector. The two duel with their magical powers, and the barong's supporters draw their krises and rush in to attack the witch. The rangda puts them in a trance and the men try to stab themselves, but the barong also has great magical powers and casts a spell that stops the krises from harming the men. This is the most dramatic part of the dance – as the gamelan rings crazily the men rush back and forth, waving their krises around, all but foaming at the mouth, sometimes even rolling on the ground in a desperate attempt to stab themselves. Finally, the rangda retires defeated – good has won again. Good must always triumph over evil in Bali, and no matter how many times the spectators have seen the performance or how well they know the outcome, the battle itself remains all-important.

The end of the dance still leaves a large group of entranced barong supporters to be brought back to the real world. This is usually done by sprinkling them with holy water, sanctified by dipping the barong's beard in it.

Legong This is the most graceful of Balinese dances and, to sophisticated Balinese connoisseurs of dancing, the one of most interest.

There are various forms of the Legong but the Legong Kraton, or Legong of the palace, is the one most usually performed. A performance involves just three dancers – the two Legongs and their 'attendant' known as the *condong*. The Legongs are identically dressed in tightly bound gold brocade. So tightly are they encased that it's something of a mystery how they manage to move with such agility and speed. Their faces are elaborately made up, their eyebrows plucked and repainted, and their hair decorated with frangipanis.

The dance relates how a king takes a maiden, Rangkesari, captive. When Rangkesari's brother comes to release her, he begs the king to let her free rather than go to war. The king refuses and on his way to the battle meets a bird bringing ill omens. He ignores the bird and continues on to meet Rangkesari's brother, who kills him. The dance, however, only relates the lead up to the battle and ends with the bird's appearance. When the king leaves the stage he is going to the battle that will end in his death.

The dance starts with the condong dancing an introduction. The condong departs as the Legongs enter the stage. The Legongs dance solo, in close identical formation, and even dance in mirror-image formation when they dance a nose-to-nose love scene. They relate the king's sad departure from his queen, Rangkesari's request that he release her and the king's departure for the battle. Finally, the condong reappears with tiny golden wings as the bird of ill fortune and the dance comes to an end.

BALI

Other Dances There are a number of other dances performed in Bali:

Baris The warrior dance known as the Baris is a male equivalent of the Legong in which femininity and grace give way to the energetic, war-like martial spirit. The solo Baris dancer has to convey the thoughts and emotions of a warrior preparing for action and then meeting an enemy in battle. The dancer must show his changing moods not only through his dancing, but also through facial expression.

Janger In the Janger dance, formations of 12 young women and 12 young men perform a sitting dance, where the gentle swaying and chanting of the women is contrasted with the violently choreographed movements and loud shouts of the men.

Kebyar This is a male solo dance like the Baris, but with greater emphasis on the performer's individual abilities. There are various forms of the dance, including the seated Kebyar Duduk where the 'dance' is done from the seated position, so that movements of the hands, arms and torso, plus facial expressions, are all important.

Pendet This is an everyday dance of the temples that doesn't require arduous training and practice – a small procedure gone through before making temple offerings. You may often see the Pendet being danced by women bringing offerings to a temple for a festival, but it is also sometimes danced as an introduction and a closing for other dance performances.

Ramayana The *Ramayana* is a familiar tale in Bali, but the dance is a relatively recent addition to the Balinese repertoire. It tells much the same story of Rama and Sita as told in the Kecak but without the monkey ensemble and with a normal gamelan orchestra accompaniment. It's also embellished with many improvisations and comic additions. Rawana may be played as a classic bad guy, while the monkey god Hanuman can be a comic clown.

Sanghyang The Sanghyang Dedari is performed by two girls who dance a dream-like version of the Legong. The dancers are said to be untrained in the intricate pattern of the dance and, furthermore, they dance in perfect harmony but with their eyes firmly shut. A female choir and a male Kecak choir provide a background chant, but when the chant stops the dancers slump to the ground in a faint. Two women bring them around, and at the finish, a priest blesses them with holy water and brings them out of the trance. The modern Kecak dance developed from the Sanghyang. In the Sanghyang Jaran, a boy in a trance dances around and through a fire of coconut husks riding a coconut-palm hobby horse – it's labelled the 'fire dance' for the benefit of tourists. Once again the priest must be on hand to break the trance at the close of the dance.

Topeng The word Topeng means 'pressed against the face', as with a mask. In this mask dance, the dancers have to imitate the character their mask indicates they are playing. The Topeng Tua, for example, is a classic solo dance where the mask is that of an old man and requires the performer to dance like a creaky old gentleman. Mask dances require great expertise because the character's thoughts and meanings cannot be conveyed through the dancer's facial expressions, so the character of the unpleasant, frenetic, fast-moving demon has to be portrayed entirely through the dance.

The Gamelan

As on Sumatra and Java, Balinese music is based around the gamelan orchestra (for more details see the Java chapter). The whole gamelan orchestra is known as a *gong* – an old fashioned *gong gede* or a more modern *gong kebyar*. There are even more ancient forms of the gamelan, such as the *gong selunding*, still occasionally played in Bali Aga villages like Tenganan.

Although the instruments used are much the same, Balinese gamelan is very different from the form you'll hear in Java. The Yogyakarta style, for example, is the most reserved, formal and probably the gentlest and most 'refined' of gamelans. Balinese gamelan often sounds like everyone going for it full pelt. Perhaps a more telling point is that Javanese gamelan music is rarely heard except at special performances, whereas in Bali you seem to hear gamelans playing everywhere you go.

BALINESE SOCIETY

Traditional Balinese society is intensely communal; the organisation of villages, the cultivation of farmlands and even the creative arts are communal efforts – a person belongs to their family, clan, caste and the village as a whole. Religion permeates all aspects of life and ceremonies, and rituals mark each stage in the life cycle. The first ceremony takes place before birth, at the third month of pregnancy, when a series of

BALINESE PAINTING

The art form most influenced both by western ideas and tourist demand is painting. Traditional painting was very limited in style and subject matter and was used primarily for temple decoration. The arrival of western artists after WWI expanded painting beyond these limitations and introduced new subject matters and materials with which artists could work. The best places to see examples of Balinese painting styles are the Museum Puri Lukisan and Neka Museum in Ubud.

Traditional Painting

Balinese painting was strictly limited to three basic kinds: *langse*, *iders-iders* and calendars. Langse are large rectangular hangings used as decoration or curtains in palaces or temples. Iders-iders are scroll paintings that are hung along the eaves of temples. The calendars were usually astrological, showing the auspicious days of each month.

Most of the paintings were narratives with mythological themes, illustrating stories from Hindu epics and literature. These paintings were always executed in the *wayang* style, the flat two dimensional style that is imitative of the *wayang kulit* performances (shadow puppet play), the figures invariably shown in three-quarters view. Even the colours that artists could use were strictly limited to a set list of shades (red, blue, brown, yellow and a light ochre for flesh).

In these narratives the same characters appeared in several different scenes, each depicting an episode from the story. The individual scenes were usually bordered by mountains, flames or ornamental

Text inset: A trance dancer, surrounded by smoke and incense seeks spirits to enter her body (photograph by Gregory Adams).

Right: A traditional *wayang*-style painting.

RICHARD I'ANSON

walls. The deities, princes and heroes were identified by opulent clothing, jewellery, elaborate headdresses and by their graceful postures and gestures; and the devils and giants by their bulging eyes, canine teeth, bulbous noses and bulky bodies. Semarapura is still a centre for traditional painting – the painted ceiling of the Hall of Justice in Semarapura is a fine example of the style.

Foreign Influences

Under the influence of Walter Spies and Rudolf Bonnet, who settled in Bali in the 1930s, Balinese artists started painting single scenes instead of narrative tales and used scenes from everyday life rather than romantic legends as their themes. Even more importantly, pictures were painted for their own sake – not as something to cover a space in a palace or temple. The idea of a painting being something you could do by itself (and for which there might be a market) was wholly new.

As the 1930s-style degenerated into stale copying a new style emerged in Ubud, with particular encouragement from the Dutch painter Aries Smit. His 'Young Artists', as they were known, picked up where those of the 1930s had left off, painting Balinese rural scenes in brilliant technicolour.

Below: A selection of paintings from the Neka Museum in Ubud exhibiting the freer forms and vivid colours of modern Balinese painting.

BERNARD NAPTHINE

BERNARD NAPTHINE

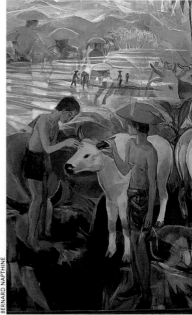

BERNARD NAPTHINE

Where are the Dances?

Denpasar Kecak every evening at the Arts Centre.

South Bali Barong during festivals on Pulau Serangan; all sorts of dances at hotels and restaurants in Sanur, Nusa Dua, Jimbaran and the Kuta region; and Ramayana ballet at Taman Festival Bali park, Sanur.

Ubud & Around All sorts of dances, Ramayana ballet and wayang kulit shadow puppets on dance stages in Ubud; Legong is famous in Peliatan, near Ubud; Barong & Rangda can be seen in Batubulan; wayang kulit can be seen at Sukawati; and Kecak is very famous at Bona.

East Bali Barong, Topeng and Legong at Candidasa.

West Bali Legong at restaurants at Tanah Lot.

offerings is made at home and at the village river or spring to ensure the wellbeing of the baby. When the child reaches puberty its teeth are filed to produce an aesthetically pleasing straight line – even teeth symbolise an even temperament, while crooked fangs are characteristic of witches and demons.

Balinese women are not cloistered away, though the roles of the sexes are fairly well delineated, with certain tasks handled by women and others reserved for men. For instance, the running of the household is very much the woman's task, while caring for animals is mostly a male preserve.

Balinese society is held together by collective responsibility. If a woman enters a temple while menstruating, for instance, it is a kind of irreverence, an insult to the gods, and their displeasure falls not just on the transgressor but on the whole community. This collective responsibility produces considerable pressure on the individual to conform to *adat* (traditional values and customs).

Households

Despite the strong communal nature of Balinese society, traditional houses are surrounded by a high wall and the compound is usually entered through a gateway backed by a small wall known as the *aling aling*. It serves a practical and a spiritual purpose – both preventing passers-by from seeing in and stopping evil spirits from entering. Evil spirits cannot easily turn corners so the aling aling stops them from scooting straight in through the gate. Inside there will be a family temple in one corner, a garden and a separate small building (bale) for each household function: cooking, sleeping, washing and the toilet.

Village Organisation

Each village is subdivided into *banjars,* which all adults join when they marry. It is the banjar that organises village festivals, marriage ceremonies and even cremations. Throughout the island you'll see the open-sided meeting places known as bale banjar – they're nearly as common a sight as temples. Gamelan orchestras are organised at the banjar level, and a glance in a bale banjar at any time might reveal a gamelan practice, a meeting, food for a feast being prepared, even a group of men simply getting their roosters together to raise their anger in preparation for the next round of cockfights.

One of the important elements of village government is the *subak*. Each individual rice field is known as a *sawah* and each farmer who owns even one sawah must be a member of the local subak. The rice fields must have a steady supply of water and it is the job of the subak to ensure that the water supply gets to everybody. It's said that the head of the local subak will often be the farmer whose rice fields are at the bottom of the hill, for he will make quite certain that the water gets all the way down to his fields, passing through everybody else's on the way!

RELIGION

The Balinese are nominally Hindus, but Balinese Hinduism is half a world away from that of India. When the Majapahits evacuated to

BALI

Bali they took with them their religion and its rituals, as well as their art, literature, music and culture. The Balinese already had strong religious beliefs and an active cultural life, and the new influences were simply overlaid on existing practices – hence the peculiar Balinese interpretation of Hinduism.

The Balinese worship the same gods as the Hindus of India – the trinity of Brahma, Shiva and Vishnu – but they also have a supreme god, Sanghyang Widi. Unlike in India, the trinity is never seen – a vacant shrine or empty throne tells all. Nor is Sanghyang Widi often worshipped, though villagers may pray to him when they have settled new land and are about to build a new village. Other Hindu gods such as Ganesh, Shiva's elephant-headed son, may occasionally appear, but a great many purely Balinese gods, spirits and entities have far more relevance in everyday life.

The Balinese believe that spirits are everywhere, an indication that animism is the basis of much of their religion. Good spirits dwell in the mountains and bring prosperity to the people, while giants and demons lurk beneath the sea, and bad spirits haunt the woods and desolate beaches. The people live between these two opposites and their rituals strive to maintain this middle ground. Offerings are carefully put out every morning to pay homage to the good spirits and nonchalantly placed on the ground to placate the bad ones. You can't get away from religion in Bali – there are temples in every village, shrines in every field and offerings made at every corner. Although it enforces a high degree of conformity, it is not a fatalistic religion – there are rules and rituals to placate or drive out the bad spirits, and ensure the favour of the gods and the good spirits.

Temples

The word for temple is *pura*, which is a Sanskrit word literally meaning a space surrounded by a wall. As in so much of Balinese religion the temples, though nominally Hindu, owe much to the pre-Majapahit era. Their *kaja*, *kelod* or *kangin* (alignment to-

wards the mountains, the sea or the sunrise) is in deference to spirits that are more animist than Hindu.

Almost every village has at least three temples. The most important is the *pura puseh*, or temple of origin, which is dedicated to the village founders and is at the kaja end of the village. In the middle of the village is the *pura desa* for the spirits that protect the village community in its day-to-day life. At the kelod end of the village is the pura dalem, or temple of the dead. The graveyard is also here and the temple will often include representations of Durga, the terrible incarnation of Shiva's wife.

Families worship their ancestors in family temples, clans in clan temples and the whole village in the pura puseh. Certain special temples in Bali are of such importance that they are deemed to be owned by the whole island rather than by individual villages. These include Pura Besakih (Besakih Temple) on the slopes of Gunung Agung, the most revered place in Bali, often called 'The Mother Temple'.

The simple shrines or thrones you see, for example in rice fields or next to sacred old trees, are not real temples as they are not walled. You'll find these shrines in all sorts of places, often overlooking crossroads, intersections or dangerous curves in the road, to protect road users.

Temple Design Balinese temples usually consist of a series of courtyards entered from the kelod side. In a large temple the outer gateway will generally be a *candi bentar*, modelled on the old Hindu temples of Java. These gateways resemble a tower cut in halves and moved apart, hence the name 'split gate'. The first courtyard is used for less important ceremonies, and will have a number of bale for preparing food and holding meetings. There will also be a *kulkul* (alarm drum) tower in this outer courtyard and perhaps a banyan or frangipani tree.

The innermost and holiest courtyard (small temples may have just two courts) is entered by another candi-like gateway. A passage through the middle of it symbolises

Nyepi

The major festival for the Hindu Balinese is Nyepi, usually held around the end of March or early April. It celebrates the end of the old year and the start of the new year, according to the *saka* (local Balinese calendar based on the lunar cycle), and usually coincides with the end of the rainy season. Visitors are welcome to join in the celebrations, but the lack of transport can cause interruptions to travel plans.

Ceremonies The day before Nyepi, ceremonies known as *pratima* are held at town squares and sports grounds at different times throughout the island (with a guide and vehicle you may be able to witness several). Later that afternoon, at about 4 pm, the villagers, all dressed up in traditional clothing, gather somewhere central, such as the market. While men play Balinese instruments, locals offer gifts of food and flowers to the *ogoh-ogoh*, a huge monster doll.

Then the *ngrupuk* march starts, where young men lift the ogoh-ogoh by poles and walk around the village (or immediate suburban area) two or three times, passing major buildings and important temples. This is followed by prayers and speeches. When it gets dark, evil spirits are noisily chased away with anything that makes enough noise. With flaming torches and bonfires, the ogoh-ogoh is then burnt, and much drinking and revelry ensues. The best place to see this is Denpasar.

For the Visitor The day of Nyepi (which officially lasts for 24 hours from 6 am) is one of complete and utter inactivity – so that when the evil spirits do descend, they decide that Bali is uninhabited and therefore leave the island alone for another year. With very, very few exceptions, *everything* all over Bali will close or stop during Nyepi: all road, air and sea transport on, and to, Bali will cease; all shops, bars and restaurants will close; and no-one (including foreigners) is allowed to leave the environs of their hotel – police patrols will strictly enforce this. Only the international air terminal, special airport buses and taxis, and emergency rooms at hospitals will function during this 24 hour period. Stock up on snacks, or stay at a hotel with a restaurant, which should provide simple meals for guests. Government offices, banks and many shops also close the day before Nyepi, and some shops remain closed the day after.

For visitors, Nyepi is a day for catching up on sleep, writing letters or washing. Others may wish to plan a side-trip to Lombok (which is predominantly Muslim, and won't close for the day), but you will miss out on the festivities prior to Nyepi. While some may resent this interruption to their travel plans, the Balinese ask that you respect their customs for this short time.

the holy mountain through which you must pass to enter the inner court. This gateway will be flanked by statues of guardian figures or by small protective shrines.

In the inner court there will usually be two rows of shrines, the most important on the kaja side and the lesser on the kangin side. These shrines vary in number and design from temple to temple, although there are detailed rules to cover all of them. In the major temples the shrines will include multi-roofed thatched pagodas known as *meru*. The number of roofs are, apart from some rare exceptions, always odd and the holiest meru will have 11 roofs. The inner court may also contain simple little thrones for local and less important gods to use.

Visiting Temples Except on rare occasions anyone can enter a temple, but you are expected to be politely dressed. You normally need to wear a temple scarf – a sash tied loosely around your waist – and a sarong, long dress or long pants. Many of the larger, more touristed temples rent scarves and sarongs (if you're wearing short pants or a short dress) to visitors for about 1000Rp. You can buy a cheap sarong or scarf yourself, and they make nice souvenirs.

Priests should be shown respect, particularly at festivals. They're the most important people and should, therefore, be on the highest plane. Don't put yourself higher than them by climbing up on a wall to take photographs. There will usually be a sign outside temple entrances asking you to be well dressed, wear a temple scarf and be respectful, and also requesting that women not enter the temple during menstruation.

Nearly every temple (or other site of interest to tourists) will levy an entry charge or ask for a donation from foreigners – any non-Balinese is a foreigner. Usually this is around 1000Rp to 2000Rp. If there is no fixed charge and a donation is requested, 1000Rp is a suitable amount, though the donation book may indicate that people have paid thousands – zeros are sometimes added afterwards.

Temple Festivals For much of the year Balinese temples are deserted, but on holy days the deities and ancestral spirits descend from heaven to visit their devotees, and the temples come alive with days of frenetic activity and nights of drama and dance. Temple festivals come at least once every Balinese year – 210 days. Because most villages have at least three temples, you're assured of at least five or six annual festivals in every village. The full moon periods around the end of September to the beginning of October or early to mid-April are often times of important festivals. One such festival is Galungan, which takes place throughout the island. During this 10 day period all the gods, including the supreme deity, Sanghyang Widi, come down to earth for the festivities.

Funerals

A Balinese funeral is an amazing, colourful, noisy and exciting event. Basically it's a happy occasion, as it represents the destruc-

tion of the body and the release of the soul so that it can be united with the supreme god.

The body is carried to the cremation ground in a high multi-tiered tower made of bamboo, paper, string, tinsel, silk, cloth, mirrors, flowers, and anything else bright and colourful. Carried on the shoulders of a group of men, the tower represents the cosmos, and the base, in the shape of a turtle entwined by two snakes, symbolises the foundation of the world. On the base is an open platform where the body is placed – in the space between heaven and earth. The size of the group carrying the body and the number of tiers on the tower varies according to the caste of the deceased.

On the way to the cremation ground, the tower is shaken and run around in circles to disorient the spirit of the deceased so that it cannot find its way home. A gamelan sprints along behind, providing a suitably exciting musical accompaniment and almost trampling the camera-toting tourists. (Tourists are accepted in the procession because they add to the noise and confusion, further disorienting the spirits.) At the cremation ground the body is transferred to a funeral sarcophagus and the whole lot – funeral tower, sarcophagus and body – goes up in flames. Finally, the colourful procession heads to the sea (or a nearby river if the sea is too far away) to scatter the ashes.

LANGUAGE

Balinese language, as distinct from Indonesian, the national language, reflects caste distinctions. Traditionally there are five forms of the language, with the usage governed by the social relationship between the two people having a conversation. Modern usage is described in terms of three forms: Low Balinese (Ia) is used between intimates and equals and when talking to inferiors; Polite or Middle Balinese (Ipun) is used when speaking about superiors, or when addressing superiors or strangers, mainly when one wishes to be very polite but doesn't want to emphasise caste differences; and High Balinese (Ida) is used when talking to superiors, particularly in the context of religious ceremonies.

EMBASSIES & CONSULATES

Only Australia and Japan (the citizens of which together make up nearly half of all visitors to Bali) have proper consular facilities. Most places below are open Sunday to Thursday, from about 8 am to noon and 1 to 4 pm, and will be closed on Indonesian and their own national holidays. Many have pager systems for emergency calls. All telephone area codes are ☎ 0361.

Australia
(☎ 235092/3, 234139 ext 3311 for emergencies, fax 231990,
email ausconbali@denpasar.wasantara.net.id)
Jalan (Jl) Mochammad Yamin 4, Renon,
Denpasar – responsible for all Commonwealth citizens, and, at a pinch, Irish citizens
France
(☎/fax 285485 – the same for emergencies)
Jl Bypass Ngurah Rai, Sanur
Germany
(☎ 288535 – the same for emergencies,
fax 288826)
Jl Pantai Karang 17, Sanur
Netherlands
(☎ 751517, 753174 for emergencies,
fax 752777)
Jl Raya Kuta 599, Kuta
USA
(☎ 233605, 234139 ext 3575 for emergencies, fax 222426)
Jl Hayam Wuruk 188, Renon, Denpasar

MONEY

In general, travellers who don't need air-conditioning and hot water will discover they can get good rooms almost anywhere in Bali for under 40,000Rp; sometimes as little as 25,000Rp will get you a fine 'economy' room in a mid-range hotel. Transport is equally affordable – remember that Bali and Lombok are small islands. Public minibuses, buses and bemos are the local form of public transport and they're very cheap. With the current favourable exchange rate, hiring your own car or motorbike is now a very attractive idea.

A few automatic teller machines (ATMs) are starting to appear in Bali, but they are primarily for customers (normally Indonesians) with an account at that particular (Indonesian) bank. A few larger banks accept major international credit cards for cash advances. The Kuta area has the most number of ATMs.

POST & COMMUNICATIONS

Bali is one of the best places in Indonesia, and South-East Asia, to send and receive mail, and to communicate by email – if you have the expertise, and the recipient has the technology. There are Internet centres in Ubud, Kuta/Legian, Sanur, Nusa Dua and Lovina. There are also poste restante services at the main post offices around Bali, and Home Country Direct Dial telephones in Kuta, Ubud, Denpasar, Sanur and at the airport.

BOOKS

The classic work is *Island of Bali* by Mexican artist Miguel Covarrubias. First published in 1937, it's still available as an Oxford in Asia paperback. Despite many changes, much of Bali is still as Covarrubias describes it, and few people have come to grips with the island so well.

Colin McPhee's *A House in Bali* is a lyrical account of a musician's lengthy stay in Bali to study gamelan music. *The Last Paradise* by Hickman Powell and *A Tale from Bali* by Vicki Baum also date from that heady period in the 1930s, when so many westerners 'discovered' Bali. K'Tut Tantri's *Revolt in Paradise* again starts in the 1930s, but this western woman who took a Balinese name remained in Indonesia through the war and during part of the subsequent struggle for independence from the Dutch.

Our Hotel in Bali by Louis G Koke tells of the original Kuta Beach Hotel established by Americans Robert and Louis Koke during the 1930s. Hugh Mabbett's *The Balinese* is an interesting collection of anecdotes, observations and impressions, and *In Praise of Kuta* is a sympathetic account of that much maligned beach resort.

For a rundown on Balinese arts and culture, look for the huge and expensive *The Art & Culture of Bali* by Urs Ramseyer. An economical and useful introduction to Balinese painting can be found in *The Development of Painting in Bali*, published by the

Neka Museum. *Balinese Paintings* by AAM Djelantik is a concise and handy overview of the field.

There's a growing number of large-format, well-illustrated coffee-table books on Bali. *Bali High – Paradise from the Air* has some stunning photographs of Bali taken from a helicopter. *Balinese Textiles*, by Brigitta Hauser, Marie-Louise Nabholz-Kartaschoff & Urs Ramseyer, is a large and lavishly illustrated guide to various styles of weaving and their significance.

Bookshops in the Kuta region, Sanur and Ubud have a wide range of English-language novels and books, particularly on Indonesia. Big hotels, some supermarkets and various tourist shops and galleries have more limited selections, and numerous bookshops and small hotels sell second-hand books.

GETTING THERE & AWAY

Air

Bali's airport is actually a few kilometres to the south of Kuta. Officially the airport is named Ngurah Rai, after a hero of the struggle for independence from the Dutch.

The airport has a hotel-booking counter, which covers only the more expensive places. There's also a tourist information counter, a left-luggage room, several moneychangers, an expensive duty-free shop and some souvenir shops, an ATM machine for international credit cards and a Home Country Direct Dial telephone.

International Refer to the introductory Getting There & Away chapter for details of international flights to/from Bali. The international departure tax is 50,000Rp.

If you're flying out of Bali, reconfirm your bookings at least 72 hours before departure. Most international airline offices are at the Grand Bali Beach Hotel in Sanur, or based at the airport. The telephone and fax numbers are below – all have ☎ 0361 telephone area codes.

Air France
  ☎ 288511 ext 1105, fax 287734
Air New Zealand
  ☎ 756170

ANA (All Nippon Airways)
  ☎ 761102, fax 761107
Ansett Australia
  ☎ 289636, fax 289637
Cathay Pacific
  ☎ 286001, fax 288576
Continental Micronesia
  ☎ 287774, fax 287775
JAL (Japan Airlines)
  ☎ 287577, fax 287460
KLM (Royal Dutch Airlines)
  ☎ 756124-7, fax 753950
Korean Air
  ☎ 289402, fax 289403
Lufthansa
  ☎/fax 287069
MAS (Malaysian Airlines)
  ☎ 285071, fax 288716
North-West Airlines
  ☎ 287841, fax 287840
Qantas
  ☎ 288331, fax 287331
Singapore Airlines
  ☎ 288511 ext 1587
Thai Airways
  ☎ 288141, fax 288063

Domestic Bali is well-connected to most of Indonesia. The main airline is Merpati Nusantara Airlines, which has regular, direct flights to Surabaya, Yogyakarta, Jakarta, Mataram, Bima, Maumere, Kupang, Dili, Ambon and Manado. Also, Mandala has daily flights to Yogyakarta; Garuda Indonesia flies many times a day to Jakarta; Sempati and Bouraq have daily flights to Surabaya and Jakarta; and Bouraq also has irregular flights to Waingapu, Maumere and Kupang. Domestic departure tax is 11,000Rp.

Fares, which are almost identical for each airline, have increased considerably in recent years, but flights are still good value. Current schedules are listed in English in the Indonesian-language daily *Bali Post*. The airline offices (with ☎ 0361 area codes) are:

Bouraq
  (☎ 241397)
  Jl Jenderal Sudirman, Blok A47-48, Denpasar
Garuda
  (☎ 225245, 227824-5 for bookings and reconfirmations)
  Jl Melati 61, Denpasar
  (☎ 751179)

Kuta Beach Hotel
(☎ 289135)
Sanur Beach Hotel
(☎ 288243)
Grand Bali Beach Hotel, Sanur
(☎ 771864)
Nusa Indah Hotel, Nusa Dua
(☎ 730681)
Bali Imperial Hotel, Seminyak
Mandala
(☎ 222751)
Jl Diponegoro 98, Blok D/23, Denpasar
Merpati
(☎ 261238)
Jl Melati 57, Denpasar
Sempati
(☎ 288511, ext 1587)
Grand Bali Beach Hotel, Sanur

Sea

Java Ferries travel between Gilimanuk in
western Bali and Ketapang (Java) every 15 to
30 minutes, 24 hours a day. The actual crossing takes under 30 minutes. The fare is 1000/
300Rp for adults/children. A bicycle costs
1400Rp; a motorcycle, 2700Rp; and a car
or jeep, 10,550Rp.

Lombok Refer to the Lombok Getting
There & Away section in the Nusa Tenggara
chapter for details.

Other Indonesian Islands Four Pelni
boats stop at Pelabuhan Benoa, Bali: the
Tatamailau links Bali with southern Sulawesi, Maluku and Irian Jaya; the *Dobonsolo*, with Java, Nusa Tenggara, Maluku and
Irian Jaya; and the *Awu* and *Tilongkabila*,
with Nusa Tenggara and southern Sulawesi.
You can inquire and book at the Pelni office
(☎ 721377) at Pelabuhan Benoa, which is
open Monday to Friday from 8 am to 4 pm
and Saturday until 12.30 pm.

Public Bus

Java Many buses from numerous bus companies travel daily between the Ubung terminal in Denpasar and major cities in Java, but
most travel overnight. Fares vary between
operators, and depend on what sort of comfort you want – a decent seat, and even air-
conditioning, are worth paying extra for.

From Denpasar, the average fare to Surabaya
(10 to 12 hours) is about 32,000Rp; to Yogyakarta (15 to 16 hours), about 58,000Rp; and
as far as Jakarta (26 to 30 hours), about
90,000Rp. Some companies avoid Denpasar
altogether, and travel directly between Java
and Padangbai or Singaraja, via Lovina.

In Bali, you can buy tickets in advance at
travel agencies in the tourist centres for a
little more than the normal price; directly
from the bus company offices in Denpasar;
or at the Ubung terminal. If you just turn up
at the Ubung terminal, you will probably
get on a bus within an hour or so, but it's advisable to book at least one day ahead.

Lombok Plenty of public buses also travel
between Denpasar and Mataram. Refer to
the Lombok Getting There & Away section
in the Nusa Tenggara chapter for details.

Tourist Shuttle Bus

A few companies offer more expensive
tourist shuttle buses between Bali and
Surabaya, Yogyakarta and Jakarta – the
Kuta-based company Peram has the most
reputable and extensive service. Before you
buy a ticket in Bali, however, make sure it
is a *direct* shuttle bus service, and not just a
shuttle bus to the Ubung terminal in Denpasar, and then a public bus the rest of the
way to Java. Most shuttle buses leave from
either Ubung or Kuta, and cost about
45,000Rp to Surabaya, 65,000Rp to Yogyakarta and 100,000Rp to Jakarta.

The Lombok Getting There & Away section in the Nusa Tenggara chapter has details about tourist shuttle bus services
between Bali and Lombok.

GETTING AROUND

Bali is a small island with good roads and
regular, inexpensive public transport. Traffic is heavy from Denpasar south to the
Kuta region and Sanur, east about as far as
Semarapura and west as far as Tabanan.
Over the rest of the island, the roads are remarkably uncrowded. If you rent your own
vehicle it's easy to find your way around –
roads are well signposted and maps are

BALI

readily available. Off the main routes, most roads are surfaced but often very potholed.

To/From the Airport

The Ngurah Rai airport is just south of Kuta Beach. From the official counters, just outside the international and domestic terminals, pre-paid airport taxis cost:

Destination	Fare (Rp)
Kuta Beach	8000 to 10,000
Legian	11,500
Seminyak	12,500
Denpasar	15,000
Jimbaran	17,500
Sanur	17,500
Nusa Dua	17,500
Tanjung Benoa	18,500
Ubud	47,000

The impecunious should walk across the airport car park and continue a couple of hundred metres to the airport road, from where public *bemos* (minibuses) go to Denpasar's Tegal terminal via Kuta throughout most of the day. You could walk all the way to Kuta – it's only a few kilometres on the Tuban road or along the beach.

Bemo

Most of Bali's public transport is provided by minibuses, usually called bemos, but on some longer routes the vehicle may be a full-sized bus. Denpasar is the transport hub of Bali and has bus/bemo terminals for the various destinations – see the Denpasar section later in this chapter for details. Unfortunately, travel in southern Bali often requires travelling via one or more of the Denpasar terminals, and this can make for an inconvenient and time-consuming trip.

The fare between main towns may be posted at the terminals, or you can ask around for the right price. You can also flag a bemo down pretty much anywhere along its route, but you may be charged the *harga turis* (tourist price) – Bali bemos are notorious for overcharging tourists. Ask a local the correct fare before embarking on a journey,

and pay the exact amount when you get off. If you ask the correct fare, they'll know that you don't know and they may try to overcharge you. It's better to watch what other passengers pay, or make your best estimate of the correct fare.

You can charter a whole vehicle for a trip, or by the day for around 70,000Rp to 90,000Rp depending on the distance; the price should include driver and petrol. In tourist areas, you can only charter vehicles with yellow plates; regular bemos are only licensed to work fixed routes. In non-tourist areas, this doesn't seem to be enforced, and bemo charter is cheaper but you usually have to pay for petrol and buy food for the driver.

Beware of pickpockets on bemos – they often have an accomplice to distract you, or use a package to hide the activity.

Tourist Shuttle Bus

Tourist shuttle buses travel between the main tourist centres in Bali. There are three main routes, and they don't go anywhere west of Tabanan or Bedugul:

• Kuta-Legian to Ubud, via Sanur
• Kuta-Legian to Lovina via Ubud and Kintamani or Bedugul
• Kuta-Legian to Lovina, via Ubud, Gianyar, Semarapura, Padangbai, Candidasa, Tirta Gangga, Culik (for Amed), Tulamben, Yeh Sanih and Singaraja

Shuttle buses are more comfortable and reliable than public transport, but considerably more expensive. They are generally cheaper than chartering a bemo or hiring a car, but if you're travelling in a group of three to five, chartering a bemo will be cheaper per person than taking a shuttle bus, and will give you more flexibility regarding the departure time and route.

Several shuttle bus companies operate out of Kuta-Legian, but the most reliable and established company, with the widest network, is Perama. Always try to book a ticket at least one day before you want to leave. You can book at any of the hundreds of travel agents in the tourist centres. Shuttle buses will normally pick you up outside the travel agent where you booked or another pre-determined spot – or even from outside your hotel if it's convenient for them.

Taxi

Metered taxis are common in Denpasar and the tourist areas of southern Bali. They are a lot less hassle than haggling with bemo drivers, but dearer, of course. They are almost always cheaper than the private 'transport' operators. You can always find a taxi at the airport, and you will hear them beep their horns at you if you walk anywhere around a tourist centre. Don't get in a taxi if the driver says the meter isn't working – it may suddenly 'fix' itself. Taxis cost 2000Rp for the first kilometre and then 900Rp for each subsequent kilometre.

Car & Motorcycle

Road Rules & Risks Road rules in Bali are the same as for the rest of Indonesia. Remember to have your International Driving Permit (IDP) and the vehicle's registration papers with you at all times. Cops will stop vehicles on some very thin pretexts in order to extract 'on-the-spot fines'. Most matters can be settled for about 50,000Rp, but don't make any offers – wait for the cop to ask.

Driving is risky. If you have a serious accident, it may be wise to go straight to the nearest police station rather than confront an angry mob of locals. If it's a minor accident, you may be better off negotiating a cash settlement on the spot than spending the rest of your holiday hassling with police and lawyers.

Rental More and more car-rental places are springing up. The usual rental vehicle is a Jimny, a small Suzuki jeep. Typical costs for a Suzuki are around 50,000Rp to 75,000Rp a day, including insurance and unlimited kilometres; a larger, more comfortable Toyota Kijang costs from around 85,000Rp per day. It's substantially cheaper by the week. You can also find regular cars, but they cost more and are not as well suited to steep, rough, winding roads.

Motorcycles are a popular way to get around Bali, but can be dangerous. Most rental motorcycles are between 90cc and 125cc, with 100cc the usual size. Rental charges vary with the bike, period of hire and demand. The longer the hire period the lower the rate; the bigger or newer the bike the higher the rate. Typically you can expect to pay from around 17,500Rp to 25,000Rp a day. This incudes a flimsy helmet, which is compulsory and provides protection against sunburn but not much else.

Simply look for a travel agent, restaurant, losmen or shop with a sign 'motorbike for rent'. The Kuta region is the main motorcycle-hire place but you'll have no trouble finding a motorcycle in any of the tourist centres. Check it over before riding off – some are very poorly maintained.

Licence You must have an IDP to rent a car; to rent a motorcycle you should have an IDP endorsed for motorcycles. If not, technically you should obtain a local motorcycle licence, which is valid for three months in Bali, Lombok and Sumbawa. Some rental agencies don't bother asking foreigners about their IDP, and many readers who have been stopped on a rented motorcycle by police claim that the police are happy with their standard, nonendorsed IDP. While this is a little risky, a fine is still probably cheaper than getting a local motorcycle licence. The situation is very unclear, so discuss it with a reputable motorcycle rental agency before you drive anywhere.

The cost of a local motorcycle licence is a ridiculous 150,000Rp, so most foreigners don't bother getting one. If you want one, the rental agency/owner will take you to the police station in Denpasar. You pay your money and complete a written test in English with multiple-choice answers – the agency/owner will help you with any tricky questions. The whole process can take as little as 20 minutes if the agency/owner has 'friends' at the police station.

Under no circumstances should you drive a motorcycle or car without an IDP. Your insurance company will disown you if you have an accident, and enforcement is strict. The fine for riding without a licence is at least 2,000,000Rp. Some police may let you off with an 'on-the-spot fine' but don't count on it. They can impound the motorcycle and put you in jail until you pay up.

Insurance Insurance is not obligatory for cars or motorcycles, but rental agencies or owners require it, so if insurance is not included in your rental price and agreement, you will have to pay extra. For a motorcycle, insurance can be expensive; and for a car, the cost for a single day can run to 25,000Rp (less per day for longer rental). Whether it actually does you much good if worst comes to worst is not entirely clear. Your travel insurance may provide some additional protection, although liability for motor accidents is specifically excluded from many policies. Make sure that your personal travel insurance covers you for injuries incurred while driving or motorcycling. Some policies specifically exclude coverage for motorcycle riding, or have special conditions.

Bicycle

In the main tourist areas it's quite easy to rent a pushbike by the hour or the day, and it's a good way to get around locally. Mostly they're 10 speed mountain bikes, and they are rented for around 5000Rp per day. Check the bike carefully – many are in bad condition and few are perfect.

Touring the island by bicycle is quite popular and a great way to see Bali. If you want to try it, it's probably best to bring your own bike with you; airlines will generally carry a bike as part of your 20kg baggage allowance. Otherwise be prepared to spend some time looking for a good machine to rent, and/or some effort making it suitable for long-distance touring. Good brakes, seat, tyres and a lock are essential; bells, lights and luggage racks are desirable.

You can usually get a bemo to take you and your bike up the bigger mountains (the bike goes on the roof and costs the same as a passenger), though this is more difficult with the newer bemos. Bicycles are used extensively

by the Balinese, and even the smallest village has some semblance of a bike shop. Some shops will allow you to borrow tools to work on your own bike. The best shops for extensive repairs are in Denpasar.

Once you're out of the congested southern region, traffic is relatively light and the roads are not too bad, particularly if you invest in a good, padded seat. You can accomplish a beautiful 200km circle trip of Bali, level or downhill almost the whole way, with a couple of bemo rides.

Bicycle Tour This 200km route is designed to take in the greatest number of points of interest with the maximum amount of level or downhill roads. For convenience, the tour is divided into six days of actual riding in a clockwise direction, which takes advantage of evening stops where there are convenient losmen.

Day 1 – Kuta to Bedugul (57km) The first 37km is level cycling, but from the village of Luwus it's uphill, so you can catch a bemo – on a good bicycle even this section is quite manageable. Estimated riding time is seven hours.

Day 2 – Bedugul to Singaraja (30km) Estimated riding time is three hours, a steep climb then downhill most of the way. You can detour to the Lovina beaches.

Day 3 – Singaraja to Penelokan (60km) The 24km from the coast up to Penulisan is very steep, so a bemo is recommended. The first 10km and the final 10km are fine. Detour down to Danau Batur and Toya Bungkah to climb Gunung Batur.

Day 4 – Penelokan to Semarapura via Rendang (31km) You can detour to Pura Besakih by bemo, but the direct ride is only about four hours. An alternative would be via Tampaksiring to Ubud.

Day 5 – Semarapura to Denpasar (40km) Estimated riding time is six hours. This road has heavy traffic.

Day 6 – Denpasar to Kuta If you go via Sanur and Benoa this is a 24km ride and estimated riding time is five hours. Again there are some stretches of heavy traffic on this run.

Boat

Small boats go to a number of islands around Bali, notably those in the Nusa Penida group.

Usually they will pull up to a beach, and you have to wade to and from the boat with your luggage and clamber aboard over the stern. Details of boat services are given in the relevant chapters.

Organised Tours

Many travellers end up taking one or two organised tours because it can be such a quick, convenient and cheap way to visit a few places, especially where public transport is limited (eg Pura Besakih) or nonexistent (eg Tanah Lot after sunset). All sorts of tours are available from the tourist centres, and there is an extraordinarily wide range of prices, from 45,000Rp to US$60 per person for basically the same sort of tour.

The cheaper tours may use less comfortable vehicles, have less qualified guides and be less organised, while higher priced tours may include a buffet lunch, an English-speaking guide and air-conditioning, but generally a higher price is no guarantee of higher quality. Some tours make long stops at craft shops, so you can buy things and earn commissions for the tour operator. Tours are typically in an eight to 12 seat minibus or jeep that picks you up and drops you off at a major hotel or pre-determined place.

Some agencies also arrange more specialised trips, such as diving trips to Pulau Menjangan (Menjangan Island) or cultural trips to Tenganan village. All tours can be booked at a travel agency or hotel in a tourist centre. But remember: if you can get together a group of four or more, most tour agencies will arrange a tour to suit you, or you can easily create your own tour by chartering or renting a vehicle.

Tours to Other Islands Several companies in the tourist centres in Bali offer organised tours of one, two or three days to Java to see the magnificent Gunung Bromo and Borobudur Buddhist temple near Yogyakarta, with some sightseeing in western Bali en route (if travelling by bus). Prices range from about US$100 to US$200 per person per day, depending on whether you take a private bus or fly.

The shuttle bus company, Perama, offers interesting two-day trips between Lovina and Bromo for 100,000Rp per person, all inclusive. Spice Island Cruises (☎ 0361-286283, fax 286284) is one of several companies with upmarket cruises to Nusa Tenggara and Komodo from about US$150 per person per night. All of these trips can be booked at any travel agency in Bali.

Refer to the Lombok Getting There & Away section in the Nusa Tenggara chapter for details about organised tours from Bali to Lombok and Nusa Tenggara.

Denpasar

☎ 0361

The capital of Bali, Denpasar, has been the focus of a lot of the growth and wealth over the last 20 years. It has an interesting museum, an arts centre and lots of shops. Denpasar means 'next to the market', and the main market (Pasar Badung) is said to be the biggest and busiest in Bali. Denpasar was formerly the capital of the Badung district, but the city and surrounding area, including Sanur, Pelabuhan Benoa port and Pulau Serangan, was split off in 1992 to become a self-governing municipality. Denpasar still has some tree-lined streets and pleasant gardens, but the traffic, noise and pollution make it a difficult place to enjoy.

Many of Denpasar's residents are descended from immigrant groups, such as Bugis mercenaries and Chinese, Arab and Indian traders. More recent immigrants have been attracted by the wealth in Denpasar, including Javanese civil servants, tradespeople and workers, and Balinese from all over the island. They give the city a cosmopolitan air, and it is increasingly a Java-oriented modern Indonesian city rather than a parochial Balinese capital. As the city grows it is engulfing the surrounding villages, but their banjars and village life continue amid the urbanisation. The recent immigrants tend to occupy detached houses outside the family compounds, and may eventually supplant the traditional communal way of life.

BALI

BALI

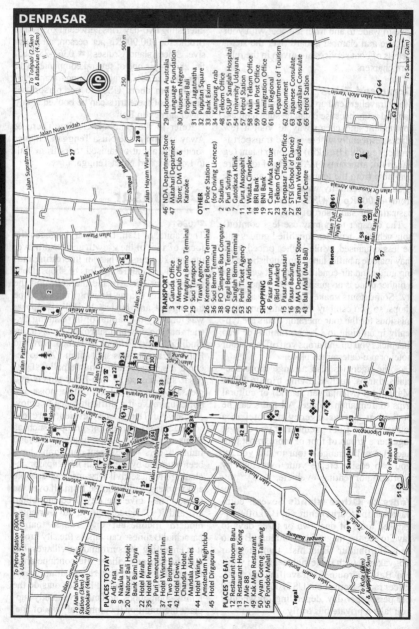

DENPASAR

TRANSPORT
3 Garuda Office
4 Merpati Office
10 Wangaya Bemo Terminal
25 Suci Transport
   Travel Agency
26 Kereneng Bemo Terminal
36 Suci Bemo Terminal
38 PO Simpatik Bus Company
40 Tegal Bemo Terminal
52 Sanglah Bemo Terminal
53 Pelni Ticket Agency
55 Bouraq Airlines

SHOPPING
6 Pasar Burung
  (Bird Market)
15 Pasar Kumbasari
16 Pasar Badung
39 MA Department Store
43 Bali Mall (Mal Bali)

46 NDA Department Store
47 Matahari Department
   Store; DM Club &
   Karaoke

OTHER
1 Police Station
  (for Driving Licences)
2 Stadium
5 Puri Sutriya
7 Gatotkaca Klinik
11 Pura Maospahit
14 Wisata Cineplex
18 BRI Bank
19 BNI Bank
21 Catur Muka Statue
23 Telkom Office
24 Denpasar Tourist Office
27 STSI (School of Dance)
28 Taman Wedhi Budaya
   Arts Centre

29 Indonesia Australia
   Language Foundation
30 Museum Negeri
   Propinsi Bali
31 Pura Jagatnatha
32 Puputan Square
33 Bank Exim
48 Telkom Office
51 RSUP Sanglah Hospital
54 University Udayana
58 Main Telkom Office
59 Petrol Station
60 Main Post Office
61 Immigration Office
62 Bali Regional
   Department of Tourism
   Monument
63 Japanese Consulate
64 Australian Consulate
65 Petrol Station

PLACES TO STAY
8 Adi Yasa
9 Nakula Inn
20 Natour Bali Hotel;
   Bank Bumi Daya
22 Hotel Mirah
35 Hotel Pemecutan;
   Puri Pemecutan
37 Hotel Wisnasari Inn
41 Two Brothers Inn
42 Hotel Dewi
   Chandra Hotel;
   Mandala Airlines
44 Hotel Viking;
   Amsterdam Nightclub
45 Hotel Dirgapura

PLACES TO EAT
12 Restaurant Atoom Baru
13 Restaurant Hong Kong
17 Mie 88
49 Kak Man Restaurant
50 Ayam Goreng Taliwang
56 Pondok Melati

Orientation

The main road, Jl Gunung Agung, starts at the western side of town. Further east, it changes to Jl Gajah Mada in the middle of town, then Jl Surapati and finally Jl Hayam Wuruk. One infuriating aspect of visiting – and driving around – Denpasar is that roads regularly change names, often every time they cross another road.

Another problem is the proliferation of one-way traffic restrictions, sometimes for only part of a street's length, which often change and are rarely marked on any maps. The traffic jams can be intense and parking can be difficult so avoid driving around Denpasar if you can. If you have rented a vehicle, think about parking it outside town, or leaving it in Kuta or Sanur, and using taxis, bemos and your feet around Denpasar. The city is pretty flat, so a bicycle would be good – if you could survive the traffic.

In contrast to the rest of Denpasar, the Renon area, south-east of the town centre, is laid out on a grand scale, with wide streets, large car parks and huge landscaped blocks of land. This is the area of government offices, many of which are impressive structures, built with lavish budgets in modern Balinese style.

Information

Tourist Offices The Denpasar Tourist Office (☎ 234569, fax 223602) deals with tourism in the Denpasar municipality, which includes Sanur. It offers (free) copies of the valuable *Calendar of Events* booklet, which is relevant for all over Bali; the interesting *Bali Kini* tourist magazine; and the handy *Discover Denpasar* brochure. The office is open Monday to Thursday from 7 am to 2 pm, Friday until 11 am and Saturday until 12.30 pm.

The Bali Regional Department of Tourism, Post and Telecommunications (☎ 222 387, fax 226313) in Renon is mainly a bureaucratic facility, but if you go to the back of the main building, staff happily hand out a few brochures and maps. It has the same opening hours as the Denpasar Tourist Office.

Money Most branches of major Indonesian banks are located near or on the corner of Jl Gajah Mada and Jl Arjuna. Bank Exim is one of the best for changing money and arranging transfers from overseas. The rates offered by the moneychangers along the northern end of Jl Diponegoro are better than those offered by the banks, but not as good as rates available in Kuta.

Post & Communications The main post office (☎ 223565), with the poste restante service, is inconveniently located in Renon, but open from 8 am to 8 pm.

The main Telkom office is also inconveniently located in Renon, but there are *wartels* (public telephone offices) all over town. For telephone calls and faxes, the smaller Telkom offices just north of the Denpasar Tourist Office, and along Jl Teuku Umar, are handy. The Denpasar Tourist Office has a Home Country Direct Dial telephone.

Bookshops One of the best bookshops in Bali is the Gramedia Book Shop in the basement of the Matahari department store. It boasts a large range of expensive souvenir books about Bali in English, French, German and Japanese, numerous Lonely Planet guides, and a range of useful maps of Bali, Lombok and the rest of Indonesia.

Emergency If you must get sick or injured, do it in Denpasar. The city's main hospital, Rumah Sakit Umum Propinsi (RSUP) Sanglah (☎ 227912-5), is open 24 hours a day, has English-speaking staff, and is regarded by expats as the best on the island. Three private medical practices that deal with foreigners are Surya Husadha Clinic (☎ 233786-7), Jl Pulau Serangan 1-3, just south of RSUP Sanglah; Gatotkaca Klinik (☎ 223555), Jl Gatotkaca; and Manuaba Clinic (☎ 426393), Jl Cokroaminoto. The ambulance number is ☎ 118. There are plenty of pharmacies around town.

To make any general complaint, or to get a motorcycle licence, contact the police station (☎ 228690) on Jl Pattimura. The general police emergency number is ☎ 110.

Museum Negeri Propinsi Bali

The Bali Provincial State Museum (☎ 222 680) comprises several buildings and pavilions, including examples of the architecture of both the *puri* (palace) and pura, with features like a candi bentar and a kulkul tower.

The **main building** has a collection of prehistoric pieces downstairs, including stone sarcophagi, and stone and bronze implements. Upstairs are examples of traditional artefacts, including types still in everyday use. The **northern pavilion** houses dance costumes and masks, including a sinister rangda, a healthy looking barong and a towering barong landung figure. The **central pavilion** is like the palace pavilions of the Karangasem kingdom (based in Amlapura) where rajahs held audiences. The **southern pavilion** has a varied collection of textiles, including *endek* (a Balinese method of weaving with pre-dyed threads), double *ikat* (cloth in which the pattern is produced by dyeing individual threads before weaving), *songket* (silver and gold-threaded cloth, hand woven using a floating weft technique) and *prada* (the application of gold leaf or gold or silver thread in traditional Balinese clothes).

Tickets cost 750Rp. The museum is open from 8 am to 3.45 pm on Sunday, Tuesday, Wednesday and Thursday; it closes a little earlier on Friday and Saturday.

Pura Jagatnatha

Next to the museum, the state Jagatnatha Temple was built in 1953, and is dedicated to the supreme god, Sanghyang Widi. Part of its significance is its statement of monotheism. The *padmasana* (shrine) is made of white coral, and consists of an empty throne (symbolic of heaven) on top of the cosmic turtle and two *naga* (mythological serpents) that symbolise the foundation of the world. The walls are decorated with carvings of scenes from the *Ramayana* and *Mahabharata*. Pura Jagatnatha is more frequently used than many Balinese temples, with local people coming every afternoon to pray and make offerings. For this reason it can often be closed to the public.

Taman Wedhi Budya

This arts centre (☎ 222776) was established in 1973 as an academy and showplace for Balinese culture, but it doesn't seem to have much purpose these days. Still, it's a quiet and shaded respite from the maddening traffic, and is worth a look around.

The centre does hold entertaining Kecak dances (6000Rp) every evening from 6.30 to 7.30 pm, as well irregular temporary art exhibits. From mid-June to mid-July, the centre hosts the Bali Arts Festival (see the 'Bali Arts Festival' boxed text later in this section). You may need to book tickets at the centre for more popular events.

It's open Tuesday to Sunday from 8 am to 5 pm, and entry is free. If you don't fancy the long walk, the Kereneng-Sanur bemo will drop you off at the nearby corner of Jl Hayam Wuruk and Jl Nusa Indah. You can enjoy a meal or drink after the evening dance at the handful of *warungs* (food stalls) opposite the main gate.

Places to Stay

There are plenty of hotels in Denpasar, but the standards are lower and the prices are higher than in most other places around Bali. And finding somewhere quiet, away from the incessant traffic, is not easy. It may be wise to pre-book a room during the busier times in July, August, around Christmas and Idul Fitri (the end of Ramadan). Most places include breakfast.

Places to Stay – Budget

Adi Yasa (☎ 222679, Jl Nakula) is central and friendly, but the cheaper singles/doubles for 12,500/15,000Rp are like a sauna (ie there's no fan) and have a shared bathroom. The newer rooms, for 15,000/20,000Rp, are far nicer, but often full. Just a few metres west, *Nakula Inn* (☎ 226446) is better, and worth the few extra rupiahs. The large rooms have a private bathroom and ceiling fan, and are located in a cool, shaded setting. They cost 25,000/30,000Rp, plus 5000Rp for breakfast.

Handy to the Tegal terminal is *Two Brothers Inn* (☎ 222704) – look for the sign

Bali Arts Festival

The annual Bali Arts Festival is based at the arts centre in Denpasar, and lasts for about one month over June and July. It's a great time to be in Bali, and is an easy way to see an enormous variety of traditional dances, music and crafts. The productions of the *Ramayana* and *Mahabharata* dances are grand, and the opening ceremony and parade in Denpasar is particularly colourful.

Details about events and times are available at tourist offices in the tourist centres of south Bali, or check the Web site (www.baliwww.com). You can easily take a day trip to Denpasar from Kuta, Ubud, Sanur and Nusa Dua.

off Jl Imam Bonjol. This standard losmen is quiet, but also fairly inconvenient, and the staff can be a bit surly. Small rooms, with a shared bathroom, cost 15,000/20,000Rp.

The central *Hotel Mirah* (☎ 240321, Jl Kaliasem 1) is run by a friendly family, and good value. Clean rooms, with a portable fan and private bathroom, cost 20,000/40,000Rp (more for air-con and TV), and are reasonably quiet despite the location. Another good option is the clean, central and surprisingly quiet *Hotel Wismasari Inn* (☎ 222437, Jl Sutoyo 1). The better rooms at the back cost 30,000Rp; the cheerless rooms inside are 20,000Rp.

Places to Stay – Mid-Range

Most mid-range places are on or near busy Jl Diponegoro, and mainly cater to Indonesian business travellers. They are handy to the local shops, but to nothing else. *Hotel Viking* (☎ 223992, Jl Diponegoro 120) has very noisy 'economy' rooms for 30,000Rp, and better, quieter rooms at the back for 65,000Rp with air-con. A little further south, *Hotel Dirgapura* (☎ 226924, Jl Diponegoro 128) is better value, and more suited to budget travellers. It has dozens of rooms, so there's usually a vacancy, and many rooms are away from the main road. Singles/doubles cost

15,000/20,000Rp and triples cost 25,000Rp, but you will have to ask for a portable fan. Among other noisy, mid-range places along Jl Diponegoro are *Hotel Dewi* (☎ 226720) and *Chandra Hotel* (☎ 226425).

Hotel Pemecutan (☎ 423491), on corner of Jl Imam Bonjol and Jl Hasanudin, is an unusual, atmospheric place in the middle of a palace with a pretty garden. It is good value for 50,000/60,000/75,000Rp, with air-con, satellite TV and a private bathroom, but ask for a room at the back if you want any sleep. The entrance is on Jl Thamrin, and the reception is a little hard to find.

Places to Stay – Top End

There are no luxury hotels in Denpasar; if you want a top notch place, stay in the Kuta region, Sanur or Nusa Dua. The government-owned *Natour Bali Hotel* (☎ 225681, fax 235347, Jl Veteran 3) dates from the Dutch days. There are some nice Art Deco details (look at the light fittings in the dining room), but incongruous Balinese decorations have since been added. Prices are still currently quoted in rupiah, so it's not that outrageous at 200,000/217,500Rp, with satellite TV, pool and hot water – but prices are much higher for the 'suite'.

Places to Eat

Most places cater for local people and Indonesian visitors and immigrants, so they offer a good selection of authentic food at reasonable prices. Naturally, the cheapest places are the *warungs* at the bemo/bus terminals, and the Pasar Kumbasari and Pasar Burung markets. They serve food until 10 pm, after most restaurants in town have closed.

Restaurant Atoom Baru (Jl Gajah Mada 108) is a typical Asian (as opposed to western) Chinese restaurant. The vast menu has loads of seafood and other dishes for 7000Rp to 12,000Rp. Across the road, the classy *Restaurant Hong Kong* boasts an inordinately wide range of Chinese and Indonesian dishes from 10,000Rp to 15,000Rp per dish, and 9500Rp for a large beer (although it is served in an ice-cold glass).

BALI

Better value can be found at *Mie 88*. Although the menu is not extensive, prices are very reasonable (from 4500Rp to 6500Rp), and the beer is cheap (6500Rp for a large one). There is not much to choose from in Renon, but *Pondok Melati (Jl Raya Puputan)* has good, cheap seafood, although the setting is noisy.

A number of places along Jl Teuku Umar cater mainly for passing motorists, so if you don't have your own transport, get a bemo. Some, like *Kak Man Restaurant*, serve real Balinese food, as well as standard Indonesian fare. Almost opposite, *Ayam Goreng Taliwang* does Lombok-style food – very *pedas* (spicy). Most of the shopping centres have upstairs *eateries*, which serve cheap Indonesian and Chinese food in air-conditioned comfort.

Entertainment

The younger, more affluent denizens of Denpasar congregate around the shopping centres in the evening, and often later around a local cinema. *Wisata Cineplex (☎ 423023)* has five screens, and shows recent western movies in the original language, sub-titled in Bahasa Indonesia. Tickets cost about 6500Rp.

Many discos, bars and nightclubs can be found along Jl Diponegoro, such as *Amsterdam Nightclub*, which features live music later in the week; or around the Matahari department store, such as *DM Club & Karaoke*. The only cultural performances are the evening Kecak dance at the *Taman Wedhi Budaya* arts centre (see its entry earlier in this section).

Shopping

Markets The pungent Pasar Badung is reputedly the largest and oldest market in Bali. It's very busy in the morning and evening, and a great place to browse and bargain, except for the unsolicited guides/commission takers who sometimes attach themselves to you. Most visitors head to the clothing and handicrafts section on the top floor.

Pasar Kumbasari, along the opposite side of the river from Pasar Badung, has handicrafts, fabrics and gold work. Pasar Burung is a bird market with hundreds of caged birds and small animals for sale as pets – although they hardly make practical souvenirs. It's lovely to listen to and very colourful to see, but some visitors may be upset with the cruel conditions.

Jl Sulawesi, east of Pasar Badung, has many shops with batik, ikat and other fabrics. There are plenty of gold shops *(toko emas* or *toko mas)* in the area known as Kampung Arab.

Shopping Centres The western-style shopping centres are quite a recent innovation. The MA department store was one of the first, but has since been eclipsed by bigger, newer places such as Matahari, with a wide range of clothes, cosmetics, leather goods, sportswear, toys and baby things; NDA; and the newest and biggest, Bali Mall (Mal Bali). Most places have western fast-food restaurants and an eatery (see Places to Eat earlier in this section), and amusement centres for the kids (and the young at heart).

Getting There & Away

Air It's not necessary to come to Denpasar to arrange bookings, tickets or reconfirmation of flights. Most airlines are based in Sanur anyway, and the travel agencies in the Kuta region, Sanur, Ubud and other tourist centres can provide these services. Airline offices based in Denpasar are listed in the general Getting There & Away section earlier in this chapter.

Public Bus The usual route for land travel to Java is from Denpasar to Surabaya, although some buses go as far as Yogyakarta and Jakarta. They usually travel overnight. There are also regular buses from Denpasar to Mataram (Lombok), and further east to Sumbawa, but it's generally better to do this trip in individual stages.

In Denpasar, the bus companies have offices along Jl Hasanudin and the top of Jl Diponegoro; alternatively, you can book directly at the Ubung terminal. To Surabaya or even Jakarta, you may get on a bus within an hour of arriving at Ubung, but at busy times you should buy your ticket at least one day ahead.

Tourist Shuttle Bus None of the shuttle bus companies travel to or from Denpasar, because so few tourists come here, and public transport is frequent and reliable.

Bemo Denpasar is *the* hub for bemo transport around Bali. Unfortunately, the city has several confusing terminals, so you'll often have to transfer from one terminal to another. Most travellers will probably only need to know the terminals that link the Kuta region and Sanur with other tourist centres, such as Ubud and Padangbai. Each terminal has regular bemo connections to the other terminals in Denpasar for about 400Rp to 700Rp.

Ubung North of the town centre, on the road to Gilimanuk, Ubung terminal is the terminal for northern and western Bali.

Destination	Price (Rp)
Bedugul (for Danau Bratan)	2100
Gilimanuk (for the ferry to Java)	3900
Kediri (for Tanah Lot)	850
Mengwi	900
Negara	2500
Singaraja (via Pupuan or Bedugul)	3400
Tabanan	1000

Batubulan This is the terminal for eastern and central Bali, although it does also offer a new, useful service (priced for foreigners) directly to Nusa Dua in the south. The terminal is about 6km north-east of Denpasar.

Destination	Price (Rp)
Amlapura	2500
Bangli	1100
Besakih	1700
Candidasa	1900
Gianyar	1000
Kintamani (for Danau Batur)	2500
Nusa Dua	2300
Padangbai (for the ferry to Lombok)	1700

	Price (Rp)
Semarapura	1100
Singaraja (via Kintamani or Amlapura)	3500
Tampaksiring	1000
Tirta Gangga	2100
Tulamben	2400
Ubud	700

Tegal On the road to Kuta, Tegal is the terminal for all of southern Bali, except Suwung and Pelabuhan Benoa.

Destination	Price (Rp)
Airport	500
Jimbaran	700
Kuta	500
Legian	450
Nusa Dua/Bualu	500
Sanur	500
Ulu Watu	1100

Kereneng East of the town centre, Kereneng has bemos to every other terminal in Denpasar, including Sanglah, as well as Sanur.

Sanglah From this terminal near the main hospital, bemos go to Kereneng, Suwung and Pelabuhan Benoa.

Suci Not really a terminal, but more a stop on the side of the road, bemos link Suci with the other local terminals.

Wangaya From this tiny terminal, bemos go up the middle of Bali to Pelaga (1300Rp), via Sangeh and Petang; and to Ubung and Kereneng terminals.

Getting Around

To/From the Airport The Getting Around section at the start of this chapter has information about how to travel between the airport and Denpasar.

Bemo The main form of public transport is the bemo, which takes various circuitous routes from and between the domestic bemo terminals. Bemos line up for various destinations at each of the terminals, or you can

BALI

hail them from anywhere along the main roads – look for the destination sign above the driver's window. The lists under Bemo in the previous Getting There & Away section indicate which bemos you will need from one terminal to another. The Tegal-Sanur bemo is handy for Renon, the NDA and Matahari department stores, and Jl Diponegoro; and the Kereneng-Sanur bemo travels along Jl Gajah Mada, past the museum and Denpasar Tourist Office. You can also charter bemos from the various terminals. Prices are negotiable, of course.

Taxi Many taxis prowl the streets of Denpasar looking for fares; you will hear them beep at you constantly. Prices are negotiable, because few of them have meters. If you want to order a metered taxi, try Praja Bali Taxis (☎ 701111), Airport Taxi (☎ 751011, ext 1611) and Ngurah Rai Taxis (☎ 289090), which should use their meters.

AROUND DENPASAR
☎ 0361
If you are based in Denpasar, it's easy to take day trips to anywhere south of the city and as far as Padangbai, Ubud and Tanah Lot on any form of public or private transport.

Sidakarya
There is nothing particularly interesting about this village, about 5km south of Denpasar, unless you stay at *Bali International Youth Hostel* (☎ 720812, Jl Mertesari 19). There's a *restaurant*, and a small pool, but the rooms are not cheap: they cost 40,000Rp with a fan and 56,000Rp with air-con. Give the hostel a ring and ask if it offers a free pick-up from the Kuta region, Denpasar or the airport. You won't meet a lot of travellers here, however.

South Bali

The southern part of Bali, south of the capital Denpasar, is the tourist end of the island. The overwhelming mass of visitors to Bali is concentrated here. Nearly all the package-tour hotels are found in this area and many tourists only get out on day trips; some never get out at all.

KUTA
☎ 0361
The Kuta region is overwhelmingly Bali's largest and tackiest tourist beach resort. Most visitors come to the Kuta region sooner or later because it's close to the airport, and has the best range of budget hotels, restaurants and tourist facilities. Some find the area overdeveloped and seedy, but if you have a taste for a busy beach scene, shopping and nightlife, you will probably have a great time – but go somewhere else if you want a quiet, unspoilt tropical hideaway.

It is fashionable to disparage the Kuta region for its rampant development, low-brow nightlife and crass commercialism, but the cosmopolitan mixture of beach-party hedonism and entrepreneurial energy can be exciting. It's not pretty, but it's not dull either, and the amazing growth is evidence that a lot of people find something to like in Kuta.

The *kelurahan* (local government area) of 'Kuta' extends for nearly 8km along the beach and foreshore. Visitors have a choice of basing themselves in, and/or visiting, four different areas:

Kuta has the greatest choice of hotels, restaurants, shops and nightclubs, and the best beach – but the worst traffic and most annoying hawkers.

Legian, to the north, is a slightly quieter version of Kuta, with less of everything, including hotels and hawkers.

Seminyak, north of Legian, somehow retains a small town atmosphere, with little traffic and no hawkers, but the beach is scruffy in parts and it's isolated from the 'action' in Kuta.

Tuban, between Kuta and the airport to the south, is newly developed, with a good beach in most places, many upmarket hotels and large shopping centres.

History
Mads Lange, a Danish copra trader and adventurer, established a successful trading enterprise near modern Kuta, and had some success in mediating between local rajahs

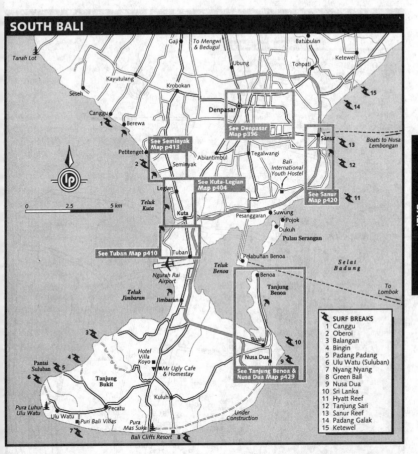

SOUTH BALI

Tanah Lot

Gaji
To Mengwi
& Bedugul
Batubulan
Ketewel

Kayutulang
Ubung
Tohpati

Seseh
Krobokan

Canggu
Denpasar

1
Berewa

See Denpasar
Map p396

See Seminyak
Map p413

Petitenget
Abiantimbul
Tegalwangi

2
Seminyak

Sanur
13
Boats to Nusa
Lembongan

Bali
International
Youth Hostel
12

Legian
See Kuta-Legian
Map p404

Teluk
Kuta

Kuta
See Sanur
Map p420
11

Pesanggaran
Suwung
Pojok
Dukuh
Pulau Serangan

See Tuban Map p410
Tuban

Pelabuhan Benoa
Selat
Badung

Ngurah Rai
Airport

Teluk
Benoa

Benoa

To
Lombok

Teluk
Jimbaran
Jimbaran

Tanjung
Benoa

3

Hotel
Villa
Koyo

Mr Ugly Cafe
& Homestay

10

Pantai
Suluban

4
5

Tanjung
Bukit

Bualu

Nusa Dua

9

See Tanjung Benoa &
Nusa Dua Map p429

6

Kuluh

Pura Luhur
Ulu Watu

Pecatu

Ulu Watu
Puri Bali Villas
Pura
Mas Suka

Under
Construction

7
Bali Cliffs Resort 8

SURF BREAKS
1 Canggu
2 Oberoi
3 Balangan
4 Bingin
5 Padang Padang
6 Ulu Watu (Suluban)
7 Nyang Nyang
8 Green Ball
9 Nusa Dua
10 Sri Lanka
11 Hyatt Reef
12 Tanjung Sari
13 Sanur Reef
14 Padang Galak
15 Ketewel

BALI

0   2.5   5 km

and the Dutch, who were encroaching from the north. His business soured in the 1850s, and he died suddenly, perhaps murdered. His grave, and a monument erected later, are near Kuta's night market.

The original Kuta Beach Hotel was started by a Californian couple in the 1930s, but closed with the Japanese occupation of Bali in 1942. In the late 1960s, Kuta became known as a stop on the hippie trail between Australia and Europe, and an untouched 'secret' surf spot. Accommodation opened and, by the early 1970s, Kuta had a delightfully laid-back atmosphere. Enterprising Indonesians seized opportunities to profit from the tourist trade, often in partnership with foreigners who wanted a pretext for staying longer. When Kuta expanded, Legian further north became the quiet alternative, but now you can't tell where one ends and the other begins. Legian has now merged with Seminyak, the next village north. To the south, new developments in Tuban are filling the area between Kuta and the airport.

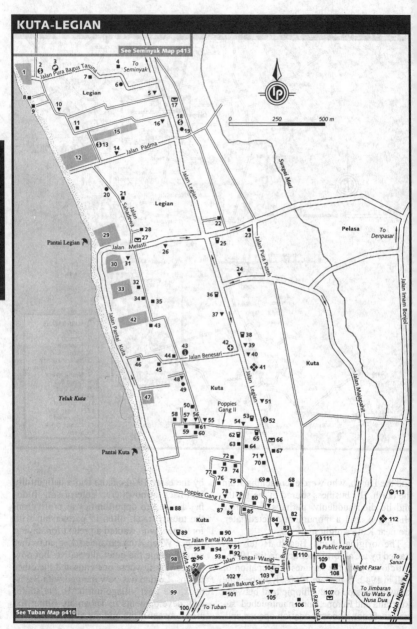

KUTA-LEGIAN

See Seminyak Map p413

Jalan Pura Bagus Taruna

To Seminyak

Legian

Jalan Padma

Jalan Sahadewa

Legian

Jalan Legian

Pantai Legian

Jalan Melasti

Jalan Pantai Kuta

Teluk Kuta

Jalan Benesari

Kuta

Poppies Gang II

Pantai Kuta

Poppies Gang I

Kuta

Jalan Pantai Kuta

Kuta Square

Jalan Tengai Wangi

Jalan Bakung Sari

To Tuban

See Tuban Map p410

Sungai Mati

Pelasa

To Denpasar

Jalan Pura Puseh

Kuta

Jalan Majapahit

Jalan Imam Bonjol

Jalan Buni Sari

Public Pasar

Night Pasar

To Sanur

To Jimbaran
Ulu Watu &
Nusa Dua

Jalan Raya Kuta

Jalan Ngurah Rai

0   250   500 m

KUTA-LEGIAN

PLACES TO STAY
1 Hotel Jayakarta
4 Losmen Made
  Beach Inn;
  Bamboo Palace
7 Baleka Beach Hotel
8 Puri Tantra Beach
  Bungalows
9 Bali Kelapa Hotel
11 Sinar Indah; Bali Sani
  Hotel
12 Bali Padma Hotel
15 Three Brothers Inn
21 Suri Wathi Beach
  House
22 Surfers Paradise
28 Sorga Beach Inn
29 Legian Beach Hotel
30 Bali Intan Legian
32 Adus Beach Inn
33 Resor Kul Kul
34 Hotel Camplung Mas
  (Ocean Blue)
35 Hotel Puri Tanahlot
44 Kuta Bungalows
45 Un's Hotel
46 Komala Indah II
  & Restaurant
47 Hotel Istana Rama
50 Suka Beach Inn
58 Bounty Hotel
59 Poppies Cottages II
60 Bali Sandy Cottages
61 Hotel Barong
63 Ronta Bungalows
  & Warung
64 Jus Edith
67 Sri Kusuma Hotel
  & Bungalows
68 Penginapan Maha
  Bharata
70 Paradiso Beach Inn
72 Sari Bali Bungalows
73 Suji Bungalow
74 Puri Ayodia Inn
75 Kempu Taman Ayu
76 Rita's House
77 Berlian Inn
80 Komala Indah I
85 Poppies Cottages I
87 Masa Inn
88 Hotel Aneka Kuta
90 Budi Beach Inn
92 Ida Beach Inn
93 Asana Santhi
  Homestay (Willy I)

94 Kuta Suci
  Bungalows
95 Yulia Beach Inn
98 Natour Kuta Beach
100 Melasti Bungalows;
  Karthi Inn
101 Hotel Ramayana
106 Bamboo Inn; Zet Inn;
  Jensen's Inn II

PLACES TO EAT
5 Glory Bar
  & Restaurant
10 Poco Loco
14 Joni Sunken Bar
  & Restaurant
16 Warung Kopi
24 Yanie's
26 Orchid Garden
  Restaurant
31 Taman Garden; Legian
  Garden Restaurant;
  Restaurant Puri
  Bali Indah
37 Aroma's Cafe
39 Mama Luccia
  Italian Restaurant
40 Gemini
48 Brasil Bali Restaurant
51 Mama's German
  Restaurant; Norm's
  Sports Bar; Lips
54 Batu Bulong
55 Twice Pub
56 Warung 96; Warung
  Dewi; The Corner
  Restaurant
57 Warung Nanas;
  Warung Ziro
71 Mini Restaurant;
  Expresso Bar
  & Pizzeria
78 Nusa Indah Bar &
  Restaurant
79 TJ's; Bamboo Corner;
  Bali Asi
81 Poppies Restaurant
82 Sushi Bar Kunti
84 Made's Warung
86 Fat Yogi's
91 Lenny's Seafood;
  The Bookshop
102 Dayu I
103 Bali Aget
105 Agung Cafe;
  Agung Supermarket

BARS & NIGHTCLUBS
25 Peanuts
36 Bounty I
38 001 Club
53 SC (Sari Club)
62 Tubes Bar
65 The Maccaroni Club
89 Hard Rock Cafe
  & Hard Rock
  Beach Club
104 The Pub
110 Casablanca Bar

OTHER
2 Bank Bali
3 Swiss & Austrian
  Consular Agents; Swiss
  Restaurant
6 Bali@Cyber Cafe
  & Restaurant
13 Bank Bali
17 Postal Agency
18 ATM Machines
19 The Bookstore
20 Legian Cyber Cafe
23 Bali Bungy
27 Postal Agent;
  Ant Pasar
41 Matahari Department
  Store; Timezone;
  McDonald's; Cinema
42 Legian Medical Clinic;
  Subway Restaurant
43 Bali Tourist Office
49 Adrenalin Park
52 Bank Panir
66 Postal Agency
69 Perama Office
83 Bemo Corner
96 Kambodja Wartel &
  Internet Centre
97 Kuta Square; Matahari
  Department Store;
  McDonald's; KFC;
  Timezone; Banks
99 Kuta Art Pasar;
  Artists Cafe
107 Main Post Office
108 Chinese Temple
109 Badung Tourist Office;
  Police Station
111 BCA Bank
112 Galeal de Wata
  Shopping Centre; KFC
113 Bemos to Nusa Dua;
  Petrol Station

BALI

All this development has taken its toll, and the area is now a chaotic mixture of shops, bars, restaurants and hotels on a confusing maze of streets and alleys, often congested with heavy traffic, thick with fumes and painfully noisy. Kuta is trying to move upmarket, and shopping is the big growth area. Nearly all the clothing sold in Kuta is locally made, and a growing Balinese garment industry is exporting worldwide. Lots of expatriate businesspeople rent houses or bungalows around Seminyak; many are married to Balinese and are permanent residents.

Modern Kuta is an international scene, but a traditional Balinese community remains. The religious practices are observed, and the banjars are still active in governing the local community. Temples are impressive and well kept, processions and festivals are elaborate and the offerings are made every day. The observance of *nyepi*, the day of stillness when no work is done (see the 'Nyepi' boxed text earlier in this chapter), has left many tourists perplexed at the closure of their favourite bar or restaurant.

Orientation

The Kuta region is a disorienting place – it's flat, with few landmarks or signs, and the streets and alleys are crooked and often walled on one or both sides so it feels like a maze. The busy Jl Legian runs roughly parallel to the beach from Seminyak in the north through Legian to Kuta. It's a two way street in Legian but in most of Kuta it's one way going south, except for an infuriating block near Jl Melasti where it's one way going north.

Between Jl Legian and the beach is a tangle of narrow streets, tracks and alleys, with an amazing hodgepodge of tiny hotels, souvenir stalls, warungs, bars, building construction sites and even a few remaining stands of coconut palms. A small lane or alley is known as a *gang*; most are unsigned, and too small for cars, although this doesn't stop some drivers trying. The best known are known locally as Poppies Gang I and II – use these as landmarks.

Most of the bigger shops, restaurants and nightspots are along Jl Legian and a few of the main streets that head towards the beach. There are also dozens and dozens of travel agencies, souvenir shops, banks, moneychangers, motorcycle and car rental places, postal agencies and wartels (public telephone offices) – everything a holiday maker could need or want within a few hundred metres walk. No wonder so many visitors never make it out of the Kuta region – which is a shame, of course, because Bali has so much to offer.

Information

Tourist Offices The Badung Tourist Office (☎/fax 756176) is responsible for Badung province, ie the Kuta region, Nusa Dua and Tanjung Bukit (but not Sanur). It is open daily except Sunday from 7 am to 6 pm. The Bali Tourist Office (☎ 754090, fax 758521) is responsible for the whole of the island, but is unhelpful and uninformed, so it's not worth trying to find (it's at the back of the Century Plaza building). It is open daily from 8 am to 9 pm.

Money There are many banks around the Kuta region, mainly along Jl Legian and at Kuta Square. However, the numerous moneychangers are faster, more efficient, open longer hours and offer better exchange rates. The rates for moneychangers are advertised on boards on paths or windows outside the shops or offices, but look around because rates do vary enormously. In or near upmarket hotels and modern shopping centres, the rates are absurdly low – about 20% lower than places around the corner. There are also plenty of ATMs, especially in and around the Kuta Square shopping area.

Post The main post office is on a dirt road east of Jl Raya Kuta. It's small, efficient and has an easy, sort-it-yourself poste restante service. It is open Monday to Thursday from 8 am to 2 pm, until noon on Friday and 1 pm on Saturday. This post office is the best place in Bali from which to send any large packages back home. There are also postal agencies along the main roads.

Telephone There are wartels about every few hundred metres along Jl Legian, the main roads between Jl Legian and the beach, and along Jl Dhyana Pura in Seminyak. Home Country Direct Dial telephones are located on the ground floor of the Matahari department store at Kuta Square, and near the left luggage counter at the international terminal at the airport.

Email & Internet Access There are cybercafes sprouting up everywhere. Three of the best are:

Bali@Cyber Cafe & Restaurant
  (bi-cafe1@idola.net.id)
Kambodja
  (kambodiana@denpasar.wasantara.net.id) –
  the most expensive
Legian Cyber Cafe
  (cyleg1@idola.net.id)

Bookshops For quality books about Bali, the best bookshop is M-Media on the 4th floor of the Matahari department store at Kuta Square. It also sells maps, and Lonely Planet guides to Asia, Australia and beyond.

Emergency Of the several private clinics in the Kuta region, the most accessible and modern is Legian Medical Clinic (☎ 758 503). It operates 24 hours a day, and also has an ambulance and dentist service. It charges 50,000Rp for a consultation in the clinic, or 250,000Rp for an emergency visit to your hotel room.

The local police station (☎ 751598) is next to the Badung Tourist Office, and there are one or two temporary tourist police posts along Jl Legian. If you have any major problem, or need a local driving licence, head for the main police station in Denpasar.

Dangers & Annoyances Theft is not an enormous problem, but visitors do lose things from unlocked hotel rooms or from the beach. Going into the water and leaving valuables on the beach is simply asking for trouble. There are also some snatch thefts, so hang on to your bag and keep your money belt under your shirt – wearing a bumbag over your shirt is not a great idea.

It is generally safe to walk around the streets in the Kuta region at any time, but there are occasional reports of robberies and assaults on the beaches and around nightclubs late at night, so please be careful. Assaults on women are still rare, but these days the main threat often comes from drunken foreign men rather than local males.

The surf can be very dangerous, with a strong current on some tides, especially in Legian. Lifeguards patrol swimming areas of the beaches at Kuta and Legian, indicated by red-and-yellow flags. If they say the water is too rough or unsafe to swim in, they mean it. There have also been unsubstantiated reports of sewage flowing into the sea near Kuta, especially after heavy rain.

For most visitors, hawkers, touts and wannabe guides are *the* major annoyance; and sadly they will leave an everlasting impression on many. Beach selling is now restricted to the upper part of the beach, where professionals with licence numbers on their conical hats will importune you to buy anything from a cold drink to a massage or a hair-beading job. Closer to the water, you can lie on the sand in peace – you'll soon find out where the invisible line is.

A number of scams also seem to be in operation in Bali (see Scams under Dangers & Annoyances in the Facts for the Visitor chapter).

Activities
From the Kuta region you can easily go surfing, sailing, diving, fishing or rafting anywhere in southern Bali, and be back for the start of the evening happy hour.

Surfing The Kuta-Legian coast has good reef and beach breaks, and the beach break at Kuta is the best place to learn surfing. Beginners can rent surfboards/boogie boards on the beach, or from losmen near the beach, for about 20,000/15,000Rp per day, and even get surfing lessons from 50,000Rp per day.

BALI

For more experienced surfers, there are great surf breaks around the south-western tip of Tanjung Bukit, most notably at **Pantai Suluban** (Suluban Beach), 3km west of Ulu Watu (see Ulu Watu later in this section for more information), **Padang Padang**, **Bingin** and **Balangan**.

On the southern coast are two more breaks, much more exposed and potentially dangerous. Both are accessible because they are next to top-end hotels. **Nyang Nyang** is reached by a track down the cliffs near Puri Bali Villas, and **Green Ball** is beside Bali Cliffs Resort (see the South Coast entry later in this section).

Most of these surfing spots are accessible by a driveable road, followed by a short walk from a car park. These are some of the prettiest beaches in Bali, and better still, they're practically deserted when the surf isn't working. They are worth exploring even if you're not into surfing, but they are rarely suitable for swimming.

A few surf shops near Tubes Bar, and along or just off Jl Legian, also hire surfboards and boogie boards, and can arrange repairs, lessons and shuttle buses to nearby surfing spots.

Activities for Children Popular activities for kids include the slides, pools and water sports at Waterbom Park in Tuban, and Timezone video arcades, located in the two Matahari department stores. There is also bungee jumping, mini golf and horse riding. The best idea is to grab a handful of brochures from any travel agent, which will also happily book most activities for you.

Places to Stay

Kuta, Legian, Tuban and Seminyak have hundreds of places to stay, so we can't possibly list them all. We have tried to list some (but not all) places that have character, and are convenient and quiet – at a good price. There is a 10% tax on all accommodation. In the cheaper places this is normally included in the price, or not payable at all, but check first. More expensive places add it on, along with an individual service charge of 5% to

15%, which can add substantially to your bill. If you're staying for a few days (or longer), you should always ask for a discount.

In all categories, the hotels are grouped by location, from Tuban to Seminyak, and then listed alphabetically.

Places to Stay – Budget

The best type of losmen is a relaxed, family-run place built around an attractive garden. Look for a place that is far enough off the main road to be quiet, but close enough so that getting to the beach, shops and restaurants is no problem. Many cheaper losmen offer breakfast, even if it's only a couple of bananas and a cup of tea.

There will be many other places of similar standard and price in the same areas as the ones listed here, so if your first choice is full, there will be others within walking distance.

Tuban There are mostly mid-range and top-end places south of Kuta. The only budget place is *Mandara Cottages* (☎ 751775, fax 761770, Jl Segara). It is within walking distance of the airport, the rooms are set back from the road and there's a pool. The rooms have huge beds, hot water and cost a very reasonable 45,000Rp.

South Kuta There are a number of cheap places on, or just south of, Jl Pantai Kuta, although anywhere close to the road will be noisy.

Bamboo Inn (☎ 751935), just off Jl Bakung Sari, is a traditional little losmen that is quiet and friendly, but often full. Simple rooms cost 25,000Rp. *Budi Beach Inn* (☎ 751610, Jl Pantai Kuta) is an old-style losmen with a garden and large, airy singles/doubles for a negotiable 39,000/44,000Rp to 77,000/88,000Rp with air-con. It is central and nicer than it looks from the entrance.

Jensen's Inn II (☎/fax 752647), just off Jl Bakung Sari, is quiet, friendly and central, so it's often full. Clean rooms cost US$12/15, but try to negotiate a more sensible price, and in rupiah. *Kuta Suci Bungalows* (☎/fax 753761, email kutasuci@denpasar.wasantara.net.id) is a little noisy and the rooms could do with some renovations, but it's good value at 22,000/27,500/38,500Rp for singles/doubles/triples, or slightly more for a bungalow.

Central Kuta Cheap places can be found along the tiny alleys and lanes between Jl Legian and the beach, but a few are also on the eastern side of Jl Legian. This is the best place to base yourself: it's quiet, only a short walk from the beach, and there are plenty of shops and restaurants nearby, so you rarely have to venture into the chaos of Jl Legian.

Adus Beach Inn (☎ 755326) is a new, family run place that is quiet, spotlessly clean and excellent value for 25,000/30,000Rp.

Bali Sandy Cottages (☎ 753344) is secluded and close to the beach. Its rooms are pleasant and good value for 35,000/50,000Rp. It's in a large, quiet garden, where a pool ought to be, but isn't.

Jus Edith is a no-frills place that charges a no-frills 15,000/20,000Rp. Some rooms are better than others, and if you looked around elsewhere you could do better.

Kempu Taman Ayu (☎ 751855) is a friendly little place with rooms for 16,000/25,000Rp (although the rooms are not particularly private).

Komala Indah I (☎ 751422) is clean and great value, considering the location. A room with a squat toilet and *mandi* (a large water tank from which you ladle water to pour over yourself like a shower) costs 15,000Rp.

Komala Indah II (☎ 754258) is still set among the coconut palms that typified Kuta only 30 years ago. Some rooms are better than others, but priced at a bargain 15,000/20,000Rp. The attached restaurant is excellent. (One female reader did complain, however, about unwarranted attention from sleazy staff.)

Masa Inn (☎ 758507, fax 752606) is friendly and very good value, so it's often full. The pool is an attraction, and rooms are cheap at 24,000/27,000Rp, or 35,000/45,000Rp with fan and hot water. Air-con family rooms are 45,500Rp.

Penginapan Maha Bharata (☎ 756754) is a quiet place with large, pleasant rooms for

20,000/25,000Rp. Look for the sign from the main road.

Puri Ayodia Inn is a small, standard losmen in a quiet but convenient location, and is good value for 15,000/20,000Rp.

Rita's House (☎ 751760) is not fancy, but it's good value for 20,000/25,000Rp. It continues to get rave reviews from long-stay travellers. More rooms are being built, which will detract from the general cosiness.

Ronta Bungalows (☎ 754246) is clean, has a nice garden and is central, but it's often full. At 15,000/20,000Rp, it's not hard to understand why. The restaurant is also good, and popular.

Suka Beach Inn (☎ 752793) is a popular place, and better than others in the immediate area. Decent rooms cost only 15,000/20,000Rp.

Legian A few places are crowded along the two busy main roads in Legian, Jl Padma and Jl Melasti, or in areas between. Jl Pura Bagus Taruna is a quieter stretch of road.

Losmen Made Beach Inn (☎ 752127) is excellent value. Rooms cost 35,000Rp.

Sinar Indah (☎ 755905) is a standard losmen that is handy to the beach, but try to negotiate because 55,000Rp per room, with fan and hot water, is a little high.

Sorga Beach Inn (☎ 751609) is good value at 15,000/20,000Rp. The garden is shady, but the crickets will probably keep you awake at night.

Surfers Paradise (☎ 751103) is a quiet bed & breakfast that is good value at 30,000/35,000Rp, or 70,000Rp with air-con. The setting is pleasant, but the rooms could do with some renovation.

Seminyak There are very few budget places in Seminyak.

Kesuma Sari Beach Bungalows (☎ 730575) is a small, friendly place that is tucked away. It has character-filled rooms with enormous beds, hot water and a sort of alfresco bathroom for 45,000Rp.

Mesari Beach Inn (☎ 751401) is quiet and next to some stables (where you rent horses). Rooms only cost 20,000/25,000Rp, and

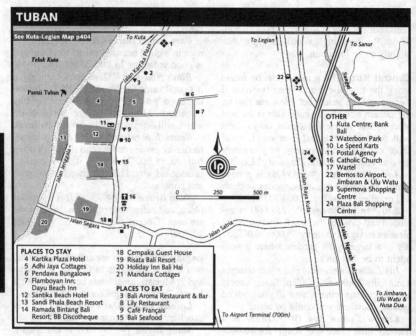

TUBAN

See Kuta-Legian Map p404

To Kuta

To Legian

To Sanur

Teluk Kuta

Pantai Tuban

Jalan Kartika Plaza

Jalan Tengkulu

Jalan Segara

Jalan Satria

Jalan Raya Kuta

Jalan Ngurah Rai

Sungai Mati

0   250   500 m

To Jimbaran,
Ulu Watu &
Nusa Dua

To Airport Terminal (700m)

PLACES TO STAY
4 Kartika Plaza Hotel
5 Adhi Jaya Cottages
6 Pendawa Bungalows
7 Flamboyan Inn;
   Dayu Beach Inn
12 Santika Beach Hotel
13 Sandi Phala Beach Resort
14 Ramada Bintang Bali
   Resort; BB Discotheque
18 Cempaka Guest House
19 Risata Bali Resort
20 Holiday Inn Bali Hai
21 Mandara Cottages

PLACES TO EAT
3 Bali Aroma Restaurant & Bar
8 Lily Restaurant
9 Café Français
15 Bali Seafood

OTHER
1 Kuta Centre; Bank
   Bali
2 Waterbom Park
10 Le Speed Karts
11 Postal Agency
16 Catholic Church
17 Wartel
22 Bemos to Airport,
   Jimbaran & Ulu Watu
23 Supernova Shopping
   Centre
24 Plaza Bali Shopping
   Centre

charming bungalows 50,000Rp, which is why it's often full.

Puri Mangga Bungalows (☎ 730447, fax 730307) is pleasant and has rooms with hot water and fan, which the manager is willing to negotiate down to only 25,000Rp.

Places to Stay – Mid-Range

The best of the mid-range hotels are former budget places that have improved their facilities. These places are normally family-owned and understand the need to occupy a room, so prices are more negotiable. Many of the new package-tour hotels are featureless and dull, with standard features like air-conditioning and a swimming pool, but nothing in the way of Balinese style. All hotels listed below offer air-conditioned rooms and hot water, and most of the ones priced in US dollars have swimming pools.

Tuban *Adhi Jaya Cottages* (☎/fax 753607, Jl Kartika Plaza) is nothing special. Fan-cooled singles/doubles/triples cost US$15/20/25, while the air-conditioned cottages for US$30/35/42 are better value.

Cempaka Guest House (☎ 751621, fax 753529, Jl Kartika Plaza) is a noisy family-run place close to the airport. Singles/doubles with air-con, TV and hot water can be easily negotiated down to 60,000/65,000Rp.

Rooms at ***Flamboyan Inn*** (☎/fax 752610) normally costs US$36/42/55 with air-con, but the manager is willing to negotiate. The place is quiet and is recommended for families.

Pendawa Bungalows (☎ 752387, fax 757 777) is one of several decent places along a quiet laneway. It has a spacious garden, and six types of rooms priced from US$19/23/29 to US$48/58/79.

Sandi Phala Beach Resort (☎ 7537708, fax 754889) has rooms in a neat two storey block facing directly onto the beach, and cost US$35/42.

South Kuta The new Kuta Square shopping development has revived this end of town, and it's a good place to base yourself if you love shopping.

Asana Santhi Homestay (Willy I) (☎ 751281, Jl Tengai Wangi) is attractive and surprisingly quiet and relaxed. The well-kept rooms have interesting furnishings, and the staff are very helpful. Rooms cost about US$30.

The rooms at *Ida Beach Inn* (☎ 751205, fax 751934, Jl Tengai Wangi) are squashed together, but the place is quiet and has a nice garden. It's a little hard to find, down a laneway. Rooms cost from US$33.

Melasti Bungalows (☎ 751335, fax 751 563, email melasti@denpasar.wasantara .net.id, Jl Kartika Plaza) is a top-end hotel with a number of mid-range rooms for a reasonable US$30/36, with fan and hot water. Other rooms are priced at up to US$120/145.

Yulia Beach Inn (☎ 751893, fax 751055, Jl Pantai Kuta) is a long-running, friendly, quiet place with basic rooms starting at US$7/10. A bungalow with hot water costs US$20/25/29.

Central Kuta The back lanes between Jl Legian and the beachfront road have a number of mid-range places that are handy to everything. They don't carry much traffic, so it's a relatively quiet area.

The rooms in the *Hotel Barong* (☎ 751 804, fax 761520) are too close together, but it's new, central and offers almost permanent discounts of 50% or more on its normal rates of US$78/85/110.

Berlian Inn (☎ 751701) is good value, being quiet, friendly and central. Rooms are priced from US$8/10 to US$22/27.

Kuta Bungalows (☎ 754395, fax 753748) is popular and central, and costs US$34/40/ 50. There are substantial discounts for longer stays.

Paradiso Beach Inn (☎ 752270, fax 751 781) is far more inviting than the entrance

suggests. There is not much of a garden, but it's quiet. Rooms cost US$20/25/37, or US$30/35/50 with air-con.

Poppies Cottages II (☎ 751059, fax 752364, email info@bali.poppies.net.id) is the original Poppies (despite the name) and is neither as fancy nor as central as Poppies I. There are only a few cottages, but guests can use the pool at Poppies I. At US$30/36/51, this is no longer good value.

Hotel Puri Tanahlot (☎ 752281, fax 755 626) has stylish bungalows set around a pleasant garden and pool. It's quiet and rates are negotiable: standard rooms are US$8/10, and bungalows only US$25/30.

Sari Bali Bungalows (☎ 753065) has nice bungalows and rooms in a spacious garden with a good pool. Prices are 50,000/70,000Rp with fan and cold water, and 100,000/ 120,000Rp with air-con.

The pleasant *Sri Kusuma Hotel & Bungalows* (☎ 751201, fax 756567) is central and clean, and has plenty of rooms for US$20/30/ 38. Bungalows with satellite TV, air-con and private balconies are US$30/40/50.

Suji Bungalow (☎/fax 752483) is a family-run place with a perfect little garden around a pool. The rooms have decent patios, offering some privacy, and cost a negotiable 60,000/80,000/100,000Rp, or 95,000/115,000/135,000Rp with air-con and hot water.

Un's Hotel (☎ 757409, fax 758414, email unshotel@denpasar.wasantara.net.id) is quiet and secluded, and features wide patios for shade and plenty of foliage around the pool. Standard rooms cost US$17/20/24 with fan and hot water, while rooms with air-con are US$22/30/35. A family room with cooking equipment, fridge and satellite TV costs only a few dollars more.

Legian *Baleka Beach Hotel* (☎ 751931, fax 753976, Jl Pura Bagus Taruna) is a good place with a pleasant pool. Rooms with a fan cost a reasonable 75,000/ 90,000Rp, while rooms with air-con are 125,000/175,000Rp.

Bali Kelapa Hotel (☎ 754167, fax 754 121), also known as Bali Coconut Hotel, is

BALI

friendly, very close to the beach and has rooms for only 80,000Rp.

The charming *Puri Tantra Beach Bungalows* (*π/fax 753195*) is a handful of traditional cottages. It's often full, because it's such good value at US$40/45.

Suri Wathi Beach House (*π 753162, fax 758393*) is off the main road, so it's very quiet, and there are plenty of rooms and a swimming pool. Rooms are excellent value for US$8/10, or US$12 for a bungalow.

The popular *Three Brothers Inn* (*π 751 566, fax 756082*) has rooms scattered around a gorgeous garden, but the newer rooms have less character than the originals. Prices are US$22 with fan and hot water, and US$38 with air-con.

Seminyak In this area there are also houses and bungalows to rent by the week or month if you look around – ideal for families. If you pre-book a room by phone or fax, staff may pick you up from the Kuta region or the airport for free.

Dewi Tirta Cottages (*π 730476*) has decent rooms (not cottages) for 65,000/75,000Rp with fan/air-con. It's quiet, and one of the few places willing to negotiate, but it lacks some character.

Prince of Legian Cottages (*π 730733, fax 732144, Jl Double Six*) has fully equipped bungalows that sleep up to four and are popular with long-term visitors, especially families. Its rates are US$40 per bungalow, but reductions of US$10 per night are possible for longer stays. Bookings are recommended.

Sarinande Beach Inn (*π/fax 730383*) is a delightful little hideaway. It's secluded, but it offers free transfers to the Kuta region and airport. Rooms, including satellite TV, air-con and fridge, are excellent value for US$35/40/48.

Places to Stay – Top End

Kuta, Legian, Tuban and Seminyak also have plenty of places in the top-end category, all with hot water, satellite TV, air-con and a swimming pool (or two). Most visitors stay at top-end places as part of a package tour, with special rates considerably lower than the 'published prices' listed below – these 'published prices' are rarely negotiable for independent travellers, however. Some hotels have the cheek to add variable 'high season supplements' in peak times (July-August and December-January).

Tuban There are many top-end places along the main road through Tuban, but not all are on the beach.

Holiday Inn Bali Hai (*π 753035, fax 754 549, email holidayinn@denpasar.wasantara .net.id, Jl Segara*) has excellent Balinese architecture as well as a beautiful pool and gardens. Rooms are priced from US$175, bungalows from US$333.

The large *Kartika Plaza Hotel* (*π 751 067, fax 752475, email kartikaplz@denpasar .wasantara.net.id, Jl Kartika Plaza*) is right on the beach, has a gigantic pool and charges from US$181.

Risata Bali Resort (*π 753340, fax 753354, Jl Segara*) has nice rooms set around a pool in a garden. It's a short walk from the beach, but it's a fair way from most of the shops and nightlife. Prices start at US$96/108.

Santika Beach Hotel (*π 751267, fax 751 260, email santika@denpasar.wasantara .net.id, Jl Kartika Plaza*) has a beach frontage, swimming pools, tennis courts and a variety of rooms priced from US$145.

Kuta *Hotel Aneka Kuta* (*π 752067, fax 752 892, email anekuta@denpasar.wasantara .net.id, Jl Pantai Kuta*) is directly opposite the beach and has rooms for US$66/72. For the privacy of a villa you pay US$78/85. The 'full suite' costs US$303.

Bounty Hotel (*π/fax 753030*) is central but a little way from the beach. Despite its distinctive black-tiled pool, it's not as luxurious as others in this range. Prices start at US$121, but discounts of 50% are not uncommon for independent travellers.

Hotel Camplung Mas (*π 751580, fax 751869*) is marketed to young Aussie package tourists. Its nice semi-detached cottages have high fences affording some privacy and cost US$59/61 for a twin/triple.

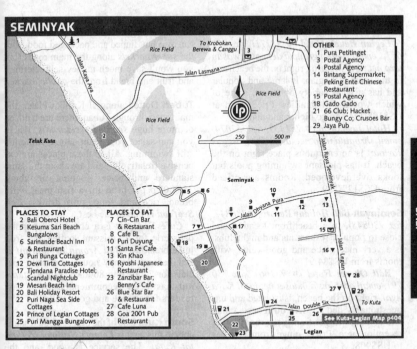

SEMINYAK

Teluk Kuta

Rice Field

Rice Field

Rice Field

To Krobokan,
Berewa & Canggu

Jalan Lasmana

Jalan Kaya Aya

Jalan Raya Seminyak

Jalan Dhyana Pura

Jalan Legian

Jalan Double Six

Seminyak

Legian

To Kuta

0   250   500 m

See Kuta-Legian Map p404

OTHER
1 Pura Petitinget
3 Postal Agency
4 Postal Agency
14 Bintang Supermarket;
Peking Ente Chinese
Restaurant
15 Postal Agency
18 Gado Gado
21 66 Club; Hacket
Bungy Co; Crusoes Bar
29 Jaya Pub

PLACES TO STAY
2 Bali Oberoi Hotel
5 Kesuma Sari Beach Bungalows
6 Sarinande Beach Inn & Restaurant
9 Puri Bunga Cottages
12 Dewi Tirta Cottages
17 Tjendana Paradise Hotel; Scandal Nightclub
19 Mesari Beach Inn
20 Bali Holiday Resort
22 Puri Naga Sea Side Cottages
24 Prince of Legian Cottages
25 Puri Mangga Bungalows

PLACES TO EAT
7 Cin-Cin Bar & Restaurant
8 Cafe BL
10 Puri Duyung
11 Santa Fe Cafe
13 Kin Khao
16 Ryoshi Japanese Restaurant
23 Zanzibar Bar; Benny's Cafe
26 Blue Star Bar & Restaurant
28 Cafe Luna
28 Goa 2001 Pub Restaurant

Hotel Istana Rama (☎ 752208, fax 753078, Jl Pantai Kuta) is a huge, impressive place opposite the beach, and charges less than others for the same sort of luxuries: from US$102 a room.

Natour Kuta Beach (☎ 751361, fax 753958, Kuta Square) is the successor to the original Kuta Beach Hotel, but this rebuilt version has no sense of history. There are nice views and the location is very central, however. Rooms are priced from US$108/121 to a massive US$363 for the 'executive' suite.

Poppies Cottages I (☎ 751059, fax 752364, email info@bali.poppies.net.id) has an exotically lush garden and beautifully built cottages, with a quasi-alfresco bathroom and a sitting room. It's cheaper than most top-end places, and with a lot more character: US$93/99/114 for singles/doubles/triples. Make a reservation – it's very popular.

Hotel Ramayana (☎ 751864, fax 751866) is well established and close to Kuta Square. Lots of rooms are fitted into a limited space. Prices start at US$60/72 (20% more for a room closer to the pool).

Resor Kul Kul (☎ 752520, fax 752519, email kulkul@indosat.net.id, Jl Pantai Kuta) is a huge and popular hotel that has two and three-storey blocks of rooms plus bungalows in relatively spacious grounds. Rooms start at US$114/127.

Legian Close to the beach, the *Bali Intan Legian* (☎ 751770, fax 751891, email intan@denpasar.wasantara.net.id, Jl Pantai Kuta), is a standard package-tour hotel with rooms in two-storey blocks from US$96/108, and garden cottages for US$121/133.

Bali Padma Hotel (☎ 752111, fax 752149, email padma@denpasar.wasantara.net.id, Jl Padma) is a huge hotel by the beach, with lush gardens and lots of lotus ponds. Prices start at a whopping US$169/193.

Legian Beach Hotel (☎ 751711, fax 752 651, email legiangroup@denpasar.wasan tara.net.id, Jl Melasti), right on the beach and in the heart of Legian, is large and popular and has a wide variety of rooms, some of which would suit families. Prices start at US$108/121 and go higher and higher.

Hotel Jayakarta (☎ 751433, fax 752074, email jhrbali@indo.net.id, Jl Pura Bagus Taruna) is an enormous place right on the beach. It has pleasant swimming pools but looks overdeveloped. Rooms are priced from US$127/139.

Seminyak *Bali Holiday Resort (☎ 730847, fax 730848)*, in a beachfront location and close to popular restaurants and nightclubs, is a very nice place and good value, with rooms from US$84/91.

Bali Oberoi Hotel (☎ 751061, fax 730 791, email obrblres@indosat.net.id, Jl Kaya Aya), right on the beach, is isolated and unquestionably hedonistic. You'll need a map and compass to get from your room to the reception area. Prices range from US$393 to US$908.

Puri Bunga Cottages (☎ 730334), in the heart of Seminyak, is well set up, if a little overdeveloped, and good value for US$66/72.

Puri Naga Sea Side Cottages (☎ 730761, fax 730524, Jl Double Six) is a comfortable, well-located hotel with rooms from US$78/90 for a standard/deluxe.

Tjendana Paradise Hotel (☎ 753573, fax 730518, Jl Dhyana Pura), also known as Hotel Bali Saphir, has an impressive Balinese foyer that belies a standard layout of three-storey motel-style rooms from US$96/109.

Places to Eat

If you want to eat cheaply, try the places that cater to local workers. Every afternoon, *food carts* appear at the end of the roads leading to Legian Beach; along the esplanade, opposite the Hard Rock Cafe in Kuta; and even along the chaotic Jl Legian. There are also cheap *warungs* in the back streets near the

post office, and a few dotted around the alleys between Jl Legian and the beach in Kuta. You can also buy tinned and packaged food from the *supermarkets* along the main roads (but you won't save much money self-catering), and fruit and bread from the *public market*.

Tuban Dotted along Jl Kartika Plaza, the main road through Tuban, there are a dozen or more huge *seafood restaurants*, where you can select your main course while it's still swimming. All of these places are expensive (relatively), and are about the same standard and price – count on about 35,000Rp per head for a fish meal, with bread, rice and soup, plus drinks. *Bali Seafood* is one of the best.

Café Français is a classy and popular patisserie for a croissant, coffee and fruit juice breakfast. *Bali Aroma Restaurant & Bar* has very happy hours, and daily specials for 7000Rp to 8000Rp. *Lily Restaurant* has been recommended by a few readers for service and good value.

South Kuta One of the best seafood restaurants in this area is *Lenny's Seafood (Jl Pantai Kuta)*. The service is good, and the seafood dishes are not as pricey as you would imagine – from 9000Rp to 13,000Rp. *Bali Aget* has a good range of cheap breakfasts, pizza specials at lunch time and a long happy hour – so you could stay there the whole day!

East along Jl Bakung Sari, there are several good, inexpensive restaurants including *Dayu I*. Above *Agung Supermarket*, which has a lot of western food items for sale, *Agung Cafe* serves Korean barbecue dishes and other Korean standards. In Kuta Square, there is a *McDonald's*, *KFC* and a few other fast-food joints.

Central Kuta Poppies Gang I is named for *Poppies Restaurant (☎ 751059)*, one of the oldest and most popular in Kuta. The prices are around 15,000Rp for main courses, and the food is well prepared and presented. The garden setting and atmosphere are delightful – make a reservation. A few metres west, *TJ's (☎ 751093)* is a deservedly popular

Mexican restaurant, with a good ambience and main courses cost 10,000Rp. Bookings may also be necessary.

Bamboo Corner is quaint, and a good place to try seafood specials (about 7000Rp), or something from the range of Chinese and Indonesian dishes for around 5000Rp. One of the best is *Bali Asi*. The service is friendly, and specials include lunch time pizzas for about 5000Rp, and fish specials in the evening for about 7500Rp. It also boasts one of the cheapest and longest happy hours.

Nearby, *Nusa Indah Bar & Restaurant* is excellent for seafood specials (costing a very reasonable 6000Rp), has a friendly atmosphere, and serves ice-cold Carlsberg and San Miguel beers for the same price as a Bintang. Other recommended places in the general area are *Fat Yogi's*, which does tasty Italian meals for about 10,000Rp and decent pizzas for slightly more; and the popular *Made's Warung*, which offers delicious meals for 10,000Rp to 15,000Rp.

Poppies Gang II has dozens of cheap eateries. *Batu Bulong* is tasty and cheap, as is *Warung Nanas*, which is popular for its very happy hour and specials from 4500Rp to 9000Rp. Next door, the daily specials for 6000Rp to 7000Rp at *Warung Ziro* are excellent value, and it's not as crowded as others in the area. *Twice Pub* has been recommended by a few readers. These, and many others nearby, have laser video movies at night, which can detract from the ambience and service.

The lane heading north from Poppies Gang II has sprouted several good, cheap eateries to satisfy those staying in the budget hotels nearby. The service is friendly, and the daily fish specials are excellent, especially at *Warung 96*, while *Warung Dewi* (try the excellent sandwiches) and *The Corner Restaurant* (or Bali Corner) are also deservedly popular. Further up, one of the best value places has to be *Brasil Bali Restaurant*. It offers an extraordinary range of very cheap Brazilian, Indonesian and western-style dishes and breakfasts, and the drinks are always inexpensive. Many travellers end up eating there time and time again.

Along Jl Legian The possibilities along Jl Legian seem to be endless. Most of the time the road is an almost continuous traffic jam, however, and a table near the road can mean you have to shout to be heard. Just north of Bemo Corner, *Sushi Bar Kunti* offers set menus with delicious Japanese treats for 25,000Rp. *Mini Restaurant* is a huge place despite the name. It serves Chinese dishes for 10,000Rp to 12,000Rp, and also specialises in seafood. You can choose your intended meal from the tanks next to the street. Next door, *Expresso Bar & Pizzeria* has pizzas for 13,250Rp in a pleasant setting.

Continuing north, *Mama's German Restaurant* has authentic German food with *sauerbraten*, bratwurst and pork knuckles, and expensive draught beer. The Chinese *Gemini Restaurant* continues to be recommended by readers, despite its bare and basic appearance. *Mama Luccia Italian Restaurant* is classy, with meals from about 15,000Rp to 22,000Rp.

Aroma's Cafe was awarded Bali's Best Restaurant, and we continue to get lots of rave reviews from readers. It's a mid-priced vegetarian restaurant with good food and a delightful garden setting – the desserts and fruit drinks are particularly tasty. A little further north and just east of Jl Legian is *Yanie's*, a popular place with good burgers, pizzas and steaks, as well as Indonesian standards. It's inexpensive, opens till late and has a good, fun atmosphere.

Legian Jl Padma and Jl Melasti, and the laneway between them, have numerous mid-range restaurants and bars; it's a great place to look around for buffet breakfasts (from 5000Rp) and daily specials (from 7500Rp), and to hunt out cheap happy hours.

Some of the classier, but more expensive, places specialising in Chinese food and seafood are *Orchid Garden Restaurant*; *Legian Garden Restaurant*, which has an excellent happy hour and cheap breakfasts; and *Restaurant Puri Bali Indah*, with very tasty Chinese food. *Taman Garden* is very popular for its delicious food, happy hours and effusive staff; it attracts a lot of repeat customers. At *Joni Sunken Bar & Restaurant*, you can eat and drink while semi-immersed in a swimming pool. It also offers live music, and good-value buffet breakfasts for 8500Rp.

Further north, things get more expensive but the standards are higher – this is the fashionable end of town. *Poco Loco* is a popular, upmarket Mexican restaurant and bar. *Warung Kopi (Jl Legian)* is well re-garded for its varied menu of European, Asian and vegetarian dishes, good break-fasts and tempting deserts – prices start at around 9500Rp for a main dish. The long-standing *Glory Bar & Restaurant (Jl Legian)* does various buffets on various nights; its Balinese buffet (about 20,000Rp) is one of the few recommended places to try authentic local cuisine.

Seminyak There is nothing cheap in Semin-yak. *Goa 2001 Pub Restaurant (Jl Legian)* is where trendy expats choose from a multi-cultural menu and a long list of fancy drinks – all at fancy prices. Also recommended are *Ryoshi Japanese Restaurant (Jl Legian)* and *Cafe Luna*, nearby, for a range of meals from about 10,000Rp. Further north along Jl Legian, *Kin Khao* is the best place for Thai food. Nearby, a few *warungs* serve cheap and tasty Indonesian fare for local workers, but foreigners are always welcome.

Along Jl Dhyana Pura, *Santa Fe Cafe* is a pretty, and a pretty expensive, option for US south-western dishes; and *Puri Duyung* is also charming – dishes start at about 11,000Rp. *Cin-Cin Bar & Restaurant* has sensible prices (dishes start at about 8500Rp) and *Cafe BL* is also pretty good. It's a pleasant walk to *Sarinande Beach Inn*, where you can enjoy some cold drinks and snacks by the hotel pool for reasonable prices. Along Jl Double Six, *Blue Star Bar & Restaurant* is one of the best value places, and offers tasty daily specials from 7000Rp.

On the beachfront, it's hard to go past *Zanzibar Bar*, which also serves meals. Bet-ter still and worth a trip to Seminyak is *Benny's Cafe*, a great place for breakfast or a beer and a meal while watching the sunset

at the end of a 'hard day'. Even better is the classy *La Lucciola*, on a beach track past the Oberoi, near Pura Petitenget. Its meals are more international than strictly Italian, and its prices are a little high but not excessive. People rave about this place.

Entertainment

Around 6 pm the sunset at the beach is the big attraction, perhaps with a drink at one of the beach bars. After a good dinner, many visitors are happy with a video movie, an-other drink (or two) and a stroll in the cooler evening air. But a lot of people are here to party, and around the Kuta region that means lots of drinking, loud music and late nights. Check out the 'What's On in Bali' sections of the English-language newspapers, *Jakarta Post* and *The Observer*, to find out what's happening, and what's trendy.

Bars, Clubs, Nightclubs & Discos Bars are usually free to enter, and often have spe-cial drink promotions and 'happy hours' be-tween about 6 and 9 pm – sometimes longer. For the serious drinker, the biggest concen-tration of bars is on Jl Legian, while Jl Melasti and Jl Padma have a lot of Aussie-style bars. Plenty of party animals go on the (in)famous *Peanuts Pub Crawl* (☎ 754226) on Tuesday and Saturday night. Special buses (5000Rp a ticket) go to a handful of local watering holes – you can also book at Peanuts or anywhere the Crawl is advertised.

Some popular places along Jl Legian in-clude *Lips*, a sleazy country & western bar; *001 Club*, a self-proclaimed 'rage spot' with an all-you-can-drink offer of 30,000Rp; and *Norm's Sports Bar*, a long-established Aussie favourite that is looking neglected these days. One of the most popular places is *Sari Club* (or *SC*), which features a giant video screen, dance music and a young crowd – but drink prices are high. Around the cor-ner, *Tubes Bar* is where surfers drink beer, play pool and watch surfing videos. Further up Jl Legian is *Bounty I*, built in the shape of a sailing ship and easy to spot. It gets people in early with happy hours, and packs them onto the dance floor till the wee hours.

BALINESE TEMPLE SCULPTURE

Architecture and sculpture are inextricably bound together in Bali. A temple gateway is not just erected, instead every square centimetre of it is intricately carved in sculptural relief and a diminishing series of demon faces is placed above it as protection. Even then, it's not complete without several stone statues to act as guardians.

The level of decoration varies. In small or less important temples, sculpture may be limited or even nonexistent. In other temples, particularly some of the temples with exuberant detail in northern Bali, the relief sculpture may be almost overwhelming in its intricacy and interest. Sometimes a temple is built with minimal decoration in the hope that sculpture can be added when more funds are available. The sculpture can also deteriorate after a few years and is restored or replaced as resources permit – it's not uncommon to see a temple with old carvings, which are barely discernible, next to newly finished work.

Sculpture often appears in set places in temples. Door guardians – representations of legendary figures like Arjuna or other protective personalities – flank the steps to the gateway. Similar figures can often be seen at bridge openings. Above the main entrance to a temple, Kala's monstrous face often peers out, sometimes a number of times – his hands reaching out beside his head to catch any evil spirits foolish enough to try to sneak in.

Elsewhere other sculptures make regular appearances – the front of a *pura dalem* (temple of the dead) will often feature images of the *Rangda* (witch) and sculptured relief panels may show the horrors that await evildoers in the afterlife.

Text inset: Temple detail (photograph by Sara-Jane Cleland).

Right: Examples of vibrant Balinese temple decoration.

Colourful purification ceremony held on the beach, with temple umbrellas aloft.

Ramayana performance, Ubud.

Barong performer, Ubud Palace.

Monkey-god, Hanuman, Ubud.

Festival at Pura Besakih, the most revered temple in Bali, known locally as the Mother Temple.

Along Jl Legian, in Seminyak, *Goa 2001 Pub Restaurant* is where a lot of people start the evening with a meal and a few drinks. Alternatively, *Jaya Pub* is a place for an older crowd to enjoy relaxed music and conversation, while *Cafe Luna* has streetside tables where you can see and be seen.

Later on, the action shifts to the beachside *66 Club* (pronounced 'double six'), particularly on Saturday night, or the chic *Gado Gado*. They both have a cover charge (about 10,000Rp) which should include one drink. When there aren't many people in town, these two seem to alternate, with only one open on a given night. For something a little more sophisticated, try *Scandal Nightclub* at Tjendana Paradise Hotel.

Live Music Jl Melasti has a few loud bars that feature some Indonesian bands singing decent reggae and top 40 hits in passable English. One of the newest and most extraordinary places is *The Macaroni Club (Jl Legian)*, which features live jazz every night except Sunday from 10.30 pm, and even invites guests to jam with the musos on Friday night. Entry is free, but prices for drinks and meals are not cheap. *Joni Sunken Bar & Restaurant (Jl Padma)* is one place which constantly features decent acoustic guitar music.

More upmarket venues, attracting older customers, include the glossy, new *Hard Rock Cafe (Jl Pantai Kuta)*, with live music most nights and pricey drinks. Several upmarket hotels have something a bit more sophisticated. In Tuban, *Santika Beach Hotel* has pianists and singers most nights, and *Ramada Bintang Bali Resort* regularly features top-40-type bands. On the beach in Seminyak, *Crusoes Bar* normally has live music on Wednesday, Friday and Saturday, and happy hours every evening.

Video Movies & Sports Telecasts Large-screen laser disc video movies are featured at an increasing number of restaurants and bars, particularly along or near Poppies Gang II. Many start at about 3 pm daily, and different movies run about every two hours.

For anyone who can't survive without seeing their favourite sport on TV, many bars and restaurants, particularly around Poppies Gang II and along southern Jl Legian, show live telecasts of foreign sports.

Cinema The modern three screen *cinema complex* on the 4th floor of the Matahari department store on Jl Legian shows recent western movies, usually in the original language with Indonesian sub-titles. Tickets cost 6500Rp, and shows start at 6 pm.

Balinese Dance Large hotels and restaurants put on tourist versions of the best known Balinese dances, and these are well publicised. They are usually included in a set menu, which can cost up to US$25 per head. Hotels that regularly hold dances include *Bali Padma*, Legian; *Ritz-Carlton*, Jimbaran (see Tanjung Bukit later in this chapter); and *Kartika Plaza*, Tuban.

Shopping

Parts of the Kuta region are now almost door-to-door shops and over the years these have become steadily more sophisticated. There are still many simple stalls where T-shirts and beach wear are the main lines. Often these are crowded together in 'art markets' like the one at the beach end of Jl Bakung Sari, and on Jl Melasti. Many of the shops come and go, and the price you pay often depends on your ability to bargain, so recommending any particular shops is not worthwhile.

For everyday purchases, like food, toiletries and stationery, there are shops and mini-markets along the main streets. Many visitors end up going to one or both of the two enormous Matahari department stores. Kuta Square is easily the largest and most sophisticated group of shops in Bali. In these shopping centres, and along the main streets around the Kuta region, you can also buy slide and print film, and have it developed quickly and cheaply.

Kuta shops have arts and crafts from almost every part of the island, from woodcarvings to paintings to textiles and just about everything else in between. They also offer many interesting pieces from other parts of Indonesia, and it can be difficult to assess their authenticity and value – many of the 'Irian Jaya antiques' are made locally and recently. Some of the best areas in which to shop are the public market and the Kuta Art Market.

More and more music shops are springing up, offering an enormous range of cassette tapes and compact discs of western, Indonesian and Balinese music – all at fixed prices. Tapes cost about 15,000Rp (less for local music), while CDs cost about 90,000Rp.

Getting There & Away

Air If you want to buy or change an airline ticket, you should visit the relevant airline office in Sanur, in Denpasar or at the airport (details are listed in the general Getting There & Away section at the beginning of this chapter). The myriad of travel agencies in the Kuta region will reconfirm your flight for a small fee, but any decent hotel should do this for its guests for nothing.

Public Bus Lots of travel agents in the Kuta region sell bus tickets to Java and Lombok, but these are for the same public buses that leave Ubung terminal in Denpasar, so you must still get to Ubung yourself. Tickets will be slightly cheaper if you buy them at Ubung, but you won't save any money by going especially to Denpasar to buy the tickets.

Tourist Shuttle Bus Several times a day, tourist shuttle buses travel between Kuta and Legian and almost every place you want to go in Bali. You can also get shuttle bus/boat connections to Lombok (including the Gili Islands), and Java directly from Kuta/Legian. (See under Gili Islands in the Lombok section of the Nusa Tenggara chapter.)

Perama (☎ 751551, fax 751170) is the best known operator in Kuta, and around Bali. Other shuttle bus companies have similar fares, and may offer more suitable times. Perama has a convenient office on Jl Legian, but you can also book tickets for Perama and other shuttle bus companies at any travel agent.

Bemo Public bemos regularly travel between Tegal terminal in Denpasar for about 500Rp (but tourists are generally charged slightly more). Most 'S' bemos go only to the terminal area in Kuta, just beyond Bemo Corner, but the S1 does a loop around Jl Pantai Kuta.

If the public bemos will not stop for you in the tourist areas, you may have to go to Jl Pantai Kuta, east of Bemo Corner, for a trip to Denpasar; or Jl Raya Kuta, outside the Supernova shopping centre, in Tuban, for a trip to anywhere south of Tanjung Bukit and the airport. For all other places, go to Tegal terminal first, from where you'll probably need a connection to another terminal in Denpasar, and yet another to your destination.

Car & Motorcycle There are many car and motorcycle rental places around the Kuta region, so prices here are the most competitive in Bali – as long as you look around. The general Getting Around section at the start of this chapter has details about prices and standards in the Kuta region.

Getting Around

To/From the Airport The general Getting There & Away section at the start of this chapter has details about getting *from* the airport to the Kuta region. Going *to* the airport, you can take a shuttle bus (5000Rp), charter a bemo for about 6000Rp (haggle hard) or take a metered taxi (about 7500Rp). Alternatively, catch a bemo from the corner of Jl Raya Kuta and Jl Bakung Sari, or possibly even from outside the Supernova shopping centre in Tuban, and walk for a few minutes to the airport terminal from the bemo stop. A chartered bemo, metered taxi or tourist shuttle bus is more convenient.

Public Bemo Dark blue bemos do a loop from Bemo Corner, along and up Jl Pantai Kuta, along Jl Melasti, then up Jl Legian for a short while and then return down Jl Legian to Bemo Corner (about 500Rp for the loop). Bemo drivers are sometimes reluctant to pick up tourists (the transport mafia influence), and bemos are less frequent and more expensive in the afternoon and evening. For many short trips, and certainly at night, you'll probably have to charter a taxi or private car.

Chartered Bemo Bemos available for charter are easy to find – offers of 'transport' follow any tourist on foot. They don't have meters so you have to negotiate the fare before you get on board. You should be able to get from the middle of Kuta to the middle of Legian for around 4000Rp, but bargain hard. A full-day charter should run to about 90,000Rp, and you can estimate a price for shorter trips on a proportional basis.

Taxi There are plenty of taxis around the Kuta region. Most use their meters and are quite cheap – in fact, a metered taxi will often cost the same (or even less) than a chartered (unmetered) bemo or car, especially if you aren't good at haggling with bemo drivers. Taxis are very useful for trips around town at night, when they cost a little more, and they can be hired for trips to anywhere in southern Bali and even as far as Ubud.

Bicycle To find a bicycle, ask your hotel and look around the streets. Bicycles only cost about 5000Rp per day, and for such a low price the agencies aren't interested in renting by the hour. The agency should provide a lock and key. Beware of thieves who might snatch things from the basket or luggage rack.

AROUND KUTA
☎ 0361
Berewa
This greyish beach, secluded among stunning paddy fields, is a few kilometres up the coast from Kuta. There is no public transport in the area, but the hotels do provide shuttle services to/from the Kuta region. The turn-off is along the road heading west from Krobokan.

There are three luxury resorts with pools, all next to each other along the beach. *Bolare Beach Hotel (☎ 730258, fax 731663, email bolare@indosat.net.id)* has a great beachfront location, and singles/doubles cost US$72/85. *Legong Keraton Beach Cottages (☎ 730280, fax 730285)* has very nice

individual cottages, set in a pretty garden right by the beach, for US$78/97. *Dewata Beach Hotel (☎ 730263, fax 730290)* has restaurants, tennis courts and a disco. The rooms are comfortable, but nothing special, and start at US$108/121.

You can eat in the *hotel restaurants*, or in the *cafes* and *warungs* in the village, about 200m up from the resorts.

Canggu
A popular surf spot with right and left-hand breaks, Canggu is surprisingly undeveloped. Surfers naturally congregate at the unnamed *warung* a few metres from the beach, but the only place to stay is the ultra-expensive *Hotel Tugu Bali (☎ 731701, fax 731704, email bali@tuguhotels.com)*. It offers all the luxuries you would expect for US$302 to US$545. To get to Canggu, go west at Krobokan and south at Kayutulang, but you'll need your own transport.

SANUR
☎ 0361
Sanur is an upmarket alternative to the Kuta region for those coming to Bali for sea, sand and sun, and a downmarket alternative to Nusa Dua for those who want a package-tour holiday in an air-conditioned hotel with a swimming pool. Good, inexpensive eateries abound, so you don't have to swallow the high prices at hotel restaurants. Other tourist services are here, with some charming craft, clothing, art and antique shops.

The beach is wide and white, and sheltered by a reef. At low tide, it's very shallow, and you have to pick your way out over rocks and coral through knee-deep water. At high tide, the swimming is fine and there's also a classic but fickle surf break. An array of water sports is available – windsurfing, snorkelling, water-skiing, parasailing, paddle boards etc – all for a price.

Sanur doesn't have the noise, confusion and traffic of the Kuta region, and you're not constantly badgered to buy things – badgered yes, but not constantly. The nightlife is sedate by comparison, but you can always go over to the Kuta region for a wild night.

Orientation

Sanur stretches for about 3km along an east-facing coastline, with the landscaped grounds and restaurants of expensive hotels fronting right onto the beach. The conspicuous Grand Bali Beach Hotel is at the northern end of the strip. West of the beachfront hotels is the main drag, Jl Danau Tamblingan. It runs roughly parallel to the beach, with the hotel entrances on one side and wall-to-wall tourist shops and restaurants on the other side. For some reason, most of the streets are named after Indonesian lakes, such as Jl Danau Tamblingan and Jl Danau Buyan.

Information

Sanur is part of the Denpasar municipality, so you'll have to go to the Denpasar Tourist Office for information, although your hotel may have some local maps and information.

Money The exchange rates offered by moneychangers in Sanur, especially in the big hotels, are poor – at least 10% lower than in the Kuta region. The main American Express office in Bali is in the Grand Bali Beach Hotel. There are a couple of banks along the main road; Bank BCA, near Made's Kitchen restaurant, does cash advances on Visa cards.

Post & Communications Sanur's post office is on the southern side of Jl Danau Buyan; more convenient postal agencies are listed in the Sanur map key. There's a Home Country Direct Dial telephone in the area where the airline offices are located at the Grand Bali Beach Hotel, and several wartels dotted along the main road. The Internet centre in the Grand Bali Beach is very expensive; the one at the Santai Hotel is far better value.

Emergency The nearest hospital is in Denpasar, but there is a medical clinic (☎ 288 271) in the Bali Hyatt hotel. The police station (☎ 288597) is on Jl Bypass Ngurah Rai.

Museum Le Mayeur

The Belgian artist Adrien Jean Le Mayeur de Merpes lived in this house from 1935 to

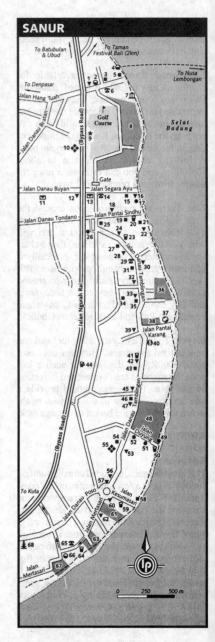

SANUR

PLACES TO STAY	PLACES TO EAT	7	Museum Le Mayeur;
3 Watering Hole	1 Si Pino Restaurant		Water Sports Kiosk
Homestay & Restaurant	12 Splash Bakery	9	Police Station
5 Ananda Hotel	16 Warungs	10	Supermarket
8 Grand Bali Beach Hotel;	18 Kalimantan Bar	11	Main Post Office
Airline Offices; Amex	& Restaurant	13	Postal Agent
Office	22 Mango Bar & Restaurant;	14	Telkom Wartel
15 Desa Segara	Benno's Corner Cafe	17	Sanur Beach Pasar;
19 Queen Bali Hotel	24 Bali Hai Bar & Restaurant		Sanur Beach Pasar Bar
& Restaurant	28 Warung Wina		& Restaurant; Water Sports
21 Natour Sindhu Beach	(Vienna Cafe)		Kiosk
25 Puri Mango Guest	30 Kuri Putih	20	Rumours Nightclub
House & Restaurant	32 Cumi Cumi	23	Bali Janger
27 Homestays Yulia,	33 Taman Bayu	26	Pasar Sindhu Night
Luisa & Coca	39 Swastika II Restaurant		Pasar & Art Pasar
31 Made's Homestay	42 Made's Kitchen; Bank BCA	29	Wartel
& Pub; Wartel	45 Cafe Batu Kimbar;	37	German Consulate
34 Prima Cottages	Postal Agency	40	Bank Danamon
35 Keke Homestay	47 Melanie's Restaurant;	41	No I Club
36 Santrian Beach Resort	Wartel	44	Petrol Station
38 Laghawa Beach Inn	53 Warung Agung	49	Surya Water Sports
43 Santai Hotel; Kafe Jali	56 Oka's	50	Banjar Club
Tiwa; Internet Centre	57 Kafe Jepun	51	Duyung Art Pasar
46 Penginapan Jati;	60 Cafe Ketut	52	Supermarket
Warung Bali Sun	62 Tropika Kafe; Jaya	55	Double U Shopping Centre
48 Bali Hyatt; Medical Clinic	Kesuma Art Market	59	Bali International
54 Penginapan Lestari			Sports Club
58 Villa Kesumasari II	OTHER	64	Trophy Pub; Postal Agency
61 Sativa Sanur Cottages	2 Bemo Stop; Perama Office	65	Wartel
63 Puri Santrian Hotel	4 Boats to Nusa Lembongan	66	Bemo Stop; Warungs
67 Hotel Sanur Aerowisata	6 Wartel	68	Pura Belangjong

1958, when Sanur was a quiet fishing village. The house must have been a delightful place then – a peaceful and elegant home right by the beach – but today it's squeezed between the Grand Bali Beach and Diwangkara Beach hotels. The museum is worth a quick look, but it's nothing special.

The home displays paintings and drawings by Le Mayeur; some are interesting impressionist-style paintings from his travels in Africa, India, Italy, France and the South Pacific. Paintings from his early period in Bali are romantic depictions of Balinese daily life and beautiful Balinese women, but unfortunately, many of them are yellowed, dirty and badly lit.

Tickets cost 750/250Rp for adults/children. The museum (☎ 286201) is open Sunday to Wednesday from 8 am to 2 pm, until 11 am on Friday and until 12.30 am on Saturday.

You must take off your shoes when you enter the buildings.

Activities

There are numerous activities in Sanur, and all around southern Bali. The diving off Sanur is not great, but there is a good variety of fish on the reef; at low tide, they're in water shallow enough for snorkellers. There are three good surf breaks on the reef but mostly they need a big swell to work, and they're only good in the wet season, when winds are offshore.

You can organise any number of water sports at one of three kiosks (indicated on the Sanur map). Other popular activities include bowling and golf at the Grand Bali Beach Hotel complex. The kids will enjoy the Taman Festival Bali nature reserve, north of Sanur.

BALI

Places to Stay

There are a few rock-bottom places in Sanur and a handful of cheap mid-range hotels, but Sanur is primarily a medium to high-price resort – a place of 'international standard' hotels for package tours. Most budget and mid-range places include breakfast. Many hotels are on the main road, Jl Danau Tamblingan.

Places to Stay – Budget

The three cheapest places are huddled together, and behind little art shops (which is where the staff will probably be). For these prices, in this part of Bali, don't expect much, but you may get a good deal on some batik or carvings. *Yulia Homestay* (☎ 288 089) charges 30,000Rp per room, while *Luisa Homestay* (☎ 289673) and *Coca Homestay* (☎ 287391) charge 25,000Rp. The best in this range is *Keke Homestay* (☎ 287 282). Run by a friendly, English-speaking family, and set off the main road, its singles/doubles are quiet, clean and cost 30,000/40,000Rp.

Places to Stay – Mid-Range

Most places that charge US dollars will have a swimming pool, but you will only be a few minutes walk away from a glorious beach anyway.

In the northern part of Sanur, *Watering Hole Homestay* (☎/fax 288289, Jl Hang Tuah), opposite the Grand Bali Beach Hotel entrance, has clean, pleasant rooms for 50,000/80,000Rp with fan/air-con; and 100,000Rp for a large, family-sized room with air-con. It's a friendly, family-run place, with a good restaurant downstairs. Just down the road, *Ananda Hotel* (☎ 288327) is recommended: charming, clean and quiet singles/doubles are great value for 40,000/50,000Rp. It's the best place to base yourself before or after catching a boat to Nusa Lembongan.

Also good value is *Penginapan Lestari* (☎ 288867), where rooms with fan/air-con cost 50,000/75,000Rp. None of the rooms has hot water, but it's quiet and friendly, and has some character. One the best value

places in this price range is *Penginapan Jati* (☎ 289157), although it doesn't have a pool. The outside decor is a bit ornate, but the staff are friendly and it's clean and quiet. Rooms costs US$15; the rooms for US$20 have a small kitchen.

Worth checking out is *Made's Homestay* (☎/fax 288152), at the back of the pub with the same name. It's a bit garish, but the staff are affable, and there's a small pool. Singles/doubles cost US$20/25 with a fan; US$25 per room with air-con, bath and fridge. *Villa Kesumasari II* (☎ 287824, fax 288876) is in a perfect, tranquil position, right on the beach, but is overpriced at 70,000/100,000Rp for fan/air-conditioned rooms. Try to bargain with the manager if business is slow. *Prima Cottages* (☎ 286 369, fax 289153) is in a scruffy area, but the cottages are good value for a negotiable US$20/30 with fan/air-con.

Santai Hotel (☎ 287314) is a clean, comfortable two storey place with singles/doubles facing a pool for US$30/37. It has been recommended by several readers for its 'environmental awareness', and decent library. Among other good hotels with rooms for about US$35/45, including air-con, are *Laghawa Beach Inn* (☎ 288494, fax 289 353); *Puri Mango Guest House* (☎ 288411, fax 288958), although it's on a noisy main road; and *Queen Bali Hotel* (☎ 288054), which also offers better bungalows for slightly more.

Places to Stay – Top End

Most of the top-end hotels are on or near the beach, and some are in southern Sanur, along Jl Mertasari. The prices given here are the low-season 'published rates' (including taxes and service charges), but prices will be considerably cheaper if you come on a package tour. Some places add a 'high supplement' in peak season (July-August and December-January).

Bali Hyatt (☎ 281234, fax 287693, email byhatt@dps.mega.net.id) blends in remarkably well. Singles/doubles start at around US$205/242, and you'll pay even more if you want a decent view.

Desa Segara (☎ 288407, fax 287242, email segara@denpasar.wasantara.net.id) has good facilities for kids. Rooms start at US$78/90, but the family bungalow for US$154 is steep.

Grand Bali Beach Hotel (☎ 288511, fax 287917, email gbb@indosat.net.id) was Bali's first 'big' hotel and is still one of the biggest on the island. Dating from the mid-60s, it was built as a Miami Beach-style rectangular block facing the beach. Managed by the government Natour group, it has all the usual facilities from bars, restaurants and a nightclub to swimming pools and tennis courts, as well as a golf course and bowling alley. Prices start at US$230, and the 'Presidential Suite' will set you back a mere US$4356.

Natour Sindhu Beach (☎ 288351, fax 289268, email nsindhu@denpasar.wasantara.net.id) is right on the beach and well set up. It has rooms at a reasonable US$90/97 and bungalows for US$115/121.

Puri Santrian Hotel (☎ 288009, fax 287101, email santrian@denpasar.wasantara.net.id) is an attractive place with private cottages in a lush garden, two pools and beach frontage. It charges a comparatively reasonable US$121/128.

Santrian Beach Resort (☎ 288009, fax 288185) features a great beach frontage, two swimming pools and tennis courts. Rooms start at US$80/85 and bungalows cost US$100/105.

Sativa Sanur Cottages (☎/fax 287881) is also on the beach and has stylish rooms, attractively arranged around a swimming pool and gardens, for US$82/95.

Hotel Sanur Aerowisata (☎ 288011, fax 287566, email sanurbch@dps.mega.net.id) is a vast place with rooms from US$170/182, as well as a full range of sporting facilities and entertainment options.

Places to Eat

All top-end hotels have their own restaurants, snack bars, coffee bars and cocktail bars – all at top-end prices, of course. A few restaurants along Jl Danau Tamblingan feature menus in German (probably because the German consulate is nearby.) Because Sanur is so spread out, most visitors end up choosing a restaurant close to their hotel.

Northern Sanur The best places to grab a cheap meal are the *food stalls* and *warungs* at the beach end of Jl Segara Ayu, and around the Pasar Sindhu Night Market.

On the Bypass road, *Splash Bakery* has a good selection of bread, cakes and pastries, as well as commendable local versions of the great Australian meat pie.

One of the best hotel restaurants is at *Queen Bali Hotel* (Jl Pantai Sindhu) – starters are about 4000Rp and western dishes 9500Rp to 12,000Rp, but Chinese and Indonesian meals are a lot less. *Kalimantan Bar & Restaurant* (Jl Pantai Sindhu) (aka the Borneo) has main dishes for about 12,000Rp, in a tranquil, shady setting, and offers something called a 'Wyoming Cowboy breakfast'.

The restaurant in *Watering Hole Homestay* (Jl Hang Tuah) is popular for good meals at decent prices. It also features a fantastic Indonesian buffet with Legong dancing on Thursday night for about 20,000Rp per person. Along the same street, *Si Pino Restaurant* is also good.

Along Jl Danau Tamblingan, it's hard to go past *Bali Hai Bar & Restaurant*, especially during happy hours. Main meals cost 9000Rp to 11,000Rp, and the three-course set menus for about 19,000Rp are very tempting. *Lotus Pond Restaurant* (☎ 289 398) has an expensive à la carte menu, and features a *rijstaffel* (a banquet of Dutch-style Indonesian food) buffet nightly for 50,000Rp, including free transport within Sanur if you ring first. *Warung Wina*, aka Vienna Cafe, has good prices, and will appeal to German speakers, because the menu is also in that language. *Puri Mango Guest House* has a restaurant that serves pizzas for 10,000Rp; and good-value three-course menus for about 19,000Rp.

Most of the walkway along central Sanur is cluttered with cafes and restaurants, where you can catch a sea breeze (some places don't have fans, anyway). The major disappointment is that you won't see the classic sunsets of the Kuta region, but the seafood in most places is very tasty. *Mango Bar & Restaurant* is friendly, although the servings can be small. *Benno's Corner Cafe*, next door, is excellent for snacks and drinks. *Sanur Beach Market Bar & Restaurant* is not bad value, and very popular; meals cost 9000Rp to 12,000Rp. Dotted among these are some cheap *warungs* and *rumah makans* (restaurants), mainly for local workers, but anyone can try a delicious *nasi cap cai* (rice with fried vegetables), for example, for about 3500Rp.

Southern Sanur Heading south along Jl Danau Tamblingan there are dozens of great places to try. You may want to just walk along and choose somewhere you fancy, or try one of the following places. *Kuri Putih* has surprisingly reasonable prices for its 'mexi-bali' lunches (about 9000Rp), but prices are higher at night when it often features Balinese dances. *Taman Bayu* (aka *Bayu Garden*) is classy, with main courses for about 15,000Rp, and has Balinese dancing most nights. *Cumi Cumi* has tasty seafood in pleasant surroundings.

Also along Jl Danau Tamblingan, other good budget places include: *Warung Bali Sun*, popular for sensible prices in a friendly atmosphere; *Warung Agung*; *Cafe Batu Kimbar*; and *Made's Kitchen*, a charming and cheap place for snacks and drinks. The vegetarian restaurant, *Kafe Jali Tiwa*, in Santai Hotel, has been recommended by several readers. *Melanie's Restaurant* has decent prices, eg pizzas for 10,000Rp and great Thai food for about 9500Rp, and a menu in English and German.

Near the roundabout, there are about a dozen cheap *rumah makans* where authentic Indonesian food can be found for less than 5000Rp. In this area, *Tropika Kafe* has a menu in English and Swedish, but specialises in Balinese cuisine and seafood. The half-priced drinks during happy hour is an added attraction. Another place worth checking out is *Cafe Ketut*, which offers sensibly priced meals (8000Rp to 12,000Rp). *Kafe Jepun* doesn't seem to specialise entirely in

Japanese food these days, but the pastas for 12,000Rp, and Indonesian food for 10,000Rp, are worth trying. *Oka's* has a pretty setting, but meals are pricey.

Entertainment

Balinese Dance & Music You can see tourist-oriented – but still charming and traditional – Balinese dances in tourist restaurants and hotels all over Sanur, or go on special tours to Denpasar, Batubulan or Bona. Taman Festival Bali park, near Sanur, also features regular performances of the *Ramayana* ballet.

Restaurants featuring regular dances include: *Swastika II Restaurant, Kuri Putih, Watering Hole Homestay* and *Taman Bayu*. At the big hotels, a dinner show will cost around US$25 per person, plus drinks. *Grand Bali Beach Hotel, Bali Hyatt* and *Hotel Sanur Aerowisata* have some of the most lavish productions.

Bars, Clubs, Nightclubs & Discos *Rumours Nightclub (Jl Pantai Sindhu)* probably attracts the youngest crowd, mainly tourists plus some local beach boys. The slick *Bali Janger* disco is popular with Denpasar yuppies, but tourists also come along with bar girls and local boys. *No 1 Club (Jl Danau Tamblingan)* is one of Sanur's more popular nightspots, with flashy light shows and expensive drinks. These three places all have a cover charge of about 10,000Rp, and don't get going much before midnight.

Trophy Pub (Jl Mertasari) is a British-style pub with a pool table, bar food and reasonably priced beer. Unashamedly catering to the Aussie sports fan, *Bali International Sports Club* promises 'ice cold beer from the esky' and sports telecasts from all over the world.

Shopping

Shops on the Bypass road are worth a browse, especially for antiques. For souvenirs and clothes, it's best to head to the Jaya Kesuma Art Market, the small Double U shopping centre, Sanur Beach Market, Pasar Sindhu Art Market or Duyung Art Market.

For serious spending sprees, it's easy to commute to the modern shopping centres in Denpasar, Kuta and Nusa Dua. There's also a supermarket on the Bypass road and another near the Bali Hyatt. A few other supermarkets were being built along Jl Danau Tamblingan at the time of research, and should be finished soon.

Getting There & Away

Public Bemo There is an official bemo stop at the southern end of Sanur, and another directly outside the entrance to the Grand Bali Beach Hotel, but you can normally hail a bemo anywhere along Jl Danau Tamblingan and Jl Danau Poso.

Different bemos operate between Sanur and Denpasar. From Sanur, blue bemos go through the Renon area and across town to Tegal terminal (change here for a bemo to Kuta). Green bemos sometimes go through Denpasar, but usually they go through the eastern outskirts straight to Kereneng terminal. The current fare is 500Rp, but don't be surprised if you're charged much more.

Chartered Bemo You can easily charter a bemo from the bemo stop outside the Grand Bali Beach Hotel to anywhere in southern Bali. A chartered bemo is much faster and more convenient than a public bemo, and cheaper than a shuttle bus if you share with three or more people, but it may not be cheaper than a metered taxi if you don't bargain hard with the bemo driver.

Tourist Shuttle Bus Perama operates regular shuttle bus services to Kuta (5000Rp), and to Ubud (5000Rp) on the way to Lovina (12,500Rp), via Bedugul (7500Rp) or Kintamani (10,000Rp). A few other operators with slightly different prices and departure times also operate to/from Sanur. You can book tickets for Perama buses at the Perama office, or book for Perama, and other operators, at any of the shops and travel agencies along the main road.

Boat Public and shuttle boats to Nusa Lembongan leave from in front of the Ananda Hotel. The Nusa Penida section later in this chapter has details.

Getting Around

To/From the Airport The general Getting Around section at the start of this chapter has information about how to get from the airport to Sanur. From Sanur *to* the airport, a metered taxi will cost about 8500Rp, and a tourist shuttle bus 5000Rp.

Public Bemo Bemos go up and down Jl Danau Tamblingan and Jl Danau Poso for 500Rp. If the bemo is empty, make it clear that you want to take a public bemo, and not charter it.

Car, Motorcycle & Bicycle Numerous agencies along the main road in Sanur rent cars, motorcycles and bicycles. Vehicle rental is about 10% more expensive in Sanur than the Kuta region, and some heavy bargaining is often necessary. It is probably worth going to the Kuta region and renting something there.

AROUND SANUR
Pulau Serangan

South of Sanur is Pulau Serangan (Turtle Island). The beaches on Serangan's east coast were, for many years, turtle nesting sites, and some of the islanders made a living catching turtles and collecting their eggs. Unfortunately, uncontrolled exploitation resulted in the complete elimination of the Serangan turtles over the last few decades, and none survive to lay eggs on the beach.

The island has two villages, Pojok and Dukuh, and an important temple, **Pura Sakenan**, a 1km walk south from the boat landing. Walking around Serangan is quite pleasant, because there are no cars. The southern end of the island has nice **beaches**, and there's good **snorkelling** off the east coast.

Getting There & Away The easiest, but most expensive, way to the island is on an organised diving trip from one of the diving or water sports agencies in Sanur, Tanjung Benoa or Nusa Dua. A one hour trip costs

BALI

BALI

about US$15 per person, but allows no time to really explore the island. During low tide, you may even be able to walk (albeit quickly) across to the island from Suwung.

The boat terminal for Serangan is at Suwung, a scruffy mangrove inlet south of Jl Bypass Ngurah Rai. The starting price for chartering a boat (which holds up to 10 people) is 25,000/50,000Rp one way/return. There are occasional public boats (2000Rp per person).

Pelabuhan Benoa

Benoa is actually in two parts: Pelabuhan Benoa port, to the north, is connected by a 2km causeway to the main Kuta to Sanur road; and Benoa village is on Tanjung Benoa to the south – see the Tanjung Benoa section later in this chapter. Pelabuhan Benoa consists of a wharf and a variety of offices. It is the port for ships run by Pelni, the fast *Mabua Express* boat to Lombok and many luxury cruises, and fishing, diving and surfing trips.

Visitors must pay a toll at a gate at the start of the causeway – 250Rp for pedestrians and 600Rp per vehicle. Public bemos (1000Rp) leave from Sanglah terminal in Denpasar (the driver pays the toll). A chartered bemo or taxi from the Kuta region or Sanur should cost around 8000Rp one way, plus the toll.

JIMBARAN
☎ 0361

Just beyond the airport, south of Kuta, Teluk Jimbaran (Jimbaran Bay) is a superb crescent of white sand and blue sea. Jimbaran itself is a busy fishing village, somehow squeezed between the airport and a number of luxury hotels. Enjoying the sunset and scenery, with a cool drink and a fresh fish on the fire, is a truly wonderful way to spend an evening.

Places to Stay

Puri Indra Prasta (☎ 701544) is uninspiring, noisy and overpriced, but there is a pool. Try to bargain down from 60,000/125,000Rp for a room, including breakfast, with fan/air-con. *Nelayan Jimbaran Cafe & Homestay* (☎ 702253) is better value,

with small, clean singles/doubles for 75,000/90,000Rp, excluding breakfast.

Puri Bambu Bungalows (☎ 701377, fax 701440) has air-conditioned rooms in three-storey blocks around a pool, but it does have some character and the staff are friendly. Room prices start at US$66/78, and 30% discounts are easy to obtain in quieter times.

Pansea Puri Bali (☎ 701605, fax 701320) has a full range of facilities and services, including a huge swimming pool, two bars and two restaurants. Accommodation in air-con bungalows costs US$193/220, but this includes breakfast, dinner and water-sports facilities.

Four Seasons Hotel (☎ 701010, fax 701 020) has over 100 individual villas spreading down a hillside on the southern edge of the bay The accommodation is so spread out that little golf buggies are provided to transport guests between their villas and the reception area, restaurants, tennis courts and the beach. The villas are beautifully finished with great views and yours from US$500 per night.

Between Jimbaran and the airport is the peaceful and eco-friendly *Udayana Lodge* (☎ 261204, fax 701098, email lodge@denpasar .wasantara.net.id), set in 70 hectares of bushland, with a swimming pool. Rooms with air-con cost US$45 with breakfast.

Places to Eat

Many open-sided *warungs* along the beach serve delicious fresh seafood every evening; it's a perfect place for dining, sea breezes and sunset watching. The warungs are located along the northern part of the beach, and along the quieter southern part, not far from the entrance to the Four Seasons Hotel.

The standard deal is a whole fish, plus rice, bread, salad and, maybe, a dessert for 12,000Rp to 15,000Rp – the price depends on whether there are any seats (sitting on the sand is authentic and cheaper), and the cost of the day's catch. You pick your own fish from an ice box, and it's barbecued over coconut husks while you wait.

The rooftop cafe at the *Nelayan Jimbaran Homestay* has spectacular views, but is more expensive than the beachside warungs. There are also some unexciting *warungs* along Jl Ulu Watu. The big hotels all have their own *restaurants*, but expect to pay at least US$15 for lunch, and US$20 for dinner, plus drinks.

Getting There & Away

Public bemos travel between Denpasar's Tegal terminal and Jimbaran (700Rp) on a southern loop from Kuta, but it's easier to catch any bemo heading towards Ulu Watu. Bemos don't run in the evening, however, so if you come for an evening meal you'll need a taxi or chartered transport to get back. Taxis hang around the two beachside warung areas for this very reason.

ULU WATU
☎ 0361

Pura Luhur Ulu Watu is one of several important temples to the spirits of the sea along the southern coast of Bali. The temple is perched at the south-western tip of the peninsula, where sheer cliffs drop precipitously into the clear blue sea. The real attraction is the location, but watch out for the local monkeys, which like to snatch spectacles and sunglasses, as well as handbags, hats and anything else they can get. One attraction is that Ulu Watu is not nearly as touristy as Tanah Lot.

The temple complex is open daily, but the small temple itself is only open to Hindu worshippers. Tickets cost 1000Rp (which includes rental of a sarong and sash), and 300Rp to park a vehicle.

On Wednesday and Saturday evening, an enchanting Kecak dance is held during sunset (from about 6 to 7 pm) in the temple grounds. It's the cheapest (7000Rp a ticket), and one of the best settings, of any Balinese dance in Bali. A useful leaflet, included with the ticket, explains in English who are the baddies and goodies in this complex performance.

Surfing

The Ulu Watu area (specifically Pantai Suluban) is Bali's surfing mecca, featured in several classic surfing films. Before the car park for Pura Luhur Ulu Wat, the road turns off to the Suluban Surf Beach, from where it's about 3km down a rocky road (passable for most vehicles). From the car park, continue on foot another 250m, down to the small gorge along a shaky path, to the beach. Half a dozen warungs give great views of the various surf breaks and the awesome sunsets, and serve simple meals, drinks and allow you to doss down for the night on the floor for about 5000Rp. You can also get ding repair stuff, and a massage, depending on what you need most.

There are other great surf breaks around the south-western tip of Tanjung Bukit, most notably **Padang Padang**, **Bingin** and **Balangan**. On the southern coast are two more breaks, much more exposed and potentially dangerous. Both are accessible because they are next to fancy hotels. **Nyang Nyang** is reached by a track down the cliffs near Puri Bali Villas, and **Green Ball** is beside Bali Cliffs Resort.

A few surf shops around Tubes Bar in Kuta offer shuttle bus services to surf spots around the peninsula for 25,000Rp return.

Places to Stay & Eat

On Jl Ulu Watu, a few kilometres south of Jimbaran, there are a couple of places to stay that are convenient and have good views. *Hotel Villa Koyo* (☎ 702927) is a modern mid-range hotel that asks US$75 for a room, but may offer a 50% discount if business is slow (which is often). *Mr Ugly Cafe & Homestay* has small, but comfortable, rooms for about 35,000Rp; the *cafe* is a good stop for a drink or a snack.

There are other *restaurants* along Jl Ulu Watu, and plenty of *food stalls* in the incongruous shopping complex at the temple car park sell drinks and simple meals. It's nicer to stop for a meal or drink at Jimbaran.

Getting There & Away

Bemos travel between Tegal terminal in Denpasar and Ulu Watu village and temple (1100Rp), via Kuta (the stop is on Jl Raya Kuta, outside the Supernova shopping centre) and Jimbaran. However, public transport stops in the late afternoon, so to see the Kecak dance you'll have to go on an organised tour, or use private transport. Many travel agencies in the Kuta region and Sanur arrange sunset trips to the temple, with a side trip to one or two nearby beaches, for about 20,000Rp per person – plus an extra 10,000Rp waiting time for the dance. If you're travelling in a group of two or more it's cheaper to charter a taxi or car.

SOUTH COAST
☎ 0361

Bali Cliffs Resort (☎ *771992, fax 771993, email bcr@indosat.net.id*) is a huge, luxury hotel perched on a cliff top at the very south of Tanjung Bukit. Two transparent elevators go down the cliff to a restaurant, bar and beach. It's very expensive, of course: rooms are priced from US$235 to a whopping US$2662 for the 'Presidential Suite'. If that's just a *little* out of your range, you can enjoy an expensive meal at the restaurant, which includes free use of the incredible elevator and the swimming pool.

A much smaller luxury option is *Puri Bali Villas* (☎ *701362, fax 701363*), accessible by the road to the Nyang Nyang surf spot. It offers about six large private villas for US$250 per night, each with a magnificent view over a grassy field to the ocean.

NUSA DUA
☎ 0361

Nusa Dua is better known as Bali's top-end beach resort, a collection of suitably sumptuous five-star hotels, successfully isolated from the realities of everyday life in Bali, with no schools, banjars or independent developments inside the enclave. This is where tourists pay almost exclusively in US dollars (and lots of them) to live where no hawkers are allowed, but the drawbacks are the lack of shops, other than the expensive shopping centre, and the general isolation.

Less exclusive hotels are proliferating along the peninsula of Tanjung Benoa (see later in this chapter), while the village of Bualu, home to many hotel staff, is a burgeoning Indonesian town.

Orientation
In the middle of the resort is the enormous Galleria shopping centre, with everything you will probably need: banks and moneychangers; ATMs, which accept foreign credit cards; a postal agency; travel agencies; an American Express office (☎ 773334, fax 773306), which will keep mail for customers; and plenty of restaurants.

There is an Internet centre (sansan@indosat.net.id) in Bualu village. The Klinik Gawat Darurat medical clinic (☎ 771118) is modern and well equipped, as you would expect, and should not be confused with the Nusa Dua Clinic in Tanjung Benoa.

Activities
The best surfing at Nusa Dua is on the reef to the north and south of the two 'islands'. 'Sri Lanka' is a right hander in front of Club Med. The other breaks are reached by boat from the beach south of the Hilton. They work best with a big swell during the wet season. Most diving and water sports are based in nearby Tanjung Benoa (see that section later in this chapter). The Bali Golf & Country Club (☎ 771791, fax 771797) has 18 holes; and for something a little different, try a one hour Camel Safari (☎ 773377) for US$33/17 for adults/children.

Places to Stay
There is nothing even remotely cheap in Nusa Dua, but most visitors stay as part of a package tour anyway. Some places are so exclusive that you may have to prove that you're a guest to get past the front gate, or that you can at least afford to pay for a meal or drink inside.

Bali Hilton International (☎ *771102, fax 771199*) is massive and the most southerly hotel. It has a full range of convention and leisure facilities, and rooms from US$175 to US$275; heaps more for suites.

Hotel Bualu Village (☎ *771310, fax 771313*) is away from the beach and not as elegant as the others, but has a more friendly, informal atmosphere. Most sporting facilities are included in the prices, which are comparatively modest at US$100/120.

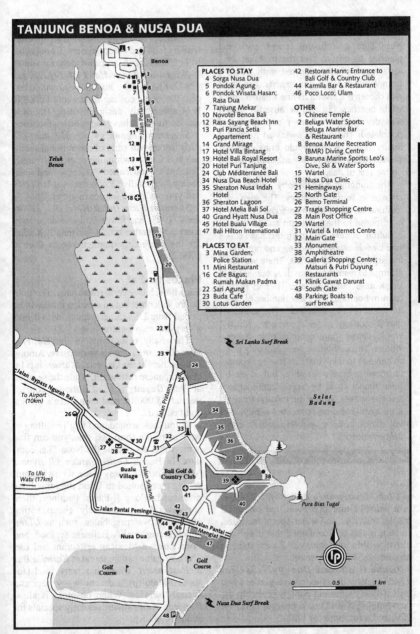

TANJUNG BENOA & NUSA DUA

PLACES TO STAY
4 Sorga Nusa Dua
5 Pondok Agung
6 Pondok Wisata Hasan; Rasa Dua
7 Tanjung Mekar
10 Novotel Benoa Bali
12 Rasa Sayang Beach Inn
13 Puri Pancia Setia Appartement
14 Grand Mirage
17 Hotel Villa Bintang
19 Hotel Bali Royal Resort
20 Hotel Puri Tanjung
24 Club Méditerranée Bali
34 Nusa Dua Beach Hotel
35 Sheraton Nusa Indah Hotel
36 Sheraton Lagoon
37 Hotel Melia Bali Sol
40 Grand Hyatt Nusa Dua
45 Hotel Bualu Village
47 Bali Hilton International

PLACES TO EAT
3 Mina Garden; Police Station
11 Mini Restaurant
16 Cafe Bagus; Rumah Makan Padma
22 Sari Agung
23 Buda Cafe
30 Lotus Garden

42 Restoran Hann; Entrance to Bali Golf & Country Club
44 Karmila Bar & Restaurant
46 Poco Loco; Ulam

OTHER
1 Chinese Temple
2 Beluga Water Sports; Beluga Marine Bar & Restaurant
8 Benoa Marine Recreation (BMR) Diving Centre
9 Baruna Marine Sports; Leo's Dive, Ski & Water Sports
15 Wartel
18 Nusa Dua Clinic
21 Hemingways
25 North Gate
26 Bemo Terminal
27 Tragia Shopping Centre
28 Main Post Office
29 Wartel
31 Wartel & Internet Centre
32 Main Gate
33 Monument
38 Amphitheatre
39 Galleria Shopping Centre; Matsuri & Putri Duyung Restaurants
41 Klinik Gawat Darurat
43 South Gate
48 Parking; Boats to surf break

Benoa

Jalan Pertama

Teluk Benoa

Jalan Bypass Ngurah Rai

To Airport (10km)

Jalan Pratama

Sri Lanka Surf Break

Selat Badung

To Ulu Watu (17km)

Bualu Village

Jalan Srikandi

Bali Golf & Country Club

Pura Bias Tugal

Jalan Pantai Peminge

Jalan Pantai Mengiat

Nusa Dua

Golf Course

Golf Course

Nusa Dua Surf Break

0   0.5   1 km

BALI

Tourism – Nusa Dua Style

Nusa Dua is a luxury tourist enclave planned to ensure that the mistakes of Kuta would not be repeated, with advice from World Bank tourism experts. The site was chosen not just for its fine weather and white beaches, but also because the area was dry, relatively barren and sparsely populated. The objective was an isolated luxury resort, which would bring in the tourist dollars while having minimal impact on the rest of Bali.

The underlying philosophy reflected a change in tourism strategy. The idea of 'cultural tourism', which emerged in Ubud in response to the hedonism and 'cultural pollution' of Kuta, was to protect Bali's culture by selectively promoting and presenting aspects of it to tourists. There was an attempt to restrict tourism development to the Kuta-Sanur-Ubud area, but as mass tourism boomed, the sheer number of visitors was seen as a problem. The solution was a strategy of 'elite tourism', which would derive more revenue from fewer visitors. The authorities were probably not so naive as to think that rich tourists would be more culturally sensitive, but at least their impact could be largely confined to resort enclaves, where the cultural tourist attractions could be re-created with visiting dance troupes, gamelan muzak and Balinese decor.

Club Méditerranée Bali (π/fax 771521) is a package-tour operation that offers all meals, activities and water-sports facilities. In fact, it's so self-contained that it's an enclave within an enclave. Rates start at around US$157 per person.

Grand Hyatt Nusa Dua (π 771234, fax 772038), which has extensive gardens and a river-like swimming pool, is probably the best hotel in Nusa Dua. It charges US$193/ 220, and a lot more for villas.

Hotel Melia Bali Sol (π 771510, fax 771 360) offers some Mediterranean touches with its food and entertainment. Rooms cost from US$212/240, and a lot more for suites.

Nusa Dua Beach Hotel (π 771210, fax 771229) has all the luxuries you would expect for rooms costing from about US$200. It is attractively designed using Balinese architecture, and has good sporting facilities.

Sheraton Lagoon (π 771327, fax 772 326) features all sorts of recreational facilities and a vast swimming pool with 'sandy beaches', landscaped 'islands' and cascading 'waterfalls'. Rooms start at US$280, and you pay more for ocean views.

Sheraton Nusa Indah Hotel (π 771906, fax 771908) has fewer Balinese decorative touches than other hotels, and mainly pitches for the conference market; rooms start at US$225.

Places to Eat

Each hotel has several restaurants. The public are welcome, but an evening meal will be priced from US$25 per person, with drinks a very expensive extra.

The many restaurants in the *Galleria shopping centre* are also expensive. Among many others at the Galleria, *Matsuri* is a 1st class Japanese restaurant, while the seafood at *Putri Duyung* is good, although courses start at 25,000Rp, and then there's drinks, and tax, and ...

If you look around, and you're willing to walk or take a short taxi ride, you can find some value outside of the Nusa Dua complex. In Bualu, *Lotus Garden (Jl Bypass Ngurah Rai)* is a classy place, with a tranquil setting more suited to Ubud than this busy main road. Along Jl Pantai Peminge, there are several comparatively cheap eating places and watering holes, such as *Ulam*, which serves quality Balinese seafood, and *Poco Loco*, a Mexican restaurant and bar. The best value can be found at *Karmila Bar & Restaurant*, which has tasty food (for about 10,000Rp), a decent happy hour and friendly service. When business is slow, *Restoran Hann* advertises daily specials for about 10,000Rp.

Entertainment

The *Galleria shopping centre* offers Kecak and Legong dances and live shows – and all for free, whether you're staying at Nusa Dua or not. Hotels in Nusa Dua will know the current schedule of attractions, or ask someone at the information booth (☎ 771662) at the shopping centre. Major hotels like the Grand Hyatt, Putri Bali and Hilton feature Balinese dances in their restaurants during the evening.

Shopping

Nusa Dua is a market-free and hawker-free zone, but bordering the edges of Nusa Dua, especially along Jl Pantai Peminge, there are a few good souvenir shops with sensible prices.

The Galleria shopping centre, with its 70 or more shops, is designed to ensure that visitors to Nusa Dua do not need to go anywhere else. It lacks the charm and bustle (and also the hawkers) of the Kuta region, and prices are higher. A free shuttle bus (☎ 771662) connects all Nusa Dua hotels with the shopping centre about every hour. The Traiga shopping centre is the poor man's alternative to the Galleria, but it does boast ATMs that accept foreign credit cards, a good bookshop, a decent supermarket, and heavenly air-conditioning.

Getting There & Away

It is easy enough to get a taxi to/from the airport. Public bemos travel between Denpasar's Tegal terminal and the terminal at Bualu (the bemo also goes through Bualu village) for 500Rp – from Bualu, it's about 1km to most hotels. There's also a new bemo service between Batubulan terminal in Denpasar and Nusa Dua (2300Rp). Perama has tourist shuttle buses between Kuta and Nusa Dua several times a day for 5000Rp.

Getting Around

Firstly, find out what shuttle bus services your hotel provides; the Galleria provides a free shuttle bus to the shopping centre. Otherwise, you'll have to order taxis, walk or rent a bicycle to get around. The bigger hotels, and a few places in the Galleria, rent bicycles

for US$2/20 per hour/day (about 30 times the cost of rental in the Kuta region).

TANJUNG BENOA
☎ 0361

The peninsula of Tanjung Benoa extends north from Nusa Dua, past Bualu village, and to Benoa village. Benoa village is one of Bali's multi-denominational corners, with an interesting **Chinese temple** as well as a mosque and Hindu temple nearby.

It is best to base yourself in the northern part of the peninsula; the area between the Villa Bintang and Club Med hotels is comparatively run down, and lacks shops and restaurants. The wartels, police station and well-equipped Nusa Dua Clinic (☎ 771324) are on Jl Pertama, while the post office is on Jl Bypass Ngurah Rai.

Activities

There are four reputable diving agencies, and water-sports agencies for parasailing, jet-skiing and water-skiing: Beluga Water Sports (☎/fax 771997), a long-established, upmarket outfit that also runs cruises; BMR (Benoa Marine Recreation, ☎/fax 771757), a reliable operator with a range of water sports, and diving and fishing trips; Leo's Dive, Ski & Water Sports (☎ 771592, fax 771989), which offers just about every possible water sport, and reasonably priced diving; and Baruna Marine Sports. You can rent full snorkelling gear at BMR. Several of these agencies also offer one-hour cruises in a glass-bottom boat and fishing trips.

Places to Stay

Four cheap places are adjacent, so you can check them all out easily. *Pondok Agung* (☎/fax 771143) is now more in the mid-range, but prices are negotiable. It charges US$20/25 for a fan-cooled/air-conditioned room with hot water and satellite TV, and there's a swimming pool. *Tanjung Mekar* (☎ 772063) is a small guesthouse, with nice rooms for 30,000Rp. *Rasa Dua* (☎ 773515) offers a few rooms in the home of one of the local boat operators for 35,000Rp. *Pondok Wisata Hasan* (☎ 772456) is another friendly, quiet option. Rooms with a fan cost 30,000Rp, while those with air-con and hot water cost 60,000Rp.

Rasa Sayang Beach Inn (☎ *771643*) is friendly and clean, and great value at 30,000/ 37,500Rp for fan-cooled singles/doubles, and 48,000/60,000Rp with air-con. For a bit more comfort, try the quiet *Puri Pancia Setia Appartement* (☎ *772243*), where rooms (which aren't apartments) cost 50,000Rp with air-con, but no hot water.

In Benoa village, *Sorga Nusa Dua* (☎ *771 604, fax 771394*) is an attractive place, with a pool, gardens and tennis court. Rooms cost US$96/103. *Novotel Benoa Bali* (☎ *772 239, fax 772237, email novobenoa@denpasar .wasantara.net.id*) straddles both sides of the road and costs about the same. *Grand Mirage* (☎ *771888, fax 772148, email gmirage@denpasar.wasantara.net.id*) is another huge complex with all the trimmings for US$220/235. *Hotel Villa Bintang* (☎ *772 010, fax 772009, email vl_bintang@denpasar .wasantara.net.id*) is another popular place for package tours. Rooms cost US$102/115.

Heading further south, after passing some construction sites, you reach *Hotel Bali Royal Resort* (☎ *771039, fax 771885*), a small place with a pretty garden and air-conditioned suites from US$170. *Hotel Puri Tanjung* (☎ *772121, fax 772424*) is a little bigger, and a comparative bargain at US$73/110.

Places to Eat

There are several beachfront restaurants in or near Benoa village, such as *Mini Restaurant*, with a pleasant outdoor setting and meals for under 12,000Rp; and *Mina Garden*, a long-time favourite. For something really classy, *Beluga Marine Bar & Restaurant* has meals for about 15,000Rp, which is not outrageous considering the decor, location and service.

Cafe Bagus is away from the beach, but pretty cheap, with some interesting items on the menu: the 6000Rp buffet breakfast is incredible value compared with the US$13 alternatives offered by most nearby hotels. *Rumah Makan Padma* has sensible prices

(about 10,000Rp for seafood dishes), and a menu in German. *Sari Agung* is another standard tourist restaurant and bar.

Right on the 'border' with Nusa Dua, *Buda Cafe* often has daily specials, such as fish and chips and a small beer for 10,000Rp, but other prices are normally high. Nearby, cheap *warungs* cater to hotel staff and offer the best value for money.

Getting There & Away

Refer to the previous Nusa Dua section for details about how to get to Bualu by public bemo and tourist shuttle bus. From Bualu, green bemos hurtle along the Tanjung Benoa road, but not very often. It may be easier to take a taxi from Nusa Dua, Kuta or Sanur.

Getting Around

Travelling by taxi, or on foot, is the main way to get around, because bemos are not frequent. A bicycle would be ideal along the flat and relatively quiet Tanjung Benoa road. However, no bikes are available for rent in Tanjung Benoa (budding local entrepreneurs, please take note of this deficiency), although there are some in Nusa Dua.

Denpasar to Ubud

The road from Denpasar to Ubud, via Batubulan, Celuk, Sukawati, Batuan and Mas, is lined with places making and selling handcrafts. Many tourists stop and shop along this route, but there are some quieter back roads where much of the craft work is done in small workshops and family compounds. There are regular bemos along this route, but if you want to stop at craft workshops and buy things, it's more convenient to have your own transport.

BATUBULAN

Stone carving is the main craft of Batubulan, which means 'moon stone'. You'll see hundreds of statues beside the road, and you're welcome to come in and watch the workers, many of them young boys, chipping away at big blocks of soft volcanic stone. The temples around Batubulan are noted for their fine stone sculptures. **Pura Puseh**, about 200m to the east of the busy main road, is worth a visit. Batubulan is also a centre for antiques and a variety of crafts, textiles and woodwork, and has some well-regarded dance troupes.

Batubulan is best known, however, as the bemo terminal for eastern and central Bali – see Getting There & Away in the earlier Denpasar section above for details.

TAMAN BURUNG BALI BIRD PARK & RIMBA REPTIL PARK

This bird park boasts over 1000 birds, including rare *cenderawasih* (birds of paradise), and highly endangered Bali starlings. There are also Komodo dragons, and a fine collection of tropical plants among two hectares of landscaped gardens. Next door, Rimba Reptil reptile park has about 20 species of slithery creatures from Indonesia and Africa, as well as turtles and crocodiles.

Tickets are relatively expensive: 39,000/ 19,000Rp to either for adults/children, or 70,000/35,000Rp for a combined ticket to both parks. Many organised tours stop at the parks; alternatively, you can take a Denpasar to Ubud bemo, get off at the obvious junction at Tegaltamu, and follow the signs north for about 800m.

CELUK

Celuk is a silver and goldsmithing centre, with numerous jewellery specialists and a wide variety of pieces on sale. The bigger showrooms are for tour groups. Most of the work is done in tiny family workshops in the back streets.

SUKAWATI

Before the turn-off to Mas and Ubud, Sukawati is a centre for the manufacture of wind chimes, temple umbrellas and *lontar* (palm) baskets, dyed with intricate patterns. Sukawati has a busy **craft market**, an obvious, two storey building on the eastern side of the main road – public bemos stop right outside. Every type of quality craftwork and touristy trinket is on sale, at cheap prices for

those who bargain hard. Across the road is the colourful morning **produce market**, with the old **royal palace** behind.

Sukawati is also renowned for its **traditional dances** and *wayang kulit* (shadow puppet) performances. **Puaya**, about 1km north-west of Sukawati, specialises in making high quality leather shadow puppets and topeng masks.

BATUAN

Batuan is a noted painting centre with a number of **art galleries**. It came under the influence of Bonnet, Spies and the Pita Maha artists' co-operative at an early stage. Traditionally, Batuan painters produced dynamic black-ink drawings, but the newer 'Batuan style' of painting is noted for including a large number of different subjects in a single canvas, even the odd windsurfer or a tourist with a video camera. Batuan is also noted for the ancient *gambuh* dance performed in the **Pura Puseh** every full moon.

MAS
☎ 0361

Mas means 'gold', but it's woodcarving, particularly mask carving, that is the craft practised here. The road through Mas is almost solidly lined with craft shops which do business by the tour-bus load, but there are plenty of smaller carving operations in the back lanes. The bigger and more successful outlets are often lavishly decorated with fine woodcarvings.

Along the main road, *Taman Harum Cottages* (☎ *975567, fax 975149*) has elegant individual bungalows, and a swimming pool. Prices range from US$79 for a standard room to US$145 for a family room. Opposite, *Bima Cottages* (☎ *974538*) charges US$25/ 35 for quiet single/double bungalows, with air-con and hot water, and the management is very willing to negotiate.

BLAHBATUH

Blahbatuh is a detour from the more direct road to Ubud. Its **Pura Gaduh** has a 1m-high stone head said to be a portrait of Kebo Iwa, the legendary strongman and minister to the

BALI

last king of the Bedulu kingdom (see Bedulu and Gunung Kawi in the Around Ubud section later in this chapter). Gajah Mada, the Majapahit prime minister, realised that he could not conquer Bedulu, Bali's strongest kingdom, while Kebo Iwa was there, so he lured him away to Java (with promises of women and song) and had him killed. The stone head is thought to be very old, but the temple is a reconstruction of an earlier temple destroyed in the great earthquake of 1917.

Kutri

North of Blahbatuh, Kutri has the interesting **Pura Kedarman** (also known as Pura Bukit Dharma). If you climb Bukit Dharma hill behind the temple, you'll find a panoramic **view** and a **hilltop shrine** with a stone statue of the eight armed goddess Durga killing a demon-possessed water buffalo.

Bona

Bona, on the back road between Gianyar and Blahbatuh, is credited with being the modern home of the **Kecak dance**. Kecak and other dances are held here several times a week. Most visitors come from Ubud on organised tours. Bona is also a **basket-weaving centre** and many other articles are also woven from lontar leaves.

Nearby, **Belega** is a centre for bamboo furniture – roadside workshops and showrooms are stacked with the bamboo chairs, tables, beds and wardrobes that are standard issue in many of Bali's hotels.

Ubud

☎ 0361

Perched on the gentle slopes leading up towards the central mountains, Ubud is the centre of 'cultural tourism' in Bali, and it has attracted visitors interested in Balinese arts ever since Walter Spies was here in the 1930s. Apart from the many places of interest in Ubud itself, there are also numerous temples, ancient sites and interesting craft centres around the town.

Ubud has undergone tremendous development in the past few years, and now has problems of traffic congestion in the town centre and urban sprawl on the edges. It's still a pretty relaxed place though, especially in a secluded family compound or in one of the delightful open-air restaurants, where the fragrant evenings are still quiet enough to hear a frog in a rice field. There's an amazing amount to see in and around Ubud. You'll need at least a few days to appreciate it properly, and Ubud is one of those places where days can become weeks and weeks become months.

Orientation

The once small village of Ubud has expanded to encompass its neighbours – Campuan, Penestanan, Padangtegal, Peliatan and Pengosekan are all part of what we see as Ubud today. The centre of town is the junction where the market and bemo stops are located. The main thoroughfare, Monkey Forest Rd, runs south to, naturally, the Monkey Forest Sanctuary – the road is one way heading south until the junction with Jl Dewi Sita.

The main east-west road is Jl Raya. West of Ubud, the road drops steeply down to the ravine at Campuan, where an old suspension bridge, next to the new one, hangs over Sungai Wos. Nearby, is the pretty village of Penestanan, famous for its painters. East and south of Ubud proper, the villages of Peliatan, Pengosekan and Nyuhkuning are known variously for painting, traditional dance and woodcarving. North of Ubud it's less densely settled, with picturesque rice fields interspersed with small villages, many of which specialise in a local craft.

Information

Tourist Offices The tourist office, or Yaysan Bina Wisata (☎ 96285), is open daily from 8 am to 8 pm. It doesn't hand out any maps or many brochures, but the staff are friendly and can answer most questions. They can tell you about authentic traditional dances and ceremonies in the region, and sell tickets to tourist-oriented dance and music performances. The tourist office is a local venture, set up in an effort to protect the village from the tourist onslaught by providing a service aimed at informing and generating a respect among visitors for Balinese culture and customs.

Money All the major banks are represented in central Ubud, and most will change cash and travellers cheques. The dozens of moneychangers along the main roads offer better rates and better service than the banks, however. The exchange rates are comparable to Kuta, but they often vary considerably from one moneychanger to another, so look around.

Post & Communications The charming little post office has a sort-it-out-yourself poste restante. The post office is inconvenient for most visitors, but there are several other handy postal agencies along the main roads.

The few wartels can be used for local and international telephone calls and faxes, and there's a main Telkom office along the eastern end of Jl Raya. Home Country Direct Dial telephones can be found outside the main Telkom office, Ary's Warung and the main post office.

Email & Internet Access A few Internet centres are starting to pop up, and their prices are some of the lowest in Bali. Three cheap and reliable centres are:

Balinet
(yakin@deps.mega.net.id)
Pondok Pekak Library & Resource Center
(pondok@denpasar.wasantara.net.id)
Roda Tourist Service
(rodanet@denpasar.wasantara.net.id)

Bookshops Ubud is the best place in Bali to buy new and second-hand novels, and new books about Bali. Ubud Bookshop and the bookshop in the Pandawa Homestay sell a few foreign newspapers and magazines. Ganesha Bookshop has a good selection of titles about travel, women's issues, arts and music, including a few titles in French. Ary's Bookshop has a fair stock of books

and maps about Bali and Indonesia. Some of the museums mentioned later also have decent bookshops.

Libraries Pondok Pekak Library & Resource Center (☎ 976194) is a very relaxed and friendly place with Internet facilities (see Email & Internet Access in this section); a service for cheaply refilling plastic bottles with mineral water; a library and second-hand bookshop; and a useful message board. It is open daily from 9 am to 9 pm, except Sunday, when it closes at 3 pm.

Emergency The Ubud Clinic (☎ 974911, mobile 081 1396069) is the best and most well-equipped medical centre in the region. It is open all day, every day, and charges 75,000Rp for a consultation at the clinic – more for a visit to your hotel. The *puskesmas* (community health centre, ☎ 974415) is pretty basic. The police station (☎ 975316) is in Andong.

Museums

Museum Puri Lukisan This Palace of Fine Arts was established in the mid-1950s and displays excellent examples of all schools of Balinese art. The modern Balinese art movement started in Ubud, where artists first used modern materials, were influenced by foreign styles and began to depict scenes of everyday Balinese life. Rudolf Bonnet, who played such an important role in this change, helped establish the museum's permanent collection in 1973.

It's a relatively small museum, but has some excellent art. You enter the museum by crossing a river gully beside the road and wander from building to building through beautiful gardens with pools, statues and fountains.

The museum has been restored in the last few years, and the paintings are well preserved, and satisfactorily labelled in English. It's open from 8 am to 4 pm daily, and admission is 5000Rp. There are exhibitions of art for sale in other buildings in the gardens and in a separate display just outside the main gate.

BALI

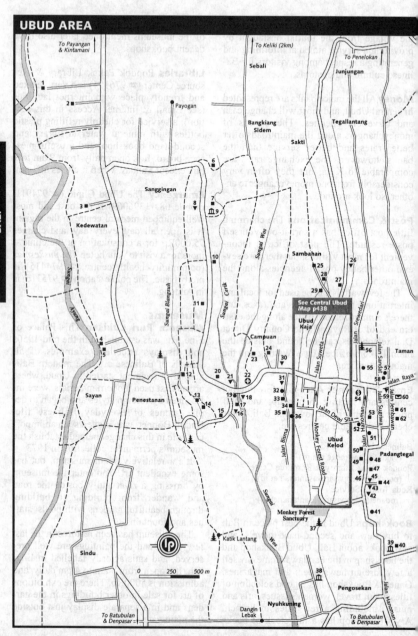

UBUD AREA

To Payangan & Kintamani

To Keliki (2km)

To Penelokan

Sebali

Junjungan

Payogan

Bangkiang Sidem

Tegallantang

Sakti

Sanggingan

Kedewatan

Sambahan

Campuan

Ubud Kaja

See Central Ubud Map p438

Taman

Sayan

Penestanan

Ubud Kelod

Padangtegal

Monkey Forest Sanctuary

Sindu

Katik Lantang

Pengosekan

To Batubulan & Denpasar

Dangin Lebak

Nyuhkuning

To Batubulan & Denpasar

To Payangan

0   250   500 m

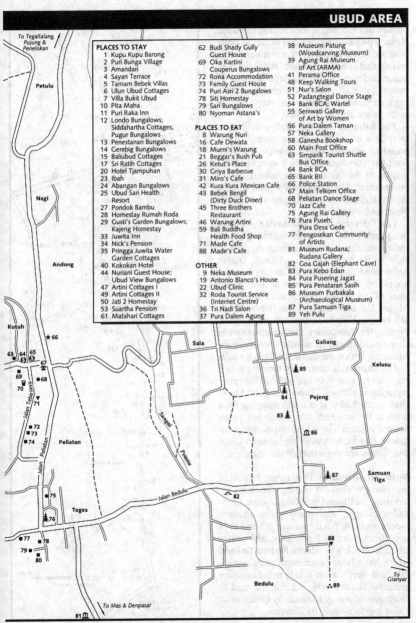

UBUD AREA

PLACES TO STAY
1 Kupu Kupu Barong
2 Puri Bunga Village
3 Amandari
4 Sayan Terrace
5 Tamam Bebek Villas
6 Ulun Ubud Cottages
7 Villa Bukit Ubud
10 Pita Maha
11 Puri Raka Inn
12 Londo Bungalows;
  Siddahartha Cottages;
  Pugur Bungalows
13 Penestanan Bungalows
14 Gerebig Bungalows
15 Baliubud Cottages
17 Sri Ratih Cottages
20 Hotel Tjampuhan
23 Ibah
24 Abangan Bungalows
25 Ubud Sari Health
  Resort
27 Pondok Bambu
28 Homestay Rumah Roda
29 Gusti's Garden Bungalows;
  Kajeng Homestay
33 Juwita Inn
34 Nick's Pension
35 Pringga Juwita Water
  Garden Cottages
40 Kokokan Hotel
44 Nuriani Guest House;
  Ubud View Bungalows
47 Artini Cottages I
49 Artini Cottages II
50 Jati 2 Homestay
53 Suartha Pension
61 Matahari Cottages

62 Budi Shady Gully
  Guest House
69 Oka Kartini
  Couperus Bungalows
72 Rona Accommodation
73 Family Guest House
74 Puri Asri 2 Bungalows
78 Siti Homestay
79 Sari Bungalows
80 Nyoman Astana's

PLACES TO EAT
8 Warung Nuri
16 Cafe Dewata
18 Murni's Warung
21 Beggar's Bush Pub
26 Ketut's Place
30 Griya Barbecue
31 Miro's Cafe
42 Kura Kura Mexican Cafe
43 Bebek Bengil
  (Dirty Duck Diner)
45 Three Brothers
  Restaurant
46 Warung Artini
59 Bali Buddha
  Health Food Shop
71 Made Cafe
88 Made's Cafe

OTHER
9 Neka Museum
19 Antonio Blanco's House
22 Ubud Clinic
32 Roda Tourist Service
  (Internet Centre)
36 Tri Nadi Salon
37 Pura Dalem Agung

38 Museum Patung
  (Woodcarving Museum)
39 Agung Rai Museum
  of Art (ARMA)
41 Perama Office
48 Keep Walking Tours
51 Nur's Salon
52 Padangtegal Dance Stage
54 Bank BCA; Wartel
55 Seniwati Gallery
  of Art by Women
56 Pura Dalem Taman
57 Neka Gallery
58 Ganesha Bookshop
60 Main Post Office
63 Simparik Tourist Shuttle
  Bus Office
64 Bank BCA
65 Bank BII
66 Police Station
67 Main Telkom Office
68 Peliatan Dance Stage
70 Jazz Cafe
75 Agung Rai Gallery
76 Pura Puseh;
  Pura Desa Gede
77 Pengosekan Community
  of Artists
81 Museum Rudana;
  Rudana Gallery
82 Goa Gajah (Elephant Cave)
83 Pura Kebo Edan
84 Pura Pusering Jagat
85 Pura Penataran Sasih
86 Museum Purbakala
  (Archaeological Museum)
87 Pura Samuan Tiga
89 Yeh Pulu

BALI

Neka Museum The Neka Museum was opened in 1976, and is the creation of Suteja Neka, a private collector and dealer in Balinese art. It has an excellent and diverse collection that is well exhibited, and is the best place to learn about the development of painting in Bali. A helpful pamphlet detailing the exhibits is provided on entry, and the pictures are all well labelled.

The **Balinese Painting Hall** provides an overview of local painting, many influenced by wayang kulit puppetry. The **Arie Smit Pavilion** features Smit's works and examples of the 'Young Artist' school, which he inspired. The **Lempad Pavilion** houses Bali's largest collection of works by I Gusti Nyoman Lempad.

The **Contemporary Indonesian Art Hall** has paintings by artists from other parts of Indonesia, many of whom have worked in Bali. Works by Abdul Aziz, Affandi, Dullah and Anton Kustia Wijaya are among the most appealing. The upper floor is devoted to the work of foreign artists, such as Louise Koke, Miguel Covarrubias, Rudolph Bonnet, Donald Friend, Han Snel and Antonio Blanco. Finally, the **Temporary Exhibition Hall** has changing displays of mostly contemporary paintings, with some items available for sale.

The museum is open daily from 9 am to 5 pm. Tickets cost 5000Rp, and no flash photography is allowed. There is a good **bookshop** in the lobby. It is worth stopping for a drink at the attached cafe, which has views normally found with a US$100-a-night bungalow. Any bemo travelling between Ubud and Kintamani stops outside the museum.

Museum Rudana This large, imposing museum (☎ 976479) in Teges contains interesting traditional paintings, some Lempad drawings, and many more modern pieces from Affandi, among others. It is open from 8 am to 5 pm daily, and tickets cost 2500Rp. It's beside the **Rudana Gallery**, which has a large selection of paintings for sale, and there's a small cafe in the museum grounds. The museum is along the road to Denpasar, and easy to reach by bemo, or as a side trip to Bedulu by bicycle.

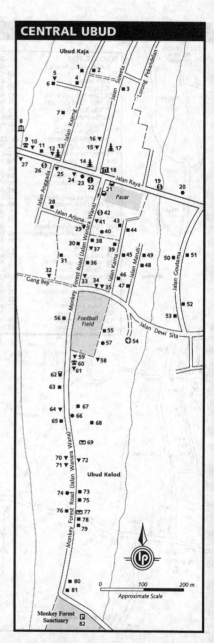

CENTRAL UBUD

CENTRAL UBUD

PLACES TO STAY
1 Artja Inn
2 Arjana Accommodation
3 Suci Inn
4 Shanti Homestay
6 Siti Bungalows
7 Roja's Bungalows
11 Puri Saraswati Bungalows
28 Anom Bungalows;
Jungut Inn
30 Alit's House
31 Oka Wati Hotel
36 Gayatri Bungalows
38 Pandawa Homestay
& Bookshop
39 Gandra House
40 Hibiscus Bungalows
43 Yuni's House
44 Pondok Wisata
Puri Widiana
45 Wija's House
46 Ning's House
47 Budi Bungalows
48 Dewi Putri
Accommodation
49 Sayong House
50 Darta Homestay
51 Shana Homestay
52 Donald Homestay
53 Agung Cottages
55 Wahyu Bungalows
56 Bendi's 2 Accommodation
& Bendi's Restaurant
63 Ubud Village Hotel
65 Pertiwi Bungalows

67 Puri Garden Bungalows
68 Rice Paddy Bungalows
73 Ubud Bungalows
75 Saren Inn
76 Hotel Argasoka
78 Fibra Inn
79 Ubud Inn
80 Monkey Forest Inn
81 Hotel Champlung Sari

PLACES TO EAT
5 Han Snel's Garden
Restaurant
10 Mumbul's Cafe
12 Lotus Cafe
15 Bumbu Restaurant
16 Coconut Cafe;
Cafe Angkasa
24 Ary's Warung
25 Ryoshi Japanese Restaurant
27 Casa Luna
29 Kul Kul Restaurant
32 Lillies Garden Restaurant
33 Cafe Tirta; Ibu Rai
Bar & Restaurant
34 Bamboo Restaurant
35 Tutmak Cafe
37 Gayatri Cafe
41 Canderi's Warung
58 Cafe Bali
59 Noni Orti; Milano Salon
61 Yogyakarta Cafe
64 Cafe Wayan
70 Dian Cafe; Lotus Lane
Restaurant; Mendra's Cafe

71 Jaya Cafe
72 Monkey Cafe

OTHER
8 Museum Puri Lukisan
9 Wartel
13 Pura Taman Saraswati
14 Pura Desa Ubud
17 Pura Merajan Agung
18 Ubud Palace
19 Bank Danamon
20 Lempad's Home
21 Bemo Stops;
Pasar Seni (Art Market)
22 Yayasan Bina
Wisata (Tourist Office)
23 Ary's Bookshop
26 Bank Bali;
Toko Tino Supermarket;
Ubud Bookshop
42 BNI Bank
54 Puskesmas (Community
Health Centre)
57 Pondok Pekak Library
& Resource Center
(Internet Centre)
60 Wartel
62 Putra Bar
66 Balinet Internet
Center
69 Postal Agency
74 Meditation Shop
77 Postal Agency
82 Carpark (for Monkey
Forest Sanctuary)

BALI

Agung Rai Museum of Art (ARMA)

This new museum (☎ 976659) has two vast buildings housing works lent by Agung Rai. It's a good idea to visit ARMA late in the afternoon, have dinner nearby and then watch some **traditional dances** inside the ARMA grounds in the evening – inquire and book at ARMA. There are also two coffee shops in the grounds, and a good **bookshop** with surprisingly low prices.

ARMA is open daily from 9 am to 6 pm. Tickets cost 5000Rp. The main entrance is along the eastern road to Samuan Tiga, although you can also enter from a gate along Jl Hanoman. If travelling by public transport, catch the Ubud to Gianyar bemo

which travels along both roads – the museum is easy to reach from either road.

Galleries

There are countless galleries and shops exhibiting artwork for sale, but three are particularly interesting. The **Neka Gallery** is owned by Suteja Neka (sponsor of the Neka Museum). It has a huge variety of work, generally of a very high quality, in all the Balinese styles, as well as work by European residents like Snel and Smit. Most works are for sale, often at pretty high prices.

Also important is the **Agung Rai Gallery** at Peliatan. Again, the collection extends for room after room and covers the full range of

Balinese styles, plus works by artists like Blanco, Smit, Snel, Meier and Affandi.

The **Seniwati Gallery of Art by Women** has a good selection of paintings for sale, with a variety of styles and a uniformly high standard. They are by Balinese, Indonesian and foreign women artists who live in Bali and make use of the facilities at the nearby Seniwati Sanggar workshop.

Artists' Homes

The home of **I Gusti Nyoman Lempad** is in the main street of Ubud. There are lots of paintings for sale, but the only Lempad works are some attractive but weathered stone sculptures.

Walter Spies and Rudolf Bonnet both lived for some time at Campuan, near the suspension bridge. **Spies'** home is now one of the rooms at the Hotel Tjampuan, and can be inspected if it's not in use; you can even stay there if you book well ahead.

Beside the Campuan suspension bridge, a driveway leads to the superbly theatrical house of **Antonio Blanco**, who came to Bali from Spain via the Philippines. Blanco's speciality is erotic art and illustrated poetry. Tickets to the house costs 3500Rp, and it's open daily from 8 am to 5 pm.

Arie Smit and Han Snel are well known western artists residing in Ubud. In the 1960s, Smit sparked the 'Young Artists'' school of painting in Penestanan. Snel's work can be seen at his **Siti Bungalows** and at **Han Snel's Garden Restaurant** (see Places to Stay and Places to Eat later in this section).

Walks Around Ubud

It's interesting to walk through the fields and to surrounding villages, where you frequently see artists at work in open rooms and verandahs on the quieter streets.

Monkey Forest Monkey Forest Rd is lined with hotels, restaurants and shops for its whole length, but at the far end, at the bottom of the hill, is the **Monkey Forest Sanctuary**. It's inhabited by a handsome band of monkeys ever ready for passing tourists who just might have peanuts to hand out. Be warned –

the monkeys can put on ferocious displays of temperament if you don't come through with the goods, and quickly. The interesting old **pura dalem agung** (temple of the dead) is in the sanctuary – look for the rangda figures devouring children at the entrance to the inner temple. Tickets cost 1100Rp, and it's open daily during daylight hours.

The road swings east at the Monkey Forest, and you can follow it around to Padangtegal or Pengosekan. Nyuhkuning is a small village south of the monkey forest, noted for its woodcarving; a small **museum patung** (woodcarving museum) here keeps irregular hours.

Campuan At the confluence of Sungai Wos and Sungai Cerik is Campuan, which means 'where two rivers meet'. An obvious path passes the marvellous Ibah hotel and leads north along the ridge between the rivers towards the Neka Museum and Bangkiang Sidem village.

Penestanan The road bends sharply as it crosses the river at Campuan and then runs north, parallel to the river. If you take the steep uphill road that bends away to the left of the main road you reach Penestanan. Along this road are **galleries**, many of them specialising in paintings of the Young Artists' style, and several places to stay and eat.

Sayan & Kedewatan West of Penestanan is Sayan, the site for Colin McPhee's home in the 1930s, so amusingly described in *A House in Bali*. North of Sayan is Kedewatan, another small village where a road turns east and swings back towards Ubud via Campuan. Just west of the villages and the main road is Sungai Ayung. The deep gorge of the swift-flowing river Ayung offers magnificent panoramas. Several expensive hotels, and the homes of a number of modern-day McPhees, are perched on the edge.

Petulu In the late afternoon, you can enjoy the spectacle of thousands of herons arriving home in Petulu. They nest in the trees along the road through the village and make a spectacular sight as they fly in and commence squabbling over the prime perching places.

A good route there is along Jl Suweta, north of Ubud's bemo terminal, which continues to the village of Junjungan, heavily into the carving of garudas. Petulu is southeast of Junjungan – the turn-offs are signposted, but ask if you're unsure.

Activities

Ubud is close enough to southern Bali for you to enjoy some diving at Tanjung Benoa, or surfing at Kuta, for the day, but most visitors prefer more relaxed activities in the glorious countryside, or perhaps something soothing for the soul or body.

Budget-priced bicycle and hiking trips can be arranged with Keep Walking Tours, based at Tegun Galeri shop (☎/fax 96361, email balitrade@denpasar.wasantara.net.id), Jl Hanoman.

The legendary Victor Mason still runs the wonderful (but expensive) Bali Bird Walks (☎ 975009) from the Beggar's Bush Pub. Ubud is a great place to base yourself while you go rafting down the mighty Sungai Agung. For these activities, pick up a brochure from (and book at) any travel agency in Ubud.

Ubud has a few health and beauty salons where you can really pamper yourself. Milano Salon, Tri Nadi Salon and Nur Salon have all been recommended by very satisfied customers. For the ultimate treatment, you can stay at Ubud Sari Health Resort (see Places to Stay later in this section).

Courses

Ubud is the sort of relaxed place where it's easy to spend a few weeks and learn a bit about Balinese and Indonesian culture, music, dancing, language and cooking. Some of the more interesting courses are at ARMA (see Museums earlier in this section), which offers courses in Balinese painting, music and dance, and children's programs; Noni Orti and Casa Luna restaurants, which conduct Balinese cooking courses; Pondok Pekak Library, which has classes in Bahasa Indonesia; and Ganesha Bookshop, which

holds music workshops. To find out what courses are currently on offer, check out the notice boards at the Pondok Pekak Library, Casa Luna restaurant, Bali Buddha Health Food Shop and tourist office.

Organised Tours

Taking an organised tour or two is not a bad idea because a lot of attractions around Ubud are quite difficult to reach by public transport, and finding your way around this part of Bali isn't easy even with your own vehicle.

All travel agencies in Ubud can arrange organised tours, but it's worth shopping around because some prices include entrance fees and some don't. The more interesting local half-day trips take in Mengwi, Alas Kedaton, Bedugul and Tanah Lot; or go to Goa Gajah, Pejeng, Gunung Kawi, Tampaksiring and Kintamani.

Places to Stay

Ubud has hundreds of places to stay. We can't possibly mention them all, but we have tried to list a range of charming and stylish places that are good value. A simple, clean room within a family home compound will be priced from around 15,000/20,000Rp, usually including a private bathroom and a light breakfast. It is often worth paying a little more, however: for about 25,000/40,000Rp, including breakfast, you can get a very nice room or bungalow.

A tax of 10% is added to the cost of a room, and fancier places add another 5% to 11% more for service. In the low season, or if you're staying for a few days or longer (as many visitors do), it's certainly worth asking for a discount.

Places to Stay – Budget

Central Ubud The cheapest places are near the northern end of Monkey Forest Rd, but there are nicer places a few minutes walk away. These places are not very appealing, but they are central and only cost about 10,000/15,000Rp for singles/doubles. The best are *Pandawa Homestay* (☎ 975698), and *Anom Bungalows* and *Jungut Inn*, both along the quieter Jl Arjuna.

BALI

Off the main road, *Rice Paddy Bungalows* is one of three secluded, tranquil places with almost identical settings and prices: 30,000Rp, or 35,000Rp for upstairs rooms with the best views. Across from the football field, *Wahyu Bungalows* (☎ 975055) is clean, shady and quiet. Rooms, with an alfresco-style bathroom, start at 20,000Rp, and climb to 80,000Rp with hot water, balcony and views. *Bendi's 2 Accommodation* (☎ 96410) has a quiet garden setting. The manager is open to negotiation, so rooms are available for as little as 25,000Rp with hot water. *Saren Inn* (☎ 975704) is a mid-range place struggling to attract guests, so the management happily offers big discounts. For 30,000/40,000Rp with hot water and a fridge, this can be excellent value.

Also recommended are *Gayatri Bungalows* (☎ 96391), with an immaculate garden and spacious rooms for 20,000/25,000Rp, and *Monkey Forest Inn*, which is friendly and excellent value with rooms for 15,000/20,000Rp including hot water.

Along Jl Maruti, *Dewi Putri Accommodation* (☎ 96304) is quiet, with a babbling brook at the back, and very good value with rooms for 10,000/15,000Rp. *Sayong House* (☎ 96305) is at the end of a quiet lane, with rooms for 20,000/30,000Rp; 50,000Rp for a double with hot water. Also, *Budi Bungalows* is clean, quiet and comfortable, and has rooms for only 15,000/20,000Rp.

Jl Karna has several good places, although the noise from the motorcycles going to and from the market can be a little annoying at times. *Wija's House* has rooms for 50,000Rp with hot water, but these prices will probably increase once the new swimming pool is completed. For about 15,000/20,000Rp, there's *Gandra House* (☎ 976529); the charming *Ning's House* (☎ 973340); *Pondok Wisata Puri Widiana*, with a shady garden; and the friendly *Yuni's House* (☎ 975701). Nearby, along Gang Narada, *Hibiscus Bungalows* is pretty, but a little pricey with rooms for a negotiable 25,000/50,000Rp.

Jl Goutama is another cheap, quiet and central place to stay, where there are a dozen or more losmen. *Shana Homestay* is good value: large rooms, some with private patios, cost 15,000/20,000Rp. *Donald Homestay* (☎ 977156) is better than it looks from the outside. The setting is pretty, the staff are friendly and the rooms cost a negotiable 35,000/40,000Rp. *Darta Homestay* is good value, with a real farmyard atmosphere, and rooms for 10,000/15,000Rp.

East of Ubud There is not that much on offer along Jl Hanoman, which is a shame considering its central location and the number of cheap places to eat nearby. *Suartha Pension* (☎ 974244) has a charming, traditional family setting, and rooms for 15,000/20,000Rp. A little off the main street, *Jati 2 Homestay* (☎ 975550) has a small number of delightful rooms for 20,000/25,000Rp, and views of rice fields that upmarket hotels charge the earth for. *Artini Cottages I* (☎ 975348) is a cheaper version of its more expensive partner across the road, and has rooms in an ornate setting from 25,000/40,000Rp.

A side road off Jl Hanoman leads to about six more peaceful places. The wonderful views of the rice paddies from the more expensive room upstairs are worth a splurge. The recommended *Ubud View Bungalows* (☎ 974164) charges 40,000/50,000Rp per double for downstairs/upstairs rooms – all with hot water. Also worth trying is *Nuriani Guest House* (☎ 975346), where rooms in another lovely garden cost 20,000/35,000Rp for downstairs/upstairs; or 30,000/40,000Rp with hot water.

Jl Jembawan is yet another delightful street, with a number of good-value places close to central Ubud. The new and spacious *Budi Shady Gully Guest House* (☎ 975033) charges 25,000/30,000Rp for singles/doubles with hot water, which is excellent value. Another good place is *Matahari Cottages* (☎ 975459), which has a charming setting. Bungalows cost 30,000/35,000Rp, and larger rooms with three beds are 50,000Rp.

A little further east, Jl Tebesaya is reminiscent of a village street, and still reasonably central; the places on the eastern side, overlooking the creek, are particularly attractive.

Puri Asri 2 Bungalows (☎ 96210) has a lovely garden, and clean rooms for 20,000Rp with cold water and a bargain 30,000Rp with hot water. *Rona Accommodation* (☎ 973229) is a well-established favourite, not least for its bookshop and travel agency. Good rooms cost 20,000Rp to 40,000Rp with hot water. Another gem is the popular *Family Guest House* (☎ 974054). Set in a pleasant garden, it has friendly staff and rooms for 25,000/35,000Rp; 30,000/50,000Rp with hot water. There are another eight or so other good places along the same street.

North of Ubud Many visitors ignore anywhere north of Jl Raya, so this area is normally quiet and good value, but still close to central Ubud. *Suci Inn* (☎ 975304, Jl Sutewa) is a long-established favourite. It's a friendly, relaxed place that is quiet yet very close to the action. Clean rooms cost 15,000/20,000Rp (see the Central Ubud map). Further up, *Pondok Bambu* (☎ 96421) charges 40,000Rp for a large room with hot water, and is one of several friendly, cheap and family-run places up this street.

Jl Kajeng is another good place to base yourself, although it's barely wide enough for one vehicle. *Shanti Homestay* (☎ 975421) is a good option, with rooms for 20,000/30,000Rp, or 40,000Rp for an upstairs room with hot water. *Roja's Bungalows* (☎ 975107) costs 25,000/30,000Rp for rooms in a friendly atmosphere, but try to negotiate as this price is a little high. *Arjana Accommodation* (☎ 975583) has nice rooms for 15,000/20,000Rp with an alfresco-style bathroom. *Artja Inn* is also friendly, and offers tasty breakfasts and endless tea. With some negotiation, rooms for as little as 10,000Rp per person are possible. (See the Central Ubud map for the previous four accommodation options.)

There are a few more places further up Jl Kajeng. *Homestay Rumah Roda* (☎ 975 487) is a very friendly, popular place. Bungalows cost 25,000/30,000Rp, but it's on the wrong side of the road for the views. Opposite, *Kajeng Homestay* (☎ 975 018) has a stunning setting – one of the nicest in the budget range in Ubud. Rooms with cold water cost 20,000/30,000Rp, but hot water costs only 5000Rp extra per person.

South of Ubud Going down Jl Peliatan, south of the junction with Jl Bedulu, there is a cluster of decent places charging about 12,000/15,000Rp for singles/doubles. These include *Siti Homestay* (☎ 975599), *Sari Bungalows* (☎ 975541), and *Nyoman Astana's* (☎ 975661) which has the nicest garden and the optional extra of hot water for its 20,000/25,000Rp rooms.

West of Ubud For seclusion, within walking distance of Ubud, many travellers find the places around Campuan and Penestanan very appealing, but most of the dozen or more places dotted around the rice fields are now priced in the mid-range market. They are accessible by very steep steps from the main road west of Ubud, or along a driveable road from Penestanan.

Among the better in the budget range are the popular *Londo Bungalows* (☎ 920361), with rooms for 40,000Rp, including hot water; the fairly charmless *Siddahartha Cottages* (☎ 975748), with rooms for 50,000Rp, without hot water; and *Pugur Bungalows* (☎ 976672), which is overpriced, but often full, with rooms for 45,000/70,000Rp, including hot water.

A little closer to town, Jl Bisma has a real countryside atmosphere. Of the handful of places stretching southwards, *Juwita Inn* (☎ 976056, fax 975162) is the closest and one of the best. It offers bungalows, with hot water, almost lost in a luscious garden, for a reasonable 35,000/55,000Rp.

Places to Stay – Mid-Range
There are dozens of decent mid-range places from 40,000/50,000Rp for singles/doubles, and a growing number of new or renovated hotels for around US$40/50, almost always equipped with a swimming pool, hot water and air-con. The places that charge US$ are often never close to full, so prices are usually negotiable, especially if you're staying a few days.

BALI

Central Ubud Straddling the budget and mid-price ranges are two recommended places along Monkey Forest Rd. *Hotel Argasoka* (☎ 96231) has lovely gardens, spacious rooms and hot water, and is excellent value with rooms for 50,000/60,000Rp. *Ubud Bungalows* (☎/fax 975537) also has spacious rooms starting at 50,000Rp, and 80,000Rp for a pleasant family room.

Central, pleasant and well kept is *Puri Saraswati Bungalows* (☎/fax 975164, Jl Raya). Rooms start at US$40/48/56 for singles/doubles/triples. The quiet *Oka Wati Hotel* (☎ 96386, fax 975063, email okaati@ mmm.net) still has a rice paddy in view, but is now a little overpriced with rooms from US$33 to US$55. One gem is *Agung Cottages* (☎ 975414, Jl Goutama), which is set in a lovely, quiet garden and has friendly staff. Huge, spotless rooms cost 75,000Rp with hot water.

Along Monkey Forest Rd, *Ubud Village Hotel* (☎ 9975701, fax 75069) has pleasantly decorated rooms, each with a separate garden entrance, for US$40/45; US$65/75 with air-con. *Puri Garden Bungalows* (☎ 975 395), with its lush garden, is a pleasant place to stay for US$23/29. *Pertiwi Bungalows* (☎ 975236, fax 975559, email pertiwi@indo sat.net.id) has comfortable rooms, plenty of outdoor space for kids and a swimming pool, but there's nothing that special about it. Rooms cost from US$42/48, and double that for the deluxe rooms.

Also along Monkey Forest Rd, the well-established *Ubud Inn* (☎ 975071, fax 975188, email ubud-inn@indosat.net.id) has bungalows and rooms from US$30/40 to US$50/60, dotted around a spacious garden and swimming pool. Next door, *Fibra Inn* (☎/fax 975451) has a pool, and pleasant and comfortable bungalows from US$52/60. Several readers have recommended it.

East of Ubud Close to central Ubud, *Artini Cottages II* (☎ 975689, fax 975348, Jl Hanoman) has a stunning set-up with a pool. Its rooms for 100,000/150,000Rp are excellent value. The central *Oka Kartini Couperus Bungalows* (☎ 975193, fax 975759, Jl Raya)

may have an unusual name, but it has good-value rooms for US$20/25 and a pool.

North of Ubud To the north, there is nothing much in the mid-range, but one majestic place is worth booking ahead. *Gusti's Garden Bungalows* (☎ 96311, Jl Kajeng) may look unassuming from the street, but it opens up to a stunning garden, where large rooms, with hot water, are perched overlooking a swimming pool. Normally, you would expect to pay US$50 or more for this sort of place, but it only charges between 50,000Rp and 90,000Rp per double, depending on the view.

Another place where bookings are essential is *Ubud Sari Health Resort* (☎ 974 393, fax 976305, email ubudsari@denpasar .wasantara.net.id, Jl Kaleng). It offers a range of health treatments, massages and courses, and the three charming bungalows are great value from 45,000/50,000Rp to 100,000Rp for three people, including breakfast and hot water.

West of Ubud Along or just off Jl Bisma, there are several stunning places. One of the best and most popular is *Nick's Pension* (☎ 975526). It has a pool, and a tranquil setting, far from any main road, with rooms from US$20 to US$35 (with hot water). *Abangan Bungalows* (☎ 975977, fax 975082), up a steep driveway north of Jl Raya, has a lovely setting with a pool, and is still close to Ubud. The small rooms cost US$20; larger rooms in the rice-barn style are US$30 to US$35.

In the rice fields around Penestanan, a few more mid-range places are being built. One of the better ones is *Baliubud Cottages* (☎ 975058, fax 974773), which has a pool, and rooms from US$35/46 to US$69/78 with air-con. Secluded, picturesque and boasting a swimming pool is *Penestanan Bungalows* (☎ 975603, fax 288341). *Gerebig Bungalows* (☎ 974582) has rooms with hot water for a negotiable 70,000Rp, and wonderful views, but if you can live without hot water, there is better value nearby. *Sri Ratih Cottages* (☎ 975638, fax 976650) has a pool and is popular with tour groups. Rooms normally cost US$30/35, but are negotiable when business is quiet.

Places to Stay – Top End

Central Ubud There are very few top-end places in central Ubud. *Hotel Champlung Sari* (☎ 974686, fax 975473, Monkey Forest Rd) is convenient and has nice views, but the singles/doubles are ordinary and cost US$95/106.

North & South of Ubud Just off Jl Kajeng, one of the nicest places in Ubud is artist Han Snel's *Siti Bungalows* (☎ 975 699, fax 975643). The individual cottages are decorated with the artist's own work, and cost from US$57 to US$115. Some are perched right on the edge of the river gorge – it's worth making a reservation for these (see the Central Ubud map).

The only convenient top-end place south of Ubud is *Kokokan Hotel* (☎ 975742, fax 975332), owned by Agung Rai, patron of the ARMA museum nearby. It features nice views, fascinating architecture and fine decor. There is a range of singles/doubles/triples from US$109/121/145, or you can get the complete 'Pondok Manis' house for US$302.

West of Ubud The long-established *Hotel Tjampuhan* (☎ 975368, fax 975137) is beautifully situated above the confluence of the Cerik and Wos rivers. The hotel is built on land surrounding artist Walter Spies' home built in the 1930s. Individual bungalows in a wonderful garden cost from US$63/73. The Spies' House (which accommodates four) costs US$174, but you'll have to make a reservation for this.

Ibah (☎ 974466, fax 974467, email ibah@denpasar.wasantara.net.id) has a charming location overlooking a lush valley, and offers spacious and stylish individual suites from US$235, and US$423 for the 'Ibah Suite'. The delightful garden is decorated with stone carvings, handcrafted pots and antique doors, and the swimming pool is set into the hillside beneath an ancient looking stone wall.

Very close to central Ubud, *Pringga Juwita Water Garden Cottages* (☎/fax 975 734) has ponds and a swimming pool in one of the prettiest gardens in Ubud. Standard rooms cost from US$69/79; the luxurious deluxe rooms cost about US$15 more per person.

In Sanggingan, *Villa Bukit Ubud* (☎ 975371, fax 975767) is not bad value with rooms for US$73/85. *Puri Raka Inn* (☎/fax 975213) has been recommended by readers, not least for its enormous bath and excellent swimming pool. It's struggling for business, so offers substantial discounts: standard rooms can cost only 100,000Rp, while luxurious 'superior' rooms are 300,000Rp.

Pita Maha (☎ 974330, fax 974329, email pitamaha@dps.mega.net.id) is dramatically situated on the edge of Sungai Cerik. The individual villas, each in a small private compound, cost from US$302 to US$484 per night, but not all of them enjoy the best views. *Ulun Ubud Cottages* (☎ 975024, fax 975524) has bungalows beautifully draped down the hillside overlooking the valley. The whole place is decorated with wonderful carvings, paintings and antiques. Standard rooms are good value for US$45/55, while bungalows cost US$50/65 and family rooms, US$110/90.

In the village of Kedewatan, *Amandari* (☎ 975333, fax 975335) has superb views over the rice paddies or down to the Ayung, and the main swimming pool seems to drop right over the edge. Rooms start at US$556, and go much, much higher.

A little further north is *Kupu Kupu Barong* (☎ 975478, fax 975079). Clinging precariously to the steep sides of the Ayung gorge, the beautiful two-storey bungalows cost from US$405 to US$845. The views from the rooms, pool and restaurant are unbelievable, as you would hope for the price. *Puri Bunga Village* (☎ 975448, fax 975 073) has a similarly dramatic location, but less spectacular prices: rooms start at US$139/195.

More affordable, and also overlooking the Ayung, are two good places. *Sayan Terrace* (☎ 974384, fax 975384) has a brilliant view

BALI

and attractive rooms for US$30/48, and family rooms for US$70. *Taman Bebek Villas* (☎ *975385, fax 976532, email tribwana@ dps.mega.net.id)* has a choice of elegant rooms, and villas with kitchenettes, starting from an affordable US$44; suites are US$100 or more.

Places to Eat

For the cheapest meals, the market has *food stalls* – but they often close early in the evening. The price of meals in restaurants and warungs is considerably cheaper in areas where budget travellers normally stay. In unassuming little places along the roads heading north of Jl Raya, and along Jl Sugiwa, Jl Hanoman and Jl Jembawan, you can pay as little as 2500Rp for a *nasi goreng*, 3500Rp for a passable spaghetti and 4500Rp for a fish meal with the trimmings. You can easily pay three times this at many places along Jl Raya and Monkey Forest Rd – not including pricey drinks.

Along Jalan Raya *Ary's Warung* is one place that has moved steadily upmarket, but remains incredibly popular. It serves a wide variety of excellent food, including dips, omelettes and wholemeal sandwiches, for about 7500Rp; main meals start at 15,000Rp. Nearby, *Ryoshi Japanese Restaurant* is one of a chain of upmarket Japanese eateries across Bali, and is always popular with Japanese visitors – which is a good sign.

Across the road, *Lotus Cafe* was for a long time *the* place to eat. A leisurely meal overlooking the lotus pond is still an Ubud institution: main meals start at 15,000Rp. *Casa Luna* features a superb international menu, and is so popular that you may be lucky to find a table in the evening. It also sells bread and pastry from its own bakery, great desserts (try the 'Death by Chocolate' cake) and half serves for kids. The service is efficient, and the atmosphere is pleasant and friendly. *Mumbul's Cafe* is the best place in Ubud for ice cream and scrumptious treats like sundaes and banana splits

North of Jalan Raya One of Ubud's real dining pleasures is *Han Snel's Garden Restaurant* (see the Central Ubud map), just off Jl Kaleng. The setting is beautiful, with frogs croaking in the background. The food is exquisite and prices start at 12,000Rp a dish, and the servings generous.

Ketut's Place (☎ *975304, Jl Suweta)* still runs the weekly Balinese Feast – for inquiries and bookings, contact Suci Inn, closer to town (see the previous Places to Stay entries). For 35,000Rp per person, you get a great meal of Balinese specialities that is also an excellent introduction to Balinese life and customs. There's usually an interesting group, so it's very sociable.

Also along Jl Suweta are *Coconut Cafe*, and *Cafe Angkasa* (which rivals the Tutmak Cafe as Ubud's best coffee house). *Bumbu Restaurant* is popular with people staying in the area. The Indian and Indonesian food is cheap and tasty, and served in a pleasant setting.

Along Monkey Forest Rd Many places are now overpriced, but a few good cheapies remain. *Canderi's Warung*, run by the irrepressible Ibu Canderi, is an old Ubud institution. It offers large serves of Indonesian, western and vegetarian dishes at reasonable prices. *Kul Kul Restaurant* is also popular for its large serves at good prices. *Bendi's Restaurant*, in Bendi's 2 Accommodation, features authentic Balinese food, and is one of the few places that offers breakfast and an upstairs room. The *gado gado* (salad with peanut sauce, 6500Rp) is particularly good. *Cafe Tirta* is also cheap and friendly, although the service is slow if it's busy. For something a little nicer for which you won't have to delve too deeply into your pockets, *Gayatri Cafe* is excellent: seafood specials cost about 7500Rp, and it has a comfortable upstairs area.

For sheer elegance, in a wonderful setting, it's hard to go past *Ibu Rai Bar & Restaurant*. Prices are not as steep as you may imagine: pasta dishes are about 10,000Rp, while a large beer is 6500Rp. *Noni Orti* is about the same sort of standard and price. For something a little more authentic, just as elegant but a little cheaper (9000Rp to 12,000Rp a dish), *Lillies Garden Restaurant* and *Cafe Bali* are romantically set among the rice fields.

Further south, *Cafe Wayan* is popular and relaxed: meals start at 15,000Rp and go higher – the smoked duck is particularly good, but expensive. It offers regular Balinese feasts (60,000Rp), and baked goodies to rival Casa Luna. Close by are three good places virtually next to each other: *Mendra's Cafe* has cheap beer, but the serves are small; *Dian Cafe* has a good range and reasonable prices; and *Lotus Lane Restaurant* is one of the chain of classy places dotted around Bali.

Yogyakarta Cafe looks unassuming from the outside, but it has a huge indoor and outdoor setting. It specialises in barbequed seafood priced from 8500Rp – you'll see the smoke, and smell the food, from the street. The new *Monkey Cafe* has a superb setting and is the best place for vegetarian food at reasonable prices (6000Rp to 9000Rp).

Along Jl Dewa Sita, *Bamboo Restaurant* has inexpensive Balinese dishes, pizzas (9500Rp), coconut pies (2500Rp) and a breezy upstairs setting. *Tutmak Cafe* is a stylish place that serves pasta, and about the best coffee in Ubud – use it to wash down some delicious chocolate cake.

East of Ubud Along Jl Hanoman, especially further south, many cheerful *restaurants* and *warungs* serve authentic and tasty Indonesian food for about 4000Rp, and western food, such as pasta and pizza, for about 6500Rp. This is one of the best value areas in Ubud, and worth a short walk if you're not staying nearby. *Three Brothers Restaurant* is unpretentious, and offers simple food at honest prices, in a friendly atmosphere. *Warung Artini* has also been recommended by several readers.

Along Jl Tebesaya, there are also a few good and inexpensive places, including *Made Cafe*, where the Italian food will not disappoint you. Just down Jl Jembawan, the new *Bali Buddha Health Food Shop* is a popular place to meet other travellers and

relax with something healthy to drink or eat. It also features a useful notice board for messages and ads about current and future courses and events.

South of Ubud Padangtegal has some interesting options. *Bebek Bengil* (aka Dirty Duck Diner, *Jl Hanoman*) does delectable deep-fried duck dishes in a delightful dining area. Going south, *Kura Kura Mexican Cafe* has substantial Mexican main dishes from around 8000Rp – you can smell the chilli wafting across the main road.

West of Ubud Up the slope south of Jl Raya, *Miro's Cafe* has a varied menu and a cool garden setting. Well-prepared Indonesian dishes cost about 7500Rp and other main courses about 10,500Rp, and it has a good vegetarian selection. *Griya Barbecue* (*Jl Raya*) serves very good pork, chicken, steak and fish dishes for about 20,000Rp, but pasta and Indonesian dishes are more reasonably priced at about 10,000Rp.

Continuing towards Campuan, *Murni's Warung* is an old Ubud favourite, with a four level dining room and bar. Prices are squarely set for the upmarket tourist, however. Opposite, *Beggar's Bush Pub* probably has the best views in Ubud. Meals start at 9000Rp for a snack and 12,000Rp for a main meal, and the food is tasty and the serves are large.

Long-term stayers in Penestanan usually eat at their losmen, but the new *Cafe Dewata* is attracting plenty of customers for its good prices and breezy setting. *Amandari* has excellent food in a sophisticated atmosphere and *Kupu Kupu Barong* has superb views – reservations for both are recommended, especially at lunch time. Further out, *Warung Nuri* is the place for drinks, meals and 'English breakfasts' before or after visiting the Neka Museum. Or visit *Indus*, a newish restaurant serving delicious meals in a spectacular setting at very reasonable prices. It's across the road from Ananda Cottages.

Entertainment
Balinese Music & Dance Within one week in Ubud, you can see Kecak, Legong and

BALI

Barong dances, *Mahabharata* and *Ramayana* ballets, wayang kulit puppets and gamelan orchestras on a number of stages in Ubud and surrounding villages. The Agung Rai Museum of Art (see Museums earlier in this section) also holds regular traditional dances – for these, book at ARMA.

You can buy tickets (10,000Rp to 15,000Rp) from any of the travel agencies or hotels around Ubud, the tourist office or the touts who hang around outside Ubud Palace. The most attractive and accessible setting is the central Ubud Palace, but if you want to get a seat in the front few rows, you'll have to get there at least 30 minutes before starting time. If the performance is held in a small local village, transport is usually included in the ticket price.

Bars Probably the closest thing to a bar is *Beggar's Bush Pub (Jl Raya)*, built on four levels – so take your pick of the best views. Glasses of draught beer cost 6000Rp. Op-posite, *Murni's Warung* has an intimate lounge bar with high-priced drinks.

Yogyakarta Cafe (Monkey Forest Rd) also serves draught beer for 6500Rp in a classy setting, but the only views are of the TV and video screen. Happy hours are more of a 'Kuta thing', but *Jaya Cafe (Monkey Forest Rd)* and nearby *Mendra's Cafe* offer discounted drinks in the evening. Jazz fans will want to visit *Jazz Cafe (Jl Tebesaya)* for its relaxed atmosphere, excellent food (about 12,000Rp for tasty pasta), live music on Tuesday, Thursday and Saturday evenings and jam sessions on Saturday afternoons.

Videos & Sports Telecasts Some of the central places that feature videos nightly are *Casa Luna (Jl Raya)*, which also shows children's movies in the afternoon; *Bamboo Restaurant*; *Coconut Cafe (Jl Suweta)*; and *Putra Bar (Monkey Forest Rd)*, which also boasts live international sports telecasts by satellite.

Shopping

Paintings The main galleries have excellent selections, and they're very interesting to look through, but prices are typically well over the US$100 mark – you will get better prices directly from the artist or an artist's workshop. If your budget is limited, look for a smaller picture of high quality, rather than something that resembles wallpaper in size and originality. The common Balinese landscape paintings, with intricate wooden frames, make great souvenirs, and are available at many of the hundreds of art shops around Ubud. Prices start at 50,000Rp and depend on quality.

Woodcarvings Small shops by the market and along Monkey Forest Rd often have good woodcarvings, particularly masks. There are other good woodcarving places along Jl Bedulu (between Pengosekan and Teges), and along the road between Nyuhkuning and the southern entrance to Monkey Forest Sanctuary.

Surrounding villages also tend to specialise in different styles or subjects. Along

JENNY BOWMAN

Rangda, the witch-widow, the adversary of the barong in the Barong & Rangda dance.

JULIET COOMBE

he sea temple of Tanah Lot – venerated by the Balinese and photographed by the tourists.

PAUL BEINSSEN

ice harvest.

JULIET COOMBE

A face like a dragon ...

ANDREW BROWNBILL

Rice fields near Tirtagangga, East Bali.

RICHARD I'ANSON

Rice – the staple of Balinese life.

PAUL BEINSSEN

Perahu (outrigger) fishing boat, Padangbai.

GREG ELMS

Cremation tower – ashes are scattered in the sea

PAUL BEINSSEN

The village of Amed on the north-east coast is a tranquil place to spend some time.

the road from Teges to Mas, look for masks and some of the most original carved pieces with natural wood finishes. North of Ubud, look for carved garuda birds in Junjungan, and painted flowers and fruit in Tegallalang, about 1km east of Petulu. Near the ARMA Museum, wood chimes are a common item for sale.

Other Items The two storey Art Market (Pasar Seni) sells a wide range of clothing, sarongs, footwear, and souvenirs of variable quality at negotiable prices. Some other decent souvenirs include leather goods, batiks, baskets and silverware (but the range is far better at Celuk).

Toko Tino Supermarket is reasonably large, and sells most things. In central Ubud, several photography shops sell slide and print film, and develop your snaps quickly. Ubud's colourful produce market, adjacent to the art market, operates every third day. It starts early in the morning, but winds up by lunch time.

Getting There & Away

Bemo Ubud is only on two bemo routes. Small orange bemos travel from Gianyar to Ubud, and on to Pujung, and larger brown bemos travel from Batubulan terminal in Denpasar to Ubud, and then head to Kintamani via Payangan. Official fares are 700Rp to Gianyar, 1500Rp to Denpasar and 2000Rp to Kintamani, but don't be surprised if you're overcharged a little. To get to Bedugul, go back to Denpasar; to get to Lovina, get a connection in Kintamani. Surprisingly, Ubud doesn't have a bemo terminal; bemos stop at one of two convenient points, north and west of the market in the centre of town.

Tourist Shuttle Bus Shuttle buses are very useful for places that are not particularly easy to reach by public transport, such as Sanur, Kuta, Lovina and Bedugul. Plenty of companies offer shuttle buses at regular times; just check out the billboards outside the dozens of shops, travel agencies and hotels along the main roads in Ubud,

particularly on Monkey Forest Rd, and buy your ticket a day in advance.

Car & Motorcycle With numerous nearby attractions, many of which are difficult to reach by bemo, renting a vehicle is an attractive idea. The ubiquitous Suzuki *Jimny* jeep costs about 50,000/60,000Rp per day without/with insurance; the larger Toyota Kijang costs from 70,000/80,000Rp. A motorcycle costs from 15,000/20,000Rp; it's about 5000Rp more per day for something newer. Cars and motorcycles can be easily rented from one of the numerous agencies, most of which are found on Monkey Forest Rd, Jl Hanoman and Jl Raya. You may also be able to rent one from your hotel.

Taxi There are very few taxis in Ubud – those that honk their horns at you have usually dropped off passengers in Ubud from southern Bali and are hoping for a fare back. They should use their meters, but check first.

Getting Around

To/From the Airport Pre-paid taxis from the airport to Ubud are reasonably expensive, but taxis are not always available in Ubud. If your plane leaves at an unreasonable hour, you'll have to pre-book a taxi at your hotel or at a travel agency in Ubud for about 40,000Rp, or you can charter transport yourself. There are also shuttle buses to the airport (7500Rp), but they are hard to organise from the airport.

Bemo Bemos don't directly link Ubud with nearby villages; you'll have to catch a bemo going to Denpasar, Gianyar, Pujung or Kintamani and get off at the appropriate place. Small orange bemos to Gianyar travel along eastern Jl Raya, down Jl Peliatan and east to Bedulu. Bemos to Pujung head east along Jl Raya and then north through Andong and past the turn-off to Petulu. Larger brown bemos to Denpasar go east along Jl Dewi Sita and down Jl Hanoman. To Kintamani, they travel along western Jl Raya, past Campuan and turn north at the junction after Sangginan.

BALI

Bicycle Many shops, agencies and hotels in central Ubud rent mountain bikes. The standard charge is 5000Rp per day, or 4000Rp per day for a longer rental.

Around Ubud

The region east and north of Ubud has many of the most ancient monuments and relics in Bali. Many of them predate the Majapahit era and raise as yet unanswered questions about Bali's history. Some sites are more recent, and in other instances newer structures have been built on and around the ancient remains. They're interesting to history and archaeology buffs, but not that spectacular to look at – with the exception of Gunung Kawi, which is very impressive. Perhaps the best approach is to plan a whole day walking or cycling around the area, stopping at the places that interest you, but not treating any one as a destination in itself.

If you're travelling by public transport, start early and take a bemo to the Bedulu intersection, and another to Tirta Empul (about 15km from Ubud). See the temple of Tirta Empul, then follow the path beside the river down to Gunung Kawi. From there you can return to the main road and walk downhill about 8km to Pejeng, or flag down a bemo going towards Gianyar. The temples and museum at Pejeng and the archaeological sites at Bedulu are all within about 3km of each other.

BEDULU
☎ 0361

Bedulu was once the capital of a great kingdom. The legendary Dalem Bedaulu ruled the Pejeng dynasty from here, and was the last Balinese king to withstand the onslaught of the powerful Majapahits from Java. He was eventually defeated by Gajah Mada in 1343. The capital shifted several times after this, to Gelgel and then later to Semarapura.

Goa Gajah
Only a short distance east of Teges is Goa Gajah (Elephant Cave). The origins of the cave are uncertain – one tale relates that it was created by the fingernail of the legendary giant Kebo Iwa. It probably dates back at least to the 11th century, and it was certainly in existence at the time of the Majapahit takeover of Bali. In modern times the cave was discovered by Dutch archaeologists in 1923; the fountains and bathing pool were not unearthed until 1954.

The cave is carved into a rock face and you enter through the cavernous mouth of a demon. The gigantic fingertips pressed beside the face of the demon push back a riotous jungle of surrounding stone carvings. Inside the T-shaped cave you can see fragmentary remains of *lingam*, the phallic symbols of the Hindu god Shiva, and its female counterpart the *yoni*, plus a statue of the elephant-headed god Ganesh. In the courtyard in front of the cave are two square bathing pools with water gushing into them from waterspouts held by six female figures. To the left of the cave entrance, in a small pavilion, is a statue of Hariti, surrounded by children. In Buddhist lore, Hariti was an evil woman who devoured children, but under the influence of Buddhism she reformed completely to become a protector of children and a symbol of fertility.

From Goa Gajah you can clamber down through the rice paddies to Sungai Petanu where there are crumbling **rock carvings** of stupas (domes for housing Buddhist relics) on a cliff face, and a small **cave**.

Goa Gajah is open daily from 8 am to 6 pm. If you're travelling independently arrive before 10 am, when a number of large tourist buses start to arrive. Admission costs 1100Rp – plus extra for cameras, videos, car parking and renting a sarong.

Yeh Pulu
This 25m, carved cliff face is believed to be a hermitage dating from the late 14th century. Apart from the figure of elephant-headed Ganesh, the son of Shiva, there are no obviously religious scenes here. The energetic frieze includes various scenes of everyday life, though the position and movement of the figures suggests that it

could be read from left to right as a story. One theory is that they are events from the life of Krishna, the Hindu god.

The Ganesh figures of Yeh Pulu and Goa Gajah are quite similar, indicating a close relationship between the two sites. You can walk between the sites, following small paths through the rice fields, but you might need to pay a local kid to guide you. If travelling by car or bicycle, look for the signs to 'Relief Yeh Pulu' or 'Villa Yeh Pulu' east of Goa Gajah.

The entrance fee is 1100Rp – more for cameras, videos and sarong rental. The ticket includes a small brochure with an explanation in English, but if you want more information about Yeh Pulu buy *The Talking Stones* by Madi Kertonegoro, available from bookshops in Ubud.

Next to the entrance, *Made's Cafe* offers cold drinks and snacks, and you can stay at *Pondok Wisata Lantar* (☎ 942399), which has small, clean rooms for 15,000Rp, including breakfast.

Pura Samuan Tiga

The majestic Pura Samuan Tiga (Temple of the Meeting of the Three) is about 200m east of the Bedulu junction. The name is possibly a reference to the Hindu trinity, or it may refer to meetings held here in the early 11th century. Despite these early associations, all the temple buildings have been rebuilt since the 1917 earthquake. The imposing main gate was designed and built by I Gusti Nyoman Lempad, one of Bali's most renowned artists and a native of Bedulu.

Museum Purbakala

This Archaeological Museum (☎ 942447) has an ill-assorted collection of artefacts from all over Bali. Next to the pond inside the complex, a notice board offers a reasonable explanation of the exhibits in English. The museum is open Monday to Thursday from 8 am to 2 pm, and on Friday and Saturday until noon. It is about 500m north of the Bedulu junction, and easy to reach by bemo or bicycle.

Getting There & Away

About 3km east of Teges, the road from Ubud reaches a junction where you can turn south to Gianyar or north to Pejeng, Tampaksiring and Penelokan. Any Ubud to Gianyar bemo will drop you off at the Bedulu junction, from where you can walk to the attractions. The road from Ubud is reasonably flat, so coming by bicycle is a good option.

PEJENG

Further up the road to Tampaksiring is Pejeng and its famous temples. Like Bedulu, Pejeng was once an important seat of power, the capital of the Pejeng kingdom, which fell to the Majapahit invaders in 1343.

Pura Kebo Edan

Also called the Crazy Buffalo Temple, this is not an imposing structure but is famous for its 3m-high statue, known as the Giant of Pejeng, thought to be about 700 years old. The temple is on the western side of the road. You might have to pay 1000Rp to enter.

Pura Pusering Jagat

The large Pura Pusering Jagat (Navel of the World Temple) is said to be the centre of the old Pejeng kingdom. Dating from 1329, this temple is visited by young couples who pray at the stone lingam and yoni. Further back is a large stone urn, with elaborate but worn carvings of gods and demons searching for the elixir of life in a depiction of the *Mahabharata* tale 'Churning the Sea of Milk'. The temple is on a small track running west of the main road.

Pura Penataran Sasih

This was once the state temple of the Pejeng kingdom. In the inner courtyard, high up in a pavilion and difficult to see, is the huge bronze drum known as the **Moon of Pejeng**. The hourglass-shaped drum is more than 2m long, the largest single-piece cast drum in the world. Estimates of its age vary from 1000 to 2000 years, and it is not certain whether it was made locally. Even in its inaccessible position, you can make out these patterns and the distinctive heart-shaped face designs.

BALI

TAMPAKSIRING

Tampaksiring is a small town with probably the most impressive ancient monument in Bali, and a large and important temple, with public baths.

Gunung Kawi

On the southern outskirts of town a sign points east off the main road to the wondrous Gunung Kawi. From the end of the access road a steep stone stairway leads down to the river, at one point making a cutting through an embankment of solid rock. There, in the bottom of this lush green valley, is one of Bali's oldest, most charming and certainly largest ancient monuments.

Gunung Kawi consists of 10 rock-cut candi (shrines), memorials cut out of the rock face in imitation of actual statues. They stand in 7m high sheltered niches cut into the sheer cliff face. A solitary candi stands about 1km further down the valley to the south; this is reached by a trek through the rice paddies on the western side of the river. Each candi is believed to be a memorial to a member of 11th century Balinese royalty, but little is known for certain. Legends relate that the whole group of memorials was carved out of the rock face in one hard working night by the mighty fingernails of Kebo Iwa.

The five monuments on the eastern bank are probably dedicated to King Udayana, Queen Mahendradatta, their son Airlangga and his brothers Anak Wungsu and Marakata. While Airlangga ruled eastern Java, Anak Wungsu ruled Bali. The four monuments on the western side are, according to this theory, to Anak Wungsu's chief concubines. Another theory is that the whole complex is dedicated to Anak Wungsu, his wives, concubines and, in the case of the remote 10th candi, to a royal minister.

Admission to Gunung Kawi is 1100Rp, plus extra for camera and video. It is open daily from 7 am to 5 pm.

Tirta Empul

A well-signposted fork in the road north of Tampaksiring leads to the holy springs at Tirta Empul. Founded in 962 AD, the springs are believed to have magical powers, so the temple is important. The springs are a source of Sungai Pakerisan, which rushes by Gunung Kawi only 1km or so away. The actual springs bubble up into a large, crystal-clear tank within the temple and gush out through waterspouts into a bathing pool. Despite its antiquity, the temple is glossy and new – it was totally restored in the late 1960s.

There is an admission charge (1100Rp), and an additional fee for a video or camera. You must wear a sarong or long pants, and you may also need to rent a scarf. The complex is open from 8 am to 6 pm; come early in the morning or late in the afternoon to avoid the tourist buses. You can also use the clean, segregated and free **public baths** in the grounds.

Overlooking Tirta Empul is Soekarno's palace, **Istana Negara**. It's an unspectacular, single storey structure, designed by Soekarno himself and built in 1954 on the site of a Dutch rest house.

Getting There & Away

Tampaksiring is an easy day trip from Ubud, or a stopover between Ubud and Danau Batur. If travelling by bemo, get a connection in Bedulu. Tirta Empul and Gunung Kawi are easy to find along the Penelokan to Ubud road, and are only about 1.5km apart. There is nowhere to stay in Tampaksiring.

East Bali

The eastern end of Bali is dominated by the mighty Gunung Agung, the 'navel of the world' and Bali's 'mother mountain'. Towering at 3142m, Agung has not always been a kind 'mother' – in 1963 there was a disastrous eruption (see 'The 1963 Eruption' boxed text later in this section). Today, Agung is quiet but the 'mother temple', Pura Besakih, perched high on the slopes of the volcano, attracts a steady stream of devotees – and tourists.

The main route east goes through Gianyar and Semarapura (also known as Klungkung), then close to the coast past Kusamba,

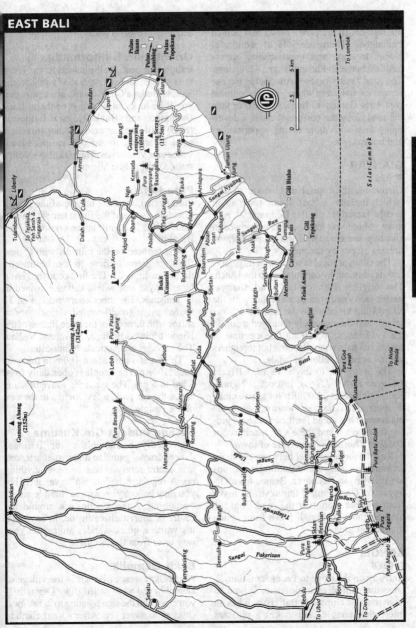

EAST BALI

the bat-infested temple of Goa Lawah, and the turn-off to the pretty beach and port of Padangbai. There are lots of wonderful places to stay, and great diving opportunities, between Padangbai and Candidasa. The road finally reaches Amlapura, another former capital, from where you can continue past Tirta Gangga to the east coast, or take the road along the north-east coast, a developing area with more diving opportunities and bungalows.

GIANYAR
☎ 0361
Gianyar is the capital of Gianyar district (which includes Ubud). It has some small **textile factories**, on the Denpasar side of town, where you can see ikat being woven and buy some material made up as shirts, dresses etc, or by the metre.

The Gianyar royal family saved its palace, and its position, by capitulating to the Dutch. The original 18th century **Puri Gianyar** palace was destroyed in a conflict with the Klungkung kingdom in the mid-1880s, was rebuilt and then severely damaged again in the 1917 earthquake. It's a fine example of traditional palace architecture, but foreigners are not normally allowed inside.

The best place to stay is *Pondok Wisata Gianyar 1 (☎ 942165)*, just off Jl Ngurah Rai, which costs 22,000Rp for small, clean double rooms. Gianyar's *warungs* along the main street are noted for their fine *babi guling* (roast pig); and there's an incongruous *Dunkin' Donuts* in the centre of town.

Regular bemos travel between the main terminal in Gianyar and Batubulan terminal (1000Rp) in Denpasar. Bemos from Gianyar to Ubud and Tampaksiring leave from another stop over the road from the market; those to Bangli leave from inside the market area.

BANGLI
☎ 0366
Halfway up the slope to Penelokan, Bangli, once the capital of a kingdom, is said to have the best climate in Bali. Bangli has an interesting temple, and makes a pleasant base for exploring the area, but its range of accommodation is poor.

Orientation & Information
Bangli is a neat, well-planned town. There is a tourist office (☎ 91537) inside the Sasana Budaya Giri Kusuma arts centre, but you'll be lucky to find anyone there. Bank Danamon and Bank Negara Indonesia (BNI) will change cash but not travellers cheques, and the former will accept cash advances on Visa cards. There is also a police station, and public hospital.

Pura Kehen
Pura Kehen, the state temple of the Bangli kingdom, is one of the finest temples in east Bali; a little like a miniature version of Pura Besakih.

It is terraced up the hillside, with a great flight of steps leading to the beautifully decorated entrance. The first courtyard has a huge banyan tree with a kulkul entwined in its branches. The inner courtyard has an 11 roofed meru (multi-roofed shrine), and a shrine with thrones for the three figures of the Hindu trinity –. Brahma, Shiva and Vishnu. The carvings are particularly intricate.

Tickets at a gate about 100m to the west cost 1100Rp. The temple is open daily from 8 am to 5 pm. The requisite souvenir stalls are at the car park, a few metres to the east of the temple gate.

Sasana Budaya Giri Kusuma
Supposedly a showplace for Balinese dance, drama, gamelan and visual arts, this arts centre rarely seems to have anything on. A regular schedule isn't available, but you may be lucky enough to stumble across something. Alternatively, ask around the centre or tourist office inside. In any case, it's worth a quick wander around on your way to or from the temple.

Bukit Demulih
About 3km west of Bangli is the village of Demulih, and a hill called Bukit Demulih. If you can't find the sign pointing to it, ask local children to direct you. After a short climb to

the top, you'll see a small **temple** and good **views** back over Bangli and southern Bali.

On the way, a steep side road leads down to Tirta Buana, a **public swimming pool** in a lovely location deep in the valley.

Places to Stay & Eat
Artha Sastra Inn (☎ *91179*), opposite the bemo terminal, is a former palace residence. It's pleasant, friendly and popular, and singles/doubles start at 15,000/20,000Rp. *Bangli Inn* (☎ *91419*), next to the market, is the most comfortable place in town, and quite good value for a negotiable 25,000Rp per room. *Losmen Dharmaputra*, just north of the bemo terminal, has unappealing rooms with a shared bathroom for 10,000Rp.

Bangli has very few restaurants, but it does boast good *food stalls* and *warungs* in the market area.

Getting There & Away
Bangli is easy to reach: it's on the main road between Denpasar's Batubulan terminal (1100Rp) and Gunung Batur, via Penelokan. Bemos also regularly leave Gianyar and go up the road to Bangli, although it's often quicker to get a connection at the junction near Peteluan. Tourist shuttle buses travelling between Ubud and Gunung Batur usually go via Tampaksiring, and bypass Bangli.

SEMARAPURA (KLUNGKUNG)
☎ 0366

Semarapura was once the centre of Bali's most important kingdom, and a great artistic and cultural focal point. Today, it's a major public transport junction, with an interesting palace and a busy market. It's a reasonable place to base yourself while you explore the surrounding area, although the range of accommodation is not good. The town is still commonly called Klungkung, but has been officially renamed Semarapura, and this new name appears on most signs and maps these days.

Information
Bank Danamon, Bank BCA and Bank Pembangunan will change cash. There is also a post office, wartel and police station, all along the main road.

Semara Pura
When the Dewa Agung dynasty moved here in 1710, a new palace, the Semara Pura, was established. Most of the original palace and grounds were destroyed during Dutch attacks in 1908, and the **Pemedal Agung**, the gateway on the southern side of the square, is all that remains of the palace itself – it's worth a close look to see the carvings. The complex is open daily from 7 am to 6 pm, and tickets cost 2000Rp.

Kertha Gosa The 'Hall of Justice' was effectively the supreme court of the Klungkung kingdom, where disputes and cases that could not be settled at the village level were eventually brought. This open-sided pavilion is a superb example of Klungkung architecture, and its ceiling is completely covered inside with fine paintings in the Klungkung style. The paintings, done on asbestos sheeting, were installed in the 1940s, replacing cloth paintings that had deteriorated.

Bale Kambang The ceiling of the beautiful 'Floating Pavilion' is painted in Klungkung style. Again, the different rows of paintings deal with different subjects. The first row is based on the astrological calendar; the second, on the folk tale of Pan and Men Brayut and their 18 children; and the upper rows on the adventures of the hero Sutasona.

Museum Semarajaya This museum has some archaeological pieces, and some quite interesting contemporary accounts of the 1908 puputan. It's nothing special, but entry is included in the ticket to the whole complex, so you might as well have a quick look.

Places to Stay & Eat
Loji Ramayana Hotel (☎ *21044, Jl Diponegoro*), on the road to Amlapura, is pleasant, with a restaurant in a pavilion out the back, and reasonably quiet. The better rooms are

quite big, and cost a negotiable 30,000Rp. Directly opposite, *Losmen Cahay Pusaha* (☎ 22118) has noisy rooms from 15,000Rp.

Apart from the charming *restaurant* in the Loji Ramayana, the adjacent, Chinese *Bali Indah* and *Sumber Rasa* restaurants on Jl Nakula are both neat, clean and cheap.

Getting There & Away

Very frequent bemos and minibuses from Denpasar (Batubulan terminal) pass through Semarapura (1100Rp) on the way to Padangbai and Amlapura. Bemos heading north to Rendang and Besakih leave from the centre of Semarapura; most other bemos leave from the inconvenient Klod terminal, about 2km south.

Tourist shuttle buses travelling between southern Bali or Ubud and Padangbai or Candidasa will stop in Semarapura on request. The town is also a regular stop-off on organised bus tours around eastern Bali.

AROUND SEMARAPURA
☎ 0366

Gelgel

Once the seat of Bali's most powerful dynasty, Gelgel's decline started in 1710 when the court moved to Klungkung (Semarapura), and finished when Dutch ships bombarded the place in 1908. **Pura Dasar** is not particularly attractive, but its vast courtyards are a clue to its former importance, and festivals here attract large numbers from all over Bali. A little to the east, the **Masjid Gelgel** is the oldest mosque in Bali.

Gelgel is about 3km south of Semarapura, past the intersection by the Semara Pura complex, and accessible by bemo.

Kamasan

Another quiet, traditional village, Kamasan is where the Kamasan style of classical painting originated. A number of artists have workshops and small showrooms along the main streets. To get here from Semarapura, head south towards Gelgel and look for the turn-off to Kamasan. It's easiest to reach this village using your own transport.

Museum Seni Lukis Klasik

Nyoman Gunarsa, one of the most respected and successful modern artists in Indonesia, established this museum and arts centre near his home town of Banda. The three storey building houses a wide variety of older pieces, including stone and wood carvings, architectural antiques, masks, ceramics and textiles. The museum is open Tuesday to Sunday from 9 am to 5 pm, and admission is 5000Rp. It is about 6km from Semarapura, near a bend on the road to Denpasar – look for the mannequin policemen at the base of a large statue nearby.

Sidemen Road

A less travelled route goes north-east from Semarapura, via Sidemen and Iseh, to the Rendang to Amlapura road. The area boasts marvellous **scenery** and a delightful rural character, and is easily accessible by bemo from Semarapura, although most of the road is fairly rough.

Sidemen was a base for Swiss ethnologist Urs Ramseyer, and is also a centre for traditional culture and arts, particularly songket, a cloth woven with threads of silver and gold. German artist Walter Spies lived in **Iseh** for some time from 1932 onwards. Later, the Swiss painter Theo Meier, nearly as famous as Spies for his influence on Balinese art, lived in the same house.

Places to Stay & Eat In Sidemen, *Sidemen Pondok Wisata* (☎ 23009) is pleasantly old-fashioned, with four-poster beds and great views. Rooms cost 50,000Rp per person with breakfast, or 70,000Rp per person with three meals. *Subak Tabola Inn* (☎ 23015), along a small track 1.5km to the right heading south from Sidemen, is set among rice fields and has a lovely outlook. It has a small pool and comfortable rooms from US$35 – more with full board.

Another wonderful place in Sidemen is *Sacred Mountain Sanctuary* (☎/fax 23456, email sacredmt@dps.mega.net.id). It has a small pool, and rooms cost about 150,000Rp, including breakfast.

Pondok Wisata Patal Kikian (☎ 23001) is delightful, and offers almost total seclusion, tranquillity and awesome views of Gunung Agung. Stylish singles/doubles cost US$25/50, but you should book first to ensure it has adequate staff and food. Look for the poorly signposted turn-off on the left, not far south of Iseh.

Kusamba

A side road goes south to this fishing and salt-making village, where you'll see lines of colourful fishing *perahus* (outriggers) lined up on the beach. Fishing is normally done at night and the 'eyes' on the front of the boats help navigation through the darkness. Regular boats travel to the islands of Nusa Penida and Nusa Lembongan, clearly visible from Kusamba. East and west of Kusamba, there are thatched roofs of salt making-huts along the beach.

Pura Goa Lawah

About 3km east of Kusamba is the Bat Cave Temple. The cave in the cliff face is jam-packed full of bats, and the complex is equally overcrowded with tour groups later in the day. The temple itself is small and unimpressive, although it's very old and of great significance to the Balinese.

The cave is said to lead all the way to Besakih, but it seems nobody has volunteered to confirm this: the bats provide sustenance for the legendary giant snake Naga Basuki, which is also believed to live in the cave. The cave and temple are open daily, and admission is 500Rp. Sashes are available for rent.

PURA BESAKIH

Perched nearly 1000m up the side of Gunung Agung is Bali's most important temple, Pura Besakih. In fact, it is an extensive complex of 23 separate but related temples, with the largest and most important being **Pura Penataran Agung**. It's most enjoyable during one of the frequent festivals, when hundreds, perhaps thousands, of gorgeously dressed devotees turn up with beautifully arranged offerings. The panoramic view and the mountain backdrop are impressive

too, but try to arrive early, before the mist rolls in, along with the tour buses.

Despite its importance to the Balinese, Besakih can be a disappointment. The architecture is not especially impressive, tourists are not allowed inside any of the temples, the views are usually obscured by mist, and the number of entry charges, hustlers and souvenir sellers can be infuriating. The tourist information office can answer basic questions, but has no printed information and does nothing to make the site more comprehensible.

You pay to park (600Rp per car; 200Rp for a motorcycle) and then to enter (1100Rp per person). You can buy tickets at the front entrance of the complex, or at a bus lay-off about 1km before the complex. If you don't have a sarong you'll have to rent one for 2000Rp to 3000Rp, although demands of 5000Rp are frequent. The best time to come is at about 8 am, before the souvenir stalls open and the tourist buses start to unload their passengers. The complex is open daily, during daylight hours.

Warning Many unofficial and unscrupulous guides hang around the temple. If someone latches on to you, let them know quickly whether you want their services and for how much. There are a few minor scams. Some 'guides' claim that you need to pay a 5000Rp 'fee' for going further into the temple complex during a festival, but this is not true.

Places to Stay & Eat

Staying at Besakih is useful if you want to start climbing Gunung Agung early (see the following Gunung Agung section), but surprisingly there is nowhere decent or central to stay. There are some unsigned losmen within the complex, though you'll have to ask at the tourist office or the gate for directions. One place, *Homestay Kobar*, offers basic doubles for 15,000Rp.

There are many inexpensive *warungs* around the car park, and plenty of shops selling food along the road inside the complex. Naturally, there are several pricey *restaurants* along the main roads to the temple complex.

BALI

About 7km below Besakih, *Lembah Arca Restaurant & Accommodation* (☎ 0366-23076) is a reasonable place to stay and eat, and only a short bemo ride from Besakih. It's prettily situated in a valley by a bend in the road, but the singles/doubles are average and overpriced for 25,000/40,000Rp.

Getting There & Away

Most people travel from Semarapura to Besakih by minibus or bemo (1500Rp). Ask the driver to take you to the temple entrance, not to the village of Besakih about 1km south of the temple complex. It may be quicker to get a connection in Rendang or Menanga. You may prefer to charter a vehicle, because public transport is not frequent and has all but ceased by 3 pm.

GUNUNG AGUNG

Gunung Agung is Bali's highest and most revered mountain, an imposing peak that can be seen from most of southern and eastern Bali, although it's often obscured by cloud and mist. Most books and maps give its height as 3142m, but some say it lost its top in the 1963 eruption and is now only 3014m. The summit is an oval crater, about 500m across, with its highest point on the western edge above Besakih.

Climbing

It's possible to climb Agung from various directions, but the two shortest and most popular routes are from the temple at Besakih, and up the southern flank from Selat or Muncan. The latter route goes to the lower edge of the crater rim, but you can't make your way from there around to the very highest point: you'll have great views south and east, but you won't be able to see central Bali. If you want to say you've been to the very top, or if you want the 360° view, climb from Besakih.

To have the best chance of seeing the view before the clouds gather, get to the top before 8 am; if you want to see the sunrise, you'll have to get to the summit by 6 am.

Start your climb well before dawn and plan it so that you'll be walking when there is some moonlight. Take a strong torch (flashlight) and plenty of water and food, waterproof clothing, a warm jumper and extra batteries – just in case.

You should take a guide for either route, although it's not strictly necessary. Before you start, or early in the climb, the guide will stop at a shrine to make an offering and say some prayers. This is a holy mountain and you should show respect. (Besides, you will want to have everything going for you.)

It's best to climb during the dry season (April to September); July, August and September are the most reliable months. At other times, the paths can be slippery and dangerous, and you probably won't see anything of the view. Climbing Agung is not permitted when major religious events are being held at Besakih (which generally occur in April). No guide will take you up at festival times, regardless of whether you are hoping to set off from Besakih, Selat or Muncan: there are horror stories about those who defied the ban and came to a sticky end on Agung.

From Selat or Muncan This route involves the least walking because there is a driveable road from Selat or Muncan to Pura Pasar Agung (Agung Market Temple), high on the southern slopes of the mountain. From the temple, you can climb to the top in as little as two hours, but allow at least three or four – it's a pretty demanding trek. You must report to the police station at Selat before you start out from either town, and again when you return. You should arrange a guide in Muncan or Selat – ask around the markets in either town, or contact the helpful guys at the police station in Selat. A guide will charge about 35,000Rp per person, including food – transport will cost extra.

You can stay the night near Muncan or Selat (see the following Rendang to Amlapura section), and drive up early in the morning, or drive up the day before and stay overnight at the temple. If so, a donation and some devotions are appropriate. Pura Pasar Agung has been greatly enlarged and improved, in part as a monument to the 1963 eruption that devastated this area.

The 1963 Eruption

The most disastrous volcanic eruption on Bali this century took place in 1963, when Gunung Agung blew its top in no uncertain manner at a time of considerable prophetic and political importance.

The culmination of Eka Desa Rudra, the greatest of all Balinese sacrifices and an event which only takes place every 100 years on the Balinese calendar, was to be on 8 March 1963. At the time of the eruption, it had been more than 100 Balinese years (115 years on the lunar calendar) since the last Eka Desa Rudra, but there was dispute among the priests as to the correct and most propitious date.

Naturally the temple at Besakih was a focal point for the festival, but Agung was already acting strangely as preparations were made in late February. The date of the ceremony was looking decidedly unpropitious, but Soekarno, then the president of Indonesia, had already scheduled an international conference of travel agents to witness the great occasion as a highlight of their visit to the country, and he would not allow it to be postponed. By the time the sacrifices began, the mountain was glowing, belching smoke and ash, and rumbling ominously, but Gunung Agung contained itself until the travel agents had flown home.

On 17 March Agung exploded. The catastrophic eruption killed more than 1000 people (some estimate 2000) and destroyed entire villages – 100,000 people lost their homes. Streams of lava and hot volcanic mud poured right down to the sea at several places, completely covering roads and isolating the eastern end of Bali for some time. The entire island was covered in ash and crops were wiped out everywhere.

Torrential rainfall followed the eruptions, and compounded the damage as boiling hot ash and boulders were swept down the mountain side, wreaking havoc on many villages, including Subagan, just outside Amlapura, and Selat, further along the road towards Rendang. The whole of Bali suffered a drastic food shortage, and many Balinese were resettled in western Bali and Sulawesi.

Although Besakih is high on the slopes of Agung, only about 6km from the crater, the temple suffered little damage from the eruption. Volcanic dust and gravel flattened timber and bamboo buildings around the temple complex, but the stone structures came through unscathed. The inhabitants of the village of Lebih, also high up on Agung's slopes, were all but wiped out. Most of the people killed at the time of the eruption were burnt and suffocated by searing clouds of hot gas that rushed down the volcano's slopes. Agung erupted again on 16 May, with serious loss of life, although not on the same scale as the March eruption.

The Balinese take signs and portents seriously – that such a terrible event should happen as they were making a most important sacrifice to the gods was not taken lightly. Soekarno's political demise two years later, following the failed Communist coup, could be seen as a consequence of his defiance of the volcanic deity's power. The interrupted series of sacrifices finally recommenced 16 years later in 1979.

Start climbing from the temple at around 3 or 4 am. There are numerous trails through the pine forest, which is why you need your guide, but after an hour or so you climb above the tree line. The ground is stony and the surface can be loose and broken towards the summit. Allow yourself plenty of time to get down again. From the temple you can walk down to Sebudi and catch a bemo. Alternatively, arrange for a chartered bemo to pick you up at the temple.

From Besakih This climb is tougher than the climb from the south. You must leave no later than 6.30 am if you want to get back down again before nightfall; it's best to leave at midnight if you want a clear view before the clouds close in. Allow five to six hours for the climb, and four to five hours for the descent. The starting point is Pura Pengubengan, north-east of the main temple complex, but it's easy to get lost on the lower trails, so hire a guide. The tourist information office near the car park at Besakih can arrange guides, but it charges around US$25 per person, which is way too much, so try to negotiate. Arrange a guide the day before, and stay in a losmen at or near Besakih so you can start early.

RENDANG TO AMLAPURA

A scenic road goes around the southern slopes of Gunung Agung from Rendang to near Amlapura. It runs through some superb countryside, descending more or less gradually as it goes further east. You can do it in either direction, but if you are travelling by bicycle, you are better off heading eastward.

Starting in the west, **Rendang** is an attractive town, easily reached by bemo from Semarapura or via a particularly pretty minor road from Bangli. About 4km along a winding road is the old-fashioned village of **Muncan**, the buildings in which have quaint shingle roofs. The road then passes through some of the most attractive rice country in Bali before reaching **Selat**, where you turn north to get to Pura Pasar Agung, a starting point for climbing Gunung Agung (see the previous section for details). You can stay at *Pondok Wisata Puri Agung*, on the road between Selat and Duda. It has clean and comfortable rooms for 40,000Rp.

Further on is **Duda**, where another scenic route branches south-west via Sidemen to Semarapura (see the Around Semarapura section earlier in this chapter). Further east, a side road (about 800m) leads to **Putung**, which has a car park, some souvenir stalls and *Pondok Hilltop Resort (☎ 0366-23039)*, where you can enjoy wonderful views down the southern slopes to the coast. The resort

charges US$20/25 for very ordinary singles/doubles, all in dire need of renovation. It is still worth coming for the views, and a meal (about 9000Rp to 15,000Rp) or an expensive drink.

This area is superb for **hiking**: there's an easy-to-follow track from Putung to **Manggis**, about 8km down the hill. Continuing east, **Sibetan** is famous for growing *salaks*, the delicious fruit with a curious 'snakeskin' covering that you can buy between December and April from stalls along the road. Nearby, a poorly signposted road leads north to Jungutan, with its **Tirta Telaga Tista**, a pleasant pool and garden complex built for the water-loving old rajah of Karangasem.

The scenic road finishes at Bebandem, where there's a **cattle market** every three days, with plenty of other stuff for sale as well. Bebandem and several nearby villages are home to members of the traditional metal workers caste, which includes silversmiths and blacksmiths.

In **Abian Soan**, the delightful *Homestay Lila* is a good place to base yourself while you hike around the area; you can arrange a guide at the homestay. Very basic rooms, in a friendly atmosphere, cost 10,000/15,000Rp. For more information about hiking in this area, see the Hiking Around Tirta Gangga section later in this chapter.

PADANGBAI
☎ 0363

Located on a perfect little bay, Padangbai is the port for ferries between Bali and Lombok, and passenger boats to Nusa Penida. It is also a popular place to break a journey and relax while you plan your assault on Bali or Lombok (depending on which way you're heading), and it's a better option than Candidasa.

Information
The tourist information booth is rarely open or staffed, but check it out if you need some information – you may be lucky. The moneychangers along the main streets and at the hotels offer very poor rates – check the rates at Bank Rakyat Indonesia (BRI) first.

Hiking

If you walk south-west from the ferry terminal and follow the trail up the hill, you'll eventually come to the idyllic **Pantai Kecil** (Little Beach) on the exposed coast outside the bay. Be very careful in the water, because there may be strong currents.

On a headland, at the north-eastern corner of the bay, a path uphill leads to three **temples**, including Pura Silayukti.

Diving

There's some pretty good diving on the coral reefs around Padangbai, but the water can be a little cold and visibility is not always ideal. Many of the operators based in Sanur, Kuta, Tulamben and along the north-east coast organise dives around Padangbai, but one local agency has started. Gecko Dive Centre on Jl Silayukti, will take you to the main sites, including Pura Jepun and the Blue Lagoon.

Places to Stay

Along the beach road, Jl Silayukti, *Hotel Puri Rai* (☎ 41385, fax 41386) has a collection of two-storey cottages looking rather like traditional rice barns. Considering the other choices it isn't great value: US$20 to US$30 for fan-cooled rooms; US$30 to US$40 with air-con. Next door, *Made's Homestay* (☎ 41441) is popular, and the English-speaking manager is a mine of information, but at 30,000/50,000Rp for singles/doubles, you can do better.

Kerti Beach Inn (☎ 41391) has basic rooms at the front for a bargain 10,000Rp, and double-storey thatched cottages for 20,000Rp. The popular *Padangbai Beach Homestay* (☎ 41517) is the only place with genuine, individual bungalows, but they could do with some renovation. They cost a reasonable 25,000Rp. At the end of the bay, *Topi Inn* (☎ 41424) is in a serene location.

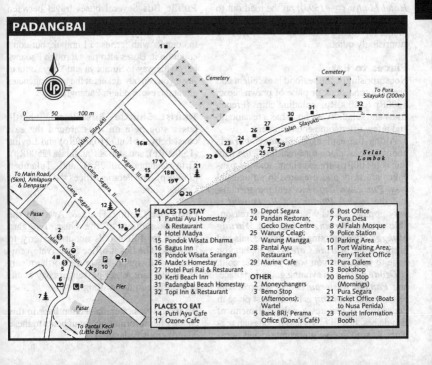

PADANGBAI

PLACES TO STAY	19 Depot Segara	6 Post Office
1 Pantai Ayu Homestay & Restaurant	24 Pandan Restoran; Gecko Dive Centre	7 Pura Desa
4 Hotel Madya	25 Warung Celagi; Warung Mangga	8 Al Falah Mosque
15 Pondok Wisata Dharma	28 Pantai Ayu Restaurant	9 Police Station
16 Bagus Inn	29 Marina Cafe	10 Parking Area
18 Pondok Wisata Serangan		11 Port Waiting Area; Ferry Ticket Office
26 Made's Homestay	**OTHER**	12 Pura Dalem
27 Hotel Puri Rai & Restaurant	2 Moneychangers	13 Bookshop
30 Kerti Beach Inn	3 Bemo Stop (Afternoons); Wartel	20 Bemo Stop (Mornings)
31 Padangbai Beach Homestay		21 Pura Segara
32 Topi Inn & Restaurant	5 Bank BRI; Perama Office (Dona's Café)	22 Ticket Office (Boats to Nusa Penida)
PLACES TO EAT		23 Tourist Information Booth
14 Putri Ayu Cafe		
17 Ozone Cafe		

Cemetery

Cemetery

To Pura Silayukti (200m)

Jalan Silayukti

Selat Lombok

To Main Road (5km), Amlapura & Denpasar

Gang Segara III

Gang Segara II

Gang Segara

Jalan Pelabuhan

Pasar

Pier

Pasar

To Pantai Kecil (Little Beach)

0   50   100 m

BALI

The bamboo building has small doubles upstairs for 15,000Rp, and some dorm beds for a very reasonable 3000Rp per person.

Away from the beach there are also several good alternatives. *Pantai Ayu Homestay* (☎ 41396) is very friendly and has great views (although the cemetery does spoil them somewhat). Singles cost 15,000Rp, and doubles cost 20,000Rp to 25,000Rp. In the village, there are three tiny places down an alley called Gang Segara III. *Pondok Wisata Dharma* (☎ 41394) is probably the best, with rooms for a negotiable 12,000/17,000Rp; rooms upstairs are slightly more expensive.

Pondok Wisata Serangan (☎ 41425) charges 40,000Rp for clean rooms upstairs, with a large balcony, but will soon be overshadowed by the unfinished, two storey *Pondok Wisata Kembar Inn* next door. The friendly *Bagus Inn* (☎ 41398) is simple but excellent value with rooms for 8000/ 12,000Rp, and the mosquito nets are a bonus. *Hotel Madya* (☎ 41393), on the road out to Amlapura, is clean and good value, with rooms for 15,000/20,000Rp – the rooms are surprisingly quiet.

Places to Eat

Not surprisingly, the seafood is excellent and cheap: a tuna steak or plate of prawns costs 4000Rp to 6000Rp, including chips (French fries) and salad. Every hotel has a restaurant, and a few offer some entertainment.

Along the esplanade, *Depot Segara* is about the best place for breakfast – the fruit juices (1500Rp) are excellent, and the pancakes are tasty and prepared in an unusual way. *Putri Ayu Cafe* has seafood specials, and the related *Pantai Ayu Restaurant* is very popular for its wide range and reasonable prices. *Warung Celagi* and *Warung Mangga* offer tempting seafood specials and pizzas, while *Marina Cafe* is cheap, but you have to specify if you want your beer cold.

Ozone Cafe is an evening gathering place, and *Pandan Restoran* is also relaxed. The restaurant at *Topi Inn* is the fanciest place in Padangbai. It features a colourful menu of fish dishes, health foods and Indonesian regulars, as well as live guitar music and occasional Balinese dancing. It's the perfect place for a late night dessert and coffee. The quaint restaurant on top of *Pantai Ayu Homestay* offers great food and views.

Entertainment

Hotel Puri Rai has the town's only video show.

Getting There & Away

Bemo Padangbai is 2km south of the main Semarapura to Amlapura road. For no particular reason, there are two bemo stops. The one used before noon is along the esplanade, while in the afternoon bemos congregate along the road out of town. Regular bemos go to Amlapura (1500Rp) via Candidasa (1000Rp), Semarapura (1500Rp) and occasionally on to Denpasar (1700Rp). Alternatively, walk along the shady road to the main road and hail down a passing bemo.

Public Bus Several buses travel between Denpasar (Batubulan terminal) and Padangbai (2200Rp) daily. These theoretically are timed to connect with ferries to Lombok, but don't count on it. Buses also pass through Padangbai on the way to Surabaya and Yogyakarta in Java; you can buy tickets at the travel agencies along the esplanade in Padangbai.

Tourist Shuttle Bus Perama shuttle buses stop here on trips around the east coast between Kuta (10,000Rp) and Lovina (15,000Rp), and stop at Candidasa (2500Rp), Tirta Gangga (5000Rp) and Tulamben (7500Rp). The Perama office (☎ 41419) is at Dona's Cafe.

Ferry See Getting There & Away in the Lombok section of the Nusa Tenggara chapter for full details about the ferry to Lombok. The ticket office for private vehicles is well signposted in the northern part of the car park; other passengers pay at another office in the waiting area.

Boat The Nusa Penida section later in this chapter has information about boats to these islands from Padangbai.

PADANGBAI TO CANDIDASA
Buitan (Balina)
☎ 0363

Balina is the name bestowed on the tourist development in the village of Buitan. The beach is pretty and quiet, but beach lovers may be disappointed with the black sand and rocks. To find the turn-off, look for the small yellow sign 'Balina' from the main road.

Places to Stay & Eat From the street to Buitan, it's easy to follow the signs to the various accommodation options. *Balina Beach Resort* (☎ 41002, fax 41001) has a variety of rooms, including some very attractive cottages. The pretty gardens and pool face a reasonably good bit of beach, but it's no longer good value: doubles cost from US$66 to US$85. Opposite, *Puri Buitan* (☎ 41021) has modern, motel-style singles/doubles from US$30/35 to US$65/75, but it often offers substantial discounts.

If you walk east along the beach (access is not so easy from the main road), you'll find two pleasant, budget places. *Matahari Beach Bungalows* (☎ 41008) offers charming, secluded bungalows for 35,000Rp, or 75,000Rp with air-con and hot water. *Pondok Purina* (☎ 41029) is another pleasant collection of bungalows costing US$7/10/15 for singles/doubles/triples.

You will probably end up eating at your hotel or another hotel, but the main street through Buitan does have a couple of decent, tourist-oriented *warungs*.

Sengkidu & Mendira
☎ 0366

Mendira also has a few hotels and losmen. Purists may be disappointed with the black sand, which all but disappears at high tide, but it's a pretty area and a quieter alternative to Padangbai or Candidasa.

The friendly little *Homestay Dewi Utama* (☎ 41053) offers basic accommodation, but the price can't be beaten: 12,000Rp per room, including bathroom and breakfast. Just a little further up the road, *Pondok Wisata Pisang* (☎ 41065) has simple bungalows that cost 15,000/ 25,000Rp for singles/doubles. *Amarta Beach Inn Bungalows* (☎ 41230) has a gorgeous location and friendly atmosphere, and is excellent value with rooms for 25,000/ 30,000Rp, including breakfast. *Anom Beach Inn Bungalows* (☎ 41902, fax 41998) is a bit fancier, and has a pool. It offers a huge range of rooms and bungalows from US$25/31. The 'superior bungalow' is US$49/61.

There are a couple of cheap *warungs* in the main street, such as the one belonging to Homestay Dewi Utama, but you'll probably end up eating at your hotel, or another one nearby. Exquisite seafood awaits you.

TENGANAN

Tenganan is occupied by Bali Aga people, descendants of the original Balinese who inhabited Bali prior to the Majapahit arrival. The village is surrounded by a wall, and consists basically of two rows of identical houses stretching up the gentle slope of the hill. The Bali Aga are reputed to be exceptionally conservative and resistant to change but even here the modern age has not been totally held at bay – a small forest of TV aerials sprouts from those oh-so-traditional houses. The most striking feature of Tenganan, however, is its exceptional neatness, the hills providing a beautiful backdrop.

A peculiar, old-fashioned version of the gamelan known as the *gamelan selunding* is still played here, and girls dance an equally ancient dance known as the Rejang. There are other Bali Aga villages nearby, including **Asak**, where another ancient instrument, the *gamelan gambang*, is still played.

Getting There & Away

Tenganan is at the end of a road 4km uphill from a turn-off just west of Candidasa. At the turn-off, a posse of *ojeks* (motorcycles taking paying pillion passenger) offers rides to the village for about 1500Rp; otherwise you can wait for an infrequent bemo at the turn-off. The best idea is to take an ojek or bemo up there, and enjoy the gentle walk back downhill to the main road.

BALI

CANDIDASA
☎ 0363

Until the 1970s, Candidasa was a just a quiet little fishing village, then beachside losmen and restaurants sprang up and suddenly it was *the* new beach place in Bali. Now it's shoulder to shoulder tourist development, and many find it overbuilt and unattractive. The main drawback is the lack of a beach, which, except for the far eastern stretch, has eroded away as fast as the new hotels have been erected. Most of the coastline has breakwaters, so you can't even walk along any of the coastline.

Despite this, some visitors enjoy Candidasa, especially the eastern part – it's less hectic than the Kuta region and is a good base to explore eastern Bali. The budget and midrange accommodation is surprisingly good value, and it's also popular with divers (scuba and snorkelling), although beach-lovers will prefer Padangbai, Mendira or Buitan.

Information

Just about everything in Candidasa is along the main Gianyar to Amlapura road. Candidasa boasts a tourist office that was open, but never staffed, each time we visited – you may have better luck. Easily found along the main road are bookshops, postal agencies and wartels. The rates offered by the many moneychangers along the main road are not particularly attractive; Bank Danamon usually has a better rate.

Diving & Snorkelling

Gili Tepekong, which has a series of coral heads at the top of a sheer drop-off, is perhaps the best diving site. Three reputable agencies arrange dives all over eastern Bali. Costs are fairly high, but discounts are certainly possible. Baruna has a kiosk (☎ 41185), and an office (☎ 41217) in the Puri Bagus Candidasa Hotel. Calypso Bali Dive (☎ 41126, fax 41537) is based inside the Candidasa Beach Bungalows II; and Stingray Diver Services (☎ 41063) is in the Puri Bali Bungalows. A few hotels and shops along the main road rent snorkel gear. With the sheltered breakwaters, it's safe to snorkel, even for children, although tragically there is not much coral near the shore to admire.

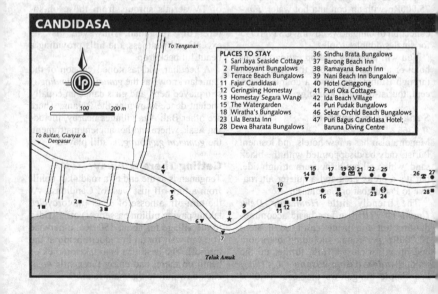

CANDIDASA

To Tenganan

0   100   200 m

To Buitan, Gianyar & Denpasar

PLACES TO STAY
1   Sari Jaya Seaside Cottage
2   Flamboyant Bungalows
3   Terrace Beach Bungalows
11 Fajar Candidasa
12 Geringsing Homestay
13 Homestay Segara Wangi
15 The Watergarden
18 Wiratha's Bungalows
23 Lila Berata Inn
28 Dewa Bharata Bungalows
36 Sindhu Brata Bungalows
37 Barong Beach Inn
38 Ramayana Beach Inn
39 Nani Beach Inn Bungalow
40 Hotel Genggong
41 Puri Oka Cottages
42 Ida Beach Village
44 Puri Pudak Bungalows
46 Sekar Orchid Beach Bungalows
47 Puri Bagus Candidasa Hotel;
    Baruna Diving Centre

Teluk Amuk

Places to Stay

Easily the best place to base yourself is the original fishing village hidden in the palm trees east of the lagoon: it's far quieter than the rest of Candidasa and there is a beach, but the lack of transport in the area means a short walk to most restaurants and public transport. Most places in the budget range include breakfast in their prices.

Places to Stay – Budget

There are three reasonable places to check out on the western side of town, but this is far from the centre of Candidasa and the beach. *Sari Jaya Seaside Cottage* (☎ 41212) charges 20,000Rp for decent individual bungalows; *Flamboyant Bungalows* (☎ 4127) is reasonable, charging 12,500/15,000Rp for singles/doubles; and *Terrace Beach Bungalows* (☎ 41232) is the nicest of the bunch and charges 15,000/20,000Rp for its rooms.

Geringsing Homestay (☎ 41084) has attractive cottages in a quiet garden from 10,000/12,000Rp – excellent value. Next door, *Homestay Segara Wangi* (☎ 41159) has rooms for 15,000Rp; the rooms closer to the shore are better. Continuing east, the inexpensive rooms at *Wiratha's Bungalows* (☎ 41973) are also good value at 15,000/30,000Rp.

In the centre of town, the popular *Lila Berata Inn* (☎ 41081) is a no-frills place charging 8000/10,000Rp for its rooms; don't stay here if you are put off by traffic noise, squat toilets or chickens in the garden. Immediately east of the lagoon is a good place to check out a few alternatives: *Sindhu Brata Bungalow* (☎ 41825) has rooms and bungalows for 36,000/45,000Rp; and *Pandawa Bungalows* (☎ 41925) has a quaint corridor of rooms for 20,000/25,000Rp.

In the eastern part of Candidasa there are several good options. *Barong Beach Inn* (☎ 41137) is quiet and laid back, and has rooms from 20,000/30,000Rp, depending on the view. *Ramayana Beach Inn* has rooms for a negotiable 15,000/25,000Rp and is very quiet, with great views from the tiny garden. *Nani Beach Inn Bungalow* (☎ 41829) has quaint, spotless rooms with something that could be described as a 'beach' in front of them for 40,000/50,000Rp. *Hotel Genggong*

BALI

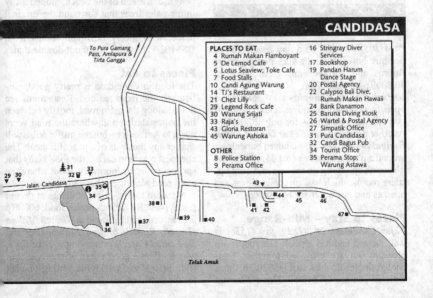

CANDIDASA

To Pura Gamang
Pass, Amlapura &
Tirta Gangga

PLACES TO EAT
4 Rumah Makan Flamboyant
5 De Lemod Cafe
6 Lotus Seaview; Toke Cafe
7 Food Stalls
10 Candi Agung Warung
14 TJ's Restaurant
21 Chez Lilly
29 Legend Rock Cafe
30 Warung Srijati
33 Raja's
43 Gloria Restoran
45 Warung Ashoka

OTHER
8 Police Station
9 Perama Office

16 Stringray Diver
   Services
17 Bookshop
19 Pandan Harum
   Dance Stage
20 Postal Agency
22 Calypso Bali Dive;
   Rumah Makan Hawaii
24 Bank Danamon
25 Baruna Diving Kiosk
26 Wartel & Postal Agency
27 Simpatik Office
31 Pura Candidasa
32 Candi Bagus Pub
34 Tourist Office
35 Perama Stop;
   Warung Astawa

Jalan Candidasa

Teluk Amuk

Um, What Happened to the Beach?

The answer lies a few hundred metres offshore where the Candidasa reef used to be. To help with the construction of new hotels in Candidasa, the reef was dug up, ground down and burnt to make lime for cement. Without the protection of the reef, the sea soon washed the beach away.

Mining of the coral reef stopped completely in 1991, but the erosion continues, even a dozen kilometres along the coast. A series of large and intrusive T-shaped piers have been built, ironically constructed out of concrete blocks. Sand has started to rebuild itself against these piers, providing some nice, sheltered bathing places if the tide is right – but it's not the palm-fringed beach it was just 25 years ago.

Concrete seawalls protect the foreshore from further erosion, but even these are being destroyed in places by the sea. At least it has been a lesson in the fragility of coastal environments, which has not been lost on other beach resorts.

(☎ 41105) actually has a tiny beach (full of perahus, however) and a very pretty garden. Rooms and cottages are great value at 30,000Rp to 40,000Rp.

Puri Pudak Bungalows (☎ 41978) is open to negotiation and excellent value if you can get a bungalow for only 20,000Rp. Another great option is *Sekar Orchid Beach Bungalows* (☎ 41977). Standard bungalows around a pleasant garden cost 35,000Rp, but it's worth splurging on the one and only upstairs room, which has gorgeous views, sea breezes and hot water for 65,000Rp.

Places to Stay – Mid-Range

Fajar Candidasa (☎ 41539, fax 41538) is well located and has a pool. The rooms are pleasant but are crowded together. Fan-cooled singles/doubles cost US$30/36; those with air-con are US$48/60. *Dewa Bharata*

Bungalows (☎ 41090, fax 41091) has a pool, bar and restaurant, and is good value with rooms for US$23/28, including breakfast.

The more pleasant eastern end of Candidasa has *Puri Oka Cottages* (☎ 41092, fax 41093), with nice rooms and a small beach and pool. Prices are normally US$36/40 but can be negotiated down.

The nicest place in Candidasa is *Ida Beach Village* (☎/fax 41096), which has six tastefully decorated bungalows in a huge garden, with scattered palm trees. At only 35,000Rp to 45,000Rp per room, including breakfast, this place is very popular, so bookings are essential.

Places to Stay – Top End

The Watergarden (☎ 41540, email watergarden@denpasar.wasantara.net.id) is delightfully different, with a swimming pool and fish-filled ponds that wind around the buildings and through the lovely garden. The rooms are tasteful, and cost from US$85/96, or double that for a two-bedroom suite.

Puri Bagus Candidasa Hotel (☎ 41131, email pbcandi@denpasar.wasantara.net.id) is right at the end of the beach, hidden away in the palm trees that surround the original fishing village. It's a handsome beachfront place, with nicely designed rooms from US$102/115; villas are about double that.

Places to Eat

The food in Candidasa is pretty good, particularly the fresh seafood. Restaurants are dotted along the main road, mostly between the police station and where the road veers north to Amlapura – but the traffic noise will shatter any thoughts of a peaceful meal. The cheapest places to eat are the *food stalls* that spring up nightly, normally about where the main road almost crashes into the sea.

Standard tourist-oriented dishes at decent prices (4000Rp for Indonesian food; 6000Rp for seafood) can be found at *Rumah Makan Hawaii*, *Rumah Makan Flamboyant* and *De Lemod Cafe*. Worth trying is *Toke Cafe*, which offers a good range of meals at sensible prices, and an idyllic setting (except for the traffic noise). *Warung Astawa* offers seafood specials for 6500Rp, and continues to get rave reviews from readers who appreciate the music, service and food. *Warung Srijati* promises 'the best Balinese food in town'. For only about 4000Rp a dish, it's worth a visit to find out if you agree with this assessment.

More expensive is *Lotus Seaview*, which is part of the Bali-wide chain of upmarket tourist restaurants and has a wonderful outlook. *TJ's Restaurant* is related to the popular TJ's in Kuta, but the food is not as Mexican or as good. At *Raja's*, the seafood is average, so it's best to stick with what it knows best: pizzas for about 12,500Rp.

If you're based in eastern Candidasa, you'll have to walk to the main road for meals, eat at a nearby hotel or try one of two decent places: the classy *Warung Ashoka* or *Gloria Restoran*.

Entertainment

Barong, Topeng and Legong dances take place at 9 pm on Tuesday and Friday at the *Pandan Harum dance stage* in the centre of Candidasa. Tickets cost 6000Rp. Some restaurants, such as *Candi Agung Warung*, and a number of places where the main road turns north, offer free Legong dances most nights. Notice boards around town advertise current performances.

Some restaurants, like *Raja's* and *Chez Lilly*, show video movies most evenings; these are advertised outside, or on notice boards along the main road. *Legend Rock Cafe* has live music and dancing some nights, but less often in the low season when Candidasa is very quiet. Sports fans will want to visit *Candi Bagus Pub* for live satellite telecasts of their favourite sports, or to play pool.

Getting There & Away

Candidasa is on the main road between Amlapura and Denpasar, so plenty of bemos and buses hurtle along the main road and stop in Candidasa. There is no bus or bemo terminal, so hail down public transport anywhere along the main road.

Most visitors prefer the more comfortable and direct tourist shuttle buses that travel between Kuta (about 10,000Rp) and Lovina (about 15,000Rp) and stop anywhere in between. Check around because prices do vary considerably. Perama has an office (☎ 41114) at the western end of the strip, but has a pick-up/drop-off point near the lagoon; and Simpatik (☎ 41262) is next to the Candi Loka restaurant. It is easier to book a ticket at just about any hotel, restaurant or shop.

You can also rent cars and motorcycles from agencies along the main road.

AMLAPURA
☎ 0363

Amlapura is the main town and transport junction in eastern Bali, and the capital of the Karangasem district. It is not worth staying here overnight, especially considering the lack of accommodation, but it's worth a detour from nearby Tirta Gangga or a visit while driving along the main road skirting eastern Bali.

Information

Amlapura has a confusing array of one-way streets. The friendly staff at the tourist office (☎ 21196) will be more than surprised if a tourist wanders in for information, but they will be more than happy to help; and there's a police station. BRI and Bank Danamon will change money.

Puri Agung Karangasem

Amlapura's three palaces along Jl Teuku Umar are decaying reminders of Karangasem's period as a kingdom in the late 19th and early 20th centuries. Only the Puri Agung Karangasem has been restored and is open to visitors, but you can wander around the other two.

Outside Puri Agung Karangasem, there's an impressive three tiered entry gate and beautiful sculptured panels. After you pass through the entry courtyard a left turn takes you to the Bale London, so called because of the British royal crest on the furniture. The main building is known as Maskerdam, after Amsterdam in the Netherlands, because it was the Karangasem kingdom's acquiescence to Dutch rule that allowed it to hang on

BALI

long after the demise of the other Balinese kingdoms. On the other side is the Bale Kambang, surrounded by a pond. The ornately decorated Bale Pemandesan, in between Maskerdam and the pond, was used for royal tooth-filing and cremation ceremonies.

Puri Agung Karangasem is open daily from 8 am to 6 pm, and admission is 2000Rp. Ask for an explanation sheet at the entrance, which tells you all you need to know (in English). You don't need a sarong, because it's more a museum than a place of worship.

Places to Stay & Eat

There is very little reason to stay here, especially considering the far better options in Tirta Gangga, only 6km away. *Homestay Lahar Mas (☎ 21345, Jl Diponegoro)* in the south-western part of town is basic and noisy, but clean enough, with singles/doubles for 13,500/15,000Rp.

There's the usual collection of *warungs* around the main bus/bemo terminal, plus the *Sumbar Rasa (Jl Teuku Umar)* restaurant in town, and *Rumah Makan Lumayan* next to the Lahar Mas. Amlapura tends to shut down early, so don't leave your evening meal until too late.

Getting There & Away

Amlapura is the major transport hub in eastern Bali. Buses and bemos regularly ply the main road to Batubulan terminal (2500Rp) in Denpasar, via Candidasa, Padangbai and Semarapura. Plenty of buses also go around the north coast to Singaraja (about 2500Rp), via Tirta Gangga, Amed and Tulamben, but these leave from the special terminal in the south-west of town.

TAMAN UJUNG

About 5km south of Amlapura, Taman Ujung is an extensive, picturesque and crumbling ruin of a once-grand water palace complex. The last king of Karangasem completed this grand palace in 1921, but it has been deteriorating for some time and was extensively damaged by an earthquake in 1979. You can wander around the remnants of the main pool or admire the **views** from the pavilion higher up the hill. Regular bemos leave from the main terminal in Amlapura.

TIRTA GANGGA
☎ 0363

The tiny village of Tirta Gangga (Water of the Ganges) is an increasingly popular place to stop off and relax for a day (or more) while touring around eastern Bali. It is quiet (if you stay away from the main road), there's a good selection of cheap restaurants and hotels, excellent trekking in the region (see the following Hiking Around Tirta Gangga entry) and a pretty palace to admire. Almost everything is within a few hundred metres along the main road from the palace.

Taman Tirta Gangga

Amlapura's water-loving rajah, after completing his masterpiece at Ujung, later had another go at Tirta Gangga. It isn't grand, but it's still a place of beauty and a reminder of the former power of the Balinese rajahs. The palace has a **swimming pool**, as well as ornamental ponds. It never closes, but the ticket office is only open between 7 am and 6 pm, daily. Tickets cost 1100Rp; it's an extra 4000Rp to swim in the nice, clean 'pool A'.

Places to Stay

Opposite the water palace, *Hotel Rijasa (☎ 21873)* is a small and simple place where extremely neat and clean bungalows cost 15,000/20,000Rp for singles/doubles; a little more for hot water. Actually within the palace compound, *Tirta Ayu Homestay (☎ 22697)* has individual bungalows for 30,000/40,000Rp, and more spacious ones for 60,000/70,000Rp. This is worth a splurge for the superb setting, and you can use the swimming pools for free.

Right by the palace, the peaceful *Dhangin Taman Inn (☎ 22059)* is a relaxed place. The cheaper rooms are fairly ordinary and a bit claustrophobic, but cheap at 10,000/15,000Rp; the larger rooms have some character for 25,000/30,000Rp. Every room is different, so look around.

Just up the road from the palace, on the left, a driveway leads to *Puri Sawah Bungalows*

(☎ 21847, fax 21939), which has a handful of comfortable rooms with great views. The standard rooms cost 65,000Rp; the larger two-room bungalows with hot water for 120,000Rp are ideal for families.

About 200m further up the hill, some very steep steps on the left lead to *Kusuma Jaya Inn* (☎ 21250). It boasts wonderful views, and rooms for a negotiable 15,000Rp for singles, and 20,000Rp to 30,000Rp for doubles. The staff are friendly, and some readers have raved about the food. Finally, another 600m further up, *Prima Bamboo* (☎ 21316) also offers outstanding views (and easier steps), but it's close to the main road and noisy. The rooms are reasonably pleasant, however, for 20,000/25,000Rp.

Places to Eat
About a dozen *warungs* cluster around the entrance to the water palace, and serve usual fare at cheap prices. The best of the bunch are the unassuming *Warung Rawa*, on the main road, and *Tirtagangga Cafe*, near the entrance to the palace, which serves good pizzas (about 12,000Rp) and ice-cold beer. The restaurants in the *Pura Sawah Bungalows* and *Tirta Ayu Homestay* are worth a splurge for great views and ambience. One reader claimed that *Good Karma* served 'the best food in Indonesia'. This place and *Genta Bali* are the trendiest places to hear western music and meet other travellers.

Entertainment
Hotel Rijasa often holds traditional Balinese dances on Sunday night for 5000Rp.

Getting There & Away
Regular bemos and minibuses travelling between Amlapura and Singaraja stop at Tirta Gangga, right outside the water palace, or any hotel further north. The fare to Amlapura should be 500Rp, but beware of blatant overcharging.

Perama tourist shuttle buses pass through once or twice a day in either direction to Lovina (12,500Rp) and Kuta (12,500Rp). Several shops in Tirta Gangga sell tickets – look for the notice boards.

HIKING AROUND TIRTA GANGGA
The rice terraces around Tirta Gangga are some of the most beautiful in Bali. They sweep out from Tirta Gangga, almost like a sea surrounding an island. A few kilometres beyond, on the road to the east coast, there are more dramatically beautiful terraces, often seen in photographs of Bali. From Tirta Gangga, or Abian Soan (see the Rendang to Amlapura section earlier in this chapter), tiny paths take you to many picturesque traditional villages. Some of the more interesting places to hike to are Pura Lempuyang (768m), one of Bali's nine directional temples (five hours return from Ngis); Bukit Kusambi, a small hill with a big view (a short hike from Abian Soan); and Budakeling village, home to several Buddhist communities (about six hours return from Tirta Gangga).

Most villages are connected by obvious roads or paths, but to ensure a warm welcome in the smaller villages, and to find your way there from Tirta Gangga, you may want a guide. You can arrange this at your hotel at Tirta Gangga, or contact Nyoman Budiasa, who operates the only trekking agency (☎ 0363-22436) in Tirta Gangga, based at the Genta Bali warung. Another good place to arrange hikes is Homestay Lila in Abian Soan.

THE NORTH-EAST COAST
The north-east coast from Amed to Selang is starting to attract a number of visitors, who come for the secluded seaside accommodation and excellent, accessible diving and snorkelling. The down side is that public transport is infrequent, facilities are limited, the beach is often black and rocky, and there are no telephones on the coast that you can use to book accommodation or diving directly.

Diving & Snorkelling
The best diving spots are Jemeluk, with coral reefs only minutes away by boat, Tulamben (see the following section), the shipwreck near Lipah, and the coral gardens and fish at Selang. By chartering a local boat, you can also dive around the

BALI

three tiny islands east of Selang. The main operators along the coast are Mega Dive (email, in Denpasar, megadive@dps.mega .net.id), based at Amed Beach Cottage; Arni Dive Centre, at Hotel Indra Udhyana; and Eco-dive, at Jemeluk, which is cheaper than most operators in eastern Bali.

Snorkelling is excellent at several places along the coast, and nowhere better than at Jemeluk where you can admire stunning coral only 10m from the beach. Almost every hotel rents snorkelling equipment for about 10,000Rp per day.

Places to Stay & Eat

About 1km east of Amed, **Pondok Kebun Wayan** offers small but charming rooms for 15,000Rp, with outside toilet, or 30,000Rp if you want a bathroom, mosquito net and fan. About 500m further on, **Divers Cafe** has a delightful restaurant on the beach, and two bungalows for 30,000Rp. The village of Jemeluk is another 500m on. Here, **Eco-dive** has some simple bungalows. They are overpriced at 28,000Rp, but this is a wonderful area for snorkelling.

Less than 1km further east is **Amed Beach Cottage**, on a small, rocky beach. This tranquil place charges a reasonable 20,000/ 30,000Rp for spacious, if a little airless, singles/doubles. Another 100m further along, **Kusumajaya Indah Bungalows** has more character and a prettier garden than others in this range. Its rooms cost 35,000/ 45,000Rp. It's another 1.5km to Bunutan, from where public transport to the south-east is hard to find.

About 800m past Bunutan, the very classy and very expensive **Hotel Indra Udhyana** (bookings: ☎ 0370-26336, fax 36797) has grabbed the best location along the coast. The 33 luxurious cottages, with all the mod cons, cost US$120 to about US$350. In Lipah, which has some white sand (but not much), there are several **warungs** and more hotels: **Wawa-Wewe Bar**, **Restaurant & Bungalows** and **Tiyung Petung Cafe Homestay**, both of which charge 30,000Rp per room. The latter has a lovely **cafe**, and often features live music.

Nearby, **Hidden Paradise Cottages** (bookings: ☎ 0361-431273, fax 423820) has cottages around a picturesque pool, but it can't compete with other places for value: US$35/46 for rooms with fan/air-con. Also in Lipah, the popular **Pondok Vienna Beach** is probably the best in the mid-range. It is right on the beach and has charming rooms for 60,000Rp.

Finally, close to Selang, the most popular place along this coast is **Good Karma Bungalows**. Overlooking a black beach, Sulawesi-style bungalows are sprawled all over the place. They cost 30,000Rp to 60,000Rp for singles and 40,000Rp to 75,000Rp for doubles; 'homes' sleeping up to six people are 115,000Rp.

Getting There & Away

Plenty of minibuses and bemos run to Culik from Singaraja and Amlapura, sometimes with a detour to Amed. Tourist shuttle buses will also drop you off at Culik. About every hour in the morning, a bemo goes from Culik to the T-junction in the middle of Bunutan. Further south-east, you can continue on an ojek, or take an ojek all the way from Culik – they congregate at the turn-off to Amed. From Selang to Ujung, via Seraya village, public transport is very limited, and allow plenty of time to get around – it may even be quicker to walk.

TULAMBEN

Tulamben is becoming a popular stopover. The major attraction is the submerged wreck of the US cargo ship *Liberty* – probably the most popular dive site in Bali. Tulamben also offers clear water for swimming and snorkelling, and a few restaurants and places to stay, but the grey rocky beach is disappointing. There are no telephones in this area, so no hotel or diving agency can be contacted directly.

Diving & Snorkelling

The wreck of the *Liberty* is a few metres out from a parking area that has a change room, shop and the Puri Madhya Bungalows. You can swim straight out from here, and you'll see the stern rearing up from the depths. Many divers commute to Tulamben from Candidasa or Lovina, and it can get quite crowded between 11 am and 4 pm, with up to 50 divers around the wreck at a time. It's better to stay the night in or near Tulamben and get an early start. You will want at least two dives to really explore the site.

Every hotel has a diving centre attached, but not all of them are particularly reliable or cheap. The best are Mimpi Tulamben Dive Centre (bookings: ☎ 0361-701070, fax 701074), at the Mimpi Resort; PT Tulamben Segara Wisata, based at the Puri Madhya Bungalows and right at the jump-off point to the wreck; and PT Wisnu Dewa Segara, based at the new Bali Coral Bungalows and probably the best value, because it normally negotiates.

Most hotels and dive centres rent snorkelling gear for anything from 15,000Rp to US$5 per day.

Places to Stay & Eat

All *warungs* and hotels – all of which have *restaurants* – are situated along a 3km stretch of the main road.

The first hotel as you approach from Lovina, and the only one right by the wreck, is *Puri Madhya Bungalows*. It has a few small, clean rooms with sea views for 30,000Rp. If you use its dive centre for two or more dives, it will often provide free accommodation.

About 400m further south-east, *Bali Coral Bungalows* has a cluster of new and clean bungalows for 40,000Rp, with a fan and mosquito net, or US$15 if you want views and hot water. It's worth negotiating because right next door is *Gandu Mayu Bungalows*, which also has clean and comfortable rooms, but they're more spread out and cheaper: 15,000Rp to 25,000Rp per room. Both places have excellent restaurants, worth visiting if you're only coming for the day.

Another 500m east, there are three places in a row. *Paradise Palm Beach Bungalows (bookings: ☎ 0363-41052)*, also known as *Bali Sorga Cottages*, has a large number of neat and clean bungalows, with verandahs overlooking a pretty garden. They cost

Wreck of the *Liberty*

On 11 January 1942, the armed US cargo ship USAT *Liberty* was torpedoed by a Japanese submarine off the south-western coast of Lombok. It was then towed by two naval ships with the intention of beaching it on the coast of Bali, and retrieving its cargo of raw rubber and railway parts. When its condition looked perilous the crew were evacuated and the ship was successfully beached. The rapid spread of the war through Indonesia prevented the cargo from being salvaged, but everything which could be taken was stripped in the ensuing years.

The *Liberty* sat on the beach at Tulamben until 1963 when the violent eruption of Gunung Agung toppled it beneath the surface of the water. Or at least that's one version of the story. Another relates that it sank some distance offshore and the lava flow from the eruption extended the shoreline almost out to the sunken vessel.

Much of the ship remains intact, and is now a haven for diverse marine life that astounds biologists and divers alike.

30,000Rp to 35,000Rp (US$35 if you want hot water, air-con and the best views). *Matahari Bungalows*, also known as Puri Tulamben Bungalows, is the least appealing option, but cheap with rooms for 20,000Rp to 25,000Rp. The luxurious and very comfortable *Mimpi Resort (bookings: ☎ 0361-701070, fax 701074)* offers a range of upmarket singles/doubles for US$66/90, and charges up to US$180 for a seaside cottage.

Getting There & Away

Plenty of minibuses, buses and bemos travel between Amlapura and Singaraja and stop anywhere in Tulamben, though they tend to be less frequent after 2 pm. Perama tourist shuttle buses, with an office at the Gandu Mayu Bungalows, will drop you off anywhere along the main road on its daily trip in either direction between Kuta (15,000Rp) and Lovina (10,000Rp).

TULAMBEN TO YEH SANIH

The only place to stay along this stretch of road is *Alamanda* in Sambirenteng. It is a tasteful place on the beach with a fine coral reef just offshore. It boasts its own diving centre, a pretty pool and very attractive bungalows in a garden setting for US$45/50 for singles/doubles, and some cheaper rooms for US$30/36. The beachfront *restaurant* is an excellent place to stop for lunch.

Les is home to a lovely **waterfall**, reputedly one of Bali's highest. Bemos or minibuses may make the 1.5km detour south of the main road to Les; if not, walk or look for an ojek at the turn-off. To get to the waterfalls, follow the main road for 500m from the right of the market place, temple and public baths in Les, and then continue along the obvious path that virtually hugs the stream for another 2.5km.

The next main town is Tejakula, famous for its **horse bath**. Although it was actually built as a place to wash horses, it's now the town's public bathing place, and has quite graceful but somewhat run-down rows of white arches. Apart from this, it's a quaint village, with some finely carved **kulkul towers**.

Nusa Penida Region

Nusa Penida, an administrative region within the Semarapura district, comprises three islands – Nusa Penida itself, the smaller Nusa Lembongan to the north-west and tiny Nusa Ceningan between them. Nusa Lembongan is a wonderful place, where surfers and non-surfers alike can get away from the relative chaos of mainland Bali and enjoy its surf, seclusion and quiet beaches. The island of Nusa Penida has several villages, but is right off the tourist track and has few facilities for visitors, whereas Nusa Ceningan is very sparsely populated.

Economic resources are limited on the islands. It has been a poor region for many years and there has been some transmigration from here to other parts of Indonesia. Thin soils and a lack of fresh water make it impossible to cultivate rice, but other crops are grown. Maize, cassava and beans are staples here. The cultivation of sea grass *(rumput laut)* is the main crop on Lembongan.

Diving

There are great diving possibilities around the islands, but no dive operators. You will have to arrange a trip with a dive centre in Sanur, Candidasa or the Kuta region. Stick with the most reputable operators, because diving here is demanding. The water is cold and the currents difficult, so local knowledge is essential.

NUSA PENIDA

Clearly visible from anywhere along Bali's south-eastern coast, the island of Nusa Penida is a limestone plateau, and was once used as a place of banishment for criminals and other undesirables from the kingdom of Klungkung. The population is predominantly Hindu, although there are some Muslims (and a mosque) in Toyapakeh. The culture is distinct from that of Bali: the language is an old form of Balinese no longer heard on the mainland, and there are also local types of dance, architecture and craft, including a unique type of red ikat weaving.

Sampalan

There's nothing inspiring about Sampalan, the main town on Penida, but it's quiet and pleasant, with a market, schools and shops strung out along the curving coast road. The market area, from where the bemos congregate, is in the middle of town. Pelabuhan Buyuk, where the boats leave for Padangbai, is a few hundred metres west of the market.

Between the market and the harbour is a small side road, where the friendly *Losmen Made* charges about 15,000Rp for a small clean room. The government rest house, *Bungalow Pemda*, opposite the police station, a few hundred metres east of the market, also has rooms for 15,000Rp. There are a few simple *warungs* along the main road and around the market. *Kios Dewi*, east of the market, serves Padang-style food.

Toyapakeh

If you come by boat from Lembongan you'll probably be dropped at (or just off) the beach at Toyapakeh, a pretty town with lots of trees. The **beach** has clean white sand, clear blue water and Gunung Agung as a backdrop. Step up from the beach and you're at the roadhead, where bemos can take you to Sampalan. Few travellers stay here, but *Losmen Terang*, near the waterfront, has singles/doubles for 7500/10,000Rp.

Around the Island

A trip around the island, following the north and east coasts, and crossing the hilly interior, can be completed in a few hours by motorcycle.

About 6km south of Sampalan, steps go up on the right side of the road to the narrow entrance of **Goa Karangsari** caves. There are usually people who will provide a pressure lantern and guide you through the cave for about 5000Rp. The limestone cave extends over 200m through the hill and emerges on the other side to overlook a verdant valley.

Continue south past several charming **temples** to Suana. Here the main road swings inland and climbs up into the hills, while a very rough side track goes south-east, past more interesting temples to **Semaya**, a fishing village with a sheltered **beach** and one of Bali's best **dive sites** offshore.

A scenic ridge-top road goes north-west from Tanglad. At Batukandik, a rough road leads to a spectacular *air terjun* (waterfall). Sheer limestone cliffs drop hundreds of metres into the sea, with offshore rock pinnacles surrounded by crashing surf. At the base of these cliffs, underground streams discharge fresh water into the sea. You can go down the cliff face on an exposed metal stairway. Back on the main road, continue to Batumadeg, past Bukit Mundi (the highest point on the island at 529m) and through Sakti which has traditional stone buildings. Return to the north coast at Toyapakeh.

The important temple of **Pura Dalem Penetaran Ped** is near the beach at Ped, a few kilometres east of Toyapakeh. It houses a shrine to the demon Jero Gede Macaling, the source of power for practitioners of black magic. From there, the road is straight and flat back to Sampalan.

Getting There & Away

The shuttle boat between Sanur and Nusa Lembongan (see the following section) is the best way to the islands, but you can go to Nusa Penida directly from Padangbai on a public boat. At Padangbai, the boats leave at about 8 am from the beach, just northeast of the car park for the Bali to Lombok ferry. The ticket office is not signposted. On Penida, the boats land at Pelabuhan Buyuk, just west of Sampalan.

Slower perahus carry goods and occasional passengers between Sampalan and Kusamba, the closest port to Semarapura, the district capital. The boats leave when they're full, weather and waves permitting, and cost about 3000Rp one way. This is only for the adventurous.

Some public boats travel between Sampalan or Toyapakeh and Jungutbatu on Nusa Lembongan. They tend to travel in both directions between 5 and 6 am. You can charter a whole boat between the two islands for around 25,000/50,000Rp one-way/return, but bargain hard.

Getting Around

Bemos regularly travel along the sealed road between Toyapakeh and Sampalan, and sometimes on to Suana and up to Klumpu, but beyond these areas the roads are rough or nonexistent and transport is very limited. You may be able to rent a motorcycle or negotiate an ojek, but they're expensive.

NUSA LEMBONGAN

The most developed island for tourism is Nusa Lembongan. Most visitors come for the surf that breaks on the reefs, or the quiet beach, but it's still a great place to relax even if you're not into swimming, surfing or diving. The island has a range of good budget accommodation, most with its own patch of glorious beach.

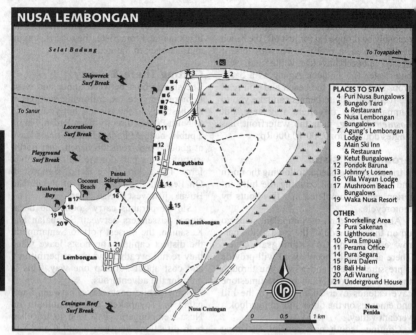

NUSA LEMBONGAN

Selat Badung

To Toyapakeh

Shipwreck
Surf Break

To Sanur

Lacerations
Surf Break

Playground
Surf Break

Mushroom
Bay

Coconut
Beach

Pantai
Selegimpak

Jungutbatu

Nusa Lembongan

Lembongan

Ceningan Reef
Surf Break

Nusa Ceningan

Nusa
Penida

0   0.5   1 km

PLACES TO STAY
4 Puri Nusa Bungalows
5 Bungalo Tarci & Restaurant
6 Nusa Lembongan Bungalows
7 Agung's Lembongan Lodge
8 Main Ski Inn & Restaurant
9 Ketut Bungalows
12 Pondok Baruna
13 Johnny's Losmen
16 Villa Wayan Lodge
17 Mushroom Beach Bungalows
19 Waka Nusa Resort

OTHER
1 Snorkelling Area
2 Pura Sakenan
3 Lighthouse
10 Pura Empuaji
11 Perama Office
14 Pura Segara
15 Pura Dalem
18 Bali Hai
20 Adi Warung
21 Underground House

Information

There are very limited facilities on the island. For information about diving trips and other happenings, check out the notice board at the Main Ski Inn, or ask around your hotel. There's a doctor on the island who specialises in coral cuts and surfing injuries – he can be contacted through your hotel. Electricity is available from 5 pm to 7 am (from noon on Sunday), and only the upmarket places will have generators. Don't expect to change any money on the island.

Lembongan Village

About 4km south-west along the sealed road from Jungutbatu is Lembongan village. Leaving Jungutbatu you pass the Balinese-style **Pura Segara** temple with an enormous banyan tree outside; then a steep climb up a knoll offers a wonderful view back over the beach. It's possible to con-

tinue right around the island, following the rough track that eventually comes back to Jungutbatu, but the roads are steep for cyclists and walkers. As you enter Lembongan, you may want to ask directions to the bizarre **Underground House**, a labyrinthine dwelling with many meandering passages.

Surfing

The best time to surf is in the dry season (April to September), when the winds come from the south-east. There are three main breaks on the reef, all aptly named: **Shipwreck** is a right-hand reef break named for the remains of a wreck that is clearly visible from the shore; **Lacerations** is a fast hollow right that breaks over shallow coral; and **Playground** is an undemanding left-hander. Most surfers (and snorkellers) stay at, or hang around, the Main Ski, Agung Lembongan and Puri Nusa hotels.

Snorkelling

There's good snorkelling on the reef, especially off the north of the island, and some spots are accessible from the beach. To reach other snorkelling spots you need to charter a boat, which costs about 15,000Rp per hour per boat. Also ask around the hotels – particularly the Puri Nusa and Main Ski – about organised trips. A half day/one day trip will cost about 20,000/30,000Rp per person. Snorkelling gear can be rented at the Puri Nusa and Main Ski hotels, or from locals who hang around nearby.

Cruises

Some visitors come for the day, seeking sun, surf and diving, and then return to Sanur, Nusa Dua or the Kuta region in the evening. There are a number of cruise operators, offering cruises ranging from US$35 to US$86 per person. Most leave from Pelabuhan Benoa in Bali and sail to a beach on, or a large pontoon just off, Nusa Lembongan, where you can enjoy a substantial buffet lunch and water activities. Cruises can be booked through any travel agency in southern Bali.

Places to Stay

Most of the accommodation is along a beach on the north-west coast, so that's where many visitors go. Prices are negotiable and do vary, depending on the season and how long you want to stay. Peak season is around Christmas and from July to August. There are no telephones on the island, but some places have offices in Bali that can be contacted by radio from the island, so you can book ahead.

Jungutbatu In the village, about 30m up a laneway, *Johnny's Losmen* is a classic Indonesian losmen, first opened 17 years ago. It's basic but quite OK, and very good value at 3000/6000Rp for singles/doubles. The obvious, light-green *Pondok Baruna* has friendly staff, and a few spotless rooms for 20,000/25,000Rp. It doesn't have a lot of character, but it's quieter than the party-oriented places to the north.

North-West Coast *Main Ski Inn & Restaurant* (☎ 0361-289213) is very popular with surfers and all budget travellers. Bungalows cost 20,000Rp to 50,000Rp, depending on the season and whether you want an upstairs room with views and breezes.

Agung's Lembongan Lodge (☎ 0361-422266) has cheap doubles from 20,000Rp, and bungalows for 40,000Rp. The bungalows are a little close together, denying much privacy, but it's a friendly and popular place. *Nusa Lembongan Bungalows* is a hotch-potch of unexciting bungalows for about 30,000Rp, but some readers have commented favourably about friendly staff. *Bungalo Tarci* has rooms for 25,000Rp, and two-storey bungalows for 40,000Rp – but prices will be higher in the peak season. One place not overrun with surfers and divers is the friendly, family-run *Ketut Bungalows*, with clean and quiet rooms from 25,000Rp to 40,000Rp.

At the far northern end of the beach, *Puri Nusa Bungalows* (☎/fax 0361-298613) is more upmarket, but very popular with surfers and divers, especially those from Japan. Smart rooms in a solid, two storey block cost 25,000Rp at the back to 50,000Rp at the front.

Mushroom Bay The only cheap place is *Mushroom Beach Bungalows*, a collection of charming Balinese-style bungalows with a five star setting, overlooking a gorgeous beach. Prices range from a very reasonable US$10 to US$15, including breakfast. The very classy thatched bungalows at *Waka Nusa Resort* (☎/fax 0361-261130) cost about US$157 a night, plus meals.

Pantai Selegimpak A little more realistic in price is *Villa Wayan Lodge* (☎ 0361-724545) on Pantai Selegimpak. Rooms cost US$21 to US$28 a night. The food is excellent, and the management can arrange snorkelling trips and transport to/from Bali.

Places to Eat

Every hotel, except Johnny's Losmen, has a *restaurant*. The two storey restaurant at

BALI

Main Ski Inn, right on the beach, serves tasty, reasonably priced western and Indonesian food. It has stupendous views, and often features movies on the island's only video machine. The restaurant at *Bungalo Tarci* has a great cook.

At Mushroom Bay, you can eat at your hotel, and there are also a couple of warungs along the main street, such as *Adi Warung*.

Getting There & Away

There is no jetty on Nusa Lembongan – boats land at Jungutbatu (and sometimes Mushroom Bay) and you have to jump off into the shallow water. The strait between Bali and Lembongan is very deep and huge swells can develop during the day. You may get wet with spray, so be prepared.

Most boats from Kusamba or Padangbai go to Toyapakeh on Nusa Penida, but sometimes they also go to Jungutbatu. Ask the boatmen around the beach near Johnny's Losmen and Pondok Baruna on Lembongan for details.

A public boat leaves daily at about 8 am from the northern end of Sanur Beach, in front of the Ananda Hotel. The fixed 'tourist price' to Jungutbatu is 15,000Rp. The trip takes about 1½ hours – more if conditions are unfavourable. Perama has at least one shuttle bus/boat trip daily, with good connections to all tourist centres in Bali. The company normally uses its own boat rather than the public one (but double-check this with Perama). The Perama boat also leaves from in front of the Ananda Hotel in Sanur, and lands in front of the Perama office (well, hut) at Jungutbatu.

Getting Around

There is a main road as far as the hills and mangroves will allow, stretching from Pura Sakenan in the north to the bridge to Nusa Ceningan. You can walk around the island in about three hours, which is just as well because finding a motorcycle to rent is not easy. A bicycle is a better option, although still not cheap: 5000Rp per hour from Ketut Bungalows, or about 15,000Rp per day from one of the villagers who may approach you. And be warned: the hills can be steep.

NUSA CENINGAN

A narrow suspension bridge crosses the lagoon between Nusa Lembongan and Nusa Ceningan, so it's quite easy to explore its network of tracks on foot or a rented motorcycle or bicycle – not that there's much to see. There's also a fishing village and several small agricultural plots. The island is quite hilly and you'll get glimpses of great scenery as you go around the rough tracks.

West Bali

Most of the places regularly visited in west Bali, like Sangeh or Tanah Lot, are easy day trips from Denpasar, Ubud or the Kuta region. The rest of the west tends to be a region travellers zip through on their way to or from Java, but it does offer a few secluded places to stay, the West Bali National Park (Taman Nasional Bali Barat) and long stretches of wide black-sand beach and rolling surf. Countless tracks run south of the main road, usually to fishing villages which rarely see a tourist despite being so close to a main transport route.

TANAH LOT
☎ 0361

The spectacularly located Tanah Lot is possibly the best known, and most photographed temple, in Bali. The tourist crowds here are phenomenal, especially at sunset, and the commercial hype is appalling, but the temple, perched on a little rocky islet, looks superb – whether delicately lit by the dawn light, or starkly outlined at sunset.

For the Balinese, Tanah Lot is one of the important and venerated sea temples, but it's a well-organised tourist trap. Around the car park (parking costs 350Rp), dozens of souvenir shops are on a sort of sideshow alley, which you can easily bypass. Follow the crowds past the entrance (tickets cost 1100Rp) and down to the sea. You can walk over to the temple itself at low tide, or climb up to the left and sit at one of the many tables along the cliff top. Order an expensive drink, or a more expensive dinner, get your camera ready – and wait for 'The Sunset'.

Places to Stay & Eat

Losmen Puri Lukisan, directly opposite the entrance to the car park, charges 20,000/25,000Rp for simple singles/doubles. Better is *Pondok Wisata Astiti Graha* (☎ 812955), about 800m before the car park. Decent rooms away from the main road cost 45,000Rp.

Dewi Sinta Restaurant & Villa (☎ 812 933, fax 813956) is on souvenir shop alley, not far from the ticket office. Rooms are clean, but unexciting, and cost US$14/19; US$28/36 with air-con. Just inside the entrance, the slightly better *Mutiara Tanah Lot* (☎ 812939) charges 175,000Rp per double.

One of the most controversial hotels in Bali is *Le Meridien Nirwana Golf Spa & Resort* (☎ 815900, fax 815901), which continues to have a detrimental effect on the local environment and community. It offers an 18 hole golf course, three swimming pools and everything else imaginable. Rooms cost US$250 to US$1080.

There are oodles of *warungs* around the car park, and expensive *restaurants* inside the grounds. *Dewi Sinta* has an elegant restaurant, with set menus from 16,000Rp to 20,000Rp, and Legong dances on Saturday and Thursday nights.

Getting There & Away

Bemos leave regularly for Tanah Lot from Kediri (600Rp), which has good connections to Denpasar's Ubung terminal (850Rp). Bemos have usually stopped running by nightfall, so if you stay for the sunset, you may need to stay nearby, charter a vehicle or walk back to Kediri. Tanah Lot is the main attraction of the many *very* popular organised tours, which often include other sites such Bedugul, Mengwi and Sangeh.

MENGWI
☎ 0361

The huge state temple of **Pura Taman Ayun**, surrounded by a wide, elegant moat, was the main temple of the Mengwi kingdom, which survived until 1891, when it was conquered by the neighbouring kingdoms of Tabanan and Badung. The large and spacious temple was originally built in 1634, and extensively renovated in 1937. It is a lovely place to wander around, especially before the tour buses arrive.

Across the moat from the temple is a rather lost-looking **Mandala Wisata Arts Centre**. There's also a small **museum**, featuring unspectacular and uninformative dioramas of Balinese festivals. *Sari Royal Garden Restaurant*, overlooking the moat, is not too expensive considering the charming view. The complex is open daily from 8 am to 6 pm, and admission is 1000Rp.

Any bemo between Denpasar (Ubung terminal) and Bedugul or Singaraja can drop you off at a roundabout in Mengwi, where signs indicate the road (250m) to the temple. Pura Taman Ayun is a stopoff on many organised tours from Ubud and southern Bali.

MARGA

Marga is an attractive area of traditional family compounds. North-west of the village, **Margana memorial** commemorates the battle of Marga. On 20 November 1946, a force of 96 independence fighters was surrounded by a much larger and better-armed Dutch force fighting to regain Bali as a colony after the departure of the Japanese. The outcome was similar to the puputan of 40 years before. There was, however, one important difference: this time the Dutch suffered heavy casualties too, and this may have helped weaken their resolve to hang on to the rebellious colony.

Also on the site is a small **museum**, with a few photos, home-made weapons and other artefacts from the conflict. The whole complex is open daily from 9 am to 5 pm, and tickets cost 1000Rp. Get off any bemo between Denpasar and Bedugul or Singaraja, about 6km north of Mengwi, and walk westward about 2km through Marga. Even with your own transport, it's easy to get lost, so ask directions.

BALI

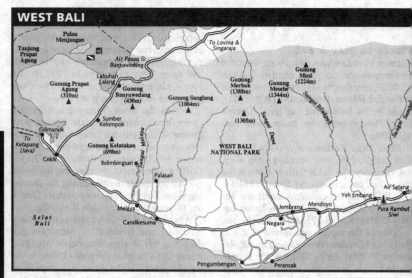

WEST BALI

SANGEH

About 20km north of Denpasar, near the village of Sangeh, stands the **monkey forest** of Bukit Sari. It is featured, so the Balinese say, in the *Ramayana*. There's a unique grove of nutmeg trees in the monkey forest and a temple, **Pura Bukit Sari**, with an interesting old Garuda statue.

Take care: the monkeys will jump all over you if you've got a pocketful of peanuts and don't dispense them fast enough. The Sangeh monkeys have also been known to steal hats, sunglasses and even thongs from fleeing tourists. This place is touristy, but the forest is cool, green and shady, and the monkeys are cute as well as cheeky. The souvenir sellers are restricted to certain areas and are easy to avoid.

The monkey forest area is open daily from 7.30 am to 6.30 pm, and tickets cost 1100Rp. You can reach Sangeh on any bemo from Denpasar's Wangaya terminal. There is also road access from Mengwi and Ubud, but no public transport. Most people visit on an organised tour.

TABANAN
☎ 0361

Tabanan is the capital of the district of the same name. It's a large, well organised place with shops, a hospital, a police station (☎ 91210) and a market, but little specifically for tourists, such as decent accommodation

Things to See & Do

The **Gedung Marya arts complex** was named after a famous dancer Mario, and is the venue for an arts fair every June. You can also visit the limited ruins of the ancient **Puri Tabanan** royal palace. **Subak Museum** has displays on the irrigation and cultivation of rice, and the intricate social systems that govern it. The museum is up a steep road on the left just before you come into town from the east – look for the sign 'Mandala Mathika Subak'. It's officially open daily from 8 am to 7 pm, but hours are somewhat erratic.

Places to Stay & Eat

Hotel Taruna Jaya (☎ 812478), about 1km south of the hospital, was closed at the time of research. The only alternative, the very

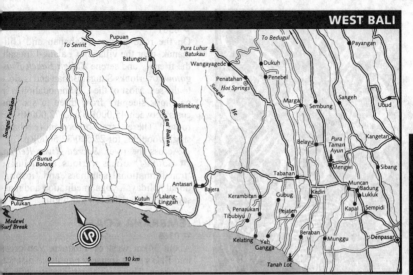

WEST BALI

BALI

dreary *Hotel Sederhana* a further 50m south, charges 30,000Rp for an airless cubicle. There are plenty of *warungs* along the main road through town.

Getting There & Away

All bemos and buses between Denpasar and Gilimanuk stop at the main terminal at the western end of Tabanan. The bemo terminal in the town centre has transport to the main terminal and nearby villages.

SOUTH OF TABANAN
☎ 0361

In **Kediri** is the Pasar Hewan, one of Bali's busiest **cattle markets**. The town is also the terminal for bemos to Tanah Lot (see that section earlier in this chapter). About 10km south of Tabanan is **Pejaten**, a centre for the production of **traditional pottery**, including elaborate, ornamental roof tiles. A little west of Tabanan, a road goes south via Gubug to the secluded coast at **Yeh Gangga**, where *Yeh Gangga Beach Bungalows (bookings: ☎ 261354)* provide stylish accommodation for about US$40 a double.

The next road turns down to the coast through **Kerambitan**, a village noted for its beautiful old buildings, including two 17th-century **palaces**; a tradition of wayang-style painting; and its own styles of music and dance, particularly *tektekan* (a ceremonial procession).

A small road leads about 4km from southern Kerambitan to **Tibubiyu**, where you'll find *Bee Bees Bungalows & Restaurant*, an isolated, tranquil and tasteful place, with two-storey thatched bungalows for about 40,000/50,000Rp for singles/doubles. It's surrounded by rice fields, the beach is close and it serves good meals.

NORTH OF TABANAN
☎ 0361

Another monkey forest, **Alas Kedaton**, is a stopoff on many organised tours from Ubud and southern Bali. It is open daily from 7.30 am to 6.30 pm, and admission is 1100Rp, including a guide. In the village of Wanasari, **Taman Kupu Kupu Bali** (☎ 814282) features thousands of pretty, indigenous butterflies in a huge, enclosed area.

JENNY BOWMAN

Pejaten, south of Tabanan, is noted for its traditional ceramics, including terracotta tiles.

The northern road then reaches a fork: take a left to **Pura Luhur Batukau** (see the Central Mountains section later in this chapter), via the **hot springs** at Penatahan. There are several pools where you can soak, and you can stay at *Yeh Panes* (☎ 262356), where well-finished singles/doubles cost US$144/178.

The road to the right continues to Penebel, and then to **Dukuh**, where *Taman Sari Bungalow & Coffee House* (☎ 812898) has rooms for US$10. It's a friendly and secluded place, and an ideal base for exploring the area if you have your own vehicle.

LALANG-LINGGAH
☎ 0361

On the road between Tabanan and Gilimanuk, near the village of Lalang-Linggah, the friendly and serene *Balian Beach Bungalows* overlooks Sungai Balian and is close to the sea. Most of the accommodation is in pavilions sleeping from three to six, and costs between 45,000Rp and 72,000Rp per room. There are other more basic singles/doubles for 22,500/32,5000Rp.

Across the river, *Sacred River Retreat* (☎ 730904) offers various all-inclusive 'transformational seminars' and 'inspirational holidays', yoga, meditation and massage for about US$250 per night.

JEMBRANA COAST
☎ 0365

About 34km west of Tabanan, you cross into Bali's most sparsely populated district, Jembrana. There are some interesting back roads to the north coast, but the main road follows the southern coast most of the way to Negara, the district capital.

Medewi

Along the main road, a large sign points down the paved road (200m) to Pantai Medewi. The beach is black and rocky, but Medewi is noted for its *long* left-hand wave. It works best at mid to high tide on a 2m swell – get there early before the wind picks up.

Medewi Beach Cottages (☎ 40029, fax 41555) dominates the beach. It's a pleasant place to relax awhile, and the pool is an added attraction. Standard singles/doubles for US$17/23, and a cheaper restaurant, are located on one side of the road; the more expensive rooms, from US$46/52, and a classier restaurant, are on the other. Traditional dancing is held during evening meals on Sunday.

The unsignposted *Homestay Gede*, about 50m west of the Cottages, has a few very basic rooms for 10,000Rp, with a shared bathroom, but they are almost permanently full of surfers.

A few hundred metres west of the turn-off to Medewi, *Tinjaya Bungalows* has pleasant rooms in two-storey grass-and-bamboo cottages (25,000/30,000Rp downstairs/upstairs), and some small rooms inside for 20,000Rp.

Pura Rambut Siwi
Picturesquely situated on a cliff top overlooking a long, wide stretch of beach, this superb temple is one of the important coastal temples in southern Bali. The effusive caretaker rents sarongs, and provides a rapid-fire commentary about the temple in passable English for which he wants a 'donation'. The temple is at the end of a 300m paved road, and is not particularly well signposted – look for the turn-off at the predictable cluster of *warungs* along the main road. Any of the regular bemos and buses between Denpasar and Gilimanuk will stop at the turn-off.

NEGARA
☎ 0365
Negara is a friendly, prosperous little town, and not a bad place to break up a journey. Most banks change money, but you're more likely to be successful at BNI. The town is most famous for the bull races nearby (see the following Around Negara section).

Places to Stay & Eat
The central *Hotel Ana (☎ 41063, Jl Ngurah Rai)* is the cheapest place in town: singles/doubles without a bathroom cost 7000/9000Rp; with a bathroom they cost 9000/11,000Rp.

There are many cheap options on the noisy Denpasar to Gilimanuk road, Jl Sudirman, which bypasses the town centre; the quietest and friendliest is *Hotel Ijogading*, which charges 10,000/15,000Rp for its rooms.

The best place in town is *Hotel Wira Pada (☎ 41161, Jl Ngurah Rai)*. The grounds are spacious and it has off-street parking. Pleasant, quiet rooms cost 20,000/25,000Rp with a fan and 35,000/40,000Rp with air-con.

The restaurant at the Wira Pada serves good food, although it's a little pricey. *Rumah Makan Puas*, 200m further east, offers decent Padang-style food, and there are many *warungs* in the market area. Hardy's Supermarket, just west of the Wira

Pada, has a small *eatery*, *CFC* fried chicken stall and a cheap roof-top *bar*.

Getting There & Away
Negara is a stopoff for every type of bemo, bus and minibus travelling between Gilimanuk and the Ubung terminal (2500Rp) in Denpasar.

AROUND NEGARA
☎ 0365
Perancak
This is the site of Nirartha's arrival in Bali in 1546, commemorated by a small temple, **Pura Gede Perancak**. **Taman Wisata Perancak (☎ 42173)** is a tourist spot where **bull races** and Balinese buffets are sometimes staged for organised tours from southern Bali. If you're travelling independently, give the park a ring before you go out there. In Perancak, ignore the depressing little zoo, and go for a walk along the picturesque **fishing harbour**.

Jembrana
Once capital of the region, Jembrana is the centre of the *gamelan jegog* (a gamelan using huge bamboo instruments that produce a very low-pitched, resonant sound). Performances often feature a number of gamelan groups engaging in musical contest. To see and hear them in action, time your arrival with a local festival, or ask in Negara where you might find a group practising.

Belimbingsari & Palasari
Christian evangelism in Bali was discouraged by the Dutch administration, but sporadic missionary activity resulted in a number of converts, many of whom were rejected by their own communities. There was little room for them in Denpasar, so in 1939 they were encouraged to resettle in these two Christian communities.

Belimbingsari was established as a Protestant community, and now has the largest Protestant church in Bali. Palasari is the Catholic community, and its cathedral is also large and impressive, and shows Balinese touches.

The network of back roads and tracks to the villages is confusing and poorly mapped and signposted, so be prepared to get lost and ask for directions. Otherwise, get a bemo or bus to drop you near one of the turn-offs, where you can arrange an ojek.

WEST BALI NATIONAL PARK

Taman Nasional Bali Barat covers 19,003 hectares of the western tip of Bali. In addition, 50,000 hectares are protected in the national park extension, as are nearly 7000 hectares of coral reef and coastal waters.

At the **park headquarters** (☎ 0365-40060), right at the junction in Cekik, you can organise guides for local trekking and check out the relief map of the park. The headquarters is open daily from 7 am to 4 pm. There is also a small **visitors' centre** (no telephone) at Labuhan Lalang, which is the starting point for trips to Pulau Menjangan (see the Pulau Menjangan entry later in this section).

The main roads to/from Gilimanuk go through the national park, but you don't have to pay an entrance fee just to drive through. If you want to visit Pulau Menjangan or trek in the park, however, you must buy a ticket at Labuhan Lalang. Tickets cost 2000Rp per person per day.

Flora & Fauna

Most of the natural vegetation in the park is not tropical rainforest, which requires rain all year, but coastal savanna, with deciduous trees that become bare in the dry season. The southern slopes have more regular rainfall, and hence more tropical vegetation, while the coastal lowlands have extensive mangroves. Over 200 species of plants can be found around the park.

Local fauna includes black monkeys, leaf monkeys and macaques (seen in the afternoon along the main road near Sumber Kelompok); and barking, sambar, mouse, Java and muncak deer. You may also see squirrels, wild pigs, buffaloes, iguanas, pythons and green snakes. The bird life is prolific, with many of Bali's 300 species represented, including the very rare Bali starling.

Trekking

A few day hikes are possible in the park, but all trekkers must be accompanied by an authorised guide. It's best to arrive the day before you want to trek, and make inquiries at the park headquarters at Cekik, the visitors' centre at Labuhan Lalang or any hotel in Gilimanuk, or along the coast east of Gilimanuk. A guide may miraculously appear at your hotel within minutes of your arrival, anyway – but make sure he is authorised.

The cost of hiring a guide is negotiable, but expect to pay about 10,000Rp per hour per group (of up to four), plus transport and food. Early morning is the best time to start – it's cooler and you're more likely to see wildlife.

Following are some of the more popular treks: walk around the mangroves in Teluk Terima, then partially follow the Sungai Terima into the hills and back down to the road along the steps at Makam Jayaprana (two to three hours); walk from Kelatakan to Ambyasari via the microwave tower on Gunung Kelatakan (four hours); and between about June and September (when the sensitive Bali starlings move further inland), trek around some of the Prapat Agung peninsula.

Pulau Menjangan

This uninhabited island boasts what is believed to be Bali's oldest temple, **Pura Gili Kencana**, dating back to the Mahajapit period in Java. You can walk around the island in an hour or so, but the attractions are mainly underwater. The **diving** is excellent: there is great visibility and superb unspoiled coral. Snorkellers can find some decent spots not far from the jetty on the island. Diving trips to the island can be arranged with most dive operators throughout Bali, but it's more accessible from the dive centres at Pemuteran, Pulaki or Lovina.

The jetty for boats to Menjangan is at Labuhan Lalang, where there are several *warungs*. Local boat owners have a strict arrangement: it costs 60,000Rp for a four hour trip to the island (and 5000Rp for every subsequent hour) in a boat holding 10 people, or five scuba divers with equipment. No negotiation is possible. You can rent snorkelling gear at Lalang (10,000Rp for four hours).

Makam Jayaprana

A short walk up some stone stairs from the southern side of the road, a little west of Labuhan Lalang, will bring you to the grave of Jayaprana, the foster son of a 17th century king. There are fine **views** to the north at the top.

Places to Stay

There is nowhere to stay within the national park. The closest hotels are in Gilimanuk and along the north-west coast (see the North-West Coast entry later in this section).

Getting There & Away

Refer to the following Gilimanuk section below for details about public transport.

GILIMANUK
☎ 0365

Gilimanuk is the terminus for ferries that shuttle back and forth across the narrow strait to Java. There is a bank offering horrendously low rates, a post office, wartels and an uninformative tourist office underneath the unmistakably hideous stone *thing* stretching across the road. There are also masses of voracious mosquitos, so take precautions.

Places to Stay & Eat

Most places are on Jl Raya, the busy main road between Cekik and the terminal/port. If you have a tent, you can *camp* in the grounds of the park headquarters at Cekik for free. The grounds are not pristine, but the bathroom is clean enough.

Penginapan Nusantara II is closest to the ferry terminal, and has a view over the bay that is magic at sunrise. However, the rooms are dingy, airless and overpriced for 25,000Rp. The best place in the centre of town is *Sampurna Hotel* (☎ 61250), which charges 15,000Rp to 25,000Rp for a room with a fan, 55,000Rp for a room with air-con. If you have your own transport, *Lestari Homestay* is a good option. It has a range of

rooms from 12,000Rp for grotty doubles to 50,000Rp for plush, new bungalows.

There are *warungs* and *rumah makans* around the market and the ferry terminal (such as *Rumah Makan Murah Meriah*), but the best in Gilimanuk is *Rumah Makan Elmina*, near the bemo terminal.

Getting There & Away

Buses frequently hurtle along the road between the main terminal in Gilimanuk and Ubung terminal (3900Rp) in Denpasar, and along the north coast to Singaraja (2700Rp). Cheaper minibuses and bemos leave from outside the market in Gilimanuk, but they're very crowded and will stop at every place along the way.

Refer to the general Getting There & Away section at the beginning of this chapter for information about the ferry between Gilimanuk and Ketapang in Java.

NORTH-WEST COAST
☎ 0362

The road from Gilimanuk to Lovina is sparsely populated, but a few resorts and dive centres take advantage of the secluded beaches and coral reefs.

Pemuteran

There are three local dive operators in Pemuteran: Yos Diving Centre at Pondok Sari; Arkipelago at Taman Sari; and Reef Seen Aquatics (☎/fax 92339, email reefseen@ denpasar.wasantara.net.id). All rent snorkelling gear.

Reef Seen also organises sunset and sunrise cruises, glass-bottom boat trips and horse riding.

The spacious *Taman Sari Hotel* (bookings: ☎ 0361-288096, fax 286297) faces its own pretty beach. Gorgeous bungalows in the dramatic foothills start at US$40, but 20% discounts are possible in the low season. Next door, *Pondok Sari* (☎ 92337) also has an attractive setting overlooking this beach, and has a similar set-up for a very similar price. Not far away, *Taman Selini Beach Bungalows* (☎/fax 93449) costs US$57, but it's not as nice as the other two options.

Pulaki

Pura Pulaki is a coastal temple that was completely rebuilt in the early 1980s and is home to a large troop of monkeys. A few hundred metres east of the temple, a well-signposted paved road (3km) leads to **Pura Melanting**, set dramatically in the foothills and gloriously devoid of tourists and hawkers.

The elegant *Matahari Beach Resort (☎ 92312, fax 92313)* has beautifully finished bungalows in attractive gardens, with a big pool and direct beach frontage. Singles/doubles cost from US$165/192 and go much higher. It's also the base for David's Dive Sport, and offers tennis, windsurfing and mountain-biking.

Central Mountains

Most of Bali's mountains are volcanoes; some are dormant, but some are definitely active. The mountains divide the gentle sweep of fertile rice land to the south from the narrower strip to the north. North-west of Gunung Agung is the stark and spectacular caldera that contains the volcanic cone of Gunung Batur (1717m), the lake of Danau Batur and numerous smaller craters. In central Bali, around Bedugul, is another complex of volcanic craters and lakes, with much lusher vegetation. A string of smaller mountains stretches off to the sparsely inhabited western region.

The popular round trip to the north coast crosses the mountains on one route (eg via Gunung Batur) and returns on the other (from Singaraja, via Bedugul), thus covering the most interesting parts of the central mountain region. You can do the circuit easily in either direction, but getting to more remote areas by public transport is a little tricky, though not impossible.

GUNUNG BATUR
☎ 0366

Most day-trippers come on organised tours and stop at the crater rim at Penelokan for views and lunch; most overnight visitors stay in the villages around the lake.

Information

Tourist Office The tourist information office, or Yayasa Bintang Danu (☎ 23370), at Penelokan has some limited information about local transport fares and trekking routes. It is open daily from 9 am to 3 pm. The ticket offices at Kubupenelokan, Penelokan and Toya Bungkah also act as quasi-tourist offices.

Entry Tickets If you arrive by private vehicle from the south (but not from Singaraja), you will be stopped at ticket offices at Penelokan or Kubupenelokan. Tickets, valid for one visit to anywhere along the road between Penelokan and Penulisan, cost 1100Rp, plus more for a car (1000Rp), motorcycle (200Rp), camera (1000Rp) and video (2500Rp). If you then travel to Toya Bungkah, you have to pay the same amount *again* – valid for one visit to the village. Keep the tickets if you drive back and forth around the crater rim, or you may have to pay again.

Money You can change money at BRI in Kintamani; at Hotel Segara in Kedisan; Jero Wijaya travel agency and another money-changer in Toya Bungkah; and Lakeview Hotel and several nearby stalls in Penelokan.

Dangers & Annoyances Gunung Batur has a well-deserved reputation as a money-grubbing place where visitors (mainly around Penelokan) are hassled by hawkers as persistent as they are in the Kuta region, and by plenty of wannabe guides (mainly around the lake area). It is not uncommon for tourists to pay US$60 *each* for a four hour trip up the volcano. This is more than a school teacher makes in a month, so it's not surprising that guides are prepared to spend days or weeks trying to catch just one group of gullible trekkers.

Guides will usually provide breakfast on the summit, and this often includes the novelty of cooking eggs or bananas in the steaming holes at the top of the volcano. Unfortunately, the practice has resulted in an accumulation of litter – egg shells, banana

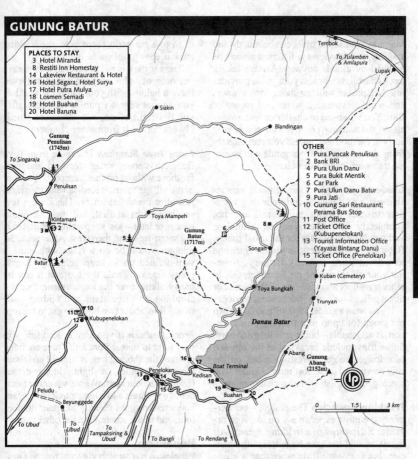

GUNUNG BATUR

PLACES TO STAY
3 Hotel Miranda
8 Restiti Inn Homestay
14 Lakeview Restaurant & Hotel
16 Hotel Segara; Hotel Surya
17 Hotel Putra Mulya
18 Losmen Semadi
19 Hotel Buahan
20 Hotel Baruna

OTHER
1 Pura Puncak Penulisan
2 Bank BRI
4 Pura Ulun Danu
5 Pura Bukit Mentik
6 Car Park
7 Pura Ulun Danu Batur
9 Pura Jati
10 Gunung Sari Restaurant; Perama Bus Stop
11 Post Office
12 Ticket Office (Kubupenelokan)
13 Tourist Information Office (Yayasa Bintang Danu)
15 Ticket Office (Penelokan)

peels, plastic bags etc – around the summit. Please take out your rubbish.

Also, keep an eye on your gear and don't leave valuables in your car, especially at any car park at the start of a volcano trail.

Organised Tours This area is a main attraction for many organised tours, which is why Penelokan is chock-a-block with expensive restaurants and hawkers. You can easily book day tours from any travel agency in Ubud or southern and northern Bali.

Climbing Gunung Batur

Soaring up in the centre of the huge outer crater is the cone of Gunung Batur (1717m) and a cluster of smaller cones. You can take one route up and another one down, then get a bemo back to your starting point. Start early (depending on which route you take), before mist and cloud obscure the view. Ideally, you should get to the top for sunrise (about 6 am) – it's a magnificent sight, although it can get crowded; throngs of about 100 on top are not uncommon in the high season.

You should think twice before taking a longer route in the wet season (October to March), because the trails can be muddy and slippery, and the views will almost always be blocked by clouds anyway. Always take a torch (flashlight), unless your guide provides one, hat, proper walking shoes, long trousers and jumper (sweater), water and plenty of film. You will need to charter or rent a vehicle to the starting point if you climb very early in the morning, unless you start directly from Toya Bungkah. Your guide will organise transport for an extra charge.

Guides If you have a strong torch, reasonable sense of direction and your own transport to the starting point, and it's not completely dark when you start climbing, you won't need a guide for the usual routes. But a guide is still useful if you can hire one for a decent price – not easy. Before you commit yourself to anyone on the street, talk to other travellers and visit one of the tourist or ticket offices for some independent advice.

If you want a guide, 15,000Rp to 20,000Rp per group (of up to four people), plus transport, is reasonable – but haggle long and hard. Some trips include breakfast at the top and take longer, more interesting routes on the way down, and these cost more. Guides who speak good English will also charge more.

Trekking Agencies The easiest – but certainly the most expensive – option is to organise a trip through a trekking agency. All hotels around the lake have trekking agencies, but many are little more than a guide in a room with a telephone.

Routes You can reach the summit from Batur village or Kintamani, but most travellers use one of three routes.

From the North-East The easiest route is from the north-east, where a track enables you to use private transport within about 45 minutes walk of the top. From Toya Bungkah, take the road north-east towards Songan and take the left fork after about 3.5km, just before Songan. Follow this small

road for another 1.7km to a well-signposted track on the left, which climbs another 1km or so to a car park. From here, the walking track is easy to follow to the top.

The car park is not secure, so don't leave anything of value in your car; don't even leave a helmet with your motorcycle. Also, you cannot rely on public transport after you finish the climb, but you could probably ask for a lift from other climbers.

From Toya Bungkah The route from Toya Bungkah is pretty straightforward, and ideal for those without private transport. Walk out of the village towards Kedisan and turn right just after the ticket office. There are a few separate paths at first, but they all rejoin sooner or later – just keep going uphill, tending south-west and then west. After about 30 minutes you'll be on a ridge with quite a well-defined track; keep going up. It gets pretty steep towards the top and it can be hard walking over the loose volcanic sand – climbing up three steps and sliding back two. Allow about two hours to get to the top.

From Kedisan If you stay at Kedisan, you may want to start at Pura Jati. There are three options: the shortest trek is straight up (about three hours return); a slightly longer detour (about four hours return) goes via crater number two or three; and a longer trek (five or six hours return) goes directly to crater number four, and to the summit via the other two.

Penelokan

Penelokan has superb **views** across to Gunung Batur and down to the lake at the bottom of the crater. It is basically a junction, with a large hotel, several restaurants and numerous pushy souvenir sellers. Don't be put off by the touts, hawkers and tourist buses if you plan to stay in a village around the lake.

Places to Stay & Eat *Lakeview Restaurant & Hotel* (☎/fax 51464) has firmly gone upmarket, and now charges US$36 for a 'superior' room, and US$48 for 'deluxe' rooms with the best views.

The road around the rim has a crowd of *restaurants* geared to bus-loads of tour groups. They all have fine views, and offer buffet-style lunches for 20,000Rp to 25,000Rp, plus 21% tax. À la carte alternatives are still very expensive. Dotted among the restaurants are *warungs* with similar views, and decent meals for about 5000Rp.

Batur & Kintamani

The village of Batur used to be down in the crater. A violent eruption in 1917 killed thousands of people and destroyed more than 60,000 homes and 2000 temples. The village was rebuilt, but Gunung Batur erupted again in 1926. This time the lava flow covered all but the loftiest temple shrine. The village was relocated up on the crater rim, and the surviving shrine was also moved up and placed in the temple, **Pura Ulun Danu**.

Places to Stay & Eat The only hotel, *Hotel Miranda*, is very basic but cheap at 10,000/20,000Rp for singles/doubles. It does provide good food, an open fire at night and the friendly, informative owner also acts as a guide (of course).

Penulisan

At a bend in the road, several steep flights of steps lead to Bali's highest temple, **Pura Puncak Penulisan**, at 1745m. The **views** from the temple are superb: facing north you can see over the rice terraces clear to the Singaraja coast. It costs 1000Rp to enter, and you can rent a sash and/or sarong from someone outside the entrance.

Kedisan

A hairpin-bend road winds its way down from Penelokan to Kedisan on the shore of the lake. The road is longer (about 4km) than it looks on the map, and very steep. There are a few places to stay in the immediate area, and it's more pleasant than Toya Bungkah.

Places to Stay & Eat Not actually in the village, but around the corner towards Toya Bungkah, are two good places. *Hotel Surya* (☎ 51378) has a number of clean, comfort-able rooms for 20,000Rp, or 30,000Rp with hot water. The staff are friendly, and the views from the restaurant are superb. The 'economy' rooms at *Hotel Segara* (☎ 51136) next door are the same price and standard, but the better rooms for 50,000Rp to 80,000Rp have extra attractions like satellite TV and hot water. Closer to the village, *Hotel Putra Mulya* has slightly nicer 'economy' rooms than the Surya or Segara for 20,000Rp. *Losmen Semadi* is the same price as the Putra Mulya, but not as clean.

All the hotels have *restaurants*, and include breakfast in their rates. Opposite the boat terminal in Kedisan, *Cafe Segara* is good for breakfast and lunch, but closes at 7 pm. Fish is obviously a speciality, and costs about 6500Rp.

Buahan

A little further around the lake (a pleasant 15 minute stroll from Kedisan) is Buahan, a friendly village with market gardens right down to the lake shore. *Hotel Baruna* (☎ 512 21) is the best place to stay: it's friendly and almost guaranteed 'guide-free'. Simple, clean singles/doubles cost 20,000/25,000Rp. *Hotel Buahan* (☎ 51217) is good value for 30,000Rp with hot water, and the rooms are new and clean, but views are obstructed by a brick wall.

Trunyan & Kuban

The village of Trunyan is squeezed tightly between the lake and the outer crater rim. This is a Bali Aga village, inhabited by descendants of the original Balinese, the people who predated the Majapahit arrival. Unlike the other well-known Bali Aga village, Tenganan (in eastern Bali), this is not an interesting or friendly place.

A little beyond Trunyan and accessible only by boat (there's no path) is the **village cemetery** at Kuban. The people of Trunyan do not cremate or bury their dead – they lie them out in bamboo cages to decompose, although strangely there is no stench.

The only way to reach Kuban, and the main way to Trunyan, is by chartered boat from Kedisan (see the Boat entry under

BALI

Getting Around later in this section). Sadly, both places (and the boat trip) are blatant tourist traps: touts and guides want large tips for a three minute, barely comprehensible explanation.

Toya Bungkah

The major village on the lake is Toya Bungkah, also known as Tirta, with its hot springs – *tirta* and *toya* both mean 'water'. Toya Bungkah is a scruffy little village, but despite this many travellers stay here so they can climb Gunung Batur early in the morning – then most get out as quickly as possible afterwards.

The hot springs bubble out in a couple of spots, and feed an unattractive **public bathing pool** before flowing out into the lake. The water is soothingly hot, ideal for aching muscles after a volcano climb, but if you use the *very* public baths, you may be stared at by locals and hassled by hawkers. Alternatively, you can pay through the nose at the new **Tirta Sanjiwani Hot Springs Complex**.

Places to Stay Many places offer similar prices and standards, and include breakfast. For about 15,000/20,000Rp for singles/doubles, the following options on the road from Kedisan are good value: *Hotel Dharma Putra* (☎ 51197), which has a mandi (ie no shower) and squat toilet; *Under the Volcano I* (☎ 51666), which has large, clean rooms around a small garden; and *Nyoman Pangus Bungalows* (☎ 51667). *Arlina's Bungalows* (☎ 51165) is clean, comfortable and friendly but now overpriced: standard rooms are 45,000Rp, while those with hot water are 60,000Rp.

The main attraction of *Bali Seni Toyabungkah Hotel* (☎ 51173) is the quiet location off the main road, and the fact that you may be the only guest. The rooms need some renovation, and cost 20,000/30,000Rp. Down the hill, *Pualam Homestay* is cheap, clean and its rooms cost a negotiable 10,000/15,000Rp. *Wisma Tirta Yastra* has the best location on the waterfront, but the rooms are very basic for 12,000Rp.

The path leading to the Lakeside Cottages is quiet, but most budget places here are not good value. Costing about 25,000Rp with cold water or 30,000Rp with hot water are rooms at *Under the Volcano II* (☎ 51666) and the motley bunch of poorly maintained rooms at *Awangga Bungalows*.

Lakeside Cottages (☎ 51249, fax 51250) is popular with package tours. Standard rooms cost US$8/10, while 'superior' rooms with hot water and satellite TV are US$20/25. Dominating the village, the incongruous *Hotel Puri Bening Hayato* (☎ 51234, fax 51248) has modern, comfortable rooms for US$54/66, or US$84/96 with everything, including the best views.

Places to Eat A few *warungs* huddle around the car park, and all the hotels have *restaurants*, mostly with similar menus and prices. *Amertha's Restaurant*, on the waterfront, has the best views, especially of the chaos at the public bathing pool in the late afternoon, but prices are a little high. *Arlina's Bungalows* has a popular restaurant, which offers large serves at reasonable prices. *Setana Boga Grill House*, near Wisma Tirta Yastra, has fish dishes for about 6000Rp.

Songan

The road continues from Toya Bungkah around the lake to Songan, a large and interesting village with some old buildings and market gardens that extend to the edge of the lake. At the end of the road is **Pura Ulun Danu Batur**. From the temple, you can climb to the top of the outer crater rim in about 20 minutes and see the north-east coast. It's an easy downhill stroll (about 6km) to the coastal road at Lupak.

The only place to stay in Songan is the small *Restiti Inn Homestay* on the left, past the centre of the village. A clean, simple room costs 15,000Rp.

Getting There & Away

Bemo From Batubulan terminal in Denpasar bemos regularly travel to Kintamani, via Ubud and Payangan, for 2500Rp. These bemos do not come through Penelokan, but it's easy enough to find transport to the lake. If you're coming from eastern Bali, catch one of the regular bemos from Gianyar or Bangli, via Penelokan. Buses and minibuses also frequently travel from Singaraja, through Kintamani and Penelokan (2000Rp).

Tourist Shuttle Bus A shuttle bus will minimise the hassle of changing bemos and carrying luggage. Perama has a service at least once a day from Kuta and Sanur (10,000Rp from both places). It travels via Ubud (7500Rp), stops at the Gunung Sari Restaurant near Kubupenelokan and continues to Lovina (7500Rp). If you pre-arrange it with the driver, he will drop you anywhere between Kubupenelokan and Penulisan, but not to anywhere else.

Getting Around

Bemo From Kintamani, via Penelokan, public bemos run to Kedisan (500Rp), Toya Bungkah (1000Rp) and Songan (1500Rp). They run about every half-hour in the morning, and hourly in the afternoon. Orange bemos regularly shuttle back and forth around the crater rim between Penelokan and Kintamani (200Rp). To get to Penulisan, catch a bus or minibus going to Singaraja.

Ojek One quick and easy way to get around is by ojek. Although not necessary between Penulisan and Penelokan, they are very handy for the roads around the lake and volcano. Drivers don't like to negotiate, but when travelling from Penelokan try not to pay more than 2000Rp to Kedisan, 3000Rp to Buahan and 5000Rp to Toya Bungkah.

Boat A chartered trip around the lake on a motorised wooden boat is very enjoyable, but certainly overpriced. Boats leave from a large terminal in Kedisan, where there is a ticket office, car park and persistent hawkers. The fare allows you to visit the tourist traps of Trunyan and Kuban (see the Trunyan & Kuban section earlier in this section), but if you also want to go to Toya Bungkah, you'll have to negotiate an extra payment.

The trip takes less than two hours, and costs a minimum of 40,000Rp per boat, plus about 2000Rp in fees and insurance per person. A maximum of seven people can share one boat, but it may be hard for you to find others to share the cost. The terminal opens at 8 am, and the last boat leaves at about 4 pm. Try to go before 10 am, when the waves are less choppy and the mighty Gunung Batur is most photogenic.

DANAU BRATAN

Coming from the south, you gradually leave the rice terraces behind and ascend into the cool, damp mountain country around Danau Bratan. This lovely area is an excellent place to relax and use as a base for hiking around the other lakes and surrounding hills (mentioned later in this section). It also has a picturesque temple, botanical gardens, colourful market and golf course, and you can participate in a variety of water sports on the lake itself. Thankfully, the area lacks the tourists and touts found around Gunung Batur.

Bedugul

Bedugul is the name of the area at the southern end of the lake, sometimes known as Taman Rekreasi Bedugul, or Bedugul Recreation Park. There's a hotel and restaurant (see Places to Stay in this section), souvenir shops and facilities for a number of water sports.

Kebun Raya Eya Karya Bali

At the intersection in Candikuning, a road (1km) leads to these pretty botanical gardens. They cover more than 120 hectares on the lower slopes of Gunung Pohon, and boast an extensive collection of trees and some 500 species of orchid. It's a lovely place – cool, shady and scenic. Tickets costs 1000Rp, and it's open daily from 7 am to 6 pm (but try to avoid Sunday).

Pura Ulun Danu Bratan

This Hindu/Buddhist temple was founded in the 17th century, and is dedicated to Dewi Danu, the goddess of the waters. While you cannot enter the temple itself, it is definitely worth visiting for the surrounding,

BALI

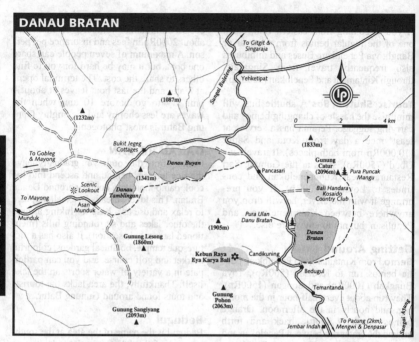

DANAU BRATAN

To Gitgit &
Singaraja

Yehketipat

(1087m)

(1232m)

Sungai Baldena

0   2   4 km

(1833m)

To Gobleg
& Mayong

Bukit Jegeg
Cottages

Danau Buyan

Gunung
Catur
(2096m)   Pura Puncak
Mangu

Scenic
Lookout

Danau
Tamblingan

(1341m)

Pancasari

Bali Handara
Kosaido
Country Club

To Mayong

Asah
Munduk

Munduk

Gunung Lesong
(1860m)

(1905m)

Pura Ulan
Danu Bratan

Danau
Bratan

Kebun Raya
Eya Karya Bali

Candikuning

Bedugul

Temantanda

Gunung
Pohon
(2063m)

Gunung Sangiyang
(2093m)

To Pacung (2km),
Mengwi & Denpasar

Jembar Indah

Sungai Ayung

immaculate **gardens**, and **views** of the majestic, and often permanently cloud-covered, Gunung Catur. The gardens are open daily from 8.30 am to 6 pm, but if you come any time after 6 am (for the sunrise) someone will still want the entrance fee of 1000Rp.

Activities

Wherever there's a lake in Bali, a variety of water sports are normally available; the advantage here is that prices are geared towards Balinese and Indonesian visitors. Paddling a rowing boat across part of the lake is a wonderful experience, especially at sunrise (about 6 am). You can organise boats and water sports at the temple gardens; from near the lane leading to the Ashram Guest House (see Places to Stay in this section); and, best of all, at Bedugul Recreation Park (Taman Rekreasi Bedugul) at Bedugul.

From the Goa Jepang (Japanese Cave), a well-marked path ascends to the top of Gunung Catur (2096m). It takes about two hours from the caves and about one hour back down.

One of the most spectacular golf courses in the world must be the Bali Handara Kosaido Country Club (☎ 0362-22646, fax 23048), located on the outskirts of the volcano near Pancasari.

Places to Stay

Bedugul Opposite the turn-off to Bedugul is *Bukit Strobeli (☎ 0368-21265)* – also known as Strawberry Hill. It has a huddle of uninspiring, but cheap, rooms for 22,000Rp, although the noise from the main road is deafening. A little further west, *Hotel Bukit Permai (☎/fax 0368-21445)* is away from the road and has excellent views, but it lacks some character and charm. Rooms cost

50,000Rp to 100,000Rp (with the best views and satellite TV). In the recreation park, **Bedugul Hotel** (☎ 0368-21197, fax 21198) has motel-style rooms and bungalows in a good location, but without much charm, for 84,000/108,000Rp for singles/doubles; however, regular discounts of up to 50% make this an attractive option.

Candikuning Along the road to the botanical gardens, signs point to several cheap hotels, mostly about 100m or so off the road. **Penginapan Cempaka** (☎ 0368-21042), near the entrance to the gardens, has clean, quiet rooms for 25,000Rp to 40,000Rp. Next door, the simple **Pondok Permata Firdous** (☎ 0368-21531) is reasonable value for 20,000Rp a double.

Pondok Wisata Dahlia Indah (☎ 0368-21233), in the village and along a lane near the road to the gardens, is a decent mid-range option, with comfortable rooms for a negotiable 40,000Rp. **Sari Artha Inn** (☎ 0368-21022) costs 15,000Rp to 20,000Rp for simple and very noisy rooms. Better bungalows further away from the main road and with hot water cost 35,000Rp, but their walls are paper thin. The Perama tourist shuttle bus stops here, so it is convenient.

The two best places are closest to the lake. **Ashram Guest House** (☎ 0368-21450, fax 21101) gets mixed reviews from travellers, and is often busy in the peak season so book ahead. It has a range of rooms starting at 15,000Rp with a shared bathroom, no hot water and no breakfast, rising to 30,000Rp with private bathroom, cold water and breakfast. If you want hot water, breakfast and views, you'll pay 70,000Rp. Opposite, **Lila Graha Bungalows** (☎ 0368-21446) is charming and better value, but has limited views. The rooms are clean, have real sheets and a huge bathroom, and cost 35,000/40,000Rp. The staff are friendly, but a little work-shy.

Next to the temple, the new **Enjung Beji Resort** (☎ 0368-21490, fax 21022) has many clean and pleasant cottages, and a tennis court, but the cottages lack character and few actually face the lake. All come with satellite TV, and start at a reasonable, and negotiable,

100,000Rp but climb to 300,000Rp. Next door, but not even facing the lake, **Wisma Beratan Indah** (☎ 0368-21342) is cheap, but fairly cheerless. Rooms cost 30,000Rp to 60,000Rp for a family room with a TV and garage, but no views.

Pancasari Further north, and further up the price range, are a few places, such as **Pancasari Inn** (☎/fax 0362-21148), which has rooms for US$42. If you are really flush with funds, you can stay at **Bali Handara Kosaido Country Club** (☎ 0362-22646, fax 23048), where 'standard bungalows' start at US$91, while rooms start at US$121 and go as high as US$423. The attraction is obviously the golf course (see Activities early in this section), but it also boasts a sauna, tennis court, fitness centre and traditional Japanese bath.

Places to Eat

The cheapest places are the **food stalls** at the Candikuning market, and at the car park overlooking the lake, but they tend to close by about 7 pm. Naturally, there are plenty of **warungs** along the road to the botanical gardens, and outside the entrance to the gardens at Pura Ulun Danu Bratan. In Candikuning, **Rumah Makan Ananda** has the best range and prices for Indonesian food, while closer to the lake, **Bedugul Cafe** has cheap snacks, cold beer and fish meals (6500Rp).

All **hotel restaurants** are open to the public. The restaurant at **Ashram Guest House** is overpriced and has a limited menu, while the restaurant at **Lili Graha Bungalows** has better prices, better service and a bigger range of meals. **Bukit Strobeli** has an excellent restaurant, and is worth the walk if you're not staying there.

Inside the temple gardens, **Restoran Ulun Danu** offers a large à la carte menu or a buffet lunch for 20,000Rp. It is a perfect place for a relaxing drink, but is not open for dinner. **Bedugul Restaurant** overlooks the lake and has superb views. However, the à la carte menu is deliberately limited and overpriced, so you're almost forced to accept the buffet for 24,000Rp.

Getting There & Away

Bemo, Minibus & Bus The regular bemos, minibuses and buses travelling between Denpasar's Ubung terminal and Sukasada terminal in Singaraja stop anywhere along the main road between Bedugul and Pancasari. To get to Ubud, you'll have to change bemos in Denpasar; to get to Gunung Batur, get connections in Singaraja – or walk.

Tourist Shuttle Bus A shuttle bus run by Perama, and a few other operators, is the easiest way to the region, especially from Ubud. They start in Kuta and Sanur (7500Rp from both places), stop at Ubud (7500Rp) and continue to Lovina (7500Rp). The Perama stop is at Sari Artha Inn in Candikuning, but the driver may drop you off anywhere between Bedugul and Pancasari if you ask nicely.

Getting Around

If you are staying in Candikuning, it is walking distance to Bedugul and the temple. To travel anywhere else, jump on one of the very frequent blue Denpasar to Singaraja bemos; the trip will cost about 500Rp.

DANAU BUYAN & DANAU TAMBLINGAN

North-west of Danau Bratan are two more lakes, Buyan and Tamblingan. Neither lake is developed like Bratan, nor particularly pretty. There's a hiking trail around the southern side of Buyan, then over the saddle to Tamblingan and on to Asan Munduk, but the paved road towards Munduk is better for hiking: it is flat and elevated, and runs parallel to the lakes for about 7km, offering stunning views. Take a Denpasar to Singaraja bemo to the turn-off, wait for irregular transport to anywhere near Asan Munduk and then walk back to the Denpasar to Singaraja road.

MUNDUK
☎ 0362

When the Dutch took control of northern Bali in the 1890s they experimented with commercial crops in these mountains, establishing plantations for coffee, vanilla, cloves and cocoa. Quite a few old Dutch buildings remain along the road in Munduk and further west, and there are some **Bali Aga villages** in the region.

The 'environmental trekking centre' at Puri Lumbung Cottages offers a series of two to three-hour **hikes** to nearby coffee plantations, waterfalls and villages, as well as around Tamblingan and Buyan lakes. The guides charge about 15,000Rp per hour.

Places to Stay & Eat

Puri Lumbung Cottages (☎/fax 92810), on the right side of the road as you enter Munduk from Bedugul, is jointly run by the local community. It's a delightful place to stay, and has well-finished, thatched bungalows for US$60/66/97 for singles/doubles/family rooms. *Warung Kopi Bali* restaurant in the hotel has a wonderful outlook and serves excellent lunches and dinners, with main courses starting at around 8000Rp.

The other charming option is one of the seven spotless, renovated Dutch villas run by *Penginapan Guru Ratna (☎ 92812, fax 92810)* and Puri Lumbung Cottages. Prices range from 40,000Rp per double, with a shared bathroom, to US$24 for a mini-home with a kitchen – large enough for a family. These prices are high, but this is a lovely village, and the managers are very helpful and friendly. The meals (about 10,000Rp) have been described by readers as a real 'Balinese feast'. If this is out of your price range, ask around the village for a room in other former *Dutch villas* for about 20,000Rp per person.

Getting There & Away

There is no regular public transport to Munduk, but if you take the Denpasar to Singaraja bemo to the turn-off and wait, some form of public transport will eventually arrive. From Seririt, transport is even scarcer. You may have to charter a bemo from Candikuning or Seririt.

PELAGA & PETANG
☎ 0361

A scenic road heads north from Ubud, via Sangeh and Petang, and finishes at the pretty village of Pelaga. Pelaga holds infrequent **bull races**, and is a wonderful place for **hiking** to Danau Bratan and Gunung Catur. The views from Petang of Gunung Agung are glorious, and you can go hiking, or swimming in nearby rivers.

In Pelaga, ***Pondok Wana Plaga*** *(☎ 702 218)* is a delightful place – prices were not available at the time of research but rooms should cost about US$10 per person. In Petang, you can stay at the unnamed ***losmen*** *(☎ 232550)*, just outside the village, for US$20 per person, including three meals.

Bemos from Wangaya terminal in Denpasar (1300Rp) occasionally travel up this road, but it's best to have your own transport.

GUNUNG BATUKAU

Gunung Batukau (2276m) is the third of Bali's three major mountains and the holy peak of the western end of the island. If you want to climb it, you'll need a guide because there are many false trails and it's easy to get lost. From the temple, a guide will charge 70,000Rp to 100,000Rp. It takes about five or six hours to get to the top, and four hours to get down, through quite thick forest.

On the slopes of Batukau, **Pura Luhur Gunung Batukau** was the state temple when Tabanan was an independent kingdom. There are several routes to the temple, but none of them are particularly high-class roads – it's a remote place. The most straightforward way to get there is to follow the road north from Tabanan to Wangayagede, the last village before the temple.

ROUTES THROUGH PUPUAN

The two most popular routes between the southern and northern coasts are the roads via Kintamani and Bedugul, but there are two other routes over the mountains. Both branch north from the Denpasar to Gilimanuk road, one from Pulukan and the other from Antasari, and meet at Pupuan before dropping down to Seririt, west of Lovina. Both are accessible by bemo, but there is nowhere to stay along the way.

The Pulukan to Pupuan road climbs steeply up from the coast providing fine views back down to the sea. The route runs through spice-growing country. At one point, the narrow and winding road actually runs right through an enormous bunut tree, which bridges the road. Further on, the road spirals down to Pupuan through some of Bali's most beautiful rice terraces. It is worth stopping off at the magnificent **waterfall** at Pujungan, a few kilometres south of Pupuan.

The road from Antasari initially travels through rice paddies, then climbs into the spice-growing country and finally descends through the coffee plantations to Pupuan. If you continue another 12km or so towards the north coast you reach Mayong, where you can turn east to Munduk and on to Tamblingan and Buyan lakes.

North Bali

North Bali, the district of Buleleng, is an interesting contrast to the south of the island. The Lovina beaches are popular with budget travellers, boasting a wide variety of places to stay and eat without the chaos of the Kuta region. Many travellers coming from Java go straight from Gilimanuk to the north coast, preferring this to taking the south-coast road, which would take them to Denpasar or, horror of horrors, Kuta.

Buleleng has a strong artistic and cultural tradition. Its dance troupes are highly regarded and a number of dance styles have originated here, including Joged and Janger. Gold and silver work, weaving, pottery, musical-instrument making and temple design all feature distinctive local styles. The Sapi Gerumbungan is a bull race in which style is as important as speed. This is a Buleleng tradition, and quite different from the races of Negara in south-west Bali. Events are held at villages near Lovina, on Independence Day (17 August), Singaraja Day (31 March) and other occasions.

SINGARAJA
☎ 0362

Singaraja (which means Lion King) is Bali's second largest city, but it's orderly,

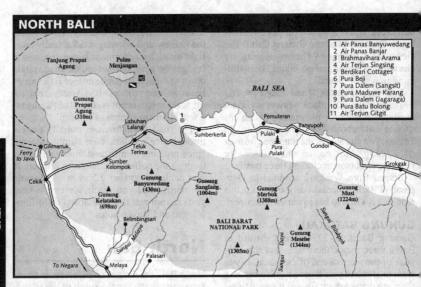

NORTH BALI

BALI SEA

Tanjung Prapat Agung

Pulau Menjangan

Gunung Prapat Agung (310m)

Labuhan Lalang

Pemuteran

Banyupoh

1 Air Panas Banyuwedang
2 Air Panas Banjar
3 Brahmavihara Arama
4 Air Terjun Singsing
5 Berdikari Cottages
6 Pura Beji
7 Pura Dalem (Sangsit)
8 Pura Maduwe Karang
9 Pura Dalem (Jagaraga)
10 Pura Batu Bolong
11 Air Terjun Gitgit

Gilimanuk

Ferry to Java

Teluk Terima

Sumberkerta

Pulaki

Pura Pulaki

Gondol

Grokgak

Cekik

Sumber Kelompok

Gunung Banyuwedang (430m)

Gunung Sanglang (1004m)

Gunung Merbuk (1388m)

Gunung Musi (1224m)

Gunung Kelatakan (698m)

Belimbingsari

BALI BARAT NATIONAL PARK

Gunung Mesehe (1344m)

Sungai Melaya

Sungai Daya

Sungai Bilukpoh

(1305m)

Palasari

To Negara

Melaya

even quiet, compared to Denpasar. Singaraja was the centre of Dutch power in Bali and remained the administrative centre for the Lesser Sunda Islands (Bali through to Timor) until 1953. It is one of the few places in Bali where there are visible reminders of the Dutch period, but there are also Chinese and Muslim influences.

Orientation & Information

The main commercial areas are in the northeast part of town (immediately south of the old harbour) and along Jl Pramuka and Jl Ngurah Rai. Most hotels, restaurants and offices of bus companies are along Jl Ahmad Yani. Traffic does a few complicated one way circuit of the town, but it's easy enough to get around on foot or by bemo.

The main banks will change money, as will the moneychanger on Jl Pramuka. The tourist office (☎ 25141), on the corner of Jl Veteran and Jl Gajah Mada, is reasonably helpful. The largest hospital in northern Bali is the RSUP Umum (☎ 22046), and there is a major police station (☎ 41510).

Things to See & Do

Pelabuhan Buleleng, just north of Jl Erlangga, is an interesting area to walk around. The conspicuous **Yudha Mandala Tama** monument commemorates a freedom fighter who was killed by gunfire from a Dutch warship early in the struggle for independence. Nearby is a colourful **Chinese temple**.

Tourists are welcome to visit the small historical library (☎ 22645), Gedung Kirtya, next to the tourist office, but it's more of interest to scholars. This small institution has a vast collection of old Balinese manuscripts written on *lontar* (palm) leaves. It is open Monday to Thursday from 7 am to 2 pm, and closes a little earlier on Friday and Saturday.

The impressive **Pura Jagat Natha** is Singaraja's main temple and the largest in northern Bali. It's not usually open to visitors, but from the outside you can appreciate its majesty and admire the elaborate carved stone decorations.

Places to Stay

On Jl Ahmad Yani, *Hotel Sentral* (☎ 21 896) is OK at 15,000Rp a room; *Hotel Duta*

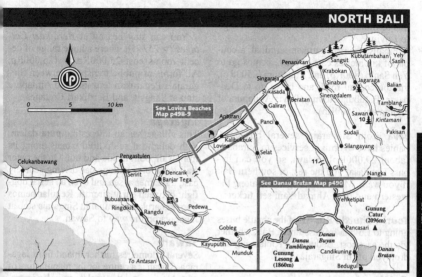

NORTH BALI

Karya (☎ 21467) is slightly better at 17,500/
20,000Rp for singles/doubles, or 35,000/
40,000Rp with air-con; and *Hotel Saku
Bindu (☎ 21791)* and *Hotel Gelar Sari (☎ 21
495)* are both reasonable value at 15,000/
20,000Rp. The only place to offer any peace
in this area is the basic *Losmen Darma
Setu (☎ 23200)*, with rooms for 10,000/
12,000Rp. Look for the sign in eastern Jl
Ahmad Yani.

*Wijaya Hotel (☎ 21915, fax 25817, Jl
Sudirman)* is the most comfortable and convenient place in town. Standard rooms with
a fan and outside bathroom cost 20,000/
25,000Rp; rooms with a private bathroom
and air-con are 60,000/65,000Rp.

Places to Eat
There is not a great range of places to eat in
Singaraja; you'd be better off taking a 10
minute bemo ride to one of the many restaurants in Lovina. In the evening, there are
food stalls in the night market on Jl Durian,
while during the day they are at the main
market on Jl Ahmad Yani. There are always
warungs around the bemo/bus terminals.

Opposite Wijaya Hotel, *Rumah Makan
Hebring* serves cheap, traditional Indonesian food in a family atmosphere, but it's
often closed in the evenings. *Cafe Lima
Lima* is one of three places in a huddle
along Jl Ahmad Yani that serve cheap un-
memorable Indonesian food and seafood,
but no beer. *Cafetaria Sari Rosa (Jl Imam
Bonjol)* is probably the best of the lot in the
centre of town.

Getting There & Away
Bemo & Bus Singaraja is the transport hub
for the northern coast and has three main
bemo/bus terminals. From the main Sukasada
terminal, on the southern side of town,
minibuses go to Denpasar (Ubung terminal,
3400Rp), via Bedugul, about every half-hour
between 6 am and 4 pm; and to Semarapura
(3000Rp) via Kintamani. (There is also a tiny
bemo stop next to the *puskesmas* (community
health centre) in Sukasada village, with services to Gitgit.)

From Banyuasri terminal, buses and minibuses leave for Gilimanuk (2700Rp) and
Seririt, and buses go to Denpasar (Ubung

terminal) about every 20 minutes. From this terminal, plenty of blue bemos also go to Lovina.

Finally, from Penarukan terminal, a couple of kilometres east of town, bemos go to Yeh Sanih (800Rp) and Amlapura (2500Rp), via the coastal road; and buses go to Denpasar (Batubulan terminal), via Amlapura or Kintamani (3500Rp).

Java From Singaraja, several bus companies have overnight services to Surabaya (about 29,000Rp) in Java, so you can bypass Denpasar and the rest of southern Bali if you want. Many travel agencies along the western end of Jl Ahmad Yani sell tickets.

Tourist Shuttle Bus All of the shuttle buses going to Lovina from southern Bali, whether via the east cost, Bedugul or Kintamani, can drop you off in Singaraja.

Getting Around
Plenty of bemos link the three main bemo/bus terminals, and hurtle along all main roads in between. The bemos are all well signed and colour-coded, and charge about 500Rp for a ride anywhere around town. For shorter trips, take a *dokar* (pony cart). There are also plenty of ojeks around the place.

AROUND SINGARAJA
☎ 0362
Interesting sites around Singaraja include some of Bali's best known temples. The north-coast sandstone is very soft and easily carved, allowing local sculptors to give free rein to their imagination. You'll find some delightfully whimsical scenes carved into a number of the temples here.

Sangsit
A few kilometres east of Singaraja, there is an excellent example of the colourful architectural style of northern Bali. Sangsit's **Pura Beji** is a subak temple, dedicated to the goddess Dewi Sri, who looks after irrigated rice fields – it's about 500m off the main road towards the coast. About 500m north-east of Pura Beji is a **pura dalem** that shows scenes

of punishment in the afterlife, and other pictures that are humorous and/or erotic.

You can stay nearby at **Berdikari Cottages** (☎ 25195), where a huge range of decent rooms cost 25,000Rp to 125,000Rp. All forms of public transport between Singaraja's Penarukan terminal and Amlapura stop at Sangsit, and Berdikari Cottages.

Jagaraga
This village has an interesting **pura dalem**, with delightful sculptured panels along its front wall, both inside and out. On the outer wall look for a vintage car driving sedately past, a steamer at sea and even an aerial dogfight between early aircraft. Regular bemos from Penarukan terminal in Singaraja stop at Jagaraga on the way to Sawan.

Sawan
Several kilometres further inland from Jagaraga, Sawan is a centre for the manufacture of gamelan gongs and complete gamelan instruments. The strange looking **Pura Batu Bolong** is worth a look. Around Sawan are **cold water springs** believed to cure all sorts of illnesses. Regular bemos travel from Penarukan terminal in Singaraja to Sawan.

Kubutambahan
About 1km east of the turn-off to Kintamani is **Pura Maduwe Karang** (Temple of the Land Owner). Like Pura Beji at Sangsit, the temple is dedicated to agricultural spirits, but this one looks after unirrigated land. This is one of the best temples in northern Bali, and is particularly noted for its sculptured panels, including the famous bicycle panel depicting a gentleman riding a bicycle with flower petals for wheels. The temple is easy to find in the village. Kubutambahan is on the Singaraja to Amlapura road, and there are regular bemos and buses.

Yeh Sanih
About 15km east of Singaraja, Yeh Sanih (aka Air Sanih) is a popular spot where freshwater springs are channelled into some pleasant **swimming pools** before flowing into the sea. The area is attractively laid out

with pleasant **gardens** and a restaurant (see the following Places to Stay & Eat section). Admission to the springs and pool is 450Rp, and it's open from 8 am to 6 pm daily. The inevitable hotels, restaurants and warungs stretch along the main road for about 2km east of the springs.

Places to Stay & Eat The first place on your right, as you come from Singaraja, is *Puri Rena Restaurant & Bungalows* (☎ *26589*). It offers quiet singles/doubles in a lovely garden on a hill for 15,000/ 25,000Rp. The *restaurant* is secluded and has great views. Opposite, *Puri Sanih Bungalows* (☎ *23508*) has a picturesque *restaurant* inside the gardens, overlooking the pools, and two sets of bungalows nearby. The cheaper ones are closer to the pools, and to the main road, and cost 20,000Rp, while the better ones have views, huge beds and tranquillity for 55,000Rp.

About 300m further east, the two charming and luxurious bungalows at *Cilik's Beach Garden* (☎*/fax 26561*) are very attractively laid out in a lovely, quiet garden. They cost US$55/70.

Getting There & Away Yeh Sanih is on the main road along the northern coast. It's an easy trip with your own vehicle; and frequent public transport between Singaraja (800Rp) and Amlapura stops right outside the gardens.

Gitgit

About 11km south of Singaraja, are the pretty, and pretty touristy, **Air Terjun Gitgit** waterfalls. The well-signposted path (800m) from the main road in the village is predictably lined with souvenir stalls, but the workers are quite friendly. The 40m falls are pretty, and a great place for a picnic, but not pristine. You buy a ticket (1100Rp) about halfway down the path. There is another small waterfall, sometimes called **Gitgit Multi-Tier Waterfall**, about 2km further up the hill from the main falls and about 600m off the main road.

Opposite the path to Air Terjun Gitgit falls, *Gitgit Hotel & Restaurant* (☎ *26212,*

fax 41840) has clean, uninteresting and overpriced rooms from 50,000Rp. The restaurant is also way overpriced. It's cheaper, and more atmospheric, to eat at one of the *warungs* along the path to the main falls.

Regular buses and minibuses travel between the main Sukasada terminal in Singaraja and Denpasar (Ubung terminal), via Bedugul, and stop at Gitgit. More regular and direct bemos to Gitgit (700Rp) also leave from outside the puskesmas in Sukasada village (see Getting There & Away in the previous Singaraja section).

LOVINA
☎ 0362

West of Singaraja is a string of coastal villages – Tukad Mungga, Anturan, Kalibukbuk and Temukus – which have become a popular beach resort collectively known as Lovina. There are plenty of shops, bars, hotels and other tourist facilities, but the place isn't totally overrun (yet) by tourist developments and, surprisingly, rice paddies still dominate the area. Lovina is a convenient base for trips around the northern coast, a good place to meet other travellers and there's a bit of nightlife if you look hard.

The sand is black and volcanic, and not the white stuff found in the south. The beaches are also thin and don't offer much privacy, but they're mostly clean and fine to walk along (although where there are no hotels, the beaches are quite scruffy). There is no surf, as a reef ensures that the water is calm most of the time. The sunsets here are as spectacular as those in the Kuta region, and as the sky reddens, the lights of the fishing boats appear as bright dots across the horizon.

Orientation

It's hard to know where one village ends and the next one begins, but the signposts along the main road indicating the location of the various hotels and restaurants are good landmarks. The tourist area stretches out over about 8km, but the main focus of Lovina is Kalibukbuk, 11km west of Singaraja.

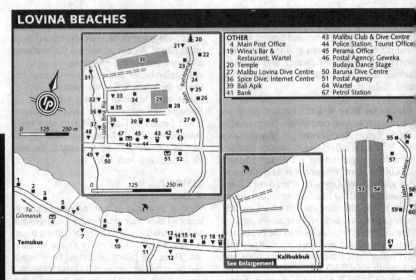

LOVINA BEACHES

OTHER
4 Main Post Office
19 Wina's Bar &
   Restaurant; Wartel
20 Temple
27 Malibu Lovina Dive Centre
36 Spice Dive; Internet Centre
39 Bali Apik
41 Bank

43 Malibu Club & Dive Centre
44 Police Station; Tourist Office
45 Perama Office
46 Postal Agency; Geweka
   Budaya Dance Stage
50 Baruna Dive Centre
51 Postal Agency
64 Wartel
67 Petrol Station

Information

The tourist office, which shares the same premises as the police station, is not worth visiting: it has a poor map of Lovina on the wall, and staff offer limited information. There are plenty of moneychangers around Lovina; their rates are better than the solitary bank.

The main post office is inconvenient for most visitors, but postal agencies and wartels are dotted along the main road. Spice Dive Center (spicedive@singaraja.wasantara.net.id) runs an Internet centre for a reasonable 500Rp per minute. The friendly folk at Warung Karma (karma@singaraja.wasantara .net.id) also have an Internet centre for visitors.

A few shops in Kalibukbuk offer a cheap, and environmentally friendly, Aqua mineral water refill service; it costs 1000Rp to refill a 2L bottle.

Boat Trips

Dolphin trips are Lovina's special tourist attraction. There is no evidence that the dolphins are harmed by the attention, but there is some suggestion that boats have to travel further and further to see fewer dolphins. At times, tourists are hassled by touts selling dolphin trips. It is best to buy a ticket the day before; your hotel is as good a place as any. The price of a trip is supposedly fixed at 15,000Rp per person by a boat-owners' arrangement, but competition is often so intense that discounts are possible. Some operators will give a refund of 50% if you don't see dolphins. Others offer breakfast and/or beverages on the boat – but some readers have reported being ripped off with these 'offers'.

Snorkelling

Generally, the water is clear and the reef is good for snorkelling. The coral here is not the best you'll find, but it's not bad. In many places you can simply swim out from the beach, or get a boat to take you out; the boatman should know where the best coral is found. Various organised snorkelling tours are available from your hotels and travel agencies. Full snorkelling gear can be rented from numerous shops along the main streets of Kalibukbuk, and possibly from your hotel.

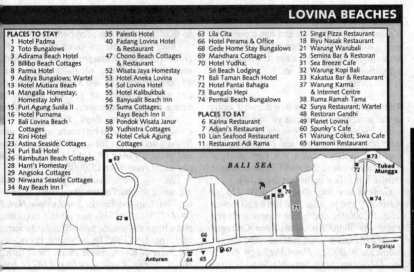

LOVINA BEACHES

PLACES TO STAY
1 Hotel Padma
2 Toto Bungalows
3 Adirama Beach Hotel
5 Billibo Beach Cottages
8 Parma Hotel
9 Aditya Bungalows; Wartel
13 Hotel Mutiara Beach
14 Mangalla Homestay;
   Homestay John
15 Puri Agung Susila II
16 Hotel Purnama
17 Bali Lovina Beach
   Cottages
23 Astina Seaside Cottages
24 Puri Bali Hotel
26 Rambutan Beach Cottages
28 Harri's Homestay
29 Angsoka Cottages
30 Nirwana Seaside Cottages
34 Ray Beach Inn I

35 Palestis Hotel
40 Padang Lovina Hotel
   & Restaurant
47 Chono Beach Cottages
   & Restaurant
52 Wisata Jaya Homestay
53 Hotel Aneka Lovina
54 Sol Lovina Hotel
55 Hotel Kalibukbuk
56 Banyualit Beach Inn
57 Suma Cottages;
   Rays Beach Inn II
58 Pondok Wisata Janur
59 Yudhistra Cottages
62 Hotel Celuk Agung
   Cottages

63 Lila Cita
66 Hotel Perama & Office
68 Gede Home Stay Bungalows
69 Mandhara Cottages
70 Hotel Yudha;
   Sri Beach Lodging
71 Bali Taman Beach Hotel
72 Hotel Pantai Bahagia
73 Bungalo Hepi
74 Permai Beach Bungalows

PLACES TO EAT
6 Karina Restaurant
7 Adjani's Restaurant
10 Lian Seafood Restaurant
11 Restaurant Adi Rama

12 Singa Pizza Restaurant
18 Biyu Nasak Restaurant
21 Warung Warubali
25 Semina Bar & Restoran
31 Sea Breeze Cafe
32 Warung Kopi Bali
33 Kakatua Bar & Restaurant
37 Warung Karma
   & Internet Centre
38 Ruma Ramah Tama
42 Surya Restaurant; Wartel
48 Restoran Gandhi
49 Planet Lovina
60 Spunky's Cafe
61 Warung Cokot; Siwa Cafe
65 Harmoni Restaurant

BALI SEA

BALI

Anturan · To Singaraja

Diving

Scuba diving on the local reef is nothing special, but this is a good area for beginners. Local dive centres arrange trips to other sites in the area, particularly Pulau Menjangan, off the west coast, and Tulamben or Amed to the east. The most reputable and long-running operators in Lovina also run introduction and PADI certificate courses. They are: Baruna Dive Centre (☎ 41084), one of the branches of a well-regarded Bali-wide company; Malibu Lovina Dive Centre (☎/fax 41225) and the associated Malibu Dive Centre (☎ 41310); and Spice Dive Centre (☎ 41305; email spicedive@singaraja.wasantara.net.id), which has a very good reputation.

Places to Stay

The first hotel is only about 6km from Singaraja; the last is about 8km further west. During peak times (July to August and December to January) accommodation may be tight and prices are higher, sometimes even double the prices listed in this section. Generally, the cheapest places are away from the beach.

There are so many places along the Lovina Beach strip that it's impossible to give a complete and up-to-date list. We have tried to include places that are good value, close to the beach and away from the busy main road.

Singaraja to Anturan Starting from the Singaraja end, a road leads to Pantai Happy, more traditionally called Tukad Mungga. Here, business is often slow because it's far from Kalibukbuk and parts of the beach are scruffy, so prices are low and negotiable.

Bungalo Hepi (☎ 41020), which has a pool surrounded by unkempt gardens, is excellent value at 15,000/30,000Rp a single/double, or 30,000Rp a double with air-con. At the end of the road, *Hotel Pantai Bahagia* (☎ 41017, formerly Happy Beach Inn) is a very cheerful place, and has pleasant rooms from 15,000/20,000Rp. *Permai Beach Bungalows* (☎ 41471, fax 41224) has a nice setting and a pool. The rooms are normally expensive – 50,000/ 70,000Rp with fan/air-con – but prices are often negotiable, especially if you use its dive centre.

Facing the main road is the upmarket **Bali Taman Beach Hotel** (☎ *41126, fax 41840*). It's small, but attractive, and has a pool and nice gardens. Prices range from US$13/17 for a single/double with a fan to US$125 for a luxurious family suite, and it's good value in this range.

Anturan Continuing west, a turn-off leads to the scruffy little fishing village of Anturan, which now has an excess of places to stay. Most of the rooms and bungalows are crowded together, but it's a popular spot (probably because the small Perama tourist shuttle bus office is just up the road).

Gede Home Stay Bungalows (☎ *41526*) is friendly and popular, and has small rooms from 15,000Rp, and better rooms with hot water for 30,000Rp. **Mandhara Cottages** (☎ *41476*) has a good location and decent rooms for 50,000Rp. **Hotel Yudha** (☎ *41183, fax 41160*, formerly Simon's Seaside Cottages) has a cluster of singles/doubles for 50,000/55,000Rp, which seems a lot because there's no pool. Recommended, especially for families, is **Sri Beach Lodging** (☎ *42235*). It boasts a great beachfront location, but the rooms, which cost up to 30,000Rp for a family, are small.

Back on the main road, **Hotel Perama** (☎ *41161*), at the back of the small Perama office, has cheap but unexciting rooms for 10,000/15,000Rp; 40,000Rp for a bungalow.

Anturan to Kalibukbuk Continuing west from Anturan, the next turn-off leads to **Lila Cita**, right on the beachfront. This place is quiet and charming, and has singles/doubles for 15,000/25,000Rp. On the way, **Hotel Celuk Agung** (☎ *41039, fax 41379*) has rooms from US$25/30, including air-con, fridge, hot water, satellite TV, tennis courts and a pool. Discounts of up to 30% are possible, so it's good value.

Jl Loviana has about a dozen hotels, and is a good place to look around for something suitable. The pleasant **Hotel Kalibukbuk** (☎ *41701*) has rooms from 35,000Rp with fan and 50,000Rp with air-con. Back from the beach, **Banyualit Beach Inn** (☎ *417889,*

fax 41563) has a pool, and fan-cooled doubles for 30,000Rp, cottages with air-con for 65,000Rp and a range of options in between.

Other budget places along this road include **Yudhistra Cottages** (☎ *41552*), with rooms set around a pleasant garden for 15,000Rp with a fan and 35,000Rp with air-con and hot water; the friendly and quiet **Suma Cottages** has rooms for a negotiable 25,000/30,000Rp; **Rays Beach Inn II** (☎ *41088*), with a bit more space than Suma's and rooms for 25,000Rp; and **Pondok Wisata Janur** (☎ *41056*), with a small cluster of rooms for 15,000/20,000Rp.

The only two upmarket places in Lovina are along this part of the main road, but extend back to the beach. **Sol Lovina Hotel** (☎ *41775, fax 41659*) has all the luxuries, and a huge swimming pool. Standard rooms cost from US$100/110, while the Presidential Suite is much, much more. Next door, **Hotel Aneka Lovina** (☎/*fax 23827*) has similar facilities, a huge pool in a lovely garden and rooms priced from US$85/95.

Kalibukbuk About 11km from Singaraja, the 'centre' of Lovina is the village of Kalibukbuk. Many visitors choose to stay here because it's convenient and central.

Down Jl Ketepang, **Rambutan Beach Cottages** (☎ *41388, fax 41057*) has a swimming pool set in charming gardens, but there is little that is authentically 'Balinese' about it. It offers 'budget' singles/doubles/triples for US$10/12/17, or US$20/20/25 with hot water. It's recommended for families. The rooms at **Puri Bali Hotel** (☎ *41485*) have hot water, and cost a negotiable 40,000Rp with fan or 100,000Rp with air-con.

Close to the beach is the clean and well-run **Rini Hotel** (☎ 41386). Normally a popular, budget-priced option, it recently underwent renovation and now features a saltwater pool, so check the latest prices. The long-standing **Astina Seaside Cottages** (☎ *41187*) has some character, and a garden setting, and is still good value. Rooms cost from 17,000/20,000Rp with a shared bathroom to 35,000/40,000Rp for a cottage with a bathroom.

Along the busy main road, the cosy *Wisata Jaya Homestay* has reasonable rooms for 11,000/12,000Rp. Further west, *Chono Beach Cottages* is central, but noisy, yet the negotiated rate of 15,000/20,000Rp is good value if you are able to achieve it.

The next turn-off, Jl Bina Ria, has a handful of bars and restaurants before it ends at the beach. A driveway leads to the rambling *Nirwana Seaside Cottages* (☎ 41288, fax 41090), on a large slab of privileged beachfront property. Rooms start at 45,000/75,000Rp with a fan and hot water; 85,000/100,000Rp for an air-conditioned bungalow. The rooms and bungalows are pleasant, but the service could be better.

A side track goes to *Angsoka Cottages* (☎ 41841, fax 41023), which has a pool and a range of rooms from 20,000/40,000Rp with a fan to 105,000Rp with air-con and hot water. *Ray Beach Inn I* (☎ 41087) has rooms in a cell block-style for 15,000Rp, and is a last resort. *Palestis Hotel* (☎ 41035) has the most ornate outside decorations, a welcome pool inside and promises 'a good sleep'. Rooms are good value, and start at 40,000Rp with a fan. Another small track, next to the Palestis, leads to several other cheap, pleasant places, such as the family-run *Harri's Homestay* (☎ 41152), with rooms for 15,000/25,000Rp; and *Padang Lovina Hotel*, with doubles for 30,000Rp.

West of Kalibukbuk Back on the main road there's a string of other cheapies. Among them is *Hotel Purnama* (☎ 41043), with rooms for 15,000Rp; *Mangalla Homestay*, with rooms for the same price; the popular but small *Homestay John* (☎ 41260), north of the Mangalla and actually on the beach, which has rooms for 25,000Rp; *Puri Agung Susila II* (☎ 41080), about the cheapest around with rooms for 10,000Rp; and *Hotel Mutiara Beach* (☎ 41132), which has rooms for a reasonable 20,000Rp for a room upstairs.

Parma Hotel (☎ 41555) has cottages from 20,000/25,000Rp, and cheaper rooms (15,000Rp) by the road, all set in a garden extending down to the beach. Further along,

Billibo Beach Cottages (☎ 41358) charges 45,000/80,000Rp for rooms with satellite TV, air-con and hot water, while the nearby *Adirama Beach Hotel* (☎/fax 41759) charges US$15 to US$30 for rooms with air-con and satellite TV. Near the bend in the road, *Toto Bungalows* (☎ 41107) has very basic rooms for 10,000/15,000Rp.

Further west there are even more places – secluded or isolated, depending on your point of view. One of the best is the new *Hotel Padma* (☎ 41140). It is noisy, but until it's better known the rooms are good value at 20,000Rp to 60,000Rp for a mid-range place. The pool is a real attraction.

Places to Eat

Just about every hotel has a restaurant and bar, and the public is always welcome. Some of the dozens and dozens of places to eat are listed here, but you'll do well to just look around and eat somewhere that takes your fancy. Even the nicest looking restaurants will have main courses for under 8000Rp. Always keep an eye out for daily specials.

Anturan Starting from the Singaraja end, *Harmoni Restaurant* has delicious fresh fish and other seafood dishes, but the service is often slow, so be ready for a leisurely meal. Further west, *Warung Cokot* serves good, cheap Balinese food, such as *babi guling* (roast pig), while the swish *Siwa Cafe* caters more for the passing bus tour crowd, and charges accordingly. *Spunky's Cafe* may have a corny name, but it's a bright, friendly place, with good food for about 6000Rp. It is one of several newer places along Jl Loviana.

Kalibukbuk Along the main road, *Surya Restaurant* is very popular, and has reasonable pizzas (5000Rp) for lunch and tasty seafood specials (about 7500Rp) all day long. *Malibu Club* next door has a bakery and serves pizzas, but it's overpriced and more interested in catering for the night-time crowd. *Chono Beach Restaurant* is also popular, perhaps because of the happy hour as much as the food.

BALI

On Jl Ketepang, *Semina Bar & Restoran* has buffets, Balinese dancing and a reasonably priced à la carte menu in a nice setting. The road finishes at the wonderful *Warung Warubali*, one the best places to watch the sunset during a happy hour. It is open 24 hours a day, and meals cost 10,000Rp to 13,000Rp.

On Jl Bina Ria, the popular *Ruma Ramah Tama* features a more imaginative menu than many other places, including a wide range of vegetarian dishes and children's serves. Further down, *Kakatua Bar & Restaurant* offers Mexican, Thai and Indian cuisine, as well as pizzas, so most people should be catered for. Directly opposite, *Warung Kopi Bali* is deservedly very popular and gets a lot of repeat business. The servings are large, the food is tasty and prices are reasonable (8000Rp to 12,500Rp). At the end of the road, *Sea Breeze Cafe* has very tasty food, and a wonderful outlook.

West of Kalibukbuk Back on the main road, and heading west, the once popular Arya's Cafe has become *Planet Lovina*, which does not quite capture the atmosphere found in the similarly named chain of US restaurants. *Restoran Gandhi* and *Biyu Nasak Restaurant* both specialise in vegetarian food, as well as seafood, with most dishes about 7500Rp.

Further along, *Singa Pizza Restaurant* is one of the best places for pizzas (about 9500Rp). *Adjani's Restaurant* is a popular place for genuine Indonesian and Balinese food (for about 6500Rp) in a friendly atmosphere, and the owners run cooking classes. If you're staying in the western part of Lovina, *Restaurant Adi Rama* and *Karina Restaurant* are OK, while the seafood dishes (about 11,500Rp) at *Lian Seafood Restaurant* are worth a short bemo ride.

Entertainment

Balinese Dancing Some of the hotel restaurants offer Balinese dancing with a Balinese buffet meal, or Dutch-style *rijstaffel* (banquet). At about 15,000Rp for entertainment and unlimited food, this is very good value and worth a splurge at least once. These evenings are held at the restaurant at *Rambutan Beach Cottages* on Wednesday and Sunday; and at least weekly at *Chono Beach Restaurant* and *Semina Bar & Restoran*. Otherwise, try to find out what's happening at *Geweka Budaya Dance Stage* along the main road in Kalibukbuk.

Bars & Nightclubs Lovina's social scene seems to centre on *Malibu Club*, which has pulsating discos on Wednesday and Saturday nights, and live music on other nights. Another bar, which only seems busy in the tourist season, is *Wina's Bar & Restaurant*. *Bali Apik* and several places nearby, such as *Surya Restaurant*, have started a happy-hour war, much to the delight of thirsty patrons. From about 6 to 9 pm, large Bali Hai beers cost from 4500Rp.

Video Nights Especially popular with families are the video nights. Admission is free, but prices of drinks and food will be higher than elsewhere. *Warung Karma*, the restaurant at *Padang Lovina Hotel*, *Malibu Club* and *Bali Apik* advertise current and future attractions on notice boards along the main road, and on notices nailed to the trees around Lovina.

Shopping

Lovina isn't nearly as well set up for shopping as Sanur, Candidasa and the Kuta region. There are a few shops, but little in the way of souvenirs, art markets and sarong shops. So, you'll find shopping in Lovina a pleasure, rather than a chore, but prices are not as competitive as other tourist centres in Bali.

Getting There & Away

Public Bus & Bemo To get to Lovina from southern Bali by public transport, you will probably need to get a connection in Singaraja (see that section earlier for details). The normal fare on the regular blue bemos from Banyuasri terminal in Singaraja to Kalibukbuk is 800Rp, but don't expect any change from 1000Rp.

Java There are direct public buses between Surabaya (Java) and Singaraja, so if you're coming from the west you can get off anywhere along Lovina rather than backtrack from Singaraja. To Java, catch a bus in Singaraja (see that section earlier). Alternatively, catch a regular public bus from Singaraja to Gilimanuk (or hail it down along the main road in Lovina), and take the ferry to Java.

Many travel agencies in Lovina sell 'tourist bus' trips to major cities in Java, but beware: these are often just tourist shuttle buses from Singaraja all the way to Ubung terminal in Denpasar, and then a deluxe public bus (which is still reasonably comfortable) to Java.

Tourist Shuttle Bus Lovina is the most northern and western point for all shuttle bus services in Bali. At least once a day, Perama buses link Lovina with Kuta, Sanur and Ubud (all for 12,500Rp), via Bedugul (7500Rp) or Kintamani (7500Rp).

The main Perama office (☎ 41104) is next to the tourist office, and there's another small office in Anturan. Simpatik (☎ 21 234) and Marga Sakti Transport (no telephone) have identical shuttle bus runs for about the same price as Perama. These buses can be booked at your hotel or at the numerous shops-cum-travel-agencies along the streets. And remember: these buses don't go any further west than Kalibukbuk.

Getting Around

The Lovina strip is *very* spread out, but you can easily travel back and forth on bemos. The standard fare is 500Rp, but foreigners are regularly overcharged by a few hundred rupiahs. Several shops in Kalibukbuk rent bicycles for about 6000Rp per day. Lovina is an excellent base from which to explore northern and central Bali, and rental prices for cars and motorcycles are quite reasonable.

AROUND LOVINA
☎ 0362
All of the attractions listed in the earlier Around Singaraja section are also easily accessible from Lovina.

Air Terjun Singsing
About 5km west of Kalibukbuk, a sign leads to Air Terjun Singsing. The waterfall is not huge, but the pool underneath is good for **swimming**. The water isn't crystal clear, though it's cooler than the sea and very refreshing. You can clamber further up the hill to another **waterfall** (Singsing Dua), which is slightly bigger and has a **mud bath** that is supposedly good for the skin. This waterfall also cascades into a deep pool in which you can swim. Both falls are more spectacular in the wet season, of course, and may be reduced to a trickle in the dry season.

Banjar
Brahmavihara Arama Bali's only Buddhist monastery is vaguely Buddhist-looking, with colourful decorations, a bright orange roof and statues of Buddha, but it has very Balinese decorative carvings and door guardians. You need a sarong, but this can be rented for a small donation. The monastery doesn't advertise any regular courses or programs, but visitors are welcome to meditate in special rooms. The temple is about 4km from an obvious turn-off from the main road. If you don't have your own transport, charter an ojek at the turn-off.

Air Panas Banjar These hot springs are beautifully landscaped with lush tropical plants. You can relax here for a few hours and have lunch at the restaurant, or even stay the night and *really* indulge yourself.

Eight carved stone *nagas* (mythical snake-like creatures) spew water from a natural hot spring into the first bath, which then overflows (via the mouths of five more nagas), into a second, larger pool. In a third pool, water pours from 3m-high spouts to give you a pummelling massage. You must wear a (modest) swimsuit and you shouldn't use soap in the pools, but you can do so under an adjacent outdoor shower.

Buy your ticket (1000Rp) from the little office at the end of the road, and cross the bridge to the baths. There are changing rooms under the restaurant, on the right side. The complex is open daily from 8 am to 6 pm.

Places to Stay & Eat The wonderful *Pondok Wisata Grya Sari* (☎ 92903, fax 92966) is set in the hills, very close to the baths and is one place where you may wish to splurge on a night's accommodation. Very nice singles/doubles start at US$36/41; the suites are twice as expensive, but only slightly better. The Grya Sari has an expensive *restaurant* in a lovely setting. The Indonesian food at *Restoran Komala Tirta*, overlooking the baths, is also pretty good and inexpensive.

Getting There & Away The monastery and hot springs are both well signposted along separate roads south of the main road. If you don't have your own transport, it's easy to catch a bemo to the turn-off to Banjar Tega village, then get an ojek up to the monastery first. From there you can walk to the hot springs – it's about 3km and mostly downhill. Look for signs and/or ask for directions.

Alternatively, go back down to Banjar Tega from the monastery, and turn left along Jl Sekar in the centre of the village. The small road runs west and then north for about 2km to Banjar village. From there, it's only a short distance uphill before you see the 'air panas 1km' sign on the left. Follow the road to the car park, where you'll be shown a place to park (200Rp). From the springs, you should be able to get an ojek back to the main road (2.4km), or it's a pleasant walk.

CELUKANBAWANG
☎ 0362

Celukanbawang, the main cargo port for northern Bali, has a large wharf. Bugis schooners, the magnificent sailing ships that take their name from the seafaring people of Sulawesi, sometimes anchor here. There are two hotels: *Hotel Puri Mustika Permai* (☎ 93444) has rooms from 50,000Rp to 100,000Rp; and the dreary *Hotel Drupa Indah* (☎ 93242) has doubles for 25,000Rp.

Sumatra

Sumatra is an island with an extraordinary wealth of natural resources, abundant wildlife, evocative Islamic and colonial architecture, and breathtaking mountains, lakes and rivers. It is also home to people of diverse cultures: the majority Malays; the former head-hunters and cannibals of the Batak regions; the matrilineal Muslim Minangkabau; and the indigenous groups of Pulau Nias (Nias Island) and the Mentawai Islands who, until early this century, had little contact with the outside world.

Sumatra is almost four times the size of neighbouring Java, but supports less than a quarter of the population. During Dutch rule it provided the world with large quantities of oil, rubber, pepper and coffee. Its seemingly inexhaustible resources continue to prop up the Indonesian economy today.

HISTORY

Knowledge of Sumatra's pre-Islamic history is sketchy. Mounds of stone tools and shells unearthed north of Medan indicate that hunter-gatherers were living along the Straits of Melaka 13,000 years ago, but otherwise there is little evidence of human activity until the appearance about 2000 years ago of a megalithic culture in the mountains of western Sumatra. The most notable remains are in the Pasemah Highlands near Lahat. A separate megalithic cult developed at about the same time on Pulau Nias.

Sumatra had little contact with the outside world until the kingdom of Sriwijaya emerged as a regional power at the end of the 7th century. Presumed to have been based near the modern city of Palembang, Sriwijayan power was attained through control of the Straits of Melaka – the main trade route between India and China. At its peak in the 11th century, Sriwijaya controlled a huge slab of South-East Asia, covering most of Sumatra, the Malay peninsula, southern Thailand and Cambodia. Sriwijayan influence collapsed after the kingdom

- Visit the Bohorok Orang-utan Rehabilitation Centre in Bukit Lawang, or trek through the jungle of nearby Gunung Leuser National Park and get a good look at the personable primates.

- Danau Toba is a laid-back place to unwind. The largest lake in South-East Asia, it occupies the caldera of a volcano that collapsed 100,000 years ago.

- Bukittinggi, the cultural heart of the matrilineal Minangkabau people, is the place to organise treks to the isolated villages of the Mentawai Islands.

- Aceh is home to popular snorkelling and diving haven Pulau Weh, and to the long, isolated beaches of the wild west coast.

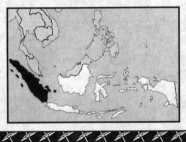

was conquered by the south Indian king Ravendra Choladewa in 1025. For the next 200 years, the void was partly filled by Sriwijaya's main regional rival, the Jambi-based kingdom of Malayu.

After Malayu was defeated by a Javanese expedition in 1278, the focus of power moved north to a cluster of Islamic sultanates on the east coast of what is now the province of Aceh. These sultanates began life as ports servicing trade through the Straits of Melaka. Many of the traders were

SUMATRA

505

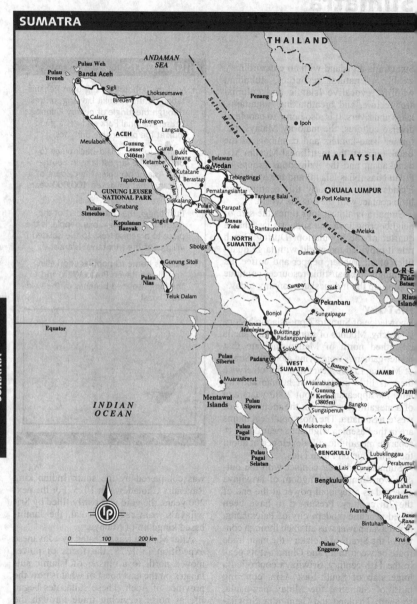

SUMATRA

THAILAND

ANDAMAN
SEA

Pulau Weh
Banda Aceh
Pulau
Breueh

Sigli

Lhokseumawe

Penang

Bireuen

Ipoh

Calang

Takengon

ACEH

Langsa

Meulaboh

Gunung
Leuser
(3404m)

Gurah
Bukit
Lawang

MALAYSIA

Ketambe

Belawan
Medan

KUALA LUMPUR
Port Kelang

Tapaktuan

Kutacane
Berastagi

Tebingtinggi

GUNUNG LEUSER
NATIONAL PARK

Sidikalang

Pematangsiantar

Tanjung Balai

Melaka

Pulau
Simeulue

Sinabang

Pulau
Samosir

Parapat

Kepulauan
Banyak

Singkil

Danau
Toba

Rantauparapat

NORTH
SUMATRA

Sibolga

Dumai

SINGAPORE
Pulau
Batam

Gunung Sitoli

Sungai

Siak

Riau
Island

Pulau
Nias

Pekanbaru

Teluk Dalam

Bonjol

Sungaipagar

RIAU

Equator

Danau
Maninjau

Bukittinggi
Padangpanjang

Padang

Solok

WEST
SUMATRA

Batang Hari

JAMBI

Pulau
Siberut

Muarabungo
Gunung
Kerinci
(3805m)

Jambi

Muarasiberut

Bangko

Mentawai
Islands

Pulau
Sipora

Sungaipenuh

INDIAN
OCEAN

Pulau
Pagai
Utara

Mukomuko

Sungai Musi

Pulau
Pagai
Selatan

Ipuh
BENGKULU

Lubuklinggau

Perabumul

Lais

Curup

Lahat

Bengkulu

Manna

Pagaralam

Bintuhan

Danau
Rana

Pulau
Enggano

Krui

0   100   200 km

Selat Malaka

Strait of Malacca

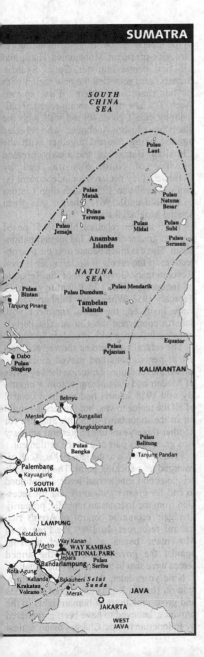

SUMATRA

SOUTH
CHINA
SEA

Pulau
Laut

Pulau
Matak

Pulau
Natuna
Besar

Pulau
Terempa

Pulau
Jemaja

Pulau
Midai

Pulau
Subi

Pulau
Serasan

Anambas
Islands

NATUNA
SEA

Pulau Mendarik

Pulau
Bintan

Pulau Dumdum

Tambelan
Islands

Tanjung Pinang

Equator

Pulau
Pejantan

Dabo
Pulau
Singkep

KALIMANTAN

Belinyu

Mentok

Sungailiat

Pangkalpinang

Pulau
Bangka

Pulau
Belitung

Tanjung Pandan

Palembang

Kayuagung

SOUTH
SUMATRA

LAMPUNG

Kotabumi

Metro

Way Kanan

WAY KAMBAS

Jepara

NATIONAL PARK

Pulau
Seribu

Bandarlampung

Kota Agung

Kalianda

Bakauheni Selat

Krakatau
Volcano

Sunda

Merak

JAVA

JAKARTA

WEST
JAVA

SUMATRA

Muslims from Gujarat (west India), and the animist locals were soon persuaded to adopt the faith of their visitors – giving Islam its first foothold in the Indonesian archipelago.

These traders also provided the island with its modern name. Until this time, the island was generally referred to as Lesser Java. The name Sumatra is derived from Samudra, meaning 'ocean' in Sanskrit. Samudra was a small port near modern Llokseumawe that became the most powerful of the sultanates. As Samudran influence spread around the coast of Sumatra and beyond, the name gradually came to refer to the island as a whole. Marco Polo spent five months in Samudra in 1292, corrupting the name to Sumatra in his report.

After the Portuguese occupied Melaka (previously known as Malacca) on the Malay peninsula in 1511 and began harassing Samudra and its neighbours, Aceh took over as the main power base on Sumatra. Close to what is now Banda Aceh, at the strategic northern tip of Sumatra, Aceh carried the fight to the Portuguese and carved out a substantial territory of its own, covering much of northern Sumatra as well as large chunks of the Malay peninsula. Acehnese power prevailed until the reign of Sultan Iskandar Muda at the beginning of the 17th century, when Dutch traders began their probings into Sumatra. The Dutch based themselves in the West Sumatran port of Padang, but made little effort to militarily impose themselves on Sumatra until the post-Napoleonic War phase of their empire building.

After the war, the Dutch returned to find that their influence in Sumatra had all but evaporated. The British ruled in Bencoolen (now Bengkulu, founded in 1685), and had also established themselves on the island of Penang in the Straits of Melaka. American traders were monopolising pepper exports from Aceh, and the Chinese were exploiting the rich reserves of tin on the islands of Bangka and Belitung, east of Palembang.

The subsequent Dutch campaign to control Sumatra resulted in some of the most protracted fighting of the colonial era. It began with a failed attempt to capture Palembang in

1818; a second attempt in 1825 succeeded, but fighting dragged on in the South Sumatran interior until 1847.

In West Sumatra, Dutch designs on the Minangkabau lands were threatened by the rise of the Islamic fundamentalist Padri movement. The Padris were so called because their leaders had made their pilgrimages to Mecca via the Acehnese port of Pedir. They had returned fired up with a determination to establish a true Islamic society, which put them at violent odds with supporters of Minangkabau *adat* (traditional law). Fighting broke out in 1803, and by 1821, when the Dutch entered the fray in support of the traditional leaders, the Padris had won control of much of the highlands.

Bukittinggi's fort, Benteng de Kock, was the Dutch headquarters for a war that dragged on until 1837, when they finally captured the equator town of Bonjol, stronghold of the Padri leader Imam Bonjol – whose name adorns street signs all over Indonesia.

The Dutch needed three military expeditions – in 1847, 1855 and 1863 – to establish authority over Pulau Nias, whereas diplomacy persuaded the British to vacate Bengkulu (which was traded for Melaka). Treaties and alliances brought other areas of Sumatra under Dutch rule, and the war with the Bataks ended in 1872 – although Batak resistance continued until 1895.

The war with the Acehnese, however, proved to be the bloodiest and the longest lasting. The Acehnese turned back the first Dutch attack in 1873 before succumbing to a massive assault two years later. They then took to the jungles to wage a guerrilla struggle that lasted until 1903, when the Acehnese sultan Tuanku Muhamat Dawot surrendered. Even after the surrender, the Dutch were forced to keep a military government in the area until 1918. They were booted out of Aceh in 1942 immediately before the WWII Japanese occupation of Sumatra and did not try to return during their post-war effort to reclaim their empire. From 1945 until Indonesia achieved independence in 1949, Aceh was ruled by Daud Beureueh, the leader of an Islamic modernist movement.

Sumatra contributed several key figures to the independence struggle, including future vice-president Mohammed Hatta and the first prime minister, Sutan Syahrir. Sumatra also provided the new nation with its fair share of problems. First up was Aceh. The new nation's living-together philosophy didn't go down too well with the staunchly Muslim Acehnese, who rebelled against being lumped together with the Christian Bataks in the newly created province of North Sumatra. Led by Beureueh, they declared an independent Islamic republic in 1953. Aceh didn't return to the fold until 1961, when it was given special provincial status.

The Sumatran rebellion of 1958-61 posed a much greater threat to Indonesian nationalism. There is much debate over the true objectives of the rebels in declaring their rival Revolutionary Government of the Republic of Indonesia (PRRI) in Bukittinggi on 15 February 1958. While many local grievances were involved, the main argument with Jakarta concerned the Communist Party's growing influence with President Soekarno.

The central government showed no interest in negotiations and moved quickly to smash the rebellion, capturing the key cities of Medan and Palembang within a month. By mid-1958 Jakarta had regained control of all the major towns, but the rebels fought on in the mountains of South Sumatra for another three years until a general amnesty was granted as part of a peace settlement.

From the 1970s to the late 1990s, Aceh re-emerged as a sticking point. The province's religious and intellectual leaders continued to call for greater autonomy and for secession from the Indonesian republic, primarily to regain economic control of Aceh's rich natural resources. In 1989 the Free Aceh Movement began a low-level uprising against the government, and the armed forces were sent in to 'monitor' the situation.

Nine years later, the National Commission on Human Rights uncovered atrocities and gross violations of human rights in the province, believed to have been perpetrated by Indonesian troops. Charges made against the military included massacre, rape, looting and house burning, and several mass graves were uncovered. The Habibie government responded by ceasing military operations in Aceh and beginning a withdrawal of combat troops, but moves to grant independence seem unlikely.

GEOGRAPHY

Stretching nearly 2000km and covering an area of 473,607 sq km, Sumatra is divided neatly in two by the equator just north of Bukittinggi.

The main feature is the Bukit Barisan mountains which run most of the length of the west coast, merging with the highlands around Danau Toba (Lake Toba) and central Aceh in the north. Many of the peaks are over 3000m (the highest is Gunung Kerinci at 3805m). Spread along the range are almost 100 volcanoes, 15 of them active. The mountains form the Sumatra's backbone, dropping steeply to the sea on the west coast, but sloping gently to the east. The eastern third of the island is low-lying, giving way to vast areas of swampland and estuarine mangrove forest bordering the shallow Straits of Melaka. It's traversed by numerous wide, muddy, meandering rivers, the biggest being the Batang Hari, Siak and Musi.

The string of islands off the west coast, including Pulau Nias and the Mentawai Islands, are geologically older than the rest of Sumatra.

CLIMATE

Sitting astride the equator, Sumatra's climate is about as tropical as tropical gets. Daytime temperatures seldom fail to reach 30°C on the coast, but fortunately most of the popular travellers' spots are in the mountains where the weather is appreciably cooler. Places like Berastagi, Bukittinggi and Danau Toba get cool enough at night to warrant a blanket.

The time to visit Sumatra is during the dry season, from May to September. June and July are the best months. The timing of the wet season is hard to predict. In the north, the rains start in October, and December/January are the wettest months; in the south, the rains start in November, peaking in January/February. Bengkulu and West Sumatra are the wettest places, with average rainfall approaching 3500mm.

FLORA & FAUNA

Large areas of Sumatra's original rainforest have been cleared for plantations, but some impressive tracts of forest remain – particularly around Gunung Leuser National Park (Taman Nasional Gunung Leuser) in the north and Kerinci Seblat National Park in the central west.

The extraordinary *Rafflesia arnoldii*, the world's largest flower, is found in pockets throughout the Bukit Barisan – most notably near Bukittinggi – between August and November.

Sumatra's forests are home to a range of rare and endangered species, including the two-horned Sumatran rhino, the honey bear and the Sumatran tiger. Unfortunately, the Sumatran tiger, the only surviving tiger species in Indonesia since the extinction of the Bali and Java tigers, remains under threat from illegal hunting and habitat destruction, despite being protected.

Gunung Leuser National Park is one of the world's last strongholds of the orangutan, with more than 5000 living in the wild. The rehabilitation centre at Bukit Lawang is one place where you can be sure of seeing one.

ECONOMY

Sumatra is enormously rich in natural resources and generates the lion's share of Indonesia's export income. The biggest earners are oil and natural gas. The fields around the towns of Jambi, Palembang and Pekanbaru produce three-quarters of Indonesia's oil. Llokseumawe, on the east coast of Aceh, is the centre of the natural gas industry.

Rubber and palm oil are the next biggest income earners. Timber is another heavily exploited resource, and the forests of the eastern Sumatran lowland are disappearing rapidly into an assortment of pulp mills and

SUMATRA

plywood factories. Other crops include tea, coffee, cocoa beans and tobacco. Sumatra was noted as a source of prized black pepper by the Chinese more than 1000 years ago and it remains a major crop in southern Sumatra.

POPULATION & PEOPLE

Sumatra is the second-most populous island in the archipelago, with 40 million people. Population density is, however, but a fraction of Bali's or Java's.

Continuing transmigration from these two islands has added to Sumatra's remarkably diverse ethnic and cultural mix. (See the entries on the Bataks in the Danau Toba section, the Acehnese in the Aceh section, the Minangkabau in West Sumatra, the Mentawaians in the Mentawai Islands section and the Kubu in the Jambi section.)

FOREIGN CONSULATES

Several countries have a consulate general or honorary consulate in Sumatra, all in Medan (area code 061). These include:

Australia
  Honorary Consulate:
  (☎ 557810/324520)
  Australia Centre, Jl RA Kartini 32
Germany
  Honorary Consulate:
  (☎ 537108)
  Jl Karim MS 4
India
  Consulate General:
  (☎ 531308/326452)
  Jl Uskup Agung Sugiopranoto 19
Malaysia
  Consulate General:
  (☎ 535271/531342)
  Jl Diponegoro 43
Netherlands
  Honorary Consulate:
  (☎ 536130)
  Jl Monginisidi 45T
Singapore
  Consulate General:
  (☎ 513366)
  Jl Tengku Daud 3
UK
  Honorary Consulate:
  (☎ 518699/519992)
  Jl Ahmad Yani 2

GETTING THERE & AWAY

The international airports at Banda Aceh, Batam, Medan, Padang and Pekanbaru are visa-free, as are the seaports of Belawan (Medan); Dumai; Batu Ampar, Nongsa and Sekupang (Pulau Batam); Tanjung Pinang (Pulau Bintan); and Tanjung Balai (Pulau Karimun).

Most travellers arrive and depart through Medan, either by air on the daily connections to Kuala Lumpur, Penang and Singapore, or by sea on the high-speed catamarans that run between Penang and Belawan. Most of northern Sumatra's main attractions are within easy reach of Medan.

Another approach is to travel by boat from Singapore to Batam in the Riau Islands (where you clear customs), and then buy a boat/bus combination fare to the mainland city of Pekanbaru. There are also regular flights from Batam to Medan, Padang and a host of other destinations.

Coming from Jakarta, the main route is by bus and ferry from Merak to the southern Sumatran ferry terminal of Bakauheni, and then north by bus on the Trans-Sumatran Hwy. A popular alternative, which eliminates the long haul by bus, is to catch the weekly Pelni boat from Jakarta to Padang.

If you're heading to Sumatra from the Americas, Europe or Oceania, a good way to travel is to reach Kuala Lumpur, Penang or Singapore first. They are much closer to Medan than Jakarta, and open up more options for onward travel.

Malaysia

Air Medan is Sumatra's major international airport and has the widest choice of destinations. Malaysian Airlines flies to Penang daily for US$55 and to Kuala Lumpur for US$60. Regional Malaysian airline Pelangi flies Medan-Ipoh four times a week (US$60). Pelangi is the main international operator out of Padang with five flights a week, priced in Malaysian ringgit, to Kuala Lumpur (RM348) – two of these flights go via Johor Bahru (RM279). Silk Air flies thrice weekly from Pekanbaru to Melaka (RM156) and Pekanbaru to Kuala Lumpur (RM265).

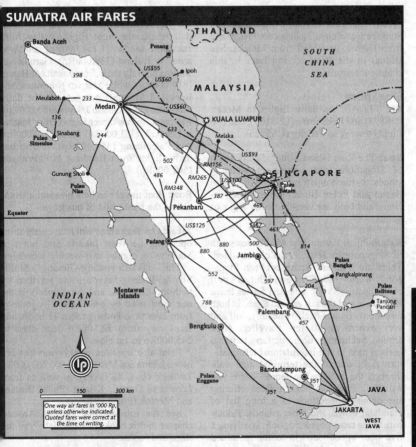

SUMATRA AIR FARES

THAILAND

SOUTH
CHINA
SEA

Banda Aceh

Penang

398

US$55

Ipoh

US$60

MALAYSIA

Meulaboh — 233 —

Medan

US$60

136

KUALA LUMPUR

Sinabang

Pulau
Simeulue

244

633

Melaka

US$93

502

RM156

SINGAPORE

Gunung Sitoli

486

RM265

US$100

Pulau
Nias

RM348

387

Pulau
Batam

Equator

Pekanbaru

465

US$125

461

457

Padang

880

500

814

880

Jambi

204

552

Pulau
Bangka

INDIAN
OCEAN

Mentawai
Islands

597

Pangkalpinang

Pulau
Belitung

788

Palembang

217

Tanjung
Pandan

457

Bengkulu

Bandarlampung

351

Pulau
Enggano

351

JAVA

351

JAKARTA

WEST
JAVA

0   150   300 km

One way air fares in '000 Rp,
unless otherwise indicated.
Quoted fares were correct at
the time of writing.

SUMATRA

Boat The main ferry route between Malaysia and Sumatra is the one from Penang to Medan's port of Belawan. However, the route between Melaka and Dumai is becoming increasingly popular.

Penang to Belawan The high-speed ferries _Ekspres Selasa_ and _Ekspres Bahagia_ take about four hours to complete the run across the Straits of Melaka. Between them, there are departures from Penang daily, except Sunday, for RM90. On Tues-

day, Thursday and Saturday there are 9 and 10 am departures, while on Monday, Wednesday and Friday there is one departure, at 9 am. The Ekspres Bahagia's Penang office (☎ 04-2631943) is on Jl (Jalan) Pasara King Edward; tickets for the Ekspres Selasa can be bought at the Kuala Perlis-Langkawi Ferry Service (☎ 04-2625630), ground floor, PPC bldg, Jl Pasara King Edward. See the Medan Getting There & Away section for Medan-Penang ferry information.

Melaka to Dumai Ferries travel daily between Melaka and Dumai, a visa-free port on Sumatra's east cost. Tickets cost 110,000Rp from Dumai, or RM80 from Melaka. See Dumai in the Riau section later in this chapter for details.

Singapore

Air Silk Air has daily flights to Medan (US$93) and Pekanbaru (US$100), and two flights a week to Padang (US$125).

Boat The Riau Islands, immediately south of Singapore, are convenient stepping stones to the Sumatran mainland. Pulau Batam and Pulau Bintan are the main islands, and both are visa-free entry and exit points.

Batam Pulau Batam, just 45 minutes south of Singapore by ferry, is the closer island. There are frequent ferries between Singapore's World Trade Centre and Batam's port of Sekupang (S$17). The first ferries leave at 7.30 am and the last around 8 pm, in both directions. Batam itself is deathly dull and very expensive, so few travellers stick around. Sekupang's domestic ferry terminal is right next to the international terminal – turn right out of the terminal and walk through the hole in the fence. There you will find a row of ticket offices offering speedboat connections to a long list of mainland towns and other islands. Pekanbaru is the most popular option, involving a five hour speedboat trip to the mainland bus/ferry terminal of Tanjung Buton followed by a four hour bus trip. Fares for the combined ticket start at 50,000Rp. Most services to Pekanbaru leave before 9 am, so you will need to leave Singapore early to avoid getting stuck on Batam.

See the Pulau Batam Getting There & Away entry in the Riau section later in this chapter for more details.

Bintan There are numerous daily services between Pulau Bintan and Tanah Merah in Singapore, costing S$20. Bintan is the best place to find boats to the outer Riau islands.

Java

Air Between Garuda Indonesia and Mandala, there are eight flights a day from Jakarta to Medan (1,157,000Rp) and three a day to Padang (788,000Rp). Garuda and Bouraq both fly daily from Jakarta to Batam (814,000Rp), while Merpati Nusantara Airlines and Mandala compete on the daily runs from Pekanbaru to Jakarta (880,000Rp) Merpati also has direct flights from Jakarta to Bengkulu (351,000Rp), Jambi (597,000Rp) and Palembang (457,000Rp). It also has daily flights from Bandung to Palembang (502,000Rp).

Boat Boat travel can be a pleasant alternative to the hard grind of bus travel.

Jakarta to Sumatra Pelni has several ships operating between Jakarta and ports in Sumatra on regular two-weekly schedules

The Jakarta-Padang-Gunung Sitoli-Sibolga-Padang-Jakarta route serviced by both the *Kambuna* and the *Lambelu* is the one most used by travellers. The journey from Jakarta to Padang takes 41 hours and fares vary from 72,500Rp deck class to 245,000Rp in 1st class.

Pelni also operates weekly services between Jakarta and Medan (107,000/363,000Rp 1st/deck class, 45 hours), as well as from Jakarta to Dumai, Kijang (Pulau Bintan) and Mentok (Pulau Bangka).

See the introductory Getting Around chapter in this book for more details of the ships and routes.

Merak to Bakauheni Ferries operate 24 hours a day between Merak in Java and Bakauheni at the southern tip of Sumatra. They depart every 36 minutes. The trip across the narrow Sunda Strait takes two hours. You're better off travelling deck class (3000Rp) and enjoying the breeze than sitting in the smoke-filled 1st class lounge (5000Rp). If you travel by bus between Jakarta and destinations in Sumatra, the price of the ferry is included in your ticket.

There's also a 'Superjet' service that does the crossing in 30 minutes for 8000Rp. It leaves Bakauheni every 70 minutes from 8.40 am to 4.50 pm.

The Bahauheni ferry terminal is surprisingly modern and efficient, and there are buses waiting to take you north to Bandarlampung's Rajabasa bus terminal (2000Rp, two hours). There are also share taxis that will take you to the city destination of your choice from 6000Rp.

Elsewhere in Indonesia

Air There are occasional direct flights between Pontianak (Kalimantan) and Medan (1,152,000Rp) or Batam (572,000Rp); otherwise, getting to Sumatra by air means changing planes in Jakarta.

Boat Pelni boats can get you from Sumatra to the furthest reaches of the archipelago. The *Lambelu*, for example, sails from Padang to Jakarta and on to Surabaya, Ambon (capital of Maluku) and Bitung, on Sulawesi's northern tip. See the introductory Getting Around chapter for more details of the ships and routes.

GETTING AROUND

Travelling around Sumatra is pretty straightforward these days, thanks largely to a greatly improved road network. Most travellers follow a well trodden trail across Sumatra, starting from Medan and stopping at Bukit Lawang, Berastagi, Danau Toba, Pulau Nias, Bukittinggi, Padang and then on to Java.

Air

An hour on a plane is an attractive alternative to many hours on a bus. Merpati is the main operator within Sumatra; Bouraq and Mandala compete on a handful of routes. Sample Merpati fares include Padang-Medan for 172,700Rp, Medan-Banda Aceh for 398,000Rp, Batam-Padang for 465,000Rp and Medan-Pekanbaru for 502,000Rp. Small airlines like Sabang Merauke-Raya Air Charter (SMAC) and Deraya Air fly to minor destinations that the bigger airlines don't bother with. SMAC, for example, has flights from Medan to Gunung Sitoli on Pulau Nias for 244,000Rp.

Bus

Bus is the most common mode of transport and, in many cases, the only option for intercity travel. Nowadays, the going is relatively easy on the main traveller routes, especially if you take the air-con coaches or tourist minibuses. A lot of money has been spent improving Sumatra's primary roads in the past 10 years, particularly the Trans-Sumatran Hwy.

However, getting off the beaten track still means hours of bone-shaking bus horror. On the backroads travel can be grindingly slow, uncomfortable and thoroughly exhausting, particularly during the wet season when bridges are washed away and the roads develop huge potholes. Avoid seats at the rear of the bus, where the bouncing is worst.

Numerous bus companies cover the main routes and prices vary greatly, depending on the level of comfort. Tickets can be bought from the bus company or from an agent, who will typically charge 10% more. In some towns, agencies are the only places to buy tickets. It pays to shop around, especially in the main tourist areas.

The best express air-con buses have reclining seats, toilets, video and (unfortunately) even karaoke. The only problem is that many of them do night runs, so you miss out on the scenery. A normal bus (without air-con) can be of virtually any standard, from a reasonably comfortable former 1st class bus without air-con to a rusty heap with no doors, broken windows and a goat on the roof. It might be harder going, but the latter is usually more fun.

Tourist Bus Many travellers take the convenient 'tourist' buses that do the Bukit Lawang-Berastagi-Parapat-Bukittinggi run. You may feel like you're in a tour group at times, and 'tourist' doesn't mean 'comfortable', but these buses do take some scenic routes that normal ones don't cover. They also pick up and drop off at hotels, travel during the day so you can see the scenery and stop at points of interest on the way. The cost and journey times are about the same as air-con buses.

Train

Sumatra has a very limited rail network. The only useful service runs from Bandarlampung in the south to Palembang, and then on to Lubuklinggau. There are also passenger trains from Medan to Pematangsiantar, Tanjung Balai and Rantauparapat.

Boat

Sumatra's rivers are major transport routes which teem with a motley but colourful collection of multipurpose vessels: rowing boats, speedboats, outriggers, ferries, junks and large cargo vessels. Boats are usually available for charter and will take you almost anywhere.

Taking a boat is both a welcome respite from bus travel and another way of seeing Sumatra. There are many places you can't get to any other way – islands that don't have an airstrip, or river villages not connected by road.

Jambi, Palembang and Pekanbaru are important towns for river transport. There are also regular links to surrounding islands, such as Banda Aceh to Pulau Weh, Padang to Pulau Siberut, Pekanbaru to Pulau Batam, Sibolga to Pulau Nias and Singkil to the Banyak Islands.

Public Transport

The usual Indonesian forms of transport – *bemos* (small passenger-tucks), *opelets* (minibuses), *becaks* (bicycle-rickshaws) and *dokars* (horse-drawn carts) – are available for getting around towns and cities in Sumatra. The base rate for a bemo is 300Rp, while the minimum fare for becaks and dokars is 1500Rp.

There are numerous tales of woe involving becak riders and demands for outrageous amounts of money, almost always as a result of breaking the golden rule of becak travel: agree on the fare beforehand and, if there is more than one passenger, clarify how many people are covered by the fare.

On bemos, hang back and watch what the locals pay if you are not certain of the fare, or check the price with other travellers.

North Sumatra

The province of North Sumatra is home to many of Sumatra's most popular attractions, including the jewel in the crown, Danau Toba. Other attractions are the Orang-utan Rehabilitation Centre at Bukit Lawang, the Karo Batak Highlands around Berastagi, and Pulau Nias off the west coast.

The province's 70,787 sq km straddle Sumatra from the Indian Ocean in the west to the Straits of Melaka in the east, bordered by Aceh to the north and West Sumatra and Riau to the south. It has a population of more than 11 million, with Medan and Pematangsiantar the main cities.

The main ethnic groups in North Sumatra are the coastal Malays who live along the Straits of Melaka; the five Batak groups from the highlands around Danau Toba and Pulau Samosir; the Pesisirs (central Tapanuli) along the Indian Ocean coastline; and the people from Pulau Nias. These ethnic groups all have their own dialects and religious beliefs, traditional customs, arts and cultures.

North Sumatra produces more than 30% of Indonesia's exports. Fine tobacco is grown around Medan. Oil, palm oil, tea and rubber are also produced in large quantities and exported from the port of Belawan, about 26km from Medan.

MEDAN
☎ 061 • pop 2 million

Medan is the capital of North Sumatra and the third largest city in Indonesia. Most people's abiding memory of Medan is of battered old motorcycle becaks belching fumes into the already heavily polluted air – that and the humidity. Most treat the city strictly as an entry and exit point.

History

Medan is an Indonesian word variously translated as 'field', 'battlefield' or 'arena'. It was on the fertile swamp at the junction of the Deli and Babura rivers (near Jl Putri Hijau) that the original village of Medan Putri was founded by Rajah Guru Patimpus in 1590.

From the end of the 16th century to the early 17th century, Medan was a battlefield in the power struggle between the kingdoms of Aceh and Deli. It remained a small village until well into the 19th century. In 1823 a British government official, John Anderson, found a population of only 200.

The town began to grow after the arrival of the Dutch. An enterprising planter named Nienhuys introduced tobacco to the area in 1865 and Medan became the centre of a rich plantation district. In 1886 the Dutch made it the capital of North Sumatra. By the end of Dutch rule, the population had grown to about 80,000 – still a far cry from today's huge, sprawling city.

The solid Dutch buildings of the affluent older suburbs inspire images of bloated bureaucrats and fat European burghers from the colonial era, while jerry-built lean-tos house the bulk of today's population.

Orientation

Finding your way around Medan presents few problems, although the traffic can be horrendous. Most places of importance are on or around the main street, Jl Ahmad Yani, which runs north-south through the city centre. South of the city centre, it becomes Jl Pemuda and then Jl Katamso; to the north, it becomes Jl Soekarno-Hatta, Jl Putri Hijau and then Jl Yos Sudarso.

Travellers arriving in Medan from Parapat and points south will find themselves deposited at the giant Amplas bus terminal, 6.5km from town on Jl Sisingamangaraja (often written as SM Raja). It runs into the city centre parallel to Jl Katamso.

Information

Tourist Offices The North Sumatran tourist office (☎ 538101), Jl Ahmad Yani 107, has friendly staff who speak English well. The office is open from 7.30 am, closing at 2.30 pm Monday to Thursday, at noon on Friday and at 1 pm on Saturday. It is closed on Sunday. The Medan City tourist office (☎ 525248), among the travel agencies at Jl Katamso 43E, is less helpful: it has a glass cabinet full of brochures and maps.

There is also an information desk at the domestic arrival terminal at the airport.

Money Medan has branches of just about every bank operating in Indonesia. Unfortunately, only a handful of them deal in foreign exchange these days, or only do so at their head office branches. Your best bet is to head to the intersection of Jl Diponegoro and Jl H Zainal Arifin, where Bank Central Asia (BCA) and Bank Internasional Indonesia (BII) have headquarters. Both offer competitive rates on cash and travellers cheques in several currencies. Two hundred metres east on Jl Zainal Arifin, Bank Bali also has rates worth comparing.

Outside banking hours, try changing cash or travellers cheques at one of the travel agencies on Jl Katamso, such as Trophy Tours at 33D, or at one of the big hotels.

Amex is represented by Pacto (☎ 510 081) at Jl Katamso 35G. Diner's Club International has an office (☎ 513331) at the Hotel Dharma Deli.

ATMs have sprung up all over Sumatra recently and Medan seems to have one on every corner. MasterCard and Cirrus are the most commonly accepted; for Visa, try BII bank machines.

If you're heading south, it's a good idea to change plenty of money because you won't find good exchange rates again until you hit Bukittinggi.

Post & Communications The main post office is in an unusual old Dutch building on the main square, Taman Kebawan. Fax, photocopy and parcel services are available, and you can surf the Net for 5000Rp an hour. The post office is open daily from 8 am to 8 pm, and the Internet facilities conveniently stay open until 11 pm.

Internet services are also available at the Novotel Soechi Medan's air-con Internet centre and at Indo.net's student-packed office at Jl Katamso 32F.

International calls can be made at several *wartels* (telephone offices) around town, including a 24 hour centre at the Simpang Raya plaza. The Novotel, Hotel Danau Toba

SUMATRA

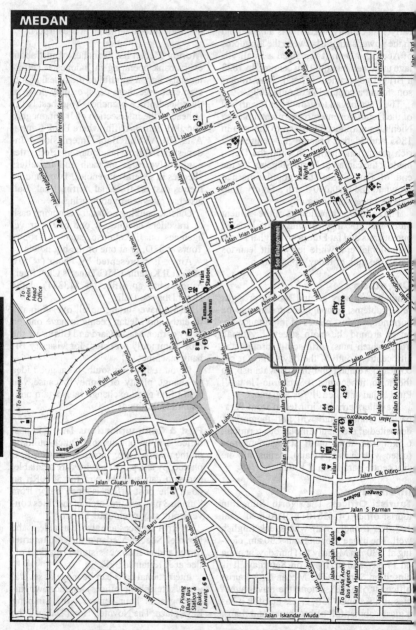

MEDAN

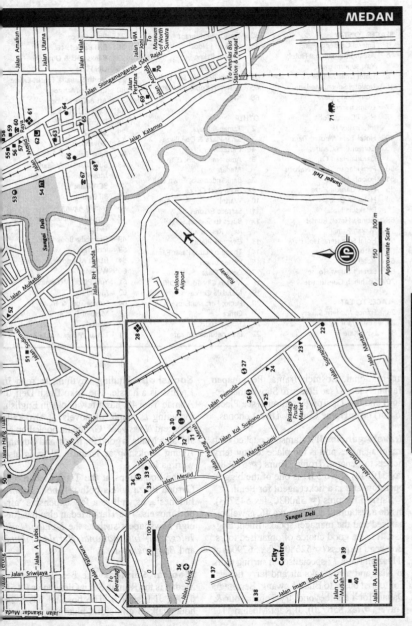

SUMATRA

MEDAN

PLACES TO STAY
1. Emeral Gardenia Hotel
5. Asean International Hotel; Yuki supermarket
8. Hotel Dharma Deli
15. Novotel Soechi Medan; Hong Kong Plaza
37. Losmen Irama
38. Hotel Danau Toba International
40. Hotel Tiara Medan; Tiara Convention Centre; Garuda Head Office
50. Penginapan Taipan Nabaru
51. Polonia Hotel
55. Hotel Garuda Plaza
56. Hotel Sri Deli; Dhaksina Hotel
58. Ibunda Hotel; Rumah Makan Famili
59. Hotel Sumatera; Hotel Garuda Citra
63. Hotel Zakia
69. Sarah's Guest House
70. Shahibah Guesthouse

PLACES TO EAT
23. France Modern Bakery
24. Restaurant Agung
31. Lyn's Kafe
32. Tip Top Restaurant
35. G's Koh I Noor
48. Medan Bakers
52. Pizza Hut
57. Taman Rekreasi Seri Deli
65. Restoran Kubang Padang
68. KFC

OTHER
2. Taman Budaya
3. Sinar Plaza & Deli Plaza
4. Clocktower
6. Amusement Park (Site of Medan Fair)
7. Bank Indonesia; Town Hall
9. Main Post Office
10. Wartel
11. Satsaco Ekspres
12. Buses to Singkil; Singkil Raya Restaurant
13. Olympia Plaza
14. Thamrin Plaza; Pasar Ramai
16. Water Tower
17. Gelora Plaza
18. Medan City Tourist Office
19. Mandala Office
20. Pacto; Perdana Express Office
21. Trophy Tours
22. Indo.net Internet cafe
25. Pelni Office
26. BNI Bank 1946
27. Banks SBU & Duta
28. Uni Plaza
29. North Sumatra Tourist Office
30. Chinese Mansion
33. Art & Craft Shops
34. Bank Bali ATM
36. Rumah Sakit Gleneagles
39. Silk Air
41. Governor's Office
42. Bank Bali
43. Bukit Barisan Military Museum
44. BCA Bank
45. BII Bank
46. Mesjid Agung
47. Parisada Hindu Dharma Temple
49. Gramedia Bookshop
53. Inda Taxi
54. Istana Maimoon
60. Wartel
61. Yuki Plaza; McDonalds
62. Mesjid Raya
64. Sukma Tour & Travel
66. Merpati Office
67. Wartel
71. Taman Margasawata Zoo

International, Losmen Irama, Penginapan Tapian Nabaru (see Places to Stay in this section) and the Tip Top Restaurant (see Places to Eat) have Home Country Direct phones.

Travel Agencies Jl Katamso is packed with travel agencies and is the place to buy ferry tickets to Penang. Trophy Tours (☎ 514888, fax 510340) at No 33D is one of the biggest operators and is a ticket agent for Pelni.

Satsaco Ekspres (☎ 550030, fax 545763), inside a restaurant at Jl Bangka 46, is well organised and the manager speaks fluent English. It has a good choice of organised tours. Boraspati Express (☎ 526802, fax 567906) at Jl Dazam Raya 77 specialises in surfing tours to Nias and also books air and ferry tickets. For tourist buses to Bukit Lawang, Berastagi, Danau Toba and beyond, try Tobali Tour & Travel (☎/fax 856770), Jl Kapt Muslim 111.

Bookshops Finding anything to read in English is a hassle. The Toko Buku Deli, Jl Ahmad Yani 48, has a few books in English, including a couple of novels. It also sells *Time* and *Newsweek*. Gramedia bookshop on Jl Gajah Mada is good for maps, and Gunung Agung bookshop at Thamrin Plaza is also worth a look.

The bookshops at the Tiara Medan and Garuda Plaza hotels both sell books about Indonesia, as well as a few expensive 'airport' novels. The Tiara Medan also has foreign newspapers such as the *London Daily Telegraph*, *International Herald Tribune* and *Bangkok Post*.

Medical Services The best hospital in Medan is the Rumah Sakit Gleneagles (☎ 56 6368), Jl Listrik 6. The hospital has a 24 hour walk-in clinic and pharmacy, as well as English-speaking doctors and specialists. For an ambulance, dial ☎ 118.

Dangers & Annoyances Theft is a growing problem in Medan, and it is commonly carried out by thieves on motorbikes. One traveller reported having his backpack stolen in this way while he negotiated a fare with a becak driver, while another traveller had her pack ripped from her shoulders as she walked down the street in a large group.

Istana Maimoon & Mesjid Raya
The city's two finest buildings are within 200m of each other. The crumbling Istana Maimoon (Maimoun Palace) on Jl Katamso was built by the sultan of Deli in 1888, and the family still occupies one wing.

The magnificent black-domed Mesjid Raya (Grand Mosque) is nearby at the junction of Jl Mesjid Raya and Jl Sisingamangaraja. It was commissioned by the sultan in 1906. Both buildings are open to the public and ask for donations rather than charging an entrance fee. Dress modestly when visiting the mosque – women are asked to cover their heads with the scarves provided.

Museums
The **Museum of North Sumatra** (☎ 716 792), Jl HM Joni 51, is open Tuesday to Sunday from 8.30 am to noon and 1 to 5 pm. Admission for tourists is by donation but you may be asked to buy a 750Rp student ticket anyhow. The museum has good coverage of North Sumatran history and culture. Most exhibits are well marked.

The **Bukit Barisan Military Museum**, near the Hotel Danau Toba International on Jl H Zainal Arifin has a small collection of weapons, photos and memorabilia from WWII, the War of Independence and the Sumatran rebellion of 1958.

Hash House Harriers
Medan's two branches of the Hash House Harriers continue an eccentric approach to exercise that dates back to the mad-dogs-and-Englishmen days of the British in South-East Asia.

The run takes the form of a game of hare and hounds, a pursuit that has its origins in the hunting traditions of the British aristocracy. A 'hare' is selected to lay a trail for the 'hounds' to follow – dotted with false leads and other tricks.

The prime objective is to work up a thirst. Both sets of Harriers meet at Lyn's Kafe at Jl Ahmad Yani 98, where you can get information about the next run.

Other Attractions
Some fine European buildings are dotted along Jl Soekarno-Hatta opposite Taman Kebawan (Kebawan Park), including the **Bank Indonesia**, the **Town Hall** and the **post office**. Look out for the splendidly ornate **Chinese mansion** opposite the Tip Top Restaurant on Jl Ahmad Yani and the similarly eye-catching **Parisada Hindu Dharma** temple on the corner of Jl Teuku Umar and Jl H Zainal Arifin.

Breaking the Medan skyline are modern edifices like **Yuki Plaza**, three floors of neon-lit shopping arcades straight out of Singapore. The top floor has a lively **amusement park** with some good rides for small children. North of town, Deli Plaza's amusement centre has **dodgem cars** for the bigger kids.

A bemo ride south along Jl Katamso takes you to Medan's depressing zoo, **Taman Margasawata**. No attempt has been made to recreate the animals' habitats and most cages are missing basic amenities such as watering holes. The carnival atmosphere on Sunday, with cabaret-style singers, food stalls and donkey rides is horribly incongruous. Entry costs 1350Rp; 2100Rp on weekends. The widely promoted **crocodile farm** at Asam Kumbang, 5km south-west of the city centre, makes the zoo look like Club Med. Literally piled on top of one another in filthy concrete cells, the dehydrated crocs look like bizarre surrealist sculptures as they await their next incarnation as fashion accessories. Hardly worth the 1500Rp entry fee and the taxi fare there (around 10,000Rp return).

Places to Stay
Every becak driver in Medan seems to tout for one or other of the travellers' haunts.

Their favourite hunting ground is around the travel agencies on Jl Katamso, where buses drop new arrivals at the end of the ferry trip from Penang. They will tell any number of stories to divert you from the hotel of your choice: the place you want to go to doesn't exist; it's closed for repairs, full, dirty or too expensive; or it's changed its name – to the place they represent.

Places to Stay – Budget

The best travellers' places are south of the city centre off Jl SM Raja. The *Hotel Zakia* (☎ 722413), across from Mesjid Raya on Jl Sipiso-Piso, is the most popular joint. It has dorm beds for 7000Rp; doubles with fan cost 14,000Rp, or from 18,000Rp with bathroom and fan. Prices include a breakfast of roti and coffee.

Further south is the family-run *Sarah's Guest House* (☎ 743783), tucked away at Jl Pertama 10. Doubles with fan cost 15,000Rp; 20,000Rp with bathroom. The owner offers free transport to the airport. This place should not be confused with the nearby *Shahibah Guesthouse* (☎ 718528, Jl Armada 3), home of the most persistent becak touts. It has dorm beds for 7000Rp and massive doubles with bathroom for 25,000Rp.

The *Losmen Irama* (☎ 326416, Jl Palang Merah 1125) is on an easy-to-miss alley opposite the Hotel Danau Toba International – look for the guys selling live bats nearby. With some of the city's grottiest rooms and most unhelpful staff, its sole virtue is its proximity to the city centre. It charges 6000Rp per person, and has a Home Country Direct phone for international calls.

Penginapan Tapian Nabaru (☎ 512155, Jl Hang Tuah 6) occupies an old timber house on the banks of the Sungai Deli (Deli River). It's a quiet place, with dorms for 5000Rp and doubles with shared bath for 8000Rp, but it's a long way out.

Places to Stay – Mid-Range

There is a string of mid-range places north of the Mesjid Raya on Jl SM Raja, and it's worth bargaining your way along this competitive strip before you decide. Just ask to look at a room and the published rate will drop substantially.

The charming *Hotel Sri Deli* (☎ 713571) at No 30 has comfortable doubles with fan and bathroom for 35,000Rp, and air-con rooms from 60,000Rp. Breakfast is included. The labyrinthian *Dhaksina Hotel* (☎ 720000, fax 740113) at No 20 has some grotty budget rooms, but its air-con rooms starting at 50,000Rp are very comfortable. Across the road at No 31, the *Ibunda Hotel* (☎ 745555, fax 740772) is a large, popular place above the Rumah Makan Famili (see Places to Eat later in this section). Air-con singles/doubles start at 50,000/60,000Rp.

Nearby at No 27, the formidable-looking *Hotel Garuda Citra* (☎ 717733) has basic air-con doubles for 66,000Rp and much better rooms in its new wing for 94,000Rp. Prices include breakfast, and discounts are common. *Hotel Sumatera* (☎ 721551) at No 35 has seen better days – its air-con doubles from 45,000Rp are in need of an upgrade.

Places to Stay – Top End

Medan's best hotels are of international standard. They all offer such luxuries as fitness centres, swimming pools and 24 hour room service. Very few of these places quote their rates in US dollars any more, which is a bonus for travellers.

The monolithic *Hotel Danau Toba International* (☎ 557000, Jl Imam Bonjol 17) has massively discounted its prices, with standard doubles dropping from US$89 to 88,000Rp. The *Hotel Garuda Plaza* (☎ 771 1411, fax 714411, Jl SM Raja 18) also has good deals, but it takes a bit of bargaining. Other international-standard hotels include the new *Novotel Soechi Medan* (☎ 561234, 76A Jl Cirebon), the *Hotel Tiara Medan* (☎ 516000, Jl Cut Mutiah) and *Asean International Hotel* (☎ 575888), on the corner of Jl Gatot Subroto and Jl Glugur Bypass.

Places to Eat

Medan has the most varied selection of cuisines in Sumatra, from basic Malay-style *mie* (noodle) and *nasi* (rice) joints, to top-class Chinese, Japanese and western restaurants.

The *Taman Rekreasi Seri Deli*, opposite the Mesjid Raya, is a slightly upmarket approach to stall dining. You just sit down and waitresses bring round a menu that allows you to choose from the offerings of about 20 stalls.

The Dutch-style *Tip Top Restaurant* (Jl Ahmad Yani 92) is an old favourite with foreign visitors. Its colonial wood finish and slowly revolving ceiling fans make it a pleasant spot to relax, in spite of the continuous traffic outside. It serves European, Chinese and Padang food, and has a Home Country Direct phone. *Lyn's Kafe* nearby has western meals and is a popular expat watering hole.

For Padang food, try the *Restaurant Agung* (Jl Pemuda 40) or the *Restoran Kubang Padang* (Jl IR Juanda 63). The popular *Rumah Makan Famili* (Jl SM Raja 31) below the Ibunda Hotel, has bowel, brain or heart with coconut on its menu, as well as other more standard offerings.

Vegetarians looking for something other than *gado gado* should check out *G's Koh I Noor*, a family-run Indian restaurant at Jl Mesjid 21. Other good Indian places are *Maharaja* and the *Cahaya Curry House* on Jl Cik Ditiro.

The Hotel Danau Toba International (see Places to Stay earlier in this section) has some fine restaurants, including *Osaka* (Japanese), *Riung Lembur* (Javanese and Sundanese) and the popular expat hang-out *The Tavern*, which specialises in grills (and beers). The Novotel's high-class Chinese restaurant and reasonably priced buffets are also recommended.

Medan's first *McDonald's* has boldly positioned its golden arches in Yuki Plaza, directly opposite the arches of the Mesjid Raya, while *KFC* has two branches: one on the corner of Jl IR Juanda and Jl Katamso, and one at Deli Plaza. *Pizza Hut* (☎ 519 956), on the corner of Jl Multatuli and Jl Suprapto, offers free delivery to your home or hotel.

Jl Semarang, east of the train line between Jl Pandu and Jl Bandung, is a great place to have a quick and cheap Chinese meal at night.

Fruit is surprisingly hard to find. The main fruit market is *Pasar Ramai* (Ramani Market), next to Thamrin Plaza on Jl Thamrin. *Brastagi Fruits Market*, an upmarket, air-con shop rather than a market, is more conveniently located on Jl Kol Sugiono. It has a great selection of local and imported tropical fruit, as well as apples and oranges.

There are some excellent bakeries awaiting the sweet-toothed traveller. Two to check out are the *France Modern Bakery* (Jl Pemuda 24C), and *Medan Bakers* (Jl H Zainal Arifin 150), just beyond the Hindu temple.

Entertainment

The *amusement park* (taman ria) on Jl Gatot Subroto is the site of the Medan Fair in March/April.

Shopping

Medan has a number of interesting arts and crafts shops, particularly along Jl Ahmad Yani. Try Toko Asli at No 62, Toko Rufino at No 56 or Toko Bali Arts at No 68. They all have a good selection of antique weaving, Dutch pottery, carvings and other pieces. Jl Ahmad Yani is also a good place to buy sporting equipment and musical instruments, though whether the brand-named items are legitimate is another question.

Clothes, shoes, jewellery, electrical goods and cosmetics can be found at any one of Medan's multi-level air-con shopping arcades. Most of these arcades also have well stocked supermarkets.

Getting There & Away

Medan is Sumatra's main international arrival and departure point.

Air There are daily international flights from Medan to Singapore, Kuala Lumpur and Penang. See the introductory Getting There & Away section in this chapter for details.

There are numerous direct flights to Jakarta (1,157,000Rp). Garuda does the trip five times daily, and Mandala has three flights daily. Garuda also has daily flights to Banda Aceh (398,000Rp). Merpati flies daily to Padang (486,000Rp) and Batam

(633,000Rp), and three times a week to Pekanbaru (502,000Rp). It also has three flights a week to Pontianak in Kalimantan (1,152,000Rp). SMAC flies from Medan to Gunung Sitoli (244,000Rp) on Pulau Nias three times a week.

Airlines with offices in Medan are as follows:

Garuda Indonesia
Head office: (☎ 514877) Tiara Convention Centre, Jl Cut Mutiah
Branch office: (☎ 516400) Hotel Dharma Deli, Jl Balai Kota 2
General Inquiries: ☎ 327747
Malaysian Airlines
(☎ 519333) Hotel Danau Toba International, Jl Imam Bonjol 17
Mandala
(☎ 516379) Jl Katamso 37E
Merpati Nusantara Airlines
(☎ 321888) Jl Katamso 219
Silk Air
(☎ 537744) 6th floor, Bank Umum Servitia bldg, Jl Imam Bonjol
SMAC
(☎ 537744) Jl Imam Bonjol 23 (close to the airport)
Thai Airways International
(☎ 510541) Hotel Dharma Deli, Jl Balai Kota 2

Bus There are two main bus stations. Buses to Parapat, Bukittinggi and other points south leave from the huge Amplas terminal, 6.5km south of the city centre along Jl SM Raja. The best companies for long-distance travel south are ALS and ANS. Their offices are in a separate building behind the main block. They charge similar fares – 25,000Rp for air-con services to Parapat (for Danau Toba) and 55,000Rp to Bukittinggi. Of course, less reputable companies (with less comfortable buses) are cheaper. Almost any opelet heading south on Jl SM Raja will get you to Amplas.

Buses to the north leave from Pinang Baris bus station, 10km west of the city centre on Jl Gatot Subroto. Get there by taxi (around 10,000Rp) or by opelet down Jl Gatot Subroto. There are public buses to both Bukit Lawang (2000Rp, three hours) and Berastagi (3000Rp, two hours) every half hour between 5.30 am and 6 pm. Buses

to Banda Aceh leave from 8 am to 11 pm - get tickets from Pinang Baris or buy one in advance from the booking agents west of town on Jl Gajah Mada. The journey takes anything up to 13 hours in daytime, but the express night buses do the trip in about nine hours. Fares cost 35,000Rp, up to 45,000Rp for the latest luxury buses with reclining seats. The same bus companies also sell tickets to Bireuen (23,000Rp), the change-over point for buses to Takengon and the Gayo Highlands.

Tobali Tour & Travel (see Travel Agencies earlier in this section) also runs 'tourist' buses (not all are air-con) to popular destinations south of Medan. The trips include stops at interesting sites along the way. Fares are 20,000Rp to Bukit Lawang, 17,000Rp to Berastagi and 25,000Rp to Pulau Samosir (ferry transfer included).

A minibus goes daily to Singkil (25,000Rp, eight hours), the departure point for boats to the Banyak archipelago (see the Aceh section in this chapter for details). The bus leaves at 2 pm from outside the Singkil Raya restaurant on Jl Bintang, one block east of Olympia Plaza.

Train There are passenger services twice a day to Pematangsiantar (10,000/16,000Rp for *bisnis/eksekutif* class) and Tanjung Balai (3500Rp, *ekonomi* class only), and three times a day to Rantauparapat (15,000/28,000Rp, bisnis/eksekutif only).

Taxi There are several long-distance taxi operators in Medan. Inda Taxi (☎ 516615), Jl Katamso 62, has share taxis to Parapat (17,000Rp) and Sibolga (22,000Rp). Top-end hotels can arrange charter taxis for four people to places like Berastagi and Bukit Lawang (around 100,000Rp).

Boat High-speed ferries to Penang now run daily from the port of Belawan, around one hours drive from Medan. Tickets can be bought from agents in town (RM96) and the fare includes bus transport to the port. The ferries all depart at 10 am; buses from Medan leave around 8 am.

Sukma Tours (☎ 720421), Jl SM Raja 92A, and Pacto (☎ 510081), Jl Katamso 35G, handle tickets for the *Ekspres Bahagia*, which sails Monday to Saturday. Perdana Express (☎ 545803), Jl Katamso 35C, sells tickets for the *Ekspres Selasa*, which leaves on Wednesday, Friday and Sunday. For ferry information from Penang to Medan, see the main Getting There & Away section earlier in this chapter.

Every five days Pelni's *Umsini* sails to Jakarta (107,000/363,000Rp for deck/1st class) via Batam (55,000/185,000Rp). The trip to Jakarta's Tanjung Priok takes 45 hours. The main Pelni office (☎ 622526) is 8km north of the city centre at Jl Krakatau 17A – but don't head out there thinking the staff will be more helpful than those at the centrally located branch office (☎ 518 899), Jl Sugiono 5. Those wanting a Pelni timetable will have their work cut out for them.

Getting Around

To/From the Airport Airport taxis operate on a coupon system – get a ticket first from the taxi desk. Most trips to central Medan cost 8000Rp. Becaks are not allowed into the airport area.

Public Transport Medan's taxis are a convenient way of getting around – but they can be expensive, depending on the traffic and on how far you want to go. For short distances it may well work out cheaper to insist that the driver use the meter; for longer distances it is usually more economical to agree to a price *before* you get in the car. After bargaining you should be able to charter a taxi for a few hours for around 10,000Rp per hour.

Opelets are the main form of public transport. They cost 500Rp, although you may be asked to pay double if you have a large backpack. Just stand by the roadside and call out your destination.

For becaks, reckon on paying about 1000Rp per kilometre – which means that most journeys around the city centre should cost no more than 3000Rp.

BUKIT LAWANG
☎ 061

Bukit Lawang, 96km north-west of Medan, is on the eastern edge of the giant Gunung Leuser National Park. The country is wild and enchanting, with dense jungle and clear, fast-flowing rivers.

It is also the site of the famous Bohorok Orang-utan Rehabilitation Centre, which has made this once-remote village one of the most popular spots in Sumatra. Many tourists opt to spend four or five days here.

During the week, foreign tourists have the place pretty much to themselves; those seeking solitude would be best to avoid Bukit Lawang on the weekend, when busloads of Medan holiday-makers hit town. Accommodation can be hard to find on Friday and Saturday nights, when quiet coffee shops suddenly transform into blaring disco joints.

For more information on Gunung Leuser National Park, see the Aceh section later in this chapter.

Orientation & Information

The town exists almost solely to service the tourist industry. The bus stops where the road ends: at a small square surrounded by shops and a few offices. There are a couple of restaurants by the river where you can sit and take stock. The closest accommodation is on the opposite side of the river, but the prime locations are a 15 minute walk upstream. There is a small tourist office in the white building at the back of the bus lot. There isn't much information available, but the staff are helpful and speak English.

Money Change money before you arrive. There are no banks in Bukit Lawang and the rates at the local moneychangers are appalling.

Post & Communications There is no post office, but you can buy stamps from the shops and there are some post boxes. There is a small Telkom wartel across the river from the Wisma Leuser Sibayak, and Wisma Bukit Lawang Cottages has a card phone.

SUMATRA

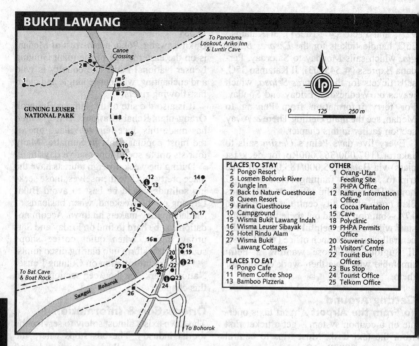

BUKIT LAWANG

To Panorama
Lookout, Ariko Inn
& Luntir Cave

Canoe
Crossing

GUNUNG LEUSER
NATIONAL PARK

0   125   250 m

To Bat Cave
& Boat Rock

Sungai Bohorok

To Bohorok

PLACES TO STAY
2 Pongo Resort
5 Losmen Bohorok River
6 Jungle Inn
7 Back to Nature Guesthouse
8 Queen Resort
9 Farina Guesthouse
10 Campground
15 Wisma Bukit Lawang Indah
16 Wisma Leuser Sibayak
26 Hotel Rindu Alam
27 Wisma Bukit
   Lawang Cottages

PLACES TO EAT
4 Pongo Cafe
11 Pinem Coffee Shop
13 Bamboo Pizzeria

OTHER
1 Orang-Utan
   Feeding Site
3 PHPA Office
12 Rafting Information
   Office
14 Cocoa Plantation
15 Cave
18 Polyclinic
19 PHPA Permits
   Office
20 Souvenir Shops
21 Visitors' Centre
22 Tourist Bus
   Offices
23 Bus Stop
24 Tourist Office
25 Telkom Office

Medical Services Minor medical problems can be dealt with by the nurse at the polyclinic next to the PHPA (national park) permits office.

Dangers & Annoyances The PHPA requires tourists to employ a guide to enter the park, but the only qualification a guide needs is the ability to pay the registration fee. As a result, some guides know little about the flora and fauna, they leave rubbish behind, have no first aid skills (and don't carry a kit) and they feed the orangutans in the forest for the amusement of tourists (which isn't allowed). Consult other travellers and quiz your guide before handing over your hard-earned cash.

More disturbing are recent reports of sexual harassment – and in some cases sexual assault – of female travellers, usually during overnight trekking trips. Women, including those travelling in pairs, are strongly advised to join larger groups for treks – legitimate and responsible guides will team you up with other travellers if you insist.

Another downside of Bukit Lawang's boom is petty theft. Take care with valuables and use hotel safety boxes where available.

Bohorok Orang-Utan Rehabilitation Centre

Bukit Lawang's famous Orang-utan Rehabilitation Centre was set up in 1973 to help primates readjust to the wild after captivity or displacement through land clearing. That was the original intention. These days the tourist industry that has grown up around the centre would be devastated if the animals failed to front for the cameras.

Newly arrived primates are quarantined, given a medical checkup, and treated for any illnesses or diseases they may have

Going Ape

Gunung Leuser National Park is one of the orang-utan's last remaining strongholds, with more than 5000 animals thought to be living in the wild.

The orang-utan is found today only in Sumatra and Borneo, although fossilised remains show that its habitat once extended to China and Java.

It is the world's largest arboreal mammal, large males weighing up to 90kg. Despite its size, the orang-utan moves through the jungle canopy with great agility and assurance, swinging on vines and branches or using its weight to sway saplings back and forth to reach the next.

The name *orang hutan* is Malay for 'person of the forest', and there are numerous myths and legends surrounding the creature. Stories were told of how the orang-utan would carry off pretty girls. Others told of how it could speak, but refused to do so because it did not want to be made to work.

Orang-utans have a long life-span, but tend to breed slowly. Females reach sexual maturity at about the age of 10 years. Orang-utans have few young and stay around their mothers until they are between seven and 10 years old. The females remain fertile until about the age of 30 and, on average, have only one baby every six years.

Orang-utans tend to be quite solitary creatures.

They are primarily vegetarians, their normal diet comprising fruit, shoots and leaves, as well as nuts and tree bark that they grind up with their powerful jaws and teeth. They occasionally eat insects, eggs and small mammals.

Despite their remarkably human expressions, orang-utans are considered to be the most distantly related to humans of all the great apes.

Outside Gunung Leuser National Park, orang-utans can be found in the Tanjung Puting and Kutai national parks, in the Gunung Palung and Bukit Raja reserves in Kalimantan, as well as in neighbouring Sarawak and Sabah.

JENNY BOWMAN

contracted through human contact. Many animals, after spending years as caged pets, must re-learn how to climb trees, find food and make a nest. When they are ready, the orang-utans are released into the forest near the centre, where they can access twice-daily feedings of milk and bananas until they can fully fend for themselves. The aim of the monotonous diet is to encourage the orang-utans to search for natural forest fodder and become self-sufficient.

Still, the feedings are hugely popular. They take place at a platform in the jungle on the west bank of the Sungai Bohorok. The river crossing to the site (by dugout canoe) is included in the cost of the PHPA

permit required to enter the park (4000Rp, plus 500Rp insurance). The permit is valid for one day and is available from the PHPA permit office in Bukit Lawang, open from 7 am daily. Feeding times are from 8 to 9 am and 3 to 4 pm, and the river crossings operate between 7.30 and 8 am and 2.30 and 3 pm. These are the only times visitors are allowed to enter the national park other than with a guide or on an organised trek. Make sure you leave yourself enough time to make the 30 minute walk from the permit office in town to the canoe crossing upstream.

Most days about half a dozen orang-utans turn up to be fed, but fewer show up if there is an abundance of forest food available. It's best to get there early so that you can see the orang-utans arrive, swinging through the trees. It is forbidden to touch or feed the animals.

Occasionally, orang-utans can be seen by the river opposite the Jungle Inn and Losmen Bohorok River, where they come down to check out the tourists.

Bukit Lawang Visitors' Centre

This fine establishment is run by the World Wide Fund for Nature (WWF). It has good displays of flora and fauna found in Gunung Leuser National Park and a section to explain the orang-utan rehabilitation program. It's backed up by some stunning photographs. The centre sells a small but very informative booklet about the national park by New Zealand writer and photographer Mike Griffiths. It's a good investment if you plan to spend some time in the park. The centre is open daily from 8 am to 3 pm.

Rafting

The Back to Nature Guesthouse organises whitewater rafting trips down the Alas and Wampu rivers from $US20 a day. It also arranges combined rafting/trekking trips. The Rafting Information Office, run by the area's search and rescue crew, has similar deals. Both operations provide helmets, life jackets and safety gear.

Trekking

Almost every losmen advertises trekking, and half the losmen workers seem to be guides – without whom you are not allowed into the park. They offer a range of tours around Bukit Lawang, as well as three- and five-day walks to Berastagi.

Around Bukit Lawang, expect to pay US$10 for a three hour trek, US$15 for a day trek (9 am to 3 pm) and US$35 for a two day trek, including overnight camping in the jungle. Prices include basic meals, guide fees, camping equipment and the park permit.

Bring along mosquito repellent, sunscreen and a large water bottle, and wear sturdy shoes with good grip. Lightweight long pants and long-sleeved tops are recommended as added protection against mosquitos and leeches (tiny, yellow and all-too-ready to suck your blood). A sarong is useful as a sheet for sleeping or as a towel, and a pair of thongs (flip-flops) is good for crossing rivers. Reasonable fitness is required, particularly during the wet season when tracks become muddy and slippery.

While many visitors are happy with their trekking experience (or exhilarated at simply having survived), others are disappointed. Talk to other travellers and chose a guide who is recommended. The guides working at the rehabilitation centre have a good reputation.

Short Walks

There are a number of short walks that don't require guides or permits. A 20 minute walk to the south-west of town gets you to a **bat cave**. It's signposted behind the Wisma Bukit Lawang Cottages. The 2km walk passes through rubber plantations and patches of forest.

A lot of the forest trees are durians, so take care in late June and July when the spiked fruits crash to the ground (there are signs warning people not to linger). You'll need a torch (flashlight) to explore the caves.

There are more bat caves a further 4km downstream at a site called **Boat Rock**, but entry without a guide is not allowed.

The Panorama Lookout walk starts just north of the Jungle Inn. The path through the rainforest is very steep and slippery. **Gua Luntir** (Luntir Cave), about 20 minutes walk from the lookout, is another bat hang-out.

Tubing

Many of the losmen rent out inflated truck inner tubes (around 2000Rp per day) which can be used to ride the rapids of Sungai Bohorok. Several people have got into difficulties on the river, and life jackets are not available.

Places to Stay & Eat

Bukit Lawang has an abundance of good, cheap losmen spread out along the river. Accommodation is concentrated in two main areas: along the river bank opposite

Trekking Lightly

Trekking is the best way to see the local flora and fauna up close and it can be a wonderfully rewarding experience. The rainforest at Bohorok is home to birds, reptiles, a range of tropical plants and, of course, primates. What you see depends largely on chance – but how you see it is another story.

While the majority of guides are responsible, unfortunately, some of them are attempting to remove any element of chance on their treks. The orang-utan is the main target – by establishing their own private feeding sites in the forest, unscrupulous guides make certain they can deliver what they promise. While it may be good for tourism, feeding the orang-utans in the jungle encourages dependence on human handouts and undermines the long-running rehabilitation program. The only time the orang-utans are supposed to be fed is at the twice-daily sessions near the rehabilitation centre; at all other times they must find their own food.

The illegal feeding has caused other problems. While most orang-utans are not aggressive, some have learnt to demand food from trekking groups, usually by forcefully shoving their outstretched hands in tourists' faces. Others have resorted to theft, pinching backpacks from tourists because they expect every bag to be full of food. Guides are usually quite adept at getting the bags back, but it can still be a frightening ordeal.

Irresponsible guides also let tourists touch the orang-utans they lure down from the trees. While it may be an appealing opportunity at the time, remember that orang-utans are highly susceptible to human illness and disease, including the flu. A sick orang-utan can spread illness throughout the wild population; that's why new arrivals at the rehabilitation centre are quarantined and the sick kept in cages.

Lastly, trekking creates rubbish, and that rubbish sometimes gets left behind. Food (including fruit) scraps may well decompose, but piles of the stuff attract flies and ants and harbour disease. Make sure it is cleaned up and removed for proper disposal.

Be aware of your impact and let your guide know, in the nicest possible way, if his behaviour is harmful to the environment. The orang-utans in Bohorok have been rescued from logging plantations and the illegal pet trade to provide them with a new life – don't let their future be spoiled by tourism.

SUMATRA

the town and upstream along the path to the orang-utan feeding site. Almost all of the losmen have associated restaurants.

The downstream accommodation is dominated by the *Wisma Bukit Lawang Cottages* (☎ 545061) and the *Wisma Leuser Sibayak* (☎ 550576), two large bungalow complexes offering a range of rooms. The Sibayak has some cheapies for 5000Rp, as well as comfortable modern rooms by the river for 35,000Rp. Bukit Lawang Cottages has stylish traditional-style rooms from 10,000Rp to 40,000Rp, including some with beautiful tropical garden bathrooms. Both also have good restaurants.

A little further upstream, the *Wisma Bukit Lawang Indah* is the typical travellers' haven, with very basic 5000Rp bungalows, a laid-back balcony restaurant and a menu with all the old favourites. Many of the trekking guides seem to be stationed here.

The accommodation near the canoe crossing, about a 15 minute walk upstream from town, is quieter. The renovator's bug has hit a couple of places, improving the range and quality of rooms offered; however, there have been local concerns that the efforts to attract travellers to this area could destroy the natural environment. While 5000Rp rooms were still available at the time of research, there were plans to set the price of the cheapest rooms in this area at 10,000Rp.

The *Jungle Inn*, with its creative carpentry and incredibly relaxed style, is very popular. It has basic doubles for 10,000Rp, and an eclectic range of other rooms cost 45,000Rp to 80,000Rp. Host Indra and his Australian-born wife Khadijah must be doing something right – Jungle Inn also attracts a lively crew of Thomas Leaf monkeys, who like to swing from little perches inside the restaurant.

The *Back to Nature Guesthouse* nearby has 7500Rp doubles and a new wing was under construction when we visited. Rooms are expected to cost 30,000Rp to 50,000Rp, and there are plans for an Internet cafe and bakery on the same site. The *Losmen Bohorok River* has grotty doubles with share *mandi* (Indonesian-style bath) for 10,000Rp, and much better rooms overlooking the river for 15,000Rp. *Queen Resort* has doubles with mosquito nets for 15,000Rp, and the *Farina Guesthouse*, opposite the camping ground, is good value with large, clean doubles for 10,000Rp.

For those who really want to get away from it all, *Ariko Inn*, a steep 20 minute climb up the steps past the canoe crossing, is the place. Doubles start at 5000Rp. A top-end option is the *Pongo Resort*, in the national park near the rehabilitation centre. Smart doubles with breakfast and permit included are 50,000Rp to 75,000Rp. *Pongo Cafe*, also on the national park side of the river, is good for a pre-orang-utan watching snack.

The swankiest place in town is *Rindu Alam (☎ 545015)*, where 75,000Rp gets a spotless modern double with TV and breakfast. Of the non-guesthouse eateries, *Pinem Coffee Shop*, near the camping ground, and *Bamboo Pizzeria* are worth trying.

Durian trees are abundant in and around Bukit Lawang. They are as fresh and as cheap as you'll find anywhere, from 750Rp for a small one.

Getting There & Away

There are direct buses to Medan's Pinang Baris bus station every half hour between 5.30 am and 6 pm (2000Rp, three hours). Public minivans also leave for Medan throughout the day. They cost 2500Rp and are usually quicker than (but just as crowded as) the large buses. A chartered taxi to Medan costs 100,000Rp.

The tourist minibuses are heavily promoted. They leave early in the morning for Medan (20,000Rp), Berastagi (25,000Rp) and Danau Toba (23,000Rp).

BERASTAGI (BRASTAGI)
☎ 0628

Berastagi is a picturesque hill town in the Karo Highlands, 70km from Medan on the back road to Danau Toba. At an altitude of 1300m, the climate is deliciously cool after the heat of Medan. The setting is dominated by two volcanoes: Gunung Sinabung to the west and the smoking Gunung Sibayak to the north.

Berastagi itself is not wildly exciting, but it is a well set-up base for trekking and other adventure activities. Architecture buffs will enjoy trips to nearby traditional Karo Batak villages.

Orientation

Berastagi is essentially a one-street town spread along Jl Veteran. The colourful **Tugu Perjuangan** (Combat Memorial), commemorating the Bataks' struggle against the Dutch in the 1800s, marks the centre of town. The hill to the north-west of town is Bukit Gundaling, a popular picnic spot and mid-range accommodation area.

Information

Tourist Offices The Karo regional tourist office (☎ 91084), next to the memorial in the centre of town, is friendly and helpful. The best sources of travellers' information, however, are the noticeboards at the Wisma Sibayak.

Money You can change US dollars (cash and travellers cheques) at the Bank Rakyat Indonesia (BRI) at the southern end of Jl Veteran. It's open Monday to Friday from 8 am to noon and 1 to 3 pm. You can

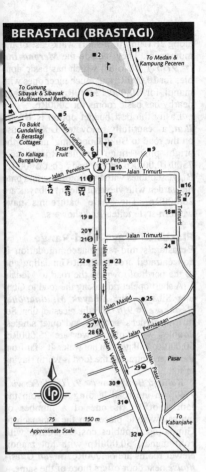

BERASTAGI (BRASTAGI)

PLACES TO STAY
1   Rudang Hotel
2   Hotel Bukit Kubu
4   Hotel International Sibayak
5   Wisma Ikut
7   El Shaddai Hotel
9   Ginsata Guesthouse
10 Ginsata Hotel
16 TS Lingga
17 Trimurty
18 Merpati Inn
23 Losmen Sibayak Guesthouse
24 Losmen Pusat
32 Wisma Sibayak

PLACES TO EAT
8   Rendezvous Restaurant
15 Raymond Steakhouse; Tobali Tour & Travel
19 Jane & Tarzan Coffee Shop; Rumah Makan
    Muslimin; Torong Inn
20 Asia Restaurant
26 Eropah Restaurant
27 Villa Flores

OTHER
3   Power Station
6   Petrol Station
11 Tourist Office
12 Police
13 Telkom Office
14 Post Office
21 BNI Bank ATM
22 Public Health Centre
25 Ria Cinema
28 BRI Bank
29 Bus & Opelet Terminal
30 Mini Market
31 Chemist

change other currencies at any of the many moneychangers, but the rates are terrible. Bank Negara Indonesia (BNI) has Berastagi's only ATM, near the Asia Restaurant at Jl Veteran 22. It accepts Cirrus and MasterCard.

Post & Communications The post office and Telkom wartel are side by side near the memorial at the northern end of Jl Veteran. The Telkom wartel is open 24 hours and has a Home Country Direct phone.

Things to See & Do

Several travel agents and budget hotels advertise guided **treks** along the well trodden trails through **Gunung Leuser National Park** to Bukit Lawang. Prices start at $US50 for a three day/two night trip. Accommodation is provided in villages along the way. **Rafting** on Sungai Alas is another option, with four-day trips costing $US110, meals and accommodation included. Of course, most people come to Berastagi to climb nearby **Gunung Sibayak** and/or **Gunung Sinabung** – see the Around Berastagi section later for details.

There's not a lot to do in town. **Golf** can be played at the Hotel Bukit Kubu (see Places to

Stay later in this section). Green fees are 20,000Rp for the nine par-three holes and you can hire a set of clubs for 25,000Rp. The hotel charges 4500Rp for a game of **tennis**, plus 7000Rp for racket hire.

Kampung Peceren is a cluster of traditional houses on the northern outskirts of Berastagi. Most of the houses are still occupied. Any opelet heading north can drop you there (300Rp). There's a 400Rp entry fee to the village (and 300Rp more if you need to use the toilet!) and if you're lucky, someone might even invite you inside their house for a peek.

There are good views from **Bukit Gundaling**, particularly at sunset. A round-tour of the hill by horse-drawn *sado* (cart) costs 7000Rp.

Those suffering post-trekking aches and pains might like to try the traditional **herbal sauna** (3500Rp for as long as you like) and **massage** (7000Rp per hour) at TS Lingga guesthouse (see Places to Stay).

Places to Stay – Budget

The original Berastagi guesthouse, *Wisma Sibayak* (☎ 20953) is one of the old-style Asian traveller haunts. Dilapidated, dingy, but laid-back, it offers dorm beds for 5000Rp, small singles/doubles for 6000/10,000Rp, and larger rooms for 15,000Rp. It's packed with travellers, and the guest books are full of useful and amusing information about sightseeing, festivals, transport, walks, climbs and other things to do in the area. The Sibayak's back-up budget place is *Losmen Sibayak Guesthouse* (☎ 91122, Jl Veteran 119), which has more pleasant rooms but lacks Wisma Sibayak's good vibe.

There are several reasonable places up near the Tugu Perjuangan. The *Ginsata Hotel* (☎ 91441, Jl Veteran 27) has clean doubles with shower for 20,000Rp; try to get one of the better rooms on the 2nd floor. Around the corner is the co-owned *Ginsata Guest House*, a pleasant old timber building with rooms from 10,000/12,000Rp. The friendly *El Shaddai Hotel* (☎ 91023, Jl Veteran 3) has clean green doubles for 7500Rp, and rooms with mandi for 15,000/20,000Rp.

There is a cluster of tiny guesthouses along Jl Trimurti, a short walk east of the monument. They include the *Merpati Inn* (☎ 91157) at No 68, which has basic doubles for 10,000Rp and much nicer ones with mandi for 10,000/12,000Rp. *TS Lingga* nearby has basic rooms for 5000Rp.

Easily the best budget option is *Wisma Ikut*, a beautifully renovated Dutch house on the road to Bukit Gundaling, next to the bright pink Hindu temple. Rooms cost 7500/10,000Rp; dorm beds cost 5000Rp. Bigger doubles with balconies opening onto the garden with views of Mount Sibayak are 20,000Rp. The share bathrooms have western-style toilets and showers.

Places to Stay – Mid-Range

Berastagi's mid-range accommodation is concentrated around Bukit Gundaling and to the north of town on the road to Medan.

A short opelet ride along the road to Gunung Sibayak, the *Sibayak Multinational Resthouse* (☎ 91031) is the nicest option. Set in lush gardens, spotless and quiet singles/doubles with cold shower are 25,000Rp; 50,000Rp will get you hot water. It's far from the town centre, but the food is worth staying in for.

Kaliaga Bungalow (☎ 91116, Jl Perwira 219), on the road leading west from the tourist office, is one of a number of bungalow-style places on the approach to Gundaling. Doubles cost 20,000Rp with cold mandi; 30,000Rp with hot mandi. Newer rooms are 60,000Rp. *Sagan Guesthouse* next door offers more of the same.

The *Hotel Bukit Kubu* (☎ 20832), just north of town on Jl Sempurna, was originally a guesthouse owned by the Dutch oil company Batavia Petroleum. It sits on a small hill set back from the road, surrounded by its own nine-hole golf course. Rates are 50,000/60,000Rp for large rooms; 135,000Rp for a bungalow.

Places to Stay – Top End

Three- and four-star hotels are springing up everywhere, aimed largely at the Malaysian and Singaporean package-tour markets.

They all have swimming pools, tennis courts and fitness centres. The cheapest doubles are listed at about 120,000Rp, but this is very negotiable. The biggest is the *Hotel International Sibayak* (☎ 91301) on the road to Bukit Gundaling. The smaller-scale but lovely *Berastagi Cottages* (☎ 91725) has a range of stylish rooms from 140,000Rp.

Places to Eat

Berastagi is famous for its *fruit and vegetable markets*. The rich volcanic soils of the surrounding countryside supply much of North Sumatra's produce. Passionfruit is a local speciality. You'll find both the *marquisa bandung*, a large, sweet, yellow-skinned fruit, and the *marquisa asam manis*, a purple-skinned fruit that makes delicious drinks.

At night, try delicious *cakes* made from rice flour, palm sugar and coconut, steamed in bamboo cylinders. You can buy them at the stall outside the Ria Cinema.

Most of the budget hotels have restaurants. The restaurant at the *Wisma Sibayak* serves good food, while the Torong Inn's *Jane & Tarzan Coffee Shop* and the *Ginsata Guest House* serve typical travellers' fare. Newcomer *Raymond Steakhouse* (*Jl Veteran 49*) has delicious fruit lassis and great food, including New Zealand steak (25,000Rp). *Villa Flores* (*Jl Veteran 73*) has pizza, steak, pasta, falafel and even paella on its menu.

There's Padang food at the *Ginsata Hotel* and at the *Rumah Makan Muslimin*, downstairs from the Torong Inn.

The *Eropah Restaurant* (*Jl Veteran 48G*) serves good, cheap Chinese food. The aircon *Asia Restaurant* at No 9-10 is bigger and more expensive.

Shopping

There are a number of interesting antique and souvenir shops along Jl Veteran. Crispo Antiques has particularly interesting items.

Getting There & Away

Berastagi's bus terminal is on Jl Veteran. There are frequent buses to Medan (2000Rp, two hours). Daily tourist buses also head to Medan, leaving at 2 pm (17,000Rp).

Getting to Parapat (for Danau Toba) by public bus is a hassle. See Parapat's Getting There & Away entry later in this section for details. The easy option is to catch one of the tourist buses making the Bukit Lawang-Parapat run. Berastagi is the midpoint, and buses going in both directions stop here for lunch. It costs 25,000Rp to Bukit Lawang (leaving Berastagi at 2 pm) and 23,000Rp to Parapat (leaving at 1 pm). Raymond Steakhouse is the booking office for Tobali Tour & Travel. It runs daily buses in both directions.

Berastagi is the southern approach for visits to Gurah and Gunung Leuser National Park. Unfortunately, the only way to get there is a long haul on public buses, first to Kabanjahe (500Rp), then to Kutacane (7000Rp) and finally to Gurah (2500Rp). For more details, see the Gurah & Gunung Leuser National Park entry in the Aceh Province section.

Getting Around

Opelets leave from the bus terminal on Jl Veteran. They run every few minutes between Berastagi and Kabanjahe (500Rp), the major population and transport centre of the highlands. You need to go to Kabanjahe, 16km south of Berastagi, to get to many of the villages mentioned in the following section.

Horse-drawn sados charge from 1500Rp for rides around town. Villa Flores restaurant hires pushbikes for 10,000Rp a day.

AROUND BERASTAGI
Gunung Sibayak

Many people come to Berastagi to climb Gunung Sibayak (2094m), probably the most accessible of Indonesia's volcanoes. It's best to avoid going on Sunday, when day-trippers from Medan are out in force.

You need good walking boots because the path is steep in places and is slippery year-round. It can be cold at the top, so bring something warm to wear as well as food, drink and a torch (flashlight), in case you get caught out after dark. The guest books at Wisma Sibayak are full of information about this climb, and include numerous warnings about the dangers of sudden weather

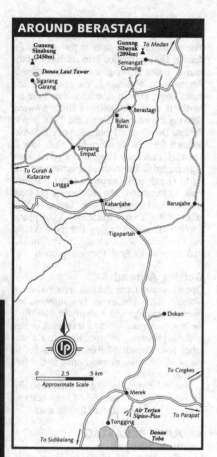

AROUND BERASTAGI

Gunung Sinabung (2450m)

Danau Laut Tawar

Sigarang Garang

Gunung Sibayak (2094m)   To Medan

Semangat Gunung

Berastagi

Bulan Baru

Simpang Empat

To Gurah & Kutacane

Lingga

Kabanjahe   Barusjahe

Tigapartah

Dokan

To Cingkes

0   2.5   5 km
Approximate Scale

Merek

Air Terjun Sipiso-Piso   To Parapat

Tongging   Danau Toba

To Sidikalang

changes. People are strongly advised not to climb alone.

There are three ways to tackle the climb, depending on your energy level. The easiest way is to take the track which starts to the north-west of town, a ten minute walk past the Sibayak Multinational Resthouse. It's 7km to the top (about three hours). Pay 500Rp entry at the small hut.

Alternatively, you can catch a local bus (1500Rp) to Semangat Gunung at the base of the volcano, from where it's a two hour climb to the top. There are steps part of the way but the track is narrower and in poorer condition than the one from Berastagi.

The longest option is to trek through the jungle from Air Terjun Panorama (Panorama Waterfall) on the Medan road, about 5km north of Berastagi. Allow at least five hours for this walk. It is best to take a local guide, as it is very easy to get lost.

Whichever route you choose, on the way down it's worth stopping for a soak in the **hot springs** (500Rp to 1500Rp), a short ride from Semangat Gunung on the road back to Berastagi.

Gunung Sinabung

Gunung Sinabung (2450m) is considerably higher than Sibayak and the views from the top are spectacular.

The climb takes six hours up and four hours down, starting from the village of Sigarang Garang. Sigarang Garang is 30 minutes by opelet from Kabanjahe (1500Rp), so you will need to start early or join an organised walk with a guide. Again, you'll need good shoes, warm clothing, food, drink and a torch. It's unwise to go alone – a solo Danish traveller died on Sinabung in July 1995 after getting lost in a storm and falling.

Air Terjun Sipiso-Piso

This impressive waterfall is at the northern end of Danau Toba, 24km from Kabanjahe and about 300m from the main road. The tourist bus from Bukit Lawang stops at the falls. To make your own way there, take a bus from Kabanjahe to Merek (1000Rp) and then walk or hitch a ride on a motorbike.

Traditional Villages

There are some fine examples of traditional Karo Batak architecture in the villages around Berastagi. Most of the houses are no more than 60 years old – or possibly 100 – but certainly not 400, as claimed by some guides. It's surprising that no-one has asked one family in Cingkes to take down the carved plaque stating that their ancient-looking home was built in 1936!

The Bataks

British traveller William Marsden astonished the 'civilised' world in 1783 when he returned to London with an account of a cannibalistic kingdom in the interior of Sumatra that, nevertheless, had a highly developed culture and a system of writing. The Bataks have remained a subject of fascination ever since.

According to Batak legend, all Bataks are descended from Si Radja Batak, who was born of supernatural parentage on Bukit Pusuk, a mountain on the western edge of Danau Toba.

According to anthropologists, the Bataks are a Proto-Malay people descended from Neolithic mountain tribes from northern Thailand and Myanmar (Burma) who were driven out by migrating Mongolian and Siamese tribes.

When the Bataks arrived in Sumatra they did not linger long at the coast but trekked inland, making their first settlements around Danau Toba, where the surrounding mountains provided a natural protective barrier. They lived in virtual isolation for centuries.

The Bataks were among the most warlike peoples in Sumatra, and villages were constantly feuding. They were so mistrustful of each other (not to mention outsiders) that they did not build or maintain natural paths between villages, or construct bridges.

They practised ritual cannibalism in which the flesh of a slain enemy or a person found guilty of a serious breach of *adat* (traditional law) was eaten.

Today, there are more than six million Bataks and their lands extend 200km north and 300km south of Danau Toba. They are divided into six main groupings: the Pakpak Batak to the north-west of Danau Toba, the Karo Batak around Berastagi and Kabanjahe, the Simalungun Batak around Pematangsiantar, the Toba Batak around Danau Toba, and the Angkola and Mandailing Bataks further south.

The name 'Batak' was certainly in use in the 17th century, but its origins are not clear. It could come from a derogatory Malay term for robber or blackmailer, while another suggestion is that it was an abusive nickname, coined by Muslims, meaning 'pig eater'.

The Bataks are primarily an agricultural people. The rich farmlands of the Karo Highlands supply vegetables for much of North Sumatra, as well as for export.

In contrast to the matrilineal Minangkabau, the Bataks have the most rigid patrilineal structure in Indonesia. Women not only do all the work around the house, but also much of the work in the fields.

Although there is an indigenous Batak script, it was never used to record events. It seems to have been used only by priests and *dukuns* (mystics) in divination and to record magic spells.

Religion & Mythology

The Bataks have long been squeezed between the Islamic strongholds of Aceh and West Sumatra. The Karo Batak in particular were constantly at odds with the Islamic Acehnese to the north, who several times tried to conquer them and convert them to Islam.

Interestingly, after long years of resistance to the Acehnese, the Karo were easily subdued by the Dutch, who brought with them Christianity.

The majority of today's Bataks are Protestant Christians, especially in the north around Danau Toba and the Karo Highlands. Islam is the predominant religion in the south.

Most Bataks, however, still practise elements of traditional animist belief and ritual. Traditional beliefs combine cosmology, ancestor and spirit worship and *tondi*. Tondi is the concept

SUMATRA

The Bataks

of the soul – the essence of a person's individuality – which is believed to develop before birth. It exists near the body and from time to time takes its leave, which causes illness. It is essential for Bataks to make sacrifices to their tondi to keep it in good humour.

The Bataks believe the banyan to be the tree of life and relate a creation legend of their omnipotent god Ompung:

One day Ompung leant casually against a huge banyan tree and dislodged a decayed bough that plummeted into the sea. From this branch came the fish and all the living creatures of the oceans. Not long afterwards, another bough dropped to the ground and from this issued crickets, caterpillars, centipedes, scorpions and insects. A third branch broke into large chunks that were transformed into tigers, deer, boars, monkeys, birds and all the animals of the jungle. The fourth branch, which scattered over the plains, became horses, buffalo, goats, pigs and all the domestic animals. Human beings appeared from the eggs produced by a pair of newly created birds, born at the height of a violent earthquake.

Architecture

Traditional Batak houses are built on stilts, 1 to 2m from the ground. Finishing touches vary from region to region, but all follow the same basic pattern. They are made of wood (slotted and bound together without nails) and roofed with sugar palm fibre or, more often these days, rusting corrugated iron. The roof has a concave, saddleback bend, the ends rising in sharp points, which from certain angles look like the buffalo horns they are invariably decorated with. The gables are usually extravagantly embellished with mosaics and carvings of serpents, spirals, lizards and monster heads complete with bulbous eyes.

The space under the main structure is used for rearing domestic animals like cows, pigs and goats. The living area, or middle section, is large and open with no fixed internal walls and is often inhabited by up to a dozen families. This area is usually sectioned off with rattan mats, which are let down at night to provide partial privacy. It is dark and gloomy inside, the only opening being a door approached by a wooden ladder. A traditional village is made up of a number of such houses, similar to the villages of the Toraja people of central Sulawesi.

There are many interesting traditional villages around Berastagi. The houses have very high roofs and are much larger than those of the Toba Batak. A traditional Toba village (huta) has only one gateway, and is always surrounded by a moat and bamboo trees to protect the villagers from attack. The houses in the village are lined up to the left and right of the king's house. In front of the houses is a line of rice barns used for storing the harvest.

Culture

The strong Indian influence running through Batak culture is evident in the cultivation of wet-field rice, the type of houses, chess, cotton and even the type of spinning wheel.

A purely Batak tradition is the sigalegale puppet dance, once performed at funeral ceremonies, but now more often a part of wedding ceremonies. The puppet, carved from the wood of a banyan tree, is a life-sized likeness of a Batak youth. It is dressed in the traditional costume of red turban, loose shirt and blue sarong. A red ulos (a piece of rectangular cloth traditionally used to wrap round babies or around the bride and groom to bless them with fertility, unity and harmony) is draped from the shoulders.

The Bataks

The sigalegale stand up on long, wooden boxes through which ropes are threaded and operated like pulleys to manipulate its jointed limbs. This enables the operator to make the sigalegale dance to gamelan music accompanied by flute and drums. In some super-skilled performances the sigalegale weeps or smokes a cigarette. Its tongue can be made to poke out and its eyelids to blink. The sigalegale is remarkably similar in appearance to the *tau tau* statues of Tana Toraja in central Sulawesi, although the tau tau do not move.

One story of the origin of the sigalegale puppet concerns a loving, but childless, couple who lived on Pulau Samosir. Bereft and lonely after the death of her husband, the wife made a wooden image of him. Whenever she felt intensely lonely she hired a *dalang* (puppeteer-storyteller) to make the puppet dance and a dukun to communicate with the soul of her husband through the puppet.

The other story goes that there was once a king who had only one child, a son. When his son passed away the king was aggrieved because he now had no successor. In memory of his dead son, the king ordered a wooden statue to be made in his likeness and when he went to see it for the first time, he invited his people to take part in a dance feast.

Whatever its origins, the sigalegale soon became part of Batak culture and was used at funeral ceremonies to revive the souls of the dead and to communicate with them. Personal possessions of the deceased were used to decorate the puppet, and the dukun would invite the deceased's soul to enter the wooden puppet as it danced on top of the grave. At the end of the dance, the villagers would hurl spears and arrows at the puppet while the dukun performed a ceremony to drive away evil spirits. A few days later the dukun would return to perform another ceremony, sometimes lasting 24 hours, to again chase away evil spirits.

Arts & Crafts

Traditionally, the Bataks are skilled metalworkers and woodcarvers; other materials they use are shells, bark, bone and horn. Their work is decorated with fertility symbols, magic signs and animals.

One particularly idiosyncratic art form developed by the Toba Bataks is the magic augury book, *pustaha*. These books comprise the most significant part of their written history. Usually carved out of bark or bamboo, the books are important religious records that explain the established verbal rituals and responses of priests and mourners. Other books, inscribed on bone or bamboo and ornately decorated at each end, document Batak myths.

Porhalaan are divining calendars – 12 months of 30 days each – engraved on a cylinder of bamboo. They are used to determine auspicious days on which to embark on certain activities, such as marriage or the planting of the fields.

Music

Music is as important to the Bataks as it is to most societies, but traditionally it was played as part of religious ceremonies rather than for everyday pleasure. Today the Bataks are famous for their powerful and emotive hymn singing. Most of their musical instruments are similar to those found elsewhere in Indonesia – cloth-covered copper gongs in varying sizes struck with wooden hammers; a small two stringed violin, which makes a pure but harsh sound; and a kind of reedy clarinet.

SUMATRA

Lingga The best known of these villages is Lingga, a few kilometres north-west of Kabanjahe. Unfortunately, the place is on every tour itinerary and is overrun with tourists. There are about a dozen traditional houses with characteristic horned roofs. Some, such as the *rumah rajah* (king's house), are occupied and in good condition; others, including the *sapo ganjang* (the house for young, unmarried men), have almost collapsed.

Admission to the village is 500Rp. There are English- and German-speaking guides who will show you around for 2000Rp (1000Rp per person for groups). The villagers, especially the women, do not like being photographed. There are regular opelets to Lingga from Kabanjahe (500Rp).

Barusjahe There are only three traditional houses still standing in Barusjahe and their dilapidated condition suggests that they won't be around much longer. It's hardly worth the 30 minute opelet journey from Kabanjahe (1000Rp).

Dokan It's amazing that tour groups have yet to discover the charming little village of Dokan, about 16km south of Kabanjahe. Traditional houses are still in the majority here and most are in good condition.

There are no admission charges, guides or children wanting pens, money etc. You can get there either by the occasional direct opelet from Kabanjahe (1000Rp) or by catching any service heading south to Danau Toba and then walking the last 1.5km from the turn-off.

Cingkes Very few travellers make it to Cingkes, about 35km south-east of Kabanjahe via Seribudolok. It's the largest of the villages and well worth the effort to get there. At first glance the place doesn't appear overly exciting, but a bit of exploration reveals at least two dozen traditional houses – all occupied and in good condition. There are regular opelets from Kabanjahe (1500Rp, one hour), but the road is very bad. Wednesday is market day and a good time to visit.

PARAPAT
☎ 0625

Tumbling down a hillside on the eastern shore of Danau Toba is the resort town of Parapat, a pleasure spot for the wealthy set from Medan, 176km to the north. Unmoved by tourist literature that describes it as the 'most beautiful mountain and lake resort in Indonesia', most travellers linger only long enough to catch a ferry to Pulau Samosir.

It is, however, a good place to buy Batak handcrafts, and the lively lakeside markets on Wednesday and Saturday are worth a visit.

Orientation
Parapat is divided into two parts. The line of restaurants and shops along the Trans-Sumatran Hwy (Jl Sisingamangaraja) are about 1.5km from the ferry dock and main market place. The two are linked by Jl Pulau Samosir, which becomes Jl Harranggaol for the final stretch to the market. The bus terminal is about 2km east of town on the Trans-Sumatran Hwy – an opelet will get you there.

Information
Tourist Offices There is a fairly unhelpful tourist office on Jl Pulau Samosir near the highway.

Money You can change money at the BNI bank on the highway, which now has an ATM with Cirrus and MasterCard access. Exchange rates are poor for currencies other than US dollars, but marginally better than you'll find on Pulau Samosir.

Post & Communications The post office is on Jl Sisingamangaraja. It's open at 7.30 am and closes at 3 pm from Monday to Thursday, at 11 am on Friday and at 1 pm on Saturday. International calls can be made from the wartels on the highway and on Jl Harranggaol. The Natour Hotel has a Home Country Direct phone in the lobby.

Markets
The produce markets by the ferry dock on Wednesday and Saturday are the main events of the Parapat week.

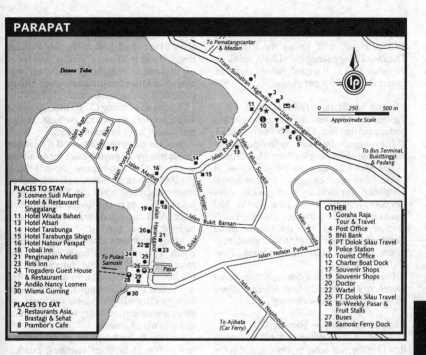

PARAPAT

Danau Toba

To Pematangsiantar & Medan

Trans-Sumatran Highway

Jalan Sisingamangaraja

Approximate Scale

To Bus Terminal, Bukittinggi & Padang

Jalan Ikan Mas

Jalan Ikan

Jalan Pora_pora

Jalan Manhat

Jalan Pulau Samosir

Jalan Tahun Sung.it

Jalan Spigo

Jalan Haranggaol

Jalan Srikki

Jalan Bukit Bansan

Jalan Nelson Purba

Jalan Pemuda

Jalan Karmel Napitupulu

To Pulau Samosir

Pasar

To Ajibata (Car Ferry)

PLACES TO STAY
3 Losmen Sudi Mampir
7 Hotel & Restaurant Singgalang
11 Hotel Wisata Bahari
13 Hotel Atsari
14 Hotel Tarabunga
15 Hotel Tarabunga Sibigo
16 Hotel Natour Parapat
18 Tobali Inn
21 Penginapan Melati
23 Riris Inn
24 Trogadero Guest House & Restaurant
29 Andilo Nancy Losmen
30 Wisma Gurning

PLACES TO EAT
2 Restaurants Asia, Brastagi & Sehat
8 Prambor's Cafe

OTHER
1 Goraha Raja Tour & Travel
4 Post Office
5 BNI Bank
6 PT Dolok Silau Travel
9 Police Station
10 Tourist Office
12 Charter Boat Dock
17 Souvenir Shops
19 Souvenir Shops
20 Doctor
22 Wartel
25 PT Dolok Silau Travel
26 Bi-Weekly Pasar & Fruit Stalls
27 Buses
28 Samosir Ferry Dock

SUMATRA

Organised Tours

PT Dolok Silau, which has offices on the Trans-Sumatran Hwy and down by the ferry dock, can organise tours for groups to local coffee, tea, ginger, clove and cinnamon farms, as well as other places of interest in and around Parapat. Goraha Raja Tour & Travel (☎ 41728), Jl Sisingamangaraja 44, has tours to places as far away as the Banyak Islands.

Special Events

The week-long Danau Toba Festival is held every year in mid-June. Canoe races are a highlight of the festival, but there are also Batak cultural performances.

Places to Stay – Budget

Travel agent *Andilo Nancy* (☎ 41534) has singles/doubles for 7500/10,000Rp above its office by the ferry dock and more rooms

next to its office at the bus terminal. There are several places to stay on Jl Haranggaol just uphill from the market. The *Penginapan Melati* (☎ 21174) at No 37 has basic 15,000Rp doubles, and much better 20,000Rp rooms with attached mandi. The bar downstairs sometimes has live music.

Wisma Gurning (☎ 41327) is a simple, friendly place right on the lake with doubles for 20,000Rp. It's on a raised pathway to the left of the ferry dock as you face the lake. The *Trogadero Guest House* (☎ 41148, Jl Harranggaol 112) is a notch better, with small bungalows for 20,000/25,000Rp. Further up Jl Harranggaol is friendly *Tobali Inn*, with spotless rooms with mandi for 10,000/15,000Rp and triples for 20,000Rp. It also has a range of excellent mid-range rooms from 35,000Rp.

There are a couple more budget places near the junction of the highway and Jl

Pulau Samosir. Directly opposite the lake-side turn-off is the small and dismal *Losmen Sudi Mampir*, with rooms for 20,000Rp. The *Hotel Singgalang* (☎ 41260), uphill on the other side of the road, has much better rooms at 10,000Rp per person.

Places to Stay – Mid-Range

Parapat has countless mid-range hotels, but nothing outstanding. The *Riris Inn* (☎ 41392, Jl Harranggaol 39), near the ferries, has un-remarkable clean doubles from 25,000Rp.

The *Hotel Tarabunga* (☎ 41700) on Jl Pulau Samosir charges from 65,000/70,000Rp for old-style singles/doubles (95,000/110,000Rp with lake views), and has a restaurant overlooking the lake. Don't confuse this place with the nearby *Hotel Tarabunga Sibigo* (☎ 41665), a giant, run-down concrete box with rooms from 70,000/80,000Rp.

Further up Jl Pulau Samosir, the *Atsari Hotel* (☎ 41219) and *Hotel Wisata Bahari* (☎ 41302) are pleasant enough.

Places to Stay – Top End

The *Hotel Natour Parapat* (☎ 41012, Jl Mar-ihat 1) is the best hotel in town, and also the oldest. It occupies a prime site with fine views over the lake. Prices start at 185,000Rp for a double, but you'll need to fork out 220,000Rp for a lake view. Nonguests can enjoy the hotel's beautiful private beach for a 3500Rp 'cover charge'.

Places to Eat

The highway strip is well equipped to feed the passing traveller. There are several *Padang* food places and no less than five Chinese restaurants, the best of which is the *Singgalang* – below the hotel of the same name. There's another string of basic restaurants along Jl Haranggaol. The *Trogadero Guest House* has a good restaurant right by the lake serving mainly Chinese meals. For a younger, traveller-friendly vibe, *Prambor's Cafe* on the highway has cheap western and Indonesian meals, Guinness beer, and posters of rock legends on the walls.

Getting There & Away

Bus The bus terminal is on the highway, about 2km east of town on the way to Bukit-tinggi. Buses to Medan (7000Rp, four hours) are frequent, although services taper off in the afternoon. Other destinations include Sibolga (15,000Rp, six hours), Bukittinggi (29,000Rp, 18 hours) and Padang (32,000Rp, 20 hours). These services are normal (without air-con) and mostly leave in the morning.

You can cut several hours off the journey to Bukittinggi by paying extra for an air-con services. The non-express air-con buses (40,000Rp) take 16 hours, while the express 'super executive' buses (95,000Rp) take 13 hours. They bypass Sibolga and travel at night. ANS has a good reputation; it has an office at the bus terminal.

Many travellers use the tourist mini-buses. There are daily buses north to Be-rastagi (22,500Rp, four hours), Medan (25,000Rp) and Bukit Lawang (35,000Rp), and south to Bukittinggi (50,000Rp) and Sibolga (30,000Rp). Tickets for these ser-vices are advertised everywhere in Parapat and on Pulau Samosir.

Getting to Berastagi by public bus is a real hassle. It involves changing buses at Pematangsiantar and Kabanjahe, and can take up to six hours.

Boat See Getting There & Away in the Danau Toba section for details of ferries to Pulau Samosir.

Getting Around

Opelets shuttle constantly between the ferry dock and the bus terminal (300Rp).

AROUND PARAPAT
Labuhan Garaga

The village of Labuhan Garaga, 25km south-east of Parapat, is a centre for the weaving of cotton Batak blankets, *kain kulos*, which are widely sold in Parapat and on Pulau Samosir. The colours and patterns vary from region to region, but most have vertical stripes (rust-red and white are the predominant colours) on a background of ink-blue. They're not cheap, but they are attractive and practical buys. Prices start at 30,000Rp and rise to 150,000Rp for the best quality cloth.

DANAU TOBA & PULAU SAMOSIR

☎ 0625

Danau Toba is one of Sumatra's most spectacular sights. It occupies the caldera of a giant volcano that collapsed in on itself after a cataclysmic eruption about 100,000 years ago. Measurements of ash deposits indicate that the blast made Krakatau's 1883 effort look like a hiccup. The flooding of the resultant crater produced the largest lake in South-East Asia, covering an area of 1707 sq km. The water is 450m deep in places.

Out of the middle of this huge expanse of blue rises Pulau Samosir, a wedge-shaped island almost as big as Singapore – created by a subsequent upheaval between 30,000 and 75,000 years ago. The island has long been North Sumatra's premier attraction for foreign travellers, although it acquired a bad reputation for hustling in the late 1980s

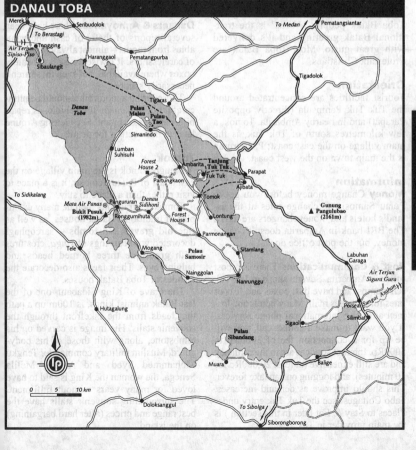

DANAU TOBA

SUMATRA

and early 1990s. Things have quietened down a bit these days, and it's a good place to relax. At an altitude of 800m, the air is pleasantly cool – and you couldn't ask for a more spectacular setting.

Most foreigners stay in touristy Tuk Tuk, but those with a serious interest in Toba Batak culture will gain more satisfaction from scrambling over the mountain ridge to the villages on the other side of the island.

Visitors to the west will discover that Samosir isn't actually an island at all. It's linked to the mainland by a narrow isthmus at the town of Pangururan – and then cut again by a canal.

Danau Toba is the home of the outgoing Toba Batak people. '*Horas*' is the traditional Batak greeting and it's delivered with great gusto. Most Toba Batak are Protestant Christians.

Orientation

Tourist facilities are concentrated around the Tuk Tuk Peninsula (directly opposite Parapat) and in nearby Ambarita. Tomok, a few kilometres south of Tuk Tuk, is the main village on the east coast; Pangururan is the main town on the west coast.

Information

Money Change money before you get to Pulau Samosir. Exchange rates at the island's hotels and moneychangers are lousy. The BRI bank in Ambarita doesn't change money, but the post office does.

Post & Communications There is a post office in Ambarita. Several shops in Tuk Tuk sell stamps, and have post boxes and lists of rates for overseas mail. Many hotels and losmen advertise international phone services. If you want to make a collect call, you will be up for a connection fee of 3000Rp to 5000Rp. Internet services are in their infancy and are still expensive (at least 20,000Rp for 10 minutes), and logging on can take forever. This should improve as demand increases. Tabo Cottages (see the Tuk Tuk entry under Places to Stay & Eat later in this section) is the main provider in Tuk Tuk.

Bookshops There are several places on the Tuk Tuk Peninsula selling or leasing second-hand books. The Gokhon Library and Bagus Bay Homestay & Restaurant have the best collections.

Medical Services The small health centre close to the turn-off to Carolina's (see the Tuk Tuk entry under Places to Stay & Eat later in this section), at the southern end of the Tuk Tuk Peninsula, is equipped to cope with cuts and bruises and other minor problems.

Emergency There is a small police station at the top of the road leading to Carolina's.

Dangers & Annoyances There have been several reports of thefts of cash and valuables from rooms – almost always the result of carelessness. It's wise to use hotel safety boxes where available, but even these aren't necessarily secure.

Those hiring a motorbike should be ultra-careful not to damage the vehicle, as repair bills can be exorbitant. See Getting Around later in this section for details.

Tomok

Although Tomok is the main village on the east coast of Pulau Samosir, it is a place to visit rather than a place to stay.

Tomok's attractions include many examples of traditional **Batak houses**, as well as fine old **graves** and **tombs** – sarcophagi decorated with carvings of *singa*, creatures with grotesque three horned heads and bulging eyes. Their faces also decorate the facades of Toba Batak houses.

The grave of King Sidabatu, one of the last Batak animist kings, is 100m up a path that leads from the lakefront through the souvenir stalls. His image is carved on his tombstone, along with those of his bodyguard, Muslim military commander Tengku Mohammed Syed, and Anteng Melila Senega, the woman the King is said to have loved for many years without fulfilment. The surrounding souvenir stalls have the best range and prices (after hard bargaining) on the island.

Nearby, a traditional house has been turned into a small **museum**. There are a few interesting items among the Christian religious photos and paintings.

Tuk Tuk

This once-small village is now a string of hotels and restaurants stretching right around the peninsula, just above the lake's waters. Pointed Batak roofs have been plonked on many of the new concrete-block hotels; otherwise, traditional Batak culture is not much in evidence. Still, the living is easy and very cheap. There are lots of places renting bicycles and motorcycles, making Tuk Tuk a good base from which to explore the rest of the island.

Ambarita

A couple of kilometres north of the Tuk Tuk Peninsula, Ambarita has a group of **stone**

chairs where village matters were discussed and wrongdoers were tried. Guides love to spin a colourful yarn about how serious wrongdoers were led to a further group of stone furnishings in an adjoining courtyard and beheaded. A 'donation' of 1000Rp is required.

Simanindo

Simanindo, at the northern tip of the island, can lay claim to being Pulau Somosir's cultural centre.

There's a fine old traditional house that has been meticulously restored and now functions as a **museum**. It was formerly the home of the Batak king Rajah Simalungun, and his 14 wives. Originally, the roof was decorated with 10 buffalo horns, which represented the 10 generations of the dynasty.

The museum has a very small collection of brass cooking utensils, weapons, Dutch

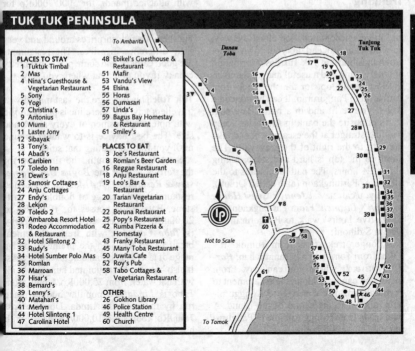

TUK TUK PENINSULA

To Ambarita

Danau Toba

Tanjung Tuk Tuk

PLACES TO STAY
1 Tuktuk Timbal
2 Mas
4 Nina's Guesthouse & Vegetarian Restaurant
5 Sony
6 Yogi
7 Christina's
9 Antonius
10 Murni
11 Laster Jony
12 Sibayak
13 Tony's
14 Abadi's
15 Caribien
17 Toledo Inn
19 Dewi's
23 Samosir Cottages
27 Anju Cottages
27 Endy's
28 Lekjon
29 Toledo 2
30 Ambaroba Resort Hotel
31 Rodeo Accommodation & Restaurant
32 Hotel Silintong 2
33 Rudy's
34 Hotel Sumber Polo Mas
35 Romlan
36 Marroan
37 Hisar's
38 Bernard's
39 Lenny's
40 Matahari's
41 Merlyn
44 Hotel Silintong 1
47 Carolina Hotel

48 Ebikel's Guesthouse & Restaurant
51 Mafir
53 Vandu's View
54 Elsina
55 Horas
56 Dumasari
57 Linda's
59 Bagus Bay Homestay & Restaurant
61 Smiley's

PLACES TO EAT
3 Joe's Restaurant
8 Romlan's Beer Garden
16 Reggae Restaurant
18 Anju Restaurant
19 Leo's Bar & Restaurant
20 Tarian Vegetarian Restaurant
22 Boruna Restaurant
25 Popy's Restaurant
42 Rumba Pizzeria & Homestay
43 Franky Restaurant
45 Many Toba Restaurant
50 Juwita Cafe
52 Roy's Pub
58 Tabo Cottages & Vegetarian Restaurant

OTHER
26 Gokhon Library
46 Police Station
49 Health Centre
60 Church

Not to Scale

To Tomok

SUMATRA

and Chinese crockery, sculptures and Batak carvings. Entry is 1000Rp.

There are very polished displays of **Batak dancing** in an adjoining traditional village compound from Monday to Saturday at 10.30 and 11.45 am, and on Sunday at 11.45 am only. The show costs 7500Rp.

Pangururan

Samosir's major population centre is a dusty old town where tourism takes a welcome back seat. While there's nothing much in Pangururan itself, the surrounding **villages** and hillsides dotted with colourful multi-storey **Batak graves** are worth exploring. Pangururan is next to the narrow isthmus connecting Samosir to the mainland, and so has transport links to Berastagi. It's not a popular route and the road is very poor as far as Tele. There are **hot springs** on the mainland near Pangururan.

Trekking

A couple of treks across the island are popular with the energetic. Both are well trodden and there's accommodation along the way, so you can proceed at your own pace. Gokhon Library in Tuk Tuk has information about trekking and a useful map of Samosir.

Most people opt for the short trek from Ambarita to Pangururan. It can be done in a day if you're fit and in a hurry. The path starts opposite the bank in Ambarita. Keep walking straight at the escarpment and take the path to the right of the graveyard. The climb to the top is hard and steep, taking about 2½ hours. The path then leads to the village of Partungkaon (also called Dolok), where you can stay at *Jenny's Guest House* or *John's Losmen*. From Partungkaon, it's about five hours' walk to Pangururan via Danau Sidihoni.

A longer trek starts from Tomok. It's 13km from Tomok to a pasanggrahan, *Forest House 1*, where you can stay. From there, you can walk along the escarpment to Partungkaon, or cut across to Ronggurnihuta, almost in the centre of the island. A path leads from Ronggurnihuta to Pangururan via Danau Sidihoni.

You can avoid the initial steep climb on both these treks by starting from Pangururan. Either way, you don't need to take much with you, but wet-weather gear may make life more comfortable. The Samosir Bataks are hospitable people and, although there are no *warungs* (food stalls), you can buy cups of coffee at villages along the way. It may also be possible to arrange accommodation in the villages.

Neither walk takes you through jungle or rainforest. In fact, most of Pulau Samosir is either pine forest or plantation – cinnamon, cloves and coffee.

Places to Stay & Eat

Samosir has some of the best-value accommodation in Indonesia. Losmen have moved steadily upmarket over the years and most places offer a range of rooms. The majority tend to be of the concrete-box variety, but you can still find a good-sized clean box, usually with attached mandi, for 5000/7000Rp for singles/doubles.

Every losmen and hotel has a restaurant, but there are few surprises around and very little difference in prices. The restaurants are good earners, and some places get pretty cranky if you don't eat where you stay.

Tuk Tuk This is where the vast majority of travellers stay. The shoreline is packed solid with hotels and losmen of every shape and size. The best advice is to wander around until you find something that suits.

Starting in the south, the first stop for the ferries is near the *Bagus Bay Homestay & Restaurant* (☎ 41482). It has a good restaurant, and a range of doubles in part-stone, Batak-style houses for 10,000Rp to 20,000Rp; dorm beds cost 3800Rp. Nearby is *Tabo Cottages*, with fresh wholemeal bread baked daily on the premises, and a range of tasty vegetarian burgers and snacks. It also has six well appointed bungalows, all with hot water, from 25,000Rp. Uphill from Tabo is *Linda's*, a popular budget place run by the energetic Linda. Doubles cost 7,000Rp; rooms are 10,000/15,000Rp with hot water.

Second stop for the ferries is the long-running *Carolina Hotel* (☎ 41520), easily the most stylish place on the island. It attracts a varied crowd, but seems most popular with couples. Carolina's older bungalows start at 20,000Rp, or 50,000Rp for hot water. Modern doubles cost from 60,000Rp, family units cost 150,000Rp. The food is a bit hit-and-miss. You'll find a more basic but homely setting next door at *Ebikel's*, where 10,000Rp gets you a clean room with mandi. Run by an exuberant family, this place also serves up consistently good food.

Rumba Pizzeria & Homestay has very basic singles/doubles for a low 4000/5000Rp. The focus here is the pizza and the atmosphere, particularly at night. Further north, the restaurant at *Bernard's* is recommended, and the 14 clean rooms out back are good value at 15,000Rp, 25,000Rp with hot shower.

The *Romlan* (☎ 41557) is set on its own small headland with a private jetty. Run by a friendly German woman, it has basic rooms for 5000Rp and better doubles in Batak-style houses for 12,000Rp. Beyond Romlan is a cluster of package-type hotels, including the giant *Toledo Inn*. Among them are a couple of good mid-range places: *Samosir Cottages* (☎ 41050) and *Anju Cottages* (☎ 41348) both have good standard rooms with cold shower for 10,000Rp, and larger new rooms with hot water from 20,000Rp. Nearby is *Leo's Bar & Restaurant*, advertising the cheapest cold beer on the island.

The north-west coast of the peninsula beyond the Toledo Inn is occupied by a string of budget places, many with simple Batak-style huts. *Tony's* (☎ 41209) and the friendly *Sibayak* next door have quiet rooms right by the lake for 6000/8000Rp; doubles with hot water cost 15,000Rp.

There are half a dozen more places dotted along the road to Ambarita. *Tuktuk Timbul* is a great spot for people who want to get away from it all, although it's looking a bit worse for wear these days. Rooms cost from 8000Rp to 20,000Rp.

Ambarita If you find Tuk Tuk a bit hectic, there are some quiet guesthouses on the lakeside north of Ambarita. They include *Barbara's* (☎ 41230) and *Thyesza* (☎ 41443), side by side on a pleasant swimming beach. Barbara's has 5000Rp dorm beds and 15,000Rp doubles; Thyesza has lovely doubles for 10,000Rp. Both have better rooms with hot water for 25,000Rp. A giant step up from these is the swanky blue-roofed *Sanggam Resort Hotel*. Great for families (there's a playground on the grassy grounds), doubles start at 100,000Rp.

If you're really serious about getting away from it all, *Le Shangri-La* is the place, 6km past Ambarita. Clean Batak-style bungalows face a sandy beach and cost 15,000Rp; dorm beds cost 6000Rp. The ferries no longer stop here, so catch a Simanindo-bound bus from Ambarita (500Rp) and tell the driver where you need to get off. Le Shangri-La is signposted from the road.

Tomok There are plenty of restaurants and warungs here for day-trippers who come across on the ferry from Parapat, but no hotels in the town centre. The only places to stay are a few kilometres south of town. *Sobo Agape* has reasonable dorm beds for 5000Rp and overpriced doubles from 35,000Rp. Further along is *Toba Beach Hotel* (☎ 41275), a three-star resort-style place with a swimming pool right on the lake. The 85,000Rp standard rooms are nothing special, but the 150,000Rp rooms are worth splashing out on.

Pangururan Right in the middle of town, *Mr Barat Acomodation* (☎ 20053, Jl Sisingamangaraja 2/4) has extremely basic rooms for 7000Rp per person and a restaurant with a tourist menu. The nearby *Hotel Wisata Samosir* (☎ 20050) is a better choice; economy rooms cost 6000Rp per person and good doubles cost from 20,000Rp. On the main street, *Roma Restaurant* offers western, Indonesian and Batak food, and cold Guinness for 8000Rp.

Entertainment
The *Bagus Bay Restaurant* on the Tuk Tuk Peninsula stages Batak dancing on Wednesday and Saturday nights at 8 pm and shows

SUMATRA

free videos on other nights. It also offers free transport back to your losmen at the end of the night. *Roy's Pub*, also on the peninsula, pumps out rock music at night and sometimes has bands.

Shopping

Pulau Samosir's souvenir shops carry a huge range of cheap cotton goods, such as brightly coloured T-shirts that let folks back home know where you've been for your holidays. Most of it is the standard stuff found in tourist shops throughout Indonesia.

Something a bit out of the ordinary is the embroidery produced by locals, such as the Gayo, living north and east of Danau Toba. The work decorates a range of bags, cushion covers and place mats.

Toba Batak musical instruments for sale include the *grantung*, consisting of several slats of wood strung out on a harness and hit with sticks – like a xylophone.

Bamboo divining calendars *(porhalaans)* are on sale everywhere around Tomok, Tuk Tuk and Ambarita.

Getting There & Away

Bus See the Parapat section earlier in this chapter for information on bus travel to/from Danau Toba. There are daily buses from Pangururan to Berastagi (10,000Rp, four hours) via Sidikalang, from where it's possible to get buses to Kutacane, Sabulus Salam (for Singkil), and Tapaktuan on the west coast.

Boat There is a constant stream of ferries between Parapat and various destinations on Samosir. Ferries between Parapat and Tuk Tuk operate roughly every hour. From Parapat, the first ferry leaves around 9.30 am and the last at about 7.30 pm. The first ferry from Pulau Samosir leaves at 7.15 am and the last around 4.30 pm, but check the exact times with your hotel. The fare is 1500Rp one way, paid on board – ignore the touts trying to sell you a ticket in Parapat at triple the price. Some ferries serve only a certain part of Tuk Tuk, so check at Parapat and you will be pointed to the appropriate boat. Tell the staff where you want to get off

on Samosir when you pay your fare, or sing out when your hotel comes around – you'll be dropped off at the doorstep or nearby. When leaving for Parapat, just stand out on your hotel jetty and wave a ferry down.

Five ferries a day shuttle vehicles and people between Ajibata, just south of Parapat, and Tomok. The departure times from Tomok are 7 and 10 am, and 1, 4, and 7.30 pm. In the other direction, a ferry leaves every three hours from 8.30 am to 8.30 pm. Cars cost 17,500Rp, and places can be booked in advance through the Ajibata office (☎ 41194) or Tomok office (☎ 41157). The passenger fare is 950Rp.

Every Monday at 7.30 am a ferry travels from Ambarita to Haranggaol (3000Rp, 2½ hours) via Simanindo. There are buses from Haranggaol to Kabanjahe (for Berastagi).

Getting Around

It is astounding that public transport services the whole of Pulau Samosir *except* the Tuk Tuk Peninsula. There are regular minibuses between Tomok and Ambarita (500Rp), continuing to Simanindo (1000Rp) and Pangururan (1750Rp). Services dry up after 3 pm.

Ferries sail from Tomok to Tuk Tuk (1000Rp), but you can't catch one going in the reverse direction. The odd ferry goes from Tuk Tuk to Ambarita. The only other options for getting around and out of Tuk Tuk are to walk or ride a pushbike or motorbike. You can rent motorcycles in Tuk Tuk for 30,000Rp to 40,000Rp a day. They come with a free tank of petrol but no insurance – so take care. There are lots of stories about travellers who have been handed outrageous repair bills – even for a scratch – so check the bike over carefully before taking it. Bicycle hire costs from 6000Rp a day for a rattler to 10,000Rp for a flash mountain bike.

SIBOLGA
☎ 0631

The departure point for boats to Pulau Nias, Sibolga is a west-coast port town with a well earned reputation for hustling tourists. If it's not the becak drivers, it's the touts and black marketeers who appear around the harbour at nightfall and try to offload ferry tickets at outrageous prices. Still, most travellers get through it all pretty easily, and the only thing you are likely to lose is a few rupiah and your temper.

Orientation & Information

There are two harbours, and the town centre lies midway between the two. Boats to Pulau Nias leave from the harbour at the end of Jl Horas. You can change money at the BNI bank at the beach-end of Jl Katamso, where there's also an ATM with Cirrus and MasterCard access.

Bangun, who runs the small tourist office (☎ 21734) directly opposite the Hotel Wisata Indah on Jl Katamso, specialises in helping westerners who want to spend as little time in town as possible. He is a wealth of reliable information, and his office sells tickets for the boats to Nias and for the tourist minibuses. Bangun also takes travellers to the boats from his office in the town centre.

Dangers & Annoyances Tales of woe about rip-offs by becak drivers are a dime a dozen, and surfers weighed down with bags and boards are favourite targets. It is essential to agree on the fare and destination before you start – and bargain hard. Becaks theoretically cost about 1500Rp for most distances in town.

If you arrive in Sibolga after the ticket office and Tourist Information Service have shut, you may have to deal with the ticket sellers at the harbour. The key is to be firm and insistent and not let their badgering get to you. Bargain them down to a reasonable price, and remember you are not required to pay extra for luggage, including surfboards.

Beaches

Pantai Pandan is a popular white sand beach at the village of the same name, 11km north of Sibolga. After a swim, 10,000Rp will buy you a meal of excellent grilled fish at one of the seafood restaurants.

A few hundred metres from Sibolga is **Pantai Kalangan**, which has a 750Rp entry fee. Both beaches get very crowded on weekends, but are good places to pass the time while you're waiting to catch a boat from Sibolga. Opelets run all day between Sibolga and both beaches (500Rp).

Places to Stay & Eat

If you need to stay the night, the best cheapies are along Jl Horas near the port. Both the *Hotel Karya Samudra* at No 134 and *Losmen Bando Kandung* have singles/doubles for 10,000/15,000Rp.

The best place to head is the *Hotel Pasar Baru* (☎ 22167), a clean place at the corner of Jl Imam Bonjol and Jl Raja Junjungan. It charges 20,000Rp for small doubles with fan; 50,000Rp for air-con doubles. There's Chinese food at the restaurant downstairs. The *Ikan Bakar Siang Malam* (*Jl Katamso 45*), near the BNI bank, serves delicious grilled fish for lunch and dinner – just as the name suggests. Reckon on about 8000Rp per head, including rice and vegetables.

The *Hotel Prima Indah* (☎ 22872, *Jl Katamso 45A-B*) is a big white wedding-cake of a hotel, with doubles from 55,000Rp to 80,000Rp. Across the road is the fanciest place in town, *Hotel Wisata Indah* (☎ 23688), which overlooks the sea. Doubles start at 98,000Rp.

Getting There & Away

Bus Sibolga is a bit of a backwater as far as bus services are concerned. The express buses that travel the Trans-Sumatran Hwy bypass Sibolga by taking a shortcut inland between the towns of Tarutung and Padangsidempuan. There are still plenty of buses, but the going is painfully slow. Typical fares and journey times from Sibolga are Bukittinggi (17,000Rp, 12 hours); Padang (20,000Rp, 14 hours); Medan (18,000Rp, 11 hours); and Parapat (14,000Rp, six hours).

All this makes the door-to-door tourist minibuses an attractive option. There are several each day to Medan (22,000Rp, nine hours), via Parapat (20,000Rp, five hours), and to Bukittinggi (30,000Rp, nine hours) and Padang (35,000Rp, 10 hours). Tickets can be booked through Bangun at the tourist office.

SUMATRA

Boat Ferries to Pulau Nias leave from the harbour at the end of Jl Horas. There are boats to Gunung Sitoli, in the north of Nias, at 8 pm nightly, except Sunday. Two companies operate on this route. PT Simeulue sells deck/cabin class tickets on its rickety old wooden ferry for 13,500/21,000Rp. ASDP runs a modern steel ferry, which also takes vehicles, 15,000Rp deck class and 19,500Rp for an aircraft-style seat in an aircon room. ASDP does not sell tickets for cabins, but it's possible to negotiate with the crew for their beds once you're on board. Around 25,000Rp per person is reasonable.

Getting to Teluk Dalam, where most travellers want to go, is often a challenge. PT Simeulue is the only operator on this route and its service has been scaled down to just three trips a week – in theory. According to the schedule, a boat leaves for Teluk Dalam at 8 pm on Tuesday, Thursday and Saturday. Tickets cost 18,000Rp deck class, 23,000Rp for a cabin bed. Cancellations are common, however, as the company refuses to sail unless the boat is reasonably full. Even more sporadic is PT Simeulue's ferry to Pulau Tello (22,000/27,000Rp deck/cabin class).

ASDP has a ticket office in town (☎ 22721), Jl Let-Jend S Parman 34, next door to the BNI bank on the corner of Jl Katamso. It also has a harbour office that is conveniently open from 7 am to 8 pm, after the central office has closed. Unfortunately, PT Simeulue does not have an office at the harbour and its town office (☎ 21497), Jl Pelabuhan 9, closes at 6 pm. After that time, you'll have to track down Bangun from the tourist office (see the Orientation & Information entry earlier in this section) or bargain at the harbour.

A Pelni boat sails from Gunung Sitoli to Sibolga every second Saturday, continuing to Padang and Jakarta.

Pulau Nias

Pulau Nias, an island almost the size of Bali, is 125km off the west coast of Sumatra. Magnificent beaches, a legendary surf break and an ancient megalithic culture combine to make it one of Sumatra's most exotic destinations.

It still takes quite an effort to get to Nias, but it's no longer off the beaten track. Teluk Lagundri (Lagundri Bay) is now part of the world professional surfing circuit but it remains low-key, with only one large-scale development.

History

Local legend has it that Niassans are the descendants of six gods who came to earth and settled in the central highlands.

Academics have come up with a host of theories to explain such customs as the use of stone to produce monumental works of art. Niassans have been linked to the Bataks of Sumatra, the Naga of Assam in India, the aborigines of Taiwan and various Dayak groups in Kalimantan.

Head-hunting and human sacrifice once played a part in Niassan culture, as it did in Batak culture.

The Niassans developed a way of life based mainly on agriculture and raising pigs. Hunting and fishing, despite the thick jungle and the proximity of many villages to the coast, was of secondary importance. The Niassans relied on the cultivation of yams, rice, maize and taro. Pigs were a source of food and of wealth and prestige; the more pigs you had, the greater your status in the village. Gold and copper work, as well as woodcarving, were important village industries.

The indigenous religion was thought to have been a combination of animism and ancestor worship, with some Hindu influences. Today the dominant religions on Pulau Nias are Christianity and Islam – overlaid with traditional beliefs. Christianity was introduced by the missionaries who followed the arrival of the Dutch military in the 1860s.

Traditionally, Niassan villages were presided over by a village chief, heading a council of elders. Beneath the aristocratic upper caste were the common people, and below them the slaves, who were often traded.

PULAU NIAS

Selat Nias

To Sibolga →

Pantai Ladara
Tuhemberua
Gunung Mazlaya ▲
Lahewa
Muara Indah
Pelabuhan Baru
Sihireo Siwahili
Gunung Sitoli
Sungai Susua
Sungai Muzai
Tumori
Sungai Mou
Hiliduho
Puncak Indah Laowomaru
Pulau Mause
Ombolata
Hilimbawodesolo
Lapangan Terbang (Binaka Airport)
Sungai Oyo
Lolofitu
Binaka
Hiliweto
Pulau Wunga
Pulau Onolimbu
Pulau Semambawa
Sungai Moros
Mandrehe
Id Gewo
Tetehosi
INDIAN OCEAN
Olayama
Sungai Mola
Tetesua
Gunung Lolomatua ▲
Sirombu
Tundrumbaho
Pulau Asu
Pulau Hinako
Lolowa'u
Gomo
Sungai Susui
Tetegewo
To Sibolga
Pulau Bawa
Sungai Morio
Lahusa
Sungai Meoya
Sungai Eto
Sungai Gema
Hilisimaetano
Sungai Sa'o
Bawomataluo
Lagundri
Teluk Dalam
Pantai Sorake
Teluk Lagundri

0   10   20 km

SUMATRA

Sometimes villages would band together to form federations, which were often at war with one another. Prior to the Dutch conquest, inter-village warfare was fast and furious, usually spurred on by the desire for revenge, slaves or human heads. Heads were needed when a new village was built, for the construction of a chief's house and for the burial of a chief. In central Nias, heads were required components of wedding dowries. Today you can still see samples of the weapons used in these feuds:

vests of buffalo hide or crocodile skin; helmets of metal, leather or plaited rattan; spears; swords; and shields.

Until the first years of the 19th century, when people like the Englishman Sir Stamford Raffles began to send back reports about the island, Nias was little-considered. When it was mentioned, it was as a source of slaves. It did not come under full Dutch control until 1914. Today's population of just under 600,000 is spread through more than 650 villages, most inaccessible by road.

Orientation

Most of the interesting places on Pulau Nias are in the south, and that's where most travellers head. The port of Teluk Dalam is the main town of the south. Gunung Sitoli, in the north, is the island's biggest town. The only airport is at Binaka, near Gunung Sitoli.

Information

Money Changing money is no longer the hassle it once was, but rates are pretty bad. The BPDSU bank in Teluk Dalam and the BNI bank in Gunung Sitoli change US dollars (cash and travellers cheques).

Health Chloroquine-resistant malaria has been reported on Nias, so take appropriate precautions.

Organised Tours

Nias Megalithic Adventures (☎ 0639-21460) at Miga Beach Bungalows just south of Gunung Sitoli, offers a range of guided tours and treks. Guides can also be hired through the tourist office in Gunung Sitoli if you want to set your own program.

Getting There & Away

Air SMAC has flights from Medan to Binaka airport, 17km south of Gunung Sitoli, every Monday, Wednesday and Saturday for 244,000Rp one way/return. Flights leave Medan at 7 am and Gunung Sitoli at 8 am. The SMAC office is at Jl Lagundri 46 (☎ 0639-21010) in Gunung Sitoli.

Boat There are two boats from Gunung Sitoli to Sibolga every night except Sunday, and one from Teluk Dalam to Sibolga every Monday, Wednesday and Friday. In theory, all the services leave at 8 pm, but in practice they seldom set sail before 10 pm. See Sibolga's Getting There & Away entry in the previous section for fares and important boat details.

In Gunung Sitoli, the ASDP ticket office (☎ 0639-21554) is at the harbour at the end of Jl Yos Sudarso. PT Simeulue is on Jl Sirau, opposite the Bintang Terang restaurant. In Teluk Dalam, PT Simeulue can be found at Jl Ahmad Yani 41 (☎ 0639-21295).

Pelni provides a weekly link between Gunung Sitoli and Jakarta. Two ships do the journey, operating on alternate Saturdays. Every second week, the *Kambuna* goes to Jakarta (108,000/369,000Rp deck class/1st class) via Padang (36,000/120,000Rp), departing at 1 pm. Every other week, the *Lambelu* sails for Jakarta (112,000/383,000Rp) via Sibolga and Padang (38,500/128,500Rp), departing at 8 am. Check the timetable at the Pelni office (☎ 0639-21846), by the seafront at Jl Cengkeh 38.

Getting Around

Getting around Nias is not difficult, although bus travel can still be painfully slow as even 'new' roads seem to be perpetually potholed. Fortunately, most of the interesting places in the south are fairly close together.

A new road down the east coast is now the main route from Gunung Sitoli to Teluk Dalam via Tetehosi and Lahusa. While it is an improvement on the old 'Trans-Niassan Hwy' across the central mountains, the new road is already deteriorating. The 128km trip takes a good three hours by car, or four hours by public bus – still, it's preferable to the five or more hours on the old route.

Local buses operate around the two major towns; elsewhere, you can catch rides on trucks or negotiate pillion rides on motorcycles. Chartering a car and driver is another option, but it can be costly.

GUNUNG SITOLI

☎ 0639   • pop 27,000

On the north-eastern coast of Nias, this is the island's main town. It's a fairly innocuous little place with a certain seedy, tropical charm.

Orientation

Most places of importance to tourists are grouped around the parade ground at the northern end of town. The port is about 2km north of town, and the bus terminal is around 1.5km south, beyond the bridge.

Information

Tourist Offices There is a small tourist office (☎ 21545) behind the parade ground at

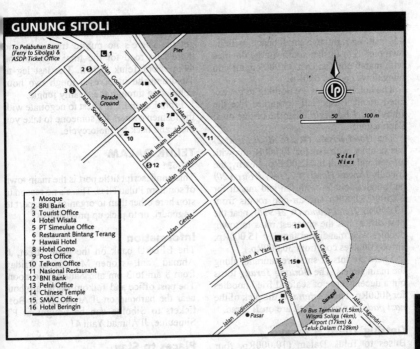

GUNUNG SITOLI

To Pelabuhan Baru
(Ferry to Sibolga) &
ASDP Ticket Office

Pier

Parade
Ground

Jalan Gomo
Jalan Soekarno
Jalan Hatta
Jalan Sirao
Jalan Imam Bonjol
Jalan Supratman
Jalan Cereja
Jalan A Yani
Jalan Diponegoro
Jalan Cengkeh
Jalan Sudirman
Jalan Lagundri

Selat
Nias

Sungai Nou

To Bus Terminal (1.5km),
Wisma Soliga (4km),
Airport (17km) &
Teluk Dalam (128km)

Pasar

0   50   100 m

1 Mosque
2 BRI Bank
3 Tourist Office
4 Hotel Wisata
5 PT Simeulue Office
6 Restaurant Bintang Terang
7 Hawaii Hotel
8 Hotel Gomo
9 Post Office
10 Telkom Office
11 Nasional Restaurant
12 BNI Bank
13 Pelni Office
14 Chinese Temple
15 SMAC Office
16 Hotel Beringin

Jl Soekarno 6. The staff are friendly and a
couple of them speak English, but the office
can't even offer a map of town.

Money The only place to change money is
the BNI bank (☎ 21946) on Jl Imam Bonjol.

Post & Communications The post office
is on the corner of Jl Gomo and Jl Hatta. International phone calls can be made from the
24 hour Telkom wartel on Jl Hatta, where
there's a Home Country Direct phone.

Medical Services There is a public hospital (☎ 21271) on Jl Ciptmangunkusumo.

Things to See
About the only feature of Gunung Sitoli that
warrants a second look is the bizarre, bright
yellow model of a northern Niassan home
that sits on the roof of the **Hotel Gomo**.

There are some fine examples of the real
thing at the nearby villages of **Sihireo Siwahili** and **Tumori**. Sihireo Siwahili is
smaller but easier to get to. Opelets from
Gunung Sitoli to Hiliduho can drop you at
the turn-off (500Rp), leaving a walk of
about 200m.

Places to Stay & Eat
Most travellers head for *Wisma Soliga*
(☎ 21815), 4km south of town, and for good
reason. It's clean, spacious and has a good
restaurant that specialises in seafood. Doubles with mandi and fan start at 25,000Rp,
or from 50,000Rp with air-con. The manager can organise various tickets and transport. If you're coming from the south, ask
to be dropped off; otherwise, you'll be up
for 3000Rp for a becak from town, or
1000Rp for two opelets – one to the bus terminal and one to the hotel.

SUMATRA

The same transport arrangements apply to nearby *Miga Beach Bungalows* (☎ 21 460), sitting right on a small beach, with its own pier 1km further south. Large doubles with mandi and fan cost 35,000Rp; air-con bungalows cost 60,000Rp.

The hotels in town are nothing to get excited about – especially cheapies like the filthy *Hotel Beringin*, near the bridge on Jl Diponegoro.

The *Hotel Wisata* (☎ 21858, Jl Sirao 2) has doubles with fan for 20,000Rp or with air-con and mandi for 42,000Rp. Nearby, the friendly *Hawaii Hotel* (☎ 22147, Jl Sirao 20) has singles/doubles with fan and mandi for 17,500/25,000Rp and air-con rooms from 40,000Rp. *Hotel Gomo* (☎ 21 926), near the post office, has the cheapest rates in town; doubles with mandi and fan cost 15,000Rp; air-con doubles cost from 30,000Rp.

There are lots of small restaurants along the main streets. The *Bintang Terang* turns out a decent serve of seafood fried noodles for 4000Rp. The *Nasional* is the pick of the *nasi padang* places. Both are on Jl Sirao.

Getting There & Away

Buses to Teluk Dalam (10,000Rp, four hours) leave from the bus terminal south of town (500Rp by opelet). Services dry up in the afternoon, so aim to leave before noon. You will probably need to change buses in Teluk Dalam for Teluk Lagundri.

Getting Around

SMAC operates a minibus between Binaka airport and Gunung Sitoli (6000Rp). Buses meet the boats at the port.

GOMO

The most famous reminders of the island's megalithic past are the *menhirs* (single standing stones) and stone carvings around Gomo in the central highlands of southern Nias.

The best examples of these stone wonders are at **Tundrumbaho**, 5km from Gomo. Some are believed to be more than 3000 years old. There are more carvings at **Lahusa Idanotae**, halfway between Gomo and Tundrumbaho, and at **Tetegewo**, 7km south of Gomo.

Getting There & Away

Unfortunately, Gomo is not an easy place to get to. There's no public transport, and there's no road for the final eight of the 44km from Teluk Dalam. The last leg to Tundrumbaho involves a tough two hour uphill slog through the steamy jungle.

From Lagundri, it's best to negotiate with the losmen owners for someone to take you there and back by motorcycle.

TELUK DALAM
☎ 0631

This nondescript little port is the main town of southern Pulau Nias. There's no reason to stop here other than to organise transport to Lagundri, or to pick up provisions.

Information

The BPDSU bank on the main street, Jl Ahmad Yani, is open Monday to Friday from 8 am to 3 pm and Saturday to noon. The post office and Telkom wartel are both near the harbour, on Jl Ahmad Yani. Boat tickets to Sibolga can be bought at PT Simeulue, Jl Ahmad Yani 41.

Places to Stay

You are better off heading straight to Lagundri. No-one in their right mind would consider staying at the disgusting Wisma Jamburae on the waterfront.

Getting There & Away

Taking a truck or opelet to Lagundri, about 13km away, costs 1500Rp for a pillion ride. Motorcyclists ask 5000Rp for a pillion ride. Buses to Gunung Sitoli cost 10,000Rp, or you can charter a car for 150,000Rp and sightsee along the way.

There are occasional buses to the villages of Bawomataluo and Hilisimaetano (1500Rp).

TELUK LAGUNDRI
☎ 0630

The perfect horseshoe bay at Lagundri is Nias' main attraction. The surfing break is at the mouth of the bay off Pantai Sorake, and there is good swimming at the back of the bay on Pantai Lagundri.

There's not much to do here except surf, swim, walk and bask in the sun, so bring books, cards and games to keep yourself amused when you get tired of the beach. Lagundri is a good base for treks to traditional villages.

Information

The Nias Surf Club Secretariate, at Dolin Losmen, provides surfing information and can organise charter fishing boats to breaks at nearby islands. Sea Breeze Losmen is another good source of information.

The only working phone is at Sorake Beach Resort and, not surprisingly, calls are expensive. The resort promotes itself as the place to confirm and book SMAC flights from Gunung Sitoli, but the staff are surprisingly unhelpful and vague if you actually try to do so. You'd be better off confirming your ticket yourself – if you do book a flight through the hotel, don't head for the airport unless you have a ticket in your hand.

Lagundri also has a police station, and a small clinic that can handle minor medical problems.

Dangers & Annoyances Petty theft seems to have reached epidemic proportions. It frequently takes the form of local boys 'finding' valuables and wanting a reward for their safe return. People are advised not to leave *anything* lying around, and to keep their money and travellers cheques on them at all times. Security tends to be poorest at the cheaper bungalows.

Another scam involves friendly 'guides' offering to save you time and stress by organising a boat or aeroplane ticket for you. One such guide recently made off with more than half a million rupiah given to him by a group of travellers who wanted tickets for the ferry back to the mainland.

Surfing

Pantai Sorake stages a leg of the World Qualifying Series in June/July, attracting some of the best young surfers in the Southern Hemisphere. The surf is at its best from June to October. For the rest of the year, the waves are perfect for beginners. Several places hire boards and snorkelling gear, and offer repair services. Sea Breeze has the biggest range of equipment.

Popular surf destinations off Nias include the islands of Asu, Bawa and Hinako, which can be reached only by chartering a boat. Most losmen will do this for you or you can bargain directly with local fishermen. Pulau Tello, further south towards the Mentawai Islands, is an up-and-coming destination that can be reached by charter boat, or by occasional boat from Sibolga (see Getting There & Away in the Sibolga section earlier).

Places to Stay & Eat

The bay is ringed by dozens of places to stay. The majority of lodgings are basic palm-thatch huts, but there are a few more luxurious options.

Each place comes with its own restaurant, and for the owner, meals are the cash cow. Some losmen offer ridiculously cheap (sometimes free!) rooms just to get customers for their restaurants. Not surprisingly, they get very peeved if you then eat elsewhere. It's worth paying a bit more to be a free agent.

The most popular cheapies (5000Rp) are those closest to the surf break, such as *Olayama* and *Sun Beach*. The *Damai*, tucked around the corner to the west of the headland, offers comparative seclusion.

The *Sea Breeze* (☎ 21224), close to the judging tower, is a bit upmarket from these. It has decent doubles with mandi and fan for 20,000Rp, and more basic 10,000/15,000Rp singles/doubles.

Non-surfers often prefer to stay near the swimming beach, where the cheapies include the long-running *Risky* and *Magdalena*. The *Lantana Inn* (☎ 21048), on the Teluk Dalam road, is a mid-range place with doubles from 33,000Rp and a good seafood restaurant.

The only top-end option, the *Sorake Beach Resort* (☎ 21195), is on the headland beyond the surf break. Listed rates start at 200,000Rp for very stylish timber bungalows, but bargaining can get you a 50% discount in the off-season.

The best non-losmen eatery is **Toho Bar & Restaurant**, on the road behind the surf break. It does delicious barbecue pork and is a popular watering hole in the evenings.

It's also possible to buy **fresh fish** and **lobster** cheaply on the beach from local fishermen and get it cooked at your losmen.

Getting There & Away

Lagundri is about 13km from Teluk Dalam: 1500Rp by truck or opelet, or 5000Rp by motorcycle. Some buses from Gunung Sitoli go directly to Lagundri (12,000Rp), but most stop in Teluk Dalam, where you must change.

SOUTHERN VILLAGES

The architecture of southern Nias is fascinating. Traditional villages, with their very wide, straight, cobblestone streets and rows of ship-like wooden houses, remain a striking testament to the past.

Built on high ground with defence in mind, villages are typically surrounded by stone walls and reached by dozens of stone steps. The preferred material for almost everything, stone was used to carve bathing pools, staircases, benches, chairs and memorials.

While the houses of northern Nias are free-standing oblong structures on stilts with thatched roofs, the houses of the south are built shoulder to shoulder on either side of a long, paved courtyard. Emphasising the roof as the primary feature, southern Niassan houses are constructed using pylons and cross-beams slotted together without the use of bindings or nails.

Bawomataluo

This is the most famous, and the most accessible, of the southern villages. It is also the setting for **stone jumping** *(lompat batu)*, featured on Indonesia's 1000Rp note.

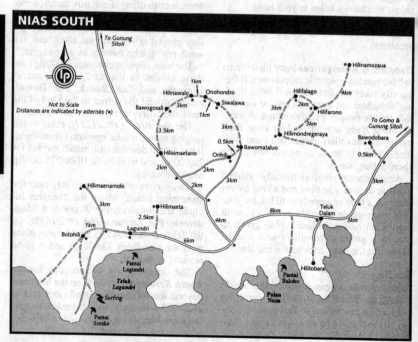

Bawomataluo translates as 'sun hill'; as its name suggests, the village is perched on a hill about 400m above sea level. The final approach is up 88 steep stone steps.

Houses are arranged along two main stone-paved avenues that meet opposite the impressive **chief's house**, thought to be the oldest and largest on Nias. Outside are stone tables where dead bodies were once left to decay, and nearby is the 1.8m stone structure for jumping. The houses themselves look like rows of washed-up Spanish galleons.

Although it's still worth exploring, Bawomataluo is on every tourist itinerary and villagers are accustomed to viewing foreigners as money jars waiting to be emptied.

Don't arrive expecting to take a casual stroll while studying the architecture; it's likely that from the moment you set foot in the village you'll be hounded by scores of kids trying to unload statues, beads and other knick knacks.

The typical tourist fare at Bawomataluo includes fairly half-hearted **war dances** (traditionally performed by young, single males, but these days by any able-bodied person), and stone jumping. Once a form of war training, the jumpers had to leap over a 1.8m-high stone wall traditionally topped with pointed sticks. These days the sticks are left off – and the motivation is financial.

The village is 15km from Teluk Dalam and is accessible by public bus (1500Rp).

Hilisimaetano
There are 140 **traditional houses** in this large village, 16km north-west of Teluk Dalam. **Stone jumping** is performed here most Saturdays. Hilisimaetano can be reached by public transport from Teluk Dalam (1500Rp).

Orihili
From Bawomataluo, a **stone staircase** and trail leads downhill to the village of Orihili. From Bawomataluo you can see the rooftops of Orihili in a clearing in the trees.

Botohili
This is a smaller village on the hillside above the peninsula of Pantai Lagundri. It has two

rows of traditional houses, with a number of new houses breaking up the skyline. The remains of the original entrance, stone chairs and paving can still be seen.

Hilimaeta
This village is similar to Botohili and also within easy walking distance of Lagundri. The stone-jumping pylon can still be seen and there are a number of stone monuments, including benches and a four-legged stone table. In the middle of the paved area stands a 2m-high **stone penis**. A long pathway of stone steps leads uphill to the village.

Hilimaenamolo
This small village is in poor condition. Much of the paving has been ripped up and many stone monuments have either collapsed or been dismantled.

Aceh

Few travellers make it to Indonesia's northernmost province. Many people are under the impression that the Acehnese are Islamic zealots fiercely hostile to the presence of foreigners. Not so. The provincial capital, Banda Aceh, is a relaxed place by Indonesian

> **WARNING**
>
> There has been a resurgence of activity since April 1999 by the Free Aceh Movement, which has been fighting for an independent Islamic state since the 1970s. At the time of writing, there are 150,000 refugees in Aceh, as people flee their villages to escape violent conflicts between the separatist rebels and Indonesian troops. Anyone travelling to Aceh should check the safety situation with their embassy in Jakarta. Particular trouble spots include the districts of North Aceh (specifically the north-western industrial city of Llokseumawe), Pidie and East Aceh.

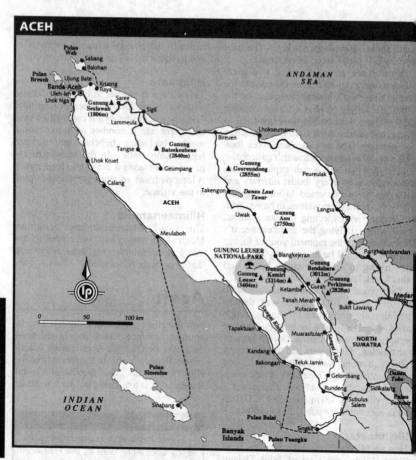

ACEH

Pulau Weh
Sabang
Balohan
Pulau Breueh
Ujung Bate
Banda Aceh
Uleh-leh
Lhok Nga
Krueng Raya
Saree
Gunung ▲ Seulawah (1806m)
Sigli
Lammeula
ANDAMAN SEA
Lhokseumawe
Tangse
Gunung ▲ Bateekeubeue (2840m)
Bireuen
Lhok Kruet
Geumpang
Gunung ▲ Geureundong (2855m)
Peureulak
Calang
Takengon
Danau Laut Tawar
ACEH
Uwak
Gunung Anu (2750m) ▲
Langsa
Meulaboh
GUNUNG LEUSER NATIONAL PARK
Blangkejeran
Gunung ▲ Bendahara (3012m)
Pangkalanbrandan
Gunung ▲ Leuser (3404m)
Gunung Kemiri (3314m) ▲
Ketambe
Gurah
Gunung ▲ Perkinson (2828m)
Medan
Tanah Merah
Bukit Lawang
Kutacane
Tapaktuan
Muarasitulam
Sungai Kluet
NORTH SUMATRA
Kandang
Bakongan
Teluk Jamin
Sungai Alas
Gelombang
Danau Toba
Rundeng
Sidikalang
Pulau Simeulue
Subulus Salem
Pulau Samosir
INDIAN OCEAN
Sinabang
Pulau Balai
Singkit
Banyak Islands
Pulau Tuangku

0   50   100 km

SUMATRA

city standards and the Acehnese tend to leave people alone. Women travellers may find they get a little more attention than usual, but this can largely be avoided by taking fashion tips from the locals and covering up the arms and legs.

Alcohol is not available as openly as elsewhere in Indonesia. If you really need a tipple, beer is served in most Chinese restaurants. You can also try the better hotels.

Aceh's attractions include laid-back Pulau Weh, the deserted beaches of the rugged west

coast, and the forest of Gunung Leuser National Park in the central mountains.

History

I am the mighty ruler of the Regions below the wind, who holds sway over the land of Aceh and over the land of Sumatra and over all the lands tributary to Aceh, which stretch from the sunrise to the sunset.

This extract is from a letter sent in 1585 by the Sultan of Aceh to Queen Elizabeth I of England, which marked the beginning of a trade agreement between Aceh and England that lasted until the 19th century. The letter gives insight into the extent of Aceh's sphere of influence as a trading nation, and provides a colourful assessment of Aceh's importance.

Years before Melaka fell to the Portuguese, Aceh was its chief trade competitor. Rivalry between the two was intensified by religious hostility, as Aceh was one of the earliest centres of Islam in the archipelago.

Religious tensions and the harsh Portuguese rule spurred people of different nationalities – Islamic scholars, Egyptians and Arabians, craftspeople from India and goldsmiths from China – to abandon Melaka and set themselves up in Aceh.

This influx of traders and immigrants contributed to Aceh's wealth and influence. Aceh's main exports were pepper and gold; others were ivory, tin, tortoiseshell, camphor, aloe-wood, sandalwood and spices. The capital, Banda Aceh, was also important as a centre of Islamic learning and as a gateway for Muslims making the pilgrimage to Mecca.

Aceh's history is particularly interesting because despite its early and strong allegiance to Islam, there have been four women rulers (although it is possible that real power lay with a council of 12 men). However, such a state of grace did not last and in 1699 a legal recommendation from Mecca condemned rule by women as contrary to Islamic practice. The last female ruler was deposed and replaced by a government headed by religious leaders.

Aceh's power began to decline towards the end of the 17th century, but it remained independent of the Dutch for a long time. Singapore and Aceh were active trading partners with the help of a long-standing secret treaty with Britain.

That came to an end in 1871 when the Dutch occupied Aceh after negotiating with the British. The Acehnese responded by negotiating with both the Italian and US consuls in Singapore, but before any new deals were struck the Dutch declared war.

The war went on for 35 years before the last of the sultans, Tuanku Muhamat Dawot,

surrendered. Even then, no Dutch area was safe from sabotage or guerrilla attack by the Acehnese until the Dutch surrendered to Japan in 1942.

The Japanese were welcomed at first, but resistance soon sprang up when local institutions were not respected. During this time, the Islamic Party, which had been formed in 1939 under the leadership of Daud Beureueh, emerged as a political force.

In 1951 the central Indonesian government incorporated Aceh's territory into the province of North Sumatra under a governor in Medan. Angered at being lumped together with the Christian Bataks, Daud Beureueh proclaimed Aceh an independent Islamic Republic in September 1953. This state lasted until 1961, when military and religious leaders had a falling out.

The central government resolved the conflict by giving Aceh provincial status and granting autonomy in matters religious, cultural and educational. However, many Acehnese continue to push for full independence from Indonesia, believing Jakarta robs the province of the profits from its abundant natural resources, leaving them impoverished.

BANDA ACEH
☎ 0651

Banda Aceh, the capital of Aceh, is a sprawling city at the northern tip of Sumatra. It's an odd mix of faded grandeur and modern architecture. A highly religious place, the city virtually stops dead at important prayer times, as local mosques take centre stage.

Orientation

Banda Aceh is split in two by the Sungai Krueng Aceh. The city's best-known landmark, the Mesjid Raya Baiturrahman, lies on the southern side. Behind the mosque is the huge central market, and adjoining the market is the main opelet terminal.

The city north of the river is centred around the junction of Jl Ahmad Yani and Jl Khairil Anwar. There are lots of hotels and restaurants in this area.

SUMATRA

BANDA ACEH

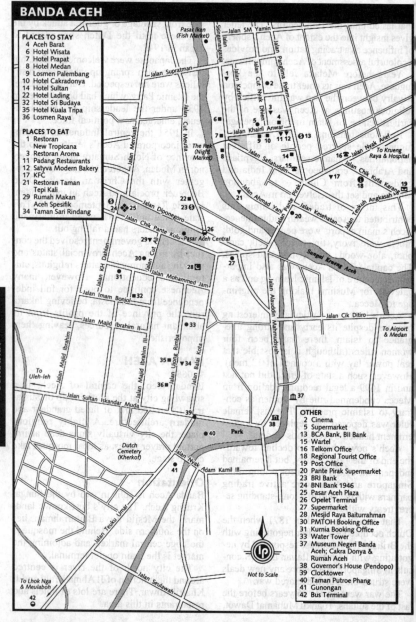

PLACES TO STAY
4 Aceh Barat
6 Hotel Wisata
7 Hotel Prapat
8 Hotel Medan
9 Losmen Palembang
10 Hotel Cakradonya
14 Hotel Sultan
22 Hotel Lading
32 Hotel Sri Budaya
35 Hotel Kuala Tripa
36 Losmen Raya

PLACES TO EAT
1 Restoran
   New Tropicana
3 Restoran Aroma
11 Padang Restaurants
12 Satvya Modern Bakery
17 KFC
21 Restoran Taman
   Tepi Kali
29 Rumah Makan
   Aceh Spesifik
34 Taman Sari Rindang

OTHER
2 Cinema
5 Supermarket
13 BCA Bank, BII Bank
15 Wartel
16 Telkom Office
18 Regional Tourist Office
19 Post Office
20 Pante Pirak Supermarket
23 BRI Bank
24 BNI Bank 1946
25 Pasar Aceh Plaza
26 Opelet Terminal
27 Supermarket
28 Mesjid Raya Baiturrahman
30 PMTOH Booking Office
31 Kurnia Booking Office
33 Water Tower
37 Museum Negeri Banda
   Aceh; Cakra Donya &
   Rumah Aceh
38 Governor's House (Pendopo)
39 Clocktower
40 Taman Putroe Phang
41 Gunongan
42 Bus Terminal

Not to Scale

Information

Tourist Offices The Dinas Parawisata (DIPARDA, ☎ 23692) is at the back of a government building at Jl Chik Kuta Karang 3 – it's signposted from the street. Although they don't speak much English, the staff are friendly and hand out free copies of an excellent guidebook to the province if you fill in a form.

Money The best rates are to be found at BCA bank, Jl Panglima Polem 38-40. The BNI bank, Jl KH Dahlan, has reasonable rates for US dollars (travellers cheques and cash), and has an ATM for MasterCard and Cirrus. The BII bank next door won't change foreign currency, but its ATM is useful for Visa cardholders. The BRI bank on Jl Cut Meutia will change only US dollars (cash).

Post & Communications The main post office is on Jl Teukuh Angkasah and Internet facilities are available for 5000Rp an hour. International phone calls can be made nearby at the 24 hour Telkom wartel, Jl Nyak Arief 92. It has a Home Country Direct phone.

Cultural Centres A cultural complex behind the governor's official residence, Pendopo, stages dances and theatre on special occasions. The complex was built in 1981 for the National Koran Reading Competition.

Medical Services The Rumah Sakit Dr Zainal Abidur (☎ 26090/22606) on Jl Nyak Arief is one of the best hospitals in town.

Mesjid Raya Baiturrahman

With its brilliant white walls and liquorice-black domes, the Mesjid Raya is a dazzling sight on a sunny day. The first section of the mosque was built by the Dutch in 1879 as a conciliatory gesture towards the Acehnese after the original one had been burnt down. Two more domes – one on either side of the first – were added by the Dutch in 1936 and another two were built by the Indonesian government in 1957. Two new minarets were added in 1994. Non-Muslims are not allowed to enter any part of the mosque.

Gunongan

For a contrast in architectural styles, check out the Gunongan, on Jl Teuku Umar. Built by Sultan Iskandar Muda (who reigned from 1607-36) as a gift for his Malay princess wife, it was intended as a private playground and bathing place. Its three levels each resemble an open leaf or flower. The building consists of a series of frosty peaks with narrow stairways and a walkway leading to ridges, which represent the hills of the princess' native land.

Directly across from the Gunongan is a low, vaulted gate, in the traditional Pintu Aceh style, which gave access to the sultan's palace – supposedly for the use of royalty only.

These architectural curiosities, plus a few whitewashed tombs, are about all that remains to remind today's visitor of the past glories of the Acehnese sultanates.

Dutch Cemetery (Kherkhof)

Close to the Gunongan is the last resting place of more than 2000 Dutch and Indonesian soldiers who died fighting the Acehnese. The entrance is about 250m from the clocktower on the road to Uleh-leh. Tablets set into in the walls by the entrance gate are inscribed with the names of the dead soldiers.

Museum Negeri Banda Aceh

The museum, Jl Alauddin Mahmudsyah 12, has a good display of Acehnese weaponry, household furnishings, ceremonial costumes, everyday clothing, gold jewellery and calligraphy. Open Tuesday to Saturday, entry costs 750Rp.

In the same compound is the **Rumah Aceh** – a fine example of traditional Acehnese architecture, built without nails and held together with cord and pegs. It contains more Acehnese artefacts and war memorabilia. In front of the Rumah Aceh is a huge cast-iron bell, the **Cakra Donya**, said to have been a gift from a Chinese emperor in the 15th century.

Markets

Market lovers will enjoy the colourful **Pasar Aceh Central**, just north of the Mesjid Raya

The Acehnese

As a result of a history of extensive and mixed immigration, Aceh's population is a blend of Indonesian, Arab, Tamil, Chinese and indigenous groups. Curiously, some of the tallest people in Indonesia live in the province. Ethnic groups include the Gayo and Alas in the mountains, the Minangkabau on the west coast, the Kluetin in the south, and Javanese and Chinese throughout.

Religion

Aceh is the most staunchly Muslim part of Sumatra, with Christians and Buddhists comprising only a small percentage of the population.

Nevertheless, animism is also part of the everyday fabric of Acehnese life. There is a prevailing popular belief in the existence of spirits who dwell in old trees, wells, rocks and stones. Ghosts and evil spirits are said to be particularly malicious around dusk, when they can wreak havoc on all those they come in contact with. *Dukuns* (mystics) are still called in to help solve grievances, cure illnesses and cast spells on enemies.

Rituals are still observed at significant times of the agricultural year, such as harvest, and dreams and omens are interpreted. In some parts of Sumatra, pilgrimages are made to the tombs of Acehnese scholars and religious leaders.

Weapons

Metallurgy was learned early from Arab and Persian traders and, because of Aceh's continued involvement in wars, weapon-making became a highly developed skill. Acehnese daggers and swords comprise three parts: blade, handle and sheath. The blade can have both edges sharpened or just one, and can be straight, concave or convex. The handles of weapons are usually made of buffalo horn, wood or bone. They are carved in the form of a crocodile's mouth, a horse's hoof or a duck's tail and embellished with

MARSDEN'S HISTORY OF SUMATRA

between Jl Chik Pante Kulu and Jl Diponegoro (see Shopping later in this section).

The **Pasar Ikan** (fish market) on Jl Sisingamangaraja is one of the liveliest in Sumatra. At the rear, by the river, you can see the boats unloading their cargoes of shark, tuna and prawns. Nearby, running off Jl SM Yamin, is 'Jalan Pisang' (Banana Street), an alley full of banana stalls. It's a great place for people-watching.

Places to Stay – Budget

There are no bargains in Banda Aceh. You're better off staying clear of the cheap

losmen along Jl Khairil Anwar. Places like the *Aceh Barat* and the *Losmen Palembang* look interesting, but seem to have no interest in foreign guests.

You'll be made much more welcome at *Losmen Raya* (☎ 21427, Jl Ujong Rimba 30), an old Dutch building 500m from the Mesjid Raya. Doubles with fan cost 15,000Rp, or from 20,000Rp with private bathroom. Rates include breakfast. If it's full, try the similarly priced *Hotel Sri Budaya* (☎ 21751) nearby, on the corner of Jl Imam Bonjol and Jl Syech Mudawali. It also has a few air-con doubles for 40,000Rp.

The Acehnese

gold or silver. The sheaths are made of rattan, silver or wood and fastened with bands of a mixture of gold, brass and copper called *sousa*.

The best example of this art form is the *rencong*, a dagger which has a convex iron and damascene (etched or inlaid) blade with one sharpened edge. Less well known Acehnese weapons are the *siwah* (knife) and *pedang* (pointed sword).

Jewellery

While there is a long tradition of fine gold and silver jewellery craft – stemming from the early days of the sultanate – there is almost no antique jewellery to be found in Aceh today. Much of it was sold to raise money for the war against the Dutch. Excellent gold and silver jewellery is still produced, but there is not much variation in design.

Weaving & Embroidery

Despite its long history and prominent reputation, Acehnese weaving is rapidly disappearing. On the other hand, embroidery is a vital art form. Areas around Sigli, Meulaboh and Banda Aceh are renowned for embroidery using gold-coloured metallic thread (*soedjoe*) on tapestry, cushions, fans and wall hangings. The main motifs are flowers, foliage and geometric designs. The finished work is decorated with mirrors, golden paillettes, sequins and beads, in an effect known as *blet blot*.

Mendjot beboengo is a kind of embroidery from the Gayo and Alas regions south of Takengon, traditionally done only by men. Stylised motifs of geometric flowers in red, white, yellow and green thread are embroidered on a black background.

Music

Typical Acehnese instruments include a three stringed zither (called an *arbab*) made of the wood of the jackfruit tree, with strings of bamboo, rattan or horsetail hair; and bamboo flutes (*buloh merindu, bangsi, tritit* and *soeling*). Gongs made of brass (sometimes dried goatskin) are also common; they come in three sizes: *gong, canang* and *mong-mong*, and are struck with padded wooden hammers. Tambourines (*rapai*) are made of goatskin.

Places to Stay – Mid-Range

Three places on Jl Ahmad Yani offer the best mid-range value. *Hotel Medan* (☎ 25 001) at No 15 looks nothing special, but has clean, comfortable air-con doubles with TV from 45,000Rp.

Next door at No 19, the popular *Hotel Prapat* (☎ 22159) has doubles with mandi and fan for 30,000Rp, and rooms with air-con and TV for 45,000Rp.

Next along, the new *Hotel Wisata* has the nicest, cleanest rooms; doubles cost 30,000Rp with fan, 45,000Rp with air-con and TV.

South of the river, the sprawling *Hotel Lading* (☎ 23006, Jl Cut Meutia 9) has a range of rooms, including slightly grotty doubles with outside bathroom for 17,500Rp and doubles with air-con and TV for 50,000Rp. The hotel can also accommodate three to five people to a room.

Places to Stay – Top End

The best hotel in town is the three star *Kuala Tripa* (☎ 24535, Jl Ujong Rimba 24), where the cheapest double costs 196,000Rp. You can pay 2000Rp to use the pool if you're not staying there.

SUMATRA

The *Hotel Sultan* (☎ 22469), in a small alley off Jl Panglima Polem, somehow also rates three stars despite being relatively faded. The nearby *Hotel Cakradonya* (☎ 33 633, Jl Khairil Anwar 10) gets just one star for a very similar standard of facilities – and is cheaper, with doubles from 70,000Rp.

Places to Eat

The square at the junction of Jl Ahmad Yani and Jl Khairil Anwar is the setting for Banda Aceh's lively night food market, the *Rek*. If there's nothing here that takes your fancy, the *Restoran Aroma* on Jl Cut Nyak Dhien does cheap but tasty Chinese food.

On the western side of the Mesjid Raya, *Rumah Makan Aceh Spesifik* serves top-notch Acehnese cuisine, but it can be expensive. The *Restoran New Tropicana* (Jl Ahmad Yani 90-92) is a smart air-con Chinese place specialising in seafood.

If you're staying south of the river, the place to go is the *Taman Sari Rindang*. It serves cheap meals, and is very popular with Banda Aceh's young crowd in the evenings. Not far from the Rek, on the riverbank, the *Taman Tepi Kali* is similar.

Satyva Modern Bakery (Jl Khairil Anwar 3) has cakes and pastries, and *Pante Pirak supermarket*, on the street of the same name, is well stocked and open daily until 10 pm.

Shopping

Aceh is well known for its colourful embroidery, which adorns anything from a hat to a wallet. Anita Souvenirs in Pasar Aceh Plaza on Jl Diponegoro is a good place to look.

There are some interesting places to browse along Jl Chik Pante Kulu on the other side of the market. H Keucik Leumik at No 115 specialises in Acehnese antiques and also has a good selection of old Dutch and Chinese porcelain. Close by, Toko Daud deals in traditional weaponry. The goldsmiths at the jewellery shops along Jl Chik Pante Kulu can turn out any design you care to nominate.

Getting There & Away

Air Garuda has one flight a day from Banda Aceh to Medan (398,000Rp). The Garuda office is at the Hotel Sultan (☎ 32523). At the time of research, Pelangi had temporarily ceased its flights to Penang and Kuala Lumpur.

Bus The Terminal Bus Seuti is on Jl Teuku Umar at the southern approach to town. There are numerous buses to Medan; take the express night buses, which cut the trip from 13 hours to about nine hours. Tickets cost 25,000Rp to 40,000Rp. Kurnia and PMTOH are both recommended. The PMTOH office (☎ 21215), Jl Cut Ali 58, is on the west side of the Mesjid Raya, and Kurnia (☎ 32922) is around the corner at Jl Mohammed Jam 48.

Heading down the west coast, PMTOH and Aceh Barat run buses from Banda Aceh to Calang (10,000Rp, three hours), Meulaboh (15,000Rp, five hours) and Tapaktuan (28,000Rp, 11 hours). From Tapaktuan, it's possible to continue to Sidikalang and then complete a loop of northern Sumatra to Medan via Berastagi.

Boat For information on transport to Pulau Weh, see that section further on.

Getting Around

To/From the Airport Airport taxis charge 20,000Rp for the 16km ride into town, and 25,000Rp to Krueng Raya (for Pulau Weh).

Public Transport Opelets (known as *labi-labi*) are the main form of transport around town and cost 500Rp. The main terminal, on Jl Diponegoro, is mayhem – touts may try to usher you onto their vehicles even if they're not going where you want to go. For Krueng Raya (2500Rp), take labi-labi No 02H; No 01D goes to the airport (2000Rp) via Jl Cik Ditiro.

AROUND BANDA ACEH
Uleh-leh

Five kilometres west of Banda Aceh is the old port of Uleh-leh, where you can while away a few interesting hours watching the traders come in from outlying islands. There are some attractive **villages** around Uleh-leh and an unattractive, exposed black sand beach.

Lhok Nga

Lhok Nga, 17km west of Banda Aceh, is a popular weekend picnic spot, despite the nearby operations of a cement company.

There's a beautiful white sand Indian Ocean beach at **Lampu'uk**, a few kilometres south. Women should dress modestly – most local women swim fully clothed.

Places to Stay Both *Pondok Wisata Darlian* and *Pondok Wisata Mitabu* have basic doubles for 10,000Rp.

The place to go if you want to relax in comfort is the *Taman Tepi Laut Cottages* (☎ 44210, fax 44202). Immaculate rooms and cottages cost from 50,000/60,000Rp on weekdays/weekends.

Hugely popular as a swimming & surfing spot is *Aceh Bungalows*, set on a 2km stretch of beach at Lampu'uk, just past Lhok Nga. A double costs 8000Rp. The place is regularly full, but the owners can usually find you somewhere to crash until a bed becomes available.

Getting There & Away Take labi-labi No 04 (1000Rp) from the opelet terminal in Banda Aceh for both Lhok Nga and Lampu'uk.

PULAU WEH

☎ 0625 • pop 24,000

This beautiful little island just north of Banda Aceh is the main reason most travellers come to Aceh. It has some magnificent palm-fringed beaches, good diving and snorkelling and a rugged, jungle-covered interior; however, malaria has been reported on the island.

Most of Pulau Weh's population lives in the main town of Sabang. During Dutch rule, Sabang was a major coal and water depot for steam ships, but with the arrival of diesel power after WWII, it went into decline.

During the 1970s this was a duty-free port, but this status was eliminated in 1986 and Sabang became a sleepy fishing town again. The only industry – other than fishing – is rattan furniture.

Weh's main drawcard is the beaches at Gapang and Iboih. Picking the best time to visit is difficult, as rain is never far away. November to January are the wettest months, and July is supposedly the driest.

Information

In Gapang and Iboih, the dive shops and most guesthouses have information about things to see and do. In Sabang, try Losmen Irma or the Stingray Dive Centre. The post office is in Sabang at Jl Perdagangan 66, and the 24 hour telephone office is next door. It has a Home Country Direct phone. BRI bank on Jl Perdagangan changes Amex travellers cheques, US and Australian dollars, UK pounds and Dutch guilders.

Sabang

The island's main township has a couple of attractions. **Pantai Paradiso**, a white sand beach shaded by coconut palms is a ten minute walk away. A little further is **Pantai Kasih** (Lover's Beach) and about 30 minutes from town is **Pantai Sumur Tiga**, a popular picnic spot.

Less than 2km from town is **Danau Anak Laut**, a serene freshwater lake that supplies the island's water. From the nearby hills it is possible to see the port and Teluk Sabang.

Gunung Merapi is 17km from town. This semi-active volcano holds boiling water in its caldera and occasionally emits smoke.

Iboih

The most popular beach on Pulau Weh is at Iboih, about 20km north-west of Sabang. Atmospheric and lively, Iboih is unfortunately succumbing to the effects of too much growth, too fast. At the time of research, plans were afoot to install running water and electricity, which will hopefully improve the village's poor hygiene and lack of amenities.

Opposite Iboih, 100m offshore, is **Pulau Rubiah**, a densely forested island surrounded by spectacular coral reefs known as the **Sea Garden**. It is a favourite snorkelling and diving spot. Many losmen organise trips to the island, but you can head out there yourself if you are a strong swimmer.

Adjacent to the Sea Garden is the **Iboih Forest nature reserve**. It has coastal caves that can be explored by boat.

Gapang

The beach at Gapang, around the headland from Iboih, attracts people who prefer a quieter, more contemplative environment. Good for **swimming** and **snorkelling**, there are far fewer bungalows, only a couple of restaurants and, of course, fewer people.

Diving & Snorkelling

There's no reason to dive with second-rate equipment – brand new gear with all the safety features is available, usually for the same price, so compare what's on offer before deciding on a dive.

At Iboih there's Rubiah Tirta Divers. At Gapang the Stingray Dive Centre competes with the excellent Lumbalumba, run by an enthusiastic Dutch couple. In Sabang, there's the original Stingray office (☎ 21265), on the corner of Jl Teuku Umar and Jl Perdagangan. All companies charge $US40 for a day trip, including two dives, lunch and equipment hire. Beginners' open-water dive courses, run over several days, cost around $US250.

Snorkelling gear can be hired almost anywhere for around 3000Rp per piece per day.

Places to Stay

Sabang Sabang has a couple of reasonable cheapies. *Losmen Irma* (☎ 21148, Jl Teuku Umar 3) and *Losmen Pulau Jaya* (☎ 21344), a few doors up, both charge 7500/14,000Rp for basic singles/doubles. The Pulau Jaya also has large doubles with fan and mandi for 32,000Rp and air-con rooms for 40,000Rp.

On the street opposite Losmen Irma, *Losmen Sabang Marauke* has the cheapest beds in town, at 5000Rp. It has single, double and triple rooms.

The nicest place in town is the *Samudera Hotel* (☎ 21503), an old Dutch villa up the hill on Jl Diponegoro. Doubles cost 25,000Rp with fan, 35,000Rp with fan and mandi, and from 45,000Rp with air-con.

Out at Pantai Kasih, the new *Pantai Kasih Guesthouse* (☎ 21066, Jl Hasanud-

din 10) has basic doubles for a pricey 30,000Rp, or 40,000Rp with fan and mandi.

Iboih Palm-thatch bungalows, mostly without attached mandi, are all you'll find at Iboih. *Horas*, *Arina*, *Dolphin*, *Fatimah* and *Mama* bungalows all charge 10,000/ 12,000Rp for basic singles/doubles, though huts on the water's edge are dearer. Competition among the bungalow owners is stiff and bargaining is expected.

Gapang The *bungalows* at Gapang are spread out along the shoreline, offering far more privacy than at Iboih. They cost 7000Rp to 12,000Rp, depending on their condition. Hopefully, the arrival of the pink, box-like *Sultan Hotel* won't spell disaster for the quiet cove. Under construction at the time of research, the hotel's tiny upstairs rooms were expected to cost 30,000Rp, rooms with fan and mandi 75,000Rp, and characterless air-con doubles an exorbitant 200,000Rp. Much nicer are pleasant traditional-style rooms at the *Gapang Beach Hotel*, on the road out of Gapang, from 50,000Rp.

Places to Eat

Sabang Sabang has plenty of restaurants along the main street, Jl Perdagangan, serving cheap Padang food. The *Dynasty Restaurant* at No 54 offers something a bit different, with upmarket Chinese food. It does a steak for 6000Rp – and you can wash it down with a cold beer for 5000Rp.

The *Restaurant Sabang* at No 27 serves up a huge portion of sweet and sour fish for 5000Rp.

Yulie Coffie Cafe, downstairs from Losmen Irma, has a range of pancakes and breakfast goodies aimed at the tourist market.

Iboih & Gapang Each cluster of bungalows at Iboih and Gapang has its own small restaurant offering basic meals, such as rice, fish and vegetables from 4000Rp.

Getting There & Away

Ferries to Pulau Weh leave from Krueng Raya, 33km east of Banda Aceh. There are regular labi-labi from Banda Aceh opelet terminal to the port (2500Rp, 45 minutes). Ferries leave Krueng Raya daily at 3 pm, but you should get there by 1.30 pm to get a ticket. Ferries from Pulau Weh's port of Balohan return to Krueng Raya at 8 am the next morning. The two hour trip costs 5750/7300Rp deck/1st class from Krueng Raya and, strangely, 5400/6950Rp from Balohan.

Getting Around

From Balohan there are regular bemos for the 15 minute ride to Sabang (2000Rp, 15 minutes). For those who want to skip Sabang, a bunch of minibuses await the boat each evening to ferry new arrivals straight to Iboih and Gapang (8000Rp a person). In the reverse direction, 6 and 7 am minibuses take beached-out travellers from Gapang and Iboih to the port via Sabang. Getting from Sabang to Gapang and Iboih can be difficult but there are usually minibuses at 11 am and 5 pm, leaving daily from outside the Stingray Dive Centre.

Pulau Weh has a good road network and motorcycles are the ideal way to get around if you want to see a bit of the island. They can be rented from Yulie Coffie Cafe in Sabang or from various bungalows in Iboih and Gapang.

BANDA ACEH TO SINGKIL

Very few travellers make it to the remote west coast of Aceh, with its seemingly endless Indian Ocean beaches backed by densely forested hills.

The journey from Banda Aceh to Singkil, the southernmost point in Aceh, used to be an endurance test on degraded, twisting roads. These days, it's plain sailing as far south as Teluk Jamin, although the final stretch to Singkil via Subulus Salem is still arduous, particularly in the wet season.

It's best to take the journey in stages, stopping off to enjoy the attractions en route.

Calang

Calang is a fairly nondescript small town 140km south of Banda Aceh, but the **beaches** along this part of the coast are superb.

About 15km north of Calang is the small village of **Lhok Geulumpang**, home of the popular *Sunset Beach Flower Guesthouse*, also known as Hasan's, after the charming host. No electricity makes for atmospheric evenings at the open-air communal dinner table, where delicious home-cooked meals are served. Bungalows are 7500/15,000Rp for singles/doubles. New bungalows with bathrooms were close to completion at the time of research. If Hasan's is full, *Camp Europa* next door has a similar set-up but without the good cheer. The first bungalow-style accommodation in the area, Camp Europa has not been the same since its expat German owner Dieter apparently left the country.

Getting There & Away PMTOH and Aceh Barat operate regular buses to Calang from Banda Aceh (10,000Rp, three hours) and Meulaboh (4000Rp, two hours). Drivers know the stop and Camp Europa is signposted from the main road.

Meulaboh
☎ 0655

Almost 250km from Banda Aceh on the south-western coast is the small, sleepy town of Meulaboh. You can't change money here, but the local BNI bank has an ATM for Cirrus and MasterCard.

There's good **surf** nearby, although strong currents make the beaches close to town dangerous for swimming. **Lhok Bubon**, 16km north, is a safe swimming beach.

There are half a dozen losmen in Meulaboh. The *Hotel Tiara* (☎ 21531, Jl Teuku Umar 157) has fan singles/doubles for 10,000/17,500Rp and air-con rooms from 37,000Rp. The tiny *Mustika* (☎ 21033, Jl Nasional 78) has very basic 11,000Rp rooms, 22,000Rp rooms with fan and 37,500Rp air-con doubles.

The *Losmen Pelita Jaya* next to the bus terminal on Jl Singgahmata looks grotty and won't accept female guests.

Getting There & Away There are regular buses to Meulaboh from Banda Aceh (15,000Rp, five hours) and Tapaktuan

SUMATRA

(12,000Rp, six hours). SMAC flies between Medan and Meulaboh twice a week (233,000Rp), continuing from Meulaboh to Sinabang (136,000Rp) on Pulau Simeulue.

Pulau Simeulue

The isolated island of Simeulue, about 150km west of Tapaktuan, is known for its clove and coconut plantations and not much else. The island is said to be restful and the people friendly. There are few shops and no luxuries, but there is plenty of fruit, coffee, rice, noodles and fish.

Getting There & Away There are occasional boats from Meulaboh to Sinabang, as well as three flights a week from Medan (136,000Rp) via Meulaboh.

Tapaktuan
☎ 0656

The sleepy seaside town of Tapaktuan, 200km south of Meulaboh, is the main town in South Aceh. It's very laid-back by Sumatran standards and is a pleasant place to hang out for a couple of days.

Information Most places of importance are on the main street, Jl Merdeka, which runs along the coast. Flamboyant Tour & Travel (☎ 21351) at No 134, and Widuri Tours & Travel (☎ 21574) a few doors down are the main source of information about the town and its surrounds. Flamboyant has folders full of information about the Banyak Islands, but the staff readily admit it's out of date. Much more reliable is their information about jungle treks around Tapaktuan and trips to local caves and waterfalls.

Things to See & Do The town can be used as a base to explore the lowland **Kluet region** of Gunung Leuser National Park, about 45km south. Kluet's unspoilt swamp forests support the densest population of **primates** in South-East Asia and are also good sites for **bird-watching**. It may be possible to hire guides through the national park office in Kandang, 38km south of Tapaktuan.

Pantai Tu'i Lhok, 18km north of Tapaktuan, is the best of several good beaches in the area. There is a small **waterfall** behind the beach where you can rinse off after swimming. There's a much larger waterfall at **Pantai Air Dingin**, just south of Tu'i Lhok.

Places to Stay & Eat Most places to stay are along the main road, Jl Merdeka.

Tiny *Pondok Wisata Kanada* (☎ 21209), above a shop at No 52, has a few basic doubles for 8000Rp. The *Losmen Bukit Barisan* (☎ 21145) occupies an old Dutch house at No 37. It has cheap singles/doubles at the back for 10,000/12,500Rp and better rooms inside for 15,000Rp. *Hotel Panorama* (☎ 21004) next door is a modern two storey place with doubles from 11,000Rp. Rooms with air-con, TV and breakfast cost 35,000Rp. The *Hotel Dian Rana* (☎ 21444) on Jl Angkasah may be the most expensive place in town, but the plumbing is shocking and it's right on the busy highway. Still, its 45,000Rp air-con doubles are comfortable enough.

Jl Merdeka is also a good place to find a bite to eat. Being a fishing port, there are several *restaurants* selling delicious grilled fish. Expect to pay about 6000Rp for a decent feed. After dark, the focus switches to the *night market* by the main pier, opposite Hotel Panorama.

Getting There & Away It's a long haul to Tarpaktuan from Banda Aceh (18,000Rp, 11 hours) and most people prefer to break their journey at Meulaboh (12,000Rp, six hours). The journey from Medan (18,000Rp, 10 hours) via Berastagi and Sidikalang is about 80km shorter than from Banda Aceh. Many travellers opt for the air-con night buses on these routes; tickets cost 30,000Rp.

There are also frequent buses south to Subulus Salem (9000Rp, four hours), from where there are buses to the port of Singkil (10,000Rp, four hours) and north to Sidikalang (5000Rp, two hours). From Sidikalang it is possible to get a direct bus to Pengururan (5000Rp, two hours) on the west coast of Pulau Samosir, or to head to Parapat on the eastern shore of Danau Toba.

Teluk Jamin

The tiny coastal village of Teluk Jamin, 70km south of Tapaktuan, is a designated departure point for boats to the Banyak Islands – in theory. The services had all but dried up at the time of research, but ask around for current schedules.

Pak Ambrin, who operates one of the boats, can reportedly organise a *room* in a private house if you need somewhere to stay overnight. The nearest losmen is the *Karya Baru* at Bakongan, 11km north-west.

Getting There & Away Teluk Jamin is on the main coast road so there are frequent buses – both north to Tapaktuan and south to Subulus Salam and Sidikalang. The bus from Medan to Tapaktuan passes by at about 4 am.

Singkil

Singkil is a remote port at the mouth of the Sungai Alas. It merits a mention only as the main departure point for boats to the Banyak Islands.

Catching a boat will mean spending a night at one of Singkil's four losmen. The *Indra Homestay*, *Harmonis* and *Purnama* have basic doubles for 7000Rp. The rooms at *Favourit* are a shade more upmarket at 10,000Rp.

Getting There & Away There are daily minibuses from Medan to Singkil (25,000Rp, eight hours), leaving at 2 pm from outside the Singkil Raya restaurant on Jl Bintang (behind Olympia Plaza). If you're travelling from Berastagi, Danau Toba or Tapaktuan, you will need to change buses at Sidikalang and Subulus Salem.

The economic crisis has taken its toll on the boat service to Pulau Balai, the main island drop-off point for the Banyak archipelago. At the time of research the schedule was in disarray, and boats left only when there were enough people to make it profitable. Weather also plays havoc with the boat timetable, particularly in the wet season, so be prepared to wait. Theoretically, boats leave for Pulau Balai on Monday, Wednesday and Friday at 7 am, returning on Thursday and Sunday at 3 pm. The journey takes four to five hours and costs 7500Rp one way. Chartering a boat is an alternative but prices are high (from 250,000Rp one way) and you must arrange for the boat captain to pick you up.

BANYAK ISLANDS

The Banyak ('many') Islands are a cluster of 99 islands, most uninhabited, about 30km west of the Acehnese port of Singkil. A few years ago the islands were right off the beaten track; these days they are popular with travellers keen on adventure and a back-to-basics lifestyle.

Malaria has been reported on the islands, so take suitable precautions.

Orientation & Information

Desa Balai, on Pulau Balai, is where boats from the mainland will deposit you. It is the only settlement of any size – it even has electricity in the evenings. It has a post office and a telegram office, but there is nowhere to change money, so bring enough with you. The Nanda restaurant, close to where the boats dock, has information about accommodation, and boats to other islands.

Things to See & Do

The setting is perfect for hanging out. The islands are ringed by pristine palm-fringed **beaches** and there is excellent **snorkelling** on the surrounding coral reefs. **Diving** can be organised at The Point bungalows (see Places to Stay & Eat) on Pulau Palambak Besar. There is good **trekking** through the virgin **jungles** of the largest island, Pulau Tuangku.

Conservationists are campaigning to save the **turtles** of Pulau Bangkaru from poachers. Green turtles can be seen year-round, and giant leatherback turtles in January and February. A group called the Turtle Foundation organises three-day trips to Bangkaru for small groups (200,000Rp, including food and accommodation), leaving every Saturday. Tours should be booked in Desa Balai on arrival.

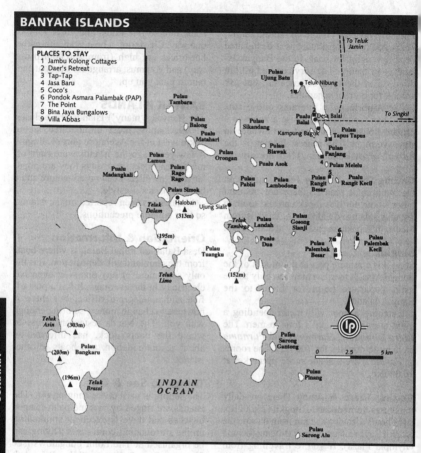

BANYAK ISLANDS

PLACES TO STAY
1 Jambu Kolong Cottages
2 Daer's Retreat
3 Tap-Tap
4 Jasa Baru
5 Coco's
6 Pondok Asmara Palambak (PAP)
7 The Point
8 Bina Jaya Bungalows
9 Villa Abbas

Places to Stay & Eat

There are half a dozen islands with accommodation – mostly in small, palm-thatch bungalows by the beach. In the low season places often close, but open again to meet demand; check on arrival at Desa Balai. Every place has its own kitchen, usually charging about 10,000Rp for three set meals. Fish, rice and vegetables feature prominently.

Few people bother to stick around on Pulau Balai, although there is some accommodation. *Daer's Retreat* has basic singles/doubles for 4000/6000Rp, or 8000/10,000Rp with private bathroom.

The most popular destination is Pulau Palambak Besar, which has three good places to choose from. The biggest of them is aptly named *The Point*, and has rooms for 4000/6000Rp. Its nine rooms make it one of the few places large enough to offer a choice in its restaurant. It also has a generator, which means cold drinks. *Bina Jaya Bungalows*, and *Pondok Asmara Palambak* (commonly known as PAP) are the other options.

There's also accommodation on Pulau Palambak Kecil *(Villa Abbas)*, Pulau Rangit Besar *(Coco's)*, Pulau Panjang *(Jasa Baru)*, Pulau Tapus Tapus *(Tap-Tap)* and Pulau Ujung Batu *(Jambu Kolong Cottages)*. Visitors to Pulau Tuangku can stay with the Lukman family at the *health centre* in Haloban for 2500Rp per person.

Getting There & Away
There are regular boats between Pulau Balai and the mainland ports of Singkil (7500Rp, four hours) and Teluk Jamin (10,000Rp, six hours). See the Singkil entry earlier in this chapter for details.

As it stands, the boat timetable to Teluk Jamin doesn't appear to make much sense. The Wisma Sibayak in Berastagi and Flamboyant Tours in Tapaktuan may have the latest timetable information.

Getting Around
Boats to the various beach bungalows can be arranged through the Nanda restaurant on Pulau Balai. Sample fares include 3500Rp to Pulau Rangit Besar and 5000Rp to Pulau Palambak Besar.

BANDA ACEH TO MEDAN
People who catch the express night buses on this route aren't missing anything.

The small hill town of Saree, about 1½ hours south of Banda Aceh, sits in the shadow of **Gunung Seulawah** (1806m). One of Sumatra's last **wild elephant herds** lives around Seulawah for part of the year.

From Saree, the road descends to the coastal town of Sigli, where there is a concrete factory.

Llokseumawe is a major industrial city 274km south-east of Banda Aceh that was the scene of unrest during the political upheaval of the late 1990s. Unless you have an interest in natural gas liquefaction facilities, fertiliser factories or paper mills, there is no point stopping here.

GAYO HIGHLANDS
The road from Takengon to Blangkejeran, the main towns of the Gayo Highlands in the central mountains of Aceh, is astoundingly picturesque. The Gayo, who number about 250,000, lived an isolated existence until the advent of modern roads and transport. Farming is the main occupation. Pressure for land to grow coffee and tobacco led to some serious overclearing, the evidence of which is still visible. The Gayo also grow rice and vegetables.

Like the neighbouring Acehnese, the Gayo were renowned for their fierce resistance to Dutch rule. They are also strict Muslims.

It's said that one way of telling you are in Gayo country is by the number of water buffalo, which replace the hump-necked *bentang* cattle preferred by the Acehnese.

Takengon
☎ 0643
The Dutch made Takengon, on the shores of Danau Laut Tawar, their base when they arrived at the beginning of the 20th century. Much of the town centre dates from that time. Yet to be discovered by the tourist throng, it is the largest town in the highlands, but is still pleasantly provincial. At an altitude of 1100m, the climate is cool.

Danau Laut Tawar is 26km long, 5km wide and 50m deep in places, and is surrounded by steep hills rising to volcanic peaks of more than 2500m. Gunung Geureundong, to the north, rises 2855m.

Orientation & Information The Mesjid Raya is in the centre of town on Jl Lebe Kadir, which is where you'll find the post office, Telkom wartel and police station, as well as shops and restaurants. You can change US dollars (cash and travellers cheques) at BRI bank on Jl Yos Sudarso. The Hotel Buntu Kubu doubles as a traveller information centre and can organise guides and overnight trips for two or more people.

Things to See & Do Takengon's main attractions are natural. Admire the views, cruise around the lake in a *perahu* (dugout canoe), or explore caves, waterfalls and the three-peaked **Burni Telong** volcano.

SUMATRA

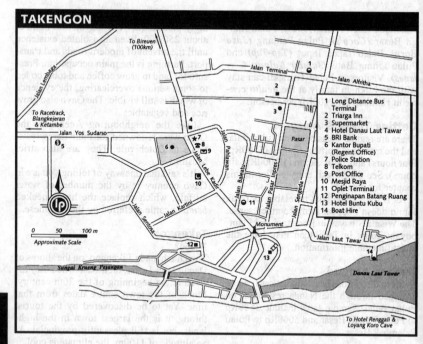

TAKENGON

1 Long Distance Bus Terminal
2 Triarga Inn
3 Supermarket
4 Hotel Danau Laut Tawar
5 BRI Bank
6 Kantor Bupati (Regent Office)
7 Police Station
8 Telkom
9 Post Office
10 Mesjid Raya
11 Oplet Terminal
12 Penginapan Batang Ruang
13 Hotel Buntu Kubu
14 Boat Hire

There are stalagmites and lots of bats at **Loyang Koro** (Buffalo Caves), which are by the lake, 6km from town beyond Hotel Renggali. Get there by labi-labi from Jl Baleatu and take a torch (flashlight).

Four kilometres past Loyang Koro are the **Loyang Putri Pukes**, caves which are said to contain a rock that was once a woman. The woman, Putri Pukes, turned to stone when she ignored her mother's advice and looked back at her village as she left to marry an outsider. Unfortunately erosion has removed any distinguishing features from the rock.

The sulphurous **hot spring** at Simpang Balik is said to cure skin diseases. Take a labi-labi headed to Bireuen and get off at Simpang Balik, around 15km north of Takengon. The springs are 100m from the main road.

A man-made wonder is the intricately **carved house** of the region's last traditional ruler at the village of Kebayakan, on the lakeside just north of Takengon.

In the week following Independence Day (August 17), Takengon hosts a regional **horse racing** carnival, held at the track to the west of town. The jockeys, 12-year-old boys who ride bareback, come from all over the Gayo Highlands.

Places to Stay & Eat The best budget place by far is the *Hotel Buntu Kubu* (☎ 22254, Jl Malem Dewa), perched on a hill overlooking Danau Tawar. The hotel has a varied history; a former Dutch official residence, museum and Indonesian military post, it has been lovingly restored. Doubles with mandi start at 20,000Rp. The hotel is the only traveller-oriented place in town, and the only place to get information.

The *Penginapan Batang Ruang* (☎ 21 524, Jl Mahkamah 7) may have doubles for

10,000Rp, but the share mandis are a disgrace and the management is unfriendly.

The **Triarga Inn** (☎ 21073) is a good mid-range place off Jl Pasar Inpres, right near the bus terminal. The cheap (15,000Rp) doubles are not worth looking at, but there are some good doubles upstairs for 25,000Rp to 45,000Rp with hot water. **Hotel Danau Laut Tawar** (*Jl Lebe Kadir 35*), opposite the parade ground, has rooms for 20,000Rp.

The **Hotel Renggali** (☎ 21144), perched on the lakeside 2.5km out of town, looks pretty flash from a distance. Close up, it's too tatty to be asking 78,000Rp for its standard doubles, although the 96,000Rp rooms in the new building are reasonable.

Padang food and Chinese-style **noodle dishes** can be found all along Jl Lebe Kadir, Jl Pasar Inpres and around the bus terminal. Delicious fresh Gayo coffee is available everywhere. A local speciality is *kopi telor kocok* – a raw egg and sugar creamed together in a glass and topped up with coffee.

Shopping Takengon is the place to buy traditional-style Gayo/Alas tapestry, which is made into clothes, belts, purses and cushion covers. Keramat Mupakat, Jl Lebe Kadir 24, has a good range.

At the market, it's sometimes possible to buy highly decorated engraved pottery called *keunire*, which is used in wedding ceremonies.

Getting There & Away PMTOH has two buses a day to Medan: a 6 am normal bus (15,000Rp) and a 'deluxe' air-con bus at 7.30 am (29,000Rp, 11 hours). To Banda Aceh there's an air-con bus at 7.30 am and 7.30 pm (19,000Rp, eight hours).

There are also regular buses north to Bireuen, 218km south-east of Banda Aceh on the Trans-Sumatran Hwy. The 100km journey to Bireuen (4000Rp, three hours) passes through spectacular country. Heading south, there are regular buses on the much-improved road to Blangkejeran (15,000Rp, seven hours) and Gurah/Ketambe (19,000Rp, nine hours).

Getting Around Labi-labi leave from the southern end of Jl Baleatu. Fares around town cost 300Rp. Perahus for lake cruising can be hired at the pier at the end of Jl Laut Tawar. Count on around 15,000Rp per day, or 2000Rp per hour.

Blangkejeran

Blangkejeran is the main town of the remote southern highlands. The area is recognised as the Gayo heartland and it is possible to hire guides to take you out to some of the smaller **villages**.

There are several small guesthouses: **Penginapan Juli** (*Jl Kong Buri 12*); **Wahyu** (*Jl Blawar 9*); and **Penginapan Mardhatillah**, on Jl Besar.

There are regular buses north to Takengon and south to Gurah and Kutacane.

GURAH & GUNUNG LEUSER NATIONAL PARK
☎ 0629

Gurah, in the heart of the Alas Valley, is one of the main access points to Gunung Leuser National Park. The Gurah area lies between the towns of Blangkejeran and Kutacane, on the east bank of the Sungai Alas. Directly across the river is Ketambe, home to a world renowned conservation research station – but it is off limits to tourists. For more information, see the Ketambe Research Station boxed text in this section.

Gunung Leuser National Park is one of South-East Asia's greatest flora and fauna sanctuaries. Within the park's boundaries live four of the world's rarest animals – tigers, rhinoceros, elephants and orang-utans. There are an estimated 500 tigers, 100 rhinos and 300 elephants in the park, but your chances of seeing them are extremely remote. You can, however, be sure of encountering plenty of primates. The most common is the white-breasted Thomas Leaf monkey, which sports a splendid, crested punk hair-do.

Habitats range from the swamp forests of the west coast to the dense lowland rain-forests of the interior. Above 1500m, the permanent mist has created moss forests rich in epiphytes and orchids.

SUMATRA

Rare flora includes two members of the rafflesia family, *Rafflesia acehensis* and *R. zippelni*, which are found along the Sungai Alas.

More than 300 bird species have been recorded in the park, including the bizarre rhinoceros hornbill, and the helmeted hornbill, which has a call that sounds like maniacal laughter.

Crocodiles used to be common in the lower reaches of Sungai Alas/Bengkung, but have been virtually wiped out by poachers.

Information

You are not allowed to enter the park without a permit and a guide. Both are available from the PHPA office in Tanah Merah, about an hour by labi-labi from Gurah, or 15 minutes from Kutacane. Permits cost 2000Rp per day and you will need three photocopies of your passport (there's a photocopier at the office). Guides can be hired from the PHPA office or from any guesthouse in Gurah. Some guides are still based in Kutacane. Guides construct shelters at night, cook food, carry baggage, cut through the trails (or what's left of them) and show you the wildlife.

Kutacane, 43km from Gurah, is the closest town of any note and is the place to go for supplies, and post and telephone facilities.

Gurah Recreation Forest

The *hutan wisata* (recreation forest) at Gurah is like a park within the national park.

Gurah's 9200 hectares have been set up with a network of walking tracks and viewing towers to give visitors an introduction to **rainforest** life. The most popular walk involves a two hour (5km) hike from Gurah to **hot springs** by Sungai Alas. If you want to spend a night in the jungle, there is a camping ground halfway to the springs. There's also a 6km walk to a **waterfall**.

Gurah and nearby Balailutu offer a range of bungalow and guesthouse accommodation (see Places to Stay later in this section).

Trekking

As well as supplying guides and permits, the PHPA office in Tanah Merah also has

Ketambe Research Station

The Ketambe Research Station has been conducting extensive studies of the flora and fauna of Gunung Leuser National Park for more than 20 years.

The immediate area is home to a large number of primates, as well as Sumatran tigers, rhinoceros, sun bears, hornbills and snakes. Positioned on the west bank of the Sungai Alas, accessible only by dugout canoe, the station is off-limits to almost everyone but those people working there. A small team of ecologists, behavioural scientists and student volunteers from the universities of Banda Aceh, Jakarta and Utrecht in the Netherlands, work and live at the site. Most venture out only to make phone calls to family and friends or to visit the PHPA office in Tanah Merah to renew their long-term national parks permits. As a result, the station has a tightly-knit family atmosphere.

In the early 1970s Ketambe was home to Sumatra's orang-utan rehabilitation program, but the project was relocated to the now-famous site at Bukit Lawang to allow researchers to study the Ketambe region without the disruption of tourists.

Nowadays the station's primary concern is hard-core conservation. Tourists cannot visit the station or its surrounding forest – in fact, it is forbidden to even cross the river.

The ongoing mission of the station is to record all the species of fauna in the park – still an unknown quantity. More-specific conservation projects are also conducted, targetting animals that are seriously threatened by the changing environment and human encroachment.

The national parks' primate population, particularly orang-utans and Thomas Leaf monkeys, has suffered greatly at the hands of poachers, who catch and sell the animals as pets. Logging too has taken its toll. Rare birds are also in need of protection.

The PHPA hopes to start a program to educate locals about the long-term consequences of stripping the forest of trees and native wildlife to make a quick buck.

information about a variety of treks, from short walks to 14 day hikes through the jungle to the tops of the park's mountains.

Gunung Kemiri At 3314m, it is the second highest of the peaks in Gunung Leuser National Park. The return trek takes five to six days, starting from the village of Gumpang, north of Gurah. It takes in some of the park's richest **primate habitat**, with orang-utans, macaques, siamangs and gibbons.

Gunung Leuser The park's highest peak is, of course, Gunung Leuser (3404m). Only the fit should attempt the 14 day return trek to the summit. The walk starts from the village of Angusan, west of Blangkejeren.

Gunung Perkinson Allow seven days for the return trek to the summit of Gunung Perkinson (2828m), on the eastern side of the park. There is a **rafflesia** site at about 1200m and some spectacular moss forest.

Gunung Simpali The trek to Gunung Simpali (3270m) is a one week round trip starting from the village of Engkran and following the valley of Sungai Lawe Mamas. **Rhinos** live in this area. The Lawe Mamas is a wild, raging river that joins the Alas about 15km north of Kutacane.

Rafting
If you're after whitewater thrills, don't bother with the regular US$150 three-day/two-night trips down the Sungai Alas that start from Muarasitulan, south of Kutacane. There's some magnificent scenery along the way, lots of birds and monkeys, but only one stretch of water vaguely resembling a rapid. You'll be longing for an outboard motor by the time you get to Gelombang on the third afternoon.

Serious rafters should start further upstream, eg at Angusan, near Blangkejeran.

Places to Stay & Eat
Gurah Accommodation is scattered along the only road through the area. Each guesthouse has its own small *restaurant*. Coming from the south, Pondok Wisata Ketambe is the first and best budget option. Owned by the regional national parks chief, it is the only place with modern communications equipment (a CB radio). Bungalows set in the forest range from 10,000Rp to 50,000Rp; all have inside mandis. Hot showers are also available. The restaurant here is the best place to meet other travellers.

Next door, *Wisma Sadar Wisata* has basic 7500Rp bungalows and a range of newer ones across the road from 15,000Rp. *Cinta Alam Guesthouse*, also known as Mr Ali's after the elderly owner, has its bungalows perched on the edge of paddy fields out back. Check out the rooms on the river (20,000Rp to 40,000Rp) among the banana trees.

Three kilometres up the road, the comfortably appointed *Gurah Bungalows* is the only upmarket option, with 25,000Rp to 85,000Rp rooms set deep in the forest, right on the river.

Kutacane The original base for exploring the national park, Kutacane has taken a back seat since travellers discovered the guesthouses in Gurah. Only a handful of losmen have survived, and they are all pretty shabby. You can find basic doubles for as little as 5000Rp at places on the main street (known by locals as Jl Besar), like *Wisma Renggali* (☎ 21386) and *Wisma Rindu Alam*. *Wisma Wisata* (☎ 21406) at No 93 is a clean place on the edge of town, with basic doubles for 7500Rp. The *Hotel Bru Dihe* (☎ 21444, Jl Guru Leman 14), near the mosque, is easily the best place in town. Large doubles cost 20,000Rp with mandi and fan, or 45,000Rp with air-con.

There are lots of restaurants near the bus terminal. *Sapo Bawan* has good nasi and mie goreng. If you're after Padang food, *Anita*, opposite Wisma Renggali, is worth a try, or stroll down the main street to *Roda Baru*, *Damai Baru* or *Nasional*.

Getting There & Around
Long-distance buses leave from the terminal in Kutacane. The Pinem company has daily direct buses from Medan's Pinang Baris terminal to Kutacane via Kabanjahe (10,000Rp,

SUMATRA

six hours). Many travellers head to Gurah from Berastagi, which means catching an opelet to Kabanjahe (500Rp), then one of the frequent buses to Kutacane (7000Rp, four hours). Along the way there are fine views of Gunung Sinabung and the Alas Valley. From Kutacane there are countless labi-labi to Tanah Merah (500Rp) and Gurah (2500Rp).

There are also buses heading north to Blangkejeran and beyond. This road is a lot better than it used to be, but is still prone to wash-out in the wet season. The northbound buses pass through Gurah and you can try hailing one down, or buy a ticket in advance from Pondok Wisata Ketambe. The losmen adds a small commission but it rings ahead to Kutacane to make sure the bus picks you up.

West Sumatra

The province of West Sumatra is like a vast and magnificent nature reserve, dominated by volcanoes, with jungles, waterfalls, canyons and lakes. This is the homeland of the Minangkabau, one of Indonesia's most interesting and influential ethnic groups. They make up 95% of the province's population of 3½ million.

Padang is the provincial capital. The other major cities are Payakumbuh, Bukittinggi, Padangpanjang, Solok and Sawahlunto. There are four large lakes in West Sumatra: Singkarak near Solok; Maninjau near Bukittinggi; and Diatas and Dibawah, east of Padang.

The fascinating Mentawai Islands are also part of West Sumatra. Only recently emerged from their stone-age isolation, the inhabitants of these islands are quite different from the people of mainland Sumatra.

The economy of West Sumatra, although predominantly based on agriculture (coffee, rice, coconuts and cattle), is strengthened by industries like coal mining.

History

Legend has it that the Minangkabau are descended from none other than that wandering Macedonian tyrant, Alexander the Great.

According to legend, the ancestors of the Minangkabau arrived in Sumatra under the leadership of King Maharjo Dirajo, the youngest son of Alexander, more commonly known in Indonesia as Iskandar Zulkarnair. They settled in the Padangpanjang area and gradually spread out over western Sumatra.

Anthropologists suggest that the Minangkabau arrived in West Sumatra from the Malay peninsula some time between 1000 and 2000 BC, probably by following the Sungai Batang Hari upstream from the Straits of Melaka to the highlands of the Bukit Barisan mountains. Little is known about the area's history, however, until the arrival of Islam in the 14th century. The abundance of megalithic remains around the towns of Batusangkar and Payakumbuh indicate that the central highlands supported a sizeable community some 2000 years ago.

There's evidence that the Jambi-based kingdom of Malayu and its subsequent Majapahit conquerors controlled the area between the 11th and 14th centuries. It was about this time that Islam first arrived on the local scene, and that the region was split into small Muslim states ruled by sultans. By the time the Europeans arrived in the early 17th century, West Sumatra's power base comprised little more than a few small-time rajahs who ruled minuscule village-states.

It remained this way until the beginning of the 19th century, when war erupted between followers of the Islamic fundamentalist Padri movement and supporters of Minangkabau *adat* (traditional law). The Padris were so-named because their leaders were *hajis* (pilgrims) who had made their way to Mecca via the Acehnese port of Pedir. They returned determined to establish a true Islamic society. Their frustration at the lax pre-Islamic ways of their fellows boiled over into open conflict in 1803. The Dutch arrived in 1821 and supported the traditional leaders against the Padris, who by this time had won control of much of the highlands.

The fighting dragged on until 1837, when the Dutch overcame the Padri strongholds. Today, a curious fusion of traditional beliefs and Islam is practised in West Sumatra.

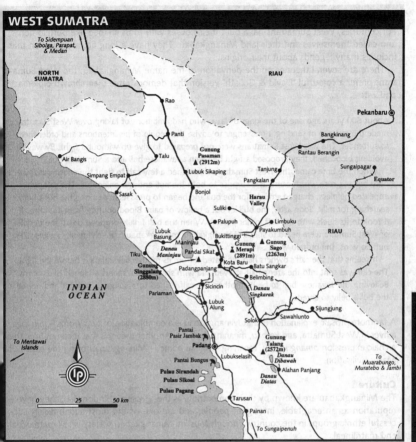

WEST SUMATRA

Flora & Fauna

The *Rafflesia arnoldi* can be seen around the small village of Palupuh, 16km north of Bukittinggi, between August and November. West Sumatra is also famous for its many orchid species.

Tigers, rhinoceros, sun bears, elephants and various species of monkey and deer are all native to West Sumatra. Of particular interest in the Mentawai Islands is *Siamang kerdil*, a rare species of black-and-yellow monkey usually called *simpai mentawai* by

the locals. They are strictly protected. The province is also home to diverse bird-life.

Special Events

In addition to the dances performed by the Minangkabau, there are several important cultural and sporting events in West Sumatra.

Boat Racing A colourful annual boat race is held in Padang to commemorate Independence Day, 17 August.

The Minangkabau

For centuries, West Sumatrans have built their houses with roofs shaped like buffalo horns, and called themselves and their land Minangkabau. They have a long literary tradition that includes many legends about their origins.

There are several theories on the derivation of the name Minangkabau; the West Sumatrans prefer a colourful 'David & Goliath' version that demonstrates their shrewd diplomacy and wit:

About 600 years ago one of the kings of Java, who had ambitions of taking over West Sumatra, made the mistake of sending a messenger to advise the people of his intentions and order them to surrender. The wily West Sumatrans were not prepared to give up without a fight. By way of avoiding bloodshed, they proposed a fight between a Javanese bull and a Sumatran bull.

When the time came, the West Sumatrans dispatched a tiny calf to fight the enormous Javanese bull – a ruse which came as a surprise to both the bull and the onlookers. The calf, which appeared helpless, charged straight for the bull and began to press its nose along the bull's belly, searching for milk. Soon after, the bull let out a bellow of pain. Blood pouring from its stomach, it took to its heels with the calf in hot pursuit. When the bull finally dropped dead, the people of West Sumatra were heard to shout, 'Minangkabau, minangkabau!', which literally means 'The buffalo wins, the buffalo wins!'.

It seems that the calf's owners had separated it from its mother several days before the fight. The calf was sent into the arena half-starved and with sharp metal spears attached to its horns. Believing the Javanese bull to be its mother, the calf rushed to assuage its hunger and ripped the bull's belly to shreds.

A far more prosaic explanation is that Minangkabau is a combination of two words – *minanga*, a river in West Sumatra, and *kerbau*, meaning 'buffalo'. Another theory is that it comes from the archaic expression *pinang kabhu*, meaning 'original home' – Minangkabau being the cradle of Malay civilisation.

Culture

The Minangkabau are known by their compatriots as the 'gypsies of Indonesia'; they have a reputation as an adaptable, intelligent people, and are one of the most economically successful ethnic groups in the country. Though Muslim, Minangkabau society is still matriarchal and matrilineal.

According to Minangkabau *adat* (customary law), men have no rights over their wives other than to expect them to remain faithful. The eldest living female is the matriarch and holds the power in her household, which can be as many as 70 people descended from one ancestral mother, living under the same roof. She is deferred to in all matters of family politics.

Every Minangkabau belongs to his or her mother's clan. At the basic level of the clan is the *sapariouk*, those matri-related kin who eat together. These include the mother, grandchildren and son-in-law. The name comes from the word *periouk* (rice pot). A number of genealogically related sapariouk make up a lineage, or *sapayung*. The word *payung* means 'umbrella'.

Children, by right of birth, are members of their mothers' sapayung. All progeny from a marriage is regarded as part of the mother's family group and the father has no say in family affairs. Ancestral property, although worked collectively, is passed down the female line rather than down the male line.

The Minangkabau

The most important male member of the household is the mother's eldest brother, who replaces the father in being responsible for the children's education and offers them economic advice as they grow older. He also discusses, and advises them on, their prospective marriages.

Arts & Crafts

West Sumatra has a reputation for exquisite, handloomed songket cloth, and fine embroidery. Songket weaving uses gold and silver threads (imitation these days) to create patterns on a base of silk or cotton, depending on the budget. The designs are usually elaborate floral motifs and geometric patterns. One of the most popular designs, used in both weaving and embroidery, incorporates stylised flowers and mountains in an ornate pattern known as *gunung batuah*, or 'magic mountain'.

The woven material is traditionally used as a sarong, shawl or wrap. Expect to pay more than 200,000Rp for a sarong of good quality. It's also widely available in the form of cushion covers, bedspreads, handbags, wallets and other such items.

Songket weaving is a widely practised in West Sumatra. Kubang, 13km from Payakumbuh near the Riau provincial border, is the centre for commercial weaving.

The village of Silungkang, on the Agam Plateau near the coal town of Sawahlunto, specialises in vividly coloured silk songket sarongs and scarves. Other weaving villages in this area include Balai Cacang, Koto Nan Ampek and Muara.

Pandai Sikat, near Padangpanjang on the main road between Padang and Bukittinggi, is known for the quality of its cloth and for its decorative woodcarving.

Traditional weavers use another, unusually painstaking, technique called 'needle weaving'. The process involves removing certain threads from a piece of cloth and stitching the remaining ones together to form patterns. These patterns include identifiable motifs such as people, crabs, insects, dogs and horses. This cloth is traditionally used to cover the *carano* – a brass *sirih* (stand) with receptacles for betel nut, tobacco and lime – which is used for ceremonial occasions. You're unlikely to find any examples for sale.

The Minangkabau are also renowned for their fine embroidery. Villages specialising in this are Koto Gadang, Ampek Angkek, Naras, Lubuk Begalung, Kota Nan Ampek and Sunguyang.

Another highly developed art found in West Sumatra is silverwork. Filigree jewellery, as fine as spider webs, is a speciality. Koto Gadang, near Bukittinggi, is the place to go if you're interested.

Dance & Music

Dance is an important part of Minangkabau culture. Dances include the colourful Tari Payung (Umbrella Dance), a welcome dance about a young man's love for his girlfriend; the dazzling Tari Lilin (Candle Dance), a miracle of physical coordination in which female dancers are required to rhythmically juggle and balance china saucers – with burning candles attached to them – while simultaneously clicking castanets; and the dramatic Tari Piring (Plate Dance), which involves the dancers leaping barefoot on piles of broken china.

The most popular of the Minangkabau dances is the Randai, a unique dance-drama performed at weddings, harvest festivals and other celebrations. The steps and movements for the Randai developed from the Pencak Silat, a self-defence routine that exists in various styles. The dance is learnt by every Minang boy when he reaches the age at which he is considered too old to remain in his mother's house but too young to move into another woman's.

SUMATRA

The Minangkabau

The Randai combines the movements of Pencak Silat with literature, sport, song and drama. Every village in West Sumatra has at least one Randai group of 20 performers. Both female and male roles are played by men in traditional *gelambuk* trousers and black dress. The traditional version tells the story of a woman so wilful and wicked that she is driven out of her village before she brings complete disaster on the community. The drama is accompanied by gamelan music.

It is the custom for Minang youths to spend some time in a *surau* (prayer house), where they are taught, among other things, how to look after themselves. This includes learning the Pencak Silat. The style of Pencak Silat most often performed is the Mudo, a mock battle that leads the two protagonists to the brink of violence before it is concluded. It is a dramatic dance involving skilled technique, fancy footwork and deliberate pauses which follow each movement and serve to heighten the tension.

Harimau Silat, the most aggressive and dangerous style of Pencak Silat, originated in the Painan district of West Sumatra. The steps for the Harimau Silat imitate a tiger stalking and killing its prey. With their bodies as close to the ground as possible, two fighters circle menacingly, springing at each other from time to time.

The percussion instruments used to accompany most of the dances are similar to those of the Javanese gamelan and are collectively called the *telempong* in West Sumatra. Two other instruments frequently played are the *puput* and *salung*, kinds of flute that are usually made out of bamboo, reed or rice stalks.

Bullfighting Known locally as *adu kerbau*, bullfighting is popular West Sumatran entertainment. It bears no resemblance to Spanish bullfighting – there is no bloodshed (except by accident) and the bulls, which are water buffaloes *(kerbau)*, don't get hurt.

Two animals of roughly the same size and weight are made to lock horns in a trial of strength. Once horns are locked, the fight ends when one animal tires and runs off, pursued by the winner. It often ends up with both beasts charging around a muddy paddock, scattering onlookers in all directions.

The original intention was to help develop buffalo breeding in the region. As a spectator sport, the main focus is betting. It's an interesting insight into local culture and well worth seeing.

The centres for bullfighting are the villages of Kota Baru and Batagak, between Padang and Bukittinggi. The host village in each district is rotated every six months or so. The first bullfight in a new location is an important day for the host village, which kicks off proceedings with a meeting of village elders, followed by a demonstration of *pencak silat* (Minangkabau martial art) dancing.

Bullfights are held every Tuesday afternoon at about 5 pm around Kota Baru and every Saturday from 4 pm around Batagak. There are bemos to the bullfights from Bukittinggi's Aur Kuning bus terminal for 600Rp each way. Entry is another 600Rp. Alternatively, travel agencies in Bukittinggi charge 10,000Rp for the round trip plus admission.

Horse Racing Horse racing in Sumatra is a vivid, noisy spectacle. Horses are ridden bareback and jockeys are dressed in the traditional costume of their region or village – the aim is to gain prestige for the district where the horse is bred and raised. Padang, Padangpanjang, Bukittinggi, Payakumbuh and Batu Sangkar each stage one meeting a year, normally over two days.

Tabut Festival The highlight of the West Sumatran cultural calendar is the colourful Islamic festival of Tabut, staged at the seaside town of Pariaman, 36km north of Padang.

It takes place at the beginning of the month of Muharam to honour the martyrdom of Mohammed's grandchildren, Hassan and Hussein, at the battle of Kerbala. Because the date is fixed by the Islamic lunar calendar, it moves forward 10 days each year.

Central to the festival is the *bouraq*, a winged horse-like creature with the head of a woman, which is believed to have descended to earth to collect the souls of dead heroes and take them to heaven.

Nearby villages create painted effigies of bouraqs and adorn them with gold necklaces and other paraphernalia. The effigies are carried through the streets with much merriment, dancing and music, and are finally tossed into the sea. Spectators and participants then dive into the water and grab whatever remains of the bouraqs, the most valued memento being the gold necklace. When two bouraqs cross paths during the procession, a mock fight ensues. Each group praises its own bouraq, belittling and insulting the other at the same time.

People from all over Indonesia come to witness or take part in the festival. Admission to the area is by donation.

Other West Sumatran towns also celebrate Tabut, but usually on public holidays, such as Independence Day (17 August) and Hero Day (10 November).

PADANG
☎ 0751 • pop 700,000

Padang is a flat, sprawling city (the name means 'field') on the coastal plains between the Indian Ocean and the Bukit Barisan mountains. It is West Sumatra's capital, and Sumatra's third largest city.

Many travellers use Padang as an entry or exit point to Sumatra, taking the Pelni boats between the city and Jakarta to bypass southern Sumatra. Tabing airport is one of Indonesia's visa-free entry points, with direct connections to Kuala Lumpur, Johor Bahru and Singapore.

Padang is an easy-going place with some fine colonial architecture, wide clean streets (the city has won numerous awards for tidiness) and a fascinating old quarter near the docks. There are palm-fringed beaches nearby and mountains a few hours away. The unique Mentawai Islands are off the coast. The road between Padang and Solok affords views of some of the most picturesque scenery in Sumatra: exquisite high-peaked Minangkabau houses and lush, terraced rice paddies.

Orientation & Information
Padang is easy to find your way around and the central area is quite compact. Jl M Yamin, stretching from the bus terminal corner at Jl Pemuda to Jl Azizchan, is the main street. The main bus and opelet terminals are both across from the market.

Tourist Offices The West Sumatran government office (DIPARDA, ☎ 34232) is at Jl Sudirman 43 and the regional tourist office (☎ 55231) is further north at Jl Khatib Sulaiman 22. Both are very helpful and have English-speaking staff. They have the same opening hours: from 7.30 am to 2.30 pm Monday to Thursday; until 11.30 am on Friday; and until 1 pm on Saturday. The regional office is a fair way from the city centre, but easily reached by orange *biskota* (city bus) 14A. There is also a small Padang city office (☎ 34186) at Jl Samudera 1.

Money Padang has branches of all the major Indonesian banks. BCA bank is on Jl Agus Salim. Amex is represented by Pacto (☎ 37678), Jl Tan Malaka 25. There's a 24 hour moneychanging service – with reasonable rates – at the Dipo International Hotel (see Places to Stay). ATMs are found all over town, and there's one inside the post office.

Post & Communications The post office, Jl Azizchan 7, is near the corner of Jl M Yamin. It has Internet facilities for 10,000Rp an hour. The huge Minangkabau-style Telkom wartel is on the corner of Jl Ahmad Dahlan and Jl Khatib Sulaiman,

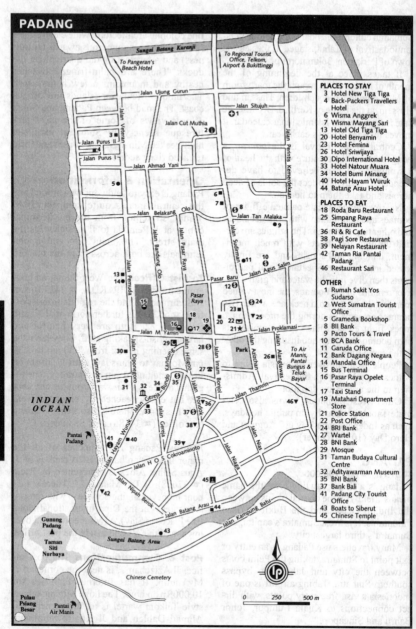

PADANG

PLACES TO STAY
3 Hotel New Tiga Tiga
4 Back-Packers Travellers Hotel
6 Wisma Anggrek
7 Wisma Mayang Sari
13 Hotel Old Tiga Tiga
20 Hotel Benyamin
23 Hotel Femina
26 Hotel Sriwijaya
30 Dipo International Hotel
33 Hotel Natour Muara
34 Hotel Bumi Minang
40 Hotel Hayam Wuruk
44 Batang Arau Hotel

PLACES TO EAT
18 Roda Baru Restaurant
25 Simpang Raya Restaurant
36 Ri & Ri Cafe
38 Pagi Sore Restaurant
39 Nelayan Restaurant
42 Taman Ria Pantai Padang
46 Restaurant Sari

OTHER
1 Rumah Sakit Yos Sudarso
2 West Sumatran Tourist Office
5 Gramedia Bookshop
8 BII Bank
9 Pacto Tours & Travel
10 BCA Bank
11 Garuda Office
12 Bank Dagang Negara
14 Mandala Office
15 Bus Terminal
16 Pasar Raya Opelet Terminal
17 Taxi Stand
19 Matahari Department Store
21 Police Station
22 Post Office
24 BRI Bank
27 Wartel
28 BNI Bank
29 Mosque
31 Taman Budaya Cultural Centre
32 Adityawarman Museum
35 BNI Bank
37 Bank Bali
41 Padang City Tourist Office
43 Boats to Siberut
45 Chinese Temple

SUMATRA

north of the city centre. The staff can organise collect calls. The wartel in the town centre, Jl Imam Bonjol 15H, is the place to make international or collect calls. Both Telkom and the wartel are open 24 hours.

Medical Services If you need a hospital, try the privately owned Rumah Sakit Yos Sudarso on Jl Situjuh.

Things to See & Do

The **Adityawarman Museum**, 500m from the bus terminal on Jl Diponegoro, is built in the Minangkabau tradition with two rice barns out the front. It has a small but excellent collection of antiques and other objects of historical and cultural interest. The museum is open daily, except Monday, from 8 am to 6 pm; admission is 250Rp.

The nearby **Taman Budaya Cultural Centre** stages regular dance performances as well as poetry readings, plays and exhibitions of paintings and carvings.

There's an **amusement park** with slides, swings and dodgem cars, by the beach at the Taman Ria Pantai Padang (see Places to Eat).

The old **train line** from Padang to Bukittinggi has been re-opened for tourist trains. Every Sunday, there is a train up the coast to Pariaman departing at 8.30 am and returning at 2.30 pm. Tickets are 3000/4000Rp one way/return; 4000/6000Rp in the air-con carriage. Regular services to the Anai Valley, near Padangpanjang, have ceased but group bookings can be made by contacting ☎ 32200 or fax 28046.

Organised Tours

Rimbun Tours, at the Hotel Bumi Minang (☎ 37572, email rimbun@indosat.net.id), runs half-day historic tours of Padang, and day trips to offshore tropical islands and Bukittinggi. Mr Arzein at the regional tourist office can organise tours and treks to off-the-beaten-track destinations.

Surf charters to the Mentawai Islands operate out of Padang from March to October. Good Sumateran Surf Tours, based at the Dipo International Hotel (☎/fax 34261), is a popular US company. The Surf Travel

Company, based at the same hotel, is a long-running Australian operation; its Web site is www.surftravel.com.au.

Places to Stay – Budget

Unusually for a major city, there are a few reasonable budget hotels. The *Hotel Sriwijaya (☎ 23577)* on Jl Alanglawas has clean singles/doubles from 15,000/20,000Rp. Its location is quiet and close to the city centre. Another good place is the spotless *Hotel Benyamin (☎ 22324, Jl Azizchan 19)*, down the lane next to Hotel Femina. Rooms cost 20,000/30,000Rp and all have fans – a good investment in steamy Padang.

Opposite the bus terminal, the dilapidated *Old Tiga Tiga* has prison-like rooms on the ground floor for 10,000/12,000Rp and comfortable large rooms upstairs for 25,000/33,000Rp. Much cleaner is the *New Tiga Tiga (☎ 22173, Jl Veteran 33)*, a couple of kilometres north of the city centre. Tiled rooms with fan, mandi and breakfast cost 20,000/25,000Rp, or from 25,000/32,000Rp with air-con.

Nearby, the *Back-Packers Travellers Hotel (☎ 35751, Jl Purus I 2)* is a spotless new place with dorm beds for 15,000Rp, fan doubles from 24,000Rp and air-con rooms from 48,000Rp. The hotel is in a difficult-to-find street north of the town centre; luckily, there's free transport from the co-owned Dipo International Hotel (see the following entry).

Places to Stay – Mid-Range

Some pleasant old Dutch villas along Jl Sudirman have been converted into hotels. The nicest is the friendly, guesthouse-style *Wisma Mayang Sari (☎ 22647)* at No 19. It has clean, well appointed singles/doubles with air-con, hot water and TV from 45,000/50,000Rp. The nearby *Wisma Anggrek (☎ 32 785)* at No 39 has a reputation as a 'love hotel'. Nevertheless, it's friendly, and doubles with air-con, TV and mandi start at 40,000Rp.

The *Dipo International Hotel (☎ 34261, Jl Diponegoro 25)* is the most traveller-friendly of the mid-range places. It has a 24 hour restaurant and moneychanger, a Home Country Direct phone, Internet facilities and nightly entertainment. The cheapest rooms could do with a lick of paint, but are still reasonable value at 60,000/65,000Rp.

One of the nicest options is the *Hayam Wuruk* (☎ 21726, Jl Hayam Wuruk 16), near Pantai Padang. Modern singles/doubles with air-con start at 55,000/85,000Rp, including use of the swimming pool and gym.

Places to Stay – Top End
The *Hotel Bumi Minang* (☎ 37555, Jl Bundo Kandung 20-28) is Padang's No 1 establishment, with a swimming pool and flood-lit tennis courts. Singles/doubles start at 350,000/400,000Rp and rise to 5,000,000Rp. The *Natour Muara* (☎ 35600, Jl Gereja 34) has more modest doubles from 180,000Rp. *Pangeran's Beach Hotel* (☎ 51333, Jl Ir Juanda 79) has doubles from 130,000Rp, breakfast and dinner included.

The *Batang Arau Hotel* (☎ 27400, Jl Batang Arau 33) oozes romance and style. It occupies an old Dutch bank, built in 1908, right on the riverbank near the warehouses and temples of the old quarter. It's more of a guesthouse than a hotel, with just seven rooms – all individually decorated with beautiful colonial and traditional furniture and fittings. Some have balconies overlooking the river. Doubles cost US$70, including breakfast.

Places to Eat
Travellers with a taste for Padang food have hundreds of restaurants to choose from. The best include *Roda Baru* (Jl Pasar Raya 6) upstairs in the market; *Simpang Raya* (Jl Azizchan 24) opposite the post office; and *Pagi Sore* (Jl Pondok 143).

Jl Pondok also has a cluster of Chinese-Indonesian restaurants. The *Ri & Ri Cafe* at No 86 is a pleasant little place that opens in the evenings.

The *Restaurant Sari* (Jl Thamrin 71B) is an upmarket Chinese place that also serves good seafood. Expect to pay at least 20,000Rp per person. Serious seafood fans wanting to splurge should head to the *Nelayan Res-*

taurant (Jl Hos Cokroaminoto 44). Prices are not listed, so ask before you order.

Stretching along Pantai Padang at the southern end of Jl Samudera, the *Taman Ria Pantai Padang* has dozens of outdoor food stalls selling Padang and other Indonesian snacks, drinks and ice cream. Very popular at night, it's not the most picturesque seaside scene but it makes for a nice change.

Getting There & Away
Air International flights from Padang are covered in the Getting There & Away section at the beginning of this chapter.

Garuda flies twice daily to Jakarta (788,000Rp); Mandala does the trip once a day for the same price. Merpati has the busiest domestic schedule, with four flights a week to Pulau Batam (465,000Rp) and Medan (486,000Rp), and three week to Palembang (552,000Rp).

Merpati and Pelangi Air are based at the Hotel Natour Muara (☎ 38103). Silk Air (☎ 38120) has an office at the Hotel Bumi Minang. Garuda (☎ 30737) is at Jl Sudirman 2, and Mandala is opposite the bus terminal on Jl Pemuda.

Bus Padang's bus terminal is conveniently central. Every north-south bus comes through here, so there are loads of options.

There are frequent, but normal, buses to Bukittinggi (3500Rp, two hours). You can get all the way to Jakarta in 30 hours for 51,000Rp/120,000Rp normal/air-con. Fares to Parapat (for Danau Toba) are 27,500/41,000Rp; it's 30,000/49,000Rp to Medan. Other destinations include Bengkulu (25,000Rp), Sibolga (20,500Rp) and Sungaipenuh (11,000Rp) in Kerinci Seblat National Park.

Taxi Angkasa Taxi (☎ 55800) has charter cars to Bukittinggi (70,000Rp) and Danau Maninjau (85,000Rp). Charters are slightly cheaper if booked from the desk at the airport.

Boat Pelni ships call at Padang's Teluk Bayur port every Friday en route to Gun-

Padang Cuisine

Padang is the home of Padang food, the Minangkabau cuisine that is popular across Sumatra and the archipelago. Apart from being some of the spiciest food in Indonesia, it would also have to qualify as one of the world's fastest 'fast foods'.

There are no menus in a Padang restaurant. You simply sit down and almost immediately a waiter will set down at least half a dozen bowls of various curries and a plate of plain rice. Watching him carry the bowls, stacked high along one arm, is half the fun. You pay only for what you eat, and you can test the sauces free of charge.

The most famous Padang dish is *rendang*, chunks of beef or buffalo simmered slowly in coconut milk until the sauce is reduced to a rich paste and the meat becomes dark and dried. Other popular dishes include egg dusted with red chilli *(telor balado)*, fish baked in coconut and chilli *(ikan panggang)* and red mutton curry *(gulai merah kambing)*. Locals like to wash it all down with a cup of sweet tea or lukewarm water. Unfortunately, Padang cuisine is not vegetarian-friendly but the restaurant will usually come up with some green beans, eggs and spinach if you ask. Fresh fruit, usually pineapple and bananas, is offered for dessert.

The food is normally displayed in the front window so you can take a look at what you're going to eat before entering and go somewhere else if you don't like what you see. Don't be overly concerned about the odd fly cruising around the food on display – you'll go hungry if you try to find a restaurant without flies.

One thing to note: when your food arrives, so does a small bowl of water. This is for washing your right hand – the traditional Padang eating utensil – before the meal. The left hand should be kept out of sight, as it is considered unclean. Many westerners find eating this way difficult at first, but with persistence it becomes second nature. Some travellers even say that once they've mastered the technique, eating meals with cutlery just doesn't taste as good.

Food and sauces should be spooned onto your plate of rice, then mixed together with the fingers. After some practice, you can extract tiny bones from fish and meat one-handed, and knead the rice into small balls so you can pop them in your mouth. If you just can't bear to do it, ask for a spoon – the other patrons will be mildly amused, but after all, you are a foreigner. When you are finished eating, use the water to wash your hand.

ung Sitoli on Pulau Nias (36,500/120,500Rp for deck/1st class). They stop again every Sunday on the way south to Jakarta (72,500/245,000Rp), Surabaya, Ujung Pandang and beyond. The Pelni office (☎ 33624) is out at Teluk Bayur, but you can buy commission-free tickets from Ina Tour & Travel at the Dipo International Hotel.

Boats to Pulau Siberut leave from the harbour on Sungai Batang Arau (also known as Sungai Muara), just south of Padang's city centre. See the Mentawai Islands section later in this chapter for full details.

Getting Around

To/From the Airport Tabing airport is 9km north of the centre on the Bukittinggi road. Airport taxis charge a standard 10,000Rp for the ride into town. The budget alternative is to walk from the airport terminal to the main road and catch any opelet into town for 500Rp. Heading out to the airport, city bus *(biskota)* 14A is the best one to get.

Public Transport There are numerous opelets and *mikrolets* (small opelets) around town, operating out of the Pasar Raya terminal off Jl M Yamin. The standard fare is 500Rp.

AROUND PADANG
Air Manis

The fishing village of Air Manis is 4km from Padang, just south of Sungai Batang Arau. You can get there by opelet, but a more interesting route is to take a perahu across the river from Jl Batang Arau, where the boats to Siberut leave. There's a **Chinese cemetery** overlooking the town, and then it's a 1km walk to Air Manis. According to local mythology, the rock at the end of the beach is what remains of Malin Kundang (a man who was transformed into stone when he rejected his mother after making a fortune) and his boat. There are opelets from Air Manis back to Padang for 500Rp.

Beaches

There are some good beaches around Padang. **Pantai Bungus**, 22km south of Padang, remains a popular spot despite the plywood mill dominating the northern end. The southern end is palm-fringed and postcard-pretty. *Losmen Carlos* (☎ 30353) is a laid-back place to hang out, though the popular method of relaxation won't suit everyone. Basic rooms cost 15,000Rp, and rooms with mandi are from 25,000Rp. Quiet *Tin Tin Homestay* is similar. A shade more upmarket is *Carolina Beach* (☎ 37900), with large fan/aircon doubles for 40,000/50,000Rp. Even more upmarket is *Cavery Beach Hotel* (☎ 30356), with stylish wooden bungalows overlooking the beach for 90,000Rp; some cheaper rooms were being renovated at the time of research. All the losmen organise **snorkelling** trips to nearby islands and have information on local attractions. There are regular opelets to/from Padang (1000Rp).

Pasir Jambak is the best of several beaches north of Padang. You can stay at *Uncle Jack's* for 25,000Rp per person with meals. Jack can organise snorkelling trips to nearby Pulau Sawo. Opelet 423 will get you there for 500Rp.

Islands

There are a number of islands just offshore from Padang. **Pulau Pisang Besar** (Big Banana Island) is the closest, only 15 min-

utes out; boats run there from the Sungai Batang Arau (Muara) harbour. Other islands include **Pagang**, **Pasumpahan**, **Sirandah** and **Sikoai**, where you can stay at the expensive *Pusako Island Resort*. Boats can be chartered from Muara, though Pantai Bungus is the usual departure point.

Carolina Beach hotel owns *bungalows* on Pulau Pasumpahan (20,000Rp a night).

PADANG TO BUKITTINGGI

There's some magnificent scenery on the 90km trip from Padang to the hill town of Bukittinggi, thanks to a combination of rich volcanic soil and ample rainfall. The road climbs through a vast patchwork of rice paddies and pockets of lush tropical rainforest. Looming in the background are the peaks of the Merapi and Singgalang volcanoes.

Along the way is the **Lembah Anai Nature Reserve**, renowned for its waterfalls, wild orchids and giant rafflesia flowers.

Padangpanjang

Padangpanjang, 19km from Bukittinggi, is the main town along the way. It's interesting for its **conservatorium** (ASKI) of Minangkabau culture, dance and music. This is the best place to get accurate information on live dance and theatre performances. It has a fine collection of musical instruments, which includes Minangkabau and Javanese *gamelan* (percussion orchestra) outfits. There are also excellent costume displays, with particularly interesting bridal jewellery and ornaments like the headdress, necklace and the deceptively light bracelet called *galang-gadang*.

Places to Stay The modern *Wisma Singgalang Indah* (☎ 82213), on the Padang-Bukittinggi road, has clean doubles from 55,000Rp.

Getting There & Away Padangpanjang is a comfortable morning or afternoon trip from either Padang or Bukittinggi. There are regular buses between Bukittinggi, Padang and Padangpanjang.

Danau Singkarak

About 15km south-east of Padangpanjang, Singkarak is the largest of West Sumatra's crater lakes. Despite its easy accessibility, it remains virtually undiscovered by tourists.

Places to Stay The *Singarak Sumpur Hotel* (☎ 0752-82533) is a small resort hotel at the northern tip of the lake, near the village of Sudut Sumpur. It has comfortable doubles overlooking the water for 50,000/85,000Rp.

Getting There & Away There are frequent opelets from Padangpanjang to the villages around the lake (500Rp). Most continue to Solok.

BUKITTINGGI
☎ 0752

The easy-going hill town of Bukittinggi is one of the most popular traveller centres in Sumatra. Many travellers heading north from Java make Bukittinggi their first stop. It's easy to spend a week here checking out the town and surrounding attractions. At 930m above sea level, it can get quite cold at night.

Bukittinggi was a Dutch stronghold during the Padri Wars (1821-37), and it was here that Sumatran rebels declared their rival government in 1958. Today it is a busy market town with a small university, and is a centre for Minangkabau culture.

The town is sometimes referred to as Kota Jam Gadang (Big Clock Town), after its best-known landmark – the Minangkabau-style clocktower that overlooks the large market square. Another name is Tri Arga, after the three majestic mountains – Merapi, Singgalang and the more distant Sago – that lie south.

Orientation

The town centre is conveniently compact. Most of the cheap hotels, restaurants and travel agencies are at the northern end of the main street, Jl Ahmad Yani. The clocktower and markets are at the top end. Jl Sudirman runs south from the clocktower to the post office and bus terminal.

Its rusty iron roofs make Bukittinggi look remarkably like the hill station towns of India; the changes in the town's level, and the connecting steps, can be a little confusing.

Information

Tourist Offices The tourist office is tucked away behind rows of market stalls, just north of the clocktower. The helpful staff have some useful local transport information, as well as a number of good-value tours and treks. The office is open Monday to Thursday from 8 am to 2 pm, Friday until 11 am, and Saturday until 12.30 pm. The government tourist office, Jl Lenggogeni 1, opposite the BNI bank, is less helpful.

Money BNI bank, on the corner of Jl M Yamin and Jl Lenggogeni, is the place to change money. You can get there from the market by heading down the steps to the left of the tourist office. After hours, try money-changer Toko Eka on Jl Minangkabau.

Post & Communications The main post office is on Jl Sudirman. Internet facilities are available for 15,000Rp an hour. The Telkom wartel nearby no longer acts as a call centre, but international calls can be made from dozens of wartels around town. Reverse charge calls can be made from the Home Country Direct phone at Rendezvous Coffee Shop (see Places to Eat).

Travel Agencies Bukittinggi has plenty of travel agencies, most of them along Jl Ahmad Yani. It's a good idea to stroll along the street and check out what they can offer. One of the better ones is Mitra Wisata Tours & Travel (☎ 21133) at Jl Ahmad Yani 99.

Pasar Atas

Pasar Atas is a large and colourful market crammed with stalls of fruit and vegetables, clothing and crafts. It's open daily, but the serious action is on Wednesday and Saturday, when the stalls overflow down the hill. There are some good antiques and arts and crafts to be found around the market.

SUMATRA

BUKITTINGGI

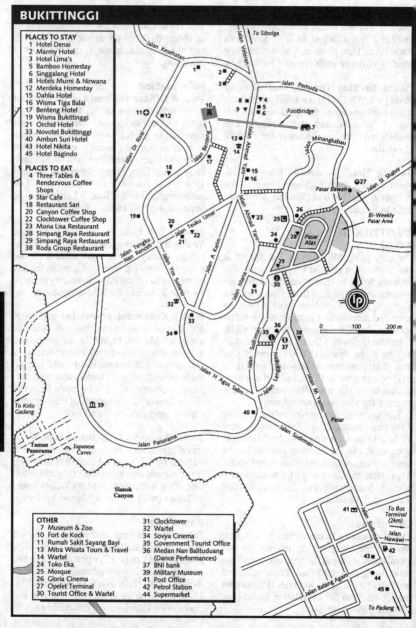

PLACES TO STAY
1 Hotel Denai
2 Marmy Hotel
3 Hotel Lima's
5 Bamboo Homestay
6 Singgalang Hotel
8 Hotels Murni & Nirwana
12 Merdeka Homestay
15 Dahlia Hotel
16 Wisma Tiga Balai
17 Benteng Hotel
19 Wisma Bukittinggi
21 Orchid Hotel
33 Novotel Bukittinggi
40 Ambun Suri Hotel
43 Hotel Nikita
45 Hotel Bagindo

PLACES TO EAT
4 Three Tables &
   Rendezvous Coffee
   Shops
9 Star Cafe
18 Restaurant Sari
20 Canyon Coffee Shop
22 Clocktower Coffee Shop
28 Mona Lisa Restaurant
28 Simpang Raya Restaurant
29 Simpang Raya Restaurant
38 Roda Group Restaurant

OTHER
7 Museum & Zoo
10 Fort de Kock
11 Rumah Sakit Sayang Bayi
13 Mitra Wisata Tours & Travel
14 Wartel
24 Toko Eka
25 Mosque
26 Gloria Cinema
27 Opelet Terminal
30 Tourist Office & Wartel
31 Clocktower
32 Wartel
34 Sovya Cinema
35 Government Tourist Office
36 Medan Nan Balituduang
    (Dance Performances)
37 BNI bank
39 Military Museum
41 Post Office
42 Petrol Station
44 Supermarket

To Sibolga
Jalan Kesehatan
Jalan Veteran
Jalan Pemuda
Footbridge
Jalan Ahmad Yani
Jalan Minangkabau
Jalan St Shahir
Pasar Bawah
Bi-Weekly
Pasar Area
Jalan Benteng
Jalan Dr Rivai
Jalan Teuku Umar
Jalan Ahmad Yani
Pasar Atas
Jalan Tengku
Nan Renceh
Jalan Yos Sudarso
Jalan A Karim
Jalan Istana
Jalan Sudirman
Jalan Lenggogeni
Jalan H Agus Salim
Jalan M Yamin
To Koto
Gadang
Taman
Panorama
Japanese
Caves
Sianok
Canyon
Jalan Panorama
Pasar
Jalan Sudirman
To Bus
Terminal
(2km)
Jalan
Nawawi
Jalan Batang Agam
To Padang

0   100   200 m

An electrical fire burnt down the main building of Pasar Atas in 1997 and stall-holders set up in the laneways surrounding the market's charred shell. The site was supposed to be repaired by 1999, but at the time of research there was still no sign of action.

Benteng de Kock, Museum & Zoo

Apart from the defensive moat and a few rusting cannons, not much remains of the fort, Benteng de Kock, built by the Dutch during the Padri Wars. It does, however, provide fine views over the town from its hilltop position.

A footbridge leads from the fort over Jl Ahmad Yani to Taman Bundo Kandung, site of the museum and zoo. The museum, built in 1934 by the Dutch 'controleur' of the district, is a superb example of Minangkbau architecture, with its small amphitheatre and colourful statues out the front. It is the oldest museum in the province and has a good collection of Minangkabau historical and cultural exhibits.

The zoo is a sad place, with a pair of elephants and a pair of camels that look like they've just emerged from seven nights on Noah's Ark. There's a 1000Rp entry fee to see the fort and zoo, plus an extra 300Rp for the museum.

Taman Panorama & Japanese Caves

Taman Panorama, on the southern edge of the town, overlooks the deep Sianok Canyon (Ngarai Sianok) to the west of town. From the park you can enter the extensive grid of caves built in WWII by the Japanese, using slave labour. Many of the tunnels open onto the cliff face of the canyon. Entry to the park is 300Rp and entry to the Japanese Caves (Lobang Jepang) costs a further 500Rp.

Military Museum

Next to the Minang Hotel, overlooking Taman Panorama, is the Military Museum, the final resting place of a collection of faded photographs from the war of independence against the Dutch. There are some gruesome photos from the attempted coup of 1965, plus souvenirs from Indonesia's war against the Fretilin guerrillas in East Timor.

Organised Tours

Almost every hotel, coffee shop and travel agency offers tours of the district. Most places now charge in US dollars, although the tourist office still quotes rates in rupiah.

Standard offerings include visits to the bullfights, excursions to the Harau Valley, Danau Singkarak, Danau Maninjau, trips to traditional Minangkabau villages, and treks to nearby mountains and volcanoes. Six- or 10-day trips to Pulau Siberut, in the Mentawai Islands, are extremely popular. Most places charge US$120 for six days (five nights) and US$150 for 10 days (nine nights), including meals, transport and accommodation. See the Mentawai Islands section later in this chapter for more information.

Places to Stay – Budget

Bukittinggi's budget hotels are a pretty charmless lot, but they're certainly cheap. Most are close together at the northern end of Jl Ahmad Yani. The friendly *Bamboo Homestay* has doubles with shared mandi for 8000Rp. *Murni* has the cheapest doubles in town (7000Rp). *Wisma Tiga Balai* asks 10,000/15,000Rp for singles/doubles. *Nirwana* has basic 10,000Rp doubles and much larger rooms with inside mandi for 20,000Rp. The *Singgalang Hotel* (☎ 21 576), next to the bank, is a popular place, with doubles for 10,000Rp and free tea and coffee all day.

There are several good places on the road to Benteng de Kock. Friendly *Wisma Bukittinggi* (☎ 34008, Jl Yos Sudarso 25) has basic rooms for 7500/12,000Rp and rooms with mandi and views of Gunung Singgalang from 12,000/20,000Rp. One of the nicest places is *Merdeka Homestay* (☎ 21 253), on the corner of Jl Dr Rivai and Jl Yos Sudarso. A solid Dutch house with original tilework throughout, Merdeka has large clean rooms with inside mandi for 15,000/20,000Rp.

SUMATRA

Places to Stay – Mid-Range

Mid-range places have popped up all over Bukittinggi, and clean, new rooms with hot water and TV are readily available.

A popular option is the often-full *Orchid Hotel (☎ 32634, Jl Teuku Umar 11)*, with pleasant doubles from 35,000Rp. Near the budget places on Jl Ahmad Yani, the *Dahlia Hotel (☎ 22185)* has three storeys of spotless tiled rooms set around rather elaborate hallways. Singles/doubles with shared bathroom cost 20,000/30,000Rp; self-contained rooms start at 40,000Rp.

The *Marmy Hotel (☎ 23342, Jl Kesehatan 30)* is a very central option, with enormous rooms for 40,000/45,000Rp, many of which are perfect for families. A few doors down, *Hotel Lima's (☎ 22641)* has less inviting doubles for 50,000Rp.

At the intersection of Jl Sudirman and Jl Panorama, the *Hotel Ambun Suri (☎ 34 406)* has comfortable carpeted rooms from 50,000Rp, including breakfast. Once the best mid-range place in town, the *Benteng Hotel (☎ 21115)*, right near the fort, is looking too faded to be asking 60,000/65,000Rp for its rooms, although some have nice views.

Past the post office, the *Nikita Hotel (☎ 31 629, Jl Sudirman 55)* has very flash doubles from 55,000Rp and discounts can be bargained for. Nearby *Hotel Bagindo (☎ 23 100, Jl Sudirman 45)* has older doubles with hot water from 30,000Rp.

Places to Stay – Top End

Hotel Denai (☎ 32920, Jl Dr Rivai 26) has comfortable singles/doubles from 94,000/ 110,000Rp. Up a giant notch is the *Novotel Bukittinggi (☎ 35000)*, a curious Arab/ Moghul-style building at the southern end of Jl Yos Sudarso. A standard double costs 305,000Rp plus 21% tax and service.

Places to Eat

The restaurants among the cheap hotels on Jl Ahmad Yani feature all the favourite travellers' fare. There are half a dozen different ways to have your breakfast egg, as well as various pancakes, muesli, fruit salad and buffalo-milk yoghurt.

Star Cafe and *Rendezvous Coffee Shop* are the most popular haunts, and are good places to pick up information. The Rendezvous has a Home Country Direct phone. The pace is a bit slower on Jl Teuku Umar, where the *Clocktower* and *Canyon* coffee shops draw the crowds.

Many people reckon the best food in town is at the *Restaurant Sari*, near the fort on Jl Benteng. The menu is predominantly Chinese. The long-running *Mona Lisa (Jl Ahmad Yani 58)* also serves Chinese food.

Naturally enough, Padang food is plentiful. *Roda Group* and *Simpang Raya* are big names in the nasi padang business, with branches all over Sumatra. Simpang Raya has two branches in the market; Roda Group has replaced its fire-gutted branch with one in the new Jl M Yamin market area opposite BNI bank.

A number of places, including the western-oriented coffee houses, do the local speciality, *dadiah campur*, a tasty mixture of oats, coconut, fruit, molasses and buffalo-milk yoghurt.

Entertainment

There are performances of Minangkabau dance/theatre every night in the *Medan Nan Balinduang hall*, Jl Lenggogeni, behind BNI bank. A different group performs each night from 8.30 pm. Tickets cost 12,500Rp.

Shopping

Bukittinggi is a good place to go shopping. There are a number of interesting antique, souvenir and curio shops around. Try Kerajinan, Jl Ahmad Yani 44, or Aladdin at No 14. There are more shops around the market area.

Box collectors can look out for a couple of Minangkabau versions. *Salapah panjang* (long boxes) are brass boxes used for storing lime and tobacco; *salapah padusi* are silver boxes used for storing betel nut and lime.

The market shops are crammed with beautiful embroidered Minang garments in rich reds and golds. Pillow cases and slippers are easy-to-carry souvenirs, as are ceremonial wedding sashes and gold hair adornments.

Getting There & Away

If you're arriving in Bukittinggi from the north (Parapat) or east (Pekanbaru), get off the bus near the town centre and save the hassle of an opelet ride back from the bus terminal.

The Aur Kuning bus terminal is about 2km south of the town centre, but easily reached by opelet from Jl Ahmad Yani (300Rp). There are heaps of buses to Padang (3500Rp, two hours), Danau Maninjau (1500Rp, one hour) and Solok (2000Rp, two hours), as well as frequent services east to Pekanbaru (8000Rp, five hours). Sinar Riau company runs direct buses to the port of Dumai (15,000Rp economy or 30,000Rp air-con, 10 hours), where you can catch a boat to Melaka.

All buses travelling on the Trans-Sumatran Hwy stop at Bukittinggi. Heading south, you can catch a bus right through to Jakarta from 45,000Rp/76,000Rp normal/air-con. There are a few buses to Bengkulu, Jambi and Palembang, but most services leave from Padang.

Heading north, you can cut hours off the journey by catching one of the express air-con buses that bypass Sibolga via a shortcut between Padangsidempuan and Taratung. They will get you to Parapat in 13 hours for 55,000Rp. The trip to Medan takes 18 hours and costs 25,000Rp to 55,000Rp. There are also regular buses to Sibolga (18,000Rp, 11 hours). The tourist office has a list of bus companies, and ticket prices – which vary quite a lot between travel agencies, so shop around. You can also buy tickets at the bus terminal.

Air-con tourist minibuses leave for Parapat every morning (40,000Rp). Tickets can be booked at a number of travel agencies in town. The buses stop just outside Bonjol at the equator, site of a tacky monument and stalls selling 'I Crossed The Equator' T-shirts.

Getting Around

Opelets around Bukittinggi cost 250Rp for three-wheelers or 300Rp for the four-wheel variety. The four-wheelers run to the bus terminal. *Bendis* (horse carts) cost from 1500Rp, depending on the distance.

AROUND BUKITTINGGI
Koto Gadang

This village, known for its silverwork, is an hour's walk south-east of Bukittinggi through Sianok Canyon. Turn left at the bottom of the road just before the canyon and keep going – *don't* cross the bridge.

Pandai Sikat

Its name means 'clever craftsmen' and the village is famous for its **songket weaving** (gold and silver threads woven into patterns on a base of silk or cotton) and ornate **woodcarving** – too ornate for many western tastes. The village is only 13km from Bukittinggi and easily accessible by bemo (500Rp) from Aur Kuning bus terminal.

Ngalau Kamanga

The 1500m-long **cave** at Ngalau Kamanga, 15km north-east of Bukittinggi, was used as a base for guerrilla attacks against the Dutch in the late 19th and early 20th centuries. The cave is dripping with stalactites and stalagmites and has a small, clear lake.

Batu Sangkar

The bustling town of Batu Sangkar, 41km south-east of Bukittinggi, lies at the heart of traditional Minangkabau country. **Benteng der Capellen**, now the police station, was a Dutch stronghold during the Padri Wars.

The spectacular **Rumah Gadang Payaruyung** in the village of Silinduang Bulan, 5km north of Batu Sangkar, features on all the Bukittinggi tour itineraries. The palace is a scaled-down replica of the former home of the rulers of the ancient Minangkabau kingdom of Payaruyung. The original appears on the 100Rp coin.

There are lots of more modest examples of **traditional architecture** in the villages around here, particularly at Belimbing. The houses are supposed to have been built in the 16th century, but they certainly appear more recent than that.

Rafflesia Sanctuary

The sanctuary is signposted near the village of Palupuh, about 16km north of Bukittinggi.

SUMATRA

Rafflesia normally bloom between August and November. The tourist office in Bukittinggi can tell you if there are flowers around.

Gunung Merapi

Looming large over Bukittinggi to the east is the smouldering summit of Gunung Merapi (2891m). Merapi is one of Sumatra's most restless volcanoes and is occasionally deemed too dangerous to climb. The last major eruption was in 1979. The tourist office in Bukittinggi can tell you when the mountain is off limits (which probably won't stop the staff offering their services as guides).

The climb begins at the village of Kota Baru (of bullfighting fame). It's a one hour climb to the forestry station shelter and then another four hours to the top. Most people climb at night, with the aim of being on the summit at dawn. You'll need good walking boots, warm clothing, a torch (flashlight), food and drink.

There have been several reports of people getting lost on Merapi. It's very unwise to attempt the climb alone, and people are advised to take a guide or join a group. Travel agencies in Bukittinggi do guided trips to Merapi for US$15 per person.

Harau Valley

The Harau Valley, 15km north-east of Payakumbuh, is a popular local beauty spot that is included on many tour itineraries. The valley is enclosed by spectacular, sheer 100m cliffs. The cliffs are popular with rock-climbers – anyone interested should contact Dodi at the Harau Cliff Coffee Shop in Bukittinggi. Otherwise, there's walks and waterfalls. Harau village is 3km up the valley.

Getting There & Away The Harau Valley is not an easy place to get to. Plenty of one- to four-day tours are available from Bukittinggi travel agents, but independent travellers will need to catch an opelet from Bukittinggi to Payakumbuh (800Rp), then another from Payakumbuh to the Harau Valley (500Rp) or Sari Lamak (from where it's a 5km walk to the valley). The easiest

day to get out there is Sunday, but the place is normally packed with day-trippers.

Limbuku

The village of Limbuku, near Payakumbuh, must be the only place on the planet to stage **duck racing** – the ducks are trained to fly, of course! It is customary for young village girls to attend the race in traditional costume, with the idea of attracting a suitor. The racing is usually held in July. Ask at the tourist office in Bukitinggi.

DANAU MANINJAU
☎ 0752

Maninjau, 38km west of Bukittinggi, is another of Sumatra's beautiful mountain crater lakes. The final descent to Danau Maninjau, on the road from Bukittinggi, is unforgettable. The road twists and turns through 44 numbered hairpin bends, and offers stunning views over the shimmering blue lake and surrounding hills.

Maninjau caters for travellers of all ages and persuasions, but remains relatively unspoiled. At 500m above sea level, the air is pleasantly cool. The lake is 17km long, 8km wide and 480m deep in places.

Orientation & Information

The only village of any size is called Maninjau. Most people arrive from Bukittinggi; get off at the junction outside Telkom if you want to stay in town. Most buses continue around the lake to Bayur.

To the south of the junction is Jl H Udin Rahmani. Here are Maninjau village's handful of shops, restaurants and guesthouses.

To the north of the junction is Jl SMP, which leads off around the lake. The majority of Danau Maninjau's losmen are stretched along the next 1.5km of road; a new crop of budget places has opened a further 2km along at Bayur village. The bank, post office, telephone office and police station are in Maninjau village.

Money BRI bank will change US dollars only – cash or travellers cheques.

MANINJAU

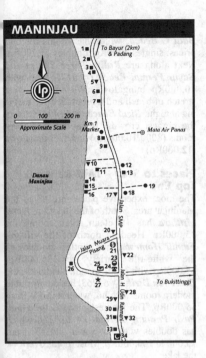

PLACES TO STAY
1   Happy Homestay
2   Ananda Homestay
3   Tropikal Baru
4   Palanta Homestay
6   Abang Homestay
7   Hotel Pasir Panjang Permai
8   Hotel Tan Dirih
9   Famili Homestay
11 Dangau Impian Homestay
13 Alam Maninjau Guesthouse & Restaurant
14 Beach Guesthouse
15 Febby
16 Riak Danau
26 Maninjau Indah Hotel
30 Srikandi Homestay
31 Pondok Impian
33 Pillie Homestay; Hotel Mutiara

PLACES TO EAT
5   Palanta Cafe
10 Cafe 44
17 Blues Cafe
20 Cafe Kawa
22 Bagoes Cafe; Indowisata Travel
28 Three Tables Coffee House
29 Bobo Coffee House
32 Srikandi Restaurant

OTHER
12 Glory Bookshop
18 PT Maninjau Wisata
19 Khethek Batik; Barong Cafe
21 BRI Bank
23 Bus Stop
24 Telkom Office
25 Post Office
27 Police Station
34 Mosque

SUMATRA

Post & Communications The post office is on the road running down to the lake. International calls can be made from the Telkom wartel next to the bus stop.

Travel Agencies Indowisata Travel (☎ 61 418), part of Bagoes Cafe in Maninjau village, sells tickets for the tourist minibuses and Pelni ships leaving from Padang. It also offers a range of tours and activities, including rafting. Further north, PT Maninjau Wisata (☎ 61295) offers similar services.

Things to See & Do

Hanging out by the lake is the reason most people come to Maninjau. The water is considerably warmer than at Danau Toba, so it's a good place for **swimming**. Some guesthouses hire dugout canoes or inflated truck inner tubes. Generally, the further away you travel from town, the cleaner the water.

If you're feeling energetic, it takes about six hours to **cycle** around the lake (see Getting Around). The road is fairly flat, but almost three-quarters of the 70km is unsealed. There are also some good walks. Fit people only should attempt the strenuous three hour hike to **Sakura Hill** and **Lawang Top**, which have excellent views of the lake and surrounding area. It's much easier to do this hike in reverse, catch a Bukittinggi-bound bus as far as Matur and climb Lawang from there before descending to the lake on foot.

Learn how to **make batik** at Khethek/ Barong Cafe, up the path next to the PT Maninjau Wisata travel agency. It costs 50,000Rp per piece, and you can take as long as you like to complete it. All materials are provided.

Places to Stay – Budget
There are dozens of cheap guesthouses to choose from, and there is not much between them. The most popular traveller haunts are in Bayur, but the original places just north of Maninjau village are still good value.

Maninjau Right in the village, *Pillie Homestay* (☎ 61048), and *Srikandi Homestay* (☎ 61630) on Jl H Udin Rahmani, charge 10,000Rp for basic doubles. Much nicer, but twice the price, are doubles at *Pondok Impian* nearby.

Heading north on Jl SMP, there's little difference between the *Riak Danau*, *Febby* and *Beach Guesthouse*, next to each other on the lake's edge, 500m from town. All have singles/doubles for 8000/10,000Rp and newer rooms with mandi from 15,000Rp.

On the opposite side of Jl SMP, *Alam Maninjau* (☎ 61069) has a range of doubles in impressive wooden houses up the hillside, offering great views of the lake. Rooms start at 20,000Rp, but you'll pay double that for the best rooms and views.

About 1.5km from town are the *Palanta Homestay*, *Tropikal Baru*, and *Ananda* and *Happy* homestays. Tiny family-run places, they all offer simple doubles for 10,000Rp, and rooms with bathrooms inside for around 15,000Rp.

Bayur Beyond Bayur village is a cluster of guesthouses set way back from the road along the edge of the lake. Most have a little patch of beach and canoes for hire. To get to them, follow the tiny tracks through the paddy fields; each place has its own sign on the road pointing the way. Once you're down by the lake, it's possible to cut across to other guesthouses by taking the network of dykes and tracks that rim the paddy fields.

First up past the village is oddly named *Batu C Beach*, which has rooms for odd prices: singles 7900Rp, doubles 11,700Rp. Next along are *Rully*, *Three Tables* and *Bayur Permai Beach* (☎ 61215), all with 10,000Rp bungalows. With the longest stretch of beach and a reputation for partying at night, *Rizal Beach* (☎ 61404) attracts the biggest crowds. It has six homestay rooms (8000/10,000Rp) and six bungalows (12,000Rp).

Places to Stay – Mid-Range & Top End
The more expensive places are all in the Maninjau area. South of the junction, *Hotel Mutiara* has 10 clean, tiled rooms for 35,000Rp. Heading north of the village, *Famili Homestay* has spotless doubles of the white-tile variety for 35,000Rp, 45,000Rp with inside mandi. Next door, the *Hotel Tan Dirih* (☎ 61263) has comfortable modern rooms with hot water and TV from 55,000Rp. The fanciest place is the *Hotel Pasir Panjang Permai* (☎ 61022), which has doubles with hot water and TV from 75,000 to 100,000Rp. Most rooms overlook the lake.

Places to Eat
Most of the *guesthouses* serve basic meals like mie/nasi goreng, western favourites and freshly caught fish.

In Maninjau village, the long-running *Three Tables Coffee House* (there are more seats upstairs) has an extensive menu. Just down the road at the nicely decked-out *Srikandi Restaurant*, a grilled *ikan mas* (carp) large enough for two costs 15,000Rp and a plate of sweet and sour fish costs 10,000Rp.

Also in the village, *Cafe Bagoes* has nice wooden decor and all the usual traveller fare, as well as beef *rendang* (meat simmered in spices and coconut milk), fried tofu and grilled fish. A few hundred metres north, *Alam Maninjau* has an excellent open restaurant, beautifully lit at night. A real treat is the breadfruit juice, made with fruit from the family's prized tree.

Entertainment

The excellent evening shows at *Alam Maninjau* showcase a range of activities from jumping on broken glass to traditional music and dance. Shows are held every second Tuesday, or by request for groups. The 7,500Rp entry includes a snack and a drink.

Getting There & Away

There are hourly buses between Maninjau and Bukittinggi (1500Rp, one hour) and a daily 6 am bus to Padang (7000Rp, 3½ hours), which goes via the coast. The travel agencies also sell tickets for the tourist buses. Fares include 35,000Rp to Padang, 40,000Rp to Sibolga and 75,000Rp to Pulau Samosir (Danau Toba).

Getting Around

Several places rent mountain bikes for 6000Rp a day and motorcycles for 35,000Rp. Buses travel throughout the day between Maninjau and Bayur – just stand by the road and hail one.

Mentawai Islands

The remote Mentawai Islands are off the west coast of Sumatra. The largest island, Siberut, is home to the majority of the Mentawais' population of 30,000, and it has become a popular trekking destination. The other islands – Sipora, Pagai Utara and Pagai Selatan – are seldom visited.

After being isolated for thousands of years, change is now coming to the Mentawais at an alarming rate. Tourism is but a minor development alongside the transmigration schemes and pro-logging policies of the Indonesian government.

Trekking has become big business on Siberut, with a steady stream of travellers coming to catch a glimpse of an ancient jungle 'lifestyle' that is fast disappearing. The villagers, their bodies covered with ritual tattoos, and wearing little but loincloths, decorative bands and rings, are a photogenic lot who have found tour groups to be good sources of extra income.

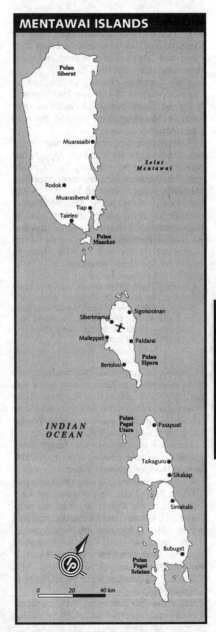

SUMATRA

History

Very little is known about the origins of the Mentawaians but it is assumed that they emigrated from Sumatra to Nias and made their way to Siberut from there.

They remained virtually undisturbed by other cultures until the late 19th century, when the Dutch permitted Protestant missionaries to attempt to convert them to Christianity.

There are several pre-19th century western references to the islands. It appears that in 1621 Siberut was the only island inhabited. The Mentawaians are mentioned in a scientific paper presented in 1799 by the Englishman John Crisp. Sir Stamford Raffles seems to have been particularly impressed by the Mentawaians and their culture. In one of the many reports he wrote urging the British government to compete with the Dutch in colonising Indonesia, he states:

> Formerly, I intended to write a book to prove that the Niassans were the most contented people on earth. Now I have to acknowledge the fact that the people of the Mentawai Islands are even more admirable and probably much less spoiled than we.

In 1864 the Mentawai archipelago was nominally made a Dutch colony, but it was not until 1901, during the Russo-Japanese War, that the Dutch placed a garrison on the islands to prevent another foreign power using them as a naval base.

It was the missionaries who had the most influence on the people, creating fundamental changes in their culture.

The first permanent mission was set up in 1901 on Pagai Utara, by German missionary August Lett. Eight years later Lett was murdered by the locals, but the mission survived and by 1916, 11 baptisms had been recorded. There are now more than 80 Protestant churches throughout the islands. Over half the population claims to be Protestant, 16% Catholic, 13% Muslim, while the rest have no official religion.

More than 50 years after the Protestants, Catholic missionaries moved in to vie for converts. They opened a mission in south Siberut, a combined church, school and clinic. Free medicines and clothes were given to any islander who became a Catholic, and by 1969 there were almost 3000 converts.

Islam began to make inroads when government officials were regularly appointed from Padang during the Dutch era. To complicate religious matters further, the Baha'i faith was introduced in 1955. For more information on the Mentawaians, see the boxed text in this section.

Economy

Taros and bananas are the staple crops of the Pagai islands and Sipora, while on Siberut, sago is also cultivated. Traditionally, women own the taro fields and are responsible for planting and maintaining them. The banana plantations belong to the men – some are worked by one or two families, others by an entire *uma* (communal house). The Mentawaians also grow cassava, sweet potato and other crops. Their diet is supplemented by hunting and fishing.

SIBERUT

Although Siberut has been a popular destination for several years, conditions on the island remain basic. Siberut's port of Muarasiberut is the only town of any size. It has shops, where you can stock up on provisions, as well as the island's only losmen.

About two-thirds of the island is still covered with tropical rainforest and it's surrounded by magnificent coral reefs teeming with fish.

When to Go

May is generally the driest month, but it can rain on Siberut any time of year. The seas between Siberut and the West Sumatran coastline can get very rough in June and July, when it can be too dangerous to sail. October and November tend to be the wettest months on Siberut.

What to Bring

If you're heading off independently, you will need your own food supplies. Essential

The Mentawaians

Although the distance between the mainland and the Mentawai Islands is not great, strong winds, unpredictable seas and coral reefs made navigation to the islands difficult in past centuries. The result was that the Mentawaians had very little contact with the outside world and remained one of the purest indigenous Indonesian societies until early in the 20th century when the missionaries arrived. The Mentawaians had their own language, adat and religion. They were skilled in boat building but had not developed any kind of handicraft nor cultivated rice.

Physically, the Mentawaians are slim and agile. Traditional clothing is a loincloth made from the bark of the breadfruit tree for men and a bark skirt for women. They wear bands of red-coloured rattan, beads and imported brass rings on their arms, fingers and toes. Traditionally, Menatawaians sharpened their teeth and were decorated with tattoos. The government has banned tattoos, sharpened teeth and long hair. Although the ban has not been enforced, it's now rare to see people looking like this, except in the more remote villages.

Culture

Villages are built along river banks and consist of one or more *uma* (communal house) surrounded by single-storey family houses *(lalep)*. Several families live in the same building. Bachelors and widows have their own quarters, known as *rusuk*, identical to the family longhouse except they have no altar. Traditionally, the houses stand on wooden piles and are windowless.

Although essentially patriarchal, society is organised on egalitarian principles. There are no inherited titles or positions and no subordinate roles. It is the uma, not the village itself, that is pivotal to society. It is here that discussions affecting the community take place. Everyone is present at meetings, but the prominent men make most of the major decisions, including choosing a *rimata* (the person who leads religious affairs and is the community's spokesperson to the outside world), building an uma, clearing forests or laying out a banana plantation.

On such occasions the people of the uma carry out a religious festival known as *punen*. This usually involves ritual sacrifices of both pigs and chickens and, depending on the importance of the occasion, the festival can last for months on end, sometimes years. All kinds of everyday jobs and activities become taboo; work in the fields is stopped and strangers are denied access to the uma – its isolation being marked by a cordon of palm leaves and flowers.

Religion

The native Sibulungan religion is a form of animism, involving the worship of nature spirits and a belief in the existence of ghosts, as well as the soul. The chief nature spirits are those of the sky, sea, jungle and earth. There are also two river spirits: Ina Oinan (Mother of Rivers) is beneficent, while Kameinan (Father's Sister) is regarded as evil. Apart from these nature spirits, all inanimate objects have spirits *(kina)* that give them life. Although the sky spirits are considered the most influential, there is no hierarchy among the spirits.

The worship of the soul is of utmost importance, being vital to good health and longevity. The soul is believed to depart the body at various times during life before its ultimate escape at death. Sickness, for example, is the result of the temporary absence of the soul from the body; dreams also signify that the soul is 'on vacation'.

When the soul leaves the body at death it is transformed into a ghost *(sanitu)*. Mentawaians try to avoid these ghosts, whom they suspect of malevolently attempting to rob the living of their souls. To protect themselves, they place fetish sticks at every entrance to the village. This tactic is considered foolproof, provided no-one has committed a ritual sin or broken a taboo.

SUMATRA

items for jungle living are a mosquito net, insect repellent, torch (flashlight) and plastic bags for keeping things dry. You can buy most supplies in Muarasiberut, but they are much cheaper in Padang.

The smaller your backpack, the easier it will be to carry in the jungle and to transport in the *sampans* (small longboats).

You will also need to bring things for barter and gifts. Pens, pencils and paper are perhaps better choices than cigarettes, which unfortunately are the accepted gift currency. Drugs – either prescribed or recreational – should never be given as gifts.

The demand for gifts has become a constant hassle. Many islanders seem to think that westerners are rich fools who willingly part with anything asked of them. It's wise to give things only to people who have helped.

Information

Information on Siberut is hard to come by. Syahruddin's Homestay in Muarasiberut is the place to ask questions, organise guides etc (see Places to Stay & Eat). Quiz other travellers and the guides in Bukittinggi before you set off.

Permits Permits for the islands are issued upon landing in Muarasiberut and cost 2000Rp. Bring three photocopies of your passport.

Money There are no banks and no official moneychangers. While some villagers prefer gifts as payment, most places on the well trodden tourist trail definitely prefer cash. You'll need cash in Muarasiberut.

Post & Communications There is a post office in Muarasiberut. If you're desperate, and very patient, the wartel may be able to get you a phone line to the outside world.

Health Chloroquine-resistant malaria is a common problem and each year many locals die from it. There are plenty of snakes around, but they are not likely to be a problem. The rivers are used for washing and as running toilets, and therefore are a source of disease. Never drink water unless it has been boiled or purified.

Dangers & Annoyances Theft can be a problem, but normally only small items left lying around go missing. Also remember that elderly people dislike cameras and are afraid of flashes. Don't arrive at a village with camera at the ready.

Things to See & Do

The traditional settlement of **Sakelot** is only 1km from Muarasiberut and easily accessible on foot. The other villages close to the main town are new – a legacy of the government's policy of moving the people out of the jungle and setting them up along the coastal strip.

The main reason people come to Siberut is to visit the villages of the interior, where the way of life is slowly adapting to modernity. One of the easiest villages to get to from Muarasiberut is **Tiap**, two hours by boat along a narrow branch of jungle river. A more adventurous, but still comparatively easy, trip is to **Rodok**, where people live in small, traditional houses. It takes between five and six hours to get there and back by boat.

Two more remote villages are **Sakudai** and **Madobak**. The journey to Sakudai takes two days – one day by boat and the other trekking through the jungle. The trip to Madobak takes six hours by boat.

Organised Tours

Most travellers take the easy option and join the organised tours, which operate out of Bukittinggi. It is also the cheap option, as chartering boats on your own is expensive.

Typically, a 10 day tour out of Bukittinggi costs US$150, and a six day tour US$120. Keep in mind that three days are spent getting to and from Siberut, so the six-day trips are not great value. The tour price includes a guide, accommodation (in village huts), food and transport.

Every coffee shop, losmen and travel agency promotes the tours. Before you hand over your cash, spend some time in the coffee shops talking to travellers who have done a trip, and read the comment books. It's worth asking about the size and composition of a group before signing up.

The treks usually include plenty of mud-slogging, river crossings and battles with indigenous insects, so don't expect a gentle jaunt through the jungle.

The reward for your suffering is the chance to experience unspoiled rainforest and the local culture of Siberut. Most, but not all, people come away happy with their trekking package.

Places to Stay & Eat

The only losmen on Siberut is *Syahruddin's Homestay* in Muarasiberut. It has good doubles for 10,000Rp. In more remote areas, it's often possible to stay at *missionary buildings*, *schools* or with *local families*. You will have to negotiate payment for your lodgings – either a cash 'donation' or a gift. The situation is much the same for food.

Getting There & Away

Air The only airport is on Pulau Sipora, but there are no scheduled flights.

Boat Getting to the Mentawai Islands can be a hassle, particularly in the wet season. Two companies used to run boats to the islands, but at the time of research only PT Simeulue (☎ 39312) was still in business – the other operator, PT Rusco, had lost both its vessels in accidents at sea. PT Simeulue sets sail only once a week, on Thursday at 6 pm, but cancellations are common in the wet season. Tickets cost 18,000/23,500Rp for deck/cabin class and can be bought at PT Simeulue's office, Jl Arau 7, in an alley that runs directly behind Jl Batang Arau. The journey takes 10 to 12 hours.

If you are booking a tour from either Padang or Bukittinggi, find out whether your guide is planning to use the scheduled service, as you could find your departure is delayed. It's more reliable to join a guide who charters a boat.

Getting Around

If you're planning on making your own way around Siberut, the biggest expense will be transportation. The roads on the island are little more than logging tracks and there are no buses.

Boats, used both around the coast and on rivers, are the main form of local transport. Getting to villages that are off the beaten track will mean chartering boats as well as hiring your own guide. You need to bargain hard.

Riau

The province of Riau is split into two distinct areas, mainland Riau and the Riau Islands.

Mainland Riau covers a huge expanse of eastern Sumatra's sparsely populated east coast and has the modern oil town of Pekanbaru as its capital. It has Indonesia's richest oil fields, and huge deposits of tin and bauxite. Much of the land is dense forest or mangrove swamp – too low-lying and poorly drained for agriculture. The jungle is home to such rare creatures as the Sumatran rhinoceros and tiger, as well as bears, tapirs and elephants.

Several animistic and nomadic peoples (including the Sakai, Kubu and Jambisal) still live in the jungle, mostly around the port of Dumai.

Offshore Riau is made up of more than 3000 islands spread over more than 1000km of ocean. The islands' capital is the town of Tanjung Pinang, on Pulau Bintan southwest of Singapore. The islands are home to a third of Riau's population of 2.7 million.

Mosquitos are rife throughout Riau and a strain of chloroquine-resistant malaria has been reported.

History

Before the advent of air travel, Riau's position at the southern entrance to the Straits of Melaka, the gateway for trade between India and China, was strategically significant.

From the 16th century, the Riau Islands were ruled by a variety of Malay kingdoms, which had to fight off constant attacks by pirates and the opportunistic Portuguese, Dutch and English. The Dutch eventually

SUMATRA

SUMATRA

RIAU

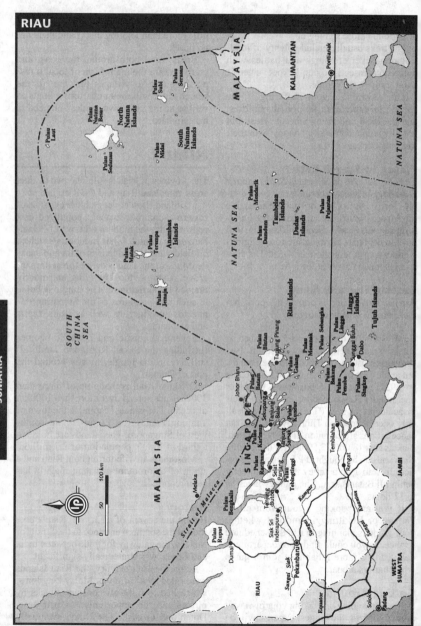

won control over the Straits of Melaka, and mainland Riau (then known as Siak) became their colony in 1745 when the Sultan of Johor surrendered.

Dutch interest lay in ridding the seas of pirates so they could get on with the serious business of trade rather than in developing the region, so they left Riau alone.

Oil was discovered around Pekanbaru by US engineers before WWII, but it was the Japanese who drilled the first well at Rumbai, 10km north of Pekanbaru. Rumbai is now the base for Caltex Pacific Indonesia. The country around Pekanbaru is crisscrossed by pipelines connecting the oil wells to refineries at Dumai because ocean-going tankers cannot enter the heavily silted Sungai Siak.

PEKANBARU
☎ 0761 • pop 500,000

Before the Americans struck oil, Pekanbaru was little more than a sleepy river port on the Sungai Siak. Today it is a bustling modern city, and Indonesia's oil capital. Most travellers wisely treat the place as no more than an overnight stop between Singapore and Bukittinggi.

Orientation

The main street of Pekanbaru is Jl Sudirman. Almost everything of importance to travellers – banks, hotels and offices – can be found here or close by. Speedboats leave from the wharf at the northern end of Jl Sudirman. The bus terminal is at the other end of town on Jl Nangka, off Jl Sudirman.

Information

Tourist Offices The tourist office (☎ 40356), Jl Sudirman 200, is south of the city centre on the way to the airport. The staff have little to offer other than dusty pamphlets.

Money Most of the city's banks are spread along Jl Sudirman. BCA bank is at No 448. The BII branch near the bus terminal, Jl Nangka 4, changes US and Singapore dollars (cash and travellers cheques) and has an ATM for Cirrus, MasterCard and Visa.

Post & Communications The main post office is on Jl Sudirman, between Jl Hangtuah and Jl Kartini. Internet services are available at 8000Rp per hour. The Telkom wartel is about 1km north along Jl Sudirman.

Travel Agencies Kota Piring Kencana Travel (☎ 21382), Jl Sisingamangaraja 3, does plane and bus bookings as well as tours. Most of the staff speak English.

Things to See

If you've got time to burn, check out the **Museum Negeri Riau** and neighbouring **Riau Cultural Park**, towards the airport on Jl Sudirman. Both are open from 8 am to 2 pm Monday to Thursday, and Saturday, and to noon on Friday.

The **Balai Adat Daerah Riau**, on Jl Diponegoro, has displays of traditional Malay culture and is open the same hours as the museum. The **Mesjid Raya**, near the river on Jl Mesjid Raya, dates back to the 18th century, when Pekanbaru was the capital of the Siak sultans. The courtyard holds the graves of the fourth and fifth sultans.

Places to Stay – Budget

For years travellers have headed to *Poppie's Homestay* (☎ 33863), Jl Cempedak II, a few minutes walk from the bus terminal. The ceiling fans barely stir the hot air and there's the odd rodent, but the owner arranges boat tickets to Batam and buses to Bukittinggi, even if you arrive late at night. All rooms cost 15,000Rp; breakfast is 3500Rp extra. To get there from the bus terminal, cross Jl Nangka and head down Jl Taskurun. Take the second street on the left (Jl Kuini), and Jl Cempedak II is the first street on the right. If you are coming from the port, phone for a free pick-up.

Places to Stay – Mid-Range

The *Hotel Linda* (☎ 36915), down a small alleyway opposite the bus terminal, has a good choice of rooms. Doubles with mandi and fan are 30,000Rp; 75,000Rp gets you a large double with air-con, hot water and TV.

SUMATRA

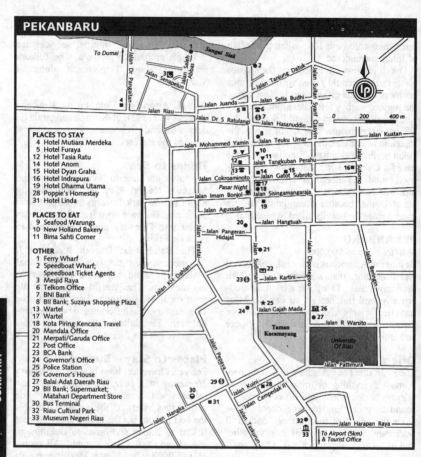

PEKANBARU

PLACES TO STAY
4 Hotel Mutiara Merdeka
5 Hotel Furaya
12 Hotel Tasia Ratu
14 Hotel Anom
15 Hotel Dyan Graha
16 Hotel Indrapura
19 Hotel Dharma Utama
28 Poppie's Homestay
31 Hotel Linda

PLACES TO EAT
9 Seafood Warungs
10 New Holland Bakery
11 Bima Sahti Corner

OTHER
1 Ferry Wharf
2 Speedboat Wharf;
  Speedboat Ticket Agents
3 Mesjid Raya
6 Telkom Office
7 BNI Bank
8 BII Bank; Suzaya Shopping Plaza
13 Wartel
17 Wartel
18 Kota Piring Kencana Travel
20 Mandala Office
21 Merpati/Garuda Office
22 Post Office
23 BCA Bank
24 Governor's Office
25 Police Station
26 Governor's House
27 Balai Adat Daerah Riau
29 BII Bank; Supermarket;
  Matahari Department Store
30 Bus Terminal
32 Riau Cultural Park
33 Museum Negeri Riau

Taman Kacamayang

University Of Riau

To Airport (5km) & Tourist Office

0   200   400 m

The *Hotel Anom* (☎ 36083), on the corner of Jl Sudirman and Jl Gatot Subroto, has modern rooms set around a courtyard. Aircon doubles with mandi start at 57,000Rp.

Hotel Dharma Utama (☎ 21171, Jl Sisingamangaraja 10) has a range of singles/doubles from 25,000/35,000Rp with fan and mandi, or 30,000/50,000Rp with air-con.

Places to Stay – Top End

Supply far exceeds demand in this category, which means that there are some good deals to be had. Discounts of 50% on listed rates are freely available at big hotels. The best of them is the conveniently central *Hotel Dyan Graha* (☎ 26851, Jl Gatot Subroto 7), with doubles from 251,000Rp to 680,000Rp. Its main rivals in this price bracket are the nearby *Hotel Indrapura* (☎ 36233, Jl Dr Sutomo 86), and the *Hotel Mutiara Merdeka* (☎ 31272), Jl Dr Pangaitan, which is a long way from anything else of interest.

A notch below this lot, but better value, are *Hotel Tasia Ratu* (☎ 33225, Jl Hasyim

Ashari 10) and ***Hotel Furaya*** *(☎ 26688, Jl Sudirman 72)*. Doubles at both places start at 110,000Rp.

Places to Eat

There are innumerable cheap places to eat along Jl Sudirman, particularly at night around the market at the junction with Jl Imam Bonjol. The restaurant at the *Hotel Anom* does good Chinese food, while there's a choice of sate, *martabak* (sweet or savoury omelettes) or Chinese food at *Bima Sahti Corner* on Jl Tangkuban Perahu.

There is cheap seafood at the two *warung makanan laut* on Jl Wolter Monginsidi, easily spotted by the marine creatures adorning their awnings. The *New Holland Bakery (Jl Sudirman 153)* has a fine selection of cakes and pastries, as well as hamburgers and ice cream. It also serves good fresh fruit juices.

Getting There & Away

Air Simpang Tiga is a visa-free entry point, and one of the busiest airports in Sumatra. Pelangi Air flies three times a week to Kuala Lumpur (RM265) and Melaka (RM156); Silk Air flies daily to Singapore (US$100).

Merpati has direct flights to Jakarta (880,000Rp), Batam (387,000Rp) and Medan (502,000Rp). Flights to Palembang go via Batam. Mandala has daily flights to Jakarta, for the same price as Merpati. The Merpati/Garuda office (☎ 21575) is at Jl Sudirman 343. Pelangi Air is represented by Kota Piring Kencana Travel (see Travel Agencies earlier in this section); Mandala (☎ 20055) is at Jl Sudirman 384.

Bus Bukittinggi is the main destination and there are frequent departures from the Mayang Terurai terminal, Jl Nangka. The 240km trip takes about five hours and costs from 7500Rp. Buses north to the port of Dumai take five hours and cost from 6000Rp.

Boat Agencies all around town sell tickets for the boats to Pulau Batam. There are a bunch of agencies around the bus terminal, and more near the speedboat wharf. Tickets include the bus fare to Tanjung Buton and the speedboat from there to Batam, usually via Selat Panjang. There is not a lot of difference between the speedboat services, though prices vary from 50,000Rp to 57,000Rp. The journey takes about nine hours, reaching Batam at about 5 pm – in time to catch a ferry to Singapore.

Other speedboat destinations include Tanjung Pinang on Pulau Bintan (85,000Rp), Tanjung Balai on Pulau Karimun (45,000Rp) and Tanjung Samak on Pulau Rangsang (45,000Rp). It's also possible to go by speedboat down Sungai Siak to Tanjung Buton (15,000Rp) and Selat Panjang (32,500Rp).

Share Taxi Several companies run comfortable air-con minibus 'taxis' south to Bukittinggi and Padang and north to Dumai. Reliable operators are CV Karya Maju (☎ 22 839), Jl Sudirman 290, and Bukittinggi Wisata Express (☎ 26104), Jl Sudirman 134.

Getting Around

To/From the Airport Airport taxis charge 15,000Rp for the 12km trip into town. It's a 1km walk to the main road if you want to catch an opelet (500Rp) into town.

Public Transport Opelets around Pekanbaru cost a standard 500Rp.

DUMAI
☎ 0765

Most of Pekanbaru's oil exits through the port of Dumai, 158km north of Pekanbaru. The only reason to come here is that it's a visa-free entry point with daily ferry links to the Malaysian port of Melaka.

Ferries leave Melaka at 9 am and return at 1 pm, but you must check in at the respective ports two hours before departure to clear immigration. Tickets cost 110,000Rp from Dumai and RM80 from Melaka. Port taxes are extra. The trip takes two hours.

Ferries travel daily to Pulau Batam (56,500Rp, seven hours), stopping en route at Pulau Bengkalis (15,000Rp), Selat Panjang (30,000Rp) and Pulau Karimun (45,000Rp).

SUMATRA

Two Pelni boats call at Dumai in the course of their fortnightly circuits to Jakarta (97,000/327,000Rp deck/1st class). The *Bukit Siguntang* goes via Kijang on Pulau Bintan (38,000/123,000Rp), and the *Sirimau* stops in Kijang, and Mentok on Pula Bangka. The ships depart from Dumai on alternate Sundays at 4 pm.

There are frequent buses from Dumai to Pekanbaru (7000Rp, four hours), as well as some door-to-door minibus share taxis to Bukittinggi (40,000Rp) and Padang (45,000Rp). CV Karya Maju (☎ 35239), Jl Sukajadi 110, and CV Nusantara Jaya (☎ 37 815), Jl Sudirman 411, are reliable.

If you get stuck in town, head to Jl Sudirman. Very basic *Wisma Hang Tua*, at No 431, and *Penginapan AA* across the road have doubles with fan from 11,000Rp. A big notch up is the *City Hotel (☎ 21550)* at No 445, with air-con doubles from 60,000Rp. The *Royal Dumai Hotel (☎ 34888)* at No 58 is the fanciest place in town, with doubles from 139,000Rp.

SIAK SRI INDERAPURA

Some 120km downriver from Pekanbaru is Siak Sri Inderapura, site of the beautiful **Asserayah el Hasyimiah Palace**, built in 1889 by the 11th sultan of Siak, Sultan Adbul Jalil Syafuddin. The palace was restored five years ago as a museum. The site also houses a dazzling white **mosque** with a silver dome.

The *Penginapan Monalisa*, by the dock in Siak, has basic singles/doubles for 7500/11,000Rp.

Siak can be reached from Pekanbaru by a various forms of river transport, including speedboats that will do the trip in two hours for 10,000Rp.

RIAU ISLANDS

The Riau Islands are scattered like confetti across the South China Sea. The locals say there are as many islands as there are grains in a cup of pepper (3214 islands in all, more than 700 of them uninhabited and many of them unnamed).

The modern administrative region of Riau includes the islands immediately south-west of Singapore (eg Batam, Bintan, Rempang, Galang, Karimun and Lingga), as well as the remote South China Sea islands of Anambas, Natuna and Tambelan.

Tanjung Pinang on Pulau Bintan is the traditional capital of the islands, but Pulau Batam is being (over) developed as a soulless and expensive industrial extension of Singapore.

History

The early history of the Riau Islands suggests a wave of migration from southern India. Around 1000 AD, Pulau Bintan emerged as a separate kingdom, which was enlarged by a propitious marriage to the son of a king of Palembang. A capital was built in Temasik (now Singapore) and the principality was renamed Bintan Temasik Singapura.

By 1500 the kingdom of Melaka held sway over the islands of Kundur, Jemaja, Bunguran, Tambelan, Lingga and Bintan. The Portuguese ruled Riau for a brief period following their conquest of Melaka, but from 1530 to the end of the 18th century the archipelago was a stronghold of Malay civilisation, with its main centres at Penyenget and Lingga.

In 1685 Sultan Mahmud Syah II was coerced into signing an agreement with the Dutch, which greatly diminished his authority. The Dutch assumed full control of the archipelago on the death of the rajah in 1784.

Opposition to the Dutch did not really re-emerge until the early 1900s, when the Rusydiah Club was formed by the last sultan of Riau-Lingga. This was ostensibly a cultural and literary organisation, but later assisted in the struggle for Indonesian independence.

People

Most of the inhabitants of the islands are of pure Malay origin, but there are several indigenous groups like the *orang laut* (sea gypsies) of the Natuna Islands, the Mantang peoples of Penuba and Kelumu islands and the Baruk people of Sunggai Buluh on Pulau Singkep.

Bintan is the largest and most populous of the Riau Islands. The majority its of people

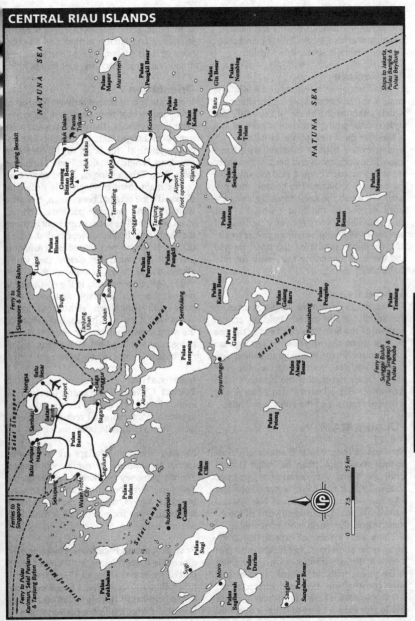

are of Malay origin, but the ethnic melting pot includes Sumatran Bataks and Minangkabau, as well as a large Chinese community. The population is about 90% Muslim.

Architecture

The traditional architecture of the Riau Islands is called *rumah lipat kijang* (hairpin), which refers to the shape of the roof. The style is undergoing a revival at present and is used for most new public buildings.

Houses are usually adorned with carvings of flowers, birds and bees. Often there are wings on each corner, said to symbolise the capacity to adapt. The houses' four pillars have much the same meaning: the capacity to live in the four corners of the universe. The flowers convey a message of prosperity and happiness from owner to visitor, the birds symbolise the one true god and the bees symbolise the desire for mutual understanding.

Special Events

The islanders of remote Pulau Serasan in the South Natuna Islands hold an annual **Festival of the Sea**. Packets of sticky rice are hung on trees near the beach, then logs are cut from the forest, loaded into canoes and dropped into deep water to appease the gods of the ocean and protect the islanders from drowning. The islanders also observe the principal festivals of the Islamic calendar.

PULAU BATAM
☎ 0778

Nowhere in Indonesia is the pace of development more rapid than on Pulau Batam. Until the island was declared a free-trade zone in 1989, it was a backwater comprising little more than the shanties of Nagoya and coastal villages. After several years of frantic construction, the island is unrecognisable.

There are a number of expensive golf resorts on the north coast, but for the most part there's a distinct frontier-town atmosphere to the place, with ridiculously high prices, ugly construction sites and characterless housing estates. There's no reason to pause any longer than it takes to catch a boat out.

Batam has largely usurped Bintan's traditional role as the transport hub of the Riau Islands. Hang Nadim airport and the seaports of Batu Ampar, Nongsa and Sekupang are all visa-free entry and exit points.

Orientation

Most travellers to Batam arrive at the port of Sekupang by boat from Singapore. After you clear immigration, there are counters for money exchange, taxis and hotels. The domestic terminal, for boats to the Sumatran mainland, is right next door. Ferries to Bintan leave from Telaga Punggur in the south-east.

The main town of Nagoya is decidedly sleazy. It's the original boom town, complete with bars and massage parlours. The old shanties can still be seen peeping out between the flash new hotels, offices and shopping centres. Nagoya's port area of Batu Ampar is just north of town. Batam Centre, the island's administrative centre, is to the south.

The Nongsa Peninsula in the north-east is ringed by beautifully manicured golf resorts built with Singapore visitors in mind. Waterfront City is a half-baked resort on the west coast that mostly attracts Singaporeans on weekend bungy-jumping, nightclubbing or indoor skiing jaunts.

Information

Tourist Offices The Batam Tourist Promotion Board (☎ 322871) has a small office outside the international terminal at Sekupang. It can help with hotel bookings.

Money Singapore dollars are as easy to spend as Indonesian rupiah on Batam. There's a money exchange counter at the Sekupang ferry building, but the rates are better in Nagoya, where all the major banks are based. They include the BCA bank on Jl Sakura Anpan.

Post & Communications The main post office is in Batam Centre, but there is a small post office near the Nagoya Plaza Hotel on Jl Imam Bonjol. International phone calls can be made from the Telkom wartel on Jl Imam Bonjol and from card phones everywhere.

Places to Stay – Budget
Budget accommodation on Batam is some of the worst in Indonesia – filthy and outrageously expensive. The utterly rock-bottom places are little more than brothels and are impossible to recommend. There are some more reasonable places around Komplek Nagoya Business Centre, Blok VI. *Wisma Batam Indah* (☎ 424531) has doubles with fan from 50,000Rp; rooms with air-con and mandi (but no window) cost 90,000Rp. Two doors down, *Wisma Sri Purnama* (☎ 42 1819) has air-con rooms only for 80,000Rp. Nearby, the *Famili Inn* (☎ 455802, Komplek Nagoya Point, Blok D, No 10-11) has doubles with fan from 55,000Rp.

Places to Stay – Mid-Range
Mid-range accommodation is similarly overpriced, but at least there are some reasonable options. One of the best is *Hotel Singapura* (☎ 459842, Komplek Tanjung Pantun, Blok U No 10-12) near McDonald's on Jl Imam Bonjol. Spotless doubles with air-con and mandi start at 130,000Rp. Next to the Melia Panorama Hotel, the *Wisma Wisatam* (☎ 454117) has air-con rooms with TV from 100,000Rp. The friendly *Wisma Furama* (☎ 455276, Komplek Nagoya Business Centre, Blok VI No 33) is similar. At the top end of this bracket, the centrally located *Horisona* (☎ 457111, Jl Sultan Abdul Rachman) has plush rooms for S$45/60.

Places to Stay – Top End
Flash new hotels and golf resorts are springing up everywhere, even though supply already appears to far exceed demand. It's certainly worth bargaining or asking about current discounts.

There are some smart-looking places on Jl Imam Bonjol in Nagoya. They include *Nagoya Plasa* (☎ 459888) and *Harmoni* (☎ 459308), both charging from S$125 for the cheapest doubles.

Out at Nongsa, places like the *Palm Springs Golf & Country Club* (☎ 459899) and the *Turi Beach Resort* (☎ 310075) won't give you much change from S$200 for a double.

Places to Eat
In Nagoya the best place to head is the *night markets* along Jl Raja Ali Haji or the big and raucous *Pujasera Nagoya* food centre.

Seafood-loving Singaporeans head for the *kelongs* (restaurants built out over the sea on stilts) that dot the coast. The *Batam View Kelong* at Nongsa keeps its catch live in tanks. Everything is charged by the kilo.

Getting There & Away
Air Hang Nadim airport is international in name only.

Garuda and Bouraq have daily direct flights to Jakarta (814,000Rp). Merpati destinations include Medan (633,000Rp), Padang (465,000Rp), Palembang (461,000Rp) and Pekanbaru (387,000Rp). Merpati also flies to Pontianak in Kalimantan (572,000Rp).

Garuda's office (☎ 458620) is in the Bank Pembangunan Bdg, Jl Imam Bonjol. Bouraq (☎ 458344) has offices at the Harmoni Hotel and Merpati (☎ 457288) is at Jodoh Square Blok A1.

Boat There are numerous services to Singapore, as well as daily links to the Sumatran mainland.

Singapore Ferries shuttle constantly between Singapore's World Trade Centre and Sekupang (S$17, 45 minutes). In both directions, the first ferries leave Singapore and Sekupang at 7.30 am, while the last ferries leave at around 8 pm.

There are less-frequent services from Singapore to Batu Ampar, Nongsa and Waterfront City. See the introductory Getting There & Away section earlier in this chapter for more details.

Malaysia Several boats leave daily from Batu Ampar for Johor Bahru. Prices start at 90,000Rp.

Pulau Bintan The ferry dock at Telaga Punggur, 30km south-east of Nagoya, is the main port for speedboats to Tanjung Pinang on neighbouring Pulau Bintan. There's a steady flow of departures from 8.15 am to 5.15 pm.

The trip takes 45 minutes and costs 11,000Rp one way, plus 1500Rp port tax. There are three boats a day to Tanjung Pinang (25,000Rp) from Sekupang. It's also possible to travel from Telaga Punggur to Lagoi (16,000Rp), in the north of Pulau Bintan. Departures are at 8 and 10.30 am and 3 pm.

Elsewhere in Indonesia The main reason travellers come to Batam is its links to Pekanbaru on the Sumatran mainland. Boats leave from the domestic wharf at Sekupang, next to the international terminal. The trip to Pekanbaru (50,000Rp) involves a five hour boat trip to Tanjung Buton on the Sumatran mainland, via Selat Panjang on Pulau Tebingtinggi, followed by a four hour bus ride. There is no point in breaking the journey en route. The boat to Pekanbaru leaves sometime between 8.30 and 9 am, so to make it you'll need to catch the first ferry on its way from Singapore.

Other destinations from Sekupang include Pulau Karimun (21,000Rp); Pulau Kundur (20,000Rp); Dumai (56,000Rp); and Kuala Tungkal, on the Jambi coast (80,000Rp).

Pelni ships pass through Batam every few days, on their way to Belawan (55,000/185,00Rp deck/1st class) or Jakarta (107,000/363,000Rp). Tickets can be bought at the domestic ferry terminal or at travel agencies in Nagoya.

Getting Around

Fixed-fare taxis operate from the airport and the ports of Sekupang and Telaga Punggur. Sample fares from Sekupang include 25,000Rp to Nagoya and 30,000Rp to Telaga Punggur. From the airport it's 20,000Rp to Nagoya and 35,000Rp to Sekupang.

There is a token bus service between Nagoya and Sekupang (1000Rp), but most people use the share taxis that cruise the island: just stand by the roadside and call out your destination. Sample fares from Sekupang include 1500Rp to Nagoya and 6000Rp to Telaga Punggur. You will need to make it clear that you are paying for a seat, not the whole taxi.

PULAU BINTAN
☎ 0771

Bintan is twice as large as Batam and many times more interesting. Singapore-centric development is low key, with the exception of a cluster of golf resorts on the north coast around Lagoi. The main attractions are the old town of Tanjung Pinang (a visa-free entry/exit point), nearby Pulau Penyenget and the relatively untouched white sand beaches of the east coast.

Tanjung Pinang may be the largest town in the Riau Islands but it retains much of its old-time charm, particularly the picturesque, stilted section of town that juts over the sea around Jl Plantar II. The harbour hosts a constant stream of vessels, from tiny sampans to large freighters.

Orientation

Speedboats from Pulau Batam and Singapore deliver you to the main pier in Tanjung Pinang. Everything of importance to travellers is within 10 minutes walk of the pier.

Information

Tourist Offices There's no point trekking 2km around the coast to the regional tourist office. It hasn't even got a brochure, let alone anything useful like a map. Bong's Homestay (see Places to Stay) is a much better source of information.

Money BCA bank has a branch on Jl Temiang, and BNI bank and Bank Dagang Negara are opposite each other on Jl Teuku Umar. The BII bank ATM at the post office accepts Visa, MasterCard and Cirrus. Outside banking hours, you will have to accept much poorer rates at the numerous moneychangers.

Post & Communications The post office is near the harbour on Tanjung Pinang's main street, Jl Merdeka. International phone calls can be made from the wartel on Jl Hangtuah.

Travel Agencies There are a couple of travel agencies in Tanjung Pinang that can book airline tickets out of Batam and organise tours around Bintan. Pinang Jaya

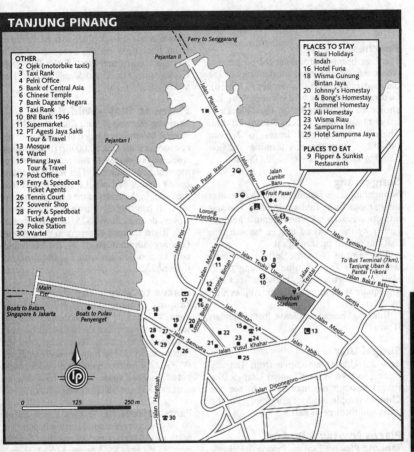

TANJUNG PINANG

OTHER
2 Ojek (motorbike taxis)
3 Taxi Rank
4 Pelni Office
5 Bank of Central Asia
6 Chinese Temple
7 Bank Dagang Negara
8 Taxi Rank
10 BNI Bank 1946
11 Supermarket
12 PT Agesti Jaya Sakti
   Tour & Travel
13 Mosque
14 Wartel
15 Pinang Jaya
   Tour & Travel
17 Post Office
19 Ferry & Speedboat
   Ticket Agents
26 Tennis Court
27 Souvenir Shop
28 Ferry & Speedboat
   Ticket Agents
29 Police Station
30 Wartel

PLACES TO STAY
1 Riau Holidays
   Indah
16 Hotel Furia
18 Wisma Gunung
   Bintan Jaya
20 Johnny's Homestay
   & Bong's Homestay
21 Rommel Homestay
22 Ali Homestay
23 Wisma Riau
24 Sampurna Inn
25 Hotel Sampurna Jaya

PLACES TO EAT
9 Flipper & Sunkist
   Restaurants

Ferry to Senggarang
Pejantan II
Pejantan I
Jalan Plantar II
Jalan Pasar Ikan
Jalan Pasar
Jalan Gambir Baru
Fruit Pasar
Jalan Ketapang
Lorong Merdeka
Jalan Pos
Jalan Merdeka
Jalan Teuku Umar
Jalan Temiang
To Bus Terminal (7km),
Tanjung Uban &
Pantai Trikora
Jalan Bakar Batu
Lorong & Bintan
Jalan Teratai
Jalan Gereja
Volleyball Stadium
Jalan Bintan
Jalan Mesjid
Jalan Samudra
Jalan Yusuf Khahar
Jalan Tabib
Jalan Diponegoro
Jalan Hangtuah

Main Pier
Boats to Batam,
Singapore & Jakarta
Boats to Pulau
Penyenget

0   125   250 m

SUMATRA

Tour & Travel (☎ 21267), Jl Bintan 44, is the agent for Garuda/Merpati; PT Agesti Jaya Sakti Tour & Travel (☎ 21377), further up the street, is the agent for Bouraq.

Pulau Penyenget

A short hop across the harbour from Tanjung Pinang, tiny Penyenget was once the capital of the Riau rajahs. The island is believed to have been given to Rajah Riau-Lingga VI in 1805 by his brother-in-law, Sultan Mahmud, as a wedding present.

It is a charming place, littered with reminders of its past. The coastline is dotted with traditional Malay stilted houses. The ruins of the **old palace** of Rajah Ali and the **tombs** and graveyards of Rajah Jaafar and Rajah Ali are clearly signposted inland. The most impressive site is the sulphur-coloured **mosque**, with its many domes and minarets. You won't be allowed into the mosque if you're wearing shorts or a short skirt.

There are frequent boats to the island from Bintan's main pier for 1000Rp per person. There's a 500Rp entry charge on weekends.

Beaches

The best beaches are along the east coast, where there is also good **snorkelling** outside the monsoon season (November to March). Getting there can be a hassle, but there is a choice of accommodation (see Places to Stay) at the main beach, **Pantai Trikora**. There are occasional buses to Trikora (4000Rp) from the bus terminal outside Tanjung Pinang. Taxis cost 30,000Rp.

Senggarang

Senggarang is a fascinating village across the harbour from Tanjung Pinang. The star attraction is an old **Chinese temple** held together by the roots of a huge banyan tree that has grown up through it.

The temple is to the left of the pier, where boats from Tanjung Pinang dock. Half a kilometre along the waterfront is a big square with three Chinese temples side by side.

Boats to Senggarang leave from Pejantan II wharf.

Sungai Ular

You can charter a sampan from Tanjung Pinang to take you up Sungai Ular (Snake River) through the mangroves to see the **Chinese temple**, with its gory murals of the trials and tortures of hell.

Places to Stay – Budget

Tanjung Pinang Tanjung Pinang has plenty of budget accommodation. Lorong Bintan II, a small alley between Jl Bintan and Jl Yusuf Khahar, is the place to look. The popular *Bong's Homestay* at No 20 has six tiny doubles for 20,000Rp, including breakfast. *Johnny's Homestay*, next door at No 22, acts as an overflow. *Rommel Homestay* (☎ 21 081), on the corner of Lorong Bintan II and Jl Yusuf Khahar, has dingy rooms for 15,000Rp. *Ali's*, opposite, is much the same. *Hotel Surya* (☎ 21811) on Jl Bintan is more substantial with clean, simple rooms with fan/mandi for 24,000/27,500Rp.

Pantai Trikora Out at Pantai Trikora, *Yasin's* (☎ 26770), near the village of Teluk Bakau, is a laid-back place with half a dozen palm huts right on the beach for S$5 to S$10, including breakfast. *Bukit Berbunga Cottages* next door and *Shady Shack*, 1km south, offer similar.

Places to Stay – Mid-Range

Tanjung Pinang *Wisma Riau* (☎ 21023, Jl Yusuf Khahar 8) is a faded old place with air-con rooms starting at 50,000Rp (80,000Rp on weekends). *Sampurna Inn* next door is even more shabby-looking. The *Riau Holidays Indah* (☎ 22644), off Jl Plantar II, sits over the water in the midst of the old stilted part of town. It has slightly musty but comfortable air-con doubles from S$25, including breakfast. Right in front of the main pier, *Wisma Gunung Bintan Jaya* (☎ 29288) has brand-new air-con doubles with TV and breakfast from S$23.

Places to Stay – Top End

Tanjung Pinang The *Hotel Sampurna Jaya* (☎ 21555, Jl Yusuf Khahar 15) is a reasonable one star place that desperately needs renovation to justify its pricey doubles, starting at S$52. The brand new *Hotel Furia* (☎ 311226) on the main street lacks charm but offers good value. Spotless tiled doubles start at S$38 (or S$42 on weekends).

Pantai Trikora The *Trikora Beach Resort* (☎ 24454), set on a quiet private beach 1km north of the budget bungalows, has doubles from S$55 (from S$65 on weekends). There's a swimming pool, tennis court and private island offshore.

Places to Eat

There are several pleasant coffee shops with outdoor eating areas in front of the volleyball stadium on Jl Teuku Umar – try *Flipper* or *Sunkist*. There are some good *Padang food* places along Jl Plantar II where you can get a tasty fish curry or jackfruit curry (*kare nangka*).

The colourful *fruit market* is at the northern end of Jl Merdeka.

Getting There & Away

Boat is the only way to get to/from Bintan now the airport at Kijang has closed. While Batam is the main link to the Sumatran mainland, Tanjung Pinang has retained its connections to some of the more remote islands of the Riau archipelago. It also has links to Singapore and Malaysia. Most services leave from the main pier at the southern end of Jl Merdeka, but check when you buy your ticket. There are dozens of ticket agents at the main pier and along Jl Merdeka.

Pulau Batam Regular speedboats leave from the main pier for Telaga Punggur on Batam (11,000Rp, 45 minutes) from 7.45 am to 4.45 pm daily. Three boats a day go direct to Sekupang – one speedboat (25,000Rp) and two ferries (18,000Rp).

Elsewhere in Sumatra A daily 6 am express service goes to Pekanbaru (80,000Rp), with a changeover in Batam. The occasional slow boat reaches Pekanbaru via Sungai Siak.

There are two fast boats a day to Tanjung Balai (31,500Rp, 2½ hours) on Pulau Karimun and one a day to Pulau Penuba (28,000Rp), and Sunggai Buluh (37,500Rp, four hours) on Pulau Singkep. Pulau Bangka and Pulau Belitung can be reached on the weekly fast boats to Jakarta (see the following Jakarta entry). The Anugra Makmur company runs bi-monthly boats to the remote Natuna islands.

Malaysia There are three boats a day to Johor Bahru (115,000Rp).

Singapore Several companies run services to Tanah Merah in Singapore (S$20). In all there are around 10 trips a day.

Jakarta Pelni (☎ 21513), Jl Ketapang 8, Tanjung Pinang, offers two routes to Jakarta (107,000Rp deck class, 28 hours). The *Bukit Siguntang* and *Sirimau* sail on alternate weeks from the southern port of Kijang.

The alternative is the *Samudera Jaya*. It leaves Tanjung Pinang every Thursday (92,000Rp, 18 hours), stopping en route at Pulau Bangka (62,000Rp) and Tanjung Pandang on Pulau Belitung (82,000Rp). *Telaga Express* does a similar run (95,000Rp), leaving Tanjung Pinang every Monday.

Getting Around

The bus terminal has been inconveniently relocated 7km out of Tanjung Pinang, an opelet ride (500Rp) along the road to Pantai Trikora. There aren't many buses and unless you happen to turn up when one is leaving, you'll have to bargain for a driver to take you to your destination. Hiring a taxi in Tanjung Pinang is more convenient and won't cost much more. Count on 30,000Rp to Pantai Trikora.

Tanjung Pinang is crawling with orange-helmetted *ojek* (motorbike taxi) drivers, who are fine for shorter distances.

OTHER RIAU ISLANDS

Few travellers make it to the remote outer islands of Riau. Getting there is half the problem, especially since local airline SMAC ceased flights in the region. Head to the better-serviced islands first, and you can usually organise to island-hop from there.

Pulau Singkep

Pulau Singkep is the third-largest island in the archipelago. The place has become even more of a backwater since the closure of the huge tin mines that provided most of the island's jobs. Much of the population has now gone elsewhere in search of work.

The main town, **Dabo**, is shaded by lush trees and gardens and is clustered around a central park. A large **mosque** dominates the skyline. **Batu Bedua**, not far out of town, is a white sand beach fringed with palms. It's a good place to spend a few hours. The fish and vegetable **markets** near the harbour are interesting, and Jl Pasar Lamar is a good browsing and shopping area.

If you decide to stay, try *Wisma Sri Indah* on Jl Perusalaan, *Wisma Gapura Singkep* opposite, or *Wisma Sederhana*. Some travellers have reported very good deals at the smartest place in town, the *Hotel Wisma Singkep*, which overlooks the town.

SUMATRA

You can eat at the *markets* behind Wisma Sri Indah or try any of the warungs on Jl Pasar Lama and Jl Merdeka. *Food stalls* and *warungs* pop up all over the place at night.

Getting There & Around There's one boat a day to Tanjung Pinang on Bintan (37,500Rp) and daily ferries to Daik on Pulau Lingga. Boats dock at Singkep's northern port of Sunggai Buluh, from where there are buses to Dabo. Several shops in Dabo act as ticket agencies.

Pulau Penuba

Penuba is a small island wedged between Pulau Lingga and Pulau Singkep. It's an idyllic place to do nothing but swim, walk and read. The main settlement on this island is the village of the same name, which is tucked into a small bay on the south-east coast.

The **Attaqwa Mosque** stands in the centre of the village. Several good **beaches** are within 10 minutes walk and there are more fine beaches near the north coast village of **Tanjung Dua**.

A house next to the Attaqwa Mosque is now used as a *guesthouse* for foreign visitors. Ask around for the caretaker. There are several *warungs* along Jl Merdeka, the main street.

A daily boat travels to Pulau Penuba from Tanjung Pinang (28,000Rp), or you can charter a boat from Pulau Singkep for the half hour trip.

Pulau Lingga

Not much remains of the glory that was once Lingga except a few neglected ruins. The arrival point is Daik, which is hidden 1km up a muddy river. It has the all-enveloping atmosphere of oppressive humidity and tropical seediness that pervades many of Somerset Maugham's stories.

Daik is pretty much a single street, some cargo wharves and about a dozen Chinese shops, with dirt roads and tracks branching out to the Malay villages around the island. You must report to the police as soon as you arrive.

Things to See The main site of historical interest is the ruin of the **palace** of Rajah Suleiman, the last rajah of Lingga-Riau. Next to the palace are the foundation stones of the building, said to have housed the rajah's extensive harem. Otherwise, there's not much left. The surrounding jungle hides overgrown bathing pools and squat toilets. The ruins are a two hour walk from Daik and you'll need someone to guide you through the maze of overgrown forest paths.

A half hour walk from Daik is the **Makam Bukit Cenckeh** (Cenckeh Hill Cemetery), where you'll find the crumbling graves of Rajah Abdul Rakhman (ruled 1812-31) and Rajah Muhammed (ruled 1832-41).

On the outskirts of Daik is the **Mesjid Sultan Lingga**, in the grounds of which is the tomb of Rajah Mahmud I, who ruled in the early 19th century.

Inland is **Gunung Daik**, its three peaks looking like a crown. The central peak is said never to have been climbed.

Places to Stay & Eat There is one *hotel* in Daik, near the ferry dock on the main street. Expect to pay about 8000Rp for a double. There are a few small *warungs* on the main street.

Getting There & Around There are daily boats for the two hour trip from Daik to Dabo on Pulau Singkep, and occasional boats between Tanjung Pinang and Daik. There's no public transport on Lingga – or transport of any kind, for that matter.

Pulau Karimun

Karimun is a small island to the south-east of Singapore with a few resort hotels catering to visitors from the city-state. The main centre is the port of **Tanjung Balai**.

Tanjung Balai has a few small *losmen* with doubles from 20,000Rp, as well as the *Hotel Holiday Karimun* (☎ 21065, Jl Trikora Laut 1), with air-con doubles for 75,000Rp.

Most speedboat services between Batam and Pekanbaru call at Tanjung Balai (21,000Rp). There are two boats a day from Tanjung Pinang (31,500Rp, 2½ hours).

Natuna Islands

These islands are right off the beaten track and difficult to reach.

The population of **Pulau Natuna Besar** is fairly small, although there's an extensive transmigration program on Sungai Ulu, with settlers from Java growing cash crops such as peanuts and green peas.

The islands are noted for fine basket-weave **cloth** and various kinds of **traditional dance**. One particularly idiosyncratic local dance is a kind of *Thousand & One Arabian Nights* saga, incorporating episodes from Riau-Lingga history.

Getting There & Away Every second Sunday the *Anugra Makmur* leaves Tanjung Pinang on Bintan, stopping at several of the islands, including Pulau Midai (35,000Rp), Pulau Sedanau (39,000Rp) and Pulau Serasan (41,000Rp).

Jambi

The province of Jambi occupies a 53,435 sq km slice of central Sumatra, stretching from the highest peaks of the Bukit Barisan mountains in the west to the coastal swamps facing the Straits of Melaka in the east.

Sumatra's highest peak, Gunung Kerinci (3805m), is on the border of Jambi and West Sumatra. Sumatran tigers – Jambi's faunal mascot – and rhinos still inhabit the forests of the surrounding Kerinci Seblat National Park.

Huge expanses of rubber and palm oil plantation cover the eastern lowlands. Timber is also big business, with two large mills guzzling the remaining lowland forest at a fast pace. Jambi is also emerging as an important oil producer; its main field is south-east of its capital on the South Sumatran border.

The province is sparsely populated, with around two million people, many of them migrants from Java and Bali.

History

The province of Jambi was the heartland of the ancient kingdom of Malayu, which first rose to prominence in the 7th century.

Much of Malayu's history is closely and confusingly entwined with that of its main regional rival, the Palembang-based kingdom of Sriwijaya. The little that is known about Malayu has mostly been gleaned from the precise records maintained by the Chinese court of the time.

It is assumed that the temple ruins at Muara Jambi mark the site of Malayu's former capital, the ancient city of Jambi – known to the Chinese as Chan Pi. The Malayu sent their first delegation to China in 644, and the Chinese scholar I Tsing spent a month in Malayu in 672. He reported that when he returned 20 years later, Malayu had been conquered by Sriwijaya. The Sriwijans appear to have remained in control until the sudden collapse of their empire at the beginning of the 11th century.

After Sriwijaya's demise, Malayu re-emerged as an independent kingdom. It stayed that way until it became a dependency of Java's Majapahit empire, which ruled from 1278 until 1520. It then came under the sway of the Minangkabau people of West Sumatra.

In 1616 the Dutch East India Company opened an office in Jambi and quickly formed a successful alliance with Sultan Muhammed Nakhruddin to protect its ships and cargoes from pirates. It also negotiated a trade monopoly with Nakhruddin and his successors. The major export was pepper, which was grown in great abundance. In 1901 the Dutch East India Company moved its headquarters to Palembang and effectively gave up its grip on Jambi.

JAMBI
☎ 0741

The capital of Jambi is the city of the same name, a busy river port about 155km from the mouth of Sungai Batang Hari. Unless you're working in the oil or paper industries, there is little reason to visit. It's a long way from anywhere else of interest.

Orientation

Jambi sprawls over a wide area, a combination of the old Pasar Jambi district spreading

SUMATRA

south from the port, and the new suburbs of Kota Baru and Telanaipura to the west. Most of the banks, hotels and restaurants are in Pasar Jambi near the junction of Jl Gatot Subroto and Jl Raden Mattaher, while government buildings are out at Kota Baru.

Information

Tourist Offices It's hardly worth the haul out to Kota Baru to visit the regional tourist office (☎ 25330), Jl Basuki Rahmat 11. The Hotel Jambi Raya (see Places to Stay) keeps a stock of brochures.

Money BCA bank is conveniently located on Jl Raden Mattaher. The BNI bank has a branch on Jl Sutomo.

Post & Communications The main post office is near the port at Jl Sultan Thaha 9. You can make international phone calls from the wartel on Jl Raden Mattaher. The main Telkom wartel is on Jl Dr Sumantri in Telanaipura.

Travel Agencies Mayang Tour & Travel (☎ 25450), Jl Raden Mattaher 27, and Saung Bulian Tour & Travel (☎ 25621), Jl Hailim Perdana Kusuma 19, are both reliable.

Museum Negeri Propinsi Jambi

The museum, one of the city's few attractions, is out in Telanaipura on the corner of Jl Urip Sumoharjo and Jl Prof Dr Sri Sudewi. It has a good section on costumes and handicrafts, as well as a small historical display.

Organised Tours

Mayang Tour & Travel (☎ 25450), Jl Raden Mattaher 27, includes the museum, and the temples at Muara Jambi (see later under Things to See in the Muara Jambi section) in its city tour. It also organises tours to the Kerinci Valley and to the Kubu settlements at Bukit Duabelas.

Places to Stay – Budget

The cheap hotels are on the market streets by the port. They are rock-bottom, survival-only places. The *Hotel Sumatra* (Jl Kartini 26)

has doubles for 10,000Rp and looks marginally less uninviting than the others.

Places to Stay – Mid-Range

If you can afford it, step up a notch to somewhere like the *Hotel Pinang* (☎ 23969, Jl Dr Sutomo 9), 100m from the river. Clean doubles with fan/air-con cost 30,000/50,000Rp. The *Hotel Kartika Jaya* (☎ 22 699), opposite the Pinang on the corner of Jl Hos Cokroaminoto, has air-con singles/doubles from 35,000/50,000Rp.

Places to Stay – Top End

The ever-expanding *Hotel Abadi* (☎ 25 600, Jl Gatot Subroto 92) is the only three-star hotel in town. Its owners have a novel approach to hotel management: don't renovate, just build a new wing. The oldest singles/doubles look decidedly tatty these days, at 70,000/90,000Rp. The latest wing has comfortable modern rooms for 180,000/250,000Rp. There is a sleazy disco downstairs that belts out rock music into the small hours.

Things are a bit quieter at the nearby *Hotel Jambi Raya* (☎ 34971, Jl Camar 1), tucked away on a small alleyway. It has small, modern air-con doubles for 78,000Rp; much larger rooms cost 150,000Rp.

Places to Eat

There's a reasonable choice of food stalls at the small *night market* on Jl Sultan Iskandar Muda. The market is opposite the well stocked *Mandala Supermarket*. The *Saimen Perancis* is an excellent bakery on Jl Raden Mattaher that also serves meals. *Simpang Raya* (Jl Raden Mattaher 22) and *Safari* (Jl Veteran 29) serve good Padang food.

For a treat, try the top-notch Chinese food at *Restaurant Abadi*, adjoining the Hotel Abadi.

Shopping

The Sanggar Batik dan Kerajinen (Batik and Art Centre), near the museum on Jl Dr Sri Sudewi in Telanaipura, produces and sells traditional Jambi batik featuring striking floral motifs. The centre also has a range of handicrafts from all over the province, including songket weaving and finely woven split-rattan baskets. The centre was set up by the local PKK (family welfare movement) to provide employment for local women.

Getting There & Away

Air Merpati has daily direct flights to Jakarta (597,000Rp); its office is at the Hotel Abadi.

Bus Jambi is not on the Trans-Sumatran Hwy, but there are reasonable sealed roads linking the city to Pekanbaru and via the highway at Muarabungo and Saralungun. The road to Palembang is in bad repair. Intercity services use the Simpang Kawat bus terminal on Jl M Yamin.

There are frequent buses to Palembang (20,000Rp, seven hours) and Padang (from 25,000Rp, 10 hours). Ratu Intan Permata (☎ 60234), near the bus terminal on Jl M Yamin, has door-to-door services to Pekanbaru (50,000Rp, eight hours).

Boat Ratu Intan Permata (see the preceding Bus entry) also operates connecting services from Jambi to the coastal town of Kuala Tungkal (8000Rp, two hours), from where there's a daily speedboat service to Pulau Batam (80,000Rp, seven hours).

Getting Around

Airport taxis charge a standard 10,000Rp for the 8km run into town. Local transport comprises the usual assortment of taxis, opelets and becaks. Rawasari opelet terminal, off Jl Raden Mattaher in the centre of town, is where all opelets start and finish their journeys. The standard fare is 500Rp.

MUARA JAMBI

The large temple complex at Muara Jambi, 26km downstream from Jambi, is the most important Hindu-Buddhist site in Sumatra. It is assumed that the temples mark the location of the ancient city of Jambi, capital of the kingdom of Malayu 1000 years ago. Most of the temples, known as *candi*, date from the 9th to the 13th century, when Jambi's power was at its peak.

For centuries the site lay abandoned and overgrown in the jungle on the banks of the Batang Hari. It was 're-discovered' in 1920 by a British army expedition sent to explore the region.

Things to See

It's easy to spend all day at Muara Jambi. The site covers 12 sq km, stretching more than 7km along the north bank of the Batang Hari. Much of the area is covered in forest.

Eight temples have been identified so far, each at the centre of its own low-walled compound. Some are accompanied by *perwara candi* (smaller side-temples). Three of the temples have been restored to something close to their original form. The site is dotted with numerous *menapo* (smaller brick mounds) that are thought to be the ruins of other buildings – possibly dwellings for priests and other high officials.

The entrance is through an ornate archway in the village of Muara Jambi. Admission is by donation, although there's a 500Rp charge to bring a vehicle in. Most places of interest are within a few minutes walk of here.

The restored temple straight ahead of the donation office is **Candi Gumpung**. Check out the fiendish *makara* (demon head) that guards the steps. Excavation work here yielded some important finds, including a *peripih* (stone box) containing sheets of gold inscribed with old Javanese characters. The writing dates the temple back to the 9th century. A statue of Prajnyaparamita found here is now the star attraction at the small **site museum** nearby.

Candi Tinggi, 200m south-east of Candi Gumpung, is the finest of the temples uncovered so far. It dates from the 9th century but is built around another, older temple. A path leads east from Candi Tinggi to **Candi Astano**, 1.5km away, passing **Candi Kembar Batu** and lots of **menapo** along the way.

The temples on the western side of the site are yet to be restored. They remain pretty much as they were found – minus the

SUMATRA

jungle, which was cleared in the 1980s to allow archaeologists to have a look. The western sites are signposted from Candi Gumpung. First stop, after 900m, is **Candi Gedong Satu**, followed 150m further on by **Candi Gedong Dua**. They are independent temples despite what their names may suggest. The path continues west for another 1.5km to **Candi Kedaton**, the largest of the temples, then a further 900m north-west to **Candi Koto Mahligai**.

The dwellings of the ordinary Malayu folk have long since disappeared. According to Chinese records, they lived along the river in stilted houses or in raft huts moored to the bank.

Getting There & Away

Boats to Muara Jambi (5000Rp one way, two hours) leave from the river bank opposite the Pelni office in Jambi. There are lots of boats on weekends, when Muara Jambi is a popular picnic spot. On other days you may be forced to charter a boat (50,000Rp return).

Another option is to charter a taxi (50,000Rp) and go by road. Reckon on a minimum of two hours waiting time.

KERINCI
☎ 1748 • pop 300,000
Kerinci is a cool mountain valley tucked away high in the Bukit Barisan on Jambi's western border. It is one of the most beautiful places in Sumatra. Towering over the valley to the north is Gunung Kerinci, an active volcano and, at 3805m, Sumatra's highest mountain. Picturesque Danau Kerinci is nestled at the southern end of the valley. The Sungai Kerinci waters the rich farmland in between, and the whole area is surrounded by the lush forests of Kerinci Seblat National Park. Kerinci tea is a hugely profitable crop, and dense plantations can be seen throughout the region.

The valley's population is found in some 200 villages. The main town and transport hub is **Sungaipenuh** (Full River), but many travellers opt to stay in the tiny village of Kersik Tuo, the departure point for treks to Gunung Kerinci. While Kerinci is in Jambi province, culturally the people are unmistakably Minangkabau West Sumatran, with the same matrilineal social structure.

More than 100 people were killed when an earthquake measuring 7.0 on the Richter Scale rocked the valley in October 1995, although Sungaipenuh suffered little damage. Gungung Kerinci last erupted in 1934.

Orientation & Information

Despite being a regional centre, Sungaipenuh retains a quiet provincial feel. Most places of importance are near the large sports field in the centre of town.

You can change US dollars (cash and travellers cheques) at the BNI bank branch on Jl Ahmad Yani, directly opposite Hotel Matahari. The post office, Jl Sudirman 1, is nearby and the Telkom wartel is around the corner on the southern side of the sports field.

If you're heading for the national park, you'll need to call in at the national parks office (☎ 22500, 22240), Jl Basuki Rahmat 11, for a permit (1500Rp). Ranger guides can be hired for 50,000Rp per day for treks to Gunung Kerinci and Danau Gunung Tujuh. The office is open Monday to Thursday from 8 am to 2.30 pm, Friday until 11 am and Saturday from 7.30 am to 12.30 pm. Permits are valid for 10 days.

Kerinci Seblat National Park

The park protects 1½ million hectares of prime equatorial rainforest spread over four provinces. It covers a 350km swathe of the Bukit Barisan mountains from near Padang (West Sumatra) in the north to near Curup (Bengkulu) and Lubuklinggau (South Sumatra) in the south. Almost 40% of the park falls within Jambi's boundaries, and Sungaipenuh is the only real access point – enabling Jambi's tourist people to promote the park as their attraction.

Unfortunately, there is not much to promote. Facilities within the park are virtually nonexistent. Most of the park is dense rainforest, its inaccessibility the very reason it is one of the last strongholds of endangered species like the Sumatran tiger and Sumatran rhinoceros. Trekking opportunities are

The Kubu

The Kubu are the indigenous people of southern Sumatra, nomadic hunter-gatherers who once lived throughout the region's lowland forests. They are descended from the first wave of Malays to migrate to Sumatra.

Today their domain is restricted to a reserve called Bukit 12 – 287 sq km of forest to the east of the Trans-Sumatran Hwy town of Bangko.

The traditional Kubu way of life came to an end when large-scale transmigration from Java and Bali began. The migrants cut down forests for plantation farming and brought with them diseases like measles and tuberculosis.

The Kubu steadfastly resisted attempts to persuade them to settle in government-built villages. In 1985 they were granted the forest reserve around Bukit 12. It is home to about 1000 people, divided into five groups. Each group is led by a *temenggung* (chief).

A road leads off towards the reserve from the town of Limbur, on the main highway about 25km east of Bangko. There are buses to Limbur from Bangko, where you can stay at the ***Bangko Indah Hotel*** on Jalan Lintas.

restricted to a few points on the fringe of the park; descriptions follow.

Gunung Kerinci

It's a tough two day climb to the summit of Sumatra's highest mountain, starting from the village of Kersik Tua, 43km from Sungaipenuh among the tea plantations of the 60 sq km Kayo Aro estate.

The mountain lies within the national park, so you'll need a permit – get one in Sungaipenuh, or your guide can organise it for you. It is a sensible precaution to take a guide – available in Kersik Tua and Sungaipenuh – and very foolish to tackle the climb alone. Many people also hire a porter

(50,000Rp per day) to ease the burden. Although the path to the top is clearly defined (unfortunately by scattered rubbish), weather conditions can change very suddenly on the mountain. Also, parts of the mountainside are covered in scree, making it easy to slip. You'll need to bring food, a water bottle, a tent and a sleeping bag (easily hired in Kersik Tua), as it can get as low as 2°C at night.

The 16km from the village to the top is normally tackled in two stages. It takes about six hours to climb to a camping ground at about 3000m, where most people spend the night before setting off for the final two hour climb to the summit at dawn. At the top you'll find a greenish crater lake measuring about 120m by 400m.

There are **cave paintings** in the Gua Kasah on the lower slopes, 5km from Kersik Tua. On the way back you can stop at the **hot springs** near the Kayo Aro plantation. It's too hot to swim in the main pool, but you can get a private room with a hot-water mandi.

Danau Gunung Tujuh

Tranquil Danau Gunung Tujuh (1950m) is the highest volcanic lake in South-East Asia. It takes 3½ hours to climb to the lake from the village of Pelompek, 8km beyond Kersik Tua. The lake lies within the park; permits are available in Pelompek.

Danau Kerinci

Danau Kerinci, 20km south of Sungaipenuh, is a small lake nestled beneath Gunung Raja (2543m). **Stone carvings** in the villages around the lake suggest that the area supported a sizeable population in megalithic times. The best-known of these stone monuments is **Batu Gong** (Gong Stone), in the village of Muak, 25km from Sungaipenuh. It is thought to have been carved 2000 years ago.

Sengering Caves

The extensive network of caves outside the village of Sengering includes the celebrated **Gua Tiangko**. Obsidian flake tools found in the cave show that it was occupied by some of Sumatra's earliest-known residents some 9000 years ago. The caves are also known for their stalactites and stalagmites. Sengering is 9km from Sungai Manau, a village on the road to Bangko.

Mesjid Agung Pondok Tinggi

This fine old mosque, with its pagoda-style roof, stands at the northern edge of Sungaipenuh in the village of Pondok Tinggi. It looks nothing special from the outside, but the interior is a different story, with elaborately carved beams and old Dutch tiles. Not a single nail was used when it was built in 1874. You need permission to go inside.

Places to Stay & Eat

Sungaipenuh The best place for travellers is the *Hotel Matahari* (☎ 21061, Jl Ahmad Yani 25), a sprawling colonial-era guesthouse. Clean doubles with outside bathroom cost 15,000Rp, and there is a useful wall map of the area and transport information. The 1960s-style *Hotel Yani* (☎ 21409, Jl Murandi 1) has carpeted doubles from 13,500Rp. The new *Aroma Hotel* (☎ 21142, Jl Imam Bonjol 14) has some cheap rooms, as well as doubles with hot water and TV from 45,000Rp. There's good Padang food at *Minang Soto* on the main street. The *Dendeng Batokok* restaurant a few doors down is named for the local speciality – charcoal-grilled strips of smoked beef.

Kersik Tua There are five small homestays in Kersik Tua, the best of which is *Subandi Homestay* (☎ 357009). It costs 7500Rp per person in clean comfortable rooms, but the real attraction is Pak Subandi, who is also a guide. A wealth of knowledge on the Kerinci area, he is a keen bird-watcher and environmentalist.

The other homestays are *Keluarga Paiman* (☎ 357030), *B Darmin* (☎ 357070), *Wandi* and *Keluarga Timan*. Their rates are similar to Subandi's.

Getting There & Away

The shortest approach to Sungaipenuh is from the West Sumatran capital of Padang, a journey of 246km via the coast road (from 12,500Rp, eight hours). There is also a breathtakingly scenic back route that takes the mountain road past Gunung Kerinci and follows the valleys south. If you're coming on the inland road and want to get off at Kersik Tua (an hour north of Sungaipenuh), let the driver know, as it's easy to miss.

Sungaipenuh has a new long-distance bus station 5km from town in Kumun, but everyone, including the bus companies, seems to be ignoring it. The huge lot is empty and only a couple of ticket agents have set up shop. All buses still set off from the terminal in town. There are frequent buses east to Bangko (9000Rp, four hours) on the Trans-Sumatran Hwy, as well as direct buses to Bengkulu (15,000Rp) and Bukittinggi (15,500Rp).

Getting Around

You can get almost anywhere in the valley from the bus terminal in Sungaipenuh market. Sample destinations and fares include Danau Kerinci (500Rp), Kersik Tua (2000Rp) and Pelompek (2000Rp).

Dokars cost 1500Rp for most rides around Sungaipenuh.

Bengkulu

Nothing much seems to have changed in Bengkulu for years – except prices. It remains Sumatra's most isolated province, cut off from its neighbours by the Bukit Barisan, particularly during the rainy season from December to March, when land transport can cease completely.

Few tourists come to Bengkulu. There is not a lot to do apart from adjust to the slower pace of life.

History

Little is known of Bengkulu before it came under the influence of the Majapahits from Java at the end of the 13th century.

Until then, it appears to have existed in almost total isolation, divided between a number of small kingdoms such as Sungai Lebong in the Curup area. It even developed its own cuneiform script, *ka-ga-nga*.

In 1685, after having been kicked out of Banten in Java three years previously, the British moved into Bengkulu (Bencoolen, as they called it) in search of pepper. The venture was not exactly a roaring success. Isolation, boredom and constant rain sapped the British will, and malaria ravaged their numbers.

The colony was still not a likely prospect in 1818 when Sir Thomas Stamford Raffles arrived as its British-appointed ruler, taking the title Lieutenant-General of Fort Marlborough. In the short time he was there, Raffles made the pepper market profitable and planted cash crops of coffee, nutmeg and sugar cane. In 1824 Bengkulu was traded for the Dutch outpost of Melaka and a guarantee not to interfere with British interests in Singapore.

From 1938-41 Bengkulu was a home-in-domestic-exile for Indonesia's first president, Soekarno.

Flora

Bengkulu's rainforests are home to both the *Rafflesia arnoldi* and the world's tallest flower, *Amorphophalus titanum*.

The rafflesia is found in a number of sites throughout the Bukit Barisan mountains, most notably around Bukittinggi in West Sumatra. But it was in Bengkulu, in 1818, that Raffles and a British government botanist named Arnold first set eyes on the flower – hence the plant's botanical name. The rafflesia is found at a number of sites dotted around Bengkulu's mountains, the most accessible being close to the main road halfway between Bengkulu and Curup.

The lily-like *Amorphophalus titanum*, Bengkulu's floral emblem, flowers only once every three years, when it throws up a spectacular flower spike than can stand over 2m high. The flower is a rich red, with a huge yellow stamen protruding from its core. The plant is a member of the same family as the taro, the starchy tuber that is a staple food in parts of Asia and the Pacific islands. Known locally as *kibut* or *bunga bangkai*, it is found mainly in the Rejang Lebong district north of Curup.

BENGKULU
☎ 0736 • pop 60,000
Bengkulu, a relaxed town, is the capital of the province of the same name.

Orientation & Information

Although Bengkulu is by the sea, most of the town is set back from the coast, touching only near the fort, Benteng Marlborough. The coast is surprisingly quiet and rural, just a kilometre or so from the town centre.

Jl Suprapto and the nearby Pasar Minggu Besar are in the modern town centre, which is connected to the old town area around the fort by the long, straight Jl Ahmad Yani/Jl Sudirman.

All manner of supplies can be found at the well stocked Mini Market 88 on the corner of Jl Suprapto and Jl Sudirman.

Tourist Offices The Bengkulu tourist office (☎ 21272), Jl Pembangunan 14, is inconveniently situated to the south of town. There's not much material in English but the staff are friendly.

Money The best place to change money is BCA bank, Jl Suprapto 150, near the Gandhi Bakery. You can also change money at Bank Dumi Daya, Jl R Hadi 1. Amex and US dollars (cash and travellers cheques) can be changed at BNI bank on Jl S Parman.

Post & Communications The main post office (and poste restante) is south of the town centre on Jl S Parman, but there is another post office on Jl Ahmad Yani. The Telkom wartel is at the intersection of Jl Suprapto and Jl Soekarno-Hatta.

Benteng Marlborough

Fort Marlborough became the seat of British power in Bengkulu after 1719, when it replaced nearby Fort York, of which nothing but the foundations remain.

The fort was restored and opened to the public in 1984 after a long period of use by the Indonesian army. It's not a hugely impressive structure, but its historical value and pleasant setting overlooking the Indian

BENGKULU

INDIAN OCEAN

Jalan Teluk Segara

Jalan Panjaitan

Jalan Benteng

Jalan Tengiri

Pasar Barukota

Jalan Khadijah

Thomas Parr Monument

Daerah Monument

Jalan Ditra

Jalan Ahmad Yani

Jalan Veteran

Jalan Santoso

Jalan Sudirman

European Cemetery

Jalan M. Hasan

Jalan Santoso

Jalan Kerapu

Monumen Inggris

Jalan Samudera

Jalan Cendrawasih

Jalan Pantai Nala

Pasar Minggu Besar

Jalan MT Haryono

Jalan Irian

Jalan Suprapto

To Lias & Ipuh

Jalan Soekarno-Hatta

Jalan Fatmawati

Jalan S Parman

0   250   500 m

To Post Office, Museum,
Airport, Bus Terminal,
Pulau Baai Harbour &
Tourist Office

To Curup &
Trans-Sumatran
Hwy

PLACES TO STAY
2 Losmen Samudera
9 Wisma Balai Buntar
11 Vista Hotel
14 Rio Asri Hotel
15 Wisma Rafflesia
28 Wisma Bumi Endah
31 Hotel Pantai Panjang
32 Horison Hotel
33 Permata Gading Resor

PLACES TO EAT
13 Rumah Makan Srikandi
17 Tassa Cafe
18 Rumah Makan Si Kabayan
19 Warung Makanan Laut Dedi
25 Gandhi Bakery

OTHER
1 Fort Marlborough
3 Mosque
4 Wartel
5 Post Office
6 Police
7 Governor's House
8 Bank Indonesia
10 Pelni Office
12 San Travel
16 Fruit Shop
20 Merpati Office &
   Hotel Samudera Dwinka
21 Mesjid Jamik
   (Bung Karno Mosque)
22 Putra Rafflesia Bus Office
23 Mini Market 88
24 BCA Bank
26 Telkom
27 BNI Bank 1946
29 Soekarno's House
30 Mosque

SUMATRA

Ocean compensate for that. A small museum houses a few interesting old engravings and copies of official correspondence from the time of British rule, and the old British gravestones at the entrance make poignant reading. Admission is 250Rp.

The fort was attacked and fell twice. It was overrun by a local rebellion as soon as it was completed in 1719, and was captured briefly by the French in 1760.

Bengkulu has a few other British reminders, including the **Thomas Parr monument** in front of the Pasar Barukota, erected in memory of a British governor beheaded by locals in 1807. The **Monumen Inggris** near the beach is dedicated to Captain Robert Hamilton, who died in 1793 'in command of the troops'.

Soekarno's House

Soekarno was exiled to Bengkulu by the Dutch from 1938 until 1941. The small villa in which he lived on Jl Soekarno-Hatta is maintained as a museum. Exhibits include a few faded photos, a wardrobe and even Bung's trusty bicycle.

The house is open Sunday and Tuesday to Thursday from 8 am to 2 pm, Friday to 11 am and Saturday to noon; it is closed Monday. Admission is 250Rp.

Other Things to See

During his stay Soekarno, who was an architect, designed the **Mesjid Jamik** at the junction of Jl Sudirman and Jl Suprapto. It is commonly known as the Bung Karno mosque.

The **Bengkulu Museum Negeri** is near the tourist office on Jl Pembangunan – bring your own light bulbs if you want to see anything. The graves in the **European cemetery** behind the small church on Jl Ditra are testament to the colonialists' vulnerability to malaria.

Bengkulu's main beach, **Pantai Panjang**, hardly rates as an attraction – it's long, grey, featureless and unsafe for swimming.

Places to Stay – Budget

As in most major towns, the cheap hotels are pretty unappealing. The **Losmen Samudera** (☎ 343831), opposite the fort entrance on Jl Benteng, at least has location going for it, but the rooms are extremely basic. Tiny fan doubles cost 10,000Rp. **Wisma Rafflesia** (☎ 31650, Jl Ahmad Yani 924) has equally grotty doubles from 10,000Rp.

The best option is the **Vista Hotel** (☎ 20 820), among the bus agents on Jl MT Haryono. Its many and varied rooms include 12,500Rp and 15,000Rp doubles with mandi, as well as some mid-range choices.

Places to Stay – Mid-Range

The **Wisma Balai Buntar** (☎ 21254, Jl Khadijah 122) offers the best value in town. The old Dutch villa's huge, clean rooms cost 22,000Rp, including breakfast.

A good alternative is the **Wisma Bumi Endah** (☎ 21665, Jl Fatmawati 29), a small family-run guesthouse of the white-tile variety. Doubles with mandi and fan cost 25,000Rp, or 45,000Rp for larger air-con rooms.

By the beach on Jl Samudera, the **Hotel Pantai Panjang** (☎ 24001) has private wooden bungalows from 40,000Rp. Air-con starts at 60,000Rp. Heading south, **Permata Gading Resor** (☎ 21855) has bright blue bungalows with air-con and TV for 65,000Rp. A third or fourth person can be accommodated for an extra 7500Rp each.

Places to Stay – Top End

The fanciest hotel in town is the **Horison** (☎ 21722, Jl Pantai Nala 142). Facilities include swimming pool and snooker room; doubles start at 181,000Rp.

The **Rio Asri Hotel** (☎ 21952, Jl Veteran 63) has air-con doubles from 127,000Rp. There's a gym, and a swimming pool non-guests can use for 4000Rp.

Places to Eat

Rumah Makan Srikandi on Jl Ahmad Yani does excellent southern Sumatran food very cheaply. **Rumah Makan Si Kabayan** (Jl Sudirman 51) serves Sundanese food and is considered the best restaurant in town – but it's not cheap. Seafood fans should head straight to the wonderful **Warung Makanan Laut Dedi**, also on Jl Sudirman.

On either side of Laut Dedi are several cheap mie and nasi joints, including **Buffet Kubang**, which makes fabulous martabak filled with vegetables or beef and served with sweet chilli sauce.

Nearby, the wonderfully decked-out **Tassa Cafe** is the only traveller-style place in town, and is a good place to meet Bengkulu's younger generation. **Gandhi Bakery** on Jl Suprapto has a fine selection of ice creams and cakes.

Getting There & Away

Air Merpati has five flights a week to Jakarta (351,000Rp). The Merpati office (☎ 27 111) is in the Hotel Samudera Dwinka, Jl Sudirman 246.

Bus Panorama terminal, the long-distance bus terminal, is several kilometres east of town, but all services continue to the various company depots in town.

SUMATRA

Tickets can be bought from the bus company offices on Jl MT Haryono, which becomes Jl Bali further along. Putra Rafflesia (☎ 20313), Jl MT Haryono 12, and Bengkulu Indah (☎ 22640), Jl Bali 57, service a wide range of destinations. San Travel (☎ 21811), Jl MT Haryono 73, is also recommended.

Fares include 27,500Rp (32,500Rp aircon) to Padang, and 49,000Rp (from 80,000Rp air-con) to Jakarta. Sriwijaya Express, Jl Bali 36, runs buses up the coast to Sungaipenuh in the Kerinci Valley (15,000Rp).

Habeco, Jl Bali 67, at the northern edge of town, has daily buses along the coast road to Padang (20,000Rp, 16 hours) via Lais (1500Rp), Ipuh (4500Rp) and Mukomuko (9000Rp).

Boat Ask about services to Pulau Enggano at the Pelni office (☎ 21013), Jl Khadijah 10, near the fort.

Getting Around

Airport taxis charge a standard 10,000Rp to town. The airport is 200m from the main road south, and there are regular opelets to town for 500Rp. Tell the driver you want to go to the *benteng* (fort). Opelets also greet buses when they arrive at Jl MT Haryono/Jl Bali. The fare to almost anywhere in town is 500Rp, regardless of anything the drivers may tell you.

NORTHERN BENGKULU

The coast road (Jl Manusurai Pantai), running north from Bengkulu to Padang, offers a number of possibilities for travellers.

The road is now sealed all the way and the journey takes about 16 hours – a reasonable alternative to the usual trip inland via Lubuklinggau and the Trans-Sumatran Hwy. However, in the wet season the coast road is prone to wash-out and even landslides.

The journey can be done in a number of short hops. The first town north of Bengkulu is **Lais**. The beach is only 100m from the road, and you can stay at *Elly's House* (Jl Utama 21), on the main road opposite the post office.

There are reputed to be elephants further north near **Ipuh**, around the mouth of the Sungai Ipuh. *Wisma Rindu Alam (Jl Protokol 1)*, opposite the soccer pitch, has very basic singles/doubles for 7000/12,000Rp. The owner also rents out a nearby four bed *villa* on the banks of the Sungai Batang Muar (25,000Rp per night).

Mukomuko, 200km north of Bengkulu, was the northern outpost of the British colony of Bencoolen. **Benteng Anna** (Fort Anna) survives as a reminder.

CURUP

Curup is a small town in the foothills of the Bukit Barisan, halfway between Bengkulu and Lubuklinggau. It is a launching pad for visits to the attractions of the surrounding Bukit Barisan. The town itself is in a valley watered by the upper reaches of the Sungai Musi, which eventually flows through Palembang.

There's nowhere to change money in Curup, although it is possible to draw money on Visa or MasterCard from the BCA bank on Jl Merdeka.

Things to See

There are many fine examples of **rumah adat** (traditional stilted wooden houses) in the villages around Curup. Volcanic **Gunung Kaba**, 19km east of Curup, has two large sulphurous craters surrounded by dense rainforest. The **hot springs** and **waterfall** at Suban are popular with weekend picnickers.

Places to Stay & Eat

There are a number of cheap losmen, including *Losmen Nusantara (Jl Merdeka 794)*, which has doubles for 7000Rp.

Much better is the *Hotel Aman Jaya* (☎ 21 365, Jl Dr AK Gani 10). Standard doubles with shower and fan cost 30,000Rp; huge rooms upstairs with hot water and air-con cost 40,000Rp. It's a friendly place, with information on surrounding attractions and how to get to them.

The busy *Restaurant Sari Buan (Jl Merdeka 120)* serves Padang food. Palembang food (see Places to Eat in the Palembang section later in this chapter) can be found around the corner at **Warkop Ramanda** *(Jl Cut Nyak Dhien 1)*.

Getting There & Away
There are frequent connections to Bengkulu and Lubuklinggau (both 5000Rp, three hours). Buses leave from the busy central market.

PULAU ENGGANO
Pulau Enggano is a remote island with an area of 680 sq km, 100km off the coast of southern Bengkulu. It is so isolated that until as recently as 100 years ago, some Sumatrans believed it was inhabited entirely by women. Apparently these women miraculously managed to procreate through the auspices of the wind, or by eating certain fruit.

The island is featured on a map of Asia drawn in 1593. Enggano is Portuguese for 'deceit' or 'disappointment', which suggests that the Portuguese were the first Europeans to discover it. It wasn't until three years later that Dutch navigators first recorded it.

The original inhabitants are believed to have fled the Sumatran mainland when the Malays migrated there. The present-day inhabitants live by cultivating rice, coffee, pepper, cloves and copra. Wild pigs, cattle and buffaloes are abundant.

There are five villages on the island: **Banjar Sari** on the north coast; **Meok** on the west coast; **Kaana** and **Kahayupu** in the east; and **Malakoni**, the harbour. The island is relatively flat (the highest point is Bua Bua, at 250m) and the coastline is swampy. It's worth visiting only if you are a keen anthropologist and/or a real adventurer with plenty of time.

Places to Stay
The only place to stay is the *Losmen Apaho* in Malakoni.

Getting There & Away
Pelni operates occasional boats from Bengkulu to Malakoni. If the schedules don't work out, you will need to go to the small port of Bintuhan, about 225km south of Bengkulu, and ask at the harbour.

Getting Around
The villages on the island are connected by tracks originally made by the Japanese and not very well maintained since. The only way of getting around is to walk.

South Sumatra

The province of South Sumatra stretches from the high peaks of the Bukit Barisan mountains in the west to the vast mangrove swamps of the coastal lowlands facing the shallow Selat Bangka (Bangka Strait) in the east. It also includes the large islands of Bangka and Belitung. All roads and rivers (and the train line) lead to Palembang, the provincial capital.

PALEMBANG
☎ 0711 • pop 1.5 million
Palembang, Sumatra's second-largest city, is huge, heavily polluted and industrial. The main industries are oil refining, fertiliser production and cement manufacture.

People glancing at a map could be forgiven for not realising that Palembang, 80km from the mouth of the Sungai Musi, is also a major port. When Sumatra's oil fields were discovered and opened in the early 1900s, Palembang quickly became South Sumatra's main export outlet hub. As well as oil, the port also handles exports from the province's seemingly endless rubber, coffee, pepper and pineapple plantations.

Palembang has little to offer travellers apart from transport connections.

History
A thousand years ago Palembang was the centre of the highly developed Sriwijaya civilisation. The Chinese scholar I Tsing spent six months in Palembang in 672 and reported that 1000 monks, scholars and pilgrims were studying and translating Sanskrit there.

Few relics from this period remain – no sculpture, monuments or architecture of note – nor is there much of interest from the early 18th century, when Palembang was an

SUMATRA

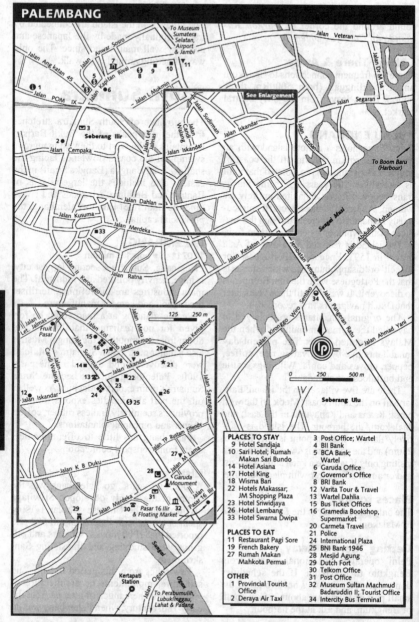

PALEMBANG

To Museum Sumatera Selatan, Airport & Jambi

Jalan Veteran

Jalan Dr Ista

Jalan Ang katan 45

Jalan Anwar Sosro

Jalan Kapitan Rival

Jalan L Mukmin

Jalan POM IX

Jalan Segaran

See Enlargement

Jalan Sudirman

Jalan Candi Walang

Jalan Iskandar

Jalan Tendean

To Boom Baru (Harbour)

Seberang Ilir

Jalan Let. Jalmas

Jalan Cempaka

Jalan Iskandar

Jalan Dahlan

Sungai Musi

Jalan Kusuma

Jalan Merdeka

Jalan Abdullah

Ashan

Jalan Il Keronggo

Jalan Ratna

Jalan Kedaton

Jembatan Ampera

Jalan Kironggo Wiro Sentiko

Jalan Pangeran Ratu

Jalan Ahmad Yani

Jalan Let. Jalmas

Fruit Pasar

Jalan Kol Atmo

Jalan Dempo

Jalan Meru

Jalan Sudirman

Jalan Candi Walang

Jalan Iskandar

Jalan Sayangan

Jalan Iskandar

Seberang Ulu

Jalan TP Rustam Effendy

Jalan M Lama

Garuda Monument

Jalan K B Duku

Jalan Merdeka

Pasar 16 Ilir & Floating Market

Sungai

Kertapati Station

Jalan Ogan

To Perabumulih, Lubuklinggau, Lahat & Padang

SUMATRA

0   125   250 m

0   250   500 m

PLACES TO STAY
- 9 Hotel Sandjaja
- 10 Sari Hotel; Rumah Makan Sari Bundo
- 14 Hotel Asiana
- 17 Hotel King
- 18 Wisma Bari
- 22 Hotels Makassar; JM Shopping Plaza
- 23 Hotel Sriwidjaya
- 26 Hotel Lembang
- 33 Hotel Swarna Dwipa

PLACES TO EAT
- 11 Restaurant Pagi Sore
- 19 French Bakery
- 27 Rumah Makan Mahkota Permai

OTHER
- 1 Provincial Tourist Office
- 2 Deraya Air Taxi
- 3 Post Office; Wartel
- 4 BII Bank
- 5 BCA Bank; Wartel
- 6 Garuda Office
- 7 Governor's Office
- 8 BRI Bank
- 12 Varita Tour & Travel
- 13 Wartel Dahlia
- 15 Bus Ticket Offices
- 16 Gramedia Bookshop, Supermarket
- 20 Carmeta Travel
- 21 Police
- 24 International Plaza
- 25 BNI Bank 1946
- 28 Mesjid Agung
- 29 Dutch Fort
- 30 Telkom Office
- 31 Post Office
- 32 Museum Sultan Machmud Badaruddin II; Tourist Office
- 34 Intercity Bus Terminal

Islamic kingdom. Most of the buildings of the latter era were destroyed in battles with the Dutch.

Palembang translates as 'gold from the ground', which probably stems from the city's name in Sriwijayan times, Swarna Dwipa, which translates as 'Golden Island'.

Orientation

Palembang sits astride the Sungai Musi, once the city's pride but now suffering badly from industrial waste. Some of the streams feeding into the Sungai Musi look not merely polluted, but positively corrosive. The city's skyline is dominated by the giant Jembatan Ampera (Ampera Bridge), built in the 1960s, that links the two halves of the city.

A hodgepodge of wooden houses on stilts crowd both banks of the Sungai Musi. The south side, Seberang Ulu, is where the majority of people live.

Seberang Ilir, on the north bank, is the city's better half, where you'll find most of the government offices, shops, hotels and the wealthy residential districts.

The main street is Jl Sudirman, which runs north-south to the bridge. The bus terminal and train station are both on the southern side.

Information

Tourist Offices The Palembang city tourist office (☎ 358450) is at the Museum Sultan Machmud Badaruddin II, off Jl Sudirman near the bridge. The South Sumatran provincial tourist office (☎ 357348) is among the government offices on Jl POM IX.

Money Palembang has branches of all the major banks. BCA and BII banks have the best rates. Their main offices are on Jl Kapitan Rivai.

Outside banking hours, the bigger hotels are a better bet than moneychangers like Dharma Perdana, Jl Kol Atmo 446 (opposite Hotel Lembang), which will change only US and Singaporean dollars (cash) at poor rates.

Post & Communications The post office is close to the river, next to the Garuda

monument on Jl Merdeka. Internet facilities are available for 6000Rp per hour. International phone calls can be made next door at the Telkom wartel. The only place to make collect calls is Wartel Dahlia, on Jl Iskandar near the intersection with Jl Sudirman.

Dangers & Annoyances The pickpockets in Palembang are notoriously crafty. Be especially careful around shopping malls and market areas – a lock on your daypack is recommended. Many of the pickpockets are young children who work in groups. The old trick, whereby one person bumps into you while a partner relieves you of your belongings, is common.

Things to See

The **Museum Sumatera Selatan** is well worth a visit. It houses finds from Sriwijayan times, as well as megalithic carvings from the Pasemah Highlands, including the famous *batu gajah* (elephant stone). Check out the magnificent **rumah limas** (traditional house) behind the museum. The museum is about 5km from the town centre off the road to the airport. It's open Sunday to Thursday from 8 am to 4 pm and on Friday until 11 am; admission is 250Rp.

The dust-covered exhibits at the **Museum Sultan Machmud Badaruddin II**, near Jembatan Ampera, are not so interesting. However, the staff can organise boat trips (25,000Rp an hour) on the Sungai Musi to songket-weaving villages and floating houses downstream.

Other attractions include the colourful **floating market** on the river near the Ampera Bridge and imposing **Mesjid Agung**, built by Sultan Machmud Badaruddin at the beginning of the 19th century.

The remains of a late 18th century **Dutch fort**, occupied today by the Indonesian army, can be seen to the north of Jl Merdeka. Sections of the outside walls still stand.

Organised Tours

Varita Tours & Travel (☎ 372034), Jl Iskandar 541, specialises in tours to Danau Ranau. Carmeta Travel (☎ 321388), east on

Jl Iskandar, is the mainland booking agent for trips to Pulau Bangka.

Special Events

Palembang's annual tourist event is the *bidar* (canoe) race held on the Sungai Musi in the middle of town every 17 August (Independence Day). A bidar is about 25m long, 1m wide and is powered by up to 60 rowers.

Places to Stay – Budget

Palembang's cheap hotels are nothing to look forward to – and they're not particularly cheap. The best place to look is around the junction of Jl Sudirman and Jl Iskandar. The *Hotel Asiana (☎ 365016, Jl Sudirman 45E)* isn't quite as grim as it looks from the street. Basic singles/doubles with fan are 20,000/25,000Rp. There's no proper sign, just the word 'Penginapan' written above a doorway; take the steps up. The *Hotel Makassar (☎ 359565, Jl Iskandar 561)*, in an alley next to the JM Shopping Plaza, has clean doubles with fan from 18,000Rp.

Places to Stay – Mid-Range

Palembang has a number of faded old mid-range places that continue to be popular. *Hotel Sriwidjaja (☎ 355555, Jl Iskandar 31)* sits at the end of a cul-de-sac, about 50m from the Hotel Makassar (the street numbers are confusing). Large doubles cost from 20,000Rp with fan; or 52,000Rp with air-con, hot water and TV.

Another old gem is the *Sari Hotel (☎ 31 3320)*, on the corner of Jl Sudirman and Jl Kapitan Rivai. Singles/doubles start at 54,500/60,000Rp, all with air-con, TV and refrigerator.

Wisma Bari (☎ 315666), well positioned in a small lane right beside the Hotel King, is one of the new breed of mid-rangers. Modern air-con rooms with TV start at 65,000Rp. *Hotel Wisata (☎ 352681, Jl Iskandar 105-7)* is similar.

Places to Stay – Top End

The four star *Hotel Sandjaja (☎ 310675)*, on Jl Kapitan Rivai, is the smartest of a growing band of upmarket hotels catering for

businesspeople. It has rooms from US$80, a swimming pool and a choice of restaurants.

The central *Hotel King (☎ 362323, Jl Kol Atmo 623)* and *Hotel Lembang (☎ 363333, Jl Kol Atmo 16)* both have doubles from US$40. The *Hotel Swarna Dwipa (☎ 313322, Jl Tasik 2)*, some distance west of the city centre, has singles/doubles from 110,000/140,000Rp. Facilities include a gym and swimming pool.

Places to Eat

Palembang is hardly a name to make the taste buds tingle in anticipation, but the city does lend its name to the distinctive cuisine of southern Sumatra (including Lampung and Bengkulu) in the same way Padang lends its name to West Sumatran fare.

The best-known dish is *ikan brengkes* (fish served with a spicy durian-based sauce). *Pindang* is a spicy clear fish soup. Another Palembang speciality is *pempek*, also known as *empek-empek*, a mixture of sago, fish and seasonings that is formed into balls and deep fried or grilled. Served with a spicy sauce, pempek are widely available from street stalls and warungs for 250Rp each.

Palembang food is normally served with a range of accompaniments. The main one is *tempoyak*, a combination of fermented durian, *terasi* (shrimp paste), lime juice and chilli that is mixed up with the fingers and added to the rice. *Sambal buah* (fruit sambals), made with pineapple or sliced green mangoes, are also popular.

A good place to try Palembang food is *Rumah Makan Mahkota Permai (Jl Mesjid Lama 33)*, near the junction with Jl Sudirman.

If you're hooked on Padang food, *Rumah Makan Sari Bundo*, part of the Sari Hotel set-up, and the *Pagi Sore (Jl Sudirman 96)*, opposite, are both good – but can be pricey, especially for seafood.

The main *night food market* is on Jl Sayangan, to the east of Jl Sudirman, with dozens of noodle and sate stalls. The *French Bakery*, opposite Hotel King on Jl Kol Atmo, also sells noodle dishes and other simple meals.

Getting There & Away

Air Merpati (☎ 312132), in the Hotel Sandjaja, has three flights a day to Jakarta (457,000Rp) and one to Pangkalpinang (204,000Rp). Other Merpati services include three flights a week to Medan (880,000Rp), Pulau Batam (461,000Rp) and Pekanbaru (500,000Rp), and one daily to Bandung in Java (502,000Rp).

Deraya Air Taxi (☎ 371878), Jl Kapitan Rivai 27, has daily flights from Palembang to Tanjung Pandan on Pulau Belitung (217,000Rp). Another small airline, Serunting Sakti, flies to Lubuklinggau on the Trans-Sumatran Hwy near Bengkulu, every Wednesday and Sunday (156,000Rp).

Bus The main bus terminal is south of the Sungai Musi at the junction of Jl Pangeran Ratu and Jl Kironggo Wiro Sentiko. Most of the bigger bus companies have ticket offices on Jl Kol Atmo, just north of and opposite Hotel King. ALS is a reliable company, with daily air-con buses north to Bukittinggi (50,000Rp, 18 hours), Medan (62,000Rp) and through to Banda Aceh (95,000Rp). It also has daily buses to Jakarta (from 35,000Rp, 20 hours) and points east.

There are several services to Jambi (20,000Rp, seven hours). Sriwijaya has daily buses to Bengkulu (26,000Rp, 15 hours).

Train The Kertapati train station is on the south side of the river, 8km from the city centre. Any opelet marked 'Kertapati' will get you there. There are three trains a day to Bandarlampung; the 10.30 am train is ekonomi class only (6000Rp, 7½ hours); the 8.30 am and 9 pm services are eksekutif class only (35,000Rp, 6½ hours). There are three trains to Lubuklinggau – 8, 11 am and 8 pm – which stop at Lahat (for the Pasemah Highlands – see this section later in this chapter). It's four hours to Lahat and seven to Lubuklinggau, but the fares are the same: 6000Rp ekonomi (11 am service only), 16,000Rp bisnis and 36,000Rp eksekutif.

Boat There are four 'jetfoil' services and one ferry a day from Palembang's Boom Baru jetty to Mentok on Pulau Bangka. The jetfoil services (25,000Rp, four hours) leave between 7 and 8.30 am. The ferry (15,000Rp, 10 hours) leaves at 5 pm.

Getting Around

To/From the Airport Sultan Badaruddin II airport is 12km north of town. Taxis cost a standard 15,000Rp.

Public Transport Opelets around town cost a standard 500Rp. They leave from around the huge roundabout at the junction of Jl Sudirman and Jl Merdeka (there is no city centre opelet terminal). There are lots of metered taxis, or you can charter one for 10,000Rp an hour.

DANAU RANAU

Remote Danau Ranau, nestled in the middle of the Bukit Barisan mountains in the southwestern corner of South Sumatra, is one of the least accessible – and least spoiled – of Sumatra's mountain lakes. It is around 300km (about eight hours by bus) from Palembang.

Temperatures at Ranau seldom rise above a comfortable 25°C. It is a good place to relax or go hiking in the surrounding mountains. It's possible to climb Gunung Seminung (1881m), the extinct volcano that dominates the region.

The main town and transport hub of the area is Simpangsender, about 10km northwest of the lake. Bandar Agung, at Ranau's northern tip, is the main lakeside settlement. Change money before you get there.

Organised Tours

Varita Tours & Travel (☎ 0711-372034), Jl Iskandar 541, Palembang, specialises in tours to Danau Ranau.

Places to Stay & Eat

There are several small hotels in Bandar Agung, including the **Hotel Seminung Permai** *(Jl Akmal 89)*, with clean doubles for 10,000Rp. Jl Akmal is the main street leading down to the lake. Padang food is about all you'll find in the restaurants.

Tour groups head for the *Wisma Danau Ranau*, south of the village of Simpang-sender on the lake's western shore. Lakeside bungalows cost 80,000Rp; large doubles in the main building cost 50,000Rp. Rooms can be booked through Varita Tours & Travel (see the preceding Organised Tours entry).

Getting There & Away

Most routes to Danau Ranau go through the Trans-Sumatran Hwy town of Baturaja. There are two buses a day to Baturaja from the main bus terminal in Palembang (7500Rp, four hours). The Palembang-Bandarlampung train line stops at Baturaja, which is about 3½ hours south of Palembang.

There are regular buses for the remaining 120km from Baturaja to Simpangsender (4000Rp, three hours), where you can pick up an opelet for the final 18km to Bandar Agung (500Rp). It's a good idea to arrive in Baturaja as early as possible to give yourself plenty of time to get a bus out again. If you do get stuck, there are dozens of uninspiring budget losmen to choose from.

PASEMAH HIGHLANDS

The highlands, tucked away in the Bukit Barisan west of Lahat, are famous for the mysterious megalithic monuments that dot the landscape. The stones have been dated back about 3000 years, but little else is known about them or the civilisation that carved them. While the museums of Palembang and Jakarta now house the pick of the stones, there are still plenty left *in situ*.

Orientation & Information

The main town of the highlands is Pagaralam, 68km (two hours by bus) south-west of the Trans-Sumatran Hwy town of Lahat.

Lahat's regional tourist office (☎ 22496), Jl Amir Hamzeh 150, is a complete waste of time. The best source of information about the highlands is the Hotel Mirasa in Pagaralam (see Places to Stay). There's nowhere to change money, so bring enough rupiah to see you through.

Megalithic Sites

There are two distinct styles of ancient sculpture in the highlands. The early style dates from almost 3000 years ago and features fairly crude figures squatting with hands on knees or arms folded over chests. The best examples of this type are at a site called **Tinggi Hari**, 20km west of Lahat west of the small river town of Pulau Pinang.

The later style, incorporating expressive facial features, dates from about 2000 years ago and is far more elaborate. Examples include carvings of men riding, and groups of people standing next to, buffaloes and elephants, two men battling with a snake, a man struggling with an elephant lying on its back, and a couple of tigers – one guards a representation of a human head between its paws. The natural curve of the rocks was used to create a three dimensional effect, though all the sculptures are in bas-relief.

Sculptures of this style are found throughout the villages around Pagaralam, although some take a bit of seeking out. **Tegurwangi**, about 8km from Pagaralam on the road to Tanjung Sakti, is the home of the famous **Batu Beribu**, a cluster of four squat statues that sit under a small shelter by a stream. The site guardian will wander over and lead you to some nearby dolmen-style stone tombs. You can still make out a painting of three women and a dragon in one of them.

The village of **Berlubai**, 3km from Pagaralam, has its own **Batu Gajah** (Elephant Stone) sitting out among the rice paddies, as well as tombs and statues. There is a remarkable collection of stone carvings among the paddies outside nearby **Tanjung Aru**. Look out for the one of a man fighting a giant serpent.

Gunung Dempo

This dormant volcano is the highest (3159m) of the peaks surrounding the Pasemah Highlands. It's a tea-growing area, and there are opelets from Pagaralam to the tea factory.

Places to Stay

Pagaralam Few travellers stop overnight in Pagaralam, even though it's much cooler than

The fantastic natural textures of laid-back Pantai Trikora on Pulau Bintan, part of the Riau Islands.

Stall holder – Bukittinggi markets.

Clock tower, Bukittinggi.

A modern home in Karo Batak style, Berastagi.

PETER PTSCHELINZEW

The impressive structure of the black-domed Mesjid Raya (Grand Mosque), Medan.

SARA-JANE CLELAND

Danau Maninjau, like Danau Toba, is one of Sumatra's magnificent volcanic crater lakes.

Lahat and there are half a dozen places to stay. The **Hotel Mirasa** (☎ 21266) is the place to base yourself. It has a range of doubles from 15,000Rp, and the owner can organise transport to the sites. The hotel is on the edge of town on Jl Mayor Ruslan, about 2km from the bus terminal. There are cheaper places in town, such as the **Hotel Telaga** (☎ 21236) on Jl Serma Wanar. It has doubles for 8000Rp.

Lahat There are lots of hotels in Lahat. The super-cheapies are grouped together close to the train station on Jl Stasiun, but most of them appear to be in the massage business. The places on the main street, Jl Mayor Ruslam III, are much better. The **Hotel Permata** (☎ 21642) at No 31 is conveniently close to both the bus terminal and the train station. It has a few basic doubles for 7000Rp and aircon doubles for 30,000Rp. The best rooms in town are 50m down the road at the **Nusantara Hotel** (☎ 21336), where air-con doubles with hot water cost up to 60,000Rp.

Getting There & Away
Every bus travelling along the Trans-Sumatran Hwy calls in at Lahat, nine hours north-west of Bandarlampung and 12 hours south-east of Padang. There are regular buses to Lahat from Palembang (6000Rp, five hours), and the town is a stop on the train line between Palembang and Lubuklinggau. There are frequent small buses between Lahat and Pagaralam (2000Rp, two hours).

Getting Around
There are opelets to the villages around Pagaralam from the *stasiun taksi* (taxi station) in the centre of town. All local services cost 300Rp.

PULAU BANGKA
☎ 0717
Western visitors are few and far between on Bangka, a large, very sparsely populated island 25km off the east coast of Sumatra. Tourist authorities are trying hard to promote the place, in particular the beaches of the east coast. They've got their work cut out for them: the beaches are miles from anything

else of interest, a hassle to get to, and there are no cheap places to stay. All the beach hotels are priced with wealthy visitors from Singapore and Malaysia in mind, but they, too, appear to be staying away in droves.

The island's name is derived from the word *wangka* (tin), which was discovered near Mentok in 1710. The island is covered with old mine workings. Tin is still mined on the island, although operations have been greatly scaled down in recent years.

There are only small pockets of natural forest left on Bangka. Rubber, palm oil and pepper are major crops.

Orientation & Information
Pulau Bangka's main town is Pangkalpinang, a bustling business and transport centre with a population of about 50,000 people. Most places of importance to travellers are close to the intersection of the main streets, Jl Sudirman and Jl Masjid Jamik. The bus terminal and markets are nearby on Jl N Pegadaian.

You can change money at BCA bank, Jl Masjid Jamik 15, or at BNI bank, Jl Sudirman 119. The post and telephone offices are at the northern end of Jl Sudirman, some way from the town centre.

There is a small tourist office (☎ 92496) just south of Sungailiat, the island's administrative centre. Mentok, on the north-western tip of the island, is the port for boats to Palembang.

Pangkalpinang
The fact that the **cemetery** is listed as one of the main attractions is a fair comment on the health of the tourist industry. That said, it is a huge cemetery, and there are some extravagant looking graves. There are supposedly 100,000 people buried there.

Pantai Pasir Padi is a beach 2.5km south of town, easily reached by opelet (300Rp). The swimming is poor and the main attraction is the seafood restaurant.

Travel agents tempt keen Asian golfers with packages that include a round at the **golf course** on the southern edge of town, kindly constructed by the island's tin company.

Mentok

Few people bother to stay here longer than it takes to get on a bus to Pangkalpinang.

Near Mentok's lighthouse is a **memorial** to 22 Australian nurses who were shot dead by the Japanese during WWII. The nurses had survived the sinking of the SS *Vyner Brooke* during the evacuation of Singapore.

From February until July 1949, during independence negotiations, the hilltop guesthouse at nearby **Gunung Menumbing** (445m) served as a home-in-domestic-exile for then-future President Soekarno and Vice-President Hatta.

Beaches

The best are **Pantai Parai Tenggiri**, 4km from Sungailiat, which is monopolised by the Parai Beach Hotel; and the deserted **Pantai Matras**, 5km further up the coast.

Places to Stay

Pangkalpinang There are quite a few cheap losmen around the centre of town. A good choice is *Penginapan Srikandi (☎ 21884, Jl Masjid Jamik 42)*, which has singles/doubles with mandi and fan from 10,000/16,000Rp. Immediately opposite is *Bukit Shofa Hotel (☎ 21062)*. It's a clean, modern place with rooms from 11,000/20,000Rp with mandi and fan, and doubles with air-con for 50,000Rp.

The *Sabrina Hotel (☎ 22424)* is a good mid-range place on Jl Diponegoro, a quiet side street off Jl Sudirman. Comfortable doubles with air-con, TV, hot water and breakfast cost 50,000Rp.

The *Menumbing Hotel (☎ 22991, Jl Gereja 5)* is supposedly the best hotel in town, but these days it looks too grubby to justify two stars. Doubles start at 80,000Rp, and there is a swimming pool nonguests can use for 2500Rp.

Mentok Near the harbour, *Losmen Mentok (Jl Ahmad Yani 42)* has rooms for 6000Rp. Overlooking the market, the splendid-sounding *Tin Palace Hotel (Jl Major Syafrie Rahman 1)* has rooms with mandi and fan for 20,000Rp, and with air-con for 30,000Rp.

Beaches The beaches east of Sungailiat are tourist resort territory. The *Parai Beach Hotel (☎ 92335)* is the best of this lot, with air-con bungalows by the beach. Few guests would be paying the advertised prices, which start from 110,000Rp, and peak at 300,000Rp for suites.

Places to Eat

There are lots of small restaurants in Pangkalpinang, including plenty of places along Jl Sudirman and in the markets near the main junction.

For Padang-style food, try *Sari Bundo (Jl Sudirman 77)*. Nearby, opposite Video Queen, is a small *restaurant* serving *pempek* (fish balls), the Palembang speciality. The flashiest restaurant in town is the *Tirta Garden (Jl Sudirman 3)*, an upmarket Chinese and seafood restaurant about 3km from the town centre.

If it's seafood that you're after, the place to go is *Restaurant Asui Seafood*, on Jl Kampung Bintang behind the BCA bank. *Gebung*, known locally as 'chicken fish' because of the firmness of its flesh, is worth sampling.

Getting There & Away

Air Merpati has one flight a day from Pangkalpinang to Palembang (204,000Rp).

Boat There are four daily jetfoil services between Palembang and Mentok (25,000Rp; three hours, depending on conditions). There's also a daily ferry from Palembang (15,000Rp, 10 hours).

The Pelni liner *Sirimau* stops at Mentok on the Dumai-Jakarta route. There are departures to Jakarta (47,500Rp deck class) every second Sunday. The Pelni office (☎ 22 743) in Mentok is outside the port gates.

Getting Around

To/From the Airport Airport taxis charge 6000Rp for the 7km run into Pangkalpinang, or you can walk to the main road and catch an opelet for 300Rp.

Public Transport There is regular public transport between Bangka's main towns, but most opelets stop running in mid-afternoon. After that, taxis are the only option.

There are public buses from Mentok to Pangkalpinang (6000Rp, four hours) and Sungailiat (6500Rp).

Lampung

Sumatra's southernmost province was not given provincial status by Jakarta until 1964. The Lampungese, however, have a long history as a distinct culture.

There's evidence that Lampung was part of the Palembang-based Sriwijayan Empire until the 11th century, when the Jambi-based Malayu kingdom became the dominant regional power.

Megalithic remains at Pugungraharjo, on the plains to the east of Bandarlampung, are thought to date back more than 1000 years and point to a combination of Hindu and Buddhist influences. The site is believed to have been occupied until the 16th century.

Lampung is famous for its pepper, a prized crop that attracted the West Javanese sultanate of Banten to the area at the beginning of the 16th century. Banten introduced the Islamic faith to Lampung.

Lampung's pepper also interested the Dutch, and the Dutch East India Company built a factory at Menggala in the late 17th century in a failed attempt to usurp the pepper trade.

When the Dutch finally took control of Lampung in 1856, they launched the first of the transmigration schemes that have sought to ease the chronic overcrowding in Java, moving large numbers of people from West Java to farm the fertile plains of eastern Lampung. The Javanese brought gamelan and *wayang* (shadow puppetry) with them.

Transmigration has made east Lampung something of a cultural melting pot. Some newcomers came from Hindu Bali, and trips to 'Balinese villages' are on some organised tour agendas.

The majority of the province's eight million people live in the main city, Bandarlampung, and in the transmigration settlements to the east. Very few people live on Lampung's rugged western seaboard, most of which is taken up by Bukit Barisan Selatan National Park.

Today, coffee is Lampung's most important income earner, closely followed by timber. Pepper remains a major crop, and there are also large areas of rubber and palm oil plantation.

The main tourist attractions are the volcano at Krakatau and the elephants of Way Kambas National Park.

BANDARLAMPUNG
☎ 0721   • pop 600,000
The major city and administrative centre of Lampung is Bandarlampung, at the northern end of Teluk Lampung.

Bandarlampung is a new name that marks the official merger of the old towns of Telukbetung (coastal) and Tanjungkarang (inland), which have grown together over the years. The merger has produced the fourth largest city in Sumatra.

When Krakatau erupted in 1883, almost half the 36,000 victims died in the 40m-high tidal wave that funnelled up Teluk Lampung and devastated Telukbetung. A huge steel maritime buoy was erected as a memorial on a hillside overlooking the city – the position it came to rest after the wave had receded (see Things to See later in this section).

Few travellers venture out of the bus terminal on their way to/from Jakarta, and there's little reason to.

Orientation
Most places of relevance to travellers are in Tanjungkarang, including the train station and the bulk of the hotels. The Rajabasa bus terminal is on the northern edge of town and the airport is a 30 minute drive further north.

Information
Tourist Offices There's a temporary regional tourist office upstairs at the main post office on Jl KH Dahlan. Several of the staff speak English. Yaman Aziz at the Lampung Provincial Tourist Office (☎ 428565), Jl WR Supratman 39, is very helpful.

SUMATRA

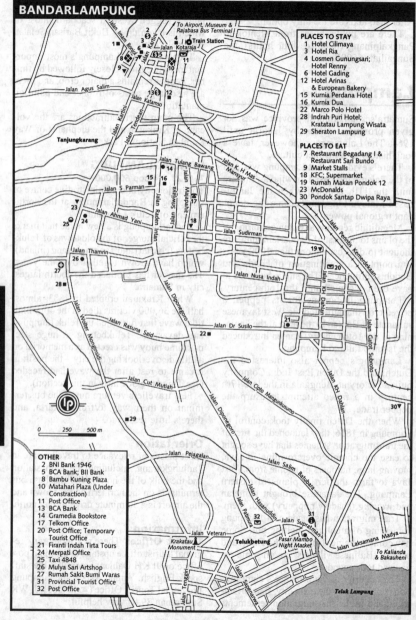

BANDARLAMPUNG

To Airport, Museum & Rajabasa Bus Terminal

Train Station

Tanjungkarang

Teluk Lampung

To Kalianda & Bakauheni

Teluk Lampung

PLACES TO STAY
1 Hotel Cilimaya
3 Hotel Ria
4 Losmen Gunungsari;
   Hotel Renny
6 Hotel Gading
12 Hotel Arinas
   & European Bakery
15 Kurnia Perdana Hotel
16 Kurnia Dua
22 Marco Polo Hotel
28 Indrah Puri Hotel;
   Kratatau Lampung Wisata
29 Sheraton Lampung

PLACES TO EAT
7 Restaurant Begadang I &
   Restaurant Sari Bundo
9 Market Stalls
18 KFC; Supermarket
19 Rumah Makan Pondok 12
23 McDonalds
30 Pondok Santap Dwipa Raya

OTHER
2 BNI Bank 1946
5 BCA Bank; BII Bank
8 Bambu Kuning Plaza
10 Matahari Plaza (Under
   Constraction)
11 Post Office
13 BCA Bank
14 Gramedia Bookstore
17 Telkom Office
20 Post Office; Temporary
   Tourist Office
21 Firanti Indah Tirta Tours
24 Merpati Office
25 Taxi 4848
26 Mulya Sari Artshop
27 Rumah Sakit Bumi Waras
31 Provincial Tourist Office
32 Post Office

Jalan Imam Bonjol
Jalan Kartini
Jalan Kotaraja
Jalan Agus Salim
Jalan Katamso
Jalan Kartini
Jalan Tendean
Jalan Tulang Bawang
Jalan K. H Mas Mansyur
Jalan Majapahit
Jalan Wijaya
Jalan S Parman
Jalan Ahmad Yani
Jalan Raden Intan
Jalan Sudirman
Jalan Thamrin
Jalan Nusa Indah
Jalan Perintis Kemerdekaan
Jalan Kh Dahlan
Jalan Gatot Subroto
Jalan Diponegoro
Jalan Rasuna Said
Jalan Dr Susilo
Jalan Wolter Monginsidi
Jalan Cut Mutiah
Jalan Cipto Mangunkusumo
Jalan KH Dahlan
Jalan Pejagalan
Jalan Salim Batubara
Jalan Diponegoro
Jalan Hasanuddin
Jalan Palmira
Jalan Supratman
Jalan Veteran
Jalan Laksamana Madya
Jalan Teuku Umar
Jalan Sisamatwa

Krakatau Monument
Telukbetung
Pasar Mambo Night Market

SUMATRA

0   250   500 m

Post & Communications The main post office is inconveniently located halfway between Tanjungkarang and Telukbetung on Jl KH Dahlan. You can surf the Net there for 6000Rp per hour. There is a small post office on Jl Kotaraja, near the train station. International telephone calls can be made from the 24 hour Telkom wartel on Jl Majapahit, which has a Home Country Direct phone.

Money Like many banks, BCA has branches in Tanjungkarang (Jl Raden Intan 98) and Telukbetung (Jl Yos Sudarso 100). ATMs are everywhere.

Things to See
There's virtually nothing to see in town. The **Krakatau monument**, a huge steel maritime buoy washed out of Teluk Lampung by the post-eruption tidal waves, is worth a look only to satisfy curiosity about the scale of what happened in 1883. The monument is in a small park off Jl Veteran in Telukbetung.

The **Lampung Provincial Museum**, 5km north of central Tanjungkarang on Jl Teuku Umar, houses a dusty collection of bits and pieces – everything from Neolithic relics to stuffed animals.

Organised Tours
Krakatau Lampung Wisata (☎ 263625/ 486666), Jl Kartini 25, and at the Sheraton, offers tours to Way Kambas National Park and Way Kanan, as well as to Krakatau. Similar programs are offered by Firanti Indah Tirta (☎ 269267), Jl Dr Susilo 91, and Elendra Tour & Travel (☎ 704737), Jl Sultan Agung 32. All tours include an English-speaking guide, lunch and transport, and cost around US$35 per person for a couple (US$20 per person for groups).

Places to Stay – Budget
Things are grim at the budget end of the scale. There are a couple of rock-bottom places on Jl Kotaraja, less than 100m from the train station. The **Losmen Gunungsari** at No 21 has dingy doubles for 12,500Rp. Down the alley next door is **Hotel Renny**, with airless doubles and a putrid share mandi for 15,000Rp. The **Hotel Cilimaya** (☎ 263504, Jl Imam Bonjol 261) is a step up from these. It has basic rooms for 12,000Rp, or 17,000Rp with mandi and fan.

Places to Stay – Mid-Range
Things start to improve rapidly if you are prepared to spend a bit more. A good place to look is around the junction of Jl Raden Intan and Jl S Parman.

The **Kurnia Perdana Hotel** (☎ 262030, Jl Raden Intan 114) has very clean rooms with air-con, TV and breakfast from 45,000Rp. Across the road at the **Kurnia Dua** (☎ 25 2905, Jl Raden Intan 75), air-con rooms start at 40,000Rp; doubles with fan and mandi cost 30,000Rp.

In the centre of town, off Jl Kartini at No 72, is the **Hotel Gading** (☎ 255512), with fan doubles from 25,000Rp; air-con rooms cost from 35,000Rp. The **Hotel Ria** (☎ 253974, Jl Kartini 79) around the corner has interesting wood-panelled doubles with mandi and fan from 31,500Rp, 45,000Rp with air-con.

At the top end of this bracket, centrally located **Hotel Arinas** (☎ 266778, Jl Raden Intan 35A) has clean, modern singles/ doubles from 66,000/73,000Rp, all with air-con, TV and hot water.

Places to Stay – Top End
The most stylish place in town is the impressive **Sheraton Lampung** (☎ 486666, Jl Monginsidi 175). The cheapest doubles are US$105.

All the creature comforts can be had for much less. At the **Marco Polo Hotel** (☎ 26 2511, Jl Dr Susilo 4), 128,000Rp will get you a room with a view of Teluk Lampung and use of the Olympic-size pool. The plush **Indrah Puri Hotel** (☎ 258258, Jl Monginsidi 70) has beautiful singles/doubles from US$62/75.

Places to Eat
There are some good restaurants in Bandarlampung, with many serving regional food. The unremarkable-looking **Rumah Makan Pondok 12**, opposite the main post office on Jl KH Dahlan, specialises in Palembang food.

SUMATRA

Pondok Santap Dwipa Raya is an upmarket Palembang-style place on Jl Gatot Subroto. It serves a delicious *sayur asam* (sour vegetable soup). *Sari Bundo* and *Begadang I* (one of four in town) are a couple of popular Padang restaurants near the markets on Jl Imam Bonjol.

European Bakery & Restaurant (Jl Raden Intan 35) is particularly strong on pastries.

Fast-food fans can get their fill at *KFC* on Jl Sudirman, or *McDonald's* on Jl Kartini.

The *Bambu Kuning Plaza* on Jl Imam Bonjol, near the corner of Jl Kartini, has some small food outlets. The *market stalls* around the plaza offer a wide range of snacks.

Shopping

Lampung produces weavings known as ship cloths (most feature ships), which use rich reds and blues to create primitive-looking geometric designs. Another type is *kain tapis*, a ceremonial cloth elaborately embroidered with gold thread. Mulya Sari Artshop, Jl Thamrin 85, has a good collection of both, but Lampung Art, opposite the Telkom towers on Jl Kartini, is more convenient.

Getting There & Away

Air Merpati (☎ 263419) has three flights a day to Jakarta (351,000Rp). The office is on Jl Ahmad Yani, near the corner of Jl Kartini.

Bus The city's sprawling Rajabasa bus terminal is one of the busiest in Sumatra. There's a constant flow of departures, 24 hours a day, south to Jakarta and north to all parts of Sumatra.

There are buses to Palembang (from 22,500Rp, 10 hours) and Bengkulu (from 25,000Rp, 16 hours), but most people heading north go to Bukittinggi – a 22 hour haul that costs 45,000Rp for regular buses, up to 125,000Rp for the best air-con services.

The trip to Jakarta takes eight hours. Tickets range from 27,000Rp to 55,000Rp (air-con), and include the price of the ferry between Bakauheni and Merak.

Train This is one of the few places in Sumatra where it is possible to catch a train. Unfortunately, the train only goes to Palembang – a place most travellers avoid.

If you do want to go there, there are daily departures. The 8.30 am and 9 pm trains have bisnis (24,000Rp) and eksekutif (40,000Rp) class only and take eight hours. The 10.30 am train has ekonomi seats only (6000Rp) and takes 1½ hours longer.

The train station is at the end of Jl Kotaraja in the heart of Tanjungkarang. The ticket office is open from 7 am to 5 pm.

Taxi Share taxis shuttle between Bandarlampung and Bakauheni (6000Rp), Jakarta (50,000Rp) and Palembang (50,000Rp). Reputable companies include Taxi 4848 (☎ 255388), Jl Monginsidi 34, and Dynasty Taxi (☎ 485674), Jl KH Dahlan 53 and Rajabasa terminal.

Getting Around

To/From the Airport The airport is 22km north of town. Airport taxis charge 30,000Rp for the ride to/from town.

Public Transport There are frequent opelets between the city and Rajabasa bus terminal (500Rp). Taxis charge a standard 10,000Rp for the trip.

WAY KAMBAS NATIONAL PARK

This national park occupies 1300 sq km of coastal lowland forest around the Sungai Way Kambas on the east coast of Lampung, 110km from Bandarlampung.

The park is home to five pairs of rhinos, the occasional Sumatran tiger and – the main attraction – elephants.

Elephants

Way Kambas is home to about 350 Sumatran elephants *(Elephas maximus sumatrensis)*, a subspecies of the Asian elephant found only in Sumatra and Kalimantan. About 250 still live in the wild – but don't expect to see any of them. What you'll find is something much closer to a circus than a brush with nature: the Way Kambas elephant training centre.

The centre was set up to do something about the 'problem' of wild elephants that has been created by the clearing of elephant habitat for farming.

The elephants are rounded up and get to earn their living by performing useful tricks like playing soccer. Elephantine football is very popular with local tourists, many of whom seem overcome with emotion at the wonder of it all.

Given a day's notice, the tourist offices in Bandarlampung can organise elephant rides. It costs 25,000Rp for an hour's ride, which is quite long enough for the average behind.

Way Kanan

The Way Kanan 'resort', as the tourist blurb calls it, is little more than a small guesthouse and a few ramshackle huts in a jungle clearing on the banks of the Sungai Way Kanan, about 13km from the entrance to the national park.

An official guide is based at the camp during daylight hours. Guided activities include three-hour jungle treks and two-hour canoe trips on the Sungai Way Kanan and surrounding waterways.

Judging by the piles of evidence on the road, elephants visit Way Kanan from time to time. There's certainly more chance of seeing an elephant than a Sumatran tiger, sightings of which are extremely rare. What you will see – and hear – are lots of primates and birds.

There is very little virgin forest in the national park. The only parts the loggers left alone were the parts they couldn't get to. There are, however, a few big trees. They include some massive scaly-barked meranti trees with trunks rising as straight as an arrow for 30m before the first branches.

Organised Tours

Day trips to Way Kambas and Way Kanan are covered in Bandarlampung's Organised Tours entry earlier. Some tours also include a stop at Pugungraharjo archaeological site.

Places to Stay & Eat

There is a small *guesthouse* at the elephant training centre with basic doubles for 25,000Rp, and there are *food stalls* to cater for day-trippers. The stalls close after dark, so you'll need to bring food if you're staying the night. Conditions are even more basic at the *Way Kanan Guesthouse*, and 25,000Rp for a double is way over the top. You'll need to bring your own food, but cooking facilities and utensils are provided.

Otherwise, the nearest accommodation is the *Losmen Lindung* at Jepara, 10km south of the turn-off to Way Kambas, where singles/doubles cost 10,000/15,000Rp.

If you turn up late at the park entrance, the staff will normally let travellers bunk down somewhere.

Getting There & Away

The Putri Candi and Ratu Dewata companies run buses from Bandarlampung's Rajabasa bus terminal to Jepara (5000Rp, 2½ hours). They go past the entrance to Way Kambas, an arched gateway guarded by a stone elephant in the village of Rajabasalama, 10km north of Jepara. Alternatively, you can catch a bus to Metro (2000Rp, one hour) and then another to Rajabasalama (2500Rp, 1½ hours).

From the park entrance, it is easy to find someone to take you into the park by motorcycle. The going rates are 10,000Rp to Way Kambas and 15,000Rp to Way Kanan. You will need to negotiate a time to be picked up again.

KALIANDA
☎ 0727

Kalianda is a quiet little town 30km north of the ferry terminal at Bakauheni. It has a great setting overlooking Teluk Lampung, with Gunung Rajabasa as a backdrop. There are boats from nearby Canti to Krakatau and other islands in Teluk Lampung.

Things to See & Do

The main reason for stopping here is to visit **Krakatau**, but there are a couple of other things you can do while you organise that.

Gunung Rajabasa (1281m) is a **volcano climbing** opportunity, and there are **hot springs** on the tide line at Wartawan Beach, just beyond Canti. An opelet to the beach costs 1000Rp.

SUMATRA

There are scheduled boats from Canti to the nearby islands of **Sebuku** (2000Rp) and **Sebesi** (2500Rp), leaving at 11 am and 2 pm. It is reportedly possible to **camp** on both islands and there are bungalows on Sebesi, built by the owner of Hotel Beringin.

Organised Tours

Hotel Beringin organises a range of tours for small groups, including overnight trips to Krakatau, and Gunung Rajabasa climbs.

Places to Stay & Eat

Close to the centre of town, *Hotel Beringin (☎ 2008, Jl Kesuma Bangsa 75)* is an old Dutch villa with high ceilings and fans slowly stirring the air. Huge singles/doubles with mandi cost 11,000/16,500Rp; smaller rooms without mandi cost 6500Rp. The manager is very friendly and has lots of information about local attractions.

The upmarket option is the *Kalianda Hotel (☎ 2392)*, on the way into town from the highway. Air-con doubles start at 33,000Rp.

Just past the harbour at Canti, *Hotel Riung Gunung* has clean and comfortable units from 27,500Rp, and there's a great seawater swimming pool built into the coastline.

The *food stalls* that appear in Kalianda's town centre at night are the best places to eat. There's Padang food at the *Rumah Makan Palapa* on Jl Raya.

Getting There & Away

There are regular buses between Kalianda and Bandarlampung's Rajabasa bus terminal (2000Rp, 1½ hours). Most buses don't go right into Kalianda, but drop you off along the highway at the turn-off to Kalianda. From there, simply cross the road and wait for an opelet into town (500Rp). There are a few direct buses from the Bakauheni ferry terminal to Kalianda (3000Rp), but it's usually quicker to catch any north-bound bus from Bakauheni, get off at the Kalianda turn-off and catch an opelet into town for 1000Rp.

Getting Around

There are regular opelets from Kalianda to Canti (1000Rp) and along the road that

rings Gunung Rajabasa via Gayam and Pasuruan. Motorcycles can be rented from the Hotel Beringin (40,000Rp per day).

GUNUNG KRAKATAU

The movie moguls decided that Krakatau was East of Java. They should have opted for South of Sumatra. The Indonesian government considers Krakatau to be Sumatran, and Lampung promotes the volcano as its attraction. It's certainly cheaper and reportedly safer to get to Krakatau from Lampung than from Java.

For the story of Krakatau and details on the area, see the Krakatau section in the Java chapter.

Getting There & Away

Bandarlampung The Lampung provincial tourist office can arrange speedboat charter for up to six passengers (600,000Rp). The trip takes 1½ hours each way. Tour operators charge from US$60 per person (four or more people) to US$115 per person (two people) to take you by bus to Canti and then by boat to Krakatau. See Bandarlampung's Organised Tours section earlier in this chapter for more details.

Kalianda/Canti Hotel Beringin in Kalianda is a good place to meet up with other travellers wanting to see Krakatau. The hotel's tour costs 65,000Rp per person and includes visits to Sebuku and Sebesi islands, Pulau Anak and Krakatau itself. It includes transport, food and camping. The hotel can also organise independent charter boats, including an eight-seater (300,000Rp), a two person boat (130,000Rp), and a speedboat (260,000Rp). Boat charters from Canti (three hours each way) cost the same.

BAKAUHENI

Bakauheni is the major ferry terminal on Sumatra's southern tip, and the main transit point between Java and Sumatra. There are ferries between Bakauheni and Merak (Java) 24 hours a day, leaving frequently. See the introductory Getting There & Away section earlier in this chapter.

Nusa Tenggara

Nusa Tenggara (the name means 'South-East Islands') is quite different from the rest of Indonesia. As you travel east, the climate becomes drier, so people tend to raise corn, sago and taro rather than rice; the flora and fauna are more evocative of parts of Australia than of tropical Bali; the people are poorer than those elsewhere in Indonesia; and there is a great variety of cultures and religions.

Each island has its own peculiar sights, some of which rival anything seen in Java or Bali. The great stone-slab tombs and traditional villages of Sumba, the intricate *ikat* weaving of Sumba and Flores, the brilliantly coloured lakes of Kelimutu in Flores and the dragons of Pulau Komodo (Komodo Island) rate as some of the finest attractions in South-East Asia. The region also has good beaches and fine coral.

Although a steady stream of travellers passes through, until recently the lack of transport confined most of them to a limited route. There are now more opportunities for off-the-beaten-track explorations and the lack of tourists will mean that your reception is more natural. It does create one problem, though: you will constantly be the centre of attention. It's not unusual to attract an entourage of 50 children in a small village, all programmed to yell 'hello mister' until either they or you collapse from exhaustion. At the other extreme, in more isolated areas you will cause kids to scatter in all directions!

Living in one of the poorer and less developed regions of Indonesia, the people of Nusa Tenggara were ill-equipped to handle the monetary crisis which swept the country in the late 1990s. Yet despite galloping inflation, drought and poor yields, political uncertainty and other problems, Nusa Tenggarans remain remarkably stoic about their own hardships and incredibly hospitable to curious westerners. If you ever find yourself in need, stranded or without sustenance, it is likely that you'll be rescued by kind-hearted strangers willing to share what little they have.

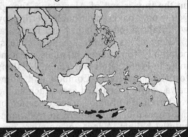

Nusa Tenggara is divided into three provinces: West Nusa Tenggara (comprising Lombok and Sumbawa), with its capital at Mataram in Lombok; and East Nusa Tenggara (comprising Flores, Sumba, Timor and a number of small islands), with the capital at Kupang in Timor.

Only about 4% of the Indonesian population live in Nusa Tenggara, but there are so many different languages and cultures that it's impossible to think of these people as one group. There are several languages

NUSA TENGGARA

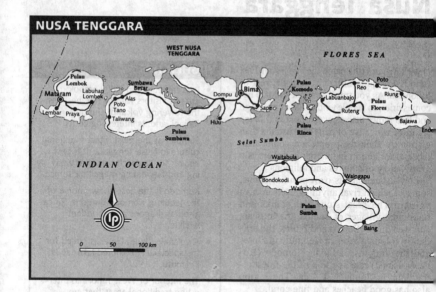

NUSA TENGGARA

on the tiny island of Alor alone, though you won't have any trouble getting by with Bahasa Indonesia in Nusa Tenggara.

Many of its people are now at least nominally Christian; Christians predominate in Flores, Roti and Timor. Muslims form a majority in Lombok and Sumbawa, while in isolated areas such as the western half of Sumba, a large section of the population still adhere to traditional animist beliefs. A layer of animism persists alongside Christianity in other areas, with customs, rituals and festivals from this older tradition still very much a part of life.

Even the wildlife of Nusa Tenggara is different from that of western Indonesia. Nusa Tenggara is definitely a transition zone between Asian and Australian flora and fauna. A 300m deep channel (one of the deepest in the archipelago) runs between Bali and Lombok, and extends north between Kalimantan and Sulawesi. The channel marks the Wallace Line – see the special colour section 'The Wallace Line' in the Kalimantan chapter.

GETTING THERE & AROUND

Transport in Nusa Tenggara has improved immensely in the past decade, with more surfaced roads, and more regular ferries and buses. Travel can still be arduous, but on the whole, if you stick to the main routes, you shouldn't have much trouble. Most people who travel right through Nusa Tenggara by surface transport are quite happy not to repeat the experience and unless travelling to/from Australia fly back to their starting point.

Air

Merpati Nusantara Airlines flies between Darwin (Australia) and Kupang, and Kupang is an international gateway (no visa is required for most western nationalities).

Soaring costs have played havoc with Merpati's more marginal routes. Cancellations are common, even on flights to the main hubs of Kupang, Maumere (Flores) and Mataram (Lombok). For other airports, the less used and less profitable the run, the greater the chance of a cancellation, often blamed on 'technical problems'.

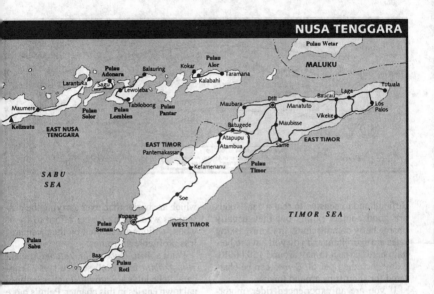

NUSA TENGGARA

Nusa Tenggara is not well connected to the other island groups. Most flights to/from Nusa Tenggara are via Bali. Direct flights from Ujung Pandang (Sulawesi) to Maumere have stopped, but may resume as the economy improves. There are no direct flights from Nusa Tenggara to Maluku and Irian Jaya.

It's wise to book early and reservations are essential in the peak August tourist season. The most popular routes are Mataram-Bima-Labuanbajo and Maumere-Denpasar. Overbooking sometimes occurs, so make sure your booking is confirmed when you buy your ticket and always reconfirm. On the other hand, if you've been told a flight is full, it can sometimes be worth going to the airport before the flight leaves. Many Merpati offices don't have computers, so no-show seats are not re-offered.

Bus

Though the roads have improved enormously, bus travel is still uncomfortable. Air-con express coaches run right across Lombok and Sumbawa, but elsewhere small, hot buses with limited leg room are crammed with passengers and all manner of produce. They constantly stop to drop off and pick up passengers and, if buses are not full, they will endlessly loop around town searching for passengers until they are full. Even if the road is paved, it is usually narrow and winding, and there are always sections under repair that will rattle your fillings. Don't underestimate journey times – a trip of only 100km may take three hours or more – and don't overestimate your endurance abilities.

Most buses leave in the morning around 7 or 8 am, so be prepared for early starts. Where buses leave later in the day, they are limited and less patronised so they often spend longer looking for passengers. Some night buses, leaving around 5 pm, are available between major towns, but you miss out on the scenery. Long-distance buses usually meet the main ferries if you want to travel straight on to other destinations.

Car & Motorcycle

Self-drive cars can be found at reasonable rates in Lombok. Elsewhere it is much more

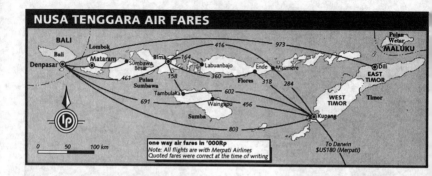

NUSA TENGGARA AIR FARES

one way air fares in '000Rp
Note: All flights are with Merpati Airlines
Quoted fares were correct at the time of writing

To Darwin
$US180 (Merpati)

difficult and expensive to rent a car. Hotels are good contact points but they usually charge hefty commissions. In Flores, asking rates are exorbitant and you will have to bargain hard. Expect to pay around 150,000Rp a day, including petrol. *Bemos* can be chartered for short trips around towns.

If you are an experienced rider, motorcycling is great way to see Nusa Tenggara, and you can transport your bike on ferries between most of the islands. It's best to bring your own machine. It's possible to find short-term hires in a few large towns, but it's difficult to convince anyone to let you take their bikes to other islands. Traffic is relatively light, even on the main highways, but the usual hazards of villages crowded with pedestrians, chickens and goats apply.

Bicycle

Bicycles can be rented around the main centres of Lombok, but they are not a popular form of transport anywhere in Nusa Tenggara. Long-distance cycling is a possibility on the undulating terrain of Sumba and Sumbawa. Cycling on hilly Flores or Timor requires legs of iron and a well geared mountain bike; however, the quiet roads and spectacular scenery compensate for the steep inclines. Lombok, with its light traffic, is good for cycling.

Boat

The economic problems that beset the airlines have proved a boon for the ferries,

which are busier than ever carrying the passengers who can no longer afford to fly or whose options are limited by the closure of less profitable air routes.

Pelni's *Awu*, *Dobonsolo*, *Tatamailau* and *Tilongkabila* ferries all service Nusa Tenggara. Schedules are provided under individual town entries in this chapter. Pelni's more basic Perintis cargo ships, and freighters, cover many routes and are an option if you get stuck. Ask at the office of the harbour master *(syahbandar)* or at the shipping offices. Conditions are primitive, but you can often negotiate to rent a cabin.

Most of the islands are connected by ferries, which are regular, if rarely comfortable. There are several trips daily between Bali and Lombok, and Lombok and Sumbawa. Between Sumbawa and Flores one ferry goes daily (except Friday), usually stopping at Pulau Komodo along the way. Ferries go twice a week between Timor and Larantuka in Flores, and three times a week between Timor and Alor and between Timor and Sabu. A ferry connects Kupang with Ende (Flores), Waingapu (Sumba) and Sabu. All of these ferries take cars as well as passengers and, in addition, there are smaller boats from Flores to the islands of Adonara, Solor and Lembata, from Kupang to Roti and a few other possibilities. Details are provided in the relevant sections of this chapter.

For shorter hops, chartering sailing boats or small motorboats is often an option. A popular way of travelling between Flores and Lombok is on a five day boat tour out of Labuanbajo, stopping at Komodo and other islands along the way. Some Bugis schooners find their way right down into Nusa Tenggara, for those who want a really different way of getting to Sulawesi.

Lombok

Lombok has both the lushness of Bali and the starkness of outback Australia. Parts of the island drip with water, while pockets are chronically dry and droughts can last for months, causing crop failure and famine, but recent improvements in agriculture and water management have made life in Lombok less precarious.

The indigenous Sasak people make up about 90% of the population. They follow the Islamic religion, but have a culture and language unique to Lombok. There is also a significant minority who have a Balinese culture, language and religion – a legacy of the time when Bali controlled Lombok. Balinese-style processions and ceremonies are conducted, and there are several Balinese Hindu temples.

History

Islam may have been brought to the island from Java, but there's no firm evidence that Java controlled the island. Not much is known about Lombok before the 17th century, at which time it was split into numerous, frequently squabbling petty states, each presided over by a Sasak 'prince' – a disunity which the neighbouring Balinese exploited.

Balinese Rule In the early 17th century, the Balinese state of Karangasem took control of western Lombok. At the same time, Sumbawans (effectively vassals of the Makassarese) crossed the straits from their colonies in Sumbawa and established settlements in eastern Lombok. The war of 1677-78 saw the Makassarese ejected off the island and eastern Lombok temporarily reverted to the rule of the Sasak princes. Balinese control was soon reasserted, and by 1750 the whole island was in Balinese hands. Squabbles over royal succession soon had the Balinese fighting among themselves and Lombok split into four separate kingdoms. By 1838 the Mataram kingdom had subdued the other three kingdoms, which included reconquering eastern Lombok. Mataram forces then crossed to Bali via the Lombok Strait and overran Karangasem, reuniting Karangasem and Lombok.

In western Lombok, where Balinese rule dated from the early 17th century, the relations between the Balinese and the Sasaks were relatively harmonious. The traditional Sasak village government had been replaced with the direct rule of the *rajah* (king), or by a landowning Balinese aristocrat. The Sasak peasants assimilated Balinese Hinduism and participated in Balinese religious festivities. Intermarriage between Balinese and Sasaks was common, and Sasaks were organised in the same irrigation associations *(subak)* that the Balinese used for wet-rice agriculture.

Things were very different in eastern Lombok, where the Balinese maintained control from garrisoned forts. Although the traditional Sasak village government remained intact, the village chief became little more than a tax collector for the local Balinese *punggawa* (district head). Villagers were reduced to the level of 'serfs' and the aristocracy had its power and landholdings slashed. The hostility the Sasaks felt towards the Balinese enabled the eastern Lombok aristocracy to lead several peasant rebellions.

There were further revolts in 1855 and 1871, which the Balinese also suppressed.

Dutch Involvement During an uprising in 1891, the Sasak chiefs sent envoys to the Dutch officials in Bali, asking for help and inviting the Dutch to rule Lombok. The Dutch were initially reluctant to take military action, but their resolve strengthened when van der Wijck became governor general of the Dutch East Indies in 1892. He made a treaty with the rebels in eastern Lombok in June 1894. With the pretext of

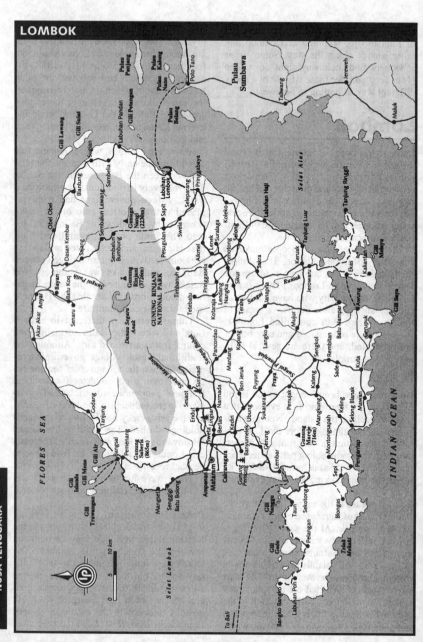

LOMBOK

freeing the Sasaks from tyrannical Balinese rule, he sent a large army to Lombok. The Balinese rajah in Lombok capitulated to the Dutch demands, but the younger Balinese princes overruled him and attacked and routed the Dutch.

It was a short-lived victory; the Dutch army dug in at Ampenan, and in September 1894 reinforcements began arriving from Java. The Dutch counter-attack began: Mataram was overrun and the Balinese stronghold of Cakranegara was bombarded with artillery. Finally, the rajah surrendered and a large group of Balinese, including members of the aristocracy and the royal family, marched into the Dutch guns and were killed in a traditional *puputan* (ritualised fight to the death).

Dutch Rule By maintaining the support of the remaining Balinese and the Sasak aristocracy, the Dutch were able to maintain their hold on more than 500,000 people, using a police force that never numbered more than 250. Although there were several village uprisings, they were localised and short-lived, and lacked the leadership of the Sasak aristocracy. Most villagers lived in fear of being evicted from their land.

Despite the privations of the period, the Dutch are well remembered in Lombok as liberators from Balinese domination.

During Dutch rule, from the early 20th century to full independence in 1949, villagers were forced to sell more and more of their rice crops to pay the taxes imposed by the Dutch. The amount of rice available for consumption declined and famines ravaged the island from 1938 to 1940, and in 1949.

Post-Colonial Lombok Even after Indonesia attained its independence from the Dutch, Lombok continued to be dominated by its Balinese and Sasak aristocracy. In 1958 Lombok became part of the new province of Nusa Tenggara Barat (West), and Mataram became its administrative capital. Following the attempted coup in Jakarta in 1965 (see the History section in the Facts About Indonesia chapter), Lombok (like other places in Indonesia) experienced mass killings of communists and ethnic Chinese. Details of the mass killings in Lombok are still obscure.

Lombok Under Soeharto Under former president Soeharto's 'New Order', there was stability and some growth, but nothing like the booming wealth and development of Java or Bali. Crop failures led to famine in 1966, and to severe food shortages in 1973. People moved away from Lombok under the *transmigrasi* program (for more information see the Population & People section in the Facts about Indonesia chapter). There are, however, several foreign aid agencies that continue to try to improve water supply, agricultural output and health.

Geography

Lombok is a small island, just 80km from east to west and about the same distance from north to south. Gunung Rinjani (Mt Rinjani) dominates the northern part of the island, and streams on the volcano's southern flank water the rich plains of central Lombok. The far south and east is drier, with scrubby, barren hills. The majority of the population live on the central plain and in the wetter, more fertile western coastal areas.

Economy

The rice grown in Lombok is noted for its excellent quality, but due to the drier climate, the productivity is not as high as in Java or Bali. There are also small and large plantations of coconut palms, coffee, kapok and cotton; new crops such as cloves, vanilla, pineapple and pepper have been introduced, but tobacco is probably the biggest cash crop. Quarrying of pumice stone has also been a good earner in recent years.

Tourism Tourist development only started around 1980, when Lombok became 'Indonesia's best kept secret' and 'an undeveloped, unruined alternative to Bali'. A few lessons about the effects of unrestrained development in the tourist centres in Bali have been learnt and put into practice in Lombok, but tourism still has a dramatic effect on the local environment and community: in Seng-gigi, Kuta and the Gili Islands, large stretches of coastline have been commandeered for luxury resorts, but often for speculative purposes so hotels are rarely built; sewerage and rubbish is often not disposed of properly; boats and scuba divers around the Gilis often damage fragile coral reefs; top-end hotels create chronic water shortages, especially in the dry area around Kuta; and there is often conflict between conservative Islamic and western values caused by foreigners who drink alcohol and don't dress 'properly'.

Population & People

The latest Census figures show Lombok has a population of 2.4 million, the majority living in and around the main centres of Mataram, Praya and Selong. Almost 90% of the people are Sasak, about 10% are Balinese, and there are minority populations of Chinese, Javanese and Arabs. Some Sumbawanese live in the east of the island, and Buginese along the coast.

Sasaks Physically and culturally, the Sasaks have much in common with the Javanese, the Balinese and the Sumbawanese. Basically hill people, the Sasaks are now spread over central and eastern Lombok, and are generally much poorer than the Balinese minority. Most Sasaks are nominally Muslims, but many retain elements of the ancient animist beliefs (see Religion in the Facts about Indonesia chapter for further information).

Chinese Most of Lombok's Chinese live in Ampenan or Cakranegara. The Chinese first came to Lombok with the Dutch, as a cheap labour force. They were later fostered as economic intermediaries between the Dutch and the Indonesian population and were allowed to set up their own businesses. When the Dutch were ousted in 1949, the Chinese stayed and continued to expand their business interests.

The economic success of the Chinese did not necessarily make them popular. In the aftermath of the 1965 purge, many of Lombok's Chinese were murdered en masse along with the thousands that were killed throughout the country. Racism and economic jealousy resurfaced in early 1998, and the Chinese bore the brunt of several protests in Mataram.

Arts

Lombok has an indigenous music style and a number of traditional dances, but they are mainly performed in the context of seasonal or life-cycle ceremonies, and have not been developed as tourist attractions.

Dance The popular Cupak Gerantang tells the story of Panji, a romantic hero. The dance, which is usually performed at celebrations and festivals, probably originated in Java in the 15th century. The Kayak Sando, another version of the Panji story, in which the dancers wear masks, is found only in central and eastern Lombok.

The Gandrung is about love and courtship – *gandrung* means being in love, or longing. It's a social dance, usually performed by the young men and women of the village. Everyone stands around in a circle and then, accompanied by a full *gamelan* (orchestra), a young girl dances by herself for a time before choosing a male partner from the audience to join her. It's performed in Narmada, Lenek and Praya.

The Oncer is a war dance performed vigorously by men and young boys in central and eastern Lombok. Participants play a variety of musical instruments in time to their movements, and wear severe black costumes with crimson and gold waistbands, shoulder sashes, socks and caps.

The Rudat, with a combination of Islamic and Sasak influences, is performed by pairs of men dressed in black caps and jackets and black-and-white checked sarongs. They're backed by singers, tambourines and cylindrical drums called *jidur*.

Music The Tandak Gerok is an eastern Lombok performance which combines dance, theatre and singing to music played on bamboo flutes and on the bowed lute called a *rebab*. A unique feature of the Tandak Gerok is that the vocalists imitate the sound of the gamelan instruments. It's usually performed after harvesting or other hard physical labour, but is also staged at traditional ceremonies.

The Genggong involves seven musicians using a simple set of instruments, including a bamboo flute, a rebab and knockers; they accompany their music with dance movements and stylised hand gestures.

Handicrafts There's little of the purely decorative art so common in Bali, but traditional Lombok handicrafts are sought after by collectors and tourists. They are mainly objects of everyday use, like baskets, pottery and textiles, made with great skill using traditional technology (eg hand and foot operated looms, and old kilns) and natural, local materials (eg bamboo, grass and clay).

Villages specialise in certain crafts and it's interesting to travel to a number of them, seeing hand weaving in one village, basketware in another and pottery in a third.

Society & Conduct
Traditional Culture *Adat* (traditional law) is still fundamental to the way of life in Lombok today, particularly customs relating to birth, circumcision, courtship and marriage.

JENNY BOWMAN
Penujak village is well known for its traditional *gerabah* pottery made from a local clay.

Sasaks show a fascination with heroic trials of strength, physical prowess and one-on-one contests. Peresehan is a fight between two men using long rattan staves and small rectangular shields. Lanca, originally from Sumbawa, is another trial of strength, this time between men who use their knees to strike each other.

Avoiding Offence Most of Lombok is conservative, and immodest dress and public displays of affection between couples can cause offence. Both men and women should cover their knees, upper arms and shoulders – brief shorts and tank tops should not be worn away from Senggigi and the Gilis (even Kuta is conservative). Nude or topless bathing anywhere is also very offensive.

Many people in Lombok fast during Ramadan. During this time, it is insensitive and offensive for foreign visitors to eat, drink or smoke in public during the day. For more information see Public Holidays and Special Events in the Facts for the Visitor chapter.

Islamic law forbids drinking alcohol and, although booze is widely available in Lombok, public drunkenness is frowned upon. It's particularly offensive to drink alcohol near a mosque.

Religion
Islam and Balinese Hinduism are the two main religions in Lombok, but there are also Wektu Telu adherents and small numbers of Christians and Buddhists. For further information see Religion in the Facts about Indonesia chapter.

Wektu Telu Wektu Telu is an indigenous religion, which is unique to Lombok and thought to have originated in the northern village of Bayan. The number of adherents is officially quite small (less than 30,000), although this may be understated, as it is not one of Indonesia's officially recognised religions.

In the Sasak language, *wektu* means 'result' and *telu* means 'three'. The name probably denotes the complex mixture of Hindu, Islamic and animist influences that make

NUSA TENGGARA

up this religion; and the concept of a trinity is embodied in many Wektu Telu beliefs, for example the sun, moon and stars (representing heaven, earth and water) and the head, body and limbs (representing creativity, sensitivity and control).

The Wektu Telu observe only three days of fasting during Ramadan. They do not pray five times a day as laid down by Islamic law, they do not build mosques and they have no objection to eating pork. Their dead are buried with their heads facing Mecca, but Wektu Telu do not make pilgrimages there. In fact, the only fundamental tenets of Islam to which the Wektu Telu seem to hold firmly are the belief in Allah, and that Muhammed is Allah's prophet. They regard themselves as Muslims, but are not accepted as such by orthodox Muslims and relations between the two groups have not always been good. The number of Wektu Telu has been declining as more young people adhere to orthodox Islam.

Religious Festivals Most of the Wektu Telu religious festivals take place at the beginning of the rainy season (from October to December), or at harvest time (April to May), with celebrations in villages all over the island. Many of these ceremonies and rituals are annual events but, as they do not fall on specific days, getting to see one is a matter of luck and word of mouth.

Lombok's Muslims celebrate the various events in the Islamic calendar (see Public Holidays and Special Events in the Facts for the Visitor chapter), especially the end of Ramadan.

Post & Communications

The main post office on Jalan (Jl) Sriwijaya in Mataram is the only one with a poste restante service.

There is a Home Country Direct Dial telephone inside the waiting room at the airport. Most of Lombok has the 0370 telephone area code, but much of east Lombok, including Tetebatu, has the 0376 code. There are Internet centres in Senggigi, and on Gili Air (see the Senggigi section later for details).

Activities

Trekking Gunung Rinjani (3726m) and its surroundings are a superb area for trekking. Other shorter hikes include the villages of central Lombok; waterfalls around Tetebatu; villages around Mataram; and the remote coastline east and west of Kuta.

Diving The diving and snorkelling off the Gili Islands is great, but less exciting near Senggigi. A few dive centres are located on the Gilis and in Senggigi. In the current economic climate, large discounts are often possible, so diving is usually cheaper than in Bali.

Surfing The southern and eastern coasts get the same swells that generate the big breaks on Bali's Bukit Peninsula. The most accessible surfing beach is Kuta; other south-coast places that you can get to by land, with a little difficulty, include Selong Blanak, Mawan and Ekas.

Organised Tours

Organised tours provide a quick introduction to the highlights of the island. Tours are normally half-day trips around Mataram, or full-day trips to Kuta and the south coast; the central craft villages; or the Gili Islands and north coast. Prices start from about 25,000/40,000Rp per person for a half-day/full-day tour. You can arrange a tour with any travel agency in Senggigi or Mataram, or ask the West Lombok tourist office in Mataram for some suggestions.

Many companies organise tours around Lombok from Bali. They normally use the speedy *Mabua Express*, and then tear through Senggigi, Kuta and several handicraft villages in central Lombok by bus. From Bali, day trips cost about US$75 per person, and can be booked at any travel agent in Bali.

Boat trips from Lombok to the islands further east are widely promoted. The main destination is Pulau Komodo, near Flores, to see the giant Komodo dragons (lizards), but boats also stop at other islands for snorkelling, trekking and beach parties. Some of these trips are pretty rough, with minimal safety provisions. Perama, is usually reliable, although its trips get mixed reviews from readers.

Getting There & Away

Air Merpati is now the only domestic airline flying to/from Lombok. Currently, there are 10 flights a day from Denpasar to Mataram, and return, for 85,000Rp. From Mataram, Merpati also has direct flights daily to Sumbawa Besar (107,000Rp) and Bima (202,900Rp) in Nusa Tenggara, and Surabaya (190,400Rp) in Java. The Singapore Airlines subsidiary, Silk Air, has direct flights from Singapore five times a week for US$220/321 (one way/return), but given the economic situation at the time of writing this flight may be cancelled in the future.

Airline Offices The offices for the airlines currently represented in Lombok are:

Bouraq
   (☎ 27333) Hotel Selaparang, Mataram
Garuda Indonesia
   (☎ 32305) Hotel Lombok Raya, Mataram
Merpati
   Main office: (☎ 36745) Jl Selaparang, Mataram
   Agency: (☎ 33844) Jl Selaparang, Mataram
Silk Air
   (☎ 93877) Jl Raya Senggigi, Senggigi

Public Bus Many public buses travel daily between Mandalika terminal in Bertais (Mataram) and the major cities in Sumbawa, Java and Bali. For long-distances, book your ticket one or two days ahead at the terminal, or from a travel agency along Jl Pejanggik/Selaparang in Mataram. If you get to the terminal before 8 am, there may be a spare seat on a bus going in your direction, but this is risky during any major public holiday.

Some sample fares are: Bima (16,100/27,500Rp economy/luxury class, 12 hours); Denpasar (20,000Rp luxury, six hours); Jakarta (90,000Rp luxury, two nights); Ruteng (60,000Rp economy, 20 hours); Sumbawa Besar (8950/15,000Rp, five hours); Surabaya (40,000Rp luxury, 20 hours); and Yogyakarta (70,000Rp luxury, 30 hours).

Tourist Shuttle Bus/Boat The Bali-based company Perama has tourist shuttle bus/boat services between the main tourist centres in Lombok (ie Senggigi, the Gili Islands and Kuta) and most tourist centres in Bali (eg Ubud, Sanur and the Kuta region). A few other companies offer similar services at similar prices. Tickets can be booked directly, or at any travel agency in Lombok or Bali, and include boat or ferry charges.

Boat Many travellers come to Lombok by ferry from Sumbawa or Bali, or by Pelni liner from elsewhere in Indonesia.

Bali Ferries travel between Padangbai (Bali) and Lembar (Lombok) every 60 to 90 minutes, 24 hours, daily. VIP (1st) class costs 9000/5000Rp for adults/children; *ekonomi* (2nd) class costs 5500/2900Rp. Bicycles cost an extra 700Rp; motorbikes, 6200Rp; and cars and jeeps, 35,700Rp. The trip takes at least four hours, sometimes up to seven.

The luxury jet-powered *Mabua Express* (☎ 81225, Bali ☎ 0361-721212) travels daily in both directions between the Pelni port at Lembar and Pelabuhan Benoa (Bali). The fare is US$25/17.50 for 'diamond/emerald' (1st/2nd) class, but at the time of writing this was dearer than flying between Bali and Lombok, so prices were slashed to 80,000Rp, for one class only. You can book directly, or at travel agencies in Lombok or Bali.

Sumbawa Ferries travel between Labuhan Lombok (Lombok) and Poto Tano (Sumbawa) every 45 to 60 minutes, 24 hours, daily. Ekonomi A (1st) class costs 3650/2000Rp for adults/children; ekonomi B (2nd) class costs 2350/1550Rp. Motorbikes cost an extra 6050Rp, and cars, 36,900Rp. If you're coming from Sumbawa, start early so you can reach Labuhan Lombok by 4 pm because public transport is limited after this time.

Other Islands Every two weeks the Pelni liners, *Awu* and *Tilongkabila*, link Lembar with other islands of Nusa Tenggara, and with Kalimantan and Sulawesi. Tickets can be bought at the Pelni office (☎ 37212) in

Mataram Monday to Thursday and Saturday from 8.30 am to noon, and 1 to 3 pm, and until 11 am on Friday.

Getting Around
There is a good road across the middle of the island, between Mataram and Labuhan Lombok, and fairly good roads in most other populated areas. Public transport is generally restricted to the main routes; away from these, you have to hire a *cidomo* (pony cart), charter an *ojek* (pay to be a pillion passenger on a motorcycle) or walk. During the wet season, remote roads are often flooded or washed away, and others become impassable because of fallen rocks and rubble – and often the damage may not be repaired until the dry season.

Bus & Bemo The main terminal, Mandalika, is at Bertais, 6km south-east of central Mataram; other regional terminals are in Praya, Anyar and Pancor (near Selong). You may have to go via one or more of these terminals to get from one part of Lombok to another. For main routes, fares are fixed by the provincial government, and a list should be displayed at the terminals. The bus and bemo drivers may still try to overcharge. Most public transport becomes scarce in the afternoon and normally ceases after dark, often earlier in more remote areas.

Chartering a bemo by the day can be convenient and reasonably cheap – about 80,000Rp per day (including petrol), depending on distance. Some bemos are restricted to certain routes or areas. For example, the yellow bemos that shuttle around Mataram cannot be chartered for a trip to Lembar.

Tourist Shuttle Bus Shuttle buses link the main tourist centres in Lombok. Currently, this service only links Mataram with Kuta, Senggigi, Bangsal and Tetebatu – so you cannot travel from, say, Kuta to Bangsal, without changing shuttle buses first in Mataram, but you can normally connect on the same day. From Senggigi, there are also shuttle boats to the Gili Islands (see the Gili

Islands section later in this chapter). Perama is the most established operator, with the widest network.

Car & Motorcycle Hotels in Mataram and Senggigi can often arrange car or motorbike rental, and there are a few 'official' car rental companies with a wider range of vehicles, but these tend to be more expensive. A small vehicle such as a Suzuki Jimny costs about 60,000Rp per day, and Toyota Kijangs cost about 90,000Rp – plus petrol and insurance. If you rent for a few days, you should get a discount.

You can rent motorbikes in Mataram and Senggigi for around 17,500Rp per day, all inclusive. If your International Driving Permit is not endorsed for motorbikes, the police in Lombok don't seem to mind – no-one has a definite policy on the matter. It's best to ask the rental agency/owner about the current requirements. If you get a motorbike licence in Bali, it's also valid for Lombok.

Bringing a Vehicle from Bali A reputable rental agency in Bali should allow you to take a car or motorbike to Lombok for up to one week. As cars in Bali are only registered for driving around that island, you will need a special permit (25,000Rp) from the police in Denpasar – the rental agency can arrange this easily. No special permit is required to take a rented motorbike from Bali to Lombok.

Bicycle Bicycles can be rented at most of the tourist centres, although they're not always in good condition. With its limited traffic, Lombok is ideal for bicycle touring. Two interesting routes are: Mataram to Banyumulek, via Gunung Pengsong and return; and along the coastal road from Mataram to Pemenang, via Senggigi – and if you feel energetic, return via the steep road through Pusuk Pass.

MATARAM
The capital, and main city in Lombok, is Mataram, although it's actually a conglomeration of four separate towns – Ampenan (the port); Mataram (administrative centre); Cakranegara (business centre), which is

often shortened to Cakra; and Bertais (where the main bus terminal is located). Some travellers use Mataram as a base to organise trips elsewhere around the island, but most head straight to Senggigi or the Gili Islands.

Orientation

The four towns are spread along one main road that starts as Jl Pabean in Ampenan, quickly becomes Jl Yos Sudarso, then changes to Jl Langko, Jl Pejanggik and travels through Sweta to Bertais as Jl Selaparang. It's a one way street all the way, running west to east. A parallel one way road, Jl Tumpang Sari-Panca Usaha-Pancawarga-Pendidikan, brings traffic back towards the coast.

Information

Tourist Offices The tourist office (☎ 21 658) responsible for West Nusa Tenggara province, which includes Lombok, is on Jl Suprato, just north of the museum. It is overflowing with helpful staff, but is only worth visiting if you need some information and maps about Sumbawa.

The tourist office (☎ 31730), Jl Langko, for West Lombok, ie Mataram and Senggigi, actually serves as an unofficial tourist office for all of Lombok. The staff are friendly and well informed, and it's worth visiting to check the latest airline and Pelni schedules, and to book organised tours.

Money There are a number of banks along the main road in Cakra. Most will change money and travellers cheques, although it may take some time (about an hour). There are also moneychangers in Ampenan and in Mataram's Cilinaya shopping centre, which are efficient, open for longer hours and have slightly better rates than the banks – but the rates in Senggigi will generally be better. You can also change money at the airport.

Post & Communications The main post office on Jl Sriwijaya is inconvenient, but it does have the only poste restante service in Lombok. A more convenient post office is located opposite the West Lombok tourist office.

The Telkom office, Jl Langko, in Ampenan has telegram and fax services, and is open 24 hours. There are other *wartels* (public telephone offices) around town, and a Home Country Direct Dial telephone in the waiting room of the airport.

Emergency The two best hospitals in Lombok are: the Rumah Sakit Umum Mataram (☎ 21345), Jl Pejanggik, which has English-speaking doctors; and the Catholic Hospital (☎ 21397) at Jl Pabean, in Ampenan.

The main police station (☎ 110), where you may have to go for a local motorbike licence (if you haven't got one from Bali), is on Jl Langko.

Museum Negeri Nusa Tenggara Barat

This modern museum has exhibits on the geology, history and culture of Lombok and Sumbawa. If you intend buying any antiques or handicrafts have a look at the kris (traditional daggers), *songket* (silver or gold-threaded cloth), basketware and masks for comparison. It's open Tuesday to Thursday and on weekends from 8 am to 2 pm, until 11 am on Friday and is closed on Monday. Tickets cost 2500Rp.

Mayura Water Palace

This palace was built in 1744, and was once part of the Balinese kingdom's royal court in Lombok. Its main feature is a large artificial lake, with a *bale kambang* (floating pavilion) in the centre, connected to the shoreline by a raised footpath. This pavilion was used as both a court of justice and a meeting place for the Hindu lords. There are other shrines and fountains in the surrounding park.

The entrance to the walled enclosure of the palace is on the western side (tickets cost 500Rp). It's a pleasant retreat, but in 1894 the palace was the site of bloody battles as Dutch and Balinese forces fought for the control of Lombok.

Pura Meru

Pura Meru is the largest temple in Lombok. It was built in 1720 under the patronage of

NUSA TENGGARA

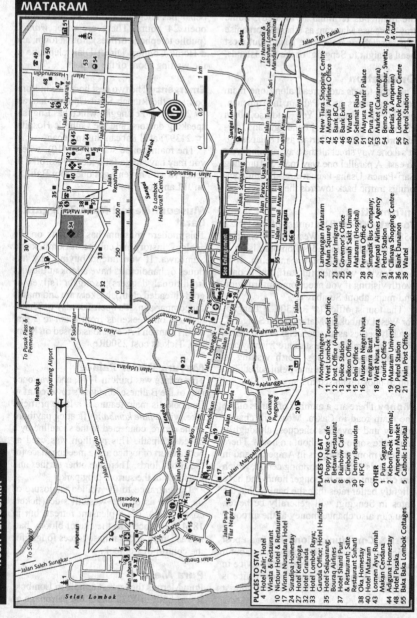

MATARAM

1 km
0.5
0

500 m
250
0

To Pusuk Pass &
Pemenang

To Senggigi

To Narmada &
Labuhan Lombok
Mandalika Terminal

To Praya
& Kuda

To Lombok
Handicraft Centre

Selaparang Airport

Rembiga

Ampenan

Selat Lombok

NUSA TENGGARA

PLACES TO STAY
4   Hotel Zahir; Hotel
    Wisata & Restaurant
10 Nitour Hotel & Restaurant
17 Wisma Nusantara Hotel
24 Suradipa Homestay
27 Hotel Kertajoga
32 Hotel Granada
33 Hotel Lombok Raya;
    Garuda Office; Hotel Handika
35 Hotel Selaparang;
    Bourag Airlines
37 Hotel Shanti Puri
    & Restaurant; Sate
    Restaurant Suharti
38 Oka Homestay
40 Hotel Mataram
43 Losmen Ayu; Rumah
    Makan Cendana
44 Adiguna Homestay
48 Hotel Pusaka
55 Baka Baka Lombok Cottages

PLACES TO EAT
3   Poppy Nice Cafe
6   Betawi Restaurant
8   Rainbow Cafe
9   Cirebon
30 Denny Bersaudra
47 KFC

OTHER
1   Pura Segara
2   Kebon Roek Terminal;
    Ampenan Market
5   Catholic Hospital
7   Moneychangers
11 West Lombok Tourist Office
12 Post Office (Ampenan)
13 Police Station
14 Telkom Office
15 Pelni Office
16 Museum Negeri Nusa
    Tenggara Barat
18 West Nusa Tenggara
    Tourist Office
19 Mataram University
20 Petrol Station
21 Main Post Office
22 Lapangan Mataram
    (Main Square)
23 Kantor Imigrasi
25 Governor's Office
26 Rumah Sakit Umum
    Mataram (Hospital)
28 Perama Office
29 Simpatik Bus Company;
    Merpati Airlines Agency
31 Petrol Station
34 Cilinaya Shopping Centre
36 Bank Danamon
39 Wartel
41 New Tiara Shopping Centre
42 Merpati Airlines Office
45 Bank BCA
46 Bank Exim
49 Wartel
50 Selamat Riady
51 Mayura Water Palace
52 Pura Meru
53 Market (Cakranegara)
54 Bemo Stop (Lembar, Sweta;
    Bertais & Ampenan)
56 Lombok Pottery Centre
57 Petrol Station

the Balinese prince Anak Agung Made Karang of the Singosari kingdom as an attempt to unite all the small kingdoms in Lombok, and as a symbol of the universe, dedicated to the Hindu trinity of Brahma, Vishnu and Shiva.

The outer courtyard has a hall housing the wooden drums that are beaten to call believers to festivals and special ceremonies. In the middle courtyard are two buildings with large raised platforms for offerings. The inner court has one large and 33 small shrines, as well as three *meru* (multi-roofed shrines), which are in a line: the central meru, with 11 tiers, is Shiva's house; the meru to the north, with nine tiers, is Vishnu's; and the seven tiered meru to the south is Brahma's. The meru are also said to represent the three great mountains, Rinjani, Agung and Bromo.

The temple is open daily, and a donation is expected (about 500Rp) for the caretaker, who will lend you a sash, and sarong if you need one. (If you are wearing shorts, you'll need to wear a sash or sarong when entering a Hindu temple.) A major festival is held here every June – ask either tourist office in Mataram for details.

Places to Stay – Budget

Although some budget places in Ampenan and Mataram are cheap and popular, Cakranegara is the most central, convenient and pleasant place to base yourself.

Cakranegara The quaint and popular *Oka Homestay* (☎ 22406, Jl Repatmaja) has a quiet garden, and singles/doubles for 12,500/15,000Rp. *Adiguna Homestay* (☎ 25946, Jl Nursiwan 9) is another good place, with rooms from 12,500/15,000Rp. The popular *Losmen Ayu* (☎ 21761, Jl Nursiwan 20) is well set up for budget travellers. It offers comfortable rooms for 12,500/15,000Rp, and a range of better, cleaner and newer rooms over the road for 20,000/25,000Rp; rooms with air-con cost more. It has a kitchen that guests can use. *Hotel Shanti Puri* (☎ 32649, Jl Maktal) has rooms for 20,000/25,000Rp; more expensive rooms with air-con and hot water cost 45,000/50,000Rp.

It's on a quiet street and is a good place to meet other travellers.

Ampenan The unassuming *Hotel Zahir* (☎ 34248, Jl Koperasi 9) has singles/doubles and triples, with a small verandah facing a central courtyard, for 8000/10,000/15,000Rp. The staff are friendly and helpful, and can arrange cheap motorbike rental. *Hotel Wisata* (☎ 26971, Jl Koperasi 19) has a good choice of clean and comfortable rooms from 12,500/15,000Rp to 35,000/40,000Rp with air-con, but it lacks character.

Mataram The cheapest in the city is *Suradipa Homestay* (☎ 24576, Gang Macan VII alley) – look for the sign from Jl Cockroaminoto. Don't expect too much luxury, but it's very good value at 7500/10,000Rp for singles/doubles with a fan and private bathroom. Conveniently close to the Perama office, *Hotel Kertajoga* (☎ 21775, Jl Pejanggik) is noisy but good value, with fan-cooled rooms for 19,500/23,000Rp and better rooms with air-con for 27,500/33,000Rp. The central *Wisma Nusantara Hotel* (☎ 23 492, Jl Suprapto 28) has a large number of clean but noisy rooms – you're always guaranteed a bed. The rooms cost US$11, but the manager is willing to negotiate.

Places to Stay – Mid-Range

Cakranegara *Hotel Selaparang* (☎ 32670, Jl Pejanggik 40) has a good range of singles/doubles from 25,410/30,250Rp with a fan to 51,425/57,475Rp with air-con, hot water and satellite TV. The management will happily offer discounts of about 20%. *Hotel Mataram* (☎/fax 34966, Jl Pejanggik 105) has a small pool and cluster of standard rooms for 30,000/37,500Rp; air-con rooms with hot water cost 40,000/45,000Rp.

Ampenan *Nictour Hotel* (☎ 23780, fax 36579, Jl Yos Sudarso) is quiet and offers air-con in all rooms. 'Superior' rooms cost 90,000/110,000/130,000Rp for singles/doubles/triples, and another 30,000Rp per person for the 'deluxe' rooms. Discounts of up to 40% are possible at quiet times.

NUSA TENGGARA

Mataram *Hotel Granada (☎ 36015, Jl Bung Karno 7)* is a little inconvenient, but it's pleasant enough. All rooms have air-con, hot water and satellite TV, and there's a swimming pool. Room prices start from 70,950/76,450Rp for singles/doubles; ask for a low season discount regardless of the time of year. Nearby, the new **Baka Baka Lombok Cottages** *(☎ 25378, Jl Bung Karno 31)* has a range of quaint, clean and large cottages for 57,500Rp, all with hot water. This is currently excellent value; no doubt an introductory offer to entice guests.

Hotel Handika (☎ 33321, Jl Panca Usaha 3) is in a noisy part of town. It has fan-cooled rooms from US$8/10 to US$28/30, but the management is happy to offer discounts of 50%. The central **Hotel Pusaka** *(☎/fax 33 119, Jl Sultan Hasanuddin 23)* has rooms with air-con and satellite TV from 47,500/ 55,000Rp to 100,000/125,000Rp.

Places to Stay – Top End
Hotel Lombok Raya (☎ 32305, fax 36478, Jl Panca Usaha 11, Mataram) offers attractively furnished, fully equipped rooms and a big swimming pool. Its rooms, from US$55/ 60 for singles/doubles, are pretty good value.

Places to Eat
Ampenan There are several decent Indonesian and Chinese restaurants along Jl Pabean, including the popular *Cirebon*, with a standard menu and dishes from around 5000Rp. A little further west, **Rainbow Cafe** is a cheap, friendly little place with reggae-inspired decor, cold beer and reasonable food. *Poppy Nice Cafe* is as appealing as its name, with a good range of well prepared dishes and hospitable management. **Hotel Wisata** and *Nictour Hotel* also have decent restaurants.

The best place is **Betawi Restaurant** *(Jl Pabean)*. From the seats upstairs, you can look down and watch Ampenan go about its business. There is a good range of Indonesian, Chinese and western dishes (for about 7500Rp), and the beer is cold.

Mataram *Denny Bersaudra* is a good place to try authentic Sasak-style food from

about 6000Rp a dish. Look for its sign at the roundabout along western Jl Selaparang.

Cakranegara *Hotel Shanti Puri (☎ 32649, Jl Maktal)* is a friendly place with a wide range of tasty food. The nearby **Sate Restaurant Suharti** *(Jl Maktal)* is worth visiting for its selection of delicious *sates* from 3500Rp to 5000Rp per plateful. Near the junction of Jl Selaparang and Jl Hasanuddin, and around the nearby market, there are many Javanese-style **rumah makans** (eating houses), but none are memorable or worth recommending.

Rumah Makan Cendana (Jl Nursiwan) is handy to the Ayu and Adiguna losmen, and offers a good range of meals from 3500Rp. There are also decent **restaurants** in most of the hotels along Jl Selaparang, and some cheap **eateries** in the New Tiara shopping centre. Most visitors, and affluent locals, end up at the conspicuous **KFC** *(Jl Selaparang)*.

Shopping
Two areas in Ampenan have a good selection of handicraft shops and are interesting to browse around: the west side of Jl Saleh Sungkar (which heads north to Senggigi), and around Hotel Zahir. An excellent place to look for local products is the market off Jl Hasanuddin.

The Lombok Pottery Centre has a vast range from all of the main pottery places around the island, and the prices are reasonably competitive. A couple of weaving factories operate in Cakra, where you can see dyeing and weaving, and buy ikat or hand woven songket sarongs. Selamat Riady is a shop that sells textiles and a few other crafts.

Getting There & Away
Bus & Bemo Mandalika terminal in Bertais is the main bus and bemo terminal for the entire island. It is also the terminal for long-distance buses to Sumbawa, Bali and Java (see Getting There & Away at the start of the Lombok section), and is the eastern terminus for local bemos from Ampenan.

The terminal is fairly chaotic, so you may have to rely on the touts to show you which bus or bemo to catch. Long-distance buses leave from behind the main terminal building, while bemos and smaller buses leave from one of two car parks on either side. Any vehicle without a destination sign on top can usually be chartered for a negotiable price.

Kebon Roek terminal in Ampenan is for bemos to Bertais and Senggigi.

Ojek You can also arrange a trip around Mataram, or anywhere else in Lombok, by ojek. Ask around the hotels in Ampenan, or look for motorcyclists hanging around the markets in Cakra and Ampenan. The Hotel Zahir can arrange daytrips by ojek for 35,000Rp per day.

Getting Around

To/From the Airport Lombok's Selaparang airport is convenient. Taxis from the airport cost 7500Rp to anywhere in Mataram; 12,000Rp to Senggigi; 26,000Rp to Bangsal and Lembar; and 41,000Rp to Tetebatu. Alternatively, you can walk out of the airport car park to Jl Adi Sucipto and either take one of the No 7 bemos that run frequently to the terminal at Ampenan, or a cidomo to Mataram from the corner of Jl Sutomo and Jl Sudirman.

Bemo Mataram is *very* spread out, so don't plan to walk from place to place. Yellow bemos constantly shuttle back and forth between Kebon Roek terminal in Ampenan and Mandalika terminal in Bertais. These terminals are good places to charter bemos. Outside the market in Cakra, there is a handy bemo stop for services to Bertais, Ampenan and Lembar.

Car & Motorcycle Most hotels in the city can arrange car and motorbike rentals. Several rental agencies are based along Jl Pendidikan and Jl Pancawarga, and near Hotel Zahir in Ampenan. The West Lombok tourist office can also help. However, you're better off renting in Senggigi where the prices are more competitive and the range of vehicles is larger.

AROUND MATARAM

Not far east of Bertais there are some gorgeous areas of villages, rice fields and temples; reminiscent of some of the best landscapes and scenery that Bali has to offer.

Taman Narmada

Laid out as a miniature replica of the summit of Gunung Rinjani and its crater lake, Taman Narmada (Narmada Park) was built in 1805 and takes its name from a sacred river in India. The temple, **Pura Kalasa**, is still used, and the Balinese Pujawali celebration is held here every year in honour of the god Batara, who dwells on Gunung Rinjani. There are also two swimming pools in the grounds.

This is a beautiful place to spend a few hours, but don't visit on Sunday when it's very crowded. The park is open from 7 am to 6 pm daily. Tickets cost 500Rp, plus another 500Rp to swim in the pools.

Narmada is on a hill about 6km east of Sweta, on the main east-west road crossing Lombok. Frequent bemos from the terminal in Bertais take you to the Narmada market, which is directly opposite the entrance to the gardens.

Pura Lingsar

This large temple complex, built in 1714, is the holiest in Lombok. It combines the Bali Hindu and Wektu Telu religions in one complex. Designed in two separate sections and built on two different levels, the Hindu temple in the northern section is higher than the Wektu Telu temple in the southern section.

The Wektu Telu temple is noted for its small enclosed pond devoted to Lord Vishnu, and the holy eels which can be enticed from their hiding places with hardboiled eggs (available at stalls outside). You will be expected to rent a sash and/or sarong (or bring your own) to enter the temple, but not to enter the outside buildings.

Places to Stay & Eat *Pura Lingsar Homestay*, 500m from the temple, and on the road towards Suranadi, has pleasant singles/doubles for 15,000/20,000Rp. There are basic *food stalls* and shops in the parking area.

Getting There & Away Pura Lingsar is not on the main east-west road from Bertais. First take a bemo from Bertais to Narmada, and another to Lingsar. Ask to be dropped off near the entrance to the temple complex, which is 300m down a well marked path from the main road.

Suranadi

Suranadi is a pleasant village in the sort of gorgeous countryside that is becoming difficult to find in Bali. **Pura Suranadi** is one of the holiest Hindu temples in Lombok. Set in pleasant gardens, it's noted for its bubbling, icy cold spring water and restored baths with ornate Balinese carvings. Opposite the village market is a small forest sanctuary, **Hutan Wisata Suranadi**. Although neglected, it's a shady and quiet area for short hikes and bird watching.

Places to Stay & Eat *Suranadi Hotel* (☎ 33686, fax 35630) has decent rooms for US$30, and overpriced cottages for US$60. There are two swimming pools, tennis courts, a restaurant and a bar. It's a lovely place to stay awhile, especially if you can negotiate a better price. The public can swim in the hotel pool.

Pondok Surya has basic rooms, a nice outlook and an excellent restaurant, which mainly serves guests. It's casual and friendly, and the rooms, which are a bit dark, cost 15,000Rp per person. Look for the sign at the market. A little further away (charter a bemo), *Teratai Cottages* has bungalows from 30,000Rp to 60,000Rp, and a swimming pool and tennis court.

Several upmarket *restaurants* are dotted along the main road, opposite the entrances to the temple and forest. You can also eat at cheap *warungs* (food stalls) at the market.

Getting There & Away You will have to wait for an infrequent public bemo from Narmada; if that fails, charter one.

Sesaot

About 5km from Suranadi is Sesaot, a charming market town on the edge of a forest.

There are some gorgeous picnic spots and you can swim in the river. The water is very cool and is considered holy as it comes straight from Gunung Rinjani. There is regular transport from Narmada, and you can eat at the *warungs* along the main street.

Air Nyet

Further east, Air Nyet is another pretty village with more places for swimming and picnics. Ask directions for the unsigned turn-off in the middle of Sesaot. The bridge and road to Air Nyet are rough, but it's a lovely stroll (about 3km) from Sesaot. You could also charter a vehicle from Sesaot or Narmada.

GUNUNG PENGSONG

This Balinese temple is 9km south of Mataram, and has great views of rice fields, volcanoes and the sea. The whole area was used by retreating Japanese soldiers in WWII to hide, and remnants of **cannons** can be found, as well as plenty of pesky monkeys. Try to get there early in the morning before the clouds envelop Gunung Rinjani. There's no set admission charge, but you'll have to tip the caretaker about 500Rp. There is very little direct public transport from Bertais, so you'll have to charter or rent a vehicle.

BANYUMULEK

This is one of the main **pottery centres** in Lombok, specialising in decorated pots and pots with a woven fibre covering, as well as more traditional urns and water flasks. It's close to the city, a couple of kilometres west of the Sweta-Lembar road.

LEMBAR

Lembar is the port for Pelni liners, the *Mabua Express* and ferries to/from Bali.

Places to Stay

Sri Wahyu (☎ 81048) is just off the main road, about 1km north of the port – look for the sign along the main road. Reasonable singles/doubles cost 8800/9900Rp, and better rooms are 13,200/14,800Rp. About 200m further north along the same road, and opposite the weighbridge, *Serumbung Indah* (☎ *81153*) is a better option, with good rooms for 20,000Rp.

Getting There & Away

Plenty of bemos go to Lembar from the terminal in Bertais, or you can catch one at the stop at the market in Cakra. From Lembar, plenty of public transport heads to Bertais. See Getting There & Away at the start of the Lombok section for details on the ferries and boats between Bali and Lembar.

SOUTH-WESTERN PENINSULA

A road from Lembar goes round the east side of the harbour and then heads south, some distance inland, and after almost 20km reaches a T-junction at Sekotong. From there, the road to the left cuts across the peninsula and ends at Sepi on the southern coast, while the other road follows the coast, more or less, around Lombok's south-west peninsula. The further you go on this road, the rougher it gets and it may become impassable for ordinary cars past Labuhan Poh.

Taun has a stunning, white, sandy beach. Nearby, *Sekotong Indah Beach Cottages* has comfortable accommodation near a beach; basic singles/doubles with a shared bathroom cost 15,000/20,000Rp; better rooms are 20,000/25,000Rp; and individual cottages are good value for about 30,000Rp. If you keep following this track, you'll eventually reach **Bangko Bangko**; from there it's about 2km to **Desert Point**, which is a famous surf break.

There are two groups of picturesque islands off the north coast of this peninsula – **Gili Nanggu** and **Gili Gede**. You can reach them by chartered *perahu* (outrigger boat) from Lembar, Taun or Labuhan Poh. The only tourist accommodation is on Gili Nanggu, where *Cempaka Cottages (Mataram* ☎ *22898)* charges about 45,000Rp per person, including all meals.

Further west, Gili Gede is the largest island in the second group. It has several **traditional villages**, where Bugis settlers make a living from boat building, more glorious beaches and clear water for snorkelling.

SENGGIGI

On a series of sweeping bays, north of Mataram, Senggigi is the most developed tourist area in Lombok, with a range of tourist facilities and accommodation options. Senggigi has experienced a lot of development in the last few years, and much of it is still pretty raw. With the dearth of tourists in the current economic climate, Senggigi is also looking quite forlorn, with empty shops, hotels and restaurants – though this could mean discounts for visitors.

Senggigi has fine beaches, although they slope very steeply into the water, and there are signs that erosion is starting to eat away the foreshore. There are beautiful sunsets over the Selat Lombok (Lombok Strait) that can be enjoyed from the beach, a nearby temple or one of the beachfront restaurants. As it gets dark the fishing fleet lines up offshore – each boat has bright lanterns.

Orientation

The area known as Senggigi is spread out along nearly 10km of coastal road. Most of the shops and other facilities, and a fair concentration of hotels, are on the main road, Jl Raya Senggigi, which is about 6km north of Mataram.

Information

You can change money and travellers cheques at most of the big hotels, but you're better off using one of the moneychangers along Jl Raya Senggigi.

The Telkom office is inconveniently positioned north-west of the main shopping area, but there are other wartels along Jl Raya Senggigi. There are two Internet centres: Bulan Cybercafe (bulan@mataram .wasantara.net.id), which also has a message board, an Aqua mineral water refill service and a fax machine; and Planet Internet (planet@mataram.wasantara.net.id).

The nearest hospitals are in Mataram, but there's a medical clinic in the Hotel Senggigi Aerowisata complex, which is available to guests and the public. The police station (☎ 110) is along the northern stretch of central Senggigi.

SENGGIGI BEACH

To Pondok Damai,
Windy Cottages, Bangsal,
Pemenang & Mangset

Jalan Raya Senggigi

Kampung
Krandangan

Selat Lombok

PLACES TO STAY
1 Hotel Puri Mas
2 Santai Beach Inn
   & Restaurant
3 Alang Alang
   & Restaurant
4 Bale Kampung
6 Puri Saron
7 Pacific Beach Cottages
9 Sheraton Senggigi Hotel
11 Hotel Puri Bunga
14 Lombok Intan Laguna
   & Restaurant
15 Pondok Shinta Cottages
16 Sonya Homestay;
   Kafe Expresso
23 Hotel Elen; Warungs
25 Pondok Wisata Rinjani
29 Hotel Senggigi Aerowisata;
   Medical Clinic
30 Mascot Berugaq Elen
   Cottages
34 Raja's Bungalows

35 Bukit Senggigi Hotel;
   Albatross Dive Centre;
   Blue Coral Dive Centre
38 Dharma Room & Bungalow
39 Lina Cottages & Restaurant
42 Graha Beach Hotel
43 Pondok Senggigi & Restaurant
44 Melati Dua Cottages
45 Bumi Aditya
47 Batu Bolong Cottages

PLACES TO EAT
5 Cafe Johan
19 Princess of Lombok ;
   Down Under Pub; Wartel
22 Malibu
24 Arlina Restaurant;
   Bayan Restaurant
31 Taman Senggigi
40 Sunshine Restaurant
46 Dynasty & Kafe Alberto
   Restaurant
48 Cafe Wayan

OTHER
8 Pura Kapusan
10 Telkom Office
12 Police Station
13 Pasar Seni (Art Market);
   Gede's Warung; Warung Lino
17 Galleria Shopping Centre
18 Pacific Supermarket;
   Silk Air; Kafe Bucu
20 Shopping Centre (Empty)
21 Post Office
26 Planet Internet
27 Gossip Cafe
28 Chartered Boats to Gili Islands;
   Snorkelling Gear Rental;
   Food Stalls
32 Bulan Cybercafe
33 Mosque
36 Perama Office
37 Marina
41 Wartel
49 Pura Batu Bolong

To Mini-Golf
Sambhu

Jalan Palma Raja

Jalan Raya Senggigi

To Atithi
Sanggraha Beach
Cottages, Pondok
Asri, Pondok Wisata
Sita Hawa, Hotel
Jayakarta &
Ampenan

0   250   500 m

Pura Batu Bolong

This temple is on a rocky point that juts into the sea about 1km south of central Senggigi. As a Balinese temple, it's oriented towards Gunung Agung, Bali's holiest mountain. There's a good view of Senggigi from the point, and it's a great place to watch the sun set. During the day, you will be urged to 'donate' 5000Rp in return for renting a sash before you enter, but 1000Rp is enough. At other times, you can wander in and out like the locals.

Activities

There's reasonable snorkelling off the point, in the sheltered bay around the headland, and in front of Windy Cottages, a few kilometres north of Senggigi. The best time for snorkelling is June to September. You can rent snorkelling gear (7500Rp per day) from several spots along the beach near the Hotel Senggigi Aerowisata, or from the dive centres.

Dive trips from Senggigi normally only visit the Gili Islands, so it's better and cheaper to base yourself there, unless you prefer Senggigi's swankier hotels. There are two reputable dive centres along the main road: Albatross (☎ 93399, fax 93388) and Blue Coral (☎ 93441, fax 93251, email blue_coral@mataram.wasantara.net.id).

Places to Stay – Budget
South Senggigi *Pondok Wisata Siti Hawa* *(☎ 93414, fax 23912)* is a funky little home-stay fronting a fantastic beach, run by a local community group. The bamboo cottages cost 10,000/13,0000Rp for singles/doubles. It caters for budget travellers: there are cheap home-cooked meals, and you can rent motorbikes, bicycles and boats.

Atithi Sanggraha Beach Cottages (☎ 93 070) is also worth checking out. The cottages are clean, quiet and dotted around a small garden with its own beach. The cottages may lack character, but for 20,000/25,000Rp they're excellent value. Not as good, but still cheap, *Pondok Asri* (☎ 93 075) has rooms, which are a little noisy, from 15,000Rp to 25,000Rp.

Central Senggigi The oft-ignored *Melati Dua Cottages (☎ 93288, fax 93028)* has quaint individual cottages from 30,000Rp to 60,000Rp with air-con (no hot water), but they are close to the main road.

Pondok Wisata Rinjani (☎ 93274) has cottages in a pretty garden for 15,000/20,000Rp a single/double, but the whole complex is looking rather neglected these days. *Sonya Homestay (☎ 63447)* is a basic, family-run losmen that has been recommended by several readers. The atmosphere is friendly, and the small rooms (which are clustered together) are only 15,000Rp. Close by, *Pondok Shinta Cottages* is a last resort: very ordinary rooms, with no fan and next to the main road, cost 8000/10,000Rp. One of the best is *Hotel Elen (☎ 93014)*, which is easy to miss behind the Hero Photo shop. Clean, modern rooms with a ceiling fan and some style cost 17,500/25,000Rp.

Well off Jl Raya Senggigi, *Bumi Aditya* has bamboo bungalows that are small, clean and appealing from 15,000Rp to 25,000Rp. You may have to look hard for a member of

staff sometimes. *Raja's Bungalows (☎ 93 569)* is recommended for seclusion and a friendly atmosphere. It's about 200m up a path past the mosque – look for the hotel sign from the main road.

North Senggigi In Kampung Krandangan, *Bale Kampung* provides cheap food and good information about the local attractions – it's not too far away from the sea, but seems like light years from the 'Senggigi scene'. Rooms cost 16,500/21,000Rp for singlesdoubles, and can fit up to four people; quaint but tiny bungalows cost 14,300/17,600Rp. The bathrooms are rustic and have squat-style toilets. You can walk east from Bale Kampung to the edge of the Gunung Rinjani National Park (Taman Nasional Gunung Rinjani).

Places to Stay – Mid-Range
South Senggigi *Batu Bolong Cottages (☎ 93065, fax 93198)* has spacious, well finished bungalows on both sides of Jl Raya Senggigi, from 35,000Rp to 86,000Rp (with hot water and air-con). This is very good value when compared to some of the soulless new, concrete places nearby.

Central Senggigi *Lina Cottages (☎ 93 237)* is central, friendly and good value – which is why it's often full (so book ahead). Singles/doubles cost 40,000/50,000Rp; a bungalow with sea views, hot water and air-con is still reasonable value for Senggigi at 100,000Rp.

Pondok Senggigi (☎ 93273) has gone steadily upmarket. It has a nice swimming pool and the rooms run off a long verandah and face a pleasant garden. Prices start at US$9/12, but most rooms cost at least twice this amount – with air-con and hot water the cost is US$39/45. In the centre of town, *Dharma Room & Bungalow (☎ 93050)* has a lovely garden that leads onto the beach. The rooms with a fan for 45,000Rp are often full; bungalows with air-con and hot water cost 130,000Rp.

Graha Beach Hotel (☎ 93101, fax 93400) has a good, central beachside location, but the rooms are small and lack character. They cost US$45 (US$50 for an ocean view), with air-con, phone and satellite TV. *Mascot Berugaq Elen Cottages* (☎ 93365, fax 93 236) has almost top-end facilities and location for a mid-range price. It offers pleasant 'Sasak-style' and 'Seaview' bungalows for US$42 and US$49 respectively. The rooms have air-con, hot water and phone, but the best feature is the quiet garden setting that extends to the beach.

North Senggigi *Santai Beach Inn* (☎ 93 038) has a cosy atmosphere and a lush garden. There's a good library and book exchange, and it serves traditional meals in a pleasant pavilion. Economy bungalows cost 26,000/33,000Rp for singles/doubles and standard bungalows (with fan) are 40,000/52,000Rp. There is one family room, which has hot water and costs 80,000Rp. Advanced bookings are recommended.

Next door, the classy *Hotel Puri Mas* (☎/fax 93023) has attractively decorated bungalows and villas surrounded by trees and shrubs, and a pretty pool. Prices range from US$23 for the 'standard bungalow' to US$143 for the 'villa'.

The spacious and charming *Windy Cottages* (☎ 93191, fax 93193) charges a very reasonable 60,000Rp for standard rooms; and 75,000Rp to 90,000Rp for bigger bungalows with hot water. It's a great spot for snorkelling.

In Mangset, *Pondok Damai* (☎ 93019) is a quiet, seaside retreat. It has a comfortable, charming collection of cottages for 40,000/55,000Rp, but there's no hot water. Although not great value, it's cheap for this part of the beach.

Places to Stay – Top End

Senggigi has acquired a few luxury hotels. None of them are well patronised, even in the high season, so discounts on the 'published' (official) prices listed here are often available.

The huge *Hotel Jayakarta* (☎ 93045, fax 93043, email jayakarta@mataram.wasantara. net.id) is impossible to miss; the central lobby

building is absolutely massive. The rooms are plain, but well furnished, and cost US$85/97 for singles/doubles. The first 'international standard' hotel built at Senggigi, *Hotel Senggigi Aerowisata* (☎ 93210, fax 93200, email senggigi@lombokisland.com), is operated by Garuda and has a beautiful setting, lovely garden, tennis courts, swimming pool and other mod cons. Rooms cost US$157, but discounts of 30% are regularly advertised.

Lombok Intan Laguna (☎ 93090, fax 93 185, email intan@mataram.wasantara.net.id) is a large and handsome hotel, with a big pool. Rooms start at US$121, and cost double for suites. *Bukit Senggigi Hotel* (☎ 93 173, fax 93226, email bukit@mataram.was antara.net.id) has motel-like rooms staggering up the side of a small hill – some have views over the sea. Prices start at US$90/97, but 40% discounts are often available. There's also a swimming pool, a disco and a karaoke lounge.

Further north, *Sheraton Senggigi Hotel* (☎ 93333, fax 93140, email ssbr_sgg@ mataram.wasantra.net.id) is the best hotel in Senggigi, and also the most expensive, with rooms starting at US$181. *Pacific Beach Cottages* (☎ 93006, fax 93027) has all the standard luxuries, but the rooms are ordinary and its limited character. Rooms cost US$55 and bungalows are US$67.

Holiday Inn Resort (☎ 93444, fax 93092, email hirlo@mataram.wasantara.net.id) offers all the comforts you would expect for US$170, but offers 50% discounts in the low season. The small number of luxury bungalows at *Alang Alang* (☎ 93518, fax 93 194) overlook the ocean, but they're close to the main road. They cost US$70.

Continuing north along the coast, a few upmarket options offer character and style. One in particular, *Hotel Nusa Bunga* (☎ 93 035), has a splendid beachfront position, a pool and comfortable, air-con bungalows in a pretty garden from US$55/65.

Places to Eat

Beachside dining is a Senggigi speciality. It is especially delightful in the evening, with cool sea breezes, blazing sunsets and great views, but the hawkers on the beach can be annoying. Some of the restaurants north and south of Senggigi have minibuses that cruise along the main road in the evening hoping to pick up (and later drop off) some customers – it's a free service and worth considering. There's not much at the budget end of the scale, except a couple of *warungs* along the main road near the mosque and a few *food stalls* along the beach, particularly at the end of the road past the Hotel Senggigi Aerowisata.

South Senggigi The upmarket *Cafe Wayan* (☎ 93098) is owned by the same people who run the excellent Cafe Wayan in Ubud. Pizzas cost 10,000Rp, but the other meals cost considerably more. The freshly baked pastries and cakes are delightful.

Two long-term favourites, *Dynasty Restaurant* and *Kafe Alberto* (☎ 93313), have joined forces to provide Chinese and Italian food with wonderful views for reasonable prices – it costs from 9000Rp to 13,000Rp for seafood and other meat dishes.

Central Senggigi The restaurant at *Pondok Senggigi* is not the cheapest, but it's still popular from breakfast until late at night. The large open dining area is comfortable and convivial, and there's a wide selection of well prepared western, Indonesian and Sasak food.

The beachfront restaurant at *Lina Cottages* is also very good. Meals start at 10,000Rp, the setting is superb and the happy hours make drink prices competitive. Next door, *Sunshine Restaurant* has cheap drinks while the sun sets, and meals are priced from about 10,000Rp. For sea views and sea breezes – at similar prices – try *Gede's Warung* and *Warung Lino*. Both are hidden at the back of the Pasar Seni (Art Market).

Princess of Lombok has a bar downstairs and a pleasant open dining area upstairs. It offers good Mexican food – most dishes are 17,500Rp, and steaks cost 20,000Rp. *Arlina Restaurant* is central and reasonably priced, with meals from 6000Rp to 10,000Rp. For decent coffee, as well as pasta and Indonesian

food, try *Kafe Expresso*, near the Sonya Homestay. *Malibu* has decent happy hours and meals for 9,000Rp to 14,000Rp. It remains popular because of the fresh seafood that you can choose from the table along the roadside, and the friendly staff.

Most days *Lombok Intan Laguna* offers buffets of seafood or *sates*, or a *rijsttafel* (a banquet of Dutch-style Indonesian food), for about 30,000Rp per person – this is worth a splurge at least once. The two storey *Taman Senggigi* is popular and stylish, but most meals cost about 20,000Rp.

North Senggigi *Alang Alang* and *Cafe Johan* offer superb views and the prices aren't too bad – from 10,000Rp for Chinese and Indonesian food. The restaurant at *Windy Cottages* is further up the coast in an open-sided pavilion facing the sea. It's a scenic area and the beach is nice – a trip up here for lunch makes a lovely outing. The vegetarian restaurant at *Santai Beach Inn* (☎ 93038) is also worth a trip north. Bookings are essential.

Entertainment
Pondok Senggigi, *Kafe Bucu*, *Bayan Restaurant* and *Marina* often have live music. The late afternoon happy hour at *Lombok Intan Laguna* usually coincides with live traditional music; more upbeat dance bands normally feature later in the evening. *Dynasty Restaurant* and *Kafe Alberto* sometimes have traditional dancing and, conversely, karaoke nights. A couple of the pubs can be quite sociable – the *Down Under Pub* at the Princess of Lombok has good music and pool tables. *Gossip Cafe* often has a disco.

Getting There & Away
Regular bemos travel to Senggigi from the Kebon Roek terminal in Ampenan (500Rp), and usually continue north as far as Pemenang or Bayan. There are also occasional bemos to Senggigi from the Mandalika terminal in Bertais (600Rp). Don't be surprised if you're overcharged a little on any bemo going to Senggigi.

The Perama company has several tourist shuttle bus/boat services daily between Senggigi and the main tourist centres in Bali – eg to the Kuta region (20,000Rp) and Ubud (17,500Rp); and the main tourist centres in Lombok, via Mataram – eg Bangsal (5000Rp), Tetebatu (7500Rp) and Kuta (10,000Rp).

Getting Around
A pre-paid taxi from the airport to Senggigi costs 12,000Rp; from Senggigi to the airport, a metered taxi will cost far less. Taxis regularly ply Jl Raya Senggigi looking for customers.

GILI ISLANDS
Off the north-west coast of Lombok are three small, coral-fringed islands – Gili Air, Gili Meno and Gili Trawangan – each with superb, white sandy beaches, clear water, coral reefs, brilliantly coloured fish and the best snorkelling in Lombok. The islands have become enormously popular with visitors, who come for the very simple pleasures of sun, snorkelling and socialising. It's cheap, and the absence of cars, motorbikes and hawkers adds greatly to the pleasure of staying on the Gilis. Although known to travellers as the 'Gili Islands', *gili* actually means 'island', so this is not a local name.

Dangers & Annoyances
There are occasional thefts on the islands, which are not always dealt with effectively. There are no police on any of the Gilis, so report any theft to the island *kepala desa* (village head), and if there is no response, go to the police station in Tanjung or, better, Mataram.

Gili Trawangan has a reputation as the 'party island'. With poorly lit beach parties, alcohol and no police, it's perhaps not surprising that a few foreign women have complained about minor (so far) cases of sexual harassment and assault from Indonesian and foreign men.

Although not common, stonefish are found on coral reefs where they are camouflaged and almost invisible. If you stand on one, the venomous spines can cause excruciating pain and sometimes death. Don't walk on coral reefs. Also, jellyfish are common when strong winds blow from the mainland, and they can leave a painful rash. See the boxed text 'Marine Life to Watch Out For' in the Health section of the Facts for the Visitor chapter.

Accommodation
The Gilis standard is a plain little bamboo bungalow on stilts, with a thatched roof, a small verandah out the front and a concrete bathroom block at the back. Inside, there will be one or two beds with mosquito nets. When the islands are busy (July, August and around Christmas) owners increase room prices – possibly double the prices quoted later in this section.

Touts often meet the boats as they land. Once they take your luggage, you're normally committed to wherever they take you.

Getting There & Away
All boats pull up on the beaches, so you'll have to wade ashore with your luggage. The weather can often be rough, the trips slow and the conditions a little primitive at times:

> The sea was so rough that the boat couldn't reach the beach, so luggage and passengers went from the beach one by one in a small canoe. The captain and the two boatmen got more and more serious, non-smiling and stressed. After one hour, the rudder broke off. We took four hours to reach Gili Trawangan from Bangsal.
>
> **Moura Modiman**

Public Bemo & Boat Firstly, catch a bus or bemo to Pemenang, from where it's about 1km by cidomo to the harbour at Bangsal. The North Lombok section later in this chapter has more information on Bangsal.

The Koperasi Angkutan Laut (Sea Transport Co-operative) is the boat owners' cartel which monopolises public transport between Bangsal and the islands. It's a matter of sitting and waiting until there's a full boat load, ie about 15 people. Public boats normally start leaving Bangsal and each of

DIVING & SNORKELLING IN THE GILIS

There are three islands just off Lombok's west coast that are a favourite haunt for day-trippers of all diving levels, with varied terrain and surprising marine life – turtles and seasonal manta rays can be seen at most dive sites. The Gilis – Gili Air, Gili Trawangan and Gili Meno – are low, sandy islands with shallow blue waters and nice beaches. The water depth is 6 to 27m. The Gili Air dive described below is a boat dive, but all dive sites can be snorkelled safely by staying between the dive boat and the shore.

Diving in the Gilis is pleasant, especially if you're into invertebrates. Off Gili Air, there's a nifty channel that allows a shallow and easy drift dive. The slope is sandy with patch coral and flowing soft corals. Sea anemones are common among the cantankerous percula clownfish. Clownfish live within the stinging tentacles of the anemone, free from harm through a coating that their body develops.

Text inset: Clownfish (photograph by Michael Aw).

Top left to right: Diver watching fish in plate coral; Hawksbill turtle.

Bottom left to right: Panda clownfish; Schooling Jacks.

MICHAEL AW

Diving & Snorkelling in the Gilis

There are a couple of local bamboo fish traps planted here. While the 'free Willy' spirit urges us to break these and set the fish free, we need to remember that this is a food source for local families. Enjoy the drift here and stop when you see something of interest. The channel looks as though there should be something big swimming by occasionally, and whitetip sharks have been seen here, so keep an eye on the blue void. There are big elephant ear sponges as well.

The diving is even better off Gili Trawangan. To the north and west there is a rocky shoreline and a point. The area around the point can be rough and churned up, but the sloping shelf nearby contains large coral heads, big patches of staghorn, and other acropora (hard corals) and occasional valleys that are home to fish schools. There are cuttlefish in abundance here and they can be approached quite closely. Watch as they react to you. They will change colours in a furious progression that ranges from wild bioluminescent to stark pale. The boulders that are scattered around provide refuge for big snappers that can weigh 35 to 45kg.

Tim Rock from Lonely Planet's *Diving & Snorkeling Bali & the Komodo Region*

Top left to right: Crown of Thorns sea star; Thorny oyster.

Middle left to right: Lombok seascape; Turnicats on sea sponge.

Bottom left to right: Pink Flatworm; Pink Nudibranch.

Coral Conservation

In the past, fish bombing and the careless use of anchors resulted in the damage of coral reefs. There is greater awareness of this now and the rehabilitation of damaged reefs is possible. Unfortunately, many visitors are unwittingly causing more damage by standing and walking on the reefs, often while snorkelling, boating or windsurfing. Perfectly formed corals are easily broken and take years to recover; the reef ecology is very sensitive.

If you're not into conservation, then think about the stonefish. These fish – with their venomous spines – are well camouflaged on the coral reefs of the Gilis, and at times they are virtually invisible. Standing on a stonefish can cause excruciating pain and sometimes death. So keep off the reefs! See the boxed text 'Marine Life to Watch Out For' in the Health section of Facts for the Visitor.

the three islands at about 8 am – but check the departure times at the Koperasi's offices the day before. Boats normally stop running by 4 pm. From Bangsal, the one way fare is 1200Rp to Gili Air, 1500Rp to Gili Meno and 1600Rp to Gili Trawangan.

Tourist Shuttle Bus & Boat The main shuttle service operator, Perama (Senggigi ☎ 93007), is reliable and well established. It has a service to the Gilis that leaves Senggigi at 9 am and returns at 3 pm, so you can do a day trip from Senggigi. This boat normally connects with tourist shuttle bus services to tourist centres in Lombok and Bali.

From Senggigi, the fare per person to Gili Trawangan is 10,000/20,000Rp (one way/return), and it will also go to Gili Meno (12,500/25,000Rp) and Gili Air (15,000/30,000Rp) if requested by passengers. Sunshine (based at the restaurant of the same name in Senggigi) also has a daily boat service to the Gilis, which leaves at the same time and for the same price.

Perama and a few other operators also offer direct shuttle bus/boat services to the Gilis from Kuta, Ubud and most tourist centres in Bali. However, this service often involves a shuttle bus to Padangbai, the public ferry to Lembar, a shuttle bus to Mataram or Senggigi (where you may have to stay the night at your own expense) and a shuttle boat to the Gilis the next morning. Check the exact details before you book.

Chartering a Boat To charter a boat from Bangsal to the Gilis, the Koperasi charges 15,000/25,000Rp (one way/return) to Gili Air; 18,000/35,000Rp to Gili Meno; and 21,000/40,000Rp to Gili Trawangan.

To visit all three islands from Bangsal will cost about 60,000Rp return, plus a negotiable extra cost for waiting. The Perama offices on the three islands can also arrange chartered boats, but they cost more.

You can also charter a boat to the Gilis for the day from in front of the Hotel Senggigi Aerowisata in Senggigi. The non-negotiable cost is 100,000Rp for a four person boat or 200,000Rp for a 10 person boat.

Island Hopping Perama runs a convenient shuttle boat service between the islands, so you can stay on one island and look around the others. (The schedule does not allow you to visit two other islands in one day.) The fares are 4000Rp between Gili Air and Gili Trawangan, and 3000Rp between Gili Meno and the other two islands. The boats do two runs a day at about 9 am and 3 pm – check the times, and book with the individual Perama offices, or at any of the shops-cum-travel agencies on the islands.

Gili Air

Gili Air is the closest island to the mainland, and has the largest population. There are beaches around most of the island, but some are not suitable for swimming because they're quite shallow and have a sharp coral bottom. Because the hotels and restaurants are so scattered, the island has a pleasant, rural character and it's a delight to wander around.

NUSA TENGGARA

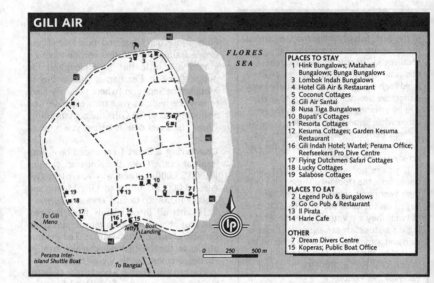

GILI AIR

FLORES SEA

PLACES TO STAY
1 Hink Bungalows; Matahari Bungalows; Bunga Bungalows
3 Lombok Indah Bungalows
4 Hotel Gili Air & Restaurant
5 Coconut Cottages
6 Gili Air Santai
8 Nusa Tiga Bungalows
10 Bupati's Cottages
11 Resorta Cottages
12 Kesuma Cottages; Garden Kesuma Restaurant
16 Gili Indah Hotel; Wartel; Perama Office; Reefseekers Pro Dive Centre
17 Flying Dutchmen Safari Cottages
18 Lucky Cottages
19 Salabose Cottages

PLACES TO EAT
2 Legend Pub & Bungalows
9 Go Go Pub & Restaurant
13 Il Pirata
14 Harie Cafe

OTHER
7 Dream Divers Centre
15 Koperas; Public Boat Office

To Gili Meno

Jetty   Boat Landing

Perama Inter-island Shuttle Boat

To Bangsal

0   250   500 m

Information The Perama office (☎ 36341) and wartel are next to the Gili Indah Hotel, and the Koperasi boat operators have an office next to the jetty. Pondok Cafe has an Aqua mineral water refill service, and a small book exchange; and the Hotel Gili Air has a fax and 'e-mile' service (giliair@mataram .wasantara.net.id).

At budget-range hotels and restaurants without generators, electricity comes on at about 6 pm. You can change money at the better hotels, but the rates are lousy.

Snorkelling & Diving There's quite good snorkelling off the east and north side of the island. There is also excellent diving within a short boat ride, with lots of whitetip sharks and underwater canyons. It's best to deal with the two main diving centres: the German-run Dream Divers Centre (☎ 93738); or Reefseekers Pro Dive (☎/fax 34387).

One local company (☎ 64018) operates glass bottom boat tours to the other two islands between 5.30 pm and midnight, including snorkelling (gear is provided) and a barbecue fish dinner.

Places to Stay Although the staff at *Lombok Indah Bungalows* are fairly lackadaisical, the setting overlooking the beach is superb. The bungalows are Gili-standard and cost 15,000Rp. Another good option is the bungalows at the back of the *Legend Pub*, which cost 12,000/15,000Rp for singles/doubles – but they may not be too quiet if the pub gets rowdy.

On the east coast, *Coconut Cottages* (☎ 35 365) has a set of charming cottages in a pretty garden from 25,000Rp to 50,000Rp. *Gili Air Santai* (☎ 641022) is a little classier than most places, but still good value with bungalows from 20,000Rp to 40,000Rp. These two places are perfect for anyone who wants a western-style bathroom and regular electricity.

On the south-west coast, *Lucky Cottages*, *Flying Dutchman Safari Cottages* and *Salabose Cottages* are close to the main drag, but still secluded. Simple bungalows cost about 12,500/15,000Rp.

On the far north-west coast, there are three places in a row, totally secluded from the rest of the island – but not from each other. *Matahari Bungalows* is the best, but dearest, for 18,000/20,000Rp.

There are more places in the centre of the island. *Resorta Cottages* is the most basic and cheapest place on the island with rooms for 7000/10,000Rp. *Bupati's Cottages* has good, quiet bungalows for a negotiable 15,000Rp. *Nusa Tiga Bungalows* is also quiet, spacious and very good value with rooms for 12,000/15,000Rp.

Gili Indah Hotel (☎ 36341) is the biggest place on Gili Air. It features a variety of bungalows in a wonderful garden, virtually on the beach. The 'standard' bungalows are not particularly good value for 20,000/25,000Rp, but it's worth booking ahead and splurging on the 'superior' bungalows (50,000/60,000Rp).

On the nicer, northern end of the island, *Hotel Gili Air (☎/fax 34435, email giliair@ mataram.wasantara.net.id)* is another up-market option. The attractive beautiful bungalows in a large garden, facing a superb beach, cost US$23/28 to US$28/34 with hot water and air-con.

Places to Eat Most hotels and losmen have decent restaurants. The restaurant at *Hotel Gili Air* has a delightful setting and is worth the walk – take a torch (flashlight) at night. The unique *Il Pirata Restaurant* serves very ordinary pasta (from 10,000Rp) on something that looks like a pirate ship (well, it does after a few Bintang beers).

In the central part of the island, *Garden Kesuma Restaurant* has a lovely ambience, especially in the evening, and good prices (daily specials are about 6500Rp). *Pondok Cafe* is popular with long-stayers and a good place to meet other travellers, and *Harie Cafe* is always popular. Several places along the east coast serve decent pizzas and other western food.

Legend Pub and *Go Go Pub & Restaurant* offer about the only nightlife on the island, which is fairly tame compared to Gili Trawangan and Senggigi.

Gili Meno

Gili Meno, the middle island, has the smallest population. It is perfect for anyone who wants almost total seclusion and a chance to wallow on a private beach.

Information You can make telephone calls at the wartel near the Gazebo Hotel, and change money at the Kontiki Meno Bungalows and the Gazebo Hotel. While normal food and drink supplies are adequate, there are no real shops on the island, so stock up on anything else you may need.

Activities Locals can organise fishing, dolphin and boating trips if you can find enough passengers to share the costs. The beach on the eastern side of the island is very nice, and there's good snorkelling just offshore and further north – you can rent gear from most losmen for about 7500Rp per day. The most reputable dive centre is Albatross Diving Centre, based at Casablanca Cottages.

Places to Stay All places on the north coast and many cheapies all over the island have no electricity or generators, which means no fans for the heat or mosquitoes.

Pondok Meno is quiet and relaxed, although the garden is scruffy. Simple bungalows cost 15,000Rp. *Pondok Santai* is very similar in standard and price, while *Pondok Karang Baru* looks newer and sturdier and is worth paying a little more: 20,000/25,000Rp for singles/doubles. *Zoraya Pavilion (☎ 27 213)* has a variety of interesting rooms in a large shady area. The prices are negotiable, and cost 25,000Rp to 70,000Rp.

The most central and convenient places are also the most uninspiring. *Malia's Child Bungalows* charges 16,500/20,000Rp for its bungalows, but the bathroom and toilet are outside. *Rusty's Bungalows* is probably the best of the lot for 15,000/20,000Rp.

Janur Indah Bungalows (☎ 33284) is clean, and has bungalows with a ceiling fan and an unusual sunken bathroom for 50,000Rp. This is priced for the just-come-off-the-boat-crowd who land in front of the hotel, so try to negotiate a better price. *Casablanca Cottages (☎ 33847, fax 93482)* is back from the beach, but is nicely set up with a garden and small swimming pool.

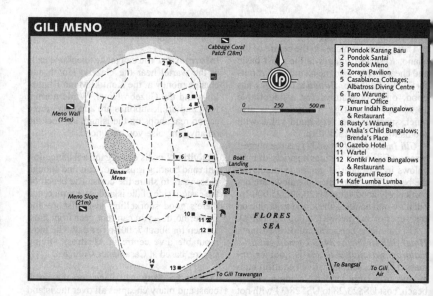

GILI MENO

Cabbage Coral
Patch (28m)

Meno Wall
(15m)

Danau
Meno

Meno Slope
(21m)

Boat
Landing

FLORES
SEA

To Gili Trawangan

To Bangsal

To Gili
Air

0   250   500 m

1 Pondok Karang Baru
2 Pondok Santai
3 Pondok Meno
4 Zoraya Pavilion
5 Casablanca Cottages;
   Albatross Diving Centre
6 Taro Warung;
   Perama Office
7 Janur Indah Bungalows
   & Restaurant
8 Rusty's Warung
9 Malia's Child Bungalows;
   Brenda's Place
10 Gazebo Hotel
11 Wartel
12 Kontiki Meno Bungalows
   & Restaurant
13 Bouganvil Resor
14 Kafe Lumba Lumba

The quaint cottages cost US$11/14 with a fan to US$50 with air-con and hot water.

Gazebo Hotel (☎/fax 35795) has tastefully decorated bungalows with private bathrooms and air-con, comfortably spaced among shady coconut trees. Cottages cost US$45/55; more for full-board. It's closed from mid-January to mid-March. *Kontiki Meno Bungalows* (☎/fax 32824) has standard wooden bungalows for 30,000Rp, as well as more expensive brick bungalows for 50,000Rp – all with fans.

The upmarket *Bouganvil Resor* (☎/fax 35295) has a swimming pool and large comfortable rooms with air-con and hot water from US$30 to US$72 – considerably more in the high season.

Places to Eat *Janur Indah Bungalows* has reasonable prices: 4000Rp to 7000Rp for most dishes. *Brenda's Place*, the beachfront restaurant at Malia's Child Bungalows, has a wide range of cheap western and Indonesian food, and a breezy upstairs area. *Rusty's Warung* is deservedly popular for good value western and Indonesian meals

from 3000Rp to 7000Rp. *Kontiki Meno Bungalows* has pretty good food in a big pavilion, but it's more expensive than other places. Although it's a fair walk, *Kafe Lumba Lumba* has decent Padang-style food, and promises outstanding sunsets, as well as live music most nights.

Gili Trawangan
The largest island, Trawangan, has the most visitors and facilities, and a reputation as the 'party island' of the group. The island is about 2km long and 1½km wide – you can walk right around it in about two hours.

Information Several places will change money or travellers cheques, but you'll get a far better rate at Senggigi. The Blue Marlin Dive Centre may give cash advances on Visa or MasterCard for a 3% commission (but don't count on it); and it has an expensive fax service. The wartel sells stamps (there is no post office), and there are a few bookshops in the Pasar Seni. Perama boats normally beach outside its office; other boats anchor near (but not at) the jetty.

Activities Trawangan is great for wandering around. There are some remains of an old **Japanese cannon** behind the Dewi Sri Bungalows, and the hill in the south-west corner is a good place to enjoy the view across the straits to Bali's Gunung Agung, especially at sunset.

One or two local outfits run four-hour trips on a glass bottom boat to the other two islands – inquire and book at any shop-cum-travel agency. If you ask around, you can rent a boat holding up to 10 people for 80,000Rp to 100,000Rp per day.

The best area for snorkelling is off the north-east coast. Snorkelling gear can be rented from the shacks near the boat landing. Some excellent diving sites are within a short boat ride, especially off Trawangan's west coast. You should choose one of the three long-established centres: Blue Marlin Dive Centre (☎ 32424, fax 93043, email

bmdc@mataram.wasantara.net.id); Albatross (☎ 38134); and Blue Coral (☎ 34497).

Places to Stay The cheapest places are the homestays a few hundred metres from the beach, such as *Alex Homestay* and *Losmen Eky*, which cost 8000/10,000Rp for singles/doubles.

For some isolation, *Sudi Mampir Cottages* costs 10,000/15,0000Rp; *Pondok Santai*, spread out in a nice garden, has doubles for 15,000Rp; and *Dewi Sri Bungalows*, a tidy place well away from everything, has bungalows for 15,000Rp. *Sunset Cottages* has been recommended by readers and has rooms for about 25,000/35,000Rp.

For something closer to the 'action', there are a number of central, clean but unexciting places, such as *Danau Hijau Cottages,* with rooms for 20,000Rp to 30,000Rp; *Halim Bungalows*, basic but cheap, with rooms for

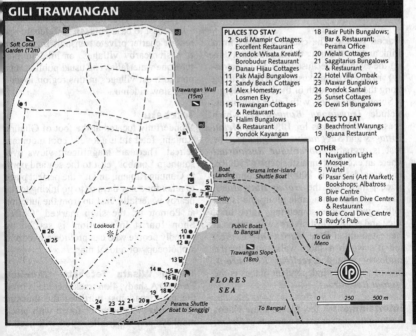

GILI TRAWANGAN

Soft Coral Garden (12m)

Trawangan Wall (15m)

Boat Landing

Perama Inter-island Shuttle Boat

Jetty

Public Boats to Bangsal

To Gili Meno

Trawangan Slope (18m)

Lookout

FLORES SEA

Perama Shuttle Boat to Senggigi

To Bangsal

0   250   500 m

PLACES TO STAY
2 Sudi Mampir Cottages; Excellent Restaurant
7 Pondok Wisata Kreatif; Borobudur Restaurant
9 Danau Hijau Cottages
11 Pak Majid Bungalows
12 Sandy Beach Cottages
14 Alex Homestay; Losmen Eky
15 Trawangan Cottages & Restaurant
16 Halim Bungalows & Restaurant
17 Pondok Kayangan
18 Pasir Putih Bungalows; Bar & Restaurant; Perama Office
20 Melati Cottages
21 Saggitarius Bungalows & Restaurant
22 Hotel Villa Ombak
23 Mawar Bungalows
24 Pondok Santai
25 Sunset Cottages
26 Dewi Sri Bungalows

PLACES TO EAT
3 Beachfront Warungs
19 Iguana Restaurant

OTHER
1 Navigation Light
4 Mosque
5 Wartel
6 Pasar Seni (Art Market); Bookshops; Albatross Dive Centre
8 Blue Marlin Dive Centre & Restaurant
10 Blue Coral Dive Centre
13 Rudy's Pub

NUSA TENGGARA

10,000/15,000Rp; the ordinary *Mawar Bungalows,* which charges about 20,000Rp; and *Pasir Putih Bungalows*, with an attached, noisy bar. One of the best is *Saggitarius Bungalows*, set out in a pretty garden. Rooms cost 15,000Rp; bungalows are 25,000Rp.

A number of newer, characterless concrete 'bungalows' are located along the main strip. Priced from 25,000Rp to 40,000Rp per room, they are generally clean, friendly and safe, and offer fans and modern bathrooms. *Pak Majid Bungalows* and *Sandy Beach Cottages* have rooms for identical prices (30,000Rp) and similar facilities, but are nothing special. *Pondok Wisata Kreatif (☎ 34 893)* and *Trawangan Cottages (☎ 23582)* are overpriced with rooms for 35,000/40,000Rp, but are both popular and friendly.

Hotel Villa Ombak (☎ 22093) features stylish lumbung-style rooms with a fan for US$35, and better bungalows for US$50. It has a nice garden, but no swimming pool – it finds it very hard to compete, so prices are negotiable.

Places to Eat The cheapest places for a drink and meal during the day (but not during the evening, because there's no electricity) are any of the makeshift *warungs* strung along the beach, north of the boat landing.

Some of the hotels with better restaurants include *Trawangan Bungalows*, which does passable pizzas for 10,000Rp, *Melati Cottages* and *Saggitarius Bungalows*. The best is arguably *Borobudur Restaurant* where an excellent tuna steak costs 7500Rp, and a cold beer is 8000Rp. A couple of places, including the *Halim Bungalows*, offer fresh fish on a table along the island path – just choose something, agree on a price and enjoy. Most divers swap stories at the restaurant at *Blue Marlin Dive Centre*, and it's worth a short walk north to the modestly named *Excellent Restaurant*. One of the better independent places is the *Iguana Restaurant*.

Entertainment A few places show videos most nights, such as the restaurants at *Halim*, *Melati* and *Pasir Putih* hotels. Each screening starts at 7 pm. The major 'rage spot' is *Rudy's Pub*, which advertises upcoming attractions on trees along the path.

Getting Around You can rent a cidomo for a short trip, or to go around the island. A cartel of bicycle owners at the beachfront warungs have set the price of rental at a ludicrous 5000Rp per hour, or 20,000Rp per day. It only takes about one hour to cycle around the island – if the bike works, and the tracks aren't too sandy.

CENTRAL LOMBOK

The area on the southern slopes of Gunung Rinjani is well watered and lush, and offers opportunities for scenic walks through the rice fields and jungle. Towards the southern coast the country is drier, and dams have been built to provide irrigation during the dry season. Most of the places in central Lombok are more or less traditional Sasak settlements, and several of them are known for particular types of local handicrafts.

It is best to base yourself in Tetebatu and rent or charter private transport from there to visit nearby villages, or hike to picturesque waterfalls. The usual public transport to most villages in this region is on a very slow cidomo.

Tetebatu

Wonderfully located at the foot of Gunung Rinjani, Tetebatu is a lovely, cool mountain retreat. There are magnificent views over southern Lombok, east to the sea and north to Gunung Rinjani, and it's the perfect place to relax for a few days or to go hiking to the nearby waterfalls. Just up from the junction at Pomotong, the shop marked 'Coffee Shop Tourist Information' is staffed by friendly people who can provide advice and a photocopy of a local map.

Taman Wisata Tetebatu (Monkey Forest)
A shady, 4km track that leads from the main road just north of the mosque heads into this pocket of forest with black monkeys and waterfalls – you will need a

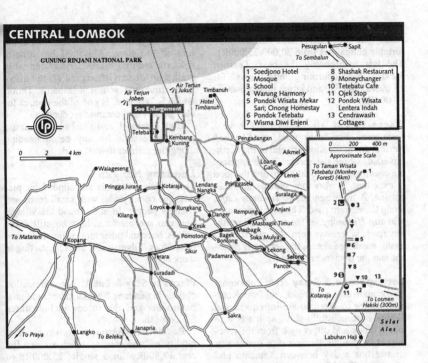

CENTRAL LOMBOK

GUNUNG RINJANI NATIONAL PARK

Pesugulan — Sapit
To Sembalun

1 Soedjono Hotel
2 Mosque
3 School
4 Warung Harmony
5 Pondok Wisata Mekar
   Sari; Onong Homestay
6 Pondok Tetebatu
7 Wisma Diwi Enjeni
8 Shashak Restaurant
9 Moneychanger
10 Tetebatu Cafe
11 Ojek Stop
12 Pondok Wisata
   Lentera Indah
13 Cendrawasih
   Cottages

Air Terjun Joben
Air Terjun Jukut
Timbanuh
Hotel Timbanuh

See Enlargement

Tetebatu
Kembang Kuning
Pengadangan
Aikmel

0   2   4 km

0   200   400 m
Approximate Scale

To Taman Wisata
Tetebatu (Monkey
Forest) (4km)

Waiageseng
Pringga Jurang   Kotaraja   Lendang   Pringgasela
                           Nangka
Loyok   Rungkang   Danger   Rempung
Kilang   Kesik
Kopang   Pomotong   Bagek   Masbagik
                           Bontong
                  Sikur   Padamara
Terara
Suradadi

Lenek
Loang
Gali
Suralaga
Anjani
Masbagik Timur
Suka Mulya
Lekong
Selong
Pancor

To Mataram

To Losmen
Hakiki (300m)

To
Kotaraja

Sakra

To Praya   Langko   Janapria
           To Beleka

Labuhan Haji

Selat
Alas

NUSA TENGGARA

guide to find them (ask at your losmen). Alternatively, you could take an ojek from the turn-off. A tiny, unmarked path at the end of the track leads to *Kios Monkey Forest*, a compound with a few huts where a handful of visitors can stay and eat (for a donation).

Waterfalls On the southern slopes of Gunung Rinjani National Park there are two waterfalls. Both are only accessible by private transport, or on a lovely 1½ hour walk (one way) through the rice fields from Tetebatu. If walking, even in a group, for safety reasons *be sure* to hire a reputable guide (ask at your losmen). There have been reports of muggings in this area.

Locals believe that water from **Air Terjun Jukut** (aka Jeruk Manis and Air Temer) will increase hair growth. The falls are a steep 2km walk from the car park at the end of the road. To the north-west, **Air Terjun Joben**

(aka Otak Kokok Gading) is more of a public swimming pool; locals believe the water here can cure all sorts of ailments.

Places to Stay There is a string of small, friendly losmen along the two main roads. Almost identical in price (about 15,000/20,000Rp for singles/doubles) and standard are four places next to each other along the northern road: *Pondok Wisata Mekar Sari*; *Pondok Tetebatu*; *Wisma Diwi Enjeni*, with the best views and setting; and the friendly *Onong Homestay*. The road ends at the charming, colonial *Soedjono Hotel*. It has great views, a large swimming pool (empty at the time of writing) and a range of rooms: bungalows cost 16,500/22,000Rp and 'superior' rooms are 55,000/66,000Rp.

Along the road heading east, *Cendrawasih Cottages* is newer and cleaner than most, and good value with cottages for

15,000/20,000Rp. *Pondok Wisata Lentera Indah* (aka Green Orry) has a range of comfortable bungalows from 20,000/25,000Rp. The last is probably the best: *Losmen Hakiki* has charming bungalows for 15,000/25,000Rp, and larger bungalows for 30,000Rp.

Places to Eat All hotel's listed have a *restaurant*. For Sasak food, try *Shashak Restaurant* at the southern end of the northern road, where the service is slow, prices are cheap (3000Rp to 6000Rp) and the food is excellent. It also runs classes in Sasak cuisine. A little trendier is *Tetebatu Cafe*, along the eastern road. The best is probably *Warung Harmony*, at the top of the northern road, where western, Indonesian and Sasak meals are cheap, the setting is pleasant and the owners are friendly.

Getting There & Away From Pomotong, on the main east-west road, and from Kotaraja, bemos to Tetebatu are infrequent and cidomos are painfully slow, so it's best to take a quick and direct ojek from the junction at Pomotong. Perama runs one tourist shuttle bus a day between Tetebatu and Mataram (7500Rp) – book at Pondok Wisata Lentera Indah.

Getting Around Pondok Wisata Lentera Indah rents mountain bikes (8000Rp per day), but the roads are steep. Motorbikes can be rented from Warung Harmony, Shashak Restaurant, Pondok Wisata Lentera Indah and Pondok Tetebatu.

Loyok & Rungkang

Loyok is noted for its fine **handicrafts**, particularly basketware and weaving with natural fibres, like bamboo. Rungkang is known for its **pottery**, which is made from a local black clay. The pots are often finished with attractive cane work, which is woven all over the outside for decoration and greater strength. From Pomotong, take a bemo or ojek to Rungkang, from where you can either walk or hire a cidomo 1km to Loyok.

Masbagik

Quite a large town on the main road at the turn-off to Selong, Masbagik has a daily colourful morning market, and a huge **cattle market** on Monday afternoon. There's also a post office and wartel. Masbagik Timur, which is 1km east, is one of the centres for clay **pottery** and ceramic production.

Both Masbagik and Masbagik Timur are easily accessible by any bemo heading along the main east-west road.

Lendang Nangka

This Sasak village is surrounded by picturesque countryside, with small roads and friendly people. In and around the village, you can see blacksmiths who still make knives, hoes and other tools using traditional techniques. Silversmiths are also starting to work here.

Places to Stay & Eat All accommodation options in Lendang Nangka have communal bathrooms and the prices include three Sasak meals.

Radiah's Homestay offers simple hospitality and the rooms, which are scruffy, cost 17,500Rp for a single; 25,000Rp to 30,000Rp for a double. About 200m west of Radiah's, *Pondok Wira* is a little better, and has rice barn-style singles/doubles for 20,000/25,000Rp, and better bungalows for 25,000/30,000Rp. About 2km further towards Kotaraja, *Pondok Sasak* has more character, but the staff can be unhelpful. Simple rooms cost 15,000Rp per person.

Getting There & Away Catch a bus or bemo to Masbagik, on the main east-west road, then take a cidomo to Lendang Nangka. Otherwise, hire an ojek from Pomotong or Tetebatu.

Pringgasela

This village is a centre for **traditional weaving** on simple looms. The cloth produced here features beautifully coloured stripes running the length of the cloth. You can watch the weavers in action and buy the end-product of their work, such as sarongs and blankets.

Akmal Homestay and *Rainbow Cottages* offer simple, family-style accommodation with communal bathroom facilities and the prices include three Sasak meals. Both are on the road heading north to Timbanuh. Akmal Homestay is run by a friendly family and charges 15,000/20,000Rp for singles/doubles. Next door, Rainbow Cottages is not as welcoming, and charges 15,000Rp per person.

If you don't have your own transport, take a bemo to Masbagik or Rempung, and then a cidomo or ojek to Pringgasela.

Timbanuh

At the end of a road up the southern slope of Gunung Rinjani sits the Dutch colonial *Hotel Timbanuh*, a cool respite where the views are simply glorious. The place has seen better days, however, and the rooms are uninspiring for 15,000/25,000Rp for singles/doubles. You will have to prearrange meals with the staff after you arrive, and charter or rent your own transport to get there.

Loang Gali

At Loang Gali, there's a public swimming pool fed by springs in the forest. There are also plenty of **hiking trails** begging to be explored. Overlooking the pools, *Loang Gali Cottages* charges 15,000Rp per person. Loang Gali is at the end of an unsigned dirt road, off the main road north of Lenek. You will need your own transport, and will probably have to ask directions.

SOUTH LOMBOK

South Lombok is appreciably drier than the rest of the island; it is also sparsely populated, and has limited roads and public transport. Most visitors head for Lombok's more serene version of Kuta, but if you have your own transport, and especially if you're into surfing, you can visit several excellent surfing spots and enjoy stunning coastal scenery.

Praya

Praya is the main town in the south-west. It's quite attractive, with spacious gardens, tree-lined streets and a few old **Dutch buildings**.

The bemo terminal, on the north-west side of town, is the transport hub for the region.

Dienda Hayu Hotel (☎ 54319, Jl Untung Surapati 28), just up from the market, is clean and comfortable. Economy rooms cost 27,500Rp and VIP rooms, with air-con, cost 38,500Rp. There aren't a lot of reasons to stay in Praya, unless you use it as a base to explore local craft villages.

Sukarara

Sukarara is a 'traditional weaving centre', though it doesn't look very traditional. The main street is given over to touristy, commercial craft shops, but it's still worth a visit to see the various styles of weaving. Get a bemo to Puyung (where a huge market is held every Sunday), along the main road. From there, hire a cidomo or walk 2km to Sukarara.

Penujak

Penujak is well known for its traditional *gerabah* pottery made from a local clay with the simplest of techniques. The elegantly shaped pots range in size up to 1m high, and there are kitchen vessels of various types and decorative figurines, usually in the shape of animals. The **traditional pottery** is a rich terracotta colour, unglazed, but hand burnished to a lovely soft sheen. Penujak is on the main road from Praya to the south coast; any bemo to Sengkol or Kuta will drop you off.

Rembitan & Sade

The area from Sengkol down to Kuta is a centre of traditional **Sasak culture**. There are regular bemos on this route, especially in the morning.

Rembitan is on a hill just west of the main road. It's a slightly sanitised Sasak village, but is nevertheless an authentic cluster of thatched houses and *lumbung* (rice barn) surrounded by a wooden fence. On top of the hill is **Masjid Kuno**, an old thatched-roof mosque. A little further south is Sade, another 'traditional' village that some say was constructed just for tourists, but it may have been merely an extensive renovation. Donations to both villages are 'requested'.

NUSA TENGGARA

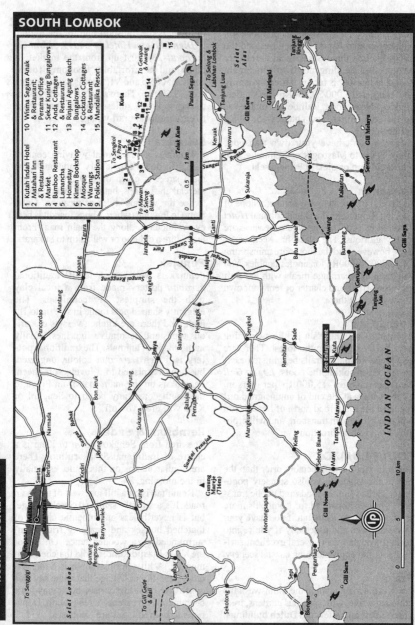

SOUTH LOMBOK

1 Kutah Indah Hotel
   & Restaurant
2 Matahari Inn
   & Restaurant
3 Market
4 Bamboo Restaurant
5 Lamancha
   Homestay
6 Kimen Bookshop
7 Mosque
8 Warungs
9 Police Station
10 Wisma Segara Anak
   & Restaurant;
   Perama Office
11 Sekar Kuning Bungalows
12 Anda Cottages
   & Restaurant
13 Rinjani Agung Beach
   Bungalows
14 Cockatoo Cottages
   & Restaurant
15 Mandalika Resort

Kuta

The best known place in this region is Kuta (sometimes spelt 'Kute'), a magnificent stretch of white sand and turquoise sea with rugged hills rising around it. It has far, *far* fewer tourists and facilities than the (in)famous Kuta Beach in Bali, but there are big plans to develop a whole stretch of the superb south coast with luxury hotels. People flock to Kuta for the annual *nyale* fishing celebration (see the boxed text 'Nyale Fishing Festival' in this section). The main tourist season is August; for the rest of the year, Kuta is quiet and laid back.

Information Guests can change money at Matahari Inn, Mandalika Resort and Kuta Indah Hotel, while anyone can change money at the Anda Cottages and Wisma Segara Anak (which is also a postal agency). New books can be bought at Wisma Segara Anak, and old paperbacks at Kimen Bookshop. There are telephones in the hotels, but no wartel. The mosquitoes can be bad at times, so come prepared.

Surfing Plenty of good waves break on the reefs – many are supposedly secret. There are 'lefts' and 'rights' in the bay in front of Kuta, and some more on the reefs east of Tanjung Aan. Local boatmen will take you out for a negotiable fee. About 7km east of Kuta is the fishing village of Gerupak, where there are several potential breaks on the reefs at the entrance of Teluk Gerupak (Gerupak Bay). Again, access is by local fishing boat. There are more breaks further out, but nearly all require a boat. The current charter rate is about 80,000Rp per day.

For surfing tips, repairs and surfboard/boogie-board rentals (15,000/10,000Rp per day), visit the office belonging to the Ocean Blue surf shop.

Places to Stay Most places are along the esplanade and are fairly similar: bamboo cottages (often semi-detached) on stilts, in a scruffy garden, with an attached concrete bathroom and a small balcony. They should provide a fan and mosquito net.

Nyale Fishing Festival

On the 19th day of the 10th month in the Sasak calendar – generally February or March – hundreds of Sasaks gather on the beach at Kuta, Lombok. When night falls, fires are built and young people sit around competing with each other in rhyming couplets called *pantun*. At dawn the next day, the first *nyale* (a worm-like fish), are caught, after which it's time for the teenagers to have fun. In a colourful procession boys and girls sail out to sea – in different boats – and chase one another with lots of noise and laughter. The nyale are eaten raw or grilled, and are believed to have aphrodisiac properties. A good catch is a sign that the rice harvest will also be good.

Around a spacious garden, *Anda Cottages* (☎ 54836) is good value at 12,500/15,000Rp for singles/doubles. The modern rooms for 25,000/35,000Rp are large and clean. *Sekar Kuning Bungalows* (☎ 54856) is very similar. *Wisma Segara Anak* (☎ 54834) is well set up, although possibly a little complacent because it is popular and convenient. Bungalows cost 10,000/15,0000Rp.

Rinjani Agung Beach Bungalows (☎ 54849) has rooms for 15,000Rp, and bungalows for 20,000Rp. The bungalows with air-con are good value for 30,000Rp. *Cockatoo Cottages* (☎ 54830) is a little more secluded, and good value. Simple bungalows cost 7000/10,000Rp; the one modern bungalow for 20,000Rp is worth asking for. The quiet and cosy *Lamancha Homestay* is not on the beach, but has one lovely bungalow for 20,000Rp, and a few smaller, dreary rooms for 15,000Rp.

The two mid-range places are a short walk from the beach. *Kuta Indah Hotel* (☎ 53781, fax 54628) charges US$21/26 to US$42/49 for decent rooms around a grassy area. The pool is probably the main attraction. The hotel also provides free transport to local beaches and surfing spots. The shady and

NUSA TENGGARA

popular *Matahari Inn (☎ 54832, fax 54909, email matahari@mataram.wasantara.net.id)* is jointly managed by Swiss expats. The economy rooms for 25,000/30,000Rp are decent, but often full; the range of rooms with air-con and hot water are excellent value for 60,000Rp to 110,000Rp.

The brand, spanking new *Mandalika Resort (☎ 53333, fax 53555, email novotel@ lombokonline.com)* is run by Novotel, and has a range of rooms from US$156. Children are welcome and well catered for.

Places to Eat There are several cheap *warungs* along the esplanade, and each hotel has a restaurant. *Cockatoo Cottages* is probably the best value, with western meals for 8000Rp and tasty Indonesian dishes for about 6000Rp. *Wisma Segara Anak* is large, breezy and has the only happy hour in town (large beers are 7000Rp), but the meals are a little overpriced. *Matahari Inn* offers reasonable pizzas from 10,000Rp, and *Anda Cottages* is popular with tour groups because of its airy setting and reasonable prices. *Bamboo Restaurant* is also good value, but some items may be *habis* (unavailable).

Getting There & Away Public transport directly to Kuta from the Mandalika terminal in Bertais (Mataram, 1250Rp) is not frequent; you may have to catch a bemo to Praya, and then another to Kuta. Travel early or you may get stuck and have to charter a vehicle some of the way. Perama (☎ 54846), based at Wisma Segara Anak, has one tourist shuttle bus per day to Mataram (10,000Rp).

Getting Around Surprisingly, the only place that rents motorbikes is Matahari Inn (17,000Rp per day), but this may change in the future. The occasional cidomo plods along the main road; otherwise, saunter around like everyone else.

East of Kuta

Quite good roads traverse the coast to the east, passing a series of beautiful bays that are punctuated by headlands. There's public transport, but you will see more with

your own transport – a mountain bike would be good (but bring your own).

Pantai Segar (Segar Beach) is about 2km east around the first headland, and you can easily walk there. An enormous rock another 2km further east offers superb views across the countryside if you climb it early in the morning. From Kuta the road goes 5km east to **Tanjung Aan**, where there are two classic beaches with very fine, powdery white sand. The road continues another 3km to the fishing village of **Gerupak**, where there's a market on Tuesday. Alternatively, turn north-east just before Tanjung Aan and go to **Awang**, a fishing village with a sideline in seaweed harvesting. You could take a boat from Awang across to **Ekas**, or to some of the other not-so-secret surf spots in this bay.

West of Kuta

The road west of Kuta is sealed as far as **Selong Blanak**, which is a lovely sandy bay. The road doesn't follow the coast closely, but there are regular and spectacular ocean vistas. In between are more fine beaches like **Mawan**, **Tampa** and **Mawi**, but you have to detour to find them. They are all known to have surfing possibilities in the right conditions.

For accommodation, the isolated *Selong Blanak Cottages*, 1.5km north of Selong Blanak, has a variety of rooms from 35,000Rp, and a decent restaurant, but the place is looking neglected these days.

From Pengantap, you climb across a headland to descend to another superb bay, which you follow around for about 1km. Look carefully for the turn-off west to **Blongas**, which is a very steep, rough and winding road with breathtaking scenery. There are some good places for surfing and diving, but you'll need to charter a boat to find them. This is as far west as you can go on this road.

EAST LOMBOK

All that most travellers see of the east coast is Labuhan Lombok, the port for ferries to Sumbawa, but improvements to the road around the north-east and east coast make a round-the-island trip quite feasible and enjoyable. Similarly, the once-remote south-eastern peninsula is becoming more accessible, particularly to those with their own transport.

Labuhan Lombok

Labuhan Lombok, also known as Labuhan Kayangan, is the port for ferries and boats to Sumbawa. The town of Labuhan Lombok, 3km from the ferry terminal, is a scruffy place. If you're on your way to or from Sumbawa, there's no need to stay overnight, and the choice of hotels is very poor.

Places to Stay & Eat In the village, *Losmen Dian Dutaku* has very depressing singles/doubles for 5000/10,000Rp – a last resort only. On the road to the port, *Losmen Munawar* is also noisy and uninspiring, but a little better with rooms for the same price. The best option, *Hotel Melati Lima Tiga*, has rooms for 12,500/18,000Rp, but is still noisy. There are some *warungs* in the town, and around the ferry terminal.

Getting There & Away Frequent buses and bemos travel between Labuhan Lombok and the Mandalika terminal in Bertais (Mataram), and also head north from Labuhan Lombok to Anyar. Note that public transport to/from Labuhan Lombok is often marked 'Labuhan Kayangan' or 'Tanjung Kayangan'. Buses and bemos that do not go directly to Labuhan Lombok, but just travel the main road along the east coast, will only drop you off at the port entrance, from where you'll have to catch another bemo to the ferry terminal. Don't walk; it's too far.

See Getting There & Away at the start of the Lombok section in this chapter for information about the ferry to Sumbawa.

South of Labuhan Lombok

The capital of the East Lombok administrative district, **Selong**, has some Dutch colonial buildings. On the road towards the sea, *Hotel Erina* (☎ 0376-21297, Jl Pahlawan) is not a bad place to stay; decent rooms cost 15,000Rp to 20,000Rp.

The transport junction for the region is **Pancor**, where you can stay at *Hotel Melati*, about 2km north of the bemo terminal.

On the coast is **Labuhan Haji**, which is accessible from Selong and Tanjung Luar by bemo. The black sand beach here is a bit grubby, but the water is OK for swimming. *Melewi's Beach Hotel* (☎ 0376-21241), almost on the beach, about 300m from the bemo stop, is isolated and has great views across to Sumbawa. Pleasant bungalows cost 20,000/25,000Rp for singles/doubles.

Tanjung Luar is one of Lombok's main fishing ports and has lots of Bugis-style houses on stilts. From there, the road swings west to **Keruak**, where wooden boats are made, and continues past the turn to **Sukaraja**, a traditional Sasak village where you can buy woodcarvings. Just west of Keruak a road leads south to **Jerowaru** and the south-eastern peninsula. You'll need your own transport, but it's easy to lose your way and the roads go from bad to worse. A sealed road branches west past Jerowaru – it gets pretty rough but eventually reaches **Ekas**, from where you can charter a boat to Awang across the bay.

On the east coast of the peninsula, **Tanjung Ringgit** has some large caves, which according to a local legend are home to a demonic giant. The road there is rough, and may be impassable after heavy rains. It might be easier to charter a boat from Tanjung Luar.

NORTH LOMBOK

The sparsely populated northern part of Lombok is very scenic, with a variety of landscapes and seascapes, few tourists and even fewer facilities. Public transport is not frequent, nor does it detour from the main road. With your own transport, however, you can stop along the way to admire the views, and make side trips to the coast, waterfalls and inland villages. The major attraction is unquestionably the mighty Gunung Rinjani.

Bangsal to Bayan

The road from Senggigi to Bangsal is scenic, especially the inland route through Pusuk Pass. But continuing north from Bangsal, the road is winding and often steep and public

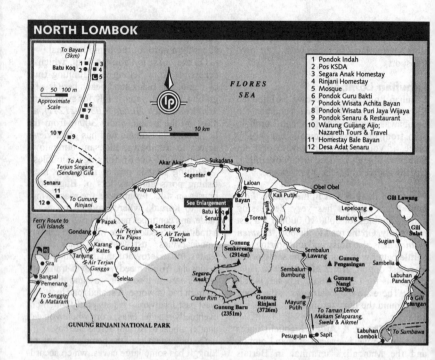

NORTH LOMBOK

To Bayan (3km)
Batu Koq
0   50   100m
Approximate Scale
To Air Terjun Singang (Sendang) Gila
Senaru
To Gunung Rinjani

1 Pondok Indah
2 Pos KSDA
3 Segara Anak Homestay
4 Rinjani Homestay
5 Mosque
6 Pondok Guru Bakti
7 Pondok Wisata Achita Bayan
8 Pondok Wisata Puri Jaya Wijaya
9 Pondok Senaru & Restaurant
10 Warung Guijang Aijo; Nazareth Tours & Travel
11 Homestay Bale Bayan
12 Desa Adat Senaru

FLORES SEA

0   5   10 km

Akar Akar   Sukadana
Segenter   Anyar
Kayangan   Laloan
Bayan   Kali Putih   Obel Obel   Gili Lawang
See Enlargement   Batu Koq   Torean
Senaru   Lepeloang
Blantung   Gili Sulat
Ferry Route to Gili Islands   Papak   Santong   Gunung Senkereang (2914m)   Sajang   Sugian
Gondang   Air Terjun Tiu Pupas   Air Terjun Tiuteja   Sembalun Lawang
Karang Kates   Gangga   Gunung Pengasingan   Sambelia
Sira   Air Terjun Gangga   Selelas   Sembalun Bumbung   Gunung Nangi (2330m)   Labuhan Pandan
Tanjung   Segara Anak
Bangsal   Pemenang   To Senggigi & Mataram   Crater Rim   Gunung Baru (2351m)   Gunung Rinjani (3726m)   Mayung Putih   To Taman Lemor Makam Selaparang, Swela & Aikmel   To Gili Petangan
GUNUNG RINJANI NATIONAL PARK
Pesugulan   Sapit   Labuhan Lombok   To Sumbawa

transport is less frequent. Several minibuses a day go from Mandalika terminal in Bertais (Mataram) to Bayan, and make stops along the way, but you may have to get connections in Pemenang and/or Anyar.

Bangsal The junction for boats to the Gili Islands has shaded warungs, money-changers, shops and travel agents – all taking advantage of the fact that travellers often have to wait there. If you get stuck, *Taman Sari Guesthouse*, at the entrance to the port, has clean singles/doubles for 20,000/25,000Rp.

From the boat terminal, walk about 800m straight up the road for a bemo along Jl Raya Tanjung to Bayan (for Senaur connections). To the south, take a cidomo to Pemenang, which is well connected to Senggigi and Mataram by bemo. You can avoid the hassles of public transport, and enjoy the scenery, by

chartering a bemo or jeep at Bangsal – a vehicle to Senaru costs about 35,000Rp.

Tanjung This village and transport terminal is quite large and attractive, and has a big cattle market on Sunday. Just before Tanjung is the *Manopo Homestay (fax 32688)*, aka Le Club des Explorateurs. It has eccentric management, a lovely seaside location and several basic rooms from 15,000Rp to 25,000Rp.

Karang Kates A little further north-east, Karang Kates (Krakas) has springs that spurt out freshwater from the sea bed offshore – the locals collect their drinking water from the sea. The road sign announcing 'Water in the Sea' is not quite as daft as it appears. It's a great area for snorkelling, but bring your own gear or rent something in Senggigi.

continued on page 676

NUSA TENGGARA

CLIMBING GUNUNG RINJANI

Rinjani is the highest mountain in Lombok and the second-highest in Indonesia; at 3726m it soars above the island. Its huge crater contains a large crescent-shaped lake, Segara Anak (Child of the Sea), which is about 6km across at its widest point.

Rinjani has a series of natural hot springs (*mata air panas*) known as **Kokok Putih**, on the north-eastern side of this crater, which are said to have healing powers, particularly for skin diseases. The lake is 600 vertical metres below the crater rim, and in the middle of its curve is the new cone, Gunung Baru (also known as Gunung Barujari), which is only a couple of hundred years old. Rinjani is an active volcano and erupted as recently as 1994, changing the shape of this inner cone and sprinkling ash over much of Lombok.

Both the Balinese and Sasaks revere Rinjani. To the Balinese, it is equal to Gunung Agung, a seat of the gods, and many Balinese make an annual pilgrimage here. In a ceremony called *pekelan* the people throw jewellery into the lake and make offerings to the spirit of the mountain. Some Sasaks make several pilgrimages a year – full moon is their favourite time for paying respects to the mountain and curing ailments by bathing in its hot springs.

The climb to the crater lake is not to be taken lightly. Don't try it during the wet season (November to April), because the tracks will be slippery and dangerous; in any case you would be lucky to see anything more than mist and cloud. June to August is the only time you are guaranteed (well, almost) no rain or cloud. There are a few possibilities, from a strenuous dash to the rim and back, to a five day trek around the summit. Most visitors stay in Senaru and climb the northern route to the crater lake and return the same way – this route is easily accessible and has better services for trekkers. Alternatively, start from Sapit or trek between Senaru and Sembalun Lawang on the eastern side. It should be noted that in mid-1999, travellers reported being robbed and attacked by gangs armed with machetes at a campsite along the trail and at a hotel in the area. Check the latest situation and camp at the more popular areas.

Organised Tours

A number of agencies in Mataram and Senggigi can organise all-inclusive treks. They are expensive (from US$120 per person for two to three days, minimum of two), but they save time and hassle. Prices include transport to the start, equipment, an English-speaking guide, porters, food and water. Established operators include: Discover Lombok (☎ 36781), Pasar Seni art market, Senggigi; Nazareth Tours & Travel, with offices in Senggigi, Ampenan (Mataram) and Senaru (☎ 31705); Perama, from their offices in Mataram and Senggigi; and Segara Anak Trekking Club, based at Segara Anak Homestay, Senaru.

Text inset: Illustration by Mick Weldon.

Do-it-Yourself

You can organise a trek yourself in Sapit, Senaru or Sembalun Lawang for about one-fifth of the cost charged by trekking agencies. In Sapit, contact Hati Suci Homestay; in Senaru, contact any of the losmen, particularly Pondok Indah, Pondok Guru Bakti and Homestay Bale Bayan, which are helpful and have equipment to rent; or contact the two losmen in Sembalun Lawang.

Guides & Porters

You can trek from Senaru to the hotsprings and back without a guide – the trail is well defined. From Sembalun Lawang the starting point is clear, but after that there are a number of trails branching off and you could get lost. Climbing to the summit of Rinjani is generally undertaken in the dark to meet the sunrise, so it's best to have someone with you who knows the way.

In Senaru, guides cost about 30,000Rp per day and porters cost 20,000Rp; in Sembalun Lawang and Sapit, the standard costs are 40,000/25,000Rp for a guide/porter. You also have to provide food, water and transport for them, and probably cigarettes as well.

Equipment

There are some very crude shelters on the way, but don't rely on them – a sleeping bag and tent are essential. In Senaru, a two/four person tent will cost about 15,000/30,000Rp; a sleeping bag, 6000Rp; and sleeping mattress, 3000Rp – prices are for a two night/three day trek. A stove (so you don't deplete the limited supply of firewood and also so you can boil water) will cost 10,000Rp to 15,000Rp in Senaru for three days, plus fuel. Rental prices in Sapit and Sembalun Lawang are slightly more, because there is little or no competition. You'll also need to bring your own solid footwear, some layers of warm clothing, and wet weather gear.

Food & Supplies

Take rice, instant noodles, sugar, tea, coffee, eggs, biscuits or bread, some tins of fish or meat (and a can opener!), onions, fruit and anything else that keeps your engine running. It's better to buy most of these supplies in Mataram or Senggigi, where it's cheaper and there's more choice, but there's a fair range in Senaru. Take plenty of water (there are some water sources along the way, however), matches and a torch (flashlight).

The Climb

The walk is usually done from Senaru in the north. Independent trekkers usually go halfway and then back to Senaru, but you can walk from Senaru to Sembalun Lawang and then take public transport or charter a bemo back to Senaru. The trail from Pelawangan II (*pelawangan* means gateway and refers to one of the few places that you can access the crater rim) to Lawang is indistinct. A guide is strongly recommended for this section and essential if starting in Lawang.

Facing page from left to right: The view from the flank of Gunung Rinjani, hot springs.

PETER TURNER

PETER TURNER

PETER TURNER

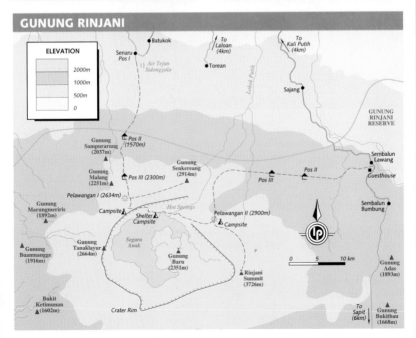

GUNUNG RINJANI

ELEVATION

2000m
1000m
500m
0

Batukok
Senaru
Pos I
Air Tejun
Sidonggala

To
Laloan
(4km)

To
Kali Putih
(4km)

Torean

Lokok Putih

Sajang

GUNUNG
RINJANI
RESERVE

Gunung
Sampurarung
(2037m)

Pos II
(1570m)

Gunung
Malang
(2251m)

Pos III (2300m)

Gunung
Senkereang
(2914m)

Pos II

Pos III

Sembalun
Lawang

Guesthouse

Pelawangan I (2634m)

Gunung
Marungmeriris
(1892m)

Campsite

Shelter
Campsite

Hot Springs

Pelawangan II (2900m)

Campsite

Sembalun
Bumbung

Gunung
Buanmangge
(1916m)

Gunung
Tanaklayur
(2664m)

Segara
Anak

Gunung
Baru
(2351m)

Rinjani
Summit
(3726m)

0   5   10 km

Gunung
Adas
(1893m)

Bukit
Ketimunan
(1602m)

Crater Rim

To
Sapit
(6km)

Gunung
Bukitbau
(1668m)

Climbing Gunung Rinjani

PETER TURNER

PETER TURNER

Masochists in a hurry could walk from Senaru to Lawang (or vice versa) in two full days with one night at the hot springs, but the first day would be very difficult and it doesn't include the climb to the top. More usual is a three day walk to the hot springs and return from Senaru, or a four or five day full-circuit including the ascent of Rinjani. The minimum time for the full circuit is three days/two nights.

The last day of the full circuit is a long slog, but is downhill all the way after the hard climb to Rinjani. Many walkers return to Senaru, after climbing the summit, for a five day trip that includes another night at the hot springs.

Senaru to Hot Springs
Day 1 Senaru to Pos III (five to six hours)
Day 2 Pos III to Kokoh Putih (three to four hours)
Day 3 Hot Springs to Senaru (eight to nine hours)

Top: View from Pelawangan II.

Bottom: View of Gunung Agung and Gunung Batur from the Rinjani summit.

Full Circuit
Day 1 Senaru to Pos III (five to six hours)
Day 2 Pos III to Kokoh Putih (three to four hours)
Day 3 Hot Springs to Pelawangan II (three to four hours)
Day 4 Pelawangan II to Rinjani summit and further on to Sembalun (10 to 11 hours)

Senaru to Pos III (5-6 hours)
At the end of the village is the PHPA post (Pos I on some maps, 860m) where you register and pay a fee (2000Rp). Just beyond the post is a small *warung* and then the trail forks – continue straight ahead on the right fork. The trail steadily ascends through scrubby farmland for about half an hour to the sign at the entrance to Gunung Rinjani National Park (Taman Nasional Gunung Rinjani). The wide trail climbs for another 2½ hours until you reach Pos II (1570m), where there are two shelters. Water can be found 100m down the slopes from the trail, and is the most reliable source on the ascent – but it should be treated or boiled.

Another 1½ hours steady walk uphill brings you to Pos III (2300m), where there's another two shelters in disrepair. Water is 100m off the trail to the right, but sometimes dries up in the dry season. Pos III is the usual place to camp at the end of the first day.

Pos III to Pelawangan I (1½-2 hours)
From Pos III, it takes about 1½ hours to reach the rim, Pelawangan I, at an altitude of 2634m. Set off very early to arrive at the crater rim for the stunning sunrise. It's possible to camp at Pelawangan I. You can extend yourself to walk here at the end of the first day for a spectacular sunset and an equally spectacular sunrise the next morning. The drawbacks are that level camp sites are limited, there is no water and it can be very blustery.

Pelawangan I to Segara Anak & Hot Springs (2-3 hours)
It takes about two hours to descend to Segara Anak and around to the hot springs. The first hour is a very steep descent and involves low-grade rock climbing in parts. At the bottom of the crater wall, it is then an easy one hour walk across undulating terrain around the lake edge.

There are several places to camp, but most hikers prefer to be near the hot springs to soak their weary body and recuperate. Two dilapidated shelters are beside the lake, but the nicest camp sites are at the lake's edge. Fresh water can be gathered from a spring near the hot springs.

Some hikers spend two nights, or even more, at the lake but most head back to Senaru the next day. The climb back up the rim is certainly taxing – allow at least three hours and start early to make it back to Senaru in one day. Allow five hours from the rim down to Senaru. The last bemo down the mountain from Senaru leaves at around 4 pm.

Rather than retrace your steps, the best option is to press on to Sembalun Lawang if you can work out what to do with your gear.

Hot Springs to Pelawangan II (3-4 hours)

The trail starts beside the last shelter at the hot springs and heads away from the lake for about 100m before veering right. The trail traverses the northern slope of the crater, away from the lake, and it's an easy walk for one hour along the grassy slopes. Then it's a steep and constant climb; from the lake it takes about three hours until you finally reach the crater rim.

At the rim a sign points the way back to Segara Anak. Water can be found down the slope near the sign. The trail forks here – go straight on to Lawang or continue along the rim to the campsite of Pelawangan II (2900m). It's only about 10 minutes more to the campsite on a bare ridge.

Pelawangan II to Rinjani Summit (5-6 hours return)

Gunung Rinjani stretches in an arc above the campsite at Pelawangan II and looks deceptively close. The usual time to start the climb is at 3 am in order to reach the summit in time for the sunrise before the clouds roll in.

It takes about 45 minutes up to the ridge that leads to Rinjani. The steep trail is slippery and hard to find in the dark unless you have a guide or you checked it out the evening before. Don't try to climb to the peak when strong winds are blowing; the winds are icy, dust swirls in your eyes and it can upset your balance. Once on the ridge it's a relatively easy walk gradually uphill, for an hour or so. After about an hour heading up towards what looks like the peak, the real summit of Rinjani looms behind and towers above you.

The trail then gets steeper and steeper. About 500m before the summit, the scree is composed of loose, fist-sized rocks – it is easier to scramble on all fours. This section can take one hour. The views from the top are truly magnificent on a clear day. The descent is much easier, but take it easy on the scree. In total it takes three hours or more to reach the summit, two to get back down.

Pelawangan II to Sembalun Lawang (5-6 hours)

After having negotiated the peak it is possible to reach Lawang the same day. After a two hour descent, it is a long and hot three hour walk. Head off early to avoid as much of the heat of the day as possible and make sure you have plenty of water to reach Lawang.

From the camp site head back to the main trail and follow it for only a couple of hundred metres. The trail almost becomes a road but don't keep following it – the trail to Lawang is a small and unsigned side trail that branches off. Keep looking over the edge until you find it – it follows the next ridge along from Rinjani, not the valley. Once on the trail, it's easy to follow and takes around two hours to reach the bottom.

At the bottom of the ridge the trail levels out and crosses undulating to flat grassland all the way to Lawang. An hours walk will bring you to Pos III, a relatively new shelter, and then it is another 30 minutes to Pos II. Long grass obscures the trail, which was once a road, and in places you cannot see it more than a couple of metres ahead. About

30 minutes beyond Pos II the trail crosses a bridge and then crosses a small rise to a lone tree. The trail seems to fork here; take the right fork.

Having orientated Lawang firmly in your mind, experienced hikers with plenty of water should be able to reach it without too much difficulty – as a general rule the trail follows the flank of Rinjani before swinging around to Lawang at the end. However, a guide is strongly recommended for this part of the trip.

Starting from Sembalun Lawang, it is six or seven hours to Pelawangan II and *a guide is essential*. It is much harder to get your bearings walking up the mountain, and the trail is all but impossible to find on your own. This is an easier walk to the rim than from the Senaru side, with only a three hour walk up the ridge. Before starting off, sign in at the Departemen Kehutanan (Forest Department) office on the main road in Lawang, where the road to Rinjani starts, and pay the 2000Rp fee. Horses can be hired to take you to Pos III for 30,000Rp.

A Night Climb

If you travel light and climb fast you can reach the crater rim from Senaru in about six hours – it's approximately a 1770m altitude gain in 10km, approximately. With a torch and some moonlight, and/or a guide, set off at midnight and you'll be there for sunrise. Coming back takes about five hours. Take lots of snack food and water.

Around the Rim

If you reach Pelawangan I early in the day, you can follow the crater rim around to the east for about 3km to Gunung Senkereang (2914m). This point overlooks the gap in the rim where the stream from the hot springs flows out of the crater and north-east towards the sea. It's not an easy walk, however, and the track is narrow and very exposed in places.

Other Routes on Rinjani

You can climb up to the crater from Torean, a small village south-east of Bayan. The trail follows Sungai Putih (the stream that flows from Segara Anak and the hot springs), but it's hard to find – you'll need a guide.

You can also climb the south side of Rinjani from either Sesaot or Tetebatu. Either route will involve at least one night camping in the jungle and you may not see any views at all until you get above the tree line. Again, a guide is essential. A better option from the south is from Sapit to Pelawangan II.

Gunung Baru (2351m) is the 'new' cone in the middle of Segara Anak and it may look tempting but *it's a very dangerous climb*. The track around the lake to the base of Baru is narrow and people have drowned after slipping off it. The climb is over very loose surface and if you start sliding or falling there is nothing to stop you and nothing to hang on to. Also, many of the tracks around here were wiped out in the 1994 eruption.

continued from page 670

Godang In this village, *Suhardi Home Stay* has simple but pleasant singles/doubles for about 15,000/25,000Rp. It's the best place to base yourself while you explore the nearby beaches and waterfalls.

Air Terjun Tiu Pupas This 30m waterfall is about 4km inland along a rough track from Gondang. There are other nearby waterfalls on the northern slopes of Gunung Rinjani, but they're only worth seeing up until the beginning of the dry season, and most are very difficult to reach.

Segenter This traditional Sasak village is a bit hard to find, but worth the effort. A track (usually not accessible by car) heads south off the main road, about 1km west of Sukadana. The village is neatly laid out, with rows of identical rectangular houses facing each other and communal pavilions in between. Afterwards you should make a donation and sign the visitors' book.

Bayan This northernmost part of Lombok's coast is the birthplace of the Wektu Telu religion, and also a home for traditional Muslims. The **mosque**, on the road east of the junction at Bayan, is possibly the oldest in Lombok – perhaps over 300 years old.

Banyan to Labuhan Lombok

This road has limited public transport. The road east from the main northern junction at Anyar is very steep and windy. There are isolated black sand beaches along the way, particularly at Obel Obel.

Further south, the pleasant and secluded *Siola Cottages*, just before the village of Labuhan Pandan, is set in a coconut grove on the seashore. Bungalows cost about 20,000Rp; more including meals. You can also stop there for a meal or a snack at the restaurant. About 2km south, *Gili Lampu Cottages* has simple bamboo bungalows a bit back from the beach for 15,000Rp.

From Labuhan Pandan, or further north at Sugian, you can charter a boat to the unin-

habited **Gili Sulat** and **Gili Pentangan**. Both islands have lovely white beaches and good coral for snorkelling, but no facilities. As you approach Labuhan Lombok, look for the giant trees about 5km north of the harbour.

Senaru

This picturesque village is the usual starting point for a climb up Gunung Rinjani, but even if you're not interested in climbing, Senaru is still worth a visit. There is a good range of budget accommodation, some with superb views over the valley to the east and up to the rim of Gunung Rinjani.

Air Terjun Singang (Sendang) Gila Make sure you visit these magnificent waterfalls. From the entrance to the falls, it's a pleasant 30 minute walk, partly through forest and partly alongside an irrigation canal that follows the contour of the hill, occasionally disappearing into tunnels where the cliffs are too steep.

Another 30 minutes or so further up the hill are more waterfalls, where you can go swimming. The track is steep and tough at times, so it's a good idea to take a guide. Some boys will probably approach you and offer their services (for a negotiable fee, of course).

Desa Adat Senaru The traditional village compound of Senaru has an air of untainted antiquity, but it has become a bit of a tourist trap lately. You must report to the village head, sign a visitors' book and make a 'donation' – at least 5000Rp is 'urged', but 1000Rp is enough.

Places to Stay & Eat Most losmen are similar in standards and price, and are located along the main road through the village. *Segara Anak Homestay* has good views and a helpful manager who charges 15,000Rp a room. *Pondok Guru Bakti* and *Pondok Indah* have rooms for about 15,000Rp and are good places to organise treks.

Other good options are: *Rinjani Homestay*, which is basic but a little cheaper than most others (10,000Rp); *Pondok Wisata Achita Bayan*, which costs 10,000/12,000Rp for singles/doubles; and *Pondok Wisata Puri Jaya Wijaya*, which is the cheapest with rooms for 7500/10,000Rp. *Homestay Bale Bayan*, opposite the 'traditional village', is quite atmospheric and the closest to the trailhead. Decent rooms cost 15,000Rp. The rooms at *Pondok Senaru (Mataram ☎ 22 868)* are large, quaint and offer views from the small patios, but the hotel caters to tour groups, and charges 50,000Rp.

Every losmen has a *restaurant* or 'coffee shop' (a common term in the village). The best for views is the restaurant at *Pondok Senaru*, which also has good food at surprisingly reasonable prices. The only independent restaurant is the basic *Warung Guijang Aijo*.

Getting There & Away From the west, catch a bemo to Anyar, from where bemos travel to Senaru about every 20 minutes until 4 pm. If you're coming from, or going to, eastern Lombok, get off at the junction near Bayan (your driver will know it), from where bemos go to Senaru.

Sapit

Sapit has stunning views across to Sumbawa, with Gunung Rinjani forming a spectacular backdrop. Even if you're not climbing Gunung Rinjani, Sapit is still worth visiting if you want somewhere cool and relaxing to hang out.

Between Swela and Sapit, a side road goes to **Lemor Park**, where there's a refreshing spring-fed swimming pool, and a few pesky grey and black monkeys. Tickets cost 400Rp, and it's open from 8 am to 4 pm daily. Further down the road towards Pringgabaya, another side road goes to **Makam Selaparang**, the burial place of ancient Selaparang kings. Neither place is particularly exciting, but it's a good excuse for some hiking.

You can also visit a few **hot water springs** and small **waterfalls** near Sapit. Ask either homestay for directions.

Places to Stay & Eat *Hati Suci Homestay (Mataram ☎ 36545, fax 35753)* has several pleasant bungalows in a splendid location.

The bungalows cost 20,000/35,000Rp to 30,000/50,000Rp for singles/doubles. The restaurant is worth a visit, if only for the breeze and views. Not as good, but cheaper, is the associated *Balelangga Bed & Breakfast* (same contact details as the Hati Suci). Simple bungalows, with outside bathroom facilities, cost 15,000/25,000Rp. It is about 700m past the Hati Suci Homestay.

Getting There & Away First get a bus to Pringgabaya, which is on the main road between Labuhan Lombok and Mataram. From Pringgabaya catch a bemo to Sapit.

Sembalun Lawang & Sembalun Bumbung

On the eastern side of Gunung Rinjani is the beautiful Sembalun valley. The inhabitants of the valley claim descent from the Hindu Javanese, and a relative of one of the Majapahit rulers is said to be buried here. Sembalun Bumbung is a sprawling and relatively wealthy village lying just off the main road. It is often referred to simply as Sembalun; the 'Bumbung' is used to differentiate it from Sembalun Lawang, 2.5km north along the main road. Lawang is a satellite village, but it's at the start of a trek to Gunung Rinjani, and the better place to stay.

Places to Stay & Eat Along the main road to the start of the trail in Sembalun Lawang are two places, which also serve meals and arrange guides, porters and hiking gear. *Pondok Sembalun* is an attractive place where small bungalows cost 10,000/12,500Rp for singles/doubles. *Wisma Cemara Siu (☎ 03 76-21213)* has good rooms in a spacious, spotless house with views of the mountain for 10,000/15,000Rp.

In Sembalun Bumbung, *Puri Rinjani* has basic rooms in the house for 10,000Rp or new bungalows out the back for 15,000Rp. Horse riding can be arranged for around 15,000Rp, and there are plans to provide mountain bikes for guests.

Getting There & Away From Kali Putih to the north, a few bemos run along the rough road to both villages, usually only in the morning. From Aikmel to the south, a scenic, sealed road twists over the mountains, normally only as far as Bumbung.

Sumbawa

Between Lombok and Flores, and separated from them by narrow straits, is the rugged land mass of Sumbawa. Larger than Bali and Lombok combined, Sumbawa is a sprawling island of twisted and jutting peninsulas, with a coast fringed by precipitous hills and angular bights, and a mountain line of weathered volcanic stumps stretching along its length.

Sumbawa is a scenic island, with plenty of scope for exploring off the beaten track. Few visitors venture beyond Sumbawa Besar, Bima or Hu'u, mainly because once off the highway, transport is infrequent or excruciatingly uncomfortable. To get out into the countryside you really need to charter transport or rent a motorcycle.

The mountain and coastal regions in the south – which were not converted to Islam

until around the late 19th century – and the Tambora Peninsula in the north are rarely visited by travellers. If you're in the right place at the right time (on holidays and during festivals), you might see traditional Sumbawan fighting, a sort of bare-fisted boxing called *berempah*. Horse and water buffalo races are held before the rice is planted.

Towards the east end of the island, the narrow Teluk Bima (Bima Bay) cuts deep into the north coast, forming one of Indonesia's best natural harbours. It's surrounded by fertile lowlands, which reach west into the rich interior Dompu plains.

History

For centuries Sumbawa has been divided between two linguistically and, to some extent, ethnically distinct peoples: the Sumbawanese speakers, who probably reached the west of the island from Lombok; and the Bimanese speakers, who independently occupied the Tambora Peninsula and the east. The squatter, darker-skinned Bimanese are more closely related to the people of Flores, while the western Sumbawans are closer to the Sasaks

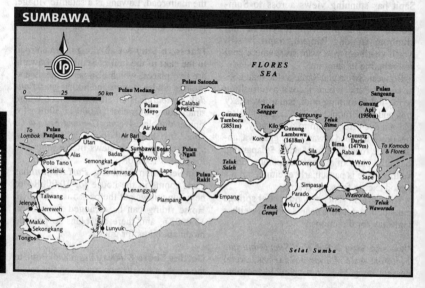

SUMBAWA

of Lombok. Both languages have considerable variation in dialect, but the spread of Bahasa Indonesia has made communication easier in the last couple of decades.

Sumbawa, with its rich timber resources in the west, was probably an early trading call for Javanese merchants on the way to the Spice Islands in Maluku. Bima and parts of western Sumbawa are said to have been under the control of the Javanese Majapahit empire.

Along the western coastal lowlands, the local population expanded and petty kingdoms developed along the entire length of the island. In eastern Sumbawa, the areas around Teluk Bima and the Dompu plains became the leading centres for the Bimanese-speaking population. Before 1600 these were probably animist kingdoms.

There appears to have been some intermarriage between the Balinese and western Sumbawanese aristocracies, which may have linked the islands from the 15th or 16th centuries. In the early 17th century, the Islamic Makassarese states of southern Sulawesi undertook a military expansion, and by 1625, the rulers of Sumbawa had been reduced to Makassarese vassals and had nominally converted to Islam.

Makassar's rise was halted by the Dutch East India Company (Vereenigde Oost-Indische Compagnie; VOC), whose forces occupied it in 1669. Soon afterwards treaties were made between the Dutch and the rulers of Sumbawa by which Dutch hegemony was recognised and tribute was paid to the Dutch. For their part, the Dutch maintained only a distant supervision of what they considered to be a politically unstable island with poor commercial possibilities, taking more or less direct control only in the 1900s.

The western Sumbawans, meanwhile, held nominal control over neighbouring Lombok from the middle of the 17th century until 1750, when the Balinese took it over. Then followed 30 years of sporadic warfare between the Sumbawans and the Balinese, including at least one large-scale Balinese invasion of western Sumbawa. It was only through the intervention of the VOC, which was interested in maintaining the status quo, that the Balinese were turned back.

Barely had the wars finished, when Gunung Tambora in Sumbawa exploded in April 1815 killing 10,000 or more people in a shower of choking debris. In one of the greatest eruptions of modern times, the volcano vented 150 cubic kilometres of ash and pumice. By the time it ended, the 4200m peak had shrunk to approximately 2850m. Agricultural land was wrecked and livestock and crops wiped out. It's estimated that another 82,000 people, a large portion of Sumbawa's population, either died of starvation and disease or fled their lands. See the special colour section 'Fire Mountains' in the Java chapter.

By the middle of the 19th century, immigrants from other islands were brought in to help repopulate the blighted coastal regions. The people of Sumbawa are therefore a diverse lot – in coastal regions there are traces of Javanese, Makassarese, Bugis, Sasak and other ethnic groups.

In 1908 the Dutch government sent administrators and soldiers to Sumbawa Besar and Taliwang to head off the prospect of a war between the three separate states that comprised western Sumbawa. This inaugurated a period of far more direct Dutch rule.

The sultans kept a fair degree of their power under the Dutch, but after Indonesian independence their titles were abolished; now their descendants hold official power only when they are functionaries of the national government.

Little evidence remains of the Dutch presence, and the only traces of the old sultanates are the palaces in the towns of Sumbawa Besar and Bima.

Climate

Sumbawa is at its best at the end of the wet season around April/May. As the dry season progresses, the greenery dies off and much of the island becomes brown and dusty under the increasingly sweltering heat.

Religion

Sumbawa is the most predominantly Muslim island anywhere east of Java or south of

Sulawesi. Christian missionaries never even bothered to try here and Islam seems to have overshadowed Sumbawa's indigenous traditions, though outside the cities older animist traditions still exist under the veneer of Islam.

Special Events

Check out the 'horse racing', which is a big local event across Sumbawa from August to October. It's not quite the Royal Ascot, but what these boys on ponies lack in stature, they make up for in enthusiasm.

Getting Around

Sumbawa's single main road runs all the way from Taliwang (near the west coast) through Sumbawa Besar, Dompu and Bima to Sape (on the east coast). It's surfaced all the way. Fleets of buses, some of them luxurious by Nusa Tenggara standards, link all the towns on this road.

POTO TANO

Poto Tano is a hodgepodge of stilt houses beside a mangrove-lined bay, 10km off the main highway. Apart from providing a port for ferries to/from Lombok, there is no reason to stop here.

Getting There & Away

The ferries run (roughly) hourly, 24 hours a day, between Lombok and Poto Tano (2350/3650Rp 1st/2nd class, 1½ hours). The through buses from Mataram to Sumbawa Besar, Taliwang or Bima include the ferry fare.

Buses also meet the ferry and go to Taliwang (1500Rp, one hour) and Sumbawa Besar (3000Rp, two hours).

TALIWANG
☎ 0372

During the 19th century, Taliwang was one of the 'vassal states' of the kingdom of Sumbawa based in Sumbawa Besar. This region has its own dialect and, through migration, is closely linked to Lombok.

Today Taliwang is an oversized village, with friendly people and few tourists. It lies close to the west coast of Sumbawa, 30km south of Poto Tano along a narrow road

winding through the hills. Taliwang is prospering from activity generated by a huge gold mine near Maluk to the south, but the pace remains pretty sleepy.

Lebok Taliwang, a lake close to the Poto Tano road near Taliwang, is quite a picture when covered in water lilies. **Poto Batu**, 6km from Taliwang, is a local sea resort with a cave/blow hole and a decent beach. **Labuhan-balat**, a Bugis stilt fishing community of just eight houses on a very pretty bay, is 7km from Taliwang; take a truck or bemo there.

Places to Stay & Eat

Taliwang's market is next to the bus terminal. Behind the market and directly opposite the mosque, the friendly but spartan *Losmen Azhar* has rooms for 7500Rp per person. *Hotel Taliwang Indah* (☎ 81014, Jl Jenderal Sudirman) has a 1st floor porch overlooking the hills and a friendly manager who speaks good English. Rooms cost 15,000Rp. The attached restaurant has a long menu and excellent food. On the same street, opposite the cinema, *Losmen Tubalong* (☎ 81018) has singles/doubles with *mandi* (Indonesian shower) for 15,000/25,000Rp.

Getting There & Away

Buses from Taliwang to Poto Tano cost 1000Rp and you can buy tickets with connections right through to Mataram (12,000Rp, five hours). Most buses leave between 6 and 9 am. Direct buses also go from Taliwang to Sumbawa Besar (4000Rp, three hours).

SOUTH-WEST SUMBAWA

Many of the small trickle of visitors who make it to the Taliwang area are surfers in search of the good waves along this coast. The area has many beautiful, but isolated, white sand beaches.

From Taliwang, bemos and trucks run 11km south over a good, paved road to Jereweh, from where it is 6km to the beach at Jelenga. The *Pondok Wisata Jelenga* has bungalows for 20,000Rp.

Maluk

A popular surfing destination, Maluk is 30km south of Taliwang. The superb beach has white sand framing turquoise and deep blue waters. Its isolation had kept the number of visitors to a trickle, but a massive mining project near Maluk is driving a wave of development.

The open cut gold mine about 30km inland is the biggest thing to hit Sumbawa since Islam. Apart from a new road into the mine, the road to Sejorong will be pushed right through to Lunyuk. Access will be much improved and a large number of workers will use Maluk's wonderful beach for rest & recreation. Maluk is still sleepy and the beach untouched, but local developers are building small restaurants and new bungalows.

Ten kilometres further south, **Sekongkang** also has a fine surfing beach and the kepala desa offers accommodation. New losmen are planned. The beach is at Sekongkang Bawah, 2km downhill from Sekongkang Atas where some buses stop.

Places to Stay & Eat *Surya Beach Bungalows (Jl Pasir Putih)* is 400m from the beach at the southern end of Maluk village. For a long time the only place to stay, it has slightly worn bungalows with shared mandi for 15,000Rp and a restaurant. The *Maluk Beach Bungalows* is 200m closer to the beach and has new, more substantial singles/doubles with shared mandi for 10,000/15,000Rp. *Iwan's* is another new place further north and has similar accommodation for the same price. *Hotel Trophy*, run by an Australian, is a new place with great facilities.

Kafe & Rumah Makan Bisma has the best food around, a convivial owner and plenty of cold beer in the evenings. Expatriate mine workers flock here after work. For some jaw-dropping conversation, ask them how much they earn. *Rumah Makan Rasate*, further south, is another new addition with standard fare and a few open-sided bungalows for *lesahan* (traditional style, on straw mats) dining.

Getting There & Away At least five buses a day leave Taliwang for Maluk (2500Rp, 1½ hours) between 5 am and 7 pm. Some continue on to Sekongkang (1500Rp) and further to Tongos.

The mine operates a ferry to Lombok. The ferry is only for its workers, but the port may become a public utility and private ferries may start running.

SUMBAWA BESAR
☎ 0371

At one time the name 'Sumbawa' only applied to the western half of the island, which fell under the sway of the sultan of the state of Sumbawa; the eastern half of the island was known as Bima. Almost all that remains of the old western sultanate is the wooden palace in Sumbawa Besar, the showpiece of the town.

Sumbawa Besar is the chief town of the western half of the island, a laid-back, friendly place where cidomos still outnumber bemos and where Muslims flood out of the mosques after midday prayer. There are some lovely tree-lined boulevards around the new palace, but the town has no remarkable attractions except for the old palace. A trip out to **Pulau Moyo** or to nearby villages can be rewarding, but they can be difficult to reach. For most travellers Sumbawa Besar is just a rest stop on the journey across the island.

Apart from the steady stream of travellers that pass through Sumbawa Besar on their way to or from Komodo and Flores, the area is also popular with luxury cruises from Bali that dock at the small port of Badas, west of the town.

Orientation

Sumbawa Besar is small; you can easily walk around most of it, except maybe to the main post office, which is only a bemo or cidomo ride away.

Information

Tourist Offices The tourist office (☎ 23 714, Jl Bungur 1) is 100m south of the main post office on the edge of town, just off Jl Garuda. It has helpful staff and some useful

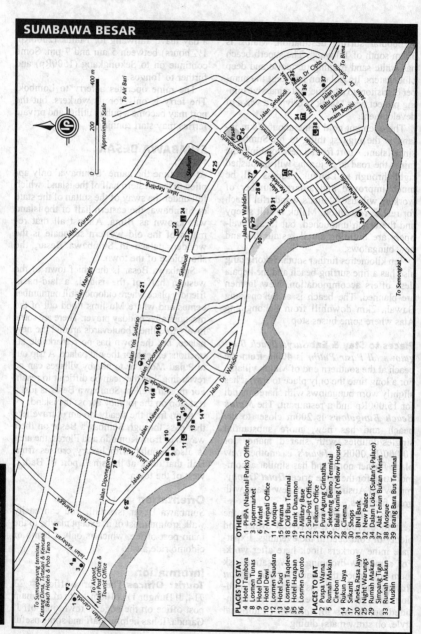

SUMBAWA BESAR

Approximate Scale

400 m

200

To Air Bari

To Bima

To Sumurpayung terminal,
Karang Dima, Tirtasari & Kencana
Beach Hotels & Poto Tano

To Airport,
Main Post Office &
Tourist Office

To Semongkat

PLACES TO STAY
4 Hotel Tambora
8 Losmen Tunas
9 Hotel Dian
10 Hotel Dewi
12 Losmen Saudara
13 Hotel Suci
16 Losmen Taqdeer
35 Hotel Harapan
36 Losmen Garoto

PLACES TO EAT
2 Puspa Warna
5 Rumah Makan
Cirebon
14 Rukun Jaya
17 Srikanti
20 Aneka Rasa Jaya
25 Night Warungs
29 Rumah Makan
Simpang Tiga
33 Rumah Makan
Mushin

OTHER
1 PHPA (National Parks) Office
3 Supermarket
6 Wartel
7 Merpati Office
11 Mosque
15 Perama
18 Old Bus Terminal
19 Bank Danamon
21 Military Base
22 Sub-Post Office
23 Telkom Office
24 Pura Agung Girinatha
26 Seketeng Bemo Terminal
27 Balai Kuning (Yellow House)
28 Cinema
30 Shops
31 BNI Bank
32 New Palace
34 Dalam Loka (Sultan's Palace)
37 Alat Tenun Bukan Mesin
38 Mosque
39 Brang Bara Bus Terminal

brochures. Take a yellow bemo past the airport and post office and get off at the 'Dinas Pariwisata'. The office is open Monday to Thursday from 7 am to 2 pm, until 11 am on Friday, and until 1 pm on Saturday.

The national park service Perlindungan Hutan dan Pelestarian Alam (PHPA, ☎ 21 358) has its office at the Direktorat Jenderal Kehutanan, Jl Garuda 12. It has information about Pulau Moyo, but you'll probably be referred to one of the tour companies for arrangements. The office is open Monday to Friday from 8 am to 2 pm.

Money The Bank Negara Indonesia (BNI) at Jl Kartini 10 is open Monday to Friday from 8 am to 2.30 pm, and until noon on Saturday. It changes a range of currencies at reasonable rates. Bank Danamon is just off Jl Diponegoro and gives credit card cash advances.

Post & Communications The main post office for poste restante is on Jl Garuda, about 1.5km from the Hotel Tambora. For stamps, a sub-post office is near the town centre on Jl Yos Sudarso. Both are open Monday to Thursday from 7 am to 2 pm, on Friday until 11 am and on Saturday until 12.30 pm.

The Telkom office on Jl Setiabudi is open 24 hours, and there is a Telkom wartel at Jl Hasanuddin 105.

Dalam Loka (Sultan's Palace)

Back in the early 1960s, Helen and Frank Schreider passed through Sumbawa Besar in their amphibious jeep and later described the remnants of this palace in their book *The Drums of Tonkin*:

> Sumbawa Besar ... had a sultan. A small man with tortoise-shell glasses and a quiet, friendly dignity ... his old palace, now deserted except for a few distant relatives, was a long barn-like structure of unpainted wood that seemed on the point of collapsing. Beneath the ramshackle entrance, a rusted cannon from the days of the Dutch East India Company lay half-buried in the ground ... Mothers and fathers and naked little children made the palace shake as they followed us up the ramp into a great empty room that was once the audience chamber ... Only when the

few remaining court costumes, the faded silver brocade kains, the gold-handled krises and the long gold fingernails that were a sign of royalty's exemption from labour were modelled for us did we have any idea of the extravagance of this past era. By government decree, the sultans are no longer in power.

Built in 1885, the palace was restored in the early 1980s, but only a few of the original pillars and carved beams remain. It is usually locked – ask around for the caretaker, who speaks English and can show you around. Inside are a few illustrations, explanations in Indonesian and an old palanquin, but otherwise it is empty. A small donation towards the upkeep is customary, but not obligatory.

The descendants of the sultans now live at the **Balai Kuning** (Yellow House) on Jl Wahidin and they have numerous artefacts from the days of the sultanate. By calling the tourist office and giving notice, visits can be arranged for groups (contact the tourist office). Again, a small donation is expected.

New Palace

The imposing building with the bell tower at its gate on Jl Merdeka is the headquarters of the *bupati* (head government official) of West Sumbawa. It's built in imitation of the style of the old sultan's palace; a reminder that the national government now holds the power that was once the sultans'.

Pura Agung Girinatha

This Balinese Hindu temple is on Jl Yos Sudarso, near the corner of Jl Setiabudi. Next door is a *banjar*, which is a Balinese community hall.

Places to Stay

The *Losmen Taqdeer* (☎ 21987), down a residential lane off Jl Kamboja near the old bus terminal on Jl Diponegoro, is a clean little place with rooms from 6000Rp. Another cheap option, right on the doorstep of the sultan's palace, is the *Losmen Garoto* (☎ 22062, Jl Batu Pasak 48). Clean singles/doubles upstairs cost 4000/7000Rp or larger rooms with mandi cost 8000/12,000Rp. Next door is a small restaurant.

Other cheap hotels are clustered along Jl Hasanuddin close to the mosque (and therefore a dawn wake-up call): *Hotel Suci* (☎ *21 589*), where large double rooms with private mandi around a neat courtyard cost 17,500/22,500Rp, or 50,000/55,000Rp with air-con; *Losmen Saudara* (☎ *21528*), with small, clean rooms from 10,000/15,000Rp; or the less clean *Losmen Tunas* (☎ *21212*) for 10,000/12,000Rp. *Hotel Harapan* (☎ *21629, Jl Dr Cipto 7*) is another option and costs 10,000/15,000Rp for rooms with mandi.

The place with the best set up for tourists is the *Hotel Tambora* (☎/fax *21555, Jl Kebayan*). There's a wide range of rooms, all with attached bath, starting at 12,600/ 21,000Rp and running through to deluxe rooms with air-con, hot water and TV for 93,000/120,000Rp, including tax. The hotel is helpful with information, makes bus bookings, and has a restaurant and a small supermarket next door.

Of equal standard, *Hotel Dewi* (☎ *21170, Jl Hasanuddin 60*), is a bright hotel with stark tilework everywhere. The rooms are spotless and good value, and cost 12,500/ 16,500Rp (27,500/33,000Rp with air-con) to 55,000Rp for deluxe rooms. There's also a restaurant here.

A 10 minute bemo ride north-west from town, *Tirtasari Hotel* (☎ *21987*) is a reasonable option right on the beach opposite the new bus terminal. The beach is not great, but the water is clean. The hotel has spacious grounds, but is a little run down and a long way from town. Economy doubles cost 12,500Rp, larger bungalows are 25,000Rp with fan or 35,000Rp with air-con, and VIP bungalows with hot water are 40,000Rp and 45,000Rp.

The most luxurious hotel is the *Kencana Beach Hotel* (☎ *22555*) on the highway, 11km west of town. Under the same management as the Hotel Tambora, it has a swimming pool, restaurant and poolside bar. Attractive bungalows fronting the beach cost US$30/35 with fan, US$45/55 with air-con, or deluxe bungalows cost US$65/75. The beach has black sand, but is very pleasant. The clear water is good for snorkelling.

Places to Eat

The cheapest food can be found at the streetside *warungs* that set up in front of the stadium in the evenings. *Soto ayam* (chicken soup), sate, *bakso* (meatball soup) and other Madurese fare are sold. The *Rukun Jaya (Jl Hasunuddin)*, close to many of the hotels, is a small restaurant with cheap food.

Rumah Makan Mushin (Jl Wahidin 31) is a spotless little cafe with Lombok/ Taliwang dishes. Meals are simple, but very tasty, and the *ayam bakar* (grilled chicken) is excellent. The more adventurous can try the *jeroan ayam* (chicken intestines).

Sumbawa Besar has two very good Chinese restaurants: the *Aneka Rasa Jaya (Jl Hasanuddin 14)* and the *Puspa Warna (Jl Cendrawasih 16)*. Both have extensive menus and specialise in seafood, including grilled whole fish.

The restaurant in the *Tambora Hotel* is very good and the *Dewi* and *Tirtasari* hotels also have good food.

Getting There & Away

Air Merpati (☎ 21416) on Jl Diponegoro has three flights a week to/from Mataram and on to Denpasar (Bali).

Bus Sumbawa Besar's main long-distance bus station is the Sumurpayung terminal at Karang Dima, 5.5km north-west of town on the highway, although some morning buses to Bima leave from the Brang Bara terminal on Jl Kaharuddin. Fares and approximate journey times from Sumbawa Besar include: Sape (11,500Rp, 7½ hours); Bima (10,000Rp, seven hours); Dompu (7500Rp, 4½ hours); Taliwang (4000Rp, three hours); and Poto Tano (3000Rp, two hours).

Buses to Bima leave between 7 and 9 am and at 8 pm, but between these times you have to hope for a seat on a bus coming through from Lombok. You can buy combined bus and ferry tickets from Sumbawa Besar through to Mataram (25,000Rp) or Bali. Buses to Lombok leave at 6, 8 and 9 am and 3 pm. Hotels, such as the Tambora, sell tickets and can arrange pick-up.

Boat Pelni's *Tatamailau* stops every two weeks at the small port of Badas, 7km west of Sumbawa Besar, on its loop through the eastern islands. The Pelni office is at Labuhan Sumbawa, the town's fishing port, 3km west of town on the Poto Tano road.

Getting Around

To/From the Airport The airport is only 500m from the Hotel Tambora and you can easily walk into town. Turn to your right as you exit the airport terminal and cross the bridge. Alternatively, take a yellow bemo (500Rp).

Bemo The streets here, apart from the bemo speedway along Jl Hasanuddin, are relatively stress free. Bemos and cidomos cost 500Rp for trips anywhere around town.

The local Seketeng bemo terminal is on Jl Setiabudi, in front of the market; cidomos congregate along Jl Urip Sumoharjo near where it meets Jl Setiabudi. For trips to villages around Sumbawa Besar, there are public bemos. Get to the terminal early in the morning as there's often only one bemo daily; after that you'll have to charter (prices are negotiable).

AROUND SUMBAWA BESAR

A number of attractions can be visited around Sumbawa Besar. All are difficult to reach by public transport – hire a motorcycle and preferably a guide in Sumbawa Besar.

Pulau Moyo

Two-thirds of Pulau Moyo, an island off the coast just north of Sumbawa Besar, is a nature reserve with good coral reefs teeming with fish. Moyo rises to 648m; its centre is composed mainly of savanna with stands of forest. The reserve is inhabited by wild cattle, pigs, deer and several varieties of birds, though its main attractions are diving and snorkelling.

Accommodation is limited and Pulau Moyo's good diving and snorkelling has to be arranged through operators. It is possible, but difficult, to visit Moyo independently on a day trip. For travel to the island,

the PHPA office in Sumbawa Besar has information and a good map of Moyo.

The normal access is from Air Bari, which is on the coast north of Sumbawa Besar. Public bemos (2000Rp, one hour) run to Air Bari three or four times daily to no fixed schedule, starting at around 7 am. They leave from the turn-off to Air Bari, at the far end of Jl Sudirman. Otherwise, you'll have to charter a bemo.

From Air Bari, you can hire a motorised outrigger or fishing boat for the half-hour, 3km crossing to the south coast of the island. You must bargain – 10,000Rp each way is a good price, petrol included. Ask for Pak Lahi if you are having problems finding a boat. The boats can take you to Air Manis, which has reasonable snorkelling, or Tanjung Pasir, just to the east, which has better snorkelling. Good reefs with a plunging wall can be found all around the island if you are prepared to charter a boat. Some of the best diving is around the Amanwana Resort on the west coast.

If getting there independently sounds like too much trouble, tour operators or the hotels in Sumbawa Besar can arrange trips. The Hotel Tambora's sibling hotel, Kencana Beach Hotel, has a good speedboat that takes up to 15 people for 350,000Rp per day.

Just to the north-east of Pulau Moyo is the small **Pulau Satonda**, which also has good beaches, snorkelling and a salt-water lake in the middle of the island. It is three hours by boat from Air Bari.

Places to Stay A forestry worker runs basic bungalows in the south of Moyo for 25,000Rp a day. Arrange your return journey from Moyo with whoever takes you there. There are also four PHPA guard posts on Moyo; one at the south end, the others in villages, where you can stay overnight for a donation, but take your own food and water.

The *Amanwana Resort* (☎ 22330) on the western side of the island is an ultra-exclusive resort run by the Aman chain. Most guests come on package tours from the Aman hotels in Bali. Princess Di stayed here and could no doubt afford the rates.

The US$720 a day price is incredible when you consider that accommodation is in tents, though admittedly they're luxurious tents on platforms.

Other Attractions

Some of the best songket sarongs are made in the village of Poto, 12km east of Sumbawa Besar (1000Rp by bus or bemo) and 2km from the small town of Moyo. Traditional designs include the *prahu* (outrigger boat) and ancestor head motif. Modern Balinese-style ikat is also woven on handlooms; head into the village across from the football field and ask around to see it being made.

The hills south of Sumbawa Besar are home to a number of **traditional villages** and **hiking** possibilities. One of the more interesting villages is Tegel, from where horses can be hired to venture higher into the forest.

Near Batu Tering are megalithic sarcophagi believed to be the 2000 year old **tombs** of ancient chiefs. Footprints in the stones are said to be those of the gods. Batu Tering is about 30km by bemo from Sumbawa Besar, via Semamung. The sarcophagi are 4km on foot from the village, and then it is another 2km to **Liang Petang** (Dark Cave).

Ai Beling is a pretty waterfall in the southern mountains. Take the road south through Semamung a further 8km to Brangrea, then the turn-off to the falls, from where it is 6km along a rough road with many forks. You need a guide.

Buffalo races, **wedding ceremonies** and *karaci* (traditional **stick fighting**) are staged regularly at Pamalung village, 7km from Sumbawa Besar. They are put on for the cruise ships from Bali, usually on Tuesday and Saturday.

CENTRAL SUMBAWA

It's a beautiful ride from Sumbawa Besar to Bima. After Empang you start moving up into the hills through rolling green country, which is thickly forested, with occasional sprays of palm trees along the shoreline.

Gunung Tambora

Dominating the peninsula, which juts north in central Sumbawa, is the 2850m volcano Gunung Tambora. The huge crater contains a two coloured lake, and there are views as far as Gunung Rinjani (Lombok). It can be climbed from the western side. The base for ascents is the small logging town of Calabai, which is five hours by a very crowded bus from Dompu or an hour by speedboat from Sumbawa Besar. Few people bother though, because from Calabai it is a hard three day return walk.

Tambora's peak was obliterated in one of the greatest volcanic explosions of modern times, the eruption of April 1815 (see Sumbawa History earlier in this section), but since then all has been quiet. The eruption wiped out the entire population of Tambora and Pekat (two small states at the base of the mountain), as well as devastating much of the rest of Sumbawa.

Dompu
☎ 0373

The seat of one of Sumbawa's former independent states, Dompu is now the third-biggest town on the island. If you're travelling between Sumbawa Besar and Bima, you don't get to see it: buses detour via the Ginte bus terminal (on a hill 2km from Dompu). From there, bemos run into town (500Rp). The town has a colourful market snaking through its back streets, but otherwise it's just a stopover.

Change money at the BNI bank, which opens Monday to Friday from 7.30 am to 3 pm and Saturday from 8.30 am to noon.

Hotel Pusaka (☎ 21577) and *Wisma Praja (☎ 21699)* are both near the centre on Jl Soekarno-Hatta. Singles/doubles at the Wisma Praja cost 15,000/17,500Rp, or 20,000/25,000 with mandi. Hotel Pusaka charges a flat 25,000Rp per room. Also central is the spic and span *Wisma Samada (☎ 21417, Jl Gajah Mada 18)*. It is the best in town, and charges 25,000Rp for a room with a fan or 40,000Rp with air-con.

Buses run from Ginte bus terminal to Bima (2000Rp, two hours), Sape (6500Rp,

3½ hours) and Sumbawa Besar (7500Rp, 4½ hours). You can also get a combined aircon bus/ferry ticket through to Mataram.

Hu'u & Lakey's Beach

Hu'u is best known as a stronghold of surf culture. Several hotels have sprung up along Lakey's Beach, 3km from Hu'u village, to cater to surfers who have been coming here since the early 1980s. The best waves are between June and August.

Lately an attempt has been made to woo the average garden-variety tourist to the long stretch of palm tree lined, white sand beach at Hu'u.

Information A few of the hotels will change US and Australian dollars at poor rates. Bring enough rupiah with you. Lakey's only telephone is at a wartel opposite the entrance to Lakey Peak Bungalows. It can book and reconfirm flights with Merpati in Bima (best of luck) or hotels, such as Primadona, can do it for you via two-way radio links to contacts in Dompu.

Places to Stay & Eat Lakey's accommodation is mostly wedged together adjacent to the main surf breaks: Lakey Peak, Lakey Pipe and Nangas. The sole exception is *Periscopes*, a basic camp adjacent to a surf break of the same name 1.5km north of the main beach.

Mona Lisa Bungalows is a good place to start looking. It has a good restaurant and a range of well-appointed bungalows for 20,000/30,000Rp with fan, through to bungalows with air-con for 50,000/65,000Rp. Like all the places here, prices drop outside the May to August peak season.

Heading south from Mona Lisa, *Hotel Aman Gati* is popular but pricey, with the best bungalows in Lakey. Its restaurant has a huge TV screen showing non-stop surfing videos. Bungalows with fan and bathroom cost US$8/10, or US$18/20 with air-con.

Next along, *Lakey Peak* has a dowdy restaurant, but good bungalows for 20,000/35,000Rp. *Balumba* has big clean rooms for 20,000/30,000Rp.

Intan Lestari is the one of the original surf camps, with a rustic little restaurant, and rooms for 20,000/25,000Rp with mandi. The position is hard to beat – right in front of Lakey Peak and Lakey Pipe. Motorbikes are available for rent.

South of Intan Lestari, *Anton Malingi* has basic rooms for 20,000Rp per person. The big and breezy *Puma Bungalows* next door are worth the 30,000/45,000Rp asking price.

Next is the French-managed *Fatmah Restoran*, which is the best on the beach. The only drawback is that the service can be slow when the crowds pile in. There are a few new rooms out back for 35,000Rp, and surf boards and snorkelling masks for hire.

A couple of hundred metres north of Mona Lisa, *Primadona Lakey Cottages* has a huge restaurant and rooms with fan for 15,000/20,000Rp, or 25,000/35,000Rp with air-con. The wooden bungalows with mandi and fan are better value at 20,000/25,000Rp.

Further north, the dusty *Kambera Cottages* cost 20,000Rp with mandi.

Getting There & Away It is an almighty effort to reach Hu'u by public transport. From Sumbawa Besar or Bima take a bus to Dompu's Ginte bus terminal on the northern outskirts of town, then a bemo (500Rp) to the central market. From here take a cidomo (500Rp per person) to the Lepardi bus terminal on the southern outskirts, from where several buses a day run to Rasabau (1500Rp, 1½ hours). From Rasabau you then have to take an incredibly crowded bemo to the beach (750Rp).

Try doing this with a surfboard and you'll soon see why so many people take a taxi from Bima airport. The taxi price is fixed at 85,000Rp, but it may be possible to negotiate a lower price outside the terminal.

Donggo

From Rato/Sila, on the Dompu to Bima road, infrequent buses run to the village of Donggo. It is 4km along a good road and then 10km on a rough road up the mountain. It may be possible to stay with the kepala desa in Donggo. The village has a few traditional houses and superb views. The Dou Donggo (Mountain People) living in these highlands speak an archaic form of the Bima language and may be descended from the original inhabitants of Sumbawa. Numbering about 20,000, they've adopted Islam and Christianity over their traditional beliefs in the last few decades, with varying degrees of enthusiasm; they're being absorbed into Bimanese culture and will probably disappear as a distinct group. The most traditional village is Mbawa where, at least until a few years ago, people still wore distinctive black clothes, and a few *uma leme* (traditional houses whose design was intimately connected with the traditional region) were still standing.

BIMA & RABA
☎ 0374

Bima and Raba together form the major town in the eastern half of Sumbawa. Bima, Sumbawa's chief port, is the main centre; Raba, a few kilometres east, is the departure point for buses east to Sape, where you get the ferry to Komodo or Flores.

The Bima region has been known since the 14th century for its sturdy horses, which were exported to Java. Local tradition claims that before the 17th century, when Bima fell to the Makassarese and its ruler was converted to Islam, this region had some sort of political control over Timor, Sumba and parts of western Flores.

Today, the former sultan's palace apart, Bima is a rather practical place. It has a good range of services and shops, and the *pasar malam* (night market) on Jl Flores is worth a wander.

Information
Tourist Office The tourist information office, Dinas Pariwisata (☎ 44331), is next to the Kantor Bupati on Jl Soekarno Hatta in Raba, about 2km from Bima past the Hotel Parewa. It is open Monday to Friday from 7 am to 3 pm, and until noon on Saturday.

Money The BNI bank on Jl Sultan Hasanuddin changes foreign currency and travellers cheques, as does the Bank Rakyat

Indonesia (BRI) on Jl Sumbawa. Both are open Monday to Friday until 1 pm. If you're heading east, this is the last place to change money before Labuanbajo (Flores).

Post & Communications The main post office is on Jl Sultan Hasanuddin, about 500m east of the Hotel Sangyang. Opening hours are Monday to Saturday from 8 am to 2 pm. The main 24 hour Telkom office is adjacent to the tourist office on Jl Soekarno Hatta. It's also possible to make international calls from the Telkom Warpostel Remaja on Jl Lombok, in the centre of Bima.

Sultan's Palace
The former home of Bima's rulers is now partly a museum. The building itself is less impressive than its counterpart in Sumbawa Besar, but the exhibits inside (mail shirts, sedan chairs, battle flags, weapons, a chart comparing the alphabets of Indonesian languages with the Latin alphabet) hold some interest. Built in 1927, the palace had fallen into complete disrepair by the late 1950s, but has been restored. The royal family recently added some impressive artefacts to the collection. You can see the royal bedchamber (with its four poster bed, and Koran on the dressing table) and photos of the tombs of some early Bima rulers; the tombs still stand in the hills outside town.

The museum is open Monday to Saturday from 8 am to 6 pm. Admission is 5000Rp for tourists.

Horse Racing
Horse races are held every Sunday throughout the dry season (May to October) at the Desa Panda horse stadium, 14km from town on the airport road. There's a large grandstand, a gaggle of warungs and plenty of cheering as boys on horses thunder around a dusty track. The height of the racing season is 17 August.

Places to Stay
Bima is compact, and most hotels are in the middle of town. The friendly *Wisma Komodo* (☎ 42070, Jl Sultan Ibrahim) is often full, but

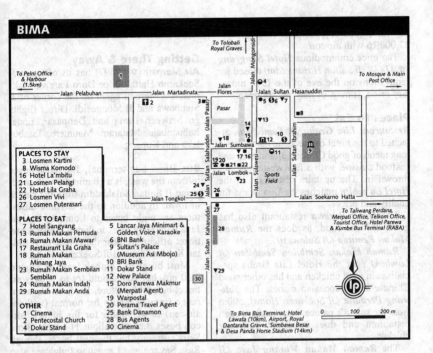

BIMA

PLACES TO STAY
3 Losmen Kartini
8 Wisma Komodo
16 Hotel La'mbitu
21 Losmen Pelangi
22 Hotel Lila Graha
26 Losmen Vivi
27 Losmen Puterasari

PLACES TO EAT
7 Hotel Sangyang
13 Rumah Makan Pemuda
14 Rumah Makan Mawar
17 Restaurant Lila Graha
18 Rumah Makan Minang Jaya
23 Rumah Makan Sembilan Sembilan
24 Rumah Makan Indah
29 Rumah Makan Anda

OTHER
1 Cinema
2 Pentecostal Church
4 Dokar Stand
5 Lancar Jaya Minimart & Golden Voice Karaoke
6 BNI Bank
9 Sultan's Palace (Museum Asi Mbojo)
10 BRI Bank
11 Dokar Stand
12 New Palace
15 Doro Parewa Makmur (Merpati Agent)
19 Warpostal
20 Perama Travel Agent
25 Bank Danamon
28 Bus Agents
30 Cinema

To Tolobali Royal Graves
To Pelni Office & Harbour (1.5km)
To Mosque & Main Post Office
To Taliwang Perdana, Merpati Office, Telkom Office, Tourist Office, Hotel Parewa & Kumbe Bus Terminal (RABA)
To Bima Bus Terminal, Hotel Lawata (10km), Airport, Royal Dantaraha Graves, Sumbawa Besar & Desa Panda Horse Stadium (14km)

0   100   200 m

is well run and the manager speaks excellent English. Rooms are worn and cost 10,000Rp or 15,000Rp with mandi.

Hotel Lila Graha (☎ 42740, Jl Lombok 20) has a great restaurant and remains popular despite sliding standards and rising prices. The rates cost 11,000/15,000Rp for dingy singles/doubles with shared mandi, or 16,500/20,000Rp with mandi, to 42,500Rp for air-con double rooms in its new wing. Add 10% tax to the rates, but breakfast is included.

Hotel La'mbitu (☎ 42222, Jl Sumbawa 4), situated next door to Lila Graha's new wing, is a smart well-run place that gives the apathetic management next door a run for its money. Well appointed rooms with fan and hot water cost 30,000Rp, and air-con rooms start at 47,500Rp.

Bima has a number of cheaper but seedy hotels. **Losmen Pelangi** (☎ 42878, Jl Lombok), has 'boxy' doubles for 10,000Rp, or 15,000Rp with mandi. So too the friendly, but dowdy, **Losmen Puterasari** (Jl Soekarno Hatta 7). **Losmen Vivi** across the road from the Puterasari, is the cheapest in town at 6000Rp per person. **Losmen Kartini** (☎ 42 072, Jl Pasar 11), charges 7500Rp per person. It's not a bad place to stay, but it is used as a base by sex workers.

Hotel Parewa (☎ 42652, Jl Soekarno Hatta 40), 1km from the town centre, is a comfortable mid-range hotel with a good upstairs restaurant, but has seen better days. Economy rooms with fan cost 27,500Rp, or standard rooms with air-con and TV go for 44,000Rp. All have attached bathrooms, but the plumbing is hopeless.

The most luxurious hotel is the **Hotel Lawata** (☎ 43696, Jl Sultan Salahuddin), 10km from town on the airport road. It has a swimming pool, an excellent restaurant

NUSA TENGGARA

and attractive bungalows perched over the bay for 49,000/55,000Rp, or from 69,300/77,000Rp with air-con.

The once commodious *Hotel Sangyang* (☎ 41438, Jl Sultan Hasanuddin) closed for renovations on the eve of the 1998 monetary crisis. It may, or may not, re-open.

Places to Eat

Restaurant Lila Graha (Jl Sumbawa), attached to the hotel of the same name, has a long menu of good Chinese, Indonesian and seafood cuisine, with a few western dishes thrown in. The upstairs restaurant in the *Hotel La'mbitu* matches the Lila Graha for quality and price.

The *Hotel Parewa* restaurant also has good Chinese food, as does the *Rumah Makan Pemuda (Jl Sulawesi)*.

Rumah Makan Sembilan Sembilan (Jl Lombok) near the Hotel Lila Graha specialises in fried chicken and has other good Chinese and Indonesian dishes. The *Taliwang Perdana (Jl Soekarno Hatta)*, 500m from the sultan's palace, is a pleasant, open restaurant and does excellent Taliwang chicken.

The *Rumah Makan Minang Jaya (Jl Sumbawa)* is a good, clean Padang eatery, while a couple of more basic restaurants, the *Rumah Makan Indah* and *Rumah Makan Anda*, are along Jl Sultan Salahuddin. The *pasar* has stalls selling interesting snacks and on the same street is the *Rumah Makan Mawar*, a very popular local haunt.

Entertainment

Though Bima is a small, conservative city like most others in Indonesia, it has undeservedly acquired a reputation as some sort of outpost of Islamic fundamentalism. In reality, compared to the towns in Flores, it is almost a swinging city. Well, it has a couple of slightly seedy karaoke bars, both on Jl Sultan Hasanuddin: the *Ayoedia Karaoke* and the *Golden Voice Karaoke* above the Lancar Jaya Minimart.

The most popular choice, though, is a lively sporting scene on the fields in front of the Sultan's Palace, where crowds gather at dusk to support their soccer or volleyball teams and chew the fat.

Getting There & Away

Air Merpati (☎ 42697) has its office at Jl Soekarno Hatta 60, or Doro Parewa Makmur is a Merpati agent on the corner of Jl Sumbawa and Jl Mongosidi. Direct flights go between Bima and Denpasar, Ende, Labuanbajo, Mataram, Maumere, Tambulaka and Kupang.

Bus Bima bus terminal, for most buses to/from the west, is a 10 minute walk south along Jl Sultan Salahuddin from the centre of town. In addition to the daytime buses, there are night buses to Lombok, Bali or Java with ferry fares included. Several bus ticket offices are near the corner of Jl Sultan Kaharuddin and Jl Soekarno Hatta.

Most buses to Lombok leave at around 7.30 pm, but you should try to book your ticket before departure. Fares to Mataram range from 24,000Rp for normal (without air-con) to 42,500Rp for the luxury, air-con buses that take about 11 hours. Bima Setia currently has the best buses, though Rasa Sayang and Langsung Indah are also good. Many continue on to Denpasar (80,000Rp to 85,000Rp), arriving at 11 am the next morning, or you can even continue right through to Surabaya and Jakarta.

Destinations in Sumbawa are mostly serviced by smaller, crowded, normal buses that are the local supply line, stopping anywhere and everywhere. They run between 6 am and 5 pm. Destinations from Bima include Dompu (2000Rp, two hours) and Sumbawa Besar (10,000Rp, seven hours).

Buses east to Sape go from Kumbe bus terminal in Raba, a 20 minute (500Rp) bemo ride east of Bima. You should be able to pick up a yellow bemo easily on Jl Sultan Kaharuddin or Jl Soekarno Hatta. Buses leave Kumbe terminal for Sape (2500Rp, two hours) from about 6 am until 5 pm. Don't rely on these local buses to get you to Sape in time for the morning ferry to Komodo or Flores. Alternatively, the big buses coming though Bima from Surabaya at 4 am go through to Sape for 4000Rp. The other alternative is a chartered bemo, which will do the run in 1½ hours and cost 40,000 Rp to 50,000Rp, depending on your bargaining skills.

Boat The Pelni office is at Bima's port at Jl Pelabuhan 103. The *Kelimutu* calls at Bima twice a fortnight; one week sailing on to Waingapu, Ende and Kupang, and the next week sailing to Lembar.

Getting Around
To/From the Airport Taxi prices are fixed at 17,500Rp for the 16km, 20 minute trip to the town centre or 85,000Rp to Hu'u.

The airport is amid salt pans by the highway, so you can walk out to the main road about 100m in front of the terminal and catch a bus there. Any local bus from Dompu or Sumbawa Besar can take you into town, but they can be very crowded.

Local Transport A bemo around town costs 400Rp per person; horse-drawn *dokar* (known locally as 'Ben Hur') are 300Rp.

EASTERN SUMBAWA
Few visitors to Eastern Sumbawa venture far from Bima and Sape, partly because there are few traditional areas to explore. However, the coastline to the south is quite beautiful and developers are eyeing several sites along it.

South Coast
The sparsely populated south coast has some wonderful beaches. The white sand beach at **Rontu**, has accommodation, but is difficult to reach. The turn-off is at Simpasai, halfway along the road to Parado. From Simpasai it is 5km along a terrible road to the large village of Sondo, from where the road becomes sealed again. Buses run between Bima and Sondo (2000Rp), but for the last 9km to Rontu you'll have to hire a horse-drawn dokar for 1500Rp per person. *Rontu Beach Bungalow* is a new place with a large, impressive

restaurant, but the rooms are very simple for 25,000Rp. If you can be bothered making the long journey, you'll probably be the only guests.

Wawo
On the main highway between Bima and Sape, the Wawo area is noted for its traditional houses, *uma lengge*. The most impressive are at **Maria**, just off the highway, and can be seen from the bus on the way to Sape. Maria is possibly the most visited 'traditional' village in Sumbawa, but the houses are no longer inhabited.

The Dou Wawo people are considered ethnically distinct from the Bimanese but Islam and modernisation have long penetrated these villages.

SAPE
Sape is a pleasant little town with amiable people and an immense number of dokar, which (as in Bima) the locals call 'Ben Hur'. These jingling little buggies with their skinny, pompomed horses don't look much like Roman chariots, but the drivers obviously think they're Charlton Hestons as they race each other along the main street after dark.

There are two colourful daily markets in town; one right in its centre and the other behind the bus terminal. Sape's hotels and restaurants are basic, but it is a more convenient place to stay overnight than Bima if you want to catch the ferry to Komodo or Flores. The ferry leaves from Pelabuhan Sape, about 4km down the road. There's lots of boat building going on along the street running towards the port.

Information
The PHPA Komodo Information Office is about 2.5km from the town centre along the road to Pelabuhan Sape. The office has some interesting brochures and maps, and is open daily.

Places to Stay
The most convenient place to wait for the ferry is *Losmen Mutiara*, nestled just outside

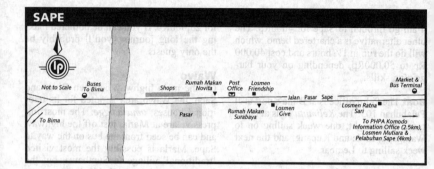

the entrance to the port. The best rooms are upstairs, with access to a balcony overlooking the harbour. All have shared mandi and cost 7500/10,000Rp for singles/doubles. There are a couple of small warungs opposite the hotel.

In town, *Losmen Friendship* lives up to its name. Clean doubles with shared mandi cost 8,000Rp, or 10,000Rp with private mandi. Two cheaper, more basic places are the *Losmen Ratna Sari* and the *Losmen Give* with rooms from 7000Rp.

Getting There & Away

Bus Buses always meet the ferries arriving at Pelabuhan Sape; they are usually express services direct to Lombok or Bali.

For most destinations in Sumbawa, you will need to go to Bima for an onward bus. Buses leave from both bus terminals every half hour for Raba (2500Rp, two hours) until around 5 pm. From Raba take a bemo to Bima (500Rp, 20 minutes). Taxi drivers may tell you that the buses have stopped running and you must charter a taxi to Bima – walk away and ask someone else. If you're travelling from Mataram to Sape, make sure your bus doesn't terminate in Bima.

Boat The ferries to Labuanbajo usually stop at Komodo Island, but be sure to confirm this when you buy your ticket as Komodo sometimes gets by-passed, particularly when one of the ferries is in dry dock. The ferries leave from Pelabuhan Sape at 8 am daily except Friday. Tickets can be purchased at the pier about one hour before departure.

The ferries to/from Flores stop at Komodo but can't dock at the island, so small fishing boats shuttle to Loh Liang for an extra 2000Rp. Sape to Komodo costs 10,000Rp, or to Labuanbajo 11,500Rp. Taking a bicycle through to Labuanbajo costs an extra 3000Rp, 11,000Rp for a motorcycle or a 179,000Rp for a car.

The duration of the crossing varies with the tides and weather, but allow five to seven hours to Komodo and eight to 10 hours to Labuanbajo. Two companies operate on alternate days – the ferry leaving Sape on Monday, Wednesday and Saturday is the biggest and is slightly faster.

Ferries have been known to break down and be out of action for weeks, and a few years back passengers were stranded at Sape when a party of government officials commandeered a ferry for a jaunt to Komodo. Check the schedules in Bima.

You can also charter your own boat to Komodo – Bima travel agents have well equipped boats based at Pelabuan Sape – but this is usually easier and cheaper to organise from Labuanbajo.

Getting Around

A dokar between Sape and the ferry pier will cost around 500Rp per person, if you share the ride.

Komodo & Rinca Islands

A hilly, desolate island sandwiched – along with Padar and Rinca – between Flores and Sumbawa, Komodo's big attraction is lizards – 3m, 100kg monsters, known as *ora* to the locals and tagged 'Komodo dragons' by westerners. The island is surrounded by some of the most tempestuous waters in Indonesia, fraught with riptides and whirlpools. From the sea it looks a far more fitting habitat for a monstrous lizard than for the few hundred people who live in the island's lone village.

Komodo gets a constant stream of visitors these days, but to understand how far off the beaten track it used to be, read *Zoo Quest for a Dragon*, by naturalist and adventurer David Attenborough, who filmed the drag-

ons in 1956. Dragons also inhabit Rinca, Padar and coastal western Flores. Some people now prefer to visit Rinca than Komodo, since it's closer to Flores, has fewer visitors and dragon-spotting is less organised.

Orientation & Information

Komodo The only village is Kampung Komodo, a fishing village in a bay on the east coast. On the same bay and a half-hour walk north of the village is **Loh Liang**, the tourist accommodation camp run by the PHPA. You pay a 20,000Rp park entrance fee on arrival at Loh Liang, valid for seven days. If you are going on to Rinca, keep your park entrance ticket as Rinca is part of the same national park.

The PHPA warns you not to walk outside the camp without one of its guides. Longer treks around the island can be organised, and the PHPA office has a list of guides' fees

KOMODO & RINCA

FLORES SEA

Gili Banta
Tanjung Beru
Pulau Sabola Besar
Batugosok
Teluk Gili Lawa
Selat Sape
Gunung Satalibo (740m)
Pulau Kukusan Besar
Pulau Bidadari
Warcicu
Pulau Sebayur
Pulau Kanawa
Pulau Bajo
Labuanbajo
Pulau Tatawa
Pulau Pungu
Gunung Ara (826m)
Poreng Valley
Loh Sebita
Banu Nggulung
Loh Liang
Komodo National Park
Kampung Komodo
Pantai Merah
Gunung Komodo (655m)
Pulau Lasa
Pulau Punya
Pulau Komodo
Selat Lintah
Teluk Kima
Kampung Rinca
Doro Raja (340m)
Teluk Logo
Loh Wau
Pulau Padar
Teluk Kerbau
Loh Kima
Loh Buaya
Kampung Loh Karora
Pulau Flores
Doro Lankai (520m)
Pulau Langkoi
Tanjung Torolangki
Pulau Tata
Pulau Rinca
Teluk Baru
Doro Ora (670m)
Kampung Loh Baru
Selat Molo
Loh Tongker
0 5 10 km
Gili Dasampi
Gili Motong

NUSA TENGGARA

for them. Though the dragons are a docile bunch for the most part, a lot of emphasis is put on 'danger' – this includes encounters with Komodo dragons that can snap your leg as fast as they'll cut a goat's throat, or having a cobra spit poison at you. Several years ago an elderly European wandered off alone and was never found. Locals are attacked periodically, most commonly while sleeping out in the open. The guides will happily fill you in on the latest casualties.

Rinca The PHPA tourist camp is at **Loh Buaya** and it's possible to camp in some of the villages. The park entrance fee here is also 20,000Rp and PHPA guides cost

6000Rp. Again, keep your entrance ticket if you're going on to Komodo.

Dragon Spotting

Komodo You're likely to see dragons all year at Banu Nggulung, a dry river bed about a half-hour walk from Loh Liang. The ritual feeding of dragons with goats provided by tourists is a thing of the past and dragons are now only fed when the PHPA wants to do a head count. The watering hole at Banu Nggulung still attracts dragons, but since the feeding stopped less dragons are turning up. More than likely you will see a dragon, but in the future sightings may not be guaranteed as before.

Komodo Dragons

There were rumours of these awesome creatures long before their existence was confirmed in the west. Fishers and pearl divers working in the area had brought back tales of ferocious lizards with enormous claws, fearsome teeth and fiery yellow tongues. One theory holds that the Chinese dragon is based on the Komodo lizard. The first Dutch expedition to the island was in 1910; two of the dragons were shot and their skins taken to Java, resulting in the first published description.

The Komodo dragon is actually a monitor lizard. Monitors range from a tiny 20g and 20cm long to the granddaddy of them all, the Komodo dragon (Varanus komodoensis). All monitors have some things in common: the head is tapered; the ear openings are visible; the neck is long and slender; the eyes have eyelids and round pupils; and the jaws are powerful. But the dragons also have massive bodies, four powerful legs (each with five clawed toes) and long, thick tails (which function as rudders but can also be used for grasping or as a potent weapon). The body is covered in small, nonoverlapping scales; some may be spiny, others raised and bony.

The monitors' powerful legs allow them to sprint short distances, lifting their tails as they run. Many species stay in or near the water and can swim quite well, with an undulating movement of the trunk and tail. When threatened they'll take refuge in their normal resting places – holes, trees (for the smaller monitors) or water. They *are* dangerous if driven into a corner and will then attack even a much larger opponent. They threaten by opening the mouth, inflating the neck and hissing. The ribs may spread or the body expand slightly, making the monitor look larger. It often rises up on its hind legs just before attacking and the tail can deliver well-aimed blows that will knock down a weaker adversary. Their best weapons are their sharp teeth and dagger-sharp claws, which can inflict severe wounds.

All monitors feed on other animals: small ones on insects; larger ones on frogs and birds; and the *ora* (the local name for the Komodo dragon) on deer, wild pig and even water buffalo that inhabit the islands. The ora also eat their own dead. They can expand their mouth

A little 'grandstand' overlooks the river bed where the dragons gather. Spectators are fenced off from the dragons – don't expect to walk up to the dragons and have them say 'cheese'. A telephoto lens is handy, but not essential. A guide costs 6000Rp, or 2000Rp per person for groups of more than three. The PHPA prefers to organise fixed times and take large groups, though smaller groups are less zoo-like.

You might spot dragons on some of the other walks and a few lazy ones can often be seen around the camp looking for food.

Rinca There are no established dragon feeding places on Rinca, but there are often a few

monitors hanging around the jetty and PHPA camp at Loh Buaya. The guides know spots where the dragons are likely to sun themselves, but spotting them can still be a matter of luck. But other wildlife is much more abundant than on Komodo: there are several monkey colonies, wild water buffalos, deer, horses, pigs, bush turkeys and eagles.

Other Activities

Most visitors stay one night at Komodo and only visit Banu Nggulung, but Komodo has a number of other things to do and it is quite easy to spend two or more days on the island.

Other walks include the climb to **Gunung Ara** (538m), about 3½ hours return. The

Komodo Dragons

cavity considerably, enabling them to swallow large prey; the ora can push practically a whole goat into its throat.

Being such a large reptile, the ora rarely moves until warmed by the sun. They seem to be stone deaf, but have a very keen sense of smell. Of all the monitors, the ora lays the largest eggs – up to 12cm long and weighing around 200g. The female lays 20 or 30 eggs at a time and usually buries them in the wall of a dry river, where they hatch by themselves nine months later.

Monitors are *not* relics of the dinosaur age; they're remarkably versatile, hardy modern lizards, if not exactly sensitive and new age. Why they exist only on and around Komodo Island is a mystery, as is why males outnumber females by a ratio of 3.4 to one. Populations of the ora vary, though there has been a decline on Komodo from 3336 in 1990 down to an estimated 1600 in 1996. About 800 are found on Rinca and fewer in the other locations.

The villagers never hunted the monitors, which weren't as good to eat as the numerous wild pigs on the island and for other reasons not too hard to imagine! Today the ora is a protected species.

JENNY BOWMAN

NUSA TENGGARA

chances of seeing a dragon are slim, but there are expansive views from the top. **Poreng Valley**, 5.5km from Loh Liang, is another favourite dragon haunt and has a more out-in-the-wild feeling than Banu Nggulung. You can also continue on to **Loh Sebita**. Even if you do not spot dragons, you will see plenty of other wildlife such as wild buffalos, deer, wild pigs and some of Komodo's bird life.

Kampung Komodo is a half-hour walk from park headquarters along the beach. It's a friendly Muslim Bugis village of stilt houses infested with goats, chickens and children. The inhabitants are said to be descendants of convicts who were exiled to the island last century by one of the sultans in Sumbawa.

Komodo is very hot most of the year; take water on the walks.

The national park has a dive cooperative and diving and snorkelling can be arranged at Loh Liang. Mask and fins for snorkelling cost US$8 and boat rental is US$30 for four people. Dive packages start at US$150 for two divers. Good snorkelling can be found at **Pantai Merah** (Red Beach) and the small island of **Pulau Lasa** near Kampung Komodo.

Bomb fishing has destroyed much of the reefs in the national park. The areas around Pulau Tata and Gili Dasampi are less affected and offer some of the best diving in the park, but the currents can be ferocious. The southern tip of Pulau Padar also has reasonable diving. Dolphins are common in the seas between Komodo and Flores, and the area is also on a whale migration route from the Indian Ocean to the South China Sea.

To view coral without getting your feet wet, take the glass-bottom boat that cruises the bay around Loh Liang and Pantai Merah; it costs US$8 per person.

Places to Stay & Eat

On Komodo, the *PHPA camp* at Loh Liang is a collection of large, spacious wooden cabins on stilts with front balconies. Each cabin has four or five rooms, a sitting area and two mandi. Rooms are spartan with mattresses on the floor, but are comfortable and have plenty of rustic charm. Singles/doubles cost 15,000/20,000Rp, but single rooms are limited and you'll usually have to pay the extra for a double. A few more luxurious rooms cost 25,000/35,000Rp. During the peak tourist season – around July/August – the rooms may be full, but the PHPA will rustle up mattresses for you to sleep on even if you can't be guaranteed a room. Electricity, produced by a noisy generator, operates from 6 to 10 pm.

There's also a restaurant at the camp, with a limited menu of *nasi/mie goreng* (fried rice/noodles) for around 8000Rp, fish and other simple meals, plus some drinks (including beer and drinking water). Bring other food yourself, or pick up basic supplies at Kampung Komodo.

On Rinca, accommodation at the *PHPA camp* at Loh Buaya is similar to that on Komodo, at the same prices, but there's no restaurant so bring your own food. The PHPA guides are very friendly; they don't get many people staying at the camp and are glad of the company.

Getting There & Away

Komodo From Sape (Sumbawa), a ferry departs at 8 am daily, except Friday, and costs 10,000Rp for the five to seven hour journey, depending on the sea conditions and the ferry (one ferry is faster than the other). Going the other way, the Labuanbajo-Komodo-Sape ferry departs from Labuanbajo at 8 am daily, except Friday, and costs 5500Rp for the three hour journey. Tickets can be purchased at the harbours in Sape and Labuanbajo one hour before departure.

The ferries cannot dock on Komodo so they stop about 1km out to sea, from where small boats transfer you to Loh Liang for an extra 2000Rp.

Leaving Komodo, the small boats depart at 10 am to meet the Labuanbajo-Sape ferry, and at noon to meet the Sape-Labuanbajo ferry.

Boats to Komodo can be chartered from Labuanbajo or Sape. It is easier and cheaper to arrange in Labuanbajo, although it is becoming increasingly expensive to charter a boat, and hotels and boat operators prefer to sell tours. If you can arrange it yourself, boats cost 80,000Rp to 150,000Rp for a day trip for up to six people, or from 150,000Rp for a two day trip with an overnight stay on the boat. Labuanbajo to Rinca takes two or three hours in an ordinary boat. Labuanbajo to Komodo takes three to four hours. Komodo is also included on the boat tours between Lombok and Labuanbajo. See the Labuanbajo entry in the following Flores section for more details.

Rinca There are no regular passenger ships or ferries to Rinca, so the only option is to charter a boat. It's only two or three hours by motorboat from Labuanbajo to Rinca; a charter boat costs around 80,000Rp for up to six people. Ask at the hotels or around the harbour.

Flores

Flores is a big, rugged and remarkably beautiful island. Dominated by a string of volcanoes, the long-impenetrable terrain has divided the island into many distinct ethnic groups. You'll find some interesting cultures here, with layers of traditional beliefs beneath the prevalent Christianity.

Flores has a thriving ikat-weaving tradition, a developing beach spot at Labuanbajo and fine snorkelling off some parts of the coast. The island has attracted a steady flow of visitors in recent years, but has nothing like the tourist scene in Bali or Lombok.

History

Flores owes its name to the Portuguese, who called its easternmost cape Cabo das Flores, meaning 'Cape of Flowers'. The island's diverse cultures have enough similarities to suggest that they developed from a common type, differentiated by geographical isolation and the varying influence of outsiders. Long before Europeans arrived in the 16th century, much of coastal Flores was firmly in the hands of the Makassarese and Bugis from southern Sulawesi. The Bugis even

established their own ports as part of a trading network throughout the archipelago. They brought gold, coarse porcelain, elephant tusks (used as currency), a sort of machete known as *parang*, linen and copperware, and left with rubber, sea cucumber (much of it fished from the bay of Maumere), shark fins, sandalwood, wild cinnamon, coconut oil, cotton and fabric from Ende. Bugis and Makassarese slave raids on the coasts of Flores were a common problem, forcing people to retreat inland.

Javanese chronicles dating from the 14th century place Flores (rather imaginatively) within the Majapahit realm. In the 15th and 16th centuries, most of western and central Flores is thought to have become a colony of the Makassarese kingdom of Gowa in southern Sulawesi, while eastern Flores came under the sway of Ternate in Maluku.

As early as 1512, Flores was sighted by the Portuguese navigator Antonio de Abreu, and Europeans had probably landed by 1550. The Portuguese, involved in the lucrative sandalwood trade with Timor, built fortresses on Pulau Solor and at Ende, and in 1561 Dominican priests established a mission on Pulau Solor. From here the Portuguese Dominicans extended their work to eastern Flores, founding over 20 missions by 1575. Despite attacks by pirates, local Islamic rulers and raiders from Gowa, the missionaries converted, it is claimed, tens of thousands of Florinese. The fortress at Ende was overrun in 1637 by Muslims and the mission abandoned, as eventually were all the other missions in southern Flores. The growth of Christianity continued, however, and today a church is the centrepiece of almost every village.

In the 17th century, the VOC kicked the Portuguese out of Flores and the surrounding area and concentrated on monopolising the trade in sappanwood (used to make a red dye) and wild cinnamon. The local slave trade was also strong; a Dutch treaty with Ende outlawed it in 1839, but it was reported to exist into the 20th century.

Though Ternate and Gowa ceded all their rights on Solor, Flores and eastern Sumbawa

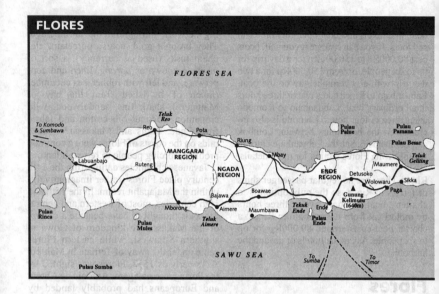

FLORES

FLORES SEA

To Komodo & Sumbawa

Labuanbajo · Ruteng · Reo · Pota · Riung · Mbay

Teluk Reo

MANGGARAI REGION

NGADA REGION

Mborong · Bajawa · Aimere · Boawae · Maumbawa · Maumere

Teluk Aimere

Pulau Rinca · Pulau Mules

ENDE REGION

Ende · Detusoko · Wolowaru · Paga · Sikka · Maumere

Gunung Kelimutu (1640m)

Pulau Palue · Pulau Pamana · Pulau Besar

Teluk Geliting

Teluk Ende · Pulau Ende

SAWU SEA

Pulau Sumba

To Sumba · To Timor

---

to the Dutch in the 17th century, Flores was too complex and isolated for the Dutch to gain real control. Around 1850 the Dutch purchased Portugal's remaining enclaves in the area, including Larantuka, Sikka and Paga in Flores. Dutch Jesuits then took over missionary work in Flores and founded their new bases in Maumere and Sikka, which are still their centres in Flores today.

Even into the first decade of this century, the Dutch were constantly confronted with rebellions and inter-tribal wars. The unrest continued until a major military campaign in 1907 subdued most of the tribes of central and western Flores. Missionaries moved into the isolated western hills in the 1920s.

Geography

The island's turbulent volcanic past has left a complicated relief of V-shaped valleys, knife-edged ridges, and a collection of active and extinct volcanoes. One of the finest volcanoes is the caldera of Kelimutu in central Flores, with its three, coloured lakes. There are 14 active volcanoes in Flores;

only Java and Sumatra have more. The central mountains slope gently to the north coast, but along the south coast the spurs of the volcanoes plunge steeply into the sea.

The island is part of one of the world's most geologically unstable zones, and earthquakes and tremors hit every year. In December 1992 an earthquake measuring 6.8 on the Richter scale, and the massive tidal wave that followed it, killed around 3000 people in eastern Flores and flattened much of Maumere.

The rugged terrain makes road construction difficult; although Flores is only about 375km long, its main east-west road winds, twists, ascends and descends for nearly 700km and heavy wet-season rains, as well as the frequent earthquakes and tremors, mean that it has to be repaired year-round.

Climate

The rainy season (November to March) is more intense in western Flores, which receives the brunt of the north-west monsoon and has the highest mountains. Ruteng, near Flores' highest peak (the 2400m Gunung

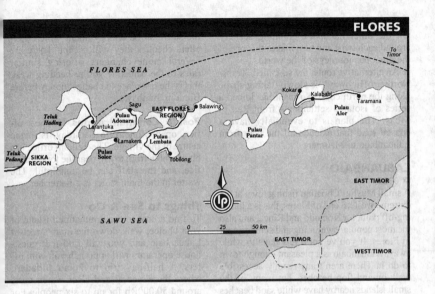

FLORES

Ranaka), gets an average 3350 mm of rain every year, but Ende has only 1140 mm and Larantuka just 770 mm.

Population & People

Difficulties of communication have contributed to the diversity of Flores' cultures. In the more remote areas, you'll find older people who don't speak a word of Bahasa Indonesia and whose parents grew up in purely animist societies.

Physically, the people at the western end of the island are more Malay, while the other inhabitants of Flores are more Melanesian. The island's 1½ million people are divided into five main language and cultural groups. From west to east, these are: the Manggarai (main town Ruteng); the Ngada (Bajawa); the closely related Ende and Lio peoples (Ende); the Sikkanese (Maumere); and the Lamaholot (Larantuka).

Religion

Around 85% of the people are Catholic (Muslims tend to congregate in the coastal towns), but in rural areas particularly, Chris-

tianity is welded onto traditional beliefs. Animist rituals are still important here for a variety of occasions, ranging from birth, marriage and death to the building of new houses, or to mark important points in the agricultural cycle. Even educated, English-speaking Florinese still admit to the odd chicken, pig or buffalo sacrifice to keep their ancestors happy when rice is planted or a new field opened up. In former times, it took more than animal blood to keep the gods and spirits friendly; there are persistent tales of children or virgin girls being sacrificed.

Getting Around

What one Indonesian tourist leaflet charitably calls the 'Trans-Flores Highway' loops and tumbles nearly 700km from Labuanbajo to Larantuka, at the eastern end of the island. The main road is paved all the way, but buses are often small, cramped and overcrowded, and the road is narrow and forever winding. Floods or landslides in the rainy season are not uncommon, and the latest trouble spots are attended by scores of workers doing back-breaking work in difficult conditions –

NUSA TENGGARA

it must seem like patching a crumbling dyke. On the other hand, the stunning scenery around each twist and turn makes this one of the great bus journeys of the world.

An alternative route, the so-called 'Trans-Northern Highway', is slowly taking shape along the north coast. So far it has joined a series of isolated settlements from Reo to Mbay. The plan is to eventually have a coastal road that extends all the way from Labuanbajo to Maumere.

LABUANBAJO
☎ 0385

A small Muslim/Christian fishing town at the extreme western end of Flores, this is a jumping-off point for Komodo and Rinca, and also the most popular swimming and sunning spot in Flores. If you've got a few days to while away, Labuanbajo is a pleasant enough town to do it. There aren't any readily accessible walk-on-and-flop beaches, but many of the small islands nearby have white sand beaches and good snorkelling. The harbour is littered with outrigger fishing boats and is sheltered by the islands, giving the impression that you're standing on the shores of a large lake.

Information
Tourist Offices The tourist office, Dinas Pariwisata, (☎ 41170) for the Manggarai region has helpful staff who speak English. It is out of town on the airport road, near the Telkom office, and is open Monday to Thursday from 7 am to 2 pm, Friday until 11 am and Saturday until 2.30 pm.

The PHPA administers Komodo National Park, which takes in Komodo and Rinca islands and other parts of western Flores, including the Riung area. The PHPA information booth provides practical information for Komodo and Rinca islands, and is attended by members of the local guide association (☎ 41066). The main PHPA office is a little out of town.

Money The BNI and BRI banks on the main street are open Monday to Friday from 8 am to 3.30 pm. The BNI bank also opens on Saturday morning. For currencies other than US$, expect a poor exchange rate, and the staff can be choosy about which travellers cheques they will accept. There are several moneychangers offering similar rates to the banks. If you're heading west, this is the last place to change money before Bima in Sumbawa.

Post & Communications The post office, open Monday to Saturday, is in the centre of the village. The Telkom office is a bit of a hike from town, near the tourism office, and the staff can be unhelpful. The wartel in the main street is a better bet.

Things to See & Do
To find a boat to the uninhabited island of your choice, walk down the main street of Labuanbajo and you will find that guesthouse operators will approach you with offers. A half-day trip to **Pulau Bidadari**, where there's coral and clear water, costs around 50,000Rp for up to six people. For divers, there's good coral between the islands of **Sabolo Besar** and **Sabolo Kecil**. Operators such as Dive Komodo Alor Safari (☎ 41277), the Bajo Dive Club and CN Dive offer dive trips; Dive Komodo is the most established operator.

Beaches worth lounging on are at **Batugosok**, **Weicucu** and on **Pulau Kanawa**, which all have accommodation. Transport is free if you stay there. Most boats leave from the shoreline at the northern end of the main street. They generally charge for day trippers. **Pantai Weicucu** is not much of a beach, but there's a white sand beach and reef on the small island opposite.

Batu Cermin (Mirror Rock) is a limestone outcrop with an impressive series of caves about 4km from town. The main cave is in the centre of the outcrop – take the ladder walkway up and around into the longest canyon. An unmarked cave lies in the centre. If you're going into the cave a torch (flashlight) is essential. You will have to stoop to enter, but can stand once inside. Walk through a series of chambers to where the cave opens into a towering, narrow canyon. This is the 'Mirror Rock' that gives

LABUANBAJO

FLORES SEA

Football Field

PLACES TO STAY
9 Homestay Gembira
13 Gardena Hotel
18 Mutiara Beach Hotel
20 Bajo Beach Hotel
25 Chez Felix
26 Sony Homestay
28 Mitra Hotel
31 Hotel Wisata
36 New Bajo Beach Hotel
37 Cendana Beach Hotel

PLACES TO EAT
15 Dewata Ayu Restaurant
17 Borobudur
29 Arto Moyo
33 Papaya Restaurant
35 New Tenda Nikmat

OTHER
1 Boats to Waecicu Beach
 & Batugosok
2 CN Dive
3 Ferry Office
4 Harbour Master's Office
5 Dive Komodo
6 Pelni Agent
7 Church
8 Mosque
10 PHPA Information Booth
11 Wartel
12 Wannen Tours
14 Sinbad Shuttle &
 Waecicu Beach Office
16 Kanawa Bungalows office
19 Mega Buana Bahari
21 Viewpoint
22 BRI Bank
23 Post Office
24 Puri Bagus Komodo Office
27 Bajo Dive Club;
 Pungu Hotel office
30 Wartel
32 BNI Bank
34 PHPA Main Office
38 Telkom Office
39 Tourist Office
40 Merpati Office
41 Batu Cermin Caves

Pantai Wae Rana

To Pantai Waecicu & Batugosok

To Pearl Farm

Pantai Binongko

Not to Scale

Pasar

To Danau Dolat

To Ruteng

To Ruteng

the outcrop its name; around mid-morning, the sun shines into the canyon and reflects off the walls. To get there, take the road east of the airport. Walk, or charter a bemo. There's a 1500Rp entrance fee.

Organised Tours

A popular way to travel between Labuanbajo and Lombok is on boat tours. A typical itinerary takes in one of the islands – Bidadari or Kanawa – then Rinca. You sleep overnight on the open deck of the boat, usually at Pulau

Kalong (Flying Fox Island; a mangrove island covered in bats) then head for Pulau Komodo to see the dragons and take in some snorkelling. The boats then head along the north coast of Sumbawa making several snorkelling stops off islands, including Pulau Moyo and Pulau Satunda off Sumbawa, before docking at Labuhan Lombok.

Local companies have formed a cooperative that sells tours on a range of small to mid-sized boats through Mega Buana Bahari (☎ 41289). Fares are typically around

250,000Rp for a four day, three night trip. Entry to the Komodo National Park and bus transfers to Mataram are often included. Shop around and find out exactly what is included – scheduled stops, equipment, what sort of food is served, sleeping arrangements (always on the boat, but check where) etc. Most companies proffer written itineraries. It may pay to have the captain initial these clauses on departure to avoid arguments about whether you have an 'old' brochure, but more experienced operators will explain the deal upon departure.

Independent operators also offer cheaper tours and it is especially important to check out arrangements with these. Almost all the hotels arrange tours, either through the main companies or smaller operators. The cheapest hotels usually offer the cheapest tours.

Travellers rate the trips from excellent to dismal – much depends on the boat, the crew and your fellow travellers, who you are stuck with for up to a week.

If the ferry schedule to Komodo is not convenient, tours are available. A two day tour, sleeping overnight on the boat, to Komodo, Rinca and Kalong starts at around 50,000Rp per person on a fishing boat that takes eight people. Many hotels can arrange boats for day trips to Komodo or Pulau Sabolo, which has good snorkelling. Small boats for a day trip to Komodo start at around 75,000Rp for up to six people, which will give you about three hours wandering around the island. Charter boats can also be taken to Bidadari and Sabolo – large boats will cost around 60,000Rp.

Places to Stay

Stay in Labuanbajo itself or at one of the beach hotels. Price wars between the hotels can see rates drop to ridiculously low levels in the low season. Rates quoted here should be viewed as a guide to high season prices and can change from week to week. All hotel rates include breakfast.

Central Area The *Mutiara Beach Hotel* is one of Labuanbajo's original hotels and has a waterfront restaurant with a harbour view.

The asking price for upstairs rooms without mandi but with a view is 15,000Rp, or dark downstairs rooms with mandi is 20,000Rp. Both are negotiable.

The well appointed *Bajo Beach Hotel* (☎ 41009) across the road has rooms ranging from basic economy single/double rooms with outside mandi for 10,000/15,000Rp, through to pleasant rooms with fan and shower for 25,000Rp.

The *Gardena Hotel* (☎ 41258) has a hill-top position above the main road and an attached restaurant serving good food. Basic bungalows around a garden, some with great harbour views, cost 20,000/30,000Rp.

The *Mitra Hotel* (☎ 41003) is a switched-on budget place offering a variety of services, including tours. Simple but clean rooms cost 10,000/12,500Rp or 12,500/15,000Rp with mandi. It is well geared for travellers and also rents out motorcycles for 30,000Rp per day.

The *Hotel Wisata* (☎ 41020) competes with the Bajo Beach to be the best in town and has better service. Rooms with shower and fan cost 15,000/20,000Rp; larger, double rooms facing the courtyard cost 25,000Rp. The restaurant is good.

Labuanbajo also has a number of homestays. The best of these is *Chez Felix*, run by a friendly family that speaks good English. There's a pleasant porch area for eating and the rooms are clean, with large windows, and cost 15,000/20,000Rp with shared bath, 20,000/30,000Rp with mandi and 25,000/35,000Rp with fan and mandi.

Nearby is the quiet *Sony Homestay*, with a nice hilltop view. Basic but clean rooms with private bath are 8000/10,000Rp. Labuanbajo has plenty of other basic, anonymous losmen such as the *Losmen Sinjai* and *Homestay Gembira* next to the mosque.

Beach Hotels You'll need to take a boat ride – free for guests – to get to most of these hotels from Labuanbajo.

Kanawa Island Bungalows is on Pulau Kanawa, one hour by boat from Labuanbajo. The beach and snorkelling are very good, and simple bungalow accommodation costs 15,000/20,000Rp, or 20,000/25,000Rp for new rooms.

The *Waecicu Beach Hotel* is a 20 minute boat ride north of Labuanbajo at Waecicu Beach. Boats each way leave three times a day; the last boat leaves at dusk. The calm waters are good for swimming and the small island opposite offers a white sand beach and good snorkelling. The price, 25,000Rp per person for a basic bamboo bungalow or 30,000Rp with attached mandi, includes three meals.

Puri Bagus Komodo (☎ 41030) at Batu-gosok is set on a fine white beach on the mainland, a half hour boat ride from town. This is far and away the classiest accommodation in Labuanbajo. Two storey bungalows and lodge rooms are very attractive, but expensive at US$75. The resort has a good restaurant and a dive shop. Boats supposedly leave Labuanbajo at 6, 9 and 11 am, and 7 pm, but inquire at the resort office in Labuanbajo.

The *New Bajo Beach Hotel* (☎ 41047) is 2.5km south of town and is the best hotel that can be reached by road. Air-con double rooms cost 70,000Rp. The beach is pleasant enough, but no world-beater.

The *Cendana Beach Hotel*, 2km past the New Bajo Beach, is on a nondescript beach. This large hotel has become run down, but the rooms are spacious and reasonably priced at 10,000/20,000Rp with fan and shower; and there's better rooms for 15,000/25,000Rp.

Pungu Hotel (☎ 41083) on Pulau Pungu is a new place with simple bungalows a half hour boat ride from Labuanbajo. Bungalows cost 15,000Rp. The booking office is near the Arto Moro restaurant.

Places to Eat

Labuanbajo has a few good restaurants specialising in seafood at reasonable prices. The pick of the crop is the *Borobudur*, set above the road with lovely views. It has excellent fish, prawns, a few Thai dishes, steaks and even schnitzel. It's more expensive than most, but worth it. The Chinese owner worked as a cook in Australia, so western dishes are a speciality.

The *Dewata Ayu Restaurant* next door serves good seafood and cheaper Indonesian dishes. The *Arto Moro* has a prime position on the harbour side of the road, overlooking the water, but the menu is limited. The *Papaya Restaurant* is worth a look, and the *New Tenda Nikmat* has pleasant bamboo decor and serves a mean grilled fish. Otherwise, the restaurants in the *Gardena*, *Bajo Beach* and *Wisata* hotels all have long menus and reasonable prices.

Getting There & Away

Air Merpati has direct flights between Labuanbajo and Bima (164,200Rp) four days a week, with connections on to Mataram (407,600Rp), Denpasar (457,900Rp) and further afield. The Merpati office is between Labuanbajo and the airport, about 1.5km from the town. It opens Monday to Saturday from 7.30 am to 1 pm, and daily (including Sunday) from 4 to 5 pm.

Bus & Truck Buses to Ruteng (7500Rp, four hours) leave at 7.30 am and around 4 pm, when the ferry arrives from Sape and Komodo. Other Ruteng buses are supposed to go at 11 am and 2 pm, but don't count on them. Chances are they will cruise town endlessly and, if they still don't have enough passengers, will wait for the ferry.

Buses to Bajawa (15,000Rp, 10 hours) leave at 6.30 am and a bus also usually meets the ferry. The Damri bus to Ende (27,500Rp, 14 hours) meets the ferry, if you are desperate to get to Kelimutu in a hurry. You can buy tickets from hotels, or from buses around the pier. If you get an advance ticket, the bus will pick you up from your hotel.

Passenger trucks also ply the route to Ruteng. They are less comfortable, but cost the same. If you do find yourself on a truck, it's imperative to get a seat in front of the rear axle; the positions behind are good approximations of ejector seats.

Boat The ferry from Labuanbajo to Komodo (5500Rp, three hours) and Sape (11,500Rp, eight to 10 hours) leaves at 8 am daily, except Friday. You can get tickets from the harbour master's office (in front of the pier) one hour before departure. Bicycles, motorcycles and cars can be taken on the ferry. See the Sape entry in the previous Sumbawa section for more details. The ferry doesn't dock at Komodo, but small boats shuttle to the park headquarters for an extra 2000Rp.

The Pelni passenger ships *Tatamailau*, *Tilongkabila* and *Pangrango* all stop at Labuanbajo. From Labuanbajo, the *Tilongkabila* heads to Ujung Pandang, then up the east coast of Sulawesi.

Getting Around

To/From the Airport The airfield is 2.5km from the town and hotels can arrange a taxi (2000Rp). A crush of touts meets each plane to offer free lifts to the hotel of your choice.

REO

Set on an estuary a short distance from the sea, Reo's focal point is the large Catholic compound in the middle of town. This straggling town used to be important for boat connections. When the Trans-Flores Hwy was impassable in the wet season, regular boats ran between Labuanbajo and the port of Kedidi, just outside town, but these boats are now rare as road transport has improved.

Reo has a couple of cheap losmen and a few small eateries. The centrally located *Losmen Teluk Bayur (Jl Mesjid 8)* has basic rooms for 10,000Rp and is near the mosque. The *Hotel Nisangnai (Jl Pelabuhan)*, on the road to Kedindi, is a notch better.

The 60km bus trip from Reo to Ruteng takes 1½ hours and costs 5000Rp. The road from Reo to Riung is improving, enabling travellers to get to Riung via the north coast, which has some good beaches around Pota.

RUTENG
☎ 0385

A market town and meeting point for the hill people of western Flores, Ruteng is the heart of Manggarai country, which is the region extending to the west coast from a line drawn north from Aimere. The town is surrounded by rice fields on gentle slopes beneath a line of volcanic hills.

Ruteng is a pleasantly cool town that has no attractions in itself, but has points of interest in the areas around the town. Unlike Bajawa, which has a well developed tourist industry, Ruteng only sees overnight visitors who stop to break the bone-shaking bus journey.

Ruteng's lively, sprawling market on Jl Kartini is a meeting place for people from the surrounding hills.

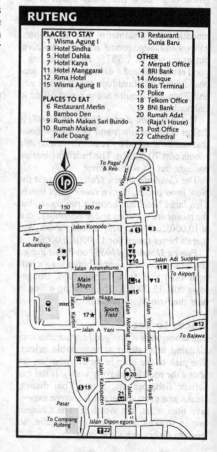

RUTENG

PLACES TO STAY	
1	Wisma Agung I
3	Hotel Sindha
5	Hotel Dahlia
7	Hotel Karya
11	Hotel Manggarai
12	Rima Hotel
15	Wisma Agung II

PLACES TO EAT	
6	Restaurant Merlin
8	Bamboo Den
9	Rumah Makan Sari Bundo
10	Rumah Makan Pade Doang
13	Restaurant Dunia Baru

OTHER	
2	Merpati Office
4	BRI Bank
14	Mosque
16	Bus Terminal
17	Police
18	Telkom Office
19	BNI Bank
20	Rumah Adat (Raja's House)
21	Post Office
22	Cathedral

To Pagal & Reo

0   150   300 m

Jalan Waeces

To Labuanbajo

Jalan Komodo

Jalan Amenehuno

Jalan Adi Sucipto

To Airport

Main Shops

Jalan Niaga

Jalan Kartini

Sports Field

To Bajawa

Jalan A Yani

Jalan Motang Rua

Jalan Yos Sudarso

Jalan S Riyadi

Jalan Kabupaten

Jalan Baruk

Pasar

To Compang Ruteng

Jalan Dipon egoro

The calm blue waters of Gili Air, Lombok – island-hop or stay put and enjoy the rural ambience.

And the beat goes on ...   Fisherman – Labuanbajo, Flores.   Mobile market – Kuta, Lombok.

Labuanbajo harbour, Flores, dotted with *perahu* (outrigger fishing boats).

Ceremonial *caci* whip fighter, Flores.

One of the few mosques in animist Sumba.

Quiet village with the *putih merah* flying, Sumba.

Mother and child, Flores.

Information

The BNI bank on Jl Kartini has the best rates for cash and travellers cheques. The BRI bank on Jl Yos Sudarso is reasonable for US dollars, but has low rates for other currencies. Banks are open Monday to Friday from 7.15 am to noon and 1 to 3 pm.

The post office at Jl Baruk 6 is open Monday to Saturday from 7 am to 2 pm and for limited postal services on Sunday. The Telkom office on Jl Kartini is open 24 hours.

Places to Stay

The main backpackers' choice is the *Rima Hotel* (☎ 22196, Jl A Yani 14). It's on the ball with information and arranges bus tickets and tours to the surrounding attractions. Economy singles/doubles with shared mandi cost 10,000/15,000Rp, or a few lighter and more spacious rooms cost 15,000/25,000Rp and 25,000/35,000Rp. It has a reasonable restaurant, but make sure you order early.

The *Hotel Karya (Jl Motang Rua)* is Ruteng's original hotel, and looks it. It's cheap at 7500Rp per person, but the rooms are dank.

The well run *Hotel Sindha* (☎ 21197, Jl Yos Sudarso) is central and a good option. The rooms with outside mandi for 10,000Rp are bright, roomy and better value than those with mandi for 15,000Rp. Spacious rooms with western bath, TV and balcony are 37,500Rp. New VIP rooms with hot water showers cost 50,000Rp. The attached restaurant serves good Chinese food and has satellite TV if you're desperate for news.

Wisma Agung I (☎ 21080, Jl Waeces 10), is one of the town's best hotels and good value, but is a 15 minute walk from the town centre. Pleasant economy rooms with shared mandi are 10,000/15,000Rp, or good renovated rooms with bathroom are 15,000/20,000Rp. The new section next door, Agung III, has spacious, well appointed rooms for 40,000Rp.

Wisma Agung II (☎ 21835, Jl Motang Rua), behind a shop with the same name (Toko Agung), is basic, clean and right in the town centre. Rooms with mandi are 15,000/20,000Rp.

The *Hotel Manggarai* (☎ 21008, Jl Adi Sucipto) is close to the town centre and is reasonable value. The rooms with outside mandi go for 11,000/16,000Rp, and the rooms with mandi cost 14,000/18,000Rp.

The *Hotel Dahlia* (☎ 21377, Jl Kartini) is a fancy-looking hotel. Very ordinary rooms for 20,000Rp without mandi, or 30,000Rp with mandi, are overpriced, but the VIP rooms with hot water for 35,000Rp are among the most luxurious in Ruteng.

Places to Eat

On Jl Motang Rua, the cosy and friendly *Bamboo Den* next to the Hotel Karya has fried chicken, sate and other dishes. *Rumah Makan Sari Bundo* next door is a Padang restaurant serving big prawns and good *rendang* (curry). *Warungs* around the market serve Padang food, buffalo soup and sate.

Ruteng has some good Chinese restaurants, such as the *Restaurant Dunia Baru (Jl Yos Sudarso 10)*, and the *Rumah Makan Pade Doang (Jl Motang Rua 34)*. The *Restaurant Merlin (Jl Kartini)* near the Hotel Dahlia is also good. Also, many of the hotels have their own restaurants.

Getting There & Away

Air Merpati had a small plane making twice-weekly flights to Bima and Kupang, but tight margins play havoc with the schedules. Check the current state of play with the Merpati agent (☎ 21197), which is out in the rice paddies, about a 10 minute walk east from the town centre.

Bus Buses will drop you at hotels on your arrival in Ruteng. Buses to Labuanbajo (7500Rp, four hours), Bajawa (8000Rp, five hours) and Ende (17,500Rp, nine hours) leave around 7.30 am. There are noon buses to Bajawa and Labuanbajo, and the Agogo bus to Ende at 5 pm costs 17,500Rp, but is quicker than the day buses and will drop you at your hotel in Ende. You can buy tickets for the morning buses at the bus terminal or from the ticket agencies scattered around town. Alternatively, most hotels will get them for you and arrange for the bus to pick you up.

NUSA TENGGARA

Buses, trucks and bemos run frequently until noon to Reo (5000Rp, 1½ hours). A front seat will cost an extra 500Rp, but is worth it on the bad road. You can catch buses at the bus terminal or as they circle the streets.

Getting Around

The airport is about 2km south-east from the town centre, about a half-hour walk. The Hotel Sindha offers guests free transport to the airport. Otherwise, you can charter a bemo.

AROUND RUTENG

Like Bajawa, many travellers stop at Ruteng for an introduction to the traditional cultures around it. A good starting point is **Compang Ruteng**, a traditional village 3km from Ruteng. The compound is centred on its *compang*, the traditional ancestor altar composed of a raised stone burial platform of rocks and ringed by a stone wall. Facing the altar are two renovated *rumah adat* (traditional houses). One is the Mbaru Gendrang, a meeting house for the village elders and all ceremonies begin here. It also holds many sacred heirlooms, including a gold and silver *panggal*, the buffalo horn shaped headdress used in ceremonial *caci* (a martial art in which participants duel with whips and shields).

The *penti* ceremony, held in August between the rice harvest and the next planting, is the most important Manggarai ceremony. It honours the ancestors and involves caci fights, dancing and the slaughter of buffalo and pigs.

The village receives a steady trickle of tourists and the occasional tour group. You will be asked to sign the visitors' book and make a sizeable donation. Ask around Ruteng for information on the ceremonies that are held further afield.

Golo Curu, a hill to the north of Ruteng, offers spectacular early morning views of the hills, valleys, rice paddies, terraced slopes and distant mountain valleys. Walk down the Reo road and when you're 20 minutes past the Hotel Karya you should turn right at the small bridge. There's a

The Manggarai

The Manggarai hill people are perhaps the best known and most interesting of the many 'traditional' ethnic groups in Flores. They tend to be shy, but friendly – you'll see many around Ruteng in their distinctive black sarongs, trailing black-haired pigs into market or herding beautiful miniature horses. The Manggarai language is unintelligible to the other people of Flores.

Makassarese from Sulawesi have mixed with the coastal Manggarai for well over 100 years and the Bimanese dominated the area for at least 300 years until early this century, when the Dutch took over all of Flores. Christianity now predominates among the upland Manggarai, and Ruteng has several large Christian schools and churches. Traditional animist practices still linger, but are dwindling – traditionally, the Manggarai would carry out a cycle of ceremonies, some involving buffalo or pig sacrifices, to ask favours from ancestor and nature spirits and the supreme being, Mori. In some villages you can still find the *compang*, a ring of flat stones on which offerings were placed, or you may be shown ritual paraphernalia used during sacrificial ceremonies.

Trials of strength and courage known as *caci* still take place in Ruteng during the national Independence Day celebrations (17 August). The two combatants wear wooden masks like uptilted welder's helmets. One carries a rawhide oval shield and 1m-long whip, the other a short, springy stick and a thick cloth wrapped around his forearm.

The Manggarai traditionally practised slash-and-burn agriculture. They were introduced to rice cultivation around 1920 by the Dutch, but only in the last few decades has the area been devoted to permanent rice terraces. Maize (sweet corn) is the other main crop, though other crops (such as coffee and onions) are grown for export. The Manggarai also raise fine horses and large water buffalo, the latter primarily for export.

derelict shrine on the hilltop, with a statue of the Virgin Mary on a pedestal. Further north, 6km from Ruteng, near Cancar, is the **Waegarik waterfall**.

Manggarai sarongs are black with pretty embroidered patterns. You can find them in the main Ruteng market, or visit the weaving village of **Cibal**. Cibal is difficult to reach and good weaving is more easily seen at **Pagal**, 21km north of Ruteng on the main road to Reo. It's about a 5km walk east over the hill to Cibal.

The 2140m **Gunung Ranaka**, an active volcano that erupted in 1987, can be reached by road – take an eastbound bus along the highway to the turn-off at the 8km mark. It is then a 9km walk along the old Telkom road to the abandoned transmitter station at the top. The road is flanked by 2 to 3m high regrowth, so views are limited, but it's a pleasant enough walk. You can charter a bemo from Ruteng for around 10,000Rp, but drivers may not be willing to go right to the top. The paved road is in bad repair, especially the last 2km. There are good views from the top, but you can't reach the active crater, further down the slopes as it's too dangerous.

Danau Ranamese, which is a lake that is known as 'little Kelimutu' to locals, is 22km from Ruteng, right next to the main Bajawa road. This small lake is a pleasant picnic spot surrounded by jungle-clad hills. It has a visitors' centre, with bare accommodation. There are a few short trails around the visitors' centre and lake. At the time of writing, longer trails were being developed.

BAJAWA
☎ 0384   • pop 15,000

The small hill town of Bajawa is the centre of the Ngada people, one of the most traditional groups in Flores. The town is at an altitude of 1100m and is surrounded by volcanic hills, with the 2245m Gunung Inerie (to the south) predominant. Bajawa is cool, low key and clean. It also has a good range of restaurants and accommodation, making it a popular place to spend a few days exploring the countryside and making trips to the Ngada villages.

Information
Bajawa's tourist office (☎ 21554), Jl Soekarno Hatta, is helpful, but its information is dated and not so useful.

The BNI bank just off Jl Basoeki Rahmat is the best place to change money. The rates at the BRI bank on Jl Soekarno Hatta are lousy. The post office is on Jl Soekarno Hatta, north of the latter, and is open Monday to Saturday from 8 am to 2 pm.

Places to Stay
Bajawa has a surprising number of hotels for its size and new places are opening all the time. All include breakfast in the price. The newcomers include *Hotel Sehati* (☎ 21 431, Jl Basoeki Rahmat), which is more a homestay than a hotel but it's trying hard with singles/doubles with mandi for 25,000/ 30,000Rp. It has one 'spring bed', which is the talk of the town.

Edelweis (☎ 21345, Jl Ahmad Yani 76) is next to the popular Carmellya Restaurant. Its rooms cost 15,000Rp, or 20,000Rp with mandi.

Across the road, the *Hotel Korina* (☎ 21 162, Jl Ahmad Yani 81) is one of the better places, with friendly and efficient staff. Room rates range from 20,000/25,000Rp to 30,000/35,000Rp, but avoid the room next to the noisy pig pen.

The long-running *Homestay Sunflower* (☎ 21236), on a small path off Jl Ahmad Yani, was one of the first to run trips to traditional villages. It is now looking run down, but it's still an informative place and has a pleasant balcony overlooking the valley. Small and often dark rooms cost 15,000/20,000Rp with attached mandi.

The small *Hotel Ariesta* (☎ 21292, Jl Diponegoro) is bright, clean and a good choice. The rooms at the front or around the pleasant courtyard area at the back cost 30,000/35,000Rp with mandi.

The *Elizabeth Hotel* (☎ 21223, Jl Inerie) is a short hike from the centre of town. Spotless, bright rooms in this family-run establishment cost 35,000/40,000Rp.

Nearby, the staff at *Stela Sasandy* (☎ 21 198), just off Jl Soekarno Hatta, are friendly

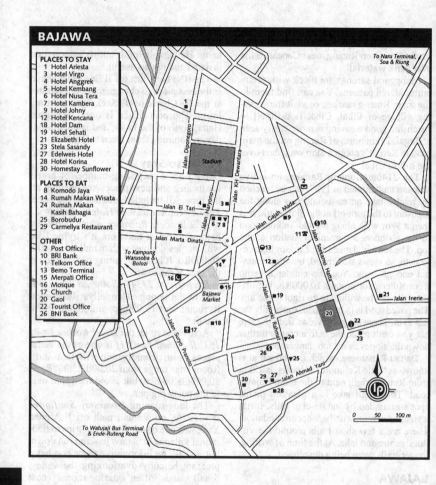

BAJAWA

PLACES TO STAY
1 Hotel Ariesta
3 Hotel Virgo
4 Hotel Anggrek
5 Hotel Kembang
6 Hotel Nusa Tera
7 Hotel Kambera
9 Hotel Johny
12 Hotel Kencana
18 Hotel Dam
19 Hotel Sehati
21 Elizabeth Hotel
23 Stela Sasandy
27 Edelweis Hotel
28 Hotel Korina
30 Homestay Sunflower

PLACES TO EAT
8 Komodo Jaya
14 Rumah Makan Wisata
24 Rumah Makan
    Kasih Bahagia
25 Borobudur
29 Carmellya Restaurant

OTHER
2 Post Office
10 BRI Bank
11 Telkom Office
13 Bemo Terminal
15 Merpati Office
16 Mosque
17 Church
20 Gaol
22 Tourist Office
26 BNI Bank

To Naru Terminal,
Soa & Riung

Jalan Diponegoro

Stadium

Jalan KH Dewantara

Jalan Haryono

Jalan El Tari

Jalan Marta Dinata

Jalan Gajah Mada

Jalan Soekarno Hatta

Jalan Inerie

Jalan Basoeki Rahmat

To Kampung
Warusoba &
Bolozi

Bajawu
Market

Jalan Surjo Pranoto

Jalan Ahmad Yani

To Watujaji Bus Terminal
& Ende-Ruteng Road

0   50   100 m

---

and helpful, with rooms for 15,000Rp or 20,000/25,000Rp with mandi.

The **Hotel Dam** (☎ 21045) is a quiet and delightful little place near the church, run by a friendly family. Rooms with attached bath cost 8800Rp per person, or there are two cheaper rooms with shared mandi at 6600Rp per person.

The friendly **Hotel Kencana** (*Jl Palapa 7*) has basic rooms for 10,000Rp with mandi.

A group of hotels can be found close to the centre of town, west of the market. The **Hotel**

Anggrek (☎ 21172, Jl Letjend Haryono) is probably the best value in town with clean rooms with mandi for 10,000Rp per person. The restaurant here serves excellent food.

The largest hotel is the **Hotel Kembang** (☎ 21072, Jl Marta Dinata), which has well appointed double rooms with private bath for 22,500Rp and 25,000Rp.

Places to Eat
For a small town, Bajawa has a great range of restaurants.

NUSA TENGGARA

The travellers' favourite is the small and friendly *Carmellya Restaurant (Jl Ahmad Yani)*. It has good maps of the area and lots of other information. The food isn't bad either, even stretching to a few Indonesian-style Italian, Swiss and Mexican dishes. The guacamole is great, but avoid the 'potato' rosti.

The hot competition is the *Borobudur*, which is around the corner in Jl Basoeki Rahmat. This is a branch of the Labuanbajo restaurant of the same name and it has a similar menu.

An old favourite, the *Rumah Makan Kasih Bahagia*, is a good Chinese restaurant with cold beer and decent food at reasonable prices. Its move to Jl Basoeki Rahmat is giving both the Carmellya and Borobudur a run for their money.

Rumah Makan Wisata (Jl Gajah Mada) is near the market and has passable Indonesian and Chinese fare, but slow service. Two smaller Padang restaurants right in the market are the *Rumah Makan Pondok Salero* and *Rumah Makan Roda Baru*.

The *Komodo Jaya* has an extensive menu with a wide variety of good noodle and seafood dishes.

The *Hotel Anggrek* and *Hotel Kambera* have attached restaurants with long menus – the Hotel Anggrek, in particular, serves excellent home-style cooking.

Shopping

Bajawa market is busy and colourful. Lots of women from the Ngada area and further afield wear ikat cloth, some of which is for sale. The better examples are black with white motifs, often depicting horses. The fruit here is plentiful and of good quality.

Getting There & Away

Air Bajawa no longer has a reliable air service. At the time of writing Merpati was considering a weekly flight to link Bajawa with Bima and Ende. The Merpati office (☎ 21 051) is adjacent to the Bajawa market.

Bus Long-distance buses leave from Watujaji terminal, 3km south of town near the Ende-Ruteng road. The bus to Labuanbajo

(15,000Rp, 10 hours) leaves around 7 am. The buses to Ruteng (7500Rp, five hours) leave on a more frequent basis. Buses to Ende (7500Rp, five hours) leave at 7 am and noon, and there is a through bus to Moni and Maumere (15,000Rp). Morning and midday buses also run to Riung (5000Rp, 2½ hours) along the newly completed road. Most hotels arrange bus tickets.

Bemo & Truck The town's bemo terminal is on Jl Basoeki Rahmat. Regular bemos travel from here to Soa, Mangulewa, Mataloko, Langa and Boawae. A bemo to Bena runs perhaps once or twice a day, depending on passenger demand, but not to any schedule. There is also at least one truck a day that runs to Jerebuu, passing through Bena. The bemos roam around town a lot, so you can also pick them up on the street.

Boat There's a ferry that runs from Aimere, on the coast near Bajawa, to Waingapu on Friday (18,000Rp) and to Kupang on Monday (27,000Rp), but this is not a popular route and may not last. Take a bemo from the Watujaji terminal to Aimere (2500Rp) and buy your ticket on the ferry.

Getting Around

To/From the Airport The airport is 25km from Bajawa and about 6km outside Soa. Bemos from the Bajawa market cost 2500Rp, but make sure you don't get stranded in Soa.

Bemo Yellow bemos cruise around town for 500Rp, but you can walk to almost everywhere except the bus terminals.

AROUND BAJAWA

The main attraction in Bajawa is the chance to get out into the countryside and explore the traditional villages. You can visit the villages by yourself, but you may get more out of your visit if you go with a guide. A good guide will provide an introduction, explain local customs and give an insight into village life. Members of the local guiding association offer tours at 30,000Rp per person for a day trip to the villages, including lunch

The Ngada

Sixty thousand Ngada people inhabit both the upland Bajawa plateau and the slopes around Gunung Inerie stretching down the south coast. They were subdued by the Dutch in 1907 and Christian missionaries arrived about 1920. Older animistic beliefs remain strong and the religion of many Ngada, to a greater extent than in most of Flores, is a fusion of animism and Christianity.

The most evident symbols of continuing Ngada tradition are the pairs of *ngadhu* and *bhaga*. The ngadhu is a parasol-like structure about 3m-high consisting of a carved wooden pole and thatched 'roof', and the bhaga is like a miniature thatch-roof house. You'll see groups of them standing in most Ngada villages, though in the less-traditional ones some of the bhaga have disappeared.

The functions and meanings of ngadhu are multiple, but basically they symbolise the continuing presence of ancestors. The ngadhu is 'male' and the bhaga is 'female', and each pair is associated with a particular family group within a village. Though the carved trunks of ngadhu often feel like solid stone, their tops are usually dilapidated. Some are said to have been built to commemorate people killed in long-past battles over land disputes and may be over 100 years old. Periodically, on instruction from ancestors in dreams, a pair of ngadhu and bhaga is remade according to a fixed pattern, accompanied by ceremonies that may involve buffalo sacrifices.

The main post of a ngadhu, known as *sebu*, should come from a tree that is dug up complete with its main root, then 'planted' in the appropriate place in the village. Each part of the post has specific designs carved on it on different days: an axe and a cassava on the top part; a dragon head in the form of a flower in the middle; and a geometric design around the base. The three parts are also said to represent the three classes of traditional Ngada society: from top to bottom, the *gae*, *gae kisa* and *hoo*. A crossbeam with two hands holding an arrow and a sword links the top of the pole to the roof. The walls of the bhaga must be cut from seven pieces of wood. Near the ngadhu there's usually a small stone post which is the 'gate keeper', while the bases of both ngadhu and bhaga are often surrounded by circles of stones, said to symbolise meeting places.

The traditional Ngada village layout – of which there are still a few examples left – is two rows of high-roofed houses on low stilts. These face each other across an open space that contains ngadhu and bhaga and groups of human-high stone slivers surrounding horizontal slabs. The latter, which appear to be graves of important ancestors, have led to some exotic theories about the Ngada's origins.

Traditionally, the Ngada believe themselves to have come from Java and they may have settled here three centuries ago. But stone structures which are in varying degrees similar to these 'graves' crop up in other remote parts of Indonesia – among them Pulau Nias, Sumatra's Batak Highlands, parts of Sulawesi, Sumba and Tanimbar – as well as in Malaysia and Laos. The common thread is thought to be the Dongson culture, which arose in southern China and

and public transport. You can also charter a bemo for around 80,000Rp per day or a car (such as a Kijang) for 120,000Rp. All guides are local and knowledgeable. The main difference is their proficiency in English (a few also know a little Dutch, German and/or French). Talk to your guide beforehand.

The villages are now quite used to tourists. If visiting, it is customary to sign the visitors' book and make a donation of 1000Rp or so.

The Ngada

northern Vietnam about 2700 years ago then migrated into Indonesia, bringing, among other things, the practice of erecting large monumental stones (megaliths). This practice, it's thought, survived only in isolated areas that were not in contact with later cultural changes.

Some writers also claim to have recognised Hindu, Semitic and even Caucasian elements in Ngada culture; one theory seeking to explain apparent similarities between Indonesian and Balkan culture suggests that the Dongson culture originated in south-east Europe!

What makes the Ngada unusual today is their preservation of animistic beliefs and practices. 'Straight' Christianity has made fewer inroads in the villages than in Bajawa itself. In addition to ngadhu, bhaga and the ancestor worship that goes with them, agricultural fertility rites continue (sometimes involving gory buffalo sacrifices) as well as ceremonies marking birth, marriage, death or house building. The major annual festival is the six day Reba ceremony at Bena, 21km from Bajawa, held around late December/early January, which includes dancing, singing, buffalo sacrifices and the wearing of special black ikat costumes. The highest god in traditional Ngada belief is Gae Dewa who unites Dewa Zeta (the heavens) and Nitu Sale (the earth).

JENNY BOWMAN

Taking photos is usually okay, but ask first and remember that entering a village is like entering someone's home. Bena and Wogo are the most traditional and impressive villages. Bena has fine views.

Kampung Bolozi

Only a 30 to 45 minute walk west from Bajawa, Kampung Bolozi has some *ngadhus* (a parasol like structure consisting of a carved wooden pole and thatched roof), a

AROUND BAJAWA

Kuruboko | To Poma & Riung
Nagarawe
Waepana | Bajawu Airport | Mangeruda Mata Air Panas
Meli | Piga | Loa
Menge | Tarawaja
Not to Scale | Soa | Radawae | To Boawae, Aegela & Ende
Surisina | Zau
Zepe | Roa
Bolozi | Bajawa | Sarasadu
To Aimere & Ruteng | Watujaji | Boua
Bomuzi | Borado | Mangulewa | Malanuza
Langa | Wolobobo | Warikeo | Mataloko
Gunung Inerie (2230m) | Bela | Dena | Welu | Wogo | Toda | Reko
Watumeze | Dadawau | Kampung
Bena | Doka | Wogo Lama
Jerebuu | Malanage Mata Air Panas | Were | Laja
Nage | Maumbawa
Waebela | Utaseko

SAWU SEA

Bajawa to Watujaji	3km
Bajawa to Mangulewa	5km
Mangulewa to Bena	10km
Watujaji to Langa	4km
Langa to Bena	12km
Bena to Malanage	6km

few traditional houses and an old tomb. See the Around Bajawa map for directions; if in doubt, ask for Kampung Warusoba, which is on the way to Kampung Bolozi.

Langa & Bela

There are ngadhus and *bhagas* (miniature thatch-roofed houses) in Langa, which is 7km from Bajawa, but this village is fairly modern. Bemos travel here from Bajawa's bemo terminal. Bela is more interesting and traditional and is a couple of kilometres away, off the road. **Borado** is 3km from Langa and is another traditional village.

Bena

At the base of **Gunung Inerie** (2230m), 19km from Bajawa, Bena is one of the most traditional Ngada villages and its stone monuments are a **protected site**. Houses with high thatched-roofs line up in two

rows on a ridge, with the space between them filled with ngadhus, bhagas and strange megalithic tomb-like structures. Some of these 'tombs' are said to contain hoards of treasure. The house of the leading family in each part of the village has a little model house on top of its roof. A small Christian shrine sits on a mound at the top of the village and behind it a recently built shelter offers a spectacular view of the Inerie volcano and the south coast. Gunung Inerie can be climbed from Watumeze, between Langa and Bena, in about four hours.

Bena is the most visited village and weavings and souvenir stalls line the front of the houses. Despite it being crowded when tour buses arrive, traditional beliefs and customs are still strongly followed. It may be possible to stay with the kepala desa for around 10,000Rp to 15,000Rp (not including meals).

Getting There & Away Bena is 12km from Langa. Bemos travel from Langa to Bena occasionally, but more often they finish in Langa and want you to charter the rest of the way. Otherwise, you have to walk. Direct bemos run from Bajawa via Mangulewa roughly every hour throughout the day.

Nage

Nage is a traditional village on a plateau about 7km from Bena. It has great views of Gunung Inerie. Several well maintained ngadhus, bhagas and tombs lie between two rows of high-roofed houses. About 2km before Nage are the **Malanage Hot Springs**, where a fast flowing and hot, emerald-green river mixes with a cold water stream.

Getting There & Away You can walk from Nage to Bena; just continue north on the paved road through the village. Otherwise, one bemo in the morning and one in the afternoon runs from Bajawa via Bena and Mangulewa.

Wogo

Wogo is a large village with eight or nine sets of ngadhu and bhaga, ringed by traditional houses. This is one of the area's largest and most traditional villages, though a few signs of modernity can be seen. The original village, Wogo Lama, was abandoned many years ago when the villagers decided to move closer to the main road and the delights of modernity, such as electricity.

About a kilometre further on from Wogo, turn off at the Dadawea sign and follow the track off to the left to Wogo Lama, where vast groups of jagged stones jut from the ground. These megalithic **ancestor tombs** are still important for use in ceremonies.

Getting There & Away Wogo is 1.5km from Mataloko, which is 18km from Bajawa on the Ende road and easily reached by bus or bemo. Mataloko is famous for its huge seminary on the highway.

Soa

Soa, about 20km north of Bajawa, is a transitional cultural region whose people are related to the Bajawanese and the Boawaenese. Interesting sites in this area include: **Loa**, where traditional *sagi* fights with lumps of wood are held around June; and the developed **hot springs** at Mangaruda, past the airport on the back road to Boawae. Entry to the springs costs 2500Rp (but the staff may ask for double this amount). Tours from Bajawa visit the springs.

BOAWAE

Boawae is 41km from Bajawa on the highway to Ende and is the centre of the Nage-Keo people (related to, but distinct from, the Ngada). It sits at the base of **Gunung Ebulobo**. This smoking volcano can be climbed with a guide hired in the village and usually involves an overnight stop on the mountain then a two hour ascent early the next morning.

Boawae is the source of most of the best Bajawa-area ikat. Gory buffalo-sacrifice rituals take place here and an equally messy form of boxing called *etu* is part of the May to August harvest festivities. The boxers wear garments made of tree bark that has been painted with animal blood. Their gloves may be studded with broken glass!

Places to Stay

Few visitors bother to stop at Boawae, but the *Wisma Nusa Bunga* on the highway has clean, simple rooms from 12,000Rp. A much better option is the *Hotel Sao Wisata*. To get there take the road next to the Wisma Nusa Bunga and follow it for 1.5km down to the river and then around to the left near the church. In lush gardens by the river, this delightful guesthouse has doubles for 25,000Rp and meals are available.

RIUNG

This small fishing village is one of the few places in Flores with access to white sand beaches and excellent snorkelling over intact reefs. The main village itself is fairly nondescript, although there's a Muslim Bugis stilt village built around the harbour. Most of the action is on the islands and getting to them requires a charter boat. About seven of the 17 **uninhabited islands** off Riung have white sand beaches. Most of the homestays can arrange day trips to several of the islands (about 20,000Rp per person for up to six people, including lunch).

RIUNG

To Seventeen Islands Marine Park

Pulau Pata

FLORES SEA

0   125   250 m
Approximate Scale

❶ Local Guide Association

Hotel Nur Iklas

Homestay Tamri Beach

Mbou

Persona Riung

PHPA Office

Church

Pondok SVD

Rumah Makan Cilegon

Riung Market

Homestay Madona

Liberty Homestay

To Watujapi Hill, Mbay & Ende

Homestay Florida Inn

To Bajawa Road

NUSA TENGGARA

The **giant iguanas** are another attraction and can be seen further north along the mainland coast at Torong Padang. The beasts have yellow markings and are more brightly coloured than Komodo dragons. Some readers reported seeing an iguana that was 3m long. A day trip that combines snorkelling and lizard watching can be arranged in Riung.

Watujapi Hill, about 3km from Riung, offers a magnificent view of the 17 Islands Marine Park. If you count them there are actually more than 21 islands, but the government authorities decided on the number as a neat tie-in with Independence Day (17 August).

Information

The PHPA office is near the Homestay Tamri Beach and has information about the Riung area. You normally don't have to use one of its guides, but you must sign in and pay 7500Rp before going to the islands. There's a well organised local guide association with an office on the beach near the Nur Iklas homestay. It's a good place to arrange boats and guides, and for information generally.

Places to Stay & Eat

There are several homestays in Riung and they all offer bed-and-meal deals for around 10,000Rp to 15,000Rp per person. The best choice for information and originality is *Nur Iklas*, which is right next to the harbour in the Bugis stilt village. The building was originally a traditional stilt house and features precarious stepladders and a large 1st floor balcony. The manager speaks excellent English.

Liberty Homestay has a nice balcony area and large rooms. *Homestay Madona* is nearby and is run by a friendly couple. *Homestay Tamri Beach* is popular with travellers and has good maps and information. *Hotel Nur Jaya* (☎ 21252, Jl Yani 20) is a quiet, family run place.

Homestay Florida Inn is on the road into town and is a bit far from the harbour. *Persona Riung* is government owned and a notch up in quality, but not as good value.

The most salubrious accommodation is found at the *Pondok SVD*, otherwise known as the 'Missionaries', on the road coming into town. Its spacious rooms are comfortable but comparatively pricey at 60,000Rp.

Also a little out of town is the popular *Crystal Bungalows*, which is 3km out on the Bajawa road and has rooms for 15,000Rp. One of the owners is French.

Getting There & Away

From Ende (5000Rp, four hours), a bus leaves every morning at 6 am from Ndao terminal. The only other alternative is to take a bus at 1 pm to Mbay and then a bemo to Riung. Buses from Bajawa (5000Rp, 2½ hours) leave at 8 am and midday, and the newly paved road is excellent.

ENDE

☎ 0381

The people gathered in south-central Flores, in and around the port of Ende, have a mix of Malay and Melanesian features. The aristocratic families of Ende link their ancestors through mythical exploits and magical events to the Hindu Majapahit kingdom of Java. Today most of the 60,000 people living in Ende are Christians but there are also many Muslims.

Ende is a pleasant town that is surrounded by fine mountain scenery. The cone of **Gunung Meja** (661m) rises almost beside the airport, with the larger **Gunung Iya** occupying a promontory south of Gunung Meja. Ende is primarily a stopover to eastern Flores or a launching pad to Sumba, though trips to the nearby villages are worthwhile.

The December 1992 earthquake caused extensive damage in Ende, but things are now back to normal.

Ende is very hot and dusty towards the end of the dry season.

Orientation

Ende is at the neck of a peninsula jutting south into the sea. The old port and most of the shops are on the western side of the neck. The main port, Pelabuhan Ipi, is on the eastern side.

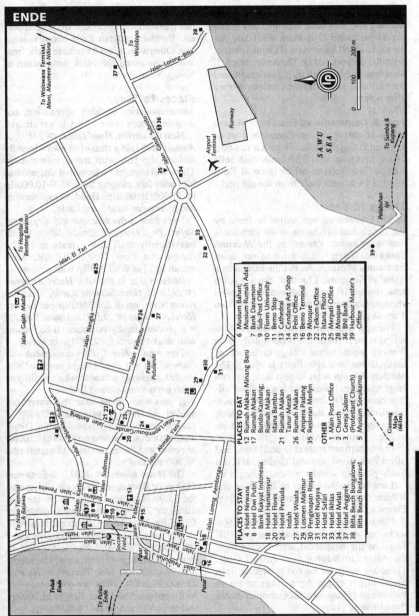

ENDE

To Wolotopo

To Wolowona Terminal, Moni, Maumere & Ndona

Jalan-Lorong-Bitta

Jalan Gatot Subroto

Airport Terminal

Runway

SAWU SEA

To Sumba & Kupang

Pelabuhan Ipi

To Hospital & Benteng Baranu

Jalan El Tari

Jalan Gajah Mada

Jalan Cajah Mada

Jalan Nangka

Jalan Kelimutu

Pasar Potulando

Jalan Banteng

Jalan Legampusu/Garuda

Jalan Ahmad Yani

Jalan Pahlawan/Sukarni

Jalan Sudirman

Jalan Yos Sudarso

Jalan Kartini

Jalan Pewira

To Nabo Terminal & Bajawa

Jalan Hatta

Jalan Baku

Jalan Sockamo

Jalan Palbean

Soccer Field

Pasar Pasar

Jalan Pasar

Jalan Pelabuhan

Jalan Lorong Aembonga

Jalan Kemakmuran

Telak Ende

To Pulau Ende

Gunung (661m)

PLACES TO STAY
4 Hotel Nirwana
8 Hotel Dwi Putri;
  Bank Rakyat Indonesia
18 Hotel Hamansyur
20 Hotel Flores
24 Hotel Persuda
  Indah
27 Hotel Wisata
29 Losmen Makmur
30 Penginapan Rinjani
31 Hotel Nurjaya
32 Hotel Safari
33 Hotel Ikhlas
34 Hotel Melati
37 Hotel Anggrek
38 Bitta Beach Bungalows;
  Bitta Beach Restaurant

PLACES TO EAT
12 Rumah Makan Minang Baru
17 Rumah Makan
  Bundo Danamon;
  Rumah Makan
  Istana Bambu
21 Rumah Makan
  Tanur Merah
26 Rumah Makan
  Ampera Padang
35 Restoran Merlyn

OTHER
1 Main Post Office
2 Church
3 Gereja Salom
  (Protestant Church)
5 Musium Soeukarno
6 Musium Bahari;
  Musium Rumah Adat
7 Bank Danamon
9 Sub-Post Office
10 Flores University
11 Bemo Stop
13 Cathedral
14 Cendana Art Shop
15 Pelni Office
16 Bemo Terminal
19 Mosque
22 Telkom Office
23 Istana Photo
25 Merpati Office
28 Mosque
36 BNI Bank
39 Harbour Master's
  Office

Information

Money The BRI bank is in the same building as the Hotel Dwi Putri on Jl Yos Sudarso. The BNI bank is on Jl Gatot Subroto, near the airport. Bank Danamon is on Jl Soekarno and is worth trying for credit card transactions. Hotel Ikhlas changes money after hours.

Post & Communications The main post office is out in the north-eastern part of town on Jl Gajah Mada. There's a sub-post office opposite the BRI bank that sells stamps. The Telkom office is on Jl Kelimutu, a 15 minute walk from the old port.

Things to See

In 1933 Soekarno was exiled to Ende by the Dutch and his house on Jl Perwira is now a museum, known as the **Musium Soekarno**. There's not a lot to see apart from some photographs but the caretaker, a friend of Soekarno's brother, can tell you a few stories if your Indonesian is good enough. It's open Monday to Saturday from 7 am to noon.

The new **Musium Bahari** (Maritime Museum) is on Jl Hatta and is open daily from 7 am to 8 pm. It has a large collection of seashells but little else. Entry is 500Rp. The **Musium Rumah Adat** is next door and is a large traditional house with a stylised village compound in front that has a *tubu musu* (sacrificial stone altar). It's worth a look and is open Monday to Saturday from 8 am to 2 pm. Entry is 500Rp.

The **waterfront market** is on Jl Pasar and offers fruit, food, tea and clothes, and is a lively place to wander around. There's an **ikat market** on the corner of Jl Pabean and Jl Pasar that sells a large variety of ikat from Flores and Sumba.

The Ende area has its own style of ikat weaving, mostly using abstract motifs. Some of the best local stuff comes from the village of **Ndona**, 8km east of Ende. There are irregular bemos to Ndona from Ende, but it might be quicker to go to Wolowana (5km) and take another bemo from there to Ndona.

Wolotopo is about 8km east of Ende and has traditional houses built on several levels. Bemos run from Ende about twice a day. Otherwise, it's a 45 minute walk from Wolowana along the black sand beach of Nanga Nesa.

Places to Stay

Accommodation is fairly spread out, but frequent bemos make it easy to get around.

Near the airport, *Hotel Ikhlas (☎ 21695, Jl Ahmad Yani)* is in a class of its own – friendly and on the ball with travel information. There's an excellent selection of singles/doubles with fans ranging from 7500/10,000Rp to 15,000/20,000Rp. Good, cheap western and Indonesian food is available.

Next door is the spacious and airy *Hotel Safari (☎ 21997, Jl Ahmad Yani)*, which has friendly staff and a restaurant. The rooms cost from 20,000/40,000Rp with mandi to 75,000/90,000Rp with air-con.

Better value is the new *Hotel Anggrek (☎ 22538, Jl Gatot Subroto, Km 3)*, which has rooms with mandi for 7500Rp per person. *Hotel Nur Jaya (☎ 21252, Jl Ahmad Yani 20)* is a pleasant family-run place. It has rooms with shared mandi for 7500Rp per person.

The small *Hotel Persada Indah (Jl Garuda 39)* is a good budget hotel with an English speaking manager who can fill you in on excursions around Ende.

If you want to be near the waterfront market, the *Hotel Hamansyur (☎ 21373, Jl Loreng Aembonga 11)* is reasonable. Dingy rooms in the old building cost 7000/12,500Rp or newer and better rooms with mandi cost 10,000/15,000Rp.

The *Hotel Flores (☎ 21075, Jl Sudirman 28)* has 1st floor economy rooms with mandi for 15,000Rp, clean rooms with fan and mandi for 25,000Rp and air-con doubles for 40,000Rp. There's a small restaurant as well.

The large and spotless *Hotel Dwi Putri (☎ 21685, Jl Yos Sudarso)* is the best in town and has a good restaurant. The rooms with fan, shower and flushing toilet cost 25,000/30,000Rp. The air-con rooms are well appointed and cost 50,000/55,000Rp, and large VIP rooms cost 100,000Rp.

The quiet *Hotel Wisata* (☎ *21368, Jl Ke-limutu*) is another more upmarket hotel. Its rooms cost 10,000/15,000Rp with mandi, 17,500/22,500Rp with fan and 30,000/40,000Rp to 45,000/60,000Rp with air-con. It also has a TV lounge and restaurant.

Bitta Beach Bungalows (☎ *21965, Jl Lorong Bitta*) is fine but suffers from its proximity to the Bitta Beach Restaurant, which is next door and has karaoke throughout the week and disreputable late night crowds on weekends. Bungalows with air-con cost 40,000Rp.

The *Hotel Melati* (☎ *21311, Jl Gatot Subroto 21*) is just around the corner from the airport and has rooms for 10,000/16,000Rp, but other hotels have more appeal. The *Hotel Nirwana* (☎ *21199, Jl Pahjawan 29*) is quiet and a better class of hotel, while the *Losmen Makmur* and *Penginapan Rinjani* (*Jl Ahmad Yani*) are seedy and cheap.

Places to Eat
The waterfront market area has the biggest concentration of rumah makans including the *Rumah Makan Bundo Kandung*, which serves Padang food. The *Rumah Makan Istana Bambu*, next door, is one of Ende's best restaurants with a long menu of Indonesian, Chinese and seafood dishes.

Most other restaurants serve Padang cuisine, such as the *Rumah Makan Minang Baru* on Jl Soekarno and the *Rumah Makan Ampera Padang* at Jl Kelimutu 31.

Restoran Merlyn is near the airport on Jl Gatot Subroto and is a fancy and slightly expensive Chinese restaurant. The remote *Bitta Beach Restaurant* is past the airport and down a dusty road to the beach. It's a local favourite, as much for the karaoke as the food.

The *Pasar Potulando* is a night market on Jl Kelimutu that sells snacks, fruit and vegetables.

Getting There & Away
Air Merpati (☎ 21355) is on Jl Nangka, which is a 15 minute walk from the airstrip. From Ende there are twice-weekly flights to Bima and on to Denpasar. There are also direct flights to Kupang. This office is hopeless at organising bookings on through flights originating in other cities. The staff will probably tell you to try your luck at the airport just before departure, as seats are often available.

Bus Buses to eastern Flores leave from Wolowana terminal, which is 4km from town. Buses to Moni (3000Rp, two hours) depart between 6 am and 2 pm or alternatively you can take a Wolowaru bus that passes through Moni. Buses to Maumere (7000Rp, five hours) leave around 8 am and 5 pm. Maumere buses will drop you in Moni, but charge for the full fare through to Maumere. A bus to Nggela leaves at 7 am and a through bus to Larantuka leaves at 8 am.

Buses heading west leave from Ndao terminal, 2km north of town on the beach road. The departures from Ende are: Bajawa (7500Rp, five hours) at 7 and 11 am; Ruteng (17,500Rp, nine hours) at 7.30 am; Labuanbajo (27,500Rp, 14 hours) at 7 am; and Riung (5000Rp, four hours) at 6 am.

Boat Ende is a popular place to get boats to Sumba, with a few connections per week. There are also direct boats to Kupang. Ships dock at Pelabuhan Ipi, which is the main port, 2.5km south-east from the town centre.

The schedules listed here are definitely subject to change. The ferry to Waingapu (22,000Rp, 10 hours) leaves Ende on Tuesday, returns to Ende on Wednesday, and goes to Kupang (29,000Rp, 16 hours) on Thursday and Saturday.

Pelni's *Pangrango* stops in Ende every two weeks and sails to Waingapu (22,000Rp ekonomi, eight hours) every two weeks and Sabu (23,000Rp) on alternate weeks. The *Awu* also sails from Waingapu to Ende and then to Kupang (38,500Rp, 11 hours) every fortnight. The Pelni office (☎ 21043), on the corner of Jl Pabean and Jl Kemakmuran, is open Monday to Saturday from 8 am to noon and 2 to 4 pm.

Other boats sail irregularly to these and other destinations; for details ask at the harbour master's office at Pelabuhan Ipi.

Getting Around

Bemos run frequently to just about everywhere in town (even Pelabuhan Ipi) for a flat rate of 500Rp. You can easily flag a bemo on the street; if not, pick one up at the bemo stop on Jl Hatta (near the old port).

You can charter a car to Kelimutu for up to six people for 100,000Rp – ask at your hotel. The Hotel Ikhlas can arrange minibuses to Kelimutu and the attractions around Ende.

KELIMUTU

Of all the sights in Nusa Tenggara, the coloured lakes of Kelimutu are the most spectacular. The three lakes are set in deep craters at an altitude of 1600m and are near the summit of the Kelimutu volcano (*keli* means mountain). They have a habit of changing colour and most recently the largest was a light turquoise, the one next to it was olive green and the third one was black. A few years ago the colours were blue, maroon and black, while back in the 1960s the lakes were blue, red-brown and *cafe au lait*. Colours can also change in the rainy season, when they may be less spectacular.

No-one has managed to explain the cause of the colours or why they change, except to suppose that different minerals are dissolved in each lake. The moonscape effect of the craters gives the whole summit area an ethereal atmosphere. There's a story among the locals that the souls of the dead go to these lakes: young people's souls go to the warmth of the green lake; old people's to the cold of the milky turquoise lake; and those of thieves and murderers to the black lake.

Kelimutu has attracted sightseers since Dutch times and today there's a paved road up to the lakes from Moni, 13.5km away at the base of the mountain. You even get an occasional bus-load of tourists and a small helipad has been constructed for VIP guests. There's a staircase up to the highest lookout point, from where you can see all three lakes.

There's a wonderfully spacious feeling up there and you can scramble around the perimeters of two of the lake craters for a bit of solitude. Hope for a sunny day – sunrise is stunning and the turquoise lake

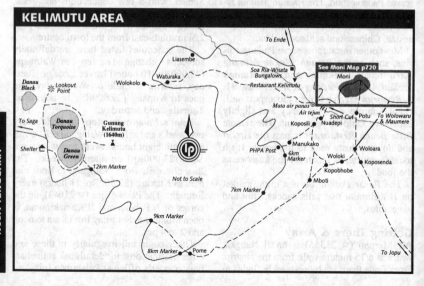

KELIMUTU AREA

To Ende
Liasembe
Waturaka
Soa Ria-Wisata Bungalows
See Moni Map p720
Moni
Restaurant Kelimutu
Wolokolo
Danau Black
Lookout Point
Mata air panas
Ait tejun
Short Cut
Potu
To Wolowaru & Maumere
Koposili
Nuadepi
To Saga
Danau Torquoise
Gunung Kelimutu (1640m)
Manukako
PHPA Post
Woloki
Woloara
Shelter
Danau Green
6km Marker
Koposenda
12km Marker
Kopobhobe
Not to Scale
Mboti
7km Marker
9km Marker
8km Marker
Pome
To Jopu

reaches its full brilliance in the sunlight. If the weather is bad, come back the next day because it really is worth seeing.

Getting There & Away

Moni is 52km north-east of Ende and is the usual base for visiting Kelimutu. From Moni you can assess the weather before going up to the lakes for sunrise, though even if it looks clear in Moni there can be cloud cover at Kelimutu.

Most visitors make their way up to the top at 4 am on trucks or minibuses, which are arranged by either the hotels or bars for 6000Rp per person. The truck returns to Moni at about 7 am, which can be a little hurried, so you may want to linger until the sun brings out the full brilliance of the lakes and then walk down. The sun rises earlier at the top than in the valley below. Later in the day, clouds roll in and block out the view.

The walk down takes about 2½ hours and isn't too taxing. Some hardy souls also walk up the 13.5km of winding (but not too steep) road. There's a PHPA post at a house where you have to pay 2000Rp per person (more if you've hired a vehicle). Beware of false 'PHPA posts', which have been known to set up further down the road. A shortcut (Jl Potong) leaves the Moni-Ende road about 750m from the centre of Moni and comes out on the Kelimutu road beside the PHPA post. This cuts about 6km off the journey but is easier to follow in daylight, so most people only use it on the way down unless they've checked it out the day before.

Another path branches off the shortcut at Koposili and goes via the villages of Mboti and Pome, reaching the Kelimutu road about 5.5km from the summit. It's no shorter but it passes through villages where enterprising villagers serve drinks and breakfast.

Occasionally a kindly old man will point out a 'shortcut' back to Moni. This route is even longer but the hope is that you might buy some ikat along the way. It's a pleasant hike but prepare yourself for the fact that it may take longer than walking on the main road.

MONI

Moni is a pretty village and the gateway to Flores' main tourist attraction, Kelimutu. It is cooler than the lowlands, scenic and a good place for walks.

The village is strung alongside the Ende-Maumere road and is the heart of the Lio region, which extends from just east of Ende to beyond Wolowaru. Lio people speak a dialect of the Ende language and are renowned for their ikat weaving. A colourful market spreads over the playing field in front of Moni's church every Monday morning. The local ikat is attractive, with bands of blue and rusty-red. Cloth from the Nggela and Maumere regions can be bought here. There are also a few stalls along Moni's main street.

Things to See & Do

In the kampung opposite the market, the high-thatched rumah adat serves as a cultural centre of sorts. Traditional dance performances are held in front of it every evening and cost 12,500Rp.

Apart from the trek to/from Kelimutu there are several other walks from Moni. About 750m along the Ende road from the centre of Moni, paths lead down to a 10m **air terjun**, with a pool big enough for swimming and a couple of **hot springs**. This is the village mandi and you can also bathe here – men to the left pool, women to the right. Another short walk is out past the church to **Potu** and **Woloara** (about 2.5km from Moni). From Woloara you could continue on through several villages to **Jopu** (about 5km). If you're energetic and well prepared either walk on to **Wolojita** and **Nggela** or you can loop back to Wolowaru and catch a bus or truck back to Moni.

Places to Stay

Coming from Ende, the first place you encounter is the government-owned *Sao Ria Wisata*, which is a collection of bungalows perched in splendid isolation on the hillside above Moni. The clean air and expansive views are a real tonic. Its 20,000Rp rooms are shabby, but the airy 25,000Rp rooms are OK.

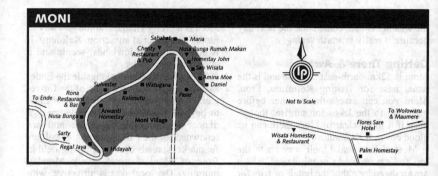

Continue 1.5km down a steep hill into Moni village, where there's a collection of homestays of a similar basic standard, charging similar prices. New, simple bungalows are sprouting everywhere. Most places are within five minutes' walk of each other, so it's worth checking a few out. The going rate is around 10,000Rp per room or 15,000Rp with attached mandi. Breakfast is usually included.

Hidayah is the homestay at the entrance of the village. It has shaky bamboo huts overlooking a burbling brook and pretty rice fields. *Regal Jaya* and *Nusa Bunga* are also reasonable options across the road.

Arwanti Homestay is newer and more solid than most places in Moni. *Sulvester* has cheap simple rooms, as has *Kelimutu*. *Watugana* is marginally more expensive, but is one of the better places with new rooms and simple bungalows. The higher the price, the more substantial the breakfast.

The next cluster of places on the bend at the bottom of the village starts with *Sahabat* and *Maria*, which are homestays with attractive aspects a little off the main road, up behind the Nusa Bunga. *Homestay John*, *Sao Wisata*, *Amina Moe* and the clean and tidy *Daniel* are on the main road at the Maumere end of the village. Amina Moe tends to be the most aggressive discounter. Sao Wisata is a notch above the rest, with larger rooms.

About 500m beyond the main village is the *Wisata Homestay & Restaurant*, which

has a large restaurant and rickety bamboo bungalows. Further along the road to Maumere is the *Flores Sare Hotel*, which is a stark cement block with Moni's most comfortable rooms at 75,000Rp. There's also a decent restaurant. A simpler option is the nearby *Palm Homestay*, which is on a side road to Woloara.

Places to Eat

Many of the homestays do simple but tasty buffet meals that are usually vegetarian.

The choice of restaurants is pretty good too. *Rona Restaurant & Bar* has an expansive choice, including vegetarian fare, and is a popular drinking spot at night. The noise and action often gravitates to the *Chenty Restaurant & Pub*, which is above the main road between the two clusters of homestays.

Next to the Homestay John is the cheap and cheerful *Nusa Bunga*. The *Sarty* is inconveniently located on the outskirts of town, but is worth a look. *Restaurant Kelimutu* is just down from Sao Ria Wisata and has reasonable food. The slow service gives you time to enjoy the fantastic view.

Getting There & Away

Moni is 52km north-east of Ende and 96km west of Maumere. For Ende (3000Rp, two hours), buses start at around 7 am. Other buses come through from Maumere or Wolowaru until about noon. Late buses come through at around 9 pm. Many buses and trucks leave on Monday, Moni's market day.

For Maumere (7500Rp, four hours) the first buses from Ende start coming through at around 9 or 10 am and then later in the evening around 7 pm.

As most of the buses stop mid-route in Moni they can be crowded and it's first come, first served for a seat. Sometimes you'll be sitting in the aisle on a sack of rice or a pig if you're lucky. Some of the home-stays make 'bookings', which usually means they will hail a bus for you.

AROUND MONI
Detusoko & Camat
On the highway between Detusoko and Camat, 35km from Ende, *Wisma Santo Fransiskus* is a quiet and peaceful guest-house. Individuals are no longer encouraged because, incredibly, a number of visitors have sought to haggle with the sisters for a room. The sisters do expect a rather large donation as a contribution to the school fund, but this is not a hotel. Groups that make prior arrangements are welcome. There are some lovely walks around the area and it should even be possible to walk along foot trails all the way to Kelimutu.

Wolowaru
The village of Wolowaru, straggling along the Maumere road just 13km south-east of Moni, can be used as a base for trips to the ikat-weaving villages of Jopu, Wolojita and Nggela. The road to these villages branches off from the main road in Wolowaru. The daily market winds down around 9 am, except on Saturday, the main market day.

Hotel Kelimutu (☎ 41020) is the most convenient place to stay and has simple rooms for 5500Rp per person. It is right next to the *Rumah Makan Jawa Timur*, Wolowaru's premier dining establishment. The *Losmen Setia* is near the market and has basic rooms for the same price.

Getting There & Away All Maumere-Ende buses stop in Wolowaru, with fares and departure times much the same as for Moni. A few morning buses originate in Wolowaru – ask at the Rumah Makan Jawa

Timur. All the through buses stop at the Jawa Timur, usually for a meal break.

Nggela, Wolojita & Jopu
Beautiful ikat sarongs and shawls can be found in these and other villages between Wolowaru and the south coast. Impromptu stalls will spring up before your eyes as you approach the villages.

Nggela is worth a visit for its hilltop position above the coast, but the chief attraction is the weaving, usually done by hand and still using many natural dyes. The weaving is among the finest in Flores and you'll be able to watch the weavers at work. In former times the size, colour and pattern of the ikat shawls of this region indicated the status of the wearer. Nggela ikat typically has black or rich, dark-brown backgrounds, with patterns in earthy red, brown or orange. Bargain hard and watch out for brighter synthetic dyes,

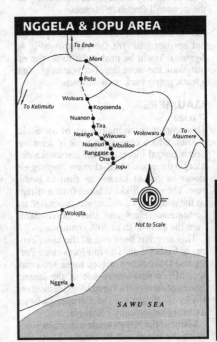

NGGELA & JOPU AREA

To Ende
Moni
Potu
Woloara
To Kelimutu
Koposenda
Nuanon
Tira
Neanga   Wiwuwu   Wolowaru   To Maumere
Nuamuri   Mbuliloo
Ranggase
Ona   Jopu
Wolojita
Not to Scale
Nggela
SAWU SEA

which are becoming more common (you should pay less if the dyes aren't natural).

In Nggela, the *Homestay Nggela Permai* costs 5500Rp per person.

Wolojita is about 7km inland from Nggela and has similar-quality weavings, but not Nggela's fine location. At Jopu, 6km further inland (and the same distance from Wolowaru), weaving has been declining in the last few years.

Getting There & Away A road branches off the Ende-Maumere road at Wolowaru and heads to Jopu (6km), Wolojita (12km) and Nggela (19km). One bus per day leaves Ende at 5.30 am for Nggela, passing Moni at about 7.30 am and then Wolojita. Otherwise, it's a good half day's walk to Nggela from Wolowaru. It's only two or 3km further from Moni via Woloara, so you could just as easily start from there. The volcano-studded scenery is beautiful, particularly on the downhill stretch to Nggela.

From Wolojita to Nggela, you can either follow the road or take a short cut past the hot springs (ask for the *jalan potong ke Nggela*). You'd be pushing it to do the return walk the same day, but you might find a truck going back to Wolowaru.

MAUMERE
☎ 0382

This seaport is the main town of the Sikka district, which covers the neck of land between central Flores and the Larantuka district (in the east). The Sikkanese language is closer to that of Larantuka than to Endenese. The name Sikka is taken from a village on the south coast, which was controlled by Portuguese rulers and their descendants from the early 17th to 20th centuries.

This area has been one of the chief centres of Catholic activity in Flores since Portuguese Dominicans arrived some 400 years ago. Missionaries were one of the largest groups of foreigners to establish themselves in Flores. Nowadays the European priests are being replaced by Florinese.

Many of the priests made important studies of the island and its people. They also encouraged local arts & crafts, and helped the Florinese with improved tools and seeds for agriculture. Until recent decades many Florinese were tilling the soil with sharpened sticks, and slash-and-burn farming is still common.

In December 1992 Maumere was devastated by an earthquake and the ensuing 20m-high tidal waves killed thousands. Maumere was only 30km from the epicentre of the quake, which almost flattened the entire town. Most of the town has now been rebuilt but there is little to tempt travellers to linger.

There's a strong ikat-weaving tradition in the Maumere region and some interesting trips can be made out of town.

Information
The tourist office (☎ 21652) on Jl Wairklau is well out of the way and has little in the way of literature. The BNI bank on Jl Soekarno Hatta is the best place to change money. The BRI bank also handles foreign exchange. Try Bank Danamon on Jl Pasar Baru Barat for credit card cash advances.

The post office is next to the soccer field on Jl Pos and the Telkom office is further south from the town centre, opposite the BNI bank on Jl Soekarno Hatta.

Places to Stay
Maumere has a number of hotels, most with a wide variety of rooms. Cheap rooms tend to be dismal, while better rooms with mandi are expensive compared to other towns in Flores.

The *Gardena Hotel* (☎ 22644, Jl Patirangga) is the pick of the cheap hotels and is on a quiet street close to the centre. It's clean, friendly and has singles/doubles for 15,000/22,500Rp with mandi and fan or 25,000/30,000Rp with air-con (plus tax). It is a good place to contact guides and to get information on the sights around Maumere.

The *Hotel Senja Wair Bubuk* (☎ 21498, Jl Yos Sudarso) is near the seafront and gets a steady stream of travellers. It offers tours and motorcycle and car rental. Grubby rooms with fan and mandi range from 11,000/16,500Rp to 25,000/31,000Rp.

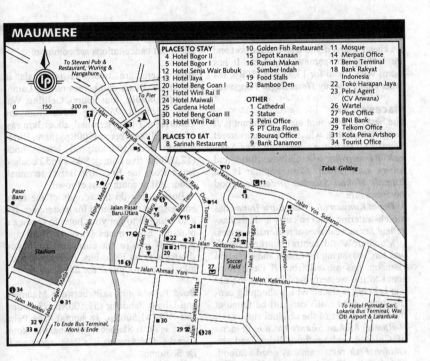

MAUMERE

PLACES TO STAY
4 Hotel Bogor II
5 Hotel Bogor I
12 Hotel Senja Wair Bubuk
13 Hotel Jaya
20 Hotel Beng Goan I
21 Hotel Wini Rai II
24 Hotel Maiwali
25 Gardena Hotel
30 Hotel Beng Goan III
33 Hotel Wini Rai

PLACES TO EAT
8 Sarinah Restaurant

10 Golden Fish Restaurant
15 Depot Kanaan
16 Rumah Makan
    Sumber Indah
19 Food Stalls
32 Bamboo Den

OTHER
1 Cathedral
2 Statue
3 Pelni Office
6 PT Citra Flores
7 Bouraq Office
9 Bank Danamon

11 Mosque
14 Merpati Office
17 Bemo Terminal
18 Bank Rakyat
    Indonesia
22 Toko Harapan Jaya
23 Pelni Agent
    (CV Arwana)
26 Wartel
27 Post Office
28 BNI Bank
29 Telkom Office
31 Kota Pena Artshop
34 Tourist Office

The small and friendly *Hotel Jaya (☎ 21 292, Jl Hasanuddin 26)* is a good buy and has rooms with fan and mandi for 15,000/25,000Rp, including breakfast.

A little far from the centre but close to the Ende (west) bus terminal, the well run *Hotel Wini Rai (☎ 21388, Jl Gajah Mada 50)* has basic, economy rooms with shared mandi for 12,500/17,500Rp and substantial rooms with private mandi and fan for 25,000/30,000Rp, or 37,500/42,500Rp with air-con.

The new *Hotel Wini Rai II (☎ 21362, Jl Soetomo)* is a smaller offshoot in the centre of town. This is a good hotel for information and to contact guides. The rooms are spotless, if a little dark. Basic rooms at the back cost 12,500/17,500Rp with shared mandi. Much better rooms at the front are 20,000/25,000Rp with mandi or 32,500/37,500Rp with air-con.

Hotel Maiwali (☎ 21220, Jl Raja Don Tomas 40) is the best choice close to the town

centre. Rooms with fan and mandi cost 18,000/27,000Rp, or 35,000/50,000Rp with air-con. It also arranges car hire.

The fanciest place is the *Hotel Permata Sari (☎ 21171, Jl Sudirman 1)*, which is on the waterfront about 2km from the town centre. Standard rooms and cottages with shower and fan cost 27,000/35,000Rp, while air-con rooms cost 33,000/44,000Rp to 99,000/115,00Rp.

There's an open-air restaurant near the water. To get there, take a bemo heading east.

The central *Hotel Beng Goan I (☎ 21041, Jl Moa Toda)* is a popular local hotel. Standard rooms cost 6000/10,000Rp without mandi and 11,000/17,500Rp with mandi. The new rooms with air-con are good and cost 25,000/30,000Rp and 35,000/50,000Rp. *Hotel Beng Goan III* is still undergoing post-earthquake restoration, which may eventually make it one of the better hotels.

NUSA TENGGARA

Other hotels include the Muslim-run *Hotel Bogor II* (☎ 21137, *Jl Slamet Riyadi*), which is a cheap option if you arrive at the port and are looking for somewhere close. It has rooms with mandi for 13,750/18,150Rp. It's better than the seedy *Hotel Bogor I* opposite.

Places to Eat
The best place to hunt out a restaurant is Jl Pasar Baru Barat, which is the main street running down to the waterfront. The *Sarinah Restaurant* has Chinese food and serves good squid. Most popular is the *Rumah Makan Sumber Indah* for good Javanese fare.

Depot Kanaan (*Jl Pasar Baru Timur*) has mouth-watering chicken curry and other excellent Javanese dishes at reasonable prices.

Maumere's old central market, which was torched during a Muslim and Christian flare up, has moved from Jl Pasar Baru Barat to the western outskirts and the old site is being replaced with a shopping centre. A few *food stalls* can still be found at the southern side of the original site.

Rumah Makan Shanty has a long menu of Chinese and seafood dishes and the *Golden Fish* restaurant has good seafood. The *Bamboo Den* is near the Hotel Wini Rai and has slow service but good cheap Indonesian food, fish and cold beer.

The *Stevani Pub & Restaurant* has karaoke and pricey western and Indonesian dishes but is situated 6km west of town. *Shinta Karaoke* is 3km east of town on the beach and 1km past the Hotel Permata Sari. It competes with the Stevani Pub in the noise stakes but has good Chinese food.

Shopping
Toko Harapan Jaya on Jl Pasar Baru Timur has the most comprehensive collection of ikat (from Flores and other islands) that you'll find anywhere in Nusa Tenggara except Sumba. You can also buy carvings and other artefacts here.

Getting There & Away
Air Merpati (☎ 21342, *Jl Raja Don Tomas 18*) has five flights a week from Kupang

and on to Bima and Denpasar, and five a week directly from Denpasar and on to Kupang, but cancellations are common.

Bus There are two bus terminals in Maumere. Buses and bemos east to Larantuka (10,000Rp, four hours), Geliting, Waiara, Ipir and Wodong leave from the Lokaria (or Timur) terminal, about 3km east of town. Take a bemo (500Rp) there. Buses west to Moni (10,000Rp, 3½ hours), Ende (12,000Rp, five hours), Sikka and Ledalero leave from the Ende (or Barat) terminal, about 1.5km south-west of town.

Buses often do the rounds of the town endlessly in their search for passengers. It's also possible to get your hotel to arrange a pick-up. Ende buses leave at 8 am and 5 pm. If you're travelling to Moni you should take an Ende bus. Buses to Larantuka leave throughout the day.

Boat Pelni's *Awu* sails between Maumere and Ujung Pandang (51,500Rp, 23 hours) and Dili (41,500Rp, 18 hours). The Pelni office is on Jl Slamet Riyadi, next to Hotel Lareska. CV Arwana is a Pelni agent on Jl Dr Soetomo.

Getting Around
To/From the Airport Maumere's Wai Oti airport is 3km from town, 800m off the Maumere-Larantuka road. A taxi to/from town is 6000Rp. Otherwise, it's about a 1km walk out of the airport to the Maumere-Larantuka road to pick up a bemo (500Rp) into town.

Bemo Bemos run around town regularly and cost 500Rp anywhere within the city.

Car & Motorcycle A car will cost around 100,000Rp per day around town or 150,000Rp further afield. If you hire a car to Moni and further east you should agree on an itinerary and schedule of staggered payments before you go. A few places around town hire out motorcycles for around 35,000Rp per day; ask at your hotel or the travel agencies.

AROUND MAUMERE
Ledalero & Nita
Many Florinese priests studied at the Roman Catholic seminary in Ledalero, which is 19km from Maumere on the Ende road. The chief attraction here is the **museum** run by Father Piet Petu, who is Florinese. It houses a collection of historic stone implements and Florinese ikat – you'll see designs and natural dyes that are either rare or no longer produced, including softly textured, pastel-coloured old Jopu sarongs. It's a good place to try to piece together the jigsaw of Florinese culture. Admission is free but you might leave a donation.

Nita is 2km beyond Ledalero on the main road and has a Thursday market. Bemos to Ledalero and Nita leave from Maumere's Ende terminal.

Sikka
On the south coast, 27km from Maumere, Sikka was one of the first Portuguese settlements in Flores, dating from the early 17th century. Its rulers dominated the Maumere region until the 20th century. Today it's interesting mainly as the home of Sikkanese ikat, and women draped in this style of ikat will descend on you. Sikka has a beautiful church dating from 1899.

The road to Sikka leaves the Ende road 20km from Maumere. Take a bemo from Maumere to Sikka (1500Rp, 45 minutes).

About 4km before Sikka is **Lela**; another weaving centre with a Catholic population. It has a few colonial buildings and a long and rocky black sand beach.

Geliting
Geliting, about 10km east of Maumere on the Larantuka road, has a huge, colourful market on Friday. There's lots of beautiful ikat around – more being worn than for sale – and thousands of people come from surrounding villages. Get there by bemo from Maumere's east terminal.

Watublapi
Watublapi is in the hills 20km south-east of Maumere and is a large Catholic mission.

From here, you can walk to **Ohe**, where you can see both coasts of Flores. **Bola** is a large village 6km from Watublapi, and 2km further on is the traditional coastal weaving village of **Ipir**. Market day in Ipir is Monday and bemos go there from Maumere (2000Rp, 1½ hours). On other days bemos usually finish at Bola. You should be able to stay with villagers or the kepala desa in Bola or Ipir.

Waiara
Waiara is just off the Larantuka road 13km east of Maumere and is the jumping-off point for the Maumere 'sea gardens'. Once regarded as one of Indonesia's best dive destinations, the 1992 earthquake and the tidal wave destroyed many of the reefs. The fish and reefs around Pulau Pemana and Pulau Besar are still worth the effort.

Waiara has two resorts. The *Sea World Club (Pondok Dunia Laut,* ☎ *0382-21570, fax 21102)* is run by missionaries. It has spotless comfortable cabin rooms costing from US$10/15 a single/double to US$30/35 for air-con. Dive packages start at US$70 per day for cabin rooms and include all meals and two dives. A tax and service charge of 15% is added to all rates.

The desolate *Flores Sao Resort (*☎ *21555)* was once the best hotel in Flores. Renovations are planned and badly needed. Until then the cheaper US$25/30 rooms are unavailable and you'll be directed towards the US$55/60 rooms.

To get there, catch a Talibura bus from Maumere to Waiara (1000Rp) or take a bemo to Geliting and walk 1.5km along the Larantuka road. You'll see the signs for the turnoff to Sea World Club first and Flores Sao Resort is about 500m further along the road. The resorts charge 10,000Rp per person to drop off or pick up guests from Maumere.

Wodong & Waiterang
Waiterang beach is 28km east of Maumere and just outside Wodong village. It's a pleasant place to while away a few days. Attractions include diving spots west of the nearby **Pulau Besar** and the beaches and snorkelling at **Pulau Pangabatang**. Boats

can be chartered in Wodong village but are easier to arrange with homestays in Waiterang. Boats cost 60,000Rp for a full-day trip or some of the homestays have guided trips for around 15,000Rp per person.

Nangahale is about 10km north-east of Wodong and is an interesting boat building village settled by survivors from Pulau Babi after the 1992 earthquake. It is easily reached by bemo or bus from Waiterang. On the way to Nangahale the road passes **Patiahu**, 33km from Maumere, which has the best white sand beach on this stretch of coast.

The landscape south-west of Waiterang is dominated by the smoking **Gunung Egon** (1703m). This active volcano can be climbed from Blidit in around three hours; slightly less coming down. There is little shade, so start early to avoid the heat of the day. It is a relatively easy climb apart from the final scramble to the top. Blidit is 6km from Waiterang – 15,000Rp by chartered bemo. Guides to take you up Egon can be arranged in Waiterang for around 10,000Rp.

Places to Stay & Eat *Flores Froggies* is near Wodong village and is a popular homestay started by a French couple. Unfortunately the couple has left and it is now a little run down. Simple huts cost 6000/7500Rp for singles/doubles and bungalows are 8000/ 12,000Rp or 12,500/14,500Rp with mandi. All rates include breakfast. Although the French specialties are no longer on the menu, the beachside restaurant is still good.

On the eastern side of Froggies, *Pondok Praja* is the most substantial place and the friendly owner speaks good English. Its large bungalows are Waiterang's best and cost 17,500Rp and 25,000Rp.

Waiterang Beach Cottage is west of Froggies and is a well kept place with small bungalows for 5000/10,000Rp. You can eat at its pleasant restaurant.

Further along is *Ankermi*, which is the pick of the places to stay. It has attractive grounds, a good restaurant and lots of information on nearby attractions. The owner is switched-on and used to run Moni's best restaurant – the story of his departure provides fascinating insights into the local tourism industry. Bungalows cost 7000/10,000Rp or 12,000/17,500Rp with mandi and there is also a dorm bungalow with two mattresses per room for 5000Rp per person.

Another good option is *Wodong Beach Homestay*, which is off by itself further around the headland. It's under Belgian management and houses the funky little Coral Bar. It also runs good trips to the islands. Tiny bungalows are 6000Rp and larger bungalows are 10,000Rp, or 15,000Rp with mandi.

Getting There & Away Wodong is right on the Maumere-Larantuka road. Take any Talibura, Nangahale or Larantuka bemo or bus from Maumere's Lokaria terminal (1300Rp). A bemo from Wodong to Waiterang costs 600Rp. Through buses to Larantuka can be picked up in Wodong but are often hopelessly crowded; to get a seat it is better to first go to Maumere. Heading west, a direct bus to Moni passes Wodong around 10 am.

LARANTUKA
☎ 0383 • pop 30,000
A busy little port at the eastern end of Flores, Larantuka nestles around the base of the **Ili Mandiri volcano**, separated by a narrow strait from Pulau Solor and Pulau Adonara. Larantuka is the departure point for boats to the Solor Archipelago (east of Flores) and for a twice-weekly ferry to Kupang.

This corner of Indonesia, though always isolated, was one of the first to attract European interest. Lying on sea routes used by the Portuguese seeking sandalwood from Timor, the Larantuka-Solor area saw Portuguese forts and over 20 Dominican missions being built by 1575. Portugal maintained a few enclaves until the mid-19th century, among them Larantuka, which was the centre of a community of Topasses (from *tupassi*, a south Indian word for 'interpreter'), the descendants of Portuguese men and local women. The Topasses are still a significant group in Larantuka today.

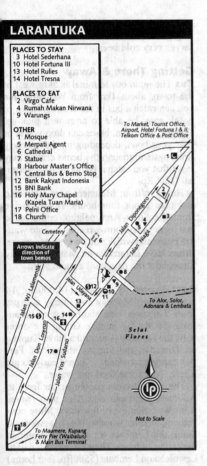

LARANTUKA

PLACES TO STAY
3 Hotel Sederhana
10 Hotel Fortuna III
13 Hotel Rulies
14 Hotel Tresna

PLACES TO EAT
2 Virgo Cafe
4 Rumah Makan Nirwana
9 Warungs

OTHER
1 Mosque
5 Merpati Agent
6 Cathedral
7 Statue
8 Harbour Master's Office
11 Central Bus & Bemo Stop
12 Bank Rakyat Indonesia
15 BNI Bank
16 Holy Mary Chapel
   (Kapela Tuan Maria)
17 Pelni Office
18 Church

To Market, Tourist Office, Airport, Hotel Fortuna I & II, Telkom Office & Post Office

Cemetery

Arrows indicate direction of town bemos

To Alor, Solor, Adonara & Lembata

Selat Flores

Not to Scale

To Maumere, Kupang Ferry Pier (Waibalun) & Main Bus Terminal

Orientation & Information

Hotels, the ferry pier, shipping offices and the main bus terminal are in the southern part of town. Further north-east are the homes, mosques and fishing boats of the local Muslims, and post office, Telkom office and airport. The Kupang boat pier is to the south. The BNI and BRI banks change money.

Things to See

Portuguese-style Catholicism flourishes in Larantuka. There's a large **cathedral**, and the smaller **Kapela Tuan Maria** (Holy Mary Chapel) contains Portuguese bronze and silver known as *ornamento*. On Saturday in this chapel, women say the rosary in Portuguese. On Good Friday a statue of the Virgin Mary is carried from the chapel in procession around the town to the accompaniment of songs in Latin.

Larantuka's **market** has some weaving – look for ikat from Lembata, Adonara and Solor.

Places to Stay

The family-run *Hotel Rulies* (☎ 21198, Jl Yos Sudarso 44) has the best set up for travellers. Clean singles/doubles with shared bath cost 15,000/26,000Rp and food is available. The manager speaks English and the staff can answer most queries.

The *Hotel Tresna* (☎ 21072) is along the road and is a reasonable place. The rooms cost 11,000/16,500Rp, 17,600/27,500Rp with mandi or 44,000/58,300Rp with air-con.

The *Hotel Fortuna III* is above the shops in the centre of town. Smart new rooms with shared mandi cost 15,000/20,000Rp. *Hotel Sederhana* on the same street has rooms for the same price, but may not take travellers.

The *Hotel Fortuna I* (☎ 21140, Jl Diponegoro 171) is inconveniently located about 2km north-east of town near the Telkom office. The rooms for 8000/12,000Rp with mandi are cramped and dreary, while much better rooms with fan cost 22,000/27,500Rp.

Its newer offshoot, the *Hotel Fortuna II* (☎ 21383), is a small place directly across the road with the best rooms in town. Large and bright rooms with fan are 25,000/30,000Rp or quite plush rooms with air-con are 40,000/60,000Rp.

Places to Eat

Eating possibilities are limited, but a few *warungs* set up in the evening along Jl Niaga. *Rumah Makan Nirwana* is a decent Chinese restaurant and the best in town. Also good is the tiny *Virgo Cafe*, which is behind a shop and hair salon. The entertaining owner specialises in fish and chips

NUSA TENGGARA

The Lamaholot

The Larantuka area has long had closer links with the islands of the Solor Archipelago – Adonara, Solor and Lembata – than with the rest of Flores. It shares a language, Lamaholot, with the islands. The whole area, particularly outside the towns, fascinates anthropologists because of its complex social and ritual structure, which in some parts survives pretty well intact.

There's a web of myths about the origins of the Lamaholot people: one version has them descended from the offspring of Watowele (the extremely hairy goddess of Ili Mandiri) and a character called Patigolo, who was washed ashore, got Watowele drunk, cut her hair (thus removing her magic powers and discovering that she was female) and made her pregnant. Alternatively, locals believe their forbears came from Sina Jawa (China Java), Seram or India – take your pick.

At some stage, probably before the 16th century, the Lamaholot area became divided between two groups known as the Demon and the Paji. The Demon, associated with the 'Rajah' of Larantuka, were mainly grouped in eastern Flores and the western parts of Adonara, Solor and Lembata; the Paji, with their allegiance to the 'Rajah' of Adonara, were centred in the eastern parts of the three islands. Anthropologists tend to believe that the conflict between the two groups was mainly a ritual affair or, as one writer puts it, 'two groups representing the two halves of the universe engaged in regular combat to produce human sacrifices for the securing of fertility and health'. Such a pattern was not uncommon in eastern Indonesia. Today, people still know who is Paji and who is Demon, but ritual warfare has subsided. Other animist rites survive, including those for birth, name-giving, marriage, the building of a new house, the opening of new fields in *ladang* (slash-and-burn) agriculture and the planting and harvesting of crops.

and political analysis. He speaks excellent English, with an Australian accent, and serves very cold beer.

Getting There & Away

Bus The main bus terminal is 5km west of the town, about 1km from Waibalun, but you can catch a bus in the centre of town or hotels may be able to arrange a pick-up. Coming into town, buses can drop you at or near your hotel, depending on the one way street system, though the bemo drivers may insist that you catch a bemo from the terminal (1000Rp).

Buses to/from Maumere cost 10,000Rp and take about four hours. If you arrive from the Solor Archipelago, enthusiastic bus jockeys will arm-wrestle you into waiting buses and whisk you away to Maumere. Buses leave Larantuka for Maumere hourly throughout the day, until around 5 pm.

Boat Ferries to Kupang (14,000Rp, 14 hours) depart Monday and Friday at 2 pm from Waibalun, 4km south-west of Larantuka (500Rp by bemo). Going the other way, the ferries to Larantuka leave Kupang on Thursday and Sunday afternoons. Ferries can get crowded, so board early to get a seat. Take some food and water.

The slow Persero passenger/car ferry to Adonara, Lembata and Alor also leaves from Waibalun every few days. More convenient, smaller wooden boats to Adonara, Solor and Lembata leave from the pier in the centre of town. They run twice a day to Lewoleba on Lembata (5500Rp, four hours) at around 7 am and noon, stopping at Waiwerang (Adonara) on the way. There's no morning boat to Lewoleba on Monday. A boat goes once a week to Lamalera on Lembata (7000Rp, seven hours), on Lembata, on Friday at 9 am.

The Pelni passenger ship *Tatamailau* calls in at Larantuka on its route from Labuanbajo to Dili (35,000Rp ekonomi) and Pulau Ambon (Maluku), returning in the opposite direction. The *Sirimau* stops at Larantuka on its fortnightly run from Kupang to Ujung Pandang and Java. The Pelni office on Jl Yos Sudarso has details on other Pelni boats and it is worth asking around the pier and harbour master's office on Jl Niaga for other possibilities.

Getting Around
Bemos run up and down Jl Niaga and Jl Pasar, and to outlying villages. Bemos in town cost 500Rp.

AROUND LARANTUKA
Six kilometres north of Larantuka is a white sand beach at **Weri**; get there by bemo from the central bemo stop in Larantuka. **Lewoloba** is near the village of Oka and puts on traditional dancing when tour boats arrive. **Mokantarak** is 10km from Larantuka on the road to Maumere and is a traditional village with a rumah adat.

Solor & Alor Archipelagos

A chain of small islands stretches out from the eastern end of Flores. These volcanic and mountainous specks, separated by swift and narrow straits, can be visited by a spectacular ferry ride from Larantuka. Andonara and Solor are where the Portuguese settled in the 16th century and are close to Larantuka. Further east, Lembata is the main island of interest because of the traditional whaling village of Lamalera. These islands form the Solor Archipelago, which has close cultural links with the Larantuka area; together their people are known as the Lamaholot.

Beyond Lembata are the main islands of the Alor Archipelago, Pantar and Alor, whose people were still head-hunting in the 1950s.

The scenery is spectacular, all the islands (notably Lembata) produce distinctive ikat weaving and there are some almost purely animist villages, despite the spread of Christianity and (to a lesser degree) Islam.

In remote villages the people are poor and not used to westerners; children will follow you in excited bunches. On the other hand, many Lamaholot travel far afield to seek their fortunes (there are so few opportunities locally) and it is not uncommon to meet people who have worked as labourers or domestic help in Malaysia and Singapore.

The food quality is generally bad. If you can't deal with all this, limit your stay to the urban centres of Kalabahi (Alor) and Lewoleba and make a few day trips into the surrounding countryside.

One thing you should bring is plenty of money. You can only change money in Kalabahi.

History
European contact was made as early as 1522 when the only remaining ship of the explorer Magellan's fleet sailed through the Lembata-Pantar strait. By the middle of the century, the Dominican Portuguese friar Antonio Taveira had landed on Solor to set about spreading Catholicism. The Solor mission became the base for extending Christianity to mainland Flores and a fort was built to protect the converts from Muslim raids. The Portuguese were eventually forced out of Solor by the Dutch, but until the mid-19th century, Portugal held on to Wurek (Adonara) and Pamakajo (Solor).

Getting Around
Alor has some bemos and ancient buses, but most of the islands have only one decent road and transport to more isolated areas is limited to a few trucks per week. Asking around the ports may prove more fruitful; on Alor and Lembata the most reliable transport to their south coasts is by boat.

SOLOR
Rita-Ebang is the main town and the easiest to reach. Lohojong is a few kilometres west of Menanga on the north coast and has the ruins of the **Portuguese fort**. Lamakera (on the north-eastern tip) is a whaling village, but is not really set up to accommodate visitors.

Getting There & Away
From Larantuka there are boats to Rita-Ebang every morning at about 7 am. From Waiwerang boats cross to Menanga,

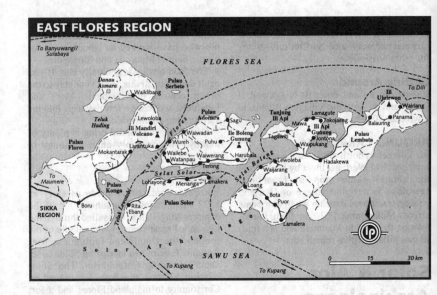

EAST FLORES REGION

Lahayong and Lamakera on Monday and Thursday. No regular bemo travels across the island from west to east.

ADONARA

Adonara was known as the 'Island of Murderers' because of a feud between two clans. The feud apparently ran for hundreds of years, with people in the hills being killed and houses burned – very likely a case of ritual conflict between the Demon and Paji groups (see the boxed text 'The Lamaholot' in the Flores section). Though extremes of animism have died out, there are villages in the hinterland where Christianity has only the loosest of footholds. One traveller reported placing her hands on a sacred rock above one village and being unable to remove them. The chief settlements are Wailebe (on the west coast) and Waiwerang (on the south coast). A few bemos link the main villages.

Waiwerang

Waiwerang's markets on Monday and Thursday attract villagers from throughout

the island and from Solor. Waiwerang has a post office, a wartel and a bank, but money cannot be changed. The places to stay include the very basic *Losmen Taufiq*, run by a friendly Muslim woman. The *Hotel Asri* is basic, but a notch above the Taufiq and has a pleasant front porch. The *Hotel Ile Boleng (Jl Pasar Baru)* is the pick of the town's hotels. English is spoken and meals can be arranged. The rooms at back have great views across the water.

Getting There & Away All the boats to Lewoleba on Lembata call in at Waiwerang on the way. The trip takes about two hours and costs 3000Rp. Passenger ferries dock at the main wharf in the centre of town, but at low tide they may dock at the car ferry port a kilometre west of town. The boat to Lamalera leaves on Friday evenings around 11 pm.

Small boats run between Waiwerang and the towns of eastern Solor (Lamakera, Menanga and Lohayong) on Monday and Thursday. Otherwise you can charter a boat to Solor for up to six people for around 100,000Rp.

LEMBATA

Lembata is well known for the whaling village of Lamalera and for the volcano, **Ili Api**, which towers over the main town of Lewoleba. As in the rest of the Lamaholot region, many Lembata villagers still use the slash-and-burn method of clearing land. Corn, bananas, papayas and coconuts are grown, but most rice is imported.

Lewoleba

Despite the ominous smoking of Ili Api in the background, the chief settlement on Lembata and 'capital' of Solor regency is a relaxed little town. A couple of larger government buildings and a Telkom office are all that distinguishes it from any other scruffy village.

Boats unload you at a pier about a 10 minute walk west of the town – take a *mikrolet* (small taxi) or *becak* (trishaw) for 500Rp. Below town, on the water, is a Bajo stilt village built out over the sea. Some of its people are pearl divers and you can arrange to go out with them on diving trips. Have a good look at the pearls you're offered in town as many are just shells. Locals will take you out by sampan to a sandbank off Lewoleba – it's the closest place to town for a swim in beautifully clear water.

Orientation & Information The centre of Lewoleba is the market place, which comes alive every Monday with buyers and sellers from around the region.

The post office is off the main street near the south side of the market. There is a bank, but it does not change money so bring sufficient funds. If you are stuck, the Flores Jaya shop opposite the post office will change US dollars at very poor rates. The Telkom office is 1km west of town along the main street and closes around 11 pm (you cannot make collect calls).

Places to Stay & Eat Halfway between the ferry wharf and the town, near the cemetery, the *Lile Ile* is a switched-on homestay with plenty of information on Lembata. The rooms in a separate building to one side

have a long porch with stunning views of the volcano across the water. Singles/doubles cost 10,000/18,000Rp, plus 4000Rp for great home-cooked meals served on the huge open deck of the main house. There is even a selection of videos at 5000Rp per movie. The owner grew up in the Netherlands and speaks fluent Dutch and English.

The *Hotel Rejeki* is right in the middle of town, opposite the market. Clean rooms with outside mandi cost 10,000/18,500Rp downstairs and are better than the wooden rooms upstairs for the same price. Newer rooms with attached mandi cost 20,000/37,500Rp. The meals are generous and cheap, and there's always fresh seafood on the menu. Good information on Lembata is provided and transport can be hired.

Another good choice is the *Hotel Lewoleba* (☎ 41012, Jl Awololong 15) – take the road opposite the Hotel Rejeki past the post office. It has a few rough rooms for 5000Rp per person and much better rooms with mandi for 12,500Rp per person. The air-con rooms for 35,000/45,000Rp are luxurious in this part of world.

The Hotel Rejeki has far and away the best food in town. There are also a few dismal rumah makans near the market. *Rumah Makan Hosana* has Padang food or *Rumah Makan Bandung* has passable Javanese fare.

Getting There & Away

The main road across the island is now sealed and a regular host of mikrolet and buses run to destinations around Lewoleba, including Waipukang, Loang and Puor (for Lamalera). Buses to the east run to Hakadewa and direct to Balauring (5000Rp, two hours) on Lembata. Some of the rough back roads are plied by infrequent trucks. Buses terminate next to the ferry dock or you can catch them in Lewoleba in front of the market.

Small passenger ferries ply daily between Lewoleba and Larantuka (5500Rp, four hours). They leave around 7 am and noon (there's no morning boat on Monday) from Lewoleba (and at the same times from Larantuka), stopping at Waiwerang on the way. They can be crowded but there's usually no problem getting a seat. It is a spectacular journey through the islands past smoking volcanoes.

The large and slow passenger/car ferries to Kalabahi from Larantuka stop at Lewoleba every few days (schedules are subject to change). They depart from Lewoleba at 11 am for Balauring (four hours) in north-eastern Lembata where they stop for the night. Balauring has a reasonable losmen or you can sleep on the deck of the boat. At 7 am the next morning the ferry continues on to Kalabahi (12,500Rp, nine hours) via Baranusa (6000Rp, four hours) on Pantar. There are usually plenty of seats, though the ferry can fill up on Pantar. Bring food and water.

A more comfortable option is to take a bus to either Balauring or Wairiang on Tuesday and catch the small wooden *Diana Express* boat, which leaves for Kalabahi either early Wednesday or Thursday. The drivers of the white *Diana* buses from Lewoleba know the *Diana Express* schedule.

Getting Around You can take mikrolet around town and to the ferry dock, or Lewoleba has a few becaks imported from Ujung Pandang and Java, which cost 500Rp anywhere around town.

Around Lewoleba

Lembata's best ikat, recognisable by its burgundy-coloured base and highly detailed patterning, comes from the villages on the slopes of Ili Api, 15 to 20km from Lewoleba. **Atawatun** and **Mawa** are on the north coast and are two of the best places to see fine ikat. **Jontona** is on the east side of the deep inlet on Lembata's north coast. It's possible to stay there with the kepala desa. An hour's walk from Jontona towards Ili Api is the **Kampung Lama** (Old Village), with many traditional houses. These contain sacred and prized objects, including a huge number of elephant tusks, but are occupied by villagers only for ceremonies such as the *kacang* (bean) festival in late September/early October. It is possible to climb **Ili Api** – it takes about six hours to the top. Take a guide.

Lembata has some good **beaches**. You can take a mikrolet to Tagawiti and then it is a 2km walk to the beach where there is reasonable snorkelling out on the reef. The eastern bay on the way to Hakadewa also has some good snorkelling closer to shore. Sunbathing is difficult – the crowds of kids block out the sunlight. It pays to be able to speak some Indonesian if venturing further afield.

Lamalera

Like characters out of *Moby Dick*, the people who live in this village on the south coast of Lembata still use small boats to hunt whales. The whaling season is limited from May to October, when the seas aren't too rough. Even then the whales are infrequent, with only about 15 to 25 caught each year. The villagers probably qualify as subsistence whalers and are therefore exempt from international bans on whaling.

The meat is shared according to traditional dictates. The heads go to two families of original landowners, which is a custom observed, it is said, since the 15th century. The blubber is melted to make fuel for

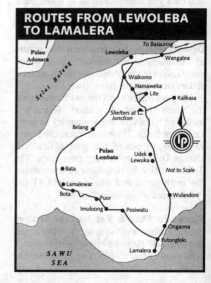

ROUTES FROM LEWOLEBA TO LAMALERA

Lamalera

The villagers of Lamalera are thought to have originated from Lapan Batan, a small island in the straits between Lembata and Pantar that was destroyed by a volcanic eruption. The ancestors arrived in boats that each clan has kept as the model for all future boats. While the original boats have been repaired and extended over generations, the villagers consider them to be the same boats. To the villagers, each boat is a living being and a physical link to the ancestors and the ancestral home.

The loss of boats from the village is more than an economic blow to the villagers – it means losing an important part of their heritage. Most recently, in March 1994, two small boats from Lamalera sank after being dragged almost to Timor by a wounded whale, a distance of around 80km. The crew of the two boats was later picked up by a third boat from the village and the 36 men then drifted for several days before being rescued by a P & O cruise ship.

The loss of the boats sent the village into a two month period of mourning in which no whaling was allowed. When the mourning period finished, a ceremony took place to 'let the boats go'.

lamps and some is traded for fruit and vegetables in a barter-only market in the hills.

Most of the whales caught are sperm whales, though smaller pilot whales are occasionally taken. When whales are scarce the villagers harpoon sharks, manta rays and dolphins, which are available year-round. Using nets is alien to these people and fishing rods are used only for sharks.

The whaling boats are made entirely of wood and held together with wooden dowel instead of nails. Each vessel carries a mast and the sail is made of palm leaves, but these are lowered during the hunt, when the men (usually a crew of 12) row furiously to overtake the whale. As the gap between the

boat and the whale narrows, the harpooner takes the 3m long harpoon and leaps onto the back of the whale. An injured whale will try to dive, dragging the boat with it, but cannot escape since it has to resurface.

Your chances of actually seeing a whale hunt, or the bloody business of butchering a whale, are quite small. Otherwise Lamalera is just another fishing village. A steady trickle of travellers make their way here and tourism is certainly welcome as an economic alternative to whale hunting. For around 15,000Rp you can combine the two and go out in the boats on a whale hunt.

On Saturday there's an interesting **barter-only market** at Wulandoni, about a 1½ hour walk along the coast from Lamalera. Another nice walk along the coast is to **Tapabali**, where you can see local weaving. In Lamalera, common ikat motifs are whales, manta rays and boats.

Places to Stay & Eat There are four small homestays in Lamalera, all costing around 15,000Rp per day, including meals. *Guru Ben's* is above the village, perched on a hill overlooking the shoreline. Pak Ben speaks good English and is a gracious host. The slightly more salubrious *Bapa Yosef's*, also known as the 'White House', is right on the point at the end of the beach. This small house sleeps four and someone will come in three times a day to cook meals. *Mama Maria's Homestay* is right in the heart of the village, behind the shady town square. *Abel Beding* is on the main path through the village, past the town square, and is on-the-ball with information.

Getting There & Away The easiest way to get to Lamalera is by boat from either Lewoleba or Larantuka. The boat from Lewoleba to Lamalera (5000Rp, six hours) leaves after the Monday pasar malam (usually 1 am or later, but be there 10.30 pm for a spot). From Larantuka, a boat leaves on Friday, stopping in Waiwerang on the way.

Otherwise take a Surya Kasih or Taruna truck from Lewoleba to Puor, from where it's a 2½ hour walk, mostly downhill. Bring plenty of water for the walk. Trucks leave around 7 to 9 am. From Lewoleba, the bemos leave at 7 am and run only as far as Bota – a 45 minute walk before Puor.

Leaving Lamalera, the truck from Puor leaves around 10 am, so start the walk early. The market ferry from Lewoleba returns on Monday morning and the boat to Waiwerang and Larantuka leaves on Wednesday. Because of connections and Lamalera's isolation, you really need five days or more to visit Lamalera from Larantuka.

Balauring

This small town is predominantly Muslim and is on the peninsula at the eastern end of Lembata. Ferries linking Alor and Lembata stop here for the night, which is the only reason to visit. There are wonderful views of Ili Api as you come into Balauring.

Stay at the *Losmen Telaga Sari*, a friendly dilapidated guesthouse run by two welcoming ancients. The 20,000Rp per head tariff includes meals, but by her own admission the woman in charge is not a great cook. Walk straight down the road leading off the end of the pier and the losmen is the second last building on the street. There's also a scruffy *homestay* right by the pier for 5000Rp per person, but it rarely has beds. Otherwise, you can sleep on the boat – the crew may be able to provide you with a mat to sleep on the deck.

Small buses (5000Rp, two hours) run the 53km from Balauring over the paved road to Lewoleba. Buses also run to **Wairiang** on the far eastern coast, a 45 minute journey by bus. The small *Diana Express* boat to Kalabahi usually leaves Balauring on Wednesday (sometimes Thursday), calling in at Wairiang. Lie back on the wooden deck and enjoy the spectacular view. With luck you will see one of the many pods of dolphins that frequent these waters.

ALOR

East of the Solor group are Pulau Alor and Pulau Pantar. Alor is quite scenic and has a wide mix of cultures in a small area. Diving spots around the island are reputedly among the best in South-East Asia. The island is so rugged and travel there so difficult that the roughly 140,000 inhabitants of Alor are divided into some 50 tribes, with about as many different languages. To this day there is still some isolated, occasional warfare between the tribes.

Although the Dutch installed local rajahs along the coastal regions after 1908, they had little influence over the interior whose people were still taking heads in the 1950s. The mountain villages were steep hilltop fortresses and during the rainy season the trails became impassable. The different tribes had little contact with each other except during raids.

When the 20th century came, the warriors put western imports to good use by twisting wire from telegraph lines into multibarbed arrowheads over the tip of which they pressed a sharpened, dried and hollowed chicken bone. When the arrow hit the bone would splinter deep inside the wound.

The coastal populations are predominantly Muslim. Christianity has made inroads, primarily through Dutch Protestant missionaries, but indigenous animist cultures still survive, mainly because travel around the island has been very difficult. New roads now cross the island, but boats are still a common form of transport.

Kalabahi
☎ 0386
Kalabahi is the chief town on Alor and is located at the end of a long and spectacular palm-fringed bay on the west coast. It's a cliched tropical port – lazy and slow-moving, with boats scattered around the harbour. The sea breezes make Kalabahi cooler than most other coastal towns in Nusa Tenggara.

Kalabahi is relatively prosperous, but outside the town living conditions are poor. There are a few interesting villages and nice beaches nearby. Some of the beaches have spectacular snorkelling and diving, but also dangerous currents.

It's worth strolling around the Pasar Inpres in Kalabahi. It has a huge variety of fruit and you'll see women making bamboo mats.

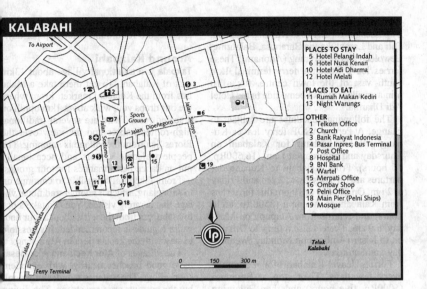

KALABAHI

PLACES TO STAY
5 Hotel Pelangi Indah
6 Hotel Nusa Kenari
10 Hotel Adi Dharma
12 Hotel Melati

PLACES TO EAT
11 Rumah Makan Kediri
13 Night Warungs

OTHER
1 Telkom Office
2 Church
3 Bank Rakyat Indonesia
4 Pasar Inpres; Bus Terminal
7 Post Office
8 Hospital
9 BNI Bank
14 Wartel
15 Merpati Office
16 Ombay Shop
17 Pelni Office
18 Main Pier (Pelni Ships)
19 Mosque

Money Cash and travellers cheques can be cashed at the BNI and BRI banks. The Ombay shop is one block back from the port and will change US dollars outside banking hours at reasonable rates.

Places to Stay The central *Hotel Adi Dharma (☎ 21049, Jl Martadinata 12)* is on the waterfront near the main pier. It has the best set-up for travel information and has great views across the harbour from the porch, especially at sunset. Rooms are 12,000/18,000Rp for singles/doubles with shared mandi, 14,000/20,000Rp with fan and bath or 40,000/45,000Rp with TV and air-con.

The nearby *Hotel Melati (☎ 21073, Jl Soetomo)* has a shady garden and old rooms for 8000/14,000Rp or 12,500/19,000Rp with mandi. The new block has better rooms for 16,500/22,000Rp or 30,000/35,000Rp with air-con.

Out near the bus terminal, *Hotel Pelangi Indah (☎ 21251, Jl Diponegoro 100)* has the best rooms in town and the attached restaurant is a definite bonus. Spotless rooms with verandah, fan and mandi cost 20,000/25,000Rp, while those with air-con and shower are 40,000/50,000Rp. Any bemos going to the bus terminal can drop you there.

The *Hotel Nusa Kenari (☎ 21119, Jl Diponegoro 11)* is nearby and has good rooms for 15,000Rp with mandi or 25,000Rp and 30,000Rp with air-con and shower.

Places to Eat Kalabahi has the best dining in the Solor and Alor archipelagos, which isn't saying much. The best option and Kalabahi's only restaurant is in the *Hotel Pelangi Indah*. The *Rumah Makan Kediri* is close to the pier and serves excellent *nasi campur* (rice 'with the lot') and other reasonable fare. There is also a grungy *Padang restaurant* opposite the market on Jl Diponegoro.

At night, a few streetside *warungs* and *kaki limas* (push cart-style food stalls) set up on the southern side of the sports ground. Sate, soto ayam and other Javanese fare are on offer. This meagre collection is about the closest thing to nightlife in Kalabahi, which otherwise closes down around 8 pm.

NUSA TENGGARA

Getting There & Away Kalabahi is linked by passenger/car ferries to Kupang, Atapupu, Dili and Larantuka via Baranusa, Balauring, Lewoleba and Weiwerang (Adonara). These ferries leave from the ferry terminal 1km south-west of the town centre. It's a 10 minute walk or 500Rp bemo ride to the Hotel Adi Dharma.

The following schedules are subject to change. A Perum ASDP ferry leaves Kupang's Bolok harbour for Kalabahi on Thursday and Saturday at 1 pm (16,500Rp, 16 hours). From Kalabahi to Kupang departures are on Tuesday at 2 pm and Friday at 2 pm. On Sunday at 10 pm this ferry runs from Kalabahi to Atapupu (8500Rp, eight hours) and returns from Atapupu on Monday at 9 am. There's also a ferry to Dili and on to Kisar (Ambon) on Monday, Wednesday and Saturday.

Ferries leave Kalabahi for Larantuka every few days. They stop at Baranusa (5000Rp, five hours) and then Balauring (12,500Rp, nine hours) where they stop overnight. Balauring has a *losmen*. The next day at 7 am ferries continue from Balauring to Larantuka (nine hours) via Lewoleba and Waiwerang. Take food and water as there's usually none on the boat.

Pelni boats leave from the main pier in the centre of town. The Pelni ship *Awu* calls in at Kalabahi twice every fortnight, sailing on to Dili and Kupang. Pelni cargo ships also regularly run from Kalabahi to Dili and Kupang and take passengers. Check at the Pelni office.

Cargo ships are slow (14 hours to Dili) and the conditions are not the best. It pays to rent a cabin from one of the crew members for about 15,000Rp.

Other small boats from the central wharf make their way to the other islands of the Alor Archipelago. A boat also travels once a week to Wairiang on the north-eastern tip of Lembata.

Getting Around Transport around town is by bus and bemo (500Rp), which finish by 7 pm. It's also possible to rent a motorcycle through the Hotel Adi Dharma or the Toko Kencana shop opposite the market on Jl Diponegoro for around 30,000Rp per day.

Around Kalabahi

Takpala is a traditional village about 13km east of Kalabahi. To get there take a Mabu bus from the Kalabahi market. From where the bus drops you, walk about 1km uphill on a sealed road. There are several traditional high-roofed houses and the view over the Flores Sea from the village is stunning. The people welcome visitors and occasionally put on dance performances for tour groups.

From Takpala it's possible to continue on to **Atimelang**, which is another traditional village that is rarely visited. You can take a bus to Mabu, but from there it's about a four hour walk; a guide is recommended. It's possible to stay with the kepala desa in Atimelang.

The villages of **Alor Kecil** and **Alor Besar** have good beaches nearby, with excellent snorkelling. The water is wonderfully cool, but the currents are very strong. The diving around the islands is superb, but is best arranged in Kupang. Alor Kecil has some weavings and offers great views across to other islands. This area is being promoted as a potential diving resort. Buses to Alor Kecil and Alor Besar leave from the Kalabahi Pasar Inpres or catch them outside the Hotel Melati.

Near the airport at the northernmost tip of the island is **Mali**, which is a lovely white sand beach with good snorkelling. It's possible to rent a boat for a tour of the area and at high tide you can walk to **Pulau Suki**, off the beach at Mali. There's an old grave there, said to be that of a sultan from Sulawesi.

PANTAR

The second largest island of the Alor group, Pantar is about as far off the beaten track as you can get. The Perum ferries between Larantuka and Alor stop at **Baranusa**, which is the main town and a sleepy little place with a straggle of coconut palms and a couple of general stores. Baranusa's only accommodation is the friendly *Homestay Burhan*, with just one room that costs 10,000Rp including meals.

Moko

Alor's chief fame lies in its mysterious *mokos* – bronze drums about 0.5m high and 0.33m in diameter, tapered in the middle like an hourglass and with four ear-shaped handles around the circumference. They're closed at the end with a sheet of bronze that sounds like a bongo when thumped with the hand. There are thousands of them on the island – the Alorese apparently found them buried in the ground and believed them to be gifts from the gods.

Most mokos have decorations similar to those on bronze utensils made in Java in the 13th and 14th century Majapahit era, but others resemble earlier South-East Asian designs and may be connected with the Dongson culture that developed in Vietnam and China around 700 BC and then pushed its influence into Indonesia. Later mokos even have English or Dutch-influenced decorations.

Theories about the mokos' origins usually suggest they were brought to Alor from further west by Indian, Chinese or Makassarese traders, but this doesn't explain why they were buried in the ground. Maybe the Alorese buried them in some long-forgotten times as an offering to spirits at a time of plague or to hide them during attacks.

Today mokos have acquired enormous value among the Alorese and families devote great time and energy to amassing collections of them, along with pigs and land. Such wealth is the only avenue to obtaining a bride in traditional Alorese society. In former times, whole villages would sometimes go to war in an attempt to win possession of a prized moko.

The export of mokos is restricted by the government.

The main reason to visit Pantar is to climb **Gunung Sirung**, which is an active volcano with an impressive smouldering crater.

From Baranusa take a truck to Kakamauta, from where it is a three hour walk to Sirung's crater.

The only other island of note is the lightly populated **Pulau Pura**, sandwiched between Pantar and Alor. It is dominated by a towering, forested peak topped by a small crater lake.

Roti & Sabu

The small islands of Roti and Sabu (also spelled Sawu), between Timor and Sumba, are little visited but, with their successful economies based on the lontar palm, have played a significant role in Nusa Tenggara's history and development and now preserve some interesting cultures. Roti, in particular, has a few beautiful coastal villages and some of the best surf in Nusa Tenggara.

ROTI

Off the west end of Timor, Roti (Rote) is the southernmost island in Indonesia. The lightly built Rotinese speak a language similar to the Tetum of Timor, though Bahasa Indonesia is almost universally understood.

Traditionally, Roti was divided into 18 domains. In 1681 a bloody Dutch campaign placed their local allies in control of the island and Roti became the source of slaves and supplies for the Dutch base at Kupang. In the 18th century, the Rotinese began taking advantage of the Dutch presence, gradually adopted Christianity and, with Dutch support, established a school system that eventually turned them into the region's elite.

The Rotinese openness to outside influences is the main reason their culture is no longer as strong as Sabu's, though there are still areas where people adhere to the old traditions. At some festivals, families cut chunks from a live buffalo and take them away to eat.

Ikat weaving on Roti today uses mainly red, black and yellow chemical dyes, but the designs can still be complex: floral and *patola* (traditional geometric ikat design) motifs are typical. One tradition that hasn't

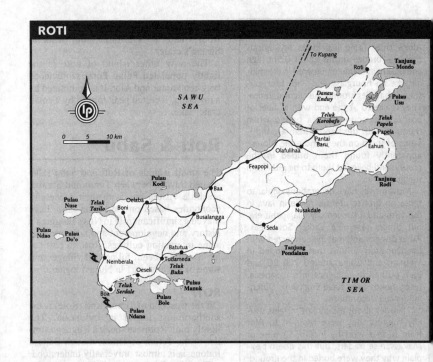

ROTI

disappeared is the wearing of the wide-brimmed lontar hat, ti'i langga, which has a curious spike sticking up near the front like a unicorn's horn (perhaps representing a lontar palm or a Portuguese helmet or mast). Rotinese also love music and dancing; the traditional Rotinese 20 stringed instrument, the *sasando*, features on the 5000Rp note.

Baa

Roti's main town is Baa, on the north coast. The main street, Jl Pabean, is close to the ocean and some houses have boat-shaped thatched roofs with carvings (connected with traditional ancestor cults) at various points. The coast from the ferry port at Pantai Baru to Baa is lightly populated and has some superb coral beaches. There is an excellent, deserted beach just 3km from Baa.

Apart from a bustling market on Saturday, Baa has little to offer and most travellers

pass straight through on their way to Nemberala. The BRI bank in Baa does not change money.

Places to Stay & Eat The *Pondok Wisata Karya* (☎ 71290, Jl Kartini 1) just off Jl Pabean, has clean rooms with outside mandi for 7500Rp per person. The manager speaks good English and will change money at a reduced rate if you're desperate.

Hotel Ricky (☎ 71045) is a few doors down, although the main entrance is around the corner on Jl Gereja. This is Baa's best hotel – it has a variety of rooms, all with mandi. Rates start at 7500/10,000Rp for singles/doubles. It has a good restaurant and can arrange car hire at high rates.

Further along Jl Pabean is the *Hotel Kezia* (☎ 71038). It is dark but cool and has reasonable rooms with mandi from 10,000/15,000Rp.

Rumah Makan Karya and *Warung Makan Lumayah*, both on Jl Pabean near the town centre, serve basic meals, or the *Hotel Ricky* has the fanciest restaurant. Shops sell the local delicacy, *susu goreng*, made from buffalo milk that's cooked until it becomes a brown powder. It doesn't look much, but it is sweet and very tasty.

Papela

This Muslim Bugis fishing village in the far east of Roti is set on a beautiful harbour. Every Saturday, it hosts the biggest market on the island. There is one hotel, the *Wisma Karya (Jl Lorong Asem)*, which costs 25,000Rp per person. Buses go to Papela from Baa and Pantai Baru over the best road on the island.

Nemberala

A surfers' secret for a few years, Nemberala is a relaxed little coastal village with white sand beaches and good surf between April and July, earning it the title of T-land. A long coral reef runs right along the main beach, with snorkelling possibilities. Nemberala has some good accommodation and is the only real tourist centre on the island. Nemberala can be used as a base to explore other points of interest on Roti, but you need to charter transport or hire a motorbike.

Places to Stay & Eat Nemberala has a small selection of simple homestays, which all charge about 10,000Rp to 15,000Rp per person. The price is variable and depends on the season. As you come into Nemberala, the road swings around to the left and near the corner is *Mr Tomas Home-stay*, one of the most popular places. Small and family-run, it has old rooms in the original house and a new block of good rooms with shared mandi.

If you turn right at the corner and head north along the dirt road for 500m you reach *Tirosa*, right near the beach. Run by the kepala desa and his family, who speak good English, this simple losmen also operates the town's bus.

A few hundred metres south of Mr Tomas, *Losmen Anugurah* is set back from the beach, but is close to the main surf break. This surfers' favourite has cold beer and rooms with and without mandi.

A little further south and right on the beach is *Nemberala Beach Resort (Kupang, ☎ 23073)*, a very pleasant but expensive mid-range option. Bungalows are 65,000/105,000Rp plus tax for singles/doubles, including meals served in the restaurant-bar. Family quads are 210,000Rp. It also operates yacht and surfing tours to Roti from Australia (book through Indah Travel in Darwin) and organises trips around Roti.

Around Nemberala

About 8km from Nemberala, **Boa** has a spectacular white sand beach and good surf. You should be able to charter a motorcycle to Boa in Nemberala. Further east, **Oeseli** also has a superb beach, but is more easily approached from Tudameda to the east.

Pulau Ndana is an island which can be reached by boat from Nemberala – the Nemberala Beach Resort runs day trips. Legend has it that the island is uninhabited because the entire population was murdered in a revenge act in the 17th century and the small lake on the island turned red with the victims' blood. The island is populated by wild deer, a wide variety of birds and (reportedly) turtles, which come to lay their eggs on the beaches.

Boni is about 15km from Nemberala near the north coast and is one of the last villages on Roti where traditional religion is still followed. Market day is Thursday. To get there you can charter or perhaps rent a motorcycle in Nemberala.

The tiny **Pulau Ndao** is another ikat-weaving and lontar-tapping (see 'The Lontar Economy' boxed text in this chapter) island, 10km west of Nemberala. Although administratively part of Roti, the people are very different and speak a language related to Sabunese. Ndao is famous for its gold and silversmiths and also produces some fine ikat.

A small ferry leaves Namosain near Kupang on Wednesday and stops in at Nemberala on Thursday before continuing on to Ndao. It runs in the reverse direction on

NUSA TENGGARA

Monday. It's possible to charter a boat to Ndao in Nemberala.

Getting There & Away

Boat Ferries run to Kupang daily except Friday, leaving at 1 pm (in reality 2 pm). The four hour trip costs 8500Rp. The ferries are fairly reliable, but the unexpected cancellation of services has occurred.

Getting Around

A pack of buses and bemos greet the ferry at Pantai Baru and run to Baa (1½ hours), Nemberala (3½ hours), Papela (one hour) and other towns in the south. Most bus transport around the island relies on the ferry timetable. Buses leave Baa for Pantai Baru around 11 am to meet the ferry. In the other direction, buses to Nemberala from the ferry pass through Baa, otherwise connections around the island are limited.

Regular bemos do run from Baa to Busalangga and at least one bemo runs to Papela in the morning, while trucks service more remote locations. Baa also has a few ojek, which mainly shuttle between Baa and the ferry, but will take you anywhere, including Nemberala.

The Hotel Ricky in Baa and the Nemberala Beach Resort in Nemberala can arrange a car and driver, but it will cost at least 150,000Rp a day. It is cheaper to charter a bemo for the day, but that will probably set you back 100,000Rp. Nemberala has no bemos to charter – the nearest are in Busalangga.

In Nemberala, you can hire a motorbike or the Nemberala Beach Resort rents bicycles.

SABU

Midway between Roti and Sumba, but with closer linguistic links to Sumba, the low, bare island of Sabu (also spelled Sawu) is still a stronghold of animistic beliefs collectively known as *jingitui*. These persist even though Portuguese missionaries first arrived before 1600 and their work was continued by the Dutch.

Sabu's population (about 60,000 people) is divided into five traditional domains; the main settlement, **Seba** (on the north-west coast), was the centre of the leading domain in Dutch times. Sabunese society is divided into clans, named after their male founders, but it is also divided in half – into the 'noble' and 'common' halves, which are determined by the mother's lineage. The halves are called *hubi ae* (greater flower stalk) and *hubi iki* (lesser flower stalk). Sabunese women have a thriving ikat-weaving tradition. Their cloth typically has stripes of black or dark blue interspersed with stripes decorated with floral motifs, clan or hubi emblems.

A group of stones near **Namata** is a ritual site: animal sacrifices, followed by the whole community sharing the meat, take place around August to October. Another festival in the second quarter of the year sees a boat pushed out to sea as an offering.

There are three places to stay on Sabu: *Ongka Da'i Homestay*, *Makarim Homestay* and *Petykuswan Homestay*. Seba has a market, and a handful of trucks provide the island's transport, although you can hire a motorcycle at reasonable rates.

Getting There & Away

Boat Ferries leave Kupang's Bolok harbour for Sabu on Tuesday and Wednesday (14,000Rp, nine hours), and continue on to Waingapu. From Sabu, ferries to Kupang leave on Tuesday and Wednesday. Ferries from Waingapu to Sabu leave on Monday and Saturday, and in the reverse direction on Sunday and Thursday.

Pelni passenger ships also call in at Sabu. The *Pangrango* sails Kupang-Roti-Sabu-Ende and back every two weeks.

Sumba

A great ladder once connected heaven and earth. By it, the first people came down to earth in Sumba and settled at Cape Sasar, on the northern tip of the island – or so the myth goes. Another Sumbanese tale recounts how Umbu Walu Sasar, one of their two ancestors, was driven away from Java by the wars. Transported to Sumba by the powers of heaven, he came to live at Cape Sasar. The other ancestor, Umbu Walu Mandoko, arrived by boat, travelled to the east and lived at the mouth of the Sungai Kambaniru.

Such myths may come as near to the truth as any version of the origins of a people who are physically of Malay stock with a tinge of Melanesian; whose language falls into the same bag that holds the Bimanese of eastern Sumbawa, the Manggarai and Ngada of western Flores and the Sabunese of Sabu; whose death and burial ceremonies are strongly reminiscent of Tana Toraja in Sulawesi; and whose brilliant ikat textiles, fine carved stone tombs and high, thatched clan houses suggest common origins with similar traditions scattered from Sumatra to Maluku.

Wherever they came from, the island on which the Sumbanese have ended up is – south of Flores and midway between Sumbawa and Timor – far from Indonesia's main cultural currents. Sumba's isolation has helped preserve one of Indonesia's most fascinating cultures, particularly in its wetter, more fertile and more remote western half, which is home to about two-thirds of the island's 400,000 people.

Right up until this century, Sumbanese life was punctuated by periodic warfare between a huge number of rival princedoms. Though Christianity and (to a lesser extent) Islam have now made inroads, around half the people in the west and a significant minority of people in the east still adhere to the animist *marapu* religion, and old conflicts are recalled every year at western Sumba's often-violent Pasola festivals, which involve mock battles between teams of mounted horse riders.

The 'mock' battles sometimes become real, as in August 1992, when two villages went to war and several people were killed and over 80 homes were burned down.

Many Sumbanese men still carry longbladed knives in wooden sheaths tucked into their waistbands. They wear scarves as turbans and wrap their brightly coloured sarongs to expose the lower two-thirds of their legs, with a long piece of cloth hanging down in front. A woman may have her legs tattooed after the birth of her first child

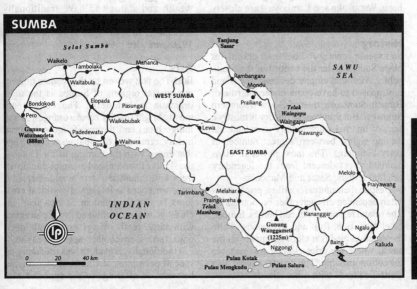

SUMBA

Selat Sumba

Tanjung Sasar

Waikelo
Tambolaka
Mananca
Waitabula
Rambangaru
Mondu
WEST SUMBA
Elopada
Pasunga
Prailiang
Bondokodi
Teluk Waingapu
Pero
Waikabubak
Lewa
Waingapu
Gunung Watumandeta (888m)
Padedewatu
Kawangu
Rua
Waihura
EAST SUMBA
Melolo
Praiyawang
Tarimbang
Melahar
Praingkareha
Teluk Mambang
Kananggar
INDIAN OCEAN
Ngalu
Gunung Wanggameti (1225m)
Baing
Kaliuda
Nggongi
Pulau Kotak
Pulau Mengkudu
Pulau Salura

0   20   40 km

SAWU SEA

as a recognition of status; often it will be the same motifs that are on her sarong. Another custom, teeth filing, has all but died out, but you'll still see older people with short, brown teeth from the time when jagged white teeth were considered ugly.

The last 20 years have seen an increasing flow of visitors to Sumba, many attracted by the ikat cloth of eastern Sumba. Other Sumbanese traditions are much stronger in the west, where you'll see exotic houses, ceremonies and tombs. The tombs are a constant reminder that, for a Sumbanese, death is the most important event in life. Against this background, the most recent attraction of Sumba – surfing – hardly seems to fit.

Despite their warlike past, the Sumbanese are friendly, but more reserved than many other peoples in Nusa Tenggara. Foreigners should consider hiring a guide when going to villages, at least until they learn some visitor behaviour.

Though at least some Bahasa Indonesia is spoken everywhere, Sumba has six main languages. Kambera is spoken throughout East Sumba. The five main languages of West Sumba – Anakalang, Weyewa, Mamboru, Wanukaka and Lamboya – are closely related.

History

Fourteenth century Javanese chronicles place Sumba under the control of the Majapahits. After that empire declined, the island is supposed to have come under the rule of Bima in Sumbawa, then of Gowa in southern Sulawesi. But Sumbanese history is mostly a saga of internal wars, mainly over land and trading rights, between a great number of petty kingdoms. The most powerful clans claimed direct descent from the legendary original settlers, Sasar and Mandoko.

Despite their mutual hostility, princedoms often depended on each other economically. The inland regions produced horses, lumber, betel nuts, rice, fruit and dyewoods, while the much-valued ikat cloth was made on the coast, where the drier climate was suitable for cotton growing. The coastal people also controlled trade with other islands.

The Dutch initially paid little attention to Sumba because it lacked commercial possibilities. The sandalwood trade conducted in the 18th century was constantly interrupted by wars among the Sumbanese. Only in the mid-19th century did the Dutch arrange a treaty permitting one of their representatives to live in Waingapu, buy horses and collect taxes. Towards the end of the century, Sumba's trade with other islands through Waingapu led to extensive internal wars as various princes tried to dominate it and, in the early 20th century, the Dutch decided to secure their own interests by invading the island and placing it under direct military rule.

Military rule lasted until 1913, when a civilian administration was set up, although the Sumbanese nobility continued to reign and the Dutch ruled through them. When the Indonesian republic ceased to recognise the native rulers' authority, many of them became government officials, so their families continued to exert influence.

Sumba's extensive grasslands made it one of Indonesia's leading horse-breeding islands. Horses are still used as transport in more rugged regions; they are a symbol of wealth and status and have traditionally been used as part of the bride-price. Brahmin bulls, first brought to Sumba in the 1920s, are also bred.

Arts

Ikat The ikat woven by the women of eastern coastal regions of Sumba is the most dramatic in Indonesia. The colours are mostly bright (earthy *kombu* orange-red and indigo blue) and the motifs are a pictorial history, reminders of tribal wars and an age that ended with the coming of the Dutch – the skulls of vanquished enemies dangle off trees and mounted riders wield spears. A huge variety of animals and mythical creatures is also depicted in Sumba ikat, including *nagas* (crowned snake-dragons with large teeth, wings and legs), deer, dogs, turtles, crocodiles, apes and eagles.

Traditionally, ikat cloth was used only on special occasions: at rituals accompanying harvests; as offerings to the sponsors of a festival; or as clothing for leaders, their relatives and their attendants. Less than 90 years ago, only members of Sumba's highest clans and their personal attendants could make or wear it. The most impressive use of the cloth was at important funerals, where dancers and the guards of the corpse were dressed in richly decorated costumes and glittering headdresses. The corpse was dressed in the finest textiles, then bound with so many more that it resembled a huge mound. The first missionary in Sumba, DK Wielenga, described a funeral in 1925:

> The brilliant examples of decorated cloths were carefully kept till the day of the burial. The prominent chief took 40 or 50 to the grave with him and the rajah was put to rest with no less than 100 or 200. When they appeared in the hereafter among their ancestors, then they must appear in full splendour. And so the most attractive cloths went into the earth.

The Dutch conquest broke the Sumbanese nobility's monopoly on the production of ikat and opened up a large external market, which in turn increased production. Collected by Dutch ethnographers and museums since the late 19th century (the Rotterdam and Basel museums have fine collections), the large cloths became popular in Java and the Netherlands. By the 1920s, visitors were already noting the introduction of nontraditional designs, such as rampant lions from the Dutch coat of arms.

A Sumbanese woman's ikat sarong is known as a *lau*. A *hinggi* is a large rectangular cloth used by men as a sarong or shawl.

Traditional Culture

Old beliefs fade, customs die and rituals change: the Sumbanese still make textiles, but no longer hunt heads; 25 years ago the bride-price may have been coloured beads and buffalos – today it might include a bicycle. Certainly though, the bride dowry can be high and many Sumbanese men migrate just to find wives that don't expect a dowry.

Churches are now a common sight, and in some areas traditions are dying, but elsewhere, particularly in the west, they thrive.

Villages A traditional village usually consists of two more or less parallel rows of houses facing each other, with a square between. In the middle of the square is a stone with another flat stone on top of it, on which offerings are made to the village's protective *marapu* (spiritual forces). These structures, spirit stones or *kateda*, can also be found in the fields around the village and are used for offerings to the agricultural marapu when planting or harvesting.

The village square also contains the stone-slab tombs of important ancestors, usually finely carved, but nowadays often made of cement. In former times the heads of slain enemies would be hung on a dead tree in the village square while ceremonies and feasts took place. These skull trees, called *andung*, can still be seen in some villages today and are a popular motif on Sumbanese ikat.

A traditional Sumbanese dwelling is a large rectangular structure raised on piles; it houses an extended family. The thatched (or nowadays often corrugated-iron) roof slopes gently upwards from all four sides and in the loft are placed *marapu maluri* objects. See Religion in this section for further details.

Rituals accompanying the building of a house include an offering, at the time of planting the first pillar, to find out if the marapu agree with the location; one method is to cut open a chicken and examine its liver. Many houses are decked with buffalo horns or pigs' jaws from past sacrifices.

Visiting Villages Many Sumbanese villages these days are accustomed to tourists, but even those that get a steady stream sometimes have difficulty understanding the strange custom of westerners who simply want to observe 'exotic' cultures. If you're interested in their weavings or other artefacts, the villagers can put you down as a potential trader. If all you want to do is chat and look around, they may be puzzled about why you've come, and if you simply turn up with a camera and start putting it in their faces, they're likely to be offended.

On Sumba, giving *sirih pinang* (betel nut) is the traditional way of greeting guests or

Betel Nut – The Peacekeeper

One traditional custom that still thrives in parts of Nusa Tenggara, particularly Sumba and Timor, is the chewing of betel nut, or *siri pinang*. Apart from the obvious reason for chewing it – it gives you a little pep up to help you through the day – there are more complex social and cultural reasons.

Chewing betel is a statement of adulthood, and the three parts that make up the 'mix' that are chewed together have symbolic meaning. The green stalk of the siri represents the male, the nut or pinang the female ovaries and the lime *(kapor)* is symbolic of sperm. The lime causes the characteristic flood of red saliva in the mouth, and when the saliva is spat out, it is believed to be returning the blood of childbirth back to the earth.

Betel nut traditionally played an important role in negotiation and discussion between different clans. Betel nut would always be offered to visitors to a village as a gesture of welcome. If a male entering a village did not accept the betel offered, it was tantamount to a declaration of war.

Even today, if you're offered betel nut never refuse it! Some foreigners have really caused offence by saying, 'No, I don't want to buy it'. If you don't want to chew it, just put it in your pocket or bag. Most foreigners find betel nut pretty disgusting – it tastes a bit like bark. It gives you a mild buzz and a bright red mouth. It also creates an amazing amount of saliva, so if you're going to be embarrassed about spitting constantly, you'd better not have any. Whatever you do, don't swallow it – or you're likely to really embarrass yourself!

A stylised betel nut holder.

hosts. It's a good idea to take some with you – it's cheap and can be bought at most markets in Sumba. Offer it to the kepala desa or to any other 'senior' looking person.

Some villages have grown used to foreigners arriving without sirih. In these places, appointed representatives keep a visitors' book, which they'll produce for you to sign and you should donate 2000Rp or so. In off-the-beaten-track kampungs, offering money or cigarettes is also OK, especially if you make it clear that you're offering it because you don't have any sirih. This way you still conform to the give-and-take principle.

Whatever the circumstances, taking a guide, at least to isolated villages, is a big help. A guide smooths over any language difficulties and through them you should learn enough about the behaviour expected of guests to feel confident visiting villages alone. No matter where you go, taking the time to chat with the villagers helps them to treat you more as a guest than a customer or alien. Remember that when you enter a village, you're in effect walking into a home.

Religion

The basis of traditional Sumbanese religion is marapu, a collective term for all the spiritual forces, including gods, spirits and ancestors. The most important event in a person's life is death, when they join the invisible world of the marapu, from where they can influence the world of the living. *Marapu mameti* is the collective name for all dead people. The living can appeal to them for help, especially to their own relatives, though the dead can be harmful if irritated. The *marapu maluri* are the original people placed on earth by god; their power is concentrated in certain places or objects, much like the Javanese idea of *semangat*.

Death Ceremonies On the day of burial, horses or buffalos are killed to provide the deceased with food for their journey to the land of marapu. Ornaments and a sirih bag are also buried with the body. The living must bury their dead as richly as possible to avoid being reprimanded by the marapu mameti. Without a complete and honourable ceremony, the dead cannot enter the invisible world and roam about menacing the living. It has been said the dead travel to Cape Sasar to climb the ladder to the invisible world above.

One Sumbanese custom that parallels the Torajan customs of central Sulawesi is the deliberate destruction of wealth to gain prestige, often by sponsoring festivals where many buffalos are slaughtered. Funerals may be delayed for several years, until enough wealth has been accumulated for a second burial accompanied by the erection of a massive stone-slab tomb. In some cases the dragging of the tombstone from outside the village is an important part of the procedure. Sometimes, hundreds are needed to move the block of stone and the family of the deceased feed them all. A *ratu* (priest) sings for the pullers, which is answered in chorus by the group. The song functions as an invocation to the stone.

When the Indonesian republic was founded, the government introduced a slaughter tax in an attempt to stop the destruction of livestock. This reduced the number of animals killed, but didn't alter basic attitudes. The Sumbanese believe you *can* take it with you.

WAINGAPU
☎ 0387 • pop 25,000

The largest town in Sumba, Waingapu became the administrative centre after the Dutch military 'pacified' the island in 1906. It had long been the centre of the trade controlled by the coastal princedoms, with textiles and metal goods brought in by traders from Makassar, Bima and Ende, and the much-prized Sumba horses, dyewoods and lumber being exported.

Waingapu is the main entry point to Sumba, but the island's attractions lie in the west and south-east. The town does have a large group of ikat traders who run shops or hang around outside hotels (see Shopping later in this section).

Orientation & Information

Waingapu has two centres: the older, northern one focuses on the harbour; the southern one is around the main market and bus terminal, about 1km inland.

The BNI bank is on Jl Ampera near the market, or the BRI bank is on Jl Ahmad Yani. The post office on Jl Hasanuddin is open Monday to Friday from 8 am to 4 pm. The Telkom office on Jl Tjut Nya Dien is open 24 hours.

Places to Stay

Hotel Permata Sari (☎ 61516) is otherwise known as Ali's and is handy if arriving by ferry. It has harbour views – from the bathrooms! Large rooms with attached mandi are 7500Rp per person. Basic meals are available and Ali, the owner, is a good source of information. A Hindu temple 50m away provides background music in the evenings.

If the Permata Sari is full, as it sometimes is when the ferries dock, the nearby *Hotel Lima Saudara* (☎ 61083, Jl Wanggameti 2) is a bit of a dive but has singles/doubles with mandi and midget-sized beds at 10,000/16,000Rp.

The other hotels are in the new part of town. The *Hotel Elvin* (☎ 62097, Jl Ahmad Yani 73) is well run and has a good restaurant. Large rooms with mandi cost 20,000/30,000Rp, or 30,000/40,000Rp with air-con.

NUSA TENGGARA

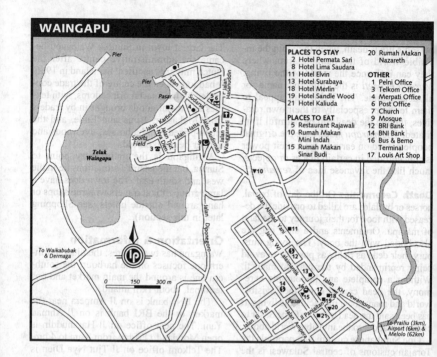

WAINGAPU

PLACES TO STAY		20	Rumah Makan
2	Hotel Permata Sari		Nazareth
8	Hotel Lima Saudara		
11	Hotel Elvin	**OTHER**	
13	Hotel Surabaya	1	Pelni Office
18	Hotel Merlin	3	Telkom Office
19	Hotel Sandle Wood	4	Merpati Office
21	Hotel Kaliuda	6	Post Office
		7	Church
PLACES TO EAT		9	Mosque
5	Restaurant Rajawali	12	BRI Bank
10	Rumah Makan	14	BNI Bank
	Mini Indah	16	Bus & Bemo
15	Rumah Makan		Terminal
	Sinar Budi	17	Louis Art Shop

The **Hotel Sandle Wood** (☎ 61199, Jl Panjaitan 23) is an attractive, popular hotel close to the bus terminal. It has a landscaped garden and an art shop. Small, run-down rooms with outside mandi cost 15,000/20,000Rp, but much better rooms with attached mandi for 20,000/30,000Rp are good value; air-con rooms are 45,000/55,000Rp.

The **Hotel Merlin** (☎ 61300, Jl Panjaitan 25) has better service and is the top hotel. Rooms with shower, intercom and comfy beds start at 27,000/33,000Rp. The intercom is not a complete joke; the stairs were made for a breed of mythical gigantic tourists. Air-con rooms with TV are 44,000/55,000Rp and the VIP rooms at 66,000/77,000Rp have hot water. The 4th floor restaurant has great views and the hotel has an art shop attached.

Nearby is the quiet, friendly **Hotel Kaliuda** (☎ 61264). Rooms with shared bath are 19,250Rp, or 22,000Rp with attached bath.

The **Hotel Surabaya** (☎ 61125, Jl El Tari 2) has efficient service, but is uncomfortably close to the mosque. Rooms with attached mandi go for 14,000/24,000Rp.

Places to Eat

Waingapu is not over endowed with eateries.

The **Rumah Makan Mini Indah** (Jl Ahmad Yani 27) is a simple place with very tasty food – choose from the selection in the showcase. **Restaurant Rajawali** (Jl Sutomo) is a reasonable choice in the old part of town. The **Rumah Makan Sinar Budi**, behind the market, serves Padang food.

Otherwise, eat at the hotels. **Hotel Merlin** has a restaurant with Indonesian and western food and great views. **Hotel Elvin** has a spick-and-span restaurant with a wide variety of Indonesian and Chinese dishes. The slightly grotty **Hotel Surabaya** has cold beer and cheap servings of Chinese food.

Shopping

Waingapu has several 'art shops' selling ikat from the villages of south-eastern Sumba and artefacts from the west of the island. Traders will also set up impromptu stalls in front of your hotel – some will squat there patiently all day. You can get an idea of the range of quality, design and price before heading out into the villages. Prices in town are higher, though not necessarily by that much, and the range is good.

Two art shops worth a look in Waingapu are Louis, Jl W J Lalaimantik 15, near the Hotel Sandle Wood, and Savana, near the Hotel Elvin on Jl Ahmad Yani. The Hotel Sandle Wood has a huge collection of ikat tucked away in a musty back room and the Hotel Merlin also has a decent range.

Getting There & Away

Air Merpati (☎ 61329), Jl Soekarno, has flights from Kupang (455,700Rp) and on to Denpasar (691,000Rp) on Monday, Wednesday and Friday mornings. Flights in the other direction stop at Waingapu on Tuesday, Thursday and Friday afternoons.

Bus The terminal is in the southern part of town, close to the market. Buses to Waikabubak (6500Rp, four hours) depart around 8 am, noon and 3 pm. A few of the morning and noon buses continue through to Waitabula. The road to Waikabubak goes through Lewa (a horse breeding centre) and Anakalang. It's an excellent road, paved all the way.

Buses head south-east to Melolo, Rende and Baing. Several travel through the morning and afternoon to Melolo, with a few continuing on to Rende, Ngalu and Baing. Most return to Waingapu the same day.

There are also daily buses north-west to Prailiang and south-west to Tarimbang.

Car The hotels rent cars with driver for out-of-town trips, but may require bargaining. Count on 150,000Rp for a full day's touring around eastern Sumba.

Boat Waingapu is well serviced by Perum ASDP ferries sailing to/from Ende and Aimere, and to/from Sabu and on to Kupang. All depart from the old pier in the centre of town. Schedules are subject to change – check them at the harbour.

The *Ile Ape* departs Ende for Waingapu (12,000Rp, 10 hours) on Sunday at 7 pm and continues to Sabu (13,500Rp, nine hours) on Monday at 2 pm. From Sabu it continues on to Kupang on Tuesday at 2 pm. It returns from Sabu on Thursday and sails from Waingapu to Ende on Saturday at 2 pm.

Rokatenda sails from Ende to Waingapu on Tuesday at 7 pm and returns to Ende on Wednesday at 7 pm. *Ile Mandiri* does a Sabu-Waingapu-Aimere run, leaving Sabu on Sunday and returning from Aimere on Thursday.

Pelni ships leave from the newer Dermaga dock to the west of town – a bemo to this pier is 500Rp per person. The *Pangrango* calls in every two weeks at Waingapu on its way to/from Labuanbajo (27,000Rp economy) and Ende (22,000Rp, seven hours). The *Awu* runs from Lembar to Waingapu and on to Ende and in the reverse direction comes from Ende and goes to Bali (68,500Rp).

Getting Around

To/From the Airport The airport is 6km south of town on the Melolo road. A taxi into town costs 3000Rp, or cars from the Elvin, Sandle Wood and Merlin hotels usually meet incoming flights and offer a free ride to intending guests.

Bemo A bemo to any destination around town will cost 500Rp.

AROUND WAINGAPU

Three kilometres out of Waingapu, **Prailiu** is an ikat-weaving centre that's worth a look. You should be able to see at least some aspects of production going on there. Bemos to Prailiu run from Waingapu's main bus and bemo terminal (500Rp).

Kawangu is 10km from Waingapu and about 300m off the road south to Melolo. It has some stone-slab tombs. Traditional houses may be seen at **Maru**, on the coast north-west of Waingapu. Buses go there daily, and there's a big market on Monday.

NUSA TENGGARA

Prailiang, another traditional village on the road between Waingapu and Maru, sees few visitors.

EAST SUMBA

A number of the traditional villages southeast of Waingapu can be visited from Waingapu. The stone ancestor tombs are impressive and the area produces some of Sumba's best ikat. The villages are quite used to tourists. Almost every village has a visitors' book and a donation of 2000Rp or so is expected. Ikat for sale will appear.

Melolo

The small town of Melolo, 62km from Waingapu and close to some interesting villages, has one losmen, the friendly and security-conscious *Losmen Hermindo*. Clean rooms with mandi cost 7500Rp per person. The losmen can arrange car hire for a day trip around the area. Basic meals are available on request; otherwise there's one small *warung* in town. Ten minutes' walk through mangroves from Losmen Hermindo, there's a long, sandy beach, although the water's a bit murky.

The market is about 3km out of town on a lonely, dusty hill. The main market day is Friday, when you might see some good ikat and also *hikung* cloth (distinguished from ikat by its woven, not dyed, patterns). Bemos run regularly from town to the market (400Rp).

Getting There & Away Buses to Melolo from Waingapu (2500Rp, 1½ hours) run hourly until around 4 pm along an excellent, paved road that crosses mainly flat grasslands. From Melolo the road continues on to Baing. Another road from Melolo crosses the mountains to Nggongi; trucks run along this road, at least in the dry season.

Praiyawang

Seven kilometres towards Baing from Melolo, Praiyawang is a traditional compound of Sumbanese houses and is the central village of Rende. It has an imposing line-up of big stone-slab tombs and makes fine quality ikat. You'll be shown some magnificent ikat, but the prices are high. Though Rende still has a rajah, other traditions have declined due to the cost of ceremonies and the breakdown of the marapu religion.

The largest tomb at Praiyawang is that of a former chief. It consists of four stone pillars 2m high, supporting a monstrous slab of stone about 5m long, 2½m wide and 1m thick. Two stone tablets stand atop the main slab, carved with human, buffalo, deer, lobster, fish, crocodile and turtle figures. A massive Sumbanese house with concrete pillars faces the tombs, along with a number of older rumah adats. It's possible to stay, but remember that these are members of a royal family, not hotel staff. Act accordingly!

Getting There & Away Several buses go from Waingapu to Rende, starting at about 7 am (3000Rp); otherwise take a bus to Melolo, from where bemos and trucks run throughout the day. The last buses back to Waingapu leave around 2.30pm.

Umabara & Pau

Like Rende, these two villages, about 4km south-west of Melolo, have traditional Sumbanese houses, stone tombs and weavings. At Umabara, the largest tombs are for relatives of the present rajah, who speaks some English and is quite friendly. Weavings, mostly hikung cloth, are available for purchase.

From Melolo, bemos can drop you at the turn-off to the villages on the main Waingapu-Melolo road. Walk for about 20 minutes then, at the horse statue, fork right for Umabara or left for Pau, both just a few minutes further on. A trail also links the two villages. From Waingapu, ask the bus driver to drop you at the turn-off.

Mangili

The Mangili district, centred on the villages of **Ngalu** and **Kaliuda**, is famed for its fine weaving. Kaliuda ikat is reputedly the best in Indonesia and is noted for its rich natural colours and the fine lines of its motifs. You might have trouble finding what you want

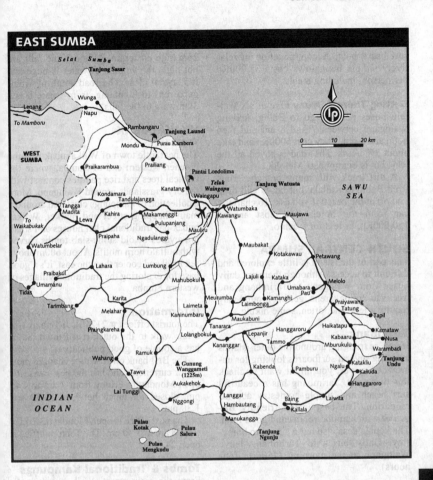

EAST SUMBA

Selat Sumba
Tanjung Sasar

Lenang
To Mamboru

Wunga
Napu
Rambangaru
Tanjung Laundi
Mondu
Purau Kambera
Prailiang

WEST SUMBA

Praikarambua

Pantai Londolima

Praipaha
Kanatang
Teluk Waingapu
Waingapu
Tanjung Watuata

SAWU SEA

Kondamara
Tandulajangga
Tangga Madita
Lewa
Kahira
Makamenggit
Pulupanjang
Mauliru
Watumbaka
Kawangu
Maujawa

To Waikabubak

Praipaha
Ngadulanggi

Maubakat
Kotakawau
Petawang

Watumbelar
Lahara
Lumbung
Lajuli
Kataka
Umbara Pau
Melolo

Praibakul
Umamanu
Tidas
Tarimbang
Karita
Melahar
Mahubokul
Meurumba
Laimeta
Kaninumbaru
Kamanghi
Laimbonga
Maukabuni
Praiyawang
Tatung
Tapil

Praingkareha
Tanarara
Lolangbokul
Lepanjir
Hanggaroru
Haikatapu
Kamataw
Nusa

Ramuk
Kananggar
Tammo
Kabaaru
Mburukulu
Warambadi

Wahang
Tawui
▲ Gunung Wanggameti (1225m)
Aukakehok
Kabenda
Pamburu
Ngalu
Katakliu
Kaliuda
Tanjung Undu

Lai Tunggi
Nggongi
Langgai
Hambautang
Manukangga
Baing
Kallala
Laiwita
Hanggaroro

INDIAN OCEAN

Pulau Kotak
Pulau Salura
Pulau Mengkudu
Tanjung Ngunju

0   10   20 km

as much of the best stuff gets bought up in large quantities and shipped off to Bali. Still, the villagers are happy to chat and you may see some of the work being produced, even if the prices make you weep. Kaliuda also has some stone-slab tombs. About six buses a day leave from Waingapu and pass through Melolo and Ngalu, the first leaving Waingapu at about 7 am. From Melolo, the trip takes about 1½ hours and costs 2000Rp. Kaliuda is a 3km walk from Ngalu towards the coast.

Baing

Baing is the main village of the Waijelu district, 124km from Waingapu. This spread out, sleepy settlement has little of interest, but **Kallala**, 2km away on the coast, has a wide, white sand beach and good surf between May and August. An Australian, the renowned Mr David (as he is referred to throughout East Sumba), has lived in Sumba for 20 years, is a mine of information and has set up bungalow accommodation at Kallala (also known as Watulibung).

NUSA TENGGARA

It mostly attracts surfers, but the seas are also renowned for game fishing and the resort has a boat. Accommodation in relatively simple bungalows costs 35,000Rp per person, including meals.

Getting There & Away Five or six Waijelu buses per day go to Baing, leaving Waingapu between 7 and 8 am and then noon and 1 pm. They cost 6000Rp and take about 3½ hours. The road is paved all the way, but is bumpy past Melolo.

A dirt track with many branches runs from Baing to Kallala, but buses will drop you off at the beach if you ask. To charter a car from the hotels will cost around 150,000Rp, or less for a bemo.

SOUTH-CENTRAL SUMBA

This part of the island is little explored and difficult to access. Although there are daily buses from Waingapu to Tarimbang and trucks to Praingkareha, getting around may require a jeep and, often, some hiking.

Tarimbang

If you're trudging around the outer islands carrying several surfboards looking for uncrowded waves, you might want to check this place out. Tarimbang has a beautiful surf beach and simple homestay accommodation. The best is the friendly *Bogenvil* with bamboo rooms and good food. The kepala desa also has a six room homestay. Daily buses to Tarimbang leave Waingapu in the morning (4500rp, four hours).

Praingkareha

Praingkareha's big attraction in the wet season is the 100m high **Air Terjun Laputi**. There's a pond with eels above the falls and a beautiful pool at the base. Tradition forbids women to look into the pool, but an exception is made for foreigners.

The falls are about 3km from the village. If you walk via the valley, a guide is advisable. Otherwise follow the main road to a fork, take the old road to the left and walk down a steep path to the falls.

Lumbung

As at Praingkareha, there is a spectacular 25m high **air terjun**. Although the falls are not high, the volume of water is huge and it's crystal clear. The road south of Waingapu runs to Lumbung, from where it is a 3km walk to the falls.

WAIKABUBAK
☎ 0387

The neat little town of Waikabubak is at the greener, western end of Sumba, where the tropical trees and rice paddies contrast with the dry grasslands around Waingapu. More a collection of kampungs clustered around a main shopping street and market, Waikabubak has traditional clan houses and small graveyards of old stone-slab tombs carved with buffalo horn motifs. About 600m above sea level and cooler than the east, it's a good base for exploring the traditional villages of western Sumba.

Information

The tourist office (☎ 21240), Jl Teratai 1, is a fair walk to the outskirts of town, but it has a couple of good publications.

The BNI bank on Jl A Yani changes most major currencies and has the best rates. It's open Monday to Friday from 7 am to 4.45 pm, closed for lunch between 12.30 and 1.30 pm.

The post office is open Monday to Friday from 8 am to 3.30 pm. The Telkom office is open 24 hours.

Tombs & Traditional Kampungs

From the main street, Waikabubak looks like any other unprepossessing Indonesian town of shops, houses and concrete, but right within the town are very traditional kampungs with stone-slab tombs and thatch houses.

Kampung Tambelar has very impressive tombs – you could spend days travelling to a remote village and not see better – but the most interesting kampungs are on the western edge of town. It's only a short stroll from most hotels to **Prai Klembung** and then up the ridge to **Tarung** and **Waitabar**.

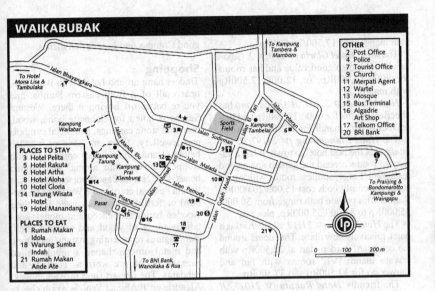

WAIKABUBAK

To Kampung
Tambera &
Mamboro

To Hotel
Mona Lisa &
Tambulaka

Kampung
Waitabar

Sports
Field

Kampung
Tambelar

Kampung
Tarung

Kampung
Prai
Klembung

Pasar

To Praiijing &
Bondomarotto
Kampungs &
Waingapu

To BNI Bank,
Wanokaka & Rua

OTHER
2 Post Office
4 Police
7 Tourist Office
9 Church
11 Merpati Agent
12 Wartel
13 Mosque
15 Bus Terminal
16 Algadrie
Art Shop
17 Telkom Office
20 BRI Bank

PLACES TO STAY
3 Hotel Pelita
5 Hotel Rakuta
6 Hotel Artha
8 Hotel Aloha
10 Hotel Gloria
14 Tarung Wisata
Hotel
19 Hotel Manandang

PLACES TO EAT
1 Rumah Makan
Idola
18 Warung Sumba
Indah
21 Rumah Makan
Ande Ate

0   100   200 m

Kampung Tarung, reached by a path off Jl Manda Elu, is the scene of an important month long ritual sequence, the *Wula Podhu*, each November. This is an austere period when even weeping for the dead is prohibited. Rites consist mainly of offerings to the spirits (the day before it ends hundreds of chickens are sacrificed) and people sing and dance for the entire final day. Tarung's monuments are under official protection.

Plenty of other kampungs are dotted around Waikabubak, such as those on the road to the Hotel Mona Lisa and just off the road at Puunaga, but these are more modern kampungs with concrete tombs.

Other interesting kampungs occupying ridge or hilltop positions outside town include **Praiijing** and **Bondomarotto**. Kampung Praiijing is especially scenic, perched on a hilltop about 4km from town. There are five neat rows of traditional houses and large stone tombs. **Kampung Prairami** and **Kampung Primkateti** are also beautifully located on adjacent hilltops. You can take a bemo to the turn-off to Praiijing (500Rp).

Another major kampung worth visiting is **Tambera**, 10km north on the road to Mamboro.

Some of these kampungs are more traditional and visiting them is less formalised than many further out – perhaps because most can only be reached on foot along narrow paths, while others further out of town are accessible by vehicle. At most of the kampungs around Waikabubak, locals are accustomed to the eccentric behaviour of tourists, so you can see some traditional culture without offending somebody. It is customary to give 2000Rp and you may be invited to chew betel nut.

Places to Stay

Tarung Wisata Hotel (☎ *21332, Jl Pisang 26*) has singles/doubles with shared mandi for 6000/10,000Rp and rooms with mandi for 10,000/15,000Rp to 20,000/25,000Rp plus tax. There's a restaurant and rooftop sitting area, and staff are on the ball with travel information.

The friendly *Hotel Aloha* (☎ *21245, Jl Sudirman 26*) is a popular budget choice with good food and information on western Sumba. Spotless singles/doubles with private mandi cost 17,500/25,000Rp.

The small *Hotel Gloria* (☎ 21024, Jl Gajah Mada 14) is also good value and has rooms for 8000/12,000Rp, or 12,000/17,500Rp with mandi.

Hotel Pelita (☎ 21104, Jl Ahmad Yani) has cheerless rooms for 6000/10,000Rp and better rooms with mandi for 15,000/20,000Rp.

The *Hotel Manandang* (☎ 21197, Jl Pemuda 4) is the best hotel in town. It has a variety of rooms around the garden and a good restaurant. Large, spotless rooms with washbasin and comfy beds cost 15,000/20,000Rp. Rooms with private bath range from 30,000/ 35,000Rp to 50,000/55,000Rp, plus tax.

The *Hotel Artha* (☎ 21112, Jl Veteran) is a quiet, relatively new place. The rooms around the courtyard garden start at 22,500Rp with private mandi. VIP rooms with fan and shower go for 32,500Rp and 37,500Rp.

The friendly *Hotel Rakuta* (☎ 21077, Jl Veteran) is dowdy and deserted, but has ambitious building plans. For now, rooms with mandi cost 25,000Rp.

The *Hotel Mona Lisa* (☎ 21364, Jl Adhyaksa) competes with the Manandang to be Waikabubak's best, but it is 2.5km from town. Well appointed bungalows overlooking the rice paddies cost 25,000/35,000Rp to 40,000/55,000Rp with TV and fridge. A few spotless rooms with shower cost 15,000/ 25,000Rp. Add 10% tax to all prices.

Places to Eat

The *Hotel Manandang* has the best restaurant in town, even if it is a little expensive. Most of the other hotels serve food, which is just as well because dining options elsewhere are limited. The *Warung Sumba Indah* near the Telkom office is a small, Balinese-run place with a wide variety of tourist services and tasty Balinese food.

There are a few grotty *warungs* on the main road opposite the mosque, but the sate is good and you can see it cooked. Otherwise Waikabubak has some decent rumah makan. *Rumah Makan Ande Ate* is cheap and popular with locals. The small *Rumah*

Makan Idola, at Jl Bhayangkara 55, is a long walk from the centre of town, but has good Chinese and Indonesian dishes.

Shopping

Traders hang around hotels with ikat cloth, nearly all of it from eastern Sumba, and you're better off buying it there. Western Sumba is noted for elaborate bone, wood, horn and stone carvings, and metal symbols and jewellery. There are bone or wooden betel nut and *kapor* (lime) containers with stoppers carved into animal and human heads; knives with Pasola horsemen (see the Pasola Festival entry in the West Sumba section) or fertility symbols carved into their wooden handles; tobacco and money containers made of wood and coconut shell; stone figures representing marapu ancestors; and metal omega-shaped symbols called *mamuli*, which are worn as earrings and pendants. The one art shop in Waikabubak, Algadrie on Jl Ahmad Yani, is worth checking before you go out to villages. Mostly poor quality souvenirs at high prices are on display – the good stuff is held at the back.

Getting There & Away

Air The Merpati agent (☎ 21051) is above a shop at Jl Ahmad Yani 11. There are flights from Kupang (602,000Rp) to Tambulaka and on to Denpasar (618,500Rp) on Thursday and Sunday mornings. Thursday's flight to Denpasar goes via Bima (157,600Rp). Flights from Denpasar to Kupang stop at Tambulaka on Thursday and Sunday afternoons. Sunday's flight from Denpasar stops at Bima en route to Tambulaka. Airport tax is 5500Rp.

Bus The bus terminal is central. Buses run to Waingapu (6500Rp, five hours) at 8 am, noon and 3.30 pm, and throughout the day to Waitabula (2000Rp, one hour). There are frequent bemos to Anakalang (1500Rp, 40 minutes), Wanokaka (1000Rp) and Lamboya (1500Rp), and less frequent and less certain minibuses and trucks to other villages. To Kodi, take a bus to Waitabula and catch a truck or bemo from there.

Getting Around

To/From the Airport The airport is at Tambolaka, 42km north-west of Waikabubak. The Bumi Indah bus is supposed to go every flight day at 7 am, but it's not reliable. If it hasn't picked you up at your hotel by 7.30 am, you'd better get a taxi or charter a bemo, which will cost a nasty 60,000Rp. It's not a bad idea to check the flight list at Merpati the day before; if you find out who is going and where they are staying, you can arrange to split the cost.

Bus Minibuses, bemos and trucks service most other towns and villages in western Sumba; for details, see under individual village entries. Generally, it's best to get them early when they tend to fill up and depart more quickly.

Car & Motorcycle Waikabubak is an excellent place to rent a motorbike for exploring West Sumba. Experienced guides are hard to find, though you can probably get someone to go with you for around 15,000Rp per day.

The friendly Warung Sumba Indah (☎ 21 633), at Jl Patimura 7, has a variety of motorcycles for rent for 30,000Rp and 35,000Rp. They are in most demand on weekends. A car and driver can also be hired. Most hotels can also find a motorcycle for rent, and the Mona Lisa and Manandang hotels rent vehicles with driver at high rates.

WEST SUMBA

The traditional village culture of western Sumba is one of the most intact in Indonesia. Kampungs of high-roofed houses are still clustered on their hilltops (a place of defence in times past), surrounding the large stone tombs of their important ancestors. Away from the towns, old women with filed teeth still go bare breasted and men in the traditional 'turban' and short sarong can be seen on horseback. The agricultural cycle turns up rituals, often involving animal sacrifices, almost year-round, and ceremonies for events like house building and marriage can take place at any time. Some kampungs are unaccustomed to foreigners; taking betel nut and cigarettes is a good way to get a friendly reception.

You should give yourself at least a few days around western Sumba; once you have learned some basic manners as a guest arriving in a village, hopefully armed with some Indonesian, it's possible to do without a guide.

Pasola Festival

The most famous of Nusa Tenggara's festivals sees large teams of colourfully clad horse riders engaging in mock battles. Its pattern is similar to that of other ritual warfare that used to take place in Indonesia – the cause not so much a quarrel between opposing forces as a need for human blood to be spilled to keep the spirits happy and bring a good harvest. Despite the blunt spears that the combatants now use and the efforts of Indonesian authorities to supervise the events, few holds are barred; injuries and sometimes deaths still occur.

The Pasola is part of a series of rituals connected with the beginning of the planting season. It takes place in four different areas in February or March each year, its exact timing determined by the arrival on nearby coasts of a certain type of sea worm called *nyale*. Priests examine the nyale at dawn and from their behaviour predict how good the year's harvest will be. Then the Pasola can begin: it's usually fought first on the beach and then, later the same day, further inland. The opposing 'armies' are drawn from coastal and inland dwellers.

The nyale are usually found on the eighth or ninth day after a full moon. In February Pasola is celebrated in the Kodi area (centred on Kampung Tosi) and the Lamboya area (Kampung Sodan); in March it's in the Wanokaka area (Kampung Waigalli) and the remote Gaura area west of Lamboya (Kampung Ubu Olehka).

Anakalang & Around

Right beside the main road to Waingapu at Anakalang, 22km east of Waikabubak, **Kampung Pasunga** boasts one of Sumba's most

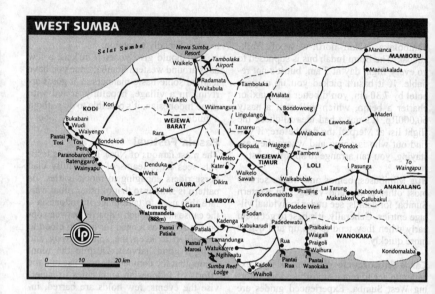

impressive tomb line-ups. The grave of particular interest consists of a horizontal stone slab with a vertical slab in front of it. The vertical slab took six months to carve with the figures of a man and a woman. The tomb was constructed in 1926; five people are buried here and 150 buffalo were sacrificed during its construction. You can see it from the road.

The more interesting villages are south of town. Walk 10 minutes along the road past the market to **Kabonduk**, home to Sumba's heaviest tomb weighing in at 70 tonnes. It is said 2000 workers took three years to chisel the tomb out of a hillside and drag it to the site.

From Kabonduk, it is a very pleasant 15 minute walk across the fields and up the hill to **Makatakeri** and, five minutes further, to **Lai Tarung**, the original ancestral village for the area. The ancestral village of 12 local clans is now mostly deserted except for a few families that act as marapu caretakers, and a couple of the houses have collapsed. There are impressive views over the surrounding countryside to the coast and several tombs scattered around. There's also a

government-built 'showroom' traditional house and some marapu houses. Lai Tarung comes alive for the Purungu Takadonga Ratu – a festival honouring the ancestors – held every year around June.

At **Gallubakul**, 2.5km down the road from Kabonduk, the Umba Sawola tomb is a single piece of carved stone about 5m long, 4m wide and nearly 1m thick. You'll be asked to sign in and pay 1000Rp to take photos.

Market days at Anakalang are Wednesday and Saturday.

Getting There & Away Regular minibuses run between Waikabubak and Anakalang (fewer after 1 pm) or buses to Waingapu can drop you on the highway.

South of Waikabubak

The Wanokaka district, centred on Waigalli about 20km south of Waikabubak, has numerous traditional kampungs and is the scene of one of the March Pasolas. The Watu Kajiwa tomb in **Praigoli** is said to be one of the oldest in the area. **Kampung Sodan** is the centre for the Lamboya Pasola (further west), but fire destroyed the village some years ago and it is not of interest as a traditional village.

The south coast has some fine beaches. **Pantai Rua** has a beach with swimming spots, but the best beaches and surf in the area are at **Ngihiwatu** and further west at **Pantai Marosi** near Lamandunga – you need a vehicle to get there.

Homestay Mete Bulu is at Watukarere, 1.5km from Pantai Marosi on foot. It has very basic rooms for 15,000Rp including meals. The *Homestay Ahong* is on the beach in the village of Rua. The *Sumba Reef Lodge* is an exclusive hotel on the south coast that never really got off the ground.

Getting There & Away

Wanokaka district buses run south-east to Waigalli from where it is a 5km walk to Praigoli. Lamboya district buses cover the towns of the south-west and run through Padede Watu to Kadenga, Kabukarudi and Walakaka, but they don't usually run to the beaches. Buses leave roughly ever hour throughout the day from Waikabubak.

By far the best way to visit the area is by car or motorcycle. Most roads are sealed and traffic is light. The hills south of Waikabubak are a very taxing ride for cyclists.

Kodi

Kodi is the westernmost region of Sumba, and the small town of Bondokodi, about 2km from the coast, is the centre of this district. The Kodi area offers plenty of attractions: villages with incredible, high-peaked houses and unusual megalithic tombs; long, white sand beaches with waves pounding off coral reefs; and the opportunity to see or buy some fascinating local wood, bone and horn carvings. If you're on foot, you won't see much of the region unless you stay a couple of days.

The biggest **market** in the region is at Kori, held every Wednesday; to get there, people from around the region hang off any vehicle they can get hold of, so it must be good. A couple of buses run from Bondokodi in the morning, before 8 am.

Pero

Pero is a friendly coastal village situated on spectacular coastline just a few kilometres from Bondokodi.

To visit traditional kampungs, go either north or south along the coast. To get to **Ratenggaro**, first cross the freshwater pool that runs to the coast below Pero. At low tide you can wade across; otherwise, small boys will get you across in canoes. From the other side, follow the dirt track for about 3km along Pantai Radukapal, a long stretch of white sand beach, until you come to the fenced kampung of Ratenggaro. It is possible to stay with the kepala desa.

The view from Ratengaro along the coastline is breathtaking – coconut palms fringe the shoreline and the high roofs of Wainyapu peep out above the trees across the river. On the near side of the river mouth, unusual stone tombs occupy a small headland. To get to **Wainyapu**, you'll probably have to wade across the river at low tide.

On the way to Ratenggaro you'll probably notice the roofs of **Kampung Paranobaroro** through the trees, about 1km inland. The houses there have even higher roofs, stone statues, and there is an elaborate example with pig jaws and numerous buffalo horns hanging from its verandah. During the day, only women and children are in the village – women are often weaving and happy to chat.

Another way to reach Paranobaroro is to head south from Bondokodi market for about 1km and take a dirt road to the right past the school. Keep forking right towards the coast; you'll reach Paranobaroro after about 2km.

To reach **Tosi**, about 6km north and the scene of the Kodi Pasola in February, head north from Bondokodi market along the paved road. If you are coming from Pero, it's simply left at the T-intersection. About 1km along the road you'll see a track on your left. Follow it for 5km, past a series of tombs. Many people report aggression here, so perhaps bypass the village itself and take a 10 minute walk to the beach. From there a track runs all the way back to Pero.

Place to Stay *Homestay Stori* in the centre of Pero is clean and cosy. The cost is 13,000Rp per person, including three meals. At night, an impromptu art shop may set up on the front porch. The carvings of bone, horn, wood and stone are unique to the area.

Getting There & Away From Waikabubak there are direct buses to Waitabula and frequent bemos and trucks from there.

Waitabula

This sleepy market town, on the main highway between Tambolaka airport and Waikabubak, is a transit point with frequent connections to Bondokodi/Pero, Waikelo and Waikabubak. Direct buses run all the way to Waingapu. *Losmen Anggrek* is on the main road opposite the Catholic church. There is no sign – ask for Ibu Imanudu if you draw a blank. Well kept rooms at the back cost 8000Rp per person or 10,000Rp with attached mandi. Meals are not provided, but Waitabula has a couple of basic *warungs* in the centre of town. Bemos to the airport are 500Rp.

Waikelo

This small, predominantly Muslim town north of Waitabula is the main port for West Sumba. Although there are rumours of a planned Pelni service to Bima starting operation, as yet only cargo ships go to other ports in Nusa Tenggara.

The town has a superb beach and you can find relative solitude if you walk west around the bay. Regular buses and bemos run between Waikelo and Waitabula and a few continue on to Waikabubak. *Newa Sumba Resort (Jakarta ☎ 525 1685)* is a mid-range resort 3km east of Waikelo down a rough road, or it is slightly closer to the airport along an equally rough road. Bungalows are very comfortable and attractive, but overpriced at US$45/60 to US$75/90 – expect discounts. The resort is on a fine stretch of beach and has a restaurant, but because of its isolation and lack of a telephone it rarely gets any guests.

West Timor

Kupang is the main city and is very Indonesian, with its buzzing streets and honking horns. West Timor is not touristy, although it's very scenic with some traditional areas in the south-west that are off the track and worth exploring. New interest for travellers was added to the island of Timor in 1989 when East Timor, a former Portuguese colony, was opened up to foreign tourists for the first time since Indonesia invaded in 1975. In August 1999, in a United Nations sponsored referendum, the people of East Timor (including the enclave of Oucussi situated within West Timor) voted in favour of independence. See the East Timor chapter for more information.

West Timor's landscape is unique, with its spiky lontar palms, rocky soils and central mountains dotted with villages of beehive-shaped huts. It has some fantastic coastline and rugged, scenic mountains. There are no tourist-type beach spots yet, though you can take trips from Kupang to nearby islands for swimming and snorkelling.

The island of Timor is 60% mountainous; Tatamailu is the highest peak and stands at 2963m. Along the north coast, the mountains slope right into the sea. Aggravated by dry winds from northern Australia, the dry season is distinct and results in hunger and water shortages. To remedy the water problem, there is an intensive program of small dam building. Maize is the staple crop, but coffee and dry rice are important and some irrigated rice is grown in the river valleys.

Thanks to Merpati's twice weekly flights between Kupang and Darwin, more travellers to/from Australia are passing through Timor. There are also interesting options for onward travel from Kupang on to Roti, Sabu and Sumba.

Apart from Kupang (one of the largest and most prosperous towns in Nusa Tenggara), West Timor is poor. It has a population of 1.3 million and East Timor about 850,000. Much of West Timor is still very traditional. Modern Indonesian education has permeated the towns, but elsewhere Bahasa Indonesia may not even be spoken.

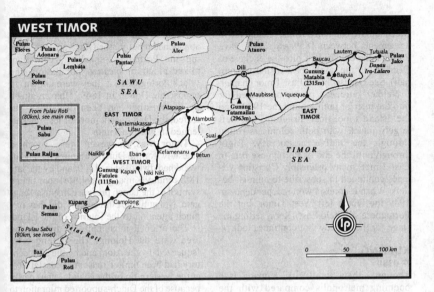

Small children may even cry at the sight of an *orang putih* (foreigner).

Christianity is widespread, though still fairly superficial in some rural areas; the old animistic cultures have not completely disappeared. In the hills of the centre, villagers still defer to their traditional chiefs. In the mountain areas, traditional ikat dress is common, and betel nut and *tuak* (village liquor) are still preferred. On the southern coast of central West Timor and East Timor, it is rumoured that internecine wars between tribes continue and the occasional head is still taken.

About 14 languages are spoken on the island, both Malay and Papuan types, though Tetum (the language of the people thought to have first settled in Timor in the 14th century) is understood in most parts.

History

The Tetum of central Timor are one of the largest ethnic groups on the island. Before the Portuguese and Dutch colonisation, they were fragmented into dozens of small states. Skirmishes between them were frequent, with head-hunting a popular activity,

although when peace was restored, the captured heads were kindly returned to the kingdom from which they came.

The Atoni group are thought to be the earliest inhabitants of Timor. A theory is that they were pushed westward by the Tetum. The Atoni form the predominant population of West Timor and, like the Tetum, were divided into numerous small kingdoms before the arrival of Europeans. It's thought that their traditional political and religious customs were strongly influenced by Hinduism, possibly due to visits by Javanese traders, but they held to strong animist beliefs.

The first Europeans in Timor were the Portuguese, perhaps as early as 1512, the year after they captured Melaka. Like Chinese and western Indonesian traders before them, the Portuguese found the island a plentiful source of sandalwood (prized in Europe for its aroma and for the medicinal santalol made from the oil). In the mid-17th century the Dutch occupied Kupang, Timor's best harbour, beginning a long conflict for control of the sandalwood trade. In the mid-18th century the Portuguese withdrew to the eastern half of Timor. The division of the island between the two colonial powers, worked out in agreements between 1859 and 1913, gave Portugal the eastern half plus the enclave of Oecussi (on the north coast of the western half). See Oecussi in the East Timor chapter.

Neither European power penetrated far into the interior until around the 1920s and the island's political structure was left largely intact, with both colonisers ruling through the native aristocracy. Right through until the end of Portuguese rule in East Timor, many ostensibly Christian villages continued to subscribe to animist beliefs. When Indonesia won independence in 1949 the Dutch left West Timor, but the Portuguese still held East Timor, setting the stage for the tragedy that continues today.

KUPANG
☎ 0380

Though only a small city, Kupang is a booming metropolis compared with the overgrown villages that pass for towns in other parts of Nusa Tenggara. It is the capital of East Nusa Tenggara (Nusa Tenggara Timur, NTT) Province, which covers West Timor, Roti, Sabu, the Solor and Alor archipelagos, Sumba, Flores and Komodo. As such it comes equipped with footpaths, brightly coloured bemos with sophisticated sound systems and a nightlife of sorts.

The city centre is busy, noisy and untidy; the wealthier residential areas are in the suburbs; and the eastern outskirts are experiencing a building boom of oversized government buildings.

Merpati's twice weekly flights between Darwin and Kupang are attracting many short-term tourists from Australia and have put Kupang well and truly on the South-East Asia travellers' route. It's not a bad place to hang around for a few days – English naval officer Captain William Bligh did after being cast adrift by the mutinous crew of his ship the *Bounty* in 1789.

History
The VOC occupied Kupang in the middle of the 17th century, mainly in an attempt to gain control of the sandalwood trade. The Portuguese had built a fort at Kupang but abandoned it before the Dutch arrived, leaving the Portuguese-speaking, Christian, mixed-blood or *mestizo* population (the 'black Portuguese', as they were known) to oppose the Dutch. In 1849, after an attack by the mestizo had been decisively defeated, the Dutch went more or less unchallenged in western Timor.

Timor was, however, very much a sideshow for the Dutch. Supplies of sandalwood had dwindled by 1700, and by the late 18th century Kupang was little more than a symbol of the Dutch presence in Nusa Tenggara. Not until the 20th century did they pay much attention to the interior of the island.

The original inhabitants of the Kupang area were the Helong. The Helong were 'squeezed' by the Atoni and by the 17th century had been limited to a small coastal strip at the western tip of the island. Later, partly because of the Dutch-supported migration to Kupang of Roti islanders, most of the Helong migrated to Semau (off Kupang).

Orientation
Kupang is hilly and the central area hugs the waterfront. The central bemo terminal, Kota Kupang (or simply Terminal), almost doubles as a town square, though you're not likely to stroll leisurely across it with bemos coming at you from all directions. Many of the shops and restaurants are around here. Kupang's El Tari airport is 15km east of town; Tenau harbour is 10km west.

Information
Tourist Offices The regional government tourist office (☎ 21540) is way out of town, grouped with other government offices east of Kupang. The office is helpful for maps and a few brochures, but that's about it. To get there, take bemo No 10 or 7. Get off at Jl Raya El Tari at the SMP5 secondary school and walk 200m east. The office is open Monday to Thursday from 7 am to 3 pm.

Money Kupang is the best place to change money in Nusa Tenggara outside Mataram.

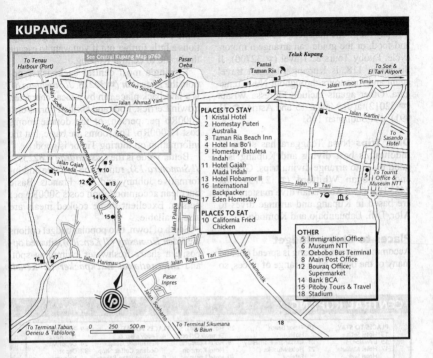

KUPANG

PLACES TO STAY
1 Kristal Hotel
2 Homestay Puteri Australia
3 Taman Ria Beach Inn
4 Hotel Ina Bo'i
9 Homestay Batulesa Indah
11 Hotel Gajah Mada Indah
13 Hotel Flobamor II
16 International Backpacker
17 Eden Homestay

PLACES TO EAT
10 California Fried Chicken

OTHER
5 Immigration Office
6 Museum NTT
7 Oebobo Bus Terminal
8 Main Post Office
12 Bouraq Office; Supermarket
14 Bank BCA
15 Pitoby Tours & Travel
18 Stadium

The Bank Dagang Negara (BDN), Jl Urip Sumohardjo 16, is central, but most banks have good rates. You can get cash advances on Visa or MasterCard from the Dagang Negara. The currency exchange office at Kupang airport is open when flights arrive from Darwin.

Post & Communications Poste restante mail goes to the main Kantor Pos Besar at Jl Palapa 1 – take bemo No 5. You can also send and receive email from there too. A branch post office is at Jl Soekarno 29. The Telkom office is at Jl Urip Sumohardjo 11.

Museum NTT
The East Nusa Tenggara Museum is near the tourist office and is worth a look to see what you're heading into or to round out your Nusa Tenggara experience. It houses a collection of arts, crafts and artefacts from all over the province. Aurora Arby is an anthropologist who will be happy to show you around. To get there, take a No 10 bemo from the Terminal. It's open Monday to Saturday from 8 am to 3 pm. Entry is free, but drop a donation in the box as you leave.

Markets
The main market is the rambling Pasar Inpres off Jl Soeharto in the south of the city. To get there, take bemo No 1 or 2 and follow the crowd when you get off. It's mostly fruit and vegetables, but some crafts and ikat can be found. A lesser market is on Jl Alor, which is 2km east of town.

Organised Tours
Village Visits Many fascinating traditional villages can be visited in Timor but Indonesian, let alone English, is often not spoken so a local guide is necessary. Guides will find

you and will ask around 30,000Rp per day. You pay for public transport, accommodation and food, or the guide can arrange a motor-cycle. Pitoby Tours & Travel (☎ 32700), Jl Sudirman 118, is Kupang's biggest travel agent and runs tours throughout Nusa Tenggara. Other agents include Floressa Wisata (☎ 32012) at Jl Mawar 15 and Astria (☎ 31 991) at Jl Sudirman 146.

Dive Trips Nusa Tenggara has some of Indonesia's best diving and Kupang is a good place to arrange diving trips. Graeme and Donovan Whitford (☎ 21154, fax 24833) are two Australian dive masters who are based in Kupang and arrange dives to Alor, Dili, Labuanbajo and Komodo.

Places to Stay – Budget

Accommodation in Kupang is spread out and many of the hotels have a range of prices, so the budget, mid-range and top end overlap to some extent. There are also some good options a little further out if you want to escape the bustle of central Kupang.

Kupang's most central backpacker option, the *L'Avalon* (☎ 32278, Jl Sumatera 8), is a laid-back place run by a local character, Edwin Lerrick. Four and six-bed dorms cost 5000Rp per person, or the double rooms cost 12,000Rp. The rooms are basic, but the information on touring Timor is good.

Better value is the *Cassandra* (☎ 822392, Jl Sumatera 13), run by the amiable and informative Johnny and Etty Francis. Basic but clean accommodation costs 5000Rp per person. Excellent home cooked meals are also available.

South of town, two popular budget options are *Eden Homestay* (Jl Kencil 6), situated opposite a shady freshwater swimming spot, and *International Backpacker* (Jl Kencil

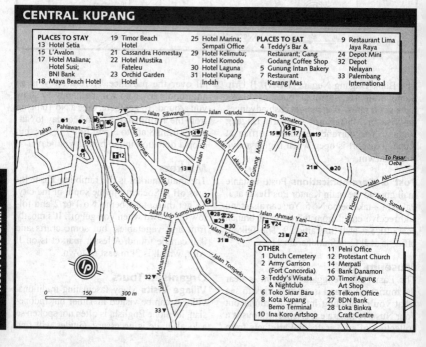

CENTRAL KUPANG

PLACES TO STAY
13 Hotel Setia
15 L'Avalon
17 Hotel Maliana; Hotel Susi; BNI Bank
18 Maya Beach Hotel
19 Timor Beach Hotel
21 Cassandra Homestay
22 Hotel Mustika Fateleu
23 Orchid Garden Hotel
25 Hotel Marina; Sempati Office
29 Hotel Kelimutu; Hotel Komodo
30 Hotel Laguna
31 Hotel Kupang Indah

PLACES TO EAT
4 Teddy's Bar & Restaurant; Gang Godang Coffee Shop
5 Gunung Intan Bakery
7 Restaurant Karang Mas
9 Restaurant Lima Jaya Raya
24 Depot Mini
32 Depot Nelayan
33 Palembang International

OTHER
1 Dutch Cemetery
2 Army Garrison (Fort Concordia)
3 Teddy's Wisata & Nightclub
6 Toko Sinar Baru
8 Kota Kupang Bemo Terminal
10 Ina Koro Artshop
11 Pelni Office
12 Protestant Church
14 Merpati
16 Bank Danamon
20 Timor Agung Art Shop
26 Telkom Office
27 BDN Bank
28 Loka Binkra Craft Centre

To Pasar Oeba

0   150   300 m

37B). Both have beds for 5000Rp per person. Eden's bungalows are basic, but this friendly place has a shady garden and offers meals and cheap tours. International's dormitories and small rooms are more substantial, the staff are friendly and there are meals. To get there from the Terminal, catch a No 3 bemo.

The *Homestay Batulesa Indah (☎ 32 863, Jl Johar 1/5)* used to be popular, but has drifted under new management. Singles/doubles cost 10,000/15,000Rp.

The *Taman Ria Beach Inn (☎ 31320, Jl Timor Timur 69)* is on the beachfront about 3km from the Terminal – catch a No 10 bemo. The beach is pleasant and the restaurant is good. Rooms with mandi and fan cost 25,000Rp per person.

Homestay Puteri Australia (☎ 25532) is down a lane opposite the Taman Ria Beach Inn and is a small, comfortable homestay run by an Australian and her Sumbanese husband. A share room costs 5000Rp a bed and a double with shared mandi is 12,000Rp, including breakfast.

Fateleu Homestay (☎ 31374, Jl Gunung Fateleu 1) is a friendly place close to the city centre. Basic rooms cost 10,000/17,000Rp with fan and shared bath; rooms with private mandi cost 18,500/25,000Rp.

The central *Hotel Setia (☎ 23291, Jl Kosasih 13)* is clean and quiet. It costs 10,000Rp per person or 13,500Rp with mandi.

Places to Stay – Mid-Range

Along the waterfront on Jl Sumatera, a short bemo ride from the Terminal, are four hotels, but the *Timor Beach Hotel (☎ 31651)* stands out for its restaurant with panoramic sea views. Singles/doubles situated around an elongated courtyard are a little dark, but good value at 17,500/22,500Rp with fan and bath, or 30,000/35,000Rp with air-con.

Across the road the large *Maya Beach Hotel (☎ 32169, Jl Sumatera 31)* is the best mid-range hotel in this stretch with air-con rooms costing from 40,000Rp with bath to 62,500Rp with hot water. Nearby, *Hotel Maliana (☎ 21879, Jl Sumatera 35)* has rooms with fan and mandi for 23,000/

28,000Rp, and air-con from 32,000/37,000Rp to 35,000/40,000Rp. The *Hotel Susi (☎ 22 172, Jl Sumatera 37)* is next door and has rooms with shared mandi in its old section for 12,500Rp, rooms with fan from 20,000/22,000Rp and air-con rooms for 30,000/35,000Rp plus tax. Concrete cancer is getting the better of the Susi, but the views from the third floor are excellent.

The *Hotel Ina Bo'i (☎ 33619, Jl Kartini 4)* has a bar, restaurant and spacious grounds. This former government guesthouse is relatively new and its comfortable rooms are good value at 15,000/25,000Rp or 35,000/42,000Rp with air-con. The only drawback is that it's 4km from town – take bemo No 10 or ring for free pick-up.

Clustered on Jl Kelimutu close to the city centre is a group of hotels: the *Hotel Kelimutu (☎ 31179, Jl Kelimutu 38)*; *Hotel Komodo (☎ 21913, Jl Kelimutu 40)*; and the *Hotel Laguna (Jl Kelimutu 36)*. Standards are similar and competition keeps the prices down. The very clean and relatively new Kelimutu is a notch ahead of the pack and has good service. Rooms with bath and fan cost 30,000/40,000Rp and air-con rooms cost 40,000/50,000Rp.

Another option is the friendly *Hotel Marina (☎ 22566, Jl Ahmad Yani 96)*. Spacious rooms with fan and shared bath cost 25,000/30,000Rp or 30,000/35,000Rp with fan and private bath. Air-con costs 40,000/50,000Rp.

Places to Stay – Top End

Orchid Garden Hotel (☎ 33707, fax 33669, Jl Gunung Fateleu 2) is a small hotel with excellent bungalows built around a Balinese-style garden. It has a swimming pool and singles/doubles with hot water, TV and minibar cost 147,400/169,600Rp.

Hotel Flobamor II (☎ 33476, Jl Sudirman 21) is a declining hotel with a tiny pool next to the restaurant. Large rooms are comfortable but pricey at US$26/40 plus tax.

The *Sasando Hotel (☎ 33334, fax 33338, Jl Kartini)* is out in the middle of nowhere about 5km east of town. It is Kupang's biggest hotel and it has a pool, restaurant and disco. It is built on a ridge with great views across the sea. Rooms with all the trimmings, including fridge, start at 90,000Rp. Add 21% tax to the rates, but similarly sized discounts may be available.

Kupang's newest and best hotel is the **Kristal Hotel** (☎ 25100, fax 25104, Jl Timor Timur 59), on the beach, 2km east of the town centre. The beach is not great but this three star hotel has a pool, restaurant and disco. Well appointed rooms cost US$70/80 to US$180, plus 21%. Big weekend discounts apply.

Places to Eat

Kupang has a greater variety of food than most places in Nusa Tenggara, so tuck in while you can.

Visiting Darwinites head to **Teddy's Bar & Restaurant** (Jl Ikan Tongkol 1-3) for a meat pie and chips or sizzling steaks and a great view across the water. The food is so-so, but neither staff nor patrons seem to care. Cheaper and tastier is the **Gang Godang Coffee Shop** next door, with an excellent selection of western and Asian dishes. The Australian owner has an accent as broad as the Timor Gap, a sense of fun and an endless supply of icy cold beer. There is also a book exchange and information on surfing tours.

The **Restaurant Karang Mas** (Jl Siliwangi 88) hangs over the water and is a favourite spot to take in the sunset over a beer. It has seen better days, but the food is OK and the beer is cheaper than at the similar **Pantai Laut Restaurant** nearby.

Around the Terminal, **Restaurant Lima Jaya Raya** (Jl Soekarno 15) has Chinese and Indonesian food and a loud, sweaty nightclub upstairs. When you can't eat another noodle or grain of rice, step into the **Gunung Intan Bakery** (Jl Pahlawan) and sniff the air. It has a delicious selection of pastries, doughnuts and buns. **California Fried Chicken** (Jl Mohammed Hatta) is a KFC clone.

The **Depot Mini** (Jl Ahmad Yani) is a spotless restaurant with good, cheap Chinese food. The **Depot Nelayan** (Jl Mohammed Hatta 14) has Chinese seafood and great ikan bakar (grilled fish), but lots of road noise.

Further along the same road, the **Palembang International** (Jl Mohammed Hatta 54) is packed every night and serves excellent Chinese and Indonesian food, including pigeon and giant prawns.

The **Timor Beach Hotel** has one of Kupang's better restaurants, with a varied menu and an elevated position overlooking the water. The drawback is that it's often booked out with function and wedding groups and the service is slow at the best of times.

You'll see night **warungs** around town, particularly around the Terminal. Try the **bubur kacang** (mung beans and black rice in coconut milk). Some of these warungs sell **RW** (dog meat).

Entertainment

Kupang's nightclubs can be a bit seedy and it pays to keep your wits about you.

The round, thatched bar at **Teddy's** attracts tourists and expats and is open until the wee hours on weekends for a drink in quieter surrounds. Teddy's also has a loud and very dark nightclub attached to the travel agent across the road.

Other seedy nightclubs include the **Surya Disco**, 6km east of town near the beach, and the **Kupang Pub**, which is 4km out on the same road and set back from the road on the right. The **Restaurant Lima Jaya Raya** on Jl Soekarno also has a loud and sweaty nightclub of sorts on weekends and attracts a local crowd.

Discos that are more upmarket can be found at the **Sasando Hotel** and the **Kristal Hotel**.

Shopping

Timorese ikat is colourful and display a huge variety of designs, and there are lots of other embroidered textiles. Purists will be disappointed that natural dyes are now rare in Timor but, interestingly, the tourist trade is starting to create a demand for them. You may also see some at Kupang's market, Pasar Inpres, where villagers sometimes sell their weavings.

Several shops in Kupang sell ikat, handicrafts, old silver jewellery, ornamental betel nut *(sirih)* containers and more. Bizarre hats *(ti'i langga)* from Roti make a fun purchase, but try fitting one in your backpack. These shops also have ikat from other parts of East Nusa Tenggara, including Roti and Sabu. Prices are quite high and bargaining won't bring them down dramatically, but Timorese crafts are hard to find elsewhere in Nusa Tenggara.

Try Dharma Bakti at Jl Sumba 32, out towards Jl Tim Tim, for local craft work. Toko Sinar Baru is at Jl Siliwangi 94, opposite the Terminal, and has an interesting range, but it's hard to shift prices. Ina Koro Artshop also has a good selection and is on Jl Pahlawan, near the Pelni office.

Getting There & Away
Kupang is the transport hub of Timor, with buses to/from the rest of the island and regular passenger boats and flights to many destinations in Nusa Tenggara and beyond.

Air Merpati (☎ 33833), Jl Kosasih 2, has direct flights to Denpasar (803,300Rp), Waingapu (455,700Rp) and Tambolaka (602,000Rp) on Sumba, Maumere (284,100Rp) and Ende (318,200Rp).

Merpati also flies to/from Darwin (Australia) on Wednesday and Saturday. From Kupang the fare is around US$180 one way – shop around the travel agents for the best deal.

Bus & Bemo Long-distance buses depart from the Oebobo terminal near the museum – take a No 10 bemo. Departures include: Soe (5000Rp, three hours) and Niki Niki (6500Rp, 3½ hours) every hour or two from 5 am to 6 pm; Kefamenanu (9500Rp, 5½ hours) from 7 am to 3 pm; and Atambua (12,500Rp, eight hours) and Dili (22,000Rp, 12 hours) at 7.30 and 8 am, and 7 and 8 pm. Bemos to villages around Kupang go from the central terminal, Kota Kupang.

Boat Pelni ships depart from Tenau, 10km south-west of Kupang (1000Rp, bemo No 12). Ferries leave from Bolok, 13km south-west of Kupang (1500Rp, bemo No 13).

Pelni (☎ 22646) is at Jl Pahlawan 3, near the waterfront. Pelni's *Dobonsolo* runs directly from Bali to Kupang, and on to Dili, Kota Ambon and Irian Jaya. The *Awu* sails from Kupang to Ende, Waingapu, Kalabahi and Dili. The *Sirimau* sails between Kupang and Larantuka and Ujung Pandang. The *Pangrango* sails from Kupang to Ujung Pandang, via Roti, Sabu, Ende, Waingapu and Labuanbajo. It returns via the same ports.

Perum ASDP is Nusa Tenggara Timur's major ferry company, with passenger/car ferries operating throughout the province. The ferry schedules are subject to change, but unfortunately the Kupang office has closed and you'll have to go to Bolok harbour to get the latest sailing times. The better tourist hotels in Kupang have the latest schedules. Buy tickets at the harbour at least half an hour before departure – the ticket windows can get very crowded. Perum currently has ferries from Bolok to: Larantuka (22,000Rp, 14 hours) on Tuesday, Thursday and Sunday afternoons; Kalabahi (24,000Rp, 16 hours) on Tuesday and Saturday; and Ende (18,500Rp, 16 hours) on Monday and Friday. The Ende ferry continues on to Waingapu.

Daily ferries to Roti (8500Rp, four hours) leave from Bolok. The scheduled departure is at 7 am, but they invariably leave around 8 am. Ferries also go from Kupang, and Pulau Sabu and Pulau Ndau off the Timor coast (see the Roti & Sabu section later in this chapter).

Getting Around
To/From the Airport Kupang's El Tari airport is 15km east of the town centre. Taxis from the airport cost a fixed 22,500Rp, or 15,000Rp to the airport. By public transport, turn left out of the terminal and walk 1km to the junction with the main highway, from where bemos to town cost 1000Rp. Going to the airport take bemo No 14 or 15 to the junction and then walk.

Bemo Around town, bemos cost a standard 500Rp and are fast, efficient, brightly painted and incredibly noisy – drivers like the bass high and a multi-speaker stereo system is *de rigueur*. They stop running by 9 pm.

Kupang is too spread out to do much walking. The hub of bemo routes is the Kota Kupang terminal, usually just called 'Terminal'. Bemos are numbered, with the main bemo routes as follows:

Nos 1 & 2 Kuanino-Oepura passing the following hotels: Maya; Maliana; Timor Beach; Fateleu; Orchid Garden; Marina; and Flobamor

No 3 Aimona-Bakunase to Eden Homestay and Backpackers

No 5 Oebobo-Airnona-Bakunase passing the main post office

No 6 Oebobo-Oebufu to the stadium but not to the bus terminal

No 10 Kelapa Lima-Walikota from the Terminal to the Taman Ria Beach Hotel, tourist information office and Oebobo bus terminal

No 12 Tenau

No 13 Bolok

Nos 14 & 15 Penfui (useful for getting to the airport)

No 17 Tarus to Pantai Lasiana

Car & Motorcycle It's possible to rent a car with a driver for around 100,000Rp or a motorcycle for 25,000Rp per day. Ask at your hotel or travel agent. Teddy's taxis charge 10,000Rp for destinations in town, 15,000Rp to the airport and 20,000Rp to Bolok harbour. Chartering around town costs 15,000Rp per hour (minimum two hours).

AROUND KUPANG
Pulau Semau

Semau is visible to the west of Kupang and has some decent beaches where you can snorkel. Though not one of Asia's great island paradises, it makes a pleasant day trip from Kupang. International Backpacker, Eden Homestay and Taman Ria Beach Inn can arrange trips (see Places to Stay in the Kupang section), as do local tour companies. A day trip will cost about 25,000Rp, including lunch. Irregular local boats go from Namosaen village, west of Kupang. Teddy's Bar in Kupang has some run-down bungalows on the island costing 60,000Rp to 100,000Rp, including meals. *Flobamor Bungalows* is a better choice, with substantial rooms for 125,000Rp a day including meals. Hotel Flobamor II in Kupang han-

dles bookings and can arrange diving and fishing trips from Semau.

Pulau Kera

Pulau Kera (Monkey Island) is the blob of trees and sand that is visible from Kupang. This small and uninhabited island has sandy beaches and clear water. Taman Ria Beach Inn, L'Avalon and some of the other homestays organise day trips, or talk to the people operating the fishing boats.

Beaches

Kupang's beaches are grubby, but get better the further you go from town. The beach at Taman Ria is 3km from the town centre and is OK, or keep heading out to **Pantai Lasiana**, which is about 10km east of Kupang by bemo No 17. It's in a lovely setting but is a busy picnic spot on weekends, when drink and snack stalls and litter are the order of the day. Outside the wet season, the water is clear.

There are great beaches near Tablolong, 27km south-west of Kupang. From the village, head south-west around the headland and walk along and find your own deserted beach, such as **Air Cina**, a beautiful stretch of white sand. Air Cina can also be reached via a dirt track that turns off the main road 3km before Tablolong. Bring plenty of food and water, and check when the last bemo goes back to Kupang.

Oenesu

This waterfall lies off the Kupang-Tablolong road. The turn-off is 13km from Kupang near Tapa village, which is serviced by regular bemos from Tabun. From the main road you'll have to walk 2.5km to the falls. Take the road to Sumlili and past the Imanuel Church is the turn to the falls, which is 800m away along a rough road.

Baun

A small village 30km south-east of Kupang in the hilly Amarasi district, Baun is an ikat-weaving centre with a few Dutch buildings. You can visit the *rumah raja*, the last rajah's house, which is now occupied by his widow. She loves to chat to foreigners and will show you her weavings and rose garden. Market day in Baun is Saturday. From Baun to the south coast is a solid day's hike; there's a good surf beach down there.

To get to Baun, take a bemo from Kupang's Terminal Sikamuna or Pasar Inpres.

Sandalwood Factory

One kilometre past Oesapa, take the turn-off to the airport (Jl Adisucipto) and just around the corner is the CV Horas sandalwood factory. This small factory processes the wood into pulp, which is then made into oil at the Tropical Oil factory in Batuplat, south-west of Kupang. The second factory is probably more interesting, but it cannot be visited. After you have sniffed a lump of sandalwood and seen the woodchip machine you can buy souvenirs at the office – sandalwood oil, pens, rosaries and small statues carved in Bali. The factory is open Monday to Saturday from 8 am to 4 pm.

Noelbaki

At the Km 17 mark on the Kupang-Soe road, take the left turn and then turn left again over the ramshackle bridge. *Hotel Noelbaki* (☎ *23302*) is 300m along this road and is a little oasis in the dry landscape. Owned by Teddy's Bar in Kupang, it has a tiny swimming pool, bar and satellite TV showing the latest football or cricket matches from Australia. Simple rooms are A$18, deluxe rooms are A$26 with fan or A$32 with air-con, and backpackers accommodation is planned. Tours can be arranged.

Oebelo

Oebelo is 22km from Kupang on the Soe road and is where Pak Pah and his family have set up a workshop (look for the Home Industri Sasando sign) producing the traditional 20 stringed Rotinese instrument, the *sasando* (featured on the 5000Rp note). They also make the Rotinese lontar-leaf hat, ti'i langga. If you're interested, Pak Pah will play the Rotinese version of *Waltzing Matilda* for you. **Oesau** is another 6km down the road and has a war memorial dedicated to the 2/40th Australian Infantry Battalion.

CAMPLONG

From Oesau the road to Soe winds up the hills to Camplong, which is a cool, quiet hill town, 46km from Kupang. One kilometre from town, towards Soe on the highway, the **Taman Wisata Camplong** is a forest reserve that has some caves and a spring-fed swimming pool. It's a tough 7km walk to **Gunung Fatuleu**, which attracts botanists interested in the unique montane flora found on the slopes.

The Camplong convent at the reserve, *Wisma Oe Mat Honis* (☎ *50006*), has excellent rooms for 10,000Rp per person. See Sister Krista, who can also arrange all your meals for a donation (around 15,000Rp per day is appropriate).

Camplong is at the edge of the Dawan territory and 5km further towards Soe and is where you'll see the first of many Dawan houses.

Regular buses run from Kupang's Oebobo terminal (2000Rp) to Camplong and on to Soe.

SOE
☎ 0388

The road from Kupang passes through rugged, scenic hill country that is reminiscent of the Australian bush, to the regional centre of Soe. At an elevation of 800m, it's cool at night but hot enough for shorts and T-shirts during the day. Soe is an excellent base for side trips to traditional villages and colourful markets around the area. Soe itself is a dull sprawl of modern houses but has a large market, where you'll see people in their traditional garb.

Like most of rural Timor, the Soe district is poor. Australian aid projects in the area include building dams to cope with the water shortages and health education programs.

Outside Soe, you'll see the beehive-shaped houses (*ume kebubu*), which give the region a distinctive character. With no windows and only a metre high doorway, lopo are small and smoky and the authorities have instituted a program to replace them. The locals, however, consider their new houses unhealthy, as they're cold, so they construct new lopo behind the approved houses. Ume kebubu are

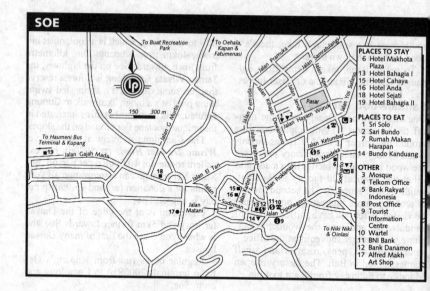

```
SOE
```

To Buat Recreation Park
To Oehala, Kapan & Fatumenasi
To Haumeni Bus Terminal & Kupang
Jalan Gajah Mada
To Niki Niki & Oinlasi

0   150   300 m

Jalan Pramuka
Jalan Samratulangi
Jalan G. Murtis
Jalan Pemuda
Jalan Jeruk
Jalan Kihajar Dewantara
Jalan Hayam Wuruk
Jalan Yos Sudarso
Pasar
Jalan Ketumbar
Jalan Merdeka
Jalan Brahmana
Jalan Proklamasi
Jalan Soeharto
Jalan El Tari
Jalan Kartini
Jalan Sudirman
Jalan Diponegoro
Jalan Matani

PLACES TO STAY
6 Hotel Makhota Plaza
13 Hotel Bahagia I
15 Hotel Cahaya
16 Hotel Anda
18 Hotel Sejati
19 Hotel Bahagia II

PLACES TO EAT
1 Sri Solo
2 Sari Bundo
7 Rumah Makan Harapan
14 Bundo Kanduang

OTHER
3 Mosque
4 Telkom Office
5 Bank Rakyat Indonesia
8 Post Office
9 Tourist Information Centre
10 Wartel
11 BNI Bank
12 Bank Danamon
17 Alfred Makh Art Shop

also designed to store grain, particularly corn, which is kept up high, and the smoke from kitchen fires keeps the bugs away.

Information

The Tourist Information Centre (☎ 21149) on the main street, Jl Diponegoro, has good information on the surrounding area and can arrange guides. Pae Nope is a knowledgeable guide who can be contacted through the centre. Change money at the BNI bank opposite.

Places to Stay

The travellers' favourite is the *Hotel Anda* (☎ 21323, Jl Kartini 5). This would have to be the most eccentric losmen in Indonesia, with the gaudy statuary and dazzling paint job at the front, and replica of a warship at the back. Rooms with shared mandi are fairly basic, but the rooms in the ship are cute. The cost is 8000Rp per person or 10,000Rp with mandi. Pak Yohannes is a wonderful host who speaks English, Dutch and German, and is a wealth of knowledge on the area's history and attractions.

If this is full, the *Hotel Cahaya* (☎ 21087) next door has clean rooms for 7500Rp per person, or 10,000Rp with mandi.

Soe has a few mid-range hotels. The *Hotel Bahagia I* (☎ 21015, Jl Diponegoro 72) is the best value and has rooms with outside mandi for 35,000Rp. Singles/doubles with mandi cost 35,000/45,000Rp and VIP rooms are 47,000Rp. *Hotel Bahagia II* (☎ 21095) is on the way in from Kupang and is a long hike from the town centre, but is Soe's best hotel. Air-con rooms cost from 44,000Rp to 87,500Rp and cottages from 150,000Rp to 200,000Rp.

The *Hotel Makhota Plaza* (☎ 21068, Jl Soeharto 11) is a busy place with rooms from 27,500/33,000Rp. The *Hotel Sejati* (☎ 21 101, Jl Gajah Mada 18) is dowdy but cheap enough at 15,000Rp, or 20,000Rp with mandi. The price includes breakfast.

Places to Eat

There are a few good restaurants on Jl Soeharto, including the *Rumah Makan Padang* and the nearby *Rumah Makan Suka Jadi* (with Javanese food); the *Rumah Makan*

NUSA TENGGARA

Harapan (serving tasty, good-value Chinese food – try the *ikan tauco*, fish with sweet sauce); and the *Hotel Makhota Plaza*. *Hotel Bahagia I* also has a decent restaurant. Other recommended restaurants are near the market on Jl Hayam Wuruk, including the *Sri Solo* for Javanese food and the *Sari Bundo* for Padang food.

Shopping

The shop attached to the Hotel Bahagia I has a good but expensive range of weaving and carvings. Bargaining is essential. Toko Timor Sakti is on Jl Diponegoro 70 and has an excellent range of Timorese arts but is expensive, or visit the house of Alfred Makh, Jl Cendana 11, who also has a great collection.

Getting There & Away

The Haumeni bus terminal is 4km west of town (500Rp by bemo). Regular buses run from Soe to Kupang (5000Rp, three hours), Kefamenanu (4500Rp, 2½ hours) and Oinlasi (2500Rp, 1½ hours), while bemos cover Niki Niki (1500Rp) and Kapan (1000Rp). Buses from the east can drop you off at a hotel, as can the evening buses from Kupang.

AROUND SOE
Oinlasi

Regular buses from Soe make the 51km trip along a winding mountain road to Oinlasi in around 1½ hours. Its Tuesday market is one of the biggest and best in West Timor and attracts villagers from the surrounding hill districts, many wearing their traditional ikat. Weavings, carvings, masks and elaborately carved betel nut containers can be found, but get there early. The market starts early in the morning and continues until 2 pm, but it is at its best before 10 am. A direct bus from Kupang makes the trip in about four hours.

Boti

In an isolated mountain valley, 12km from Oinlasi along a rugged mountain road, the village of Boti is presided over by the sprightly 80-year-old Rajah of Boti. The rajah speaks only in the local dialect through a translator and talks with all the flourish of a self-styled potentate, even though his 'kingdom' comprises only some 220 villagers.

Christianity never penetrated here and the rajah maintains strict adherence to *adat* (tradition). Only clothes made from locally grown cotton may be worn and the villagers wear homespun shirts, ikat sarongs and shawls. Boti is one of the last remaining villages in Timor where men let their hair grow long, but only after they are married. Indonesian education is shunned, as is Christianity.

The adherence to tradition is a wise one it seems for the village now attracts a steady stream of visitors, including the occasional tour group. The village welcomes visitors as they provide a source of income.

On arrival you will be lead to the rajah's house where, traditionally, betel nut should be placed in the tray on the table as a gift. It's possible to stay with the rajah in his house with all meals provided for around 15,000Rp per person. Day trippers are also expected to contribute a sizeable donation. You can see ikat being hand woven in the village's cooperative and, at night, there may be performances of traditional dance. Pay at the security post when you sign the visitors' book or place it in the box provided for offerings at the rajah's house rather than handing it directly to the rajah.

The rajah will proudly show you his bizarre collection of name cards and photos. If asked to add to the collection, telephone cards, old credit cards, backpackers' discount cards etc would seem to suffice.

The village requests that you bring a guide conversant with Boti adat, though it is unlikely you will be turned away without one. However, a guide really is essential to get there and to converse with villagers. Only a few villagers speak any Bahasa Indonesia.

Getting There & Away From Oinlasi, you can take a bus south on the main road for 2km to the turn-off to Boti. It is then 9km on a dry, rocky and hilly road. Motorcycles and cars can negotiate the road or it is a three hour walk – take plenty of water. The road crosses a wide, stony river bed that may be impassable in the wet season after heavy rain.

The road passes through the seven gates of Bele village. The system of gates and fences is designed to keep the animals in, for in these parts if a farmer catches an animal eating his crops he has the right to kill it. The amount of crop damage is then assessed and meat is distributed to the farmer as compensation and the owner of the animal keeps the rest.

It is also possible to catch a bus from Soe to Oenai and then follow the tracks along the river for two hours. A guide is essential. Bring water from Soe. Alternatively, you can charter a bemo in Soe; count on about 80,000Rp for a full day trip to Boti.

Niki Niki

Niki Niki is 34km east of Soe along the Soe-Kefa road and is the site of some old royal graves. It has a busy market on Wednesday, which is as large and interesting as the Oinlasi market but easier to reach, being on the main highway. Niki Niki has a couple of restaurants, but no accommodation. Regular buses and bemos run to Niki Niki from Soe (1000Rp).

Kapan

Kapan is 21km north of Soe and has an interesting market on Thursday, when the roads are blocked with stalls. The village is situated on steep slopes, from where you can see **Gunung Mutis** (2470m). From Kapan, some trucks run to **Futamenasi**, which is 20km away and has even more spectacular alpine scenery, or you can take a bemo there from Soe.

On the way to Kapan is the **Buat Recreation Park**, which has a swimming pool, playground and viewing tower (not that there is a lot to see). The government has recently built two comfortable bungalows there, costing US$25 each, but unless you have a car there is little reason to stay way out there. The park is 3km north of Soe on the Kapan road and then 2km west.

Also on the way to Kapan are the **Oahala Falls**, 10km from Soe. The Kapan buses will drop you on the highway, from where it is a 2.5km walk to the falls.

Kolbano

The village of Kolbano is on the south coast 110km from Soe and has white sand beaches and good surf between May and August. The easiest access is by bus from Noilmina on the Kupang-Soe road (about six hours over a decent road). From Soe, there are regular buses to Se'i along a twisting, dipping road that goes through isolated communities. Se'i buses sometimes continue on to Kolbano. A joint Australian-US-Indonesian oil research project has begun in the area.

KEFAMENANU

Kefamenanu is 217km from Kupang and is cool and quiet, with some pleasant walks to the surrounding hills. The town is very Catholic and has a few impressive churches. It's known as 'Kefa' to the locals and once had a reputation as a place to buy fine rugs. Though this tradition declined, it is gradually being revived. Locals bring around reasonable ikat to the losmen and you could strike a bargain.

Oelolok is a weaving village 26km from Kefa by bus and a further 3km by bemo. It has a Tuesday market. The Istana Rajah Taolin in Oelolok is a fine Dutch bungalow that served as the 'palace' of the local rajah.

Orientation & Information

Kefa is fairly spread out. The old market (Pasar Lama) is a few kilometres north of the bus terminal and is the town centre. The tourist office, Dinas Pariwisata (☎ 21520), is on Jl Sudirman opposite the playing field north of the highway, but has little to offer. The post office is on Jl Imam Bonjol, opposite the market. The Telkom office is nearby on Jl Sudirman.

Places to Stay & Eat

Losmen Soko Windu (☎ 31122, Jl Kartini) is a clean, friendly place. It's a short bemo ride from the bus terminal, but is close to the centre of town. Large, clean rooms with shared bath cost 10,000Rp per person.

The *Hotel Ariesta* (☎ 31007, Jl Basuki Rachmat) looks upmarket, but is good value. Clean doubles with shared mandi are

20,000Rp or 33,000Rp to 38,500Rp with bathroom. It also has a good restaurant.

The *Hotel Cendana* (☎ *31168, Jl Sonbay)* is a friendly, quiet retreat that offers rooms with mandi and fan at 22,000Rp, or air-con rooms for 44,000Rp to 55,000Rp. The staff can help you charter bemos and rent motorcycles.

The central *Losmen Setangkai* (☎ *31217, Jl Sonbay)* is basic and cramped, but cheap at 8500Rp per person for rooms without mandi.

The *Stella Maris* is on the corner of Jl El Tari and Jl Sudirman and has good Chinese food. On the main road around the centre of town are the *Rumah Makan Sari Bundo*, which serves Padang food and the *Rumah Makan Kalasan*, which serves good fried chicken. The *Hotel Ariesta* and the *Hotel Cendana* also serve meals.

Getting There & Away
The main bus and bemo terminal, Terminal Bus Kefa, is a few kilometres south of the town centre. Buses to Soe, Kupang and Atambua leave from there, but the bus to Oecussi (East Timor) leaves from the Pasar Lama, in the centre of town. Buses to Kefa leave Kupang (9500Rp, 5½ hours) early in the morning. From Kefa to Kupang, there are several buses in the morning and a few at night. The last bus leaves at 8 pm from the Rumah Makan Minang Jaya, near the Hotel Cendana. Regular buses run to/from Soe (4500Rp, 2½ hours) and Atambua (4000Rp, two hours). Five buses a day go to Oecussi (3500Rp, three hours) between 8 am and 4 pm.

Getting Around
Within Kefa there are no regular bemo routes; just tell the driver where you are going. Bemos cost 500Rp around town.

TEMKESSI
Temkessi is a traditional village around 50km north-east of Kefa. It has seen few travellers because of its isolation. Sitting high on a hilltop, its only entrance is a small passage between two huge rocks. The village has about 18 families and 25 traditional

houses. The rajah's house sits on top of rocks overlooking the village. There's lots of weaving but little Indonesian is spoken, so a guide may be necessary.

To get there, regular buses run from Kefa to Manufui, about 8km from Temkessi. On market day in Manufui (Saturday) trucks or buses should run through to Temkessi. Otherwise, it may be possible to charter a bemo in Manufui.

ATAMBUA
☎ 0389
Atambua is the major town at the eastern end of West Timor. It's quite a cosmopolitan place; the shops have a wide range of goods and the streets are lively at night. Since the bus route to Dili has changed to the coast road, it's only a three hour journey between the two cities.

Atambua is the capital of Belu Province, which borders East Timor. The district is mainly dry farming, using traditional time-consuming methods, though there are some wet paddy lands on the south coast. Belu has some beautiful scenery and traditional villages.

Betun is a prosperous town 60km south, near the coast, which has a couple of losmen and restaurants. A few intrepid travellers visit the nearby villages of **Kletuk**, **Kamanasa** and **Bolan** – you can see flying foxes and watch the sun set over the mountains at Kletuk.

Information
The tourist office (☎ 21483), at Jl Basuki Rahmat 2, has no brochures and the staff speak no English, but will try to answer queries. Money can now be changed in Atambua at the BNI bank. Most major currencies can be exchanged but US and Australian dollars, and Netherlands guilders attract the best rates. The bank is open weekdays from 8.30 am to 3.30 pm. The BDN bank also changes money.

Places to Stay & Eat
All hotels offer a free breakfast. You can ask the bus to drop you at a hotel.

The best budget choice is the central *Hotel Kalpataru* (☎ 21351, Jl Gatot Subroto 3). Pak Manik speaks English and Dutch and his colonial-style house is an oasis of hospitality. Simple, well kept rooms with outside mandi cost 11,000Rp per person.

Next door, the *Hotel Liurai* (☎ 21084, Jl Gatot Subroto 4) doesn't have the same atmosphere, but is a good hotel. Rooms with share mandi cost 6500Rp per person. Singles/doubles with attached mandi cost 12,500/18,000Rp; newer rooms for 18,000Rp per person are much better.

Hotel Nusantara (☎ 21377, Jl Soekarno 42) is also central. The rooms are OK, but badly need a coat of paint. Rooms with mandi cost 15,000/25,000Rp.

Hotel Merdeka (☎ 21197, Jl Merdeka 37) has reasonable rooms with mandi at 20,000Rp in a big jailhouse block at the back. The *Hotel Klaben* (☎ 21079, Jl Dubesi Nanaet 4) costs 15,000/20,000Rp or the *Hotel Minang* (☎ 21379, Jl Soekarno 129) has large, bare rooms with shared mandi for 15,000Rp per person.

The best of the central hotels is the sparkling *Hotel Intan* (☎ 21343, Jl Merdeka 12). Good rooms cost 32,000/42,000Rp with outside mandi, 42,000/52,000Rp with attached mandi and 63,000/74,000Rp with air-con.

The best hotel is the *Hotel Nusantara Dua* (☎ 21773, Jl Kasimo), which is close to the bus terminal but a fair walk from the town centre. Rooms with bathroom cost 25,000/35,000Rp or 45,000/60,000Rp with air-con. Meals can be ordered and the staff speak fluent English.

The *Rumah Makan Moro Senang* has excellent Chinese and Indonesian food and serves great fried prawns. *Rumah Makan Estry* (Jl Merdeka 11) also has reasonable Chinese food. Atambua has two good Padang restaurants: the *Padang Raya* on Jl Soekarno and the *Minang*, on the opposite side of the street in the hotel of the same name.

Getting There & Away

Bus The bus terminal is 1km north of town (500Rp by mikrolet No 3 or 4). Buses include: Kupang (13,000Rp, eight hours); Dili (7500Rp, three hours); and Atapupu (1500Rp, 40 minutes). Buses to Dili leave regularly until about 11 am and you can easily arrange for the bus to pick you up at your hotel in the morning.

The trip to Dili is quite scenic, hugging the coast most of the way (sometimes closer than you'd like).

Boat The ferry from the port of Atapupu, 25km from Atambua, to Kalabahi (Alor) sails Monday morning at 10 am and costs 8500Rp for the eight hour crossing. You might find boats here to other islands.

East Timor

This is a beautiful land and the Portuguese influence, though fading, gives East Timor a unique character. Dili is a graceful city with many reminders of Portugal. Most visitors only make it to Dili, but it is well worth venturing into the countryside.

The north coast is the driest part of Timor and is almost a desert in the dry season. It has some fine beaches and colonial towns such as Baucau. In contrast, rugged mountains run the length of East Timor and the interior is lush. Old Portuguese forts dot the countryside and former colonial hill stations provide a cooling break from the heat of the coast.

HISTORY

Until the end of the 19th century, Portuguese authority over their half of Timor was never strong. Colonial influence was undermined by shifting alliances of Timorese rulers or *liurai*, who were backed to varying degrees by the Topasses (influential traders of mixed Portuguese and Timorese decent), Dominican missionaries and others wary of Portuguese rule. A series of rebellions between 1893 and 1912 led to bloody and conclusive 'pacification' by the colonial authorities.

The colony's fading fortunes tracked the long decline of the sandalwood trade. When Portugal fell into a depression after WWI,

HIGHLIGHTS

- The charming town of Baucau has fine examples of Portuguese architecture, and gorgeous beaches nearby.
- The hill town of Maubisse makes a pleasant and relaxing break from the heat of the coast.

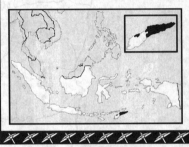

East Timor drifted into an economic torpor. Neglected by Portugal, it was notable only for its modest production of high-quality coffee and as a distant place of exile for opponents of Portugal's Salazar regime. The ordinary Timorese were subsistence farmers, with maize the main crop.

In 1941 Australia sent a small commando force into Portuguese Timor to counter rising Japanese influence, deliberately breaching the colony's neutral status. Although the military initiative angered Portugal and dragged East Timor into the Pacific War, its success in containing Japanese expansion suited Australia's security interests.

The Australians' success was largely due to the support they received from the East Timorese, for whom the cost was phenomenal. Japanese soldiers razed whole villages, seized food supplies and killed Timorese in areas where the Australians were operating. In other areas the Japanese had incited rebellion against the Portuguese, which resulted in horrific

WARNING

In August 1999, following the results of the East Timor referendum, violence escalated, destroying much of Dili and Baucau's infrastructure and leaving many homeless. At the time of writing, an international peacekeeping force Inter-FET is in control of East Timor. Travellers should contact their embassy or consulate in Jakarta or Bali before travelling to East Timor.

EAST TIMOR

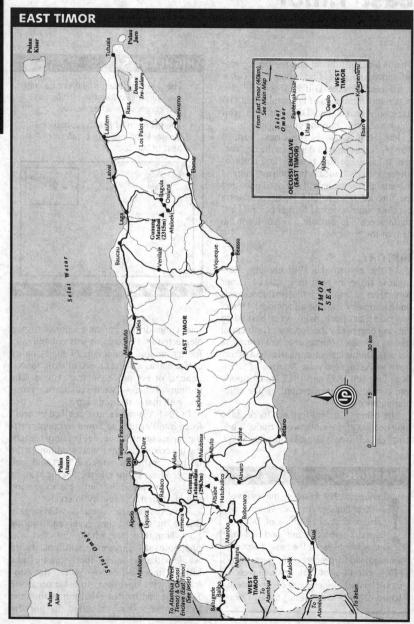

EAST TIMOR

repression when the Japanese left. By the end of the war, between 40,000 and 60,000 East Timorese had died.

The dictatorship that ruled Portugal from 1932 to 1974 suddenly gave way to a bloodless coup in April 1974. The new government set about discarding the remnants of its empire as quickly as possible. With independence now a real possibility, three political forces emerged: Fretilin, which favoured early independence; the Uniao Democratica Timorense (UDT), which wanted Portugal to oversee a gradual transition to independence; and Apodeti, a minor player with no popular support that advocated integration with Indonesia. Fretilin and the UDT formed an alliance in January 1975 and began to negotiate with Portugal on transition to independence.

As the political situation deteriorated in mid-1975, Indonesia signalled that it could not accept leftist Fretilin rule in East Timor. The UDT-Fretilin alliance split and the UDT, fearing the increasingly popular Fretilin would stage a coup, seized power in a pre-emptive coup on 11 August 1975. The ensuing civil war forced the Portuguese out and brought Indonesian troops to the border.

Within a month Fretilin had control of most of the country and proved surprisingly effective in getting things back to normal, but by then Indonesia was preparing for a takeover. On 28 November 1975 Fretilin declared independence for East Timor. The UDT and Apodeti denounced Fretilin's action and declared East Timor's integration with Indonesia. Portugal refused to recognise either declaration. On 7 December, the day after a US presidential visit to Jakarta, Indonesian forces invaded.

East Timor and Fretilin faced Indonesia alone. Despite public utterances about the importance of self-determination for the people of East Timor, Australia signalled its reluctance to 'become bogged down in another futile argument over sovereignty'. Like the US, it seems that Australia had advance notice of Indonesia's plans to invade yet made no attempt to persuade Indonesia to back off.

UDT exiles and Indonesian irregulars spearheaded the well armed invasion force.

The poorly equipped defenders put up a good fight, but soon lost control of Dili and other key centres. Many retreated to East Timor's rugged interior and began a protracted guerrilla campaign against Indonesian rule.

Indonesia 'integrated' East Timor as its 27th province in July 1976, a claim never recognised by the United Nations. The cost of the takeover to the East Timorese was immense. International humanitarian organisations estimate that at least 100,000 people died in the hostilities and the disease and famine that followed. Large sections of the population were moved from the fertile highlands to arid coastal areas for 'security reasons', exacerbating famine and increasing dependence on Indonesian hand-outs.

Integration relied on a two-fold strategy: the ruthless repression of any resistance; and the generous provision of aid. In contrast to Portugal's long neglect of East Timor, Jakarta poured a fortune into health, communications, basic utilities and other infrastructure. Education, virtually nonexistent under the Portuguese, became a priority. Jakarta built and staffed hundreds of schools, a university and a modern polytechnic, giving its new province the best education facilities east of Ujung Pandang.

The guerrilla movement was eventually subdued, but not eliminated. The grim reality for pro-independence strategists was that any resistance against the Indonesian military risked provoking brutal reprisals against the civilian population. Military activity receded and by 1989 Indonesia was confident enough to open East Timor to foreign tourists.

Indonesia's battle on the diplomatic front was less successful. Australia is one of only a handful of nations to formally recognise Indonesia's claim to the territory. In signing a border treaty with Indonesia in 1989 to divide the oil-rich waters between Timor and Australia, Australia's only mention of East Timor's unresolved claim for self-determination was when its foreign minister, Gareth Evans, dryly conceded that 'the world is a pretty unfair place'.

Then on 12 November 1991, about 1000 Timorese staged a rally at the Santa Cruz cemetery in Dili where they had gathered to commemorate the death of an independence activist two weeks earlier. Indonesian troops opened fire on the crowd and East Timor was once again in the world headlines. The severely embarrassed Indonesian government initially admitted to 19 deaths, then to 51, but other reports claimed many more.

UN-sponsored talks on the territory's future continued to languish. Jakarta shunned conciliatory proposals from all quarters, including its own military strategists, the Bank of Indonesia, the moderate Bishop Carlos Belo of Dili and East Timorese independence activists. Tensions remained high. When an Indonesian officer reportedly attended a Christian mass and desecrated the host in September 1995, rioting spread across East Timor as the people vented their anger against the military presence. A similar incident occurred in Baguia in June 1996 and spread to Baucau. The 1997 Indonesian general elections prompted widespread protests and guerrilla activity, including the bombing of an army truck.

In 1996 Bishop Belo and Jose Ramos-Horta, Fretilin's UN representative, were awarded the Nobel Peace Prize for their efforts to find a peaceful resolution to East Timor's struggle. The Indonesian government responded by reiterating its stance that it would never consider independence for East Timor.

The economic and political drama that brought about President Soeharto's removal from office in 1998 finally forced some concessions. The caretaker Habibie government promised a reduction in troop numbers, an end to military business monopolies, moves towards a truly civilian government and a vote on limited autonomy. As a sign of goodwill, 1000 troops were withdrawn from Dili amid much fanfare. However, within months an extra 3000 or more soldiers quietly entered near Los Palos in the east.

In July 1999, Indonesia and Portugal agreed to endorse an August 8 UN-sponsored referendum to vote on autonomy or independence for East Timor. This was postponed to August 30 because of a continuing deterior-

ation of the security situation, namely harassment and intimidation by pro-Jakarta militias. The results of the peaceful election confirmed without doubt that the East Timorese rejected Indonesian rule – 78.5% of registered voters opted for independence. Celebrations were short-lived, however: pro-integrationalists alleged voting irregularites, while pro-Jakarta militia torched buildings and attacked pro-independence and Church leaders. In September 1999, InterFET, an international peacekeeping force arrived in East Timor. See the boxed text 'End of an Occupation, Birth of a Nation' later in this chapter.

BOOKS

Paul Ryan's *Timor: A Travellers Guide* is an inspiring travel guide to Timor and essential reading for exploring Timor in depth. It is hard to find in East or West Timor, but may be available in Darwin, Australia.

Probably the best account of events surrounding the Indonesian invasion of East Timor is John Dunn's *Timor: A People Betrayed*. Dunn was the Australian consul in East Timor from 1962 to 1964; he was also part of a 1974 Australian government factfinding mission to East Timor, and returned in 1975, just after the Fretilin-UDT war. *Timor, The Stillborn Nation*, by Bill Nicol, tends to criticise Fretilin's leaders and places much more blame on the Portuguese. For the inside story from the Fretilin point of view, read *Funu: The Unfinished Saga of East Timor*, by Jose Ramos-Horta.

NORTH COAST TO DILI

The first town in East Timor, 4km over the border from West Timor, is **Batugede**, 111km from Dili. The Portuguese fort has massive walls and a couple of old cannons, but is locked. There's a police checkpoint where you may have to show your passport, but they don't usually bother with foreigners. If you are turned back (this is rare), it is possible to enter East Timor via the Atambua-Suai road.

From Batugede the twisting, dipping road hugs the cliffs around the coast. **Maubara** is 49km west of Dili and has a 17th century Portuguese fort and an impressive church.

End of an Occupation, Birth of a Nation

East Timor's historic vote for independence, in a self-determination process organised by the United Nations, was a rare high point in the territory's bloody struggle towards nationhood. The ballot had been threatened by escalating violence and intimidation by pro-Jakarta thugs, who took over the streets and threatened further mayhem if the vote did not go their way. Yet in a moving act of quiet defiance, 98.6% of registered voters cast their ballots on 30 August 1999. An overwhelming majority of 78.5% opted to end Indonesia's brutal 24 year occupation.

Despite the appalling devastation, looting and massacres that followed, many East Timorese regard their vote for freedom as a triumph. On the day of the referendum, voters emerged in huge numbers, including thousands who had been in the highlands hiding from pre-vote intimidation and violence. By the time the 200 polling stations across the territory opened at 6.30am, half of East Timor's 450,000 registered voters were already waiting outside. By day's end, a huge majority of eligible voters had filed quietly through the booths.

The ballot asked the East Timorese to accept or reject an offer of political autonomy within Indonesia, with Jakarta retaining control of the territory's foreign affairs, defence, national taxation and financial institutions. When the results of the vote became known, Indonesia's caretaker President BJ Habibie promised Indonesia would endorse East Timor's decision to secede.

The majority vote assured East Timor's prospects for independence, but at a terrible price. Militia groups, orchestrated by elements of the Indonesian military establishment, unleashed a reign of terror that killed thousands of unarmed civilians, displaced much of the population and devastated the territory's infrastructure. The scale of violence rivalled Indonesia's invasion and subjugation of East Timor in 1975. No-one was safe. Churches across East Timor initially provided some sanctuary, but even they were attacked as the militia and their uniformed masters implemented a 'scorched earth' policy to empty the territory and flatten its towns.

Within days of the vote, Dili and Baucau lay in ruins and the unarmed UN mission had been reduced to a token presence. Survivors of the many atrocities either fled to the hills or sought refuge in neighbouring provinces. Some were forced to evacuate, many ending up in poorly run refugee camps in West Timor, where they remained vulnerable to militia violence.

A horrified world responded by demanding that Jakarta's fragile civilian administration reign in the hardcore military elements backing the rampage in East Timor. As daily reports of fresh atrocities continued to emerge and starvation threatened the survivors hiding in the highlands, Indonesia reluctantly agreed to allow the UN to intervene. Three weeks after the ballot, an Australian-led international peacekeeping force entered East Timor with a strong UN mandate to take whatever measures were necessary to restore order.

The overwhelming result in favour of independence shocked an Indonesian public which had been kept in ignorance about the humanitarian situation for so many years. Its vote to secede challenged long-standing attitudes about Indonesia's 'liberation' of this remote province.

The territory's ongoing relationship with Indonesia will be a critical factor in determining its longer term fortunes. Despite years of occupation, East Timor can ill-afford to sever all contact with its nearest and biggest neighbour. Indonesia's attitude to the fledgling nation on its doorstep will probably depend on the influence of its reform movement, particularly reformers within the military establishment.

An independent East Timor faces a difficult future. The most pressing task for independence leaders will be to reconcile the divisions created by 24 years of oppressive Indonesian rule. East Timor's vote for independence was just the beginning of a nation-building process.

Brendan Delahunty

It was here, in 1893, that a series of revolts took place, eventually leading to the bloody pacification of the island by the Portuguese.

Liquica is 35km west of Dili and is a large, shaded town with some reasonable beaches. The town has some fine Portuguese buildings, including the governor's office and the hospital. The eastern edge of town has a lively market. There are regular Dili-Liquica-Maubara return buses for day trips from Dili.

At **Aipelo**, 29km from Dili, the *Bekas Penjara Aipelo* is a 19th century Portuguese jail. The walls still stand, but it's in ruins.

INLAND ROAD TO DILI

Until the coast road was completed, the main road to Dili used to go from Batugede inland through the mountains.

From Batugede the road heads up into the hills and **Balibo**, which has a Portuguese fort. In 1976, five Australian-based journalists reporting the war were executed by Indonesian soldiers in Balibo, but Indonesia has never admitted responsibility.

Buses from Batugede run the 40km to **Maliana**, a busy market town at the edge of the Nunura Plains, a fertile flood plain and rice-growing district. This region still produces some fine ikat. Buses run to Atambua in West Timor, usually via the coast, though there is a back road across the border to Atambua via Weluli.

Bobonaro is 20km east of Maliana and is a hill town with a straggling market where you might find some ikat. Just east of town is the turn-off to **Marobo**, 3km along a rough road. Marobo was once a Portuguese hot spring resort. Although the hotel has gone, there is a large swimming pool fed by the spring in a beautiful setting. Further north-east in the hills is the market town of **Atsabe**, and a high air terjun is just outside town. This region also produces ikat.

Ermera is 62km south-west of Dili and is a major coffee producing area. Coffee brought wealth to the town and good examples of Portuguese architecture can be seen, including the beautiful church.

DILI
☎ 0390

Dili was once the capital of Portuguese Timor. Though it had been a popular stop on the Asian trail, it was off-limits from 1975 to 1989 and only now are visitors starting to trickle in again. Dili is a pleasant, lazy city. Centred on a sweeping harbour, with parkland edging the waterfront on either side, it still has the feel of a tropical Portuguese outpost. A number of Portuguese buildings survive, you can sample Portuguese food and wine, and everything closes down for the afternoon siesta from noon until 4.30 pm.

The dry season is *really* dry in this part of Timor, but it makes for some spectacular scenery, with rocky, brown hills dropping right into a turquoise sea lined with exotic tropical plants. To top it off, Dili has some beautiful sunsets over the harbour.

Information
Tourist Offices The tourist office, Dinas Pariwisata (☎ 21350), is on Jl Kaikoli. A staff member, Pedro Lebre, speaks English and the office has some good brochures and maps.

Money The BDN bank, next to the New Resende Inn, and the BNI bank, in Jl Calmera, change US and Australian dollar travellers cheques and cash in other currencies. The Bank Danamon can process credit card cash advances.

Portuguese Dili
Dili was never a jewel in the crown of the Portuguese colonial empire and it lacks lavish public buildings. When the English scientist Alfred Russel Wallace spent several months here in 1861, he noted Dili as:

> ... a most miserable place compared with even the poorest of Dutch towns ... After three hundred years of occupation there has not been a mile of road made beyond the town, and there is not a solitary European resident anywhere in the interior. All the government officials oppress and rob the natives as much as they can, and yet there is no care taken to render the town defensible should the Timorese attempt to attack it.

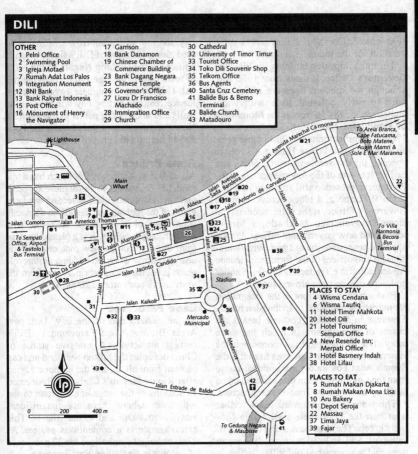

DILI

Despite Wallace's unflattering assessment, Dili has some graceful reminders of colonial rule. Many buildings remain, especially along the waterfront, which was once the preserve of colonial officials and the well-to-do. Many buildings were inhabited by the Indonesian armed forces, which commandeered them after the takeover.

You can take a pleasant stroll taking in most of the sights, preferably in the morning or late afternoon to avoid the heat of the day.

Starting east of the harbour, the old **Chinese Chamber of Commerce** is a delightful Portuguese villa. Dili once had a large Chinese population and its merchants conducted much of the city's trade, though many fled in 1975. The building served as the Taiwanese consulate before the takeover and is now naval headquarters. Underneath the Indonesian crest the original Portuguese lettering has been painted over, but is still visible.

Further along is the old **Garrison**, built in 1627, with massive, thick walls and heavy, wooden-shuttered windows. Portuguese cannons grace the front of the building on Jl Antonio de Corvalho. It now serves as the garrison for the Indonesian army.

The most imposing building in Dili is the **Governor's Office**. It dates from 1960 and, although the modern lines are plain, it is built in early colonial style with wide, arched verandahs. In front is the **Monument of Henry the Navigator**, also erected in 1960 to commemorate the Portuguese presence in Asia and Prince Henrique's role in opening up the sea lanes some 500 years earlier. It is one of the few memorials to the Portuguese presence still standing in Dili.

On Jl Formosa, a block across from the Governor's Office, is the solid, neoclassical **Liceu Dr Francisco Machado**, a former school and now government offices. On the opposite corner are the old **godowns** (warehouses) and offices of the former Sociedade Agricola Patria e Trabacho (SAPT). Similar godowns can be seen around town.

Back on the waterfront is the **Integration Monument**, a memorial to Indonesian rule. A Timorese in traditional costume breaks the chains of colonialism, in much the same tacky style as the Free Irian monument (the Howzat man) in Jakarta. Across from it is the **Rumah Adat Los Palos**, a traditional house from the Los Palos region that has been taken as the symbol of East Timorese architecture.

The waterfront boulevard leads further west past the Portuguese style **Igreja Motael** church. The road runs along the beachside park and is lined with shady banyan trees and whitewashed old villas, which is some of Dili's prime real estate, to the still-functioning old **lighthouse**.

Back in town towards the stadium, one of Dili's major attractions is the **Mercado Municipal** (City Market). From the outside it looks for all the world like a piece of Portugal or South America, though renovations to the interior are modern Indonesian and not *simpático*. The market is a lively focal point and well worth a browse. It has the usual offerings – vegetables, clothes etc – but a few peddlers will sidle up to you offering Portuguese (sometimes Mexican) coins.

Other Portuguese buildings include the simply styled **Matadouro**, the still-functioning city abattoir with tomorrow's *bifstek* tethered alongside. One of Dili's finest colonial edifices is the **Gedung Negara** to the south of town not far past the Balide bemo terminal. This former Portuguese governor's residence features jutting bay windows, solid walls and ancient fan palms in the gardens. Now the government guesthouse, the Pope stayed here on his visit to Timor.

Areia Branca

About 4km east of town, this beach has white sand (*areia branca* in Portuguese or *pasir putih* in Indonesian), clear water and sweeping views of the harbour and the hills to the south. It has the feel of an abandoned resort, with small thatched shelters. It is a pleasant escape from the city, but the new motocross circuit nearby is noisy when the budding motorcycle grand prix champions let rip. A taxi from the town centre costs around 2000Rp.

Cape Fatucama

At the eastern end of the bay, 1km past Areia Branca, Cape Fatucama is Dili's newest attraction. A massive statue of Christ occupies the hilltop headland and can be seen from all around the harbour. Styled after Rio de Janiero's Christ the Redeemer, 14 stations of the cross line the road to the top, from where there are magnificent views across Dili and to the islands. This extravagance is a contentious project. At 27m, its height symbolised the 27 provinces of Indonesia (including East Timor).

There's a good beach around the headland.

Places to Stay

The only backpackers' hostel is the *Villa Harmonia* (☎ 23595), 3km from town on the way to the Becora bus terminal. This friendly, well-run establishment is the best place for information. The manager, Pedro Lebre from the tourist office, speaks excellent English. Singles/doubles with outside mandi cost 14,000/18,000Rp. Food and drinks are available. Mikrolet I (400Rp) run to the Becora terminal past the Villa Harmonia.

The other vaguely cheap options tend not to take foreigners. The **Wisma Taufiq** (☎ 21934, Jl Americo Thomas) has reasonable rooms for 15,000/25,000Rp or 20,000/30,000Rp with mandi. **Hotel Basmery Indah** (☎ 22151, Jl Estrade de Balide), opposite the University of Timor Timur, has large but run down rooms with mandi from 20,000Rp for a double. The more expensive **Wisma Cendana** (☎ 21141, Jl Americo Thomas) is a large hotel with a garden and faded rooms for 75,000Rp.

Hotel Tourismo (☎ 22029, Jl Avenida Marechal Carmona) is on the waterfront and is a Dili institution. Apart from the Villa Harmonia, almost all foreigners stay here, with good reason. It has a good restaurant, satellite TV and a pleasant garden eating area. The cheapest rooms need maintenance, but the others are good. The rooms with fan and shower go for 36,300/45,100Rp or 50,600/59,400Rp with a sea view; air-con bumps the price up to 64,900/75,900Rp, and more expensive rooms and suites are available.

Hotel Dili (☎ 21871, fax 313081, Jl Avenida Sada Bandeira 25) was taken over by the military after the 1975 invasion and badly neglected. Its owners, the Favaro family, finally regained control in September 1998 and have ambitious renovation plans. For now, rooms cost 40,000Rp.

New Resende Inn (☎ 22094, Jl Avenida Bispo de Medeiros 5) is a well appointed hotel on a par with the Tourismo. The rooms with air-con and bath cost from 80,000/85,000Rp to 95,000/100,000Rp.

Hotel Lifau (☎ 24880, Jl Belarmino Lobo 10) takes foreigners but is nothing special. Its relatively large, new double rooms cost 30,000Rp.

Hotel Mahkota Plaza (☎ 21662, Jl Alves Aldeia) is a big soulless hotel that is favoured by government officials. Air-con doubles with shower, TV, phone and minibar start at 85,000/96,000Rp, plus 15% tax.

Places to Eat

Dili has some of the best dining in Nusa Tenggara. One legacy of the army is that East Timor imports cheap Portuguese, French and US wines and Tiger beer directly from Singapore. Wine (tintu) can be bought in Dili's Chinese shops.

Timorese Portuguese food is a real treat; you can get good steaks, stews and salads with olive oil dressing. Dili's best Portuguese restaurant is the moderately priced **Massau**, which is a fair hike from the town centre. The pleasant bamboo decor and excellent food is best appreciated with a bottle of Portuguese wine – bring your own.

For delicious ikan bakar (grilled fish) try one of the waterfront restaurants on Jl Pasir Putih, about 3km east of town: the **Boto Matene**, **Angin Mamri**, **Sole E Mar** and **Marannu** are great places to sit with a drink and enjoy cool sea breezes in the evening.

Budget eats are confined to Javanese, Padang and other introduced fare. **Kaki limas** offer the cheapest food – soto, bakso, mie etc – and can be found on the waterfront near the Hotel Dili or around the Integration Monument.

The **Rumah Makan Mona Lisa** on Jl Alberqueque has cheap and tasty Javanese food – the kering tempe (crispy tempe) is good. The **Depot Seroja** on Jl Alves Aldeia, next to the cinema, has reasonable nasi/mie dishes and cold drinks in clean surroundings. In the town centre, the more upmarket **Rumah Makan Djakarta**, just off Jl Alberqueque, has Indonesian food and a cool interior. For cakes and pastries try the **Aru Bakery** on Jl Alberqueque.

The **Hotel Tourismo** has one of the best restaurants in town with a lovely garden setting. As well as Chinese and Indonesian food, Portuguese dishes are featured. The **New Resende Inn** also has a decent restaurant with a similar menu.

There are a few good Chinese restaurants on Jl 15 Oktober, including the **Lima Jaya** or the fancier **Fajar**, which has an extensive menu and dark interior.

Getting There & Away

Air Merpati (☎ 21880) is next to the New Resende Inn and has daily direct flights to Bali (972,700Rp).

EAST TIMOR

Bus Coming into East Timor on the bus from West Timor, Indonesians are required to show their identity cards at police checkpoints along the way, but they usually don't bother with foreigners.

Terminal Tasitolo, to the west of town past the airport, has buses to towns in the west such as Atambua (11,000Rp, 3½ hours) and Kupang (22,000Rp, 12 hours). Tickets can be bought in advance from agents opposite the Mercado Municipal.

Buses east to Baucau (4500Rp, three hours), Los Palos (10,000Rp, seven hours) and Viqueque (10,000Rp, seven hours) leave from Terminal Becora, 4km east of town. Buses and bemos to Maubisse (4000Rp, three hours), Suai (10 hours) and other southern towns leave from the Balide terminal, 1km south of town. Most buses leave before 8 am.

Boat The Pelni office (☎ 21415) is on Jl Sebastian de Costa 1, which is the road to the airport near the town centre. The *Awu* travels from Kupang to Kalabahi, Dili, Maumere and Ujung Pandang and in the reverse direction. The *Dobonsolo* sails from Kupang to Dili and then Ambon before continuing on to Irian Jaya. It travels in the reverse direction two weeks later. The *Tatamailau* comes from Labuanbajo via Larantuka to Dili and continues on to southern Maluku and Irian Jaya, and then reverses its route. Economy fares from Dili include: Kalabahi for 25,500Rp; Larantuka, 34,000Rp; Kupang, 37,500Rp; Ambon 52,500Rp; Waingapu, 69,500Rp; and Ujung Pandang, 77,500Rp.

Pelni's Perintis cargo ships also have some interesting routes along the Timor coast and to neighbouring islands.

Getting Around

Dili's Comoro airport is 5km west of town; the standard taxi fare is 7500Rp. Buses A or B (400Rp) stop on the main road outside the airport and also go to Terminal Tasitolo. From Terminal Tasitolo the Mikrolet I (500Rp) runs to the Villa Harmonia and Becora bus terminal, through the centre of town.

Dili's beat-up taxis cost a flat 2500Rp around town, but are hard to find after 7 pm. New taxis with meters are also beginning to appear.

DILI TO THE SOUTH COAST
Maubisse

Maubisse is 70km south of Dili and sits high in rugged mountains. Its large market is at its most active on Sunday when villagers come from miles around. This small hill town is an easy day trip from Dili and the drive via **Aileu** is spectacular. It makes a delightful break from the heat of the coast, and you can stay at the fine old Portuguese guesthouse on the hill above the market. The guesthouse is usually locked, but the caretaker lives nearby. Rooms cost 20,000Rp, or 30,000Rp for more modern rooms. Eat in the places around the market.

Direct buses leave Balide terminal in Dili for Maubisse (4000Rp, three hours) between 6 and 9 am. Later buses may finish in Aileu, where you should be able to find a bemo going through to Maubisse. Return buses finish around noon, or take a bemo to Aileu and then another to Dili. Buses and bemos also go to Ainaro, Same and Suai.

Hatubuilico

The road south from Maubisse has spectacular scenery. Just before **Aitutu** is the turnoff to Hatubuilico, the base for climbing **Gunung Tatamailau**, Timor's highest peak at 2963 m. The 15km track to Hatubuilico is rough and there is no regular public transport. Charter a bemo in Maubisse or be prepared for a long walk.

Hatubuilico has a well run government losmen, but no restaurants. Its shops sell basic supplies. The hike to Tatamailau is a steady, long haul to the top rather than a steep climb and takes around three hours.

Ainaro

The trip to Ainaro, 45km south of Maubisse, is also stunning. Ainaro has a large church and a few other Portuguese buildings. You can stay at the *Semar Inn* for 15,000Rp per night and the town also has a few small restaurants. Direct buses run to/from Dili and south to Suai.

Same

Same is also 45km from Maubisse along a scenic route. During the late 19th and early 20th century, this was a centre of revolts led by Boaventura, the *liurai* (native ruler) of Same. There's one losmen in town.

Betano is a coastal village about 20km from Same and has a long, black sand beach. Regular bemos run the 40 minute trip from Same, but there is little to see along the south coast heading east from here to Viqueque.

Suai

Suai is a sprawling town on the move due to imminent offshore oil drilling. It can be reached by road from Ainaro (buses stop either side of a river crossing east of Suai to exchange passengers) and is also easily reached from Dili by a direct bus that goes via Atambua and Betun in West Timor (the quickest route from Dili). There are checkpoints on the road from West Timor, but these are often deserted.

In September 1999 during the militia inspired violence following the East Timor ballot approximately 100 people, including two Catholic priests, were massacred by militia inside a wooden church in Suai where they had been seeking refuge.

Suai Loro (South Suai) is 4km from town and has a spectacular black sand beach and expansive vistas. There's good swimming at high tide, but the currents can be treacherous.

Mikrolet run from Suai's *mercado* (market) to villages in the district, including **Tilomar**, which has an old residence of the Portuguese governor and superb views over the coast. Further on is **Fatalulik**, which has a large, three level traditional house.

Places to Stay In Debos, the centre of Suai, *Losmen Sabor* has basic rooms at 15,000Rp. *Hotel Cendana* has doubles with mandi from 16,500Rp and a family unit for 45,000Rp. The very clean and comfortable *Wisma Covalima* has four rooms with fan or air-con from 25,000Rp.

Down by the beach in Suai Loro, *Wisma Suaidah* has comfortable rooms for around 15,000Rp with mandi. There is a shop, but no cooking facilities. Regular mikrolet run into town or you could hitch a lift.

Places to Eat *Wadang Surya*, opposite Telkom, offers good Javanese food. *Warung Surabaya* next door, is just as tasty. Opposite the market, *Warung Bali* is a good place for a feed of pork with crackling. Next door, *Warung Sinar* has sate and fresh iced juices of avocado, coconut and tomato. Next along, the *Muli* shop sells hot *pao* (Portuguese bread rolls), a nice treat for breakfast.

At the crossroads on the way to Kamanasa and Suai Loro, is the *Rumah Makan Priangan*, the town's best restaurant. It features a changing menu and good chicken and eggplant dishes.

BAUCAU

The second largest centre of what was Portuguese Timor, the charmingly raffish colonial town of Baucau has many Portuguese buildings (of which the Mercado Municipal is the most impressive) and Japanese caves left over from WWII. Baucau once had an international airport, 8km west of the town centre, but until recently it was used by the Indonesian military. The altitude makes Baucau pleasantly cool and the beaches, 5km sharply downhill from the town, are breathtakingly beautiful. To get to them you might need to charter a bemo.

Places to Stay & Eat

In Kota Baru, *Hotel Los Amigos* (☎ 21252, *Jl Kota Baru*) is a basic Timorese-run losmen (no sign). Recently it closed for renovation, but ask for Jose Antonio Suares, who speaks English and Portuguese. Even if the place isn't open, Jose will put you up in his house in Kota Lama for 7500Rp per person. Jose and his sons are fine hosts.

About 1.5km past the Los Amigos is the *Hotel Antika* (☎ 21193, *Jl Kota Lama*), above the Padang restaurant of the same name. This new hotel has well kept rooms with shared mandi for 20,000Rp.

Behind the hospital, *Hotel Bella Vista (Jl Tirilolo)* has magnificent views down to the Kota Lama and across the ocean. Rooms with outside mandi cost 15,000Rp.

At the central *Hotel Baucau* nothing seems to work. The restaurant is closed, it often has no water and service is non-existent. Rooms with mandi cost 20,000Rp. Large and more gracious rooms in the historic older building cost 30,000Rp with shared mandi.

Except for the Hotel Baucau, all hotels provide food. The *Padang restaurant* in the Hotel Antika is the pick of the very limited dining options in Kota Lama. Kota Baru has a few basic *rumah makan*, a long way from anywhere.

Getting There & Around

Dili to Baucau is a three hour bus trip (4500Rp) along the coast. The bus stops briefly at Manatuto on the way. Buses and bemos run from Baucau to Los Palos for 10,000Rp. Bemos around town cost 400Rp. You should check in at the police station when you arrive, otherwise they may come looking for you to give them an English lesson.

AROUND BAUCAU

A good road heads south over the mountains from Baucau to Viqueque, which is near the south coast. **Venilale**, about 25km from Baucau, has Portuguese architecture, a large school and Catholic orphanage. It is possible to stay at the *orphanage* with the nuns, who come from Timor, Italy and the USA.

Around 70km from Baucau, **Viqueque** is a large, regional town with a notable army presence. The very average *Wisma Wisata* costs 20,000Rp per night. You can usually reach Viqueque, which is serviced by direct buses from Dili (seven hours), but the army is unlikely to let you venture further along the south coast.

BAUCAU TO TUTUALA

There's an old Portuguese fort at **Laga**, on the coast about 20km beyond Baucau. From Baucau you can continue on to **Los Palos**,

the main plateau town of the Lautem regency. The traditional, high-pitched houses of the Fataluku people in the area are a symbol for all East Timor and grace every tourist brochure.

The *Losmen Pui Horo Jaya* (otherwise known as the Losmen Verrisimo) is basic, friendly and costs 10,000Rp. The government-run *Wisma Wisata*, opposite the police station, is well kept and good value at 20,000Rp.

You can hire guides in Los Palos to explore the surrounding countryside. The pretty village of **Rasa**, on the main road 11km from Los Palos, is easily reached by bemo and has a number of traditional houses.

From Los Palos, early morning buses go along a bad road to **Tutuala** on the eastern tip of the island. Tutuala is perched on cliffs high above the sea. The government *rest house* (which costs 20,000Rp a night) has breathtaking views along the coast. A road down the cliffs to the pretty beach leads to **caves** that house ancient, primitive paintings.

OECUSSI (AMBENU)

The isolated former Portuguese coastal enclave of Oecussi (referred to by Indonesia as Ambenu) is part of East Timor, but geographically and culturally it is a part of West Timor. Pantemakassar is a sleepy little settlement, and the rest of the population (50,000 people) is scattered throughout the province in traditional hamlets.

Oecussi was the first Portuguese colony in Timor. Dominican missionaries first settled in 1556 at Lifau, on the coast 5km west of Pantemakassar, but it was not until 1656 that it became a colony with a Portuguese administrator. In 1701, a governor was appointed, but was driven out by the Topasses who controlled Lifau. The Portuguese returned, but finally abandoned the colony in favour of Dili in 1769.

The area was not formally part of Portuguese Timor until the treaty of 1904 with the Dutch. In 1911 a rebellion broke out against Portuguese forced labour policies and the brutal Portuguese response sent many Dawan refugees fleeing to West Timor.

The colony was integrated into Indonesia without resistance in 1976. The people are keenly aware of events further east – politically Oecussi is very much a part of East Timor. Portugal neglected Oecussi and so has Indonesia. While the eastern part of East Timor has good roads to transport the army, Oecussi only has one neglected road from Kefamenanu to Pantemakassar and one partly sealed coastal road.

Pantemakassar

Pantemakassar was the first permanent Portuguese settlement in Timor. However, the locals never accepted Portuguese rule, rebelling and forcing the colonists to flee to Dili in 1769. It was later recaptured by the Portuguese, and a fort, garrison and mission were built. Today Pantemakassar is a sleepy coastal town of around 8000 people sandwiched between hills and the coast. It is a pleasant place to wind down for a few days.

Many Portuguese buildings are scattered around the town, including the old garrison known as **Fatusuba**, which is 1.5km south of town on the hill. **Poto Tano** is 12km east on the Kefa road and has a large, colourful market on Tuesday.

There is a good beach at **Lifau**, 5km west of Pantemakassar, which is the site of the original Portuguese settlement. A memorial marks the spot where the Portuguese supposedly first landed on 18 August 1540.

The swimming here is good, but if you are just after a swim **Pantai Mahata**, 2km east of the town past the port, is a better beach and easier to reach.

Information The post office is on the corner of Jl Integrasi and Jl Jose Osorio. The Telkom office is further east, past the fountain, on Jl Santa Rosa. The town has a bank, but it does not change money.

Places to Stay & Eat The town has one hotel, the friendly and clean *Hotel Aneka Jaya* (☎ 2128, Jl Soekarno). Singles/doubles with mandi are 11,000/16,000Rp. The hotel is also an agent for the Dili-Atambua-Oecussi bus. The hotel has a handy restaurant next door or the small, basic *Rumah Makan Sami Jaya* is just around the corner, one block east of the hotel on Jl Merdeka. The only other place to eat is the *Rumah Makan Arema*, which is west of town on Jl Integrasi.

Getting There & Away Five buses leave every morning at 7 am for Dili (12,500Rp, six hours), via Kefa (3500Rp, three hours) and Atambua. Bemos also run east along the coast to Wini, just over the border. The coastal road from Wini to Atambua is in shocking condition and is not serviced by regular public transport, but a new road is being built.

Kalimantan

Kalimantan is the southern two-thirds of the island of Borneo. Of the 12 million people on Borneo, about nine million live in Kalimantan, most in settlements along its rivers. Mountains stretch across Borneo's interior, and heavy rainfall and poor drainage have produced a broad rim of dense, inhospitable wetlands along much of the island's coast and river basins.

Timber and mining interests have penetrated deep into Kalimantan, bulldozing and chainsawing at an alarming rate. Growing pressure for tighter controls over natural resource exploitation seems to have spurred millers and miners to accelerate the pace and make the most of lax environmental law enforcement, as well as to meet the demand for jobs and development. In addition to timber and mining interests, plantation development for palm oil and other cash crops is also depleting the forests. Indigenous Dayak requests to preserve traditional lands have attracted some government sympathy, yet vast tracts of rainforest continue to fall, rivers are being fouled and indigenous cultures are reeling from the social and economic intrusions of the 20th century.

In fact, deepest, darkest Borneo is becoming increasingly remote. You certainly won't find it on the streets of Balikpapan, Samarinda, Banjarmasin or Pontianak, all of which are typical Indonesian cities complete with bustling traffic, department stores and fast-food chains. Travellers in search of unlogged jungle and traditional Dayak hospitality find themselves having to travel further and further afield, often at great expense. There are pockets of accessible indigenous culture, wildlife and jungle close to major waterways – the highway system of Kalimantan – but these are increasingly rare.

The visions of Eden that colour popular imagery of Borneo probably stem from the accounts of early European explorers. Anxious to justify their expensive exploits, they filed reports to their sponsors with exaggerated claims of the island's fertility and great commercial potential. It seemed one could simply clear the jungle and, with minimal effort, grow anything. Later works by naturalist Alfred Wallace and novelists such as Joseph Conrad added considerably to Borneo's mystique.

Kalimantan's unique cultures, unusual wildlife and spectacular flora remain the main attractions for the trickle of tourists with the time, money and energy required to explore this region. Wetlands and mountains provide a buffer to the ravages of development, and it's here that you'll find truly wonderful remnants of pre-colonial Kalimantan.

HIGHLIGHTS

- River travel and the bewildering array of watercraft is a definite highlight, particularly along the Sungai Mahakam.

- The Orang-utan Rehabilitation centres at Tanjung Harapan and Camp Leakey, within Tanjung Puting National Park, are probably the best in Indonesia.

- Samarinda and its river life is perhaps the main tourist attraction in Kalimantan.

- Kalimantan is one of the least visited parts of Indonesia, so it's a great place to get off the beaten track.

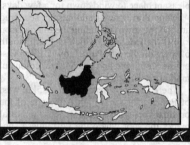

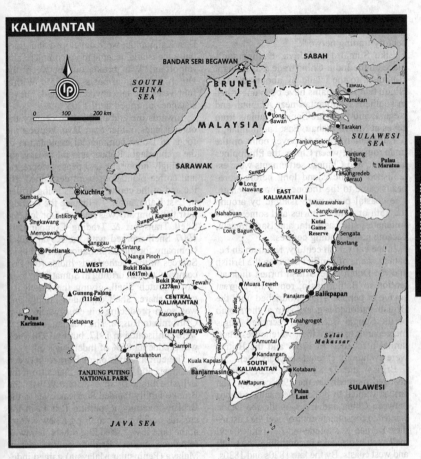

KALIMANTAN

The orang-utan rehabilitation centres and diverse forest reserves at Tanjung Puting National Park (Taman Nasional Tanjung Puting) are a world-class attraction. So too is the river life along the Sungai Mahakam (Mahakam River) and the remote Kayan and Kenyah settlements in the Apokayan Highlands and around Long Bawang. Even in tourist precincts such as Tanjung Isuy in East Kalimantan, where visitors pay by the hour to see 'primitive' culture, there are still many who believe in the old ways. Take a walk in any Dayak village late at night, listen for the drumbeat of a healing or harvest ceremony and learn about the old ways first hand.

HISTORY

Although the pace of economic and social change has accelerated dramatically in recent years, there was considerable activity long before the multinationals moved in. The powerful kingdoms of Brunei, Kutai and Banjarmasin were built on a thriving trade in jungle products and, before then, there is evidence that Borneo was an integral part of the Sriwijaya kingdom's 5th century trading network.

Like Sumatra and Java, Kalimantan's place on the India-China trade axis brought Hinduism to the island by about 400 AD. Hindu temple remains have been unearthed in southern Kalimantan near Amuntai and Negara, and there are Sanskrit tablets from caves at Muara Wahau, East Kalimantan.

Kalimantan was a stopover point on the trade routes between China, the Philippines and Java, and Chinese settlements were established on the island long before Europeans came to the Indonesian archipelago. The coastal ports were Islamic by around the 15th or 16th centuries and some of the sultanates, such as Kutai and Banjarmasin, became major trading centres.

In the early 17th century, Kalimantan became a scene of conflict between the British and the Dutch. The British turned their attention to Banjarmasin, reputedly a great source of pepper. Trade flourished until the British stationed a guard ship at the mouth of the Sungai Barito and recruited Bugis mercenaries to guard their warehouses. Banjarmasin rebelled in 1701, and the British were eventually evicted six years later.

British and Dutch interest in Borneo changed markedly in the 19th century. The British wanted to protect their sailing routes between China and India, while the Dutch wanted to consolidate control over the East Indies. Borneo was a hide-out for 'pirates' and the Dutch had a stake in controlling the south and west coasts. By the late 1820s and 1830s, the Dutch had concluded treaties with various small west-coast states. Parts of the Banjarmasin sultanate were signed over to the Dutch in the early 1800s, but the Dutch didn't establish garrisons or administrative offices.

In 1839 the Dutch were jolted by the arrival of English adventurer James Brooke, who established a private colony at Kuching, Sarawak. With Brooke's arrival, the spectre of intervention by other private colonists and European powers suddenly became a reality for the Dutch. In the 1840s and 1850s they put down several internal disputes and established new treaties with local rulers. New coal mines in South and East Kalimantan were developed and gradually the island became more commercially important. War broke out between the Dutch and Banjarmasis in 1859. Within four years the latter were defeated, but resistance continued until 1905.

Towards the end of the 19th century the outer islands, rather than Java, became the focus of Dutch commercial exploitation of the archipelago. Rubber and oil became increasingly important, and pepper, copra, tin and coffee plantations were developed. By the end of the century, oil was being drilled in East Kalimantan. To finance the drilling, a British company was set up in London, the Shell Transport & Trading Company. In 1907 Shell merged with the Royal Dutch Company for the Exploitation of Petroleum Sources in the Netherlands Indies (the first company to start drilling in Sumatra) to form Royal Dutch Shell, giving the Dutch the greater share. Shell expanded rapidly and was soon producing oil everywhere from California to Russia. The Russian properties were confiscated in 1917, but by 1930 Shell was producing 85% of Indonesia's oil.

The current division of Borneo between Indonesia and Malaysia originates from the British-Dutch rivalry. After WWII the Brooke family handed Sarawak over to the British government, putting Britain in the curious position of acquiring a new colony at the time it was shedding others. Sarawak remained under British control when Malaya (Peninsular Malaysia) gained independence in 1957.

Sabah was also once part of the Brunei sultanate. It came under the influence of the British North Borneo Company as Brunei declined. In 1888 North Borneo's coast became a British protectorate, although fighting did not end until the death of the Sabah rebel leader, Mat Salleh, in 1900. After WWII, the administration of Sabah was handed over to the British government. In 1963 Sarawak and Sabah joined with the Malay peninsula – and, temporarily, Singapore – to form the nation of Malaysia.

Indonesia's President Soekarno, suspicious of Britain's continuing influence in Malaysia, challenged the newly independent state with military confrontations. Long after 'Konfrontasi' was abandoned, anti-Malaysian Chinese guerrillas of the Sarawak People's Guerrilla Troops, originally trained and armed by Indonesia, remained in Kalimantan. The so-called emergency also provided a convenient, officially sanctioned excuse for Dayak people to resume head-hunting.

East Kalimantan has become one of Indonesia's prime *transmigrasi* (transmigration) targets. The transmigrants tend to settle on marginal lands, replacing diverse tracts of jungle with extensive monocultures of rubber and pulp-wood trees. The newcomers also provide the mining and logging industries with a ready supply of willing young labourers. Transmigrants occasionally clash with Dayak groups, whose indigenous land-use regimes and land rights are rarely recognised. In West Kalimantan, this tension has been particularly acute, where violent outbreaks between local Dayaks and Madurese have occurred in recent years.

Not everyone goes to Kalimantan on government-sponsored schemes. A major group in East Kalimantan are the Bugis of southern Sulawesi, continuing a transmigration tradition spanning 400 years. The Kahar-Muzakar rebellion in 1951 spurred Bugis to emigrate from Sulawesi. After the rebellion was suppressed, another wave of Bugis transmigrants joined their relatives in Kalimantan, tempted by the prospect of a better life.

FLORA & FAUNA

The strangest and perhaps the most intriguing inhabitants of Kalimantan are the orang-utans, whose almost human appearance and disposition puzzled both Dayaks and early European visitors. The English Captain Daniel Beeckman visited Borneo early in the 18th century and wrote:

> The natives do really believe that these were formerly men, but metamorphosed into beasts for their blasphemy. They told me many strange stories of them ...

Today, one of the last orang-utan refuges is the Tanjung Puting National Park in Central Kalimantan, which also has a program to reintroduce captive orang-utans back into the wild. In East Kalimantan, the Wanariset Orang-utan Reintroduction Centre in East Kalimantan, was established in the early 1990s for the same purpose, though with a somewhat different approach.

The deep waters of the Sungai Mahakam in East Kalimantan are home to freshwater dolphins; there are proboscis monkeys and crab-eating macaques and crocodiles in the mangrove swamps; while the forest is the haunt of gibbons clouded leopards, giant butterflies and hornbills, including the legendary black hornbill.

The Dayaks traditionally believe that the black hornbill carries the human soul, but because of its feathers and huge beak it was almost hunted into extinction. Beaks and bony humped skulls are still immersed in water overnight, to give whoever drinks the water special spiritual powers. Some Dayaks keep juvenile hornbills as pets, releasing them when they become old enough to mate.

The variety of plants found in Kalimantan is mind boggling; there are an estimated 5000 different species of trees alone, including many belonging to the Dipterocarpaceae family, which make up the tall canopy of the rainforest. The durable ironwood tree *(Eusideroxylon zwageri)* was first used by the Dayak tribes as the foundation posts for their traditional longhouses and carvings. Today the wood is used for docks, boardwalks, boat hulls and roof shingles all over Kalimantan. Botanical creations range from the sublime and delicate, such as the hundreds of species of orchids native to the island, to the world's largest flower, the rafflesia, a corpulent parasitic blossom that looks like something from a science-fiction movie.

POPULATION & PEOPLE

The population of Kalimantan is approximately nine million. The three biggest ethnic groups are the recently arrived Malay-Indonesians who tend to follow Islam and

KALIMANTAN

The Great Fires

Indonesia was the subject of intense media coverage in 1997 when it suffered the disastrous effects of raging forest fires in Kalimantan. The fires pumped enough smoke into the air to blanket the entire region in haze. This black haze reached as far as southern Thailand and the Philippines, with Malaysia and Singapore particularly badly affected. Freak weather conditions meant that the impact was felt not only by the local rural communities but also by urban dwellers throughout South-East Asia.

Some fires were a result of the slash-and-burn agriculture still practised by some of Kalimantan's indigenous peoples. Despite the ban by then-president Soeharto in 1997, this method is the easiest, fastest and cheapest way to clear land. Other fires were started by recent settlers to clear land for agriculture; still more were set by illegal loggers to cover their activities. The ferocity of the fires was greatly exacerbated by the unusually dry conditions caused by El Niño. The unmitigated catastrophe impacted upon the environment, wildlife, human health and the region's economy.

Large areas of forest and peatland were destroyed, which had an untold effect on wildlife and endangered species. The incidence of human respiratory disease rose dramatically in affected areas. Smog caused massive disruption to transport systems. Rain became dangerously acidic, causing damage to freshwater and marine ecosystems. Furthermore, biomass burning is a major source of trace gases in the atmosphere, which contributes considerably to global warming.

The fires burned out of control again in 1998, the second year of what might prove to be the worst El Niño-related drought ever recorded in Indonesia. The lengthy drought affected food supples, worsening the plight of rural communities already reeling from the effects of fires, haze and the Asian economic crisis.

Indonesia has a history of fire-related disasters and concern about the problem is escalating. The Great Fire of Borneo in 1983 was scarcely reported in the world's press but this response is no longer the case. Concern has spread throughout the Association of South East Asian Neighbours (ASEAN) region and around the world. ASEAN has requested that Indonesia intensify enforcement against slash-and-burn practices and encourage zero-burning by the plantation industry.

Fire is a natural, inevitable and often essential part of many ecosystems but fire mismanagement is one of the most serious problems facing forests throughout the world. The events in Indonesia have served to focus attention on this global crisis and to generate possible solutions to prevent a repeat of this environmental catastrophe.

Lucy Williams

---

live in settlements along the coasts and the main rivers; the Chinese, who have controlled trade in Kalimantan for centuries; and the Dayaks, the collective name for the indigenous inhabitants of the island.

The Dayaks

The tribes do not use the term Dayak. Although considered by some to be a slightly pejorative term, it's still the most common word used by Indonesians to designate Kalimantan's indigenous people. The tribes prefer to use their separate tribal names, such as Kenyah, Kayan, Iban and Punan etc.

Most 'Dayaks' were probably coastal dwellers until the arrival of Malay settlers drove them inland to the highlands and river banks. Some also live in neighbouring Sabah and Sarawak. Tribal dialects have linguistic characteristics that suggest Dayaks may be descendants of peoples from southern China or South-East Asia.

Swidden or so-called 'slash and burn' agriculture is the mainstay of Borneo's agricultural economy. Dry fields are cleared then burnt to provide ash to enrich the poor soils, crops are grown for one or two seasons, then the blocks are left to fallow for a number of years. There are also reserves set aside for hunting, traditional medicines and extraction of jungle products such as honey and rattan. Many tribes maintain small reserves of untouched rainforest to provide emergency food supplies during periods of extreme drought.

When population growth puts too much pressure on the land, whole villages may uproot to find new land. One such mass migration was the recent exodus of large groups of Kayan and Kenyah from the Apokayan Highlands to valleys in the Mahakam basin and across the border to Sarawak. The Apokayan's population has dropped from 30,000 in the 1950s to about 5000 today. The introduction of government-subsidised transport and basic services has stabilised the situation, but arable land is still scarce and goods are expensive.

Another, as yet unexplained, migration started in the mid-16th century when Iban groups began to abandon their agricultural settlements in the Kapuas basin in West Kalimantan and move north, most to the Batang Lupar region in Sarawak. The pattern changed again after James Brooke suppressed their 'piracy' and recruited Iban forces to pacify inland tribes elsewhere in his expanding colony. Violent Iban incursions drove other tribes, notably the Kenyah and Kayan, further upstream.

The most striking feature of many older Dayak women is their pierced ear lobes, stretched with the weight of heavy gold or brass rings. This custom is increasingly rare among the young. Older Dayaks, influenced by missionaries, often trim their ear lobes as a sign of conversion.

It was once the custom for all women to tattoo their forearms and calves with bird and spirit designs. Tattooing of young women has almost disappeared, except in tribes deep in

JENNY BOWMAN

A Kenyah Dayak woman with traditional pierced earlobes.

the interior. It's still seen among men, although traditionally men in many Dayak cultures were expected to earn their tattoos by taking heads.

Like those of many indigenous cultures around the world, Dayak traditions and belief systems have taken a beating in the 20th century. Pressure from the Indonesian government, increasing development and Protestant Christian missionaries continue to weaken the backbone of Dayak tribal cultures.

In the past, many Dayak tribes lived in large communal buildings on tall posts above the ground, mainly for defence. For the most part, this tradition has gone by the wayside in the last 50 years, though the Indonesian government has subsidised the construction of many new longhouses after recognising that they had a certain attraction for visiting tourists. There are many different names for longhouses depending on the region, but *rumah suku dayak* is a general term used in Indonesian.

Not all Dayaks live in villages. The Punan are nomadic hunter-gatherers who still live off the forest, although some stay in longhouses at the height of the rainy season and

KALIMANTAN

many have settled in permanent riverside villages. To other Dayaks, the Punan are the ultimate jungle dwellers. As logging and ethno-religious evangelism push them deeper into the interior, they can be difficult to find.

BOOKS

Borneo, Change and Development by Mark Cleary and Peter Eaton is a rich compilation of contemporary research on Borneo and on humanity's accelerating impact on the island. It provides excellent historical and environmental data for researchers or eco-tourists.

The Periplus Edition of *Kalimantan: Indonesian Borneo* by Kal Muller is full of information on places to visit, with particular emphasis on Dayak culture.

A Field Guide to the Mammals of Borneo, Junaidi Payne, *et al*, is another must for eco-tourists.

Stranger in the Forest is an inspiring account of Eric Hansen's six month trek across Borneo in 1982.

Into the Heart of Borneo by Redmond O'Hanlon is an entertaining read, recounting the almost slapstick adventures of a naturalist and an English poet as they made their way to Gunung Batu (Mt Batu) in Kalimantan, via Sarawak. It gives a good account of interior travel.

Travellers to Tanjung Puting will find *Reflections of Eden* by Biruté Galdikas, an interesting read, describing the years the author spent studying orang-utans which culminated in the creation of the rehabilitation centre at Tanjung Puting. Equally absorbing is *The Follow* by Linda Spalding, a recent book that questions Galdikas' approach to saving the orang-utans, as well as revealing some of the deeper problems facing the park.

GETTING THERE & AWAY

Visa-free entry is now possible for visitors entering Indonesia by road at Entikong or by air at Pontianak and Balikpapan. To enter or exit Indonesia by air, sea or land elsewhere in Kalimantan you need to obtain a visa in advance. Tarakan, in East Kalimantan, accepts new arrivals as long as they already have visas.

Singapore

Silk Air has two flights a week to Balikpapan. Merpati Nusantara Airlines previously flew to Kalimantan destinations from Singapore but recently cancelled the service. Check in Singapore to see if flights have resumed. A convenient option is to take one of the frequent jet boats from the World Trade Centre in Singapore to the Indonesian island of Batam (one hour), from where Merpati flies three times a week to Pontianak. Tickets can be booked in Batam through Merpati.

Malaysia

The border post at Entikong became an official international entry point in January 1994 and the same rules apply as at major airports and seaports. To get a 60 day tourist pass (see Visas & Documents in the Facts for the Visitor chapter). It's advisable to have an onward ticket, though no-one seems to check.

There's still much confusion concerning travel between Sabah and East Kalimantan. Flights and boats go between Tawau and Tarakan, but Tarakan is not yet an official international entry point. This may well change in the near future, as it has become much easier to make the border crossing. In the meantime, Indonesian visas can be obtained at Indonesian embassies in Sabah at Tawau or Kota Kinabalu. If you entered Indonesia on a 60 day tourist pass and want to leave this way, officially you should do your paperwork in Jakarta before immigration will let you through at Nunukan. Nowadays, however, it seems that most travellers are getting through without this formality – check with the authorities before making the trip, though sometimes they give conflicting answers depending on where you inquire.

Air Malaysian Airlines flies three times a week between Pontianak and Kuching in Sarawak for US$74. Bali-Air has a charter that flies between Tarakan and Tawau twice a week for 527,500RP, but you may need the proper exit permit and visa.

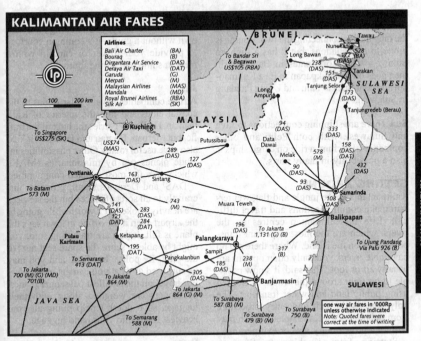

KALIMANTAN AIR FARES

Airlines

Bali Air Charter	(BA)
Bouraq	(B)
Dirgantara Air Service	(DAS)
Deraya Air Taxi	(DAT)
Garuda	(G)
Merpati	(M)
Malaysian Airlines	(MAS)
Mandala	(MD)
Royal Brunei Airlines	(RBA)
Silk Air	(SK)

0   100   200 km

BRUNEI

To Bandar Sri & Begawan US$105 (RBA)

Tawau
Nunukan
Long Bawan   177   528 (BA)
238 (DAS)   Other
Tarakan
151 (DAS)
Tanjung Selor

SULAWESI SEA

Long Ampung
173 (DAS)

Tanjungredeb (Berau)

MALAYSIA

Kuching

To Singapore US$275 (SK)

US$74 (MAS)

Putussibau

289 (DAS)

127 (DAS)

Data Dawai   94 (DAS)   333 (DAS)   158 (DAS)

Melak   578 (M)   (DAT)

90 (DAS)   432 (DAS)

93 (DAS)

108 (DAS)   Samarinda

Pontianak   163 (DAS)   Sintang

743 (M)

Muara Teweh

To Batam 573 (M)

141 (DAS)   283 (DAS)
121 (DAT)   284 (DAT)

196 (DAS)   To Jakarta 1,131 (G) (B)

Balikpapan

Pulau Karimata

Ketapang

195 (DAT)

Palangkaraya

Sampit

317 (B)

To Ujung Pandang Via Palu 926 (B)

Pangkalanbun   185 (DAS)   238 (M)

305 (DAS)

To Jakarta 700 (M) (G) (MD) 701(B)

To Semarang 413 (DAT)

To Jakarta 864 (M)

Banjarmasin

SULAWESI

To Jakarta 864 (G) (M)

JAVA SEA

To Surabaya 587 (B) (M)

To Surabaya 479 (M)

To Surabaya 750 (M)

one way air fares in '000Rp unless otherwise indicated
Note: Quoted fares were correct at the time of writing

To Semarang 588 (M)

KALIMANTAN

Land Air-con buses from Pontianak to Kuching cost 50,000RP and take about 10 hours. Bookings can be made at agencies around Pontianak and at some hotels.

Sea Strictly speaking, to leave Indonesia by sea via Nunukan in East Kalimantan (to Tawau, Sabah), you need an exit permit from the immigration office in Jakarta if you entered Indonesia at a visa-free port (the exit permit isn't necessary if you entered Indonesia on a one month visa paid for in advance). But in practice this rule doesn't seem to be applied as rigorously as it once was. There's no guarantee of getting through, however, if your paperwork is not in order.

Speedboats depart frequently every morning from Tarakan to Nunukan (41,000Rp) and from Nunukan to Tawau (55,000Rp). Buy tickets on the dock in Tarakan.

Brunei

Air Royal Brunei Airlines flies to Bandar Seri Begawan three times a week from Balikpapan (US$105) with connections to Kuala Lumpur and Manila.

Elsewhere in Indonesia

Travel across some parts of Kalimantan is possible only by air or on foot. It's often much easier to go from Kalimantan to Sulawesi or Java than from one part of Kalimantan to another. For example, Pelni boats from Pontianak to Kumai will first go to Semarang on Java then to Kumai.

Air Merpati and Garuda Indonesia have the best connections with the rest of Indonesia, while Dirgantara Air Service (DAS), Deraya Air Taxi and Missionary Aviation Fellowship (MAF) are often your only options on many routes within Kalimantan. Banjarmasin and

Balikpapan are the busiest and best-connected airports but, curiously, Bouraq is the only airline connecting the two. Bouraq is prone to cancellations, but it has a flight to Sulawesi which originates in Banjarmasin then goes on to Balikpapan in East Kalimantan and continues to Palu and Ujung Pandang in Sulawesi.

Sea There are shipping connections to Java and Sulawesi, with both Pelni and other companies. Hitching a ride on cargo ships is also a possibility in many ports.

GETTING AROUND

Kalimantan's dense jungle and flat, wet terrain make communications and travel difficult. Life in Kalimantan centres on the rivers, which are the most important transport routes on the island. Where there are no navigable rivers, your only other options are usually air or foot. That said, it's now possible to go right around the whole of Borneo using public land and water transport. The only snag is the exit and entry procedure from Sabah to East Kalimantan, which may require a proper entry visa or exit permit.

Starting from Kuching in Sarawak (Malaysia), for example, go by bus to Pontianak then take a jet boat to Ketapang and a combination of bus and river travel to Pangkalanbun in Central Kalimantan. From there go overland by bus to Palangkaraya and on to Banjarmasin by public speedboat. From Banjarmasin, a good paved road leads to Samarinda, and from Samarinda take a ferry or bus to Berau, though the ferry route is much more comfortable. The route from Berau to Tarakan can be covered by a combination of bus and speedboat or ferry, and from Tarakan there are speedboats to Nunukan on the border with Sabah.

The area around Pontianak has the best roads, stretching north along the coast, inland to Sintang and across the border to Kuching. Apart from these, and the highways from Samarinda to Banjarmasin and from Muara Teweh to Banjarmasin, there are few continually sealed roads, but this is changing fast.

Chartering a boat or vehicle is common in Kalimantan and if you're doing it on your own without a guide, it's common courtesy to provide your driver or captain with a meal at some part of the journey.

Air

Airline companies have regular flights to the coastal cities and into the interior of Kalimantan. DAS now carries the bulk of the traffic, but Merpati, Bouraq and Deraya Air Taxi also have useful routes. Other possibilities include planes run by missionaries (MAF), which serve the most isolated communities.

DAS' and Deraya's small, propeller aircraft fly to all sorts of places but the services are heavily booked. It's worthwhile going to the airport even if the office in town says the plane is full. If you are travelling solo, you might be able to score the spare seat next to the pilot. Be polite, but firm, and you may be surprised at what you can get away with. For travel on the smallest passenger planes, passengers are weighed along with their luggage, so it doesn't help piling all your heaviest items into your hand luggage.

Bus

Bus services are continuing to expand in Kalimantan as more roads become passable. Check for new bus routes that have been added after this travel guide was published. There are a couple of comfortable air-conditioned routes, such as Pontianak to Sintang and Banjarmasin to Balikpapan or Samarinda. Other than that, most bus trips in Kalimantan are hot, crowded and, well, interesting. During the rainy season vehicles often get stuck in mud holes, which is a good excuse for everyone to get out and help push.

The Bahasa Indonesia word '*bemo*' to describe minibus transport will generally be met with blank looks of incomprehension in Kalimantan. The term for this type of transport varies depending on the region: *opelet*, Colt and taxi are the most commonly used names.

Boat

There are a number of variations on the river ferry theme. The *feri sungai* (river ferry/

cargo boat), also known as a *kapal biasa*, carries both cargo and passengers; the *taxi sungai* (river taxi) carries cargo on the lower level and has rows of wooden bunks (sometimes with mattresses and pillows) on the upper level; and the *bis air* (water bus) has rows of seats. Most boats on longer rides have an enclosed toilet rigged up at the stern.

Along Sungai Kapuas in Pontianak are the *bandung*, large cargo-cum-houseboats that take up to a month to move upriver to Putussibau. A bis air covers the same distance in about four days. A *long bot*, as the name indicates, is a longboat – a narrow vessel with two large outboard motors at the rear and bench seats in a covered passenger cabin. Speedboats commonly ply the Barito, Kapuas, Pinoh, Kahayan and Kayan rivers and elsewhere. Don't get too hung up on the terminology; what is called a bis air in one province may be a taxi sungai in another.

West Kalimantan

West Kalimantan is dissected by Indonesia's longest waterway, the Sungai Kapuas (1143km), which is the main transport artery for rafts of logs and other heavy cargo to and from the interior. Roads and buses are rapidly superseding the river as the main mode of moving people.

The province has about four million inhabitants, including the highest concentration of ethnic Chinese people in Indonesia. The proportion of Chinese residents is estimated to be 35% in Pontianak and 70% in Singkawang. Everything has a Chinese flavour and even the major Muslim festivals are celebrated with Chinese firecrackers.

Beyond the activity on the coast and along the Kapuas, the province's interior is relatively unexplored. There are many Iban settlements north of the Kapuas, and Punan and Kenyah-Kayan villages in the mountainous eastern part of the province. Contact with neighbouring Sarawak is increasing now that border restrictions have been relaxed.

PONTIANAK
☎ 0561

Situated right on the equator, Pontianak lies astride the confluence of the Sungai Landak and Sungai Kapuas, the latter joining the Sungai Kapuas further upriver. The city was founded in 1770 by Arab trader Abdul Rahman Al Gadri, who used a barrage of cannon fire to frighten off the resident *pontianak* (spirits), clearing the way for human settlement. The discovery of sizeable gold deposits north of Pontianak a few decades later gave the young settlement a great economic and demographic boost.

Pontianak is a sprawling city with a giant indoor sports stadium, a large university and two big girder bridges upstream from the city centre. Like Banjarmasin it really needs to be seen from the canals and riverside boardwalks. Charter a boat or walk over the Kapuas Bridge from Jalan (Jl) Gajah Mada for a sweeping view of the river and brilliant orange sunsets.

The road north from Pontianak along the coast passes a number of beaches on the way, including Pasir Panjang (Long Beach), just back from the Pontianak-Singkawang road. The small Mandor Nature Reserve is 70km to the north-east and is known mainly for its orchids. The town of Mandor also has a war memorial for the 20,000 people, among them the Sultan of Sambas, massacred by the Japanese in 1942. South of Pontianak is Ketapang, which is a little south of the Gunung Palung (also spelled Paleng on some maps) wildlife reserve. For most travellers, Pontianak is the starting point for trips along the Kapuas, which terminate in Putussibau in the north-eastern corner of the province. From Putussibau, at the edge of Kalimantan's shrinking frontier country, you can walk to the headwaters of Sungai Mahakam in East Kalimantan.

Orientation

The commercial hub of Pontianak is in the north of town, particularly on Jl Rahadi Usman in the area around the city passenger ferry. Here you'll find several markets, the main opelet (public minibus) terminal

KALIMANTAN

WEST KALIMANTAN

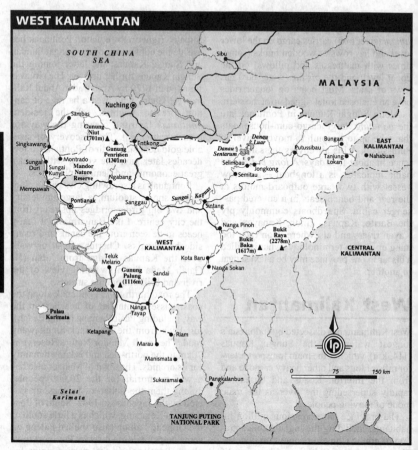

(Kapuas Indah), banks and moneychangers. Between here and Jl Pattimura there are numerous places to eat and shop. A good landmark is the Santo Yoseph church clock tower on Jl Pattimura.

Information

Tourist Offices The Kalimantan Barat tourist office (☎ 36172, fax 43104) is way out at Jl Ahmad Sood 25. It has fine intentions and a few brochures on West Kalimantan, but not much useful information. The big hotels

and private travel agencies often offer better advice. For maps of Pontianak and West Kalimantan try the bookshops on Jl Juanda, such as Toko Juanda at No 32 and Toko Buku Budaya upstairs at No 8-10.

Immigration & Consulates The immigration office (☎ 34516) on Jl Sutoyo, near the Museum Negeri Pontianak, handles visa extensions, but it's easier to take a bus to Kuching and return via the border post at Entikong for a new two month pass.

The Malaysian Consulate, Jl Ahmad Yani 42, is open weekdays. A visa is not needed for Sarawak, nor is an exit permit from Indonesian immigration.

Money Banking hours are Monday to Friday from 8 am to 3 pm. Bank Negara Indonesia (BNI) on Jl Tanjungpura changes most major currencies and its ATM takes Cirrus and MasterCard. Bank Internasional Indonesia (BII) on the corner of Jl Tanjungpura and Jl Diponegoro also has an ATM.

Moneychangers offer better rates than the banks. A couple are located across from the banks on Jl Tanjungpura, or try PT Safari on Jl Nusa Indah III 45 and at Jl Tanjungpura 12.

Sintang and Putussibau do not have international banking facilities. Change money in Pontianak before heading upriver.

Post & Communications For poste restante, the main post office, at Jl Sultan Abdur Rahman 49, is open Monday to Saturday from 7.30 am to 9.30 pm and Sunday 8 am to 2 pm.

The main post office has 10 Internet terminals, with access costing 8000Rp per hour, available Monday to Saturday 8 am to 9 pm. The Tanjungpura University campus, east of the museum on Jl Ahmad Yani, has a cybercafe near the library, behind the big white Rektorat building. Open 7 am to 11 pm, it charges 10,000Rp per hour.

Travel Agencies Plenty of travel agencies book airline and coastal boat tickets but English is not often spoken. Ateng Tour (☎ 32683, fax 36620, email ateng@pontianak.wasantara.id), Jl Gajah Mada 201, is an exception. It also organises expensive tours to places such as Gunung Palung with a couple of weeks' notice. Another large agent nearby is PT Putra Tanjung Angkasa Tours & Travel (☎ 34011), Jl Gajah Mada 212.

A number of travel agents are opposite the passenger harbour entrance on Jl Pa'kasih. Staff at PT Titian Kapuas (☎ 31187, fax 49468), just up from Jl Pa'kasih on Jl Husanuddin at the roundabout, are very friendly and speak some English.

No-one speaks English at CV Perintis (☎ 32967), Jl Kapten Marsan 345, on the ground floor of the Kapuas Indah building, but the congenial staff can help with bus, boat and plane tickets.

River Life

Pontianak's wealth stems from its river trade and the best vantage point from which to view river activity is from the water. The attractive park and gazebo dock on Jl Rahadi Usman between the ferry crossing and the Kartika Hotel is a good place to get your bearings. Hire a sampan (rowboat) or motorised canoe for an hour or two from the docks next to the ferry terminals or behind the Kapuas Indah building.

For an interesting experience of riverfront life, take a walk from the Mesjid Abdurrakhman (Abdurrakhman Mosque) along the wobbly wooden boardwalks past the stilt houses at washing time, either early or late in the day. The people of the *kampung* (village) are friendly and curious. Take your camera. There are plenty of willing models, especially the kids.

South along Jl Sultan Muhammad on the riverfront is the *pinisi* (schooner) harbour, where the Bugis-style sailing schooners dock alongside the large houseboats, or bandung, peculiar to West Kalimantan. Bandungs function as floating general stores that ply Sungai Kapuas, trading at villages. Their family owners live on board and a typical run up the Kapuas might last as long as a month.

Mesjid Abdurrakhman

Also known as the Mesjid Jami, this was the royal mosque of Syarif Abdul Rahman (in Indonesian, Abdurrakhman), who reigned as Sultan of Pontianak from 1770 until his death in 1808. The Sumatran-style mosque has a square-tiered roof and is made entirely of wood. Beautiful inside and out, it's worth the short canoe trip across the river from the pinisi harbour. Charter a boat for 3000Rp to 5000Rp or wait for a shared canoe taxi for 500Rp per person.

PONTIANAK

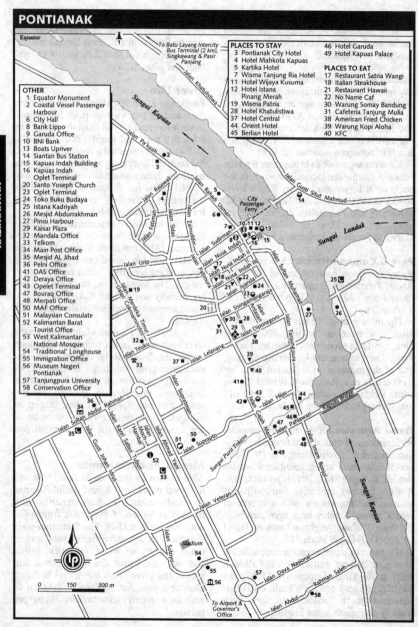

PLACES TO STAY
3 Pontianak City Hotel
4 Hotel Mahkota Kapuas
5 Kartika Hotel
7 Wisma Tanjung Ria Hotel
11 Hotel Wijaya Kusuma
12 Hotel Istana
   Pinang Merah
19 Wisma Patria
28 Hotel Khatulistiwa
37 Hotel Central
44 Orient Hotel
45 Berlian Hotel
46 Hotel Garuda
49 Hotel Kapuas Palace

PLACES TO EAT
17 Restaurant Satria Wangi
18 Italian Steakhouse
21 Restaurant Hawaii
22 No Name Caf
30 Warung Somay Bandung
31 Cafeteria Tanjung Mulia
38 American Fried Chicken
39 Warung Kopi Aloha
40 KFC

OTHER
1 Equator Monument
2 Coastal Vessel Passenger
   Harbour
6 City Hall
8 Bank Lippo
9 Garuda Office
10 BNI Bank
13 Boats Upriver
14 Siantan Bus Station
15 Kapuas Indah Building
16 Kapuas Indah
   Oplet Terminal
20 Santo Yoseph Church
23 Oplet Terminal
24 Toko Buku Budaya
25 Istana Kadriyah
26 Mesjid Abdurrakhman
27 Pinisi Harbour
29 Kaisar Plaza
32 Mandala Office
33 Telkom
34 Main Post Office
35 Mesjid AL Jihad
36 Pelni Office
41 DAS Office
42 Deraya Office
43 Opelet Terminal
47 Bouraq Office
48 Merpati Office
50 MAF Office
51 Malaysian Consulate
52 Kalimantan Barat
   Tourist Office
53 West Kalimantan
   National Mosque
54 'Traditional' Longhouse
55 Immigration Office
56 Museum Negeri
   Pontianak
57 Tanjungpura University
58 Conservation Office

Istana Kadriyah

About 100m south of the sultan's mosque is his former palace, a two storey ironwood building which is now an interesting museum. It displays the personal effects of the sultan's family. Eight sultans reigned after the death of the first in 1808. The last died in 1978. Visiting hours are from 8.30 am to 6 pm daily. There's no admission fee, but a donation is encouraged.

Museum Negeri Pontianak

Near Tanjungpura University, south of the city centre on Jl Ahmad Yani, this recently built national museum has a collection of *tempayan*: South-East Asian ceramics (mostly water jugs) from Thailand, China and Borneo. The jugs displayed vary in size from tiny to tank-like and date from the 16th century.

Tribal exhibits include diorama of the clothing, musical instruments, tools and crafts of the Dayak cultures of West Kalimantan. The museum is open Tuesday to Sunday from 9 am to 1 pm. Around the corner on Jl Sutoyo is a replica of a Dayak longhouse.

Equator Monument

The official monument marking the equator was originally erected in 1928 as a simple obelisk mounted with a metallic arrow. In 1930 a circle was welded to the arrow, in 1938 another circle was added in the other direction and its subsequent incarnation is unintentionally funny, looking like a giant gyroscope on a pillar. The caretakers then encased the original in a building in 1991 and built a huge replica. On 23 March and 23 September the sun is supposed to be directly overhead.

To get to the monument, take an opelet (500Rp) from the Siantan bus terminal heading north-west on the highway. The monument is right on the highway and even if you can't get your tongue around the name for equator, *khatulistiwa*, taken from Arabic, people will know what you mean.

Special Events

Pontianak's proximity to the equator has given rise to an annual Equator and Culture Festival, to promote tourism in West Kalimantan. Usually it's held in late March, to coincide with the sun's position overhead and features Dayak and Malay traditional dancing, singing and games. Ask at the hotels or tourist office for the exact dates.

Places to Stay – Budget

Good budget accommodation is hard to come by in Pontianak. The **Wisma Patria** (☎ 36063, *Jl Merdeka Timur 497*) has rooms for 19,000Rp with fan and *mandi* (bath) or for 30,000Rp with air-con. The staff are friendly, but check out the rooms first. Standards for cleanliness seem to have dropped with the rupiah.

Backing on to the river opposite the Kapuas Indah building is the **Hotel Wijaya Kusuma** (☎ 32547, *fax 39032, Jl Kapten Marsan 51-53*), which has seen better days. It has dormitory beds for 14,300Rp and windowless economy rooms for 22,000Rp with fan and shared mandi. Rooms with mandi and air-con cost from 30,800Rp.

Next door, the **Hotel Istana Pinang Merah** (☎ 38840, *fax 39032*) is not much better. Singles/doubles cost 30,000/36,000Rp, with mandi and air-con. The neighbourhood around here is a bit seedy and is notorious for its gambling and prostitution.

Probably the best deal in Pontianak is at the **Wisma Tanjung Ria** (☎ 34371, *Jl Rahadi Usman 1*). Spotlessly clean rooms are available with air-con and shared mandi for 30,000Rp and 35,000Rp, as well as rooms with air-con and mandi from 40,000Rp. The only catch is that this is a hostel run by the Indonesian military (note the cannons out front). Depending on your political outlook, you may not want to patronise their premises.

Places to Stay – Mid-Range & Top End

Despite its location, which straddles two busy roads, the **Hotel Central** (☎ 37444, *fax 34993, Jl Merdeka Timur 232*), is clean and friendly and has rooms with air-con and mandi from 44,000/55,000Rp. A small breakfast is included and a fridge in the lobby has cold beer, water and soft drinks.

KALIMANTAN

Hotel Khatulistiwa (☎ 36793, fax 34930, Jl Diponegoro 56 and Jl Sisingamangaraja 126) is a sprawling place with clean economy rooms for 40,700Rp with air-con and mandi, and better rooms for 55,000Rp. Don't be put off by the small alleys that lead to the hotel from either Jl Diponegoro or Jl Sisingamangaraja.

The *Pontianak City Hotel (☎ 32495, fax 33781, Jl Pak Kasih 44)* is in the north of town, near the harbour for coastal passenger boats. Clean economy air-con rooms cost 33,000/45,000Rp and standard rooms cost 50,000Rp to 55,000Rp. A small breakfast is included.

At the opposite end of town, the *Orient Hotel* – if they haven't fixed the sign yet, it will say 'Orien' – *(☎ 32650, fax 40651, Jl Tanjungpura 45)* has rooms with air-con and bath starting at 46,000Rp. The staff are very friendly, but the place is a bit run-down and you're probably better off somewhere else.

A little further out of town from the Orient, the *Hotel Garuda (☎ 36890, fax 39001, Jl Pahlawan 40)* has clean air-con rooms with shower for 80,000Rp and deluxe/family rooms with bath and fridge for 105,000/140,000Rp, plus a 10% government tax. The only drawback here is the noisy location.

The *Kartika Hotel (☎ 34401, fax 38457, Jl Rahadi Usman)* has similar rates and is better situated, right on the river near the centre of town. Rooms are priced from 90,000Rp, with air-con, shower, fridge and breakfast included. Rooms with river views start at 125,000Rp. A 20% tax is added to all room prices but try for a 25% discount instead.

The recently renovated *Hotel Kapuas Palace (☎ 36122, fax 34374, Jl Imam Bonjol)* has a fitness centre, tennis court, bar and western-style coffee shop, and a 100m swimming pool. The surrounding grounds are a pleasant respite from Pontianak's chaotic traffic. Room prices start at 165,000Rp and rise to 285,000Rp for business suites and 525,000Rp for the presidential suite. Prices do not include a 20% tax, though discounts are common.

The *Hotel Mahkota Kapuas (☎ 36022, fax 36200, Jl Sidas 8)* is still the best place

in town and often offers discounts. Studio rooms are good value at 128,000Rp and standard singles/doubles are 176,000/208,000Rp. Suites are 400,000Rp and the presidential suite goes for 920,000Rp. All prices include breakfast, but not the 21% tax and service charge. There's a wide range of facilities, including a bar, a coffee shop, an excellent restaurant, a disco and a swimming pool.

Places to Eat

The local coffee is excellent and the numerous *warung kopis* (coffee shops) around town are central to life in Pontianak, though they are generally frequented by a mostly male clientele. The best place to seek them out (the coffee shops, not the men) is in the centre of town on the side streets between Jl Tanjungpura and Jl Pattimura. The *Warung Kopi Aloha* opposite the KFC is a good place for coffee and snacks. A little place on Jl Antasari opposite the Restoran Hawaii has fried *roti* (bread) for breakfast as well as delicious coffee. There's no discernible name, but the exterior is festooned with Nescafé signs.

The popular *Warung Somay Bandung*, inside the car park on Jl Sisingamangaraja, serves delicious Chinese-style *bubur ayam* (sweet rice porridge with chicken) and the house speciality, *somay*, a tasty concoction of potatoes, tofu, hard boiled egg and spicy peanut sauce for 3500Rp.

The best fare is at the countless warungs, especially those lining Jl Pattimura. The *Cafeteria Tanjung Mulia*, opposite the Kaisar Plaza department store, is a lively place serving a variety of dishes, including delicious *sate ayam* (grilled chicken sticks served with a spicy peanut sauce) with peanut sauce. Night warungs on Jl Sudirman and Jl Diponegoro dish up steaming plates of rice noodles, crab, prawns, fish and vegetables, and goat sate – all fried up in a wok for 4000Rp. For riverside dining, try the *Sinar Ria Restaurant*, floating on a dock beside the Kapuas Indah, or the glassed-in restaurant in the *Kartika Hotel*, which is air-conditioned.

Pontianak has a large Chinese population and excellent Chinese food. The *Restoran Hawaii (Jl Nusa Indah III 80)* is a good choice for Chinese food, as is *Restaurant Satria Wangi* on Jl Nusa Indah II. There's a Chinese flavour to everything – even the traditional *gado gado* is served on noodles rather than rice.

For a western food fix, there's a *KFC (Jl Gajah Mada 54)* and the *Italia Steakhouse (Jl Nusa Indah II 109)*, which has hamburgers, spaghetti and steak, as well as Japanese style hotpot at reasonable prices. More expensive western fare can also be found at the Hotel Mahkota Kapuas and the Hotel Kapuas Palace.

Pontianak has a few large supermarkets with various goodies. The supermarket on the ground floor of the *Kaisar Plaza* department store on Jl Pattimura is the most central. You'll find a good bakery next door.

Shopping

It's worth looking out for *kain songket* (material with silver or gold thread woven into it) from the town of Sambas. The **souvenir and material shops** on Jl Nusa Indah III sell it, as do the **market stalls** lining Jl Pattimura. Prices are often cheaper than those at Sambas. Some of these shops also stock selections of old (and reproduction) trading beads, cheap bags of rough-cut gems, and beautiful old Chinese and Dutch china and glassware. For last minute purchases at the airport, a very good **gem shop** is in the departure lounge. The owner, Abdul Rahim, speaks perfect English and is a trained gemologist.

Getting There & Away

Air Garuda (☎ 34142), Jl Rahadi Usman 84, is open weekdays from 8 am to 4 pm, Saturday until 1 pm, and Sunday from 9 am to noon. Merpati (☎ 40035), Jl Imam Bonjol 89, has similar hours. DAS (☎ 31166), Jl Gajah Mada 67, Deraya (☎ 37670), Jl Gajah Mada 197, Bouraq (☎ 30882), Jl Pahlawan 3A, and Mandala (☎ 34488), Jl Merdeka Timur 178, also service Pontianak. At the time of writing, the only international flight out of Pontianak was with Malaysian Airlines (☎ 37327), whose office is in the Hotel Mahkota Kapuas.

Due to the economic crisis, flights to Kalimantan have been cut back, so check with the airlines or travel agents for current schedules. Daily flights between Pontianak and Jakarta cost around 700,000Rp with Garuda, Merpati, Mandala or Bouraq.

Merpati has three flights a week to Batam (572,300Rp), from where it's easy to make a boat connection to Singapore or Medan (1,150,900Rp). There are also direct Merpati flights to Balikpapan (742,800Rp) three times a week.

Malaysian Airlines flies to Kuching on Monday, Wednesday and Friday for US$74, and has connections to Kuala Lumpur and Singapore.

DAS has daily flights to Ketapang (140,500Rp) as does Deraya (120,700Rp). Deraya also has small Cessna planes that fly daily to Pangkalanbun (247,200Rp) while DAS (282,400Rp) makes the trip four times a week on a larger 28-passenger aircraft. Deraya also has a daily flight to Semarang (412,200Rp).

DAS flies between Pontianak and Sintang (162,500Rp) and Putussibau (289,000Rp) with eight-passenger planes. DAS also flies to Banjarmasin (525,200Rp) from Pontianak once a week.

MAF (☎ 33476), Jl Letjen Suprapto 50A, flies to various places in West Kalimantan but it's better to contact them to find out the most recent schedules. Fares for regular flights and charters are quite expensive. There's no sign on the office in Pontianak, but it's around the corner from the Malaysian Consulate.

Bus Pontianak's intercity bus terminal is in Batu Layang, north-west of town. Take a ferry to Siantan (200Rp) and a white opelet to Batu Layang (500Rp) or take one of the opelets (1000Rp) that make the trip from the terminal on Jl Sisingamangaraja near the SJS office. From Batu Layang, buses go north along the coast to Singkawang (5000Rp, 3½ hours) and Sambas (8000Rp) and inland to Sanggau (9000Rp) or Sintang (13,000Rp).

For longer hauls to Kuching and Sintang, book early at bus offices such as SJS (☎ 34626, fax 4427), Jl Sisingamangaraja

KALIMANTAN

155, or Tebakang Express (☎ 34559), Jl Diponegoro 105. Air-con buses go to Kuching (50,000Rp, 10 hours) and to Sintang (25,000Rp, nine hours). These buses leave from the ticket offices in Pontianak. Agents around the Kapuas Indah also sell tickets for economy buses going to Putussibau (40,000Rp), but it's a gruelling 20 hour ride.

Car & Motorcycle Renting a car and driver in Pontianak is the perfect way to see coastal West Kalimantan at your own pace, but it's not cheap. Travel agencies or your hotel can arrange a car for about 200,000Rp to 300,000Rp per day. You might get a better price by bargaining with the taxis that wait around the entrance to the Kapuas Indah opelet terminal near the Garuda office. Motorcycles are an option for experienced riders only and cost around 50,000Rp a day.

Boat There are two Pelni ships that sail regularly between Pontianak and Java. The *Lawit* makes a weekly run to Jakarta (30 hours). Economy class costs 85,000Rp, not including a mattress, which is usually an extra 2000Rp. Twice a month the *Lawit* goes to Semarang (30 hours) from Pontianak then backtracks to Kumai (18 hours) in Central Kalimantan. Twice a month, the *Bukit Raya* goes from Pontianak to Surabaya (40 hours). Tickets in economy are 95,000Rp. The Pelni office (☎ 48124, fax 48131) is located away from the harbour on Jl Sultan Abdur Rahman 12, near the main post office. Ticket sales take place in the morning. Agents around town also sell tickets.

Another boat service to Jakarta is the *Kapuas Express*, which leaves three times a week. The journey takes about 20 hours and first-class tickets are 225,000Rp, which includes a bunk. Second-class tickets are 190,000Rp for a reclining seat. Tickets can be booked through most travel agents.

Daily jet boats go to Ketapang (six hours) and have reclining seats in first class for 60,000Rp and economy seats for 50,000Rp. All the above coastal boat services, including Pelni, leave from the harbour area on Jl Pa'kasih north of the Kartika Hotel.

Riverboats up Sungai Kapuas leave from the dock at the back of the Kapuas Indah building. Tickets are sold here for regularly scheduled boats, though the long runs up the Kapuas leave only once a week, having largely been replaced by bus travel. The 800km journey from Pontianak to Putussibau is 44,000Rp and takes about four days. A boat to Sintang (about 400km by river from Pontianak) costs 22,000Rp per person and takes two days and one night. This includes basic meals, but you're well advised to supplement the meagre fish and rice diet with food from Pontianak.

You could also try to get on an unscheduled boat, like the houseboat bandungs. The bandungs don't usually take passengers, but they may make exceptions for curious foreigners.

Getting Around

To/From the Airport A counter at the airport sells tickets for taxis into town (20,000Rp). Alternatively, walk down the road in front of the terminal building to the main road into Pontianak, where you should be able to get an opelet for 500Rp. It's a half-hour drive from the airport to the Kapuas Indah opelet terminal. Hotels can arrange taxi rides to the airport for the regular 20,000Rp fare. For early morning flights, it's a good idea to book the night before.

Public Transport The main opelet terminals are in the middle of the city: the Kapuas Indah terminal near the waterfront, a terminal on Jl Sisingamangaraja, and a terminal off Jl Gajah Mada. There are taxis for hire next to the Garuda office at the road entrance to Kapuas Indah, and *becaks* (bicycle rickshaws) aplenty. A tour of the city and environs by taxi is 15,000Rp per hour with a two hour minimum.

The best and most fun way to get around is by public opelet. All rides cost 500Rp regardless of the distance.

Motorised canoes depart from piers next to the Kapuas Indah building on the river. Crossing the river to the Istana Kadriyah and Siantan ferry terminal is 500Rp per person or about 3000Rp to charter. A car and passenger ferry 100m downstream from the Kapuas Indah building takes passengers to the other side for 200Rp.

SUNGAI KAPUAS

Pontianak is the launching point for riverboat services along Indonesia's longest river. From the air the many curves and oxbow lakes of the Kapuas basin make it a geographical spectacle; but at ground level, the primary attraction is the life on the river itself and the vessels plying their way up or down. As elsewhere in Kalimantan, take a slow boat to see and photograph the river activity.

Boats of all shapes and sizes journey the Kapuas, but the standard is a boat with a lower deck (no seats) where passengers stake out their territory, and a roof full of cargo. Cheap, fast and reliable buses from Pontianak to Sintang have reduced the need for regular passenger services along the Kapuas and riverboats leave only once a week. Even the road to Putussibau has improved to the point that buses have now replaced speedboats. Beyond Putussibau, however, or along tributaries, boats remain the dominant mode of moving people, though this usually means waiting around for enough people to fill a boat or chartering one yourself at considerable expense. In general, motorised canoes are less expensive (and slower) than speedboats, but still count on paying an average of 50,000Rp per hour for the journey.

Sintang
☎ 0565

A wave of transmigration brought 15,000 new farming families to the Sintang area in the early 1980s, but most migrants since then have come to service the logging boom. During the rainy season, the streets of Sintang's waterfront are flooded, rising just shy of the floor level of the hotels and shops flanking the street. Don't be surprised if you have to wade knee deep through the water or teeter on planks to get around.

The nearby **Gunung Kelam** monolith offers a challenging hike through the jungle, a waterfall *(air terjun)*, butterflies and panoramic views of the surrounding countryside. Take a white opelet to Pasar Impres (500Rp) and then a Kelam opelet to the base (2000Rp). A road circles the hill and you can be dropped off at the gaudy park entrance. The stepped path to the top has steel ladders over more difficult rock faces and the going can be difficult.

Take a boat across the river (500Rp) to visit the **Dara Janti Museum** which has various items from the former sultan's palace, including Dayak artefacts, gamelan and Portuguese cannons. Ask around to get the keeper to let you in and leave him a small donation. Boats to the other side of the river congregate in front of the coffee shops and shops facing the river.

Guides Daniel Madu (☎ 21815), Jl Sugiono 4, is an experienced guide who speaks excellent English and the local Dayak dialects. He specialises in a variety of trips, including one south down the Pinoh River, west across to the headwaters of the Mahakam in East Kalimantan and north to the lakes and rivers of West Kalimantan. Contact him two weeks to a month before your trip to arrange a trek.

Places to Stay The *Sesean (☎ 21011, Jl Katamso 1)*, a friendly place on the waterfront, has tiny singles for 11,000Rp with fan and shared mandi, and large twin rooms for 18,000Rp. Doubles with mandi and air-con cost 35,000Rp. The covered veranda facing

SINTANG

1 Sesean
2 Losmen Setia
3 Ranah Minang
4 Losmen Central
5 Motorised Canoe Hire
6 Warkop Valentine
7 Flamboyan
8 Selera Kita Restaurant
9 Bakso 33
10 Bus Terminal

Riverboat Dock

Sungai Kapuas

Jalan Katamso

Jalan Panjaitan

Pasar

Jalan Supratman

Jalan Sugiono

To Sei Ukoi Bus Terminal (10km) & Airport

0   50   100 m

the river is a great place to sit in the evening. The nearby **Losmen Setia** (☎ *21611*) is cheaper than the Sesean, but a little run down. Singles/doubles cost 7000/8000Rp without fan or mandi and 12,000/16000Rp with fan. Rooms with mandi and fan are 19,000Rp, and with air-con, 27,500Rp. The **Losmen Central**, at the corner of Jl Katamso and Jl Sugiono is cheaper still, with rooms for 7000Rp and 8000Rp, but it's hard to find anyone in charge at the reception.

The **Flamboyan** (☎ *21111*) is the ugly white building on the corner of Jl Sugiono and Jl Panjaitan. It charges 22,000Rp for a twin-room with fan and mandi and 44,000Rp with air-con and is *not* an attractive place. Further south-east down Jl Panjaitan, construction is under way for what is expected to become Sintang's best hotel.

Places to Eat For strong coffee, reasonable food and a view of the riverside activity, join the rest of the gossips at **Warkop Valentine**. **Bakso 33** has conventional Indonesian fare and the **Selera Kita** next door has Chinese food. Back on the waterfront on Jl Katamso the **Ranah Minang** has passable Padang food. Otherwise there are coffee and cake stalls around the market.

Getting There & Away

DAS flies to Sintang (160,000Rp) and Pontianak (289,000Rp) on Monday, Wednesday, Friday and Saturday, but only if there are enough passengers to make the trip worthwhile. You can try booking tickets at the Flamboyan Hotel, but it's probably better to go out to the airport, either by opelet or motorcycle, from the Sintang bus terminal.

The long distance bus terminal is called Sungai Ukoi (or abbreviated as Sei Ukoi). It's about 10km south-west of Sintang and can be reached by public opelet (500Rp) from the Sintang bus terminus. Buses leave from Sungai Ukoi to Nanga Pinoh (1000Rp, one hour). Just to confuse things, however, buses to Putussibau and Pontianak (including the air-con night bus) leave from the Sintang bus terminal.

Riverboats stop by the dock in front of Jl Katamso. Speedboat charters are also available here.

Putussibau
☎ 0567

The Dutch were conspicuous by their absence from much of inland Kalimantan until the turn of the century. Even then, the colonial presence tended to be for security rather than economic reasons. The first district officer was stationed in Putussibau in 1895.

Today Putussibau is a pretty and quiet but still important market town. A few kilometres upstream are traditional attractions, such as the longhouse villages of **Melapi I** and **Sayut** (also known as **Melapi II**) on the Kapuas. Along the Sungai Mendalam is a new longhouse at **Semangkok I** and a much older one just upstream at **Semangkok II**. Chartering a boat to the longhouses costs about 50,000Rp per hour. A cheaper way to the Melapi longhouses is by public opelet for 2000Rp, which leaves from the car park on the waterfront. The Melapi longhouses accept overnight guests, but payment for

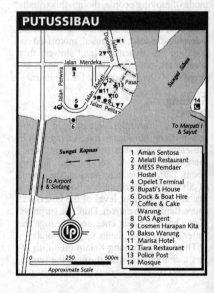

PUTUSSIBAU

1   Aman Sentosa
2   Melati Restaurant
3   MESS Pemdaer Hostel
4   Opelet Terminal
5   Bupati's House
6   Dock & Boat Hire
7   Coffee & Cake Warung
8   DAS Agent
9   Losmen Harapan Kita
10 Bakso Warung
11 Marisa Hotel
12 Tiara Restaurant
13 Police Post
14 Mosque

0   250   500m
Approximate Scale

food is expected and it is customary to give gifts or pay for any photographs you take.

Guides Guides will probably appear after the news gets around that travellers have arrived, but not many speak English well. Jahari (☎ 21534) is a guide with a ready smile and is very easygoing, though with limited English. Mochtar Umar is another guide who works out of Putussibau and Tanjung Lokan. Prices will vary depending on the length of your trip. See the Putussibau to Long Apari entry later in this chapter for approximate guide prices.

Places to Stay The *MESS Pemdaer* (☎ 21 010, Jl Merdeka) is a government hostel which is often full, but, apart from a noisy TV lounge at the front, it's great value. Clean rooms with private mandi and aircon are 15,000Rp. A new hotel, the *Aman Sentosa* (☎ 21691, Jl Diponegoro 14), is a bit more expensive but very clean. Economy rooms with fan and shared mandi cost 20,000Rp and other rooms with air-con and mandi cost from 40,000Rp.

The accommodation next to the waterfront is less appealing. The *Marisa Hotel* on Jl Melati has a sad-looking bar and restaurant downstairs, and small rooms upstairs for 15,000Rp and 20,500Rp with fan and mandi. Air-con rooms are 35,000Rp. The somewhat sleazy but friendly *Losmen Harapan Kita* (☎ 21157, Jl Pelita) faces the river and has singles with shared mandi for 10,000Rp. Doubles with mandi cost 15,000Rp and 20,000Rp.

Places to Eat The *Tiara* (Jl Melati 5), next door to the Marisa Hotel, has excellent sate, green vegetables, rice and mixed dishes. The *Melati* (Jl Diponegoro 7) also has good food and beer. Look for the prominent Guinness sign in front of the restaurant. The *warung* down the boardwalk past the DAS agent serves strong coffee and cake.

Getting There & Away
In Putussibau or Pontianak check to see whether the missionary airline, MAF, has resumed flying to Putussibau and Tanjung Lokan. Transport to the airport is by motorcycle (10,000Rp) or opelet (15,000Rp).

The road is partly paved from Sintang to Putussibau, but heavy rains still create the odd mud hole that swallows up buses. Depending on the weather the journey can take six to eight hours and costs 20,000Rp. The bus to Pontianak takes 20 hours and costs 40,000Rp.

Putussibau is the last stop for scheduled riverboats from Pontianak, arriving and departing once a week. They stop at the dock in front of the house of the *bupati* (district head). The journey takes two days to Sintang (22,000Rp) and four days to Pontianak (44,000Rp).

To continue on to the village of Tanjung Lokan it's necessary to charter a boat. The two day trip costs 1,000,000Rp.

Putussibau to Long Apari
The hardy, intrepid and wealthy (expenses are considerable) can begin a river and jungle trek eastwards from Putussibau, across the West-East Kalimantan border through the Muller Range to Long Apari at the headwaters of the Mahakam.

From Putussibau (or Sintang), the first step is to arrange a knowledgable guide – the bupati can assist or try asking at the DAS agent. Would-be guides will also find you; they will certainly be willing to take your cash, but may have little knowledge of the track and local languages. The village of Tanjung Lokan also has guides. *Do not* attempt the trip beyond Tanjung Lokan alone, as trails are not well marked.

In Putussibau, stock up on provisions for you and your guide(s) – allowing about 20,000Rp per person per day for sugar, coffee, eggs, canned fish and tobacco. Then charter a motorised canoe (500,000Rp) to make the one day trip to Nanga Bungan. From there you must charter a smaller canoe for about the same amount for another day's travel to **Tanjung Lokan**. Fuel is *very* expensive.

In Tanjung Lokan, find guides to lead you through the jungle into East Kalimantan and the village of Long Apari. Some claim the walk takes two or three days, but allow for five or six. Guides will ask for up to 300,000Rp each, often more. From Long Apari, you have to charter a boat down the first part of the Mahakam. Regular public boat services begin at Long Bagun.

The trek to Long Apari from Tanjung Lokan goes through rough country so travel light. You need food, a set of dry clothes to sleep in, basic medicines, cooking equipment and a sheet of strong waterproof material for shelter. Allow plenty of time each day for guides to set up camp and hunt or fish for extra protein.

NANGA PINOH

An interesting side trip off the Sungai Kapuas is from Sintang to Nanga Pinoh, which is a one hour bus ride from Sintang (1000Rp). In Nanga Pinoh it's possible to continue by bus to Kota Baru and Nanga Sokan, but taking a speedboat is more fun. Despite the heavy logging in the area, the forest cover by the river, along with sections of rapids, make it a scenic trip. Public speedboats leave when there are enough passengers to fill the boat and cost 30,000 per person. The trip takes three hours to Kota Baru. Chartering a speedboat will cost about 500,000Rp for a round trip to Kota Baru. From Kota Baru it's a half hour speedboat ride to Nanga Sokan where you can continue on to Central Kalimantan by a combination of trekking and river travel, though it's advisable to take a guide.

SINGKAWANG
☎ 0562

This predominantly Hakka Chinese town boomed in the early 18th century, when mines from Sambas to Pontianak accounted for about one-seventh of total world gold extraction. Powerful Chinese associations ran the show, especially on the rich Montrado fields, and an agricultural infrastructure soon sprang up to supply the miners. Hakka is still the lingua franca. Singkawang is also the site of Chinese ceramic workshops making reproductions of Ming dynasty water jars and other items that have featured prominently in the history of Kalimantan.

Apart from the ceramic workshops, Singkawang's main attraction is nearby **Pasir Panjang**, a 3km stretch of white sand and calm water with few people except on public holidays. Pasir Panjang is a 20 minute drive out of Singkawang just off the Singkawang-Pontianak road. (See Pasir Panjang under Around Singkawang later in this chapter.)

Places to Stay

The hotel precinct is in the noisy commercial hub at the northern end of Jl Diponegoro near the main mosque and Chinese temple. The *Hotel Khatulistiwa Plaza* (☎ 31697, Jl Selamat Karman 17) has rooms on the third floor priced at 12,500Rp with fan and mandi, but the rooms on the second floor for 15,000Rp and on the first floor for 20,000Rp are much better value.

The best budget rooms are at the *Hotel Kalbar* (☎ 34128, Jl Kepol Machmud) which has clean doubles for 15,500Rp with fan and shared mandi. Rooms with air-con and mandi cost 26,500Rp and 50,000Rp. Another budget option is the *Hotel Duta Putra Kalbar* (☎ 31430, Jl Diponegoro 32) diagonally opposite the Hotel Khatulistiwa Plaza. Small rooms with fan and mandi cost 17,500Rp and air-con rooms cost 25,000Rp and 35,000Rp. The *Hotel City* (☎ 32212, Jl Yos Sudarso 27) is a large place with a disco and clean rooms with fan and mandi for 25,000Rp and air-con rooms for 50,000Rp and 75,000Rp.

About 1km south of town is Singkawang's best mid-range accommodation, the *Hotel Paseban* (☎ 31449, Jl Ismail Tahir 41). It's a pleasant, clean place, if a little isolated. Rooms with fan and mandi cost 22,000Rp and 29,000Rp. Air-con rooms range from 41,000Rp to 67,000Rp plus 10% tax. The most upmarket accommodation in town is the *Hotel Mahkota Singkawang* (☎ 31244, fax 31491, Jl Diponegoro 1) which has a swimming pool, disco and air-con rooms from 94,000Rp to 158,000Rp plus 21% government tax.

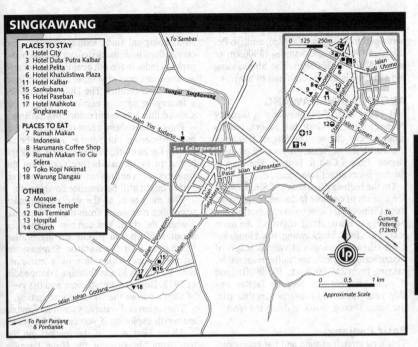

SINGKAWANG

PLACES TO STAY
1 Hotel City
3 Hotel Duta Putra Kalbar
4 Hotel Pelita
6 Hotel Khatulistiwa Plaza
11 Hotel Kalbar
15 Sankubana
16 Hotel Paseban
17 Hotel Mahkota Singkawang

PLACES TO EAT
7 Rumah Makan Indonesia
8 Harumanis Coffee Shop
9 Rumah Makan Tio Ciu Selera
10 Toko Kopi Nikimat
18 Warung Dangau

OTHER
2 Mosque
5 Chinese Temple
12 Bus Terminal
13 Hospital
14 Church

Places to Eat

Chinese food is your best bet. The *Rumah Makan Tio Ciu Selera (Jl Diponegoro 106)* serves *kue tiaw goreng* (fried rice noodles), loaded with shrimp, squid, wheat gluten and freshly made fishballs. Most of its dishes are prepared in the savoury Chiu Chao (Chao Zhou) style and the beer (9000Rp) is ice cold.

Also on Jl Diponegoro are the *Bakso 68*, *Bakso 40* and *Bakso Sapi Ideal* noodle shops, serving variations on *bakso* (meatball soup) with *mie* (wheat noodles), *bakmi* (egg noodles) and *kue tiaw* (rice noodles). The *Rumah Makan Indonesia* on the same street serves mostly Javanese food.

The *Toko Kopi Nikmat* on Jl Sejahtera has excellent coffee, along with a variety of cakes and bread with a rich butter spread. Just south past the Rumah Makan Indonesia on Jl Diponegoro the *Harumanis* coffee shop also has good coffee and cakes.

Across from the Hotel Makhota on the road to Pontianak the *Warung Dangau* (☎ 33 410) is a large outdoor restaurant in a pleasant setting which has Chinese and Indonesian food at reasonable prices.

Getting There & Away

From Pontianak, cross the Sungai Kapuas by city passenger ferry (200Rp) to the Siantan bus terminal and then take a white opelet (500Rp) from there to the Batu Layang terminal. Opelets also go directly to Batu Layang (1000Rp) from the terminal on Jl Sisingamanga in Pontianak. Buses to Singkawang (5000Rp, 3½ hours) leave throughout the day. From Singkawang to Gunung Poteng (see Around Singkawang), catch a Bengkayang bus east for the 12km trip (700Rp). Let the driver know where you're going and he'll let you off at the foot of the hill

Beyond Singkawang there are buses to Sintang (14,000Rp, nine hours) and Colts north-east to Sanggau (6000Rp), north to Pemangkat (700Rp) and Sambas (3000Rp) or east to Mandor (3000Rp). The Singkawang bus terminal is in the south part of town.

AROUND SINGKAWANG

Just 12km east of Singkawang is **Gunung Poteng**, once a minor hill resort, but its hotel is now closed. The largest flower in the world, the rafflesia, grows wild on these slopes. Take a Colt to Poteng. The hike to the top takes about two hours.

On the highway just south of Singkawang are a series of **ceramic factories** which make huge Chinese jars with colourful motifs. The Semanggat Baru, about 100m off the main road, 5km from Singkawang, has a long, ancient kiln and ceramics at various stages of manufacture. Prices are quite reasonable, ranging from 250,000Rp to 400,000Rp, and if you like what you see, the factory can ship your purchase to Jakarta. Another kiln, the Sinar Terang, is 400m down the road.

Pasir Panjang

This long stretch of sand and flat grassy picnic area 12km south of Singkawang is deserted on weekdays but crowded on weekends and public holidays. The *Palapa Beach Hotel* has clean twin rooms with fan and mandi for 40,000Rp and 75,000Rp. Small cottages with air-con, mandi and mini-bar fridge are 100,000Rp; more comfortable cottages are 150,000Rp. The hotel also runs overnight snorkelling tours to a tiny, deserted island beyond Pulau Lemukutan called Pulau Randayan, but getting there can be quite expensive and accommodation on the island is 50,000Rp and 100,000Rp for simple rooms.

Getting There & Away

From Singkawang take any opelet heading south on the highway from the Singkawang bus terminal (1000Rp, 20 minutes) and get off at the Taman Pasir Panjang (Long Beach Park) gate or at the warung 200m further on. It's a 500m walk to the beach. A motorcycle taxi from Singkawang is about 10,000Rp.

SAMBAS
☎ 0562

Archaeological finds indicate Sambas had connections with the Sriwijaya kingdom and perhaps India in the 6th century, and became an important port city in its own right from the late 13th century. The Dutch established a factory in Sambas between 1608-10, but showed little interest in colonising the area.

Palace ruins show a hint of the city's former prosperity, but Sambas is now better known for its cloth, kain songket. Check the prices in Pontianak before taking on the weavers or vendors at Sambas market. Prices might still be cheaper down south.

The market is at the end of the main street that runs north from the bus terminal towards the river. You can hire a canoe for about 1000Rp and paddle on the Sungai Sambas to visit the **Keraton Sambas**, the former palace which is now a museum, built by Sultan Mulia Ibrahim Tsjafioeddin in 1933. Both the architecture and the view of Sambas from the river are enchanting.

The region and waterways around Sambas are worth exploring if you can find a guide.

About 1km west of the market, on the road from Singkawang, the *Hotel Parades* (☎ 91182, Jl Gusti Hamzah) has spotless rooms with fan and shared mandi for 17,000Rp, rooms with fan and mandi for 23,000Rp and air-con rooms for 42,000Rp.

Colts from Singkawang to Sambas (3000Rp, three hours) leave regularly from the Singkawang bus terminal.

Central Kalimantan

Central Kalimantan was formed in 1957, after a Dayak revolt calling for greater autonomy from centuries of domination by Banjarmasin. It remains the only province with a predominantly Dayak population, mostly Ngaju, Ot Danum and Ma'anyan peoples. It's also the least populated province in Kalimantan, with just 1.57 million people.

Bahasa Ngaju is the most widely spoken dialect, and is the language of the Kapuas, Palangkaraya and southern Barito regencies.

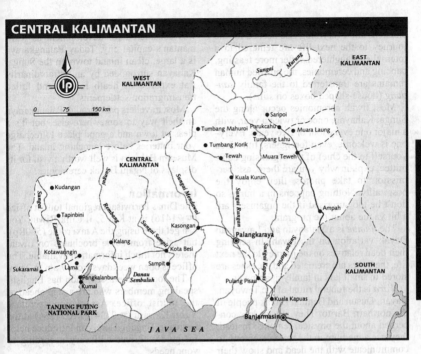

CENTRAL KALIMANTAN

The main faith is nominally Islam, but *kaharingan* (meaning 'life') is still widely observed. Kaharingan is an indigenous tradition passed between generations through story telling, rituals and festivals. Jakarta recognises the creed as a kind of 'Hinduism', the name used for any religion that won't fit neatly into an officially recognised category. Every few years a major intertribal religious festival called a *tiwah* takes place in Central Kalimantan (see the Society & Conduct entry later) and features a month of feasting, drinking and ritual dancing.

The northern reaches of Central Kalimantan are mountainous, while the rest of the province is low, flat and poorly drained. Timber extraction has stripped much of the province of its forest cover. Natural attractions include the mountains north of Muara Teweh and Tanjung Puting National Park near Pangkalanbun in the south.

The major river thoroughfares run roughly parallel from the northern hills to the coast. Five canals built in the Dutch era join the Kahayan with the Kapuas and two lower branches of the Barito, cutting the distance from Banjarmasin to Palangkaraya significantly.

Special Events
Tiwah, Ijambe & Wara Ceremonies

The region is famous for its tiwah: colourful interment ceremonies in which dozens of Ngaju Dayak families retrieve the remains of their dead from temporary graves and send them on their way to the next life, according to the traditions of the kaharingan faith. Groups of villages participate, dispatching up to 150 or more long-dead 'spirits' in a month of feasting and ceremonies. The peak of activity is when bones are taken from the graves, and washed and purified to cleanse the spirit of sins. Water buffalo, pigs, chickens and everything else needed for the journey to the next life are tethered to a totem then slaughtered. After more feasting, dancing and ceremonies, the purified human remains are transferred to the family *sandung* (house-shaped boxes on stilts).

Most tiwah ceremonies occur along the Sungai Kahayan, once or twice a year, with a major one every four or five years. Everyone is welcome, even foreigners. Introduce yourself to the chief of the organising committee, explain why you are there, ask permission to take photos, then enjoy the hospitality. Nothing happens in a hurry, so don't be too surprised if the organisers are a bit vague about the program.

The *ijambe* is a Ma'anyan and Lawangan Dayak variation on the tiwah. In sending their dead relatives on the journey to the next life, the bones are cremated and the ashes are stored in small jars in family apartments.

Wara is the funeral ritual of the Tewoyan, Bayan, Dusun and Bentian Dayak people of the northern Barito. They are far less concerned about the physical remains; instead, they use a medium in the wara ceremony to communicate with the dead and show their spirits the way to Gunung Lumut, the nirvana of this branch of the kaharingan faith.

Potong Pantan Ceremony Another kaharingan tradition is the *potong pantan* welcoming ceremony in which important guests are met by the head of the village, offered a machete and invited to cut through *pantan* –lengths of wood blocking the entrance to the village. As they cut, guests introduce themselves and explain the purpose of their visit to purge themselves of bad spirits. *Tapung tawar* is an extension of the potong pantan, in which guests have their faces dusted with rice flour and their heads sprinkled with water to protect them from bad spirits and illness.

PALANGKARAYA
☎ 0536 • pop 133,800

Palangkaraya (Great and Holy Place), was built on the site of the village of Pahandut and quickly developed into a modern, regional centre. During the Soekarno period it was considered for development as Kalimantan's capital city. Today Palangkaraya is a large, clean inland town on the Sungai Kahayan surrounded by an extraordinarily flat expanse of heath forests and failed transmigration settlements.

Most travellers pass through Palangkaraya on their way to somewhere else, but it's a pleasant town and a good place to recharge your batteries before launching inland. The Museum Balanga is well worth a visit for its displays of Ngaju Dayak ceremonies.

Information
The Dinas Pariwisata regional tourist office (☎ 21416) is at Km 5, Jl Cilik Riwut. You can get there using the A taxi route (500Rp), but aside from some brochures on tiwah, there's not much information available. The office is open weekdays from 7 am to 2 pm.

The local guide association has English-speaking members who are a step ahead of the tourist office. Association secretary Yusuf Kawaru (☎ 23341, fax 21254) at the Dandang Tingang Hotel can introduce helpful guides. Prices will vary according to your needs.

It's difficult to find accurate maps of Central Kalimantan, but try the Bali Indah Photo on Jl Ahmad Yani 77.

Money The best place to change money is at the Bank Dagang Negara (BDN) on Jl Ahmad Yani, open weekdays from 7.30 am to 2.30 pm. Most of the banks in Palangkaraya will exchange travellers cheques only up to US$300.

BNI bank has two ATM machines that accept Cirrus or MasterCard. One is at their main branch near the main post office on Jl Imam Bonjol. The other is on Jl Dharmasugondo just south of the night market.

Post & Communications The main post office is on Jl Imam Bonjol, south of the roundabout on the D taxi route. The post office is open daily from 7.30 am to 2.15 pm. Their Internet service has two terminals (10,000Rp per hour).

PALANGKARAYA

PLACES TO STAY		26 Hotel Payang	25 Nina's	10 Telaga Biru
1 Dandang Tingang		27 Losmen Mahkota		Supermarket
7 Hotel Virgo		28 Losmen Harapan	OTHER	11 Merpati Office
8 Hotel Dian Wisata		29 Losmen Putri Sinta	2 Post Office	13 BDN Bank
12 Hotel Lampang		30 Hotel Mina	3 BNI Bank	14 Mosque
15 Hotel Sakura		31 Losmen Ayu	4 Mandala Wisata	18 Minibus Station
16 Hotel RachmanYanti			(Traditional House)	21 Souvenir Shops
17 Adidas Hotel		PLACES TO EAT	6 Temporary Dock	23 Sandung of
19 Hotel Laris		5 Simpang Raya	(Upstream Boats)	Pahandut Village Head
20 Hotel Halmahera		22 Ruman Makan	9 Flamboyan Pier	32 Rambang Pier
24 Hotel Melati Serasi		Almukminum	(Upstream Boats)	(Downstream Boats)

KALIMANTAN

Things to See

On the south side of Jl Panjaitan, on the C Taxi route, the **Mandala Wisata** is a model of a traditional longhouse and includes an art centre. For wandering around, try the lively **pasar malam** (night market) on the corner of Jl Jawa and Jl Halmahera.

The **Museum Balanga** is at Km 2.5, Jl Cilik Riwut and is *officially* open Tuesday to Thursday from 8 am to 1 pm and until 10 am on Friday (closed Monday and weekends). If everything is closed, don't despair. Wander around and see if there are any staff in the office. Sri Utami, Education Coordinator for the museum, may be there. She speaks excellent English and can help find someone to take you around the museum or she'll take you around herself. Admission is free. The A taxi route (500Rp) goes past the museum.

The main building has good displays of Ngaju ceremonies, performed to celebrate the cycle of birth, marriage and death. The displays give the visitor a better appreciation of the Ngaju culture and the kaharingan faith.

Places to Stay – Budget

There are a cluster of cheap hotels by Rambang Pier where the longboats, river ferries and speedboats depart for Banjarmasin. *Hotel Mina* (☎ 22182, Jl Nias 17) is cool, clean and friendly and the best of the bunch in this neighbourhood. Singles/doubles with fan cost 13,000/17,500Rp or 15,000/20,000Rp; air-con rooms cost 28,000/37,000Rp. Next door is the *Losmen Putri Sinta* (☎ 21132, Jl Nias 15). It's a good budget option – rooms with fan and shared mandi range from 8000Rp for singles through to 23,000Rp for quads. There are also rooms with fan and mandi ranging from 12,000Rp for singles to 30,000Rp for quads. Closer to the dock, *Losmen Ayu* (☎ 34747, Jl Kalimantan 147) is small and grotty, but cheap. Singles cost from 7500Rp and doubles cost 10,000Rp with shared mandi.

Further up from the dock, near Jl Dharmasugondo, the *Hotel Laris* (☎ 22741, Jl Madura 18) has basic rooms for 10,000Rp and 15,000Rp with fan and shared mandi. Nearby, the *Hotel Melati Serasi* (☎ 23682, Jl Dr Murjani 54) has clean singles/doubles/

triples with fan and shared mandi for 9,000/ 16,000/25,000Rp and with private mandi for 15,000/20,000/30,000Rp. The lobby has a fridge with cold drinks.

Places to Stay – Mid-Range

The *Losmen Mahkota* (☎ 21672, Jl Nias 5), in the Rambang Pier vicinity, has singles/ doubles with air-con and mandi for 25,000/ 35,000Rp. Up the road, the *Hotel Payang* (☎ 24993, Jl Nias 6) is overpriced and full of mosquitoes. Rooms range from 15,000Rp to 35,000Rp, but there's much better accommodation elsewhere.

The hotels along Jl Ahmad Yani offer some of the best accommodation in Palangkaraya. At the western end of the street the *Hotel Dian Wisata* (☎ 21241, Jl Ahmad Yani 56) opened in 1998 and has spotless rooms in a pleasant setting. Economy rooms cost 30,000Rp; rooms with fan and mandi cost 40,000Rp; and rooms with air-con cost 50,000Rp. Breakfast is included. Farther west, the *Hotel Virgo* (☎/fax 21265, Jl Ahmad Yani 13) has rooms with fan, mandi and breakfast for 22,000/27,500Rp. Air-con singles are 44,000Rp and 66,000Rp and doubles are 55,000Rp and 77,000Rp.

The *Hotel Rachman Yanti* (☎ 21634, Jl Ahmad Yani 82A) has rooms with fan and mandi for 30,000/35,000Rp. Air-con rooms are 45,000/50,000Rp. The reception is on the second floor. The friendly *Hotel Sakura* (☎ 21680, Jl Ahmad Yani 87) has air-con singles starting at 55,000Rp and doubles for 102,000Rp. All prices include breakfast.

Places to Stay – Top End

The *Dandang Tingang* (☎ 21805, fax 21254, Jl Yos Sudarso 13) is getting a little run down but is still the best hotel in Palangkaraya. The staff are helpful and some of them speak English, basic French and Japanese. It's outside the town centre, but the C taxi route goes by the gate. There's a good restaurant, a bar and a disco. Air-con singles/doubles range from 35,000/ 55,000Rp to 225,000/275,000Rp, including breakfast but not the additional 20% government tax.

Although it lacks the large grounds and ambience of the Dandang Tingang, the new *Hotel Lampang* (☎ 20002, fax 22220, Jl Irian 2) has nice, clean air-con rooms from 70,000/80,000Rp to 80,000/95,000Rp with breakfast included. The 20% tax is additional. Some of the staff speak English. Further east along Jl Ahmad Yani, the *Adidas Hotel* (☎ 21770, fax 25328, Jl Ahmad Yani 90) has air-con rooms for 75,000/90,000Rp that are good value. The price includes coffee, tea and snacks but not the 20% tax.

Places to Eat

Barbecued fish and freshwater crayfish hold pride of place in Palangkaraya cuisine. In the Jl Dharmasugondo area, the *Ruman Makan Almukminum* has three small restaurants, all virtually around the corner from each other, two on Jl Madura and one on Jl Dharmasugondo. All serve delicious barbecued fare, including crayfish, *patin* fish (considered a delicacy upriver) and chicken. You can't beat the price here: a full meal with iced drink can be had for less than 10,000Rp.

The Almukminum trio face stiff competition from a lively, colourful *pasar malam* on Jl Halmahera and Jl Jawa, where you'll find plenty of cheap noodle and rice dishes, plus a colourful range of seasonal fruit. For morning coffee there are a few *warungs* on Jl Nias towards Rambang Pier.

At the intersection of Jl Suprapto and where Jl Ahmad Yani becomes Jl S Parman, the *Simpang Raya* has decent Padang food. There is also a string of restaurants on the north side of Jl S Parman up to Jl Panjaitan. The *Banama Restaurant* in the Dandang Tingang hotel is a good place for an air-conditioned respite, with cold beer and drinks, and excellent food.

For self-catering, the *Telaga Biru* supermarket on Jl Ahmad Yani has all kinds of things, including cold drinks and delicious cakes.

Shopping

There's not a lot to buy in Palangkaraya in the way of special crafts, but the souvenir shops along Jl Madura west of Jl Dharmasugondo have some nice baskets and mats in the 17,000Rp to 35,000Rp range. The market has tubular rattan or bamboo fish weirs for sale, just like the ones in the museum.

Getting There & Away

Air Merpati (☎ 21411, fax 22113) has an office at Jl Ahmad Yani 69 and DAS (☎ 21550) is at Jl Milono 2. CV Wartel Permata (☎ 28 552, fax 26198) at Jl S Parman 7 also books airline tickets, as does PT Mulio Angkasa Raya (☎ 21031, fax 23723) on Jl Ahmad Yani 55.

Merpati has direct flights to Jakarta (863,800Rp) on Tuesday, Thursday and Sunday, and flies with a stopover in Banjarmasin (237,900Rp) on the other days of the week. Merpati also flies to Surabaya (596,500Rp) three times a week.

DAS flies daily to Muara Teweh (196,000Rp) and Buntok (142,000Rp), and thice weekly to Kuala Kurun (142,000Rp).

Bus & Jeep Yessoe Travel (☎ 23466) has an office on Jl Pahgrango 27 on the D taxi route (500Rp) from where morning and evening buses depart for Pangkalanbun (35,000Rp). The road is paved all the way except for about two hours near Pangkalanbun where, if there are heavy rains, buses can get stuck and prolong the journey. CV Eka Perkasa (☎ 21052) at Jl Dharmasugondo 2, near the taxi terminal, also sells bus tickets for Yessoe buses. Maduratna Perdana (☎ 25086) on Jl Nias 8 beside the Hotel Payang has buses going to Pangkalanbun for the same price.

CV Eka Perkasa has Kijang services to Banjarmasin, with eight people crammed into a jeep for 35,000Rp each. The speedboat to Banjarmasin is a better option, being both cheaper and faster.

Boat Boats downstream to Banjarmasin leave from Rambang Pier (Dermaga Rambang) near the hotel cluster. Speedboats cost 27,600Rp to Banjarmasin (and take about six hours), 24,600Rp to Kuala Kapuas and 22,000Rp to Pulang Pisau. Boats leave on the hour from 7 am to 11 am. Buy your ticket from the office at the pier.

Boats heading upstream normally leave from Flamboyan Pier (Dermaga Flamboyan) but the dock has been moved temporarily because of the March 1998 fire that swept through most of the stilt house neighbourhood. To get to the pier, go down a trail just west of the Hotel Virgo, marked by the misspelt sign 'speedboad'. Daily speedboats go to Tewah (five hours) and cost 60,000Rp per person. Slow boats to Tewah (26,500Rp) take one night and one day.

Handmade Bridges

Until recently road transport in the outer islands of Indonesia was notoriously unreliable, especially during the wet season. Buses and trucks could pick their way around landslides, fallen trees, huge potholes and other obstacles, but rivers often presented an insurmountable barrier. Even highways usually depended on a fragile series of wooden bridges, tiny river ferries and precarious causeways and fords. Monsoon rains routinely made long routes impassable.

Reliable links to isolated areas started to become a reality from the early 1980s with the appearance of durable steel truss bridges, many the result of an Australian aid initiative. The bridges are now a common feature of highways across Indonesia with, literally, a box of tools and an instruction manual in Bahasa Indonesia. They are designed to be built with unskilled labour and minimal construction equipment, making them ideal for remote regions.

The bridges proved so useful that Indonesia now buys dozens of kits at a time. According to the Australian designers, Transfield-MBK, if all their Indonesian bridges were put end to end, they would extend for over 130km and the steelwork alone would weigh more than 185,000 tonnes.

Brendan Delahunty

Getting Around

To/From the Airport The airport is on the edge of town, but there are no direct roads so it takes a good fifteen minutes to get there. Taxis cost 15,000Rp.

Public Transport Efficient taxi buses – marked A, B, C or D – cost 500Rp. The taxi terminal is at the intersection of Jl Ahmad Yani and Jl Dharmasugondo.

Kijang charter is 15,000Rp an hour (minimum two hours). An *ojek* (motorcycle) is about half that. Becak drivers congregate around the dock and along Jl Halmahera at the night market.

INTO THE INTERIOR

The main challenge is to get beyond the logged areas or find pockets of forest that have escaped the ravages of the chainsaw. Palangkaraya guide association members (see Information under Palangkaraya earlier) can assist at a reasonable price, but travel to the interior is always an uncomfortable, expensive proposition and prices will vary according to river conditions.

One route is to take a speedboat from Palangkaraya to **Tewah** (60,000Rp), charter a *klotok* (motorised river canoe) to **Batu Suli Hill** and on to the longhouse settlement of **Tumbang Korik** (six hours, 200,000Rp or more) on the Sungai Hamputung, via river rapids and **Tumbang Miri**. From Tumbang Korik you can to trek to **Tumbang Mahuroi** (spending a night in the jungle), and then head back downstream to Tewah or on to **Kuala Kurun**. Count on at least five or six days to do this trip.

Another option involves travelling by motorcycle and can be done in three days. Go from Tewah to **Tumbang Miri**, by motorcycle south to **Tumbang Rahuyan** or the gold-mining area near **Sungai Antai** (three hours), then down the river by boat to **Tumbang Baringei** (three hours), on to **Tumbang Malohoi** (the site of a longhouse) by motorcycle and then by klotok or speedboat south to **Tangkiling** and on to Palangkaraya.

Alternatively, for a four to five day trip, take a motorcycle from Kuala Kurun north to **Seihanyu**, a klotok to the upper reaches of the Kapuas to **Sungai Mendaun** and on to **Jarak Masuparia**. Hike from there to **Masuparia**, a gold-rush field in a natural depression in the jungle. Continue by motorcycle to **Tumbang Masao** then by klotok downstream to **Purukcahu** and **Muara Teweh** or continue from Tumbang Masao to the Sungai Barito headwaters, past a series of rapids north of **Tumbang Tuan**, and into territory so far untouched by the logging companies. These last options are the most difficult and expensive, but well worth considering if you have the cash and the stamina.

MUARA TEWEH AREA
☎ 0519

Deep in the heart of logging country, Muara Teweh is the last riverboat stop on the Sungai Barito, unless the water is high enough for the boats to get up to **Purukcahu**. From Purukcahu you can journey farther north by boat and hire Dayak guides for treks into the north-eastern mountains and forest. Near Gunung Pacungapung, on the border of Central and East Kalimantan, a cement pillar marks the geographical centre of Borneo.

Information

The main settlement of Muara Teweh is on the north bank of the Barito. The road parallel to the river, Jl Panglima Batur, is where most accommodation is located.

Muksin Hussein (☎ 22342) is a school teacher who speaks English and can help arrange guides. In Purukcahu, look for Mahrani, a Siang Dayak who also speaks English and is a good person to ask about trips further inland, though he may be unable to guide you himself.

Places to Stay & Eat

Muara Teweh has a lot of accommodation to choose from. A floating guesthouse, the *Penginapan Betang Danum* (☎ 21612, Jl Panglima Batur) has clean rooms for 10,000Rp with shared mandi. Access to the hotel is marked by a signpost, about 50m west of the Barito Hotel. The *Barito Hotel* (☎ 21080, Jl Panglima Batur 43) is also a good place to stay. Singles/doubles/triples with fan and shared mandi cost 7700/12,100/15,400Rp. Singles/doubles with private mandi are 22,000/27,5000Rp. At the eastern end of Jl Panglima Batur, before the market, the *Wisma Tewe Raya* (☎ *21053, Jl Panglima Batur 92)* has singles starting at 6000Rp and quads from 24,000Rp, all with shared mandi. Singles/doubles with mandi and fan are 17,500/30,000Rp.

The best hotel in Muara Teweh is the *Wisma Pacifik* (☎ *21231, Jl Panglima Batur 87),* which has comfortable beds in air-con rooms with mandi for 66,000Rp. Next door, the *Hotel Gloria* (☎ *21126, Jl Panglima Batur 79)* has air-con rooms priced from 35,000/40,000Rp. On the hill above town, the *Penginapan Gunung Sintuk* (☎ *21088, Jl Surapati)* has nice air-con rooms for 33,000/44,000Rp. Cheaper rooms with shared mandi are 6,000/10,000Rp.

There are a couple of *warungs* along Jl Panglima Batur west of the Barito Hotel, one or two up the hill on Jl Surapati and also further along near the market. *Wisma Pacifik* has a good restaurant with reasonable prices.

In Purukcahu there are a couple of *losmen* with rooms costing around 10,000Rp, or you can also stay in the longhouse at Konut, about 10km from Purukcahu.

Getting There & Away

Air DAS links Muara Teweh with Palangkaraya daily (196,000Rp). The airport is 5km north of town and transportation from the airport is by motorcycle (5000Rp) unless you can hitch a ride with someone else. An opelet or Kijang from town to the airport is about (10,000Rp), depending on your bargaining skills.

Boat It's 56 hours by riverboat from Banjarmasin to Muara Teweh (16,500Rp) and another 24 hours to Purukcahu, river conditions permitting. Most boats have bunk beds and a warung, but bring your own food as well. Speedboats from Muara Teweh to Purukcahu take about three hours and cost 25,000Rp. The dock is opposite the Hotel Gloria on Jl Panglima Batur.

Bus Buses leave daily and nightly for an uncomfortable 12 hour trip to Banjarmasin (15,000Rp). The bus terminal is 3km west of town across the bridge.

Opelets go to Purukcahu (15,000Rp, three hours) from the terminal on Jl Surapati.

MUARA TEWEH TO SAMARINDA

From Muara Teweh you can trek overland to **Long Iram** in East Kalimantan and then catch a boat down the Sungai Mahakam to Samarinda. (See Samarinda and Long Iram under East Kalimantan later.) A number of different routes are possible, depending on whether you want to trek through the jungle or just follow logging roads. Logging roads head east from Muara Teweh or Muara Laung upriver. The trek takes up to two weeks and can be done on your own, following logging roads – a depressing way to see the jungle, or you can also try hitching rides on trucks, if they come by, or motorcycles. Be sure to take sun protection and iodine to purify your water. There are more interesting trails upriver from Purukcahu. Hire a guide along the way or bring one from Palangkaraya, Banjarmasin, Muara Teweh or Purukcahu.

PANGKALANBUN
☎ 0532
Pangkalanbun is a necessary stopover to register with the police if you intend to visit Tanjung Puting National Park. Most travellers avoid Pangkalanbun and head for Kumai, but it's a good place to stock up on food and the people are friendly.

Orientation & Information

Pangkalanbun is not a big town – it has a small central area between Jl P Antasari and Jl Kasumayuda but it's a bustling place. BNI bank, near the passenger pier on Jl P Antasari, will exchange US dollar travellers cheques and cash, but at very low rates. It's open weekdays from 7.30 am to 3 pm and Saturday until 11 am. The ATM machine there takes Cirrus and MasterCard. The Bank Rakyat Indonesia (BRI), 150m east of BNI bank on Jl P Antasari, has slightly better rates.

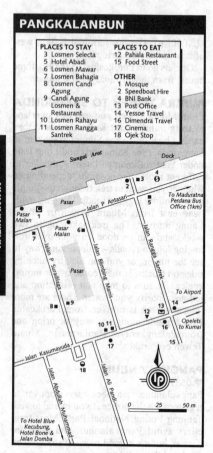

PANGKALANBUN

PLACES TO STAY	PLACES TO EAT
3 Losmen Selecta	12 Pahala Restaurant
5 Hotel Abadi	15 Food Street
6 Losmen Mawar	
7 Losmen Bahagia	**OTHER**
8 Losmen Candi	1 Mosque
Agung	2 Speedboat Hire
9 Candi Agung	4 BNI Bank
Losmen &	13 Post Office
Restaurant	14 Yessoe Travel
10 Losmen Rahayu	16 Dimendra Travel
11 Losmen Rangga	17 Cinema
Santrek	18 Ojek Stop

Try PT Dimendra Travel (☎ 21170) on Jl Kasumayuda for air and boat tickets, as well as information about river trips and guides. Talk to Leo Pumasara, when he's not across the lane making hamburgers. Nearby, Yessoe Travel (☎ 21212) sells buses tickets to Sampit and Palangkaraya, as well as air tickets. It can also suggest guides. Maduratna Perdana (☎ 22129) on Jl Antansari 17 has bus services to Palangkaraya. Their office is 1km east of BNI bank.

Places to Stay – Budget

The choice is not brilliant at this end of the market. Once you have restocked and made onward travel arrangements, consider staying at Kumai. (See the Tanjung Puting National Park section later.)

Losmen Selecta (☎ 21526), near the dock, is basic but central and has singles/doubles for 15,000/20,000Rp. Another budget option is *Losmen Candi Agung* (☎ 22 259, Jl P Suradilaga). It has two wings, on either side of the road, and a restaurant. Singles/doubles/triples with shared mandi are 10,000/20,000/25,000Rp. Some singles are available with mandi for 15,000Rp. The *Losmen Bahagia* (☎ 21226, Jl P Antasari 100) is also decent, with singles/doubles for 16,000/25,000Rp with fan and mandi.

Places to Stay – Mid-Range & Top End

The *Hotel Abadi* (☎ 21021, Jl P Antasari 150) has rooms with fan and mandi for 30,000Rp and air-con rooms for 50,000Rp and 75,000Rp. It's good value and has a restaurant next door. Away from the town centre is *Hotel Bone* (☎ 21213, Jl Domba 21) next door to the Hotel Blue Kecubung. Clean rooms with fan and mandi are 24,000Rp including breakfast. Air-con rooms are 42,000Rp and more comfortable rooms are 72,000Rp.

The *Hotel Andika* (☎ 21218, fax 21923, Jl Hasanudin 51A) is on the road from the airport into town. It's clean, the staff are helpful and the restaurant is good. They have singles for 30,000Rp and 45,000Rp with fan and mandi and doubles for 35,000Rp plus 21% tax. Air-con rooms are 60,000Rp.

The *Hotel Blue Kecubung* (☎ 21211, fax 21513, Jl Domba 1) has well kept economy rooms for 60,000/75,000Rp, standard rooms for 88,500/111,000Rp and deluxe rooms for 114,000/138,000Rp. All rooms have air-con. Given the state of the hotel, it's a little overpriced, but even so, it's still the best in town. The Blue Kecubung also runs the Rimba Lodge in the national park.

Places to Eat

Beside the post office on Jl Kasumayuda the *Pahala Restaurant* is breezy and clean and has good iced drinks, *tempe*, (fermented soybean cake), *nasi goreng* (fried rice) and the usual fare. You'll find barbecued chicken and friendly service at the *warung* adjoining Losmen Candi Agung, and loads of snacks in the *small supermarkets* on Jl P Antasari.

A *food street* up from Jl Rangga Santrek at Jl Kasumayuda, has hamburgers and pizza. Leo of Dimendra Travel doubles as a hamburger chef.

Getting There & Away

Air The Merpati and DAS offices are on Jl Hasanuddin, near Hotel Andika. The Deraya Air Taxi agency is at Jl P Antasari 51, near the swampy market.

DAS flies from Pangkalanbun to Banjarmasin (305,500Rp) five times a week and to Pontianak (282,400Rp) four times a week. Deraya flies daily to Pontianak (247,200Rp) and Ketapang (195,000Rp) and Merpati has three flights a week to Semarang (587,700Rp).

Bus Both Yessoe Travel and Maduratna Perdana have buses leaving from their offices to Palangkaraya for 30,000Rp and 35,000Rp (air-con). The trip takes 12 hours, depending on road conditions.

Boat Pelni passenger ships from Semarang and Surabaya call at Kumai, the access point for Tanjung Puting National Park alternately about once a week. The trip takes a full day and night from either Semarang or Surabaya, and economy fares are 45,000Rp and 48,500Rp, respectively. You need to book cabins a week in advance. Try Dimendra Travel or contact PT Wisana Angkasa Travel (☎ 0531 21904) in Sampit. Pelni boats also go to Java from Sampit.

Getting Around

A taxi from the airport to town costs 20,000Rp, or 40,000Rp for a two hour charter. A taxi from the airport to Kumai is 40,000Rp and includes a stop at the Pangkalanbun market to photocopy your

passport and visa, and at the Pangkalanbun police station for your registration to enter the reserve. Near the Losmen Selecta and on corners around town, ojeks can be hired, but bargain hard. A trip out to Kumai costs around 10,000Rp.

Colts to Kumai (2000Rp) leave from near the roundabout on the hill leading up from Jl Kasumayuda. A Kijang to Kumai costs about 20,000Rp.

Pangkalanbun to West Kalimantan

Public speedboats leave from the dock near the Losmen Selecta for **Kotawaringin Lama** (15,000Rp) up the Sungai Lamandau. From there, 4WDs go to **Sukamara** (15,000Rp), from where you can take a speedboat to **Manismata** and further on up to **Riam** in West Kalimantan. You can continue up to **Ketapang** from Riam.

TANJUNG PUTING NATIONAL PARK

The **orang-utan rehabilitation centres** at Tanjung Harapan and Camp Leakey are like nowhere else in Indonesia. They are sanctuaries for all primates, including humans. Juvenile orang-utans orphaned or rescued from captivity are reintroduced to the jungle at these centres, under the supervision of rangers. As the orang-utans grow and learn to live in the wild, they spend longer and longer away from the camps. However, some adults can't kick the habit and usually return at dawn and dusk feeding times. The increasing destruction of the orang-utans' natural habitat due to logging and mining, worsened by the fires of 1997, has made it even more difficult to fully rehabilitate the animals to the wild. Indeed, the orang-utans at Tanjung Puting are increasingly becoming 'bicultural' which poses a problem for park management.

What sets Tanjung Puting apart is the sense of refuge, the relative absence of litter and the obvious affection the staff have for the animals they work with. Canadian researcher Dr Biruté Galdikas – known locally as '*ibu* (mother) professor' – began taking in rescued orang-utans in the early 1970s with

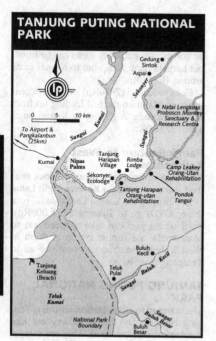

TANJUNG PUTING NATIONAL PARK

0 5 10 km

To Airport & Pangkalanbun (25km)

Gedung Sintok
Aspai
Sungai Sekonyer
Sungai Kumai
Natai Lengkuas Proboscis Monkey Sanctuary & Research Centre
Sungai Sekonyer
Kumai
Nipas Palms
Tanjung Harapan Village
Rimba Lodge
Sekonyer Ecolodge
Camp Leakey Orang-Utan Rehabilitation
Tanjung Harapan Orang-utan Rehabilitation
Pondok Tangui
Buluh Kecil
Teluk Pulai
Sungai Buluh Kecil
Tanjung Keluang (Beach)
Teluk Kumai
National Park Boundary
Buluh Besar
Sungai Buluh Besar

the assistance of the Leakey Foundation, the US philanthropic foundation which sponsors research on all great apes.

The orang-utans in Borneo and Sumatra are the only great apes outside Africa, and Dr Galdikas probably knows more about them than anyone. In the early days of her research, she would spend weeks tracking wild orang-utans and was the first to document, for instance, that the birth interval for orang-utans is about once in every eight years, making them vulnerable to extinction.

Tanjung Puting National Park encompasses more than 305,000 hectares of tropical rainforest, mangrove forest and wetlands, and is home to a vast variety of fauna, including crocodiles, hornbills, wild pigs, bear cats, crab-eating macaques, orang-utans, proboscis monkeys, gibbons, pythons, dolphins and mudskippers (a kind of fish that can walk and breathe on land). This is also a

habitat for the dragon fish, an aquarium fish worth 700,000Rp and highly valued by Chinese collectors throughout South-East Asia.

Most visitors go straight to the research centre at Camp Leakey, or the quieter rehabilitation centre at Tanjung Harapan which was established in 1989 to cope with the overflow from Camp Leakey. At **Natai Lengkuas**, further up the Sungai Sekonyer, a project is under way to research the large populations of proboscis monkeys and gibbons. Those with enough time can consider exploring the southern section of the park along the Sungai Buluh Besar. Far upstream there's a **lake** known for its abundance of bird life but requires a special permit from the PHPA office. On the way back to Kumai, take a detour to visit the deserted beach of **Tanjung Keluang**, which is said to be a fine vantage point to enjoy a lovely sunrise and sunset.

For more information on the orang-utan research and rehabilitation work in Tanjung Puting contact the Orangutan Foundation International (OFI), 822 S Wellesley Ave, Los Angeles, CA, USA 90049, (☎ 310 207 1655, fax 207 1556, email redape@ns.net). Or check its Web site: www.ns.net/orangutan. The OFI publishes *A Guidebook to Tanjung Puting National Park* packed with information about Tanjung Puting, written by Drs Biruté Galdikas & Gary Shapiro. It can be ordered through the foundation.

Orientation & Information

A trip into the park begins at the Pangkalanbun police station, where you must register and give the police a bit of English practice. Make sure you have photocopies of the photo page of your passport and of the page with your current immigration stamp.

Then head to Kumai, on the banks of Sungai Kumai about 25km south-east of Pangkalanbun, and register at the riverside conservation office (PHPA) a short way north of the Jl H M Idris and Jl Gerliya intersection. It's open weekdays from 7 am to 2 pm and Saturday until 1 pm (closed Sunday). Registration costs 2000Rp per person per day and 2000Rp a day for a boat 'parking' fee. You *must* provide a copy of your police letter from Pangkalanbun and a photocopy of your passport. The park office will give you three letters: one for you; one for the ranger stationed at Tanjung Harapan (or whichever other post you choose to visit inside the park); and the third for the ranger at the Orang-Utan Research & Conservation Project at Camp Leakey.

For more information contact the Director of Tanjung Puting National Park, PHPA (☎/fax 61187), Jl H M Idris 735, Kumai, Kalimantan Barat.

Guides

The PHPA may advocate hiring a guide or two, but they're really not necessary as the boat crews know where to go and the rangers in the park can accompany you on walks if you ask nicely. However, some PHPA guides speak a little English, have a lot of knowledge about the area and will also cook on overnight trips. The official PHPA guide rate is 50,000Rp per day, but they may ask more. Use your discretion. It can be good to have a guide along as a companion, but as is always the case with guides, go with your intuition as to whether you are compatible.

It's possible to trek through the park from Camp Leakey to Tanjung Harapan, or vice versa, but this requires a special permit from the PHPA and a guide. The office does not provide equipment.

In Kumai, freelance guides will track you down and it can get a bit annoying after a while. Patience is an asset. Hamu Dani, who often works on the Satria boat and will take travellers on a trip to Dayak villages up the Sungai Lamandau, is highly recommended. Jien Joan is another guide who speaks excellent English and also works as a cook for the Baso family on their Garuda boats. (See the Klotok Hire entry later in this section for contact information.)

Rules & Conduct

Regardless of whether you have a guide or not, the park has certain rules of conduct that unfortunately not all visitors or even all staff follow. No matter what the boat crew

or rangers do, don't succumb to the temptation to feed the orang-utans or initiate contact with them. The younger ones especially are *very* hard to resist picking up and cuddling, but let them come to you.

The orang-utans look cute, but they are also strong animals who will grab your camera, bag, or anything else that is hanging off your body.

Kumai
☎ 0532

Kumai is a small port town with freighters and Bugis and Madura schooners tied up to the docks. The main street, Jl H M Idris, is parallel to the river, and most of the hotels are near the intersection with Jl Gerliya. At the southern end of Jl H M Idris is the Pelni office, shops, wartels and market. The nearest bank that changes money is in Pangkalanbun, where rates are very poor. Change plenty of money in a major town before setting out.

Pangkalanbun is better for onward travel arrangements, but the Anggun Jaya Travel Agency (☎ 61168) at Jl Gerilya 383 near the Garuda Hotel can book airline tickets and sells bus and Pelni economy tickets.

Places to Stay & Eat

There are a few budget and mid-range hotels in Kumai, and there's usually no problem getting a room, *except* the night before a Pelni boat comes into town. Overnight, Kumai turns from a sleepy port into a boom town, swelled with gold miners, loggers and many others from elsewhere in Indonesia trying to make a living in this part of Kalimantan.

Most travellers frequent the *Aloha* (☎ 61238, Jl H M Idris 465) at the intersection with Jl Gerliya, where small clean singles/doubles with fan and shared mandi cost 15,000/20,000Rp. It has a restaurant run by the owners.

Opposite the Aloha, there are two hotels in the same building. Downstairs the *Losmen Melati* (☎ 61122) is friendly but has airless rooms; with mandi they cost 12,500Rp. Upstairs, the *Hotel Mutiara* has pleasant, large rooms with fan and mandi for 17,500Rp. The reception for both hotels is downstairs.

South on Jl H M Idris past the Pelni office, the *Losmen Cempaka* (☎ 61030) has rooms upstairs with fan and shared mandi for 15,000Rp. Heading west about 400m up Jl Gerliya from the intersection with Jl H M Idris, the *Losmen Kumara* (☎ 61562) has basic rooms with fan and shared mandi for 15,000Rp. Right across the street, the *Hotel Garuda* (☎ 61145, Jl Gerliya 377) has the only air-con rooms available in Kumai. They cost 45,000Rp plus 10% tax. Rooms with fan and mandi are 30,000Rp and 35,000Rp. It's a clean and friendly place.

For luxury accommodation, you have to head up the Sungai Sekonyer to the *Rimba Lodge*, a very comfortable and tastefully designed hotel inside the park, across from Tanjung Harapan. Room prices range from $US24 to $US58 and come with fan, mosquito net and western-style toilets except for the cheapest rooms, which have squat toilets. The setting is magical and a good option for travellers who may want to experience the park by klotok but need a more comfortable place to sleep. Bookings can be made through the Hotel Blue Kecubung in Pangkalanbun (☎ 21211, fax 21513).

Downstream directly across from the Tanjung Harapan dock, the *Sekonyer Ecolodge* (fax 22991) also has rooms for $US40/50. Contact the lodge directly by fax or through Kalpataru Adventure in Jakarta (☎/fax 021-880 2218). Both the Rimba and Sekonyer lodges can arrange tours and boat hire.

Places to Eat

Kumai is not blessed with great restaurants. There's not much to recommend in terms of *warung* fare since they all serve about the same: noodles, sate, bakso etc. You'll find them scattered along Jl H M Idris towards the market. There are some gado gado places on Jl Gerliya beside the Garuda Hotel. In the evening, vendors come out to sell *terang bulan* and *martabak* pancakes, which are delicious.

One exception to Kumai's dearth of cuisine and a comfortable place to eat is the *Depot Asri* restaurant on Jl Gerliya, roughly halfway between the Losmen Kumara and the Jl H M Idris intersection. It's clean and pleasant, and has cold drinks (no beer), but have your dinner early as it closes at 7 pm.

Klotok Hire

Tanjung Puting is one of the highlights of travelling in Kalimantan and by far the best way to see it is by hiring a klotok for a few days (or more). It serves as your transportation, accommodation and restaurant. At night the crew moors the boat well away from settlements, allowing passengers to enjoy the sunsets and wildlife in peace. Sleep on mattresses on the upper and lower deck, wake to the haunting cries of gibbons at dawn and watch for the telltale splash of big crocodiles. Swim and wash in the river pool at Camp Leakey, but avoid the contaminated waters of Sungai Sekonyer. Mercury used in the gold mining upstream at Aspai is dumped directly into the river. Allow time to explore the forest reserves around the rehabilitation camps and plan your river movements for dawn or dusk, when various primates come down to the river's edge.

There are currently eight different families operating klotoks for tourists to hire, identified by their boat names: Garuda, Satria, Cahaya Purnana, Sampurna, Kalimantan, Omega, Harapan Mina and Gunung Berlian. At the time of writing, the standard price was 150,000Rp per day, not including food. Decide beforehand with the captain whether you are paying for their food as well, which is usually the case. Some travellers have had problems with crew members dipping into food supplies that were not part of the deal and this can lead to bad feelings on the boat.

The Baso family's *Garuda I, Garuda II* and *Garuda III* have been around the longest and the two brothers Yatno and Yadi are excellent captains. Their boats are in high demand around school and public holidays – which is probably the only time a reservation is required. To book, call ☎ 61174 or write to *Garuda Boat*, Baso (Yatno & Yadi), Jl H M Idris (Rt 6) 705, Kumai Hulu 74181, Pangkalanbun, Kalimantan Tengah. Another popular boat with travellers is *Satria*, which can be booked at

Jl H M Idris 600. Agencies in Banjarmasin such as Indo Kalimantan Travel and Arjuna can also arrange a booking for klotok hire.

Plan for at least three days on the river. That way you can work your way slowly up the river to the various stations. It takes two hours to get to Tanjung Harapan from Kumai and four to five hours to Camp Leakey.

Getting There & Away

Colt Kumai is about 30 minutes away from Pangkalanbun by Colt (2000Rp), which depart from the hill on Jl Kasumayuda, just past the roundabout. An ojek from Kumai to Pangkalanbun or the airport will cost 10,000Rp. A Kijang costs 20,000Rp.

Boat Pelni ships call at Kumai from Semarang and Surabaya alternately once a week. The Pelni office in Kumai is a short walk south from the Aloha Hotel, on the riverside. An economy ticket to Semarang costs 45,500Rp, and 48,500Rp to Surabaya.

Getting Around

Speedboat Speedboats can reach Camp Leakey in less than two hours and cost about 250,000Rp, but there's little point in visiting Tanjung Puting if you have only one day. Public speedboats are constantly ferrying people up to the gold-mining site of Aspai for between 10,000Rp and 20,000Rp per person. The main speedboat dock is 75m south of the Pelni office.

Canoe Wooden canoes with crew can be hired at some of the stations for about 20,000Rp per day. This is a better way to explore Sungai Sekonyer and its shallow tributaries. The canoes are also much quieter so you're likely to see more wildlife, including crocodiles if you're lucky – or unlucky, depending on your viewpoint. Bring an umbrella or hat and lots of water.

South Kalimantan

South Kalimantan (Kalimantan Selatan, or Kal-Sel) is Kalimantan's smallest and most densely populated province, covering an area of 37,660 sq km and with a population approaching three million. Kal-Sel is an important centre for diamond mining, rattan processing and, of course, timber. It is the centre of Banjarese culture and a good starting point for treks into Central and East Kalimantan.

Traditional Banjarese clothing is made from *kain sasirangan*, cloth produced by a striking tie-dyeing process. The traditional Banjar-style house is the 'tall roof' design and the best examples can be seen in the town of Marabahan, 50km north of Banjarmasin on the Sungai Barito. There are still a few around Banjarmasin and Banjarbaru, the remains of some in Negara and some impressive public buildings such as the governor's office on Jl Bali which draw on this style.

In the mountainous north-eastern interior of South Kalimantan are groups of Dayaks said to be descendants of the original Banjar race. These original Banjars may have been families from the Barito delta area who fled to the mountains to avoid Muslim conversion in the 15th and 16th centuries.

SOUTH KALIMANTAN

KALIMANTAN

Communal houses *(balai)* accommodate up to 30 or more families and serve as a ritual centre for these mountain villages.

The province also has one million hectares of wetlands, including 200,000 hectares of tidal marshland, and 500,000 hectares of freshwater swamp. As elsewhere in Kalimantan, these rich reserves are heavily exploited and becoming degraded, but their sheer size still makes them a valuable refuge for wildlife.

BANJARMASIN
☎ 0511

Banjarmasin is easily one of Kalimantan's most interesting cities. Indeed, it may be the only city in Kalimantan worth lingering in for a few days. The main attraction is its waterlogged suburbs traversed by canals; the residents of Banjarmasin are up to their floorboards in water and much of the city's commerce occurs on water. Many houses are perched on stilts or ride the tides on bundles of floating logs. Don't leave town without taking a tour of the canals and making an early morning visit to the floating market.

History
The upstream city of Negara is the site of the region's first kingdom. Banjarmasin rose to prominence in 1526 when Pangeran Samudera, a descendant of one of Negara's Hindu kings, overthrew the ruler in Negara and moved the capital to Bandar Masih, the present site of Banjarmasin. The sultanate became an important commercial power, on par with Brunei.

Competing English and Dutch interests each established factories in Banjarmasin between 1603 and 1814. Trouble erupted in 1701 after the British stationed a warship on the Sungai Barito to guard their warehouses. The Banjars revolted and took six years to evict the foreigners.

The Dutch felt the sting of Banjar resistance after placing an unpopular prince on the Banjarmasin throne in 1857. A fullblown rebellion followed, leading to the Banjarmasin War of 1859-63. Rural Islamic leaders led a courageous resistance, heavily

taxing Dutch financial and human resources. The Dutch declared the sultanate to be 'lapsed' in 1860. By 1863 they were back in control, but sporadic resistance continued until 1905.

More recently, even prior to the 1998 protests in Jakarta, Banjarmasin was a political powder keg. Riots and looting occurred during the May 1997 regional election campaign and more than a hundred people died. The Hotel Kalimantan and massive Mitra Plaza Shopping Centre were gutted by fire and have yet to be re-opened.

Orientation
Banjarmasin is big, but just about everything you might need is packed into the city centre around the Pasar Baru (Baru market) along Jl Pasar Baru. Most of the big banks are along Jl Lambung Mangkurat. Travellers arriving by ship can catch small yellow *bis*

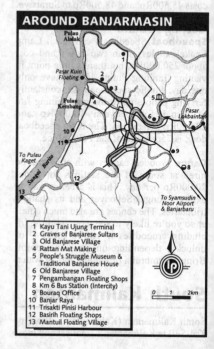

AROUND BANJARMASIN

1 Kayu Tani Ujung Terminal
2 Graves of Banjarese Sultans
3 Old Banjarese Village
4 Rattan Mat Making
5 People's Struggle Museum & Traditional Banjarese House
6 Old Banjarese Village
7 Pengambangan Floating Shops
8 Km 6 Bus Station (Intercity)
9 Bouraq Office
10 Banjar Raya
11 Trisakti Pinisi Harbour
12 Basirih Floating Shops
13 Mantuil Floating Village

kota (literally, city minibus) direct to Jl Hasanuddin (600Rp), but most others terminate at Pasar Antasari, a few hundred metres east of the city centre. The Sungai Barito lies to the west of the city centre.

Information

Tourist Offices The South Kalimantan regional tourist office (☎/fax 52982) at Jl Panjaitan 34, near the Grand Mosque, is open Monday to Thursday from 7.30 am to 2.30 pm and Friday until 11.30 am. The helpful staff can introduce guides from the South Kalimantan Tourist Guide Association. There's also a city tourist office next to the Banjarmasin city hall on Jl Pasar Baru, and an information counter at the airport.

Money BDN bank, next to the Telkom office on Jl Lambung Mangkurat, has the best rates for travellers cheques, but will only change up to US$300. Rates are less generous at the moneychanger at the Diamond Homestay. BNI bank, also on Jl Lambung Mangkurat, next to the Hotel Mentari, has an ATM that takes Cirrus or MasterCard.

Post & Communications The Telkom office for long distance phone calls is at Jl Lambung Mangkurat 4. The main post office is further south at the Jl Pangeran Samudera intersection. The post office has three terminals for Internet use. The service is open from 8 am to 9 pm and charges 10,200Rp an hour.

Travel Agencies Adi Angkasa Travel (☎ 66 300), Jl Hasanuddin 27, is run by friendly and informative Pak Mariso who, along with his staff, speaks English. It also has local tours and can arrange trekking trips. The Borneo Homestay (see Places to Stay later in this section) has a travel agency – Indo-Kalimantan Tours (☎ 66545, fax 57515, email borneo@banjarmasin.wasantara.net.id) – that books air tickets and arranges tours and trekking throughout Kalimantan. Arjuna (☎ 53150, fax 54944, email arjuna@ bjm.mega.net.id) is on the ground floor of the Arjuna shopping plaza and runs the

Amadit Lodge in Loksado and has tours up the Sungai Mahakam in East Kalimantan and elsewhere. The Diamond Homestay (see Places to Stay later in this section) can book flights and runs a tour and trekking service as well.

Guides The going rate for guides is about 20,000Rp per hour for local tours (including transport to nearby Pulau Kaget, the floating markets or Pulau Kembang) or 40,000Rp to 50,000Rp per day for jungle tours (eg to Loksado). Indo-Kalimantan tours is a good local source for trekking information and has a team of excellent guides.

Bookshops Maps of South and Central Kalimantan are available at Toko Cenderawasih Mas, Jl Hasanuddin 37, a drafting supply store between the Merpati office and Jl Pos. Across the street, the Toko Buku Merdeka on Jl Hasanuddin 44 has city and provincial maps, as does the Gramedia bookshop on Jl Veteran 55-61.

Mesjid Raya Sabilal Muhtadin

The giant modern mosque on Jl Sudirman is hard to miss, with its copper-coloured flying saucer dome and five minarets with lids and spires. Also called the Grand Mosque, it was completed in 1981 at the monumental cost of US$4.5 million and is the second largest in Indonesia. Despite the gaudy exterior, the interior is a work of art. Proper attire is mandatory: visitors must wear long pants and suitable shirts to be able to enter. Women wearing sleeveless shirts will not be allowed in.

There's a small **zoo** in the park adjacent to the mosque, with young orang-utans, some proboscis monkeys, macaques and sun bears pacing their cages frantically. There are also different species of birds, a huge python and a komodo dragon on display. The animals look healthy, but if you are easily depressed by zoo visits, don't go.

Floating Markets

The floating markets are groups of boats, large and small, to which buyers and sellers

KALIMANTAN

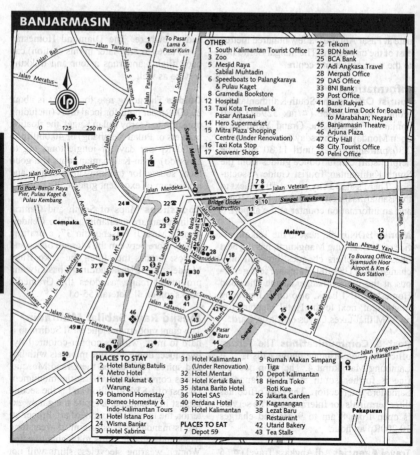

BANJARMASIN

OTHER
1 South Kalimantan Tourist Office
3 Zoo
5 Mesjid Raya Sabilal Muhtadin
6 Speedboats to Palangkaraya & Pulau Kaget
8 Gramedia Bookstore
12 Hospital
13 Taxi Kota Terminal & Pasar Antasari
14 Hero Supermarket
15 Mitra Plaza Shopping Centre (Under Renovation)
16 Taxi Kota Stop
17 Souvenir Shops
22 Telkom
23 BDN bank
25 BCA Bank
27 Adi Angkasa Travel
28 Merpati Office
29 DAS Office
33 BNI Bank
39 Post Office
41 Bank Rakyat
44 Pasar Lima Dock for Boats to Marabahan; Negara
45 Banjarmasin Theatre
46 Arjuna Plaza
47 City Hall
48 City Tourist Office
50 Pelni Office

PLACES TO STAY
2 Hotel Batung Batulis
4 Metro Hotel
11 Hotel Rakmat & Warung
19 Diamond Homestay
20 Borneo Homestay & Indo-Kalimantan Tours
21 Hotel Istana Pos
24 Wisma Banjar
30 Hotel Sabrina
31 Hotel Kalimantan (Under Renovation)
32 Hotel Mentari
34 Hotel Kertak Baru
35 Istana Barito Hotel
36 Hotel SAS
40 Perdana Hotel
49 Hotel Kalimantan

PLACES TO EAT
7 Depot 59
9 Rumah Makan Simpang Tiga
10 Depot Kalimantan
18 Hendra Toko Roti Kue
26 Jakarta Garden
37 Kaganangan
38 Lezat Baru Restaurant
42 Utarid Bakery
43 Tea Stalls

paddle in canoes. Trading begins at dawn and is usually over by 9 am. **Pasar Kuin** at the junction of the Kuin and Barito rivers is one of the most commonly visited markets during the floating market tours. For breakfast, pull up beside the canoe cafe and, using a bamboo pole with a nail pushed through the end, spike your choice from the generous smorgasbord.

East of the town centre, another floating market, **Pasar Lokbaintan**, takes longer to get to but is also worthwhile.

Canal Trips
Everything in Banjarmasin happens on or around the waterways. Chartering a motorised canoe costs about 7500Rp per hour. Try the riverside adjacent to Jl Pos. Two or three hours should be enough to include a dawn visit to one of the two floating markets. Start from the mosque, go to Pasar Kuin where the Sungai Kuin runs into the Sungai Barito, perhaps stop at Pulau Kembang, head past the sawmills of the Sungai Alalak and back to town via the Sungai Andai.

Arjuna, Indo-Kalimantan Tours and Diamond Homestay all have tours starting at around 30,000Rp depending on the size of the party and how long you plan to go for.

Pulau Kembang

Pulau Kembang is an island 20 minutes from the city centre by boat. It is home to a large tribe of long-tailed macaques who congregate at a decrepit Chinese temple near the shore. On Sunday, Chinese families bring gifts of eggs, peanuts and bananas for the monkeys. The temple is a decidedly minor attraction and, if you've fed monkeys with peanuts before, it can be safely dropped from your itinerary. Otherwise, proceed with caution and *don't* touch the monkeys. Macaques can be quite aggressive when they're feeling peckish.

Pulau Kaget

About 12km downstream from Banjarmasin is a wetland reserve inhabited by the comical, long-nosed proboscis monkeys. Indonesians call them *kera belanda* (Dutch monkeys), because of their long noses, red faces and pot bellies. Ask at the tourist office for the best time to leave Banjarmasin (this depends upon the tide) to reach the island when the monkeys come out to feed. Have the captain cut the engines and glide beneath the trees so the monkeys won't flee.

Speedboat operators at the pier at the end of Jl Pos ask 50,000Rp to 100,000Rp for a round trip. A klotok takes two hours each way and costs 30,000Rp to 40,000Rp. Smaller boats can take you south via Banjarmasin's narrow canals. On the river, you can see Banjarmasin's giant plywood mills, most of which were built after a total ban on log exports in the late 1980s.

Special Events

During Ramadan, the Muslim month of fasting, Banjarmasin is the site for the festive *pasar wadai* (cake fair). Dozens of stalls sell South Kalimantan's famous Banjarese pastries near the city hall or the Grand Mosque. Muslims don't eat these delicious pastries until after sundown, of course, but non-believers can gorge themselves all day. The cake fair is at its most lively at the beginning and the end of Ramadan.

Banjarmasin is a good place to be on August 17, national Independence Day. There are boat races on the Sungai Martapura, and celebrations throughout the city.

Places to Stay – Budget

The **Borneo Homestay** (☎ 66545, fax 57 515, email borneo@banjarmasin.wasantara. net.id, Jl Hasanuddin 33, Rt 20) is down an alley off Jl Hasanuddin and is a good place to meet other travellers. The owner, Johan, speaks excellent English and also runs Indo-Kalimantan Tours. A bar (with cold beer) and rooftop lounging area overlooks the river upstairs. Single rooms without fan and shared mandi cost 15,000Rp and doubles with fan cost 20,000Rp. Rooms with air-con and mandi cost 40,000Rp. There's a 10% tax on all room prices. Breakfast is an additional 4000Rp.

Another favourite place with budget travellers, the **Diamond Homestay** (☎ 66100, fax 66200, Jl Hasanuddin 58), is on the next alley east from Borneo Homestay. Singles with fan and shared mandi are 18,000Rp and 20,000Rp, and doubles are 25,000Rp and 27,000Rp, not including 10% tax.

If these places are full, the nearby **Hotel Istana Pos** (☎ 59955, fax 362268, Jl Pos 3) is an old Dutch warehouse that has recently been turned into a hotel. Their cheaper rooms are upstairs and include fan and mandi for 30,000Rp. Air-con rooms with mandi cost 65,000Rp and up.

The **Hotel Kalimantan** (☎ 54483, Jl Haryono MT 106) – not to be confused with former luxury Hotel Kalimantan, which is still under renovation – is less central but another good budget option. Singles/ doubles/triples with shared mandi and fan are 15,000/20,000/25,000Rp. It caters to local travellers.

The **Wisma Banjar** (☎ 66293, Jl Suprapto 5) is near the Grand Mosque and is often full. Singles/doubles with fan and mandi cost 17,500/25,000Rp. There are also air-con rooms for 25,000/35,000Rp.

KALIMANTAN

Places to Stay – Mid-Range

The best mid-range place in Banjarmasin is the quiet and friendly *Hotel SAS (☎ 53054, Jl Kacapiring Besar 2)*. It is less centrally located but has large, comfortable singles/ doubles with fan and mandi priced from 33,000/36,300Rp. Air-con rooms start at 48,400Rp. All room prices include breakfast, but not the 10% tax.

The *Hotel Sabrina (☎ 54442, Jl Bank Rakyat 21)* is near the centre of town and has rooms for 25,000/33,000Rp with fan and shared mandi and air-con singles/doubles/ triples for 44,000/49,500/55,000Rp. All prices include breakfast. If it's full, you'll probably be directed to the nearby *Perdana Hotel (☎ 68029, fax 67988, Jl Katamso 8)*, which is friendly but whose rooms are buggy and stuffy and cost 34,800/39,600Rp with fan and mandi. They also have more expensive air-con rooms. All prices include breakfast but this hotel has seen better days.

The *Hotel Kertak Baru (☎ 54638, Jl Haryono MT 1)* is a clean place next to the Hotel Istana Barito. Air-con rooms with immaculate mandi start at 60,000Rp.

West of the Grand Mosque, the *Hotel Metro (☎ 52427, Jl Sutoyo 26)* is cheaper, with rooms with fan and mandi for 24,000/ 33,000/36,000Rp. Air-con rooms cost from 36,000/42,000/48,000Rp.

Places to Stay – Top End

The *Hotel Istana Barito (☎ 67300, fax 52240, Jl Haryono MT 16-20)* is the top place to stay in Banjarmasin and often offers up to 35% discounts. Its facilities include a number of fine restaurants, a swimming pool, a coffee shop, a bar and a disco. Rooms start at 250,000Rp and go up to 580,000Rp for family suites, plus 21% tax. The daily 'American' breakfast buffet is 15,000Rp.

The recently renovated *Hotel Mentari (☎ 68944, fax 53350, Jl Lambung Mangku-rat)* has friendly staff. Its standard air-con rooms cost 121,000Rp and its suites are 199,650Rp, not including 21% tax. The hotel has a coffee shop, restaurants, a disco, a bar and a pharmacy. Another good option is the

Hotel Batung Batulis (☎ 66269, fax 66 270, Jl Jend Sudirman 1), on the north side of the Grand Mosque. Clean air-con rooms with fridges are 90,950Rp and suites are 121,200Rp, including tax.

Places to Eat

Banjarmasin's excellent array of *kueh* (cake) includes deep-fried breads – some with delicious fillings – and sticky banana rice cakes, both cheap but tasty options for breakfast at the tea stalls. Stuff yourself for 500Rp to 1000Rp, or even less at the *canoe warung* at the floating markets. A local speciality is *ayam panggang* (chicken roasted and served in sweet soy sauce), but fish and freshwater crayfish hold pride of place in Banjar cuisine.

There is a string of eateries along Jl Pangeran Samudera – try the *Kaganangan (Jl Pangeran Samudera 30)* for local dishes. As with most regional cuisine, you pay only for what you eat. The *Lezat Baru* on the same street has good Chinese food at reasonable prices.

On Jl Veteran near the Gramedia book-shop, the *Depot Kalimantan (Jl Veteran 19)* and *Depot 59 (Jl Veteran 59)* have tasty and moderately priced Banjar food. Nearby, the *Rumah Makan Simpang Tiga (Jl Veteran 22)* has Chinese and Indonesian food.

For a taste of street culture, eat at the *tea stalls* along Jl Niaga Utara between Jl Katamso and Jl Pangeran Samudera near Pasar Baru. Kalimantan's version of the night market is called *belauran*. Banjarmasin's is a huge affair at the Antasari terminal, where you will find more cheap *eateries*.

Western food is available at the *Rama Steak House* in the Arjuna shopping complex on Jl Lambung Mangkurat. Grilled fillets are 20,000Rp. The *Jakarta Garden* on Jl Hasanuddin serves seafood and has cold beer for 12,000Rp a bottle.

For pastries, cookies, bread and ice cream, check out the famous *Utarid* (also called the *Menseng Bakery (Jl Pasar Baru 22-28)*, near the Jl Antasari bridge. At Jl Hasanuddin and Jl Sudimampir the *Hendra Toko Roti Kue* is another good place for bread, cakes and cold drinks while the *Hero Supermarket (Jl Sugiyono)* is a dream come true for self-caterers.

Shopping

If you're a hat freak, the central market (Pasar Baru) area sells hats of every shape, colour and material.

The city is famous for its kain sasirangan, a kind of colourful tie-dye batik. A few shops along Jl Hasanuddin and some stalls in the market near the Jl Antasari bridge sell sasirangan, but mostly as material. Clothes are sold in stores at Km 3.7, Jl Ahmad Yani but large sizes are difficult to find.

Polished stones are a hot item on the streets of Banjarmasin. Just as touts fling boxes of wrist watches at you in Kuta Beach in Bali, the touts here will show you their stones. Most are polished and cut for bulky jewellery, but some offer cut crystals, agates and other interesting bits. Don't fork out too much money if you know little about stones – there are a lot of fakes about.

Getting There & Away

Air The Garuda office (☎ 54203, fax 59063) is in the Hotel Istana Barito. Merpati (☎ 66 203) is at Jl Hasanuddin 31 and is open Monday to Thursday from 7 am to 4 pm and weekend mornings. Bouraq (☎ 52123) is inconveniently located at Jl Ahmad Yani 343, 4km from the city centre. DAS (☎ 52902), Jl Hasanuddin 6, Blok 4, is across the road from Merpati.

Bouraq has daily flights to Balikpapan (317,000Rp). It also services Surabaya (479,000Rp), Denpasar via Surabaya (766,500Rp) and Jakarta (864,000Rp).

Garuda and Merpati have direct flights to Jakarta (864,000Rp) and connecting flights from there. Merpati has flights twice a week to Surabaya (479,800Rp) and three times a week to Palangkaraya (237,900Rp). DAS flies to Pangkalanbun (305,000Rp) five times a week and on to Pontianak (549,400Rp).

Adi Angkasa Travel at Jl Hasanuddin 27 is a good place to buy air tickets and offers some discounts.

Bus Buses and orange Colts depart frequently from the Km 6 terminal for Martapura and Banjarbaru (1750Rp). Air-con night buses to Balikpapan (35,000Rp, 12 hours) and Samarinda (40,000Rp, 14 hours) leave daily around 5 pm. About four different companies do the route and all have luggage compartments. Economy buses leave from Km 6 during the day for Balikpapan (22,500Rp) and Samarinda (25,000Rp). Regular day buses go to Muara Teweh (17,500Rp, 12 hours) and Batulicin (10,000Rp, six hours).

Besides the Colts for Martapura, it's easy to find Colts at the Km 6 terminal to various places in South Kalimantan. They are parked under signs marking their destinations. Colts go to Kandangan (6000Rp, three hours), Negara (8000Rp, four hours), Barabai (7000Rp, four hours), Margasari (6000Rp, three hours) and south to Pagatan (11,500Rp, five hours). Take a yellow taxi kota to Km 6 from the Jl Antasari terminal for 600Rp.

One bus leaves daily to Marabahan from Km 6, but it's easier to go to Kayu Tani Ujung in the north section of Banjarmasin. Colts leave frequently from there for Marabahan (3000Rp), a journey of about 1½ hours. There's an extra 250Rp charge for the short ferry crossing. Take a taxi kota to Kayu Tani Ujung (600Rp) from the Jl Antasari terminal.

Boat All sorts of vessels leave from Banjarmasin to Java and inland by river.

Passenger Ship Pelni ships leave for Surabaya twice a week (18 hours) and Semarang once a week (24 hours) from the Trisakti pinisi harbour. Take a taxi kota from the terminal on Jl Antasari for 600Rp. The route goes past the harbour master's and various ticket offices. Pelni tickets are also sold at the Pelni office (☎ 53077) on Jl Martadinata 10 and at many of the travel agencies in town. Pelni fares from Banjarmasin to Surabaya are 50,000Rp in economy, 134,000Rp in 2nd class and 163,500Rp in 1st class. Fares to Semarang are 56,500/152,500/186,000Rp.

The Dharma Kencana (☎ 51419) ferry to Surabaya is at Jl Yos Sudarso 8 near the harbour. The air-conditioned ferry leaves every other day in the afternoon and takes 20 hours. Tickets are 48,000Rp for seats. There is a cafeteria on board.

Sailboat Schooners constantly ply the route from Banjarmasin to Surabaya. First, go to the harbour master's office for information and for permission to sail, which you are more likely to get if you have a demonstrated interest in sailing, or want to photograph or write about the trip. Then approach the individual captains. The harbour master's office, known as Kantor KPLP (☎ 54775), is on Jl Barito Hilir at Trisakti.

Ferry & Speedboat The trip from Banjarmasin to Palangkaraya goes up three rivers – the Barito, the Kapuas and the Kahayan – and through the two artificial canals that link them. Speedboats to Palangkaraya (27,700Rp, six hours) leave daily from a dock where Jl Lambung Mangkurat meets Jl Pos. At the time of writing, a new bridge was being constructed at this intersection.

Bis air to Palangkaraya (10,000Rp, 18 hours) depart from the Banjar Raya pier on the Sungai Barito, as do boats going up the Barito to Muara Teweh (17,500Rp, 56 hours) in Central Kalimantan. Take a yellow taxi kota (600Rp) to the end of Jl Sutoyo Siswomiharjo, west of the city centre.

Riverboats from the wharf at Pasar Lima go to Negara and Marabahan. The seemingly impenetrable market is at the intersection of Jl Niaga Utara and Jl Pasar Baru. Walk through to the river. Boats leave twice a week to Negara (5000Rp, 12 hours) and daily to Marabahan (2500Rp, four hours).

Getting Around

To/From the Airport Banjarmasin's Syamsudin Noor airport is 26km from town on the road to Banjarbaru. Take a taxi kota from Pasar Baru or the terminal at Jl Antasari to the Km 6 terminal. From there catch a Martapura-bound Colt, get off at the branch road leading to the airport and walk

the 1.5km to the terminal. A taxi all the way to the airport costs 15,000Rp to 20,000Rp. They cluster near the Hotel Sabrina.

From the airport to the city, buy a taxi ticket at the counter in the terminal, or walk out of the airport, through the car park, past the MiG aircraft, turn left and walk to the Banjarmasin-Martapura highway. From there pick up one of the frequent Colts to Banjarmasin.

Public Transport It is possible to hire a boat operator to navigate the canals. Expect to pay about 7500Rp per hour without a guide.

Onshore, the area around Pasar Baru is very small and easy to walk around and most of the hotels, taxi terminals, airline offices etc are nearby. Taxis are 100,000Rp a day or 15,000Rp per hour and there are plenty of becaks, ojeks and *bajaj* (three-wheeled motorised taxis). A bajaj from the city centre to Banjar Raya pier is around 5000Rp; by motorcycle it costs about 3000Rp.

The yellow minibuses are called taxi kota and they go to various parts of town, including the Km 6 terminal, which is the departure point for buses to Banjarbaru, Martapura and Balikpapan. The standard fare is 600Rp.

MARABAHAN & MARGASARI

For a glimpse of river life, take a boat 65km up the Barito from Banjarmasin to Marabahan, a small town with some old, traditional Banjar-style wooden houses. The losmen on the river, such as the **Hotel Bahtera**, have adequate accommodation with rooms from 10,000Rp to 20,000Rp, with shared mandi.

From Marabahan you can charter a boat to Margasari, a handicraft village which produces lots of rattan and bamboo products, such as fans, hats and maps. Colts from there to Banjarmasin (6000Rp) take about three hours.

BANJARBARU
☎ 0511

The chief attraction of this town, on the road from Banjarmasin to Martapura, is its museum collection of Banjar and Dayak artefacts, and statues found at the sites of Hindu temples in Kalimantan. Exhibits include a replica of Banjar riverboat equipment used in traditional Banjar circumcision ceremonies (including an antibiotic leaf and a cut-throat razor), cannons, swords and other artefacts from wars with the Dutch, a small cannon used by British troops in Kalimantan, and Dayak and Banjar swords, knives and other pointy things.

Probably the most interesting exhibit is of items excavated from the Hindu Laras Temple and Agung Temple in East Kalimantan, including a Nandi bull and a *lingam* (the phallic symbol of the Hindu god Shiva). The remains of the Laras Temple are in Margasari village, near Rantau. Agung Temple is near Amuntai, 150km from Banjarmasin. Unless you're a hardcore archaeology freak, it's not worth going all the way to these villages to view what are mainly heaps of rubble.

The museum (☎ 92453) is on the Banjarmasin–Martapura highway at Jl Ahmad Yani 36. Ask the Colt driver to drop you off. It's open daily from 8.30 am to 2.30 pm, but closes at 11 am on Friday and 1.30pm on Saturday.

MARTAPURA
☎ 0511

Martapura is a little east of Banjarbaru. The large Friday market here is a photographer's paradise, with every type of food on sale and lots of colourfully dressed Banjar women.

You can't miss the recent addition to the market area: a brilliant white building with blue roofing built in traditional style. The choice of uncut gems, silver jewellery and trading beads – both strung and unstrung – is excellent, but be prepared to bargain hard. The old market is behind the new building. The Kayu Tangi diamond-polishing factory behind the market on Jl Sukaramai is open to visitors. Beware of spending money on diamonds unless you know what you're doing.

Backing on to the market is *Wisma Penginapan Mutiara* (☎ 91762, Jl Sukaramai 91) where quite decent singles/doubles with shared mandi cost 15,000/25,000Rp.

Colts leave frequently for Martapura (1750Rp, 45 minutes) from the Km 6 terminal in Banjarmasin.

CEMPAKA

The Cempaka diamond fields are a short detour off the Martapura road and a good place to see some of the smaller diamond and gold digs and the conditions people are willing to endure in the hope of finding treasure lying within the soil. The mines are, in fact, silt-filled, water-logged holes dug from muddy streams. The diggers at the bottom of the shaft can spend the day up to their necks in water, passing up baskets full of silt which is washed away in the search for gold specks, diamonds or agates. There are also larger ponds at the site where water and silt are sucked out and dredged.

There are records of 20-carat diamonds from these fields as far back as 1846 – a 106.7 carat monster in 1850 and, the biggest of all, the 167.5 carat Tri Sakti (Thrice Sacred) found in August 1965. Most diamonds are a fraction of the size, but the hope of another big find keeps the miners focused on the job.

Diggers usually work in teams of 10 to 15, digging one day, sluicing the next, with men and women sharing the back-breaking work. Typically, a 'chief' pays the miners 2500Rp a day lunch money to work the claim. If and when there's a find, 10% of the dividend usually goes to the land owner, 10% to the chief, 15% to the pump operator and wood cutter, 10% for tax and the remaining 55% is divided among the team. By-products such as sand and large stones are sold for building and road construction. The activity on the fields tends to follow the big finds. There are touts aplenty to show you the way and sell you polished stones. It's customary to give a 1000Rp to 2000Rp tip to these 'guides'.

To get to Cempaka, take a Banjarmasin-Martapura Colt and ask to get off at the huge roundabout just past Banjarbaru (1750Rp). From there take a green taxi to Alur (600Rp) and walk the last 1km along a dirt road off the main road to the diamond digs. Chartering a minibus taxi from Martapura costs 15,000Rp for a round trip. The diamond mines and polishing centres are closed Friday morning.

KANDANGAN
☎ 0517

This is a transit town 135km from Martapura, with a busy, central minibus terminal and a remarkable old marketplace built in the colonial era.

Kandangan has excellent accommodation at the *Bangkau Hotel* (☎ *21455, Jl Suprapto 2)*, around the corner from the central minibus terminal. Rooms with fan and mandi cost 15,000Rp, or 20,000Rp for bigger rooms. Air-con singles/doubles cost 35,000/45,000Rp. Up the street about 100m on the opposite side, the *Losmen Loksado* (☎ *21 352, Jl Suprapto)* is cheap and friendly. Rooms cost 10,000Rp with fan and shared mandi and 15,000Rp with mandi. There are also three losmen on the main street, Jl Antasari, but they do not welcome foreigners.

Food stalls at the minibus terminal have excellent *nasi bungkus* (take-away rice parcels) with chicken or liver but the best thing to eat in Kandangan is *ketupat*, a delicious local specialty that features sticky rice triangles and broiled *harawan*, a river fish, covered over with a coconut sauce and a squeeze of lime. Restaurants serving the dish are abundant, but a favourite with drivers is *Warung Ketupat Mandagi* about 1km north-west of the minibus terminal on the road to Barabai.

Colts from Banjarmasin's Km 6 terminal to Kandangan cost 6000Rp and take about three hours. There's a bus terminal 2km east of Kandangan where daily night buses stop on the way from Banjarmasin to Balikpapan and Samarinda, usually at around 7 pm. To get out to the station, catch a minibus heading to Negara, or take an ojek for 5000Rp.

NEGARA

Not far from Kandangan, the town of Negara lies to the west, propped up on stilts along the Sungai Negara. This north-western section of South Kalimantan is mostly wetlands and, towards the end of the wet season, water surrounds Negara making the city look like a very waterlogged island. The only land above water is the road, but even that disappears occasionally.

Negara (also spelt on some maps as 'Nagara') was the capital of South Kalimantan's first kingdom, the Hindu realm of Negara Dipa, first ruled by Maharaja Empu Jatmika. In 1526 Pangeran Samudera, a descendant of one of Negara's Hindu kings, overthrew his uncle – Pangeran Tumenggung – and moved the capital to Bandar Masih, the present site of Banjarmasin.

One amazing Negara custom is the raising of water buffalo herds on wooden platforms. They are released daily for grazing and drinking, swim up to 5km and are herded home by 'canoe cowboys'. The wetlands are also remarkable for their prolific fish and bird life, the occasional snake and plenty of ducks. Apart from trading in water buffalo the locals make a living fishing for serpent fish, a popular freshwater fish eaten throughout South-East Asia. They have a distinctive method of catching the fish using live ducklings as bait.

Tour the town by boat – it may be as much as 50,000Rp for half a day depending on your bargaining skills, but that should be enough to visit the wetland buffalo, small sawmills, wharves and other river life. Back on land, ask to see the sword-making. Local craftsmen forge beautiful swords, machetes and kris (daggers) in a variety of styles, complemented by remarkably decorative sheaths.

Surprisingly for such a large town, Negara has no hotel. Ask around for *homestay* accommodation, which should cost 5000Rp to 10,000Rp a night. Negotiate a rate in advance. There are a few small *warung* that serve ketupat and ayam panggang. For breakfast, look out for the *eateries* with trays of doughnut-style kueh.

Getting There & Away

Colts from Banjarmasin to Negara (8000Rp) leave from the Km 6 terminal and take four hours. From Kandangan to Negara there's the option of public minibus taxi (2000Rp), shared Japanese compact taxi with four people (3000Rp per person), chartered taxi (15,000Rp) or ojek (5000Rp). Twice-weekly boats leave from the Pasar Lima pier in Banjarmasin for Negara (5000Rp) and take 12 hours.

LOKSADO

About 40km east of Kandangan in the Muratus Mountains, a collection of villages are the remnants of an animist Banjar society that may have moved here from the Barito delta to avoid the Javanese immigration of the 15th and 16th centuries. About 20 villages are spread over 2500 sq km between Kandangan and Amuntai to the west and the South Kalimantan coast to the east. Loksado is an important market village accessible by road and a good base for trekking in the area.

Places to Stay & Eat

The *small island* on the river running through Loksado has basic accommodation available, if you can find anyone in charge. Rooms cost 15,000Rp to 20,000Rp. The Loksado *kepala desa* (village head) takes guests for about 10,000Rp per person, which includes dinner. Some travellers have also stayed in a ***house*** near the Protestant Christian church, the *geraja etrata*. Ask at the church, which is north along the main path of the town about 300m from the bridge. Give a donation to the church if you stay.

Those looking for a little luxury in this neck of the woods should check out the ***Amandit River Lodge***, just off the road before arriving in Loksado. The pleasant rooms are fan-cooled and there's a garden and a coffee shop. Rates start from US$35/40 for singles/doubles. Arjuna Travel in Banjarmasin takes reservations.

Eateries along the main lane from the suspension bridge are basic and shut down shortly after dusk. The best breakfast is roti from the wok at a ***warung*** about 20m from the bridge.

Getting There & Away

There's a good road to Loksado, terminating just before the suspension bridge. Colts and pick-ups leave the Kandangan minibus

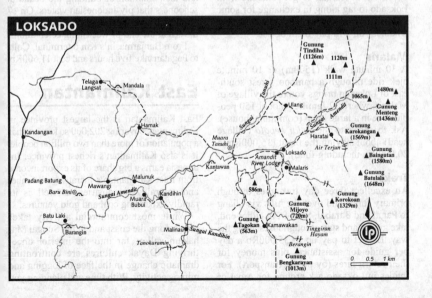

LOKSADO

0   0.5   1 km

KALIMANTAN

terminal for Loksado (4000Rp) in the afternoon, and leave Loksado for Kandangan early in the morning, departing from the main bridge. The trip takes 1½ hours.

Coming back from Loksado, many travellers charter a bamboo raft and pole down Sungai Amandit. The usual drop-off point is Muara Tanuhi, two hours downstream (40,000Rp), where there are also **hot springs** (bring your bathing suit). Continuing on to Bubuhi a few more hours downstream is feasible, but costs a lot more. From the nearby road at Bubuhi, minibus taxis and ojeks go back to Kandangan.

AROUND LOKSADO
From Loksado there are hundreds of paths through mountain garden plots to other villages over the hills, many crossing mountain streams via suspension bridges. Follow the path upstream on the Sungai Amandit for three hours (8km) to a series of **air terjun** just past Balai Haratai. It's easy enough to find the first waterfall, but local knowledge is handy if you want to climb to the middle and top falls, and find the nearby cave. Ask at Haratai or get someone from Loksado to tag along in exchange for some English practice or at least make it clear whether you will pay them or not.

Malaris
A 30 minute walk (1500m) or 10 minute ojek ride through a bamboo forest southeast of Loksado brings you to the village of Malaris, where 32 families (about 150 people) live in a large balai (communal house). Ask to speak to the *balai kepala* (village head) about staying the night (15,000Rp to 20,000Rp, including food).

Treks
An excellent three day trek goes through primary forest and over the hills via Ulang to **Pagat** and **Barabai**. Start from either end, take guides and stay at longhouses along the way. Expect to pay up to 35,000Rp a day per guide for assistance, plus money for their return fares (by public transport). For guides in Loksado ask around for Amat or

Korlan, who speak English. Travel agencies in Banjarmasin also arrange treks to Loksado or try asking at the Hotel Bankau or Losmen Loksado.

Barabai has an excellent losmen, the **Fusfa Hotel** (☎ 41136, Jl Hasan 144) with a restaurant and immaculate singles/doubles/triples with fan and mandi for 18,150/27,225/36,300Rp. Air-con rooms cost 42,350/51,425/60,500Rp. From Barabai, taxi minibuses go to Kandangan (2000Rp, one hour).

Treks can also be made over the hills from Loksado to the coast. The trek to **Kota Baru** on Pulau Laut takes three or four days by a combination of foot, minibus and boat, passing through hillside gardens, forests and over Gunung Besar, the province's highest peak at 1892m.

SOUTH COAST
An alternative route between Banjarmasin and Balikpapan is the coastal route via **Pagatan** and **Batulicin**. Buses to Batulicin (10,000Rp) take six hours. From Batulicin, Pelni boats go to Ujung Pandang in Sulawesi.

Pagatan is known for its Bugis community and their tradition of building the beautiful schooners that ply Indonesian waters. On 17 April each year, local Bugis make offerings to the sea at the end of week-long celebrations.

From Banjarmasin's Km 6 terminal, Colts to Pagatan take five hours and cost 11,500Rp.

East Kalimantan

East Kalimantan is the largest province in Kalimantan, covering 202,000 sq km, and has a population of more than two million people. It is also Kalimantan's richest province: Indonesia earns a big share of its export income from East Kalimantan's lucrative oil, timber and natural gas industries, as well as its rapidly expanding coal and gold ventures.

While most commercial activity takes place along the coast and in the Sungai Mahakam valley, far into the interior once-thriving Dayak cultures are confronting dramatic change in the face of logging and mining activity. With time and planning you

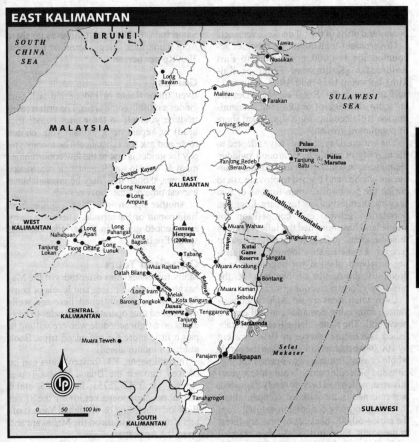

EAST KALIMANTAN

SOUTH CHINA SEA

BRUNEI

MALAYSIA

Long Bawan

Malinau

Tawau

Nunukan

Tarakan

SULAWESI SEA

Tanjung Selor

Pulau Derawan

Tanjung Redeb (Berau)

Tanjung Batu

Pulau Maratua

Sungai Kayan

EAST KALIMANTAN

Long Nawang

Long Ampung

Sambaliung Mountains

WEST KALIMANTAN

Nahabuan

Long Apari

Long Pahangai

Long Bagun

Long Lunuk

Tiong Ohang

Tanjung Lokan

Gunung Menyapa (2000m)

Tabang

Muara Wahau

Sangkulirang

Kutai Game Reserve

Sangata

Sungai Wahau

Sungai Belayan

Muara Ancalung

Mua Raritan

Datah Bilang

Sungai Mahakam

Bontang

Long Iram

Melak

Muara Kaman

Sebulu

Barong Tongkok

Kota Bangun

Danau Jempang

Tanjung Isuy

Tenggarong

Samarinda

CENTRAL KALIMANTAN

Muara Teweh

Selat Makasar

Panajam

Balikpapan

SOUTH KALIMANTAN

Tanahgrogot

SULAWESI

0 50 100 km

can reach places that rarely see a foreign face, and enjoy pockets of wilderness, but loggers and the military are ever-present.

Fifth century Sanskrit inscriptions found in the Wahau Valley north of Tenggarong are all that remains of one of Indonesia's oldest Hindu kingdoms and the area's contact with Indian and Sriwijaya merchants. Its successor, the Sultanate of Kutai, was founded in the 13th century with the assistance of refugees from strife-torn East Java. Kutai became an important regional trading power

and its capital, Tenggarong, remained East Kalimantan's largest and busiest urban centre until eclipsed by Samarinda and Balikpapan in the 20th century.

The region has had its share of opportunists, such as the pirate Arung Singkang, a descendant of the Bugis royal family of Wajo in Sulawesi Selatan.

Full-scale exploitation of the Mahakam delta's oil reserves began in 1897, shifting the focus of commerce to the oil refineries at Balikpapan. By 1913 the province was producing more than half of the East Indies' oil output and Balikpapan has been riding the booms and busts of the oil market ever since.

Government transmigration schemes accounted for 114,000 newcomers to East Kalimantan (Kalimantan Timur or Kal-Tim) between 1954 and 1985, with over half settling in the Kutai regency. Despite an acute shortage of arable land, transmigration still accounts for a significant share of population growth.

The various Dayak tribes have adapted to the scarcity of arable land through swidden techniques, in which plots of secondary jungle are slashed and burned to provide ash to enrich the poor soils, sown for one or two seasons, then left fallow for years. Logging, population growth and competition for arable land has shortened the fallow periods in some areas, giving the land less time to recover. Unsustainable logging and farming has been blamed for degrading hundreds of thousands of hectares of the province's forests to poor grassland.

Even when areas are set aside for conservation, competing demands can still exact a heavy toll. The Kutai Game Reserve, established as a nature reserve in 1936, was cut by 100,000 hectares in 1968 when the park's whole coastal frontage was opened for logging and oil exploration. Within a few years this area, which had been severely degraded, was returned to the park as 'compensation' for a new logging concession excised from the park – 60,000 hectares of primary forest in the south. Fires in 1982-83 then claimed a big share of the remnants of the park's undisturbed forests. In 1997 and early 1998, more fires in the reserve and the surrounding area drove out wildlife and further ravaged the remaining forest.

DAYAK VILLAGES

Probably the best starting point for visits to inland Dayak villages is Samarinda. Longboats leave from here to ply the Mahakam, Kedang Kepala and Belayan rivers. DAS flies from Samarinda to Long Ampung, close to the source of the mighty Sungai Kayan.

The relatively acculturated Kenyah Dayak village of **Pampang** is 26km from Samarinda. Public taxi minibuses go there from Samarinda's Segiri terminal for about 3000Rp per person.

Guides

Even those fluent in Indonesian will find guides a must in some areas. The drill is to introduce yourself to the *camat* (subdistrict head) or kepala desa, explain your chosen route and ask for assistance. The money you pay for guides is one of the few opportunities many folk get to supplement their subsistence incomes, though they may be unavailable at harvest time or other busy periods.

Another option is to take a guide from Balikpapan or Samarinda. There are many experienced guides in Samarinda who also speak English.

Organised Tours

Many travel agencies offer tours of the Mahakam at varying prices and levels of comfort. The ones mentioned here are well-established tour operators who cater to travellers on a tight schedule who are willing to pay a little more for organised trips. Book at least a month ahead.

In Balikpapan, PT Tomaco Tours can be booked through the Buana Wisata Travel Agency (☎ 0542-22751, fax 33683, email buanabpn@bpp.mega.net.id) in the Hotel Benakutai building on Jl Ahmad Yani. It offers a number of tours on the Mahakam and up to the Apokayan.

Mesra Tours (☎ 0541-38787, fax 41017, email mesra@smd.mega.net.id) has an office in the Hotel Mesra in Samarinda, managed by Lucas Zwaal, who speaks Dutch, German, English and Indonesian. Mesra offers a number of tours, which include trips up the Mahakam, as well as treks to West Kalimantan, the Apokayan, Loksado in South Kalimantan and tours to Tanjung Puting in Central Kalimantan.

Arjuna Tours and Travel (☎ 0511- 58150, fax 54944, email arjuna@bjm.mega.net.id) in Banjarmasin also runs tours up the Mahakam from Samarinda.

BALIKPAPAN
☎ 0542 • pop 365,000

Balikpapan is an air-con oil boomtown with little to recommend it to the average traveller. Accommodation is expensive and there's little to see around town. For up-market travellers, on the other hand, Balikpapan has the best hotels and restaurants in Kalimantan and an active nightlife scene. The huge oil refinery dominates the city and, while flying in, you can see stray tankers and offshore oil rigs. This is the centre of Kalimantan's oil business and the chief city of the province. There are frequent flights to Jakarta and a couple of five star hotels with world-class standards.

Balikpapan's oilfields made it a strategic target in the Japanese invasion of 1941, and again in the Allied advances in 1944-45. Australians occupied Balikpapan after a bloody invasion and suppressed anti-colonial unrest. A memorial stands on the boulevard meridian near Pertamina Hospital for the 229 Australians who died here and there's a memorial for Japanese soldiers near the beach at Lamaru east of the airport on the way to Manggar.

Balikpapan's fortunes soared with the oil price shocks of the 1970s, but then plummeted with an oil glut and falling prices in the 1980s, crippling the city's enclave economy. The subsequent upturn in oil, coal and timber prices restored confidence and stimulated new activity.

Today, even in the wake of Indonesia's economic crisis and suffering once more from low oil prices, Balikpapan has an air of easy, yet oddly artificial, affluence that you won't find anywhere else in Kalimantan. The central area is mainly given over to shops, hotels and restaurants. The Pertamina, Union Oil and Total residential areas are insulated from the rest of town. The neighbourhood near the market north of the oil refinery is by far the most interesting precinct, built on stilts over tidal mudflats, with uneven, lurching wooden walkways.

Balikpapan also supports an ongoing effort to rescue orang-utans from the surrounding area, especially since the devastation of the nearby forests during the fires of 1997 and early 1998. The Wanariset Orangutan Reintroduction Centre was established with the assistance of the Balikpapan Orangutan Survival Foundation (BOS). BOS and the Wanariset Centre are grateful for donations, but unlike Tanjung Puting, the centre is not open to the public. For more information, contact BOS (☎ 413069, fax 410365), PO Box 447, Balikpapan, East Kalimantan 76103. Or see its Web site: www.redcube.nl/bos/.

Orientation & Information

The best landmark is the beachfront Balikpapan Centre on the corner of Jl Sudirman and Jl Ahmad Yani. This large shopping complex is at the axis of the commercial and hotel district. Head north along Jl Ahmad Yani to find the restaurants, east along the shore to get to the airport, or west along Jl Sudirman to find the immigration, government and post offices. Jl Sudirman joins Jl Minyak, which loops past the seaports and oil refinery areas.

The Gramedia bookshop in the Balikpapan Centre has maps of Balikpapan and other areas in Kalimantan.

Money There's no shortage of banks in Balikpapan, but most of them seem to close on the weekends. Bank Rakyat at Jl Sudirman 37, a grey multistorey building near the post office, changes major travellers cheques and currencies. The bank is open weekdays from 8 am to 3 pm. Bank Duta, on the corner of Jl Ahmad Yani and Jl Sudirman, has similar hours and changes cash, but not travellers cheques. Bank Bali's ATM, by the Balikpapan Centre, allows Cirrus and MasterCard cash withdrawal, as does BNI bank across from the Blue Sky Hotel on Jl Suprapto. The PT Haji La Tunrung Star Group at Jl Ahmad Yani 51, close to the intersection with Jl Sudirman, changes cash and travellers cheques and is open daily from 7 am to 9 pm.

Post & Communications The post office is on Jl Sudirman, west of the city centre and is open Monday to Saturday from 8 am

BALIKPAPAN

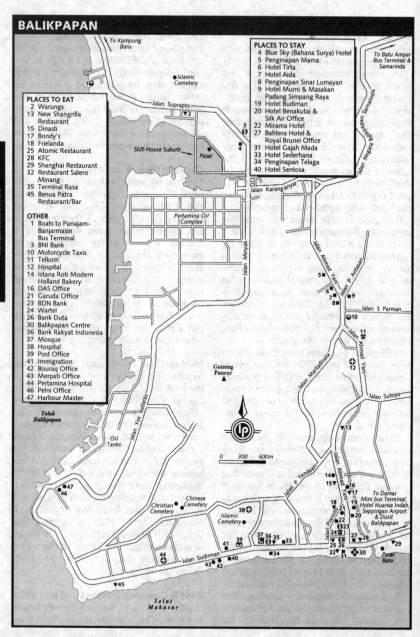

To Kampung Baru

To Batu Ampar Bus Terminal & Samarinda

Islamic Cemetery

Jalan Suprapto

Stilt-House Suburb

Pasar

PLACES TO STAY
4 Blue Sky (Bahana Surya) Hotel
5 Penginapan Mama
6 Hotel Tirta
7 Hotel Aida
8 Penginapan Sinar Lumayan
9 Hotel Murni & Masakan Padang Simpang Raya
19 Hotel Budiman
20 Hotel Benakutai & Silk Air Office
22 Mirama Hotel
27 Bahtera Hotel & Royal Brunei Office
31 Hotel Gajah Mada
33 Hotel Sederhana
34 Penginapan Telaga
40 Hotel Sentosa

PLACES TO EAT
2 Warungs
13 New Shangrilla Restaurant
15 Dinasti
17 Bondy's
19 Frielanda
25 Atomic Restaurant
28 KFC
29 Shanghai Restaurant
32 Restaurant Salero Minang
35 Terminal Rasa
45 Benua Patra Restaurant/Bar

OTHER
1 Boats to Panajam-Banjarmasin Bus Terminal
3 BNI Bank
10 Motorcycle Taxis
11 Telkom
12 Hospital
14 Istana Roti Modern Holland Bakery
16 DAS Office
21 Garuda Office
23 BDN Bank
24 Wartel
26 Bank Duta
30 Balikpapan Centre
36 Bank Rakyat Indonesia
37 Mosque
38 Hospital
39 Post Office
41 Immigration
42 Bouraq Office
43 Merpati Office
44 Pertamina Hospital
46 Pelni Office
47 Harbour Master

Jalan Karanganyar

Pertamina Oil Complex

Jalan Minyak

Jalan Negara Balikpapan-Samarinda

Jalan Ahmad Yani

Jalan P Antasari

Jalan S Parman

Jalan Ahmad Yani

Jalan Martadinata

Jalan Ahmad Yani

Jalan Sutoyo

Gunung Pancur

Teluk Balikpapan

Oil Tanks

Jalan Yos Sudarso

0   300   600m

To Damai Mini bus Terminal, Hotel Nuansa Indah, Seppingan Airport & Dusit Balikpapan

Jalan P Tendean

Jalan Ahmad Yani

Jalan Pranoto

Christian Cemetery

Chinese Cemetery

Islamic Cemetery

Jalan Sudirman

Pasar Baru

Selat Makasar

to 8 pm. The Internet service charges 5000Rp an hour and is open daily from 8 am to 4 pm. East of Jl Ahmad Yani, the Cyber Sadena at Jl Sudirman 325 charges 8000Rp per hour for Internet access.

The Telkom office is at Jl Ahmad Yani 418 and is open 24 hours.

Travel Agencies A good place to buy air tickets is PT Totogasono Sekawan (☎ 24 516, fax 23722) at Jl Ahmad Yani 40, close to the Garuda office. The staff speak English well and are very friendly and efficient. For Pelni tickets try CV Pelita Agung (☎ 44 0790, fax 32298) at Jl Ahmad Yani 21, across from the Hotel Murni.

Organised Tours
Several travel agencies in Balikpapan organise all-inclusive visits to Dayak villages. See Organised Tours under Dayak Villages earlier for details.

Places to Stay – Budget
Budget travellers are better off skipping Balikpapan altogether and heading up to Samarinda, where there are much better deals. In Balikpapan most of the cheaper accommodation is north of the city centre on Jl Ahmad Yani, which is on taxi route No 3. Cheapest of the bunch is the *Hotel Murni* (☎ 25290, Jl Pangeran Antasari 1), a bright blue, three storey building that has singles with fan and mandi for 15,000Rp and doubles for 22,000Rp to 25,000Rp. The rooms are clean but the place suffers from traffic noise. Across the street, the *Penginapan Sinar Lumayan* (☎ 36092, Jl Ahmad Yani 49) has similar prices, as well as triples for 35,000Rp.

Up the road, the *Hotel Aida* (☎ 21006, Jl Ahmad Yani 29) has airless economy rooms costing 20,500Rp with shared mandi and 30,500Rp with mandi. Rooms with air-con cost 53,500Rp and 65,500Rp.

Another good budget option is the friendly *Penginapan Telaga* (☎ 33071, Jl Sudirman Complex Cemera 44) down near the shore. Singles/doubles/triples on the top floor cost 25,000/30,000/35,000Rp with fan and shared mandi. The rooms are

basic, but clean. Air-con doubles/triples with mandi cost 50,000/60,000Rp. Prices include breakfast.

Places to Stay – Mid-Range
The *Hotel Gajah Mada* (☎ 34634, fax 34646, Jl Sudirman 14), beside the Balikpapan Centre, has singles/doubles with fan and mandi for 30,000/40,000Rp, but the best value are air-con rooms for 60,000/75,000Rp. They also have more expensive rooms. All prices include breakfast but not the 21% tax. The *Hotel Sederhana* (☎ 22564, Jl Sudirman 45) is a reasonable mid-range option west of the Balikpapan Centre. Singles with air-con are 42,350/48,400Rp, doubles are 48,400/54,450Rp and triples are 54,450/60,500Rp, including taxes and breakfast.

The *Hotel Budiman* (☎ 36030, fax 23811, Jl Ahmad Yani) has seen better days but has adequate air-con doubles with mandi starting at 50,000Rp, breakfast included. A 21% tax is added. Nearby, the *Mirama Hotel* (☎ 33 906, fax 34230, Jl Pranoto 16) is more expensive but very comfortable. Rooms with air-con, bath and minibar range from 80,000Rp to 150,000Rp, plus a 21% tax surcharge. Facilities include a coffee shop, pharmacy and meeting rooms. A new wing of the hotel is across the street.

The *Hotel Tirta* (☎ 22772, fax 22132), further north at Jl Ahmad Yani 8, has a mind boggling variety of rooms and cottages that, along with discounts of between 10% and 25%, make it another mid-range option. Standard rooms with air-con, bath and fridge start at 82,000Rp and cottages by the pool cost 137,000Rp. All prices include breakfast, but a 21% tax is added. Another place offering considerable discounts is the *Hotel Sentosa* (☎ 35908, fax 35958, Jl Sudirman Blok B, 31-34). Air-con rooms with bath cost from 45,000Rp to 95,000Rp.

The *Hotel Nuansa Indah* (☎ 418555, fax 412138, Jl Sudirman 1), near the Damai minibus terminal, opened in 1997 and has air-con rooms for 68,000Rp, 78,000Rp and 88,000Rp. All prices include breakfast but not the 21% tax. Some of the staff speak English.

Places to Stay – Top End

The top hotel in Balikpapan, and indeed in Kalimantan, is the *Dusit Balikpapan* (☎ 20155, fax 20150, Jl Sudirman). It has a fitness centre, tennis courts, a jogging track, swimming pool, Chinese, Thai, Indonesian and western dining, one of the most popular bars in town and top-notch service standards. Rates start from US$135 plus taxes, though discounts are sometimes available.

Hotel Benakutai (☎ 31896, fax 31823, Jl Ahmad Yani) was formerly the best hotel in town and still maintains high standards. Rooms start at US$95/110, plus tax. Substantial discounts are occasionally available. There's an international-style bar/restaurant with great coffee.

The central *Bahtera Hotel* (☎ 22563, fax 31889, Jl Sudirman 2) is a slightly cheaper option, with economy rooms for US$50, standard rooms for US$70 and superior rooms for US$85, but don't expect quite the same standards as at the Dusit Balikpapan or the Benakutai. The *Blue Sky Hotel (Bahana Surya)* (☎ 35845, fax 24094, Jl Suprapto 1) has a fitness centre, squash court, swimming pool and Japanese and Chinese restaurants. Singles/doubles in the older wing cost US$50/60, while rooms in the new wing cost from US$75/85, plus a 21% tax.

Places to Eat

Balikpapan has some excellent restaurants. *Bondy's* on Jl Ahmad Yani offers seafood and hearty meals of western fare in an open courtyard. It's not cheap, but well worth a splurge. Look for the big red and white rooftop sign and venture through the sterile street-front bakery to the courtyard and its broad balconies where you'll find good food, attentive staff and a pleasant atmosphere. The seafood is much better than the steak.

On the road to the airport, western-style food is also served at *Martha's Steakhouse*, also known as the *Borneo Steakhouse (Jl Sudirman Rt 46)* from 10 am to 11 pm. Past the airport and along taxi route No 7 (watch for the blue sign) *Lila's Restoran (Jl Mulawarman 56)*, also known as *Jack's Bar*, serves a variety of western dishes and is well

worth the trip – for the setting on the beach as much as the food. Walk 100m from the highway towards the ocean

For inexpensive Indonesian-style Chinese fare, try the string of restaurants, including *Frielanda*, near the Mirama Hotel. The *Atomic* on Jl Pranoto close to Jl Sudirman has more authentic Chinese food and is air-conditioned. The *Dinasti* on Jl Ahmad Yani appeared to be temporarily closed at the time of writing but may have reopened by now. Further up the street, the *Restoran Shan-grilla (Jl Ahmad Yani 29)* is another popular place for locals. For more upmarket Chinese dining, try the *Shanghai Restaurant* on Jl Sudirman, east of the Balikpapan Centre.

The *Masakan Padang Simpang Raya*, next to the Hotel Murni, serves Padang food. So too does the *Restaurant Sinar Minang* on Jl Sudirman, beside the Hotel Gajah Mada. The latter serves *dang galah* (giant river prawns).

The *Benua Patra* on Jl Yos Sudarso has a splendid view of the ocean and serves both western and Indonesian food. Both the *Dusit Balikpapan* and the *Benakutai* hotels have excellent upmarket western and Asian restaurants. For fast food, there's a *KFC* next door to the Bahtera Hotel and a *Texas Fried Chicken* in the Balikpapan Centre. The *Pacifica Food Fair*, in the back section of the centre, offers a wide range of Asian and western fast food and is a good place to recuperate from the searing heat outside.

The *Hero Supermarket* in the Balikpapan Centre has everything from cheese to chocolate chip cookies. The *Istana Roti Modern Holland Bakery* on Jl Ahmad Yani near the Dinasti restaurant is a good place for pastries and bread.

Entertainment

Balikpapan is an R&R centre for oil workers and other expats working in mining and logging upriver. Consequently, there's a large number of bars and discos in town, though the latter began to be referred to as 'music pubs' after discos were closed down in Balikpapan in the aftermath of the 1998 riots in Jakarta. Things may have returned to normal by the time of publication. One of the better options is the ***Borneo Pub*** at the Dusit Balikpapan. For a pub crawl, try the rather seedy karaoke places near the Hotel Sentosa and make your way out to the more western-style ***Joy's Bar*** on Jl Sudirman out of town, beside Martha's Steakhouse. The ***Benakutai*** and ***Blue Sky Hotel*** also have live music venues.

A crocodile farm at Teritup, east of the airport, where visitors can feed crocodiles a chicken for 10,000Rp, might be entertaining for some people. Take a route No 7 taxi (2000Rp) from the Damai terminal

Getting There & Away
Air Garuda (☎ 22300), at Jl Ahmad Yani 14, is opposite the Hotel Benakutai. Merpati (☎ 24452) is at Jl Sudirman 32. Bouraq (☎ 31 475) has an office nearby on Jl Sudirman 13 and DAS (☎ 24286) is at Jl Ahmad Yani 33. For international flights, the Silk Air office is in the Benakutai Hotel and Royal Brunei Airlines has an office in the Bhatera Hotel.

Garuda has two flights a day to Jakarta (1,131,000Rp) and Bouraq flies to the capital three times a week.

Merpati has useful flights to Pontianak (742,000Rp) three times a week and flights to Tarakan (578,000Rp) daily. Bouraq flies to Banjarmasin (317,000Rp) four times a week, to Surabaya (749,600Rp) daily and to Ujung Pandang (926,000Rp) four times a week. DAS flies to Samarinda (107,500Rp) and on to Berau (355,00Rp) and Tarakan (470,500Rp) daily except Sunday.

Silk Air flies to Singapore (US$275) twice a week and Royal Brunei flies to Bandar Seri Begawan (US$105) three times a week with connections to Manila and Kuala Lumpur.

Bus From Balikpapan buses head north to Samarinda or south to Banjarmasin. Buses to Samarinda (4700/6000Rp normal/air-con, two hours) depart from the Batu Ampar bus terminal north of the city accessible by taxi on routes 1, 2 or 3 for 1200Rp (it's a long way). Tickets are sold on the bus and at the terminal.

Buses to Banjarmasin (22,500/35,000Rp, 12 hours) depart from the bus terminal on the opposite side of the harbour to the city. To get there, take route No 6 taxi from Jl Sudirman near the Balikpapan Centre to the pier on Jl Monginsidi. You'll know you've arrived because kids mob the minibus to solicit passengers for speedboat charters. Speedboats cost about 2000Rp per person, or around 10,000Rp to charter, and take 10 minutes.

Air-con buses to Banjarmasin also leave from a stand on Jl Soekarno-Hatta on the way to the Batu Ampar terminal.

Boat The Pelni liners *Kambuna* and *Tidar* call alternately about every four days, connecting Balikpapan with Pantoloan, Pare Pare and Ujung Pandang (Sulawesi), and Surabaya (Java) and beyond. There's a fortnightly run to Tarakan.

In Balikpapan the Pelni office (☎ 24171) is at Jl Yos Sudarso 76. Economy fares are: Pantoloan (34,500Rp); Pare Pare (45,500Rp); Ujung Pandang (50,000Rp); Surabaya (107,000Rp); and Tarakan (67,500Rp).

The Kharma Kencana company (☎ 22 194) has a car and passenger ferry service to Mamuju in Sulawesi that departs every second day. The journey takes 16 hours and costs 33,000Rp for foot passengers. Tickets are sold at the dock at Kampung Baru at the end of Jl Monginsidi. To get there take a taxi to the end of route No 6.

At the next dock over, the Tanjung Selamat Express leaves twice a week for Pare Pare (50,000Rp, 24 hours). Tickets are sold at the dock between 10 am and 2 pm or at the agency office (☎ 34516) nearby at Rt 1, Jl Monginsidi 4, about 500m from the docks.

Getting Around
To/From the Airport Seppingan airport is a 15 minute drive from Pasar Baru. A taxi from the airport to town costs a standard 10,000Rp, or 15,000Rp for air-con, if you buy a taxi ticket in the terminal.

A short walk from the airport, you can catch route No 7 taxis on the highway going to the Damai minibus terminal. Transfer to a route No 1 or 3 taxi to get into town (600Rp).

Taxi Minibuses Colour-coded as well as numbered, these taxi minibuses cut a circular route around the town and are a perfect way to get around. The usual price within town is 600Rp, but watch out for overcharging. The trip out to the Batu Ampar bus terminal costs 1200Rp.

For more personalised service at a budget price, ojeks cost from 3000Rp to 5000Rp per ride.

SAMARINDA
☎ 0541   • pop 470,000

As oil is to Balikpapan, so timber is to Samarinda. Both cities are important trading ports, but although it is just a couple of hours from Balikpapan by bus, Samarinda is a different place entirely. Samarinda is less obviously affluent, less expat-oriented and more Indonesian than its neighbour. For travellers it's a good place to arrange inland journeys up the Sungai Mahakam to Dayak areas.

Most of the people who have settled in Samarinda are Banjars from South Kalimantan, so the main dialect is Banjarese. There are also many Kutais, a grouping that includes the indigenous people of this area.

On the south side of Sungai Mahakam, in the part of town called **Samarinda Seberang**, you can visit cottage industries where Samarinda-style sarongs are woven. The traditional East Kalimantan wraparound is woven from *doyo* leaf.

Orientation
The main part of Samarinda stretches along the north bank of the river. The best orientation point is the enormous Mesjid Raya Darussalam on the riverfront. Most of the offices and hotels are concentrated in the area north of the riverfront. Another useful landmark is the Mesra Indah shopping centre.

Information
Tourist Office The Kantor Pariwisata tourist office (☎ 41669, fax 37697) is at Jl Harmonika 1, just off Jl Kesuma Bangsa. Some of the staff speak English well and are very knowledgable about the area.

Samarinda city maps and regional maps can be found in the Gramedia bookshop in the Mesra Indah shopping centre.

Money BNI bank, on the corner of Jl Sebatik and Jl Panglima Batur, changes only US dollars (cash and travellers cheques). It's open weekdays from 8 am to 3 pm and Saturday mornings. It also has an ATM that takes Cirrus and MasterCard, as does Bank Bali on the corner of Jl Panglima and Jl Sulawesi.

Near the post office, Bank Central Asia (BCA) on Jl Sudirman changes US cash and travellers cheques, as well as Hong Kong and Singapore dollars, but is closed on weekends.

Post & Communications The main post office is on the corner of Jl Gajah Mada and Jl Awang Long and is open daily from 7.30 am to 8 pm. Internet access is available for 8000Rp an hour. The Wartel Helma, on Jl Basuki Rahmat 22, west of Jl Agus Salim, also has an Internet service for 10,000Rp per hour.

Guides In 1998, following widespread forest fires the year before and in the aftermath of the Asian economic crisis, there were more guides in Samarinda than travellers and the tourist market had virtually dried up. Guides keep a check on who is in town through the budget hotels and their rates vary enormously depending on the kind of trip you are planning. For real adventure, don't expect anything in the way of a bargain, but most travellers find something to suit their budget and ambitions.

Mokhta (☎ 273554), who works out of the Aida Hotel, is a reliable and enthusiastic guide and a mine of information on treks up-river. He often meets the buses at the Sungai Kunjang ferry terminal. Try his phone number or you can leave a message at the hotel.

Jailani and his brother Rusli (☎/fax 74 7376, email jailani@smd.mega.net.id) are experienced guides. They can organise customised trips along the Mahakam, across into West Kalimantan or into the Apokayan, at very reasonable rates. If you can't reach them by phone, leave a message at the Hotel Hidayah I on Jl Mas Tumenggung.

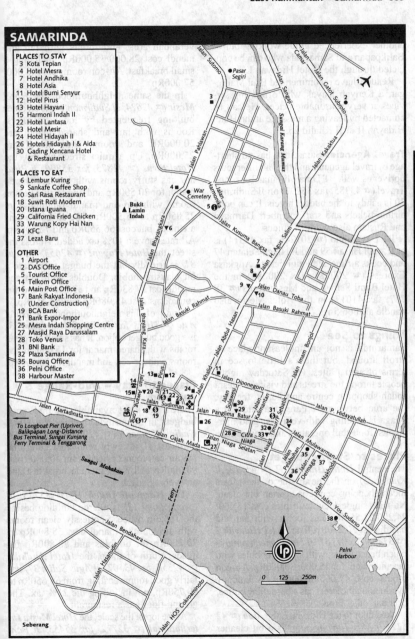

SAMARINDA

PLACES TO STAY
3 Kota Tepian
4 Hotel Mesra
7 Hotel Andhika
8 Hotel Asia
11 Hotel Bumi Senyur
12 Hotel Pirus
13 Hotel Hayani
15 Harmoni Indah II
22 Hotel Lantasa
23 Hotel Mesir
24 Hotel Hidayah II
26 Hotels Hidayah I & Aida
30 Gading Kencana Hotel
   & Restaurant

PLACES TO EAT
6 Lembur Kuring
9 Sankafe Coffee Shop
10 Sari Rasa Restaurant
18 Suwit Roti Modern
20 Istana Iguana
29 California Fried Chicken
33 Warung Kopy Hai Nan
34 KFC
37 Lezat Baru

OTHER
1 Airport
2 DAS Office
5 Tourist Office
14 Telkom Office
16 Main Post Office
17 Bank Rakyat Indonesia
   (Under Construction)
19 BCA Bank
21 Bank Expor-Impor
25 Mesra Indah Shopping Centre
27 Masjid Raya Darussalam
28 Toko Venus
31 BNI Bank
32 Plaza Samarinda
35 Bouraq Office
36 Pelni Office
38 Harbour Master

Suryadi (email surya57@hotmail.com) is another experienced guide working out of Balikpapan and Samarinda who can be contacted through the Hotel Hidayah I.

Readers have recommended Paul Mauregar, a Kenyah Dayak who offers his services at very reasonable prices. He can be contacted by leaving a message at the Hotel Hidayah II at Jl Khalid 25.

Travel Agencies Samarinda has no shortage of travel agencies and they all offer tours upriver as well. PT Duta Miramar Tours and Travel (☎ 43385, fax 35291) on Jl Sudirman 20 is handy to the budget hotels. It can book airline tickets and staff members Darmawi and Rustam also work as guides.

PT Dayakindo (☎ 201246, fax 43314) is at Jl Abul Hasan 59 and Jl Niaga Selatan 47 and books airline and Pelni tickets. Angkasa Express (☎ 200281, fax 200280) in the Hotel Bumi Senyur and Mesra Tours (☎ 38 787, fax 41017) in the Hotel Mesra also handle air bookings.

Things to See

Samarinda is not an unpleasant place to stroll around, but there's little to see in terms of actual sites. On Saturday nights, people throng the streets and visit the Mesra Indah shopping centre and during the day, the area between Jl Panglima and Citra Niaga is bustling with vehicles, gold merchants, food stall operators and fruit sellers.

Places to Stay – Budget

The central *Hotel Hidayah II* (☎ 41712, Jl Khalid 25) on the north side of the Mesra Indah shopping centre is spartan but clean. No frills singles/doubles/triples cost 15,400/ 24,200/33,550Rp and rooms with fan and mandi cost 30,250Rp. The *Hotel Hidayah I* (☎ 31408, fax 37761, Jl Mas Tumenggung) is much better value, with singles/doubles with fan and mandi for 25,000/ 30,000Rp. Air-con rooms cost 47,000/58,000Rp. A balcony overlooking the street has a bar selling coffee, beer and other drinks.

Next door to the Hidayah I, the *Aida* (☎ 42 572, Jl Mas Tumenggung) is a bit cleaner

and also good value. It has a coffee shop verandah area, and rooms with fan and mandi cost 28,000/35,000Rp, including a small breakfast. Air-con rooms cost 48,000/ 57,000Rp.

In the same neighbourhood, the *Hotel Mesir* (☎ 42624, Jl Sudirman 23) is an older building frequented by local travellers. Rooms with fan and shared mandi are 20,000Rp and rooms with mandi are 25,000Rp. Up a quiet street nearby, the *Hotel Pirus* (☎ 41873, fax 35890, Jl Pirus 30) has stuffy rooms with fan and shared mandi for 20,500Rp and one to five person rooms with fan and mandi ranging from 25,850Rp to 45,500Rp. The air-con rooms are nicer, but cost 66,550Rp and 72,600Rp. All rates have a 10% tax added. Across the street, the *Hotel Hayani* (☎ 42653, Jl Pirus 31) is friendly but the budget rooms are a bit claustrophobic. Doubles with fan and mandi cost 27,830Rp and 33,880Rp and air-con rooms cost 45,980Rp and 54,450Rp.

North of this neighbourhood, the *Hotel Asia* (☎ 31013, fax 31476, Jl Agus Salim 33) is a good budget option. It has small but clean rooms with shared mandi for 15,000Rp and rooms with air-con and mandi for 20,000Rp.

Places to Stay – Mid-Range & Top End

There's not a lot available for mid-range budgets in Samarinda, but try the *Hotel Gading Kencana* (☎ 41043, fax 31954, Jl Sulawesi 4), a newly renovated hotel that has air-con rooms priced from 40,000Rp to 90,000Rp. All rates include breakfast and an evening snack.

The *Harmoni Indah II* (☎ 35775, Jl Awang Long 12) is a large building beside the Telkom office. Spotlessly clean rooms with air-con and mandi cost 58,800Rp to 79,200Rp for doubles and 88,800Rp for quads. North of there, the *Hotel Andhika* (☎ 42358, fax 43507, Jl Agus Salim 37) has fairly good rooms costing from 66,650Rp to 90,750Rp, not including the 21% tax. The ground floor has a restaurant.

At the top of the scale, the *Hotel Mesra International* (☎ 32772, fax 35453, Jl Pah-

lawan 1) is worth visiting for its beautiful setting alone. It offers the full complement of services, including tennis courts, a large swimming pool, restaurants, jogging track and golf links in a very tastefully designed arrangement. Standard rooms are priced from US$47/56 to US$91/102; luxury suites and cottages cost US$102/115. Add a 21% tax to all prices. Package deals are often available.

The *Hotel Bumi Senyur (☎ 41443, fax 38014, Jl Diponegoro 17-19)* doesn't quite have the same setting as the Mesra, but is very central and offers similar amenities, including a golf course outside town. Not including the 21% tax, standard room rates start at US$85, superior rooms start at US$105 executive suites start at US$210. Try asking for a 40% discount.

Places to Eat

Samarinda's chief gastronomic wonder is the *udang galah* (giant river prawn) found in the local warungs. The Citra Niaga hawkers' centre off Jl Niaga, a block or two east of the mosque, is a crowded pedestrian precinct with an excellent range of Padang food, seafood, sate, noodle and rice dishes, fruit juices, and warm beer. Establish prices in advance.

The *fast food* place in front of the Hero supermarket inside the Mesra Indah shopping centre serves some surprisingly good simple meals. Try the *ayam bakmi* (chicken with egg noodles).

For good, albeit not cheap, Chinese fare, dine at *Lezat* on Jl Mulawarman. The *Haur Gading Restaurant* in the Hotel Gading Kencana serves Chinese and Indonesian food in nice surroundings. Across from the Telkom office, the *Istana Iguana (Jl Awang Long 22)*, is an airy, clean place with great food. Other recommended restaurants are the *Lembur Kuring* near the Hotel Mesra and the *Sari Rasa (Jl Agus Salim 26)* near the Hotel Asia.

For a splurge, the *Mesra* and *Bumi Senyur* hotels have good western, Japanese and Chinese food.

For sticky pastries and bread, try the *Suwit Roti Modern (Jl Sudirman 8)* and for cheese

and other western goodies there's always the Hero supermarket in the Mesra Indah shopping centre. Travellers craving a fast-food fix can try the *California Fried Chicken* joint on Jl Sulawesi, with an adjacent ice-cream parlour, or the *KFC* on Jl Mulawarman. For breakfast with croissants and cappuccino, try the *Sankafe* on Jl Agus Salim near the Hotel Asia. Another good coffee and bakery place is the *Warung Kopi Hai Nan (Jl Niaga Utara 50)* but it doesn't open until 10 am.

Entertainment

There are some karaoke bars on Jl Dermaga near the harbour and around the sleazy Kaltim Theatre complex on Jl Sebatik. Nearby, the Plaza Samarinda houses the *Diskotek Gardena*, which is open from 11 pm to 3 am with a cover charge of 10,000Rp for men. Women get in for free. The only alcohol served is beer.

The *Mesra* and *Bumi Senyur* hotels have western-style bars, but it's more fun to hang out on the veranda of the *Aida* and *Hidayah II* hotels and watch the world go by on the street below.

Shopping

Rattan goods, doyo leaf cloth, carvings and other jungle products are available from a string of souvenir shops west along the riverfront on Jl Slamat Riadi and Jl Martadinata. At Jl Sudirman 10, the Fitriah Souvenir shop has a good selection of items, but they are rather expensive.

If you are planning on sleeping outside during trips inland, you may want a sleeping bag, available at Toko Venus (☎ 33255), Citra Niaga, Blok C1, for about 175,000Rp. They also have snorkelling and other outdoor equipment.

Getting There & Away

Air DAS (☎ 35250), Jl Gatot Subroto 92, has heavily subsidised and heavily booked flights to the interior. Fares are 92,100Rp (plus tax) to Data Dawai (twice a week) and 93,100Rp to Long Ampung (once a week) in the Apokayan. It's advisable to book two to three weeks in advance, but seats are sometimes nabbed by getting your name on the waiting list and hanging around the DAS office the day before the flight.

DAS also has flights to Tarakan (432,000Rp, daily except Sunday) that stop in Berau (151,000Rp). There are also flights to Melak and Tanjung Selor. For all DAS flights, it's best to deal directly with its office, on the B taxi route. It's open daily to 9 pm.

MAF (☎ 23628), Jl Ruhui Rahaya 1, also has flights to Long Ampung and Data Dawai but they are much more expensive. Check for other destinations. The MAF office is a bit difficult to get to, located north of town near the university. It's open weekdays from 8 am to 4 pm.

Merpati and Garuda flights from Balikpapan can be booked at PT Duta Miramar (☎ 43385) at Jl Sudirman 20. The Bouraq office (☎ 41105) is at Jl Mulawarman 24.

Bus From Samarinda you can head northwest to Tenggarong or south to Balikpapan. The long-distance bus terminal is adjacent to the riverboat terminal at Sungai Kunjang, on the north side of the river a couple of kilometres upstream from the bridge. Take a green A taxi from the centre of town. There are daily buses to Balikpapan (4700/6000Rp normal/air-con, two hours) and frequent buses to Kota Bagun (5000Rp, three hours), where you can catch boats going upriver.

Another way to shorten travel time on the river is to take a Colt to Sebulu (2000Rp, 45 minutes) or Tenggarong (2000Rp, one hour). Colts to Tenggarong leave from Harapan Baru, the terminus for the orange G taxi (1000Rp), which leaves from Citra Niaga. Colts to Sebulu leave from Citra Niaga.

Buses to Bontang (6000/7000Rp, three hours) leave from the Lempake terminal north of the city, at the end of the B taxi route (1000Rp). There are also buses or Kijangs that make the 12 hour trip north to Berau for 60,000Rp.

Taxi Chartered taxis go directly to Balikpapan for around 75,000Rp and take less than two hours, leaving from the Sungai Kunjang terminal or the KFC on Jl Mulawarman.

Boat Both coastal ships and riverboats leave from Samarinda.

Passenger Ship Pelni (☎ 41402) is at Jl Yos Sudarso 40-56. The *Binaiya* does a fortnightly run from here to Toli-Toli (54,000Rp economy), Tarakan (86,000Rp) and Nunukan (95,000Rp), and south to Pare Pare, Batulicin and Surabaya.

Apart from Pelni services, a ferry goes once a week to Pare Pare (40,000Rp, 21 hours). The *Teratai* leaves every two days for Berau (50,000Rp, 27 hours). Ticket sellers hang around on Jl Yos Sudarso outside the harbour passenger terminal or you can go to the Lambung Mangkurat agency (☎ 20 3671) at Jl Antasari 58.

For information on which boat leaves when, check with the harbour master at the Kantor Administrator Pelabuhan on Jl Yos Sudarso 2, about 200m east of Jl Nakhoda.

Riverboat Boats up the Sungai Mahakam leave from the Sungai Kunjang ferry terminal south-west of the town centre, reached by taking a green A taxi. The fare is 1000Rp, but if you get in an empty taxi they may try to make you charter – insist on *harga biasa* (the usual price).

A boat to Tenggarong takes four hours, to Melak 24 hours and to Long Iram one day and a night (20,000Rp). If conditions permit it's another 12 hours to Long Bagun (30,000Rp). Most boats have a sleeping deck upstairs, which costs an additional 5000Rp, as well as a sleeping deck and simple canteen on the lower level.

Speedboats go to Melak and back for 2,000,000Rp.

Getting Around

To/From the Airport The airport is quite literally *in* the suburbs. Tickets are 7500Rp for a ride into town. Alternatively, walk 100m down to Jl Gatot Subroto, turn left and catch a reddish-brown Colt – a B taxi – all the way to the waterfront (500Rp).

Public Taxis City minibuses, called taxis, run along several overlapping routes, designated A, B and C. Route C goes past Hotel Mesra and the university area, route B goes past the airport. Most short runs cost 500Rp. Route A goes to the Sungai Kunjang ferry terminal for boats going upriver and the long-distance bus terminal for 1000Rp.

AROUND SAMARINDA
Kutai Game Reserve
This wildlife reserve is home to orang-utan and other exotic species, and can be visited either in a tour booked through agencies in Balikpapan and Samarinda or on your own. Other than a monument to Bontang's location on the equator, some wooden houses on stilts and an immense liquefied natural gas plant, there's little reason to spend much time in the town. The fires of 1997-98 caused tremendous devastation in the reserve so ask around in Samarinda to see if it's worth visiting. Guide services cost about 20,000Rp per day.

Places to Stay The best place to stay in Bontang is the comfortable *Equator Hotel* (*☎ 0548-41878, fax 41215*). Three-bedroom air-con bungalows with kitchen and private mandi cost 300,000Rp. Other rooms cost 125,000Rp and 150,000Rp. The government *Kutai Guesthouse* in the reserve offers beds for 10,000Rp to 15,000Rp. Basic Indonesian food is available, but you should bring some of your own.

Getting There & Away Take a bus from the Lempake terminal in Samarinda (see the Getting There & Away section under Samarinda) to Bontang for 6000Rp or 7000Rp with air-con (three hours) and then charter a boat from the PHPA office (100,000Rp for the round trip).

TENGGARONG
☎ 0541   ● pop 48,000
On the Sungai Mahakam, 39km from Samarinda, Tenggarong was once the capital of the mighty sultanate of Kutai. Today it's a pleasant and quiet riverside town. The chief attractions of Tenggarong are the Erau Festival, which occurs every year in late September if there's enough money in the budget,

and the former sultan's palace museum, built earlier this century with royalties from early oil exploitation. The trip to Tenggarong from Samarinda is currently about one hour, but will be cut in half when the new bridge being built downstream is completed.

Orientation & Information
A tourist office (*☎ 61042, fax 61093*), flanked by souvenir shops, is on Jl Diponegoro in the centre of town, but offers little other than information on whether the

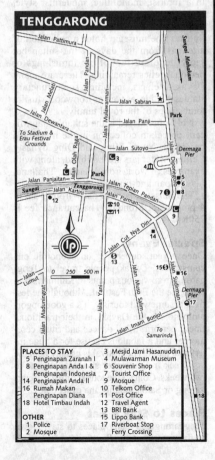

TENGGARONG

PLACES TO STAY		3	Mesjid Jami Hasanuddin
5	Penginapan Zaranah I	4	Mulawarman Museum
8	Penginapan Anda I &	6	Souvenir Shop
	Penginapan Indonesia	7	Tourist Office
14	Penginapan Anda II	9	Mosque
16	Rumah Makan	10	Telkom Office
	Penginapan Diana	11	Post Office
18	Hotel Timbau Indah	12	Travel Agent
		13	BRI Bank
OTHER		15	Lippo Bank
1	Police	17	Riverboat Stop
2	Mosque		Ferry Crossing

KALIMANTAN

Erau Festival will be held or not. A travel agent (☎ 61184) at Jl Kartini 35 can book tickets for onward flights from Samarinda or Balikpapan.

Lippo Bank on Jl Sudirman between the riverboat dock and the centre of town has an ATM that takes Cirrus and MasterCard. The other banks in town don't exchange foreign currency.

Mulawarman Museum

The former sultan's palace is now a museum. It was built by the Dutch in the 1930s in a futurist, monolithic, modernist style, replacing what, by all accounts, had been a marvellous wooden palace until destroyed by fire. The museum holds a collection of artefacts from the days of the sultan but sadly there are few of his furnishings or personal relics remaining. There are many Dayak artefacts, including some funerary statues outside, as well as ironwood Muslim tombstones of the royal family.

Not to be missed is the sultan's magnificent porcelain collection in the museum's basement. Yuan, Ming and Qing dynasty Chinese water jars are exhibited, along with examples of work from Vietnam, Thailand, Java, Japan and Europe.

The museum is open daily from 8 am to 4 pm except Monday. The entrance fee is 750Rp.

Special Events

Once a year, depending on economic circumstances, Dayak people travel to Tenggarong from various points in Kalimantan to celebrate the Erau Festival. Although the festival is somewhat touristy, it's a good opportunity to see the Dayaks in their traditional finery perform tribal dances and ritual ceremonies and a fabulous excuse for a huge intertribal party. The festival is usually held the last week in September and lasts for one to two weeks. Contact the tourist office in Tenggarong or Samarinda for the exact dates.

Places to Stay & Eat

Tenggarong has many places to stay. Down on the waterfront, the *Penginapan Indonesia*

(☎ 61221, Jl Diponegoro 44) is clean and has singles/doubles with fan and shared mandi for 7500/15,000Rp. Rooms with more comfortable beds are 15,000Rp. Next door, the *Penginapan Anda I* has rooms for 7500Rp per bed with shared mandi. The *Penginapan Zaranah I* is cheaper still with beds for 5000Rp, thought these last two places are a bit gloomy.

Across the small bridge, the *Penginapan Anda II* (☎ 61409, Jl Sudirman 65) has small rooms with shared mandi. Rooms without fan are 12,000/15,000Rp; and with fan are 18,000/25,000Rp. Much nicer air-con rooms are in the new wing out back beside a quiet and shady lane. Rooms with mandi are 52,000/63,256Rp. The staff here are very friendly.

Probably the best budget option is the *Penginapan Diana* (☎ 611610, Jl Sudirman 18). Rooms with fan and shared mandi cost 10,000/20,000Rp. There's also a *restaurant* and a veranda facing the river.

The *Hotel Timbau Indah* (☎ 61367, Jl Muksin 15) has good mid-range accommodation although it's about 2km downstream from the centre of town, on the road to Samarinda. Air-con rooms start at 60,500/78,650Rp and go up to 121,000/151,000Rp, including tax. A *restaurant* faces the river, but food is not usually prepared unless the hotel has enough guests.

A number of *warungs* are on Jl Cut Nya Din, near the intersection with Jl Sudirman, and a grocery store on Jl Sudirman near the same corner is well stocked with food and cold drinks. The *restaurant* attached to the Penginapan Indonesia is a great place for breakfast, serving coffee and *roti bakar* (toasted bread).

Getting There & Away

Colts to Tenggarong from Samarinda take one hour and cost 2000Rp. They deposit passengers at the Petugas terminal on the outskirts of Tenggarong, about 5km from the centre of town. From here taxi kota go to the centre of Tenggarong for 700Rp. Ojeks will take you for 2000Rp. Colts from Petugas also go to Kota Bagun (2 hours, 3500Rp).

There are no direct buses or Colts from Tenggarong to Balikpapan, but south of Samarinda, a couple of kilometres before the bridge, get out and hail a bus from the roadside. Sedan taxis hang around the pier and will go to Balikpapan for about 100,000Rp.

SUNGAI MAHAKAM

Rivers are the highways of Kalimantan and the Sungai Mahakam is the busiest of all. Daily riverboats ply the Mahakam from Samarinda all the way to Long Bagun, three days and 523km upstream. When conditions are right, it's possible to charter or share a ride on motorised canoes from Long Bagun to Long Pahangai, a one to two day trip through gorges and rapids. The return trip to Long Bagun takes just six or seven hours. *Never* tackle this stretch without local assistance. These waters can be lethal.

Beyond Long Pahangai, there are motorised canoes through to Long Apari, and from there you can walk through to Tanjung Lokan on the Sungai Kapuas headwaters in West Kalimantan.

If the Mahakam is low, boats may not be able to get any further than Long Iram, 114km short of Long Bagun. If the river is too high, the same may apply since the currents may be too swift.

Many of the towns and villages along the Mahakam are built over wooden walkways that keep them above water during the wet season. Often there will be a budget hotel or a longhouse where travellers can stay – the standard price is about 10,000Rp per person, more when food is included.

Kota Bangun

Kota Bangun is a dusty stop at the start of the Mahakam lake country, about three hours by bus from Samarinda along a paved road. Coal, rubber and transmigration are the major local activities.

The friendly *Penginapan Muzirat (Jl Mesjid Raya 46)* is directly opposite the main mosque. Small rooms with fan and shared mandi are 7,500/15,000Rp. A pleasant veranda faces the river. It's a short walk to where the buses stop or to the boat dock.

The *Sri Bagun Lodge* is virtually deserted and is somewhat forlorn with its empty lawns and tennis court. It closed down in 1998, but if you walk up and talk to the friendly caretaker, he can give you an air-con room (with enormous tiled bathrooms) for 35,000Rp or 50,000Rp for a triple. It's about 1km upstream from the boat dock.

From Kota Bagun, it's fun to hire a *ces* (a motorised canoe with a long propeller shaft) to visit Muara Muntai, Tanjung Isuy and Mancong. You'll have to bargain, but it should be around 30,000Rp to Muara Muntai (one hour), 65,000Rp to Tanjung Isuy (three hours) or 100,000Rp to Mancong (six hours). A local schoolteacher in Kota Bagun, Maskur, speaks English well and offers his service as a guide. There is abundant bird life as well as macaque and proboscis monkeys (in the early morning or late evening) and if you're *very* lucky, you may see *pesut* – the freshwater dolphins this area is famous for.

There are five buses a day to Samarinda (5000Rp) between 7 am and 3 pm.

Muara Muntai

Muara Muntai is a Kutai market town built over mudflats in the heart of the Mahakam's lake country. The streets are spotlessly clean boardwalks, but mind the mosquitoes. It doesn't look much from the water, but its beautifully built and maintained boardwalks are an attraction in themselves. Join the hordes promenading at night, and check out the Bappeda's (Agency for Regional Development) fine, old, wooden house and huge portico, straight ahead from the dock.

Places to Stay & Eat There are two losmen. Turn left at the boardwalk parallel to the dock and walk about 20m to the *Penginapan Nita Wardana*. Small basic rooms are 7500Rp per person. The *Penginapan Etam Sri Muntai Indah*, 50m down the boardwalk, is much the same.

The *warung* between the two losmen serves *sop Muara Muntai*, a filling soup with rice, chicken, noodles, cabbage and a squeeze of lime. *Warungs* opposite the Nita Wardana sell fried rice, noodles etc.

KALIMANTAN

Getting There & Away Public boats leave for Tanjung Isuy via Jantur and Danau Jempang every morning and return from Tanjung Isuy in the early afternoon, but some of these public services are highly irregular, so be prepared to charter a ces. The price for the public boat is 7000Rp, provided there are five or more passengers. For charter, a full day on the lakes costs about 100,000Rp.

Express boats from Samarinda to Muara Muntai take 13 hours; slower boats take 18 hours. The fares are 5000Rp, more or less.

Tanjung Isuy

Tanjung Isuy is on the shores of Danau Jempang in Banuaq Dayak territory. Half the fun is getting there, via spectacular wetlands, shallow lakes and **Jantur**, a Banjar village built on a flooded mudflat. Jantur's **mosque** stands alone on a bend in the river, accessible only by boats and high gangplanks. Beside it is the cemetery, the highest point in town but still just 20cm above the water level at the end of the wet season. Bodies buried here must be anchored in their watery graves to prevent them bobbing to the surface.

Tanjung Isuy is a favoured destination for tour groups in search of an 'authentic' Dayak experience. Most arrive in speedboats from Samarinda, mob the souvenir stalls in the longhouse, watch a mix of Dayak dancing and zoom back. Activity focuses on the **Taman Jamrot Lamin**, a longhouse vacated in the late 1970s, and rebuilt by the provincial government as a craft centre and tourist hostel. Despite the commercial nature of these pay-by-the-hour performances, they are lively, rhythmic and loads of fun for the whole town. The mix of Kenyah, Kayan and Banuaq dancing is confusing, but very entertaining. Solo travellers could commission a dance for about 150,000Rp though it may be more authentic to forego the dancing and join families watching satellite TV in the evening when the electricity comes on.

Places to Stay & Eat The best place to stay is the *Taman Jamrot Lamin* on Jl Indonesia Australia, 500m from the jetty. Unlike a real longhouse it has private guest rooms with mosquito nets and comfortable beds at 10,000Rp per person with shared mandi. The main problem with staying in Tanjung Isuy overnight is the rapacious mosquitoes.

Another option is the one budget hotel in Tanjung Isuy – the *Penginapan Beringan*, which also costs 10,000Rp per person. The couple who run the Beringan also prepare and serve food downstairs.

A *cafe* a few doors down from the Taman Jamrot Lamin has basic fare, but the *sop ayam* is delicious. Make sure you go out to eat swathed with mosquito repellent.

Shopping There are some nice doyo weavings and *mandau* (machetes) with carved handles available in the craft centre next door (as well as a lot of junk), offered at reasonable prices. Back down the road towards the dock, there's a house across from the first intersection that also sells carvings and weavings.

Getting There & Away Riverboats leave for Samarinda (24 hours) twice a week, stopping in Muara Muntai (five hours). There are public ces to Muara Muntai leaving daily in the early afternoon (7000Rp and up, depending on the number of passengers), but check at the dock. You can charter a ces direct to Kota Bangun (65,000Rp), catch a bus and be in Samarinda or Balikpapan that night.

Mancong

A trip to Mancong is recommended, but plan to be on the river in the early morning or evening. Hire a ces to get from Tanjung Isuy to Mancong via the Sungai Ohong, past flocks of magnificent water birds and a gorgeous stretch of riverside jungle. Allow about three hours to get there. Chartering a ces for a round trip costs about 75,000Rp, or you can return to Tanjung Isuy by motorcycle for between 10,000Rp and 15,000Rp. The trip takes about half an hour.

On the river it's essential to go slowly to spot proboscis monkeys, snakes (if you're lucky) and bird life, including hornbills. Near villages and towns on the water large ibis hang around the house docks hoping for a free feed.

In Mancong a grand, wooden, two storey **longhouse** was built by the government in 1987 as a tourist attraction and, as such, it's a bit depressing. Only one family appears to be living in it. The statues outside the longhouse are worth the visit, however, as is Mancong itself for its quiet riverside charm. Banuaq weavers here make cloth from the doyo leaf and sell it at reasonable prices. Folk dances are occasionally held at the longhouse for ritual purposes or for tourist groups. Austere *rooms* are available in the longhouse for 5000Rp per person.

THE UPPER MAHAKAM
Melak & Around
Melak is the biggest town on the upper Mahakam, famous for the nearby **Kersik Luwai Orchid Reserve**, where 72 different species of orchid grow, including the extremely rare green-black *Cologenia pandurata* orchids.

The best time to see the orchids is supposedly January to February, but don't get your hopes up. The reserve is about 16km from Melak and may be reached by chartering a 4WD or ojek.

Inquire whether any funerals, weddings or harvest ceremonies are being held while you are there – they can be fascinating experiences, often including the ritual slaughter of water buffalo. Healing ceremonies are most frequently held in March, April and June, according to locals.

Barong Tongkok is a small village at the centre of the plateau, with a few *warungs*, most serving Padang food, and a new hotel, the *Putri Tanjung*. Rooms with fan and mandi are 25,000Rp.

In nearby **Eheng** an unusually long **Banuaq longhouse** and cemetery are worth visiting. The longhouse was started in the 1960s and is home to 32 families. It may well be the

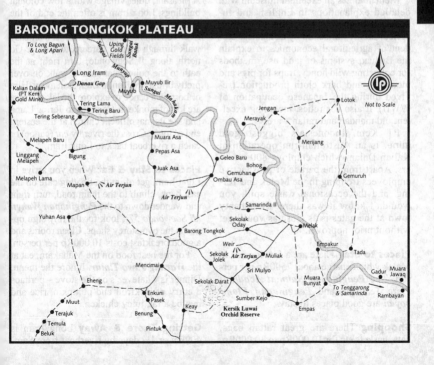

BARONG TONGKOK PLATEAU

MELAK

Sungai Mahakam

Jalan Ahmad Yani

Jalan Piere Tendean

0 25 50 m

To Post Office,
Orchid Reserve
& Tering

Pasar

1 Penginapan
   Flamboyan
2 Warung Pangkalan
3 Padang Restaurant
4 Penginapan Rahmat
   Abadi
5 Penginapan Bahagia
6 Rumah Makan ACC
7 Boat Schedules
   & Information
8 Village Square

last real Kalimantan longhouse built without government subsidy. Market day is Monday, the best day to visit. From Melak a public minibus goes to Barong Tongkok that continues on to Eheng, or you can hire an ojek in Melak for about 50,000Rp a day.

Mencimai has an excellent museum with detailed explanations in English and Indonesian of the local systems of shifting agriculture. It was set up by a Japanese student of agricultural economics to explain the Banuaq systems of land use, methods for collecting wild honey, traps for pigs and monkeys, and bark cloth production (revived during the Japanese occupation of WWII). It also has relics, including excellent old mandau and rattan ware.

PT Kem, Indonesia's biggest **gold mine**, is an Australian-run operation at Kalian Dalam which employs 800 workers. Apart from the parade of prospective employees trooping in via Melak and Tering, and the occasional waste spill, you wouldn't know it was there. The shanty town at the gates is as close as you'll get without prior approval.

Places to Stay There are a few losmen in Melak which charge about 7500Rp per person. The *Penginapan Rahmat Abadi*, Jl Piere Tendean, and *Penginapan Flamboyan* are good places to stay.

Shopping There are great rattan bags, hats, baskets etc for 10,000Rp to 30,000Rp,

depending on size and quality. You might find a few old mandau as well. You will also see some beautiful trading beads, but most are not for sale.

Getting There & Away Boats from Samarinda leave on the 325km trip at 9 am and arrive in Melak at around 10 am the next day. The fare is 17,500Rp per person on the lower deck and 20,000Rp on the upper.

Getting Around Transport charter is expensive – between 200,000Rp and 250,000Rp a day for cars or 4WDs and 50,000Rp a day for ojeks.

There are regular public minibuses between Melak and Tering, as well as between Barong Tongkok and Eheng. The fare to Tering is 5000Rp and takes about an hour.

Long Iram

A pleasant, quiet village with a few colonial buildings, Long Iram is often the end of the line for many would-be explorers because of river conditions or lack of time. It's an easy walk through market gardens to Tering. Go north along Jl Soewondo, turn right at the path to the police station and walk on over pretty bridges to Danau Gap, 3km away. Hire or borrow a canoe to explore the lake – there are lots of monkeys. Continue to Tering Lama and see its magnificent church at the eastern end of town. Cross the river by *cat* (canoe) or catch a riverboat back to Long Iram.

Places to Stay & Eat When you arrive in Long Iram, get off at the floating cafe on the east bank, climb to the main road, turn right and wander down to the *Penginapan Wahyu (Jl Soewondo 57)*; look for the tiny sign opposite the two-storey shops. Clean rooms and a good breakfast costs 10,000Rp per person.

For the best food on the Mahakam, eat at the *Warung Jawa Timur*. Ignore the menu. Dinner is whatever's on the stove – perhaps a curry of jackfruit and pumpkin, rice and maybe a fat, juicy chicken.

Getting There & Away Long Iram is 409km or 1½ days by riverboat from Samarinda. The fare is 20,000/25,000Rp on the lower/upper deck.

Long Iram to Banjarmasin

A few intrepid travellers have trekked overland west of Long Iram (a week to 10 days) to a tributary of the Sungai Barito in Central Kalimantan and, from there, worked their way downriver to South Kalimantan and Banjarmasin. It's not exactly a jungle experience, as much of this area has been logged and travel is often via logging roads. There's a logging road from nearby Tering to **Tanjung Balai** in Central Kalimantan. You may be able to hitch a ride to Tanjung Balai and then to **Muara Teweh**. From there public river and road transport goes to Banjarmasin.

Datah Bilang to Muara Merak

If conditions allow you to ferry upriver beyond Long Iram, places of interest include Datah Bilang, where there's a Protestant community of **Kenyah Dayak** who moved here from the Apokayan in the 1970s. The older women have the traditional long earlobes and will charge 10,000Rp per photograph. A reader has recommended the Bahau

A Kenyah godly mask from the
Apokayan Highlands of Kalimantan.

JENNY BOWMAN

Dayak village of **Long Hubung**, 45 minutes north of Datah Bilang by motorised canoe.

Less than 25km downstream is Muara Merak, a **Punan** settlement. There's good trekking in this area, especially along the Sungai Merak to the north-east. With a Punan guide hired in Muara Merak, you could trek overland east for five or six days to Tabang and then travel down the Sungai Belayan to Kota Bangun, where you can catch a boat or bus back to Samarinda.

Long Bagun to Long Apari

Long Bagun is a **longhouse** settlement and the end of the line for regular longboat services from Samarinda along the Mahakam. The journey costs 30,000Rp to 35,000Rp and takes three days, conditions permitting. The boat docks in Long Iram one night each way while the crew sleeps, since night navigation can be tricky this far upriver.

From Long Bagun you must charter motorised canoes from village to village or trek through the forests. River conditions must be optimal because of river rapids between Long Bagun and the next major settlement, **Long Pahangai**. Under normal conditions, it's a one or two day canoe trip from Long Bagun to Long Pahangai, then another day to Long Apari. **Long Lunuk**, between Long Pahangai and Long Apari, is a good place from which to visit Kenyah villages or alternatively, stay at **Tiong Ohang**, two hours upstream from Long Lunuk.

Long Apari is the uppermost longhouse village on the Mahakam and is beautiful. The longboat trip from Long Lunuk takes five to six hours. Dinner in Long Apari is often greasy pig and bony fish – tasty supplements from the city make welcome presents. The village is the stepping off point for treks to West Kalimantan.

Getting There & Away To start your trip from the top, fly to Data Dawai, an airstrip near Long Lunuk. DAS flies twice a week (92,100Rp), but you often need to book weeks in advance. From there you can work your way downriver back to Samarinda, or trek overland to the Apokayan highlands.

KALIMANTAN

SUNGAI TELEN

There are regular longboat services up the Telen, which branches north off the Mahakam near **Muara Kaman**, from Samarinda to **Muara Wahau**. This trip takes three days and two nights, and goes via the Kenyah and Bahau villages of **Tanjung Manis**, **Long Noran** and **Long Segar**. Nearby caves were the site of 5th century Sanskrit finds, now in the museum at Tenggarong.

An alternative route from Samarinda to Berau (see the Berau entry later in this chapter) is to take a boat north from Muara Wahau to **Miau Baru** and try hitching a ride to the Dayak village of **Marapun**, two hours away. From Marapun, take a 12 hour boat ride down the Kelai to **Berau/Tanjung Redeb**.

SUNGAI BELAYAN

Another adventurous trip is up the Sungai Belayan to **Tabang**. The Belayan branches north-west off the Mahakam at Kota Bangun and longboats take about three days to reach Tabang from Samarinda.

Tabang can also be reached on foot from the town of **Muara Merak** on the Mahakam. Hire a Punan guide in either Tabang or Muara Merak to lead you through the extensive rainforests that are nomadic Punan territory.

SUNGAI KAYAN & THE APOKAYAN

South of Tarakan is **Tanjung Selor** at the mouth of the mighty Sungai Kayan. Regular longboat services go up the Kayan as far as the Kenyah villages of **Mara I** and **Mara II**, but a long section of rapids – Kalimantan's wildest whitewater – prevents boats from reaching the headwaters of the Kayan in the Apokayan Highlands.

The Apokayan Highlands has some good trekking; you could also trek overland to the Mahakam headwaters from here in about a week with a guide from Long Ampung. Guides in Samarinda lead easy or vigorous treks to Dayak longhouses from Long Ampung.

One of Jailani's (see Guides in the Samarinda section earlier) most picturesque tours consists of the following itinerary: first a flight from Samarinda to Long Ampung on DAS, then a 2½ hour easy walk to stay overnight at the longhouse of **Long Uro**. The next day involves a 45 minute walk to the longhouse of **Lidung Payau** where you catch a boat back to Long Ampung for the flight back to Samarinda. Hardy travellers may include a difficult five hour jungle walk from Lidung Payau to **Long Sungai Barang**. Nights are cold and longhouse verandahs can be hard, so pack a sleeping bag.

Getting There & Away

DAS flies from Samarinda to Tanjung Selor daily, and has a government-subsidised flight from Samarinda to Long Ampung in the Apokayan area once a week for 93,100Rp.

LONG BAWAN

Another inland option is the picturesque area around Long Bawan. Like the Apokayan, it's too far above the rapids to be of much interest to logging companies – yet. Also like the Apokayan, there's a noticeable military presence and prices are high, even for the simplest commodities. Any presents from the city will be welcome – booze, toys, sweets, sugar etc.

Getting There & Away

Air DAS flies daily to Long Bawan from Tarakan for 238,000Rp.

BERAU (TANJUNG REDEB)

☎ 0554 • pop 105,000

People use the names Berau and Tanjung Redeb interchangeably. Strictly speaking, Tanjung Redeb is the spit of land between the Segan and Kelai rivers, whereas Berau refers to the whole urban area. It doesn't seem to matter which you use. Fans of Joseph Conrad might prefer to think of Berau as the village Patusan featured in *Lord Jim*, and Sambir in *Almayer's Folly*; it was the setting for both. Berau is best known today for its riverside coal fields downstream and timber operations.

Berau was once the seat of two minor kingdoms, Gunung Tabur, with its palace *(kraton)* on the banks of the Segan, and

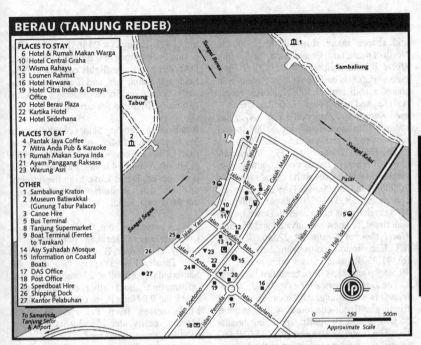

BERAU (TANJUNG REDEB)

PLACES TO STAY
6 Hotel & Rumah Makan Warga
10 Hotel Central Graha
12 Wisma Rahayu
13 Losmen Rahmat
16 Hotel Nirwana
19 Hotel Citra Indah & Deraya Office
20 Hotel Berau Plaza
22 Kartika Hotel
24 Hotel Sederhana

PLACES TO EAT
4 Pantak Jaya Coffee
7 Mitra Anda Pub & Karaoke
11 Rumah Makan Surya Inda
21 Ayam Panggang Raksasa
23 Warung Asri

OTHER
1 Sambaliung Kraton
2 Museum Batiwakkal (Gunung Tabur Palace)
3 Canoe Hire
5 Bus Terminal
8 Tanjung Supermarket
9 Boat Terminal (Ferries to Tarakan)
14 Asy Syahadah Mosque
15 Information on Coastal Boats
17 DAS Office
18 Post Office
25 Speedboat Hire
26 Shipping Dock
27 Kantor Pelabuhan

To Samarinda, Tanjung Selor & Airport

Approximate Scale
0   250   500m

KALIMANTAN

Sambaliung, with a palace on the Kelai. The palaces face each other across Tanjung Redeb. Gunung Tabur's moment in history came towards the end of WWII when the palace was mistaken for a Japanese military post and flattened by Allied bombers. The Sambaliung palace was untouched, supposedly because of the spiritual power of two cannons.

The Gunung Tabur palace was rebuilt, belfry and all, and is now a museum. It contains a few relics, including an old cannon found in the jungle by the very first rajah; however, its spiritual powers have been in doubt since the Allied bombing.

In the bungalow beside the palace lives Putri Kanik Sanipan, the daughter of the last rajah of Gunung Tabur. She is a graceful woman in her late 70s who speaks fluent Dutch and Indonesian. She occasionally takes tea with visitors and talks of the old

days – that is, if you speak Dutch or Indonesian. Her collection of photographs includes many of the former palace and of state occasions. Locals often ask her to bless their children, light incense and say prayers in the traditional Gunung Tabur way. Get there by regular canoe ferry (500Rp).

The **Sambaliung Kraton** is now a private residence, occupied by the grandson of the last rajah and his relatives. Get there by canoe, or walk across the Sungai Kelai by the bridge near the bus terminus.

Places to Stay

Berau has a lot of budget and mid-range accommodation to choose from. The *Hotel Citra Indah* (☎ 21171, *Jl Antasari*) is a cavernous place with large, clean rooms with shared mandi for 15,000Rp. Its air-con rooms with mandi cost 38,500Rp. The staff are friendly.

Across the street, the *Kartika Hotel (☎ 21 379, Jl Antasari)* has singles/doubles with fan and shared mandi for 11,000/22,000Rp. North of there, on Jl Gajah Mada, the friendly *Hotel Wisma Rahayu (☎ 21142, Jl Pangalang Batur)* is basic, but clean. Rooms with shared mandi cost 11,500/22,000Rp; rooms with fan and mandi cost 27,500Rp. The *Losmen Rahmat (Jl Pangalang Batur 472)* has rooms with shared mandi for 20,000Rp and rooms with fan and mandi for 25,000Rp.

The *Hotel Nirwana (☎ 21893, Jl Aminuddin 715)* is one of Berau's nicest hotels, with singles/doubles/triples with fan and mandi for 20,000/25,000/30,000Rp. They also have aircon rooms for 37,500/40,000/45,000Rp. A 10% surcharge is not included. Down on the waterfront, the newly renovated and friendly *Hotel Central Graha (☎ 22580, Jl Yani)* has clean air-con rooms with shared mandi for 41,250Rp and rooms with mandi for 49,500Rp and 88,000Rp, breakfast included.

The *Hotel Berau Plaza (☎ 23111, Jl Antasari)* is a new hotel with clean rooms and friendly staff. Air-con rooms with mandi are 55,000Rp and 90,000Rp, including breakfast. The *Hotel Sederhana (☎ 21353, Jl Antasari)* was under renovation at the time of writing, but management expect to have rooms with fan and mandi for 24,200/ 36,300Rp and air-con rooms for 48,400Rp.

Places to Eat

There are a number of warungs on Jl Niaga near the intersection with Jl Yani that have barbecued fish and chicken. Try the clean and friendly *Warung Asri*. It also serves breakfast, including the very spicy *pecel* which is similar to gado gado. The *Ayam Panggang Raksasa* next to the Hotel Berau Plaza specialises, oddly enough, in ayam panggang.

Try the martabak stalls on Jl Yani. Eat on the harbour wall and chat with the passers-by enjoying the evening breeze off the river. The *Pantak Jaya* is a coffee place near the canoe pier. Stores along Jl Yani are well-stocked with food supplies but the best place is the *Tanjung Supermarket* on Jl Niaga. For cold beer and entertainment of sorts try the *Mitra Anda Pub & Karaoke* on Jl Gajah Mada.

Getting There & Away

Air The DAS office (☎ 21210) is at Jl Pemuda 411. Deraya (☎ 21363) has an office beside the entrance to the Hotel Citra Indah. DAS has two daily flights each to Tanjung Selor and Samarinda, and flights to Tarakan daily except on Sunday. Deraya also has two daily flights to Samarinda.

Bus Buses to Tanjung Selor (25,000Rp) take 3½ hours over 124km of mostly unpaved road. The 355km journey to Samarinda (45,000Rp) takes 14 hours. Most of the road is not paved. Buses leave from the terminal on Jl Hari Isa just south of the bridge crossing the Sungai Kelai.

Boat A passenger boat, the *Starlight*, leaves from Berau to Tarakan (37,000Rp, 11 hours) once a week. Buy tickets on the boat. The *Teratai* leaves every two days for Samarinda (50,000Rp, 27 hours). To find information about other coastal vessels check the PT Naga Pertu office on Jl Gajah Mada across from the Asy Syahadah Mosque, easily identified by its beautiful, red-tiled, three-tiered roof.

The boat to Tarakan stops at Tanjung Batu, where you can hitch a lift on local boats going out to Pulau Derawan. Supposedly, a public boat goes daily from Berau to Tanjung Batu, but good luck finding it! Speedboats for hire congregate at the dock at the end of Jl Antasari. A speedboat to Pulau Derawan (three hours) will cost about 250,000Rp one way. In the early morning or evening look for proboscis and macaque monkeys on the banks of the river as you head towards the mouth of the Sungai Berau.

Getting Around

To/From the Airport Taxi tickets for a trip into town bought at the airport cost 15,000Rp, but you can charter a taxi minibus for 10,000Rp. The airport is about 9km south-west of town off the road to Samarinda.

For short trips on the waterways around Berau, charter a motorised canoe for between 10,000Rp and 15,000Rp per hour.

PULAU DERAWAN
☎ 0551

Derawan is part of the Sangalaki Archipelago, a marine reserve off Tanjung Batu between Berau and Tarakan. There are dive resorts on Derawan and Sangalaki islands, and their popularity is growing despite their isolation.

Derawan is a beautiful tear-shaped speck of land with a village around the fringe, spotless white sand beaches, coconut plantations in the centre and a good supply of fresh water. Schools of *tongkol* (tuna fish) surround the island and cause feeding frenzies near the surface where birds dive for spoils. Rare green turtles lay eggs on the beach near the Derawan Dive Resort.

There are no cars, no motorcycles and electricity generators run for only a few hours in the evening. The main entertainment is the volleyball and badminton matches in the early evening, and satellite TVs.

Other islands in the group include **Sangalaki**, which divers visit to see manta rays and green turtles; **Karaban**, which has an ecologically intriguing lake in its centre, caves with swallows' nests and a population of huge coconut crabs; and **Maratua**, which has a population of 2100 in four villages, set around a lagoon. There's also a military patrol stationed here to keep 'pirates' in check.

Activities
The island's main attractions, snorkelling and diving, are conducted from the Derawan Dive Resort (see the Places to Stay & Eat entry). The charge for three dives off Pulau Derawan is US$75, plus tank and equipment hire. Dives off Pulau Sangalaki and other outer islands cost more. Renting snorkelling equipment is US$6 a day. Besides the Derawan Resort, Borneo Divers of Kota Kinabalu, Malaysia (☎ 60 88 222226, fax 221550, email bdivers@po.jaring.my) also run trips to the outer islands or you can try hiring boats in the village. Readers have recommended a captain named Adin for trips out to the outer islands.

Places to Stay & Eat
Pulau Derawan Most visitors to Pulau Derawan come on package diving tours and stay at the **Derawan Dive Resort** (☎ 23275, fax 23274, email derawan@bpp.mega.net.id). There's an office and dive shop in the Hotel Benakutai in Balikpapan. Four-day, three-night packages cost US$470 and include three dives per day, accommodation and meals. Seven-day, six-night packages cost US$990 for the same deal. A minimum of two people is required. The resort is very comfortable, with air-con cottages and buffet meals.

For cheaper accommodation there's the **Djamhari Homestay** with five rooms in a pleasant building near the Derawan Dive Resort. Rooms with shared mandi and three meals a day cost 35,000Rp. Further west along the village's main path, the **Losmen Ilham** has clean rooms with fan (when the electricity is on) and shared mandi for 20,000Rp and larger rooms for 40,000Rp. An additional 20,000Rp per person includes three meals a day.

Near the public pier at the north end of the island, the **Penginapan Yogi Mas** is a new building with singles/doubles with fan and shared mandi for 20,000/40,000Rp.

There are a couple of *warungs* in the village, and buffet meals at the **Derawan Dive Resort** are US$10 per meal, not including cold drinks and beer. It's a good idea to bring along fruit and snacks from Berau or Tarakan for variety.

Tanjung Batu If you are stuck in Tanjung Batu waiting for a boat, the **Losmen Famili** has rooms with shared mandi (no fan) for 15,000Rp.

Getting There & Away
The weekly Berau-Tarakan boat drops passengers at Tanjung Batu, a fishing village with a couple of warungs and a losmen. From there you have to hitch a ride to Derawan. Besides taking a speedboat from Berau, another option is chartering a speedboat from Tarakan to Derawan for around 300,000Rp. The journey takes about two hours.

TARAKAN

☎ 0551 • pop 130,000

Just a stepping stone to other places, Tarakan is an island town close to the Sabah border. It was the site of bloody fighting between Australians and Japanese at the end of WWII. Unless you're really enthusiastic about Japanese blockhouses, or want to try exiting Indonesia to Sabah, there's little of interest. It's not a bad town, just dull. Some of the houses have old Japanese cannon shells painted silver and planted in their front yards like garden gnomes.

The battle at Tarakan was one of a series of battles fought by Australian soldiers in Indonesia and New Guinea from mid-1944 onwards. There's an interesting argument put forward by Peter Charlton in *The Unnecessary War – Island Campaigns of the South-West Pacific 1944-45* that these battles had no value in the defeat of the Japanese. The capture of Tarakan (after six weeks of fighting and the deaths of 235 Australians) was carried out to establish an air base that was never used. After the Tarakan operation Indonesia was effectively bypassed, yet in July 1945 an assault was made on Balikpapan. This last large amphibious landing of the war managed to secure a beach, a disused oil refinery, a couple of unnecessary airfields and the deaths of 229 Australians.

There's a memorial *(kuburan Australia)* to the Australian soldiers on the grounds of the Indonesian military barracks, right in front of their volleyball courts. A gravesite *(kuburan Jepang)* lies in the hills nearby for the Japanese who were killed, alongside old bunkers.

Pantai Amal is a swimming beach outside of town. Get there by public minibus (500Rp) or charter a taxi for 2000Rp. Locals will suggest visiting the **Pembinan Hutan** tourist attraction just outside of town, but it consists of a pathetic collection of animals, including bears and monkeys, in small cages.

Information

BDN bank on Jl Yos Sudarso will change US travellers cheques and currency. BNI bank, next door, has an ATM that takes Cirrus or MasterCard. The Kantor Imigrasi Tarakan (☎ 21242) is on Jl Sumatra, just opposite the golf course, about 5km from the centre of town. Officials here say you can't exit Indonesia from Tarakan or Nunukan with a free two month visa, nor can they provide an exit permit. Immigration officials in Jakarta, on the other hand, claim you can exit from Tarakan and Nunukan with a free visa. Try it to see who's right!

Staff at the tourist office (☎ 32100), outside town on Jl Martadinata 171, can

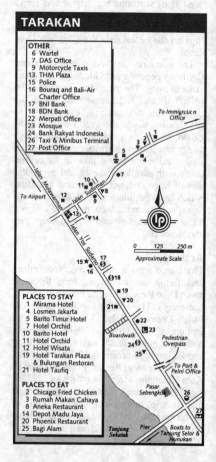

TARAKAN

OTHER
6 Wartel
7 DAS Office
9 Motorcycle Taxis
13 THM Plaza
15 Police
16 Bouraq and Bali-Air Charter Office
17 BNI Bank
18 BDN Bank
22 Merpati Office
23 Mosque
24 Bank Rakyat Indonesia
26 Taxi & Minibus Terminal
27 Post Office

0 125 250 m
Approximate Scale

PLACES TO STAY
1 Mirama Hotel
4 Losmen Jakarta
5 Barito Timur Hotel
7 Hotel Orchid
10 Barito Hotel
11 Hotel Orchid
12 Hotel Wisata
19 Hotel Tarakan Plaza & Bulungan Restoran
21 Hotel Taufiq

PLACES TO EAT
2 Chicago Fried Chicken
3 Rumah Makan Cahaya
8 Aneka Restaurant
14 Depot Madu Jaya
20 Phoenix Restaurant
25 Bagi Alam

To Immigration Office
To Airport
Boardwalk
Pedestrian Overpass
To Port & Pelni Office
Pasar Sebengkok
Tanjung Sekatak
Pier
Boats to Tanjung Selor & Nunukan

recommend guides for trips inland, such as a Mr Hery (☎ 32981), who speaks English and has taken many groups for trips on the Sungai Kayan.

Travel Agencies The agent for the Derawan Dive Resort and Borneo Divers in Tarakan is PT Tanjung Harapan Mulia (☎ 21572, fax 51376), at Jl Yos Sudarso 38. It also books air and boat tickets. PT Sampurna Andal Mandiri (☎ 21975), near the Hotel Tarakan Plaza on Jl Yos Sudarso, is another place for air and boat tickets, as is PT Angkasa Express (☎ 51 789, fax 23326) near the THM Plaza at Jl Yos Sudarso THM Complex, Blok D-5.

Places to Stay – Budget

The best budget place is the *Losmen Jakarta (☎ 21704, Jl Sudirman 112)*, but that's not saying a lot. Singles/doubles without fan or mandi cost 7000/14,000Rp. Doubles/triples with fan and mandi cost 16,000/24,000Rp and triples with fan and shared mandi cost 21,000Rp. The *Barito Hotel (☎ 21212, Jl Sudirman 129)*, is a bit more expensive but has fairly nice rooms, starting at 25,000Rp with fan and shared mandi and 30,000Rp with mandi. Air-con rooms are 35,000Rp and 40,000Rp.

Next door, the *Hotel Anggrek (☎ 21664, Jl Sudirman 171)* is a little run down. Rooms with fan and shared mandi are 17,000/22,000Rp. Rooms with mandi are 26,000/28,000Rp. Near the intersection with Jl Yos Sudarso, the *Hotel Wisata (☎ 21245, Jl Sudirman 46)* is very friendly but this doesn't make up for the small, grubby rooms full of mosquitoes. Rooms with fan and shared mandi are 15,000/19,800Rp and with mandi are 22,800/29,400Rp. The air-con rooms for 38,400Rp aren't much better. There's also a 20% tax.

Places to Stay – Mid-Range and Top End

The *Barito Timur Hotel (☎ 21181, Jl Sudirman 133)* is run by the same people as the Hotel Barito, but is a much nicer place. Rooms with shower and air-con are 60,000Rp and 65,000Rp and rooms with

bathtubs are 70,000Rp and 80,000Rp. A breakfast of cake, coffee or tea is included. Further east up Jl Sudirman, the *Mirama Hotel (☎ 21637, Jl Sudirman 3)* is clean and pleasant. Air-con singles/doubles with mandi are 60,000/65,000Rp, not including a 10% tax.

The *Hotel Tarakan Plaza (☎ 21870, fax 21029, Jl Yos Sudarso)* is the closest thing Tarakan has to a top-end hotel. Air-con rooms cost 143,000/154,000Rp and VIP rooms cost 176,000Rp. There's a good restaurant and bar downstairs and the staff speak English well.

Places to Eat

Food and fruit stalls are plentiful around the THM Plaza at the corner of Jl Yos Sudarso and Jl Sudirman, and the *Depot Madu Jaya* is a cosy warung. Inside the THM Plaza there's a *supermarket*.

The *Rumah Makan Cahaya* on Jl Sudirman has good octopus, *cap cai* (fried vegetables) and nasi goreng. The *Phoenix Restaurant* on Jl Yos Sudarso and the *Aneka Restaurant* on Jl Sudirman are other good choices for Chinese food. For *ikan bakar* (barbecued fish) try the *Bagi Alam* near the BRI Bank on Jl Yos Sudarso. It's easy to spot by the fish painted on the gable of the restaurant's roof.

The most comfortable place to eat is the air-conditioned *Bulungan Restoran* in the Hotel Tarakan Plaza. They have delicious Chinese, Western and Indonesian food at reasonable prices, though it's more expensive than you'll find on the street.

For entertainment and a cold beer there are two places on Jl Mulawarman about 500m north-west of the THM Plaza. The *Nirwana* and the *Goldstar (bintang mas* in Bahasa Indonesia) have a bar, disco and other diversions. For a more sedate drinking environment, try the bar at the Hotel Tarakan Plaza.

Getting There & Away

Air Merpati flies daily to Balikpapan (578,000Rp) and DAS flies to Samarinda (432,000Rp) daily except Sunday with a stopover in Berau (173,000Rp). DAS has

KALIMANTAN

daily flights to Long Bawan (238,000Rp), Tanjung Selor (151,000Rp) and Nunukan (171,300Rp) and a flight once a week to Malinau (64,600Rp). MAF has scheduled flights to Long Nawang, Long Bia, Long Bawan, Malinau and other out of the way places. Prices are at least twice as much as DAS flights.

Bali-Air flies once a week to Tawau (527,500Rp) in Malaysia but you may have problems without an exit permit.

Merpati (☎ 21911, fax 23396) is at Jl Yos Sudarso 10 and is open daily from 8 am to 1 pm. The DAS office (☎ 51578) is at Jl Sudirman 9 and is open daily from 7 am to 9 pm. The MAF office (☎ 51011) is in the lobby of the Barito Timur Hotel and you should check there for schedules.

At the time of writing, the Bali-Air office was in the Bouraq office (which is not currently flying out of Tarakan) beside the police station on Jl Yos Sudarso.

Boat The Pelni office (☎ 51169) is at the main port across from the Pertamina complex on Jl Yos Sudarso. Take a taxi minibus (500Rp) almost to the end of Jl Yos Sudarso. The Pelni ship *Tidar* calls into Tarakan on its Pantoloan-Balikpapan-Pare Pare-Surabaya run. The *Binaiya* comes from Toli-Toli then to Nunukan, back to Toli-Toli and then on to

Samarinda. The *Awu* comes from Ujung Pandang then up to Nunukan and back to Ujung Pandang. The office is open from 8 am to noon, but travel agencies also sell Pelni tickets.

The other pier is roughly halfway between the Pelni office and the THM Plaza, from where boats go to other destinations in East Kalimantan. The *Starlight* goes to Berau once a week (36,000Rp, 11 hours), stopping at Tanjung Batu (26,000Rp). Speedboats leave frequently for Tanjung Selor (18,500Rp, one hour), Nunukan (41,000Rp, three hours) and Malinau (61,000Rp, five hours). Daily slow boats go to Tanjung Selor (11,000Rp, four hours) and Malinau (46,000Rp, 20 hours). Buy tickets at the office on the pier.

Getting Around

To/From the Airport Tickets for taxis into town are 6000Rp though you might be able to bargain for a cheaper ride outside. Walk out about 200m to the highway and try catching a public minibus for a 500Rp, 5km ride into town.

The standard price for public minibuses is 500Rp. As is the case in Balikpapan, the drivers here sometimes take you for a ride, so to speak, and overcharge. Taxi charter is about 10,000Rp an hour. There are also ojeks for hire at various street corners.

Sulawesi

The strangely contorted island of Sulawesi sprawls across the sea between Kalimantan and Maluku. It was first referred to as Celebes by the Portuguese, but the origins of the name are unclear. One derivation is from the Bugis words *selihe* or *selire*, meaning 'sea current', or from *si-lebih*, meaning 'more islands'. Others say Celebes could be a corruption of *Klabat*, the name of the volcano that towers over Minahasa in the north. The modern name Sulawesi (and possibly Celebes too) seems to come from *sula* (island) *besi* (iron), which is a reference to the iron deposits around Danau Matano (Lake Matano), the richest in South-East Asia.

The 227,000 sq km island is divided into four provinces: South (which includes Tana Toraja and the Mamasa Valley); South-East; Central (which includes the Togean Islands); and North Sulawesi.

A popular route, which includes most of the highlights, is Ujung Pandang-Tana Toraja-Danau Poso-Togean Islands-Manado, but there is plenty more to see and enjoy in Sulawesi.

POPULATION & PEOPLE
The interior of the island has always provided a refuge for some of Indonesia's earliest inhabitants, some of whom preserved elements of their idiosyncratic cultures well into the 20th century. The Makassarese and Bugis of the south-west peninsula, and the Christian Minahasans of the far north, are the dominant groups of Sulawesi – they have also had the most contact with the west. In Central Sulawesi, the Toraja, with their unique traditions, architecture and ceremonies, are fascinating.

Other minorities, particularly Bajau sea nomads, have played an integral role in the island's history. The rise of the kingdom of Gowa – Sulawesi's first major power – from the mid-16th century was partly due to its trading alliance with the Bajau. The Bajau

- Tana Toraja's unique culture with its colourful ceremonies is Sulawesi's best known attraction.

- The mountains of Tana Toraja are serenely beautiful, as are those of Central Sulawesi. Trekkers can explore the unusual megaliths of the Bada Valley, and see unique wildlife in many of Sulawesi's national parks.

- The reefs around Pulau Bunaken offer some of the best snorkelling and diving, while the pristine Togean Islands are an untouched tropical wonder.

supplied valuable sea produce, especially the Chinese delicacy *trepang* (sea cucumber), tortoiseshell, birds' nests and pearl, attracting international traders to Gowa's capital, Makassar (now Ujung Pandang).

Makassar quickly became known as a cosmopolitan, tolerant and secure entrepôt that allowed traders to bypass the Dutch monopoly over the spice trade in the east – a considerable concern to the Dutch. In 1660 the Dutch sunk six Portuguese ships in Makassar harbour, captured the fort and forced Gowa's ruler, Sultan Hasanuddin, into an alliance. Eventually, the Dutch managed to exclude all other foreign traders from Makassar, effectively shutting down the port.

SULAWESI

857

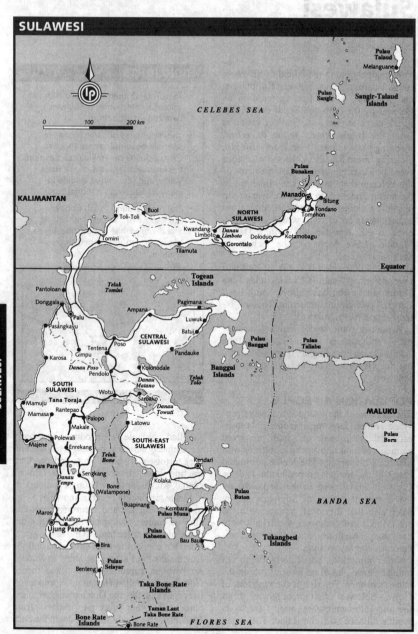

The Bajau

Nomadic Bajau 'Sea Gypsies' still dive for *trepang* (sea cucumbers), pearls and other commercially important marine produce, as they have done for hundreds, perhaps thousands, of years. The Bajau are hunter-gatherers who spend much of their whole lives on boats, travelling as families wherever they go.

There are several permanent Bajau settlements around the Togean Islands, and even some stilt villages on offshore reefs, but the itinerant character of Bajau culture still survives. Newlyweds are put in a canoe and pushed out to sea to make their place in the world. When they have children, the fathers dive with their three-day-old babies to introduce them to life on the sea.

The rare intrusions from the outside world can sometimes result in tragedy. When Bugis and Chinese traders introduced air compressors to enable the Bajau to dive longer and deeper for trepang, the lethal nature of caisson disease ('the bends') was rarely explained properly and 40 men were killed, and many more crippled, in one area alone. These days, the Bajau divers' only concessions to modernity are goggles fashioned from wood and glass, and handmade spearguns.

Even after Indonesia won its independence, ongoing civil strife stultified Sulawesi's attempts at post-war reconstruction until well into the 1960s. Sulawesi is now enjoying its first decades of uninterrupted peace, which has delivered unprecedented and accelerating development. This rapid growth is particularly evident in Manado and Ujung Pandang, which seem to belie the economic crisis affecting the rest of Indonesia.

CLIMATE

Although temperatures are relatively constant all year, Sulawesi's mountainous terrain plays havoc with local rainfall patterns. The wettest months along the west coast tend to be late November, December and early January, when north-westerly and westerly winds prevail, while south-easterly winds dump heavy falls along the eastern regions in late April, May and early June.

Mountain ranges at right angles to the prevailing winds tend to have heavy rainfall on the windward side, and little on the leeward. Valleys with a north-south orientation receive little rain at any time of year, making the Palu Valley in Central Sulawesi one of the driest areas in Indonesia.

FLORA & FAUNA

Sulawesi's landscape is strikingly beautiful, and the island is home to 127 indigenous mammals; 61% are found only on Sulawesi. Excluding 62 species of bats, the proportion of endemic mammal species rises to 98% – but many are in danger of extinction.

The biggest (and among the rarest) mammal is the 1m-high dwarf buffalo *(anoa)*. Also endemic is the *babi rusa* (deer pig), which has long legs and tusks that curve upwards like horns, and the *tarsier*, the world's smallest primate (see the boxed text 'Tarsiers'). Popular locals not yet considered at risk of extinction include the shy, but very cute, *cuscus*, and the black-crested macaque also known as the *yaki*.

Of the 328 known species of birds, 27% are endemic, but many are also endangered. Around the Togean islands and Manado, divers will be able to see dugongs, dolphins and turtles. However, the pristine coral and

The Maleo

One of Sulawesi's endemic, and most endangered, birds is also one of its least attractive. The maleo *macrocephalon maleo* has a black and white crest and an orange beak, but otherwise it is the same size, and has the same characteristics, as an ordinary chicken. Maleo lay huge eggs in nests in the ground near hot springs, but the eggs are often collected by locals for ceremonies and food.

SULAWESI

marine life around Kepulauan Spermonde (near Ujung Pandang), Pulau Bunaken (Bunaken Island) and the Togean islands (Central Sulawesi) are under constant threat from scuba diving, bad fishing practices and tourism (see the boxed text 'Conservation of the Togeans' later in this chapter).

GETTING THERE & AWAY
Air
International Silk Air flies between Manado and Singapore twice a week (currently Monday and Sunday) for US$420/799 (one way/return). Bouraq flies between Manado and Davao in the southern Philippines (ideal if you want another Indonesian visa) on Monday and Friday for US$156/262. It is important to note that you need an outward ticket (eg Manado-Davao-Manado on Bouraq) before you can enter the Philippines (or even buy a ticket to Davao).

Silk Air flies between Ujung Pandang and Singapore for US$250/361 on Monday and Thursday; and Malaysia Airlines flies between Ujung Pandang and Kuala Lumpur on Tuesday and Friday for US$180/320.

Tickets for all international flights from Ujung Pandang and Manado are often cheaper at travel agencies.

Domestic The three transport hubs are Ujung Pandang and Manado, which are well connected with the rest of Indonesia, and Palu, which has flights to Balikpapan in Kalimantan. See the individual sections, and the Sulawesi Air Fares chart in this chapter, for details about all domestic flights.

Sea
Sulawesi is well connected: 14 of Pelni's 20 liners stop at Ujung Pandang, Bitung (the seaport for Manado), Pare Pare and/or Toli-Toli, as well as a few minor towns. (Pelni no longer sails to the Philippines.)

Some of the more important boats which stop at Ujung Pandang, and sometimes Bau Bau, at least every two weeks are:

Awu – to Nusa Tenggara, Bali and eastern Kalimantan

Bukit Siguntang – to southern Maluku, southern Irian Jaya and Java

Ciremai – to northern Maluku, northern Irian Jaya and Java

Kambuna, *Kerinci* and *Tidar* – to Java and eastern Kalimantan

Lambelu – to Java and southern and northern Maluku

Rinjani – to southern Maluku and southern and northern Irian Jaya

Sirimau – to Nusa Tenggara, Java and eastern Kalimantan

Tatamailau – to southern Irian Jaya, southern Maluku, Bali and Nusa Tenggara (this boat has a four weekly route)

Tilongkabila – to Nusa Tenggara and Bali

GETTING AROUND
Air
In the current economic crisis, the number of flights around Sulawesi has been reduced dramatically. Merpati Nusantara Airlines is the main carrier, but Bouraq, Garuda Indonesia and Mandala also have a few flights. See the individual Getting There & Away entries, and the Sulawesi Air Fares chart in this chapter, for details of flights around Sulawesi.

Bus, Bemo & Kijang
Regions around Ujung Pandang and the south-west peninsula, and around Manado and the north-east peninsula, have excellent roads and frequent, comfortable buses. Elsewhere, roads are often rough, distances are long, and public transport is often crowded and uncomfortable. Allow plenty of time to travel overland in central Sulawesi, especially in the wet season. In the south-east and south-west peninsulas, sharing a Kijang (a type of 4WD taxi) is a quick, but not necessarily more comfortable, way of getting around.

Boat
The few Pelni ships that link towns within Sulawesi are a comfortable alternative to long and rough bus trips. Every two weeks (the *Tatamailau* has a four weekly route) the following boats sail from Ujung Pandang: the *Kambuna* and *Kerinci* go to Toli-Toli and Pantoloan (for Palu); the *Bukit Siguntang*, *Lambelu*, *Rinjani* and *Tatamailau* go to Bau Bau; the *Ciremai* goes to Bau Bau,

SULAWESI AIR FARES

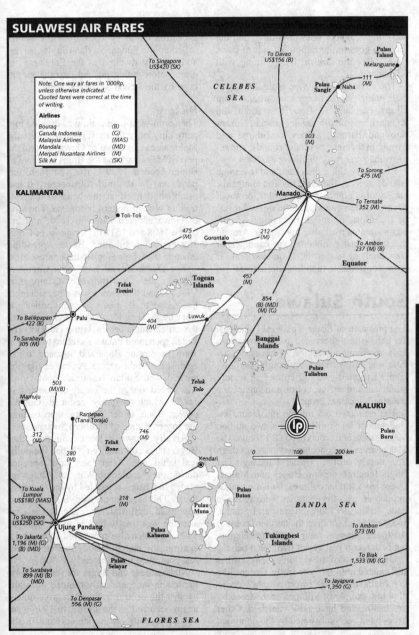

Note: One way air fares in '000Rp,
unless otherwise indicated.
Quoted fares were correct at the time
of writing.

Airlines

Bouraq	(B)
Garuda Indonesia	(G)
Malaysia Airlines	(MAS)
Mandala	(MD)
Merpati Nusantara Airlines	(M)
Silk Air	(SK)

CELEBES SEA

To Singapore US$420 (SK)

To Davao US$156 (B)

Pulau Talaud
Melanguane

Pulau Sangir — Naha — 111 (M)

303 (M)

To Sorong 475 (M)

KALIMANTAN

Toli-Toli

Manado

To Ternate 352 (M)

475 (M)

Gorontalo

212 (M)

To Ambon 237 (M) (B)

Equator

457 (M)

Togean Islands

Teluk Tomini

854 (B) (MD) (M) (G)

To Balikpapan 422 (B)

Palu

404 (M)

Luwuk

Banggai Islands

To Surabaya 305 (M)

Pulau Taliabun

503 (M)(B)

MALUKU

Mamuju

Rantepao (Tana Toraja)

Teluk Tolo

Pulau Buru

312 (M)

746 (M)

Teluk Bone

280 (M)

Kendari

N

0   100   200 km

To Kuala Lumpur US$180 (MAS)

318 (M)

Pulau Muna

Pulau Buton

BANDA SEA

To Singapore US$250 (SK)

Ujung Pandang

Pulau Kabaena

To Ambon 573 (M)

To Jakarta 1,196 (M) (G) (B) (MD)

Pulau Selayar

Tukangbesi Islands

To Biak 1,533 (M) (G)

To Surabaya 899 (M) (B) (MD)

To Jayapura 1,350 (G)

To Denpasar 556 (M) (G)

FLORES SEA

SULAWESI

the Banggai islands and Bitung (for Manado); the *Lambelu* goes to Bitung; and the *Sirimau* goes to the remote islands of Bone Rate. Also, the *Umsini* links Bitung with Kwandang.

The most useful service is the *Tilongkabila*, which sails every two weeks from Ujung Pandang to Bau Bau, Raha and Kendari; up to Kolonodale, Luwuk, Gorontalo and Bitung; across to Tahuna and Lirung in the Sangir-Talaud islands; and returns the same way to Ujung Pandang.

Elsewhere along the coast, and to remote islands such as the Togeans and Banggais, creaky old cargo/passenger ships, or *kapal kayu* (wooden boats), are the normal mode of transport, although occasional speedboats are also available for charter. Around the south-east peninsula, the *kapal cepat* (fast boat) or 'super-jet' is quicker and far more comfortable than the alternatives.

South Sulawesi

The province of South Sulawesi (Sulawesi Tengah; often shortened to Sulteng) is a lush, mountainous region of caves, waterfalls and large (but surprisingly shallow) lakes. Irrigated-rice agriculture is widely practised, and coffee, cotton and sugar cane are also important crops.

The estimated 6.5 million inhabitants include about four million Bugis, two million Makassarese and around 500,000 Toraja. The Makassarese are concentrated in the southern tip, mainly around Ujung Pandang. The Bugis (centred around Bone) and Makassarese have similar cultures; both are seafaring people who for centuries were active in trade, sailing to Flores, Timor and Sumba, and even as far south as the northern coast of Australia. Islam is their dominant religion, but both retain vestiges of traditional beliefs.

Descendants of the region's earliest tribes still existed until fairly recently. Groups like the Toala (meaning 'forest people') dwindled to a couple of villages near Maros by the 1930s, and have now vanished. Other tribes have been subsumed by the dominant groups. Torajan mythology suggests that its ancestors came by boat from the south, sailed up the Sungai Sa'dan (Sa'dan River) and initially dwelled in the Enrekang region, before being pushed into the mountains by the arrival of other groups.

History

The south-west peninsula was divided into petty kingdoms; the most powerful were the Makassarese kingdom of Gowa (around the port of Makassar) and the Bugis kingdom of Bone. Around 1530 Gowa started to expand, and by the mid-16th century it had established itself at the head of a major trading bloc in eastern Indonesia. The king of Gowa adopted Islam in 1605, and between 1608 and 1611 the kingdom of Gowa attacked and subdued Bone, spreading Islam to the whole Bugis-Makassarese area.

The Dutch United East India Company (Vereenigde Oost-Indische Compagnie, VOC) found that Gowa was a considerable hindrance to its plans to monopolise the spice trade. They found an anti-Gowa ally in the exiled Bugis prince Arung Palakka. The Dutch sponsored Palakka's return to Bone in 1666, prompting Bone and Soppeng to rise against the Makassarese. A year of fighting ensued, and Sultan Hasanuddin of Gowa was forced to sign the Treaty of Bungaya in 1667, which severely reduced Gowa's power. Bone, under Palakka, then became the supreme state of southern Sulawesi.

Rivalry between Bone and the other Bugis states continually reshaped the political landscape. After their brief absence during the Napoleonic Wars, the Dutch returned to a Bugis revolt led by the Queen of Bone. This was suppressed, but rebellions continued until Makassarese and Bugis resistance was finally broken in 1905-06. In 1905 the Dutch also conquered Tana Toraja, again in the face of bloody resistance. Unrest continued until the early 1930s.

Makassarese and Bugis are staunchly Islamic and independently minded – revolts against the central Indonesian government again occurred in the 1950s. In 1996 a series of protests on the streets, and in the

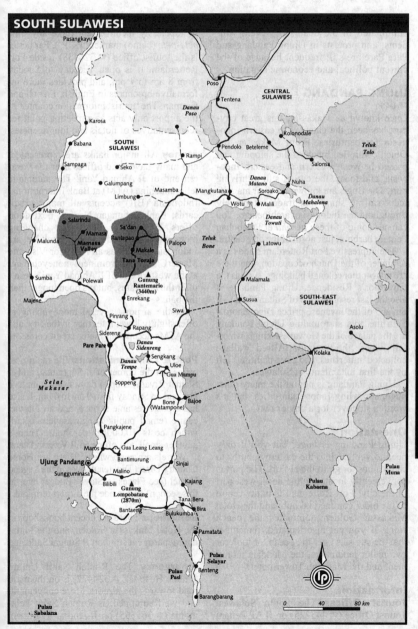

SOUTH SULAWESI

university campuses, of Ujung Pandang culminated in the deaths of several students; and protests in Ujung Pandang and Pare Pare are still frequent because of the current political and economic situation.

UJUNG PANDANG
☎ 0411

Once known as Makassar, this great city-port has been the gateway to eastern Indonesia for centuries. From Makassar, the Dutch controlled much of the shipping that passed between western and eastern Indonesia, and today, the city is still a thriving port. The Bugis are known for their magnificent sailing ships that trade extensively throughout the Indonesian archipelago. You can see some of these *perahu* at Pelabuhan Paotere harbour, just north of the city centre.

The impressive Fort Rotterdam stands as a reminder of the Dutch occupation, and there are many other colonial buildings, such as the Governor's Residence. Ujung Pandang is also the last resting place of Sultan Hasanuddin and of the Javanese prince Diponegoro.

In the area surrounding Ujung Pandang are the palace of the Gowanese kings, waterfalls where the naturalist Alfred Wallace collected butterflies, and cave-paintings left by the first inhabitants of Sulawesi.

Ujung Pandang is not unlike many other huge, sprawling Indonesian cities, but it's worth a stopover for a day or two.

Orientation

Ujung Pandang is *huge*, but you'll only need to venture into the eastern suburbs to catch a bus, or go to the airport. The port is conveniently located in the north-west part of the city; Fort Rotterdam is in the centre of the older commercial hub; and the Hotel Makassar Golden dominates the beach front. If you get disorientated, remember that the sun sets over the ocean, or look for two major landmarks, the Mandala monument and the Marannu Tower hotel.

Information

Tourist Offices The South Sulawesi Tourist Office (☎ 443225) on Jl AP Pettani

is friendly, but has limited information and is hopelessly inconvenient (take any blue *pete-pete* (bemo) marked 'IKIP'). Far better is the tourist office (☎ 320438) inside Fort Rotterdam. It is open Tuesday to Sunday from 8 am to 4 pm, and provides more informative brochures in English, French and German. The 'tourist information counter' at the airport only acts as a meeting point for representatives of hotels and tour agencies.

Money All major banks are represented, and many have head offices near the western end of Jl Ahmad Yani. The automatic teller machine (ATM) at Bank Internasional Indonesia (BII) accepts all major credit cards; Bank Tabungan Negara, next door, offers competitive rates for changing money; and the head office of Bank Negara Indonesia (BNI) has an ATM for Visa and MasterCard. The prominent moneychanger at the western end of Jl Ahmad Yani doesn't offer the best rates, but it's open longer than the banks.

At the airport, several moneychangers offer slightly lower rates than in the city; and the ATMs accepts all major credit cards.

Post & Communications The main post office, on the corner of Jl Supratman and Jl Slamet Riyadi, is open daily from 8 am to 8 pm, and on Sunday from 9 am to 4 pm. It also has a poste restante service, and an Internet centre (email publik@upg.wasantara.net.id) which costs 10,000Rp per hour. There's another small post office on Jl Veteran Utara.

Wartels are everywhere. There are Home Country Direct Dial telephones in the Legend Hostel (see Places to Stay – Budget later in this section) and inside the airport terminal.

Bookshops There are decent bookshops in the Hotel Makassar Golden, and the Matahari department store on Jl Sungai Saddang.

Emergency The Rumah Sakit Umum (Public Hospital, ☎ 324427) is on the main road towards the airport. More convenient, and well equipped, is Rumah Sakit Pelamonia (☎ 365365) on Jl Jendral Sudirman.

THE WALLACE LINE

Detailed surveys of Borneo and Sulawesi by English naturalist Alfred Russel Wallace in the 1850s resulted in some inspired correspondence with Charles Darwin. Wallace was struck by the marked differences in wildlife, despite the two islands' proximity and similarities in climate and geography. His letters to Darwin, detailing evidence of his theory that the Indonesian archipelago was inhabited by one distinct fauna in the east and one in the west, prompted Darwin to publish similar observations from his own travels. The subsequent debate on species distribution and evolution transformed modern thought.

Wallace refined his theory in 1859, drawing a boundary between the two regions of fauna. Wallace's Line, as it became known, divided Sulawesi and Lombok to the east, and Borneo and Bali to the west. He believed that islands to the west of the line had once been part of Asia, and those to the east had been linked to a Pacific-Australian continent. Sulawesi's wildlife was so unusual that Wallace suspected it was once part of both, a fact that geologists have since proven to be true.

Other analyses of where Australian-type fauna begin to outnumber Asian fauna have placed the line further east. Lydekker's Line, which lies east of Maluku and Timor, is generally accepted as the western boundary of strictly Australian fauna, while Wallace's Line marks the eastern boundary of Asian fauna.

Alfred Russel Wallace from *On the Zoological Geography of the Malay Archipelago*, 1859
'... the western and eastern islands of the Archipelago ... belong to regions more distinct and contrasted than any other of the great zoological divisions of the globe. South America and Africa, separated by the Atlantic, do not differ so widely as Asia and Australia: Asia with its abundance and variety of large Mammals and no Marsupials, and Australia with scarcely anything but Marsupials; ... Asia the poorest tropical region in Parrots, Australia the richest ...'

PAUL BEINSSEN

JASON EDWARDS

ANDREW BROWNBILL

A sick orang-utan at a rehabilitation centre.

ANDREW BROWNBILL

For many Kalimantan kids, their backyard is a river.

DAVID ANDREW

Sci-fi Rafflesia – the world's largest flower.

MARIE CAMBON

Negara, a stilt village in South Kalimantan – best toured by boat ...

There is also a police station (☎ 110) on Jl Ahmad Yani; and an immigration office, near the port.

Fort Rotterdam

One of the best preserved examples of Dutch architecture in Indonesia, Fort Rotterdam continues to guard the harbour of Ujung Pandang. A Gowanese fort dating back to 1545 once stood there, but failed to keep out the Dutch. The original fort was rebuilt in Dutch style after the Treaty of Bungaya in 1667. Parts of the crumbling wall have been left untouched, and provide an interesting comparison to the restored buildings.

Inside the fort, **Museum Negeri La Galigo** has an assortment of exhibits, including rice bowls from Tana Toraja, kitchen tools, musical instruments and various costumes. The Fort is open daily from 8 am to 6 pm, and a 'donation' is expected (1000Rp is enough). The museum is open Tuesday to Sunday from 8 am to 12.30 pm, and costs another 350Rp. The entrance is at Km1, Jl Pasar.

Makam Pangeran Diponegoro

Prince Diponegoro of Yogyakarta led the Java War (1825-30), but his career as a rebel leader came to a sudden halt when he was tricked into going to the Dutch headquarters to negotiate peace, and was taken prisoner and then exiled to Sulawesi. He spent the last 26 years of his life imprisoned in Fort Rotterdam. His grave and monument can be seen in a small cemetery on Jl Diponegoro.

Old Gowa

Remnants of the former kingdom of Gowa, on the south-eastern outskirts of Ujung Pandang, include the **Tomb of Sultan Hasanuddin** (1629-70), ruler of Gowa in the mid-17th century. Outside the tomb compound is the **Pelantikan Stone**, on which the kings of Gowa were crowned.

About a 15 minute walk from the tomb (ask directions if walking) is **Mesjid Katangka** (Katangka Mosque). Another mosque was built here in 1603, but a modern building now occupies the site. More interesting is the attached **cemetery** with its large crypts, each containing several graves.

Benteng Sungguminasa (Sungguminasa Fort), once the seat of the Sultan of Gowa, is a few kilometres further south at Sungguminasa. The former royal residence, now known as **Museum Balla Lompoa**, houses a collection of artefacts similar to those in the Fort Rotterdam museum. Although the royal regalia can only be seen on request, the wooden Bugis-style palace itself is the real attraction.

To Old Gowa and Sungguminasa, take a red pete-pete marked 'S. Minasa' from Makassar Mall, and asked to be dropped off, or, better, charter a taxi.

Other Attractions

Pelabuhan Paotere (Paotere Harbour), a short *becak* (bicycle rickshaw) ride north of the city centre, is where the Bugis sailing ships berth. Tourists are charged 350Rp to enter Paotere. There is usually lots of activity on the dock, and in the busy **fish market** a few streets south.

A large number of ethnic Chinese Indonesians live in Ujung Pandang. New and old **Chinese temples** are dotted along Jl Sulawesi; the most ornate is on the corner of Jl Sulawesi and Jl Serui Sama.

Taman Anggrek CL Bundt (Clara Bundt Orchid Garden) is hidden away behind a home at Jl Mochtar Lufti 15. It contains exotic hybrids, some up to 5m high, and a huge collection of shells. Admission is free, and you can have a look, but the public aren't that welcome these days.

The towering **Monumen Mandala** is a smaller version of Jakarta's Monas (National Monument), and celebrates the 'liberation' of Irian Jaya. Further south along Jl Jendral Sudirman, there is an incongruous herd of spotted deer in the gardens of the Governor's Residence.

Places to Stay – Budget

Some really cheap places often don't take foreigners, and many double as brothels.

The bottom of the line is *Hotel Nusantara* (☎ 323163, Jl Sarappo 103), where hot, noisy sweatboxes go for 15,000Rp. Just

UJUNG PANDANG

PLACES TO STAY
4 Hotel Nusantara
6 Hotel Murah
11 Hotel Yasmin
12 Hotel Yasmin
13 Legend Hostel
24 Hotel Aman
27 Hotel Ramayana Satrya
28 Marlin Hotel
32 Hotel Surya Berlian
34 Marannu Tower;
   Marannu City Hotel; Cafe 69
35 Pondok Suada Indah
36 Hotel Celebes
37 Hotel Purnama
39 Hotel Pantai Gapura
40 Hotel Makassar Golden; Pier 52
41 Hotel Losari Beach,
45 Hotel Riantira
47 Hotel Surya Indonesia

49 Penginapan Surya
50 Hotel Puri Wisata
51 Hotel Delta
52 Hotel Losari Metro
53 Hotel Radisson
54 Richardson Homestay
56 Hotel Victoria Internasional,
   Coffee Shop; Jazz Pub

PLACES TO EAT
33 Candy Bakery
42 Kafe Kareba;
   Kios Semarang
43 KFC; Swensen's,
   Kantin Baik dan Murah;
   Galael Supermarket
60 Matahari Department
   Store; KFC
62 Pizza Kafe Ria;
   Supermarket

OTHER
1 Pelabuhan Makasar
   (Pelni Port)
2 Port Entrance
3 Immigration Office
5 Jameson Supermarket
7 Diponegoro Tomb
8 Mandala Office
9 Makassar Mall;
   Matahari Department Store
10 Chinese Temple
14 BKI Bank
15 Moneychanger
16 Police Station
17 Fort Rotterdam
18 Garuda Office
19 Main Post Office
20 Wartel
21 Bank Tabungan Negara
   & BII bank

22 BNI Bank
23 Bioskop Artis
25 Al Markas al Islami
   Mosque
26 Merpati Office
29 Post Office
30 Rumah Sakit Pelamonia
31 Monumen Mandala
38 Benteng Theatre
44 Istana Cinema
46 Wartel
48 BNI Bank
55 Taman Anggrek CL
   Bundt
57 Wartel
58 Pelni Office
59 Governor's Residence
61 Mandala Office
63 Studio 21
64 Bouraq Office

across the road, *Hotel Murah* (☎ *323101, Jl Sarappo 60)* is not much better: windowless rooms cost 10,000Rp to 20,000Rp.

Another cheapie is *Hotel Aman* (☎ *322554, Jl Mesjid Raya)* for 20,000Rp per room, but it's noisy and inconvenient. *Hotel Purnama* (☎ *323830, Jl Pattimura 3A)* has dismal rooms with a bathroom for 20,000Rp, but it's quietish, central and cheap. At least *Penginapan Surya (Jl Mochtar Lufti Sawerigading 15)* is central and quiet, but still nothing great. Rooms cost 15,000Rp.

Legend Hostel (☎ *328203, fax 328204, Jl Jampea 5G)* is cheap, clean, popular and friendly, but the rooms are dreary and noisy. Doubles, with a fan and shared bathroom, cost 17,500Rp; beds in a dorm are 7000Rp. The attractions are the service, book exchange, noticeboard, guest book and chance to meet other travellers. Just up the road, *Losmen Semeru* (☎ *318113, Jl Jampea 27)* offers ordinary rooms, but for 17,500Rp per double, with air-con, this is very good value. It is understandably popular, and often full.

Hotel Ramayana Satrya (☎ *442478, fax 442479, Jl Gunung Bawakaraeng 121)* has been recommended by many travellers. Economy rooms with a fan and bath cost 22,000Rp; and singles/doubles with air-con and hot water cost 33,600/44,800Rp to 61,600/72,800Rp. It's quiet, despite the noisy location, and has a good restaurant, but is inconvenient. Opposite, *Marlin Hotel* (☎ *444975, Jl Bawakaraeng 120)* desperately needs renovation, and the rooms are very noisy, but each one has several beds so it's good for small groups. Rooms with a fan cost 32,500/37,500Rp; with air-con, 43,000/50,000Rp.

Recommended for its friendly, cosy atmosphere is *Richardson Homestay* (☎ *32 0349, Jl Mochtar Lufti Sawerigading 21)*. It offers quiet, comfortable rooms, with a shared bathroom, for 35,000/40,000Rp with fan/air-con.

Places to Stay – Mid-Range
The choice of mid-range hotels is excellent, especially in the residential precinct south of the fort. All rooms have air-con, satellite TV

and breakfast (unless stated otherwise), and most have budget-priced economy rooms.

Pondok Suada Indah (☎ *317179, fax 312856, Jl Hasanuddin 12)* is highly recommended. This small, spacious hotel has the feel of a colonial guesthouse. Well furnished singles/doubles start at 48,400/60,500Rp. The popular *Hotel Riantira* (☎ *324133, Jl Ranggong 10)* is on a quiet street. Rooms with a fan cost 27,000Rp to 37,000Rp; with air-con 44,000/49,000Rp.

The five storey *Hotel Surya Indonesia* (☎ *327568, fax 311498, Jl Daeng Tompo 3)* offers breezy views of the city and harbour islands. Rooms are small, but comfortable, and cost from 61,710/76,230Rp. The associated *Hotel Surya Berlian* (☎ *327208, fax 3312 52, Jl Amannagappa)* is charming, central and quiet. Rooms, set around a courtyard, cost 47,000/57,000Rp. Also central and good value is *Hotel Yasmin* (☎ *320424, fax 3282 83, Jl Jampea 5)*, with rooms from 78,000Rp to 139,000Rp for the 'suite'. It is well signed, and easy to find from Jl Ahmad Yani.

Hotel Puri Wisata (☎ *312344, fax 312783, Jl Hasanuddin 36)* has fan-cooled rooms for 40,000/50,000Rp, and more luxurious rooms with air-con from 72,000/85,000Rp; and the nearby *Hotel Delta* (☎ *312711, fax 312655, Jl Hasanuddin 43)* costs from US$51/63 – but ask for a discount, and try to pay in rupiah.

Places to Stay – Top End
A glut of empty rooms in a glut of top-end hotels means substantial discounts. At the time of writing, three or four-star hotels were offering singles/doubles for the rupiah equivalent of about US$10/15. Inquire at the hotel reception or, if you arrive by air, talk to one of the hotel representatives at the airport.

One of the few places with style is *Hotel Pantai Gapura* (☎ *325791, fax 316303, email hotelpg@upg.mega.net.id, Jl Pasar Ikan 10)*. It offers a range of luxury cottages, overlooking the sea, and a stunning swimming pool. This is all yours for US$108/121 – but 50% discounts are very common. Nearby, *Hotel Makassar Golden* (☎ *314408, fax 320951, Jl Pasar Ikan 50)* is a landmark, with rooms from 181,500Rp to 363,000Rp.

SULAWESI

Also close to the water and city centre is **Hotel Losari Beach** (☎ 326062, fax 313978, Jl Penghibur). It has a range of rooms from US$40 in the guesthouse or hotel, but it's not great value unless you get a discount (which is often possible). **Hotel Celebes** (☎ 320770, fax 320769, Jl Hasanuddin 2) is good value because it charges rupiah – from 215,000Rp to 373,000Rp for the 'suite'.

Marannu Tower and **Marannu City Hotel** (☎ 327051, fax 321821, Jl Hasanuddin 3) almost occupy an entire city block, and is another landmark. The hotel complex has rooms from 338,800/363,000Rp, but management offers discounts to about 100,000/150,000Rp.

Other decent top-end places, which should offer substantial discounts, include: (☎ 331133, fax 331188, Jl Khairilanwar 19) with rooms for US$88/100; **Hotel Victoria Internasional** (☎ 328888, fax 312368, Jl Sudirman 24) with rooms for US$102/120; and **Hotel Radisson** (☎ 333111, fax 333222, Jl Somba Opu), with room from US$170.

Places to Eat

Home to Indonesia's foremost seafaring peoples, Ujung Pandang has an abundance of good seafood; barbecued fish and octopus are especially popular. Because of the sizeable Chinese population, Ujung Pandang is also a good place for Chinese food. Local specialities include *coto makassar* (soup made from buffalo innards) and the odd, but sweet, blend of avocadoes, condensed milk and chocolate syrup.

The hundreds of **night warungs** (food stalls) lining the waterfront south of the Hotel Makassar Golden make Pantai Losari (Losari Beach) the longest dining strip on Sulawesi. Here you can buy any sort of fresh and cheap Indonesian and Chinese meal, enjoy a cold drink and watch Ujung Pandang's famous sunset.

The other restaurants in the area can be disappointing, however. Many are sleazy, pick-up joints with karaoke machines, and all of them are along the noisy main road (Jl Penghibur). One of the best is **Kios Semarang**, which has decent food, surprisingly

cheap drinks (large beers, 7000Rp) and great views. Nearby, **Kafe Kareba** has live music, western food (such as burgers for 9000Rp and baked fish for 12,000Rp) and breezes, but the views aren't great.

Jl Pattimura boasts a few decent **fish restaurants**. None are any better than the others, but the fish is fresh and the prices are reasonable (about 10,000Rp).

For cakes and pastries, try the **Candy Bakery** (Jl Baumassepe). The popular **coffee shop** (Jl Ranggong) on the ground floor of Toko Baji Pamai, next to Hotel Riantira, also has plenty of cheap, tasty pastries, and hot and cold drinks.

Fast food junkies will go to **KFC** (Jl Hasanuddin), or enjoy an ice cream at **Swensen's** or cheap Indonesian food at **Kantin Baik dan Murah** in the same building. All three are above the **Galeal Supermarket**, which sells all sorts of 'necessities', like chocolate, ice cream and cheese. In the Matahari department store on Jl Sungai Saddang, there is a decent **eatery** and another **KFC**, and the Indonesian equivalent, **CFC**, is nearby. Around the corner, **Pizza Kafe Ria** (Jl G Latimojong) was part of the Pizza Hut chain, and has tasty pizza, pasta and self-serve salads for less than 10,000Rp each. There is a well-stocked **supermarket** downstairs.

Of the hotels (see the Places to Stay entry in this section), **Hotel Victoria Internasional** has a pleasant coffee shop, with decent prices; **Hotel Delta** has a small restaurant; and **Hotel Losari Beach** has main courses between 10,000Rp and 15,000Rp, but it's impossible to escape the karaoke machine. The Japanese **Shogun Restaurant** is next door.

Entertainment

Along the esplanade, **Kafe Kareba** is a bar and restaurant that features live bands most nights. Jazz fans should head for **Jazz Pub** at the Hotel Victoria Internasional, which also offers plenty of interesting traditional dances and poolside parties. **Cafe 69**, a small, outside bar in the Marannu hotel complex, sometimes features live bands. For the sunset, there are several so-so bars along the esplanade, such as **Kios Semarang** and the huge *Pier 52*, which is part of Hotel Makassar Golden, with its unmistakable Toraja-style architecture. Pier 52 offers western food, pastries, great views and high prices (small beers for 8000Rp).

The modern *Studio 21 (Jl Sam Ratulangi)* cinema has five screens showing current, western films in their original language (with Indonesian subtitles). *Benteng Theatre (Jl Pasar Ikan)* also shows decent, new films, but older places, such as *Bioskop Artis (Jl Gunung Lompobatang)* and *Istana Cinema (Jl Hasanuddin)*, show Indian and Chinese films in less comfort. Check Ujung Pandang's daily (Indonesian language) *Fajar* newspaper for screening details.

Shopping
Jl Somba Opu has plenty of shops with great collections of jewellery, 'antiques' and touristy souvenirs, including crafts from all over Indonesia, such as Kendari filigree silver jewellery, Torajan handicrafts, Chinese pottery, Makassarese brass work, and silk cloth from Sengkang and Soppeng. Shopping centres are appearing everywhere, from the amorphous bazaars in and around Makassar Mall, to the huge Matahari department stores at Makassar Mall and on Jl S Saddang.

Getting There & Away
Air Shop around and check for the current prices with both airlines and agents; there is usually competition and some agents discount, especially for international flights. All airlines charge the same price for the same domestic flights.

Merpati Nusantara Airlines (☎ 442480) flies directly and regularly to Ambon (573,400Rp), Denpasar (555,800Rp), Jakarta (1,196,000Rp), Biak (1,532,600Rp), Manado (853,900Rp) and Surabaya (899,300Rp). There are less regular flights to Kendari, Luwuk, Mamuju, Palu and Rantepao – see the relevant sections in this chapter for details.

Garuda Indonesia (☎ 322705) flies directly to Manado, Denpasar and Jakarta daily; and to Biak and Jayapura (1,350,000Rp) four times a week. Bouraq (☎ 452506) flies four times a week to Balikpapan (923,400Rp) via

Palu; and to Manado, Surabaya and Jakarta five days a week. Mandala flies daily to Surabaya and Jakarta, and to Manado most days. Mandala has two offices: one (☎ 324288) along Jl S Saddang, and another (☎ 33 3888) along Jl Cokroaminoto.

Malaysia Airlines (☎ 330888) is in the Marannu hotel complex; and Silk Air (☎ 32 6733) is in the Hotel Makassar Golden. See the introductory Getting There & Away section at the start of this chapter for details about international flights to/from Ujung Pandang.

Bus & Kijang The terminals for buses, bemos and Kijangs are surprisingly chaotic, unorganised and very inconvenient. All this may change when Terminal Daya, about two-thirds along the main road to the airport, becomes the main terminal. The best idea is to check with the tourist office at Fort Rotterdam, or hire a taxi and ask the driver to take you to the correct terminal.

Terminal Gowa (Terminal Sungguminasa) is about 10km south-east of the city centre; take a red pete-pete marked 'S. Minasa' from the city centre. From here, buses go to places within South Sulawesi province – eg Pare Pare (8500Rp); Bone (9600Rp); Sengkang (13,300Rp); Rantepao (16,000Rp to 35,000Rp); and Palopo (21,500Rp).

Terminal Panaikang is in the eastern suburbs, but most services are due to move to Terminal Daya later. From Panaikang, there are currently Kijangs to Bone, Bantimurung and the Gua Leang Leang (Leang Leang Caves); and buses to the rest of Sulawesi, eg Tana Toraja, Palu, Poso, Gorontalo and Manado. To Panaikang, catch the special blue pete-pete from town.

Terminal Mallengkeri is another distant terminal with a few Kijangs and buses to parts of southern Sulawesi, such as Pantai Bira and Pulau Selayar. It's best to hire a taxi to this terminal.

Boat Ten Pelni boats stop in Ujung Pandang about once a week, mostly on the way to Surabaya and Jakarta, eastern Kalimantan and/or Ambon.

The most useful services are the *Tidar* to Balikpapan for 49,000/162,500Rp (economy/1st class); the *Sirimau* to Kupang (98,500/333,500Rp) in Nusa Tenggara; and the *Tilongkabila* to Bau Bau and then up the east coast to Kendari (55,000/183,000Rp), Kolonodale, Luwuk, Gorontalo and Manado.

The efficient, and computerised, Pelni office (☎ 331401), Jl Sam Ratulangi, is open Monday to Saturday from 8 am to 2 pm. You can also buy tickets at any Pelni agency around town, some of which are linked by computer to the Pelni office. The chaotic Pelabuhan Makassar port, which is used by Pelni boats, is only a becak ride from most hotels.

Getting Around

To/From the Airport Pete-petes from Makassar Mall to Ujung Pandang's Hasanuddin airport (22km) pass by Terminal Daya for 1500Rp. The Damri bus to Maros (see Bantimurung later in this section) also stops along the main road, outside the gate to the airport (which is 500m from the terminal).

Pete-pete and Damri buses *to* the city stop outside the main gate, although you may need to change to another pete-pete at Terminal Daya.

A pre-paid taxi from the airport to the city costs a hefty 23,000Rp, plus the toll (1000Rp) for the short cut from the north. To the airport, a metered taxi costs about 19,000Rp. The driver will normally take the longer route to the east, but it's cheaper to pay the toll, and use the short cut.

Public Transport Ujung Pandang is too hot to walk around – you'll need a becak, pete-pete or taxi. Annoying becak drivers kerb-crawl, hoping you'll succumb to their badgering and/or the heat. They want anything up to 10,000Rp; locals pay about 1000Rp around town. The main pete-pete terminal is at the Makassar Mall, and the standard fare around town is 500Rp. Airconditioned taxis use meters and are worth using; 5000Rp will get you across town in comfort.

AROUND UJUNG PANDANG

Pulau Samalona

A tiny speck just off Ujung Pandang, Pulau Samalona is popular for fishing and snorkelling, particularly on Sunday. Otherwise, there's nothing much to do – it takes about two minutes to walk around the island.

A few of the houses have scruffy *rooms* for rent for a hefty 50,000Rp per person, including meals, such as the unsigned *Rati Losmen* and *Mirna Losmen*. If you ask around, you can buy expensive cold drinks, and fresh fish meals. Snorkelling gear is also available.

You will have to charter something for about 50,000Rp one way or return from the special jetty in Ujung Pandang and, if you stay, pre-arrange to be picked up later. On Sunday, you can probably share a boat with some day-trippers; otherwise, Legend Hostel (see Places to Stay under Ujung Pandang earlier in this chapter) often organises trips.

Pulau Kayangan

☎ 0411

This tiny island is more of a circular promenade than a beach, and is not great for swimming (although plenty of locals do). It's very busy on Sunday, but almost completely empty for the rest of the week.

The cabins are part of *Wisata Bahari Pulau Kayangan* (☎ 315752). The rooms are stuffy and have private bathrooms, and cost about 30,000Rp per double. Some of the *restaurants* around the island are positioned over the water, and many are perfect for sunsets. Prices are better than anywhere along the esplanade in Ujung Pandang.

Boats travel from the special jetty in Ujung Pandang every 15 minutes (5000Rp per person return) until 10 pm – perfect for a sunset cruise followed by a meal on the island.

Bantimurung

Air Terjun Bantimurung (Bantimurung Falls) are set amid lushly vegetated limestone cliffs. It's crowded with day-trippers on weekends and holidays; at other times it's a wonderful retreat. Entrance to the reserve costs 2000Rp; and the small **butterfly museum** inside costs another 750Rp.

Upstream from the main waterfall, there's another smaller waterfall and a pretty, but treacherous, pool. The interesting **Gua Mimpi** caves are nearby – bring a torch (flashlight). Bantimurung is also famous for its beautiful butterflies. The naturalist Alfred Wallace collected specimens here in the mid-1800s.

Catch a Damri bus (one hour) to Maros from outside the main post office or Makassar Mall in Ujung Pandang, and a pete-pete to Bantimurung (30 minutes).

Gua Leang Leang

A few kilometres before the Bantimurung turn-off is the road to caves, which are noted for their ancient paintings. The age of the paintings is unknown, but relics from other nearby caves have provided glimpses of life from 8000 to 30,000 years ago. There are 60 or so known caves in the Maros district, but most are dry. A notable exception is **Salukan Kalang**, the largest known cave on Sulawesi at 11km long – but access is restricted.

Catch a pete-pete from Maros (see the Bantimurung entry earlier in this chapter) to the 'Taman Purbakala Leang-Leang' turn-off on the road to Bone, and then walk the last couple of kilometres. Alternatively, charter a pete-pete from Maros, and combine it with a trip to Bantimurung.

Malino
☎ 0417

Malino is a hill resort, once famous as the meeting place of Kalimantan and East Indonesian leaders who endorsed the Netherlands' ill-fated plans for a federation – the influence of the Dutch is still visible in the town's architecture. There are many scenic walks, and the spectacular **Air Terjun Takapala** are set amid rice fields, 4km east of town.

One place to spoil yourself is *Resort Celebes (☎ 21134, Jl Hasanuddin 1)*. This luxurious place is set in a pretty garden, with rooms from 75,000Rp – but most cost 120,000Rp upwards. Direct pete-petes leave from Terminal Gowa in Ujung Pandang.

Sulawesi Seafarers

The Bugis are Indonesia's best known sailors, trading and carrying goods on their magnificent wooden schooners throughout Indonesia.

The Bugis' influence expanded rapidly after the fall of Makassar, resulting in a diaspora from southern Sulawesi in the 17th and 18th centuries. They established strategic trading posts at Kutai (Kalimantan), Johor (north of Singapore) and Selangor (near Kuala Lumpur), and traded freely throughout the region. Bugis and Makassarese boats are still built along Sulawesi's and Kalimantan's south coasts, using centuries-old designs and techniques.

The Bajau, Bugis, Butonese and Makassarese seafarers of Sulawesi have a 500 year history of trading and cultural links with the Aborigines of northern Australia. British explorer Matthew Flinders encountered 60 Indonesian schooners at Melville Bay in 1803; and today many more still make the risky (and illegal) journey to fish reefs in the cyclone belt off the northern coast of Australia.

Many Minahasans of north Sulawesi, relative newcomers to sailing folklore, work on international shipping lines across the world. Like their Filipino neighbours, the Minahasans' outward looking culture, plus their language and sailing skills, make them the first choice of many captains.

SOUTH COAST

This area is remarkably barren compared to the peninsula's rich agricultural hinterland. The climate is drier, rice gives way to maize and *lontar* (palm), and boat building, fishing and salt-making are the main activities.

Any bemo or bus along the south coast from the Gowa or Mallengkeri terminals in Ujung Pandang will drop you off at any place listed later in this section. The road between Ujung Pandang and Pantai Bira is a popular cycling route, but the road is narrow, busy and the region is very hot.

SULAWESI

Bantaeng

Bantaeng is a Makassarese boat-building centre with a rich maritime history. It was a dependency of the Javanese kingdom of Majapahit, and its ships were mentioned in 14th century Javanese poetry. Just north of Bantaeng (charter a pete-pete) is an impressive waterfall.

It's better to continue to Pantai Bira or Ujung Pandang, but you can stay at the decent *Hotel Alam Jaya*, along the main road in the far eastern end of town, for 25,000/35,000Rp for singles/doubles. Plenty of *rumah makans* (restaurants) nearby offer fresh fish for passing travellers.

Bulukumba
☎ 0413

The Bugis and Makassarese villages on the coastline near Bulukumba are known for traditional boat building. The modern *Malboro Hotel* (☎ 81458), along the main road, costs 35,000/55,000Rp with fan/air-con, but it's better to stay in Pantai Bira.

Bulukumba is the junction for public transport to Pantai Bira, and one of the departure points for ferries to Pulau Selayar (see Getting There & Away under Pulau Selayar later in this chapter). Bulukumba's busy terminal is a few kilometres from town, and has all sorts of vehicles that travel to Ujung Pandang (9000Rp), Pantai Bira (2500Rp) and Bone (7000Rp).

PANTAI BIRA
☎ 0413

Fishing, boat building and weaving are the primary commercial activities in Pantai Bira, but the gorgeous white sand beaches are now drawing travellers off the main Ujung Pandang-Tana Toraja tourist trail. Pantai Bira is a very relaxed spot (except on Sunday), where goats outnumber vehicles (and, often, tourists). Pantai Bira has reasonable facilities, but the settings of most accommodation options are disappointing.

Orientation & Information

Almost everything is located along a small section of the main road into Pantai Bira, Jl

Kapongkolang. Foreign tourists must pay 1000Rp per person, per visit, at a gateway at the start of the road. The Bira Beach Hotel has a wartel, which also acts as a postal agency, Pelni agency and moneychanger.

Things to See

Boat builders use age-old techniques to craft **traditional ships** at Marumasa near Bira village. Boats of various sizes are at various stages of construction.

Weavers gather under raised Bugis houses to work and gossip. You can hear the click-clack of their looms as you walk along the streets in Bira village. Near the entrance gate, a collection of tiny souvenir stalls stand empty – a sad indication of the dearth of tourists. There is a small market in the village.

A short hike takes you to the top of **Pua Janggo**, a small hill above Tanateng village, with great views. Nearby, there are some **caves** with plenty of frisky monkeys – from Bira Beach Hotel, turn left at the tennis court, walk another five minutes, then walk back towards the beach for about 20 minutes.

Diving

The diving around Pantai Bira is not exceptional, but you'll see (harmless) sharks, manta rays and huge groupers, and superb coral at several dropoffs. The best spots are around Marumasa, northern Pulau Lihukan, and southern and eastern Pulau Betang – your boatman will know where to go.

The only dive centre is at Bira Beach Hotel, which charges US$50 for two dives; or US$300/340 for a package of 12/24 dives. Staff will negotiate when business is quiet (which is most of the time). Another company, Antara Tour (☎ 0411-327522, fax 325625), based at Marannu Pavilion Hotel, Jl Thamrin 2, Ujung Pandang, is a German-run outfit which offers expensive diving trips around Pantai Bira, and other parts of southern Sulawesi.

Snorkelling

Snorkelling is also good, but you'll have to charter a boat to find the best spots. A trip

AROUND BIRA

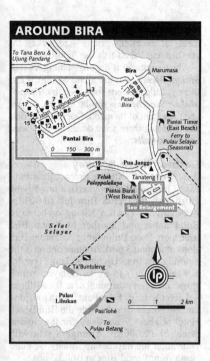

To Tana Beru &
Ujung Pandang

Bira   Marumasa

Pasar
Bira

Pantai Timur
(East Beach)
Ferry to
Pulau Selayar
(Seasonal)

Jalan Kapongkolang

Pantai Bira

0   150   300 m

Pua Janggo

Teluk
Paloppalakaya   Tanateng
Pantai Barat
(West Beach)
See Enlargement

Selat
Selayar

Ta'Buntuleng

Pulau
Lihukan   0   1   2 km

Pasi'lohé

To
Pulau Betang

AROUND BIRA

PLACES TO STAY
2   Sunrise Guesthouse
5   Hotel Purnama Bira
6   Pondok Wisata Tanjung Bira
8   Riswan Bungalows
10 Anda Bungalows
11 Riswan Guesthouse
12 Nusa Bira Indah Cottage
13 Bira View Inn Restaurant
14 Pondok Wisata Bahagia
16 Bira Beach Hotel & Restaurant;
    Wartel; Dive Centre & Restaurant
17 Hotel Sapolohe
19 Malboro Cottages

PLACES TO EAT
7   Rumah Makan Sederhana
9   Rumah Makan Melati

OTHER
1   Harbour
3   Entrance Gate
4   Souvenir Shops
15 Boats (for Pulau Lihukan)
18 Monkey Caves

around Lihukan and Betang islands will cost about 60,000Rp per day. The beach in front of Bira View Inn is good, but don't venture too far because the currents can be surprisingly strong. Equipment can be rented from most hotels, including Riswan Bungalows, Bira View and Bira Beach hotels, from 10,000Rp to US$5 per day.

Swimming

The tides can be severe, but Pantai Barat (West Beach) is a perfect stretch of beach, about 100m north-west of Bira Beach Hotel. Along this beach, you can hire huge inflatable rubber tyres, and enjoy the serenity – except on Sunday, when the place is usually crawling with day-trippers from Ujung Pandang.

Places to Stay

Most accommodation is in small, well-furnished and clean individual cottages, with private bathrooms and verandahs. However, very few have genuine seaviews and many are cluttered around a 'garden' of limestone.

Bira View Inn (☎ 82043, fax 81515) has a row of clean, modern cottages on a cliff overlooking the bay, and is the only hotel to really exploit its superb location. The standard cottages for 65,000Rp are overpriced, but the two-storey Bugis-style 'houses' for 75,000Rp are excellent.

Bira Beach Hotel (☎/fax 81515) has a large collection of bungalows at negotiable prices. The cheaper bungalows for 38,500/49,500Rp without/with fan are pleasant, but most have unexciting settings. The overpriced 'Seaview Cottages' cost 93,500/104,500Rp with fan/air-con, but have no real 'seaviews'.

Hotel Sapolohe (☎/fax 82128) has a beautiful Bugis-style house, but very few rooms take advantage of the views. The deluxe rooms with views, air-con, TV and hot water are way too high at 212,000Rp; the clean, comfortable bungalows out the back for 90,750Rp are not great value either. Further

SULAWESI

around, *Malboro Cottages* (formerly Tanjung Bira Cottages) is another motley bunch of clean, simple bungalows around a limestone 'garden' with no views for 20,000Rp. It is accessible along a road north of Pantai Bira, or by walking along the beach. The rooms at *Nusa Bira Indah Cottage (☎/fax 0411-85 5125)* are very clean and well furnished, but the setting, around the usual limestone 'garden', is unexciting. Standard rooms cost 40,000Rp; 60,000Rp for the 'eksekutif' with TV and fan.

Riswan Bungalows (☎ 82127) has simple cottages facing the main road for 20,000/25,000Rp for singles/doubles. The associated, and popular, *Riswan Guesthouse (☎ 82 127)* is a huge Bugis house with a breezy porch overlooking the sea. Rooms cost 20,000Rp per person with a shared bathroom, including three meals. There is a convivial atmosphere, where you're likely to meet other like-minded travellers.

If the other places are full, try *Anda Bungalows (☎ 82125)*, with rooms for about 20,000/25,000Rp; *Pondok Wisata Tanjung Bira (☎ 82753)*, with rooms for 30,000Rp; opposite, *Hotel Purnama Bira*, which is slightly better, with rooms for 35,000Rp; and *Pondok Wisata Bahagia*, with a multi-coloured collection of uninspiring cottages for 40,000Rp.

Sunrise Guesthouse, on a cliff overlooking Pantai Timur (East Beach), has good views, but the rooms are nothing special for 30,000Rp. (The area is known for its dawn views and the monkeys that appear in the wee hours.) The guesthouse intends to build more rooms to take advantage of its new-found convenience to the huge new harbour just below (see Boat section under Getting There & Away).

Places to Eat

Most of the hotels have simple *restaurants*, but only the Bira Beach Hotel and Bira View Inn offer views (the sunsets are superb). Both serve good breakfasts (9000Rp); a range of western food, and seafood for about 9000Rp; and cold beer. The breezy *restaurant* in front of Nusa Bira Indah Cottage has

delicious fruit drinks and a range of tasty meals at excellent prices – pancakes for 2000Rp and baked fish for 7000Rp.

Always popular is the unassuming *Rumah Makan Melati*, but the menu is limited and there is little western food. Nearby, *Rumah Makan Sederhana* is similar in price, service and the extent of its menu. Opposite the Bira Beach Hotel, there are a dozen or more food and drink *stalls*.

Getting There & Away

Bus, Bemo & Kijang From Ujung Pandang (Terminal Mallengkeri), a few Kijang go directly to Pantai Bira for 10,000Rp. Alternatively, catch a Kijang or bemo to Bulukumba, and another to Pantai Bira (transport from Bulukumba to Pantai Bira stops at around 3 pm). Another option is the morning bus from Ujung Pandang (Terminal Mallengkeri) to Pulau Selayar, which stops at the ferry terminal near Bira village.

Direct Kijangs from Pantai Bira to Ujung Pandang leave from outside the Bira Beach Hotel at about 9 am daily for the 'tourist price' of 12,000Rp. Arrange a seat with your hotel the day before; otherwise get a bemo from Pantai Bira to Bulukumba.

Boat The harbour near Pantai Timur is being extended. Local hoteliers are hoping (perhaps optimistically) that ferries from as far as Kendari, Ujung Pandang and Bali will bring boatloads of tourists to Pantai Bira. See Pulau Selayar for details about ferries to that island.

Getting Around

Bemos link Pantai Bira with Bulukumba, via Bira village, mainly in the morning. A bicycle would be a good way to get around, but sadly none of the hotels have anything to rent. In any case, it's a pleasant area to walk around.

There aren't many boats for hire at Pantai Bira, but if you ask your hotel, or someone at the boat landing (ask the day before you intend to travel) at the end of Jl Kapongkolang, you can rent boats for about 60,000Rp per day.

PULAU LIHUKAN

Weavers at **Ta'Buntuleng** make heavy, colourful cloth on hand looms under the houses in the village. On the pretty beach west of the village there is an interesting old graveyard, and off the beach there are acres of sea grass and coral, but mind the currents and sea snakes. To see the best coral, which is further out, you'll need a boat.

There is no regular transport, but if you wait a public boat will leave from the end of Jl Kapongkolang in Pantai Bira eventually. Alternatively, charter a boat to visit, and snorkel around, Lihukan and the nearby, uninhabited **Pulau Betang**.

PULAU SELAYAR
☎ 0414

This long, narrow island lies off the southwestern peninsula of Sulawesi, and is inhabited by Bugis and Makassarese. Most reside along the infertile west coast and in **Benteng**, the main town. Like Pantai Bira, Selayar's long coastline is a repository of flotsam from nearby shipping lanes, perhaps accounting for the presence of a 2000-year-old Vietnamese Dongson drum, kept in an annexe near the former **Benteng Bontobangun** (Bontobangun Fort), a few kilometres south of Benteng.

Selayar's other attractions are its sandy beaches and picturesque scenery. The snorkelling near small **Pulau Pasi**, opposite Benteng, is good, but you'll have to bring your own equipment (or rent from Pantai Bira) and charter a boat.

Places to Stay & Eat

Most visitors stay and eat at *Hotel Berlian* (☎ 21129), Jl Sudirman in Benteng. It offers a range of decent rooms from 17,500Rp to 37,500Rp with air-con and private bathroom.

Getting There & Away

The season determines the departure point for ferries to the island. From about September to February, ferries (2500Rp, 2½ hours) travel between the new harbour near Pantai Bira and Pamatata; and from about March to August, between the beach at Bulukumba

and Benteng. A ferry leaves both Pantai Bira/Bulukumba and Pamatata/Benteng at about 8 am, and sometimes also at 2 pm. (The timings are no good for a day trip.) Your hotel, or bemo driver, will know the current schedules. Buses leave Terminal Mallengkeri in Ujung Pandang each morning to link with the ferry from Bulukumba or Pantai Bira.

TAKA BONE RATE

South-east of Pulau Selayar, and north of Pulau Bone Rate, is the 2220 sq km Taka Bone Rate, the world's third largest coral atoll. (The largest, Kwajalein in the Marshall Islands, is just 20% bigger.) Some of the islands, and extensive reefs, in the region are now part of **Taman Laut Taka Bone Rate**, which is a marine reserve that has a rich variety of marine and bird life.

There is no official accommodation on the islands, but you can stay with villagers if you ask the *kepala desa* (village head) at Bone Rate on Pulau Bone Rate. Alternatively, take a tent and camp on a beach. The Pelni liner *Sirimau* links Bone Rate with Ujung Pandang and Kupang every two weeks.

BONE (WATAMPONE)
☎ 0481

Bone (Watampone) was a semi-autonomous state under the overlordship of Gowa, the strongest anti-Dutch power in the East Indies. The authoritarian ruler, Arung Palakka, and his followers returned from exile in 1666 and rallied the Bugis of Bone and Soppeng for a long overland campaign, forcing Hasanuddin to cede territory, including Bone. Palakka emerged the most powerful man in south Sulawesi, creating a system of unprecedented autocratic rule.

Today, Bone is a particularly charming country town; one of the nicest in southern Sulawesi. It's a pleasant place to break up a journey, and there's a good range of accommodation.

Things to See & Do

A statue of Arung Palakka dominates the square. South of the town centre is **Pusat Kebudayaan Bola Soba**, a huge Bugis house

BONE (WATAMPONE)

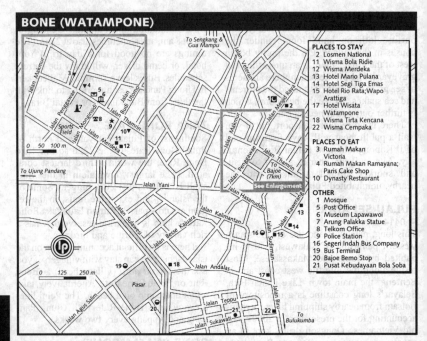

To Sengkang &
Gua Mampu

To Ujung Pandang

To
Bajoe
(7km)

See Enlargement

Jalan Yani

To
Bulukumba

PLACES TO STAY
2   Losmen National
11 Wisma Bola Ridie
12 Wisma Merdeka
13 Hotel Mario Pulana
14 Hotel Segi Tiga Emas
15 Hotel Rio Rata; Wapo
    Arattiga
17 Hotel Wisata
    Watampone
18 Wisma Tirta Kencana
22 Wisma Cempaka

PLACES TO EAT
3   Rumah Makan
    Victoria
4   Rumah Makan Ramayana;
    Paris Cake Shop
10 Dynasty Restaurant

OTHER
1   Mosque
5   Post Office
6   Museum Lapawawoi
7   Arung Palakka Statue
8   Telkom Office
9   Police Station
16 Segeri Indah Bus Company
19 Bus Terminal
20 Bajoe Bemo Stop
21 Pusat Kebudayaan Bola Soba

built in 1881, and now used sparingly for cultural events. You can't normally enter, but ask your hotel about any local events being held there.

Museum Lapawawoi is a former palace housing one of Indonesia's most interesting regional collections, including an odd array of court memorabilia, and dozens of photographs of state occasions. One of the inner rooms is reserved for offerings to Bone's former kings. The museum is open Monday to Saturday from about 8 am to 2 pm; and is free to enter.

Places to Stay

Wisma Bola Ridie (☎ 21412, Jl Merdeka 8) is a former royal residence, built in the Dutch colonial style. Small rooms facing a rear courtyard cost 17,500Rp; and there are huge, charming and airy singles/doubles, with private bathroom in the main building,

for 25,000/35,000Rp. Next door, *Wisma Merdeka* (☎ 21298, Jl Merdeka 4) is more modern and has huge rooms in the main house for 20,000Rp. You may have to hunt down staff at both places.

Losmen National (☎ 21545, Jl Mesjid Raya 86) is a large, old-style mansion divided into simple rooms, starting from 15,000/25,000Rp without/with a bathroom. High ceilings compensate for the lack of fans and the noisy location, but it's convenient and friendly. *Hotel Segi Tiga Emas* (☎ 21718, Jl Kawerang 14) is recommended for good service, and clean rooms for 30,000/45,000Rp with fan/air-con; and there's a few good economy rooms with fan for only 20,000Rp.

Wisma Tirta Kencana (☎ 21838, Jl Sulawesi 63) is close to the bus terminal but still quiet, and is highly recommended. It offers a range of large, comfortable and airy singles/doubles from 19,500/22,500Rp with a private bathroom, but no fan. With a fan and bathroom they cost 24,500/27,800Rp. Other rooms cost up to 70,600/76,500Rp.

Other ordinary cheapies include: *Wisma Cempaka (☎ 21414, Jl Biru 36)* with rooms for 20,000/35,000Rp with fan/air-con; *Hotel Rio Rata (Jl Kawerang 8)* with rooms for 25,000Rp with a fan; and *Hotel Mario Pulana (☎ 21098, Jl Kawerang 16)* with rooms for 50,000Rp with air-con.

The upmarket place in town is the comfortable *Hotel Wisata Watampone (☎ 21 362, fax 22367, Jl Sudirman 14)*. The cheapest rooms are 65,340Rp and have hot water and a fan, while the other singles/doubles cost from 94,380/116,160Rp – all come with air-con, hot water and satellite TV. There's a swimming pool, and discounts of 20% are often given, without asking.

Places to Eat

There is a cluster of simple *rumah makans* in the market area, and *night warungs* and Padang *rumah makans* along the main shopping street, Jl Penggawae. Along Jl Penggawae, *Rumah Makan Victoria* serves generous plates of standard Chinese-Indonesian fare; and *Rumah Makan Ramayana* is the best place in town. It offers a range of meals, such as tasty *gado-gado* (4500Rp), but specialises in spicy barbecued chicken pieces (5000Rp).

Just around the corner, *Dynasty Restaurant (Jl Thamrin)* has a menu longer than its karaoke song list. A few shops have tasty baked pastries and cakes; the best is *Paris Cake Shop*, which is conveniently next to the Rumah Makan Ramayana. The new *Wapo Arattiga (Jl Sudirman)* is run by a couple of effusive ladies, who offer cheap Indonesian food, and delicious drinks, in a modern setting.

Getting There & Away

Bus & Bemo Bone is not a major transport junction, but several buses and Kijangs travel daily to Bulukumba, Palopo, Pare Pare, 'Polmas' (ie Polewali and Mamasa), Malili and Sengkang; and more regularly to Ujung Pandang (Terminal Gowa) for 9600Rp. Try to get

to the convenient, and reasonably organised, terminal in Bone by 8 am.

To Rantepao, get a connection in Palopo; buy a seat on the direct daily bus from the Segeri Indah bus company office on Jl Sudirman; or see what's waiting at the bus terminal at the end of the causeway in Bajoe if you arrive by ferry from Kolaka. Several bus agencies along Jl Besse Kajuara, either side of the bus terminal, sell tickets for the bus/ferry/bus to Kendari.

Boat Three ferries ply the route between the nearby port of Bajoe and Kolaka in South-East Sulawesi. Plenty of agencies along Jl Besse Kajuara and opposite the bus terminal sell tickets for Pelni ships from Ujung Pandang and Pare Pare.

AROUND BONE
Bajoe

Bajoe is the major regional port, 7km from Bone. You could charter a canoe from the wharf to see the **floating village**, but everyone understandably heads straight to Bone or on the ferry to Kolaka.

Getting There & Away From Bajoe, three ferries (eight hours) leave every evening at 5, 8 and 11 pm for Kolaka, the gateway to the south-east peninsula. All departure and arrival times are for the benefit of those travelling to/from Ujung Pandang or Kendari.

Tickets cost 13,600/17,600Rp for deck/economy class, but you're unlikely to get much sleep in either class, unless you find a quietish, breezy spot at the front. If you get to the boat two hours early, members of the crew will offer one of their below-deck, one-person cabins for about 35,000Rp. These are comfortable, and normally have fans, but are unbearably stuffy.

From Bone, bemos head to Bajoe every few minutes from a special stop behind the market (as indicated on the Bone map). From the bus terminal at the end of the incredibly long causeway in Bajoe, buses head off to most places, including Ujung Pandang and Rantepao, just after the ferry arrives – but it's better to stay overnight in Bone and

SULAWESI

catch something from there. As soon as you get off the ferry, you can jump on a becak to Bajoe; or an ojek, bus or bemo to Bone.

Gua Mampu

James Brooke (later the Raja of Sarawak) visited these caves in 1840 hoping to find statues and remnants of an ancient civilisation. According to legend, a princess dropped a spool and promised to marry whoever could return it. The spool was retrieved by a dog, which demanded the princess honour her promise. When she refused, many people were suddenly turned to stone statues through a subsequent curse. Brooke was disappointed to learn, however, that the 'statues' were only fallen stalactites.

A tour of the caves requires some imagination, as the guide points out shapes and names them inappropriately. The whole lot is covered by slippery, smelly bat guano, which is scraped, and used as fertiliser, by local women. Take a bemo to **Uloe** from Bone or Sengkang; the caves are about 7km south of Uloe, along another road. You may have to hike this last 7km, so it's easier to charter your own transport.

SENGKANG
☎ 0485

Sengkang is a pleasant town, with a scenic lake nearby, silk weaving and several good hotels (and it's a better place to stay than Pare Pare). BNI bank will change money.

Danau Tempe

Danau Tempe is a large, shallow lake fringed by wetlands, with floating houses and magnificent birdlife. Geologists believe the lake was once a gulf between southern Toraja and the rest of southern Sulawesi. As they merged, the gulf disappeared and geologists believe the lake will eventually disappear too.

There are no organised boat tours, so find the longboat terminal (at the end of a laneway marked 'Setapak 7', opposite a sports field along Jl Sudirman) and charter a boat for about 10,000Rp per hour. In about two hours, you can speed along **Sungai Walanae**, visit **Salotangah village** in the middle of the lake,

go across to **Batu Batu village** on the other side, and come back. A boat trip is particularly charming at dusk. Staff at the Apada, Eka and Al Salam II hotels (see Places to Stay in this section) can also arrange trips and recommend places to visit.

Silk Weaving

Sengkang's other attraction is its *sutera* (silk) weaving industry. You can visit silk workshops, but most are located in remote villages, with little or no reliable public

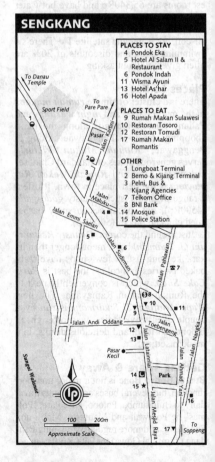

SENGKANG

PLACES TO STAY
4 Pondok Eka
5 Hotel Al Salam II & Restaurant
6 Pondok Indah
11 Wisma Ayuni
13 Hotel As'har
16 Hotel Apada

PLACES TO EAT
9 Rumah Makan Sulawesi
10 Restoran Tosoro
12 Restoran Tomudi
17 Rumah Makan Romantis

OTHER
1 Longboat Terminal
2 Bemo & Kijang Terminal
3 Pelni, Bus & Kijang Agencies
7 Telkom Office
8 BNI Bank
14 Mosque
15 Police Station

To Danau Temple
To Pare Pare
Sport Field
Pasar
Jalan Kartini
Jalan Maluku
Jalan Emmi Saelan
Jalan Sudirman
Jalan Pahlawan
Jalan Andi Oddang
Jalan Toebengeng
Pasar Kecil
Jalan Latamтаmla
Jalan Ahmad Yani
Jalan Mesjid Raya
Jalan Nangka
Sungai Walanae
Park
0   100   200m
Approximate Scale
To Soppeng

transport. Ask the staff at your hotel to recommend some workshops, and charter a pete-pete from the terminal. Alternatively, just walk around the market in Sengkang, where a gorgeous silk shawl costs about 30,000Rp and a sarong about 50,000Rp.

Places to Stay

There are three excellent places to stay. *Hotel Apada* (*☎/fax 21053, Jl Nangka 9*) is well set up, charming and has a friendly atmosphere. Rooms with a fan start from 33,000Rp; from 55,000Rp with air-con. The management is helpful, and can arrange traditional dances.

Just as good is the bright, friendly *Pondok Eka* (*☎/fax 21296, Jl Maluku 12*). Large, airy rooms, mostly around a large courtyard, cost 30,000Rp with fan; air-con rooms cost 40,000Rp to 60,000Rp (with a huge bath and hot water). The staff are happy to show you the local attractions.

A little off the main road is the quiet *Hotel Al Salam II* (*☎ 21278, fax 21893, Jl Emmi Saelan 8*). Clean singles/doubles with a bathroom and fan cost from 22,000/33,000Rp, but the 'VIP' rooms with air-con are not great value for 66,000/77,000Rp.

If the latter places are full, try: *Wisma Ayuni* (*☎ 21009, Jl Ahmad Yani 31*), an old Dutch house, with rooms for 15,000/20,000Rp; *Hotel As'har* (*☎ 21299, Jl Latainrilai*), with rooms from 20,000Rp to 55,000Rp with air-con; and *Pondok Indah* (*☎ 21430, Jl Sudirman 30*), with rooms for 25,000/35,000Rp with fan/air-con.

Places to Eat

There is a cluster of decent *rumah makans* near the corner of Jl Latainrilai and Jl Andi Oddang: *Restoran Tomudi* serves good Indonesian and Chinese food; *Rumah Makan Sulawesi* specialises in baked fish; and *Restoran Tosora* is a little more expensive, but worth a visit for a wide range of tasty food.

Rumah Makan Romantis, just down from Hotel Apada, has good, cheap food and cold beer in an upmarket setting. *Hotel Al Salam II* has an informal restaurant and

bar inside the complex, which is open to the public, and also serves good breakfasts.

Getting There & Away

Sengkang is readily accessible from Pare Pare (two hours) by bus or Kijang. To/from Rantepao (six hours), you may need a connection in Palopo. There are plenty of buses and Kijangs along the rough, horrible road to Bone, and on to Bajoe; and very regular buses to/from Terminal Gowa in Ujung Pandang (13,300Rp). Pete-petes to local destinations leave from the main terminal in Sengkang, on Jl Kartini. Agencies for long-distance buses and Kijangs, and Pelni boats (from Pare Pare and Ujung Pandang), are a few metres up (south) of the terminal.

SOPPENG (WATANSOPPENG)
☎ 0484

The pretty district capital of Soppeng (Watansoppeng) is the other big silk producer in the region, and the source of silk-worm eggs for Sengkang's silk industry. It's a pleasant detour, but there isn't a great deal to see or do.

If you want to stay: *Hotel Kayangan* (*Jl Kayangan 4*) is inconvenient and has basic rooms from 15,000Rp; *Hotel Makmur* (*☎ 21038, Jl Kemakmuran 104*) is on the main road from Sengkang, and has pleasant rooms from 22,500Rp; and *Hotel Aman* (*☎ 21206, Jl Merdeka 92*) is an old Dutch house, with rooms from 22,000Rp. Ask your pete-pete to drop you off at your hotel.

From Soppeng, plenty of buses and Kijangs go to Ujung Pandang (Terminal Gowa) and Sengkang. Minibuses to Sengkang also leave from the main street in Pare Pare.

PARE PARE
☎ 0421

Pare Pare is a smaller, greener version of Ujung Pandang, and a quiet stopover between Tana Toraja or Mamasa and Ujung Pandang – but there is a dire lack of decent accommodation, so you're better off detouring to Sengkang. Pare Pare is the second largest port in the region, so some people come here to catch boats to the east coast of Kalimantan.

SULAWESI

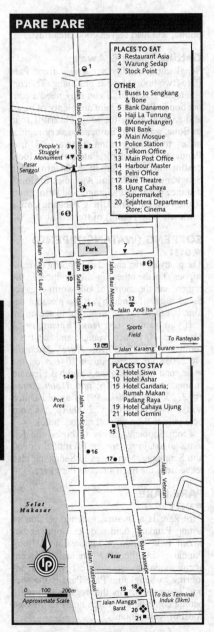

PARE PARE

PLACES TO EAT
3   Restaurant Asia
4   Warung Sedap
7   Stock Point

OTHER
1   Buses to Sengkang & Bone
5   Bank Danamon
6   Haji La Tunrung (Moneychanger)
8   BNI Bank
9   Main Mosque
11 Police Station
12 Telkom Office
13 Main Post Office
14 Harbour Master
16 Pelni Office
17 Pare Theatre
18 Ujung Cahaya Supermarket
20 Sejahtera Department Store; Cinema

People's Struggle Monument

Pasar Senggol

Park

Sports Field

To Rantepao

PLACES TO STAY
2   Hotel Siswa
10 Hotel Ashar
15 Hotel Gandaria; Rumah Makan Padang Raya
19 Hotel Cahaya Ujung
21 Hotel Gemini

Port Area

Selat Makasar

Pasar

0   100   200m
Approximate Scale

To Bus Terminal Induk (3km)

Jalan Baso Daeng Patompo
Jalan Pinggir Laut
Jalan Sultan Hasanuddin
Jalan Bau Massepe
Jalan Andi Isa
Jalan Karaeng Burane
Jalan Andicammi
Jalan Veteran
Jalan Mangga Barat
Jalan Matirotasi

Orientation & Information

Pare Pare is stretched out along the waterfront. At night, the esplanade turns into a lively pedestrian mall with warungs and stalls. Most of what you need is on the streets running parallel with the harbour. Haji La Tunrung moneychanger has competitive rates, although the major banks also change money. The main post office, on Jl Karaeng Burane, plans to have an Internet centre in the future.

Places to Stay

The choice of hotels is so bad, that a detour to somewhere else (eg Sengkang) is worth considering.

The best is *Hotel Gemini* (☎ 21754, Jl Bau Massepe 451). It's a small cluster of rooms, close to the main road, but is clean, airy and popular, with rooms for 15,000Rp to 25,000Rp depending on size. *Hotel Cahaya Ujung* (☎ 22810, Jl Mangga Barat) has a range of airless, dark rooms from 15,125Rp to 54,450Rp with air-con and TV – the outside looks far nicer than the rooms inside.

On a busy main road, *Hotel Gandaria* (☎ 21093, Jl Bau Massepe 395) is good value with rooms for 15,000Rp with a fan, and 40,000Rp with air-con and TV. *Hotel Ashar* (Jl Sultan Hasanuddin) is along a quiet street (with a loud mosque opposite), but most rooms are dark and airless. They start at 20,000Rp; it's worth paying extra (50,000Rp) for the rooms with air-con. *Hotel Siswa* (☎ 21374, Jl Baso Daeng Patompo 30) has some charm, and is good value with rooms for 12,500/17,500Rp without/with bathroom, but don't expect much privacy or peace.

Places to Eat

There are several small *rumah makans* along Jl Baso Daeng Patompo, in the vicinity of Hotel Siswa. At night, *warungs* line the esplanade, each with exactly the same choice of rice and noodle dishes. *Stock Point* has a small range of tasty doughnuts, cakes and cold drinks. *Restaurant Asia (Jl Baso Daeng Patompo)* has a vast array of Chinese and Indonesian food, and excellent, but pricey, seafood from 20,000Rp.

Next door, **Warung Sedap** specialises in *ikan bakar* (baked fish), but check the price before you order your fish.

Getting There & Away

Bus Pare Pare is on the main road between Ujung Pandang and Rantepao, and plenty of buses and Kijangs go to Ujung Pandang (Terminal Gowa) for 8500Rp, Rantepao and Bone. Most buses travel through Terminal Induk several kilometres south of the city, but it's often easier to hail a bus as it flies through town. Buses to Bone (15,000Rp), via Sengkang (10,000Rp), also leave from a convenient agency, just up from Hotel Siswa.

Boat The main reason to come to Pare Pare is to catch a ship to eastern Kalimantan. Every two weeks, Pelni (☎ 21017) has the *Tidar* to Pantoloan, near Palu, for 42,000/139,500Rp (economy/1st class); and the *Binaiya* and *Leuser* to Samarinda (46,000/153,500Rp). All three then go to Tarakan (115,000/392,000Rp) and on to Nunukan.

Every one or two days, several decent passenger boats travel between Pare Pare and Samarinda and Balikpapan (both 40,000Rp, 22 hours) and Nunukan (75,000Rp, two nights). Details and bookings are available from agencies near the port, and just north of Restaurant Asia.

POLEWALI
☎ 0428

Polewali is the gateway to the Mamasa Valley. There is no need to stay, but **Guest House Melati** (☎ 21075, *Jl Ahmad Yani 91*) has a range of decent rooms from 15,000Rp to 60,000Rp. The touts at the bus terminal will assume you're going to Mamasa or Rantepao, and will help you find a connecting bus. See Getting There & Away under Mamasa later in this chapter for details about travelling to 'Polmas', the common abbreviation for Polewali and Mamasa.

MAJENE
☎ 0422

Most of the pleasure in visiting Majene is getting there, along a coast road with stunning vistas of sand, sea and mountains. The town itself is a centre for fishing and boat building. There's a couple of basic losmen: **Wisma Cahaya** (☎ 22105, *Jl Rahman 2*) has rooms for 15,000Rp; and, if you need air-con, stay at **Penginapan Bogor** (☎ 21109, *Jl Monginsidi 13*). There are a few simple *warungs* along Jl Syukur Rahim. Majene is a stopoff for any bus travelling between Pare Pare and Mamuju.

MAMUJU
☎ 0426

Mamuju used to be the end of the road, literally and metaphorically. These days, it's still not easy to reach, and the trip is long and rough.

Mamuju has a couple of reasonable places to stay: **Penginapan Mirna** (☎ 21258, *Jl Yos Sudarso 24*) is the cheapest with rooms from 15,000Rp to 25,000Rp; and **Wisma Rio** (☎ 21 014, *Jl Kemakmuran 28*) has rooms for 65,000Rp with air-con. Each hotel has, or is close to, a *restaurant*.

There are regular buses from Makale and Rantepao (25,000Rp, 12 hours), and plenty of buses from Ujung Pandang and Pare Pare. To save the rough trip, Merpati flies once a week (312,300Rp) from Ujung Pandang – the local agency is at Jl Jembatan Udara. You can also walk to and from Mamuju – see Mamasa to Mamuju in the Around Mamasa section later.

PALOPO
☎ 0471

This Muslim port is the administrative capital of the Luwu district. Before the Dutch, it was the centre of the old and powerful Luwu kingdom. The former palace is now the tiny **Museum Batara Guru** on Jl Andi Jemma, opposite the police station, and contains relics of the royal era. On the waterfront is a **Bugis village**, and a long pier where you can get a closer look at the fishing boats.

Palopo is a sprawling town, with an inordinate number of becaks. There is no reason to come here, except to catch public transport between the east coast of the southwest peninsula and Tana Toraja.

Places to Stay & Eat

Hotel Risma (☎ 21178, Jl Andi Jemma 14) has singles/doubles, clustered around a small garden, from 10,000/20,000Rp with a fan to 35,000/50,000Rp with air-con. *Hotel Adifati (☎ 21437, Jl Andi Jemma 86)* has decent rooms with a fan around a small garden for about 17,500Rp, and 35,000Rp with air-con. The best is *Buana Hotel & Restoran (☎ 22 164, Jl Dalan 89)*. Rooms cost 22,500/26,000Rp with a fan, and 45,000Rp to 52,000Rp with air-con; the rooms upstairs are far nicer. The added attraction is the *restaurant*.

Most *rumah makans* are located around the central market, bus terminal and Luwu Plaza shopping centre. The best is *Rumah Makan Sulawesi*, near the bus terminal and next to the dreary Hotel Palopo.

Getting There & Away

Vehicles regularly leave from just outside Terminal Bolu in Rantepao for the *very* winding trip to Palopo (5000Rp, two hours). From Palopo's organised terminal, plenty of buses and minibuses go to Rantepao, Pare Pare, Ujung Pandang, Mamasa (via Siwa and Polewali), Soroako (via Malili), Sengkang and Bone. The road between Palopo and Bone (six hours) is initially good, but disappears into huge potholes for the last two hours.

Boats irregularly travel between Palopo and Malili, but the buses are faster and more frequent. There is a daily ferry from Siwa, south of Palopo, and isolated Susua on the south-east peninsula.

MALILI & SOROAKO

Malili, and nearby Soroako, are mining towns, built near a series of mountain-fringed lakes linked by rivers and streams. Soroako is on the shores of the 16,400 hectare Danau Matano, Sulawesi's deepest lake. Danau Towuti is the second largest lake in Indonesia, with an area of 56,100 hectares – only Danau Toba in Sumatra is bigger. The lakes support impressive birdlife and other fauna.

There is nowhere to stay in either town, but you can ask for a room in a home, or camp by the lakes if you have your own tent

and transport. There are many buses daily from Rantepao, Palopo and Wotu. Those travelling light could take the ferry across Danau Matano to Nuha, and hitch a ride on anything going north towards Kolonodale.

Tana Toraja

Tana Toraja is undoubtedly the most popular destination in Sulawesi. It's a vast, pretty and mostly unspoilt area of traditional villages, unique architecture and fascinating cultures, but it's also very busy, especially during the height of funeral (and tourist) season in July and August. At this time, Toraja working throughout Indonesia return home for celebrations, followed by hoards of tourists whose presence sends Rantepao hotel prices into orbit. To avoid the big tour groups (and big prices), visit Tana Toraja between the end of the wet season (ie late March) and the onset of the tourist season.

Maps

If you're doing some serious hiking, pick up a copy of the detailed *Tana Toraja* (1:85,000) map, published by Periplus. *Tana Toraja*, published by Travel Treasure maps, is colourful, but not accurate nor detailed enough for hiking. Both are available in Rantepao (for about 50,000Rp).

Books

In the souvenir shops and supermarkets in Rantepao, you can buy a few decent locally produced guides: *A Guide to Toraja* by AT Marampa is available in English, German and French, and lists dances, ceremonies and some local walks; *Toraja – An Introduction to a Unique Culture* by LT Tangdilintin and M Syafei is written in their own unique style; and *Life & Death of the Toraja People* by Stanislaus Sandarupa is readable and informative.

Taxes

The South Sulawesi government has levied a fee of 3500Rp per tourist per visit to 'fund the development of Tana Toraja'. The fee is

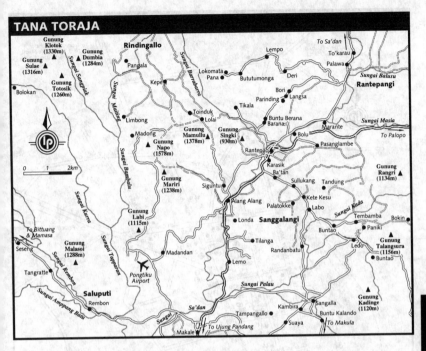

TANA TORAJA

Gunung Klotok (1330m)
Gunung Dumbia (1284m)
Gunung Sulae (1316m)
Gunung Totosik (1260m)
Bolokan
Rindingallo
Pangala
Kepe
Sungai Sungaiak
Sungai Maling
Sungai Barrobarri
Lempo
To Sa'dan
To'karau
Palawa
Lokomata Pana
Bututumonga
Deri
Sungai Balusu
Rantepangi
Bori
Parinding
Langsa
Tikala
Limbong
Toinduk
Lolai
Buntu Berana
Barana
Marante
Sungai Masia
To Palopo
Madong
Gunung Mamullu (1378m)
Gunung Singki (930m)
Bolu
Pasanglambe
Gunung Napo (1578m)
Rantepao
Karasik
Ba'tan
Sungai Bambalu
Gunung Mariri (1238m)
Siguntu
Sullukang
Tandung
Gunung Rangri (1134m)
Alang Alang
Palatokke
Labo
Kete Kesu
Sungai Kada
Tembamba
Bokin
Gunung Labi (1115m)
To Bittuang & Mamasa
Seseng
Londa
Sanggalangi
Tilanga
Randanbatu
Buntao
Ledo
Paniki
Gunung Talangsura (1156m)
Buntao
Gunung Malasoi (1288m)
Sungai Kurra
Sungai Tapparan
Tangratte
Madandan
Lemo
Saluputi
Rembon
Sungai Ampang Batu
Pongtiku Airport
Sungai Palau
Sa'dan
Sungai
Tampangallo
Makale
To Ujung Pandang
Kambira
Suaya
Sangalla
Buntu Kalando
To Makula
Gunung Kadinge (1120m)

0   1   2km

SULAWESI

included in pre-booked organised tours, and airline tickets, but is rarely collected any other way. Also, every single tourist attraction charges at least 1250Rp, sometimes up to 5000Rp, so make sure you have plenty of small change. There is also a 10% tax on all food and accommodation in Tana Toraja, although some cheaper hotels and restaurants already include the tax, or don't bother with it.

RANTEPAO
☎ 0423

Rantepao is the largest town and commercial centre of Tana Toraja, and the main travellers' centre on Sulawesi. Although a bit scruffy in parts, it's the obvious place to base yourself while you explore the lush, green countryside. Rantepao has cool evenings and rain throughout the year – even in the dry season.

Information
Tourist Offices The Government Tourist Office (☎ 23374) in the town square is a waste of time – staff are more interested in playing table tennis (ping pong) than dealing with nuisance visitors. Instead, go to the Tourist Information Service (☎ 23369), Jl Pao Pura, just down (south) from the hospital, where friendly staff can provide accurate, independent information about local ceremonies, festivals and other activities.

Money It's a good idea to stock up on rupiah before you arrive. Bank Rakyat and BNI bank change money, but offer lower rates than banks in Ujung Pandang; and Bank Danamon won't change travellers cheques. The best rates are available from the moneychangers, eg in Hotel Indra Toraja II, Rachmat Restoran and the Abadi Moneychanger.

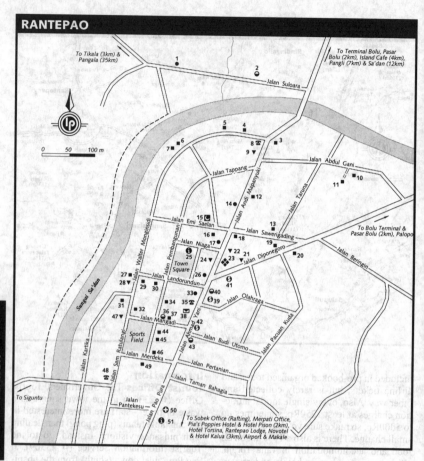

RANTEPAO

Post & Communications The tiny post office on Jl Ahmad Yani is open Monday to Saturday from about 8 am to 3 pm. Next door, the Telkom office is open 24 hours, and has a Home Country Direct Dial telephone, and a fax service. There are several pricey wartels along Jl Ahmad Yani, and a useful collect call service at Toraja Permai travel agency.

Emergency The main hospital is Rumah Sakit Elim (☎ 21258) – but you're better off getting injured or sick elsewhere on Sulawesi because facilities here are very basic.

Markets

Rantepao's main market is held about once a week (but still operates in a reduced capacity daily). The main market is a very big and very social occasion that attracts crowds from all over Tana Toraja. The commerce is lively, but incidental to the real business of the day – endless coffee, *kretek* (clove cigarettes) and gossip. Ask around Rantepao for

RANTEPAO

PLACES TO STAY

3	Wisma Nirmala	37	Hotel Te Bas	15	Mosque
4	Losmen Wisma	44	Pondok Wisata	17	Bus Company Offices
5	Wisma Imanuel	45	Hebron Inn	23	Toko Abadi Supermarket;
6	Wisma Surya	46	Homestay Padatindo		Toraja Permai Travel
7	Wisma Wisata	49	Wisma Anata		Agency
10	Wisma Irama			25	Government Tourist Office
11	Wisma Monton	**PLACES TO EAT**		26	Souvenir Shops
12	Wisma Indo Grace;	9	Rima Restoran	33	JET Tourist Service
	Rumah Makan Indo Grace	21	Rumah Makan Santai	35	Telkom Office;
13	Duta 88 Cottages	22	Restaurant Setia Kawan		Bank Danamon
16	Losmen Flora;	24	Saleko Cafe	36	Bemos to La'bo
	Restoran Flora	28	Restoran Mambu	38	Post Office
18	Hotel Victoria	47	Mart's Cafe;	39	Bank Rakyat
19	Wisma Tanabua		PT Panorama Indah	40	Kijangs to Makale;
20	Marura Hostel				Rachmat Restoran
27	Hotel Indra Toraja (II)	**OTHER**		41	Abadi Moneychanger
29	Hotel Indra Toraja (I)	1	Indo Sella	42	Bank BNI
30	Indra City Hotel		(Rafting & Trekking)	43	Bemos to Madandan
31	Wisma Monika	2	Bemos to Sa'dan &	48	Wartel
32	Wisma Maria I		Tikala	50	Rumah Sakit Elim
34	Homestay Rainbow	8	Wartel		(Hospital)
		14	Bus Company Offices	51	Tourist Information Service

the exact day, or seek out other markets in the area. Pasar Bolu is 2km north-east of town, and easily accessible by bemo.

Places to Stay

Rantepao has a competitive selection of cheap hotels and comfortable homestays, but all prices rise in the tourist season of June to August, when some private homes also accept guests. Most budget and mid-range places include breakfast, but they won't offer (nor do you really need) a fan or air-conditioning.

Views, setting and hot water are often a selling point for mid-range places. Plenty of these mid-range hotels are located along the road between Rantepao and Makale, and just north of Rantepao. They cater almost exclusively for tour groups with their own transport, but individuals are always welcome, and rates are often negotiable at quieter times.

Places to Stay – Budget

Hebron Inn (☎ 21519, Jl Pembangunan 35) is better than others in the immediate area, and has singles/doubles, around a small courtyard, for 30,000/35,000Rp. (If the staff

are absent, come back later.) The staff at **Hotel Te Bas** (☎ 21415, Jl Mangadi) are also often missing. The hotel is central and the rooms face a garden, but for 30,000Rp per double, you can probably do better.

Along quiet Jl Monginsidi, there are a few decent, cosy and convenient places. **Losmen Wisma** (Jl Monginsidi 66) has comfortable rooms with a private bathroom for 25,000Rp. **Wisma Wisata** (☎ 21746, Jl Monginsidi 40) is the cheapest place in town and excellent value with rooms for 10,000Rp per person. The best is the large, friendly **Wisma Surya** (☎ 21312, Jl Monginsidi 36). The rooms are decent, although they could do with some renovation, and cost 25,000/30,000Rp.

Homestay Rainbow (Homestay Pelangi, ☎ 21753, Jl Pembangunan 11A) is delightful. Pleasant rooms cost 20,000/50,000Rp, and the staff are friendly. **Wisma Maria I** (☎ 21 165, Jl Sam Ratulangi 23) is just off the main road, so it's quieter than the others, and the rooms overlook a large garden. The staff can be nonplussed, but its rooms are good value for 15,000/25,000Rp, or 30,000/40,000Rp for a better standard of room with hot water.

Over the road, *Wisma Monika (☎ 21216, Jl Sam Ratulangi)* has good, clean and comfortable rooms upstairs for a negotiable 25,000Rp.

Two adjacent, modern and quiet places are worth checking out. *Wisma Irama (☎ 21371, Jl Abdul Gani 16)* has a range of clean rooms downstairs for 25,000/35,000Rp and upstairs for 35,000/45,000Rp, with hot water (not always reliable). The garden is pretty, and the service is efficient. Almost next door, *Wisma Monton (☎/fax 21675, Jl Abdul Gani 14A)* is a three storey place down a quiet lane. The service is good, and the rooms cost 30,000Rp to 60,000Rp for the top floor, which has the best views and hot water.

Along the noisy main road is *Wisma Indo Grace (☎ 21291, Jl Andi Mapanyuki)*. Rooms cost 17,500Rp, but it's often full. *Indra City Hotel (☎ 21163, Jl Landorundun)* has a range of comfortable rooms with balconies from 34,800/40,600Rp to 40,600/46,400Rp, although the rooms are a little clustered together. For 25,000Rp, *Wisma Tanabua (☎ 21072, Jl Diponegoro 43)* is central and has good value rooms.

About 1.5km south of town are two excellent, adjacent places, both virtually in the countryside. They also offer book exchange and information about local attractions. The popular *Pia's Poppies Hotel (☎ 21121)* has charming rooms, some with boulders for floors and even aquariums, for a reasonable 27,500/38,500Rp. Next door, *Hotel Pison (☎/fax 21344)* is also recommended. Rooms cost 27,500/49,500Rp, or 66,000Rp a double if you want to splurge on a 'spring mattress'. All rooms come with hot water, and have small, private balconies with views.

There are plenty of other cheapies, but they're nothing special: *Wisma Anata (☎ 21 356, Jl Merdeka 5)* has rooms for 20,000Rp; *Homestay Padatindo (☎ 21793, Jl Pembangunan 31)* costs 20,000Rp for its rooms but is often surprisingly full; and *Pondok Wisata (☎ 21595, Jl Pembangunan 23)* has dark rooms for 30,000Rp to 45,000Rp, and unhelpful staff. Absolute last resorts for about 15,000/25,000Rp for rooms are the noisy *Losmen Flora (☎ 21586, Jl Emi Saelan)*;

Wisma Nirmala (☎ 21319, Jl Andi Mapanyuki 18); *Hotel Victoria (☎ 21038)*, on the corner of Jl Sawerigading; and *Marura Hostel (Jl Diponegoro)*.

Places to Stay – Mid-Range

A lot of mid-range places are strewn around the valleys, but there are three good places clustered together, just off the main road (Jl Pao Pura) about 3km south of Rantepao – by the turn-off to Kete Kesu. *Hotel Torsina (☎ 21293)* has comfortable singles/doubles with a fan and hot water, along a verandah with views, for a negotiable 60,000/80,000Rp. One attraction is the swimming pool. Similar in standards and price is *Hotel Kalua (☎ 21485)*, but without the pool. *Rantepao Lodge (☎ 23717, fax 21248)* charges US$42/48 for the same sort of rooms as the others, but will negotiate if you point out to the management that the other two cost considerably less. The rooms are charmingly built in Toraja style, surrounding a pretty garden and swimming pool.

Hotel Indra Toraja (☎ 21163, fax 21547, Jl Landorundun) has two annexes, opposite each other in a central location. Rooms have hot water, and start from US$35/44, but this is far too much. The only place in Rantepao that offers traditional-style housing is the new *Duta 88 Cottages (☎ 23477, Jl Sawerigading 12)*. The rooms are charming, but a little clustered together, and good value for 50,000Rp with hot water and satellite TV. The only mid-range place to offer river views is *Wisma Imanuel (☎ 21416, Jl Monginsidi 16)*. Its rooms, with satellite TV and hot water, are very comfortable, and excellent value for 40,000Rp to 60,000Rp.

Places to Stay – Top End

The only top-end place close to Rantepao is the new *Novotel Coralia Hotel (☎ 21192, fax 21666, email novotour@upg.wasantara. net.id)*, set in the countryside, a 20 minute walk from the turn-off to Kete Kesu along the Rantepao-Makale road. Huge, tongkonan-style rooms officially cost US$121/151 for singles/doubles, but discounts to 239,500Rp per room are already being offered.

Places to Eat

Many of the eateries in Rantepao serve Torajan food, but they often require at least two hours notice – perhaps, order dinner while you're having lunch. 'The Toraja' section in this chapter details the sort of local cuisine that is often available.

Some *warungs* and *rumah makans* along Jl Andi Mapanyuki, such as *Restaurant Setia Kawan* and *Saleko Cafe*, and Jl Suloara offer excellent baked fish, and other local staples, for considerably less than the tourist-orientated restaurants along the main roads. The several *balok* (palm wine) bars around town welcome foreigners (especially anyone with musical talents), but not in big numbers.

Mart's Cafe (Jl Sam Ratulangi) is an elegant place with tourist-oriented prices, and a wide range of Indonesian, Torajan and western food. Try the Torajan beef (13,000Rp): it's far better than the baked fish. Just up the road (north), the charming *Restoran Mambu* is recommended for its vast menu, including western fare, even if the service is a little slow at times.

The restaurant at *Homestay Rainbow (Jl Pembangunan 11A)* caters well for foreigners who prefer jaffles, pancakes and Coke; it also offers cheap Indonesian and Chinese food. Another decent place for meals and coffee is *Rumah Makan Santai (Jl Diponegoro)*.

Rumah Makan Indo Grace (Jl Andi Mapanyuki) is popular and convenient to most hotels, and has a range of meals, such as baked fish (9000Rp), and large beers for 8000Rp. Also popular is the unassuming *Rima Restoran*, just up the road (north), which has tasty food (most meals cost about 10,000RP). It's particularly good for Torajan food. The best value in town is at *Restoran Flora (Jl Emi Saelan)*, under the losmen of the same name. All the food, including omelettes, sandwiches and salads, are very reasonably priced, and delicious.

Island Cafe, a few kilometres north of town by bemo, offers large serves of Indonesian and western food. The breezy dining deck overlooks small rapids, and it's a good place to meet other travellers. The upmarket place in town is *Rachmat Restoran (Jl Ahmad Yani)*, which caters unashamedly for tour groups, and is priced accordingly (10,000Rp for a *nasi goreng*), but the food is good and the public are welcome.

The best supermarket is *Toko Abadi*, on Jl Andi Mapanyuki, which sells food for hiking and some of life's 'necessities', eg chocolate and ice cream.

Shopping

Woodcarving, weaving and basketry are the main crafts of Tana Toraja – some villages are noted for particular specialities, such as Mamasan boxes (used to store magic, as well as salt, betel nut etc), huge horn necklaces and wooden figurines. Woodcarvings include panels, clocks and trays, carved like the decorations on traditional houses and painted in the four traditional colours – black, white, yellow and brown. The carvers at Kete Kesu, not far from Rantepao, and Londa, are renowned for the quality of their work.

The hard part is separating the good stuff from the mass produced 'schlock' made for the tourist market. Artefacts sold in the souvenir shops, especially around the market building in town, include mini replicas of Torajan houses with incredibly exaggerated overhanging roofs; hand spun Toraja weaving (especially good in Sa'dan); and the longer cloths of the Mamasa Valley. Necklaces made of plant seeds and chunky silver and amber or wooden beads festoon the gift shops, but the orange beaded necklaces are the authentic Torajan wear. Black and red velvet drawstring bags are popular with tourists, much to the amusement of locals who use them for carrying betel nut ingredients to funerals.

Getting There & Away

Air Flying – especially *into* Tana Toraja – provides a dramatic look at the landscape and architecture of traditional villages. The only carrier, Merpati, has slashed its service from at least once a day to once a *week* (currently Monday) for 279,700Rp. Therefore, it's vital to book this flight as soon as possible, and reconfirm it several times. The Merpati office (☎ 21615) is based at Ramayan

SULAWESI

Satyra Travel Agency, about 2km south of Rantepao, along the main road to Makale.

Bus & Bemo Most long-distance buses leave from (and tickets are bought at) bus company offices along, or just off, Jl Andi Mapanyuki. There is an impressive number of services: the most comfortable buses (with the slightly higher prices) are Litha, Batutumonga and Sumber Indah. Try to book your ticket one or two days in advance.

To the north, there are plenty of buses to Pendolo (25,000Rp, 10 hours), Tentena (25,000Rp, 12 hours), Poso (30,000Rp, 13 hours) and Palu (35,000Rp, 20 hours). To the south, even more buses head to Pare Pare (10,000Rp, five hours). To Terminal Gowa in Ujung Pandang (10 hours), buses often run at night, and prices range from 16,000Rp to 35,000Rp for something quick, spacious and comfortable. Various companies also have services to Mamuju via Polewali, from where there are connections to Mamasa. The only direct bus between Tana Toraja and Mamasa leaves from Makale – see Getting There & Away under Mamasa later in this chapter.

From Terminal Bolu, 2km north of Rantepao, there are regular vehicles to Palopo, and several buses a day to Soroako, via Malili. From outside Rachmat Restoran, Kijangs leave every minute to Makale (1000Rp, 20 minutes). The Around Tana Toraja entry later in this section has more details about transport between Rantepao and other places in Tana Toraja. Plenty of bemos travel between Terminal Bolu and the main streets of Rantepao.

Boat Of course, you can't actually catch a boat to Tana Toraja, but you can buy tickets on Pelni ships from Ujung Pandang and Pare Pare at agencies around Rantepao (and Makale). The agencies charge a fee of about 20,000Rp, and the tickets take about two days to arrive in Rantepao (or Makale) from either city.

Getting Around
To/From the Airport From the airport, squeeze into whatever vehicle is available –

normally a Kijang (5000Rp per person), which goes to Rantepao, via Makale, and will drop you off anywhere in between. To the airport, tee up transport with the Merpati office when you reconfirm; take a bemo to Madandan, and arrange for a detour to the airport; or charter a bemo or Kijang.

Public Transport Rantepao is small and easy to walk around. Becaks start at 1000Rp, but some drivers are cunning enough to ask up to 5000Rp.

MAKALE
☎ 0423
Makale is the administrative capital of Tana Toraja, but has very few of the amenities of Rantepao. It's a small, pretty town built around an artificial lake and set amid cloud-shrouded hills. The town also boasts white-washed churches atop each hill, a fascinating market and Dutch houses in the older part of town. A quieter alternative to the comparative 'hustle and bustle' of Rantepao, Makale is well connected to most of Tana Toraja by bemo. Bank Rakyat may change money, but you're better off trying in Rantepao.

Things to See
Makale's **market** is a blur of noise, colour and commotion. On the main market day, held about once a week, you'll see pigs, strapped down with bamboo strips for buyers' close inspection, buckets of live eels, piles of fresh and dried fish, and a corner of the market reserved for *balok* (palm wine) sales.

Heading out of the market towards Tondon, there are a few **tau tau** hidden in a rock face. You can then explore the hills behind Makale, or continue along the road to **Sangalla**.

Places to Stay – Budget
There are several homestays along the road from Rantepao, but they're noisy and inconvenient. About a kilometre north of town, *Wisma Merry (☎ 22174, Jl Pongtiku 100B)* is OK with rooms for 20,000Rp, but you're better off in Makale. *Wisma Fajar (☎ 22022, Jl Merdeka 11)* is a good option in the middle

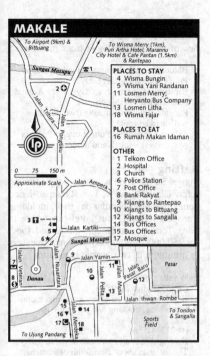

MAKALE

To Airport (9km) &
Bittuang

To Wisma Merry (1km),
Puri Artha Hotel, Marannu
City Hotel & Cafe Pantan (1.5km)
& Rantepao

Sungai Masupu

Jalan Trilura
Jalan Pongtiku

PLACES TO STAY
4 Wisma Bungin
5 Wisma Yani Randanan
11 Losmen Merry;
Heryanto Bus Company
13 Losmen Litha
18 Wisma Fajar

PLACES TO EAT
16 Rumah Makan Idaman

0   75   150 m
Approximate Scale

Jalan Ampera

OTHER
1 Telkom Office
2 Hospital
3 Church
6 Police Station
7 Post Office
8 Bank Rakyat
9 Kijangs to Rantepao
10 Kijangs to Bittuang
12 Kijangs to Sangalla
14 Bus Offices
15 Bus Offices
17 Mosque

Jalan Kartiki

Sungai Masupu

Jalan Nusantara
Jalan Veteran

Jalan Yamin

Jalan Pasar Baru
Jalan Pelita
Jalan Musa

Pasar

Danau

Jalan Ihwan Rombe

To Tondon
& Sangalla

Sports
Field

Jalan Merdeka

To Ujung Pandang

of town and has double rooms for 15,000Rp.
Other budget choices are convenient, but
very noisy: **Losmen Litha** (☎ 22 441, Jl
Pelita) has rooms for 15,000Rp per person;
and **Losmen Merry** (☎ 22013, Jl Yamin) has
rooms for the same price.

The best two places are next to each other
and close to town. **Wisma Bungin** (☎ 22255,
Jl Nusantara 35) is good value with rooms
for 16,500Rp, but get one at the back to
avoid the constant traffic noise. Next door,
Wisma Yani Randanan (☎ 22409, Jl Nusantara 33) is a little better with decent rooms
(with three beds) for 22,000Rp per room.

Places to Stay – Mid-Range &
Top End

About 1.5km north of town, **Puri Artha
Hotel** (☎ 22470, fax 22047, Jl Pongtiku 114)
is the best mid-range hotel in Makale. The
cheaper rooms for 48,300/62,100Rp for

doubles/triples are not great value, but the
top rooms with satellite TV, fridge and hot
water for 83,375Rp are worth a splurge.
Next door is **Marannu City Hotel** (☎ 22221,
fax 22028, Jl Pongtiku 116) with singles/
doubles from US$73/85, although heavy
discounts are usually possible. The main attraction is the swimming pool, which the
public can use for 5000Rp anyway.

Places to Eat

The local specialty is *pa'piong*, smoked in
bamboo tubes in the market through the day
and sold in **warungs** around the market at
night. Throughout the day seasonal fruit and
kue kue (cakes), such as banana fried in a
shortcrust pastry, are available from **food
stalls** along the lanes near the market.

North of town, **Cafe Pantan**, in front of
the Marannu City Hotel, is breezy and reasonably priced. The only restaurant in town
is **Rumah Makan Idaman**, a small, friendly
place which serves the usual Indonesian fare,
as well as excellent baked fish (5500Rp). It
is Muslim-run, so no alcohol is served.

Getting There & Away

See Getting There & Away under Rantepao
earlier in this chapter for information about
flights to Tana Toraja.

Every minute from dawn to dusk, Kijangs
race between Rantepao and Makale
(1000Rp, 20 minutes). Most of the bus companies based in Rantepao also have offices
near the corner of Jl Merdeka and Jl Ihwan
Rombe in Makale. Buses will pick up pre-
booked passengers in Makale for any destination listed in Getting There & Away
under Rantepao. The only direct bus connection between Tana Toraja and Mamasa
leaves from Makale – see the Mamasa section later in this chapter.

See Around Tana Toraja for details about
regional public transport from Makale.

AROUND TANA TORAJA

Most of the following places can be reached
on day trips from Rantepao and Makale, but
you can make longer trips by staying
overnight in villages, or camping out. You

SULAWESI

can use public transport, go on organised tours, hire a motorbike or mountain bike, charter a vehicle with a driver-cum-guide or, best of all, walk. The roads to major towns, such as Makale, Palopo, Sa'dan, Batutumonga, Madandan and Bittuang, are paved, but many other roads around Tana Toraja are constructed out of compacted boulders – you don't get stuck, but your joints get rattled loose. Walking is often the only way to reach the remote villages.

Guides

Guides are useful if you have a common language, but in some ways it's better to explore the region without one if you're travelling independently. If you have a sense of direction, a decent map (see Maps at the beginning of this section), know a few relevant phrases of Bahasa Indonesia and are not going too far off the beaten track, you won't go too wrong.

However, a guide will help facilitate visits to remote and traditional villages, arrange accommodation and pass on information about ceremonies. A guide/porter should cost about 40,000Rp/25,000Rp per day – plus their transport, food and accommodation. Guides and porters can be hired around Rantepao (you'll probably be approached in the street); from tourist agencies in Rantepao; from hotels in Rantepao and Makale; or ask around villages along the way.

Hiking

Hiking is the best way to reach isolated areas, and to really get a feel for the countryside and people. Always take good footwear; a water bottle and food; a strong torch (flashlight) in case you walk at night, stay in villages without electricity or want to explore caves; and an umbrella or raincoat – even in the dry season, it's more likely than not to rain. If you take advantage of Torajan hospitality, bring gifts or pay your way.

If you prefer a professional trekking company, contact the operators listed under Rafting later in this section. As an example, Indo Sella charges US$20 per person (minimum of two) for an all-inclusive two day trek.

Shorter hikes are mentioned in the individual sections later in this chapter, but a few of the popular longer treks include:

- Batutumonga-Lokomata-Pangala-Baruppu-Pulu Pulu-Sapan (three days)
- Bittuang-Mamasa (three days) – see Around Mamasa later in this chapter
- Pangala-Bolokan-Bittuang (two days) – a well-marked trail
- Sa'dan-Sapan-Pulu Pulu-Baruppu-Pangala (three days) – tough and mountainous

Rafting

Sungai Sa'dan river has 20 rapids, including a few Class IV and V. Two Rantepao-based companies offer popular day trips, including transport to/from your hotel (anywhere in Tana Toraja), equipment, guide and food, for 250,000/1,200,000Rp for one/three days (a minimum of two people is required):

Indo Sella
    (☎ 25210, fax 23605)
    Jl Suloara 113; also offers kayaking, mountain biking, trekking and paragliding.
Sobek
    (☎ 21336)
    Jl Pongtiku; is an Indonesia-wide company. The office is about 2km south of Rantepao, on the road to Makale.

Organised Tours

Most organised tours are pre-booked from overseas, as part of a packaged tour around Sulawesi and/or eastern Indonesia. Tana Toraja is not somewhere you can just turn up at a travel agency and expect to join a tour, like on Bali.

A few travel agencies are springing up in Rantepao (but not in Makale). They offer a range of services, including organised tours of the region – but you will need to find others to help share the cost. You could probably charter a vehicle (from your hotel, or the bemo terminal), with a driver, for about 70,000Rp per day. But for about 85,000Rp to 100,000Rp per day most travel agencies can organise a more comfortable vehicle, with a knowledgeable driver-cum-guide who speaks a common language, and a comprehensive itinerary (if you don't know where to go).

Four decent, long-running agencies in Rantepao, which can arrange tours, vehicles and guides are:

Indo Sella
(☎ 25210, fax 23605)
Jl Suloara 113
JET Tourist Service
(☎ 21145, fax 23227)
Jl Landorundun 1; probably the most knowledgeable and helpful
PT Panorama Indah
(☎ 25276, fax 25522)
Jl Sam Ratulangi 40, near Mart's Cafe
Toraja Permai
(☎ 21784, fax 21236)
Jl Andi Mapanyuki 10

Getting Around

Mountain bikes can be rented at a few travel agencies and shops around Rantepao for a standard, but expensive, 20,000Rp per day. The main roads out of Rantepao and Makale are good, but often windy and steep, and always narrow, so you spend more time worrying about not falling off the bike than enjoying the scenery. Bikes can be used along some walking trails, but the trails are often too rocky. The most ecologically sound method of transport is by horse, but they're rarely available for hire anyway.

Motorbikes (only available in Rantepao) are better value at 40,000Rp per day, including insurance – plus petrol. The walking trails are often rough for motorbikes, but motorbikes are far more flexible than cars. It's more comfortable, and cheaper for three people or more, to charter a bemo or Kijang (see Organised Tours earlier in this section), but some places will be less accessible.

The two junctions for public transport are not surprisingly in Rantepao and Makale. From the scruffy and muddy Terminal Bolu in Rantepao, there are regular bemos and Kijangs to all main villages, but the vehicles are poorly signed so you have to ask around the terminal. As indicated on the Rantepao and Makale maps, some public transport also leaves from designated places in these towns.

Some of the more useful services from Rantepao (and Makale) are to:

• Bittuang – for treks to Mamasa and only leaves from Makale
• La'bo – via Kete Kesu
• Lempo – useful for hiking up to Batutumonga
• Madandan – can detour via the airport for a little extra
• Pangala – via Batutumonga
• Sangalla – only leaves from Makale
• Sa'dan – usually via Tikala

Batutumonga

Batutumonga, about 20km north of Rantepao, is a haven on the slopes of Gunung Sesean, with panoramic views of Rantepao and the Sa'dan valley, including stunning sunrises. You can stay there, or easily day trip from Rantepao or Makale – perhaps do some hiking and enjoy lunch at one of the restaurants.

Places to Stay & Eat The first place as you come from Rantepao is *Mama Siska's Homestay*, a steep 15 minute walk up the hill, just before Batutumonga. There are no views, and staff are often absent, but the food makes up for the very basic accommodation, which costs about 25,000Rp per person, including meals. Next up the hill is *Mentirotiku*. It offers simple, but comfortable, accommodation in tongkonan-style houses for 25,000Rp per person; and better, individual rooms with views for 50,000Rp per double.

The upmarket place is the new *Sesean Mountain Lodge*. The rooms should be finished by the time you get there, but expect to pay about US$50 for a large, traditional tongkonan-style cottage. Opposite, the charming *Landorondin Homestay* has small, comfortable wooden rooms, with a private bathroom, but no views, for 20,000Rp per person. Nearby, *Betania Homestay* (Mama Ria's) boasts the best views. The accommodation is just a mattress on a floor in a tongkonan for 25,000Rp per person including meals, but the setting is superb.

All the hotels, expect Mama Siska's, have a *restaurant*, which is open to the public. The cheapest, and best for views, is at Betania

Homestay, while the most elegant is currently at Mentirotiku. There will also be a classy new restaurant at Sesean Mountain Lodge.

Getting There & Away Simply take a bemo to Lempo from Terminal Bolu in Rantepao, and walk 2km (uphill); or 1km towards Pangala, and get off anywhere along the main road in Batutumonga. The walk from Batutumonga to Lempo is short, pleasant and downhill.

North of Rantepao

From Batutumonga, you can walk to **Loko-mata**, and return on the same day. Lokomata has cave graves hewn into a rocky outcrop, and outstanding scenery. The return hike to Rantepao is an easy hike down the slopes to **Pana**, with its ancient hanging graves, and a few baby graves in nearby trees. You can see tiny villages with towering tongkonan, women pounding rice, men scrubbing their beloved buffalo and children splashing happily in pools. The path ends at **Tikala** and, from there, regular bemos go to Rantepao.

Alternatively, backtrack through Lempo to **Deri**, the site of rock graves, walk down to the Rantepao-Sa'dan road and catch a bemo back to Rantepao. This is a very pleasant downhill walk (five hours) through some of the finest scenery in Tana Toraja.

At 2150m above sea level, **Gunung Sesean** is not the highest peak on Sulawesi, but one of the most popular for hiking. The summit is accessible via a trail beginning behind Landorondin Homestay in Batutu-monga. The return trip to the summit takes five hours. A guide might be useful, but you can manage on your own.

Beyond Gunung Sesean, the sleepy village of **Pangala** (35km from Rantepao) is noted for its fine dancers, as is nearby **Baruppu**. Pangala's main accommodation is *Losmen Sando*, a surprisingly elegant place with comfortable rooms, and a spacious restaurant overlooking a coffee plantation. Rooms cost from 17,500Rp per person, and staff can offer good advice about local trekking.

Pangli (7km north of Rantepao) has tau tau and house graves. About 2km further north,

the traditional village of **Palawa** is just as attractive, but less popular, than Kete Kesu, with tongkonan houses and rice barns. In the dry season, you can walk south-west from Palawa to **Bori** (6km), fording a river and walking through rice fields. Bori is the site of an impressive *rante* (ceremonial ground) and some towering megaliths. About a kilometre south of Bori, **Parinding** has tongkonan houses and rice barns that you pass on the walk (two hours) between Bori and Tikala.

Further north is the weaving centre of **Sa'-dan** (12km north of Rantepao), where local women set up a market to sell their woven cloth. It's all handmade on simple looms, but not all is produced in the village (some of the blankets come from the west, particularly Mamasa). You can stop for food at the *River Cafe* on the way back to Rantepao – check out the crafts for sale next door.

West of Rantepao

About 2km west across the river from Rantepao, **Gunung Singki** (930m) is a steep hill. There's a slippery, overgrown hiking trail to the summit, which has panoramic views across Rantepao and the surrounding countryside. From the hill, continue walking down the dirt road to **Siguntu** (7km from Rantepao), which offers more superb views of the valleys and Rantepao. The path is not obvious so keep asking directions.

The walk (3km) from Siguntu to the main road at Alang Alang is also pleasant. Stop on the way at the traditional village of **Mendoe**. At Alang Alang, where a covered bridge crosses the river, you could head to **Londa**, back to Rantepao or Makale, or remain on the western side of the river and continue walking to the villages of **Langda** and **Madandan**.

South of Rantepao

On the outskirts of Rantepao, just off the road leading to Makale, is **Karasik**, with traditional-style houses arranged around a cluster of megaliths. The houses may have been erected some years ago for a single funeral ceremony, but some are now inhabited.

continued on page 902

THE TORAJA

People

Despite the isolation caused by the rugged landscape of central Sulawesi, traditional cultures have existed in the territory bordered by the Bugis to the south-west, the Paul district in the north, and the Loinang and Mori peoples in the east. The people in this vast area are collectively referred to as the Toraja. The name is derived from the Bugis word *toriaja* (literally, men of the mountains), but the connotations of the name are something like 'hillbilly' – rustic, unsophisticated highlanders.

Customarily, the Toraja have been split by ethnologists into western, eastern and southern groups. To some extent these divisions represent the varying degrees of influence the old kingdoms of Luwu, Gowa and Bone have had on the Toraja. They don't reflect any political organisation among the Toraja. Of all the Toraja peoples, the best known to the western world are the southern Toraja, also known as the Sa'dan or Saqdan Toraja. Most live in, and around, the towns of Rantepao and Makale.

Before the Dutch came, there were several groups of head-hunters in the archipelago, including the Toraja. Their head-hunting was not on any great scale and their raids were basically tests of manhood for the young men of the tribe. Head-hunting was also necessary to find heads for a chief's death-feast to provide slaves for his afterlife. If enough

Text inset: Toraja woman (photograph by Greg Elms).

Right: Harvest time.

GREG ELMS

enemies could not be captured in raids, the chief's family would buy slaves and sacrifice them. Under Dutch rule, the wars and raids came to an end.

Buffaloes are a status symbol for the Toraja, and are of paramount importance in various religious ceremonies. Pigs and chickens are slaughtered at many rituals, such as the consecration of new *tongkonan* houses (see Architecture later in this section), but buffaloes are usually saved for the biggest celebrations of all – funeral feasts (see Funerals later in this section). Dogs are eaten in some parts of Tana Toraja, and sold for meat like regular livestock. Coffee (reputedly the best in Indonesia) is the main cash crop, and fish are farmed in ponds in the rice fields.

History

The Bugis traded Indian cloth, Dutch coins and porcelain with the Toraja in return for coffee and slaves. The Bugis possibly introduced cockfighting to the Toraja, who incorporated the sport into the death rituals of their noble class. Islam brought a new militancy to the Bugis, and under Arung Palakka they attacked the Toraja in 1673 and 1674. However, Islam never spread much further than the southern Toraja areas, probably because of the people's fondness for pork and palm wine.

The Toraja did not come into serious contact with the west until the early 20th century. Torajan life and culture had survived the constant threat from the Bugis, but in 1905 the Dutch began a bloody campaign to bring central Sulawesi under their control. The Toraja held out against the Dutch for two years, until the last substantial resistance was wiped out in the mountains around Pangala, north-west of Rantepao.

The missionaries moved in on the heels of the troops, and by WWII many of the great Torajan ceremonies (with the exception of funeral celebrations) were disappearing. Tourism, mining and migration have aided the destruction that began with the missionaries.

Religion

Despite the strength of traditional beliefs, the Christian Church of Toraja is a very active force. One of the first questions asked of you will be your religion, and Protestants are given immediate approval as *saudara* (sister/brother).

Physical isolation and the lack of a written language resulted in considerable variations in beliefs, customs and mythology, although theancestor cult has always been very strong. Prior to the arrival of Christianity, the Toraja believed in many gods, but worshipped one in particular as the special god of their family, clan or tribe. Puang Matua was the nearest the Toraja originally came to the concept of a supreme being, and early missionaries began prayers in their churches with his name.

The Toraja have a long and involved mythology dividing creation into three worlds, each watched over by its own god. The Sa'dan Toraja also had a rigid caste system and a slave class. Although the Dutch abolished slavery, its effects continued long after. Christianity undermined some traditional Toraja beliefs, but the ceremonies are still a vital part of life.

Although one of the five pillars of the Pancasila is the belief in one god, the Toraja gained official sanction to maintain their polytheistic beliefs (AluIh Todolo), possibly because Toraja beliefs were considered similar to those of the Balinese Hindus, for whom an exception had already been made. Like the followers of traditional faiths elsewhere in Indonesia, the Toraja are officially listed as 'Hindu'.

Architecture

One of the most noticeable aspects about Tana Toraja is the size and grandeur of tongkonans, the traditional houses, raised on piles and topped with massive roofs. These houses are closely bound up with Torajan traditions – one of their important functions is as a constant reminder of the authority of the original noble families whose descendants alone have the right to build such houses. The state of a tongkonan also symbolises the unity of a clan. It is the meeting place for family gatherings, and may not be bought or sold.

Tana Toraja is one of the few places in Indonesia where traditional houses are still being built, and the skills to make them survive. The owners often live in modern houses, keeping the tongkonan for ceremonies and as a symbol of the family's status. The tourist trade has also inspired the renovation of some older houses, and construction of new

Traditional *tongkonan* dwellings are common sights in the villages of Tana Toraja.

SIMON ROWE

ones. Most tongkonan have rice barns, surrounded by several ordinary bungalows on stilts, like the houses of the Bugis and Makassarese.

The roof, rearing up at either end, is the most striking aspect. Some believe the house represents the head of a buffalo and the rising roof represents the horns; others suggest that the roof looks more like a boat, and that the raised ends represent the bow and stern. The houses all face north – possibly because ancestors of the Toraja came from the north by boat, and inverted the boats to use as shelters. Others maintain that the north (and east) is regarded as the sphere of life, the realm of the gods.

The high gables are supported by poles, and the wall panels are decorated with painted engravings. Each geometrical design has an individual name and meaning. On these panels, red (the colour of blood) symbolises human life; white (the colour of flesh and bone) is the symbol of purity; yellow represents God's blessing and power; and black symbolises death and darkness. Traditionally, the colours were all natural – black is the soot from cooking pots, yellow and red are coloured earth, and white is lime. Artisans would decorate the houses, and be paid in buffaloes. A realistic carving of a buffalo's head decorates the front part of each house. Numerous buffalo horns, indicating the wealth of the family, are attached to the front pole that supports the gable.

The beams and supports are cut so they all neatly slot or are pegged together; no metal nails are used. The older houses have roofs of overlapping pieces of bamboo, but newer ones use corrugated metal sheets. Standing on thick solid piles, the rectangular body of the house is small in contrast to the roof, and consists of two or three dark rooms with low doors and small windows. If necessary, the whole house can actually be put on runners and moved to another location.

Torajan houses always face a line-up of rice barns – wealthy owners may have a whole fleet of barns. The barns look like miniature houses, and the rice storage area is surprisingly small. They have a small door at one end, and the surface of the walls and the high gables are usually decorated. The rice storage chamber is raised about 2m off the ground on four smooth columns of wood, polished to prevent rats climbing up them.

About 60cm from the ground is a wooden platform stretched between the pillars, an important meeting place to sit and while away the hours, as well as a shelter from downpours. Who sits where depends on status, so be careful not to offend elders by taking their place at ceremonies. The boat-shaped roof shelters an area about twice the size of the rice chamber.

Traditional Sports

The unique form of unarmed man-to-man combat is called *sisemba*. It's something like Thai boxing, except that use of the hands is banned and you can't kick your opponent when he's down (very sporting).

GREG ELMS

GREG ELMS

Top: Exquisite tiered rice fields.
Bottom: Rice workers.

SIMON ROWE

SIMON ROWE

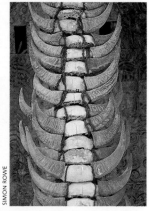

SIMON ROWE

SIMON ROWE

Top: A Tana Toraja funeral ceremony, 7km north of Rantepao. Cakes made from black sugar and coffee are presented to relatives of the deceased by women from a neighbouring village.

Middle left to right: A sacrificial buffalo on its death march; rows of buffalo horns from ceremonies past represent gifts given and honour bestowed on the deceased ancestors.

Bottom: Relatives of the deceased approach the family house during the funeral ceremony.

Top: Musicians and dancers are often hired for funeral ceremonies in Tana Toraja.

Middle: A wooden buffalo head above a Rantepao hotel.

Bottom: Ceremonial umbrellas stand outside a house near Rantepao during a funeral ceremony.

Carved wooden effigies of the dead at a traditional Toraja burial site.

GREG ELMS

Now more a feat of strength and endurance, the original aim of the contest was to instil courage in Torajan youths – a useful attribute for a people once hemmed in by their coastal enemies, and occasionally at war with each other.

These fights are held at the time of the rice harvest, or just after (June to early August), which is also the most popular time for funerals and house ceremonies. Fights are held between individuals, or teams of two or more, and the women look on and cheer their favourites. When the men of one village challenge another, anything up to 200 a side is possible.

The Toraja had another contest known as *sibamba*, in which the contestants used wooden clubs to hit each other, protecting themselves from the blows with a bull-hide shield (similar to the contests found on Lombok, eastern Bali and Sumbawa). It was probably banned during Dutch rule.

Funerals

Tomate (funeral) literally means 'dead person', and of all Torajan ceremonies the most important are those concerned with sending a dead person to the afterworld. Without proper funeral rites the spirit of the deceased will cause misfortune to its family. The funeral sacrifices, ceremonies and feasts also impress the gods with the importance of the deceased, so that the spirit can intercede effectively on behalf of living relatives. Funerals are sometimes held at the *rante*, funeral sites marked by one or more megaliths. In Tana Toraja, there are several arcs or groups of roughly hewn stone slabs around villages, and each stone possibly represents a member of the noble class who lived and died there. Some are as high as 4m, symbolising the importance of the deceased. The efforts to raise even one stone involves scores of men dragging the stone to the designated place with ropes, and a sacrificial slaughter to celebrate the new megalith – part of the complex funeral preparations for nobles.

At a funeral, bamboo pavilions for the family and guests are constructed around a field. The dead person 'presides' over the funeral from the high-roofed tower constructed at one end of the field. The Toraja generally have two funerals, one immediately after a death and an elaborate second funeral after preparations (ie raise the necessary cash, obtain livestock, gather relatives from afar and so on). For this reason tomate are usually scheduled during the dry season from July to September, when family members have free time.

The corpse remains in the house where the person died. These days, it's preserved by injection instead of traditional embalming herbs. Food is cooked and offered to the dead person; those of noble birth have attendants who stay in their immediate presence from the hour of death to the day of their final progress to the tomb. An invitation to visit the deceased is an honour (but a polite refusal won't cause offence). If you accept, however, remember to thank the deceased and ask permission of the deceased when you wish to leave – as you would a living host. You won't be expected to pray, but might be invited to take photos, an indication that the deceased is still an important part of the family.

The souls of the dead can only go to *puya*, the afterworld, when the entire death ritual has been carried out. A spirit's status in the afterlife is the same as its owner's status in the present life; even the souls of animals follow their masters to the next life – hence the animal sacrifices at funerals. They believe the soul of the deceased will ride the souls of the slaughtered buffaloes and pigs to heaven. The trip to puya requires a strong buffalo, because the long and difficult journey involves crossing hundreds of mountains and thousands of valleys.

Sons and daughters of the deceased have an equal chance to inherit their parents' property, but their share depends on the number of buffaloes they slaughter at the funeral feast. The buffalo has traditionally been a symbol of wealth and power – even land could be paid for in buffaloes. The more important the deceased, the more buffaloes must be sacrificed: one for a commoner, four, eight, 12 or 24 as you move up the social scale. The age and status of the deceased also determines the number of animals slaughtered. Large ceremonies, where more than 100 buffaloes are slaughtered, are spoken of with awe for years afterwards. The type of buffalo is also significant – the most prized is the *tedong bonga* (spotted buffalo), which may cost many millions of rupiah per head.

The temptation to sacrifice dozens of buffaloes to honour the dead and impress the living prompted the Indonesian government to levy a tax on each slaughtered animal to limit the destruction of wealth. However, funeral ceremonies have lost none of their ostentation and are still a ruinous financial burden on families. Some now refuse to hold tomate, despite their social obligation to do so.

Visitors with strong stomachs can see freshly killed pigs roasted on open fires to scorch the skin before the pig is gutted and the meat mixed with piles of vegetables and stuffed into bamboo tubes. The bamboo tubes are cooked slowly over low flames to produce tasty *pa'-piong* (see Food later in this section). Cuts of buffalo meat are also distributed – the funeral season is the only time of year families are guaranteed regular supplies of meat.

Funerals can be spread out over several days and involve hundreds of guests (and many tourists). The wooden effigies, known as *tau tau* (see Graves & Tau Tau later in this section), can cost nearly a year's wages for many Indonesians. Bamboo pavilions are constructed specially for the occasion, with a death tower at one end.

After the guests display their presents of pigs and buffaloes, the traditional *mabadong* song and dance is performed. This is a ceremonial re-enactment of the cycle of human life and the life story of the deceased. It's a slow-moving circular dance performed by men in black sarongs, who stand shoulder to shoulder and chant for hours. It also bids farewell to the soul of the deceased, and relays the hope that the soul will arrive in the afterworld safely.

Ceremonies may include buffalo fighting, in which the bulls, agitated by the insertion of chilli up their behinds, lock horns and strain against each other. The winner is the one which makes its opponent slide backwards. The crowd urges them on with frenzied whoops and yells, but is ready to scatter in case one breaks loose and charges in panic (so don't get too close to the action!). You might also see sisemba (see Traditional Sports earlier in this section), and maybe cockfights at the end of the ceremony.

As well as the mabadong, orchestras of school children often play painted bamboo wind instruments. The programme might also include dances like the *maranding*, a war dance performed at the burial service of a patriotic nobleman to remind the people of his heroic deeds, or the *makatia*, which reminds the people of the deceased's generosity and loyalty. Songs may also be sung to console the bereaved family, or convey their grief to the other guests at the funeral.

Other Ceremonies

The Toraja have a number of other ceremonies connected with the construction of a tongkonan house (see Architecture earlier in this section). Construction is preceded by the sacrificial killing of a chicken, pig or buffalo; and the successful completion of the house is celebrated with a large feast in which many pigs and at least one buffalo are killed. You can also attend weddings and harvest ceremonies, each usually involving special traditions and ritual slaughter, *but you must be invited* – not formally, but at least by someone who knows someone. And please remember to dress conservatively.

At these celebrations, there is usually plenty of traditional Torajan dancing, graceful routines to the beat of a large drum (or sometimes taped music). What the dance lacks in complexity is more than made up for by the enthusiasm of the audience, who dash forward to stuff rupiah notes into the performers' headbands. The women's clothes accentuate the strength and power of Torajan women: they wear flame-coloured dresses with beaded decoration hanging from the waist and shoulders. The family *kris* (dagger) is tucked into the waistband – in other areas of Indonesia, only men may wear a kris.

Graves & Tau Tau

The Toraja believe that you can take possessions with you in the afterlife, and the dead generally go well equipped to their graves. Since this led to grave plundering, the Toraja started to hide their dead in caves or hew niches out of rock faces.

These caves were hollowed out by specialist cave builders who were traditionally paid in buffaloes, and since the building of a cave would cost several buffaloes, only the rich could afford it. Although the exterior of the cave grave looks small, the interior is large enough to entomb an entire family. The coffins go deep inside the caves, and sitting in balconies on the rock face in front of the caves are the tau tau – life-size, carved wooden effigies of the dead.

Tau tau are carved only for the upper classes; their expense alone rules out their use for poor people. Traditionally, the statues only showed the gender of the person, not the likeness, but now they attempt to imitate the likeness of the person's face. The making of tau tau appears to have been a recent innovation, possibly originating in the late 19th century. The type of wood used reflects the status and wealth of the deceased; *nangka* (jackfruit) wood is the most expensive. After the deceased has been entombed and the tau tau placed in front of the grave, offerings are placed in the palm of the tau tau. You can see the carvers at work at Londa.

If there are no rocky outcrops or cliff faces to carve a niche in, wooden house graves are created, in which the coffin is placed. Most of the hanging graves, where the wooden coffins are hung from high cliffs, have rotted away. Sometimes the coffins may be placed at the foot of a mountain. Babies who have died before teething are placed in hollowed-out sections of living trees. Examples of these graves can be seen at Pana.

Most tau tau seem to be in a permanent state of disrepair, but in a ceremony after harvest time the bodies are re-wrapped in new material and the clothes of the tau tau replaced. Occasionally left lying around the more obscure cave graves is a *duba-duba*, a platform in the shape of a traditional house which is used to carry the coffin and body of a nobleman to the grave.

There are many tau tau at Lemo and a few elsewhere, but it's becoming increasingly difficult to see tau tau in Tana Toraja. So many have been stolen that the Toraja now keep many of them in their own homes.

Food

Attending ceremonies, or going to a local restaurant, is the best time to try Torajan food. The best known is pa'piong, the spinach-like vegetable with pork, chicken or fish cooked in bamboo tubes. Chicken pa'piong has the added flavour of coconut; pork pa'piong tends to have a high fat content, because fat is considered as tasty as the meat. If you want to try pa'piong in a restaurant, order several hours in advance because it takes time to cook. *Pamerasan*, buffalo meat in a black sauce, is delicious if the meat is tender.

Fresh fish is rushed from Palopo on motorcycles, laden with huge pannier baskets. *Ikan mas* (gold fish) and *ikan belut* (eels) are caught in local rice fields and barbecued.

You can also indulge your sweet tooth with *kue baje*, cakes of sticky rice and palm sugar rolled in a dry corn leaf. *Kue deppa* are triangular rice flour cakes bought loose from street stalls, and *kacang goreng* is a very sweet concoction of peanuts and treacle wrapped in corn leaves.

A rare delicacy is *kolak*, a sweet banana soup with coconut milk and palm sugar, spiced with ginger.

Drinks

Rantepao and Makale markets have whole sections devoted to the sale of the alcoholic 'palm wine' known locally as *balok*. Every few months the palm, with its huge, dark metallic-green fronds and untidy black-haired trunk, produces a great cluster of round, dark fruit. The stem is pierced close to the fruit and if sugary sap flows from the wound the fruit cluster is cut off and a receptacle is hung to catch the juice dripping from the amputated stump. This ferments naturally, producing one of creation's finest brews. The sap can also be boiled down to produce crystalline red sugar – *gula merah*.

Balok, known nationally as *tuak* and internationally as *toddy*, is sold in huge jugs in tiny warungs around town. It comes in a variety of strengths and colours, from lemonade coloured to orange or red (made by adding tree bark). Balok also ranges from sweet to bitter, depending on its age. It doesn't keep for more than a day, so be wary of buying blends of old and new. Women in markets often mix and blend fresher, sweeter alcoholic *induk* with the older, more alcoholic brews.

Coffee is Toraja's other famous brew, an excellent antidote to a night of balok tasting. *Robusta* is the most widely available variety, drunk strong and black with equal portions of coffee and sugar. The aromatic *arabica* is also available at much higher prices. It is largely produced for export, and you can see the whole process of growing, harvesting, drying and roasting throughout Tana Toraja. In villages, coffee is sometimes roasted with ginger, coconut or even garlic for an unusually fragrant taste.

Language

Bahasa Toraja (and variations of it) remains the predominant language, despite the lack of books written in the language. Although Indonesian is widely spoken and understood, some people, mainly older folk in remote villages, do not speak Bahasa Indonesia at all. The following phrases will guarantee instant laughter and appreciation. If you can't get your tongue around the characteristic glottal stop (indicated with an apostrophe), there will be a crowd of teachers to help.

How are you?	*Apa kareba?*
I'm well.	*Kareba melo.*
Good/fine.	*Melo.*
Thank you.	*Kurre sumanga.*
You're welcome.	*Bole paria.*
How much is this?	*Se pira te' indok?*
Where are you going?	*Umba me sule?*
I'm just going for a walk.	*Su malong-malong.*
I don't have any sweets!	*Ta'e ku ampui gula-gula!*

continued from page 892

Just off the road to Kete Kesu is **Buntu Pune**, where there are two tongkonan houses and six rice barns. According to local legend, one of the two houses was built by a nobleman named Pong Marambaq at the beginning of the 20th century. During Dutch rule, he was appointed head of the local district, but planned to rebel and was subsequently exiled to Ambon (Maluku), where he died. His body was returned to Tana Toraja, and buried at the hill to the north of Buntu Pune.

About 1km further along from Buntu Pune is **Kete Kesu** (6km from Rantepao), reputed for its woodcarving (see Shopping under Rantepao earlier in this chapter). On the cliff face behind the village are some grave caves and very old hanging graves. The rotting coffins are suspended on wooden beams under an overhang. Others, full of bones and skulls, lie rotting in strategic piles. Along the vague trail heading uphill is another grave cave. One of the houses in the village has several tau tau on display. The village is a tourist museum – no-one seems to live here any more – but it's still an interesting site.

From Kete Kesu, you can walk to **Sullukang**, which has a rante marked by a number of large, rough-hewn megaliths, and on to **Palatokke** (9km from Rantepao). In this beautiful area of lush rice paddies, and traditional houses, there is an enormous cliff face containing several grave caves and hanging graves. Access to the caves is difficult, but the scenery makes it worthwhile. From Palatokke, you can walk to La'bo, **Randanbatu**, where there are more graves, and then continue to Sangalla, Suaya and Makale.

At **Londa** (6km south of Rantepao) is a very extensive burial cave at the base of a massive cliff face. You can hire lamps for a good look around. A bemo between Rantepao and Makale will drop you at the turn-off, about 2km from the cave. Go in the morning for the best photos.

The entrance to the cave is guarded by a balcony of tau tau. Inside the cave is a collection of coffins, many of them rotted

away, with the bones either scattered or thrown into piles. Other coffins hold the bones of several family members – it's an old Toraja custom that all people who have lived together in one family house should also be buried together in a family grave. A local myth says that the people buried in the Londa caves are the descendants of Tangdilinoq, chief of the Toraja when they were pushed out of the Enrekang region, and forced to move into the highlands.

Kids hang around outside the Londa caves with oil lamps to guide you around (about 5000Rp). Unless you've got a strong torch, you really do need a guide with a lamp. Inside the caves, the coffins and skulls have been placed in strategic locations for the benefit of sightseers. If you're thin, and don't suffer from claustrophobia, squeeze through the tunnel connecting the two main caves, past some interesting stalactites and stalagmites. Londa is also famous for its wood carvers.

Further south, 2km (east) off the Rantepao-Makale road, is **Tilanga** (10km from Rantepao), a lovely, natural cool-water swimming pool. You can swim, but don't be put off if some friendly eels come to say hello. From Makale, it's an interesting hike (11km) along muddy trails and rice paddies to Tilanga, but ask directions once you leave the main road.

Lemo (10km south of Rantepao) is probably the most interesting burial area in Tana Toraja. The sheer rock face has a whole series

---

The Graves of Lemo

According to local legend, these graves are for descendants of a Toraja chief who reigned over the surrounding district hundreds of years ago and built his house on top of the cliff into which the graves are now cut. Because the mountain was part of his property, only his descendants could use it. The chief himself was buried elsewhere because the art of cutting grave caves had not yet been developed.

of balconies for tau tau. The biggest balcony has a dozen figures, with white eyes and black pupils and outstretched arms like spectators at a sports event. It's a good idea to go before 9 am for the best photos. A Rantepao-Makale bemo will drop you off at the turn-off to the burial site, from where it's a 15 minute walk to the tau tau.

East of Rantepao

Marante is a fine traditional village, just north of the road to Palopo. Near Marante, there are stone and hanging graves with several tau tau, skulls on the coffins and a cave with scattered bones. From Marante, you can cross the river on the suspension bridge and walk to pretty villages, set in rice fields.

In the same direction, but further off the Palopo road, is the traditional village of **Nanggala** (16km from Rantepao). It has a particularly grandiose traditional house and an impressive fleet of 14 rice barns. The rice barns have a bizarre array of motifs carved into them, including soldiers with guns, western women and cars. Keep an eye out for a colony of huge black bats hanging from trees at the end of the village.

From Nanggala, you can walk south to **Paniki**, a tough hike (five hours) along a dirt track up and down the hills. The trail starts next to the rice barns, and along the way you'll see coffee-plantation machines grinding and packing coffee into sacks. From Paniki, walk (two hours) to **Buntao** (15km from Rantepao), which has some house graves and tau tau. Alternatively, catch a bemo from Paniki to Rantepao. About 2km from Buntao is **Tembamba**, which has more graves and is noted for its fine scenery.

East of Makale

Sangalla has the simple *Homestay Kalembang Indah* for 25,000Rp per person, including meals. Just south of Sangalla, are the hot springs at **Makula**, well signed from the Rantepao-Makale road. At Makula, you can stay at the upmarket *Hotel Sangalla* (☎ 24112) for US$33/38 for single/doubles. The public can use the hot springs swimming pool for 3000Rp.

There are over 40 tau tau at **Tampangallo**, between Sangalla and Suaya. The graves belong to the chiefs of Sangalla, descendants of the mythical divine being Tamborolangiq, who is believed to have introduced the caste system, death rituals and agricultural techniques into Torajan society. The former royal families of Makale, Sangalla and Menkendek all claimed descent from Tamborolangiq, who is said to have descended from heaven by a stone staircase. Take a Kijang from Makale to Sangalla, get off about 1km after the turn-off to Suaya, and walk 500m through the rice fields to Tampangallo.

Mamasa Valley

The Mamasa valley is often referred to as West Tana Toraja, but this overstates the connection between Mamasa and Tana Toraja. Mamasan tongkonan have heavy, wooden roofs, quite different from the exaggerated U-shaped bamboo roofs to the east. Torajan ceremonies and funerals survive in the Mamasa valley, but on the whole these are far less ostentatious affairs than those around Tana Toraja.

Mamasans have embraced Christianity with unfettered enthusiasm: choir groups regularly meet up and down the valley, flexing their vocal chords in praise of God. *Sambu* weaving is a craft which still thrives in the hills around Mamasa village. These long strips of heavy woven material are stitched together to make blankets, which are ideal insulation for the cold mountain nights.

Like Tana Toraja, the best way to explore the valley is on foot. The paths tend to follow the ridges, giving hikers stunning views of the clean, mountain-fringed countryside. There are few roads, and many paths to choose from, so you'll need to constantly ask directions, or hire a guide in Mamasa village, or in other villages as you go along. The other source of confusion is that village districts, such as Balla, cover broad areas and there are few villages per se. Even centres within the village area, such as Rante Balla, Balla Kalua and Buntu Balla, are very spread out.

SULAWESI

MAMASA

Mamasa is the only large village in the valley. The air is cool and clean, and the folk are hospitable. The rhythm of life has a surreal, fairytale-like quality for those used to the hustle of Indonesia's big cities. The highlight of the week is the **market**, where hill people trade their produce. Look for locally made woven blankets, a must for those cold mountain nights. While walking through hill villages, trekkers will also be offered plenty of fine-looking blankets direct from weavers so take money or gifts to barter with.

Places to Stay & Eat

Losmen Mini (Jl Ahmad Yani) is a rambling mountain lodge in the heart of town, with sunny upstairs doubles for 22,500Rp, or darker rooms out the back for 15,000Rp. *Mantana Lodge (Jl Emmy Saelan)* has a bright interior; singles start at 15,000Rp, and doubles cost 20,000Rp to 27,500Rp. It has a good restaurant with cold beer, and souvenirs for sale.

Losmen Marapan (Jl Ahmad Yani) is one of the older and more charming places.

Small economy rooms cost 11,500Rp, and the better rooms with a fan cost about 25,000Rp. *Mamasa Guest House (Jl Buntu Budi)* has views of the surrounding mountains and Mambulilin waterfall. Doubles cost 22,500Rp. *Wisma Mamasa*, just off Jl Monginsidi, is an old Dutch house on a rise overlooking the town. Pleasant rooms cost 15,000Rp a double.

Mamasa Cottages is built over hot springs at Kole, 3km north of Mamasa. It offers lovely rooms for a negotiable 100,000Rp, and may be worth a splurge – hot spring water flows to every bathroom.

Most losmen serve reasonably priced food – *Mantana Lodge* has one of the best restaurants in town.

Getting There & Away

On a map, Mamasa looks tantalisingly close to Rantepao, but there's no direct transport because the road is so bad. You can travel from Makale to Bittuang by Kijang or bemo, but from Bittuang you'll have to walk (see the Mamasa to Bittuang entry later in this section).

The only direct connection between Tana Toraja and Mamasa is the bus (15,000Rp, 12 hours), which travels three times a week from the Heryanto Bus Company, next to Losmen Merry, in Makale. Otherwise, from Tana Toraja (or anywhere else), catch a bus towards

MAMASA

PLACES TO STAY
1 Mamasa Guest House
6 Losmen Marapan
8 Losmen Mini
9 Mantana Lodge & Restaurant
11 Wisma Mamasa

OTHER
2 Hospital
3 Motorcycle Depot
4 General Store
5 Mosque
7 Pasar; Bus/Bemo Terminal
10 Post Office
12 Police Station
13 Church Toraja Mamasa

Majene or Mamuju and get off at Polewali, from where plenty of creaky minibuses go to Mamasa (three hours) along a rough road, which is often prone to mudslides.

AROUND MAMASA

The countryside surrounding Mamasa is strikingly beautiful. You can hire motorbikes for a negotiable 45,000Rp per day from the guys hanging around the garage on Jl Rambu Saratu in Mamasa. You can charter a bemo or Kijang along the valley's couple of main roads, but footpaths and very slender suspended bridges are the only access to most villages.

The following places (with distances in kilometres from Mamasa in brackets) are easy to reach from Mamasa, but take warm clothes and gifts for your hosts if you plan to stay overnight. As most people grow their own coffee here, in return for any hospitality bring condensed milk, chocolate, sugar, *kreteks* (clove cigarettes) and other goods from town.

North of Mamasa

Rante Buda (4km) has an impressive 25m-long tongkonan house known as Banua Layuk (High House), an old chief's house with colourful motifs. This tongkonan is one of the oldest and best preserved in the valley, built about 300 years ago for one of five local leaders, the chief of Rambusaratu. A donation (about 2000Rp) is expected.

Kole (3km) has hot springs, also tapped for the guests at Mamasa Cottages (see Places to Stay & Eat in the Mamasa section earlier). **Loko** (4km) is a traditional village with old houses, set in the jungle. The only way there is to hike via Kole or Tondok Bakaru. Hardy hikers can continue from Loko up the steep hill to **Mambulilin**

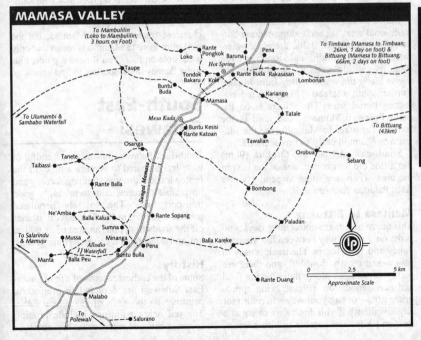

MAMASA VALLEY

To Mambulilin (Loko to Mambulilin; 3 hours on Foot)

To Timbaan (Mamasa to Timbaan; 26km, 1 day on foot) & Bittuang (Mamasa to Bittuang; 66km, 2 days on foot)

Loko
Rante Pongkok
Baruna
Pena
Taupe
Hot Spring
Tondok Bakaru
Rante Buda
Rakasasan
Lombonan
Buntu Buda
Kariango
Mamasa
To Ulumambi & Sambabo Waterfall
Mesa Kada
Tatale
Buntu Kesisi
Rante Katoan
To Bittuang (43km)
Osanga
Tawalian
Tanete
Orobua
Sebang
Taibassi
Rante Balla
Bombong
Ne'Amba
Balla Kalua
Rante Sopang
Paladan
Sumna
To Salarindu & Mamuju
Mussa
Minanga
Allodio Waterfall
Pena
Balla Kareke
Manta
Balla Peu
Buntu Bulla
Sungai Mamasa

0   2.5   5 km
Approximate Scale

Rante Duang
Malabo
To Polewali
Salurano

SULAWESI

Sarambu (Mambulilin Waterfall), and on to the peak of **Gunung Mambulilin** (9km). **Taupe** (5km) is a traditional village with jungle walks and panoramic views.

South of Mamasa

Rante Sopang (9km) is a busy centre for weaving and retailing crafts. The path up the hill from the roadside craft shop leads to a few workshops, where women weave long strips of heavy cloth for Mamasa's distinctive, colourful blankets.

Osango (3km) is the site of *tedong-tedong* (burial houses), supposedly up to 200 years old. There are lots of paths and the village is *very* spread out, so ask for directions along the way. **Mesa Kada** (2km) are hot springs, which are nice for a swim.

Tanete (8km) has mountain graves under a cave. Tanete, and nearby **Taibassi**, are also centres for traditional weaving and carving. **Rante Balla** (12km) has big beautiful tongkonans, and is also a centre for weaving blankets and baskets.

Buntu Balla (15km) has beautiful views, traditional weaving and tedong-tedong burial sites. Near Buntu Balla, there's a waterfall at **Allodio**; a traditional village at **Balla Peu**; megalithic remains at **Manta**; and views along the whole valley from **Mussa**. Further south, **Malabo** (18km) has tedong-tedong burial sites. The village is on the main Polewali-Mamasa road, and is the turn-off for hikes to Mamuju (see the Mamasa to Mamuju entry in this section).

South-east of Mamasa, **Orobua** (9km) has a fine old tongkonan, one of the best in the area. There are more sweeping views from **Paladan** further south.

Mamasa to Bittuang

This 66km hike takes about three days, and is the only direct way between the Mamasa valley and Tana Toraja. The track is easy to follow and mostly downhill, and there are plenty of villages along the way for food and accommodation. (Please bring appropriate gifts – or pay your way – in return for any hospitality if you don't stay or eat at a losmen.) You may be able to hire a horse,

with a guide, some of the way for around 30,000Rp per day – ask your hotel in Mamasa or around Bittuang. The area is chilly at night, so come prepared.

The usual route is:

Day 1 – Mamasa to Timbaan (26km) This start is mostly uphill. Take a break at Rakasasan (two to three hours), lunch at Lombonan (four hours) and stop overnight at Timbaan, where there are two *losmen*.

Day 2 – Timbaan to Paku (24km) At Bau, there is usually somewhere to eat. At Ponding, you can stay at **Homestay Papasado**; or continue to Paku, and stay at **Mountain Homestay**.

Day 3 – Paku to Bittuang (16km) It's easier to walk (three hours), but there may be some public transport from Paku to Bittuang. There are three simple *losmen* at Bittuang, but you're better off catching a bemo or Kijang to Makale, from where there are Kijangs to Rantepao.

Mamasa to Mamuju

The hike to Mamuju takes from three days to one week, depending on your luck with transport. Salarindu, the halfway mark, can be reached by irregular public transport (or by chartered transport) from Mamasa, but the trail from there to Mamuju is rough and only accessible on foot. You'll need a guide, plus some fluency in Indonesian, to find your way.

South-East Sulawesi

South-East Sulawesi rewards the handful of travellers prepared to venture a little off the beaten track with some stunning scenery and hospitable cultures, and surprisingly good transport links. The sparsely populated province, including the Tukangbesi islands off the southern tip, has an area of 38,000 sq km, and is inhabited by diverse ethnic groups.

History

Some of the earliest records of life in South-East Sulawesi are depicted in prehistoric paintings on the walls of caves near Raha. The red ochre paintings include hunting scenes, boats and warriors on horseback.

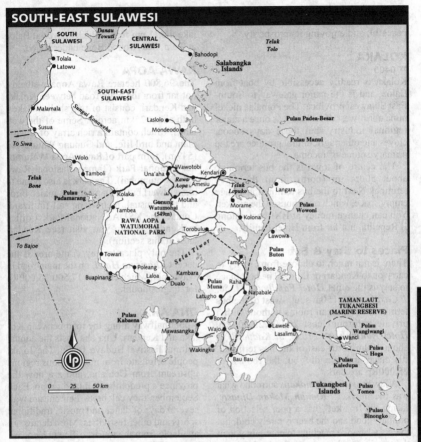

SOUTH-EAST SULAWESI

SULAWESI

The region's most powerful pre-colonial kingdom was Buton, based at Wolio, near Bau Bau. Its control and influence over other regional states was supported by the Dutch colonialists. Buton came under direct Dutch rule after the fall of Makassar in 1669, and was granted limited autonomy in 1906.

Other local trading centres maintained a low profile, probably for reasons of self-defence. Kendari was one of the busiest, but the island of Bungkutoko at the mouth of

Kendari harbour hid the town so well it was not really 'discovered' by the Dutch until 1830. At that time, the inland regions were dominated by the Tolaki people, traders of agricultural and forest produce who originated in the valley upstream from Una'aha and gradually forced other inland tribes southwards.

The civil strife of the 1950s and 1960s was a time of extreme hardship for the people of the province. Farms and villages were plundered by rebel and government forces alike, decimating the region's agricultural sector. Now, South-East Sulawesi is peaceful, and enjoying its prosperity.

KOLAKA
☎ 0405

Kolaka is readily accessible by boat from Bajoe, and is the major gateway to South-East Sulawesi province. The Pomalaa nickel mine north-west of Kolaka was once a major regional industry, but these days cocoa, cloves and other agricultural produce are the primary source of income.

The centre of town is the bus terminal, about 500m up (north) from the ferry terminal. Next to the bus terminal is a huge empty space, which once housed the market. You can change money at BNI bank, along Jl Repelita, not far from Hotel Family.

Places to Stay & Eat
There is not much to choose from, so try to carry on to Kendari or Bajoe. The best place to stay is the quiet *Hotel Family (☎ 21350, Jl Cakalang 6)*, 150m south-west of the bus terminal. Airy, clean rooms without/with a private bathroom cost 20,000/25,000Rp. *Hotel Rahmah (☎ 21036, Jl Kadue 8)* is about 100m north-east of the bus terminal. It's clean and friendly, but the rooms for 25,000Rp are dark.

A few basic *rumah makans* surround what was the 'market'. *Rumah Makan Dinasty*, facing the 'market', has a poor selection of ordinary food and the beer is rarely cold, but there's a karaoke machine to entertain you in the evening while you wait for the ferry.

Getting There & Away
Bus, Bemo & Kijang All day and night, plenty of buses, bemos and Kijangs travel between Kolaka and Kendari (10,000Rp, six hours). You may be able to find a spare seat on a bus going directly to Kendari, or Ujung Pandang, while on the ferry.

Boat Three ferries travel overnight from Kolaka to Bajoe (eight hours), the main port on the east coast of the south-west peninsula. The ferries leave at 5, 8 and 11 pm, and are

all timed for a convenient arrival in Ujung Pandang. If you want to stopover at Bone, take the 11 pm ferry, which arrives at Bajoe at 7 am. See Around Bone under Bajoe.

RAWA AOPA
The 96,800 hectare Rawa Aopa wetlands, not far from the main road between Kolaka and Kendari, consist of two shallow lakes, both about 25km across. Some of the wetlands, which contain a rich array of aquatic plant and bird life, and Gunung Watumohai (549m), form part of **Rawa Aopa Watumohai National Park** (Taman Nasional Rawa Aopa Watumohai). The park is also home to *anoa* (dwarf buffalo), macaque, maleo birds and the unusual, metre-long sail-fin lizard. Contact the KSDA (National Parks) office in Kendari before you visit (see Kendari later in this section).

The only place to stay in the area is the decent *Kharisma Hotel*, on the main road in Wawotobi, which charges 17,500/25,000Rp for singles/doubles.

UNA'AHA
About halfway along the road between Kolaka and Kendari, Una'aha hosts the annual cultural Festival Budaya Tolaki. The Tolaki people originate from mountainous regions upstream from Una'aha, and are now the province's predominant inland group. Each September, they celebrate their culture with several days of dance and music, traditional sports and other festivities. More details are available from the tourist office in Kendari.

KENDARI
☎ 0401

The capital of South-East Sulawesi province has long been the key port for trade between the inland Tolaki people and seafaring Bugis and Bajau traders. Little was known of Kendari's history before its 'discovery' by a Dutch explorer in 1830, and its isolation continues to cushion it from dramatic developments elsewhere. Kendari is a bustling town with little to recommend it, except the range of decent accommodation that makes it a good place to break up a journey.

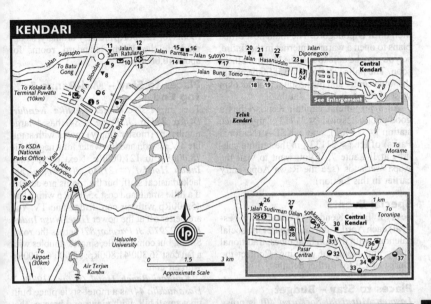

KENDARI

PLACES TO STAY
9 Hotel Duta
12 Hotel Memilwin
14 Hotel Nusa Indah II
15 Nusa Indah Hotel I
16 Hotel Kartika Kendari
20 Hotel Sultra
21 Kendari Beach Hotel
23 Hotel Cendrawasih
30 Losmen Murni
31 Hotel Nirwana

PLACES TO EAT
8 Rumah Makan Marannu
11 Dhiba Bakery & Camel Cafe
17 Rumah Makan Ayam Goreng Raja; Toko Sinar Jaya
18 Restoran Karina
19 Night Warungs
22 Rumah Makan Gemini
27 Rumah Makan Ayam Goreng Sulawesi

OTHER
1 PLN Gembol (Handicrafts)
2 Dekranasda (Handicrafts)
3 Terminal Pasar Baru
4 Al-Kautbar Mosque
5 Tourist Office
6 Terminal Mandonga; Pasar
7 Cinemas
10 Main Post Office
13 Hospital
24 Bank Danamon; Vina Cafe
25 BNI Bank
26 Police Station
28 Telkom Office; Bus Agency for Ujung Pandang & Bone
29 Merpati Office
32 Central Bemo Terminal
33 Pelni Dock
34 Kendari Theatre
35 Superjet Office
36 Pelni Office
37 Dock (Slow Boats)

Orientation

Kendari begins in a tangle of lanes in the old *kota* (city) precinct adjacent to the original port in the east, and becomes progressively more modern as each era has tacked another suburb to the west. The one very, *very* long main road has most of the facilities, except the bus terminals. The main road's many names are confusing, especially at the kota end where 'Jl Sudirman' and 'Jl Soekarno' are used interchangeably.

Information

The tourist office (☎ 26634) is rarely worth visiting; it's inconvenient (you'll need to take a taxi) and the staff are unhelpful. The best place to change money is Bank Dana-mon on Jl Diponegoro. The main post office plans to open a warung Internet in the future, so you may be able to surf the Net from there soon. The police station is on Jl Sudirman in the town centre and the hospital is about 6km west of town on Jl Sam Ratulagi.

As a provincial capital, Kendari has a good public hospital (☎ 21773); large police station (☎ 21461); and a KSDA (National Parks) office (☎ 21133), in the remote sub-urbs at Jl Laute 7, if you want to visit the Aopa wetlands (see the Rawa Aopa entry earlier in this section).

Special Events

Festival Teluk Kendari (Kendari Bay Fes-tival) each April is the highlight of the social calendar, with dragon boat races, traditional music and plenty of partying. Contact the tourist office for further details.

Places to Stay – Budget

Losmen Murni (Jl Soekarno 40) is noisy and basic, but dirt cheap for 10,000Rp per room. Opposite, and just off the main road (so there's some chance of sleep), is *Hotel Nirwana (☎ 21647, Jl Soekarno 51)*. The rooms also cost 10,000Rp, but it's a little more congenial than Losmen Murni.

Just off the road, the quietish *Hotel Cen-drawasih (☎ 21932, Jl Diponegoro 42)* is one of the best places to stay and the service is very good. The rooms with a fan cost 33,000Rp and offer pleasant views, and wel-come breezes can be enjoyed from the pri-vate balconies. The rooms with air-con for 55,000Rp are not as good. *Hotel Memilwin (☎ 21924, Jl Sam Ratulangi)* has small rooms, and it's a little noisy, but the place is clean and central. Rooms with a fan cost 33,000Rp; 55,000Rp with air-con and satellite TV.

In a good location, but also along the noisy main road, is *Hotel Sultra (☎ 21484, Jl Hasanuddin 91)*. Large singles/doubles with a fan cost 30,250/38,000Rp; 41,250/49,500Rp with air-con. The service is good, and it's opposite the warungs along the es-planade. *Hotel Duta (☎ 21053, Jl A Silondae)* is easy to miss, but central and reasonably quiet, up a small embankment. The economy rooms for 22,500Rp are very ordinary, so up-grade to the decent 'standard' rooms for about 40,000Rp.

Places to Stay – Mid-Range & Top End

The impressive *Hotel Kartika Kendari (☎/fax 25116, Jl Parman 84)* has a large number of (mostly empty) rooms with satel-lite TV, air-con and hot water for a negotiable 73,000Rp to 121,000Rp. Next door, *Nusa Indah Hotel I (☎ 21146, Jl Parman)* has lackadaisical staff, but the rooms are decent, if a little small, and cost 35,000Rp with a fan; 45,000Rp with air-con, fridge and TV. You are better off at the newer *Hotel Nusa Indah II (☎ 22970, Jl Parman 87)* across the road. Small, but comfortable, singles/doubles with a fan cost 36,300/41,800Rp; 55,000/61,500Rp with air-con.

Kendari Beach Hotel (☎/fax 21988, Jl Hasanuddin 44) is a motel-style place built up a small hill, with views and breezes that can be enjoyed from the private balconies. All rooms have air-con and satellite TV, and start from a very reasonable 71,500Rp. The better rooms cost 82,500Rp to 104,500Rp and have hot water and the best views.

Places to Eat

The *night warungs* along the esplanade are a popular hang-out in the evening. They offer cheap Indonesian food, and excellent (free) views of the bay. The warungs about 200m further west specialise in tasty baked fish. Nearby, *Restoran Karina* is not as expensive as the setting suggests: seafood costs about 15,000Rp; Chinese and Indonesian meals, 12,000Rp; and large beers, 9000Rp.

Restaurants serving fried chicken, rather than seafood, are scattered at various inter-vals along the main road, including *Rumah Makan Ayam Goreng Sulawesi*, *Rumah Makan Ayam Goreng Raja* and *Rumah Makan Gemini*. Three quiet (karaoke-free!) cafes are *Vina Cafe*, in the hotel of the same name, and the trendy and modern *Dhiba Bakery* and *Camel Cafe*, both in the same building.

Rumah Makan Marannu (Jl A Silondae) serves decent Chinese food (for under 10,000Rp), but the seafood is expensive. The restaurant at *Kendari Beach Hotel* overlooks the bay, and offers breezes and an extensive menu at surprisingly competitive prices. Seafood costs about 9000Rp; a large cold beer, the same price. There are several well-stocked supermarkets along the main road, including *Toko Sinar Jaya*.

Entertainment
A drink watching the sunset at Restoran Karina, or a nearby warung, is pleasant, and there are plenty of *karaoke bars* and *nightclubs* along the main road. The *Kendari Theatre* shows sleazy movies. More comfortable and enjoyable is the modern *cinema complex*, not far from the tourist office.

Shopping
The National Handicrafts Council, Dekranasda, sells handicrafts from around the province, including ornate Kendari silver work, woven cloth and beautiful baskets. Nearby, PLN Gembol village is a line of workshops and showrooms that fashion outrageously bulky tables, clocks and other odds and ends from teak roots. Take a pete-pete to the corner of Jl Ahmad Yani and Jl Haryono and then walk; or take a taxi.

Getting There & Away
Air Merpati flies between Kendari and Ujung Pandang daily for 318,200Rp. The Merpati office (☎ 22242) is along the main road, just in front of the market. Don't forget to ask the staff about transport to the remote airport (see Getting Around later in this section).

Bus, Bemo & Kijang The main terminal is at Puwatu, about 10km west of Hotel Duta. From there, plenty of buses, bemos and Kijangs go to Kolaka. You can take pot luck and jump on a bus to Ujung Pandang or Bone at Terminal Puwatu, but it's more convenient to book a ticket (and board the bus) at one of the agencies along the main road – several are located about 200m east of the Telkom office. Most buses leave Kendari at about 1 pm to

link with the 8 pm ferry (which means arriving in Bajoe/Bone at about 4 am). The fare to Bone/Ujung Pandang is 35,000/45,000Rp, and includes the ferry trip in 'deck' class but you can upgrade to 'economy' class, or rent a cabin, once on board.

Southbound minibuses leave from Terminal Pasar Baru at about 6 am and 11 am to the port of Torobulu (three hours), in time to link with the 10 am or 3 pm ferry to Tampo on Pulau Muna (three hours), from where bemos leave for Raha (one hour). The fast boat is a far better option to Raha.

Boat Kendari is not well serviced by Pelni, but is relatively close to the major port of Bau Bau. Every two weeks, the *Tilongkabila* heads up the coast to Kolonodale (52,500/144,500Rp for economy/1st class), and on to Bitung for Manado (109,500/303,500Rp); and to Raha (20,000/54,500Rp) and Ujung Pandang The Pelni office (☎ 21 915) is adjacent to a church on top of a hill, just up from a roundabout near the Kendari Theatre.

The 'super-jet' *kapal cepat* (fast boat) leaves the Pelni dock at Kendari at about 7 am and noon daily for Raha (20,000Rp, 3½ hours) and Bau Bau (28,500Rp, five hours). You can buy your ticket directly from the super-jet office (☎ 24514), just around from the Pelni dock at Jl Sukowati 8, or from agencies just outside the Pelni dock.

A slow, noisy, old *kapal kayu* (wooden boat) leaves Kendari at 1 pm daily for Raha (eight hours) for 13,000/19,000/21,000Rp for deck/room/VIP class; and Bau Bau (12 hours) for 20,000/28,000/31,000Rp. It leaves from the special dock (indicated on the map); the ticket office is opposite the dock entrance. This boat is very slow and very uncomfortable, so take the fast boat.

Getting Around
To/From the Airport Contact the Merpati office about transport to the airport (30km south-west of Kendari). From the airport, you'll have to jump on anything available, but make sure it's a shared vehicle; anything chartered will be very expensive.

Public Transport Kendari is *very* spread out. For short distances, take a becak; for anything along the main road, take a pete-pete; to anywhere else, catch an air-conditioned taxi. Pete-petes link the kota end of town with Mandonga terminal and market every few seconds, and many continue on to Terminal Puwatu.

AROUND KENDARI
Air Terjun Kambu
The closest attraction to Kendari is the Kambu waterfalls at the foot of Gunung Kambu, 3km upstream from the campus at Haluoleo University. Walk from the university, or charter a pete-pete.

Air Terjun Morame
More impressive is the multi-tiered Morame waterfalls, 100m of tumbling water set amid ebony, teak and banyan trees on the Sungai Kali Osena, 65km south of Kendari. There is a deep pool at the base of the falls, which is excellent for **swimming**.

Take a bus from Terminal Pasar Baru (one hour), or charter a boat (about two hours) from near the Pelni dock in Kendari. If you have a boat, arrange a slight detour to Teluk Lapuko bay, a great spot for **swimming** and **snorkelling**, with white sand beaches and clear water.

Pulau Hari
This tiny island, 18km off the Kendari coast, is a **nature reserve** with white sand beaches, and opportunities for **snorkelling** and **walking**. Bokori Diving Centre (☎ 0401-26634, fax 27435), based at the tourist office in Kendari, runs diving and snorkelling trips to Hari, and other nearby islands. Alternatively, get a group together, and charter a boat from near the Pelni dock in Kendari. It should cost about 70,000Rp for the day, but bring your own snorkelling gear.

RAHA
☎ 0403
Raha, the main settlement on Pulau Muna, is a quiet backwater, about halfway between Kendari and Bau Bau. Raha is famous for its horse fighting, cave paintings and lagoons – see Around Raha later in this chapter.

Raha suffers from electricity shortages, and restrictions for about six hours a day (at varying times). You can change money at Bank Danamon and BNI bank, but don't, ahem, 'count' on it.

Places to Stay
Hotel Raudhah (☎ 21088, Jl Yos Sudarso 25) is a bit dark, but good value for 20,000/35,000/50,000Rp for singles/doubles/triples. *Hotel Alia* (☎ 21218, Jl Sudirman 5) is quiet, breezy and close to the causeway. Rooms cost 20,000Rp to 65,000Rp. *Hotel Ilham* (☎ 21070, Jl Jati 16) is friendly and pleasant. The rooms with a fan and bathroom for 25,000Rp are nothing special, but the air-con rooms for 50,000Rp are nice.

The new *Hotel Permata Sari* (☎ 21164, Jl A Yani 67) is conveniently opposite the bus/

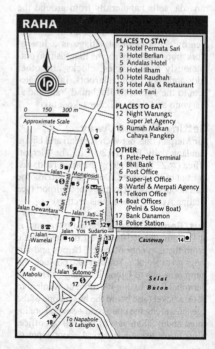

RAHA

0   150   300 m
Approximate Scale

PLACES TO STAY
2 Hotel Permata Sari
3 Hotel Berlian
5 Andalas Hotel
9 Hotel Ilham
10 Hotel Raudhah
13 Hotel Alia & Restaurant
16 Hotel Tani

PLACES TO EAT
12 Night Warungs;
   Super Jet Agency
15 Rumah Makan
   Cahaya Pangkep

OTHER
1 Pete-Pete Terminal
4 BNI Bank
6 Post Office
7 Super-jet Office
8 Wartel & Merpati Agency
11 Telkom Office
14 Boat Offices
   (Pelni & Slow Boat)
17 Bank Danamon
18 Police Station

Jalan Monginsidi
Jalan Sukawati
Jalan Dewantara
Jalan Jati
Jalan A Yani
Jalan Yos Sudarso
Jalan Wamelai
Jalan Sudirman
Jalan Sutomo
To Mabolu

Causeway

Selat Buton

To Napabole & Latugho

bemo terminal, but is still reasonably quiet. Large, clean singles/doubles cost 17,500/30,000Rp. As a last resort try: **Hotel Tani** (☎ 21168, Jl Sutomo 18); **Hotel Berlian** (☎ 22530, Jl Sukowati 77); and **Andalas Hotel** (☎ 21076, Jl Sukowati 62).

Places to Eat

There are a handful of unexciting *night warungs* at the start of the causeway, and several unappealing *rumah makans* serving coto makassar near the pete-pete terminal.

The best option in Raha is **Rumah Makan Cahaya Pangkep** (Jl Sudirman), where excellent baked fish, rice and soup costs 6000Rp. *Hotel Alia* has a small restaurant which is open to the public.

Getting There & Away

Bemo Pete-petes to Tampo depart from the terminal in Raha in time to meet the two ferries for Torobulu, from where minibuses go to Kendari. Minibuses also go to the very bottom of Pulau Muna for the boat to Bau Bau. Current information about bus/ferry schedules is available at the information office at the front of the terminal in Raha. For Kendari and Raha, the 'super-jet' boat is far better.

Boat Raha is the only stop between Kendari and Bau Bau on both the fast 'super-jet' and the slow wooden boat. For the 'super-jet', buy tickets the day before your departure at the agency, in the unsigned shack at the start of the causeway, or from the main office (☎ 22018) along Jl Dewantara. These boats are scheduled to leave for Kendari at about 9 am and 3 pm; and for Bau Bau at about 10.30 am and 3.30 pm. Ask around the office at the end of the causeway for the current schedule of the daily wooden boat (see Getting There & Away under Kendari earlier). For both services, have your elbows ready for the onboard scramble to claim a seat.

Every two weeks, the Pelni liner *Tilongkabila* stops at Raha on its way up (via Kendari) and down (via Bau Bau) the east coast of Sulawesi. The Pelni office is at the end of the causeway.

Getting Around

Raha is easy enough to walk around, but if you're going to the bus/bemo terminal, or the end of the causeway with heavy luggage, take a becak. Ojeks are also a handy way to get around, and to visit the places listed under Around Raha.

AROUND RAHA
Napabale

Raha's main attraction is Napabale, a pretty lagoon at the foot of a hill. The lagoon is linked to the sea via a natural tunnel, so you can paddle through when the tide is low. It is a great area for hiking and swimming, and you can hire boats to take you around the lake. Napabale is a scenic ride (15km) from Raha. You can reach it by ojek, or by regular pete-pete to Lohia village, from where the lagoon is another 1.5km walk, at the end of the road. There are usually a couple of *food stalls*, and often a few more on Sunday, when it's often crowded. On other days, you may have this gorgeous place to yourself.

Pantai Melerua

Not far from Napabale, Melerua beach has superb scenery and unusual rock formations. Although you can swim and snorkel (bring your own gear), there isn't a sandy beach as such. Take the regular pete-pete towards Lohia and ask the driver to drop you off at the unmarked turn-off. From here walk (or go by ojek) about 7km until the very rough path finishes.

Gua Mabolu

The solid 10km walk through plantations, and pretty walled gardens, from Mabolu village is probably more interesting than the caves themselves. The caretakers can take you to a selection of the best caves, starting with **Liang Metanduno**, which includes paintings of a horse with two riders, headless warriors and some boats. There used to be coffins and bones in some of the caves, until scientific papers describing them in 1983-84 prompted a team of archaeologists from Jakarta to plunder the site.

SULAWESI

From Raha, catch (or charter) a pete-pete to Mabolu, and ask the driver to drop you off at the path to the caves. The paths are not clear, so you'll need someone from Mabolu to show you the way to the caves, and to the caretakers who live nearby.

Horse Fighting

Festival Danau Napabale (Napabale Lake Festival) is held each June at the village of **Latugho**, 30km inland from Raha. The festival features horse fighting, as well as the more gentle spectacle of kite flying. Horse fighting is a Muna tradition with a robust following – it's not for the tenderhearted.

BAU BAU
☎ 0402

Bau Bau is the main settlement on Pulau Buton, and is strategically situated at the southern entrance of Selat Buton (Buton Strait). It was once a fort, the seat of the former sultanate of Wolio, which reigned over the scattered settlements on Buton and the neighbouring islands of Muna, Kabaena, Wowini and Tukangbesi. Bau Bau is a pleasant town, with a few things to see, and the regular Pelni connections make it an interesting way of entering or leaving Sulawesi.

Orientation & Information

Most of what you need is along Jl Kartini, which starts to the right (west) as you leave the port and is about two blocks from the sea and the esplanade, Jl Yos Sudarso. As you head left (east) from the port, the offices for the tourist department (☎ 23588), Telkom and Pelni are within 1.5km. BNI bank, opposite the pete-pete terminal, just off the western end of Jl Kartini, will change money. There are a few taxis, ojeks and, of course, hundreds of becaks.

Things to See

About 3km up the steep hill from town (charter a taxi or ojek) is the fascinating **Benteng Keraton**, an abandoned 16th century Wolio fort, which also offers superb views. Another 2km further from town are some wonderfully restored traditional houses and the

Pusat Kebudayaan Wolio, a cultural centre and museum in a restored palace. The centre is also the focal point of Bau Bau's Festival Kraton each September, a celebration of the craft, culture and former glory of the Wolio kingdom. Also worth visiting is the **Pantai Nirwana**, 11km south of Bau Bau.

Places to Stay

The cheapest is *Losmen Hanny* (☎ 21403, Jl Cut Nyak Dien 3) with basic rooms for 30,000Rp; it's about 500m east of the port. Far better for this price is *Wolio Homestay* (☎/fax 21189, Jl Betoambari 92), run by friendly folk who only charge 20,000Rp a double – take a taxi.

Hotel Debora (☎ 21203, Jl Kartini 15) is convenient, friendly and clean, and has a range of rooms from 33,000Rp to 66,000Rp with air-con and TV. Opposite, *Hotel Lilyana* (☎ 21197, Jl Kartini 18) is pleasant and quietish, but not as good with rooms for 33,000Rp to 55,000Rp.

One of the most spectacular places in southern Sulawesi is the *Highland Resort (House on the Hill,* ☎ 21189, fax 21200, email trvlindo@upg.mega.net.id). Built on top of a hill, 7km from town (take a taxi), it offers outstanding views of the sea and mountains. The handful of comfortable rooms, with a shared bathroom, cost 45,000Rp, plus 20,000Rp for meals (almost mandatory, because there's nowhere nearby to eat).

Hotel Mira (☎ 22911, Jl Mawar 7) is one of a few places along a non-existent 'beach', a short taxi ride from town. It has a range of new, modern rooms for 35,000Rp with a bathroom but no fan; and 50,000Rp to 75,000Rp with air-con.

Places to Eat

Night warungs spring up every evening along the esplanade, a few hundred metres west of the port. The best restaurant is *Warung Pangkep*, a large place along the esplanade, which serves outstanding baked fish meals for 5000Rp, and can even rustle up a cold beer for a thirsty traveller. Opposite, *Restaurant Vita* is more upmarket, and not as friendly or cheap. If you're sick of fish, try *Ayam Goreng Silwana* along Jl Kartini, halfway between the port and Hotel Debora.

Getting There & Away

Bus & Bemo From the terminal, about 2.5km west of the port, next to the bridge, regular pete-petes go to regional villages, including Lasalimu, for the ferry to the Tukangbesi islands (see the Tukangbesi Islands later in this section).

Boat The fast 'super-jet' boat takes 1½ hours to Raha (14,500Rp) and five hours to Kendari (28,500Rp), and leaves at 7 am daily (sometimes another leaves around noon). Demand can often be greater than supply, so book ahead (from 5 pm the day before) at the office (☎ 22497), which is opposite Warung Pangkep, about 500m west of the port.

A slow, wooden boat (see Getting There & Away under Kendari earlier in this chapter) leaves most days from a jetty not far from BNI bank for Raha and Kendari. You can also take the 8 am ferry from the same jetty to Pulau Muna, and then a bus to Raha – but the fast boat is better.

Every two weeks, the Pelni liners *Bukit Siguntang*, *Ciremai*, *Lambelu*, *Rinjani* and *Tatamailau* (every four weeks) link Bau Bau with Ujung Pandang for 41,300/139,500Rp (economy/1st class), and most also go to Ambon, southern Maluku and/or Irian Jaya. Every two weeks, the *Tilongkabila* goes up and down the east coast of Sulawesi, stopping off at Raha, Kendari and Bitung (for Manado), among other places.

TUKANGBESI ISLANDS

This string of remote islands off the far southeast coast are difficult to reach, but offer superb diving, isolated beaches and stunning landscapes. Most of the islands are now part of **Taman Laut Tukangbesi** marine reserve.

A few intrepid travellers are heading to Pulau Hoga. There is a friendly *homestay* (satellite ☎ 00872-761-480-862) for 35,000Rp per person per day, including meals. The homestay also arranges snorkelling and diving trips. Other simple homestays are being built on the island. Check the availability of accommodation, and travel arrangements, with Highland Resort or Wolio Homestay (see Places to Stay under Bau Bau earlier in this chapter), or PT Wolio Tours & Travel (☎/fax 0402-21200), Jl Betoambari 92, Bau Bau, before you head to Hoga.

The British-based NGO (nongovernment organisation), Operation Wallacea (email op_wal_hoga@compuserve.com) also organises 'volunteer' programs for those interested in marine conservation. The public are welcome, but trips must be pre-booked and are not cheap.

Getting to Hoga is not easy. From Bau Bau, catch (or charter) a pete-pete to Lasalimu, where you'll probably have to stay the night at the town's only *losmen*. Early the next morning, take the daily ferry to Wanci on Pulau Wangiwangi, and wait around for another boat (or charter one) to Hoga.

Central Sulawesi

Most of Central Sulawesi's population live in its coastal towns, so the province's 63,000 sq km hinterland is sparsely populated. But it's these mountains, lakes and valleys that attract most visitors. While the star attractions are the megaliths around Bada and Besoa valleys, the rugged landscape and hospitable highland cultures throughout Central Sulawesi make a detour worthwhile. Few other places in Indonesia can boast such an interesting and accessible juxtaposition of nature, culture, history and landscapes.

History

Undated remains from a cave near Kolonodale indicate a long history of human settlement. The most spectacular prehistoric remains are the Bronze Age megaliths found throughout Central Sulawesi, but the meaning and creators of these statues, cylindrical vats, urns and mortars are unknown. The highest concentration is along Sungai Lariang in the Bada Valley, and there are others throughout the region and down to Tana Toraja.

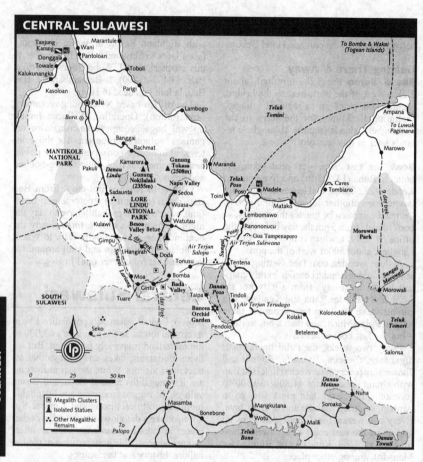

CENTRAL SULAWESI

Legend:
- ■ Megalith Clusters
- ▲ Isolated Statues
- ∴ Other Megalithic Remains

0   25   50 km

There was no single dominant power in the area. The Portuguese built a fort at Parigi at the eastern end of Teluk Tomini in 1555, and were followed by two Muslim Minangkabau traders who settled in Palu and Parigi in 1602 to trade gold and propagate their faith.

Ternate (northern Maluku), competing with Gowa for dominance of Sulawesi, had extended its influence over Palu and Toli-Toli by 1680. Ternate held some sway over the Banggai islands; and at one time a royal dynasty of Javanese origin ruled there, subject to the sultanate of Ternate. After the Dutch took over the Banggais in 1908, indigenous rulers were set up to run the islands.

The Dutch settled at Gorontalo in the late 17th century, and at Parigi in 1730. Along with Makassar, these were the principle Dutch settlements of the time. (The rest of the island was controlled by local tribes.) In the late 1780s, the Dutch attempted to take Toli-Toli, because of its fine harbour, but without success.

DANAU POSO

Indonesia's third largest lake, Danau Poso, covers an area of 32,300 hectares and reaches an average depth of 450m. The lake is 32km long, 16km wide and 600m above sea level – so the evenings are pleasantly cool without being too cold.

Danau Poso is the main reason to stop at Tentena and/or Pendolo (see their separate entries further in this section). You can hike in the countryside around the lake, or take boat trips, but boats are surprisingly hard to arrange in either town. There's a handful of narrow beaches around Tentena, but these disappear when the tide is high. The beaches near the jetty at Pendolo are better.

Things to See

The lake is also famous for its wild orchids, especially in **Taman Angerek Bancea** (Orhid Park). It is accessible on foot (about 11km), by chartered vehicle, or by irregular bemo to Taipa from Pendolo.

Air Terjun Salopa, near Tentena, is a crystal clear series of pools, cascades and falls set amid unspoilt forest. A path to the left of the falls leads to upper levels, and some pristine swimming holes. Mornings are the best time for photos. Take a bemo heading west across the bridge from Tentena, ask to be dropped off at the turn-off and walk 3km through rice fields. A chartered bemo from Tentena will cost around 20,000Rp return.

Air Terjun Sulewana is a sunken gully of steaming white water, 10km from Tentena. Take any bemo heading north from Tentena and walk 3km west from the sign (on the left as you head north).

If requested, the daily Tentena-Pendolo boat will stop at Tindoli, along the south-east shore of the lake, near **Air Terjun Terudago**.

Special Events

The undisputed highlight of Central Sulawesi's social calendar is the annual Festival Danau Poso in late August. Villagers from far afield gather for a colourful celebration of culture, with dancing, song, traditional sports and other activities. More details are available from the tourist offices in Poso and Palu.

PENDOLO

Pendolo is a sleepy village on the southern shore of Danau Poso. It is a charming spot, but has far fewer facilities than Tentena.

Places to Stay & Eat

All hotels are huddled together in two separate areas.

Only metres from the boat landing, about a kilometre east of the village centre is **Pendolo Cottages**. This rustic place overlooks mangroves, but is still pleasant, and gets rave reviews from readers. Rooms cost 17,500Rp to 20,000Rp, but the bungalows for 15,000/25,000Rp for singles/doubles are nicer – and a hearty breakfast is included. About 50m to the east, **Mulia Hotel** has a range of modern and comfortable rooms from 69,000Rp to 92,000Rp. It is used by tour groups, and has a surprisingly elegant **restaurant** with reasonable prices.

Along Jl Pelabuhan, which runs from the bus stop to the lake, there are a handful of unexciting options – the best are **Homestay Petezza** and **Penginapan Rizqun**, with rooms for about 10,000Rp per person.

At the end of this road, overlooking the lake, are two excellent places. The modern **Homestay Masamba** has rooms from 20,000Rp, and an old jetty for sunbaking. Over the road, **Losmen Victory** has rooms for about 20,000/25,000Rp. Both have excellent **restaurants** overlooking the lake.

Getting There & Away

Bus & Bemo Pendolo is on the main Palopo-Poso highway, but there is no bus terminal as such. Getting onward transport is normally a matter of hailing down a passing bus from the junction of the main road and Jl Pelabuhan – but most buses are full. Between Pendolo and Tentena, take the boat; if heading further north, take the boat to Tentena, from where there are regular buses to Poso and Palu.

From Rantepao, you could charter a bemo for about 200,000Rp. Split among a few people, this is not unreasonable – it cuts hours off the journey, and you can see the pretty Wotu to Pendolo stretch in daylight hours.

SULAWESI

Boat Most people take the Pendolo-Tentena boat (10,000Rp, three hours) to enjoy the views and fresh air – but it's no fun in rough weather (and the roof leaks when it rains). The boat leaves Pendolo daily at 8 am from the jetty, near the Mulia Hotel, and is more reliable and scenic than the bus.

TENTENA
☎ 0458

Tentena, at the northern end of the lake, is larger and prettier than Pendolo, and is surrounded by clove-covered hills (from June to November the cloves are particularly aromatic). Tentena has excellent accommodation and a varied cuisine, but lacks Pendolo's fine beaches.

Travel Agencies

Organised treks to Lore Lindu and Taman Morowali parks can be arranged in Tentena (also see the separate sections for Lore Lindu and Morowali later in this chapter). Most hotels double as local tour operators and trekking agencies: Hotel Sinar Abadi and Pondok Wisata Ue Datu are reliable sources of information; PT Wisata Gautama Putra Indah (☎ 21356), near Natural Cottages, is somewhere to meet guides and mull over trekking itineraries; and Hotel Victori has a map of Morowali on the wall, heaps of trekking advice about Lore Lindu and current information about visiting the Togean islands.

Things to See & Do

The pretty, covered 210m bridge marks where the lake ends and the outflowing Sungai Poso begins its journey to the coast. V-shaped **eel traps** north of the bridge snare the two-metre monsters Tentena is famous for. Live specimens are available for inspection and sale at warungs in the centre of town. Just off the road to Kolonodale, **Gua Latea** contains bones and skulls from burials long ago. Closer to town is **Gua Pamona**. A lookout nearby offers wonderful views.

Places to Stay

Hotel Victori (☎ 21392, *Jl Diponegoro 18*) is quiet and popular. It offers a book exchange, advice and guides for local tours and trekking, and a convivial outdoor sitting area.

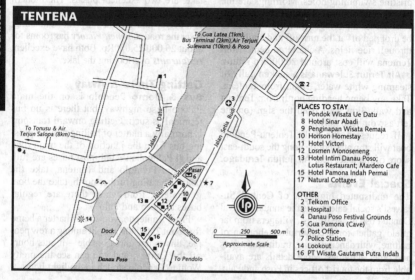

TENTENA

To Gua Latea (1km),
Bus Terminal (2km), Air Terjun
Sulewana (10km) & Poso

To Tonusu & Air
Terjun Salopa (8km)

To Pendolo

Danau Poso

PLACES TO STAY
1 Pondok Wisata Ue Datu
8 Hotel Sinar Abadi
9 Penginapan Wisata Remaja
10 Horison Homestay
11 Hotel Victori
12 Losmen Monoseneng
13 Hotel Intim Danau Poso;
   Lotus Restaurant; Mardero Cafe
15 Hotel Pamona Indah Permai
17 Natural Cottages

OTHER
2 Telkom Office
3 Hospital
4 Danau Poso Festival Grounds
5 Gua Pamona (Cave)
6 Post Office
7 Police Station
14 Lookout
16 PT Wisata Gautama Putra Indah

0   250   500 m
Approximate Scale

Pasar

SULAWESI

Rooms start at 22,500Rp, but the rooms for 70,000Rp, without air-con and hot water, are not great value.

The most charming place is *Pondok Wisata Ue Datu* (☎ 21322, fax 21212, Jl Ue Datu 93). Although it's a short walk from the town centre, and doesn't have perfect lake views, it boasts a friendly, country village atmosphere. Very well furnished individual cottages cost 35,000Rp; and other rooms cost 15,000Rp to 25,000Rp. Canoe rental, and traditional meals and dancing, can be arranged for guests.

One of the best value places is *Natural Cottages* (☎ 21356, Jl Yos Sudarso 32). It has three huge bungalows, each with two 'futon-style' double beds, hot water and private verandah with lake views. For only 30,000Rp a room, this is worth booking ahead. (Some travellers have complained about thefts from the rooms, however, so be careful.) Right next to the jetty is *Hotel Pamona Indah Permai* (Jl Yos Sudarso 25). The cheaper rooms for 17,500Rp and 30,000Rp are uninspiring, but the rooms for 50,000Rp with satellite TV, fan and hot water are worth a splurge.

Other cheapies, with no lake views or atmosphere, include: *Horison Homestay* (☎ 21 038, Jl Setia Budi 6), with pleasant rooms for 17,500Rp; *Hotel Sinar Abadi* (☎ 21031, Jl Yos Sudarso), with prison-cell-like singles/doubles for 15,000/20,000Rp; *Penginapan Wisata Remaja* (☎ 21301, Jl Yos Sudarso), with unexciting rooms for 15,000Rp; and *Losmen Monoseneng* (☎ 21165, Jl Diponegoro), with dreary cubicles for 17,500Rp.

The upmarket place, *Hotel Intim Danau Poso* (☎ 21345, fax 21488, Jl Yos Sudarso) boasts the best lake views. The economy rooms, with a shared bathroom, cost 15,000Rp to 30,000Rp, and are good value – some even have lake views. The large, modern rooms for 70,000/80,000Rp for the 'mountain'/'sea' views are worth a splurge, and the landlady often offers a 30% discount.

Places to Eat

The local speciality is *sugili* (eel), one to two-metre monsters from the river flowing out of the lake. You could buy a few to take home, but it's a little easier to try it at the hotel restaurants listed in this section (for about 10,000Rp). You can buy tasty *pisang molen* (banana fried in a sweet pastry) at stalls in front of the eastern part of the bridge.

The restaurant at *Hotel Pamona Indah Permai* offers lake views and breezes, and mouthwatering baked fish for a reasonable 10,000Rp, as well as plenty of other dishes. It's the best place to have lunch while waiting for the boat. In the grounds of Hotel Intim Danau Poso, the *Lotus Restaurant*, and the breezy and cheaper *Mardero Cafe*, are decent places for a meal and drink.

Getting There & Away

Bus & Bemo Plenty of buses and bemos make the bumpy run to Poso (2500Rp, two hours) and Palu. They leave from the terminal at the fork of the roads to Pendolo and Poso (2km north of Tentena), and sometimes from the market in central Tentena. For longer distances, eg to Rantepao, you can also book tickets at the bus offices around Tentena. Some buses, eg to Kolonodale, originate in Poso, so you have to hail one down from outside the terminal.

Jeep The availability and price of jeeps to Gintu in Lore Lindu National Park depends on the condition of the road. The price should be around 35,000Rp per person by public jeep; up to 300,000Rp to charter one.

Boat Every day at 3 pm a boat chugs across the lake to Pendolo (10,000Rp, three hours) from Tentena. The schedule allows you to catch a bus/bemo to Tentena from Poso; look around Tentena and have lunch at a lakeside restaurant; and continue to Pendolo on the same day. The boat is more scenic, and reliable, than the bus for travel between Tentena and Pendolo.

POSO

☎ 0452

Poso is the main town, port and terminal for road transport on the northern coast of central

SULAWESI

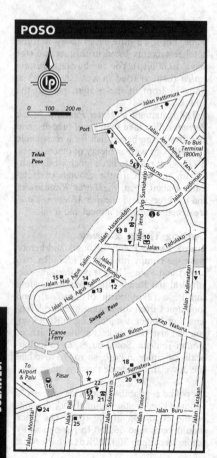

POSO

POSO

PLACES TO STAY
4   Losmen Lalang Jaya; Rumah Makan
    Lalang Jaya
12 Losmen Sulawesi
13 Penginapan Delie
14 Hotel Kalimantan
15 Hotel Bambu Jaya
18 Losmen Aluguro; Aluguro Bus Company
20 Losmen Beringin
25 Hotel Alamanda

PLACES TO EAT
2   Night Warungs
9   Rumah Makan Pelangi
11 Padang Raya
19 Rumah Makan Pemuda; Beringin Theatre
22 Rumah Makan Surabaya

OTHER
1   Pelni Office
3   Boat Offices
5   Bank BNI
6   Tourist Office
7   Telkom Office
8   Bank Dagang Negara
10 Post Office
16 Bemo Terminal
17 Police Station
21 Wartel
23 Bank Danamon
24 Jawa Indah Bus Company

Poso has a friendly tourist office (☎ 21839) at the back of some government buildings, just off Jl Sudirman, but it does little more than hand out a few brochures. For information about Lore Lindu and Morowali parks, you should get information, guides etc from somewhere closer, ie Kolonodale, Tentena or Palu. Poso is the last chance for Togean and Tentena-bound travellers to change money; the best is BNI bank, near the port.

Places to Stay
Losmen Beringin (☎ 21851, Jl Sumatera 22) has bright and comfortable singles/doubles from 8250/13,750Rp to 27,500/33,000Rp with a bathroom and fan. However, the staff and guests are noisy, and there is a small mosque *inside* the hotel. Opposite, the modern *Losmen Aluguro* (☎ 23736, Jl Sumatera 20) is back from the busy road, and has a

Sulawesi. For most travellers, it's a transit point and somewhere to change money. Many folk head for the beaches (see Around Poso later in this chapter) or go to Ampana (for the boat to the Togean islands), but Poso is a pleasant place to break up a journey.

Orientation & Information
The northern part of Poso, around the Hotel Bambu Jaya, is more like a small village – it has limited shops and restaurants. Most facilities are along, or near, Jl Sumatera.

range of decent rooms from 16,500/24,750Rp to 40,000Rp per double with air-con.

Central, quiet and friendly is *Hotel Alamanda* (☎ 21233, Jl Bali 1). Rooms with a fan cost 15,000/22,000Rp; and 35,000Rp to 50,000Rp with air-con. One of the best is *Losmen Lalang Jaya* (☎ 22326, Jl Yos Sudarso), conveniently next to the port. Rooms overlooking the sea are creaky and smallish, but very atmospheric. They cost 35,000Rp with a private bathroom.

In 'northern' Poso, *Hotel Bambu Jaya* (☎ 21570, Jl Haji Agus Salim 101) overlooks the sea, and is breezy, so fans are often not needed. Rooms are clean, quiet and cost 25,000/33,000Rp without/with a fan; and 49,500Rp with air-con. In the same area, there are a few basic, family-run places with singles/doubles for about 7500/15,000Rp: *Penginapan Delie* (☎ 21 805, Jl Haji Agus Salim 12); opposite, *Hotel Kalimantan* (Jl Haji Agus Salim 13); and the slightly better *Losmen Sulawesi* (☎ 21294, Jl Imam Bonjol 3).

Places to Eat
Every afternoon, *night warungs* are set up along the breezy esplanade, Jl Pattimura, east of the port. There are a few unexciting rumah makans along Jl Sumatera, such as *Rumah Makan Pemuda* and *Rumah Makan Surabaya*. The large *Padang Raya* (Jl Kalimantan) has Padang food; and *Rumah Makan Pelangi* on Jl Tadulako is the best in the older part of town.

The best in Poso is the charming *Rumah Makan Lalang Jaya*, part of the losmen of the same name. Built over the sea, it has superb views, reasonably priced food (baked fish from only 3500Rp) and cold drinks.

Getting There & Away
Bus & Bemo From the bus terminal, about 800m north of the post office, there are regular buses to Ampana (8000Rp, five hours), Luwuk (22,500Rp, 20 hours), Kolonodale (15,000Rp, eight hours), Rantepao (35,000Rp, 13 hours), Ujung Pandang (45,000Rp) and Manado (about 55,000Rp). From the terminal, minibuses also regularly go to Tentena

(2500Rp, two hours), and occasional Kijangs go to Kolonodale (14,000Rp).

To Palu (10,000Rp, six hours), most buses leave from offices along Jl Sumatera – the best companies are Jawa Indah and Alugoro. It's worth paying a little more for the 'eksekutif' class buses, because the stretch from Toboli to Palu is *very* rough. From the terminal, next to the market, bemos go to nearby villages and beaches.

Boat The port is easy to reach by bemo, and has a ticket office for boats to the Togean islands, via Ampana. (see Getting There & Away in the Togean Islands section later in this chapter for full details about boats between Poso and the Togean islands.) The Pelni office (☎ 21190) is just outside the port. No Pelni liner comes to Poso, but the office sells tickets for boats from Pantoloan, near Palu.

Getting Around
Poso is a small, tidy town, and you can get to most places on foot. Bemos ply the streets and run flexible routes for 500Rp. Behind the market, a tiny motorised canoe connects 'northern Poso' with its southern half for 150Rp.

AROUND POSO
There are plenty of good places for swimming and snorkelling around Poso. **Pantai Madale** is a snorkelling spot, 5km east of Poso; **Pantai Matako** is a white sand beach, about 20km further east; and **Pantai Toini**, 7km west, has a few *rumah makans* for great seafood. All three can be reached by bemo from the terminal near the market in Poso.

Also, **Tombiano**, 40km east, has huge wet caves occupied by bats; about 47km west, **Maranda** offers a small waterfall and hot water spring for swimming; and **Gua Tampenaporo** is a cave off the main road to Tentena, 22km south. Hop on any bus from the main bus terminal in Poso heading in the relevant direction, and ask the driver to drop you off.

Lembomawo, 4km south of Poso, is renowned for its ebony carving. Take a bemo

SULAWESI

from the terminal at the market in Poso. If you cross two hanging bridges (ask directions) from Lembomawo, a circular walk (about 4km) to **Ranononucu** (which also has some shops selling ebony) will bring you back to the main road to Poso.

LORE LINDU NATIONAL PARK

Covering an area of 250,000 hectares, this large and remote national park has been barely touched by tourism. It's a wonderful area for trekking – the park is rich in exotic plant and animal life, including butterflies larger than a human hand. It's also home to several indigenous tribes, most of whom wear colourful clothing – at least for traditional ceremonies. Other attractions include ancient megalithic relics, mostly in the **Bada**, **Besoa** and **Napu** valleys; remote peaks, some over 2500m; bird watching around **Kamarora**; and the 3150 hectare lake, **Danau Lindu**, with the tiny **Pulau Bola**.

Food is readily available in the villages, but it's

wise to bring other necessities, such as mosquito repellent and sunblock lotion, plus gifts to repay any hospitality. If trekking, you may have to sleep under roofs of covered bridges, which can get cold. Conversely, during the day it can get very hot, so the wildlife will be in hibernation in the forest, and is often very difficult to see.

Visiting the Park

Before you visit the park, you should go to the Balai Taman Nasional Lore Lindu office (☎/fax 0451-23439), Jl Tanjung Manimbayan 144, Palu. At this office, you can ask questions, check out the detailed map on the wall and buy your permit (1500Rp per person per day). You can also buy permits at the small field offices (which have no accommodation) at Kulawi and Wuasa, but if you're coming from Tentena try to buy your permit later.

The main national park office, rangers' station and visitors' centre are about a 1km walk from Kamarora village. Some *guesthouses* are being built near the visitors' centre, and visitors can also stay in the spare *rooms* at the rangers' station.

Guides

For long-distance trekking, a guide is compulsory, and also necessary if you're intent on finding the megaliths, most of which are concentrated around Gintu and Doda. You can organise a guide with most of the travel agencies listed in the Tentena section, or the Masamba, Victory and Petezza hotels in Pendolo, but they mainly want to sell expensive, all-inclusive trips. An organised trek from Tentena, for example, will cost 350,000Rp to 600,000Rp per person (depending on group size) for four to five days, including food, transport and accommodation.

If travelling independently, arrange a guide at the visitors' centre (Kamarora); the two field offices (Kulawi or Wuasa); the tourist office in Poso; or the tourist office or national park office in Palu – see the relevant sections in this chapter for details. If you're coming from Tentena, try in Bomba. Guides will cost about 40,000Rp per day.

The stylised ancient megaliths of the Lore Lindu area are said to be related to ancestor worship.

Trekking

The rangers at Kamarora can show you the start to several short trails, for which you don't need a guide – eg to the 10m **waterfall** about 2km from Kamarora, and the hot water springs at **Kadidia** (3km). To reach the summit of the 2355m **Gunung Nokilalaki** (6km), you'll need a guide.

Other longer hikes (with a guide) include Rachmat to Danau Lindu (six hours one way) and Sadaunta to Danau Lindu (four hours one way). An exciting alternative is to go on horseback; and horses and handlers are available for about 50,000Rp per day at Watutau and Gimpu.

The main trekking trail is Tonusu to Gimpu, via Tuare and Moa, or Doda and Hangirah – or vice versa. Unless you're planning to return to your starting point, send all non-essential gear ahead by car or bus. To start, take a public (or chartered) bemo to Tonusu or Gimpu, and then tackle the trail like this:

Tonusu to Gintu From Tonusu, walk for two days, sleeping under covered bridges. You'll need to carry food and water-purification tablets. You could shorten the hike, and charter a motorbike to Peatua (26km) and walk to Malei bridge (six hours). The next day, hike from Malei to Bomba (18km), and look for the Bomba, Bada and Sepe megaliths. At Bomba, stay at the friendly *Ningsi Homestay*. From there, it's about 10km to Gintu, where you can stay at *Losmen Merry*.

Gintu to Moa It's an easy three hour walk to Tuare, where you can stay with the kepala desa. **Moa** is four hours further on, over two difficult rivers. Moa's kepala desa also takes guests. (There is a path from Gintu to **Doda**, a lesser centre for megalithic remains, where you can stay at the unexciting *Losmen Rindu Alam*.)

Moa to Gimpu It's a strenuous eight hour hike, over two rivers with poor bridges, to Gimpu, where you can stay at the pleasant *Losmen Santo*. From Gimpu, you can hike into the Besoa Valley, or travel back by public (or chartered) transport to Palu.

Getting There & Away

There are three main approaches to the park. Firstly, the trekking trail from Tonusu to Gintu. Secondly, the road from Palu to

Gimpu (100km) – charter a vehicle, or take the twice daily bus (currently 8 am and 2 pm) from Terminal Masomba. The road between Palu and Gimpu is paved, but deteriorates into a muddy track south of Gimpu. Lastly, the paved road (with irregular public transport) from Palu to Betue, via Rachmat, Kamarora, Wuasa and Watutau. South of Betue, the road is terrible.

Roads within the park consist chiefly of mud and holes, and transport is by jeep, horseback and foot.

PALU
☎ 0451

Palu, the capital of Central Sulawesi, only came to prominence during the Japanese occupation in WWII. Situated in a rain shadow for most of the year, it's one of the driest places in Indonesia. Generally days are hot, nights are tolerably cool, and the brilliant sunshine is ideal for swimming, diving and getting sunburnt.

Many travellers don't detour to this part of Sulawesi, unless they're trekking in Lore Lindu National Park, or heading on to Tanjung Karang.

Information

Tourist Offices The helpful tourist office (☎ 21795) on Jl Raya Moili has plenty of brochures and maps of the city, and is an excellent place to get independent information about Lore Lindu National Park. It's open Monday to Thursday and Saturday from 7.15 am to 4 pm, and Friday until 11.30 am.

National Parks Office For permits, maps and information about Lore Lindu, visit the Balai Taman Nasional Lore Lindu office, a few metres off Jl Tanjung Manimbayan.

Money Most banks are represented in Palu. Bank Exim and BNI bank are the best and most convenient for changing money.

Post & Communications The main post office is inconveniently located on Jl Yamin, but it does have a small Internet centre (customer@palu.wasantara.net.id),

PALU

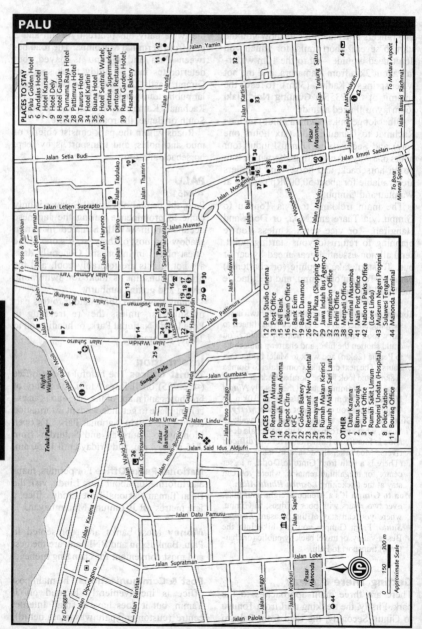

PLACES TO STAY
5 Palu Golden Hotel
6 Andalas Hotel
7 Hotel Karsam
9 Hotel Dely
18 Hotel Garuda
24 Purnama Raya Hotel
28 Pattimura Hotel
30 Taurus Hotel
34 Hotel Kartini
35 Buana Hotel
36 Hotel Sentral; Wartel;
Sentasa Supermarket;
Sentasa Restaurant
39 Rama Garden Hotel;
Hasana Bakery

PLACES TO EAT
10 Restoran Marannu
14 Rumah Makan Aroma
20 Depot Citra
21 KFC
22 Golden Bakery
23 Restaurant New Oriental
25 Ramayana
27 Palu Plaza (Shopping Centre)
31 Rumah Makan Kerinci
37 Rumah Makan Sari Laut

OTHER
1 Datu Karama
2 Banua Souraja
3 Tourist Office
4 Rumah Sakit Umum
Propinsi Undata (Hospital)
8 Police Station
11 Bouraq Office
12 Palu Studio Cinema
13 Post Office
15 BNI Bank
16 Telkom Office
17 Bank Exim
19 Bank Danamon
26 Mosque
29 Jawa Indah Bus Agency
32 Immigration Office
33 Pelni Office
38 Merpati Office
40 Terminal Masomba
41 Main Post Office
42 National Parks Office
(Lore Lindu)
43 Museum Negeri Propinsi
Sulawesi Tengala
44 Manonda Terminal

which charges a reasonable 6000Rp per 30 minutes. There is another handy post office on Jl Sudirman. The main Telkom office is conveniently located on Jl Ahmad Yani and the staff are efficient. There is also a good wartel in the Hotel Sentral complex.

Emergency Palu has a large and reasonably well-equipped hospital, Rumah Sakit Umum Propinsi Undata (☎ 21270), Jl Suharso; a police station (☎ 21015), Jl Sam Ratulangi; and immigration office (☎ 21433), Jl Kartini.

Things to See & Do

The large, provincial **Museum Negeri Propinsi Sulawesi Tengah** (☎ 22290) features interesting traditional art, and other geological and archaeological items. It is open daily from about 8 am to 2 pm, and entry costs 750Rp – but it is inconveniently located. The **Banua Souraja** traditional house, and **Datu Karama** mausoleum nearby, are mildly interesting, but also hard to reach, and you'll have to find someone next door to open them up.

Pantai Palu is neither clean or nice. Fortunately, there is an excellent beach and reefs at Tanjung Karang (see Diving & Snorkelling in the Donggala & Tanjung Karang section later).

If you have time, you can also visit the **Bora mineral springs**, 12km south of Palu; and the springs at **Taman Mantikole** nature reserve, about 25km south of town.

Places to Stay – Budget

The best of a bad lot is **Purnama Raya Hotel** (☎ 23646, Jl Wahidin 4), which is central, clean and good value at 15,000/25,000Rp for singles/doubles with a bathroom and fan. The knowledgeable manager also doubles as a local guide. **Hotel Karsam** (☎ 21776, Jl Suharso 15) has rooms for 15,000Rp but on our last visit the staff were unhelpful.

Another depressing option is **Hotel Garuda** (Jl Hasanuddin 29), which is noisy and has rooms for 17,500Rp. Opposite, **Taurus Hotel** (☎ 29699, Jl Hasanuddin 32) is better. It's still noisy, but the rooms with a fan and bathroom are OK for 20,000Rp.

There's decent views from the bar-cum-cafe upstairs. **Andalas Hotel** (☎ 22332, Jl Raden Saleh) is better than most, with rooms for 17,500/25,000Rp.

Places to Stay – Mid-Range & Top End

There are three decent, adjacent places along Jl Kartini. **Hotel Sentral** (☎ 22789, fax 22418, Jl Kartini 6) is large, efficient and aptly named. All rooms have air-con and satellite TV, and cost 40,000Rp for smallish ones to 80,000Rp for the 'deluxe' with hot water and a fridge. Next door, the airy **Buana Hotel** (☎ 21475, Jl Kartini 8) is not quite as nice, but is still good value: rooms with air-con and satellite TV cost 40,000Rp to 80,000Rp. **Hotel Kartini** (☎ 21964, Jl Kartini 12) is the cheapest, but is now run down. Dark, unexciting rooms cost 25,000Rp with a fan; and 45,000Rp with air-con.

Just around the corner is the new **Rama Garden Hotel** (☎ 29500, fax 29300, Jl Monginsidi 81). The rooms are well furnished, and cost 35,000Rp to 70,000Rp. The outdoor seating area downstairs is an attraction. **Pattimura Hotel** (☎ 21775, fax 24493, Jl Pattimura 18) is on a noisy street, but good value. All rooms have air-con and satellite TV, and cost 45,000Rp for uninspiring dark rooms to 60,000Rp for the better 'deluxe' ones. **Hotel Dely** (☎ 21037, Jl Tadulako 17) is in a quiet neighbourhood, and has impeccable service, but is inconveniently located. Economy singles/doubles cost 36,300/42,350Rp, and the '1st class' rooms are 60,500/72,600Rp with air-con and satellite TV.

The main attraction of **Palu Golden Hotel** (☎ 21126, fax 23230, Jl Raden Saleh 1) is the excellent swimming pool, but there's nothing else to justify the room rates of US$55 upwards – although you can often pay in rupiah at a more favourable rate.

Places to Eat

There are plenty of **night warungs** along the breezy esplanade, Jl Raja Moili. Jl Hasanuddin II is also a busy thoroughfare with several places to eat. **Restaurant New Oriental**

SULAWESI

is large, clean and has a vast menu, including pigeon and frogs, but prices are high. Better is *Depot Citra*, where the baked fish is large, prices are cheap and the service is friendly. Popular with locals is *Rumah Makan Sari Laut (Jl Monginsidi)*. It offers superb baked fish meals, with the trimmings, for about 12,000Rp, plus ice-cold drinks.

Golden Bakery (Jl Wahidin) has scrumptious cakes, small burgers, simple Indonesian food and delicious fruit juices. *Hasana Bakery (Jl Monginsidi)*, near the Rama Garden Hotel, also has tempting treats. More affluent locals, and visiting fast food junkies, head to *KFC (Jl Hasanuddin)*.

Along Jl Wahidin, *Ramayana* and *Rumah Makan Aroma* serve all sorts of Indonesian and Chinese food. The upmarket *Restoran Marannu (Jl Setia Budi)* is one of many places for expensive, but tasty, seafood and Chinese cuisine. The Padang-style *Rumah Makan Kerinci (Jl Kartini)* is large and popular.

Several hotels have *eateries* offering Padang food, which are open to the public. In the Hotel Sentral complex, the *Sentosa Supermarket* is well stocked; and, above it, *Sentosa Restaurant* is breezy, and offers a large menu, including western food.

Getting There & Away

Air Merpati (☎ 21172) flies from Palu to Luwuk (404,000Rp) and Manado (456,800Rp) twice a week; and to Ujung Pandang (503,000Rp) three times a week. Bouraq (☎ 27795) flies to Ujung Pandang for the same price, four times a week; and has a handy flight to Balikpapan (422,000Rp) most days.

Bus & Shared Taxi Buses to Ampana (15,000Rp), Gorontalo (35,000Rp), Poso (10,000Rp), Rantepao (35,000Rp) via Palopo, Manado (about 50,000Rp), Ujung Pandang (50,000Rp) and Luwuk (27,000Rp) all leave from Terminal Masomba. A few others also leave from inconvenient bus company offices dotted around the distant suburbs of Palu. One handy agency is Jawa Indah, opposite the Bank Exim building.

Minibuses and shared taxis to places like Pantoloan (for Pelni boats) and Donggala (for Tanjung Karang) leave from Terminal Manonda.

Boat Travelling by boat can avoid long and uncomfortable bus rides through central Sulawesi. Palu is also well connected to eastern Kalimantan.

Every two weeks, the Pelni liners *Kambuna* and *Kerinci* sail to Balikpapan for 33,500/109,000Rp (economy/1st class) and Ujung Pandang (73,000/245,500Rp); and the *Tidar* goes to Nunukan, Tarakan and Ujung Pandang. These boats dock at Pantoloan, 22km north of Palu, accessible by shared taxi from Terminal Manonda in Palu, or metered taxi (about 12,000Rp). The Pelni office (☎ 21696) in Palu is efficient; there's another at Pantoloan.

Smaller, less comfortable ships along the northern coast to Toli-Toli and Kwandang leave from Wani, 2km north of Pantoloan. You can book these boats at a small agency in Terminal Masomba in Palu.

Getting Around

To/From the Airport Mutiara airport is 7km east of town. Public transport is awkward to arrange, so take a metered taxi for about 5000Rp from the city centre.

Public Transport Transport around Palu is by bemo – 500Rp gets you anywhere. Routes are not signed and are flexible, so flag down one that looks like it's going your way. There are occasional ojeks; and becaks and *bendis* (horse and cart) near the terminals and markets, but they can't take you far. Taxis are cheap, air-conditioned and drivers always use the meters.

DONGGALA & TANJUNG KARANG
☎ 0457

As the administrative centre under the Dutch, Donggala was briefly the most important town and port in central Sulawesi. When the harbour silted up, ships used the harbours on the other side of the bay, and Palu became the regional capital. Today, Donggala is a quiet backwater – somewhere to pass through on the way to Tanjung Karang.

Diving & Snorkelling

The main attractions are sun, sand and water at **Tanjung Karang** (Coral Peninsula), about 5km north of Donggala. The reef off the Prince John Dive Resort is a delight for snorkellers and beginner divers, but you may not be welcome if you're not a guest. The only dive centre is at Prince John, which arranges individual dives for US$27; snorkelling/diving day trips for about US$20/82; and PADI courses. Diving and snorkelling equipment can be rented. Most of the homestays listed in the Places to Stay & Eat entry also rent snorkelling gear.

Places to Stay & Eat

There are four places to stay in Tanjung Karang (nowhere in Donggala). All except the Marlyna have pretty *restaurants* overlooking the sea, which the public can use. All hotels include three meals in their rates.

Just off the start of the road to Tanjung Karang, *Prince John Dive Resort (☎ 71710, fax 23027)* has now gone firmly upmarket. The beach is white and clean, the bungalows have superb settings and most have excellent views, but for US$17/22 to US$23/30 for singles/doubles you would expect (but don't get) hot water and air-con.

Better value is available at *Harmoni Cottages (☎ 21573)* at the end of the road. Right on the white sand, these basic, individual cottages with communal bathrooms, have views and friendly service for 30,000Rp person. Staff can also organise local hikes. Close by, *Natural Cottages (Palu ☎ 0451-25020)* also has rickety, wooden cottages, with private bathrooms, in a gorgeous seaside setting, for 35,000Rp per person. Behind these, *Marlyna Cottages* are nicer inside, but they have no views, are cluttered together and cost too much (60,000Rp per person).

Getting There & Away

From Terminal Manonda in Palu, shared taxis leave regularly for the pretty ride to

Donggala (2500Rp). Alternatively, charter a creaky old Toyota Corolla to Donggala for about 12,500Rp, or a newer Kijang for about 15,000Rp. From Donggala terminal to Tanjung Karang, it's a pleasant 30 minute walk (but ask directions through the village), or you can charter a vehicle from Donggala terminal or directly from Palu.

TOLI-TOLI
☎ 0453

Continuing up the thin peninsula towards Manado is Toli-Toli. There are a few islands to explore just offshore, but most visitors understandably bypass this remote area and travel via the Togean islands. The best places to stay are *Hotel Anda (Jl Mansyur)*, with rooms for 25,000Rp, and *Penginapan Salamae (Jl A Yani)*, which has rooms for 35,000Rp. There are some decent *rumah makans* along Jl Katamso.

Merpati no longer flies to Toli-Toli. Every two weeks, the Pelni liners *Binaiya*, *Kambuna*, *Kerinci* and *Leuser* stop by, usually on the way to eastern Kalimantan and/or Pare Pare. The Pelni office is at Jl Yos Sudarso 106.

KOLONODALE
☎ 0452

Kolonodale is a small tangle of long, dusty streets set on the stunning Teluk Tomori, and is the gateway to Taman Morowali nature reserve (see the Taman Morowali entry later in this section). Rainfall in the bay area is heavy and constant, and the best time to visit is from September to November.

Most accommodation, shops and the market are adjacent to the main dock. The intersection in front of the market serves as the bus/bemo terminal. There is a small post office behind the main mosque, and a 24 hour Telkom office, up the hill from the Pelni office.

Places to Stay & Eat

Losmen Jungpandang (☎ 21091, Jl Yos Sudarso) is convenient to the dock, and has small, basic singles/doubles for about 8000/12,500Rp, with shared bathroom. The attached *restaurant* offers simple Indonesian fare. *Penginapan Sederhana (☎ 21124, Jl Yos Sudarso 64)* is also basic, with rooms from 10,000Rp, and is managed by the local environmental group, Sahabat Morowali (Friends of Morowali). About 200m north of the Sederhana, *Penginapan Lestari (☎ 21044)* is a nice, old place with rooms for 17,500Rp per person, including meals. *Penginapan Rejeki Jaya (Jl Hasanuddin 73)*, 250m south of the town centre, offers clean rooms with meals for the same price.

There are basic *warungs* around the bus terminal and market, but you're better off getting a room rate including meals.

Getting There & Away

Bus Several buses a day travel between Kolonodale and Poso (15,000Rp, eight hours), via Tentena. You may also find a Kijang in Kolonodale going as far as Poso. From the south, cross Danau Matano by boat from Soroako to Nuha, rent a motorbike or jeep to Beteleme, and then wait for a bus to Kolonodale.

Boat The Pelni liner *Tilongkabila* stops at Kolonodale once a week on its way to Luwuk or Kendari. *Perahu* (traditional outrigger boats) leave the main dock most days at about 11 pm for the overnight trip east to Baturube and Pandauke, from where there are buses to Luwuk (five hours).

TELUK TOMORI

Most visitors to Kolonodale head straight to Morowali, so they miss much of the stunning beauty of the islands and inlets around Tomori bay, where limestone cliffs plunge into emerald waters, and unbroken forests cover islands and surrounding hills. To properly explore the bay, rent a boat from Kolonodale: for around 70,000Rp per day, you can charter a small 'Johnson' (dugout canoe with an outboard motor), or for about 120,000Rp, a larger boat holding up to 10 people.

Sights include a **limestone cliff** across the water from Kolonodale with faint painted outlines of prehistoric handprints and fossils embedded in the rock; the oddly shaped 'mushroom rock'; tiny **fishing villages**; and some fine **beaches** on uninhabited islands at the mouth of the bay. There are also **coral reefs** with plenty of marine life, but the visibility can be poor.

TAMAN MOROWALI

This 225,000 hectare nature reserve was established in 1980 on the eastern shore of Teluk Tomori after Operation Drake, a British-sponsored survey of the endangered species in the area. The reserve includes islands in the bay, accessible lowland plains and densely vegetated peaks up to 2421m high.

Taman Morowali is also home to about 5000 Wana people, who live mostly by hunting and gathering, and through shifting agriculture. The park is rich in wildlife, such as *anoa* (dwarf buffalo), maleo birds, *babi rusa* (pig deer) and the world's tiniest bat, but dense jungle is often all you'll see.

Trekking

You will need at least four days to properly visit the park, plus a few extra to get there and back – and the going can be tough. Treks can be organised through travel agencies in Tentena for 350,000Rp to 600,000Rp per person (depending on group size), including transport, food and accommodation, for a five to six-day trek. You may also be able to organise something in Pendolo (see Guides under Lore Lindu National Park earlier in this chapter).

However, if you want to travel independently, and you need a guide (which is necessary to see the wildlife), wait until you reach Kolonodale. In Kolonodale, guides may approach you in the street; or you can organise one through your hotel, or visit the KSDA (National Parks) office – where you must register and buy a permit (1500Rp per day) anyway. A good source of independent advice, and a good place to organise guides, is Friends of Morowali (☎ 0465-21124) on Jl Yos Sudarso 64, a local environmental group.

From Kolonodale, it's a two hour boat trip across Teluk Tomori and up Sungai Morowali to drop-off points for hikes to **Kayu Poli**,

A squealing, smiling, squirming mass of young Bajau boys, Togean Islands.

Dolong, a small fishing village on Pulau Walea Kodi, Togean Islands.

Central Sulawesi has some spectacular scenery.

Bajau stilt house built over a reef, Togean Islands.

Finely crafted sailing ships, Pelabuhan Paotere.

Bajau 'sea gypsies' are water hunter-gatherers.

Volcanoes to climb – Pulau Siau, North Sulawesi.

a small Wana settlement. You can stay in a local home there or at another village, and spend some time with the Wana people to observe their way of life. West of Kayu Poli (three hours) is the eerily silent **Danua Rahu**, which takes about five hours to cross by canoe. You can leave the park via Sungai Rahu, and return to Kolonodale by boat.

A far longer trek from Kayu Poli east to Taronggo, visiting highland villages, takes five to seven days. Another useful starting point is to catch the regular night ferry from Kolonodale to Baturube, and enter the reserve from the east. Particularly hardy trekkers can hike north across the peninsula all the way to Marowo, accessible by bemo to Ampana, in nine days.

LUWUK
☎ 0461

Luwuk is the biggest town on Sulawesi's isolated eastern peninsula, and the stepping-off point for the Banggai Islands. Nearby attractions include the 75m high waterfall **Air Terjun Hengahenga**, 3km west of Luwuk; and **Taman Bangkiriang** nature reserve, 80km south-west of Luwuk, home to central Sulawesi's largest maleo bird population.

Places to Stay & Eat

For about 15,000Rp per room, you can stay at *Hotel Kota*, near the bus terminal; *Penginapan Rahmat*; or *Homestay Senang Hati*. The best of a motley bunch is *Ramayana Hotel (☎ 21073, Jl Danau Lindu)* with decent singles/doubles for 22,500/34,500Rp; its seaside *restaurant* is pleasant. The newest place is *Maleo Cottage (☎ 21101, fax 23661, Jl Lompobattang)*; no further details were available at the time of writing.

Getting There & Away

Merpati (☎ 21123) has flights to Manado (456,800Rp) three times a week; to Palu (404,000Rp) twice weekly; and to Ujung Pandang (746,100Rp) once a week. The Merpati office (☎ 21123) is at Jl Imam Bonjol 3.

Every week, the Pelni liner *Tilongkabila* links Luwuk with Kolonodale or Gorontalo, and is an excellent way to travel to this remote part of Sulawesi. The Pelni office (☎ 21888) is at Jl Dewi Sartika 373.

There are also buses to Pagimana, Poso and Bunta for connections to Ampana.

BANGGAI ISLANDS

With a *lot* of time and patience you could visit the wild and remote Banggai Islands. It's a superb area for swimming, diving and marine life, such as whales and *dugong* (sea cows). Boats can be chartered from most villages, but bring your own diving gear.

The largest and most populous island is Pulau Peleng, with the main settlements at Tataba and Salakan. Parts of some of the islands have been snapped up by speculators, so things may start to change for the islands. Currently, there is no official accommodation, but you can stay at a local home in any village if you check with the kepala desa first.

There is a daily ferry between Luwuk and Tataba. The Pelni liner *Ciremai* links Tataba with Ujung Pandang or Bitung (for Manado) once a week.

PAGIMANA

Pagimana is the starting and finishing point for the ferry to Gorontalo (see Getting There & Away under Gorontalo later in this chapter). It's a good idea to continue to Ampana or Luwuk, but if you get stuck ask for Pak Oki's home, which has cheap *rooms* for rent. To Ampana, you'll probably have to get a connection at Bunta. To Luwuk, catch a local bemo.

TANJUNG API NATIONAL PARK

The 4246 hectare Cape Fire National Park is home to anoa, babi rusa, crocodiles, snakes and maleo, but most people come to see the burning coral cliff fuelled by a leak of natural gas. Try cupping the gas bubbling through the water and putting a match to it. You need to charter a boat around the rocky peninsula from Ampana. It's more interesting at dusk.

AMPANA
☎ 0464

The main reason travellers come to Ampana is to catch a boat to/from the Togean islands,

SULAWESI

but it's a laidback, pleasant town and a good stopover while you recover from, or prepare for, your assault on the Togeans.

The main Poso-Luwuk road goes through Ampana, and is called Jl Hatta. Many hotels are along Jl Hatta, which heads towards the sea from Jl Hatta. The main dock, market and bus terminal are all close to Jl Kartini.

Places to Stay & Eat

Along Jl Kartini, there are several budget places. *Penginapan Mekar* (☎ *21058*) has simple, well-furnished rooms from 12,500Rp to 30,000Rp with a bathroom. It's also the reservation agency for Kadidiri Paradise Bungalows on Pulau Kadidiri (in the Togeans). *Losmen Irama* (☎ *21055*) is good value with quiet rooms for 10,000/14,000Rp without/with fan (and you'll need the fan), or 20,000/40,000Rp for singles/doubles with air-con.

Other basic places include: *Hotel Palasa* (☎ *21091*), along the other end of Jl Kartini and across the main road, with pokey rooms for 20,000Rp; and the new, but noisy, *Penginapan Family* (☎ *21034, Jl Hatta 37*), with rooms for 12,000Rp per person.

Marina Cottage (☎ *21280*) is in Labuhan village, a 10 minute bendi ride from Ampana. It's on a very rocky beach, but the seaside setting is pleasant. Cottages with a bathroom cost 35,000Rp to 55,000Rp. The *restaurant* is worth visiting for the sunsets alone.

Of the couple of unexciting rumah makans along Jl Kartini, the best is *Rumah Makan Mekar* at the end of the road. Nearby, *night warungs* spring up later in the afternoon. *Rumah Makan Ikan Bakar*, near Penginapan Family, rarely has baked fish (despite its name), and the *mie goreng* is terrible, but the beer is cold.

Getting There & Away

Bus & Bemo Ampana is on the main road between Poso and Luwuk. Several buses travel each day to Poso (8000Rp, five hours), often continuing to Palu (15,000Rp, 11 hours). To Luwuk, catch a bemo from the terminal, opposite the main dock in Ampana, to Bunta and then another to Luwuk.

Boat Boats to Poso, Wakai and beyond leave from the main boat terminal at the end of Jl Yos Sudarso, in the middle of Ampana. Boats to Bomba leave from a jetty in Labuhan village, next to Marina Cottage.

Togean Islands

This archipelago of pristine coral and volcanic isles in the middle of Teluk Tomini is a riot of blue, gold and green. The undisturbed jungle shelters a variety of wildlife. The islands' reefs support a rich diversity of marine life, and the seven or so ethnic groups sharing this place are hospitable. Although the islands are difficult to reach, and the facilities are basic, many travellers fall in love with the Togeans, and their lifestyle – and often end up staying a lot longer than they anticipated.

Information

The Togeans are changing rapidly, and more bungalows are being built on more islands. In fact, nobody (certainly not the tourist authorities in the provincial capital, Palu) know where they all are. The best source of current information about homestays, transport and activities is obviously other travellers, but it's also worth asking staff and checking out the noticeboards at:

Ampana
    Togean Information Centre (☎ 0464-21520), Jl Kartini 16, opposite Hotel Irama, is run by a local environmental NGO, and is worth visiting for free, independent advice.
Gorontalo
    Information and boat schedules are freely available at Melati Hotel, and less so at Hotel Saronde.
Manado
    Smiling Hostel has a whole noticeboard full of useful information.
Poso
    The manager of Losmen Lalang Jaya is helpful, and the hotel is next to the port for boats to the Togeans.

Diving & Snorkelling

The Togeans are the only place in Indonesia where you can find all three major

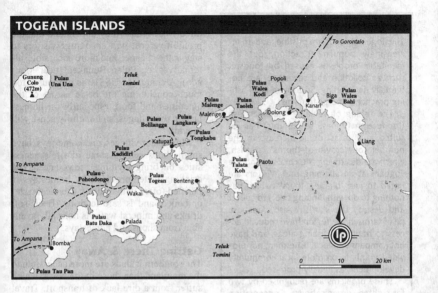

TOGEAN ISLANDS

To Gorontalo

Gunung Colo (472m)

Pulau Una Una

Teluk Tomini

Popoli

Pulau Walea Kodi

Pulau Malenge

Pulau Taoleh

Biga

Pulau Walea Bahi

Malenge

Kanari

Pulau Bolilangga

Pulau Langkara

Dolong

Pulau Tongkabu

Katupat

Pulau Kadidiri

Liang

To Ampana

Pulau Pohondongo

Pulau Togean

Benteng

Pulau Talata Koh

Paotu

Wakai

Pulau Batu Daka

Palada

To Ampana

Bomba

Teluk Tomini

Pulau Tau Pan

0   10   20 km

reef environments – atoll, barrier and fringing – in one location. Two atolls and their deep lagoons lie off the north-west of Pulau Batu Daka. Barrier reefs surround many islands at the 200m depth contour (five to 15km offshore), and fringing reefs surround all of the coasts, merging with the sea grass and mangroves. There is also at least one sunken WWII bomber plane, which is a couple of hours by speedboat from Kadidiri.

The mix of coral and marine life is spectacular and unusually diverse. The more conspicuous residents include gaily marked coral lobsters, a colony of dugong, schools of a hundred or more dolphins, the occasional great whale, commercially important species of trepang and natural pearls.

You can rent snorkelling gear from most homestays, but it's always better to bring your own. The only dive centres are on Kadidiri and Walea Kodi islands; and they are reliable and safe. Details are listed later under Pulau Kadidiri and Pulau Walea Kodi sections.

Places to Stay & Eat

Most of the rooms are wooden and in individual cottages, along or near a beach. The cottages are generally spartan, but comfortable, and have a mosquito net but no fan because the sea breezes keep everything cool. Most places have rustic, communal bathroom facilities. All prices mentioned in this entry

SULAWESI

Warning

Sadly, several travellers have reported thefts (usually money) from rooms, boats (while snorkelling or diving) and homestays (after depositing a money belt with staff for safe-keeping). It is imperative that you either lock up your valuables or leave them with someone you trust. If you're depositing something into the care of homestay staff, you should *fully* list your money, travellers cheques and credit cards on paper, and have it countersigned by a staff member. The cottages are easy to break into, and there are no police on the islands.

Conservation of the Togeans

The Togean Islands are pristine, and an increasingly popular attraction, but the inevitable problems caused by tourism, such as pollution and sewerage, are potentially devastating. So too are local fishing practices, and pearl farms.

The fishing of valuable Napolean fish (for foreign Chinese restaurants) has resulted in a catastrophic increase in the number of 'crown-of-thorns' starfish, which are destroying the coral around the Togeans at an alarming rate. Visitors are urged to join 'bintang tours' (which has nothing to do with Bintang beer) to collect and destroy the starfish. Also, Japanese pearl farms in the region have reduced access to traditional fishing areas, and have not compensated local fisherman, nor provided grants to promote local community development, as initially promised.

These problems are recognised by two far-sighted organisations: Conservation International, Indonesia (☎ 021-799 3955, fax 794 7731, email ciip@cbn.net.id); and Toloka Foundation (☎ 0464-21520, email toloka@palu.wasantara.net.id). They aim to educate local fishermen about sustainable fishing practices; educate local children about marine conservation; lobby the Indonesian government to declare the Togeans a protected nature and marine reserve; help conserve endangered turtles, crabs and other marine life; and limit the development of local tourism.

are per person, and all rates include meals (unless stated otherwise) of fish, vegetables and rice. If that bores you, bring some supplements.

As part of a (seemingly narrow-minded) 'Let's Go Central Sulawesi' tourism campaign, the authorities in Palu want to introduce a standard, minimum charge of US$10 (payable in rupiah; currently 60,000Rp) per person for accommodation, including meals. The more savvy homestay owners plan to oppose (or even ignore) the directive, because they understand that the prohibitive cost will encourage visitors to stay at the cheaper, and more accessible, alternatives, eg Pulau Bunaken (near Manado). A charge of US$10 is obviously too much considering the basic nature of the amenities and food, especially for homestays in the villages, so hopefully sense will prevail.

Most major villages, and homestays, have small shops selling some of life's necessities, but bring anything else you need. The drinking water provided by homestays is purified (often with a strong chemical taste) or boiled, and is safe to drink. Beer, soft drinks and mineral water is normally available from shops and homestays.

Getting There & Away

The southern islands are more accessible to the mainland than those in the north, which suffer from a dire lack of transport. Travel to the Togeans can be long, uncomfortable and rough, especially during 'wave season' (December and January).

Ampana A public boat (known as a *bodi*) leaves at 10 am every day for Wakai (6500Rp). From a separate jetty at Labuhan village, another boat leaves for Bomba (5000Rp) at the same time. But for some reason, the boat to Wakai does not stop at Bomba.

Currently, wooden cargo/passenger boats also travel between Ampana and the major settlements of Bomba, Wakai, Katupat and Malenge three times a week. Once a week, one of the boats also stops at Tongkabu and Dolong.

If you ask around the main port at Ampana, the port in Wakai or at the Wakai Cottages, you could charter a 10 person boat between Ampana and Wakai or Kadidiri for about 250,000Rp. From Bomba to Ampana, this is not as easy to arrange, but is still possible for about 150,000Rp.

Gorontalo Once a week, one wooden boat ploughs the waters between Gorontalo and

Poso, via Dolong, Malenge, Katupat, Wakai and Ampana. It currently leaves Gorontalo on Friday at 9 pm (more likely at around midnight), stops overnight (Saturday) at Wakai, and continues to Ampana and Poso. Tickets are available from the office at the relevant terminal in Gorontalo (see Getting There & Away in the Gorontalo section later in this chapter for details). The trip from Gorontalo to Wakai costs 22,750Rp, and takes about 17 hours.

The boat leaves Poso on Monday night at about 10 pm, and from Ampana on Tuesday at about 10 pm, but does not stop overnight en route. Tickets are available at offices in the harbours at Poso and Ampana.

At Gorontalo, Poso and Ampana, you can usually rent one of the handful of tiny two-berth cabins from the crew – tee this up during the afternoon before you leave. The crew ask (and normally get) an extortionate 60,000Rp per cabin. Cabins will be far harder to arrange anywhere en route, especially if there are many travellers getting on at somewhere like Wakai.

The only other option is the regular overnight ferry to Pagimana (see Getting There & Away in the Gorontalo section later for details), which is five hours by bus from Ampana.

Marisa Anyone loaded with rupiah (about one million rupiah) can charter a speedboat between Marisa (about 150km west of Gorontalo) and Wakai or Kadidiri; but it may take a day or two to arrange.

Getting Around
Allow plenty of time to get around, because transport within the Togeans is a chronic problem. Regardless of where you stay, you need boats to get there and away, and to reach swimming and snorkelling spots. Schedules for public boats are unreliable, and trips are long and uncomfortable, so chartering something is a good way to get around, although not many boats are available for rent.

Public Boat Ask your homestay, or anyone around the village, about the current timetables for boats to other islands, or further on to Ampana and Gorontalo. The locals rely heavily on these boats, so they always know what is going where and when.

Chartered Boat If you're in a hurry, flushed with cash and/or in a small group, chartering a boat is not that expensive. Charters are not hard to arrange in Wakai, Bomba and Kadidiri, but it's far more difficult in smaller settlements because there are simply not many boats around. You'll often have to accept anything that's available, from a nifty speedboat to a ponderous wooden trawler.

The rates should be negotiable but are often fairly standard among the cartel of local operators; eg 100,000Rp from Wakai or Kadidiri to Bomba on a speedboat, and 150,000Rp from Bomba to Ampana on a wooden trawler.

PULAU BATU DAKA
The largest, and most accessible, populated and visited island is Pulau Batu Daka, which is home to the two main villages, Bomba and Wakai.

Bomba
Bomba is a tiny outpost at the south-western end of the island, which most travellers sail past on the way to and from Wakai (for Pulau Kadidiri). Bomba is a decent alternative to Kadidiri and, although the setting is not as picturesque, there's decent swimming and snorkelling close by, and you won't be overrun by other travellers.

There are **bat caves** in the hills behind Bomba, but you'll need a guide. It's a pleasant walk, and take a torch (flashlight) for the cave. There are other pleasant **walks**, and **prolific birdlife** around this part of the island.

Places to Stay In the village, *Losmen Poya Lisa* is an obvious place, built over the water, with basic rooms for 20,000Rp. However, you're better off at one of the places nearby, which are all accessible by chartered boat from the village.

Built on a rocky outcrop, two minutes by boat, is the friendly *Sisilea Bungalows* has basic cottages for 20,000Rp. There is no beach nearby, but the snorkelling close to the jetty is fantastic. On another minuscule island, 300m from Sisilea's, *Poya Lisa Cottages* is built on a pretty beach and boasts some of the best facilities in the Togeans. Cottages cost from 35,000Rp.

The most extraordinary place in the Togeans is *Homestay Tondongi Reef*, built in the Bajau style in the middle of the ocean (but protected by a nearby islet), 10 minutes from Bomba. Follow the sign in Bomba for bookings (☎ 0464-21371) and transport, or book at the agency at Jl Pulau Papa 3, Ampana. Rooms cost about 30,000Rp.

Several slightly upmarket new bungalows, such as the *Island Retreat*, are being built five minutes away by boat on the gorgeous beach, Pasir Putih.

Wakai

The largest settlement in the Togeans is Wakai. It's mainly used as the departure point for boats to Pulau Kadidiri, but there are two decent hotels and several well-stocked general stores. A small **waterfall**, a few kilometres inland from Wakai, is a pleasant hike – ask directions in the village.

Places to Stay & Eat *Wakai Cottages* is pleasant, friendly and run by the owners of Wakai Cottages on Pulau Kadidiri. Clean bungalows cost 25,000Rp. Turn right as you walk off the jetty, and ask directions through the village – it's a 15 minute walk.

Togian Islands Hotel is a huge, airy weatherboard hotel built over the water, near the jetty. The rooms cost 25,000Rp to 60,000Rp, without meals, but a *restaurant* is attached to the hotel.

The cheapest place is a room at the back of the *Rumah Makan Cahaya Sidrap*, close to the jetty. Rooms cost 10,000Rp, with a shared bathroom, excluding meals. There's a basic *restaurant* upstairs, which offers (unbelievably) a karaoke machine.

PULAU KADIDIRI

The *in* place in the Togeans is the beach on Pulau Kadidiri, a short boat trip from Wakai, which boasts a perfect beach, dozens of cheap bungalows, supreme snorkelling and swimming only metres from your room, and superb diving further out.

A short walk west of the beach eventually brings you to a series of craggy coral cliffs, home to coconut crabs the size of small footballs. Put your hand into any hole in the sand, and you may never see it again!

Activities

Kadidiri is the most popular destination in the Togeans, and a range of activities are now on offer. But there is some animosity among homestay operators, so if you're staying at Wakai Cottages, you may not be able to use the facilities or activities offered by Kadidiri Paradise Bungalows – and vice versa.

Kadidiri Paradise and Wakai Cottages rent snorkelling gear for about 10,000Rp per day. The dive centre at Kadidiri Paradise has been heartily recommended by many satisfied customers, and charges a reasonable US$25 per dive including transport.

Wakai Cottages can arrange hikes around the island for 25,000Rp per person; treks to Pulau Una Una (see later in this section); and boat hire for about 60,000Rp per day to visit nearby islands, and for snorkelling.

Coconut Crabs

Coconut crabs, the world's largest terrestrial arthropods, once lived on islands throughout the western Pacific and eastern Indian oceans, but unsustainable human exploitation has reduced stocks to a handful of isolated islands, including the Togeans. Mature crabs weigh up to 5kg, and their large-clawed legs can span 90cm.

Despite popular myth, there is little evidence to support stories of crabs climbing trees to snip coconuts off, removing the husk and then carrying the nut up again to drop from a great height. However, there *is* evidence that humans are eating these crabs to the edge of extinction, so please make a more sustainable choice from the menu.

Places to Stay

In the high season (July to August), it pays to check with the owners of Wakai Cottages and Togian Islands Hotel in Wakai, and Penginapan Mekar in Ampana, about the availability of rooms on Pulau Kadidiri because bungalows are limited and some folk do stay a long time.

There are three places in a row along the beach at Pulau Kadidiri, so you should look around. All places have a small book exchange, which is just as well because you'll do a lot of reading. For anyone who wants almost total seclusion, there are also homestays on Pulau Kota and Pulau Taipi, both only a few minutes by boat from Kadidiri.

Pantai Kadidiri The unsigned *Wakai Cottages* is run by the same people who own Wakai Cottages in Wakai. It occupies most of the beach (to the right as you face the beach), and all cottages are separate, have seaviews and cost 20,000/25,000Rp without/with a bathroom. Further to the right, as you face the beach, *Pondok Lestari* has a few simple cottages for 20,000Rp, with a shared bathroom. Some travellers have raved about the meals and friendly service.

To the left is *Kadidiri Paradise Bungalows* – bookings can be made at the Penginapan Mekar (☎ 0464-21058) in Ampana. This place is well set up, with a small selection of good bungalows along the beach, and many more less appealing bungalows away from the beach. All have shared bathrooms and cost 30,000Rp per bungalow.

Pulau Kota *Laguna Homestay* is wonderfully located overlooking a lagoon in the middle of Kota island. The cottages cost 30,000Rp. The Homestay is run by Kadidiri Paradise Bungalows, so check with the staff about availability and transport.

Pulau Taipi Taipi has a pretty, sandy beach, and is close to some awesome snorkelling spots. *Taipi Cottages* has rooms for 40,000Rp which can also be booked (or transport arranged) at Kadidiri Paradise Bungalows.

Getting There & Away

The public boats sail tantalisingly close to Kadidiri, but won't stop, so you must go to Wakai first (see the general Getting There & Away section at the start of this chapter). After the boat arrives in Wakai, hop on the boat to Kadidiri – it is owned by Wakai Cottages, so you may be charged 2500Rp if you decide not to stay at Wakai Cottages on Kadidiri. Once or twice a day, the same boat also delivers fresh water and supplies to Kadidiri from Wakai; ask your homestay in Kadidiri or Wakai about the schedules. You can also charter a boat between Wakai and Kadidiri for about 15,000Rp one way.

PULAU UNA UNA

The Togeans are part of an active volcanic belt. **Pulau Una Una**, which consists mostly of Gunung Colo (472m), was torn apart in 1983 when the volcano exploded for the first time in almost 100 years. Ash covered 90% of the island, destroying all of the houses, animals and most of the crops, but Una Una's population had been safely evacuated. You can trek to the top of volcano (three hours), and admire the awesome lava landscapes all around the island.

A public boat leaves Wakai about four times a week, but there is currently nowhere to stay on Una Una. Wakai Cottages on Pulau Kadidiri organises guided treks up the volcano, and snorkelling along the way, for 200,000Rp per 10 person boat.

PULAU TOGEAN

The main settlement on this island is the very relaxed Katupat village, which has a small market and a couple of shops. Around the island there are more magical **beaches**, and some decent **hikes** for anyone sick of swimming, snorkelling and diving.

Near the jetty in Katupat, *Losmen Melati* offers simple accommodation, although it's overpriced at 40,000Rp per room. *Fadhila Cottages*, on a tiny island just across from Katupat, offers excellent food and superb snorkelling for 35,000Rp. Other places are springing up around the island, such as the recommended *Losmen Bolilanga Indah*, so

SULAWESI

check with other travellers, and the places mentioned in Information under Togean Islands earlier in this chapter.

PULAU MALENGE

Malenge is remote, and not readily accessible, but is secluded and has wonderful **snorkelling** just offshore from the village. Some locals, with the aid of NGOs, have established excellent **walking trails** around the mangroves and jungles to help spot the incredibly diverse fauna, including macaque, tarsier, hornbill, cuscus and salamander.

Near the jetty in Malenge village, **Losmen Malenge Indah** and **Losmen Lestari** are nicely situated over the water, and have rooms for 25,000Rp. Further around, and only accessible by chartered boat, a few more places are being built, such as **Honeymoon Beach Bungalows** (☎ 0452-21336).

PULAU WALEA KODI

Dolong is a busy fishing village, and the only settlement on the island. Facilities are basic, transport is limited, and the island doesn't offer the picturesque beaches and snorkelling found elsewhere.

The friendly **Hotel Lima** is an unsigned home about five minutes walk, heading left, as you leave the jetty. It costs 25,000Rp, and is not nearly as exotic as other places in the Togeans. Several **rumah makans** around the jetty cater for the rush of hungry ferry passengers.

On an island, just off Walea Kodi, is the first of what may be many upmarket diving resorts: the Italian-run **Walea Dive Center Resort** (bookings ☎/fax 873-682-421370). Package deals, including cottage, three meals, transport and three dives a day, cost about US$121 per person per day.

North Sulawesi

North Sulawesi is the most developed region on the island, and probably the most egalitarian in Indonesia; its people have a long history of trade and contact with the outside world. With the Sangir-Talaud island group,

North Sulawesi forms a natural bridge to the Philippines, providing a causeway for the movement of peoples and cultures, and as a result the language and physical features related to the Philippines can be found among the Minahasans.

The three largest distinct groups in the province are the Minahasans, Gorontalese and Sangirese, but there are many more dialects and subgroups. The kingdoms of Bolaang Mongondow, sandwiched between Minahasa and Gorontalo, were important political players too.

The Dutch have had a more enduring influence on this isolated northern peninsula than anywhere else in the archipelago: Dutch is still spoken among the older generation, and well-to-do families often send their children to study in the Netherlands.

History

The Minahasans have never been subject to dynastic rule. Pressure to institute royalty led to a meeting of the linguistically diverse Minahasan states around 670 AD at a stone now known as Watu Pinabetengan (near Kawangkoan). That meeting paved the way for a durable system of independent states. Threats from outside forces, notably the neighbouring kingdoms of Bolaang Mongondow, unified the Minahasans from time to time. Bolaang Mongondow expansionism led to a strong Minahasan backlash in 1655; one of the few occasions when the independent states were forced into a defence alliance.

At the time of the first contact with Europeans in the 16th century, northern Sulawesi had strong links with the sultanate of Ternate (northern Maluku) and Bugis traders from southern Sulawesi. The Portuguese used Manado as a supply stop, and Portuguese missionaries had some success in Minahasa and Sangir-Talaud islands in the 1560s. The Dutch then toppled the Ternate sultanate, and were keen to collude with the local powers to throw out their European competitors. In 1677 the Dutch occupied Pulau Sangir and, two years later, a treaty (possibly forced) with the Minahasan chiefs led to Dutch domination for the next 300 years.

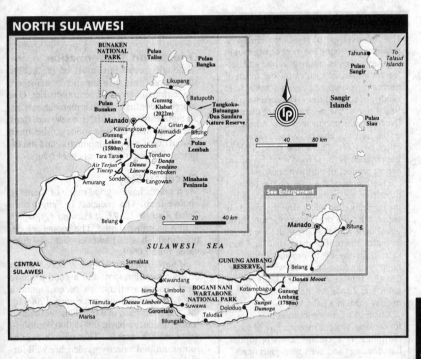

NORTH SULAWESI

SULAWESI

Although relations with the Dutch were often less than cordial, and the region did not actually come under direct Dutch rule until 1870, the Dutch and Minahasans eventually became so close that the north was often referred to as the 'twelfth province of the Netherlands'. (A Manado-based political movement called Twaalfe Provincie even campaigned for Minahasa's integration into the Dutch state in 1947.)

Christianity became a force in the early 1820s, and the wholesale conversion of the Minahasans was almost complete by 1860. Because the school curriculum was taught in Dutch, the Minahasans had an early advantage in the competition for government jobs and positions in the colonial army. The Minahasans also fought alongside the Dutch to subdue rebellions in other parts of the archipelago, notably the Java War of 1825-30.

The Minahasan sense of being different became a problem for the Indonesian government after independence. In March 1957, military leaders of both southern and northern Sulawesi launched a confrontation with the central government with demands for greater regional autonomy, more local development and a fairer share of the revenue. The Minahasan leaders were dissatisfied with the subsequent negotiations, and declared their own autonomous state of North Sulawesi in June 1957. The Indonesian government then bombed Manado in February 1958, and, by June, Indonesian troops had landed in northern Sulawesi. Rebel leaders retreated into the mountains, and the rebellion was finally put down in mid-1961.

Like most export-oriented commodity-producing regions in Indonesia, North Sulawesi province has done well under the subsequent stability and pro-development

Coconut Economy

The inhabitants of northern Sulawesi province are among the most prosperous in Indonesia. Cloves, nutmeg, vanilla and coffee are important cash crops, but much of northern Sulawesi is covered by a solid canopy of coconut trees. The coconut palm tree is one of the most important plants in the tropical economy, not only producing edible fruit but also oil, waxes, fibres and other products. Copra, the dried flesh of the coconut, is the second most important export product of northern Sulawesi.

Like bamboo, the uses of the coconut palm tree are manifold. You can eat the meat, drink the juice, dry the meat as copra, burn the dried husks for fuel, build your house with the timber, use the fronds to thatch the roof or make mats and baskets, burn the oil to provide lighting at night, make rope and mats with the fibre, use the thin centre spine of the young palm leaf to weave hats, and bag your midday meal in a palm leaf.

Coconut oil, made from copra, is used for cooking, and the manufacture of soaps, perfumes, face creams, tanning lotions, hair dressings and even nitro-glycerine.

orientation of modern Indonesia. The province's infrastructure is probably the best in Indonesia, and export demand for its varied cash crops has offset the disadvantage of distance from domestic markets. Visitors to North Sulawesi will see little evidence of the economic crisis affecting the rest of Indonesia.

GORONTALO
☎ 0435

The port of Gorontalo is the second-largest centre in the province, and has the feel of a large, friendly country town, where bendis outnumber *mikrolets* (bemos). The town features some of the best preserved colonial houses on Sulawesi.

Gorontalo's local hero is Nani Wartabone, an anti-Dutch guerilla, and there is a large statue of him in the sports field adjacent to the Melati Hotel.

Orientation & Information
Although spread out, most of the hotels, shops and other life-support systems are concentrated in a small central district. One source of confusion is that many streets are ambiguously named. BNI bank and Bank Danamon will change money. The main post office is a useful landmark, and the efficient Telkom office is open 24 hours.

Places to Stay
Most places have a good range of rooms to choose from. The cheapest is *Penginapan Teluk Kau* (☎ 22093, Jl Parman 42), which is in a charming home. The rooms are depressingly basic, however, but are good value for 10,000Rp.

Melati Hotel (☎ 22934, Jl Gajah Mada 33) is a popular spot, and a good place to meet other travellers. It's based around a lovely old home, built in the early 1900s for the then harbour master. The 'economy' rooms inside are basic for 35,000/45,000Rp without/with meals. The new block of rooms, around a pretty garden, are well furnished, but overpriced at 55,000/90,000Rp for singles/doubles with a fan, and 75,000/115,000Rp with air-con. However, the service, local information and breakfast are excellent.

Hotel Saronde (☎ 21735, fax 22677, Jl Walanda Maramis 17), just across the field from the Melati, is very good value, and offers some useful travel information in the foyer. The rooms cost 16,500/23,650Rp to 33,000/40,700Rp with air-con and satellite TV; and the newer wing has better, but more expensive, rooms. *Hotel Wisata* (☎ 21736, fax 24807, Jl 23 Januari 19) is also good value, and helpful. The cheapest rooms cost 13,750/19,800Rp, and the rooms for 38,500/49,500Rp, with air-con and satellite TV, are nicely furnished but dark.

Hotel Imam Bonjol (☎ 26240, Jl Imam Bonjol 14) is a quiet, central new place with rooms from 21,000/30,000Rp with fan to 30,000/42,500Rp with air-con. *Lika Hotel*

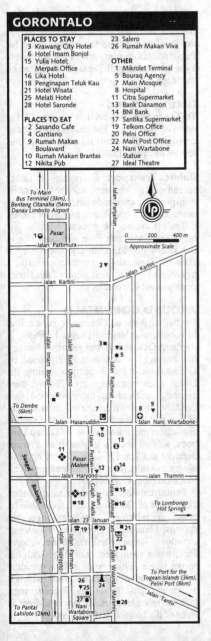

GORONTALO

PLACES TO STAY
3 Krawang City Hotel
6 Hotel Imam Bonjol
15 Yulia Hotel;
   Merpati Office
16 Lika Hotel
18 Penginapan Teluk Kau
21 Hotel Wisata
25 Melati Hotel
28 Hotel Saronde

PLACES TO EAT
2 Sasando Cafe
4 Gantiano
9 Rumah Makan
   Boulavard
10 Rumah Makan Brantas
12 Nikita Pub

23 Salero
26 Rumah Makan Viva

OTHER
1 Mikrolet Terminal
5 Bouraq Agency
7 Main Mosque
8 Hospital
11 Citra Supermarket
13 Bank Danamon
14 BNI Bank
17 Santika Supermarket
19 Telkom Office
20 Pelni Office
22 Main Post Office
24 Nani Wartabone
   Statue
27 Ideal Theatre

To Main
Bus Terminal (3km),
Benteng Otanaha (5km),
Danau Limboto Airport

Pasar

Jalan Pattimura

Jalan Panjaitan

0   200   400 m
Approximate Scale

Jalan Kartini

Jalan Kartini

Jalan Imam Bonjol

Jalan Budi Utomo

Jalan Rachmat

To Dembe
(6km)

Jalan Hasanuddin

Jalan Nani Wartabone

Sungai

Balango

Jalan Pertiwi

Pasar
Malem

Jalan Haryono

Jalan Thamrin

Jalan Gajah Mada

Jalan 23 Januari

Jalan Ahmad Yani

To Lombongo
Hot Springs

Jalan Suprapto

Jalan Parman

Jalan Walanda Maramis

To Port for the
Togean Islands (3km),
Pelni Port (8km)

Jalan Tantu

To Pantai
Lahilote (2km)

Nani
Wartabone
Square

(☎ 21296, Jl Ahmad Yani 20) has quiet, old-fashioned rooms from 18,150/23,650Rp to 31,900/42,350Rp with satellite TV and air-con. As a last resort, **Krawang City Hotel** (☎ 22 437, Jl Rachmad 31) has noisy rooms with a fan for 15,000Rp; 27,500Rp with air-con.

The top-end hotel is surprisingly good value. **Yulia Hotel** (☎ 828395, Jl Ahmad Yani 26) offers rooms with air-con, satellite TV and hot water from 88,000/99,000Rp.

Places to Eat

The local delicacy is *milu siram*, which is a corn soup with grated coconut, fish, salt, chilli and lime. Look for it at the **stalls** around the market at night, or try it at Melati Hotel, if you're a guest. The **night market** has a vast number of warungs selling cheap and tasty food.

There is a surprising dearth of decent restaurants in Gorontalo, but no traveller will starve. **Rumah Makan Brantas** (Jl Hasanuddin) is a depot of delights, with an exquisite selection of cakes and pastries. **Rumah Makan Boulavard**, near the hospital, has a varied selection of fish and Chinese food, and is worth the walk. **Gantiano** (Jl Rachmad) is a Padang restaurant with an airy seating area. Another decent Padang place is **Salero** (Jl Ahmad Yani). Handy to some hotels, **Rumah Makan Viva**, just off Jl Gajah Mada, does an excellent *gado-gado*, but little else.

The flashest places are **Nikita Pub** (Jl Haryono) and **Sasando Cafe** (Jl Panjaitan) – the latter advertises itself as a 'Singing Hall', so you've been warned. Of the hotels, only **Yulia Hotel** has a public restaurant with decent food at reasonable prices.

Entertainment

The *Ideal Theatre* shows decent foreign movies every night for 2500Rp.

Shopping

Souvenirs of the area include the soft and very colourful *krawang* embroidery, available at several shops along Jl Gajah Mada, Jl Ahmad Yani and Jl Budi Utomo.

SULAWESI

If heading directly to the Togean islands by boat or ferry, stock up on life's necessities at either the Santika or Citra supermarkets.

Getting There & Away

Air Merpati now only flies to/from Manado, three times a week (212,000Rp). The Merpati office (☎ 828395) is in the Yulia Hotel. Bouraq no longer flies to Gorontalo, but it has an agency (☎ 21070) for other flights, eg Manado to Ujung Pandang.

Bus The main bus terminal is 3km north of town, and accessible by bemo, bendi or ojek. There are direct buses to Palu (50,000Rp), Poso (55,000Rp) and Tentena (60,000Rp) along the bone-crunching road through the thin peninsula of northern Sulawesi. Buses to Manado (16,000/25,000Rp for normal/ air-con, 10 hours) leave every hour, and about every two hours to Kotamobagu (10,000/12,500Rp, eight hours).

From the terminal, next to the market, mikrolets go in all directions to regional villages.

Boat Every two weeks, the Pelni liner *Tilongkabila* links Gorontalo with Bitung (for Manado) for 32,500/98,000Rp (economy/1st class), continues north to Lirung and Tahuna (55,000/178,000Rp) in the Sangir-Talaud islands and then heads south to Luwuk. The Pelni (☎ 21089, corner of Jl 23 Januari and Jl Gajah Mada) office is efficient and convenient. The *Umsini* stops at Kwandang nearby (see the Kwandang section later).

Every second day, a large, stable ferry crosses the gulf from Gorontalo to Pagimana, and returns on the alternate day. It leaves both places at about 9.30 pm, and arrives at about 6 am. Tickets cost 20,500/ 17,500Rp for A/B class. You can also rent a two-berth cabin for a negotiable 50,000Rp extra from the crew, and mattresses can be rented on board for 2000Rp. This ferry is a more comfortable and regular (but more time consuming) way of travelling between Gorontalo and the Togean islands.

Direct boats to the Togeans (see the Togean Islands earlier for details) leave from

a port, about 3km east of the post office. Another 5km further along the same road is the Pelni port, where ferries also leave for Pagimana. Both ports are easily accessible by mikrolet along Jl Tantu (as indicated on the map).

Getting Around

To/From the Airport The airport is 32km north of Gorontalo. The best way from, and certainly *to*, the airport is on the special bus run by Merpati (15,000Rp).

Public Transport Gorontalo is rather spread out, so you may want to use public transport. For shorter distances, take a ubiquitous bendi or becak; and for longer routes, mikrolets cruise the streets. Also, a few ojeks seem to come from nowhere late in the afternoon. Surprisingly, there are no taxis in Gorontalo, but you can charter a mikrolet or ojek to visit some of the attractions around Gorontalo.

AROUND GORONTALO

On the outskirts of Gorontalo, on a hill at Lekobalo, overlooking Danau Limboto, is **Benteng Otanaha**. It was probably built by the Portuguese and supposedly used by Gorontalo kings as a bastion against the Dutch when relations soured. Today, there are the remains of just three towers. Take a bendi or mikrolet from the mikrolet terminal to a path at the foot of the hill. Otanaha also offers panoramic views of **Danau Limboto**, a 5600 hectare lake with an average depth of just 7m. The lake is easily accessible by mikrolet (one hour), along an excellent road from Gorontalo.

Pantai Lahilote is a white sandy beach 2km south of Gorontalo, and accessible by bendi or mikrolet. The **Lombongo hot springs**, 17km east of Gorontalo, at the western edge of Bogani Nani Wartabone National Park, has a swimming pool filled with hot spring water. A nicer spot is the swimming hole at the foot of a 30m waterfall, which is a 3km walk past the springs. To the springs, take the mikrolet marked 'Suwawa' from in front of the hospital in Gorontalo.

KWANDANG

Kwandang is a port on the north coast of the peninsula, not far from Gorontalo. On the outskirts of the town, along the Gorontalo-Kwandang road, are the remains of two interesting fortresses of obscure origins. **Benteng Ota Mas Udangan** stands on flat ground, and appears to be badly placed to defend anything. One suggestion is that the ocean once came right up to the fort, but has since receded. **Benteng Oranje** lies on a hill some distance back from the sea, and has only been partly restored, so it's not as interesting.

To Kwandang, take a bus from the Gorontalo bus terminal (two hours). Once a week, the Pelni liner *Umsini* stops at Kwandang on the way to Bitung (for Manado) or Balikpapan (eastern Kalimantan).

KOTAMOBAGU
☎ 0434

Kotamobagu (or 'Kota') was once the seat of power for the pre-colonial Bolaang Mongondow kingdoms, but is now a prosperous market town set in a fertile valley of towering coconut plantations. There isn't much to do, but it's the ideal stopover between Manado and Gorontalo, and the gateway to the Bogani Nani Wartabone National Park.

Orientation & Information

The main road from the Bonawang bus terminal is Jl Adampe Dolot. This turns into Jl Ahmad Yani, through the centre of town, and has several well-stocked supermarkets and a BNI branch (which changes money). Parallel to this street is Jl Borian.

The small tourist office is at Jl Ahmad Yani 188; and the office for the Bogani Nani Wartabone National Park (☎ 22548) is along Jl AKD, the road to Doloduo, about 5km from central Kotamobagu.

Things to See & Do

About 23km east of Kotamobagu, **Danau Mooat** is a crater lake 800m above sea level. The lake is surrounded by dense forest, providing refuge for a variety of birdlife and other fauna. There is also a small crater lake at **Gunung Ambang** (1780m), 27km north of Kotamobagu. The mountain is part of **Taman Gunung Ambang**, a large nature reserve, with hot mud pools, tree ferns and flowering shrubs.

Places to Stay & Eat

The best place to stay is *Hotel Ramayana* (☎ 21188, Jl Adampe Dolot 50), which has clean, quiet singles from 11,000Rp to 16,500Rp, and doubles from 16,500Rp to 22,000Rp. Almost opposite, and often full, *Hotel Wijaya* (☎ 21621, Jl Adampe Dolot 193) has a range of rooms from 15,000Rp to 30,000Rp.

Hotel Ade Irama (☎ 21216, Jl Ade Irama) is friendly, and on a quietish street two blocks behind the Bank Rakyat building on Jl Ahmad Yani. The rooms are dark, however, and they're overpriced at 25,000Rp per person. *Hotel Karya Dua* (☎ 21327, Jl Borian 8), about 50m down from the Serasi bemo terminal, has singles/doubles with a shared bathroom for 8000/15,000Rp; or 30,000Rp with a bathroom and air-con.

Several unimpressive rumah makans serving Padang food are located along Jl Ahmad Yani – the best is *Putra Minang Restaurant* at the roundabout. For something fresher, *Rumah Makan Nasional*, on Jl Ahmad Yani, serves cheap, simple Indonesian food. The nicest restaurant in town is *Rumah Makan La Rose*, next to Hotel Wijaya.

Getting There & Away

The main Bonawang bus terminal is a few kilometres from Kotamobagu, in the village of Monglonai, and accessible by mikrolet. Buses to Manado (three hours) cost about 6000/7000Rp for normal/air-con, and to Gorontalo (eight hours), 10,000/12,500Rp. You can buy tickets at the terminal, or from the ticket office at the Paris Supermarket on the roundabout on Jl Ahmad Yani, Kotamobagu.

From the central Serasi bemo terminal on Jl Borian in Kotamobagu, Kijangs go to Manado (12,500Rp per person) and bemos head to Doloduo.

BOGANI NANI WARTABONE NATIONAL PARK

About 50km west of Kotamobagu, this national park (193,600 hectares) has the highest conservation value in North Sulawesi, but it's mostly inaccessible. The park (formerly known as Dumoga-Bone) is at the headwaters of Sungai Dumoga, and was established to protect large irrigation projects downstream from flooding, silting and polluting the water. It later became a haven for rare flora and fauna, including black-crested macaque *(yaki)*, and a species of giant fruit bat only discovered in 1992. Finding rare fauna requires patience and luck, but you should see plenty of hornbills and tarsiers.

Visiting the Park

You should first visit the Kantor Balai Taman Nasional Bogani Nani Wartabone office in Kotamobagu. At this office, you can buy a permit (2500Rp per visit), pick up some useful tips, pore over decent trekking maps and ask lots of questions. You can also enter the park, and buy a permit at Limboto, near Gorontalo, but this is a long way from the main hiking trails.

You could day trip from Kotamobagu with private transport, but it's best to base yourself in the park in order to appreciate the scenery, and spot wildlife, while hiking at dawn and/or dusk. The area around the park entrance at Kosinggolan village has several trails, lasting from one to nine hours, and there are various options for overnight jaunts through the jungle if you have camping equipment.

You can stay at the budget *Niko Guest House* in Kosinggolan. Another possibility is to either hike (9km) or catch the occasional mikrolet to Toraut, and stay at the similar *Wisma Cinta Alam*.

To Kosinggolan, take a regular mikrolet to Doloduo from the Serasi terminal in Kotamobagu. Then walk about 2km west (or ask the bemo driver to continue) to the ranger station at Kosinggolan, just inside the park, where you must register and pick up a compulsory guide for 12,500Rp per short hike (more for longer trips).

Tarsiers

Tarsiers are tiny, nocturnal creatures of the genus *Tarsius*, which live in primary and secondary rainforests in Indonesia and the Philippines. Their bodies, which vary in colour from light grey to dark brown, are only about 12cm long, but their tail is often twice that length. They have a comparatively large head, which they can rotate 180°, and huge eyes and sensitive ears, allowing them to locate the tastiest insects.

Tarsiers live in family groups of up to eight, and spend most of the day in trees, often strangler fig trees. They have a curious 'song' which they use when defending their territory. The best places to see these delightful creatures is Tangkoko-Batuangas Dua Saudara, and Lore Lindu, national parks in Sulawesi. But they are tiny, and sleep a lot, so you'll have to look long and hard.

Stefan Merker

MANADO
☎ 0431

In 1844 Manado had been levelled by earthquakes, so the Dutch redesigned it from scratch. Fourteen years later, the famous naturalist Alfred Wallace visited, and described the city of Manado as 'one of the prettiest in the East'. Today, this large provincial capital is clean, confident and cosmopolitan, with the highest standard of living in eastern Indonesia. The locals are affable and the kids won't hound you with constant assaults of 'Hello Misteerrrr'.

There are many attractions near Manado that can be visited as day trips, but some travellers prefer to stay in places like Tomohon (see the Tomohon section later in this chapter).

History

The original Minahasans are said to originate from Lumimuut, who rose from the sea and gave birth to Toar. After many years' separation, mother and son met again. Not recognising each other, they married and their descendants populated the region. Minahasan lands and languages were divided by the god Muntu Untu at Watu Pinabetengan (the 'dividing stone'), a carved rock near Kawangkoan.

Rice surpluses from Minahasa's volcanic hinterland made Manado a strategic port for European traders sailing to and from the 'Spice Islands' (Maluku). Spain established a fort at Manado in 1627, but by 1643 the Manado rulers wanted their unruly and corrupt Spanish guests out, and appealed to the Dutch VOC on Ternate for help. The Dutch and their Minahasan allies eventually gained the upper hand in 1655, built their own fortress in 1658 and expelled the last of the Spaniards a few years later.

The Dutch helped unite the linguistically diverse Minahasan confederacy, and in 1693 the Minahasans scored a decisive military victory against the Bolaang to the south. By the mid-1800s, compulsory cultivation schemes were producing huge crops of cheap coffee for a Dutch-run monopoly. Minahasans suffered immensely from this 'progress', yet economic, religious and social ties with the colonists continued to intensify. Minahasan mercenaries put down anti-Dutch rebellions on Java and elsewhere, earning them the name *anjing Belanda* (Dutch dogs).

The Japanese occupation of 1942-5 was a period of deprivation, and the Allies bombed Manado heavily in 1945. During the war of independence that followed, there was bitter division between pro-Indonesian unitarians and those favouring Dutch-sponsored federalism, and the city was bombed by Indonesian troops in 1958.

These days, Manado is a vibrant city, which seemingly belies the economic crisis affecting the rest of Indonesia. Development of Bitung's deep sea port, and direct air links with the Philippines and Singapore, have opened Manado to the outside world, and trade and tourism continue to flourish.

Orientation

Along Jl Sam Ratulangi, the main road running north-south, you'll find upmarket restaurants, hotels and supermarkets. The esplanade, Jl Piere Tendean, is a surprisingly dreary thoroughfare but this is slowly changing with new breakwaters, dive centres and a hole in the ground that promises to be another huge shopping centre with a McDonalds hamburger joint.

Information

Tourist Offices The North Sulawesi Tourism Office (☎/fax 864911), just off Jl 17 Agustus (look for the sign), is open from 8 am to 2 pm Monday to Thursday; until 11 am on Friday and until noon on Saturday. Far more helpful is the Tourist Information Counter at the airport: it has good maps on the wall, and plenty of hotel brochures with current price lists. Don't be fooled by the 'Tourism Information Service' sign outside the Culture, Art and Tourism Department (☎ 851723), just down from the Merpati office. It can provide a few dated brochures, but nothing more.

National Parks Office The KSDA office (☎ 862688, fax 864296) has informative

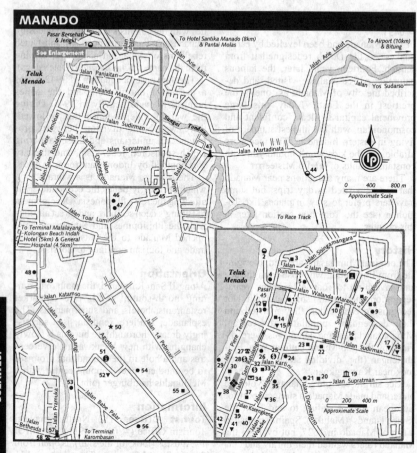

MANADO

brochures and advice about trekking in Tangkoko-Batuangus Dua Saudara National Park.

Philippines Consulate Most foreigners don't need a visa to visit the Philippines, but you can check with the consulate (☎ 862181, fax 855316) or with the Bouraq office (which sells tickets to Davao). It is nigh impossible to buy Filipino pesos at the banks in Manado, but you could try at the consulate. See the general Getting There &

Away section at the start of this chapter for more information about travelling to the Philippines.

Money Manado is overflowing with banks, and it's the best place in the region to change money. Bank Central Asia (BCA) probably has the best rates, and quickly provides cash advances of up to three million rupiah on Visa and MasterCard. Other good banks include: BII bank, which accepts Visa, MasterCard, Alto and Cirrus cards for

MANADO

PLACES TO STAY			
3	Smiling Hostel; Celebes Hotel	41	Dolphin Donats
7	New Angkasa Hotel	42	Rumah Makan Green Garden
8	Rex Hotel; Hotel Regina	52	Hilltop Restaurant
10	Manado Plaza Hotel; Ebony Disco		

PLACES TO STAY
- 3 Smiling Hostel; Celebes Hotel
- 7 New Angkasa Hotel
- 8 Rex Hotel; Hotel Regina
- 10 Manado Plaza Hotel; Ebony Disco
- 14 Kawanua Sahid Hotel
- 20 Biteya City Hotel
- 22 Hotel Kawanua
- 23 Manado Bersehati Hotel
- 30 Novotel Manado
- 33 Hotel Jawa Timur
- 37 Hotel Mini Cakalele
- 39 Hotel Jeprinda
- 40 Hotel New Queen
- 49 Hotel Minahasa
- 55 Hotel Sahid Manado

PLACES TO EAT
- 15 Rumah Makan Ria Rio
- 17 KFC; Galael Supermarket
- 18 Rumah Makan Raja Oci
- 36 Restoran Surabaya
- 38 Bacarita Restoran

- 41 Dolphin Donats
- 42 Rumah Makan Green Garden
- 52 Hilltop Restaurant

OTHER
- 1 Boats to Bunaken
- 2 Pelabuhan Manado (Port)
- 4 Ticket Offices (Boats from Manado Port)
- 5 President Complex (Shops & Cinema)
- 6 Kienteng Ban Hian Kiong
- 9 Manado Cinema
- 11 Town Square
- 12 Wisata Disco
- 13 Benteng Cinema
- 16 Oriental Bar & Karaoke
- 19 Museum Negeri Propinsi Sulawesi Utara
- 21 Garuda Office
- 24 Silk Air Office
- 25 Bank Rakyat
- 26 Pelni Office
- 27 Telkom Office

- 28 Bank BII
- 29 Blue Banter; Sunset Cafe
- 31 Matahari Department Store; KFC; Timezone; Batavia Restoran
- 32 Bank BCA
- 34 Main Post Office; Internet Centre
- 35 Bouraq Office
- 43 Toar Limimuut Monument
- 44 Terminal Paal 2
- 45 Philippines Consulate
- 46 Culture, Art & Tourism Department
- 47 Merpati Office
- 48 Mandala Office
- 50 Police Station
- 51 North Sulawesi Tourism Office
- 53 Studio 21 Cinema
- 54 Immigration Office
- 56 KSDA (National Parks Office)
- 57 Sam Ratulagni Monument
- 58 Wartel

SULAWESI

cash advances; Bank Rakyat; and BNI bank, at the airport, which accepts Visa and MasterCard.

Post & Communications The main post office, on Jl Sam Ratulangi, is open from about 8 am to 7.30 pm Monday to Friday, but closes at 6 pm on weekends. It has a very popular and efficient Internet centre (guest_@manado.wasantara.net.id – place a number from 1 to 6 before the (@), which charges a very reasonable 2000Rp per 15 minutes. The efficient 24 hour Telkom office is nearby, also on Jl Sam Ratulangi. Numerous wartels around town offer competitive long-distance rates.

Emergency The general hospital, Rumah Sakit Umum (☎ 853191), is on Jl Monginsidi in Malalayang; and there is an emergency number for ambulances (☎ 118). Both the main police station (inquiries ☎ 852916, emergencies ☎ 110) and immigration office (☎ 863491) are on Jl 17 Agustus.

Things to See

Most of the main attractions are outside the city, but the provincial **Museum Negeri Propinsi Sulawesi Utara** (☎ 892685, Jl Supratman) is worth a look. It features a large display of traditional costumes, housing, implements and so on, with captions in English. It costs 750Rp to enter, and is open from 8 am to 2 pm, Sunday to Thursday; until 11 am on Friday and until midday on Saturday.

The 19th century **Kienteng Ban Hian Kiong** is the oldest Buddhist temple in eastern Indonesia and hosts a spectacular festival in February (variable dates). Standing on Jl Panjaitan, it makes for a colourful landmark.

There seem to be monuments on every second corner dedicated to Minahasan and Indonesian heroes. The **Sam Ratulangi monument** honours the first republican governor of east Indonesia, hailed as the 'father to the Minahasan people' after his death in June 1949. **Toar Lumimuut monument** depicts the Adam and Eve characters of Minahasan mythology, Lumimuut and her son-husband, Toar.

Activities

There are a few sporting activities in and around Manado. Blue Banter (see Diving under Pulau Bunaken later in this chapter) offers jet-skiing (US$36, 30 minutes) and half-day fishing trips (US$100 per person). Affluent locals, and golf-crazy visitors, head to the driving range, which is on the road to the airport. For relief from the incessant heat, the public can use the swimming pool at Kawanua Sahid Hotel for 6500Rp.

Special Events

Minahasans love an excuse to party. Watch out for festivals, such as: the Tai Pei Kong festival, which is held at Kienteng Ban Hian Kong in February; Pengucapan Syukur (Minahasan Thanksgiving Day) in June/July/August; Bunaken Festival in July; the Anniversary of Manado on 14 July; traditional horse races in the second week of August; and the anniversary of North Sulawesi province on 23 September.

Places to Stay – Budget

Manado is one place where you can find comfortable, mid-range accommodation for a budget price.

Smiling Hostel (☎ 868463, Jl Rumambi 7), in a charmless, cement block backing on to the old harbour, is cheerful, central, popular and clean – and, best of all, there's information aplenty from staff, other travellers and message boards. Dorm beds cost 7500Rp, basic singles/doubles are 11,000/17,000Rp and the 'deluxe' rooms for 22,500Rp have a private bathroom. The rooftop *cafe* does a brisk trade in jaffles, pancakes, fried rice and beer – all the basic food groups.

The friendly **Rex Hotel** (☎ 851136, fax 867706, Jl Sugiono 3) is modern and clean, and has economy rooms for 12,500/17,500Rp, and air-con rooms for 35,000Rp. **Manado Bersehati Hotel** (☎ 855022, fax 857238, Jl Sudirman 1) is a Minahasan-style house, set about 20m off the main road. The staff are efficient and helpful (although one reader did warn us about the dishonest manager), but all the rooms are tiny. The cheapest rooms, for 12,500/21,000Rp, are basic;

the rooms with a bathroom and fan are 21,000/27,500Rp; and better rooms with air-con cost from 42,500Rp. Another quiet, central option is the friendly **Hotel Jawa Timur** (☎ 851970, Jl Kartini 5). Basic rooms cost 13,200Rp, and other tiny rooms with private bathroom cost 27,500/44,000Rp with fan/air-con.

Hotel Kawanua (☎ 863842, fax 861974, Jl Sudirman II/40) is a decent place, but often full. Rooms with shared bathrooms cost 21,850Rp; singles/doubles with a bathroom and fan are 26,450/32,300Rp; and 36,800Rp with air-con and hot water. **Hotel Jeprinda** (☎ 864049, Jl Sam Ratulangi 33) is cheerful, but noisy. The standard rooms with air-con and satellite TV are average, but cheap, for 39,500/46,000Rp; the 'superior' rooms for 62,500Rp are spacious and well furnished. Nearby, the comfortable **Hotel Mini Cakalele** (☎ 852942, fax 86 6948, Jl Korengkeng 40) is great value. It has rooms with verandahs around a courtyard for 25,850Rp with a fan; 38,500Rp with air-con and satellite TV. Suites are luxurious and only cost 77,000Rp.

Hotel Minahasa (☎ 862559, 862059, Jl Sam Ratulangi 199) is an elegant hotel with a colonial atmosphere that is constantly recommended by readers. The friendly manager speaks Dutch and English. Spotlessly clean rooms with a fan cost 39,600/52,800Rp; 82,500/95,700Rp with air-con. It's a little inconveniently located, however.

Other good, quiet and mid-range options, with budget prices, include: **Biteya City Hotel** (☎ 866598, Jl Supratman), with rooms for 34,650/42,350Rp with a fan and 42,350/50,050Rp with air-con; and **New Angkasa Hotel** (☎ 864062, Jl Sugiono 10) with large, well-furnished rooms for 35,000Rp with a fan, and 45,000Rp with air-con and satellite TV – further discounts of 25% are possible.

Places to Stay – Mid-Range

Next to Smiling Hostel, **Celebes Hotel** (☎ 870425, fax 859068, Jl Rumambi 8A) has a large range of rooms at good prices. The cheapest rooms from 25,000Rp to 45,000Rp are comfortable and clean, but have a shared bathroom. The better rooms, from 59,950Rp to 79,850Rp, have private bathrooms with hot water. The cafeteria has great views over the chaotic fish market. *Hotel Regina (☎ 85 0090, fax 867706, Jl Sugiono 1)* is a brand, spanking new, but charmless, place with spotless rooms for 88,000Rp with air-con, hot water and satellite TV.

Hotel New Queen (☎ 855551, fax 853049, Jl Wakeke 12) is clean and on a quiet street. It's one of the best mid-range places in Manado, with singles/doubles from US$54/61, but it will accept rupiah at a very favourable rate.

Manado Plaza Hotel (☎ 851124, fax 86 2940, email plaza@mdo.mega.net.id, Jl Walanda Maramis 1) is an ageing landmark in the heart of town. Motel-style rooms with satellite TV, air-con and hot water start from only 60,000Rp, and it's very good value. Free entrance to its sleazy Ebony disco and karaoke room may not be a major selling point for some folk.

The classy *Kolongan Beach Indah Hotel (☎/fax 853001, Jl Walter Monginsidi)* in Malalayang is a quiet alternative to Manado, and very handy to the Malalayang bus terminal (about 100m away). Rooms with hot water and air-con (some with views) cost 60,000/75,000Rp, and the *restaurant* is a good place to wait for your bus.

Places to Stay – Top End
Kawanua Sahid Hotel (☎ 67777, fax 65220, Jl Sam Ratulangi 1) was Manado's top establishment, but is now looking a bit dated. It charges from US$61/73 for singles/doubles, but does accept rupiah at favourable rates. The associated *Hotel Sahid Manado (☎ 851688, fax 863326, Jl Babe Palar)* is huge, but inconvenient, and has a range of rooms for about the same price as its 'cousin'.

Along the esplanade, the newest and most expensive is *Novotel Manado (☎ 855555, fax 851174, email novotel@mdo.mega.net.id, Jl Piere Tendean)*. The rooms start from US$139, and stop at a lazy US$1198 for the 'Presidential Suite'. It is almost permanently empty, so big discounts are often advertised.

Hotel Santika Manado (☎ 858222, fax 858666, email santika@mdo.mega.net.id), about 8km north of Manado, is one of several super-expensive resorts along nearby beaches. The rooms start at US$108/121.

Places to Eat
Manado is a Mecca for adventurous diners. Regional delights include *kawaok*, translated into Indonesian as *tikus hutan goreng* (fried forest rat). The name is unfortunate, because this heavily spiced dish is quite tasty. There's also tough *gamy rintek wuuk* (spicy dog meat), *lawang pangang* (stewed bat), tender and tasty freshwater *ikan mas* (gold fish) and *tinutuan* (vegetable porridge). However, most restaurants in Manado only offer the latter two dishes on their menu. One popular place that does offer some decent traditional food is *Rumah Makan Green Garden (Jl Sam Ratulangi)*.

The drinks of choice are *saguer*, a very quaffable fermented sago wine, and Cap Tikus (literally, rat brand), the generic name for distilled saguer. Cap Tikus is sold as No 1, No 2 or No 3, referring to its strength and when it was removed from the distillation process. It is best diluted and served over ice. Durian lovers should try crushed durian in saguer.

The *night warungs* along the esplanade near Pasar 45, and further south along Jl Piere Tendean, offer a good selection of cheap Indonesian food. A number of breezy *restaurants* strung along the esplanade serve fresh seafood and other cuisine, and cold drinks – perfect for admiring the awesome sunsets. The best, and most accessible, is probably the badly signed *Bacarita Restoran*, just south of the Novotel; and it's open 24 hours. Overlooking the water, opposite the Novotel, *Sunset Cafe* has the best setting in Manado. If you stick to soft drinks and Indonesian food, it's surprisingly good value; but the western food (pizzas and burgers from 18,000Rp) and alcoholic drinks are not cheap.

For delicious food and great views, stop at one of the restaurants in the Lokon foothills, along the road to Tomohon (see Places to Eat under Tomohon later in this

SULAWESI

chapter). More convenient, with similarly gorgeous views, the *Hilltop Restaurant* has reasonably priced drinks, but most meals start from 20,000Rp. The entrance is unsigned and opposite the tourist office.

For fresh seafood, try *Rumah Makan Ria Rio (Jl Sudirman 5)* or *Rumah Makan Raja Oci*, which is further east along Jl Sudirman. *Restoran Surabaya (Jl Sarapung)* has a long and varied menu, but caters more for the upmarket local clientele.

There is a *KFC* above *Galael Supermarket* on Jl Sudirman, and another next to the Matahari department store on Jl Sam Ratulangi. For pastries, hot and cold drinks and simple Indonesian food, try *Batavia Restoran*, a few metres north of the Matahari department store.

One of the best is certainly *Dolphin Donats (Jl Sam Ratulangi)*. It specialises in doughnuts, but also offers a large range of delicious Indonesian, Chinese and western food, such as steaks (17,500Rp) and burgers (8000Rp). It is clean, has good service and is ideal for families.

Entertainment

As in the nearby Philippines, music is a way of life for the Minahasans. They love jazz, and there are always small concerts and backroom gigs, so ask around. The discos tend to look like crowded airport lounges early in the evening, but when the smuggled flasks of Cap Tikus are drained, the crowds loosen up and mob the dance floor.

The young crowd heads to *Wisata Disco*, near Pasar 45. It has it all: a pub, restaurant, disco and karaoke. *Ebony Disco* in the Manado Plaza Hotel complex can be a bit of a pick-up joint. *Oriental Bar and Karaoke* is one of several karaoke joints along Jl Sudirman – enter at your own risk. The younger set hang around the *Timezone* video arcade in the Matahari department store.

Studio 21 Cinema is modern and features recent western releases (with Indonesian subtitles). More convenient, but not as comfortable, are the *Manado* and *Benteng* cinemas. The local (Indonesian-language) *Manado Post* lists screening details.

Getting There & Away

Air Merpati (☎ 853213) flies daily to Jakarta (1,873,600Rp), via Ujung Pandang (853,900Rp) and Surabaya (1,421,800Rp); almost daily to Ternate (352,300Rp), with connections to Ambon; and less regularly to Sorong (475,000Rp), Luwuk, Palu, Gorontalo, and Naha and Melanguane (Sangir-Talaud islands). See the individual sections, and the Sulawesi Air Fares chart, in this chapter for details.

For the same price as Merpati, Garuda (☎ 852154) flies daily from Manado to Jakarta, via Ujung Pandang, with same day connections to Denpasar; and Bouraq (☎ 841470) and Mandala (☎ 851743) fly to Jakarta, via Ujung Pandang and Surabaya, five times a week.

Tickets for domestic flights often cost slightly less at travel agencies, and agencies often sell international tickets at substantial discounts. Several reliable travel agencies are located around Rumah Makan Green Garden, on Jl Sam Ratulangi.

See the introductory Getting There & Away section in this chapter for details about international flights on Bouraq and Silk Air (☎ 863744) to/from Manado.

The international departure tax is 25,000Rp.

Bus There are three reasonably orderly terminals for long-distance buses and local mikrolets.

To Tomohon, Tondano and other places south of Manado, they leave from Terminal Karombasan, south of the city. From the far southern Terminal Malalayang, very regular buses go to Kotamobagu (6000/7000Rp for normal/air-con, three hours) and Gorontalo (16,000/25,000Rp, 10 hours), and others leave at least every hour all the way to Ujung Pandang (95,000/105,000Rp, two days), via Palu (50,000/55,000Rp) and Poso (55,000/60,000Rp). Tickets on all long-distance buses can (and should) be booked one day in advance at the terminals.

From Terminal Paal 2, at the eastern end of Jl Martadinata, varied public transport runs to Bitung, the airport and Airmadidi.

Boat All Pelni boats use the deep-water port of Bitung, 55km from Manado. Five Pelni liners call by once or twice a week: the *Umsini* goes to Kwandang (36,500/112,000Rp for economy/1st class), Balikpapan (96,500/327,00Rp) and Ujung Pandang (134,000/456,500Rp); the *Lambelu*, to Ternate (26,000/83,000Rp), Ambon (82,500/250,500Rp) and Ujung Pandang (134,000/456,500Rp); the *Ciremai*, to Banggai islands, Ternate (26,000/83,000Rp) and Sorong (91,000/307,500Rp); the *Kambuna*, to Balikpapan (96,500/327,00Rp) and Ujung Pandang (134,000/456,500Rp); and the *Tilongkabila*, to Tahuna (29,500/95,000Rp), Lirung (43,500/143,500Rp), Gorontalo (32,500/98,000Rp) and other ports along the south-eastern coast. There is no longer any Pelni service to Davao, in the southern Philippines.

The Pelni office (☎ 62844, Jl Ratulangi) is open for ticket sales Monday to Friday from 8.30 am to 2.30 pm. On Saturday, you can buy tickets at the Pelni office in the port complex at Bitung; and on Sunday, you'll have to wait until Monday.

From the port in Manado, small, slow and uncomfortable boats leave every day or two for Tahuna and Lirung in the Sangir-Talaud islands; and to Mangole, Sanana and Ambon in Maluku. Tickets are available from the stalls outside the port. From Bitung, four overnight ferries a week also travel to Ternate in northern Maluku. These boats are strictly for the frugal and adventurous.

Getting Around
To/From The Airport Mikrolets from Sam Ratulangi airport go to Terminal Paal 2 (500Rp), where you can change onto a mikrolet heading to Pasar 45 (400Rp) or elsewhere in the city. From the airport to the city (13km), drivers want 20,000Rp, but it'll cost about 13,000Rp if they use the meter.

Public Transport About 70% of all vehicles in Manado are mikrolets, so finding one with a spare seat is a matter of waiting a second or two. They're not too hard to work out: look for the sign on top of the vehicle, check the direction it's going and double-check the tiny sign on the window. For example, a mikrolet marked Malalayang on top, but Pasar 45 in the window, heading north, will go up Jl Sam Ratulangi. Most mikrolets heading north go through Pasar 45, and past the Pasar Jengki fish market, but some go directly to Terminal Paal 2 along Jl Sudirman. Mikrolets heading to Terminal Malalayang go down Jl Sam Ratulangi or Jl Piere Tendean; and to Terminal Karombasan, they often go along Jl 17 Agustus. The fare for any destination around town is 400Rp.

Private taxis are reasonably cheap, wonderfully air-conditioned and drivers will use the meter if you insist.

PULAU BUNAKEN
☎ 0431
The wildly varied shapes and colours of the fringing coral off Pulau Bunaken have become an international snorkelling and diving attraction. The 808 hectare island is part of the 75,265 hectare Bunaken National Marine Park, which includes: Manado Tua (Old Manado), the dormant volcano that can be seen from Manado, and climbed (four hours) following a path; Nain and Mantehage islands; and Pulau Siladen, which has a homestay (see Places to Stay & Eat later in this section). The national park headquarters (near the jetty at Pantai Liang) is often closed, and is not interested in being a quasi-tourist office.

Most of Pulau Bunaken's residents live in Bunaken village at the southern tip. The scarcity of fresh water has limited the island's development, and villagers must import their drinking water from Manado. (Washing water is drawn from small, brackish wells.) And, unfortunately, tourism has exacted a heavy toll: westerly winds often sweep alarming piles of garbage on to Pantai Liang, sometimes turning picturesque tropical beaches into refuse heaps overnight.

Before you go to Bunaken, visit Smiling Hostel (see Places to Stay – Budget under Manado earlier in this chapter): the message board is a veritable goldmine of current information for, and by, fellow travellers.

SULAWESI

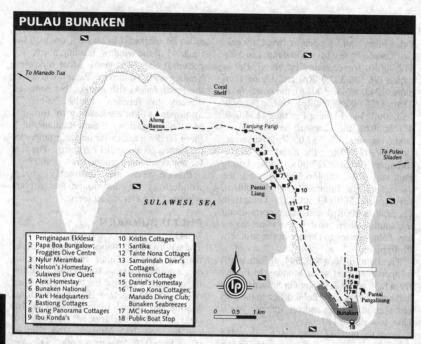

PULAU BUNAKEN

To Manado Tua

Coral Shelf

Alung Banua

Tanjung Parigi

To Pulau Siladen

Pantai Liang

SULAWESI SEA

1 Penginapan Ekklesia
2 Papa Boa Bungalow;
   Froggies Dive Centre
3 Nylur Merambai
4 Nelson's Homestay;
   Sulawesi Dive Quest
5 Alex Homestay
6 Bunaken National
   Park Headquarters
7 Bastiong Cottages
8 Liang Panorama Cottages
9 Ibu Konda's
10 Kristin Cottages
11 Santika
12 Tante Nona Cottages
13 Samurindah Diver's
   Cottages
14 Lorenso Cottage
15 Daniel's Homestay
16 Tuwo Kona Cottages;
   Manado Diving Club;
   Bunaken Seabreezes
17 MC Homestay
18 Public Boat Stop

Pantai Pangalisang

Bunaken

0 0.5 1 km

Diving & Snorkelling

Bunaken boasts some of the world's most spectacular and accessible coral drop-offs, caves and valleys, full of brightly coloured sponges and fish – you may also be lucky enough to see turtles, eels and dolphins. Knowledgeable dive operators can also take you to some fascinating WWII plane wrecks. The most accessible site is the flat coral off Pantai Liang, which takes a dramatic 90° turn less than 100m offshore, plummeting from one to 2m depths to dark oblivion.

The best snorkelling and diving sites are listed on maps in most homestays on Bunaken, and any decent boatman will know where to take you. Pantai Liang and in front of Daniel's Homestay (Pantai Pangalisang) are good, accessible spots if you don't have a boat. Well-worn snorkelling equipment can be rented from warungs, dive centres and most homestays on

Bunaken for about 20,000Rp per day, but it's best to bring your own.

The rates for dive trips do vary, but it's obviously very important to use a qualified centre with well-maintained equipment. Trips around Bunaken, and nearby islands, including most equipment, transport, lunch and a guide, will cost about US$50/60 for one/two dives; US$20 for subsequent dives; and US$250 to US$400 for PADI courses. There is some competition on the island, so discounts are always possible, especially when it's quiet.

There are several reliable dive centres on Bunaken. At Pantai Liang is the impressive Froggies Dive Centre (email manado@ divefroggies.com), based at Papa Boa Bungalow and linked with Smiling Hostel in Manado; and the well-established Sulawesi Dive Quest (☎ 870253), also based at Kolongan Beach Indah Hotel in Manado At

Pantai Pangalisang, the best are Manado Diving Club, which charges a bargain US$18/33/47 for one/two/three dives, and has been recommended by readers; Daniel's Homestay; Bunaken Seabreezes (also recommended by readers); and Samurindah Diver's Cottages.

The best dive centres are on the mainland: Baracuda Diving Resort (☎ 862033, fax 864848) at Pantai Molas beach, north of Manado; Blue Banter (☎ 851174, fax 86 2135, email b_banter@mdo.mega.net.id) on Jl Piere Tendean, Manado, which is part of Novotel so it's reliable, but expensive; the well-regarded Nusantara Diving Centre (☎/fax 860638, email ndc@mdo.mega.net .id), Pantai Molas, which is committed to local marine conservation; and the recommended, Italian-run Manado Seagarden Adventures (☎/fax 861100, email kudalaut@ indonet.net.id) in Manado.

Boat Trips

For those with less time and more money, a few operators organise expensive day trips to Bunaken on yachts, glass-bottom boats and quasi-submarines. For example, Blue Banter (see Diving & Snorkelling earlier in this section) charges from US$30 for half-day trips by 'submarine' or boat. Bunaken is also a very easy day trip from Manado – see Getting There & Away in this section for details.

Places to Stay & Eat

Most tariffs are negotiable, and should include a fan and/or mosquito net. All prices in this section are per person (unless stated otherwise), and all rates include three meals.

The homestays at Pantai Liang are a little close together, which means impromptu beach parties are more likely, and Liang has the better beach. The homestays at Pantai Pangalisang mostly overlook ugly mangroves, but are only metres from extraordinary snorkelling sites and very close to the island's best beach at Bunaken village. All homestays between Bunaken village and the jetty at Pangalisang are connected by a concrete path, but the homestays south of the jetty at Liang are a little hard to reach. Only the places at Liang have telephones.

Pantai Pangalisang At the end of the jetty **Samurindah Diver's Cottages** is the most recent, and expensive, place to stay. It has a neat row of modern bungalows, with hot water, for 100,000Rp, but this is overpriced compared to other places nearby. Heading south, **Lorenso Cottage** is run by a friendly, easy-going family. Cottages cost 35,000Rp. The biggest place, **Daniel's Homestay** (Manado ☎/fax 0431-866311) has older cottages for 30,000Rp, and well furnished, new cottages closer to the sea for 40,000Rp. It is popular and well set up, so it's a good place to meet other travellers.

Tuwo Kona Cottages is run by a women's co-operative, and is highly recommended. Pleasant cottages around spotless grounds cost 35,000Rp.

Also good is the **Manado Diving Club**. Cottages around a lawn, with no mangroves in sight, cost 30,000/40,000Rp for singles/ doubles with a ceiling fan; and up to 60,000/ 75,000Rp for larger, nicer cottages. Diving and accommodation packages are available.

Bunaken Seabreezes (Manado ☎ 0431-864117) is very well set up, with a small beach, decent bar and satellite TV – the closest thing to a 'party atmosphere' at Pangalisang. Cottages cost 33,000Rp to 60,000Rp.

Almost in Bunaken village, the last homestay has the best beach. **MC Homestay** has ordinary cottages, but the setting is superb, and the prices are reasonable (from 35,000Rp). One satisfied guest claimed that it 'served the best food in Sulawesi'.

Pantai Liang Right at the jetty is **Bastiong Cottages** (☎ 853566). The rooms are pleasant, if a somewhat clustered together; and more were being built at the time of writing. They are a little more expensive at 60,000Rp, but are well furnished – the only truly 'mid-range' option.

Continuing north are several cheap places of similar standard and price. **Alex Homestay** is cheap at 30,000Rp, but it's worth paying a little more for something better.

Nelson's Homestay (☎ 856288) is decent with a range of rooms at good prices: from 20,000Rp for ramshackle huts to 40,000Rp for something newer and sturdier. *Nylur Merambai (☎ 869015)* has nice rooms for 40,000Rp, which overlook a mangrove, but the *restaurant* has far better seaviews.

Papa Boa Bungalow (☎ 850434) is a popular place with a decent selection of pleasant cottages. With a communal, outside bathroom, the cottages cost 30,000Rp; the better cottages with private bathrooms are 40,000Rp. Often ignored, and last in line (so it's quieter), are the two rooms at *Penginapan Ekklesia (☎ 869271)* for 40,000Rp.

About 300m south of the jetty, in 'upper Liang', beach frontage is sacrificed for superb views above the rocks. Most places are poorly signed, and you'll have to look for staff and for steps up to the cottages. Most are only two or three bungalows, with a tiny restaurant, and cost about 30,000Rp. Of these, *Tante Nona Cottages* continues to get rave reviews for friendly service and outstanding meals; and many travellers have enjoyed their stay at *Liang Panorama Cottages*, *Santika*, *Kristin Cottages* and *Ibu Konda's*.

Pulau Siladen *Martha Homestay* is in the fishing village on nearby Pulau Siladen. It is a basic, but pleasant, alternative to Bunaken, and rooms cost 25,000Rp.

Getting There & Away

Every day at about 3 pm, except Sunday, a public boat (5000Rp, one hour) leaves the harbour, near Pasar Jengki fish market in Manado, for Bunaken village and Pulau Siladen. The boat doesn't normally stop at Liang or Pangalisang, so you'll have to walk from the boat landing in Bunaken village (near the huge church) to your homestay, or charter something directly from Manado to the jetties at Liang or Pangalisang beaches. The boat leaves Bunaken between 7 and 8 am daily (except Sunday), so you can't day trip from Manado using the public boat.

Most travellers charter a boat. Boatmen will approach you when you walk along the road towards Pasar Jengki; on Bunaken, ask around the beach or your homestay. Boatmen are now used to big-spending foreigners, so you'll have to pay about 25,000Rp per boat (holding about 10 people) for a one way trip, or about 80,000Rp per boat per day (or about 12,000Rp per hour) to Bunaken, and the best snorkelling and swimming sites around the nearby islands. Chartering is worth it, especially to the remote islands and reefs, such as those around Manado Tua.

KAWANGKOAN

During WWII, the Japanese dug caves into the hills surrounding Manado to act as air-raid shelters, and as storage space for ammunition, food, weapons and medical supplies. One accessible **Japanese cave** is 3km from Kawangkoan.

About 5km from Kawangkoan is **Watu Pinabetengan**, a place of immense spiritual significance for the Minahasans. It is a stone on a summit, said to be the place where the lands of Minahasa were first divided around 670 AD in a pact to establish the region's system of independent states. Unfortunately, much of the stone and its obscure markings has been smothered by Indonesia's love affair with the bag of cement.

Mikrolets to Kawangkoan leave from Terminal Karombasan in Manado. From Kawangkoan, you can get another towards Kiawa village to see the caves; or take a bendi to Pinabetengan village. It takes you as far as the turn-off that leads to Watu Pinabetengan, and then you'll have to walk (4km).

TOMOHON
☎ 0431

Tomohon is a pleasant, cool respite from Manado, with a stunning setting below Gunung Lokon volcano. It's popular with city folk on weekends; and for travellers, it's a popular alternative to Manado, and an ideal base to explore the many nearby attractions.

Places to Stay

Happy Flower Homestay (☎ 352787, email blume@manado.wasantara.net.id), at the foot of Gunung Lokon volcano, is justifiably applauded by all for its simple accommodation, pretty garden with ponds, and cheerful hospitality. Basic singles/doubles are unbeatable for 10,000/15,000Rp; newer, individual cottages are more private and pleasant, and cost 27,500Rp to 50,000Rp. Catch the Manado to Tomohon bus, and get out at 'Gereja Pniel', a few kilometres before Tomohon. Take the path opposite the church, walk 300m and look for the homestay tucked away in trees to the right.

Kawanua Cottages (☎ 52688, fax 52060) is a collection of comfortable cottages, set around an immaculate garden, for 75,000Rp – discounts of 20% are frequently available. It is about 4km south of Tomohon, on the road to Sonder.

Homestay Tomohon (☎ 352260, Jl Pangolombian 604) is a new, but charmless, collection of brightly coloured buildings, and is very good value at 35,000Rp per double. It is not far from Kawanua cottages; look for the sign along the main road to Sonder. On the road to Uluindano, *Hotel Wawo (☎/fax 352449)* has been recommended by readers. It costs a bargain 40,000Rp per double, with hot water and satellite TV.

There are several mid-range places, all about 5km north of Tomohon, and well signed from the road to Manado. They are all set amid well-groomed gardens with gorgeous views of Lokon, and are serene (except on weekends). It's worth chartering a taxi from Tomohon to check out a few places. One of the best is *Lokon Resting Resort (☎ 351203, fax 351636)* where superb cottages cost from 96,250Rp.

Places to Eat

Minahasa's extraordinary cuisine is served in a string of restaurants on a cliff overlooking Manado, just a few kilometres before Tomohon. The food at *Tinoor Indah* and *Pemandangan* is as incredible as the spectacular views. The bus from Manado to Tomohon will drop you off at any restaurant, but buses back to Manado are often full. Most hotels in Tomohon have *restaurants*, open to the public, and there are plenty of simple *rumah makans* around town.

Getting There & Away

From Terminal Karombasan in Manado, mikrolets and minibuses regularly travel to Tomohon (1000Rp, 40 minutes). From the terminal in Tomohon, based around an abandoned petrol station along the main road, buses go to Manado, and mikrolets go to Tondano and various other towns.

Getting Around

There are a few bendis around town, but a good way to see local sights in quick time is to charter a mikrolet, or a more comfortable, but expensive, taxi. The taxis are lined up opposite the mikrolet terminal.

AROUND TOMOHON

Gunung Lokon volcano (1580m) contains a constantly simmering crater lake of varying hues, which takes about three hours to reach (another hour to the peak) from Tomohon. Before climbing any volcano in the area, report to the **vulcanology centre** in Tomohon. The centre can provide advice about the hike, and it also has spectacular photographs of other volcanoes, including Gunung Colo in the Togeans. Happy Flower Homestay in Tomohon can help arrange this, and other hikes in the area, for guests.

There are numerous other wonderful places to explore from Tomohon, and all are accessible by mikrolet from Tomohon. **Danau Linow**, a small, highly sulphurous lake, which changes colours with the light, is home to extensive birdlife. Take a mikrolet to **Sonder**, get off at **Lahendong** and walk (1.5km) to the lake. From Danau Linow, you can also hike (8km) to **Danau Tondano**, but you'll need to ask directions.

There are also hot springs, private mineral baths and nice walks near **Langowan**. From Tondano village, take a mikrolet to Langowan, and ask the driver to drop you off nearby. Several kilometres out of Tomohon, on the road to **Tara Tara**, are caves, which were used by Japanese forces during WWII. **Komplex Walepapetaupan Toar-Lumimuut** is a park, swimming pool and landscaped garden dedicated to the Minahasans' origin myth in Sonder. From Sonder, occasional mikrolets go to **Tincep**, from where it's a short walk to more pretty waterfalls.

DANAU TONDANO

This lake, 30km south-west of Manado, is 600m above sea level. It's a beautiful area for hiking, and popular with Manado's upper class who flock there for Sunday lunch. Just before **Remboken** village, along the road around the lake, **Objek Wisata Remboken** has a swimming pool, a wonderful *restaurant* overlooking the lake and some gardens to wander around. There are also several decent *restaurants* along the road around the lake, where fresh fish is, naturally, the speciality.

Surprisingly, the only place to stay around the lake is *Hotel Bethseda (☎ 0431-855368, fax 864721)*, along the main road, just before Remboken. The rooms are large and comfortable, but a little overpriced at 75,000Rp, and the hotel boasts its own hot water spring.

Some of the best **Japanese caves** are just outside Tondano village on the road to Airmadidi. A bus from Airmadidi to Tondano will get you to the caves in 45 minutes. From the caves, you can hitch or walk (one hour) to the mikrolet terminal in Tondano village.

From Terminal Karombasan in Manado, mikrolets regularly leave for Tondano village (1350Rp), or you can get there by mikrolet from Tomohon. From Tondano, catch another mikrolet to Remboken, and get off anywhere you like along the main road around the lake. From Tondano, you can also take a leisurely bendi to Objek Wisata Remboken, or anywhere in between.

AIRMADIDI

Airmadidi (Boiling Water) is the site of mineral springs. Legend has it that nine angels flew down from heaven on nights of the full moon to bathe and frolic here. One night a mortal succeeded in stealing a dress belonging to one of them – unable to return to heaven, she was forced to remain on earth. The public baths make a refreshing stop after an overnight hike to the peak of nearby Gunung Klabat.

Airmadidi's real attraction is the odd little **pre-Christian tombs** known as *warugas*. Corpses were placed in these carved stone boxes in a foetal position with household articles, gold and porcelain, but most have been plundered. There's a group of these tombs at Airmadidi Bawah, a 15 minute walk from Airmadidi mikrolet terminal. You can see more warugas at Likupang, at the tip of the peninsula.

Mikrolets to Airmadidi leave from Terminal Paal 2 in Manado, and there are connections between Airmadidi and Tondano and Bitung.

GUNUNG KLABAT

Gunung Klabat (2022m) is easily the highest peak on the peninsula. The obvious path to the crater at the top starts behind the police station at Airmadidi, where you must register and take a guide. The climb (about four hours to the top, two for the descent) goes through superb rainforest flora and fauna, but it's a tough hike.

It's best to stay overnight near the top, in a tent or makeshift shelter, and be there for the sunrise and the stupendous views across the whole peninsula. Try to avoid Sunday, when the mountain can be surprisingly crowded with local hikers. This area was the last hideout for the anti-Indonesian rebels in the late 1950s and early 60s; and it's easy to see how they evaded capture for so long.

BITUNG
☎ 0438

Sheltered by Pulau Lembah, Bitung is the chief regional port, and home to many factories. Despite its spectacular setting, the town is very unattractive, so if you arrive by boat, head to Manado, Tomohon or anywhere else as soon as possible.

Places to Stay & Eat

Regardless of what time you arrive by boat in Bitung, there will be buses to Manado, but if you leave Bitung by boat early in the morning, it may be prudent to stay overnight. *Samudra Jaya (☎ 21333, Jl Sam Ratulangi 2)* is cheap and central, with rooms from

17,500Rp. *Penginapan Minang* (☎ 21333), a bit further along the same road, is a dark hovel above a restaurant of the same name, with rooms for about 20,000Rp. The fanciest place in town is *Dynasty Hotel* (☎ 22111, Jl Sudarso 10), with doubles from 66,000Rp.

There are plenty of unexciting *rumah makans* in the town centre, and near the port.

Getting There & Away

Bus Bitung is connected by a surfaced race-track along which mikrolet drivers often attempt to break land speed records. All sorts of vehicles leave regularly from Terminal Paal 2 in Manado (1600Rp, one hour). The driver stops at Terminal Mapalus, just outside Bitung, from where you have to catch another mikrolet (10 minutes) to town or the port.

Boat See Getting There & Away under Manado earlier in this chapter for details about boats to Bitung. The port is in the middle of Bitung, and the Pelni office (☎ 21 167) is in the port complex.

TANGKOKO-BATUANGAS DUA SAUDARA

Tangkoko is one of the most impressive and accessible nature reserves in Indonesia, and includes some coastline and coral gardens offshore. About 30km from Bitung, the 8800 hectares are home to black macaques, cuscus and tarsiers; maleo birds and endemic red knobbed hornbills, among other fauna; and rare types of rainforest flora. Tangkoko is also home to a plethora of midges called *gonones*, which bite and leave victims furiously scratching for days afterwards. Always wear long trousers, tucked into thick socks, and take covered shoes.

To enter the park, you need a permit from the KSDA (National Parks) field office in Batuputih, which currently costs 750Rp (the cost may increase for foreigners later). The office can organise knowledgeable guides to lead you along designated hiking trails (about 6km each) to view wildlife, and boat trips to nearby islands to see the preserved nesting grounds of maleos. The KSDA office in Manado (see the National Parks

office under Manado earlier in this chapter) is a good source of information, and worth visiting before heading to Tangkoko.

You could day trip from Manado with your own transport, but it's worth staying in, or near, the park so you can hike at dawn and/or dusk – easily the best times to see the wildlife. There are four basic losmen in Batuputih village – the best is probably *Mama Ruus*, with rooms for 25,000Rp, including three meals. Inside the park, you can also stay at *Ranger Homestay*, which as rooms for 17,500Rp, plus meals. If you have a tent, you can *camp* on the pleasant, black sand beach.

The main entrance is at Batuputih. From Manado, take a bus to Bitung, get off at Girian and catch a mikrolet to Batuputih. Some of the dive centres in or near Manado, as listed under Diving & Snorkelling under Pulau Bunaken earlier in this chapter, also run expensive day trips to the park from Manado.

SANGIR-TALAUD ISLANDS
☎ 0432

Strewn across the sea between Indonesia and the southern Philippines are the volcanic island groups of Sangir and Talaud. They offer dozens of unspoilt sandy beaches; a few crumbling **Portuguese forts**; several **volcanoes** to climb; many caves and waterfalls to explore; and some superb diving and snorkelling (bring your own gear). But like most wonderfully pristine places, the islands are not easy to reach.

There are 77 islands, of which 56 are inhabited. The main islands in the Sangir group are **Sangir Besar** and **Siau**; and the main islands in the Talaud group are **Karakelong**, **Salibabu** and **Kaburuang**. The capital of the group is **Tahuna** on Sangir Besar; the other major settlement is **Lirung** on Pulau Salibabu. The tourist office (☎ 22219) is on Jl Tona, Tahuna.

Places to Stay & Eat

In Tahuna, *Hotel Nasional* (☎ 21185, Jl Makaampo 58) has a range of decent rooms from 20,000/45,000Rp with fan/air-con. The best place, *Hotel Victory Veronica*

SULAWESI

(☎ 21494, Jl Raramenusa 16), has rooms with a fan for 25,000Rp, and up to 65,000Rp with air-con. **Penginapan Bintang Utara** (☎ 21 375, Jl Pahlawan) has fan-cooled rooms for 20,000Rp. The Nasional boasts the best **restaurant** in town, while the Victory Veronica has the decent **Deniest Coffee Shop**. **Manalagi Restoran** (Jl Imam Bonjol) is also OK.

In Lirung, for about 17,500/22,500Rp for singles/doubles, there is **Penginapan Chindy** and **Penginapan Sederhana**, but don't expect too much luxury or privacy. There are some **warungs** near the port, but nothing else to satisfy the tastebuds.

Getting There & Away

Air Once a week (currently Saturday), Merpati flies from Manado to Naha (302,800Rp),

which is about 20km from Tahuna; and on to Melanguane, which is near Lirung in the Talaud group. The flight to Melanguane costs 413,900Rp from Manado, or 111,100Rp from Naha. The Merpati office (☎ 21037) is on Jl Makaampo, Tahuna.

Boat Travelling by boat provides a look at the stunning set of volcanic islands along the way. From Bitung (near Manado), the Pelni liner **Tilongkabila** stops at Tahuna (29,500/95,000Rp for economy/1st class) and Lirung (43,500/143,500Rp) once every two weeks. Pelni is far more comfortable than the other options, such as the **Pulo Teratai** and the **Agape Star**, which sail between Manado and Lirung (15 hours), often via Tahuna (11 hours), every one or two days. Book at the boat offices near the port in Manado.

Maluku

From Halmahera in the north to Wetar off the north-eastern end of Timor, hundreds of islands make up the province of Maluku (previously called The Moluccas). Sprawled across a vast area of ocean, but representing only a tiny proportion of Indonesia's land area, what these islands lack in size they more than make up for in historical significance. These were the fabled 'Spice Islands' to which Indian, Chinese, Arab and later, European traders, came in search of the cloves, nutmeg and mace which grew only there. These islands bore the brunt of the first European attempts to wrest control of the Indonesian archipelago and the lucrative spice trade.

HISTORY
Pre-Colonial Times
Before the arrival of Europeans, the sultanate of Ternate held tenuous sway over some of the islands and parts of neighbouring Sulawesi and Irian Jaya, but there was little political unity. When the Portuguese reached the Indonesian archipelago, Maluku was known to them as Jazirat-al-Muluk (Land of Many Kings), from which the name Maluku apparently originated. (Another explanation is that Maluku is derived from the words *yasiratul jabal malik*, which loosely translated mean 'mountainous'.)

The spice trade goes back a lot further than the Portuguese and Dutch presence. The Roman encyclopaedist Pliny described trade in cinnamon and other spices from Indonesia to Madagascar and East Africa and from there to Rome. By the 1st century AD, Indonesian trade was firmly established with other parts of Asia, including India and China, and spices also reached Europe through the caravan routes from India and the Persian Gulf.

The Portuguese
Apart from Marco Polo, and a few wandering missionaries, Portuguese sailors were the first Europeans to set foot on Indonesian soil.

HIGHLIGHTS

- Between them, the islands of Ambon, Seram, Saparua, Halmahera, Morotai and Bacan have lots to offer – great beaches, diving, hiking, crumbling forts, WWII wrecks and traditional cultures.

- The Banda Islands are the highlight of Maluku, with magnificent forts, a volcano, stunning diving and snorkelling, and small islands to explore.

- Ternate has awesome volcanic scenery, black-sand beaches and forts.

- The Kai Islands boast some of the best beaches east of Bali.

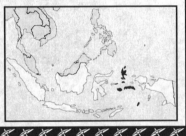

Their first small fleet and its 'white Bengalis' (as the local inhabitants called them) arrived in Melaka (Malaysia) in 1509. Their prime objective was to reach the Spice Islands of Ternate, Tidore, Ambon, Seram and the Banda Islands.

A master plan was devised for the Portuguese to bring all the important Indian Ocean trading posts under Portuguese control. The capture of Melaka in 1511, then Goa (India), preceded the Portuguese attempt to wrest control of the Spice Islands. Ternate and Tidore, the tiny, rival clove-producing islands, were the scene of the greatest Portuguese effort. The islands were

MALUKU

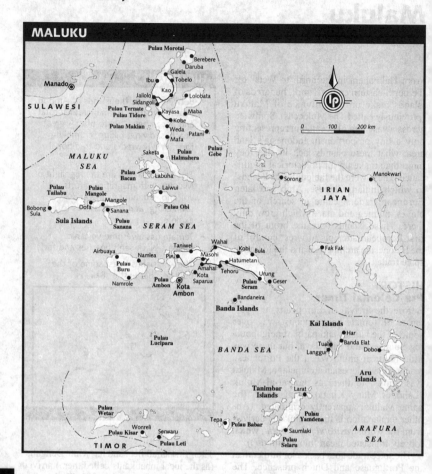

MALUKU

ruled by sultans who controlled the cultivation of cloves and policed the region with fleets of war boats with sails and more than a hundred rowers each. But the sultans had no trading boats of their own – cloves had to be shipped out, and food and other goods imported, on Malay and Javanese ships.

Early in the 16th century, Ternate granted the Portuguese a monopoly over its clove trade in return for help against Tidore. The Portuguese built their first fortress on Ternate the following year, but relations with the Muslim sultan were continually strained and they began fighting each other. The Portuguese were finally thrown out in 1575 after their fort was besieged for several years. Undeterred, they ingratiated themselves with the sultan of Tidore, and built another fort on that island.

Meanwhile, Ternate continued to expand its influence under the fiercely Islamic and anti-Portuguese Sultan Baab Ullah and his son Sultan Said. The Portuguese never succeeded in monopolising the local clove trade, so they moved south to Ambon, Seram and the Bandas, where nutmeg and mace were also produced. Again, they failed to establish a monopoly and in any case lacked the shipping and labour force to control trade in the Indian Ocean. By the end of the 16th century, the Dutch arrived with better guns, bigger ships, larger financial backing, and a more lethal combination of courage and brutality.

The Dutch

The first Dutch fleet reached Maluku in 1599, and returned home with enough spices to produce a massive profit. More ships followed, and the various Dutch companies eventually merged in 1602 to form the Vereenigde Oost-Indische Compagnie (VOC). VOC ships sailed back to Maluku and later exterminated many of the inhabitants of the Bandas.

By 1630 the Dutch were established on Ambon, in the heart of the Spice Islands, with their headquarters at Batavia (Jakarta) in the west. Melaka fell to them in 1641, but a monopoly of the spice trade eluded them for many years; they first had to fight the Ternateans, and then the Ambonese with their Makassarese allies (from Sulawesi). By around 1660, the Dutch finally succeeded in wiping out all local opposition to their rule in Maluku; and in 1663 they forced the Spanish, who had established a small presence on Ternate and Tidore, to evacuate their remaining posts. Inevitably, the importance of the islands as an international supplier of spices faded, as European competitors established plantations in other countries.

After a brief British occupation of the Dutch East Indies during the Napoleonic Wars, the Dutch returned in 1814 – but soon encountered rebellious activity. The first was led by Pattimura (Thomas Matulessy) in 1817. The uprising lasted only a few months, and ended with the capture and execution of Pattimura.

He is now regarded as one of Indonesia's national heroes – Ambon's university and airport are called Pattimura, as is one of the city's main streets. In Kota Ambon, a giant

statue depicts Pattimura as a warrior of superhuman proportions. A Christian, he came from Pulau Saparua (Saparua Island), near Pulau Ambon, and had been a sergeant-major in the British militia when the British occupied Ambon during the Napoleonic Wars.

After Independence

When the Dutch left Indonesia after WWII, Maluku was to become part of the State of East Indonesia. However, when it became apparent that the mainly Christian Maluku was going to be part of a predominantly Muslim Javanese republic, the independent Republic of the South Moluccas, or Republik Maluku Selatan (RMS), was proclaimed on Pulau Ambon in 1950. It was apparently supported by most of the 2000 or more Ambonese KNIL troops on the island. (A number of

MALUKU

Ambonese at the time were soldiers in the Royal Netherlands Indies Army, KNIL.)

A few months later, Indonesian troops occupied Pulau Buru and parts of Pulau Seram and, by the end of September 1950, had landed on Ambon. By November, most resistance on Ambon had been put down and the RMS 'government' soon fled to the Seram jungles (where many RMS troops had already gone).

At this time there were still several camps of Ambonese KNIL soldiers and their families in Java. Initially the Dutch intended to demobilise them and send them back to Ambon, but it was feared the soldiers may be massacred. Instead, the Dutch sent them, numbering about 12,000, to the Netherlands with the aim of repatriation when the RMS was suppressed, but most remained in the Netherlands. Today, at least 40,000 Malukans and their descendants live in the Netherlands; few have returned to live in Maluku.

On Seram, there continued to be pockets of RMS resistance until the mid-1960s. The dream of an independent 'South Moluccas' still has its adherents among some Malukans in the Netherlands, as well as in Maluku. There was a Maluku-related train hijack in the Netherlands in the mid-1970s, but there has been negligible activity since.

Maluku Today

In January 1999, a few months after the writing of this chapter, there were violent clashes between Muslims (mostly from Java and Sulawesi) and Christians (mostly Ambonese) on Pulau Ambon. These clashes continued for several days, often exacerbated by the violent reactions of the military and police forces, and by a seemingly uncaring central government. Muslim-Christian clashes are not uncommon in Indonesia, and Pulau Ambon has, until now, always been regarded by the Indonesian government and people as a showpiece of religious harmony.

According to media reports, many buildings in Kota Ambon were destroyed during the clashes, and many villages around Pulau Ambon were demolished. At least 200 people were killed by opposing groups, or by the police, and tens of thousands of residents fled the island. The violence also spilled over into the nearby islands of Seram and Saparua, and was particularly bad in the Kai Islands.

See the 'Warning' boxed text earlier in this chapter for information regarding how these clashes may affect travel to, and within, Maluku.

GEOGRAPHY

Maluku has an area of 850,000 sq km, of which 90% is water and 10% islands – 1027 of them at last count. The largest islands, Halmahera and Seram, are the most undeveloped and underpopulated, while the smallest, Ambon and the Banda Islands, are the most populated and developed, mainly because of the colonial spice trade.

The islands are mostly forested and mountainous, with the exception of the swampy Tanimbar and Aru islands in the south-east. The highest mountain is Gunung Binaya (Mt Binya; 3027m) on Seram, while many islands, such as Ternate (700m), are simply volcanoes with villages perched precariously around the side. Over 70 serious volcanic eruptions in Maluku have been recorded in the past few hundred years and earthquakes around the region are not uncommon.

Cloves and nutmeg are still cultivated around the islands, although the quantity and value is far lower than a few centuries ago. Businesses – mostly owned by non-Malukan Indonesians – export cocoa, coffee and fruit, such as bananas, and fishing is a big industry around Pulau Halmahera and the southern islands. On Seram, ironwood is heavily logged (as is ebony and teak on Pulau Buru), and oil is also produced.

The province contains four districts: North Maluku (the capital is Kota Ternate on Pulau Ternate); the oddly shaped and curiously conciliatory Central Halmahera (the capital is Soa Siu on Pulau Tidore); Central Maluku (the capital is Masohi on Pulau Seram), which does not include Kota Ambon or areas of Pulau Ambon, which are part of a separate municipality; and South-East Maluku (the capital is Tual in the Kai Islands).

CLIMATE

Timing a visit to Maluku is different from the rest of Indonesia. In central and southern Maluku, what is referred to as the 'dry monsoon season' (average maximum temperature of 30°C) lasts from October to March; the 'wet monsoon season' (average maximum temperature of 23°C) is from May to August; and the months in between are called the 'transition periods'. However, northern Maluku has its 'wet monsoon' from December to March.

Maluku is not somewhere you can rely on strictly defined wet or dry seasons. Try to avoid the 'wet monsoon season', when it may rain for days, but also be prepared for rain at any time anywhere in the region. To add to the confusion, there are slight climatic variations between each island group, and even on the coasts of Ambon, Halmahera and Seram it can be clear and dry while the mountainous interiors are cloudy and wet. If you're trekking in the hinterlands of these islands be prepared for a lot of rain.

FLORA & FAUNA

Vegetation is luxuriant and includes some species common to Australia such as *kayu putih* (eucalypts), as well as the usual tropical Asiatic species. Maluku hardwoods, such as amboina, are prized by timber companies. Ambon and Tanimbar islands are famous for their wild orchids, and Pulau Ternate has brilliantly coloured bougainvillea. And, of course, the nutmeg plant – which has caused so much strife in the past – is still cultivated on parts of Ambon and Saparua islands, as well as on the Bandas.

Maluku's seas teem with life such as dugongs, turtles, trepang, sharks, and all sorts of tropical fish and shellfish. In the forests, cuscus and long-nosed bandicoots thrive. In more open spaces there are wallabies, miniature tree kangaroos and Timor deer, while crocodiles and monitor lizards are found in the mangrove regions of South-East Maluku. Pulau Bacan is famous for its unique species of tail-less monkeys. All over the province, insect life abounds, and the butterflies are particularly beautiful.

The birdlife around Pulau Seram, particularly in Manusela National Park (Taman Nasional Manusela), is abundant; many species of the bright, noisy *nuri* parrot and a species of cockatoo are endemic to the island. And with some patience and guidance, you may encounter the shy *cenderawasih* (bird of paradise) in the Aru Islands. See the boxed text 'Birds of Paradise' in the Irian Jaya chapter for more detail.

POPULATION & PEOPLE

Maluku has a population of over two million people – only about 1% of Indonesia's total population. The islands are in the 'transition zone' between the Malays of Asia and the Papuans of Polynesia, resulting in a unique ethnicity. There is European ancestry, particularly Portuguese, among the Ambonese, Ternateans and southern Halmaherans; descendants of people from Polynesian islands as far as Hawaii live in northern Seram; and Javanese, Buginese (from Sulawesi) and Chinese have intermarried in many places around Maluku over the centuries.

When the Javanese first traded in the region, they often called the indigenous people

JENNY BOWMAN

In the Tanimbar Islands, antique gold jewellery is said to possess ancestor spirits.

MALUKU

alifuro, a less than endearing term meaning 'uncivilised'. The word is now an accepted way to describe the traditional Papuan Alfuro people who inhabit the interiors of Halmahera, Seram and Buru islands. Pulau Seram is home to the Nuala people, who are also of Papuan descent.

Forty-five percent of Malukans are Christians, who live mainly in the central and southern area. The remaining population comprises Muslims, who live primarily in the north, and non-indigenous Malukans.

BOOKS

The 19th century naturalist Alfred Wallace spent six years roaming the Indonesian archipelago, spending much of that time in Maluku. His record of the journey, *The Malay Archipelago*, still makes fascinating reading. Marika Hanbury-Tenison's *A Slice of Spice* details a visit to Ambon and the wilds of Seram in the early 1970s.

For a readable history of the province, pick up *Indonesian Banda* by Willard A Hanna and *Turbulent Times Past in Ternate and Tidore* by Hanna & Des Alwi. Both are only available in Bandaneira, however.

For an account of the tourist scene in the Banda Islands in the 1970s, read the relevant chapter of Annabel Sutton's *The Islands In Between*. Shirley Deane's *Ambon, Island of Spices* is an enjoyable account of her time on Ambon, and her travels around Maluku.

SPECIAL EVENTS

With some planning, you could witness a festival or ceremony while in Maluku. Many are not tourist oriented, but you'll still be made very welcome by locals. Check the current dates with the tourist office in Kota Ambon.

January-March
New Year
 Hila on Pulau Ambon celebrates the Christian New Year with feasts and songs throughout January.
Ceremony in Mamala and Morela (Pulau Ambon)
 Men beat each other with sticks and test the curative powers of coconut oil, one week after the end of Ramadan.

Sasi Lompa
 A similar sort of ceremony is held at Pelauw (Pulau Haruku) every three years.

April-June
Anzac Day
 A commemoration is held at the Commonwealth War Cemetery in Kota Ambon on 25 April.
Traditional Canoe Races
 Races are held in the Banda Islands in April.
Pattimura Day
 Commemorates the leader of an uprising against the Dutch in the early 19th century (see The Dutch under History earlier in this chapter); celebrated by villagers on Ambon and Saparua islands on 14 and 15 May.

July-September
Darwin to Ambon Yacht Race
 Finishes each July or August at Amahusu on Pulau Ambon, with a pageant and lots of partying.
Anniversary of Pulau Ambon
 Celebrated on 7 September with traditional ceremonies and dances.

October-December
Anniversary of Soa Siu
 The anniversary of the founding of the city is celebrated on 31 October at Pulau Tidore.
Anniversary of Masohi
 Celebrated on 3 November, features traditional performances and kite competitions.
Purification Ceremony
 A traditional ceremony involving purification of the souls of the villagers; held on the second Friday of December in Soya Atas on Pulau Ambon.
Canoe Races
 Held in Nolloth on Pulau Saparua on 28 December.

ACTIVITIES

Ninety percent of Maluku is ocean, so it's not surprising that the diving and snorkelling is spectacular, particularly around the Banda Islands, Pulau Ambon, and the neighbouring islands of Seram, Saparua and Nusa Laut. However, only Ambon and the Bandas have dive centres, while snorkelling gear is available for rent on Ambon, the Bandas and Saparua.

Most of the other 10% of the province is mountainous, with unlimited trekking opportunities. There is a recognised trek across Seram and some smaller trails around Pulau Ambon, while northern Halmahera, with its fantastic volcanoes, lakes and traditional villages, is begging to be explored. It's also relatively easy to scramble to the top of volcanoes in the Bandas and on Pulau Ternate for indescribable views. However, always be prepared for lots of rain and mud wherever you go.

Some of the most beautiful beaches in Indonesia can be found in Maluku, and many are all but deserted. Beaches around Pulau Ambon are easy to reach; around Pulau Ternate they often have black volcanic sand; and around the Lease Islands, they are picturesque. But the prize goes to the Kai Islands, where the beaches have powder-white sand, coconut palms and turquoise waters.

GETTING THERE & AWAY
Air
Kota Ambon is connected daily to most major cities in Indonesia – in fact, with the exception of the Ternate-Manado flight, all flights to Maluku come to Ambon. Merpati is the major airline, but Mandala also offers flights between Ambon and Jakarta, via Ujung Pandang and Surabaya.

See the Maluku Air Fares chart, and Getting There & Away in the Kota Ambon and Kota Ternate sections later in this chapter, for full details of flights to and from Maluku.

Sea
Several Pelni liners connect Maluku reasonably well with the rest of Indonesia. All (with the exception of the *Tatamailau*) have a two-weekly route.

Bukit Siguntang – links Ambon and the Bandas to southern Sulawesi and Java.
Ciremai – links Ternate with Sorong and northern Irian Jaya, and Sulawesi.
Dobonsolo – links Ambon with Dili and Nusa Tenggara, Bali, Java and the northern Irian Jaya.
Lambelu – links Ambon with southern Sulawesi, Java and Kalimantan.
Rinjani – links Ambon, the Bandas and South-East Maluku with northern Irian Jaya and southern Sulawesi.

Umsini – links Ternate with northern Sulawesi, Kalimantan and northern Irian Jaya.
Tatamailau – links Ambon and South-East Maluku with southern Sulawesi, Nusa Tenggara and southern Irian Jaya.

Other non-Pelni passenger boats connect Maluku (mainly Pulau Ambon and Pulau Ternate) with Sulawesi (Bau Bau and Bitung) and Irian Jaya (Fak Fak and Timika), but trips across the seas around Maluku on slow, wooden vessels are strictly for the adventurous and frugal. It is far better to wait for a Pelni liner or fly.

Yacht If you have some sailing experience (and an Australian visa if heading to Darwin), you may be able to hitch a lift on a yacht during the annual Darwin to Ambon Yacht Race (see Special Events earlier in this section). Further details are available

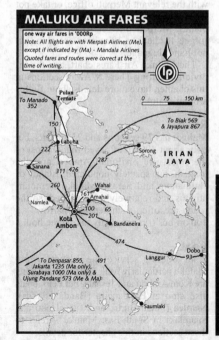

MALUKU AIR FARES

one way air fares in '000Rp
Note: All flights are with Merpati Airlines (Me), except if indicated by (Ma) - Mandala Airlines. Quoted fares and routes were correct at the time of writing.

To Manado 352
Pulau Ternate
150
222
Labuha
Sanana
311 426
260
Namlea
75
Wahai
161
Amahai
100 65
201
Kota Ambon
Bandaneira
287
Sorong
IRIAN JAYA
To Biak 569 & Jayapura 867
474
Langgur
Dobo 93
To Denpasar 855, Jakarta 1235 (Ma only) & Surabaya 1000 (Ma only) & Ujung Pandang 573 (Me & Ma)
491
Saumlaki

0   75   150 km

MALUKU

from Restoran Halim in Ambon (☎ 0911-52177, email hlm@ambon.wasantara.net.id) and Darwin Sailing Club in Darwin (☎ 61-89-811700).

GETTING AROUND
Air
Merpati has an extensive network of flights around Maluku, all of which start and finish at Ambon or Ternate. Just about every developed and populated island in Maluku is connected by air to both places, but the number of flights has been recently reduced. Flying to more remote destinations, including the Bandas, can be problematic – small Merpati Twin-Otter or Cassa planes are sometimes cancelled or delayed for no apparent reason.

You cannot book return flights from remote islands at the Merpati offices in Ambon and Ternate – you'll have to telephone and book a return or onward ticket with the relevant Merpati office, or take pot luck when you arrive. On the smaller planes, Merpati often has (but sometimes forgets to check) a 10kg limit on cabin (but not hand) luggage.

The Maluku Air Fares chart, and the individual Getting There & Away sections in this chapter, have more details about flights around Maluku.

Road
Maluku has 79 seaports and 25 airports, but only about 400km of paved roads. Most of the roads are on Pulau Ambon and the longish, but sparsely populated, islands of Halmahera and Seram. Maluku is mountainous and relatively undeveloped, so the roads are often potholed and narrow – a 100km bus trip can easily take three hours.

Boat
Pelni doesn't service the islands *within* Maluku particularly well. The two main ports are Kota Ambon and Ternate, but Pelni boats also stop at Bandaneira (Banda Islands), Namlea (Pulau Buru), and Tual, Dobo and Saumlaki in South-East Maluku – refer to these sections in this chapter for details.

If you want to go to more remote places, or can't wait for the Pelni boat, a plethora of other services is available. Perintis is a reliable service, with a wide range of boats. Other boats are slower, less comfortable and less seaworthy, but cheaper than Pelni. Schedules for non-Pelni boats are erratic, so make inquiries at the relevant harbours, and be prepared for rough conditions.

Speedboat Between neighbouring islands, and among villages on islands with no roads, speedboats (often called *spid*) are often the only mode of transport – especially along northern Pulau Seram, between islands in South-East Maluku, and all over Pulau Halmahera. These boats often only travel when there are enough passengers, but they can always be chartered.

Pulau Ambon

Barely a dot on a map of Indonesia, the island of Ambon is the economic and transport centre of Maluku. Its landscape is dramatic and mountainous, with little flat land for cultivation or roads. There are a few good beaches, some old forts (one is superbly renovated) and pretty villages, as well as coral reefs and plenty of opportunities for hiking. To appreciate the island and its culture, you need to get out into the villages where there's a definite Polynesian feel.

The island is just 48km by 22km, with an area of 770 sq km. The larger northern peninsula is known as Leihitu and the smaller arrowhead-shaped southern peninsula is Leitimur. Kota Ambon, the capital, lies on the Leitimur peninsula, on the southern side of Teluk Ambon (Ambon Bay).

History
Ambon had the misfortune to be almost at the dead centre of the Spice Islands. The original trade intermediary between central Maluku and western Indonesia was the sultan of Ternate, who brought Islam to Ambon and had some influence in reducing the incidence of head-hunting between

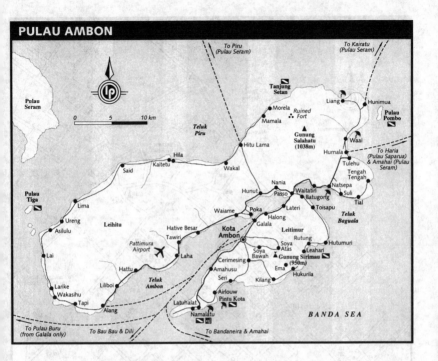

PULAU AMBON

To Piru (Pulau Seram)
To Kairatu (Pulau Seram)

Pulau Seram

0   5   10 km

Tanjung Setan
Morela
Ruined Fort
Mamala
Liang
Hunimua
Pulau Pombo

Teluk Piru

Gunung Salahatu (1038m)

Hitu Lama
Waai

Hila
Kaitetu
Wakal
Hurnala
To Haria (Pulau Saparua) & Amahai (Pulau Seram)

Said
Tulehu
Tengah Tengah

Nania
Natsepa
Suli

Pulau Tiga
Hunut
Passo
Waitatiri
Tial

Lima
Waiame
Poka
Batugong
Lateri
Toisapu
Teluk Baguala

Ureng
Leihitu
Halong
Galala
Leitimur

Asilulu
Hative Besar
Tawiri
Kota Ambon
Rutung
Hutumuri

Lai
Pattimura Airport
Soya Atas
Leahari

Hattu
Laha
Cerimesing
Soya Bawah
Gunung Sirimau (950m)

Larike
Liliboi
Amahusu
Seri
Ema
Hukurila

Wakasihu
Teluk Ambon
Kilang

Tapi
Alang
Airlouw
Pintu Kota

Latuhalat

Namalatu

BANDA SEA

To Pulau Buru (from Galala only)
To Bau Bau & Dili
To Bandaneira & Amahai

indigenous tribes. The Javanese also showed some interest in the island, and established a base at Hitu Lama on the north coast. At this time the island grew no spices, but was still an important stopover between Ternate and the nutmeg-producing Banda Islands.

The Ternatean rulers were displaced on Ambon by the Portuguese in 1512, who were then expelled by the Dutch in 1599. When the Portuguese fort in Kota Ambon was about to be attacked, the Portuguese appear to have simply surrendered and sailed away. The Dutch occupied the fort, renamed it Victoria and made Ambon their spice trade base.

The British first settled on the island in 1615, even though it was under Dutch control, and then captured the island completely in 1796. Ambon was then re-captured by the Dutch in 1802, taken over again by the British in 1810 during the Napoleonic Wars, but returned to the original 'owners' in 1814.

The Dutch probably wished they hadn't bothered when rebellions by some Malukans started five years later.

During WWII, Kota Ambon became a Japanese military headquarters and prisoner of war camp. The city was bombed extensively by Allied planes, destroying most of its colonial and pre-colonial architecture. In 1950 Ambon was the centre of the South Malukan independence movement before it was extinguished by an Indonesian military force a few months later.

Pulau Ambon was the scene of horrific clashes between Muslims and Christians in early 1999 (see Maluku Today under History earlier in this chapter).

KOTA AMBON
☎ 0911

Founded by the Dutch in 1517, Kota Ambon, the capital of Maluku, was once a

MALUKU

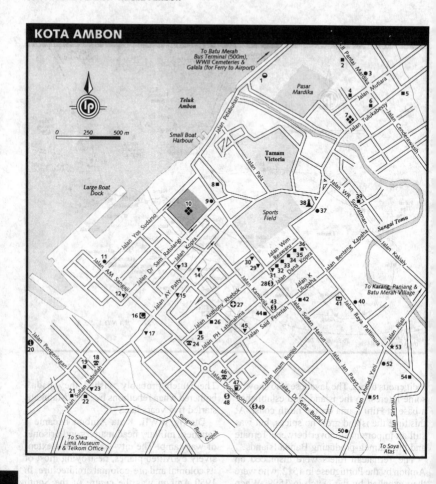

KOTA AMBON

pleasant colonial town before it was bombed during WWII and haphazardly rebuilt. Sitting in the foothills and overlooking a busy harbour, the city is not unlike many others in Indonesia, belying its common moniker *Ambon manise* or 'beautiful Ambon'. The city doesn't have a great number of attractions, but its good facilities make it ideal as a base while exploring the island and the rest of Maluku, or as a stopover between Sulawesi and Irian Jaya.

Orientation

The main streets for shops, restaurants and offices are Jalan (Jl) Yos Sudarso (one way heading north-east), Jl Dr Sam Ratulangi (one way heading south-west) and Jl AY Patty (one-way heading north-east). The main harbour is at the junction of Jl Yos Sudarso and Jl AM Sangaji. Along Jl Sultan Babullah, past the Mesjid Al-Fatah (Al-Fatah mosque), the 'Muslim quarter' is a noisy, vibrant place, with cheap hotels and restaurants.

KOTA AMBON

PLACES TO STAY
2 Hotel Mardika
4 Wisata Hotel
5 Simponi Hotel
6 Hotel Josiba
8 Hotel Sumber Asia
19 Penginapan Wisma Jaya
21 Penginapan Nisma
22 Abdulalie Hotel
25 Penginapan Gamalama
26 Hotel Elenoor
32 Hotel Baliwerti
33 Hotel Hero
34 Penginapan Beta
35 Hotel Rezfanny
36 Hotel Mutiara
39 Pondok Wisata Avema Lestari
42 Hotel Amboina
44 Limas Hotel
51 Wisma Game
54 Hotel Ramayana

PLACES TO EAT
12 Ratu Gurih
13 Andre's Donuts & Bakery
14 Studio Kafe
15 Restoran Amboina
17 Rumah Makan Jawa Timur
23 Rumah Makan Ai Madura II
29 Halim Restoran
30 Restaurant Sakura
31 Pondok Cita Rasa
45 Rumah Makan Ujung Pandang

OTHER
1 Terminal Mardika
3 PT Aihauhihina Agency
7 Citra Supermarket & Cafeteria
9 Amboina Theatre
10 Ambon Plaza; Eatery; Cinemas; Timezone; Matahari Department Store; KFC & CFC

11 Port Entrance
16 Mesjid Al-Fatah
18 Wartel
20 Government Tourist Office
24 Wartel
27 Rumah Sakit GPM (Hospital)
28 BCA Bank
37 Pelni Office
38 Pattimura Memorial
40 Rinamakana
41 Main Post Office; Internet Centre
43 BNI Bank
46 Wartel
47 Planet 2000
48 Bank Danamon
49 Bank BII
50 Merpati Nusantara Airlines Office
52 Mandala Office
53 Police Station

Information

Tourist Offices The Government of Maluku Tourist Office (☎ 52471, fax 43303) is on the 2nd floor of a large building without signage at the end of Jl Pengeringan, which runs towards the coast from the Abdulalie Hotel. The friendly staff speak good English, have plenty of useful maps and brochures on-hand, and will happily answer questions about travelling around Maluku. The office is open Monday to Thursday from 7.30 am to 2 pm, and closes at 11.30 am on Friday and 1 pm on Saturday. The information booth at the airport is officially open daily between 7 am and 4 pm but is rarely staffed.

Other Offices If you need to obtain visa extensions, the immigration office (☎ 53066) is on Jl Dr Kayadoe, in the outer suburbs. Contact the Forestry Department (☎ 41189) for information on trekking on Pulau Seram, and permission for camping on Pulau Pombo (see Around Pulau Ambon later in this chapter). It's on Jl Kebun Cengkeh, near Batu Merah village.

Money Stock up with plenty of rupiah before you arrive, or while you're in Kota Ambon. (Kota Ternate is the only other place in Maluku where you can change money.) You can't change money at the airport, but there are several decent banks in town. Bank Central Asia (BCA) and Bank Internasional Indonesia (BII) will change major currencies in cash and travellers cheques. BCA also offers cash advances of up to three million rupiah on Visa, and BII has an automatic teller machine (ATM) for MasterCard, Visa and Cirrus cards. The best is Bank Negara Indonesia (BNI), which has an ATM for Visa and Cirrus cards, offers the best exchange rates and is open for longer hours.

Post & Communications The main post office is open Monday to Friday from 8 am to 8 pm, until 4 pm on Saturday and 3 pm on Sunday. It has a haphazard, self-service poste restante which somehow works. It also boasts the only Internet centre in Maluku (publik@ambon.wasantara.net.id), which charges 7500Rp per 30 minutes.

MALUKU

The modern Telkom office on Jl Dr JB Sitanala in the western part of the city is open 24 hours. You'll need to take a *becak* (bicycle-rickshaw) or a LIN III yellow *bemo* (minibus). More convenient *wartels* (public telephone offices) are along the main roads, and there are telephones at the post office.

Emergency The police station (☎ 110) is on the corner of Jl Rijali and Jl Raya Pattimura. The best hospitals are Rumah Sakit Umum (☎ 43438) on Jl Dr Kayadoe in the suburbs; and the more central Rumah Sakit GPM (☎ 52373) on Jl Anthony Rhebok. There's also an ambulance service (☎ 118).

Museum Siwa Lima

This museum (☎ 42841) contains a fascinating collection of Malukan, Indonesian and colonial artefacts, housing and clothing, and marine animals, with most captions in English. There are also nice views from the museum, and the countryside nearby is great for hiking.

Take the Amahusu bemo, and ask the driver to let you off. The museum is a 10 minute walk at the top of a steep road. It's usually open daily except Monday from 9 am to 2 pm, but it's worth ringing first to make sure. Entrance costs 750Rp; 1500/3000Rp extra for a camera/video.

War Memorials

Tugu Doolan (Doolan Monument) is a memorial dedicated to a heroic Australian WWII serviceman, and generally to other unknown Australian WWII soldiers – it's a small monument and probably of little interest to many travellers. Take the bemo towards Kudamati to reach it.

The far more interesting **Commonwealth War Cemetery**, in the suburb of Tantui, has stones and plaques for over 2000 Australian, Dutch, British and Indian servicemen killed in Sulawesi and Maluku during WWII. The gardens and layout are superb, and it's worth a visit if only for the peace and quiet. A ceremony is held here every Anzac Day (25 April). A Tantui bemo will

take you straight past the cemetery; it circles back to the main bemo terminal, so pick it up on your return leg.

On the same road, closer to the city, the humbler **Taman Makam Pahlawan Indonesia** (Indonesian Heroes Cemetery) is dedicated to Indonesian servicemen killed fighting Malukan rebels during the 1950s and 1960s.

Other Attractions

The **Pattimura Memorial** stands at one end of the sports field. Pattimura – really called Thomas Matulessy – rallied against the Dutch in 1817, only to be betrayed by one of the village chiefs on Pulau Saparua who took him prisoner and delivered him to the Dutch on Ambon. The monument stands on the site where he and his followers were hanged. Nearby, **Taman Victoria** (Victoria Park) offers some welcome space and greenery.

In the suburb of Karang Panjang, the **Martha Christina Tiahahu Memorial** honours another Maluku freedom fighter. Tiahahu's father supported Pattimura against the Dutch and, after they were both captured, her father was executed on Pulau Nusa Laut and she was put on a ship to Java. Grief-stricken by her father's execution, she starved herself to death and her remains were thrown into the sea. Tiahahu's story is far more exciting than the memorial, but the views of the city from here are captivating. Take the bemo marked KarPan.

Places to Stay

Because of the favourable exchange rate and intense competition among poorly patronised hotels, Ambon is good value. All hotels in Ambon now add a government tax of 10% on all room rates (which has been included in this section). Most budget and mid-range places have a private mandi and toilet, rather than a (cold) shower, and include breakfast.

A number of hotels are also springing up around the island. They are generally quieter and better value than those in Kota Ambon, and still easily accessible to the city. Refer to Around Pulau Ambon later in this chapter for details.

Also refer to the 'Warning' boxed text at the beginning of this chapter.

Places to Stay – Budget

Penginapan Gamalama (☎ 53724, Jl Anthony Rhebok 27) is friendly and central, and has decent singles/doubles for 19,250/27,500Rp. Ask for quieter rooms upstairs and try to get there early because it's often full. Next door, *Hotel Elenoor (☎ 52834)* is about the same standard and price. *Penginapan Beta (☎ 53463, Jl Wim Reawaru 14)* is deservedly popular, and one of the best value places in town – it hasn't increased its rates for several years. Clean rooms along a pleasant verandah cost 15,000/22,000Rp. Next door, *Hotel Rezfanny (☎ 42300)* has rooms for 20,000/22,000Rp with a shared bathroom, 27,500/30,000Rp with a private bathroom and 66,000Rp with air-con. However, all rooms are fairly cheerless and airless.

Behind the police station, a good option is *Hotel Ramayana (☎ 53369, Jl Sirimau)*. Although some rooms are a bit seedy and have no outside windows, they are good value for 27,500Rp with bathroom and air-con. *Wisma Game (☎ 53525, Jl Ahmad Yani 35)* continues to be a popular choice. It has decent rooms for 14,300/22,000Rp without/with a private bathroom.

The 'Muslim quarter', about 500m southwest of the main mosque, has several good, cheap places, although the area is a little inconvenient and noisy. *Abdulalie Hotel (☎ 52057, fax 52796, Jl Sultan Babullah IV/7)* has a range of rooms – the dreary ones cost 14,500/20,400Rp. The better rooms cost 27,000/33,600Rp with fan, to 72,000/84,000Rp with air-con and TV. Opposite, *Penginapan Nisma (☎ 53942, Jl Sultan Babullah SK 44/35)* has comfortable, though noisy, rooms with fan for 25,300/33,000Rp or 36,300/48,400Rp with air-con.

The quieter *Penginapan Wisma Jaya (☎ 41545, Jl Sultan Babullah SK 45/30)* is actually about 100m down a lane from Jl Sultan Babullah – look for the sign from the main road. The air-conditioned rooms on the ground floor for 33,000/38,500Rp are tiny and cheerless, but the rooms upstairs with fan and shared bathroom are better value for 20,350/27,500Rp.

Convenient to the bemo terminal is *Pondok Wisata Avema Lestari (☎ 55596, Jl WR Supratman)*, a cosy place run by a friendly woman. The rooms are large and spotless, and cost 20,000/35,000Rp, or 50,000Rp for triples, all with a shared bathroom. Add an extra 5000Rp per person for rooms with a private bathroom. Rooms with air-con cost 35,000/50,000Rp.

Places to Stay – Mid-Range

Hotel Hero (☎ 42978, fax 52493, Jl Wim Reawaru 7B) is good value. All rooms are clean, feature satellite TV and air-con, and cost 49,500Rp to 88,000Rp (with hot water). Next door, the modern and comfortable *Hotel Baliwerti (☎ 55996, Jl Wim Reawaru 9)* has rooms with air-con and satellite TV from 66,000Rp, but the management is normally willing to negotiate because it's often empty.

Limas Hotel (☎ 48233, Jl Kamboja 16) is quiet and central, and costs 27,500Rp for basic rooms; 36,000/46,000Rp with fan/air-con. *Hotel Sumber Asia (☎ 56587, Jl Pala 34)* is conveniently close to the small boat harbour and bemo and bus terminals, but is in a seedy area. The rooms are bright and airy, and cost 18,200Rp with fan and shared bathroom; 28,000Rp to 45,000Rp with fan and satellite TV; and 56,000Rp with air-con and TV.

Near the Mardika terminal and market are several convenient places, but they aren't great value. *Wisata Hotel (☎ 53567, fax 53592, Jl Mutiara 16)* is neat and comfortable. Rooms with hot water and air-con start from 59,500Rp; 105,600Rp with TV and fridge. *Hotel Josiba (☎ 41280, Jl Tulukabessy 27)* offers rooms with similar standards and service from 33,000Rp to 55,000Rp. Opposite, *Simponi Hotel (☎ 54305)* is the cheapest in this area. Rooms cost 22,000/38,500Rp, but it still isn't great value. The best in this area, *Hotel Mardika (☎ 41460, Jl Pantai Mardika)*, is convenient and friendly but a little noisy. It has rooms with air-con from 38,500Rp to 60,000Rp with satellite TV and hot water.

MALUKU

Airport To avoid an early morning chartered taxi to the airport from Kota Ambon, or if you're just transiting Ambon overnight, *Hotel Maluku* (☎ *61415*) on the main road in Tawiri is a good place to stay. It's about three minutes by bemo or a 20 minute walk east from the airport, otherwise, ring from the airport and hotel staff will pick you up and also return you to the airport the following day (for free). Large, clean rooms cost from 40,000Rp; (negotiable).

Places to Stay – Top End

The city has a surprising number of top-range hotels. All have the modern conveniences you would expect for the high prices, but they are very poor value unless you can pay in rupiah. *Hotel Amboina* (☎ *41725, fax 55723, Jl Kapitan Ulupaha 5A*) has a range of rooms from 78,000Rp to 300,000Rp for the 'suite' – with management willing to offer further 40% discounts. *Hotel Mutiara* (☎ *53075, fax 521711, Jl Raya Pattimura 12*) also accepts rupiah, and charges from 144,000/163,000Rp for singles/doubles.

Some resorts around the island are better value – see Around Pulau Ambon later in this chapter.

Places to Eat

For genuine Ambonese food – such as *colo colo*, a sweet and sour sauce particularly delicious on baked fish, and *kohu kohu*, an unusual fish salad – you will probably have to visit the villages around the island.

The cheapest places are the *food stalls* around the market, the bemo and bus terminals and along the waterfront near the small boat harbour. During the evening a few women along the footpath of Jl AM Sangaji sell huge plates of *nasi campur* (fried rice 'with-the-lot') from around 2500Rp. On Jl Said Perintah, there are several good places for Padang-style food (Sumatran cuisine), such as *Rumah Makan Ujung Pandang*. Near BII, along southern Jl Diponegoro, there are several reasonable *Chinese restaurants*, although none are particularly memorable.

Halim Restoran (*Jl Sultan Hairun*) is always popular, but the service and food never seems to justify its popularity. Chinese dishes cost around 10,000Rp, and the beer is always ice-cold, making it especially popular with its frequent Australian clientele. Next door, *Restaurant Sakura* serves genuine Chinese food, and is quieter and cheaper than Halim's. *Ratu Gurih* (*Jl AM Sangaji*), near the port, is popular with locals. Great tasting baked fish for about 10,000Rp is a speciality.

Restoran Amboina (*Jl AY Patty*) has simple decor, but is recommended for the quality and range of its meals, ice creams and cakes, though the beer is never really cold. *Andre's Donuts & Bakery* (*Jl Kopra*), just off Jl AY Patty, has delicious assorted donuts, ice cream and pizza slices. *Pondok Cita Rasa* (*Jl Wim Reawaru*) is handy if you're staying somewhere along the same street. It has a pleasant open-air setting and serves baked fish from around 12,500Rp, and other Indonesian food for about 8000Rp.

The *eatery* at the back of the 3rd floor of the Ambon Plaza is an air-conditioned retreat. It features a wide range of Asian meals from about 5000Rp, and more expensive western dishes such as spaghetti and steak from 15,000Rp. The cafeteria in the basement of *Citra Supermarket* (*Jl Tulukabessy*) has a tempting range of cheap dishes such as nasi campur for 3500Rp, as well as chilled soft drinks and cakes.

KFC has an outlet in the Ambon Plaza, as does its Indonesian equivalent, *CFC*, which is – surprisingly – more expensive. You can also get decent burgers for about 7500Rp, as well as Indonesian food, at the trendy new *Studio Kafe* (*Jl AY Patty*).

Opposite the main mosque, *Rumah Makan Jawa Timur* (*Jl Sultan Babullah*) has a vast selection – the baked fish for 8000Rp is particularly good. One of the best places in the 'Muslim quarter', *Rumah Makan Ai Madura II* (*Jl Sultan Babullah*) serves good, reasonably priced Javanese food – the *sate* (charcoal-grilled skewered meat with spicy peanut sauce) dishes are particularly tasty. These sort of places never serve alcohol, of course.

Entertainment

Amboina Theatre shows some sleazy films, but the two *cinemas* on the 4th floor of the Ambon Plaza offer far better films in more comfort for 6000Rp. On the same floor, the noisy *Timezone* video arcade is popular with local kids.

A number of particularly seedy *bars*, most with (the dreaded) karaoke machines, are located around the bemo and bus terminals; better and more convenient *bars* are along Jl Diponegoro, including the trendiest place in town, *Planet 2000*. This massive place has four (!) floors of karaoke machines and discos (the discos have a 15,000Rp entrance charge). There are also a few *nightclubs* for dancing and drinking along Jl AY Patty.

Shopping

The bemo and bus terminals are based in and around the noisy and dirty Mardika and Batu Merah markets. The daily food market in the village of Batu Merah, between the bus terminal and the main north-east road, is far quieter and is the closest 'village market' to the city.

Along Jl Yos Sudarso, towards the port, masses of people sell masses of things, including fresh fish. Jl AY Patty is lined with dozens of shops selling just about every conceivable tacky souvenir. Interesting 'sculptures' made from cloves are priced from around 30,000Rp.

Exquisite, but often a little garish, portraits made from oyster shells (see the boxed text 'Oyster Shell Art' in this section) are also for sale. A framed mid-sized portrait of two birds of paradise might cost about 100,000Rp – after bargaining. Oyster shell brooches are cheaper at around 5000Rp, and a little easier to carry around. Some turtle-shell products are still for sale, but please don't encourage this illegal industry by buying any (see Environmental Concerns under Responsible Tourism in the Facts for the Visitor chapter).

It's worth a look around the small Rina-makana shop opposite the post office, where you can pick up some authentic artefacts from all over Maluku (handy if you're not going to places such as the Kai Islands).

Oyster Shell Art

If you spend any time in Kota Ambon you'll notice and probably admire portraits made from oyster shells *(kulit mutiara)*. Oyster shell art, which possibly dates back to the 15th century, flourished during the Japanese occupation in WWII and has since resurfaced with the growth of the tourist industry.

The oyster shells are carefully broken, painstakingly sliced into various shapes and then glued onto black velvet to make portraits – usually of birds of paradise, Dutch galleons, horses and symbols from the Koran.

The village of Batu Merah, now part of Kota Ambon's sprawling mass, is the centre for this ancient and complicated art. You can see the portraits being made at several workshops around the Batu Merah mosque, along the main north-east road out of the city – and everything you see is for sale, of course.

Getting There & Away

Air From Ambon, Merpati flies to most major islands in Maluku – but not that regularly, and flights are often delayed and cancelled. For details of flights to places *within* Maluku, refer to the Maluku Air Fares chart at the start of this chapter, and the individual Getting There & Away entries in this chapter for each destination.

Four times a week, Merpati stops in Ambon on flights between Denpasar (855,000Rp) and Jayapura (867,100Rp), via Biak (569,000Rp) and Ujung Pandang (573,400Rp). This flight also occasionally detours to Sorong (287,400Rp). The Merpati office (☎ 52481) is open daily from 8 am to 5 pm, except Sunday and public holidays, when it's open from 9 am to 3 pm. It will also handle bookings for Garuda flights elsewhere in Indonesia, but you must book return or onward flights from remote islands within Maluku at the relevant Merpati offices yourself.

MALUKU

Merpati also has five flights a week between Ambon and Ternate (426,000Rp), with connections to Manado. Tickets are only available at the unsigned PT Aihauhihina agency (☎ 51942), opposite Hotel Amans on Jl Pantai Mardika, or from a travel agent.

Mandala (☎ 48888) flies between Ambon and Jakarta (1,235,000Rp), via Ujung Pandang (573,400Rp) and Surabaya (1,000,500Rp). This flight is popular with savvy Indonesians.

Boat Five Pelni boats travel to Ambon on a regular basis. Every two weeks, the *Dobonsolo* goes to Dili, East Timor, for 53,500/178,000Rp (economy/1st class) and Sorong, for the same price; the *Bukit Siguntang* and *Rinjani* go to Bandaneira (28,000/90,000Rp) and to Bau Bau, southern Sulawesi (61,500/205,500Rp); and the *Lambelu* goes to Bau Bau, Namlea (18,500/57,000Rp) and Ternate (70,000/235,000Rp). Every four weeks, the *Tatamailau* goes to Bau Bau and Amahai (17,500/47,500Rp).

Pelni boats leave from the main city port. (Some travellers have unfortunately reported bag-snatching during the chaotic disembarkations of boats in Kota Ambon, so be careful.) Pelni (☎ 48219) has a new office, opposite the Pattimura Memorial. You can buy tickets daily from 8 am to noon from the back of the building. To avoid the hassle of lining up, you can also buy Pelni tickets from numerous agencies (which are open longer hours) around the port area.

Other more basic boats going to lesser islands in Maluku leave from the small boat harbour, near the end of Jl Pala. A board at the harbour entrance indicates destination and departure schedules. The individual Getting There & Away entries in this chapter have further details on boats run by Perintis and other shipping lines to/from Kota Ambon. Also refer to the sections on Buru, Haruku, Seram and Saparua islands for boat travel info between these islands and Pulau Ambon.

Getting Around
To/From the Airport Pattimura airport is on the other side of the bay from Kota Ambon

– allow one hour for all forms of transport. Official taxis from a special counter in the arrivals hall cost 25,000/30,000Rp for normal/air-con vehicles. You should be able to arrange something to the airport for about the same price from your hotel.

There may be a comfortable Damri airport bus at the bus terminal in the city, or waiting in the airport car park – but don't count on it. The quickest, cheapest and most reliable form of public transport is a combination of the regular Poka-Laha bemo from the airport to the port of Poka (500Rp), the vehicle/passenger ferry across to Galala (350Rp) and a bemo (400Rp) to Terminal Mardika.

Public transport is not reliable between about 6 am and 6 pm, so early morning check-ins (which are common from Ambon) may require an expensive chartered taxi. You can avoid this by staying at the hotel near the airport the night before your departure (see Places to Stay – Mid-Range earlier in this section).

Becak The city has thousands of *becak*s (bicycle-rickshaws), with same colour becaks operating on different days of the week. A short trip costs about 1000Rp, but foreigners are usually charged 2000Rp or more. Becaks cannot travel along busy Jl Yos Sudarso, Jl Dr Sam Ratulangi or Jl AY Patty, and cannot go anywhere near the bus or bemo terminals. Instead, they stop and congregate around the Wisata Hotel, and at the back of Batu Merah village. From both stops, it's a 200m to 500m walk to the bus or bemo.

Bemo Yellow bemos around the city are cheap (about 300Rp), but their routes are confusing. It's best to use them if you're only going to the bus or bemo terminals. Along the streets heading that way, listen for the shout of '*terminal!!*' or '*pasar!!*' (market) from the bemo jockeys. Throughout the city, bemos can only stop at designated places – you can't just flag one down from anywhere – and most bemos from the villages will only drop you off at the terminal.

From Terminal Mardika, which is the most confusing mass of vehicles in eastern Indonesia, bemos go to most places on the southern peninsula (Leitimur). Bemos are well marked, colour coded and go something like this:

Yellow To Galala, Tantui, Karang Panjang and Kudamati, all for about 500Rp.
Red To Hunut (1200Rp), Tawiri (1400Rp) and places towards (but often not going to) the airport.
Green Along the southern road to Amahusu (500Rp), Namalatu and Latuhalat (800Rp), Airlouw (1000Rp) and Seri (1200Rp).
Blue To eastern villages, such as Leahari and Hutumuri (1200Rp), and up to Passo (1300Rp).
Orange To Soya Atas (800Rp).

Bus From Terminal Batu Merah, a 10 minute walk further east of Terminal Mardika, buses and minibuses (and even a few bemos, just to add to the confusion) go everywhere else on the island, and to Masohi on Pulau Seram. The vehicles are well signed (but can be any colour), and leave from specific lanes. Just keep walking along the front of the terminal until you find the lane with your bus.

The following buses, minibuses and bemos leave from Terminal Batu Merah:

Hila & Kaitetu Direct minibus (1500Rp)
Liang & Hunimua Direct minibus (1200Rp)
Mamala & Morela Direct minibus (1250Rp)
Hitu Lama Direct minibus (1100Rp)
Natsepa Bemo to Suli (700Rp)
Tulehu & Hurnala Direct minibus or any vehicle to Waai, Hunimua or Liang (1000Rp)
Waai Direct bus or bus/minibus to Liang or Hunimua (1000Rp)
Waitatiri Direct bemo or bemo to Suli; or any vehicle to Tulehu, Liang or Hunimua (600Rp)

AROUND PULAU AMBON
☎ 0911
Pulau Ambon was once two separate islands, but is now joined at Passo by a short isthmus between the southern peninsula (Leitimur) and northern peninsula (Leihitu). There is plenty to see around the island, and it's easy enough to day trip from Kota

Ambon once you get the hang of the bemo system and bus terminals.

Around Leihitu, public transport goes as far as Larike via the northern road, and as far as Liliboi along the southern road. To more remote places in the far west, such as Alang, boats leave daily from the small boat harbour in Kota Ambon. In the north-east, the main road and public transport finishes at Liang and Morela.

Around Leitimur, roads and public transport connect the city with Latuhalat, Namalatu, Seri and Leahari. Along the south coast, between Leahari and Seri, roads and public transport are often not reliable, and sometimes non-existent.

Chartering a bemo and driver for around 12,000Rp per hour is an excellent way to see the island, especially if you can get a group together. Ask around the bemo terminal or ask the staff at your hotel. More expensive jeeps with drivers are available from around Jl Sultan Hairun in Kota Ambon, or can be arranged at your hotel.

Diving & Snorkelling
Pulau Ambon and nearby Seram and Saparua islands offer outstanding reefs and marine life. Diving is available year-round, but the roughest time (when some dive trips may be unavailable) is between April and June.

Two recommended agencies are: Ambon Dive Centre (☎ 62101, fax 62104), opposite the entrance to Pantai Namalatu (Namalau Beach); and PT Singa Laut Diving Centre (☎ 62107, fax 62108), based at Lelisa Beach Resort in Latuhalat, and run by a friendly Dutch-born Malukan.

Both offer trips to Namalatu, Pintu Kota and Leahari in the south; Tanjung Setan (Devil's Point) and Pulau Pombo in the north; Pulau Tiga in the south-west; and Seram and Saparua islands. The prices for trips around Pulau Ambon are about the same for both dive centres: US$70 for two dives; US$40 for one night-dive; and about US$250 for a five day certificate course. Transport and guides are included, but check whether all equipment is also included.

MALUKU

A few places offer some decent snorkelling, such as Amahusu, Namalatu and Pulau Pombo, but you'll have to bring your own equipment or hire gear from the two diving agencies.

Leitimur

Amahusu Amahusu is famous as the finishing point and dock for the annual Darwin to Ambon Yacht Race (see Special Events earlier in this chapter). There is really no beach as such, but the coral around here is reasonable for snorkelling.

Hotel Tirtha Kencana (☎ 42324, fax 47961) has comfortable bungalow-style accommodation with air-con, hot water and TV from 90,000Rp to 150,000Rp. The hotel is a good place for a meal or a drink while watching the sunset.

Namalatu & Latuhalat Along the south coast, Namalatu (Kings Name) is the pleasant public beach near the village of Latuhalat (King of the West). There's good **diving** (organised by the diving agencies mentioned in the Diving & Snorkelling entry in this section) and snorkelling on coral reefs offshore and in nearby coves. Ambonese like to buy gifts made of cloves from villagers in Latuhalat, although it's surprisingly hard to find anyone offering these to tourists – you may have to look around Kota Ambon instead.

Penginapan Santai Beach (☎ 62109), just off the main road in Latuhalat, has a small artificial sandy beach (which is available to non-guests for 500Rp); a small pool (usually empty); and decent rooms from 77,000Rp to 110,000Rp. Nearby, *Lelisa Beach Resort* (☎ 62106, fax 62108), along the main road, is spacious, but has no beach. Rooms cost 99,000Rp and pleasant cottages are 132,000Rp.

Opposite the Lelisa, the cosy *Homestay Europa* (☎ 62105) is popular. The prices are comparatively good value – about 40,000/50,000Rp for singles/doubles – and the owners are helpful and friendly. Ring before heading out there in July and August, because it may be closed. Non-divers can

stay at the *homestay* behind the Ambon Dive Centre, opposite Pantai Namalutu. Simple rooms cost 25,000Rp.

Pintu Kota The signposted road past the Penginapan Santai Beach leads to this small rocky beach, with some outstanding **diving** (beware of strong currents), and plenty of rocks to clamber around and admire the views. There is no public transport, so you'll have to walk from Latuhalat (about 20 minutes) or from **Airlouw** (40 minutes), which is famous for its brick-making. Both places are connected to Kota Ambon by bemo. If you walk further north for a few kilometres from Airlouw, you reach the traditional village of **Seri**, also connected by bemo to the city.

Soya Atas Infrequent bemos go to the pretty village of Soya Atas, perched on the slope of **Gunung Sirimau** (950m), and famous for its purification ceremonies (see Special Events earlier in this chapter). The quaint Protestant **church** opposite the village square was apparently first built in 1546.

The narrow, obvious path from the village to the top of the hill (about 30 minutes) offers some stupendous views of the city and harbour. Local folklore says that at the top there is a **sacred urn** known as *tempayang setan* (devil's urn), permanently filled with water. If you are lucky enough to see this mythical urn magically fill with water, you'll be guaranteed instant good fortune.

From the top of the hill, gentle, narrow **hiking trails** (you'll need to ask locals for exact directions) lead past **WWII trenches** to villages on the south coast, such as Kilang and **Hukurila**, (in)famous for the distillation of liquor made from sugar palm leaves.

The **hike** along Jl Sirimau, which starts behind the police station in Kota Ambon, to the top of Sirimau shouldn't take more than a couple of hours. It's best to catch a bemo up to Soya Atas and walk back down to the city.

Leihitu

Waitatiri Although there isn't much of a beach, several hotels have been built in Waitatiri. The cheapest is *Hotel Holiday Beach*

Inn (☎ *61406*), which actually does have a small, decent beach. The dreary rooms inside are very cheap for 10,000Rp; air-con rooms for 25,000Rp are better, but still not great. *Penginapan Suli Indah* (☎ *61209*) has decent, clean bungalows overlooking an ugly breakwater for 35,000/50,000Rp for singles/doubles.

The best of the top-end range is *Baguala Beach Resort* (☎ *61476, fax 62277*), a spacious and clean place with a swimming pool – it's perfect for families. Luxurious rooms/ cottages cost US$44/50, but it does accept rupiah at very favourable exchange rates. The *restaurant* is excellent and worth visiting.

Natsepa Natsepa Indah Recreation Park (Taman Rekreasi Natsepa Indah) is a lovely swimming beach with great views and several *warungs* (food stalls). On Sunday it's crowded but entertaining; on other days it's virtually empty. Just down the road, **Taman Lunterse Boer** features another beach, more shade and a beachside *restaurant*.

In the Natsepa beach complex, *Vaneysa Natsepa Paradise* (☎ *61451*) offers seclusion and wonderful views. Simple rooms cost 22,000Rp; the large rooms (which sleep four people) are very pleasant and cost 44,000Rp. The *restaurant* serves delicious and cheap Indonesian food, and is worth a trip out from Kota Ambon. Over the road, *Sea View Restaurant* is a little more upmarket and serves cold beer. At the back, *Ponpana Cottages* (☎ *62218*) has several new, pleasant but charmless bungalows. They cost 50,000Rp to 70,000Rp for a family room with air-con.

Along the main road, *Penginapan Miranda* (☎ *61244*) is friendly but reasonably noisy and has no views. Rooms cost 20,000/ 30,000Rp with fan/air-con. *Taman Lunterse Boer* (☎ *61366*) has several new bungalows which are overpriced – but negotiable – for 80,000Rp; even so the seaside setting and views are charming.

Hurnala & Tulehu Hurnala is the port for ferries and speedboats to Haruku, Saparua and Seram islands – refer to those sections in this chapter for details. If you're catching one of these boats from Kota Ambon, make sure you get off at the ferry terminal or nearby speedboat terminal at Hurnala, about 1km north of Tulehu, and not in Tulehu itself.

About 3km up the hill from Tulehu (ask directions from a local) is **Air Panas Hatuasa** (Hatuasa Hot Springs).

Waai Continuing north, Waai has a nice **beach**, but is more famous as the home of the sacred eels in **Kolam Waiselaka** (Waiselaka Pond). The over-fed eels are enticed out from under the rocks by a villager with an egg. The eel very quickly darts out and sucks out the yolk from a hole in the shell. If you see the eel (and you probably will), it's meant to bring good luck. The pool is behind the large church, which is on the main road and opposite the port.

Liang & Hunimua The road continues as far as Liang (via Hunimua), where some very pretty, deserted beaches stretch several kilometres. Hunimua is the terminal for ferries to/from Pulau Seram – refer to that section in this chapter for details.

Pulau Pombo This tiny, alluring island off the north-east coast is now part of Pulau Pombo Reserve (Taman Pulau Pombo). The combination of low tides and clear water provide astounding diving and snorkelling around pristine coral reefs. Ask the two diving centres (see Diving & Snorkelling earlier in this section) what trips they can organise, otherwise bring or rent some snorkelling equipment.

You can stay free of charge in some decrepit **huts**, or **camp** (if you have a tent) on the island, but you need permission first from the Forest Department (Departemen Kehutanan) in Kota Ambon (see Other Offices under Information in the earlier Kota Ambon section). You must also bring your own food and water. You can only reach the island by chartered boat, which will be expensive (about 60,000Rp either one way or return) from Tulehu, Waai or Liang.

MALUKU

Morela & Mamala These remote villages are home to an unusual annual ceremony – see Special Events earlier in this chapter.

Hila & Kaitetu Hila's strategic position on the north coast, overlooking Pulau Seram (once a serious rival) has resulted in a long and fascinating history.

The magnificently restored **Benteng Amsterdam** (Amsterdam Fort) is grandly positioned along the pretty coast. Originally built by the Portuguese in 1512, then taken over by the Dutch VOC in the early 17th century, the fort is one of the best restored in Maluku and is definitely worth a visit. It's also famous as the former residence of the respected, blind Ambonese naturalist and author, GE Rumphius. Ask the guard at the office, next to the small **museum**, to show you inside the old spice warehouse.

Almost next door, the quaint Protestant **Immanuel Church** is claimed by villagers to be the oldest church in Indonesia. Built in 1580 by the Catholic Portuguese, but then taken over by a Protestant Dutch governor 200 years later, the church has since been extensively restored. A helpful notice in English inside the church explains its history. It is, of course, most atmospheric during services on Sunday mornings.

At the intersection where Christian Hila and Muslim Kaitetu meet, a five minute walk from the church, is **Mesjid Wapaue**. Originally built in 1414 on nearby Gunung Wawane, the mosque was transferred to the present site in 1664. According to a local legend, the mosque was moved by supernatural powers.

If you hire a guide, they can take you to a beautiful **waterfall** near Hila. Beware – the pool may look inviting, but it's actually full of harmful snakes.

Tawiri The *Hotel Maluku (☎ 61415)* is close to the airport – ideal if you're just transiting Ambon overnight (see Places to Stay – Mid Range in the earlier Kota Ambon section). If you ask directions in the village, or at the hotel, you can visit two nearby **WWII memorials** for Australian and Japanese soldiers.

Central Maluku

Several islands surround Pulau Ambon, and form most of the district of Central Maluku. Although not far from Ambon, and easy to reach, these islands are not well developed for tourism; however, Pulau Buru does offer unspoilt landscapes, Pulau Seram has some rugged trekking and Pulau Saparua has a majestic fort. Seram and Saparua islands also have excellent diving spots, but trips and equipment must be arranged on Pulau Ambon.

PULAU BURU
☎ 0913

The large island immediately west of Ambon has always been renowned as an exile for undesirable prisoners – a sort of Indonesian Alcatraz. These days, Buru attracts the occasional adventurous traveller seeking secluded beaches, pretty waterfalls and gorgeous lakes. However, many of these natural attractions are only accessible by hiking; your hotel will have more information, and be able to arrange guides. The two main towns are Namlea and Namrole.

Places to Stay & Eat
Namlea has a couple of simple places to stay with rooms from 15,000Rp to 50,000Rp, including three meals, such as *Hotel Asia Jaya (☎ 21048)* and *Hotel Pattimura*. In Namrole, *Mess Kesehatan* has rooms for 10,000Rp per person, while *Hotel Labuang* charges 25,000Rp per room.

Getting There & Away
Merpati flies twice a week between Ambon and Namlea (75,100Rp). The Merpati agency (☎ 21078) is at Jl Sakura 5, Namlea.

The more convenient ferry leaves Galala (Pulau Ambon) every night at 10 pm for the 10 hour trip to Namlea, and another travels in the opposite direction at the same time. Once a fortnight the Pelni liner *Lambelu* also travels between Ambon and Namlea. From the small boat harbour in Kota Ambon, other less comfortable passenger boats travel most days to Namlea and often on to Namrole and other small villages.

Lease Islands

PULAU SAPARUA
☎ 0931

Pulau Saparua is the most populated, developed and accessible of the Lease Islands, which also include Haruku and Nusa Laut islands. Saparua is where the revered independence hero, Pattimura, fought the Dutch, but was later betrayed. He was handed over to the Dutch and hanged in Kota Ambon.

Saparua is an alluring place, so quiet and relaxed compared to Ambon. With its stunning fort and captivating beaches, Saparua is an enjoyable day trip from Ambon – but it's worth staying a few more days. Kota Saparua is the only town of any size on the island; Haria is the port.

Benteng Duurstede

Only one block from the main road in Kota Saparua, this large Dutch fort was built in 1676 primarily to guard against Portuguese invasion. It is well restored, and sits majestically overlooking **Pantai Waisisil**, the site of battles between Pattimura's troops and the Dutch. You can wander around the fort and visit the **museum** opposite, which has dramatic dioramas of this and other pertinent episodes of Malukan history. All captions are in Indonesian; even so, it's interesting enough. You may have to find someone to open it all up for you – ask at the museum or Hotel Duurstede.

Ouw

The friendly village of Ouw is famous for its traditional earthenware **pottery**; if you look hard or ask around, you can watch local women in small workshops at the back of their homes – it's all for sale if you feel like buying something. One pottery shop is next to a small, overgrown **fort** which locals and historians appear to have forgotten.

The road to Ouw is dotted with pretty beaches for snorkelling and swimming – just choose somewhere nice from the window of the bemo and get off. There are also some great hiking trails south of Ouw.

Kollor

In front of Putih Lessi Indah Cottages, the coral and marine life is good for snorkelling – equipment can be rented from the Cottages (see the following Places to Stay & Eat entry for details). A few hundred metres inland (ask directions at the Cottages) is **Gua Tujuh Puteri** (Seven Daughters Cave) with a small, refreshing freshwater swimming pool. The Cottages can also organise other local hikes for guests.

Places to Stay & Eat

In Kota Saparua, *Penginapan Lease Indah* (☎ 21040, Jl Benteng, aka Jl Muka) is a few minutes' walk from the bemo terminal. Comfortable rooms cost 30,000/40,000Rp with fan/air-con. It also rents snorkelling equipment. *Hotel Duurstede* (☎ 21510) has a stunning setting, right on the beach and next to the fort – probably the best location in Maluku, outside of the Banda Islands. New, clean rooms are a little pricey at 40,000Rp including breakfast, but worth it. No fan or air-con is provided, but neither is necessary because of the welcome sea breezes.

A few places are starting to pop up around the island at the same rate that others are closing down. One of the best is the new *Putih Lessi Indah Cottages* (☎ Ambon 0911-54815), set on a pretty beach and described by one reader as 'an absolute gem'. Individual bungalows around a small garden are large and clean, and cost 35,000Rp

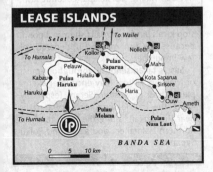

LEASE ISLANDS

To Wailei
Selat Seram
To Hurnala
Kollor
Nolloth
Pelauw
Pulau
Saparua
Mahu
Kabau
Pulau
Haruku
Hulaliu
Kota Saparua
Haruku
Sirisore
Haria
Ouw
Ameth
To Hurnala
Pulau
Molana
Pulau
Nusa Laut

BANDA SEA

0   5   10 km

MALUKU

per person, including good meals. It's along the main road, just south of Kollor, about 700m from the local boat terminal.

Another recommended place is *Laino Bungalows* near Haria, which is encouragingly involved in community development and local conservation. Bungalows cost 35,000Rp to 50,000Rp; great meals are about 8000Rp extra.

There's a decent *rumah makan* (restaurant) at the bemo terminal in Kota Saparua, but the few visitors usually eat at *Rumah Makan Andalas (Jl Benteng)*, halfway between the Penginapan Lease Indah and the terminal. Both offer little more than nasi campur, however.

Getting There & Away

Most boats travel between Hurnala (Pulau Ambon), and Haria, about ten minutes by bemo from Kota Saparua.

A ferry (4500Rp, two hours) leaves the ferry terminal at Hurnala daily at about 9 am; another ferry leaves the ferry terminal at Haria at the same time. There are also ferries on market days (Wednesday and Saturday) between Hurnala and Wailei (Pulau Seram), via Pelauw (Pulau Haruku) and Kollor (Pulau Saparua).

Speedboats (6000Rp, 1½ hours) travel between the ferry or speedboat terminal (about 300m from the ferry terminal) in Hurnala and the Haria speedboat terminal (about 200m from the ferry terminal). They leave when there are about 15 passengers, ie about once an hour in the morning. From Haria, speedboats sometimes head to Amahai or Masohi (Pulau Seram) and Pelauw (Pulau Haruku).

Getting Around

All bemos around the island start and finish at the terminal in Kota Saparua. They are marked: 'Hatawono' for the north-east road to Nolloth; 'Haria' for the main port; and 'Tenggara' for the south-east road to Ouw. There are only a few minibuses each day to Kollor. Bemo services are infrequent, so chartering a bemo is a good idea. There are also a few becaks around Kota Saparua.

PULAU HARUKU

Haruku was once another Dutch stronghold – the forts **Benteng New Zeland** and **Benteng Neuw Horn** are now decrepit, but still fascinating to wander around. The island, which boasts some beautiful, secluded beaches, such as Pantai Hulaliu, was also the site of some fierce fighting in WWII. Every three years Pelauw village hosts the **sasi lompa ceremony** (the last one was held in January 1997). See the Special Events earlier in this chapter for details.

There are no *penginapan* (simple lodging houses) to stay in, but some form of accommodation will be found if you contact the *kepala desa* (village head) at Pelauw.

Sasi

A belief unique to most of Maluku is known as *sasi*, a formal warning created to protect property and safeguard against the theft of precious plants, fruit and animals. To disobey sasi used to result in a spell against the offender, but these days a fine, such as repaying (by a multiple of ten) the theft or damage is more common. The placement of sasi warnings and the enforcement of punishment are carried out by a villager called a *kewang*.

The difficulty is recognising the warning. It may be an intricate symbol of palm leaves hiding some potentially harmful bamboo sticks, but often the kewang simply attaches a sign, for example, to a coconut tree stating *sasi kelapa* (coconut sasi), to stop people pinching the coconuts. A sign stating *sasi lompa* would attempt to stop locals pinching small fish from a pond, because the fish may be undersized, or few in number.

Sasi is taken seriously throughout most of Maluku. Visitors may encounter examples of sasi in western Seram (especially along the trail leading to the waterfalls near Rumahkai), along the main roads in northern Halmahera and all around Pulau Saparua.

On Wednesday and Saturday, ferries sail between Hurnala (Pulau Ambon) and Wailei (Pulau Seram), and stop at Kollor (Pulau Saparua) and Pelauw. You may be lucky and find a speedboat between Pelauw and Amahai or Masohi (Pulau Seram), or perhaps Haria (Pulau Saparua).

PULAU NUSA LAUT

Nusa Laut offers more unspoiled beaches, the ruin of an old **church** in the village of **Ameth** and the decrepit Dutch fort **Benteng Beverwyk**. The father of the famous Maluku freedom fighter, Martha Christina Tiahahu, was captured on this island during the rebellions against the Dutch.

Again, there is nowhere to stay, but if you contact the kepala desa at Ameth, a room can usually be arranged. The only public transport to the island is between Haria (Pulau Saparua) and Ameth on market days (Wednesday and Saturday). Alternatively, charter a boat from Haria.

PULAU SERAM

☎ 0914

Maluku's second largest island (171,151 sq km), Seram is wild, mountainous and heavily forested. The Malukans call it Nusa Ina (Mother Island) because they believe the ancestors of central Maluku came from Seram. Much of the interior is home to the indigenous Alfuro and Nuaula peoples, who are

both of Papuan descent. The south and west coasts of Seram are populated by Malays, and there are transmigrants scattered around the island from Java and Sulawesi.

A very tough four to seven day trek between the north and south coasts takes you through some of Manusela National Park, home to many species of birds, including the *nuri* parrot. The island is surrounded by coral reefs and you'll often see *lumba lumba* (dolphins). The capital, Masohi, is the only town of any size.

Getting There & Away

Air Merpati flies twice a week between Ambon and Amahai (100,400Rp), near Masohi, on its way to/from the Banda Islands. In fact, the Amahai-Bandaneira flight is subsidised by the local government – tickets cost only 65,000Rp – a good reason to detour to Pulau Seram on the way to/from the Bandas. Every week, Merpati also flies directly, and some would say less reliably, between Ambon and Wahai (160,900Rp) in northern Seram.

Bookings for flights to/from Seram should be made with the Merpati office in Kota Ambon, but there is also a Merpati agency on Jl Pemda Maluku Tengah, Masohi (no telephone), and in Wahai (☎ 21118).

Bus From Terminal Batu Merah in Kota Ambon, buses leave every morning to Masohi (17,500Rp, six hours), Taniwel and Tehoru. For villages along the north coast,

PULAU SERAM

buses marked 'Saleman' leave from outside Mesjid Al-Fatah in Kota Ambon. All buses between Pulau Ambon and Pulau Seram use the ferry between Hunimua (Ambon) and Waiprit (Seram); the cost of the ferry is included in the bus ticket.

Ferry One or two vehicle/passenger ferries travel daily between Hunimua, near Liang (Ambon), and Waiprit, near Kairatu (Seram). You can take the bus to Hunimua and catch the ferry yourself, but it's easier and just as cheap to take a bus/ferry/bus package from Kota Ambon.

A ferry also travels on market days (Wednesday and Saturday) between Hurnala (Ambon) and Wailei (Seram), via Pelauw (Pulau Haruku) and Kollor (Pulau Saparua). Another boat (7000Rp, four hours) travels between Hurnala and Amahai (Seram) every evening, but travelling at night is no fun.

Every four weeks, the Pelni liner *Tatamailau* travels between Ambon and Amahai (Seram) in both directions, but it isn't worth waiting for. Every few days, slow, cheap and crowded boats also leave from the small boat harbour in Kota Ambon and crawl along the north coast of Pulau Seram to Taniwel, Wahai, Kobi and Geser.

Speedboat Speedboats are a lot faster than ferries, but only leave when there are enough passengers, which can be 15 or 25, depending on the size of boat. They travel between Amahai and the speedboat terminal in Hurnala (15,000Rp, two hours); and sometimes between Amahai, or Masohi, and Haria (Saparua) and Pelauw (Haruku). Speedboats can be chartered for 150,000Rp to 250,000Rp (depending on the size of the boat and your negotiation skills) between Amahai and Hurnala. One large 'super-jet' (seating up to 50 people) leaves Hurnala at 7 am and Amahai at 10 am daily, sometimes doing another return trip in the afternoon.

The port in Masohi is 200m down from Penginapan Nusantara, and the port in Amahai is at the market/bemo terminal.

Getting Around

You will probably have to charter a bemo to/from the airport at Amahai (around 10,000Rp), or hang around the terminal and wait for other passengers to share the cost.

Masohi is the centre for most bus travel around the island, while the main port and airport are in nearby Amahai. The bus terminal in Masohi is quite organised; buses are well marked and wait patiently under destination signs. They regularly go to Kairatu (for Waiprit harbour) and Saka (the buses are marked 'Saleman'), but less frequently to other places. Buses to the east of the island leave from Amahai, so get a bemo there first from along the main road in Masohi.

Along some sections of the north coast, boats are common; speedboats are covered, faster and more expensive than the slower uncovered longboats, but you may not have much choice anyway. There is a road, and daily bus, between Wahai and Kobi on the north-east coast.

Masohi

Masohi is the capital of the Central Maluku district, which includes the Banda Islands, and oddly, parts of northern Pulau Ambon. It's a quiet place with wide, empty streets, and there isn't a lot to do but respond to the inevitable shouts of 'Hello Mister!!!' and, more interestingly, 'I love you!!!'.

Orientation & Information Just about everything you'll need is on a 300m stretch of the main street, Jl Abdullah Soulissa, which heads towards Amahai from the bus terminal/market. Along this street, Bank Danamon, almost opposite Hotel Masohi Manise, changes money and provides cash advances on Visa and MasterCard, but don't count on it. The post office is on the parallel street, Jl Imam Bonjol.

If you're planning a trip to Manusela National Park, you'll need to visit the Forest Department (☎/fax 22164) for a visitor permit (1000Rp). The office is at Jl Imam Bonjol 27, the Amahai end of that street and a becak ride from most hotels. The staff here are more cluey than the tourist office and can provide an interesting brochure, and guides if the tourist office can't.

The Kantor Bupati (Provincial Office) with the mildly useful tourist office (☎ 21462) is also on Jl Imam Bonjol. It's open from 7.30 am to 2.30 pm daily except Sunday; it closes a little earlier on Friday and Saturday.

Places to Stay All *losmen* (basic accommodation) are within walking distance of the bus terminal, although there are plenty of becaks around. *Penginapan Nusantara (☎ 21119, Jl Abdullah Soulissa)* is central, but noisy and uninspiring, with singles/ doubles with bathroom from 18,150/ 25,300Rp; 38,500/46,200Rp with air-con. It has a number of triple rooms, also. The popular *Wisma Sri Lestari (☎ 21178, Jl Abdullah Soulissa)* has clean, basic rooms for 25,000Rp. The newest place in town is *Hotel Masohi Manise (☎ 21820, Jl Abdullah Soulissa)*, which has quiet, clean economy rooms for 35,000Rp, and rooms with air-con and satellite TV from 44,000/ 66,000Rp.

The best value is at the quiet *Penginapan Nusa Ina (☎ 21221)* on the corner of Jl Cengkeh and Jl Pala, two blocks north-west from the market. Simple but decent rooms with bathroom cost 15,000Rp; 30,000Rp for the 'family room' which sleeps four people. Check out a few rooms because some are better than others. *Penginapan Mujuh (☎ 21229, Jl Rambutan 27)* is in the middle of the market area, and a little noisy, but decent enough with rooms for 16,000/ 22,500Rp with shared bathroom; 25,000/ 31,000Rp with private bathroom. Also, a staff member at the tourist office rents out *rooms* in the back of his house for 15,000Rp – inquire at the tourist office.

Places to Eat On one side of Wisma Sri Lestari, *Vieta Bar & Restoran* opens after 8 pm for upmarket meals and drinks; on the other side, *WM Surabaya* and, virtually opposite, *Rumah Makan Madura*, serve excellent, cheap Indonesian food. *Rumah Makan Borobudur*, a few metres past the market in the opposite direction from

Amahai, is the best place for huge baked fish meals for about 12,000Rp. The restaurant on the 2nd floor of *Hotel Masohi Manise* is surprisingly good value, and it also has a rooftop *bar*. Cheap *warungs* and *teahouses* huddle around the busy and pleasant market.

Northern Seram

The bus marked 'Saleman' (10,000Rp, three hours) travels between Masohi (and Kota Ambon) and the tiny, busy port of Saka every one or two hours (more in the morning) – but this road is rough, and almost impassable if it has been raining. From Saka, public longboats and speedboats service the north coast, including Sawai and Wahai. Boats leave when there are enough passengers, or you can charter one easily enough – but bargain

---

Bird Tribes of Seram

Lusiala

A scattering of villagers on the north coast of Pulau Seram believe their ancestors are descended from a unique species of tiny birds called *lusiala* that live in a cave above their village. According to the legend, another area of Seram was originally inhabited by an aquatic tribe of humans which gradually dispensed with its marine features. A couple from this tribe continually prayed for a child, but eventually the female gave birth to two birds, similar to bats, except they had human heads. Shocked, the couple left their village, rowed to a village on the north coast and cared for their bird-children in a cave. Many people along the north coast still fear the lusiala birds, and regularly interpret their activities as omens.

Bati

Some Bati people in southern Seram claim they can fly. They are said to have piercing eyes and the power during certain times of the year to pick up a human and carry them around the sky. Many Ambonese and Seramese continue to believe in the powers of the Bati.

MALUKU

hard. To get a boat between Wahai and Sawai, you'll probably have to head back to Saka.

Sawai The friendly village of Sawai is an exhilarating 30 minute longboat ride from Saka. From Sawai, you can rent a boat with a driver/guide from around 60,000Rp per day and visit two islands – **Pulau Sawai** for swimming and **Pulau Raja** to see its colony of bats. It's also fun to rent your own canoe for about 5000Rp per day and explore some underwater caves, complete with enormous turtles; or go to tiny **Pantai Ora**, which is great for swimming and snorkelling.

Pondok Wisata Lisar, built on stilts literally on top of the clear water, is worth a trip in itself. Simple rooms with stunning views cost 30,000Rp per person including meals and lots of complimentary tea. Other places are being built nearby, as well as at Pantai Ora – and will probably cost at least 50,000Rp per room.

Wahai Wahai, 90 minutes by longboat from Saka, is the main town on the north coast. Two **Portuguese cannons** dated 1785 in the main square indicate a colonial past which most historians seem to have ignored. Wahai has plenty of shops if you need to stock up on food and water for the trek to Manusela National Park.

Penginapan Taman Baru (☎ 222), opposite the Telkom building (ask directions), costs 15,000Rp per person for basic rooms with share bathroom; 23,000Rp with three meals. On the main street, *Penginapan Sinar Indah (☎ 255)* is nicer than it looks from the outside – a good room with share bathroom, costs 20,000Rp; 28,500Rp with three meals.

Bonara

Along the road east of Masohi, the traditional village of Bonara is inhabited by the Nuaula people of Papuan descent who are recognisable by their bright red cloth hats. (You'll probably see more Nuaulans along the road to Saka.)

You may be disappointed if you visit Bonara, however, because the villagers resent being a tourist attraction; in fact, they actively discourage tourism by being unfriendly, and insist on exorbitant amounts for photos. The village has only a dozen **traditional houses** and many villagers are away working during the day anyway. Take the bemo towards Tehoru; it's a rough road, but the scenery along the way is very pretty.

Western Seram

Three hours by bus along the rough, western road from Masohi are picturesque **waterfalls**, just outside the village of Rumahkai. It's a lovely walk to the falls and the setting is superb, but it's a long day trip from Masohi – start early. The bus between Kota Ambon and Masohi goes past the entrance to the falls, so you can get off and leave your gear at the small *rumah makan* at the gate.

Another hour further west, the road passes the village of **Kairatu**; ferries to Hunimua on Pulau Ambon leave from Waiprit nearby. There are several cheap losmen in Kairatu such as *Penginapan Sudi Hampir*, about 2km towards Masohi on the main road.

Manusela National Park

A large part of Pulau Seram's centre is designated as Manusela National Park (189,000 hectares). It's officially protected, but the park management has to contend with locals who want to use the area for logging, farming and building.

Manusela means 'bird of freedom' in the local Alfuro/Nuala languages, and the park hosts an abundance of birdlife, such as the bright nuri, cassowary and cockatoo. There are also endemic bandicoots, forest rats and cuscus. Traditional Alfuro and Nuaula people live in the main villages. The park has no shortage of rugged scenery, including thundering waterfalls, swampy mangroves, thick rainforests and, among it all, wild orchids.

The only way into the park is on foot, and trekking between the north and south coasts is a very, very tough, muddy, steep slog. Generally, the best time to trek is between July and September as there is less rain, but the weather will still probably be miserable most of the time.

Food & Accommodation Bring all your cooking gear and loads of wet weather stuff. You can buy food in Wahai or Hatumetan, or bring it from Masohi. You may be able to stay in huts in the villages – check with the kepala desa first. There are also some wooden shelters along the way and some caves that are possible to sleep in. Otherwise, bring your own (very waterproof) tent.

Guides & Porters Guides are compulsory and can be arranged through the tourist office in Masohi – the staff aren't experts on trekking, so don't expect to have all your questions answered. The standard price for a guide is 30,000Rp per day. A porter is also recommended and costs around 15,000Rp per day, but they will only trek from one village to another as there's still a lot of animosity and distrust between villages.

Permits You'll also need a visitor permit (1000Rp) from the Manusela National Park unit (☎/fax 22164) of the Forest Department in Masohi. See the Orientation & Information entry under Masohi earlier in this section.

Trekking Ironically, most of the recognised trail doesn't actually go through much of the park, but you wouldn't know – it's all jungle. From the south, the trail starts from Hatumetan, accessible by public or chartered boat from Tehoru. From the north, you can start from Wahai, or save two days hike by chartering a boat from Wahai or Sawai to the logging centre of Opin. From Opin, you'll have to wait for the daily truck to Roho. (Check the current situation with the Forest Department in Masohi.)

Theoretically, the trek between Roho and Hatumetan can be completed in four days, but you should allow about seven, and a few extra days to get to/from the start and finishing points. The normal itinerary goes something like this:

Roho to Kanikeh – seven hours.
Kanikeh to Solumena to Manusela village – six hours.

Manusela village to a place known as **Rumah Batu (Rock House)** – seven hours. From the north, this is the most difficult section as you climb to about 2000m.
Rumah Batu to Hatumetan – six hours. From the south, this section is very steep.

Banda Islands

South-east of Ambon lies the tiny cluster of gorgeous islands known as the Banda Islands. The group consists of ten islands, with a total area of 55 sq km. The three main islands are Pulau Neira, where the only town of any size, Bandaneira, and the airport are located; the largish, crescent-shaped Pulau Banda Besar (Big Banda Island); and the volcano, Pulau Gunung Api (Fire Mountain Island), looming menacingly from the sea. The other seven islands are sparsely populated, if at all, and are harder to reach.

The Bandas are littered with deserted forts, as well as functioning nutmeg plantations and charming Dutch villas. The islands are surrounded by superb beaches, and you can easily snorkel around some of the most stunning coral reefs you will ever see. If that isn't enough, there's a volcano, Gunung Api, to climb. The Bandas are understandably, and deservedly, an increasingly popular place to visit and to stay awhile.

History

The first Europeans to arrive in the Banda Islands were the Portuguese in 1512. Next came the Dutch – a fleet arrived in Maluku in 1599 with orders to seek out spices at their source and circumvent the Portuguese monopoly. Part of the Dutch fleet came to the Bandas, loaded a cargo of spices, alarmed the Portuguese and returned to the Netherlands. Soon afterwards the Dutch forced the Portuguese out of the spice trade, but the Dutch also had rivals. In 1611 the British East India Company set up a fort on Pulau Run in the Bandas, and in 1606 the Spanish took Ternate and Tidore islands in northern Maluku.

The turning point came in 1619 when Jan Pieterszoon Coen, the new governor-general

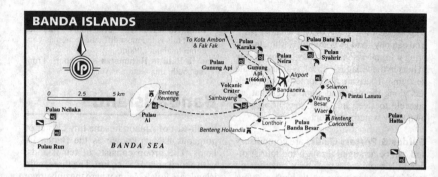

BANDA ISLANDS

To Kota Ambon & Fak Fak

Pulau Karaka

Pulau Batu Kapal

Pulau Syahrir

Pulau Neira

Pulau Gunung Api

Gunung Api (666m)

Airport

Selamon

Bandaneira

Pantai Lanutu

Volcanic Crater

Sambayang

Waling Besar

Waer

Benteng Revenge

0   2.5   5 km

Pulau Neilaka

Pulau Ai

Lonthoir

Pulau Banda Besar

Benteng Concordia

Pulau Hatta

Benteng Hollandia

Pulau Run

BANDA SEA

of the VOC, envisaged a Dutch commercial empire in the east. He seized control of the Bandas, killed many of the 'unhelpful' Bandanese and started producing nutmeg using imported slaves and labourers with Dutch overseers.

In 1621 Coen attacked Pulau Lonthor (now Pulau Banda Besar), the most important island of the group, and in revenge for the murder in 1609 of Admiral Verhoeven, Coen ordered the massacre of 44 village chiefs in front of Benteng Nassau (Nassau Fort) in Bandaneira. Many other Bandanese were killed or fled to the Kai Islands. Coen then returned to Batavia (Jakarta) and announced that the VOC would accept applications for land grants in the Bandas. The applicants had to settle permanently on the islands and produce spices exclusively for the company at fixed prices. They became known as *perkeniers*, from the Dutch word for 'garden'. Nearly 70 plantations were established, mostly on Banda Besar and Ai islands.

This agreement was not broken until almost 200 years later. The Bandas, like other Dutch-held parts of the archipelago, were occupied by the English during the Napoleonic Wars, at which time nutmeg seedlings were shipped off to Sri Lanka, Sumatra and Penang. By 1860 these areas were almost as important as the Banda Islands for producing nutmeg and mace. The invention of refrigeration, however, which allowed meat to be kept without the heavy use of spices, saw the end of the spice trade. Today the

Bandas still produce nutmeg and mace for use in Indonesia, but more is now grown in northern Sulawesi.

The islands continued to be ignored by the Dutch in the 19th and 20th centuries, and, thankfully, by the Japanese during WWII – who saw no use for nutmeg or the Bandas. Only since the early 1980s have the Banda Islands been 'rediscovered' by foreigners – this time by less destructive ones – tourists.

Books

Indonesian Banda by Willard A Hanna is an engaging book which details the occupation of the Bandas by the various European powers. *Turbulent Times Past in Ternate and Tidore*, co-written by Hanna & Banda supremo Des Alwi, is only available in Bandaneira, either at the shop opposite Hotel Maulana or at Rumah Budaya (see the Bandaneira entry later in this section). Both are small, expensive paperbacks.

Diving & Snorkelling

Chartering a boat (and boatman) is the ideal way to visit other islands to find the best diving and snorkelling sites. Boat trips are not organised on a regular basis, so ask staff at the popular homestays about any trips, and ask other guests about sharing costs. Some homestays urge you to deal with certain boatmen, but to avoid this and obtain lower prices, deal directly with someone at the fish market. The best season for all water activities is between October and March.

MALUKU

Some of Indonesia's most extraordinary diving and snorkelling can be found at nearly 50 dive sites around the Bandas, including:

Bandaneira Just off the jetty in front of the VOC Governor's Residence.

Sambayang and the lava around Pulau Gunung Api Excellent for tabletop coral and brightly coloured fish, accessible by canoe from Bandaneira.

Selamon Near the northern tip of Pulau Banda Besar. Stunning sponges and coral in clear water about 50m from the shore.

Pulau Ai Has a huge drop-off, three homestays to stay in and boats to hire.

Pulau Karaka Just offshore from a pretty beach.

Pulau Syahrir Only a few metres from a charming beach with a homestay.

Diving More distant islands with rougher waters are more suitable for scuba diving. Pulau Run boasts a vast number of fish in a lagoon and a drop-off; Pulau Nelaka has a coral reef which attracts serious divers; and Pulau Hatta, with the pristine Skaro reef nearby, is superb.

The only dive centre in the Bandas is opposite Hotel Maulana in Bandaneira. Technically the centre is only available to guests of the Maulana and the associated Hotel Laguna, but if you ask the dive instructor directly, he will usually accept your money. However, several divers have reported serious concerns about the poor maintenance of equipment. The dive centre charges about US$80 for a half-day trip to nearby islands including two dives, a guide, equipment and transport. A full day trip with two dives to more remote islands costs about US$90.

Snorkelling Some homestays in Bandaneira, such as the Flamboyan, Delfika 1, Gamalama and Pondok Wisata Matahari, and one or two shops around the port, rent full snorkelling gear for about 20,000Rp per day. To reach nearby snorkelling sites you can rent a one or two-person canoe from homestays such as Pondok Wisata Matahari, or from the fish market, for about 20,000Rp per day; 30,000Rp with a guide/paddler.

For longer trips, you can charter a boat (comfortably holding eight to 10 people) for a full day to visit Karaka, Gunung Api, Syahrir and Banda Besar islands. This will cost about 80,000Rp per boat per day; 100,000Rp to include Pulau Ai. Snorkelling equipment, and perhaps a fresh coconut on the beach, is extra. Your hotel should provide a free lunch as part of its room rate.

Swimming A good local beach for swimming and snorkelling is **Pantai Malole**, a 40 minute stroll north of Bandaneira along a shady path – you may need to ask directions along the way. Another decent beach is **Pantai Kolamroton** – walk about 1km north of the airport, along the eastern coast.

BANDANEIRA
☎ 0910

The main island in the Bandas is Pulau Neira. It has the only village, Bandaneira, and most of the attractions, as well as the port and airport. In its heyday, Bandaneira was a thriving town of spacious mansions, some of which are being slowly restored, while today, it's a charming, sleepy, friendly place. Bandaneira is the best place to base yourself, although there is accommodation on Pulau Syahir and Pulau Ai (see Other Islands later in this section).

Orientation & Information

Facilities in Bandaneira are more suited to the village it is, and not (thankfully) to the tourist trade. There is still no travel agency or bank, nor anywhere to change money – so stock up on rupiah in Pulau Ambon. There is a community health centre *(puskesmas)*, and a police station in a lovely, restored villa along Jl Pantai.

The tourist counter at the airport sometimes hands out brochures, but it's usually closed. Your hotel is the best source of current local information. The comparatively large and modern Telkom office is a becak ride away in the 'suburbs' on Jl Rajawali, and is open 24 hours. In contrast, the quaint post office is often closed.

One frustrating aspect about exploring Bandaneira is that the museum, 'exile houses' and forts are often closed, and have

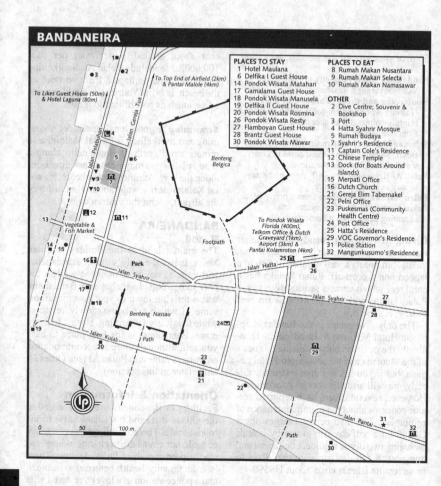

BANDANEIRA

PLACES TO STAY
1 Hotel Maulana
6 Delfika I Guest House
14 Pondok Wisata Matahari
17 Gamalama Guest House
18 Pondok Wisata Manusela
19 Delfika II Guest House
20 Pondok Wisata Rosmina
26 Pondok Wisata Resty
27 Flamboyan Guest House
28 Brantz Guest House
30 Pondok Wisata Mawar

PLACES TO EAT
8 Rumah Makan Nusantara
9 Rumah Makan Selecta
10 Rumah Makan Namasawar

OTHER
2 Dive Centre; Souvenir & Bookshop
3 Port
4 Hatta Syahrir Mosque
5 Rumah Budaya
7 Syahrir's Residence
11 Captain Cole's Residence
12 Chinese Temple
13 Dock (for Boats Around Islands)
15 Merpati Office
16 Dutch Church
21 Gereja Elim Tabernakel
22 Pelni Office
23 Puskesmas (Community Health Centre)
24 Post Office
25 Hatta's Residence
29 VOC Governor's Residence
31 Police Station
32 Mangunkusumo's Residence

To Top End of Airfield (2km) & Pantai Malole (4km)

To Likes Guest House (50m) & Hotel Laguna (80m)

Benteng Belgica

To Pondok Wisata Florida (400m), Telkom Office & Dutch Graveyard (1km), Airport (3km) & Pantai Kolamroton (4km)

Footpath

Vegetable & Fish Market

Park

Jalan Syahrir

Benteng Nassau

Jalan Kujali

Path

0   50   100 m

---

very irregular opening hours. The best time to find anything open is before noon on a weekday – or ask your hotel staff to find the caretaker and/or key.

Rumah Budaya

The Rumah Budaya (Culture House) on Jl Gereja Tua is an old Dutch villa with a small collection of cannons, muskets, helmets, coins, maps and china. On the walls, paintings graphically portray past wars and massacres, and in another room a useful display

neatly shows the layout of the Banda Islands. At the time of writing, the museum housed a fascinating but temporary display on the history of the Bandas (with excellent captions in English). Hopefully, the display will become permanent. The museum also sells the book *Indonesian Banda*, as well as a few T-shirts and postcards. Entry costs 5000Rp.

Benteng Nassau

The original stone foundations of this fort were built by the Portuguese around 1529 when they sent troops from their base in Pulau Ternate (northern Maluku). The fort, however, wasn't completed and the foundations were abandoned. In 1608 a powerful Dutch fleet under Admiral Verhoeven arrived with orders to annexe the Banda Islands. When negotiations stalled, Verhoeven simply confronted the Bandanese with a *fait accompli* by landing soldiers on Pulau Neira and building a fort on the old Portuguese foundations. Benteng Nassau was restored for use as a warehouse by the British in the early 19th century, but it eventually lapsed into ruin.

Sadly, the fort is overgrown – only three walls and a gateway remain, and an old cannon lies on the ground. Still, it's pleasant enough for a clamber around and there are nice views of Benteng Belgica. The best place to appreciate the size and shape of Nassau is from Belgica; in fact, there is supposedly a hidden tunnel between Nassau and Belgica.

Benteng Belgica

The construction of this Dutch fort began in 1611, under the direction of Pieter Both. He had been appointed governor-general of the region to create a monopoly and expel the English. Faced with the prospect of a Banda-English alliance, his men erected, at a staggering cost, the imposing Benteng Belgica on the ridge overlooking Benteng Nassau. It was maintained as a military headquarters until 1860, and then lapsed into ruin until it was magnificently restored a few years ago.

With Gunung Api looming on the island nearby, the fort's setting is quite stunning. It's a marvellous place to wander around and imagine its former opulence. At the entrance, where you must report and pay a small donation, a room has a small display of artefacts, photos and diagrams. All captions are in Indonesian, but you still get an idea of the incredible effort that went into its restoration.

Exile Houses

In 1936 two nationalist leaders, Mohammed Hatta and Sutan Syahrir, who had both proved troublesome for the Dutch, were transferred from the horrors of the Boven Digul prison (in central Irian Jaya) to Bandaneira – clearly showing how little respect the Banda Islands received at the time from the Dutch administration.

In 1942 the Dutch suddenly called them back to Java in an effort to counter Japanese control of Indonesia. At the time of the proclamation of independence in 1945, Hatta became Indonesia's vice-president and, later, Syahrir became prime minister.

Hatta's Residence features some old typewriters, furniture and clothes left over from his stay. There's a huge old urn half-buried in the back garden. **Syahrir's Residence** has been nicely restored and contains some interesting furniture and memorabilia from that era.

Another lesser-known nationalist leader was also exiled in Bandaneira between 1928 and 1940. **Dr Tjipto Mangunkusumo's Residence** has also been restored, but is basically empty and lacking in any of the doctor's personal memorabilia.

Other Attractions

The quaint Dutch Protestant **Gereja Tua (Old Church)** on the appropriately-named Jl Gereja Tua (Old Church Street) was built in 1852, after the original church was destroyed in an earthquake. The church has been extensively restored since, and still holds services. A large number of people are buried beneath the floor. There is another charming but closed old church, **Gereja Elim Tabernakel** along Jl Kujali, which nobody seems to know much about.

Also called the Istana Mini, the 19th century **VOC Governor's Residence** was once the home of the infamous Jan Pieterszoon Coen. It's majestically located just back from the waterfront, with a walkway jutting out to the sea. Although empty, it's worth wandering around; also have a look at the unrestored barracks at the back. A guest book must be signed, and a small donation is 'encouraged'.

Captain Cole's Residence has also been lovingly restored, but is often closed. Cole was the commander of the British Marines who captured Benteng Belgica in 1810 during the interlude of the Napoleonic Wars.

MALUKU

Not far from the Telkom office, a **Dutch graveyard** has tombstones dating back to the 17th century – take a becak or ask directions. The **Chinese Temple** on Jl Pelabuhan is about 300 years old, but is rarely used.

Places to Stay

All accommodation is in Bandaneira, with the exception of one homestay on Pulau Syahrir and three on Pulau Ai (see Other Islands later in this section). Prices for accommodation listed here include meals (except Hotels Laguna and Maulana), which invariably comprise fish, vegetables and rice. However, the price of fish in the Banda Islands is now very expensive (most of it is sold to refrigerated boats from Taiwan and Hong Kong), so fish is sometimes not offered.

Many places are cheap homestays, or *pondok wisatas*, which are usually a few rooms at the back of a friendly family home; others are converted Dutch villas with a few new rooms around a small garden. Most hotels will pick you up at the airport if you prearrange it, and some hotel touts at the airport provide free transport. If you're staying awhile, it's worth negotiating a cheaper rate; and if you don't want meals included, ask for a reduction of about 10,000Rp per single or double per day.

Places to Stay – Budget

The convivial and helpful *Pondok Wisata Rosmina* (☎ 21145, Jl Kujali 25) has comfortable rooms and good food for 25,000Rp per person. For about the same price, *Pondok Wisata Mawar* (☎ 21083, Jl Kujali), near the VOC Governor's Residence, is a real find – a great location in a friendly atmosphere. For antique furniture in huge (musty) rooms and sparkling service, *Pondok Wisata Florida* (☎ 21086, Jl Hatta), a two minute walk east of Hatta's Residence, is recommended. Most rooms have two or three beds, so it's ideal for small groups or families, and it's good value for 30,000Rp per person.

Likes Guest House (☎ 21089, Jl Pelabuhan), between the Maulana and Laguna hotels, is one of the few places that offer dramatic views of Pulau Gunung Api. It has some ordinary rooms inside this friendly family home for 35,000Rp person; the one room with views is sensational for 40,000Rp per person. *Pondok Wisata Matahari* (☎ 21050), along a path parallel to Jl Pelabuhan, has several decent singles/doubles with terrific views for 50,000/60,000Rp, and some uninspiring cheaper rooms (with views of nothing) for 30,000/40,000Rp. However, several travellers have been disappointed with the food.

In the village, *Gamalama Guest House* (☎ 21053, fax 21309, Jl Gereja Tua) has large, clean rooms (good for families or small groups), efficient staff and tasty food. Many rooms are upstairs and hence breezy. Rooms cost 50,000/60,000Rp with fan; 65,000/75,000Rp with air-con. Opposite, *Pondok Wisata Manusela* (☎ 21149) is about the same standard and very good value at 30,000Rp per room; the better rooms at the back are 40,000Rp.

Delfika I Guest House (☎ 21027, Jl Gereja Tua) is a long-term favourite, with good food and friendly service. It's an old Dutch villa, with rooms set around a small garden (with noisy caged birds). The ordinary rooms inside the main building cost 40,000/65,000Rp; the very comfortable, newer rooms are good value for 55,000/80,000Rp. The newest place is *Delfika II Guest House* (☎ 21127), along a footpath in the village, near the corner of Jl Pelabuhan and Jl Kujali. The views are superb, but its rooms are a little pricey for 50,000/75,000Rp; 75,000/100,000Rp with the best views.

Flamboyan Guest House (☎ 21233, Jl Syahrir) serves great food, has a lovely garden setting and clean rooms for 50,000Rp per person – generous discounts are common. In a renovated villa opposite, the popular *Brantz Guest House* (☎ 21068) has the nicest garden among the budget hotels, and rooms for a negotiable 50,000Rp per person; 70,000Rp with air-con. The hotel is a good source of local information, and can organise tours. There are also a couple of other cheaper pondok wisatas only a few metres away.

Pondok Wisata Resty (☎ 21060, Jl Hatta) is owned by the local Merpati manager, who may persuade you to stay there if you book a return flight from Bandaneira by telephone. The rooms are new and clean, and the food is tasty; rooms cost 40,000Rp per person. It's currently unsigned but is new, white and easy to spot.

Places to Stay – Mid-Range & Top End

At the top end of the scale is *Hotel Maulana* (☎ 21022, fax 21024, Jl Pelabuhan). While you get good views and the rooms are comfortable, there is nothing else to justify its rates: from US$60/72 excluding meals. Part of the same group, but cheaper, is *Hotel Laguna* (☎ 21018, Jl Pelabuhan), a few metres up the road. It offers decent singles/doubles for a comparatively reasonable 180,000/300,000Rp.

Places to Eat

There is not a great choice of places to eat in Bandaneira, which is why most homestays offer meals (or is it the other way around?). It's cheaper to eat at your hotel, but if you want to try some local restaurants, negotiate a reduction in your room rate.

The following restaurants are next to each other along Jl Pelabuhan, and offer some alternatives to the standard offered at homestays. *Rumah Makan Namasawar* has a nice outdoor setting, and sells reasonably good ice cream and pancakes, as well as hot chips. *Rumah Makan Selecta* offers the same sort of food, but the setting and service isn't quite as good. *Rumah Makan Nusantara* has basic but delicious Indonesian food from 3500Rp. One or two other cheap *rumah makans* congregate around the port and opposite the Maulana.

Getting There & Away

Air Merpati flies between Pulau Ambon and Bandaneira (200,500Rp) three times a week; twice a week via Amahai, near Masohi, on Pulau Seram. The flight between Bandaneira and Amahai is far cheaper (65,000Rp) because it's subsidised by the local government – a good reason to take a sidetrip to Seram.

In the wet season, some services are cancelled through lack of passengers, and/or

bad weather; and in the dry (and tourist) season, some flights are heavily booked. You may have to wait in Ambon for a while for an available flight or seat, or you could get stuck in the Banda Islands for a few days. Allow plenty of time.

The pretty Bandaneira airport has been extended and can cater for larger planes, but most flights are on tiny planes which seat about 15 people; the flight from Bandaneira to Amahai can only take about eight passengers. Also, there is a limit of 10kg per person, but this is generally ignored if you're only a few kilograms over.

It is important to note that you cannot book, or buy, a return ticket from the Bandas in Masohi or Ambon. You must: (a) ring the Merpati office in Bandaneira, book a return ticket and pay for it as soon as you arrive; (b) take pot luck and book and buy your return ticket as soon as you arrive, even at the Bandaneira airport while you're waiting for your luggage; or (c) time your visit so you can travel one way on a Pelni liner (see the Boat entry following).

The Merpati office (☎ 21041) on Jl Pelabuhan in Bandaneira is officially open from 7.30 am to 1 pm daily, and until 11 am on Friday – but the office is closed when a flight is arriving or departing. The office can be a very frustrating place: overbooked or cancelled flights, misplaced luggage and an 'underhand' system of dubious ticketing is not uncommon.

Boat Two Pelni liners stop at Bandaneira: the *Bukit Siguntang* and *Rinjani* sail from Kota Ambon to Bandaneira (28,000/90,000Rp economy/1st class, seven hours), and back again, every two weeks. The *Rinjani* also travels to the equally delightful Dutch colonial town of Fak Fak, on the south coast of Irian Jaya, and back – making Fak Fak an appealing side trip. Because Pelni can sometimes be more reliable than Merpati, a boat is a good option for travel to, and especially from, the Bandas.

The Perintis boat *Iweri* is a reasonable alternative, and goes to many of the same places as the Pelni liners. In Bandaneira, the new Pelni office (☎ 21122), which also handles bookings for Perintis boats, has a helpful schedule for all passenger boats on a wall outside.

Uncomfortable cargo and passenger boats also link Bandaneira with Kota Ambon (12 hours), most places in south-east Maluku, and Agats (for the Asmat Region of Irian Jaya) every two or three weeks. The harbour master's office at Bandaneira port has the current schedules.

Getting Around

To/From the Airport Sometimes public bemos and becaks wait for all incoming flights, but most transport is provided free by a hotel tout. (Don't worry: their frantic hassling of visitors is not the least bit indicative of the Banda Islands.) The road past Delfika I Guest House turns into a footpath and leads to the western end of the runway in 15 minutes; or via the main road, past Hatta's Residence, it takes about 30 minutes on foot. To reach the airport, tee up transport with your hotel, take a becak or walk.

Public Transport Bandaneira and Pulau Neira are very small, easy and pleasant to walk around. Many locals ride bicycles, but Delfika I has the only bicycle for rent on the island and charges a hefty 50,000Rp per day. Hopefully, more homestays will see the benefit of bicycle rental and more will become available soon.

Boat Motorised boats are the only form of inter-island transport (see the following Other Islands entry). A canoe for one or two people costs about 20,000/30,000Rp without/with a paddler or guide. These canoes are often harder to steer than you think, but are useful for visiting snorkelling sites around Neira, Gunung Api and Karaka islands. Ask your hotel staff or ask someone at the fish market.

OTHER ISLANDS

Except for daily passenger boats between Bandaneira and Banda Besar and Ai islands, there is no regular public transport between any of the islands. Boats holding eight to 10

people can be rented for a very negotiable price of about 12,000Rp per hour depending on tourist demand, distance (the most important factor being petrol cost) and length of hire. All boats leave Bandaneira from around the fish market – the exact location varies a little, so ask around.

Pulau Gunung Api

This volcano has been a constant threat to Bandaneira and to the villages perched around its fertile slopes. Gunung Api (666m) has erupted numerous times over the centuries, often when a fleet of ships planned to attack Bandaneira – something which was always regarded by the colonialists as a bad omen. The most recent eruption was in 1988, when three people were killed, over 300 houses were destroyed and ash covered the sky for days afterwards.

The volcano can be climbed in about 1½ hours; allow about one hour for coming down. The first part is relatively easy with some wooden steps (often broken) and resting places; the top bit involves a tough scramble up steep, loose ground. This part is also particularly tricky on the way down. At the top, be careful of hot rocks and craters.

To see the sunset and reach the top before the early morning cloud covers the indescribable views for the rest of the day, start at 5.30 am – but the volcano can be climbed at any time of the day. Try to time your stay at the top so you can watch the tiny Merpati plane circle the volcano before it lands – an extraordinary sight.

Guides are available for about 15,000Rp, but are not necessary unless you want someone to carry your gear – ask around at your hotel in Bandaneira, or at the fish market. A chartered canoe from Bandaneira to the island will cost about 5000Rp return. The boatman will know where you should start the climb and he will somehow be there when you come down.

Gunung Api also has some extraordinary coral along the north coast. The boatman should know where to find the best snorkelling spots (see also Diving & Snorkelling earlier in this section).

Pulau Karaka

Off the northern end of Pulau Gunung Api, Pulau Karaka (Old Woman's Island) has a small beach and some fine coral reefs in shallow water near the shore. It's close enough to paddle from Bandaneira in a canoe if you're fit and competent, and will take at least an hour.

Pulau Banda Besar

The largest island of the Banda group is worth a trip or two from Bandaneira. The main village and dock, Lonthoir, has a series of steep steps (260 in all) leading to **Benteng Hollandia** (Hollandia Fort), erected in 1624. About halfway up, on the right, is a **sacred well** known as Perigi Keramat (or Perigi Pusaka). If you then turn left at the top of the stairs and ask directions, you'll find Benteng Hollandia. Placed high on the central ridge of the island, with great views of the surrounding islands and Lonthoir, the fort was once enormous, but an earthquake destroyed it in 1743. What little remains is derelict and overgrown, and is a disappointment after Benteng Belgica. Someone will ask you to sign the visitors' book and you'll be obliged to pay a small donation.

A path heads along the north coast, east of Lonthoir, initially over some rocks, and then passes small swimming beaches, wild clove trees and spotless villages. If you continue on, there's an interesting, old **colonial nutmeg plantation** around Waling Besar.

Near Waer, on the east coast, is the decrepit fort, **Benteng Concordia**. Further north, **Pantai Lanutu**, behind Selamon village, is a magical area for swimming and snorkelling. If there are some boys hanging around the beach, ask one to pick a fresh coconut from a nearby palm tree and open it for you. The only way to Waer is on foot from Lonthoir (not really recommended without a guide), or by chartering a boat directly from Bandaneira.

To get to Lonthoir, charter a boat (about 8000Rp one way) or take the regular public boat (800Rp, 25 minutes) from the Bandaneira fish market. Less regular public boats also leave Bandaneira for Waling

Besar and other villages, but often only when there's enough demand. There are no vehicles or transport on the whole island.

Pulau Syahrir

Also known as Pulau Pisang because of its banana shape, and home to a leper colony during Dutch times, Syahrir has a lovely sandy beach, stunning coral (with a big drop-off) and colourful fish. You can wander uphill to the small village behind the beach.

Homestay Mailena has a few rooms right on the beach, which are comfortable and offer almost total seclusion. You should book a room and check the price before you get there, however, because some visitors without bookings have been charged as much as 80,000/100,000Rp without/with meals – which is way too high. The problem is locating the owner of Homestay Mailena in Bandaneira – ask around for Pak Ahmat Kediri at the *ashrama polisi* (police hostel), about 200m east of the police station.

Syahrir is about 40 minutes by boat from Bandaneira. There are very few public boats, so you'll have to charter one (and arrange for it to pick you up later) for about 40,000Rp one way or return.

Pulau Hatta

This island is virtually ignored by travellers, but it has another lovely beach. You can stay in a village home, but a homestay may be built on the island soon. Public transport to this remote island will always be difficult to find, however, and chartering a boat will always be expensive.

Pulau Ai

This delightful island is where the British attempted to gain some ascendancy over the Banda Islands and the spice trade in 1610. With its secluded beaches, snorkelling sites, unhurried villages, 36 abandoned nutmeg plantations and old fort, Pulau Ai is a popular alternative to the comparative 'hustle and bustle' of Bandaneira.

Things to See & Do From the boat ramp, head right for a few minutes to **Benteng**

MALUKU

Revenge. Built by the British, then captured by the Dutch, the fort is decrepit, with only the walls remaining. More interesting nearby is the former **Dutch plantation house**, Welvaren, which is also mostly in ruins. The Welvaren plantation was established in the mid-18th century, and once covered about one-third of the island.

Ask your boatman or someone at your hotel to point out the best **snorkelling** spots – many are close to the homestays and only a short swim from the shore. Homestay Weltevreden can organise snorkelling trips, and you can rent snorkelling gear from the Weltevreden and Revenge homestays.

Places to Stay & Eat The island has three homestays. Prices include three meals of (you guessed it) fish, vegetables and rice; most rooms have a communal bathroom, and prices are certainly negotiable for longer stays. It's worth checking all three before deciding. Another homestay is slowly being built right by the boat ramp.

The best is *Homestay Weltevreden*, at the top of the lane from the boat ramp. The rooms are simple but clean, and cost 25,000/30,000Rp for singles/doubles; or 35,000/45,000Rp with a private bathroom. *Homestay Revenge* is a popular, pleasant place with rooms for 30,000/50,000Rp including good meals. From the boat ramp, head right and walk for two minutes; it's in front of the fort. Finally, *Homestay Welvaren* is the newest, and cheapest with rooms for 25,000/40,000Rp. The family is nice, but the rooms are stuffy. It's at the back of the village; walk past the fort, turn left at Welvaren and then left again.

Getting There & Away Two or three passenger boats (5000Rp, one hour) leave from a spot a few metres south of the Pondok Wisata Matahari in Bandaneira anytime between noon and 1 pm for what is sometimes a rough trip. Boats leave Ai for Bandaneira any time between 7 and 9 am (check with your homestay). Unfortunately, the timing prevents you from day-tripping by public boat to Ai from Bandaneira, but you can

always charter a boat from Bandaneira for about 60,000Rp return; this includes several hours for exploring and snorkelling.

Pulau Run

Run, once the centre of English activity in the Bandas, is mainly famous as one of the greatest swaps in history. After the Treaty of Breda in 1667, the British gave Run to the Dutch in exchange for another little island – Manhattan. There's a decrepit **English fort** on a spit of half-exposed coral rock on **Pulau Neilaka**, which lies just off Run, and some stunning diving offshore.

There are a couple of villages, but no official accommodation. Occasional public boats go to Run from Pulau Ai, or charter a boat from Ai or Neira islands.

South-East Maluku

The islands of South-East Maluku province are dispersed across the sea between Timor and Irian Jaya. The three main groups are the Kai, Aru and Tanimbar islands. West of the Tanimbars, two arcs of smaller, sparsely populated islands stretch across to Timor: a southern arc consisting of the Babar and Leti groups, Kisar and Wetar, and a northern arc of volcanic, wooded islands, including Serua, Nila, Teun, Damar and Romang.

The centre for transport to the islands is the provincial capital, Tual, in the Kai Islands. These islands remain undeveloped with limited facilities, but they do boast some of the most magnificent beaches in Indonesia. You'll need a lot of time to really explore the region, and be prepared for some uncomfortable boat rides across rough seas and/or infrequent and delayed flights.

KAI ISLANDS
☎ 0916

Also known as the 'Thousand Islands' (although there are really only 287), the word 'Kai' probably originates from the Portuguese word for 'stone'. The three main islands are Pulau Kai Kecil (known locally as Nuhu Roa), Pulau Dullah, and the very

Iconic and isolated Indonesian paradise – Pulau Syrahir in the Banda Islands – a great diving location.

A view of Pulau Tidore from Pulau Ternate.

Catholic church, Kota Ternate.

Market at Rum, Pulau Tidore.

'Hello Mister' brigade, Ternate.

Hilltop view of Soa Siu, Pulau Tidore – the only town on the island.

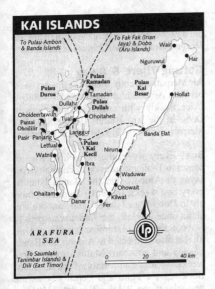

KAI ISLANDS

To Pulau Ambon & Banda Islands

To Fak Fak (Irian Jaya) & Dobo (Aru Islands)

Wair
Nguruwul
Har
Pulau Ramadan
Pulau Duroa
Tamadan
Pulau Kai Besar
Hollat
Dullah
Pulau Dullah
Ohoideertawun
Pantai Oholilir
Tual
Ohoitaheit
Pasir Panjang
Langgur
Banda Elat
Letfual
Pulau Kai Kecil
Nirun
Watnil
Ibra
Waduwar
Ohowait
Ohaitam
Danar
Kilwat
Fer

ARAFURA SEA

To Saumlaki Tanimbar Islands) & Dili (East Timor)

0   20   40 km

mountainous and sparsely populated Pulau Kai Besar (aka Nuhu Yut). The main towns on Pulau Kai Kecil and Pulau Dullah are, respectively, **Langgur** and **Tual**. Pulau Kai Besar is home to many Bandanese people, who fled the Banda Islands during colonial times and still speak Bandanese (a language which has all but disappeared in the Bandas).

Information

The helpful tourist office (☎ 21805) can provide useful information. It's badly signposted, just off the lane at the end of Jl Pattimura in Tual. Neither bank in Langgur changes money.

Pulau Kai Kecil

Seventeen kilometres from Tual, **Pasir Panjang** is an isolated, unspoiled beach with sparkling-blue water, powdery-white sand and thousands of coconut palms. It's the best and most accessible beach in the Kais. Not far away, **Ohoideertawun** has another fine beach, and the intriguing **Gua Luwat** (Luwat Cave) has some unexplained and unusual paintings.

Pulau Dullah

The pretty village of Dullah claims to have the **Belang Museum**, which is nothing more than three decaying longboats *(kora-kora)*. On the way to Dullah, **Taman Anggrek** (Orchid Garden) has the small **Danau Ngadi** (Ngadi Lake) and some pleasant picnic spots. The beach at Tamadan has some Japanese **WWII wrecks**.

Pulau Kai Besar

Wildlife enthusiasts should head to this island. Its unspoilt flora and coastline are a haven for birdlife, while its **traditional villages**, such as Ohowait, are wonderful to explore.

Places to Stay

Most cheap places are in Tual. The following have basic rooms with a shared bathroom: the 'old' *Rosemgen I* (☎ 21045, Jl Karel Sadsustubun) costs 18,000Rp per person, or 25,000Rp with simple meals – plus lots of mosquitoes; *Losmen Nini Gerhana* (☎ 21343, Jl Pattimura) is noisy but friendly for 22,500Rp per room; and *Mirah Inn* (☎ 21172, Jl Mayor Abdullah) costs about 14,500Rp per person. The quiet but inconveniently located *Linda Mas Guest House* (☎ 21271, Jl Antoni Rebok) has comfortable rooms for around 25,000Rp, and more expensive rooms with air-con and TV from 52,500Rp.

The only place to stay in Langgur is the quiet, 'new' *Rosemgen II* (☎ 21477, Jl Merdeka Watdek), where singles/doubles start at 36,000/48,000Rp with fan and bathroom. Ask for a room with a river view.

On the west coast of Pulau Kai Kecil, *Coaster Cottages* at Pantai Ohoililir has a delightful setting and snorkelling opportunities nearby (it rents equipment). It's isolated and isn't easy to reach, but this appeals to many visitors. Expect to pay about 50,000Rp per double, including meals – current details and bookings are available at Mirah Inn in Tual. For about the same price, *Savana Cottages* (☎/fax 22390) at Ohoideertawun is another picturesque collection of bamboo cottages with an idyllic

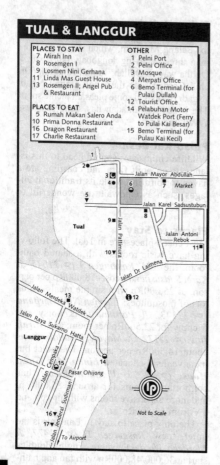

TUAL & LANGGUR

PLACES TO STAY
7 Mirah Inn
8 Rosemgen I
9 Losmen Nini Gerhana
11 Linda Mas Guest House
13 Rosemgen II; Angel Pub & Restaurant

PLACES TO EAT
5 Rumah Makan Salero Anda
10 Prima Donna Restaurant
16 Dragon Restaurant
17 Charlie Restaurant

OTHER
1 Pelni Port
2 Pelni Office
3 Mosque
4 Merpati Office
6 Bemo Terminal (for Pulau Dullah)
12 Tourist Office
14 Pelabuhan Motor Watdek Port (Ferry to Pulai Kai Besar)
15 Bemo Terminal (for Pulau Kai Kecil)

setting – current details and bookings are available at Losmen Nini Gerhana in Tual.

Places to Eat

There are plenty of *warungs* around the markets in both Langgur and Tual, but hotel food is probably your best bet.

In Tual, *Rumah Makan Salero Anda* and *Prima Donna Restaurant* offer poor food and little variety. In Langgur, *Angel Pub & Restaurant* at Rosemgen II has cold beer, live music and a great river view – though

for a good dinner you must order earlier in the day. Along Jl Jenderal Sudirman are the *Dragon* and *Charlie* Chinese restaurants.

Getting There & Away

Air Merpati currently flies three times a week between Ambon and Langgur (474,400Rp); twice weekly with onwards connections to Dobo in the Aru Islands (93,000Rp). The Merpati agency (☎ 21376) is on Jl Pattimura.

Boat Every week, the Pelni liner *Rinjani* comes to Tual, and goes on to Fak Fak (Irian Jaya) or Ambon, via the Banda Islands; every two weeks, the *Bukit Siguntang* travels to Dobo (Aru Islands) and Ambon; and about once a week, the *Tatamailau* goes to Dobo, Saumlaki (Tanimbar Islands) or Dili. Tual is also connected to Ambon, the Banda Islands and southern Maluku every three weeks by less comfortable Perintis boats. Bookings for Pelni and Perintis boats are possible at the Pelni office (☎ 21181) in Tual. Other crowded boats regularly sail between the Kai and Tanimbar islands.

Getting Around

From Langgur's Dumatabun airport, take a public bemo from the main road, or charter one. Reasonable roads link the major villages throughout Kai Kecil and Dullah islands, but there is no regular public transport around Kai Besar. Chartering a bemo will cost about 15,000Rp per hour.

The *Tanjung Burang* ferry sails between Banda Elat on Pulau Kai Besar and Tual's Pelni port three times a week; and at least one ferry sails daily between Banda Elat and Pelabuhan Motor Watdek port in Tual.

TANIMBAR ISLANDS
☎ 0918

The 66 islands forming the Tanimbars were 'discovered' by the Dutch in 1629, but not settled for nearly 300 years because of a lack of fresh water. The islanders are renowned for their carving, painting and other handicrafts, while the islands are known for beautiful, wild orchids; but the islands remain undeveloped. Transport to and around the Tanimbars can be rough and irregular. The main town, Saumlaki, on Pulau Yamdena is little more than a 200m stretch of road called Jl Bhineka.

Things to See & Do
At **Sangliat Dol**, a 30m-high stone staircase leads up from the beach to an 18m-long boat-shaped carved stone platform. The stone structures are interesting enough, but it's a long, uncomfortable ride (1½ hours) from Saumlaki. On the way, Ilngei has a pretty swimming beach. Nearer Saumlaki, charter a bemo to the lovely, tropical **Pantai Leluan**.

Places to Stay & Eat
There are only three places to stay, all along Jl Bhineka in Saumlaki. *Penginapan Ratulel* (☎ 21014) is the cheapest at 25,000/30,000Rp for singles/doubles; add on an extra 15,000Rp for three meals. The best is *Penginapan Harapan Indah* (☎ 21019), which has small upstairs rooms for 36,000Rp with a shared bathroom (more for air-con and TV), including excellent meals.

Hotel food is definitely recommended, although it's the usual simple fare. There are a few *warungs* and Padang-style *rumah makans* around the market, but nothing else.

Getting There & Away
Merpati flies between Ambon and Saumlaki (490,900Rp) weekly. The Merpati office (☎ 21017) is in Penginapan Harapan Indah. The Pelni liner *Tatamailau* connects Saumlaki with Tual every two weeks, and there are regular boats between Kai and Tanimbar islands. Perintis also services Dobo, Tual, Bandaneira and Ambon. The Pelni office is near the port, just off the main street in Saumlaki.

Getting Around
From the tiny Olilit airport, you can share or charter a bemo, or get a lift with the friendly guys from Merpati.

The one main road on Pulau Yamdena goes up the east coast from Saumlaki as far as Arui. The road is rough and may be impassable in the wet season. All buses leave from the huge Yamdena Plaza in Saumlaki. Chartering transport for about 15,000Rp per hour will offset inevitable waiting.

ARU ISLANDS
☎ 0917

The Aru Islands are little more than a collection of swampy islands in the 'transition zone' between Australia, New Guinea and Asia. A national reserve, the South-East Aru Marine Reserve in the south is home to a diminishing number of birds of paradise, but crocodiles and deer are common all over the Arus. Pearl farming and fishing are being developed by foreign interests.

The Arus are difficult to get to and almost impossible to explore, so they receive very few visitors. In the main town, Dobo, there are two simple losmen: the best is *Vanesya Homestay* (☎ 21071).

Merpati (Dobo ☎ 21007) flies between Ambon and Dobo (547,000Rp), via Tual/Langgur (93,500Rp), twice a week. Dobo is a regular stop for boats between Ambon and the southern coast of Irian Jaya. The Pelni ships *Tatamailau* and *Bukit Siguntang* link Dobo with Ambon, Timika and Tual, and Perintis boats stop regularly.

TANIMBAR ISLANDS

Pulau Molu

Pulau Maru

Larat — Pulau Larat

Lamdesar

Pulau Wuliaru

Watmuri

Pulau Yamdena — To Tual (Kai Islands), Dobo (Aru Islands), the Banda Islands & Pulau Ambon

Arui

Pulau Sera — Bukrane

Sangliat Dol

Olilit Airport — Amdasa

Inglei

Wasletan — Pantai Leluan

Pulau Matkusa — Saumlaki

Pulau Astubun

Pulau Nustabun

Pulau Selaru

0   25   50 km

ARAFURA SEA

MALUKU

Northern Maluku

Of the 353 islands in northern Maluku, the most famous and interesting are the original 'Spice Islands', Ternate and Tidore. These two islands were among the first areas in which the Portuguese, and later the Dutch, established themselves in Maluku. Once bitter rival sultanates, the two islands are scattered with the ruins of forts, surrounded by black sand beaches, and full of beautiful volcanic and tropical scenery.

If you have the time, it's also worth exploring the remote Sula Islands, the pretty Bacan Islands, the oddly shaped Pulau Halmahera, and Pulau Morotai, with its WWII history and pristine landscape.

PULAU TERNATE
History

Well before the Europeans came, the sultanate of Ternate was one of the most important in Maluku, with influence as far south as Ambon, west to Sulawesi and east to Irian Jaya. Ternate's prosperity came from its abundant production of cloves, which allowed it to become a powerful regional military force.

In 1511 the Portuguese were the first to settle in the region and establish a monopoly of the spice trade, but in 1575 they were expelled by the Ternateans. Five years later, the British under the command of Francis Drake visited the wealthy port, but no further British interest was taken in the islands.

Then came an endless series of invaders: the Dutch re-established a local monopoly in 1599; the Spanish became the chief foreign power in Ternate and Tidore for much of the 17th century; the British took control during the Napoleonic Wars; the Dutch returned soon after; and the Japanese occupied the islands during WWII.

KOTA TERNATE
☎ 0921

The town of Ternate in contrast to Kota Ambon is a relaxed place, only occasionally interrupted by rumblings from the huge, still-smoking Gunung Api Gamalama, the volcano on which all villages on the island cling. The market, near the bemo terminal, is one of the busiest and most colourful in Maluku, and is certainly worth a look around. (Some traders around the market may offer Dutch colonial coins, but only an expert could guarantee their authenticity.)

With its regular transport connections with Manado in northern Sulawesi, Ternate is an ideal place to stopover before heading to Sulawesi, Pulau Ambon or Irian Jaya.

Information

Tourist Offices The tourist office (☎ 21044, ext 65) is on the ground floor of the Governor's Office (Kantor Bupati) on Jl Pahlawan Revolusi. The friendly staff speak English, and have a few brochures and maps available. The office is open Monday to Thursday from 7.30 am to 2.30 pm, until 11 am on Friday and 1 pm on Saturday. You should visit the

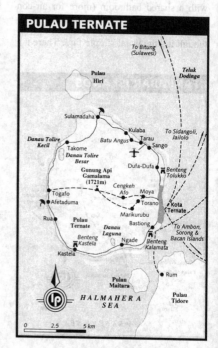

PULAU TERNATE

office for advice and current information before attempting to climb Gunung Api Gamalama (see Around Pulau Ternate later in this section for details).

Money Ternate is the only place in Maluku (besides Kota Ambon) where you can change money. The best banks are BNI (which will give cash advances on Master-Card and Cirrus Cards), Bank Exim and Bank Danamon. They are all open weekdays from about 8 am to 2 pm.

Post & Communications The main post office is open from 8 am to 8 pm daily, and has a useful poste restante. Next door, the Telkom office is open 24 hours.

Kedaton Sultan
Built around 1250, the Sultan's Palace is now a **museum** containing an absorbing collection of Portuguese cannons, Dutch helmets and armour, and memorabilia from the reigns of past sultans. The sultans' crown, which supposedly has magical powers (including the ability to stop Gamalama from erupting), is only displayed on special occasions.

The museum is officially open from 8 am to 4 pm weekdays, but you're more likely to find it open in the mornings. It is regarded as a holy place, so shoes must be removed before entering the main rooms. A small donation is expected. The museum is just back from Jl Sultan Babullah, the road leading to the airport. It's an easy 1.5km walk north of the terminal, or catch any bemo heading north.

Benteng Oranye
Opposite the bemo terminal, this fort was built by the Dutch in 1607 on top of an undated Malay fort, which explains its former name, Benteng Malayo. The fort was the headquarters of the entire VOC operation until about 1619, when it was transferred to Batavia (Jakarta), and was the residence of the Dutch governors in Ternate.

The fort has now been taken over by the Indonesian military and police, although you can still have a look around. It hasn't

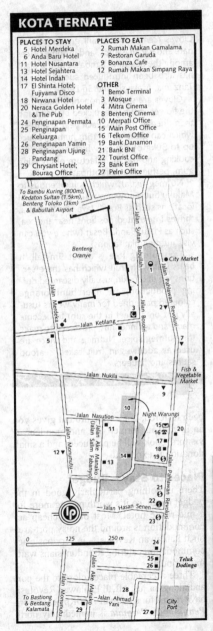

KOTA TERNATE

PLACES TO STAY
5 Hotel Merdeka
6 Anda Baru Hotel
11 Hotel Nusantara
13 Hotel Sejahtera
14 Hotel Indah
17 El Shinta Hotel; Fujiyama Disco
18 Nirwana Hotel
20 Neraca Golden Hotel & The Pub
24 Penginapan Permata
25 Penginapan Keluarga
26 Penginapan Yamin
28 Penginapan Ujung Pandang
29 Chrysant Hotel; Bouraq Office

PLACES TO EAT
2 Rumah Makan Gamalama
7 Restoran Garuda
9 Bonanza Cafe
12 Rumah Makan Simpang Raya

OTHER
1 Bemo Terminal
3 Mosque
4 Mitra Cinema
8 Benteng Cinema
10 Merpati Office
15 Main Post Office
16 Telkom Office
19 Bank Danamon
21 Bank BNI
22 Tourist Office
23 Bank Exim
27 Pelni Office

Spicy Cengkeh & Pala

Cloves (cengkeh) are still grown on Ternate and Bacan islands, and in some places among the beautiful Bandas, but the plant has also been introduced successfully to Tanzania, Malaysia and Sri Lanka.

Cloves are simply unopened buds from the flower of the tree, picked by hand and then dried in the sun. Each year, the trees, which can grow up to 15m high, produce up to 30kg of cloves, which are used for cooking and the manufacture of chewing gum, perfumes and toothpaste.

Nutmeg (pala), which is indigenous to Maluku but is now grown in other tropical locations such as Brazil, Java and Sumatra, thrives in elevated positions near the sea, such as Pulau Banda Besar (where you can visit nutmeg plantations).

The nutmeg tree is about 9m tall. It bears yellowish fruit which has three sections: an outer skin, usually discarded during production; an inner burnt-orange coloured part, dried for many weeks (usually just on a sheet in the sun) to become mace; and an inner nut, processed to make the nutmeg spice. Nutmeg and mace are used as additives in fruit cakes, seafood sauces and liqueurs.

been restored, but a walk around gives you an idea of its former size and grandeur. A visitors' book will be produced, and a small donation is expected.

Places to Stay – Budget
There is nothing particularly good in the budget range, so it's worth paying more for a mid-range hotel. Most of the cheap accommodation is around the noisy port area on Jl Pahlawan Revolusi – ie very basic accommodation catering to Indonesians waiting for boats.

Three acceptable places close to the port and along, or just off, Jl Pahlawan Revolusi, have rooms for a bargain 7500Rp per person. *Penginapan Permata* is immediately north of the mosque, about 20m from the main road, and is the best of the bunch; *Penginapan Keluarga* (☎ 22250) is just south of the mosque, 50m off the main road (look for the sign); and *Penginapan Yamin* (☎ 21929) is the noisiest of the lot. Slightly better, and more expensive, is *Penginapan Ujung Pandang* (Jl Ahmad Yani), but it's often full.

A couple of family-run places on Jl Ake Manako (also known as Jl Salim Fabanyo) aren't great value, but they're friendly and central. Rooms have a bathroom and fan, but are invariably noisy. *Hotel Sejahtera* (☎ 21139) costs 20,000/35,000Rp for tiny singles/doubles; and *Hotel Nusantara* (☎ 21086) also has small, dreary rooms for 30,000/35,000Rp.

One of the cheapest in this range, *Anda Baru Hotel* (☎ 21262, Jl Ketilang), has rooms with fan and bathroom for 20,000/25,000Rp, but rooms with air-con from 35,000 to 50,000Rp aren't good value. The mosque over the road can be deafening at times, and the hotel staff are a little eccentric. The old *Hotel Merdeka* (☎ 21120, Jl Merdeka 19) is the best budget place: it has charm, friendly staff and a pleasant outdoor seating area. Rooms with fan cost 22,500/27,500Rp; 37,500 to 47,500Rp with air-con.

Places to Stay – Mid-Range
There are three similar, adjacent places on Jl Pahlawan Revolusi, so you can check out each of them. *El Shinta Hotel* (☎ 21059) has noisy singles/doubles at the front for 30,250/41,250Rp, and better rooms at the back for about 66,000/77,000Rp with air-con and satellite TV – the latter is good value because it include meals. All rooms at *Neraca Golden Hotel* (☎ 21668) have air-con, TV and hot water, and are well furnished, if a little dark. Prices range from 66,000 to 82,500Rp, and discounts are regularly offered. *Nirwana Hotel* (☎ 21787) is a bit of a rabbit warren, but the rooms are large, quiet and clean. Prices start at 44,000Rp; 'superior' rooms with satellite TV, hot water and air-con are good value for about 65,000Rp, but make sure everything works first.

Hotel Indah (☎ 21334, Jl Bosoiri 3) has recently been renovated, and raised its prices accordingly, so it's no longer great value. The cheapest rooms for 27,500/38,500Rp are small; the rooms with air-con and hot water for 44,000/55,000Rp aren't bad. The friendly *Chrysant Hotel (☎ 21580, Jl Ahmad Yani 131)* has quiet rooms, but many badly need some renovation. Prices are 30,000/50,000Rp; 55,000Rp with satellite TV and air-con.

Places to Eat

There is not a great choice. Dozens of *warungs* spring up every evening around Jl Bosoiri; there's a collection of cheap *food stalls* along the waterfront, just north of the tourist office; and several good *rumah makans* serve Padang food at the bottom-end of Jl Pahlawan Revolusi. The large *Rumah Makan Simpang Raya (Jl Monunutu)* is also worth trying for Padang food.

Restoran Garuda (Jl Pahlawan Revolusi) is recommended for its selection, reasonable prices (about 8000Rp for Indonesian food) and cold drinks, but don't sit at the back of the restaurant in the evening unless you just 'luurve' karaoke. Nearby, *Rumah Makan Gamalama* is good and cheap. A large plate of *nasi ikan* (rice with fish) costs 2500Rp, for example, but cold drinks aren't available. For the best fruit drinks and assorted *kue-kue* (cakes) in Maluku, head immediately to *Bonanza Cafe (Jl Nukila)*.

Bambu Kuring (Jl Sultan Babullah) is a 10 minute stroll north of the bemo terminal. The reasonably priced menu (from 10,000Rp) is vast, and the private tables are surrounded by rattan decor and ponds (with lots of mosquitoes, so come prepared).

Entertainment

Several times a day, two good cinemas show English or Chinese-language films (with Indonesian subtitles); *Mitra Cinema*, Jl Ketilang, has better sound and films than the *Benteng Cinema* (Jl Bosoiri). For karaoke, late night drinking and dancing, the only places to be seen are the *Fujiyama Disco* in the El Shinta Hotel, and *The Pub* in the Neraca Golden Hotel.

Getting There & Away

Air Ternate is the hub for all air transport in northern Maluku. Merpati has flights to Manado in Sulawesi (352,300Rp) almost daily, and to Ambon (461,000Rp) five times a week. Tickets for both can be purchased at the Merpati office (☎ 21651), daily from 8 am to noon and 3 to 4.30 pm; 10 to 11.30 am on Sunday.

Flights to Galela and Kao on Pulau Halmahera and Pulau Morotai are temporarily on hold. Flights to Labuha on the Bacan Islands, and Pulau Gebe (east of Pulau Halmahera) are irregular and unreliable; and tickets for both destinations are available at a separate office (current details are available from the Merpati office).

Bouraq no longer flies between Ternate and Manado, but the Bouraq office in the Chrysant Hotel (☎ 21288) in Ternate sells tickets for other Bouraq flights, such as Manado-Ujung Pandang.

Boat Ternate is also the major port for northern Maluku – but take note of the different ports.

Every two weeks, the Pelni liners *Umsini* and *Ciremai* link Ternate with Bitung (for Manado) for 25,500/82,500Rp, and Sorong (58,000/195,000Rp); and the *Lambelu* links Ternate with Ambon (70,000/235,000Rp), via Namlea. The Pelni office (☎ 21434) is located in the city port area. Tickets are normally available about two days before the boat arrives.

There is a multitude of other boats: some go up the north coast of Pulau Halmahera to Daruba, Tobelo and Pulau Gebe every week or so; there are milk runs to Pulau Bacan, the Sula Islands, Pulau Buru and Ambon, among other places, every couple of weeks; larger boats go to the Sulas and Ambon every week; smaller boats crawl south to Pulau Obi and the Bacan Islands about twice a week; overnight boats sail to Tobelo, via Daruba, about every week; and all sorts of vessels go to Bitung every day or so.

The three ports can be confusing, as two of the ports are at Bastiong (a few kilometres south of the city and accessible by bemo) and are only a few hundred metres apart. The 'first' port as you come from Kota Ternate has most slow and fast boats to Bacan and Obi islands and southern Halmahera; and speedboats to Rum (Pulau Tidore).

The 'second' port, a little further south of the 'first', is for speedboats to Sidangoli, the nearest port on Halmahera; ferries to Rum and Sidangoli; and the overnight ferry to Bitung (23,250/29,750Rp for 2nd (B) class/1st (A) class, four times a week). You can also buy tickets for buses and Kijang (Toyota 4WDs) to anywhere along the Sidangoli-Galela road, on northern Halmahera, from near this port.

The largest port in the city, at the end of Jl Pahlawan Revolusi, caters for Pelni and Perintis boats; most boats and speedboats to northern Halmahera; and boats to Sulawesi, the Sula Islands and Ambon.

Noticeboards outside the shipping offices in the city port and along the entrances of the two Bastiong ports give boat schedules. Tickets for most boats (except speedboats and ferries) can, and should, be bought at least one day before departure. The Pulau Tidore, Pulau Halmahera and Bacan Islands sections later in this chapter also have details.

Getting Around

The Babullah airport is just north of Kota Ternate. From the airport, you'll have to pay 10,000Rp for a shared taxi (you can charter one to the airport for far less); or walk about 1km from the airport terminal to the university and catch a public bemo (500Rp) to the terminal. The city is small and you can easily walk to most places. Bemos around town cost 400Rp, and a *bendi* (horse-drawn cart) usually costs about 1000Rp to any place in town.

AROUND PULAU TERNATE

It's easy to visit all the sights around the tiny island in one or two-day trips from the city. Most of the circular, paved road is covered by public bemos. They go infrequently as far as Takome (750Rp) via the north road, and Togafo (900Rp) via the south road; but not between the two villages, because the area is so sparsely populated.

Therefore, you can't completely circle the island by public transport.

Chartering a bemo for about 12,000Rp per hour is a good option. If chartering, allow at least two hours to quickly see the sights; a couple of hours more if you really want to explore the lakes, climb forts and take a swim. It will take considerably longer by public bemo. Few of the attractions are signposted, so ask your diver to drop you off at the less obvious places. The places in this section are listed starting anti-clockwise from the city.

Benteng Tolukko

Built by the Portuguese in 1512 and restored by the Dutch in 1610, this fort (also known as Benteng Holandia) is the best on the island. The seaside setting and the views are superb, and it has recently been well restored. Ask the woman next door to let you in. She will produce the inevitable visitors' book, and a small donation is expected (2000Rp is enough). The fort is about 300m east of the main road to the airport. It's a pleasant 3km walk north of the bemo terminal, or take any bemo heading that way.

Batu Angus

Batu Angus (Burnt Rock) is a volcanic lava flow caused by the eruption of Gunung Api Gamalama in 1737. It's a huge area of black rocks heaped on top of each other as far as you can see, and is great for clambering around and admiring the view of Pulau Hiri. The rocks are located on both sides of the main road, not far past the airport.

Sulamadaha

At the top of the island, Sulamadaha has a scruffy black beach and pretty views of Pulau Hiri. If you walk north from the beach, initially over some rocks, for 15 minutes, there's a tiny **coral beach** where the water is better for swimming and the snorkelling is good (bring your own gear). From the Sulamadaha port, down a lane off the main road before the beach, public motorboats (1000Rp) leave several times a day for the tiny villages on **Pulau Hiri**; or you can charter a motorboat for about 40,000Rp return.

Just before the beach, the friendly *Hotel Pantai Indah (☎ 21659)* has clean singles/doubles with bathroom and fan for 35,000/40,000Rp, including three meals. It's a pleasant, quiet alternative to the city.

Danau Tolire Besar

Ignore Danau Tolire Kecil, the smaller, dirtier lake next to a black sand beach, and head straight for Danau Tolire Besar. An easy-to-follow, but unsigned, 500m trail from the main road leads to this stunning, deep volcanic lake which contains crocodiles, fish and, according to local legend, the wreck of a WWII plane. The lake and foothills are great for hiking. Public bemos go as far as Takome, from where you'll have to walk a few kilometres; alternatively charter transport from the city.

Afetaduma

This popular and clean black sand beach is especially crowded on Sunday, when you are far more likely to get a public bemo.

Kastela

This tiny village boasts the fort, **Benteng Kastela**, built in 1522. It's next to the main mosque, but is overgrown, in ruins and virtually unrecognisable. There is a decent beach just off the main road.

Danau Laguna

This large volcanic, spring-fed lake near Ngade is covered with lotuses and is another great area for hiking. The main entrance is usually closed, so take the dirt track down to the lake from the start of the wall as you come from the city.

Opposite the main entrance to the lake, **Taman Eva** (Eva Park) is a popular spot for Ternateans on Sunday. It has a pleasant garden, a small *cafe* and splendid views across the bay to Pulau Tidore. You can scramble down to the rocks below and dive into the sea.

Benteng Kalamata

About 1km south of Bastiong, this fort is also known as Benteng Kayu Merah (Red Wood Fort). Built in 1540 by the Portuguese, and rebuilt by the Dutch in 1610, its location by the sea is spectacular, but the fort has been over-restored and has consequently lost a lot of its charm. Still, it's worth a look around. A visitors' book must be signed, and a donation given (about 2000Rp).

Gunung Api Gamalama

This active volcano (1721m) is, in fact, the island of Ternate. It has erupted fiercely many times over the centuries, often resulting in mass evacuations and loss of life. In 1840 it destroyed almost every house on the island. The most recent eruptions were in 1980, 1983 and 1994, when hot ash sprayed 300m above the crater.

You can wait for an irregular public bemo (or charter one) to **Marikurubu** village on the slopes of Gamalama. Although it's close to the city, many people in the area still maintain their old customs and live in **traditional housing**. This is great country for **hiking**, but beware: a white face will certainly cause a large gathering; you'll need a guide if you plan to do any walking in the area; and a few big black hairy spiders set webs for unsuspecting tourists.

If you take a bemo to Marikurubu, get off at Torano and then walk 1km or so (ask directions), you'll find the enormous **Cengkeh Afo** (clove tree) on the slopes of the volcano. Almost 400 years old and claimed to be the oldest clove tree in the world, it still produces up to 400kg of cloves each harvest.

The summit of Gamalama takes about four hours to reach and is not difficult if plenty of rest stops are taken. Start at about 5 am to ensure breathtaking views before clouds cover the top of the volcano for the rest of the day. You must talk to the tourist office in Kota Ternate before you plan anything. To find the trails, you'll need a guide (about 40,000Rp). Ask at the tourist office, or try a hotel like the Merdeka.

You can start the trek from: Marikurubu (the quickest way); Moya (longer, but you can visit Cengkeh Afo on the way); or Togafo (the longest trek, and transport is irregular). Be careful, especially at the top, because some tourists without guides have disappeared while climbing the volcano.

PULAU TIDORE
☎ 0921

Tidore was also once part of the pre-colonial spice trade and, like Ternate, a great Islamic sultanate which claimed parts of Halmahera and areas as far as Irian Jaya. Rivalry between the neighbouring sultanates resulted in frequent wars, and only in 1814 was peace finally established. To placate potentially troublesome modern Tidoreans, the oddly shaped Central Halmahera district was created by the Indonesian government.

Ternate has far better facilities for visitors, but Tidore is an easy and enjoyable day trip from Ternate. Soa Siu is the capital of the district, and the only town on the island.

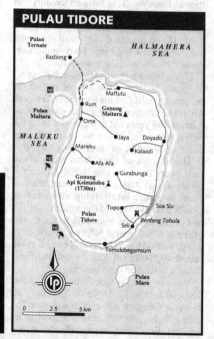

PULAU TIDORE

Pulau Ternate

HALMAHERA SEA

Bastiong ●

Maftutu

● Rum

Gunung Maitara ▲

Pulau Maitara

● Ome

MALUKU SEA

● Jaya   Doyado ●

● Marieku   Kalaodi ●

● Afa Afa

● Gurabunga

Gunung Api Keimatubu ⏚ (1730m)

Topo ●   Soa Siu ●

Pulau Tidore   Benteng Tohula

Seli ●

● Tomolobegamsum

Pulau Mare

0   2.5   5 km

Things to See & Do

The port for ferries and speedboats to Ternate, **Rum**, is a busy, friendly village where nutmeg is still cultivated. From Rum, you can charter a sailboat, or take a public boat, to the gorgeous island of **Pulau Maitara**, which has clear, blue waters for snorkelling and swimming.

Along the Rum-Soa Siu road, you'll see plenty of pretty beaches, foundations of abandoned **colonial houses** and snorkelling spots – just get on and off the bemo as you like.

Just before you arrive in Soa Siu, ask to be dropped off at **Sonyine Malige Sultan's Memorial Museum** which contains a small but intriguing collection of sultanate memorabilia. If it isn't open, ask at the office at the side of the building. Only 50m from the museum, at the fork in the road, the ruins of the 17th century Spanish fort **Benteng Tohula** stand enticingly. Ask a local child to show you how to climb up there.

Bemos leave irregularly from the Soa Siu market/terminal to the small village of **Gurabunga** perched on the side of **Gunung Api Keimatubu** (1730m). The views from there are superb. If you take a bemo up to the village, it's a pleasant walk (one hour) back to the main road. If you want to climb the volcano, ask the kepala desa for help with finding a guide and for current information. The climb to the top can be tricky in parts and takes about five hours to the peak.

Places to Stay & Eat

There is no need to stay on Tidore, but there are a few homestays. Near the Soa Siu market, *Johra Penginapan* is the cheapest at around 10,000Rp per person. Also in Soa Siu, the friendly *Jangi Homestay* (☎ 21131, Jl Malawat 32) is the best place at about 18,000Rp per person. For both places, ask the bemo driver to drop you off, or take a becak from the market. Ask your hotel to provide meals; alternatively there are plenty of *warungs* at the market/terminal in Soa Siu.

Getting There & Away

The best way is by speedboat (1250Rp, 10 minutes). They travel every few minutes between the 'first' Bastiong port, south of Kota Ternate, and Rum. From the 'second' Bastiong port, there are also wooden boats to Rum, and ferries (six daily) to Rum and Sidangoli (Pulau Halmahera), but both forms of transport are very slow and infrequent.

Getting Around

The road between Rum and Soa Siu is virtually one long village, and bemos regularly travel between both places (1200Rp, 40 minutes). Bemos are less frequent from Soa Siu to Maftutu in the north, and non-existent from Maftutu back to Rum, so you cannot completely circle the island without chartering transport (12,000Rp per hour).

PULAU HALMAHERA

The largest island in Maluku (17,780 sq km), Pulau Halmahera is unusually shaped with four peninsulas and dozens of islands off its western coast. Its population is mainly Muslim and, like the people of Ternate and Tidore, is a mix of Portuguese, Gujarati (from western India), Arab, Malay and Dutch – a result of long contact with foreign spice traders.

Only the northern peninsula has any infrastructure, large villages or places to stay – although there is one *losmen* in Weda, at the northern part of the southern peninsula, and another *losmen* nearby in Payahe. Halmahera is an interesting and easy diversion from Ternate. It has plenty of beaches, volcanoes, islands and WWII remnants to explore, as well as opportunities for some **trekking** in the mountains and visits to **traditional villages** between Ibu and Daru.

Getting There & Away

Air Frequent and cheap bus transport within Halmahera has severely affected the reliability and number of flights to the island. Currently, all commercial flights to/from Halmahera have been cancelled.

Boat About once a week, one or two boats connect Tobelo with Manado; otherwise, all boats to Halmahera start and finish at Ternate. Boats used to regularly link Ternate

with Tobelo (15 hours), and Daruba on Pulau Morotai (12 hours), but these now sail once a week only.

Sidangoli is the closest port on Halmahera to Ternate. Every few minutes, speedboats (5000Rp, 30 minutes) hurtle between Sidangoli and the 'second' port at Bastiong (Pulau Ternate), although from Sidangoli, boats often drop passengers off at a jetty in the fish and vegetable market. The ferry between Sidangoli, the 'second' port at Bastiong and Rum (Pulau Tidore) is cheaper, but takes far longer and only travels six times daily. A ferry and speedboat also travel daily between Jailolo and the city port in Kota Ternate.

Getting Around

Public Transport From Sidangoli, a good road heads up the west coast through Jailolo as far as Ibu. The 176km road along the east

PULAU HALMAHERA

coast between Sidangoli and Galela, via Kao and Tobelo, is slowly improving, and is even excellent in some parts. You have the choice of a bus, or a Kijang which is more comfortable, marginally more expensive, but not necessarily faster.

From Sidangoli to Kao (15,000Rp, three hours) or Tobelo (17,500Rp, five hours), it's better to buy a ticket for the bus or Kijang at the 'second' port at Bastiong before you get on the ferry or boat from Ternate to Sidangoli – this avoids the pandemonium of finding a seat in a vehicle at the Sidangoli terminal after the ferry arrives from Ternate. At Tobelo, buy a return ticket at an agency along the main road the day before you leave. Unfortunately, all buses and Kijangs leave Tobelo at 4 am to catch the Sidangoli-Bastiong ferry, although most people use the speedboat. In Kao, you'll have to hail down any passing vehicle, which is not easy because they're often full.

Boat The lack of roads means that most travel around the island is by speedboat or longboat. For places on the north-east peninsula, boats travel between Daru and Fayaui, and a large ferry travels most days between Tobelo, Daruba and Subaim. Roads cover most of the north-west peninsula, but boats from Jailolo travel to places further north such as Ibu and Pulau Morotai. For the southern peninsula, the hub for boat transport is Saketa, which is regularly linked with Bacan and Ternate islands.

Sidangoli

Sidangoli is little more than a terminal for boats to Ternate and buses to Kao or Tobelo, but it's pleasant enough to stay while you plan your assault on Halmahera. You can easily day trip from Ternate and combine it with a visit to Jailolo.

Penginapan Sidangoli Indah, only 50m from the bus terminal, sometimes doubles as a brothel, but the place is reasonably nice – large rooms with a bathroom cost 30,000Rp. A small *restaurant* is attached. Almost in the market area, along the main road parallel to the sea, the new *Penginapan Indah Fanny*

has clean rooms for 25,000Rp. Opposite, the best place to eat, *Indah Fanny*, serves simple Indonesian food and cold beer, but has a blasted karaoke machine.

Jailolo

Jailolo was once one of four sultanates in the region, but the village is not quite as grand these days. Very few white faces detour to this part of Halmahera, so crowds of onlookers can be a little disconcerting. Jailolo's one *penginapan* is unmarked and unnamed in the market area. Huge rooms with antique furniture cost 25,000Rp, including meals. Jailolo is a nice day trip from Sidangoli or Ternate – the ride between Sidangoli and Jailolo (40 minutes, frequent) by bemo is delightful.

Kao

Kao is worth a stopover if you have plenty of time, or want to break up the journey between Ternate and Tobelo. It's a friendly, dusty town with a nice swimming beach nearby. Plenty of **WWII** remnants, including the **shipwreck** of the *Dai Nippon*, clearly show that Kao was a major Japanese WWII base (with up to 60,000 troops).

Penginapan Dirgahayu has average rooms with bathroom (and plenty of mosquitoes) for 17,500Rp per person, including three decent meals. Next door, *Dua Puteri* is the only place to eat, serving basic Indonesian food.

Tobelo
☎ 0924

Tobelo is the hub for buses and boats servicing northern Halmahera and Pulau Morotai, and is a pleasant place to base yourself while exploring the area. Virtually everything you need is along, or just off, Jl Kemakmuran, part of the main road south to Kao and north to Galela. The banks here are reluctant to change money, so stock up in Ternate.

Tobelo is easy to walk around, although a becak (around 500Rp) is useful from the port to your hotel. The bus may drop you off at a new terminal out of town (but Kijangs normally don't). If so, take another short bemo ride to your hotel.

Places to Stay & Eat It's worth paying a little more for a quiet, decent room. *Hotel Karunia (☎ 21202, Jl Kemakmuran)*, and *Penginapan Asean* on the road to the port, are basic and noisy but good value for 12,500Rp per room. The best in the budget range is *Penginapan Alfa Mas (☎ 21543)*, which has spotlessly clean, quiet rooms with bathroom from 20,000Rp to 40,000Rp with air-con. Look for the sign off the main road.

Penginapan Sengkanaung (☎ 21865) is good value: large rooms for 25,000/35,000Rp with fan/air-con are quiet and clean, but the small windows are reminiscent of a prison cell. It's just off the southern main road; look for the sign. Just off the northern main road, *Hotel Pantai Indah (☎ 21064, Jl Iman Sideba)* is the best in the mid-range category. Large singles/doubles with a fan cost 38,500/66,000Rp; 66,000/88,000Rp with air-con and satellite TV. The price includes three excellent meals, or pay 10,000Rp less per person without meals. Nearby, *President Hotel (☎ 21312, Jl Kemakmuran)* has clean rooms with air-con, but it's not great value these days: 45,000/60,000Rp. The *restaurant* is good and open to the public.

If you don't eat at your hotel, a few uninteresting *warungs* around the market/bemo stop serve Padang food. About 150m up from the President Hotel on the main road, *Rumah Makan Almufid* serves excellent baked fish and chicken meals for about 5000Rp.

Around Tobelo

Along the road between Tobelo and Galela (45 minutes), which hugs the pretty coastline and is lined with swaying palms, there are a few interesting things to see. **Pantai Luari**, a small, semi-developed tourist beach (for Indonesian tourists) is nice enough for swimming and relaxing under the trees. From the bridge in Mamuya village, an 800m trail leads to small **hot water springs**, which are definitely worth a dip. From Mamuya, you can go trekking up the **Mamuya and Do volcanoes**. Each one takes about six hours to reach the summit, and you can organise a guide at the volcanology office (Kantor Guning Api) in Mamuya.

Closer to Galela, there are some interesting **WWII shipwrecks** at Pune. About 50m down a lane behind a church on the main road sit two untouched and overgrown Japanese cannons *(meriam jepang)*. To find other WWII remnants, you'll have to do some asking and exploring.

The road finishes at **Galela**, a sleepy Muslim village with nowhere to stay or eat. Nearby there's a series of stunning **volcanic lakes**. The largest, **Danau Duma**, complete with small crocodiles, is superb and worth exploring. A good road circles the lake and starts only 3km from Galela. If walking, ask directions to the correct paths and allow about three hours from Galela to the lake. Alternatively, charter a bemo or take public bemos from Galela to the pretty villages on the lake, such as **Igobul** and **Soa Konora**.

From Danau Duma it's about 5km to the smaller, pretty **Danau Makete** – full of lotus flowers and friendly women doing their laundry. You can walk (ask directions), or take a bemo to Makete village, from Galela. This is another excellent area for **hiking**.

PULAU MOROTAI

Morotai was an important Japanese base during WWII before it was captured by the Allies and used by General MacArthur to plan Allied offensives across the Pacific. Today, the sparsely populated 1600 sq km island offers unexplored tropical beaches, unused WWII airports, WWII wrecks, and unlimited diving and snorkelling opportunities (bring your own gear).

The major town and transport centre, **Daruba**, is an unexciting and poor village. The only main road on the island doesn't go far out of Daruba, but there are still plans for an extension as far as Berebere. The island is fairly flat, so it's a good place for **hiking** along beaches and through jungle and isolated villages.

The best and most accessible place to stay is *Penginapan Panber*, an unsigned light-yellow building along Jl Yasan. It has passable rooms for 25,000Rp per person, including meals. Daruba has a few *warungs*, but it's best to eat at the hotel.

A large ferry leaves Tobelo daily at about 8 am for Daruba (three hours), and often then continues to Subaim on the north-east peninsula. The ferry stops in Daruba for little more than an hour, so it's not much of a day trip from Tobelo, especially because the ferry ride is dull. The ferry's arrival in Tobelo is not timed to connect with buses or Kijangs from Tobelo to Sidangoli.

BACAN ISLANDS
☎ 0927

The Bacan Islands, at the southern end of Halmahera, include Mandioli and Kasiruta islands, but most development, facilities and transport are on Pulau Bacan, where Labuha is easily the largest town. Bacan is a pleasant detour (or possibly a day trip) from Ternate, or a stopover between Ternate and Ambon.

Benteng Barnevald

This fort was originally built by the Portuguese to counter the expanding Spanish empire, but was soon captured by the Dutch in 1609. Complete with a moat and several cannons, the fort is entirely overgrown but still discernible, and definitely one of the most fascinating in Maluku. It's about 500m behind a Protestant church in Labuha – if in doubt ask directions.

Air Belanda (Dutch Water), a pretty area with a stream and **waterfall**, is worth a 3km stroll from the centre of Labuha – again ask directions, or charter a bemo.

Places to Stay & Eat

In the centre of Labuha, *Pondok Indah* (☎ 21048) has clean, quiet rooms for 30,000Rp, including meals. *Penginapan Borero* (☎ 21 024) is worth paying a little extra for. Decent singles/doubles cost 35,000/50,000Rp, including meals.

If you don't eat at your hotel, *Eka Ria Restaurant* and *Sibela Cafetaria*, near both hotels, serve reasonable meals.

Getting There & Away

Merpati has two flights a week between Ternate and Labuha (149,500Rp), which go on to Ambon (310,500Rp) – but flights are often cancelled. Several boats sail between Bacan and Ternate islands daily, but these travel at night which means you miss the spectacular mountain, volcano and island scenery.

The 'super-fast' *Kie Raha Express* (five hours) leaves the 'first' Bastiong port on Ternate daily at about 8 am for Babang, except Sunday. This normally allows you time for a short day trip from Ternate – but check the return time from Babang first at Bastiong. Bacan's port, Babang, is about 30 minutes by public bemo from Labuha.

SULA ISLANDS
☎ 0929

South-west of Pulau Halmahera are the remote Sula Islands. They are sparsely populated, densely forested and ignored by just about every traveller to Maluku. If you want to really get away from the tourist trail and visit unexplored diving (bring your own gear) and hiking spots among traditional villages and rugged terrain, then the Sulas may be for you.

The best place to base yourself is Sanana, although most boat transport goes to/from Mangole on Pulau Mangole. Sanana is a very relaxed place, with a large, decrepit **Dutch fort** near the port.

Along the main road, the unmarked *Penginapan Sula Indah* costs from 25,000Rp per person; 15,000Rp extra for three meals. One of the few places to eat, the bizarrely named *Rumah Makan Elvis Raya* (The Great Elvis Restaurant), opposite the port, serves simple, cheap Indonesian food.

Merpati flies twice a week from Ambon to Sanana (259,900Rp), and sometimes on to Ternate, via Labuha (222,000Rp) on Pulau Bacan. The Merpati offices are on Jl Pantai, Sanana (☎ 21078), and PT Anugerah Jaya, Mangole (no telephone).

Boats sail to Mangole, and less often to Sanana and Dofa, from Babang (Pulau Bacan), Ternate and Ambon every day or so (inquire at the relevant harbours), but the seas around these islands can be very rough. Roads are almost non-existent on the Sulas – boats are the major form of transport within and between each island.

Irian Jaya

Irian Jaya, the western half of the island of New Guinea, was only 'acquired' by the Indonesians after the Dutch surrendered control in the 1960s. Over three times larger than Java and Bali combined, Irian Jaya's 421,981 sq km is mainly impenetrable jungle where traditional tribes still manage to survive harsh conditions and modern intrusions.

Almost all visitors head to Baliem Valley (the only part of the interior generally accessible to tourists), some include a side-trip to Pulau Biak (Biak Island) and/or the capital, Jayapura. Irian Jaya has a lot more to offer, but it still suffers – and will for some time – from limited transport due to geographic inaccessibility and excessive government travel regulations.

When the Portuguese sighted New Guinea in 1511 they called it Ilhas dos Papuas (Island of the Fuzzy Hairs), from the Malay word *papuwah*. Later, Dutch explorers called it New Guinea because the black-skinned people reminded them of the people of Guinea in Africa. *Irian* is a word from the Biak language meaning 'hot land rising from the sea'. Under the Dutch, Irian Jaya was known as Dutch New Guinea and when sovereignty was transferred to Indonesia it was renamed Irian Barat (West Irian), then Irian Jaya (*jaya* means 'victorious' in Bahasa Indonesia). Other names used internationally include West Irian and West Papua.

HISTORY
Dutch Rule

In 1660 the Dutch recognised the Sultan of Tidore's sovereignty over New Guinea and as the Dutch held power over Tidore (the Sultan's territory), New Guinea was now theoretically Dutch. The British were also interested in the region and unsuccessfully attempted to establish a settlement in the north-west near Manokwari in 1793. In 1824 Britain and the Netherlands agreed that the Dutch claim would stand and Irian Jaya became part of the Dutch East Indies.

HIGHLIGHTS

- With its unique culture and trekking opportunities, the Baliem Valley is Irian Jaya's major tourist attraction.
- Pulau Biak is popular for its beaches, diving and WWII relics.
- Sentani is a great base to explore magnificent Danau Sentani.
- Manokwari and Nabire, on the north coast, make pleasant bases to explore nearby islands, mountains and lakes.

In 1828 the Dutch established a token settlement in western Irian Jaya in Lobo (near Kaimana) but it also failed miserably. The Dutch did not develop the province until 1896, when settlements were set up in Manokwari and Fak Fak in response to perceived Australian claims from the eastern half of New Guinea. In 1855 the first missionaries, Germans, established a settlement on an island near Manokwari. The province continued to be virtually ignored, except by mining companies from the USA and Japan, which explored the rich oil reserves during the 1930s. However, all mining was halted during WWII and later stalled because of the struggle for control of the province.

As part of the Dutch empire during WWII, Irian Jaya was occupied by the Japanese before being liberated in 1945. After WWII, the

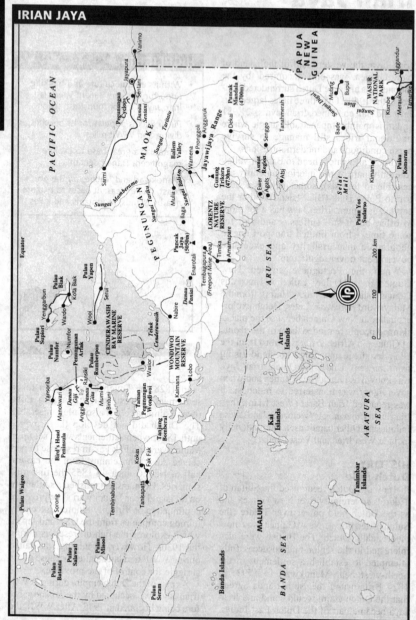

IRIAN JAYA

Dutch used the region as a place of exile and set up the Boven Digul camp (in what is now Tanahmerah) as a prison for Indonesian nationalists.

Due to international pressure, the Dutch were forced to withdraw from Indonesia after WWII, but still clung to Dutch New Guinea. In an attempt to stop Indonesia from gaining control, the Dutch encouraged Irian Jayan nationalism and began building schools and colleges to train Papuans in professional skills, with the aim of preparing them for self-rule by 1970.

Indonesia Takes Over

Following WWII many Indonesian factions – whether Communist, Soekarnoist or Soehartoist – claimed the western side of New Guinea as part of Indonesia. Their argument was that all the former Dutch East Indies should be included in the new Indonesian republic. Throughout 1962 Indonesian forces infiltrated the area, but with little success. The Papuan population failed to welcome them as liberators and either attacked them or handed them over to the Dutch. However, US pressure eventually forced the Dutch to capitulate abruptly in August 1962.

A vaguely worded agreement in that year under United Nations (UN) auspices required that Indonesia allow the Papuans of West Irian to determine, by the end of 1969, whether they wanted independence or to remain within the Indonesian republic. This 'Act of Free Choice' was 'supervised' by the UN in 1969. The Indonesian government, however, announced that it would use the procedure of *musyawarah*, by which a consensus of 'elders' would be reached.

In July 1969 the Indonesian government announced that the assemblies in the Merauke, Jayawijaya and Paniai districts, where the greater part of the population lived, had unanimously decided to become part of Indonesia. Irian Jaya became Indonesia's 26th province, consisting of nine districts, with capitals at Sorong, Manokwari, Biak, Serui, Nabire, Jayapura, Merauke, Wamena and Fak Fak.

Irian Jaya during WWII

After the bombing of Pearl Harbour, the Dutch declared war on Japan; Irian Jaya, then part of the Dutch East Indies, inevitably assumed importance in the battle for the Pacific. (Ironically, some Indonesians welcomed the Japanese as Asian liberators who would eradicate the hated Dutch colonialists.)

In early 1944 a four-phase push, led by General Douglas MacArthur, was launched from New Guinea (now Papua New Guinea) to liberate Dutch New Guinea (as Irian Jaya was called) from Japanese occupation. The Allies were far from optimistic: this part of the world was almost completely undeveloped, inhospitable and unchartered.

Phase one – the capture of Hollandia (Jayapura) – was the biggest amphibious operation of the war in the south-western Pacific and involved 80,000 Allied troops. (There are several WWII monuments around Jayapura, and rusting wrecks along nearby beaches.) The second phase – to capture Sarmi – saw strong resistance from the Japanese. The third phase was the capture of Pulau Biak – primarily to control the airfield (now the domestic airport) – and nearby Pulau Numfor, on the way to Sorong. Several hard battles were fought on Biak, not assisted by a severe underestimation by Allied intelligence of the Japanese strength. The fourth and final phase was the successful push to the Japanese air bases on Pulau Morotai, off northern Halmahera, and then towards the Philippines.

Along the south coast, the Allies fought for control of Merauke because of fears that it would be used as a base for Japanese air attacks against Australia. (Fak Fak, which was also the site of battles with the Japanese, has probably the best range of untouched WWII relics in Irian Jaya.)

Papuan Opposition

Even before the 'Act of Free Choice', the Indonesians faced violent opposition from the Papuans. In 1969 rebellions broke out on Pulau Biak and at Enarotali in the highlands. Between 1977 and the mid-1980s there was occasional conflict in the highlands around the Baliem Valley, Tembagapura (site of the US-run Freeport copper mine in central Irian Jaya) and in remote areas of the Paniai district.

After a lull of a few years, anti-Indonesian activity recommenced in the mid-1990s. In 1995 members and sympathisers of the major independence group, the Free Papua Movement or Organisasi Papua Merdeka (OPM), stormed the Indonesian consulate in Vanimo, just over the border in Papua New Guinea (PNG), and rioted in Tembagapura and Timika. In 1996 about 5000 Irianese rioted for several days and burned Pasar Abepura (Abepura Market) in Jayapura, resulting in several deaths. In the same year, several European and Indonesian researchers were kidnapped in a remote part of the Baliem Valley. The Europeans were released unharmed four months later, but two Indonesian hostages were killed by the OPM.

In 1998 separatist activities such as raising independence flags and holding public rallies took place in Jayapura, Biak and Wamena. The participants were harshly and often violently dealt with by the Indonesian authorities, but a few months later the post-Soeharto government indicated a willingness to listen to separatists, and has reduced the military presence in the province.

The Irianese anti-Indonesian feeling is provoked by the use of their land for logging, mining and other commercial purposes without compensation or consultation; resentment about the unequal distribution of wealth from these enterprises; transmigration, which brings large numbers of western Indonesians to Irian Jaya; attempts to 'Indonesianise' traditional people; and occasional brutal responses to political dissent.

Transmigration

The Indonesian policy of transmigration is one of the reasons for continuing unrest in Irian Jaya. Possibly up to one-third of Irian Jaya's population originates from outside the province, mainly from Java, Bali and Sulawesi. Most of the transmigrants live in settlements near the main towns of Jayapura, Merauke, Manokwari, Nabire and Sorong.

As Irian Jaya represents about 22% of Indonesia's total territory, but only about 1% of its population, the Indonesian government continues to plan to move hundreds of thousands of people to Irian Jaya from other, overcrowded, islands. Poor locations and lack of planning for many existing settlements indicate that the main thrust of transmigration is less for the benefit of the transmigrants than to make the province truly 'Indonesian'.

GEOGRAPHY

The 640km-long Penungunan Maoke (Maoke Mountains) is the backbone of Irian Jaya. Incredibly, the province's highest peak, Puncak Jaya (Jaya Peak, 5050m) and other mountains such as Puncak Mandala (4700m) have permanent snowfields and small glaciers. Alpine grasslands, jagged bare peaks, montane forests, rainforests, ferocious rivers, gentle streams, stunning rock-faces and gorges all add to the varying landscape of the highlands. The most cultivated areas of the highlands are around Danau Paniai (Paniai Lake) and Baliem Valley to the east.

Swamps with sago palms and low-lying alluvial plains of fertile soil dominate the south-eastern section around Merauke, while around the Asmat region swamps stretch 300km inland.

The northern coastal plain is much narrower, with larger-than-life tropical vegetation – jungle in other words. White sandy beaches fringed with coconut palms along the north coast and on the islands of Biak, Numfor and Yapen means that this small region matches travellers' expectations of 'tropical' Indonesia.

CLIMATE

Generally the driest and best time to visit Irian Jaya is between May and October, although it can and does rain anywhere, anytime. (Rain falls in Kota Biak up to 25 days a month.) Strong wind and rain is more common along the north coast from November to March. Along the south coast, however, it can be wet and windy from April to October; but this is the dry season in Merauke, the only part of Irian Jaya with distinct seasons. The best time to visit the Baliem Valley is between March and August when the days are drier and cooler – nights are usually cold year-round. Coastal towns are generally always hot and humid, while it's often cooler in the highlands.

FLORA & FAUNA

About 75% of Irian Jaya is forest, so it's no surprise that its flora is as varied as its geography. The usual lush collection of Asiatic species (some endemic to New Guinea island) lie in this transition zone between Asia and Australia. The south coast's vegetation includes mangroves and sago palms (especially around the Asmat region), as well as eucalypts, paperbarks and acacias in the drier south-eastern section. Highland vegetation ranges from alpine grasslands and heath to unique pine forests, bush and scrub. Orchid species are also prevalent.

Animals are largely confined to marsupials, such as bandicoots, ring-tailed possums, pygmy flying phalangers, large cuscuses, tree kangaroos and, in the south-east, wallabies. Reptiles include snakes (many of which are poisonous), frill-necked and monitor lizards, and crocodiles. The spiny anteater is also found. Insect life is abundant with Irian Jaya host to about 800 species of spiders. Penungunan Arfak is known for its colourful butterflies.

Despite large-scale plunder, Irian Jaya's exquisite birdlife is still famous and an increasingly popular attraction for serious bird lovers. There are more than 600 species, including the elusive bird of paradise *(cenderawasih)*, found on the appropriately named Bird's Head Peninsula and Pulau Yapen; cassowaries around the southern coastal region; and bowerbirds, cockatoos, parrots, kingfishers and crowned pigeons all over Irian Jaya.

Some 20% of Irian Jaya is designated as conservation area. With some effort you can visit several national parks: Supiori Island

Reserve (Taman Pulau Supiori) on Pulau Biak; Wasur National Park (Taman Nasional Wasur) near Merauke; and Cenderawasih Bay Marine Park (Taman Laut Teluk Cenderawasih). Lorentz Reserve between Timika and the Asmat region, remains virtually inaccessible and is currently off limits to tourists.

POPULATION & PEOPLE

Approximately two million people live in Irian Jaya. The interior is predominantly populated by pure-blood Papuans, while along the coast there has been intermarriage with Melanesians and Malays. The most populated and interesting traditional areas have varying degrees of accessibility: the Baliem Valley is the easiest place to visit, while most of the Paniai district is currently off limits and the Asmat region is difficult to reach.

The Dani of Baliem Valley are a gentle people who live in compounds of huts made from trees and mud, where they raise their precious pigs. They often still use stone implements to farm their dietary/agricultural staple, the sweet potato.

A little less accessible are the Manikom and Hatam people near the lakes at Anggi, and the Kanum and Marind near Merauke. With considerably more time and effort you can visit the Asmat people, who are renowned for their carvings. Further inland from the Asmat region, the Kombai and Korowai people live in truly extraordinary treehouses, sometimes up to dozens of metres high, to avoid tides, wild animals and tribal invasion. Incredibly, the Indonesian media reported in mid-1998 that two 'new tribes' which use sign language to communicate had been 'found' in very remote parts of the interior.

Christianity is the major religion. Churches of all denominations are dotted around the interior, but (despite what missionaries may say) indigenous people enjoy a combination of traditional beliefs and Christianity. Centuries-old trade with Malays (and transmigration from western Indonesia) ensures that Islam is strong in many coastal towns.

Estimates of the number of languages in Irian Jaya vary from 200 to over 700 – there has been very little study of the linguistics of the region. There is no doubt, however, that Irian Jaya and neighbouring PNG, with a combined population of only a few million, speak an inordinately high percentage of the world's languages.

VISAS & DOCUMENTS

Currently, the only way to travel between PNG and Irian Jaya is on a boat between Vanimo and Jayapura. It is very important to note that Jayapura is not a visa-free port, so you must obtain an Indonesian tourist visa (valid for four weeks, but often extendable) before you leave Vanimo. Indonesian visas are easy to obtain in Vanimo or Port Moresby. Most visitors need a PNG visa (available in Jayapura).

Surat Jalan

For political and bureaucratic reasons, foreigners must obtain a travel permit known as a *surat jalan* before they can visit many places in Irian Jaya, particularly the interior.

Currently, you can visit Jayapura, nearby Sentani, and Sorong without a surat jalan. Depending on the whim of the local police, you may need one for Pulau Biak, Nabire and Manokwari, but you can get one easily after you arrive at these places. For other areas, such as Merauke and the vicinity, Agats and the Asmat region, Pulau Yapen, Timika, Fak Fak, and Wamena and the Baliem Valley, you must have a surat jalan before you go. Foreigners are currently not permitted to go anywhere near the PNG border, Gunung Trikora (Mt Trikora), the Paniai district, Sungai Mamberamo (Mamberamo River) or Ilaga. To go anywhere else, it's safe to assume that you will need a surat jalan.

A surat jalan lasts from one week to one month depending on the amount of time you request, the expiry date of your visa and the mood of the policeman but one surat jalan will normally cover all travel around Irian Jaya. If you have a normal 60 day tourist card (the sort provided on arrival in Indonesia), you can apply for a surat jalan at a local police station *(polres)*; if you have a Business Visa or any other type of visa, you'll have to visit a branch of the provincial police force *(polda)*, possibly in Jayapura. Surat jalan are normally available at any district capital, and are particularly easy to get in Kota Biak and Jayapura, where staff are used to foreigners. Some police stations may be reluctant to issue a surat jalan allowing you to visit a more remote area of another district, so you may have to apply for a separate permit at the particular district capital.

When you apply for a surat jalan, give the policeman two passport-size photos (black & white is OK) and ask him to list on the permit every destination you may possibly travel to. It will take about one hour to process and there is often an 'administration fee' of about 5000Rp. The permit stipulates (in English) that the 'certificate must be returned to [wherever you obtained it] when the purpose has been accomplished' – but thankfully this isn't necessary. The whole process may sound overwhelming, but don't be concerned: the police are invariably helpful and friendly, and as bored with the paperwork as you are. To save time and hassle, a travel agent or hotel in Irian Jaya may be able to arrange the permit for a negotiable fee; if you're on an organised tour, the permit should be arranged by your travel agency.

In places where a surat jalan is needed, your hotel, guide or travel agency (if you're on a tour) may request your permit and send it to the local police for registration and stamping. If not, you'll have to report to the police station yourself, preferably as soon as you arrive; certainly within 24 hours. In remote areas, including the Baliem Valley (but not Wamena), you'll need to report and show your permit to police or village authorities wherever you stay overnight. Always have a few photocopies of your permit handy to give to police or to your hotel, guide or travel agency.

BOOKS

Peter Matthiessen's *Under the Mountain Wall* chronicles his daily life among the Kurulu tribe of the Baliem Valley in 1961.

Robert Mitton's *The Lost World of Irian Jaya* was compiled from his letters, diaries, maps and photographs after his death in 1976. It bitterly criticises the reckless way that Irians have been forced into the modern world.

Norman Lewis visited Irian Jaya in the 1980s to research his book *An Empire of the East*, in which he provides insights into the Baliem Valley and the Freeport copper mine. George Monbiot's *Poisoned Arrows* details a remarkable journey to the wilds of Irian Jaya with the objective of uncovering the truth about transmigration and the nature of anti-Indonesian resistance.

The Asmat is a collection of photographs of the Asmat people and their art, taken by Michael Rockefeller in 1961. *Irian Jaya: The Timeless Domain* written in the late 1980s by Julie Campbell is an informative narrative with photos, and mainly focuses on the Baliem Valley and Asmat region. It is available in Irian Jaya but is expensive.

Islands in the Clouds by Isabella Tree is part of Lonely Planet's travel literature series, Journeys. The book deals mainly with visits to remote regions of the PNG highlands; however, the author offers some entertaining insights into Jayapura and the Baliem Valley.

SPECIAL EVENTS

Festivals and ceremonies are an integral part of Irianese traditional culture but very few are officially programmed or advertised. If you ask around when you arrive in a town or village, you may be lucky enough to witness something truly special.

January
Irian Jaya Tourism Week
Traditional ceremonies and cultures from all over Irian Jaya are on display each year at different district capitals; held in mid-January.

August
Baliem Festival
This spectacular festival features mock tribal fighting, traditional dancing and plenty of feasting; it's held in Yetni, generally between 9-14 August. Check with the tourist office in Wamena for more details. See the boxed text 'Baliem Festival' later in this chapter.

Independence Day
In Assologaima in the north-west, Indonesian Independence Day (17 August) is marked with traditional dancing, cooking, and pig feasts.
Munara Festival
This Biak festival features fire walking, traditional dancing and boat races; held in mid-August.

October
Asmat Art & Culture Festival
Held in Agats and Merauke, the festival features woodcarving and traditional dancing.

November
Festival in Fak Fak
Involving traditional dancing, *kora-kora* (canoe) races and sporting events, this festival is held on 15-17 November annually.

ACTIVITIES

Not surprisingly, most activities centre on the coast, the mountains and the traditional people.

Diving

Biak and Yapen islands, and Cenderawasih Bay Marine Reserve boast some astonishing coral and marine life and there are an unknown number of WWII ship and plane wrecks waiting to be explored – or even discovered – close to Sorong and Manokwari. These areas have the potential to rival northern Sulawesi, but Biak, Sorong and Jayapura have the only dive centres. The best time for diving along the north coast is between April and September.

Trekking

Trekking is the best way to see the interior, but if the harsh terrain and very limited transport doesn't deter you, then draconian government regulations may.

Currently the Baliem Valley is the only place in the interior where long-distance trekking is allowed, but this region does offer more than enough to satisfy. With a lot of planning, time and money, you can organise serious expeditions as far as the south Asmat coast (with the aid of river transport).

Some limited trekking is also permitted around Pegunungan Arfak and Anggi, near

Manokwari; Pegunungan Cyclop and Danau Sentani; and Wasur National Park and the flood plains near Merauke. It may also be possible to (if you obtain a special permit) trek around the Wondiwoi Mountains Reserve (Taman Pegunungan Wondiwoi) near Wasior, and Tanjung Bomberai near Fak Fak, but enticing areas such as Paniai and Habbema lakes and Gunung Trikora are off limits.

See the Hiking and Trekking entry under Around the Baliem Valley for information on what to bring.

GETTING THERE & AWAY

Most visitors to Irian Jaya head straight to Jayapura through Biak and/or Ujung Pandang (Sulawesi) for a connection to Wamena in the Baliem Valley, but there are several other interesting ways to enter Irian Jaya:

- Fly to Port Moresby (capital of PNG), then travel by air to Vanimo and catch a boat to Jayapura.
- Take a Pelni liner via Fak Fak or Agats to Timika or Merauke, and fly to Jayapura.
- Take a boat or plane from Sorong, or a boat from the Banda Islands to Fak Fak, then fly to Nabire and on to Biak and Jayapura.
- Take a boat and/or plane along the north coast to Jayapura, stopping at Manokwari, Biak, Nabire and/or Serui.

Air

Unless you have a lot of time, flying is the best way to get to Irian Jaya. Merpati Nusantara Airlines and Garuda Indonesia regularly connect the main regional centres (Sorong, Biak and Jayapura) with internal flights to major western Indonesian centres, such as Ambon, Ujung Pandang, Denpasar and Jakarta. See the Irian Jaya Airfares Chart in this chapter.

PNG Air Nuigini no longer flies between Vanimo and Jayapura. The only route between Irian Jaya and PNG is now by boat. The PT Kuwera Jaya travel agency (see Organised Tours under Jayapura later in this chapter) is the agency in Irian Jaya for Air Nuigini flights within PNG.

Sea

Indonesia Pelni regularly links the north coast of Irian Jaya (as far as Jayapura) with Indonesia, but less often with the south coast. Every Pelni liner listed below has a two week schedule except the *Tatamailau*, which runs every four weeks.

Ciremai – links the north coast with southern and northern Sulawesi, Ternate (northern Maluku) and Java.
Dobonsolo – links the north coast with Ambon, Nusa Tenggara, Bali and Java.
Rinjani – links the north coast and Fak Fak with southern Sulawesi and south-east Maluku.
Umsini – links the north coast with Ternate, northern and southern Sulawesi and Kalimantan.
Tatamailau – has a complicated schedule which links the south coast with south-east Maluku, Ambon, southern Sulawesi, Bali and Nusa Tenggara.

Perintis also has a few boats which regularly link the north coast of Irian Jaya with northern Maluku and Sulawesi, and the south coast with south-east Maluku. Any other type of boat will be slow and uncomfortable; it's best to wait for a decent boat, or fly.

PNG The only way to travel between PNG and Irian Jaya is by boat. The MV *Naremo Express* travels between Vanimo in PNG and the Pelni port in Jayapura, and back again each Monday and/or Wednesday (depending on demand). From PNG the trip takes about two hours and costs 60 kina plus 30 kina departure tax; from Jayapura it costs about 125,000Rp plus 20,000Rp departure tax. In Jayapura, schedules and bookings are available from the boat office (☎ 0967-31449) or the PNG Consulate in Vanimo.

The only alternative is to charter a boat (seating six) for about 500,000Rp one way from Jayapura. Ask around the port, or at PT Kuwera Jaya travel agency in Jayapura (see Organised Tours under Jayapura); the travel agency will also help you wade through immigration procedures. Before you charter a boat, however, check with the PNG Consulate about immigration regulations.

The Visa & Documents section earlier in this chapter has information on obtaining an

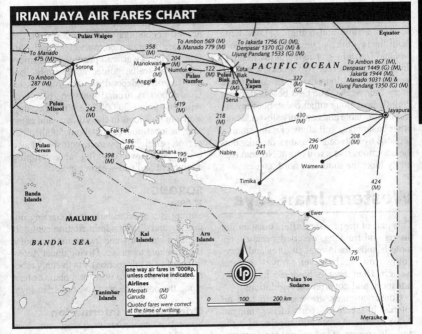

IRIAN JAYA AIR FARES CHART

Equator

Pulau Waigeo

To Manado 475 (M)

358 (M)

To Ambon 569 (M) & Manado 779 (M)

To Jakarta 1756 (G) (M), Denpasar 1370 (G) (M) & Ujung Pandang 1533 (G) (M)

Sorong

Manokwari 204 (M)

34 (M)

Numfor

122 (M)

Kota Biak

PACIFIC OCEAN

To Ambon 867 (M), Denpasar 1449 (G) (M), Jakarta 1944 (M), Manado 1031 (M) & Ujung Pandang 1350 (G) (M)

To Ambon 287 (M)

Anggi

Pulau Numfor

Pulau Biak 80 (M)

Pulau Yapen

327 (M) (G)

Pulau Misool

242 (M)

419 (M)

Serui

Jayapura

Pulau Seram

Fak Fak

186 (M)

218 (M)

430 (M)

296 (M)

208 (M)

398 (M)

Kaimana

195 (M)

Nabire

241 (M)

Wamena

Banda Islands

Timika

424 (M)

MALUKU

Ewer

Kai Islands

Aru Islands

BANDA SEA

one way air fares in '000Rp, unless otherwise indicated.
Airlines
Merpati (M)
Garuda (G)
Quoted fares were correct at the time of writing.

75 (M)

0   100   200 km

Tanimbar Islands

Pulau Yos Sudarso

Merauke

Indonesian visa in PNG; and the Jayapura section later has information on obtaining PNG visas in Irian Jaya.

GETTING AROUND

Very few roads have successfully crossed the seemingly impenetrable terrain of Irian Jaya. Roads between Jayapura and Wamena, and Sorong and Manokwari, are due to be completed in a few years, but construction problems continue to occur. Boats are slow and infrequent, and often uncomfortable, so flying is the popular option.

Air

The centres for internal flights are Sorong for the north-west; Biak for the Teluk Cenderawasih (Cenderawasih Bay) region; Jayapura for the Baliem Valley; and Merauke for the south-east coast. In the current economic crisis, the main carrier, Merpati,

has severely reduced the number of Irian Jaya flights; flights may also be cancelled due to lack of passengers. Always allow plenty of time to travel around and be prepared for delays and cancellations. Most Merpati planes are small and have a 10kg baggage limit per person (usually ignored if you're over by a few kilograms).

Between Jayapura and Wamena, you can fly on a cargo plane operated by Trigana; it charges more than Merpati, but is usually more reliable. The Protestant-run Mission Aviation Fellowship (MAF) and the Catholic-run Associated Mission Aviation (AMA) organisations fly to/from many remote places and they sometimes accept tourists. However, their primary concern is missionary business so you'll need to book at least one week in advance; their prices are high. You can also often charter their planes at exorbitant rates.

Boat

Travelling around Irian Jaya by boat will take some time and planning. Four large Pelni liners – the *Dobonsolo*, *Ciremai*, *Rinjani* and *Umsini* – stop in major towns along the north coast every two weeks; the *Tatamailau* crawls along the south coast twice every four weeks. The next best option is a Perintis boat along either coast, but they are less comfortable and certainly slower. Many other basic boats sail along certain, smaller sections of both coasts, and as far inland as the enormous rivers will allow. No boat regularly links the south and north coasts.

Western Irian Jaya

This part of the province offers outstanding diving and trekking, deserted beaches, remote islands, traditional cultures and easygoing towns; however, travel around western Irian Jaya is hindered by limited transport, and government regulations.

Conservationists are starting to take an interest in the area – parts of Pegunungan Arfak (home to over 300 species of birds and 320 species of butterflies) are now protected under the Arfak Mountains Wildlife Preservation (CAPA) program. CAPA is assisted by the World Wide Fund For Nature (WWF), whose office is on the main road about 3km before the airport in Manokwari.

Diving

The coast near Manokwari has numerous WWII ship and plane wrecks, while the Raja Empat Islands near Sorong boast some of the best coral and marine life in Indonesia. Both areas are fairly sheltered, and diving is possible year-round.

The only dive operator based in western Irian Jaya is Irian Diving (☎ 0951-25274, fax 27371), Jl Gunung Gamalama 3, Sorong. It offers a range of professional diving, trekking and bird-watching trips, but concentrates on pre-booked organised tours rather than day trips. It charges a little more than US$100 per person per day, including accommodation, food and all diving costs.

Trekking

There are unlimited trekking possibilities around Pegunungan Arfak and Wasior, but there are no organised tours. The tourist office in Manokwari can provide good information on trails, guides and permits, but this can often depend on who you talk to. Guides/porters around western Irian Jaya will cost about 30,000/15,000Rp per day. You can buy food in the villages and often stay in local houses for about 5000Rp per person per night; however, you should also bring your own cooking and camping equipment and wet-weather gear.

SORONG
☎ 0951

Sorong is a spectacularly uninteresting oil, logging and district administration centre. It is also a base for some increasingly popular birdwatching tours (see Diving under Activities earlier in this section), but the only other reason to come is to wait for a plane or boat along the north or south coast of Irian Jaya.

Orientation & Information

Sorong is enormously spread out. You should base yourself around the small boat harbour near Hotel Indah, where there are cheap hotels, restaurants and shops. To reach banks, government offices, the main port, the *angkot* (bemo) terminal and Merpati office, take a public or chartered angkot.

Bank Bumi Daya (BBD) on Jl Ahmad Yani will change money. The police station (☎ 23210) is on Jl Basuki Rahmat. A surat jalan isn't needed for Sorong, but is required for travel to the interior or to any island off the coast. The Merpati office (☎ 21402) is in the Hotel Grand Pacific, Jl Raja Ampat 105.

Things to See & Do

Pantai Casuari is a good beach nearby for swimming and snorkelling (bring your own gear) and is accessible by public angkot from the terminal. The best outing from Sorong is to **Pulau Jefman** by speedboat or ferry – the island has some walking trails and nice beaches. **Pulau Doom** can be reached by public or chartered boat from the small boat harbour. An engaging walk around the island takes about 40 minutes (but be prepared – there are more 'hello misters' here per second than anywhere else in Indonesia!).

You can also rent a boat for 150,000Rp per day to visit nearby islands such as **Pulau Batanta** for its birdlife; **Pulau Matan** for swimming, snorkelling among shipwrecks and hiking; and **Pulau Kafiau** for diving.

Places to Stay & Eat
The best of the budget places is the central *Losmen Mulia Indah (☎ 22772, Jl Sam Ratulangi 68)*, which costs from 22,500Rp for a tiny room. Several reasonable hotels offer singles/doubles with fan and bathroom priced from about 24,500/32,500Rp, such as *Irian Beach Hotel (☎ 23782, Jl Yos Sudarso)*; *Hotel Batanta (☎ 21569, Jl Barito)*, opposite the football ground; and *Hotel Indah (☎ 21514, Jl Yos Sudarso 4)*, conveniently positioned opposite the small boat harbour.

Every evening *warungs* (food stalls) set up along the waterfront. For spectacular sunsets and delectable baked fish, try the restaurant in the *Irian Beach Hotel* or *Rumah Makan Ruta Sayang* next door.

Getting There & Away
Air Sorong is a regular stopover on Merpati flights between Jayapura and the rest of Indonesia. There are flights most days to Jayapura (657,000Rp), Ambon (287,400Rp) and Biak (357,800Rp); a few days a week to Fak Fak, Kaimana and Timika; and less often to Manado (see the Irian Jaya Airfares Chart in this chapter). There is currently no direct flight to Manokwari.

Boat Sorong is the hub for boat travel along the south and north coasts. Every two weeks the *Rinjani* goes to Manokwari on the way to Jayapura and to Fak Fak and Ambon; the *Ciremai* to Jayapura and Ternate (northern Maluku); and the *Dobonsolo* to Ambon and Jayapura. Other (non-Pelni) boats head in all directions. The Pelni office (☎ 21716) and dock, both on Jl Ahmad Yani several kilometres from Hotel Indah, also handle bookings for Perintis boats.

Getting Around
Jefman airport is spectacularly, but inconveniently located on Pulau Jefman. From the airport, take a speedboat or longboat to the small boat harbour. To reach the airport check with the Merpati office about the infrequent ferry. Small planes to/from Fak Fak and other regional centres leave from Minland airport about 5km from Sorong.

Yellow angkots travel frequently along the main roads, and can be chartered for a negotiable 15,000Rp per hour.

FAK FAK
☎ 0956
The first successful Dutch settlement in Irian Jaya, Fak Fak – yes, it *is* pronounced *that* way – is a quaint, colonial town, nestled among the foothills and overlooking several sparkling bays. Except for the mosque, the main street along the waterfront is reminiscent of a small seaside European village. Fak Fak is close and accessible to Pulau Ambon and the Banda Islands by sea, and to Sorong by air, so it's an easy and pleasant place to start or finish a visit to Irian Jaya.

Orientation & Information
Many facilities are on or close to the main street, Jl Izaak Telussa, which hugs the coast. On Jl Izaak Telussa, Bank Exim changes money on weekday mornings only. The street leads to the tidy Pasar Tamburani, which is worth a wander around, and to the *mikrolet* (bemo) terminal.

Some other official businesses are on the streets rising sharply behind Jl Izaak Telussa. The tourist office (☎ 22828) on Jl Nuri is open weekdays from 7.30 am to 3 pm and is worth a visit. It can arrange speedboats for charter, and has accommodation at Kokas (see Around Fak Fak later in this section) and on Pulau Tulir Seram. The post office is on Jl Letjen Haryono, and the 24 hour Telkom office and the hospital are on Jl Cenderawasih.

You should report to the police (☎ 22200) on Jl Tamburani, opposite Hotel Sulinah, after you arrive. You need a surat jalan for Fak Fak; preferably get one before you arrive (try Sorong).

Pulau Tulir Seram

The best excursion is to tiny, uninhabited Pulau Tulir Seram in the harbour. The island offers short **walking trails**, a huge monument with a **museum** underneath (ask for the key from the tourist office in Fak Fak before you go), and some superb views. A two-room *guesthouse* offers absolute seclusion (also organise this with the tourist office and bring your own food). To get there, ask around Danaweria village just east of Fak Fak about chartered longboat hire (about 25,000Rp return).

Places to Stay & Eat

The best places are all along, or just off, Jl Izaak Telussa. The central *Hotel Tembagapura* (☎ 22447) at No 16 is quiet and often full. Rooms with bathroom cost from 21,500/33,000Rp; more for air-con. The friendly *Hotel Marco Polo* (☎ 22537) is on an unnamed lane opposite the mosque. Dorm-style beds cost 20,000Rp per person; about 50,000Rp for individual rooms. *Hotel Sulinah* (☎ 22447) on Jl Tambaruni at the western end of the main street, has very clean rooms for 43,500Rp including meals.

Strung along Jl Kartini, just above Jl Izaak Telussa, several *warungs* serve mouthwatering baked fish meals from 3500Rp. *Rumah Makan Sahabat* on the main street is recommended for drinks and cakes, and *Hotel Tembagapura* has a good public restaurant. *Amanda Restaurant*, at the bend on Jl Izaak Telussa, has good service plus, of course, a karaoke machine. The seafood is particularly tasty and costs about 12,500Rp a dish.

Getting There & Away

Fak Fak is linked four days a week to Sorong (242,000Rp) and Kaimana (186,000Rp) as part of the Merpati route between Sorong and Nabire. The Merpati office (☎ 71275), Jl Isak Telussa 9, is open irregularly.

Every two weeks, the Pelni liner *Rinjani* sails to Sorong and to the Bandas; twice every four weeks, the *Tatamailau* goes to Ambon and the south coast of Irian Jaya. Perintis boats stop at Fak Fak every two or three weeks during their crawl along the south coast and around south-east Maluku. The port is centrally located at the eastern end of Jl Izaak Telussa, but the Pelni office (☎ 22335) is on the steep rise on Jl SMA Negeri.

Getting Around

Torea airport was somehow carved out of the hillside and the runway is frighteningly short. From the airport take a shared taxi into town; to reach the airport, you can usually get a public mikrolet from Terminal Tamburani. The streets of Fak Fak are extremely steep so unless you like mountain climbing take a mikrolet.

AROUND FAK FAK

Travel to most places near Fak Fak is hindered by limited local transport. Around the village and beach at **Kokas**, on the north coast of the peninsula, there is a plethora of Japanese WWII cannons, tunnels and shipwrecks, and a mosque built in 1870. You'll have to charter a boat from Fak Fak to inspect ancient rock paintings along the coast as far as **Goras**, to visit the **Ugar Islands** for diving, or to see the magnificent **Air Terjun Madedred** (Madedred Waterfalls).

With permission from the tourist office in Fak Fak, you can stay in the *guesthouse* at Kokas – but watch out for the huge coconut crabs! Kokas is a four to six hour (often rough) trip by chartered boat; or you can wait a week or so for a passenger ship; or a year or two for the 42km road from Fak Fak to be completed.

MANOKWARI
☎ 0986

The first place in Irian Jaya to be settled by missionaries, Manokwari ('Old Village' in Biak) is a pleasant base from which to explore Teluk Cenderawasih. It is also easy to get around and has good facilities. Manokwari and Pegunungan Arfak are famous for unique species of butterflies.

Orientation & Information

Most of the town hugs the small Teluk Doreri. The eastern side of the bay is the best and most convenient place to base yourself.

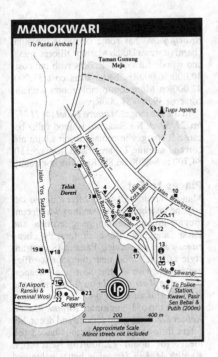

MANOKWARI

PLACES TO STAY
2   Hotel Maluku
3   Hotel Pusaka Sederhana
8   Losmen Apose
10 Hotel Arfak & Restaurant
19 Hotel Mulia; Post Office
20 Mutiara Hotel & Restaurant

PLACES TO EAT
1   Rumah Makan Kebun Sirih;
    Rumah Makan Hawai
4   Warung Solo
6   Rumah Makan Hosana
18 Rumah Makan Blitar; Wartel

OTHER
5   Merpati Office
7   Wartel
9   Bioskop Intim (Cinema)
11 Goa Jepang
12 Bank Exim
13 Tourist Office
14 Main Post Office
15 Pelni Office
16 Pelni Port
17 Cargo Port; Temporary Pelni Office
21 Terminal Sanggeng
22 Bank Exim
23 Small Boat Harbour

The tourist office (☎ 21230) on Jl Merdeka is reasonably useful and worth visiting if you plan to trek in Pegunungan Arfak. It's open Monday to Friday from 8 am to 2 pm and until 1 pm on Saturday. A surat jalan is not needed for Manokwari, but is necessary for anywhere else in the immediate vicinity. You can get one at the police station (☎ 21359) on Jl Bayangkhara, about 200m past the port, or in Biak. Better still, arrange one through the tourist office in Manokwari.

The Bank Exim branches will change money on weekday mornings. The main post office is near the port; a smaller one is next to the Hotel Mulia.

Tugu Jepang & Taman Gunung Meja

A reasonably flat 3km walk takes you through Taman Gunung Meja (Table Mountain Park), a protected forest with plenty of birds and butterflies. Take a *taksi* (bemo) to Amban (a pleasant university town) from Terminal Sanggeng, and get off at the sign to Tugu Jepang. The Japanese memorial is 1km before the end of the well-marked trail; it's not terribly interesting, but offers great views. The trail ends not far from Hotel Arfak.

Goa Jepang

This is more a series of tunnels (built by the Japanese in WWII) than a cave. The entrance, which you can look at but not really explore, is on the lane leading to Hotel Arfak. The tunnel is a disappointment. However, if you're going to Pulau Biak, make sure you see the Japanese cave (Gua Binsari) near Bosnik (see Around Pulau Biak later in this chapter).

Pulau Mansinam & Pulau Lemon

Try to visit these two islands, set majestically in the bay under Penungunan Arfak.

Two German missionaries settled on Mansinam in 1855, and became the first in Irian Jaya to spread the 'Word'. Mansinam is a picturesque little island, with a small village, the ruins of an **old church**, a **memorial** to the missionaries and a pleasant **beach**. It's best to report to the village head *(kepala desa)* before wandering around.

Nearby Pulau Lemon has some **beaches**, huts, and **WWII wrecks** ideal for **snorkelling** around (bring your own gear), but isn't as enticing or accessible as Mansinam. A passenger boat from the jetty at Kwawi (a five minute walk past the port) goes to Mansinam three or four times a day. It's more fun to ask a boy in Kwawi to take you in his canoe (around 10,000Rp return to Mansinam or 12,000Rp return to both islands).

Beaches
Pasir Sen Bebai and adjacent **Pasir Putih** are pleasant beaches but a little untidy. Take a taksi from Terminal Wosi, about 4km from Manokwari. The other nearby beach, **Pantai Amban**, is 5km from Amban village. It's perfect for surfing, though the water reportedly has sea lice, and public transport is limited.

Places to Stay
One of the best value places is the central *Hotel Pusaka Sederhana (☎ 21263, Jl Bandung 154)*. The cheapest singles/doubles cost 12,000/17,500Rp; 25,000/30,000Rp with fan; and 35,000/45,000Rp with air-con. Opposite Merpati, the friendly *Losmen Apose (☎ 21369, Jl Kota Baru)* is also a good option. Rooms for 20,000/25,000Rp with fan and outside bathroom are cheerless, but the rooms with air-con for 30,000/55,000Rp are better. The *Hotel Maluku (☎ 21948, Jl Sudirman 52)* has quiet rooms (but some are dark) for 20,000/25,000Rp with share bathroom; 35,000/50,000Rp with private bathroom, air-con and TV.

Clean, friendly and quiet (except for noise from the nearby mosque), but not particularly great value, *Hotel Mulia (☎ 21320, Jl Yos Sudarso)* has rooms with fan for 30,000/42,500Rp; 45,000/60,000Rp with air-con; and triples with fan/with air-con for 55,000/75,600Rp. *Hotel Arfak (☎ 21293, Jl Brawijaya 8)* has some decaying, colonial charm (it was a Dutch Marine Officers' mess) and wonderful views. Rooms with fan costs 30,000/36,000Rp; better ones cost 33,000/42,000Rp. More comfortable rooms with air-con cost 39,000/51,000Rp.

In the top range, *Mutiara Hotel (☎ 21777, fax 21152, Jl Yos Sudarso)* is good value because it charges in rupiah. Rooms with air-con and satellite TV are priced from 66,550/84,700 to 84,700/96,800Rp (with hot water).

Places to Eat
Manokwari doesn't really offer much to satisfy the tastebuds. The *warungs* which congregate around the Sanggeng terminal and Pasar Sanggeng offer basic fare; the cheap *rumah makan* serving Padang (Sumatranstyle cuisine) food near the tourist office are better. Two of the best and cheapest places are *Warung Solo* on Jl Sudirman and *Rumah Makan Blitar* on Jl Yos Sudarso.

At the top of Jl Sudirman, *Rumah Makan Kebun Sirih* has good service and decor, but offers little more than delicious baked fish meals for about 12,500Rp. Next door, *Rumah Makan Hawai* is better value and has a good variety of meals from 5000Rp to 10,000Rp. One of the more popular places is *Rumah Makan Hosana* on Jl Kota Baru, where good Indonesian food costs about 7500Rp and seafood about twice that.

The restaurant at the *Mutiara Hotel* has the best service in Manokwari and there is often live music in the evenings. Main meals cost about 10,000Rp; it serves good, western-style breakfasts. The charmless restaurant at the back of *Hotel Arfak* is open to the public and serves decent food at good prices.

Getting There & Away
Air Merpati flies once or twice a week to Nabire (419,400Rp) and Anggi (34,400Rp); and several times a week to Jayapura (430,400Rp) via Biak (203,800Rp). There are no flights to/from Sorong. The Merpati agency (☎ 21133) on Jl Kota Baru is open Monday to Saturday from 7.30 am to 1 pm; Sunday from 6 to 8 pm.

Boat Manokwari is a stop on the fort-nightly run along the north coast to Sorong (37,000/119,500Rp for economy/1st class), Biak (26,500/83,500Rp) and Jayapura (68,500/228,500Rp) on the Pelni liners *Ciremai*, *Dobonsolo*, *Rinjani* and *Umsini*. The Pelni office handles tickets for all major boats. It is temporarily located in the cargo port area, but will move back into its renovated office soon.

Getting Around

Rendani airport is about a ten minute drive from most hotels. Drivers of chartered tak-sis may initially ask 20,000Rp, but will quickly go down to 10,000Rp. Alterna-tively, walk straight outside the terminal and catch a public taksi to Terminal Wosi, another to Terminal Sanggeng and, if neces-sary, another to your hotel.

From Terminal Wosi, about 4km west of Manokwari, public taksis regularly leave for the airport, beaches and nearby villages. Terminal Sanggeng in Manokwari is mainly a transit point for taksis into town and has frequent services linking both sides of Teluk Doreri.

ANGGI LAKES

In Penungunan Arfak, at an elevation of 2030m, **Danau Giji** and **Danau Gita** are very clear and more than 100m deep, and they offer exquisite scenery and wildlife, as well as excellent **hiking** and **swimming**. The Manikom and Hatam people of this region lead a traditional lifestyle.

The two- or three-day trek to the lakes from Ransiki follows Sungai Momi to Siwi, and then involves some climbing, and hiking along muddy trails to the lakes. It is essential that you have a guide; ask the district office in Ransiki (see the Ransiki entry later in this section). You can sleep in local *huts* along the way for about 7000Rp per person, or the district office in Anggi can arrange accom-modation for about 12,000Rp per person. You should take your own food, although you can buy vegetables along the way.

Merpati flies between Manokwari and Anggi twice a week (currently Tuesday and

Sunday) for 34,400Rp. The MAF service can be more reliable than Merpati, but you'll need to give MAF at least one week's notice. MAF flies to Irai, about 1km north-east of Anggi, for 105,000Rp, but may charge tourists US dollars in the future. The MAF office (☎ 21155) is in an unsigned hangar at the end of the airport in Manok-wari. Flights to/from Anggi are sometimes cancelled because of fog.

RANSIKI

Crowded taksis leave every hour or so from Terminal Wosi in Manokwari for the pleas-ant transmigration town of Ransiki (8000Rp, two hours). It's a rough trip – and often im-passable in the wet season (November to March) – but the scenery through the jun-gle, along the coast and past villages is su-perb. Even if you're not going to Anggi lakes, the trip to Ransiki is still worthwhile.

The district office in Ransiki allows trav-ellers to stay in its *guesthouse* (15,000Rp per person), which is especially useful if you're going on to Anggi or Pulau Rumberpon.

CENDERAWASIH BAY MARINE RESERVE
☎ 0986

The 14,300 sq km marine reserve is the largest in Indonesia, with 18 islands and over 500km of coastline. It is home to en-dangered species of giant clams, turtles and dugongs, and offers some of the best **div-ing** (130 species of coral), **bird-watching** (150 species) and **trekking** imaginable but, as in most of Irian Jaya, the possibilities are severely limited by lack of transport, and government regulations.

The larger **inhabited islands** in the area are Rumberpon, Mioswaar, Roon and An-grameos. You can explore the coastline from either Nabire or Ransiki for about 150,000Rp per day by speedboat, or base yourself on Pulau Rumberpon or Wasior (although neither are strictly in the park).

Before venturing too far into the reserve, permission and advice should be obtained from the WWF (email wwfnabire@jayapura. wasantara.net.id), Jl Martadinata 15, Nabire.

Pulau Rumberpon

From Rumberpon, you can **snorkel** among superb coral and marine life, and charter boats to islands, such as **Pulau Wairondi** with its untouched **turtle** population, and **Pulau Auri**. Rumberpon also offers some jungle **hiking**.

A room at the unnamed *eco-tourism resort (☎ 22731, PT Wamesa Alam Wisata, Manokwari)* costs from US$30/40, plus meals and transport; snorkelling gear is available for rent. Bookings must be made at least two weeks in advance. If you ask someone important in the village, you can probably *camp* on the beach for a few days (bring your own tent and cooking gear), or stay in a *village hut*.

Public speedboats leave Ransiki for Rumberpon most days (about two hours).

Wasior

From Wasior, you can charter boats to islands in the marine park, or organise a trek in **Wondiwoi Mountains Reserve**, home to over 100 species of birds; (this requires special permission from the district office in Wasior). There is no official accommodation in Wasior, but finding somewhere to stay shouldn't be a problem; however, getting a surat jalan to cover this area may be (try the tourist office in Manokwari). Overnight ferries travel between the Pelni port in Manokwari and Wasior most days.

Central Irian Jaya

PULAU BIAK

The centre for transport, commerce and tourism in central Irian Jaya is Pulau Biak. Horrific WWII battles between the Allies and Japanese took place here, but today the island is an important Indonesian naval base and a hub for sea and air travel along the north coast of Irian Jaya. The island has a great deal to offer and is a worthy stopover, especially if you're a WWII buff or into diving; but other pleasant towns, such as Nabire and Serui, are also good bases for exploring Teluk Cenderawasih and the countryside.

Diving & Snorkelling

Pulau Biak and the Teluk Cenderawasih area have the potential to compete with northern Sulawesi in the diving stakes, with the added bonus of being cheaper and less overrun by tourists. However, the diving industry in Biak is nascent and there is nowhere else in central Irian Jaya to organise diving or snorkelling trips, or to rent equipment.

Janggi Prima Tours & Travel can organise very good value diving trips (minimum of two people), but lack of equipment means it cannot currently cater for large groups. The Biak Diving Centre offers all-inclusive trips with one/two dives for US$60/83 (see Organised Tours under Kota Biak later in this section). Also talk to the effusive staff at the tourist office in Kota Biak.

The best places for diving near Biak are:

Padaido Islands Especially Rurbas and Pakreki islands (see Around Pulau Biak later in this section).
Tanjung Barari The cape at the far east of the island (not accessible by public transport).
Pulau Meosindi On the way to Pulau Yapen.
Pulau Rani Off the west coast of Biak, accessible by boat from Kota Biak.
Pulau Mapia The very best. Far off the northwest coast of Pulau Supiori, and takes some real effort and money to reach.

If you have your own equipment and transport, some spots off Nabire and Numfor and Yapen islands are also excellent. Also, the Cenderawasih Bay Marine Reserve (see under Western Irian Jaya earlier in this chapter) is not that far away.

Snorkelling is far less hassle and still great fun. Notable spots around Biak are near Bosnik; the Padaido Islands, particularly Nusi and Mansurbabo islands; and around Korem. You can rent snorkelling gear in Kota Biak from the Biak Art Shop (☎ 0981-22913), in the pasar on Jl Selat Makassar; from Janggi Prima for about 15,000Rp per day; and from the Biak Diving Centre near Bosnik for considerably more. (See Organised Tours in the following Kota Biak section.)

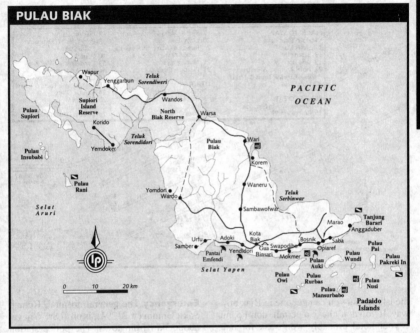

PULAU BIAK

(Map labels:) Wapur; Yenggarbun; *Teluk Sorendiweri*; Wandos; Supiori Island Reserve; Pulau Supiori; Korido; North Biak Reserve; Warsa; *PACIFIC OCEAN*; *Teluk Sorendidori*; Yemdoker; Pulau Insubabi; Pulau Rani; Pulau Biak; Wari; Korem; Waneru; *Teluk Serbinwar*; Yomdori; Wardo; *Selat Aruri*; Sambawofwar; Marao; Tanjung Barari; Anggaduber; Samber; Urfu; Adoki; Kota Biak; Swapodibo; Bosnik; Saba; Pulau Pai; Pantai Emfendi; Yendidori; Gua Binsari; Mokmer; Opiaref; Pulau Wundi; Pulau Pakreki In; *Selat Yapen*; Pulau Auki; Pulau Owi; Pulau Rurbas; Pulau Mansurbabo; Pulau Nusi; Padaido Islands

0   10   20 km

KOTA BIAK
☎ 0981

Kota Biak, the only town of any size on the island, is a relaxed place and the ideal base to explore nearby attractions and the Teluk Cenderawasih region. There is no accommodation elsewhere on the island (except for a luxury hotel near Bosnik), and transport is limited in the north, but most places of interest can be visited on day trips from the city.

Only 1° south of the equator, Biak is always hot and humid, and rain often falls in sudden, short spells; it's a good idea to start your day early and hibernate like the locals between 1 and 4 pm.

Orientation
Kota Biak is a compact town. A lot of what you'll need is along Jl Ahmad Yani (which joins Jl Prof M Yamin from the airport), Jl Sudirman (which goes past the port) and Jl

Imam Bonjol, all of which intersect at the Bank Exim. The majority of places to stay and eat are around this area, but a few offices, the terminal for taksis (bemos) and buses, and the pasar are a short taksi ride away.

Information
Tourist Offices The helpful tourist office (☎ 21663) is on Jl Prof M Yamin, opposite a sports field about halfway along the road to the airport – take the taksi marked 'Ambroben'. The office happily hands out free brochures about other places in Irian Jaya in English, Japanese and German, but sometimes runs out of ones about Biak; staff speak a little English. It's open Monday to Thursday from 7 am to 3 pm, until 11 am on Friday and 1 pm on Saturday.

Documents According to the police in Biak, foreigners need a surat jalan to visit

IRIAN JAYA

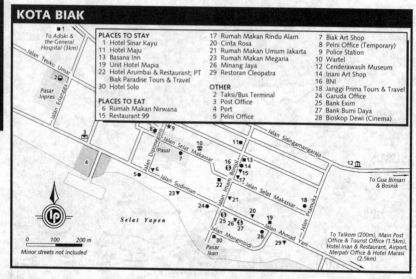

KOTA BIAK

To Adoki & the General Hospital (3km)

Jalan Teuku Umar

Pasar Inpres

Jalan Erlangga

PLACES TO STAY
1 Hotel Sinar Kayu
11 Hotel Maju
13 Basana Inn
19 Unit Hotel Mapia
22 Hotel Arumbai & Restaurant; PT Biak Paradise Tours & Travel
30 Hotel Solo

PLACES TO EAT
6 Rumah Makan Nirwana
15 Restaurant 99

17 Rumah Makan Rindu Alam
20 Cinta Rosa
21 Rumah Makan Umum Jakarta
23 Rumah Makan Megaria
26 Minang Jaya
29 Restoran Cleopatra

OTHER
2 Taksi/Bus Terminal
3 Post Office
4 Port
5 Pelni Office

7 Biak Art Shop
8 Pelni Office (Temporary)
9 Police Station
10 Wartel
12 Cenderawasih Museum
14 Iriani Art Shop
16 BNI
18 Janggi Prima Tours & Travel
24 Garuda Office
25 Bank Exim
27 Bank Bumi Daya
28 Bioskop Dewi (Cinema)

Jalan Sisingamangaraja

Jalan Diponegoro

Jalan Selat Makassar

Pasar

Jalan Sudirman

Jalan Imam Bonjol

Jalan Selat Makassar

Jalan Pramuka

Selat Yapen

Jalan Monginsidi

Jalan Ahmad Yani

Pasar Ikan

To Gua Binsari & Bosnik

To Telkom (200m), Main Post Office & Tourist Office (1.5km), Hotel Irian & Restaurant, Airport, Merpati Office & Hotel Marasi (2.5km)

0   100   200 m
Minor streets not included

---

the island, but you can get one in Biak anyway. If you don't have a permit, don't panic – your hotel probably won't ask for one. Biak is a very handy place to obtain one for the Baliem Valley and places such as Pulau Yapen and Nabire. The friendly guys at the 'intel' section of the police station on Jl Diponegoro will need two photographs and an 'administrative fee' of about 5000Rp, and can issue the permit in an hour or two.

Money You can change money at Bank Exim and BBD bank, but the new Bank Negara Indonesia (BNI) is the best. The bank at the domestic airport also changes money, but the rates aren't good.

Post & Communications The main post office is a taksi ride away on the road to the airport, opposite the tourist office. It has a poste restante service and is open daily from 8 am to 6 pm. A smaller post office is opposite the port. The modern 24 hour Telkom office is on Jl Yos Sudarso, about 200m east of Unit Hotel Mapia. There are other *wartels* (public telephone offices) around town.

Emergency The general hospital, Rumah Sakit Umum (☎ 21294), is on Jl Sri Wijaya, about 3km from town. The police station (☎ 21005) is on Jl Diponegoro.

Cenderawasih Museum

Built in traditional Biak architectural style, this museum has a small and mildly interesting assortment of Biak, Indonesian and colonial artefacts. There are a few Japanese WWII exhibits, but the collection at Gua Binsari is far better (see Around Pulau Biak later in this section). The museum was temporarily closed at the time of writing.

Organised Tours

Biak is the place to organise diving (see Diving & Snorkelling earlier in this section) and bird-watching tours anywhere between Sorong and Jayapura. There are three reliable agencies:

Biak Diving Centre (☎ 81050, fax 81051)
  Hotel Biak Beach, Marao, near Bosnik has a range of expensive tours of Pulau Biak; and snorkelling, fishing and diving trips.

The Asmat region, one of the few truly unexplored areas left in the world.

Shrewd businessmen – expect to pay for a photo.

Irian Jayan florist, Wamena.

Penis sheaths *(horim)* – Dani male *de rigueur*.

Dani *honay* (thatch-roofed hut), Baliem Valley.

A *mumi* – a form of Dani ancestor-worship.

Traditional ceremony, Mingima, Baliem Valley.

Aerial view of a Dani village, Baliem Valley.

The Big One on Biak

Pulau Biak was hit by a massive earthquake in February 1996. The main mosque in Kota Biak was completely destroyed and the airport tower damaged, but the subsequent tsunami caused the most destruction. Pretty seaside villages, such as Bosnik, Wardo and Korem were all but devastated – the flimsy wooden huts and shops stood no chance. Approximately 150 people died, many more went missing, and an estimated 10,000 were left homeless. The island is slowly recovering.

Janggi Prima Tours & Travel (☎/fax 22973), Jl Pramuka 5, Kota Biak is an impressive one-man outfit which offers an interesting range of trekking and diving tours around Biak and Yapen islands. The manager speaks good English.

PT Biak Paradise Tours & Travel (☎ 21835), Hotel Arumbai, Kota Biak has a range of pricey tours around Pulau Biak.

Places to Stay – Budget

Biak is not endowed with many cheap places. The huge, rambling **Hotel Sinar Kayu** (☎ 21333, Jl Sisingamangaraja 89) has tiny but quiet singles/doubles with outside bathroom for 15,600/31,200Rp. Dark rooms with bathroom cost 24,000/42,000Rp; better ones with air-con cost 50,400/60,000Rp. Food is available to hotel guests for 6000Rp per meal.

The more central **Hotel Solo** (☎ 21397, Jl Monginisidi 4) has tiny, dreary rooms with paper-thin walls for 14,500/25,000Rp with share bathroom. The new rooms at the back with private bathrooms for 30,000/35,000Rp are better, but still not great value. Triples cost 37,5000/40,000Rp with share/private bathrooms.

The large **Unit Hotel Mapia** (☎ 21383, Jl Ahmad Yani 23) is really rundown, but remains popular. Very ordinary economy rooms cost from 15,730/24,200Rp; better rooms with bathroom and fan cost 25,410/32,670Rp; 32,670/41,140Rp with bathroom and air-con. Breakfast costs an extra 3000Rp.

Hotel Maju (☎ 21841, Jl Imam Bonjol 45) remains the best option in this range. Smallish but comfortable rooms with bathroom and fan cost 24,200/35,100; 48,400/60,500Rp with air-con; 42,350Rp for triples. Ask for the quieter rooms at the back.

Places to Stay – Mid-Range & Top End

The two places across from and either side of the airport are good value. On the western side towards Kota Biak, **Hotel Irian** (☎ 21939, fax 21458) is a charming old place with a bar and restaurant; it has a vast number of rooms. Singles/doubles overlooking the garden cost 38,720/55,660Rp with fan; 83,490/117,370Rp with sea views and air-con; 68,970/139,150Rp for triples with fan/air-con. It's an appealing place to have a drink while waiting for a connecting flight, though it's expensive. To the east, **Hotel Marasi** (☎ 22345, fax 21496) is modern and clean, and the tariff includes three good meals. Rooms cost 46,400/71,600Rp with fan; 61,000/88,000Rp with air-con.

Basana Inn (☎ 22281, fax 21988, Jl Imam Bonjol 46) is the best mid-range choice. Clean, quiet rooms with air-con, set around a delightful garden, cost 47,000/57,000Rp; 87,000/92,000Rp with satellite TV.

Hotel Arumbai (☎ 21835, fax 22501, Jl Selat Makassar 3) is the best in the top end and is very good value when it charges in rupiah. Luxury accommodation with air-con, swimming pool, hot water and airport transfers costs from 118,000/152,000Rp; deluxe rooms and suites will do considerably more damage to your wallet, however.

Overlooking the beach in Marao village near Bosnik, the enormous **Hotel Biak Beach** (☎ 81005, fax 81003) has all the luxuries, views and service you'd expect at US$108 for a standard room and a trifling US$610 for the 'Cenderawasih Suite'. The hotel is, not surprisingly, almost permanently empty, so discounts of 50% are regularly offered.

Places to Eat

To sample some traditional *barapen* cooking, you'll have to be invited to a traditional party in a village. Barapen cuisine is food cooked under hot rocks, on which some of the braver (and possibly more intoxicated) divers attempt some impromptu fire walking.

Biak is surprisingly devoid of good, cheap warungs – try *Pasar Inpres* and the *pasar* on Jl Selat Makassar. Some places along Jl Sudirman, such as *Rumah Makan Megaria,* serve large plates of Indonesian food for about 5000Rp, but other dishes are not good value. The best spots for Padang food are *Rumah Makan Rindu Alam* on Jl Imam Bonjol, and *Minang Jaya* on Jl Ahmad Yani.

The pick of the bunch is the unsigned *Cinta Rosa*, almost opposite the BBD bank. Popular with locals, but only open in the evenings, it serves tasty baked fish and chicken meals from about 5000Rp. On the other side of the road, with a noisy outdoor setting, *Restoran Cleopatra* offers an impressive range of meals from 5000Rp. For cold drinks and assorted *kue-kue* (cakes), head straight to *Rumah Makan Nirwana*, near the port.

Along Jl Imam Bonjol are the clean and modern *Rumah Makan 99* and *Rumah Makan Umum Jakarta*. They serve decent Indonesian food for about 8000Rp and seafood for about 12,000Rp, but the karaoke machine invariably cranks up in the evening. For western food at western prices (spaghetti costs 17,500Rp), try the restaurant at *Hotel Arumbai*. The food at *Hotel Irian* is nothing special, but the setting is very pleasant – but watch out for the annoying 21% 'tax'. There are several well stocked *supermarkets* along Jl Imam Bonjol.

Entertainment

There is no shortage of places offering beer and karaoke machines, and there are several billiard rooms around the streets, but no bars or nightclubs to speak of. *Bioskop Dewi* is the only cinema in town. It mainly shows violent foreign films (with Indonesian subtitles), but there may be something quieter and more comprehensible playing when you visit. A pricey drink in the garden of *Hotel Irian* during the late afternoon is very pleasant indeed.

Shopping

There are two markets in town. Several shops in the pasar on Jl Selat Makassar sell locally made items such as batik, carvings and souvenirs made from shells, as well as Asmat and Baliem carvings, which are often imitations. The scruffy Pasar Inpres, next to the taksi/bus terminal, mainly sells food and clothing, but it's worth wandering around for some atmosphere.

The best souvenir shop is Iriani Art Shop on Jl Imam Bonjol. It has a great selection of local and other Irianese art, carvings and jewellery at reasonable (and often fixed) prices.

Getting There & Away

Air Biak is the major centre for air travel throughout Irian Jaya. Merpati flies to Manokwari (203,800Rp) and Sorong (357,800Rp) several times a week. Biak is a stopover on its regular flights between Jayapura (327,000Rp) and Jakarta (1,755,900Rp), with stops at Ambon (569,000Rp), Ujung Pandang (1,532,600Rp), Denpasar (1,369,800Rp), and sometimes Timika (241,200Rp). Merpati also flies to Nabire, Serui (Pulau Yapen) and Yemburwo (Pulau Numfor); see the Irian Jaya Airfares Chart in this chapter.

The Merpati office (☎ 21386) is across the road from the airport. It's open Monday to Friday from 7.30 am to 4.30 pm and weekends from 9 am to 2 pm; closed for lunch daily from noon to 1 pm.

Garuda stops in Biak four times a week on flights between Jayapura and Jakarta, via Ujung Pandang, for the same price as Merpati. The Garuda office (☎ 21416) is open weekdays from 7.30 am to 4.45 pm and in the morning only on weekends.

Boat Biak should be a natural stop for all Pelni services along the north coast of Irian Jaya, but surprisingly the *Rinjani* and *Umsini* pass close by without stopping. Every two weeks the *Ciremai* and *Dobonsolo* do stop at Biak on the way to Jayapura (49,000/163,000Rp for economy/1st class) and Manokwari (26,500/83,500Rp).

The Pelni office (☎ 22469) is temporarily located opposite the police station, while a new office is being built opposite Rumah Makan Nirwana. The office is normally open Monday to Saturday from 7.30 am to 4.30 pm, but is open longer when a boat is to due to arrive or depart. When a Pelni boat is in town, it's worth paying a little extra for a ticket from one of the agencies that spring up from nowhere around the port, rather than wait in line at the Pelni office for hours.

Perintis boats and a few others also stop at Biak; current schedules and tickets are available at the port.

Getting Around
To/From the Airport Public taksis marked 'Ambroben' frequently link the Frans Kaisiepo airport with any place in Kota Biak for 500Rp; simply walk outside the front door of the airport terminal. A private taxi from the airport to a hotel in the city officially costs 10,000Rp.

Public Transport The terminal for public taksis which service the entire island is next to Pasar Inpres, a few blocks from most hotels. A few more comfortable, but less regular buses leave from outside the terminal for more distant places. Taksis can take some time to fill up, so chartering one for about 15,000Rp per hour is a good idea.

Taksis are well marked, but their destinations can be confusing:

South-West Coast The 'Yendidori/Adoki' taksi goes to Yendidori (700Rp) and Adoki (1000Rp); and 'Urfu/Samber' continues to Samber (1200Rp) ie as far as the road goes.
South-East Coast 'Ibdi/Bosnik' and 'Kajasi/Saba' go to Bosnik (1200Rp); 'Kajasi/Marao' to Bosnik and Marao (1600Rp); 'Mokmer/Parai' to beaches close to the city; and 'Anggaduber/Mnurah' to the end of the road (2000Rp).
North-East Coast 'Maneru/Korem' goes to Korem (1700Rp); and 'Wari/Moos' continues to Wari (2500Rp).
North-West Coast 'Yomdori/Wardo' goes to Wardo (3000Rp).
Far North & Pulau Supiori The bus marked 'Kota Supiori Utara' goes as far as Yenggarbun (8500Rp).

AROUND PULAU BIAK
There are many fascinating places around Pulau Biak, but irregular public transport is a hindrance. Public buses and taksis traverse the rough roads as far south-west as Samber; Marao in the south-east; Wardo in the north-west; and Yenggarbun on Pulau Supiori in the far north. North of Wardo and around most of Supiori, trucks, boats and feet are the main forms of transport. Remember that towns on the island may look biggish on a map, but none are really more than a handful of village huts with no accommodation or food for travellers.

Adoki
Past the lovely beach at **Yendidori**, the village of Adoki is famous for its fire walking. While women dance around the fire, men take an hour to stoke it with coral and wood. About five men, aged between 12 and 70 years, walk across the fire and back again – it's all over in about three minutes. An exhibition of fire walking has to be arranged days in advance and costs about 250,000Rp. Ask around the market on Jl Selat Makassar in Kota Biak, or in the village. Next to Adoki, **Pantai Emfendi** has white sand and great views. It's especially popular with locals on Sunday.

Urfu & Samber
From Adoki, the road continues for another bumpy 20 minutes to the village of Urfu, surrounded by amazing **rock formations**. The road finishes near the pretty fishing village of Samber. If you ask directions to the steps from the main road, you can wander around the friendly place. There are some reminders of a seemingly forgotten Dutch colonial past and of the WWII Japanese occupation.

Wardo
At the end of the bumpy north-west road is the small group of huts called Wardo ('deep water' in Biak language) set on a picturesque bay. From Wardo, you can charter a boat to **Air Terjun Wapsdori**. The 12m waterfalls are appealing and you can have a refreshing dip at the top (watch out for the very unstable

ladder), but the ride along the peaceful, overgrown **jungle river** is the highlight.

The two hour return trip to the falls from Wardo by motorboat (holding up to four) will cost about 30,000Rp per boat. Cheaper, slower and more fun is a trip by canoe for about half this. Bargain hard as the locals are used to tourists.

Gua Binsari

This Japanese cave is known locally as Gua Binsari (*binsar* means grandmother in the Biak language) because an old woman apparently lived there many decades ago. The cave (actually a tunnel) is a chilling reminder of the day in 1944 when 3000 to 5000 Japanese were killed by US bombs and fires. There are still many rusting remnants of the war around the place. The tunnel leads to Bosnik several kilometres away. Locals refuse to go into the dark cave – believe their warnings about snakes and bats!

Foreigners are charged 5000Rp, which should include a tour in English. A small **museum** over the road has a remarkable collection of Japanese WWII weapons and photos. If the museum is unattended, ask someone at the house next door to open it. Chartering a taksi from Kota Biak is a good idea; otherwise, take a public taksi towards Bosnik and ask to be dropped off at the unsigned road that leads about 800m up the hill to the cave.

Mokmer

Mokmer has a decent **beach** and the road through the village, parallel to the main road, is a pleasant walk. Take the bemo towards Bosnik and ask the driver to let you off at the unsigned turn-off.

Bird & Orchid Garden

About 4km east of Mokmer, on the main road to Bosnik, is the Taman Burung & Anggrek (Bird & Orchid Garden). The pleasant gardens contain 72 types of orchids and about 50 species of caged birds, such as the cenderawasih (which is probably as close as you'll ever get to one); and if you're really lucky, the Double Eyed Fig Parrot. Sadly, several birds died in a recent drought. The entrance

fee seems to vary for foreigners, but it should be 3000Rp. The gardens are open Monday to Saturday from 7.30 am to 3 pm.

Bosnik & Marao

Bosnik was the Dutch capital of the island, a landing site for the Allies in WWII and it's now the starting point for trips to the Padaido Islands. Some **WWII relics** lie near the sandy **beach**, and a small, busy **pasar** is held every Wednesday and Saturday.

The south-eastern road continues past a beach at Opiaref, and then heads up a hill to the small village of Marao, where the huge *Hotel Biak Beach* stands incongruously (see Places to Stay – Mid-Range & Top End under Kota Biak earlier). Even if you can't afford to stay there, it's worth a splurge on a meal or drink amid the sheer luxury. A trail continues along the coast past more charming and deserted beaches until the village of **Anggaduber**.

Padaido Islands

This stunning cluster of 30 islands (only 13 are inhabited) is wonderful for **diving**, **snorkelling** and **swimming** (see Diving & Snorkelling under Central Irian Jaya earlier).

Owi and Auki islands are the closest to Bosnik. They are also the most populated, so you're more than likely to find a passenger boat from Bosnik and be able to stay in a *local hut*. Public boats travel between Bosnik and some of the islands on Bosnik's market days (Wednesday and Saturday). If you ask around and bargain hard, it's possible to charter a boat (holding five people) from Bosnik or the *pasar ikan* (fish market) in Kota Biak, but you may have to pay whatever they ask to get back.

Pulau Supiori

Separated from Pulau Biak by a narrow channel, most of Supiori is designated as **Supiori Island Reserve**, an area of mangroves and montane forests with endemic species of parrots and cockatoos. The north-east road from Biak goes past Korem and Wandos, and stops at the channel. The bridge over the channel is often broken, so a pontoon with an ingenious pulley system takes passengers and even taksis across the water.

The only road on Supiori continues as far as Wapur and a few buses travel each day between Kota Biak and Yenggarbun. If you have the time, soaking up the scenery on a day trip by public (or chartered) taksi from the city to the channel and back is worthwhile.

PULAU NUMFOR
Part of the Biak-Numfor district, this irresistible, unspoilt and undeveloped island is about halfway between Biak and Manokwari. There is no official travellers' accommodation, but you can easily arrange to stay with a local family if you contact the kepala desa in Kameri or Yemburwo (the two main villages); alternatively organise something with the tourist office in Kota Biak.

There are dozens of unexplored **snorkelling** and **swimming** spots around the island, such as Pantai Asaibori in western Numfor and Pantai Pakreki in the south. From Kameri, you can charter a boat (20 minutes) to the heavenly Pulau Manem, where there's no shortage of **birdlife**, sandy **beaches** and Japanese **WWII wrecks**.

Merpati flies from Biak to Yemburwo (122,400Rp) twice a week (currently Monday and Friday). Most days (depending on demand) speedboats leave for the rough 12 hour trip to Yemburwo from the pasar ikan or port in Kota Biak.

PULAU YAPEN
☎ 0983
This elongated mountainous island south of Biak offers **bird-watching** around its northern shores, and great **diving** at nearby Pulau Arumbai. Although Yapen is pleasant enough, it has limited facilities and transport, and there is little to justify a detour unless you're a bird lover, or have an adventurous streak.

The only town of any size is Serui, the district capital. A surat jalan, which is needed for a visit to Serui and anywhere else on the island, can be easily obtained in Kota Biak.

Places to Stay & Eat
There are only three places to stay on the island, all in Serui. *Bersaudara Hotel* (☎ 31420, Jl Jendral Sudirman 56) and *Marina Hotel* (☎ 31062, Jl Wolter Monginsidi) offer ordinary rooms for about 30,000Rp per person, including meals. The best is *Merpati Inn* (☎ 31154, Jl Yos Sudarso). It's a bit noisy, but is good for information on chartered boats and Merpati flights. Singles/doubles (including meals) cost 33,000/48,500Rp with fan; 48,500/59,500Rp with air-con.

You will probably end up eating at your hotel. If not, some night *warungs* and a couple of *rumah makans* serving Padang food are located in the port area.

Getting There & Away
Merpati flies between Biak and Serui (79,500Rp) every day. The Merpati office (☎ 31620) is on Jl Yos Sudarso, next to (you guessed it) Merpati Inn. Every two weeks, the Pelni liners *Rinjani* and *Umsini* stop on their way to Jayapura and Nabire. The overnight ferry *Teluk Cenderawasih I* sails to Nabire and Biak twice a week.

An interesting alternative is a chartered boat from Biak. Ask around the port in Kota Biak or contact one of the travel agencies there about what they can offer (see Organised Tours under Kota Biak earlier).

AROUND PULAU YAPEN
Cenderawasih still manage to survive in the north of the island. To look for some, charter a boat (holding about 10 people) from Serui for about 100,000Rp per day, plus about 15,000Rp per hour for fuel. A guide (about 25,000Rp per day) will arrange for you to stay with villagers (around 10,000Rp per night). There is also a 'protection fee' of about 50,000Rp levied on each group looking for the birds.

General **bird-watching** tours can be arranged with Best Tours & Travel and Dani Sangrila Tours (see Organised Tours under Jayapura later in this chapter); Irian Diving (see Diving under Western Irian Jaya earlier); and Janggi Prima Tours & Travel in Biak (see Organised Tours under Kota Biak earlier).

IRIAN JAYA

Birds of Paradise

THE MALAY ARCHIPELAGO, ALFRED WALLACE

Over 40 different species of the bird of paradise (*cenderawasih*) are found in small areas of northern Irian Jaya and southern Maluku, as well as in Papua New Guinea. Cenderawasih were first taken to Europe following colonial exploration around the East Indies. Their feathers fetched remarkable prices as fashionable accessories and the birds soon faced extinction. As their legs and wings were often removed by traders to highlight their beautiful plumage, and as several early colonial explorers only saw them in flight and never on land, Europeans originally thought that the birds had no feet and always flew.

The male bird is usually more brightly coloured than the female and displays its magnificent plumage during mating, often hanging upside down from branches to show off its colours; it does this alone or in groups called *leks*. Cenderawasih mostly nest in open parts of a tree; feed on fruit and insects; usually have remarkable thin, curled 'tail-wires' up to 30cm long with colourful tips; and often have loud calls.

The birds are scarce and very difficult to find, but with some patience, lots of time and a good guide it may be possible. Locating the birds will involve chartering boats, organising guides and camping out on Waigeo, Misool, Batanta and Salawati islands, off the coast of Sorong; along sections of the aptly named Teluk Cenderawasih (Bird of Paradise Bay); the northern coast of Pulau Yapen; and in the remote Aru Islands of south-east Maluku. Organised tours can be arranged through travel agencies in Sorong, Biak, Wamena and Jayapura. The less adventurous can admire several of these creatures in aviaries at the Bird & Orchid Garden near Bosnik on Pulau Biak.

Pulau Arumbai offers superb **snorkelling** (bring your own gear) among coral and dolphins, and is home to thousands of cockatoos and hornbills. There are also decent beaches at **Pantai Mariadei** and **Pantai Ketuapi**; and the scenery around **Danau Sarawandori** is pretty. You must charter a boat to Arumbai from Serui, but the beaches and lake are accessible by public bemo from Serui.

Infrequent buses go as far as Wooi in the west and Manawi in the east. Chartering for about 15,000Rp per hour is a quicker way

of getting around. All roads on Yapen are rough and the terrain is mountainous.

NABIRE
☎ 0984

Nabire is the capital of the Paniai district and ignored by most travellers. However, it's a pleasant town with wide streets, nearby beaches and islands to explore, and is a worthwhile stopover on the way to/from Biak or Jayapura. And for some reason, noone in Nabire has yet learnt how to yell 'Hello Mister!!!!'.

Orientation & Information

The post office, taksi terminal and most shops are along Jl Yos Sudarso, parallel to the waterfront. Nearby, Jl Pepera has a few offices, including the 24 hour Telkom office and Bank Exim, which will change money. The airport is walking distance (ask directions) from the hotels listed.

It's a good idea to have a surat jalan for Nabire – you will certainly need one for any trips into the interior. Organise it at the police station (☎ 21110) on Jl Sisingamangaraja, or in Kota Biak.

Things to See & Do

Like most of Irian Jaya, the accessibility of nearby attractions is limited by irregular transport, rough roads and travel restrictions. You can charter a boat for an hour or two to islands such as **Pulau Moor**, **Pulau Papaya** and the very tiny **Pulau Nusi**, where some travellers reported staying in a hut for a week and having a great time. Boats to these and other islands usually leave from the MAF beach at the end of Jl Sisingamangaraja. A chartered taksi can take you to some **hot springs** near the port; and **Pantai Wahario** is good for snorkelling (bring your own gear) and swimming, and can be reached by public taksi.

Places to Stay & Eat

The best of a limited choice is *Hotel Nusantara (☎ 21180, Jl Pemuda 20)*. It has a large range of rooms, good service and a nice setting. Simple, clean doubles without bathroom cost 43,000Rp; considerably more with air-con and TV. All prices include three meals. The next best, *Hotel Anggrek (☎ 21066, Jl Pepera 22)*, has rooms starting at 23,500Rp without meals or bathroom; it's also set around a lovely garden.

Most of the restaurants are congregated around the taksi terminal – the best are rumah makans *Sari* and *Kebun Sirih*. For some of the most mouthwatering baked fish you will ever taste, try the *warungs* along the waterfront, opposite the taksi terminal. *Lucky Supermarket* on Jl Yos Sudarso is well stocked.

Getting There & Away

Air Merpati flies every day to Biak (218,100Rp) and several times a week to Jayapura (430,400Rp). From Nabire, there are also flights to Kaimana and on to Fak Fak and Sorong (see the Irian Jaya Airfares Chart). Book as soon as you can and be prepared for delays and frustrations. The Merpati office (☎ 21591) on Jl Pemuda next to the Hotel Nusantara is open from 8 am weekdays and closes when it feels like it.

Boat Every two weeks, the Pelni liners *Rinjani* and *Umsini* stop in Nabire's Samabusa port on the way to Serui and Manokwari. Perintis boats crawl along the north coast and stop in Nabire every week or so. About twice a week, the *Teluk Cenderawasih I* goes to Serui (12 hours) on Pulau Yapen and on to Biak. Samabusa port is about 20km east of Nabire; taksis are frequent when boats arrive and depart. The Pelni office (☎ 21350) is on Jl Sam Ratulangi behind the taksi terminal.

TIMIKA
☎ 0901

Timika exists almost entirely to service the Freeport copper and gold mine in Tembagapura, approximately 60km to the north. Visiting the mine is not possible unless you have been 'invited' by a Freeport employee living in Tembagapura. You will need a surat jalan before you can enter Timika.

Timika is even more expensive than Wamena in the Baliem Valley. The overpriced *Hotel Surya (☎ 21860)*, opposite the market, has cubicles for 32,500Rp; while *Losmen Amole Jaya (☎ 21125, Jl Pelikan)* is comparatively good value at 43,500Rp a room. Several top end places, such as the *Sheraton Hotel (☎ 59494)*, cater almost exclusively for visiting foreign workers, but the public is welcome.

Timika serves as a useful entry point to Irian Jaya. The regular Jayapura-Biak flight on Merpati often detours through Timika, so you can see the awesome Freeport mine and the snow-capped Puncak Jaya, Irian Jaya's highest mountain, from the plane. There are also three flights a week between Timika

The Freeport Mine and Traditional People

Not far from Puncak Jaya in the southern highlands, the US-run PT Freeport Indonesia Company owns the world's second largest copper mine, and its largest gold deposits. The minerals were discovered in the 1930s, but mines were not opened until the 1960s; Freeport has since built the modern town of Tembagapura (Copper Town) and a staggering complex of tunnels and private roads carved through a mountain range. Over 78,000 tonnes of ore are extracted per day and Freeport is continuing to explore several other areas of Irian Jaya for further mining.

There are serious concerns, however: Freeport continues to enjoy a 'special relationship' with the Indonesian government, and there was never any serious consultation with, or compensation for, the local Amungme and Komoro people; Freeport employs about 16,000 people (easily the largest private employer in Irian Jaya), but only about 10% are Irianese; copper tailings cause enormous environmental damage and affect the health of villagers through contamination of sago palms and drinking water; Freeport moves entire villages with thousands of indigenous people from their homelands to undertake further mining; and the Indonesian military presence in the area has resulted in instances of human rights abuse.

Yet Jakarta is likely to remain unmoved. Freeport is Indonesia's largest foreign taxpayer (it has paid an estimated US$760 million in taxes since 1989) and contributes about US$1 billion a year to the Indonesian – but not necessarily the Irianese – economy.

In recent years, riots and sabotage in Tembagapura and the nearby service town of Timika have halted production from the mine – which makes a *profit* of over US$1 million per day. Local Irianese have demanded scholarships and other employment schemes for local youths; 1% of profits for local community projects; and changes to local Freeport and Indonesian security and community-development personnel.

To its credit, Freeport does spend millions of dollars each year on the local community – Jakarta, meanwhile, is happy to collect the huge taxes and continues to allow Freeport to act as a quasi-local government responsible for community development and welfare.

and Sorong via Biak. The Merpati office (☎ 54021) is on Jl Tamora.

The Pelni liner *Tatamailau* stops at nearby Amamapare port three times every four weeks on its way to Merauke, Agats and south-east Maluku.

The Baliem Valley

The Baliem Valley is easily the most popular destination in Irian Jaya and the most accessible place in the interior. While the Dani people who inhabit most of the inner valley have adopted some western conveniences, and the main town, Wamena, has a few modern facilities, the valley remains one of the last truly fascinating, traditional areas in the world.

The first white men chanced upon the valley in 1938, a discovery which came as one of the last and greatest surprises to a world that had mapped, studied and explored the mystery out of its remotest corners. WWII prevented further exploration and it was not until 1945, when a plane crashed there and the survivors were rescued, that attention was again drawn to the region.

The first Dutch missionaries arrived in 1954, the Dutch government established a post at Wamena in 1956, and changes to the Baliem lifestyle soon followed. Today Indonesia has added its own brand of colonialism, bringing schools, police, soldiers, transmigrants and shops, but the local culture has in many ways proved very resilient.

The Baliem Valley is 1554m above sea level, about 60km long and 16km wide, with Wamena at its centre. Running through the valley is the mighty Sungai Baliem, which drops 1500m in less than 50km on its way to the Arafura Sea on the south coast.

Climate

The best time to visit is between March and August, when it rains less (but be prepared for rain anytime of the year). The days are fine (up to 26°C) and the evenings are cool

(about 12°C) – but it's always colder in higher areas, such as around Danau Habbema. The best season coincides with the European summer which means that the Baliem Valley is often busy at this time, especially in August. The wet season is from about September to January, when trekking in some parts may be wet and unpleasant.

Special Events

The main event on the calendar is the Baliem Festival held in August. On Indonesian

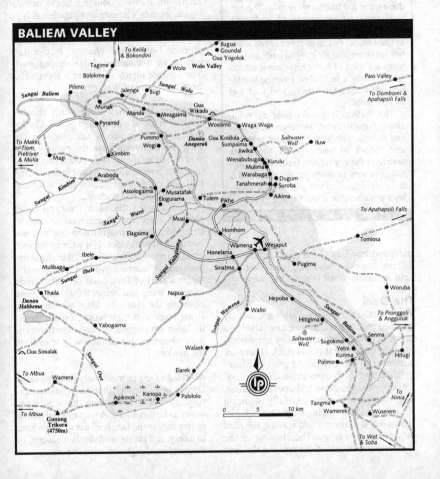

BALIEM VALLEY

IRIAN JAYA

Baliem Festival

To coincide with the busiest time for tourism (the European summer holidays), a festival is held in the Baliem Valley, generally between 9-14 August. Check with the tourist office in Wamena for current details – the dates and activities vary little from year to year, however.

With the encouragement of the Indonesian government and local missionaries, the highlight of the festival is the mock 'tribal fighting', where men from villages dress up in full traditional regalia. The festival also features plenty of traditional dancing by both men and women, as well as Dani music. Feasts of pigs cooked using hot rocks are also an integral part, and pig races are a lot of fun. Other lesser attractions include a festival of flowers, exhibitions of traditional archery, and foot and bicycle races.

The festival is usually held at Yetni, along Sungai Yetni, between Sugokmo and Kurima. Although it is tourist oriented and there's no shortage of foreigners watching the events, the festival is a magical (and very photogenic) occasion and is the only chance to see several of the valley's attractions in a short space of time.

Independence Day (17 August), traditional dancing, cooking and pig feasts are also held in Assologaima in the north-west.

The Dani

The tribes of the Baliem Valley are usually grouped together under the name 'Dani' – a rather pejorative name given by neighbouring tribes, but one that has stuck. There are a number of other highland groups, distinguished from each other by language, physical appearance, dress and social customs. The Dani are farmers, skilfully working their fertile land, digging long ditches for irrigation and drainage, and leaving the land fallow between crops. The clearing of the land and the tilling of the soil for the first crop is traditionally men's work; the planting, weeding and harvesting is women's.

Food The sweet potato *(erom)* is the staple food in the highlands. The Dani recognise 70 different types – some varieties can only be eaten by a particular group, such as pregnant women or old men, and ancestor spirits get the first erom from every field.

Houses Traditional Dani villages comprise several self-contained fenced compounds, each with its own cooking house, men's house, women's houses and pigsties. A typical compound might be home to four men and their families, perhaps 20 people. A traditional Dani house *(honay)* is circular, topped by a thatched dome-shaped roof. You can see plenty of honay a short stroll from the centre of Wamena.

Clothing Dani men wear penis sheaths *(horim)* made of a cultivated gourd. The Indonesian government's campaign in the early 1970s to eradicate the penis gourds was mostly a failure. Many Dani (mainly in the more remote areas) wear pig fat in their hair and cover their bodies in pig fat and soot for health and warmth.

Traditionally the men wear no other clothing apart from ornamentation such as string hair nets, cenderawasih feathers and cowry shell necklaces. If a woman wears a grass skirt it usually indicates that she is unmarried. A married woman traditionally wears a skirt of fibre coils or seeds strung together, hung just below the abdomen and covering the buttocks. Dani women carry string bags with their heads, usually heavily laden with vegetables and even babies or pigs when they are on their way to or from the market.

Marriage Despite missionary pressure many Dani have maintained their polygamous marriage system – a man may have as many wives as he can afford. A man must give four or five pigs to the family of the girl he wishes to marry; and his social status is measured by the number of pigs and wives he has.

Dani men and women sleep apart. The men of a compound sleep tightly packed in one hut, and the women and children sleep in the other huts. After a birth, sex is taboo for the mother for two to five years, apparently to give the child exclusive use of her milk. As a result of this care, the average Dani life expectancy is 60 years, which is relatively high among traditional peoples. This practice also contributes to polygamy and a high divorce rate.

Customs One of the Dani's more unusual (now prohibited) customs is to amputate one or two joints of a woman's finger when a close relative dies – you'll see many older women with fingers missing up to the second

JENNY BOWMAN

Despite campaigns by the Indonesian government, the Dani prefer traditional modes of dress.

joint. Dani women will often smother themselves with clay and mud at the time of a family death. Cremation was the traditional method of disposing of the deceased, but sometimes the body is kept and dried.

Fighting between villages or districts seems to be partly a ritual matter to appease the ancestors and attract good luck, and partly a matter of revenge and settling scores. In formal combat, fighting was carried out in brief clashes throughout the day and was not designed to result in carnage. After a few hours the opposing groups tended to turn to verbal insults instead. The Indonesian government and foreign missionaries, through sponsored mock battles during the annual Baliem Festival (see the boxed text earlier), have done their best to stamp out Dani warfare, with a fair amount of success. However, a clash between the Wollesi and Hitigima districts in 1988 led to about 15 deaths, and there have been unsubstantiated reports of tribal fighting north of the Baliem Valley throughout the 1990s.

Language The northern and western Dani speak a dialect of Dani distinct from that spoken in the Wamena area. Around Wamena, a man greeting a man says *nayak*; if greeting more than one man, *nayak lak*. When greeting a woman, a man says *la'uk*; if greeting more than one woman, *la'uk nya*. Women say *la'uk* if greeting one person; *la'uk nya* if greeting more than one person. *Wam* means 'pig'; *nan* is 'to eat'; *i-nan* is 'to drink'; *an* is 'I'; and *hano* is 'good'. Most Dani speak Bahasa Indonesia, but they appreciate a greeting in their own language.

The Dani are friendly but can be shy. Long handshakes allowing time to really feel the other's hand are common. Throughout the region, locals request 200Rp to 500Rp or a cigarette or two if you want to take their photo, but sometimes up to 5000Rp is asked if they're dressed up in feathers or other ceremonial costumes.

Surat Jalan

Currently, a surat jalan is essential if you want to stay more than one or two days in

IRIAN JAYA

Tourism in the Baliem

Only in the last 10 years has tourism started to make an impact on the Baliem Valley, with about 70% of tourists arriving from Europe, often in August. In 1988, 758 foreigners visited – by 1995 over 6000 had visited. The Indonesian authorities hoped to double that figure in a few years, but tourism suffered in 1998 because of instability throughout Indonesia.

While the number of tourists may not seem large, the impact of tourism is substantial. Wamena struggles to dispose of sewage and rubbish, and pollution from public transport is bad. Gua Wikuda, near Wosilimo, has been developed by indigenous people (with profits returning to them also), but generally the tourist and transport industries, with the exception of guides, are run by non-Irianese.

There are ways for visitors to minimise the impact of tourism and improve the standard of living for indigenous people, such as staying at places run by local people; taking out everything you bring when trekking; urging guides and porters to look after local flora when building shelters and making tracks; underplaying your comparative wealth by not flashing around loads of money and western goods; be sensitive when taking photos – ask first and don't begrudge your photo opportunity a few hundred rupiah or a cigarette or two; and not contributing to local inflation by overpaying guides and porters.

Tourism does sometimes benefit the indigenous people. Interest in the valley, for example, and travel within it, ensures that the Indonesian government does not mistreat indigenous Irianese; traditions are often maintained, if only for the sake of tourist dollars; and some money does trickle back to help local community development.

Wamena and travel around the Baliem Valley – but regulations regarding the travel permit are less stringent each year.

You cannot obtain a surat jalan in Wamena, but it's easy to get one from police stations in Jayapura and Biak. Take a few photocopies of the permit to give to regional police stations around the valley. There are shops with photocopy machines along Jl Trikora and in Pasar Nayak in Wamena. The Visas & Documents section earlier in this chapter has more information about the permits.

In Wamena, your hotel, guide or travel agency (if on an organised tour) should take your surat jalan, and report your presence, to the police station. If not, you should report to the police station on Jl Safri Darwin within 24 hours. It is painless but necessary.

In the countryside, you should report personally and show your surat jalan to police stations or village authorities if you stay anywhere outside Wamena eg the district centres of Jiwika, Kurima and Kimbim. Reporting to the police is often neither necessary nor possible if you're trekking to remote areas, but still try to report to village authorities as you go along. Some more remote areas in the region may be off limits to foreigners; the police in Wamena will let you know about the current situation.

WAMENA
☎ 0969

The main town in the Baliem Valley, and the capital of the Jayawijaya district, Wamena is a dusty, sprawling place. Although there's not much to do in the town itself, it provides a good base for exploring nearby villages and the countryside. Wamena is expensive compared to the rest of Indonesia, but this is understandable as *everything* has to be flown in from Jayapura, where most goods arrive from western Indonesia by boat or plane.

Orientation

Many hotels, places to eat and offices are along Jl Trikora, only one block from the airport. The centre of town is the scruffy, crowded Pasar Nayak – which is *still* due to transfer to Homhom, about 3km north of its current location, sometime in the future. While the market and taksi terminal areas

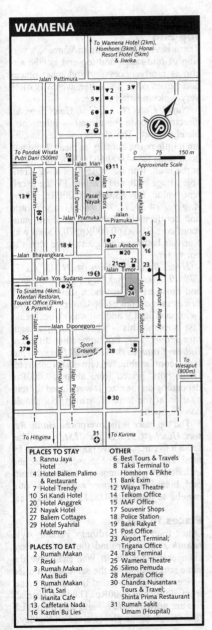

WAMENA

To Wamena Hotel (2km),
Homhom (3km), Honai
Resort Hotel (5km)
& Jiwika

Jalan Pattimura

To Pondok Wisata
Putri Dani (500m)

Jalan Irian

0   75   150 m
Approximate Scale

Jalan Safri Darwin

Pasar
Nayak

Jalan Trikora

Jalan Angkasa

Jalan Thamrin

Jalan Pramuka

Jalan
Pramuka

Jalan Ambon

Jalan Bhayangkara

Jalan Yos Sudarso

Jalan Timor

To Sinatma (4km),
Mentari Restoran,
Tourist Office (3km)
& Pyramid

Airport Runway

Jalan Gatot Subroto

Jalan Diponegoro

Jalan Thamrin

Sport
Ground

To
Wesaput
(800m)

Jalan Achmad Yani

Jalan Panjaitan

To Hitigima

To Kurima

PLACES TO STAY	OTHER
1 Rannu Jaya Hotel	6 Best Tours & Travels
4 Hotel Baliem Palimo & Restaurant	8 Taksi Terminal to Homhom & Pikhe
7 Hotel Trendy	11 Bank Exim
10 Sri Kandi Hotel	12 Wijaya Theatre
20 Hotel Anggrek	14 Telkom Office
22 Nayak Hotel	15 MAF Office
27 Baliem Cottages	17 Souvenir Shops
29 Hotel Syahrial Makmur	18 Police Station
	19 Bank Rakyat
PLACES TO EAT	21 Post Office
2 Rumah Makan Reski	23 Airport Terminal; Trigana Office
3 Rumah Makan Mas Budi	24 Taksi Terminal
5 Rumah Makan Tirta Sari	25 Wamena Theatre
9 Irianita Cafe	26 Silimo Pemuda
13 Caffetaria Nada	28 Merpati Office
16 Kantin Bu Lies	30 Chandra Nusantara Tours & Travel; Shinta Prima Restaurant
	31 Rumah Sakit Umam (Hospital)

are not pleasant, just a few blocks to the west some lovely, quiet streets, such as Jl Thamrin are worth wandering around. Take a torch (flashlight) at night, because there are few street lights; many streets are also poorly sign-posted.

If your hotel or guide doesn't take your surat jalan to the police station (☎ 31072) you'll have to report there yourself. The friendly officers are a good source of trekking information and will tell you of any places off limits.

Information

Tourist Offices The tourist office (☎ 31365) is worth a visit as soon as you arrive to get current information about markets, ceremonies and trekking. It's open Monday to Saturday from 7.30 am to 2 pm, but closes at 11 am on Friday and 1 pm on Saturday. The office is inconveniently located almost at the top of Jl Yos Sudarso, about 3km from the Bank Rakyat building. A taksi towards Sinatma, or a becak along nearby, parallel Jl Bhayangkara, will save a walk.

The tourist information booth at the arrivals area in the airport seems to be permanently closed these days.

Money Bank Exim on Jl Trikora and the huge, incongruous Bank Rakyat on the same street will change money, but their rates are about 20% lower than the same banks in Biak and Jayapura. You are well advised to stock up on rupiah before coming to the Baliem Valley. There is nowhere else in the valley to change money.

Post & Communications The post office on Jl Timor is open Monday to Thursday and Saturday from 8 am to 2 pm, and until 11 am on Friday. The Telkom office on Jl Thamrin is open 24 hours a day; more convenient wartels are located along Jl Trikora close to the market.

Emergency Rumah Sakit Umum (☎ 31152) is a hospital along the southern end of Jl Trikora. Travellers have reported that service and advice is of a low standard.

IRIAN JAYA

Places to Stay

Even though Wamena is one of the most expensive places in Indonesia, this is currently less discouraging because of the favourable exchange rate. Still, the only way to live cheaply is to 'go Dani' and stay in a cheap Dani-style hut in a village near Wamena (see Around the Baliem Valley later in this section). All budget and cheaper mid-range places include breakfast.

Places to Stay – Budget

The cheapest place is *Hotel Syahrial Makmur* (☎ 31306, Jl Gatot Subroto 51), a two minute walk south of the airport. Singles/doubles cost 24,000/30,000Rp or 33,000/42,000Rp, depending on room size, so it's not great value.

Hotel Trendy (☎ 31092, Jl Trikora 112) has a terrible name, but it's a decent place. Comfortable, clean rooms (better ones at the front) cost 44,000/55,000Rp. Triples are good value at 66,000Rp, and there's a convivial lounge area. *Sri Kandi Hotel* (☎ 31367, Jl Irian 16) is a little inconvenient, but is quiet and friendly. The rooms (most with huge bathrooms) aren't great value for 40,000/55,00Rp, but the 'family rooms' are a better price at 60,000/75,000Rp for doubles/triples.

One of the nicest places is *Pondok Wisata Putri Dani* (☎ 31223, Jl Irian 40), about 500m west of the Sri Kandi. Spotless, comfortable rooms in a family home cost 45,000Rp, or rooms with bathroom cost 60,000Rp. *Rannu Jaya Hotel* (☎ 31257, fax 31900, Jl Trikora 109) is quiet, central and provides a decent breakfast. The cheapest rooms cost 43,200Rp, but there are better ones at the back with satellite TV for 60,000Rp.

For some peace and seclusion and a pretty garden, *Wamena Hotel* (☎ 31292) is worth considering – but the rooms priced at a negotiable 50,000/60,000Rp badly need some renovation. It's about 2km north of the cutely-named Hotel Trendy; take a becak. The hotel provides free transport to a restaurant of your choice in the evening.

Places to Stay – Mid-Range & Top End

There is very little value in Wamena's version of mid-range and top-end hotels; aircon is rarely necessary and most places don't even offer hot water, which is often very welcome after a hike.

Nayak Hotel (☎ 31067, Jl Gatot Subroto) directly opposite the airport is often completely empty. The cheaper singles/doubles are a little noisy, but they're clean, large and good value for 44,000/66,000Rp. The 'suites' at the back, with hot water (not always reliable), huge bath, and satellite TV are excellent value for 88,000/110,000Rp. *Hotel Anggrek* (☎ 31242, Jl Ambon) is also central and comfortable. Rooms with share bathroom cost 50,000/60,000Rp; 70,000Rp with a private bathroom; all guests have access to hot water.

Hotel Baliem Palimo (☎ 31043, fax 31 798, Jl Trikora) has large, modern rooms and most are set around a nice courtyard. Prices range from 58,664Rp to 150,350Rp (with satellite TV and hot water), but breakfast is extra. This is where many package-tour groups stay. For something different, *Baliem Cottages* (☎ 31370, Jl Thamrin) has large, comfortable, western-style (concrete) Dani 'huts' priced from about 50,000Rp, depending on the size. It was closed for renovation at the time of writing, but should now be open.

The top place is the overpriced *Honai Resort Hotel* (☎ 31515, fax 31513) in Pikhe, about a five minute drive north of Wamena by taksi. The rooms are, of course, very nice and include hot water, transport to/from the airport, breakfast and dinner, but there is nothing else to justify the US$125/140 price tag.

Places to Eat

Other than a few ordinary Padang-style *rumah makans* around the market, most cheaper restaurants in Wamena serve the same sort of food for the same sort of price – rice- and noodle-based Indonesian meals from 5000Rp to 8000Rp. The local specialties are prawns (*udang*) and baked goldfish (*ikan mas*). Some places close on Sunday.

Rumah Makan Mas Budi on Jl Pattimura is badly signed, but is deservedly popular and probably the best place in Wamena. The food and service is good and the free fruit for desert is a nice touch, but soft drinks are reasonably expensive. The comfortable and clean *Rumah Makan Reski* on Jl Trikora offers Indonesian food for 8000Rp to 10,000Rp; fish and prawn dishes cost 20,000Rp. Some readers have recommended *Rumah Makan Tirta Sari* on Jl Trikora, but it was closed every time we walked past – you may have better luck.

In the western 'suburbs' of Wamena, *Caffetaria Nada* on Jl Thamrin is worth trying; in the southern 'suburbs', *Shinta Prima Restaurant (Jl Trikora 17)* is worth a short walk, although it gets mixed reviews from readers. The prices aren't too bad, but the service is a bit scrappy.

The new, barn-like *Irianita Cafe*, just off Jl Trikora, is the only place serving western food such as steak and chicken (about 15,000Rp), but the ambience is often shattered by the karaoke machine. The friendly *Kantin Bu Lies* on Jl Angkasa, next to the airport, is recommended for simple Indonesian food. It's the best place to wait for your flight.

The only place with any real style and reasonable prices is the delightful *Mentari Restoran (Jl Yos Sudarso 47)*. It's a 20 minute walk from downtown Wamena; alternatively, take a taksi towards Sinatma (becaks do not run at night, nor along Jl Yos Sudarso during the day). The elegant restaurant inside *Hotel Baliem Palimo* is open to the public and worth a splurge.

Wamena is designated a 'dry' area, so no alcohol should be brought into the capital by travellers. If you are desperate, however, some of the more expensive hotels may be able to find you a bottle of something at an outrageous price.

Entertainment

Wamena isn't the most exciting place in Indonesia. Incredibly (but inevitably) most restaurants have karaoke machines, but thankfully (probably because no alcohol is available), they aren't really popular among local patrons. Most nights *Wijaya Theatre* and *Wamena Theatre* show films in their original languages (with Indonesian subtitles), with varying degrees of comfort and sound and picture quality.

Shopping

The Dani (traditionally the men) are fine craftspeople, so it's no surprise that a wide selection of souvenirs is available. Usually it's cheaper to buy directly from the Dani in the villages, but they can strike a hard bargain, so also check out prices in the shops and markets. A number of traders will approach you on the streets of Wamena or hang around the doorways of popular hotels and restaurants. Bargaining is essential if you want a good price and bartering is acceptable in the villages.

Several reasonable souvenir shops have sprung up along Jl Trikora and there are several co-operatives, apparently run by indigenous people, near the corner of Jl Trikora and Jl Ambon. Silimo Pemuda, on Jl Thamrin, is a genuine co-operative of Dani people making and selling carvings, weaving and pottery in stalls. It's a good idea, but it looks neglected and the goods on sale are tacky.

The cost of stone axe blades *(kapak)* depends on the size and the labour involved in making each one; blue stone is the hardest and considered the finest material, and is thus more expensive – from at least 20,000Rp (up to 250,000Rp for something large and authentic). *Sekan* are thin, intricately hand-woven rattan bracelets which cost from 3000Rp. *Noken* are bark-string bags made from the inner bark of certain types of trees and shrubs, which is dried, shredded and then rolled into thread. The bags are coloured with vegetable dyes, resulting in a very strong smell, in patterns which vary according to their origin. They cost 5000Rp to 15,000Rp.

Other handcrafts include: various head and arm necklaces *(mikak)* of cowry shells, feathers and bone; grass skirts *(jogal* and *thali)*; assorted head decorations *(suale)*, often complete with the horns of a wild pig and – gruesomely – an entire squashed parrot, for up to 50,000Rp; woven baskets for around 10,000Rp; carved spears and arrows for about 8000Rp each; and woven place mats for about 5000Rp. Asmat woodcarvings, shields and spears are also available in the souvenir shops, but be very wary of price and quality.

Of course the most popular souvenir is the penis gourd, held upright by attaching a thread to the top and looping it around the waist or chest. These are priced from 2000Rp to 30,000Rp depending on size (!) and quality of materials, craftmanship and your bargaining ability.

Getting There & Away

Air Merpati flies between Sentani (Jayapura) and Wamena 10 times a week for 208,000Rp. As flying is the only way in and out of the valley, services are heavily booked in August during peak season, but are sometimes cancelled through lack of passengers during the rest of the year. Always allow a couple of days' leeway for inevitable delays when catching flights to/from Sentani.

It is important to note that the Merpati office in Jayapura (or anywhere else in Indonesia) cannot book tickets from Wamena to Sentani – you will have to book a ticket by telephone before you arrive in Wamena, or contact Merpati in Wamena as soon as you arrive. The Merpati office (☎ 31488) is open daily from 7 am to 3 pm and until 2 pm on Sunday.

Cargo planes also fly between Sentani and Wamena, and are a useful and often more reliable alternative to Merpati. Trigana is now the only cargo service selling passenger tickets. The price from Wamena to Sentani (240,000Rp) is a lot less than Sentani-Wamena (340,000Rp), when the planes are jam-packed with cargo. It has an efficient office (☎ 31611) in the Wamena airport, and in Sentani (see the Sentani entry later in this chapter).

The MAF service (☎ 31263) flies between Sentani and Wamena once or twice a day. As they charge US$104 per person, it's clear it's not interested in becoming an alternative airline. MAF also flies to more obscure destinations – schedules are posted outside its offices in Wamena and Sentani. The Indonesian army (TNI) also has several cheap flights a day between Sentani and Wamena – these are for locals and the military – but it's another possibility if you beg hard enough.

Getting Around

Becak Almost all hotels in Wamena are within walking distance of the airport. For longer trips around town, take a becak. The official price is about 500Rp per kilometre, but foreigners are always charged more. Any trip around town should cost 1000Rp to 1500Rp; about 2000Rp to Wamena Hotel; and about 3000Rp to Wesaput. Becaks hang around the market and can be hailed from the street, but they don't run at night and they're not allowed along Jl Yos Sudarso – they also seem to disappear when it rains!

Bicycle One new and pleasant way of getting around the immediate area is on a mountain bike. These can be rented from Best Tours & Travels (see Organised Tours under Around the Baliem Valley later) for 15,000Rp per day; or about 12,500Rp for longer rental. Mountain bikes are good for visiting villages along main roads, but hopeless along most walking trails. Best Tours & Travels also arranges mountain bike tours, but these are expensive.

AROUND THE BALIEM VALLEY

Trekking is certainly the best way to see particular scenery, witness special ceremonies and visit people in more-remote areas, but if you don't have the time, money or inclination to trek, don't be put off coming to the Baliem Valley. With an increasing number of places to stay in the valley and more transport along new and improving roads, visitors can see most of the traditional people, villages and customs, as well as all the mummies, markets, scenery, hanging bridges and wild pigs they want on day trips from Wamena, Jiwika, Manda and Kurima – and for a lot less than the cost of trekking.

Getting Around

Public Taksi Hopelessly overcrowded taksis go as far south as Kurima (18km); north on the western side of the valley to Pyramid (35km); and north on the eastern side to Manda (32km). Public transport tends to slow down to a trickle all around the valley after about 3 pm, and is less plentiful on Sunday. Almost no village or tourist attraction is signposted, so ask your taksi driver (or guide) to let you know when to get off.

The destinations of taksis are marked (and often coded), but they can still be confusing:

Baliem Valley – near Wamena 'Sinatma' taksis (code DK) go up Jl Yos Sudarso to the terminal at Sinatma (500Rp); 'Homhom/Pikhe' (HP) go to places just north of Wamena, as far as Pikhe (500Rp), but these taksis normally leave from a special stop along northern Jl Trikora. 'Wesaput' (aka Waisaput) (KW) go to Wesaput (500Rp) via Jl Pattimura.

Baliem Valley – South 'Sugokmo' taksis (SG) go to Hitigama (1500Rp) and Sugokmo (2000Rp). 'Kurima' go to that village (2500Rp) via Yetni.

Baliem Valley – West 'Kimbim' taksis (KP) travel to Kimbim (3000Rp). 'Pyramid' (4000Rp) go to that village, although you may need a connection in Kimbim. 'Ibele' (also KP) go to that village (2000Rp) via Elagaima (1500Rp).

Baliem Valley – East Taksis marked 'Wosilimo', 'Kurulu' and 'Tanahmerah' (all coded WL) stop near Aikima (1500Rp), and at Jiwika (2000Rp) and Wosilimo (2500Rp). 'Manda' (also WL) goes to Manda (3000Rp).

Chartered Taksi Chartering a taksi for about 15,000Rp per hour (a lot more for remote and rougher roads) is worth considering to avoid these sardine-cans-on-wheels, or to go to more-remote places. Paying for empty seats will always hurry up your departure (and make you very popular with other impatient passengers).

Mummies

Black, wizened mummies *(mumi)*, most at least 200 years old, are located in several villages around the region. They are worth a look, but one is pretty much the same as another. You will have to pay up to 10,000Rp to see one, and the display by the villagers is often disappointingly contrived and tourist-oriented. The most accessible mummy is at Sumpaima, just north of Jiwika. The one at Aikima is a bit broken, as is the one at Musatafak. The mummy at Pummo is the best preserved, but has reportedly been moved. If you wish to see more, ask the tourist offices for locations.

Markets

Attending a market in the countryside is a great way to meet locals, buy souvenirs and witness some Dani culture. (Don't be put off by the scruffy market in Wamena.) It's a good idea to check the market day with the tourist office in Wamena before you take a long trip out to a remote village. Markets usually start early and may be over, or less interesting, by noon. Markets are normally held in:

town	day
Bolokme	(Monday and Friday)
Jiwika	(Sunday)
Kelila	(Tuesday, Thursday and Saturday)
Kimbim	(Tuesday and Saturday)
Kurima	(Tuesday and Friday)
Manda	(Monday and Thursday)
Pyramid	(Saturday)
Tagime	(Tuesday and Friday)
Wosilimo	(Monday)

Hiking & Trekking

Wandering around the valleys and hills brings you into close contact with the Dani and makes even Wamena seem a distant metropolis! The Baliem Valley is outstanding hiking country, but travel light (or hire a porter) because the trails are often muddy and slippery. You have to clamber over stiles, often cross rivers by dugout canoe or log raft and traverse creeks or trenches on quaint footbridges, single rough planks or slippery logs. You can take one day or half-day trips, with or without a guide, from Wamena, Jiwika, Manda and Kurima, or go for longer guided treks around the Baliem Valley staying in villages or camping as you go.

IRIAN JAYA

Day Hikes – Without a Guide If you follow designated paths and/or roads, you can easily take a few short hikes without a guide. Some other possible short hikes are mentioned in the Pugima, Sinatma, Pikhe, Suroba & Dugum, Jiwika, Danau Anegerak and Manda entries later in this section.

Aikima-Suroba-Dugum-Mulima (four hours) – follow the foothills from Aikima to Dugum, then head back to the main road as far as Mulima.

Elagaima-Ibele (three hours) – just follow the main road.

Kimbim-Pummo (four hours) – mostly flat countryside.

Kelila-Bokondini (four hours) – you need to arrange transport to/from Wamena, but there's somewhere to stay in Kelila (see the Kelila entry later in this section).

Manda-Bugi (two hours).

Sugokmo-Kurima (two hours) – just follow the main road; there's somewhere to stay in Kurima (see the Kurima entry later).

Wamena-Hitigama (three hours) – walk down Jl Ahmad Yani from Wamena.

Day Hikes – With a Guide Only a few of the many possible day hikes are listed here. For these, you'll need a guide to find the best and most direct paths and bridges. You can hire a guide in Wamena, or a more knowledgeable one at the village you starting from.

Assologaima-Meagaima (four hours).

Bolokme-Tagime-Kelila (seven hours) – there's somewhere to stay in Kelila (see the Kelila entry later).

Kurima-Hitugi (three hours) – there's somewhere to stay in Kurima (see the Kurima entry later).

Meagaima (or Manda)-Bugi-Wolo (four hours).

Meagaima-Manda-Munak-Pyramid (four hours).

Pyramid-Pummo-Meagaima (four hours).

Sugokmo-Tangma (six hours).

Wolo-Ilugua (three hours) – about two-thirds of the way, a side track to the right leads around a huge sinkhole and down to **Gua Yogolok** and **Goundal**, a tiny village on the floor of an awesome canyon.

Wosilimo-Meagaima (two hours).

Longer Treks Following are just a few of the many possible two to seven day hikes around the Baliem Valley. You will need guides for these treks, and you'll have to arrange transport at one or both ends, or rely on public transport. Longer and more difficult treks to Danau Habbema, Yali country, Gunung Trikora and towards the Asmat region are described later in this section.

Pyramid-Tagime-Kelila (three to four days).

Kurima-Tangma-Wuserem-Senma-Sugokmo (four days).

Pyramid-Pietriver (three days).

Wamena-Kurima-Hitugi-Pugima-Wamena circle (two days).

Wosilimo-Pass Valley-Dombomi-Apahapsili Falls (seven days) – you may even see cenderawasih along this trail.

Guides & Porters A real cut-throat trekking industry has emerged in Wamena (although this does depend on the number of tourists in town). Guides will latch onto you as soon as you arrive off the plane in Wamena (and even in Sentani) and, if you show any interest, they will never let you go. Many travellers are being overcharged, and guides sometimes refuse to finish the trek until they're paid more than initially agreed. The situation is becoming so bad that the police station in Wamena intends to maintain a register of 'blacklisted' guides (but this is unlikely to work, because the guides will simply use different names when they approach you).

Before committing yourself to a guide: decide if you really want to go trekking (as opposed to taking day trips from Wamena and other villages); seek advice from other travellers and/or ask if they want to join you and share costs; visit the tourist office; and decide where you want to go and for how long.

If you're going off the main roads or paths, a guide is essential. There are no decent maps of the area and a guide can help decide where to go, facilitate communication with locals, find (or even create) places to stay, make sure you're on the right path and generally keep you informed about ceremonies, festivals etc. In addition, you'll get to know a local person. The tourist office in Wamena has a small list of 'licensed' guides, but the whole licensing and registration of guides is extremely haphazard.

The prices for guides have increased with the number of (often wealthy) tourists visiting the region. The 'official' price (according to the tourist office) is 50,000Rp per day for a 'professional' guide – one who has trekking experience; speaks English (sometimes Dutch) and several local languages; and genuinely knows the area you want to visit. Other guides who may not speak English will charge about 30,000Rp per day.

For more distant and difficult trekking, the rate increases by about 20,000Rp per day for any sort of guide. For shorter hikes in the countryside, you can usually hire a guide for about 5000Rp per hour – ask around the police station, village headquarters or market. The guide won't speak any English, but will know the area. If you hire a guide from Jayapura or Sentani, you may be liable for all his travel and accommodation expenses, before and after the trek.

Porters are a very good idea. In fact, you may need two porters per trekker: one for a backpack and another for camping and cooking gear, food etc. They cost about 15,000Rp per day. A cook (if your guide or porter refuses to cook) costs another 20,000Rp per day. You will have to provide enough food for all guides, porters and cooks, and anything left over at the end should be distributed among the 'staff'. A 10% tip at the end of a trek is expected.

You can organise a guide and a trek yourself, but bargain long and hard, and allow a couple of days in Wamena to arrange things. It's not a bad idea to test out a guide on a short hike before hiring him for a longer trek; also ask other travellers for recent recommendations of reliable guides.

Of course, the hassle can be avoided if you take an organised trek through a travel agency (see Organised Tours, following). Depending on your bargaining skills, knowledge of trekking in the valley and which agency you deal with, using a trekking company may not be much dearer than organising things yourself.

Organised Tours Several good – and not so good – travel and tour agencies are starting to spring up in Wamena (and in Jayapura and Sentani), catering to the lucrative organised trekking market. An agency can arrange (and pre-arrange with notice) completely packaged, all-inclusive trekking tours if you don't want the hassle of organising everything yourself, but they are usually more expensive. Don't forget that the tourist office is willing to provide impartial, free advice on anything to do with trekking.

A few reliable agencies, with the best range of treks around the Baliem Valley (and the Asmat region), are listed here.

Best Tours & Travels (☎ 32101, fax 32102), Jl Trikora, Wamena. Although still one of the more impressive outfits, Best is now seriously overpriced (about US$50 per person for day hikes around Wamena, and more for longer treks). It also has a branch at Sentani airport.

Chandra Nusantara Tours & Travel (☎ 31293, fax 31299), Jl Trikora 17, Wamena, is the original agent in town, and still one of the best value.

Dani Sangrila Tours & Travel arranges pricey trips from its office in Jayapura for about US$50 per person per day; less in a larger group.

Janice B Lani (☎ 31292) is a one-man agency, based at the Wamena Hotel in Wamena. He can arrange treks for a reasonable, but negotiable 70,000Rp per person per day.

What to Bring You can buy most things you need from Wamena's market and shops, such as food, bottled water and cooking gear. Everything is naturally more expensive in Wamena, so try stocking up in Sentani or Jayapura, or bring your own equipment and supplies from home. Take a torch (flashlight) if you want to explore any of the caves in the area. The nights are always cold and usually wet, so bring warm clothes and waterproof gear. And please make an effort to take out everything you bring in, and encourage your guides and porters to do the same.

The only place which rents trekking equipment is Best Tours & Travels (see Organised Tours earlier in this section), but prices are high: two-person tents are US$15 per day and sleeping bags are US$5. Eating equipment (cutlery and crockery) can also be hired, but not cooking equipment such as camping stoves.

Maps The only half-decent map is the *Tourist Map* (15,000Rp), available at Rannu Jaya Hotel. However, do *not* use it as a substitute for a knowledgeable guide: the map is not completely accurate, nor is it detailed enough for trekking.

Accommodation There are simple Dani-style huts in a few villages (see individual destination entries later in this section). Also, in many villages you can find a wooden bed in the house of a teacher or a leading family for about 10,000Rp per person, including basic meals. Ask at the village police station (if there is one) or ask the kepala desa (there is always one of these) where you should report. Your guide should know where to stay. Sleeping on the floor of Dani huts is also possible, but make sure you've been invited before entering a compound or any particular hut.

Missions can put you up in one or two places, but you're generally advised to try somewhere else. Guides can make temporary shelters from trees and rocks, but please ask them to respect the environment. The best idea is to bring or hire a tent because Dani huts and compounds are havens for all sorts of nasty insects. One traveller reported being badly bitten by fleas (from pigs) and she was still madly scratching fleabites two months later!

Food & Water Some larger villages have kiosks selling biscuits, canned drinks, noodles and rice. The last reliable supplies are at Manda on the north-east side of the valley; Kimbim on the north-west; and Kurima to the south. You can buy sweet potatoes along the way and a few other vegetables and eggs (and maybe a chicken) at local markets, but you'll need to bring other food yourself. Your guide should know where to find drinking water – bring tablets or filters to purify it, or cooking equipment to boil it. Bottles of mineral water are available in Wa-

mena, but very expensive and very heavy – and they inevitably end up littering the trails.

Baliem Valley – Near Wamena

Wesaput Almost a 'suburb' of Wamena, Wesaput is just across the other side of the airport. Take a path across the runway just before Hotel Syahrial Makmur and head south; or a path from the small cemetery at the end of Jl Gatot Subroto, then walk north. You'll need to clamber over the airport fence (like everyone else) and look for the huge, fading orange clock marking the start of the road to Wesaput. Alternatively, take a becak (about 3000Rp) or a public taksi.

About 300m along the road to Wesaput, on your right, is the indigenously run but poorly signed, *Wio Silimo Tradisional Hotel*, the best Dani-style place in the valley. The rooms cost 20,000Rp and are simple but varied, so ask to see a selection. It provides free transport in the evening to a restaurant of your choice in Wamena. One traveller was amused because the place is sometimes used by Dani couples for 'forbidden love affairs'.

At the end of the road, the traditionally-built and unmarked **Palimo Adat Museum** displays a small, interesting collection of Dani clothing, decorations and instruments. It's worth a look, if only because there's no other museum in the valley. A donation is expected (2000Rp should be enough) and it's open daily from 8 am to 4 pm, except Sunday.

At the back of the museum, the nearest **hanging bridge** to Wamena, strung across Sungai Baliem, is about 50m long and unstable at times. A tiny, impromptu **Dani market** is often set up by the bridge.

Pugima A one hour walk from the bridge at Wesaput leads to Pugima, which has a few Dani compounds (past the huge church). Although Pugima is not particularly interesting, the flat trail (with one small hill) provides an easy and convenient glimpse of Dani farms, villages and people, and of the magnificent scenery. Halfway along, behind a small lake with fish, you can explore **Gua Pugima**, an eerie cave.

Sinatma At the end of Jl Yos Sudarso, about 4km from Pasar Nayak, is the 'suburb' of Sinatma. Pasar Silimo, opposite the taksi terminal, is contrived and fairly dull. From the terminal, head right as you face Wamena and some easy **walking trails** take you to the raging Sungai Wamena, some pretty Dani compounds and dense woodlands. Near the small hydroelectric power station further up the hill, you can cross the river on a treacherous **hanging bridge**.

Baliem Valley – South
The area south of Wamena, hugging Sungai Baliem, probably has the most dramatic mountain scenery in the whole valley.

Hitigima Hitigima has a school and mission. A sign on the right as you head south, a few hundred metres past the church, leads to some **saltwater wells** *(air garam)*, similar to the ones at Jiwika (see the Jiwika entry later).

Sugokmo Near the bridge is a small **memorial** to a Japanese tourist and his Dani guide who drowned when a hanging bridge collapsed. A little further on is **Yetni** (the site of the Baliem Festival – refer to the boxed text earlier in this chapter).

Kurima The southern road finishes at Kurima. This charming village is a perfect base for **hiking** around the southern valley. *Kuak Cottages* can put you up for about 15,000Rp per person (meals are extra). It's a basic place, with a stunning setting overlooking Sungai Baliem. It's about 300m along the path from the end of the road in the village.

Baliem Valley – East
The road heading north along the eastern side of the valley is paved most of the way, but is terrible between Aikima and Mulima. Public transport stops at Manda.

Pikhe The area near the bridge in Pikhe is excellent for short **hikes**. Just before the bridge is the upmarket Honai Resort Hotel (see Places to Stay in the Wamena section earlier).

Aikima About 8km north of Wamena (further by road), just to the east of the road to Jiwika, is the fairly nondescript village of Aikima. It's famous for its 300-year-old **mummy**, but you will have to ask around and pay to see it – the mummy near Jiwika is more accessible and just as good.

Suroba & Dugum Just east of the main road, the pretty villages of Suroba and Dugum are worth exploring. Get off at the sign to Pondok Wisata Suroba Indah (see the Places to Stay entry later). The walk (15 minutes) along the path to the homestay goes through some of the nicest scenery you'll see around Wamena, and over two fascinating and intricate **hanging bridges** – one for locals and a more stable one for timid foreigners. At a clearing nearby, traditional **pig feasts** and **dancing** can be pre-arranged at substantial cost, mainly for packaged tours.

Jiwika Jiwika (pronounced 'Yiwika') is a local administrative centre, a pleasant base from which to explore the eastern valley, and a cheap, quiet alternative to Wamena. Ask around the village and you may be able to arrange a mock **fighting ceremony** between some villagers for about 60,000Rp.

About one hour up a steep path (with some scrambling at the top) from Jiwika, there are some **saltwater wells**. To extract the salt, banana stems are beaten dry of fluid and put in a pool to soak up the brine. The stem is then dried and burned and the ashes are collected and used as salt. If a local boy in Jiwika doesn't offer his services as a guide, ask one to show you the way and ask him if anyone will be working at the wells. Start the hike from Jiwika before 10 am. Tickets cost 1500Rp.

Places to Stay A few Dani-style places along the road between Aikima and Jiwika offer simple *local accommodation* – often just a wooden bed (maybe with no mattress), a floor full of straw and very basic, communal toilets. (Bathing is by bucket or in a nearby stream.) Beds cost 5000Rp to 10,000Rp per person; meals are extra.

The pretty and authentic *Pondok Wisata Suroba Indah* is just off the main road in Suroba, and one of the best – look for the sign from the main road. *Pondok Wisata Dani Homestay* on the main road near Wenabubuga, about 1km south of Jiwika, also has a nice setting, and rooms rather than huts – but it looks very neglected nowadays. *Wiyuk Huts* on the main road in southern Jiwika is authentic and well set up.

Losmen La'uk in Jiwika is not good value: very basic rooms without a bathroom cost 11,000Rp per person, and slightly better singles/doubles with bathroom cost 20,000/35,000Rp. Decent meals (10,000Rp) are available for guests if pre-ordered.

Jiwika to Wosilimo The road between Jiwika and Wosilimo is flanked by rocky hills full of unexplored **caves** and superb views of the valley. Although the road can be a little steep at times, the area is great for **hiking**.

Sumpaima, a few hundred metres north of Jiwika (look for the blue sign), has one of the better **mummies** near Wamena. The going price to view it is about 5000Rp.

At the back of an attractive Dani compound, **Gua Kotilola** apparently contains the bones of victims of a past tribal war. It costs 3000Rp to enter and is on the right as you head north, before Waga Waga, about 22km from Wamena. Ask the taksi driver to drop you off outside the compound and yell for someone to open the gate.

Wosilimo Wosilimo (or 'Wosi') is a major village with a few shops. **Gua Wikuda**, 500m along the trail to Pass Valley, have been developed by indigenous people who can take you for a tour inside. The entry fee is 3000Rp.

One hour on foot from Wosi, along a small path behind the church and over a hanging bridge, is **Danau Anegerak**. This lake is another great area for **hiking**, and locals rent basic **fishing** equipment and arrange simple accommodation in a Dani-style **hut** (about 10,000Rp per person, including meals).

Pass Valley A rough road continues from Wosi to Pass Valley. There is no public transport along this road, but it's a popular place for **trekking** (see Hiking & Trekking earlier in this section).

Manda Public transport stops at Manda, where there is a shop, loads of friendly people and some wonderful scenery to admire and **hike** around. You can stay in an authentic *Dani hut* for 10,000Rp per person, including meals; it's just behind the market, but isn't signposted.

Wolo Valley This is one of the most spectacular side valleys of Sungai Baliem. Inspired by a strong strain of Evangelical Protestantism, Wolo is a nonsmoking place with lovely flower gardens. There are plenty of great **hikes** in the area (see Hiking & Trekking earlier).

Baliem Valley – West

This side of the valley isn't as scenic for hiking or as interesting for day trips from Wamena by taksi; the road from Wamena to Pyramid is fairly dull (about a seven hour walk).

Kimbim Kimbim is a local administrative centre and is pleasant enough, with a few shops and a busy **market**. You may be able to find somewhere to stay if you ask at the police station or district office. Not far from Kimbim (ask directions), the village of **Araboda** has a mummy called 'Alongga Hubi'.

Pyramid About 3km from Kimbim, Pyramid is a graceful missionary village with churches, a theological college, an amazing airstrip carved from the hill and a bustling market. Some taksis from Wamena go directly to Pyramid, but you may have to get a connection in Kimbim. The road to Makki and beyond to Tiom has recently been completed, but public transport currently still stops at Pyramid.

Danau Habbema

Danau Habbema (3450m above sea level) offers wonderful **trekking** among unique flora (including orchids). You can walk around the lake and to nearby caves, such as **Gua Simalak** (or even to Gunung Trikora depending on regulations). Allow about five days return from Wamena and bring everything you need.

There are two ways to the lake: a trekking trail (about 50km) starts from Elagaima and goes through Ibele (where some taksis go) and Thalia; or a shorter, but rough, vehicular road starts from Sinatma and continues to Walaek, from where the road is sometimes passable as far as Pabilolo.

At the time of writing the lake was generally off limits to foreigners because of the activities of the Free Papua Movement (OPM). Some enthusiastic trekkers did manage to go there recently by hiring a police officer from Wamena as a guide-cum-escort – but allow a week to organise special permits in Wamena.

Gunung Trikora

At around 4750m, Trikora is just 300m shy of Puncak Jaya (5050m), Irian Jaya's highest peak. Experience, good equipment and a guide are essential – and a special permit is also required (the ordinary surat jalan for Irian Jaya specifically excludes permission to visit Trikora). A special permit can only be obtained from the army headquarters in Jakarta. Given plenty of notice, the tour agencies listed in the Jayapura and Around the Baliem Valley sections may be able to organise trips to Trikora.

NORTH OF THE BALIEM VALLEY

From Manda a decent road continues as far as Bolokme, but sturdy vehicles can continue to Kelila or even Bokondini, without too many problems. However, you will have to hitch, trek or charter something to go anywhere further than Manda. In Kelila, the pleasant *Pondok Wisata Dogobak* offers simple accommodation for about 15,000Rp per person, plus meals. About 20km west of Bokondini is Karubaga, which is linked to Wamena once a week by Merpati.

LANI COUNTRY (WEST DANI)

West along Sungai Baliem, upstream from Pyramid, is the country of the Western Dani who call themselves Lani. There are tracks to **Magi** from Kimbim, Pyramid and Bolokme. Between Sungai Pitt and Kuyawage, the Baliem disappears underground for 2km. **Ilaga**, about 60km west of Kuyawage, beyond the western Baliem watershed, is accessible by missionary flight from Nabire, Sentani and Wamena, but check whether your surat jalan will allow you to travel this far.

YALI COUNTRY

East and south of the Dani region are the Yali people, who live in rectangular houses and whose men wear 'skirts' of rattan hoops, with their penis gourds protruding from underneath. Missionaries are at work, but the Indonesian presence is thinner than in the Baliem Valley. Bordering the Yali on the east are the Kim-Yal people, who practised cannibalism up until the 1970s.

Reaching Yali country on foot involves plenty of ups and downs along steep trails. **Pronggoli**, the nearest centre from Wamena as the crow flies, is a three-day hard slog by the most direct route, with camping necessary along the way. From Pronggoli to **Angguruk** takes another day. It's then relatively easy trekking from Angguruk to nearby villages, such as **Panggele**, **Psekni**, **Tulukima** and **Tenggil**.

Easier but longer (about seven days) is a southern loop through Kurima-Tangma-Wet-Soba-Ninia, then north to Angguruk. Another popular trek includes Kosarek-Serkasi-Telambela-Membahan-Helariki-Angguruk (about six days). You can reduce this tough trek by trying to get on a missionary flight (more likely if you're on an organised tour) to Kosarek or Angguruk. You can usually rely on a *hut* belonging to a local family or a teacher's house for somewhere to stay in the region, but bring all your own food.

FAR SOUTH

It's at least a two-week trek from Wamena down to Dekai via Soba, Holuon and Sumo. From **Dekai**, it is possible to **canoe** downriver as far as Senggo on the fringes of the Asmat region, and then take a motorboat to

Agats on the south coast of Irian Jaya. You will need a special surat jalan, and be on an organised (and expensive) tour.

Eastern Irian Jaya

Many travellers come to this part of Irian Jaya just to get a connection to Wamena in the Baliem Valley, but Sentani and Jayapura and the surrounding areas, as well as the interior near Merauke have a lot to offer. Adventurous travellers with loads of time and money are also starting to trickle down to the remote, swampy Asmat region, with its unique people and culture.

JAYAPURA
☎ 0967

In Dutch times, Jayapura was known as Hollandia (it then became Soekarnopura and Kota Baru), and was deliberately placed just a few kilometres from the border with German New Guinea to emphasise the Dutch claim to the western half of the island. In April 1944 the Allies stormed ashore at Hamadi and captured the town after only token resistance from the Japanese (see the boxed text 'Irian Jaya during WWII' earlier in this chapter).

As the capital of Irian Jaya, Jayapura is dominated by non-Irianese and looks similar to most medium-sized Indonesian cities, although it is pleasantly situated around Teluk Yos Sudarso and is surrounded by steep hills. There's little reason to stay in Jayapura, because Sentani is nicer and more convenient, but you'll probably have to visit to book air or boat tickets, and collect a surat jalan for the Baliem Valley.

Orientation

Just about everything you will need – most hotels, shops, restaurants, airline offices, and the police station – is confined to the parallel main streets of Jl Ahmad Yani and Jl Percetakan. Along the waterfront, Jl Koti leads to Hamadi in the east, past the port; and Jl Sam Ratulangi heads north towards Tanjung Ria, past some government buildings,

to areas called Dok I to Dok V. A few other facilities, most government buildings and the taksi terminal are strung along the main road to Abepura.

Information

Tourist Offices The tourist office (☎ 33381, ext 2441) can provide brochures (which are often unavailable in the individual district tourist offices) in English, Dutch, German and Japanese about most districts in Irian Jaya. It's on the ground floor at the far southern end of the Governor's Office (*Kantor Gubernor*) complex at Jl Soa Siu, Dok II. It's open weekdays from 7 am to 2.30 pm. Take a chartered or public taksi north along Jl Sam Ratulangi.

Documents A surat jalan is not required if you visit only Jayapura and Sentani, but Jayapura is the final place to obtain one for the Baliem Valley and many places further south or west. The permit is easy to get, usually while you wait.

Go to the Foreigners' Service office at the back of the local polres (☎ 31027) on Jl Ahmad Yani. Give the police officer a photocopy of the inside page of your passport (ie with your personal details) and your Indonesian tourist card, two passport-sized photos, and a 2500Rp to 5000Rp 'administration fee' (depending on how quickly you want the permit processed).

The office is open Monday to Friday from 7 am to 3 pm but if you ask nicely and pay an extra 'fee' the permit can be obtained up until 7 pm weekdays, and during normal working hours on weekends. If you're in a real hurry or unsure of the process, some travel agencies and hotels in Sentani and Jayapura may be able to obtain a surat jalan, even at short notice, for a negotiable fee. Go to the provincial polda station on Jl Sam Ratulangi for a surat jalan if you have a Business Visa, or any other type of special visa (ie not a tourist card).

A few shops in central Jayapura and Sentani take passport photos and it's a good idea to take a few photocopies of your surat jalan for the police after you arrive in Wamena.

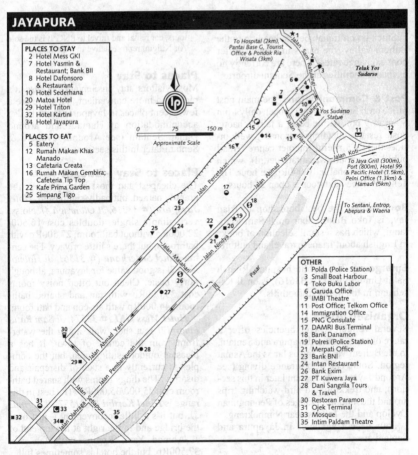

JAYAPURA

PLACES TO STAY
2 Hotel Mess GKI
7 Hotel Yasmin & Restaurant; Bank BII
8 Hotel Dafonsoro & Restaurant
10 Hotel Sederhana
20 Matoa Hotel
29 Hotel Triton
32 Hotel Kartini
34 Hotel Jayapura

PLACES TO EAT
5 Eatery
12 Rumah Makan Khas Manado
13 Cafetaria Creata
16 Rumah Makan Gembira; Cafeteria Tip Top
22 Kafe Prima Garden
25 Simpang Tigo

OTHER
1 Polda (Police Station)
3 Small Boat Harbour
4 Toko Buku Labor
6 Garuda Office
9 IMBI Theatre
11 Post Office; Telkom Office
14 Immigration Office
15 PNG Consulate
17 DAMRI Bus Terminal
18 Bank Danamon
19 Polres (Police Station)
21 Merpati Office
23 Bank BNI
24 Intan Restaurant
26 Bank Exim
27 PT Kuwera Jaya
28 Dani Sangrila Tours & Travel
30 Restoran Paramon
31 Ojek Terminal
33 Mosque
35 Intim Paldam Theatre

To Hospital (2km), Pantai Base G, Tourist Office & Pondok Ria Wisata (3km)

Teluk Yos Sudarso

Yos Sudarso Statue

To Jaya Grill (300m), Port (800m), Hotel 99 & Pacific Hotel (1.5km), Pelni Office (1.3km) & Hamadi (5km)

To Sentani, Entrop, Abepura & Waena

Approximate Scale
0   75   150 m

Jalan Sam Ratulangi
Jalan Halmahera
Jalan Koti
Jalan Ahmad Yani
Jalan Percetakan
Jalan Matahari
Jalan Nirdya
Jalan Ahmad Yani
Jalan Pembangunan
Jalan Setiapura
Jalan Olahraga
Pasar

PNG Consulate The consulate of Papua New Guinea (☎ 31250), Jl Percetakan 28, (look for the flag) is open weekdays from 8 am to noon and 1 to 4 pm. Currently a PNG visa for a maximum of two months can be issued to most nationalities within 24 hours. You will need one photograph, 20,000Rp and proof of a ticket out of PNG (either by boat or plane).

Immigration The Immigration Office (*Kantor Imigrasi*, ☎ 21647), Jl Percetakan

15, is open weekdays from 8 am to 4 pm. You will probably have to go there to collect an exit stamp if you take the boat to Vanimo – check with the PNG Consulate first.

Money Changing money at Bank Exim or at Bank Danamon is quick and painless. The best banks are on Jl Percetakan: BNI bank, which also accepts cash advances and has an automatic teller machine (ATM) for MasterCard and Cirrus cards; and Bank Internasional Indonesia (BII), next to Hotel

Yasmin, which offers the same facilities for Visa, MasterCard and Alto cards.

Stock up on rupiah before heading to the Baliem Valley (the banks in Wamena offer poor exchange rates). There are currently no exchange facilities at the Sentani airport.

Post & Communications The main post office on Jl Sam Ratulangi is open daily from 8 am to 9 pm. At the back, a fairly chaotic poste restante functions reasonably well; inside, there's a useful Internet centre (email publik@jayapura.wasantara.net.id), which charges a reasonable 10,000Rp per hour. The Telkom office next door is open 24 hours.

Bookshops The best bookshop in Irian Jaya is Toko Buku Labor on Jl Sam Ratulangi, which has a small selection of books in English about Irianese travel and culture.

Emergency The public hospital, Rumah Sakit Umum Pusat (☎ 33616), is on Jl Kesehatan in the northern foothills.

Organised Tours

Several reliable travel agencies offer a range of tours around Jayapura and Sentani, to the Baliem Valley and as far as the Asmat region. Some can also arrange diving (see Around Jayapura & Sentani later in this section); and trekking and bird-watching trips around the mountain ranges of Penungunan Cyclop and the forests near Nimbokrang.

Four decent agencies in Jayapura and Sentani are:

Best Tours & Travels is one of the best organised, but now most expensive, agencies for tours to the Baliem Valley. It has an office at Sentani airport (☎/fax 91861), which is only staffed when a plane arrives, and an office in Wamena.

Dani Sangrila Tours & Travel (☎ 31060, fax 31529), Jl Pembangunan 19, Jayapura, is good for expensive tours to the Baliem Valley and Asmat region.

Grand Irian Tours & Travel (☎ 36459, fax 36387, email g_irian@jayapura.wasantara.net.id), Jl Batu Putih 49, Jayapura, runs pricey day trips around Jayapura and Sentani (about US$45 per person) and trips to the Baliem Valley for about US$80 per person per night.

PT Kuwera Jaya (☎ 31583, fax 32236), Jl Ahmad Yani 39, Jayapura, is especially good for diving tours, car rental and travel to PNG. It is the sole Air Nuigini representative in Irian Jaya.

Places to Stay

Most visitors stay in Sentani because it's nicer and more convenient, but there are a few decent places in Jayapura. There is also accommodation at Hamadi and around Danau Sentani (see Around Jayapura & Sentani later in this section).

Places to Stay – Budget

The cheapest and most basic place is the grandly named, but badly signposted, *Hotel Jayapura* (☎ 33216, Jl Olahraga 4). Noisy, very simple singles/doubles cost 16,500/22,000Rp without bathroom; 27,500Rp with bathroom, but there's little privacy. The central *Hotel Sederhana* (☎ 31561, Jl Halmahera 2) is good value for Jayapura, although fairly basic. Clean but often noisy rooms cost 33,000Rp with fan and shared bathroom; 44,000Rp with air-con and bathroom.

Hotel Mess GKI (☎ 33574, Jl Sam Ratulangi 12) is a short walk along the waterfront from the centre of town. It has a pleasant outdoor sitting area, but the complex is currently in a state of disrepair and disarray. The dingy rooms with shared bathroom cost 25,000/35,000Rp. The best in this range is *Hotel Kartini* (☎ 31557, Jl Perintis 2), but it's a little inconvenient – just over the bridge and to the right at the top end of Jl Ahmad Yani. Rooms with fan cost 37,500Rp, but the hotel is sometimes full.

Places to Stay – Mid-Range & Top End

One of the best in the mid-range is the central and helpful *Hotel Dafonsoro* (☎ 31695, fax 34055, Jl Percetakan 20). All rooms have air-con, and singles/doubles cost from 69,300/82,500; triples cost 99,000Rp. *Hotel Triton* (☎ 33218, Jl Ahmad Yani 50) is old and the staff are perennially surly, but it's popular with visiting Indonesians. Rooms with air-con and satellite TV cost from 49,500/71,500Rp to 88,000/99,000Rp for the 'suite'.

On the road to Hamadi, only a few minutes by taksi from Jayapura, two places have the potential for great views, but most rooms don't have any. *Hotel 99* (☎ 35689) has tiny rooms priced from 27,500/42,000Rp without bathroom; better rooms cost 55,000/77,500Rp with air-con and bathroom. Next door, *Pacific Hotel* (☎ 35427) has a good range of rooms (many will have views if the renovations are ever completed) starting from a reasonable 45,000Rp, with air-con.

The flashiest place is *Matoa Hotel* (☎ 31633, fax 31437, Jl Ahmad Yani 14). Rooms start from 132,000/174,000Rp, which is not that expensive these days; the 'suite' costs 278,000Rp. It's far better value than the new *Hotel Yasmin* (☎ 33222, Jl Percetakan 8), which officially charges from US$50 per room, but negotiation and payment in rupiah is possible.

Places to Eat

Along Jl Ahmad Yani, and around the waterfront, *warungs* serve cheap and tasty *gado gado* (vegetables with spicy peanut sauce) and *nasi campur* (rice 'with the lot'). Plenty of *food stalls* along Jl Nindya also sell delicious, filling nasi campur and baked fish from about 4000Rp. Along the top of Jl Pembangunan there are several *rumah makans* huddled together, but none of them are particularly good; there's also an undercover *eatery* opposite the Garuda office.

Along Jl Percetakan, *Rumah Makan Gembira* and *Cafetaria Tip Top* next door are cheap and unpretentious places for decent Indonesian food, as is *Simpang Tigo*, down the road. *Cafetaria Creata* on Jl Irian also serves cheap Indonesian food and tasty fruit drinks. Scrumptious cakes and strong Irianese coffee or Indonesian tea can be enjoyed at the quaint and relaxed *Kafe Prima Garden* on Jl Ahmad Yani.

Of the hotels, the restaurant in *Hotel Dafonsoro* is one of the best value places for range, price and setting. Indonesian food costs about 8000Rp; other dishes are 10,000Rp to 14,000Rp. The restaurant in *Hotel Yasmin* is stylish but expensive – western food costs 15,000Rp to 22,000Rp.

For a splurge – seafood dishes from 12,000Rp and great views across the harbour – try *Jaya Grill*, on the way to the port. For the same views, but without the high prices, cosy *Rumah Makan Khas Manado* on Jl Koti is recommended. *Pondok Ria Wisata*, on the other side of the bay opposite the tourist office, is also worth trying.

Entertainment

Karaoke machines are big business in Jayapura. You'll find them, as well as 'hostess girls', at bars on Jl Percetakan, such as *Restoran Paramon* and *Intan Restaurant*. *IMBI Theatre* on Jl Halmahera and *Intim Paldam Theatre* on Jl Setiapura show newish films with Indonesian subtitles.

Getting There & Away

Air As the capital of Irian Jaya, Jayapura is well connected to the rest of Indonesia. Several times a week, Merpati flies between Jayapura and Denpasar (1,449,000Rp) or Jakarta (1,944,300Rp), with stops at Biak (327,000Rp), Ambon (867,000Rp), Manado (1,031,000Rp), Timika (296,200Rp) and/or Ujung Pandang (1,350,000Rp). Merpati also has daily flights to Wamena (see the Wamena entry later in this section); and several a week to Nabire and Merauke. The efficient Merpati office (☎ 33220) on Jl Ahmad Yani is open every day from about 7.30 am to noon and 1 to 7 pm.

Four times a week, Garuda flies between Jayapura and Denpasar, with stops at Biak and Ujung Pandang, for the same price as Merpati – but Garuda planes are considerably more comfortable. The Garuda office (☎ 36217) is open Monday to Saturday from 9 am to 6 pm and until 3 pm on Sunday.

All flights leave from the Sentani airport in nearby Sentani (see the Sentani entry later).

Wamena Merpati is the only passenger airline, but the cargo service, Trigana, is a useful alternative. Trigana's unimpressive office (☎ 91343) is in a hangar in Sentani (see the Sentani map). The missionary service AMA (☎ 91009) has flights to Nabire and more obscure places like Ilaga and

Enarotali, but not to Wamena; MAF (☎ 91109) flies to Wamena. Both offices are in Sentani.

See Getting There & Away in the Wamena section earlier in this chapter for full details about flights to/from Wamena.

Boat Naturally, all boats head west from Jayapura. Every two weeks, the Pelni liners *Ciremai* and *Dobonsolo* go to Biak (59,000/170,500Rp for economy/1st class); and the *Rinjani* and *Umsini* stop at Serui and Nabire – but not Biak.

The port is about 800m east of the Yos Sudarso statue, and the new Pelni office is about 500m further on – a public taksi to Hamadi will take you to both places. It is easier to buy Pelni tickets from agencies around the port or in town eg Dani Sangrila (see Organised Tours earlier in this section) for an extra fee.

Perintis boats also leave Jayapura every week or so and stop at Serui, Nabire, Biak and Manokwari – they normally leave from the main Pelni port. Other smaller boats to Sarmi, Serui, Nabire and Biak leave from the small boat harbour along Jl Sam Ratulangi.

PNG Air Niugini recently cancelled flights between Jayapura and Vanimo, so the only way to cross the 'border' is by boat – the introductory Getting There & Away section of this chapter has details.

Getting Around
To/From the Airport A private taxi from Sentani airport to Jayapura will cost a whopping 40,000Rp. Try sharing with other equally stunned passengers or take a public taksi (see the Sentani section later).

Bus & Taksi Taksis to all places near Jayapura leave every second or two from stops along Jl Ahmad Yani and Jl Sam Ratulangi. Trips around the city cost about 500Rp. See Getting Around under Sentani later for details about catching public taksis between Jayapura and Sentani.

Twice a day, large Damri buses travel between Jayapura and the remote transmigration centres of Genyem and Demta, via Sentani. These buses save the hassle of changing taksis between Jayapura and Sentani (or vice versa), but travel times are infrequent and inflexible. Schedules are available at the DAMRI terminal in Jayapura, and at Toko Angkasa, on the main road in Sentani, where the bus stops.

Ojek A ride on an *ojek* (a motorbike taking paying pillion passengers) is a quick and easy way to get around. There is an ojek terminal opposite the mosque, at the southern end of Jl Ahmad Yani.

SENTANI
☎ 0967
Sentani, a small town 36km west of Jayapura, with the airport and magnificent Danau Sentani nearby, is a better place to stay than Jayapura – it's quieter, cooler and more convenient, and has most (but not all) of the facilities you'll need.

Orientation
Sentani is very compact, and easy to walk around. Most shops, restaurants and offices are on the main road to Jayapura, Jl Kemiri Sentani Kota. The market and taksi terminal are a short ride to the west by taksi or ojek.

Information
The information booth at the Sentani airport is open daily from 5 am to 5 pm, and useful for general inquiries. The police station (☎ 91105) is at the entrance to the airport, but you must go to Jayapura for a surat jalan for the Baliem Valley. Bank Exim changes money on weekday mornings, and Rumah Makan Mickey will change crisp new US dollar notes for an acceptable wad of rupiah.

The post office (with a poste restante) is open Monday to Saturday from 8 am to 5.30 pm. The 24 hour Telkom office is one block behind it. See Organised Tours in the Jayapura section earlier for a list of reliable travel agencies in Jayapura and Sentani.

Places to Stay
Many places in Sentani will give you a free lift to/from the airport if you pre-arrange it,

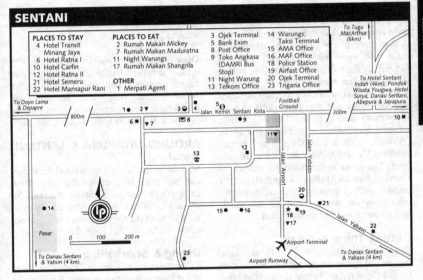

SENTANI

PLACES TO STAY	PLACES TO EAT
4 Hotel Transit Minang Jaya	2 Rumah Makan Mickey
6 Hotel Ratna I	7 Rumah Makan Maduratna
10 Hotel Carfin	11 Night Warungs
12 Hotel Ratna II	17 Rumah Makan Shangrila
21 Hotel Semeru	
22 Hotel Mansapur Rani	**OTHER**
	1 Merpati Agent

3 Ojek Terminal
5 Bank Exim
8 Post Office
9 Toko Angkasa (DAMRI Bus Stop)
11 Night Warung
13 Telkom Office
14 Warungs; Taksi Terminal
15 AMA Office
16 MAF Office
18 Police Station
19 Airfast Office
20 Ojek Terminal
23 Trigana Office

To Tugu MacArthur (6km)

To Hotel Sentani Indah (4km), Pondok Wisata Yougwa, Hotel Surya, Danau Sentani, Abepura & Jayapura

To Doyo Lama & Depapre

Jalan Kemiri Sentani Kota

Football Ground

Jalan Yabaso

Jalan Airport

Pasar

Airport Terminal

Airport Runway

To Danau Sentani & Yahim (4 km)

To Danau Sentani & Yabaso (4 km)

---

or ring them from the airport. In any case, most hotels are within a 15 minute walk of the airport. The main road through Sentani is very busy, so any hotel nearby will be noisy. There is also accommodation at Danau Sentani (see Around Jayapura & Sentani later in this section).

Hotel Ratna I (☎ 91435, Jl Kemiri Sentani Kota 7) has air-conditioned singles/doubles, often without outside windows, for 33,000/44,000Rp, but this isn't good value. If you need a surat jalan in a hurry, staff here have 'connections'. The newer version, *Hotel Ratna II* (☎ 92277, fax 91200), has sparkling rooms with air-con and satellite TV for 71,500/93,500Rp (104,500Rp per double with hot water), but they overlook a charmless courtyard.

Just off the main road, *Hotel Transit Minang Jaya* (☎ 91067) offers friendly, helpful service. Small rooms, some without windows, cost 38,500/44,000Rp with shared bathroom; 44,000/49,500Rp with bathroom. The rooms with air-con for 55,000/66,000Rp are the nicest. The best in the budget range was *Hotel Mansapur Rani* (☎ 91219, Jl Yabaso 113), but it apparently burnt down. At the time of writing, new rooms at the back were being built, but they will probably cost from 50,000Rp.

Hotel Semeru (☎ 91447, fax 92098, Jl Yabaso), a three minute walk from the airport is recommended. Clean, comfortable rooms with hot water cost 44,000Rp with fan; 59,500Rp with air-con; and 71,500Rp with air-con and satellite TV. *Hotel Carfin* (☎ 91478) is on the main road, about 800m east of the post office. Rooms with air-con and TV are modern but dark, and aren't particularly good value for 68,000/80,000Rp.

The top-notch place is *Hotel Sentani Indah* (☎ 91900, fax 92828), an extraordinary, incongruous monstrosity about 4km from Sentani, on the road to Jayapura. The rooms are luxurious, but the official rate of US$102/116 is not good value, although it's worth considering if you can pay in rupiah ie 255,000/285,000Rp.

Places to Eat

Around the market and opposite the football ground, just back from the main road, *night warungs* set up for dinner in the late afternoon. There are a few nondescript Padang-style *rumah makans* along the main road. A few other places along, or just off, the main road serve baked fish with rice and vegetables for around 5000Rp – the best is *Rumah Makan Maduratna*.

Rumah Makan Mickey remains the most popular place for travellers and expats. Indonesian food costs 5000Rp to 8000Rp; western food, such as seafood and steak costs 16,000Rp to 22,000Rp. It also boasts satellite TV and a reliable supply of cold beer. The latter two attractions cannot be found at *Rumah Makan Shrangila*, but it's understandably popular with missionaries who enjoy the (average) pizzas and excellent Chinese and Indonesian food.

Getting There & Away
The Merpati agent (☎ 91314) can take money for bookings already made, but to book a flight (eg to Wamena) go to the Merpati office in Jayapura. Refer to Getting There & Away in the Jayapura section earlier for details about travelling by plane to Sentani and by boat to Jayapura.

Getting Around
To/From the Airport A private taxi from the airport to Sentani costs 7500Rp, but you can easily walk to most hotels, or arrange for hotel staff to collect you.

Public Taksi Public transport to regional villages leaves from the taksi terminal in western Sentani, but vehicles take some time to fill up before leaving.

Travelling from Sentani to Jayapura (and vice versa) involves a confusing combination of taksis. Firstly, catch one from anywhere along the streets of Sentani towards the terminal in Abepura (1200Rp); get off along the main road, just before the terminal, and hop on another to the chaotic terminal in Entrop (700Rp); and get off just before this terminal, and take another to central Jayapura (500Rp). It may sound complicated, but it works relatively easily (many locals will be doing it too), and takes

about one hour. If in doubt, tell the boy who takes your money in the taksi where you want to go.

Ojek A convenient way to get around is by ojek. The drivers can take you to Yabaso or the taksi terminal and market in Sentani for 1000Rp, or anywhere else, such as Tugu MacArthur (see Gunung Ifu under Around Jayapura & Sentani), for a negotiable fare.

AROUND JAYAPURA & SENTANI
☎ 0967
Several interesting places around the region can be easily reached on day trips from Jayapura or Sentani. Chartering a taksi for about 15,000Rp per hour is an easy way to visit some of the more remote places, or see a few nearby sights in one day.

Diving & Snorkelling
PT Kuwera Jaya (refer to Organised Tours in the Jayapura section earlier) is still trying to establish regular diving trips around the region. Currently they charge about US$50/85 for half-day/one day trips, including equipment and transport to/from your hotel in Jayapura or Sentani. Two excellent spots for diving and snorkelling among stunning coral and fish are around Tanjung Ria (aka Pantai Base G) and Depapre (see Depapre later in this section).

Museums
Museum Loka Budaya (Cultural Museum) contains a fascinating range of Irianese artefacts, including the best collection of Asmat carvings outside of Agats. It's open weekdays from 7.30 am to 4 pm; entry is 1500Rp (5000Rp for a video or still camera). It's in the grounds of Cenderawasih University (in the closest building to Jayapura, on the western side of the road) in Abepura. Take the Sentani-Abepura taksi, almost as far as the Abepura terminal.

Museum Negeri (State Museum) in Waena is also worth a visit. There is a small but excellent selection of carvings, clothing, boats and weaving, and artefacts from all over Irian Jaya, as well as from the Dutch colonial past.

AROUND JAYAPURA & SENTANI

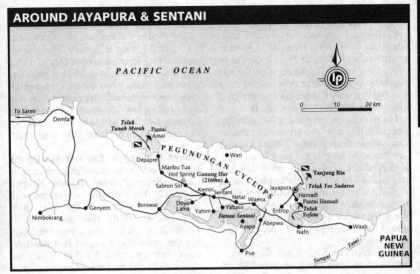

Captions are in English. The museum is still being developed and will take several years to complete. A small shop inside sells souvenirs and books; entry costs 750Rp.

Next door, **Taman Budaya** (Cultural Park) consists of neglected traditional houses representing each of the nine districts of Irian Jaya. Entry is free, so have a look around if you're going to the Museum Negeri.

The Museum Negeri and Taman Budaya have the same opening hours – Tuesday to Saturday from 8 am to 4 pm; Sunday from 10 am to 4 pm. They are on the main road between Sentani and Abepura, and are easy to spot from the taksi.

Pantai Base G

Made famous by General MacArthur, Base G Beach is known locally as Pantai Tanjung Ria. The beach is wide, and desolate except on Sunday when locals come in their hundreds for a picnic and walk. Taksis regularly head north along Jl Sam Ratulangi in Jayapura for the pleasant trip to Tanjung Ria; ask to be dropped off at the beach, which is a 10 minute walk down the hill.

Depapre

Set under the dramatic mountain ranges of Pegunungan Cyclop, the pretty village of Depapre is an enjoyable and easy day trip. From the village jetty you can charter boats or canoes to explore the sheltered Teluk Tanah Merah for some **snorkelling** (bring your own gear). A 5km track from the back of the village leads to the secluded **Pantai Amai**.

Taksis (one hour) leave about every hour from the taksi terminal in Sentani. You can easily stop along the way and visit other pretty villages, such as **Maribua Tua**, and the **hot springs** at Sabron Siri.

Danau Sentani

The magnificent Danau Sentani is in itself worth a trip to Jayapura/Sentani. As you fly into Sentani you will see the 9,630 hectare lake, its 19 islands, and fishing villages such as Ayapo, full of wooden houses precariously raised on stilts above the water. No organised tours are available, so you'll have to explore the lake yourself – but it's certainly worth the effort. The lake is particularly beautiful and photogenic at dusk and dawn.

IRIAN JAYA

Boat Trips A boat trip is the best way to enjoy the lake and visit some of the islands and villages. From Yahim harbour, a short ride south of the taksi terminal in Sentani, motorboats with room for five people can be rented for about 30,000Rp per hour, but you may have to spend some time looking for a boat and boatman. Canoes are also available and cost far less, but you can't go far.

The most convenient and reliable option, especially if you're in a group, is to charter a motorboat from Pondok Wisata Yougwa (see Places to Stay & Eat later in this section). A reliable boat holding up to nine people, and a knowledgeable guide, can be hired for a reasonable 60,000Rp per hour. From Pondok Wisata Yougwa, you can also hire a *sepeda air* (water bicycle) to paddle around for 5500Rp to 8500Rp per hour (depending on size).

By boat, you can visit simple, friendly villages such as **Doyo Lama**, renowned for the manufacture of impressive, large **woodcarvings** and for 'unexplained' **rock paintings** nearby. Taksis to Doyo Lama leave from the terminal in Sentani two or three times a day, except Sunday. Alternatively, take a regular taksi to Kemiri, along the main road to Depapre, and walk about 4km to Doyo Lama.

Hiking The other way to really explore the lake is to hike. From Hotel Mansapur Rani in Sentani, continue along Jl Yabaso, virtually parallel to the runway, for an easy 40 minute stroll. The path goes through the village of **Yabaso**, then to the shores of the lake and continues around the lake for another few kilometres through several villages. At the end of the path (90 minutes from Sentani), you may find a public boat (or charter one) across the lake to a point close to Pondok Wisata Yougwa (see under Places to Stay & Eat later in this section).

Gunung Ifar For breathtaking views of Danau Sentani, visit **Tugu MacArthur** on top of Gunung Ifar. Here, as the legend goes, MacArthur sat and contemplated his WWII strategies – a plaque states (a little strangely): 'Here stood the Headquarters of General Douglas MacArthur and Task Force reckless during the Pacific War'.

The road to the top (about 500m east of the football ground in Sentani) is unmarked and is a very steep 6km (don't try to walk). Taksis to the top are irregular, but more frequent on Sunday when the area is a popular picnic spot. Alternatively, charter a taksi or ojek. Just before you reach the monument you may have to report to a local military office and deposit your surat jalan or passport.

Places to Stay & Eat Overlooking the lake, just off the Sentani-Abepura road, is the charming *Pondok Wisata Yougwa* (☎ 71570). The sparkling new rooms, with lake views (but close to the noisy main road) are 85,000Rp (the largest one is 125,000Rp), and includes a great breakfast. For this price you'd expect (but don't receive) hot water and TV, but the air-con works well. The *restaurant* has wonderful views and is definitely worth visiting for lunch or dinner. Meals are reasonably priced; the fresh fish meals for 9500Rp are heartily recommended. The hotel is unmarked, just past the '23km to Jayapura' sign from Sentani.

Also on the Sentani-Abepura road (about 1km towards Jayapura from Pondok Wisata Yougwa) is *Hotel Surya* (☎ 71429). It's on the opposite side of the road from the lake and the rooms for 33,000/44,000Rp with fan/air-con have no views.

Hamadi

Hamadi's bustling, scruffy daily **market** is one of the most fascinating in the area. Plenty of stalls along the main road sell souvenirs, including tacky mass-produced Baliem and Asmat art (you'll find better stuff in Wamena). From Hamadi, you can charter a boat to one of the tiny islands, such as **Kayu Pulau** (curiously not called, as expected, Pulau Kayu).

Pantai Hamadi, the site of a US amphibious landing on 22 April 1944, is another two minutes' drive past the market. The beach is pleasant, if a little dirty, but it has some inviting **islands** close by, rusting **WWII**

wrecks along the beach to explore, and a **WWII statue** not far away. At the start of the trail to the beach, you'll have to report to the military station and deposit your surat jalan.

On both sides of the noisy main road in Hamadi, *Hotel Asia (☎ 35478)* has rooms from 33,000Rp with fan and bathroom; 49,500Rp with TV and air-con. Overlooking the sea, *Mahkota Beach Hotel (☎ 32997)* costs from 137,500/176,000Rp for luxurious singles/doubles. If you feel like a splurge in a splendid setting, the *restaurant* is not too expensive – about 15,000Rp for seafood, and 8000Rp for Indonesian food.

A taksi heads along Jl Koti in Jayapura to Hamadi every few seconds; you can also catch one directly to Hamadi from the terminal at Entrop.

Temples

Halfway along the Abepura-Entrop road, it's worth getting off the taksi and looking around two temples, if only for the magnificent views of Teluk Yofeta. The Buddhist **Vihara Arya Dharma** temple was not built in any classical style, but the setting and views are worth climbing up the steep, short trail.

About 300m further towards Jayapura, on the other side of the road, a Hindu temple, **Pura Agung Surya Bhuvana,** is also fairly standard, but the views and setting are also more than enough reason to walk up there.

MERAUKE
☎ 0971
Merauke is a pleasant, laid-back place, renowned as the most eastern town in Indonesia. There is very little to do, but it's a starting point for trips into the interior, particularly to the Asmat region. **Pantai Lampu Satu**, a 5km walk (or take an irregular mikrolet) west of the Bank Exim building in Merauke, is great for sunsets. If you don't mind an audience, you can also bathe in the **hot springs**, about 200m in front of Hotel Asmat.

Orientation & Information

Merauke has no town centre and virtually everything you will need is on the *very* long Jl Raya Mandala. Bank Exim at the bottom

of Jl Raya Mandala is the only place to change money. A surat jalan is needed before you arrive (get it in Jayapura). The police station (☎ 21706), near Hotel Nirmala, handles extra permits for the interior. The tourist office (☎ 21388) is on Jl A Yani.

Places to Stay & Eat

Losmen Merauke (Jl Raya Mandala 340) offers very, very basic singles/doubles without bathroom for 22,000/25,000Rp. *Hotel Asmat (☎ 21065, Jl Trikora 3)* is the best place, and has comfortable rooms with character for 24,500/32,500Rp; slightly more with bathroom. Along Jl Raya Mandala, air-con rooms priced at about 45,000/60,000Rp can be found at *Hotel Megaria (☎ 21932)* at No 166; *Hotel Nirmala (☎ 21 849)* at No 66; and *Flora Hotel (☎ 21879)* at No 294.

Plenty of *warungs* around the port serve simple, cheap meals, and *food stalls* at Pasar Ampera sell delicious nasi campur. Along Jl Raya Mandala, *Beautiful Nusantara Restaurant*, near the Flora, is good, but has a blasted karaoke machine; *Rumah Makan Sari Laut*, near the Megaria, serves delicious baked fish for about 5000Rp.

Getting There & Away

Air Merpati flies between Merauke and Jayapura (423,800Rp) four times a week; and weekly to regional centres, such as Ewer (for the Asmat region). The Merpati office (☎ 21242) is at Jl Raya Mandala 226. There continues to be speculation about sea and air links between Merauke and nearby Darwin and/or Cairns in northern Australia; unfortunately they are still only rumours.

Boat Merauke is not particularly well serviced by Pelni. The *Tatamailau* stops once every four weeks, on the way up the coast to Agats, Timika, Kaimana and Fak Fak. Perintis boats are the next best option. Uncomfortable wooden boats make fortnightly runs up and down the coast to Kimam (Pulau Yos Sudarso), Bade, Agats, and – incredibly – as far inland as Tanahmerah. The Pelni office (☎ 21591), Jl Sabang 318, is only open a few days before a Pelni or Perintis boat arrives or departs.

Getting Around

Mopah airport is about 5km from Hotel Asmat. Take a private taxi for about 10,000Rp, or a mikrolet outside the airport will take you down the main road for 700Rp. Hundreds of mikrolets go up and down the few roads and cost about 500Rp a trip.

AROUND MERAUKE
Wasur National Park

This national park is the joint project of the WWF and the indigenous people, mainly the Kanum and Marind, who contribute to, and benefit from, the park and its management. The 4,260 sq km park features huge anthills, wetlands, traditional villages, and wildlife such as cuscuses and even kangaroos – but the fauna is often very difficult to see. The best time to visit is during the dry season from April to October; the wet season (November to March) severely restricts travel within the park.

The WWF asks that travellers report to its Merauke office first; it can arrange guides and/or transport, if necessary, and take payment for accommodation. Its office (☎/fax 21397, PO Box 284, Merauke) is on the corner of Jl Biak and Jl Missi, behind the Flora Hotel.

The park offices at the two entrances (at Wasur and Ndalir villages), where you must register and pay 5000Rp, provide good local information. From **Yanggandur**, inside the park, you can hire a horse or go on foot to explore the wetlands, where there are reported to be cenderawasih.

There is no public transport to, or around, the park. A mikrolet for a day trip from Merauke will cost about 80,000Rp per day, or take an organised tour with YAPSEL (see the Sungai Bian & Muting entry later in this section). Some of the travel agencies listed under Organised Tours in the Jayapura and Around the Baliem Valley sections earlier can arrange guided tours around Wasur, but they are expensive and rarely run by local, indigenous people.

Sungai Bian & Muting

As an alternative to the comparatively overrun Baliem Valley, several areas near Merauke are worth visiting. The most accessible is an area 200km north of Merauke (mainly around Muting, and villages strung along Sungai Bian), with rainforests, wildlife and traditional people. Getting there will involve chartering vehicles, trekking (it's flat) and canoe trips, and you will need special permits from the police in Merauke – your guide or travel agency should arrange this.

Foreigners are not permitted to visit this area independently. Tours can be arranged at the indigenously-run YAPSEL agency (☎ 0971-21489, fax 21610, PO Box 283, Merauke) on Jl Missi, a few hundred metres from the WWF office. A 10 day, all-inclusive tour for a group of four will cost around 850,000Rp per person.

THE ASMAT REGION

The Asmat region is an inconceivably huge area of mangroves, pandanus, and rivers with huge tides. It remains almost completely undeveloped and one of the few truly unexplored regions left in the world. The Asmat people are justifiably famous for their woodcarvings and less so for their past headhunting exploits. They are semi-nomadic and their lives are dictated by rivers, which are a necessary source of transport and food.

To appreciate what the Asmat region has to offer definitely takes a lot of time and a lot of money. Individuals with a limited budget and no real interest in the regional culture may be very disappointed with how little they can see; Agats and the Asmat region is nowhere near as developed or accessible as Wamena and the Baliem Valley.

Very limited air and sea transport means the region is difficult to reach. Some of the travel agencies listed under Organised Tours in the earlier Jayapura and Around the Baliem Valley sections can arrange expensive trips to the Asmat region and to inland areas where the Kombai and Korowai people live in extraordinary treehouses. Expect to pay about US$100 per person per day, plus air fares.

The Asmat People

The name *asmat* comes from either *as akat* meaning 'right man' or *osamat* meaning 'man from tree'. The people refer to themselves as *asmat-ow*, or the 'real people'.

Trees feature heavily in Asmat symbolism, which is not surprising given the immense jungles in the region. The Asmat believe that humans are the image of a tree: their feet are its roots; the torso its trunk; the arms are the branches; and the fruit represents the head. Also an important element of their belief is that no person – except the very young and the very old – dies for any other reason than through tribal fighting or magic. So, each death of a family member must be 'avenged' if the spirit of the recently deceased can rest in the spiritual world known as *safan*. Not long ago, this 'avenging' took the form of head-hunting raids, and while it is now more ceremonial, it's still taken seriously.

The Asmat people centre their beliefs on the figure of Fumeripitisj who first carved wooden figures, so 'creating' the Asmat people. Through their carvings, the Asmat remain in contact with their ancestors. Each village appoints a *wow ipits* (woodcarver) based on his skills. Carvings are traditionally made only for use in ceremonies and are then left to rot in the jungle, but these days, inevitably, there is strong tourist demand for them.

Funeral ceremonies involve decorated shields which represent and avenge the dead relative, ancestor poles *(bis)* and ancestor figures *(kawe)*. Other ceremonial items include wooden masks, drums made from lizard skins, spears, paddles, and horns, which were once used to herald the return of head-hunting raids and to frighten enemies.

Agats

Facilities in the Asmat region are very limited and almost nonexistent outside Agats, which has two hotels, no daytime electricity, no telephones and limited fresh water. Due to the extraordinary tides and the location, the 'streets' are simply raised, broken wooden walkways – so watch your step. A surat jalan is necessary for Agats and the Asmat region, and must be obtained before you arrive. On your arrival, report to the police station (well, hut).

Things to See & Do The **Pusat Asmat & Pusat Pendidikan Asmat** (Asmat Education Centre & Asmat Centre) is an impressive collection of buildings which are of interest for their architecture if nothing else (they are usually empty). **Museum Kebudayaan & Kemajuan** (Museum of Culture & Progress) offers some interesting, varied displays, but with few or no explanations. It's open from 8 to 10 am daily except Sunday.

Places to Stay & Eat There are only two places to stay. Singles/doubles at the *Asmat*

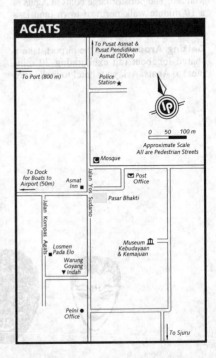

AGATS

To Pusat Asmat & Pusat Pendidikan Asmat (200m)

To Port (800 m)

Police Station ★

0   50   100 m

Approximate Scale
All are Pedestrian Streets

Mosque

To Dock for Boats to Airport (50m)

Asmat Inn ■

Post Office

Jalan Yos Sudaso

Pasar Bhakti

Jalan Kompas Agats

Losmen ■ Pada Elo

Warung Goyang ▼ Indah

Museum 🏛 Kebudayaan & Kemajuan

Pelni ● Office

To Sjuru

Inn cost 22,000/39,500Rp; 28,000/45,500Rp with bathroom. Good food (8500Rp per meal) and cold beer is available for guests if ordered well in advance. For about the same price, *Losmen Pada Elo* has friendly service, good local information and standard rooms. Guests can order food in advance for about 7500Rp a meal.

Getting There & Away Tiny Merpati planes fly weekly (currently Thursday) between Merauke and the grass airfield at nearby Ewer for 75,100Rp. Missionary planes can also be chartered from Merauke or Timika for huge sums.

The Pelni liner *Tatamailau* comes by once or twice every four weeks (depending on the tides) on the way to Timika and Merauke. Other less comfortable Perintis boats come by every week or so and travel up the south coast of Irian Jaya and to south-east Maluku. The port for large boats at Agats is a 10 minute walk north of town (and is a great place to watch sunsets).

Getting Around From the airport, take a shared longboat (an exhilarating 20 minutes) to Agats. Ask your hotel to make sure you get on a boat back to the airport when the plane returns.

Motorboats are the only form of local transport. Expect to pay at least 250,000Rp per day for a reputable boat with a driver. The boats take between 10 and 15 passengers, but Agats never attracts enough visitors to 'get a group together' to share the cost. Cheaper prices are possible – maybe 180,000Rp per day – if you ask around the village of Sjuru, a 10 minute walk from Agats.

Canoes are a far cheaper alternative, but you obviously cannot go far. They cost about 8000Rp per hour, plus 6000Rp per hour for each rower. Ask around Sjuru or at the losmen.

AROUND THE ASMAT REGION

To explore the region properly will take many days. In addition to the exorbitant boat hire, add about 40,000Rp per day for a guide and 25,000Rp for a porter or cook. Take all your own supplies with you (Agats has some basic shops). There are no hotels outside of Agats, but in the larger villages, such as **Senggo** and **Ayam**, you can sleep at missions or schools for about 10,000Rp per person. Alternatively, bring your own camping gear.

Language

The 300 plus languages spoken throughout Indonesia, except those of northern Pulau Halmahera (Halmahera Island) and most of Irian Jaya, belong to the Malay-Polynesian group. Within this group are many different regional languages and dialects. Sulawesi has at least six distinct language groups and the tiny island of Alor in Nusa Tenggara has no fewer than seven. The languages of the Kalimantan interior form their own distinct sub-family. Sumatra is no less diverse, and languages range from Acehnese in the north, to Batak around Danau Toba (Lake Toba). In southern Sumatra the main language is Bahasa Melayu (Malay Language) from which Bahasa Indonesia is derived.

There are three main languages in Java: Sundanese (spoken in West Java), Javanese (spoken in Central and East Java), and Madurese (spoken in parts of East Java and on the island of Madura, off the north coast of Java). The Balinese have their own language.

BAHASA INDONESIA

Today, the national language of Indonesia is Bahasa Indonesia, which is almost identical to Malay. Most Indonesians speak Bahasa Indonesia as well as their own regional language.

A few Bahasa essentials are included in this guide but you'll find a far more comprehensive overview in Lonely Planet's *Indonesian phrasebook*. It's structured to provide a good working knowledge of basic Bahasa Indonesia, with emphasis on the day-to-day vocabulary needed for travel around the country. John Barker's *Practical Indonesian* is another phrase book focusing on travel vocabulary.

For serious students, *Bahasa Indonesia: Langkah Baru – a New Approach*, Book I by Yohanni Johns, is a school text, which, though designed for self study, provides a substantial vocabulary and a solid grounding in Indonesian grammar.

A good Indonesian-English/English-Indonesian dictionary can also be very useful. Cheap pocket dictionaries abound in Indonesian bookshops but are often riddled with errors and omissions. The best are *Tuttle's Concise Indonesian Dictionary*, widely available in Indonesia, and *MIP Concise Indonesian Dictionary*, on sale overseas.

The most comprehensive dictionaries are *An Indonesian-English Dictionary* and its companion volume *An English-Indonesian Dictionary* by John Echols and Hassan Shadily. Unfortunately they're expensive (especially outside Indonesia) and quite weighty. *Kamus Lengkap* by S Wojowasito and Tito Wasito is a complete Indonesian-English/English-Indonesian dictionary in one volume. Despite a number of odd and inaccurate translations, it's the best comprehensive travel-size dictionary, and is cheap if purchased in Indonesia. Bilingual dictionaries in French, German, Dutch and Japanese are also available.

Pronunciation

a	as in 'father'
e	as in 'bet' when unstressed; when stressed, as the 'a' in 'may'
i	as the 'i' in 'marine'
o	as in 'bow'
u	as in 'flute'
ai	as in 'Thai'
au	a long 'ow', as in 'cow'
ua	at the start of a word, as 'w', eg *uang* (money), pronounced 'wang'

The pronunciation of consonants is very straightforward. Most sound like their English counterparts, except:

c	as the 'ch' in 'chair'
g	as in 'garden'
ng	as in 'singer'
ngg	as the 'ng' in 'anger'
j	as in 'join'
r	trilled, as in Spanish *pero*

h	like English 'h', but a bit stronger; almost silent at the end of a word
k	like English 'k', except at the end of the word, when it's more a closing of the throat with no sound, eg *tidak* (no/not), pronounced 'tee-dah'
ny	as the 'ny' in 'canyon'

Greetings & Civilities

Good morning.	*Selamat pagi.* (until 11 am)
Good day.	*Selamat siang.* (11 am to 3 pm)
Good afternoon.	*Selamat sore.* (3 to 7 pm)
Good evening.	*Selamat malam.*
Goodbye. (said by the person leaving)	*Selamat tinggal.*
Goodbye. (said by the person staying)	*Selamat jalan.*
Please. (asking for help)	*Tolong.*
Please open the door.	*Tolong buka pinta.*
Please. (giving permission)	*Silakan.*
Please come in.	*Silakan masuk.*
Thank you (very much).	*Terima kasih (banyak).*
It's nothing. (You're welcome.)	*Kembali, sama sama.*
Yes.	*Ya.*
No/Not.	*Tidak.* *Bukan.* (used to negate nouns and pronouns)
I'm sorry.	*Ma'af.*
Excuse me.	*Permisi.*
Welcome.	*Selamat datang.*
How are you?	*Apa kabar?*
I'm fine.	*Kabar baik.*
What's your name?	*Siapa nama anda?*
My name is ...	*Nama saya ...*
Where are you from?	*Dari mana asal saudara?*
I'm from ...	*Saya dari ...*
Are you married?	*Sudah kawin?*
I'm not married yet.	*Saya belum kawin.*
I'm married.	*Saya sudah kawin.*

Language Difficulties

Do you speak English?	*Bisa berbicara bahasa Inggris?*
I understand.	*Saya mengerti.*
I don't understand.	*Saya tidak mengerti.*
Please write that word down.	*Tolong tuliskan kata itu.*

Getting Around

I want to go to	*Saya mau pergi ke ...*
Where is ...?	*Di mana ada ...?*
Which way?	*Ke mana?*
How many kilometres?	*Berapa kilometer?*

What time does the ... leave/arrive?	*Jam berapa ... berangkat/tiba?*
bus	*bis*
train	*kereta api*
ship	*kapal*
aeroplane	*pesawat terbang*

Stop here.	*Berhenti disini.*
Straight on.	*Terus.*
Turn left.	*Belok kiri.*
Turn right.	*Belok kanan.*
Please slow down.	*Pelan-pelan.*

station	*stasiun*
ticket	*karcis/tiket*
first class	*kelas satu*
economy class	*kelas ekonomi*

Where can I hire a ...?	*Dimana saya bisa sewa ...?*
car	*mobil*
motorcycle	*sepeda motor*
bicycle	*sepeda*

Accommodation

Is there a room available?	*Ada kamar kosong?*
What's the daily rate?	*Berapa tarip hariannya?*
May I see the room?	*Boleh saya lihat kamar?*
I'd like to pay now.	*Saya mau bayar sekarang.*

hotel	*hotel*
price list	*daftar harga*
bed	*ranjang/tempat tidur*
room	*kamar*
quiet room	*kamar tenang*
bathroom	*kamar mandi*
with private bath	*kamar mandi didalam*
with shared bath	*kamar mandi diluar*
air-con	*ac ('ah-say')*

Around Town

bank	*bank*
chemist/pharmacy	*apotek*
market	*pasar*
police station	*kantor polisi*
post office	*kantor pos*
postage stamp	*perangko*
telephone	*telepon*
telephone number	*nomor telepon*
toilet	*kamar kecil/ WC ('way say')*
town square	*alun-alun*

| What time does it open/close? | *Jam berapa buka/ tutup?* |
| What is the exchange rate? | *Berapa kursnya?* |

Shopping

How much is it?	*Berapa harga?*
Can you lower the price?	*Boleh kurang?*
cigarettes	*rokok*
film	*filem*
matches	*korek api*
mosquito coil	*obat nyamuk*
mosquito net	*kelambu*
soap	*sabun*
toilet paper	*kertas WC*
towel	*handuk*

Health

Where is a ...	*Dimana ada ...?*
chemist/ pharmacy	*apotik*
dentist	*dokter gigi*
doctor	*dokter*
hospital	*rumah sakit*

Emergencies

Help!	*Tolong!*
Call a doctor!	*Panggil dokter!*
Call the police!	*Panggil polisi!*
It's an emergency!	*Keadaan darurat!*
I'm lost.	*Saya kesasar.*
Thief!	*Pencuri!*
Fire!	*Kebakaran!*
Go away!	*Pergi!*
hospital	*rumah sakit*

I'm sick	*Saya sakit.*
I feel nauseous.	*Saya mau muntah.*
I keep vomiting.	*Saya muntah terus.*
I'm pregnant.	*Saya hamil.*

headache	*sakit kepala*
sore throat	*sakit tenggorokan*
stomachache	*sakit perut*
medicine	*obat*

I'm allergic to ...	*Saya alergi ...*
antibiotics	*antibiotika*
penicillin	*penisilin*

Time & Days

What is the time?	*Jam berapa?*
7 o'clock	*jam tujuh*
5 o'clock	*jam lima*
How many hours?	*Berapa jam?*
five hours	*lima jam*
When?	*Kapan?*
today	*hari ini*
tomorrow	*besok*
yesterday	*kemarin*
rubber time	*jam karet*
hour	*jam*
week	*minggu*
month	*bulan*
year	*tahun*

Monday	*Hari Senin*
Tuesday	*Hari Selasa*
Wednesday	*Hari Rabu*
Thursday	*Hari Kamis*
Friday	*Hari Jumat*
Saturday	*Hari Sabtu*
Sunday	*Hari Minggu*

Numbers

1	*satu*
2	*dua*
3	*tiga*
4	*empat*
5	*lima*
6	*enam*
7	*tujuh*
8	*delapan*
9	*sembilan*
10	*sepuluh*

After the numbers one to 10, the 'teens' are *belas*, the 'tens' are *puluh*, the 'hundreds' are *ratus* and the 'thousands' *ribu*. Thus:

11	*sebelas*
12	*duabelas*
13	*tigabelas*
20	*duapuluh*
21	*duapuluh satu*
25	*duapuluh lima*
30	*tigapuluh*
90	*sembilanpuluh*
99	*sembilanpuluh sembilan*
100	*seratus*
200	*duaratus*
250	*duaratus limapuluh*
254	*duaratus limapuluh empat*
888	*delapanratus delapanpuluh delapan*
1000	*seribu*
1050	*seribu limapuluh*

one million	*sejuta*

A half is *setengah*, which is pronounced 'stengah', (eg half a kilo is *stengah kilo*). 'Approximately' is *kira-kira*.

FOOD

A few basic words and phrases will help make ordering a meal easier.

restaurant	*rumah makan*
food stall	*warung*
breakfast	*makan pagi*
lunch	*makan siang*
dinner	*makan malam*
the menu	*daftar makanan*

the bill	*bon*
food	*makanan*
take-away food	*nasi bungkus*
drink	*minuman*
delicious	*enak*
sweet	*manis*
sweet and sour	*asam manis*
cold	*dingin*
hot (temperature)	*panas*
spicy hot	*pedas*
barbecued	*bakar*
boiled	*rebus*
fried	*goreng*

Where is a (cheap) restaurant?	*Dimana ada rumah makan (murah)?*
I want ...	*Saya mau ...*
to eat	*makan*
to drink	*minum*

Please bring ...	*Boleh minta ...*
the menu	*daftar makanan*
a glass of water	*segelas air putih*
the bill	*bon*
a knife	*pisau*
a fork	*garpu*
a spoon	*sendok*

I can't eat ...	*Saya tidak boleh makan ...*
milk and cheese	*susu dan keju*
eggs	*telur*
meat	*daging*
prawns	*udang*

Not too spicy, please.	*Jangan terlalu pedas.*

Food Glossary

abon – spiced and shredded dried meat often sprinkled over *nasi rames* or *nasi rawon*

acar – pickle; cucumber or other vegetables in a mixture of vinegar, salt, sugar and water

apam – a delicious pancake filled with nuts and sprinkled with sugar

ayam – chicken; *ayam goreng* is fried chicken

babi – pork; since most Indonesians are Muslim, pork is generally only found in market stalls and restaurants run by Chinese, and in areas where there are non-Muslim populations, such as Bali, Irian Jaya and Tana Toraja on Sulawesi

bakar – barbequed, roasted

bakmi – rice-flour noodles, either fried *(bakmi goreng)* or in soup

bakso or *ba'so* – meatball soup

bawang – onion

blimbing – star fruit

bubur ayam – Indonesian porridge with chicken; the porridge is generally sweetened and made froxm rice, black sticky rice or mung beans

bubur kacang – mung bean porridge cooked in coconut milk

buncis – beans

cap cai ('chap chai') – Chinese mix of fried vegetables, although sometimes with meat as well

cassava – known as tapioca in English; a long, thin, dark brown root which looks something like a shrivelled turnip

cumi cumi – squid

daging babi – pork

daging kambing – goat or mutton

daging sapi – beef

dragonflies – popular Balinese snack; caught with sticky sticks and then roasted

durian – green spikey fruit with an overpowering smell

emping – powdered and dried *melinjo* nuts, fried and served as a snack or with a main meal

es krim – ice cream; in Indonesia you can get western brands like Flipper's and Peters, and also locally manufactured varieties

fu yung hai – a sort of sweet and sour omelette

gado gado – another very popular Indonesian dish of steamed bean sprouts, various vegetables, served with a spicy peanut sauce

garam – salt

gula – sugar

gula gula – lollies (sweets, candy)

gulai/gule – thick curried-meat broth with coconut milk

ikan – fish; if you're buying fresh fish (you can often buy it at a market and get your hotel to cook it up), the gills should be a deep red colour, not brown, and the flesh should be firm to touch

ikan asam manis – sweet and sour fish

ikan bakar – barbecued fish

ikan belut – eels; another Balinese delicacy; kids catch them in the rice paddies at night

ikan danau – freshwater fish

ikan laut – saltwater fish

jahe – ginger

jeruk – citrus fruit

kacang – bean or pea; peanut (also *kacang tanah*)

kacang hijau – mung bean sprouts; these can be made into a sweet filling for cakes and buns

kacang tanah – peanuts

kare – curry, as in *kare udang* (prawn curry)

kecap asin – salty soy sauce

kecap manis – sweet soy sauce

keju – cheese

kentang – potatoes; used in various ways, including in dishes of Dutch origin and as a salad ingredient

kepiting – crab; features in quite a few dishes, mostly of Chinese origin

kodok – frog; plentiful in Bali and caught in the rice paddies at night

kroket – mashed potato cake with minced meat filling

krupuk – shrimp with cassava flour, or fish flakes with rice dough, cut into slices and fried to a crisp

krupuk melinjo (emping) – seeds of the melinjo fruit *(gnetum-gnemon)*, pounded flat, dried and fried to make a crisp chip and served as a snack

kueh – cake

lemper – sticky rice with a small amount of meat inside, wrapped up in a banana leaf and boiled; a common snack served throughout the country

lombok – chilli. There are various types: *lombok merah* (large, red); *lombok hijau* (large, green); and *lombok rawit* (rather small but deadliest of them all, often packaged with *tahu* etc).

lontong – rice steamed in a banana leaf

lumpia – spring rolls; small fried pancake filled with shrimp and bean sprouts

madu – honey

martabak – sold all over the archipelago by street vendors; it's similar to a pancake and comes in two varieties: the most common one seems to be the very sweet version, but (at least in Java) you can also get a delicious savoury martabak stuffed with meat, egg and vegetables

mentega – butter

mentimun – cucumber

merica – pepper

mie goreng – fried wheat-flour noodles, sometimes with vegetables, sometimes with meat

mie kuah – noodle soup

nanas – pineapple

nasi – rice

nasi campur – steamed rice topped with a little bit of everything – some vegetables, some meat, a bit of fish, a krupuk or two; a good, usually tasty and filling meal

nasi goreng – fried rice. A very common dish, popular at any time of day, including breakfast. A basic nasi goreng may be little more than fried rice with a few scraps of vegetable to give it some flavour, but sometimes it includes meat.

nasi goreng istimewa (special) – usually nasi goreng with a fried egg on top

nasi gudeg – unripe jackfruit cooked in *santan* (squeezed grated coconut) and served up with rice, pieces of chicken and spices

nasi Padang – Padang food, from the Padang region of Sumatra. It's popular all over Indonesia, and is usually served cold; it consists of rice with a range of side dishes, including beef, fish, fried chicken, curried chicken, boiled cabbage, and sometimes fish and prawns. The dishes are laid out before you and your final bill is calculated by the number of empty dishes left when you've finished eating. Nasi Padang is traditionally eaten

with the fingers and it's also traditionally very hot *(pedas* not *panas); sometimes hot enough to burn your fingers, let alone your tongue! It's also one of the more expensive ways to eat in Indonesia but can be well worth it.

nasi pecel – similar to gado gado, with boiled papaya leaves, tapioca, bean sprouts, string beans, fried soybean cake, fresh cucumber, coconut shavings and peanut sauce

nasi putih – white *(putih)* rice, usually steamed; glutinous rice is mostly used in snacks and cakes

nasi rames – rice with a combination of egg, vegetables, fish or meat

nasi rawon – rice with spicy hot beef soup, fried onions and spicy sauce

nasi uduk – rice boiled in coconut milk or cream

opor ayam – chicken cooked in coconut milk

pempek (also *empek-empek*) – deep fried/grilled fish and sago balls (form Palembang in Sumatra)

pete – a huge spicy broad bean, often served in the pod

pisang goreng – fried banana fritters; a popular streetside snack

rijsttafel – Dutch for 'rice table'; Indonesian food with a Dutch interpretation. It consists of many individual dishes with rice. Rather like a glorified *nasi campur* or a hot *nasi Padang*. Bring a big appetite.

rintek wuuk – spicy dog meat; a Minahasan (Sulawesi) delicacy

roti – bread; nearly always snow white and sweet

sago – a starchy, low protein food extracted from a variety of palm tree. Sago is the staple diet of Maluku.

sambal – a hot, spicy chilli sauce served as an accompaniment with most meals

sambal pedas – hot sauce

sate – one of the best known Indonesian dishes, sate (sah-tay) are small pieces of various types of meat grilled on a skewer and served with a spicy peanut sauce

saus tomat – tomato sauce; ketchup

sayur – vegetable

sayur-sayuran – mixed vegetables

sayur asem – sour vegetable soup

sop – clear soup with mixed vegetables and meat or chicken

soto – meat and vegetable broth, often a main meal eaten with rice and a side dish of sambal

tahu – tofu or soybean curd. It varies from white and yellow to thin and orange-skinned. It's found as a snack in *warungs* and is sometimes sold with hot chillies or with a filling of vegetables.

telur – egg

tempe – made from whole soybeans fermented into cake; rich in vegetable protein, iron and vitamin B

tempe goreng – pieces of tempe fried with palm sugar and chillies

ubi – sweet potato; it has pulpy yellow or brown skin and white to orange flesh

udang – prawns or shrimps

udang karang – lobster

Drinks Glossary

air – water. You may receive a glass of water with a restaurant meal. It should have been boiled (and may not have cooled down since), but often it won't be boiled at all. Ask for *air putih* (literally, white water), or alternatively, drink tea. Hygienic bottled water is also available everywhere.

air jeruk – citrus fruit juice

air minum – drinking water

Aqua – the most common brand of mineral water, highly recommended if you're dubious about drinking the local water, although it's not cheap.

arak – a stage on from *brem*. It's usually home-produced, although even the locally bottled brands look amateurish. It makes quite a good drink mixed with lemonade. Taken in copious quantities it has a similar effect to being hit on the head with an elephant.

brem – rice wine; either home produced or commercially bottled *(Bali Brem)*. A bit of an acquired taste, but not bad after a few bottles!

es buah – more a dessert than a drink; a curious combination of crushed ice, condensed milk, shaved coconut, syrup, jelly and fruit.

es juice – although you should be a little careful about ice and water, the delicious fruit drinks are irresistible. They're made with either one or two types of tropical fruit and crushed ice, which is then blended. You can request mind-blowing combinations of *jeruk manis* (orange), *pisang* (banana), *nanas* (pineapple), *mangga* (mango), *nangka* (jackfruit) or whatever else is available.

Green Sands – a pleasant soft drink, made not from sand, but from malt, apple and lime juice

jeruk manis – orange juice

jeruk nipis – lime juice

kopi – coffee. Indonesia produces excellent coffee. The best kopi comes from Sulawesi, though Sumatra, Bali and Java also produce some fine brews. Like Turkish coffee, it's made from powdered coffee beans, but spooned straight into a glass before sugar and boiling water are added. Served sweet and black with the coffee granules floating on top, it is a real kick start in the mornings. Most restaurants that travellers frequent have adopted the odd (by Indonesian standards) habit of serving kopi without sugar.

kopi susu – white coffee, usually made with sweetened, condensed milk

stroop – cordial

susu – milk. Fresh milk is found in supermarkets in large cities, although long-life milk in cartons is more common. Cans of condensed milk are also sold in Indonesia and are very sweet.

teh – tea. Some people are not enthusiastic about Indonesian tea but if you don't need strong, bend-the-teaspoon-style tea you'll probably find it's quite OK.

teh manis – tea with sugar

teh pahit or *teh tawar* – tea without sugar

tuak – an alcoholic drink fermented from the sap of a species of palm tree

Glossary

See the Food section in the Language chapter for a food and drinks glossary.

ABRI – Angkatan Bersenjata Republik Indonesia; the armed forces

adat – traditional laws and regulations

adu domba – ram-butting fights (West Java); opposing sides against one another

agung – high, noble

air – water

Airlangga – 11th century king, who founded a dynasty and the great kingdoms of East Java, and is also of considerable historical and legendary importance in Bali

air panas – hot springs

air terjun – waterfall

aling aling – guard wall behind the entrance gate to a Balinese family compound; demons can only travel in straight lines so the aling aling prevents them from entering

alun-alun – main public square of a town or village, usually found in front of the *bupati's* (governor's) residence; traditional area for public meetings and ceremonies; nowadays they tend to be deserted, open grassed areas

anak – child

andong – horse-drawn passenger cart

angklung – musical instrument made of differing lengths and thicknesses of bamboo suspended in a frame

angkot or *angkota* – short for *angkutan kota* (city transport), these small minibuses cover city routes

angkudes – short for *angkutan pedesaan*, these minibuses run to nearby villages from the cities, or between villages

anjing – dog

argo – taxi meter

Arja – particularly refined form of Balinese theatre

Arjuna – hero of the *Mahabharata* epic and a popular temple gate guardian image

Ayodya – Rama's kingdom in the *Ramayana*

Babad – early chronicle of Balinese history

bagang – fishing platform

Bahasa Indonesia – Indonesia's national language

bajaj – motorised three wheeler taxi found in Jakarta

balai – Dayak communal houses (Kalimantan)

bale – Balinese pavilion, house or shelter; a meeting place

Bali Aga – 'original' Balinese, who managed to resist the new ways brought in with *Majapahit* migration

balian – female shaman of the Tanjung Dayak people in Kalimantan

bandar – harbour, port

bandar udara – airport; often shortened to bandara

bandung – large cargo-cum-houseboats

banjar – local area of a Balinese village in which community activities are organised

banyan – see *waringin*

bapak – father; also a polite form of address to any older man

barat – west

baris – Balinese warrior dance

Barong – mythical lion-dog creature; star of the Barong & Rangda dance and a firm champion of good in the eternal struggle between good and evil

barong kekat – holiest of *barongs*

barong landung – enormous puppets known as the 'tall barong'; these can be seen at an annual festival in Serangan, Bali

barong tengkok – a mobile form of *gamelan* used for wedding processions and circumcision ceremonies (Lombok)

batik – cloth made by coating part of the fabric with wax, then dyeing it and melting the wax out; the waxed part is not coloured and repeated waxings and dyeings builds up a pattern

batik cap – batik crafted with a *cap* or metal stamp

batik tulis – handmade batik

becak – trishaw (bicycle-rickshaw)

Belanda – Dutch; or in colloquial usage – a foreigner

belauran – night markets (Kalimantan)

belian – spiritual healer

bemo – minibus, a form of local transport. Originally a small, three wheeled pick-up with a bench seat down each side in the back, these have mostly disappeared in favour of small minibuses. Bemo (a contraction of *becak* and *motor)* is no longer widely used in Indonesia, but still common in Bali and some other areas as a generic term for minibus.

bendi – two person horse-drawn cart used in Sulawesi, Sumatra and Maluku as transport (see also *dokar*)

bensin – petrol

benteng – fort

berempah – traditional Sumbawan barefisted boxing

betang – communal house in Central Kalimantan

Betawi – original name of Batavia (now Jakarta); the name of an ethnic group indigenous to Jakarta

bhaga – miniature thatched-roof house dedicated to the ancestors of the Ngada people of Flores

bis – bus

bis air – water bus

bis malam – night bus

bisnis – business; ie business class ticket

Bodhisattvas – a divine being worthy of nirvana who remains on earth and offers guidance for others to reach nirvana

bouraq – winged horse-like creature with the head of a woman; also the name of the domestic airline which mostly services the outer islands

Brahma – the creator; one of the trinity of chief Hindu gods, along with Shiva and Vishnu

bukit – hill

bupati – government official in charge of a *kabupaten* (regency)

caci – a ceremonial martial art in which participants duel with whips and shields

camat – government official in charge of a *kecamatan* (district)

candi – shrine, or temple, usually an ancient Hindu or Buddhist temple of Javanese design

candi bentar – split gateway entrance to a Balinese temple

cap – metal stamp used to apply motifs to batik

catur yoga – ancient manuscript on religion and cosmology

cenderawasih – bird of paradise

ces – a motorised canoe with a long propeller shaft (Kalimantan)

cidomo – horse-drawn cart (Nusa Tenggara)

cinchona bark – medicinal bark which yields quinine

Condong – Legongs' attendant (see *Legong*)

cuscus – large nocturnal possums from North Australia, Papua New Guinea and nearby islands, with dense fur, prehensile tails and large eyes; also *kuskus*

dalang – puppeteer and storyteller of *wayang kulit* shadow puppet performances

danau – lake

dangdut – popular Indonesian music characterised by wailing vocals and a strong beat

Departemen Kehutanan – Forest Department

desa – village

Dewi Sri – rice goddess

dilman – horse-drawn passenger cart

dinas pariwisata – tourist office

dokar – horse cart, still a popular form of local transport in many towns and larger villages

dukun – faith healer and herbal doctor or mystic

dwipa mulia – moneychanger

ekonomi – economy; ie economy class ticket

eksekutif – executive; ie executive class ticket

Gajah Mada – famous Majapahit prime minister

Galungan – great Balinese festival, an annual event in the 210 day Balinese *wuku* calendar

Gambuh – classical form of Balinese theatre
gamelan – traditional Javanese and Balinese orchestra, usually almost solely percussion, with large xylophones and gongs
Ganesha – The Hindu god Shiva's elephant-headed son
gang – alley or footpath
Garuda – mythical man-bird, the vehicle of Vishnu and the modern symbol of Indonesia; also the name of Indonesia's international airline, Garuda Indonesia
gereja – church
gili – islet or atoll
gringsing – rare double *ikat* woven cloth in Tenganan, Bali
gua – cave; the old spelling, *goa*, is also common
gunung – mountain
gunung api – volcano (literally 'fire mountain')

haji, haja – Muslim who has made the pilgrimage *(haj)* to Mecca. Many Indonesians save all their lives to make the haj, and a haji (man) or haja (woman) commands great respect in the village.
halus – refined
harga biasa – standard price
harga touris – tourist price
homestay – small family-run *losmen*
huta – Batak village (Sumatra)
hutan – forest, jungle

ibu – mother; also polite form of address to any older woman; often shortened to *bu*
ikan – fish
ikat – cloth in which the pattern is produced by dyeing the individual threads before weaving; see also *gringsing*

jadwal – timetable
Jaipongan – relatively modern, West Javanese dance incorporating elements of *pencak silat* and *Ketuktilu*
jalan – street or road; *Jl* is the written abbreviation
jalan jalan – to go for a stroll
jalan potong – short cut
jam karet – 'rubber time'
jamu – herbal medicine; most tonics go

under this name and are supposed to cure everything from menstrual problems to baldness
jembatan – bridge
jidur – large cylindrical drums played widely throughout Lombok
jilbab – Muslim head covering worn by women
Jl – abbreviation of *jalan* (street or road); sometimes written as Jln
jukung – see *perahu*

kabupaten – regency
kain – cloth
kain songket – cloth with silver or gold thread woven through it
kaja – towards the mountains (Balinese)
kaki lima – mobile food carts; literally 'five feet' – the three feet of the cart and the two of the vendor
kala – demonic face often seen over temple gateways
kamar kecil – toilet, the traditional variety being a hole in the ground with footrests either side
kampung – village, neighbourhood
kantor – office, as in *kantor imigrasi* (immigration office) or *kantor pos* (post office)
Kantor Bupati – Governor's Office
karang – coral, coral reef, atoll
kartu chip – grey telephone card embedded with an electronic chip
kartu telepon – Telkom telephone card
kasar – rough, coarse, crude
kateda – spirit stones (Sumba)
Kawi – Bahasa Kawi (old Javanese)
kebaya – women's long-sleeved blouse with front pinned together; usually worn with a sarong
kebun – garden
kecapi – Sundanese (West Javanese) lute
kehutanan – forestry
kelurahan – local government area
kepulauan – archipelago
keliling – driving around (buses and bemos) to pick up passengers
kepala balai – Dayak village head (Sumatra)
kepala desa – village head
kepala stasiun – station master

kepeng – old Chinese coins with a hole in the centre that were the common currency during the Dutch era; they can still be bought from shops and antique dealers

kepiting – crab

ketoprak – popular Javanese folk theatre

Ketuktilu – traditional Sundanese (Java) dance in which professional female dancers dance for male spectators

kijang – a type of deer; also a very popular brand of Toyota 4WD vehicle, Kijang, often used for taxis

kina – quinine

KKN – the acronym for Korupsi, Kolusi and Nepotisme (Corruption, Collusion and Nepotism); one of the buzz words of the post-Soeharto reform era

klotok – canoe with water-pump motor used in Kalimantan

Konfrontasi – catchphrase of the early 1960s when Soekarno embarked on a confrontational campaign against western imperialism aimed at Malaysia

kopi – coffee

kora-kora – canoe (Irian Jaya)

KORPRI – Korp Pegawai Republik Indonesia, the Indonesian bureaucracy

kramat – shrine

kraton – or *keraton*; walled city palace

kretek – Indonesian clove cigarette

kris – wavy-bladed traditional dagger, often held to have spiritual or magical powers

krisis moneter – monetary crisis, often shortened to *krismon*

KSDA – Konservasi & Sumber Daya Alam; ie National Parks office

kueh – cakes

kulit – leather

kulkul – alarm drum (Bali)

Kuningan – holy day celebrated throughout Bali 10 days after *Galungan*

labi-labi – small intra-city minibus, usually with side benches in the back (Aceh, Sumatra)

ladang – non-irrigated field, often using slash-and-burn agriculture, for dry-land crops

lamin – communal house in East and West Kalimantan

langsam – crowded, peak-hour commuter train to the big cities

lapangan – field, square

laut – sea, ocean

Legong – classic Balinese dance performed by young girls

lesahan – traditional style of dining on straw mats

longbot – high-speed motorised canoe used on the rivers of Kalimantan

lontar – type of palm tree; traditional books were written on the dried leaves of the lontar palm

lopo – beehive-shaped meeting house (Timor)

losmen – basic accommodation, though not always, and usually cheaper than hotels and often family-run

lumba lumba – dolphins

MAF – Mission Aviation Fellowship; Protestant missionary air service which operates in remote regions

Mahabharata – venerated Hindu holy book, telling of the battle between the Pandavas and the Korawas

Majapahit – last great Javanese Hindu dynasty, pushed out of Java into Bali by the rise of Islamic power

mandau – machetes (Kalimantan)

mandi – common Indonesian form of bath, consisting of a large water tank from which water is ladled over the body

marapu – Balinese term for all spiritual forces, including gods, spirits and ancestors

menara – minaret, tower

Merpati Nusantara Airlines – major domestic airline

meru – multi-roofed shrines in Balinese temples; they take their name from the Hindu holy mountain, Mahameru; the same roof style also can be seen in ancient Javanese mosques

mesjid – mosque

mikrolet – small taxi; a tiny *opelet*

moko – bronze drum from Alor (Nusa Tenggara)

muezzin – those who call the faithful to the mosque

muncak – 'barking deer' found in Java

naga – mythical snake-like creature

ngadhu – parasol-like, thatched roof; ancestor totem of the Ngada people of Flores

nusa – island, as in Nusa Penida

nuri – parrot

Nyai Loro Kidul – Queen of the South Seas

Nyepi – Balinese day of stillness (see the boxed text 'Nyepi' in the Bali chapter)

Odalan – temple festival held every 210 days, the Balinese 'year'

ojek – (or *ojeg* in some areas) motorcycle that takes passengers

oleh-oleh – souvenirs

opelet – small intra-city minibus, usually with side benches in the back

OPM – Organisasi Papua Merdeka; ie Free Papua Movement, the main group which opposes Indonesian rule of Irian Jaya

ora – Komodo dragon

orang putih – white person; commonly used to mean foreigner; also *bule*

Padang – city and region of Sumatra which has exported its cuisine to all corners of Indonesia (see the colour special section 'Indonesian Cuisine' for more information)

paduraksa – covered gateway to a Balinese temple

pak – shortened form of *bapak*

pandanus – palm plant used to make mats

pantai – beach

Pantun – ancient Malay poetical verse in rhyming couplets

parkir – parking attendant

pasar – market

pasar malam – night market

pasar terapung – floating market

pasir – sand

patas – express ie express bus

patih – prime minister

patola – *ikat* motif of a hexagon framing a type of four pronged star

PDI-P – Indonesian Democracy Party of Struggle

peci – black Muslim felt cap

pedanda – high priest

pegunungan – mountain range

pelabuhan – harbour, port, dock; also *bandar*

pelan pelan – slowly

Pelni – Pelayaran Nasional Indonesia, the national shipping line with a fleet of passenger ships operating throughout the archipelago

pemangku – temple priest

pencak silat – form of martial arts originally from Sumatra, but now popular throughout Indonesia

pendopo – large, open-sided pavilion in front of a Javanese palace that serves as an audience hall

penginapan – simple lodging house

perahu – boat

perahu lading – longboat

perahu tambing – ferry boat

perbekel – Balinese government official in charge of a *desa* (village)

peresehan – popular form of physical combat peculiar to Lombok, in which two men fight armed with a small hide shield for protection and a long *rattan* stave as a weapon

perkeniers – 18th century transmigrants to Maluku who produced spices exclusively for the VOC; from Dutch 'gardener'

Pertamina – huge state-owned oil company

pesanggrahan – lodge for government officials where travellers can usually stay; also *pasanggrahan*

pete-pete – a type of *mikrolet* or *bemo* found in Sulawesi

pinang – betel nut

pinisi – Makassar or Bugis schooner

PHPA – Perlindungan Hutan dan Pelestarian Alam; the Directorate General of Forest Protection and Nature Conservation that manages Indonesia's national parks

PNG – Papua New Guinea

pompa bensin – petrol station

pondok – guesthouse or lodge (also called *pondok wisata*); hut

prasada – see *candi*

pulau – island

puputan – warrior's fight to the death; honourable, but suicidal, option when faced with an unbeatable enemy

pura – Balinese temple, shrine

pura dalem – Balinese temple of the dead

pura puseh – Balinese temple of origin

puri – palace

pusaka – sacred heirlooms of a royal family

puskesmas – short for 'pusat kesehatan masyarakat', ie community health centre (Bali)

rafflesia – gigantic flower found in Sumatra and Kalimantan, with blooms spreading up to a metre

raja – lord, prince or king

Ramadan – Muslim month of fasting, when devout Muslims refrain from eating, drinking and smoking during daylight hours

Ramayana – one of the great Hindu holy books, stories from the *Ramayana* form the keystone of many Balinese and Javanese dances and tales

rangda – witch; evil black-magic spirit of Balinese tales and dances

rattan – see *rotan*

Ratu Adil – the Just Prince who, by Javanese prophecy, will return to liberate Indonesia from oppression

rawa – swamp, marsh, wetlands

rebab – two stringed bowed lute

reformasi – 'reform'; refers to political reform after the repression of the Soeharto years

RMS – Republik Maluku Selatan; ie South Maluku Republic, the main group which opposed Indonesian rule of southern Maluku

rotan (rattan) – hardy, pliable vine used for handcrafts, furniture and weapons, such as the staves in the spectacular trial of strength ceremony, *peresehan*, in Lombok

rudat – traditional *Sasak* dance overlaid with Islamic influence (Lombok)

rumah adat – traditional house

rumah makan – restaurant or *warung* (eating house)

rumah sakit – hospital, literally 'sick house'

Sanghyang – trance dance in which the dancers impersonate a local village god

Sanghyang Widi – Balinese supreme being, never actually worshipped as such; one of the 'three in one' or lesser gods stand-in

santri – orthodox, devout Muslim

saron – xylophone-like *gamelan* instrument, with bronze bars struck with a wooden mallet

sarong (sarung) – all-purpose cloth, often sewn into a tube, and worn by women, men and children

Sasak – native of Lombok

sawah – an individual rice field, or the wet-rice method of cultivation

selat – strait

selatan – south

selendang – shawl

selimut – blanket

Sempati – domestic airline which flies to Kalimantan, southern Sumatra and Java

Shiva – the destroyer; one of the trinity of chief Hindu gods, along with Brahma and Vishnu

sirih – betel nut, chewed as a mild narcotic

sisemba – form of kick-boxing popular with the Torajan people of Sulawesi

situ – lake (Sundanese)

songket – silver or gold-threaded cloth, hand woven using floating weft technique

spid – Maluku colloquial term for 'speedboat'

stasiun – station

sudra – lowest or common caste to which most Balinese belong

suling – bamboo flute

sungai – river

surat jalan – travel permit (Irian Jaya)

syahbandar – harbour master

taman – ornamental garden, park, reserve

taman laut – marine park/reserve

taman nasional – national park

tari topeng – type of masked dance peculiar to the Cirebon area, Java

tarling – musical style of the Cirebon (Java) area, featuring guitar, *suling* and voice

tau tau – life-sized carved wooden effigies of the dead placed on balconies outside cave graves in Tana Toraja, Sulawesi

taxi sungai – cargo-carrying river ferry with bunks on the upper level

tedong-tedong – tiny structures over graves that look like houses (Sulawesi)

telaga – lake

telepon kartu – telephone card
teluk – bay
timur – east
tirta – water (Bali)
toko (e)mas – gold shops
tomate – Torajan funeral ceremony
tongkonan – traditional Torajan house (Sulawesi)
topeng – wooden mask used in funerary dances
toyo – water
transmigrasi – government-sponsored scheme to encourage settlers to move from overcrowded regions to sparsely populated ones
trepang – sea cucumber

uang – money
ular – snake
utara – north

Vishnu – the 'pervader' or 'sustainer'; one of the trinity of chief Hindu gods, along with *Brahma* and *Shiva*
VOC – Vereenigde Oost-Indische Compagnie; ie United East India Company, the Dutch trading monopoly which controlled much of Indonesia before the Dutch government assumed direct control in 1799

wali songo – 'nine holy men' who propagated Islam in Java

Wallace Line – hypothetical line intersecting Bali and Lombok and Kalimantan and Sulawesi, which marks the end of Asian and the beginning of Australasian flora and fauna
wantilan – open pavilion used to stage cockfights
waringin – banyan tree; a large and shady tree with drooping branches which root and can produce new trees. It was under a banyan *(bo)* tree that Buddha achieved enlightenment, and *waringin* are found at many temples in Bali and in village squares in Java and elsewhere.
warpostel or *warpapostel* – private telephone office *(wartel)* that also handles postage
wartel – private telephone office (shortened from *warung telekomunikasi*)
waruga – pre-Christian Minahasan (Sulawesi) tomb
warung – food stall
wayang kulit – shadow-puppet play
wayang orang – Javanese theatre or 'people wayang'; also known as wayang wong
wayang topeng – masked dance-drama
Wektu Telu – religion peculiar to Lombok that originated in Bayan and combines many tenets of Islam and aspects of other faiths
wisma – guesthouse or lodge
wuku – local Balinese calendar made up of 10 different weeks, between one and 10 days long, all running concurrently

Acknowledgments

THANKS

Many thanks to the travellers who used the last edition and wrote to us with helpful hints, useful advice and interesting anecdotes:

A Blackwell, A Hirschfeld, AM Schermbrucker, Aaron & Vanessa Petty, Aaron Ringer, Adrian James, Aeneas Precht, Afnan Soesantio, Aine Canavan, Aine Doyle, Alan Hart, Alex & Ursi, Alex Clear, Alex Gorissen, Alex Wright, Alexandra E Perry, Alexandra Fraedrich, Alice Pennisi, Alice Pitty, Alison Butler, Alison Emery, Allan Craig, Allan Wong, Amy Kolczak, Andre Hoeksma, Andrea Bindel, Andrew Riseley, Andrew Woolnough, Anette Brandt, Angela Harris, Angeline Khoo, Anika Stokkentre, Ann Virgin, Anna Bonomini, Anna Maspero, Anne Boxhall, Anne Suteras, Annette Low, Annick Donkers, Annie Russell, Annie Schalkwijk, Ans ter Woerds, Anthony Jukes, Ariane Frey, Arne Pijnakker, Aruna Subramamian, Axel Brugger, Bannon Rees, Barbara Schulte, Barry O'Keeffe, Barry Satz, Basil Condos, Ben Blackburn, Ben Hillman, Bern K Bartlau, Bernd Siedel, Beruta Sunaklis, Beth Brown, Bethan Psaila, Betty Wilson, Betty Wood, Beverley JM King, Bill Willoughby, Bjarne Bak, Bob McGuigan, Bobbie Quibell, Bonini Luciano, Bonny van de Boutenstein, Boyd Gilchrist, Bram & Martine, Brendan Ross, Brendan Shaw, Brett Wigdortz, Brian Dudden, Brian Hancock, Brian Ware, Bruce McNellie, CS Mak, Carol O'Gorman, Caroline Peer, Cathy Populin, Cedric Lechat, Cen Idris-Trans, Charles Babatsikos, Charles Kalish, Charlotte Phillips, Chester Gudowski, Chester Gudzowski, Chris & Tracy Bastian, Chris Bain, Chris Burgess, Chris Douglas, Chris Dunning, Chris Gymer, Chris King, Chris Majors, Chris Moore, Chris Perez, Christel Janke, Christian Rausch, Christine Dubos, Christine Laurence, Christine Whitehead, Christopher Edwards, Chu Chin Yi, Chua Mok You, CJM van Leirop, Claire Ellis, Colleen Duplock, Corey Fletcher, Cornelie Marks, Craig Davies, Craig Steed, Cristin Murphy, Curtis Andressen, D Chong, D Nicol, Dan Lloyd, Dane Doleman, Daniel Gondo, Daniel Madu, Daniela Gianazza, Darren Scott, Dave Aughton, Dave Evans, Dave Scarlet, David Bradbury, David Grieve, David Hardacre, David Levin, David McKeown, David Steel, Dean Myerson, Dean Tolhurst, Deane Tunaley, Debra Kadner, Dee Mahan, Deivier Berlemont, Denis Ho, Denise Buser, Dennis Billingham, Dennis Collins, Dennis Lowden, Dineke de Wit, Ditte Mortensen, Don Kossuth, Donna Pitetti, Doris Dredisel, Dorothy Jacobes, Doug Kreuzer, Dr David Thomas, Dr David Yates, Dr J Oldhoff, Dudley McFadden, Duncan Priestley, Duncan Thompson, Ed Sleebos, Eddie & Alouisa, Eddy Hill, Edward Reilley, Elaine Chow, Elaine McKenna, Elaine Morgan, Elena Siniscalco, Elizabeth Dove, Emanuela Bram, Emile Schenk, Emily Bremers, Eran Stark, Eric Findlay, Eric P van Velzen, Erik Agterhuis, Eskil Sorensen, Eva Gotsis, Evian ti, Fiona Beth Scott, Floris van Hovell, Freddy Agustian, Frederic Frantz, Frederick Schneider, GJ Hargreaves, Gareth Barkin, Gary Sim, Gavin Blue, Gavin John Croll, Gaynor M Evans, Geertje Korf, Genia Findeisen, Gentry Stephens, George Scholz, George Stevensen, Georgina Cranston, Gerard & Gillian Lemmens, Gerard Kostermans, Gert Lutke Schipholt, Gill Weston, Gizela Bedford, Glen Ewers, Glen Real, Govert Jan Repelaer van Driel, Graeme Ireland, Grag Dare, Graham Chrisp, Graham Robertson, Graham Sanders, Greg Jones, Guen Sublette, Guido Faes, Gunter Quaisser, Gunter Wehner, Gunther Heinrichs, Guy & Janet Pinneo, Guy Katznelson, Gwenn Flaux, HR Gibbons, Hamish Jenkins, Hans Bouhuys, Hans Rietveld, Hans van der Bergh, Hayley Cameron, Hayley McMillan, Heather Tanguay, Helen & Scott Sisk, Helen A Pastoriza, Helen Ebbens, Helen Wootton, Hendrik Levsen, Henrietta Somers, Henry Brownrigg, Henry Symonds, Herman Hiel, Herman van der Gun, Herman van der Kuil, Hilde Brontsema, Honest John, I Ketut Urindo, I P Zweip, Ian Alexander, Ian Hawkins, Ian McMatu, Ian Stephan, Ilja Rijnen, Ilkka Koskinen, Indrani Ganguly, Inge Sterk, Ino Spirit, Isabel Sabugueiro, Istvan Cole, Ita Kane, J Pickles, James Cringle, James Downey, James Haire, James Trotman, Jan Marshall, Jane Simon, Jason Murray, Jay J Stemmer, Jay Tanane, Jeannette Klaassen, Jeff Wall, Jemma Metcalfe-Gibson, Jennie Brundin, Jennifer Campbell, Jenny Byeshahass, Jenny Katauskas, Jeremy Polmear, Jerome Comment, Jerre Cramer, Jerry van Veenendaal, Jessica Kerstjens, JGH Oldeheuvel, Jhoni Adri, Jim Christopherson, Jim Holmboc, Jo Hunt, Jo Lynch, Joakim Magnusson, Jochen Lippert, Jodie Tranter, Jody Riley, Joe Verbiest, Joh Harrison, Johan Blok, Johan Flynn, Johan Rotsaert, Johanna de Bresser, Johannes Faber, John & Margaret Northcote, John Brickwood, John Lett, John Niron, John Pilgrim, John Reed, John Stevenson, John Youle, Jon Noble, Jonathon Potts, Jordan Thompson, Jorg Ausfelt, Jose M Lomas, Julia Crausay, Julia Kennaway, Julie Mayhew, KL Robison,

K Stokes, Karen Goddard, Karen Hashimoto, Karen Sanger, Karin Bischoff, Karin Flink, Karin Meijboom, Karin Stahel, Karl Thaiss, Kartini Slamet, Katarina Dobrovic, Kate Bysouth, Kath Mitchinson, Katherine Reed, Kathleen Kamiska, Kathleen Williams, Kathryn Sharpe, Kathy Dusi, Katie Brayne, Kees Botschuijver, Keir Jones, Keith Adams, Keith Downham, Keith Fletcher, Kelly Bassettt, Kennerly Clay, Kent Curry, Kerri Secombe, Kevin Hessee, Kevin Queen, Kiirsty Leiigh, Kim Hoffman, Kitty Stillufsen, Klaus D Hempfing, Koen van Gurp, Kristina Brodrick, Kurniadi Wijaya, Kym Gentry, LS Molodynski, Lance Gatchell, Lars Abildgaard, Laslo Wagreer, Laura Baar, Leigh Billett, Lennie Beattie, Leo van Reimsdyk, Leonard Koichi Bonarek, Leonie Stockwell, Lester Brien, Liam Guilar, Linda Burgin, Linda Croglia, Lisa Hirst, Lisa Kosewahr, Liz Brinkley, Liz McKechnie, Lorna O'Connell, Louise Wiseman, Low Puay Hwa Roger, Low Tian Hong, Luca Frangipane, Lucio Bonini, Lucy Thewlis, Lyle Bartlett, Lynn O'Donaghue, Lynne Bateman, M&K Hempfing, M Albinson, M Blyth, ME Hawkes, MM Sethi, M Nussbaum, M Phippard, M Trenerry, Maey Verbeek, Magdelene Lim, Maike Juta, Manfred Lepp, Marc Luysterburg, Marcel Kroes, Marcia Arens, Marcin Wielicki, Marco Cassinis, Marco Minelli, Marely Latchford, Margaret Dallas, Margaret Traeger, Margriet Nolet, Margrit Schafer, Maria Andrea Olcese, Marie Bell, Mark & Courtney Murrell, Mark Canavan, Mark Jackson, Mark Ogden, Mark Ogilvie, Mark Robinson, Mark Russell, Mark Townson, Mark V Erdmann, Markus Ogilvie, Marlies Havik, Martianne Sullivan, Martin & Christina Semler, Martin Covell, Martin Hobson, Martin Sherwood, Martin Spitaler, Martin Weston, Martine & Billy MacMillan, Martine Vallieres, Masato Uemori, Matt & Eileen Erskine, Matt Chabott, Maurice Hoeneveld, Maurice Jones, Melanie Calcari, Meldrum Duncan, Melinda Jollie, Michael Cartsonis, Michael Carver, Michael Foster, Michael Kohn, Michael O'Neill, Michele & Tiziana Bindi, Michele Bennett, Michele Lillie, Michelle Brisban, Michelle Keun, Michelle Stilz, Michelle Walder, Mieke Horst, Mike Dargan, Mike Dziedzic, Mike Frost, Mike Wallace, Mimmo Nuvina, Miriam Goodwin, Monal Capellone, Monica Nowacka, Morten Broberg, Mr & Mrs Altabas, Murray Sharman, N Poutney, Nadine Fogale, Nadine Guitton, Nadine White, Naomi Geer, Natalie Ilardi, Nathalie van der Slikke, Nerida Phelan, Nhu Truyen, Nick Redfearn, Nick Richards, Nick Thompson, Nicole Khodr, Nicolle Bea Fox, Nigel Searle, Norman Wake, Nuria & Jur Vanstaen, Ny S Tukan, Olav Pelger, P&R Sullivan, PA Olofsson, P Shuitemaker, Pam Olink, Pascal Carrae, Patrizia Masetti, Paul & Edith Breevaart, Paul Bigland, Paul de Vries, Paul Fletcher, Paul Jones, Paul Lawlor, Paul Mitchell, Paul Mullen, Paul Tolton, Paul Weghordt, Paul Wright, Penny Richards, Peter Bell, Peter Blumtritt, Peter Fugger-Kraka, Peter Laws, Peter Nilhill, Peter Ottevaere, Peter Roberts, Peter Smith, Peter Weijland, Phil Loxton, Philip Bale, Philippe Heurtault, Phillip & John Jongs, Phyllis Palmer, Piergiorgio Pescali, Piet van Midden, Pieter Verhulst, Polly Walker, R&J Perriber, R&M Cobden, RJ Adams, RJ Bromley, RM Cobden, RN McLean, R Sriram, RW McGuigan, RZ German, Rachel Dobson, Rachel Jaspers, Rainer Gritzka, Rais Richard Zaidi, Ralf Fahrner, Ramakant C Wakdar, Raymond Ang, Rebecca Perkin, Rehan Hasan, Reinhard Ankenbauer, Reinhold Klink, Renko Karruppannan, Rich Fuller, Richard & Lyn Durham, Richard Cooper, Richard Essex, Richard Giles, Richard Pickvance, Richard Willis, Rick & Gadis Pollard, Rick Handley, Ricky Nuyens, Rob Harling, Rob McCormack, Robby Niwarlangga, Robert Brenner, Robert Patterson, Robin G Hilton, Robin Nagy, Robin Petri, Robyn Haines, Roger Wicks, Roland Mayer, Roland Wagner, Ron Miller, Ronald Wolff, Ross Biggum, Ross Gager, Ross MacKenzie, Rosy & John Parsons, S&S LaHay, SL Moh, Sahabuddin Nur, Said Jelassi, Sally Anne Watson, Sally Taylor, Sandra Munster, Sandra van der Pas, Sara Stahl, Sarah Baxendale, Sarah Nettleton, Sascha Muller, Saskia & Tom De Bruin, Scot Bird, Seonaid Rait, Sheryl Jackson, Shirley Waldron, Simon & Penny Noble, Simon Waters, Simon Weber, Simpson Family, Sonya Plowman, Stanley Stork, Stefan Di Bucian, Steffen Henkel, Steffen Pedersen, Stephanie Liveroche, Stephanie Tufts, Stephen Aguilar, Stephen Erider, Stephen Tuff, Steve Layton, Steve Lyndon, Steve Mabey, Steve Marcus, Steve Rhodes, Steven Obrie, Stuart Cooke, Stuart McLay, Stuart Strong, Sue Frost, Sue Masters, Sue Roberts, Sue Smith, Susan Pettifer, Susanne Rose, Susie Schmitt, Suzanne Veletta, Svend Erik Hansen, Sybout Porte, T Kolesnikow, Tamara Hewett, Tamara Whyte, Tan Chee Keong, Tania Buffin, Tara Bgattie, Tatyana Tsinberg, Teck Tan, Thea Mulder, Theo Miltenburg, Thierry Tardy, Thng Hui Hong, Thomas Hinterseer, Thomas Knabe, Thomas Knutsson, Tim Birkett, Tim Crakanthorp, Tim Preston, Tim Suatan, Timothy Easterday, Todd & Younghee Lumpkin, Tony & Hana Korab, Toon & Anita, Torben Jarl Jorgensen, Tracy Pearl, Trev Clarke, Trevor Hopper, Trevor Willson, Trish Gerald, Tuesday Gutierrez, Ture Alsvik, Van Der Steen Herman, Veri Hardjono, Veri Hardjono, Vern Yen, Veronique Paccou, W Hicks, W Lown, Wanja Flantua, Wendy Silva, Wilco Pruysers, Will Hall, Willemijn Berg, Willie Monk, Willy Putzeys, Wim Van Hoorn, Win Stroud, Winston Bamford, Y Gooselink, Yasu Ohyagi, Yeok-siew, Yigal Dayan, Ym Shoen Liang, Yoav Parag.

LONELY PLANET

Phrasebooks

Lonely Planet phrasebooks are packed with essential words and phrases to help travellers communicate with the locals. With colour tabs for quick reference, an extensive vocabulary and use of script, these handy pocket-sized language guides cover day-to-day travel situations.

- handy pocket-sized books
- easy to understand Pronunciation chapter
- clear & comprehensive Grammar chapter
- romanisation alongside script to allow ease of pronunciation
- script throughout so users can point to phrases for every situation
- full of cultural information and tips for the traveller

'...vital for a real DIY spirit and attitude in language learning'
— *Backpacker*

'the phrasebooks have good cultural backgrounders and offer solid advice for challenging situations in remote locations'
— *San Francisco Examiner*

Arabic (Egyptian) • Arabic (Moroccan) • Australian *(Australian English, Aboriginal and Torres Strait languages)* • Baltic States *(Estonian, Latvian, Lithuanian)* • Bengali • Brazilian • British • Burmese • Cantonese • Central Asia • Central Europe *(Czech, French, German, Hungarian, Italian, Slovak)* • Eastern Europe *(Bulgarian, Czech, Hungarian, Polish, Romanian, Slovak)* • Ethiopian (Amharic) • Fijian • French • German • Greek • Hebrew phrasebook • Hill Tribes • Hindi/Urdu • Indonesian • Italian • Japanese • Korean • Lao • Latin American Spanish • Malay • Mandarin • Mediterranean Europe *(Albanian, Croatian, Greek, Italian, Macedonian, Maltese, Serbian, Slovene)* • Mongolian • Nepali • Pidgin • Pilipino (Tagalog) • Quechua • Russian • Scandinavian Europe *(Danish, Finnish, Icelandic, Norwegian, Swedish)* • South-East Asia *(Burmese, Indonesian, Khmer, Lao, Malay, Tagalog Pilipino, Thai, Vietnamese)* • South Pacific Languages • Spanish (Castilian) *(also includes Catalan, Galician and Basque)* • Sri Lanka • Swahili • Thai • Tibetan • Turkish • Ukrainian • USA *(US English, Vernacular, Native American languages, Hawaiian)* • Vietnamese • Western Europe *(Basque, Catalan, Dutch, French, German, Greek, Irish)*

Lonely Planet Journeys

JOURNEYS is a unique collection of travel writing – published by the company that understands travel better than anyone else. It is a series for anyone who has ever experienced – or dreamed of – the magical moment when they encountered a strange culture or saw a place for the first time. They are tales to read while you're planning a trip, while you're on the road or while you're in an armchair in front of a fire.

These outstanding titles explore our planet through the eyes of a diverse group of international writers. JOURNEYS books catch the spirit of a place, illuminate a culture, recount a crazy adventure or introduce a fascinating way of life. They always entertain, and always enrich the experience of travel.

ISLANDS IN THE CLOUDS
Travels in the Highlands of New Guinea
Isabella Tree

This is the fascinating account of a journey to the remote and beautiful Highlands of Papua New Guinea and Irian Jaya: one of the most extraordinary and dangerous regions on the planet. Tree travels with a PNG Highlander who introduces her to his intriguing and complex world, changing rapidly as it collides with twentieth-century technology. *Islands in the Clouds* is a thoughtful, moving book.

SEAN & DAVID'S LONG DRIVE
Sean Condon

Sean and David are young townies who have rarely strayed beyond city limits. One day, for no good reason, they set out to discover their homeland, and what follows is a wildly entertaining adventure that covers half of Australia.

'a hilariously detailed log of two burned out friends' – *Rolling Stone*

DRIVE THRU AMERICA
Sean Condon

If you've ever wanted to drive across the USA but couldn't find the time (or afford the gas), *Drive Thru America* is perfect for you. In his search for American myths and realities – along with comfort, cable TV and good, reasonably priced coffee – Sean Condon paints a hilarious road-portrait of the USA.

'entertaining and laugh-out-loud funny' – *Alex Wilber, Travel editor, Amazon.com*

BRIEF ENCOUNTERS
Stories of Love, Sex & Travel
edited by Michelle de Kretser

Love affairs on the road, passionate holiday flings, disastrous pick-ups, erotic encounters . . . In this seductive collection of stories, 22 authors from around the world write about travel romances. Combining fiction and reportage, *Brief Encounters* is must-have reading – for everyone who has dreamt of escape with that perfect stranger.

Includes stories by Pico Iyer, Mary Morris, Emily Perkins, Mona Simpson, Lisa St Aubin de Terán, Paul Theroux and Sara Wheeler.

Lonely Planet Travel Atlases

Lonely Planet has long been famous for the number and quality of its guidebook maps. Now we've gone one step further and produced a handy companion series: Lonely Planet travel atlases – maps of a country produced in book form.

Unlike other maps, which look good but lead travellers astray, our travel atlases have been researched on the road by Lonely Planet's experienced team of writers. All details are carefully checked to ensure the atlas corresponds with the equivalent Lonely Planet guidebook.

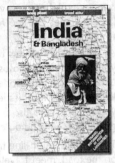

- full-colour throughout
- maps researched and checked by Lonely Planet authors
- place names correspond with Lonely Planet guidebooks
- no confusing spelling differences
- legend and travelling information in English, French, German, Japanese and Spanish
- size: 230 x 160 mm

Available now: Chile & Easter Island ● Egypt ● India & Bangladesh ● Israel & the Palestinian Territories ● Jordan, Syria & Lebanon ● Kenya ● Laos ● Portugal ● South Africa, Lesotho & Swaziland ● Thailand ● Turkey ● Vietnam ● Zimbabwe, Botswana & Namibia

---

Lonely Planet TV Series & Videos

Lonely Planet travel guides have been brought to life on television screens around the world. Like our guides, the programs are based on the joy of independent travel, and look honestly at some of the most exciting, picturesque and frustrating places in the world. Each show is presented by one of three travellers from Australia, England or the USA and combines an innovative mixture of video, Super-8 film, atmospheric soundscapes and original music.

Videos of each episode – containing additional footage not shown on television – are available from good book and video shops, but the availability of individual videos varies with regional screening schedules.

Video destinations include: Alaska ● American Rockies ● Argentina ● Australia – The South-East ● Baja California & the Copper Canyon ● Brazil ● Central Asia ● Chile & Easter Island ● Corsica, Sicily & Sardinia – The Mediterranean Islands ● East Africa (Tanzania & Zanzibar) ● Cuba ● Ecuador & the Galapagos Islands ● Ethiopia ● Greenland & Iceland ● Hungary & Romania ● Indonesia ● Israel & the Sinai Desert ● Jamaica ● Japan ● La Ruta Maya ● The Middle East (Syria, Jordan & Lebanon) ● Morocco ● New York ● Northern Spain ● North India ● Outback Australia ● Pacific Islands (Fiji, Solomon Islands & Vanuatu) ● Pakistan ● Peru ● The Philippines ● South Africa & Lesotho ● South India ● South West China ● South West USA ● Trekking in Uganda ● Turkey ● Vietnam ● West Africa ● Zimbabwe, Botswana & Namibia

The Lonely Planet TV series is produced by: Pilot Productions
The Old Studio
18 Middle Row
London W10 5AT, UK

LONELY PLANET

Lonely Planet On-line

Whether you've just begun planning your next trip, or you're chasing down specific info on currency regulations or visa requirements, check out Lonely Planet On-line for up-to-the minute travel information.

As well as mini guides to more than 250 destinations, you'll find maps, photos, travel news, health and visa updates, travel advisories, and discussion of the ecological and political issues you need to be aware of as you travel. You'll also find timely upgrades to popular guidebooks which you can print out and stick in the back of your book.

There's also an on-line travellers' forum where you can share your experience of life on the road, meet travel companions and ask other travellers for their recommendations and advice.

And of course we have a complete and up-to-date list of all Lonely Planet travel products including travel guides, diving and snorkeling guides, phrasebooks, atlases, travel literature and videos, and a simple on-line ordering facility if you can't find the book you want elsewhere.

Lonely Planet Diving & Snorkeling Guides

Beautifully illustrated with full-colour photos throughout, Lonely Planet's Pisces Books explore the world's best diving and snorkeling areas and prepare divers for what to expect when they get there, both topside and underwater.

Dive sites are described in detail with specifics on depths, visibility, level of difficulty, special conditions, underwater photography tips and common and unusual marine life present. You'll also find practical logistical information and coverage on topside activities and attractions, sections on diving health and safety, plus listings for diving services, live-aboards, dive resorts and tourist offices.

LONELY PLANET

Guides by Region

Lonely Planet is known worldwide for publishing practical, reliable and no-nonsense travel information in our guides and on our Web site. The Lonely Planet list covers just about every accessible part of the world. Currently there are thirteen series: travel guides, shoestring guides, walking guides, city guides, phrasebooks, audio packs, city maps, travel atlases, diving and snorkeling guides, restaurant guides, first-time travel guides, healthy travel and travel literature.

AFRICA Africa – the South ● Africa on a shoestring ● Arabic (Egyptian) phrasebook ● Arabic (Moroccan) phrasebook ● Cairo ● Cape Town ● Cape Town city map● Central Africa ● East Africa ● Egypt ● Egypt travel atlas ● Ethiopian (Amharic) phrasebook ● The Gambia & Senegal ● Healthy Travel Africa ● Kenya ● Kenya travel atlas ● Malawi, Mozambique & Zambia ● Morocco ● North Africa ● South Africa, Lesotho & Swaziland ● South Africa, Lesotho & Swaziland travel atlas ● Swahili phrasebook ● Tanzania, Zanzibar & Pemba ● Trekking in East Africa ● Tunisia ● West Africa ● Zimbabwe, Botswana & Namibia ● Zimbabwe, Botswana & Namibia travel atlas
Travel Literature: The Rainbird: A Central African Journey ● Songs to an African Sunset: A Zimbabwean Story ● Mali Blues: Traveling to an African Beat

AUSTRALIA & THE PACIFIC Auckland ● Australia ● Australian phrasebook ● Bushwalking in Australia ● Bushwalking in Papua New Guinea ● Fiji ● Fijian phrasebook ● Islands of Australia's Great Barrier Reef ● Melbourne ● Melbourne city map ● Micronesia ● New Caledonia ● New South Wales & the ACT ● New Zealand ● Northern Territory ● Outback Australia ● Out To Eat – Melbourne ● Papua New Guinea ● Papua New Guinea (Pidgin) phrasebook ● Queensland ● Rarotonga & the Cook Islands ● Samoa ● Solomon Islands ● South Australia ● South Pacific Languages phrasebook ● Sydney ● Sydney city map ● Tahiti & French Polynesia ● Tasmania ● Tonga ● Tramping in New Zealand ● Vanuatu ● Victoria ● Western Australia
Travel Literature: Islands in the Clouds ● Kiwi Tracks ● Sean & David's Long Drive

CENTRAL AMERICA & THE CARIBBEAN Bahamas and Turks & Caicos ● Bermuda ● Central America on a shoestring ● Costa Rica ● Cuba ● Dominican Republic & Haiti ● Eastern Caribbean ● Guatemala, Belize & Yucatán: La Ruta Maya ● Jamaica ● Mexico ● Mexico City ● Panama ● Puerto Rico
Travel Literature: Green Dreams: Travels in Central America

EUROPE Amsterdam ● Amsterdam city map ● Andalucía ● Austria ● Baltic States phrasebook ● Barcelona ● Berlin ● Berlin city map ● Britain ● British phrasebook ● Brussels, Bruges & Antwerp ● Budapest city map ● Canary Islands ● Central Europe ● Central Europe phrasebook ● Corsica ● Croatia ● Czech & Slovak Republics ● Denmark ● Dublin ● Eastern Europe ● Eastern Europe phrasebook ● Edinburgh ● Estonia, Latvia & Lithuania ● Europe ● Finland ● France ● French phrasebook ● Germany ● German phrasebook ● Greece ● Greek phrasebook ● Hungary ● Iceland, Greenland & the Faroe Islands ● Ireland ● Italian phrasebook ● Italy ● Lisbon ● London ● London city map ● Mediterranean Europe ● Mediterranean Europe phrasebook ● Norway ● Paris ● Paris city map ● Poland ● Portugal ● Portugal travel atlas ● Prague ● Prague city map ● Provence & the Côte d'Azur ● Romania & Moldova ● Rome ● Russia, Ukraine & Belarus ● Russian phrasebook ● Scandinavian & Baltic Europe ● Scandinavian Europe phrasebook ● Scotland ● Slovenia ● Spain ● Spanish phrasebook ● St Petersburg ● Switzerland ● Trekking in Spain ● Ukrainian phrasebook ● Vienna ● Walking in Britain ● Walking in Ireland ● Walking in Italy ● Walking in Switzerland ● Western Europe ● Western Europe phrasebook
Travel Literature: The Olive Grove: Travels in Greece

INDIAN SUBCONTINENT Bangladesh ● Bengali phrasebook ● Bhutan ● Delhi ● Goa ● Hindi/Urdu phrasebook ● India ● India & Bangladesh travel atlas ● Indian Himalaya ● Karakoram Highway ● Kerala ● Mumbai ● Nepal ● Nepali phrasebook ● Pakistan ● Rajasthan ● Read This First: Asia & India ● South India ● Sri Lanka ● Sri Lanka phrasebook ● Trekking in the Indian Himalaya ● Trekking in the Karakoram & Hindukush ● Trekking in the Nepal Himalaya
Travel Literature: In Rajasthan ● Shopping for Buddhas

Index

Abbreviations

Text

Bold indicates maps.

H

Bold indicates maps.

Bold indicates maps.

Bold indicates maps.

Boxed Text

MAP LEGEND

BOUNDARIES

▬ · ▬ · ▬	...............International
▬ · · ▬ · ·	.......................State
▬ ▬ ▬	..................Disputed

HYDROGRAPHY

	...............Coastline
	............River, Creek
	.........................Lake
	.........Intermittent Lake
	...................Salt Lake
	.........................Canal
◎ ⟫	...........Spring, Rapids
⫫ ⪦	.................Waterfalls
	.........................Swamp

ROUTES & TRANSPORT

	.........................Freeway
	.........................Highway
	......................Major Road
	......................Minor Road
═══════	...............Unsealed Road
	...................City Freeway
	...................City Highway
	.......................City Road
	.................City Street, Lane

	...............Pedestrian Mall
⟩══════	.........................Tunnel
⊢⊢⊢⊶⊢⊢	...Train Route & Station
▬ ▬ Ⓜ ▬	..........Metro & Station
	.........................Tramway
╫═╫═╫═	..... Cable Car or Chairlift
	...............Walking Track
· · · · · ·	................Walking Tour
	.........................Ferry Route

AREA FEATURES

	.........................Building
✿	...............Park, Gardens
+ × ×	...................Cemetery

	.........................Market
	...............Beach, Desert
	.........................Urban Area

MAP SYMBOLS

✪	**CAPITAL**	...............National Capital	✈	.........................Airport	♣ ☀	.. National Park, Lookout
◉	**CAPITAL**	...............State Capital		....Ancient or City Wall	)(	.........................Pass
●	**CITY**	.........................City	∴	...........Archaeological Site	★	.........................Police Station
●	**Town**	.........................Town	❸	.........................Bank	✉	.........................Post Office
●	**Village**	.........................Village	🏃 🏄	...... Beach, Surf Beach	⚓	.........................Shipwreck
○		.........Point of Interest	∩	.........................Cave	❖	...............Shopping Centre
			🏛 🏠	.........................Church	⋀	.........................Stupa
■		.........................Place to Stay		.........Cliff or Escarpment	🏊	.........................Swimming Pool
⚠		...........Camping Ground	◣ ▣	.... Dive Site, Snorkelling	☎	.........................Telephone
⌖		...............Caravan Park	❷ ⊕	.......Embassy, Hospital	🛕	...............Temple (Balinese)
⌂ ⌂		...............Hut, Shelter	☀	.........................Lighthouse	⬛	..........Temple (Other)
			◉ 🗼	..... Mosque, Monument	❶	.........Tourist Information
▼		.........................Place to Eat	▲ 🗻	...... Mountain, Volcano	●	.........................Transport
⬤		.........................Pub or Bar	🏛 🏛	.. Museum, Stately Home	🐾	.........................Zoo

Note: not all symbols displayed above appear in this book

LONELY PLANET OFFICES

Australia
PO Box 617, Hawthorn, Victoria 3122
☎ 03 9819 1877 fax 03 9819 6459
email: talk2us@lonelyplanet.com.au

USA
150 Linden St, Oakland, CA 94607
☎ 510 893 8555 TOLL FREE: 800 275 8555
fax 510 893 8572
email: info@lonelyplanet.com

UK
10a Spring Place, London NW5 3BH
☎ 020 7428 4800 fax 020 7428 4828
email: go@lonelyplanet.co.uk

France
1 rue du Dahomey, 75011 Paris
☎ 01 55 25 33 00 fax 01 55 25 33 01
email: bip@lonelyplanet.fr
www.lonelyplanet.fr

World Wide Web: www.lonelyplanet.com *or* AOL keyword: lp
Lonely Planet Images: lpi@lonelyplanet.com.au